SMITH, BAILEY & GUNN
ON
THE MODERN ENGLISH LEGAL
SYSTEM

LAf
(ELSM)
Bai
Std

ster@lawcol.co.uk

AUSTRALIA
Law Book Co.
Sydney

CANADA and USA
Carswell
Toronto

HONG KONG
Sweet and Maxwell Asia

NEW ZEALAND
Brookers
Auckland

SINGAPORE and MALAYSIA
Sweet & Maxwell Asia
Singapore and Kuala Lumpur

SMITH, BAILEY AND GUNN
ON
THE MODERN ENGLISH LEGAL SYSTEM

Fifth Edition

by

S.H. BAILEY, M.A., LL.B.,

*Professor of Public Law at the
University of Nottingham*

J.P.L. CHING, M.A. (Cantab.), FHEA

*Solicitor and Reader at
Nottingham Trent University*

N.W. TAYLOR, M.Phil., LL.B.

*Senior Lecturer in Law at the
University of Leeds*

LONDON
SWEET & MAXWELL
2007,

First Edition 1984
Second Impression 1986
Third Impression 1987
Fourth Impression 1988
Second Edition 1991
Second Impression 1992
Third Impression 1994
Fourth Impression 1995
Third Edition 1996
Second Impression 1998
Third Impression 1999
Fourth Edition 2002
Fifth Edition 2007

Published in 2007 Sweet & Maxwell Limited of
100 Avenue Road, Swiss Cottage, London NW3 3PF
http://www.sweetandmaxwell.co.uk
Computerset by Interactive Sciences Ltd, Gloucester
Printed by Ashford Colour Press Ltd

A CIP Catalogue Record
for this book is available
from the British Library

ISBN 978–0–421–90910–6

PREFACE

This edition, like its predecessors, has necessitated much revision and rewriting. There have also been changes in the team of authors. Michael Gunn and David Ormerod were unable to contribute to this edition because of their many other commitments. Stephen Bailey and Jane Ching are very pleased to have been joined by Nick Taylor of the University of Leeds, who has assumed responsibility for the chapters on the criminal process.

The pace of change in the legal system at the instigation of the Labour government has remained high. There are indeed many complaints about the vast quantity of new primary and secondary legislation affecting many areas. The period since the last edition has seen the working through of reforms in the wake of the Auld and Leggatt reports, in the contexts of the criminal and tribunals processes. It has also seen many new developments. These include some fundamental restructuring within the legal system, with restriction of the role of the Lord Chancellor and the establishment of the Department of Constitutional Affairs, followed only a few years later (and after the book went to press) of the Ministry of Justice. A new Supreme Court of the United Kingdom, taking over the judicial role of the House of Lords and the devolution jurisdiction of the Judicial Committee of the Privy Council, is due to start work in 2009. New machinery for the appointment of judges is already in place. It is remarkable and unfortunate that serious public consultation and debate as to both the general desirability and the detail of these changes followed rather than preceded the decision that they should happen. Other features of the period have included annual Criminal Justice Bills, continued and controversial steps to constrain the legal aid budget which are, at the date of writing, being aired in court proceedings, decisions to introduce in the future significant changes to the regulation and structure of the legal profession (or professions) contained in the Legal Services Bill as well as in the *Solicitors' Code of Conduct 2007* and many important cases on the Human Rights Act 1998.

We have endeavoured to state the position at the end of April 2007, but have been able to mention some further developments either in the text or below.

The authors wish to thank the publishers for their support and for preparing the Tables and Index. Stephen Bailey wishes to thank Nick Wikeley and officials of the Ministry of Justice for help on a number of points. Responsibility for the finished product remains with us.

S.H. Bailey

J.P.L. Ching

N.W. Taylor

August 8, 2007

Recent developments

Para.1–018 The Ministry of Justice. The creation by Mr Blair of the Department of Constitutional Affairs in 2003 proved in the event to be a staging post on the road to the establishment, as one of his last acts, of a Ministry of Justice in May 2007. An idea that had been debated on and off for much of the last century was in the event introduced after largely internal discussions lasting a matter of months. The lack of consultation was severely criticised by the Select Committee on Constitutional Affairs (Sixth Report, 2006–07 H.C. 466, *The creation of the Ministry of Justice*) and the HL Select Committee on the Constitution (see below).The appointment of a heavyweight Commons minister (Jack Straw MP) as Lord Chancellor and Secretary of State (the MoJ website has it this way round) was both inevitable, given the size and importance of the new Ministry, and welcome. The reform provoked a further dispute with the judges, who were concerned in particular that the budget for the courts would now come under pressure from the demands for resources from the prison system. Mr Straw moved quickly to reassure the judges that he would defend judicial independence, emphasising that what ministers "must not do is gratuitously to criticise individual judgments, nor show a lack of respect for the institution of the judiciary or its members. After all, it is we in Parliament who ultimately make the law, and therefore have to accept its consequences." As to resources, he said "It is my job to ensure that the resources are adequate. But long experience tells me that different structures are not themselves guarantors of resources. I do of course appreciate your concerns regarding resources, but I hope that the judiciary will understand that I need time to consider the situation" (Speech to the Lord Mayor's Annual Dinner for the Judges, July 17, 2007).

The first ministerial team comprised the Lord Chancellor and Secretary of State for Justice, two Ministers of State (David Hanson MP and Michael Wills MP) and three Parliamentary Under Secretaries (Lord Hunt of Kings Heath (the spokesman in the House of Lords), Maria Eagle MP and Bridget Prentice MP).

The Ministry's objectives are set out in *Justice—a new approach* (MoJ 1/07, May 2007). See also the Secretary of State for Justice Order 2007 (SI 2007/2128).

Para.1–021 The role of the Attorney General. The government has noted that there has been public comment in recent years in particular around the position of a Government Minister as chief legal adviser and the position of the Attorney in the role of guardian of the public interest. It intends to consult on possible ways of alleviating these conflicts (or the appearance of them): *The Governance of Britain* (Cmnd. 7170, 2007), p.24. The Select Committee on Constitutional Affairs (Fifth Report, 2006–07 H.C. 306, *The Constitutional Role of the Attorney General*) has recommended that the current duties of the Attorney General be split in two: the purely legal functions should be carried out by an official who is outside party political life; the ministerial duties should be carried out by a minister in the Ministry of Justice.

Para.1–028 The Law Commission. By virtue of the Tribunals, Courts and Enforcement Act 2007, s.60, there is now a formal requirement that the Chairman of the Law Commission be a current judge of the High Court or the Court of Appeal in England and Wales.

Para.1–033 Annual Report. The Lord Chief Justice intends to lay an Annual Report on the Judiciary before Parliament: see HL Select Committee on the Constitution, Sixth Report, 2007–07 H.L. 151, *Relations between the executive, the judiciary and Parliament*, para.139. The Committee conducted a wide ranging review of the current position.

Para.2–022 Youth Courts. The Youth Courts (Constitution Rules) 1954 are replaced by the Youth Courts (Constitution of Committees and Right to Preside) Rules 2007 (SI 2007/1611). There is to be a youth panel for each local justice area.

Para.2–025 Family proceedings in the magistrates' courts. Provision is made by the Family Proceedings Courts (Constitution of Committees and Right to Preside) Rules 2007 (SI 2007/1610) for the establishment of a family panel for each local justice area and for the chairmanship of family proceedings courts. The Family Proceedings Courts (Constitution) Rules 1991 and the Family Proceedings Courts (Constitution) (Greater London) Rules 2003 are revoked.

Para.2–031 Employment judges. By virtue of the Tribunals, Courts and Enforcement Act 2007, Sch.8, para.36, inserting s.3A in the Employment Tribunals Act 1996, in force from a day to be appointed, a member of the panel of chairmen for Employment Tribunals may be referred to as an "Employment Judge".

Para.2–075 The Judicial Committee of the Privy Council. From Monday April 2, 2007, the PCO Secretariat and the Office of the Judicial Committee moved, retaining their separate and independent identity, to the Constitution Directorate of the Ministry of Justice, whilst continuing to report to the Lord President of the Council.

Chapter 3 Legal Services Bill. By the time this book reaches you, it is entirely possible that the Legal Services Bill will have come into force, with the potential entirely to change the landscape of legal services provision in this country.

Paras 4–008, 4–009 Magistrates' training. The arrangements are now covered by the Justices of the Peace (Training and Development Committee) Rules 2007 (SI 2007/1609). A new development is that a Family Training Development Committee is established for Greater London and FDTCs may be established elsewhere.

Paras 4–008, 4–017, 4–032, 4–040 Judicial conduct. The Office for Judicial Complaints has published its first Annual Report (for 2006–07: see JCO website). 1674 complaints were received; 51 per cent related to judicial decisions; disciplinary action was taken in respect of two mainstream judges, two tribunal office holders and 28 magistrates; one tribunal office holder and 15 magistrates were removed from office; nine review bodies sat during the year. The Judicial Appointments & Conduct Ombudsman has also published his first (2006/07) Annual Report: see *www.judicialombudsman.gov.uk*.

In July 2007, the conduct of Peter Smith J was referred to the OJC by the Lord Chief Justice and the Lord Chancellor. His conduct in hearing a case, including a refusal to recuse himself, had been severely criticised by the Court of Appeal: *Howell v Lees Millais* [2007] EWCA Civ 720. The applicants were trustees, one of whom was a partner in a solicitors firm, Addleshaw Goddard. The judge had been in discussions with AG about a proposal that he join them; AG had decided not to proceed, and the judge had responded in emails expressing "disappointment and some animosity" towards AG and a partner (see Sir Anthony Clarke M.R. at para.[13]). The Court of Appeal held that the judge should have recused himself and was critical of "intemperate" remarks by him at the recusal hearing.

Para.4–011 Justices' Clerks. The HMCS has published a *Report following a consultation on a model for the provision of Justices' Clerks in England and Wales* (May 2007). It sets out a national model specifying the number of Clerkships in each area and endorses the principle that legal and administrative functions should normally be separated. If adopted, the total number would fall from 69 to 51. The rules for assistants have been amended by the Assistants to Justices' Clerks (Amendment) Regulations 2007 (SI 20076/1448).

Para.4–020 Honorary Recorders. The Lord Chief Justice has encouraged borough councils to exercise their power under s.54 of the Courts Act 1971 to appoint honorary recorders: see *The Lord Chief Justice's Guidelines for the Appointment of Honorary Recorders* (www.judiciary.gov.uk, August 1, 2007).

Paras 4–020, 4–025 Judicial working dress. The Lord Chief Justice has announced changes (www.judiciary.gov.uk, News Release, July 12, 2007). The only change in criminal proceedings is that High Court judges will wear the existing winter robes throughout the year. In civil and family proceedings, wigs, wing collars and bands will no longer be worn; Circuit judges will continue to wear their existing gown and, otherwise, a simpler gown will be used for all judges.

Para.5–009 A draft legislative programme. The government has for the first time published a draft legislative programme: see *The Governance of Britain —The Government's draft legislative programme* (Cmnd.7175, 2007). The Queen's Speech at the start of the Parliamentary session remains the occasion when the legislative programme for that session is formally announced.

Para.8–002 Territorial application of the HRA. The House of Lords in *Al-Skeini v Secretary of State for Defence* [2007] UKHL 26 has held that the Human Rights Act 1998 does apply to acts of a public authority abroad, but only where the claimant is within the jurisdiction of the UK within the meaning of Art 1, ECHR (as where he or she is in the custody of the armed forces). The House was unanimous that the Act did not apply to claims in respect of five persons killed by (or allegedly killed by) soldiers on patrol in Basra, Iraq, but held by four to one that it did apply in respect of a person held in a British detention centre in Iraq.

Para.8–011 "Public authority" under the HRA. The House of Lords in *YL v Birmingham City Council* [2007] UKHL 27 held that a private care home was not a public authority for the purposes of the Human Rights Act 1998.

Para.8–028 A British Bill of Rights and Duties. The government has announced its intention to begin exploring the issues on the introduction of a British Bill of Rights and Duties (that would apparently include the rights under the ECHR and thus remain Convention compliant) and a Constitution: *The Governance of Britain* (Cmnd.7170, 2007), pp.60–63.

Paras 10–006, 10–022 "Unified Contract". In *R. (on the application of the Law Society) v Legal Services Commission* [2007] EWHC 1848 (Admin), the first stage of the Law Society's application for judicial review of the legal aid reforms, it was held that the proposed "unified contract" for legal aid provision fell foul of the Public Contracts Regulations 2006.

Para.14–048 Judicial Review and the Decision to Prosecute. *R. (on the application of Dennis) v DPP* [2006] EWHC 3211 (Admin) provides an example of circumstances in which a decision by the CPS not to prosecute might successfully be challenged by judicial review.

Para.14–062 Police Bail. The Police and Justice Act 2006 (Commencement No. 2, Transitional and Saving Provisions) Order 2007 (SI 2007 No. 709) has brought into force s.10 and Sch.6 of the Act. These provisions amend PACE in relation to bail granted by a constable elsewhere than at a police station and bail granted at a police station.

Para.14–099 The (re) emergence of terrorism. In July 2007, the Prime Minister announced details of a consultation process over a new counter terrorism bill which could affect areas such as pre charge detention, post charge questioning, data sharing, stop and question and intercept evidence. Further, see: *http://security.homeoffice.gov.uk/* .

Paras 15–011ff The Bill has been enacted as the Tribunals, Courts and Enforcement Act 2007.

Para.15–014 Provisions as to attachment of earnings orders now appear in ss.91 and 92 of the Tribunals, Courts and Enforcement Act 2007.

Para.15–015 Provisions as to charging orders now appear in ss.93 and 94 of the Tribunals, Courts and Enforcement Act 2007.

Chapter 17 Criminal Procedure Rules. A number of changes have been made to aspects of the Criminal Procedure Rules and these can be found in The Criminal Procedure (Amendment Rules) 2007, SI 2007/699, supplemented by the fifteenth amendment to the Consolidated Practice Direction. A number of changes to the indictment are contained in Pt 14 of the Crim.P.R.

Para.17–022 The arraignment. The Court of Appeal in *R. v Kepple* [2007] EWCA Crim 1339, held that where the defendant absconds before arraignment it remains possible for the trial to proceed. The defendant may waive his right to arraignment just as he may waive his right to remain in court during the trial.

Para.17–023 Double Jeopardy. In *R. v K* [2007] EWCA Crim 971, the Court of Appeal considered the meaning of conviction and acquittal for the purposes of autrefois and emphasised that issues falling outside that narrowly defined scope can be dealt with under the well established doctrine of abuse of process.

Para.17–027 Abuse of Process. Where evidence has been lost or destroyed but a fair trial remains possible the judge must give clear directions: see *R. v Ali* [2007] EWCA Crim 691.

Para.17–031 The Prosecution Case. In *R. v Collins* [2007] EWCA Crim 854, the Court of Appeal emphasised that the practice of inviting a jury to acquit before the end of the trial has been "comprehensively disapproved". It may be exercised only in the most exceptional circumstances.

Para.17–043 The Guilty Plea. The Sentencing Guidelines Council has produced a revised guideline on reductions in sentence available following a guilty plea. See: *www.sentencing-guidelines.gov.uk/docs/Reduction%20in%20Sentence-final.pdf.*

Para.17–067 The Role of the Judge. The need for the court to "actively manage the case" was given some meaning in *R v Jisl* and this has been reiterated in *R. v L* [2007] EWCA Crim 764.

Para.17–081 Sentencing. In *R v Seed* [2007] EWCA Crim 254, Lord Phillips C.J. (at para.[6]) stated that "Unless imprisonment is necessary for the protection of the public the court should always give consideration to the question of whether the aims of rehabilitation and thus the reduction of crime cannot better be achieved by a fine or community sentence rather than by imprisonment and whether punishment cannot adequately be achieved by such a sentence."

Para.18–018 References by the Criminal Cases Review Commission. In *R. v Cottrell*; *R. v Fletcher* [2007] EWCA Crim 2016, the Court of Appeal stated that it would be contrary to the intention of Parliament for the law and practice of the Court of Appeal to be ignored by the CCRC when it was exercising its judgment whether tyo refer a conviction to the court. Doubt was cast upon the decision in *R. (on the application of Director of Revenue and Customs Prosecutions) v Criminal Cases Review Commission* (2007) 1 Cr.App.R. 30.

ACKNOWLEDGMENTS

The authors and publishers would like to thank the following for permission to reproduce materials from publications in which they have copyright.

Crown copyright. Reproduced with the permission of the Controller of HMSO.

Extracts from various law reports reproduced with kind permission of the Incorporated Council of Law Reporting for England and Wales.

Court Service forms reproduced by kind permission of the Solicitors' Law Stationery Society Limited for educational purposes only.

While every care has been taken to establish and acknowledge copyright, and contact the copyright owners, the publishers tender their apologies for any accidental infringement. They would be pleased to come to a suitable arrangement with the rightful owners in each case.

CONTENTS

PART I: COURTS, PERSONNEL AND SOURCES OF LAW

PART II: SOLVING LEGAL PROBLEMS

PART III: PRE-TRIAL PROCEDURE

PART IV: THE HEARING

TABLE OF CASES

TABLE OF STATUTES

TABLE OF STATUTORY INSTRUMENTS

PART I

COURTS, PERSONNEL AND SOURCES OF LAW

INTRODUCTION

A. THE ENGLISH LEGAL SYSTEM

The study of the English legal system is a vital part of any law student's course. **1–001** Not only are the legal institutions and processes integral to every other legal course he or she will study, they are also the subject of necessary scrutiny for assessing how well the law provides solutions to the problems it is intended to meet.

Law students are not always aware of the social context in which the rules of law they learn about will actually operate. Some of their teachers are more enthusiastic than others about ensuring that their study is not directed solely to the rules of law contained in statutes or gleaned from the decisions of the superior courts. In respect of the institutions, processes and people of the English legal system in particular, some students affect impatience at the study of matters which they think are better left to social scientists. Some even have the mis-guided belief that the study of the institutions and processes of our law does not carry the intellectual challenge of other legal subjects. Yet a failure to understand the English legal system will make much of what the student learns of those other subjects either incomprehensible or misleading.

For example, those studying the law of negligence need to know the basic elements of the tort and their respective functions. They will discover that until the 1950s its scope was confined to cases of physical damage to person or property and that the great majority of cases actually brought arise out of accidents on the road or at work. Liability in tort will be compared with other sources of accident compensation, such as social security, and related to the insurance position. As regards a tort claim, however, the student should not only be aware of the rules which prescribe who has a right to bring a claim for damages, but also of the processes whereby legal rights are actually vindicated, and indeed the enormous practical difficulties that face potential claimants. These processes form an important part of the subject matter of this book.

Almost every aspect of life in the modern state is regulated or affected in some way by law. There are laws which provide for the remedying of defined griev-ances (e.g. by the payment of damages in respect of accidentally inflicted injuries), laws which prohibit anti-social activities and provide for the imposition of penal sanctions for breach (e.g. the criminal law of murder or theft), laws which regulate potentially harmful activities by, for example systems for licens-ing, registration or inspection, usually in conjunction with the prescription of standards (e.g. liquor licensing, the protection of health and safety at work), laws which confer state benefits upon individuals (e.g. education, highways, social security, national health service) and laws which facilitate private arrangements (e.g. marriages, contracts, wills).[1] In a sense, the whole body of English law could be said to constitute the English legal system. However, we use the term in a narrower sense to cover the distinctive legal institutions and processes that come into operation when for some reason there is doubt or disagreement as to how the law applies in a given situation: there may be recourse to a lawyer or some other agency for legal advice, or, usually as a last resort, involvement in litigation before a court or tribunal.

The label "English legal system" is convenient, but has to be treated with a little care. For one thing, it extends to both England and Wales (Scotland, Northern Ireland, the Isle of Man and the Channel Islands have separate sys-tems). It should, however, be noted that the content of legislation as it affects Wales, particularly subordinate legislation, is more frequently diverging from that applicable in England, and a case is developing for Wales to be recognised at least for some purposes as a separate jurisdiction.[2] For another, it is not as systematically organised as a "system" perhaps should be.

---

[1] These five legal techniques were distinguished by R. Summers, "The Technique Element in Law," 59 Calif. L.R. 733 (1971). See also J. Farrar and A. M. Dugdale, *Introduction to Legal Method* (3rd edn, 1990), Ch.2, who distinguish two further techniques: the "constitutive" technique whereby the law recognises a group of people as constituting a legal person (e.g. a company) and the "fiscal" technique whereby the government raises money by taxation.

[2] See T. H. Jones, J. H. Turnbull and J. M. Williams, "The Law of Wales and the Law of England and Wales" (2005) 23 Stat. L.R. 135.

B. SOME BASIC CONCEPTS

There is not room here for an introduction to the theoretical background of the   **1–002**
role of law in society.[3] There are, however, certain concepts that will appear at
various points in this book and require some explanation here.

1. "COMMON LAW" AND "CIVIL LAW"

The "common law" was the term that came to be used for the laws and customs   **1–003**
applied by the royal courts which emerged after the Norman Conquest, and
which progressively replaced local laws and customs applied in sundry local
courts.[4] As the decisions of these courts came to be recorded and published, so
the practice developed whereby past decisions would be cited in argument before
the courts, and would be regarded as being of persuasive or even binding
authority.[5] The point that decisions of the superior courts are a source of law in
their own right is a distinctive feature of "common law systems", the term here
being used to distinguish such systems from continental, "civil law",[6] systems
based in origin upon Roman law but now upon a series of codes established in
the nineteenth and twentieth centuries. The basic elements of English law have
become established in a number of Commonwealth countries (most notably
Australia, New Zealand and Canada, excluding Quebec) and the United States
(except Louisiana).

2. "COMMON LAW" AND STATUTE

Apart from its use as a convenient label for one kind of legal system, the term   **1–004**
"common law" is used, in a narrower sense, for one of a number of distinct
sources of law that exist within such a system. Laws enacted by the Queen in
Parliament ("Acts of Parliament" or "statutes"), or made under delegated powers conferred by statute, have come to be of arguably greater significance than the
decisions of the courts.[7] The common law has always been particularly associated with the protection of such matters as personal freedom, rights of property
and contract, and individual interests in reputation and bodily security. However,
the nineteenth and twentieth centuries have seen a substantial expansion of the
accepted role of government to include the pursuit of such collective purposes as
the protection of public health and welfare, and the direction of the economy. The
National Health Service, state education and social security are all examples of
services established and regulated by legislation. It has also come to be felt that

---

[3] See B. Roshier and H. Teff, *Law and Society in England* (1980); P. S. Atiyah, *Law and Modern
Society* (2nd edn, 1995); R. Cotterrell, *The Sociology of Law: An Introduction* (2nd edn,
1992).

[4] See below, paras 2–003, 2–004 on the growth of the royal courts.

[5] See Ch.7.

[6] This usage of the term "civil" should be distinguished from its uses "as opposed to: (i)
ecclesiastical; (ii) criminal; (iii) military": *Osborn's Concise Law Dictionary* (9th edn, 2001).

[7] See Chs 5 and 6.

important changes in areas still dominated by the common law are more legit-imately made by statute than by judges, although the vein of judicial creativity is by no means exhausted.[8]

The term "common law" is thus used to denote rules derived from decisions of the superior courts in contrast to those derived from statute. There is, however, one usage that is narrower still. Only some judge-made rules are rules of the common law in this narrower sense—the others are rules of "equity" which are of distinct historical origin.

3. "COMMON LAW" AND "EQUITY"

1–005   By the thirteenth century, the Crown had, in effect, delegated its inherent power to dispense justice to the judges of three royal courts: the Exchequer, the Common Bench—or as it came to be known in Tudor times, the Common Pleas—and the King's (or Queen's) Bench.[9] At this time, the Common Bench was by far the busiest court as regards civil cases, with jurisdiction over matters between subject and subject, such as disputes over rights to land and actions for debt.[10] Proceedings were commenced by the plaintiff's purchase of a writ from the Chancery.[11] The Chancery was originally the royal secretariat, the place where all kinds of royal documents were prepared and authenticated by the Great Seal. Its head was the Chancellor,[12] whose office came to be one of the great offices of state. In medieval times, most Chancellors were bishops and graduates in civil or canon law. Some holders of the office were in effect the King's chief minister.

The claimant was obliged to obtain a writ in a form appropriate to the claim. At first, if there was no precedent the Chancery would be prepared to draft a new one, but by the end of the thirteenth century this could no longer be done. Once the writ was obtained it governed the detailed form the action would take; if the wrong one had been chosen, the plaintiff was required to recommence proceedings.

Among the duties of the Chancellor were those of determining questions relating to Crown property, hearing common law actions concerning his clerks, servants and officials, and entertaining "petitions of right" (i.e. claims against the Crown). In addition, the Chancellor came to deal exclusively with petitions addressed to the King or the Council in respect of grievances which for some reason were not redressed or redressible by proceedings in the common law

---

[8] See paras 4–041—4–044.

[9] See further below, paras 2–003—2–004 on the development of these courts.

[10] The King's Bench shared with the Common Bench cases of "trespass" (the term then simply meaning "wrong" as in the Lord's Prayer) and heard proceedings to correct errors in the Common Bench and local courts. Its main function was to deal with what are now called criminal cases—pleas of the Crown. By the end of the sixteenth century it had by a series of procedural devices obtained a civil jurisdiction comparable with the Common Pleas.

[11] Proceedings in the King's Bench were commenced by a petition known as a "bill" addressed directly to the court by the claimant, a simpler and cheaper procedure.

[12] Where a Chancellor was not appointed, the Great Seal could be entrusted to temporary "Keepers of the Seal". Occasionally, a permanent appointment was made to the office of "Lord Keeper of the Great Seal" where it was wished not to make an appointment to the more dignified office of Lord Chancellor; the powers of the two offices were the same.

courts. This might be because of corruption or undue influence affecting proceedings (e.g. the bribery of jurors), or because in a particular case strict common law requirements for proof appeared to lead to injustice, or because the matter did not fall within the scope of writs recognised by the common law. The Chancellor would give relief in particular cases by an order directed to the parties, his intervention being based on the dictates of their consciences judged in accordance with his own view of what was just. Proceedings before the Chancellor were simpler, and were in other respects advantageous when compared with the procedures of the common law courts. Moreover, the Chancellor developed several remedies which were not available in other courts, most notably specific performance and the injunction—an order requiring the person to whom it is addressed to perform or to refrain from performing a stated act. When performing these judicial functions, the Chancellor came to be regarded as constituting a court: the Court of Chancery.

The standard illustration of how the Chancellor operated was provided by the **1–006** person who borrowed money, acknowledged the debt by entering into a bond under seal, subsequently paid the debt, but failed to have the bond cancelled. For a common law court, the sealed bond provided incontrovertible proof of the existence of the debt: the court would enforce a second payment if proceedings were instituted by the creditor. However, the Chancellor could restrain such unconscionable action on the part of the creditor by an injunction directed to him, and order that the bond be cancelled.

At first it was not thought that there were separate systems of "law" and "equity". The Chancellor was frequently advised by the common law judges, and there were suggestions that the common law courts could take account of matters of conscience. However, tensions developed. The arguments on each side indeed reflected what is an inevitable dilemma in any system of law, the problem of reconciling the competing demands of justice and certainty. The more general a rule, the less likely it is to do justice in all the particular cases to which it applies; moreover, an attempt to construct in advance the qualifications to the rule necessary to do justice in all cases would lead to a system of rules of enormous complexity, even if all the problems could be foreseen. Hence the need for some means whereby particular cases could be dealt with justly. Ad hoc decision-making can however be unjust if like cases are treated differently and, in any event, tends to be unpredictable.[13] The Chancellors reacted to criticisms from common lawyers and to the need to introduce regularity into the processing of an increasing caseload by developing principles of "equity" or justice from their ad hoc interventions. At times, however, the tensions also reflected personal difficulties between the Chancellor and common lawyers. In the sixteenth century Cardinal Wolsey caused much discontent among common lawyers by his preference for his own robust "common sense" over legal learning, and in the early seventeenth century a dispute between Lord Chancellor Ellesmere and Sir Edward Coke, the Chief Justice of the King's Bench, was settled by King James I in favour of the former. The Chancellor's power to issue injunctions preventing

---

[13] This point was made in the seventeenth century by John Selden (*Table Talk*, edited by F. Pollock, 1927)—"Equity is a roguish thing, for law we have a measure, knowing what to trust to. Equity is according to the conscience of him that is Chancellor, and as it is larger or narrower so is equity. It is all one as if they should make the standard for the measure we call a foot to be the Chancellor's foot; what an uncertain measure would this be; one Chancellor has a long foot, another a short foot, a third an indifferent foot; it is the same thing in the Chancellor's conscience." These matters are considered further, below, paras 1–014—1–016.

a litigant from suing at common law or enforcing a judgment obtained at law was confirmed.[14] By the end of the century the common lawyers had given up the struggle. By this time it was also the established practice for lawyers rather than ecclesiastics to be appointed to the office of Lord Chancellor,[15] and, indeed, men trained in English common law and equity rather than civil law.

1–007   The principles of equity were progressively refined and developed, most notably during the course of the seventeenth and eighteenth centuries. Of fundamental significance was the development of the concept of the "trust", whereby property could be legally owned by one person, but held by that person for the benefit of another, the latter's rights being recognised and enforced by the Court of Chancery. By the nineteenth century the organisation of the Court of Chancery was totally incapable of dealing with the business, and a series of reforms increased the number of judges sharing the work of the court with the Lord Chancellor. It was also obvious that the presence of two systems with separate courts was highly inconvenient for litigants. Further reforms in the middle of the century made some of the procedural devices of the Court of Chancery (discovery of documents, injunctions) available in the common law courts, allowed those courts to consider equitable defences, and empowered the Chancery to decide questions of common law, receive oral evidence, determine issues of fact by jury trial and award damages. One aspect of the general reorganisation of the superior courts by the Supreme Court of Judicature Acts 1873 and 1875[16] was the *procedural* fusion of law and equity. Matters of both law and equity can now be determined in the course of one set of proceedings: if there is any conflict between rules of law and rules of equity, the latter are to prevail.[17] In most instances there are differences between the operation of law and equity rather than conflict. For example, different remedies may be available in respect of what both systems acknowledge to be a wrong (e.g. damages (common law) and an injunction (equity) in respect of a nuisance). Equity may impose additional obligations on a person while recognising his or her rights at common law (e.g. by accepting that a trustee is the legal owner of property while requiring him or her to hold it for the benefit of another).

4. "Law" and "Fact"

(a) Historical background

1–008   Today, English law is expounded to law students as a system of substantive rules, derived from the common law and statute, which confer rights, impose obligations, create immunities, confer legal powers and so on. This is, however, a comparatively modern way of looking at the law.[18]

The earliest methods of conducting a law suit, adopted by royal courts from the practice of local courts, involved the intervention of the Almighty. The

---

[14] See J. H. Baker, "The Common Lawyers and the Chancery: 1616" (1969) 4 Ir. Jur. (N.S.) 368.

[15] It became customary for the Chancellor to be ennobled.

[16] See below para.2–003.

[17] 1873 Act, s.25(11). See now the Supreme Court Act 1981, s.49.

[18] On the historical background see J. H. Baker, *An Introduction to English Legal History* (4th edn, 2002), Chs 4, 5; S. F. C. Milsom, *Historical Foundations of the Common Law* (2nd edn, 1981), Chs 2, 3.

claimant was required to state his claim in the appropriate form. The defendant would make a formal denial of the claim. One of them, usually the defendant, would then be required to swear on oath that his cause was just, and the oath would be tested, or put to proof. This might be done by "compurgation", whereby a fixed number of persons (eventually 12) swore oaths in his support; by "battle" where a party or a person swearing an oath in his support could be compelled to prove his veracity by successfully defending himself in a fight, it being presumed that God would aid the righteous, or by "ordeal"—

> "we find that the person who can carry red-hot iron, who can plunge his hand or his arm into boiling water, who will sink when thrown into the water, is deemed to have right on his side."[19]

By the thirteenth century all these methods were regarded with disfavour although compurgation lingered on as the method of proof in actions of debt and detinue (i.e. actions to recover money owed or property) for several centuries beyond. In such systems there was comparatively little scope for legal learning outside the forms of writs and the correct formulation of claim and defence.

These modes of proof were replaced in both civil and criminal cases by trial by jury, whereby the sheriff (a local officer appointed by the Crown) was required to bring 12 men before the court to inquire into the disputed matter and state the truth of it. At first the "jurors" might be aware of this matter themselves or might be informed before they came to court, but it came to be the rule that they should only act upon evidence given in open court, and that their verdict should be unanimous. The development of the jury caused an elaboration of legal technique in disputes as to what was the material question to be put to the jury.

In civil cases, the material question would be an issue of fact, alleged in **1–009** pleadings on behalf of the plaintiff and denied by the defendant, which would decide the case one way or another. The lawyers appearing on behalf of each party could debate with the judges in court the appropriate wording of their pleas before they were formally enrolled in the court records. Furthermore, a party was entitled to admit all the facts alleged by his or her opponent but claim that they did not give rise to a good claim: this process of "demurrer" raised an issue of law for the judges to decide. Again, it was possible for tentative demurrers to be debated in court. These debates provided the opportunity for an increasing level of sophistication in legal argument. The judges were, however, reluctant to commit themselves to formal legal exceptions to general rules. Where possible, parties were encouraged to "plead the general issue", i.e. simply to deny all the allegations put forward by the opponent. This form of plea remains the standard form of plea in a criminal trial ("not guilty") but originally it was the norm in civil trials as well. This meant that many matters that today would be reflected in detailed rules of law were left to the jury for it to do justice on the facts of the particular case. The best example was the issue of whether a defendant was liable in trespass if he or she was not at fault. For a long time it was thought that the absence of any legal rule on the point meant that liability was strict—the better view held today is that the jury was entitled to acquit the defendant if he or she was not at fault, but that was never recorded as it was not then a matter for the

---

[19] Sir William Holdsworth, *A History of English Law* (7th edn, 1956), Vol.1, p.310. The person who sunk in water was of course rescued—this was not a medieval "Catch-22" situation. See also R. Bartlett, *Trial by Fire and Water* (1986).

lawyers. By contrast "special" pleas were only permitted where there was a serious chance that the jury was likely to go wrong if the "general issue" was left to it. Much of the lawyers' debate in court would, in practice, turn on whether a special plea was permitted in the given situation rather than on the substantive question of which of the parties in that situation ought to "win".

1–010   In the sixteenth century, the judges evinced a much greater willingness to refine and determine questions of law. Pleadings became written rather than oral, and were entered before the appearance in court rather than at it. Informal, tentative discussions of pleas before formal enrolment were replaced by procedures that enabled matters of law to be raised at Westminster after the jury trial.[20] These procedures[21] enabled the lawyers to argue and the judges to determine the legal implications of facts that had already been found: there could be, for example, an objection to the opponent's plea or to the direction on the law given by the judge for the guidance of the jury. The court at Westminster could order that the plaintiff or defendant should succeed notwithstanding the jury verdict against him or her. A later development was the power to order a new trial.[22] In the same period demurrers became much more common and the judges permitted greater use to be made of the "special verdict" whereby the jury would answer specific questions of fact put to them rather than return a general verdict for one or other of the parties, and the court would enter judgment in the light of these findings. Formal errors could be corrected by a "writ of error".[23] The development of procedures such as these enabled attention to be switched from matters of form to matters of the substance of the law. The distinction between matters for the judge and matters for the jury now corresponded much more closely to the present day distinction between matters of "law" and matters of "fact".

In the nineteenth century the various procedures whereby decisions could be challenged on procedural or substantive legal grounds were replaced by appeals on points of law (and in some circumstances points of fact) to the High Court, the Court of Appeal and the House of Lords,[24] and as the decisions of these courts constitute precedents for the future,[25] it is in the course of such appeals that common law and equity can be developed.

In criminal cases, special pleading was virtually never permitted, and the general plea of "not guilty" has remained the standard form of pleading for the defendant. Questions of law concerning the indictment or the evidence could be raised informally at the trial, an indictment could be removed on a *writ of certiorari* into the Queen's Bench where the defendant could challenge it for insufficiency in form, and the trial judge could adjourn a difficult case for discussion in Serjeants' Inn or the Exchequer Chamber. This last procedure was only regularised in the nineteenth century. In 1908 it was replaced by a proper appeal to a Court of Criminal Appeal.[26] The scope for the systematic development of criminal law has thus, until comparatively recent times, been limited.

---

[20] The jury trial would normally be conducted away from Westminster: see below, para.2–004.

[21] The defendant could enter a "motion in arrest of judgment" and the plaintiff a motion *non obstante verdicto*.

[22] This was of wider significance in that the court could quash a verdict that was against the weight of evidence or where there was a misdirection on a point of law.

[23] See below, paras 2–005, 18–001.

[24] See below, paras 2–005, 2–071—2–074.

[25] See Ch.7.

[26] See further below, para.2–070.

(b) The distinction today

A distinction between matters of "law" and matters of "fact" is drawn for a **1–011** number of different purposes: one of the consequent difficulties is that it is possible for the line between "law" and "fact" to be drawn in slightly different places for each of these purposes. Three areas[27] where the distinction is of importance for the operation of the English legal system are: (1) the division of function between judge and jury; (2) the rule that only a decision on a point of law can constitute a precedent that can be cited in future cases; and (3) the question whether a particular point may be raised on an appeal limited to matters of law.

The first of these situations has declined in significance with the dramatic reduction over the last 100 years in the use of the jury in civil cases.[28] In all but a tiny proportion of cases the judge determines the facts in issue, states and applies the law and decides what remedy or remedies should be given. The discursive statement of reasons delivered by the judge may well contain a mixture of factual and legal determinations, and may be arranged for convenience of exposition rather than in clearly separated sections.[29] The components of the mixture will normally, however, be appropriately "labelled", and the precedent status and the scope of any further appeal will of course vary according to the true nature of the particular determination. The judge/jury distinction remains of significance in criminal cases where the mode of trial for the numerically small proportion of contested serious cases is still trial by jury.[30]

Rights of appeal can only be created by statute, and the grounds on which an appeal may be taken are almost invariably expressed in the statute. The commonest pattern is for a person aggrieved by the decision of a court, or, in numerous but certainly not all situations, a public authority, to be given one chance to appeal on a matter of fact but several chances to raise a matter of law.[31] Appeals from tribunals are normally limited to points of law.[32]

Some aspects of the law/fact distinction are fairly clear. An issue is one of fact where its resolution depends on the reliability or credibility of direct evidence such as a witness's testimony.[33] An issue whose resolution depends on probabilities, for example by way of inference from circumstantial evidence, is also one of fact.[34] These issues normally constitute answers to the question "what happened?". By contrast, if there is a dispute as to the existence or exact scope of a rule of the common law or a dispute over the meaning of the words of a statute, it is a dispute concerning a matter of law. This leaves one kind of issue that is difficult to classify: whether facts found fall within a common law rule or

---

[27] There are others, e.g. the effect of a misrepresentation in contract, estoppel and judicial review of administrative action under the *ultra vires* doctrine.

[28] See below, para.15–007.

[29] It is today much more common for judgments to be structured under headings (and sometimes sub-headings); all judgments are now given paragraph numbers: see below, para.7–038.

[30] See below, paras 17–089—17–103. A few factual matters are determined by the judge, e.g. those relating to admissibility of evidence and those relating to mitigation.

[31] See generally Ch.18.

[32] See below, para.18–043.

[33] These are sometimes termed "primary facts". Such facts may be admitted, or "judicial" notice of them may be taken (i.e. the facts are of general knowledge or can easily be ascertained from standard reference works).

[34] These are sometimes termed "secondary facts". An example would be inferring the speed of a vehicle from tyre marks left on the road.

statutory description. This kind of question, one of "application",[35] has been variously characterised as "law", "fact", "mixed law and fact", "fact and degree", "degree" or *sui generis*. As a matter of theory it is difficult to resist the conclusion that this is really a question of law.[36] However, there have been many cases in which it has not been so categorised.

1–012   A number of arguments have been advanced to support the classification of a question of application as one of fact.

(1) The matter can as well be determined by a layman as by a trained lawyer.[37]

(2) The words to be applied are "ordinary words of the English language". This argument was used by the House of Lords in *Cozens v Brutus*.[38] Here, the application of "insulting" in s.5 of the Public Order Act 1936, which made it an offence to use threatening, abusive or insulting words or behaviour where that was conducive to a breach of the peace, was held to be a matter of fact for the magistrates. Lord Reid stressed the undesirability of courts providing definitions of "ordinary" statutory words, whether from dictionaries or otherwise:

> "we have been warned time and again not to substitute other words for the words of a statute. And there is very good reason for that. Few words have exact synonyms. The overtones are almost always different."[39]

Similarly, it has been held that whether an appropriation is "dishonest" for the purpose of the law of theft is, within certain limits, a question of fact for the jury.[40]

(3) The rule in question sets a standard, such as one of "reasonableness".[41] The best example here is whether a defendant's conduct has been "unreasonable" and accordingly in breach of a duty to take care imposed by the law of negligence. This is clearly regarded as a question of fact.[42]

---

[35] The term used by E. Mureinik, "The Application of Rules: Law or Fact?" (1982) 98 L.Q.R. 587.

[36] *ibid. Cf.* G. J. Pitt, "Law, Fact and Casual Workers" (1985) 101 L.Q.R. 217.

[37] Denning L.J. in *British Launderers' Association v Borough of Hendon* [1949] 1 K.B. 462.

[38] [1973] A.C. 854. Followed in *R v Kirk* [2006] EWCA Crim 725 (whether words, marks or designs on a postal packet were of an "indecent or obscene" character).

[39] [1973] A.C. 854 at 861. The mere fact that a word is an "ordinary English word" does not, however, prevent a judge assisting a jury with its meaning, and a dictionary definition is likely to be a sensible starting point: *R v Da Silva* [2006] 4 All E.R. 900, *per* Longmore L.J. at paras [12]–[13] (meaning of "suspicion").

[40] *R v Feely* [1973] Q.B. 530; *R v Ghosh* [1982] Q.B. 1053. See below, para.17–078. In contrast, it has been held that whether an article is an "article which has a blade" is a question of law and not the interpretation of an ordinary English word: *R v Davis (Reginald)* [1998] Crim. L.R. 564 (CA (CrD)), *cf. R v Paul (Benjamin Michael Frederick), The Times*, September 17, 1998 (trial judge to determine meaning of "humane killer" in firearms certificate; for jury to apply that definition to the facts); *R v Criminal Injuries Compensation Board, Ex p. M (a minor)* [2000] R.T.R. 21 ("ordinarily the true meaning of a public policy or scheme is for the court to decide").

[41] This is described by Glanville Williams as raising a question of "evaluative fact": [1976] Crim. L.R. 472.

[42] See *Qualcast (Wolverhampton) Ltd v Haynes* [1959] A.C. 743, below, para.7–002.

(4) The question is one of "degree". In *Edwards v Bairstow*[43] the question was whether a particular transaction was an "adventure in the nature of trade". If it was, the profit was subject to tax. Lord Radcliffe stated that this matter was one "in which the facts warrant a determination either way" and "in which it could not be said to be wrong to arrive at a conclusion either way".[44] It was a question of degree and therefore a question of fact.[45] In this situation it is held that Parliament intends the decision-maker to resolve difficulties of application, subject to control by the courts if the decision is irrational.[46]

Running through all these points is the wish to avoid the multiplication of **1–013** decisions that can be cited as a precedent, and an increase in the number of decisions that can be taken further on appeal.[47]

The view that some questions of application are to be classified as ones of fact is a classic illustration of the competing requirements of principle and pragmatism. On the one hand it is, for example, difficult to see that there is any clear distinction between matters requiring the attention of a "trained lawyer" and those that do not, or between English words that are "ordinary" and those that are not. The "ordinary English word" argument in particular has occasioned much academic criticism[48] and in practice has been ignored more often than applied.[49] On the other hand it is equally possible to appreciate the dangers of excessive complexity. It would, for example, cause chaos, even (or, indeed especially) in an age of computerised legal databases, if every decision on whether a defendant had behaved "unreasonably" for the purposes of the law of negligence could potentially be cited as an authority.

The essentially pragmatic nature of the distinction between application questions held to be questions of law and those held to be questions of fact was candidly recognised by Lord Hoffmann in *Moyna v Secretary of State for Work and Pensions*.[50] The issue here was whether a social security claimant could "prepare a cooked meal for himself"; an inability to do so gave rise to a benefit claim. Lord Hoffmann stated that Lord Reid in *Cozens v Brutus*[51] was making two "very pertinent" points. First, he was distinguishing between: (1) the meaning of a word, which depends on conventions known to the ordinary speaker of English or ascertainable from a dictionary; and (2) the meaning the author of the utterance appears to have intended to convey. The former is not a

---

[43] [1956] A.C. 14.

[44] *ibid.* at 33.

[45] For further examples, see *Ransom v Higgs* [1974] 1 W.L.R. 1594 at 1618 (meaning of "trade" in a taxing statute); *IRC v Scottish and Newcastle Breweries* [1982] 1 W.L.R. 322 at 327 (meaning of "plant" in a taxing statute); *Clark v Perks* [2001] S.T.C. 1254 (meaning of "ship", also said to be "as ordinary an English word as one could imagine" (*per* Carnwath J. at para.[25])).

[46] *Edwards v Bairstow*, above; *R v Monopolies and Mergers Commission, Ex p. South Yorkshire Transport* [1993] 1 W.L.R. 23 at 32, *per* Lord Mustill; *R v Criminal Injuries Compensation Board, Ex p. M (a minor)* [2000] R.T.R. 21.

[47] See, e.g. the statements in *Qualcast (Wolverhampton) Ltd v Haynes*, below, para.7–002, n.12.

[48] See Glanville Williams, *Textbook of Criminal Law* (2nd edn, 1983), pp.59–67 and [1976] Crim. L.R. 472 at 532; D. Ormerod, *Smith and Hogan, Criminal Law* (11th edn, 2005) pp.646, 696–702. These authors point out that many apparently ordinary words have been the subject of judicial definition for the guidance of juries.

[49] See D. W. Elliott, "Brutus v Cozens: Decline and Fall" [1989] Crim. L.R. 323.

[50] [2003 UKHL 44, [2003] 1 W.L.R. 1929, paras [20]–[28]. See also *R v Evans* [2005] 1 Cr. App. Rep. 546.

[51] Above.

question of law because it has no legal significance; it is the latter, the meaning to be ascribed to the intention of the notional legislator in using that word, which is a statement of law. Lord Reid's second point was that the application of the word "insulting" to the facts found was itself a question of fact. There was indeed high authority[52] for saying that the question whether the facts fall one side of or the other of some conceptual line is a question of fact:

> "what this means in practice is that an appellate court with jurisdiction to entertain appeals only on questions of law will not hear an appeal against such a decision unless it falls outside the bounds of reasonable judgment."[53]

In reality:

> "there are two kinds of questions of fact: there are questions of fact; and there are questions of law as to which lawyers have decided that it would be inexpedient for an appellate tribunal to have to form an independent judgment. But the usage is well established and causes no difficulty as long as it is understood that the degree to which an appellate court will be willing to substitute its own judgment for that of the tribunal will vary with the nature of the question . . . ."[54]

Accordingly, none of the arguments identified in the previous paragraph provide a determinate test; the question is better treated expressly as one of determining in all the circumstances what is the appropriate role for the appellate court.

Finally, there are two factors which further blur the distinction between law and fact. First, there may sometimes be a tendency for an appellate court, if it is satisfied that the decision on a point is wrong, to classify the point as one of law precisely to enable it to intervene. Secondly, if a decision on an undoubted question of fact is unsupported by any evidence, or is a decision which no reasonable person could have reached or is irrational or beyond the bounds of reasonable judgment, it is regarded as erroneous in point of law.[55] This convenient fiction enables an appellate court to retain control over factual determinations that are palpably wrong.

5. "Rules" and "Discretion"

1–014   As has already been touched upon, it is inherent in any decision-making process that is required to handle more than a small number of cases (1) that consistency and certainty are likely to be regarded as important objectives (albeit not the only ones) but (2) that their achievement is likely to be at the expense of an individualised consideration of and reaction to the merits of each case. This is as true of the handling of cases by courts and tribunals as it is of programmes established by government for the administration of, for example, state welfare benefits. In each of these situations it can loosely be said that the basic rules are made by

---

[52] Lord Hoffmann cited *Edwards v Bairstow* and *O'Kelly v Trusthouse Forte Plc* [1984] Q.B. 90.

[53] Para.[25].

[54] Para.[27].

[55] See below, para.18–043; *Edwards v Bairstow* and *Moyna*, above.

Parliament (statute) or under the authority of Parliament (delegated legislation) or by certain senior judges (common law), and then put into effect by others (judges, magistrates, tribunal members, administrators in government offices and so on).[56]

It will be difficult, and usually impossible, for the "rulemaker" to draft a set of rules that covers all the possible cases that may arise, and indicate with precision the outcome desired in each of them. The consequence will be that a measure of "discretion" will be conferred on the "implementer"; the word "discretion" being used here to mean an ability to choose among alternative courses of action or inaction. The inevitable imprecisions of language will be such that the persons charged with the task of implementation will have to interpret some of the words used and decide whether the words apply to the circumstances before them. Indeed, a measure of flexibility or uncertainty may be created deliberately to enable the rules to be applied to situations not anticipated by the rulemaker. This can be done by the use of words of general rather than particular meaning, or by the incorporation in the rules of a standard such as "reasonable", "fair" or "just". The element of choice that may be present here is limited.[57] The rulemaker may go further and *expressly* confer a discretion upon the implementer. This express discretion may to a greater or lesser extent be hedged around by restrictions or limits set by the rulemaker. It must be emphasised that it is not possible to draw a clear line between rule-based and discretion-based decision-making processes: the implementation of rules tends to involve the exercise of a measure of discretion, and discretions tend to be hedged around by rules. All that can be said is that the element of discretion may be weaker or stronger as the case may be.

These points may be illustrated by some examples, both real and hypothetical. **1–015** Parliament, at the instigation of the government, has enacted that a person who is injured in an "accident arising out of and in the course of his employment" is entitled to certain welfare benefits.[58] This phrase, which first appeared in the Workmen's Compensation Act 1897, has to be applied by the DWP officer who decides in the first instance whether a particular claim for benefit is made out. The issue then may be taken on appeal to a Appeals Service appeal tribunal, then to a Social Security Commissioner and then to the courts.[59] The application of the phrase has indeed given rise to a vast number of cases.[60] It would clearly be absurd to expect any person to construct a set of rules which would cover in advance all the possible circumstances that might arise where there could be doubts as to the applicability of the phrase: even assuming a perfect set of rules *could* be constructed, it would be equally absurd to expect mere mortals to find their way around them, as the rules would be of great complexity. Moreover, an attempt to spell out in detail what would count as an "accident" and the "course of employment" might prevent the extension of the right to benefit to persons injured in novel ways or when employed in novel kinds of employment, where

---

[56] The two groups overlap in the person of a High Court judge who can propound a rule of the common law and apply it in successive breaths.

[57] It is also less usual, although not incorrect, to use the term "discretion" here than in the situations about to be described.

[58] See Social Security Contributions and Benefits Act 1992, s.94. The range of benefits specially linked to this concept was reduced by the Social Security and Housing Benefits Act 1982 and subsequent legislation.

[59] See below, paras 2–037, 2–038.

[60] See N. J. Wikeley, *Wikeley, Ogus and Barendt's The Law of Social Security* (5th edn, 2002), pp.729–737.

the extension would have been desired by the rulemaker. Accordingly, a certain measure of judgment has to be exercised by those determining the applicability of the statutory phrase, and in the sense that their task is not simple and mechanical they can be said to exercise a discretion.

It would, however, have been possible for an Act of Parliament to have provided that a sum of money should be allocated to a board, and that the board could "pay such sum as it thinks fit to any person who in the opinion of the board has suffered an accident at work". This would have entailed the delegation of a considerably greater measure of discretion than is inherent in the present statutory scheme. Moreover, the wording of the board's powers could have been varied so as to increase or decrease the area of choice open to it. The area of choice could be increased by, for example, deleting the words "at work". Conversely, it could be decreased by, for example, replacing "may" by "shall", by setting a limit to the sum payable in any one case, by deleting the words "in the opinion of the board" or by listing a number of factors that the board would be required to take into account. The wider the area of choice, the better able the board would be to reach the "right" or "most appropriate" decision in each individual case (according to its own concept of "rightness" or "propriety"). On the other hand, its greater freedom of action would enable it more easily to diverge from the rulemaker's conception of justice. Even if the board were comparatively free of fetters imposed by the rulemaker it might still have wished to develop policies for its own guidance to ensure a reasonable measure of flexibility.

1–016   A good example of a discretion-based decision making process concerned the "exceptional circumstances additions" and the "exceptional needs payments" which were formerly part of the supplementary benefits scheme. These provided, respectively, for an increase in the weekly payment, or a lump sum, in "exceptional cases" at the discretion of the Supplementary Benefits Commission. In practice, the Commission produced detailed codes for the guidance of the local officials who determined the claims on a day-to-day basis, although the codes were not published.[61] These arrangements contrasted with the rule-based system of national insurance, including those for industrial injuries. Following what was the classic "rules" v. "discretion" debate, these discretions were replaced by a rule-based structure,[62] although subsequently the introduction of the Social Fund has seen in part a return to a discretion-based approach.[63]

Accordingly, among the advantages[64] of predetermined rules over discretions are that like cases will be treated alike (consistency), that persons will not in effect be punished by rules applied *ex post facto* (predictability), that the rule maker is more likely than a person exercising a discretion to be accountable to an electorate, that the implementer will have a more limited scope to deviate

---

[61] See generally, J. A. Farmer, *Tribunals and Government* (1974), pp.89–99; M. Adler and A. Bradley, *Justice, Discretion and Poverty* (1975).

[62] See N. J. Wikeley, *et al*, *Ogus, Barendt and Wikeley's The Law of Social Security* (4th edn, 1994), pp.594–595. For a spirited defence of discretion see R. Titmuss, "Welfare 'Rights', Law and Discretion" (1971) 42 *The Political Quarterly* 113; answered by R. White in P. Morris *et al.*, *Social Needs and Legal Action* (1973), pp.23–32; *cf.* M. Adler and S. Asquith (eds), *Discretion and Welfare* (1981), especially Chs 1, 7, 11.

[63] See below, para.2–040.

[64] See generally J. Jowell, "The Legal Control of Administrative Discretion" [1973] P.L. 178, 184–194; the pioneering work in the field is K. C. Davis, *Discretionary Justice, A Preliminary Inquiry* (1969) and see P. P. Craig, *Administrative Law* (5th edn, 2003), pp.536–540 and R. Baldwin, *Rules and Government* (1995), Chs 1–3.

from the rulemaker's objective by arbitrary decision-making, that such divergent decisions can more easily be challenged, that the rules will normally be open to public criticism and that decision-making processes can more easily be planned and routinised. Conversely, rules can be inflexible, and can "permit unreasoned official behaviour".[65]

The "rules" v. "discretion" issue crops up at a number of points in the English legal system. The original development of equity was a discretionary case-by-case response to the generality or inadequacy of common law rules or procedures.[66] The subsequent development of rules of equity was a response to the arbitrariness of a system which could vary as the length of the Chancellor's foot.[67] The issue also arises in debates as to the extent to which courts and tribunals should be bound by precedent,[68] the comparative merits of different styles of statutory drafting,[69] whether it is proper for a jury to acquit a defendant who would by a strict application of the rules of criminal law be liable to be convicted, and the extent to which the discretion of a criminal court as to sentence should be limited or "structured" by the provision of guidelines.[70] As the widest discretionary powers are allocated to administrative bodies such as ministers, officials and local authorities, the extent to which the courts should control or review exercises or non-exercises of power is an important feature of administrative law[71]; however, analogous principles apply to the control by appellate courts of exercises of discretion by judges.[72] The "rules" v. "discretion" issue does not admit of easy or general solutions: the appropriate balance has to be sought depending upon the precise context in which the issue arises.

6. The Rule of Law

Frequent references are found in both legal and political writing to the importance of the "the rule of law". Much is made of the proposition that the UK (or whichever country is under consideration) is organised and behaves in such a way as is consistent with or promotes respect for the rule of law. There is a very considerable literature on this concept, but no settled agreement on its exact content.[73] One fundamental difficulty is whether the rule of law is observed within any legal system in which the state and state officials act within the legal powers conferred by that legal system, whatever the substantive content of those legal powers, or whether the concept requires more than that. In particular, there are arguments that the laws of a state that purports to observe the "rule of law" should comply with substantive moral or political standards, such as respect for fundamental human rights and democracy. Of those that regard the concept as

---

[65] [1973] P.L. 178 at p.193.
[66] See above, paras 1–005—1–007.
[67] See above, para.1–006.
[68] See below, paras 7–001—7–009.
[69] See below, para.5–008.
[70] See below, para.17–086.
[71] See below, para.18–050.
[72] See below, para.18–035.
[73] See, e.g. J. Jowell, "The Rule of Law Today", in J. Jowell and D. Oliver, *The Changing Constitution* (5th edn, 2004), Ch.1; T. R. S. Allan, *Constitutional Justice: A Liberal Theory of the Rule of Law* (2001); P. P. Craig [1997] P.L. 447.

valuable,[74] the majority seem to prefer the latter to the former, without there being any consensus to what the substantive standards should be. All would agree that the concept is or at least includes the former.

The scope of the concept has assumed greater significance with the enactment of the Constitutional Reform Act 2005, which transferred the role of head of the judiciary from the Lord Chancellor to the Lord Chief Justice and provided for the establishment of a new Supreme Court in place of the House of Lords. Section 1 provides that:

> "This Act does not adversely affect—
>
> (a) the existing constitutional principle of the rule of law, or
> (b) the Lord Chancellor's existing constitutional role in relation to that principle."

The Lord Chancellor's oath includes a promise to "respect the rule of law."[75] It is understandable that no attempt was made to provide a definition. However, there are obvious interpretative difficulties: what is the *existing* principle? what is meant by the reference to it as a *constitutional* principle? which formulation of the rule of law is contemplated? Lord Falconer (Secretary of State for Constitutional Affairs and Lord Chancellor) seemed to accept that the functions of the Lord Chancellor:

> "include dealing with other Cabinet Ministers who put forward proposals that in his view offend against the rule of law."[76]

Whether this extended to "proposals" for legislation was not clear; if it did, then it recognises that the content of legislature proposals can properly be tested against some external standards.[77] What nevertheless was clear was that there was no suggestion that the rule of law could operate as "a special rule with a higher status than that of the law itself" against which the *validity* of legislation could be tested.[78] The Lord Chancellor's duty with respect to the rule of law "was a political one . . . not a duty to be enforced in the courts".[79]

In an important lecture,[80] Lord Bingham suggested that the core of the principle was:

> "that all persons and authorities within the state, whether public or private, should be bound by and entitled to the benefit of laws publicly and prospectively promulgated and publicly administered in the courts."

---

[74] Not all do. Lord Bingham in the lecture to which reference is made below cites a comment by Judith Shklar: "It may well have become just another one of those self-congratulatory rhetorical devices that grace the public utterances of Anglo-American politicians. No intellectual effort need therefore to be wasted on this bit of ruling-class chatter."

[75] s.17, inserting s.6A in the Promissory Oaths Act 1868.

[76] H.L. Deb. 7 December 2004, col.747, in debates on the Constitutional Reform Bill.

[77] The Attorney General, Lord Goldsmith, endorsed the broader view in his lecture "Government and the Rule of Law in the Modern Age" February 22, 2006, LSE: "the rule of law comprehends some statement of values which are universal and ought to be respected as the basis of a free society."

[78] *ibid.* col.739. By referring to the "existing" principle of the rule of law: col.740. See also col.748.

[79] *ibid.* col.740. Opposition spokesmen agreed that the duty (then drafted as a "duty (not cognisable in law)" to respect the existing principle in the exercise of his functions: Lord Kingsland at col. 742 and Lord Goodhart at col.743. But see below.

[80] "The Rule of Law:" the Sixth Sir David Williams Lecture, November 16, 2006, Cambridge.

This could be broken down into eight sub-rules, all of which relate to issues covered in this book. They are as follows.

First, "the law must be accessible and so far as possible intelligible, clear and predictable". This raises issues as to the volume, drafting and publication of legislation.[81] Secondly, "questions of legal right and liability should ordinarily be resolved by application of the law and not the exercise of discretion". Where there is discretion, "this should ordinarily be narrowly defined and its exercise capable of reasoned justification".[82] Thirdly, "the law of the land should apply equally to all, save to the extent that objective differences justify differentiation".[83] Thus legislation "directed to those with red hair (to adapt Warrington L.J.'s long-lived example)"[84] would be regarded as incompatible with the rule of law. Fourthly, "the law must afford adequate protection of fundamental human rights", or at least "such human rights as, within that society, are seen as fundamental".[85] Fifthly, "means must be provided for resolving, without prohibitive cost or inordinate delay, bona fide civil disputes which the parties themselves are unable to resolve". They include the right of access to the court,[86] and reaches the current difficulties over the provision of publicly funded legal services and the government's policy that the costs of the civil courts, apart from judicial salaries, should be covered by fees from litigants.[87] Sixthly, "ministers and public officers at all levels must exercise the powers conferred on them reasonably, in good faith, for the purpose for which the powers were conferred and without exceeding the limits of such powers". This reflects the "familiar grounds of judicial review".[88] Seventhly, "adjudicative procedures provided by the state should be fair", encompassing requirements of independent and impartial and fair decision-making.[89] Eighthly, "the existing principle of the rule of law requires compliance by the state with its obligations in international law, the law which whether deriving from treaty or international custom and practice governs the conduct of nations".[90]

It is submitted, with respect, that this provides a compelling framework that is likely to command general support, although there will always be room for debate about the details. It is also interesting to note that Lord Bingham[91] did not accept the views expressed in debate in the House of Lords that the Lord Chancellor's conduct in relation to the rule of law was non-justiciable: it "would

---

[81] See Ch.5. Lord Bingham singled out for mention "the torrent of criminal legislation in recent years" which "has posed very real problems of assimilation. Not all of this legislation is readily intelligible".

[82] See the discussion of rules v discretion above, paras 1–014—1–016; and of judicial review, para.18–050. There is of course room for continuing debate in particular contexts as to how the balance should be drawn.

[83] This principle is reflected in European Union Law, the law of the ECHR and domestic judicial review: paras 6–063, 8–026, 18–050. Note in particular *A v Secretary of State for the Home Department* [2004] UKHL 56, [2005] 2 A.C. 68.

[84] *Short v Poole Corporation* [1926] Ch. 66, 91.

[85] See Ch.8 on the Human Rights Act 1998 and the principle of legality, para.6–043.

[86] *cf.* Art.6(1), ECHR, para.8–021.

[87] See paras 5–031, 11–002, 11–009, 11–015.

[88] At to which see Ch.18.

[89] See Art.6, ECHR (para.8–021) and the judicial review requirements of procedural fairness (para.18–051).

[90] Reflected e.g. in principles of statutory interpretation: paras 6–036, 6–051.

[91] Transcript, p.4, n.11: "A constitutional principle that cannot be legally enforced would not appear to me to be very valuable."

no doubt be susceptible, in principle, to judicial review". It must though be remembered that the Lord Chancellor's duty does not arise from the 2005 Act but from the pre-existing principle. Apart from possible proceedings against the Lord Chancellor, the principles summarised by Lord Bingham will have particular resonance in the principle that clear words will be needed for the courts to conclude that Parliament intended to legislate in breach of the rule of law.[92]

Finally, it is also right to note the view of Lord Goldsmith, then the Attorney General, that the executive, legislative and judiciary have a shared responsibility for upholding the rule of law; and that that includes the role of the Attorney-General and Treasury Solicitor in giving legal advice to government.[93]

C. THE BASIC INSTITUTIONS OF THE ENGLISH LEGAL SYSTEM

1–017   A number of institutions are of central importance to the creation of law. Statute law is enacted by Parliament; a vast quantity of delegated legislation is made under powers conferred by Act of Parliament.[94] Both processes are heavily dominated by the government of the day; indeed, most of the delegated powers are exerciseable by government departments.[95] Legislative authority has also been accorded to institutions of the European Union: in particular the Council of Ministers and the European Parliament.[96] Decisions of the superior courts may also constitute sources of law.[97]

The administration of the legal system, in the sense of the mechanisms for the provision of legal services, the courts and tribunals established for the resolution of legal disputes and the processes for effecting law reform, is almost entirely a matter for central government. In many countries, responsibility for legal affairs is exercised by a "Minister of Justice".[98] However, in the United Kingdom, responsibility for different aspects of the legal system has been divided among separate ministries or departments of state, the main ones being the Department for Constitutional Affairs (formerly the Lord Chancellor's Department), the Home Office, the Law Officers' Departments and the Treasury.[99] In 2007, the step was taken of establishing a Ministry of Justice in the UK.[100]

---

[92] The "principle of legality": para.6–043.

[93] "Government and the Rule of Law in the Modern Age", February 22, 2006, LSE, Transcript, p.11.

[94] See Chs 5 and 6.

[95] A detailed consideration of Parliament and government may be found in such works as S. A. de Smith and R. Brazier, *Constitutional and Administrative Law* (8th edn, 1998).

[96] See below, para.5–042.

[97] See Chs 2, 7.

[98] For debate in the last century on the establishment of such arrangements for the UK, see the fourth edition of this book at para.1–033.

[99] For a general survey, see R. Brazier, "Government and the Law: Ministerial Responsibility for Legal Affairs" [1989] P.L. 64 and *Ministers of the Crown* (1997). See also G. Zellick (edn), *Law Reform and the Law Commission* (1988), App.7.

[100] See para.1–018.

1. The Lord Chancellor's Department; the Department of Constitutional Affairs; the Ministry of Justice[101]

As is mentioned elsewhere,[102] the Lord Chancellor formerly exercised a wide **1–018** range of disparate functions, including those of judge, Speaker of the House of Lords, cabinet minister and government legal adviser. He also had extensive responsibilities concerning the administration of justice, including making or advising on judicial appointments.[103] He was responsible for the Court Service, which provided administrative support for the Court of Appeal, High Court, Crown Court and county courts,[104] and supervised the schemes for the public funding and provision of legal services.[105] Responsibility for overseeing the operations of magistrates' courts was transferred to the Lord Chancellor's Department (LCD) in 1992.[106] He was also generally responsible for law reform in civil matters, although other government departments have had their own specialised areas of concern. For example, company law and employment law are within the province of the Department of Trade and Industry. In 2001, lead responsibility for human rights issues was transferred to him; and responsibility for data protection and freedom of information has also been conferred upon him. Accordingly, from the Second World War onwards, the LCD grew from a small office of personal assistants and advisers to the Lord Chancellor into a very substantial government department.

The first steps in what proved to be a complex reform were taken in the government reshuffle of June 12, 2003, in which Lord Irvine of Lairg was replaced by Lord Falconer of Thoroton, previously a minister at the Home Office. Lord Falconer was additionally appointed to the new office of Secretary of State for Constitutional Affairs, and the department became the Department for Constitutional Affairs (DCA).[107] This was intended to lead to the abolition altogether of the Office of Lord Chancellor. It was at once announced that Lord Falconer would no longer sit as a judge. There had been no previous indication that such a step was contemplated. Detailed consultation on how these changes would be affected then followed, culminating in the Constitutional Reform Act 2005. In the event, the title "Lord Chancellor" was retained, but statutory responsibilities were rearranged to enable the holder (also Secretary of State) to focus on leadership of the DCA. The main objectives of the DCA are now to: "provide effective and accessible justice for all; ensure people's rights and responsibilities; and enhance democratic freedoms by modernising the law and the constitution".[108] The department's responsibilities are set out as follows:

[101] See P. Polden, *Guide to the Records of the Lord Chancellor's Department* (HMSO, 1988), which covers the development of the department from about 1870 (systematic record keeping started in 1889) to November 1951 and D. Woodhouse, *The Office of Lord Chancellor* (2001). See also R. B. Stevens, "A View from the Lord Chancellor's Office" (1987) 40 C.L.P. 181, "The Independence of the Judiciary: The View from the Lord Chancellor's Office" (1988) 8 O.J.L.S. 222 and *The Independence of the Judiciary* (1993); Sir D. Oulton, *Counsel*, Michaelmas 1986, p.3; Lord Mackay of Clashfern, (1991) 44 C.L.P. 241.

[102] See below, para.4–025.

[103] See below, para.4–028.

[104] See below, paras 2–053, 2–066.

[105] See below Chs 10, 11. The Lord Chancellor was responsible for civil legal aid from its introduction, and responsibility for criminal legal aid was transferred from the Home Secretary in July 1980.

[106] See (1992) *The Magistrate* 74.

[107] Officially abbreviated to DCA; sometimes referred to less than respectfully as "Dcaff".

[108] *www.dca.gov.uk/dept/overview.htm.*

"Justice: We focus on driving up performance in the justice system—
across the criminal, civil and family courts, and in the other administrative
courts and tribunals including those dealing with asylum appeals. Our
responsibilites include: Her Majesty's Courts Service[109]; major improvements in the efficiency and performance of the courts; improving the
enforcement of criminal penalties; provision of an efficient asylum appeals
process.

Rights: We focus on supporting the disadvantaged and delivery for the
public. This includes reforming legal aid and legal services,[110] and tackling
the compensation culture. Our responsibilities include: the law and policy
on human rights; information rights—including freedom of information and
data protection; gender recognition.

Democracy: Our priority is to improve engagement between the citizen
and the state. Our responsibilities include: Electoral reform and
administration."

The DCA has retained a number of further responsibilities, for example for the
Land Registry,[111] the National Archives,[112] the Public Guardianship Office,[113]
and coroners, burials and cremations.[114] It has joint responsibility with the Home
Office and the Law Officers' Department for the National Criminal Justice
Board.[115] Under the arrangements for devolution, the Scotland and Wales offices
are under the DCA umbrella, although also remaining distinct entities in their
own right.[116]

Since 1992 the Department has had a junior minister in the House of Commons,[117] ending the unsatisfactory arrangement whereby the Attorney-General,
although not a member of the Department, acted as spokesman for the Lord
Chancellor. The administrative functions of the Department in relation to courts
and tribunals are now subject to review by the Parliamentary Commissioner

---

[109] See para.1–019. The Court Service became an executive agency in 1995. It became HM Courts
Service when it took over from magistrates' courts committees direct responsibility for managing
the magistrates' courts. The DCA also has responsibility for the new Tribunals Service: see
para.2–014.

[110] See below, Chs 10 and 11.

[111] Responsible for the compulsory registration of titles to land under the Land Registration Act
2002, and the maintenance of a register of land charges under the Land Charges Act 1972. It
became an executive agency in 1990 and achieved Trading Fund Status in 1993.

[112] An executive agency bringing together the Public Record Office; the Historical Manuscripts
Commission, and from October 2006 the Office of Public Sector Information and Her Majesty's
Stationery Office. See www.nationalarchives.gov.uk.

[113] See www.guardianship.gov.uk. The PGO is the administrative arm of the Court of Protection and
provides services which promote the financial and social wellbeing of people with mental
incapacity.

[114] Transferred from the Home Office in June 2005.

[115] See para.1–025.

[116] See www.scotlandoffice.gov.uk; www.ossw.wales.gov.uk. In January 2007, the Secretary of State
for Northern Ireland (Peter Hain MP) was also Secretary of State for Wales. The Secretary of
State for Transport (Douglas Alexander MP) was also Secretary of State for Scotland.

[117] See G. Drewry (1992) 142 N.L.J. 50; J. Rozenberg, The Search for Justice (1994), p.12. The first
holder of the position was John M. Taylor MP, a solicitor. In early 2007 there was one Minister
of State (Harriet Harman Q.C. MP, previously Secretary of State for Social Security and Solicitor-
General), and three Parliamentary Under-Secretaries of State (Baroness Ashton, Bridget Prentice
MP and Vera Baird Q.C.).

for Administration,[118] and the Department's policy, administration and expenditure fall within the remit of the Select Committee on Constitutional Affairs.[119]

In 2007, a Ministry of Justice was established, with effect from May 9, taking over the responsibilities of the DCA, and (from the Home office) lead responsibility for criminal justice and sentencing policy.

It is headed by the Lord Chancellor and Secretary of State for Justice, from June 28, 2007, Jack Straw M.P.

HM Courts Service

An important feature of the Beeching Report and the Courts Act 1971[120] was the establishment of a "unified court service" under the direction of the Lord Chancellor, providing administrative support to the Supreme Court,[121] including the Crown Court and county courts.[122] It was organised on a circuit basis. From 1995 it was an executive agency of the LCD. From April 1, 2005, it has been replaced by HM Courts Service (HMCS), with responsibility extended to include the administration of magistrates' courts. The Lord Chancellor has power to appoint court officers and staff and to provide accommodation for the purposes of discharging his general duty.[123] He also may enter contracts for the provision of officers, staff or services by others; however, this may not be done for the discharge of functions which involve making judicial decisions or exercising any judicial discretion, and in the case of administrative functions, only if authorised by an order made by the Lord Chancellor after consulting the Lord Chief Justice, the Master of the Rolls and the Heads of Division. HMCS is organised structured around 42 areas, matching the existing criminal justice system areas, grouped in seven regions (this seems now preferred as a term to "circuits"). There are Area and Regional Directors and overall there are over 20,000 staff. HMCS's purpose is:

1–019

> "to manage the courts' administration in England and Wales in a reformed, improved justice system that focuses on the public."[124]

Its vision is for:

> "an organisation that supports the work of independent judges and magistrates through an empowered local service, focused on local needs and priorities within a national framework, with strong leadership at national and local level . . ."[125]

---

[118] Courts and Legal Services Act 1990, s.110, providing that such functions are to be taken as the Department's functions, although there is an exception where action is taken at the direction or on the authority of a judicial officer.

[119] The LCD first came under the jurisdiction of the Home Affairs Committee in 1991, this development, having previously been resisted by the government on the unconvincing ground that such scrutiny might threaten the independence of the judiciary: see G. Drewry (1983) 133 N.L.J. 959–960. A separate Committee on the Lord Chancellor's Department was established in January 2003, and this became the current Committee from September 11, 2003.

[120] See para.2–052.

[121] But not the House of Lords. It also supported the Probate Service.

[122] Courts Act 1971, ss.27, 28.

[123] Courts Act 2003, ss.2, 3, replacing the Courts Act 1971, ss.27 and 28. For the general duty, see para.1–033.

[124] HMCS Framework Document (DCA, April 1, 2005), p.8 (see *www.hmcourts-service.gov.uk*).

[125] *ibid.* There is also an HMCS Business Strategy, an annual HMCS National Business Plan and annual business plan for each Area and for national groups (Family; High Court; Probate Service; Criminal Appeal Office and Administrative Court Office; Civil Appeals Office). Each plan contains a large number of detailed targets.

A "non-executive contribution" to the development of each area's strategy is to be made by a Courts Board. Areas are specified by an order made by the Lord Chancellor.[126] Members are also appointed by the Lord Chancellor (members who are judges after consultation with the Lord Chief Justice). Each Board must have at least one judge; two justices assigned to a local justice area in the Board's area; at least two other members who have appropriate knowledge or experience of the work of the courts for the area; at least two other members who are representative of people living in that area, and such other members in those categories as the Lord Chancellor thinks appropriate.[127] Provision is made by regulations for the appointment of members, the selection of a chairman and procedural matters.[128] Each Board must, in accordance with guidance issued by the Lord Chancellor after consulting the Lord Chief Justice,[129] scrutinise, review and make recommendations about the way in which the Lord Chancellor is discharging his general duty in relation to the court with which the board is concerned,[130] and consider draft and final business plans in relation to those courts.[131] A framework is established for interactions between HMCS and the judiciary,[132] and much emphasis on partnership working with the judiciary and with other agencies in the justice system. The systems that support the courts, and CAFCASS, are subject to inspection by HM Inspectorate of Court Administration.[133]

2. THE HOME OFFICE

1–020   The Home Office:

> "is the government department responsible for ensuring we live in a safe, just and tolerant society by putting public protection at the heart of all we do. We are responsible for the police service and the justice system in England and Wales, national security and immigration."[134]

These include functions that in other jurisdictions are divided between a Minister of Justice and a Minister of the Interior, the Home Office being unusual in combining responsibility for both policing and criminal justice. The website's claim of responsibility for the "justice system" (by which they actually mean the criminal justice system) is overstated given the role and responsibilities of the DCA, and indeed tensions between the Home Office and the LCD are said to have formed part of the background to the 2003 government reshuffle.[135] Following the dismissal of Charles Clarke as Home Secretary in May 2006 and his

---

[126] Courts Act 2003, s.4, Sch.1; Courts Boards Areas Order 2004 (SI 2004/1192), as amended by SI 2004/1303. These are the same as police areas set out in Sch.1 to the Police Act 1996.
[127] 2003 Act, Sch.1.
[128] Courts Board (Appointments and Procedure) Regulations 2004 (SI 2004/1193).
[129] *Courts Boards Guidance* (Cm. 6461, 2005).
[130] i.e. the Crown Court, county courts and magistrates' courts.
[131] 2003 Act, s.5.
[132] See para.1–033.
[133] Courts Act 2003, ss.58–61; *www.hmica.gov.uk*. This replaced HM Magistrates' Courts Service Inspectorate.
[134] *www.homeoffice.gov.uk*.
[135] See *Current Law Statutes Annotated 2005* Notes to the Constitutional Reform Act 2005 by A. Morgan.

replacement by John Reid, a revised set of six "key objectives" were issued. They all relate to protecting the public[136] and are:

"1. protecting the UK from terrorist attack
2. cutting crime, especially violent and drug-related crime
3. ensuring people feel safer in their homes and daily lives, particularly through more visible, responsive and accountable local policing
4. rebalancing the criminal justice system in favour of the law-abiding majority and the victim
5. managing offenders to protect the public and reduce re-offending
6. securing our borders, preventing abuse of our immigration laws and managing migration to benefit the UK."

Shortly after his appointment, and in the light of a number of controversial policy failures,[137] Mr Reid described the Immigration and Nationality Department as "not fit for purpose" and stated that other failings showed that the Home Office could be "dysfunctional".[138] A reform programme was announced.[139] Subsequently, Mr Reid purposed that responsibility for prisons and probation services and for criminal justice policy be transferred to the DCA, which would become a Ministry of Justice.[140] This was implemented with effect from May 9, 2007.

3. THE LAW OFFICERS[141]

The Attorney-General and the Solicitor-General are the Law Officers of the Crown for England and Wales.[142] They are members of and the chief legal   **1–021**

---

[136] Compare the markedly different emphasis in the document published in September 2005, *Our vision; developing our approach to building a safe, just and tolerant society* (Home Office, 2005). This set out five objectives: "i people are and feel more secure in their homes and daily lives; ii more offenders are caught, punished and stop offending; iii fewer people's lives are ruined by drugs and alcohol; iv legal migrants are welcomed because immigration and abuse of the asylum laws are under control; v citizens, communities and the voluntary and community sector are more fully engaged in tackling social problems, and there is more equality of opportunity and respect for people of all races and religions."

[137] Including a failure to take appropriate steps to deport foreign prisoners after release from prison.

[138] Statement to House of Commons Home Affairs Committee, May 23, 2006; BBC News, May 23, 24, 2006.

[139] See *From Improvement to Transformation. An Action Plan to reform the Home Office so it meets public expectations and delivers its core purpose of protecting the public* (Home Office, July 2006); *Rebalancing the criminal justice system in favour of the law-abiding majority. Cutting crime, reducing re-offending and protecting the public* (Home Office, July 2006); *Fair, effective, transparent and trusted. Rebuilding confidence in our immigration system* (Home Office, July 2006).

[140] *Guardian Unlimited*, January 22, 2007.

[141] See J. Ll. J. Edwards, *The Law Officers of the Crown* (1964) and *The Attorney-General, Politics and the Public Interest* (1984); T. Daintith and A. Page, *The Executive in the Constitution* (1999), pp.287–315; Sir Elwyn Jones, [1969] C.L.J. 43; S. C. Silkin, (1980) 4 Trent L.J. 21; Sir Michael Havers, (1984) 52 Medico-Legal J. 98. For a list of the Law Officers' functions see written answer by the Attorney-General; R. Brazier, [1989] P.L. 64 at 94.

[142] Since 1972, the Attorney has been Attorney-General for Northern Ireland (see Northern Ireland Constitution Act 1973, s.10). The Solicitor-General is authorised to act as his deputy (*ibid.*). See Edwards (1984), Ch.9. There are separate Law Officers for Scotland, the Lord Advocate and the Solicitor-General for Scotland: see Edwards (1984), Ch.10; following devolution they are now members of the Scottish Executive and there is a new Scottish Law Officer to the UK government, the Advocate-General for Scotland: Scotland Act 1998, ss.48, 87. The Counsel General appointed under s.49 of the Government of Wales Act 2006 is the legal adviser to the Welsh Assembly Government.

advisers to the government,[143] and are normally[144] members of the House of Commons. Occasionally the Attorney-General has been appointed to the cabinet. The Law Officers may appear on behalf of the Crown at the International Court in the Hague and the European Court of Human Rights in Strasbourg. In this country they may appear in civil litigation or conduct prosecutions. They may not, however, undertake private work.

In civil matters the Attorney may institute proceedings in the High Court for the enforcement of public rights[145] or on behalf of the interests of charity. Her consent is required for the institution of criminal proceedings for a large number of criminal offences,[146] and she may stop trials on indictment by entering a *nolle prosequi*.[147] She superintends the work of the Queen's Proctor, who has certain duties in matrimonial cases. She exercises ministerial responsibility for the Director of Public Prosecutions (DPP), the Crown Prosecution Service (CPS) and the Serious Fraud Office (SFO)[148] and, from 1989, the Treasury Solicitor's Department.[149] The Law Officers are assisted by a small staff of civil servants in the Attorney-General's Office (formerly the Legal Secretariat to the Law Officers), based in the Attorney-General's Chambers at 9 Buckingham Gate, and generally divide the duties between them according to their own preferences.[150] The Attorney is also the head of the Bar.[151]

When taking decisions in respect of criminal matters, the Attorney-General is expected to act independently of the government. While in an appropriate case she may seek the views of ministers as to the consequences of a prosecution, there should be no pressure from them in favour of or against a prosecution: the ultimate decision is hers.[152] However, it has been asserted that the position is different where the government is acting as government in civil proceedings and

---

[143] The settled constitutional practice that Law Officers' advice to government remains confidential was breached in the Westland affair: see R. Austin, (1986) 39 C.L.P. 269 at 277–278; M. Linklater and D. Leigh, *Not With Honour* (1986). After much political pressure Lord Goldsmith's controversial advice that the use of force in Iraq in 2003 was lawful was published on April 28, 2005 (see *www.lslo.gov.uk*). The Deputy Legal Adviser to the Foreign Office, Elizabeth Wilmshurst, took a different view and resigned, her resignation letter being released to BBC News under the Freedom of Information Act 1998 (BBC News March 24, 2005). Advice was disclosed for the purposes of judicial proceedings (the Scott Inquiry and the *Factortame* litigation (H.L. Deb. 6 November 2003, cols WA128–WA129)).

[144] Not invariably: the current Attorney is Baroness Scotland Q.C., and her predecessors Lord Goldsmith Q.C. and Lord Williams of Mostyn Q.C. Lord Falconer was Solicitor-General in 1997–98. The current Solicitor-General is Vera Baird Q.C., MP. It has been the usual custom for both officers to be knighted on appointment (if not already a knight or peer); this is no longer followed, at least in the case of the Solicitor-General (from the appointment of Ross Cranston MP in 1998).

[145] e.g. to seek injunction to restrain a public nuisance or to restrain repeated or threatened breaches of the criminal law.

[146] See below, para.14–031.

[147] *ibid.*

[148] See below.

[149] Following the recommendations of the *Review of Government Legal Services* by Sir Robert Andrew (HMSO, 1989). See Vol.145 H.C. Deb. January 19, 1989, cols 262–263, written answer by the Prime Minister. These departments, together with the AGO (see *www.lslo.gov.uk*), are now collectively known as the Law Officers' Departments.

[150] Technically, the Solicitor-General is the Attorney-General's deputy, but it is now provided that any function of the Attorney-General may be exercised by the Solicitor-General: Law Officers Act 1997, s.1; previously, the Solicitor-General could only act in the Attorney's place in specified circumstances: Law Officers Act 1944, s.1, repealed by the 1997 Act.

[151] This caused some difficulty in 1989 when the Bar was severely critical of the Lord Chancellor's proposals for reform of the legal profession.

[152] The classic statement of principle was made by Sir Hartley Shawcross in 1951. H.C. Deb. January

the Attorney is the nominal plaintiff: here a decision whether to proceed is the government's collectively.[153] The then Attorney, Lord Goldsmith maintained his right to be consulted by the CPS as regards the "Cash for Honours" inquiry in 2006/07, while noting that his office would appoint independent senior counsel to review all the relevant material and advise on any prosecution.[154] In the event, no prosecution was bought.

4. THE DIRECTOR OF PUBLIC PROSECUTIONS, THE CROWN PROSECUTION SERVICE AND THE SERIOUS FRAUD OFFICE

In 1879, pressure for the introduction of a system of public prosecution led to the **1–022** establishment of the office of Director of Public Prosecutions.[155] It was originally contemplated that he would be provided with a number of locally based assistants, but this development never took place. The Director and his or her staff have thus always been based in London. The first Director took a narrow view of the scope of his functions, and between 1884 and 1908 the office was combined with that of Treasury Solicitor.

The Director's responsibilities are now set out in the Prosecution of Offences Act 1985. He or she is appointed by the Attorney-General and must be a person who has a 10-year general qualification.[156] Prior to the establishment of the CPS the Director's main functions were to conduct prosecutions in serious cases and to give advice and assistance to chief officers of police respecting the conduct of other prosecutions.[157] The Director is now head of the CPS,[158] which is responsible for the prosecution of criminal cases investigated by the police.[159] The

29, 1951: see Edwards (1964), pp.220–225 and (1984), pp.318–324. The decision of the Director of the SFO (with Lord Goldsmith's concurrence) to drop a long running fraud probe into an arms deal involving BAE Systems and Saudi Arabia (HL Deb 14 December 2006, cols 1711–1717) gave rise to significant political criticism. The decision was stated to have been taken "following representations concerning the need to safeguard national and international security"; no weight had been given to commercial interests or to the national economic interest. The Prime Minister and Foreign Secretary had expressed the clear view that the investigation would cause serious damage to UK/Saudi security, intelligence and diplomatic co-operation.

[153] Sir Michael Havers (HC Deb December 1, 1986), referring to the decision not to seek an injunction to restrain publication of Chapman Pincher's book, *Their Trade is Treachery*, a decision to which he was not a party. Analogous decisions in the *Gouriet* (*Gouriet v Union of Post Office Workers* [1978] A.C. 435) and *Crossman Diaries* (*Att.-Gen. v Jonathan Cape Ltd* [1976] Q.B. 752) cases had, by contrast, been taken independently by the Attorney: see J. Michael, "The Wright Case—The Attorney-General's Role" (1986) 136 N.L.J. 1199.

[154] See the exchange of letters between Lord Goldsmith and Dominic Grieve MP (Shadow Attorney-General) at *www.attorneygeneral.gov.uk*.

[155] Prosecution of Offences Act 1879. See generally J. Ll. J. Edwards, *The Law Officers of the Crown* (1964), Chs 16, 17 and *The Attorney-General, Politics and the Public Interest* (1984), Chs 1–5; G. Mansfield and J. Peay, *The Director of Public Prosecutions* (1987); J. Rozenberg, *The Case for the Crown* (1987); Thomas Hetherington, *Prosecution and the Public Interest* (1989).

[156] 1985 Act, s.2, as amended. The current DPP is Sir Ken Macdonald Q.C., who was appointed in 2003. His immediate predecessors were Sir Theobald Mathew (1944–64), Sir Norman Skelhorn (1964–77), Sir Thomas Hetherington (1977–87), Sir Allan Green Q.C. (1987–92), Dame Barbara Mills (1992–98), and Sir David Calvert-Smith Q.C. (1998–2002). Sir David became a High Court judge in 2005.

[157] See below, para.14–031.

[158] Below, para.14–033. The CPS has not become an executive agency but was to operate according to "Next Steps" principles from April 1996: *Department Reports of The Lord Chancellor's and Law Officers' Departments: The Government's Expenditure Plans 1996–97 to 1998–99* (Cm. 3209), p.45. See *www.cps.gov.uk*.

[159] Responsibility for charging (except for the most minor cases) was transferred to the CPS from the

Service is organised into 42 Areas,[160] each headed by a Chief Crown Prosecutor. It employs over 8,100 staff, the numbers having steadily increased. It was subject to a review by Sir Iain Glidewell[161] which recommended extensive reform including the devolution and decentralisation of powers, a focus on the core business of prosecuting, with greater emphasis on the more serious cases and greater separation of management from legal work, and improved co-operation with other agencies. A Chief Executive was appointed in 1998. Also of significance has been the fact that in 2000–01:

> "it was publicly acknowledged that the Service has been chronically under resourced since its inception and had suffered as a result ever since."[162]

A CPS Inspectorate became fully operational in 1997–98 and was placed on an independent statutory basis, reporting to the Attorney-General, from October 1, 2000.[163]

The SFO was established by the Criminal Justice Act 1987 with powers to investigate any suspected offence involving serious or complex fraud, and to institute and have the conduct of any criminal proceedings appearing to relate to such fraud.[164] Its operations extend to Northern Ireland, and are wider than that of the CPS, which is only responsible for the institution and conduct of proceedings investigated by the police. It comprises lawyers and accountants, and works in close co-operation with police officers, seconded from a number of forces, who occupy the same building. The SFO came under considerable criticism following a series of high profile cases where the defendants were acquitted, or only convicted on minor charges.[165] Nevertheless, in 1995 the government accepted the recommendation of a review group headed by Rex Davie that the SFO should not be merged with the Fraud Division of the CPS, but that the work should be restructured.[166] Under revised criteria for deciding which cases should go to the SFO, the key criterion is whether the suspected fraud was such that the direction of the investigation should be in the hands of those who would be

police in 2003 ("the biggest transformation in our history": *Annual Report of the CPS for 2003–04*, p.2), by virtue of the Criminal Justice Act 2003.

[160] Reduced from 31 to 13 in 1993: see *Annual Report of the Crown Prosecution Service 1993–94* (1993–94 H.C. 444), pp.9–11, Annex B; but increased to 42 in 1999 coterminous with the areas of police authorities, except in London where the CPS Area covers both Metropolitan and City police areas.

[161] *Review of the Crown Prosecution Service* (Cm. 3972, 1998).

[162] *Annual Report of the CPS, 2000–01* (2001–02 H.C. 138).

[163] Crown Prosecution Service Inspectorate Act 2000. It inspects each CPS Area on a two-year cycle and produces thematic reviews. See *www.hmcpsi.gov.uk*.

[164] s.1. On the work of the SFO, see D. N. Kirk and A. J. J. Woodcock, *Serious Fraud: Investigation and Trial* (3rd edn, 2003); M. Levi, *The Investigation, Prosecution and Trial of Serious Fraud* (RCCJ Research Study No. 14, 1993); JUSTICE, *Serious Fraud: Securing a fair trial* (1993).

[165] e.g. the failure of the prosecution in the *Blue Arrow* case, the acquittal of George Walker in a case arising out of the affairs of the Brent Walker group and the events that led to the passing of a non-custodial sentence on Roger Levitt: see (1993) 143 N.L.J. 1701. For the argument that the criticisms were exaggerated, see J. Bayes, (1994) 144 N.L.J. 1508. Over the first seven years of the SFO's existence, the overall conviction rate on a defendant-by-defendant basis was 62%, with one or more defendants convicted in over 75% of trials: *Annual Report of the Serious Fraud Office, 1994–95* (1994–95 HC 589), p.14. In 2000–01, 93% of defendants tried were convicted or pleaded guilty to one or more charges, with an average of 70% since the establishment of the SFO: *Annual Report, 2000–01*, Pt 1. The conviction rate for the 2002–06 period was 61%: *Annual Report, 2005–06*, Pt 1.

[166] Statement by the Attorney-General. A further Fraud Review was conducted in 2006: see *www.attorneygeneral.gov.uk*.

responsible for the prosecution. Relevant factors include: of the sum at risk is estimated to be at least £1 million; cases likely to give rise to national publicity and widespread public concern; cases requiring highly specialised knowledge of, for example, financial markets and their practices; the case has a significant international dimension; there is a need for legal, accountancy and investigative skills to be brought together; the suspected fraud appears to be complex and one in which the use of the SFO's special powers under s.2 of the 1987 Act might be appropriate.[167] A Joint Vetting Committee has been established with the CPS and other organisations to decide which is the most appropriate body to investigate a suspected fraud.[168]

The DPP may be directed by the Divisional Court to appear for the prosecution on any criminal appeal to the House of Lords, and by the Court of Appeal (Criminal Division) to appear in appeals to that court from the Crown Court or from it to the House of Lords.[169] He also has the power to intervene in prosecutions.[170] This power is used rarely, for example where private prosecutions are instituted maliciously. It includes the right to discontinue proceedings.[171] Finally, the Director's consent to prosecution is required by statute in certain classes of case.[172]

5. THE TREASURY AND OTHER GOVERNMENT DEPARTMENTS

The Treasury is involved in the administration of justice at a number of points. **1–023** It has overall responsibilities for government expenditure and the organisation of the civil service. The parliamentary draftsmen are technically Parliamentary Counsel to the Treasury, and the office is described as a "cross government unit in the Cabinet Office."[173]

The Treasury Solicitor heads a large legal department which does legal work for the Treasury and for other government departments.[174] He also presides over inter-departmental management machinery for civil service lawyers and was for many years and for most purposes the *de facto* head of the civil service Civil Legal Group in England and Wales.[175] In 1989 the government legal service was reorganised following a report by Sir Robert Andrew.[176] The Treasury Solicitor was recognised as head of the service, with the responsibility of advising on the personnel management of lawyers across departments and supported by the Government Legal Service Secretariat (formerly the Lawyers' Management

---

[167] SFO Annual Report, 2005–06.
[168] SFO Annual Report, 2004–05.
[169] Prosecution of Offences Act 1985, s.3(2)(f). See below, para.14–034.
[170] *ibid.* s.6. Below, para.14–034.
[171] *Raymond v Att.-Gen.* [1982] Q.B. 839, decided under the equivalent provision (s.4) of the Prosecution of Offences Act 1979.
[172] See below, para.14–034.
[173] *www.cabinetoffice.gov.uk*: Organisation Chart.
[174] See *www.tsol.gov.uk*. The two main workstreams are divided between Litigation and Advisory Legal Services.
[175] See G. Drewry, "The Office of Treasury Solicitor" (1980) 130 N.L.J. 753 and "Lawyers in the U.K. Civil Service" (1981) 59 *Public Administration* 15; (1992) 136 S.J. 78 at 96.
[176] *Review of Government Legal Services* (HMSO, 1989). On the appointment of the inquiry see G. Drewry, "Government Lawyers under Scrutiny" (1988) 138 N.L.J. 219.

Unit).[177] The European Division of the TSol advises the Cabinet Office on Community law issues and conducts on behalf of the United Kingdom all litigation in the Court of Justice of the European Community and the Court of First Instance.[178] Other Divisions undertake litigation, deal with *bona vacantia* (administering the estates of intestates), and advisory work for governmental departments.[179] The Government Property Lawyers was established as a Next Steps executive agency of the Lord Chancellor's Department on April 1, 1993. It was located in Taunton and provided a conveyancing and lands advisory service for all government departments and other public bodies, but was closed in 1999 as declining workload had made the business non-viable.[180] The rest of the Department was established as an executive agency from 1996.[181] Legal services to government departments may be the subject of market testing in accordance with guidelines set by the Attorney-General.[182]

6. THE OFFICIAL SOLICITOR AND PUBLIC TRUSTEE; CAFCASS

1–024   While the Treasury Solicitor is concerned with the government's legal business, the Official Solicitor to the Supreme Court heads an office in that court. He is appointed by the Lord Chancellor and must be a person with a 10-year general qualification under s.71 of the Courts and Legal Services Act 1990.[183] His functions have broadly fallen into five categories[184]: the liberty of the subject (making bail applications for remand prisoners, reviewing the cases of persons committed to prison for contempt of court,[185] investigating applications for leave to issue a writ of habeas corpus); the paternalistic jurisdiction (representing wards of court in wardship proceedings, acting as guardian of a minor's estate, dealing with the affairs of mental patients); the conduct of litigation for children

---

[177] HC Deb January 19, 1989, written answer by the Prime Minister. See M. Mair (1989) L.S.Gaz. March 22, 1989, pp.12, 37: interview with the Treasury Solicitor, James Nurshaw; *www.gls.gov.uk.*

[178] See T. Daintith and A. Page, *The Executive in the Constitution* (1999), pp.317–319.

[179] There are separate divisions for the Treasury, DfES and DCMS, and a Cabinet Office and Central Advisory Division. Some government departments have in-house Legal Advisers, including the Foreign Office, the Home Office and the Ministry of Defence.

[180] *Law Officers' Departments Departmental Report, The Government's Expenditure Plans 1999–2000 to 2001–2002* (Cm. 4207, 1999), p.42.

[181] *Departmental Report of The Lord Chancellor's and Law Officers' Departments: The Government's Expenditure Plans 1995–96 to 1997–98* (Cm. 2809, 1995), pp.60–65. See Daintith and Page (1999), pp.217–220. A Quinquennial Review by Sir Quentin Thomas in 2001 reported that it should continue as an Agency: *www.tsol.gov.uk/publications.*

[182] See (1992) 136 S.J. 663. The guidelines state that it is not appropriate to use the private sector for core governmental work where ministers and legal advisers need to maintain a close confidential relationship.

[183] Supreme Court Act 1981, s.90, as amended by the 1990 Act, Sch.10, para.49; on the meaning of "general qualification" see below, para.4–022. See N. Lowe and R. White, *Wards of Court* (2nd edn, 1986), Ch.9; J. M. L. Evans, (1966) 63 L.S. Gaz. 270, 335; C. Dyer, *The Law Magazine*, June 12, 1987, p.27; D. Venables, (1990) 20 Fam. Law 53; *www.officialsolicitor.gov.uk.*

[184] M. Hinchliffe, (1989) J. of Child Law, pp.64–67.

[185] It was in this capacity that the Official Solicitor came into prominence in 1972 in obtaining the release of trade unionists committed to prison for disobedience to orders of the National Industrial Relations Court in the course of a national dock strike: *Churchman v Joint Shop Stewards Committee* [1972] I.C.R. 222; *Midland Cold Storage Ltd v Turner, The Times*, July 27, 1972. See N. Lowe and B. Sufrin, *Borrie and Lowe's Law of Contempt* (3rd edn, 1996), pp.633–635; B. A. Hepple, (1972) 1 I.L.J. 198; Lord Denning, *The Due Process of Law* (1980), pp.36–39.

and mental patients; the administration of the estates of deceased persons when there is no-one else willing or able to do so; and assisting the court (investigating the conduct of litigation, briefing counsel to appear as *amicus curiae*).

The Office of Public Trustee was created under the Public Trustee Act 1906. From 1987, it had four main business areas. The Protection and Receivership Divisions of the Public Trust Office exercised functions under the Mental Health Act protecting the property and affairs of people with mental incapacity, the former providing administrative support to the Court of Protection. The Trust Division acted as executor or administrator of deceased persons estates or trustee of wills or settlements; in practice as an executor or trustee of last resort. Court Funds work involved managing money paid into court.[186] The Office became an executive agency within the LCD in 1994. There was some overlap with the role of the Official Solicitor's Office.

Significant changes have now been made,[187] effective from April 2001. The work of the Trust Division was transferred to the Official Solicitor and Court Funds work to the Court Service. Mental Health services were to be managed by a new executive agency within the Court of Protection, the Public Guardianship Office (PGO). The PGO took over the Public Trust Office's (PTO) last resort receivership service on a reduced scale. Accordingly, the PTO was co-located with the Official Solicitor's office and the same individual holds the position of Official Solicitor and Public Trustee.

Also effective from April 2001, a new organisation, the Children and Family Court Advisory and Support Service (CAFCASS) was established to provide representation for children in family proceedings.[188] It took some responsibilities from the Official Solicitor's Office, the family court welfare function of the former 54 Probation Committees and the functions of the 57 Guardians ad Litem and Reporting Officer panels. The Official Solicitor continues to provide litigation friend (formerly guardian ad litem) services in proceedings other than under the Children Act 1989 and in certain circumstances also under the 1989 Act for parties under disability who are not the subject of proceedings.[189] Two important areas of work that involve the Official Solicitor are cases involving the sterilisation of a person who cannot consent to the operation and the discontinuance of nutrition and hydration for a patient in a vegetative state.[190] The launch of CAFCASS proved problematic, being described as "ill-planned and badly executed"[191] and having had "a diabolical start"[192] with a serious dispute with

---

[186] See *Judicial Statistics 2000*, pp.85–86.

[187] Following a *Quinquennial Review of the Public Trust Office* (1999); *Making Changes—The Future of the Public Trust Office* (LCD, April 2000); *The Way Forward and an Analysis of Consultation* (LCD, December 2000).

[188] Criminal Justice and Court Services Act 2000, ss.11–17; N. Flicker, [2000] Fam. Law 102; G. Timmis, [2001] Fam. Law 280; *www.cafcass.gov.uk.* Responsibility for CAFCASS passed from the LCD to Dfes in 2003.

[189] *www.officialsolicitor.gov.uk.* On the division of responsibilities with CAFCASS, see *Practice Note (Officers of CAFCASS Legal Services and Special Casework: Appointment in Family Proceedings)* [2001] Fam. Law 249 and *Practice Note (The Official Solicitor: Appointment in Family Proceedings)* [2001] Fam. Law 307.

[190] *RF (Mental Patient: Sterilisation)* [1990] 2 A.C. 1; *Airedale NHS Trust v Bland* [1993] A.C. 789; *Practice Note (Official Solicitor: Declaratory Proceedings: Medical and Welfare Decisions for Adults who lack capacity)* [2001] Fam. Law 551.

[191] M. Crisell, [2002] Fam. Law 310.

[192] S. Gerlis, [2002] Fam. Law 144.

former guardians[193] and a significant budget deficit. Steps were taken to address these problems,[194] but there are still concerns.[195]

7. THE "CRIMINAL JUSTICE SYSTEM"

1–025 Co-ordination of the work of the various agencies involved in the criminal justice system has long been problematic. A Criminal Justice Consultative Council was established in 1991 and a variety of other co-ordinating groups established under the umbrella (with its own website) of what was formally termed the "Criminal Justice System" (CJS). A Public Service Agreement for the CJS as a whole was published in 1998. Sir Robin Auld[196] was highly critical of these arrangements: "the whole edifice is structurally inefficient, ineffective and wasteful".[197] His terms of reference precluded "a possible reordering of the great offices of State". However, there should be a single national body, a Criminal Justice Board, to plan and direct, local Criminal Justice Boards, and a statutory Criminal Justice Council as an advisory body. One significant task for the Criminal Justice Board should be to plan the production of an integrated IT system for the whole CJS. What emerged was the establishment of a National Criminal Justice Board (NCJB), comprising the Home Secretary, the Lord Chancellor and the Attorney-General and other ministers and officials from the whole range of relevant agencies.[198] A step of some significance was taken in 2004[199] with the decision that ministerial responsibility for the CJS was formally to be shared among the three departments. There are also 42 Local Criminal Justice Boards across England and Wales and the Office for Criminal Justice Reform, a cross-departmental team that supports the National and Local Boards and all criminal justice agencies. The Criminal Justice Council remains in being, acting in the capacity of expert adviser to the NCJB.[200] The OCJR is now hosted by the Ministry of Justice.

---

[193] See V. Swenson, [2001] Fam. Law 708; *R (on the application of National Association of Guardians ad Litem and Reporting Officers) v Children and Family Court Advisory Service* [2001] EWHC Admin 693 (decision not to continue to offer the option of contracts for services (as distinct from contracts of employment) to existing guardians quashed as reasonable notice of this change of policy and an opportunity to make representations should have been afforded to the Association). Many former guardians and managers left the service, leading to increasing difficulties in handling the work: G. Timmis, [2002] Fam. Law 148.

[194] J. Tross (CAFCASS Acting Chief Executive), [2002] Fam. Law 318.

[195] See N. V. Lowe and G. Douglas, *Bromley's Family Law* (10th edn, 2006), pp.486–487.

[196] *Review of the Criminal Courts*, Ch.8.

[197] Ch.8, para.14. A study of the Strategic Planning Group reported that the diagnosis of many was that it "is not strategic and it does not plan" (para.25). The CJCC had succeeded in improving communication but was not routinely consulted and had no standing responsibility, staff or facilities (para.31). Each agency (police, CPS, magistrates' courts, Crown Court, probation and prisons) had its own, quite separate, national information technology system (para.98).

[198] See *www.cjsonline.gov.uk*.

[199] Following the report, *Criminal Justice Reform: Working Together Implementing the CJS Capacity Review* (Home Office, CPS, DCA, 2004).

[200] H.C. Deb., October 12, 2005, col. 485W, written answer, setting out the Council's membership and responsibilities and a protocol of its relationship to the NCJB. The Council's chair, Sir Igor Judge, President of the Queen's Bench Division and Head of Criminal Justice, is as chair a member of the NCJB. Curiously, the Council is not mentioned on the CJS website.

8. THE CIVIL JUSTICE COUNCIL AND THE FAMILY JUSTICE COUNCIL

The Civil Justice Council was established in 1998 as part of the Woolf **1–026**
reforms.[201] Its functions are to keep the civil justice system under review,
considering how to make the civil justice system more accessible, fair and
efficient; advising the Secretary of State for Constitutional Affairs and the
judiciary on the development of the civil justice system; referring proposal for
changes in the system to the Secretary of State and the CPR committee; and
making proposals for research.

The Family Justice Council was established by ministers in 2002 on similar
lines.[202] Its terms of reference are to facilitate the delivery of better and quicker
outcomes for families and children who use the family justice system by promoting improved interdisciplinary working, identifying and disseminating best practice, consulting government departments on current policy, providing guidance
and direction, disseminating advice and promoting inter-agency discussion,
encouraging research and making recommendations to government. There are 41
Local Family Justice Councils.

D. LAW REFORM

It is inevitable that any legal system cannot be static: there will always be aspects **1–027**
both of the substantive law and the institutional and procedural features of the
system that require change. Many aspects of the common law are developed by
the decisions of the superior courts. However, the judges seem generally to hold
the view that this power should be exercised with caution, although this caution
is from time to time thrown to the winds.[203] Commonly, a distinction is drawn
between the application of an existing principle to new circumstances, which is
regarded as a legitimate exercise for the judges, and the creation of a new
principle, which is regarded as a matter for government and Parliament.[204]

Reform by the judges is further handicapped by the fact that the accidents of
litigation may not throw up the right cases, that the precise issues in dispute are
formulated by the parties (the opinions of the judges on other matters amounting
to *obiter dicta* which are not binding in future cases),[205] and that the judges must
normally confine themselves to the arguments and information presented by the
parties. The judges cannot in any event commission empirical research and even

---

[201] Civil Procedure Act 1997, s.6; as amended by the Constitutional Reform Act 2005, Sch.4,
para.268. *www.civiljusticecouncil.gov.uk*. It is chaired by the Master of the Rolls, its Vice
Chairman is the Deputy Head of Civil Justice, and its other members include (in 2006) five
judges, eight solicitors, two barristers, two DCA civil servants, two academics (Professors J.
Peysner and M. Partington), and members from NACAB and the insurance industry.

[202] See *www.family-justice-council.org.uk*; and "The Work of the Family Justice Council" [2005]
Fam. Law 65; *Annual Report of the Family Justice Council 2005–06*. The Council is chaired by
Sir Mark Potter, President of the Family Division and Head of Family Justice. The Deputy Chair
is Thorpe L.J.

[203] See below, paras 4–041—4–044.

[204] See, e.g. Lord Pearson and Lord Salmon in *Launchbury v Morgans* [1973] A.C. 127 at 142,
151.

[205] See below, para.7–003.

the information derived from existing research is not admissible in evidence. Judicial reforms tend also to be retrospective in nature and hence potentially unfair.[206] Accordingly, most significant law reforms must be achieved by statute.

There are several mechanisms which exist or have existed to further the cause of law reform by statute, including one permanent body, the Law Commission, several part-time bodies, such as the Law Reform Committee and the Criminal Law Revision Committee, and any number of ad hoc Royal Commissions and departmental committees.

1. THE LAW COMMISSION[207]

1–028   Calls for a permanent law reform institution were answered in 1965 by the establishment of two Law Commissions, one for England and Wales and one for Scotland.[208] This move was associated particularly with Lord Gardiner L.C.[209] The Law Commission for England and Wales comprises five "persons appearing . . . to be suitably qualified by the holding of judicial office or by experience as a person having a general qualification (within the meaning of s.71 of the Courts and Legal Services Acts 1990) or as a teacher of law in a university".[210] In practice, the chairman has been a High Court judge, who works full-time for the Commission and normally subsequently receives promotion to the Court of Appeal. The pattern for the other appointments has become settled with a common law Q.C., a solicitor and two academics. There is a legal secretary, a staff of barristers and solicitors from the legal Civil Service and several parliamentary draftsmen.[211]

The Commission's task is:

> "to take and keep under review all the law with which [it is] concerned with a view to its systematic development and reform, including in particular the

---

[206] *Cf.* below, para.7–028.

[207] See generally on the work of the Law Commission, J. H. Farrar, *Law Reform and the Law Commission* (1974); G. J. Zellick (ed.), *Law Reform and the Law Commission* (1988); N. Marsh (1971) 13 William and Mary L.R. 263; L. C. B. Gower, (1973) 23 Univ. of Toronto L.J. 257; A. L. Diamond, (1976) 10 L.T. 11 and (1977) 51 A.L.J. 396; Sir Michael Kerr, (1980) 96 L.Q.R. 515; P. M. North, (1985) 101 L.Q.R. 338; S. Cretney, (1985) 48 M.L.R. 493; Sir Ralph Gibson, (1986) 39 C.L.P. 57; Sir Roy Beldam (1987) 16 Kingston L.R. 21; Brooke J. (1995) 16 Stat. L.R. 1 and [1995] Crim. L.R. 911; Staughton L.J. (1995) 16 Stat. L.R. 7; Sir Roger Toulson, (2006) 26 L.S. 321. For a discussion of the Law Commission's use of economic reasoning, see A. I. Ogus, "Economics and Law Reform; Thirty Years of Law Commission Endeavour" (1995) 111 L.Q.R. 407. The Commission reviewed the first 20 years of its operations in its 20th Annual Report, 1984–85 (Law Com. No.155), Pt I: see Editorial, (1986) 136 N.L.J. 201. For a critical account of its operations by a former member of its staff, see R. T. Oerton, *Lament for the Law Commission* (1987). For a proposal for its abolition, see A. Samuels, (1986) 136 N.L.J. 747; response by Oerton *ibid.* p.1071.

[208] Law Commissions Act 1965; Lord Chorley and G. Dworkin, (1965) 28 M.L.R. 675.

[209] He had argued the case for such a body in Ch.1 of G. Gardiner and A. Martin (eds), *Law Reform NOW* (1963) and *cf.* (1953) 69 L.Q.R. 46.

[210] 1965 Act, s.l(2), as amended by the 1990 Act, Sch.10, para.25.

[211] Sir Michael Kerr, (1980) 96 L.Q.R. 515 at 523. Four of the five senior Civil Service legal posts were, however, abolished ((1984) 134 N.L.J. 467), the Law Commission relying instead on commissioning work from academic lawyers, some of whom join it on secondment (see 21st Annual Report, 1985–86 (Law Com. No.159), pp.1–2, 17).

codification of such law, the elimination of anomalies, the repeal of obsolete and unnecessary enactments, the reduction of the number of separate enactments and generally the simplification and modernisation of the law".[212]

The topics investigated are either referred to it by the Lord Chancellor or are aspects of one of the programmes for examination of different branches of the law with a view to reform that have been approved by the Lord Chancellor and laid before Parliament.[213] The Commission is also required to provide advice and information to government and other bodies concerned with law reform.[214]

In the course of its existence the Law Commission has dealt with a large number of substantive legal topics and projects for the consolidation of statutes and the repeal of obsolete provisions ("Statute Law Reform").[215] It has also worked on the codification of the law of contract and of the law of landlord and tenant, although these tasks proved too onerous and the work was suspended indefinitely.[216] Work on codification of the criminal law has progressed further,[217] a draft code having been produced. However, it has been recognised that "the likelihood of Parliament being able to find time to consider, in a single Bill, a proposal as large as a complete Code is very remote".[218] Accordingly, the Commission aims to "progress in stages towards the long-term objective of the enactment of a complete Code", with further work on particular topics built into the base provided by the draft Code.[219] However, pressure for the introduction of a code has remained[220] and the government is now committed to codification as part of its criminal justice policy.[221] This would help to achieve "transparency and accessibility" and "certainty, speed and efficiency". This would be "a long-term commitment, not least because of the heavy demands it might make on

---

[212] 1965 Act, s.3(1).

[213] *ibid.* s.3(1)(a), (b), (2). There have been nine general programmes (approved in 1965, 1968, 1973, 1989, 1991, 1995, 1999, 2001 and 2005) with major items on criminal law, family law and private international law. The programme arrangements are considered by S. Cretney in Zellick (1988), pp.3–20. The project selection criteria are importance (the extent to which the law is unsatisfactory and the potential benefits of reform, consolidation or repeal); suitability (whether improvements can appropriately be put forward by a body of lawyers after research and consultation; this tends to exclude subjects where the considerations are shaped primarily by political judgements); and resources: *Law Commission Ninth Programme of Law Reform* (Law Com. No. 293), para.1.3. The Tenth Programme is due to start in 2007. The Commission may also consider reform proposals from other quarters.

[214] The Commission publishes on its website (*www.lawcom.gov.uk*), three times a year, a bulletin, *Law Under Review*, giving details of the progress of government law reform projects.

[215] See below, para.5–005.

[216] See A. L. Diamond, (1968) 31 M.L.R. 361; Sir Michael Kerr, (1980) 96 L.Q.R. 515 at 527–530.

[217] See J. C. Smith, [1984] Stat. L.R. 17 and [1987] Denning L.J. 137; I. Dennis, (1986) 50 J. of Crim. Law 161; *Codification of the Criminal Law: A Report to the Law Commission* (Law Com. No.143, 1985); Symposium, [1986] Crim. L.R. 285–323; *Criminal Code for England and Wales* (Law Com. No.177, 1989).

[218] 27th Annual Report, 1992 (Law Com. No.210), p.10.

[219] *ibid.* For the first steps, see the Reports under the general title *Legislating the Criminal Code, Offences against the Person and General Principles* (Law Com. No.218, Cm. 2370, 1993); *Intoxication and Criminal Liability* (Law Com. No.229, 1995); *The Year and a Day Rule in Homicide* (Law Com. No.230, 1995); *Involuntary Manslaughter* (Law Com. No.237, 1996). For a vigorous rebuttal of criticisms by F. A. R. Bennion of the drafting of the Code ((1994) 15 Stat. L.R. 108), see J. C. Smith, (1995) 16 Stat. L.R. 105. For a review of progress, see R. Toulson (2006) 27 Stat. L.R. 61.

[220] e.g. Lord Bingham, [1998] Crim. L.R. 694.

[221] White Paper, *Criminal Justice: The Way Ahead* (Cm. 5074, 2001).

Parliament's time".[222] The Commission now plans to draft a General Part of the Code covering general principles both as to the ingredients of specific offences (such as the meaning of intention) and free-standing matters (such as the defence of self-defence).[223]

A notable feature of the Law Commission's working methods in connection with the reform of a substantive legal topic is the circulation of a "working paper". This consists of a detailed statement of the present law on the topic, an account of the criticisms and supposed defects of the law, and a statement of the options for change. The Commission normally states a provisional view as to the option that should be preferred. The paper, in both full and summarised forms, is circulated widely and the views of interested parties sought.[224] Following consultation a final report is produced, which includes a draft Bill prepared by the parliamentary draftsmen seconded to the Commission.

Overall, chances of implementation are reasonably high, although they are less where the matter falls within the purview of a government department other than the Lord Chancellor's Department (now MoJ) (most notably the Home Office and the Department of the Environment).[225] Implementation rates have varied over time. By 1994, of all the Commission's law reform reports, 78 had been implemented, 13 rejected and 32 were outstanding. However, lack of implementation had reached a crisis point by 1993. In that year, the Commission reported that only four of its reports since 1990 had been implemented, for lack of parliamentary time, with only one forming part of the government's legislative programme.[226] However, the introduction of new procedures and the end of a period of non-co-operation between government and opposition whips enabled inroads to be made on the backlog, there having been a "sea-change in attitudes".[227] A record of nine reports were implemented in 1995 and eight in 1996. The next Parliament implemented only four,[228] but then 17 were implemented between 2002 and 2006.[229] A major problem lies in the competition for Parliamentary time among ministers who naturally wish to advance projects of political significance. The Legislative and Regulatory Reform Bill in 2005–06 contained express provision for the implementation of Law Commission proposals to be one of the permitted purposes for the use of regulatory reform orders. However, this element was dropped in the face of Parliamentary opposition, given the controversial nature of some Law Commission proposals. The regulatory reform

---

[222] paras 3.57, 3.59.

[223] *Eighth Programme of Law Reform*, Item 5; Ninth Programme of Law Reform, pp.6–7.

[224] See P. M. North, "Law Reform: the Consultation Process" (1982) 66 Trent L.J. 19 and (1985) 101 L.Q.R. 338 (expressing some scepticism as to the effectiveness of consultation). The Commission has not followed the example of the Australian Law Reform Commission and organised public meetings or hearings: see the paper by the ALRC Chairman, Mr Justice M. D. Kirby, "Reforming Law Reform: New Methods of Law Reform in Australia", to the 1979 Colloquium of the UK National Committee on Comparative Law, summarised in M. Zander, *The Law-Making Process* (4th edn, 1994), pp.451–455.

[225] See Lord Hailsham, "Obstacles to Law Reform" (1981) 34 C.L.P. 279; P. M. North, (1981) III (I) *Liverpool Law Review* 5 and (1985) 101 L.Q.R. 338 at 346–357; Lord Hooson Q.C., "Reform of the Legislative Process in the Light of the Law Commission's Work" (1983) 17 L.T. 67; S. Cretney, (1985) 48 M.L.R. 493; G. Drewry in Zellick (1988), pp.28–43.

[226] 28th Annual Report, 1993 (Law Com. No.223), pp.6–12.

[227] 29th Annual Report, Pt V; below, para.5–008.

[228] 36th Annual Report 2001 (Law Com. No.275), p.20.

[229] 40th Annual Report, 2005/06 (Law Com. No.299), p.11. Overall, of 177 Law reform reports, 26 were outstanding; 14 had been accepted in full or in part and a decision was awaited on 12.

order route[230] can nevertheless be used where appropriate.[231] There are also examples of the use of Law Commission proposals by the courts in developing the law.[232]

A Ministerial Committee on Law Reform has been established, chaired by an MoJ minister, to develop and co-ordinate the government's interests in law reform, with particular reference to making effective use of the Law Commission, considering how implementation can be streamlined and considering outstanding Law Commission reports and the action to be taken on them.[233]

2. THE LAW REFORM COMMITTEE[234]

A part-time Law Revision Committee was appointed by Lord Sankey in 1934 **1–029** and produced eight reports between then and 1939, most of which were implemented.[235] It was reconstituted by Lord Simonds in 1952 under the title of Law Reform Committee, and comprised judges, practising lawyers and academics. Its permanent secretariat was provided by the LCD, but it lacked research facilities and suffered from the inevitable problems of any part-time body. By 1982 it had produced 23 reports.

3. THE CRIMINAL LAW REVISION COMMITTEE

The Criminal Law Revision Committee (CLRC), the counterpart to the Law **1–030** Reform Committee, but responsible to the Home Secretary rather than the Lord Chancellor, was established in 1959, and included judges, academics and the DPP.[236] Its reports have led to important reforming legislation, most notably the Theft Acts 1968 and 1978. Perhaps the best known report was its 11th Report on Evidence, which aroused a storm of opposition, in part at least, according to its defenders, based on the misrepresentation of some of its recommendations.[237] For the purposes of its review of sexual offences, the Committee was advised by a Policy Advisory Committee comprising five members of the CRLC and 10 members from other disciplines, including probation officers, a consultant psychiatrist, a social worker and a sociologist. There was here a greater potentional

---

[230] See para.5–028.

[231] It was used for the *Report on the Execution of Deeds and Documents by or on behalf of Bodies Corporate* (Law Com. No.258, 1998): Regulatory Reform (Execution of Deeds and Documents) Order 2005 (SI 2005/1906).

[232] e.g. *Heil v Rankin* [2001] Q.B. 272 (appropriate levels of damages for non-pecuniary losses); *Kleinwort Benson v Lincoln City Council* [1999] 2 A.C. 349 (abrogation of the rule that money was generally not recoverable in restitution on the ground that it was paid under a mistake of law): see further *Eighth Programme of Law Reform*, paras 2.11–2.21.

[233] 35th Annual Report 2000 (Law Com. No.268), p.15.

[234] See E. C. S. Wade, (1961) 24 M.L.R. 3; J. H. Farrar, *Law Reform and the Law Commission* (1974), pp.9–14, 133–137; M. C. Blair, (1982) 1 C.J.Q. 64.

[235] For an account of the one that was not (the 6th Interim Report on the Statute of Frauds and the Doctrine of Consideration (Cmd. 5549, 1937)), see J. Beatson, (1992) 45(2) C.L.P.1.

[236] See generally, Glanville Williams, "The Work of Criminal Law Reform" (1975) 13 J.S.P.T.L. 183; J. C. Smith, "An Academic Lawyer and Law Reform" (1981) 1 L.S. 119.

[237] See the articles cited in the previous footnote and M. Zander in *Reshaping the Criminal Law* (P. Glazebrook ed., 1978).

for fundamental disagreement about what it is that the law should be attempting to achieve than there had been on earlier references to the CLRC.[238] The Committee has not been convened since 1985, and its work has been superseded by the Law Commission.[239]

4. Ad Hoc Committees[240]

1–031 Investigations by Royal Commissions and departmental committees have long been a familiar feature of the law reform scene. They have the advantage over part-time advisory committees of a much greater commitment of resources, both of the time of their members and in money for research. They have the disadvantage when compared with permanent bodies that, having accumulated a large amount of information and expertise, their members disperse once the body has done its work. Other points of contrast with the law reform bodies discussed above are that ad hoc committees usually have a majority, or at least a large contingent, of non-lawyers, and are more likely than those others to be employed in connection with institutional reforms. Since 1960, there have been five Royal Commissions of particular importance for the English legal system. The Royal Commission on Assizes and Quarter Sessions,[241] chaired by Lord Beeching, made proposals for the reorganisation of the criminal courts (other than magistrates' courts) which were speedily implemented.[242]

The Royal Commission on Legal Services, chaired by an accountant, Sir Henry Benson, reported in 1979.[243] Its terms of reference were:

> "to inquire into the law and practice relating to the provision of legal services in England, Wales and Northern Ireland, and to consider whether any, and if so what, changes are desirable in the public interest in the structure, organisation, training, regulation of and entry to the legal profession, including the arrangements for determining its remuneration, whether from private sources or public funds, and in the rules which prevent persons who are neither barristers nor solicitors from undertaking conveyancing and other legal business on behalf of other persons."

The report was widely regarded as a disappointment.[244] It was criticised for its pedestrian style, its paucity of reasoning, the fact that only a limited amount of research[245] was commissioned and its apparent over-dependence on the information and arguments presented by the legal profession. The *Legal Action Group*

---

[238] Criminal Law Revision Committee, 15th Report on Sexual Offences (Cmnd. 9213, 1984), pp.1, 100.

[239] Paul Goggins MP, HC Deb April 18, 2006, cols 286W–287W, written answer.

[240] A list of major reports of official committees and commissions on law reform is given in G. Zellick (ed.), *Law Reform and the Law Commission* (1988), App.6.

[241] Cmnd. 4153, 1969.

[242] See below, para.2–052.

[243] Cmnd. 7648.

[244] See C. Glasser, *L.A.G. Bull*, September 1979, p.201; M. Elliott, (1980) J.S.W.L. 1; O. Hanson and J. Levin (1979) *Yearbook of Social Policy*, Ch.12; (1980) 43 M.L.R. 543; (1981) *Windsor Yearbook of Access to Justice* 121 (T. A. Downes, P. R. Hopkins and W. M. Rees) and 179 (P. A. Thomas); P. A. Thomas (ed.), *Law in the Balance* (1982).

[245] See C. Glasser, *op. cit.*

Bulletin was tempted to ignore the report: it would certainly be kinder so shaky were its foundations.[246] Professor Zander, who had played a significant role in securing the establishment of the Commission and who had submitted a considerable body of evidence, was more welcoming: he counted well over a 100 recommendations that he thought would amount to valuable changes.[247] The only real enthusiasts were the two branches of the legal profession, which was unsurprising given that on many issues their position was endorsed by the Commission. Many of the recommendations directed at the profession were the subject of action; those directed at the government had little impact, except that responsibility for criminal legal aid was transferred from Home Secretary to Lord Chancellor.[248] Indeed, the government subsequently decided, contrary to the recommendation of a majority of members of the Royal Commission, to end the solicitors' conveyancing "monopoly", and fundamental changes followed the Lord Chancellor's White Paper, *Legal Services: A Framework for the Future*,[249] many comprised in the Courts and Legal Services Act 1990.

The Royal Commission on Criminal Procedure (RCCP)[250] provided an interesting contrast. It was established in 1978 to consider the powers and duties of the police in respect of the investigation of criminal offences and the rights and duties of suspects and accused persons, the process of and responsibility for the prosecution of criminal offences and related matters. Three features of the report were especially noteworthy. First, the Commission was much more active than the Royal Commission on Legal Services in sponsoring research. Secondly, there was a clear intention to identify basic points of principle to which the specific recommendations were to be related.[251] Thirdly, the report indicated the lines that reform should take, leaving the details to be worked out. In consequence, the Police and Criminal Evidence Bill was presented to Parliament in 1983, together with proposals for the establishment of a national prosecution service. **1–032**

In the following decades, Royal Commissions and departmental committees were conspicuous by their absence. Questions of policy tended to be determined by government, with the use of teams of civil servants, perhaps with an independent chairman or advisers, to work out the details of implementation. Examples in the context of the law included the Civil Justice Review,[252] the Magistrates' Courts Scrutiny[253] and the Working Group on the Right of Silence.[254] The Green Papers on Reform of the Legal Profession were simply published as such. This kind of approach was certainly more convenient for government. It led to a speedier conclusion, and also avoided the risk of an independent body producing unwelcome recommendations. There were, however, corresponding doubts as to the quality of the reports produced.

---

[246] November 1979, p.246.

[247] (1980) 33 C.L.P. 33, 50.

[248] See *The Government Response to the Report of the Royal Commission on Legal Services* (Cmnd. 9077, 1983). The Law Society and the Bar also published their responses: see *L.A.G. Bulletin*, December 1983, pp.3, 6.

[249] Cm. 740, 1989. See para.3–006 of the fourth edition of this work.

[250] Cmnd. 8092, 1981.

[251] The Commission applied three standards for judging both the existing system and its own recommendations: are the arrangements, actual or proposed, fair and clear; are they open, that is, not secret and is there accountability; are they workable and efficient?

[252] *Report of the Review Body on Civil Justice* (Cm. 394, 1988). See I. Ramsey, (1988) 15 J.L.S. 416.

[253] *Magistrates' Courts: Report of a scrutiny* (HMSO, 1989).

[254] *Report of the Working Group on the Right of Silence* (Home Office, 1989).

Concerns over the series of widely publicised cases where there had been a miscarriage of justice[255] led to the appointment of the Royal Commission on Criminal Justice, chaired by Viscount Runciman. Its terms of reference were:

> "to examine the effectiveness of the criminal justice system in England and Wales in securing the conviction of those guilty of criminal offences and the acquittal of those who are innocent, having regard to the efficient use of resources"

and in particular to consider whether changes were needed in the conduct and supervision of police investigations, the role of the prosecutor, the disclosure of material, the role of experts, defence arrangements, the "right to silence", the role of trial courts and the Court of Appeal and arrangements for considering allegations of miscarriages of justice. It reported in 1993,[256] and made 352 detailed recommendations, many but not all of which were accepted. It commissioned a substantial body of research.[257] However, the report received a largely critical response from academic commentators, who argued that significant findings of that research were ignored, that the report lacked a coherent or explicit theoretical base and that the thrust of the recommendations seemed to be in facilitating convictions rather than protecting the innocent.[258] Furthermore, by the time of the report, the government's major preoccupation was again the fight against crime, symbolised with the introduction, contrary to the RCCJ's recommendation, of provisions enabling inferences to be drawn from the silence of the accused, in the Criminal Justice and Public Order Act 1994.[259]

On the civil side, Lord Woolf was invited to conduct an inquiry on access to justice. His Interim Report on *Access to Justice*, published in June 1995, made 124 recommendations. The key feature was that there should be a fundamental transfer in the responsibility for the management of civil litigation from litigants and their legal advisers to the courts. These recommendations were confirmed and expanded in the Final Report on *Access to Justice*, and have generally been accepted and implemented.[260] Lord Justice Auld was commissioned on December 14, 1999, to conduct a Review of the Criminal Courts in England and Wales. The terms of reference were to inquire into:

> "the practices and procedures of, and the rules of evidence applied by, the criminal courts at every level, with a view to ensuring that they deliver justice fairly, by streamlining all their processes, increasing their efficiency and strengthening the effectiveness of their relationships with others across the whole of the criminal justice system and having regard to the interests of all parties including victims and witnesses, thereby promoting public confidence in the rule of law."

He was not expected to (and did not) cost his proposals. The process adopted was not that of a Royal Commission. Sir Robin had 12 expert consultants, but appointed after the inquiry process had started. He sought and received many

---

[255] See below, para.14–001.
[256] Cm. 2263, 1993.
[257] It published 22 research studies (see list in App.4).
[258] See below, para.14–095.
[259] See below, para.17–048—17–050.
[260] See below, Ch.12.

written submissions and held a very large series of consultation meetings. The voluminous report[261] was accordingly essentially his view of the necessary changes in the operation of the criminal courts. He commissioned relatively little research and has been criticised for making little use of previously published work.[262] The key recommendations were: that the criminal law should be codified (with codes of offences, procedure, evidence and sentencing); existing national planning and operational bodies should be replaced by a Criminal Justice Board, supported by local boards, and existing advisory and consultative bodies by a Criminal Justice Council; the Crown Court and magistrates' courts should be replaced by a unified Criminal Court with three divisions; juries should be more widely representative of local communities; allocation of cases should be the responsibility of the magistrates' court alone; there should be a significant shift of heavy work from High Court to Circuit judges; the prosecutor should assume responsibility for charges; the disclosure regime should be reformed; there should be a comprehensive review of the law of criminal evidence and reforms of the appellate structure.[263] The report was, curiously, preceded by the publication of a White Paper, *Criminal Justice: The Way Ahead*,[264] and followed by another, *Justice for All*.[265] A number of changes derived from the Auld Report and other sources were effected by the Courts Act 2003 and the Criminal Justice Act 2003. Finally, and remarkably, the abolition of the office of Lord Chancellor and the establishment of a Supreme Court was simply announced by the Prime Minister, with no prior consultation.[266]

E. THE ROLE OF THE JUDICIARY IN COURT ADMINISTRATION

Unlike the position in some other common law jurisdictions, apart from the **1–033** anomalous position of the Lord Chancellor, when he was both head of the judiciary and political head of the LCD, the judges have not played a major role in supervising the administration of the courts.[267] A strong conception of the independence of judiciary would require the judiciary to assume administrative responsibility for the operation of the courts, including control over court buildings and facilities and the organisation of business. However, while there have been judicial expressions of concern that the decisions of civil servants are having an increasingly direct (and deleterious) effect on the work of the courts, what has been sought for the judiciary is a position of greater influence, rather

---

[261] *Review of the Criminal Courts* (2001), *www.criminal-courts-review.org*.

[262] M. Zander, *Lord Justice Auld's Review of the Criminal Courts: A Response* (*www.lse.ac.uk/ Depts/law*).

[263] See further below, Chs 14, 17.

[264] Cm. 5074 (2001).

[265] Cm. 5563, 2002.

[266] See para.2–074.

[267] See I. R. Scott, "The Council of Judges in the Supreme Court of England and Wales" [1989] P.L. 379; Lord Mackay of Clashfern, (1991) 44 C. L. P. 241, 247–250; Mr Justice R. D. Nicholson, (1993) 67 A.L.J. 404, 422–424. The judges are responsible for what happens in the court room and for "the administrative penumbra immediately surrounding the judicial process" (Lord Mackay, *op. cit.* at p.247); presiding judges for each circuit and the senior presiding judge deal with the deployment and performance of the judiciary (below, para.2–055.). Otherwise, administration is in the hands of the Court Service (above, para.1–018) and while the Lord Chancellor is ultimately accountable to Parliament for the service when he was a judge he was regarded by at least some of the judges as one of "them" rather than one of "us" for these purposes (below, para.4–038.).

than a full transfer of responsibility.[268] Such a transfer would, moreover, in the opinion of Lord Mackay, be an "extremely retrograde step".[269]

The position has to an extent been modified by the transfer of the role of head of the judiciary from the Lord Chancellor, to the Lord Chief Justice, which took effect from April 3, 2006. Section 7 of the Constitutional Reform Act 2005 provides that the Lord Chief Justice holds the office of President of the Courts of England and Wales and is Head of the Judiciary of England and Wales. As President, he is responsible:

(a) for representing the views of the judiciary of England and Wales to the Parliament, to the Lord Chancellor and to ministers;

(b) for the maintenance of appropriate arrangements for the welfare, training and guidance of the judiciary of England and Wales within the resource made available by the Lord Chancellor; and

(c) for the maintenance of appropriate arrangements for the deployment of the judiciary of England and Wales and the allocation of work within courts.

The Lord Chancellor accordingly remains responsible for the provision of resources for the judiciary, the courts and the legal system generally. By virtue of s.1 of the Courts Act 2003,[270] the Lord Chancellor is under a duty (his "general duty") to ensure that there is an efficient and effective system to support the carrying on of the business of (a) the Supreme Court (to become the Senior Courts) including the district probate registries; (aa) the Court of Protection; (b) county courts; and (c) magistrates' courts and that appropriate services are provided for those courts. He is to report to Parliament annually as to the way in which he has discharged his general duty in relation to the courts. Section 3 provides for guarantees of judicial independence.[271] The Lord Chief Justice has certain statutory responsibilities under Pt 4 of the Act concerning judicial appointments and discipline.[272] Further flesh on these legislative bones is placed by the so-called Concordat agreed between the Lord Falconer L.C. and Lord Woolf C.J. in 2004 in the course of consultations in the background to enactment of the 2005 Act.[273] This paper was an extended version of statements made by the Lord Chancellor to the House of Lords on January 26, 2004, and by the Lord Chief Justice. In the sections on resources and deployment,[274] it is stated that:

> "Arrangements will be put in place to ensure that the judiciary can be effectively involved in the resource planning of the unified Courts Agency and the Department for Constitutional Affairs, to ensure that the judiciary is enabled to have early engagement with the new agency and Department at strategic level, including on issues concerning resource plans and bids."

---

[268] See below, para.4–038.

[269] *The Administration of Justice* (1994), p.48. Lord Mackay argued that there was no way that a judge with security of tenure could be accountable to Parliament for the way in which money was spent and the courts were administered; as Lord Chancellor, he had no security of tenure: *ibid.*

[270] To be amended by the Constitutional Reform Act 2005, Sch.11, Pt 2, para.4, and the Mental Capacity Act 2005, Sch.6, para.47.

[271] See para.4–034.

[272] See paras 4–028, 4–032.

[273] See *www.dca.gov.uk/consult/lcoffice/judiciary.htm* under the title *Constitutional Reform: The Lord Chancellor's judiciary-related functions: Proposals (Since referred to as "the agreement" and also "the concordat").*

[274] Paras 19 – 42. "Resources" cover financial, material and human resources: para.19.

The Courts Service Framework Document is to include provision for at least two separate bilateral discussions during the year between the Chief Executive and representatives of the Judges' Council will be held, concentrating on providing the opportunity for judicial impact into future resource planning of the Service.[275] Senior members of the judiciary were to be non-executive members of the board of HM Courts Service and on the Corporate Board of the MoJ and in Spending Review years there are to be specified meetings between DCA officials and the Lord Chief Justice or his representative when the Departmental bid and Public Service Agreement is being worked up and before final allocations are made after the settlement. Such meetings should also take place in other years focusing on the delivery arms of the DCA.

As to the principles governing deployment, the Lord Chancellor, in consultation with the Lord Chief Justice, is responsible for the efficient and effective administration of the court system, and this includes setting the framework for the organisation of the court system (such as geographical and functional jurisdictional boundaries). The Lord Chief Justice is responsible for the posting and roles of individual judges within that framework. "Real and effective partnership between the Government and the judiciary is seen as being paramount, particularly in this area." Accordingly, all significant issues should be decided after consultation (or concurrence where responsibility is equally shared).[276]

The Lord Chief Justice and the senior judiciary, and through them the serving judiciary, are supported by a new Directorate of Judicial Offices (DJO) within the MoJ. This includes support for the Lord Chief Justice's role as head of the judiciary and in relation to judicial appointments and "judges well being". The DJO comprises: (1) the Judicial Office, based at the Royal Courts of Justice[277]; (2) the Judicial Communications Office (JCO), providing external and internal communications support for all judges, tribunal members and magistrates; and (3) the Judicial Studies Board (JSB),[278] which from April 2006 reports to the Lord Chief Justice within the management structure of the Directorate.[279] The Lord Chancellor is advised on policy and appointments relating to the judiciary and magistracy by the Legal and Judicial Services Directorate of the MoJ.[280] The Office of the Lord Chief Justice is responsible for accounting to the MoJ for the expenditure allocated to him.[281]

The greater clarity of these arrangements by comparison with the situation where matters essentially were left to the Lord Chancellor as both minister and head of the Judiciary is a positive step. However, their effectiveness will be put to the test in continued debate over the resourcing of the legal system, where particular current pressures include the family justice system and expenditure on legal aid and legal services.[282]

---

[275] See *Her Majesty's Courts Service Framework Document*, April 1, 2005, Pt 2, "The Relationship with the Judiciary". This states that the HMCS Chief Executive will ensure that all of the agency's activities are in accordance with the Concordat.

[276] Further detail on the application of these principles is set out in paras 29 – 42.

[277] It in turn comprises three teams: Planning and Governance; Judicial HR Services; and Private Offices for the senior judiciary.

[278] See para.4–033.

[279] See *www.dca.gov.uk/constitution/reform/djo.htm* and *www.judiciary.gov.uk*.

[280] See *www.dca.gov.uk/constitution/reform/services.htm* and *www.justice.gov.uk*.

[281] Concordat, para.22.

[282] See Chs 10, 11. The establishment of the Ministry of Justice caused further concern to the judiciary.

At the circuit level outside London, since 1972 there have been two (or sometimes three) High Court judges appointed for each circuit as "presiding judges".[283] Their main function now is the discharge of the Lord Chief Justice's responsibility for the conduct of the business of the courts, and they are supported by Circuit Judicial Secretariats on each circuit. This includes day-to-day responsibility for the deployment in and the business of the Crown Court, the High Court outside the Royal Courts of Justice, and the county courts, the requirement for judicial appointments below the level of the High Court, personnel issues for judges below the High Court, and deployment, personnel and monitoring issues for district judges (magistrates' courts).[284] A Lord Justice of Appeal is appointed as Senior Presiding Judge and a High Court judge as Deputy Senior Presiding Judge.[285]

F. INFORMATION ABOUT THE LEGAL SYSTEM

1-034 Statistical and factual information about the operation of the English legal system can be gleaned from various official sources. Official publications are grouped into a number of classes.[286] "Command papers" are "Presented to Parliament by Command of Her Majesty"[287] and include reports of Royal Commissions, departmental committees and the Law Commission. "House of Commons" and "House of Lords Papers" are published on behalf of the respective Houses of Parliament.[288] Other documents are published as "Non-Parliamentary Publications" by The Stationery Office[289] or by the department concerned.[290]

Statistical information may be found in the series of *Judicial Statistics* (1856–1922) published by the Home Office and covering both civil and criminal matters; and *Criminal Statistics* (1922 to date) also published by the Home Office. There are also Home Office Statistical Bulletins, which provide regular statistical information on some topics, such as the use of the Prevention of Terrorism Acts (now the Terrorism Acts 2006), and occasional information on others, such as comparative figures on remands in custody by magistrates' courts in different areas. The LCD, DCA and MoJ have published various series: *Civil Judicial Statistics* (1922–1974); *Statistics on Judicial Administration* (1972–1974) and *Judicial Statistics: England and Wales* (1975 to date). Information on legal services was given in the Annual Report of the Law Society and the Lord Chancellor's Advisory Committee, first issued in 1951 and from 1974–75 termed the *Legal Aid Annual Reports*, and is now found in the Annual Reports

---

[283] Statutory authority for their appointment is now found in the Courts and Legal Services Act 1990, s.72.

[284] See *www.judiciary.gov.uk* under "The Organisation of the Judiciary".

[285] For their detailed responsibilities, see *ibid*.

[286] See generally, J. E. Pemberton, *British Official Publications* (2nd edn, 1973); D. Butcher, *Official Publications in Britain* (2nd edn, 1991).

[287] These papers are numbered in series and since 1870 have been prefixed by an abbreviation for "Command": 1st series [1]–[4222] 1833–1869; 2nd series [C.1]–[C.9550] 1870–1899; 3rd series [Cd.1]–[Cd.9239] 1900–1918; 4th series [Cmd.1–Cmd.9889], 1919–1956; 5th series [Cmnd.1–9927] 1956–1986; 6th series [Cm.1–] 1986–.

[288] These are numbered in the session of publication (e.g. 1983–84 H.C. or H.L. 1).

[289] TSO also publish Command Papers and Parliamentary Papers: see the daily, monthly and annual TSO lists.

[290] See the *Catalogue of British Official Publications Not Published by HMSO* (1980–).

of the Legal Services Commission. The Lord Chancellor was required to publish annual reports on the business of the Supreme Court and county courts,[291] and is now required to publish annual reports as to the discharge of his general duty.[292] The Master of the Rolls issues Annual Reviews of the work of the Court of Appeal (Civil Division),[293] and there are similar reviews and reports for other parts of the system.[294]

Accessibility to this and other relevant information have been transformed by its availability on the internet.[295]

G. INTERNATIONAL STANDARDS

There has been an increasing awareness that minimum standards for the opera-   **1–035** tion of aspects of the legal system are set by international law, enshrined in treaties to which the United Kingdom is a party. The most important such treaties are the European Convention on Human Rights[296] and the International Covenant on Civil and Political Rights.[297] Key articles of the European Convention include Art.5 on the right to liberty and security of person, Art.6 on the right to a fair trial, Art.7, prohibiting retrospective criminal law, and Art.14, providing that the enjoyment of Convention rights and freedoms shall be secured without discrimination on any ground such as e.g. sex, race, colour, language or religion. There have been an increasing number and variety of successful challenges to the United Kingdom under these provisions in the context of the administration of justice in England and Wales,[298] including a series of cases concerning the rights of prisoners,[299] another series of cases that has required the fundamental remodelling of arrangements for court martials in the armed forces,[300] and cases

---

[291] Courts and Legal Services Act 1990, s.l(12). See the Annual Reports of the Lord Chancellor's Department Court Service and now HMCS (MoJ website).

[292] See para.1–033.

[293] See e.g. below, para.2–071.

[294] Court of Appeal (Criminal Division); Administrative Court; County Court; Crown Court; Magistrates' Courts.

[295] Good starting points are the MoJ and Home Office websites.

[296] See below, para.2–083.

[297] See S. H. Bailey, "Rights in the Administration of Justice" in D. J. Harris and S. Joseph (eds), *The United Kingdom and the International Covenant on Civil and Political Rights* (1995), Ch.6.

[298] The lack of a right to legal representation for criminal appeals in Scotland has been held to be unlawful: *Boner v UK* (1995) 19 E.H.R.R. 246; *Maxwell v UK* (1995) 19 E.H.R.R. 97.

[299] Cases on prisoners' correspondence (e.g. *Golder v UK* (1975) 1 E.H.R.R. 524; *Silver v UK* (1983) 5 E.H.R.R. 347); disciplinary proceedings (*Campbell and Fell v UK* (1984) 7 E.H.R.R. 165); release of life sentence prisoners (*Weeks v UK* (1987) 10 E.H.R.R. 293); *Oldham v UK*, Judgment of September 26, 2000 (two-year delay between Parole Board reviews not reasonable); *Curley v UK* (2001) 31 E.H.R.R. 14 (inadequacy of review arrangements); *Hirst v UK*, Judgment of July 24, 2001 (21-month and two-year delays between reviews not reasonable); *Thynne, Wilson and Gunnell v UK* (1990) 13 E.H.R.R. 666; prisoners in psychiatric detention (*X v UK* (1981) 4 E.H.R.R. 188); and persons detained during Her Majesty's pleasure (*Hussein v UK*; *Singh v UK* (1996) 22 E.H.R.R. 1.

[300] *Findlav v UK* (1997) 24 E.H.R.R. 221; *Coyne v UK*, Judgment of 24 September, 1997; *Hood v UK* (2000) 29 E.H.R.R. 365; *Cable v UK* (2000) 30 E.H.R.R. 1032; *Moore and Gordon v UK* (2001) 29 E.H.R.R. 729; *Stephen Jordan v UK* (2001) 31 E.H.R.R. 6; changes effected by the Armed Forces Act 1996 were held not fully to have secured trial by an independent and impartial tribunal in *Morris v UK*, Judgment of February 26, 2002 (Art.6(1)).

concerning excessive delay in civil proceedings (nine years),[301] the retrospective imposition of a confiscation order following conviction for drug offences,[302] violation of the right not to incriminate oneself, by the use at trial of statements obtained under legal compulsion,[303] the disproportionate use of a police power to enter a home,[304] the automatic refusal of bail in specified circumstances,[305] failure to disclose prosecution evidence,[306] inadequate jury directions concerning inferences from silence,[307] a lack of impartiality in proceedings where two jurors had allegedly made racist jokes,[308] and the degrading treatment of a disabled person held in custody.[309]

The necessity for a statutory regime to regulate covert surveillance by law enforcement authorities has been recognised.[310] Similarly, the Civil Procedure Rules[311] introduced as part of the Woolf reforms have been drafted to secure compliance with the requirement for a public hearing; the previous approach whereby small claims arbitrations were normally to be held in private were found to violate that requirement.[312] Challenges in high-profile cases concerning the right to silence[313] and the abolition of the marital exemption from liability for rape[314] have failed. Nevertheless, it has been argued that current trends in the criminal justice process render the United Kingdom increasingly vulnerable to challenge.[315] The implementation of the Human Rights Act 1998 has added to the pressures.[316]

---

[301] *Darnell v UK*, (1994) 18 E.H.R.R. 205; *cf. Robins v UK* (1997) 26 E.H.R.R. 527 (delay in decision concerning costs); *Howarth v UK* (2000) 9 B.H.R.C. 253 (delay in Attorney-General's reference of a sentence to the Court of Appeal (Criminal Division) (Art.6(1)).

[302] *Welch v UK* (1995) 20 E.H.R.R. 247.

[303] *Saunders v UK* (1997) 23 E.H.R.R. 313; *IJL, GMR and AKP v UK*, Judgment of September 19, 2000 (Art.6(1)).

[304] *McLeod v UK*, Judgment of 23 September 1998 (Art.8).

[305] *Caballero v UK* (2000) 30 E.H.R.R. 643; *S.B.C. v UK*, Judgment of June 19, 2001 (violation of Art.5(3) conceded; these cases concerned the Criminal Justice and Public Order Act 1994 s.25, which prevented bail being granted in murder, manslaughter and rape cases (including attempts) to a person previously convicted of such an offence or culpable homicide; this was amended by the Crime and Disorder Act 1998, s.56, enabling bail to be granted in exceptional circumstances).

[306] *Rowe and Davis v UK* (2000) 20 E.H.R.R. 1; *Atlan v UK* Judgment of June 19, 2001 (Art.6(1)).

[307] *Condron v UK*, Judgment of May 2, 2000 (Art.6(1)).

[308] *Sander v UK*, Judgment of May 9, 2000 (Art.6(1)).

[309] *Price v UK*, Judgment of July 14, 2001 (Art.3).

[310] Police Act 1997; Regulation of Investigatory Powers Act 2000; violations have been found in respect of covert police surveillance under the previous arrangements: *Khan v UK* (2000) 8 B.H.R.C. 310; *P.G. and J.H. v UK*, Judgment of September 25, 2001 (Art.8).

[311] Below.

[312] *Scarth v UK*, Judgment of July 22, (Art.6(1)).

[313] See below, paras 17–048—17–050.

[314] See below, para.14–024 and para.4–042.

[315] See Liberty, *Criminal Justice and Civil and Political Liberties* (1993).

[316] See generally, Ch.8.

CHAPTER 2

COURTS AND TRIBUNALS

A. INTRODUCTION

2–001 There are several ways in which a legal dispute (which the parties also characterise as "legal") may be resolved. It may be settled by force or by agreement. The dispute may be referred informally or formally to a third party for him or her to arbitrate. Exceptionally, the dispute may be referred to one of the institutions established by the state expressly for the purpose of resolving such matters. Some of these institutions are termed "courts", others "tribunals". These terms cannot be defined with precision, and, for the most part, little turns on whether a particular institution is labelled a court or a tribunal, or whether an institution, however labelled, falls within the legal definition of a "court".

The term "tribunal" can be used very generally to mean any "judicial assembly",[1] including a court; in the present context it is commonly used for "judicial assemblies" other than courts. If established by the state they are generally described as "administrative tribunals" to distinguish them from "domestic tribunals" established by non-state institutions such as professional and sporting associations and trade unions as part of their disciplinary procedures. The label "administrative" reflects the fact that most such tribunals are established to perform judicial functions as part of the administration of some government scheme or programme.

Finally, it should be remembered that while the settlement of disputes is the main function of almost all courts and most tribunals, it is not the only one: a number of administrative functions have also been allocated to them.[2]

B. COURTS

1. SIGNIFICANCE

2–002 Apart from the police, the courts of law are perhaps the most visible feature of the English legal system. Only the courts have power to impose punishment in

---

[1] O.E.D.

[2] e.g discretionary powers of the High Court in relation to the administration of estates or the supervision of the affairs of children and of persons incapable, by reason of mental disorder, of managing their own property and affairs; *cf.* below, para.2–060.

criminal cases; reports of these, and important civil cases decided by the superior courts, commonly appear in the national and local press, and they may be covered by radio and television. Lawyers, and to an even greater extent, law students and lecturers place great emphasis on the decisions of the superior courts. It is, however, difficult to estimate the significance of the courts in the legal system as a whole. The number of cases determined by the courts is small, and by the superior courts[3] minute, in comparison with the number of disputes settled by other means. Moreover, in a high proportion of the cases dealt with by the magistrates' courts and county courts the proceedings are merely mechanical processes for, respectively, the fining of minor traffic offenders and the collection of debts, with no live issue to be determined.

On the other hand, the courts do have a much wider indirect impact, given, first, that the chances of success in legal proceedings will influence the settlement of disputes,[4] and, secondly, that the decisions of superior courts are a source of law.[5]

2. HISTORICAL BACKGROUND[6]

(a) Courts of common law and equity

As we have said, the main function of almost all courts today is the adjudication **2–003** of disputes. They can, however, trace their origins to local and central institutions in which no distinctions were drawn between the functions of administration, legislation and adjudication. At the local level in the Dark Ages there were community assemblies or "moots" which, *inter alia*, dealt with disputes according to local custom. These assemblies, apart from the smallest, village, assemblies, came to be based on administrative units established by the Crown, the shires, and their subdivisions, the hundreds and the boroughs. At the centre was the *Curia Regis* (King's Court).

Three related themes in early legal development can be discerned. First, the administration of justice came to be regarded as an adjunct of feudal lordship rather than a matter for the community as a whole. Then there was a further shift whereby it came in particular to be one of the prerogatives of the Crown. Thirdly, the administration of justice came to be differentiated from other functions of government. The strengthening of royal justice at the expense of local, communal, justice was a gradual process, and was neither intended nor planned, but it took place at all levels. This process involved the establishment of distinct royal courts, the placing of royal officials in the localities, whether temporarily or permanently, and the development of the supervisory jurisdiction of the royal courts over local courts.

At the centre, three common law courts evolved at different times out of the *Curia Regis*: the Exchequer,[7] the Common Pleas and the King's (or Queen's)

---

[3] See below, para.2–018.
[4] See below, para.11–027—11–033.
[5] See below, Ch.7.
[6] See generally J. H. Baker, *An Introduction to English Legal History* (4th edn, 2002), Chs 1–7.
[7] As well as a common law jurisdiction, this court had an established equity jurisdiction, which was transferred to the Court of Chancery as late as 1842.

Bench. They sat at Westminster Hall. The jurisdictional lines between these courts were complex. In theory, the Exchequer dealt with matters concerning the revenues of the Crown, the Common Pleas suits between subject and subject in which the Crown had no interest, and the King's Bench "pleas of the Crown" (i.e. criminal matters and civil cases involving a breach of the King's peace or some other royal interest). By the eighteenth century a variety of fictions had enabled each court to exercise a jurisdiction that was similar in substance although different in form to the others.

Parallel to the development of the common law courts at the centre was that of the Court of Chancery, and in particular its function of dealing with petitions.[8] For a time in the sixteenth and seventeenth centuries a number of "conciliar courts" also assumed importance, being courts established under the prerogative to handle judicial matters that came before the Privy Council but were not dealt with by the Chancellor. These included the Court of Star Chamber, which became notorious towards the end of its life for its handling of political crimes, the Court of Requests and several regional offshoots. They were looked on with suspicion by the common law courts and were abolished in the 1640s. The pattern of superior courts otherwise remained substantially unchanged until the nineteenth century, when some new courts were created, and there was subsequently a general reorganisation under the Supreme Court of Judicature Acts 1873–75.[9] In this reorganisation the various superior courts[10] were replaced by one Supreme Court of Judicature comprising the High Court (in five divisions) and the Court of Appeal. The intention initially was for the appellate jurisdiction of the House of Lords to be abolished, but a successful rearguard action was fought for its retention.[11]

2–004   Royal justices from the common law courts were also sent out to travel the country. Originally, they conducted all manner of governmental affairs, but they came to concentrate on judicial proceedings. There were two bases for their jurisdiction. In criminal and some civil cases they were given ad hoc commissions from the Crown. In other civil cases they sat with a jury to try issues that arose in litigation in the superior courts at Westminster: the juries technically were summoned to Westminster "unless before then (*nisi prius*) the King's justices have come" into the country. It was obviously more convenient to try the issues locally and transmit the result to London. The system came to be known as the "assize system" and continued until the 1970s,[12] and even the present arrangements have maintained the concept of High Court judges hearing cases in the provinces, albeit now reinforced by local judges.

The significant development in the handling of criminal cases less serious than those dealt with at the assizes was the appointment by the Crown of justices of the peace and the progressive widening of their criminal jurisdiction from the

---

[8] See above, paras 1–005—1–007.

[9] This followed the recommendations of the First Report of the Judicature Commission (HMSO, 1869).

[10] i.e. the Courts of Chancery, Queen's Bench, Common Pleas, Exchequer, Admiralty (see below, para.2–006), Probate (*ibid.*), and Divorce and Matrimonial Causes (*ibid.*). The London Court of Bankruptcy, originally established by an Act of 1831 to relieve the Court of Chancery of some of its business, was incorporated in 1884.

[11] See below, para.2–072.

[12] See below, para.2–052.

thirteenth century onwards.[13] Civil cases were heard by the successors of the old community assemblies, a variegated pattern of county, hundred, manorial and borough courts. These courts were subject to the supervisory jurisdiction of the superior royal courts and came to apply the common law. They declined for different reasons and at different times, although many were only formally abolished in the 1970s.[14] The important step in the establishment of a regular system of local civil courts was the creation of new, statutory, county courts in 1846.[15]

(b) Appeals[16]

Provision for appeals was complex. The record of a court's proceedings could be reviewed for error[17] by another common law court[18] or a special court, a number of which were established by statute at various times to sit in a room at Westminster Hall known as the Exchequer Chamber.[19] Error lay from the Courts of Exchequer Chamber to Parliament, this jurisdiction being exercised by the House of Lords. Another, informal, method of review was the practice of judges to reserve cases for the opinion of their brethren, expressed at meetings held in Serjeants' Inn or the Exchequer Chamber.[20] In Chancery proceedings, a case argued before the Master of the Rolls or a Vice-Chancellor[21] could be re-argued before the Chancellor, and the Chancellor could review his own previous decisions and those of his predecessors. In the seventeenth century it was established that proceedings in error lay from the Court of Chancery to the House of Lords. A Court of Appeal in Chancery with appellate judges (Lords Justices) specially appointed to it was created in 1851 to hear appeals from the Master of the Rolls and the Vice-Chancellors. This became the model for the Court of Appeal established by the Judicature Acts 1873–75. The nineteenth century also saw the replacement of proceedings in error by statutory appeals in the modern form.

2–005

(c) Other courts

Apart from the courts of common law and equity there were courts that followed civil law procedure: the High Court of Admiralty,[22] which dealt with maritime

2–006

---

[13] See below, para.4–002. The justices also had many administrative responsibilities.

[14] Courts Act 1971, ss.42, 43; Administration of Justice Act 1977, s.23, Sch.4.

[15] See below, para.2–041: These must not be confused with the old shire or county courts presided over by the sheriff.

[16] See Baker (2002), Ch.9.

[17] This process was more akin to the modern application for judicial review than statutory appeal: see Ch.18.

[18] Proceedings in error lay from the Common Pleas to the King's Bench until 1830.

[19] (1) One was established in 1357 to hear error from the Exchequer. This comprised the Chancellor and the Treasurer with judges as assistants. (2) A second was established in 1585 to hear error from the Queen's Bench, this court comprising the justices of the Common Pleas and the barons of the Exchequer. (3) In 1830 a new Court of Exchequer Chamber was established to hear error from each of the common law courts. This comprised all the judges of the superior courts, error from one court being heard by the judges of the other two.

[20] In criminal cases such meetings became formalised with the creation of the Court for Crown Cases Reserved in 1848.

[21] See below para.4–025.

[22] This court became part of the Supreme Court of Judicature in the 1873–75 reorganisation. See F. Wiswall, *The Development of Admiralty Jurisdiction and Practice Since 1800* (1971).

matters and the High Court of Chivalry,[23] a court of honour. Canon law was administered by archdeacons' courts, the bishops' consistory courts, each presided over by the chancellor of the diocese, and the archbishops' provincial courts, the Chancery Court of York and the Court of Arches.[24] Further appeals lay to the Pope or to Papal Delegates. Following the Reformation this jurisdiction passed to the Court of High Commission, which lapsed in the 1640s, and the Court of Delegates. The latter court was replaced by the Privy Council in 1832. The relationship between the ecclesiastical courts and the royal courts was stormy and complicated.[25] The jurisdiction of ecclesiastical courts over marriage, divorce and probate ended in 1857 with the creation of the Court of Divorce and Matrimonial Causes and the Court of Probate.[26] Since then, their jurisdiction has been confined to church matters. The present court structure was introduced by the Ecclesiastical Jurisdiction Measure 1963, which retained the consistory courts, but created an appellate system of gothic complexity, largely replacing the appellate jurisdiction of the Privy Council.[27] Appeals in matters of doctrine, ritual or ceremonial lie from the consistory courts to the Court of Ecclesiastical Causes Reserved, which comprises three bishops and two judges, appointed by the Queen.[28]

C. TRIBUNALS

1. INTRODUCTION

2–007 The significant role played by administrative tribunals in the adjudication of legal disputes is a development of the present century, although it is possible to find examples of similar institutions in earlier centuries.[29] For example, the General and Special Commissioners of Income Tax were established in 1799 and 1805 respectively, with both assessment and appellate functions. The Railway and Canal Commission was established in 1873, *inter alia*, to settle disputes between

---

[23] This court has sat once since 1737: *Manchester Corporation v Manchester Palace of Varieties Ltd* [1955] P. 133. See G. D. Squibb, *The High Court of Chivalry* (1959). It has jurisdiction over such questions as the right to arms, precedence and descent. In the 1955 case the corporation claimed successfully that the company should be prevented from using the former's arms in their seal and displayed above the main curtain at the Palace Theatre, Manchester.

[24] So called because it usually sat in the arched crypt of the church of St Mary le Bow in London. Its judge became known as the Dean of Arches.

[25] See Baker (2002), Ch.8.

[26] These courts became part of the Supreme Court of Judicature in the 1873–75 reorganisation.

[27] See E. Garth Moore, *An Introduction to Canon Law* (1967), Ch.XIV; L. Leeder, *Ecclesiastical Law Handbook* (1997); M. Hill, *Ecclesiastical Law* (2nd edn, 2001); *Canons of the Church of England* (6th edn), Section G (*www.cofe.anglican.org/about/churchlawlegis/canons*). Disciplinary proceedings against a priest or deacon not involving matters of doctrine, ritual or ceremonial are now heard by a bishop's disciplinary tribunal on the Vicar-General's court (in respect of a bishop or archbishop) under the Clergy Discipline Measure 2003.

[28] The first two cases before this court were *In re St Michael and All Angels, Great Torrington* [1985] Fam. 81 and *In re St Stephen's, Walbrook* [1987] Fam. 146: see J. D. C. Harte, (1988) 2 Ecc-L.J. 22.

[29] See R. E. Wraith and P. G. Hutchesson, *Administrative Tribunals* (1973), Ch.1.

railway companies and between companies and their customers, and subsequently evolved into the Transport Tribunal.

The most important factors behind the expansion of the number of tribunals and the range of their work have been the advent of the welfare state and the development of state economic controls. The National Insurance Act 1911 set up the unemployment benefit scheme. All questions concerning claims to benefit were to be determined initially by an insurance officer. A workman dissatisfied with a determination could have it referred to a "court of referees" consisting of a chairman appointed by the Board of Trade, one member from an "employers' panel" and one from a "workmens' panel". A further right of appeal lay to an "umpire"—a national appellate authority appointed by the Crown. This arrangement proved superior to alternative methods of adjudication used in legislation of the period,[30] and was adopted as the general model for many of the new tribunals established in the following decades:

> "The extension of governmental responsibility for welfare provision, regulation of the economy, employment policy and resource development has created new statutory rights, obligations and restraints. Consequently, new areas of potential dispute have opened up, the boundaries of which have been progressively extended, and which require legislative provision for adjudication. The tendency, for a variety of reasons, has been to use tribunals rather than ordinary courts for settling disputes of this kind."[31]

This is not to say that there have been clear principles governing either the decision to allocate a particular decision to a tribunal or the details of the machinery established:

> "Parliament's selection of subjects to be referred to tribunals and inquiries does not form a regular pattern. Certain basic guidelines can be detected, but the choice is influenced by the interplay of various factors—the nature of the decisions, accidents of history, departmental preferences and political considerations—rather than by the application of a set of coherent principles."[32]

These tribunals commonly determine disputes between the citizen and the state arising out of the administration of a statutory scheme.[33] In addition, some determine disputes between citizens, normally arising out of protective legislation enacted for the benefit of one of the parties.[34]

---

[30] i.e. Workmen's Compensation Act 1897: disputes concerning compensation for industrial injuries were supposed to be settled by arbitration but in practice went to county court judges and beyond on appeal; Old Age Pensions Act 1908: pensions were administered by pensions committees of local authorities, which also adjudicated disputes, with an appeal to the Local Government Board; National Insurance Act 1911, Pt I: national health insurance was administered by friendly societies with an appeal to one of four Insurance Commissioners.

[31] *The Functions of the Council on Tribunals: Special Report by the Council* (Cmnd. 7805, 1980), p.1.

[32] *ibid.* pp.1–2.

[33] e.g. disputes concerning claims to welfare benefits.

[34] e.g. disputes between landlord and tenant arising out of rent controls, and between employer and employee concerning allegedly unfair dismissals and an expanding range of other employment matters.

2. The Franks Report

2–008   A significant landmark in the development of tribunals was the 1957 report of the Committee on Administrative Tribunals and Enquiries chaired by Sir Oliver Franks.[35] Part of the terms of reference required the Committee to review the constitution and working of tribunals other than the ordinary courts of law, constituted by a minister or for the purposes of a minister's functions.[36] Among the general points made by the Committee were, first, that the special procedures within their terms of reference should be marked by the characteristics of "openness, fairness and impartiality"[37]:

> "In the field of tribunals openness appears to us to require the publicity of proceedings and knowledge of the essential reasoning underlying the decisions; fairness to require the adoption of a clear procedure which enables parties to know their rights, to present their case fully and to know the case which they have to meet; and impartiality to require the freedom of tribunals from the influence, real or apparent, of Departments concerned with the subject matter of their decisions."[38]

Tribunals should properly be regarded as machinery provided by Parliament for adjudication rather than as part of the machinery for administration.[39] Secondly, the Committee noted that tribunals as a system for adjudication had come to stay, and indeed that the tendency to refer issues arising from legislative schemes to special tribunals was likely to grow rather than to diminish.[40]

Thirdly, the Committee recommended the establishment of two permanent Councils on Tribunals, one for England and Wales and one for Scotland, to supervise tribunal and inquiry procedures.

In addition, the report made a whole series of detailed recommendations concerning both the constitution and procedures of tribunals generally and particular tribunals. Most of the proposals were implemented in the Tribunals and Inquiries Act 1958, subsequently consolidated in the Tribunals and Inquiries Acts 1971 and now 1992, and in changes of regulations and departmental practice.

3. The Council on Tribunals[41]

2–009   The 1958 Act established one Council on Tribunals, with a Scottish Committee. Its functions in respect of tribunals are:

---

[35] Cmnd. 218.
[36] The other part of the terms of reference concerned public inquiry procedures.
[37] Cmnd. 218, p.5.
[38] *ibid.* p.10.
[39] *ibid.* p.9.
[40] *ibid.* p.8.
[41] See *The Functions of the Council on Tribunals: Special Report by the Council* (Cmnd. 7805, 1980); the Council's Annual Reports; H. W. R. Wade, [1960] P.L. 351; J. F. Garner, [1965] P.L. 321; D. G. T. Williams [1984] P.L. 73 and (1990) 9 C.J.Q. 27; O. Lomas, (1985) 48 M.L.R. 694; C. Harlow and R. Rawlings, *Law and Administration* (2nd edn, 1997), Ch.14.

"(a) to keep under review the construction and working of the tribunals specified in Schedule 1 to the [1992] Act;

(b) to consider and report on particular matters referred to the Council by the Lord Chancellor and the Lord Advocate with respect to any tribunal other than a court of law whether or not specified in Schedule 1; . . . "[42]

Thus, its powers are consultative and advisory. It was not given the executive powers recommended by the Franks Report as to the appointment of tribunal members, the review of remuneration and the formulation of procedural codes.[43] Certainly it has no power to reverse or require reconsideration of specific tribunal decisions. The Council has 15 members appointed by the Lord Chancellor and the Lord Advocate, and the Parliamentary Commissioner for Administration is a member *ex officio*. The membership comprises a mixture of lawyers, both practising and academic, and non-lawyers, with the latter predominating. The Council's requests for additional powers, put forward in its Special Report of 1980, were generally not accepted. A code for consultation with government departments has been introduced,[44] but the Council still regularly complains that it is given inadequate time to comment on draft regulations. The Council has done much useful work in minor matters, securing, for example, many amendments to draft Bills, rules and regulations, and some changes in tribunal practice. It has published a Report on Model Rules for Tribunals,[45] a Code of Practice on Access for Disabled People using the Tribunal System[46] and (with Property Holdings) a Register of Tribunal Hearing Accommodation.[47] However, its political position is weak, its resources are inadequate[48] and it "remains an inconspicuous advisory committee".[49] It is still met from time to time by spurious arguments from departments why a proposed new tribunal should not be placed under its jurisdiction; it sometimes, but not always, succeeds in overcoming them.[50] Access to the deliberative stage of tribunal hearings is occasionally denied.[51]

---

[42] Special Report, p.3. It has similar, although not identical, functions in respect of procedures involving inquiries held on behalf of a minister.

[43] It must be consulted before procedural rules are made for Sch.1 tribunals, but does not make the rules itself: 1992 Act, s.8.

[44] See the Council's Annual Reports for 1980–81 (1981–82 H.C. 89), pp.6–7 and 1981–82 (1982–83 H.C. 64), p.8 and App.C. The Code was recirculated in 1986 and 1992: Annual Report for 1991–92 (1992–93 H.C. 316), p.50 and App.I and revised and republished in January 2001 (*www.council-on-tribunals.gov.uk/consultcode*).

[45] An interim revised edition, taking account of jurisprudential developments on Art.6, ECHR, was distributed to departments in 1999: Council on Tribunals Annual Reports for 1998–99, pp.7–8 and 1999–2000, para.12.

[46] A Consultation Draft of Revised Guidance was issued in June 2002.

[47] See Annual Reports for 1990–91 (1991–92 H.C. 97), pp.23–24 (and Cm. 1434); 1992–93 (1993–94 H.C. 78), pp.11–13 and App.A; and 1993–94 (1994–95 H.C. 22), pp.11–12 and App.A. A second edition was published in 1995: Annual Report for 1994–95 (1995–96 H.C. 64), pp.44–45.

[48] The Lord Chancellor's Department took over two years to consider and reject a request for additional staff: Annual Report for 1985–86 (1986–87 H.C. 42), pp.28–30.

[49] Sir William Wade and C. F. Forsyth, *Administrative Law* (9th edn, 2004), p.925.

[50] Annual Reports for 1993–94 (1994–95 H.C. 22), pp.6–8, 41–42 (supervisory jurisdiction over Police Appeal Tribunals eventually conceded). The Council's position is helped by the fact that its current chairman Lord Newton of Braintree is a member of the House of Lords, as was his predecessor, Lord Archer.

[51] *ibid.* pp.9, 24–25 (industrial tribunals in Scotland).

4. THE LEGGATT REPORT

2–010   In 2000, the Lord Chancellor appointed Sir Andrew Leggatt, a former Lord Justice of Appeal, to conduct a review of the delivery of justice through tribunals. This, the first major review since Franks, complemented Lord Woolf's review of civil justice[52] and Sir Robin Auld's examination of the criminal justice system.[53] Sir Andrew reported in March 2001.[54] The Review found that, since the Franks Report, the numbers of tribunals had increased considerably and their work had become more complex. They were "a substantial part of the system of justice" but "too often their methods are old fashioned and they are daunting to users". They were many and disparate, and achieved no economies of scale. "Most importantly, they are not independent of the departments that sponsor them." (Consideration of their compliance with the requirements of Art.6(1), ECHR was expressly made part of the Review's terms of reference.) Overall, the object of the review was to recommend a system that was "independent, coherent, professional, cost-effective and user-friendly".[55] The Review made a series of recommendations in respect of both the system as a whole and particular tribunals. Key points were as follows.[56]

2–011   First, responsibility for tribunals should not lie with those whose policies or decisions it is the tribunal's duty to consider, in order to promote the fact and appearance of independence. Accordingly, all tribunals should instead be supported by a Tribunals Service. This would also achieve economies of scale, particularly in the provision of premises, common basic training and the use of IT, and greater administrative efficiency. The Service should be part of the Lord Chancellor's Department.

Secondly, tribunals "should do all they can to render themselves understandable, unthreatening, and useful to users". Users should be able to obtain the information they need concerning venues, timetables and sources of professional advice. Decision-makers should produce reasoned decisions in plain English or Welsh and give a proper explanation of the appeal process. Every effort should be made to reduce the number of cases in which representation is needed. Voluntary and community bodies should be funded to provide legal representation for the residual category of complex cases where legal representation is necessary; legal aid should be available only as a last resort. The system required underpinning by "the judicious and well managed application of IT" (currently, in many tribunals, it is "primitive").

Finally, the position of the Council on Tribunals should be strengthened, with additional powers and a higher profile. Overall, there was a need for a "new culture, starting with improved recognition of just how daunting the tribunal experience usually is for first-time users, as most are".

---

[52] See Ch.12.
[53] See para.1–032.
[54] The report was actually published in August 2001: *Tribunals for Users: One System, One Service* (2001). See M. Adler, (2002) 9 J.S.S.L. 177 and (2004) 39 *Benefits* 14.
[55] *ibid.* p.5.
[56] *ibid.* pp.5–14.

Many of these recommendations, particularly those concerning structure and organisation, seem sensible in principle. It would seem right that the organisation of tribunals should be similar to that for courts given that the tasks they perform are broadly the same. Whether the costs of effecting structural changes could be justified was a separate matter.[57] However, it is submitted that one key element is questionable: the belief that the majority of proceedings can, through training, changes to procedures and otherwise, be made accessible to the (unrepresented) ordinary, first-time user. The fair resolution of disputes can only be based on the proper identification of the issues and the identification of the evidence that is relevant to those issues. This very commonly requires more than just the application of "common sense". We return to these matters elsewhere.[58]

The tone of the Consultation Paper on the Leggatt Report issued by the LCD[59]   **2–012**
was largely sceptical. While the government was "determined to modernise tribunals" the report's recommendations, many of which were "controversial", would be judged "against the criterion of whether they will contribute to improving the service that users receive". The government was satisfied that tribunals already complied with the requirement of independence and impartiality set out in Art.6(1), ECHR[60] and so structural changes needed justification by reference to the needs of users.

The government's final views were set out in the White Paper, *Transforming*   **2–013**
Public Services: Complaints, Redress and Tribunals.[61] This went beyond *Leggatt* to propose improvements generally to administrative justice and justice at work, adopting as a theme the need for proportionate dispute resolution. As regards tribunals, it noted that there were now some 70 tribunals in existence, some with very large workloads, but many moribund or with insignificant workloads. All had some features in common, usually those derived from courts, but there were also differences, many explicable only in historical terms. There was little by way of alternative dispute resolution.[62] There were a number of problems with the effectiveness of tribunals today[63]: lack of perceived independence; the fact that most central government tribunals were sponsored by the responsible department meant that they were not seen to be manifestly independent of those whose decisions they were reviewing; delays; the lack of provision for informal resolution; inaccessibility of hearing centres; and inaccessibility of process. Overall, the government accepted Sir Andrew Leggatt's assessment of the present system as incoherent and inefficient.[64] Reforms were needed to deliver an improved service.[65] Key elements were, first, the establishment in stages of a new unified

---

[57] See below on the government's views.
[58] Below, Ch.16.
[59] August 2001, LCD website.
[60] The terms of appointment of part-time judicial tribunal members had been changed to ensure their independence following *Starrs and Chalmers v Procurator Fiscal* (below, para.4–021); employment tribunals and school admission and exclusion appeal tribunals met the required standards (*Link v Secretary of State for Trade and Industry*, March 23, 2001 (employment tribunals); *R. (on the application of B) v Alperton Community School* [2001] EWHC Admin 229 (Art.6(1) not applicable to these panels).
[61] Cm. 6243, July 2004. For comment, see M. Adler, (2006) 13 J.S.S.L. 69.
[62] para.3.30.
[63] Ch.5.
[64] para.5.14
[65] Ch.6.

tribunal system, under the umbrella of the DCA now MoJ. There had previously been a trend for the LCD/DCA progressively to take over administrative responsibility for more tribunals.[66] Between 2006 and 2008 it would take over from the current sponsoring department responsibility for the Appeals Service (social security), the Employment Tribunal Service, the Special Educational Needs and Disability Tribunal Panel and the Mental Health Review Tribunal for England. Others would be transferred by agreement, and all new tribunals (unless devolved) would become part of the new organisation.

2–014   The new organisation would deliver a network of hearing centres, with a better geographical spread than any individual tribunal could offer. The DCA would develop a common estate and develop new ways of operating, considering possible alternatives to formal hearings. Back-office functions would be rationalised. New standardised ways of dealing with customers would be developed, such as common terminologies, common pathways through the process (where feasible) and common terms for administrative positions. There would be first-tier and appellate levels, but not a formal divisional structure, although employment tribunals and the EAT would continue to maintain a strong degree of administrative separation. There would be a single judicial officer for each level (Tribunal judge and Tribunal Appellate judge). On appointment, judges would be assigned to a jurisdiction or jurisdiction according to operational needs provided the recruitment board has assessed them as qualified for that jurisdiction. A new office of Senior President of Tribunals would be established, with standing equivalent to a Lord Justice of Appeal. The tribunals judiciary would be supported by an executive agency within the DCA, the Tribunals Service. Tribunal rules would be overhauled, and made by a tribunals procedure committee.

The Tribunals Service was launched on April 1, 2006, and described by the DCA as the biggest change to the tribunals system in almost half a century.[67] Carnwath L.J. was appointed as Senior President Designate. Six tribunals joined the new Tribunals Service from its inception.[68] The primary tasks of the Tribunals Service are: to provide a responsive and efficient tribunals administration; to contribute to the improvement of the quality of decision-making across government; to reform the tribunals justice system for the benefit of its customers and the wider public; and to promote and protect the independence of the judiciary.[69] The structures and processes by which relationships between the Tribunal Service and the former sponsoring departments of transferred tribunals are to be

---

[66] By 2005, the DCA was responsible for the Adjudicator for HM Land Registry; the Asylum and Immigration Tribunal; the Commissioners' Office; the Finance & Tax Tribunals; the Gender Recognition Panel; the Immigration Services Tribunal; the Information Tribunal; the Lands Tribunal; the Pathogen Access Appeals Commission; the Pensions Appeal Tribunal; the Proscribed Organisations Appeals Commission; the Special Immigration Appeals Commission; and the Transport Tribunal: *Judicial Statistics* 2005, Ch.8.

[67] *www.tribunals.gov.uk*. See the *Tribunals Service Framework Document* (2006). The necessary legislation was, however, delayed from the 2005–06 session: see Lord Justice Carnwath, (2006) 13 J.S.S.L. 58.

[68] Employment tribunals and the EAT (from DTI); SENDIST (Dfes); Social Security and Child Support Appeals (DWP); MHRT (DH); Criminal Injuries Compensation Appeals Panel (HO). Statutory functions were transferred administratively to the Secretary of State for Constitutional Affairs and formally to the Lord Chancellor by a Transfer of Functions Order. See *Tribunal Service: Transfer of Statutory Functions* (2006).

[69] *Framework Document*, p.6.

conducted are set out in Partnership Agreements.[70] Arrangements for resource planning discussions with the tribunals judiciary are similar to those agreed for courts.[71] A separate Memorandum of Understanding sets the relationship of the Tribunals Service to the Judicial Services Directorate of the DCA, now MoJ.[72] The necessary statutory changes are to be effected by the Tribunals, Courts and Enforcement Act 2007.[73]

5. Supposed Advantages of Tribunals as Court-Substitutes

The Franks Committee noted that tribunals have certain characteristics which **2–015** often give them advantages over the courts: "cheapness, accessibility, freedom from technicality, expedition and expert knowledge of their particular subject".[74] Generally, tribunal proceedings are cheaper, speedier,[75] and more expert than courts of law. However, accessibility is hindered by the great complexity of the system of tribunals and the lack of publicity given to their work. Moreover, the Council on Tribunals has stated that:

"Significant changes have . . . taken place in the general constitutional and administrative climate. There is, for example, a movement towards greater formalism in procedures for settling disputes. The process started with reforms following the Franks Report which, in general, made tribunals more like courts. . . . Since then the trend towards judicialisation has gathered momentum with the result that tribunals are becoming more formal, expensive and procedurally complex. Consequently they tend to become more difficult for an ordinary citizen to comprehend and cope with on his own."[76]

Associated with this movement are the Council's arguments in favour of the extension of legal aid to tribunals, the appointment of lawyer chairmen and the extension of rights of appeal to the courts. It has also been pointed out that, despite declarations by tribunals that they are not bound by precedent, the requirements of consistency and predictability of decision lead to the development of general principles and an informal *de facto* system of precedent,[77] especially as the decisions of certain tribunals are systematically reported.

Accordingly, it is perhaps more true today than ever that "such differences as there are between [courts and tribunals] are not in any sense fundamental but at

---

[70] *ibid.* p.8.
[71] *ibid.* p.9; *cf.* para.1–033.
[72] *ibid.* p.19.
[73] See para.2–017.
[74] Cmnd. 218, p.9.
[75] The problem of delays is, however, a frequently recurring theme of Annual Reports of the Council on Tribunals.
[76] *The Functions of the Council on Tribunals: Special Report by the Council* (Cmnd. 7805, 1980), p.21.
[77] J. A. Farmer, *Tribunals and Government* (1974), pp.174–180 and Ch.3; below, para.7–031.

most differences in degree ... ".[78] In particular, it is not possible to argue that courts administer rules of law while tribunals administer both law and policy:

> "[N]o such clear line can or should be drawn. Indeed it was the evolution of this myth which helped establish the tribunal system by convincing the judges of the ordinary courts that they were concerned with legal but not with policy questions .... Properly understood, tribunals are a more modern form of court. In some cases they may have more discretion than the courts, and this is particularly true of the policy oriented tribunals. But certainly they have no more discretion than the Chancery Division has in handling trusts, wards or companies."[79]

Other, more pragmatic, reasons for establishing tribunals rather than entrusting matters to courts include the need not to overburden the judiciary,[80] the avoidance of ministerial responsibility for sensitive decisions and the easing of the workload of government departments.[81]

6. The Tribunals and Inquiries Act 1992

2–016 Apart from establishing the Council on Tribunals, the 1992 Act makes provision for the selection of chairmen of certain tribunals,[82] requires reasons to be given by Sch.1 tribunals,[83] provides in many cases for an appeal on a point of law to the High Court[84] and renders inoperative most clauses in statutes passed before August 1, 1958 purporting to exclude judicial review.[85]

7. The Tribunals, Courts and Enforcement Act 2007[86]

2–017 In brief, Pt I of this Bill concerns Tribunals and Inquiries. The guarantee of continued judicial independence in s.3 of the Constitutional Reform Act 2005 to

---

[78] B. Abel-Smith and R. Stevens, *In Search of Justice* (1968), pp.224, 228. This is perhaps not true of the policy-oriented tribunals: see Farmer (1974), p.189.

[79] Abel-Smith and Stevens (1968), pp.227–228.

[80] Franks Report, Cmnd. 218, p.9. In evidence the Permanent Secretary to the Lord Chancellor had stated that the wholesale transfer of tribunal work to the courts would necessitate the creation of a large number of additional judges, particularly in the county courts. Much of the work did not need the services of a highly remunerated judge. Moreover, a dilution of the bench was undesirable. Since then, there has been a large increase in the number of such judges, but they have been directed towards criminal and not tribunal work: see below, para.4–020.

[81] See K. Hendry (1982) 1 C.J.Q. 253, 257–58, giving the immigration appeals system as an example. See also J. A. G. Griffith, (1959) 22 M.L.R. 125, 129 in relation to national insurance and rent tribunals: "the truth was that the Department did not wish to be bothered with these decisions. And this for the most obvious of reasons: that the Department did not mind what the decisions were, for no questions of policy were involved."

[82] s.6. See below, para.4–016.

[83] s.10.

[84] s.11.

[85] Such clauses are not to prevent applications for *certiorari* or *mandamus*: see below, para.18–056.

[86] Mostly in force from days to be appointed.

Tribunal judiciary not otherwise protected.[87] The Office of Senior President of Tribunals is placed on a statutory footing.[88] There is to be a First-tier Tribunal and Upper Tribunal, each comprising its judges and other members. The Upper Tribunal is to be a superior court of record.[89] Employment tribunals, the EAT and the Asylum and Immigration Tribunal continue as separate entities. The Lord Chancellor may, with the concurrence of the Senior President, make provision for the organisation of each of the First-tier and Upper Tribunals into chambers. There are to be one or two Chamber Presidents for each Chamber, and deputy and assistant Chamber Presidents can be appointed. Chamber Presidents are appointed by the Lord Chancellor, but can be appointed to a different chamber or combination of chambers by the Senior President.[90] The First-tier and Upper Tribunals may each review its own decisions (other than specified excluded decisions): correcting accidental errors in the decision or a record of the decision; amending reasons; or setting the decision aside.[91] Any party has a right to appeal, with permission, to the Upper Tribunal on any point of law arising from a decision made by a First-tier tribunal other than an excluded decision.[92] The Upper Tribunal may (but need not) set aside the decision; if it does it must either remit the case with directions for its reconsideration or re-make the decision.[93] A further appeal, on a point of law lies, with permission, to the Court of Appeal.[94] The Upper Tribunal also has a judicial review jurisdiction, and judicial review cases may be transferred from the High Court.[95]

Tribunal Procedure Rules are to be made by the Tribunal Procedure Committee.[96] The Senior President and Chamber Presidents may give directions as to practice and procedure.[97] Provision is made for the transfer of the functions of tribunals listed in Sch.6.[98]

The Lord Chancellor is under a "general duty" to ensure that there is an efficient and effective system to support the carrying on of the business of the First-tier and Upper Tribunals, employment tribunals, the EAT and the AIT and that appropriate services are provided for them.[99] The Lord Chancellor may appoint staff, provide accommodation, and prescribe fees.[100] The Council on Tribunals is to be replaced by a new Administrative Justice and Tribunals Council.[101]

---

[87] s.1, amending s.3 of the 2005 Act so as to apply to all office holders listed in Sch.14 or s.3 (7A) (7B).

[88] s.2.

[89] s.3.

[90] s.7.

[91] ss.9, 10.

[92] s.11.

[93] s.12.

[94] ss.13, 14.

[95] ss.15–19.

[96] s.22, Sch.5.

[97] s.23.

[98] ss.30–31. Ministerial responsibilities may be transferred under s.35 and powers to make procedural rules may be transferred under s.36.

[99] s.39.

[100] ss.40–42.

[101] ss.44, 45; Sch. 7. See Lord Newton (2006) 13 J.S.S.L. 98.

D. THE SYSTEM IN OUTLINE

1. COURTS

2–018   The courts structure is shown below in diagrammatic form, with a table showing the current workload. The main courts are considered in detail in section E.

2. TRIBUNALS

2–019   There are now approximately 70 types of tribunal within the jurisdiction of the Council on Tribunals,[102] and several others outside it. They may be roughly grouped according to subject matter. The table below does not, however, purport to be a comprehensive list. Some tribunals are considered in detail in the next section.

---

[102] An alphabetical list is published as an appendix to each Annual Report.

THE PRINCIPAL COURTS EXERCISING CIVIL JURISDICTION

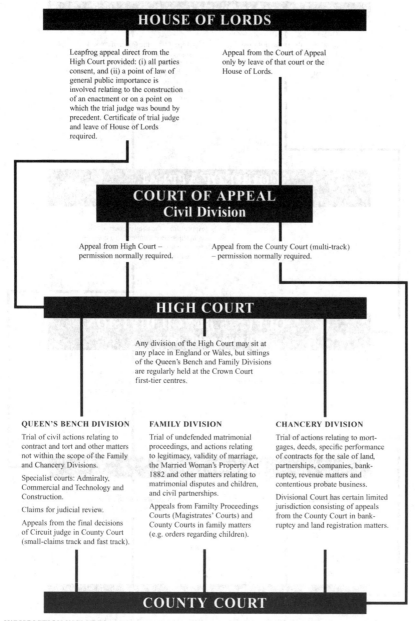

HOUSE OF LORDS

Leapfrog appeal direct from the High Court provided: (i) all parties consent, and (ii) a point of law of general public importance is involved relating to the construction of an enactment or on a point on which the trial judge was bound by precedent. Certificate of trial judge and leave of House of Lords required.

Appeal from the Court of Appeal only by leave of that court or the House of Lords.

COURT OF APPEAL
Civil Division

Appeal from High Court – permission normally required.

Appeal from the County Court (multi-track) – permission normally required.

HIGH COURT

Any division of the High Court may sit at any place in England or Wales, but sittings of the Queen's Bench and Family Divisions are regularly held at the Crown Court first-tier centres.

QUEEN'S BENCH DIVISION

Trial of civil actions relating to contract and tort and other matters not within the scope of the Family and Chancery Divisions.

Specialist courts: Admiralty, Commercial and Technology and Construction.

Claims for judicial review.

Appeals from the final decisions of Circuit judge in County Court (small-claims track and fast track).

FAMILY DIVISION

Trial of undefended matrimonial proceedings, and actions relating to legitimacy, validity of marriage, the Married Woman's Property Act 1882 and other matters relating to matrimonial disputes and children, and civil partnerships.

Appeals from Family Proceedings Courts (Magistrates' Courts) and County Courts in family matters (e.g. orders regarding children).

CHANCERY DIVISION

Trial of actions relating to mortgages, deeds, specific performance of contracts for the sale of land, partnerships, companies, bankruptcy, revenue matters and contentious probate business.

Divisional Court has certain limited jurisdiction consisting of appeals from the County Court in bankruptcy and land registration matters.

COUNTY COURT

JURISDICTION INCLUDES:

(i) Actions in contract or tort (except defamation);
(ii) Equity matters (trusts, mortgages, partnerships, etc.) where the value of the property does not exceed £30,000;
(iii) Actions for recovering land;
(iv) Undefended and some defended matrimonial cases; proceedings under the Children Act 1989; civil partnership matters;
(v) Bankruptcy.

THE COURTS EXERCISING CRIMINAL JURISDICTION

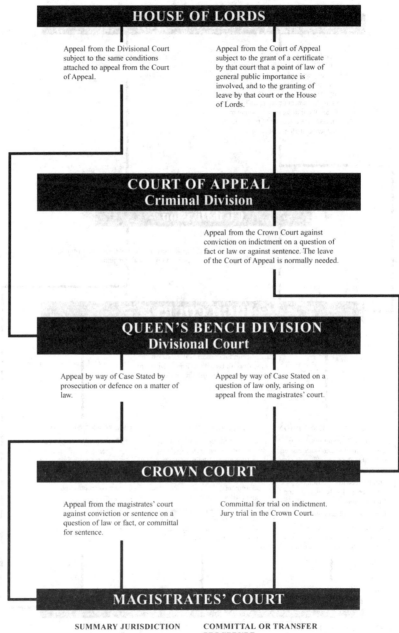

HOUSE OF LORDS

Appeal from the Divisional Court subject to the same conditions attached to appeal from the Court of Appeal.

Appeal from the Court of Appeal subject to the grant of a certificate by that court that a point of law of general public importance is involved, and to the granting of leave by that court or the House of Lords.

COURT OF APPEAL
Criminal Division

Appeal from the Crown Court against conviction on indictment on a question of fact or law or against sentence. The leave of the Court of Appeal is normally needed.

QUEEN'S BENCH DIVISION
Divisional Court

Appeal by way of Case Stated by prosecution or defence on a matter of law.

Appeal by way of Case Stated on a question of law only, arising on appeal from the magistrates' court.

CROWN COURT

Appeal from the magistrates' court against conviction or sentence on a question of law or fact, or committal for sentence.

Committal for trial on indictment. Jury trial in the Crown Court.

MAGISTRATES' COURT

SUMMARY JURISDICTION

Trial of summary offences and other offences triable summarily with the consent of the accused.

COMMITTAL OR TRANSFER PROCEDURE

Initial procedural steps in respect of cases then committed or transferred for trial in the Crown Court.

Workload of the courts: Proceedings commenced
Comparative Tables[103]

	1938	1963	1977	1989	1995	2000	2005
1. Appellate Courts							
Judicial Committee							
of the Privy Council	107	46	48	55	82	90	71
House of Lords:							
From courts in							
England & Wales	32	21	58	51	56	63	73
From elsewhere	11	18	6	12	16	16	14
Court of Appeal							
Civil Division	574	711	1,359	1,622	1,853	1,420	1,239
Criminal Division	—	2,065	6,399	7,076	8,187	7,740	7,023
High Court	263	484	1,029	2,535	4,674	4,893	7,542[104]
2. Crown Court (disposals)							
Committals for trial	—	—	53,118	101,232	88,985	72,762	77,175
Committals for sentence	—	—	12,846	13,689	11,726	28,713	32,348
Appeals	—	—	15,497	16,860	26,062	14,359	12,809
3. High Court							
Chancery Division	9,826	16,137	14,651	30,813	42,251	37,333	34,125
Queen's Bench	83,641	123,998	176,128	288,287	153,624	26,876	15,317
4. Family matters							
(High Court, County Court							
and Family Proceedings							
Courts)							
Probate (grants issues)	149,752	—	251,703	231,883	248,947	264,397	299,215
Adoption (orders made)	—	—	10,724	7,516	5,317	4,438	4,004
Public Law Applications	—	—	—	—	17,136	22,000	24,584
(Children)							
Private Law Applications	—	—	—	—	102,000	95,407	104,434
(Children)							
Dissolution of marriage	9,970	36,385	170,149	184,610	173,966	157,809	151,654
Nullity	263	919	1,095	478	881	452	436
Judicial separation	71	206	1,980	2,741	3,349	650	692
5. County courts							
Plaints entered/claims issued	1,262,402	1,543,324	1,673,966	2,615,508	2,445,248	1,871,923	1,870,374
Judgments on hearing	30,821	34,746	141,950	179,006	112,647	71,233	74,839
Trial	—	—	—	—	24,477	15,397	17,318
Arbitration/small claims	—	—	—	—	88,170	55,836	47,521
6. Magistrates' courts							
Indictable offences	—	—	470,000	539,000	497,000	493,000	423,000
Summary offences	—	—	458,000	469,000	587,000	627,000	637,000
(excluding motoring)							
Motoring offences	—	—	1,165,000	1,214,000	863,000	792,000	835,000
7. Other courts and tribunals							
Employment Appeal	—	—	748	829	1,380	1,509	783
Tribunal							
Asylum and Immigration	—	—	—	—	—	—	128,573
Tribunal[105]							

[103] Based on *Judicial Statistics 2005* and earlier volumes, and (for magistrates' courts) *Criminal Statistics 2005: England and Wales* (HOSB19/06).

[104] Includes (from 2003) stautory review under s.101, Nationality, Immigration and Asylum Act 2002.

[105] April 4, 2005 to December 31, 2005.

Table of Tribunals

General Subject Matter	Tribunal[106]	Jurisdiction	Cases decided in 2005 – England and Wales[107]	Judiciary Pool[107]	Days Sat[107]	Success Rate[107]	Oral Hearings[107]
(a) *Social Administration*							
(1) Personal Welfare	Appeals Service Tribunals	See para.2-038	210,742 (E) 15,556 (W)	1,252 (E) 274 (W)	— —	43% (E) 48% (W)	52% (E) 50% (W)
	Social Security and Child Support Commissioners	See para.2-039	5,387	17	190	53%	4%
	Mental Health Review Tribunals	Applications for discharge by mental patients	11,266 (E) 567 (W)	1,038 (E) 87 (W)	27,699 (E) 1,975 (W)	15% (E) 16% (W)	100% (E) 100% (W)
	Gender Recognition Panel		1,272	14	104	98%	0%
(2) Education	Admission Appeal Panels[108]	Appeals against admission decisions	LEA 41,070 Gov Body 18,260	—	—	38% 30%	— —
	Exclusion Appeal Panels[108]	Appeals against exclusion decisions	1,030	—	—	21%	—
	Registered Inspector of Schools Tribunal	Appeals in relation to registration of schools inspectors	3	10	3	33%	67%
	Schools Adjudicators	Adjudicators concerning school organisation plans, school establishment, closure or alteration and admissions arrangements	189	11	—	63%	0%
	Special Educational Needs and Disability Tribunal[109]	Appeals in special educational needs cases	1,078	202	225	78%	—
(3) Employment[110]	Employment Tribunals	See para.2-031	38,323	2,040	26,502	18%	90%
(4) National Health Service	PCT Discipline Committees	Alleged breaches of terms of service	—	—	—	—	—
	Family Health Services Appeal Authority	Appeals against a decision that a practitioner should be removed from the NHS	43	73	73	—	91%

(5) Immigration/Asylum	Asylum Support Adjudicators	Appeals concerning applications for support	2,534	23	1,311	27%	69%
	Asylum and Immigration Tribunal	Asylum and Immigration appeals	139,566	628	34,109	30%	76%
	Immigration Services Tribunal		15	13	18	—	—
(6) Care Standards	Care Standards Tribunals	Appeals concerning the registration of care and children's homes, the Protection of Children Act List and the registration of independent schools	118	92	101	63% (E) 50% (W)	89% (E) 100% (W)
(7) Criminal Injuries Compensation	Criminal Injuries Compensation Appeal Panel[111]	Appeals against review decisions of the Criminal Injuries Compensation Authority	3,318	74	818	50%	94%
(b) *Economic Matters* (8) Agriculture[112]	Agricultural Arbitration		4 0	139 (E) 20 (W)	— —	— —	— —
	Agricultural Land Tribunals	Disputes between landlord and tenant in respect of notice to quit and bad husbandry and drainage disputes	65 (E) 5 (W)	169 (E) 34 (W)	53 (E) 5 (W)	69% 60%	34% 40%
	Meat Hygiene Appeals Tribunals	Appeals relating to the licensing of premises	15	45	56	33%	66%
(9) Land/Housing[113]	Commons Commissioners	Determination of claims in respect of common land	3	2	1	100%	100%
	Lands Tribunal	See para.2–069	336	5	167	—	—
	Rent Assessment Panels	Appeals concerning rents; disputes about leasehold valuation	5,592	339	8,705	64%	51%
	Valuation Tribunals	Rating and Council Tax Appeals	41,391 1,258	1,177 (E) 238 (W)	2,762 (E) 468 (W)	25%	35%
	Adjudication to HM Land Registry Forestry Committee		1,215 2	13 24	156 4	— —	— —

General Subject Matter	Tribunal[106]	Jurisdiction	Cases decided in 2005 – England and Wales[107]	Judiciary Pool[107]	Days Sat[107]	Success Rate[107]	Oral Hearings[107]
(10) Commerce	Comptroller of Patents, Designs and Trade Marks	Adjudication in respect of patents, designs and trade marks	45 Patents *inter partes* 46 Patents *ex parte* 2 Designs *inter partes* 2 Designs *ex parte* 132 Trade marks *inter partes* 1,809 Trade marks *ex parte*	7 18 7 2 7 14	23 43 0 1 70 —	— — — — — —	20% 88% 0% 100% 53% 100%
	Competition Appeal Tribunal	Appeals under the Competition Act	19	34	52	85%	100%
	Office of Fair Trading[114]	Licensing decisions concerning consumer credit and estate agent activities	141	4	636	37	56
	Copyright Tribunal	Disputes between citizens concerning licences for copyright material	—	6	—	—	—
	Information Commissioner[115]	Enforcement cases	2	—	—	—	—
(11) Transport[116]	Civil Aviation Authority	Air transport and travel organisers licensing; air navigation order appeals	2	4	—	50%	100%
	Parking Adjudicators (National Parking Adjudication Service)	Appeals against Penalty Charge Notices for unauthorised vehicle parking	9,237 (E) 123 (W)	32	— —	57% (E) 52% (W)	38% (E) 32% (W)
	Parking Adjudicators (Parking and Traffic Appeals Service; London)	Appeals against Penalty Charge Notices for unauthorised vehicle parking	42,290	52	297	51%	28%
	Road User Charging Adjudicators	Appeals concerning road user charges	20,021	36	297	19%	10%
	Traffic Commissioners	Licensing of public service passenger vehicles	1,418 (E) 110 (W)	18 (E) 5 (W)	— —	—	—
	Transport Tribunal	Appeals from Traffic Commissioners	414	10	40	—	—
(c) *Revenue* (12) Taxation	General Commissioners of Income Tax	Tax appeals	26,704 (E) 1,375 (W)	1,576 (E) 150 (W)	2,080 (E) 99 (W)	4% 2%	9% 7%

Special Commissioners of Income Tax	Tax appeals	109	27	138	—	98%
Section 703 Tribunal	References concerning anti-avoidance provisions of the Income and Corporation Taxes Act 1988	0	9	0	—	—
VAT and Duties Tribunal	Appeals concerning VAT, customs and excise duties, landfill tax and insurance premium tax	675	113	934	—	—
Financial Services and Markets Tribunal	References under the Financial Services and Markets Act 2000	10	26	76	—	100%
(d) Pensions (13) Pensions[117]	Pensions Appeal Tribunals	Appeals from the Secretary of State	2,700	96	602	—	96%
	Pensions Ombudsman	Complaints and disputes concerning occupational and personal pension schemes	174	—	—	—	—
	Pensions Regulator[118]		10	8	7	10%	10%
(e) Local government	Case Tribunals	Proceedings concerning the conduct of councils	101 (E) 4 (W)	33 (E) 8 (W)	125 (E) 4 (W)	15% (E) 20% (W)	92% 100%

[106] Other miscellaneous tribunals include the Antarctic Act Tribunal, the Foreign Compensation Commission, the Horse Race Betting Levy Appeal Tribunal, the Insolvency Practitioners' Tribunal, Justice and Clerks Indemnification appointed person, the Mines and Quarries Tribunal, the Misuse of Drugs Tribunal, the National Lottery Commission Pool (no cases in 2005).

[107] Figures from Annual Report of the Council on Tribunals 2005–06. Appendix. Where a dash is shown data is either irrelevant or unavailable. "Judiciary": total number of Chairmen and members in the Tribunal's pool; "Days Sat": total number of days that a panel or arbiter sat to consider cases; "Success Rate": % of total cases decided in sample period in which the Tribunal found in favour of the appeal or in application either in whole or in part; "Oral Hearings": % of oral as opposed to "paper" hearings.

[108] Figures relate to the 2004/05 school year.

[109] There is a Special Educational Needs Tribunal for Wales which decided 49 cases in 2005.

[110] Other tribunals include the Industrial Arbitration Tribunal, the Industrial Training Levy Exemption Referees, the Police Appeals Tribunal, the Reserve Forces Appeals Tribunals (no cases in 2005) and the Reserve Forces Reinstatement Committees and Umpires (1 decision in 2005).

[111] Figures include Scotland.

[112] Other tribunals include the Controller of Plant Variety Rights, the Plant Varieties and Seeds Tribunal, the Dairy Produce Quota Tribunal and the Sea Fish Licence Tribunal (no cases in 2005).

[113] There are also London Building Acts Tribunals (no cases in 2005).

[114] Figures include Scotland.

[115] There is also an Information Tribunal (no cases in 2005).

[116] There is also an Aircraft and Shipbuilding Industrial Arbitration Tribunal (no cases in 2005).

[117] There are also Fire Service Pensions Appeal Tribunals and Police Pensions Appeal Tribunals (no cases in 2005).

[118] There is also a Pensions Regulator Tribunal.

Other tribunals of note that were not included within the jurisdiction of the Council on Tribunals included the Criminal Injuries Compensation Board, set up under the royal prerogative to consider claims for *ex gratia* compensation from the victims of crimes of violence,[119] and the Housing Benefit Review Boards set up[120] to hear appeals by claimants for rent or rates rebate or rent allowance (housing benefit) who remain dissatisfied with their local authority's determination of their claims.[121] Both areas now fall under the Council's jurisdiction. A Criminal Injuries Compensation Appeals Panel under the Council's jurisdiction was established by the Criminal Injuries Compensation Act 1995, and has dealt with applications from April 1, 1996, under a new statutory scheme.[122] The Board continued in parallel, dealing with cases arising earlier, until April 2000. Appeals in housing benefit cases were transferred to Appeal Service tribunals,[123] a change long urged by the Council on Tribunals.

E. PARTICULAR COURTS AND TRIBUNALS

2–020   In this section we consider the courts and tribunals that feature most prominently in the English legal system, by virtue either of their status in the hierarchy or their caseload. For reasons of space it is not possible to cover all tribunals in detail. We have not divided this section into "courts" and "tribunals" but have incorporated coverage of certain tribunals approximately in accordance with their position in the overall hierarchy.

1. MAGISTRATES' COURTS

(a) Introduction

2–021   Magistrates' courts are the inferior criminal courts. In addition they exercise certain family law, administrative law and minor civil functions. There is a commission of the peace for England and Wales issued under the Great Seal and addressed generally, and not by name, to all justices of the peace.[124] England and Wales is divided into "local justice areas" specified in orders made (or altered)

---

[119] See the White Paper on Compensation for Victims of Crimes of Violence (Cmnd. 2323, 1964); Annual Reports of the Board; Review of the Criminal Injuries Compensation Scheme: Report of an Interdepartmental Working Party (HMSO, 1978). The Board was due to be reconstituted as a statutory tribunal under Pt VII of the Criminal Justice Act 1988, and placed under the Council's jurisdiction, but implementation was delayed: see *R. v Secretary of State for the Home Department, Ex p. Fire Brigades Union* [1995] 2 A.C. 513, below, para.5–019, and Pt VII ultimately repealed by the Criminal Inquiries Compensation Act 1995.

[120] Housing Benefits Regulations 1982 (SI 1982/124): see the Housing Benefits (General) Regulations 1987 (SI 1987/1971), regs 81–87 and Sch.7.

[121] These Boards comprise members of the authority whose officers' decisions are in question. The claim of such Boards to be independent was not supportable, as subsequently held by the European Court of Human Rights in *Tsfayo v UK,* Judgment of November 14, 2006.

[122] Now the Criminal Injuries Compensation Scheme 2001: see *www.cica.gov.uk.*

[123] See below, para.2–038.

[124] Courts Act 2003, s.7. Formerly, commission areas were specified in primary, and then secondary legislation.

by the Lord Chancellor after consulting the Lord Chief Justice. In the case of alterations, the Lord Chancellor must also consult the justices of the peace, courts board and (unless there is only a change of name) the local authorities for the area.[125] Lay justices[126] are appointed by the Lord Chancellor on behalf and in the name of Her Majesty.[127] The Lord Chief Justice, after consulting the Lord Chancellor, must assign each lay justice to one or more local justice areas and may change an assignment.[128] The Lord Chancellor must ensure that arrangements for the exercise of these functions, so far as affecting any local justice area, include arrangements for consulting persons with special knowledge of matters relevant to the exercise of those functions in relation to that area.[129] Every lay justice is, by virtue of his or her office, capable of acting as such in any local justice area (whether or not assigned to it), but may do so only in accordance with arrangements made by the Lord Chief Justice after consulting the Lord Chancellor.[130] For each local justice area there is to be a chairman of the lay justices and one or more deputy chairmen chosen by them from among their number. Any contested election is to be made by secret ballot.[131]

(b) Criminal jurisdiction

Magistrates' courts are involved in some way in virtually all criminal prosecutions. Proceedings may be commenced by a summons or an arrest warrant issued by a justice of the peace.[132] Magistrates' courts try those offences triable only summarily, and have responsibilities in the procedure whereby persons charged with offences triable only on indictment are transferred for trial in the Crown Court. Where proceedings are brought in respect of the intermediate category of offences "triable either way", the court must decide whether the offence appears more suitable for summary trial or for trial on indictment. Once this is decided, and subject to the right of the accused to insist on trial by a jury, the court proceeds either to summary trial or the committal for trial procedure.[133] Procedural rules are made by the Criminal Procedure Rule Committee.[134]

2–022

---

[125] *ibid.* s.8, as amended by the Constitutional Reform Act 2005, Sch.14, Pt 1, paras 308, 312. See the Local Justice Areas Order 2005 (SI 2005/554), as amended by SI 2005/2949, SI 2006/1839 and SI 2006/2315. This replaced provision for the country to be divided into "petty sessions areas".

[126] i.e. justices of the peace who are not a District Judge (Magistrates' Court): s.9.

[127] *ibid.* s.10(1). See para.4–003.

[128] *ibid.* s.10(2), (6), as amended and inserted by the Constitutional Reform Act 2005, Sch.4, Pt 1, paras 308, 313.

[129] *ibid.* s.10(2A), inserted by the 2005 Act, s.106.

[130] *ibid.* s.10(3)(6), as amended or inserted by the 2005 Act, Sch.4, Pt 1, paras 308, 313.

[131] *ibid.* s.17. See the Justices of the Peace (Size and Chairmanship of Bench) Rules 2005 (SI 2005/553).

[132] Magistrates' Courts Act 1980, s.1, as amended by the Courts Act 2003, s.43 to reflect that point that each justice has a national jurisdiction. The other methods of commencing proceedings include an arrest without warrant and by a voluntary bill of indictment: see below, Ch.14. Only this last method bypasses the magistrates' court. Geographical limits to the jurisdiction of magistrates' courts have been removed: see the 1980 Act, s.2, substituted by the 2003 Act, s.44.

[133] These proceedings are explained more fully in the chapters on criminal procedure.

[134] Courts Act 2003, ss 68–74. Criminal Procedure Rules (SI 2005/384). The Lord Chief Justice may give practice directions (s.74).

A magistrates' court must be composed of at least two justices of the peace[135] unless there is express provision for a single justice to act,[136] as there is, for example, in the case of issuing a summons.[137] District Judges (Magistrates' Courts) (formerly stipendiary magistrates)[138] normally sit alone. Magistrates' courts are also responsible for the enforcement of fines.[139]

(c) Criminal proceedings concerning children

(i) Youth courts

2–023 Magistrates' courts constituted in accordance with s.45 of the Children and Young Persons Act 1933[140] or s.66 of the Courts Act 2003,[141] and sitting for the purpose of hearing any charge against a child or young person, or exercising any other jurisdiction conferred on youth courts are to be known as youth courts.[142] A justice of the peace is not qualified to sit as a member of a youth court unless he has an authorisation extending to the proceedings. Such an authorisation is given by the Lord Chief Justice, with the concurrence of the Lord Chancellor, and applies to all or designated proceedings in the youth court. The Lord Chief Justice, with the concurrence of the Lord Chancellor, may make rules about the grant and revocation of authorisations, the appointment of chairmen of youth courts and the composition of youth courts.[143] In the mean time, the existing rules as to composition continue in effect. The justices for each local justice area must at their annual meeting every three years appoint justices for the area specially qualified for dealing with juvenile cases to form a youth court panel for that area.[144] A youth court[145] must be composed of not more than three justices, and must normally include a man and a woman.[146] If the court comprises a District Judge (Magistrates' Courts) and other justices, the District Judge normally

---

[135] The office of justice of the peace is considered below, Ch.4.

[136] Magistrates' Courts Act 1980, s.121(1). Normally, three justices sit (three being the maximum: except that this rules does not apply in the case of a youth court, a family proceedings court or a licensing or betting licensing committee: SI 2005/553, r.3).

[137] *ibid.* s.26.

[138] See below, para.4–013.

[139] The collection and enforcement of fines is the responsibility of fines officers appointed by the Lord Chancellor under s.36 of the Courts Act 2003: see further *ibid.* Schs 5, 6. See NAO, *Fines Collection* (2005–06 H.C. 1049).

[140] Substituted by the Courts Act 2003, s.50.

[141] This states that the holders of specified judical offices (High Court or deputy High Court judge; Circuit or deputy Circuit judge; recorder) have the powers of a District Judge (Magistrates' Courts) in relation to criminal causes and matters and family proceedings and are qualified to sit as a member of a youth court.

[142] 1933 Act, s.45(1), as substituted.

[143] *ibid.* s.45(2)–(9), as substituted, and amended by the Constitutional Reform Act 2005, Sch.4, Pt 1, para.20. In November 2005 the DCA issued a Consultation Paper, *Authorisations to Sit in Family Proceedings Courts and Youth Courts* (CP27/05). A summary of responses was issued in September 2006.

[144] 1954 Rules, r.1, as amended by SI 2005/617, Sch., para.11.

[145] Prior to October 1, 1992, youth courts were known as juvenile courts; the change of name was effected by the Criminal Justice Act 1991, s.70. See generally Home Office Circular 30/1992, *Criminal Justice Act 1991: Young People and the Youth Court*. The main changes were that the youth court, not the magistrates' court, now deals with 17-year-olds, and new sentencing powers were conferred: see B. Gibson, (1992) *The Magistrate* 109; T. Moore and T. Wilkinson, *Youth Court Guide* (2nd edn, 2005).

[146] The Youth Courts (Constitution) Rules 1954 (SI 1954/1711), as amended, r.12. References to juvenile courts are to be construed as references to youth courts: Criminal Justice Act 1991, s.70(2).

presides.[147] A court may be held in buildings set apart for the purpose, or, as is more usually the case, in a courtroom normally used for an adult magistrates' court.[148]

(ii) *Jurisdiction*

Criminal proceedings may not be instituted against children who are under 10: it **2–024** is conclusively presumed that they cannot be guilty of any offence.[149] Where children between 10 and 14 are prosecuted it must be proved that they were children of a "mischievous discretion", i.e. that they knew that what they were doing was, legally or morally seriously wrong.[150] Young persons of 14 and over are regarded as fully responsible for their acts.

The former juvenile courts had jurisdiction in both criminal cases and care proceedings. However, the Children Act 1989 transferred care proceedings to the family proceedings courts.[151] Criminal proceedings against children and young persons[152] must normally take place in a youth court. The main exceptions are that an adult magistrates' court *must* deal with children or young persons where they are charged jointly with an adult and *may* do so where different charges are made against an adult arising out of the same or connected circumstances or where either an adult or a child or young person is charged with aiding, abetting, causing, procuring, allowing or permitting the other's alleged offence.[153] The youth court must try the case summarily except (1) where the charge is homicide or one of specified firearms offences in which case the child or young person *must* be committed for trial in the Crown Court, and (2) in the case of certain other offences where the court must commit for trial if specified conditions are established.[154]

---

[147] 1954 Rules, r.13, as amended by SI 2000/1873, r.3.

[148] Guidance on the design of youth courts is given in *The Youth Court 2001: The Changing Culture of the Youth Court: Good Practice Guide* (HO/LCD, March 2001).

[149] Children and Young Persons Act 1933, s.50, as amended by the 1963 Act, s.16(1). At common law the relevant age was seven. Section 4 of the Children and Young Persons Act 1969 provided for the age to be raised to 14, but was repealed, unimplemented, by the Criminal Justice Act 1991, s.72.

[150] The presumption that a child of this age was incapable of committing an offence, confirmed as a continuing part of the common law by the House of Lords in *C (a minor) v DPP* [1995] 2 W.L.R. 383, was abolished by the Crime and Disorder Act 1998, s.34. There is now an evidential burden on the defence to raise the issue.

[151] See below.

[152] This term applies to children and young persons under 18. For most purposes under the 1933 Act "child" is defined as a person under 14 and "young person" as a person of 14 or over but under 18: s.107, as amended. The term "child" is differently defined for other purposes: see *Halsbury's Laws of England* (4th edn), Vol.5(3), Reissue, para.3.

[153] Children and Young Persons Act 1933, s.46, as extended by the 1963 Act, s.18. Applications for bail or for a remand may be heard by any justice or justices (1933 Act, s.46(2)). The adult magistrates' court will normally try the child or young person summarily but may or may not be required to proceed with a view to committing him or her for trial in the Crown Court (Magistrates' Courts Act 1980, s.24, as amended, and to be amended by the Criminal Justice Act 2003, s.42 and Sch.3, para.9) or remit for trial (*ibid.* s.29, as amended) in the youth court.

[154] Magistrates' Courts Act 1980, s.24(1), as amended. These are: (1) that the offence is one in which the Crown Court can invoke the power under the Powers of Criminal Courts (Sentencing) Act 2000, s.91 to impose a long sentence of detention and the magistrates' or youth court considers that if the defendant is found guilty it ought to be possible for that power to be invoked; (2) that the defendant is charged jointly with an adult and the court considers it necessary in the interests of justice to commit them both for trial. There is also provision for committal of specified associated offences: s.24(1A) (inserted by the Crime and Disorder Act 1998, s.47(6)) and s.24(2), as amended.

Any person may institute criminal proceedings against a child or young person,[155] but they must notify the appropriate local authority.[156]

(iii) *Procedure*

2–025 The procedure of youth courts is less formal than for adult magistrates' courts.[157] Only members and officers of the court, the parties, their lawyers, witnesses and other persons directly concerned, press representatives, and other persons specially authorised may be present.[158] There are limits as to what may be reported.[159] In the case of children and young persons dealt with summarily the expression "finding of guilt" must be used instead of "conviction" and the expression "order made upon a finding of guilt" instead of "sentence".[160] Steps have been taken to change the culture of the youth court, with greater openness, engaging directly with the offender, feedback on the effectiveness of sentencing and a less adversarial setting.[161]

(d) Family proceedings

2–026 Magistrates have an extensive jurisdiction in family and child law matters ("family proceedings").[162] The list includes powers to make orders for financial provision for, or the protection of, parties to a marriage and children of the family, orders under the Children Act 1989, the Child Support Act 1991, the Family Law Act 1996,[163] the Crime and Disorder Act 1998,[164] and adoption orders. Proceedings concerning these matters used to be termed "domestic proceedings" and the courts when hearing them "domestic courts", but they were renamed "family proceedings" and "family proceedings courts" by the Children Act 1989. The court must be composed of two or three lay justices, or a District Judge (Magistrates' Courts) sitting as chairman with one or two lay justices, or if neither of those is practicable, a District Judge (Magistrates' Courts) sitting alone. In the case of the first two options, the court must, so far

---

[155] The provisions of s.5 of the Children and Young Persons Act 1969 which were to restrict private prosecutions were repealed, unimplemented, by the Criminal Justice Act 1991, s.72.

[156] 1969 Act, s.5(8), (9).

[157] See the Criminal Procedure Rules 2005 (SI 2005/384), Pt 38 (trial of children and young persons), Pt 44 (sentencing children and young persons).

[158] Children and Young Persons Act 1933, s.47(2) as amended by the Children and Young Persons Act 1963, s.17(2) and the Youth Justice and Criminal Evidence Act 1999, Sch.4, para.2(3).

[159] 1933 Act, s.49, as substituted by the Criminal Justice and Public Order Act 1994, s.49, and to be amended by the Youth Justice and Criminal Evidence Act 1999, Sch.2, para.3. Reporting restrictions may be lifted in the public interest: subs.(4A), inserted by the Crime (Sentences) Act 1997, s.45; for government guidance see HO/LCD Circular, *Opening up Youth Court Proceedings* (June 1998); see also *McKerry v Teesdale and Wear Valley JJ* [2001] C.O.D. 199 (power to be exercised "with great care, caution and circumspection").

[160] *ibid.* s.59.

[161] See White Paper, *No More Excuses. A New Approach to Tackling Youth Crime in England* (Cm. 3809, 1997), Ch.9; HO/LCD, *The Youth Court 2001: The Changing Culture of the Youth Court: Good Practice Guide* (2001).

[162] Defined in the Magistrates' Courts Act 1980, s.65, as amended.

[163] Pt IV, concerning family homes and domestic violence: see the Family Law Act 1996 (Pt IV) (Allocation of Proceedings) Order 1997 (SI 1997/1896).

[164] ss.11 and 12 (child safety orders).

as practicable, include both a man and a woman.[165] Magistrates' courts constituted in accordance with s.67 of the Magistrates' Courts Act 1980[166] or s.66 of the Courts Act 2003,[167] and sitting for the purposes of hearing family proceedings, are to be known as family proceedings courts.[168] A justice of the peace is not qualified to sit as a member of a family proceedings court unless authorised by the Lord Chief Justice, under arrangements similar to those for youth courts.[169]

The law relating to child care was substantially altered by the 1989 Act, which re-stated the respective powers and responsibilities of parents, courts and local authorities. The courts have power to grant, *inter alia*, "contact orders" (replacing access orders) and "residence orders" (replacing custody orders) and a variety of emergency orders; the grounds on which care or supervision orders may be granted were simplified and narrowed.[170] The magistrates' courts, county courts and High Courts have concurrent jurisdiction under the 1989 Act and the Adoption Act 1976; the Lord Chancellor has power to make orders specifying the level of court and the description of court at which different classes of proceedings should be commenced, and makes provision for the transfer of proceedings.[171] Proceedings under the 1989 Act are normally to be commenced in the magistrates' court.[172] Most orders will, however, continue to be made in divorce or matrimonial proceedings which are commenced in the county court.[173]

The courts have power to make care or supervision orders in respect of children under 17 (16 if married), if they are satisfied that (a) the child is suffering or likely to suffer significant harm; and (b) this is attributable to (i) the care given to the child, or likely to be given to him or her if the order were not made, not being what it would be reasonable to expect a parent to give; or (ii) the child's being beyond parental control.[174] The welfare of the child is the paramount consideration, and the court must take other specified matters into account.[175] Under a care order, the child is taken into the care of the local authority; a supervision order places the child under the supervision of a designated local authority.[176] Procedural Rules may be made by the Family Procedure Rule Committee.[177] Steps are being taken to establish Family Court Centres, linking the work of adjacent family proceedings courts and county courts.[178]

---

[165] 1980 Act, s.66, substituted by the Access to Justice Act 1999, Sch.11, paras 26, 27.
[166] Substituted by the Courts Act 2003, s.49(1).
[167] Concerning judges having powers of District Judges (Magistrates' Courts).
[168] 1980 Act, s.67(1).
[169] *ibid.* s.67(2)–(9), to be amended by the Constitutional Reform Act 2005, Sch.14, Pt 1, para.101; Family Proceedings Courts (Constitution) Rules 1991 (SI 1991/1405), as amended; Family Proceedings Courts (Constitution) (Metropolitan Area) Rules 1991 (SI 1991/1426), as amended.
[170] See below.
[171] Children Act 1989, s.92 and Sch.11; Courts and Legal Services Act 1990, s.9, as amended by the Constitutional Reform Act 2005, Sch.4, Pt 1, para.213.
[172] Children (Allocation of Proceedings) Order 1991 (SI 1991/1677), as amended.
[173] See below, para.2–045.
[174] Children Act 1989, Pt IV.
[175] *ibid.* s.1.
[176] *ibid.* s.31, as amended.
[177] Courts Act 2003, ss 75–80. The President of the Family Division may give Practice Directions: s.81.
[178] See e.g. the HMCS Consultation, *HMCS London Region Proposals for a Network of Family Courts Centres* (CP 16/06) and Responses (CP(R) 16/06), July 31, 2006.

(e) Civil jurisdiction

2–027   Apart from family proceedings, magistrates' courts have powers in relation to certain other civil matters, including enforcement of the payment of rates, the council tax, income tax and charges for supplies of gas, electricity and water. They also have jurisdiction in respect of the granting of licences for bookmakers, betting offices, and premises for gaming and bingo. Finally, there is a vast number[179] of statutory provisions enabling appeals to be brought against administrative decisions of various kinds.

(f) Community justice centres

2–028   A recent development has been the establishment in a number of areas, following pilots in North Liverpool, that opened in September 2005,[180] and Salford of community justice centres. The North Liverpool centre functions both as a court and as a focus for a range of community resources, directed to tacking anti-social behaviour and crime that affects the quality of life of local people. It is located within the area directly served. It is presided over by a Circuit judge, Judge David Fletcher, who works with a team from a range of agencies, including the CPS, Probation Service and Youth Offending Team and other specialist advisers. Steps are taken to develop relationships with local services and to involve local people. The CJC court can sit as a magistrates' court, with attendance by volunteer magistrates and the Circuit judge exercising the powers of a District Judge (Magistrates' Court), a Youth Court and (for sentence only) the Crown Court. In addition to dealing with particular cases, the CJC seeks to adopt a problem-solving approach, addressing the particular causes of crime in the locality. A separate, more restricted, project to deliver Community Justice principles in a mainstream magistrates' court started in Salford in November 2005. These have formed the basis for the articulation of Community Justice principles and their extension to ten more areas,[181] although it seems on a less expensive basis than in Liverpool.

(g) Appeals[182]

2–029   Appeals lie from a magistrates' court either as of right to the Crown Court,[183] where proceedings take the form of a complete rehearing, or to the High Court by a procedure whereby the magistrates state a case for the opinion of the High Court on a point of law. In family matters the appeal is heard by the Family Division, otherwise the appeal will lie to the Queen's Bench Division. Any further appeal from the High Court lies to the House of Lords in criminal cases and to the Court of Appeal and House of Lords in civil cases.

---

[179] D. Price, *Appeals* (1982) pp.53–96, including appeals against refusal of a petshop licence, or a driving licence, a notice concerning fire safety requirements and a notice requiring that an earth closet be replaced by a water closet.

[180] *http://www.communityjustice.gov.uk.*

[181] CJS, *Delivering Simple, Speedy, Summary Justice* (DCA, July 2006), Ch.6; Community Justice website. At the time of writing (February 2007) there had not been a formal evaluation.

[182] See generally, Ch.18.

[183] See below, para.2–052.

(h) Administration

Procedural rules, except in relation to any criminal cause or matter or family **2–030** proceedings, are made by the Lord Chief Justice on the advice of or after consultation with a Rule Committee, comprising the Lord Chief Justice, the President of the Family Division, the Senior District Judge (Chief Magistrate) and other persons appointed by the Lord Chancellor after consulting the Lord Chief Justice, who must include a justices' clerk, and specified lawyers.[184] Criminal cases are dealt with under the Criminal Procedure Rules 2005.[185]

The administrative arrangements were fundamentally changed by the Courts Act 2003. Previously, the administration of magistrates' courts was the responsibility of Magistrates' Courts Committees mostly comprising local justices and a small number of co-opted members, accountable to the Home Office. Whether a national agency should be set up was debated,[186] but the Police and Magistrates' Courts Act 1994 merely transferred responsibility to the LCD and tightened central controls.[187] The Courts Act 2003, based upon recommendations in the Auld Report, abolished the Magistrates' Courts Committees and brought the administration of the magistrates' courts together with that of the Court Service for superior courts (other than the House of Lords), within the newly established HM Courts Service.[188] The equivalent to the former justices' chief executive is a "designated officer".[189] The Lord Chancellor and the Lord Chief Justice must take all reasonable and practicable steps for ensuring that lay justices acting in a local justice area are kept informed of matters affecting them in the performance of their duties and for ascertaining their views on such matters.[190]

The justices continue to be supported by justices clerks and assistant clerks.[191] Justices form part of the membership of the local probation boards that are responsible, under the overall supervision of the Home Office, for the National Probation Service.[192] The objects of the Service are to assist the courts with sentencing and other decision-making in respect of persons charged or convicted of offences, and the supervision and rehabilitation of such persons. The former includes the preparation of bail information and pre-sentence reports. The latter includes giving effect to community orders, such as community rehabilitation orders (formerly probation orders), community punishment orders (formerly community service orders), supervising persons released from prison on licence, providing accommodation in probation hostels and other approved premises, and

---

[184] Magistrates' Courts Act 1980, s.144, and see also ss.145–146; s.144, as amended by the Courts and Legal Services Act 1990, Sch.18, para.25(7), and the Constitutional Reform Act 2005, Sch.4, Pt 1, para 102.

[185] SI 2005/384.

[186] See the 4th edition of this book, para.2–028.

[187] Each Committee had to appoint a Justice's Chief Executive.

[188] See para.1–019, and the White Paper, *Supporting Magistrates' Courts to Provide Justice* (Cm. 6681, 2005).

[189] i.e. designated by the Lord Chancellor in relation to a magistrates' court, justice of the peace or local justice area: 2003 Act, s.37.

[190] 2003 Act, s.21, as amended by the Constitutional Reform Act 2005, Sch.4, Pt 1, para.322.

[191] See para.4–071.

[192] See the Criminal Justice and Court Services Act 2000, ss.1–10, as amended; Local Probation Boards (Appointment) Regulations 2000 (SI 2000/3342), as amended by SI 2006/2664, Local Probation Boards (Miscellaneous Provisions) Regulations 2001 (SI 2001/786), Local Probation Boards (Appointments and Miscellaneous Provisions) Regulations 2001 (SI 2001/1035); F. V. Jarvis, *Probation Service Manual* (5th edn, 1993); *www.probation.homeoffice.gov.uk* (website of the National Probation Service).

providing reports concerning the selection of persons for early release. They are also to assist authorised persons in respect of conditional cautions and the supervision and rehabilitation of persons to whom such cautions are given. A further object is that of giving information relating to the judicial and custodial process to victims.[193] Section 69 of the 2000 Act places a duty on local probation boards to ascertain whether victims of violent or sexual offences wish to make representations about any conditions or requirements that should be placed on the offender on his release.[194] Probation officers also work in prison establishments and with youth offending teams. The Service was previously a local service provided by probation committees. The Conservative government explored the possibility of establishing a national service, but ultimately decided that it should be retained as a local service.[195] The Labour government (now with full party support) established the National Probation Service with effect from April 2001.[196] There is a National Directorate and 42 Probation Services, matching police force and CPS area boundaries throughout England and Wales, and grouped in 10 regions. The Service is subject to inspection by Her Majesty's Inspectorate of the National Probation Service,[197] first established by the Probation Services Act 1993. There is an increased emphasis on punishment and the protection of the public.[198] The 2000 Act separated out functions concerning the welfare of children and passed them to a new service, the Children and Family Courts Advisory and Support Service (CAFCASS).[199]

From 2004 the probation and prison services have been brought together as the National Offender Management Service, although they not as yet fully merged. Nine Regional Offender Managers in England and a Director of Offender Management in Wales are responsible for the commissioning of offender management services from a range of providers from public, voluntary and private sectors.[200] The Ministry of Justice has assumed responsibility for NOMS.

---

[193] 2000 Act, s.1; SI 2001/786, reg. 2.

[194] Known as "Sarah's Law" as part of a package of measures introduced following the death of Sarah Payne: see Probation Circular 62/2001.

[195] See *Organising Supervision of Punishment in the Community: A Decision Document* (Home Office, HMSO, 1991), which followed a Green Paper, *Supervision and Punishment in the Community* (Cm. 966, 1990). The Green Paper had put forward for consultation the option of establishing a single, national, centrally run probation service, but the government ultimately decided "that for the time being the service will remain locally structured" noting the overwhelming view of respondents that the service can operate most effectively as a local service: *Decision Document*, pp.2, 3.

[196] This followed the publication of figures that showed that less than half of persons who breached probation orders were returned to prison and wide variations in performance across the country. The new service would be a "unified centrally-driven service" that would develop evidence-based approaches to community punishment and public protection: Lord Bassam, HL Deb July 3, 2000, col.1286.

[197] 2000 Act, ss.6, 7, formerly Her Majesty's Inspectorate of Probation. See *www.inspectorates. homeoffice.gov.uk/hmiprobration*.

[198] Probation officers, Boards and the Secretary of State must have regard to the aims of (a) the protection of the public, (b) the reduction of re-offending, (c) the proper punishment of offenders, (d) ensuring offenders' awareness of the effects of crime on victims and the public, and (e) the rehabilitation of offenders: *ibid.* s.2. Community sentences were re-named (see above) (requiring extensive amendment to the recent consolidation measure, the Powers of Criminal Courts (Sentencing) Act 2000). Community sentences "will no longer be a soft option": J. Straw M.P., H.C. Deb March 28, 2000, col.230.

[199] 2000 Act, ss.11–17.

[200] See *www.noms.homeoffice.gov.uk*.

2. EMPLOYMENT TRIBUNALS[201]

Industrial tribunals (renamed employment tribunals in 1998[202]) were first estab-   **2–031**
lished by the Industrial Training Act 1964 to hear appeals by employers assessed
for levy payable to an industrial training board. They were then given jurisdiction
over disputes about redundancy pay. The Royal Commission on Trade Unions
and Employers' Associations[203] recommended that the tribunal's jurisdiction
should be enlarged to comprise, subject to certain limitations, all disputes
between the individual worker and employer, the primary aim being to make
available "a procedure which is easily accessible, informal, speedy and inexpensive, and which gives them the best possible opportunities of arriving at an
amicable settlement of their differences".[204] To an extent this recommendation
has been fulfilled and the jurisdiction of employment tribunals has steadily
expanded. In addition to the points already mentioned, employment tribunals
have jurisdiction in respect of complaints of unfair dismissal,[205] questions as to
terms required to be included in a contract of employment,[206] claims to equal
pay,[207] failure to allow time off for specified purposes,[208] appeals against
improvement notices or prohibition notices served by a health and safety inspector[209] and certain complaints relating to sex,[210] race,[211] disability,[212] religion[213]
and sexual orientation,[214] discrimination and a host of other matters between
employer and employee. Apart from matters arising between employer and
employee, they also handle claims by individuals against trade unions for
unreasonable exclusion or expulsion in closed shop situations and claims for
compensation in respect of pressure on the employer to take action against an
individual by reason of membership or non-membership of a union.[215] An
important development was the extension[216] and (long-delayed) implementation[217] of the Lord Chancellor's power to confer jurisdiction on employment

---

[201] See K. Whitesides and G. Hawker, *Industrial Tribunals* (1975); Sweet & Maxwell's *Encyclopedia
   of Employment Law*, Pt A7; JUSTICE Report, *Industrial Tribunals* (1987); L. Dickens, *et al.*,
   Dismissed: A Study of Unfair Dismissal and the Industrial Tribunal System (1987); A. M.
   Leonard, *Judging Inequality* (Cobden Trust, 1987); B. J. Doyle, *Employment Tribunals: The New
   Law* (1998); J. MacMillan (1999) I.L.J. 33; D. Sneath, *Employment Tribunals* (2005), *www.
   employmenttribunals.gov.uk*; *Annual Reports of the Employment Tribunals Service* (DTI, to
   2006).
[202] By the Employment Rights (Dispute Resolution) Act 1998, s.1.
[203] Cmnd. 3623, 1968: Chairman: Lord Donovan.
[204] Cmnd. 3623, 1968, para.572.
[205] Employment Rights Act 1996, ss.94–134.
[206] *ibid.* s.11, as amended.
[207] Equal Pay Act 1970, as amended.
[208] 17 Trade Union and Labour Relations (Consolidation) Act 1992 ss.168–169 (trade union duties),
   170–171 (trade union activities); Employment Rights Act 1996, ss.52–53 (to seek work during
   redundancy situation), 55–56 (ante natal care).
[209] Health and Safety at Work, etc, Act 1974, ss.21–24.
[210] Sex Discrimination Act 1975, ss.63, 72, 73.
[211] Race Relations Act 1976, s.54.
[212] Disability Discrimination Act 1995, ss.4, 6.
[213] Employment Equality (Religion or Belief) Regulations 2003 (SI 2003/1660).
[214] Employment Equality (Sexual Orientation) Regulations 2003 (SI 2003/1661).
[215] Trade Union and Labour Relations (Consolidation) Act 1992, ss.146, 150, 160.
[216] By the Trade Union and Labour Relations Act 1993, s.38. The only exclusion is a claim for
   damages or a sum due in respect of personal injuries.
[217] Employment Tribunals Extension of Jurisdiction (England and Wales) Order 1994 (SI
   1994/1623). An employment tribunal may not order the payment of an amount exceeding
   £25,000: *ibid.* art.10.

tribunals in respect of claims for damages for breach of or for a sum due under a contract of employment or other contracts connected with employment.[218]

The tribunals sit at over 50 centres, grouped under 20 Regional Offices of Employment Tribunals and the Central Office of Employment Tribunals in London.[219] There is a President of Employment Tribunals (England and Wales) who both sits as a chairman and has important administrative responsibilities in relation to the system.[220] A fully constituted tribunal has a legally qualified chairman and two "wing" members.[221] However, an increasing range of cases can be heard by the chairman sitting alone[222] or (with the consent of the parties) by the chairman and one other member.[223] In deciding (which may be at any stage) whether a case should be heard by a fully constituted tribunal, the chairman must consider whether there is a likelihood of a dispute on the facts which makes that desirable, or, conversely, where there is a likelihood of an issue of law arising which would make it desirable for the chairman to sit alone, any views of the parties and whether there are other proceedings that might be heard concurrently.[224]

A common criticism of employment tribunals has been that they have become increasingly "legalistic":

> "First, it is observed that the immense quantity of case law reported and cited in the courts is complicating the work of tribunals. Secondly, statutes, which were intended to be straightforward enactments, are increasingly being subjected to subtle lawyers' reasoning."[225]

Lord Denning M.R. suggested that some limit be placed on the reporting of cases:

> "If we are not careful, we shall find the Industrial Tribunals bent down under the weight of the law books or, what is worse, asleep under them. Let principles be reported, but not particular instances."[226]

---

[218] Employment Protection (Consolidation) Act 1978, s.131, as amended; see now the Employment Tribunals Act 1996, s.3.

[219] Regional chairmen are based at 14 of these offices.

[220] See the Employment Tribunals (Constitution and Rules of Procedure) Regulations 2004 (SI 2004/1861), reg.4, as amended.

[221] See below, para.4–016.

[222] Employment Tribunals Act 1996, s.4, as amended by the Employment Rights (Disputes Resolution) Act 1998, s.3 (the powers having previously been extended by the Trade Union Reform and Employment Rights Act 1993, s.36): these include applications for interim relief in specified unfair dismissal cases; complaints under the Pension Schemes Act 1993, s.126; proceedings concerning deductions from pay; breach of contract claims; where the parties give written consent; where the respondent is not contesting the case; proceedings concerning redundancy payments; deductions of trade union subscription or political fund contributions from wages; failure to pay remuneration under a protective award; the right to secure written particulars of employment; guarantee payments; and other specified matters.

[223] 1996 Act, s.4(1)(b), to be amended by the 1998 Act, s.4: this is to be possible (a) where such parties as are present at the beginning of the hearing in person or represented consent; or (b) where each of the parties consents.

[224] 1996 Act, s.4(5).

[225] R. Munday, "Tribunal Lore: Legalism and the Industrial Tribunals" (1981) 10 I.L.J. 146 at 147.

[226] *Walls Meat Co Ltd v Khan* [1979] I.C.R. 52 at 57, *cf.* Lawton L.J. in *Clay Cross (Quarry Services) Ltd v Fletcher* [1979] 1 All E.R. 474 at 479.

On the other hand, it has been suggested that growing "legalism" is inevitable **2–032** given that the legislation is in fact complex and interpretative difficulties unavoidable, that there is a legally qualified chairman, that legal representation is increasingly common, that in practice litigants require consistency in decision-making, and that there must be a reliable yardstick for the conciliatory procedures incorporated in the legislation to work:

> "Naturally, tribunals will continue to dispense with the flummery and much of the procedural and evidential paraphernalia of the law courts—in this sense they are informal and comparatively free. But in most important respects, tribunals do closely resemble courts. Thus, if charges of legalism mean that they interpret the law in legal fashion, one would expect to find these charges fully proven for it is quite impossible to see how else tribunals could be expected to behave."[227]

A JUSTICE Report on Industrial Tribunals[228] made a number of proposals for change. For the vast majority of cases the investigative approach should be improved, so as to reduce the need for representation, while, for a minority of cases, the adversarial system should be improved by providing legal aid for representation and establishing an upper tier Industrial Court, with senior chairmen and members, to hear them. The Industrial Court would also assume the appellate functions of the Employment Appeal Tribunal. The Committee confirmed that industrial tribunals did have a number of advantages over ordinary courts, being more accessible, less formal, more expeditious, less expensive and possessed of special expertise.[229] However, complaints of excessive "legalism" were to an extent justified. One cause was the present state of substantive employment law, which was in need of clarification and consolidation in a comprehensible form. The other main cause was the adversarial system which was a major obstacle to informality in the conduct of hearings.[230] The Committee also noted that research indicated that industrial tribunals were particularly weak in understanding and applying the legislation concerning complaints of sex or race discrimination.[231] Special training was necessary for chairmen and members who dealt with such cases.[232]

Some of those points were addressed in the Employment Rights (Dispute Resolution) Act 1998.[233] This renamed the tribunals, increased the range of cases that could be heard by the chairman alone, provided for the streamlining of the procedural rules and for the appointment of "legal officers" to carry out some of the functions of tribunal chairmen, empowered ACAS to establish an arbitration

---

[227] Munday, *op. cit.* p.159. On the procedure of employment tribunals see below, paras 13–018, 16–003.

[228] Chairman: Bob Hepple (1987). See also R. Lewis and J. Clark, *Employment Rights, Industrial Tribunals and Arbitration* (1993), which argued the case for the introduction of voluntary arbitration as an option for unfair dismissal cases, as one response to the legalism of tribunals.

[229] pp.7–9.

[230] Ch.2.

[231] V. C. Kumar, *Industrial Tribunal Applicants under the Race Relations Act 1976* (Commission for Racial Equality 1986); A. Leonard, *Judging Inequality* (1987).

[232] pp.35–38.

[233] Following the Green Paper, *Resolving Employment Rights Disputes: Options for Reform* (Cm. 2707, 1994): see D. Cockburn, (1995) 24 I.L.J. 285.

scheme for unfair dismissal disputes as a voluntary alternative to tribunal hearings and made it easier for compromise agreements to be reached. The arbitration service[234] commenced operation on May 21 and the new procedural rules[235] came into effect on July 16, 2001. Nevertheless, the government swiftly announced a further review.[236] The main proposals for change were the introduction of new procedural standards for handling disputes in the workplace, coupled with power for a tribunal to vary an award if such procedures were not in place or not used; the promotion of conciliation, introducing a fixed period for conciliation by ACAS; broadening the scope of compromise agreements and promoting the use of ADR; and the "modernisation" of employment tribunals by introducing a fast track for straightforward claims, including the possibility of a written determination, enabling the President to issue practice directions, providing clear guidance on costs, and making it easier for weak claims or responses to be struck out. Furthermore, an Employment Tribunal System Taskforce was established to advise on how the system "can be made more efficient, cost-effective and user-focused against a background of rising caseloads". The Taskforce reported in July 2002,[237] recommending greater co-ordination and consistency of practice, a new emphasis on early disclosure of information with a view to identifying the issues in dispute and their efficient resolution; an emphasis on preventive work and learning from test practice; and the use of tribunal proceedings as a last resort.[238] The government endorsed the report. The various legislative changes were effected by the Employment Act 2002[239] and revised procedure rules.[240] These were said to be the biggest change in the way employment tribunals operate since their inception.[241]

The system is clearly under enormous pressure. While claims have trebled since 1990, it has also been estimated that the number of justiciable disputes is in the range of 500,000 to 900,000 per annum, with only about 15–20 per cent of those disputes going through the employment tribunals.[242]

---

[234] See ACAS website *www.acas.org.uk.*

[235] Employment Tribunals (Constitution and Rules of Procedure) Regulations 2001 (SI 2001/1171), as amended by SI 2001/1459, *inter alia* introducing case management arrangements.

[236] *Routes to Resolution: Improving Dispute Resolution in Britain*: Consultation Document (July 2001), Government Response (November 2001).

[237] *Moving Forward: The Report of the Employment Tribunal System Taskforce* (ETST, 2002, *www.dti.gov.uk/files/file23951.pdf*).

[238] As summarised in the White Paper, *Transforming Public Services: Complaints, Redress and Tribunals* (Cm 6243, 2004), Ch.8.

[239] Including ss.22 (employment tribunals), 23 (EAT); provisions enabling procedure regulations to provide for hearings to be postponed to give an opportunity for conciliation (s.24), to enable the Secretary of State to prescribe forms (s.25), to authorise the determination of proceedings without any hearings in prescribed circumstances (s.26), to enable the President to make procedural directions (s.27), for authorising pre-hearing reviews (s.28); the introduction of statutory dispute resolution procedures and a requirement to use grievance procedures (ss.29–40; Employment Act 2002 (Dispute Resolution) Regulations 2004 (SI 2004/752), ss.22–27 and 28(1), (3) came into force on July 9, 2004 (SI 2004/1717).

[240] Employment Tribunals (Constitution and Rules of Procedure) Regulations 2004 (SI 2004/1861), as amended by SI 2004/2351, SI 2005/435 and 1865. There is now a pre-acceptance procedure to filter out ineligible claims, fixed periods for conciliation, default judgments for claims not resisted within the time limit for response and a greater focus on case management. From October 1, 2005, a prescribed form must be used. New rules of procedure for equal value claims, including case management powers, were added by SI 2004/2351.

[241] *Annual Report of the ETS*, 2005–06, p.18.

[242] *Dispute Resolution in Britain—A background paper* (2001) based in part on H. Genn, *Paths to Justice* (1999). This paper was published at the start of the *Routes to Resolution* review.

Appeals lie on a point of law[243] in most cases to the Employment Appeal Tribunal,[244] and in the others[245] to the Queen's Bench Division.

3. THE EMPLOYMENT APPEAL TRIBUNAL

The Employment Appeal Tribunal[246] was established by the Employment Protection Act 1975[247] as the successor of the politically controversial National Industrial Relations Court, inheriting the latter's appellate functions. Its membership comprises judges of the High Court or Court of Appeal[248] nominated by the Lord Chief Justice, after consulting the Lord Chancellor, at least one judge of the Court of Session nominated by the Lord President of that court, and lay members appointed by the Queen on the recommendation of the Lord Chancellor and the Secretary of State, being persons who "appear . . . to have special knowledge or experience of industrial relations, either as representatives of employers or as representatives of workers".[249] One of the judges is appointed President. Each appeal is normally heard by a judge sitting with two or, more unusually, four lay members.[250] Decisions can be by a majority, and the judge can be outvoted, even on a point of law, by the lay members. The EAT hears appeals from employment tribunals[251] and from the Certification Officer, who performs various functions in respect of trade unions, mostly on points of law. The Court of Appeal has expressed the view that the EAT has taken too wide a view of what constitutes an error of law and has thus interfered too readily with the decisions of employment tribunals.[252] It suggested that the EAT should be less ready to lay down "guidelines" for employment tribunals. For example, whether a dismissal is "fair" should essentially be regarded as a question of fact. The consequent

2–033

---

[243] Fact or law where the question is whether a person has been unreasonably excluded or expelled from membership of a trade union in a closed shop situation.

[244] See below.

[245] e.g. industrial training levy assessments, appeals against an improvement or prohibition notice.

[246] A superior court of record. See Phillips J., "Some notes on the Employment Appeal Tribunal" (1978) 7 I.L.J. 137; Browne-Wilkinson J., "The role of the EAT in the 1980s" (1982) 11 I.L.J. 69; Sir John Waite, "Lawyers and Laymen as Judges in Industry" (1986) 15 I.L.J. 32; Sir John Wood, (1990) 19 I.L.J. 133.

[247] See now the Employment Tribunals Act 1996, ss.20–28, as amended.

[248] Only the former have so far been nominated. In 2000 there were eight High Court judges (including the President) and one judge of the Court of Session nominated to the EAT. There were also nine current judges and seven Q.C.s nominated to be judicial members.

[249] The lay members do not in practice act in a partisan manner.

[250] Normally, there should be equal numbers of members whose knowledge, etc., is as representative of employers or of workers; however, an appeal may be heard by a judge and one or three members with the consent of the parties, and certain appeals may be heard by a judge alone or (in cases of national security), the President alone: Trade Union Reforms and Employment Rights Act 1993, s.37; see now the Employment Tribunals Act 1996, s.28.

[251] Including in breach of contract cases: Employment Tribunals Act 1996, s.21(1)(g), inserted by the Employment Rights (Dispute Resolution) Act 1998, Sch.1, para.17(2), correcting, with retrospective effect (para.17(3)), an oversight in the original drafting of the 1996 Act which led to the EAT dealing with such cases for a period where technically it had no jurisdiction to do so: see *Pendragon plc v Jackson* [1998] I.R.L.R. 17, EAT.

[252] See *Retarded Children's Aid Society v Day* [1978] I.C.R 437; *Methven v Cow Industrial Polymers Ltd* [1980] I.C.R. 463; *Pedersen v Camden London B.C.* [1981] I.C.R. 674; *Woods v W. M. Car Services (Peterborough) Ltd* [1982] I.C.R. 693; and the articles cited in n.246 above. See also *O'Kelly v Trusthouse Forte plc* [1983] I.C.R. 728.

advantage of greater flexibility for employment tribunals has to be balanced against the consequent inconsistency amongst them.[253]

Appeals lie on a point of law from the EAT to the Court of Appeal,[254] with the leave of either court.

4. SOCIAL SECURITY TRIBUNALS[255]

2–034   A variety of cash benefits and tax credits are available under the Social Security Contributions and Benefits Act 1992 and the Tax Credits Acts 1999 and 2002. Benefits include contributory benefits (e.g. incapacity benefit, maternity allowance, widow's benefit, bereavement benefits, retirement pension); non-contributory benefits (e.g. attendance allowance, carer's allowance, disability living allowance, guardian's allowance); industrial injuries benefit; job seeker's allowance; and income-related benefits (e.g. income support, housing benefit and council tax benefit).[256] Child benefit is payable under the Child Benefit Act 1975. Several tribunals have been established to determine questions arising in the administration of these benefits.

Two discernible trends in the development of the structure of social security tribunals have been, first, the amalgamation of different tribunal jurisdictions and, secondly, the integration of tribunals within the court system. There has at the same time been a tendency for the government to restrict rights of appeal to an independent tribunal against decisions concerning benefits, although this has to an extent been checked with the implementation of the Human Rights Act 1998.

(a) The position to 1984

2–035   Prior to 1984, a distinction was drawn between the schemes based on the insurance principle, where entitlement to benefit depended on the claimant having made appropriate contributions and otherwise falling within the rules of the scheme, and the provision of means-tested benefits involving the exercise of discretion. As regards the former, An appeal from a decision by an insurance officer or the Secretary of State lay to a National Insurance Local Tribunal,[257] comprising a legally qualified chairman,[258] a member from a panel representing employers and self-employed earners and one from a panel representing employed earners.[259] As regards the latter, tribunals were first set up in the 1930s

---

[253] 55 See Browne-Wilkinson J., *op. cit.* n.246, p.72: " . . . there are signs that . . . Industrial Tribunals are beginning to demonstrate a lack of uniformity in their approach to what constitutes fair industrial practice". His Lordship suggested that it would be desirable to aim for a middle way between the early practice of the EAT and the restrictive approach of the Court of Appeal.

[254] In Scotland, appeals lie to the Court of Session. The issue will be whether the EAT was right, not the ET: *Gover v Propertycare Ltd* [2006] 4 All E.R. 69.

[255] See generally N. J. Wikeley, *Wikeley, Ogus and Barendt's, The Law of Social Security* (5th edn, 2002), Ch.6; D. Bonner, ed., *Social Security Legislation 2006*, Vol.III, *Administration. Adjudication and the European Dimension* (Commentary by R. C. A. White and M. Rowland) (2006).

[256] 1992 Act, ss.20, 63, 94, 123, as amended.

[257] This term did not appear in the legislation, but was the title commonly used. Another label sometimes found was "Social Security Local Tribunal".

[258] This was not a legal requirement but was the almost invariable practice: see below, para.4–016.

[259] Social Security Act 1975, s.97(2): see below, para.4–016.

and subsequently evolved into Supplementary Benefit Appeal Tribunals. These comprised a chairman appointed by the Secretary of State from a panel drawn up by the Lord Chancellor, and two members.[260] The procedures and decision-making of SBATs were contrasted unfavourably with those of NILTs.[261]

(b) Social Security Appeal Tribunals

In 1980 the supplementary benefit scheme was reformed, with detailed rules of entitlement replacing discretions, thereby bringing it closer in form to the national insurance scheme.[262] The Health and Social Services and Social Security Adjudications Act 1983[263] provided for the merger of the two adjudication systems. Most claims were now submitted to an "adjudication officer" appointed by the Secretary of State for Social Security.[264] There was a Chief Adjudication Officer, who was required to advise adjudication officers and keep their work under review, and to report annually to the Secretary of State on standards of adjudication.[265]

    Appeals lay to a Social Security Appeal Tribunal,[266] which now exercised the jurisdictions formerly exercised by NILTs and SBATs. The whole system was headed by the President of Social Security Appeal Tribunals, Medical Appeal Tribunals and Disability Appeal Tribunals (subsequently generally known as the President of the Independent Tribunal Service).[267] The Lord Chancellor appointed chairmen, who had to be legally qualified. There was a single panel of members constituted by the President for the whole of Great Britain. Each tribunal comprised a chairman, nominated by the President, and two members.

2–036

(c) Other adjudicating bodies

Certain questions, including whether a person was an "earner", whether he or she was "employed" or "self-employed" and whether he or she complied with "contribution conditions" necessary for receipt of contributory benefits, were determined by the Secretary of State: in practice by a member of the DSS Solicitors' Office.[268] The Secretary of State could refer a point of law, and a dissatisfied claimant could appeal on such a point, to the High Court.

    Certain questions concerning disablement benefit were determined by "Medical Boards" of two medical practitioners, subject to a right of appeal to a Medical Appeal Tribunal, comprising a legally qualified chairman and two doctors of

2–037

---

[260] Supplementary Benefits Act 1976, Sch.4.

[261] See the first edition of this book, pp.55–57.

[262] Social Security Act 1980, Sch.2.

[263] Sch.8: in force from April 23, 1984. See J. Mesher, (1983) 10 J.L.S. 135; M. Partington, "The Restructuring of SSATs: a Personal View" in C. Harlow (ed.), *Public Law and Politics* (1986), Ch.9.

[264] Social Security Administration Act 1992, ss.20, 21, 38.

[265] *ibid.* s.39. See R. Sainsbury, "The Social Security Chief Adjudication Officer: The First Four Years" [1989] P.L. 323.

[266] *ibid.* ss.22, 40, 41, Sch.2.

[267] The first President was Judge H. J. Byrt, who held the office from 1984: see J. Fulbrook, (1989) 18 I.L.J. 177; Interview, *Legal Action*, September 1989, p.7.

[268] Social Security Administration Act 1992, ss.17, 18.

consultant status.[269] In other cases appeals on medical issues lay to a Disability Appeal Tribunal.[270]

Appeals in connection with decisions concerning the maintenance of children went before the Child Support Appeal Tribunals, whose composition was the same as for SSATs.[271] The structure mirrored that of the social security tribunals, with the President of SSATs, MATs and DATs also appointed as President of the Child Support Appeal Tribunals,[272] and provision for the appointment of a Chief Child Support Commissioner and other Child Support Commissioners.[273] These tribunals were distinctive in that they handled disputes (possibly acrimonious ones) between private individuals.

(d) Reform: The Social Security Act 1998

2–038   The Social Security Act 1998[274] introduced fundamental reforms to arrangements for decision-making and appeals under legislation relating to social security, child support, vaccine damage payments and war pensions. First, the functions of the first-tier decision-makers (adjudication officers, social fund officers and child support officers) were transferred to the Secretary of State,[275] who is now the decision-maker.[276] Accordingly, they no longer enjoy formal legal independence and the Office of the Chief Adjudication Officer has been abolished.[277] Decisions may be made or issued by an officer acting under the Secretary of State's authority or by a computer for whose operation such an officer is responsible.[278]

Secondly, the functions of social security appeal tribunals, disability appeal tribunals, medical appeal tribunals, child support appeal tribunals and vaccine damage tribunals were transferred to "unified appeal tribunals".[279] The Lord Chancellor, after consultation with the Secretary of State, may appoint a lawyer

---

[269] *ibid.* s.50, Sch.2.

[270] *ibid.* ss.33, 42, 43.

[271] Child Support Act 1991, ss.20, 21.

[272] *ibid.* Sch.3, para.1.

[273] *ibid.* s.22, Sch.4.

[274] See DSS, *Improving Decision Making and Appeals in Social Security* (Cm. 3328, 1996); N.J. Wikeley, *Current Law Statutes Annotated 1998*, (1998) 5 J.S.S.L. 104 and (1999) 6 J.S.S.L. 155; R. Sainsbury in M. Harris and M. Partington (eds), *Administrative Justice in the 21st Century* (1999), Ch.22 (arguing that the changes seemed designed to save expenditure rather than improve the lot of the average claimant).

[275] 1998 Act, s.1.

[276] *ibid.* s.8. (Tax credit decisions are, however, made by officers of HM Revenue and Customs.) Decisions may be revised (s.9) or superseded (s.10).

[277] Instead, the Secretary of State must report periodically on the standards of decision-making: 1998 Act, s.81; the President of appeal tribunals must report annually on the quality of decisions which go to appeal: Sch.1, para.10. Nevertheless, "there are obvious dangers in over-reliance on agencies being responsible for monitoring their own standards of adjudication": Wikeley (1998), pp.14–7. The 2005–06 Report noted that there did seem to be some progress in addressing issues raised in previous reports: *President's Report 2005–2006* (Tribunals Service website).

[278] Social Security Act 1998, s.2.

[279] *ibid.* s.4. The legislation did not confer a specific title on these tribunals, beyond "appeal tribunals constituted under Chapter I of Part I of the Social Security Act 1998" (see ss.1(2) and 39(1)). The side note refers to "unified appeal tribunals". The Council on Tribunals referred to them under the generic heading "The Appeals Service." They were also referred to as Appeals Service appeal tribunals or Appeals Service tribunals. From April 1, 2006, the date of transfer to the Tribunals Service, the Appeals Service changed its name to the Social Security and Child Support Appeals Tribunal: *www.tribunals.gov.uk/latest_news/latest_news.htm.*

of 10 years' standing to be (what is now) President of Social Security and Child Support Appeal Tribunals.[280] The President must ensure that appropriate steps are taken to secure the confidentiality of prescribed material, arrange for the training of tribunal members, and report to the Secretary of State.[281] There were two distinct bodies within the Appeals Service, one being the tribunals and the other being an executive agency of the Department of Work and Pensions responsible for providing administrative support. Responsibility for providing administrative support passed to the DCA's Tribunals Service on April 1, 2006.

Thirdly, the Lord Chancellor must constitute a panel of persons to act as members of appeal tribunals.[282] The panel must include persons possessing prescribed qualifications. These are lawyers, registered medical practitioners, accountants and "persons, other than registered medical practitioners, who are experienced in dealing with the needs of disabled persons—(a) in a professional or voluntary capacity; or (b) because they are themselves disabled".[283] Accordingly, other lay people are no longer eligible to be tribunal members. This change was controversial.[284] It has been argued persuasively that a minority of cases[285] are particularly suitable for determination by a tribunal including persons with knowledge or experience of conditions in the area who are representative of persons living or working in the area, and that the law should be modified accordingly.[286]

Each tribunal must comprise one, two or three members drawn by the President from the panel[287] in accordance with regulations. The member, or at least one member must be a lawyer[288] and the President must nominate the chairman, who has a casting vote.[289] The tribunal may call upon expert assistance.[290] The regulations provide that a tribunal shall comprise a legally qualified panel member, except where:

(a) the case raises issues concerning industrial injuries benefit, severe disablement allowance or a vaccine damage payment, in which case there must be,

---

[280] *ibid.* s.5, Sch.1. The qualification is a 10-year general qualification under s.71 of the Courts and Legal Services Act 1990 or an advocate or solicitor in Scotland of at least 10 years' standing. The first holder of the office was Judge Michael Harris.

[281] *ibid.* Sch.1, paras 7–10.

[282] *ibid.* s.6, as amended by the Constitutional Reform Act 2005, Sch.4, Pt 1, paras 271, 272.

[283] Social Security and Child Support (Decisions and Appeals) Regulations 1999 (SI 1999/991), Sch.3, as amended by SI 2002/1379 and SI 2005/337. In the case of medical practitioners, the Chief Medical Officer must be consulted by the Judicial Appointments Commission: s.6(3A).

[284] The Council on Tribunals expressed its concern at this change, given the valuable contribution of lay members previously: Annual Report for 1998–99, p.56. A majority of chairmen, however, were broadly content with the changes: N. J. Wikeley, (2000) 7 J.S.S.L. 88.

[285] Cases raising cohabitation, misconduct or voluntary leaving, or overpayments issues.

[286] N. J. Wikeley, (2000) 7 J.S.S.L. 88.

[287] 1998 Act, s.7(1).

[288] *ibid.* s.7(2): i.e. have a general qualification under s.71 of the Courts and Legal Services Act 1990 or be an advocate or solicitor in Scotland. The government retreated from the position that would have other members sitting alone in some cases: Wikeley (1998), pp.14–13. Opponents recalled criticisms in the past of the quality of decision making of tribunals (such as SBATs) without a lawyer.

[289] *ibid.* s.7(3). The lawyer is invariably nominated in practice, although other possibilities are not ruled out: Wikeley (1998), pp.14–13—14–14.

[290] *ibid.* s.7(4): the expert must be a panel member: s.7(5).

in addition to the lawyer, either one medical practitioner, two medical practitioners, or one medical practitioner and another panel member appointed for the purpose of training or the monitoring of standards[291];

(b) the case concerns child support or a relevant benefit[292] and raises difficult issues relating to the balance sheet of an enterprise or trust fund, in which case there must be a lawyer and an accountant; or

(c) the case concerns attendance allowance, disability living allowance or a disabled person's tax credit, in which case the lawyer must sit with a medical practitioner and a person with a disability qualification.[293]

Appeals to a tribunal lie in cases involving a relevant benefit (unless excluded by Sch.2 to the 1998 Act), other decisions (specified in Sch.3)[294] or specified cases arising under other legislation.[295] In deciding an appeal, an appeal tribunal need not consider any issue not raised by the appeal, and must not take into account any circumstances not obtaining at the time when the decision appealed against was made.[296] The former confers a discretion, and it has been argued that the latter "introduces an unwelcome element of technicality into appeals to tribunals that were once supposed to be user-friendly".[297]

An appeal lies to a Commissioner on a point of law, with the leave of the chairman or other prescribed person, or a Commissioner.[298] Where an application for leave is made to a chairman or other prescribed person, and he or she considers that the decision is erroneous in law, he or she may set it aside and refer it for redetermination by the tribunal or determination by a differently constituted tribunal; if each of the principal parties expresses the view that the decision is erroneous in law, he or she must set it aside and refer the case for determination by a differently constituted tribunal.[299]

The Secretary of State must assign a clerk to service each appeal tribunal.[300]

The functions of the Secretary of State concerning social security contributions, as exercised through the Contributions Agency, were transferred to the Treasury (policy) and the Inland Revenue, now HM Revenue and Customs (operational functions), with effect from April 1, 1999.[301] Furthermore, appeals

---

[291] In some cases it is specified that the lawyer sits with one medical practitioner.

[292] i.e. a benefit under Pts II to V of the Social Security (Contributions and Benefits) Act 1992, jobseeker's allowance, income support, working families' tax credit, disabled person's tax credit, a social fund payment, child benefit, and any other prescribed benefit: 1998 Act, s.8(3).

[293] SI 1999/991, reg.36, as amended by SI 1999/1466, reg.2, SI 2000/1596, reg.24 and SI 2004/3368, reg.2.

[294] 1998 Act, s.12; SI 1999/991, Pts IV, V.

[295] e.g. Social Security (Recovery of Benefits) Act 1997, ss.11, 12, as amended. Amendments to the child support and vaccine damage payments legislation were effected by the 1999 Acts, ss.40–47, and further amendments on child support by the Child Support, Pensions and Social Security Act 2000, ss.10, 11.

[296] 1998 Act, s.12(8).

[297] White and Rowland (2006), pp.220–227.

[298] 1998 Act, s.14.

[299] ibid. s.13. This is so, however unreasonable the parties' collective view is: see White and Rowland (2006), p.229, describing subs.(3) as "a bizarre provision".

[300] SI 1999/991, reg.37. See para.4–019.

[301] Social Security Contributions (Transfer of Functions, etc.) Act 1999.

in cases concerning housing benefit or council tax benefit now lie to appeal tribunals and then the Social Security Commissioners,[302] rather than to housing review boards, whose independence was doubtful[303] and whose establishment had been the establishment of much academic criticism.[304] One of the features of the current programme of tribunal reform has been recognition of the need to take steps to improve the quality of initial decision-making, one source of relevant information being feedback from tribunals.[305] This will reverse a trend that has, regrettably, been in the opposite direction.[306]

(e) Social Security and Child Support Commissioners[307]

The National Insurance Commissioners heard appeals from NILTs, and appeals on a point of law from Medical Appeal Tribunals and the Attendance Allowance Board. In 1980, a right of appeal on a point of law was created from SBATs to the Commissioner,[308] who were renamed Social Security Commissioners.[309] From April 23, 1984, they have heard appeals from SSATs and from 1987 these have been restricted to points of law in all cases.[310] At present there is a Chief Social Security and Child Support Commissioner, 16 Commissioners and 18

2–039

---

[302] Child Support, Pensions and Social Security Act 2000, Sch.7; Housing Benefit and Council Tax Benefit (Decisions and Appeals) Regulations 2001 (SI 2001/1002). The change was warmly welcomed by the Council on Tribunals: Annual Report for 1999–2000, para.6. One advantage of the change is that the appeal tribunals will not be influenced (as HBRBs were) by the fact that in some cases benefit payments are not fully covered by a central government subsidy: see S. Rahilly, (2001) 8 J.S.S.L. 57.

[303] Confirmed in *R. (on the application of Bewry) v Norwich City Council* [2001] EWHC Admin 657 (councillor membership of Board determining issue involving credibility; breach of common law requirement equivalent to that comprised in Art.6(1), ECHR); distinguished in *R. (on the application of Bibi) v Housing Benefit Review Board of Rochdale Metropolitan Borough Council* [2001] EWHC Admin 967 (councillor membership of Board meant that it could not be independent or expert but judicial review was a sufficient remedy given that most of the facts were not substantially in issue and that the councillors had no personal interest in their finding that a tenancy was not on a commercial basis and so did not enable a claim to be made for housing benefit). A breach of Art.6(1) was found by the ECtHR in *Tsfayo v UK*, Judgment of November 14, 2006.

[304] See N. Wikeley, (1986) 5 C.J.Q. 18; R. Sainsbury and T. Eardley, [1992] P.L. 551 (noting the very limited training of councillors); S. Rahilly in N. Harris (eds), *Social Security Law in Context* (2000), pp.424–425.

[305] White Paper, *Transforming Public Services: Complaints, Redress and Tribunals* (Cm. 6243), pp.29–30; *Tribunals Service Business Plan 2006–07*, p.35.

[306] See N. Warren, "The Adjudication Gap—A Discussion Document" (2006) 13 J.S.S.L. 110, reviewing a decline in DWP adjudication standards associated with both legislative and operational changes (*cf.* above, n.277).

[307] See Fourth Report of the Select Committee on Social Security 1999–2000 H.C. 263; R. Micklethwait, *The National Insurance Commissioners* (1976); N. Harris, (1993) 22 I.L.J. 222; D. Bonner, *et al.*, (2001) 8 J.S.S.L. 9; T. Buck, *et al.*, *Making Social Security Law* (2005). Under the 1946 legislation there was a National Insurance Commissioner and an Industrial Injuries Commissioner, each with several deputies. The same person commonly held appointments under both schemes. In 1966, these posts were merged, the National Insurance Commissioner was retitled the Chief National Insurance Commissioner, and the deputies became full Commissioners.

[308] Supplementary Benefits Act 1976, s.15A, inserted by the Social Security Act 1979, s.6. This replaced an appeal from SBATs to the High Court that had been created in 1978.

[309] Social Security Act 1980, s.14.

[310] Social Security Act 1998, s.14, re-enacting with modifications the Social Security Administration Act 1992, s.23. See also the Social Security Commissioners (Procedure) Regulations 1999 (SI 1999/1495).

Deputy Commissioners.[311] In practice three sit in Edinburgh, the others in London, although they may travel to Cardiff, Liverpool and other locations to hear cases. The Chief Commissioner may convene a Tribunal of three Commissioners to hear an appeal involving a point of law of special difficulty. He is also responsible for selecting the decisions that are to be reported. Until 1980, the only further possibility of review was an application for judicial review. There is now a right of appeal on a point of law to the Court of Appeal, with the leave of the Commissioner or the court.[312] From 1985, they have been administered by the Lord Chancellor's Department and its successors. The Social Security Commissioners have also been appointed as Child Support Commissioners under the Child Support Act 1991.[313] The Child Poverty Action Group in evidence to the Social Security Select Committee has commended the Commissioners' performance.[314]

(f) Limitation of rights of appeal

2–040   Reforms to the social security system under Pt III of the Social Security Act 1986 included the replacement of lump sum "single payments" and "urgent need payments" under the supplementary benefit legislation by payments from the, cash-limited, Social Fund. In one sense this involved a return to a system of discretionary payments. The payments, most in the form of loans, are made by social fund officers appointed by the Secretary of State. In practice, however, the detailed directions given to the officers by the Secretary of State operate very much in the manner of regulations.[315] Controversially, the government decided that there should be no rights of appeal within the tribunals system.[316] The legislation provides instead for internal review by social fund inspectors of the Independent Review Service, who are officials appointed as inspectors by the Social Fund Commissioner. The Commissioner is in turn appointed by the Secretary of State. The inspectors are subject to the guidance and directions issued to the social fund officers.[317]

---

[311] The same qualifications are specified as for appointment as President of Social Security and Child Support Tribunals above: 1998 Act, Sch.4, para.1. The current Chief Commissioner is Judge Gary Hickinbottom (2003–). (See *Tribunals*, Summer 2005, p.16). His predecessors were Judge K. A. Machin (1990–2001) and Judge Michael Harris (2001–2003).

[312] 1998 Act s.15. See *Cooke v Secretary of State* [2001] EWCA Civ 734, [2002] 3 All ER 279 where the Court of Appeal gave guidance as to the criteria for the grant of leave by that court.

[313] See the Child Support Commissioners Procedure Regulations 1999 (SI 1999/1305).

[314] Fourth Report, 1999–2000 H.C. 263, *Minutes of Evidence*, cited in D. Bonner *et al.* (2001) 8 J.S.S.L. 9 at 28.

[315] See *R. v Secretary of State for Social Services, Ex p. Stitt, The Times*, July 5, 1990.

[316] See H. Bolderson, (1988) 15 J.L.S. 279. The Council on Tribunals registered their objections in a Special Report, *Social Security—Abolition of independent appeals under the proposed Social Fund* (Cmnd. 9722, 1986). See generally R. Drabble and T. Lynes, [1989] P.L. 297; Ogus, Barendt and Wikeley, *The Law of Social Security* (4th edn, 1995), pp.684–685; J. Scampion, "The Use of Review in the Administrative Justice System: The Experience of Social Fund Reviews" summarised in M. Harris and M. Partington (eds), *Administrative Justice in the 21st Century* (1999), pp.156–160 (defending the arrangements as suitable for this context, where fair, quick and clear decision-making was needed and where the system enabled inspectors' decisions to be effectively and comprehensively monitored).

[317] Social Security Act 1998, ss.36–38; Social Fund (Application for Review) Regulations 1988 (SI 1988/34), as amended; T. Buck, *The Social Fund—Law and Practice* (2nd edn, 2000, 3rd edn, due 2007); *www.irs-review.org.uk.*

5. County Courts

(a) Establishment

The present county courts were originally established by the County Courts Act **2–041**
1846. This Act followed a lengthy campaign, which aroused hostility in several
quarters, including the Bar and certain large London solicitors' firms.[318] The
hostility was based essentially on fears of loss of business to provincial attornies
and solicitors. In the case of the Bar there was also resistance to the development
of provincial Bars, which were seen to be the only effective way of competing for
county court business.[319] The aim of the Act was to set up an effective local court
for minor cases, and, in particular, the recovery of small debts: proceedings in the
superior courts were prohibitively expensive and civil proceedings at the assizes
were prone to delay. It is ironic that similar criticisms of ordinary county court
proceedings in recent times have led to the development of new, more informal,
procedures for small claims, and arguments that a further tier of small claims
courts should be established.[320] Indeed, right from the outset the new courts were
much more heavily used by shopkeepers, traders, and other creditors than by
ordinary people, their establishment leading to "an infinite expansion of
credit".[321]

(b) Organisation

England and Wales is divided into districts and at least one court is held in each **2–042**
district.[322] The districts and locations are specified by the Lord Chancellor, after
consulting the Lord Chief Justice.[323] In 2005 there were 218 county courts; 102
had divorce jurisdiction, and 68 bankruptcy jurisdiction.[324] In 1995, about 80
offered trial facilities under which one or more judges were available on a
continuous basis to hear trials.[325] Lord Woolf recommended that arrangements
should be streamlined. Outside London, there should be three or four designated
civil trial centres on each Circuit, each with a series of satellite courts, and each
with a Senior Civil Judge appointed for each centre.[326] This has been taken
forward, subject to constraints arising from the nature of available court buildings, and with the appointment of "Designated Civil Judges" to 30 centres.[327] In

---

[318] See B. Abel-Smith and R. Stevens, *Lawyers and the Courts* (1967), pp.32–37; P. Polden, *The County Court 1846–1971* (1999).

[319] See R. Cocks, *Foundations of the Modern Bar* (1983), pp.25–26, 56–57.

[320] See below, para.12–022.

[321] Lord Westbury L.C., quoted by Abel-Smith and Stevens (1967), p.35.

[322] County Courts Act 1984, s.1; Civil Courts Order 1983 (SI 1983/713), as amended. The county court for the City of London is known as the Mayor's and City of London Court: the name is that of a court of similar jurisdiction abolished by the Courts Act 1971, on whose history see Polden (1999), Appendix. The court is maintained by the City of London.

[323] County Courts Act 1984, s.2, as amended by the Constitutional Reform Act 2005, Sch.4, Pt 1, paras 160, 161.

[324] *Judicial Statistics 2005*, p.43; Court Service website (*www.hmcourts-service.gov.uk*). Admiralty jurisdiction was removed from over 40 courts by the Civil Court (Amendment) (No.2) Order 1999 (SI 1999/1011).

[325] Lord Woolf's *Interim Report on Access to Justice* (1995), p.79. This followed a recommendation of the *Civil Justice Review* (Cm. 393, 1988), para.176.

[326] *ibid.*

[327] *Final Report on Access to Justice* (1996), Ch.8 HM Courts Service website (County Court Annual Reports). There are 10 designated "trial centres" (HMCS Courtfinder).

London, the Central London County Court hears more complex cases sent from the other London county courts.[328]

A number of centres, co-located in Northampton, have been established to handle work in bulk: the Claim Production Centre, processes claims received on magnetic media or electronically from major claimants[329]; the County Court Bulk Centre, attached to Northampton County Court, processes large volumes of debt recovery cases[330]; the Traffic Enforcement Centre, also attached to North-ampton County Court since 1997, handles the enforcement of unpaid parking charges and other matters for London and other local authorities)[331]: and a Centralised Attachment of Earnings Payments System (CAPS) deals with pay-ment processing and monitoring and, for example, enables large employers to send one payment to cover orders made in, and previously payable to, a variety of county courts.[332]

(c) Judges

2–043   Under the original arrangements the districts were grouped into 60 county court circuits, each with its own judge appointed by the Lord Chancellor from bar-risters of at least seven years' standing. On the re-organisation of the criminal courts under the Courts Act 1971[333] the existing county court judges became Circuit judges.[334] Every Circuit judge is by virtue of his or her office capable of sitting as a judge for any county court district and at least one is assigned to each district by the Lord Chief Justice after consulting the Lord Chancellor.[335] The regular sittings are normally taken by the assigned judges.

In addition, the Queen may, on the recommendation of the Lord Chancellor, appoint District judges, and the Lord Chief Justice, after consulting the Lord Chancellor, must assign each District judge to one or more districts.[336] A full-time District judge is barred from legal practice.[337] District judges were formerly called registrars; the change of title reflected the fact that their functions are now judicial. They are responsible for procedural steps in court proceedings, this responsibility being analogous to those of Masters and Registrars of the High Court, and they hear most small claims. As the small claims limit has pro-gressively been raised, the role of District judges in hearing claims has increased

---

[328] S. Webster, (1994) 138 S.J. 515. A nominated Circuit judge may issue freezing injunctions (formerly known as *Mareva* injunctions) in relation to proceedings in the List: County Court Remedies (Amendment) Regulations 1995 (SI 1995/206). The Patents County Court (below, para.2–046) moved to the Central London County Court from Wood Green.

[329] In 2005 it issued 59% of the total default claims issued; it is deemed to be part of the court in whose name the claim is issued.

[330] *Judicial Statistics 2005*, p.55. From 2001 it has included Money Claims Online, enabling claims to be made online.

[331] *ibid.*

[332] *www.hmcourts-service.gov.uk/cms/bulkcentre.htm.*

[333] See below, para.2–052.

[334] See below, para.4–020.

[335] County Courts Act 1984, s.5, as amended by the Constitutional Reform Act 2005, Sch.4, Pt 1, para.163. A judge of the Court of Appeal or the High Court or a recorder may also sit as a county court judge: *ibid.*

[336] County Courts Act 1984, ss.6–9, as amended; Courts and Legal Service Act 1990, s.74 and Sch.10 para.57. A deputy District judge is appointed as a temporary measure. The eligibility requirement is now possession of a seven-year general qualification (i.e. right of audience in any part of the Supreme Court or in all proceedings in county courts or magistrates' courts); it was formerly being a solicitor of at least seven years' standing.

[337] Courts and Legal Services Act 1990, s.75 and Sch.11.

accordingly. Their administrative functions have been transferred to the chief clerk or some other administrative officer, in accordance with the Lord Chancellor's directions.[338] County courts are administered by the HM Courts Service.[339] There are substantial staffs of clerks and bailiffs.

(d) Jurisdiction

A county court has jurisdiction in almost the whole range of civil proceedings. In some matters the jurisdiction is exclusive, in others it is exercised concurrently with the High Court. In the latter event there is in some cases a monetary limit to the county court's jurisdiction, the "county court limit", specified by Order in Council.[340] However, the High Court and County Courts Jurisdiction Order 1991,[341] following recommendations in the Civil Justice Review,[342] removed the limits for contract, tort and land law actions.

2–044

A county court may hear and determine the following matters.

(i) *Contract and tort*

An action founded on contract or tort.[343] This head of jurisdiction covers the bulk of cases brought in the county court.

(ii) *Actions in respect of land*

An action for the recovery of land or in respect of title to any hereditament.[344]

(iii) *Equity proceedings*

A variety of equity proceedings where the value of the property concerned is not more than £30,000[345]: these include proceedings for the administration of the estate of a deceased person, in respect of trusts for foreclosure or redemption of a mortgage, for the specific performance of an agreement for the sale of property, for the maintenance or advancement of an infant and for the dissolution of a partnership. These correspond to matters that would be dealt with in the Chancery Division of the High Court.

(iv) *Admiralty proceedings*

A variety of Admiralty matters,[346] such as claims for damage done by or to a ship, for loss or damage to goods carried in a ship, or for salvage, towage or

---

[338] County Court Rules 1981, Ord.1, r.3. See now CPR r.2.5 which provides generally that any act of a formal or administrative character under the CPR may be performed by a court officer.

[339] See below, para.2–055.

[340] Section 145 of the County Courts Act 1984 confers power to raise monetary limits. The current limits are set by the County Courts Jurisdiction Order 1981 (SI 1981/1123, as amended by the High Court and County Courts Juridisction Order 1991 (SI 1991/724) and s.147 of the 1984 Act.

[341] SI 1991/724. See para.1–019.

[342] Below, para.12–001.

[343] County Courts Act 1984, s.15, as amended by SI 1991/724. This head does not apply to any action where title to any toll, fair, market or franchise is in question or any action for libel or slander: *ibid.* There is a similar jurisdiction in respect of money recoverable under a statute: *ibid.* s.16.

[344] *ibid.* s.21, as amended by SI 1991/724.

[345] *ibid.* s.23. In addition, many specific powers under the Trustee Act 1925 and the Law of Property Act 1925 are conferred by the 1984 Act, Sch.2.

[346] County Courts Act 1984, ss.26, 27, as amended.

pilotage. The jurisdictional limit is £5,000, except for salvage claims, where it is £15,000. However, no county courts are currently designated by the Lord Chancellor to take Admiralty proceedings and such proceedings have to be commenced in the High Court.[347]

(v) *Probate proceedings*

Contentious matters arising in respect of the grant or revocation of probate or administration of estates where the value of the estate is not more than £30,000.[348]

(vi) *Jurisdiction by agreement*

Matters outside the monetary limits where the parties confer jurisdiction on a county court by agreement.[349]

(vii) *Family matters*

2–045 Any county court which has been designated by the Lord Chancellor, with the concurrence of the Lord Chief Justice, as a "divorce county court" has jurisdiction to hear and determine any matrimonial cause,[350] although it only has jurisdiction to try the cause if it is also designated as a court of trial.[351] A divorce county court also has jurisdiction to make orders in relation to financial relief and custody of children ancillary to proceedings for divorce, nullity or separation,[352] and, if designated by the Lord Chancellor, to make orders for financial relief where a marriage has been terminated abroad.[353] The jurisdiction of divorce county courts, so far as is exercisable by judges of such courts, is to be exercised by such Circuit judges as the Lord Chief Justice, after consulting the Lord Chancellor may direct.[354] Every matrimonial cause must be commenced in a divorce county court,[355] and will be heard there unless it is transferred to the High Court.[356] There is also provision for the transfer of family proceedings from the High Court to the county court.[357] Similar arrangements apply for the designation of "civil partnership proceedings county courts".[358] Principles governing the distribution and transfer of business between the High Court and

---

[347] See above, para.2–042 and below, para.2–062.

[348] County Courts Act 1984, s.32, substituted by the Administration of Justice Act 1985, s.51(1).

[349] *ibid*, ss.18 (Queen's Bench Division matters), 24 (many equity proceedings), 27(6) (most Admiralty proceedings).

[350] i.e. an action for divorce, nullity of marriage or judicial separation: Matrimonial and Family Proceedings Act 1984, s.32, as amended by the Family Law Act 1986, Sch.1, para.27.

[351] 1984 Act, s.33(1); Civil Courts Order 1983 (SI 1983/713), as amended. In London, the Principal Registry of the Family Division is deemed to be a county court for this purpose; see the 1984 Act, s.42, as amended by the Courts and Legal Services Act 1990, s.74(7).

[352] Under Pts II and III of the Matrimonial Causes Act 1973: 1984 Act, s.34(1)(a).

[353] Under Pt III of the 1984 Act: *ibid*. ss.33(4), 34(1)(b).

[354] 1984 Act, s.36, as amended by the Constitutional Reform Act 2005, Sch.4, Pt 1, para.173.

[355] *ibid*. s.33(3).

[356] Under *ibid*. s.39 (which applies to any family proceedings), or s.41 of the County Courts Act 1984. Prior to April 26, 1986, *all* defended causes had to be transferred to the High Court.

[357] Matrimonial and Family Proceedings Act 1984, s.38.

[358] 1984 Act, ss.36A–36D, inserted by the Civil Partnership Act 2004, Sch.27, para.92, and amended by SI 2006/1016, Sch.1, paras 5, 6(1), (2); Civil Courts (Amendment) Order 2005 (SI 2005/2923). Nine have been designated.

county courts are set out in Directions given by the President of the Family Division.[359] Other family matters may be dealt with by divorce county courts, civil partnership county courts or, in some cases, any county court. Part IV of the Family Law Act 1996[360] introduced a more coherent domestic violence jurisdiction, with powers to grant occupation orders (which can define or regulate right of occupation of the home) and non-molestation orders conferred in the High Court, county courts and magistrates' courts.[361] This is subject to the power of the Lord Chancellor to provide that certain types of proceedings be commenced in, or transferred to, a specified level of court.[362]

The jurisdiction of the county courts concerning children was remodelled on implementation of the Children Act 1989 in October 1991. There is a concurrent jurisdiction across the family proceedings courts,[363] county courts and the High Court.[364] In the county courts, the business is concentrated on particular centres and particular judges, who receive special "guidance". There are six classes of court centre. Ordinary county courts have no family jurisdiction; divorce county courts can issue all private law proceedings,[365] but contested matters are transferred to "family hearing centres" for trial; family hearing centres can issue and hear all private law family proceedings whether or not they are contested; "care centres" have full jurisdiction in private and public law[366] matters; applications under the Adoption and Children Act 2002 which are to be made to a county court must be commenced in (or transferred to) an "adoption centre"; application for a Convention adoption order must be commenced in or transferred to an "intercountry adoption centre".[367] As to the judiciary, "designated family judges" have full jurisdiction in public and private law, are based at care centres and chair local Family Court Business Committees and Family Court Forums; "nominated care judges" similarly have full public and private law jurisdiction; "circuit family judges" have full private law jurisdiction[368]; district judges can hear private law family work but have a limited jurisdiction; "nominated care district judges" have increased jurisdiction and can hear uncontested public law

---

[359] *ibid.* s.37. See *Practice Direction (Family Division: Distribution of Business)* [1992] 1 W.L.R. 586 replacing an earlier direction. A defect in the transitional arrangements led to thousands of divorces being technically invalid: see *Nissim v Nissim* (1987) 137 N.L.J. Rep. 1207; N. Wikeley, (1988) 7 C.J.Q. 97. They were retrospectively validated by the Matrimonial Proceedings (Transfers) Act 1988.

[360] Following recommendations in the Law Commission Report on *Domestic Violence and Occupation of the Family Home* (Law Com. No.207).

[361] ss.33–42A.

[362] s.57. See the Family Law Act 1996 (Pt IV) (Allocation of Proceedings) Order 1997 (SI 1997/1896): proceedings are normally commenced in a family proceedings court or county court (i.e. divorce county court, family hearing centre or care centre); provision is made for the transfer of cases.

[363] Above, para.2–026.

[364] Below, para.2–065.

[365] Above.

[366] i.e. cases usually brought by local authorities or the NSPCC, including care, supervision and emergency protection orders.

[367] *Judicial Statistics 2005*, p.60; Children (Allocation of Proceedings) Order 1991 (SI 1991/1677), as amended, Schs 1–4. The Principal Registry of the Family Division is treated as if it were all of these. The 1991 Order also provides for the transfer of cases.

[368] Deputy Circuit judges and recorders are normally only nominated for private family law proceedings, except that a recorder can be requested to act as a judge of the Family Division of the High Court and may hear public law family proceedings if nominated for them. From 2005, nominated recorders and District judges can hear care cases.

cases.[369] The detailed allocation of work is the subject of a Practice Direction.[370] Family Court Business Committees deal with administrative issues, such as the operation of the criteria for the transfer of cases; the Family Court Forums enable the professions involved in the protection and welfare of children to "discuss issues and air concerns".[371] There are also local Family Justice Councils.[372] Procedural rules are made by the Family Procedure Rules Committee.[373] Steps are being taken to establish Family Court Centres by linking specified county courts and family proceedings courts.[374]

(viii) *Other proceedings*

2–046   Jurisdiction in a large number of other matters is conferred by specific statutory provisions, including hire-purchase, consumer credit, the Rent Acts, landlord and tenant, housing and sex discrimination.[375] Designated county courts have jurisdiction in bankruptcy matters,[376] race relations,[377] and patents.[378] Appeals also lie to the county court in a number of administrative matters.[379]

(ix) *Jurisdiction of the District judge*

2–047   Any act of a county court under the CPR may, except where an enactment, rule or practice direction provides otherwise, be performed by any judge or District judge. The general jurisdiction of District judges is now set out in a Practice Direction.[380] The main features are as follows. A District judge may not:

    (1) make an injunction, except where (a) the District judge otherwise has jurisdiction, (b) the injunction is sought in a money claim not yet allocated to a track where the amount claimed does not exceed the fast track financial limit, (c) in terms agreed by the parties or ancillary to certain other orders, or (d) under specified provisions[381];

    (2) make an order committing a person to prison except where authorised by an enactment;

    (3) hear appeals under ss.204 or 204A of the Housing Act 1996;

---

[369] *Judicial Statistics 2005*, p.61.

[370] *Practice Direction: Family Proceedings (Allocation to Judiciary) Direction* 1997 [1997] 2 F.L.R. 780, [1997] Fam. Law 691, as amended.

[371] *LCD Court Service Annual Report 1991–92* (1991–92 H.C. 102), p.40.

[372] See para.1–026.

[373] See para.2–026.

[374] See *ibid*.

[375] High Court and County Courts Jurisdiction Order 1991 (SI 1991/734), Art.2.

[376] Civil Courts Order 1983 (SI 1983/713), as amended.

[377] *ibid*.

[378] A Patents County Court has been established in London under the Copyright, Designs and Patents Act 1988, ss.287–292, "to handle smaller, shorter, less complex, less important, lower value actions" than the Patents Court (below, para.2–060): *per* Sir Thomas Bingham M.R. in *Chaplin Patents Holdings Co plc v Group Lotus plc, The Times*, January 12, 1994, where the Court of Appeal upheld a decision not to transfer proceedings to the High Court.

[379] D. Price, *Appeals* (1982), pp.46–49 lists 29 situations.

[380] *Practice Direction 2b: Allocation of Cases to Levels of Judiciary*.

[381] ss.153A, 153B or 153D of the Housing Act 1996, s.3 of the Protection from Harassment Act 1997, or an order under s.1B or 1D of the Crime and Disorder Act 1998 (anti-social behaviour).

(4) try a case involving an allegation of unlawful indirect discrimination against a public authority.

On the other hand, a District judge has jurisdiction to hear any claim allocated to the small claims track or fast track or which is treated as allocated to the multi-track under CPR, r.8.9c,[382] except claims under specified Acts of Parliament; proceedings for the recovery of land, demotion claims or proceedings in respect of demoted tenancies; the assessment of damages or other sum due to a party under a judgment without any financial limit; and, with the permission of the Designated Civil Judge[383] in respect of that case, any other proceedings. A case allocated to the small claims track may only be assigned to a Circuit judge with his or her consent. Where both the Circuit judge and District judge have jurisdiction in any proceedings, the exercise of jurisdiction by the District judge is subject to any arrangements made by the Designated Civil judge for the proper distribution of business between Circuit judges and District judges.

District judges accordingly have a major role to play in hearing small claims. The court "may adopt any method of proceeding" that it "considers to be fair" and hearings are informal.[384] Prior to the Woolf reforms, District judges tried or arbitrated most small claims. Research on the handing of such cases was favourable:

"In approach and manner, district judges are decidedly down-to-earth. When dealing with litigants in person, there is no room for standing on ceremony, for airs and graces, or for pomposity . . . [S]mall claims hearings are in the main characterized by good humour and robust common sense, seasoned with large doses of legal and judicial pragmatism."[385]

(e) The boundary between High Court and County Court

The relationship between the jurisdictions of the county court and the High Court   **2–048**
was significantly altered by the Courts and Legal Services Act 1990, implementing recommendations of the Civil Justice Review.[386] The aim was to switch an increasing proportion of civil business from the High Court to county courts; a significant number of High Court civil cases was in any event being heard by Circuit judges sitting as judges of the High Court or by deputy High Court judges. Section 1 of the 1990 Act enables the Lord Chancellor to make provision by order for the allocation of business between the High Court and county courts; jurisdiction to hear applications for judicial review may not, however, be conferred on the county court. The High Court and County Courts Order 1991[387] provides that where both courts have jurisdiction, proceedings may be commenced in either, except that[388]: (1) a claim for money may only be commenced

---

[382] As to these, see below, para.12–005.
[383] See above, para.2–042.
[384] CPR r.27.8. See generally CPR, Pt 27 and *Practice Direction 27—Small Claims Track*.
[385] J. Baldwin, *Small Claims in the County Court in England and Wales* (1997), p.154.
[386] Below, para.12–001.
[387] SI 1991/734, as amended by SI 1993/1407, SI 1995/205, SI 1996/3141, SI 1999/1014, SI 2001/1387 and 2685, SI 2004/3419 and SI 2005/587. This order does not apply to family proceedings: Art.12. See I. R. Scott, (1991) 10 C.J.Q. 282.
[388] Other exceptions are that applications or appeals under the Audit Commission Act 1998, ss.17, 18 must be commenced in the High Court, and applications under s.1 of the Access to Neighbouring Land Act 1992 must be commenced in the county court.

in the High Court if the financial value of the claim[389] is more than £15,000; and
(2) personal injuries claims[390] may only be commenced in the High Court if the
financial value of the claim is £50,000 or more.[391]

In cases of concurrent jurisdiction, either court may hear the case. The
allocation of a case to the appropriate track (small claims track, fast track, multi-
track) and the appropriate court (including arrangements for transfer) is now
dealt with in the Civil Procedure Rules.[392] However, each court has power to
transfer a case to the other.[393] Indeed, if proceedings are required to be started in
the other, it must order a transfer or, if satisfied that the person bringing them
knew or ought to have known of the requirement, order that they be struck out.[394]
Orders may be made on the court's own motion or on the application of any
party. The discretion to transfer must be exercised with regard to:

(a) the financial value of the claim and the amount in dispute, if different;

(b) whether it would be more convenient or fair for hearings (including the trial)
     to be held in some other court;

(c) the availability of a judge specialising in the type of claim in question;

(d) whether the facts, legal issues, remedies or procedures involved are simple
     or complex;

(e) the importance of the outcome of the claim to the public in general;

(f) the facilities available at the court where the claim is being dealt with and
     whether they may be inadequate because of any disabilities of a party or
     potential witness;

(g) whether the making of a declaration of incompatibility under s.4 of the
     Human Rights Act 1998 has arisen or may arise;

(h) in the case of civil proceedings by or against the Crown, the location of the
     government department or officers of the Crown and, where appropriate, any
     relevant public interest that the matter should be tried in London.[395]

A review of the 1991 changes completed in 1993 "indicated that, broadly
speaking, the changes had met their objectives". In 1993–94, the number of trials
in the Queen's Bench general list which resulted in an award of £25,000 or less

---

[389] Financial values are calculated in accordance with CPR r.16.3(6): Art.9, substituted by SI
     1999/1014, Art.9.
[390] Other than negligence claims arising out of the provision of clinical or medical services (including
     dental or nursing services), which are accordingly subject to the £15,000 limit.
[391] Arts 4, 4A, 5 (Art.4(A) inserted and Art.5 amended by SI 1999/1014, Arts 4–6).
[392] Pts 26–30. See below, para.12–005.
[393] Transfers to a county court must be to such court as the High Court considers appropriate, having
     regard to the convenience of the parties and other affected persons and the state of business of the
     courts concerned: County Courts Act 1984, s.40(4).
[394] County Courts Act 1984, ss.40, 42, substituted by the Courts and Legal Services Act 1990, s.2(1),
     (3). There is also power for the High Court at any stage to order the transfer of proceedings
     commenced in (or transferred to) the county court to (or back to) the High Court: s.41, as
     amended by the 1990 Act, s.2(2). The court is not obliged to strike out an action if satisfied that
     the applicant "knew or ought to have known of the requirement"; it may instead order transfer:
     Restick v Crickmore [1994] 1 W.L.R. 420. There is also provision for the transfer of cases
     between county courts and between the Royal Courts of Justice and district registries: CPR
     r.30.2(1), (4).
[395] CPR r.30.3.

fell to 346 (compared with 1,828 in 1990–91); the percentage of trials heard by High Court judges involving an award of £5,000 or less fell to 3.8 per cent (71 per cent in 1990–91).[396] The number of writs issued in the Queen's Bench Division also declined sharply, from over 100,000 in 1991–92 to 35,000 in 1994–95.[397] There were further annual reductions to 1998–99 and then, following the introduction of the Civil Procedure Rules in April 1999, a 69 per cent reduction in the number of claims issued to 6,596 in 1999–2000 with further reductions to 5,541 in 2000–01 and 3,841 in 2005.[398] However, the number of sitting days in the Queen's Bench and Chancery Divisions has increased, as has the workload of the Family Division and the Administrative Court. This led to a further DCA consultation paper.[399] This proposed that cases should not be dealt with by High Court judges unless there were exceptional features to justify that; these features would relate to complexity, public impact, importance and significance and precedent setting. The Paper proposed a detailed structure for analysing cases for this purpose. Responses were broadly supportive.[400]

In his *Interim Report on Access to Justice*, Lord Woolf recommended that while the High Court and county courts should be retained as separate courts and the separate status of High Court judge preserved, the two levels of court should generally have the same jurisdiction and outside London should be administered together. Proceedings could be commenced in either and then transferred by the court to the appropriate level. There would be a combined set of procedural rules. The county court should have an increased small claims jurisdiction and deal with "fast track" cases.[401] Reponses to the interim review were "overwhelmingly favourable" and its recommendations were taken forward into Lord Woolf's *Final Report on Access to Justice*[402] and the government's White Paper, *Modernising Justice*.[403] A subsequent LCD consultation paper, *Modernising the Civil Courts*[404] noted that the current geographical spread of civil courts was based on the premise that the citizen would communicate with the court by attending in person or in writing. "Revolutionary changes in society and technology" make this no longer appropriate. The paper proposed the clear separation of "back office" administration and hearing centres; the Royal Courts of Justice would be the "flagship hearing centre for civil justice" and there would be a series of primary hearing centres for the management of defended cases, and a network of supplementary civil justice venues involving the best use of technology to enable remote access and joint working with Crown and magistrates' courts, tribunals, council chambers and other agencies. Streamlined, regionally based business centres would be established for administrative work, providing

---

[396] *LCD Court Service Annual Report 1993–94* (1993–94 H.C. 568), p.49.

[397] *LCD Court Service Annual Report 1994–95* (1994–95 H.C. 579), p.37.

[398] *LCD Court Service Annual Reports 1999–2000*, p.30, and *2000–01*, p.26; *Judicial Statistics 2005* p.37.

[399] *Focusing judicial resources appropriately. The Right Judge for the Right Case* (DCA CP 25/05, October 2005).

[400] Summary of responses: *www.dca.gov.uk/consult/focus/focus_resp.pdf*.

[401] Report (1995), pp.73–75, 79–81. Proposals for integration were previously considered and rejected by the Gorell Committee on County Court Procedure (1908–09 H.C. 71), the Beeching Commission on Assizes and Quarter Sessions (Cmnd. 4153, 1969), p.73, and the Civil Justice Review (Cm. 394), Ch.3. See Sir Jack Jacob, *The Reform of Civil Procedural Law* (1982), pp.7–13.

[402] HMSO, 1996.

[403] Cm. 4155, 1998, Ch.4. This followed a *Review of Civil Justice and Legal Aid* by Sir Peter Middleton (1997). See further, Ch.12.

[404] January 2001, LCD website.

customer service by telephone and email. This would be complemented by new ways of interacting with customers and supporting the judiciary using IT.

The subsequent reality has been is that there has been much less investment in modernising the civil and family courts, including the installation of appropriate IT systems than in the Crown Court and the handling of asylum appeals.[405] The Treasury has required the investment to be covered by increases in fee income, at a time when there is also encouragement for the number of claims to be reduced. Nevertheless, much of the 1991 Paper is repeated in HM Court Service's Business Strategy, acknowledging the need to address estate and IT issues.[406] The DCA has also returned to the question whether there should be a single civil court, unifying the jurisdiction of the High Court, the county courts and the family proceedings courts.[407] Reactions were mixed, although more were in favour than against. Ministers decided to adopt the merger as a long-term objective, for which primary legislation will be needed.[408]

(f) Procedural Rules and Practice Directions

2–049   Procedure in the county court was formerly governed by County Court Rules made by a committee appointed by the Lord Chancellor. By virtue of the Civil Procedure Act 1997, unified "Civil Procedure Rules" govern the practice and procedure of the Court of Appeal (Civil Division), the High Court and county courts.[409] They are made by the Civil Procedure Rule Committee, which comprises the (a) the Head of Civil Justice and the Deputy Head of Civil Justice (if there is one); (b) (appointed by the Lord Chief Justice) two or three judges of the Supreme Court, one Circuit judge, one or two District judges and a Master; and (c) (appointed by the Lord Chancellor) three persons with a Supreme Court qualification, three persons with the right to conduct litigation in relation to all proceedings in the Supreme Court, two persons with knowledge of the lay advice sector consumer affairs.[410] The power to make rules must be exercised "with a view to securing that the civil justice system is accessible, fair and efficient" and the Committee must "try to make rules which are both simple and simply expressed".[411] The rules are published on the internet,[412] and in the White Book[413] and other publications.[414] There is general statutory power to give

---

[405] See Brooke L.J., "Court modernization and the crisis facing our civil courts" (IALS, November 24, 2004), *www.dca.gov.uk/judicial/speeches/ljb241104.htm.*

[406] Brooke L.J., "The Future of Civil Justice" An address to the Civil Court Users Association, March 26, 2006 (*www.judiciary.gov.uk/publications_media/speeches/2006/sp260306.htm*): "I believe that the strategy for the future of civil justice is back on the rails. The arrangements for funding it are not."

[407] *A Single Civil Court?* (DCA, CP06/05, February 2005).

[408] *A Single Civil Court? Summary of Responses* (DCA, CP(R)06/05, October 2005). This is to be considered for implementation after 2009: *HMCS Business Strategy,* p.16.

[409] Civil Procedure Act 1997, s.1; Civil Procedure Rules 1998 (SI 1998/3132), as amended ("CPR").

[410] *ibid.* s.2 as amended. Proposed rules may be allowed or disallowed by the Lord Chancellor, and the Lord Chancellor may require the committee to include within the rules provision that would achieve a specified purpose: s.3A, inserted by the Constitutional Reform Act 2005, Sch.4, Pt 1, para.206.

[411] *ibid.* ss.1(3), 2(7).

[412] DCA website

[413] *Civil Procedure The White Book Service 2007* (Sweet & Maxwell).

[414] e.g. *The Civil Court Practice 2006* (the "Green Book") (Butterworths); *Civil Procedure Handbook 2006* (OUP).

practice directions.[415] This power can be exercised by the Lord Chief Justice, a judicial office-holder nominated by him with the agreement of the Lord Chancellor,[416] or otherwise with the approval of the Lord Chief Justice. The approval of the Lord Chancellor is also needed for all directions other than to the extent that they consist of guidance about the application or interpretation of the law or the making of judicial decisions.

(g) Register of judgments

A register recording all High Court and county court judgments, certain fines and other specified orders is maintained by a private company, Registry Trust Ltd, by agreement with the Lord Chancellor.[417]   2–050

(h) Appeals[418]

Appeals normally lie from a District judge to the Circuit judge of the county court, and from a Circuit judge to a High Court judge of the Family Division (family proceedings), a High Court judge (final decisions in the small claims track or the fast track) or the Court of Appeal (final decisions in the multi-track, decisions on a claim under CPR, Pt 8). Bankruptcy appeals lie to the Divisional Court of the Chancery Division. A second appeal to the Court of Appeal is only available if that Court considers that the appeal would raise an important point of principle or practice or that there is some other compelling reason for the Court of Appeal to hear it. Permission is normally required.[419]   2–051

6. The Crown Court[420]

(a) The Beeching Royal Commission

In 1966 the Royal Commission on Assizes and Quarter Sessions was appointed, under the chairmanship of Lord Beeching, to inquire into the arrangements for the administration of justice at assizes and quarter sessions outside London, and to report what reforms should be made for the more convenient, economic and efficient disposal of the civil and criminal business dealt with by those courts. The *assize courts* were presided over by High Court judges sent out "on circuit", a system that could be traced back to the twelfth century and which had changed comparatively little since medieval times.[421] There were seven circuits of assize towns. Assizes had jurisdiction over all indictable criminal offences and exclusive jurisdiction over some, including homicide, serious crimes of violence and   2–052

---

[415] Civil Procedure Act 1997, s.5, substituted by the Constitutional Reform Act 2005, Sch.2, Pt 2, para.6, replacing s.74A of the County Courts Act 1984.
[416] Under the Constitutional Reform Act 2005, Sch.2, Pt 1.
[417] Courts Act 2003, s.98; Register of Judgments, Orders and Fines Regulations 2005 (SI 2005/3595) replacing the County Court Register made under ss.73 and 73A of the County Courts Act 1984.
[418] See generally, Ch.18.
[419] CPR, Pt 52; *Practice Direction 52—Appeals*; Access to Justice Act 1999, ss.54–57.
[420] See I. R. Scott, *The Crown Court* (1971).
[421] See above, para.2–004. Additional "Commissioners of Assize", usually senior Q.C.s, could be appointed ad hoc.

rape. In addition, assize courts had the same civil jurisdiction as the High Court sitting in London, although priority was given to criminal cases. There were *courts of quarter sessions* for each of the 58 counties and for 93 boroughs; there were five such courts in Greater London and one for the City of London. The borough quarter sessions were presided over by a part-time Recorder, sitting alone. The county quarter sessions comprised a bench of magistrates normally with a legally qualified Chairman or Deputy Chairman, some of whom were whole-time appointments. These courts had jurisdiction to try many indictable offences with a jury, and to hear appeals from magistrates' courts and from a variety of administrative orders. In London, the *Central Criminal Court* at the Old Bailey was in effect the assize court for criminal cases. It had a number of full-time judges, including the Recorder of London and the Common Serjeant; in addition some cases would be taken by High Court judges. In 1956, new courts known as *Crown Courts* were established for Liverpool and Manchester to deal with both quarter sessions and assize work. A full time Recorder was appointed for each court. Responsibility for providing judges, court staff and court buildings was "as fragmented as the system itself".[422] The Beeching Report identified many defects of assizes and quarter sessions and recommended a fundamental reorganisation. A number of features which a good court system should provide were identified[423]:

	(a) Ease of physical access.
	(b) An early hearing.
Convenience	(c) The assurance of trial on a date of which reasonable notice has been given.
	(d) Suitable accommodation.
Quality	(e) Judicial expertise.
	(f) Adequate and dependable legal representation.
Economy	(g) Efficient use of all manpower.
	(h) Optimum use of buildings.

The restricting factors were cost and the capacity of the Bar. The report's proposals were designed to[424]:

(a) simplify the structure of the courts;

(b) deploy judge power as flexibly as possible;

(c) relate court locations to travelling facilities for the public;

(d) secure the efficient administration of all court services;

(e) ensure that courts are built and maintained as economically and efficiently as possible.

The proposals, which involved the creation of a new superior court of criminal jurisdiction, to be called the Crown Court, were largely accepted. They were

---

[422] Beeching Report, p.31.
[423] *ibid.* p.48.
[424] *ibid.* p.64.

enacted in the Courts Act 1971, substantial parts of which were re-enacted in the Supreme Court Act 1981.

(b) The constitution of the Crown Court

The Crown Court is part of the Supreme Court of England and Wales.[425] It is a single court, but sittings may be conducted at any place in England and Wales, in accordance with directions given by the Lord Chancellor, after consulting the Lord Chief Justice.[426] There are at present 92 locations.[427] The name "Central Criminal Court" has been retained for the Crown Court sitting in the City of London at the Old Bailey. There are three kinds of Crown Court centre: "first-tier" centres are visited by High Court judges, Circuit judges and recorders for the complete range of Crown Court business, and by High Court judges for High Court civil work; "second-tier" centres are the same as first-tier except that no civil business is done; "third-tier" centres are normally visited only by Circuit judges and recorders. The centres are grouped into six circuits: Midland and Oxford, North Eastern, Northern, South Eastern, Wales and Chester, and Western.[428] **2–053**

The jurisdiction of the Crown Court is exerciseable by any judge of the High Court, Circuit judge, recorder or District Judge (Magistrates' Courts).[429] In some cases one of these may sit with not more than four justices of the peace[430]: a court must normally be so comprised when hearing an appeal[431] and may be so comprised for other proceedings, but not cases listed for pleas of not guilty.[432]

The administration of the Crown Court is the responsibility of HM Courts Service.[433]

(c) Jurisdiction

The Crown Court has exclusive jurisdiction with respect to criminal trials on indictment.[434] It also has an extensive appellate jurisdiction inherited from quarter sessions, including appeals from magistrates' courts in criminal cases and appeals in a wide variety of administrative matters, such as betting, gaming and liquor licensing. Magistrates' courts may also commit convicted persons to the Crown Court for sentence. **2–054**

---

[425] Supreme Court Act 1981, s.l. The reference to the Supreme Court of England and Wales is to be replaced by one to the Senior Courts of England and Wales by the Constitutional Reform Act 2005, Sch.11, Pt 4, para.26, on establishment of the new Supreme Court. Procedural rules can be prescribed by the Crown Court Rule Committee: *ibid.* s.86, as amended by the Courts and Legal Services Act 1990, Sch.18, para.36(2) and the Constitutional Reform Act 2005, Sch.4, Pt 1, paras 114, 137.

[426] *ibid.* s.78.

[427] *Judicial Statistics 2005*, p.79.

[428] See H.L. Deb. Vol.314, col.948, January 26, 1971; H.L. Deb. Vol.321, col.572, July 1, 1971; H.L. Deb. Vol.343, col.968, June 14, 1973.

[429] Supreme Court Act 1981, s.8, as amended by the Court Act 2003, s.65(1), Sch.8, para.259. See below para.4–020.

[430] *ibid.* and see below, para.4–012.

[431] Supreme Court Act 1981, s.74, as amended by the Access to Justice Act 1999, s.79 and Sch.15 (deleting a reference to committals for sentence); Criminal Procedure Rules 2005, rr.63.7—63.9.

[432] See below, para.2–055.

[433] See para.1–019.

[434] Supreme Court Act 1981, s.46.

(d) Distribution of business

2–055   The classes of cases in the Crown Court suitable for allocation respectively to a
High Court judge, Circuit judge, recorder, or District judge (magistrates' courts)
and to a court including justices, are prescribed in directions given by the Lord
Chief Justice, with the concurrence of the Lord Chancellor.[435] For the purposes
of trial in the Crown Court, offences are grouped in four classes.

Class 1

These offences are misprision of treason and treason felony, murder, genocide,
torture, hostage-taking and offences under the War Crimes Act 1991, offences
under the Official Secrets Acts, manslaughter, infanticide, child destruction,
abortion, sedition, an offence under s.1 of the Geneva Conventions Act 1957,
mutiny, piracy and related inchoate offences. They may only be tried by (1) High
Court judge or (2) a Circuit judge, Deputy High Court judge or Deputy Circuit
judge authorised to try murder cases (or in the case of attempted murder, to try
murder or attempted murder cases), where the presiding judge has released the
case for trial by such a judge.

Class 2

These offences are to be tried by a High Court judge unless a particular case is
released by or on the authority of a presiding judge or resident judge for trial by
a deputy High Court judge, Circuit judge or deputy Circuit judge authorised to
try Class 2 cases by the Lord Chief Justice. They include rape, sexual intercourse
or incest with a girl under 13, and a series of other sexual offences.

Class 3

These offences may be listed for trial by a High Court judge, or, in accordance
with guidance given by the presiding judges, by a Circuit judge, a deputy Circuit
judge or a recorder. They comprise all offences not listed in Classes 1 or 2. A
Class 3 case is not to be listed for trial by a High Court judge except with the
consent of a presiding judge.

   For the just, speedy and economical disposal of the business of the circuits or
a circuit, the Senior Presiding Judge, or the presiding judges with his consent,
may issue guidance to resident judges[436] in relation to the allocation and management of the work at their court.

   Most other Crown Court proceedings are normally listed for hearing by a court
presided over by a Circuit judge or a recorder. Any proceedings listed for hearing
by a Circuit judge or recorder, except pleas of not guilty, are stated to be suitable
for allocation to a court comprising justices of the peace.

   Appeals from decisions of magistrates are to be heard by (i) a resident judge;
(ii) a Circuit judge, nominated by the resident judge, who regularly sits at the
Crown Court centre; (iii) an experienced recorder or Deputy Circuit judge

---

[435] Supreme Court Act 1981, s.75, as amended by the Court Act 2003, Sch.8, para.261: *Consolidated
Criminal Practice Direction*, Pt III. 21.1 and Pt IV. 33.

[436] These are Circuit judges appointed by the presiding judges to have responsibility, at one or more
centres, for seeing to the efficient and orderly running of the lists: *Civil Justice Review* (Cm. 394,
1988), para.307.

specifically approved by or under the direction of the presiding judges for the purpose; or otherwise (iv) a Circuit judge or recorder selected by the resident judge for a specific case or cases.

The same Practice Direction prescribes the general principles for the distribution of business among the different court centres geographically. Generally, the magistrates committing, transferring or sending a person for trial should select the "most convenient location" of the appropriate tier of Crown Court centre having regard to the location or locations designated by the presiding judge as the normal ones for committals from court.[437] It is possible for the location to be changed.[438] Arrangements can be made for a case to be transferred from one circuit to another.[439] Procedural rules are made by the Criminal Procedure Rules Committee.[440]

(e) Workload

The workload of the Crown Court has increased very significantly since it was established:

2–056

> "It is undoubtedly true to say that in the light of the inexorable increase in caseloads chaos would have ensued but for the implementation of the Beeching Reforms. The number of persons working in the court service is now about 10,000 and the range of quasi-judicial and administrative tasks undertaken by this bureaucracy is far greater much more sophisticated than those attempted under the pre-1971 arrangements."[441]

Between 1979 and 1989 committals for trial received by the Crown Court more than doubled, with an average annual growth rate of over 7 per cent.[442] Since 1989, the number peaked in 1991 (104,754) but has since fallen (to 80,021 in 2005).[443]

Other important factors have been the establishment of the circuit bench and the increase in the number of High Court judges, and the court-building programme. Nevertheless, the increase in workload meant that waiting times increased dramatically.[444]

(f) Appeals[445]

Appeals in relation to trials on indictment and in cases where a defendant has been committed for sentence to the Crown Court lie to the Court of Appeal (Criminal Division).[446] Appeals from an exercise of the Crown Court's appellate

2–057

---

[437] Magistrates' Courts Act 1980, s.7; Crime and Disorder Act 1998, s.51(10); *Consolidated Criminal Practice Direction*, Pt III, 21.2–11.

[438] Supreme Court Act 1981, s.76, as amended: *Practice Direction (Crown Court: Business)* [2001] 1 W.L.R. 1996, paras 12–14.

[439] *ibid.* para.9. CCPD, Pt IV, 31.1.

[440] See para.2–022.

[441] I. R. Scott, *Court Administration: The Case for a Judicial Council* (1979), p.5.

[442] *Judicial Statistics 1989* (Cm. 1154), p.67.

[443] *Judicial Statistics 2005*, p.84 The highest total ever was in 1988 (106,524) before reclassification of certain offences as summary only.

[444] See para.11–024.

[445] See generally, Ch.18, below.

[446] See below, para.2–070.

jurisdiction lie to the High Court on the same basis as appeals there from the magistrates' court.

(g) The Auld Report

2–058   Lord Justice Auld's Report on his *Review of the Criminal Courts of England and Wales*[447] recommended that the Crown Court and magistrates' courts should be replaced by a unified criminal court with three divisions.[448] The Crown Division, with the same constitution as the Crown Court, would deal with all indictable only offences and the more serious either-way offences allocated to it. The District Division would be constituted by a judge, normally a District judge or recorder, sitting with at least two magistrates, and exercise jurisdiction in respect of a mid-range of either-way matters of sufficient seriousness to merit up to two years custody. These are cases that "do not warrant the cumbersome and expensive fact-finding exercise of trial by judge and jury, but which are sufficiently serious or difficult, or their outcome is of such consequence to the public or the defendants, to merit a combination of professional and lay judges, but working together in a simpler way".[449] The Magistrates' Division would be constituted by District judges or by magistrates as magistrates' courts are today. Either-way cases would be allocated by the Magistrates' Division according to the seriousness of the alleged offence and the defendant's circumstances, looking at the possible outcome of the case at its worst and bearing in mind the jurisdiction of each Division. A dispute as to venue would be determined by the District judge after hearing representations. The defendant would have no right of election; if the current system were to continue, the current right of election should be removed.[450]

The proposal for establishment of an additional, middle tier of the unified criminal court has been criticised by Michael Zander[451] on the basis that, assuming abolition of the right of election, the existence of two forms by trial (by magistrates' court or Crown Court) was sufficient. It was not explained by the Auld Report how trial by a District judge sitting with magistrates would provide a more appropriate mode of trial for this class of case, although it would be cheaper.

7. THE HIGH COURT

(a) Constitution

2–059   The High Court of Justice is a court of unlimited civil jurisdiction and also has an important appellate jurisdiction in both civil and criminal matters. It is part of the Supreme Court of England and Wales,[452] and was created as part of the reorganisation of the superior courts under the Supreme Court of Judicature Acts

---

[447] HMSO, October 2001.

[448] Ch.7.

[449] p.277, para.26.

[450] Ch.6.

[451] Comment on the Auld Review, LCD website and *www.lse.ac.uk/Depts/law.*

[452] The Supreme Court was thus re-titled by the Supreme Court Act 1981. The Supreme Court of England and Wales is to become the "Senior Courts of England and Wales" on the establishment of the Supreme Court of the United Kingdom. The new name is curious.

1873–75. It sits at the Royal Courts of Justice in the Strand[453] and at 27 first-tier Crown Court centres outside London.[454] There are three divisions: the Chancery Division, Queen's Bench Division and Family Division,[455] headed, respectively, by the Chancellor of the High Court,[456] the President of the Queen's Bench Division[457] and the President of the Family Division.[458] Each High Court judge[459] is attached to one of the divisions, but they may be transferred to one of the others with their consent, and they may act as an additional judge of one of them at the request of the Lord Chief Justice.[460] Different classes of business are allocated for administrative convenience to each division by rules of court,[461] although technically all the jurisdiction of the High Court belongs to all the divisions alike.[462] There have been two major reorganisations. In 1881 the Exchequer and Common Pleas Divisions were merged into the Queen's Bench Division,[463] and in 1971 the Probate, Divorce and Admiralty Division was re-named the Family Division, with Admiralty business assigned to the Queen's Bench Division, probate business other than non-contentious or common form matters assigned to the Chancery Division, and wardship, guardianship and adoption jurisdiction transferred from Chancery Division to Family Division.[464]

A joint committee of High Court judges and civil servants recommended abolition of the three separate divisions of the High Court,[465] but this recommendation was not implemented. A joint committee of the Bar and the Law Society chaired by Hilary Heilbron Q.C.[466] recommended the merger of the Chancery and Queen's Bench Divisions to form a Civil Division, presided over by the Lord Chief Justice. However, Lord Woolf, in his *Interim Report on Access to Justice*, concluded that merger was not desirable, noting among other factors

---

[453] The Supreme Court moved here from Westminster Hall in 1883. See F. W. Maitland, (1942) 8 C.L.J. 2; J. Kinnard in P. Ferriday (ed.), *Victorian Architecture* (1963); M. H. Port, "The New Law Courts Competition, 1866–67" (1968) *Architectural History* 75–93.

[454] See above.

[455] Supreme Court Act 1981, s.5(l), as amended by the Constitutional Reform Act 2005, Sch.4, Pt 1, para.118. The number of divisions can be altered by Order in Council: *ibid.* s.7, as amended by *ibid.* para.120.

[456] A new office established by the 2005 Act. Previously the Lord Chancellor had formally been the head of the Chancery Division and the Vice-Chancellor the effective head.

[457] Also a new office established by the 2005 Act. Previously, the Lord Chief Justice had been head of the Queen's Bench Division. The order of precedence after the LCJ is: President of the QBD, President of the FD and Chancellor: 1981 Act, s.13, as amended by the 2005 Act, Sch.4, Pt 1, para.125.

[458] See below.

[459] See para.4–025.

[460] Supreme Court Act 1981, s.5(2), (3), as amended by the 2005 Act, Sch.4, Pt 1, para.118.

[461] Supreme Court Act 1981, s.61, as amended by the 2005 Act, Sch.4, Pt 1, para.129. Such rules are subject to any orders made by the Lord Chief Justice with the concurrence of the Lord Chancellor. See the High Court (Distribution of Business) Orders 1991 (SI 1991/1210), 1993 (SI 1993/622) and 2004 (SI 2004/3418).

[462] *ibid.* s.5(5). Any Division to which a cause or matter is assigned has jurisdiction to grant any remedy or relief sought notwithstanding that proceedings for such remedy or relief are assigned to another Division: *Practice Direction (High Court: Divisions)* [1973] 1 W.L.R. 627. Cases may be transferred between Divisions: see J. Jacob (1988) 7 C.J.Q. 94; *Barclays Bank v Bemister, Pryke v Gibbs Hartley Cooper Ltd* [1989] 1 W.L.R. 128.

[463] This was done by an Order in Council which was made on December 16, 1880 and which came into force on February 26, 1881.

[464] Administration of Justice Act 1970, with effect from August 2, 1971.

[465] Committee on the Deployment of the High Court: *Legal Action*, June 1988, p.5; (1988) L. S. Gaz. May 25, p.3.

[466] *Civil Justice on Trial—The Case for Change* (1993). See I. R. Scott, (1994) 13 C.J.Q. 9.

the distinctive nature of the specialist jurisdictions that fall under the Chancery umbrella, the team spirit among Chancery judges and their special relationship with the Chancery Bar, and the relatively small number of Chancery judges. However, judges should be assigned to lists according to their expertise, irrespective of the division to which the list belongs.[467] A further development recommended by Lord Woolf was the appointment of a senior judge as Head of Civil Justice responsible, *inter alia*, to provide leadership for the civil justice system. Civil work should be made the express responsibility of one of the two presiding judges on each circuit, and there should be a senior civil judge appointed for each trial centre.[468] In the event, a Head of Civil Justice has been appointed,[469] and a Designated Civil Judge appointed for each trial centre,[470] but it was left to the presiding judges to arrange for the discharge of responsibility for civil work, given that only one is usually on circuit at any time.[471]

Most High Court work is taken by a single judge sitting alone.[472] This should be in open court, except where under rules of court or in accordance with the practice of the court it is dealt with in chambers.[473] A proportion of the appellate and supervisory work of the High Court is dealt with by "divisional courts", which comprise two or more judges.[474]

The business is mainly conducted by the heads of division and the puisne[475] judges of the High Court. In addition, High Court work may be taken by a deputy High Court judge, a Circuit judge, a recorder, a judge of the Court of Appeal or a former judge of the High Court or the Court of Appeal.[476]

(b) The Chancery Division

2–060 The division deals with property, trusts, the administration of estates, corporate and personal insolvency partnership, companies, revenue cases, probate business other than non-contentious common form business, and other matters specifically assigned.[477]

The Patents Court established in 1977[478] is part of this division. In addition the judges of the division have been assigned to deal with the management of the property and affairs of mental patients under the Mental Health Act 1983. This

---

[467] Report, pp.76–78.

[468] *ibid.* pp.58–62.

[469] The first was Sir Richard Scott V.-C. Lord Phillips M.R. became Head of Civil Justice in 2000, and Sir Anthony Clarke M.R. in 2005. There is also a Deputy Head.

[470] See above, para.2–048.

[471] Lord Woolf, *Access to Justice—Final Report*, pp.92–94.

[472] There is provision for a judge to sit with assessors who are specially qualified in relation to the proceedings in question: 1981 Act, s.70. They are mainly used in Admiralty proceedings. See CPR, r.35.15 and para.20(1) of *Practice Direction 61—Admiralty*, below, para.2–062.

[473] Supreme Court Act 1981, s.67. Under CPR, r.39.2(1), the "general rule is that a hearing is to be in public"; this is subject to exceptions specified in r.39.2(3). This satisfies the requirements of Arts 6 and 10, ECHR: *R. (on the application of Pelling) v Bow County Court* (unreported, October 19, 2000). A hearing whether in court or in chambers may be in public or private according to the requirements of r.39.2(1) and (3).

[474] *ibid.* s.66.

[475] See below, para.4–025.

[476] *ibid.* s.9.

[477] *ibid.* Sch.1. The judges who deal with bankruptcy are referred to as the "High Court of Justice in Bankruptcy" and those who deal with company matters as the "Companies Court", but these are not formally constituted as courts under the 1981 Act. On the latter, see A. Boyle and P. Marshall, *The Practice and Procedure of the Companies Court* (1997).

[478] Patents Act 1977. The judge may sit with scientific advisers: Supreme Court Act 1981, s.70.

work is the responsibility of the "Court of Protection" which is in fact an office of the Supreme Court rather than a court.

The business is at present handled by the Chancellor and 17 puisne judges, five of whom are nominated to the Patents Court although they are available to help with the other work of the Division. One judge (Patten J.) holds the appointment of Vice-Chancellor of the County Palatine of Lancaster.[479] The judges are assisted by six Chancery masters and six registrars in bankruptcy.[480] The work is done in London and at eight centres in the provinces.[481] In the latter the work is done by the Vice-Chancellor of the County Palatine, by a High Court judge sitting at Birmingham, Bristol and Cardiff and by Circuit judges who specialise in Chancery work and who sit for this purpose as judges of the High Court.[482] The Vice-Chancellor of the County Palatine and another judge effectively act as presiding judges in relation to Chancery work outside London.[483] Steps have also been taken to transfer less onerous cases to the county court,[484] Chancery expertise for this purpose being concentrated at the Central London County Court.[485]

The administrative arrangements for the Chancery Division were substantially revised in 1982[486] following the Report of the Review Body on the Chancery Division of the High Court.[487] Amongst other matters the changes were designed to produce greater flexibility in the deployment of judges and a new approach to the drafting of orders "which should eliminate their present sesquipedalian pedantry".[488] As from October 1, 1982, orders became simpler in form and drawn by clerks (known as associates) rather than professionally qualified officers, thus bringing practice more into line with the other divisions. Further changes were effected as part of the Woolf reforms, including the introduction of case management by the court.[489]

(c) The Queen's Bench Division

This division deals mainly with claims in contract and tort, and also exercises supervisory and appellate jurisdiction over inferior courts and tribunals. The supervisory jurisdiction includes most applications for habeas corpus and all applications for judicial review.[490] The appellate jurisdiction includes appeals by case stated on a point of law from magistrates' courts and the Crown Court. Also part of this division are the Admiralty Court and the Commercial Court.[491] The

2–061

---

[479] This office, to which the appointment is made by the Chancellor of the Duchy of Lancaster, was formerly held by a Circuit judge: see para.4–020.

[480] See R. E. Ball, "The Chancery Master" (1961) 77 L.Q.R. 331. See generally, E. Heward, *Chancery Practice* (2nd edn, 1990).

[481] Leeds, Liverpool, Manchester, Newcastle-upon-Tyne, Preston, and, as from October 10, 1982, Birmingham, Bristol and Cardiff. See *Chancery Guide* (2005), para.12.1.

[482] *Chancery Guide* (2005), paras 12.4–12.6. They may also take equity work in county courts.

[483] Lord Woolf's *Interim Report on Access to Justice* (1995), p.61; *Chancery Guide* (2005), para.12.3.

[484] Under s.40 of the County Courts Act 1984.

[485] *Chancery Guide* (2005), para.13.

[486] See RSC (Amendment No.2) 1982 (SI 1982/1111); *Practice Direction (Chancery Chambers)* [1982] 1 W.L.R. 1189.

[487] Cmnd. 8205, 1981: report by Oliver L.J. and J.M. Woolf Esq.: see R. Blackford, (1981) 78 L.S. Gaz. 590.

[488] Blackford *op. cit.* p.590.

[489] See generally the *Chancery Guide* (2005) (HMCS website).

[490] Supreme Court Act 1981, s.61 and Sch.1. See below, Ch.18.

[491] Supreme Court Act 1981, s.6.

work is at present handled by the President of the Queen's Bench Division[492] and 72 puisne judges (as at December 2005). The business is done in London and at the 27 first-tier Crown Court centres in the provinces.

In London, the judges are assisted by 10[493] masters of the Queen's Bench Division.[494] Any act under the Civil Procedure Rules in relation to proceedings in the High Court may be performed by a master, except where an enactment, rule or practice direction provides otherwise.[495] Much of their work concerns matters arising before the hearing of a claim, including the case management of cases proceeding in London. A master may try a case treated as being allocated to the multi-track and proceeding under CPR, Pt 8, and (with the consent of the parties) cases allocated to the multi-track under CPR, Pt 26, and may assess damages.[496] One master sits each day as the Practice Master, to deal with procedural and practice problems arising in the Central Office and generally to supervise the work of the office. The right of audience before a master is not limited to barristers; solicitors and their clerks may appear, including unadmitted clerks. The work is normally done in chambers, which lead off from an ante-chamber generally known as "the Bear Garden".

(i) The Admiralty Court

2–062   This court has jurisdiction in a wide variety of matters concerning ships and aircraft, including claims arising out of collisions, claims for damage to cargo, for goods supplied and for repairs.[497] When necessary, it also exercises the jurisdiction of the High Court as a prize court.[498] From 1993, the practice of the Admiralty has been harmonised with that of the Commercial Court.[499]

(ii) The Commercial Court[500]

2–063   There were a number of attempts in the nineteenth century to establish some form of specialised commercial court.[501] A Commercial List was established in the Queen's Bench Division in 1895, partly as the result of dissatisfaction with

---

[492] Prior to the changes made by the Constitutional Reform Act 2005, the head of the Division was the Lord Chief Justice. However, his time in court was wholly spent on appellate work. He no longer took applications for judicial review at first instance.

[493] There is in addition the Master of the Crown Office, who is also Registrar of the Criminal Appeal Office. These offices were combined by the Courts and Legal Services Act 1990, s.78.

[494] See A. S. Diamond, "The Queen's Bench Master" (1960) 76 L.Q.R. 504; Sir Jack Jacob, "The Masters of the Queen's Bench Division" (1971) reprinted in *The Reform of Civil Procedural Law* (1982).

[495] CPR, r.2.4. Thus, for example, a master may not make a freezing order on an order authorising a person to enter land to recover, inspect or sample property, or an injunction (subject to exceptions, as where the terms are agreed by the parties).

[496] *Practice Direction 2b—Allocation of Cases to Levels of Judiciary*, paras 4.1, 4.2. See para.12–005.

[497] Supreme Court Act 1981, ss.20–24.

[498] *ibid.* ss.27, 62.

[499] *Practice Direction (Admiralty Court: Practice)* [1993] 1 W.L.R. 960; *Practice Direction (Admiralty Court: Practice)* [1996] 1 W.L.R. 127. See now CPR, Pts 49 and 61 and *Practice Direction 61—Admiralty, Admiralty and Commercial Court Guide* (7th edn, 2006).

[500] Sir Anthony Colman, V. Lyon and P. Hopkins, *The Practice and Procedure of the Commercial Court* (5th edn, 2000); *Civil Justice Review* (Cm. 394, 1988), Ch.11.

[501] Colman, Lyon and Hopkins (2000), Ch.1.

the handling of a commercial case by Lawrance J.[502] This did not, however, end the drift to arbitration.[503] The list was transformed into a court in 1970.[504] Particular features of the Commercial Court are that, in principle and court resources permitting, a hearing should take place at the earliest date for which the parties can be ready; pre-trial matters are dealt with by a judge rather than a master; and that the court "expects a high level of co-operation and realism" from the parties' legal representatives.[505] Statements of case must be "as brief and concise as possible".[506] The procedural rules have been revised to take account of the Woolf reforms.[507] A judge of the Commercial Court may be appointed as an arbitrator, provided the Lord Chief Justice agrees that he or she can be made available.[508] Less complex cases "relating to a commercial or business matter in a broad sense" and not required to proceed in the Chancery Division may be dealt with in a Mercantile Court. The London Mercantile Court is administered as part of the Commercial Court and there are Mercantile Courts at eight district registries.[509] Cases set down in them are tried by specialist Circuit judges, sitting as High Court judges, and known as Mercantile judges.[510]

A Commercial Court Committee was established in 1977 to consider and keep under review the working of the Court and the appeal procedures in arbitration proceedings, and to report to the Lord Chancellor.[511] A report of this committee[512] led to the enactment of the Arbitration Act 1979, which was designed to limit rights of appeal to the courts from the decisions of arbitrators, and thereby to halt a decline in the standing of London as a leading centre of international commercial arbitration.[513]

In recent years the workload of the Commercial Court has increased significantly, although it is still small in relation to the number of London arbitrations. Three features of its work are that in many cases either one or both litigants are businesses outside the UK,[514] that a significant part of the court's work arises out of London arbitrations, and that it is commonplace for cases to involve millions of pounds.[515]

A crisis in the early 1990s caused by the pressure of business was relieved by the appointment of additional judges: there are now 14 nominated Commercial Court judges; eight or nine are needed for most of the time.[516] The recognition

---

[502] See the 4th edition of this book at para.4–024, (1895–96) 1 Com. Cas. pp.i–x; MacKinnon L.J. (1944) 60 L.Q.R. 324–325; V. V. Veeder, (1994) 110 L.Q.R. 282; Lord Parker C.J., *History and Development of Commercial Arbitration* (1959).

[503] See G. Wilson, *Cases and Materials on the English Legal System* (1973), pp.31–43; R. B. Ferguson, "The adjudication of commercial disputes and the legal system in modern England" (1980) 7 B.J.L.S. 141.

[504] Administration of Justice Act 1970, s.3(1).

[505] *Admiralty and Commercial Court Guide* (7th edn, 2006), para.A1.

[506] *ibid*. para.C1 and App.4.

[507] See CPR, Pt 58.

[508] Arbitration Act 1996, s.93. Such appointments are rare. It is much commoner for judges of the Technology and Construction Court (para.2–064) to be appointed under s.93.

[509] Birmingham, Bristol, Cardiff, Chester, Leeds, Liverpool and Manchester.

[510] CPR Pt 59 and Practice Direction 59, *Mercantile Courts* and *Mercantile Court Guides* for each court (HMCS website).

[511] See its Annual Report for 1981, (1981) 78 L.S. Gaz. 100; Colman, Lyon and Hopkins, Ch.2.

[512] Commercial Court Committee, *Report on Arbitration* (Cmnd. 7284, 1978).

[513] See Ferguson (1980), pp.151–154; Kerr J., "The Arbitration Act 1979" (1980) 43 M.L.R. 45.

[514] About 80% in 2005: *Annual Report of the Admiralty and Commercial Court 2004–05*, pp.4–5.

[515] Goff. J., "The Commercial Court—How it Works" (1980) 77 L.S. Gaz. 1035. See generally on the working of the court, Colman and Lyon, *op. cit.*

[516] *Annual Report 2004–05*, p.7.

that the court is a "very substantial earner indeed of foreign exchange in the form of invisible earnings"[517] no doubt helped the case for additional appointments. In consequence of the Woolf reforms, a specialised procedural regime for the Commercial Court has been created within the framework of the CPR.[518] This still "differs markedly from that in the non-specialist Queen's Bench Division",[519] including different arrangements for case management. There has from time to time been concern over increasing waiting times.[520] The court aims for "lead times" (the time between the date when a hearing is fixed and the date when the hearing will take place) within specified limits.[521]

(iii) *The Technology and Construction Court*

2–064   There are five full-time Circuit judges nominated by the Lord Chief Justice, after consulting the Lord Chancellor, to deal with Technology and Construction Court claims (to October 8, 1998 known as "Official Referees' business").[522] Since 1998, a High Court judge has been appointed to take charge of the TCC specialist list.[523] Examples of TCC claims include building or other construction disputes; engineering disputes; claims by and against engineers, architects, surveyors, accountants and other specialist advisers; claims by and against local authorities relating to their statutory duties concerning the development of land or the construction of buildings; claims concerning computers, software and networks; claims relating to the quality of goods sold or hired, and work done, materials supplied or services rendered; claims between landlord and tenant for breach of a repairing covenant; claims between neighbours, owners and occupiers of land in trespass, nuisance, etc.; claims relating to the environment or fires; the taking of complicated accounts; and challenges to the decision of arbitrators in construction and engineering disputes.[524] However, to be a TCC claim it must also involve issues or questions which are technically complex or where trial by a TCC judge is desirable.[525] A TCC claim may be issued in the High Court or a specified county court,[526] and is treated as if it were allocated to the multi-track.

[517] Lord Mackay of Clashfern L.C., quoted by M. Heaney, 9(12) *The Lawyer*, March 21, 1995, p.14.

[518] CPR, Pt 58, *Practice Direction 58—Commercial Court, Admiralty and Commercial Court Guide* (7th edn, 2006).

[519] Colman, Lyon and Hawkins (2000), p.27.

[520] See F. Meisel,"Commercial Court Reform" (1986) 5 C.J.Q. 196 and "Commercial Court Reform—The Lord Chancellor's Consultation Paper" (1987) 6 C.J.Q. 95. Introduction of a £50,000 minimum jurisdictional limit has been resisted.

[521] Annual Report 2004–05, p.7.

[522] Supreme Court Act 1981, s.68, as amended by the Civil Procedure Act 1997, Sch.2, para.1 and the Constitutional Reform Act 2005, Sch.4, Pt 1, para.131. See E. Fay, *Official Referees' Business* (3rd edn, 1997); P. Coulson, *The Technology and Construction Court* (2006). The office of Official Referee, first established by the Supreme Court of Judicature Act 1873, was abolished by the Courts Act 1971. Existing holders became Circuit judges: 1971 Act, Sch.2. On each circuit other than the South Eastern Circuit judges have been appointed to conduct this business, although most is taken in London: see T. Heald, "Official Referee's Business in the Provinces" (1983) Constr. L.J. 91. There are further full time designated judges at Birmingham, Salford and Liverpool, and others elsewhere.

[523] The first was Dyson J. The current assigned judge is Jackson J. Another High Court judge sits for part of the time, and there is a panel of five reserve High Court judges: *Annual Report of the Technology and Construction Court 2006*, p.4.

[524] *Practice Direction 60—Technology and Construction Court Claims*, para.2.1.

[525] CPR, r.60.1(3).

[526] *Practice Direction 60*, paras 3.1, 3.4: Birmingham, Bristol, Cardiff, Central London, Chester, Exeter, Leeds, Liverpool, Newcastle, Nottingham and Salford.

The claim is assigned to a particular TCC judge. There is provision for a case management conference and a pre-trial review.[527] While things have not had to change as much in the TCC as elsewhere in the civil justice system, there have been some changes, "with the TCC judges apparently taking a considered and incremental approach to the development of procedure".[528] There is a Technology and Construction Court Users Committee, a Technology and Construction Bar Association (TECBAR), and a Technology and Construction Solicitors' Association (TeCSA).[529]

(d) The Family Division

This division exercises the matrimonial and domestic jurisdiction of the High **2–065** Court, which includes defended divorce cases, final dissolution matters in respect of civil partnerships, proceedings under the Children Act 1989 and matters relating to the wardship or adoption of children and declarations in medical treatment cases,[530] and deals with non-contentious or common form probate business. It also hears appeals from magistrates' courts in family proceedings.[531] The work is at present handled by the President, 19 puisne judges, and 19 District judges of the Principal Registry of the Family Division in London and at first-tier Crown Court centres.[532]

Many important aspects of High Court family work are dealt with by the District judges of the principal registry and District judges of the High Court, including decisions on ancillary matters (e.g. maintenance, adjustment of property rights and the arrangements for contact with children).

Over the years there have from time to time been proposals for the establishment of a "Family Court" with a unified jurisdiction but sitting in tiers or divisions.[533] This matter has reconsidered as part of the consultation or establishment of a Single Civil Court, and the establishment of a Family Court has been adopted as a long-term objective.[534] In the meantime steps are being taken to establish family court centres, bringing together the work of the county courts and family proceedings courts in one location, and to harmonise family procedure rules.[535]

(e) Administration

Administrative support for the High Court is provided by the Royal Courts of **2–066** Justice Group of HM Courts Service.[536] Apart from the masters, registrars and

---

[527] *ibid.* paras 6–10.
[528] A. Burr and R. Honey, "The Post-Woolf TCC: Any Change?" (2001) 17 Const. L.J. 378 at 394.
[529] HMCS website (Technology and Construction Court).
[530] See above, para.2–045.
[531] Supreme Court Act 1981, Sch.1, as amended. See above, para.2–029.
[532] Family Proceedings Rules 1991 (SI 1991/1247), r.2.32, as amended. The cases here may be dealt with by High Court judges or Circuit judges sitting as High Court judges.
[533] N. V. Lowe and G. Douglas, *Bromley's Family Law* (10th edn, 2006), pp.20–21.
[534] See "A Single Family Court" [2005] Fam. Law 935.
[535] *Annual Report of HM Courts Service 2005–06*, pp.30–31. Procedural rules are made by the Family Procedure Rules Committee: see para.2–026.
[536] The Review Body on the Chancery Division found that the establishment of the Court Service had had little impact on the Division, and were highly critical of the Division's administrative arrangements.

District judges appointed under the Supreme Court Act 1981, the officials are civil servants who are members of the Department of Constitutional Affairs In London, the principal offices include the Central Office of the Supreme Court, Chancery Chambers, the Principal Registry of the Family Division, and the Admiralty and Commercial Court Registry.

Outside London there are district registries of the High Court in 132 locations.[537] A District judge[538] is assigned by the Lord Chief Justice, after consulting the Lord Chancellor, as District judge of the High Court for one or more registry,[539] and there is provision for the appointment of deputy and assistant District judges.[540] Claims in the Queen's Bench Division may be issued in any district registry; claims in most Chancery actions may be issued out of eight Chancery district registries.[541] The other interlocutory steps are also taken here. Matrimonial causes and most other proceedings in the Family Division may be dealt with at those district registries that have a divorce county court (or, as the case may be, a civil partnerships county court) within its district,[542] although they can only be tried at the Royal Courts or designated "divorce town" or (in respect of civil partnerships) "dissolution town".[543] There are district probate registries in 11 places and sub-registries in 18 others.[544] District probate registrars are appointed by the Lord Chancellor.[545]

(f) Procedural rules

2–067   Rules for the purpose of regulating and prescribing the practice and procedure to be followed in the High Court and Court of Appeal were formerly made by the Supreme Court Rule Committee.[546] Most cases were regulated by the Rules of the Supreme Court.[547] These first appeared in 1885 and the most recent major revision was in 1965. The rules could not alter any matter of substantive law.[548] From 1999, practice and procedure in the High Court and Court of Appeal have been regulated by the Civil Procedure Rules 1998 as part of the Woolf Reforms.[549]

---

[537] Supreme Court Act 1981, s.99; Civil Courts Order 1983 (SI 1983/713), Sch. 1, as amended.

[538] See above, para.2–043.

[539] Supreme Court Act 1981, s.100, as substituted by the Constitutional Reform Act 2005, Sch.3, para.2(1).

[540] *ibid.* ss.102, 103. Formerly they were entitled district registrars.

[541] i.e. the district registries for the eight centres mentioned above, para.2–060, n.481.

[542] See the Family Proceedings Rules 1991 (SI 1991/247), r.1.2 (definition of "district registry" for the purpose of the rules), r.2.32.

[543] *ibid.*, r.1.2 (definitions of "divorce town" and "dissolution town").

[544] Supreme Court Act 1981, s.104; District Probate Registries Order 1982 (SI 1982/379), as amended.

[545] Supreme Court Act 1981, s.89, Sch.2, Pt III.

[546] Supreme Court Act 1981, ss.84, 85, as amended by the Courts and Legal Services Act 1990, Sch.18, para.36(1). See Sir Jack Jacob, "The Machinery of the Rule Committee of the Supreme Court" (1971) reprinted in *The Reform of Civil Procedural Law* (1982).

[547] The Rules were divided into Orders, rules and paragraphs, and were referred to in abbreviated form as (e.g.) RSC, Ord.1, r.1. For a transitional period, some have been retained in a Schedule to the CPR pending their replacement by new Parts of the CPR.

[548] e.g. doubts as to whether certain aspects of the "New Order 53", which introduced the "application for judicial review", were *ultra vires* were settled by the enactment of s.31 of the Supreme Court Act 1981 (see below, para.18–053).

[549] See above, para.2–049. See para.2–026 on family procedure rules.

(g) Appeals[550]

Appeals lie either to the Court of Appeal (Civil Division)[551] or direct to the **2–068** House of Lords.[552] The appeal lies direct to the House of Lords where the case has reached the High Court on appeal from a magistrates' court or the Crown Court in a criminal matter, or, otherwise, under the "leap frog" procedure.

8. THE LANDS TRIBUNAL

The Lands Tribunal was set up in 1949[553] to take over the jurisdiction of official **2–069** arbitrators to determine disputes concerning the assessment of compensation for the compulsory acquisition of land. It consists of a President, who must be a person who has held judicial office or a lawyer of at least seven years' standing, a number of members (currently four) who are lawyers of seven years' standing, and a number who are persons with experience in land valuation (i.e. qualified surveyors).[554] All are appointed by the Lord Chancellor, the valuation experts after consultation with the president of the Royal Institution of Chartered Surveyors. The Tribunal's jurisdiction may be exercised by any one or more of its members, as selected by the President, and the selection depends on the nature of the matters at issue. The Tribunal's permanent office and secretariat are in London, although it may sit in the provinces if appropriate, for example to facilitate the inspection of the relevant land and buildings. In addition to the jurisdiction in respect of compensation, it has the power to determine disputes as to the valuation of land for taxation, it hears appeals from valuation tribunals, in matters concerning disputed assessments of land and buildings for rating and disputes concerning the council tax, and from leasehold valuation and residential property tribunals, and it has a discretionary power to vary, modify or discharge restrictive covenants under s.84 of the Law of Property Act 1925. An appeal lies to the Court of Appeal on a point of law,[555] with the permission of that court. The Lands Tribunal is regarded as having a high status in the court structure, notwithstanding that, unlike the Transport Tribunal and the Employment Appeal Tribunal, it is not constituted under the 1949 Act as a court of record.[556] Its proceedings are conducted fairly formally.

---

[550] See generally Ch.18.

[551] See below, para.2–071.

[552] See below, para.2–072.

[553] Lands Tribunal Act 1949. For its rules of procedure see the Lands Tribunal Rules 1996 (SI 1996/1022), as amended. See *www.landstribunal.gov.uk*. The Tribunal is guided by the overriding objective in the CPR in exercising its powers under the Rules, although the CPR do not formally apply: *Lands Tribunal Practice Directions*, para.2.1.

[554] 1949 Act, s.2(2), as amended by the Courts and Legal Services Act, 1990, Sch.10, para.7. To be eligible, a lawyer must possess a seven year general qualification under s.71 of the 1990 Act, i.e. a right of audience in any part of the Supreme Court or all proceedings in county courts or magistrates' courts.

[555] The appeal may, but need not be, by case stated; formerly, the case stated procedure applied in all cases: see 1949 Act, s.3(4), as amended by the Civil Procedure (Modification of Enactment) Order 2000 (SI 2000/941).

[556] See *Att.-Gen. v British Broadcasting Corporation* [1981] A.C. 303 at 338 (Viscount Dilhorne). *Cf.* the *Annual Report of the Council on Tribunals, 1980–81* (1981–82 H.C. 89), p.8: "The Lands Tribunal is generally regarded as of High Court standing . . . "

9. THE COURT OF APPEAL (CRIMINAL DIVISION)

2–070 The Court of Appeal (Criminal Division) hears appeals from trials on indictment or sentences passed by the Crown Court,[557] and references by the Attorney-General under the Criminal Justice Acts 1972 and 1988.[558] It replaced the Court of Criminal Appeal[559] with effect from October 1, 1966.[560] The Lord Chief Justice is the president of the division, and the Lord Chief Justice may, after consulting the Lord Chancellor, appoint a vice-president.[561] The work is done by the Lord Chief Justice, Lords Justices and High Court judges.[562] Circuit judges may also sit at the request of the Lord Chief Justice, after consulting the Lord Chancellor.[563] For the following purposes, a court of the division must comprise an uneven number of judges not less than three[564]: (i) determining appeals against conviction; (ii) determining appeals against a verdict of not guilty by reason of insanity; (iii) determining appeals against a finding of unfitness to be tried because of a disability; (iv) determining applications for leave to appeal to the House of Lords; (v) refusing leave to appeal in situations (i), (ii), (iii) above except where the application has already been refused by a single judge; (vi) determining reviews of sentencing.

Otherwise, matters may be determined by a court comprising two judges.[565] A single judge may grant leave to appeal, grant bail and perform certain other functions.[566] Any number of courts may sit at the same time. The court gives a single judgment unless the judge presiding states that in his or her opinion the question is one of law on which it is convenient that separate judgments should be pronounced by the members of the court.[567] Procedural rules may be made by the Criminal Procedure Rules Committee.[568] The administration of criminal appeals is handled by the Criminal Appeal Office, headed by the Registrar of Criminal Appeals.[569] Appeals lie to the House of Lords, with the leave of the

[557] Criminal Appeal Act 1968, Pts I and II, as amended by the Criminal Appeal Act 1995.

[558] See below, Ch.18.

[559] Established by the Criminal Appeal Act 1907. This Act for the first time established a right of appeal for the *accused*, as distinct from the discretion of the *judge* to refer a point to his fellow judges (see above, para.1–010).

[560] Criminal Appeal Act 1966. This followed the Report of the Committee on the Court of Criminal Appeal (Chairman: Lord Donovan; Cmnd. 2755, 1965).

[561] Supreme Court Act 1981, s.3, as amended by the Constitutional Reform Act 2005, Sch.4, Pt 1, para.116.

[562] On occasion, one or more of the Law Lords (see below, para.4–025) may sit: e.g. *R. v Husseyn* (Note) (1977) 67 Cr.App.R. 131, "explained" in *Attorney-General's References* (Nos 1 and 2 of 1979) [1980] Q.B. 180, see below para.18–019.

[563] Supreme Court Act 1981, s.9, as amended by the Criminal Justice and Public Order Act 1994, s.52 and the Constitutional Reform Act 2005, Sch.4, Pt 1, para.121. Not more than one Circuit judge may sit on an appeal; a Circuit judge may not act as the single judge; 1981 Act, ss.55(6), 9(6A), inserted by the 1994 Act, s.52.

[564] Supreme Court Act 1981, s.55, as amended by the Criminal Justice Act 1988, Sch.15, para.80.

[565] *ibid.*, e.g. appeals against sentence. If the court is equally divided the case must be re-argued before an uneven number of judges not less than three: *ibid.* s.55(5).

[566] Criminal Appeal Act 1968, s.31, as amended.

[567] Supreme Court Act 1981, s.59. See *R. v Head* [1958] 1 Q.B. 132 at 137; *R. v Harz* [1967] 1 A.C. 760 at 765.

[568] See para.2–022; *Guide for Counsel/Solicitor Advocates: Hearings at the Court of Appeal Criminal Division* (2006) (HMCS website); D. Thompson and H. W. Wollaston, *Court of Appeal—Criminal Division* (1969); M. Knight, *Criminal Appeals* (1970); I. McLean, *Criminal Appeals* (2nd edn, 1986); P. Taylor, *Taylor on Appeals* (2000).

[569] This office is held in combination with that of Master of the Crown Office. See above, para.2–061,

House or the Court of Appeal, where the Court of Appeal has certified that a point of law of general public importance is involved.[570]

10. The Court of Appeal (Civil Division)[571]

The Court of Appeal was established as part of the Supreme Court by the Supreme Court of Judicature Acts 1873 and 1875. It was reconstituted with Civil and Criminal Divisions in 1966.[572] The jurisdiction of the Civil Division includes appeals from the High Court and county courts in civil matters, and from certain other courts and tribunals.[573] The Master of the Rolls[574] is president of the division, and the Lord Chief Justice may, after consulting the Lord Chancellor, appoint a vice-president.[575] The work is mainly done by the Master of the Rolls and the Lord and Lady Justices,[576] with assistance from the Lord Chief Justice, the Presidents of the Queen's Bench and Family Divisions and the Chancellor of the High Court,[577] and occasional assistance from Law Lords, High Court judges and former judges of the Court of Appeal or High Court. A court is duly constituted if it consists of one or more judges, subject to the directions of the Master of the Rolls about the minimum number of judges for specified descriptions of proceedings, and to the determination of the Master of the Rolls or a designated Lord Justice of Appeal as to the number of judges for any particular proceedings.[578] Sittings are normally held at the Royal Court of Justice, but there is a developing programme of regional sittings, which have taken place so far in Cardiff, Manchester, Exeter and Birmingham.

2–071

The work of the division is administered by the Civil Appeals Office, headed by the Head of Civil Appeals Office and Master, and two Deputy Masters. They determine certain incidental or straightforward matters.[579]

Decisions as to the composition of the courts and the allocation of the cases are made by the Head of the Civil Appeals Office acting in consultation with the Master of the Rolls. In general, the constitutions of the Court of Appeal are changed about every three weeks. Civil courts are "multi-disciplinary" rather than "specialised" (e.g. all former Chancery judges sitting on a Chancery appeal) although, where possible, no appeal on a specialist topic is listed before a court none of whose members are familiar with that speciality.[580] A small team of

---

[570] See below, para.2–072 and Ch.18.

[571] For accounts of the working of the Court of Appeal see Lord Asquith, (1947–51) 1 J.S.P.T.L. (N.S.) 350, reproduced in L. Blom-Cooper, *The Language of the Law* (1965); Sir R. Evershed, *The Court of Appeal in England* (1950); D. Karlen, *Appellate Courts in the United States and England* (1963), Ch.6; Sir John Donaldson M.R., *The Problems of a Master of the Rolls* (Holdsworth Club Presidential Address, 1985) and "The Court of Appeal" (1985) 53 Medico-Legal J. 148.

[572] Criminal Appeal Act 1966.

[573] See below, Ch.18.

[574] See below, para.4–025.

[575] Supreme Court Act 1981, s.3: for the whole court or for the Division.

[576] See below, para.4–025.

[577] Approximately three weeks a term each: *Court of Appeal Civil Division Review of the Legal Year 2004–2005*, p.5.

[578] Supreme Court Act 1981, s.54(2)–(4A), substituted by the Access to Justice Act 1999, s.59.

[579] CPR, r.52.16.

[580] Sir John Donaldson M.R., *The Problems of A Master of the Rolls* (Holdsworth Club Presidential Address, 1985), pp.9–10.

"in-house" lawyers has been appointed, each taking charge of the case management of a group of applications and appeals, defined by reference to subject
matter. They give procedural advice to litigants in person and, where necessary,
provide summaries of the issues raised for the use of judges.[581] The introduction
of greater efficiency in the administration of the Court of Appeal proved insufficient to reduce the backlog of appeals; indeed the number of cases outstanding
at the end of the year steadily increased.[582] In response, additional judges were
appointed,[583] the requirements as to documentation were revised, skeleton arguments were to be produced earlier and exchanged, and time limits were set for
oral argument in support of applications for leave to appeal and renewed applications for leave to apply for judicial review.[584] This last step moved the court
further towards the American approach whereby most emphasis is placed on the
written briefs.[585] Significant further changes were introduced as a corollary to the
Woolf reforms,[586] following a report by Sir Jeffery Bowman.[587] Appeals now lie
from final decisions of a Circuit judge in a case in the small claims or fast track
to a High Court judge instead of the Court of Appeal. The Court of Appeal
accordingly hears appeals against the decisions of the Circuit and High Court
judges in family proceedings, final decisions in cases assigned to the multi-track,
and second appeals. Second appeals where cases have been decided by the
county court or High Court can only lie where the Court of Appeal considers that
the appeal could raise an important point of principle or practice or there is some
other compelling reason.[588] Where in any proceedings in a county court or the
High Court a person appeals, or seeks permission to appeal, to a court other than
the Court of Appeal, the Master of the Rolls, or the court from which or to which
the appeal is made, or from which permission to appeal is sought, may direct that
the appeal shall be heard instead by the Court of Appeal.[589] Permission to appeal
is normally required. A Court of Appeal Users' Committee has been established
(and subsequently re-established), and young lawyers have been recruited for
fixed terms as Judicial Assistants. In 2003, a research study[590] concluded that the
most impressive change since the introduction of the new rules had been the
improvement in processing the Court's caseload, with waiting times and pending
caseloads reduced substantially. There were, however, increased pressures on the

---

[581] *Annual Review by the Master of the Rolls, 1988–89.* See *Practice Statement (Civil Appeals: Setting Down)* [1990] 1 W.L.R. 1436.

[582] Annual Review, 1992–93, p.2.

[583] *LCD Court Service Annual Report 1994–95* (1994–95 H.C. 579), pp.31–32. Three additional judges were authorised in 1994 and three more in 1996.

[584] *Practice Statement (Court of Appeal: Procedural Changes)* [1995] 1 W.L.R. 1188; *Practice Direction (Court of Appeal: Procedure)* [1995] 1 W.L.R. 1191.

[585] See Leggatt L.J., "The Future of the Oral Tradition in the Court of Appeal" (1995) 14 C.J.Q. 11, noting ominously that "it is comparatively uncommon for members of the court to change their minds about whether to dismiss or allow an appeal, once they have read the skeleton arguments" (p.15).

[586] See the Access to Justice Act 1999, ss.54–57; CPR, Pt 52; *Practice Direction 52—Appeals.*

[587] *Review of the Court of Appeal (Civil Division)* (LCD, 1997) (summary on the LCD website).

[588] 1999 Act, s.55.

[589] *ibid.* s.57.

[590] J. Plotnikoff and R. Woolfson, *Evaluation of the Impact of the Reforms in the Court of Appeal (Civil Division)* (LCD Research Study No.5/2003, DCA website). In more recent years, the numbers of cases outstanding have tended to increase although the average time between initial filing of an application and the hearing of an appeal from a High Court or county court final order continues to fall: *Court of Appeal (Civil Division) Review of the Legal Year 2004–05,* pp.15, 28.

Lords Justices, anticipated savings in legal costs had failed to materialise, and procedures were complex.

The increasing tendency of the court to deliver a single, composite opinion has attracted some criticism.[591]

Appeals lie to the House of Lords, with the leave of the court or the House, on questions of law or fact.[592]

11. THE HOUSE OF LORDS[593]

The House of Lords hears appeals (1) from the Court of Appeal; (2) in certain circumstances, direct from the High Court; (3) from the Court of Session (the highest civil court in Scotland)[594]; (4) from the Court of Appeal in Northern Ireland; (5) in certain circumstances, direct from the High Court of Justice in Northern Ireland; and (6) from the Courts-Martial Appeal Court.[595]

2–072

An appeal may not be heard or determined unless at least three from the following list are present. The historic position in this list of the Lord Chancellor and former Lord Chancellors was ended, with effect from April 2, 2006, by the Lord Chancellor (Transfer of Functions and Supplementary Provision) (No. 2) Order 2006.[596] The list today comprises the Lords of Appeal in Ordinary[597]; and any peer who has held one of the high judicial offices of member of the Judicial Committee of the Privy Council, Lord of Appeal in Ordinary, judge of the Supreme Court of England and Wales or Northern Ireland or judge of the Court of Session.[598]

Technically, it seems that all members of the House of Lords have the right to vote on appeals, but the practice has fallen into disuse. In the early nineteenth century lay peers were used to make up the necessary quorum but by the 1830s there were sufficient Law Lords[599] for a "professional" court to be possible.[600] In 1844 the convention that lay peers did not vote was established in *O'Connell v R.*[601] Daniel O'Connell appealed against a conviction for conspiracy. Three

[591] See R. Munday, [2001] C.L.J. 321. As to changes to the form of judgments, see R. Munday, [2002] C.L.J. 612.

[592] See below, and Ch.18.

[593] See L. Blom-Cooper and Gavin Drewry, *Final Appeal* (1972); R. Stevens, *Law and Politics* (1978); A. Paterson, *The Law Lords* (1982); M. Barrett, *The Law Lords* (2001); Lord Fraser of Tullybelton, 1986 S.L.T. 33; G. Dymond, House of Lords Library, Library Note, *The Appellate Jurisdiction of the House of Lords* (Updated March 2006). Brief accounts of the work of the Judicial Office in supporting the Law Lords are found in the *House of Lords Annual Reports* (to 2001–02) (Parliament website).

[594] There is no right of appeal from the highest Scottish criminal court, the High Court of Justiciary: *Mackintosh v Lord Advocate* (1876) 3 R. (H.L.) 34; Criminal Procedure (Scotland) Act 1887, s.72. See A. J. Maclean, "The House of Lords and Appeals from the High Court of Justiciary 1707–1887" 1985 J. R. 192.

[595] Appeals in English cases are considered in detail below, Ch.18.

[596] (*sic*) SI 2006/1016, Sch.1.

[597] Below, para.4–025.

[598] Appellate Jurisdiction Act 1876, ss.5, 25; Appellate Jurisdiction Act 1887, s.5. For a current list, see *www.judiciary.gov.uk*. In 1996, the internationally distinguished New Zealand judge Sir Robin Cooke was made a peer and between then and 2001 he sat on English and Scottish appeals to the House of Lords as a peer who had held high judicial office as a member of the Judicial Committee of the Privy Council; see also P. Spiller, (1996) 17 N.Z. Univ. L.R. 1.

[599] The term then covered the Lord Chancellor, the Lord Chancellor of Ireland, former Lord Chancellors, ennobled judges, and occasionally a peer who had held a minor judicial office.

[600] Stevens (1978), p.29.

[601] (1844) 11 Cl. & F. 155 at 421–426.

Law Lords were in favour of allowing the appeal, two were against it. Several lay peers purported to vote with the minority, but were persuaded to withdraw on the ground that in reality the "Court of Law" in the House was constituted by the Law Lords and interference by lay peers would greatly lessen the authority of the House. The last occasion when a lay peer attempted to vote was in *Bradlaugh v Clarke*[602] when Lord Denman[603] attended throughout the proceedings and purported to vote with Lord Blackburn against the majority of the Law Lords. His attempt was ignored by the Lord Chancellor and the Law Reports, but was noted by *The Times*.[604] In response to a question in the House of Commons, the Home Secretary stated that as the Appellate Jurisdiction Act 1876 had not excluded lay peers, it had been competent for Lord Denman to sit: had his opinion affected the result, he would have been asked to withdraw his vote on the precedent of *O'Connell's* case.[605]

Under the original arrangements for reorganisation incorporated in the Supreme Court of Judicature Act 1873 the appellate role of the House of Lords was to be abolished. The Court of Appeal was to be the final appeal court for England, and ultimately for Scotland, Ireland and the colonies. However, before the arrangements came into effect opposition developed in several quarters, the appeal to the House was retained and provision was made for the appointment of salaried Law Lords.[606]

2–073   Up to 1948, appeals to the House of Lords were heard in the Chamber of the House. In that year, the process of repairing the Palace of Westminster caused the House to commit the hearing of appeals to an Appellate Committee meeting in a committee room and this practice has been maintained ever since. The committee hears appeals and reports its conclusions to the House, where judgment is delivered at a judicial sitting.[607] The House, or the Appellate Committee, as the case may be, is presided over by the Lord Chancellor or, as is more usually the case, the senior Lord of Appeal in Ordinary present.[608] The Appellate Committee

---

[602] (1883) 8 App. Cas 354. See R. E. Megarry, (1949) 65 L.Q.R. 22–24.

[603] This was the second Lord Denman, son of the Lord Chief Justice and brother of Denman J., a High Court judge, 1872–1892. "Lord Denman was aged seventy-eight at the time of his fling, and he had been a peer for nearly thirty years and a barrister for fifty, so that his was no mere indiscretion of youth and inexperience" (Megarry (1949), p.24). He "won notoriety rather from his eccentricities than any eminent qualifications" (D.N.B.).

[604] April 10, 1883, p.4.

[605] Sir William Harcourt, H.C. Deb Vol.278, col.68, April 12, 1883.

[606] See Stevens (1979), Ch.2 and R. Stevens, "The Final Appeal: Reform of the House of Lords and Privy Council, 1867–1876" (1964) 80 L.Q.R. 343.

[607] A morning sitting in the Chamber of the House. Some appeals may be heard in the Chamber, e.g. during parliamentary recesses. In 1998, the televised hearing of the first decision of the House of Lords in the Pinochet case (*R. v Bow Street Metropolitan Stipendiary Magistrate, Ex p. Pinochet Ugarte* [1998] 4 All E.R. 897) generated interest across the world: see Barnett (2001), pp.3–6.

[608] Seniority formerly depended on the date of first appointment to the office: Blom-Cooper and Drewry (1972), p.179. From 1984, the first and second senior Law Lords have been specifically appointed as such by the Queen: H.L. Deb Vol.453, cols 914–919, June 27, 1984: see L. Blom-Cooper [1984] P.L. 376; A. A. Paterson, 1988 J.R. 235 at 251, n.59. The presiding judge may exert significant influence over the course of proceedings: Paterson (1982), pp.66–72. The most recent senior Lords of Appeal have been Lord Simonds (1954–1962); Lord Reid (1962–1975); Lord Wilberforce (1975–1982); Lord Diplock (1982–1984); Lord Fraser of Tullybelton (1984–1985); Lord Scarman (1985–1986); Lord Keith of Kinkel (1986–1996); Lord Goff of Chieveley (1996–1998); Lord Browne-Wilkinson (1998–2000); Lord Bingham of Cornhill (previously Master of the Rolls and then Lord Chief Justice immediately before his appointment as Senior Law Lord) (2000–).

must be distinguished from the "Appeal Committee" which sits to consider and report on petitions for leave to appeal and other incidental matters and which normally comprises three Law Lords.

Selection of Law Lords to sit on Appeal Committees is done by the Principal Clerk to the Judicial Office; selection of Appellate Committees, although formerly theoretically in the hands of the Lord Chancellor, was delegated to his Permanent Secretary, who consulted the Lord Chancellor in cases of difficulty.[609] Normally, the most convenient panel available is chosen; occasionally, special considerations may apply, such as the exclusion of judges with a political background from adjudicating in a case with party-political implications,[610] the strong desirability of one or both of the Scottish Law Lords sitting on an appeal from Scotland and the desirability of the presence of a Chancery judge in a Chancery appeal. The room for manoeuvre is in practice limited. The choice of panel is now left to the Senior Law Lord.[611]

Procedure on appeals to the House of Lords is regulated by Directions and Standing Orders of the House.[612] Each side must submit a "case", drawn up by counsel, which is a "succinct statement of [their] argument in the Appeal", although in practice the oral submissions of counsel and the interchange between them and the Law Lords are of greater significance.[613] The Law Lords are generally expected to confine their propositions of law to matters covered by the argument of counsel, although this view is held today less strongly than formerly.[614] Moreover, they will not normally consider a point not raised in the courts below,[615]

> "But if [the Law Lords] think it is something that really goes to the root of the thing, if they think the whole thing would be rather a mess if they did not allow it to be argued, then they would probably allow it on terms as to costs."[616]

Informal discussions among the Law Lords take place during the hearing of an appeal.[617] Judgment is invariably reserved. At the conclusion of the hearing there is a conference at which provisional opinions are expressed, and a general discussion follows. If there appears to be general agreement, it may also be agreed that a particular Law Lord should write the major opinion. Occasionally, a second conference may be convened.

---

[609] See Paterson (1982), pp.87–89. The selections have to be co-ordinated with those for the Judicial Committee of the Privy Council. There is evidence of attempts by successive Lord Chancellors, in the early years of the twentieth century, to influence the outcome of cases by their selection of panels: D. Woodhouse, *The Office of Lord Chancellor* (2000), pp.120–122.

[610] This was done for *Heaton's Transport Co v TGWU* [1973] A.C. 15. See A. Paterson, (1979) 1 B.J.L.S. 118, 126.

[611] Woodhouse (2000), p.122 (interview with Lord Irvine L.C.).

[612] See *Practice Directions and Standing Orders Applicable to Civil Appeals* (2007 edition); *Practice Directions Applicable to Criminal Appeals* (2007 edition) (House of Lords website).

[613] See A. Paterson, *The Law Lords* (1982), Chs 3 and 4.

[614] *ibid.* pp.38–45.

[615] *ibid.* pp.45–49.

[616] Lord Cross, cited by Paterson (1982), p.47.

[617] The interaction among the Law Lords is discussed by Paterson (1982), Ch.5, and Barrett (2001).

Each Law Lord is entitled to write his or her own opinion,[618] although they attempt to avoid the unnecessary multiplication of opinions. Views differ on the desirability of multiple opinions.[619] Paterson found that of those studied:

> "although in non-criminal common law cases only two active Law Lords generally favoured a single judgment in criminal appeals on a point of statutory construction, probably a majority of the active Law Lords favoured that approach."[620]

The main problem with multiple assenting judgments is that the differences in language may make it difficult to discern the *ratio decidendi*[621]; conversely, the same feature may leave subsequent judges greater scope for developing the law. The main problem with single opinions is that they may reflect an uneasy compromise. The proportion of cases with one substantive opinion with which the other Law Lords have separately concurred has increased.[622]

The House of Lords has a limited original, as distinct from appellate, jurisdiction, which includes the power to determine peerage claims and the power to conduct impeachment proceedings.[623] The right of a peer to be tried by his peers in cases of treason, felony or misprision of felony was abolished in 1948.[624]

12. THE SUPREME COURT OF THE UNITED KINGDOM

2–074 This court will take over the appellate jurisdiction of the House of Lords and the devolution jurisdiction of the Judicial Committee of the Privy Council. Legislative provision for its establishment was made by Pt 3 of the Constitutional Reform Act 2005 and it is due to open in October 2009. The context for its birth is provided by the changes to the Office of the Lord Chancellor[625] and an extended process of debate about reform of the House of Lords in general.[626]

---

[618] Occasionally the presiding judge may press for a single opinion: see *DPP v Smith* [1961] A.C. 290 and *Heaton's Transport Ltd v TGWU* [1973] A.C. 15: *cf.* the position in the Judicial Committee of the Privy Council, below. In a number of recent cases, where the Law Lords have wished to speak with one voice, there has been a single opinion of the Appellate Committee. This feature is still unusual and is found mainly in criminal cases (e.g. *R. v Forbes* [2001] 1 A.C. 473, *R v H* [2004] 2 A.C. 134) but also in cases concerning human rights (e.g. *R (on the application of Middleton) v West Somerset Coroner* [2004] 2 A.C. 182) and tax (*Barclays Mercantile v Mawson* [2005] 1 A.C. 684).

[619] See Blom-Cooper and Drewry (1972), Ch.V; R. Cross (1977) 93 L.Q.R. 378; Paterson (1982), pp.96–109 and 183–187.

[620] *op. cit.* p.185.

[621] See, e.g. *Boys v Chaplin* [1971] A.C. 356; *British Railways Board v Herrington* [1972] A.C. 877: below, pp.420–421.

[622] See P. V. Baker (1983) 99 L.Q.R. 371; Lord Diplock *In re Prestige Group plc* [1984] 1 W.L.R. 335 at 338, referring to this as "a frequent practice in this House when dealing with questions of statutory construction"; A. Bradney, "The Changing Face of the House of Lords" 1985 J.R. 178 (statistical analysis of judgments between January 30, 1974 and March 1, 1984).

[623] The last such cases were those of Warren Hastings (1788–1795: see P. J. Marshall, *The Impeachment of Warren Hastings* (1965)) and Viscount Melville (1806); *cf.* below, para.4–027.

[624] Criminal Justice Act 1948, s.30. The last trial was that of Lord de Clifford. See W. T. West, *The Trial of Lord de Clifford* 1935 (1984), and, generally, P. Marsden, *In Peril Before Parliament* (1965). A notable fictional example is provided in the film *Kind Hearts and Coronets*.

[625] See below.

[626] See A. W. Bradley and K. Ewing, *Constitutional and Administrative Law* (14th edn, pp.180–187).

The Supreme Court will consist of 12 judges appointed by the Queen,[627] and she may appoint one of the judges to be President and one to be Deputy President of the Court. The other judges will be styled "Justices of the Supreme Court".[628] The first members will be the Lords of Appeal in Ordinary immediately before commencement; the Senior Law Lord will become the President and the second senior the Deputy President.[629]

The Supreme Court will be a superior court of record.[630] An appeal will lie to it from any judgment of the Court of Appeal in England and Wales (with the permission of either court) unless excluded by an enactment; in any case where an appeal lay from a court in Scotland to the House of Lords immediately before commencement; and in other specified cases.[631] The Supreme Court has power to determine any question necessary to be determined for doing justice in an appeal to it under any enactment.[632] Nothing in Pt 3 is to affect the distinctions between the separate legal systems or the parts of the UK.[633] Accordingly, a decision of the Court on appeal from a court of any part of the UK, other than a decision in a devolution matter, is to be regarded as the decision of a court of that part of the UK.[634] A decision on a devolution matter is not binding on that Court when making such a decision, but otherwise is binding in all legal proceedings.[635]

The Supreme Court is duly constituted only if it consists of an uneven number of judges, of at least three judges, and more than half are permanent judges. This is subject to directions by the President that for specified proceedings there should be a specified number that is uneven and greater than three or that in specified description of proceedings, it is to consist of a specified minimum greater than three.[636] The Court may sit with specialist advisers.[637] The President may make Supreme Court Rules governing practice and procedure after consulting the Lord Chancellor and specified legal professional bodies.[638] The Lord Chancellor determines the date of commencement.[639]

The Court will be supported by a chief executive appointed by the Lord Chancellor after consulting the President, and to whom the President may delegate non-judicial functions, and officers and staff appointed by the President.[640] The Lord Chancellor is to provide accommodation and other

---

[627] The number can be changed by Order in Council.

[628] 2005 Act, s.23.

[629] *ibid.* s.24. As to the subsequent appointment of judges of the Supreme Court, see ss.25–31, below, para.4–028. Provision is made for tenure, salaries and allowances, resignation and retirement, medical retirement and pensions. (ss.32–37) and for acting judges and a supplementary panel (ss.38, 39).

[630] *ibid.* s.40(1).

[631] *ibid.* s.40(2)–(4), (6); Sch.9. This will presumably retain the position that no appeal was from Scotland in criminal cases, and that leave is not required for an appeal from Scotland in a civil cases (a certificate from two counsel that the point justifies an appeal is required). See generally C. Himsworth and A. Paterson, (2004) 24 L.S. 99.

[632] *ibid.* s.40(5).

[633] *ibid.* s.41(1).

[634] *ibid.* s.41(2).

[635] *ibid.* s.41(3).

[636] *ibid.* s.42. The position where one or more members is unable to continue is governed by s.43.

[637] *ibid.* s.44.

[638] *ibid.* s.45.

[639] *ibid.* s.46. The rules are to be contained in a statutory instrument.

[640] *ibid.* ss.48, 49.

resources.[641] The chief executive must ensure that the Court's resources are used to provide an efficient and effective system to support the Court.[642] The decision that there should be a Supreme Court separate from Parliament preceded the process of analysis and consultation as to how it should be done.[643] The outcome is certainly tidier from the point of view of the separation of powers, but given the general lack of involvement of Law Lords in the wider work of the House of Lords, and the existing guarantees of judicial independence, not a necessity.[644] The outcome has been for there to be as little change as possible from the previous arrangements. Alternative possibilities would have been to do nothing, abolish the judicial function of the House of Lords without replacement or to confine it to cases of real constitutional importance.[645] It remains to be seen whether the change will lead to a change in the general approaches of the judges or the extent to which it is perceived by the public as a political body.[646] Some have seen is it as a step in the move of the UK "incrementally towards a constitutionally limited political order".[647]

Other particular issues arise from the titles of the Justices[648] and the location of the new court at Middlesex Guildhall.[649]

13. THE JUDICIAL COMMITTEE OF THE PRIVY COUNCIL

2–075   The Judicial Committee of the Privy Council was established in 1833,[650] largely as the result of the efforts of Lord Brougham.[651] Previously, appeals to the Crown from the colonies, which arose out of the prerogative right of the Sovereign as the fountainhead of all justice, were dealt with by a committee of the Privy Council which did not have a regular judicial composition. The 1833 Act limited the membership almost exclusively to senior judges. The present position is that the Committee comprises the Lord President of the Council, the Lords of Appeal in Ordinary and other members of the Privy Council who hold "high judicial

---

[641] *ibid.* s.50.

[642] *ibid.* s.51.

[643] Announcement by the Prime Minister, June 12, 2003; DCA Consultation Paper, *Constitutional Reform: A Supreme Court for the United Kingdom* (CP11/03, July 2003) and Responses (DCA, January 2004); see the Special Issue of *Legal Studies* edited by D. Morgan, (2004) 24 L.S. 1–293. The case for a Supreme Court (largely based on the proposition that the Lord Chancellor should cease to sit as a judge and be head of the judiciary) was previously made by Lord Steyn, (2002) 118 L.Q.R. 382.

[644] See J. Webber, (2004) 24 L.S. 55.

[645] See Baroness Hale, (2004) 24 L.S. 36.

[646] See D. Woodhouse, (2004) 24 L.S. 134.

[647] See the discussion by J. Webber, (2004) 24 L.S. 55, *cf.* observations in the *Jackson* case, para.5–023.

[648] Note the echo of the Justices of the Supreme Court of the United States. Compare the titles of Lord and Lady Justices of Appeal in England and Wales and the point that judges of the Court of Session are styled "Lord" or "Lady", although not made peers on appointment (some, however, may have been or are subsequently made peers).

[649] Built between 1906 and 1913. Views differ as to whether this will be sufficiently impressive for one of the world's leading courts. See Lord Hope, (2005) 121 L.Q.R. 253, who does not regard the building as suitable.

[650] Judicial Committee Act 1833.

[651] See P. A. Howell, *The Judicial Committee of the Privy Council 1833–1876* (1979), Ch.12; D. B. Swinfen, "Henry Brougham and the Judicial Committee of the Privy Council" (1975) 90 L.Q.R. 396; L. P. Beth, [1975] P. L. 219. See generally D. B. Swinfen, *Imperial Appeal* (1987); M. Barrett, *The Law Lords* (2001), Ch.5.

office",[652] and former holders of these offices.[653] In addition, privy councillors who hold or have held one of a number of judicial offices in New Zealand and other Commonwealth countries may also be members.[654] The composition of the Committee in a particular case is determined by the Senior Law Lord.[655] The Judicial Committee hears appeals from certain Commonwealth countries, from the Channel Islands, in certain admiralty and ecclesiastical matters and from the regulatory body for veterinary surgeons.[656] It also has jurisdiction to determine "devolution issues".

The Commonwealth appellate jurisdiction was formerly regarded as an important unifying influence: it has now dwindled significantly as an increasing number of Commonwealth countries have abandoned the appeal.[657] For example, Canada and India abolished appeals in 1949, Sri Lanka in 1971, Malaysia in 1985, Australia (effectively) in 1986,[658] Singapore in 1994 and New Zealand in 2003. Appeals from Hong Kong ended with the territory's reversion to China in 1997.[659] The Committee's decision takes the form of advice to the Queen, to which effect is given by an Order in Council.[660] It is binding on the relevant Commonwealth courts.[661] A proportion of the cases heard by the Privy Council raise questions of constitutional interpretation. The handling of these cases has been analysed for guidance as to how the House of Lords might deal with matters arising under a written constitution with a Bill of Rights for the United Kingdom. There appeared to be a consensus that the judges seemed not to have been particularly well suited to handling such issues,[662] although the performance recently had been more impressive.[663]

---

[652] As defined by the Appellate Jurisdiction Acts 1876, ss.5, 25 and 1877, s.5. This extends the membership of the Committee to the Lords Justices of Appeal, although they rarely sit in practice.

[653] Judicial Committee Act 1833, s.l; Appellate Jurisdiction Act 1876, s.6; Appellate Jurisdiction Act 1887, s.3.

[654] Judicial Committee Amendment Act 1895, s.l, Sch.; Appellate Jurisdiction Act 1908, s.3. In 2001, there were six from New Zealand and one each from the Bahamas, Eastern Caribbean and Jamaica: Barrett (2001), p.159. For an account of the experience of the Chief Justice of New Zealand in sitting on the Privy Council, see Interview with Sir Thomas Eichelbaum, [1994] N.Z.L.J. 86.

[655] H.C. Deb, February 4, 2000, col.545W. See also the Judicial Committee (General Appellate Jurisdiction) Rules Order 1982 (SI 1982/1676), as amended.

[656] By virtue of the National Health Service Reform and Health Care Professionals Act 2002, appeals concerning health care professionals now lie to the High Court.

[657] Dominions were given the power to do this by the Statute of Westminster 1931, ss.2, 3.

[658] Australia Act 1986, s.11.

[659] See P. Wesley-Smith, (1992) 2 H.K.L.J. 118.

[660] For the republics (The Gambia, Singapore, Trinidad and Tobago) the Committee itself is the decision-making authority.

[661] At least while that country retains the appeal to the Privy Council. For example, in *Viro v R.* (1978) 18 A.L.R. 257, the High Court of Australia held that it was no longer bound by decisions of the Privy Council: see R. S. Geddis, (1978) 9 Fed. L. R. 427.

[662] P. Wallington and J. McBride, *Civil Liberties and a Bill of Rights* (1976), pp.32–33 "We come away with a rather neutral impression of the talents available"; G. J. Zellick, "Fundamental Rights in the Privy Council" [1982] P.L. 344 (criticising the decision in a case concerning the death penalty, *Riley v Attorney General of Jamaica* [1983] 1 A.C. 719); B. de Smith, "The Judicial Committee as a Constitutional Court" [1984] P.L. 557; N. S. Price, "Constitutional Adjudication in the Privy Council and Reflections on the Bill of Rights debate" (1986) 35 I.C.L.Q. 946, criticising *Robinson v R.* [1985] A.C. 956; *cf.* M. Zander, *A Bill of Rights?* (3rd edn, 1985), pp.62–64, who took a more favourable view. On the role of the Privy Council in developing the common law, see J. W. Harris, (1990) 106 L.Q.R. 574.

[663] See, e.g. *Pratt and Morgan v Attorney-General of Jamaica* [1994] 2 A.C. 1; M. Grieve, "Life after Death Row", *Counsel*, July/August 1994, p.16.

   The Judicial Committee of the Privy Council has jurisdiction to determine
questions relating to the competences and functions of the legislative and executive authorities established in Scotland and Northern Ireland and of the National
Assembly for Wales.[664] This includes power to determine as a court of first
instance whether provisions of a Bill would be within the competence of the
Scottish Parliament or Northern Ireland Assembly.[665] Otherwise, these "devolution issues" may reach the Judicial Committee on appeal or on a reference from
a superior court[666] or on a reference from a law officer[667] where such an issue is
not the subject of proceedings. In these cases the Judicial Committee must
comprise members of the Judicial Committee who hold or have held the office
of Lord of Appeal, or high judicial office in the United Kingdom. Decisions of
the Judicial Committee on devolution issues must be stated in open court and are
binding in all legal proceedings (other than proceedings before the
Committee).[668]
   As of February 2006, the Judicial Committee had determined 17 cases raising
devolution issues. All were from Scotland and raised issues concerning the
application of the ECHR; all but one[669] were criminal cases and one[670] concurred
the compatibility with the ECHR of provisions of the legislation providing for the
detention of mental patients. The composition of the Committee is effectively the
same as that of the House of Lords, with, in the cases so far heard, at least two
Scottish judges. Each judge gives a separate judgment, the main judgments

---

[664] Scotland Act 1998, s.103 and Sch.6; Northern Ireland Act 1998, s.82 and Sch.10; Government of
   Wales Act 1998, Sch.8 to be replaced by the Government of Wales Act 2006, Sch.9. See the
   Judicial Committee (Devolution) Rules Order 1999 (SI 1999/665), as amended by SI 2005/1138;
   Judicial Committee (Powers in Devolution Cases) Order 1999 (SI 1999/1320).

[665] Scotland Act 1998, s.33; Northern Ireland Act 1998, s.11. Or Welsh Assembly Measures
   (Government of Wales Act 2006, s.99). The same would apply to Bills: s.112.

[666] In specified circumstances, the Court of Session, the High Court of Justiciary, the Court of Appeal
   in Northern Ireland, the High Court and the Court of Appeal. A reference may be required by,
   inter alia, a law officer. The House of Lords may refer a devolution issue arising in judicial
   proceedings to the Judicial Committee unless the House considers it more appropriate, having
   regard to all the circumstances, that it should determine the issue.

[667] Or the Northern Ireland First Minister and deputy First Minister acting jointly in a case arising
   under the Northern Ireland Act 1998; or the National Assembly in a case arising under the
   Government of Wales Act 1998 (the Consul General under the Government of Wales Act 2006);
   or the Lord Advocate in a case arising under the Scotland Act 1998.

[668] Scotland Act 1998, s.103(1); Northern Ireland Act 1998, s.82(1); Government of Wales Act 1998,
   Sch.8, para.32; of Constitutional Reform Act 2005, s.41. It is submitted that it is the decision as
   resolving the devolution issue that is binding and that, for example, a view of the scope of a
   particular ECHR provision, even if necessary for resolution of the devolution issue, would not be
   binding in a case where this did not arise as a devolution issue.

[669] See e.g. *Montgomery and Coulter v HM Advocate and the Advocate General for Scotland* [2001]
   2 W.L.R. 779 (issues concerning the definition of "devolution issue" and the right to a fair trial
   under Art.6, ECHR in the context of pre-trial publicity); *Brown v Stott* [2001] H.R.L.R. 9, 2001
   P.C. 43 (adduction in evidence of admission by B that she was the driver at the time of an alleged
   offence, required by the Road Traffic Act 1988, s.172(2)(a), not contrary to the implied right not
   to incriminate oneself in Art.6, ECHR); *Millar v Procurator Fiscal Elgin* [2001] UKPC D4
   (hearing of criminal proceedings by temporary sheriffs appointed by the Lord Advocate contrary
   to Art.6, ECHR); *Procurator Fiscal, Linlithgow v Watson and Burrows, HM Advocate v JK*
   [2001] UKPC D1 (right to hearing within a reasonable time); *Clark v Kelly* [2003] UKPC D1 (not
   incompatible with Art.6(1) for D to be tried by court comprising a lay justice, advised on the law
   in open court by the clerk; *Kearney v HM Advocate* [2006] UKPC D1 (temporary judges
   independent and impartial for the purposes of Art.6(1)).

[670] *Anderson, Reid and Doherty v The Scottish Ministers* (DRA Nos 9, 10 and 11 of 2000) [2001]
   UKPC D5 (continued detention of restricted patients in hospital on grounds of public safety not
   dependent on their condition being capable of treatment).

normally being given by the Scottish judges. Decisions are obviously of considerable importance for the jurisdiction from which a case originates. Where not binding, they will have the same standing as a persuasive authority as a decision of the House of Lords. This jurisdiction will pass to the new supreme court.

The Committee sits in London. The recording of dissenting opinions has only been permitted since 1966.[671] Other than in devolution cases, there is either one unanimous opinion, or one for the majority and one for the minority. Lord Reid thought that the single opinion rule had led to Privy Council judgments being much inferior to speeches in the House of Lords:

> "They are perfectly adequate to decide the particular case but not often of wider importance. Yet the same Law Lords have sat and they have taken just as much trouble. The reason is that a single judgment must get the agreement of at least all in the majority so it tends to be no more than the highest common factor of all the views."[672]

Apart from the appellate jurisdiction, the Judicial Committee may entertain an application for a declaration that a person purporting to be a member of the House of Commons is disqualified by the House of Commons Disqualification Act 1975.[673] Finally, Her Majesty may refer any matter to the Judicial Committee for hearing or consideration.[674]

14. The Court of Justice of the European Communities[675]

(a) Establishment

This Court is one of the four major institutions created by the Treaties establishing the European Communities. There was originally a Court of Justice for the European Coal and Steel Community, but when the treaties establishing the European Economic Community and Euratom were concluded it was agreed that there should be one court for the three communities. The Single European Act of 1986 made provision for the establishment of a Court of First Instance to ease the Court's workload.[676]

2–076

---

[671] Judicial Committee (Dissenting Opinion) Order 1966. See D. B. Swinfen, "Single Judgment in the Privy Council 1833–1966" (1975) 20 J.R. 153.

[672] "The Judge as Law Maker" (1972) XII J.S.P.T.L. (N.S.) 22 at 29.

[673] See s.7.

[674] Judicial Committee Act 1833, s.4. See D. B. Swinfen, "Politics and the Privy Council: Special Reference to the Judicial Committee" 1978 23 J.R. 126.

[675] S. Weatherill and P. Beaumont, *EU Law* (3rd edn, 1999), Ch.6; T. C. Hartley, *The Foundations of European Community Law* (5th edn, 2003); L. Neville Brown and T. Kennedy, *The Court of Justice of the European Communities* (5th edn, 2000); Office for Official Publications of the European Communities, *The Court of Justice of the European Communities* (2006); H. Rasmussen, *On Law and Policy in the European Court of Justice* (1986); A. Arnull, *The European Union and its Court of Justice* (2nd edn, 2006).

[676] See section (f), below.

(b) Composition

2–077   The Court consists of one judge for each Member State (27),[677] assisted by eight advocates general.[678] It may sit either in "full session" (i.e. with all the judges entitled to be present), or in a Grand Chamber of 13 judges[679] presided over by the President of the Court, or in chambers of five or three.[680] The Court must sit in full session in specified cases,[681] and the Court may decide, after hearing the advocate general that a case of exceptional importance should be referred to the full Court.[682] The Court must sit in Grand Chamber when a Member State or an institution of the Communities that is party to the proceedings so requests.[683] Provision for the assignment of judges to chambers, the election of presidents of chambers and the composition of chambers is made by the Court's Rules of Procedure.[684] Only one judgment is delivered by the Chamber or Court and it is not revealed whether the decision was unanimous or reached by a majority.

The function of the advocate general is:

> "acting with complete impartiality and independence, to make, in open court, reasoned submissions on cases which, in accordance with the Statute of the Court of Justice, require his involvement."[685]

This office has no exact equivalent in any national legal system although it is loosely based on that of *commissaire du gouvernement* in proceedings before French administrative courts, especially the Conseil d'Etat. One advocate general is assigned to each case. He or she sits on the bench, next to the judges, and may put questions to the parties. His or her opinion on the case is normally expressed about three weeks after the submissions of counsel have been heard, and, unlike such submissions on behalf of a client, "the Advocate General speaks for no-one but himself".[686] The opinion sets out the facts and relevant legal provisions, analyses the issues in the light of the case law of the court and suggests the appropriate decision for the court to adopt. It tends to be longer, more informative and less bland in style than the judgments of the court. The advocate-general does not attend the deliberations of the judges. It is thought that his or her opinion is followed in about 70 per cent of cases, but this may be an overestimate.[687]

---

[677] Art.221 EC (ex Art.165 EC, as amended), as amended by the Treaty of Nice.

[678] Art.222 EC (ex Art.166 EC, as amended), as amended by the Treaty of Nice. At the request of the Court, the Council, acting unanimously may increase the number.

[679] Including the Presidents of the Chambers of five.

[680] Art.221 and Statute of the Court of Justice, Art.16.

[681] Case brought under Arts 195(2) EC (dismissal of the Ombudsman), 213(2) EC (compulsory retirement of or loss of pension for Commission member, 247(7) EC (removal of or loss of pension for member of the Court of Auditors).

[682] Art.221 and Statute of the Court of Justice, Art.16.

[683] *ibid.*

[684] Arts 9, 10, 11a–11e.

[685] Art.222 EC (ex Art.166 EC), as amended by the Treaty of Nice. See A. A. Dashwood, "The Advocate General in the Court of Justice of the European Communities" (1982) 2 L.S. 202; K. Borgsmidt, "The Advocate General at the European Court of Justice: A Comparative Study" (1988) 13 E.L.Rev. 106; T. Tridimas, (1997) 34 C.M.L. Rev. 1349.

[686] Dashwood, *op. cit.*, p.207.

[687] *ibid.* p.212.

The judges and advocates-general are chosen by agreement among the governments of the Member States. They have to be:

> "chosen from persons whose independence is beyond doubt and who possess the qualifications required for appointment to the highest judicial offices in their respective countries or who are jurisconsults of recognised competence,"[688]

and are appointed for a term of six years. A proportion[689] of the judges and advocates general are replaced every three years. The incumbents are eligible for re-appointment. The judges elect one of their number to be President for a (renewable) three-year term. The President's functions are to direct the judicial business and the administration of the court and to preside at hearings and deliberations.[690] One of the advocates general is designated as first advocate general, and performs certain administrative functions, including the distribution of cases among his or her colleagues.

There is one judge of each of the 27 nationalities.[691] There is one advocate general from each of the five largest states[692] and the remainder from the smaller states by rotation.

(c) Jurisdiction

The jurisdiction of the Court of Justice under the EC Treaty can be classified **2–078** under four main heads: (i) applications for preliminary rulings under Art.234 EC (ex Art.177 EC) in the course of proceedings in a national court or tribunal; (ii) direct actions against Member States or Community institutions; (iii) staff cases; (iv) opinions. In addition, the Council has power to confer jurisdiction on the Court in disputes relating to the application of acts adopted on the basis of the Treaty that create Community industrial property rights, and to recommend the provisions to Member States for adoption in accordance with their constitutional requirements.[693]

(i) *Applications for preliminary rulings*

These are considered in Chapter 18.

---

[688] Art.223 EC (ex Art.167 EC). See also the Protocol on the Statute of the Court of Justice.

[689] 14 or 13 judges; four advocates general.

[690] Rules of Procedure, Art.8.

[691] These were originally not legal requirements but were the consequence in practice of the need for the agreement of all the Member States. The UK judges have been Lord Mackenzie Stuart; formerly a judge of the Court of Session (1973–1988, President 1984–1988); Sir Gordon Slynn; formerly a High Court judge and then an Advocate General (1988–1992); David Edward; a Scottish Q.C. and Professor of European Institutions at the University of Edinburgh, and then judge of the Court of First Instance, 1989–1992 (1992–2004); Sir Konrad Schiemann (formerly a Lord Justice of Appeal) (2004–).

[692] France, Germany, Italy, Spain and the UK. Those from the UK have been J.-P. Warner (1973–1981); Sir Gordon Slynn (1981–1988); Prof. F. Jacobs Q.C. (1988–2006); Eleanor Sharpston Q.C., (2006–)

[693] Treaty of Nice, Art.33, inserting Art.229a EC.

(ii) *Direct actions*

2–079   (1) *Actions against Member States.*[694] Under Art.226 EC (ex Art.169 EC), if the Commission considers that a Member State has failed to fulfil an obligation imposed by the Treaty or secondary Community legislation, it must deliver a reasoned opinion on the matter, after giving the State concerned the opportunity to submit its observations.[695] If the State does not comply with the opinion within the period laid down by the Commission, the Commission may bring the matter before the Court of Justice.[696] Under (Art.227 EC (ex Art.170 EC) a Member State may bring similar proceedings against another Member State, after bringing the matter to the Commission's attention. If a breach is established the Court will make a declaratory order to that effect.[697] The Member State is required by Art.228 EC (ex Art.171 EC) to take the necessary measures to comply.[698] A large majority of cases are settled before they reach the Court.

Prior to amendments effected by the Maastricht Treaty, the sanctions were political rather than legal, and there was non-compliance in a significant number of cases. The position now is that, in such cases, the Commission after giving the Member State concerned the opportunity to submit observations, may issue a reasoned opinion specifying the points on which there has been non-compliance. If the Member State fails to take the necessary measures to comply with the original judgment within the time limit laid down by the Commission, the latter may bring the matter before the Court and the Court may impose a lump sum or penalty payment on the Member State.[699] This is an "important new power, which greatly enhances the armoury of the Court of Justice".[700]

(2) *Actions against community institutions.* These include: (1) actions under Art.230 EC (ex Art.173 EC)[701] for the annulment of, *inter alia*, acts of the Council and Commission[702]; (2) actions under Art.232 EC (ex Art.175 EC) against the Council, the Commission or the Parliament where it has, contrary to the requirements of the Treaty, failed to act[703]; (3) actions under Art.229 EC (ex Art.172 EC) to review penalties or fines imposed by the Commission; (4) actions

---

[694] Hartley (2003), Ch.10; Weatherill and Beaumont (1999), Ch.7: H. A. H. Audretsch, *Supervision in European Community Law* (2nd edn, 1986); A. Dashwood and R. White, (1989) 14 E.L.Rev. 388.

[695] A reasonable time must be allowed: Case 293/85, *Commission v Belgium* [1989] 2 C.M.L.R. 527. See A. Arnull, (1988) 13 E.L.Rev. 260.

[696] See, e.g. Case 232/78, *Commission v France* [1979] E.C.R. 2729: French ban on the import of mutton and lamb from the U.K. held to be an infringement of the Treaty; the dispute was eventually compromised.

[697] Only one case under Art.227 EC has proceeded to judgment: Case 141/78, *France v United Kingdom* [1979] E.C.R. 2923. *Cf.* the procedure under Art.88 EC (ex Art.93 EC) whereby the Commission may require a State to abolish or alter a state aid that distorts or threatens to distort competition: if the State does not comply the matter may be referred to the Court.

[698] Although Art.228 EC does not specify a time limit within which a judgment must be complied with, implementation must start immediately and be completed as soon as possible: Case 131/84, *Commission v Italian Republic* [1985] E.C.R. 3531 (unreasonable delay in implementing judgment in Case 91/81, [1982] E.C.R. 2133). Implementation must be by national provisions of a binding nature, not merely by administrative circulars or practices: Case 168/85, *Commission v Italy* [1986] E.C.R. 2945.

[699] Art.228 EC (ex Art.171 EC, as amended by Art.G(51)/TEU).

[700] Weatherill and Beaumont 1999, pp.236–237.

[701] As amended by the Treaty of Nice.

[702] See below, para.5–061. Community legislation is considered below at paras 5–036—5–064 and its interpretation at paras 6–053—6–064.

[703] See below, para.5–063.

under Art.235 EC (ex Art.178 EC) for damages based on the non-contractual (including tortious) liability of the Communities.[704]

(iii) *Staff cases*

The court has jurisdiction under Art.236 EC (ex Art.179 EC) in any dispute between the Community and its servants within the limits and under the conditions laid down in the Staff Regulations or the Conditions of Employment.

(iv) *Opinions*

The court may under Art.300 EC (ex Art.228 EC)[705] give an opinion as to whether an international agreement that the Community proposes to enter is compatible with the Treaty.

(d) Some aspects of procedure

Proceedings before the Court are governed by the Rules of Procedure[706] drawn **2–080** up by the Court with the approval of the Council. There are five stages:

(1) Written proceedings. Proceedings are commenced by filing an application specifying the subject matter of the dispute, the form of order sought, a summary of the pleas in law on which the application is based and certain other matters. A defence must be filed within one month, and a reply and rejoinder may follow.

(2) Preliminary report and assignment of cases to formations. As soon as the application is lodged, the President must designate a judge to act as rapporteur. He or she must present a preliminary report to the general meeting of the Court with recommendations as to preparatory steps, the formation to which the Court should be assigned (chamber of three or five, Grand Chambers, or full court, and whether to dispense with a hearing or an Opinion of the Advocate General.[707]

(3) Preparatory inquiries and other preparatory measures. The Court must decide whether the submission of any evidence is required, such as the oral testimony of witnesses, an expert's report or the personal appearance of the parties. These matters are dealt with at this stage. The Judge-Rapporteur then prepares a report summarising facts and arguments.

(4) Oral proceedings. The procedure includes an oral part, unless the Court determines otherwise (in cases where none of the parties gives reasons why it should be heard orally). At this stage the parties' lawyers address the Court.[708] Interchange between court and advocate is a comparatively recent

---

[704] Art.288 EC (ex Art.215 EC) provides that "the Community shall, in accordance with the general provisions common to the laws of the Member States, make good any damage caused by its institutions or by its servants in the performance of their duties".

[705] As amended by the Treaty of Nice.

[706] A codified version of the 1991 rules as amended is published on the Court of Justice website.

[707] This may be done where the Court considers that the case raises no new point of law: Statute of the Court of Justice, Art.20.

[708] Any lawyer entitled to practice before a court of a Member State may appear. Thus, either a barrister or solicitor from the UK may appear. A litigant may not normally appear in person. *Cf.* below, para.3–016.

development. The final step of this stage is the delivery of the advocate-general's opinion, which takes place in open court, normally a few weeks later.

(5) Judgment. Proceedings may be conducted in Czech, Danish, Dutch, English, Estonian, Finnish, French, German, Greek, Hungarian, Irish, Italian, Latvian, Lithuanian, Maltese, Polish, Portuguese, Slovak, Slovene, Spanish or Swedish. The language is chosen by the applicant, except where an application is made against a Member State or a natural or legal person having the nationality of a Member State, where the state's language is used, where use of another language is permitted at the joint request of the parties or at the request of one party, and in applications for preliminary rulings, which are conducted in the language of the referring court or tribunal. In practice, the working language is normally French.

There are no court fees. Costs are normally awarded to the successful party against his or her opponent. The court may grant legal aid: aid for an application for a preliminary ruling is, however, regarded as an aspect of the national proceedings, and aid will only be granted by the court if it is not available in those proceedings.

(e) Administration

2–081 This is the responsibility of the Registrar and his staff. There is a Registry, translation, library and documentation and interpretation services and an information office. In addition, three legal secretaries are attached to each judge and advocate-general.

(f) The Court of First Instance[709]

2–082 From 1974, the European Court pressed for the establishment of a separate administrative tribunal to deal with staff cases and thereby relieve the pressure on the Court. For over 20 years, nothing came of this although changes were made in the Court's procedures, including the greater use of chambers, and the number of judges and advocates general were periodically increased. Eventually, the Single European Act amended the main Treaties[710] to enable the Council, by a Decision, to establish a Court of First Instance (FI) of the European Communities, and amend the Rules of Procedure accordingly. The necessary Decision was made in 1988,[711] and provided for a Court of 12 members "attached to the Court of Justice of the European Communities" and with its seat at the Court. The Maastricht Treaty[712] amended Art.168a EC to provide directly for the establishment of the CFI. Further amendments were effected by the Treaty of

---

[709] Brown and Kennedy (2000), Ch.5; *www.curia.europa.eu.*

[710] Art.168a EC.

[711] Dec.88/591/ECSC, EC, Euratom, October 24, 1988, [1988] O.J. L 319/1 (November 25, 1988), [1989] 1 C.M.L.R. 323, as amended.

[712] Art.50. This specifically excluded only Art.177 references from the classes of action or proceeding that could be conferred on it by the Council; the original version also excluded actions brought by Member States on Community institutions.

Nice.[713] Accordingly, the CFI is to comprise at least one judge per Member State.[714] The members are appointed by common accord of the governments of the Member States for (renewable) six-year terms, and with the membership partly renewed every three years.[715] They must be "chosen from persons whose independence is beyond doubt and who possess the ability required for appointment to high judicial office". The judges "may be called upon to perform the task of an advocate general",[716] again in accordance with the Rules of Procedure. A President is elected by the judges for a (renewable) three-year term.[717] The Court also appoints a Registrar. The CFI may sit in plenary session, as a Grand Chamber or in chambers of three or five; in some cases a single judge may have jurisdiction.[718] The Council may create "judicial panels" to hear and determine at first instance certain classes of action or proceeding brought in specific areas, with appeals as prescribed on law or fact to the CFI.[719]

The Court initially exercised the jurisdiction of the European Court in (1) staff cases[720]; (2) competition cases[721]; and (3) coal and steel cases arising from the application of the ECSC Treaty.[722] Its jurisdiction has since been significantly expanded. It now includes jurisdiction to hear and determine: (1) at first instance actions or proceedings referred to in Arts 230, 232, 235, 236 and 238,[723] with the exception of those assigned to a judicial panel and those reserved in the Statute to the Court of Justice[724]; (2) actions or proceedings against decisions of judicial panels[725]; (3) questions referred for a preliminary ruling under Art.234, in specific areas laid down by the Statute.[726] Notwithstanding these developments, the backlog of cases increased in both the Court of First Instance and the Court itself.[727] The Court of First Instance has established its own Rules of Procedure, in agreement with the European Court.[728]

---

[713] Arts 30–32, inserting new Arts 224–225a EC.

[714] Art.224 EC. There currently 27. The Statute of the Court of Justice may provide for a higher number and for the CFI to be assisted by Advocates General: *ibid.* There is no such provision as yet.

[715] Art.224 EC. The first judge from the UK was David Edward Q.C. (1989–1992). He was succeeded by Christopher Bellamy Q.C. (1992–1999) and Nicholas Forwood Q.C. (1999–).

[716] Statute of the Court of Justice, Art.49.

[717] Art.224 EC.

[718] Statute, Art.50; Rules of Procedure of the CFI, Ch.2.

[719] Art.225a EC.

[720] Disputes between the Communities and their servants under Art.179 EC and Art.152 Euratom.

[721] Actions against Community institutions under Arts 173(2) and 175(3) EC relating to the implementation of the competition rules applicable to undertakings.

[722] Actions against the Commission under Arts 33(2) and 35 ECSC by undertakings or associations of undertakings concerning individual acts relating to the implication of Arts 50, 57–66 ECSC.

[723] Respectively reviews of the legality of acts; actions in respect of failure to act; compensation disputes; staff disputes; arbitrations.

[724] Art.225(1) EC.

[725] Art.225(2) EC. See below. These are, exceptionally, subject to review by the European Court where there is a serious risk of the unity or consistency of Community law being affected. The Civil Service Tribunal has been set up as a judicial panel (Council Dec. 2004/752 EC, Euratom).

[726] Art.225(3) EC. These are also subject to review by the Court on a similar basis. Where the CFI considers a case requires a decision of principle likely to affect unity or consistency, it may refer the case to the Court.

[727] Weatherill and Beaumont (1999), pp.207–209.

[728] O.J. 1991 L136, as amended.

An appeal lies to the European Court[729] against final decisions of the CFI, and decisions disposing of the substantive issues in part only or disposing of a procedural issue concerning a plea of lack of competence or inadmissibility. An appeal may be brought by: (1) any unsuccessful party (except that interveners other than Member States or Community institutions may only appeal where the Court's decision directly affects them); and (2) (except in staff cases) any non-intervening Member State or Community institution directly affected. Appeals also lie against the dismissal by the CFI of an application to intervene and the parties to proceedings may appeal against decisions of the CFI under specified Articles.[730] In cases under Art.225(2) and (3) EC, where the First Advocate-General considers that there is a serious risk of the unity or consistency of Community law being affected, he may propose that the European Court review the decision of the CFI. The appeal is limited to points of law, including lack of competence of the CFI, and a breach of procedure which adversely affects the appellant's interests. If the appeal is well founded, the European Court is to quash the decision and either itself give final judgment or remit the case to the Court of First Instance. In the latter event, the European Court's decision on points of law is binding.

15. The European Court of Human Rights[731]

2–083   Decisions of the European Court of Human Rights have become of increasing significance for the English legal system in recent years, and particularly since implementation of the Human Rights Acts 1998. The Convention for the Protection of Human Rights and Fundamental Freedoms of November 4, 1950, generally known as the European Convention on Human Rights, was one of the first achievements of the Council of Europe, an association now of 46 states. It came into force in 1953 and there are now over 40 states which are parties to the Convention.[732] Article 1 provides that these parties "shall secure to everyone within their jurisdiction" the rights and freedoms defined in Arts 2 to 18. These are mostly civil and political rights,[733] including the right to life (Art.2), the right not to be subjected to torture or to inhuman or degrading treatment or punishment (Art.3), the right to liberty and security of person (Art.5), the right to a fair trial in both civil and criminal cases (Art.6), the right to respect for private and family life, home and correspondence (Art.8), the right to freedom of thought, conscience and religion (Art.9), the right to freedom of expression (Art.10) and the right to freedom of peaceful assembly and to freedom of association with others (Art.11). Further rights are specified in the First, Fourth, Sixth and Seventh

---

[729] Arts 56–62 of the Statute of the Court of Justice, inserted by the Treaty of Nice.

[730] Arts 242 (suspensory orders); 243 (interim measures); 256(4) (suspension of enforcement).

[731] D. J. Harris, M. O'Boyle and C. Warbrick, *The Law of the European Convention on Human Rights* (1995); A. R. Mowbray, *Cases and Materials on the European Convention on Human Rights* (2nd edn, 2007); C. Gearty, "The European Court of Human Rights and Civil Liberties: an Overview" [1993] C.L.J. 89. See also *www.echr.coe.int.*

[732] The UK was the first state to ratify the Convention in 1951. Forty-six states had ratified as at June 26, 2006. Recent additions include Russia (1998), Georgia (1999), Armenia, Azerbaijan and Bosnia and Herzogovina (2002), Serbia (2004) and Monaco (2005).

[733] Economic, social and cultural rights are protected under the European Social Charter 1961: see D. J. Harris and D. D'Arcy, *The European Social Charter* (2nd edn, 2000).

Protocols to the Convention.[734] Article 13 requires that persons whose guaranteed rights are violated "have an effective remedy before a national authority".

For the purposes of enforcement the Convention established the European Commission of Human Rights and the European Court of Human Rights, each with one member in respect of each party. The Eleventh Protocol, adopted in 1994, provided for the merger of the Commission and the Court into a new European Court of Human Rights.[735] It still comprises one judge elected by the Parliamentary Assembly with respect to each party, with each sitting in an individual capacity and not as a representative of his or her country. Judges must be of high moral character and either possess the qualifications required for appointment to high judicial office or be jurisconsults of recognised competence.[736]

In particular as a result of the enormous increase in the workload, further changes are to be effected by the Fourteenth Protocol.[737] The following account assumes it is in force. Judges are elected for non-renewable nine-year terms, but must retire at 70.[738] The Court may sit in a single judge formation; in committees of three judges, in chambers of seven[739] and a Grand Chamber of 17. Provision of a single judge formation is new. A single judge cannot deal with an application against the state in respect of which he or she was elected. In cases before a Chamber or the Grand Chamber, the judge elected in respect of the state party concurred sits *ex officio*; if there is none or he or she is unable to sit, a person chosen by the President from a list submitted in advance by the state concerned sits instead. The Grand Chamber also includes the President of the Court, the Vice-President, the Presidents of the Chambers and other judges chosen in accordance with Rules of the Court.[740] A single judge may declare inadmissible or strike out of the Court's list of cases an application submitted under Art.34, where such a decision can be taken without further examination, and the decision is final. Otherwise, the judge forwards the matter to a committee.[741] A committee may declare an application inadmissible or strike it out; may declare it admissible, and may give judgment on the merits where the underlying question is subject to well-established case law of the Court.[742] Otherwise a Chamber is to decide on admissibility and merits,[743] unless released to the Grand Chamber, as may happen where a case raises serious questions of interpretation of the ECHR or its resolution before the Chamber might have a result inconsistent with an earlier judgment of the Court.[744] Where a Chamber has delivered a judgment, any

---

[734] The First Protocol came into force in 1954; all Member States except Andorra, Monaco and Switzerland were parties to it as at June 26, 2006. The UK has ratified the Sixth (abolition of the death penalty other than in time of war; May 20, 1999) and Thirteenth (complete abolition of the death penalty; February 1, 2004) but not the Fourth and Seventh. 39 states, not including the UK, are parties to the Fourth Protocol.

[735] See A. R. Mowbray, [1994] P.L. 54; D. Harris, M. O'Boyle and C. Warbrick (1995), Ch.26.

[736] Arts 21, 22.

[737] As at January 10, 2007, this had been ratified by all the states except Russia.

[738] Previously, they were elected for renewable six-year terms. The change is intended to reinforce judicial independence.

[739] The Committee of Ministers may, at the request of the plenary Court, reduce for a fixed period the size of Chambers to five.

[740] Substituted Art.26.

[741] Substituted Art.27.

[742] Substituted Art.28.

[743] Art.29, as amended by Protocol No.14, Art.9.

[744] Art.30.

party may within three months request that the case by referred to the Grand Chamber, and a panel of five judges must accept the request if the case raises a serious question affecting the interpretation or application of the ECHR or a serious case of general importance.[745]

2–084   Alleged breaches of the Convention may be raised either by a state party[746] or by any person, non-governmental organisation or group of individuals claiming to be the victim of a violation by one of the parties of rights under the ECHR.[747] The Court may only deal with the matter if all domestic remedies have been exhausted and within six months from the date when the final decision was taken. It must not deal with an anonymous application or one substantially the same as one already examined by the Court or already submitted to another procedure of international investigation or settlement. It must declare inadmissible any individual application if it considers that: (a) it is incompatible with the provisions of the Convention, manifestly ill-founded, or an abuse of the right of application; or (b) the applicant has not suffered a significant disadvantage, unless respect for human rights are defined in the Convention requires an examination of the application on the merits.[748] It may strike out an application if it concludes that the applicant does not intend to pursue the application, or the matter has been resolved, or it is otherwise no longer justified to continue the examination of the application.[749] If the Court declares an application admissible it must examine the case with the parties' representatives, and if necessary undertake an investigation. It may seek to secure a friendly settlement; if this is effected case the application is struck out.[750] Hearings are normally held in public and documents are normally accessible to the public.[751] In most cases, a declaratory judgment is given. If the Court finds there has been a violation, and if the internal law of the state concerned allows only partial reparation to be made, the Court "shall, if necessary, afford just satisfaction to the injured party".[752] In a number of cases monetary compensation has been awarded as "just satisfaction" covering costs and expenses, pecuniary losses and non-pecuniary loss. The execution of judgments and the terms of friendly settlements is supervised by the Committee of Ministers.[753] If the Committee considers in the case of a judgment that this is hindered by a problem of interpretation of the judgment, it may (if there is a two-thirds majority) refer the matter to the Court for a ruling.[754] If it considers that a state refuses to abide by a final judgment in a case to which it is a party, it may, after serving formal notice on the state, and with a two-thirds majority, refer to the Court the question whether the state has failed to fulfil its obligation (under

---

[745] Art.43.

[746] Art.33. Few such applications have been made. One example is *Ireland v United Kingdom*, Series A, No.25, judgment of January 18, 1978.

[747] Art.34. The right of individual petition is now compulsory; formerly, the state had to accept the right of individual petition (the UK first did so on January 14, 1966, with subsequent renewals).

[748] Art.35, as amended by the Fourteenth Protocol, Art.12. No case may be rejected under (b) which has not been duly considered by a domestic tribunal. Arts 14, 15. The execution of the terms of a friendly settlement are supervised by the Council of Ministers.

[749] Art.37.

[750] Arts 38, 39, as substituted by *ibid.*

[751] Art.40.

[752] Art.41.

[753] Arts 39(4) and 4(2), as substituted.

[754] Art.46(3).

Art.46(1)) to abide by such judgments. If the Court finds a violation it must refer the case to the Committee.[755]

The Court has adopted Rules of Court.[756] As from January 1, 1983, an individual applicant may be represented by an advocate authorised to practise in any of the party states or any other person approved by the President of the Chamber, or may be given leave to present his or her own case.[757]

Legal aid may be awarded.[758] The official languages are English and French.[759] There is provision for the submission of written documents and an oral hearing.[760] The Court deliberates and votes on its decision in private. A judgment of the Court is prepared: each judge is entitled to annex a separate opinion, whether concurring or dissenting, or a bare statement of dissent.[761] The workload of the Court has risen dramatically in recent years. By the end of 2005 it had registered in total 386,196 individual applications (the comparable figure in 2001 had been 77,768); 201,072 had been allocated to a decision body and Court judgments had been delivered in 5,968 cases (including 1,105 in 2005).[762] It is not thought that the changes made by the Fourteenth Protocol will be sufficient to deal with the problem and a group headed by Lord Woolf was asked to advise on possible further steps.[763] Its main recommendations include redefinition of what constitutes an application, dealing only with properly completed application forms; establishment of satellite Registry Offices in key countries; encouragement of the use of ombudsmen and ADR; and a greater use of Pilot Judgments, with repetitive cases dealt with summarily.

As of January 2002, the Court has considered on the merits 155 cases[764] **2–085** involving the United Kingdom. In 86 judgments the Court found there to be violations of one or more Articles. In the period 2002–2005, there have been a further 84 judgments with violations found in 78. Either as a consequence, or in anticipation of these findings,[765] English law has been changed in a number of significant respects.[766] For example, the law of contempt of court was amended

---

[755] Art.46(4).

[756] ECtHR Rules of Court (as in force in July 2006) (*www.echr.coe.int*).

[757] *ibid.* r.36. See P. J. Duffy, [1983] P.L. 32–33. Previously, the applicant technically had no independent right to appear although in practice his or her lawyer was permitted to address the Court as part of the Commission's case.

[758] rr.91–96.

[759] Revised Rules of Court, r.34. Another language may be used with the leave of the President of the Chamber.

[760] Revised Rules of Court, Chs II–VII.

[761] *ibid.* r.74.

[762] ECtHR, *Survey of Activities 2005*, p.33. There had been 235 judgments in total 1955–1990, and between 50 and 177 a year 1991–1999.

[763] *Review of the Working Methods of the European Court of Human Rights* (December 2005, ECtHR website).

[764] i.e. excluding cases struck out and separate applications under Art.50 where the merits have already been determined.

[765] There are also some changes that can be traced to friendly settlements or Commission decisions.

[766] See P. J. Duffy, (1980) 29 I.C.L.Q. 585–618; A. Drzemczewski, *European Human Rights Convention in Domestic Law* (1983), pp.314–322; M. P. Furmston, *et al.* (eds), *The Effect on English Domestic Law of Membership of the European Communities and of Ratifications of the European Convention on Human Rights* (1983); F. J. Hampson, "The United Kingdom Before the European Court of Human Rights" (1989) 9 Y.E.L. 121; R. R. Churchill and J. R. Young (1991) 62 B.Y.I.L. 183; D. Kinley, *The European Convention on Human Rights: Compliance without Incorporation* (1993) (arguing the case for pre-legislative scrutiny in the UK to promote compliance)); J. P. Gardiner (ed.), *Aspects of the Incorporation of the European Convention on Human Rights into Domestic Law* (1993).

following the *Sunday Times* case[767]; the law relating to the correspondence of persons in prisons has been radically altered[768]; the law in Northern Ireland concerning homosexual acts has been brought into line with the rest of the UK[769]; Isle of Man courts have been advised that birching is contrary to the European Convention[770]; phone tapping has been regulated by statute[771]; the legal regime governing courts martial has been radically revised[772]; the policy excluding homosexuals from the armed forces dropped[773]; the admission of evidence obtained under compulsion curtailed[774]; and overbroad, blanket rules excluding liability in negligence have been replaced by an approach that requires more specific attention to the policy arguments for and against liability in particular classes of case.[775] The UK is reluctantly considering changes to the blanket exclusion of prisoners from the right to vote.[776] The Convention has also had some influence in statutory interpretation,[777] although judges emphasised on a number of occasions that it was not part of English law.[778] A significant measure of incorporation has now been secured by the enactment of the Human Rights 1998, which is considered in Ch.8.

---

[767] See *Sunday Times Case*, Series A, No.30, judgment of April 26, 1979: violation of Art.10; Contempt of Court Act 1981; S. H. Bailey, (1982) 45 M.L.R. 301. It is not certain that the Act went far enough.

[768] See the *Golder Case*, Series A, No.18, Judgment of February 21, 1975; *Case of Silver*: Series A, No.61, Judgment of March 25, 1983: violations of Arts 6(1) and 8 and 3; *Case of Campbell and Fell*, Series A, No.80, Judgment of June 28, 1984; *Case of Boyle and Rice*, Series A, No.131, Judgment of April 27, 1988; G. J. Zellick, [1981] P.L. 435–438, [1983] P.L. 167–169.

[769] *Dudgeon Case*, Series A, No.45, Judgment of October 22, 1981: violation of Art.8; Homosexual Offences (Northern Ireland) Order 1982.

[770] *Tyrer Case*, Series A, No.26, Judgment of April 25, 1978; G. J. Zellick, [1982] P.L. 4–5. The UK does not now accept the rights of individual petition in respect of the Isle of Man.

[771] *Malone Case*, Series A, No.82, Judgment of August 2, 1984; Interception of Communications Act 1985 (see annotations in *Current Law Statutes 1985* by D. Foulkes). There have also been many cases arising out of the period when covert state surveillance was not regulated by the law but only Home Office guidelines: *Khan v UK*, judgment of May 12, 2000. The Convention has also influenced the law affecting mental patients, children in secure accommodation, immigration, and the right of parents to forbid the imposition by a school of corporal punishment on their children.

[772] *Findlay v UK* (1997) 24 E.H.R.R. 221: violation of Art.6(1); Armed Forces Act 1996 and many subsequent cases.

[773] *Smith and Grady v UK* (1999) 29 E.H.R.R. 493; *Lustig-Prean and Beckett v UK* (1999) 29 E.H.R.R. 548: violation of Art.8; Mowbray (2007), pp.489–495.

[774] *Saunders v UK* (1996) 23 E.H.R.R. 313; *IJL. GMR and AKP v UK*, Judgment of September 19, 2000: violation of Art.6(1); Youth Justice and Criminal Evidence Act 1999, Sch.3.

[775] *Osman v UK* (1998) 29 E.H.R.R. 245: violation of Art. 6(1), cf. *Z. v UK*, Judgment of May 10, 2001.

[776] *Hirst v UK (No.2)*, Judgment of October 6, 2005 (GC).

[777] See below, para.6–036. A. Drzemczewski, *European Human Rights Convention in Domestic Law* (1983), pp.166–187; M. Addo, (1995) 46 N.I.L.Q. 1.

[778] *ibid.* pp.314–322. See, e.g. *Malone v Metropolitan Police Commissioner* [1979] Ch. 344; *Att.-Gen. v BBC* [1981] A.C. 303 (Lord Scarman); *R. v Secretary of State for the Home Department, Ex p. Brind* [1991] 1 A.C. 696.

A. INTRODUCTION: THE "LEGAL PROFESSION"

The title "lawyer" is reserved for those who have achieved the special status of **3–001** membership of the "legal profession".[1] It is not a straightforward matter, since many people perform legal tasks even though they are not lawyers. For example, accountants may specialise in revenue law, trade union officials may appear regularly before employment tribunals on behalf of their members,[2] advice on legal matters may be given by specialist advisers on, for example, debt or immigration[3] and solicitors may delegate work to legal executives and other paralegals.[4] Conversely, many of the tasks performed by lawyers are not strictly

---

[1] Academic lawyers are not necessarily qualified, but are lawyers. See M. Partington, "Academic lawyers and legal practice in Britain: a preliminary reappraisal" (1988) 15 J.L.S. 374.
[2] See below, para.10–011.
[3] For the growing "legal advice" sector, see, for example, the National Occupational Standards for Legal Advice at *www.nos4advice.org.uk*.
[4] See below, para.3–053.

"legal".[5] Membership of the legal profession in England and Wales is still conventionally considered to involve qualification as either a barrister or a solicitor. It is usual to speak of two branches of the profession,[6] although historically it is more accurate to speak of two professions. It is entirely possible that, given the potential widening of the right to carry out activities and to provide advice hitherto conventionally confined to those two professions in the Legal Services Bill, that this is the last time that this text will be so specific about the use of the word "lawyer".

It is significant that it is accepted that lawyers are members of a "profession". Much has been written about the supposedly distinctive attributes of professions, and how and why occupational groups seek such status.[7] Medicine and law have been regarded as classic models, although there are important differences between them. A particularly significant difference has historically been that, in medicine,[8] discipline and representation of the profession lie with very different bodies, whereas until recently and as a result of external challenges discussed further in this chapter the Bar Council, for barristers, and the Law Society, for solicitors, exercised both functions.[9] A challenging statement was made by the Office of Fair Trading on this point in 2001:

> "The professions are entrusted with the delivery of services of considerable public importance. . . . Restrictions on supply in the case of professional services, just as with other goods and services, will tend to drive up costs and prices, limit access and choice and cause customers to receive poorer value for money than they would under properly competitive conditions. Such restrictions will tend also to inhibit innovation in the supply of services, again to the ultimate detriment of the public."[10]

In 1979, the Royal Commission on Legal Services recognised five main features of a profession[11]: (a) central organisation: a governing body with powers of control and discipline; (b) the primary function of giving advice in a specialised field of knowledge; (c) the restriction of admission to those with the required standard of education and training; (d) a measure of self-regulation by the profession; and (e) the paramountcy of the duty owed to the client, only subject to responsibility to the court. Increasingly, as will be seen in this chapter, the legal profession will not satisfy these elements as not all solicitors have to be

---

[5] See below, para.3–004.

[6] Although see A. M. Francis, "Legal Executives and the Phantom of Legal Professionalism: the rise and rise of the third branch of the legal profession?" (2002) 9(1) I.J.L.P. 5.

[7] See, e.g., T. J. Johnson, *Professions and Power* (1972), pp.21–38; R. Dingwall (ed.), *The Sociology of the Professions* (1983); A. Boon and J. Levin, *The Ethics and Conduct of Lawyers in England and Wales* (1999), Chs 1–3; R. O'Dair, *Legal Ethics: Text and Materials* (2001), Ch.3; H Sommerlad, "Women Solicitors in a fractured profession: intersections of gender and professionalism in England and Wales", (2002) 9(3) I.J.L.P. 213; R. L. Abel, *English Lawyers between Market and State: the Politics of Professionalism* (2003); R. L. Abel, "The Profession is Political" (2004) 11(1/2) I.J.L.P. 131; A. M. Francis, "Legal Ethics, the marketplace and the fragmentation of legal professionalism", (2005) 12(2) I.J.L.P. 173.

[8] See, however, the Department of Health White Paper, *Trust, Assurance and Safety—the Regulation of Health Professionals* (February 2007).

[9] See e.g. M. Seneviratne, *The Legal Profession: Regulation and the Consumer* (1999), Ch.7. Regulation is now handled by the Solicitors' Regulation Authority (from January 2007) and the Bar Standards Board.

[10] Office of Fair Trading, *Competition in Professions* (2001), para.1.

[11] Royal Commission on Legal Services, *Report, Vol.I* (1979), pp.28, 30.

members of the Law Society, and there is no longer any area of work that only solicitors and/or barristers can necessarily do.[12] Further, the element of self-regulation is under significant challenge in what is, at the time of writing, the Legal Services Bill.[13]

Some commentators have taken the view that the service is offered to the **3–002** public subject to self-regulation in return for considerable autonomy from external control and it is possible to see this arrangement as a form of occupational control rather than an expression of the inherent nature of particular organisations.[14] It was the view of the Royal Commission, however, that the identified features promoted the public interest, subject to points of detail, and proposed no fundamental changes. Complete self-regulation is, as we will see, removed in the regulatory scheme proposed in the Legal Services Bill.

As the OFT identified in 2001, arguments for maintaining standards tend to coincide with arguments for monopolies, restrictions on practice and high rewards.[15] Another consequence of professionalism that has historically not been addressed but is the subject of much current debate in the light of the Legal Services Bill discussed below is the extent to which it may impede the expansion of legal services.[16] So, the issue is the extent to which professionals control what they are prepared to supply rather than whether they endeavour to meet a need.[17] Aspects of professionalism that may inhibit such development are that problems tend to be defined in the professional's terms, rendering other definitions irrelevant; outsiders may be ignored on the grounds that they are not competent to assess or criticise; "specialised knowledge" may be guarded by "the creation of special forms of jargonised discourse and the fostering of an air of impenetrable mystery"[18]; emphasis on the individual lawyer-client relationship may inhibit the development of group representation and test-case strategies[19] and the proper advertising of services may be prevented.[20] However, it is also important to recognise that, whilst still thinking of themselves as professionals, the organisation of solicitors into firms, and larger and larger firms at that, is increasingly forcing them to act as businesses and business people. This drives them to consider how to maximise their existing markets, by, e.g., advertising their

---

[12] However, the individual activities of an individual within a law firm may be less than "professional" in level, "The results of specialisation in the legal profession, competition and changes in legal aid have led to a form of industrialisation within the legal sector. Legal work is often organised in a more standardised and repetitive fashion. Work is de-skilled and broken up into different activities which can be handled by lower level operatives. Many working within this new system find it easier to begin areas of highly complex work. However, long hours and the repetitive nature of the work have caused many young solicitors stress and worries about whether they have made the right choice of career": A. Sherr, "Professional Work, Professional Careers and Legal Education: Educating the Lawyer for 2010" (2000) 7(3) I.J.L.P. 325.

[13] References are to the Bill as amended in committee 6 March 2007, the most complete version at the time of writing (May 2007).

[14] Johnson (1972), p.45.

[15] See below, para.3–015.

[16] R. Cotterell, "Legal Services and Professional Ideology" (1980) Conference paper, and P. Fennell, "Solicitors, their markets and their ignorant public: the crisis of the professional ideas" in Z. Bankowski and G. Mungham (eds), *Essays in Law and Society* (1980), p.1.

[17] See, for example, S. Tomsen and M. A. Noone, "Service beyond Self-Interest? Australian lawyers, legal aid and professionalism" (2001) 8(3) I.J.L.P. 251. The issue of firms withdrawing from provision of legally aided services on economic grounds is also particularly current in the light of developments in public funding, considered further in Chs 10 and 11.

[18] Cotterell (1980), p.10.

[19] See below, para.11–016.

[20] See also Ch.8.

existing services, and to examine the potential of alternative markets. Of course, not all solicitors are motivated by business needs, but the vast majority of firms are. Private client work is rarely undertaken by large City of London firms[21] and that is particularly true of social welfare areas of work that tends to be undertaken, when undertaken by lawyers at all, by Law Centres and by private solicitors with a serious social conscience and mission.[22]

Many of the problematic features of professionalism have come under attack in recent years. The OFT produced its report on *Competition in Professions* in March 2001,[23] The status quo, preferred by the Royal Commission on Legal Services in 1979, has not prevailed as pressures to modernise, reform and provide a more societally acceptable and consumer-focused service has involved change for both barristers and solicitors.[24]

At the time of writing, however, the most pressing challenge to the nature of legal services[25] is that prompted by the Clementi review of the regulation of the provision of legal services ("Clementi"),[26] followed by proposals for action set out in the Department for Constitutional Affairs White Paper *The Future of Legal Services: Putting Consumers First*[27] and enshrined at the time of writing in a Legal Services Bill anticipated to be law by the end of 2007.[28] In October 2005, a government view of the "legal services market" was reported in *Putting Consumers First* as demonstrating "a range of increasingly fragmented and fast-moving market places, in which a wide spectrum of consumers is being supplied by an expanding range of different services, supplied by providers who may have nothing in common other than the fact that their services have some legal element".[29] The then identity of regulation and representative functions in the regulatory bodies (principally the Law Society and Bar Council) was identified as leading to the result that "[c]onsumers cannot have confidence that the organisations charged with regulating their members *and* representing them will

---

[21] See A. Sherr and J. Webb, "Law students, the external market and socialisation; do we make them turn to the City?"(1989) 16(2) *Journal of Law and Society* 16; R. G. Lee, *Firm Views: Work of and Work in the Largest Law Firms* (1999, Law Society Research Study 35).

[22] Even if a solicitor in a large firm has such a conscience and mission it is not necessarily appropriate to fulfil the firm's pro bono mission by doing some types of work because all work requires expertise and working in company/commercial areas provides little if any background for working with private clients in social welfare areas of law. Nevertheless, there is a growing commitment, even in large commercial firms, to increasing amounts of pro bono activity. For pro bono activities generally, see *www.probonouk.net* and Law Society Research Paper (2003) *The Pro Bono Work of Solicitors Findings from Omnibus Survey Nine 2002* and the website of LawWorks (previously the Solicitors' Pro Bono Group) at *www.lawworks.org.uk* and the Bar equivalent at *www,barprobono.org.uk.* and *http://www.freerepresentationunit.org.uk*

[23] See also OFT *Competition in Professions—Progress Statement* (2002).

[24] One of the effects of the OFT report was the introduction by the Bar of direct access to barristers by the public in some circumstances. It also prompted an LCD consultation paper (2002) and a DCA Report (2003) concluding that an independent review was required.

[25] "Thus we are one year away from the effective abolition of the legal profession in England and Wales . . . " K. Underwood, "The Legal Services Bill—Death by Regulation" (2007) 26(JAN) C.J.Q. 124 at 124.

[26] Clementi, D., *Review of the Regulatory Framework for Legal Services in England and Wales: a consultation paper* (March 2004) and *Report of the Review of the Regulatory Framework for Legal Services in England and Wales* (December 2004): available at: *www.legal-services-review. org.uk/content/report/index.htm.*

[27] Cm. 6679, 2005.

[28] Cm. 6839, May 2006.

[29] *op. cit.*, p.14.

put the interests of consumers above those of their members".[30] Existing regulation overall was regarded as unhelpfully complex and confusing[31] but the ultimate focus of the proposals now contained in the Legal Services Bill is in the following main areas:

(a) simplifying regulation by the creation of a Legal Services Board ("LSB")[32] with statutory objectives including the promotion of public and consumer interests, reporting to the Secretary of State for Constitutional Affairs and assisted by a Consumer Panel[33]; the LSB then regulating[34] "front line regulators" such as the new Bar Standards Board and Solicitors' Regulation Authority.[35] The "regulatory objectives" of the new structure are listed in cl.1 of the Legal Services Bill as:

"(a) supporting the constitutional principle of the rule of law;
(b) improving access to justice;
(c) protecting and promoting the interests of consumers;
(d) promoting competition in the provision of [reserved legal activities such as rights of audience and conduct of litigation];
(e) encouraging an independent, strong, diverse and effective legal profession;
(f) increasing public understanding of the citizen's legal rights and duties;
(g) promoting and maintaining adherence to the professional principles."

(b) consumer complaints in respect of all legal services will be handled by a single Office for Legal Complaints.[36]

(c) allowing for legal services to be delivered more flexibly through "alternative business structures".[37] Such organisations might include groupings of solicitors and barristers together or lawyers and non-lawyers (as, for example, insurance companies, banks, estate agents or even supermarkets).[38]

Whilst the actual effects of the Bill, assuming it is enacted in its current form, are unknown at the date of writing, the potential effects, particularly in limiting

---

[30] ibid.
[31] Vividly demonstrated in the diagram appearing on p.11 of *Putting Consumers First*.
[32] Legal Services Bill, Pt 2.
[33] ibid. cll.8–11.
[34] ibid. Pt 4.
[35] *Putting Consumers First* suggested that existing professional bodies such as the Law Society, Bar Council and Institute of Legal Executives would continue to be authorised regulators under the Legal Services Board scheme "provided they can satisfy the LSB about their governance arrangements" (p.78).
[36] Legal Services Bill, Pt 6. See also S. Young "Tomorrow's World Part 1" and "Part 2" (2006) 156(7239), N.L.J. 1351.
[37] Legal Services Bill, Pt 5.
[38] *Putting Consumers First*, pp.39 *et seq*. Three possible levels of alternative business structure, otherwise "legal disciplinary partnerships" are envisaged: type 1 (barristers and solicitors); type 2 (lawyers and ancillary professionals, e.g. legal executives or licensed conveyancers not as employees but as owners of the business); and type 3 (ownership including non-lawyers, such as banks or insurers): J. Blanes i Vidal; I. Jewitt and C. Leaver, *Legal Disciplinary Practices, A Discussion of the Clementi Proposals* (DCA, 2005). The provision of legal services through supermarkets—which have already moved into the banking and insurance fields—has been widely discussed as "Tescolaw". A legal services business has, at the time of writing, just been established by the Co-operative Group as "the Co-Operative Legal Services".

the self-regulation of the legal professions and in potentially expanding the provision of legal services very widely beyond the remit of the traditional two professions, are enormous.

B. THE LEGAL PROFESSION TODAY

1. ORGANISATION

3–003 The legal profession is conventionally divided into two branches: barristers and solicitors. The Bar has developed from the work of advocates since medieval times being based, primarily, in the four Inns of Court which still exist to-day: Gray's Inn, Inner Temple, Lincoln's Inn and Middle Temple. Solicitors have developed a line of work originally in meeting the needs of clients unable to process litigation for themselves. The Bar has been largely untouched by government, though this will change under the Legal Services Bill, and has run itself through the Inns of Court, which have been dominated by senior barristers and judges as benchers of the Inns and also through the judicial control of practice in the courts. Solicitors have been regulated by government in one way or another since a statute of 1605 subjected solicitors[39] to a measure of control to prevent overcharging and to cut their numbers: only "skilfull" and "honest" men were allowed to practise. In 1728 an Act was passed for the better regulation of solicitors and a roll of solicitors was established. In 1831, the "Society of Attorneys Solicitors and Proctors and others not being barristers practising in the Courts of Law and Equity in the United Kingdom" received a Royal Charter, and changed its name, in 1833, to the Incorporated Law Society of the United Kingdom and subsequently in 1903, to "The Law Society".[40] What is now the separate Law Society of Northern Ireland was incorporated in 1922[41] and the Law Society of Scotland was formed in 1949.[42] The remit of the Law Society of England and Wales is to

> "strive to guarantee:
>
> - To the public—access to high quality legal services.
> - To solicitors—vigorous promotion of their interests.
> - To society—a leading voice on law reform.
>
> The following standards and values govern our relationships and activities with the stakeholders. The Law Society aims to be:
>
> - Accountable
> - Objective

---

[39] The regulation was also concerned with attorneys, who performed similar functions to those of solicitors, although were more engaged in litigation. Attorneys no longer exist as separate from barristers and solicitors although those previously known as "patent agents" have recently styled themselves "patent attorneys".

[40] A history of the organisation is available at *www.lawsociety.org.uk/aboutlawsociety/whoweare/abouthistory.law*.

[41] See *www.lawsoc-ni.org/council.htm*.

[42] See *www.lawscot.org.uk/about*.

- Transparent
- Inclusive
- Fair
- Honest
- Decisive
- Collectively responsible
- Mutually respectful."

The governing body of the Bar is the General Council of the Bar of England and Wales, which defines its principal objectives as:

> "• To represent the Bar as a modern and forward looking profession which seeks to maintain and improve the quality and standard of service to all clients;
> • To maintain and enhance professional standards;
> • To maintain effective complaints and disciplinary procedures;
> • To develop an effective, fair and affordable system for recruiting, and of regulating entry to the profession;
> • To regulate education and training for the profession;
> • To combat discrimination and disadvantage at the Bar;
> • To develop and promote the work of the Bar;
> • To conduct research and promote the Bar's views on matters affecting the administration of justice, including substantive law reform;
> • To provide services for members of the Bar, e.g. Fees Collection, publications, conferences, guidance on practice management and development;
> • To promote the Bar's interests with Government, the EC, the Law Society, International Bars and other organisations with common interests."[43]

It co-operates with the Inns of Court through the Council of the Inns of Court. The independence of the Inns has been reduced as the Bar Council's policy is to be adopted if there is a disagreement with the Council of the Inns provided it has the support of two thirds of the profession.

The powers and duties of the Law Society are now derived from the Solicitors' Act 1974,[44] as amended. Membership of the Society is, perhaps surprisingly, not compulsory following qualification as a solicitor, even though it is the governing body for the profession as a whole.[45] The Master of the Rolls may only admit as a solicitor a person certified by the Society's independent Solicitors' Regulatory Authority ("SRA") to have complied with its training regulations and to be suitable for admission.[46] SRA also issues the "practising certificate" which every solicitor wishing to practise must have.[47]

---

[43] See *www.barcouncil.org.uk.*

[44] See also Courts and Legal Services Act 1990; Access to Justice Act 1999; Legal Services Bill.

[45] The effect of the Legal Services Bill may be that individual solicitors or barristers or groups of them, might find themselves working for organisations with a different regulator, that regulator still reporting to the Legal Services Board. In anticipation of the Bill, the regulatory functions of the Law Society have been vested in the Solicitors' Regulatory Authority: *www.sra.org.uk.*

[46] Solicitors Act 1974, s.3. Qualification as a solicitor is discussed in more detail below.

[47] *ibid.* ss.1 and 9–18.

2. LAWYERS AND THEIR WORK

(a) Introduction

3–004   In their study of the legal profession in the United States and England, Johnstone and Hopson identified 19 different "work tasks" performed by lawyers in the United States: giving advice, both legal and non-legal; negotiations; drafting letters and legal documents; litigation, including the preparation of cases and advocacy; investigation of facts; legal research and analysis; lobbying legislators and administrators; acting as broker; public relations; filing submissions to government and other organisations; adjudication; financing; property management; referral to clients of other sources of assistance; supervision of others' emotional support to clients; immoral and unpleasant tasks (taking care of disagreeable matters for clients which the client could do themselves but prefer to have someone else to do); acting as scapegoat; and getting business.[48] Even if this was or remains an accurate list of tasks, it is not to say that every lawyer ever or always performs all of them.[49] Some, such as advising and negotiation, are more generally significant than others. It is important to note that many, if not all, could be done by laymen. An important challenge to the legal profession in the light of the Legal Services Bill is the competition from others for services that lawyers currently provide. Whether the lawyer can be better, more efficient and provide greater value for money than other providers of legal services is a critical question for the lawyer to address urgently in the new landscape created by the Legal Services Bill.

(b) Fusion[50]

3–005   The English pattern of legal work is complicated by the division of the profession into barristers and solicitors, although the extent to which that division survives in any practical sense once the "alternative business structures" of the Legal Services Bill are in place remains to be seen. Traditionally, barristers have had an exclusive right of audience in the superior courts and have been instructed only by a solicitor client and not a lay client. Both traditions are, however, at least in principle, in a state of decline. Solicitors may obtain, currently by exemption, assessment or training and assessment, rights of audience in the higher courts (Crown Court, High Court, Court of Appeal and House of Lords)[51] and, at the time of writing, the Solicitors' Regulation Authority is considering allowing all solicitors to assert such rights of audience on qualification in any event, without

---

[48] Q. Johnstone and D. Hopson, *Lawyers and their Work* (1967), Ch.3. One might usefully compare this with the list of activities contained in the "day one outcomes" proposed by the Training Framework review of the Law Society as representing what a solicitor should be capable of at the point of qualification. See further below at para.3–051.

[49] The variety of combinations in an individual lawyer was almost endless: *ibid.* p.77.

[50] Royal Commission on Legal Services, *Report, Vol.1* (1979), pp.187–202; G. Gardiner, "Two Layers or One" (1970) 23 C.L.P. 1; M. Zander, *Lawyers and the Public Interest* (1968), pp.271–332, (1976) 73 L.S. Gaz. 882, *Legal Services for the Community* (1978), pp.170–174; F. A. Mann, "Fusion of the Legal Professions?" (1977) 93 L.Q.R. 367; P. Reeves, *Are Two Professions Necessary?* (1986).

[51] See Courts and Legal Services Act 1990, s.27 and the Law Society Higher Courts Qualification Regulations 2000. Solicitors with such qualifications are known as "solicitor-advocates".

additional training or assessment.[52] Barristers may now accept instructions otherwise than through a solicitor from members of a number of professions (whether on their own behalf or for their clients), such as accountants, architects, engineers, valuers, actuaries and insurers.[53] Barristers who have undertaken specific training in order to do so may accept instructions directly from lay clients, except in most circumstances relating to immigration and asylum, family law and crime.[54] However, there is no *kind* of work that is done by a barrister that is not done by a solicitor and very few, if any, kinds of work done by solicitors that are not also done, even if under supervision, by legal executives, paralegals and others. Advocacy in the lower courts has always been shared, indeed shared with non-lawyers in tribunals as well. Both barristers and solicitors do drafting work; and both give legal advice (solicitors directly to the client; barristers, traditionally through an oral or written opinion provided to a solicitor[55]).

The different emphases on the type of work done have led to marked differences in the geographical distribution of barristers and solicitors. Barristers have to be near the superior courts and so over 35 per cent of barristers work from chambers in central London.[56] The rest are spread through over 30 provincial centres.[57] Solicitors' offices are found throughout the country.[58] There are significant organisational differences. Barristers must be self-employed to carry out the full range of their activities. They cannot share fees nor can they—at present—employ fee-earners. To gain the advantages of working together, they congregate in chambers. Solicitors may enter partnerships, limited liability partnerships or incorporated practices.[59]

Over the years there have been many advocates for fusion of the two branches. In many other countries, including some of those originally developed from the English profession, there is no such formal distinction, rather, the individual opts to specialise in a particular area such as advocacy, rather than having to make such an election at the pre-qualification stage.

In 1977, the Royal Commission on Legal Services received submissions that **3–006** the necessity of employing a solicitor and a barrister caused inefficiency (failures in communication, delay and the return of briefs by barristers who are double-booked or whose previous cases(s) overrun); harmed the confidence of clients (barristers being regarded by some clients as too remote or insufficiently prepared) and was more expensive for clients obliged to pay for two lawyers rather than one. The Law Society and the Bar opposed fusion. In particular, it was feared that fusion would lead to a serious fall in the quality of advocacy;

---

[52] See, for example, C. Baksi, "Move to End Higher Rights" L.S.G., December 7, 2006; K. Hanley, "Access all areas" L.S.G. January 25, 2007. The Solicitors' Regulation Authority's consultation on the subject is closed in April 2007 and can be found at *www.sra.org.uk/consultations.page*.

[53] Under the Bar Council's Licensed Access Rules and Recognition Regulations. Use of a barrister under this scheme does not prevent the client being a litigant in person for costs purposes: *Agassi v Robinson (Inspector of Taxes) (Costs)* [2005] EWCA Civ 1507; D. Capper, "Costs Recovery under Bar Licensed Access Scheme" (2007) 26(JAN) C.J.Q. 23.

[54] Under the Bar Council Public Access Rules.

[55] The reason may be the peculiar expertise of the barrister, or it may be that the opinion of a barrister will carry more weight in the particular circumstances, or it may be that the solicitor is too busy and/or that the barrister's opinion is more cost effective.

[56] BDO Stoy Hayward, *Report of the 2001 Survey of Barristers' Chambers* (2001), para.3.5

[57] See below, para.3–024.

[58] See below, para.3–009.

[59] See below, para.3–008.

barristers might join solicitors' firms and become less accessible,[60] particularly because smaller solicitors' firms that could not employ barristers might find it increasingly difficult to access high quality barristers; the drift from small to larger firms might continue and reduce the number of firms in smaller towns and rural areas; smaller firms might be reluctant to refer a client on to a larger firm for fear of losing business in the longer term; and there might be a reduction in the number of specialist advocates thereby reducing standards of advocacy and also reducing the pool of persons suitable to become judges. Other arguments against fusion at that time, at least, centred on the English form of court procedure although some of the objections made on the basis of the orality of the trial must have considerably less cogency in civil procedure given the increase in written presentation of evidence inherent in the Civil Procedure Rules.[61] It was not surprising, therefore, that the Royal Commission unanimously recommended against fusion, notwithstanding the speculative nature of some of the arguments.

The fusion argument still goes on[62] in the background to many of the reforms of the legal profession and of civil and criminal procedure and practice.[63] The opening up of higher court advocacy to solicitors and removal of other monopolies historically held by the solicitors' profession, as well as the increase in barristers being employed in solicitors' firms, has led to a considerable blurring of the boundaries between the two professions. The impact of the Legal Services Bill, particularly in its promotion of "alternative business structures" as well as its further removal of monopolies, may, of course, lead not to a fused profession but to groups of solicitors and barristers, and, indeed, other professionals, working together in joint organisations.

(c) Solicitors' practices and their work

(i) *Numbers*

3–007   As at July 31, 2006, there were 131,347 solicitors on the roll (56.4 per cent men and 43.6 per cent women), of whom 104,543 had current practising certificates. Of the solicitors with practising certificates, 44,393 were women (42.5 per cent); 9,471 were from ethnic minority groups (9.1 per cent). Over a half was aged 40 or less (54.2 per cent), with the average age being 37.4 years for women and 43.7 years for men. 80,575 worked in private practice. Just under a third of those worked in small firms (1–4 partners; 31 per cent), and in middle-sized firms (5–25 partners; 30 per cent), whereas a slightly bigger proportion (39 per cent) worked in large firms (26+ partners). The 0.3 per cent of firms with 81+ partners employ 22.3 per cent of all solicitors whereas sole practices employ only 8.2 per cent of all solicitors.[64] 35.7 per cent of all solicitors are either partners or sole practitioners. 23, 968 of those with practising certificates (23 per cent) do not work in private practice, but in commerce and industry, local and national

---

[60] The law firm Herbert Smith LLP has, however, maintained an in-house advocacy unit since 2005 which contains barrister advocates and is headed by a barrister Q.C. who is also a partner in the firm. Other firms may have similar arrangements.

[61] See Mann (1977) and discussion of the Civil Procedure Rules 1998 in Chs 12 and 15.

[62] P. Knott, "Training the Next Millennium's Lawyers: Is there a Case for Joint Professional Legal Education?" (1999) 33 L.T. 50.

[63] *The Work and Organisation of the Legal Profession* (Cm. 570, 1989), *Contingency Fees* (Cm. 571, 1989), and *Conveyancing by Authorised Practitioners* (Cm. 572, 1989).

[64] These figures exclude multi-national partnerships and incorporated practices.

government (including the CPS). Since 1976, the total number of solicitors with practising certificates has grown by 234.5 per cent. Even more starkly, between 1996 and 2006, the number increased from 68,037 to 104,543.

In addition to the increasing size of the profession, important trends include increased recruitment of women and members of ethnic minorities to the profession. In recent times, women have formed the majority of new entrants, and in 2005/06 they formed 59.4 per cent of admissions to the roll. In 2005/06 1,030 of the 7,075 individuals admitted to the roll (18.9 per cent of those with known ethnicity) were from minority ethnic groups. Fewer solicitors are working in private practice, though still the vast majority do so: in 2006, 23 per cent of those with practising certificates worked outside private practice, from 15 per cent in 1990. An increasingly smaller proportion of solicitors are becoming partners or sole practitioners: in 2006, 35.7 per cent were principals, from 64 per cent in 1990.[65]

(ii) *Solicitors' firms: private practice*

Solicitors are most likely to organise as sole practitioners, partnerships or limited liability partnerships. Since the Administration of Justice Act 1985, it has been possible for them to incorporate,[66] provided there is compliance with the Solicitors' *Code of Conduct 2007*, rule 14.[67] As at July 31, 2006, there were 941 incorporated firms in England and Wales, 8,926 partnerships and 124 multinational partnerships. 42.4 per cent of all firms are based in London and the South East.[68]   **3–008**

There is no such thing as the typical firm. The range[69] includes firms which work almost exclusively in company and commercial work. These firms are often very large and are situated either in the City of London or other large conurbations where there are businesses for them to serve.[70] Some of these firms will be in "The Magic Circle" which consists of the top 10 or so firms in London.[71] A number of US firms have also, in recent years, successfully established presences

---

[65] All figures taken from *Trends in the Solicitors' Profession, Annual Statistical Report 2006* (The Law Society).

[66] Solicitors' Incorporated Practices Order 1991, SI 1991/2684.

[67] Replacing the Solicitors' Incorporated Practice Rules.

[68] *Annual Statistical Report 2006, op. cit.*

[69] One typology indicates that there are six kinds of firm: classical (follows the traditional image), managerial (strong managerial culture), political (organised around person commitment to particular types of client), routine (routine work done and little to distinguish one firm from another), large (the very big firms seeing a concentration of legal resources within them) and boutique (specialised firms operating in a narrow area of work): Boon and Levin (1999), pp.73–78, and which builds upon M. McConville, J. Hodgson, L. Bridges and A. Pavlovic, *Standing Accused: The Organisation and Practices of Criminal Defence Lawyers in Britain* (1994).

[70] These large firms will have a continuing and significant impact on the organisation and regulation of the profession. As Boon and Levin point out, some of the effects are negative because they attract corporate commercial work away from smaller firms which become less viable; they present a particular image of the profession to the public and policy makers; only they tend to attract the most able entrants to the profession; and they can effectively influence the professional bodies in particular directions. But their influence can be positive, e.g. they offer a democratic and meritocratic environment for employees: Boon and Levin (1999), pp.77–78.

[71] Variously defined. However, *The Lawyer* magazine's top 10 firms in terms of financial performance in 2006 were Clifford Chance LLP, Linklaters, Freshfields Bruckhaus Deringer, Allen and Overy LLP, Lovells, *DLA Piper UK LLP*, *Eversheds LLP*, Slaughter and May, Herbert Smith LLP, Simmons & Simmons: *www.thelawyer.com/uk100*. The firms listed in italics are national, rather than London-based, firms. Clifford Chance LLP, Freshfields Bruckhaus Deringer and Allen and Overy LLP also appear in the top 10 "global" firms.

in London. Some of these firms are not based in London, but are very large national firms (and often will undertake a very wide range of work). Niche firms specialise in particular areas of work such as shipping law and media and entertainment law. Some firms specialise in working as part of the Community Legal Service or the Criminal Defence Service (previously legal aid work). Some firms offer a generalist service. Excluding incorporated firms and multinational partnerships, in 2006, there were: 4,132 sole practitioners (46.3 per cent of all private practice firms); 3,633 firms of 2–4 principals (40.7 per cent); 793 firms of 5–10 principals (8.9 per cent); 252 firms of 11–25 principals (2.8 per cent); and 116 firms of 26 or more principals (1.3 per cent). Law Society statistics no longer include data on non-solicitor fee earners (such as employed barristers, paralegals and legal executives) or on administrative and support staff.[72] However, in 2000, 52 per cent of firm employees were administrative and support staff, and there were 30,284 non-solicitor fee earners[73]

(iii) *Solicitors' work*

3–009   There has been a continuing trend for some types of work to necessitate large firms, and this is particularly true of those firms and incorporated firms that undertake primarily company/commercial work, where the expansion has not only been domestic but also global. The clients of the large firms are often large, frequently multinational or international business organisations that demand attention and support whenever it is needed and demand specialised expertise and experience. Whilst commercial property and business/commercial affairs work forms 44 per cent of the work of 419 firms involved in the Law Society *Firms Business Survey 2003*, it forms 53 per cent of the work of the largest firms. The following table provides further information.[74]

Type of work   **Size of firm**

	Sole practitioner	2–5 solicitors	6–12 solicitors	13–40 solicitors	41–170 solicitors	All responding firms
	Mean %	Mean %	Mean %	Mean %	Mean %	Mean %
Commercial property	7	5	12	14	14	13
Business/ commercial affairs	8	8	7	15	39	31
Personal injury, accident and clinical negligence	7	6	8	21	14	14

[72] Law Society, *Annual Statistical Report 2006*, table 3.6. The Law Society fact sheet *Solicitors' Firms 2003* reports an average of 0.45 paralegals per solicitor.
[73] Law Society, *Annual Statistical Report 2000* (2001), table 4.1.
[74] Law Society, *The Solicitors' Profession in England and Wales* (2000), p.49.

	Sole practitioner	2–5 solicitors	6–12 solicitors	13–40 solicitors	41–170 solicitors	All responding firms
	Mean %	Mean %	Mean %	Mean %	Mean %	Mean %
Residential conveyancing	40	19	20	15	5	9
Probate, wills & trusts	7	5	8	10	4	6
Family law	11	7	11	8	4	5
Crime	6	14	16	5	3	5
Housing law	4	2	3	1	1	1
Welfare benefits	0	0	0	0	0	0
Personal bankruptcy insolvency & debt	0	1	1	1	1	1
Employment law	3	2	2	3	6	5
Consumer problems	0	0	0	1	0	0
Personal financial management	0	0	0	1	1	1
Other matters	6	28	9	6	8	8
No. of firms	*86*	*102*	*89*	*73*	*56*	*406*

This table confirms the importance of private litigants to the smaller firms and the location of social welfare work and Legal Services Commission funded work in smaller firms. The large firms do very little private client work. This can also be seen from the following table that forms part of the same survey, showing the average percentage of fee income from each type of client.

Type of client   **Size of firm**

	Sole practitioner	2–5 solicitors	6–12 solicitors	13–40 solicitors	41–170 solicitors	All responding firms
	Mean %	Mean %	Mean %	Mean %	Mean %	Mean %
Private individuals (not legally aided	69	50	47	47	19	28
Private individuals (legally aided)	11	29	27	11	4	9

	Sole practitioner	2–5 solicitors	6–12 solicitors	13–40 solicitors	41–170 solicitors	All responding firms
	Mean %	Mean %	Mean %	Mean %	Mean %	Mean %
Private sector firms	13	16	20	33	51	43
Public sector bodies	4	0	1	1	4	3
Other British clients	0	1	1	3	6	5
Overseas clients	2	4	4	6	17	13
No. of firms	*84*	*97*	*88*	*71*	*56*	*396*

Geographically, the spread of private practice partnerships is uneven,[75] as is clear from the following table.[76]

Size of firm by number of principals

Standard region	1	2–4	5–10	11–25	26–80	81+	Total
City of London	221	183	72	56	40	19	592
Rest of London	971	767	85	20	8	1	1,852
Rest of South East	736	460	99	40	8	1	1,344
Eastern	444	400	70	30	3	0	946
South West	311	220	67	23	8	0	629
West Midlands	299	326	70	16	3	0	714
East Midlands	179	182	44	16	4	1	425
Yorkshire and Humberside	254	260	68	18	8	2	609
North West (inc. Merseyside)	418	480	130	27	8	1	1,064
North East	115	127	38	2	2	0	284
Wales	183	228	50	4	1	0	465
England and Wales	**4,132**	**3,633**	**793**	**252**	**91**	**25**	**8,926**

3–010   Concentration of solicitors in conurbations and, indeed, in capital cities is hardly surprising. Firms need to be where the business is, whatever the nature of the business that the firm wishes to attract.[77] So, if a firm wishes to attract work from multinational companies, it is likely to need to be situated where they are;

---

[75] See C. Harding and J. Williams (eds), *Legal Provision in the Rural Environment* (1994).
[76] Law Society, *Annual Statistical Report 2006*, table 3.5.
[77] For the geographical accessibility of legal advice to individuals, see below, para.9–010.

if a firm wishes to attract business from individuals making wills and buying and selling houses, it needs to be where they live and/or work; if a firm wishes to attract criminal business, it needs to be near the courts.

Some firms have specialised in publicly funded work and now are contracted suppliers for either or both the Community Legal Service and the Criminal Defence Service established by the Legal Services Commission. Such work has been traditionally viewed as low status.[78] However, recent proposals to reform public funding, particularly in criminal cases, are highly controversial and are discussed further in Chs 10 and 11.

Firms have had to become much more business minded following the reduction in availability of publicly funded work, and will have to be even more so as the legal services market potentially expands as a result of the Legal Services Bill. The need to focus on commerciality has already been experienced by those firms that had traditionally relied upon residential conveyancing. Whilst it is still a major form of business for some firms, the profit margins are significantly reduced. Similarly, the advent of the claims management company offering "no win, no fee" arrangements in personal injury cases has caused personal injury specialist firms to reconsider their position. Other drivers of the solicitors' business include the general nature of the economy, since the more buoyant it is the more work needs to be done by solicitors in supporting the makers of goods and the providers of services,[79] developments in litigation[80] and the development of work overseas.[81]

(iv) *Solicitors' remuneration*

In 2005, the Law Society produced the following table.[82]   **3–011**

---

[78] Goriely has concluded that there is a four-stage process in relation to such work: denial of the need; lack of legal profession response; response by advice agencies; legal professional invasion of the territory: T. Goriely, "Law for the poor: the relationship between advice agencies and solicitors in the development of poverty law" (1996) 3 I.J.L. Profession 215 as discussed in Boon and Levin (1999), p.58.

[79] When times are hard, lawyers still have work to do, such as insolvency work, but it is less than when times are good.

[80] See below, Ch.11.

[81] Increasingly English law firms either have arrangements with firms in other jurisdictions or are buying such firms. A number of US firms in particular have also established a significant presence in London.

[82] Law Society, *Private Practice Solicitors' Salaries 2005, table 2.* Other salary surveys are produced by recruitment agencies such as Michael Page Legal and Chambers Guide to the Legal Profession, whose student site can be found at *www.chambersandpartners.com/Chambers Student/index.cfm.* See also R. McNabb and V. Wass, "Male-female earnings differentials among lawyers in Britain: a legacy of the law or a current practice?" (2006) 13 *Labour Economics,* 219.

		Men	Women
		£ per annum	£ per annum
Assistant/associate solicitor	Lower quartile	35,205	32,000
	Median	46,000	40,000
	Upper quartile	60,000	52,995
No.		149	195
Salaried Partner	Lower quartile	41,870	39,625
	Median	80,000	46,999
	Upper quartile	100,000	73,145
No.		25	17
Equity Partner	Lower quartile	41,000	30,000
	Median	70,000	44,250
	Upper quartile	100,000	79,719
No.		92	33

(v) *Specialisation*

3–012   There has been an increasing tendency for solicitors to specialise in certain areas of law. As the amount of new law and the areas of work have expanded, the corollary is that it is difficult to do anything but specialise and, for individuals, increasingly early in the career. This is, of course, a serious challenge for sole practitioners, who usually need to retain focus on a relatively limited range of work and so also specialise. It has become common for league tables to be devised to compare the reputation and workload of the leading firms in different areas of practice.[83] Specialisation has also had the consequence that the division of work between solicitors and barristers has been less clear, the more solicitors, especially in large firms, specialise.[84] Further, increasing specialisation has potential serious consequences for the profession as it may induce not just diversity but also a lack of professional coherence. Thus lawyers in the corporate sphere may have different approaches to other lawyers; their firms may approach similar problems in different ways; the divide between private practitioners and employed solicitors[85] may become a gulf and thus the professional bodies may have difficulty in speaking for and regulating the professions.[86] This effect is

[83] e.g. the online *Chambers Guide* which contains listings of the best firms in certain fields and lists the "leaders" in each such field: *www.chambersandpartners.com/uk/search31.aspx*.

[84] Boon and Levin (1999), pp.81–82.

[85] See below, para.3–013.

[86] See Boon and Levin (1999), pp.89–94. Of course, as they point out, one factor in all this is growth in size which produces less professional coherence in any case. It does not necessarily follow that professional coherence is always desirable.

beginning to show itself in discussion of the pre-qualification education of solicitors prompted by the Law Society's Training Framework Review.[87]

The Law Society has also been behind specialisation. Specialist panels of solicitors are intended to identify solicitors with particular competence. Solicitors not on the panel can still undertake such work, but the SRA promotes membership of a panel as a form of quality assurance[88] and panel membership is recognised by the Legal Services Commission. The panels are: Children Panel[89]; Civil and Commercial Mediation Panel; Clinical Negligence Panel; Family Law Panel; Family Law Panel—Advanced; Family Mediation Panel; Immigration Panel; Mental Health Review Tribunal Panel; Personal Injury Panel; and Planning Panel.

(vi) *Employed solicitors*

By "employed solicitors", we mean solicitors who are employees of non-solicitors.[90] The types of organisation employing solicitors outside private practice at present are demonstrated by the following table.[91]   **3–013**

Type of business	Total solicitors employed	Men	Women
Commerce and Industry	8,611	4,714	3,897
Accountancy practice	92	42	50
Nationalised Industries	59	16	43
Trades Unions	52	24	28
Government department	185	115	70

---

[87] See 3–034.

[88] "All panel members [who may include legal executives as well as solicitors] have successfully completed a range of stringent tests, examinations, interviews and role-play assessments; their fitness and suitability to be panel members has been investigated and confirmed." *http://www.law-society.org.uk/choosingandusing/specialise/accreditedpanels.law.* In addition to the panels, the SRA operates an accreditation scheme for publicly funded criminal and duty solicitor work (Criminal Litigation Accreditation Scheme); the award of rights of audience in the Higher Courts; an accreditation scheme for non-solicitors (often former police officers employed by solicitors' firms) wishing to advise clients at the police station (Police Station Representatives Accreditation Scheme) and may license individual solicitors to act as insolvency practitioners under the Insolvency Act 1986.

[89] Children Panel members may be "adult party representatives" or "children representatives". See the Law Society website for further details of panel membership and qualification.

[90] *Solicitors' Code of Conduct 2007*, rule 13: In-house practice, replacing Solicitors' Practice Rules 1990, r.4(1).

[91] Law Society, *Annual Statistical Report 2006*, table 2.7.

Type of business	Total solicitors employed	Men	Women
Local government	3,705	1,494	2,215
Court	77	37	40
Government funded services	227	89	138
Crown Prosecution Service	2,266	1,015	1,251
Advice service	395	133	262
Educational establishment[92]	199	62	137
Health Services	55	16	39
Other	552	220	332
Total	**16,475**	**7,977**	**8,498**

The numbers and importance of lawyers in industry, i.e. in-house lawyers, whose professional practice is governed by *Solicitors' Code of Conduct 2007*, rule 13,[93] have grown substantially in recent times. They are likely to be concerned with property and planning, contracts, financial services, mergers and acquisitions, company law, debt recovery, employment law, intellectual property rights, pensions law and EU law.[94] Lawyers in local government are likely to have to work over a very wide range.[95] Their primary areas of work fall into two categories. The first concerns areas of local authority responsibility, including housing, land use planning, highways and transportation, general local government work,[96] and social services.[97] The second concerns general legal work, in particular conveyancing, local planning inquiries, contracts, debt collection, criminal, and child care.[98] The activities of employed solicitors are governed by *Solicitors' Code of Conduct 2007*, rule 13, governing "in-house practice". The fact that the Legal Services Bill will allow for "alternative business structures" may require a redefinition of this concept if, for example, non-lawyers such as banks or

---

[92] As these figures represent solicitors with practising certificates, this figure will tend to represent solicitors employed in college and university legal services departments, rather than their Faculties or Schools of Law, although, of course, some teaching solicitors will maintain a practising certificate.

[93] Replacing Solicitors' Practice Rules 1990, rule 4.

[94] R. Woolfson, J. Plotnikoff and D. Wilson, *Solicitors in the Employed Sector* (Law Society Research Study No.13, 1994), table 4.3, which indicates that other work includes: consumer and advertising, building law, personal injury, taxation, natural resources, and criminal law.

[95] *ibid.* p.23 and table 4.2.

[96] i.e. all Local Government Acts, constitutional and corporate matters not falling under other headings.

[97] *op. cit.*, table 4.4(a), which also indicates that the other areas of work are: environmental health, parks, recreation and tourism, economic development, environmental protection, licensing, waste collection, agriculture, arts, libraries and museums, consumer protection, education, fire and rescue, and police. Not every level of council deals with all these issues.

[98] *ibid.* table 4.4(b) which also indicates that other areas of work are: employment (including pensions), third party claims, and judicial review.

insurance companies become owners or part-owners of law firms; or multi-disciplinary partnerships develop including, say, lawyers, accountants, and tax advisers within a single private sector organisation.

(vii) *Practice Guidance*

As a result of adverse comments made in the Clementi review about the self-regulation of the two professions, the professional conduct of solicitors is now regulated by the Solicitors' Regulatory Authority.[99] It is anticipated that this body will be an "approved regulator" of the profession under the Legal Services Bill[100] subject to the overall regulation of the Legal Services Board. It is the duty of every solicitor to comply with the *Solicitors' Code of Conduct 2007*, replacing the *Guide to the Professional Conduct of Solicitors 1999* from 1 July 2007.[101] **3–014**

The fundamental "core duties" governing the professional conduct of solicitors, registered foreign lawyers, registered European Lawyers and "recognised bodies" subject to Law Society or Solicitors Regulation Authority regulation are to be found in *Solicitors Code of Conduct 2007*, rule 1[102]:

> **"1.01 Justice and the rule of law**
> You must uphold the rule of law and the proper administration of justice.
> **1.02 Integrity**
> You must act with integrity.
> **1.03 Independence**
> You must not allow your independence to be compromised.
> **1.04 Best interests of clients**
> You must act in the best interests of each client.
> **1.05 Standard of service**
> You must provide a good standard of service to your clients.
> **1.06 Public confidence**
> You must not behave in a way that is likely to diminish the trust the public places in you or the profession."

Guidance note 10 to rule 1 adds the following: "Members of the public must be able to place their trust in you. Any behaviour within or outside your professional practice which undermines this trust damages not only you but the ability of the profession as a whole to serve society". Solicitors are also required to treat information provided to them by their clients with confidence, (subject to limited exceptions) and to avoid acting in situations of conflict of interest.[103]

Solicitors and others authorised to conduct litigation must comply with Courts and Legal Services Act 1990:

> "Every person who exercises in relation to proceedings in any court a right to conduct litigation granted by an authorised body has (a) a duty to the

---

[99] Which now has its own website: *www.sra.org.uk*.
[100] See Legal Services Bill, Sch.5, para.1.
[101] It can be found on the Solicitors' Regulation Authority website.
[102] *Solicitors' Code of Conduct 2007*, rr.15 and 16 set out the obligations of solicitors practising outside the jurisdiction, replacing the Solicitors' Overseas Practice Rules 1990, r.3.
[103] Rules 16D and 16E, amended as from 2006. See J. Jarman, "Conflicts and Confidentiality; Part 1" (2006) 150(46) Sol. J. 1560 and "Conflicts and Confidentiality: Part 2" (2006) 150(47) Sol. J. 1597.

court to act with independence in the interests of justice; and (b) a duty to comply with rules of conduct of the body relating to the right and approved for the purposes of this section; and those duties shall override any obligation which the person may have (otherwise than under the criminal law) if it is inconsistent with them."[104]

In addition, *Solicitors Code of Conduct 2007*, rule 11.01(1) provides that "[y]ou must never deceive or knowingly or recklessly mislead the court".[105]

Solicitors also have obligations to avoid discrimination and "must not in [their] professional dealings with employees, partners, members, directors, barristers, other lawyers, clients or third parties discriminate, without lawful cause, against any person, nor victimise or harass them on the grounds of: (a) race or racial group (including colour, nationality and ethnic or national origins); (b) sex (including marital status, gender reassignment, pregnancy, maternity and paternity); (c) sexual orientation (including civil partnership status); (d) religion or belief; (e) age; or (f) disability".[106]

(viii) *Monopolies*

3–015   Solicitors for a long time enjoyed certain statutory monopolies. Section 20 of the Solicitors' Act 1974 made it an offence for an unqualified person to act as a solicitor and as such to commence or conduct litigation on behalf of another. An unqualified person may not pretend to be a solicitor.[107] The principal monopolies relate to litigation, conveyancing and probate and we will consider each in turn. The initial attack on existing monopolies of solicitors and barristers was contained in the Courts and Legal Services Act 1990, whose "statutory objective" was "the development of legal services in England and Wales (and in particular the development of advocacy, litigation, conveyancing and probate services) by making provision for new or better ways of providing such services and a wider choice of persons providing them, while maintaining the proper and efficient administration of justice".[108] The comparable "regulatory objectives" of cl.1 of the Legal Services Bill include "improving access to justice; protecting and promoting the interests of consumers[109]; promoting competition in the provision of [legal] services" and "encouraging an independent, strong, diverse and effective legal profession". The regulation proposals of the Legal Services Bill, create, not monopolies, as such, but forms of legal advice activity that can only be carried out by persons—whether solicitors, barristers or others—approved and regulated under that legislation. Part 3 of the Bill first regulates "reserved legal activity"[110]—advocacy in court; conduct of litigation; "reserved instrument activity"[111]; probate and notarial activities and the administration of oaths—and then defines "legal activity", which includes reserved legal activity but also

---

[104] This provision is re-enacted in Legal Services Bill, cl.180.
[105] Replacing principle 21.01 of the *Guide* to the effect that "[s]olicitors who act in litigation, whilst under a duty to do their best for their client, must never deceive or mislead the court".
[106] Replacing Solicitors' Anti-Discrimination Rules 2004.
[107] Solicitors Act 1974, s.21. See, e.g. *Carter v Butcher* [1966] 1 Q.B. 526.
[108] s.17.
[109] The background to the current bill is explicitly consumer-focused. See the DCA paper of October 2005; *The Future of Legal Services: Putting Consumers First*.
[110] cl.12. Further definitions appear in Sch.2.
[111] Generally, documents relating to the transfer and registration of land.

includes at cl.12(3)(b) a wider range of legal advice provision that may subsequently become reserved legal activity. Under cll.14 and 16 of the Legal Services Bill, it will be an offence to conduct a reserved legal activity without being explicitly authorised by the regulatory authorities or exempt from regulation, or to pretend to be authorised or exempt.

(1) *Litigation*

Here we must distinguish the activity involved in the conduct of litigation (see Ch.12 below) from advocacy in court, particularly in the higher courts. Traditionally the first has been the preserve of the solicitor and the second that of the barrister, with some overlap in relation to advocacy in the lower courts and in pre-trial hearings. The right to conduct litigation, other than as a litigant in person acting in his or her own case,[112] is currently governed by the Courts and Legal Services Act 1990, ss.28 and 31(2)(b), granting, subject to the rules of the Law Society, all solicitors a right to conduct litigation. There is no equivalent in the Act for barristers, although s.28 of the Act allowed for other authorised bodies to grant the right to conduct litigation. As far as the Bar is concerned, as we will see, only employed barristers have been granted this right by the Bar Council. However, other professions, as, for example, intellectual property professionals such as patent and trademark attorneys have been authorised to permit their members to conduct litigation.[113] Section 28 of the Courts and Legal Services Act is replaced by cl.9 of the Bill, so that conduct of litigation, defined in Sch.2, para.3, will be "reserved legal activity", only permitted to persons or bodies authorised or exempt[114] under cl.10.

3–016

As far as advocacy is concerned, prior to the Courts and Legal Services Act 1990, rights of audience were limited by the practice of the courts and tribunals concerned rather than by rules of law. The Royal Commission on Legal Services' enthusiasm for solicitor-advocates was markedly lukewarm:

> "Many solicitors make competent advocates in magistrates' courts and some are very good. Some could achieve the same standard in the Crown Court if they could so arrange their professional lives as to enable them to concentrate on the work there."[115]

In addition to concerns about the competence of solicitors, there were concerns about the impact on the Bar, fearing a "serious and disproportionate impact on

[112] See Judges' Council Working Party, *Interim Report: Litigants in Person in the Royal Courts of Justice London* (Chair, Otton L.J.). A litigant in person may bring an adviser to court with him or her as an adviser only (a friend, a law centre employee, a trades union official) but not as an advocate, and, whilst there is a "strong presumption" that an individual should be allowed such an adviser, there is no absolute right to one: *re O (Children) (Hearing in Private: Assistance)* [2005] EWCA Civ 759. Such an adviser is known as a "McKenzie friend" after *McKenzie v McKenzie* [1971] P. 33. The Lay Representatives (Rights of Audience) Order 1999, SI 1999/1225, made under Courts and Legal Services Act 1991, s.11 allows for lay representatives in civil small claims track cases.

[113] See OFT (June 2002), *A report by the Director General of Fair Trading to the Lord Chancellor on the likely competition effects of the Institute of Trade Mark Attorneys becoming a body authorised to grant rights to conduct litigation and rights of audience.* In 1999, the Chartered Institute of Patent Agents (now the Chartered Institute of Patent Attorneys) was authorised to grant "litigator certificates" to its members to conduct intellectual property litigation.

[114] The rights of litigants in person are preserved by Sch.3, para.4 to the Bill.

[115] Royal Commission on Legal Services, *Report, Vol.1* (1979), p.212.

the income and capacity of barristers to continue in practice".[116] The Law
Society raised questions about the right of audience in 1984[117] resulting in a
practice direction allowing solicitors to appear in the High Court and Crown
Court in formal and unopposed proceedings.[118] The Marre Committee subse-
quently supported, by a majority, the extension of rights of audience in the Crown
Court to solicitors approved by a Rights of Audience Advisory Board.[119]

3–017   The Courts and Legal Services Act 1990, s.27, put rights of audience in courts
and in certain tribunals and inquiries[120] on a statutory footing. A person had a
right of audience before a court if granted through an authorised body; under
statute[121]; granted individually by the court in question; or as a litigant in person.
Section 27 came into force on January 1, 1991 and preserved any rights of
audience that had been acquired before December 7, 1989.[122] This meant that the
General Council of the Bar (s.31) and the Law Society (s.32) could continue to
grant the relevant rights.

The procedure whereby other professional bodies may become "authorised
bodies", and their qualification regulations and rules of conduct approved for the
purpose of s.27 is set out in the Courts and Legal Services Act 1990, Sch.4, Pt
I. Currently the Bar Council, the Law Society,[123] the Institute of Legal Executives, the Institute of Trade Mark Attorneys and the Chartered Institute of Patent
Attorneys are authorised bodies.[124] The National Association of Licensed Paralegals is understood to be applying at the time of writing.[125]

One of the concerns about extending rights of audience was whether the same
regulations would apply to all. It is noticeable that the Courts and Legal Services
Act 1990, s.27(2A) provides that everyone

> "who exercises before any court a right of audience granted by an author-
> ised body has (a) a duty to the court to act with independence in the interests
> of justice; and (b) a duty to comply with the rules of conduct of the body
> relating to the right and approved for the purposes of this section; and those
> duties shall override any obligation which the person may have (otherwise
> than under the criminal law) if it is inconsistent with them."[126]

Under the Legal Services Bill, cl.12 of which replaces ss.27 and 29 of the Courts
and Legal Services Act, rights of audience are "reserved legal activity", defined

---

[116] *ibid.* p.216.
[117] *Annual Statement 1983–84*, pp.48–49. See also *Abse v Smith* [1986] Q.B. 536.
[118] *Practice Direction (Solicitors: Rights of Audience)* [1986] 1 W.L.R. 545.
[119] Report of the Marre Committee, pp.149–157. See J. Hodgson (1988) 138 N.L.J. 615.
[120] The term "court" includes (a) any tribunal under the jurisdiction of the Council on Tribunals (b)
     any court-martial and (c) a statutory inquiry within the meaning of the Tribunals and Inquiries Act
     1971: 1990 Act, s.119.
[121] e.g. Customs and Excise Management Act 1979; Prosecution of Offences Act 1985, s.4.
[122] *ibid.* ss.31–33.
[123] Conduct of advocacy by solicitors in all cases is governed by the *Solicitors' Code of Conduct
     2007* Rule 11. The Solicitors' Association of Higher Courts Advocates has a website at
     www.sahca.org.
[124] Under the Legal Services Bill, Sch.5, para.1, both will continue to be "approved regulators"
     under the new regime in respect of relevant "reserved legal activities".
[125] J. Robins, "A step up the ladder", L.S.G., January 25, 2007.
[126] This provision was added by the Access to Justice Act 1999. It is re-enacted in Legal Services
     Bill, cl.180.

in Sch.2, para.2 and will be regulated under cl.10 in the same way as the right to conduct litigation.

(2) *Conveyancing*

One of the major controversies in the recent past was the abolition of the 3–018 monopoly that solicitors used to enjoy in relation to conveyancing.[127] It was particularly controversial as many solicitors were economically dependent on this type of work, but there were criticisms of the low quality of such work and relatively high charges for it.[128] A majority of the Royal Commission accepted the argument that the monopoly or closed shop was in the public interest in view of the complexity of land law and of conveyancing and the need to protect clients from dishonesty, incompetence and overcharging.[129] All were agreed that a free-for-all would not be in the public interest and a system of licensed conveyancers was introduced by the Administration of Justice Act 1985, Pt II.[130] The Council for Licensed Conveyancers, unlike the Bar Council and Law Society has always been a regulatory body rather than combining regulatory and representative functions and so has no need to separate the two functions in preparation for authorisation under the Legal Services Bill.[131] The first licences were granted on May 1, 1987, and solicitors deal with them in the same way as they would with a solicitor specialising in conveyancing. Some licensed conveyancers are employed by solicitors' firms, local authorities, banks or building societies and some are in independent practice. Conveyancing, nevertheless, remains an important element of the work of many solicitors.[132] Clause 9 of the Legal Services Bill will replace previous statutory provisions, including those in the Courts and Legal Services Act 1990 about entitlement to provide conveyancing services.

(3) *Probate*

Under the Solicitors' Act 1974, it was an offence for an unqualified person[133] to 3–019 prepare (directly or indirectly) any instrument "relating to real or personal estate,

---

[127] It had been sought by the Society of Gentlemen Practisers and was finally granted by William Pitt in 1804 as a *quid pro quo* for an increase in the tax on practising certificates and articles in the Stamp Act 1804: see R. Abel-Smith and R. Stevens, *Lawyers and the Courts* (1967), pp.22–23, Kirk (1976), Ch.7. It was moved from fiscal legislation to a Solicitors' Act in 1932. The changes appear to have been agreed because of the need to collect tax rather than in the public interest. See now Solicitors' Act 1974, s.22.

[128] M. Joseph, *Conveyancing Fraud* (1989); Royal Commission on Legal Services, *Report, Vol.1* (1979), pp.243–282.

[129] For the minority view, see *ibid.* pp.808, 809–812, 813–816.

[130] See P. Kenny, "Administration of Justice Act 1985, Part II" in *Current Law Statutes Annotated 1985*; A. Kenny (1986) 277 E.G. 262, 394.

[131] Under which it will continue to be an "approved regulator" in respect of the administration of oaths and "reserved instrument activities": Sch.5, para.1.

[132] In August 2005, 18,459 solicitors told the Law Society that they were involved in residential conveyancing: Law Society, *Categories of Work Undertaken by Solicitors 2005*. In the Law Society's Business Survey of 2003, sole practitioners reported gaining 40 per cent of their income from residential conveyancing: Law Society Fact Sheet *Solicitors' Firms 2003*.

[133] Here the term covers a person who is not a solicitor, barrister or notary public, and there are some other exclusions: Solicitors Act 1974, ss.22(2), 23(2). For some purposes, Scottish solicitors, licensed conveyancers, trade mark agents, patent attorneys and certain public officers are exempt.

or any legal proceedings",[134] to take instructions for a grant of probate or letters of administration, or to prepare papers on which to found or oppose such a grant,[135] unless he or she proved that it was not done for or in the expectation of any fee, gain or reward. An offence was committed even where the unqualified person did not personally receive the fee.[136]

However, the Courts and Legal Services Act 1990, ss.54, 55 allowed for the extension of the right to perform probate work for reward to banks, building societies, insurance companies and their subsidiaries, provided that they operated a complaints scheme which complied with requirements prescribed by regulations, and to other bodies approved under s.55 and Sch.9. The solicitors' profession was well aware of the potential consequences for its business.[137] Preparation of probate papers will be a reserved legal activity under the Legal Services Bill,[138] cl.9 of which replaces both the Solicitors' Act 1974, s.23 and the Courts and Legal Services Act 1990. The preparation of wills and similar "testamentary instruments"[139] is specifically excluded from the definition of "reserved legal activities" although as creating a will must almost inevitably involve the provision of legal advice, it will, presumably, still constitute a "legal activity" which is susceptible to becoming a reserved legal activity in the future.[140]

(4) Notarial activity[141] and the administration of oaths

3–020 In contrast to the situation in many European countries, in which the *notaire* exists as a well-established separate legal profession, notarial activity is frequently carried out by solicitors specifically empowered to do so as well as by individuals practising specifically as notaries (who describe themselves as "the oldest legal profession in England and Wales") who may carry out other legal work short of litigation.[142] In other parts of the world, legal documents are frequently required to be "notarised", that is, certified as authentic, and, consequently, documents prepared in this country may need to be notarised if they are

---

[134] Solicitors Act 1974, s.22. "Instrument" includes a contract for the sale of land, but does not include a will, an agreement not under seal, a letter of power of attorney, or a "transfer of stock containing no trust or limitation thereof": s.22(3). This restriction does not apply in the context of an exercise of a right of audience: Courts and Legal Services Act 1990, s.27(10).

[135] Solicitors' Act 1974, s.23(1).

[136] *Reynolds v Hoyle* [1976] 1 W.L.R. 207; *cf. Green v Hoyle* [1976] 1 W.L.R. 575.

[137] *Law Society Annual Statistical Report 1994*, p.45. J. Jenkins, *Wills and Probate* (Law Society Research Paper No. 6, 1998). At para.2.6, it is clear that, of those in 1994 who had made a will, 74% had the help of a solicitor, 15% had made their own, a bank advised 5% and a will-making agency wrote it in 1% of cases. The number of personal applications for probate increased by 46% between 1991 and 1996, in which time the number of solicitor applications fell by 3%: *ibid.* para.2.7.

[138] Sch.2, para.5.

[139] See, for example, Anon, "Where there's a will", *Which*, February 2007, p.26. Specialist willwriters may be members of and regulated by, for example, the Institute of Professional Willwriters (*www.ipw.org.uk*) or Society of Will Writers (*www.willwriters.com*). In addition the international Society of Trust and Estate Practitioners acts as a forum for those in this field: *www.step.org.*

[140] Sch.2, para.4(2)(a).

[141] See the Notaries Society (*www.thenotariessociety.org.uk*) and the Society of Scrivener Notaries and the Worshipful Company of Scriveners of the City of London (*www.scrivener-notaries.org.uk*).

[142] *www.thenotariessociety.org.uk.*

to be used abroad. Typical notarial tasks are described by the Notaries Society as:

> "[p]reparing and witnessing powers of attorney for use overseas; dealing with purchase or sale of land and property abroad; providing documents to deal with the administration of the estate of people who are abroad, or owning property abroad; authenticating personal documents and information for immigration or emigration purposes, or to apply to marry or to work abroad and authenticating company and business documents and transactions."

Clause 9 of the Legal Services Bill replaces Public Notaries Act 1801 and Public Notaries Act 1843 in making provision for notarial activity as a reserved legal activity.[143]

Any solicitor with a practising certificate is, by virtue of Courts and Legal Services Act 1990, s.113,[144] a "commissioner for oaths" and other individuals can be authorised to act as such[145]; entitling them to administer the oath required to "swear" an affidavit, affirmation, statutory declaration or similar document. Clause 9 of the Legal Services Bill replaces the statutory regulation of commissioners for oaths and incorporates their activity into that of "reserved legal activity".[146]

(ix) *Restrictions on practice*

(1) *Multi-disciplinary practices*

Whether there should be multi-disciplinary practices (MDPs) is a matter for the profession.[147] A solicitor may not at present form a partnership with a member of another profession although, as we have seen, it is the intention of the Legal Services Bill that they should be able to do so in the future.[148] The reasons for not allowing such partnerships in the past were summarised by the Law Society as follows[149]: **3–021**

(a) an independent legal profession has an important democratic function to defend individual liberties;

---

[143] Sch.2, para.6.

[144] See also Commissioner for Oaths Act 1889, s.1; Solicitors' Act 1974, s.81.

[145] Fellows of the Institute of Legal Executives who have paid their subscription are commissioners for oaths, as are barristers and Registered European Lawyers practising in England and Wales. Court officers are also empowered to administer oaths.

[146] Sch.2, para.7. Whilst the draft does not specifically refer to Courts and Legal Services Act 1990, the accompanying Explanatory Notes state explicitly that Commissioner for Oaths Act 1889, s.1 is replaced, s.191 of which is repealed by Courts and Legal Services Act 1990, s.113); Solicitors Act 1974, s.81 and Courts and Legal Services Act, s.113.

[147] The legislative prohibition, Solicitors Act 1974, s.39, was repealed by the Courts and Legal Services Act 1990, s.66.

[148] The restriction on "fee-sharing" with non lawyers is preserved, for the present at least, in *Solicitors Code of Conduct 2007*, Rule 8, replacing Solicitors' Practice Rules 1990, r.7. Solicitors may form partnerships with a solicitor, a registered foreign lawyer or a recognised body (that is an incorporated practice).

[149] The Law Society, *Multi-Disciplinary Practice: Consultation* (1998), section D, at *www.lawsociety.org.uk*. See also Boon and Levin (1999), pp.84–85.

(b) MDPs might reduce consumer choice, because they would gather all the best solicitors into large firms, reducing the extent of the network of firms;

(c) clients have the right to be represented by an independent lawyer;

(d) MDPs represent a surrender of independence by solicitors;

(e) there was evidence that MDPs would not take off;

(f) MDPs might lead to an increased risk of conflicts of interest and of duties;

(g) practice in an MDP could create problems with confidentiality, legal professional privilege, protection of clients' funds and professional indemnity;

(h) the conduct of non-solicitor members of an MDP could not be regulated in the same way;

(i) there might be confusion as to the nature of the MDP and the qualifications of the individuals in it.

The same Law Society document summarised the arguments for MDPs as follows:

(a) solicitors' independence would not automatically be lost through MDPs, but safeguards should be developed;

(b) MDPs could allow clients access to a range of specialists and experts under one roof;

(c) the ban on MDPs prevented solicitors competing with other professions which provide "one-stop shopping", and people would have a choice whether to go to an MDP or a traditional practice;

(d) no major adverse consequences have occurred where MDPs are permitted (e.g. Germany and New South Wales);

(e) *de facto* MDPs already exist;

(f) we should not lag behind others considering MDPs;

(g) solicitors should be entitled to choose the kind of business through which they practise;

(h) the conduct rules would remain the same for solicitors in MDPs thus removing the risks of conflicts of interest;

(i) if conflicting duties were owed, rules could prohibit an MDP undertaking both activities;

(j) MDPs would enable solicitors to give appropriate status to and so retain non-lawyer staff;

(k) solutions to regulatory problems should be sought;

(l) there was no reason to believe that other professions' standards of client care were lower;

(m) transparency to clients would avoid many of the problems;

(n) it was preferable to extend the influence of solicitors into other professions.

Substantial developments towards MDPs have already been made with the introduction of incorporated practices[150]; the sharing of fees with non-solicitor employees[151]; and the introduction of the rule that a solicitor who instructs an estate agent as a sub-agent for the sale of a property can remunerate the estate agent on the basis of a proportion of the solicitor's professional fee.[152]

Having given careful consideration to the debate, the Law Society's Council affirmed its objectives in December 1999 as "(a) the ultimate goal should be to allow solicitors who wish to do so to provide any legal service through any medium to anyone, provided that it is possible to achieve the necessary public protections; (b) the short term goal should be to investigate the ways in which it might be possible to relax the rule on fee sharing . . . ".[153] In response to this, the Law Society made its first steps towards MDPs by adopting an approach called "Legal Practice Plus".[154] "Legal Practice Plus" is a model for MDPs which would allow non-solicitors to become partners in a solicitors' practice subject to a considerable degree of regulation and providing solicitors remained in control of the partnership. In 2002, the European Court of Justice ruled that, although a regulation restricting MDPs would have effects restrictive of competition, the Bar Council making it could have reasonably considered that it was necessary for the proper practice of the legal profession in a particular member state, and so it does not breach the competition provisions of European Union law.[155] As we have seen, one of the objectives of the Legal Services Bill is to promote "alternative business structures" for the delivery of legal services which might incorporate not only solicitors and barristers but also lawyers and non-lawyers.[156] Provided there is a market demand or an advantage perceived by providers of legal services, MDPs are now inevitable.

(2) Multi-national practices (MNPs) and globalisation

Prohibitions used to apply to multi-national practices, that is solicitors engaged in practices with one or more registered foreign lawyers.[157] The pressures for   **3–022**

---

[150] Administration of Justice Act 1985, s.9.

[151] See also *Solicitors' Code of Conduct 2007*, Rule 8, replacing Solicitors' Practice Rules 1990, r.7(1).

[152] See also *Solicitors' Code of Conduct 2007*, Rule 8, replacing Solicitors' Practice Rules 1990, r.7(2).

[153] Law Society, *Multi-Disciplinary Practice: Progress Report* (1999), at *www.lawsociety.org.uk.*

[154] Law Society, *Legal Practice Plus—First Step Towards MDPs* (2000) Report of the Working Party, at *www.lawsociety.org.uk.* See also other contributions at the same site including additional interim reports of the Working Party. The Working Party suspended its operations pending clarification of what would be in the Legal Services Bill

[155] *Wouters v Algemene Raad van de Nederlandse Orde van Advocaten (Case C-309/99)* [2002] All E.R. (D.) 233.

[156] DCA, *The Future of Legal Services: Putting Consumers First* (October 2005), Ch.6. So, for example, bankers, accountants, tax specialists and lawyers might combine in a single organisation offering "one stop shop" services to business clients.

[157] As defined in the Courts and Legal Services Act 1990, s.89(9).

change came from the developing European Union,[158] the development of the Single Market, and the development of mutual recognition of professional qualifications.[159] Further, solicitors' practices have pushed business development into foreign markets. The changes were introduced after the Courts and Legal Services Act 1990, s.66.

A Registered European Lawyer (REL)[160] may practise in another member state on the same basis as lawyers qualified in that state provided he or she is registered with a competent authority in that state (in England and Wales, the Solicitors' Regulation Authority[161] or Bar Council[162]) and complies with rules of conduct of that state. Registered Foreign Lawyers (RFLs) qualified in other states may also practise in this jurisdiction under the aegis of the Solicitors' Regulation Authority[163] but only as: (a) a partner in a domestic MNP consisting of some combination of solicitors, RELs and RFLs and "non-registered European lawyers"; (b) a director of a company; or (c) a member of an LLP which is a registered body subject to Solicitors' Regulation Authority regulation. Foreign lawyers may practise as barristers subject to the consent of the Bar Council provided they comply with the Foreign Lawyers (Chambers) Rules.[164]

Thus, solicitors may practise in England and Wales in multi-national partnerships (provided there is at least one RFL and one solicitor or REL) or, as an alternative, as an incorporated practice.[165] As at July 31, 2006, there were 124 MNPs with their head offices in England and Wales.[166]

---

[158] A common Council of Bars and Law Societies of Europe (CCBE) *Code of Conduct for Layers in the European Community* (2006) can be found as annex Q to the Bar Code of Conduct and on the Law Society website.

[159] See *Morgenbesser v Consiglio dell'Ordine degli avvocati di Genova*, Case 313/01 (2003) ECJ, available at: *curia.eu.int/jurisp*. A Frenchwoman with a French law degree but not qualified to practise in France was refused a transfer to the equivalent stage in Italian pre-qualification education with a view to qualifying in Italy on the basis that she did not have an Italian law degree. It was held that the Italian Bar had to consider the experience and qualifications in the round to establish whether the applicant was entitled to proceed to qualification. In England and Wales the effect of this decision was thought to allow foreign nationals to qualify more easily than domestic students, as, for example, the foreign student could not be compelled to complete a training contract; R. Rothwell, "UK Students Denied" L.S.G. 1 December 2005. This issue has been considered as part of the Law Society's Training Framework Review, see below. The Bar Standards Board's Qualifications Committee deals with applications for the recognition of European lawyers and admission of other specially qualified applicants. The Solicitors' Regulatory Authority monitors the Qualified Lawyers' Transfer Test under the Qualified Lawyers' Transfer Regulations 1990, for some categories of foreign lawyers (and domestic barristers as well as Scottish and Northern Irish qualified solicitors, advocates and barristers) who wish to transfer into the profession. Qualified lawyers from other jurisdictions may practise in this country as Registered Foreign Lawyers or Registered European Lawyers under Establishment of Lawyers Directive 98/5/EC (see further discussion below). See also European Communities (Recognition of Professional Qualifications) Regulations 1991 and European Communities (Lawyers' Practice) Regulations (2000).

[160] See the Establishment of Lawyers Directive, 98/5/EC implemented by European Communities (Lawyer's Practice) Regulations 2000, SI 2000/1119 and Law Society, *Registered European Lawyers (RELs) and the Establishment Directive* (May 2006).

[161] *Solicitors' Code of Conduct 2007*, Rule 12.02.

[162] *Bar Code of Conduct*, Annex B, *Registered European Lawyers Rules*.

[163] *Solicitors' Code of Conduct 2007*, Rule 12.03. See also Law Society, *Registered Foreign Lawyers and Multinational Practice* (May 2006).

[164] *Bar Code of Conduct*, Annex H.

[165] Overseas practice is governed by rules 15 and 16 of the *Solicitors' Code of Conduct 2007*. Law Society, *Registered Foreign Lawyers and Multinational Practice* (May 2006), section 3.

[166] Law Society, *Annual Statistical Report 2006*, table 3.1.

(3) *Advertising*

Advertising by solicitors used to be prohibited.[167] "Touting" was regarded as **3–023** unprofessional and associated with "trade".[168] Collective advertising by the profession was acceptable. The introduction of advertising by individuals and firms was recommended both by the Monopolies Commission[169] and the Royal Commission on Legal Services.[170] The primary purpose of these recommendations was to provide information to the public rather than to drum up business. The old restrictions on advertising have, however, been swept away.[171]

The Solicitors' Publicity Code 2001 (last amended in 2003) permits advertising provided that it complies with the Practice Rules, and it cannot reasonably be regarded as being in bad taste, is not accurate or misleading in any way, and complies with any legal requirements.[172] Rule 7 of the *Solicitors Code of Conduct 2007*, replacing the Solicitors' Practice Rules 1990, states that "[y]ou are generally free to publicise your practice as a solicitor, REL or RFL, subject to the requirements of this rule". Those requirements include that publicity must not be misleading or inaccurate; that if information about fees is given it should be "clearly expressed" and state whether VAT and disbursements are included (and if services are offered as "free" they must be genuinely free) and that the solicitor must take responsibility for any publicity. Solicitors cannot make unsolicited visits or telephone calls except to a current or former client or to another lawyer or to an existing or potential professional or business connection or to a commercial or public body.[173] Advertising outside this jurisdiction must also comply with local rules about lawyers' publicity. Solicitors may name clients and the transactions carried out for clients with their consent.[174] Non-serious breaches of the rule may be dealt with by a local law society but "serious or persistent" cases will be subject to being reported to the Solicitors' Regulation Authority.

Rule 9 of the *Solicitors' Code of Conduct 2007* permits arrangements for the introduction of business, replacing rule 2 of the Solicitors' Practice Rules and the Solicitors' Introduction and Referral Code 1990.[175] The basic principle is that

---

[167] Solicitors' Practice Rules, 1936–72, r.1; see P. Fennell in P. A. Thomas (ed.), *Law in the Balance* (1982), Ch.6.

[168] "[P]rofessional ideology is not exclusively anti-entrepreneurial, but . . . incorporates elements of the value systems of both the 'pre-industrial gentleman' and the tradesman:" *ibid.* p.144.

[169] *Report on the supply of services of Solicitors in England and Wales in relation to restrictions on advertising* (1975–76, H.C. 557).

[170] Royal Commission on Legal Services, *Report, Vol.I* (1979), pp.367–373.

[171] See, for example, the notorious example of the firm of divorce lawyers who, in 2001, placed advertisements in ladies toilets with the slogan "All Men are Bastards" and in men's with "Ditch the Bitch".

[172] As for example, legislation regulating advertising such as Consumer Credit Act 1974; Consumer Protection Act 1987 and the "legal, decent, honest and truthful" requirements of the British Code of Advertising, Sales Promotion and Direct Marketing. Firms with websites must consider all of this in relation to the information placed on the website: Electronic Commerce (EC Directive) Regulations 2002. Promotion of financial services will need to comply with the Financial Services and Markets Act 2000.

[173] Where this is to an existing or former client, Data Protection Act 1998 must also be considered.

[174] For other matters contained in the Code, including letterheads and the descriptions of individual employees or the firm, LLP or company, see Rule 7.

[175] Last amended in October 2004, supplemented by *Disclosure of funding, referral and fee-sharing arrangements: important notice for all practitioners* (March 2004) and *Further Referral Fees Guidance* (December 2005). There is, at the time of writing, considerable disquiet in the media about referral fees, seen as solicitors "bidding for" or "buying" cases from, for example, claims

"[w]hen making or receiving referrals of clients to or from third parties you must do nothing which would compromise your independence or your ability to act and advise in the best interests of your clients". The requirements of an introducer should never undermine this independence.[176] Solicitors may not enter into arrangements with claims farmers acting on contingency fees for the introduction of personal injury clients. There are very specific requirements about the amount of information about the referral arrangements that has to be given to the client, including the amount of any referral fee. Breaches of these rules will be subject to investigation by the Solicitors' Regulation Authority.[177]

(d) Barristers and their work

(i) *Numbers*

3–024   In December 2005, there were 11,818 barristers (70.5 per cent of them men)[178] in self-employed practice in 360 sets of chambers (as well as 281 barristers working as sole practitioners). 212 of the sets of chambers were in London, the rest in the provinces.[179] In general, the size of the Bar has continuously increased since the early 1960s, although the rate of growth has varied. The Bar doubled in size between 1963 and 1979, and increased by almost a half between 1979 and 1989.[180] There were only 6,645 barristers in 1990. However, the rate of increase may be reducing: from 1986 to 1998 it was 4.9 per cent annually, but by 2001 had dropped to 2.0 per cent.[181] In 2005, 1,476 people were called to the Bar, of whom 51.1 per cent were men.[182]

(ii) *Work*

3–025   There is an increasing tendency for barristers to specialise, but many still have a general common law practice (contract, crime, tort (especially personal injury cases), landlord and tenant, family matters). If specialising, a barrister may do so in one of the common law areas, in Chancery work (trusts, land law, conveyancing, wills, company law, revenue matters) or in one of the other specialist areas. In London, common law chambers are concentrated in the Temple and Chancery chambers are concentrated in Lincoln's Inn. There is no rule requiring chambers to be in one of the Inns of Court. Concentrations have occurred in the Inns, because until fairly recently they have charged barristers only a proportion of the market rent, for the convenience of access to the courts and because of

---

management organisations or insurers. See Law Society, *Report on Themed Visits—Referral Fees* (July 2006). Referrals are dealt with in Rule 9 of the *Solicitors' Code of Conduct 2007*.
[176] Solicitors' Introduction and Referral Code 1990, s.1(1) replaced by the *Solicitors' Code of Conduct 2007*, Rule 9.
[177] Which began by warning all solicitors individually and in writing of a "crackdown on improper referrals" in February 2007: N. Rose, "Solicitors to get Referral Warning" L.S.G. February 1, 2007.
[178] The gender balance for employed barristers is rather more even: 54.7% of them being men: The General Council of the Bar, *Bar Statistics as at December 2005.*
[179] The General Council of the Bar, *Bar Statistics as at December 2005.*
[180] Royal Commission on Legal Services, *Report Vol.1* (1979), p.54; *Annual Report of the Bar Council 1990*, pp.20–21. See Abel (1988), pp.65–72.
[181] BDO Stoy Hayward, *Report on the 2001 Survey of Barristers' Chambers* (2001), at p.8.
[182] The General Council of the Bar, *Bar Statistics as at December 2005.*

long tradition.[183] Many sets of chambers have now opened in London, but outside the Inns.[184]

The work of barristers is, of necessity, changing. The availability of work at the criminal bar has declined, particularly as more such advocacy work is undertaken by solicitors; in general barristers no longer have a monopoly over rights of audience[185]; whilst reliance on publicly funded work has traditionally been high, the low rates of fee increases have forced barristers to look to other areas of work; and increasing specialisation has led to some new areas of work as have other pressures. Just as the Legal Services Bill will change the regulation of solicitors and open out the possibility of other organisations entering into the legal services field, so it will have an effect on the work of barristers.

The BDO Stoy Hayward survey of barristers' chambers for 2001 revealed the following about the nature of practice at that time.[186]

Type of work	2001	2000
General civil:		
Common law (Other)	3.1%	3.7%
Technology and construction court	3.3%	3.4%
Landlord and tenant (non-residential)	1.8%	1.9%
Landlord and tenant (residential)	1.6%	1.8%
Planning	1.8%	2.5%
Parliamentary and local government	2.9%	2.4%
Insolvency	2.6%	2.2%
Financial services	0.8%	1.1%
European	1.2%	0.8%
Licensing	0.3%	0.5%
Immigration	0.5%	0.5%
Personal injury	8.4%	8.0%
Professional negligence	4.6%	4.8%
Other work	2.1%	2.3%

[183] Royal Commission on Legal Services, *Report Vol.I* (1979), pp.449–450.
[184] e.g., the various sets of chambers on Bedford Row are just outside the inns, as are those on the Strand, Leadenhall Street, Fleet Street, etc.
[185] See above, paras 3–016—3–017.
[186] BDO Stoy Hayward (2001), at table 9.

Type of work	2001	2000
Total General Civil	35.0%	35.7%
Criminal	23.3%	24.7%
Commercial:		
Commercial	12.2%	11.2%
Admiralty	0.5%	0.9%
International law	0.3%	0.3%
Restrictive practices	0.2%	0.5%
Total Commercial	13.2%	12.9%
Family:		
Children	6.6%	6.9%
Other	5.1%	4.6%
Total Family	11.7%	11.5%
Chancery:		
Contentious	4.7%	4.0%
Non-contentious	2.1%	1.9%
Total Chancery	6.8%	5.9%
Employment	3.0%	3.5%
Other specialist:		
Revenue	1.7%	1.9%
Intellectual property	2.5%	2.0%
Arbitrator or Umpire	1.2%	1.3%
Defamation	1.6%	0.6%
Total Other Specialist	7.0%	5.8%
Total	100.0%	100.0%

(iii) *Remuneration*

3–026   As to remuneration, the Royal Commission on Legal Services concluded that the earnings of barristers were not out of line with those in comparable occupations, except that the earnings of barristers in the early years of practice were low.[187] A

---

[187] Royal Commission on Legal Services. *Report Vol.1* (1979), pp.507–542 and *Vol.2*, pp.579–626.

report by Coopers and Lybrand in 1985 claimed that fees for junior barristers at the criminal bar fell well below what was required to meet the principle of "fair and reasonable reward for work reasonably done".[188] The Lord Chancellor rejected the claim for a significant increase in fees, but ultimately had to raise the initial offer. However, there remain concerns about the level of fee for those barristers undertaking such publicly funded work.

The BDO Stoy Hayward survey revealed that the range of receipts for barristers was then as follows.[189]

Years' call	Receipts
0–5	£14,800–£34,300
5–10	£38,800–£78,900
Over 10	£59,300–£119,200
Q.C.s	£143,900–£278,000

Before assuming that this is a barrister's salary, some 20 per cent should be deducted for chambers expenses and a further 20 per cent on average will go on personal expenses.[190] Nevertheless, it can be noticed that some barristers make very large sums of money indeed but that some have a relatively small income. Thus, as with solicitors, there is a very wide income range.

One problem that barristers face is getting the fees paid within a reasonable time of having done the work. This problem has been a serious cause of friction. A new procedure was introduced, short of a contract,[191] and, from 2001, it became possible for barristers and solicitors to engage in a contract.[192]

(iv) *Employed barristers*

There are 2,805 barristers who are employed in commerce, industry and central **3–027** and local government as well as by firms of solicitors,[193] as, for example, in-house advocacy specialists. The General Council of the Bar provides specific *Guidance for Employed Barristers* to supplement Pt V of the Code of Conduct. There is considerable similarity in the work done by employed solicitors and barristers such that the view was expressed as long ago as 1976 that there was effective fusion between these two parts of the profession.[194] Employed barristers may now, according to para.3 of the *Guidance for Employed Barristers*: "provide advice to their employers (or, where permitted,[195] clients of their employers) and

---

[188] Annual Statement of the Senate 1985–86, p.76.
[189] BDO Stoy Hayward (2001), table 36 and p.35.
[190] *Chambers Guide to the Legal Profession 2001–2002*, p.1247.
[191] "The Terms of Work on which barristers offer their services to solicitors and the withdrawal of credit scheme 1988" in *Code of Conduct*, Annex G1.
[192] "The Contractual Terms of Work on which barristers offer their services to solicitors 2001" in *ibid.* Annex G2. A model contract was close to finalisation at the time of writing.
[193] General Council of the Bar, *Bar Statistics as at December 2005*.
[194] Chairman of the Solicitor's Commerce and Industry Group at (1976) 73 L.S. Gaz. 369.
[195] See paras 501 and 502 of the *Code of Conduct*.

undertake all the work normally undertaken by barristers. In addition, they are able to conduct correspondence on behalf of their employer, interview witnesses, take statements and hold money belonging to their employer (with the employer's consent). Special rules apply to appearing in court and conducting litigation".

Where the barrister is employed by a public authority (including the Government Legal Service), such services may also be supplied to another public authority with which the employer has an arrangement to supply legal services.[196] A Government Legal Service employed barrister may advise any Minister or Officer of the Crown.[197] A barrister employed as a justices' clerk may advise the justices.[198] Whilst acting in the course of employment, a barrister employed in a solicitors' firm or "other authorised litigator" may supply legal services to a client; a barrister employed by the Legal Services Commission may supply them to a member of the public; and a barrister employed at a Legal Advice Centre may supply services to its clients.[199] Any employed barrister may supply legal services to any person free of charge.[200] An employed barrister may conduct litigation provided he or she complies with the Employed Barristers (Conduct of Litigation) Rules.[201] There is still a reluctance to allow self-employed barristers to conduct litigation because of the restriction on conducting a client's affairs.[202] Whether this position will change as a result of the need to compete with the potential for new entrants to the field of litigation and advocacy provided by the Legal Services Bill remains to be seen.

(v) *Practice guidance*

3–028   As a result of adverse comments made in the Clementi review about the self-regulation of the two professions, the professional conduct of barristers is now regulated by the Bar Standards Board, chaired by a layperson and with an equal number of barrister and lay members. It is intended that this body will be an "approved regulator" of the Bar under the Legal Services Bill[203] subject to the overall regulation of the Legal Services Board. It is the duty of every barrister to comply with the *Code of Conduct*, now in its eighth edition.[204]

The general purpose of the Code "is to provide the requirements for practice as a barrister and the rules and standards of conduct applicable to barristers which are appropriate in the interests of justice . . . ".[205] With regard to barristers in self-employed practice (previously described as "the independent Bar"), their purpose in particular is "to provide common and enforceable rules and standards which require them: (i) to be completely independent in conduct and in professional standing as sole practitioners[206]; (ii) to act only as consultants instructed

---

[196] *ibid.* para.501(b)(i).
[197] *ibid.* para.501(b)(ii).
[198] *ibid.* para.501(c).
[199] *ibid.* para.502(a)–(c).
[200] *ibid.* para.502(d).
[201] *ibid.* para.504. The rules are at App.I of the *Code of Conduct*.
[202] *ibid.* para.401(b).
[203] See Legal Services Bill, Sch.5, para.1.
[204] *Code of Conduct*, para.105.
[205] *ibid.* para.104.
[206] The Kentridge Committee recommended that the rules against partnerships should be retained: Committee on Competition in Professions, *Report to the Bar Council* (chair S. Kentridge Q.C., 2002).

by solicitors and other approved persons (save where instructions can be properly dispensed with); (iii) to acknowledge a public obligation based on the paramount need for access to justice to act for any client in cases within their field of practice."[207] These obligations are then adjusted to the particular position of employed barristers.[208] Of the three key obligations for barristers in private practice, the second was under particular pressure from the Office of Fair Trading under competition law. In 2002, the Kentridge Committee recommended to the Bar Council that "the Bar should remove the general prohibition on direct access and allow barristers in self-employed practice to accept instructions directly from clients, subject to appropriate safeguards".[209] That process was begun with "BarDIRECT", now the "Licensed Access Scheme", which allowed members of specific professions, such as accountants, architects and engineers to instruct counsel directly either on their own behalf or that of their lay clients and was continued in July 2004 with the "Public Access Scheme" allowing barristers who have undertaken specific training to obtain instructions directly from the public (other than in immigration, family and criminal proceedings). The process of modernisation has also attacked many of the fundamental principles of the Bar, and whether the desire to maintain operation as sole practitioners can survive such pressures, particularly in the light of the challenges potentially opened by the Legal Services Bill, is open to serious doubt.[210]

All barristers must refrain from conduct which is "(i) dishonest or otherwise discreditable to a barrister; (ii) prejudicial to the administration of justice; or (iii) likely to diminish public confidence in the legal profession or the administration of justice or otherwise bring the legal profession into disrepute".[211]

All practising barristers share with others holding rights of audience "an overriding duty to the Court to act with independence in the interests of justice". They must "assist the Court in the administration of justice and must not deceive or knowingly or recklessly mislead the Court".[212] Further, they "must promote and protect fearlessly and by all proper and lawful means the lay client's best interests and do so without regard to [their] own interests or to any consequences to [themselves] or to any other person".[213] They owe their "primary duty as between the lay client and any professional client or other intermediary to the lay client and must not permit the intermediary to limit [their] discretion as to how the interests of the lay client can best be served".[214] No barrister may "discriminate directly or indirectly or victimise because of race, colour, ethnic or national origin, nationality, citizenship, sex, sexual orientation, marital status, disability,

---

[207] *Code of Conduct*, para.104(a).

[208] *ibid.* para.104(b).

[209] Kentridge Report (2002).

[210] See P. Kunzlik, "Rebuilding the Cathedral?—The partnership question and the effect of 'modernisation' on the professionalism and ethics of the English bar" (2001).

[211] *Code of Conduct*, para.301(a). In addition, a barrister must not "engage directly or indirectly in any occupation if his association with that occupation may adversely affect the reputation of the Bar or in the case of a practising barrister prejudice his ability to attend properly to his practice": *ibid.* para.301(b).

[212] *ibid.* para.302.

[213] *ibid.* para.303(a)

[214] *ibid.* para.303(b). Their primary duty is also owed to the lay client when funded by either the Community Legal Service or the Criminal Defence Service: *ibid.* para.303(c). When providing such funded services, the barrister will have to comply with any duty imposed by or under the Access to Justice Act 1999 or related provisions and with the duties in Annex E to the Code: *ibid.* para.304.

religion or political persuasion".[215] Barristers are "individually and personally responsible for [their] own conduct and for [their] professional work" and they "must exercise [their] own personal judgment in all [their] professional activities".[216] The rules emphasise further the importance of the ability to be able to practise independently of interference and inappropriate pressures.[217]

3–029　　　In order to comply with their commitment to the administration of justice, any barrister who supplies advocacy services must not withhold such services because the nature of the case is objectionable or the client's opinions or beliefs are unacceptable or because of the source of the client's funding.[218] Further, any self-employed barrister must comply with the "cab-rank rule". That is they "must in any field in which [they profess] to practise in relation to work appropriate to [their] experience and seniority and irrespective of whether [their] client is paying privately or is publicly funded: (a) accept any brief to appear before a Court in which [they profess] to practise; (b) accept any instructions; (c) act for any person on whose behalf [they are] instructed; and do so irrespective of (i) the party on whose behalf [they are] instructed (ii) the nature of the case and (iii) any belief or opinion which [they] may have formed as to the character, reputation, cause, conduct, guilt or innocence of that person".[219] There are a number of exceptions to the rule, so barristers must not accept any brief or instructions that would cause them to be "professionally embarrassed", which might arise, e.g. as a result of insufficient experience or competence, other professional commitments, or where there is a conflict of interest.[220] Further, self-employed barristers are not obliged to accept a brief or instructions, e.g. requiring them to work outside their ordinary working year; to do work other than for a proper fee; or to do any work under a conditional fee agreement.[221] Queen's Counsel are not obliged to accept instructions to settle alone any document of a kind generally settled only by or in conjunction with a junior or to act without a junior if they consider that the interests of the lay client require a junior.[222] Since 1991, the Code has required barristers to consider whether "consistently with the proper and efficient administration of justice" and "having regard to (a) the circumstances (including in particular the gravity complexity and likely cost) of the case; (b) the nature of [their] practice; (c) their ability, experience and seniority; and (d) [their] relationship with the client; the best interests of the client would be served by instructing or continuing to instruct [them]" and to advise the client if not.[223] Further, the advent of conditional fee arrangements as a means of funding litigation[224] has meant the abandonment of the cab-rank rule in this area of work.[225]

　　　It has been said that this rule "secures for the public a right of representation in the court which is a pillar of British liberty".[226] In many ways, this is true.

---

[215] *ibid.* para.305.1.
[216] *ibid.* para.306.
[217] *ibid.* para.307.
[218] *ibid.* para.601.
[219] *ibid.* para.602.
[220] *ibid.* para.603.
[221] *ibid.* para.604.
[222] *ibid.* para.605.
[223] *ibid.* para.606.1
[224] See below, para.11–007.
[225] P. Kunzlik, "Conditional fees: the ethical and organisational impact on the bar" (1999) 62 M.L.R. 850. The cab rank rule does not apply to professional clients: *op. cit.* para.604 (e).
[226] Royal Commission on Legal Services, *Report, Vol.1* (1979), p.31.

Barristers do indeed take cases about which they have concerns. However, the greater pressure to do so may be the need to keep in business rather than this rule, especially when it is noted that it is possible to avoid taking cases by being too busy or unavailable. "In real life a barrister has a clerk whose enthusiasm for the unwanted brief may not be great, and he is free to raise the fee within limits. It is not likely that the rule often obliges barristers to undertake work which they would not otherwise accept."[227]

(vi) Restrictions on practice

(1) Instructions and direct professional access

Traditionally, instructions to a barrister could only be received from a solicitor. **3–030** In addition, barristers may be appointed by the court.[228] A major change was made when it was accepted that instructions could be received from a range of professional clients. Professional client means: a solicitor (including Scottish and Northern Irish solicitors); authorised litigator; Parliamentary agent; patent agent; European Patent Attorney; trade mark agent; notary; Registered Foreign Lawyer; licensed conveyancer[229]; employed barrister or Registered European Lawyer; practising barrister or registered European lawyer acting on his or her own behalf; a foreign lawyer in a matter which does not involve the barrister supplying advocacy services and representatives of bodies giving free legal services designated by the Bar Council.[230] In 2000, LECG Ltd, working for the Office of Fair Trading, identified arguments in favour of the rule being the addition of regulatory costs if direct access were enabled, plus the need for a compensation fund, accounting rules and procedures for client care and complaints, which could be regarded as an unfair burden. The arguments for reform were that barristers would be at a competitive disadvantage if they could not offer services directly to lay clients and the requirement of the rule demands that clients employ two lawyers where that is often unnecessary.[231] Considerable developments have been made to widen access to the Bar, so that, as we have seen, a barrister may now[232] be appointed by the court, or accept instructions from a professional client or within the terms of the Licensed Access scheme[233] or the Public Access scheme.[234]

(2) Advertising and publicity

There were old and traditional restrictions on barristers advertising. Now bar- **3–031** risters "may engage in any advertising or promotion in connection with [their] practice which conforms to the British Codes of Advertising and Sales Promotion . . . ".[235] It may include photographs and illustrations of the barrister,

---

[227] per Lord Steyn in Arthur Hall v Simons [2000] 3 All E.R. 673 at 680.
[228] Kunzlik (1999), para.401(a).
[229] In a matter in which the licensed conveyancer is providing conveyancing services.
[230] Code of Conduct, para.1001.
[231] LECG Ltd, Restrictions on Competition in the Provision of Professional Services: A Report for the Office of Fair Trading (2000), paras 262–265, found as part of Office of Fair Trading, Competition in Professions (2001).
[232] Code of Conduct, para.401(a).
[233] See ibid. Annex F1.
[234] ibid. Annex F2.
[235] Code of Conduct, para.710.1.

statements of rates and methods of charging and about the nature and extent of
his or her services, and information about previous cases, provided that information is publicly available or the client's consent has been obtained.[236]

(3) *Partnerships and chambers*

3–032 The key principle for barristers in self-employed practice is their independence.
This is also one of the major rationales behind the rules on the manner in which
a barrister may practise. Self-employed barristers "must not practise from the
office of or in any unincorporated association (including any arrangement which
involves sharing the administration of [their] practice) with any person other than
a self-employed barrister or any of the following: (a) a Registered European
lawyer; (b) subject to compliance with the Foreign Lawyers (Chambers) Rules
(reproduced in Annex H) and with the consent of the Bar Council a foreign
lawyer; (c) a non-practising barrister; (d) a person who is: (i) a lawyer from a
jurisdiction other than England and Wales; (ii) a retired judge; or (iii) an
employed barrister to the extent that that person is practising as an arbitrator or
mediator".[237] The obligations upon barristers demand that they "take all reasonable steps to ensure that: (i) [their] practice is efficiently and properly administered having regard to the nature of [their] practice; (ii) proper records are kept;
[they comply] with the Terms of Work on which Barristers Offer their Services
to Solicitors . . . ".[238] They must also have "ready access to library facilities
which are adequate having regard to the nature of [their] practice". They must
also have regard to any Bar Council guidance relevant to the administration of
their practice, pupillage and training and equal opportunities issues.[239] This
principle is open to challenge, though the Kentridge Report recommended
retention of the rule against partnerships.[240] However, the changing face of civil
litigation is applying significant pressure on this position[241] and it is clear that the
drive towards "alternative business structures" in the Legal Services Bill will
challenge the principle even further.

Most self-employed barristers operate from a set of chambers involving more
than one barrister. They are not in partnership and are not sharing fees. Each
barrister contributes towards rent and towards collective expenses. Whilst some
work comes into a named barrister, other work may come into chambers and be
distributed to an appropriate barrister. Some work directed to a named barrister

---

[236] *ibid.* And see Kentridge Report (2002), which recommends that the rule against advertising
success rates should be maintained, but the advertising of fee comparisons should not be
prohibited.

[237] *Code of Conduct*, para.403.1. In combination with the restrictions upon employed barristers, this
emphasises the importance of independence.

[238] Annex G1. In a speech by the Chairman of the Bar Council given on November 4, 2006, he
indicated that a model contract for the instruction of counsel by solicitors would soon be
available.

[239] *Code of Conduct*, para.403.2.

[240] Kentridge Report (2002), recommendation (1).

[241] P. Kunzlik, "Rebuilding the Cathedral?—The partnership question and the effect of 'modernisation' on the professionalism and ethics of the English Bar" (2001), which notes a number of the
pressures pushing for partnership, notably the Woolf reforms of civil litigation, the realisation that
size matters as witnessed by the number of recent mergers and other means of increasing the size
of individual sets of chambers, the increasing difficulty, as they grow, of working in chambers in
the same way as traditionally has been the case, and the increasing need for barristers to specialise
so as to succeed.

may be passed on to a colleague in chambers.[242] A proper library can only readily be achieved by joint contributions, although any successful barrister will have his or her own directly relevant materials. There are obligations imposed upon Heads of Chambers as to the way in which chambers should operate.[243]

(4) *Queen's Counsel and junior barristers*

Another distinctive feature of practice is the division of the bar into two ranks: Queen's Counsel[244] and "junior" barristers. For many years, appointment as a Q.C. was made by the reigning monarch on the advice of the Lord Chancellor, following an extensive process of consultation amongst the judiciary and the legal professions. Concerns about the subjectivity and secrecy of the selection process have led to greater transparency such that the process is now dealt with by an independent secretariat[245]; and the process includes a competency framework setting out what is required of a Q.C.; clarity about the individuals who will see the applications; an independent selection panel including lay membership and an interview.[246]

3–033

The title Q.C. is a mark of eminence in the profession and, following the advent of higher rights of audience for solicitors, is no longer confined to members of the Bar. The Kentridge Report recommended that the Q.C. system was of value, and that it should be retained.[247] It is arguably treated as a mark of quality,[248] although the extent to which this is in fact the case is currently under investigation by the Ministry of Justice.[249] The main difference as regards work done is that Q.C.s are the skilled and experienced advocates and the expert and specialist advisers on points of law. Barrister Q.C.s do not normally do the paperwork associated with litigation unless they are acting on their own. Ordinarily, barristers "taking silk" can anticipate that their earnings will improve, but the change can be something of a gamble, although the risks are not as great as they were once thought to be. Most High Court judges are appointed from amongst the Q.C.s[250] and there are many other judicial appointments available to them.

At one time, there were rules of etiquette which prevented a Q.C. from appearing in court without a junior (the two-counsel rule) and which entitled the junior to a fee equivalent to two-thirds of that of her or his leader. The latter rule was abolished in 1966 and replaced by an entitlement to a "proper fee".[251] The

---

[242] For circumstances in which a barrister must cease to act and return his or her instructions, see *Code of Conduct* para.608.

[243] *ibid.* para.404.2.

[244] "One of our Counsel learned in the Law." Q.C.s become K.C.s when there are kings on the throne of the United Kingdom. They are frequently known as "silks" as they are entitled to wear a silk gown in court. In July 2006 175 new Q.C.s were appointed from 443 applicants. Of the successful candidates, 33 were women; 10 were of "an ethnic origin other than white" and four were solicitor-advocates: QC Appointments Secretariat press release, July 20, 2006.

[245] See the website dedicated to Q.C. application and selection at *www.qcapplications.org.uk.*

[246] See Bar Council and Law Society, *Process for QC Award for England and Wales* (November 2004) and *Summary of Revised Process for QC Award for England and Wales* (November 2006).

[247] Kentridge Report (2002), recommendation (5).

[248] S. Kentridge, *Competition in the Professions: Report to the Bar Council* (2002), para.7.7.

[249] DCA, *Quality in the Legal Services Industry, a Scoping Study* (August 2005).

[250] See below, para.4–023.

[251] Annual Statement of the Bar Council 1971–72, p.20.

two-counsel rule was placed under pressure under competition law[252] and was abrogated in 1977. Now, a self-employed barrister Q.C. "is not obliged to accept instructions (a) to settle alone any document of a kind generally settled only by or in conjunction with a junior; (b) to act without a junior if [he or she] considers that the interests of the lay client require that a junior should also be instructed".[253]

3. QUALITY OF SERVICE

3–034   Lawyers have always prided themselves on the quality of services that they provide. " . . . Most advocates are honest conscientious people who need no other incentive to comply with the ethics of their profession" and "there is the wish to enjoy a good reputation among one's peers and the judiciary".[254] This is not mere assertion of a self-satisfied profession, but reveals an important business-based truth. If barristers, who are self-employed and reliant upon the reputation and quality of their work, have a poor reputation, fewer briefs will be sent to them and so they will be under personal financial pressure to perform better. Increased competition for work between solicitors' firms and with other providers of legal services mean that, particularly for business clients, poor quality work will involve the client in taking their business to a different firm. Whilst an increasingly diverse profession reduces reliance upon accepted ethical principles,[255] it is the case that, broadly speaking, lawyers tend to adopt high standards for themselves.

However, this is no protection of quality or against bad practice. Simple membership of a profession is no longer a sufficient mark and guarantee of quality.[256] Also, there are many more members of the profession and so the likelihood of poor quality work becomes greater. It is, though, important to recognise that most legal work is transacted well and efficiently and that most clients are satisfied with the work of their lawyers.[257] There is, however, a marked move towards placing the consumer client in the driving seat as far as defining the quality of legal services is concerned,[258] apparent in the title of the White Paper preceding the Legal Services Bill (*The Future of Legal Services*: *Putting Consumers First*) and in the regulatory objectives found in cl.1 of the Legal Services Bill ("protecting and promoting the interests of consumers").

Clearly, one measure of quality is the perception of the client.[259] But that is not the only possible measure, as clients may have criteria inconsistent with those by which the profession operates. The Ministry of Justice[260] has recognised that "because few people have a deep understanding of legal issues, few consumers are in a position to know the type of legal services they need, or indeed whether they have received a good service, *even after the event*". One of the difficulties

---

[252] Monopolies Commission, *Barrister Services: A report on the supply by Her Majesty's Counsel alone of their services* (1975–6 H.C. 512).

[253] *Code of Conduct*, para.605.

[254] *per* Lord Hoffmann in *Arthur Hall v Simons* [2000] 3 All E.R. 673 at 693.

[255] See Boon and Levin (1999), at p.118.

[256] See above, paras 3–001—3–002 and see Boon and Levin (1999).

[257] See below, para.9–009.

[258] For a client's perspective, see J. Farrar, "Arrogant, incompetent, negligent and unprofessional . . . ", August 2001, *Which?*, 8.

[259] See below, para.9–009.

[260] DCA, *Quality in the Legal Services Industry, a Scoping Study* (August 2005).

is how to measure quality. The Community Legal Service's and Criminal Defence Service's "quality mark"[261] whose holders have preference when it comes to obtaining a contract to provide publicly funded legal services seeks to provide an objective standard with a logo that is intended to have client recognition.[262] Providers of legal services may acquire other external markers of quality in areas other than that of the legal services themselves, such as BARMARK (a recognition of good practice management within chambers); LexCel (the Law Society's practice management quality mark); ISO 9001:2000 and Investors in People.[263] However, it is the current view of the Ministry of Justice that quality marks are not in fact used by consumers when choosing a legal services provider, and it is conducting research into the contribution of consumers' understanding of professional qualifications (including accreditation systems such as the Solicitors Regulation Authority specialist panels) and use of referral systems to their views about quality, as well as the contribution of substantiated complaints.[264]

One major source of quality assurance, however, should be by way of the admission of appropriate, qualified personnel who are provided with good training.[265] Quality should also be assured, to some extent, by the professional practice rules[266] and the complaints systems for clients.[267] Another significant potential contribution to quality is the requirement for continuing professional development ("CPD"), which now applies to all solicitors and barristers.[268] This means that they have to demonstrate that they have been undertaking developmental activity: this ought to assist in the maintenance of the currency of practice in all its senses. Further, there is some work that can only be done if certain procedures are satisfied[269] or there are panels giving indications of expertise thereby providing some guarantee of quality.[270] When the activity is advocacy, quality assurance is supported by the role of the judges in considering

---

[261] "The Quality Mark is the quality standard that will underpin all CLS services, so that members of the public who need legal information, advice and other help can rely on receiving a quality assured service": *www.legalservices.gov.uk/civil/quality_mark.asp.*

[262] The transaction criteria underlying the quality mark were developed by the work of Professors Sherr and Paterson and Richard Moorhead. As to the Community Legal Service, see below, paras 9–005, and Ch.10. Other quality marks are promoted through the same organisations: Quality Mark for the Bar; Mediation Quality Mark (for family and community mediation); Quality Mark for Websites (legal information provided over the internet); Telephone Standards and Specialist Support.

[263] The *Solicitors' Code of Conduct 2007* creates a new Rule 5 governing "the supervision and management of a firm or in-house practice, the maintenance of competence and the internal business arrangements essential to the proper delivery of services to clients", imposing specific professional obligations on principals for supervision and compliance. See J. Jarman, "Cracking the Code: are you ready for the Law Society's new Code of Conduct?" (2006) 34 *Axiom* 14; "How lawyers can heed the Code", (2006) 103(22) L.S.G. 10 and F. Cunningham, "Get a Head Start" (2006) 8(11) *Legal Week*, 24.

[264] DCA, *Quality in the Legal Services Industry, a Scoping Study* (August 2005).

[265] See below, paras 3–051 and 3–052, and see Boon and Levin (1999), Ch.6.

[266] See below, paras 3–037 and 3–041 above.

[267] See below, paras 3–036 to 3–039 and 3–041 to 3–042.

[268] The Law Society has had a compulsory scheme for continuing professional development since 1985 and now found in the Law Society Training Regulations 1990 now administered by the SRA. The Bar Council introduced a requirement for new practitioners (i.e. in the first three years of self-employed practice) in October 1997 and a scheme for established practitioners from January 1, 2001 such that by 2005 all practising barristers (including employed barristers) were required to comply with the scheme.

[269] For example, limitations upon work in financial services as imposed by the Financial Services Act 1986.

[270] See above, para.3–012.

a barrister's or solicitor-advocate's work. Judicial comments can be beneficial or detrimental to an advocate's career; judicial comments may assist the advocate in developing advocacy and trial skills.

4. REGULATION OF AND COMPLAINTS AGAINST LAWYERS

3–035   A major debate about the regulation of the legal professions was commenced by the Legal Services Ombudsman[271] in her annual report for 2001–02. So concerned was she about the ability of the Law Society and solicitors to deal with complaints that she considered that "the time may have come for a more radical approach to the regulation of legal services".[272] As we have seen throughout this chapter, steps are currently being taken by the government in the Legal Services Bill to place the regulation of legal services under greater and more centralised control.

In her *Annual Report 2005–06*, the current ombudsman (Ms Zahida Manzoor, CBE) indicated in the context of the Legal Services Bill that:

> "[d]uring the last three years the legal profession has been through a challenging time, having an external review of its roles, responsibilities and recommendations for change . . . [that] will bring the regulation of legal services into the 21st century and place greater focus on the profession delivering a service that is in line with the expectations of its customers. If I have any concern, it is that the new structure may end up merely being an exercise in tweaking what largely exists . . . If this occurs then I do not believe that consumers would be satisfied and, in my view, the hard work, time and energy that has been devoted by many people over the past two and a half years will have been wasted".[273]

This section examines the current position as well as the proposals for change.

(a) Solicitors[274]

3–036   Problems should, in principle, be prevented from arising by the ethical norms adopted by solicitors. In effect, solicitors have accepted a general structure to their ethical commitments and this has been reflected in the way that they have regulated themselves.[275] One of the traditional means to achieve this has been control over entry to the profession and the authority to practise.[276]

---

[271] A post created under s.22 of the Courts and Legal Services Act 1990 and Legal Services Ombudsman (Jurisdiction) Order 1990, SI 1990/2485: *www.olso.org*.

[272] Legal Services Ombudsman, *Annual Report 2001–2002* (2002), at p.4. The current ombudsman also became the legal services complaints commissioner in 2004, this role involving working with the Law Society to improve its complaints system. She deemed the plan for such improvement submitted by the Law Society in 2006 to be inadequate and fined the Society £220,000 as a result: *www.olscc.gov.uk/htms/lawsocper.htm*.

[273] *Striving for Excellence Annual Report and Accounts of the Legal Services Ombudsman for England and Wales 2005–2006* (July 2006, Stationery Office, H.C. 1375).

[274] For a historical review, see M. Davies, "Solicitors—the last 20 years of self-regulation?" (2005) 21(1) P.N. 3.

[275] See Boon and Levin (1999), pp.102–104 and 106–108.

[276] See Boon and Levin (1999), pp.124–125. As described above, all solicitors wishing to practise must have a current practising certificate.

When things go wrong, there is a number of avenues open to the client affected, although there may be considerable practical difficulties in following them through. The first step is to raise the matter with the firm, company or LLP. From 1991, Practice Rule 15 on Client Care obliged all principals in private practice to have a complaints handling procedure that complied with the Solicitors' Costs Information and Client Care Code.[277] "The main object of the code is to make sure that clients are given the information they need to understand what is happening generally and in particular on (i) the cost of legal services both at the outset and as the matter progresses; and (ii) responsibility for clients' matters."[278] The Client Care Code provided standards for both client care and complaints handling. Breaches of the Client Care Code might amount to both or either disciplinary matters and evidence of inadequate professional services. The *Solicitors' Code of Conduct 2007* deals with client relations at Rule 2, providing that in respect of client care the solicitor must initially clearly identify the client's objectives; explain the issue involved and options available; agree the next steps to be taken; and keep the client informed of progress. Going further than the Client Care Code, Rule 2.02 of the *Solicitors' Code of Conduct 2007* requires the solicitor to agree an appropriate level of service and explain the responsibilities of both solicitor and client as well as provide details of the person handling the matter and the person supervising it and any conditions resulting from the involvement of a third party—such as the client's insurer—that might affect what can be done on the client's behalf. Under para.2.05, principals must ensure that the firm has a written complaints procedure; "that complaints are handled promptly, fairly and effectively in accordance with it"; that clients are told at the beginning of the relationship that they are entitled to complain, and who to and are given a copy of the complaints procedure on request. Where a complaint is made, complainants must be told in writing "how the complaint will be handled; and within what timescales they will be given an initial and/or substantive response". Solicitors will not be entitled to charge clients for investigating or dealing with complaints.

(b) Regulating solicitors' practice

The Law Society's power to make rules regulating the professional practice, conduct and discipline of solicitors (now diverted to the SRA) is subject to the concurrence of the Master of the Rolls.[279] The regulatory functions of the Law Society are now vested in the Solicitors' Regulatory Authority.[280]   **3–037**

The standards, rules and principles[281] for solicitors were set out and amplified in *The Guide to the Professional Conduct of Solicitors*[282] and are now contained

---

[277] The Client Care Code was introduced in 1999 to provide fuller and clearer guidance as to what was required in complaint handling and last amended in 2006. And see Boon and Levin (1999), pp.125–128.

[278] Client Care Code, at para.1(b). This Code also applied to RFLs and RELs registered with the Law Society. Further guidance is provided by the Law Society booklet *Your Clients; Your Business* (May 2006).

[279] Solicitors Act 1974, s.31(1).

[280] *www.sra.org.uk.*

[281] The standards usually describe important character traits such as honesty and competence; the rules prescribe particular things that must be done or not done; and the principles deal with other matters often at a fairly generalised level: see Boon and Levin (1999), p.104.

[282] The last published edition is that from 1999. Updates and amendments were until recently published on the Law Society's website but have now been divested to that of the Solicitors' Regulatory Authority.

in the *Solicitors' Code of Conduct 2007*. Some of the basic rules have already been set out, especially those governing a solicitor's general duties, publicity, introductions and referrals, complaints, employed solicitors, multi-disciplinary partnerships, and multi-national practices.[283] The rules also include important provisions about client confidentiality[284]; prevent practising solicitors from providing certain legal services other than as a solicitor; and provide safeguards to distinguish between a solicitor's practice and his or her other business.[285] The work that may be provided only through a solicitor's practice are the following services: "the conduct of any matter which could come before a court, tribunal or inquiry, whether or not proceedings are started"; court, tribunal or inquiry advocacy; instructing counsel; immigration advice; work reserved to solicitors under the Solicitors Act 1974 (as to which the Legal Services Bill will necessarily have an effect); acting as an executor, trustee or nominee in England and Wales; will drafting; giving legal advice, and any legal document drafting.[286]

There is also a requirement that a solicitor must not act for a client in situations of conflict of interest, a position clarified by Rule 3 of the *Solicitors' Code of Conduct 2007*:

> "[y]ou must not act if there is a conflict of interests (except in the limited circumstances dealt with in 3.02). (2) There is a conflict of interests if: (a) you owe, or your firm owes, separate duties to act in the best interests of two or more clients in relation to the same or related matters, and those duties conflict, or there is a significant risk that those duties may conflict; or (b) your duty to act in the best interests of any client in relation to a matter conflicts, or there is a significant risk that it may conflict, with your own interests in relation to that or a related matter. (3) For the purpose of 3.01(2), a related matter will always include any other matter which involves the same asset or liability."

Exceptions are provided, first, if "the different clients have a substantially common interest" and "all the clients have given in writing their informed consent to you or your firm acting" and, secondly, if the only conflict is that "the clients are competing for the same asset which, if attained by one client, will make that asset unattainable to the other client(s)[287]; the clients have provided informed consent and, unless the clients agree to the contrary, different individuals within the firm act for the different clients. There has always been some difficulty for many solicitors in identifying when a conflict of interests might arise and the rules in the *Solicitors' Code of Conduct 2007* are arguably no clearer. There are some conveyancing circumstances where a solicitor can act for more than one client in an apparent conflict of interest.[288] The *Solicitors' Code of Conduct 2007*, Rule 5, places obligations for the proper supervision of practices directly on principals including a threshold of management training required before an individual is "qualified to supervise", a requirement for

---

[283] See above, para.3–037.
[284] See *Solicitors' Code for Conduct 2007*, Rule 4.
[285] Solicitors' Practice Rules 1990, r.5; Solicitors' Separate Business Code 1994 and *Solicitors' Code for Conduct 2007*, Rule 21.
[286] *Solicitors' Code of Conduct 2007*, Rule 21.2, previously found in Solicitors' Separate Business Code 1994, section 3.
[287] For example, in a conveyancing contract race.
[288] Solicitors' Practice Rules 1990, r.6 replaced by *Solicitors' Code of Conduct 2007*, Rules 3.07 to 3.15.

systems for dealing with problems of conflict of interest and client confidentiality and the statement in the accompanying guidance that "[p]rincipals are responsible in law and in conduct for their firms, including exercising proper control over their staff".

Solicitors must comply with detailed rules about the holding of client's money and the maintenance of adequate book-keeping and recording systems.[289] Whether money is held by a solicitor in a separate designated client account or a general client account, he or she must account to the client for all interest earned. All interest earned in the former must be credited to the account but, in the latter, sums in lieu will be paid in except where it is very small and the solicitor may retain any interest earned over and above that required to be paid under the Accounts Rules.[290]

One form of client protection lies in the assurance that any losses or damage caused by the solicitor can be recovered by or compensated to the client. This demands that the solicitor is either sufficiently wealthy or carries sufficient insurance cover to meet such demands. This was originally achieved by the Solicitors' Indemnity Fund established by the Law Society on behalf of solicitors. However, such were the problems with the Fund, not least the cost to solicitors, that now there is simply an obligation on all practising solicitors to carry adequate professional indemnity insurance under the Solicitors' Indemnity Insurance Rules 2001.

(c) Solicitors: Professional misconduct and inadequate professional services

The power to deal with both professional misconduct and inadequate pro- **3–038** fessional services is now vested in the Solicitors' Regulation Authority, although complaints about solicitors are dealt with through the Legal Complaints Service of the Law Society.[291] Part 6 of the Legal Services Bill provides for an Office for Legal Complaints to operate a new single ombudsman scheme applicable to all those authorised to conduct reserved legal activity.

At present, however, the Legal Complaints Service provides a route to deal with complaints not resolved through the relevant firm's complaints procedure, initially by conciliation but, if necessary, by making a formal finding. Where there are substantiated complaints about inadequate professional services[292] (as opposed to disputes about bills) the Legal Complaints Service may reduce the client's bill, correct mistakes and/or pay compensation up to £15,000. "Inadequate professional services" is defined as "the provision by solicitors of services which are not of the quality which it is reasonable to expect of them".[293] The Legal Complaints Service suggests that

---

[289] See the Solicitors' Accounts Rules 1998, not affected by the *Solicitors' Code of Conduct 2007* and other relevant rules and principles. Such rules were first made in 1935 because of a number of frauds by solicitors causing public concern: Abel-Smith and Stevens (1967), pp.190–192.

[290] Solicitors' Accounts Rules, rr.24 and 25.

[291] *www.legalcomplaints.org.uk.*

[292] Although the Law Society has always had the power to deal with misconduct, it has only had the power to deal with inadequate professional services since the Administration of Justice Act 1985. See now the Solicitors Act 1974, s.37A and Sch.1A as replaced by the Courts and Legal Services Act 1990, s.93.

[293] Solicitors Act 1974, s.37A.

"[i]t is likely that you've received poor service from your solicitor if they've

- not done what you instructed them to do;
- involved you in unreasonable delays;
- given you inaccurate or incomplete information;
- failed to reply to your phone calls and letters or keep you informed about what is going on;
- failed to give you enough information about what they'll charge you before they begin your case or give you the final bill."

If the client is dissatisfied with the way that the Legal Complaints Service has investigated and dealt with the matter, further recourse is available within a three-month window to the Legal Services Ombudsman who may formally criticise, recommend reinvestigation, award compensation or, in exceptional circumstances, investigate the original complaint. In 2005–06, 89.1 per cent of the ombudsman's work was in respect of Law Society investigations and involved 1,701 reports to complainants, 492 of which involved adverse findings.[294] The ombudsman remained unhappy with the quality of Law Society complaints handling: "[o]nce again, this year, the Ombudsman's recommendations highlight repeated instances of basic errors, poor administration, poor decision making and poor service on the Law Society's part".[295]

The Legal Complaints Service may also refer matters of professional misconduct to the Solicitors' Regulatory Authority. Such matters may also be referred directly to the Solicitors' Regulatory Authority, for example by other solicitors. Breach of practice rules is not necessarily professional misconduct. "Professional misconduct" is undefined. It may be, therefore, that it is conduct that other members of the profession would regard as " 'dishonourable' or 'deplorable' "[296] The Solicitors' Regulatory Authority, whilst including amongst its key objectives that of "tackl[ing] unacceptable professional or organisational performance, misconduct and dishonesty by firm, fair and timely regulatory and disciplinary action"[297] does not seek to provide any clearer definition.

What the definition does not include is allegations of negligence by a solicitor. Negligence is conduct of a solicitor falling below a standard which may reasonably be expected of him or her and entitling the complainant to damages obtained through the courts for any loss caused. The dividing line between negligence and inadequate professional services is extremely difficult to draw and, in effect, the Legal Complaints Service deals with small negligence claims as inadequate professional services.

3–039   If there is a finding of professional misconduct, it seems to be the case that the Solicitors' Regulatory Authority has taken over the powers of the earlier Office for the Supervision of Solicitors, which include[298] reprimanding the solicitor; requiring the solicitor to pay interest on a client account[299]; refusing a practising

---

[294] *Striving for Excellence: Annual Report and Accounts of the Legal Services Ombudsman for England and Wales 2005–2006*, section 11.
[295] *ibid.*
[296] National Consumer Council, *The Solicitors' Complaints Bureau: A consumer view* (1994), p.31.
[297] *www.sra.org.uk/about/strategy.page*.
[298] See *Solicitors' Code of Conduct 2007*, Rule 20.
[299] Solicitors' Accounts Rules 1998, r.24.

certificate or issuing a conditional certificate[300]; imposing conditions on a solicitor's current practising certificate[301]; suspending, withdrawing or imposing conditions on an investment business certificate[302]; ordering an inspection of the accounts[303]; disqualifying an accountant from giving an accountant's report on the accounts[304]; intervening in a solicitor's practice[305]; or instituting disciplinary proceedings before the Solicitors' Disciplinary Tribunal.[306] Where there is a finding of undue delay, money and papers may be recovered for the client or a new solicitor. Where there is a finding of dishonesty against a solicitor and the client has suffered a financial loss, a payment may be made from the Solicitors' Compensation Fund.[307] Payments from this fund are rare, because it is a "discretionary fund of the last resort"[308] and because the more likely source of compensation is from the solicitor.[309]

(d) Disciplinary proceedings: solicitors[310]

The most serious cases are dealt with by the Solicitors Disciplinary Tribunal,[311] **3–040**
which is independent of, but currently funded by, the Law Society (although this is under review) and with both solicitor and lay membership. Its principal function is to hear and determine allegations of unbefitting conduct or breaches of the rules of professional conduct by solicitors, former solicitors, RFLS and RELs registered with the Law Society. Hearings are normally in public. The Tribunal may: strike the solicitor off the roll[312]; suspend the solicitor indefinitely or for a specified period; fine the solicitor (not more than £5,000 per allegation)[313]; reprimand the solicitor; exclude the solicitor from publicly funded work (permanently or for a specified period); terminate an open-ended period of suspension; restore a former solicitor previously struck off; prohibit the restoration of a struck-off former solicitor to the roll; or order the payment of costs.[314] In 2006, there were 212 cases before the Tribunal. The actions taken by the Tribunal were[315]:

---

[300] Solicitors Act 1974, s.12.

[301] *ibid.* s.13A.

[302] Solicitors' Investment Business Rules 1995, r.5.

[303] Solicitors' Accounts Rules, r.34.

[304] Solicitors' Accounts Rules 1998, r.37(3).

[305] Solicitors Act 1974, Sch.1.

[306] See below, para.3–040.

[307] Solicitors Act 1974, s.36 (as amended).

[308] E. Skordaki, *et al., Default by Solicitors* (1991), as quoted by Boon and Levin (1999), p.133.

[309] There used to be a Solicitors' Indemnity Fund (see Boon and Levin (1999), p.132), but now all solicitors must carry indemnity insurance, see above, para.3–038.

[310] As Boon and Levin point out, "disciplinary mechanisms [are] often a focus of criticism": Boon and Levin (1999), p.105.

[311] It was established by the Solicitors Act 1974, s.46. See Boon and Levin (1999), pp.129–132 and B. Swift, *Proceedings Before the Solicitors' Disciplinary Tribunal* (1996). Its website can be found at *www.solicitorstribunal.org*.

[312] The Court of Appeal expects that a solicitor who is found guilty of dishonesty will be struck off: *Bolton v The Law Society* [1994] 1 W.L.R. 512, but not all have been either struck off or suspended: Boon and Levin (1999), p.131.

[313] The Tribunal recommends that the level of fine should be increased: *Solicitors' Disciplinary Tribunal Annual Report 2006.*

[314] Solicitors Act 1974, ss.37A, 47 and Sch.1A Reports of the proceedings of the Solicitors Disciplinary Tribunal appear in the *Law Society's Gazette*. Appeals from the decisions of the tribunal are dealt with under CPR Pt 52 and decisions are occasionally the subject of judicial review.

[315] Boon and Levin (1999), p.131.

Struck off the roll	63
Suspended from practice	39
Fined	64
Reprimanded	16
No order, costs only order or case dismissed	10

The High Court, the Crown Court and the Court of Appeal may also exercise jurisdiction over solicitors as officers of the supreme court.[316] Clearly, of course, extreme misconduct by a solicitor may independently amount to a criminal offence.

(e) Barristers

3–041   The Bar's Code of Conduct[317] is more recent than that for solicitors. It was first published in 1981 and, in 2004, reached its eighth edition.[318] It is most readily accessible on the Bar Council website. The powers were not statutory, but predicated upon self-regulation.[319] Barristers historically self-regulated, as did solicitors, entry to the profession and the authority to practise, although these functions have now been vested in the Bar Standards Board.[320] All barristers must be called to one of the four Inns of Court (Gray's Inn, Inner Temple, Lincoln's Inn and Middle Temple). After pupillage,[321] the barrister is free to practise, subject to obtaining a practising certificate in much the same way as a solicitor.[322]

Until 1996, there were few avenues available to a lay client[323] when things went wrong.[324] Some chambers were able to deal with complaints, and the client could seek the instigation of disciplinary proceedings or go to law. A judge can be involved in discussing a barrister's practice[325] and a wasted costs order can be made against a barrister. However, there was no practice rule demanding a complaints handling system in chambers, nor a system at the level of the professional body, the Bar Council. A complaints system was introduced in 1996.[326]

---

[316] Solicitors Act 1974, ss.50–53.

[317] See above, para.3–028.

[318] Boon and Levin (1999), p.134. The Bar Council's existence was statutorily recognised in the Courts and Legal Services Act 1990, s.31.

[319] *ibid.*

[320] As to educational requirements, see below, para.3–051.

[321] *ibid.*

[322] Bar Code of Conduct, Annex D *The Practising Certificate Regulations*, made under Access to Justice Act 1999, s.46.

[323] As to the clients of a barrister, see above, para.3–030.

[324] Until the Courts and Legal Services Act 1990, s.61, a barrister could not enter a contract for his or her services and so could not be contractually bound to deliver a service and could not sue for fees. Whilst the Bar Council originally made a rule prohibiting a barrister from entering into contracts this has been ameliorated by *The Contractual Terms Of Work On Which Barristers Offer Their Services To Solicitors 2001* provision at Annex G2 of the Bar Code of Conduct, which allows for a contractual relationship. A model form of contract with solicitors is understood to be imminent at the time of writing.

[325] See above, para.3–034.

[326] Complaints System Working Party, *Report* (1995), paras 2–29.

Complaints about a barrister's professional work[327] sent to the Bar Standards Board[328] are now initially considered by the Complaints Commissioner.[329] A complaint may be about either professional misconduct or inadequate professional service. The Bar Council defines professional misconduct as "a serious error or misbehaviour by a barrister which may well involve some element of dishonesty or serious incompetence. It might include: misleading the court; failure to keep your affairs confidential; leaving a case without good reason at short notice; acting against a client's instructions or best interests".[330] Other matters that might amount to professional misconduct are listed in *Code of Conduct*, Pt IX: Compliance.

The Bar Council defines inadequate professional service as "service towards the client falling significantly below that which would normally be expected of a barrister. It is not as serious as misconduct but may well have caused significant concern or inconvenience to a client such as: delay in dealing with papers; poor or inadequate work on a case; serious rudeness to the client".[331] Complaints of negligence cannot be taken through this procedure, and the Bar Council's advice is for such a complainant to seek advice from another lawyer.[332]

The Commissioner determines, after an investigation if appropriate, whether there is a *prima facie* case, and may dismiss cases where this is lacking.[333] The Commissioner may ask the barrister for his or her comments on a complaint, which will be sent to the complainant. If the Commissioner determines that a complaint may be justified, it is referred to the Conduct Committee of the Bar Standards Board for consideration. If the complaint involves inadequate professional services, the Conduct Committee will remit the matter to an Adjudication Panel of two barristers and two laypeople. If a complaint is substantiated the panel may demand an apology, repayment of fees or order compensation of up to £5,000. The barrister may appeal.[334]

The number of complaints *received* by the Complaints Commissioner in 2005 was 422.[335] Of the 455 complaints *completed* during the year, 264 were dismissed by the Commissioner and two were completed through conciliation. Of complaints referred to the Conduct Committee, 56 were dismissed, 60 required no further action, 17 proceeded to a summary hearing and 56 were withdrawn. The Bar continues to do fairly well in its complaints handling (at least compared to the Law Society). In her 2005–06 annual report, the legal services ombudsman described 22 findings against the Bar Council and commented "[t]he Bar Council continues to deliver good results in respect of speed of service". The Legal Services Complaints Commissioner has no role in relation to the Bar Council's complaints handling procedures. Under the Legal Services Bill, the Bar will be subject to the centralised ombudsman process already described.

---

[327] Complaints about a barrister's private life or non-professional work are, therefore, not taken unless they involve an allegation of criminal or similar misbehaviour. Further, debt actions against a barrister must be pursued through the courts. Where the barrister is employed, the complaint should first be taken up with the employer and then with the Bar Standards Board.

[328] Normally a complaint must be made within six months of the complaint arising. The time limit may be extended if the matter is particularly serious or there is good reason for the delay.

[329] Currently Mr Robert Behrens, a layman.

[330] *www.barcouncil.org.uk*.

[331] *ibid*.

[332] This may result in action being taken for negligence, see below, paras 3–044—3–046. Barristers have professional indemnity insurance through the Barristers' Mutual Insurance Fund.

[333] The Commissioner also dismisses the case if it is trivial or lacks validity.

[334] Adjudication Panels and Appeals Rules, Bar *Code of Conduct*, Annex P.

[335] *Annual Report of the Complaints Commissioner 2005*, Annex B.

(f) Professional misconduct: barristers

3–042 If the Conduct Committee receives a reference from the Complaints Commissioner and agrees that the complaint may be justified and is a case involving professional misconduct, the case is referred to one of three different bodies. It may be referred to an informal hearing; a summary procedure panel; or a disciplinary tribunal. An informal hearing[336] consists of two barristers and one layperson. If it decides that the complaint is upheld, it may advise the barrister as to his or her future conduct; or admonish him or her; or impose one of the penalties for inadequate professional service.

A summary procedure panel[337] consists of one barrister, one Q.C. and one layperson. On upholding a complaint, it may do what an informal hearing may do, and, further, it can fine a barrister or suspend him or her for up to three months.

A Disciplinary Tribunal[338] is chaired by a judge with two barristers and two lay people. It deals with the most serious cases, usually sits in public and can, in addition to the penalties that the other procedures can impose, disbar a barrister or suspend him or her for an unlimited period.[339] A barrister may appeal from a summary procedure panel or a Disciplinary Tribunal to the Visitors, who are the High Court Judges.[340] The complainant has no right of appeal, although a the Complaints Commissioner or Conduct Committee may be prepared to review the matter and a complainant dissatisfied with the way the Bar Council has handled a complaint may refer the matter to the Legal Services Ombudsman.[341]

(g) The Legal Services Ombudsman[342]

3–043 The office of the Legal Services Ombudsman was created by s.21 of the Courts and Legal Services Act 1990 "to reinforce the existing system with more effective measures for dealing with complaints".[343] Both it and the role of Legal Services Complaints Commissioner will be abolished by the Legal Services Bill, cl.128, to be replaced by the Office for Legal Complaints as a single point of reference for all those involved in provision of reserved legal activity.

Until the Bill becomes law, however, the ombudsman retains the power to investigate the way in which certain professional bodies (currently the Law Society, the General Council of the Bar, the Council for Licensed Conveyancers, the Institute of Legal Executives, the Chartered Institute of Patent Attorneys[344] and the Institute of Trade Mark Attorneys) have handled complaints to them about members of their profession.[345] Secondly, where an allegation is investigated, the substance of the complaint to the professional body may also be

---

[336] Bar *Code of Conduct*, Annex J, rule 39.

[337] *ibid*. Annex L.

[338] *ibid*. Annex K.

[339] The Bar Council publishes the most serious decisions of the Tribunal once the timescale for appeal against sentence has passed.

[340] Bar *Code of Conduct*, Annex M.

[341] See below, para.3–043.

[342] See R. James and M. Seneviratne, "The Legal Services Ombudsman: Form versus Function?" (1995) 58 M.L.R. 187 and M. Seneviratne, *The Legal Profession: Regulation and the Consumer* (1999), Ch.6.

[343] Lord Chancellor's Department, *Legal Services: Framework for the Future* (Cm. 740, 1989).

[344] For complaints handling by this body, see Anon, "Complaint handling arrangements at CIPA" (2004) 33(5) C.I.P.A.J. 261.

[345] Courts and Legal Services Act 1990, s.22(1).

investigated.[346] The second power is rarely exercised, which is not surprising in view of the oversight function ascribed to the ombudsman[347]

The ombudsman cannot investigate any complaint which has been dealt with by a court or the relevant disciplinary tribunal, since the procedures in such tribunals satisfy the need for public accountability.[348] She will not investigate complaints raised more than three months after the decision of the professional body; prior to a complaint to the professional body; by lawyers about other lawyers (unless on behalf of a client); employees of lawyers or contractual disputes (as, for example, about non-payment of fees).[349]

Between 1991 and 2001, the ombudsman undertook 10,531 investigations.[350] In 2005/06, her office completed 1,701 investigations.[351] Where the ombudsman investigates,[352] upon completion of the investigation, a written report of the conclusions must be sent to the person making the allegation, any person in respect of whom the complaint was made, and the professional body concerned.[353] In 2005/06 where complaints were upheld, the results were as follows[354]:

	Law Society	Bar Council	Council for Licensed Conveyancers
Criticism	79	3	2
Lawyer to pay compensation	1	0	0
Professional body to pay compensation	253	1	6
Professional body to reconsider and pay	73	1	4
Professional body to reconsider	164	17	2
Professional body to enforce powers and pay compensation	1	0	0
Totals	571	22	14

James and Seneviratne, in 1995, concluded that, with minor reservations, the office met the four criteria essential to the work of ombudsmen, that is "independence of the ombudsman from those whom he has power to investigate;

---

[346] *ibid.* s.22(2).
[347] See James and Seneviratne (1995), p.189.
[348] Court and Legal Services Act 1990, s.22(7).
[349] *Striving for Excellence, op. cit.*
[350] Office of the Legal Services Ombudsman, *Annual Report 2001* (2002), p.4. Of those investigations, 9,456 concerned complaints about solicitors, 1,036 complaints about barristers and 39 complaints about licensed conveyancers. Some 60% of solicitors' firms and 8% of barristers have been the subject of a complaint.
[351] *Striving for Excellence, op. cit.*
[352] In some straightforward cases, there is a fast track method: James and Seneviratne (1995), p.202.
[353] Courts and Legal Services Act 1990, s.23(1). The same people must be informed if the ombudsman does not investigate: s.22(4).
[354] *Striving for Excellence, op. cit.*

effectiveness; fairness; and public accountability".[355] Their major concern was whether the ombudsman should not be more regularly, if not always, investigating the complaint at the heart of the allegation.[356] Overall, Professor Seneviratne's conclusion is that the "office is performing an excellent role, on a limited budget".[357] The Office for Legal Complaints proposed by the Legal Services Bill will continue to operate an ombudsman scheme

(h) Legal proceedings against lawyers

(i) *Negligence*

3–044   A lawyer's misconduct or incompetence may give rise to a cause of action against him or her. For example, a client may be able to sue for breach of contract,[358] breach of trust[359] or the tort of negligence. The scope of negligence liability has been wider since the decision of the House of Lords in 1963 in *Hedley, Byrne & Co Ltd v Heller & Partners Ltd*,[360] where it was established that a special relationship could give rise to a duty of care in the giving of information or advice, and that there would be liability in damages in such cases in respect of losses that were purely economic. In *Midland Bank Trust Co Ltd v Hett. Stubbs & Kemp*[361] Oliver J. stated that the case of a layman consulting a solicitor seemed: "to be as typical a case as one could find of the sort of relationship in which the duty of care described in the *Hedley Byrne* case exists."[362]

In *Ross v Caunters*,[363] Sir Robert Megarry V.-C. took matters a step further. Solicitors failed to warn a client that his will should not be witnessed by a spouse of a beneficiary and failed to notice that this had happened. They were held liable to the disappointed beneficiary whose bequest failed. This decision was upheld in *White v Jones*[364] by the House of Lords by a narrow majority. Nevertheless in *Moy v Pettman Smith*,[365] where it was suggested that a barrister, advising her client at the door of the court whether or not to accept an offer in settlement, had not given sufficient detail, Baroness Hale firmly separated the extent of the lawyer's duty to advise of risk from the extensive duty on medical practitioners when obtaining patients' consent[366]: "there is still a respectable body of professional opinion that the client pays for the advocate's opinion, not her doubts". Similarly, in *Turner v Eversheds*,[367] the claimant alleged that his solicitors had been negligent in failing to take a particular tactical step in patent proceedings.

---

[355] James and Seneviratne (1995), p.188.

[356] *ibid.* p.206 and Seneviratne (1999), p.209.

[357] Seneviratne (1999), p.209.

[358] See above for the contractual position of barristers. Solicitors may not exclude liability towards their clients but may in certain circumstances limit it to the extent of their insurance cover provided this is brought to the client's attention; *Solicitors Code of Conduct 2007*, para.2.07.

[359] e.g. *Re Bell's Indenture* [1980] 1 W.L.R. 1217.

[360] [1964] A.C. 465.

[361] [1979] Ch. 384, approved in *Henderson v Merrett Syndicates Ltd* [1994] 3 All E.R. 506.

[362] [1979] Ch. 384, at p.417.

[363] [1980] Ch. 297.

[364] [1995] 1 All E.R. 691, and see C. Kessel, "Solicitors' professional negligence" (1995) N.L.J. 499 and 537.

[365] [2005] UKHL 7.

[366] *Bolam v Frien Hospital Management Committee* [1957] 1 W.L.R. 582; *Bolitho v City and Hackney Health Authority* [1998] A.C. 232, HL.

[367] Lawtel AC9601122, February 8, 2007.

Finding that such a step, had it been taken, would not necessarily have produced any better result, the court held that the duty of the solicitors "had been to act in a professional and competent manner, not to achieve a particular result" and that they had not been negligent.

The position of victims of incompetence is further secured by the compulsory indemnity insurance requirements for both solicitors and barristers.[368] There are, however, a number of problems facing clients who wish to consider suing their lawyers. First, legal assistance is advisable, but someone whose dealings with a lawyer have been unsatisfactory, probably protracted and a source of frustration and annoyance, is unlikely to relish the prospect of involvement with yet more lawyers, although there are solicitors who specialise in such work.[369]

A greater problem used to arise from a special immunity from claims for negligence in respect of the conduct of litigation. The authorities concerned barristers, but the immunity was regarded as extending to a solicitor acting as an advocate.[370] The House of Lords in *Rondel v Worsley*[371] held that a barrister was immune from action in respect of his or her conduct at trial.[372] The immunity was justified by public policy:

> "mainly upon the ground that a barrister owes a duty to the court as well as to his client and should not be inhibited through fear of an action by his client, from performing it; partly on the undesirability of relitigation as between barrister and client of what was litigated between the client and his opponent."[373]

This immunity was subsequently limited, by the House of Lords in *Saif Ali v*   **3–045**
Sydney Mitchell and Co,[374] so that the immunity was, in effect, in respect of advocacy only and extended to pre-trial work[375] only if it was:

> "so intimately connected with the conduct of the cause in Court that it can fairly be said to be a preliminary decision affecting the way that cause is to be conducted when it comes to a hearing."[376]

This "highly controversial" immunity was abolished by the House of Lords in *J S Hall & Co (A Firm) v Simons; Woolf Seddon (A Firm) v Barrett; Roberts & Hill (A Firm) v Harris (conjoined appeals)*.[377] The public policy arguments that

---

[368] See above, paras 3–037 and 3–041.

[369] As there are specialists in defending them, previously instructed by the Solicitors' Indemnity Fund and now by firms' individual insurers.

[370] *Saif Ali v Sydney Mitchell and Co* [1980] A.C. 198 at 215, 224 and 227. The matter was put beyond doubt by the Courts and Legal Services Act 1990, s.62 which states that anyone who was not a barrister but lawfully provided any legal services had the same immunity as a barrister.

[371] [1969] 1 A.C. 191.

[372] For a history of the immunity, see M. Seneviratne, "The rise and fall of advocates' immunity" (2001) 21 L.S. 644 at 645–646.

[373] *per* Lord Wilberforce in *Saif Ali v Sydney Mitchell and Co* [1980] A.C. 198 at 212.

[374] [1980] A.C. 198.

[375] For the scope of the immunity, see Seneviratne (2001), pp.646–649.

[376] *per* McCarthy P. in *Rees v Sinclair* [1974] 1 N.Z.L.R. 180 at 187, endorsed by Lords Wilberforce, Diplock and Salmon. Lord Russell and Lord Keith favoured a wider test under which immunity would be extended to all work in connection with litigation.

[377] [2000] 3 All E.R. 673. Hereafter: *Arthur Hall v Simons*. For significant criticism of the old rule, see P. Cane, *Tort Law and Economic Interests* (2nd edn, 1996), pp.233–238 and J. Hill, "Litigation and Negligence: A Comparative Study" (1986) 6 O.J.L.S. 183.

had been said to have been in favour of the immunity were all dismissed. The arguments in favour had been (1) that the barrister[378] owed a duty to the court that transcended any duty to the client and that the necessary confidence between barristers and judges would be undermined by barristers' fear of claims; (2) that there should be a general immunity from legal action for all participants in a trial because of the adverse effects on the administration of justice if the situation were otherwise; (3) that the "cab rank rule" would be difficult to enforce if barristers had to take on clients who could then pursue actions against them; and (4) that re-litigation of cases was undesirable: the correct method of challenge was by appeal and not by collateral attack.[379] For the majority of the House of Lords,[380] none of these reasons was sufficient to warrant the retention of the immunity, though for the minority,[381] there was a public interest in maintaining the immunity for barristers involved in criminal cases. The most significant argument in favour of the immunity, and the point at which the court divided in relation to criminal procedure, was the collateral attack argument. This argument was inadequate because, whilst there was a risk of collateral attack, there are other more appropriate means whereby it could be handled through civil and criminal court procedure.[382] Weak civil cases brought against advocates could also be struck out through the summary judgment procedure,[383] and would be less likely to attract public funding as negligence cases are not supported through the Community Legal Service.[384] In any case, where there is a wrong there ought to be a remedy and there has to be a very good reason for not providing a remedy. The majority felt that no such good reason was present.[385]

3–046   The duty to the court argument (otherwise known as the divided loyalty argument) was dismissed because the duty to the court would prevail over that owed to the client. The existence of two interests that might compete was an insufficient reason for an immunity as many professionals, particularly doctors, have to handle such competing interests. It could not be negligent to act in accordance with the duty to the court, so there could not be a successful action for negligence in any such case.[386] There was no evidence[387] that there would be many cases of aggrieved clients bringing vexatious claims or that fears of such claims would have an impact upon an advocate's practice.

The remaining two arguments were dismissed readily by all the judges as not being at all strong in support of any immunity. The need to encourage freedom of speech in court has nothing to do with an advocate's immunity, so the "witness

---

[378] The principle would also apply to solicitor-advocates and others with rights of audience.

[379] See C. G. Veljanowski and C. J. Whelan, "Professional Negligence and the Quality of Legal Services—An Economic Perspective" (1983) 46 M.L.R. 700 at 711–712 and Seneviratne (2001), pp.651–657.

[380] Lords Steyn, Browne-Wilkinson, Hoffmann and Millett.

[381] Lords Hope, Hutton and Hobhouse.

[382] The applicability of this procedure in criminal cases under the House of Lords' decision in *Hunter v Chief Constable of West Midlands* [1982] A.C. 529 was particularly important for the majority, but was not sufficient for the minority, which was why they would have retained the immunity in criminal cases. There is also the wasted costs jurisdiction, see below, para.3–047.

[383] CPR Pt 24.

[384] *Arthur Hall v Simons*, at pp.680–681, *per* Lord Steyn, and pp.699–704 *per* Lord Hoffmann. For the differences on criminal cases, see pp.717–723, *per* Lord Hope, pp.726–733, *per* Lord Hutton, and pp.738–742 and 743–749 *per* Lord Hobhouse.

[385] *ibid.* p.683 *per* Lord Steyn and pp.689–690 *per* Lord Hoffmann.

[386] *ibid.* at p.687, *per* Lord Steyn, and Seneviratne (2001), at p.652.

[387] The wasted costs order had presented no such problems and, in Canada, there was no adverse consequence from the lack of an immunity: *Arthur Hall v Simons*, at pp.681–684, *per* Lord Steyn, and pp.690–697, *per* Lord Hoffmann.

analogy" argument had "no or virtually no weight at all".[388] The argument based on the cab rank rule could not justify claims for immunity by solicitors as opposed to barristers, and "its impact on the administration of justice in England is not great".[389]

Suggestions that expert witnesses might be able to claim immunity at least from disciplinary proceedings by their professional bodies have also been recently rejected.[390]

(ii) *Wasted costs order*

A wasted costs order may be made against a barrister or a solicitor, or any person **3–047** with the right to conduct litigation or advocacy.[391] Such a jurisdiction as applied to solicitors has been available since 1939.[392] The Courts and Legal Services Act 1990 extended the order to barristers and other representatives.[393] "Wasted costs" are those incurred by a litigant "as a result of any improper,[394] unreasonable[395] or negligent act or omission" by any legal or other representative,[396] and the court must consider that it is unreasonable to expect the litigant to pay them.[397] General guidance in civil cases has been provided by the Court of Appeal in *Ridehalgh v Horsefield*,[398] which also applies in criminal cases.[399] The court exercises a discretion at two stages: first in determining whether to provide the legal representative with the opportunity to show cause why an order should not be made[400] such that further proceedings will not always follow; secondly, even if the criteria are satisfied, the court is not bound to make an order, but would have to give sustainable reasons for not doing so.[401] The use of a wasted costs order as a signal to deter "like-minded" members of the profession was endorsed recently in *Morris v Roberts (Inspector of Taxes) (Wasted Costs Order).*[402]

---

[388] *Arthur Hall v Simons*, p.680 *per* Lord Steyn and pp.697–699 *per* Lord Hoffmann.

[389] *ibid.*, p.680 *per* Lord Steyn. See also pp.687–688 and 697 *per* Lord Hoffmann and p.714 *per* Lord Hope.

[390] *Meadows v GMC* [2006] EWCA 1390.

[391] The procedure for a wasted costs order in civil proceedings is found in the Civil Procedure Rules, r.48.7, which refers to "legal representatives".

[392] *Myers v Elman* [1940] A.C. 282.

[393] Supreme Court Act 1981, s.51, as amended by the Courts and Legal Services Act 1990, s.4. See S. Fennell, "Wasted costs after the Courts and Legal Services Act 1990" (1993) 9 P.N. 25.

[394] This includes conduct which would be regarded as a serious breach of professional conduct and also conduct which "according to the consensus of professional (including judicial) opinion can be fairly stigmatised [as improper]:" *Ridehalgh v Horsefield* [1994] 3 All E.R. 848, at p.861.

[395] It includes conduct which is vexatious or designed to harass the other side, and the motive for such action is irrelevant. Conduct is not unreasonable simply because it leads to the "wrong result". "The acid test is whether the conduct permits of a reasonable explanation": *Ridehalgh v Horsefield*, at pp.861–862.

[396] This need not be the litigant's *own* legal representative: *Brown v Bennett (No.1) (Wasted Costs Order)*, [2002] 1 W.L.R. 713.

[397] Supreme Court Act 1981, s.51(7).

[398] [1994] 3 All E.R. 848.

[399] *ibid.* p.868. See also *Practice Direction (Costs: Criminal Proceedings)* [2004] 1 W.L.R. 2657.

[400] If the lawyer wishes to rely on the client's instructions as a defence, complications can arise if the client refuses to waive privilege in those instructions: *Medcalf v Mardel (Wasted Costs Order)* [2002] UKHL 27.

[401] *ibid.* pp.867–868. For an example of circumstances where an order was not justified, see *Regent Leisuretime Ltd v Skerrett (Wasted Costs)* [2006] EWCA Civ 1032.

[402] [2005] EWHC 1040.

5. SOCIAL BACKGROUND, ENTRY AND TRAINING

(a) Social background

3–048   Lawyers are an "elite professional group with high status, substantial earning potential and a key role in applying and administering the law".[403] Lawyers predominantly come from middle-class homes.[404] The same is true of law students. The Law Student Survey has shown that only a minority of students' parents were engaged in working-class occupations and that a much greater proportion of them had parents who had been to university than was the case in the general population.[405] There is clear evidence that the system of admissions to law degrees perpetuates the class structure of the legal profession.[406] Most lawyers are graduates[407] and so any social imbalance seen at the academic stage of qualification maintains the social imbalance at the professional stage. Universities are meeting the challenge to broaden the basis upon which students are admitted to law schools.[408] Universities also endeavour to widen the range of students participating in education. Since 1988, there have been more women entering law schools than men.[409] Whilst there is no suggestion of illegal discrimination in the allocation of places on law degrees, the financial demands of qualification make it easier for someone from a relatively secure financial background to succeed.[410]

We turn now to consider gender and race issues in the legal profession. We do this because, as Shiner states, it matters for fairness reasons and also for the provision of legal services:

> "Laws are not created or administered in a cultural vacuum and it may be argued that the legal profession should broadly reflect the composition of the society that it serves. Opponents of such a view may reject it on the grounds that it is idealistic or even naïve. It is, however, important to distinguish between a situation in which the skewed composition of the profession reflects broad social forces (for example, those pertaining to access to higher education) and that in which biases from within the

[403] M. Shiner, "Young, gifted and blocked! Entry to the solicitors' profession", in P. Thomas (ed.), *Discriminating Lawyers* (2000), p.87, who actually made the point only about solicitors, but it applies also to barristers.

[404] See Abel (1988), pp.74–76 and 170–172 and table 2.21: Royal Commission on Legal Services, *Report, Vol.2* (1979), pp.57–61; S. Vignaendra, *Social Class and Entry into the Solicitors' Profession* (Law Society Research Study No.41, 2001).

[405] D. Halpern, *Entry into the Legal Professions* (Law Society Research Study No.15, 1994), pp.21–24; E. Duff, M. Shiner, A. Boon with A. Whyte, *Entry into the Legal Professions* (Law Society Research Study No.39, 2000); Vignaendra (2001). See also M. King, M. Israel and S. Goulbourne, *Ethnic Minorities and Recruitment to the Solicitors' Profession* (1990), pp.32–34.

[406] See Abel (1988) Ch.18, esp. pp.271–275; Vignaendra (2001); and King, Israel and Goulbourne (1990), pp.32–34 and 37–52. See also P. McDonald (1982) 9 J.L.S. 267 and R. G. Lee (1984) 18 L.T. 165.

[407] Law Society, *Annual Statistical Report 2006* 5.2, particularly table 9.7.

[408] All law schools are happy to consider applicants with non-traditional qualifications, but see C. McGlynn, *The Woman Lawyer: Making the difference* (1998), pp.10–12. Foundation degrees which allow profession into conventional LLB courses may be a means of encouraging those from non-traditional backgrounds.

[409] Law Society, *Annual Statistical Report 2006* table 9.5, para.10.5; and C. McGlynn, *The Woman Lawyer: Making the difference* (1998), p.7.

[410] See below, paras 3–051—3–052.

profession create, or reinforce, inequality. If certain communities face discrimination in the process by which the legal profession recruits its members, then how legitimate are any claims that the profession may make in terms of representing these communities? Equally, in such circumstances, what confidence can these communities have in the broader services provided by the legal profession."[411]

Both the Law Society and the Bar Council take equal opportunities[412] with **3–049** increasing seriousness. In the case of the Law Society, equality of access to the profession was a driver behind the lengthy discussions that formed the Training Framework Review from 2001. The passage of the Sex Disqualification (Removal) Act 1919 made it possible for women to become solicitors, and the theoretical possibility of women becoming barristers became a reality. However, women did not enter the profession in significant numbers until about 30 years ago. Now, more entrants are women than men[413] and the overall proportion of women in the profession is, therefore, continually growing.[414] However, the evidence indicates that women are less well paid than men.[415] Women have not been well represented at the upper echelons of both branches.[416] Women are, for example, more likely to remain as assistant solicitors than men and to take career breaks impeding their prospects for promotion. With 10–19 years' experience, 60 per cent of men have made partner (or are sole practitioners), but only 40.3 per cent of women.[417] The following table reflects the position of women solicitors

---

[411] Shiner (2000), p.87.

[412] Their equal opportunities policies are not concerned solely with discrimination on the grounds of gender and race, but also, e.g. with sexual orientation and disability.

[413] The number of women being admitted to the solicitors' roll exceeded the number of men from the early 1990s. In 2005–06 59.4% of those admitted were women: Law Society, *Annual Statistical Report 2006*, table 9.3. In 2005–06, 3,552 women were in trainee placement compared with 2,199 men. By comparison, in July 2005, of the 527 pupil barristers, 251 were women, Bar Council statistics, *www.barcouncil.org.uk*.

[414] In December 2005, there were 3,543 self-employed female barristers compared to 8,275 men. The rate of increase in the proportion of women solicitors is faster than that of women barristers: BDO Stoy Hayward (2001), table 6. For some examples of the experiences of women in both branches of the profession, see E. Cruickshank (ed.), *Women in the Law: Strategic Career Management* (2003: The Law Society).

[415] The Law Society *Annual Statistical Report 2006*, table 8.13 shows that the average starting salary for a female trainee solicitor is £20, 473, compared to that of £21,657 for a male trainee, although when considered by region, women earned more than men in the south east, east and Wales. See also R. McNabb and V. Wass, "Male-female earnings differentials among lawyers in Britain: a legacy of the law or a current practice?" (2006) 13 *Labour Economics*, 219.

[416] For solicitors, at July 31, 2006, there were 5,727 female partners (compared to 18,954 men) and 1,003 female sole practitioners (compared to 3,129 men): Law Society, *Annual Statistical Report 2006*, table 2.9. The *Lawyer Career Report* for 2005–06 found the highest percentage of female partners in any single firm to be 39%: *www.thelawyer.com/careerreport*. In July 2006, 33 new female Q.C.s were appointed from a total of 175 successful candidates: Q.C. Appointments Secretariat press release, July 20, 2006. Of the 115 members of the Bar Council in 2007, 26 were women (of whom eight were representing barristers of less than seven years' call): *www.barcouncil.org.uk*. The first (and currently only, out of 12) female member of the House of Lords, Lady Hale of Richmond, was appointed in 2004. In 2007, there were three female Lords Justices of Appeal out of 37 (Arden, Smith and Hallett L.JJ., all appointed since 2000); 11 female High Court judges (out of 108), 71 female circuit judges (out of 631): *www.judiciary.gov.uk*. Marginally better results are shown for district judges and deputy district judges in both civil and criminal courts where approximately a quarter are female. There has never been a female Chairman of the Bar Council. The first female President of the Law Society was appointed in 2002 and the current incumbent is a woman.

[417] Law Society, *Annual Statistical Report 2006*, chart 3.

as at July 31, 2006 and demonstrates that women are still finding it more difficult to make progress through the profession[418]:

Position in firm	Men		Women		Total	
	No.	%	No.	%	No.	%
Partners	18,954	39.5	5,727	17.6	24,681	30.6
Sole practitioners	3,129	6.5	1,003	3.1	4,132	5.1
Associate solicitors	5,616	11.7	5,763	17.7	11,379	14.1
Assistant solicitors	11,435	23.8	16,802	51.6	28,237	35.0
Consultants	2,713	5.6	665	2.0	3,378	4.2
Other private practice	6,177	12.9	2,591	8	8,768	10.9
All positions	48,024	100.0	32,551	100.0	80,575	100.0

Whilst the picture is constantly improving, it is not a matter about which anyone can afford complacency and some would argue that there is clear evidence of gender-based discrimination that must be tackled.[419] The idea that there is "trickle up"[420] which will solve the problem is neither sufficient nor convincing,[421] although no-one would argue for people being promoted to senior positions when not skilled sufficiently to perform the relevant tasks.

3–050   There are few formal complaints of sex discrimination, but there is evidence that fear of discrimination has, at least in the past, put off some women and ethnic minorities.[422] Both the Law Society and Bar Council have principles of professional conduct outlawing discrimination.[423] In 2005, the Law Society adopted an Equality and Diversity Policy and Strategy with the expressed objective that "we want to go beyond compliance and be at the forefront of embracing equality and diversity. We want to promote best practice in the profession and encourage the profession to be sensitive to the specific needs of the different communities to which it provides legal services. We want to promote the profession as one whose members are required to treat each other, clients and others in a fair, equal and non-discriminatory manner".[424] The Bar's Equality and Diversity Code

---

[418] Law Society, *Annual Statistical Report 2006*, table 2.9. See also, Law Society, *Women Solicitors* (2004).
[419] McGlynn (1998). For a view that the matter, in relation to law schools, is much more complicated, see F. Cownie, "Women in the Law School—shoals of fish, starfish or fish out of water?" in P. Thomas (ed.), *Discriminating Lawyers* (2000).
[420] This refers to the length of time that it takes for people to be eligible for senior positions in the law.
[421] McGlynn (1998), p.96.
[422] M. Shiner and T. Newburn, *Entry into the Profession* (1995).
[423] See also Law Society, *Career Experiences of Gay and Lesbian Solicitors* (2006).
[424] p.2.

incorporates a statement of policy on flexible working "to help barristers balance family life with practice at the Bar".

As regards opportunities for people from ethnic minorities,[425] the Royal Commission on Legal Services concluded that the position was unsatisfactory and that trends were unfavourable.[426] As with issues related to gender, there are concerns about entry to university and subsequent entry to the profession. In 2006, the percentage of ethnic minority students with a place on a law degree was relatively high.[427] However, as there may still be a bias in favour of graduates from pre-1992 universities (and in particular Oxford and Cambridge), if many of these students are in post-1992 universities, there is still likely to be a problem of access to the profession.

Ethnic group	Acceptances of students from UK		
	Male	Female	Total
White British	2,808	4,512	7,320
Black Caribbean	54	183	237
Black African	223	385	608
Black other	13	37	50
Indian	352	543	895
Pakistani	334	445	779
Bangladeshi	90	150	240
Chinese	3	82	121
Other Asian	91	130	221
Mixed white/black Caribbean	17	57	74
Mixed white/black African	14	32	46
Mixed white/Asian	51	83	134
Other mixed	39	91	130
Other	58	150	208
Unknown	249	232	481

[425] For revealing and challenging research on the perspective of Black and Asian solicitors, see S. Vignaendra, M. Williams and J. Garvey, "Hearing Black and Asian voices—an exploration of identity" in P. Thomas (ed.), *Discriminating Lawyers* (2000).
[426] Royal Commission on Legal Services, *Report, Vol.1* (1979), pp.501–504.
[427] Law Society, *Annual Statistical Report 2006*, table 6.4.

Ethnic group	Acceptances of students from UK		
	Male	Female	Total
All UK-based ethnic minority acceptances	1,375	2,368	3,743
All UK-based acceptances	4,432	7,112	11,544
% from ethnic minorities	31.0	33.3	32.4

A 1989 survey showed that 5 per cent of all lawyers were from an ethnic minority.[428] In 2005–06, 11.2 per cent of solicitors with known ethnicity[429] were from ethnic minorities (10.3 per cent of those with practising certificates). Similarly, in December 2005, 11 per cent of the practising Bar (employed and self-employed) was from an ethnic minority.[430]

(b) Entry and training

3–051   Entry to both branches of the profession is typically through a qualifying law degree or, for non-law graduates, successful completion of the Common Professional Examination (CPE) or Graduate Diploma in Law (GDL),[431] followed by a vocational educational stage and a period of on-the-job training. The Law Society and the Bar Council jointly establish, with the academic legal profession, what is to be recognised as a qualifying law degree. Although there are serious tensions between the demands of the professional bodies and what universities, as educators, wish to provide, agreement is reached on relatively broad parameters. The current *Joint Announcement on Qualifying Law Degrees*[432] requires that a degree, to comply with the Academic Stage and be a qualifying law degree, must ensure that its graduates achieve "an appropriate level of academic ability, [and have] a basic body of knowledge and understanding of English Law". This is achieved through the degree covering the "seven foundations of legal knowledge". They are: Obligations I (Contract Law); Obligations II (Law of Torts); Criminal Law; Property Law (Land Law); Public Law (Constitutional and

---

[428] General Council of the Bar, *Quality of Justice: The Bar's Response* (1989), pp.267–268.

[429] 9.7 per cent of all solicitors, including those whose ethnicity is unknown. Of solicitors with known ethnicity, 88.8 per cent were White European; 5.6 per cent Asian; 2.26 per cent Chinese; 1.7 per cent "other"; 0.9 per cent African and 0.7 per cent African-Caribbean. It is not clear how individuals of mixed race have been treated in these statistics. Law Society, *Annual Statistical Report 2006*, Table 1.5. For comparison, the 2001 census reported 7.9 per cent of the total population being of non-white ethnic origin: *http://www.statistics.gov.uk*.

[430] General Council of the Bar, *Annual Report 2005*. Calculating from statistics available on the Bar Council website and combining results for the self-employed and employed Bar (but excluding pupils) where ethnicity was known: 88.9 per cent were of White background; 4.9 per cent Asian; 3.1 per cent of Black background (including both African and African-Caribbean); 1.3 per cent "other"; 1.2 per cent of mixed background and 0.3 per cent Chinese.

[431] For an institution to offer such a course, it must have the approval, by way of a validation, of the CPE Board.

[432] *A Joint Statement issued by the Law Society and the General Council of the Bar on Completion of the Initial or Academic Stage of Training by Obtaining an Undergraduate Degree* (2001).

Administrative Law); Equity and the Law of Trusts; and the Law of the European Union (which has only been a compulsory element since 1995).[433] In addition, students must have expertise in Legal Research. To maintain the currency of knowledge and to provide some safeguard for the public, there are also time limits within which a degree may be completed.[434] Law is not taken only as the initial stage for a professional qualification, it is an academic subject in its own right and, therefore, is taught and studied for its own sake. It is a very popular subject,[435] because it is interesting, challenging and its graduates are employable (whether in the legal profession or elsewhere).

Entry to the Bar is restricted, as students, to graduates and mature students[436] and, in other cases, to the transfer of qualified legal practitioners.[437] A student entrant must join one of the Inns of Court and complete the vocational stage.[438] The academic stage, qualifying someone to be admitted as a student, is satisfied by either a qualifying law degree or a CPE/GDL pass. The vocational stage comprises the Bar Vocational Course[439] at an institution approved by the Bar Council.[440] Students who complete these two stages and comply with the keeping of terms requirements[441] are "called to the Bar".[442] At present individuals are entitled to call themselves barristers at this stage although they are not entitled to practise unless they complete 12 months' pupillage with a barrister of at least five years' standing,[443] and may not accept instructions until the second six months of pupillage.[444] The Bar Standards Board is, however, at present consulting on proposals for "deferred call" such that an individual would not be formally called to the Bar before completing pupillage, a provision that would bring barristers more into line with the solicitors' profession.

---

[433] For discussion, see P. Birks "Compulsory subjects: will the seven foundations ever crumble?" (1995) 1 *Web Journal of Current Legal Issues*; A. Bradney, "Raising the drawbridge: defending university law schools" (1995) 1 *Web Journal of Current Legal Issues*.

[434] Of course what none of this handles is the propriety or suitability of the content of law degrees or the approaches taken in teaching. For some concerns about the curriculum and other law school issues and their effects on women in the law, see C. McGlynn, *The Woman Lawyer: Making the difference* (1998), pp.12–18.

[435] In 2005, 12,084 people (7,692 women and 4,392 men) graduated in law: Law Society, *Annual Statistical Report 2006*, table 6.5. This figure refers only to those students graduating with a single honours qualifying law degree: *ibid.*

[436] The Consolidated Regulations of the Inns of Court and the General Council of the Bar (October 2005), reg.2(a) and Sch.2.

[437] *ibid.* Pt IV.

[438] *ibid.* reg.2(c).

[439] This course was introduced in 1989–90. The crucial change from the old Bar Finals Examination is the introduction and enhancement of skills training and practical exercises in addition to knowledge-based subjects.

[440] BPP Law School, Cardiff Law School, College of Law, Inns of Court School of Law, City University, Manchester Metropolitan University, University of Northumbria at Newcastle School of Law, Nottingham Law School and University of West of England at Bristol.

[441] Consolidated Regulations, reg.9, which requires attendance at 12 qualifying sessions, that is an event of an educational and collegiate nature arranged by or on behalf of an Inns of Court.

[442] Consolidated Regulations, reg.22, which requires that a student is not eligible for call (a) when under 21; (b) before satisfying the obligations about keeping of terms, passing the BVC or the other eligibility requirements for transfers; (c) before completing and signing the call declaration and paying the relevant fee; (d) until their name and description has been screened within their Inn. In order to have been admitted as a student, certificates of good character are also required: *ibid.* reg.3.

[443] *ibid.*, Pt V.

[444] *ibid.*, reg.41.2.

The costs of entry to the Bar are high. They include tuition fees for the BVC, which are between £7,750 and £11,185,[445] maintenance during that year, possibly funding during pupillage, keeping term fees and the purchase of special clothes. Barristers may not earn enough to live on for a number of years,[446] and, when paid work is done, payment may come in some considerable time later.[447] In July 2005, there were 527 pupils, but the number of pupils as compared with the number of barristers has been falling since 1999.[448] So concerned is the Bar about the cost of qualifying that, from the end of 2002, a requirement for chambers to pay pupils at least £10,000 per year plus travel expenses was introduced.[449]

3–052   Entry to the solicitors' profession consists, first, of an academic stage, by way of completion of either a qualifying law degree or a CPE/GDL pass or by way of a transfer from another profession.[450] In 2005–06, 69.9 per cent of admissions to the roll were direct entrants through their initial degree routes. This comprises 53.6 per cent or 3,791 of entrants with a qualifying law degree, and 16.4 per cent or 1,158 with a CPE/GDL pass.[451] 20.3 per cent entered as transfers: overseas lawyers (15.2 per cent of all admissions), barristers (2.9 per cent), FILEX (2.0 per cent), and justices' clerks (0.2 per cent). Secondly, all candidates, who must be student members of the Law Society, must at present take and pass a Legal Practice Course[452] at one of the institutions validated by the Law Society. In 2006–07, there were 10,325 full time places and 2,948 part time places.[453] As with qualifying as a barrister, one of the main hurdles is finance. Tuition fees range from £5,200 to over £9,000, and in addition, maintenance has to be added. Whilst there is a range of possible sources of finances including commercially available career development loans, the most likely are the student (or his or her family) or their future employer. Qualification as a solicitor is at present completed by a two-year training contract,[454] during which the Professional Skills

---

[445] It reflects the very high cost of a programme that demands considerable high level skills training.

[446] For barristers' earnings, see above, para.3–026.

[447] *ibid.*

[448] BDO Stoy Hayward (2001), p.11: in 2001 there was one pupil per 14 barristers, whereas in 1999 there was one pupil per 13 barristers.

[449] *The Times*, March 11, 2002, p.8. See also *www.legaleducation.org.uk/Pupillage*.

[450] The routes to qualification as a solicitor are: law graduate; non-law graduate (plus CPE/GDL); overseas lawyer (transfer); barrister (transfer); Scots/Northern Irish lawyers (transfer); Fellow of the Institute of Legal Executives (FILEX); and justices' clerk.

[451] Law Society, *Annual Statistical Report 2006*, table 9.7.

[452] See S. Slorach and S. Nathanson "Design and Build: the Legal Practice Course at Nottingham Law School" (1996) 30(2) *The Law Teacher* 187; N. Saunders, "From cramming to skills—the development of solicitors' education and training since Ormrod" (1996) 30(2) *The Law Teacher* 168; T. Goriely and T. Williams, *The Impact of the New Training Scheme* (1996, Law Society Research Study No. 22); A. Boon and A. Whyte, *Legal Education as Vocational Preparation?: Perspectives of Newly Qualified Solicitors* (2002, London: University of Westminster); A. Fancourt, *Hitting the Ground Running? Does the Legal Practice Course Prepare Students Adequately for the Training Contract?* (2004, UKCLE). The syllabus is currently found in *Legal Practice Course, written standards, version 10* (2004: Law Society).

[453] Law Society, *Annual Statistical Report 2006*, table 8.3.

[454] Training Regulations 1990; *Training Trainee Solicitors, The Law Society Requirements, version 2* (2004: Law Society); *Training Trainee Solicitors, Guidelines on Monitoring of Training Contracts, version 2* (2004: Law Society).
   In 2005–06, there were 5,751 traineeships registered with the Law Society, of which 61.8% were held by women and 17.5% by people from a known ethnic minority: Law Society, *Annual Statistical Report 2006*, tables 8.7 and 8.8. A significant number of these traineeships are in the

Course must be completed.[455]

In July 2001 the Law Society began consultation (the Training Framework Review) about its pre-qualification requirements, particularly in terms of access to the profession[456] (including barriers to qualification such as the cost of the LPC and that the title "solicitor" cannot be obtained without successfully obtaining and first completing a training contract with an employer). It was suggested that qualification might become dependent on demonstrating achievement of a number of defined competencies, without necessarily continuing to prescribe (or by allowing increasing flexibility as to) the means by or time period within which such competencies might be acquired. It was also necessary to address the accreditation of European qualifications[457] and the increasing specialisation within the profession. Suggestions including accepting "equivalence" to the current requirement for a degree; CPE/GDL or FILEX qualification in respect of the academic stage[458]; prescribing assessment only at the vocational stage (leaving individuals to choose whether or not to attend courses in preparation for such assessment); and promoting flexibility as to a period of "work-based learning" (not necessarily all with the same employer) to replace the training contract. Three phases of consultation and investigation took place between 2001 and 2005 and a further consultation, in respect of the period of work-based learning, took place in 2006.

The outcome, at present, is contained in the Law Society's 2006 Paper *Legal Practice Courses, Framework for authorisation, delivery and assessment.* An LPC, albeit from 2008 a new-style LPC, will continue to be mandatory. Its content will be less constrained than hitherto, and directed to achievement of the relevant aspects of a series of "day one outcomes" intended to represent the state of skill and knowledge of a solicitor at the point of qualification. There will be a minimum number of notional learning hours but class contact and allocations of time between different elements of the course will no longer be prescribed. It

---

large firms (30.7% in the firms with 81+ partners), which is why they dominate the training agenda: *ibid.* table 8.11.

[455] This course involves: advocacy and communications skills; finance and business skills; and client care and professional standards.

[456] Law Society of England and Wales *Training Framework Review Consultation Paper* (2001); *Second Consultation Paper on a New Training Framework for Solicitors* (2003); *Paper on the Training Framework Review* (19 January 2005); *Statement on the Training Framework Review* (20 January 2005); *Qualifying as a Solicitor—A Framework for the Future, a Consultation Paper* (March 2005); *A New Framework for Work Based Learning Consultation Paper* (2006); A. Boon and J. Webb, *Report to the Law Society of England and Wales on the Consultation and Interim Report on the Training Framework Review* (2002); H. Brayne, *Assessment of Legal Dispute Resolution and Legal Transaction Skills, Flexible Pathways and Assessments* (2004); S. Grace, H Thomas, C. Butcher, *Project to Support Implementation of a New Training Framework for Solicitors Qualifying in England and Wales* (2004); H. Johnson and A Bone, *Project to Support Implementation of the Law Society's New Training Framework Review for Solicitors Qualifying in England and Wales* (2004); J. Webb, M. Maughan, W. Purcell, *Project to Support Implementation of a New Training Framework for Solicitors Qualifying in England and Wales, Review of the Training Contract and Work-based Learning* (2004); J. Webb and A. Fancourt (2004) "The Law Society's Training Framework Review: on the straight and narrow or the long and winding road" (2004) 38(3) *The Law Teacher* 293.

[457] See the discussion of *Morgenbesser v Consiglio dell'Ordine degli avvocati di Genova*, Case 313/01 (2003) ECJ above.

[458] Discussion about whether or not trainees should be graduates tended to overlook the well-established FILEX route. Some criticism was quite vocal: see, for example, F. Gibb, "Lawyers split over plans for lawyers without degrees", *The Times*, February 21, 2005, in which the head of one LPC provider was quoted as commenting that "it would take longer under the plans to train as a Corgi-registered plumber than a lawyer".

may be possible to separate elective courses from the core, so that individuals might, perhaps, be able to complete their electives later or during the period of work-based learning. Courses could be tailored towards the needs of a partiuclar large firm or firms or towards Legal Services Commission work.[459] A pilot scheme for the period of work-based learning, allowing for it to take place within an accreditation training organisation such as a law firm or outside such an organisation, is planned for 2007–09. The more radical suggestions proposed during the course of consultation have, largely, failed to survive although it is possible that the more-flexible period of work-based learning may assist individuals to qualify who have had difficulty either individually or as a group in obtaining training contracts.

6. Legal Executives, Paralegals, Barristers' Clerks and Allied Professions

3–053 Most solicitors' firms employ people who are not solicitors but do professional work similar to that of solicitors. In 2000, of the 93,839 fee-earners employed by solicitors' firms, 30,284 were not solicitors.[460] Some were consultants, some were barristers. Some of these people would have been legal executives, that is, Fellows of the Institute of Legal Executives (ILEX) or working towards that status,[461] whilst others might be better described as "paralegals". Whilst a formal qualification is not yet required to work as a paralegal or in the general provision of legal advice as defined in *Putting Consumers First* and the Legal Services Bill (as at, for example, a CAB, a charity advice centre or a private sector advice service), it is now possible to obtain specific qualifications in paralegal work and this may be developing as a separate career route to that of the legal executive.[462]

A student wishing to become a legal executive takes the ILEX Professional Diploma in Law, followed by the ILEX Professional Higher Diploma in Law in the field in which he or she wishes to specialise,[463] or, if relevant, the Graduate Entry Diploma,[464] and, on successful completion, becomes a Member. He or she will become a Fellow provided he or she has had at least five years' experience under the supervision of a solicitor, including two years after passing all the

---

[459] See P. Knott and J. Janney, "Are there too many LPCs to choose from?" *The Times*, January 23, 2007.

[460] Law Society, *Annual Statistical Report 2000*, table 4.1.

[461] *www.ilex.org.uk*, which defines the organisation as "representing over 22,000 members". See also A. M. Francis, "Legal Executives and the phantom of legal professionalism: the rise and rise of the third branch of the legal profession?" (2002) 9(1) I.J.L.P. 5. At present, unlike the Bar Council and Law Society, ILEX, formed in 1963, exercises both representative and, through its Investigating Committee with lay membership, disciplinary functions.

[462] See, for example, the National Association of Licensed Paralegals, *www.nationalparalegals.com/ index.htm* which defines a paralegal as "a person qualified through education and training to perform substantive legal work that requires knowledge of the law and procedures and who is not a qualified solicitor or barrister"; Institute of Paralegals, *www.instituteofparalegals.org/index.jsp* and ILEX paralegal programmes, *www.ilexpp.co.uk*. See also J. Robins, "A step up the ladder", L.S.G., January 25, 2007.

[463] The minimum entry requirement being four CGSEs at C or above, from an approved list including English but excluding more practical craft subjects, or their equivalent including entry as a mature student on the basis of experience.

[464] Law graduates are exempt from the academic law elements of these qualifications.

examinations. Only Fellows are entitled to describe themselves as "legal executives". ILEX defines Fellows as "qualified lawyers specialising in a particular area of law. They will have passed the ILEX Professional Qualification in Law in an area of legal practice to the same level as that required of solicitors".[465] A Fellow, therefore, has a spread of knowledge and expertise in a more limited area of work than a solicitor. The contribution which a Fellow can make is highly significant: many Fellows will be at least as well versed as the majority of solicitors in their particular area of work. A Fellow may remain with that status or go on to qualify as a solicitor on completion, at present, of the Legal Practice Course and Professional Skills Course but being frequently exempted from the training contract.[466]

Students, Members and Fellows of ILEX are bound by a Code of Conduct and Guides to Good Practice. The professional standing of Fellows has been enhanced considerably[467] and, as we have seen, the Institute is authorised to grant rights of audience in the higher courts. Under the Legal Services Bill, it would potentially be possible for legal executives to set up in practice independently of solicitors' firms or other employers.[468] Complaints about the way a complaint against a Fellow has been handled by ILEX are currently within the jurisdiction of the Legal Services Ombudsman,[469] and the intention is that, the Institute will be an "approved regulator" of their activities under the Legal Services Bill.[470]

Barristers' clerks[471] have the rather different role in chambers of acting as office administrator/manager and accountant, and as business manager and agent for each individual barrister. The title "clerk" is, therefore, very misleading. Increasingly, they are being called practice managers or administrators, as these titles more accurately reflect the work that they do. There is no professional obligation to employ a clerk. The obligation on barristers is to ensure that their practice is "efficiently and properly administered having regard to the nature of [his or her] practice".[472] The clerk manipulates the flow of work in chambers by virtue of the functions of negotiating fees and arranging each barrister's time-table, and his or her relationships, built up over many years, with solicitors' firms. Increasingly, clerks are employed under formal contracts and receive salaries, rather than the traditional proportion of the barristers' fees.

One will also find other professionals working with or in support of lawyers. Legal secretaries, for example, frequently have specialist qualifications[473]; law costs draftsmen exist to draft up detailed bills of lawyers' fees, particularly when

---

[465] www.ilex.org.uk/about_ilex/default.asp.

[466] Depending on the subjects studied for the Professional Higher Diploma, a legal executive may also be required to complete parts of the G.D.L. or C.P.E. in order to cover the seven foundation subjects. It is also possible for an individual to be both a legal executive and a licensed conveyancer. Members of the Justices' Clerks Association may qualify as solicitors by a similar route.

[467] This is despite failing to convince the Royal Commission on Legal Services to adopt its proposals for profit-sharing, enhanced pay for executives with ILEX qualifications, compulsory arrangements for day release and payment for courses: Royal Commission on Legal Services, *Report, Vol.I* (1979), pp.406–417.

[468] J. Robins, "Legal Executives set to close the gap on solicitors", L.S.G. January 25, 2007.

[469] See above, para.3–043.

[470] Sch.5, para.1 in respect of rights of audience and administration of oaths.

[471] Who may be, but are not required to be, members of the Institute of Barristers' Clerks: www.barristersclerks.com. The IBC has its own code of conduct which is ancillary to that of the Bar Council and supports a BTEC Advanced Award in Chambers Administration qualification.

[472] *Code of Conduct*, para.403.2.

[473] See, for example, the Institute of Legal Secretaries and PAs: www.institutelegal secretaries.com.

they are to be assessed by the court.[474] Law librarians can be found in universities and colleges as well as in law firms and other organisations.[475] In addition, a specialist category of non-practising lawyer, generally a solicitor or barrister, has grown up in recent years and is generally described as a "professional support lawyer",[476] his or her (usually her) role differing from employer to employer but frequently involving maintenance of technical know-how and often in-house education and training. Some individuals, qualified as solicitors or barristers, may in fact now practise principally as mediators or arbitrators, others work in legal recruitment, legal publishing or as MPs or MEPs. And of course some lawyers, whether formally qualified as solicitors, barristers or legal executives or not, teach in both the commercial and the public sector.

7. CONCLUSION

3–054 The effect of the Legal Services Bill may be that this is the last edition of this text in which one can realistically speak of "the legal professions" meaning only or mainly those of the solicitor and the barrister. Other professions, including those such as accountants not previously involved in legal services may take the opportunity offered to provide many of the services traditionally associated with lawyers. This means that lawyers must look for other areas of work as well as endeavouring to ensure that they maintain a lead in terms of quality and efficacy of service over other service providers. Specialism will continue apace, though increasing size has its significant disadvantages for the control and running of firms of solicitors and sets of chambers. The large firms will not only wish to specialise even further, but also to expand their international influence as far and as wide as possible. Firms founded in other jurisdictions, notably the USA, will continue to set up shop in this country. It might be possible for such international firms or others to choose to operate under an approved regulator other than the Solicitors' Regulatory Authority or Bar Standards Board. Information technology has changed practice significantly and will continue to do so. Flexible and home-based working may become more prevalent for individual lawyers, whose means of qualification may be more diverse than ever before. The impact of the consumer in the regulation of the profession will increase. One hopes the existing professions are ready to meet the undoubted challenges, perhaps to their very existence, that lie ahead.

---

[474] See the Association of Law Costs Draftsmen: *www.alcd.org.uk.*
[475] See the British and Irish Association of Law Librarians: *www.biall.org.uk.*
[476] See, for example, J. Humphries and S. Carter, "The value of support" (2006) 8(43) *Legal Week*, 18.

CHAPTER 4

JUDGES

In this chapter we consider the men and women who are appointed to adjudicate   **4–001** upon such disputes as are referred to a court or tribunal for determination. The term "judge" is used in the title of this chapter in its wide sense to cover all such persons. More commonly, however, the term is used in a narrower sense to cover those professional lawyers who are appointed to adjudicate in the House of Lords, the Supreme Court of England and Wales (i.e. the Court of Appeal, the High Court and the Crown Court), county courts and magistrates' courts. In addition, some judicial functions are performed by officers known as "masters" and "registrars". "Magistrates" or "justices of the peace" sit in the magistrates' courts (and in some cases in the Crown Court[1]). Those persons who sit on tribunals are normally simply referred to as tribunal "chairmen" or "members",

---

[1] When they are known as "judges of the Crown Court": Supreme Court Act 1981, s.8(1).

although there are some with special designations, such as the Social Security and Child Support Commissioners,[2] and the Special and General Commissioners of Income Tax.

A. MAGISTRATES[3]

1. NUMBERS AND FUNCTIONS

4–002 On April 1, 2005 there were 28,865 active part-time lay magistrates or "justices of the peace".[4] There was also provision for the appointment of an unlimited number of District Judges (Magistrates' Courts) and deputies (formerly stipendiary magistrates).[5] Each such judge is by virtue of his or her office a justice of the peace for England and Wales.[6] In the City of London, the Lord Mayor and Aldermen used to be justices *ex officio*, but by virtue of the Access to Justice Act 1999 they are only justices if appointed by the Lord Chancellor in accordance with the Justices of the Peace Act 1997.[7] Magistrates sit in the magistrates' courts[8] and in the Crown Court,[9] perform certain administrative tasks such as the granting of betting shop licences, issue arrest and search warrants and sign various forms for members of the public.

2. HISTORICAL ORIGINS OF JUSTICES OF THE PEACE[10]

The history of the justice of the peace as a judicial officer can be traced to the Justices of the Peace Act 1361, which provided:

"First, That in every County of *England* shall be assigned for the keeping of the Peace, one Lord, and with him three or four of the most worthy in the

---

[2] See above, para.2–039.

[3] Major studies are Sir Thomas Skyrme, *The Changing Image of the Magistracy* (2nd edn, 1983); E. Burney, *J.P: Magistrate, Court and Community* (1979); M. King and C. May, *Black Magistrates* (1985); and R. Morgan and N. Russell, *The Judiciary in the magistrates' Courts* (HO, LCD, 2000). See also P. Darbyshire, "An Essay on the Importance and Neglect of the Magistracy" [1997] Crim. L.R. 627 (arguing that the magistrates' court has supplanted jury trial as the central criminal forum but that law makers and lawyers develop the common law and statute and academics shape their research and teaching around jury trial); and "For the New Lord Chancellor—Some Causes for Concern About Magistrates" [1997] Crim. L.R. 861.

[4] *Justicial Statistics 2005*, p.137.

[5] Courts Act 2003, ss.22, 24. See below, para.4–013.

[6] *ibid.* s.25.

[7] Now presumably to be taken as a reference to the Courts Act 2003: 1997 Act, s.21, repealed by the 1999 Act, Sch.15; 1999 Act, s.76(1). The Lord Mayor and Aldermen in office on September 27, 1999, were treated as having been appointed under s.5 of the 1997 Act: 1999 Act, Sch.14, para.21.

[8] Above, paras 2–021—2–030.

[9] Above paras 2–052—2–058, below, para.4–012.

[10] On the historical development of the office see E. Moir, *The Justice of the Peace* (1969); J. H. Gleason, *The Justices of the Peace in England* (1969); L. J. K. Glassey, *Politics and the Appointment of Justices of the Peace* (1979); N. Landau, *The Justices of the Peace 1679–1760* (1984); Sir Thomas Skyrme, *History of Justices of the Peace* (1994).

County, with some learned in the Law, and they shall have Power to restrain
the Offenders, Rioters, and all other Barators, and to pursue, arrest, take, and
chastise them according to their Trespass or Offence; and to cause them to
be imprisoned and duly punished according to the Law and Customs of the
Realm, and according to that which to them shall seem best to do by their
Discretions and good Advisement; and also to inform them, and to enquire
of all those that have been Pillors and Robbers in the Parts beyond the Sea,
and be now come again, and go wandering, and will not labour as they were
wont in Times past, and to take and arrest all those that they may find by
Indictment, or by Suspicion, and to put them in Prison; and to take of all
them that be not of good Fame, where they shall be found, sufficient Surety
and Mainprise of their good behaviour towards the King and his People, and
the other duly to punish, to the Intent that the People be not by such Rioters
or Rebels troubled nor endamaged, nor the Peace blemished, nor Merchants
nor other passing by the Highways of the Realm disturbed, nor put in the
Peril which may happen of such Offenders . . . [11]

The Crown had previously appointed keepers or conservators of the peace
(*Custodes Pacis*) with powers to arrest suspects and initiate criminal proceedings: the Act of 1361 gave in addition the power to determine proceedings. In
1362 the justices were required to hold formal meetings four times a year: these
became known as quarter sessions. Over the ensuing centuries, more and more
administrative duties were imposed by statute on the justices, including such
matters as the construction and maintenance of fortifications, highways, bridges
and gaols, the fixing of prices and the recruitment of soldiers. The list of
provisions to be implemented or enforced became lengthy and burdensome.[12]
Indeed, until the nineteenth century, the business of local government was largely
entrusted to the justices. Different functions were committed to one, two or three
justices or to quarter sessions. The informal meetings of two or more justices out
of quarter sessions came to be known as "petty sessions," the forerunner of
magistrates' courts.

The persons appointed in the counties were generally from the "gentry". In the
eighteenth century, the justices came into growing disrepute. The corruption of
the Middlesex Justices, described by Edmund Burke as "generally the scum of
the earth", was such that they were replaced for most purposes by metropolitan
stipendiary magistrates. Elsewhere, their administration of the Poor Law and the
Game Laws attracted much criticism. In the nineteenth century they lost most of
their administrative functions to central government departments and the new,
elected, local authorities, the process of transfer culminating in the Local Government Act 1888. At the same time, their judicial functions were extended, with
more offences becoming triable at petty sessions, and with the establishment and
development of their matrimonial jurisdiction.[13]

---

[11] This is still in force, apart from the words "and also to inform . . . in Times past".
[12] In 1485 Lambard asked, "How many Justices, think you, may now suffice, without breaking their
backs, to bear so many, not loads, but stacks of statutes?": 1 *Eirenarchia* (1581), Ch.7. F. Milton
(*The English Magistracy* (1967)) gives many examples of statutory provisions, including one
forbidding a man who was not a Lord to wear a cloak that did not "cover his privy member and
Buttocks (he being upright)" (p.9).
[13] From the Matrimonial Causes Act 1878 onwards.

3. APPOINTMENT

4-003   The Commission of the Peace is a document issued by the Crown setting out in very general terms the functions of the justices.[14] Separate Commission areas specified by statute, and then in delegated legislation made by the Lord Chancellor, have now been replaced by a single Commission area for England and Wales.[15] England and Wales has instead been divided into "local justice areas".[16] Lay justices[17] are appointed for England and Wales by the Lord Chancellor by instrument on behalf of and in the name of the Queen,[18] and assigned to one or more local justice area by the Lord Chief Justice, after consulting the Lord Chancellor.[19] Every lay justice is capable of acting as such in any local justice area, whether or not assigned to it, but may only do so in accordance with arrangements made by the Lord Chief Justice, again after consulting the Lord Chancellor.[20]

There are no formal qualifications enshrined in statute,[21] but the Guidance Notes that accompany the Application Form published by the DCA[22] specify a number that are applied in practice. Accordingly, the Lord Chancellor will consider a candidate's suitability "regardless of ethnic origin, gender, marital status, sexual orientation, political affiliation, religion or (subject to the physical requirements of the office) disability". The six key qualities sought are good character; understanding and communication; social awareness; maturity and sound temperament; sound judgement; and commitment and reliability. Applicants' health should be good enough to allow them to carry out all the duties of a magistrate, with satisfactory hearing (with or without a hearing aid) and the ability to sit and concentrate for long periods of time. Applications are welcomed from people with a disability who are able, either unassisted or with the benefit of adjustments to arrangements in accordance with the Disability Discrimination Act 1995, to carry out the range of magisterial duties.[23] Applicants must be 18 or over,[24] and people over 65[25] are not generally appointed (as there is a retiring age of 70 and five years' service is normally expected). British nationality is not

---

[14] The Crown Office (Forms and Proclamations) Rules 1992 (SI 1992/1730), Sch., Pt II, as amended by SI 2005/617, Sch., paras 153, 154.

[15] Courts Act 2003, s.7.

[16] 2003 Act, s.8. See para.2–021.

[17] i.e. a justice of the peace who is not a District Judge (Magistrates' Courts): 2003 Act, s.9.

[18] s.10(1). The appointment of magistrates is dealt with the Legal and Judicial Services Group within the DCA. The post of Secretary of Commissions is held by the Director General of this Group.

[19] s.10(2), (6), as amended by the Constitutional Reform Act 2005, Sch.4, Pt 1, para.313. The commencement of the 2003 Act, from April 1, 2005, ended the previous arrangement whereby justices of the peace for Greater Manchester, Merseyside and Lancashire were appointed by the Chancellor of the Duchy of Lancaster.

[20] s.10(3), (6), as amended by *ibid.*

[21] A requirement that the person reside in or within 15 miles of the Commission area for which he or she was appointed was removed by the Courts Act 2003 with the abolition of Commission areas, and no equivalent residential requirement introduced.

[22] Under the title *You Decide. Become A Magistrate.* See *www.dca.gov.uk/magistrates/candidates/apply.htm.*

[23] The wording has become more encouraging over time. After a pilot study, a number of blind magistrates were appointed: LCD Press Notice 224/01.

[24] A lower limit of 27 was removed in 2003: Lord Falconer, H.L. Deb. November 6, 2003, cols WA 127–WA 128.

[25] In 1997 the upper age limit was raised from 55: LCD Press Notices 143/97 and 268/98. The retiring age of 70 is enshrined in statute (2003 Act, s.13(1)) and so is exempt from the operation

a requirement, but all candidates must be willing to take the oath of allegiance.

There are then a number of "ineligibility criteria". The following will not be appointed: a serving police officer of civilian employee of a police force (or retired for less than two years), special constable or traffic warden, or their spouse or partner; anyone who has a close relative in any of these positions in the local justice area to which they might be appointed; a full-time member of HM Forces unless there is no realistic prospect of them being posted abroad in the near future; anyone whose work or community activities or those of their spouse or partner are such as to be clearly incompatible with the duties of a magistrate[26]; people employed in a penal establishment or involved in the transport of prisoners; employees of the NSPCC; security officers; a lay visitor to a police station (unless that would be given up); or a person who undertakes field work for a victim support scheme or as a Mackenzie friend in the local justice area in which they wish to serve. Also excluded are MPs, MEPs and AMs, prospective candidates and full-time party agents if part of the constituency is covered by the local justice area to which they might be appointed. There may be "other reasons for disqualification, which may be identified during the selection process". All convictions, including fixed penalty charges, or cautions, and civil proceedings involving an applicant must be disclosed.[27] Applicants who (or whose spouse or partner) have been convicted of a serious offence[28] or a number of minor offences will not be appointed if the Advisory Committee[29] does not think the public would have confidence in them as a magistrate. There are also detailed restrictions on the appointment of people with motoring convictions. All applicants are asked to disclose ethnic origin, for purpose of monitoring, and must disclose whether they are a freemason.

There are finally some restrictions in practice not mentioned in the *Notes for Guidance*. Thus the Lord Chancellor will not appoint candidates who are in the process of seeking asylum, or who are undischarged bankrupts.[30]

Candidates must answer a question on the application form:

> "Is there anything in your private or working life, or in your past, or to your knowledge in that of any member of your family or close friends, which, if it became generally known, might bring you or the magistracy into disrepute, or call into question your integrity, authority or standing as a magistrate?"

---

of the Employment Equality (Age) Regulations 2006: Harriet Harman MP, HL Deb November 23, 2006, col.179W.

[26] e.g. employees of the CPS, Probation Service, Youth Offending Team, HMCS, bailiff or member of an enforcement agency, store detective.

[27] e.g. matrimonial and bankruptcy orders must be disclosed.

[28] i.e anything other than a minor motoring conviction.

[29] See below.

[30] See *www.magistrates.gov.uk/candidates/index.htm*. Discharged bankrupts may be appointed, according to the circumstances. The automatic disqualification of undischarged bankrupts (Justices of the Peace Act 1997, s.65) was repealed by the Enterprise Act 2002, s.265.

Sexual orientation need not be disclosed. There is no property qualification[31] and women became eligible in 1919.[32]

Justices are appointed on the advice of Advisory Committees. These were first established following recommendations of the Royal Commission on the Selection of Justices of the Peace of 1910[33] in response to complaints that the Benches were dominated by Conservatives. In 2000 there were over 100 Committees with overall about 2,000 members,[34] generally one for each non-metropolitan county and metropolitan district, the City of London, some of the larger urban areas and each London commission area. Most of the county Committees have sub-committees or area panels. County Committees are normally chaired by the Lord Lieutenant; others now select their own chairmen (the name is put forward to the Lord Chancellor for appointment by him). Most Committees have eight to 10 members, and sub-committees about six to eight. The term of office is normally nine years. Appointments to a Committee are made by the Lord Chancellor, on the recommendation of an appointments committee of the Advisory Committee which comprises the chairman (or a nominee) and two other members, one of whom must be a non-magistrate.[35] A majority of Committee members are magistrates but non-magistrates form at least a third of committee membership, names being sought from the Cabinet Office public appointments unit, local businesses, employment and social groups and (usually) by local press advertisement. Committee members are given training. Bench chairmen may not be members of Advisory Committees or sub-committees or play any part in the selection process.[36] It has, indeed, been argued that magistrates generally should be excluded from membership: "Magistrates have no more business than Circuit judges to be appointing . . . their colleagues".[37] There is a need for the members of committees and sub-committees to be "drawn from a variety of backgrounds".[38] Until 1988, the names of the committee members were normally kept secret in order to keep them free from pressure and lobbying, although the name and address of the secretary was published. In that year, the Lord Chancellor, Lord Mackay, announced that he had asked the committees to take steps to make themselves known.[39]

A candidate for the magistracy can be recommended to a committee by any person or organisation, or can put himself or herself forward. In turn, the recommendations of the committee can be rejected by the Lord Chancellor.[40] All candidates are subject to a two-stage interview process, the first to determine

---

[31] This was abolished by the Liberal government in 1906: Justices of the Peace Act 1906, s.l.

[32] Sex Disqualification (Removal) Act 1919. Appointments do not, however, appear to fall within the scope of the Sex Discrimination Act 1975: see Skyrme (1983), p.51. The proportion of women to men has increased steadily—from 1.5 in 1947 to 1.1 in 1996, 1.04 in 2001, and 1.01 in 2005.

[33] Cd. 5250.

[34] 92 in England and Wales advising the Lord Chancellor; 17 advising the Chancellor of the Duchy of Lancaster: S. Humphreys, (2000) 56 *The Magistrate* 47. In 2000 there were also about 120 sub-committees. The DCA now publishes a list of the telephone numbers of Advisory Committees (*www.magistrates.gov.uk/docs/advisorycomslist.pdf*). This lists 89 committees.

[35] *ibid.*

[36] *ibid.*

[37] P. Darbyshire, [1997] Crim. L.R. 861, 866.

[38] Secretary of State and Lord Chancellor's *Directions to Advisory Committees*, para.3.9. There used to be an express requirement of political balance.

[39] Vol.499, H.L. Deb., July 20, 1988, cols 1311–1313. Lists may, for example, be available in local libraries; some are published on the Internet (e.g. Leicestershire, Staffordshire, East Sussex).

[40] In the 1980s it was reported that he had rarely rejected a recommendation on the grounds of personal unsuitability, it being unlikely that he would have information about candidates other

personal suitability, the second to test judicial aptitude by discussion of at least two case studies. Once personally suitable candidates have been identified, the Advisory Committee must then have regard to the number of vacancies and the need to ensure that the composition of the bench broadly reflects the community which it serves in terms of gender, ethnic origin, age, disability, geographical spread, occupation and industry.[41] The process is governed by the Secretary of State and Lord Chancellor's *Directions to Advisory Committees*, which were substantially revised in 1998 to take account of recommendations of the Home Affairs Select Committee.[42] They have since been reviewed by an LCD Equality Working Group[43] but there has been no in-depth empirical study of the current arrangements.[44] The *Directions* have been revised again.[45]

The main areas of difficulty have been those of politics and social and ethnic background.[46] The problems here are linked. At various points in the twentieth century lack of political balance in the magistracy (a preponderance of Conservatives) was itself a matter of political controversy led to the appointment of two Royal Commissions[47] by, respectively, a Liberal and a Labour government. Various steps were taken to try to improve the balance, with the political affiliation of candidates taken into account "only to avoid the appointment of a disproportionate number of magistrates supporting any political party".[48] In 1996, the Home Office Select Committee noted that there were still significant discrepancies.[49] The need to consider political affiliation at all was ultimately defended as the best proxy there was for social balance,[50] but this position was changed in 2003. The Lord Chancellor, Lord Falconer, announced[51] that he was amending his *Directions to Advisory Committees*. Political association had hitherto been used as an indicator of social class in seeking to achieve a Bench broadly representative of the community which they serve. However, he was satisfied that the way people vote was no longer a reliable guide to social perspective and standing. A new system was to be introduced with applicants identifying themselves against occupational and industrial groupings, based on standard classifications used by the Office for National Statistics.[52] Breakdowns of the political affiliations of Benches were given in the LCD/DCA's *Judicial*

---

than that gathered by the Advisory Committee; recommendations had, however, been rejected on grounds of occupational and political balance: King and May (1985), pp.29–30.

[41] Harriet Harman MP, H.C. Deb., October 23, 2006, col.1652W.

[42] 1995–96 H.C. 52, *Judicial Appointments Procedures*.

[43] See below, para.4–005.

[44] For earlier critical studies of the work of Advisory Committees, see Burney (1979), Chs 4 and 5; King and May (1985): see para.4–005; P. Darbyshire, [1997] Crim. L.R. 861, 866–868.

[45] They are now contained in an undated looseleaf binder (copy supplied by DCA).

[46] See R. Vogler. "Magistrates' Courts and the struggle for local democracy" in C. Sumner (ed.), *Censure, Politics and Criminal Justice* (1990), Ch.4; see the previous edition of this book at para.4–004.

[47] Royal Commission on the Selection of Justices of the Peace (Cd. 5250, 1910); Royal Commission on Justices of the Peace (Cmd. 7463, 1948).

[48] LCD, *How to become a Magistrate*

[49] Third Report, 1995–96 H.C. 52, *Judicial Appointments Procedures*, Vol.I, p.1x.

[50] LCD Press Notice 329/99. There were in any event doubts as to the reliability of the political affiliation information recorded.

[51] H.L. Deb., 6 November 2003, WA127–WA128.

[52] These are set out in the Notes for Guidance with the Application Form.

Appointments Annual Reports,[53] but were omitted from the 2004/05 Report onwards.[54]

4–004   Both Royal Commissions recommended that justices be drawn from different social backgrounds. The 1946–48 Report stated that:

> "Care must be taken to see that there are persons in the commission representative of various sections of the community. It is an advantage that a justice should have knowledge of the way of life of other classes than the class to which he belongs, and it is essential that there should be many among the justices who know enough of the lives of the poorest people to understand their outlook and their 'difficulties'."[55]

Such surveys as there have been consistently show a preponderance of professional and intermediate occupations and the under-representation of manual workers.[56] A high proportion are retired.[57]

Efforts have been made to increase the proportion of wage earners. In 1968, loss-of-earnings allowances were introduced.[58] The Employment Rights Act 1996[59] provides that an employer must give an employee magistrate reasonable time off.[60] However, as Lord Hailsham pointed out,[61] the legislation does not oblige an employer to give a magistrate a job, or to promote him or her if he or she has one. It provides no immunity from redundancy. Lord Mackay indicated that he was prepared to appoint people who were over 60 in order to complement the categories of people on the bench:

> "For example, these days it is very difficult to find people who are in levels of manufacturing industry to go on the bench during their working lives. It is important however that people with that kind of background should be on the bench.[62]

These have been proper developments, but they seem to have had relatively little effect. As already noted, attention is now paid directly to the social background of candidates by reference to the ONS groupings. It is too early to assess the consequences of this change.

4–005   It was only in the 1980s that the ethnic background of magistrates began to be properly investigated. King and May's Cobden Trust report,[63] based on research

---

[53] DCA website.

[54] Information on age, gender and ethnic background is to be published separately on the DCA website: 2004–05 Report, para.M2.

[55] para.84.

[56] See Minutes of Evidence to the Royal Commission, App.4; R. Hood, *Sentencing the Motoring Offender* (1972), Ch.3; J. Baldwin, (1976) 16 Brit. J. Criminol. 171; Skyrme (1983), p.64 (showing that in 1977 8.2% of the magistrates were manual workers); R. Henham, *Sentencing Principles and Magistrates' Behaviour* (1990), Ch.5; Morgan and Russell (2000), para.2.2.4.

[57] Morgan and Russell (2000), para.2.2.4: 26% of magistrates across eight benches surveyed; 40% according to questionnaire returns.

[58] Justices of the Peace Act 1968. See now the Justices of the Peace Act 1997, s.10.

[59] s.50(1). See A. Samuels, (1986) 42 *The Magistrate* 58. A refusal to pay the person for the time off may constitute a failure to comply with the duty: see *Corner v Buckinghamshire County Council* [1978] I.C.R. 836; *Riley-Williams v Argos Ltd*, Unreported, May 29 2003, EAT.

[60] Magistrates who are public employees are customarily given 18 days' extra paid leave to enable them to sit. Many large private firms have made similar arrangements.

[61] (1981) 37 *The Magistrate* 166.

[62] Vol.503, H.L. Deb., January 19, 1989, col.330.

[63] *Black Magistrates: A Study of Selection and Appointment* (1985), reviewed by R. Pearson, (1986) 13 J.L.S. 152.

conducted with the co-operation of the Lord Chancellor's Department, was in many respects critical, finding evidence of both direct and indirect discrimination in the selection process. A report of an LCD survey in 1987[64] showed that 1.92 per cent of magistrates were black, by comparison with 4.69 per cent of the general population, although the proportion of new appointments who were black was increasing. The absence in the survey of any local breakdown of the statistics was, however, a significant omission.[65] The Home Affairs Select Committee noted that it had not received evidence claiming that there was an acute problem with the under-representation of ethnic minorities in the magistracy.[66]

More recently, the proportion of ethnic minority appointments has increased.[67] Figures for each Bench are now published in the *Judicial Appointments Annual Report*.[68] While, overall, the composition nationally is approaching ethnic representativeness, the lay magistracy remains disproportionately white in areas with very large ethnic minorities.[69] The appointment procedures have been revised substantially since King and May's critical report in the 1980s. They were reviewed in 2000 by an Equality Working Group, established as part of the LCD's response to the report of the Stephen Lawrence Inquiry to assess the extent to which they provide equality of opportunity and supported diversity. The Group found the procedures not to be fundamentally flawed and, indeed, had many good points, but that there was room for improvement in some areas. Most Advisory Committees made concerted efforts to attract applications from people from a wide range of backgrounds. Further steps could be taken to raise the profile of the magistracy among under-represented groups and particular revisions made to the *Directions to Advisory Committees*.[70] A shadowing scheme was launched in co-operation with Operation Black Vote, a non-party political campaign supported by a broad coalition of Black organisations.[71] The Auld Report recommended that steps should be continue to be taken with a view to providing benches that reflect more broadly than at present the communities they serve.[72]

A further concerted effort was launched in 2003 with the announcement of a National Strategy for the Recruitment of Lay Magistrates (MNRS).[73] This is designed to raise the profile of the magistracy generally and develop a framework for the recruitment and retention of magistrates from under-represented groups. Elements include development of the shadowing scheme, the pilot having proved successful, the Magistrates in the Community Project, structuring PR work undertaken locally and revision of the website[74] and literature. By 2004–05, campaigns had been supported by the DCA in over 30 areas, substantial work

---

[64] Published in (1988) 44 *The Magistrate* 77–78.

[65] See N. Dholakia (1988) 44 *The Magistrate* 119, arguing in favour of regular ethnic monitoring, a proposal which had previously been rejected by Lord Hailsham.

[66] 1995–96 H.C. 52. *Judicial Appointments Procedures*, Vol.I. p.1x.

[67] From 5% to 9.3% between 1994 and 2000/01, and between 8% and 9% thereafter: *Judicial Appointments Annual Report 2004–2005*, para.M4.

[68] See Report for 2003–04, The overall statistics outside the Duchy of Lancaster were 93.6% White; 2.3% Black; 3.1% Asian; 0.8% Other; 0.2% Not known. *Cf.* 2001 Census figures for England: 90.9% White; 1.3% mixed; 4.6% Asian; 2.3% Black; 0.9% Chinese and other (CRE website)

[69] Morgan and Russell (2000), para.2.2.3.

[70] *Report of the Equality Working Group* (LCD, August 2000); The Group's recommendations were accepted.

[71] *Judicial Appointments Annual Report 2000–2001*, para.5.21.

[72] Ch.4, paras 59–68. See also J. Vennard, *et al*, *Ethnic minority magistrates' experience of the role and of the court environment* (DCA Research Series 3/04).

[73] www.dca.gov.uk/magist/recruit/natstrat_magrecruit_full.pdf.

[74] www.magistrates.gov.uk.

undertaken to engage employers, and work started on a legislative change on time off for magistrates in employment.[75]

That a political and social balance is desirable has generally been assumed or asserted rather than explained. It is possible to detect three considerations: the interests of potential appointees; the need to maintain general public confidence in magistrates' courts; and the interests of defendants. The first factor lay behind the appointment of the Royal Commissions of 1910 and 1946–48, although the Reports played down what was clearly not a respectable consideration and placed more emphasis on the second factor. For example, Lord Loreburn L.C. said in evidence to the 1910 Royal Commission:

> "I regard it as an indignity and an injustice that any section of opinion should be, in practice, excluded from a legitimate ambition, and I think that it is contrary to the public interest that the authority of the bench of justices should be weakened by any widespread suspicion that the members of it are not fairly selected."[76]

The subsequent Report[77] simply took up the second strand of this reasoning. The interests of actual defendants came a poor third. It will of course be a matter of "pot luck" whether a working-class defendant enjoys the supposed benefit of a court with one or more justices thought to be better able than the others to understand his or her outlook and difficulties. The respective social backgrounds of juries and justices do not seem to figure significantly among the considerations that affect the defendant's choice between summary trial and trial on indict-ment.[78] Lord Mackay welcomed the increasing proportion of black magistrates on the bench on the basis that

> "In addition to the special knowledge and understanding of sections of the community which black magistrates can bring to the bench, their presence in a judicial capacity can be an important factor in reassuring black defen-dants, witnesses and others connected with legal proceedings that they will be treated impartially by the courts."[79]

A study[80] of 160 newly appointed magistrates in three English counties suggested that there were no significant differences according to social class in attitudes concerning penal philosophy, sentencing practice, the causes of crime, court procedure, and the role of the magistrate. It was noted, however, that there may have been a tendency to appoint magistrates with particular views, whatever the social class. There were differences in attitude related to different political background, with Conservatives tending particularly to be more punitive in their penal philosophy. The authors concluded that "although the relationship between

[75] *Judicial Appointments Annual Report 2004–05*, paras 17–21.

[76] Minutes of Evidence. Lord Loreburn was caught between the pressure imposed by Liberal politicians and his own feelings that appointments should be made on merit without reference to politics: R. F. V. Heuston, *Lives of the Lord Chancellors* (1964), pp.153–158.

[77] Report, p.8.

[78] A. E. Bottoms and J. D. McClean, *Defendants in the Criminal Process* (1976), Ch.4. The research did show that defendants in general had a higher opinion of the Crown Court than the magistrates, for a variety of reasons.

[79] (1988) 44 *The Magistrate* 218, 219.

[80] R. A. Bond and N. F. Lemon, "Changes in Magistrates' Attitudes During the First Year on the Bench" in D. P. Farrington *et al.* (eds), *Psychology, Law and Legal Processes* (1979), Ch.8.

attitudes and behaviour is a problematic one, there is nevertheless a good prima facie case for arguing that differences in viewpoint expressed here are also likely to be expressed in some way in procedural and sentencing policies".[81] An earlier English study had not, however, found there to be such a correlation.[82] Indeed, the most significant factor seemed to be the general attitudes of the bench to which a particular magistrate belonged. Accordingly, it may well be that social and political background may neither be perceived to be of significance by defendants, nor actually of significance in affecting the way they are dealt with, although the evidence on the latter point is not entirely clear.

4. Undertakings on Appointment

A person selected to be a justice must give certain undertakings before being appointed, by completing a "Declaration and Undertaking" form.[83] These include that the magistrate will be circumspect in his or her conduct; respect confidences; complete all prescribed training (and resign if this is not completed within the time specified unless the Lord Chancellor consents to an extension); sit for at least 26 half days a year[84] (and resign if, without a reason acceptable to the Lord Chancellor he or she fails to complete the minimum number); resign if he or she becomes disqualified or unable to perform the duties of a magistrate; to inform the Chairman and Clerk to the Justices of his or her local justice area of impending criminal or civil proceedings and the outcome, disciplinary proceedings, bankruptcy and other matters; and to comply with any directions in relation to his sitting (including suspension) made by or on behalf of the Lord Chancellor.

4–006

5. Training

From 1953 it was the duty of every Magistrates' Courts Committee (MCC) to provide courses of instruction for justices in their area, in accordance with arrangements approved by the Lord Chancellor.[85] All justices appointed since

4–007

---

[81] *ibid.* p.141. *Cf.* J. Hogarth, *Sentencing as a Human Process* (1971) (survey of magistrates in Ontario); A. K. Bottomley, *Decisions in the Penal Process* (1973), Ch.4. By contrast, a study based upon simulated sentencing exercises found that differences of sentence could not be explained by the group composition of "benches" in terms of age, political affiliation, education, sex or length of experience: A. Kapardis, (1981) 145 J.P.N. 289–291.

[82] R. Hood, *Sentencing the Motoring Offender* (1972); *Cf.* Hood, *Sentencing in Magistrates' Courts* (1962), where the author's findings suggested that the social composition of a bench, in combination with particular community conditions, might affect the prison rate (pp.76–78, 119–120).

[83] Office for Judicial Complaints, *The System For Handling Magistrates' Conduct, Pastoral and Training Matters* (2006), Annex A.

[84] In practice, JPs are expected to sit more frequently: the Lord Chancellor expects an average annual attendance for each Bench of between 35 and 45 half-days: *Directions for Advisory Committees*, para.17.3. Explanations must be given in the Committee's Annual Report for each magistrate who has sat for fewer than 26 half days or for an excessive number of times (generally over 70): *ibid.*, paras 17.4, 17.5.

[85] See the Justices of the Peace Act 1997, s.64.

January 1, 1966[86] were required to attend a course of basic training. Compulsory refresher training was introduced in 1980. From January 1, 1996, no magistrate could take the chair unless he or she had taken a fully recognised Chairmanship Course based on the Judicial Studies Board (JSB) syllabus within the previous six years.[87] In the late 1990s, training was remodelled by virtue of the Magistrates' New Training Initiative. Training requirements are now centred on the acquisition of competences and not a specified number of hours of training as with the previous arrangements. Training is linked to mentoring and appraisal, through which individual training needs can be identified. Its implementation was overseen by the Judicial Studies Board Magisterial Committee. It was seen as an improvement, but there was some variation in delivery in different MCC areas and frequent criticism that it was over-complicated.[88] A revised Scheme (MNTI2) was launched in January 2004.[89]

Following the abolition of MCCs by the Courts Act 2003, it is now provided that the Lord Chief Justice, after consulting the Lord Chancellor, may make rules about the training courses to be completed before a person may exercise functions as a lay justice in any specified proceedings or class of proceedings,[90] and, more generally, rules about the training, development and appraisal of lay justices.[91] The Justices of the Peace (Training and Appraisal) Rules 2005[92] introduced a new structure. There is a Bench Training and Development Committee (BTDC) for each local justice area comprising three, six or nine justices for the area elected (or selected by a panel elected) by the justices for the area. A combined BTDC may be established for two or more local justice areas. Each BDTC must (a) establish a scheme for appraising justices; (b) identify on the training needs of justices; and (c) maintain a list of approved court chairmen. It must also report on training needs to the Magistrates' Area Training Committee (MATC) established for each Courts Board area. An approved training course must in each case be attended before sitting in or chairing the adult court, the family proceedings court, or the youth court. A justice may only be included in the list of approved court chairman if he or she has been appraised as competent to sit and completed the training course. The MATC must produce an annual training plan and report annually to the Lord Chief Justice. The JSB has been accorded a stronger role in overseeing magisterial training.

---

[86] See *The Training of Justices of the Peace in England and Wales* (Cmnd. 2856, 1967) (White Paper). The Lord Chancellor was assisted from 1974 by an Advisory Committee on Training, chaired by Boreham J. This replaced a National Advisory Council which had been set up to consider the introduction of compulsory training. The Committee was absorbed into the Judicial Studies Board (see para.4–033) with effect from 1985. The Board's functions with respect to magisterial training are discharged by its Magisterial Committee (see the *Judicial Studies Board Annual Reports*); its function in this context is to supervise the training, not (except in the case of District Judges (Magistrates' Courts)) to perform it.

[87] (1991) *The Magistrate* 139–142; (1992) *The Magistrate* 86; E. Ralphs and G. Norman, (1995) *The Magistrate* 58. See *R v Brent JJ., Ex p. Richards, The Times*, December 3, 1992, where a decision that the applicant had failed chairmanship training sessions and would not be allowed to take the chair in court was held to be invalid as being unfair and perverse on the facts.

[88] *Judicial Studies Board Annual Report 2000–2001*, Ch.6; Auld Report, pp.131–134.

[89] See JSB, *Magistrates National Training Initiative Handbook*, December 2003, and updates.

[90] Courts Act 2003, ss.10(4), 20, as amended by the Constitutional Reform Act 2005, Sch.4, Pt 1, para.321.

[91] Courts Act 2003, ss.19, 20.

[92] SI 2005/564, as amended by SI 2006/680, Sch.1, para.80. And see JSB, *Arrangements for the Organisation and Management of Magistrates' Training in the Unified Courts Administration* (CR JSB 1.0/2005, January 2005).

6. Conduct and Removal

A lay justice may resign at any time. Furthermore, the Lord Chancellor may, with **4–008** the concurrence of the Lord Chief Justice, remove a lay justice from his or her office:

(a) on the ground of incapacity or misbehaviour;

(b) on the ground of a persistent failure to meet such standards of competence as are prescribed by a direction given by the Lord Chancellor with the concurrence of the Lord Chief Justice; or

(c) if he is satisfied that the lay justice is declining or neglecting to take a proper part in the exercise of his or her functions as a justice of the peace.[93]

In addition, a supplemental list is kept in the office of the Clerk of the Court in Chancery and a lay justice whose name is entered in the list is not qualified as a JP to do any act or to be a member of a committee or other body. The name of a lay justice who reaches 70 must be entered in this list,[94] as must the name of a lay justice who applies and the application is approved by the Lord Chancellor. The Lord Chancellor may, with the concurrence of the Lord Chief Justice, direct that the name of a lay justice is to be entered in the list on the ground of incapacity.[95] In practice, a justice, even under the old provisions, would only be removed for good cause. Most who leave office have to do so because they are unable to fulfil their share of the work or because they move outside the area.[96]

The procedures for dealing with complaints against magistrates have been redesigned in the light of the Courts Act 2003 and the Constitutional Reform Act 2005, and are now set out in *The system for handling magistrates' conduct, pastoral and training matters*, published by the Office for Judicial Complaints (OJC).[97] This sets out detailed timescales and procedural steps to ensure compliance with natural justice. Overall responsibility is shared between the Lord Chancellor and the Lord Chief Justice.[98] Separate processes apply to complaints of misconduct and concerning capability. "Misconduct" includes "conduct which, in the eyes of the community as a whole, reasonably calls into question a person's suitability to sit as a magistrate".[99] The Lord Chancellor and Lord

---

[93] Courts Act 2003, s.11, as amended by the Constitutional Reform Act 2005, Sch.4, Pt 1, para.314. Under the Justices' of the Peace Act 1997 ss.5 and 7, no grounds for removal were specified. The addition of grounds is necessary to ensure sufficient safeguards of judicial independence for compliance with Art.6(1) ECHR. See also para.8–021.

[94] Where proceedings are under way, this can be delayed until they have ended if directed by the Lord Chief Justice with the concurrence of the Lord Chancellor; a chairman of lay justice can stay until his term has ended.

[95] Courts Act 2003, ss.12, 13, as amended by the Constitutional Reform Act 2005, Sch.4, Pt 1, para.315. A name must be removed if he or she ceases to be a JP. Where a name has been included on application or for reasons of incapacity, the Lord Chancellor with the concurrence of the Lord Chief Justice can direct its removal, enabling the JP to sit again: s.14.

[96] Each year, about 1% of all justices on the active list are required to resign for the first reason, and 1% for the second: Skyrme (1983), p.153.

[97] *www.judicialcomplaints.gov.uk/publications/mags_system.htm.* See para.4–032.

[98] See Section 1, Part 2.

[99] para.1.1.8.

Chief Justice "have a firm expectation that magistrates . . . will conduct themselves in such a way as to command the confidence of the communities they
serve", and magistrates must abide by the terms of their judicial oath and their
declaration and undertaking.[100] Complaints of misconduct are investigated on
behalf of the Lord Chancellor and Lord Chief Justice by Advisory Committees
and their support staff, and staff in the OJC. Competence issues are dealt with by
the BTDC. Detailed rules have been made by the Lord Chief Justice.[101] There
may be a conduct investigation hearing by a panel of members of the Advisory
Committee; if the case is substanstiated, a recommendation to the Lord Chancellor and Lord Chief Justice is formulated. A report is made through the OJC.
The Lord Chancellor and Lord Chief Justice then reach a decision. Options open
to them include requiring the magistrate to receive further training, mentoring
and/or appraisal; appointment of a judicial investigation[102]; or disciplinary action
(after a further opportunity to make representations).[103] Under the previous
arrangements,[104] justices were removed if they or a spouse were convicted of an
offence, although a conviction for a minor motoring offence would lead to a
reprimand rather than suspension or removal. Convictions for drunken driving
had in recent years led to suspension during the period of disqualification rather
than removal. Justices were also removed for refusing to apply a law he or she
found distasteful,[105] and for demonstrating outside her own courthouse in support
of a defendant on trial inside.[106]

7. Disqualification

4–009   Justices are subject to the same common law rules as to disqualification for
interest or bias as other judicial officers.[107] In addition, they are expressly

---

[100] paras 1.1.9—1.1.10.

[101] With concurrence of the Lord Chancellor: Complaints (Magistrates) Rules 2006, made with the concurrence of the Lord Chancellor under ss.115 and 117 of the Constitutional Reform Act 2005. These are set out in Section 2 of the OJC document.

[102] Under Pt 5 of the Judicial Discipline (Prescribed Procedures) Regulations 2006 (SI 2006/676).

[103] The possibilities are listed in *ibid.*, reg.26. See also s.108 of the 2005 Act.

[104] Those applicable immediately before the recent changes were summarised by S. Humphreys, (2000) 56 *The Magistrate* 56. For a successful challenge to a removal decision for non compliance with the guidelines then applicable see *R (on the application of Gill) v Lord Chancellor's Department* [2003] EWHC 156 (Admin).

[105] Colonel Delmer Davies-Evans, who disapproved of certain regulations governing the use of petrol, was removed in 1947 (see Skyrme (1983), pp.156–157). A Welsh justice who stated that she was not prepared to impose penalties on people who, non-violently, broke laws which she considered unjust to the Welsh language, resigned in 1972: R. Pearson in Z. Bankowski and G. Mungham (eds), *Essays in Law and Society* (1980), pp.89–90; see also Lord Hailsham, (1972) 28 *The Magistrate* 132–134: in a similar case, Lord Gardiner required a Welsh magistrate to resign. A number of magistrates resigned rather than enforce the community charge.

[106] Her application for judicial review of the decision was rejected: *The Times*, September 25, 1985; (1985) 135 N.L.J. 976; Lord Hailsham, (1985) 41 *The Magistrate* 149.

[107] Below, para.4–040. For cases concerning justices see *R v Altrincham JJ., Ex p. Pennington* [1975] Q.B. 549; *R v Smethwick JJ., Ex p. Hands, The Times*, December 4, 1980 (decision on allegation of statutory nuisance against local authority quashed because one of the justices was the wife of the former chairman of the housing committee); *R v Liverpool City JJ, Ex p. Topping* [1983] 1 W.L.R. 119; *R v Weston-super-Mare JJ., Ex p. Shaw* [1987] Q.B. 640 (magistrates' knowledge of other outstanding charges against the defendant: see R. Stevens, (1986) 150 J.P.N. 788; (1986) 150 J.P.N. 805); *R v Metropolitan Stipendiary Magistrate, Ex p. Gallagher* (1972) 136 J.P. 80; *R v Birmingham Magistrates' Court, Ex p. Robinson* (1986) 150 J.P. 1 (see J. N. Spencer, (1986) 150 J.P.N. 307); *R v Downham Market Magistrates' Court, Ex p. Nudd* (1988) 152 J.P. 511 (see

disqualified from acting in a case involving a local authority if they are a member of that authority.[108] A celebrated case where a magistrate was sufficiently incautious as to admit actual bias was *R v Bingham JJ., Ex p. Jowitt.*[109] The chairman of a bench hearing a speeding case, where the only evidence was that of the motorist and a police constable, said:

"Quite the most unpleasant cases that we have to decide are those where the evidence is a direct conflict between a police officer and a member of the public. My principle in such cases has always been to believe the evidence of the police officer, and therefore we find the case proved."

The conviction was quashed.

8. Legal Liability

A justice of the peace (or a justices' clerk or assistant clerk exercising the **4–010** functions of a single justice) enjoys a statutory immunity from any action for damages where he or she has acted in the execution of his or her duty and within jurisdiction. Where a justice (or clerk) has acted outside jurisdiction, but in the purported execution of his or her duty, an action will only lie if he or she has acted in bad faith.[110] The position is now similar to that of judges of superior courts.[111] A court may not order any justice, or justices' clerk or assistant clerk exercising the function of a single justice, to pay costs in any proceedings in respect of any act or omission of his or hers in the execution (or purported execution) of his or her duty; this does not, however, apply in relation to any proceedings where he or she is being tried for an offence or appealing against conviction, or in which it is proved that he or she acted in bad faith in respect of

N. A. McKittrick, (1988) 152 J.P.N. 643) (magistrates' knowledge of defendant's previous record); *R v Cambridge JJ., Ex p. Yardline Ltd and Bird* [1990] Crim. L.R. 733 (member of Bench employed as consulting surveyor by local authority conducting prosecution for demolition of listed building); *R v Romsey JJ., Ex p. Gale* (1992) 156 J.P. 567 (notes of concluding remarks prepared before all evidence heard); *R v Marylebone Magistrates' Court, Ex p. Perry* (1992) 156 J.P. 696 (magistrate signed warrants while listening to evidence); *R v Ely JJ., Ex p. Burgess* (1993) 157 J.P. 484; *R v Marylebone Magistrates Court, Ex p. Joseph, The Times,* May 7, 1993; *R v South Worcestershire JJ., Ex p. Daniels* (1996) 161 J.P. 121 (justice consulted sentencing guidelines during cross-examination of the defendant). See generally M. Beloff, (2001) 165 J.P.N. 436.
[108] Courts Act 2003, s.41.
[109] *The Times,* July 3. 1974.
[110] Courts Act 2003, ss.31 and 32 (based on provisions originally introduced by the Courts and Legal Services Act 1990, s.108). On the pre-1990 Act provisions see L. A. Sheridan, (1951) 14 M.L.R. 267; D. Thompson, (1958) 21 M.L.R. 517; "Suing the Beaks" (1990) 154 J.P.N. 212.
[111] See below, para.4–039. The Court of Appeal had stated the law of justices' immunity in similar broad terms in *Sirros v Moore* [1975] Q.B. 118, but that was disapproved by the House of Lords in *In re McC (A Minor)* [1985] A.C. 528, holding that malice and lack of cause did not have to be established where an act was done outside jurisdiction. Following the award of damages against justices in a series of cases where they had acted outside jurisdiction (*In re McC (A Minor); R v Waltham Forest JJ., Ex p. Solanke* [1986] Q.B. 983; *R v Manchester City Magistrates' Court, Ex p. Davies (No.2)* [1989] Q.B. 631), the Lord Chancellor acceded to pressure from the Magistrates' Association in favour of broadening the immunity.

the matters giving rise to the proceedings.[112] If this provision prevents a court making a costs order, the court may instead order the Lord Chancellor to make a payment in respect of costs, in accordance with regulations.[113]

In specified circumstances a justice or clerk may be (or is entitled to be) indemnified out of local funds in respect of costs reasonably incurred in or in connection with proceedings[114] in respect of any act or omission in the execution (or purported execution) of his or her duty or in taking steps to dispute any claim which might arise in such proceedings; any damages or costs ordered to be paid by him or her; and any sums payable in connection with a reasonable settlement of proceedings. There must be an indemnity in respect of criminal matters unless it is proved that the justice or clerk acted in bad faith. For other matters, the justice *may* be indemnified unless it is proved that he or she acted in bad faith; and *must* be indemnified if he or she acted reasonably and in good faith.[115]

9. JUSTICES' CLERKS[116]

4–011   Traditionally, the justices' clerk was both in charge of the administration of the magistrates' court and its chief legal adviser. Originally the clerks were the personal clerks to individual justices or benches; subsequently, they came to be appointed by the MCCs subject to the approval of the Lord Chancellor. In 1989 there were 285 clerkships in England and Wales. Of the 277 members of the Justices' Clerks' Society, 150 were solicitors, 119 barristers and eight qualified by experience.[117]

Significant changes to the administration of magistrates' courts were effected by the Police and Magistrates' Courts Act 1994,[118] which introduced the office of justices' chief executive distinct from the justices' clerk. Further changes made by the Access to Justice Act 1999 enhanced the former's role, centralising responsibility for administrative functions on him or her. Each MCC was required to appoint a justices' chief executive from a short list of one or more

---

[112] Courts Act 2003, s.34(1)–(3).

[113] 2003 Act, s.34(4), (5); Justices and Justices' Clerks (Costs) Regulations 2001 (SI 2001/1296). No order can be made in favour of a public authority or official acting on behalf of a public authority; the court must determine an amount sufficient reasonably to compensate the receiving party for costs properly incurred in the proceedings. For an example of the use of the power see *R (on the application of Osler) v Cambridge Magistrates Court* [2004] EWHC 1226 (Admin).

[114] The requirement that the proceedings be "against him" was removed from the previous legislation by the Access to Justice Act 1999, s.99(a), allowing for an indemnity in respect of judicial review and appeals by case stated. See *Liability of Judicial Officers and Others for Costs in Court Proceedings: A Consultation Paper* (LCD, 1996). The Magistrates' Association had expressed concern following the award of costs against justices in *R v Newcastle-under-Lyme JJ., Ex p. Massey* [1994] 1 W.L.R. 1684 and *R v Lincoln JJ., Ex p. Count* (1996) 8 Admin. L.R. 233 (where the justices had acted on the (erroneous) advice of their clerk).

[115] Courts Act 2003, s.54. There is no longer a discretion to grant an indemnity where there is bad faith.

[116] K. C. Clarke, [1964] Crim. L.R. 620, 697; P. Darbyshire, (1980) 144 J.P.N., 186, 201, 219, 233; P. Darbyshire, *The Magistrates' Clerk* (1984); Justices' Clerks' Society, *Administering Magistrates' Courts: The Role of the Justices Clerk* (1989); H. McLaughlin, (1990) 30 Brit. J. Criminol. 358.

[117] (1989) 45 *The Magistrate* 34.

[118] See above, para.2–030.

persons approved by the Lord Chancellor.[119] The chief executive was required to make arrangements for the efficient and effective administration of the magistrates' courts for the area to which the committee related.[120] However, the Courts Act 2003 transferred administrative responsibility for the magistrates' courts to HM Courts Service; MCCs and the office of justices' chief executive were accordingly abolished.[121] References to the justices' chief executives in legislation have been replaced by references to a "designated officer".[122]

Justices' clerks were separately appointed by MCCs, from a short list of one or more persons approved by the Lord Chancellor,[123] essentially to act as the professional legal adviser to justices. Under the Courts Act 2003,[124] with administration now the responsibility of HMCS, they are civil servants appointed by the Lord Chancellor and Lord Chief Justice, a change of status that gave rise to some resistance.[125] Accordingly, a justices' clerk is now a person appointed by the Lord Chancellor under s.2(1) of the 2003 Act,[126] and designated by him, after consulting the Lord Chief Justice, as a justices' clerk. A person may only be so designated if he or she has a five-year magistrates' court qualification,[127] or is a barrister or solicitor who has served for not less than five years as an assistant to a justices' clerk, or has previously been a justices' clerk. The Lord Chancellor must assign each justices' clerk to one or more local justice areas and may change an assignment after consulting the chairman of lay justices for the area. He may also appoint assistants to a justice's clerk with qualifications specified in regulations.[128] Justices' clerks are line managed by HMCS Area Directors.

The judicial independence of a justices' clerk is enshrined the legislation.[129] Thus a justices' clerk exercising a function exercisable by one or more justice of the peace, giving advice on matters of law, including procedure on practice, or exercising a function as a member of the Criminal or Family Procedure Rule Committees, is not subject to the direction of the Lord Chancellor or any other person. An assistant clerk is not subject to the direction of any person other than a justices' clerk. This guarantee has been criticised as too narrow, having no application to such matters as "the training of justices, the bench meetings or

---

[119] Justices of the Peace Act 1997, s.40, as amended by the Access to Justice Act 1999, ss.87 and 88(3) and Sch.12, para.11. See the Justices' Chief Executives and Justices' Clerks (Appointment) Regulations 1999 (SI 1999/2397). The 1999 Act removed a requirement that the chief executive be a person eligible to be appointed as a justices' clerk. A person could not be appointed both as a justices' chief executive and justices' clerk for a petty sessions area unless the Lord Chancellor agreed; a person so appointed could only exercise the latter's functions if authorised by the committee: s.40(6), (7).

[120] For a survey of the changes to courts management at this stage, see B. Fitzpatrick et al., (2000) 11 Criminal Law Forum 1.

[121] See para.2–030.

[122] i.e. a person appointed by the Lord Chancellor to be a designated officer in relation to a magistrates' court, justice of the peace of local justice area: Courts Act 2003, s.37. The 42 HMCS Area Directors have been so designated.

[123] Justices of the Peace Act 1997, s.42.

[124] s.27, as amended by the Constitutional Reform Act 2005, Sch.4, Pt 1, para.326.

[125] There were concerns at the threat to independence and some arguments that they should be appointed through the Judicial Appointments Commission. See Memorandum by the Justices' Clerk Society to the Select Committee on the Constitutional Reform Bill 2003–04 H.L. 125.

[126] See para.1–019.

[127] i.e. a right of audience in all magistrates' courts for five years: Courts and Legal Services Act 1990, s.71.

[128] See the Assistants to Justices' Clerks Regulations 2006 (SI 2006/3405).

[129] Courts Act 2003, s.29.

even remarks made when justices assemble for a day's duties".[130] The guarantee is, however, reflected in the fact that responsibility of the training of Legal Advisers (court clerks) is shared between HMCS and the JSB.[131]

The number of justices' clerks has been significantly reduced, to 70 in 2006.The current pattern reflects different policies of different MCC areas and is not coherent. HMCS has proposed the establishment of a model for the coherent distribution of these posts, taking account of such factors as the numbers of legal teams managed and benches served, court workload and geography.[132] The Magistrates' Association's position was that the ratio of justices' clerks to magistrates should be one to 3/400; that they should serve 1 to 6 benches and be able to sit as a Legal Adviser perhaps up to 50 per cent of the time. It was not happy with the current proposals, which might well reduce the number even further.[133] There was, however, general endorsement of the Consultation Paper's characterisation of the role of the justices' clerk as centred on responsibility for the provision of legal advice to magistrates; leadership of the legal team; the discharge of some judicial functions; ensuring that appropriate training is provided to the lay bench; liaison with the professional judiciary; and meeting court users.[134]

The functions of a justices' clerk include giving advice to justices on matters of law (including practice or procedure); furthermore, rules may be made enabling things authorised to be done by, to or before a JP to be done instead by a justices' clerk or an assistant.[135] As from October 1, 1980, a person has not been allowed to act as a court clerk unless he or she possesses one of a series of prescribed qualifications.[136] The current position is set out in the Assistants to Justices' Clerks Regulations 2006.[137] An assistant clerk may be employed as a clerk in court (increasingly commonly termed Legal Adviser) if he or she is a barrister or solicitor or has passed the necessary examinations for either profession, or has been granted an exemption in relation to any examination by the appropriate examining body. However, the Lord Chancellor may designate any person to be employed as a court clerk for a period not exceeding six months if he is satisfied that he or she is a suitable person and that no other arrangements can reasonably be made. Furthermore, the Lord Chancellor may designate an unqualified person to discharge specified out-of-court functions such as listing and case management where specifically authorised by the justices' clerk.[138] The achievement of the position long advocated that clerks offering legal advice in

---

[130] S. Baker and J. English, *A Guide to the Police and Magistrates' Courts Act 1994* (1994), p.115 (in respect of an earlier version of this provision).

[131] See HMCS, JSB, *Arrangements for the Training and Developmetn of Justices' Clerks and Legal Advisers (advice-giving functions and use of statutory powers)* (July 2006), setting out agreements between the two bodies.

[132] *A Model for the Provision of Justices' Clerks in England and Wales* HMCS Consultation Paper CP (L) 08/06, May 10, 2006.

[133] Magistrates Association Paper, January 2007.

[134] Consultation Response, August 31, 2006, Annex B.

[135] Courts Act 2003, s.28(1)–(5).

[136] Power to prescribe qualifications is conferred by the 1997 Act, s.44(3). See the Justices' Clerks (Qualification of Assistants) Rules 1979 (SI 1979/570), as amended and the fourth edition of this book at para.4–011.

[137] SI 2006/3405.

[138] This involved a return to the position as understood to be the case under the Justices of the Peace Act 1997: *The Delegation of Powers by Justices' Clerks to Non Legally Qualified Staff in Magistrates' Courts in England and Wales* (Response to Consultation CP (R) 22/05, January 20 2006, DCA).

court should be legally qualified[139] is undermined by the possibility of temporary appointment, for which no qualifications are specified in the legislation.

The justices' clerk may grant but not refuse legal aid. Under the Justices' Clerks Rules 2005[140] a justices' clerk may perform a large number of functions otherwise exercisable by a single justice, such as the issuing of a summons, adjourning a hearing with the consent of the parties, asking the accused whether he or she pleads guilty or not guilty, fixing or setting aside a date, time and place for the trial of an information, giving directions for the conduct of a criminal trial and exercising powers at an early administrative hearing, and a whole series of family matters. Similarly, an information may be laid before a justice or a justices' clerk. A justices' clerk may delegate most of these matters to an assistant.[141]

One of the issues that has caused problems since the 1940s has been the role of the court clerk or Legal Adviser in magistrates' court proceedings.[142] The clerk's function is to advise on law and procedure, but not to participate in the decision on the facts. In *R v East Kerrier JJ., Ex p. Mundy*[143] Lord Goddard C.J. stated that the clerk should not retire with the justices as a matter of course but should wait to be sent for should advice on a point of law be needed. Otherwise, observers might conclude that the clerk was influencing the justices on questions of fact, and this would constitute a breach of the principle that justice must be seen to be done. This apparently caused "alarm and despondency" in some quarters,[144] somewhat to Lord Goddard's surprise, and this led to some further "clarification",[145] or back-pedalling (depending on one's point of view). At the same time Lord Goddard C.J. threatened that justices who knowingly disobeyed the Divisional Court's directions would be reported to the Lord Chancellor.[146] The trend thereafter was for emphasis to be placed increasingly on the point that lay justices must be given proper professional advice, and less on the need to avoid the appearance that the clerk might have given an opinion on the facts.[147]

A Practice Direction was issued in 2000 by Lord Woolf C.J. with the concurrence of the President of the Family Divison.[148] The main points are as follows:

---

[139] See J.C.S., *Administering Magistrates' Courts* (1989), Ch.12

[140] S.I. 2005/545, as amended by SI 2005/2796.

[141] *ibid.* r.3, Prior to 1993 (SI 1993/1183) judical functions could not be delegated: *R v Gateshead JJ., Ex p. Tesco Stores Ltd* [1981] Q. B. 470; *R v Manchester Stipendiary Magistrate, Ex p. Hill* [1983] 1 A.C. 328. See (1992) 156 J.P.N. 435.

[142] The court clerk has been described as the "key worker in setting the tone of the courtroom atmosphere": H. Parker, M. Casburn and D. Turnbull, *Receiving Juvenile Justice* (1981), p.48.

[143] [1952] 2 Q.B. 719.

[144] (1953) 10 *The Magistrate* 65.

[145] *R v Welshpool JJ., Ex p. Holley* [1953] 2 Q.B. 403 (justices can invite the clerk to join them as they retire to advise on a point of law; the fact that he remains while the facts are discussed not sufficient to invalidate their decision); *Practice Note (Justices' Clerks)* [1953] 1 W.L.R. 1416.

[146] *R v Barry JJ., Ex p. Nagi Kasim* [1953] 1 W.L.R. 1320, 1322.

[147] N. Crampton, (1979) 129 N.L.J. 208; *R v Uxbridge Magistrates' Court, Ex p. Smith* (1985) 149 J.P. 620 (no objection where the clerk left court to advise the justices, who had retired, that certain legal submissions had been erroneous; criticised by A. Heaton-Armstrong, (1986) 150 J.P.N. 340, 357); *cf. R v Bingham JJ., Ex p. Bell*, Unreported, discussed by Heaton-Armstrong, *op. cit.* and *R v Eccles JJ., Ex p. Fitzpatrick* (1989) 89 Cr.App.R. 324 (certiorari granted where there was a reasonable suspicion of improper influence by the clerk. For the clerk's view, see A. Turner (1992) 156 J.P.N. 723). See also the joint statement by the Magistrates' Association and the Justices' Clerks' Society, (1975) 31 *The Magistrate* 4.

[148] *Practice Direction (Justices: Clerk to Court)* [2000] 1 W.L.R. 1886 (see A. Murdie, (2001) 145

1. A justices' clerk is responsible for: (a) the legal advice tendered to the justices within the area; (b) the performance of any of the functions set out below by any member of his/her staff acting as legal adviser; (c) ensuring that competent advice is available to justices when the justices' clerk is not personally present in court; and (d) the effective delivery of case management and the reduction of unnecessary delay.

2. Where a person other than the justices' clerk (a "legal adviser"), who is authorised to do so, performs any of the functions referred to in this direction he/she will have the same responsibilities as the justices' clerk. The legal adviser may consult the justices' clerk or other person authorised by the justices' clerk for that purpose before tendering advice to the bench. If the justices' clerk or that person gives advice directly to the bench, he/she should give the parties or their advocates an opportunity of repeating any relevant submissions prior to the advice being given.[149]

3. It shall be the responsibility of the legal adviser to provide the justices with any advice they require properly to perform their functions whether or not the justices have requested that advice, on: (i) questions of law (including European Court of Human Rights jurisprudence and those matters set out in s.2(l) of the Human Rights Act 1998); (ii) questions of mixed law and fact[150]; (iii) matters of practice and procedure; (iv) the range of penalties available; (v) any relevant decisions of the superior courts or other guidelines; (vi) other issues relevant to the matter before the court[151]; and (vii) the appropriate decision-making structure to be applied in any given case. In addition to advising the justices it shall be the legal adviser's responsibility to assist the court, where appropriate, as to the formulation of reasons and the recording of those reasons.

4. A justices' clerk or legal adviser must not play any part in making findings of fact but may assist the bench by reminding them of the evidence, using any notes of the proceedings for this purpose.

5. A justices' clerk or legal adviser may ask questions of witnesses and the parties in order to clarify the evidence and any issues in the case.[152]

6. A legal adviser has a duty to ensure that every case is conducted fairly.

7. When advising the justices the justices' clerk or legal adviser, whether or not previously in court, should: (i) ensure that he/she is aware of the relevant facts; and (ii) provide the parties with the information necessary to enable

---

S.J. 257; J. Guess, (2001) 165 J.P.N. 582). This revoked *Practice Direction (Justices: Clerk to Courts)* [1981] 1 W.L.R. 1163 (on which see B. Harris, (1981) 145 J.P.N. 403). *Practice Note (Justices' Clerks)* [1954] 1 W.L.R. 213, concerning the role of the clerk in domestic proceedings, remains in force. Some of these points as to the functions of a justices' clerk are also made in the Courts Act 2003, s.28(4), (5); it is stated that this subsection is not exhaustive (subs.(7)). In criminal cases the Direction now appears as Pt V. 55 of the Criminal Practice Direction.

[149] Such submissions should be heard in open court and not in some corridor or private place: *R v Chichester JJ., Ex p. D.P.P.* (1993) 157 J.P. 1042.

[150] See, e.g. *R v Consett JJ., Ex p. Postal Bingo Ltd* [1967] 2 Q.B. 9.

[151] This is regarded as referring to issues of fact and evidence, and not isues of law or mixed law and fact: *R v Uxbridge Magistrates' Court, Ex p. Smith* (1985) 149 J.P. 620 (in relation to the 1981 Statement).

[152] This proposition did not appear in the 1981 Direction. *Cf. R v Consett JJ, Ex p. Postal Bingo Ltd* [1967] 2 Q.B. 9 (clerk may ask questions in court in order to clear up ambiguities, so long as it is at the express or implied request of the bench).

the parties to make any representations they wish as to the advice before it is given.

8. At any time, justices are entitled to receive advice to assist them in discharging their responsibilities. If they are in any doubt as to the evidence which has been given, they should seek the aid of their legal adviser, referring to his/her notes as appropriate.[153] This should ordinarily be done in open court. Where the justices request their adviser to join them in the retiring room, this request should be made in the presence of the parties in court. Any legal advice given to the justices other than in open court should be clearly stated to be provisional and the adviser should subsequently repeat the substance of the advice in open court and give the parties an opportunity to make any representations they wish on that provisional advice. The legal adviser should then state in open court whether the provisional advice is confirmed or if it is varied the nature of the variation.

10. The legal adviser is under a duty to assist unrepresented parties to present their case, but must do so without appearing to become an advocate for the party concerned.[154]

This statement, which is both lengthier and clearer than its predecessors, states that advice should ordinarily be given in open court and introduces the requirement that advice given first in private be repeated in open court. This will ensure compliance with the requirements of a fair and public hearing under Art.6(1), ECHR.[155] It would seem that by virtue of the 2000 Practice Direction, specific reasons will be needed to justify departure from the general position that advice is given in open court; any generalised invocation of the confidential nature of the relationship between the justices and their professional adviser, invoked in the past by defenders of the previous arrangements,[156] will not suffice.

If justices summon the clerk when only issues of fact are involved and the clerk has made no note of evidence, a conviction may well be quashed.[157]

It has been held that it is proper for the clerk, in the absence of the justices and in conjunction with the prosecutor, to explain to an unrepresented defendant that if he or she attacks a prosecution witness his or her previous convictions can be revealed to the court.[158] However, it is not appropriate to warn the defendant and

---

[153] Similar words in the 1981 statement impliedly overruled the statements of Donaldson L.J. in *R v Guildford JJ., Ex p. Harding* (1981) 145 J.P. 174.

[154] *Cf. Simms v Moore* [1970] 2 Q.B. 327.

[155] Although in *Clark v Kelly* 2001 J.C. 16, the High Court of Justiciary held that the giving of advice in private did not breach the public hearing requirement, following *Delcourt v Belgium* (1970) 1 E.H.R.R. 355, provided that any matter on which the parties might reasonably wish to make material comment was raised in open court. The Privy Council took the same view, [2004] 1 A.C. 681.

[156] (1986) 42 *The Magistrate* 40–41; *cf.* A. Heaton-Armstrong, (1986) 150 J.P.N. 340, 357, arguing that advice on the law should always be given in open court.

[157] *R v Worley JJ., Ex p. Nash* [1982] C.L. 1932: see the comment at (1983) 147 J.P.N. 209. *Cf. R v Eccles JJ., Ex p. Fitzpatrick* (1989) 89 Cr.App.R. 324 (appearance of improper influence of decision to commit for trial) and *R v Eccles JJ., Ex p. Farelly* (1992) 157 J.P. 77 (clerk spoke to justices after they had returned from their deliberations, and then went with them when they left the court again to reconsider, without any explanation).

[158] *R v Weston-super-Mare JJ., Ex p. Townsend* [1968] 3 All E.R. 225.

a defence witness of the consequences of giving perjured evidence where such a warning has not been given to prosecution witnesses.[159]

In some areas, clerks rule on questions of the admissibility of evidence in the absence of the justices. This is generally accepted to be irregular as the clerk has no legal authority to rule on such matters. On the other hand it is also accepted that it is undesirable for the justices who are to determine guilt to determine disputed questions of admissibility, which may well involve hearing evidence which subsequently has to be disregarded as inadmissible. There is in fact no reason why the parties should not by agreement submit the issue to the clerk and, once a ruling is made, voluntarily abide by it: the real limitation is that the ruling will not technically be binding. It is likely to be in the defendant's interests for this to be done in the absence of the justices: it is unlikely that the justices could be persuaded to differ from the clerk's view on such a question.

It is also a well-established practice for lawyers to refer doubtful points of law to the clerk in advance of the hearing in order to obtain what in practice, although again not in theory, amounts to a ruling.[160]

In the case of fine default proceedings and other proceedings for the enforcement of financial orders, the court clerk may ask questions to elicit information the justice will need to make an adjudication, for example to facilitate his or her explanation for the default; however, the adviser must not act in an adversarial or partisan manner and should not seek to establish wilful refusal or neglect to pay, the duty of impartiality taking precedence over any role as collecting officer. It is for the justices' chief executive to decide whether another officer should be appointed to "prosecute".[161]

Where a justices' clerk becomes aware during the course of proceedings that a court clerk has given erroneous legal advice to the justices, he or she may be entitled to give fresh advice to the justices, although the general principle is that decisions once made should not be reversed; the matter should normally be brought to the attention of the justices' clerk by one party with notice to the other.[162]

From time to time, suggestions are made for changing the status of justices' clerks.[163] One possibility would be to appoint them to the bench, so that they, would become, in those courts where they presided, a legally qualified chairman.[164] Another possibility would be to give them the formal power to rule on points of law, while leaving the determination of the facts, as at present, to the lay justices.[165] This is virtually the present position. There is a persistent minority of cases in which lay justices exert their power to determine a point of law contrary to the clerk's advice. Lord Widgery C.J., however, warned that if justices fly in

---

[159] *R v Richmond & Gilling West Magistrates, Ex p. Steel* [1993] Crim. L.R. 711.

[160] See P. Darbyshire, (1980) 144 J.P.N. 201.

[161] *Practice Direction*, para.11, reflecting the decision of the Divisional Court in *R v Corby JJ., Ex p. Mort* (1998) 38 R.V.R. 383 that such arrangements did not give rise to a real danger of bias (the test for bias then applicable).

[162] *R v Sittingbourne JJ., Ex p. Stickings, The Times*, May 9, 1996 (justices' decision to reverse ruling that prosecution evidence was inadmissible following fresh advice from justices' clerk held to be unfair as it followed a telephone call by branch Crown Prosecutor direct to the justices' clerk).

[163] Here the suggestions are usually confined to the justices' clerk personally and do not extend to his or her assistants.

[164] Conversely, it has been proposed that District Judges (Magistrates' Courts) should normally sit without a legal adviser: Auld Report, Ch.4, para.53.

[165] See, e.g. (1992) 156 J.P.N. 433.

the face of their clerk's advice and are subsequently reversed on appeal, costs might be awarded against them.[166]

10. MAGISTRATES IN THE CROWN COURT

The Beeching Committee[167] recommended that magistrates should sit as asses-**4–012** sors with Circuit judges in the Crown Court. Before reorganisation, justices had participated in quarter sessions in the counties, but not in the assizes or borough quarter sessions. The Courts Act 1971[168] provided that justices may sit with a Circuit judge or recorder when conducting a trial on indictment and must do so when the Crown Court is hearing an appeal or dealing with a person committed there for sentence. Moreover, it provided that the justices would act as judges of the Crown Court and not merely as assessors. However, this did not prove satisfactory particular because of the pressures of time for lay justices caused by long trials.[169] Eventually, the Lord Chancellor directed that justices no longer sit in contested Crown Court trials.[170] More recently, the requirement that justices sit on committals for sentence has also been removed.[171]

The Lord Chancellor has directed that no justice should sit in the Crown Court unless he or she has demonstrated the range of competencies required by the Magistrates' New Training Initiative and has the support of the Bench chairman and justices' clerk that they have the relevant experience and competencies.[172] The justices may outvote the judge, although in the case of a tie the latter has a second and casting vote.[173] This is most likely to happen on a question of sentence, but may occur on other matters, such as the discretion to exclude evidence.[174]

11. DISTRICT JUDGES (MAGISTRATES' COURTS)

Prior to the Access to Justice Act 1999, the Queen had power to appoint up to 60 **4–013** "metropolitan stipendiary magistrates" for the inner London area,[175] and up to 56

[166] *Jones v Nicks* [1977] R.T.R. 72, 76. The advice concerned what might constitute a "special reason" for not imposing an endorsement following a speeding conviction. This step could now only be taken if the justices had acted in bad faith. See para.4–010.
[167] *Royal Commission on Assizes and Quarter Sessions* (Cmnd. 4153, 1969).
[168] ss.4, 5. See now the Supreme Court Act 1981, ss.8, 74, 75, as amended; the Criminal Procedure Rules, rr.63.7–63.9; the Crown Court Rules 1982, rr.3–5, as amended.
[169] Skyrme (1983), pp.125–130. See also G. Hawker, *Magistrates in the Crown Court* (1974): Survey by the Institute of Judicial Administration, University of Birmingham.
[170] *Practice Direction (Crime: Crown Court Business) (No.2)* [1986] 1 W.L.R. 1041 (see now above para.2–055). The change was made with the agreement of the Magistrates' Association, (1987) 43 *The Magistrate* 81, 119 (the suggestion had previously been resisted: see Skyrme (1983), pp.129–130).
[171] Access to Justice Act 1999, s.79, amending the Supreme Court Act 1981, s.74(1). For the background, see *Magistrates Sitting as Judges in the Crown Court: A Consultation Paper* (LCD, August 1998).
[172] Deputy Secretary of Commissions Circular, July 28, 2000 (Magistrates' Association website), removing a requirement for three years' experience in view of the difficulty in securing sufficient magistrates to undertake this work.
[173] Supreme Court Act 1981, s.73.
[174] *R v Smith (Benjamin Walker)* [1978] Crim. L.R. 296.
[175] Justices of the Peace Act 1997, s.16.

"stipendiary magistrates" elsewhere.[176] The former could trace their existence back to 1792, when they took over criminal jurisdiction from the largely corrupt lay justices.[177] The Metropolitan Police Courts Act 1839 provided that only barristers were to be eligible for appointment. From 1964, they shared their duties with lay justices, who, with the passage of time, have been restored to respectability.

In the provinces, stipendiaries were appointed in places where there were not enough justices to cope with the work, and where, at the same time, there was a resistance to the appointment of men who had acquired wealth through industry or trade. Boroughs might petition the Home Secretary to appoint a stipendiary; alternatively, a local Act of Parliament might provide for an appointment. The role of provincial stipendiaries was to supplement rather than to replace the lay justices. The 1948 Royal Commission noted that the determining factor behind whether a particular area had a stipendiary was "not a rational assessment of the present need but the course of past history".[178] The rationalisation of commission areas, which was a by-product of local government reorganisation, provided the opportunity for the right to take the initiative in the making of new appointments to be transferred from local authorities to the Lord Chancellor.[179] The requirements of each area were assessed by the Lord Chancellor's office.[180] Further appointments were made from time to time.[181] Where a bench was temporarily over-burdened, an acting stipendiary magistrate could be assigned to assist.[182]

The Access to Justice Act 1999[183] provided for the unification and renaming of the stipendiary bench. Accordingly, the Queen may, on the recommendation of the Lord Chancellor, appoint a person with a seven-year general qualification[184] to be a District Judge (Magistrates' Courts).[185] The Queen may designate one to be the Senior District Judge (Chief Magistrate) and may designate another as his or her deputy. A District Judge (Magistrates' Courts) may not be removed from office except by the Lord Chancellor, with the concurrence of the Lord Chief Justice, on the ground of incapacity or misbehaviour.[186] A Deputy District Judge (Magistrates' Courts) may be appointed by the Lord Chancellor for such a period

---

[176] 1997 Act, s.11, as amended by the Maximum Number of Stipendiary Magistrates Order 1999 (SI 1999/3319).

[177] See generally F. Milton, *The English Magistracy* (1967), Ch.2. Some of the existing justices managed to secure stipendiary appointments, but ministers in the early nineteenth century took greater care over appointments. See also R. Bartle, (1986) 54 Medico-Legal J. 236.

[178] Cmd. 7463, p.57.

[179] Administration of Justice Act 1973, s.2.

[180] Skyrme (1983), Ch.13.

[181] See *The Size of Benches* (HO, LCD); (1986) 42 *The Magistrate* 118; (1988) 44 *The Magistrate* 219.

[182] Popularly (or unpopularly) known as "flying stipes": they were, for example, employed in some areas during the miners' strike ((1984) 148 J.P.N. 578).

[183] s.78, inserting ss.10A–10E in the Justices of the Peace Act 1997, in turn replaced by the Courts Act 2003, ss.22–26, as amended by the Constitutional Reform Act 2005, Sch.4, paras 323–325.

[184] The appointment of solicitors had become possible under the Justices of the Peace Act 1949. The first was appointed in 1957. By 1983, 20 solicitors had been appointed, 15 in London and five elsewhere; Skyrme (1983), p.187.

[185] Candidates should normally have sat as a deputy for at least two years or have completed 30 sittings in that capacity. See further para.4–024 on changes to eligibility rules.

[186] Courts Act 2003, ss.22, 23, and see para.4–031. As at March 1, 2007, there were 139 District Judges (Magistrates' Courts) (including 33 women) (*www.judiciary.gov.uk/keyfacts*).

as he considers appropriate, subject to his power to remove him or her from office on the ground of incapacity or misbehaviour.[187] Significantly, there is now no limit on numbers and, while based at a particular court, such a judge is by virtue of his or her office a justice of the peace for England and Wales,[188] facilitating flexibility in appointment and deployment. He or she may sit alone to deal with business that would otherwise require the sitting of two or more lay justices.[189] Existing stipendiaries became District Judges (Magistrates' Courts) or Deputies.[190] The Senior District Judge (Chief Magistrate), in part the successor to the Chief Metropolitan Magistrate, is responsible for the deployment of District Judges (Magistrates' Courts) to the courts in England and Wales where they are needed.[191]

The retiring age is 70, although the Lord Chancellor may authorise a District Judge (Magistrates' Courts) to continue in office up to the age of 75.[192] The current salary is £98,900,[193] being grouped with, *inter alia*, masters and registrars of the Supreme Court and chairmen of Employment Tribunals.

Traditionally, appointment to judicial office has been on the understanding that the appointee will remain in that office. Today there is a growing trend for judicial officers to be "promoted". District Judges (Magistrates' Courts) may be invited to sit as recorders, and may now sit in the Crown Court in their own right.[194] Some have been appointed to the Circuit Bench.

The English system is unique in providing for the co-existence of both professional judges and lay justices with the same jurisdiction. Proposals have from time to time been made for a magistrates' court normally to comprise a professional judge sitting with lay justices; for lay justices to be replaced by stipendiary magistrates; and for additional stipendiaries to be appointed.[195] The whole question of the role of professional judges at this level was revisited by the government, leading to the 1999 Act reform, and by the Auld Report, following major studies[196] and a working party report.[197] The growth of the professional magistracy has generated some concerns that this may constitute a threat to the

---

[187] *ibid.* s.24. As at March 1, 2007, there were 172 Deputies (42 women) (*ibid.*).

[188] *ibid.*, s.25.

[189] *ibid.*, s.26 This does not, however, apply to proceedings: *ibid.*

[190] 1999 Act. Sch.14, paras 22, 23.

[191] *Judicial Appointments Annual Report, 2000–2001*, para.3.88.

[192] Judicial Pensions and Retirement Act 1993, s.26 and Sch.5, as amended by the Access to Justice Act 1999, Sch.II, para.41.

[193] As from November 1, 2007. In London, these is an additional salary lead of £2,000 and a London allowance of £2,000.

[194] See para.2–053.

[195] The number of provincial and acting stipendiary magistrates increased significantly through the 1990s: see P. Seago, C. Walker, D. Wall, [2000] Crim. L.R. 631, 636 (18 to 47 and 66 to 148 respectively between 1991 and 2000).

[196] P. Seago, C. Walker, D. Wall, *The Role and Appointment of Stipendiary Magistrates* (Centre for Criminal Justice Studies, University of Leeds, 1995) and "The Development of the Professional Magistracy in England and Wales" [2000] Crim. L.R. 631; R. Morgan and N. Russell, *The judiciary in the Magistrates' Courts* (HO, LCD, 2000). The evidence of the latter study was that District Judges were significantly faster and otherwise more efficient than magistrates, more interventionist and likely to sentence more heavily; most court users had confidence in both, but more in District Judges; the public generally regarded magistrates as more representative of the community.

[197] *The Role of the Stipendiary Magistracy* (the Venne Report) (LCD, February 1996); *Creation of a Unified Stipendiary Bench* (LCD Consultation Paper, 1998).

lay magistracy, with fears that the professionals may be seen as "government placemen", might act in the best interests of legal professionals rather than the public interest and might inspire less confidence as power is centralised and local autonomy lost. There seems neither any real justification for such concerns nor any political wish to disband the lay magistracy.[198] The Auld Report recommended that District judges and magistrates continue to exercise summary jurisdiction, rejecting a proposed model[199] that would have seen all minor contested cases dealt with by a mixed panel of two lay magistrates and one professional judge. Such an arrangement was, however, endorsed for the trial of less serious either-way cases.[200]

B. TRIBUNAL CHAIRMEN AND MEMBERS

4–014 There are several patterns on which the composition of a tribunal may be organised.[201] The variations reflect partly the differences in the kind of work undertaken by different tribunals and partly their diverse historical origins. Full-time appointments are commonly of similar status to one or other of the ranks of the judiciary. The Presidents of the Lands Tribunal, of SSCSATs and of Employment Tribunals and the Chief Social Security Commissioner receive a higher salary than a Circuit judge; regional chairmen of employment tribunals, senior immigration judges and Social Security Commissioners receive the same as a Circuit judge; chairmen of employment tribunals and SSCSATs and immigration judges receive the same as District judges.[202] Most appointments are part-time.[203]

It is not possible to consider here the details of appointment and tenure for all tribunals.[204] Some general observations can, however, be made.

1. WHO APPOINTS?

4–015 The Franks Committee on Administrative Tribunals and Enquiries[205] reported that appointments to tribunals were usually made by the minister responsible for

---

[198] See generally Seago *et al.*, [2000] Crim L.R. 631.
[199] A. Sanders, *Community Justice* (IPPR, 2001).
[200] Auld Report, Ch.4; see above, para.2–058.This has not been implemented.
[201] See above Ch.2.
[202] Judicial Salaries 2007–08 (DCA website).
[203] Full statistics, including breakdowns by gender and ethnic origin are given in the *Judicial Appointments Annual Reports*.
[204] R. E. Wraith and P. G. Hutchesson, *Administrative Tribunals* (1973), Ch.4; L.C.D. Memorandum on Judicial Appointments Procedures (1995), pp.42–50; *Judicial Appointments Annual Reports* (DCA website).
[205] Cmnd. 218, 1957.

the legislation under which they operated. They had received no significant evidence that any influence was in fact exerted on tribunal members by government departments, but recommended, nevertheless, that chairmen, whether legally qualified or not, should be appointed by the Lord Chancellor and members by the Council on Tribunals.[206] The position today is that the Lord Chancellor is involved in the appointment of a majority of chairmen. He either appoints the chairman directly[207] or appoints a panel from which a selection is made (normally) by the relevant President of tribunals.[208] The appointment of members has, however, not been transferred to the Council on Tribunals, and it is not argued that it should be. Most tribunal members are appointed by the relevant government department: some are appointed by the Crown or the Lord Chancellor, and some by the relevant President of tribunals. The Leggatt Review of Tribunals recommended that in view of the requirement of independence and impartiality under the ECHR, the same system should be responsible for making both judicial and tribunal appointments; the Lord Chancellor should assume responsibility for all appointments to tribunals which would otherwise be made by Westminster ministers.[209]

This is to be implemented by the Tribunals, Courts and Enforcement Act 2007.[210] The Lord Chancellor is to appoint judges and members of the Lower and members of the Upper Tribunal; and the Queen, on the recommendation of the Lord Chancellor, is to appoint judges of the Upper Tribunal. Selection is to be conducted by the Judicial Appointments Commission. A judge or member may only be removed with the concurrence of the Lord Chief Justice; salaried judges and members may only be removed by the Lord Chancellor, and on the ground of inability or misbehaviour; fees-paid judges and members hold office in accordance with their terms of appointment. The Lord Chancellor is also to have power to appoint Deputy judges of the Upper Tribunal.

2. QUALIFICATIONS FOR APPOINTMENT

The Franks Committee recommended that *chairmen* of tribunals: **4–016**

"should ordinarily have legal qualifications but that the appointment of persons without legal qualifications should not be ruled out when they are particularly suitable."[211]

---

[206] Cmnd. 218 pp.11–12.

[207] e.g. the President (and members) of the Lands Tribunal: Lands Tribunal Act 1949, s.2; chairman (and members) of Mental Health Review Tribunals: Mental Health Act 1983, s.65(2), Sch.2. Some are Crown appointments: for example, the provisions governing the appointment and tenure of Social Security Commissioners (Social Security Administration Act 1992, s.52 and Sch.2) are very similar to those governing Circuit judges (see below, para.4–020.).

[208] See the Tribunals and Inquiries Act 1992, s.6; other examples include the chairmen of Employment Tribunals and of SSCSATs (see above, paras 2–031, 2–036).

[209] Report (see para.2–010), paras 2.32, 7.7, 7.12.

[210] Schs 2, 3; Constitutional Reform Act 2005, Sch.14, to be amended by Sch.8 to the Act 2007.

[211] Cmnd. 218, p.12.

There should be no such requirement for members. The possession of a legal qualification is thought to be desirable not so much for the expertise in handling legal rules as for the qualities necessary for good chairmanship. "Objectivity in the treatment of cases and the proper sifting of facts are most often best secured by having a legally qualified chairman . . . ".[212] In the 1970s, many criticisms of Supplementary Benefit Appeal Tribunals were related to the general lack of legally qualified chairmen. They were regularly contrasted unfavourably with National Insurance Local Tribunals where a legal qualification was in practice required.[213]

In many cases, a legal qualification or legal experience is required by statute[214]: in others it is normally required as a matter of practice.[215] Even here, however, there may be criticism that appointees may not have sufficient (or any) experience in the relevant area.[216] It has also been noted that it has become more common for people to hold part-time appointments to more than one tribunal,[217] or for a full-time chairman to sit in addition as a recorder in the Crown Court.[218] A period in office as a part-time chairman is expected before appointment to a full-time position. The tenure of part-time chairmen and members has been strengthened to ensure compliance with Art.6(1), ECHR.[219]

The process of appointment has been transformed in line with changes to judicial appointments generally.[220] Each appointment exercise involves the detailed specification of both the process for appointment and selection criteria/competencies.[221] Selection (for appointment or recommendation by the Lord Chancellor) is now carried out by the Judicial Appointments Commission.[222]

---

[212] *ibid.*

[213] See the fourth edition of this book, para.4–016.

[214] e.g. Presidents of SSCSATs and Social Security Commissioners (lawyer of 10 years' standing), chairmen (now lawyer members) of SSCSATs (normally at least five years' standing), Lands Tribunal members (either lawyer or qualified surveyor) President and chairmen of Employment Tribunals (lawyers of seven years' standing), chairmen of Mental Health Review Tribunals (persons of suitable legal experience). References to standing here mean the possession of a general qualification (i.e. right of audience in any part of the Supreme Court or in all proceedings in county courts or magistrates' courts) for the appropriate number of years: Courts and Legal Services Act 1990, s.71 and Sch.10, paras 7, 27, 36, 37, 46. Age limits applied in practice have now been withdrawn: LCD Press Notice 143/02. See para.4–024 on proposed changes to eligibility rules.

[215] e.g. Immigration Adjudicators.

[216] The JUSTICE Report on *Industrial Tribunals* (1987) noted (p.47) that most appointees as chairman had little or no previous knowledge and experience of employment law and almost invariably lacked industrial experience: it recommended that preference be given to candidates with previous experience in employment law, industrial relations and tribunal work; and that there should be closer links with the Circuit bench.

[217] Wraith and Hutchesson (1973), pp.114–115; Fulbrook (1978), p.212.

[218] JUSTICE, *Industrial Tribunals* (1987), p.45.

[219] See below, para.4–021 and LCD Press Notice 284/00 announcing new arrangements for further part-time tribunal appointments, including those made by the Secretary of State for Trade and Industry to Employment Tribunals.

[220] See para.4–023.

[221] See the archived competitions on the DCA website: *www.dca.gov.uk/judicial/appointments/archapp.htm* and on the JCA website: *www.judicialappointments.gov.uk*. For some there had to be in-depth knowledge of the field on the potential (sometimes "rapidly") to acquire it (e.g. fee paid MHRT legal members 2006; fee paid immigration judge 2005; fee paid chairman of the Competition Appeal Tribunal 2005). For some there had already to be relevant experience and comprehensive knowledge (e.g. fee paid and salaried chairmen of Employment Tribunals 2005).

[222] See para.4–023.

The background of *members* will obviously be related to the nature of the tribunal's work. An obvious example is that doctors sit on SSCSATs concerning medical questions.[223] A pattern that has been commonly adopted is that of the "representative panel". For example, in Employment Tribunals, one "wing" member is taken from a panel representing employers and the other from a panel representing employed persons.[224] Similar arrangements were made for National Insurance Local Tribunals and Supplementary Benefit Appeal Tribunals.[225] However, the use of lay members in appeals service tribunals has, amid some controversy, been reduced.[226] The Leggatt Review noted widespread support for the use of lay members, but recommended that all tribunal members should be appointed "on the basis of the particular contribution which they have to make to its work". In some cases this would involve possession of a professional qualification, for example as a medical practitioner or valuer; in others, the possession of specific knowledge or experience. The criteria should be expressed in statute. It would be for Presidents and regional or district chairmen to decide whether non-lawyer members should sit on particular classes of case (or individual cases) and what is the function they are to fulfil.[227]

Comparatively little has been written about the social and political background of tribunal chairmen and members,[228] although, as with the judiciary, women and members of ethnic minorities are seriously under-represented.[229]

3. DISMISSAL

No power of a minister to terminate a person's membership of a tribunal is exercisable except with the consent of the Lord Chancellor (unless he is the minister terminating membership) and the Lord Chief Justice.[230] **4–017**

---

[223] See above.

[224] Employment Tribunals (Constitution and Rules of Procedure) Regulations 2004 (SI 2004/1861), regs 8, 9. One panel is appointed by the Secretary of State after consultation with e.g. the TUC, the other after consultation with e.g. the CBI: see JUSTICE, *Industrial Tribunals*, p.49.

[225] See the first edition of this book, pp.151–152.

[226] See above, para.2–037.

[227] Report (see para.2–010), paras 7.19—7.26.

[228] See W. E. Cavanagh and G. N. Hawker, "Laymen on Administrative Tribunals" (1974) 52 *Public Administration* 215 (Rent Assessment Panels and SBATs) and the study of NILTs by Kathleen Bell and others: (1974) 3 Journal of Social Policy 289 at pp.310–315; L. Dickens *et al.*, *Dismissed* (1985), pp.52–59 (Industrial Tribunals) and JUSTICE, *Industrial Tribunals* (1987), pp.45–50; J. Baldwin and S. Hill, (1987) 6 C.J.Q. 130 (Local Valuation Panels); J. Baldwin, *et al.*, *Judging Social Security* (1992), pp.132–140 (SSATs).

[229] See JUSTICE, *Industrial Tribunals* (1987), pp.46, 47–48, 49–50. JUSTICE proposed positive action to promote their recruitment, involving a more open, accessible and democractic appointments process for members. The processes for the appointment of General Commissioners of Income Tax have attracted strong criticism: *Report of the Equality Working Group: The Lay Magistrates and the General Commissioners of Income Tax* (June 2000, LCD).

[230] Tribunals and Inquiries Act 1992, s.7, as amended by the Constitutional Reform Act 2005, s.15(1), Sch.4, Pt I, para.225. Where the tribunal sits in all parts of the UK, the consent of the Lord President of the Court of Session and the Lord Chief Justice of Northern Ireland; where it sits in all parts of Great Britain, the LCJ and LP; where it sits in England and Wales and Northern Ireland, the two LCJs. The tribunals to which this applies are specified in Sch.1. The changes can be seen as strengthening the position of a tribunal member. As to complaints, see the Judicial Complaints (Tribunals) Rules 2006 (Judicial Complaints Office Website) and para.4–032.

4. TRAINING

4–018   The Council on Tribunals has for many years stressed the importance of training
for both chairmen and members.[231] In various contexts, shortcomings in the
quality of decision-making have been related to the absence of adequate training.[232] There were developments in the training of tribunal chairmen, although
these lagged behind developments for magistrates.[233] There was, however, little
provision of training for tribunal members. The President of the SSCSATs is
under an express duty, after consulting the Secretary of State, to arrange for such
training for chairmen and members of tribunals as he thinks appropriate.[234]

A Tribunals Committee was established as part of the enlarged JSB.[235] Its role
was seen as complementary to the Council on Tribunals, and to be that of
promoting, encouraging and advising.[236] It ran induction courses for newly
qualified chairmen, developing into a series of broader training development
seminars,[237] appointed a Tribunals' Training Co-ordinator and commenced publication of a journal, *Tribunals*.[238] A Tribunals training needs analysis was
completed in 2000, and this led to the development of a *Competence Framework
for Chairman and Members in Tribunals* (2002) and related documents.[239]

The Leggatt Review of Tribunals found that there was a particular need for
improved training in the interpersonal skills peculiar to tribunals and that national
co-ordination of training was essential. The JSB should be given responsibility
for the organisation and delivery of training for tribunal chairmen and members,
for establishing national standards and monitoring the structure and content of
training across all tribunals.[240] The White Paper, *Transforming Public Services*[241]
noted developments to date and stated that the new Tribunals Service would be
expected to work in partnership with the JSB and the Council on Tribunals. The
Senior President and other Presidents would be responsible for ensuring that all
tribunal members were properly trained. Further work would be undertaken with

---

[231] e.g. Annual Report for 1984–85 (1985–86 H.C. 54), p.11; for 1988–89 (1989–90 H.C. 114),
pp.26–27; for 1996–97 (1997–98 H.C. 376), pp.8–11 (survey of current arrangements found a
marked scarcity of tribunal training in around a quarter of the systems surveyed). In 1987, the
Council organised the first conference of Presidents and Chairmen of major tribunals falling under
its jurisdiction: Annual Report for 1986–87 (1987–88 H.C. 234), pp.6–7.

[232] e.g. in respect of General Commissioners of Income Tax (Annual Report for 1987–88, p.6);
education appeal committees (*ibid.*, p.13); industrial tribunals, especially in sex discrimination
and equal pay cases (A. Leonard, *Judging Inequality* (1987), pp.71–72; JUSTICE, *Industrial
Tribunals* (1987), pp.35–38, 48, 50).

[233] For example, there was a system for training S.B.A.T. chairmen (see Annual Report of the
Council on Tribunals for 1977–78 (1978–79 H.C. 74), pp.16–17), and some training courses were
held for chairmen of Local Valuation Courts (Report for 1978–79 (1979–80 H.C. 359), p.18).

[234] Social Security Act 1998, Sch.1, para.8. The Regional chairmen assist in this task.

[235] See below.

[236] *Judicial Studies Board Report for 1987–1991* (HMSO, 1992), p.57; *Report for 1991–1995*
(1995), Ch.6; *Annual Reports.*

[237] In 2000–01, the Committee ran courses on the effective use of small groups in training, training
the trainers, and (for new chairs in tribunals that do not as yet have their own training
programmes) tribunal skills development: *Judicial Studies Board Annual Report 2000–2001*,
paras 7.14–7.23.

[238] *ibid.*

[239] The *Framework of Standards for Training and Development in Tribunals* (2003); the *Fundamental Principles and Guidance for Appraisal in Tribunals and Model Scheme* (2003) and
Guidance on Mentoring in Tribunals (2004).

[240] Report (see para.2–010), paras 7.29–7.35.

[241] Cm. 6243, 2004, paras 6.71–6.81.

the JSB on developing the detail. All chairmen and members should be subject to an appraisal system. This has been taken forward. The JSB has developed a scheme for evaluating training and an induction framework for new chairmen and members, and has broadened its range of training programmes.[242]

5. Clerks to Tribunals[243]

The Franks Committee noted that the practice **4–019**

> "whereby the majority of clerks of tribunals are provided by the Government Departments concerned from their local and regional staffs seems partly to be responsible for the feeling in the minds of some people that tribunals are dependent upon and influenced by those Departments."[244]

They considered but rejected the possibility of establishing under the Lord Chancellor's Department a central corps of clerks for all tribunals.[245] To ensure that clerks did not exert a departmental influence, the Committee stated that their duties and conduct should be regulated on the advice of the Council on Tribunals. The duties of a clerk should generally be confined to secretarial work, taking notes of evidence and tendering advice, when requested, on points connected with the tribunal's functions. He or she should not retire with the tribunal unless sent for to advise on a specific point.

Clerks to what are now SSCSATs were from April 1984 appointed by the President, and worked from the regional offices of his organisation,[246] thus marking their independence from the Department of Social Security. The current position is that officers and staff for the President and for appeal tribunals are appointed by the Secretary of State and clerks are also assigned to tribunals by the Secretary of State,[247] being a function exercised by the Appeals Service. The role of the clerk does not appear to be problematic. A particularly important task is that of explaining the nature of proceedings to appellants; a recent study found that "tribunal clerks on the whole did a good job in difficult circumstances".[248] The Leggatt Review of Tribunals confirmed that clerks made a vital contribution to tribunal work and was critical of tribunals, particularly MHRTs, which had sought to save money by reducing the availability of clerks.[249]

---

[242] See *Annual Reports of the JSB* for 2004/05, pp.32–36 and 2005/06, pp.32–36 (*www.jsboard. co.uk*). Programmes include Tribunal skills development and advanced skills courses, a training the trainers course, appraisal skills seminars and equal treatment seminars. A *Tribunal Training Handbook* was published in 2004.

[243] See Wraith and Hutchesson (1973), Ch.5, and pp.300–306.

[244] Cmnd. 218, p.13.

[245] *ibid.* pp.13–14.

[246] Social Security Administration Act 1992, Sch.2, paras 3, 4.

[247] Social Security Act 1998, Sch.1, paras 6 and 11. See the Social Security and Child Support (Decisions and Appeals) Regulations 1999 (SI 1999/991), reg.37.

[248] J. Baldwin, *et al., Judging Social Security* (1992), pp.168–169.

[249] Report (see para.2–010), paras 4.45, 4.46; cf; similar criticisms of MHRTs in the Annual Report of the Council on Tribunals 2000–01, Ch.5, paras 13–16.

C. THE CIRCUIT BENCH

(a) Circuit judges

4–020   The Circuit Bench was created by the Courts Act 1971 as part of the reorganisation of the criminal courts following the Beeching Commission.[250] The Queen
may appoint Circuit judges and recorders on the recommendation of the Lord
Chancellor.[251] Circuit judges are appointed to serve full time in the Crown Court
and county courts, and recorders to serve as part-time judges in the Crown
Court.[252] Under the 1971 Act, only a barrister or solicitor of 10 years' standing
could be appointed as a recorder. A barrister of 10 years' standing or a recorder
who had held office for at least three years could be appointed as a Circuit judge.
A solicitor might accordingly reach the position of Circuit judge after time as a
recorder. Following changes made by the Courts and Legal Services Act 1990,[253]
the qualification for the appointment of a practitioner as a Circuit judge or
recorder became the enjoyment of general rights of audience in the Crown Court
or the county courts for 10 years. Any person who has been a District judge, or
equivalent judicial officer,[254] for at least three years, or who is a recorder, is
eligible for appointment as a Circuit judge. The requirement that a solicitor serve
three years as a recorder before becoming eligible for a Circuit judgeship was
removed. In 2000, it was decided that the post of assistant recorder should no
longer be used and appointments are now made direct to recorderships, with a
separate category of recorder in training.

On reorganisation under the 1971 Act, a number of middle-rank judges
automatically became Circuit judges, including the Vice-Chancellor of the
County Palatine of Lancaster, the Recorder of London, the Common Serjeant, the
Recorders of Liverpool and Manchester, Official Referees, the Additional Judges
of the Central Criminal Court, county court judges and the whole-time chairmen
or deputy chairmen of quarter sessions.[255] Most of these offices were abolished,
but some were retained. The Vice-Chancellor of the County Palatine of Lancaster
conducts High Court Chancery business in the North.[256] The Recorder of London

---

[250] Royal Commission on Assizes and Quarter Sessions (Cmnd. 4153, 1969).

[251] Courts Act 1971, ss.16, 21. On March 1, 2007 there were 639 Circuit judges (including 73
women) and 1365 recorders (including 201 women); of the recorders 117 were solicitors:
www.judiciary.gov.uk. The Lord Chief Justice, with the concurrence of the Lord Chancellor, may
appoint a former judge of the Court of Appeal or the High Court or a former Circuit judge as a
deputy Circuit judge: Courts Act 1971, s.24, substituted by the Supreme Court Act 1981, s.146,
as amended; to be changed again by the Tribunals, Courts and Enforcement Act 2007, s.55.

[252] 37 And to carry out such other judicial functions as may be conferred on them by statute. A
Circuit judge or recorder may be requested by the Lord Chief Justice, after consulting the Lord
Chancellor (and in the case of the High Court, only with the concurrence of the Judicial
Appointments Commission) to act as a judge of the High Court or the Court of Appeal (Criminal
Division): Supreme Court Act 1981, s.9, as amended. They are addressed as "Your Honour",
unless sitting as a judge of the High Court or at the Central Criminal Court when they are
addressed as "My Lord" or "My Lady". Circuit judges are referred to as His (or Her) Honour
Judge X and recorders as Mr (or Mrs but not Miss) recorder B: *Practice Direction (Judges: Mode
of Address)* [1982] 1 W.L.R. 101.

[253] s.71 and Sch.10, paras 31, 32.

[254] e.g. Social Security Commissioner, President of Tribunals, High Court masters, District judges:
see Pt IA of Sch.2 to the Courts Act 1971, inserted by the 1990 Act, Sch.10, para.31(2), and
amended by the Access to Justice Act 1999, Sch.11, para.19.

[255] Courts Act 1971, Sch.2, Pt I.

[256] From 1987, the post has been held by a High Court judge, rather than a Circuit judge: see above,
para.2–060.

and the Common Serjeant[257] are senior Circuit judges and sit at the Central Criminal Court. Those appointed to these offices become Circuit judges *ex officio*. In addition, the senior Circuit judges at certain large court complexes (e.g. the Recorders of Liverpool and Manchester[258] and other Senior Circuit judges, the Circuit judges at the Old Bailey, the judges of the Technology and Construction Court (formerly known as Official Referees), and the specialist Circuit judges (Chancery, Merchantile and Patents judges) are regarded as holding appointments more burdensome than that of the ordinary Circuit judge, and are paid higher salaries.[259]

The Lord Chancellor may, if he thinks fit, and if the Lord Chief Justice agrees, remove a Circuit judge from office on the ground of incapacity or misbehaviour.[260] In 1983, Judge Bruce Campbell was removed from office following his conviction for smuggling whisky and cigarettes.[261] The retiring age is 70, although the Lord Chancellor may authorise a judge to continue in office up to the age of 75.[262]

(b) Recorders

The appointment of a recorder is made by the Queen on the recommendation of the Lord Chancellor.[263] The appointment must specify the term for which the recorder is appointed, the frequency and duration of the occasions when he or she will be required to sit, and (if the Lord Chief Justice agrees) the circumstances in which the Lord Chancellor may decline to extend or terminate the appointment. The term may not last beyond the year in which he or she attains 70 (subject to continuance in office to 75 authorised by the Lord Chancellor).[264] The

4–021

---

[257] The Recorder is elected by the City, but appointed by the Crown to exercise judicial functions and the Common Serjeant is appointed by the Crown; they are paid by the City of London authorities: City of London (Courts) Act 1964, ss.7, 12. They have a number of civic duties to perform in additional to their judicial duties. The Recorder acts as the Resident Judge and the Common Serjeant the Deputy Resident Judge for the Central Criminal Court.

[258] These are honorary recorderships under the Courts Act 1971, s.54. The holders are addressed as "My Lord".

[259] £133,100, as compared with £123,200, as from November 1, 2007. There have in a number of years been difficulties in recruiting Circuit judges, with in 1987–88 three refusals for every one acceptance: salary was said to be a very important factor, especially for Q.C.s, and other factors included a perceived relative lack of status: *Review Body on Top Salaries*, Report No.28 (Cm. 581, 1989), pp.4–5. In 2005–06 "the competition for comparatively few current vacancies was fierce": *Review Body on Senior Salaries*, Report No.63, (Cm. 7030, 2007), p.62.

[260] Courts Act 1971, s.17(4), as amended by the Constitutional Reform Act 2005, Sch.4, Pt 1, paras 67, 68.

[261] *The Times*, December 6, 1983. The fact that he was removed (as distinct from resigning) enabled him to keep his pension: Rozenberg (1994), pp.111–112. Dismissal was threatened in the case of Judge James Pickles, but not effected: *ibid.*, pp.112–114 and below, para.4–032. In 1999, the Lord Chancellor accepted the resignation of Judge Richard Gee following his prosecution for conspiracy to commit offences under the Theft Act 1968 (while in practice as a solicitor) in which the jury failed to reach a verdict; he had been suspended on full pay since 1995: LCD Press Notice 389/99. Removal from office would have involved application of the civil standard of proof: *ibid.* In Scotland, Sheriff Thomson was removed in 1977 because of his political activities, and Sheriff Stewart in 1992 because of "inability to perform his judicial function": (1994) 144 N.L.J. 1651, noting the dismissal of the latter's application for judicial review.

[262] 1971 Act, s.17(1), as amended by the Judicial Pensions and Retirement Act 1993, Sch.9, para.1.

[263] See above for the eligibility rule.

[264] In practice, an appointment is not extended beyond the end of the financial year in which the recorder reaches 55: *Recorder Terms and Conditions: Guide for Applicants*, Recorder Competition 2005/06 (Judicial Appointments Commission website).

Lord Chancellor, with the agreement of the Lord Chief Justice, may terminate the appointment on the grounds of incapacity, misbehaviour or a failure to comply with specified terms of the appointment.[265] The general terms and conditions for appointment were set out in a statement by the Lord Chancellor's office.[266] Appointments are now normally for five years at a time.[267] They are required to sit judicially for at least 15 days a year and not normally for more than 30 days.[268] A daily fee, travelling expenses and subsistence allowances are payable.

The tenure in office of a recorder was to an extent precarious. Appointments were not renewed where the Lord Chancellor was not satisfied as to their continuing fitness or suitability, but the process by which this was done was not always satisfactory.[269] However, the tenure of part-time judges came under scrutiny following the decision the High Court of Justiciary[270] that Scottish temporary sheriffs, appointed by the Lord Advocate, now a member of the Scottish Executive, were insufficiently independent of the executive for compliance with the requirements of Art.6, ECHR. The Lord Chancellor reviewed the terms of service of part-time judges in England and Wales and on April 12, 2000, he announced revised terms of service for all part-time judicial appointments.[271]

Accordingly, part-time appointments are for a period of not less than five years, subject to the relevant age limit; where appointments are renewable this will normally be done automatically, except on limited and specified grounds; removal from office will likewise only be on limited and specific grounds; whenever it is administratively possible, the offer of a minimum number of sitting days will be guaranteed. Subject to statutory provision, the specified grounds for non-renewal will generally be: (a) misbehaviour; (b) incapacity; (c) persistent failure to comply with sitting requirements (without good reason); (d) failure to comply with training requirements; (e) sustained failure to observe the standards reasonably expected from a holder of such office; (f) part of a reduction in numbers because of changes in operational requirements; and (g) part of a structural change to enable recruitment of new appointees. The grounds for

---

[265] Courts Act 1971, s.21, as amended by the Judicial Pensions and Retirement Act 1993, Sch.6, para.9(1) and the Constitutional Reform Act 2005, Sch.4, Pt 1, paras 67, 69.

[266] (1971) 68 L.S. Gaz. 303.

[267] Before 2000, appointments were normally for periods of three years at a time. The change was made as part of a package designed to demonstrate the independence from the executive of the part-time judiciary: *Judicial Appointments Annual Report 1999–2000* (Cm. 4783, 2000), pp.21–22.

[268] *Recorder Terms and Conditions*, above.

[269] "Where possible, the recorder is warned in advance of any cause for concern, so as to give him a chance to improve. However, this cannot always be done": LCD, *Judicial Appointments* (1986), p.13. It was not effectively done in the case of Manus Nunan, whose appointment was not renewed in 1985: see *The Guardian*, June 13, 14 and 16, and December 2, 1986; R Brazier, *Constitutional Practice* (2nd edn, 1994), p.291; Judge James Pickles, *Straight from the Bench* (1987), pp.29–41, including notes of the interview between Nunan and Lord Hailsham L.C. The words in question were omitted from the 2nd edn of the LCD booklet.

[270] *Starrs v Procurator Fiscal, Linlithgow* [2000] H.R.L.R. 191. *Cf. Millar v Procurator Fiscal, Elgin* [2001] UKPC D4, [2002] 1 W.L.R. 1615 (*Starrs* applied; no effective waiver); *Clancy v Caird (No.1)* 2000 S.C. 441, [2000] H.R.L.R. 557 (temporary judge sufficiently independent and impartial as security of tenure was to be implied). See A. O'Neill, (2000) 63 M.L.R. 429.

[271] i.e. deputy High Court judges, deputy Circuit judges, recorders, deputy District judges, deputy masters and registrars of the Supreme Court, deputy District Judges (Magistrates' Courts) and retired Lords of Appeal, Lords Justices of Appeal and High Court judges, and the part-time judiciary who sit on tribunals or as adjudicators.

removal will generally be as at (a) to (e) and decisions not to renew or to remove will be taken by the Lord Chancellor only with the concurrence of the Lord Chief Justice and following an investigation conducted by a judge nominated by him. Decisions under (f) and (g) will be on a "first in first out" principle and again made by the Lord Chancellor with the concurrence of the Lord Chief Justice. While part-time judges already "in real terms" enjoyed significant security of tenure, the new arrangements "put beyond reasonable doubt the safeguards guaranteeing their independence".[272] As regards recorders, s.21 of the Courts Act 1971 has been amended to reflect the key elements of these conditions. Accordingly, the Lord Chancellor must extend the term of a recorder's appointment before its expiry, unless he, with the agreement of the Lord Chief Justice, declines to do so on the grounds of incapacity or misbehaviour or non-compliance with specified conditions.[273]

(c) District judges

The Lord Chancellor may appoint any person with a seven-year general qual- **4–022** ification[274] to the position of District judge or deputy District judge. The latter is a part-time appointment.[275]

(d) The judicial appointments process

The processes by which candidates are selected for appointments at all levels of **4–023** the judiciary have been transformed beyond recognition through a series of stages over the last 10 years or so. Historically, appointments were handed by the Judicial Group within the LCD. The main stages were: the acceptance by the Lord Chancellor of the need for the procedures to be much more open and transparent than formerly[276]; the introduction of annual open competitions for vacancies at the level of Circuit or District judge, assessment against published criteria and the inclusion of a lay person on the interview panel[277]; a review by Sir Leonard Peach of the processes for judicial appointments and the appointment of Q.C.s[278]; the Report of a Joint Working Party on Judicial Appointments and Silk[279]; and the establishment on Sir Leonard's recommendation, but with

---

[272] *Judicial Appointments Annual Report 1999–2000*, paras 2.14–2.18. Age limits were subsequently removed: LCD Press Notice 143/02.

[273] s.21(3)–(4C), substituted and inserted by the Constitutional Reform Act 2005, Sch.4, Pt 1, para.69.

[274] i.e. a right of audience in relation to any class of proceedings in any part of the Supreme Court or all proceedings in county courts or magistrates' courts (Courts and Legal Services Act 1990, s.71): County Courts Act 1984, s.9, as amended by the Courts and Legal Services Act 1990, Sch.10, para.57. District judges may sit in the county court or the High Court (see above, paras 2–042, 2–066). See para.4–024 for proposed changes to eligibility rules.

[275] See further para.2–042. On March 1, 2007, there were 429 District judges (including 100 women) and 734 deputies (222 women). The Tribunals, Courts and Enforcement Act 2007, s.56, will introduce new provisions whereby the Lord Chancellor's power (after a JAC selection process: see below) will only apply where a person has not previously held office as a District judge; the Lord Chancellor with the concurrence of the Lord Chief Justice, will have power to appoint a person who has been a District judge as a deputy without JAC involvement.

[276] e.g. through the publication of *Judicial Appointments: The Lord Chancellor's Policies and Procedures* (rev. edn, 1999, LCD website).

[277] LCD *Memorandum on Judicial Appointments Procedures* (1995), pp.51–60.

[278] *An Independent Scrutiny of the Appointment Process of Judges and Queen's Counsel in England and Wales* (December 1999, LCD Website). His recommendations were largely accepted.

[279] *Judicial Appointments Annual Report 1999–2000*, Annex D (Summary of recommendations).

some modifications, of a Commission for Judicial Appointments to audit the processes and investigate complaints about the way they had been applied. Sir Colin Campbell, Vice-Chancellor of the University of Nottingham (an academic legal philosopher) was appointed as First Commissioner of Judical Appointments in March 2001, and seven further Commissioners (all non lawyers) were appointed in December 2001.[280] All served part-time.

The system that ultimately evolved for appointments below the level of the High Court involved advertisement, the receipt of applications, consultation with judges and members of the profession (although the Law Society in the latter years declined to take part), the sifting of applications, interviews and assessments, and appointment personally by the Lord Chancellor.

In the event, critical reports by the Commission for Judicial Appointments (CJA) (which was less impressed with the system than Sir Leonard Peach had been) on many aspects of the arrangements, including appointments to the High Court bench, helped bring about fundamental changes. The CJA produced five annual reports, between 2002 and 2006, conducted reviews of a number of competitions and commissioned research.[281] Early on, the Prime Minister announced the decision to abolish the office of Lord Chancellor and create an independent Judicial Appointments Commission, a decision welcomed by the CJA.[282] Much of the CJA's work was directed to auditing existing processes, considering complaints and proposing changes. It acknowledged that the senior judiciary of England and Wales had "an unrivalled reputation for integrity and intellectual ability" and noted that they had seen no evidence that those appointed were "of anything other than the highest calibre".[283] Furthermore, there had since the 1990s been an increase in the proportion of the judiciary who were either women or from an ethnic minority. However, the proportions, especially in the senior judicial offices, were still significantly short of the overall proportions of women and ethnic minorities in society.[284] Nevertheless, its criticisms of the processes based on what it observed were devastating. Problems summarised in its 2006 Report, in which it looked back on its work, included inconsistencies in the ways in which candidates were selected; a lack of clear criteria for appointment, especially for silk; a lack of clarity as the role played by automatic consultation ("secret soundings"); obscurity as to how information gathered was treated and weighted; mechanisms for assessing candidates that were unrelated to the core competencies required for a post; poor interviewing techniques; systemic bias against less visible candidates, often solicitors, women and ethnic minorities; poor record keeping; and a "culture of unquestioning deference towards established judicial attitudes".[285] The LCD had responded positively, while not always in the ways recommended. Steps taken in response

---

[280] LCD Press Notice 433/01. Appointments were made by the Queen on the recommendation of the Lord Chancellor. See the Judicial Appointments Order in Council 2001, March 14, 2001.

[281] Archived at *www.webarchive.org.uk/pan/15580/20070220/www.cja.gov.uk./reports.htm.*

[282] *CJA Annual Report 2003*, p.34. The case for this was subsequently reinforced by particular criticisms by the CJA of the role of the Lord Chancellor personally in the final decisions on appointments, including "ill-advised personal interventions altering the outcomes recommended by properly constituted selection panels" (*CJA Annual Report for 2006*, pp.11, 26, 27). The criticisms were not necessarily accepted, relations between the CJA and the Lord Chancellor were at times strained and comments on the CJA in the *Judicial Appointments Annual Reports* less than effusive. Curiously, the DCA MoJ websites provide no link to the CJA archive.

[283] *Report of the Commissioners' Review of the High Court 2003 Competition* (CJA, 2004).

[284] *CJA Annual Report 2006*, p.41 See further below, para.4–029.

[285] *ibid.* pp.4–5.

had included greater transparency, the establishment of clear criteria and objective competencies; a move to an application only process, abandoning the dual system of confidential nomination and application; the introduction of assessment centres for some appointment processes; a new system for the appointment of Q.C.s; and express recognition of the value of a more diverse judiciary.[286] Nevertheless, for the future, there was still a long way to got to convince women, ethnic minorities and others that there was a judicial culture that was not "prejudiced against those perceived as not fitting the current mould"; a need for new appointments processes which "value diversity as not simply compatible with but rather integral to merit"; a need for systemic reform within the profession to produce a more diverse group of candidates; the provision of redress where complaints are upheld; and the need for work to identify more transparent and professional means to search for candidates. Overall, the system looked very different from the one inherited five years before, but it was still work in progress.[287]

As already mentioned, the decision to establish a new independent commission was taken early on in the life of the CJA. The reasons subsequently given by the government to justify the change were that it was increasingly anomalous for a minister to run the appointments process, that it was necessary for the process to command public confidence and the need to promote diversity.[288] The Constitutional Reform Act 2005 provided for the establishment of a new Judicial Appointments Commission (JAC). The Commission comprises[289] a lay chairman and 14 other Commissioners appointed by the Queen on the recommendation of the Lord Chancellor; of these, five must be judicial members, two professional members (a barrister and a solicitor), five lay members, one a tribunal member and one a lay justice member. Of the judicial members, one must be a Lord Justice, one a puisne judge, and one either of these (these are selected by the Judges' Council); one must be a Circuit judge and one a District judge or person appointed under s.89 of the Supreme Court Act 1981. The Lord(s) Justice(s) and puisne judge(s) are selected by the Judges' Council; other members must be the person (or one of the persons) selected by a special panel. Each panel comprises a person selected by the Lord Chancellor with the agreement of the Lord Chief Justice (the panel chairman), the Lord Chief Justice or his nominee, a person nominated by the panel chairman, and the JAC chairman. The JAC thus have a bare majority of lawyers (but not judges).

Section 63 of the 2005 Act applies to any selection by the JAC or a selection panel the rules that (1) selection must be solely on merit and (2) a person must not be selected unless the selecting body is satisfied that he or she is of good character. "Merit" is not defined. The JAC in performing its functions must have

---

[286] *ibid.* p.5.
[287] *ibid.* pp.6–7.
[288] DCA Consultation Paper, *Constitutional reform: a new way of appointing judges* (DCA CP 10/03. July 2003), pp.18–20.
[289] 2005 Act, Sch.12. There was an extensive debate as to the exact structure that should be adopted, the main heads of terms of the agreed position of the Lord Chancellor and the Lord Chief Justice being included as part of the 2004 Concordat: see para.1–033. See also DCA Consultation Paper, *Constitutional reform: a new way of appointing judges* and responses (DCA website); Select Committee on Constitutional Affairs, First Report 2003–04 H.C. 48, *Judicial appointments and a Supreme Court* and Third Report 2004–05 H.C. 275, *Constitutional Reform Bill [Lords]: the Government's proposals.* The CJA argued unsuccessfully for a lay majority on the JAC, and for appointments below the level of the High Court to be made (or recommended to the Queen) by the JAC: 2004–05 H.C. 275, Written Evidence.

regard to the need to encourage diversity in the range of persons available for selection for appointment, but this is subject to s.63.[290] "The aim is widening the pool, not a diverse judiciary."[291] The Lord Chancellor may issue guidance, after consulting the Lord Chancellor.

Separate processes apply to the selection of (1) the Lord Chief Justice and Heads of Division,[292] (2) Lord and Lady Justices of Appeal,[293] and (3) puisne judges and other office holders.[294] The third of these is dealt with here. This process covers the full range of appointments of judges and judicial appointments to tribunals and as arbitrator. Some are appointments by the Queen on the recommendation of the Lord Chancellor; the others are appointments by the Lord Chancellor. Where a vacancy arises, the Lord Chancellor must make a recommendation or appointment unless the Lord Chief Justice agrees that it may remain unfilled. The Lord Chancellor may request the JAC to select a person for a recommendation or appointment. The JAC must then make a selection, which must be of one person only. It must consult the Lord Chief Justice and a person (other than the LCJ) who has held the office in question or has other relevant experience. The JAC must then report to the Lord Chancellor, whose powers to reject or require reconsideration of a selection are limited. There are three possible stages. Where a person has been selected under s.88, the Lord Chancellor must (Stage 1) either accept the selection, reject it or require it to be reconsidered by the JAC. Where a person has been selected following a reconsideration or rejection at Stage 1, the Lord Chancellor must (Stage 2) accept the selection, reject it (but only if made following a reconsideration at Stage 1) or require it to be reconsidered by the JAC (but only if made following a rejection at Stage 1). Where a person has been selected following a rejection or reconsideration at Stage 2, the Lord Chancellor must (Stage 3) accept this selection, or may accept a selection previously required by him to be reconsidered at Stage 1 or 2 and not selected again.[295]

The Lord Chancellor's power to reject a selection is exercisable only on the grounds that, in his opinion, the person selected is not suitable for the office concerned or particular functions of that office. The power to require consideration is exercisable only on the grounds that in his opinion (a) there is not enough evidence that the person is suitable for the office concerned or particular functions of that office, or (b) there is evidence that the person is not the best candidate on merit. He must give written reasons for either kind of decision.[296] If the Lord Chancellor rejects a selection, the JAC may not select the person rejected, and, where the rejection follows a requirement to reconsider, may not select the person (if different) whose selection it reconsidered. If the Lord Chancellor requires a selection to be reconsidered, the JAC may select the same or a different person, but where the requirement follows a rejection, may not select the person rejected.[297] In each situation, the JAC must select a candidate unless it decides that the selection process has not identified a candidate of

---

[290] s.64.
[291] A. Morgan, *Current Law Statutes Annotated 2005*, pp.4–70.
[292] 2005 Act, ss.67–75.
[293] *ibid.* ss.76–84.
[294] *ibid.* ss.85–93, Sch.14.
[295] s.90.
[296] s.91.
[297] s.92(1)–(3).

sufficient merit; the Lord Chancellor may, however, require such a decision to be reconsidered by the JAC, and the JAC must inform him of any person selected on reconsideration.[298] The key features are, accordingly, (1) that the Lord Chancellor may not appoint a person not selected by the JAC; (2) that he may exercise the powers to reject or require reconsideration once (each) per selection process; and (3) that a person rejected by the Lord Chancellor cannot selected by the JAC. The structure seems excessively complicated (and construction of a flow chart a task for a clever person with a very large sheet of paper). The Lord Chancellor's room for manoeuvre is very limited. It remains to be seen how extensively the powers of rejection or to require reconsideration will be used.

Other points are that where the Lord Chancellor gives the JAC notice of a request he expects to make in the future, the JAC must seek to identify persons suitable for selection and report to the Lord Chancellor.[299] The Lord Chancellor may withdraw or modify a request made under s.87.[300] Where he accepts a selection he must proceed to make the appointment or recommendation, subject to the power to require a medical examination. If the person's health is not satisfactory, or he or she declines to accept appointment, or is not available within a reasonable time, the selection is disregarded and the s.87 request remains in effect.[301] The JAC must provide any assistance requested by the Lord Chancellor in connection with recommendations to be made by him or another minister as to other judicial appointments (which would include appointments to the Court of Justice of the European Communities, the European Court of Human Rights and the International Court of Justice).[302]

The JAC[303] began its work on April 3, 2006, subject to transitional arrangements whereby some competitions and appointments were seen through by the LCD or as a shared responsibility. Its initial priorities were: "(1) defining merit: that is—what makes a good judge; (2) refining and improving effective and fair methods for assessing merit; and (3) determining how best to encourage a wide range of applicants". The main elements of their new selection process (operating from October 31, 2006) are as follows. Stage 1 involves the advertisement of positions and outreach events to encourage applications; provision of a detailed information pack, including eligibility criteria; completion of a (streamlined) application form; a check by JAC of the candidate's eligibility and a character check; a qualifying test (for most appointments); and shortlisting. At Stage 2 the JAC seek references. The candidate nominates up to three (in some cases six) referees; the JAC has its own (published) list of referees. The JAC decides which referees to approach. There is then a form of face-to-face assessment which may involve an interview, role play or structured discussions. At Stage 3, the JAC decides who to recommend and carries out final checks.

The JAC has adopted a new, simplified definition of merit, identifying core qualities required for judicial office: intellectual capacity; personal qualities; an ability to understand and deal fairly; authority and communication skills; and

---

[298] ss.92(4), 93. ss.90 to 92 apply to a person selected by the JAC on reconsideration under s.93.
[299] s.94.
[300] s.95.
[301] s.96.
[302] s.98. This may include the operation of a selection process.
[303] www.judicialappointments.gov.uk. The following account is based on information provided on this website. The first chairman is Baroness Usha Prashar CBE.

efficiency. Further detail is provided under each head, and detailed guidance also provided on the implications of such matters for eligibility as convictions, insolvency and disciplinary findings.

Complaints of maladministration by the JAC or a committee of the JAC, or by the Lord Chancellor or his department, in connection with selection under Pt 4 of the 2005 Act or recommendation for appointment to an office listed in Sch.14, may be made to the JAC or the Lord Chancellor respectively, and then to the Judicial Appointments and Conduct Ombudsman.[304]

It is of course too early to assess the impact of the new arrangements. A positive feature has been the tripartite agreement of the JAC with the Lord Chancellor and the Lord Chief Justice to promote a *Judicial Diversity Strategy*.[305] This involves steps to promote judicial service and under the range of people eligible to apply; to encourage a wider range of applicants; to promote diversity through fair and open selection processes for selection to judicial office solely on merit; and to ensure that the culture and working environment for judicial office-holders encourages and supports a diverse judiciary. The processes adopted seem a refinement of what has gone before rather than a step change. The approach (including the relevant statutory provisions) maintains the position that appointment on merit and the promotion of diversity are separate concepts, with the latter subordinate to the former. The CJA supported a more nuanced position under which "merit and diversity are complementary and should be mutually reinforcing". It was "essential to reconsider the concept of merit to ensure that it takes account of all aspects of delivering justice in a pluralist society". Selection processes should test awareness of diversity issues, it being likely, but not inevitable, that minority groups would have a better understanding of these issues; the need in particular circuits or districts to improve representation might make it reasonable to factor in demographic considerations into particular competitions. They also rejected the notion that "trickle up" of women and ethnic minority practitioners from lower ranks of the profession would redress the problem.[306] The policy that has emerged is less adventurous[307]; progress will be slower and less controversial. There seems widespread agreement that positive discrimination would not be appropriate[308]; there is always room for debate as to whether a particular step crosses that line. Accordingly, the main change may prove to lie in the reduction of the personal influence of the Lord Chancellor at

---

[304] Constitutional Reform Act 2005, ss.99–105. The Ombudsman is appointed under s.62 and Sch.13 of the 2005 Act. See *www.judicialombudsman.gov.uk*. The Ombudsman's office is an associated office of the DCA but acts autonomously under the direction of the Ombudsman: *ibid*. The first holder of the office is Sir John Brigstocke KCB, a former Second Sea Lord.

[305] May 17, 2006 (JAC website). See *www.dca.gov.uk/judges/diversity.htm*, summarising the range of measures that have been adopted to encourage a wider pool of applicants. See also Opinion Leader Research, *Judicial Diversity: Findings of a Consultation with Barristers, Solicitors and Judges Final Report* (Prepared for DCA, 2006), reporting a general lack of belief that the system would ever change in a significant way. This gave rise to steps e.g. to promote judicial service, to raise awareness earlier, and to develop judicial work shadowing.

[306] *CJA Annual Reports 2002*, Ch.5 and 2005, Ch 3. The arguments for more women judges, based on equal opportunities principles and the democratic legitimacy of the judiciary, are powerfully made by Dame Brenda Hale, [2001] P.L. 489.

[307] For example, the nearest to "awareness of diversity issues" in the JAC's definition of merit is "Ability to treat everyone with respect and sensitivity whatever their background."

[308] It is not DCA or JAC policy and was not favoured by any and actively opposed by most respondents to the survey noted in n.305 above, p.3.

the last stage of the process, although it should be noted that his role attracted the criticism of the CJA in respect of a relatively small number of appointments, and there have been views that such interventions could promote diversity.[309]

Unfortunately, there have been some teething troubles. The conduct of one of the transitional competitions for Circuit judges led to complaints from a large number of applicants who were not shortlisted; the JAC accepted that in error the shortlisting panels had not been asked to consider the references; on reconsideration, 59 additional applicants were recommended for interview.[310] The processes will no doubt settle down.

(e) Changes to eligibility criteria

The Tribunals, Courts and Enforcement Act 2007[311] introduces changes to the rules as to eligibility for judicial office, as part of the government's judicial diversity strategy.[312] The main elements are: (1) discontinuance of the use of possession of rights of audience for a specified period as the basic test, as this "helped to foster the (inaccurate) perception that advocacy experience was a requirement for judicial appointment"; (2) introduction of a test based on both possession of a relevant qualification and legal experience; (3) a reduction in the number of years for which the qualification has been held and the experience gained; and (4) extension of eligibility to other legal professional groups.[313]

4–024

There will be a "judicial-appointment qualifying condition" to be "satisfied on an N-year basis" specified for each judicial office. This will be satisfied where a person has a "relevant qualification" and the total length of the person's "qualifying periods" is at least N years. A "qualifying period" is a period during which a person has a "relevant qualification" and "gains experience in law". "Relevant qualification" means (1) qualification as a barrister or solicitor, or (2) possession of a qualification awarded by the Institute of Legal Executives (ILEX) or an authorised body designated for the purposes of s.27 or s.28 of the Courts and Legal Services Act 1990. In the case of (2) the qualification must be specified in an order made by the Lord Chancellor as a relevant qualification in relation to an office or position also specified in the order.[314] A person gains experience in law during a period if it is one during which he or she is engaged in "law-related activities". These are defined very broadly to include carrying out judicial

---

[309] See the comments of the Society of Black Lawyers, quoted by the Select Committee on Constitutional Affairs, 2003–04 H.C. 48, p.37.

[310] Letter from the JAC Chairman, February 8, 2007 (JAC website); M. Berlins, *Guardian Unlimited*, February 5, 2007. Berlin notes that this created a new controversy in that it resurrected the concern that the senior judiciary might have disproportionate influence leading to a preference for candidates who happen to be known to them. See also J. Rozenberg, *www.telegraph.co.uk*, February 23, 2007. At about the same time the DCA was responsible under the transitional arrangements for a selection process for the appointment of part-time immigration judges that led to the commencement of judicial review proceedings in the High Court, which were dropped when 21 judges were reappointed: F.Gibb, *The Times*, March 13, 2007. A lawyer acting for the judges described the process as "shambolic".

[311] ss.50–52. In force from 9 days to be appointed.

[312] See paras 4–023, 4–029; DCA Consultation Paper, *Increasing Diversity in the Judiciary* CP25/04, Responses, March 2005.

[313] See Explanatory Notes, Bill 065 EN 06–07.

[314] It is intended to apply this to Fellows of ILEX, patents agents and trade mark attorneys: *ibid.*

functions of any court or tribunal; acting as arbitrator; practice or employment as
a lawyer; advising (whether or not in the course of practice or employment as a
lawyer) on the application of the law; assisting persons involved in proceedings
for the resolution of issues arising under the law; acting as mediator in respect of
issues that are or could be the subject of proceedings; drafting documents
intended to affect persons' rights and obligations; teaching or researching law;
and any other broadly similar activity. These may be done full or part time,
whether or not for remuneration and inside or outside the UK. Existing 10-year
requirements are reduced to seven years, and seven to five (the figure for Lords
of Appeal or Justices of the Supreme Court remain at 15 years).

D. JUDGES OF THE SUPERIOR COURTS[315]

1. THE CLASSES OF JUDICIAL OFFICE

4–025   Appointments to the High Court Bench are to the office of *puisne*[316] judge or
Justice of the High Court.[317] A High Court judge is almost invariably knighted
or made a Dame Commander of the British Empire upon appointment, but is
referred to as, for example, "Mr or Mrs[318] Justice Swallow".[319] Promotion to the
Court of Appeal involves elevation to the position of *Lord Justice of Appeal* or
Lady Justice of Appeal, which is normally associated with an appointment to
membership of the Privy Council. "Swallow J." becomes "Lord or Lady Justice
Swallow".[320] The next step is membership of the House of Lords as a *Lord of
Appeal in Ordinary*,[321] one of the "Law Lords". Although he or she will have
been addressed in court as "My Lord" or "My Lady" from the time of his or her

---

[315] See generally, J. A. G. Griffith, *The Politics of the Judiciary* (5th edn, 1997) and *Judicial Politics
since 1920* (1993); Lord Mackay, *The Adminstration of Justice* (1994) Ch.1; D. Pannick, *Judges*
(1987); J. Rozenberg, *The Search for Justice* (1994), Chs 1, 2.; R.Brazier, *Constitutional Practice*
(2nd edn, 1994), Ch.12; K. Malleson, *The New Judiciary* (1999); R. Stevens, *The English Judges*
(rev. edn, 2005). On the appointment, control and extra-judicial activities of the judges between
1945 and the mid-1950s, see R. B. Stevens, "The Independence of the judicary: the view from
the Lord Chancellor's Office" (1988) 8 O.J.L.S. 222.

[316] Pronounced as if it were "puny". The two words are related, a puisne judge being a "junior"
judge in the superior courts of common law.

[317] See the Supreme Court Act 1981, s.4(2).

[318] And this whether the person is married or single: *www.judiciary.gov.uk*: Forms of address for the
Judiciary.

[319] Written as Swallow J. If there are two Swallows on the bench, first names are also used.

[320] Written as Swallow L.J. The first woman appointed to this office was Dame Elizabeth Butler-
Sloss in 1988: until 1994 she was referred to as "Lord Justice", this being the designation in the
Supreme Court Act 1981, s.2(3); the usage was then changed to "Lady Justice" in anticipation
of a change to the Act: *Practice Note: Mode of Address: Dame Elizabeth Butler-Sloss* [1994] 1
F.L.R. 866. Section 2 was eventually amended by the Courts Act 2003, s.63(1).

[321] "The word 'Ordinary' is a technical term used in law to describe a judge who has jurisdiction to
hear cases by virtue of his office. In contrast to other persons who have jurisdiction only by being
peers": Lord Denning, *The Family Story* (1981), p.184.

appointment as a High Court judge, it is only at this stage (in the normal course of events) that he or she actually acquires a life peerage, as, say, "Lord Swallow of Somerset".[322]

In addition, there are several specific judicial offices. The *Lord Chancellor*[323] was for centuries regarded as the head of the judiciary in England and Wales (although not Scotland and Northern Ireland), and received formal recognition as "president of the Supreme Court".[324] He was an *ex officio* member of the Court of Appeal,[325] and was the President of the Chancery Division[326] although the effective head of that Division was the Vice-Chancellor. If he sat as a judge at all it was in the House of Lords or the Privy Council, and only Lord Hailsham of St Marylebone and Lord Mackay of Clashfern (previously a Lord of Appeal) of the recent Lord Chancellors sat at all regularly.[327] As explained elsewhere,[328] the Lord Chancellor and Secretary of State for Justice (as he now is) is no longer a judge. As was always technically the case, he or she need not even be a lawyer.[329]

The *Lord Chief Justice of England and Wales*[330] is now head of the judiciary, and President of the Courts of England and Wales.[331] The former office was created as part of the reorganisation of the superior courts under the Supreme Court of Judicature Acts 1873–75. Before then each of the superior common law courts had its own chief: the Chief Justices of the Queen's Bench and the Common Pleas, and the Chief Baron of the Exchequer. The first Lord Chief

---

[322] Lord Jenkins of Ashley Gardens apparently had wished to be styled Lord Jenkins of 24 Ashley Gardens, but was thwarted by the College of Arms. The first woman appointed as a Law Lord became Baroness Hale of Richmond. As to whether her own appointment under the Appellate Jurisdiction Act 1876 might be open to legal challenge, see Baroness Hale of Richmond, (2005) 25 L.S. 72.

[323] i.e. the Lord High Chancellor of Great Britain. When a judge written as Lord Falconer of Thoroton L.C. Incumbents since 1945 have been Lord Jowitt (1945–1951); Lord Simonds (1951–1954); Lord Kilmuir (1954–1962); Lord Dilhorne (1962–1964); Lord Gardiner (1964–1970); Lord Hailsham (1970–1974, 1979–1987); Lord Elwyn-Jones (1974–1979); Lord Havers (1987); Lord Mackay (1987–1997); Lord Irvine (1997–2003); Lord Falconer (2003–2007); and Jack Straw MP (2007–). See generally R. F. V. Heuston, *Lives of the Lord Chancellors, 1885–1940* (1964) and *1940–1970* (1987); I. S. Dickinson, "Aspects of appointments to the office of Lord Chancellor" 1988 S.L.T. 41 (which lists those appointed between 1830 and 1987); D. Woodhouse, *The Office of Lord Chancellor* (2001).

[324] Supreme Court Act 1981, s.1. He is paid £2,500 more than the Lord Chief Justice: Ministerial and other Salaries Act 1975, s.1(2), as amended.

[325] *ibid.* s.2.

[326] *ibid.* s.5(a).

[327] See G. Drewry, "Lord Chancellor as Judge" (1972) 122 N.L.J. 855; A. Bradney, (1989) 16 J.L.S. 360.

[328] See para.1–018.

[329] s.2 of the Constitutional Reform Act 2005 provides that a person may not be recommended for appointment unless he or she appears to the Prime Minister to be "qualified by experience" as to which the PM may take into account experience as a minister, member of either House, a qualifying legal practitioner, a teacher of law at a University, or other experience the PM considers relevant. Previously, there were no qualifications for appointment, but all were barristers and members of the House of Lords. Lord Mackay was the first who was not a member of the English Bar, having been Lord Advocate, a judge of the Court of Session and a Lord of Appeal. Jack Straw MP is a barrister, and the first MP to hold the office.

[330] See F. Bresler, *Lord Goddard* (1977), Ch.9. The reference to Wales was added by Lord Bingham.

[331] Constitutional Reform Act 2005, s.7. See para.1–033. A large number of powers have been conferred on him by the 2005 Act. Most include a further power to delegate their exercise to a judicial office holder nominated by him.

Justice of England appointed as such was, accordingly, Lord Coleridge,[332] Chief Justice of the Common Pleas from 1873, who took the office in 1880 following the deaths of Sir Alexander Cockburn C.J. of the Queen's Bench Division and Chief Baron Kelly.[333] From that date new incumbents have been ennobled if not already peers. The holder is referred to as Lord Phillips, Chief Justice or Lord Phillips Lord Chief Justice.[334]

The office of *Master of the Rolls*[335] dates from at least the thirteenth century. He was originally the keeper of the rolls or records of the Chancery, but with the passage of time he became recognised as a judge in the Court of Chancery: until 1813 he was the only judge in that court other than the Chancellor. After the reorganisation of the courts under the Judicature Acts 1873–75 he continued as a judge of first instance, but the man appointed in 1873, Sir George Jessel, was such an able lawyer that it was thought appropriate for the Master of the Rolls to become a judge of the Court of Appeal.[336] He is now the president of the Court of Appeal (Civil Division)[337] and Head of Civil Justice.[338] In view of the large number of important civil cases determined in that court and the power of the Master of the Rolls over the allocation of cases, the holder of that office may exert considerable influence over the development of the civil law. It was for this reason that Lord Denning, then a Lord of Appeal in Ordinary, welcomed the appointment as Master of the Rolls.[339] The holder is referred to as Sir Anthony Clarke, Master of the Rolls.[340]

The *President of the Queen's Bench Division*, *President of the Family Division* and the *Chancellor of the High Court* head, respectively, the Queen's Bench, Family and Chancery Divisions of the High Court, and are *ex officio* members of the Court of Appeal. The first of these offices was created by the Constitutional Reform Act 2005 when the Lord Chief Justice became head of the judiciary and ceased to preside over the Queen's Bench Division.[341] He is referred to as Sir Igor Judge, President,[342] and has also been appointed as Head of Criminal

---

[332] Lord Parker, (1961) 35 A.L.J. 97. Some Chief Justices of the King's Bench had styled themselves, or had been referred to informally as Lord Chief Justice of England, although this was technically incorrect. A notable example of the former was Sir Edward Coke, whose action was said to have displeased the King and to have been one of the causes of his dismissal.

[333] The opportunity was also taken to amalgamate the three common law divisions. The following have held the office: Lord Coleridge 1880–94; Lord Russell of Killowen 1894–1900; Lord Alverstone 1900–1914; Lord Reading 1914–1921; Lord Trevethin 1921–1922; Lord Hewart 1922–1940; Viscount Caldecote 1940–1946; Lord Goddard 1946–1958; Lord Parker 1958–1971; Lord Widgery 1971–1980; Lord Lane 1980–1992; Lord Taylor 1992–1996; Lord Bingham 1996–2000; Lord Woolf 2000–2005; Lord Phillips (2005–).

[334] Written as Lord Phillips C.J. or (unusually) Lord Phillips L.C.J.

[335] See Lord Denning, *The Family Story* (1981), pp.201–204; Sir John Donaldson, M.R. (1984) 17 Bracton L.J. 19 and *The Problems of A Master of the Rolls* (Holdsworth Club, 1985). The full title is "Keeper or Master of the Rolls and Records of the Chancery of England".

[336] Sir Robert Megarry, (1982) 98 L.Q.R. 370, 395.

[337] Supreme Court Act 1981, s.3(2).

[338] Courts Act 2003, s.62, substituted by the Constitutional Reform Act 2005, Sch.4, para.330.

[339] Lord Denning, *The Family Story* (1981), pp.172, 197; "the Master of the Rolls is still one of the most coveted posts in the land": *ibid.* p.204. Lord Denning also found himself "too often in a minority" in the House of Lords: *The Discipline of Law* (1979), p.287.

[340] Written as Sir Anthony Clarke M.R. It is common for the holder of the office to be ennobled, although not necessarily on appointment. Recent holders have been Lord Wright 1935–1949; Lord Evershed 1949–1962; Lord Denning 1962–1982; Sir John Donaldson (Lord Donaldson from 1988) 1982–1992; Sir Thomas Bingham 1992–1996; Lord Woolf 1996–2000; Lord Phillips 2000–2005; Sir Anthony Clarke, 2005–.

[341] See para.1–033.

[342] Written as Sir Igor Judge P.

Justice.[343] The second office was created in 1970, with the transition from the Probate, Divorce and Admiralty Division.[344] The holder is referred to as Sir Mark Potter, President,[345] and he is also Head of Family Justice.[346] He has also been appointed as President of the Court of Protection.[347] The office of Vice-Chancellor was created in 1970, the holder to be nominated by the Lord Chancellor.[348] It was made a royal appointment analogous to the other heads of division in 1982.[349] The holder was technically the vice-president of the Chancery Division,[350] but was effectively the head. He was referred to as Sir Andrew Morritt, Vice-Chancellor.[351] The title "Vice Chancellor of England" was used in the nineteenth century for the judges appointed to assist the Lord Chancellor in the Court of Chancery.[352] From 2005, the office was transformed into that of Chancellor of the High Court, following the ending of the Lord Chancellor's role as a judge. The holder is referred to as Sir Andrew Morritt, Chancellor.[353]

One of the Lord or Lady Justices of Appeal is appointed as Senior Presiding Judge by the Lord Chief Justice, with the agreement of the Lord Chancellor.[354] There is also provision for the appointment of a vice-president of both Divisions of the Court of Appeal or a vice-president for each Division[355] and of a vice-president for the Queen's Bench Division.[356]

2. MASTERS AND REGISTRARS

There are a number of officers of the Supreme Court below the ranks of the judges, who perform both administrative and judicial tasks, the latter in particular   **4–026**

---

[343] Constitutional Reform Act 2005, s.8, as amended by the Police and Justice Act 2006, Sch.14, para.61.

[344] See above, para.2–059. The old division was also headed by a President. The incumbents have been Sir Jocelyn Simon 1962–1971; Sir George Baker 1971–1979; Sir John Arnold 1979–1988; Sir Stephen Brown 1988–1999; Dame Elizabeth Butler-Sloss 1999–2005; Sir Mark Potter 2005–.

[345] Written as Sir Mark Potter P. Sir Stephen was the first who was previously a Lord Justice of Appeal; Dame Elizabeth Butler Sloss was previously a Lady Justice of Appeal, and Sir Mark Potter previously a Lord Justice. Sir Mark had not previously been a judge in the Family Division.

[346] Constitutional Reform Act 2005, s.9.

[347] Established by the Mental Capacity Act 2005, ss.45–56.

[348] Administration of Justice Act 1970, s.5.

[349] Supreme Court Act 1981, s.10(1). See generally Sir Robert Megarry, (1982) 98 L.Q.R. 370.

[350] 1981 Act, s.5(1)(a).

[351] Written as Sir Andrew Morritt V.C. Sir Andrew was the seventh and last of the modern Vice-Chancellors; the others were Sir John Pennycuick 1970–1974, Sir John Plowman 1974–1976, Sir Robert Megarry, 1974–1985, Sir Nicolas Browne-Wilkinson 1985–1991, Sir Donald Nicholls 1991–1994 and Sir Richard Scott 1994–2000. The last four holders of the office were previously Lords Justices of Appeal.

[352] 53 Geo III c. 24, 1813. In 1841 two additional Vice-Chancellors were appointed. With the death of the last Vice Chancellor of England (Sir Lancelot Shadwell) in 1850 the words "of England" were dropped. The Vice-Chancellors were transferred to the Chancery Division under the Judicature Act 1873. On their death or retirement their successors were styled as High Court justices. See A. B. Schofield, (1966) L.S. Gaz. 298; Megarry, *op. cit.*

[353] Written as Sir Andrew Morritt C. He has also been appointed as vice-president of the Court of Protection.

[354] Courts and Legal Services Act 1990, s.72.

[355] Supreme Court Act 1981, s.3(3). In 2007, Leveson L.J. was vice-president of the Criminal Division and Latham L.J. vice-president of the Civil Division.

[356] Access to Justice Act 1999, s.69. May L.J. was appointed in 2001, in succession to Kennedy L.J.

in interlocutory matters arising in the course of litigation. There are, for example,[357] a number of Masters of the Queen's Bench and Chancery Divisions, District Judges of the Principal Registry of the Family Division, Taxing Masters (cost judges) and Registrars in Bankruptcy. One of each of these groups is appointed as a "senior" or "chief".[358] A particularly important office is that of the Master of the Crown Office and Registrar of Criminal Appeals.[359] In addition, the Lord Chief Justice, after consulting the Lord Chancellor, may assign a District judge[360] to one or more district registries and while he or she is so assigned he or she is a District judge of the High Court.[361] The Lord Chancellor may appoint a deputy District judge in a district registry during such period or on such occasions as he thinks fit.[362]

3. ELIGIBILITY FOR APPOINTMENT AND NUMBERS

4–027 Prior to the Courts and Legal Services Act 1990, appointments as a judge of the Supreme Court were confined to members of the Bar. The position now is as follows[363]:

---

[357] Sch.2 to the Supreme Court Act 1981, as substituted by the Courts and Legal Services Act 1990, Sch.10, para.49, lists a number of offices. See also s.89, as amended by the 1990 Act, Sch.18, paras 37, 38 and the Constitutional Reform Act 2005, Sch.3, para.3. Appointments are now made by the Queen on the recommendation of the Lord Chancellor. As to the appointment of deputy and temporary additional masters etc see the 1981 Act, s.91, to be amended by the Tribunals, Courts and Enforcement Act 2007, s.57, cl.54. On the work of the Queen's Bench Masters see A. S. Diamond, (1960) 76 L.Q.R. 504 and Sir Jack Jacob, *The Reform of Civil Procedural Law* (1982), p.349; on Chancery Masters see R. E. Ball, (1961) 77 L.Q.R. 331.

[358] Supreme Court Act 1981, s.89(3), substituted by the 2005 Act, Sch.3, para.3(4).

[359] These were formerly separate posts, the first carrying responsibility for civil work and appeals in the Queen's Bench Division, the second for appeals to the Court of Appeal (Criminal Division). They were amalgamated by the 1990 Act, s.78. The office of Registrar of Civil Appeals has been abolished: see above, para.2–071.

[360] Appointed under s.6 of the County Courts Act 1984, as substituted by the Constitutional Reform Act 2005, Sch.3, para.1.

[361] Supreme Court Act 1981, s.100, as substituted by *ibid.*, Sch.3, para.2(1).

[362] *ibid.*, s.102, as amended by the 2005 Act, Sch.3, para.2(3). The Tribunals, Courts and Enforcement Act 2007, Sch.11, para.3, provides that the Lord Chancellor's standard power will only apply where the person has not previously been a District judge; the Lord Chancellor will be able to appoint a former District judge as a deputy without JAC involvement with the concurrence of the Lord Chief Justice.

[363] Supreme Court Act 1981, s.10(3), as amended by the Courts and Legal Services Act 1990, s.71. For proposed changes to the eligibility rules, see para.4–024.

Position	Max. Number	Qualification
Puisne judges	108[364]	10 years' High Court qualification[365] or two years' standing as Circuit judge[366]
Lords Justices of Appeal	37[367]	10 years' High Court qualification or High Court judge.
Lord Chief Justice Master of Rolls President of Queen's Bench Division President of Family Division Chancellor of the High Court	}	10 years' High Court qualification or High Court judge or judge of the Court of Appeal

In order to be qualified for appointment as a Lord of Appeal in Ordinary a person has to have: (1) been for 15 years a person who has a Supreme Court qualification in England,[368] an advocate in Scotland or a solicitor entitled to appear in the Court of Session and the High Court of Justiciary, or a member of the Bar of Northern Ireland or a solicitor of the Supreme Court of Judicature of Northern Ireland; or (2) have held for two years one or more of the "high judicial offices" judge of the High Court, Court of Appeal, Court of Session or High Court or Court of Appeal in Northern Ireland.[369] There is a maximum number of 12.[370] By convention, two of the Lords of Appeal are Scots lawyers.[371] Most of the offices below the rank of puisne judge can be held by a person with a seven or 10-year general qualification.[372] These are much in the way of minimum requirements: for example, a lawyer can expect to wait much longer than 10 years before becoming a serious candidate for appointment to the High Court.

---

[364] *ibid.* s.4(1)(e). See n.367 below.

[365] i.e. a person who has a right of audience in relation to all proceedings in the High Court: 1990 Act, s.71 (3); see further, above, para.3–017.

[366] A person of this standing is eligible for appointment as a deputy High Court judge: *ibid.* s.9(4).

[367] *ibid.* s.2(1). The number of puisne judges and Lords Justices may be increased by Order in Council, on the recommendation of the Lord Chancellor: ss.4(4) and 2(4), as amended. The maximum number of puisne judges was increased from 85 to 98 by SI 1993/1255: see H.L. Deb. vol.545, May 10, 1993, col. 1048; from 98 to 106 (anticipating implementation of the Human Rights Act 1998) by SI 1999/3138 and from 106 to 108 by SI 2003/775. The number of Lords Justices was raised from 28 to 29 in 1993; from 29 to 32 in 1994 by SI 1994/3217: see H.L. Deb., vol.559, November 30, 1994, col.686; from 32 to 35 in 1996 by SI 1996/1142. See also below, para.4–037; and from 35 to 37 by SI 2002/2837.

[368] i.e. a person with a right of audience in relation to all proceedings in the Supreme Court: 1990 Act, s.71(3)(a); see above, para.3–017.

[369] Appellate Jurisdiction Act 1876, ss.6, 25, as amended.

[370] Administration of Justice Act 1968, s.1. This number may be increased by Order in Council: *ibid.* It was raised from 11 by SI 1994/3217.

[371] This was observed notwithstanding the appointment of a Scots lawyer as Lord Chancellor: Lord Mackay was succeeded as Lord of Appeal by Lord Jauncey of Tullichettle.

[372] Supreme Court Act 1981, Sch.2, as substituted by the 1990 Act, Sch.10, para.49. A "general qualification" is a right of audience in relation to any class of proceedings in any part of the Supreme Court, or all proceedings in county courts or magistrates' courts: 1990 Act, s.71(3)(c); see above, para.3–017.

Prior to the reforms effected by the Courts and Legal Services Act 1990, solicitors were not eligible for appointment to the High Court bench and above.[373] The government argued in resisting change on this point that experience as an advocate in the Supreme Court was necessary for appointment to the bench there.[374] With the extension of rights of audience in the higher courts to appropriately qualified solicitors, the change in eligibility for judicial appointment was irresistible. However, the government also at long last accepted the case that Circuit judges should be eligible for appointment to the High Court. Such judges may be solicitors who have never had a right of audience in the higher courts; nevertheless, a successful period as a Circuit judge would seem, as a matter of common sense, to be a better demonstration of one's judicial qualities than experience as an advocate.[375] In 2000, the first appointment of a solicitor direct to the High Court was made.[376]

The expansion of eligibility for the highest judicial offices was widely welcomed during consultation on the Green Papers on Reform of the Legal Profession.[377] One concern expressed in the course of it was that if members of the Crown Prosecution Service (CPS) were to be given extended rights of audience they would thereby become eligible for a judicial appointment: it was, it was argued, wrong in principle for a person to be appointed as a judge whose experience was exclusively as a prosecutor. The White Paper[378] pointed out that it was the Lord Chancellor's current practice not to appoint serving civil servants to any paid judicial office which would involve hearing criminal cases. As appointment to a full-time judicial office had in practice to be preceded by part-time judicial experience, a member of any part of the government legal service could not become a judge without first returning to private practice for a substantial period. The Glidewell Report on the CPS recommended that this policy should be reconsidered, to improve the career possibilities for CPS lawyers.[379] The policy was changed in 2003. All government lawyers can now apply to sit as part-time judges in civil work, and CPS and SFO lawyers can become Deputy District Judges (Magistrates' Courts), but they may not sit in cases involving their own department.[380]

Academic lawyers are not appointed directly to the Bench in the UK, even if they are lawyers of the requisite standing.[381] Moreover, it seems to have become progressively less common for academic lawyers to be a member of either branch of the profession. It is generally agreed that it would not be appropriate to appoint academic lawyers as trial judges, in view of their lack of experience with the process of ascertaining the facts of cases. It is, however, arguable that academics

---

[373] See JUSTICE Sub-Committee Report on the Judiciary (1972), pp.9–20.

[374] See (1981) 131 N.L.J. 273; (1981) 79 L.S. Gaz. 193.

[375] The first solicitor Circuit judge to be promoted was Sachs J. in 1993.

[376] Lawrence Collins J., previously a partner in Herbert Smith, who was assigned to the Chancery Division. In 2007, he was the first solicitor to be appointed as a Lord Justice.

[377] See the 4th edition of this book, para.3–006.

[378] *Legal Services: A Framework for the Future* (Cm. 740, 1989), pp.42, 43.

[379] Cm. 3960, 1998, p.179.

[380] LCD Press Notice 230/03, June 3, 2003.

[381] The only reference to "practising" barristers related to eligibility for appointment as a Law Lord. The word "practising" does not appear in the qualification substituted by the 1990 Act. Professor Brenda Hoggett Q.C. was appointed to the Bench as Hale J. after moving from an academic post to a spell of almost 10 years as a Law Commissioner; in 1999 she was promoted to the Court of Appeal and in 2004 she became a Law Lord. Professor Jack Beatson FBA of the University of Cambridge, also previously a Law Commissioner, was appointed to the High Court Bench in 2003, the first to be appointed directly from a Law Faculty.

should be eligible for appointment to the Court of Appeal or the House of Lords.[382] It could not be disputed that there would be candidates with the appropriate qualities of intellect and scholarship; it would also be one method of widening the background, political and otherwise, of members of the judiciary, should that be thought to be desirable.[383]

4. METHOD OF APPOINTMENT

The methods of appointment of judges of the High Court, Court of Appeal and House of Lords and to the senior judicial offices have been completely changed by the Constitutional Reform Act 2005. **4–028**

The previous arrangements[384] were that these appointments were made by the Queen,[385] acting by convention on the advice of the Prime Minister, who in turn would have consulted the Lord Chancellor.[386] The effective voice was normally that of the Lord Chancellor, following consultation with members of the judiciary and leading members of the legal profession. The process was supported by the Judicial Group of the LCD. At different times, aspects of the arrangements gave rise to considerable controversy. For much of the nineteenth and twentieth centuries, the process was shrouded in mystery, with greater openness coming only in the closing decades of the period. The second problem was that of the calibre of some appointees. Political service was formerly a significant factor in many judicial appointments, many appointed to the High Court being sitting MPs.[387] Lord Halsbury, Unionist Lord Chancellor for three periods between 1885 and 1905, attracted particular criticism for some bad appointments, including four Conservative MPs.[388] Lord Haldane, when Lord Chancellor between 1912 and 1915, introduced a policy of appointing "only on the footing of high legal and professional qualifications",[389] and this policy, as regards puisne judgeships, was more or less maintained thereafter. The idea that the Attorney-General and Solicitor-General had a special claim should one of the higher judicial offices become vacant lasted longer, but disappeared in the middle decades of the twentieth century.[390]

Looking at the system in the latter part of the twentieth century, there was general acceptance that the calibre of appointees to the High Court was very

---

[382] The JUSTICE Sub-Committee on *The Judiciary* favoured this proposal: Report (1972), pp.21–24.

[383] A number of academics have been appointed as tribunal chairmen, recorders or deputy High Court judges; furthermore, Professor David Pearl has become a Circuit judge and John Mesher a Social Security Commissioner. Note the proposed widening of the eligibility rules: para.4–024.

[384] See the 4th edition of the book, para.4–024; D. Woodhouse, *The Office of Lord Chancellor* (2001), Ch.6.

[385] Supreme Court Act 1981, s.10(1), (2).

[386] There was some evidence that the Prime Minister on occasion overrode the Lord Chancellor's view; Lord Mackay's first choices were not necessarily accepted by Mrs Thatcher: J. Rozenberg, *Trial of Strength* (1997), pp.16–17.

[387] It should, however, be remembered that it was common for service as an MP to be combined with substantial continuing practice as a lawyer.

[388] R. F. V. Heuston, *Lives of the Lord Chancellors, 1885–1940* (1964), pp.36–66.

[389] R. B. Haldane, *An Autobiography* (1929), p.253.

[390] The key moment (at least is retrospect) being the appointment of a Law Lord, Lord Goddard, as L.C.J. in 1946, after the post had been declined by Sir Hartley Shawcross. The only Law officers subsequently appointed to the Bench were Lynn Ungoed-Thomas and Sir Jocelyn Simon, both so appointed in 1962.

high. The main criticisms articulated centred on the narrow social and educational background of the senior judiciary, and a lack of diversity, with women and ethnic minorities seriously under-represented. There were persistent complaints about the restriction of eligibility to barristers, and when that monopoly was removed,[391] about the small number of solicitors actually appointed. It was commonly suggested (although difficult to prove) that the method of appointment was a major contributory factor, in particular with its secrecy and its reliance on the personal views of the Lord Chancellor and the senior judiciary. The Constitutional Reform Act 2005 has changed the position by transferring responsibility for selecting candidates to the Judicial Appointments Commission.

The legislative structures for the appointment of: (1) the Lord Chief Justice and the Heads of Division; and (2) Lord and Lady Justices of Appeal are similar, but not identical, to those for the appointment of puisne judges and other office-holders already discussed.[392] Appointments are now made by the Queen on the recommendation of the Lord Chancellor.[393] As regards the Lord Chief Justice and Heads of Division,[394] if there is a vacancy the Lord Chancellor must make a recommendation for it to be filled unless (in the case of a Head of Division) the Lord Chief Justice agrees that it may remain unfilled. The Lord Chancellor may (after consulting the Lord Chief Justice) make a request to the JAC for a person to be selected for a recommendation. On receiving the request, the JAC must appoint a selection panel. Detailed rules apply to the composition of the panel, which will usually comprise the Lord Chief Justice, the most senior England and Wales Supreme Court judge and the chairman and a lay member of the JAC. The rest of the process is similar to that already described, except that there is no power for the JAC to determine that there is no suitable candidate. The process for appointing Lord and Lady Justices of Appeal[395] is very similar again, except that the judicial member of the selection panel other than the Lord Chief Justice (or nominee) must be a Head of Division or Lord or Lady Justice of Appeal designated by the Lord Chief Justice. Finally, the appointment of a Justice of the Supreme Court, or the President or Deputy President of the Court, under Pt 3 of the 2005 Act will be under a broadly similar structure.[396] Each selection will require a Selection Commission, normally comprising the President and Deputy of the Supreme Court, and one member each of the respective judicial appointments bodies for England and Wales, Scotland and Northern Ireland. The latter three are nominated by the Lord Chancellor or the recommendation of the body in question, and at least one must be a lay member. The Commission selects a name and reports to the Lord Chancellor, who has the same options as for other judicial appointments. The name ultimately accepted is notified to the Prime Minister who makes a recommendation to the Queen for appointment by her. In the meantime, the existing arrangements for appointing Lords of Appeal will presumably apply.[397] This appointment is made by the Queen on the recommendation of the Prime Minister, who receives advice from the Lord Chancellor. The Lord Chancellor consults serving Law Lords and other senior judges throughout the UK.[398]

---

[391] See para.4–027.
[392] See para.4–023.
[393] 1981 Act, s.10(1), (2) as amended by the 2005 Act, Sch.4, Pt 1, paras 114, 122.
[394] 2005 Act, ss.67–75. In force from October 2, 2006.
[395] 2005 Act, ss.76–84. Also in force from October 2, 2006.
[396] 2005 Act, ss.26–31, Sch.8.
[397] s.98 of the 2005 Act could be applied. See para.4–023.
[398] DCA, *Step up to a Judicial Career* (2005), p.31.

Background of appointees

Appointments to the High Court Bench have normally been made from the ranks of Queen's Counsel who have been in practice for 20 to 30 years.[399] Junior barristers may be appointed direct but the only persons normally so appointed are the Junior Counsel to the Treasury, who, indeed, are normally elevated to the bench after their period in that position. From time to time there have been promotions from the positions of Official Referee,[400] county court judge,[401] Recorder of Liverpool or Manchester, Circuit judge[402] and Registrar of the Family Division,[403] but these constitute a fairly small minority.[404] One person has been appointed to the High Court Bench and one to the House of Lords after being an advocate-general of the Court of Justice of the European Communities.[405] Those appointed are usually in their 50s, although some are appointed in their 40s.[406] Brilliance as a technical lawyer has not been regarded as a necessary precondition, although greater weight has been placed on legal ability when appointments to the Chancery Division or to the appellate courts have been considered. Formal offers of a position on the High Court bench are not usually declined, but there has been anecdotal evidence of an increasing number of members of the Bar who when approached informally indicate that they do not wish to be considered either at all or at that time.[407] A survey of deputy High Court judges revealed that 28 per cent of the respondents were unlikely to accept appointments, citing the High Court salary, the need to go on circuit, the loss of autonomy over working life and adverse impact on personal freedoms and family life as disincentives.[408]

The social and educational background of the judges has been examined in a number of surveys.[409] These show that the judges are overwhelmingly upper or upper middle class in origin, with over three-quarters having attended public school, and a similar proportion either Oxford or Cambridge University. Only 20 women have reached the High Court Bench, and one member of an ethnic

4–029

---

[399] LCD, *Judicial Appointments: The Lord Chancellor's Policies and Procedures* (1999), Senior Judicial Appointments.

[400] Sir Edward Ridley (1897). The fact that he held office was regarded as counting against him rather than for him. He was the brother of the Home Secretary, and was subsequently thought to be a poor judge: See Heuston, *Lives*, pp.49–52.

[401] The first was Sir Edward Acton (1920), the Nottingham county court judge. Ten more were elevated between 1945 and 1971.

[402] 26 were elevated between 1973 and 2000.

[403] Butler Sloss J. (1979).

[404] 26 out of 195 appointments between 1970 and 1994.

[405] Warner J. (1981); Lord Slynn (1992).

[406] The youngest in the last 50 years were Lords Hodson and Devlin who were 42 when appointed High Court judges in 1937 and 1948 respectively.

[407] This has given the Senior Salaries Review Body "grounds for concern" although there were "no major problems at present in recruiting judges of the required calibre at all levels": Report No. 51, Cm. 5389–I, 2002, para.4.33; the Review Body also recommended an additional 5.4% increase relative to the Civil Service. See further on remuneration, para.4–035.

[408] Report No.41, Cm. 4245, 1999, pp.17–19. The remuneration factor was the one most often mentioned.

[409] *The Economist*, December 15, 1956, pp.946–947; K. Goldstein-Jackson, *New Society*, May 14, 1970; H. Cecil, *The English Judge* (rev. edn, 1972), Ch.1; J. Brock (M.Phil, dissertation, quoted in the JUSTICE Sub-Committee Report on the Judiciary (1972)); F. L. Morrison, *Courts and the Political Process in England* (1973), Ch.3. The background of the Lords of Appeal appointed between 1876 and 1969 is examined in L. Blom-Cooper and G. Drewry, *Final Appeal* (1972), pp.158–169. The results of these surveys are summarised by J. A. G. Griffith, *The Politics of the Judiciary* (5th edn, 1997), pp.18–22.

minority.[410] The lack of diversity in the judiciary was the subject to adverse comment by the Commission for Judicial Appointments and is one of the priorities for attention of the new Judicial Appointments Commission and the MoJ.[411]

The process of socialisation at the Bar tends to mean that those from other backgrounds do not seem markedly different, if different at all, from the majority.[412] The extent to which judicial attitudes can be related to the social background of the judges is a large and debatable question.[413] Given the continuance for the foreseeable future (notwithstanding the establishment of the JAC) of the practice of appointing senior judges largely from the Bar, it is unlikely that there will be any significant change in the background of the people appointed. What is more plausible is that the attitudes of successive generations may gradually change.[414]

Other countries have adopted different methods of appointment. In civil law systems there is normally a career judiciary, which is part of the general civil service and separate from the legal profession. In the United States there are two basic methods of selection, *appointment* and *election*, although a compromise between the two methods is commonly applied.[415] All federal judges are appointed by the President, subject to confirmation by the Senate.[416] An appointment can in practice be vetoed by one of the candidate's home state Senators and candidates are also evaluated by the American Bar Association's influential Committee on Federal Judiciary, which makes its views known to the President and the Senate. In 1970, 82 per cent of state and local judges were elected, although real contests were rare; in 1995, only six states did not have any type of elections for judges at any level.[417] In a number of states elections are used to confirm in office judges who have been in office for a limited period following appointment by the governor, a separate Commission, or the two together.[418] It

---

[410] Elizabeth Lane J., Booth J., Butler-Sloss J. (subsequently P.) Bracewell J., Ebsworth J., Smith J. (now L.J.), Arden J. (now L.J.), Steel J., Hale J. (now a Lord of Appeal) Hogg J., Hallett J. (now L.J.), Black J., Rafferty J., Cox J., Gloster J., Dobbs J., Swift J., Pauffley J., Baron J., Macur J., Ebsworth J. was the first appointed to the Queen's Bench Division; Arden J. the first appointed to the Chancery Division. As at March 1, 2007, the numbers of judges known or believed to be of ethnic minority origin were: nine Circuit judges (1%), 58 recorders (4%), 2 recorders in training (9%), 14 District judges (3%), 30 deputy District judges (4%), 7 District Judges (Magistrates' Courts) (5%) and 9 deputy District Judges (Magistrates' Courts) (5%): *Statistics—Minority Ethnic Judges in Post* (*www.judiciary.gov.uk*).

[411] See para.4–023.

[412] As to the social background of barristers, see above, paras 3–048—3–050.

[413] See below, para.4–044.

[414] See P. McAuslan, (1983) 46 M.L.R. 1, 19.

[415] See H. Abraham, *The Judicial Process* (7th edn, 1998), Ch.2 and *Justices and Presidents* (3rd edn, 1992); L. Epstein and J. A. Segal, *Advice and Consent* (2005).

[416] The most recent example of a presidential nominee for the Supreme Court failing to obtain confirmation is Judge Robert Bork: see R. Hodder-Williams, (1988) xxxvi *Political Studies*, 613–637; Essays on the Supreme Court Appointment Process (symposium), 101 Harv. L.R. 1146–1229 (1988).

[417] Abraham (1998), p.36. In recent years a number of state judges (including Chief Justice Rose Bird and two associate justices of the California Supreme Court) have failed to obtain re-election following sustained political campaigns by opponents: see R. Reidinger, "The politics of judging" A.B.A. Journal, April 1, 1987, p.52.

[418] The "Missouri plan" is favoured by the A.B.A. A non-partisan Commission selects three candidates, one of whom the governor must then appoint. After one year in office he or she must be approved by the electorate, running unopposed in a separate, non-partisan judicial ballot: Abraham (1998), pp.38–42.

is highly unlikely that any of these methods will be introduced here,[419] although the matter would no doubt be considered should there be a move to a written constitution which accorded a general power to the Supreme Court to hold unconstitutional primary legislation invalid.

5. PROMOTION

The traditional view was that there was no system of "promotion" of judges. The **4–030** fear was that holders of judicial office might allow their promotion prospects to affect their decision-making; care might be taken to avoid offending the senior judges or the politicians responsible for making or influencing judicial appointments. Nevertheless, the trend seems to be for judges to be elevated from the Circuit Bench more regularly, and for appointments to the House of Lords and Court of Appeal to be made from the court below. Appointments are not now made direct from the Bar to the Court of Appeal[420] or the House of Lords,[421] or direct from the High Court to the House of Lords.[422] Three Lord Chancellors, Maugham, Simonds and Dilhorne, have been appointed Lords of Appeal, but the first two of these were simply reverting to an office previously held. At first, elevation to the Court of Appeal from the High Court carried no increase in salary, although membership of the Privy Council was always conferred. The salary of a Lord Justice is now roughly halfway between that of a High Court judge and a Lord of Appeal, although the differentials are small.[423] Apart from the prestige of a higher judicial office, promotion means that there is no longer the disadvantage of having to spend time away from home on circuit. There is, however, no evidence that judges are affected by "promotion sickness".

6. TENURE[424]

Every judge of the Supreme Court other than the Lord Chancellor who, even **4–031** though when a judge, held office "during the pleasure" of (in effect) the Prime Minister:

[419] An argument that the Law Lords, the Lord Chief Justice and the Master of the Rolls, but not the other judges, should be elected, under a plan similar to the "Missouri Plan" is presented by D. Pannick, (1981) 131 N.L.J. 1064.

[420] The only examples have been Slesser L.J. (1929), Scott L.J. (1935) and Somervell L.J. (1946) (all Law Officers), Duke L.J. (1918; Chief Secretary for Ireland 1916–18) and Greene L.J. (1935: leader of the Chancery bar, and subsequently Master of the Rolls). Lord Denning has written that experience as a trial judge is valuable for an appeal judge: *The Family Story* (1981), pp.169–170.

[421] Eleven examples: five Scots, two English, two Irish. The only two since 1930 have been Lord Reid (1948) and Lord Radcliffe (1949) each of whom was an outstanding judge.

[422] Seven examples: Lords Parker (1913), Tomlin (1929), Wright (1932), Porter (1938), Simonds (1944), Uthwatt (1946) and Wilberforce (1964). Lord Slynn was appointed to the House of Lords (1992) after a period as an Advocate General of the European Community; he had previously been a High Court judge.

[423] See below, para.4–035. The introduction of a differential was recommended by the Top Salaries Review Body, "in recognition of the promotion which is involved in appointment to the Court of Appeal from the High Court Bench": Report No.6, Cmnd. 5846, 1974, p.31.

[424] See Shetreet (1976), pp.1–12, 85–159; Sir Kenneth Roberts-Wray, *Commonwealth and Colonial Law* (1966), pp.484–491; W. Finnie, 1993 S.L.T. 213.

"shall hold that office during good behaviour, subject to a power of removal by Her Majesty on an address presented to Her by both Houses of Parliament."[425]

Similarly:

"Every Lord of Appeal in Ordinary shall hold his office during good behaviour but he may be removed from such office on the address of both Houses of Parliament."[426]

These arrangements date from the Act of Settlement 1700.[427] Before then judicial tenure was not regulated by statute. The King appointed on his own terms, which were usually, although not invariably, "during pleasure".[428]

The Stuarts removed or suspended a number of judges who did not conform to their expectations, James II being particularly enthusiastic in this regard.[429] From 1688, William III's appointments were made during good behaviour: the Act of Settlement took away the monarch's right to choose otherwise, although it seems that William was reluctant to see the legal position changed.[430]

It is generally accepted that under these provisions a judge may be removed from office either (1) for breach of the requirement of good behaviour, or (2) by the Crown on an address by both Houses of Parliament, irrespective of whether he or she has been of good behaviour. The "address" procedure is, theoretically, neither the exclusive procedure for removal, nor restricted to cases of misbehaviour. In cases of misbehaviour, there are indeed a number of alternative procedures for removing a judge, which do not seem to be excluded by the Supreme Court Act 1981 or any of its antecedents:

(1) Proceedings in the Queen's Bench Division commenced by the writ of *scire facias* for the repeal of the letters patent by which the office was granted.

(2) Proceedings in the Queen's Bench Division for an injunction to restrain the judge from continuing to act in an office to which he or she is no longer entitled.[431]

(3) Conviction for a criminal offence.

In these cases the "misbehaviour" must either be connected with the performance or non-performance of official duties, or, if not so connected, must involve the commission of a criminal offence of moral turpitude. Furthermore, a judge

---

[425] Supreme Court Act 1981, s.11(3). It is for the Lord Chancellor to recommend to Her Majesty the exercise of the power of removal: s.11(3A), inserted by the Constitutional Reform Act 2005, Sch.4, Pt 1, para.123.

[426] Appellate Jurisdiction Act 1876, s.6, as amended. This is in effect to be re-enacted in s.33 of the 2005 Act as regards Justices of the Supreme Court.

[427] s.3. This section was to take effect should the arrangements for ensuring the Protestant succession become operative: accordingly, the section came into operation in 1714 with the accession of George I.

[428] See C. H. McIlwain, *Constitutionalism and the Changing World* (1939), pp.294–307.

[429] See J. H. Baker, *Introduction to Legal History* (4th edn, 2002), pp.165–169; A. Havighurst, (1950) 66 L.Q.R. 62, 229; (1953) 69 L.Q.R. 522.

[430] D. Rubini, (1967) 83 L.Q.R. 343.

[431] S. A. de Smith and R. Brazier, *Constitutional and Administrative Law* (8th edn, 1998), p.381.

can be removed on any ground by an Act of Parliament, or for "high crimes and misdemeanours" by impeachment.[432] Neither would be used in preference to an address: the latter, in addition, is regarded as obsolete in the UK.[433]

Today, it is likely that the address procedure would be used in any case where a judge was to be removed, and, further, that this would only be done in a case of misbehaviour,[434] although a rather wider view might be taken of "misbehaviour" for this purpose, in particular to include private immoral conduct.[435] There have been many statements to the effect that this would be the "proper" way to proceed, notwithstanding the other possibilities.[436]

Conviction for a criminal offence does not inevitably lead to resignation or removal from office. Nine judges[437] have been convicted of driving with excess alcohol, but have continued in office.

The other methods by which a judge may leave office are:

(1) resignation[438];

(2) reaching the retiring age of 70[439];

(3) under the procedure whereby the Lord Chancellor may remove a judge who is disabled by permanent infirmity from the performance of his or her duties and is incapacitated from resigning his or her office.[440]

A retired judge may be asked to sit as a member of the Judicial Committee of the Privy Council or the House of Lords, or as a deputy judge, on an ad hoc basis. However, this is no longer possible once he or she has reached 75.[441]

---

[432] A trial by the House of Lords at the instigation of the Commons. This procedure has not been used since the trials of Warren Hastings (1788) and Lord Melville (1805). Among judges who were impeached were two Lord Chancellors, Bacon (1620) and Macclesfield (1725): see H. Cecil, *Tipping the Scales* (1964), pp.99–126.

[433] The procedure is not obsolete in the USA: President Nixon resigned rather than face impeachment; President Clinton was tried but acquitted.

[434] It seems that the address procedure can be used in cases of incapacity: see Shetreet (1976), p.274. However, resignation would be secured by informal pressure or a judge would be removed by the Lord Chancellor: see below, n.440.

[435] *Kenrick's case* (1826): Cecil (1964), pp.165–170.

[436] See Shetreet, (1976), pp.96–103.

[437] A Lord Justice in 1969, a Circuit judge in 1973, a High Court judge in 1975, two Circuit judges in 1985, a High Court Registrar in 1989 (see R. Light (1989) 139 N.L.J. 783), a District judge in 1993 (see Rozenberg (1994), p.117, and a Circuit judge in 1999. A number were severely reprimanded by the Lord Chancellor: *The Times*, June 17, 1989; Rozenberg, *op. cit.*; LCD Press Notice 209/99.

[438] Supreme Court Act 1981, s.11(7); Appellate Jurisdiction Act 1876, s.6.

[439] *ibid.* s.11(2), as amended by the Judicial Pensions and Retirement Act 1993, Sch.6, para.4. A retirement age (of 75) was first introduced by the Judicial Pensions Act 1959, but did not apply to those in office on December 19, 1959. (One of those to escape was Lord Denning M.R., who retired in 1982 aged 83.) The 1993 Act applies both retrospectively and prospectively. Judges other than High Court judges and above may be asked to continue (in annual steps) to 75: 1993 Act, s.26. A judge may retire on full pension (normally half the salary in the last 12 months of service, index-linked), (1) after 20 years' service (raised from 15 by the 1993 Act to bring it into line with the public and private sectors generally); and (2) after attaining the age of 65, or (3) if he or she is disabled by permanent infirmity; otherwise, pensions are paid pro rata. See, generally, annotations by J. Mesher in *Current Law Statutes Annotated 1993*; W. Finnie, "Judicial Tenure and Judicial Pensions" 1993 S.L.T. 213.

[440] Supreme Court Act 1981, s.11(8)(9). See A. Paterson, "The Infirm Judge" (1974) 1 B.J.L.S. 83.

[441] Judicial Pensions and Retirement Act 1993, s.26(7). Lord Bridge seemed displeased by his forced "second retirement": see *Ruxley Electronics and Constructions Ltd v Forsyth* [1995] 3 W.L.R. 118, 121 (his last case).

If a judge were, for example, to bury a meat cleaver in someone's head the address procedure for removal from office would work swiftly and surely. Judges, however, do not indulge in acts of misbehaviour that are clearly inconsistent with their remaining in office. Where matters are not clear cut, the address procedure is complex, and uncertain in some matters of detail. Charges have been presented on a number of occasions, but only one judge has been removed as a consequence. Sir Jonah Barrington, a judge of the High Court of Admiralty in Ireland, was removed in 1830 for the embezzlement of sums of money paid into court.

7. DISCIPLINE AND CRITICISM

4–032 The mechanisms for disciplining judges who misbehave are more significant in practice than the procedures for removal. Judges may be criticised in Parliament. An extreme case is that of Lord Westbury L.C., who resigned in 1865 following votes of censure passed in both Houses concerning certain appointments he had made.

Judges are often criticised in the press. "Scurrilous abuse" of a judge may, however, be punished as contempt for "scandalising the court".[442] This head of contempt must be distinguished from that concerned with publications likely to interfere with the administration of justice in particular proceedings, by, for example, influencing juries. The former head was thought to be obsolete in 1899.[443] However, proceedings were taken against the editor of the *Birmingham Daily Argus* for a spirited attack on Darling J. (an "impudent little man in horsehair, a microcosm of conceit and empty headedness").[444] He apologised, and was fined £100, with £25 costs. According to Abel-Smith and Stevens[445] "within a decade the criticism of judicial behaviour which had been so outspoken was replaced in the press by almost unbroken sycophantic praise for the judges". Similar proceedings were taken on a number of occasions in the 1920s and 1930s. Since then, press criticism of the judiciary has become more commonplace, without matching the personal insults expressed by Mr Gray. Proceedings against Quintin Hogg (as he then was), arising out of criticisms of the Court of Appeal published in *Punch*, were dismissed.[446] Salmon L.J. said.[447]

> "The authority and reputation of our courts are not so frail that their judgments need to be shielded from criticism, even from the criticism of Mr

---

[442] See S. H. Bailey, D. J. Harris and D. C. Ormerod, *Bailey, Harris and Jones, Civil Liberties: Cases and Materials* (5th edn, 2001). pp.779–786; N. V. Lowe, *Borrie and Lowe's Law of Contempt* (ed.), pp.226–247; C. J. Miller, *Contempt of Court* (3rd edn, 2000), Ch.12; C. Walker, "Scandalising in the Eighties" (1985) 101 L.Q.R. 359.

[443] *McLeod v St Aubyn* [1899] A.C. 549, 561 (a colonial judge was accused of "reducing the judicial character to the level of a clown," and "being narrow, bigoted, vain, vindictive and unscrupulous". The Privy Council held that this did not require committal for contempt).

[444] *R v Gray* [1900] 2 Q.B. 36. The full passage is printed in 82 L.T. 534. Darling was apparently "rather amused by the vigour of its expression": D. Walker-Smith, *The Life of Lord Darling* (1938), p.122.

[445] *Lawyers and the Courts* (1967), pp.126–127.

[446] *R v Metropolitan Police Commissioner, Ex p. Blackburn (No. 2)* [1968] 2 Q.B. 150.

[447] *ibid.* p.155. Mr Hogg subsequently became Lord Chancellor as Lord Hailsham of St Marylebone.

Quintin Hogg.... [N]o criticism of a judgment, however vigorous, can amount to contempt of court, provided it keeps within the limits of reasonable courtesy and good faith."

Judges are from time to time rebuked in appellate courts. Censure may be coupled with the setting aside of a conviction or the reversal of a judgment. Thus, judges have been censured for excessive interruptions,[448] threatening a jury,[449] improper behaviour on the Bench,[450] falling asleep,[451] incompetence,[452] lengthy delay (20 months) in giving judgment[453] and disloyalty to the decisions of superior courts.[454] Lord Hailsham has written that there are judges who become subject to "judge's disease, that is to say a condition of which the symptoms may be pomposity, irritability, talkativeness, proneness to *obiter dicta*, a tendency to take short cuts."[455]

There may be complaints from barristers, solicitors or litigants, either expressed in court or in private to the judge personally, or made in some other quarter. There is generally a preference for taking action privately. Confrontations in court between counsel and judge may be to the client's disadvantage; it is impossible to assess the extent to which they may also be, or be feared to be, to the barrister's future disadvantage. In particular cases the upshot has been correspondence or an interview between the Lord Chancellor and the judge,[456] or even, on occasion, a public rebuke.[457]

In 1998, the Lord Chancellor set up a Judicial Correspondence Unit with responsibility for handling complaints concerning the personal conduct of judges. He stated that he "takes a close personal interest in the handling of complaints, particularly those alleging racial or sexual discrimination" and "sees all serious complaints and cases where there is a record of similar complaints from different sources about the same judge". He replied personally to complaints in these categories and to those received from peers, MPs and members

---

[448] e.g. *Yuill v Yuill* [1945] P. 15; *Jones v N.C.B.* [1957] 2 Q.B. 55. The judge in the latter case was Hallett J., who was seen by the Lord Chancellor and resigned shortly afterwards: Lord Denning, *The Due Process of Law* (1980), pp.58–62 ("The judge who talked too much"). See generally, A. Samuels, "Judicial Misconduct in the Criminal Trial" [1982] Crim. L.R. 221.

[449] *R v McKenna* [1960] 1 Q.B. 411 (Stable J. at Nottingham Assizes threatened a jury that if they did not return a verdict within 10 minutes they would be locked up all night. They returned in six minutes with verdicts of guilty, which were quashed on appeal).

[450] *R v Hircock* [1970] 1 Q.B. 67. The judge in a criminal trial made gestures of impatience, sighed, and several times "observed in a loud voice, 'Oh God,' and then laid his head across his arm and made groaning noises" (p.71). The court did not condone this conduct but declined to quash the conviction as being unsafe and unsatisfactory.

[451] If the judge thereby misses something of importance: *R v Edworthy* [1961] Crim. L.R. 325; *R v Langham* [1972] Crim. L.R. 457.

[452] *Taylor v Taylor* [1970] 2 All E.R. 609.

[453] *Goose v Wilson Sandford & Co, The Times*, February 19, 1998. The trial judge, Harman J., resigned: LCD Press Notice 40/98.

[454] *Cassell & Co Ltd v Broome* [1972] A.C. 1027, below, para.7–014.

[455] *The Door Wherein I Went* (1975), p.255.

[456] Or an interview with the Lord Chief Justice: one such is described by Judge James Pickles in *Straight from the Bench* (1987), pp.53–57, arising out of his publication of newspaper articles.

[457] e.g. the rebuke administered to Judge Pickles by Lord Mackay L.C. for holding a press conference in a pub, and referring to the then Lord Chief Justice as a "dinosaur"; and the rebuke administered to a Circuit judge for his use of the expression "people . . . who work like niggers": LCD Press Notice 63/97. *Cf. R v Earnshaw* [1990] Crim. L.R. 53.

of devolved legislatures".[458] Outcomes were reported in the LCD/DCA *Judicial Appointments Annual Reports* (to 2002/03).[459]

The arrangements for handling complaints were remodelled in consequence of the Constitutional Reform Act 2005. This is now a joint responsibility of the Lord Chancellor and the Lord Chief Justice, supported by the newly established Office for Judicial Complaints (OJC).[460] Complaints must be lodged with the OJC. Further complaints about the handling of a complaint can be made to the Judicial Appointments and Conduct Ombudsman.[461] The procedure for dealing with complaints is set out in regulations.[462] Complaints not rejected (on specified grounds) by the OJC are referred to a judge nominated by the Lord Chief Justice with the agreement of the Lord Chancellor, who advises on whether and if so how the matter should be taken forward. The Lord Chief Justice or Lord Chancellor may decide that a case is to be investigated by an "investigating judge". Together, they ultimately decide whether the case is substantiated and, if so, whether any action should be taken. Such action may include disciplinary action or reference to a review body.

Express provision for disciplinary powers is now made by ss.108 and 109 of the Constitutional Reform Act 2005. Any power of the Lord Chancellor to remove a person from an office listed in Sch.14 to the Act[463] is exercisable only if he has complied with prescribed procedures.[464] The Lord Chief Justice has power, with the agreement of the Lord Chancellor, to give a judicial office holder formal advice, or a formal warning or reprimand, for disciplinary purposes[465]; or to suspend a person from a judicial office in specified circumstances, including power to suspend a judge where he or she is subject to criminal proceedings or convicted or a senior judge while he or she is subject to proceedings for an Address.

8. TRAINING[466]

4–033 In the late 1970s certain tentative steps were taken to introduce a measure of compulsory training for newly appointed judges. From 1963 onwards a series of

---

[458] *Judicial Appointments Annual Report 2000–2001* (Cm. 5248, 2001), pp.74–75.

[459] Typically there were c.2000 complaints; 300–400 related to personal conduct; a handful were upheld, leading to such steps as a reprimand, a discussion with a Presiding judge or a letter from the Lord Chancellor.

[460] *www.judicialcomplaints.gov.uk*; *Memorandum of Understanding between the OJC, the DCA and the Directorate of Judicial Offices for England and Wales* (April 2006).

[461] Appointed under s.62 and Sch.13 of the 2005 Act.

[462] Judicial Discipline (Prescribed Procedures) Regulations 2006 (SI 2006/676).

[463] i.e. judicial appointments other than puisne judge, Lord or Lady Justice of Appeal or Lord of Appeal (Justice of the Supreme Court) or to one of the senior judicial offices.

[464] See n.462.

[465] This does not restrict what may be done informally or for other purposes or where any advice or warning is not addressed to a particular office holder.

[466] See M. Partington, "Training the Judiciary in England and Wales" (1994) 13 C.J.Q. 319; A. Ashworth, *Sentencing and Criminal Justice* (1993), pp.49–50, 53; Judicial Studies Board: report for 1979–82 (HMSO, 1983), report for 1983–87 (HMSO, 1988) report for 1987–91 (HMSO, 1992), report for 1991–95 (1995) and subsequent annual reports; Glidewell L.J., "The Judicial Studies Board" in C. Munro and M. Wasik, *Sentencing, Judicial Discretion and Training* (1992); Judge Pitchers, *JSB Journal 1997*, Issue 3, pp.18–19; Henry L.J., *JSB Journal 1999*, Issue 8, pp.22–23; A. Rutherford, (1999) 149 N.L.J. 1120 (interview with Waller L.J.); Malleson (1999), Ch.5.

conferences and judicial seminars on sentencing were organised by the Lord Chief Justice and the Lord Chancellor's Office. Attendance at these was voluntary. However, a Judicial Studies Board was established in 1979 following the report of a Working Party chaired by Bridge L.J.[467]

From October 1985 the Board was re-established, with enlarged responsibilities beyond the criminal jurisdiction, namely the provision of training in the civil and family jurisdictions and the supervision of training for magistrates[468] and tribunal chairmen and members.[469] A Director of Studies has been appointed (the position held by a Circuit judge on secondment for two years). Executive functions are delegated to Criminal, Civil, Family, Magisterial and Tribunals committees, chaired by High Court judges.[470] An Equal Treatment Advisory Committee advises on equal treatment issues, and has issued an *Equal Treatment Bench Book*; its members ensure that equal treatment issues are included in all core seminar aims and objectives and incorporated into the training.[471]

Since 1981 it has been essential for a recorder or assistant recorder,[472] before first sitting in a criminal case, to have attended a residential induction course (now normally lasting four days) organised by the Board. The main feature is a mock trial; there are tutor group discussions of sentencing, summing up and other practical issues and some talks.[473] There is then provision for a one day seminar for newly appointed recorders and four day residential continuation seminars for Circuit judges, recorders and newly appointed High Court judges. Additional refresher seminars are organised on a Circuit basis and specialist seminars are held on such matters as serious sexual offences (a requirement for judges authorised to hear such cases) and long and complex trials.[474] Also before sitting on their own they must sit for at least a week in court with an experienced Circuit judge and there is a meeting with representatives from the Probation Service and a prison visit. The Civil and Family Committees have established training arrangements on similar lines as for the criminal jurisdiction, the main recurrent activities being induction courses for new deputy District judges and for new recorders who intend to sit in civil as well as criminal cases and for Circuit judges and recorders authorised to hear family proceedings, continuation seminars for established judges, an annual seminar for District judges and an annual President's conference for family judges. *Bench Books* have been distributed for the different categories of judge (for example, Civil, Family), and *Guidelines for the*

---

[467] *Judicial Studies and Information* (HMSO, 1978). The Working Party had received "widely felt and strongly voiced objection" to the use in their working paper of the term "judicial training", on the grounds that "training" might represent a threat to judicial independence, that appointees might resent the implication that they need to be "trained" and that the "public image of the judge" would be impaired. The Working Party accordingly adopted the term "judicial studies" and emphasised that their proposals would not involve "indoctrination" or "conditioning" (*ibid.* pp.2 and 3). Lord Devlin was caustic in his condemnation of the working paper: *The Judge* (1979), pp.18–53; *cf.* book review by E. J. Griew, [1980] Crim. L.R. 812.

[468] See above, para.4–007. From 2005 it has assumed a stronger role in the training of magistrates.

[469] See above, para.4–018.

[470] See *Judicial Studies Board: Annual Report* (www.jsboard.co.uk).

[471] *ibid.* See Brooke J, (1992–93) *The Magistrate* 194 on the work of its predecessor, the Ethnic Minorities Advisory Committee, and Dyson J., *JSB Journal 1998*, Issue 4, p.19.

[472] From April 12, 2000, no appointments as assistant recorder have been made; recorders designate must satisfactorily complete their training programme before being authorised to sit as a recorder: *Judicial Studies Board: Annual Report* 2005–06, p.11.

[473] *ibid.*

[474] *ibid.*, pp.12, 13–14.

Assessment of General Damages in Personal Injury Cases[475] and specimen directions to juries in the Crown Court have been published. The Board also publishes the *JSB Journal* three times a year. Substantial training exercises were held in relation to implementation of the Children Act 1989, the Criminal Justice Act 1991, the Human Rights Act 1998, the *Access to Justice* reforms and pension-sharing.

There has undoubtedly been a welcome increase in the scope and effectiveness of judicial training. The Royal Commission on Criminal Justice stated that "substantially more resources need to be allocated to judicial training than at present", with reductions in the intervals between refresher training.[476] The Board has been formally independent of the LCD; its secretary is not formally appointed as accounting officer but is treated as having an analogous status.[477] Lord Bingham regards it as essential for judicial independence that control of the content and form of judicial education (as it should now be called) "should rest squarely in the hands of the judges themselves, and such agencies as they may employ".[478] From April 1, 2006, responsibility for the Board, including appointments to it, transferred to the Lord Chief Justice.

9. INDEPENDENCE[479]

4–034 Much importance is rightly attached to the independence of the judiciary.[480] By that is meant independence from improper pressure by the executive, by litigants or by particular pressure groups. Reasons given in support of judicial independence are "(1) that independence is a condition of impartiality and therefore also of fair trials, and (2) that it makes for a separation of powers which enables the courts to check the activities of the other branches of government."[481] As to the first, it has been emphasised that judges must not only be impartial but appear to

---

[475] (8th edn, 2006).

[476] Cm. 2263, p.140. See also the discussion by M. Partington, (1994) 13 C.J.Q. 319, 328–336.

[477] See *Memorandum of Understanding for JSB* (1999) (*www.jsboard.co.uk*). The Board's independence in assessing the need for, and providing judicial training, including the content and nature of that training is expressly acknowledged. However, resources were allocated in the light both of the JSB's plan and of the overall resources available to the LCD.

[478] Tom Bingham, *The Business of Judging* (2000), p.67.

[479] See W. Lederman, (1956) 36 Can. Bar Rev. 769; G. Borrie, (1970) 18 Am. J. Comp. Law 697; Sir Anthony Mason, (1990) 13. U.N.S.W.L.J. 173; Justice M. D. Kirby, *ibid.*, 187; R. Stevens, *The Independence of the Judiciary: The view from the Lord Chancellor's Office* (1993), "Judges, Politics, Politicians and the Confusing Role of the Judiciary" in K. Hawkins (ed.), *The Human Face of Law* (1997), Ch.11, "A Loss of Innocence?: Judicial Independence and the Separation of Powers" (1999) 19 O.J.L.S. 365 and *The English Judges* (2005); T. Bingham, *The Business of Judging* (2000), pp.55–68; Mr Justice R. D. Nicholson, "Judicial independence and accountability: can they co-exist" (1993) 67 A.L.J. 404; K. Marks, (1994) 68 A.L.J. 173; P. Polden, (1996) 25 Anglo-Am. L.R., Malleson (1999), Ch.3 and for comparative and international perspectives, S. Shetreet and J. Deschênes, *Judicial Independence: The Contemporary Debate* (1985).

[480] Art.6(1). ECHR provides that "[i]n the determination of his civil rights and obligations or of any criminal charge against him, everyone is entitled to a fair and public hearing within a reasonable time by an independent and impartial tribunal established by law". See also Art.14(1) ICCPR, which is in similar, but not identical terms: see S. H. Bailey, in D. J. Harris and S. Joseph (eds), *The ICCPR and UK Law* (1995), pp.210–219.

[481] See T. Eckhoff, (1965) 9 *Scandinavian Studies in Law*, pp.11–48.

be impartial. Public confidence is only bolstered by "ostentatious impartiality".[482] As to the second, it has been noted with concern that the public today seem less satisfied that the judges are completely independent of the government in power.[483] An illustration of the dangers that arise when judges are dismissed where their decisions incur the displeasure of the executive is provided by the crisis in Malaysia in 1988.[484]

The extent to which judicial independence is (and should be) respected has come under increased scrutiny since the 1980s. It is generally accepted that the various factors about to be discussed are effective in securing that particular judges in deciding individual cases are protected from improper pressures. However, the relationship between the judiciary collectively and the executive has been problematic over a range of contentious issues.[485] The theme that links these is the tension between the constitutional position of the judges (particularly but not exclusively as perceived by themselves) and the "new managerialism" in the provision of public services that has become increasingly prominent in the administration of justice. We return to this below.[486] First, we consider the factors that are relevant to maintaining judicial independence; it will be noted that several are by no means clear-cut. The appointment and the tenure of judges have already been dealt with. Party political considerations seem to have been eliminated, although this does not mean that the decisions of judges are not "political" in a wider sense[487]:

> "Judges are part of the machinery of authority within the State and as such cannot avoid the making of political decisions."[488]

This point takes on an increased significance with the increased activism of the higher judiciary. "Activism" here means in particular the enhanced powers of judges under the Human Rights Act 1998 to adopt interpretations of legislative provisions that vary from a literal meaning.[489] It led to arguments that while independence and impartiality in the deciding of individual cases must vigorously be maintained, "the cloak of judicial independence can no longer be spread so widely as to inhibit the development of legitimate mechanisms of accountability". These should include further developments in the appointment process (to

---

[482] *ibid.* p.12. It has been argued that this feature has been lacking in the appointment of Scottish judges: see C. M. Campbell, 1973 J.R. 254.

[483] See D. Oliver, "The Independence of the Judiciary" (1986) 39 C.L.P. 237 and "Politicians and the Courts" (1988) 41 *Parliamentary Affairs* 13.

[484] See [1988] N.Z.L.J. 217; F. Narinan, [1988] N.Z.L.J. 266; R. H. Hickling, [1989] P.L. 20; F. A. Trindade, (1990) 106 L.Q.R. 51.

[485] Indeed one commentator has described the proposition that there is independence of the judiciary (as distinct from individual judges) as a "constitutional myth": R. Stevens (1994) 144 N.L.J. 1620, 1621.

[486] See below, para.4–037.

[487] A. Paterson, "Judges: A Political Elite" (1974) 1 B.J.L.S. 118. "Whoever can persuade the members of a society that law is inevitable or to take 'law as a given', and that the legal interpretation of a particular social situation is the only possible one, controls an important if not vital source of power in that society. In my contention British Judges are in precisely this position and that is why it is legitimate to characterize them as involved in the realm of politics": *ibid.* p.129. See also R. J. Wilson, "British Judges as Political Actors" (1973) 1 Int. Journal of Criminology and Penology 197.

[488] J. A. G. Griffith, *The Politics of the Judiciary* (5th edn, 1997), pp.292–293.

[489] *cf.* Sir Stephen Sedley's characterisation of judicial activism in the United States as "the deployment of principle and policy to enhance or defeat enacted legislation where no literal application of the constitution is possible": Foreword to Malleson (1999), p.viii.

ensure greater representativeness), training, appraisal and the handling of complaints, leading overall to increased public confidence. A number of the desirable changes were, indeed, put into effect in respect of the lower ranks of the judiciary.[490]

At the same time, there have also been arguments in varying forms in favour of a greater formal recognition of the separation of powers. An important part of the debate centred on the role of the Lord Chancellor as a member at the same time of legislature, executive and judiciary. The need to put "the relationship between the executive, legislative, and judiciary on a modern footing" was cited as one of the reasons for the Prime Minister's (hasty) decision in the context of a ministerial reshuffle that the office of Lord Chancellor should be abolished, and a new Supreme Court established, separate from the House of Lords.[491] How far the separation of powers was a principle of the UK constitution, and how far the role of the Lord Chancellor breached that principle, were contested, but there was also recognition that a continued judicial role for the Lord Chancellor would be open to challenge under Art.6(1), ECHR.[492] The proposals were initially strongly resisted by most, but not all, senior judges, led by the Lord Chief Justice:

> "Woolf declared that he believed the abolition of the post of Lord Chancellor, without creating any new constitutional safeguards, posed the biggest threat to judicial independence for hundred of years."[493]

Following negotiations, a way forward was agreed, enshrined in the so-called Concordat.[494] This in turn formed the basis of key provisions of the Constitutional Reform Act 2005.[495] During the passage of this Bill, the government conceded that the Office of Lord Chancellor should remain, alongside that of Secretary of State for Constitutional Affairs, but without the roles of judge or Speaker of the House of Lords.

One of the features of the Act was the express "Guarantee of continued judicial independence" contained in s.3. This states that:

> "The Lord Chancellor, other Ministers of the Crown and all with responsibility for matters relating to the judiciary[496] or otherwise to the administration of justice must uphold the continued independence of the judiciary."[497]

The following particular duties are imposed for the purpose of upholding that independence:

---

[490] Malleson (1999), *ibid.*

[491] See Press Notice cited by Lord Windlesham, [2005] P.L. 806, 809.

[492] See Lord Windlesham, *op. cit.* at pp.812–817.

[493] Lord Windlesham, *op. cit.* p.815.

[494] See para.1–033.

[495] The process by which this legislation was enacted is considered by Lord Windlesham in "The Constitutional Reform Act 2005: the Politics of Constitutional Reform" [2006] P.L. 35.

[496] This includes the judiciary of the Supreme Court, any other court established under the law of any part of the UK, the International Court of Justice or any other court or tribunal which exercises jurisdiction or performs functions of a judicial nature under an agreement to which the UK is a party or a UN resolution: s.3(7), (8).

[497] s.3(1).

(1) The Lord Chancellor and other ministers must not seek to influence particular judicial decisions through any special access to the judiciary.[498]

(2) The Lord Chancellor must have regard to

    (a) the need to defend that independence;

    (b) the need for the judiciary to have the support necessary to enable them
    to exercise their functions;

    (c) the need for the public interest in regard to matters relating to the
    judiciary to be properly represented in decisions affecting those
    matters.[499]

There seems no particular reason why these duties should not be enforceable
through judicial review in the unlikely event that a breach could be established,
the three particularised duties being only a duty to "have regard to" the stated
matters. The provisions seem intended to reflect current practice, but their
express recognition by statute should be helpful, and cannot be regarded as
exhaustive of both legal and conventional dimensions of the principle.

    Other relevant factors include the following.

(a) Remuneration

Judges are paid substantial salaries,[500] which are a charge on the Consolidated   **4–035**
Fund and so not subject to an annual vote in Parliament. The salaries at
November 1, 2007 are as follows: Lord Chief Justice: £230,400; Master of the
Rolls and Senior Lord of Appeal in Ordinary: £205,700; Lords of Appeal and
Heads of Division: £198,700; Lord and Lady Justices: £188,900; High Court
judges: £165,900.[501] They can be increased, but not reduced, by the Lord
Chancellor, with the consent of the Prime Minister as Minister for the Civil
Service.[502] From the time salaries became a charge on the Consolidated Fund,[503]
they could only be changed by statute, or, between 1965 and 1973, by ministerial
order.[504] Under the National Economy Act 1931, the salaries of "persons in His
Majesty's service", which term was taken to include the judges, were reduced by
20 per cent. The need to secure the independence of the judiciary was placed at
the forefront of their arguments both that the Act did not apply to them as a
matter of interpretation, and that it should not apply in principle.[505] The government

---

[498] As distinct, presumably from public abuse? Which is only barred by convention.

[499] s.3(4)–(6).

[500] Certainly by the standards of Professors of Law, and many University Vice Chancellors, but not
at all by those of leading lawyers in private practice; in 2006 the Senior Salaries Review Board
reported that the drop in the average remuneration of those recently appointed to the High Court
was over 50% after allowing for the value of the judicial pension: Report No.62, p.37.

[501] DCA website, *Judicial Salaries 2007–08*. As to pensions, see para.4–027, n.31, n.439.

[502] Supreme Court Act 1981, s.12.

[503] Judges appointed after 1786. There was no change between 1851 and 1954 (Judges' Remuneration Act 1954).

[504] Judges' Remuneration Act 1965.

[505] See Heuston, *Lives*, pp.513–519; W. Holdsworth, (1932) 48 L.Q.R. 25 and 173 L.T. 336; E. C.
S. Wade, (1932) 173 L.T. 246, 267; Stevens (1993), pp.50–62. The judges were "in a mutinous
mood" Lord Sankey L.C., quoted by Heuston, *op. cit.*, p.514. However, this "squalid incident . . .
had not reflected well on the judges. They had appeared selfish and out of touch with reality . . .
[W]hat is striking is the amateur level of argument on both sides" Stevens (1993), p.63.

restored the cuts in 1934. This argument has, however, not figured so prominently in the recent reports of the Senior (formerly Top) Salaries Review Board
on judicial salaries, in which more important considerations seem to have been
the need to attract lawyers with the right qualities and experience and the need
to maintain the judges' status in the community. Thus the Board has taken into
account both barristers' earnings and the salaries payable to Permanent Secretaries and senior military officers as "cross-checks" although there are no formal
links with either.[506] The Board conducted fundamental reviews in 1995–97,
2000–02 and 2005–06.[507] The first recommended that pay should be based on the
whole job, irrespective of the mix between judicial and administrative responsibilities; the 2000 Report recommended the upgrading of the posts of the Heads
of Division[508] the 2002 Report found the existing structure to be sound, that the
post of Senior Law Lord should be equated to that of Master of the Rolls, and that
there should be a 5.4 per cent salary increase to take account of the need to ensure
the ability to attract suitably able candidates from private practice to the High
Court bench, additional job weight since the last fundamental review and an
appropriate relationship with the pay of the senior civil service; and a further 2.5
per cent as the general increase for senior salaries. The third found that the
current structure appropriately reflected the range of job weights and the hierarchy of the judiciary; the DCA reported no difficulty in filling vacancies or in
retention; and the increased responsibilities of the senior judiciary flowing from
the Constitutional Reform Act 2005 should be recognised in modest increases in
differentials.[509] The increases recommended added 3.43 per cent to the paybill.[510]
Fears that recruitment might be adversely affected as a result of the changes to
pension arrangements introduced by the Finance Act 2004,[511] which would have
had a very significant impact on the senior judiciary, were met by the government's decision to take steps to maintain the current overall remuneration
package for the serving judiciary.[512] The Board's recommendations are normally
accepted.[513] There have been no serious allegations of corruption against English
judges for some centuries,[514] and it is not plausible that it is the level of salary
alone that is responsible. Even attempts to bribe judges appear to be rare.

It has been an accepted convention that judges may not hold paid appointments
such as directorships, or carry on any profession or business. Indeed, the holders
of full-time judicial appointments are now expressly barred from legal practice.[515] Even the few cases of judges taking business appointments on leaving the

---

[506] The Senior Salaries Review Body is of the view that there should be a "broad linkage" across the
three groups notwithstanding that this operates to limit judicial salaries by comparison with
private practice: Report No.41, Cm. 4245, 1999, p.21. This broad linkage applies through close
equivalence at the very top of the three structures: Report No.61, Cm. 6727, 2006, p.48.

[507] See Report No.39, Vol.II, Cm. 3541, 1997; Report No.51, Vol.II, Cm. 5389-II, 2002; Report
No.62, Cm. 6727, 2006.

[508] Report No.45, Cm. 4567, 2000, p.17.

[509] Report No. 62, p.41.

[510] *ibid.* p.51.

[511] Setting a limit, initially £1.5 m, on the capitalised value of a person's pension benefits, above
which further contributions are taxed at a rate of 55%.

[512] Report No.62, p.46. There were suggestions in the press that had the government failed to act
there would have been a significant number of judicial resignations.

[513] They may be staged.

[514] In November 1993, it was announced by the DPP that a police investigation had revealed no
evidence to support corruption allegations made against Tucker J., the judge appointed to preside
at the trial of Asil Nadir: see Ralph Gibson L.J. in *R v Central Criminal Court, Ex p. Guney*
[1994] 1 W.L.R. 438, 444.

[515] Courts and Legal Services Act 1990, s.75 and Sch.11, as amended.

bench have attracted criticism.[516] The Lord Chancellor has, however, decided to remove the current bar on holders of salaried judicial office returning to legal practice on ceasing to hold office, and has consulted on the conditions and safeguards to be attached.[517] It is thought that the existing restriction may deter some from applying for judicial office. However, this has met strong opposition from the Lord Chief Justice and the Judges' Council.[518]

(b) Judges and the legislature

Judges of the Supreme Court and Circuit judges are disqualified from member- **4–036** ship of the House of Commons.[519] The judges that are members of the House of Lords (commonly the Law Lords, the Lord Chief Justice and the Master of the Rolls and occasionally other judges ennobled after retirement[520]) may contribute to its debates, but by a convention established comparatively recently do not take part in political controversy.[521] They tend to confine their contributions to technical questions of a legal nature. They also play a valuable role in committees of the House.[522] However, serving judges have not felt constrained from speaking on controversial matters where they have concerned the legal system itself. This was starkly illustrated by the criticisms, sometimes expressed in intemperate language, of Lord Mackay's Green Papers on reform of the legal profession.[523] Retired Law Lords are even less inhibited. The position in the 1920s was less clear cut. In 1922 Lord Carson attacked the proposals for the establishment of the Irish Free State. He was rebuked for doing so by his former supporter, Lord Birkenhead L.C., but was defended by others.[524] The continued membership of the House of Lords of serving judges for the time being was endorsed as part of the reform of the composition of the House of Lords.[525]

---

[516] In 1970, Fisher J. resigned at the age of 52 after two-and-a-half years on the Bench in order to join a merchant bank. This provoked some criticism: see (1970) 114 S.J. 593. On the other hand, it was pointed out that a reluctant judge was unlikely to be a good one. Laddie J. resigned in 2005, taking up academic and consultancy posts: see *The Times*, May 16, 2006. The position of Lord Chancellor is arguably different, given the precariousness of office. Both Lord Birkenhead and Lord Kilmuir were criticised for taking business appointments, although the latter declined to draw the pension to which he was entitled. Lord Birkenhead defended his rights to take the pension, but assigned it to the benefit of certain hospitals (see Heuston, *Lives*, pp.396–398; J. Campbell, *F.E. Smith, First Earl of Birkenhead* (1983), pp.812–814).

[517] DCA, *Return to Practice by Former Salaried Judges* (CP 15/06. September 12, 2006).

[518] See J. Rozenberg, *www.telegraph.co.uk*, March 15 and 22, 2007; *www.judiciary.gov.uk* "Judicial views and responses".

[519] House of Commons Disqualification Act 1975, s.1 and Sch.1. There is no disqualification applicable to recorders. In 1994 there were nine recorder/MPs. Justices of the Supreme Court will be so debarred: Constitutional Reform Act 2005, s.137(1), amending the 1975 Act.

[520] A recent example is Baroness Butler-Sloss GBE.

[521] See generally L. Blom-Cooper and G. Drewry, *Final Appeal* (1972), pp.196–215.

[522] Including chairing the Law and Institutions Sub-Committee of the EU Select Committee.

[523] See the 4th edition of this book, para.3–006; G. Drewry, (1992) 45(2) C.L.P. 187, 193–194. An example is Lord Lane's comment that "oppression does not stand on the doorstep with a toothbrush moustache and a swastika armband": H.L. Deb. Vol.505, April 7 1989, col. 1331.

[524] H.L. Debs. Vol.49, cols 686–698, March 21, 1922; 715–727, March 22, 1922; and cols 931–974 March 29, 1922.

[525] White Paper, *The House of Lords: Completing the Reform* (Cm. 5291, 2001), paras 81, 82; judicial members should continue to be members of the House until 75 whether or not they sit judicially. The Royal Commission on Reform of the House of Lords (Cm. 4534, 2000), Ch.9 recommended that the Law Lords should continue to sit but that the possibility of establishing a separate supreme court be examined.

However, it was increasingly regarded as undesirable that judges should participate in the passing of legislation that they themselves may subsequently be called upon to interpret and apply. The Law Lords, responding to a recommendation by the Royal Commission, stated that:

> "they consider themselves bound by two general principles when deciding whether to participate in a particular matter, or to vote: first, the Lords of Appeal in Ordinary do not think it appropriate to engage in matters where there is a strong element of party political controversy; and secondly the Lords of Appeal in Ordinary bear in mind that they may render themselves ineligible to sit judicially if they were to express an opinion on a matter which might later be relevant to an appeal to the House.
>
> The Lords of Appeal in Ordinary will continue to be guided by these broad principles. They stress that it is impossible to frame rules which cover every eventuality. In the end it must be for the judgment of each individual Lord of Appeal to decide how to conduct himself in any particular situation."[526]

In the event, the separation of powers will be formally marked by the replacement of the Appellate Committee of the House of Lords by the new Supreme Court. Neither it nor its judges will be part of Parliament.[527] The Constitutional Reform Act 2005[528] provides that a member of the House of Lords is, while he or she holds a disqualifying judicial office,[529] disqualified from sitting or voting in the House of Lords, a committee of the House or a joint committee of both Houses. Accordingly, subject to any changes to the composition of the House, a judge who is a peer or upon whom a peerage is conferred will be a member of the House but barred from participating in its core functions. It has been stated by a minister that there will be a convention that on retirement a Justice of the Supreme Court will be offered a peerage.[530] Again, subject to any changes to the composition of the House of Lords, a judge who is made a peer will able to sit and vote once he or she leaves the disqualifying judicial office.

Associated with this change is the provision by s.5 of the 2005 Act[531] of a power for the chief justice of any part of the UK to lay before Parliament written representations on matters that appear to him to be matters of importance relating to the judiciary, or otherwise to the administration of justice, in that part of the UK.

(c) Judges and the executive

4–037 It has been generally accepted that judges other than the Lord Chancellor should not hold ministerial office or sit in the Cabinet. Both Lord Mansfield and Lord

---

[526] H.L. Deb., June 22, 2000, col.419.

[527] See para.2–074.

[528] s.137(3)–(5). In force from a day to be appointed.

[529] i.e. any of the judicial offices specified in Sch.1. Pt 1 to the House of Commons Disqualification Act 1975.

[530] Christopher Leslie MP, H.C. Deb., Vol.430, col. 760, February 1, 2005, cited by A. Morgan, *Current Law Statutes Annotated 2005*, pp.4–114.

[531] In force from April 3, 2006.

Ellenborough served in the Cabinet while Chief Justice of the King's Bench, but both cases attracted much criticism. Lord Reading C.J. performed various executive tasks for the government during the First World War, but that can be regarded as an anomalous exception to a well-established principle, which has indeed been strengthened by the practice of making non-political appointments to the position of Lord Chief Justice. This left the anomalous position of the Lord Chancellor, which has now been reconstituted unequivocally as that of a government minister by the removal from it of the roles of Speaker of the House of Lords and judge, and association with the office of Secretary of State for Constitutional Affairs, now Justice.[532]

On the other hand, there seems to be no objection to the involvement of judges with the executive in the administration of the legal system through non-executive membership of the boards of organisations such as the DCA and HM Courts Service.

One matter that has caused some controversy is the common practice of using judges as chairmen or members of Royal Commissions, Departmental Committees and Tribunals of Inquiry.[533] Indeed, judges are prominent in the ranks of "the Good and the Great". This is both expected and unexceptionable where "lawyers' law" and legal procedures are concerned. However, the subject matter of an inquiry may well be politically controversial. The judge concerned may be called upon to explain or justify the report, and indeed to argue in public the case for or against reform. The topics covered include public disorders (Red Lion Square,[534] Brixton[535]); security matters (security procedures in the public service,[536] the Vassall case,[537] the Profumo affair,[538] the D Notice affair[539]; mismanagement in the public service (the collapse of the Vehicle and General Insurance Company,[540] the Crown Agents[541]); events in Northern Ireland (disturbances in 1969,[542] interrogation methods,[543] legal procedures for dealing with terrorists,[544] the "Bloody Sunday" deaths in Londonderry,[545] the working of anti-terrorist

---

[532] See para.1–018.
[533] See D. G. T. Williams, *Not in the Public Interest* (1965), pp.188–191 and [2000] P.L. 45, 53–55; P. Hillyard (1971) 6 I.J. (n.s.) 93; G. Zellick [1972] P.L. 1; T. J. Cartwright, *Royal Commissions and Departmental in Committees in Britain* (1975); G. Rhodes, *Committees of Inquiry* (1975); Griffith (1991), Ch.2. Note the chairing of reviews of civil procedure, the criminal courts and tribunals by, respectively, Lord Woolf, Sir Robin Auld and Sir Andrew Leggatt (above, para.1–032).
[534] Cmnd. 5919, 1975: Lord Scarman.
[535] Cmnd. 8427, 1981: Lord Scarman (Inquiry under the Police Act 1964).
[536] Cmnd. 1681, 1962: Lord Radcliffe (Departmental Committee). The Security Commission is also headed by a judge; the function of this standing commission, first set up in 1964, is to investigate at the Prime Minister's request, breaches of security in the public service, and to report and advise generally on security arrangements. See I. Leigh and L. Lustgarten, [1991] P.L. 215, and Lustgarten and Leigh, *In from the Cold!* (1994), pp.476–491.
[537] Cmnd. 2009, 1963: Lord Radcliffe (Tribunal of Inquiry).
[538] Cmnd. 2152, 1963: Lord Denning. See Lord Denning, *The Due Process of Law* (1980), pp.67–73; "It was a best-seller": *ibid.* p.68.
[539] Cmnd. 3309, 1967: Lord Radcliffe (Committee of Privy Counsellors).
[540] 1971–72 H.C. 133: James J. (Tribunal of Inquiry).
[541] 1981–82 H.C. 364: Croom-Johnson J. (Tribunal of Inquiry).
[542] Cmnd. 566 (N.I.), 1972: Scarman J. (Tribunal of Inquiry).
[543] Cmnd. 4801, 1972: Lord Parker (Committee of Privy Counsellors).
[544] Cmnd. 5185, 1972: Lord Diplock (Departmental Committee).
[545] 1971–72 H.C. 220: Lord Widgery C.J. (Tribunal of Inquiry); and a further inquiry, which commenced in 1998 and is still in progress, chaired by Lord Saville of Newdigate.

legislation,[546] and police interrogation procedures[547]); the interception of communications[548]; industrial disputes (electricity supply,[549] miners,[550] and Grunwick[551]); prisons[552]; and standards in public life.[553]

Sir Richard Scott, now a Lord of Appeal, presided over a lengthy and highly contentious inquiry into the Matrix-Churchill affair where the conduct of ministers and civil servants came under close scrutiny.[554] The report of Lord Hutton's inquiry into the circumstances surrounding the death of Dr David Kelly,[555] which largely cleared the government of any wrongdoing, attracted adverse media criticism, to which Lord Hutton was moved to respond.[556] The (Saville) Bloody Sunday Inquiry has generated procedural litigation while in progress, in which rulings have been challenged successfully.[557]

The appointment of a committee is often thought to be a political delaying tactic or a mechanism for shuffling off responsibility for a controversial decision: whether or not either of these criticisms is in fact true, in a particular case it may be unfortunate for a judge to be associated with them. Moreover, the judge may find himself or herself in the midst of political controversy. He or she may be criticised for producing what is perceived by certain sections of the community, rightly or wrongly, to be a "whitewashing report",[558] or by the government for not producing such a report.[559] It is arguable that a judge is a suitable person to preside over a process for ascertaining the facts of particular incidents such as the Aberfan disaster and the Summerland fire disaster on the Isle of Man, the fire at Bradford City Football Club, the Hillsborough disaster and the activities of Dr Harold Shipman where there are no political overtones. Even here, however, there can be problems.[560] One way of minimising such problems is to use a retired High Court judge, although this may make little difference to public

---

[546] Cmnd. 5847, 1975: Lord Gardiner (Departmental Committee).

[547] Cmnd. 7497, 1979: Judge Bennett (Departmental Committee).

[548] Cmnd. 283, 1957: Birkett L.J. (Committee of Privy Counsellors).

[549] Cmnd. 4594, 1971: Lord Wilberforce (Court of Inquiry under the Industrial Courts Act 1919).

[550] Cmnd. 4903, 1972: Lord Wilberforce (Court of Inquiry).

[551] Cmnd. 6922, 1977: Scarman L.J. (Court of Inquiry).

[552] Cm. 1456, 1991, Woolf L.J. (Inquiry).

[553] Cm. 2850, 1995, Lord Nolan (standing body).

[554] See I. Leigh, "Matrix Churchill, Supergun and the Scott Inquiry" [1993] P.L. 630; R. Norton-Taylor, *Truth is a Difficult Concept* (1995); Sir Richard Scott, (1995) 111 L.Q.R. 596; [1996] P.L. Autumn Issue; D. Woodhouse, (1995) 48 *Parliamentary Affairs* 24; A. Tomkins, *The Constitution after Scott* (1998); B. K. Wintrobe, [1997] P.L. 18. While in progress the inquiry's working methods were the subject of political criticism led by Lord Howe: see Sir Louis Blom-Cooper, [1994] P.L. 1.

[555] 2003–04 H.C. 247; *www.the-hutton-inquiry.org.uk.*

[556] "The Media Reaction to the Hutton Report" [2006] P.L. 807.

[557] See *R v Lord Saville of Newdigate, Ex p. B (No.1), The Times*, April 15, 1999; *R v Lord Saville of Newdigate, Ex p. B* [2000] 1 W.L.R. 1855; *R (on the application of A) v Lord Saville of Newdigate, The Times*, December 21, 2001 (evidence of soldier witnesses should not be taken in Londonderry). See B. Hadfield, [1999] P.L. 663. This was under way when the previous edition of this book was published and is not yet complete.

[558] e.g. the adverse reaction to Lord Widgery's report on the Londonderry shootings: K. Boyle, T. Hadden and P. Hillyard, *Law and State* (1975), pp.126–129.

[559] e.g. the report of the Nyasaland Commission of Enquiry led by Devlin J. (H. Macmillan, *Riding the Storm* (1971), pp.736–738); and the refusal of Harold Wilson to accept the Radcliffe Report on the D Notice Affair: see the White Paper on the D Notice System (Cmnd. 3312, 1967).

[560] In New Zealand, Mahon J. was appointed as sole member of a Royal Commission to inquire into the Mt. Erebus aircraft disaster. Certain statements in the report were held by the Supreme Court to have been made in excess of jurisdiction, and an order for costs against the airline was quashed: *Re Erebus Royal Commission (No.2)* [1981] 1 N.Z.L.R. 618. Mahon J. resigned see [1982] N.Z.L.J. 37. An appeal to the Privy Council was dismissed: *Re Erebus Royal Commission* [1984]

perceptions.[561] It is accepted, by contrast, that a judge should not become associated with party political research committees.[562]

A stricter view of the permissible range of extra-judicial activities is taken in the United States, where the separation of powers is formally entrenched as a constitutional principle. Even the exceptional cases such as the appointment of Justice Murphy as prosecutor at the Nuremberg trials and Chief Justice Warren to investigate the assassination of President Kennedy were controversial.[563]

(d) Public statements by and about judges

Judges are expected to refrain from making party political statements; it is **4–038** sometimes said that they should refrain from criticising the policy of Acts of Parliament, but that is too restrictive. Reasoned, responsible criticism is acceptable: disparaging remarks are not. Thus, in 1978, Melford Stevenson J. was reprimanded by the Lord Chancellor, Lord Elwyn-Jones, for referring to the Sexual Offences Act 1967 as a "buggers' charter".[564] Judges were formerly inhibited by the so-called "Kilmuir rules"[565] from broadcasting on radio or television (except on special occasions, such as charitable appeals). However, these "rules" were relaxed by Lord Mackay on assuming office, judges being left to make their own decisions, after such consultation as they may think necessary.[566] Judges are now much more prepared to speak in public about their own role.[567] It is also now more common for judges, both inside and outside Parliament, to advocate changes in government policy in the legal sphere.[568] Indeed, judicial speeches have commonly been published on the DCA and MoJ websites. One consequence of the transfer of many responsibilities from the Lord Chancellor to the Lord Chief Justice has been the establishment of a Judicial

A.C. 808; see K. Keith, [1984] N.Z.L.J. 35; D. Currie, [1984] N.Z.L.J. 43; A Beck, "Trial of a High Court Judge for Defamation" (1987) 103 L.Q.R. 461.

[561] An example of the use of a retired judge to chair a highly sensitive inquiry is the *Stephen Lawrence Inquiry* chaired by Sir William Macpherson of Cluny (Cm. 4262, 1999); see L. Bridges, (1999) 26 J.L.S. 298; S. H. Bailey, D. J. Harris, D. C. Ormerod, *Bailey, Harris and Jones, Civil Liberties: Cases and Materials* (5th edn, 2001), pp.144–147.

[562] Lord Avonside, a judge of the Court of Session, resigned from a Conservative Committee on the constitutional position in Scotland following public criticism, e.g. by the Lord Advocate: see *The Times*, July 30, 1968, August 8, 1968; R. J. Wilson, "British Judges as Political Actors" (1973) 1 Int. Journal of Criminology and Penology, 197, 199–200. "A judge must expect to forgo any kind of political activity . . . ": LCD *Guidance on Outside Activities and Interests* (June 2000, LCD website).

[563] See A. T. Mason, (1953) 67 Harv. L.R. 193; (1970) 35 *Law and Contemporary Problems* (Symposium).

[564] *The Times*, July 6, 1978.

[565] A letter from the then Lord Chancellor, Lord Kilmuir, to the Director-General of the BBC in 1955, set out at [1986] P.L. 384–386. The Lord Chancellor disclaimed any disciplinary jurisdiction over judges, but stated that it was generally undesirable for judges to broadcast (it would, for example, "be inappropriate for the Judiciary to be associated with any series of talks or anything which could fairly be interpreted as entertainment . . . ").

[566] See A. W. Bradley, [1988] P.L. at p.166.

[567] See Rozenberg (1994), pp.96–103, noting, *inter alia*, the willingness of Lord Taylor C.J. and others to give press conferences.

[568] See e.g. the judicial support for incorporation of the European Convention on Human Rights into English law (e.g. Sir Thomas Bingham, (1993) 109 L.Q.R. 390; Lord Taylor C.J. "The Judiciary in the Nineties", Richard Dimbleby Lecture 1992; and continued opposition to the mandatory life sentence for murder (e.g. by Lord Lane, H.L. Deb., April 18, 1991, Vol.527 cols 1562–1564, and in his chairmanship of a Committee on the Penalty for Homicide set up by the Prison Reform Trust: see Lord Windlesham, [1993] Crim. L.R. 644, 656–657).

Communications Office and a dedicated website for the *Judiciary of England and Wales*.[569] A further legitimate route to the expression of judicial views is through one of their representative bodies.[570]

Areas where judges (especially retired judges) have been particularly outspoken have been the resourcing of the legal system and the need to protect judicial independence. Issues raised have included the failure of the executive to consult judges about resourcing decisions regarded as affecting the conduct of cases in court,[571] proposed reforms to the legal profession in the 1980s and refusals to increase the numbers of judges,[572] changes to judicial pensions,[573] cuts to eligibility to legal aid[574] and suggestions that the civil courts were on the brink of collapse.[575] However, it has also been argued that the rhetoric of judicial independence may obscure rather than illuminate resourcing issues, particularly if it is seen simply as an argument to reinforce judicial status or to resist any change.[576] The perceived challenge to judicial independence arising from the proposal to abolish the office of Lord Chancellor led to opposition in public, with no suggestion that the judges were not entitled to articulate their concerns.

Members of the executive are similarly expected to refrain from attacking judges, unless provoked. It is a rule of parliamentary practice that reflections must not be cast upon a judge's character or motives except on a substantive motion specifically criticising him or her or leading to an address for his or her removal, although reasoned arguments that a judge has made a mistake or was wrong are acceptable.[577] Furthermore, matters *sub judice* must not normally be discussed: subject to the discretion of the chair, and to the right of each House to legislate on any matter or to discuss any delegated legislation, cases in which proceedings are active in UK courts must not be referred to in any motion, debate or question, except where a ministerial decision is in question, or in the chair's opinion a case concerns issues of national importance.[578]

---

[569] *www.judiciary.gov.uk*. See evidence to the Select Committee on the Constitution's *Short Inquiry into Executive/Judiciary Relations* (2007).

[570] A Judges' Council was originally set up by statute in 1873 but met sporadically and was eventually abolished by the Supreme Court Act 1981. A Council was re-established by Lord Lane in 1988 on an extra-statutory basis (see Lord Justice Thomas, "The Judges' Council" [2005] P.L. 608; *www.judiciary.gov.uk*). There is also HM Council of Circuit Judges and the Association of District Judges. These bodies regularly respond publicly to government Consultation Papers; this may include the expression of strong opposition to proposed changes.

[571] Sir Nicholas Browne-Wilkinson, "The Independence of the Judiciary in the 1980s" [1988] P.L. 44. See also I.R. Scott, (1988) 7 C.J.Q. 103.

[572] Much fire was directed at the then Lord Chancellor, Lord Mackay: see Sir Francis Purchas (1993) 14 N.L.J. 1604, (1994) 144 N.L.J. 527, 1306; rejoinder by R. Stevens, *ibid.*, p.1620.

[573] Judicial Pensions and Retirement Act 1993, above, para.4–031, n.439.

[574] Below, paras 11–008—11–015.

[575] Judge Paul Collins on the radio programme *Law in Action*, reported by J. Rozenberg, *www.telegraph.co.uk*, February 13, 2007.

[576] See R. Stevens, (1994) 144 N.L.J. 1620 and his works cited at para.4–034, n.479.

[577] *Erskine May's Parliamentary Practice* (21st edn, 1989), pp.379–380; H.C. Deb., Vol.865, cols 1092, 1144, 1200. December 4, 1973 (criticisms of Sir John Donaldson as President of the National Industrial Relations Court; HC Deb, Vol.935, cols 1381–4, July 19, 1977; H.C. Deb., Vol.34, cols 123–126, 285–286, December 14, 15, 1982 (description by Mrs Thatcher of a 12-month sentence for the rape of a six-year-old girl as "incomprehensible" ruled to be in order).

[578] Resolution of the House of Commons, H.C. Deb., November 15, 2001, cols 1012–1018, replacing resolutions of July 23, 1963 and June 28, 1972 following a Report of the Joint Committee on Parliamentary Privilege, 1998–99 H.C. 214, paras 189–202. The new rules are similar to the previous ones, except that the exception is broader in applying in any case where a ministerial decision is under challenge and the rules expressly apply to proceedings of committees. Similar

A further cause of tension between the judges and the Labour government has been the greater willingness of particular ministers to attack publicly judicial decisions of which they disapprove.[579] Some instances have prompted intervention by the Lord Chancellor and the Attorney-General to defend the judge concerned.[580]

(e) Judicial immunity from suit[581]

At common law, every judge of a superior or inferior court is immune from liability in damages for any act that is either (1) within jurisdiction, or (2) honestly believed to be within jurisdiction.[582] The protection in (1) is available even where the judge is malicious.[583] He or she is also protected by absolute privilege in the law of defamation. Every judge:

4-039

> "should be able to do his work in complete independence and free from fear. He should not have to turn the pages of his books with trembling fingers, asking himself: 'If I do this, shall I be liable in damages?'"[584]

The rules also prevent the relitigation of the issues determined by the court.[585]

Deliberate misconduct such as corruption could lead to prosecution for a criminal offence[586] and removal from office.

(f) Disqualification for interest or bias

A judge is disqualified from hearing a case in which he or she has a direct pecuniary or proprietary interest, or in circumstances where there is a real possibility of bias on his or her part.[587] This rule applies to judges of the superior courts as much as it does to magistrates and tribunal members. Indeed, the

4-040

---

rules apply in the House of Lords. The previous rule was used to prevent debate on the Pinochet case while proceedings were in progress. See further, P. M. Leopold, "The *Sub Judice* Rule in the House of Lords" in B. Dickson and P. Carmichael, *The House of Lords: Its Parliamentary and Judicial Roles* (1999), Ch.5.

[579] Most notably, Home Secretaries, David Blunkett and John Reid. Charles Clarke, in evidence to the House of Lords Select Committee on the Constitution said it was "disgraceful" that Law Lords were not prepared to discuss the principle of new anti-terrorist laws with the Home Secretary.

[580] e.g. Lord Falconer defended the decision of a Circuit judge in sentencing a paedophile that had been attacked by John Reid as unduly lenient on the basis that it was in accordance with sentencing guidelines: *BBC News* June 15, 2006. However, he regarded Mr Reid's comments as an attack on the system rather than the judge: *Guardian Unlimited* June 15, 2006.

[581] See A. Olowofoyeku, *Suing Judges* (1993); M. Brazier, [1976] P.L. 397.

[582] *Sirros v Moore* [1975] Q.B. 118, Lord Denning M.R. and Ormrod L.J. Buckley L.J. held that if an act were outside jurisdiction a judge would only be immune if he or she had so acted as a result of a reasonable mistake of fact. See also *Rajski v Powell* (1987) 11 N.S.W.L.R. 522. (The attempt of majority of the court in *Sirros v Moore* to equate the position of judges of inferior and superior courts was subsequently disapproved: see above, para.4–010).

[583] *Anderson v Gorrie* [1895] 1 Q.B. 668.

[584] *per* Lord Denning M.R., in *Sirros v Moore*, n.582 above, at p.136.

[585] *cf.* the immunity of advocates, above, paras 3–044—3–046.

[586] *cf. R v Llewellyn-Jones* [1967] 3 All E.R. 225 (misbehaviour in a public office: misuse of funds by a county court registrar).

[587] See *R v Gough (Robert)* [1993] A.C. 646 (setting out a "real danger of bias" test); *Porter v Magill* [2002] 1 All E.R. 465 (preferring the "real possibility of bias" formulation): see further below: Sir William Wade and C. F. Forsyth, *Administrative Law* (9th edn, 2004), Ch.13.

leading case on disqualifying interests[588] concerned decrees made by Lord
Cottenham L.C. in favour of a canal company in which he held shares. The
House of Lords set aside these decrees. Lord Campbell emphasised that:

> "No one can suppose that Lord Cottenham could be in the remotest degree
> influenced by the interest ... but ... it is of the last importance that the
> maxim that no man is to be a judge in his own cause should be held
> sacred."[589]

The matters that may give rise to a possibility of bias include personal
hostility, friendship, family relationship or acquaintance with a party or with a
witness. The parties may waive the objection. The parameters of the disqualification rules have come under scrutiny in a number of recent high profile cases
which take account of the impact of Art.6(1), ECHR. There have been two major
issues. First, the division in earlier case law between support for a test that
emphasised appearances ("reasonable suspicion of bias") and one that took
greater account of the actual risks ("real likelihood of bias") was settled in
favour of the latter by the House of Lords in *R v Gough*,[590] with a preference for
the formulation "is there in the view of the court a real danger of bias?" This
approach was, however, not followed in Commonwealth cases where a test was
applied whether the events in question gave rise to a reasonable apprehension or
suspicion on the part of a fair-minded and informed member of the public that the
judge was not impartial.[591]

The *Gough* test in its application to judges was considered by the Court of
Appeal prior to implementation of the Human Rights Act 1998 in *Locabail (UK)
Ltd v Bayfield Properties Ltd* and other cases.[592] While bound by *Gough*, the
court thought is possible to apply the *Gough* test in such a way as to secure
Art.6(1) compliance. First, it would often be appropriate to inquire whether the
judge knew of the matter relied on as appearing to undermine his or her
impartiality; if it was shown that it was not the appearance of possible bias would
be dispelled. The judge might provide a written statement on the point; this
would often, but not invariably, be accepted. There would, however, be no
question of cross-examining or seeking disclosure from the judge. The court
would disregard any statement by the judge concerning the impact of any
knowledge on his or her mind or decision. Barristers sitting as judges would
know of any past or continuing personal association which might be thought to
affect their impartiality; solicitors should, before sitting in a particular case,
conduct a careful conflict search within their firm. In cases giving rise to
automatic disqualification or where, for solid reasons, he or she feels personally

---

[588] *Dimes v Grand Junction Canal Proprietors* (1852) 3 H.L. Cas. 759.

[589] *ibid.* p.793. Dimes was a "crazy attorney" who had "embarked upon interminable litigation"
against the Canal company. Cottenham died before judgment was given in the House of Lords:
"it was a common belief that Dimes had killed Lord Cottenham": J. B. Atlay, *The Victorian
Chancellors* (1906), Vol.1, p.415. *Cf. R v Mulvihill* [1990] 1 W.L.R. 438, where the Court of
Appeal held that a Circuit judge was not disqualified from presiding over a trial concerning seven
robberies of banks and building societies where he held 1,650 shares in one of the banks (the
NatWest); there was no direct pecuniary interest and no reasonable suspicion of bias (*a fortiori*,
there would be no real danger of bias under the *Gough* test, n.587 above).

[590] Above.

[591] e.g. *Webb v R* (1994) 181 C.L.R. 41, High Court of Australia.

[592] [2000] Q.B. 451. The other cases were *Locabail (UK) Ltd v Waldorf Investment Corporation;
Timmins v Gormley; Williams v H.M. Inspector of Taxes; R v Bristol Betting and Gaming
Licensing Committee, Ex p. O'Callaghan.*

embarrassed, the judge should recuse him- or herself before any objection is raised. If he or she is or becomes aware of any matter which could arguably be said to give rise to a real danger of bias, it should be disclosed to the parties. If objection is made, judgment should be exercised on it; he or she should neither yield to a tenuous or frivolous objection nor ignore an objection of substance.

The court emphasised that it could not conceive of circumstances where an objection could be soundly based on the religion, ethnic or national origin, gender, age, class, means or sexual orientation of the judge. Nor, at least ordinarily, could an objection be soundly based on his or her social or educational or service or employment background or history, nor that of any member of his or her family, or previous political associations, or membership of social, or sporting or charitable bodies; or Masonic associations; or previous judicial decisions; or extra-curricular utterances; or previous receipt of instructions to act for or against any party, solicitor or advocate engaged in a case before him or her. On the other hand, a real possibility of bias might arise from personal friendship or animosity between the judge and any member of the public involved in the case; or close acquaintance with a member of the public involved in the case, particularly where the latter's credibility was in issue; or where the judge had previously rejected the evidence of an individual whose credibility was in issue in such outspoken terms as to throw doubt on the former's ability to approach the individual's evidence with an open mind; or if the judge had previously expressed views on a question at issue in such extreme and unbalanced terms as to throw doubt on his ability to try the issue with an objective judicial mind; or if, for any other reason, there were real grounds for doubting the judge's ability to ignore extraneous considerations, prejudices and predilections. If in any case there was real ground for doubt, that doubt should be resolved in favour of recusal.[593] Applying these principles, the court held[594] that there had been neither a direct pecuniary interest nor a real danger of bias where Lawrence Collins Q.C., sitting as a deputy High Court judge, had heard a case in circumstances that, unknown to him, his firm, Herbert Smith, had acted for parties to other proceedings against the applicant's husband. On the other hand, there was such a danger in a personal injuries case where insurers were the real defendants was heard by a recorder who had published articles that expressed "pronounced pro-claimant anti-insurer views".[595]

Subsequently, the Court of Appeal in *Re Medicaments and Related Classes of Goods (No.2)*[596] held that the principles laid down in *Gough* did indeed require modification in the light of the jurisprudence of the European Court of Human

---

[593] paras [18]–[26].

[594] The *Locabail* cases. Cf. *Williams v H.M. Inspector of Taxes* (no real danger of bias where chairman of employment tribunal hearing complaint of sexual harassment and race discrimination at a Tax Office had worked for the Inland Revenue between 1958 and 1961 in a junior position); *R v Bristol Betting and Gaming Licensing Committee, Ex p. O'Callaghan* (no direct pecuniary interest and no real danger of bias where it emerged that Dyson J., who had heard judicial review proceedings concerning a £5,000 cost order arising out of objections by O'C to the renewal of a bookmaker's permit to Corals, was a non-executive director of a family company that rented premises to Corals elsewhere in the country; the judge was unaware that Corals were a tenant of the company).

[595] *Timmins v Gormley*. Cf. *Hoekstra v H.M. Advocate (No.3)* 2000 J.C. 391 (held that appeal court was not an impartial tribunal where one of the judges wrote a newspaper article, shortly after an appeal raising ECHR issues was rejected, strongly critical of incorporation of the ECHR).

[596] [2000] 1 W.L.R. 700.

Rights.[597] The difference was that when that court considers whether the material circumstances give rise to a reasonable apprehension of bias, it applies an objective test to the circumstances and does not pass judgment on the likelihood that the particular tribunal under reviewed was biased. Accordingly, an English court:

> "must first ascertain all the circumstances which have a bearing on the suggestion that the judge was biased. It must then ask whether those circumstances would lead a fair-minded and informed observer to conclude that there was a real possibility, or a real danger, the two being the same, that the tribunal was biased."

The material circumstances include an explanation given by the judge. If that explanation is accepted by the applicant for review it can be treated as accurate; if it is not, it becomes one further matter to be considered from the view point of the fair-minded observer. The court does not have to rule on whether it should be accepted or rejected.[598] The court held that there was a real danger of bias where a lay member of the Restrictive Practices Court, after the commencement of proceedings, applied for a post at a firm one of whose directors was a key expert witness for one of the parties. The House of Lords subsequently endorsed this approach, with the further modification that the "real possibility of bias" formulation should be used, and not "real danger".[599] It is generally accepted that these differences in formulation are unlikely to lead to differences in outcome in many cases. Indeed, it is arguable that the margin for differences of view as to the outcome when either version is actually applied to a concrete set of facts is broader than the difference between the two formulations.

The second issue has seen the extension of the category of automatic disqualification by the House of Lords in *R v Bow Street Metropolitan Stipendiary Magistrate, Ex p. Pinochet Ugarte*.[600] Here, the House of Lords in earlier proceedings[601] had decided by three to two[602] that a warrant for the extradition of the applicant to Chile, where he had formerly been head of state, was valid.

---

[597] *Delcourt v Belgium* (1970) 1 E.H.R.R. 355; *Piersack v Belgium* (1982) 5 E.H.R.R. 169; *De Cubber v Belgium* (1984) 7 E.H.R.R. 236; *Borgers v Belgium* (1993) 15 E.H.R.R. 92; *Gregory v UK* (1997) 25 E.H.R.R. 577.

[598] paras [83]–[86].

[599] *Porter v Magill* [2002] 1 All E.R. 465, *per* Lord Hope at paras [95]–[105]. See also *Lawal v Northern Spirit Ltd* [2003] UKHL 35, [2003] I.C.R. 856 (real possibility of bias where part-time EAT judge might appear as counsel before a tribunal having previously sat with one or more lay members of the EAT bench hearing the appeal); *AWG Group Ltd v Morrison* [2006] EWCA Civ 6, [2006] 1 All E.R. 967 (judge should have recused himself when on discovering that a proposed witness was well known to him; the problem was not solved by a decision not to call him, given his involvement in relevant events); *Gillies v Secretary of State for Work and Pensions* [2006] UKHL 2, [2006] I.C.R. 267 (no real possibility of bias simply on the ground that medical member of disability appeal tribunal also provided reports in other cases to the Benefits Agency as an Examining Medical Practitioner).

[600] [2000] 1 A.C. 119. For analysis, see D. Woodhouse (ed.), *The Pinochet Case* (2000), Chs 2 (D. Robertson), 3 (E. Grant), 4 (P. Catley and L. Claydon); Sir David Williams, [2000] P.L. 45; K. Malleson, (2000) 63 M.L.R. 119.

[601] [1998] 4 All E.R. 897. Distinguished in *Meerabux v Att Gen of Belize* [2005] UKPC 12, [2005] 2 A.C. 513 (no automatic disqualification where Bar Association's complaint against a judge was referred in accordance with the Constitution to a Council whose chairman had to be qualified to be judge and so had to be a member of the Association).

[602] Lords Nicholls, Steyn and Hoffmann, Lords Slynn and Lloyd dissenting.

Amnesty International had been given leave to intervene in the proceedings, and had supported the validity of the warrant. It subsequently emerged that one of the minority, Lord Hoffmann, was a director and chair of Amnesty International Charity Ltd, which had been incorporated to carry out AI's charitable purposes. The House unanimously set aside its earlier decision. It was not suggested that Lord Hoffmann was actually biased. The House did not reach the question whether there was a real danger or possibility of bias, but held that automatic disqualification followed where the judge's decision would lead to the promotion of a cause in which the judge was involved together with one of the parties. Here, he or she would be "a judge in his own cause", even if he or she were not technically a party.[603] It is submitted that while the outcome was right, it would have been preferable to apply the real possibility of bias test rather than by introducing an extension to the automatic disqualification rule that is uncertain in scope. Following this decision, the Lord Chancellor, as head of the judiciary, wrote to the senior law lord that "we must make every effort to ensure that such a state of affairs could not occur again". In future, the chair of a committee should ensure that its proposed members should consider together whether any of their number might appear to be subject to a conflict of interest and to require any law lord to disclose any such circumstances to the parties, and not sit if any party objects and the Committee so determines.[604]

Where a judge is not technically disqualified, he or she may well refuse to act in a case where one of the parties raises an objection. Objections, however, are not commonly made. Lord Denning M.R. withdrew from a case concerning the Church of Scientology of California as the Church felt that "there was an unconscious influence operating adversely to it" in Lord Denning's previous judgments.[605] The Church had been before Lord Denning's court on eight previous occasions, and noted that his Lordship had doubted whether it was right to call scientology a "religion" and whether the Church was entitled to call itself a church. Shaw L.J. said that it was almost impossible to resist the application for the appeal to be transferred "even though the grounds were not merely slight but non-existent". Conversely, no objection was taken to Lord Denning's acting in a case concerning the Church Commissioners, he being one of the Commissioners,[606] or to the fact that all the members of the Court of Appeal hearing the appeal in the London Transport "fares" case were both users of public transport in London and London ratepayers.[607] *Guidance on Outside Activities and Interests* has been given to the judiciary by the LCD[608] and a separate *Guide to Judicial Conduct* prepared and published by the Judges' Council.[609]

---

[603] Lord Hoffmann was not to be treated as a party as his links were to AICL and not AI itself (an unincorporated association); see Lord Browne-Wilkinson at p.134.

[604] LCD Press Notice 382/98.

[605] *Ex p. Church of Scientology of California, The Times*, February 21, 1978. Lord Lane C.J. stood down in *Moss v McLachlan* [1985] 149 J.P. 167: Pannick (1987), p.41. *Cf. Arab Monetary Fund v Hashim (No.8), The Independent*, April 30, 1993 (counsel should be satisfied that there is material on which an application for removal of a judge can properly be made).

[606] *Hanson v Church Commissioners* [1978] Q.B. 823, 831. The actual management of the estate of the Church Commissioners was vested in a separate board of governors. Various "dignitaries" including the Lord Chief Justice, the Master of the Rolls and the Lord Mayor of London, were "merely titular commissioners".

[607] *Bromley London Borough Council v Greater London Council* [1983] 1 A.C. 768, 77–777.

[608] DCA website.

[609] Revised edn 2006: *www.judiciary.gov.uk*.

10. THE JUDICIAL FUNCTION

4-041   In the course of legal proceedings, judges may be called upon to perform one or
more of the following tasks: presiding over a trial (e.g. controlling the course of
proceedings, keeping order, ruling on questions of the admissibility of evidence,
deciding when to adjourn for lunch); presiding over an appeal[610]; determining a
disputed question of fact; determining a disputed question of law; directing a jury
on the evidence and the law; deciding what remedy to award or punishment to
impose; and giving reasons for such decisions as are theirs. With the marked
decline in the use of the jury in civil cases over the last 60 years, the judicial task
of determining disputed questions of fact has correspondingly grown in significance. When considering the "nature of the judicial function", however, it is
usual to concentrate on the ways in which judges approach the determination of
disputed questions of law. Furthermore, attention is directed in particular to the
appeal courts,[611] as a higher proportion of time is spent on such questions, as the
arguments are more likely to be evenly balanced, and because the decisions of
courts at the top of the hierarchy carry most weight. In Chapters 6, 7 and 8 we
consider the principles that are applicable to the interpretation of statutes and the
handling of precedent cases and the application of the Human Rights Act 1998.
We shall see that there is considerable room for flexibility. Moreover, even where
there is no directly relevant precedent and no applicable legislation the judge
must still give an answer to any legal questions that arise.

The extent to which a judge is prepared to innovate depends upon the
respective weight attached to a number of factors[612]: the need for stability and
certainty in law (which suggests consistency with established principles and
precedents); the wish to do justice as between the parties; the need not to usurp
the role of Parliament; the need to justify a decision by reasoned argument and
not merely compromise between the parties; and the need to base a decision on
at least one of the issues raised by the parties. Differences in approach reflect
different weight attached to these factors—in particular the first two. Important
contributions to the theoretical debate have come from some of our leading
judges, speaking both extra-judicially and in decided cases. The judges' own
perceptions of the proper judicial role are equally of importance as one of the
important influences on judicial decision-making identified in empirical
studies.

Historically, the theory that held sway for the longest time was the "declaratory theory" expounded by William Blackstone and others. Blackstone wrote[613]
that:

> "it is an established rule to abide by former precedents, where the same
> points come again in litigation . . . [the judge] being sworn to determine, not

---

[610] The president of an appellate court can have a significant influence on the course of proceedings,
although his or her role is more muted than that of a trial judge sitting alone: see above,
para.2–073, n.608.

[611] There have been a number of studies of the House of Lords: L. Blom-Cooper and G. Drewry,
Final Appeal (1972); R. Stevens, *Law and Politics* (1979); A. Paterson, *The Law Lords* (1982);
D. Robertson, *Judicial Discretion in the House of Lords* (1998); P. Carmichael and B. Dickson,
The House of Lords: Its Parliamentary and Judicial Roles (1999); M. Barrett, *The Law Lords*
(2001). The nature of the judicial function is analysed in J. Bell, *Policy Arguments in Judicial
Decisions* (1983).

[612] See Paterson (1982), pp.122–127.

[613] *Commentaries*, Vol.1, pp.69–70.

according to his private sentiments: he being sworn to determine, not according to his own private judgment, but according to the known laws and customs of the land: not delegated to pronounce a new law, but to maintain and expound the old one. Yet this rule admits of exception, where the former determination is most evidently contrary to reason; much more if it be clearly contrary to divine law. But even in such cases the subsequent judges do not pretend to make a new law, but to vindicate the old one from misrepresentation. For if it be found that the former decision is manifestly absurd or unjust, it is declared not that such a sentence was *bad law*, but that it was *not law*, that is, not the established custom of the realm, as has been erroneously determined."

Thus the role of the judge is to declare what the law is, not to make it. This theory was not easy to square with the unconcealed law-making activities of particular judges such as Lord Mansfield,[614] and was abused by writers such as Bentham.[615] Nevertheless, judges in the nineteenth and early twentieth centuries generally maintained (with increasing enthusiasm) the position that their function was not to make law and, indeed, that they were not concerned with the policy implications of their rulings.[616] However, this view was held less strongly in the House of Lords than in the lower courts, some of the Law Lords, with equity or Scottish backgrounds, being more concerned with principles than precedent and more likely to advert to the likely consequences of their decisions.

After 1912, the Law Lords, who tended now to be chosen from the professional judiciary, with less regard for political affiliation:

"exhibited an increasing tendency to articulate a declaratory theory of law and to insist that the judicial function, even in the final appeal court, was primarily the formalistic or mechanical one of restating existing doctrines."[617]

At the same time there were still some judges, such as Lord Atkin and Lord Wright, who were prepared to develop private law doctrines significantly while maintaining the facade of the declaratory theory. However, there followed what Stevens terms the "era of substantive formalism" in the House of Lords:

"For the 1940s and for much of the 1950s there were no obvious signs that the Law Lords had developed rules out of broader principles of the common law or the liberal state. Indeed, there was virtually no acceptance of an element of discretion, let alone a utilitarian balancing of interests. The

---

[614] Chief Justice the King's Bench, 1756–1788. See C. H. S. Fifoot, *Lord Mansfield* (1936).

[615] *A Comment on the Commentaries* (ed. J. H. Burns and H. L. A. Hart, 1977), pp.192–206. Bentham's objections were based in part on his opposition to theories of "natural law". Moreover, he disapproved of law-making by judges, taking the view that this was a matter for Parliament.

[616] See e.g. B. Parke in *Egerton v Brownlow* (1853) 4 H.L.C. 1, 124: "It is the province of the statesman, and not the lawyer, to discuss, and of the legislature to determine, what is the best for the public good, and to provide for it by proper enactments. It is the province of the judge to expound the law only; the written from the statutes: the unwritten or common law from the decisions of our predecessors and of our existing courts, from text-writers of acknowledged authority, and upon the principles to be clearly deduced from them by sound reason and just inference; not to speculate upon what is the best, in his opinion, for the advantage of the community."

[617] Stevens (1979), p.196.

process, at best fell into Karl Llewellyn's category of judicial formalism, with opinions written 'in deductive form with an air of expression of single-line inevitability.'[618] At worst, the process was a restatement of the declaratory theory in such extreme form that it denied any purpose for a second appeal court. Legal rationality became an end in itself. The literal meaning of words was to be the only criterion of statutory interpretation."[619]

Deference to the executive in public law cases was to be expected in wartime: strong judicial challenges to the Labour government elected in 1945 with a large majority would obviously have been unwise. This approach was associated particularly with Lord Jowitt, the Labour Lord Chancellor, and Lord Simonds, a Law Lord between 1944 and 1962, apart from his period as Lord Chancellor from 1951 to 1954. A few judges stood out against this approach, notably Lord Denning,[620] but to little avail. The only developments could come with the application of established principles to novel factual situations.

Since the mid-1950s the position has changed. It has become generally accepted by the Law Lords that they may properly exercise a limited law-making function.[621] Lord Radcliffe argued that it was best if judges went about this task "on the quiet"[622]:

> "Would anyone now deny that judicial decisions are a creative, not merely an expository, contribution to the law? There are no means by which they can be otherwise, so rare is the occasion upon which a decision does not involve choice between two admissible alternatives. . . . We cannot run the risk of finding the archetypal image of the judge confused in men's minds with the very different image of the legislator. . . . [T]he image of the judge, objective, impartial, erudite and experienced declarer of the law that is, lies deeper in the consciousness of civilisation than the image of the lawmaker, propounding what are avowedly new rules of human conduct. . . . Personally, I think that judges will serve the public interest better if they keep quiet about their legislative function. No doubt they will discreetly contribute to changes in the law, because . . . they cannot do otherwise, even if they would. The judge who shows his hand, who advertises what he is about, may indeed show that he is a strong spirit, unfettered by the past; but I doubt very much whether he is not doing more harm to general confidence in the law as a constant, safe in the hands of the judges than he is doing to the law's credit as a set of rules nicely attuned to the sentiments of the day."[623]

The dominant influence in the House of Lords in this period was Lord Reid. In his well-known address entitled "The Judge as Law Maker" he swiftly disposed of the declaratory theory:

---

[618] Karl Llewellyn, *The Common Law Tradition* (1960), p.38.

[619] Stevens (1979), pp.319–320.

[620] See below.

[621] See generally A. Paterson, *The Law Lords* (1982).

[622] See Lord Radcliffe, *Not in Feather Beds* (1968), pp.265–277. Professor Atiyah has argued that most of the judges "would prefer to shelter behind the declaratory theory in public, and to confine discussion of the nature and use of the creative judicial function amongst the *cognoscenti*" (1980) 15 Israel L.R. 346, 360.

[623] Radcliffe (1968), pp.271–272, 273.

"We do not believe in fairy tales any more. So we must accept the fact that for better or worse judges do make law, and tackle the question how do they approach their task and how they should approach it."[624]

Where public opinion was sharply divided, whether or not on party lines, no judge should lean to one side or the other if it can be avoided; if it cannot:

" . . . we must play safe [and] decide the case on the preponderance of existing authority. Parliament is the right place to settle issues which the ordinary man regards as controversial."[625]

It was so improper for judges to disregard or innovate on settled law in areas **4–042** where people rely on the certainty of the law in settling their affairs, in particular in making contracts or settlements. A problem might be too complex for it to be appropriate for the judges to change some aspect of it: the only proper way forward would be for there to be legislation following a wide survey of the whole field.[626] Nevertheless, there was considerable scope for judges to mould the development of the common law, which should be done having regard to "common sense, legal principle and public policy in that order".[627] The judges did not have so free a hand when interpreting statutes as when dealing with the common law.

In the late 1950s and early 1960s there were some indications that the House of Lords was taking a freer attitude to precedents. These led to the Practice Statement in 1966 in which the Law Lords announced that they would no longer regard themselves as bound by their own previous decisions.[628] Since then, the criteria for exercising the power to overrule have been analysed in some detail. Lord Reid's views have been especially influential,[629] as they have on the wider issues concerning judicial law-making. Similarly, in the field of statutory interpretation the judges have shown a greater inclination to look at the context of the words in a statute and the statute's purpose, rather than to adopt a narrow literal approach.

Paterson shows that of the 19 Law Lords who were active between 1967 and 1973 at least 12 considered that the Law Lords had an obligation to develop the common law to meet changing social conditions. An even greater proportion of the sample of barristers interviewed by him shared this view, as did at least three of the six Law Lords appointed between 1973 and 1979.[630] Ten of 11 Law Lords interviewed accepted that they ought to be concerned with the possible social and

---

[624] (1972) 12 J.S.P.T.L. 22. For other important contributions to the debate see Diplock L.J., "The Courts as Legislators," in B. W. Harvey (ed.), *The Lawyer and Justice* (1978), p. 263; Lord Edmund-Davies, "Judicial Activism" (1975) 28 C.L.P. 1; Lord Devlin, *The Judge* (1981), Ch.1.

[625] (1972) 12 J.S.P.T.L. 22, 23.

[626] See *Myers v D.P.P.* [1965] A.C. 1001, 1022.

[627] (1972) 12 J.S.P.T.L. 22, 25.

[628] See A. Paterson, *The Law Lords* (1982), pp.143–153, and below, paras 7–026—7–028.

[629] See Paterson (1982), pp.153–169.

[630] Paterson (1982), pp.173–174. But note the view expressed by Lord Scarman in *McLoughlin v O'Brian* [1983] 1 A.C. 410, that where "principle" requires a decision which entails a degree of "policy risk", the court's function is to adjudicate according to "principle," leaving "policy curtailment" to Parliament. The policy issue as to where to draw the line in "nervous shock" cases is "not justiciable. The problem is one of social, economic and financial policy. The considerations relevant to a decision are not such as to be capable of being handled within the limits of the forensic process": pp.430–431. See, *contra*, Lord Edmund-Davies, pp.427–428.

legal consequences of their decisions, at least within the acknowledged limitations of the information available to them.[631] A majority of the Law Lords considered that there were cases coming to the Lords to which there was no single correct solution on the basis of existing legal rules and principles, and in which they had a measure of choice.[632]

In the same period, the Court of Appeal was dominated by Lord Denning M.R., who showed a greater preference for innovation than the Law Lords, albeit coupled with varying success in persuading colleagues in the Court of Appeal to agree with him.[633]

The approach of appellate judges varies according to the context. For example, continued importance has been attached by the House of Lords to the "certainty" factor in commercial and property cases, and, to a lesser extent, in criminal law cases. Here, the willingness of the House of Lords to set aside the common law rule that a man cannot be guilty of raping his wife[634] may be compared with their refusal to abolish the presumption that a child between 10 and 14 is *doli incapax*,[635] or to develop an additional qualified defence to murder to cover the case of the use of excessive force in self-defence or to prevent crime or effect an arrest, reducing the offence to one of manslaughter.[636] The former was seen as the removal of an anachronistic common law fiction, the status of women having changed out of all recognition since the rule was enunciated by Hale in the eighteenth century.[637] The latter points were much more controversial, the government having stated its intention to maintain the *doli incapax* presumption as recently as 1990,[638] and having consistently resisted proposals to change the scope of the law of murder or the mandatory life sentence for that offence.[639] By contrast, there was in the 1970s and early 1980s a marked extension of liability in such aspects of the tort of negligence as negligent mis-statement,[640] omissions,[641] nervous shock,[642] economic loss,[643] and injury to trespassers,[644]

---

[631] Paterson (1982), pp.177–178.

[632] *ibid.* pp.192–195. This runs counter to the theory developed by R. M. Dworkin that there is a right answer in all hard cases and that the judges have no discretion to make law: *Taking Rights Seriously* (1977); "No Right Answer" in P. Hacker and J. Raz (eds), *Law, Morality and Society* (1977); J. W. Harris, *Legal Philosophies* (1980), Ch.14; Bell (1983), Ch.VIII.

[633] See Stevens (1979), pp.488–505; Lord Denning, *The Discipline of Law* (1979), Pts 1 and 7.

[634] *R v R (Rape: Marital Exemption)* [1992] 1 A.C. 599. See M. Giles, [1992] Crim. L.R. 407. This decision was challenged before the European Court of Human Rights on the ground that the law was changed retrospectively, contrary to Art.7, ECHR. However, the court ruled that there was no violation as it was reasonably foreseeable by the applicant that a court might embark on the legitimate adaptation of the ingredients of the crime: *CR and SW v UK* (1995) 21 E.H.R.R. 363.

[635] *C (A minor) v D.P.P.* [1995] 2 W.L.R. 383. The presumption prevents a child being convicted of a criminal offence in the absence of clear positive evidence that the child knew that his or her act was seriously wrong, evidence of the acts amounting to the offences alone being insufficient.

[636] *R v Clegg* [1995] 1 A.C. 482.

[637] [1992] 1 A.C. 599, 616, *per* Lord Keith.

[638] White Paper, *Crime, Justice and Protecting the Public* (Cm. 965, 1990), para.8.4.

[639] See e.g. H.L. Select Committee Report on Murder and Life Imprisonment (1988–89 H.L. 78); Lord Windlesham, [1993] Crim. L.R. 644. See also A. T. H. Smith, "Judicial law-making in the criminal law" (1984) 100 L.Q.R. 46 on the supposed distinction between creating new offences (which is clearly objectionable) and extending existing offences to cover new situations.

[640] *Hedley Byrne & Co v Heller & Partners* [1964] A.C. 465.

[641] *Home Office v Dorset Yacht Co* [1970] A.C. 1004; *Anns v London Borough of Merton* [1978] A.C. 728.

[642] *McLoughlin v O'Brian* [1983] 1 A.C. 410.

[643] *Junior Books Ltd v Veitchi Co Ltd* [1983] 1 A.C. 520.

[644] *British Railways Board v Herrington* [1972] A.C. 877.

although in some of these areas, most notably economic loss, the extension of liability has been followed by retrenchment.[645] The House of Lords has now expressed a preference for developments in the scope of the tort of negligence to be incremental, by analogy with existing cases, rather than by reference to broadly expressed principles.[646] Similarly, in *Cambridge Water Co Ltd v Eastern Counties Leather plc*[647] the House declined to develop a general principle of strict liability for extra-hazardous activities, preferring instead to modify the elements of the *Rylands v Fletcher*[648] tort.[649] In public law, there has been a whole series of cases in which the courts have analysed, refined and sometimes extended the grounds upon which administrative and judicial decisions of government institutions can be challenged under the *ultra vires* doctrine.[650] In many of these, the challenges have been successful.[651] Recent high profile cases have seen the House of Lords hold that ministers of the Crown are subject to the law of contempt of court,[652] and that the government's revised criminal injuries compensation scheme was unlawful.[653] The Divisional Court found that the government allocation of aid to the Pergau Dam project in Malaysia was also unlawful.[654] Other high profile cases have been determined under the Human Rights Act 1998.[655] In others, the judges have shown restraint in circumstances where it was not obvious why restraint was any more appropriate.[656]

It is also interesting to contrast the willingness of Sir Robert Megarry V.-C. to extend the field of liability in negligence for economic loss[657] with his unwillingness to create an "altogether new right" in a case where it was claimed that there was a right to hold a telephone conversation in the privacy of one's home without molestation[658]:

---

[645] See, e.g. *Leigh and Sillavan Ltd v Aliakmon Shipping Co Ltd* [1986] A.C. 785; *Yuen Kun Yeu v Att.-Gen. of Hong Kong* [1988] A.C. 175; *D. & F. Estates Ltd v Church Commissioners for England* [1989] A.C. 177; *Murphy v Brentwood District Council* [1991] 1 A.C. 398 (over-ruling *Anns*).

[646] e.g. Lord Bridge in *Caparo Industries plc v Dickman* [1990] 2 A.C. 605, 617–618.

[647] [1994] 2 A.C. 264.

[648] (1868) L.R. 3 H.L. 330.

[649] Adding the requirement that the damage be foreseeable; making it easier for the plaintiff to establish that the defendant's user of land was "non-natural".

[650] For general surveys, see A. Lester Q.C., "English judges as law makers" [1993] P.L. 269 and Lord Woolf, "Droit Public—English Style" [1995] P.L. 57.

[651] e.g. *Ridge v Baldwin* [1964] A.C. 40 (dismissal of a chief constable held void for breach of natural justice); *Anisminic Ltd v Foreign Compensation Commission* [1969] 2 A.C. 147 (decision of the Commission struck down for misinterpretation of the relevant legislation notwithstanding a statutory clause purporting to exclude judicial review); *Padfield v Minister of Agriculture* [1968] A.C. 997 and *Laker Airways v Department of Trade* [1977] Q.B. 643 (ministerial decisions held to be abuses of discretion); *Bromley London Borough Council v Greater London Council* [1983] 1 A.C. 768 (substantial cuts in fares held to be *ultra vires*).

[652] *M v Home Office* [1994] 1 A.C. 377.

[653] *R v Secretary of State for the Home Department, Ex p. The Fire Brigades Union* [1995] 2 A.C. 513.

[654] *R v Secretary of State for Foreign and Commonwealth Affairs, Ex p. World Development Movement Ltd* [1995] 1 W.L.R. 386.

[655] See Ch.8.

[656] *R v Secretary of State for the Department, Ex p. Zamir* [1980] A.C. 930 (but cf. *R v Secretary of State for the Home Department, Ex p. Khawaja* [1984] A.C. 74); *Bushell v Secretary of State for the Environment* [1981] A.C. 75; *R v Secretary of State for the Home Department, Ex p. Brind* [1991] A.C. 696 (declining to hold that the doctrine of proportionality constituted an independent ground of challenge in English administrative law).

[657] *Ross v Caunters* [1980] Ch. 297.

[658] *Malone v Metropolitan Police Commissioner (No.2)* [1979] Ch. 344.

"No new right in the law, fully-fledged with all the appropriate safeguards, can spring from the head of a judge deciding a particular case: only Parliament can create such a right . . . The wider and more indefinite the right claimed, the greater the undesirability of holding that such a right exists."[659]

4–043   There are some apparently formidable arguments in favour of judicial restraint in law-making. The making of new law through the legislative process[660] rather than judicially is often said to be more in accordance with democratic theory[661] and is more likely to be based on a proper examination of all the relevant information. English civil procedure generally prevents anyone but the parties to litigation giving evidence[662] and enables the parties to choose what evidence to present. Moreover, there are difficulties in presenting *evidence* as distinct from *argument* about the possible social and economic implications of decisions. Conspicuous creativity in judicial law making is difficult to square with the "ostentatious impartiality" that is also regarded as desirable.[663] The judges have no written constitution to look to as a source of power.[664]

A more pragmatic reason sometimes advanced in favour of restraint is that:

"if people and Parliament come to think that the judicial power is to be confined by nothing other than the judge's sense of what is right (or, as Selden put it, by the length of the Chancellor's foot), confidence in the judicial system will be replaced by fear of it becoming uncertain and arbitrary in its application. Society will then be ready for Parliament to cut the power of the judges. Their power to do justice will become more restricted by law than it need be, or is today."[665]

---

[659] *ibid.* pp.372, 373. Compare also the extension of police powers of seizure by the Court of Appeal in *Chic Fashions Ltd v Jones* [1968] 2 Q.B. 299 and *Ghani v Jones* [1970] 1 Q.B. 693 with the refusal of the court to create a new common law power of search: *McLorie v Oxford* [1982] Q.B. 1290.

[660] See Ch.5.

[661] But see Atiyah, (1980) 15 Israel L.R. 362–365.

[662] The rules could, of course, be changed. By contrast, in the United States interest groups are much more able to institute litigation, or to present arguments in cases involving other parties.

[663] See above, para.4–034.

[664] Although here it should be noted that the power of judicial review exercised by the Supreme Court in the United States is not expressly created by the Constitution, but is itself judge-made: see *Marbury v Madison* (1803) 1 Cranch 137. Furthermore, a number of judges have expressed the view extra-judicially that in certain circumstances the courts might decline to give effect to statutes that violate fundamental constitutional principles: Lord Woolf, "*Droit Public*—English style" [1995] P.L. 57 (legislation removing or substantially impairing the High Court's powers of judicial review); Sedley J., "Human Rights: a Twenty-first century Agenda" [1995] P.L. 386, 391 ("obligation of the courts to articulate and uphold the ground rules of ethical social existence which we dignify as fundamental human rights"); Laws J., "Law and Democracy" [1995] P.L. 72 (protection of fundamental freedoms); Lord Steyn in *Att.-Gen. v Jackson* (para.5–023). These suggestions have been criticised as contrary to principle by Lord Irvine of Lairg Q.C., "Judges and decision-makers: the theory and practice of *Wednesbury* review" [1996] P.L. 59 and by J. A. G. Griffith, "Judges and the Constitution" in R. Rawlings (ed.), *Law, Society and Economy* (1997), Ch.13 ("I believe this kind of language lifts our feet off the ground and endangers more than our sense of balance": p.308) and (2000) 63 M.L.R. 159. The extent to which the judges' powers of judicial review in England and Wales are a self-standing common law creation has been the subject of extended academic debate: see C. Forsyth (ed.), *Judicial Review and the Constitution* (2000); M. Elliott, *The Constitutional Foundations of Judicial Review* (2001); A. Halpin, *Reasoning with Law* (2001), Ch.4.

[665] *per* Lord Scarman in *Duport Steels Ltd v Sirs* [1980] 1 All E.R. 529, 551. When Roger Parker Q.C. made a similar prediction in his submissions to the Court of Appeal in *Congreve v Home*

Nevertheless, restraint is not the same as complete withdrawal from the field. **4–044**
"Law reform" does not rank high in the list of priorities in the struggle for a
place in the legislative timetable: if one always waited for Parliament, one would
often wait in vain.

In his book, *The Politics of the Judiciary*[666] Professor Griffith argues that the
discussion about how creative judges should be:

> "has been and is a somewhat unreal discussion . . . What is lacking . . . is
> any clear and consistent relationship between the general pronouncements
> of judges on this matter of creativity and the way they conduct themselves
> in court."[667]

Moreover, the appellate judges:

> "have by their education and training and the pursuit of their profession as
> barristers, acquired a strikingly homogeneous collection of attitudes, beliefs
> and principles, which to them represents the public interest. . . . The judicial
> conception of the public interest . . . is three-fold. It concerns firstly, the
> interests of the State; secondly, the preservation of law and order broadly
> interpreted; and, thirdly, the judges' views on social and political issues of
> the day."[668]

They are thus concerned to preserve and protect the existing order, to serve the
prevailing political and economic forces, this being generally true of all societies
today, whether capitalistic or communist. This is not regarded by Griffith as a
matter for recrimination: his main concern is simply to dispel the myth that the
judges are "neutral".

In relation to Griffith's view that the appellate judges have acquired a homoge-
nous collection of attitudes, Lord Devlin commented[669]:

> "Since he is writing of men in their sixties and seventies whose working life
> has given them a common outlook on many questions, by no means all
> political, I have very little doubt that he is right. I have very little doubt
> either that the same might be written of most English institutions, certainly
> of all those which like the law are not of a nature to attract the crusading or
> rebellious spirit."

Office [1976] Q.B. 629, Lord Denning M.R. stated "We trust that this was not said seriously, but
only as a piece of advocate's licence." Mr Parker subsequently apologised if anything he said had
sounded like a threat. (See *The Times*, December 6 and 9, 1975.)

[666] (5th edn, 1997). For similar studies of particular areas see J. I. Reynolds, "Statutory Covenant of
Fitness and Repair" (1974) 37 M.L.R. 377 (and the rejoinder by M. J. Robinson, (1976) 39
M.L.R. 43); J. Hackney, "The Politics of the Chancery" (1981) 34 C.L.P. 113.

[667] pp.283, 284. Paterson, *The Law Lords* (1982), pp.187–189, argues that the Law Lords have been
more consistent than Griffith suggests.

[668] *ibid.* pp.295, 297. Previous editions included a reference to "the protection of property rights,"
and the third aspect of the public interest as "the promotion of certain political views normally
associated with the Conservative party". The change in wording seems to reflect in part the
disapproval by the judges of a number of policies of the Conservative government: see Griffith
(1997) pp.328–329. By 2002, it might also reflect the uncertainty as to what the views of the
Conservative party are, and the extent to which they are different from those of the Labour
government.

[669] (1978) 41 M.L.R. 501, 505–506.

However, he suggested that whether one agrees that the application of the law has been distorted depended on whether one:

> "looks at them from right or from the left . . . To my mind none of the evidence, general or specific adds much to the inherent probability that men and women of a certain age will be inclined to favour the *status quo*."[670]

He, and others, have, for instance, pointed out that in many of the cases discussed by Griffith there has been a division of opinion both between the Court of Appeal and the House of Lords, and within each court.[671]

Griffith does not suggest that anything can be done to change judicial attitudes. Lord Devlin notes that for a known bias allowance can be made:

> "[W]here novel measures are imposed by a minister or by parliament, they must be expressed in language which is emphatic enough and clear enough to penetrate the bias against them of those who are set in their ways: it is no use praying for the rejuvenation of the elderly."[672]

What these contributions to the debate do seem to suggest is that caution should be used in contemplating any dramatic extension of the powers of the judiciary, such as by the creation of a Bill of Rights on the American pattern with entrenched guarantees of civil liberties, expressed in general language, which override both legislation and administrative action. Moreover, one can be a little sceptical about claims such as those of Lord Denning[673]:

> "May not the Judges themselves sometimes abuse or misuse their power? It is their duty to administer and apply the law of the land. If they should divert it or depart from it—and do so knowingly—they themselves would be guilty of a misuse of power. So we come up against Juvenal's question, '*Sed quis custodiet ipsos custodes?*' (But who is to guard the guards themselves?) . . . Suppose a future Prime Minister should seek to pack the Bench with judges of his own extreme political colour. Would they be tools in his hand? To that I answer 'No'. Every judge on his appointment discards all politics and all prejudices. You need have no fear. The Judges of England have always in the past—and always will be vigilant in guarding our freedoms. Someone must be trusted. Let it be the Judges."

On the other hand, the adoption of a "strongly liberal viewpoint" has been identified in recent public law cases in the House of Lords and the Privy Council,[674] which does provide some corroboration for Lord Denning's view.

---

[670] *ibid.* pp.507, 509.
[671] B. Roshier and H. Teff, *Law in Society* (1980), p.67.
[672] (1978) 41 M.L.R. 501, 511.
[673] *Misuse of Power (The Richard Dimbleby Lecture 1980)*, pp.18–19. Reprinted in *What Next in the Law?* (1982).
[674] R. Gordon, "The awakened conscience of the nation," *Counsel*, March/April 1994, p.8, citing the decisions in *Pepper v Hart* (below, paras 6–037—6–041); *R v Secretary of State for the Home Department, Ex p. Doody* [1994] 1 A.C. 531 (developing the obligations of public law decision-makers to give reasons for their decisions); *M v Home Office* [1994] 1 A.C. 377 (holding that ministers may be subject to injunctions and the law of contempt); *Pratt and Morgan v Attorney-General of Jamaica* [1994] 2 A.C. 1 (holding that delay in carrying out an execution could amount to a breach of constitutional rights); and *R v Secretary of State for Employment, Ex p. Equal Opportunities Commission* (below, para.5–057).

Furthermore, both the development of a common law principle of legality[675] and the new decision-making powers and duties arising from implementation of the Human Rights Act 1998[676] are explicitly founded on the furtherance of funda-mental principles that underlie liberal democracies. These developments, coupled with the powers of the judges derived from the European Communities Act 1972,[677] have undoubtedly constituted a step change in the role of the judiciary in England and Wales. Correspondingly, interest in and concern about their decision-making has never been greater.

---

[675] See below, para.6–043.
[676] See Ch.8.
[677] See Chs 5, 6.

CHAPTER 5

LEGISLATION

A. INTRODUCTION[1]

In medieval England there was no clear distinction between legislation and other **5–001** forms of governmental action, and there was no settled procedure for enactment that had to be followed. The terminology was confusing: well-known early statutes include the "Constitutions" of Clarendon 1164, the "Great Charter" 1215, the "Statute" of Merton 1235 and the "Provisions" of Oxford 1258:

> "A statute in the region of Edward I simply means something established by royal authority; whether it is established by the King in Council, or in a Parliament of nobles, or in a Parliament of nobles and commons as well is completely immaterial."[2]

By the fifteenth century the consent of the Commons to a statute was regarded as necessary and in early Tudor times the procedure for enactment took on something like its modern form:

> "Legislation . . . was no longer the Government's vague reply to vaguely worded complaints, but rather the deliberate adoption of specific proposals embodied in specific texts emanating from the Crown or its officers."[3]

In the seventeenth century, Coke wrote that "There is no Act of Parliament but must have the consent of the Lords, the Commons and the Royal assent of the King".[4] The constitutional struggles of that century saw the end of serious attempts by the Crown to assert a legislative competence rivalling that of Parliament.[5] In the *Case of Proclamations*[6] the judges resolved that "the King by his proclamation cannot create any offence which was not an offence before" and "that the King hath no prerogative, but that which the law of the land allows

---

[1] See generally on legislation, D. R. Miers and A. C. Page, *Legislation* (2nd edn, 1990); F. A. R. Bennion, *Statute Law* (3rd edn, 1990) and *Statutory Interpretation* (4th edn, 2002); and D. Greenberg, *Craies on Legislation* (8th edn, 2004). On the history of legislation see J. H. Baker, *Introduction to Legal History* (4th edn, 2002), pp.204–212; C. K. Allen, *Law in the Making* (7th edn, 1964), pp.435–469.

[2] T. F. T. Plucknett, *Concise History of the Common Law* (5th edn, 1956), p.322.

[3] Plucknett, (1944) 60 L.Q.R. 242, 248.

[4] 4 Coke's *Institutes of the Laws of England*, p.25.

[5] See S. A. de Smith and R. Brazier, *Constitutional and Administrative Law* (8th edn, 1998), pp.73–75.

[6] (1611) 12 Co. Rep. 74.

him". However, the courts subsequently upheld the Crown's claim to a power to impose taxation incidentally to the exercise of prerogative powers such as those to conduct foreign affairs, regulate trade and take emergency measures for the defence of the realm,[7] and a power to "dispense" with the operation of a statute for the benefit of an individual.[8] James II also claimed the power to "suspend" the general operation of statutes, his target being statutes that discriminated against Dissenters and Roman Catholics. The reassertion of such claims to prerogative power after the Civil War and the Restoration led to the "Glorious Revolution" of 1688 and the Bill of Rights. The latter measure, declared to be a statute by the Crown and Parliament Recognition Act 1689, provided (*inter alia*):

> "That the pretended power of suspending of laws or the execution of laws by regall authority without consent of Parlyament is illegal ... That the pretended power of dispensing with laws or the execution of laws by regall authorities as it hath been assumed and exercised of late is illegal ...
>
> That levying money for or to the use of the Crowne by pretence of prerogative without grant of Parlyament for longer time or in other manner than the same is or shall be granted is illegal."

The prerogative powers of the Crown were in general restricted, and not abolished, but it was now clear that they could be modified or extinguished according to Parliament's wishes. Other possible rivals have also been unable to maintain any challenge to the dominance of Parliament. The Reformation Parliament established legislative supremacy over the Church.[9] In more recent times, the courts have refused to accept that a resolution of the House of Commons may alter the law of the land.[10]

Certain periods of our history have been noted for increases in legislative activity, and complaints of the difficulty of keeping abreast of the changes. Parliament passed 677 statutes in the reign of Henry VIII and these occupied almost as much space as the whole statute book had done in 1509.[11] Between 1711 and 1811 the annual number of Acts passed increased from 74 to 423. The bulk of the increase was in the number of local and private Acts. The 1811 figures included one for change of name, two for divorce, six for the settlement of private estates, 33 for inclosure and about 150 concerning local matters such as turnpike roads, canals and bridges.[12] The most dramatic increase in legislative activity has, however, been the product of the vast expansion of the activities of the state since the nineteenth century, and associated factors such as the extensive reforms in the civil service and the administrative machinery, the increasingly representative nature of Parliament, the development of political parties and the strengthening of the role of the Cabinet. The balance as regards Acts of Parliament has also shifted from private legislation to public general legislation.[13]

---

[7] *Case of Impositions: Bate's Case* (1606) 2 St. Tr. 371; *Case of Ship Money: R v Hampden* (1637) 3 St. Tr. 825.

[8] *Thomas v Sorell* (1674) Vaughan 330; *Godden v Hales* (1686) 11 St. Tr. 1165.

[9] J. H. Baker, *The Reports of Sir John Spelman Vol. II*, Introduction (1978), pp.64–70.

[10] See *Stockdale v Hansard* (1839) 9 A. & E. 1, where the Court of Queen's Bench held that the scope of Parliamentary privilege could not be extended by a resolution; *Bowles v Bank of England* [1913] 1 Ch. 57.

[11] See Baker, *op. cit.* n.9, at pp.43–46.

[12] S. Lambert, *Bills and Acts* (1971), p.52.

[13] See below, para.5–003.

Having established its legislative supremacy, Parliament was reluctant to delegate its powers.[14] In the eighteenth century, public general Acts tended "to be either overloaded with detail or to be directed to specific instances rather than to general rules".[15] However, some law-making powers had from the time of Henry VIII been entrusted to institutions such as the Commissioners of Sewers and the Justices of the Peace, and new powers were from time to time delegated by Parliament. In the eighteenth century, for example, extensive powers were granted to the Commissioners of Customs and Excise, and the Crown was given almost exclusive disciplinary powers over the Army. The following century saw a significant increase of social legislation, and a related extension of powers delegated to local and central government, but the real explosion of delegated legislation has been in the twentieth and twenty-first centuries.[16] In addition the accession of the United Kingdom to the European Communities has meant that a large body of Community legislation has become applicable in this country. A more recent development has been the introduction, in different forms, of devolution for Scotland and Wales, with the establishment of the Scottish Parliament and the National Assembly for Wales. The former institution in particular has had significant new legislative powers conferred upon it, although the powers of the latter are to be extended by the Government of Wales Act 2006. We consider in turn the various forms of legislation: Acts of Parliament, subordinate or delegated legislation and European legislation.

B. ACTS OF PARLIAMENT

1. PARLIAMENTARY SOVEREIGNTY

One of the distinctive features of the constitution of the United Kingdom is the doctrine of Parliamentary sovereignty.[17] A measure which has received the assent of the Queen, Lords and Commons, that assent being given separately and in the two Houses of Parliament by simple majorities, is accepted to have the force of law as an Act of Parliament. Its validity cannot be questioned in the courts and any earlier inconsistent legislation is repealed. Parliament (strictly the "Queen in Parliament") may pass any kind of law without restriction, except that an attempt to bind its successors either as to the content of legislation or the manner and form of its enactment cannot succeed. Acts of Parliament, thus defined, are the

5–002

---

[14] C. K. Allen, *Law and Orders* (3rd edn, 1965), Ch.2.

[15] *ibid.* p.28.

[16] In 2004 there were 38 Public General Statutes (3,470 pages: 0 General Synod measures; six local Acts). In the same year there were 3,459 statutory instruments (10,236 pages of those printed).

[17] See S. A. de Smith and R. Brazier *Constitutional and Administrative Law* (8th edn, 1998), Ch.4; A. W. Bradley and K. D. Ewing, *Constitutional and Administrative Law* (14th edn, 2007), Ch.4; Sir William Wade, *Constitutional Fundamentals* (2nd edn, 1989), Ch.3; C. R. Munro, *Studies in Constitutional Law* (2nd edn, 1999), Ch.5.

supreme form of law; the rule of judicial obedience to them is the "ultimate *political* fact upon which the whole system of legislation hangs".[18]

The definition of "Parliament" can be altered, but the process by which that can be achieved is political rather than legal. For example, there is no reason why the British people should not be able to adopt a written constitution, perhaps incorporating a Bill of Rights, which limits the powers of both government and legislature. What is unclear is how this would be done. The people of the United States did so in 1787–88 by means of a Constitutional Convention whose proposals were ratified by specially elected state conventions; the American "Bill of Rights" was added subsequently as a series of constitutional amendments. In the UK, the judges would have to be satisfied that such a change was generally accepted; a constituent assembly might provide sufficient evidence. They would look to the realities of the situation, as they did at the commencement and conclusion of the Interregnum in the seventeenth century, when they adjusted first to the absence and then to the restoration of the monarchy.

The foregoing represents the orthodox view of Parliamentary sovereignty. It has of course been argued that the definition of "Parliament" is a matter of law rather than politics, and that as such it can be altered by the existing legislative process. Parliament as at present defined could then bind its successors as to the manner and form of legislation by redefining itself either generally or for specific purposes.[19] This view, however, has had more academic support than judicial. The constitutional adviser to the House of Lords Select Committee on a Bill of Rights clearly preferred the orthodox view,[20] and this seemed to be accepted by the Committee. Moreover, the "new view" suffers from the weakness that it would enable a redefinition of "Parliament" to be effected too easily; in effect by a small partisan majority in the House of Commons.[21] For the present, Coke's definition of an Act of Parliament holds good.

This remains so notwithstanding the enactment and implementation of the Human Rights Act 1998 incorporating the European Convention of Human Rights into English law. In the case of primary legislation incompatible with Convention rights, or incompatible secondary legislation where (disregarding the possibility of revocation) primary legislation prevents removal of the incompatibility, the superior courts have powers only to make a declaration of incompatibility, and the continuing validity of the provision in question is unaffected.[22] One important qualification is, however, that at least while the European Communities Act 1972 is on the statute book the judges are prepared to recognise the primacy of European Community law over inconsistent statutes. The status of an Act of Parliament passed with the intention of overriding Community law but without repealing the 1972 Act has not, however, been tested.[23] This point has been developed and broadened by the Divisional Court in *Thoburn v Sunderland City Council*[24] in the course of holding that regulations made under s.2(2) of the

---

[18] H. W. R. Wade, [1955] C.L.J. 172, 188.

[19] See R. F. V. Heuston, *Essays in Constitutional Law* (2nd edn, 1964), Ch.1.

[20] Evidence, 1977–78 H.L. 276, pp.1–10 (D. Rippengal); Report: 1977–78 H.L. 176.

[21] Given that the House of Lords can be by-passed and that the Royal Assent by convention cannot be withheld (see below para.5–009).

[22] See below, Ch.8.

[23] See para.5–054.

[24] [2002] EWHC 195 (Admin), [2003] Q.B. 151. The "Metric Martyrs" case. See D. Campbell and J. Young, [2002] P.L.G. 399g. Marshall, (2002) 118 L.Q.R. 493. The campaign continues: *www.metricmartyrs.co.uk*.

European Communities Act 1972[25] could lawfully amend the Weights and Measures Act 1985 so as to secure a compulsory system of metric weights and measures. One point was whether the 1985 Act had impliedly repealed or restricted the scope of s.2(2). The court held that it had not. It rejected an argument[26] that the principle of EU law that EU law prevails over inconsistent laws of Member States[27] had been incorporated into English law by virtue of ss.2(1), (4) and 3(1) of the 1972 Act,[28] and that accordingly Parliament could no longer legislate contrary to EU law without withdrawing from the EU by express repeal of the 1972 Act. This argument was false as it failed to take account of the "constitutional place in our law of the rule that Parliament cannot bind its successors".[29] This rule was inconsistent with any assumption that the incorporation of EU law by the 1972 Act extended beyond laws on substantive matters to include any rule of EU law "which purports to touch the constitutional preconditions upon which the sovereign legislative power belonging to a Member State may be exercised."[30] The traditional view of sovereignty was strongly affirmed:

> "Parliament cannot bind its successors by stipulating against repeal, wholly or partly, of the European Communities Act 1972. It cannot stipulate against implied repeal any more than it can stipulate against express repeal. . . . The British Parliament has not the authority to authorise any such thing. Being sovereign, it cannot abandon its sovereignty."[31]

However, the court went on to hold that what Parliament could not do, the common law both could do and had done:

> "The common law has in recent years allowed, or rather created, exceptions to the doctrine of implied repeal: a doctrine which was always the common law's own creation. There are now classes or types of legislative provision which cannot be repealed by mere implication. These instances are given and can only be given, by our own courts, to which the scope and nature of Parliamentary sovereignty are ultimately confided."[32]

Accordingly, it was necessary to recognise a hierarchy of Acts of Parliament, "ordinary" and "constitutional", the latter being immune from implied repeal:

> "In my opinion a constitutional statute is one which (a) conditions the legal relationship between citizen and State in some general overarching manner, or (b) enlarges or diminishes the scope of what we would now regard as fundamental constitutional rights."[33]

---

[25] Below, paras 5–054—5–059.
[26] For others, see below, para.5–021.
[27] Below, para.5–054.
[28] Below, ibid.
[29] [2002] EWHC 195 (Admin), [2003] Q.B. 151, per Laws L.J. at para.[58].
[30] ibid.
[31] ibid.
[32] ibid., para.[60].
[33] ibid., para.[62]. Cf. the principle of legality, below, para.6–043.

Examples would be Magna Carta, the Bill of Rights 1689, the Acts of Union, the Reform Acts which distributed and enlarged the franchise, the Human Rights Act 1998, the Scotland Act 1998 and the Government of Wales Act 1998. Another was the European Communities Act 1972 which is "by force of the common law, a constitutional statute".[34] Repeal of such provisions could only be effected where it was clear that was the legislature's *actual* intention, and that would need "express words in the later statute" or "words so specific that the inference of an actual determination to effect the result contended for was irresistible". Repeal by implication, or by general words supplemented by a *Pepper v Hart* statement[35] would not be enough.[36] It remains to be seen whether this approach will be endorsed by the Court of Appeal and House of Lords in the future.[37] The case for it is very persuasively presented by Laws L.J. as providing an appropriate balance between the proper supremacy of EU law and the proper supremacy of the UK Parliament. It echoes Wade's "ultimate political fact" analysis by recognising an underpinning rule of the common law whose scope lies beyond the reach of Parliament and is purely to be determined by the judges. Respect for the democratic principle is preserved by the ability of the Parliament of today to legislate (by express words) as it wishes; such respect does not require, and is indeed inimical to, any possibility that the wishes of a Parliament of yesterday might have an overriding effect.

It should be noted that while the concept of "Parliamentary sovereignty" is a doctrine of great technical legal significance it should not be taken as a guide to the reality of the legislative process. First, there have always been external influences which have imposed practical restraints on the kinds of legislation which can be passed. Secondly, the legislative process is today dominated by the government and not by members of Parliament acting independently. Legislation is initiated and formulated outside Parliament, the functions of Parliament are limited to those of scrutiny and legitimisation, and governments normally enjoy a secure party majority. Thirdly, within "Parliament" the House of Commons is the dominant element.[38] Finally it must not be thought that legislation is the only method by which the government can secure its aims; much is achieved by, for example, exhortation, bargaining and the exercise of its economic power.[39]

2. PUBLIC AND PRIVATE ACTS

5–003 A distinction is drawn between public and private Acts. The former are those measures that are intended to alter the general law or deal with the public revenue

---

[34] *ibid.*

[35] Below, paras 6–037—6–041.

[36] *ibid.* para.[63].

[37] The House of Lords refused leave to appeal on July 15, 2002. In a different context, the House of Lords in *Watkins v Secretary of State for the Home Department* [2006] 2 A.C. 395 rejected the proposition that a wrongful and malicious act of a public officer that interfered with a constitutional right was actionable in tort without proof of special damage; one of the difficulties recognised was in identifying "constitutional" statutes.

[38] See below, paras 5–010—5–012.

[39] See J. J. Richardson and A. G. Jordan, *Governing under Pressure* (1979), Ch.6.

or the administration of justice.[40] The latter are of local[41] or personal[42] concern. The procedure for enactment differs in some respects[43]; a person who wishes to rely on a private Act in court must produce a Queen's Printer's copy or an examined or certified copy of the original whereas judicial notice is taken of public Acts[44]; and a private Act may be construed strictly against the interest of the promoter, although this approach is not always followed today.[45]

An important class of private legislation is that promoted by local authorities. Section 262 of the Local Government Act 1972 provided that all local legislation (with some exceptions, including protective provisions for the benefit of any person and provisions relating to a statutory undertaking), in force immediately before April 1974, would cease to have effect at the end of 1979 in metropolitan counties and at the end of 1984 elsewhere.[46] These dates were subsequently postponed by, respectively, one year and two years.[47] Local authorities wishing to preserve particular provisions were required to promote Bills to that end. Many authorities did so,[48] although the rationalisation process proved to be less straightforward and more expensive than had been anticipated.[49] Relatively few authorities now promote local Acts.[50]

---

[40] *Halsbury's Laws of England* (4th edn) Vol.34, para.729. For a useful analysis of the kinds of public Bills according to their content see I. Burton and G. Drewry, *Legislation and Public Policy* (1981), pp.32–45. The authors draw a broad distinction between innovatory "policy" Bills and non-innovatory "administration" Bills to remedy anomalies, with further sub- categories of "minor policy" Bills dealing with restricted issues within an area of public policy not otherwise intended to be changed, and "administrative reform" Bills which reorganise administrative support for an existing policy. Session-by-session surveys of legislation by Burton and Drewry have appeared in the journal *Parliamentary Affairs*. Details of the progress of Bills are set out with annual *House of Commons Sessional Information Digests* and on Parliament's website (*www.parliament.uk.*)

[41] Bills dealing with the constitution or election of local authorities or other public bodies must be introduced as public Bills: *Halsbury, ibid.*; below, para.5–013. See e.g. the London Government Act 1963; the Charlwood and Horley Act 1974.

[42] i.e. a "private bill relating to the estate, property, status or style, or otherwise relating to the personal affairs of an individual" (H.L. Standing Orders 151–174). These include Bills affecting estates, and Bills to authorise a marriage between persons within the prohibited degrees of affinity: in the case of the latter, the details are now considered by a Select Committee of the House of Lords, and not on the floor of the House: 2nd Report from the Select Committee on Procedure, 1985–86 H.L. 152, approved by the House (H.L. Deb. Vol.475, cols 709–711, June 3, 1986). Some of the prohibitions were relaxed by the Marriage (Prohibited Degrees of Relationship) Act 1986.

[43] See below, paras 5–010—5–013.

[44] The line between "public" and "private" Acts is drawn rather differently in this context: see *Halsbury's Laws of England* (4th edn) Vol.17 (Reissue), para.826. For this purpose an Act passed after 1850 is deemed to be a public Act and "to be judicially noticed as such unless the contrary is expressly provided by the Act": Interpretation Act 1978, s.3 and Sch.2, para.2. For the definition of "judicial notice" see above para.1–011, n.33.

[45] *Maxwell on Interpretation of Statutes* (12th edn, 1969), pp.262–3. See, e.g. *Allen v Gulf Oil Refining Ltd* [1981] A.C. 1001, HL.

[46] See D. Foulkes, [1976] P.L. 272; E. D. Graham, (1979) XLVII *The Table* 109; R. J. B. Morris, [1987] Stat. L.R. 2.

[47] SI 1979/969; SI 1983/619.

[48] An alternative approach, permitted in a few cases, was for the Secretary of State for the Environment to exercise the power conferred by s.262(9)(a) to exempt particular provisions from the general cesser: see SI 1986/1133; Morris, *op. cit.*, pp.26–27.

[49] Foulkes, *op. cit.*; Morris, *op. cit.*

[50] R. J. B. Morris, [1999] J.L.G.L. 122 (proposing that there should be annual Local Government (Local Provisions) Bills to enable councils to obtain legislative provisions without the need for individual local promotions).

Further work on the rationalisation of local legislation has continued under the auspices of Law Commission, leading to provisions in the series of Statute Law (Repeals) Acts.[51] Express repeal brings greater certainty than the generalised repeal effected by the Local Government Act 1972.

The scope and procedures for enactment of private legislation were considered by the Joint Committee on Private Bill Procedure in 1987–88.[52] The committee's recommendations were designed to reduce the range of private legislation by diverting matters that could be pursued by other, non-Parliamentary procedures and included recommendations on matters of detail and procedure. The outcome was the introduction by the Transport and Works Act 1992 of a new procedure for the Secretary of State to make orders in respect of such matters as rail, light rail and light rapid transit proposals and inland waterways and broadening the scope of orders in respect of harbours.[53] Orders in relation to proposals which in the Secretary of State's opinion are of national importance require the approval of both Houses of Parliament. Orders under the 1992 Act are delegated legislation and open to challenge in the courts.[54] In addition, there were some detailed changes to private Bill procedure, including the introduction of requirements as to environmental impact assessment.[55]

Public Bills which are found to affect private interests in a manner different from the way in which they affect other private interests in the same category are known as "hybrid" Bills and are subject to an amalgam of the procedural rules applicable to public and private Bills.[56]

3. GOVERNMENT BILLS AND PRIVATE MEMBERS' BILLS

5–004 A separate distinction, within the class of public general statutes, is drawn between government and "Private Member's" Bills.[57] Most of the Bills that are

---

[51] See 29th Annual Report of the Law Commission 1994 (1994–95 H.C. 244), p.51; C. S. Phipps, (1991) 22 *The Law Librarian* 60; (1992) 23 *The Law Librarian* 35.

[52] 1987–88 H.L. 97, H.C. 625.; *Private Bills and New Procedures—A Consultation Document—The Government's Response to the Report of the Joint Committee on Private Bill Procedure*, Cm. 1110, 1990.

[53] See J. Durkin, P. Lane and M. Pete, *Blackstone's Guide to the Transport and Works Act 1992* (1992).

[54] 1992 Act, s.22 (a statutory *ultra vires* clause: see below, para.18–043).

[55] See Vol.187 H.C. Deb., March 13, 1991, cols 923–925; Vol.191 H.C. Deb., May 20, 1991, cols 721–739.

[56] P. Norton, *The Commons in Perspective* (1981), p.104. In 1976 problems were caused for the government when the Speaker ruled that the Aircraft and Shipbuilding Industries Bill, which had completed its Committee stage, was prima facie hybrid: I. Burton and G. Drewry, (1978) 31 *Parliamentary Affairs* pp.151–156. Recent examples include the Cardiff Bay Barrage Act 1993, the Channel Tunnel Rail Link Act 1996 and the Crossrail Bill 2006–07.

[57] On Private Members' Bills see P. G. Richards in S. A. Walkland (ed.), *The House of Commons in the Twentieth Century* (1979), Ch.VI; P. Norton, *The Commons in Perspective* (1981), pp.99–102; P. G. Richards, *Parliament and Conscience* (1970); D. Marsh and M. Read, *Private Members' Bills* (1988); J. Gray, [1978] P.L. 242 (case study of the Unsolicited Goods and Services Acts 1971 and 1975); S. M. Cretney, "The Forfeiture Acts 1982—the Private Member's Bill as an Instrument of Law Reform" (1990) 10 O.J.L.S. 289; Sir Henry de Waal, [1990] Stat. L.R. 18. A full list of Private Members Bills passed since 1945 is contained in House of Commons Factsheet L3 (November 2006), on the Parliamentary website.

successful are introduced by the government of the day,[58] but Bills may also be introduced by individual MPs or "Private Peers". In the House of Commons certain days are set aside for Private Member's Bills and a ballot is held each session to determine which MPs may take priority on these days. A list of 20 names is drawn up; those near the top have some chance of success, although in practice a Bill will not get through without the support, or at least the benevolent neutrality, of the government.[59] There are other methods by which a private member may introduce a Bill,[60] but such Bills rarely proceed because of lack of time.[61] Some important measures have commenced life as Private Member's Bills, including the Public Bodies (Admission to Meetings) Act 1960 (sponsored by Margaret Thatcher MP), the Abortion Act 1967 (David Steel MP) and the Indecent Displays (Control) Act 1981 (Timothy Sainsbury MP). Governments tend to prefer to leave matters of conscience to Private Members' legislation: the risks generally outweigh any possible political advantages. One result is that such legislation, once in place, can become difficult to repeal or reform, as shown by the many unsuccessful attempts over the years by anti-abortionists to secure the amendment of the Abortion Act 1967.[62] A Private Member's Bill that fails may, however, provide the impetus for subsequent public legislation.[63] Overall, however, the system has been characterised as "extravagantly and egregiously wasteful both of resources and the reputation of Parliament".[64] The special features of "private Acts" mentioned above do not apply to those "public general statutes" that happen to start their life as Private Member's Bills.

---

[58] The number per session has varied between 21 and 56 in the period 1985 to 2006, depending in part on the number of sitting days in the session: see the House of Commons *Sessional Information Digests*.

[59] This point is well known to members, who should be "realistic about the prospects of success": Select Committee on Procedure (5th Report, 1994–95 H.C. 38, *Private Members' Bills*, p.xxxvii). However, the adoption by the government of procedural tactics to block the Civil Rights (Disabled Persons) Bill 1993–94 (and other Bills) where it had failed to make clear its opposition generated considerable controversy.

[60] (1) After Question Time, on notice given under S.O. No.57, or (2) under the "ten minute rule", which allows time for brief speeches for and against a Bill. Examples of the former that were ultimately successful include the Protection of Birds (Amendment) Bill 1976 (which went through all its Commons stages in 67 seconds) and the Prohibition of Female Circumcision Bill 1985 (which had been presented and had made some progress in previous sessions: see E. A. Sochart (1988) 41 *Parliamentary Affairs* 508). Examples of the latter include the Bail (Amendment) Act 1993 and the Local Government (Amendment) Act 1993.

[61] For example, in 2005–06, the numbers of Bills presented (and the number successful) were: government Bills; ballot Bills 20(3); S.O. No.57 17(0); 10-minute rule Bills 75(0); Lords' Private Members Bills 18(0). (House of Commons *Sessional Information Digest 2005–06*). The statistics for 1950–85 are given in Marsh and Read (1988), pp.22–23. The main proposal made when the Select Committee on Procedure considered them in 2002–03 (H.C. 333), was that the government should be prepared to provide drafting help for such a Bill as soon as it receives a second reading; the government agreed to make available the resources of Parliamentary Counsel wherever it appears that a Bill is likely to pass, to ensure the terms give effect to its supporters' intentions: Second Special Report of the Procedure Committee (2003–04 H.C. 610).

[62] See D. Marsh and J. Chambers, *Abortion Politics* (1981); Marsh and Read (1988), Ch.6.

[63] e.g. the Home Buyers' Bill sponsored by Austin Mitchell MP in 1983–84 (see the third edition of this book, p.120, para.6–032 and Mitchell, (1986) 39 *Parliamentary Affairs* 1).

[64] D. Oliver, D Miers and P. Evans, in P. Giddings (ed.), *The Future of Parliament* (2005), p.134. If they are not to die, possible reforms might include a reduction in numbers, a guaranteed time slot at second (and possibly third) reading with automatic closure, and a programming committee or the report stage to be taken at a general committee.

4. CONSOLIDATION, TAX SIMPLIFICATION AND STATUTE LAW REVISION ACTS[65]

5–005   On occasion, the law in a particular area is *codified*; the relevant rules as derived from both case law and existing statutory provisions are set out afresh in one statute. The leading examples are the Bills of Exchange Act 1882, the Sale of Goods Act 1893 (now consolidated in the Sale of Goods Act 1979) and the Theft Act 1968. The Law Commission's objects include that of the codification of areas of English law, but it found that this kind of work could pose great problems and could require the allocation of resources on a scale which was regarded as impossible.[66] Greater progress has, however, been made in respect of the codification of criminal law.[67]

The *consolidation* of statutory provisions on a particular topic is a process that is more modest in aim, and much more commonly achieved.[68] Here, the relevant provisions are re-enacted in one or more consolidating statutes. There are four kinds of consolidation Bill. First, there are straight consolidation Bills that simply re-enact the existing texts. Secondly, Bills presented under the Consolidation of Enactments (Procedure) Act 1949 may include "corrections and minor improvements",[69] which must be approved by a Joint Committee of both Houses on Consolidation Bills. Thirdly, improvements designed to facilitate the satisfactory consolidation, but beyond the scope of the 1949 Act may be proposed by the Law Commission; these are also considered by the Joint Committee.[70] Fourthly, consolidation with substantial amendments may be prepared by an ad hoc expert committee, or as an ordinary departmental Bill.[71] Where the consolidation process requires some amendments of substance these may be included in an ordinary Bill (normally in a Schedule)[72]; once these "pre-consolidation amend-

---

[65] See Lord Simon of Glaisdale and J. V. D. Webb, [1975] P.L. 285; I. Burton and G. Drewry, *Legislation and Public Policy* (1981), pp.205–213; Lord Simon of Glaisdale, [1985] Stat. L.R. 352. On the interpretation of consolidation legislation see below, para.6–033.

[66] Law Commissions Act 1965, s.3(l); Law Commission's 13th Annual Report 1977–78 (Law Com. 92), para.2.34 (codification of the law of landlord and tenant); *cf.* 15th Annual Report 1979–80 (Law Com. 107), para.1.4 (codification of general principles of liability in criminal law). See above, para.1–028.

[67] See above, para.1–028.

[68] *Report of a Committee appointed by the Lord President of the Council on the Preparation of Legislation* (The Renton Report: Cmnd. 6053, 1975), pp.17–18 and Ch.XTV; F. A. R. Bennion, *Statute Law* (3rd edn, 1990), Ch.6.

[69] i.e. "amendments of which the effect is confined to resolving ambiguities, removing doubts, bringing obsolete provisions into conformity with modern practice, or removing unnecessary provisions or anomalies which are not of substantial importance, and amendments designed to facilitate improvements in the form or manner in which the law is stated . . . ": 1949 Act, s.2.

[70] The Law Commission report will also cover any necessary "corrections and minor improvements." Law Commission consolidations are separate from their general law reform proposals. The Hansard Society Commission (below, para.5–009) recommended that the pace of consolidation should continue to increase and that if necessary the drafting resources of the Law Commission be strengthened to make this possible: Report, pp.110–111.

[71] For an example of the former see the *Report of the Committee on Consolidation of Highway Law* (Cmnd. 630) which led to the Highways Act 1959; (the Highways Act 1980 followed the Law Commission procedure.) For an example of the latter, see the Local Government Act 1972.

[72] Section 116 of the Companies Act 1981 enabled amendments, desirable to enable a satisfactory consolidation to be produced, to be made by Order in Council on the recommendation of the Law Commission and the Scottish Law Commission: see 19th Annual Report of the Law Commission 1983–84 (1984–85 H.C. 214), p.34. This device was used as part of the massive consolidation of companies legislation in 1985.

ments" have been passed one of the first three kinds of consolidation measure can be brought forward.[73] Large-scale consolidations include those of the Housing legislation in 1985, the Income and Corporation Taxes Act 1988,[74] the Planning legislation in 1990, Water legislation in 1991, Social Security legislation in 1992 and Education legislation in 1996.

A substantial project to rewrite primary direct tax legislation commenced in 1995. The purpose is to make the legislation easier to understand by a new, more logical structure; using plain language wherever possible; rationalising the use of definitions; omitting unnecessary and obsolete material; and using better sign-postings and layout. The Tax Law Rewrite project has a steering committee, chaired by Lord Newton, a consultative committee and multidisciplinary drafting team. The first Act in a projected series of seven was the Capital Allowances Act 2001.[75] "Exposure drafts" with a commentary were published for comment. Work is proceeding on income tax, but less extensive and formal consultation methods are to be used. The work is not simply consolidation as different language is to be employed. Some minor changes in law or approach are included, for example to correct small errors or enact an extra statutory concession.[76] A proposal to use three part numbering was rejected by the House of Lords Procedure Committee.[77] Following recommendations from the House of Commons Procedure Committee,[78] the Bills were introduced in the Commons and referred on Second Reading to a Joint Committee on Tax Law Rewrite Bills, with a Commons majority and chairman.

Various Statute Law Revision Acts have been passed at intervals from 1856 for the repeal of statutory provisions that are "obsolete, spent, unnecessary or superseded". Since 1969 the Law Commissions have prepared Statute Law (Repeals) Bills for the repeal of enactments that in their opinion are "no longer of practical utility". These are wider in scope. One was passed each year between 1973 and 1978 (inclusive) and further ones periodically thereafter.[79] Statute Law Revision Acts are no longer promoted; they were last used in relation to Northern Ireland and Isle of Man legislation. Both kinds of Bills are considered by the Joint Committee, and have made or continue to make an important contribution to the tidying up of the statute book.

The main advantage of the kinds of measures considered in this section, other than Bills for consolidation with substantial amendments, is that the Parliamentary stages, apart from consideration by the Joint Committee, are taken without debate on matters of substance.

---

[73] See, e.g. the Limitation Amendment Act 1980 and the subsequent consolidation measure, the Limitation Act 1980, and the Mental Health (Amendment) Act 1982 and the Mental Health Act 1983.

[74] The longest consolidation produced by the Law Commission and the longest Bill ever introduced.

[75] Followed by the Income Tax (Earnings and Pensions) Act 2003, the Income Tax (PAYE) Regulations 2003 (SI 2003/2682) and the Income Tax (Trading and Other Income) Act 2005.

[76] *HM Revenue & Customs: Tax Law Rewrite (www.hmrc.gov.uk/rewrite/index.htm)*; S. Hardy, (1988) 29 *The Law Librarin* 74; D. Salter, (1998) 19 Stat. L.R. 65.

[77] A decision rightly criticised by J. F. Avery Jones, [2001] B.T.R. 161.

[78] Second Report, 1996–97 H.C. 126, *Legislative Procedure for Tax Simplification Bills*; HC Standing Order No.60.

[79] Provisions identified by the Law Commission as redundant may alternatively be repealed by ordinary legislation: see the 20th Annual Report of the Law Commission 1984–85 (1985–86 H.C. 247), pp.15–16; 25th Annual Report, 1990 (1990–91 H.C. 249), p.12.

5. PROVISIONAL ORDERS AND SPECIAL PROCEDURE ORDERS[80]

5–006 In the nineteenth century, the Provisional Order procedure was introduced as a short cut to local legislation. Many statutes provided that a minister could make a Provisional Order granting certain powers to a local authority or statutory body, following the completion of certain prescribed formalities. Where there were objections there would normally be a local inquiry. One or more such Orders would then be placed before Parliament to be ratified by a Confirmation Act. Petitions against a Confirmation Bill could be submitted and they would be dealt with in the same manner as objections to a private Bill.[81] There are still some examples of Provisional Order powers on the statute book,[82] but the device has largely been superseded by the use of Orders subject to "special parliamentary procedure" under the Statutory Orders (Special Procedure) Act 1945.[83] This procedure also involves an opportunity for objections to be the subject of a local inquiry, and for petitions either against an Order generally or for amendment to be submitted to Parliament.[84] However, an Order against which no petitions are received comes into effect without a Confirmation Act; an Act is only required when a joint committee of both Houses amends the Order in a way unacceptable to the minister or reports against the Order as a whole.[85]

6. GENERAL SYNOD MEASURES[86]

5–007 The General Synod of the Church of England may pass legislative proposals ("Measures") concerning the Church. A Measure is considered by the Ecclesiastical Committee,[87] which comprises 15 members of each House nominated by the respective Speakers. The Committee reports to Parliament. A Measure approved by each House[88] is then submitted for Royal Assent, and when this is signified the Measure has the force and effect of an Act of Parliament.

---

[80] C. K. Allen, *Law and Orders* (3rd edn, 1965), pp.76–81.

[81] See below, para.5–013.

[82] See, e.g. Local Government Act 1972, ss.240, 254(8), 262(10).

[83] As amended by the Statutory Orders (Special Procedure) Act 1965, and see SI 1949/2393; SI 1962/409 and 2791. The operation of the procedure was considered by the Joint Committee on Private Bill Procedure (Report, 1987–88 H.L. 9, H.C. 625), pp.10, 50–51.

[84] For an example of a case where a minister wrongfully refused to accept a memorial from a local authority objector requiring an order to be subjected to special Parliamentary procedure, see *R v Ministry of Agriculture, Fisheries and Food, Ex p. Wear Valley D.C.* (1988) 152 L.G. Rev. 849 (the minister held erroneously that the authority was not "adversely affected" by the order).

[85] This has been done twice: the Mid-Northamptonshire Water Board Order Confirmation (Special Procedure) Act 1949 and the Okehampton Bypass (Confirmation of Orders) Act 1985. The latter was especially controversial as the Joint Committee had reported against the Orders: see the Report of the Joint Committee on Private Bill Procedure, *loc. cit.* n.83 above; H.C. Deb. Vol.87, cols 140–224, November 19, 1985, and HL Deb Vol.468, cols 1412ff, December 5, 1985.

[86] Church of England Assembly (Powers) Act 1919; Synodical Government Measure 1969. See *Hasbury's Laws of England* (4th edn) Vol.14, paras 399–411.

[87] Established by the 1919 Act, s.2.

[88] Parliament must either accept or reject a Measure: it has no power to amend: *ibid.* s.4. In 1927 and 1928 Parliament rejected proposed Measures for the revision of the Prayer Book: other rejected Measures have been the Incumbents (Vacation of Benefices) Measures 1975 and the Appointment of Bishops Measure 1984 (see H.C. Deb. Vol.64, cols 126–144, July 16, 1984).

7. ACTS OF THE NATIONAL ASSEMBLY FOR WALES

Part 4 of the Government of Wales Act 2006 (ss.103–116) provides that the **5–008**
National Assembly for Wales is to have power, within the legislative competence
prescribed by the Act, to make Acts of the National Assembly for Wales. These
powers can only take effect if commencement is supported by a referendum in
Wales, held with the approval of each House of the UK Parliament and two thirds
of Assembly Members. These Acts are a form of primary legislation and are
modelled on the arrangements for Acts of the Scottish Parliament under the
Scotland Act 1998. The government has no current plans for a referendum.

8. PREPARATION AND DRAFTING

The process by which proposals for legislation are converted into a form suitable **5–009**
for enactment is complex.[89] A government Bill originates from the relevant
ministry or department, although the ideas may be put forward from many
sources including party election manifestos, civil servants, reports of official
committees and outside interest groups, whether established to defend some
sectional interest or promote some cause. There is normally a considerable
measure of consultation. The government may issue a "Green Paper"[90] which
sets out tentative proposals and may suggest alternatives. There were over the
years some examples of pre-legislative scrutiny by select committees, and some
Bills were published in draft.[91] Following the Labour victory at the 1997 General
Election, a Select Committee on Modernisation of the House of Commons was
appointed to recommend improvements to the procedure for examining legislative proposals. One of the four themes in its reports has been improvements in
pre-legislative scrutiny.[92] The government had declared its intention to publish
more Bills in draft and the Queen's Speech now may include announcements of
draft Bills. The Committee's view was that there were significant benefits in the
consideration of draft Bills by departmental or ad hoc select committees or joint
committees, the kind of committee appropriate varying according to the circumstances. This development took place.[93] By 2006 the development was "generally acknowledged to be one of the most successful innovations in the
legislative process in recent years".[94] The proportion of government bills published in draft and scrutinised by committee generally increased until 2003–04,

[89] See Cabinet Office, *Guide to Legislative Procedures* (2004); M. Zander, *The Law Making Process*
(6th edn, 2004), Ch.1; and *A Matter of Justice* (1988), pp.236–252; D. Johnstone [1980] Stat. L.R.
67 and *A Tax Shall Be Charged* (HMSO, 1975) (preparation of VAT legislation); Miers and Page
(1990), Chs 2–4; E. A. Dreidger, *The Composition of Legislation* (2nd edn, 1976); G. C.
Thornton, *Legislative Drafting* (3rd edn, 1987); A. Graham, [1988] Stat. L.R. 4. See also B. W.
Hogwood, *From Crisis to Complacency?* (1987), Ch.5 (setting the legislative process within the
wider context of the shaping of public policy in Britain).
[90] On white paper with green covers.
[91] Miers and Page (1990), pp.43–46.
[92] First Report, 1997–98 H.C. 190, *The Legislative Process*, paras 19–30.
[93] Some pre-legislative scrutiny is conducted by a Select Committee of the House of Lords.
[94] Modernisation Select Committee, First Report, 2005–06 H.C. 1097, *The Legislative Process*, p.9.
See further, A. Kennon, [2004] P.L. 477; J. Smookler, (2006) 59 *Parliamentary Affairs* 522;
House of Commons Library Standard Note SN/PC/2822, *Pre-Legislative Scrutiny* (November 28,
2005).

but dipped thereafter.[95] The process was seen to bring the advantages of connecting with the public, including interest groups,[96] and improving the law.[97] There was, however, no conclusive evidence that it smoothed the subsequent passage of legislation; indeed the increased knowledge gained by parliamentarians as a result may give rise to additional challenge.[98] In 2007, a draft legislative programme was announced for the first time.

One legal requirement in developing the annual legislative programme is that the Secretary of State for Wales must as soon as practicable after the beginning of each Session of Parliament consult the Welsh Assembly about the UK government's programme for the Session, including one personal attendance at the Assembly.[99] More generally, the UK government has undertaken to proceed in accordance with the convention that the UK Parliament will not normally legislate with regard to devolved matters except with the agreement of the devolved legislature.[100] This applies where the devolved legislature has primary legislative powers.[101] Additional consultaion requirements appear in Guidance.[102]

Once the appropriate committee of the Cabinet[103] has approved proposals in principle, and provisionally allotted a place in the legislative programme, "Instructions" to draft are prepared by the departmental lawyers[104] and sent to the Parliamentary draftsmen: the "Parliamentary Counsel to the Treasury." The Parliamentary Counsel's office was established in 1869; there are at present 60 counsel, with chambers in Whitehall.[105] Parliamentary counsel are either barristers or solicitors. They normally work in pairs, each Bill being allocated to one of the Senior Counsel working with a Junior Counsel. As well as the drafts of a Bill, the counsel prepare government amendments and relevant motions, give advice on Parliamentary procedure, and attend conferences with ministers as well

---

[95] *ibid.* pp.10–11. The dip was to be expected immediately following a general election.

[96] Through the submission of oral and written evidence and online consultations.

[97] "There is little doubt that pre-legislative scrutiny produces better laws": *ibid.* p.12. Examples of a major impact include the draft Communications Bill where the government accepted 120 of the Joint Committee's 148 recommendations.

[98] *ibid.* p.13, citing Smookler, *op. cit.*

[99] Government of Wales Act 2006, s.33, replacing the 1998 Act, s.31.

[100] Devolution: Memorandum of Understanding (Cm. 5240, 2001).

[101] Accordingly, it applies for Scotland, enshrined in the Sewel Convention (see *www.scotland. gov.uk/Topics/Government/Sewel/KeyFacts*); following discussions between the government and the Scottish Executive, the consent of the Scottish Parliament is expressed by a Legislative Consent Motion. See A. Page and A. Batey, [2002] P.L. 501. A similar principle would apply to Northern Ireland if the Assembly were active and would presumably apply in Wales should the Assembly obtain primary legislative powers.

[102] See Devolution Guidance Notes 8, 9 and 10 and Cabinet Office, *Guide to Legislative Procedures* (2004), Ch.12.

[103] Currently the Ministerial Committee on legislation (L); see also Miers and Page (1990), pp.30–38. This Committee is chaired by the Leader of the House of Commons and includes the Secretary of State for Justice and Lord Chancellor, the Attorney General and the Advocate-General for Scotland: *Ministerial Committees of the Cabinet* (July 2007), (Cabinet Office website: *www.cabinet-office.gov.uk*).

[104] Instructions for legislation concerning the Inland Revenue are drafted by an Assistant Secretary.

[105] Of these, three are at the Law Commission, six at the HMRC Tax Law Rewrite Project (see *www.parliamentary-counsel.gov.uk*). Some appointments are part-time but the overall numbers have been significantly increased in response to the volume of work. On drafting in the nineteenth century see F. Bowers, "Victorian Reforms in Legislative Drafting" (1980) 48 *Revue D'Histoire Du Droit* 329–348. The working of the office in the 1930s and 1940s is described in Sir Harold Kent, *In on the Act* (1979).

as sittings of both Houses and their committees. They may also assist with the drafting of Private Member's Bills supported by the government or otherwise likely to become law.[106] "The hours are unpredictable and the work arduous, but correspondingly rewarding."[107] A Bill may well go through a whole series of drafts before it is presented to Parliament, clauses being revised in the light of consultation between the draftsmen and the department. Other departments including the Treasury and outside groups may also be consulted at this stage. Firm proposals may be incorporated in a government "White Paper", and this may be debated in Parliament. The actual drafts of legislation are not, however, normally circulated outside the Whitehall machine before they have been presented to Parliament.

F. A. R. Bennion, formerly one of the Parliamentary counsel, has identified a number of "drafting parameters" which the draftsman must bear in mind, and which affect the form of Bills.[108] Some of these considerations relate to the process of enactment; others to the operation of the law once it has been enacted. The "preparational" parameters include compliance with the pre-Parliamentary and Parliamentary requirements as to the form of Bills and the stages through which they must pass (*procedural legitimacy*); strict conformity with the government's timetable for legislation and other time pressures such as those imposed by emergency legislation (*timeliness*); *comprehensibility* to members of Parliament; the need to structure a Bill in such a way that the main points of policy can be debated in a rational order (*debatability*)[109]; the choice of language that will minimise objections from those involved in the legislative process (*acceptability*)[110]; and *brevity*. The "operational parameters" include the need for the text of the Bill to carry out the government's intentions (*legal effectiveness*); the desirability that the text be open to one construction only (*certainty*)[111]; *comprehensibility* to the users of the statute, who will normally be practising lawyers (judge, barrister or solicitor), public officials or non-legal professional advisers[112]; and legal compatibility with the rest of the statute book, so that inconsistent provisions are specifically repealed and that the same words mean the same thing even though they appear in different statutes.[113]

These parameters frequently conflict. The most important are procedural legitimacy, timeliness and legal effectiveness, and these may well take priority over comprehensibility and legal compatibility. "The task of making legislative

---

[106] Private Bills are generally drafted by Parliamentary Agents. Scottish Bills are drafted by members of the Lord Advocate's Department: see Lord Mackay of Clashfern, [1983] Stat. L.R. 68. In 1995, four private sector contracts were awarded to draft parts of the 1996 Finance Bill; the successful applicants were two city solicitor firms, a set of tax chambers and a former member of the Parliamentary Counsel's office working as a freelance: Treasury Press Release 109/95. The experiment was not a success and has not been repeated: Sir Geoffrey Bowman, [2005] Stat. L.R. 81.

[107] Civil Service Commission, Lawyers: *Civil Service Careers* (1980), p.27.

[108] *Statute Law* (3rd edn, 1990), pp.28–40. See also G. Engle, [1983] Stat. L.R. 7.

[109] The government may, however, wish a Bill to be drawn in such a way as to restrict opportunities for debate or amendment, for example by drawing the long title narrowly.

[110] "The red-blooded terms of political controversy are toned down. The prose style is flat." (Bennion (1990), p.34).

[111] The government may, however, intend a provision to be ambiguous.

[112] Bennion (1990), pp.37–38.

[113] "Contrary to most people's belief, however, there are no books of precedents in the Parliamentary Counsel's Office" (*ibid.* p.39).

proposals understood by non-lawyer politicians while securing their legal effectiveness is one of the most formidable faced by the Parliamentary
draftsmen."[114]

Over time there have been a number of reviews of the drafting and preparation
of legislation. In 1975, the report of the Renton Committee on the Preparation of
Legislation[115] recognised that draftsmen had to work under pressures and constraints that made it very difficult to produce simple and clear legislation. Many
statutes were well drafted, but they had received complaints about the use of
obscure and complex language, over-elaboration of detail in the quest for "certainty", the illogical structure of some statutes and problems created by the
arrangement of the statute book in a chronological series of separate Acts. There
was also criticism of the use of the "non-textual" method of amendment,
whereby the amending Act set out the substance of the change proposed to be
made without altering the text of the Act being amended. The Renton Committee
endorsed the recent change in practice whereby statutes were amended "tex-
tually" by adding words to or deleting words from the original provision
whenever convenience permitted.[116] It seems that it is now settled practice to
make the maximum possible use of textual amendment.[117]

The Renton Committee made a number of other proposals for reform. For
example, the use of statements of principle should be encouraged, with additional
guidance given where necessary in Schedules; more use could be made of
examples showing how a Bill is intended to work in particular situations;
statements of purpose should be used where they are the most convenient method
of clarifying the scope and effect of legislation; long un-paragraphed sentences
should be avoided; a statute should be arranged to suit the convenience of its
ultimate users; the typographical production should be improved, and there
should be more consolidation. They rejected suggestions that this should be on
a "one Act, one subject basis",[118] with each subject having a principal Act and
future legislation on the subject being effected by textual amendment to that Act.
The government's response to the Report was guarded. The Lord President of the
Council (Michael Foot) merely stated that the government regarded the recommendations concerning drafting practice and were taken into account by the
draftsmen.[119] Subsequent governments did not show any greater enthusiasm for
further reforms based on the Renton Report.[120]

In the early 1990s, the whole issue was the subject of a comprehensive review
by a Commission appointed by the Hansard Society for Parliamentary Government.[121] Although not an official body, the Commission consulted very widely
and generated a considerable body of information from official and other sources.

---

[114] *ibid.* p.33.
[115] Cmnd. 6053, 1975.
[116] *ibid.* Ch.XIII: Statute Law Society, *Statute Law: the Key to Clarity* (1972), pp.7–18 and *Renton
and the Need for Reform* (1979), pp.27–40.
[117] D. Johnstone, [1980] Stat. L.R. 112.
[118] Renton Report, Ch.XIV.
[119] H.C. Deb. Vol.941, col.329 written answer, December 15, 1977.
[120] Lord Simon of Glaisdale, "The Renton Report—Ten Years On" [1985] Stat. L.R. 133; H.L. Deb.
Vol.489, cols 1417–1449, summarised at [1988] Stat. L.R. 1.
[121] *Making the Law: The Report of the Hansard Society Commission on the Legislative Process*,
November 1992 (1993) (Chairman: Lord Rippon). See M. Rush, (1993) 14 Stat. L.R. 75. See also
the Report of the (Conservative Party-appointed) Norton Commission to Strengthen Parliament
(2000) which echoes some of the Hansard Commission recommendations, and A. Brazier (ed.),
Parliament, Politics and Law Making (2004).

The Commission concluded that "the legislative process in this country has been unsatisfactory for a long time and Ministers have not, up till now, shown a willingness to change it".[122] There was an "overwhelming impression" from the evidence that "many of those most directly affected are deeply dissatisfied with the extent, nature, timing and conduct of consultation on bills as at present practised".[123] The government should "make every effort to get bills in a form fit for enactment, without major alteration, before they are presented to Parliament".[124] Consultation practice should be improved and enshrined in government guidelines, including the more frequent use of independent inquiries, and more consultation on draft texts.[125] As to drafting,[126] the Cabinet's Legislation Committee should assume the wider and longer-term role of ensuring that Bills conform with the best constitutional principles and, where appropriate, have been prepared after full and genuine consultation. Ministerial responsibility for the Parliamentary Counsel, including oversight of the drafting methods and scrutiny of the drafting of government Bills, should be assigned to the Attorney-General. The number of draftsmen required should be reviewed. The drafting style adopted should be appropriate for the main users of the legislation; draftsmen should always seek for clarity, simplicity and brevity but with certainty paramount, and note the continued criticisms made by those most directly affected of the style of drafting of statute law. Ministers, civil servants and draftsmen should do all they can to eliminate unnecessary detail; some means should be found of informing the citizens, lawyers and the courts of the intention underlying the words of a statute; notes on sections should be published. The Committee also make recommendations on the Parliamentary process, access to the statute book, the programming and time-tabling of legislation and the impact of EC legislation.[127] The Conservative government's response[128] pointed to the recruitment of four additional draftsmen and an increase in the number of clauses of draft Bills published in advance for consultation.

The work of the Hansard Society Commission was built on by the Select Committee on Modernisation of the House of Commons which began its work in 1997. It accepted the general thrust of the criticisms set out in previous reports. The key elements of its recommendations have been[129]: (1) improved pre-legislative scrutiny[130]; (2) improved explanatory material[131]; (3) greater use of Special Standing Committees; (4) new arrangements for the programming of Bills; (5) the carry-over, by agreement, of some Bills from one session to the next; (6) the establishment of a parallel chamber, sitting in the Grand Committee

---

[122] *ibid.* p.138.
[123] *ibid.* p.139.
[124] *ibid.*
[125] Ch.3 and pp.139–140.
[126] Ch.4 and pp.141–142.
[127] See pp.268, 277–278.
[128] Viscount Cranborne, Leader of the House, contributing to a debate on the Commission's report, Vol.559 H.L. Deb., December 14, 1994, cols 1291ff., at cols 1321–1326.
[129] First Report, 1997–98 H.C. 190, *The Legislative Process*, approved by the House, November 13, 1997; First Report, 2005–06 H.C. 1097, *The Legislative Process*. A full set of reports is on the Parliament website. See also the HL Select Committee on the Constitution, Fourteenth Report, 2003–04 H.L. 173–I, *Parliament and the Legislative Process*; and *Government's Response*, Sixth Report, 2004–05 H.L. 114.
[130] See above.
[131] See below, para.5–010.

Room in Westminster Hall, and referred to as "Westminster Hall". Progress has been made but programming in particular has also been controversial.[132]

There is a recurrent debate on the issue whether there should be a move from the British style of "common-law" drafting to the "continental" or "civil law" method of drafting. The latter is said to be more lucid and succinct, with more emphasis on basic principles and purposes and less on detail. Proponents of such a move include Sir William Dale[133] and J. A. Clarence Smith[134]; opponents include F. A. R. Bennion[135] and Geoffrey Kolts.[136] It is claimed that civilian texts are shorter, better arranged and more easily understood by laymen; common law drafting may by contrast be "a writhing torrent of convoluted indigestion".[137] Others have argued that "civilian" texts produce a considerable degree of uncertainty, which then has to be resolved by the judges; in effect legislative power is delegated to non-elected judges and officials. "Civilian" texts can be as lengthy and complex as British statutes, and can be badly drafted.[138] Of course, the ability of each side to point to examples where the other's preferred method has gone astray proves little; generalisations as to virtues and vices are easy to make but difficult to support. It is, however, unlikely in the present climate of opinion that many English judges would wish to deal with legislative provisions that were significantly more open-textured than at present, and equally unlikely that they would be regarded by many in the community as well suited to undertake that role.[139]

9. PARLIAMENTARY PROCEDURE[140]

(a) Public Bills

5–010   The legislative timetable of Parliament is managed by the government. Detailed government Bills are examined and placed in the timetable by the Cabinet's Legislation Committee, and may be considered by the full Cabinet or the appropriate policy committee. A Bill may generally be introduced in either the House of Commons or the House of Lords, although money Bills must be

---

[132] *ibid.* The Westminster Hall experiment was made permanent in 2002. See H.C. Library Standard Note SN/PC/3939, *Modernisation: Westminster Hall* (March 6, 2006).

[133] *Legislative Drafting: A New Approach* (1977); (1981) 30 I.C.L.Q. 141; [1988] Stat. L.R. 15.

[134] Proceedings of the Ninth International Symposium on Comparative Law (1972), pp.155–178; [1980] Stat. L.R. 14.

[135] *Statute Law* (1990), pp.23–26; [1980] Stat. L.R. 61.

[136] Second Parliamentary Counsel, Canberra, Australia, [1980] Stat. L.R. 144.

[137] J. A. C. Smith, *op. cit.* n.134, at pp.158–9.

[138] See, e.g. the criticisms of a proposed directive of the European Commission on commercial agents expressed by the Law Commission in 1977 (Law Com. No.84). The text was described as badly drafted, unclear, ambiguous and internally inconsistent. *Cf.* the criticisms of M. Cults "Clearer Timeshare Act 1993" by the draftsman of the Timeshare Act 1992: E. Sutherland, "Clearer Drafting and the Timeshare Act 1992" (1993) 14 Stat. L.R. 163.

[139] See above, paras 4–041—4–044.

[140] R. Blackburn and A. Kennon, *Griffith and Ryle on Parliament* (2nd edn, 2002); P. Giddings (ed.), *The Future of Parliament* (2005); R. Rogers and R. Walters, *How Parliament Works* (6th edn, 2006), the following Reports from the Select Committee on Procedure: Second Report, 1970–71 H.C. 538, *The Process of Legislation*; First Report, 1977–78 H.C. 588; Second Report, 1984–85 H.C. 49, *Public Bill Procedure*; and the reports of the Select Committee on Modernisation of the House of Commons (above, para.5–009, n.129); G. Drewry (1972) 35 M.L.R. 289, (1979) 42 M.L.R. 80 and [1995] P.L. 203; T. St. J. Bates, [1987] Stat. L.R. 44; D. R. Miers, [1989] Stat. L.R. 26 and (1998) 29 *The Law Librarian* 87.

introduced in the Commons, and politically controversial Bills are normally introduced there. The programme is announced in the Queen's speech at the start of the session.

A government Bill introduced in the Commons is presented by a minister. It receives a formal *first reading*, when only the title is actually read out, and is ordered to be printed. A day is fixed for the *second reading*. A Bill as printed is accompanied by "Explanatory Notes". These were introduced from the start of the 1998–99 session and replaced both the brief "Explanatory Memorandum" and, where finance was involved, "Financial Memorandum" previously issued with each Bill, and the "Notes on Clauses" previously issued to MPs and peers. They are prepared by departmental officials in consultation with Parliamentary Counsel, and seek to summarise in "clear and simple English" that is "neutral in political tone rather than argumentative" the background and provisions of the Bill. They are revised when the Bill moves to the other House and after Royal Assent. They are not approved by Parliament and are not "authoritative".[141] They are published on the Internet[142] and are more helpful than the old Explanatory and Financial memoranda. Their legal status is regarded by the government as a matter for the courts.[143]

At the second reading stage the principles of the Bill are debated on the floor of the House.[144] If the Bill entails public expenditure or taxation this must be authorised by a *money resolution* moved by a minister.[145] After receiving a second reading[146] the Bill proceeds to the *committee stage*.[147] These have been either at a Standing Committee of between 15 and 60 MPs (normally about 18) that reflects the party composition of the House, or in Committee of the Whole House. The latter step is taken for Bills that are either straightforward or urgent, or, at the other extreme, politically contentious or of major constitutional significance. Greater use is made of the possibility of splitting consideration of a Bill between a Committee of the Whole House and a Standing Committee.[148] The committee examines the Bill clause by clause, first considering amendments and then the motion that the clause, as amended, "stand part of the Bill".

---

[141] Sir Christopher Jenkins, (1999) 149 N.L.J. 798. But "they can be regarded as an authoritative statement of Parliament's intention in proposing legislation": Craies (2004), p.354.

[142] *www.parliament.uk* (Bills); *www.opsi.gov.uk/legislation* (Acts).

[143] Lord Sainsbury of Turville, H.L. Deb., November 4, 1999, cols *WA99* and *WA100*; Lord Falconer of Thoroton, H.L. Deb., February 28, 2000, cols *WA43* and *WA44*. See para.6–042.

[144] Non-controversial Bills may be referred to a Second Reading Committee of between 16 and 50 MPs and Scottish Bills to the Scottish Grand Committee (members for Scottish constituencies). Law Commission Bills and Tax Law Rewrite Bills are referred automatically to Second Reading Committees unless otherwise ordered by the House: H.C. Standing Orders 59, 60. Apart from Law Commission Bills, very little use has been made of Second Reading Committees; rare examples were the Birds (Registration Charges) Bill and the Police and Firemen's Pensions Bill in 1997 and the Royal Parks (Trading) Bill 1999–2000.

[145] In the case of some Bills, such as Finance Bills, Ways and Means resolutions are passed before the Bill is introduced. Private Member's Bills rarely include provisions involving public expenditure.

[146] Only three government Bills have failed at second reading since 1905, although it is more than a mere formality and ministers do not always approach debates with closed minds: Norton (1981), pp.86–87. The Bills were the Rent Restrictions Bill in 1924, the Reduction of Redundancy Rebates Bill in 1977 (during the period of the minority Labour government) and the Shops Bill in 1986 (following a rebellion by 72 government backbenchers: see P. Regan, (1988) 41(2) *Parliamentary Affairs* 218).

[147] The committee stage for consolidation Bills may be dispensed with on a government motion, and the question on third reading put forthwith: H.C. Standing Order No.58(4).

[148] e.g. Finance Bills, the Greater London Authority Bill 1998–99, the Sexual Offences (Amendment) Bill 1998–99.

Amendments may be proposed by the minister in charge, backbenchers or the opposition; those to be taken are selected by the chairman. Proposed new clauses are then taken, followed by the Schedules, proposed new Schedules the preamble (if any) and the long title.[149]

An innovation in the early 1980s was to send some Bills to a "Special Standing Committee" with the power to question witnesses and request the submission of evidence.[150] These were for many years used sparingly, if at all, although the possibility was enshrined permanently in Standing Orders from 1986.[151] However, the work of Standing Committees was "one of the most criticized aspects of the legislative process".[152] The Modernisation Committee recommended that Special Standing Committees, renamed Public Bill Committees, become the norm for government Bills that originate in the Commons.[153] This was endorsed, with effect from the 2006–07 Session.[154] These Committees will normally[155] have power to take evidence, it being for them to decide how many evidence sessions should be held. Membership of a committee that gave pre-legislative scrutiny to a draft of the Bill is now one of the qualifications for selection for membership of a Public Bill Committee.[156] The Modernisation Committee also recommended that Public Bill Committees should normally have at least one evidence session with ministers and officials; the paperwork for meetings should be improved; there should be a pilot scheme for the use of explanatory statements for amendment; the provision of papers on-screen on laptops should be considered; and at the end the House of Commons Library should normally produce a report of the Public Bill Committee stage in order to inform debate at the report stage.[157]

Next, the House considers the Bill again at the *report stage*.[158] Any aspect of the Bill can be raised and new clauses and further amendments can be proposed. Debate is, however, confined to the contents of the Bill. Normally, the *third reading* immediately follows the conclusion of the report stage. Only minor verbal amendments can be made; if material amendments are necessary the Bill has to be considered again in committee. Third reading debates are usually short.

The Bill then proceeds to the House of Lords where the stages are repeated, with some minor procedural differences. Any amendment proposed may be moved; there is no selection. Amendments can be made at Third reading provided the issue has not been voted on at an earlier stage. The committee stage,

---

[149] See below, para.5–015.

[150] First Report from the Select Committee on Procedure, 1977–78 H.C. 588, pp.xviii–xix; H.C. Deb. Vol.991, cols 716–834, October 30, 1980.

[151] See the references in the 4th edition of this book, at para.5–008.

[152] Modernisation Select Committee, First Report, 2005–06 H.C. 1097, p.23. The evidence of the Hansard Society was that they "fail to deliver genuine and analytic scrutiny" and that "their political functions are neutered, dominated almost exclusively by government". The role of government backbenchers was merely to secure the government's majority, commonly providing an opportunity for them to deal with their own correspondence.

[153] *ibid*.

[154] H.C. Deb., November 1, 2006, cols 304–407. See H.C. Library Factsheet L6, *General Committees* (December 2006). Bills relating only to Scotland are committed to a Scottish Public Bill Committee.

[155] i.e. a committee to which a Bill, or certain provisions of, a Bill are committed by means of a programme order under S.O. No.83A. A Public Bill Committee to which other Bills are committed may have such powers if the House so resolves: S.O. No.63.

[156] S.O. No.86, as amended on November 1, 2006.

[157] First Report 2005–06, pp.28–35.

[158] There is no report stage if a public Bill considered in Committee of the Whole House is unamended.

if not dispensed with, is normally taken by a Committee of the Whole House,[159] although a Public Bills Committee can be used.[160] An interesting development was the introduction by the House of Lords of Special Standing Committees (subsequently renamed Special Public Bill Committees) to hear oral and written evidence on and then consider clause-by-clause, Bills, based on Law Commission reports, that are "largely devoid of party political controversy".[161] The position as to implementation of Law Commission Bills was somewhat (although not sufficiently) improved.[162] Bills can now be referred to a Grand Committee, which sits in parallel to the House. Any member of the House may attend; decisions have to be unanimous as no votes can be taken.

If amendments are made, the Bill is returned to the Commons for them to be agreed. The Commons respond with a message to the Lords which either signifies their agreement, gives reasons for disagreement or proposes other amendments.[163] Further messages may be exchanged[164] until either final agreement is reached, the Bill lapses at the end of a session,[165] "double insistence" is reached,[166] or the Commons resorts to the Parliament Acts procedure.[167] Provision has now been made for the carry-over of public Bills by agreement.[168] Proposals to move generally to a rolling programme have, however, been resisted.[169]

---

[159] A Bill may be referred to a Select Committee; this is normally done for Private Member's Bills rather than government Bills, although the Constitutional Reform Bill is the only recent example (and that against the government's wishes): 14th Report of the H.L. Select Committee on the Constitution, 2003–04 H.L. 173–I, *The Legislative Process*, p.35.

[160] They comprise 12–16 members and are designed to deal with "mainly technical and non-controversial government Bills"; they have largely been superseded by Grand Committees and the last was appointed in 1994: *Companion to the Standing Orders and Guide to the Proceedings of the House of Lords* (2005 edition), paras 6–98—6–100.

[161] See Report from the Select Committee on *The Committee Work of the House* (1991–92 H.L. 35–I), pp.19–22, 40–41; Select Committee on the Procedure of the House, First Report 1992–93 H.L. 11, para.6; Third Report 1993–94 H.L. 81 ("the procedure has already proved a valuable addition to the scrutiny function of the House". The procedure is not technically restricted to Law Commission Bills, but has in practice rarely been used.

[162] See above, para.1–028; 29th Annual Report of the Law Commission 1994 (1994–95 H.C. 244), pp.61–69. The Hansard Society Commission (above, para.5–009) supported these moves: Report, pp.118–119.

[163] The complexities of this process were considered by the Select Committee on Procedure, 2nd Report, 1990–91, H.C. 157.

[164] Referred to as "ping pong". The "speed and complexity of exchanges between the two Houses has increased markedly in recent years": House of Lords Procedure Committee, First Report 2004–05, p.7 (Statement by the Clerks of the Two Houses).

[165] Public Bills that have not been passed normally lapse at the end of the session: private and hybrid Bills (see below) may be carried forward.

[166] i.e. one House insists on an amendment to which the other has disagreed, and the other House insists on the disagreement; in these circumstances the Bill is lost but can be revived on a motion in the House to vary normal practice. See House of Lords Procedure Committee, First Report, 2004–05 H.L. 48.

[167] See below.

[168] See H.C. Standing Order No.80A. This has been relatively little used but has been made a permanent feature: see H.C. Procedure Committee, Fourth Report, 2003–04 H.C. 325, *Programming of Legislation*, pp.18–19. It was first done with the Financial and Market Services Bill between 1998–99 and 1999–2000. The House of Lords may carry over a Bill still in the Lords by an ad hoc motion: H.L. Select Committee on the Procedure of the House, Fifth Report, 2001–02 H.L. 148, para.7. This was done for the Constitutional Reform Bill.

[169] *Parliament and the Legislative Process: The Government's Response*, Sixth Report, 2004–05 H.L. 114, pp.5–6, rejecting a recommendation of the Select Committee on the Constitution (Fourteenth Report, 2003–04 H.L. 173–I).

5–011   In recent years, significant features of the work of the House of Lords have
included longer hours, a higher regular attendance, an increase in the proportions
of the House's time devoted to legislative business and an increase in the self-
confidence of peers.[170] The culture has changed further with the staged removal
from membership of the House of hereditary peers although defeats of the
government on important questions are still comparatively unusual.

A Bill passed in its entirety by both Houses is presented for *Royal Assent*.[171]
The monarch is expected by convention to give that assent; the last occasion on
which it was refused was in 1707 when Queen Anne refused her assent to a
Militia Bill. Assent may be signified: (1) by the monarch in person (this was last
done in 1854); (2) by Lords Commissioners in the presence of both Houses[172];
or (3) as is normally the case today, by separate notification to each House in
accordance with the Royal Assent Act 1967. The third method, unlike the others,
does not involve the interruption of proceedings in the Commons. The second
method is only used where Royal Assent coincides with prorogation.

The Parliament Acts 1911–1949 lay down special procedures whereby a Bill
may be presented for Royal Assent when it has been passed only by the
Commons.[173] A money Bill may be so presented where the Lords have failed to
pass it without amendment after it has been before them for one month; a non-
money Bill may be presented where it has been passed by the Commons in two
consecutive sessions and the Lords have failed to pass it in each of those
sessions; one year has elapsed between the Commons second reading in the first
session and third reading in the second session; the Bill has been sent to the Lords
at least one month before the end of each session and the Speaker certifies that
the requirements of the Parliament Acts have been complied with. The certificate
is conclusive for all purposes and may not be questioned in a court of law. These
procedures may not be employed in respect of Bills to prolong the maximum
duration of a Parliament beyond five years, to Provisional Order Confirmation
Bills or private Bills. Objections by the House of Lords are normally dropped
without the necessity of recourse to the Parliament Acts. The procedure has only
been used seven times,[174] but like any deterrent, its efficacy and significance are
not to be gauged by how often it has to be used.[175]

---

[170] N. Baldwin in P. Norton (ed.), *Parliament in the 1980s* (1985), Ch.5; A. Adonis, "The House of
Lords in the 1980s" (1988) 41 *Parliamentary Affairs* 380; *Report by the Group on the Working
of the House* (1987–88 H.L. 9).

[171] See F. A. R. Bennion, [1981] Stat. L.R. 133; A. Twomey, [2006] P.L. 580.

[172] Under the Royal Assent by Commission Act 1541; this was originally part of the Bill of Attainder
against Catherine Howard, which did not receive the King's assent in person to spare his hearing
once more the "wicked facts of the case". The Bill actually received the assent on February 11,
1542. The Reading Clerk reads out the title of the Bill; the Commissioners raise their hats; and
the Clerk of the Parliaments pronounces "La Reyne le Veult". In the case of money Bills the
expression is "La Reyne remercie ses bons sujets, accepte lew benevolence, et ainsi le veult"; for
personal private Acts, "Soil fait comme il est désiré". If assent were refused the expression would
be "La Reyne s'avisera".

[173] S. A. de Smith and R. Brazier, *Constitutional and Administrative Law* (8th edn, 1998,
pp.304–308).

[174] Welsh Church Act 1914 (disestablishment); Government of Ireland Act 1914 (Home Rule: the
Act was not implemented); Parliament Act 1949; War Crimes Act 1991 (see G. Ganz (1992) 55
M.L.R. 87); the European Parliamentary Elections Act 1999; the Sexual Offences (Amendment)
Act 2000; and the Hunting Act 2004. See generally, H.C. Library Standard Note SN/PC/675, R.
Kelly and C. Pond, *The Parliament Acts*. As to the status of Acts passed under these procedures,
see para.5–023.

[175] Lord Rodger of Earlsferry in *R (on the application of Jackson) v Attorney General* [2006] 1 A.C.
262, at para.[133].

For the draftsman, the first publication of the Bill after first reading is an important deadline as changes thereafter have to be made by formal amendments. Indeed, most of the amendments that are made are government amendments, and these tend to reflect second thoughts by the civil servants rather than the persuasive arguments of members. Amendments of substance proposed by back-benchers or opposition and actually agreed are few in number, and are more likely to be accepted in the Lords.[176] More amendments than usual were carried against the government during the passage of the Scotland and Wales Bills in 1977–78. These were controversial constitutional measures, and the Labour government was then in a minority in the Commons.[177] "Parliament's exposure of the successive Bills' inherent defects and illogicalities was impressive".[178] However, "the debates were poorly attended and the debating was done by a few stalwarts, with most MPs (though a smaller proportion than usual) content to live up to their image as lobby fodder".

The pressure on the Parliamentary timetable is such that where legislation is particularly contentious governments may secure the placing of limits on the time available for debate (formerly termed timetable or "guillotine" motions); this may mean that, as in the case of the Scotland and Wales Bills, important clauses are not scrutinised by the Commons, although they will normally be considered by the Lords.[179] The House of Commons Select Committee on Procedure reported in 1978 that:

"the balance of advantage between Parliament and Government in the day to day working of the Constitution is now weighted in favour of the Government to a degree which arouses widespread anxiety and is inimical to the proper working of our parliamentary democracy".[180]

Over the years, proposals for earlier timetabling have been made by various bodies but the government and opposition front benches were generally not persuaded that they were workable. However, arrangements for what is now called the "programming" of specified Bills by the House of Commons on the recommendation of a Programming Sub-Committee of the relevant Standing Committee (for proceedings in Standing Committee) were introduced in November 2000, and revised in June 2001. They have proved controversial, with every programme motion in 2000–01 being opposed and acceptance that the aim that all clauses of Bills should properly be considered had not been achieved.[181] The

---

[176] See J. A. G. Griffith, *Parliamentary Scrutiny of Government Bills* (1974); P. Norton, (1976) 57 *The Parliamentarian* 17. Where the government accepts or is unsuccessful in resisting an amendment, the version proposed in debate is usually replaced at a later stage by one drafted by a parliamentary draftsman: T. Millett, [1988] Stat. L.R. 70.

[177] I. Burton and G. Drewry, "Public Legislation: A Survey of the Sessions 1977/8 and 1978/9" (1980) 33 *Parliamentary Affairs* 173, 174–186. These sessions provided "significant evidence for the power that still belongs to backbenchers in the House of Commons", although "only in a minority Parliament may the fate of Government Bills be in serious doubt. Even then, most legislation, being inevitable whatever the Government in power, is secure, protected by the close rapport between the two front benches" (p.199).

[178] *ibid.* p.186.

[179] See G. Ganz, "Recent developments in the use of guillotine motions" [1990] P.L. 496.

[180] First Report, 1977–78 H.C. 588, Vol.1, p.viii.

[181] See Modernisation Committee: First Report, 1997–98 H.C. 190, paras 57–66, Second Report, 1999–2000 H.C. 589, First Report, 2000–01 H.C. 382, First Report, 2002–03 H.C. 1222; Procedure Committee, Fourth Report, 2003–04 H.C. 325 (*Government Response*, 2003–04 H.C. 1169).

nadir was reached with the Criminal Justice and Police Bill 2000–01 where the government secured passage of a motion that it should be deemed to have been reported to the House as if the clauses whose consideration had not been completed by the Standing Committee had been ordered to stand part of the Bill, subject to the government amendments that had been tabled but not considered. The view was expressed forcefully and persuasively that the new arrangements simply shifted the balance in favour of the government and against the Opposition and backbenchers.[182] The arrangements have continued, with some modifications; as has the opposition.[183]

As regards the subsequent stages, after second reading Bills should normally be committed to a special standing committee (able to take direct evidence).

5–012   The apparent limitations on the effectiveness of Parliamentary scrutiny have led to suggestions for the scrutiny of legislation by other bodies particularly from the technical standpoint. Sir William Dale proposed[184] the establishment of a "Law Council" to advise the government on draft Bills. "Its duty would be to examine them from the point of view of coherent and orderly presentation, clarity, conciseness, soundness of legal principle, and suitability for attaining the Government's objective", a function performed in France by the Conseil d'Etat. It would not concern itself with matters of policy, and its advice could be rejected by the government. Its membership would include judges, lawyers (practising and academic) and laymen. The Renton Committee, however, rejected proposals for formal machinery for the scrutiny of the drafting of Bills, either before or after their formal introduction in Parliament.[185] Before introduction, it was for government departments to decide what advice they should obtain as to the drafting of their Bills; after introduction, a new scrutiny stage would "impose undue strain on a Parliamentary machine which is already under great pressure, and . . . add to the labour of the draftsmen who have more than enough to do as it is to keep pace with the legislative programme".

The Renton Committee did recommend new Parliamentary procedures: (1) for incorporating improvements (including the correction of obvious inaccuracies) certified by the Speaker and the Lord Chancellor to be of a drafting nature, after the passage of a Bill by both houses and before Royal Assent[186]; and (2) for the re-enactment of statutes, in whole or in part, with drafting improvements.[187] In addition they suggested that the Statute Law Committee[188] should keep the

---

[182] Memorandum by Angela Browning MP and Richard Shepherd MP to the Modernisation Committee, 2000–01 H.C. 382, Appendix; see H.C. Deb., June 28, 2001, cols 812–890.

[183] See the Draft Report of the Modernisation Committee proposed by Richard Shepherd MP, (2003–04 H.C. 1222), pp.13–43.

[184] *Legislative Drafting: A New Approach* (1977), pp.336–337..

[185] Cmnd. 6053, pp.129–133.

[186] This was endorsed in principle by the House of Commons Select Committee on Procedure, 1977–78 H.C. 588, Vol. I, p.xxvii. A proposed procedure for the correction of errors *after* Royal Assent did not find favour with the House of Lords (Acts of Parliament (Correction of Mistakes) Bill [Lords], session 1976–77, withdrawn) and was not supported by the Select Committee (*ibid.*). See A. Samuels, "Errors in Bills and Acts" [1982] Stat. L.R. 94. This is to be distinguished from the correction of printing errors in HMSO copies of statutes: see below, para.5–022, n.262.

[187] This would be modelled on the present procedure for consolidation Bills.

[188] A committee appointed by the Lord Chancellor and first established in 1868. It met once a year and supervised the Statutory Publications Office, the form of Acts and the production of *Statutes in Force*. Most of its functions in the field of consolidation and statute law revision passed to the Law Commissions in 1965. In 1991 it was replaced by the Advisory Committee on Statute Law, to advise the Lord Chancellor on all matters relating to the publication of the statute book. Its membership now includes the Permanent Secretary to the MoJ, the Clerk of the Parliaments, the Clerk of the House of Commons, the Chairmen of the Law Commissions, First Parliamentary

structure and language of statutes under continuous review, monitor the implementation of the Renton Committee's recommendations and publish reports.
None of these proposals has been accepted, the third being rejected by the
Cabinet apparently on the grounds that the Committee was not an "appropriate
body" to discharge these functions and that the proposal to keep the statute book
under continuous review was not "likely to lead to any worthwhile improvements in the drafting of legislation".[189] More recently, there has been renewed
interest in the development of standards and checklists to aid the preparation and
Parliamentary scrutiny of legislation.[190]

Attention is now being paid to the development of mechanisms for post-
legislative scrutiny. In 2006, the Law Commission reported[191] that there had been
overwhelming support for the principle that there should be a more systematic
approach to this matter, and suggested that Parliament consider setting up a new
Joint Parliamentary Committee. Such an arrangement would see whether legislation was working in practice as intended, contribute to better regulation, improve
the focus on implementation and delivery of policy aims and identify and
disseminate good practice. Apart from this, government departments should give
routine consideration to whether and if so how legislation will be monitored and
reviewed.

(b) Private Bills[192]

Standing Orders of each House lay down a complicated series of procedural   **5–013**
requirements that must be observed before a private Bill is introduced, including
the giving of public notice. In practice, a promoter needs the professional
assistance of a Parliamentary Agent,[193] who drafts the Bill and acts on behalf of
the promoter thereafter. Petitions for private Bills must normally be deposited by
November 27 each session.[194] A local authority that wishes to promote a Bill
must resolve to do so by a majority of the whole number of council members at
a meeting of which 30 days' notice has been given in the local press; a second
meeting must confirm the decision after the deposit of the Bill in Parliament.[195]
The promoters must prove to the two "examiners", one appointed by each of the

---

Counsel (and his counterpart for Scotland) the Treasury Solicitor, the Solicitor to the Scottish
Executive, Assembly Legislative Counsel to the National Assembly for Wales, and representatives of HMSO and the MoJ: Civil Service Yearbook (2006).

[189] *Renton and the Need for Reform*, pp.7–8; H.L. Deb., col.776, March 7, 1978. The Select
Committee supported the third proposal, and urged the government to reconsider its attitude:
1977–78 H.C. 588, Vol.1, pp.xxvii–xxviii.

[190] See D. Oliver, "Improving the Scrutiny of Bills: The Case for Standards and Checklists" [2006]
P.L. 219. The scrutiny of Constitutional Bills is considered by R. Hazell, *ibid.*, p.247.

[191] Law Com. No. 302, Cm. 6945, 2006. See also Fourteenth Report of the Select Committee on the
Constitution, 2003–04 H.L.173, *Parliament and the Legislative Process*, Ch.5.

[192] F. Clifford, *History of Private Bill Legislation* (1887); O. C. Williams, *Historical Development of
Private Bill Procedure* (1948); The Study of Parliament Group, "Private Bill Procedure; A Case
for Reform" [1981] P.L. 206; Joint Committee on Private Bill Procedure, 1987–88 H.L. 97, H.C.
625; H.C. Library, Factsheet L4.

[193] See D. L. Rydz, *The Parliamentary Agents: A History* (1979) R. Owen and J. Bracken, (1998) 29
The Law Librarian 79.

[194] Personal Bills can be deposited at any time, are customarily presented first to the House of Lords
and are considered by the Personal Bills Committee of the Lords before first reading. The other
stages are similar to those for other private Bills.

[195] Local Government Act 1972, s.239. A Bill may not be promoted to change a local government
area, its status or electoral arrangements: *ibid.* s.70.

Houses, that the formalities have been observed, and this may be challenged by opponents of the Bill.

Private Bills normally proceed first in the House of Lords. The first reading is a formality; the second reading is normally so, but may be opposed. A Bill that passes the second reading is regarded as having received the conditional approval of the House. If the Bill passes the second reading opposed clauses are then referred to a Select Committee of five Lords. The House may agree to an Instruction to the Committee to the effect that the Committee should have regard to or be satisfied of certain matters before passing a particular provision. Procedure here is largely modelled on judicial proceedings: the case for and against the clause is put by counsel for the promoters and for the objectors; witnesses may be called and examined on oath; government departments may make representations and previous decisions of the Committee may be cited. Unopposed clauses are normally considered by the "Committee on Unopposed Bills", an informal meeting conducted by the Lord Chairman of Committees or his Counsel. The promoters, usually represented here by a Parliamentary Agent rather than counsel, must prove a need for the clauses. Unopposed clauses in local Bills promoted as a consequence of the Local Government Act 1972[196] were referred instead to more formal Select Committees. These applied the principles: (1) that the promoters had to prove a current need in their area that could only be met by legislation; (2) that the legislation would deal effectively with the problem; and (3) that provisions to meet a need common to all or a great number of authorities should not be included in a private Bill where the government had given a firm undertaking to introduce general legislation to meet that need.[197]

After the committee stage, the report stage is usually a formality although the Bill may be amended. The Bill is given a third reading and sent to the other House where the various stages are repeated, with some differences in detail.[198]

These procedures have been described as "cumbersome and expensive"; proceedings of private Bill committees "can be casual and their decisions unpredictable" and opposed Bill committees "tend to be legalistic and time-consuming".[199] Generally, private members take little interest in private legislation; when they do take an interest, however, their influence may be greater than in relation to public legislation as the whips are rarely applied and normally the government simply offers advice.[200]

---

[196] See above, para.5–003.

[197] See e.g. Special Report from the Select Committee on the County of South Glamorgan Bill, 1974–75 H.L. 347, Vol.366 H.L. Deb., cols 864–930, and Second Report of the Select Committee, 1975–76 H.L. 132.

[198] There are, for example, separate committees for opposed and unopposed *Bills* rather than *clauses*.

[199] The Study of Parliament Group, [1981] P.L. 206, 221. For reform proposals see *ibid.* pp.218–227 Report of the Joint Committee on Private Bill Procedure, 1987–88 H.L. 97, H.C. 628; *Government Response*, Cm. 1110, 1990.

[200] P. Norton, (1977) 30 *Parliamentary Affairs* 356.

10. Arrangement of Acts of Parliament[201]

The elements of a public general statute are normally arranged in the following order. A revised format for official versions of Bills and Acts was adopted as from the start of 2000–01 Session.[202]   **5–014**

(a) Short title

This is the title by which the statute is generally known (e.g. the "Interpretation Act 1978"). The practice of including a section providing for the citation of an Act by a short title developed in the nineteenth century; the Short Titles Act 1896[203] conferred short titles on many statutes passed before this practice became established.

(b) Year and chapter number

A statute passed today is cited by reference either to its short title or to the calendar year in which it is passed and its "chapter number" within that year. Statutes are numbered in the order in which Royal Assent is given. Until 1963[204] statutes were regarded as chapters of the legislation passed in the relevant *session* rather than *calendar year*, and were numbered accordingly.[205] Thus the Interpretation Act 1889 can be cited as "52 & 53 Vict. c. 63" (chapter 63 of the session that fell in the fifty-second and fifty-third years of the reign of Queen Victoria) and its replacement, the Interpretation Act 1978 as "1978 c. 30" (Chapter 30 of 1978).   **5–015**

(c) Long title

This describes the scope of the Act; if a Bill is amended so as to go beyond the long title as printed in the Bill the long title must be amended as well.

(d) Date

The date, given in square brackets, is that on which Royal Assent was signified.

(e) Preamble

Public Acts formerly[206] included a preamble, which could be lengthy, explaining why the Act was passed. They are still necessary for private Acts, and begin with   **5–016**

---

[201] See F. A. R. Bennion, *Statute Law* (3rd edn, 1990), Ch.3.

[202] See Second Report from the Select Committee on Procedure of the House, 1998–99 H.L. 52. The main changes were: a new format for clauses, with bold clause titles instead of side notes; Schedules in the same type size as clauses; more informative headers at the top of each page; some left alignment of internal headings; a new format for Repeal Schedules.

[203] Replacing the Short Titles Act 1892. See also the Statute Law Revision Act 1948, Sch.2.

[204] The practice was changed by the Acts of Parliament Numbering and Citation Act 1962.

[205] See G. Chowdharay-Best, "The Citation of Acts of Parliament" (2000) 21 Stat. L.R. 126 for a full analysis.

[206] Preambles are occasionally found in modern public Acts, particularly those which implement international conventions (e.g. the Oil in Navigable Waters Act 1963), public Acts of a local nature (e.g. the Towyn Trewan Common Act 1963) or legislation of a formal or ceremonial character (e.g. the John F. Kennedy Memorial Act 1964). Another example is the Canada Act 1982, which provided for the patriation of the Canadian Constitution.

the word "Whereas." For example the Parliament Act 1911 includes the following:

> "Whereas it is expedient that provision should be made for regulating the relations between the two Houses of Parliament:
>
> And whereas it is intended to substitute for the House of Lords as it at present exists a Second Chamber constituted on a popular instead of heredi-tary basis, but such substitution cannot be immediately brought into operation:
>
> And whereas provision will require hereafter to be made by Parliament in a measure effecting such substitution for limiting and defining the powers of the new Second Chamber, but it is expedient to make such provision as in this Act appears for restricting the existing powers of the House of Lords:"

(f) Enacting formula

This normally runs:

> "Be it enacted by the Queen's most Excellent Majesty, by and with the advice and consent of the Lords Spiritual and Temporal, and Commons, in this present Parliament assembled, and by the authority of the same, as follows:— "

The formula is slightly different for money Bills and Bills passed under the Parliament Acts procedures.

(g) Sections and Schedules

5–017   The body of an Act is divided into *sections* (equivalent to the *clauses* of the Bill) and *subsections*, a practice introduced by Lord Brougham's Act of 1850.[207] Each section is printed with *a marginal note* (from 2000–01, a *clause title*) indicating its content. Occasionally, errors may creep in. For example in the Married Women (Maintenance in Case of Desertion) Act 1886, a subsection (s.1(1)), which provided that a wife who had committed adultery could not claim alimony where her husband had deserted her, was printed with the marginal note "custody of children". A long Act may be divided into *Chapters* or *Parts*. Sections dealing with related subject matter may be grouped under *headings*. Matters of details are commonly included in *Schedules* at the end of the Act. Each schedule is linked to one of the preceding sections and may be divided into *Parts, paragraphs* and *sub-paragraphs*. There may also be *marginal notes* (now *paragraph titles*) and *cross-headings*. A *Schedule* may be used to set out the provisions of an earlier Act as amended.[208]

The body of the Act may include the following kinds of provisions: "defini-tions, principal provisions, administrative provisions, miscellaneous clauses, penal clauses, clauses dealing with the making of rules or byelaws, saving clauses, temporary and transitory clauses, repeals and savings, date of coming

---

[207] Interpretation of Acts Act 1850, 13 & 14 Vict. c. 21, s.2.
[208] Known as a "Keeling schedule". Examples include the Cinematograph Films Act 1948, Sch.2 and the Criminal Evidence (Amendment) Act 1997, Sch.2 (see A. Samuels, (1997) 18 Stat. L.R. 250). *Cf.* Education Act 1980, Sch.5.

into operation (if specified)" and the duration of the Act if it is limited.[209] "Common-form" clauses, those dealing with geographical extent, commencements, short title, citation and interpretation, are normally found at the end of the statute.

(h) Extent[210]

There is a presumption that an Act applies throughout the United Kingdom[211] **5-018** and not beyond.[212] "Extent clauses" are used to negative that presumption,[213] Acts which apply only to Scotland, Northern Ireland usually include the country in brackets in the short title.[214] Statutes may expressly be made to apply to transactions abroad. For example, the English courts may exercise jurisdiction in respect of murders committed by British subjects abroad[215] and some Acts extend to the territorial waters adjacent to the United Kingdom.[216]

(i) Commencement[217]

Until 1793 each Act of Parliament was deemed to come into operation from the **5-019** first day of the session in which it was passed, unless a commencement date was specified. The element of retrospectivity was seen to be unjust and the rule was changed.[218] An Act now comes into effect at the beginning of the day on which Royal Assent is given, unless some other commencement date is specified.[219] Today, it is commonly provided that the Act shall come into effect on a specified date, or on a day to be appointed, and, in the latter event, that different days may be appointed for different provisions, different purposes or different areas. The advantages of delayed commencement are that it gives those affected time to prepare, and gives ministers and departments time to draw up the necessary

---

[209] Statute Law Society, *Statute Law Deficiencies* (1972), p.6. (based on Sir Alison Russell's analysis of the general frame of a Bill.).

[210] See F. A. R. Bennion, *Statutory Interpretation* (4th edn, 2002), Pt V; Craies (2004), pp.401–413.

[211] i.e. England, Scotland, Wales and Northern Ireland but not the Channel Islands or the Isle of Man.

[212] See *R v Jameson* [1896] 2 Q.B. 425, 430; *Draper & Son Ltd v Edward Turner & Son Ltd* [1965] 1 Q.B. 424; *Air-India v Wiggins* [1980] 1 W.L.R. 815; *R (on the application of Al-Skeini) v Secretary of State for Defence* [2006] H.R.L.R. 7; *Office of Fair Trading v Lloyds TSB Bank plc* [2007] Q.B. 1.

[213] Extent clauses normally indicate expressly that an Act applies to Northern Ireland even though this is not strictly necessary.

[214] The Renton Committee recommended that where an Act affects only England and Wales this too should be indicated in the short title: Cmnd. 6053, p.124. This has not been implemented. The Transport (Wales) Act 2006 extends to England and Wales, some powers applying to transport to and from Wales. An Act that only affects England does not indicate this in the title. For the persuasive argument that Wales should be recognised as a jurisdiction, so that the extent clause of a statute can state that it only has effect in Wales, see T. H. Jones, J. H. Turnbull and J. M. Williams, (2005) 26 Stat. L.R. 135.

[215] Offences against the Person Act 1861, s.9

[216] e.g. Wireless Telegraphy Act 1949, ss.1, 6; Marine, etc., Broadcasting (Offences) Act 1967, s.1; *Post Office v Estuary Radio Ltd* [1968] 2 Q.B. 740. See generally the Law Commission's *Report on the Territorial and Extraterritorial Extent of the Criminal Law* (Law Com. No.91, 1978) and *Jurisdiction over Offences of Fraud and Dishonesty with a Foreign Element* (Law Com. No.180, 1989).

[217] See Bennion (2002), pp.229–238; Craies (2004), pp.359–381.

[218] Acts of Parliament (Commencement) Act 1793.

[219] Interpretation Act 1978, s.4. p.229.

regulations and orders after due consultation with interested parties. The main disadvantage is that it may be difficult for users to establish whether a particular provision is in force.[220] There may be many commencement orders in respect of one statute,[221] and some provisions may never be implemented at all, for reasons such as a lack of resources[222] and governmental second thoughts about the desirability of particular provisions.[223] Complaints have been voiced about the present position and various improvements proposed.[224] Governments have been exhorted to refrain from promoting legislation unless its implementation within a reasonable time can be foreseen.

In 1982 the Management and Personnel Office (the successor to the Civil Service Department) issued new guidance on the commencement of legislation.[225] Acts which do not provide for a commencement date to be appointed by order should normally provide for commencement not less than two months after Royal Assent (three months for consolidation Acts). Commencement provisions should be grouped at the end of any Bill in which that is practicable, if appropriate in a separate clause or Schedule; alternatively, a full list of commencement provisions should be published with the Act or in a press notice. Commencement dates should be specified in the Act where possible and appropriate; otherwise, every effort should be made to minimise the number of commencement orders and to rationalise their issue and the dates of commencement.

In interpreting statutes there is a presumption that statutes do not operate retrospectively so as to affect an existing right or obligation, except as regards matters of procedure.[226] Parliament may, however, use words in a statute which clearly show an intention that it should so operate.[227]

It was commonly assumed that statutory provisions that were not brought into force had no legal status or effect. However, this assumption was challenged in *R v Secretary of State for the Home Department, Ex p. Fire Brigades Union*.[228] Here, the Criminal Justice Act 1988[229] provided for a statutory criminal injuries compensation scheme to replace the scheme introduced by virtue of the royal prerogative. These provisions were, however, not brought into force. In 1993 the government announced that they would not be implemented and would be

---

[220] A most useful publication with this information is *Is it in force?*, an annual cumulative publication published in conjunction with the 4th edition of *Halsbury's Statutes of England.*

[221] See, e.g. the Consumer Credit Act 1974 and the Control of Pollution Act 1974.

[222] Examples include various provisions concerning legal advice and law centres (see below, para.10–016).

[223] Examples include the Easter Act 1928, provisions of the Children and Young Persons Act 1969, the Health and Safety at Work etc. Act 1974, s.71 (see J. R. Spencer, (1981) 131 N.L.J. 644) and the Criminal Justice Act 1988 (ss.108–117: a statutory scheme for criminal injuries compensation; see below).

[224] A. Samuels, (1979) *The Magistrate* pp.173–4; Statute Law Society Working Party on the Commencement of Acts of Parliament, [1980] Stat. L.R. 40.

[225] (1982) 79 L.S. Gaz. 968. See now the Cabinet Office, *Guide to Legislative Procedures* (2004), Ch.34.

[226] *Re Athlumney* [1898] 2 Q.B. 547, 551–552 *per* R. S. Wright J.; *Att.-Gen. v Vernazza* [1960] A.C. 965. See below, para.6–049.

[227] e.g. the War Damage Act 1965, which reversed the decision of the House of Lords in *Burmah Oil Co v Lord Advocate* [1965] A.C. 75; the Northern Ireland Act 1972, which retrospectively removed limitations on the power of the Parliament of Northern Ireland to legislate for the armed forces: see S. H. Bailey, D. J. Harris and B. L. Jones, *Civil Liberties: Cases and Materials* (4th edn 1995), pp.291–292.

[228] [1995] 2 W.L.R. 464.

[229] ss.108–117 and Schs 6 and 7.

repealed in due course[230] furthermore, the existing scheme would be replaced by a (less expensive) flat rate tariff scheme under the Royal prerogative. On an application for judicial review, the House of Lords held: (1) (unanimously) that the Home Secretary was under no legally enforceable duty to bring the 1988 Act provisions into force at any particular time[231]; but (2) (by three to two)[232] that while these provisions remained unrepealed it was under a duty to keep the question of implementation under review and it was an abuse or excess of power for him to exercise the prerogative power in a manner inconsistent with that duty. Of these two points, the first has the greater long-term significance, given that reliance on the Royal prerogative for such programmes is highly exceptional.

A statute is valid from the moment of commencement even though it has not been published. However, reliance on an unpublished statute may be open to challenge under the ECHR and the Human Rights Act 1998 on the ground that an interference with a Convention right is not "prescribed by law", and the exercise of a power conferred by an unpublished provision may be open to challenge on judicial review as unfair.[233]

(j) Definitions

Modern statutes commonly include "definition sections" in which the meaning   5–020
of words and phrases found in the statute are explained, either comprehensively (X "means" ABC) or partially (X "includes" ABC). The qualification "unless the contrary intention appears" is usually added. The Interpretation Act 1978 gives definitions of a large number of words and expressions. These are applicable where the words are found "in any Act, unless the contrary intention appears".[234] For example, "Secretary of State" means "one of Her Majesty's Principal Secretaries of State".[235] The 1978 Act also provides generally that:

"In any Act, unless the contrary intention appears—

(a) words importing the masculine gender include the feminine;
(b) words importing the feminine gender include the masculine;
(c) words in the singular include the plural and words in the plural include the singular".[236]

---

[230] Lord Browne-Wilkinson was rightly critical of this statement, noting that "It is for Parliament, not the executive, to repeal legislation" (p.474).

[231] This was "a decision of a political and administrative character quite unsuitable to be the subject of review by a court of law" (*per* Lord Keith at p.466).

[232] Lords Browne-Wilkinson, Lloyd and Nicholls, Lords Keith and Mustill dissenting.

[233] See *R (on the application of L) v Secretary of State for the Home Department* [2003] 1 W.L.R. 1230.

[234] Interpretation Act 1978, s.5 and Sch.1. They may also apply to subordinate legislation: see *ibid.* s.23.

[235] Many statutory functions are entrusted to "the Secretary of State". This device enables these functions to be switched between departments without the need for the statute to be amended. Where amendment is necessary, as where a function is given to a particular minister, it is usually effected by a statutory instrument under the Ministers of the Crown (Transfer of Functions) Act 1946. The "Secretary of State" device makes it more difficult to discover where responsibility for a particular function commonly lies.

[236] Section 6. See, e.g. *Annicola Investments v Minister of Housing and Local Government* [1968] 1 Q.B. 631, where the word "houses" was held to include a single house. Examples of cases where the "contrary intention" has appeared are those where the terms "every man" or "any person" have been held not to include women: e.g. *Chorlton v Lings* (1868) L.R. 4 C.P. 374; *Bebb v The Law Society* [1914] 1 Ch. 286.

There are also general provisions covering such matters as references to service by post, distance, time of day and the Sovereign, and the construction of subordinate legislation.[237]

(k) Amendments and repeals

5–021   Statutes commonly amend or repeal earlier enactments. Repeals are normally set out in a Schedule at the end, although important changes may also be included in the body of the Act or another Schedule. A power may be conferred by statute to repeal or modify Acts of Parliament by statutory instrument:

> "A provision by which it does so is known as a 'Henry VIII' clause, as it has been said 'in disrespectful commemoration of that monarch's tendency to absolution (*sic*)'. I doubt whether this is a just memorial to his late Majesty, who reigned 100 years before the Civil War and longer yet before the establishment of parliamentary legislative supremacy in our constitutional law. But the label is old and convenient".[238]

Such powers are controversial because they involve the transfer of power to change primary legislation to the executive, and they receive special scrutiny.[239] They are nevertheless an established feature of the statute book. A particularly important example is provided by s.2(2) and (4) of the European Communities Act 1972.[240] In *Thoburn v Sunderland City Council*[241] the Divisional Court firmly rejected the argument that a Henry VIII power, such as s.2(2) and (4) of the 1972 Act, can only lawfully be exercised in relation to Acts already on the statute book at the time when the Henry VIII power is created. Accordingly, regulations made under s.2(2) could lawfully amend the Weights and Measures Act 1985 so as to introduce a compulsory system of metric weights and measures. The court held that the 1985 Act could not be taken impliedly to have repealed or restricted the scope of s.2(2) as there was no *inconsistency* between the two measures. Furthermore, the 1985 Act was itself a consolidation of pre-1972 legislation and s.2(2) could clearly have amended that.[242] There is also no rule of law that Henry VIII powers can only be used to effect minor or modest changes in primary legislation,[243] although any doubts about the scope of such a power should be resolved by a restrictive approach.[244]

An earlier statute may also be amended or repealed by implication where the provisions of a later Act are so inconsistent that the two cannot stand together, although the courts seek to reconcile apparently inconsistent provisions where

---

[237] 1978 Act, ss.7–11.

[238] *per* Laws L.J. in *Thoburn v Sunderland City Council* [2002] EWHC 195 (Admin.), at para.[13]. See Craies (2004), pp.15–20.

[239] Below, para.5–028.

[240] Below, para.5–054.

[241] Above.

[242] "I cannot think that the law of our constitution is botched by such random consequences": *per* Laws L.J. at para.[52]. Laws L.J. also thought it "likely to be correct" that no implied repeal can be effected by a consolidation Act since it is presumed not to change the law: *ibid.*

[243] *ibid.*, at para.[73]. Similarly, there was no reason to construe s.2(2) as limited to effecting minor changes by reference to statements in Parliament; these statements fell outside the *Pepper v Hart* parameters and, apart from *Pepper v Hart*, an enforceable legitimate expectation could not be based on a statement in Parliament: para.[76].

[244] *R (on the application of Orange Personal Communications Ltd) v Secretary of State for Trade and Industry* [2001] Eu.L.R. 165, 177, *per* Sullivan J.

possible.[245] The Divisional Court has, however, held that the doctrine of implied repeal cannot apply in respect of "constitutional" statutes.[246]

At common law a repealed Act was treated as if it had never existed, except in relation to transactions past and closed, but this rule was changed in 1889.[247] For example, where an offence is committed against an existing statutory provision, criminal proceedings may now be instituted even after that provision is repealed, unless the repealing enactment provides otherwise.[248] There was also a common law rule that where statute A was repealed by statute B and statute B was subsequently repealed by statute C, statute A was regarded as reviving unless the contrary intention appeared. This rule was abolished in 1850: repealed statutes stay repealed unless expressly revived.[249] Unlike the Scots, the English have never had a rule that a statute can be disregarded on the ground that it is obsolete[250]; such provisions have to be repealed by a subsequent statute.[251]

11. ENROLLMENT AND PUBLICATION[252]

In medieval times a systematic official record of parliamentary statutes was not   **5–022** kept. An incomplete statute roll was started in the Chancery for internal purposes in 1299 and continued to the middle of the fifteenth century. *Rotuli Parliamentorum* ("Rolls of Parliament") were kept between 1290 and 1503; they contained a general record of parliamentary proceedings, but only included some

---

[245] *Vauxhall Estates Ltd v Liverpool Corporation* [1932] 1 K.B. 733; *Ellen Street Estates Ltd v Minister of Health* [1934] 1 K.B. 590. There is a presumption against implied repeal: *R v Governor of Holloway Prison, Ex p. Jennings* [1982] 1 W.L.R. 949; *Henry Boot Construction (UK) Ltd. v Malmaison Hotel (Manchester) Ltd* [2001] Q.B. 388; *Nwogbe v Nwogbe* [2000] 2 F.L.R. 744 (presumption applied even though a provision was left unenforceable); *cf. R (on the application of O'Byrne) v Secretary of State for the Environment, Transport and the Regions* [2002] H.L.R. 30, CA (provisions in the Green Belt (London and the Home Counties Act 1938 preventing the sale of land in the London green belt without ministerial consent held to be impliedly repealed by the right-to-buy provisions of the Housing Act 1985); on appeal, the House of Lords held that as a matter of construction the statutes were not in conflict [2002] 1 W.L.R. 3250. Furthermore, provisions in an Act cannot be impliedly repealed by general words in subsequent subordinate legislation: see *Hyde Park Residence Ltd v Secretary of State for the Environment and the Regions* (2000) 80 P. & C.R. 419.

[246] Above, para.5–002.

[247] Interpretation Act 1889, s.38(2); see now the Interpretation Act 1978, s.16.

[248] See *Bennett v Tatton* (1918) 88 L.J.K.B. 313; *Postlethwaite v Katz* (1943) 59 T.L.R. 248; *R v West London Stipendiary Magistrate, Ex p. Simeon* [1983] 1 A.C. 234 (repeal of the "sus" law held not to affect a prosecution for an offence committed before the repeal came into effect). *Cf. Aitken v South Hams District Council* [1995] 1 A.C. 262 (notice to abate a noise nuisance under s.58 of the Control of Pollution Act 1974 continues to be effective notwithstanding repeal of s.58 by the Environment Protection Act 1990, by virtue of s.16 of the 1978 Act).

[249] See now the Interpretation Act 1978, s.15. Similarly, the repeal of an Act does not revive anything not in force or existing at the time of the repeal: *ibid.* s.16(1)(a). Hence, if statute B modifies statute A by partial repeal or substitution of words, statute A continues in effect subject to the modification notwithstanding the repeal of statute B.

[250] Under the doctrine of desuetude, Acts of the Scottish Parliament may become obsolete and repealed by a long period of contrary practice by the community: *M'Ara v Magistrates of Edinburgh* 1931 S.C. 1059; *Brown v Magistrates of Edinburgh* 1913 S.L.T. 456, 458; *Earl of Antrim's Petition* [1967] A.C. 691.

[251] See above, para.5–002.

[252] F. A. R. Bennion, *Statutory Interpretation* (4th edn, 2002), pp.182–187.

of the Acts. From 1483 "Inrollments of Acts" (records of each Act "engrossed" on parchment) were certified by the Clerk of the Parliaments and delivered to the Chancery; the officers of the Chancery commonly termed them the "Parliament Rolls" although they are distinct from the *Rotuli Parliamentorum*. From the middle of the nineteenth century two copies of each Act have been printed on vellum; one copy is kept in the House of Lords, the other in the Public Records Office.[253]

Lawyers at first relied on private manuscript collections of statutes. These formed the basis of unofficial printed collections that began to appear from 1481 onwards. From 1483 *Sessional Volumes of Statutes* were printed and published; these came to be issued by the King's or Queen's Printer but were not technically an official series published by royal or parliamentary authority. Useful collections of *Statutes at Large* appeared in the late eighteenth century, with various editors (e.g. Pickering (1762), Ruffhead and Runnington (1786) and Tomlins and Raithby (1811)). These covered statutes from Magna Carta to date; continuation volumes, sometimes covering several sessions, and based on the King's Printer's copies, were produced in the eighteenth and nineteenth centuries under the titles of *Statutes of the United Kingdom or Public General Statutes*. The Controller of Her Majesty's Stationery Office was appointed as the Queen's Printer in 1886. From 1940 the King's or Queen's Printer's copies of statutes have been published on an annual rather than a sessional basis, with *Public General Acts and Measures* issued separately from *Local and Personal Acts*; each Act is also published individually by HMSO. From 1996, all statutes (as from 1988) have been published on the Internet as well as on paper.[254]

The first official collection of statutes was the edition of *Statutes of the Realm* prepared by the Record Commissioners and published in nine volumes between 1810 and 1828. This gave texts and translations of statutes between 1235 and 1713, excluding the Commonwealth period,[255] and while a considerable improvement on what was otherwise available, was in various respects incomplete and inaccurate.[256] Later in the century, the Statute Law Committee[257] supervised the publication of the first edition of *Statutes Revised*, which comprised the public Acts in force at the end of 1878, as amended, given in chronological order. Two further editions were produced between 1888 and 1929 and in 1950. This series was superseded by *Statutes in Force*, which was published in loose booklet form rather than in bound volumes to facilitate the substitution of revised copies of statutes that are heavily amended; there are also supplements. The volumes are arranged in 124 groups (131 were originally

---

[253] See. S. A. de Smith and R. Brazier, *Constitutional and Administrative Law* (8th edn, 1998), p.90. For an analysis of the speech acts involved in the enactment process, see B. S. Jackson, "Who enacts statutes?" (1997) 18 Stat. L. R. 177, noting that the production of neither the printed nor vellum copy is necessary for the Act to come into force. A third print is made of Measures of the General Synod.

[254] *www.opsi.gov.uk/acts.htm*. On the role of HMSO in the legislative process, see C. Tullo and A. Pawsey, (1998) 29 *The Law Librarian* 148. The trading functions of HMSO were privatised in 1996, passing to The Stationery Office (TSO). HMSO is now part of the Office of Public Sector Information (OPSI). OPSI is in turn now part of the National Archives.

[255] As to which see C. H. Firth and R. S. Rait, *Acts and Ordinances of the Interregnum* (1911).

[256] See T. F. T. Plucknett, *Statutes and their Interpretation in the Fourteenth Century* (1922), Ch.II.

[257] See above, para.5–012.

planned) according to subject-matter.[258] These official collections are supplemented by the *Index to the Statutes and the Chronological Table of the Statutes*.[259] As a matter of citation, references to another Act in a statute passed after 1889 are, unless the contrary intention appears, to be read as referring to: (a) any revised edition of the statutes printed by authority; (b) if it is not printed there, to the *Statutes of the Realm*; or (c) in other cases, to the Queen's Printer's copy.[260] Occasionally it may be necessary to go behind the published version and check its authenticity against the original source.[261] Where through a printing error a statute as printed by HMSO does not reflect the version of the vellum print, the Clerk of the Parliament authorises the issue of a correction slip. This is sometimes done where the vellum print does not reflect the version assented to Parliament.[262]

There are various departmental compilations of statutes and regulations published by HMSO and regularly revised, such as *The Taxes Acts* (for HMRC) and several works on the law of social security (for the Department of Work and Pensions). The most important current commercial collections are *Halsbury's Statutes of England* (4th edn: a revised edition arranged by subject matter) and *Current Law Statutes Annotated* (arranged in chronological order). There are also many collections on particular topics published in loose-leaf encyclopedias. An important advantage of these commercial publications is that the statutes are given in annotated form. Statutes and statutory instruments are also included in a range of databases including *LexisNexis, Westlaw* and *Lawtel*, there is a website devoted to Welsh legislation,[263] and an official UK Statute Law Database has been made available for public use from December 20, 2006.[264]

12. VALIDITY

Subject to the position that arises in consequence of the European Communities **5–023** Act 1972, the validity of an Act of Parliament may not be questioned in an English court; there is no Bill of Rights or other constitutional limitation to which legislation must conform as there is, for example, in the United States of

---

[258] The published materials are, however, significantly out of date (P. Clinch, [1994] Stat. L.R. 64) and work on revised material (as distinct from newly enacted Acts) and other tables and indexes was suspended in order to concentrate on the development of a new statute law database: Lord Mackay of Clashfern L.C., Vol.546 H.L. Deb., June 9, 1993, WA 55.

[259] This covers public and general legislation; editions since 1974 have also recorded the effect of local and personal legislation enacted since then. A *Chronological Table for Local Legislation 1797–1994* (Law Com. No.241 Scot Law Com. No.155) was published by HMSO in 1996, the culmination of 20 years' work by the Law Commission; an *Index to the Local and Personal Acts 1850–1995* was published simultaneously: see 31st Annual Report of the Law Commission 1996, pp.48–50. An online version of the Local Acts Table to the end of 2005 available at www.legislation.hmso.gov.uk/chron-tables/local/introduction-to-local-acts.htm. A *Chronological Table of Private and Personal Acts 1539–1997* (Law Com. No.256; Scot Law Com. No.170) was published in 1998. This is also on the Internet.

[260] Interpretation Act 1978, s.19.

[261] See, e.g. *R v Casement* [1917] 1 K.B. 98, 134, in relation to the Treason Act 1351, where the *Rotuli Parliamentorum* and the Statute Rolls were consulted.

[262] F. A. R. Bennion, *Statutory Interpretation* (4th edn, 2002), pp.183–185; J. J. Rankin, [1987] Stat. L.R. 53.

[263] Wales Legislation Online: *www.wales-legislation.org.uk*. See D. Miers and D. Lambert, [2002] P.L. 663.

[264] *www.statutelaw.gov.uk/Home.aspx*.

America.[265] This point has arisen in cases where it has been claimed that a private Act is invalid on the ground that parliamentary standing orders have not been observed[266] or that Parliament has been misled by fraudulent misrepresentations[267]: such claims have failed. In 1982, a taxpayer argued that the change in the status of MPs from self-employed meant that they had become employees of the Crown and so disqualified from membership. As a result, the Social Security Act 1975, which imposed on him certain obligations to pay national insurance contributions, was invalid. His argument was emphatically and summarily rejected by Nourse J.: "the court can only look at the Parliamentary roll".[268] Of much more importance was the claim of a group of Canadian Indian Chiefs that the Canada Act 1982 was *ultra vires* on the ground that the consent of the "Dominion" of Canada had not been obtained as required by s.4 of the Statute of Westminster 1931, merely the consent of the Senate and House of Commons of Canada. Sir Robert Megarry V.-C. held[269] that he owed "full and dutiful obedience" to every Act of Parliament, and that the Canada Act 1982 was such an Act. The Court of Appeal held[270] that even on the assumption that Parliament could bind its successors by a provision such as s.4, the application failed as there had been compliance with that section. Attempts to impugn statutes on the ground that they are contrary to international law have also failed.[271]

This issue arises in a different form in respect of legislation enacted through the procedure of the Parliament Acts 1911–1948. In *R (on the application of Jackson) v Attorney General*[272] opponents of the Hunting Act 2004, which banned the hunting of a wild mammal with a dog and hare coursing, sought a declaration that the Parliament Act 1949 was not an Act of Parliament and consequently of no legal effect, and accordingly the Hunting Act 2004 was not an Act of Parliament and was of no legal effect. This was rejected by the House of Lords. Among the points made were: (1) the court had jurisdiction to determine whether these Acts were indeed Acts of Parliament[273]; (2) the Parliament Acts provided an alternative way of enacting primary legislation, not a new form of sub-primary parliamentary legislation or delegated legislation; (3) the question then arose, what were the limits to s.2 of the 1911 Act? This provided that "any Public Bill (other than a Money Bill or a Bill containing any provision to extend the maximum duration of Parliament beyond five years)" could, if passed by the House of Commons in two successive sessions,[274] be presented directly for

---

[265] See above, para.5–002. The question of possible conflict with European legislation is considered below, paras 5–054—5–059. As to whether a court may exercise a jurisdiction to determine whether an *ostensibly* authentic Act of Parliament is *in fact* authentic see S. A. de Smith and R. Brazier, *Constitutional and Administrative Law* (8th edn, 1998), pp.89–93.

[266] *Edinburgh and Dalkeith Rly v Wauchope* (1842) 7 Cl. & F. 710.

[267] *Lee v Bude and Torrington Junction Railway* (1871) L.R. 6 C.P. 576; *Pickin v British Railways Board* [1974] A.C. 765.

[268] *Martin v O'Sullivan* [1982] S.T.C. 416, 419, *affirmed* [1984] S.T.C. 258.

[269] [1983] Ch. 77.

[270] *ibid.*

[271] *Mortensen v Peters* 1906 S.L.T. 227; *Cheney v Conn* [1968] 1 W.L.R. 242.

[272] [2006] 1 A.C. 262. See M. Plaxton, (2006) 69 M.L.R. 249; A. Young, [2006] P.L. 187; A. McHarg, [2006] P.L. 539; J. Jowell, [2006] P.L. 562.

[273] The case raised a matter of statutory interpretation. The certificate of the speaker under s.2(2) that the provision of s.2 have been complied with is "conclusive for all purposes, and shall not be questioned in any court of law". But this does not determine the status of that which is enacted via this route. See Lord Nicholls of Birkenhead at paras [49]–[51], Lord Hope of Craighead at paras [110]–[116], Lord Carswell at para.[169].

[274] Reduced from three by the Parliament Act 1949.

Royal Assent without the assent of the House of Lords. The members of the House of Lords were agreed on the outcome of the present case but not on the overall scope of s.2.

First, all seem agreed that a money Bill,[275] a Bill to extend the duration of Parliament or a Bill for confirming a Provisional Order[276] could not validly be enacted through this route, and the courts would have jurisdiction to declare that a purported Act of any such description was not a valid Act of Parliament.[277] These were *expressly* excluded. Secondly, a majority of the House[278] stated that a Bill to remove from s.2 the words expressly excluding Bills to extend the life of Parliament could also not validly be taken through the s.2 route. This was *impliedly* excluded.[279] Thirdly, there were differing views as to whether there could be any further *implied* exclusions. Four of the nine members of the House were clear that there could not.[280] Four members, with varying degrees of specicifity, expressly left this open.[281] The ninth judge, Lord Rodger of Earlsferry, said[282] that it was unnecessary to decide "what limits, if any, there may be to the scope of s.2(1)," but then mentioned one exception (a Bill to delete the exclusion of a Bill extending the maximum duration of Parliament) on which "I . . . specifically reserve my opinion." It is thus unclear which group was the one to which he was aligned. Nevertheless, the House unanimously rejected the argument that s.2 was subject to the particular implied limitation that it could not be used to amend the conditions which s.2(1) laid down for its use.[283] It also rejected (as unworkable) the position of the Court of Appeal (not supported in argument by any parties to the appeal) that there was an implied limitation that s.2 could be used for modest amendments to those conditions but not fundamental ones.[284]

For the future, the possibility of arguing that there are *other* implied limits to the use of s.2(1) for particular changes that might be thought to be morally

---

[275] The reason for the exclusion of a money Bill from s.2 is that it can be presented for Royal Assent under s.1 if it is not passed within one month. It is accordingly difficult if not impossible to envisage circumstances in which there would be any wish to use s.2 for this purpose.

[276] Expressly excluded from the definition of "public Bill" by s.5.

[277] See Lord Hope of Craighead at para.[118] (in respect a Bill extending the maximum duration of Parliament).

[278] See Lord Nicholls of Birkenhead at paras [58]–[59] ("This *implied* restriction is necessary in order to render the *express* restriction effectual. It is ancillary to the express exclusion."); *cf.* Lord Steyn at para.[79], Lord Hope of Craighead at para.[122], Baroness Hale of Richmond at para.[164], Lord Carswell at para.[175]. Lord Bingham of Cornhill disagreed, at paras [32], [37], noting that it would be odd if s.2 could not be used to change the period stated in s.1(1) for the submission of money Bills or to amend s.5. Lords Rodger of Earlsferry (para.[139]), Walker of Gestingthorpe (para.[141]) and Brown of Eaton-under-Heywood (para.[194]) left the point open.

[279] Lord Nicholls, *ibid.*

[280] Lord Bingham at para.[30], Lord Nicholls at para.[61], Lord Steyn at para.[88] and Baroness Hale at para.[158]. For example, the "known object of the Parliament Bill . . . was to secure the grant of Home Rule to Ireland. This was, by any standards, a fundamental constitutional change": Lord Bingham at para.[31].

[281] Lord Hope at paras [123]–[124], Lord Walker of Gestingthorpe at para.[141], Lord Carswell at paras [176]–[178] and Lord Brown of Eaton-under-Heywood at para.[194].

[282] At para.[139].

[283] Which the 1949 Act had done by reducing the number of sessions in which the Bill had passed the Commons from three to two.

[284] In any event the Court of Appeal had been wrong to conclude that the change effected by the 1949 Act was "modest": see Lord Bingham at para.[38].

objectionable, or fundamental to constitution[285] (like complete abolition of the House of Lords), does not seem effectively to have been ruled out. For those who were of the view that there was only one (or no) implied exception to s.2(1), the existence of any legal limit preventing the enactment of "outrageous" legislation would require a further change to the doctrine of parliamentary sovereignty itself.[286]

There were in the seventeenth century dicta that Acts of Parliament "against common right and reason, or repugnant, or impossible to be performed",[287] or contrary to natural justice by making a man judge in his own cause[288] could be held by the judges to be void. However, these dicta were controversial even at that time, were not acted upon, and are not accepted today: "since the supremacy of Parliament was finally demonstrated by the Revolution of 1688 any such idea has become obsolete".[289] This position was reaffirmed by Lord Scarman in *Duport Steels Ltd v Sirs*[290]:

> " ... [I]n the field of statute law the judge must be obedient to the will of Parliament as expressed in its enactments. In this field Parliament makes and unmakes the law: the judge's duty is to interpret and to apply the law, not to change it to meet the judge's idea of what justice requires. Interpretation does, of course, imply in the interpreter a power of choice where differing constructions are possible. But our law requires the judge to choose the construction which in his best judgment meets the legislative purposes of the enactment. If the result be unjust but inevitable, the judge may say so and invite Parliament to reconsider its provision. But he must not deny the statute. ... Only if a just result can be achieved without violating the legislative purpose of the statute may the judge select the construction which best suits his idea of what justice requires."

This position is not challenged by the enactment of the Human Rights Act 1998.[291] It should, however, be noted that in *R (on the application of Jackson) v Attorney General*[292] Lord Steyn[293] expressly left open the question whether in

> "exceptional circumstances involving an attempt to abolish judicial review or the ordinary role of the courts, the Appellate Committee of the House of Lords or a new Supreme Court may have to consider whether this is a constitutional fundamental which even a sovereign Parliament acting at the behest of a complaisant House of Commons cannot abolish."

---

[285] e.g. Complete abolition of the House of Lords, mentioned by Lord Brown at para.[184].

[286] See Lord Steyn's remarks, below.

[287] *Dr Bonham's Case* (1610) 8 Co. Rep. 114, 118, *per* Coke C.J.; Coke subsequently expressed a different view extrajudicially: 4 *Coke's Institutes* 37, 41.

[288] *Day v Savadge* (1614) Hob. 85, 87 *per* Hobart C.J.; *cf.* Holt C.J. in *City of London v Wood* (1701) 12 Mod. 669, 686–688.

[289] *Pickin v British Railways Board* [1974] A.C. 765, 782 *per* Lord Reid. *Cf.*, however, the extrajudicial statements by a number of judges that particular statutory provisions might not be immune from judicial scrutiny: see above, para.4–043.

[290] [1980] I.C.R. 161, 189–190.

[291] See below, Ch.8.

[292] [2006] 1 A.C. 262. See also Lord Hope of Craighead at paras [104]–[107], Baroness Hale of Richmond at para.[159].

[293] At para.[102]. No such issues arose in the present case.

C. SUBORDINATE LEGISLATION[294]

1. DELEGATION

Each year the output of subordinate[295] legislation vastly exceeds that of Acts of **5–024** Parliament. Law-making powers have been delegated by Parliament to a wide variety of public authorities, including the Crown, ministers, the National Assembly for Wales (and from 2007 Welsh ministers), local authorities and public corporations. Procedural rules may be made for the courts by Rule Committees consisting of judges and lawyers.[296]

In addition, the Crown retains certain powers to legislate by virtue of the Royal prerogative. There have been examples of the delegation of rule-making powers by Parliament for as long as Parliament has been acknowledged as the supreme law-making body. However, the nineteenth and twentieth centuries have seen an enormous increase, albeit "wayward and unsystematic",[297] in the extent of delegation, matching the extension of the powers and functions of government. Each of the World Wars saw the creation of a complex system of statutory powers, mostly contained in delegated legislation made, respectively, under the Defence of the Realm Acts 1914–15 and the Emergency Powers (Defence) Acts 1939–40; every aspect of national life was closely regulated.

The developments were at first welcomed on the ground that Parliament was thereby able to deal with the issues of importance while the details could be settled departmentally. Certain judges and academic commentators were less enthusiastic. The most extreme of the criticism was expressed by the then Lord Chief Justice, Lord Hewart, in a book entitled "The New Despotism" (1929). The main objections articulated were that wide powers were given to the executive, and that the safeguards against abuse, particularly Parliamentary safeguards, were inadequate. Some people held the view that the delegation of legislative power was unwise and might be dispensed with altogether. However, it was difficult to disentangle general objections to the extension of state power from objections to the particular form that the extension took. Delegated legislation was one of the issues considered by the Committee on Ministers' Powers, which reported in 1932.[298] The Committee expressed the view that "whether good or bad" the practice of delegation was inevitable[299]:

---

[294] See C. K. Allen, *Law and Orders* (3rd edn, 1965); Sir William Wade and C. F. Forsyth, *Administrative Law* (9th edn, 2004), Ch.22; S. A. de Smith and R. Brazier, *Constitutional and Administrative Law* (8th edn, 1998), Ch.17; K. Puttick, *Challenging Delegated Legislation* (1988); HMSO, *Statutory Instrument Practice* (4th edn, 2006); R. Baldwin, *Rules and Government* (1995), Ch.4; E. C. Page, *Governing by Numbers* (2001).

[295] Strictly, the term "subordinate" legislation covers "all legislation, permitted as well as authorised, that is inferior to statute law"; "delegated" legislation is that "authorised by Act of Parliament": HMSO, *Access to Subordinate Legislation* (House of Commons Library Document No. 5).

[296] Civil Procedure Rules; Criminal Procedure Rules.

[297] Allen (1965), p.32.

[298] Cmd. 4060. The first chairman was the Earl of Donoughmore; he was succeeded as chairman by Sir Leslie Scott.

[299] *ibid.*, p.5.

"the system of delegated legislation is both legitimate and constitutionally desirable for certain purposes, within certain limits, and under certain safeguards."[300]

It pointed to the pressure on parliamentary time, the technicality of the subject matter of modern legislation, the difficulty of working out administrative machinery in time to insert all the required provisions in the Bill, the flexibility of a system which allowed for adaptation to unknown future conditions without the necessity of an amending Act, and for the opportunity for experiment, and the need on occasion for emergency action. The Committee made a number of suggestions for improving the terminology, publication and scrutiny of delegated legislation. One of the members of the Committee, Ellen Wilkinson MP, thought that certain passages gave:

"the impression that the delegating of legislation is a necessary evil, inevitable in the present state of pressure on parliamentary time, but nevertheless a tendency to be watched with misgiving and carefully safeguarded."[301]

Nevertheless, since then the constitutional propriety of delegation has not seriously been questioned, although concern has been expressed at the growing tendency in recent years for statutory instruments to deal "no longer . . . with means but with principles".[302]

2. THE FORMS OF SUBORDINATE LEGISLATION

5–025 The nomenclature of nineteenth century subordinate legislation was varied and confusing. Different procedures were followed for making and issuing the different kinds of rules. Some kind of regularity was created by the Rules Publication Act 1893, and the position was further improved by its replacement, the Statutory Instruments Act 1946. Today, most subordinate legislation takes the form of *statutory instruments* made under the procedure laid down by the 1946 Act or *byelaws* made under the Local Government Act 1972,[303] although other forms are possible. Different names are still used for different kinds of statutory instruments; these names merely indicate the general nature of the instrument and no longer reflect any difference as to the procedure whereby they are made and promulgated. The selection of a particular title is a matter of departmental practice.

---

[300] *ibid.*, p.51.
[301] *ibid.* p.137. She felt that in the conditions of the modern state the practice "instead of being grudgingly conceded ought to be widely extended, and new ways devised to facilitate the process".
[302] Andrew Bennett, MP, Chairman of the Joint Committee on Statutory Instruments, in evidence to the Select Committee on Procedure: Second Report, 1986–87 H.C. 350, *The Use of Time on the Floor of the House*, pp.vii, 6. The Committee noted this view "with concern". See also K. Puttick, *Challenging Delegated Legislation* (1988), Ch.3.
[303] See below, para.5–029.

The following are the main kinds of subordinate legislation. *Orders in Council* are made by the Queen with the advice of the Privy Council (the "Queen in Council"). They may be made under the Royal prerogative[304]; more commonly they are made under a statutory power, in which case they are normally statutory instruments. *Proclamations* are notices given by the Queen to her subjects; again, they may be made under the Royal prerogative[305] or statute[306] and are published in the *London Gazette. Royal Warrants* are made under the Royal prerogative and normally concern the pay and pensions of members of the armed forces. *Regulations, Rules, Orders, Schemes* and *Warrants* are usually statutory instruments. The usage of these terms is imprecise although "Rules" are usually[307] the procedural rules of a court or tribunal, and the term "Warrant" is used to describe some Treasury instruments which confer an authority or an entitlement to money. *Directions* may occasionally have to be promulgated as statutory instruments. *Measures of the National Assembly for Wales* are made under Pt 3 of the Government of Wales Act 2006 (ss.93–103) within the areas of legislative competence conferred by the Act.[308] They are subject to approval by Her Majesty in Council.

3. Preparation of Subordinate Legislation

Subordinate legislation is generally drafted by lawyers in the government depart-   **5–026**
ment concerned, in the Treasury Solicitor's office where the department has no legal branch, or, in cases of exceptional importance or difficulty, by one of the Parliamentary draftsmen.[309] The "division of labour" between the Parliamentary counsel responsible for statutory drafting and departmental lawyers has been described as "a basic weakness of the system",[310] although any significant change would obviously require a large increase in the number of counsel. The "preparational parameters" mentioned above[311] in relation to statutes are not applicable to nearly the same extent, although the draftsman has to take care to ensure that the instrument is *intra vires*[312]; the "operational parameters" are, however, equally important.[313] Prior consultation between the department and advisory bodies and interest groups is a well-established practice[314]; consultation

---

[304] e.g. an Order altering the constitution of a colony. An Order in Council under the prerogative may not alter the common law or statute law: *The Zamora* [1916] 2 A.C. 77, 90.

[305] e.g. coinage proclamations.

[306] e.g. proclamations of a state of emergency under the Emergency Powers Act 1920.

[307] Not invariably: see the Immigration Rules.

[308] See ss.94, 95 and Sch.5.

[309] E. C. Page, *Governing by Numbers* (2001), Ch.6, discussing the relative contribution of lawyers and administrators, who are commonly relatively junior.

[310] F. A. R. Bennion, *Statute Law* (3rd edn, 1990), p.57.

[311] At para.5–009.

[312] See below, para.5–031.

[313] Bennion (1990), pp.57–58.

[314] See J. F. Garner, [1964] P.L. 105; A. D. Jergesen, [1978] P.L. 290; Page (2001), Ch.7, noting that the process is dominated by the executive but that interest groups do have an impact, particularly where "their case can be made in a form that fits the conception of what government officials want to achieve" (p.154).

requirements may be imposed in the parent Act.[315] Local authority byelaws are prepared by the authority concerned but must normally conform to the models issued by government departments to stand much chance of being confirmed. Important statutory instruments may be examined by the Cabinet's Legislation Committee.

4. PROCEDURES FOR MAKING SUBORDINATE LEGISLATION

(a) Statutory instruments

(i) *Procedure*

5–027 The "statutory instrument" procedure applies to delegated legislation: (1) made, confirmed or approved under a power conferred on the Crown after 1947 by statute[316] and expressed to be exercisable "by Order in Council"[317]; (2) made, confirmed or approved under a power conferred on a minister after 1947 by statute[318] or on Welsh ministers by any statute or Measure or Act of the National Assembly for Wales, and expressed to be exercisable "by statutory instrument"[319]; (3) made under a power contained in a statute passed before 1948 to make "statutory rules"[320] within the meaning of the Rules Publication Act 1893[321]; or (4) confirmed or approved under certain powers contained in pre-1948 statutes.[322] A statute may provide that a power conferred on a body other than a minister shall be exercisable by statutory instrument.[323]

(ii) *Laying before Parliament and scrutiny*

The procedural requirements for statutory instruments are prescribed partly by the parent Acts and partly by the 1946 Act. The parent Act may require that the

---

[315] A statutory duty to consult is regarded as mandatory (see below para.5–028). However, a court will not imply an obligation to consult if there is no express provision: *Bates v Lord Hailsham* [1972] 1 W.L.R. 1373.

[316] Sub-delegated legislation made under a power conferred by statutory instrument is thus not normally within the scope of the 1946 Act.

[317] Statutory Instruments Act 1946, s.1(1).

[318] See n.316 above.

[319] Statutory Instruments Act 1946, s.1(1) and (1A); s.1(1A) inserted by the Government of Wales Act 2006, Sch.10, para.2. The 1946 Act is generally applied with modifications to statutory instruments made by Welsh ministers, the role of Parliament being undertaken by the National Assembly for Wales: see 2006 Act, Sch.10, para.3.

[320] Provided, in most cases, that the rule is of a "legislative" and not an "executive" character: Statutory Instruments Regulations 1947 (SI 1948/1), reg.2(1).

[321] Statutory Instruments Act 1946, s.1(2). There are certain exceptions: see SI 1948/1, reg.2(3) and Schedule.

[322] Statutory Instruments Act 1946, s.9(1); SI 1948/1, reg.2(2); Statutory Instruments (Confirmatory Powers) Order 1947 (SI 1948/2). The rule has to be legislative rather than executive in character and subject to the requirement that it be laid before Parliament.

[323] See e.g. Wireless Telegraphy Act 2006, s.122 (orders and regulations made by OFCOM); Constitutional Reform Act 2005, s.46 (Supreme Court Rules) (this applies generally to procedural rules for courts).

instrument[324] be laid[325] before Parliament.[326] If it does it has to be laid "before it comes into operation", unless it is essential that it comes into operation sooner, in which case the Speakers of the Commons and the Lords must be informed of the reason.[327] This process merely brings the instrument to the attention of Parliament. An instrument may have to be laid in draft[328] or after it has been made. In addition, the instrument may be made subject to the "affirmative resolution" or the "negative resolution" procedure. Under the former, the instrument can only come into effect if a resolution approving it is passed, within the period (if any) specified in the parent Act, by each House (or the Commons alone if it deals with financial matters).[329] Under the latter, which is a much more common requirement,[330] but which is less efficacious in ensuring Parliamentary scrutiny, either House may within 40 days of its being laid resolve that the instrument should be annulled.[331] Since 1973 it has been possible for proceedings on statutory instruments to be taken in Commons Standing Committees on Delegated Legislation[332] (from 2006–07 known as Delegated Legislation Committees, which are now "general committees" rather than "standing committees") rather than on the floor of the House. Indeed, from 1994, all affirmative statutory instruments have been automatically referred to a standing committee, unless de-referred on a government motion, and debates on the floor of the House

---

[324] i.e. "any document by which" a power to make orders etc. is "exercised": Statutory Instruments Act 1946, s.l(l). A document referred to in regulations need not be laid provided that it is not part and parcel of the regulations: *R v Secretary of State for Social Services, Ex p. Camden London Borough Council* [1987] 1 W.L.R. 819; and see A. I. L. Campbell, [1987] P.L. 328.

[325] As to the meaning of "laying", see the Laying of Documents before Parliament (Interpretation) Act 1948. It normally involves delivery of copies to the Votes and Proceedings Office of the Commons and the Office of the Clerk of the Parliaments. Subordinate legislation other than statutory instruments may also have to be laid before Parliament, e.g. under the Immigration Act 1971; see *R v Immigration Appeals Tribunal, Ex p. Joyles* [1972] 1 W.L.R. 1390.

[326] Sometimes just the House of Commons: e.g. orders prescribing maximum rates under the Rates Act 1984: *R v Secretary of State for the Environment, Ex p. Greenwich London Borough Council, The Times*, December 19, 1985; *R v Secretary of State for the Environment, Ex p. Leicester City Council* (1985) 25 R.V.R. 31 (references in s.4(1) to "Parliament" to be read in context as to a reference to the House of Commons only). Where the power to make subordinate legislation has been transferred exclusively to Welsh ministers, any requirement as to laying, approval etc. is to be construed as referring to the National Assembly and not Parliament: Government of Wales Act 2006, Sch.11, paras 33–35 (as to the previous position, see the 1998 Act, s.44).

[327] Statutory Instruments Act 1946, s.4(1), as amended by the Constitutional Reform Act 2005, Sch.6, para.4.

[328] See *ibid.* s.6(1). The instrument may not be made within 40 days, and either House may resolve that it shall not be made.

[329] An example of a draft not approved (here, by the House of Lords) was the draft Greater London Authority (Election Expenses) Order 2000; the right not to approve/to annul was last exercised in 1968.

[330] In 1976–77 there were 127 instruments subject to affirmative procedure, 669 subject to negative procedure, 37 general instruments only required to be laid, and 197 general instruments not so required: First Report from the Select Committee on Procedure, 1977–78 H.C. 588 Vol.1, p.xxxi; an increasing proportion of instruments have been made subject to the first two procedures. In 2003–04, 207 affirmative instruments were laid before the Commons (204 considered in committee, 13 on the Floor) and 1,038 negative instruments so laid (16 considered in committee, 0 on the Floor): H.C. Sessional Returns 2003–04.

[331] Statutory Instruments Act 1946, s.5(l). This takes the form of an address to Her Majesty praying that the instrument be annulled, and is commonly termed a "prayer". A rare example of annulment by the House of Lords took place in respect of the Greater London Authority Elections Rules 2000 (SI 2000/208).

[332] Prior to 1995–96, known as Standing Committees on Statutory Instruments.

limited to $1\frac{1}{2}$ hours. Nevertheless, Parliamentary scrutiny of the merits of instruments under these procedures has not been particularly effective in either forum.[333]

From 2002–03, the House of Lords has established a Merits of Statutory Instruments Committee. It examines the merits of any statutory or other legislative instrument which is subject to the affirmative or negative procedure. It draws "to the special attention of the House" any instrument laid in the previous week which it considers may be:

(a) politically or legally important or that gives rise to issues of public policy likely to be of interest to the House;

(b) inappropriate in view of changed circumstances since the passage of the parent Act;

(c) inappropriately implementing EU legislation; or

(d) imperfectly achieving its policy objectives.

In particular cases its reports have had an impact on debates and through correspondence with the government.[334] The Committee has been critical of shortcomings in the management of the flow of instruments,[335] although the government's response was generally non-committal.[336]

An instrument may also be scrutinised by the Joint Committee on Statutory Instruments. This committee was first appointed in 1973, and replaced the separate committees of each House that had formerly undertaken this work.[337] The Chairman is an Opposition MP. The Committee examines instruments laid before either House and subject to either form of resolution procedure, other instruments of a general character and special procedure orders. It may draw the attention of Parliament to a particular instrument on any of a number of specified grounds, or on any other grounds not impinging on the merits of or policy behind the instrument.[338] The specified grounds are that:

(i) it imposes a charge on the public revenues;

(ii) it is made under an enactment excluding it from challenge in the courts;

(iii) it purports to have retrospective effect where the parent Act does not so provide;

---

[333] See First Report from the Select Committee on Procedure, 1977–78 H.C. 588, Vol. 1, pp.xxix–xxxix; J. Beatson (1979) 12 Cornell Int. L.J. 199; P. Norton, *The Commons in Perspective* (1981) pp.95–99; P. Byrne, (1976) 29 *Parliamentary Affairs* 366; A. Beith MP, (1981) 34 *Parliamentary Affairs* 165.

[334] Third Special Report, 2003–04 H.L. 73, *The Committee's Method of Working*; Sessional Reviews of the Work of the Committee: 2003–04 H.L. 206; 2004–05 H.L. 106; 2005–06 H.L. 275. In 2005–06, 22% of the affirmative and 9% of the negative instruments were reported. The first ground is by far the commonest relied on. The Committee in 2006–07 is to begin taking oral evidence on perhaps the six most significant SIs.

[335] Twenty-ninth Report, 2005–06 H.L. 149, *The Management of Secondary Legislation*. The Committee has provided *Guidance* to the departments.

[336] 2005–06 H.L. 275, pp.28–37.

[337] See the Report from the Joint Committee on Delegated Legislation, 1971–72 H.C. 45, H.L. 184.

[338] H.C. Standing Order No.151.

(iv) it has been unjustifiably delayed in publication or being laid before Parliament;

(v) it has not been notified in proper time to the Lord Chancellor and the Speaker where it comes into effect before being presented to Parliament;

(vi) it may be *ultra vires*;

(vii) it appears to make an unusual or unexpected use of the powers conferred by the parent Act;

(viii) it requires elucidation as to its form or purport; or

(ix) it is defective in drafting.

Instruments subject to House of Commons proceedings only are examined by the Commons members of the Joint Committee acting as a Commons Select Committee on Statutory Instruments. No formal steps have to be taken in either House following an adverse report by one of these committees, although such reports may be referred to in other Parliamentary proceedings concerning the instruments, and the work of these committees and their predecessors seem to have played a part in reducing delays and improving drafting.[339] A survey published in 1988 concluded that the technical process of scrutiny now appears to work as effectively as a parliamentary committee can be expected to function.[340] Nevertheless, the increasing use of delegated legislation for major policy implementation, the lack of parliamentary time for debate, the increase in decisions taken before the Committee's report is published and the emphasis on political rather than legal points in debates on the merits have led to "the reality that parliamentary scrutiny of delegated legislation is not effective democratic control".[341] The Hansard Society Commission[342] considered the "whole approach of Parliament to delegated legislation to be highly unsatisfactory. The House of Commons in particular should give its procedure for the scrutiny of statutory instruments a thorough review".[343]

The Commons Select Committee on Procedure has subsequently made some recommendations for reform, which have yet to be implemented.[344] These include proposals that: (1) a sifting committee be established to recommend

---

[339] See S. A. de Smith and R. Brazier, *Constitutional and Administrative Law* (8th edn, 1998), pp.349–351.

[340] A view confirmed by E. C. Page, *Governing by Numbers* (2001), Ch.8.

[341] J. D. Hayhurst and P. Wallington, "The Parliamentary Scrutiny of Delegated Legislation" [1988] P.L. 547, 573–576. The conclusions are Professor Wallington's. For proposals for minor procedural changes, see Hayhurst and Wallington, pp.575–576; Second Report from the Select Committee on Procedure, 1986–87 H.C. 350, *The Use of Time on the Floor of the House*, pp.vi–xi. See also T. St. J. Bates, [1986] Stat. L.R. 114.

[342] Above, para.5–009.

[343] Report, pp.89–90. Particular changes proposed include review of SIs by departmentally related select committees; the use of special standing committees on longer or more complicated SIs; more meaningful motions for debate on an SI in standing committee, including the possibility of suggesting (although not making) amendments (pp.90–94).

[344] Fourth Report, 1995–96 H.C. 152, *Delegated Legislation*; First Report, 1999–2000 H.C. 48, *Delegated Legislation*: First Report, 2002–03 H.C. 501, *Delegated Legislation: Proposals for a Sifting Committee*.

which negative instruments merited debate and which affirmative instruments did not[345]; (2) "praying time" should be extending from 40 to 60 days; (3) motions in the DL Committee should be substantive and amendable; (4) proposals for certain very complex draft orders ("super-affirmatives") should be laid for pre-legislative scrutiny by the relevant departmental select committee; (5) no decision on an SI should be made until it has been considered by the Joint Committee on Statutory Instruments (matching the position in the House of Lords). These proposals were endorsed by the Royal Commission on the Reform of the House of Lords,[346] and are eminently sensible.

5–028   A development of some significance that was in the course of being introduced when the Commission reported was the establishment by the House of Lords of a Select Committee on the Scrutiny of Delegated Powers (now the Select Committee on Delegated Powers and Regulatory Reform).[347] Its terms of reference are:

> "to report whether the provisions of any bill[348] inappropriately delegate legislative power, or whether they subject the exercise of legislative power to an inappropriate degree of Parliamentary scrutiny."

It receives memoranda from the relevant government department and may receive oral evidence and has generally been able to report to the House before the Committee stage. It has been particularly concerned with so-called "Henry VIII clauses", which enable primary legislation to be amended or repealed by subordinate legislation; the appropriate level of scrutiny (i.e. affirmative or negative procedure or no parliamentary control) has been recommended according to the circumstances.[349] It has suggested that matters that should not be left to delegation include: provisions designed to ensure compatibility with the ECHR; substantial changes to electoral law; the power to increase the severity of a sentencing power; and the establishment of quasi-judicial institutions.[350] The Committee has made a useful contribution, its reports appearing on time and commanding respect and its intervention having led to changes in the legislation proposed on a number of occasions.

---

[345] The Committee's proposals were reaffirmed in 2002–03 H.L. 501, but rejected on the unconvincing ground that this would "lead to greatly increased demands on parliamentary time and on government departments" (Second Report, 2002–03 H.C. 684, Annex A). The work of the equivalent House of Lords committee (above) provides a useful precedent.

[346] *A House for the Future*, Cm. 4534, Ch.7. It suggested that the sifting committee could be a Joint Committee (except in respect of financial matters). It also proposed that the House be given formal power to delay secondary legislation by up to three months, in place of current power of absolute veto.

[347] Its establishment was proposed by the (Jellicoe) Select Committee on the *Committee Work of the House* (1991–92 H.L. 35-I). It first conducted a general inquiry into the principles of its work (First Report, 1992–93 H.L. 57) and periodically conducts reviews of its work: most recently in its Eighteenth Report, 2004–05 H.L. 110, *Special Report Sessions 2003–04 and 2004–05: The Work of the Committee.*

[348] It does not, however, consider Consolidation or Supply Bills.

[349] See 1993–94 H.L. 90, pp.3–4. It takes the view that there should be a presumption in favour of the affirmative procedure: Third Report, 2002–03 H.L. 21, *Henry VIII Powers*, debated at H.L. Deb., January 14, 2003, cols 165–187; and see 2003–04 H.L. 9, pp.10–12.

[350] 37th Report, 1999–2000 H.L. 130, *Special Report for 1999–2000—The Committee's Work*, para.36.

(iii) *Orders under the Legislative and Regulatory Reform Act 2006*

Special arrangements for scrutiny were introduced in respect of "deregulation orders" made under Pt I of the Deregulation and Contracting Out Act 1994.[351] These orders, made by the Secretary of State, amended or repealed statutory provisions passed before the end of the 1993–94 session, in order to remove or reduce burdens on business. The procedure was thought by the government to be necessary because of the difficulty of finding time for primary legislation on such matters; however, the switch to secondary legislation aroused controversy because of the perceived inadequacy of the scrutiny arrangements. Accordingly, after a consultation stage, proposals for deregulation orders were examined by a special Deregulation Committee of the House of Commons and by the House of Lords Select Committee On Delegated Powers and Deregulation (as the Delegated Powers Scrutiny Committee became), which reported to their respective Houses. Apart from substantive scrutiny, these committees also performed the functions of the Joint Committee on Statutory Instruments in relation to proposed orders. The committees did not have the power to veto draft orders, but adverse reports were treated with the "utmost seriousness".[352] Sixty days (excluding recesses) were allowed for "Parliamentary consideration" from the day that the proposed order was laid. Orders were subject to an affirmative resolution by each House. The procedure was relatively little used in the 1997–2001 Parliament. It was, however, suggested that this procedure could form the basis for improved scrutiny of other legislation.[353] A similar procedure was indeed established in respect of remedial orders under the Human Rights Act 1998.[354]

The Regulatory Reform Act 2001 replaced the 1994 Act powers by new arrangements that were broader in scope[355] and the Commons and Committees were renamed.[356] The Orders under the 1994 Act could only be used to remove or reduce burdens. The new regulatory reform orders had to have that effect, but in addition could re-enact a provision that imposed a burden provided it was proportionate to the benefit expected to result from the re-enactment; make a new provision that imposed a burden that affected any person in the carrying on of the activity provided it was proportionate to the benefit expected to result from its creation; and remove inconsistencies and anomalies. Regulatory reform orders under the 2001 Act were also relatively little used,[357] and the legislative structure was changed again by the Legislative and Regulatory Reform Act 2006. The passage of the Bill was controversial, with criticism from many quarters[358] that

---

[351] ss.1–6. See A. Page, *Current Law Statutes Annotated 1994*; M. Royle, (1994) 15 Stat. L.R. 170.

[352] Government response (1993–94 H.C. 404) to the *Fourth Report of the Select Committee on Procedure* (1993–94 H.C. 238), p.viii. "In normal circumstances the Government would expect to submit a revised proposal or to withdraw the proposal altogether": *ibid.*

[353] See M. Ryle, "The Deregulation and Contracting Out Bill 1994—A Blueprint for the Reform of the Legislative Process?" (1994) 15 Stat. L.R. 170.

[354] See below, Ch.8.

[355] See C. Andrews, *Current Law Statutes Annotated 2001*.

[356] Deregulation and Regulatory Reform Committee (HC), from 2001–02 the Regulatory Reform Committee; Select Committee on Delegated Powers and Regulatory Reform (HL).

[357] See *A Bill for Better Regulation*: Consultation Document (Cabinet Office, July 2005).

[358] See e.g. H.C. Procedure Committee, First Report, 2005–06 H.C. 894; Regulatory Reform Committee, First Special Report, 2005–06 H.C. 878 and Government Response, 2005–06 H.C. 1004 and First Special Report, 2006–07 H.C. 160 (summarising the legislative process of the Bill).

the proposed powers were overbroad.[359] The proposed establishment of this as a special route for the implementation of Law Commission reports was dropped, and other provisions watered down.

The Act provides two order-making powers. Section 1 enables a minister by order to make any provision which he considers would serve the purpose of removing or reducing any burden,[360] or the overall burdens, resulting directly or indirectly for any person from any legislation.[361] The provision that may be made includes provision abolishing, conferring or transferring, or providing for the delegation of, functions of any description, provision creating or abolishing a body or office, and provision made by amending or repealing any enactment.[362] The second power is to make an order for securing that regulatory functions[363] are exercised so as to comply with the principles that regulatory activities should be: (a) carried out in a way which is transparent, accountable, proportionate and consistent; and (b) targeted only at cases in which action is needed.[364] Provision cannot be made (except merely restating an enactment[365]) unless the minister considers that certain conditions, where relevant, are satisfied in relation to that condition.[366] Provision cannot be made that restates an enactment unless the minister considers that it would make the law more accessible or more easily understood.[367] Other limits include that provision may not be made for the delegation of any function of legislating by any subordinate instrument; for the imposition, abolition or variation of any tax (although the Treasury has certain narrow powers to make regulations); for the creation of a new offence or increase the penalty for an existing offence above a specified level[368]; to authorise any forcible entry, search or seizure or compel the giving of evidence; or to amend or repeal Pt I of the present Act or the Human Rights Act 1998.[369]

---

[359] A letter by six Cambridge Law Professors pointed out that the Bill could be used (inter alia) to create a new offence of incitement to religious hatred, abolish trial by jury, introduce house-arrest, allow the Prime Minister to sack judges and "reform Magna Carta" (*The Times*, February 16, 2006). They were unkindly referred to in debate by Lord Lipsey as "six silly Cambridge law professors" (H.L. Deb., June 13, 2006, col.161) but their criticisms, with those of others, had effect.

[360] i.e. (a) a financial cost; (b) an administrative inconvenience; (c) an obstacle to efficiency, productively or profitability; or (d) a sanction, criminal or otherwise, which affects the carrying on of any lawful activity: s.1(3). A financial cost or administrative inconvenience may result from the form of legislation (e.g. where it is hard to understand: s.1(5)).

[361] s.1(1), (2). The Bill had proposed a power of "reforming legislation". The legislation may be primary or secondary: s.1(6).

[362] s.1(7). An order may contain consequential, supplementary, incidental or transitional provision (s.1(8)) and may bind the Crown (s.1(9)).

[363] Defined in s.32(2). It does not include any function of conducting criminal or civil proceedings: s.32(3)(b)(ii).

[364] s.2.

[365] As defined in s.2(5).

[366] s.3(1), (2). These are that the policy objective could not be secured by non-legislative means; the provision's effect is proportionate to the policy objective; the provision strikes a fair balance between the public interest and the interests of any person adversely affected by it; the provision does not remove any necessary protection; or prevent any person from continuing to exercise any right or freedom which that person might reasonably expect to continue to exercise; and is not of constitutional significance.

[367] s.3(3), (4).

[368] Two years' imprisonment (indictment); imprisonment for a term exceeding 51 weeks (summary offences) or 12 months (triable either way offences) or a fine exceeding level 5 on the standard scale.

[369] ss.4–8.

An order must be made by statutory instrument after prescribed consultation.[370] A draft order must be laid before Parliament with an explanatory document. The document must contain the minister's recommendation as to whether the order should be subject to the negative resolution procedure, the affirmative resolution procedure or the super-affirmative resolution procedure. This applies unless either House requires a more rigorous procedure.[371]

Overall, the new powers are not significantly broader their predecessors and extensive use remains unlikely. As before, a ministerial undertaking has been given that orders will not be used "to implement highly controversial reforms."[372]

(iv) *Printing and publication*

Once a statutory instrument is made it must be sent to the Queen's Printer and copies must as soon as possible be printed and sold by or under the authority of the Queen's Printer.[373] The requirements as to printing and sale do not apply to instruments classified as "local";[374] to general instruments otherwise regularly printed and published; to temporary instruments; to schedules whose printing and sale "is unnecessary or undesirable having regard to the nature or bulk of the document" and to any other steps taken to publicise them; and to confidential instruments not yet in operation.[375] The requirements may, however, be imposed by the Statutory Instruments Reference Committee appointed by the Speakers.[376] The Queen's Printer allocates statutory instruments received to the series for the calendar year in which they are made, and numbers them consecutively as near as may be in the order in which they are received.[377] They are cited by their number and year.[378] Since 1997, the full text of statutory instruments has been published on the Internet as well as on paper,[379] an arrangement that has instantly transformed their accessibility.

HMSO also publishes: (1) periodical lists of the titles of instruments issued; (2) an Annual Edition with full texts of instruments issued, an appendix of prerogative legislation and relevant lists, tables and indices; (3) the annual *Table of Government Orders*, a chronological list showing which instruments are still in force, amended or revoked; and (4) the *Index to Government Orders*, issued

---

[370] s.13.

[371] s.15. The procedures are set out in ss.16–18.

[372] Jim Murphy MP, H.C. Deb., February 9, 2006, cols 1058–1059.

[373] Statutory Instruments Act 1946, s.2(1), as amended with retrospective effect by the Statutory Instruments (Production and Sale) Act 1996 (the addition of the words "or under the authority of" regularised the position that the Queen's Printer had contracted out the printing of SIs since at least 1965).

[374] See generally on local statutory instruments, R. J. B. Morris, [1990] Stat. L.R. 28.

[375] Statutory Instruments Regulations 1947 (SI 1948/1), regs 3–8. These matters have to be "certified" by the responsible authority (i.e. minister) in each case. This must be done in proper form: *Simmonds v Newell* [1953] 1 W.L.R. 826.

[376] SI 1948/1, reg.11, as amended by SI 2006/1640. The Committee has power to determine certain other questions which may arise as to numbering, publication, classification, etc. It consists of the Lord Chairman of Committees (Lords), the Chairman of Ways and Means (Commons) and six senior officers of both Houses: *Erskine May's Parliamentary Practice* (22nd edn, 1997), p.577.

[377] SI 1948/1, reg.3.

[378] Statutory Instruments Act 1946, s.2(2).

[379] See *www.opsi.gov.uk/stat.htm*.

every two years, which lists existing powers to make delegated legislation and current exercises of those powers according to subject matter. LexisNexis Butterworths publish *Halsbury's Statutory Instruments*, which lists and summarises delegated legislation in force according to subject matter, gives the annotated text of the "more important orders, rules and regulations, selected on the basis of the likely requirements of subscriber",[380] and includes a regular updating service. Regulations are available (as amended) on such databases as *Westlaw* and *LexisNexis* and also normally included in encyclopedias on particular topics.

Rules and Orders made before 1949 are included in the series *Statutory Rules and Orders and Statutory Instruments Revised to Dec. 31st 1948*, which is arranged according to subject matter.[381]

(v) *Commencement*

The position as to the commencement of subordinate legislation is unclear. The subordinate legislation in question may expressly provide for its own commencement.[382] If it does not, there is some authority that an order can only come into effect when it is *made known*.[383] In a later case,[384] however, Streatfeild J. directed a jury as follows:

> "I do not think that it can be said that to make a valid statutory instrument it is required that all of these stages should be gone through; namely, the making, the laying before Parliament, the printing and the certification of that part of it which it might be unnecessary to have printed. In my judgment the making of an instrument is complete when it is first of all made by the Minister concerned and after it has been laid before Parliament."[385]

The defendant was prosecuted for breach of a schedule to a statutory instrument that had not been printed as required by the Act. Streatfeild J. held that it was not invalid for lack of publication.

Section 3(1) of the Statutory Instruments Act 1946 provides that regulations should be made for the publication by HMSO of lists showing the dates of issue of instruments printed and sold by the Queen's Printer; in any legal proceedings, "an entry therein shall be conclusive evidence of the date on which any statutory instrument was first issued" by HMSO.

Section 3(2) provides that in criminal proceedings for a contravention of "any such statutory instrument" it is:

---

[380] *Halsbury's Statutory Instruments: A User's Guide*, p.5.

[381] Earlier editions were published in 1896 and 1904. Up to and including 1960 the Annual Editions were also arranged by subject matter rather than chronologically.

[382] From 1947 all statutory instruments required to be laid before Parliament after being made must show the dates on which they come into operation; this does not, however, cover the whole field as not all instruments must be laid. Where a day is specified, the instrument comes into effect at the beginning of that day: Interpretation Act 1978, ss.4(a), 23.

[383] Bailhache J. in *Johnson v Sargant* [1918] 1 K.B. 101. *Cf. Jones v Robson* [1901] 1 Q.B. 673 where a requirement to give *notice* of certain orders was held to be directory (but in this case the order had been published, and the defendant knew of it).

[384] *R v Sheer Metalcraft Ltd* [1954] 1 Q.B. 586.

[385] *ibid.* p.590. (There may of course be no "laying" requirement.)

"a defence to prove that the instrument had not been issued by Her Majesty's Stationery Office at the date of the alleged contravention unless it is proved that at that date reasonable steps had been taken for the purpose of bringing the purport of the instrument to the notice of the public, or of persons likely to be affected by it, or of the person charged".[386]

It is not, however, clear whether this defence is available: (1) in respect of any instrument which has not been issued, including those exempted from publication requirements; or (2) in respect of an instrument which has not been issued in breach of a publication requirement; or (3) in respect only of the period between the making of an instrument and its issue in circumstances where such issue does subsequently take place.[387] Moreover, the statutory defence does not apply to subordinate legislation other than statutory instruments. There is much to be said for the principle of *Johnson v Sargant*[388]: "To bind a citizen by a law, the terms of which he has no means of knowing,[389] is the very essence of tyranny."[390]

(b) Local authority byelaws[391]

District and London borough councils have a general power to make byelaws for   **5–029**
the "good rule and government" of the area "and for the prevention and suppression of nuisances" therein[392] in addition there are numerous specific byelaw-making powers.[393] The procedure for making byelaws, to be followed in all cases unless specific provision is otherwise made, is laid down by s.236 of the Local Government Act 1972. Byelaws cannot take effect until they are confirmed by the appropriate minister. Public notice must be given at least one month before application is made for confirmation, and a copy must be available for inspection. The confirming authority may fix the date on which a byelaw is to come into effect; if no date is so fixed, it comes into effect one month after it is confirmed. When confirmed, a copy must be printed and deposited at the authority's offices; it must be open to public inspection without payment at all reasonable hours, and copies supplied on payment of such sum, not exceeding 20p per copy, as the authority may determine.[394]

---

[386] It has been suggested that a similar defence should be created in respect of Acts of Parliament: Statute Law Society Working Party on Commencement of Acts of Parliament [1980] Stat. L.R. 40, 51–52. The defence failed on the facts in *R v Sheer Metalcraft Ltd, loc. cit.* n.384 above.

[387] The difficulty is created by the word "such": see D. Lanham, (1974) 37 M.L.R. 510, 521–523. The *Sheer Metalcraft* case: (1) is not inconsistent with the first interpretation, but the point as to whether the defence can apply in respect of *exempted* instruments did not arise as the minister had not certified that the instrument should be exempt; (2) is inconsistent with the second interpretation; and (3) is inconsistent with the third, as there was no suggestion that the schedule was ever published.

[388] [1918] 1 K.B. 101. Lanham, (*ibid.*) argues that even where a date of commencement is specified, an instrument can only come into effect when published; *contra*: A. I. L. Campbell, [1982] P.L. 569; response by Lanham, [1983] P.L. 395.

[389] Ignorance of a published instrument would probably not be regarded as a defence: ignorance of the law is not excuse.

[390] *per* Barwick C.J. in *Watson v Lee* (1980) 54 A.L.J.R. 1, 3.

[391] Sometimes spelt "by-laws."

[392] Local Government Act 1972, s.235(1).

[393] See *Encyclopedia of Local Government Law*, App.6.

[394] Local authorities do not always seem to be aware of these obligations.

5. ARRANGEMENT OF STATUTORY INSTRUMENTS

5–030   A statutory instrument is normally arranged in the following order[395]:

(i) Year and number of the instrument.

(ii) An indication of the subject matter; this corresponds to the categories in the lists published periodically by HMSO.

(iii) Title.

(iv) The dates when the instrument was made, laid before Parliament and is due to come into operation.

(v) A recital naming the person making the instrument and the relevant enabling powers.[396]

(vi) The main provisions of the instrument. These are termed *articles* (in an Order), *regulations* or *rules* as the case may be. Subdivisions are called *paragraphs*. The instrument may be divided into *Parts* and may include a *Schedule*. Common form provisions as to title, definitions and commencement are placed at the beginning.

(vii) An indication of the minister by whom the instrument was signed.

(viii) An "Explanatory Note" stated to be "not part of" the instrument.

6. VALIDITY OF SUBORDINATE LEGISLATION[397]

5–031   All delegated legislation must conform to the limits laid down expressly or impliedly in the enabling Act; if those limits are exceeded the validity of the instrument[398] may be challenged in the courts.[399] Challenges may be made directly, for example by a claim in the High Court for a declaration that the legislation is *ultra vires*; or indirectly, for example by raising the argument that an instrument is *ultra vires* as a defence to enforcement proceedings, such as a

---

[395] See Bennion (1990), pp.55–57. Electronic templates are provided: see *Statutory Instrument Practice* Circulars.

[396] The standard formula includes the words "and of all his other enabling powers". This does not cover all powers that *could* be used but only those necessary for the SI to have effect or to conform to EU law or be compatible with Convention rights: *Polestar Jowetts v Komori UK Ltd* [2006] EWCA Civ 536.

[397] See generally Sir William Wade and C. F. Forsyth, *Administrative Law* (9th edn, 2004), pp.874–891; K. Puttick, *Challenging Delegated Legislation* (1988); T. St J. N Bates, (1998) 19 Stat. L.R. 155. Successful challenges to the *vires* of statutory instruments between 1914 and 1986 are summarised by J. D. Hayhurst and P. Wallington, [1988] P.L. 547, 566–573.

[398] Or other form of delegated legislation.

[399] The courts may also ensure that prerogative legislation falls within the scope of an existing prerogative power.

prosecution for contravening the instrument.[400] An instrument may be *ultra vires* if there has been a failure to comply with a "mandatory" procedural requirement. Some requirements are merely "directory"; the authorities are "directed" to comply with them, but compliance is not a pre-condition to the validity of the instrument. It is not easy to predict whether a court will hold a particular requirement to be mandatory or directory. In this context the duty to consult affected parties has been held to be mandatory,[401] but requirements as to publication[402] and laying[403] have been held to be directory. The scope of a consultation requirement was described as follows by Webster J. in *R v Secretary of State for Social Services, Ex p. Association of Metropolitan Authorities*[404]:

> " . . . in any context the essence of consultation is the communication of a genuine invitation to give advice and a genuine receipt of that advice. In my view it must go without saying that to achieve consultation sufficient information must be supplied by the consulting to the consulted party to enable it to tender helpful advice. Sufficient time must be given by the consulting to the consulted party to enable it to do that, and sufficient time must be available for such advice to be considered by the consulting party. Sufficient, in that context, does not mean ample, but at least enough to enable the relevant purpose to be fulfilled. By helpful advice, in this context, I mean sufficiently informed and considered information or advice about aspects of the form or substance of the proposals, or their implications for the consulted party, being aspects material to the implementation of the proposal as to which the Secretary of State might not be fully informed or advised and as to which the party consulted might have relevant information or advice to offer."

---

[400] Resort to this latter mode of proceeding is well established and in *R v Reading Crown Court, Ex p. Hutchinson* [1988] Q.B. 384, D.C. (pet. dis. [1988] 1 W.L.R. 308, HL) the Divisional Court affirmed that its availability had not been affected by the principle of *O'Reilly v Mackman* [1983] 2 A.C. 237 that matters of *vires* should normally be raised directly on an application for judicial review. The availability of collateral challenge was confirmed by the House of Lords in *Boddington v British Transport Police* [1999] 2 A.C. 143, overruling *Bugg v Director of Public Prosecutions* [1993] Q.B. 473, where the Divisional Court held that collateral challenge could only be based on a claim that the instrument was substantively as distinct from procedurally invalid.

[401] *Agricultural etc. Training Board v Aylesbury Mushrooms Ltd* [1972] 1 W.L.R. 190.

[402] *R v Sheer Metalcraft Ltd* [1954] 1 Q.B. 586; see above, para.5–028.

[403] See *Bailey v Williamson* (1873) L.R. 8 Q.B. 118; *Starey v Graham* [1899] 1 Q.B. 406, 412; *Springer v Doorly* (1950) L.R.B.G. 10 (W. Indian Court of Appeal); A. I. L. Campbell, [1983] P.L. 43; but see de Smith, Woolf and Jowell, *Judicial Review of Administrative Action* (5th edn, 1995), p.275, for the argument that laying requirements should be regarded as mandatory; *cf. Bain v Thorne* (1916) 12 Tas. L.R. 57 (Sup.Ct. of Tasmania). In 1981 Ronald Biggs escaped extradition from Barbados to the UK because the Barbados High Court held that regulations designating the UK as a country to which a fugitive could be extradited should have been laid before the Barbados Parliament: *The Times*, April 24, 1981: *Biggs v Commissioner of Police* [1982 May] W.I.L.J. 121. Note, however, that the decision turned on a provision of the Interpretation Act of Barbados to the effect that the term "shall" [i.e. in "shall . . . be laid"] was "to be construed as imperative" (*ibid.*). In *R v Secretary of State for Social Services, Ex p. Camden London Borough Council* (unreported, February 26, 1986) Macpherson J. held that a requirement that supplementary benefit regulations "shall not be made" unless a draft had been laid before Parliament and approved by each House imposed a mandatory requirement. On appeal, the Court of Appeal assumed this to be so without deciding the point ([1987] 1 W.L.R. 819).

[404] [1986] 1 W.L.R. 1, 4–5.

An instrument may also be quashed if there is unfairness in the consultation process.[405]

An instrument may be *ultra vires* if its subject matter lies beyond the scope of the enabling power. For example, in *Hotel and Catering Industry Training Board v Automobile Proprietary Ltd*[406] the House of Lords held that a power to make an order establishing a Training Board for persons employed "in any activities of industry or commerce" did not enable an order to be made in respect of members' clubs. Clear words are needed to authorise the making of subordinate legislation that interferes with fundamental rights[407] or rights conferred by other primary legislation,[408] or that amends primary legislation.[409] Subordinate legislation must be read and given effect, so far as possible, in a way that is compatible with Convention rights,[410] and public authorities will act unlawfully if they make subordinate legislation that is incompatible with such rights.[411] Subordinate legislation may also be *ultra vires* if it conflicts with directly effective Community law.[412]

The established grounds upon which byelaws may be struck down are usually said to be those of *ultra vires*, uncertainty, unreasonableness and repugnancy to

---

[405] *R v Secretary of State for Health, Ex p. US Tobacco International Inc* [1992] 1 Q.B. 353 (ban on oral snuff quashed where the sole importers were not given the details of the scientific advice on which the ban was based).

[406] [1969] 1 W.L.R. 697. See also *R v Customs and Excise Commissioners, Ex p. Hedges and Butler Ltd* [1986] 2 All E.R. 164 (power to demand production of the whole of the records of a business (including records concerning non-dutiable goods) held not to be "incidental" or "supplementary" to powers concerning the regulation of excise warehouses and dealings in dutiable goods); *R v Secretary of State for Social Services, Ex p. Cotton, The Times*, December 14, 1985; *R v Inland Revenue Commissioners, Ex p. Woolwich Equitable Building Society* [1987] S.T.C. 654; *R v Secretary of State for Trade and Industry, Ex p. Thomson Holidays, The Times*, January 12, 2000 (order required to be founded on facts found in Monopolies Commission report and not wider in its scope).

[407] In accordance with the principle of legality recognised by Lord Steyn in *R v Secretary of State for the Home Departments, Ex p. Pierson* [1997] 3 All E.R. 577, 603–607 (see below, para. 6–043); see e.g. *R v Lord Chancellor, Ex p. Witham* [1998] Q.B. 575 (Lord Chancellor's general power to fix court fees cannot be used to set such high levels that would effectively bar the poor from access to the courts), distinguished in *R v Lord Chancellor, Ex p. Lightfoot* [2000] Q.B. 597 (deposit of £250 to be paid by debtor wishing to petition for bankruptcy did not interfere with the right of access to the court) and *R v Legal Aid Board, Ex p. Duncan & Mackintosh, The Independent*, February 23, 2000 (right to choose one's legal representative not inherent in right of access to the court).

[408] *R v Secretary of State for Social Security, Ex p. Joint Council for the Welfare of Immigrants* [1997] 1 W.L.R. 275 (regulations excluding from social security benefits asylum seekers who did not claim asylum on arrival held ultra vires as this was a serious impediment to the exercise of their rights under the Asylum and Immigration Appeals Act 1993; primary legislation with retrospective effect was passed to secure this: Asylum and Immigration Act 1996, s.11).

[409] *McKiernon v Chief Adjudication Officer, The Times*, November 1, 1989; *Britnell v Secretary of State for Social Security* [1991] 1 W.L.R. 198; *R v Secretary of State for Trade and Industry, Ex p. Orange Personal Communications Ltd* (unreported, October 25, 2000); *cf. R v Secretary of State for the Environment, Transport and the Regions, Ex p. Spath Holme Ltd* [2001] 1 All E.R. 195, 202–203, *per* Lord Bingham of Cornhill.

[410] Human Rights Act 1998, s.3(1), below, para.8–006.

[411] *ibid.* s.6(1), below, para.8–010.

[412] e.g. regulations as well as primary legislation were disapplied in *R v Secretary of State for Transport, Ex p. Factortame (No.2)* [1990] 1 A.C. 603; *cf. Bourgoin SA v Ministry of Agriculture, Fisheries and Food* [1986] Q.B. 716 (revocation of licence *ultra vires*); Case C-173/99, *R (on the application of BECTU) v Secretary of State for Trade and Industry* [2001] 1 W.L.R. 2313, ECJ (Working Time Regulations failed to implement directive correctly); *Secretary of State for Social Security v Walter* [2001] EWCA Civ (regulations held not to be directly discriminatory on the ground of sex); *Oakley Ltd v Animal Ltd* [2005] EWHC 210 (Ch).

the general law,[413] although the last three grounds may also be regarded as facets of the *ultra vires* doctrine. For example, in *Staden v Tarjanyi*[414] a district council made a byelaw in respect of a pleasure ground which provided:

> "A person shall not in the pleasure ground . . . take off, fly or land any glider, manned or unmanned, weighing in total more than four kilogrammes. . . . "

The respondent flew a hang glider over the pleasure ground and was prosecuted under the byelaw. It was conceded that "in" meant "in or over". The Divisional Court held that the byelaw was invalid for uncertainty:

> " . . . anyone engaged upon the otherwise lawful pursuit of hang gliding must know with reasonable certainty when he is breaking the law and when he is not breaking the law. . . . [T]o be valid the byelaw must set some lower level below which the glider must not fly."[415]

The leading authority on the meaning of "unreasonableness" in the context of **5–032** byelaws is *Kruse v Johnson*[416] where Lord Russell of Killowen C.J. stated[417] that local authority byelaws ought to be supported if possible and "benevolently" interpreted, but might be struck down if unreasonable:

> "But unreasonable in what sense? If, for instance, they were found to be partial and unequal in their operation as between different classes; if they were manifestly unjust; if they disclosed bad faith; if they involved such oppressive or gratuitous interference with the rights of those subject to them as could find no justification in the minds of reasonable men, the Court might well say, 'Parliament never intended to give authority to make such rules; they are unreasonable and ultra vires'. . . . A by-law is not unreasonable merely because particular judges may think that it goes further than is prudent or necessary or convenient, or because it is not accompanied by a qualification or an exception which some judges may think ought to be there."

Successful challenges, on this ground are rare. It has been unclear whether a statutory instrument, as distinct from a byelaw, can be challenged for unreasonableness. In *Maynard v Osmond*[418] regulations which did not allow police officers to be legally represented in disciplinary proceedings were challenged on this ground[419]; the members of the Court of Appeal did not express any doubt as to the court's jurisdiction to entertain such a challenge, but dismissed the application on the merits.

---

[413] See *Cross on Local Government Law* (9th edn, 1996) paras 6–06—6–10.
[414] (1980) 78 L.G.R. 614.
[415] *ibid.* p.623. As to the test for uncertainty, see *Percy v Hall* [1997] Q.B. 924 discussed in *Cross*, para.6–08.
[416] [1898] 2 Q.B. 91.
[417] At pp.99–100.
[418] [1977] Q.B. 240.
[419] The Police (Discipline) Regulations 1965 (SI 1965/543); the regulations applicable to Deputy Chief Constables, Assistant Chief Constables and Chief Constables did permit legal representation (SI 1965/544). The court did not accept that this constituted "unfair discrimination".

In *R v Secretary of State for the Environment, Ex p. Nottinghamshire County Council*,[420] the council challenged the 1985–86 guidance on expenditure limits given by the Secretary of State to local authorities, under s.59 of the Local Government, Planning and Land Act 1980, *inter alia* on the ground of unreasonableness. The guidance was required to be laid before, and approved by resolution of, the House of Commons. Lord Scarman in the House of Lords said[421]:

> " . . . I cannot accept that it is constitutionally appropriate, save in very exceptional circumstances, for the courts to intervene on the ground of 'unreasonableness' to quash guidance framed by the Secretary of State and by necessary implication approved by the House of Commons. . . ."

The challenge failed on the merits. It is to be noted that the possibility of a challenge for unreasonableness was not completely ruled out. Indeed, the suggestion that Parliamentary approval would properly restrict the permissible scope of such a challenge has been doubted.[422] It is clearly the case that Parliamentary approval, other than in an Act of Parliament, does not render delegated legislation immune from challenges based on other aspects of the *ultra vires* doctrine.[423] In *R v Secretary of State for the Environment, Ex p. Hammersmith and Fulham London Borough Council*[424] the House of Lords unanimously approved Lord Seaman's view, although the list of grounds of challenge said to be permissible is so lengthy[425] that it is difficult to see what kind of challenge is ruled out.[426]

The Court of Appeal has held subsequently that the true position is that delegated legislation, whether or not approved by either or both Houses of Parliament, is indeed subject to challenge on the ground of irrationality, but that in some contexts, such as that of local government finance,

> "there is a heavy evidential onus on a claimant for judicial review to establish the irrationality of a decision which may owe much to political,

---

[420] [1986] A.C. 240. *Cf. City of Edinburgh District Council v Secretary of State for Scotland* 1985 S.L.T. 551

[421] [1986] A.C. 240, 287.

[422] Sir William Wade and C. F. Forsyth, *Administrative Law* (9th edn, 2004), pp.27, 379–380; C. M. G. Himsworth, 1985 S.L.T. 369; A. I. L. Campbell, 1986 S.L.T. 101; C. T. Reid, [1986] C.L.J. 169. A provision in the Immigration Rules was held to be unreasonable in *R v Immigration Appeal Tribunal, Ex p. Manshoora Begum* [1986] Imm. A.R. 385. The Rules "have repeatedly been held to be rules of administrative practice merely, not rules of law and not delegated legislation" but "undoubtedly have statutory force to some extent" (Wade and Forsyth (2004), p.869). They are subject to Parliamentary disapproval but are not published as statutory instruments.

[423] *R v HM Treasury, Ex p. Smedley* [1985] Q.B. 657, 666–669 (*per* Sir John Donaldson M.R. in relation to an Order in Council); *R v Secretary of State for the Environment, Ex p. Greater London Council* (unreported, April 3, 1985): discussed in the articles cited in n.422 above, and in M. Grant, *Ratecapping and the Law* (2nd edn, 1986), pp.12–13; *R v Secretary of State for the Environment, Ex p. Nottinghamshire County Council* [1986] A.C. 240, 247–251 (*per* Lord Scarman).

[424] [1991] 1 A.C. 521, 594–597.

[425] That the exercise of discretion frustrates the policy of the statute, that legally relevant considerations have been ignored or irrelevant considerations taken into account, that there is bad faith, improper motive, or manifest absurdity: see Lord Bridge at pp.596–579. *Cf.* below, para.18–050.

[426] A challenge to the merits of an exercise of discretion cannot in any event be based on the *ultra vires* doctrine.

social and economic considerations in the underlying enabling legislation".[427]

Even where there are grounds for holding delegated legislation *ultra vires*, a remedy may still be refused in the exercise of the court's discretion.[428] The court may be able to hold that an invalid part of an order can be "severed", leaving the remaining part intact.[429] Finally, the court may in an appropriate case hold that an order is invalid only in so far as it affects a particular applicant.[430]

7. QUASI-LEGISLATION[431]

In recent years, greater attention has been paid to "administrative quasi-legisla-   **5–033**
tion"[432]: administrative rules that do not have direct legal force. There has been:

> "an exponential growth of statutory and extra-statutory rules in a plethora of forms. Codes of practice, guidance, guidance notes, guidelines, circulars, White Papers, development control policy notes, development briefs, practice statements, tax concessions, Health Service Notices, Family Practitioner Notices, codes of conduct, codes of ethics and conventions are just some of the guises in which the rules appear."[433]

(a) Statutory codes

There are many variables in the structure and operation of such codes: the overall   **5–034**
picture is arguably more confused than the arrangements for delegated legislation

---

[427] *per* Auld L.J. in *O'Connor v Chief Adjudicating Officer and Secretary of State for Social Security* [1999] E.L.R. 209, 221, approved by the Court of Appeal in *R (Asif Javed) v Secretary of State for the Home Department* [2002] Q.B. 129 (Secretary of State's inclusion of Pakistan in an Order applying an expedited appeals procedure, as a country in which it appeared to him "that there is in general no serious risk of persecution" was irrational and therefore invalid); *cf. R (on the application of Tucker) v Secretary of State for Social Security* [2002] H.L.R. 27 (housing benefit regulation held not to be irrational). See to similar effect Mustill L.J. in *R v Secretary of State for the Environment, Ex p. the GLC and ILEA* (unreported, April 3, 1985).

[428] e.g. *R v Secretary of State for Social Services, Ex p. Association of Metropolitan Authorities* [1986] 1 W.L.R. 1.

[429] *Dunkley v Evans* [1981] 3 All E.R. 285; *D.P.P. v Hutchinson* [1990] 2 A.C. 783; *cf. R v Secretary of State for Transport, Ex p. Greater London Council* [1985] 3 All E.R. 300.

[430] e.g. *Agricultural etc. Training Board v Aylesbury Mushrooms Ltd* [1972] 1 W.L.R. 190 (where an order was only held to be invalid in respect of a particular organisation that had not been consulted).

[431] G. Ganz, *Quasi-Legislation: Recent Developments in Secondary Legislation* (1987); R. E. Megarry, (1944) 60 L.Q.R. 125; Lord Campbell, "Codes of Practice as an Alternative to Legislation" [1985] Stat. L.R. 127; A. Samuels, "Codes of Practice and Legislation" [1986] Stat. L.R. 29; T. St. J. Bates, [1986] Stat. L.R. 114, 120–123; H.L. Deb., Vol.469, cols 1075–1104, January 15, 1986 (debate on codes of practice); R. Baldwin and J. Houghton, "Circular Arguments: The Status and Legitimacy of Administrative Rules" [1986] P.L. 239; R. B. Ferguson, "The Legal Status of Non-Statutory Codes of Practice" [1988] J.B.L. 12; R. Baldwin, *Rules and Government* (1995), Ch.4.

[432] A term coined by Megarry, *op. cit.*

[433] Ganz (1987), pp.1–2.

were before the Statutory Instruments Act 1946. These variables include the following:

— By whom they are made: a minister; a non-governmental statutory agency; a non-statutory body.

— To whom they are directed: officials; local authorities; courts and tribunals; private organisations and citizens.

— Whether they are subject to Parliamentary scrutiny: there may be a requirement for a code to be laid before Parliament (in draft or in a final version), subject to affirmative or negative procedures.

— How they are published: by TSO, by a government department or otherwise.

— Their legal effect: there are several forms. In the case of some codes, no effect is stated, although it does not follow that they are entirely devoid of legal effect. There may be a requirement that provisions of the code be taken into account, if relevant, by a local authority, tribunal or court. It may be provided that breach of a code may be relied upon as tending to establish civil or criminal liability, and compliance as tending to negative such liability: indeed in one case as establishing liability unless the contrary is proved.

— The content: McCrudden[434] distinguishes four types of codes, although any one code may contain elements of them all:

> "Codes may include provisions (i) to codify existing non-legal practice; (ii) to codify the already existing law of the courts and/or the previous legal interpretations on a particular issue of the body making the code; (iii) to set out recommended good industrial practice; and (iv) to interpret independently those statutory provisions for which the body making the code has some responsibility."

An alternative typology is suggested by Baldwin and Houghton,[435] who distinguish: (i) procedural rules; (ii) interpretative guides; (iii) instructions to officials; (iv) prescriptive/evidential rules; (v) commendatory rules; (vi) voluntary codes; (vii) rules of practice, management or operation; and (viii) consultative devices and administrative pronouncements.

Examples include the Immigration Rules,[436] the PACE Codes of Practice,[437] the Code of Guidance concerning Homelessness,[438] the Highway Code,[439] the

---

[434] (1988) 51 M.L.R., 409, 531.

[435] [1986] P.L. 239, 240–245.

[436] Immigration Act 1971, ss.3(2); Nationality, Immigration and Asylum Act 2002, s.84(1): made by the Secretary of State, issued as a House of Commons paper, subject to annulment by Parliament and binding on the Asylum and Immigration Tribunal, no consultation requirements.

[437] See below, para.14–003.

[438] Housing Act 1996, s.182: made by the Secretary of State, published as a Circular, authorities to have regard to guidance, no laying or consultation requirements.

[439] Road Traffic Act 1988, s.38: made by the Secretary of State, who must consult such representative organisations as he thinks fit, issued via HMSO, subject to annulment by Parliament, may be relied on in legal proceedings as tending to establish or negative liability.

Sex Discrimination Code of Practice,[440] the Code of Practice on Picketing,[441] and the Approved Documents giving guidance with respect to the requirements of building regulations.[442]

The position as to Parliamentary scrutiny is different in a number of respects from that for statutory instruments. On the one hand, particular codes have been examined by the appropriate departmental select committee, which does not normally happen with other forms of legislation. On the other, the Joint Committee on Statutory Instruments only has jurisdiction to examine documents, other than statutory instruments, that require Parliamentary approval; there is no provision for the merits to be debated in a general committee; and the likelihood of a merits debate in the Chamber is low.[443]

The perceived advantages of codes of practice and the like include the use of informal, non-technical, language; flexibility; and the promotion of uniformity of practice, particularly in the public sector.[444] Their "fundamental rationale" is the adoption of a voluntary approach rather than compulsion.[445]

While there is much to be said for this where codes are based on widespread consultation and consensus, there are nevertheless difficulties.[446] Sometimes they are introduced as an unhappy compromise between statutory regulation and inaction. In some areas the voluntary approach has broken down and compulsion has replaced persuasion. There has been criticism of the use of codes with controversial provisions that go beyond existing legislation,[447] particularly given the limited effectiveness of Parliamentary scrutiny. The haphazard variety of forms and procedures is indefensible. Proposals have been made for the strengthening of Parliamentary scrutiny, a "code of practice regulating codes of practice" and the establishment of a body "to advise on the creation of quasi-legal or voluntary rules instead of legal rules and evolve criteria for their use".[448] In December 1987, the government issued Guidance on Codes of Practice and Legislation, primarily for the use of parliamentary draftsmen, and those framing legislative proposals.[449]

---

[440] Sex Discrimination Act 1975, s.56A: made by the Equal Opportunities Commission (with the approval of the Secretary of State), which must publish a draft and consider any representations made about it, consult appropriate organisations, issued via HMSO, draft subject to annulment by Parliament, to be taken into account by Employment Tribunal if it appears relevant.

[441] Trade Union and Labour Relations (Consolidation) Act 1992, ss.203–208: made by the Secretary of State, who must consult ACAS, draft to be approved by Parliament, to be taken into account by Employment Tribunal if it appears relevant.

[442] Building Act 1984, ss.6, 7: made by Secretary of State or designated body, issued via HMSO, no laying or consultation requirement, breach tends to establish and compliance to negative liability in legal proceedings.

[443] Baldwin and Houghton, [1986] P.L. 239, at pp.26–32.

[444] In the public sector, codes of practice and other forms of guidance may be used to provide a framework for the exercise of discretionary powers, so as to promote uniformity in decision-making. However, power to give guidance will not normally authorise the issue of binding directions (*Laker Airways Ltd v Department of Trade* [1977] Q.B. 643) and the recipient of such guidance must not fetter its discretion by regarding it as binding (*R v Police Complaints Board, Ex p. Madden* [1983] 1 W.L.R. 447). Conversely, such guidance is likely to be a legally relevant consideration and must at least be taken into account.

[445] Ganz (1987), pp.96–98.

[446] *ibid.* pp.98–108.

[447] Highlighted by the decision of Scott J. in *Thomas v National Union of Mineworkers* [1986] Ch. 20 to limit by injunction the number of pickets outside particular premises to six, in line with a provision of the Code of Practice on Picketing then made under s.3 of the Employment Act 1980.

[448] Ganz (1987), Ch.6; A. Samuels [1986] Stat. L.R. 29.

[449] [1989] Stat. L.R. 214.

(b) Voluntary guidance[450]

5–035 There are many examples of codes of practice, guidance and the like without any statutory backing. In the public sector, for example, guidance may be given by central government departments to local authorities in circulars and other forms of communication, and instructions are commonly given to officials within departments.[451] The effect varies widely: the legal effect may be indirect, but the practical implications of great significance.[452] In the private sector such codes have in some circumstances been adduced as evidence, for example of proper professional or technical standards, and may be incorporated into a contract.[453] They may also be recognised as appropriate by government, even without express legislative endorsement.[454] Difficulties as to their accessibility and uncertainties as to legal effect are even more pronounced here.

D. COMMUNITY LEGISLATION

1. INTRODUCTION

5–036 The accession of the United Kingdom to membership of the European Communities (the European Economic Community, the European Coal and Steel Community and the European Atomic Energy Community) meant that the vast and ever-increasing body of Community law became applicable in this country.[455] The system of Community law is founded on the provisions of the various Treaties whereby the Member States agreed to establish the Communities, new members joined ("Accession Treaties") and aspects of the original Treaties have

---

[450] Ganz (1987), pp.59–65, 75–95; R. B. Ferguson, [1988] J.B.L. 12.

[451] e.g. the government's policy to reduce the number of school places in the light of falling school rolls; the use of circulars in town and country planning to state planning policy; extra-statutory tax concessions; standing orders and circular instructions governing the management of prisons.

[452] It has been held that even non-statutory guidance, if erroneous in law, can be challenged on an application for judicial review: *Royal College of Nursing v Department of Health and Social Security* [1981] A.C. 800; *Gillick v West Norfolk Area Health Authority* [1986] A.C. 112.

[453] R. B. Ferguson, [1988] J.B.L. 12.

[454] e.g. the codes of practice for residential care homes (Centre for Policy on Ageing, *Home Life* (1984) and *A Better Home Life* (1996)) and nursing homes (National Association of Health Authorities, *Registration and Inspection Nursing Homes: A Handbook for Health Authorities* (1985)). The Secretaries of State for Social Services and for Wales asked local authorities to regard *Home Life* "in the same light" as guidance issued under s.7 of the Local Authority Social Services Act 1970 (which suggests that it is not technically guidance under the Act). The codes were in practice taken into account by local authorities, inspectors and registered homes tribunals: see D. Carson, [1985] J.S.W.L. 67, 69–70; R. Brooke Ross, [1985] J.S.W.L. 85; R. M. Jones (ed.), *Encyclopedia of Social Services and Child Care Law* (1993), para.D1–303. These have been replaced by National Minimum Standards published by the Secretary of State under s.23(1) of the Care Standards Act 2000.

[455] See L. Collins, *European Community Law in the United Kingdom* (4th edn, 1990), Chs 1 and 2; J. Usher, *European Community Law and National Law, The Irreversible Transfer?* (1981); T. C. Hartley, *The Foundations of European Community Law* (5th edn, 2003).

been changed and augmented, most notably by the Single European Act of 1986,[456] the (Maastricht) Treaty on European Union of 1992,[457] the Treaty of Amsterdam (1999) and the Treaty of Nice (2001). The Maastricht Treaty introduced changes to the structure and nomenclature of the arrangements for European co-operation. The 12 Member States established among themselves a "European Union", making "a new stage in the process of creating an ever closer union among the peoples of Europe, in which decisions are taken as closely as possible to the citizen".[458] Its task was "to organise, in a manner demonstrating consistency and solidarity, relations between the Member States and between their peoples". The Union was founded on the European Communities, supplemented by the "implementation of a common foreign and security policy" and the development of "close cooperation on justice and home affairs".[459]

The "European Communities" thus formed one part of a broader Union; it was, however, only the Communities that possessed legislative powers affecting Member States and citizens. One final complication was that while the term "European Community" had popularly been used to cover the three communities, the ECSC and Euratom no longer having independent roles, the Maastricht Treaty substituted "European Community" for "European Economic Community" throughout the Treaty of Rome.[460]

Austria, Finland and Sweden became Member States from January 1, 1995. This structure was modified by the Treaty of Amsterdam (in effect from 1999). The EU remains with three "pillars" but the two non-EC pillars were substantially revised, with some matters moved to the EC pillar and the Justice and Home Affairs pillar re-titled as "Provisions on Police and Judicial Co-operation in Criminal Matters".[461] It also renumbered the provisions of both the Treaty on European Union and the Treaty establishing the European Community.[462] The Treaty of Nice (signed in 2001) introduced further changes to take account of the substantial enlargement of the EU. Ten new countries joined in 2004,[463] and two in 2007.[464] Croatia and Turkey began membership negotiations in 2005. There are Consolidated Versions of the Treaty Establishing the European Community and the Treaty on European Union.[465] A draft Treaty establishing a Constitution

---

[456] This had the objectives of "unblocking the Community's decision making process, thereby hastening the completion of a genuine common market", enhancing the role of the Parliament in the legislative process, and establishing a formal basis for European Political co-operation: A. Arnull (1986) 11 E.L. Rev. 358; see also H.-J. Glaesner, (1986) 6 Y.E.L. 283; Symposium (1986) 23 C.M.L. Rev. 743–840; M. A. McElhenny, (1988) 39(1) N.I.L.Q. 54.

[457] This introduced further major changes, including the establishment of a timetable for progress towards economic and monetary union with a single currency and monetary policy; further changes to legislative procedures; new fields of activity, such as culture, public health and consumer protection; and citizenship of the European Union. See D. O'Keefe and P. Twomey (eds), *Legal Issues of the Maastricht Treaty* (1994); Harmsen, (1994) 45 N.I.L.Q. 109; D. Curtin, (1993) 30 C.M.L. Rev. 17.

[458] Treaty on European Union, Title I, Art.A.

[459] *ibid.* Art.B. See below, para.5–040.

[460] *ibid.* Title II, Art.G. The ECSC Treaty expired on July 23, 2002.

[461] See D. O'Keefe and P. Twomey, *Legal Issues of the Amsterdam Treaty* (1999).

[462] Note the method of citation adopted by the Court of Justice and the Court of First Instance: see the Court of Justice website, *http://curia.europa.eu/en/content/juris/index_infos.htm*.

[463] Cyprus, the Czech Republic, Estonia, Hungary, Latvia, Lithuania, Malta, Poland, Slovaki and Slovenia.

[464] Bulgaria and Romania.

[465] See N. Foster, *Blackstone's EC Legislation 2006–2007* (2006).

for Europe was signed in Rome in 2004,[466] but needs the ratification of all states, which has not been forthcoming.[467]

The Treaty provisions are sometimes termed the *primary* legislation of the Communities. The Treaties give various powers to the Council and the Commission and the Parliament to make laws by *regulation, directive* or *decision*, the resulting body of law being termed *secondary* legislation. Secondary legislation must conform to the express or implied limits set by the relevant treaty provisions.

Under Community law, a further distinction is drawn between laws (both primary and secondary) that have *direct application* or *effect* without any act of implementation by Member States and laws that require such implementation.

Under UK law, rules of international law such as treaty provisions can only take effect within our domestic legal system if expressly implemented by Act of Parliament. Accordingly, the government secured the passage of the European Communities Act 1972 to enable Community law to take effect within the United Kingdom.

In this section we consider, first, the main Community institutions, secondly, the different kinds of Community legislation and the extent to which it may be directly applicable or effective, thirdly, the question of the supremacy of Community law, fourthly, the implementation of Community law in the United Kingdom, and fifthly, the methods by which the validity of Community legislation may be challenged.

2. THE COMMUNITY INSTITUTIONS[468]

5–037   The four main institutions of the European Community, established by the EC Treaty are the Commission, the Council and the European Parliament (the political institutions) and the Court of Justice. The political institutions will be considered here.[469]

(a) The Commission[470]

The Commission comprises one national from each Member State.[471] To 2004, some Member States, including the five largest countries (France, Germany, Italy, Spain and the UK) had two each, the rest one each.[472] Each Commissioner is in effect nominated by his or her national state, but must be acceptable to all the

---

[466] *ibid.* pp.591–731.

[467] It was rejected at referenda in France and the Netherlands, and the ratification process has been postponed in a number of countries: *ibid.* p.591.

[468] See Hartley (2003) Ch.1; S. Weatherill and P. Beaumont, *EU Law* (3rd edn, 1999), Chs 2–4.

[469] The Court of Justice is considered above, para.2–076.

[470] Arts 211–219 EC; D. Spence (ed.), *The European Commission* (3rd edn, 2006).

[471] Art.213 EC and Accession Treaty 2003, Art.45.

[472] The United Kingdom adopted the practice of nominating one with a Conservative and one with a Labour political background. The UK Commissioners have been Sir Christopher Soames and George Thomson (1973–77); Roy Jenkins (1977–81); Christopher Tugendhat (1977–85); Ivor Richard (1981–85); Lord Cockfield and Stanley Clinton Davis (1985–89); Sir Leon Brittan (1989–99); Bruce Millan (1989–95); Neil Kinnock (1995–2004); Christopher Patten (1999–2004); Peter Mandelson (2004–).

Member States, and is not a "representative" of his or her own country. The procedure for appointment from 1995 has been for the governments first to nominate by common accord the President of the Commission, subject to the approval of the European Parliament, and then, in consultation with him or her, to nominate the other Commissioners; they are then subject as a body to a vote of approval by the Parliament.[473] After approval, they are all appointed by common accord of the governments of the Member States.[474] Article 213(2) EC provides:

> "The Members of the Commission shall, in the general interest of the Community, be completely independent in the performance of their duties.In the performance of these duties, they shall neither seek nor take instructions from any Government or from any other body. They shall refrain from any action incompatible with their duties. Each Member State undertakes to respect this principle and not to seek to influence the members of the Commission in the performance of their tasks. . . . "

The term of office is five years (increased from four years from 1995), and may be renewed. All the Commissioners retire together. It is for the President to decide on the Commission's internal organisation and the allocation of responsibilities, and (after obtaining the approval of the College i.e. the Commissioners) appoint Vice-Presidents. A Commissioner will have to resign if the President so requests, after obtaining the approval of the College.[475] The Commissioners are supported by over 15,000 staff, organised into a number of Directorates General, with a number of specialised services, including a Legal Service.

The main activities of the Commission are:

> "formulating proposals for new Community policies, mediating between the Member States to secure the adoption of these proposals, co-ordinating national policies and overseeing the execution of existing Community policies."[476]

Under the EC Treaty, its task is "to ensure the proper functioning and development of the common market".[477] The Commission meets in private[478] and makes decisions by a simple majority vote. Its commitment to the furtherance of

---

[473] In 1995, although not a formal part of the procedure, the Parliament held individual hearings for each nominee.

[474] By virtue of the Treaty of Nice, Art.2(22), substituting a new Art.214(2) EC, the Council acting by qualified majority nominates the President, subject to approval by the Parliament. Acting by a qualified majority and by common accord with the nominee, it is to adopt the list of other persons whom it intends to nominate as Commissioners, drawn up in accordance with the proposals of each Member State. They are then all to be subject as a body to Parliament's approval; after approval they are then to be appointed by the Council by qualified majority.

[475] Art.217 EC as substituted by the Treaty of Nice, Art.2(24).

[476] Hartley (2003) p.11.

[477] Art.211 EC; *cf.* the broader objectives of the Council: below, para.5–038.

[478] A general right of access to documents, subject to exceptions, was conferred by Commission Decision 94/90, replaced by rules under Reg.(EC) No.1049/2001 of the Parliament and the Council: see below, para.5–038, n.482.

Community interests provides a balance to the Council of Ministers, which tends to reflect national interests.

(b) The Council[479]

5–038   The Council of the European Union[480] comprises representatives of the Member States, each state sending a minister authorised to commit the government of that state. The Presidency is held by each Member State[481] in turn for a term of six months.

The Council is attended by different ministers according to the business to be dealt with. General matters are normally considered by foreign ministers; agriculture matters by agriculture ministers, financial matters by finance ministers and so on. The Council meets periodically, and normally in private.[482] It is supported by a General Secretariat, which is organised on similar lines to the Commission, but is much smaller. The Council's business is prepared by the Committee of Permanent Representatives (COREPER), which itself meets at two levels: COREPER II, comprising the heads of permanent delegations (ambassadors), which deals with matters of political importance, and COREPER I, comprising deputies, which deals with day-to-day business and technical matters. In turn there are many committees and expert working groups. The Council has six key responsibilities: (1) to pass European legislation, jointly with the Parliament in many areas; (2) to co-ordinate the broad economic policies of the Member States; (3) to conclude international agreements between the EU and other countries or international organisations; (4) to approve the EU's budget, jointly with the Parliament; (5) to develop the EU's Common Foreign and Security Policy, based on guidelines set by the European Council; and (6) to co-ordinate co-operation between the national courts and police forces in criminal matters.[483]

---

[479] Arts 202 EC–210 EC. The Merger Treaty (1965), Arts 1–8 previously provided for the merger of separate Councils for each Community.

[480] The Council adopted this title in 1993: Council Decision 93/591 of November 8, 1993.

[481] The order is decided by the Council acting unanimously.

[482] From 1993, it has held some public debates and voting outcomes have been made public, as part of a number of moves to improve the transparency of the institutions' business: *Intergovernmental Conference 1996: Commission Report for the Reflection Group* (1995), p.39. See also Council Decision 93/731/EC on public access to Council Documents, as amended by Council Decisions 96/705 and 2000/527, giving a general right of access to documents subject to a range of exceptions; access must be refused where disclosure could undermine the protection of the "public interest", of "the individual and of privacy", of "commercial and industrial secrecy", of "the Community financial interests", of confidentiality as requested by the supplier of the information (Art.4(1)) and it may be refused to protect "the confidentiality of the Council's proceedings" (Art.4(2)). Decisions under Art.4(1) must be made on a case by case basis; and under Art.4(2) a genuine balance must be maintained between the interest of the citizen in obtaining access and the interest of the Council in preserving confidentiality; the exceptions must be construed narrowly and particular reasons for refusal required: Case T-174/95, *Svenska Journalistforbundet v Council* [1998] E.C.R. II–2289. See also Art.255 EC, conferring a general right of access subject to principles to be defined by the institutions; which principles were set out in Reg. (EC) No.1049/2001 of the Parliament and Council. Under this, access was extended to documents from third parties, a document protected by an exception (other than the public interest or the protection of private life) will nevertheless be divulged if the public interest demands it, a document register is made available to the public and the time limits for replies were reduced to 15 working days.

[483] *www.europa.eu/institutions/inst/council/index_en.htm.*

Under the EC Treaty, its task is "to ensure that the objectives set out in this Treaty are attained", and to that end "ensure co-ordination of the general economic policies of the Member States" and "have power to take decisions".[484] The more important decisions are reserved to the Council rather than the Commission.[485]

The Treaties specify different voting arrangements for different kinds of Council decision. Some acts must be unanimous. Most require a "qualified majority".[486] Here the votes of Member States are weighted:

France, Germany, Italy, UK	: 29 votes each
Spain and Poland	: 27 votes
Romania	: 14 votes
Netherlands	: 13 votes
Belgium, Czech Republic, Greece, Hungary, Portugal	: 12 votes each
Austria, Bulgaria, Sweden	: 10 votes each
Denmark, Ireland, Lithuania, Slovakia, Finland	: 7 votes each
Estonia, Cyprus, Latvia, Luxembourg, Slovenia	: 4 votes each
Malta	: 3 votes

A "qualified majority" is 255 of these 345 votes, where the act is based on a Commission proposal; 255 votes with 18 Member States in favour, otherwise. The arrangements have meant that the large countries cannot outvote the smaller states and vice versa. Any Member State can request verification that the States constituting the qualified majority represent at least 62 per cent of the total population of the total population of the EU.

In many important areas the original requirement specified in the Treaties was for unanimity, the qualified majority regime only coming into effect from January 1, 1966. Even then, a convention developed whereby unanimity would be required as a matter of practice (albeit no longer as a matter of law) where "very important interests" of one or more Member States were at stake.[487] In the 1980s, this convention was applied with less force, and matters are now decided by majority votes. The Single European Act amended various Treaty provisions by substituting a qualified majority procedure for a requirement of unanimity. This process has been continued by the Maastricht and Amsterdam Treaties.

(c) The European Parliament[488]

The Parliament consists of "representatives of the peoples" of the Member States. Members are directly elected, in the following proportions[489]   **5–039**

---

[484] Art.202 EC.

[485] See further below, para.5–042.

[486] Art.205 EC.

[487] This was reflected in the so-called "Luxembourg Accords" of January 1966: a press release enshrining the part agreement/part truce that ended a dispute between France and the, then five, other Member States.

[488] Arts 189 EC to 201 EC. The Parliament was referred to as Assembly in the Treaties. It resolved to call itself the "European Parliament" in 1962, and that title was recognised in the Single European Act. See F. Jacobs, *et al.*, *The European Parliament* (6th edn, 2005); D. Judge and D. Earnshaw, *The European Parliament* (2003).

[489] Art.190(2) EC.

Germany	99
France, Italy, UK	78 each
Poland, Spain	54 each
Romania	36
Netherlands	27
Belgium, Czech Republic, Greece, Hungary, Portugal	24 each
Sweden	19
Austria, Bulgaria	18 each
Denmark, Finland, Slovakia	14 each
Ireland, Lithuania	13 each
Latvia	9
Slovenia	7
Cyprus, Estonia, Luxembourg	6 each
Malta	5
	786

This does not reflect populations: in those terms the smaller states are over-represented. Members sit in political groupings rather than by country. Much of the work is done by committees.

The Parliament exercises the powers conferred by the Treaties.[490] These have become more extensive over time. It puts Questions to the Council and the Commission, and is involved in at least a consultative capacity in the legislative process, its role here having been strengthened by the Single European Act and the Maastricht Treaty.[491] It now has a veto over the admission of new Member States, the conclusion of association agreements with other states and certain legislative proposals.[492] It has had a progressively greater say in the determination of the Community's budget.[493] Provisions added by the Maastricht Treaty enable the Parliament to request proposals from the Commission on matters on which it considers that a Community act is required to implement the Treaty and to set up temporary committees of inquiry; require it to appoint an Ombudsman; and entitle EU citizens, and other natural or legal persons resident or with a registered office in a Member State to address petitions to it on Community matters which affect him, her or it directly.[494]

(d) Other institutions

5–040   Other organs of the Community include the Economic and Social Committee,[495] with members from each Member State representing employers, workers and others (e.g. farmers, the professions and the general public), which advises both

---

[490] Art.189 EC. These are no longer described as "advisory and supervisory powers".
[491] See below, paras 5–050, 5–051.
[492] Art.49 EU; Art.300(3) EC; Art.7 EU (determination of the existence of a serious and persistent breach by a Member State of the principles mentioned in Art.6(1) EU) (see below, paras 5–050, 5–051).
[493] Hartley (2003) pp.47–51.
[494] Arts 192 EC–195 EC.
[495] Arts 257 EC–262 EC.

Council and Commission; the Court of Auditors,[496] which carries out the audit and assists the Council and the Parliament in exercising their powers of control over implementation of the budget; the Committee of the Regions which represents regional and local bodies within the EC; and the European Investment Bank.

Finally, the arrangements for a common foreign and security policy and on police and judicial cooperation in criminal matters are found, respectively, in Title V (Arts 11 EU to 28 EU) and Title VI (Arts 29 EU to 42 EU). The EU is to "define and implement a common foreign and security policy covering all areas of foreign and security policy". Its objectives include safeguarding the common values, fundamental interests; independence and integrity of the EU; strengthening the security of the EU; preserving peace and strengthening international security; promoting international cooperation and developing and consolidating democracy and the rule of law and respect for human rights and fundamental freedoms. Member States are to "support the Union's external and security policy actively and unreservedly in a spirit of loyalty and mutual solidarity".[497] The EU is represented by the Presidency in matters within the CFSP, and the Presidency in association with the Commission is responsible for the implementation of decisions.[498] The general principles of and general guidelines for the CFSP are defined by the European Council[499]; decisions necessary for defining and implementing the policy are taken by the Council.[500]

Under Title VI, the EU's objective is to provide citizens with a high level of safety within an area of freedom, security and justice by developing common action among Member States in the fields of police and judicial cooperation in criminal matters and by preventing and combating racism and xenophobia. This is to be achieved by preventing and combating crime, in particular terrorism, trafficking in persons and offences against children, illicit trafficking in drugs and arms, corruption and fraud. Cooperation is to include operational cooperation and is to be promoted through Europol. Common action is to include the facilitation of extradition. The Council may adopt joint positions on action and may draw up conventions recommended to Member States for adoption.[501] Member States may accept a new jurisdiction of the Court of Justice to give preliminary rulings in relation to certain matters arising under Title VI and to review the legality of framework discussions and decisions in actions.[502]

At the apex of these structures is the European Council—regular conferences of the Heads of State or of Government and the foreign ministers of the Member States. These were informal meetings, attended by representatives of the Commission, but a regular constitution for them was provided by Art.2 of the Single European Act and now by Art.4 EU, under which the European Council is to "provide the Union with the necessary impetus for its development" and "define the general political guidelines thereof". When discussing Community matters, the European Council acts as the Council of Ministers, but the two are technically distinct.

---

[496] Arts 246 EC–248 EC, as amended by the Treaty of Nice, Art.2(36), (37).
[497] Art.11 EU.
[498] Art.18 EU.
[499] See below.
[500] Art.13 EU.
[501] Arts 29 EU–34 EU.
[502] Art.35 EC.

3. The Kinds of Community Legislation

(a) Treaty provisions concerning Community legislation

5–041 The different kinds of Community acts are described in Art.249 EC (ex Art.189, as amended):

> "In order to carry out their task and in accordance with the provisions of this Treaty, the European Parliament acting jointly with, the Council and the Commission shall make regulations and issue directives, take decisions, make recommendations or deliver opinions.
>
> A regulation shall have general application. It shall be binding in its entirety and directly applicable in all Member States.
>
> A directive shall be binding, as to the result to be achieved, upon each Member State to which it is addressed. but shall leave to the national authorities the choice of form and methods.
>
> A decision shall be binding in its entirety upon those to whom it is addressed.
>
> Recommendations and opinions shall have no binding force."

Recommendations and opinions cannot be regarded as legislative as they do not have binding effect; it has also been suggested that decisions directed to individuals, as distinct from Member States, are administrative rather than legislative in character.[503]

The Treaties require that regulations, directives and decisions state the reasons on which they are based and refer to any proposals or opinions that were required to be obtained pursuant to other Treaty provisions.[504] Regulations, directives and decisions adopted by the Parliament and the Council jointly, regulations of the Council and the Commission, and directives of those institutions addressed to all Member States, must be published in the Official Journal. They enter into force on the date specified in them, or, if no date is specified, on the twentieth day following their publication. Other directives and decisions must be notified to those to whom they are addressed and take effect upon such notification.[505]

(b) Legislative powers[506]

5–042 Under the EC and Euratom Treaties, the major policy decisions and legislative powers are reserved to the Council; the Commission being involved with (in most cases) the formulation of legislative proposals and with the implementation of decisions. However, the Commission does have some legislative powers conferred upon it by the EC Treaty.[507] Furthermore, its position has been strengthened in two ways.

First, procedures have been developed for the delegation of functions from the Council to the Commission. A distinction is drawn between the laying down of

---

[503] Case 19/77, *Miller v Commission* [1978] E.C.R. 131, 161 *per* A. G. Warner.
[504] Art.253 EC.
[505] Art.254 EC.
[506] See Hartley (2003), pp.41–47, Ch.4; R. Baldwin, *Rules and Government* (1995), Ch.8.
[507] See T. C. Hartley, (1988) 13 E.L. Rev. 122–123; Cases 88–90/80, *France, Italy and the United Kingdom v Commission* [1982] E.C.R. 2545.

general principles and detailed implementation. Only the latter process may be delegated, but that may involve rule-making by the Commission. Such arrangements were held to be lawful by the Court of Justice.[508] Express authority was provided for them by Art.10 of the Single European Act, amending Art.145 of the EC Treaty (see now Art.202 EC). Acts adopted by the Council must confer power for the implementation of the rules laid down therein by the Commission, unless ("in specific cases") the Council reserves the right to exercise directly implementing powers itself. The Council may impose certain requirements in respect of the exercise of these delegated powers, in conformity with procedures prescribed by a Council Decision. The "Comitology" Decision was adopted in 1987,[509] and corresponded for the most part to the previous informal arrangements. It was replaced by a new Council Decision in 1999.[510] Other than in the "specific cases" mentioned above, the Council may select one of a series of procedures set out in the Decision.[511]

Each procedure requires the Commission to consult a committee comprising representatives of the Member States, and chaired by a representative of the Commission. The committee must deliver its opinion within a time limit laid down by the Chairman according to the urgency of the matter.

The "advisory procedure" involves an "advisory committee". As the name suggests, the Commission must "take the utmost account of the opinion delivered by the committee" but is not bound by it. The "management procedure" involves a "management committee", which forms an opinion acting by a qualified majority. The Commission must adopt measures which shall apply immediately, but where they are not in accordance with the committee's opinion, the Council must be informed. In that event the Commission may defer application of the measures for a period (not exceeding three months) to be laid down in each basic instrument. The Council, acting by a qualified majority, may within that period take a different decision. The "regulatory procedure" involves a "regulatory committee", again acting by a qualified majority. The Commission must adopt the measures forthwith if they are in accordance with the opinion of the committee. If they are not, or if no opinion is delivered, the Commission has to submit to the Council a proposal relating to the measures to be taken and inform the Parliament. If the Parliament considers that the proposal exceeds the implementing powers provided for in the underlying basic instrument it must inform the Council of its position. The Council may, in view of any such position, act by qualified majority on the proposal, within a period (not exceeding three months from the date of referral to the Council) laid down in the basic instrument. If it indicates opposition, the Commission must re-examine the proposal. It may submit an amended proposal, resubmit its proposal or present a legislative proposal based on the Treaty. If on the expiry of the specified period

---

[508] Case 25/70, *Einfuhr- und Vorratsstelle v Köster* [1970] E.C.R. 1161; Case 41/69, *Chemiefarma v Commission* [1970] E.C.R. 661; Case 23/75, *Rey Soda v Cassa Conguaglio Zuchero* [1975] E.C.R. 1279; *cf.* Case 264/86, *France v Commission* [1988] E.C.R. 973.

[509] Dec. 87/373, O.J. 1987, L 197/33. See K. St. C. Bradley, "Comitology and the law; through a glass, darkly" (1992) 29 C.M.L. Rev. 693.

[510] Council Dec. 1999/468 of June 28, 1999 laying down the procedures for the exercise of implementing powers conferred on the Commission: O.J. [1999] L184/23. It is reproduced in N. Foster, *Blackstone's EC Legislation 2006–2007* (17th edn, 2006) pp.156–160. See Select Community on the European Union, *Reforming Comitology*, Thirty-First Report, 2002–03 H.L. 135.

[511] The Decision also prescribes a procedure that may be applied where the Council confers on the Commission the power to decide on "safeguard measures": Art.6.

the Council has neither adopted nor opposed the proposal, the proposed implementing act must be adopted by the Commission. There is also a general provision whereby if the Parliament indicates in a resolution that any draft implementing measure would exceed the implementing powers provided for in the basic instrument, it must be re-examined by the Commission. The Commission may submit new draft measures, continue with the procedure or submit a proposal to the Parliament or the Council on the basis of the Treaty. The Commission must inform the Parliament and the Committee of the action it intends to take.

The Commission expressed reservations concerning the original version of the procedures, and complained that the Council only infrequently adopted the advisory committee procedure, preferring to use "delegation procedures which allow the national authorities to block legislation".[512] The Parliament sought to have the 1987 Decision annulled under Art.173, but the European Court held that it did not have capacity to bring such an action.[513] Subject to a reservation concerning Variant III of the original procedure (under which a simple Council majority could block a decision under the regulatory procedure), the Commission (in 1995) believed that these procedures operated satisfactorily, noting that of several thousand committee opinions adopted over the previous three years, six decisions were referred back to the Council and there were no cases where no decision was taken.[514] The 1999 Decision introduced criteria for the adoption of the appropriate procedure.[515] Thus management measures, such as those relating to the common agricultural and fisheries policies or the implementation of programmes with substantial budgetary implications, should use the management procedure. Measures of general scope designed to apply essential provisions of basic instruments (including health and safety measures) should use the regulatory procedure. Without prejudice to these guidelines, the advisory committee procedure must be used in any case where it is considered to be the most appropriate.

There were continuing concerns, particularly from the Parliament, that its role was insufficiently recognised. The 1999 decision was amended in 2006.[516] This improved arrangements for the provision of information to the Parliament and introduced a new procedure, the "regulatory procedure with scrutiny", which must be used as regards measures of general scope which seek to amend non-essential elements of a basic instrument adopted under Art.251 EC,[517] inter alia by deleting or adding such elements. This involves a Regulatory Procedure with Scrutiny Committee, which forms an opinion on the draft measures acting by a qualified majority. The detailed procedure then varies according to whether the measures are in accordance with the committee's opinion, but there is an opportunity for them to be blocked by either the Council (by a qualified majority) or the Parliament, on the ground that they exceed the implementing power provided for, or are not compatible with the aim or content of the basic instrument or do not respect the principles of subsidiarity or proportionality. If they are

[512] See Commission, 21st General Report on the Activities of the European Communities, 1987, point 4; 22nd General Report, 1988, point 9.

[513] Case 302/87, *European Parliament v Council* [1988] E.C.R. 5615 (see further, below, para.5–061).

[514] *Commission Report for the Reflection Group* (1995), p.31.

[515] Art.2.

[516] Council Decision 2006/512/EC of July 17, 2006, amending Decision 1999/488/EC.

[517] The co-decision procedure, see para.5–050.

blocked, the Commission may submit revised measures or present a legislative proposal.

The second means by which the Commission's powers have been strengthened is by the recognition by the European Court that it enjoys certain *implied* legislative powers. In *Germany v Commission*[518] the European Court held that:

> "where an Article of the EEC Treaty—in this case Article 118—confers a specific task on the Commission it must be accepted, if that provision is not to be rendered wholly ineffective, that it confers on the Commission necessarily and *per se* the powers which are indispensable in order to carry out that task."[519]

It then proceeded to hold that the Commission enjoyed all "necessary" powers (rather than "indispensable") and took a generous view of what was "necessary".[520] It has been noted that:

> "Since the EC Treaty confers many tasks on the Commission, including such wide-ranging functions as that of ensuring that the provisions of the Treaty are applied,[521] this judgment is potentially significant though so far it has not been widely applied."[522]

(c) Direct applicability and direct effect

A distinction is sometimes drawn between the terms *direct applicability* and   **5–043**
direct effect.[523] Article 249 EC provides that regulations are "directly applicable" in all Member States; they come into force without any act of implementation by Member States. No other form of Community law is expressly stated in the treaties to be directly *applicable*, and it was at first thought that those other forms of law could only take *effect* within Member States if there was an act of implementation. However, the Court of Justice developed the view that treaty provisions could in principle confer rights and impose obligations directly upon individuals irrespective of any act of implementation. In the *Van Gend en Loos* case[524] the plaintiff claimed before a Dutch tribunal that there had been an increase in import duties which was rendered illegal by Art.12[525] of the EC

---

[518] Cases 281, 283–285, 287/85, [1987] E.C.R. 3203.

[519] *ibid.* p.3253.

[520] T. C. Hartley, (1988) 13 E.L. Rev. 122.

[521] Art.211 EC.

[522] Hartley (2003), p.106. See also the "supplementary means of action" available to the Council under Art.308 EC: *ibid.* pp.106–114.

[523] See J. A. Winter (1972) 9 C.M.L.R. 425; J.-P. Warner, (1977) 93 L.Q.R. 349; A. Dashwood, (1977–78) 16 J. of Common Market Studies 229; J. Steiner, (1982) 98 L.Q.R. 229, (1990) 106 L.Q.R. 144 and (1993) 18 E.L. Rev. 3; P. Pescatore, (1983) 8 E.L. Rev 155; N. Green, (1984) 9 E.L. Rev. 295; D. Curtin, (1990) 15 E.L. Rev. 195 and (1990) 27 C.M.L. Rev. 709; P. Craig, (1992) 12 O.J.L.S. 453; G. de Búrca, (1992) 55 M.L.R. 215; N. Maltby, (1993) 109 L.Q.R. 301; Plaza Martin, (1994) 43 I.C.L.Q. 26; R. Caranta, (1995) 32 C.M.L. Rev. 703; B. De Witte in P. P. Craig and G. de Búrca (eds), *The Evolution of EC Law* (1999); C. Hilson and T. Downes, (1999) 24 E.L. Rev. 121; R. Mastroianni, (1999) 5 E.P.L. 417; C. Timmermans, (1997) 17 Y.E.L. 1.

[524] Case 26/62, *Van Gend en Loos v Nederlandse Administratie Der Belastingen* [1963] E.C.R. 1.

[525] "Member States shall refrain from introducing between themselves any new customs duties on imports or exports or any charges having equivalent effect, and from increasing those which they already apply in their trade with each other." Now, after amendment, Art.25 EC: "Customs duties on imports and exports and charges having equivalent effects shall be prohibited between Member States. This prohibition shall also apply to customs duties of a fiscal nature."

Treaty. The Court of Justice, on a reference from the tribunal, held that Art.12 was indeed directly effective, and could be relied upon by the plaintiff in this case. The court stated[526]:

> "To ascertain whether the provisions of an international treaty extend so far in their effects it is necessary to consider the spirit, the general scheme and the wording of those provisions.
>
> The objective of the EEC Treaty, which is to establish a Common Market, the functioning of which is of direct concern to interested parties in the Community, implies that this Treaty is more than an agreement which merely creates mutual obligations between the contracting states. This view is confirmed by the preamble to the Treaty which refers not only to governments but to peoples. It is also confirmed more specifically by the establishment of institutions endowed with sovereign rights, the exercise of which affects Member States and also their citizens. Furthermore, it must be noted that the nationals of the states brought together in the Community are called upon to cooperate in the functioning of this Community through the intermediary of the European Parliament and the Economic and Social Committee.
>
> In addition the task assigned to the Court of Justice under Article 177, the object of which is to secure uniform interpretation of the Treaty by national courts and tribunals, confirms that the states have acknowledged that Community law has an authority which can be invoked by their nationals before those courts and tribunals.
>
> The conclusion to be drawn from this is that the Community constitutes a new legal order of international law for the benefit of which the states have limited their sovereign rights, albeit within limited fields, and the subjects of which comprise not only Member States but also their nationals. Independently of the legislation of Member States, Community law therefore not only imposes obligations on individuals but is also intended to confer upon them rights which become part of their legal heritage. These rights arise not only where they are expressly granted by the Treaty, but also by reason of obligations which the Treaty imposes in a clearly defined way upon individuals as well as upon the Member States and upon the institutions of the Community."

Article 12 imposed a clear and unconditional negative prohibition, "ideally adapted to produce direct effects in the legal relationship between Member States and their subjects".

In this and subsequent cases the Court of Justice has elaborated the criteria by which those *treaty provisions* that are regarded as directly effective are to be distinguished from those that are not. As more provisions have come before the court for consideration, the overall picture has become clearer.[527] The criteria[528] are:

---

[526] pp.12–13.
[527] A useful table is given in Collins (1990), pp.122–126.
[528] As formulated by A. G. Mayras in Case 41/74, *Van Duyn v Home Office* [1974] E.C.R. 1337, 1354. See e.g. *Application des Gaz v Folks Veritas* [1974] Ch. 381 (Arts 85 and 86 of the EC Treaty (now Arts 81 EC and 82 EC); *Rio Tinto Zinc Corporation v Westinghouse Electric Corporation* [1978] A.C. 547 (Art.85).

"— the provision must impose a clear and precise obligation on Member States;

— it must be unconditional, in other words subject to no limitation; if, however, a provision is subject to certain limitations, their nature and extent must be exactly defined;

— finally, the implementation of a Community rule must not be subject to the adoption of any subsequent rules or regulations on the part either of the Community institutions or of the Member States, so that, in particular, Member States must not be left any real discretion with regard to the application of the rule in question."

A provision may, exceptionally, be held to have direct effect prospectively only.[529]

The Court of Justice has subsequently invoked these criteria to hold that **5–044** *decisions* addressed to Member States,[530] *directives*,[531] and agreements between the Community and non-Member States[532] can be directly effective. *Van Duyn v Home Office* concerned Art.48 of the EC Treaty (now, after amendment, Art.39 EC), which provided for the "freedom of movement" of workers, including the right to enter and stay in any Member State "subject to limitations justified on grounds of public policy, public security or public health". The scope of these limitations was further regulated by Council Directive 64/221 which provided in Art.3(1) that, "Measures taken on grounds of public policy or of public security shall be based exclusively on the personal conduct of the individual concerned". Miss Yvonne Van Duyn, a Dutch national, was refused leave to enter the United Kingdom on the ground that she was intending to work for the Church of Scientology. The government regarded scientology as socially harmful, and although it had no power to prohibit its practice it had decided to take steps, within its powers, to curb its growth. Accordingly it decided that foreign nationals such as Miss Van Duyn should be refused entry. She claimed that the refusal was not based on her "personal conduct" and challenged its validity in the High Court. Several questions were referred to the European Court, which held: (1) that Art.48 was directly effective; (2) that the relevant provision of directive

---

[529] Case 43/75, *Defrenne v Sabena (No.2)* [1976] E.C.R. 455. This case concerned the direct effect of Art.119/EEC (equal pay for men and women). The court stated: "As the general level at which pay would have been fixed cannot be known, important considerations of legal certainty affecting all the interests involved, both public and private, make it impossible in principle to reopen the question as regards the past" (p.481). See T. Koopmans, [1980] C.L.J. 287; M. Waelbroeck, [1981] 1 Y.E.L. 115. This principle was applied in Case 309/85, *Barra v Belgium* [1988] E.C.R. 355; Case 24/86, *Blaizot v University of Liege* [1988] E.C.R. 379; Case C-262/88, *Barber v Guardian Royal Exchange Assurance Group* [1990] E.C.R. I-1889; Case C-437/97, *Evangelischer Krankenhausverein Wien* [2000] E.C.R. I-1157; A. Arnull, (1988) 13 E.L. Rev. 260.

[530] See Case 9/70, *Grad v Finanzamt Traunstein* [1970] E.C.R. 325: this concerned a decision which prohibited Member States from applying specific taxes concurrently with the common turnover tax (VAT) system due to be implemented by directive.

[531] See Case 41/74, *Van Duyn v Home Office* [1974] E.C.R. 1337; Case 148/78, *Pubblico Ministero v Ratti* [1979] E.C.R. 162; Case 102/79, *Commission v Belgium* [1980] E.C.R. 1473; Case 8/81, *Becker v Finanzamt Münster-Innenstadt* [1982] E.C.R. 53. In Case 131/79, *R v Secretary of State for the Home Department, Ex p. Santillo* [1980] E.C.R. 1585, 1610–11, A. G. Warner argued that the conditions for the direct effectiveness of Treaty provisions were subject to some qualification when applied to directives. In particular, there will nearly always be some element of discretion which will not, however, prevent a directive being held to be directly effective. See generally, D. Curtin, (1990) 15 E.L. Rev. 195.

[532] Case 104/81, *Kupferberg* [1982] E.C.R. 3641.

64/221 was also directly effective; but (3) that a Member State was entitled to take into account as a matter of personal conduct that the individual was associated with an organisation whose activities were considered by the state to be socially harmful.

There are, however, limitations:

> "the European Court has held that directives can only confer rights on individuals (against the State); they cannot impose obligations on individuals (in favour of the State or other individuals). This means that directives are capable of only 'vertical' direct effect; unlike regulations and Treaty provisions, they are not capable of 'horizontal' direct effect".[533]

The leading case here is *Marshall v Southampton and South West Hampshire Area Health Authority (Teaching)*.[534] Miss Marshall was dismissed by the Authority from her post as a dietician when she was 62, although she wished to continue to 65. It was the Authority's policy that the normal retiring age for its employees was the age at which state retirement pensions became payable. For women, this was 60. (The Authority had waived its policy for two years in respect of Miss Marshall.) The Court held that Art.5(1) of Council Directive 76/207 (the "Equal Treatment Directive") was to be interpreted as meaning that a general policy involving the dismissal of a woman solely because she had attained or passed the qualifying age for state pension, which age was different under national legislation for men and for women, constituted discrimination on the ground of sex, contrary to that directive. It could be relied upon against a state authority acting in its capacity as employer: the principle was not confined to governmental acts. It was for the national court to determine whether the Health Authority was a "state authority" for this purpose, although the Court noted that in the order for reference the Court of Appeal had referred to it as a "public authority". The Court stated that as Art.189 of the EC Treaty (now Art.249 EC) provided that a directive was binding "upon each Member State to which it is addressed", it followed

> "that a directive may not of itself impose obligations on an individual and that a provision of a directive may not be relied upon as such against such a person."[535]

[533] Hartley (2003), p.213.
[534] Case 152/84, [1986] Q.B. 401, [1986] E.C.R. 723 (*Marshall I*). See A. Arnull, (1986) 35 I.C.L.Q. 939 and [1987] P.L. 383; T. Millett (1987) 36 I.C.L.Q. 616; N. Foster, (1987) 12 E.L. Rev. 222. In subsequent proceedings, the European Court held that Art.6 of the Equal Treatment directive, which required Member States to introduce measures enabling the victims of unlawful discrimination to "pursue their claims by judicial process", was directly effective, and precluded the imposition of limits to the amount of compensation recoverable or the exclusion of an element for interest: Case C-271/91, *Marshall v Southampton and South West Hampshire Area Health Authority (No.2)* [1994] Q.B. 126. Accordingly, the statutory limit to compensation for sex discrimination (Sex Discrimination Act 1975, s.65(2)) was not applicable to claims based on Community Law: see the House of Lords decision in *Marshall (No.2)*, restoring the award of the industrial tribunal: [1994] 1 A.C. 530. Section 65(2) was subsequently repealed and provision made for the award of interest by the Sex Discrimination and Equal Pay (Remedies) Regulations 1993 (SI 1993/2798).
[535] [1986] Q.B. 401, 422.

Accordingly, the Court of Justice has held that a Member State cannot base criminal proceedings against an individual on the provisions of an unimplemented directive.[536]

The ruling against "horizontal direct effect" has been criticised as having **5–045** "serious consequences for the rights of the individual".[537] It has been suggested that it can be seen as a compromise between, on the one hand, the desire to give maximum effectiveness to directives and, on the other, the argument based on the wording of Art.189 (now Art.249 EC) and doubts expressed by courts in France (the *Conseil d'Etat*) and Germany (the *Bundesfinanzhof*) to the effect that directives should not be regarded as having any direct effect.[538] In any event, the ruling has since been reaffirmed by the Court of Justice in *Paola Faccini Dori v Recreb SrL*,[539] where a consumer in proceedings with a trader sought to rely on the provisions of a directive on consumer protection.[540] The relevant events[541] took place in 1989 and the directive was only implemented in Italy in 1992. The Court held that the relevant provisions were unconditional and sufficiently precise in terms of the direct effect doctrine; however, to extend that doctrine to relations between individuals

> "would be to recognise a power in the Community to enact obligations for individuals with immediate effect, whereas it has competence to do so only where it is empowered to adopt regulations."[542]

Instead, private individuals had to rely on the principles of the *Marleasing* and *Francovich* cases.[543] In reaching this conclusion the Court declined to follow the opinion of Advocate-General Lenz,[544] who argued that directives should be accorded horizontal direct effect, albeit only for the future, in the interests of the effective, uniform application of Community law.

Notwithstanding the absence of full "horizontal direct effect" so as to impose an obligation on private individuals, an unimplemented directive may nevertheless have an "incidental effect" in litigation in a national court prejudicial to the interests of such an individual.[545] For example, a neighbour may be entitled

---

[536] Case 14/86, *Pretore di Salo v Persons Unknown* [1987] E.C.R. 2545, 2569–2570: A. Arnull, (1988) 13 E.L. Rev. 40; Case 80/86, *Kolpinghuis* [1987] E.C.R. 3969: A. Arnull, (1988) 13 E.L. Rev. 42.

[537] Arnull, (1986) 35 I.C.L.Q. 939, 943.

[538] Hartley (2003), pp.212–215.

[539] Case C-91/92, [1994] E.C.R. 1-3325. See W. Robinson, (1995) 32 C.M.L. Rev. 629; J. Coppel (1994) 57 M.L.R. 859; D. Kinley, [1995] I E.P.L. 79. The same view was expressed in Case C-192/94, *El Corte Inglés v Cristina Blasquez Rivero* [1996] E.C.R. I-1281 and Case C-97/96, *Verband Deutscher Daihatsu Händler eV v Daihatsu Deutschland GmbH* [1997] E.C.R. I-6843.

[540] Dir.85/577/EEC, concerning protection of the consumer in respect of contracts negotiated away from business premises.

[541] Ms Faccini Dori sought to rely on the directive in claiming the right to cancel a contract for an English language correspondence course concluded at Milan Central Railway Station.

[542] p.I-3356, para.24.

[543] See below, paras 5–046, 5–047.

[544] [1994] E.C.R. I-3338–I-3345.

[545] Case C-194/94, *CIA Security International SA v Signalson SA and Securitel Sprl* [1996] ECR 1-2201 (firm sought court order requiring a competitor to cease marketing a security alarm on the ground that it did not comply with a Belgian technical standard; the standard had not been notified to the Commission as required by Dir. 83/189 and could not be relied on by the state); Case C-443/98, *Unilever Italia v Central Food* [2000] ECR 1-7535 (where the effect was on a contractual relationship between two private parties; S. Weatherill, (2001) 26 E.L. Rev. 177.

to challenge a grant of planning permission to a third party on the ground that an environmental impact assessment required by Directive 85/337 had had not been carried out.[546] The claimant could rely on the failure of the UK correctly to implement the directive notwithstanding the effect on the third party[547]; there was no breach of the rule against horizontal direct affect as there was no suggestion that the Directive had imposed obligations on the third party.

A further point is that once a directive has been transposed into domestic law, individuals can still rely on the direct effect doctrine where the national implementing measures are incorrect or inadequate or national measures correctly implementing the directive are not being applied in such a way as to achieve the result sought by it.[548]

Five further points should be noted. First, it becomes necessary to determine what amounts to a "state authority". The English courts initially took a narrow view, holding that directives could give rise to legal rights

> "in employees of the State itself and of any organ or emanation of the State, an emanation of the State being understood to include an independent public authority charged by the State with the performance of any of the classic duties of the State, such as the defence of the realm or the maintenance of law and order within the realm."[549]

This did not cover the British Gas Corporation,[550] and Rolls-Royce plc[551] in the period before privatisation. Conversely, a woman police officer who was a member of the Royal Ulster Constabulary Reserve was entitled to rely on the Equal Treatment Directive (76/207) against the Chief Constable,[552] and a regulatory agency acting on behalf of local authorities was held to be an emanation of the state.[553] The Court of Justice, however, took a broader view. In *Foster v British Gas plc*[554] it held that the Court had jurisdiction in a preliminary ruling to determine the categories of person against whom the provisions of a directive may be relied on, and that it was for national courts to determine whether a party before them fell into one of the categories so defined. The categories include "a body, whatever its legal form, which has been made responsible, pursuant to a measure adopted by the state, for providing a public service under the control of the State and has for that purpose special powers beyond those which result from

---

[546] Case C-201/02, *R (on the application of Delene Wells) v Secretary of State for Transport, Local Government and the Regions*, Judgment of January 7, 2004. The failure was confirmed in Case 508/03, *Commission v UK*, Judgment of May 4, 2006.

[547] Exposing it to the risk that the planning permission be revoked or conditions modified (but note that compensation would be payable by the state). These were described by the Court (at para.57) as "mere adverse repercussions on the rights of third parties".

[548] Case 62–00, *Marks & Spencer plc v Commissioners of Customs & Excise* [2002] E.C.R. I-6325, paras 27, 28. For subsequent proceedings leading to a second reference to the ECJ see [2005] UKHL 53, [2005] S.T.C. 1254, HL.

[549] *per* Lord Donaldson in *Foster v British Gas plc* [1988] I.R.L.R. 354, 356.

[550] *Foster v British Gas plc*, above.

[551] *Rolls-Royce plc v Doughty* [1988] 1 C.M.L.R. 569, EAT.

[552] Case 222/84, *Johnston v Chief Constable of the Royal Ulster Constabulary* [1986] E.C.R. 1651, [1987] Q.B. 129; A. Arnull, (1987) 12 E.L. Rev. 56;

[553] *R v London Boroughs Transport Committee, Ex p. Freight Transport Association Ltd* [1990] C.M.L.R. 229.

[554] Case C-188/89, [1990] E.C.R. 1-3330.

the normal rules applicable in relations between individuals".[555] In the light of this ruling, the House of Lords held that British Gas, when a nationalised industry, was an emanation of the state.[556] Conversely, the Court of Appeal confirmed that Rolls-Royce plc was not,[557] concluding that the fact of state ownership of a company was not sufficient where the company was not providing a public service and had no special powers.[558] The Court of Appeal reversing the Employment Appeal Tribunal, has held that the governing body of a voluntary-aided school was an emanation of the state; they voluntarily accepted financial aid from the state and provided a public service on its behalf.[559]

Secondly, even within the implementation period of a directive, the Member States must refrain from taking any measures liable seriously to compromise the attainment of the result prescribed by the directive.[560] It is immaterial whether the rule of domestic law was adopted to implement the directive.[561]

Thirdly, the Court of Justice has held that Community law precludes Member States in proceedings against them in national courts based on unimplemented but directly effective directive provisions from relying on national procedural rules relating to time limits.[562] However, this does not prevent Member States from setting a time limit to retrospective claims for arrears of benefit based on such provisions, provided that the same time limit applies to claims to benefit arrears under national law and that the rule is not framed so as to render virtually impossible the exercise of rights conferred by Community law.[563]

Fourthly, it was of course still necessary notwithstanding *Marshall* for the United Kingdom to take legislative steps to implement the directive in question so as to extend its benefits to all employees. This was done by the Sex Discrimination Act 1986,[564] which took effect from November 7, 1987.

Fifthly, the courts have considered whether the unamended UK legislation[565] could be interpreted in accordance with the Equal Treatment Directive so as to render differential retirement ages for men and women unlawful. The House of Lords in *Duke v Reliance Systems Ltd*[566] held that it could not. This point is taken up in the following section.

Overall, Member States have tended to present arguments to the Court of Justice against direct effectiveness although there seems to have been growing acceptance; Community institutions have tended, not surprisingly, to argue in favour, given that it strengthens their position at the expense of individual

---

[555] Paras 20, 22 and the ruling. Para.18, by contrast, refers to "organisations or bodies which were subject to the authority of the state *or* had special powers beyond those which result from the normal rules applicable to relations between individuals" (emphasis added).

[556] *Foster v British Gas plc* [1991] 2 A.C. 306.

[557] *Doughty v Rolls-Royce* [1992] I.C.R. 538.

[558] Relying on the terms of the ruling of the Court of Justice in *Foster* rather than para.18, and on the subsequent approach of the House of Lords in the same case: [1991] 2 A.C. 306.

[559] *National Union of Teachers v Governing Body of St Mary's Church of England (Aided) Junior School* [1997] I.C.R. 334.

[560] Case C-129/96, *Inter-Environment Wallonie ASBL v Region Wallonie* [1997] E.C.R. I-7411.

[561] Case C-14/02, *ATRAL* [2003] E.C.R. I-4431; Case C-144/04, *Mangold v Helm* [2006] 1 C.M.L.R. 43.

[562] Case C-208/90, *Emmott v Minister for Social Welfare* [1991] E.C.R. 1-3723, in respect of the three-month time limit for applications for judicial review in Ireland.

[563] Case C-338/91, *Steenhorst-Neerings v Bestuur van de Bedrijfsvereniging voor Detailhandel, Ambachten en Huisvrouwen* [1993] E.C.R. 1-5475; Case C-410/92, *Johnson v Chief Adjudication Officer (No.2)* [1995] All E.R. (E.C.) 258.

[564] ss.2, 3. See B. Fitzpatrick, (1987) 50 M.L.R. 934.

[565] Sex Discrimination Act 1975, ss.1, 6.

[566] [1988] A.C. 618. See below, paras 5–057, 5–058.

Member States, and helps ensure that Community law applies uniformly throughout the Member States. It enables individuals to take action to enforce the requirements of Community law without having to rely on Community institutions to act. It has also been stressed that it is inappropriate for a Member State that has failed to implement a directive or decision addressed to it to rely, in proceedings between itself and an individual, on its own failure to comply with that directive or decision on the basis that it is not directly effective.[567]

It has been argued that the

> "granting of direct effect to directives has probably done more than any other initiative by the European Court to enhance the effectiveness of Community law."[568]

Although a regulation is "directly applicable" by virtue of Art.189 of the EC Treaty (now Art.249 EC), it will not necessarily create rights and obligations which may be enforced in national courts. This depends on the wording of the regulation in question[569]: it has been argued that regulations only have "direct effect" if the criteria applicable to treaty provisions and other kinds of Community secondary legislation are fulfilled.[570] In *Consorzio Del Prosciutto Di Parma v Asda Stores Ltd*.[571] Lord Hoffmann said[572] that

> "One would normally assume . . . that unless the Regulation contemplated that it would have to be fleshed out by domestic or Community legislation, it was intended to be effective to create rights or duties or both and not to be what Lord Simonds once called a 'pious aspiration'."[573]

The Court of Justice[574] ruled that a regulation creates not only rights but also obligations for individuals, on which they may rely against other individuals before national courts. However, the requirement of legal certainty means that Community rules must enable those concerned to know precisely the extent of the obligations which they impose on them; accordingly, individuals were not bound by conditions not brought to their knowledge by adequate publicity. A regulation may be held to impose obligations on individuals breach of which must be held by national courts to give rise to a civil action by an individual caused loss thereby.[575]

---

[567] Case 148/78, *Pubblico Ministero v Ratti* [1979] E.C.R. 1624, 1650: A.G. Reischl, *Marshall* [1986] Q.B. 401, 421–422.

[568] Hartley (2003), p.211.

[569] Usher (1981) *op. cit.* para.5–036, n.455, pp.18–19.

[570] A.G. Warner in Case 31/74, *Galli* [1975] E.C.R. 47 and Case 74/76, *Iannelli v Meroni; Steinike and Weinlig v Germany* [1977] E.C.R. 557, 583; A.G. Reischl in *Ratti*, n.567, above; A.G. Geelhoed in Case C-253/00, *Antonio Muñoz y Cia SA Superior Fruiticola SA v Frumar Ltd* [2003] Ch. 328, who expressly applied the case law concerning directives, while noting that such effect for a regulation could be both "vertical" and "horizontal".

[571] [2001] UKHL 7. The House referred a question to the Court of Justice whether a regulation that referred to a specification concerning Parma ham enshrined in Italian law was sufficiently accessible to give rise to a Community right.

[572] At para.[21].

[573] *Cutler v Wandsworth Stadium Ltd* [1949] A.C. 398, 407.

[574] Case C-108/01, [2003] E.C.R. I-05121.

[575] So held by the Court of Justice in *Antonio Muñoz v Frumar*, above.

Finally, it should be noted that in these and other cases in this area the Court of Justice has not been consistent in its use of the *terms* "directly applicable" and "direct effect", but has tended to use them interchangeably.[576]

(d) Indirect effect; the principle of "conform interpretation"

The limitations on the direct effect doctrine in the context of directives have   **5–046** attention on the extent to which unimplemented directives may have "indirect effect". An issue has arisen as to the extent to which national courts should have regard to an unimplemented directive in *interpreting* national legislation. Furthermore, the Court of Justice has held that the failure of a Member State to implement a directive may give rise to a liability in damages.

The Court of Justice has developed its view on the first issue over a series of cases. In *Von Colson and Kamann v Land Nordrhein-Westfalen*,[577] it stated that even where a directive does not have direct effects,

> "in applying the national law and in particular the provisions of a national law specifically introduced in order to implement Directive 76/ 207, national courts are required to interpret their national law in the light of the wording and purpose of the directive in order to achieve the result referred to in the third paragraph of Article 189."[578]

This is so whether or not the time for implementing the directive has expired.[579] It was suggested by A.G. Slynn in *Marshall v Southampton and South West Hampshire Area Health Authority (Teaching)*[580] that this principle did not apply to require a national court to interpret legislation so that it accords with a *later* directive, "unless it is clear that the legislation was adopted with a proposed directive in mind".[581] This was criticised as too restrictive an approach,[582] but it was adopted by the House of Lords in *Duke v Reliance Systems Ltd*.[583] However, in *Marleasing SA v La Comercial Internacional de Alimentación SA*[584] the Court of Justice adopted a broader view. Marleasing sought an order in the Spanish courts for the annulment of a company (La Comercial) under provisions of the Spanish Civil Code that contracts lacking cause or whose cause is unlawful have no legal effect. It was alleged that La Comercial had been established as part of a scheme to defraud the creditors of another company. However, a subsequent EC

---

[576] But see A.G. Warner in *Iannelli v Merioni* [1977] E.C.R. 557 at 583 and A.G. Slynn in Case 8/81, *Becker* [1982] 1 C.M.L.R. 499, 504–505; in *Ratti*, above, A.G. Reischl argued that the term "direct applicability" should only be used in respect of *regulations*.

[577] Case 14/83, [1984] E.C.R. 1891, 1909.

[578] This passage appears in the Court's reasoning: the operative part of the judgment refers only to legislation adopted for the implementation of the directive. The principle was invoked in the narrower context in Case 262/84, *Beets-Proper v Van Lanschot Bankiers N.V.* [1986] E.C.R. 782; A. Arnull, (1987) 12 E.L. Rev. 229. However, the Court repeated the wider formulation in Case 80/86, *Kolpinghuis Nijmegen B.V.* [1987] E.C.R. 3969; A. Arnull, (1988) 13 E.L. Rev. 42.

[579] *Kolpinghuis*, above.

[580] [1986] Q.B. 401.

[581] *ibid.* p.411.

[582] A. Arnull, [1988] P.L. 313, 317.

[583] [1988] A.C. 618, below, para.5–057 criticised by Arnull, *op. cit.* See also *Organon Laboratories Ltd v D.H.S.S.* [1990] 2 C.M.L.R. 49.

[584] Case C-106/89, [1990] I-E.C.R. 4135. See G. de Búrca, (1992) 55 M.L.R. 215; Prechal, (1990) 27 C.M.L. Rev. 451; P. Mead, (1991) 16 E.L. Rev. 490; N. Maltby, (1993) 109 L.Q.R. 301.

directive[585] set out an exclusive list of the cases in which the nullity of a company may be declared, and lack of (lawful) cause was not on the list. The Court of Justice stated[586] that:

> "the Member States' obligations arising from a directive to achieve the result envisaged by the directive and a duty under Article 5 of the Treaty to take all appropriate measures, whether general or particular, to ensure the fulfilment of that obligation, is binding on all the authorities of Member States including, for matters within their jurisdiction, the courts. It follows that, in applying national law, whether the provisions in the decision were adopted before or after the directive, the national court called upon to interpret it is required to do so, as far as possible, in the light of the wording and the purpose of the directive in order to achieve the result pursued by the latter and thereby comply with the third paragraph of Article 189 of the Treaty."

Accordingly, a national court having a case within the scope of the directive was:

> "required to interpret its national law in the light of the wording and the purpose of that directive in order to preclude a declaration of nullity of a public limited company on a ground other than those listed in Article 11 of the directive."[587]

While this is a strong statement, its limits should be noted. It must be remembered that it only arises where there is an issue of *interpretation* of national law. It cannot mean that the directive must be applied irrespective of the wording of national law, for that would be to apply the direct effect doctrine between individuals, a step that the court has consistently refused to take, as in the *Marleasing* case itself.[588] This point is confirmed by the inclusion of the words "as far as possible" in para.8 of the judgment.[589] The *Marleasing* approach has, subject to this understanding, been accepted by the English courts.[590]

5–047   Of potentially greater significance was the decision of the Court of Justice in *Andrea Francovich v Italian Republic*.[591] A 1980 EC directive[592] provided, *inter alia*, for specific guarantees of the payment of unpaid wage claims in the event of an employer's insolvency. The deadline for implementation was October 23, 1983; Italy failed to fulfil its implementation obligation.[593] A number of workers unable to recover unpaid wages from their employers brought proceedings against the state, claiming fulfilment of the guarantees by the state or, in the

---

[585] First Council Directive 68/151/EEC, March 9, 1968, Art.11.

[586] At p.1–4159, para.8.

[587] At p.1–4160, para.13.

[588] At p.1–4158, para.6.

[589] See N. Maltby, (1993) 109 L.Q.R. 301, "It does not oblige the national court to interpret national law . . . *contra legem*": A.G. Van Gerven in Case C-271/91, *Marshall v Southampton and South West Hampshire Area Health Authority (No.2)* [1993] 4 All E.R. 586, 605.

[590] *Webb v EMO Air Cargo Ltd* [1993] 1 W.L.R. 49, below, para.5–059.

[591] Cases C-6/90 and C-9/90, [1991] 1–5357. See G. Bebr, (1992) 29 C.M.L.R. 557; P. Duffy, [1992] 17 E.L. Rev. 133; R. Caranta, [1993] C.L.J. 272; P. P. Craig, (1993) 109 L.Q.R. 595; J. Steiner, [1993] 18 E.L. Rev. 3; C. Lewis and S. Moore, [1993] P.L. 151; M. Ross, (1993) 56 M.L.R. 55.

[592] Dir.80/887/EEC.

[593] Confirmed in Case 22/87, *Commission v Italy* [1989] E.C.R. 143.

alternative, compensation. The Court of Justice held: (1) that the provisions of the directive were not directly effective[594]; but (2) that in order to promote the full effectiveness of Community rules, "it is a principle of Community law that the Member States are obliged to make good loss and damages caused to individuals by breaches of Community law for which they can be held responsible".[595] A further basis for this obligation was Art.5 of the EC Treaty (now Art.10 EC), under which Member States are required to take all appropriate measures to ensure fulfilment of their obligations under Community law; among these is the obligation to nullify the unlawful consequences of a breach of Community law. The conditions for state liability depended on the nature of the breach of Community law. In the case of failure to implement directives they were:

(1) the result prescribed by the directive should entail the grant of rights to individuals;

(2) it should be possible to identify the content of those rights on the basis of the provisions of the directive;

(3) a causal link must exist between the breach of the state's obligation and the loss and damage suffered by the injured parties.

These conditions gave rise to "a right on the part of individuals to obtain reparation, a right founded directly on Community law".[596] It was on the basis of the rules of national law on liability that the state was to make a reparation and for national law to designate the competent courts and procedures, although the substantive and procedural conditions must not be less favourable than for similar domestic claims. Applying these principles, the national court was required to uphold the rights of the employee to obtain reparation for the state's failure to implement the directive, the state being obliged to make good the loss and damage.

The parameters of the *Francovich* doctrine were explored in the joined cases of *Brasserie du Pêcheur SA v Federal Republic of Germany* and *R v Secretary of State for Transport, Ex p. Factortame Ltd (Factortame III)*.[597] In Brassierie du Pêcheur, a French company claimed compensation for damage caused by German laws that prohibited marketing under the designation "bier" (beer) beers lawfully manufactured by different methods in other Member States and that prohibited the import of beers containing additives. These laws were held to be incompatible with Art.30 of the EC Treaty (now, after amendment, Art.28 EC). In *Factortame III* Spanish fishermen claimed compensation in respect of losses caused by Pt II of the Merchant Shipping Act 1988.[598] Various questions were referred to the Court of Justice by the respective national courts.

Among the points made by the Court of Justice were:

---

[594] They were sufficiently precise and unconditional as regards the persons entitled to and the content of the guarantee, but not as to the identity of the person liable to provide it.

[595] [1991] E.C.R. 1–5357, 1–5415, para.37.

[596] p.5415, paras 38–41.

[597] Cases C-46/93 and C-48/93, [1996] E.C.R. I-1029. See W. Van Gerven, (1996) 45 I.C.L.Q. 507; P. P. Craig, (1997) 113 L.Q.R. 67; J. Convery (1997) 34 C.M.L. Rev. 603; R. Crawfurd Smith in P. P. Craig and G. de Búrca (eds), *The Evolution of EU Law* (1999); J. Steiner, (1998) 4 E.P.L. 69; T. Tridimas, (2001) 38 C.M.L. Rev. 301.

[598] Below, para.5–057.

(1) that the *Francovich* doctrine is applicable where the national legislature is responsible for the breach[599];

(2) that where the legislature was acting is a field in which it had wide discretion to make legislative choices, individuals suffering loss or injury thereby are entitled to reparation where:

   (i) the Community law rule breached is intended to confer rights upon them;

   (ii) the breach is sufficiently serious; and

   (iii) there is a direct causal link between the breach and the damage suffered[600];

(3) that, subject to this, the state must make good the consequences of the loss or damage caused by the breach of Community law in accordance with its national law on liability, although the conditions laid down by the national law must not be less favourable than those laid down for similar domestic claims or framed in such a way as to make it execessively difficult to obtain reparation[601];

(4) that reparation cannot be made conditional upon fault (intentional or negligent) on the part of the state organ responsible for the breach, going beyond that of a sufficiently serious breach of Community law;

(5) that reparation must be commensurate with the loss or damage sustained and cannot exclude a claim for loss of profits; specific damages such as exemplary damages must be available if they might be awarded pursuant to similar claims founded on domestic law[602]; and

(6) the obligation to make good loss or damage cannot be limited to damage sustained after delivery of a judgment of the court finding the infringement of Community law.

Applied to the facts of the cases involved here, the laws infringed (Arts 30 and 52 of the EC Treaty (now Art.28 EC and, after amendment, Art.43 EC) were plainly intended to confer rights on individuals. The test for whether the breach of Community law was sufficiently serious was whether the Member State concerned "manifestly and gravely disregarded the limits on its powers". Relevant factors here included the clarity and precision of the rule breached; the measure of discretion[603] left by that rule to the national authorities; whether the infringement and the damage caused was intentional or involuntary; whether any error of law was excusable or inexcusable; the fact that the position taken by a Community institution may have contributed towards the omission; and the adoption or retention of national measures contrary to Community law. A breach would clearly be sufficiently serious if it had persisted despite a judgment

---

[599] i.e. where there is national legislation inconsistent with directly effective Community law, and not just where there is a failure to implement a directive that is not itself directly effective (as in *Francovich*).

[600] These principles are analogous to those established in respect of the non-contractual liability of Community institutions under Art.215 of the EC Treaty (now Art.288 EC).

[601] e.g. by the conditions required to establish the English tort of misfeasance in a public office.

[602] This may include a claim for interest: Cases C-397/98 and C-410/98, *Metallgesellschaft Ltd v Inland Revenue Commissioners* [2001] All E.R. (EC) 496.

[603] Under Community, not national, law: Case C-424/97, *Haim v KVN* [2000] E.C.R. I-5123.

establishing the infringement or a clear preliminary ruling or settled case-law on the point. These matters were for the national courts to determine, although the Court did indicate that it would be difficult to regard the (*Brasserie du Pêcheur*) breach of Art.30 of the EC Treaty by the marketing prohibition as excusable error given the settled case-law of the Court, and that the nationality condition in *Factortame* was "direct discrimination manifestly contrary to Community law".[604] The way was thereby opened for substantial awards of damages in these cases.[605] Accordingly, there is now a general principle of state liability for loss and damage caused to individuals as a result of breaches of Community law for which the State can be held responsible.[606] In subsequent cases the Court has held that it has all the necessary information to be able to assess whether the facts must be held to constitute a sufficiently serious breach of Community law.[607] Provided that the Community law rights of individuals are effectively protected, it is sufficient that reparation is provided by the responsible public law body; Community law neither requires the Member State to be liable as well nor precludes both being held liable.[608] It has been held that the principle can apply where the infringement stems from the decision of a court of last instance,[609] it being for the legal system to designate the court competent to determine disputes relating to that reparation. Liability "can be incurred only in the exceptional case where the court has manifestly infringed the applicable law". It is necessary to take into account the degree of clarity and precision of the rule infringed, whether the infringement was intentional, whether the error of law was excusable or inexcusable, the position taken, where applicable, by a Community institution, and non-compliance with the court's duty to make a reference under Art.234

---

[604] *cf.* Case C-392/93, *R v HM Treasury, Ex p. British Telecommunications plc* [1996] E.C.R. I-1631, where the Court held that the UK was not to be held liable damages where it incorrectly implemented a directive, given that the provision in question was imprecisely worded, and the UK had acted in good faith and adopted an interpretation that the provision was reasonably capable of bearing; this was not, accordingly, a "sufficiently serious breach of Community law" of the kind contemplated by *Basserie du Pêcheur and Factortame*. Subsequent cases include Cases C-5/94, *R v Ministry of Agriculture, Ex p. Hedley Lomas* [1996] E.C.R. 2553 (concerning a ban on the export to Spain of animals for slaughter) and Cases C-178, 179, 188–190/94, *Dillenkofer v Germany* [1996] E.C.R. 1-4845 (failure to implement directive by the deadline), where the Court indicated that there should be liability; Case C-283/94, *Denkavit Internationaal BV v Bundesamt für Finanzen* [1996] E.C.R. I.-5063 (breach not sufficiently serious in absence of relevant case law of the Court); and Case C-66–95, *R v Secretary of State for Social Security, Ex p. Sutton* [1997] E.C.R. I-2163, where no opinion was expressed.

[605] See *R v Secretary of State for Transport, Ex p. Factortame (No.5)* [2001] 1 A.C. 524 (where the House of Lords held that the UK's breach had indeed been "sufficiently serious" to give rise to a claim for compensatory damages (a claim for exemplary damages was not pursued before the House); the fact that the government had acted on legal advice was not conclusive in its favour and it had in any event chosen to ignore clear contrary advice from the Commission); *R v Secretary of State for Transport, Ex p. Factortame (No.7)* [2001] 1 W.L.R. 942 (claim amounts to an action for breach of statutory duty; damages for distress not recoverable); and *Brasserie du Pêcheur* [1997] 1 C.M.L.R. 971.

[606] See the summary in Case C-127/95, *Norbrook Laboratories Ltd v Ministry of Agriculture, Fisheries and Food* [1998] E.C.R. I-1531 paras 105–112. The three conditions (rule of law infringed must have been intended to confer rights on individuals; sufficiently serious breach; direct causal link) apply equally in cases involving non-implementation (e.g. *Francovich*) and inconsistent national legislation or administrative action (e.g. *Factortame*).

[607] e.g. Case C-118/00, *Larsy v INASTI* [2000] E.C.R. I-5063.

[608] Case C-302/97, *Konle v Austria* [1999] E.C.R. I-3099, paras 62–64; Case C-424/97, *Haim v KVN* [2000] E.C.R. 1-5123, paras 25–34.

[609] In the case of lower courts, the remedy would be an appeal. The court of last instance would presumably have refused to make a reference for a preliminary ruling under Art.234 EC.

EC.[610] While this can be seen as a logical application of the principle of effectiveness, it may also undermine the finality of judgments. It may also

> "produce the rather strange situation whereby the House of Lords might eventually be called upon to hear a case in State liability based on one of its own judgments."[611]

It has subsequently been held that Community law precludes national legislation which excludes liability founded on a court's interpretation of provisions of law or its assessment of facts or evidence; or which limits liability solely to cases of intentional fault and serious misconduct on the part of the court, if that were to lead to the exclusion of state liability where there was a manifest infringement of the applicable law.[612]

(e) Treaty provisions

5–048   The main treaties concerning the Communities are:

(1) the Treaty establishing the European Coal and Steel Community (Paris, 1951);

(2) the Treaties establishing the European Economic Community and the European Atomic Energy Community (Rome, 1957);

(3) the Treaty establishing a Single Council and a Single Commission of the European Communities (Brussels 1965; the "Merger Treaty");

(4) the Treaties amending certain Budgetary Provisions of the Treaties (Luxembourg, 1970 and Brussels, 1975);

(5) the Accession Treaties (Brussels, 1972: Denmark, Ireland, Norway[613] and the United Kingdom (with effect from January 1, 1973); Athens, 1979: Greece (with effect from January 1, 1981); Madrid and Lisbon, 1985: Spain and Portugal (with effect from January 1, 1986); Corfu, 1994: Norway,[614] Austria, Finland and Sweden (with effect from January 1, 1995); Athens, 2003: Czech Republic, Estonia, Cyprus, Latvia, Lithuania, Hungary, Malta, Poland, Slovenia and Slovakia (with effect from May 1, 2004); Luxembourg 2005: Bulgaria and Romania (with effect from January 1, 2007));

(6) the Treaty providing for the withdrawal of Greenland[615] (Brussels, 1984 (with effect from February 1, 1985));

---

[610] Case C-224/01, *Gerhard Köbler v Austria* [2003] E.C.R. I-10239, paras [51]–[59] (the infringement here was not of a kind that had the necessary manifest character for liability to arise).

[611] J. Steiner *et al.*, *EU Law* (9th edn, 2006), pp.158–159. Presumably the House could be composed of different members in the second case. See further P. Cabral and M. C. Chaves, (2006) *Maastricht Journal of European and Comparative Law* 109.

[612] Case C-173/03, *Traghetti del Mediterraneo SpA (in liquidation) v Italy* [2006] All E.R. (EC) 983.

[613] Norway subsequently did not ratify the Treaty.

[614] Norway again failed to ratify the Treaty.

[615] Greenland had not been a Member State, but had been part of the Community through its association with Denmark: see F. Weiss, (1985) 10 E.L. Rev. 173.

(7) the Single European Act (Luxembourg and The Hague, 1986 (with effect from July 1, 1987));

(8) The Treaty on European Union (Maastricht, 1992) (with effect from November 1, 1993);

(9) the Agreement on the European Economic Area (Oporto, 1992; Brussels, 1993);

(10) the Treaty of Amsterdam (signed in 1997, in effect from May 1, 1999);

(11) the Treaty of Nice amending the Treaty on European Union, the Treaties establishing the European Communities and certain related acts (signed in 2000, in effect from February 1, 2003).

Several of the treaties have extensive Annexes and Protocols. The treaties are published by the EC and HMSO and in various unofficial collections. There is also a series of treaties entered by the Community with non-Member States.

(f) Regulations, Directives and Decisions

Regulations are the most important form of Community secondary legislation. **5–049** Under Art.189 of the EC Treaty (now Art.249 EC) they are directly applicable without any act of implementation by Member States. Indeed, such acts of implementation are normally prohibited, in case they have the effect of altering the scope of the regulation in question. Member States may not, for example, enact measures which purport to interpret provisions contained in a regulation[616]; such interpretations might vary from state to state, and the regulation would no longer be uniform in application. This prohibition also ensures that provision of a regulation can clearly be perceived to be of Community origin and so subject to the judicial remedies available under Community law, and avoids any ambiguity as to the date of entry into force.[617] Domestic legislation may, however, make supplementary provision, for example by imposing a sanction for breach of a regulation[618] or by prescribing a limitation period for claims based on Community law.[619] Exceptionally, a regulation may itself expressly require Member States to introduce implementing measures.[620]

Directives are used where the approximation or harmonisation of national laws is sought rather than strict uniformity. They may only be addressed to Member States. Choice of method is left to the Member States, although a time limit for implementation is commonly set.

Decisions may be addressed to Member States, to corporations or to individuals. The European Court has held that:

---

[616] Case 40/69, *Hauptzollamt Hamburg v Bollman* [1970] E.C.R. 69; classification of products (turkey rumps) under an agricultural regulation; Case 34/73, *Variola v Italian Minister of Finance* [1973] E.C.R. 981.

[617] Usher (1981), p.17. Member States may not adopt "any measure which would conceal the Community nature and effects of any legal provision from the persons to whom it applies": Case 50/76, *Amsterdam Bulb v Produktschap Voor Siergewassen* [1977] E.C.R. 137, 151.

[618] *Amsterdam Bulb* case, above.

[619] Case 33/76, *Rewe v Landwirtschaftkammer Saarland* [1976] E.C.R. 1989. The periods must be reasonable and non-discriminatory.

[620] See Hartley (2003), pp.203–206; Case 128/78, *Commission v United Kingdom* [1979] E.C.R. 419.

"a decision must appear as an act originating from the competent organisation intended to produce judicial effects, constituting the ultimate end of the internal procedure of this organisation and according to which such organisation makes its final ruling in a form allowing its nature to be identified."[621]

(g) Preparation of Community secondary legislation[622]

5–050   The treaties do not lay down a uniform legislative process to be adopted in all cases. Community legislation may occasionally be made by the Commission, but is usually made by the Council or (in accordance with a procedure introduced by the Maastricht Treaty) by the Parliament and Council acting jointly. Under the basic "consultative procedure" the Commission first formulates a proposal after consulting national officials, experts and representatives of interest groups (the *avant-projet* stage). The draft proposal is then sent to the Council; Member States may at this stage refer it to their national parliaments. A copy is sent to the European Parliament so that a preliminary unofficial study can be commenced in committee. The Council may, and in some cases must[623] consult the European Parliament and the European Economic and Social Committee (a consultative body representing the various categories of economic and social activity, including industry, workers and consumers). The European Parliament debates the report of its committee in plenary session. The opinions of the Parliament and the ESC are transmitted to the Council. The Council may consider the proposal in three stages: (1) in a Working Group of national experts convened by the Council secretariat; (2) in the Committee of Permanent Representatives (COREPER); and (3) in the Council itself. The Commission proposal can be amended only if the Council is unanimous.[624] Reconsultation with the Parliament is necessary where the text finally adopted differs in essence from that on which it has been consulted, except where the amendments essentially correspond to its wishes.[625]

The Single European Act[626] introduced a new "co-operation procedure"[627] which was applicable to some of the instances in which the EC Treaty required

---

[621] Case 54/65, *Compagnie des Forges de Châtillon Commentry et Neuves Maison v High Authority* [1966] C.M.L.R. 525, 538.

[622] T. St. J. N. Bates, "The Drafting of European Community Legislation" [1983] Stat. L.R. 24; Hartley (2003), pp.41–47; Weatherill and Beaumont (1999), pp.58–67, 117–143. Ch.5; A. Dashwood, (1994) 19 E.L. Rev. 343; S. Weatherill, *Law and Integration in the European Union* (1995), Ch.3.

[623] A requirement to consult will be regarded as an essential procedural requirement: Case 138/ 79, *Roquette v Council* [1980] E.C.R. 3333; Case 139/79, *Maizena v Council* [1980] E.C.R. 3393: see T. C. Hartley, (1981) 6 E.L. Rev. 181. It is not sufficient that the opinion of the European Parliament is sought; an opinion must be received, unless the need for the legislation is urgent and the Parliament fails to respond to a request for an urgent opinion: Case C-65/93, *European Parliament v Council* [1995] E.C.R. I-643. A preliminary as opposed to definitive decision may be taken by the Council before obtaining the Parliament's opinion: Case 417/93, *European Parliament v Council* [1995] E.C.R. I-1185; See S. Boyson, (1996) 21 E.L. Rev. 145.

[624] Art.250 EC.

[625] Case C-65/90 *European Parliament v Council* [1992] E.C.R. I-4593 (*Cabotage-I*); Case C-388/92, *European Parliament v Council* [1994] E.C.R. I-2067 (*Cabotage-II*), Case C-280/93, *Germany v Commission* [1994] E.C.R. I-4973.

[626] Arts 6 and 7. See J. Fitzmaurice, (1988) 26 *J. of Common Market Studies* 389.

[627] Substituted Art.149(2) (subsequently Art.189c) of the EC Treaty. See R. Bieber, (1988) 25 C.M.L. Rev. 711. The procedure is now governed by Art.252 EC.

the Parliament to be consulted.[628] This procedure commences at the final stage of the standard legislative process. Instead of adopting the proposal forthwith, the Council adopts a "common position", acting by a qualified majority.[629] The proposal is sent to the Parliament for a second time (the "second reading"), and the Parliament (acting within three months[630]) can approve or reject it, or propose amendments.[631] If the proposal is approved, or no action is taken within three months,[632] the act will be adopted by the Council. If it is rejected, the Council (acting within three months[633]) can only adopt it by unanimity. Proposed amendments are considered by the Commission (acting within one month) and then returned to the Council. If they are approved by the Commission, the Council (acting within three months[634]) can adopt them by a qualified majority. Amendments not approved by the Commission, and any Council amendments, can only be adopted by unanimity. These arrangements constituted "a real, though small," increase in the power of the Parliament, in so far as it could, in alliance with a Member State, block a measure; as regards amendments, the arrangement in essence enshrined existing practice in legal form.[635]

The Maastricht Treaty introduced a further legislative procedure, the "co-decision" or "conciliation and veto" procedure.[636]. The role of the Parliament is here enhanced still further, the procedure providing for the adoption of legislation by the Parliament and Council jointly. It applies to specified legislative powers, including some formerly subject to the co-operation procedure.[637] It was modified by the Treaty of Amsterdam. Under the co-decision procedure[638] at the "first reading stage", the Commission submits a proposal to the Parliament and the Council. The Council, by a qualified majority and after obtaining the Parliament's opinion, either: (1) if it approves all of Parliament's amendments, may

---

[628] e.g. in respect of rules designed to prohibit discrimination on the ground of nationality (Art.6 of the EC Treaty); common rules applicable to international transport, the operation of transport services by non-resident carriers and measures to improve transport safety (Art.75 of the EC Treaty, as amended by Art.6(16) TEU); sea and air transport (Art.84 of the EC Treaty); health and safety of workers (Art.118 of the EC Treaty, as amended by Art.G(33) TEU); Community environmental policy (Art.130s EC of the Treaty inserted by Art.G(38) TEU). Following the Treaty of Amsterdam, these were all brought within the scope of the co-decision procedure (below): see now Arts 12 EC (discrimination); 71 EC (transport); 80 EC (sea and air transport); 137 EC (health and safety); 175 EC (environmental policy).

[629] No time limit is specified for this, unlike for the later stages.

[630] The period may be extended by up to one month, by common accord between the Council and the Parliament: Art.252(g) EC.

[631] The Parliament can only reject or propose amendments by an absolute majority of its members: Art.252(c) EC.

[632] See n.630 above.

[633] ibid.

[634] ibid.

[635] Hartley (2003), p.43. The evidence "shows that a significant proportion of Parliament's amendments were adopted by the Commission and ultimately by the Council": Weatherill and Beaumont (1999), p.131. Rejection of the common position was a weapon that has been "used sparingly"; four were rejected by 1992, two in 1994 and one in 1996: ibid. p.132. The co-operation procedure now applies only in a few situations: e.g. Arts 99 EC, 102 EC, 103 EC, (economic policy).

[636] Art.251 EC (ex Art.189b).

[637] e.g. legislation in respect of free movement of workers (Art.40 EC); freedom of establishment (Art.44 EC); exceptions to the right of establishment on grounds of public policy, public security or public health (Art.46 EC); mutual recognition of diplomas etc. (Art.47(1) EC): establishment of self-employed persons (Art.47(2) EC); freedom of services (Art.55 EC); consumer protection (Art.153 EC); and general environmental action programmes (Art.175(3) EC).

[638] For the full details see http://ec.europa.eu/codecision/index_en.htm. Information on the progress of legislative proposals is contained in the PreLex database.

adopt the proposed act thus amended; or (2) if Parliament does not propose any amendments, may adopt the proposed act; or (3), otherwise, must adopt a common position.

Unless the act is adopted, there follows the "second reading stage". The common position is communicated to the Parliament, together with a full statement of reasons; the Commisson must also inform the Parliament fully of its position. The Parliament (acting within three months[639]) can approve the common position, propose amendments or reject it.[640] If the common position is approved, or no action is taken within three months, the act is deemed to have been adopted. If the common position is rejected (by an absolute majority of its members) the proposed act is deemed not to have been adopted. Where amendments are proposed the amended text is sent to the Council and the Commission, and the Commission is to deliver an opinion on them. If the Commission's opinion is favourable, the Council may approve all Parliament's amendments by a qualified majority; if it is unfavourable, they may be approved unanimously; if the Council does not approve all the amendments a Conciliation Committee must within six weeks be convened by the President of the Council, in agreement with the President of the Parliament.

5–051   The Conciliation Committee comprises the members of the Council or their representatives and an equal number of representatives of the Parliament. Their task is to reach agreement on a joint text, by a qualified majority on the Council side[641] and a majority on the Parliament side. The Commission is to take part in the proceedings and must take all the necessary initiatives with a view to reconciling the positions of Parliament and Council.[642] In fulfilling their task, the Conciliation Committee must address the common position on the basis of the amendments proposed by the Parliament. If within six weeks[643] of being convened, the Committee approves a joint text, the Parliament, acting by an absolute majority of the votes cast, and the Council, acting by a qualified majority,[644] has a further six weeks[645] in which to adopt the proposal (the "third reading stage"); if either of the two fails to do so, it is deemed not to have been adopted. If the Committee does not approve a joint text, the proposal is also deemed not to have been adopted.

The significance of this procedure is that the Parliament, acting by an absolute majority, has the power of veto. The initial view of the Commission was that the procedure had worked well.[646] Between May 1, 1999, and June 30, 2006, of the total number of proposals (536), 213 were adopted at first reading, 103 at second

---

[639] The period can be extended by up to one month by common accord between the Council and the Parliament: Art.251(7) EC.

[640] The proposal of amendments and rejection (but not approval) must be by an absolute majority of the Parliament's members.

[641] The normal requirement that the Council must be unanimous in amending a Commission proposal does not apply: Art.250(1) EC.

[642] The Commission may alter its proposal at any time during the procedure, as long as the Council has not acted: Art.250(2) EC.

[643] The period can be extended by a maximum of two weeks by common accord of the Parliament and the Council: Art.251(7) EC.

[644] See n.641 above.

[645] See n.643 above.

[646] *Commission Report for the Reflection Group* (1995), p.29. By then, two measures had failed to progress: one, on voice telephony, was rejected by the Parliament following a failure to agree at the conciliation stage, because of its provisions on implementing procedures; the other, on biotechnology, was rejected by the Parliament notwithstanding agreement at the conciliation stage.

reading without amendments, 124 at second reading with amendments,[647] and 95 were agreed at the conciliation stage; two proposals were rejected by the Parliament notwithstanding agreement at conciliation.[648] A joint conference of the Council, the Parliament and the Commission in 2002 concluded that the procedure was "working even better and the dialogue between institutions is improving further".[649]

The other major legislative procedure, the "assent procedure" was extended to legislation outside the budgetary process by the Maastricht Treaty.[650] Here, the assent of the Parliament is required, usually to a proposal adopted unanimously by the Council.[651] The Commission notes that this procedure is "ill-adapted to the legislative field" as Parliament may only accept or reject the instrument as laid before it.[652]

These are the main procedures. Overall, the position is excessively complex, the EC Treaty alone prior to the Treaty of Amsterdam having 22 identifiable decision-making procedures, although not all are strictly legislative.[653] The Commission identified three major weaknesses: the continued divergence between legislative procedures and the budget procedure; the complexity of the system; and the lack of logic in the choice of the various procedures and the different fields of activity where they apply. The legislative processes "need to be radically simplified, with reference to the concept of a hierarchy of acts".[654] The Treaty of Amsterdam introduced some simplification, with, for example, the virtual abandonment of use of the co-operation procedure and the expansion of the reach of the co-decision procedure.

In 1992, the report of a group appointed by the Commission under the Chairmanship of a former Commissioner, Peter Sutherland, made (inter alia) a number of recommendations to improve the quality of EC legislation.[655] The Commission's response was favourable.[656] Recommendations accepted included the adoption of more restrictive criteria for legislative intervention (the "subsidiarity" principle); better co-ordination between different departments and committees of the Commission; earlier and wider consultation; greater use of consolidated texts; consideration of the use of (directly applicable) regulations rather than directives so that a single text (albeit in different languages) is applicable throughout the Member States; and regular monitoring of the effectiveness of legislation.

---

[647] A proposed directive on the patent ability of computer-implemented inventions was rejected at second reading by the Parliament on July 6, 2005.

[648] Proposed directives on company law concerning takeover bids (1995/0341 COD) and market access to port services (2001/0047/COD) in 2001 and 2003 respectively.

[649] Joint Press Release, Co-decision website.

[650] This applies, for example, to the conferral of specific tasks on the European Central Bank in stage three of economic and monetary union (Art.105(6) EC); and proposals on a uniform procedure for elections to the Parliament (Art.190(4) EC).

[651] The assent of the Parliament is also required to other, non-legislative proposals, such as accession treaties and international agreements that (inter alia) have important budgetary implications or entail amendment of an act adopted under Art.251 EC: Art.300(3) EC.

[652] Commission Report for the Reflection Group (1995), p.30.

[653] Commission Report for the Reflection Group (1995), Annex 8 (pp.80–83).

[654] ibid. pp.31–33.

[655] The Internal Market After 1992: Meeting the Challenge: Report to the EEC Commission by the High Level Group on the Operation of Internal Market (1992). See R. Wainwright (1994) 15 Stat. L.R. 98.

[656] Follow-up to the Sutherland Report (SEC(92)2277 of December 2, 1992).

The subsidiarity principle is now enshrined in Art.5 EC (ex Art.3b) which provides:

> "The Community shall act within the limits of the powers conferred upon it by this Treaty and of the objectives assigned to it therein.
>
> In areas which do not fall within its exclusive competence, the Community shall take action, in accordance with the principle of subsidarity, only if and in so far as the objectives of the proposed action cannot be sufficiently achieved by the Member States and can therefore, by reason of the scale or effects of the proposed action, be better achieved by the Community.Any action by the Community shall not go beyond what is necessary to achieve the objectives of this Treaty."

The principle is now applied both in the formulation of the Commission's legislative programme and in the review of the existing legislative provisions; it has led to the withdrawal of some proposals and the amendment of others.[657] Each institution must ensure compliance with the principle in exercising its own powers and reasons must be given in proposing Community legislation that demonstrate compliance. The form of Community action should be as simple as possible; other things being equal, directives should be preferred to regulations and framework directives to detailed measures. Community measures should leave as much scope for national decision as possible, consistent with securing the aim of the measure and observing Treaty requirements. The Commission must consult widely before proposing legislation, except in particular case of urgency or confidentiality.[658] The principle is useful in providing a framework for debates as to the relative effectiveness of different forms of legislation in particular contexts; it is, however, unlikely to provide a basis for direct legal challenge to the substance of legislation, as distinct from the sufficiency of the reasons given for proposing it.[659]

In order to improve transparency in the institution's business, the Commission now publishes its legislative programme on an annual basis, issues more Green and White Papers, and has promoted measures to recast, simplify and consolidate Community legislation.[660] The Parliament, Council and Commission have reached an Interinstitutional Agreement on common guidelines for the quality of drafting of Community Legislation[661] which states that "Community legislative acts shall be drafted clearly, simply and precisely". Provisions "should be concise" and "overly long articles and sentences, unnecessarily convoluted wording and excessive use of abbreviations should be avoided". Amendments to

---

[657] See *Commission Report for the Reflection Group* (1995), pp.37–38; Weatherill and Beaumont (1999), pp.27–32; the 1993 Inter-Institutional Agreement on Procedures for Implementing the Principle of Subsidiarity; the Protocol on the Application of the Principles of Subsidiarity and Proportionality annexed to the EC Treaty by the Treaty of Amsterdam (1999), reproduced in N. Foster, *Blackstone's EC Legislation 2006–2007* (17th edn, 2006), pp.112–114.

[658] Protocol on the application of the principles of subsidiarity and proportionality (1999). The Commission makes an annual report to the Council under the title *Better Lawmaking* on the application of these principles.

[659] Weatherill and Beaumont (1999), pp.27–32.

[660] *Commission Report for the Reflection Group* (1995), pp.39–40. The Parliament, Council and Commission have established accelerated procedures for consolidation proposals: O.J. C43, February 2, 1995, pp.41–43; and Interinstitutional Agreement on accelerated working method for official codification of legislative texts: O.J. C102, April 4, 1996.

[661] The Agreement was made on December 22, 1998, and published in 1999, O.J. C73, March 17, 1999.

existing legislation should be textual. Under this agreement, the institutions' legal services have produced a joint practical guide for persons involved in the drafting of legislation.[662] This has been followed by a further Interinstitutional Agreement on better law-making.[663] This covers a range of matters, and includes a commitment "to promote simplicity, clarity and consistency in the drafting of laws and the utmost transparency of the legislative process"; better coordination of the legislative process, including indicative timetabling; the Commission must ensure a proper balance between general principles and detailed provisions in drafting directives, in a manner that avoids excessive use of Community implementing measures; a commitment to both pre-legislative consultation and impact analyses; and steps to update and condense existing legislation and to simplify legislation.

(h) Publication of Community secondary legislation

Regulations, directives and decisions are published in the *Official Journal of the European Union* ("L Series").[664] An English edition has been published from January 1973; English texts of pre-1972 secondary legislation were published in Special Editions of the *Official Journal* covering the pre-accession period, and by HMSO in a 42-volume work entitled *Secondary Legislation of the European Communities: Subject Edition* (1973). HMSO supplemented this series with an annual Subject List and Table of Effects up to the end of 1979. Users must now rely on the monthly and annual indices and lists published as supplements to the *Official Journal*. The European Community also publishes periodically a *Directory of Community Legislation In Force*.[665]

5–052

(i) Arrangement and citation of Community secondary legislation

The heading of a regulation indicates the authority by which it is made, the Treaty under which it is made and its number.[666] The date on which it is made is given, followed by an indication of the subject matter (e.g. "Council Regulation (EEC) No.2194/81 of July 27, 1981 laying down the general rules for the system of production aid for dried figs and dried grapes.")

A *preamble* including an explanation of the purposes of the regulation precedes its main provisions. These comprise numbered *articles*, which may be subdivided into *paragraphs*, and grouped under *Titles*. An *annex* may be attached. Directives and decisions are similar to regulations in form.[667] There is a Manual of Precedents.[668]

5–053

---

[662] *http://eur-lex.europa.eu/en/techleg/index.htm.*

[663] O.J. C321, December 31, 2003.

[664] Since 1968 the *Official Journal* has appeared in two series, one publishing secondary legislation (the "L Series") and the other giving general information, including drafts of proposed legislation the "C series"). It was formerly the Official Journal of the European Communities. It is available on the Internet: see *http:/eur-lex.europa.eu/en/index.htm.*

[665] See also Sweet & Maxwell's *Encyclopedia of European Union Law* and the C.C.H. *European Union Law Reporter.*

[666] From 1958 to 1967 there were separate series of regulations for the EEC and Euratom; from 1968 there has been a single series. Regulations were numbered in a continuous sequence until 1963; from that time a new sequence has been started each calendar year.

[667] From 1968 they have been numbered in a single series with recommendations, opinions and financial regulations.

[668] General Secretariat of the Council of the European Union, Legal/Linguistic experts, *Manual of Precedents for Acts established within the Council of the European Union* (4th edn, 2002).

The correct forms of citation have changed several times.[669] At present they are as follows: Council Regulation (EC) No.2580/2001; Directive 2001/105/EC of the European Parliament and of the Council; Council Decision 2001/824/EC, Euratom.

4. SUPREMACY OF COMMUNITY LAW[670]

5-054 It is well established in terms of Community law that on a matter regulated by binding Community law, that law takes precedence over the municipal law of a Member State.[671] It is immaterial whether the municipal law is enacted before or after the relevant Community law,[672] and whether it forms part of that state's fundamental or constitutional law.[673] Thus in the *Van Gend en Loos* case[674] the Court of Justice spoke of the creation of a "new legal order . . . for the benefit of which the states have limited their sovereign rights".

Costa v ENEL[675] concerned the nationalisation of Italian electricity undertakings. Costa, a shareholder in one of the undertakings (Edison Volta), refused to pay an invoice for electricity sent by ENEL, and claimed that the nationalisation was contrary to prior Community law (various articles of the EEC Treaty). The European Court, on a reference from the Italian magistrate (the Guidice Conciliatore of Milan), dealt firmly with the submission of the Italian government that a national court was obliged to apply the domestic law in preference to Community law[676]:

> "By creating a Community of unlimited duration, having its own institutions, its own personality, its own legal capacity and capacity of representation on the international plane and, more particularly, real powers stemming from a limitation of sovereignty or a transfer of powers from the States to the Community, the Member States have limited their sovereign rights, albeit within limited fields, and have thus created a body of law which binds both their nationals and themselves.
>
> The integration into the laws of each Member State of provisions which derive from the Community, and more generally, the terms and the spirit of the Treaty, make it impossible for the States, as a corollary, to accord precedence to a unilateral and subsequent measure over a legal system accepted by them on a basis of reciprocity. Such a measure cannot therefore be inconsistent with that legal system. The executive force of Community law cannot vary from one State to another in deference to subsequent

---

[669] *Secondary legislation of the European Communities: Subject Edition* (HMSO, 1973) Vol.42, pp.vii–viii.

[670] See Hartley (2003), Chs 7, 8; Weatherill and Beaumont (1999), Ch.12; C. Munro, *Studies in Constitutional Law* (2nd edn).

[671] Case 26/62, *Van Gend en Loos v Nederlandse Administrate der Belastingen* [1963] E.C.R. 1.

[672] Case 6/64, *Costa v ENEL* [1964] E.C.R. 585.

[673] Case 11/70, *Internationale Handelsgesellschaft v Einfuhr-und Vorratsstelle für Getreide* [1970] E.C.R. 1125; Case 106/77, *Amministrazione delle Finanze dello Stato v Simmenthal* [1978] E.C.R. 629.

[674] Above, para.5–043.

[675] Ente Nazionale Energia Elettrica (National Electricity Board), formerly the Edison Volta undertaking.

[676] pp.593–594.

domestic laws, without jeopardizing the attainment of the objectives of the Treaty set out in Article 5(2)[677] and giving rise to the discrimination prohibited by Article 7[678] . . .

The precedence of Community law is confirmed by Article 189,[679] whereby a regulation 'shall be binding' and 'directly applicable in all Member States.' This provision, which is subject to no reservation, would be quite meaningless if a State could unilaterally nullify its effects by means of a legislative measure which could prevail over Community law.

It follows from all these observations that the law stemming from the Treaty, an independent source of law, could not, because of its special and original nature, be overridden by domestic legal provisions, however framed, without being deprived of its character as Community law and without the legal basis of the Community itself being called into question. The transfer by the States from their domestic legal system to the Community legal system of the rights and obligations arising under the Treaty carries with it a permanent limitation of their sovereign rights, against which a subsequent unilateral act incompatible with the concept of the Community cannot prevail. Consequently Article 177[680] is to be applied regardless of any domestic law, whenever questions relating to the interpretation of the Treaty arise."

In the *Simmenthal* case[681] an Italian judge was faced with a conflict between a Council regulation and Italian laws, some of which were enacted after the regulation. Under Italian law domestic legislation contrary to Community law was unconstitutional.

However, only the Constitutional Court had jurisdiction to make such a ruling; the ordinary courts could not. The Court of Justice, on a reference by the judge, held that:

"every national court must in a case within its jurisdiction apply Community law in its entirety and protect rights which the latter confers on individuals and must accordingly set aside any provision of national law which may conflict with it, whether prior of subsequent to the Community rule. . . . [I]t is not necessary for the court to request for or await the prior setting aside of such provisions by legislative or other constitutional means."[682]

The position from the point of view of Community law is thus clear; we now consider it from the standpoint of UK law. The key provisions of the European Communities Act 1972 are contained in ss.2 and 3:

"2.—(1) All such rights, powers, liabilities, obligations and restrictions from time to time created or arising by or under the Treaties, and all such remedies and procedures from time to time provided for by or under the Treaties, as in accordance with the Treaties are without further enactment to

---

[677] Now Art.10(2) EC.
[678] Repealed by the Treaty of Amsterdam.
[679] Now Art.249 EC.
[680] Now Art.234 EC.
[681] [1978] E.C.R. 629.
[682] *ibid.* pp.644, 645–646.

be given legal effect or used in the United Kingdom shall be recognised and available in law, and be enforced, allowed and followed accordingly; and the expression 'enforceable Community right' and similar expressions shall be read as referring to one to which this subsection applies.

(2) Subject to Schedule 2 to this Act, at any time after its passing Her Majesty may by Order in Council, and any designated Minister or department may by regulations, make provision—

(a) for the purpose of implementing any Community obligation of the United Kingdom, or enabling any such obligation to be implemented, or of enabling any rights enjoyed or to be enjoyed by the United Kingdom under or by virtue of the Treaties to be exercised; or

(b) for the purpose of dealing with matters arising out of or related to any such obligation or rights or the coming into force, or the operation from time to time, of subsection (1) above;

and in the exercise of any statutory power or duty, including any power to give directions or to legislate by means of orders, rules, regulations or other subordinate instrument, the person entrusted with the power or duty may have regard to the objects of the Communities and to any such obligation or rights as aforesaid.

In this subsection 'designated Minister or department' means such Minister of the Crown or government department as may from time to time be designated by Order in Council in relation to any matter or for any purpose, but subject to such restrictions or conditions (if any) as may be specified by the Order in Council . . .

(4) The provision that may be made under subsection (2) above includes, subject to Schedule 2 to this Act, any such provision (of any such extent) as might be made by Act of Parliament, and any enactment passed or to be passed, other than one contained in this Part of this Act, shall be construed and have effect subject to the foregoing provisions of this section; but, except as may be provided by any Act passed after this Act, Schedule 2 shall have effect in connection with the powers conferred by this and the following sections of this Act to make Orders in Council and regulations. . . .

3.—(1) For the purposes of all legal proceedings any question as to the meaning or effect of any of the Treaties, or as to the validity, meaning or effect of any Community instrument, shall be treated as a question of law (and, if not referred to the European Court, be for determination as such in accordance with the principles laid down by and any relevant [decision of the European Court or any court attached thereto)].[683]

(2) Judicial notice shall be taken of the Treaties, of the Official Journal of the Communities and of any decision of, or expression of opinion by, the European Court [or any court attached, thereto][684] on any such question as aforesaid; and the Official Journal shall be admissible as evidence of any instrument or other act thereby communicated of any of the Communities or of any Community institution."[685]

---

[683] Words in square brackets substituted by the European Communities (Amendment) Act 1986, s.2(a).

[684] Words added by *ibid*. s.2(b).

[685] Section 2(3) authorises the necessary expenditure; s.2(5) concerns Northern Ireland; s.2(6) concerns the Channel Islands, the Isle of Man and Gibraltar. Section 3(3)–(5) makes further provision for proof of community instruments.

Thus, directly applicable and directly effective Community laws are given **5–055** effect in the United Kingdom under s.2(1); other matters are to be dealt with by statute, or by statutory instruments under s.2(2); any question as to the meaning or effect of the treaties is to be determined in accordance with Community law of which judicial notice is to be taken (s.3). There is, however, no attempt to entrench the European Communities Act itself against repeal. It is unlikely that a court would accept that the "ultimate political fact"[686] has been redefined so as to deny effect to a statute deliberately enacted by Parliament as at present constituted which conflicts with existing Community law. It is even more unlikely that the courts would decline to recognise the express repeal of the 1972 Act.[687] Where a provision of a UK statute is followed by an inconsistent provision of Community law that is directly applicable or effective, the latter is given precedence by s.2 of the European Communities Act 1972. The position is less clear where the chronology is reversed and the UK statute is enacted after the inconsistent provision of Community law. If both laws were made before the 1972 Act, Community law is again given precedence by s.2. If the UK law is more recent, there are a number of possible situations and the position appears to be as follows:

(1) The United Kingdom legislation may be unclear, in which case an English court will endeavour to interpret it so as to comply with Community law, given the established presumption that Parliament does not intend the United Kingdom to be in breach of its international obligations (the "interpretation" issue).[688] In *Garland v British Rail Engineering Ltd*,[689] Lord Diplock said[690]:

> "My Lords, even if the obligation to observe the provisions of article 119 were an obligation assumed by the United Kingdom under an ordinary international treaty or convention and there were no question of the treaty obligation being directly applicable as part of the law to be applied by the courts in this country without need for any further enactment, it is a principle of construction of United Kingdom statutes, now too well established to call for citation of authority, that the words of a statute passed after the Treaty has been signed and dealing with the subject matter of the international obligation of the United Kingdom, are to be construed, if they are reasonably capable of bearing such a meaning, as intended to carry out the obligation, and not to be inconsistent with it. A fortiori is this the case where the Treaty obligation arises under one of the Community treaties to which section 2 of the European Communities Act 1972 applies."

(2) If the United Kingdom legislation is clear and unambiguously conflicts with prior Community law, an English court will then determine whether that conflict was intended by Parliament. In the case of inadvertent conflict,

---

[686] See above, para.5–002.

[687] For the contrary argument that there has been a binding transfer of powers see Usher (1981), pp.30–38; J. D. B. Mitchell, (1967–68) 5 C.M.L. Rev. 112, (1971) *Europarecht* 97 (1979) 56 *International Affairs* 33. A withdrawal from the Community would, however, be negotiated; the arrangement would be enshrined in a treaty which could be construed as a transfer back from the Community of those powers: Usher (1981), p.38.

[688] See below, paras 5–057—5–059, 6–036, 6–053—6–064.

[689] [1983] 2 A.C. 751.

[690] At p.771.

the Community legislation will be given priority. Where conflict is intentional, the courts will give effect to the United Kingdom legislation, and the United Kingdom will be in breach of its Treaty obligations (the "sovereignty" issue).

There have been several judicial statements, some preceding accession, which support the primacy of subsequent inconsistent Acts of Parliament, without drawing a distinction between inadvertent and intentional conflicts.[691] Both the "interpretation" and "sovereignty" issues were subsequently raised in *Macarthys Ltd v Smith*[692] A man was paid £60 a week for managing a stockroom. Four-and-a-half months after he left a woman was appointed in his place at £50 a week. She claimed that she was entitled to equal pay under provisions of the Equal Pay Act 1970 that had been inserted by the Sex Discrimination Act 1975. The Court of Appeal majority[693] held that Equal Pay Act provisions were confined to cases where a man and a woman were in the same employment at the same time. The words had to be given their natural and ordinary meaning and were clear; the terms of Art.119 of the EEC Treaty[694] could therefore not be used as an aid to construction. The question whether Art.119 was so confined was referred to the Court of Justice.

5–056   Lord Denning took a different view of the proper approach to construction of the English statute and then considered the sovereignty issue[695]:

"Under section 2(1) and (4) of the European Communities Act 1972 the principles laid down in the Treaty are 'without further enactment' to be given legal effect in the United Kingdom: and have priority over 'any enactment passed or to be passed' by our Parliament. So we are entitled— and think bound—to look at article 119 of the Treaty because it is directly applicable here: and also any directive which is directly applicable here: see *Van Duyn v Home Office* [1975] Ch. 358. We should, I think, look to see what those provisions require about equal pay for men and women. Then we should look at our own legislation on the point—giving it, of course, full faith and credit—assuming that it does fully comply with the obligations under the Treaty. In construing our statute, we are entitled to look to the Treaty as an aid to its construction: and even more, not only as an aid but as an overriding force. If on close investigation it should appear that our legislation is deficient—or is inconsistent with Community law—by some oversight of our draftsmen—then it is our bounden duty to give priority to Community law. Such is the result of section 2(1) and (4) of the European Communities Act 1972.

---

[691] e.g. Salmon L.J. in *Blackburn v Attorney-General* [1971] 1 W.L.R. 1037, 1041. Lord Denning M.R. left the point open; *Felixstowe Dock and Railway Co v British Transport Docks Board* [1976] 2 C.M.L.R. 655, *per* Lord Denning M.R. at pp.664–665.

[692] [1979] I.C.R. 785, [1981] Q.B. 180; P. Schofield, (1980) 9 I.L.J. 173; T. R. S. Allan, (1983) 3 O.J.L.S. 22. See also *Shields v E. Coomes (Holdings) Ltd* [1978] 1 W.L.R. 1408.

[693] Lawton and Cumming-Bruce L.JJ., Lord Denning M.R. dissenting on this point.

[694] "Each Member State shall during the first stage ensure and subsequently maintain the application of the principle that men and women should receive equal pay for equal work . . . ." This was amplified by Art.1 of a Council directive (Dir.75/117/EEC). Now Art.141 EC: "East Member State shall ensure that the principle of equal pay for male and female workers for equal work or work of equal value is applied."

[695] [1979] I.C.R. 785, at p.789.

I pause here, however, to make one observation on a constitutional point. Thus far I have assumed that our Parliament, whenever it passes legislation, intends to fulfil its obligations under the Treaty. If the time should come when our Parliament deliberately passes an Act—with the intention of repudiating the Treaty or any provision in it—or intentionally of acting inconsistently with it—and says so in express terms—then I should have thought that it would be the duty of our courts to follow the statute of our Parliament. I do not however envisage any such situation. As I said in *Blackburn v Attorney-General* [1971] 1 W.L.R 1037, 1040: 'But, if Parliament should do so, then I say we will consider that event when it happens.' Unless there is such an intentional and express repudiation of the Treaty, it is our duty to give priority to the Treaty."

On the sovereignty issue Lawton L.J. said[696]:

"I can see nothing in this case which infringes the sovereignty of Parliament. If I thought there were, I should not presume to take any judicial step which it would be more appropriate for the House of Lords, as part of Parliament, to take. Parliament by its own Act in the exercise of its sovereign powers has enacted that European Community law shall 'be enforced, allowed and followed' in the United Kingdom of Great Britain and Northern Ireland: see section 2(1) of the European Communities Act 1972, and that 'any enactment passed or to be passed . . . shall be construed and have effect subject to' section 2: see section 2(4) of that Act.

Parliament's recognition of European Community law and of the jurisdiction of the European Court of Justice by one enactment can be withdrawn by another. There is nothing in the Equal Pay Act 1970, as amended, to indicate that Parliament intended to amend the European Communities Act 1972, or to limit its application."

Cumming-Bruce L.J. indicated that if

"the terms of the Treaty are adjudged in Luxembourg to be inconsistent with the provisions of the Equal Pay Act 1970, European law will prevail over that municipal legislation. But such a judgment in Luxembourg cannot affect the meaning of the English statute."[697]

The Court of Justice subsequently held that Art.119 was not restricted to cases of contemporaneous employment,[698] and the plaintiff's claim was duly conceded in the English proceedings. The matter came before the Court of Appeal again on the question of costs.[699] Lord Denning M.R. said[700]:

"the provisions of Article 119 of the EEC Treaty take priority over anything in our English statute on equal pay which is inconsistent with Article 119.

---

[696] At p.796.
[697] At p.798.
[698] Case 129/79, [1981] Q.B. 180, E.C.J.
[699] [1981] Q.B. 199, CA. *Cf. Re an Absence in Ireland* [1977] 1 C.M.L.R. 5, where a national insurance commissioner allowed a claimant's appeal on two grounds, one of which involved the application of Council Regulation (EEC) No.1408/71 in preference to the provisions of the Social Security Act 1975. See also *Re Medical Expenses Incurred in France* [1977] 2 C.M.L.R. 317.
[700] At p.200.

That priority is given by our own law. It is given by the European Communities Act 1972 itself. Community law is now part of our law; and, whenever
there is any inconsistency, Community law has priority. It is not supplanting
English law. It is part of our law which overrides any other part which is
inconsistent with it."

The other members of the court agreed that the Community legislation prevailed.[701] Cumming Bruce L.J. emphasised that his comment at the earlier
stage[702] had to be read in the context of his view (shared by Lawton L.J.) that the
English statute was unambiguous. Had he been of the view that it was ambiguous, it would have been "appropriate to look at Article 119 in order to assist in
resolving the ambiguity".[703]

Accordingly, it appears that both Lord Denning M.R. and Lawton L.J. distinguish between cases of inadvertent and intentional conflict: it would seem that
there is no room in the case of inadvertent conflict for the application of an
"implied repeal rule" as there is between two inconsistent statutes, and in the
case of intentional conflicts the English statute will prevail. Furthermore, even in
the case of intentional conflicts it may be that effect would only be given to the
English statute if it amended or repealed the European Communities Act 1972:
it would not be sufficient merely that the substantive law prescribed by statute
was different from that prescribed by Community law. Lawton L.J., but not Lord
Denning M.R., appears to support this view.[704] The view that the European
Communities Act 1972, as a "constitutional" statute, is not subject to implied
repeal, has now been expressed by the Divisional Court in *Thoburn v Sunderland
City Council*.[705]

5–057   As to the issues raised in *Macarthys Ltd v Smith*,[706] it is arguable that although
the Court of Appeal approached them as if there was a *conflict* between the Equal
Pay Act 1970 and Art.119, the better view is that there was simply a difference
between them.

"Article 119 is directly effective, and Community law applies in the industrial tribunals; to the extent that it gave rights to Mrs Smith more extensive
than the Equal Pay Act 1970 (as amended by the Sex Discrimination Act
1975), there was nothing in the 1970 Act forbidding the court from giving
effect to those rights. It should follow that Mrs Smith would be entitled to
rely on whichever legal rule, art. 119 or the 1970 Act, gave her more
extensive rights."[707]

This approach was echoed by the Court of Appeal in *Pickstone v Freemans
plc*,[708] where it was held that while the relevant provision of the Equal Pay Act
1970[709] was unambiguous and could not be construed in conformity with the

---

[701] Professor Hood Phillips suggested that even in cases of inadvertent conflict, an English court
should give effect to a subsequent, unambiguous United Kingdom Act of Parliament: (1980) 96
L.Q.R. 31; *cf.* O. Hood Phillips and P. Jackson, *O. Hood Phillips' Constitutional and Administrative Law* (7th edn, 1987), pp.74–79.
[702] Set out above.
[703] [1981] Q.B. 180, 201.
[704] This view is endorsed in *Halsbury's Laws of England*, 4th edn, Vol.51, para.3.14.
[705] [2002] EWHC 195 (Admin), above paras 5–002, 5–021.
[706] Above.
[707] L. Collins, *European Community Law in the United Kingdom* (4th edn, 1990), p.32.
[708] [1989] A.C. 66.
[709] s.1(2)(c).

requirements of Community law, a claim to equal pay (for work of equal value) could instead be based directly on Art.119.[710] Similarly, the House of Lords in *R v Secretary of State for Transport, Ex p. Factortame Ltd (No.2)*,[711] following a reference to the Court of Justice,[712] accepted that Community law imposes an obligation on national courts to provide an effective interlocutory remedy to protect rights having direct effect under Community law. Accordingly, interlocutory orders should be granted against the Crown disapplying Pt II of the Merchant Shipping Act 1988[713] and restraining the Secretary of State from enforcing it and related regulations against the applicants, pending the final determination by the European Court of questions concerning the compatability of these provisions with Community law. This was so notwithstanding that, as a matter of domestic law, interlocutory injunctions could not be granted against the Crown.[714] The European Court subsequently ruled that conditions of the kind imposed by the 1988 Act were indeed contrary to Community law.[715]

The possibility of a direct challenge to UK legislation was recognised and acted upon by the House of Lords in *R v Secretary of State for Employment, Ex p. Equal Opportunities Commission*,[716] in granting declarations on the application of the E.O.C. that the differing threshold provisions for full-time and part-time workers' entitlement to unfair dismissal and redundancy payments were incompatible with Community law. The less favourable treatment of part-time workers, the great majority of whom were women, constituted indirect sex discrimination for which no objective justification could be established. The *Factortame* decision provided a precedent acknowledging jurisdiction to grant such a declaration.[717] The House did, however, refuse to make a declaration in terms that the Secretary of State was in breach of the provisions of the Equal

---

[710] The House of Lords took a different approach: see below. See also *Mediguard Services Ltd v Thame* [1994] I.C.R. 751, EAT.

[711] [1991] 1 A.C. 603, HL.

[712] Case C-213/89, *R v Secretary of State for Transport, Ex p. Factortame Ltd* [1990] E.C.R. 1-2433 (known as *Factortame I* by European lawyers but titled *(No.2)* by the Law Reports ([1991] 1 A.C. 603).

[713] The 1988 Act and associated regulations (Merchant Shipping (Registration of Fishing Vessels) Regulations 1988 (SI 1988/1926) were designed to narrow the conditions under which fishing vessels can be registered as British (and thus entitled to fish against the UK quotas): vessels would have to have "a genuine and substantial" connection with the UK (1988 Act, s.14(3)). The applicants were Spanish nationals, who controlled companies that owned ships registered as British, and which would lose that registration under the new rules.

[714] *R v Secretary of State for Transport, Ex p. Factortame Ltd* [1990] 2 A.C. 85, HL *per* Lord Bridge at pp.143–150. See N. P. Gravells, [1989] P.L. 568. The House of Lords in *M v Home Office* [1994] 1 A.C. 377 subsequently held that, notwithstanding the views of Lord Bridge in *Factortame (No.1)* the High Court did have jurisdiction to grant injunctions against officers of the Crown.

[715] Case C-221/89, *R v Secretary of State for Transport, Ex p. Factortame Ltd* [1991] E.C.R. 1-3905 known as *Factortame II* by European lawyers but titled *(No.3)* in the Law Reports: [1992] Q.B. 680. Part II of the Merchant Shipping Act 1988 was amended by the Merchant Shipping Act 1988 (Amendment) Order 1989 (SI 1989/2006) to comply with an interim order in Art.169 proceedings against the UK (Case C-246/89R, *Commission v UK* [1989] E.C.R. 1-3125; Case C-246/89, *Commission v UK* [1991] E.C.R. 1-4585). Part II of the 1988 Act was subsequently repealed and replaced by the Merchant Shipping (Registration, etc) Act 1993. Questions arising out of a claim for damages by the Spanish fishermen were referred by the Divisional Court to the Court of Justice as Case C-48/93, *R v Secretary of State for Transport, Ex p. Factortame Ltd*: see below, para.5–059.

[716] [1995] 1 A.C. 1.

[717] "Although the final result is not reported [following the ECJ decision in *Factortame II*], no doubt the Divisional Court in due course granted a declaration accordingly": *per* Lord Keith of Kinkel *cf.* above, para.5–047.

Treatment Directive which require Member States to introduce measures to abolish any laws contrary to the principle of equal treatment. This was designed to facilitate actions against the United Kingdom by individuals under the *Francovich* principle,[718] but such proceedings were said to raise different issues.[719] The relevant legislation was subsequently amended to comply with Community law.[720]

Cases since *Macarthys Ltd v Smith*[721] have for the most part raised the "interpretation issue" rather than the "sovereignty issue". The dictum of Lord Diplock in *Garland v British Rail Engineering Ltd*[722] cited above[723] has been regarded as endorsing Lord Denning's approach in *Macarthys Ltd v Smith*[724] rather than that of the majority.[725] Lord Diplock's approach was purportedly followed in two, contrasting, decisions of the House of Lords.

In *Duke v Reliance Systems Ltd*,[726] Mrs Duke was dismissed by her private sector employers shortly after attaining 60, in accordance with their policy that men should retire at 65 but women at 60. She claimed that this constituted discriminatory treatment under the Sex Discrimination Act 1975, s.6(2), but her claim was dismissed on the ground that s.6(4) preserved the right of the employer to operate discriminatory retirement ages. This said that s.6(2) did not apply to "provision in relation to death or retirement". It was clear that the later Council Directive Dir.76/207/EEC (the Equal Treatment Directive) did outlaw discrimmatory retirement ages,[727] but (1) this did not have "horizonal direct effect" between individuals,[728] and (2) the UK legislation implementing the directive, the Sex Discrimination Act 1986, did not apply retrospectively so as to apply to Mrs Duke's claim. She argued, therefore, that the expression "provision in relation to . . . retirement" should be interpreted as "provision consequent upon retirement", and therefore not applying to protect discriminatory retirement ages. This would enable English law to conform with the Equal Treatment Directive. The argument was rejected.[729] Lord Templeman, with whom the other members of the House of Lords agreed, said:

> "Of course a British court will always be willing and anxious to conclude
> that United Kingdom law is consistent with Community law. Where an Act
> is passed for the purpose of giving effect to an obligation imposed by a
> decision or other instrument a British court will seldom encounter difficulty

---

[718] See above, para.5–047.

[719] *per* Lord Keith of Kinkel.

[720] See the Employment Protection (Part-Time Employees) Regulations 1995 (SI 1995/31).

[721] Above.

[722] [1983] 2 A.C. 751, 771. This approach applies as much to the interpretation of delegated as to primary legislation: *Ken Lane Transport Ltd v North Yorkshire County Council* [1995] 1 W.L.R. 1416, D.C.

[723] At para.5–054.

[724] Above.

[725] A. W. Bradley, in J. Jowell and D. Oliver, *The Changing Constitution* (2nd edn, 1989), p.41 (a point omitted from the 3rd edn, 1994).

[726] [1988] A.C. 618. Applied by the House of Lords in *Finnegan v Clowney Youth Training Programme Ltd* [1990] 2 A.C. 418.

[727] Case 151/84, *Roberts v Tate & Lyle Industries Ltd* [1986] E.C.R. 703, [1986] I.C.R. 371; Case 152/84, *Marshall v Southampton and South-West Hampshire Area Health Authority (Teaching)* [1986] E.C.R. 723, [1986] Q.B. 401.

[728] *Marshall*, above and see para.5–044.

[729] It had previously been rejected by the Employment Tribunal and the Court of Appeal in *Roberts v Cleveland Area Health Authority* [1978] I.C.R. 370, [1979] 1 W.L.R. 754.

in concluding that the language of the Act is effective for the intended purpose. But the construction of a British Act of Parliament is a matter of judgment to be determined by British courts and to be derived from the language of the legislation considered in the light of the circumstances prevailing at the date of enactment."[730]

However, the 1975 Act was not passed in order to give effect to the (later) Equal Treatment Directive, and the words of s.6(4):

"are not reasonably capable of being limited to the meaning ascribed to them by the appellant. Section 2(4) of the European Communities Act 1972 does not in my opinion enable or constrain a British court to distort the meaning of a British statute in order to enforce against an individual a Community directive which has no direct effect between individuals. Section 2(4) applies and only applies where Community provisions are directly applicable."[731]

It is clearly the case that the 1975 Act was intended at the time to preserve differential retirement ages. Indeed the UK's position was that the Equal Treatment Directive did not prohibit discriminatory retirement ages, an argument ultimately rejected by the European Court in *Marshall I*.[732]

The reasoning in *Duke* has been cogently criticised by commentators on a **5–058** variety of grounds.[733] First, it is not obvious that the narrow reading of "in relation to" was a "distortion": it was certainly a less natural reading, but one that was arguably supportable given the requirements of the directive, and the obligation under Community law (via ss.2(4) and 3(1) of the European Communities Act 1972) to interpret national legislation where possible to conform with relevant directives. Secondly, it was incorrect to say that s.2(4) only applied to Community provisions that were "directly applicable".[734] Thirdly, it gave insufficient weight to the presumed continuing intention of the United Kingdom to comply with the requirements of Community law: it is not clear that this was properly subordinated to the contemporary intention in 1975 to preserve discriminatory retirement ages. It is important, however, to see the *Duke* decision in its context. Had Mrs Duke's argument prevailed, the position would have been as if the Sex Discrimination Act 1986 had retrospective effect, and this would undoubtedly have caused severe practical difficulties. It is to be hoped that the rather doubtful reasoning employed to secure that result is not used in subsequent cases so as to undermine proper implementation by the United Kingdom of the requirements of Community law.

The decision of the House of Lords in *Pickstone v Freemans plc*[735] is accordingly to be welcomed. Here, the House placed renewed emphasis on the need to

---

[730] [1988] A.C. 618, 638.

[731] *ibid.* pp.639–640.

[732] n.727 above.

[733] E. Ellis, (1988) 104, L.Q.R. 379; A. Arnull, [1988] P.L. 313; N. Foster, (1988) 51 M.L.R 775 and (1988) 25 C.M.L. Rev. 629; B. Fitzpatrick, (1989) 9 O.J.L.S. 336.

[734] The European Court in Case 262/84, *Beets-Proper v Van Lanschot Bankiers N.V.* [1986] E.C.R. 782 held that national legislation, designed to implement a directive that was *not* directly effective, should be interpreted so as to conform to it: See above, para.5–046: This obligation would apply to UK courts via ss.2(4) and 3(1) of the 1972 Act.

[735] [1989] A.C. 66. See A. W. Bradley, [1988] P.L. 485. *Cf. J. Rothschild Holdings v Commissioners of Inland Revenue* [1989] 2 C.M.L.R. 612.

interpret English law, where possible, so as to comply with Community law. The context of the case was significantly different from that in *Duke*. Here, the question concerned the interpretation of amendments to the Equal Pay Act 1970 specifically designed to bring English law into conformity with Community law. Prior to amendment, the Act took effect where the woman was employed (a) "on like work" or (b) on work "rated as equivalent" on a job evaluation study, with a man in the same employment.[736] The European Court held that this was inadequate to comply with Art.119 of the EC Treaty (now Art.141 EC) and Council Directive Dir.75/117/EEC (the equal pay directive), which imposed a requirement of equal pay for the same work or *work of equal value*. The latter element was not fully implemented by (b), which depended on the employer having consented to a job evaluation[737] study. Accordingly, the Equal Pay (Amendment) Regulations 1983[738] introduced a new para.(c), which allowed an "equal value" claim to be made "where a woman is employed on work, not being work in relation to which paragraph (a) or (b) above applies. . . . " Mrs Pickstone, a "warehouse operative", made a claim under para.(c), claiming her work was of equal value to that of a man employed as a "checker warehouse operative". There happened to be one man also employed as a "warehouse operative".[739] The industrial tribunal and the Employment Appeal Tribunal accepted the employer's argument that para.(a) applied to Mrs Pickstone's work, and that the words "not being work . . . ." accordingly barred her claim under para.(c). The Court of Appeal[740] held that this was indeed the position under the Equal Pay Act 1970, but that Mrs Pickstone could base her claim directly on Art.119 of the EC Treaty. The House of Lords interpreted the 1970 Act in such a way as to allow her claim to proceed under it: the exclusionary words in para.(c) were intended to have effect only where the particular man with whom she sought comparison was employed on the same work. Here, her comparator was employed on different work.

> "The opposite result would leave a large gap in the equal work provision, enabling an employer to evade it by employing one token man on the same work as a group of potential women claimants who were deliberately paid less than a group of men employed on work of equal value with that of the women. This would mean that the United Kingdom had failed yet again fully to implement its obligations under Article 119 of the Treaty and the Equal Pay Directive, and had not given full effect to the decision of the European Court in *Commission v UK*.[741] It is plain that Parliament cannot possibly have intended such a failure."[742]

A purposive, rather than a literal construction was necessary.[743] There is room for argument how far this result involves a "distortion" of the statutory language.

---

[736] s.1(2)(a), (b).

[737] Case 61/81, *Commission v United Kingdom* [1982] E.C.R. 2601, [1982] I.C.R. 578; S. Atkins, [1983] P.L. 19 and (1983) 8 E.L. Rev. 48.

[738] SI 1983/1794.

[739] [1986] I.C.R. 886.

[740] [1989] A.C. 66. See A. W. Bradley, [1988] P.L. 485, 489–491.

[741] n.737 above.

[742] *per* Lord Keith of Kinkel at pp.111–112.

[743] See below, para.6–010.

The proper approach of the English courts to the interpretation of directives in **5–059** the light of the decision of the European Court in *Marleasing*[744] has been stated as follows by Lord Keith of Kinkel in *Webb v EMO Air Cargo (UK) Ltd*[745]:

> "It is for a United Kingdom Court to construe domestic legislation in any field covered by a Community directive so as to accord with the interpretation of the directive as laid down by the European Court, if that can be done without distorting the meaning of the domestic legislation: see *Duke v GEC Reliance Ltd*.[746] This is so whether the domestic legislation came after or, as in this case, preceded the directive, see *Marleasing SA v La Comercial Internacional de Alimentación SA . . . .*[747]
>
> As the European Court has said, a national court must construe a domestic law to accord with the terms of a directive in the same field only if it is possible to do so. This means that the domestic law must be open to an interpretation consistent with the directive whether or not it is also open to an interpretation inconsistent with it."

This statement has been cited on a number of occasions.[748] In *Webb* itself, the House proceeded to make a reference to the Court of Justice. In the light of the Court's ruling, the House of Lords was able to interpret the Sex Discrimination Act 1975 to accord with Community law.

The facts were that W was engaged to replace a woman on maternity leave (but employed on an indefinite rather than a short-term contract). She was dismissed when it was discovered that she too was pregnant. Section 1(1) of the 1975 Act provides that:

> "a person discriminates against a woman in any circumstances relevant for the purposes of any provision of this Act if—(a) on the ground of her sex he treats her less favourably than he treats or would treat a man."

Section 5(3) provides that:

> "a comparison of the cases of persons of different sex . . . must be such that the relevant circumstances in the one case are the same, or not materially different, in the other."

The House of Lords held initially[749] that the dismissal here was on the basis of W's unavailability for work at the time when she had been particularly required, and that the reason for that unavailability (pregnancy) was not a relevant circumstance. However, the Court of Justice ruled[750] that Community law[751] precluded dismissal of an employee recruited for an unlimited term, with a view initially to replacing

---

[744] Above, para.5–046.
[745] [1992] 4 All E.R. 929, 939, 940. The other members of the House agreed with Lord Keith. It may accordingly be necessary to decide between interpretation and disapplication: *Fleming v Customs and Excise Commissioners* [2006] S.T.C. 864.
[746] [1988] A.C. 618, 639–640 *per* Lord Templeman.
[747] Case C-106/89, [1990] E.C.R. I-4135.
[748] See, e.g. *R v Secretary of State for the Environment, Ex p. Greenpeace Ltd* [1994] 4 All E.R. 352.
[749] n.745 above.
[750] Case C-32/93, *Webb v Emo Air Cargo Ltd* [1994] Q.B. 718, [1994] E.C.R. I-3567.
[751] Arts 2, 5 of Dir.76/207/EEC (the equal treatment directive).

another employee, on the ground of pregnancy. Accordingly, the House of Lords[752] reinterpreted the 1975 Act to clarify the reason for unavailability in such a case (pregnancy) as a "relevant circumstance", pregnancy being a circumstance that could not be present in the case of the hypothetical man. While not the preferred reading, this was properly not regarded as "distortion" of the Act.

Finally, in the *Factortame* litigation[753] it was accepted by both the parties and the courts that if the Court of Justice were to rule finally that the relevant provisions of the Merchant Shipping Act 1988 were incompatible with Community law, English courts would have to give effect to the latter, whether as a matter of interpretation of the 1988 Act[754] or by disapplying it as invalid.[755] The Divisional Court "made an order designed to give effect to [the] Court's judgment in *Factortame II* and, to give detailed particulars of their claim for damages."[756] This led to another reference to the Court of Justice and the ruling in *Factortame III*.[757]

5. IMPLEMENTATION OF COMMUNITY LAW IN THE UNITED KINGDOM

5–060 As has been seen, Community law that is directly applicable or effective takes effect in the United Kingdom under s.2(1) of the European Communities Act 1972.[758] In appropriate cases,[759] such law may give rise to defences that can be relied on in English litigation.[760] Alternatively, it may form the basis of an award of damages (e.g. for breach of statutory duty[761] or the tort of misfeasance in a

---

[752] [1995] 1 W.L.R. 1454. See also *Alabaster v Barclay's Bank plc* [2005] I.C.R. 1246 and para.5–031, n.412.

[753] See para.5–057.

[754] *per* Lord Bridge in *R v Secretary of State for Transport, Ex p. Factortame Ltd* [1990] 2 A.C. 85, 140, referring to s.2(1) and (4) of the 1972 Act: "This has precisely the same effect as if a section were incorporated in Pt II of the Act of 1988 which in terms enacted that the provisions with respect to registration of British fishing vessels were to be without prejudice to the directly enforceable Community rights of nationals of any member state of the E.E.C." Although this can be labelled as an approach based on interpretation, this would seem to be "interpretation" of a kind more radical than adopted hitherto; the words read into the statute have a very substantial modifying effect.

[755] The Court of Appeal in *Factortame* [1989] 2 C.M.L.R. 353, 396 (Lord Donaldson M.R.), 403–404 (Bingham L.J.), 408 (Mann L.J.) An Employment Tribunal has jurisdiction to disapply incompatible domestic legislation: *R (Manson) v Ministry of Defence* [2006] I.C.R. 355. Similarly, a criminal court: *R v Searby* [2003] EWCA Crim 1910.

[756] Case 48/93, *R v Secretary of State for Transport, Ex p. Factortame Ltd* [1998] E.C.R. I-1029. para.12.

[757] Above, para.5–047.

[758] Above, para.5–054.

[759] See generally, J. Steiner, "How to make the action suit the case: domestic remedies for breach of EEC law" (1987) 12 E.L. Rev. 102; P. Oliver, "Enforcing Community rights in the English courts" (1987) 50 M.L.R. 881; N. Green and A. Barav, "Damages in the national courts for breach of Community law" [1986] 6 Y.E.L. 55, 83–114; J. S. Davidson, (1985) 34 I.C.L.Q. 178.

[760] e.g. a defence to criminal proceedings: Case 63/83, *R v Kirk* [1985] 1 All E.R. 453; Case 121/85, *Conegate v Commissioners of Customs and Excise* [1987] Q.B. 254; or "Euro-defences" based on EC competition law arising in civil actions: *cf. Lansing Bagnall Ltd v Buccaneer Lift Parts Ltd* [1984] 1 C.M.L.R. 224; *Ransburg-Gema AC v Electrostatic Plant Systems Ltd* [1989] 2 C.M.L.R. 712.

[761] e.g. for a breach of Art.86 EC (abuse of a dominant position): *per* Lord Diplock in *Garden Foods Ltd v Milk Marketing Board* [1984] A.C. 130, 141: see K. Banks, (1984) 21 C.M.L. Rev. 669; F. G. Jacobs (1983) 8 E.L. Rev. 353; M. Friend and J. Shaw, (1984) 100 L.Q.R. 188; but not a breach of Art.30 (prohibition of quantitative restrictions on imports and measures having equivalent effect): *Bourgoin SA v Ministry of Agriculture, Fisheries and Food* [1985] Q.B. 716, CA; or a

public office[762]), a claim in restitution[763] or the grant of an injunction,[764] as a matter of private law, or the grant of public law remedies against the Crown or other public authority.[765]

Primary legislation has been enacted to give effect to major changes, such as those consequent on the accession of new Member States,[766] major budgetary matters,[767] the Single European Act,[768] the Maastricht Treaty,[769] the Treaty of Amsterdam,[770] and the Treaty of Nice.[771] Specific Community obligations may also be implemented by Act of Parliament.[772] Section 2(2) of the 1972 Act[773] authorises the making of subordinate legislation: (1) to implement other Community laws that are not directly applicable or effective[774]; or (2) to deal with matters related to Community laws that take effect under section 2(1).[775] Subordinate legislation may not, however: (1) provide for the imposition or increase of taxation; (2) be retrospective; (3) confer the power to enact sub-delegated

breach of Art.10 of Council Reg.1422/78: *An Bord Bainne v Milk Marketing Board* [1988] 1 C.M.L.R. 605, CA.

[762] An action that lies where loss is caused by *ultra vires* acts committed maliciously (i.e. with intent to injure the plaintiff) or with knowledge of its illegality: *Bourgoin*, n.761 above: the parties settled for £3.5 m. (Vol.102 H.C. Deb., July 23, 1986, col.116, written answer). This head of liability must now be seen as subject to the ruling of the Court of Justice in *Factortame III*, above, para.5–047.

[763] Cases C-397/98 and C-410/98, *Metallgesellschaft Ltd v Inland Revenue Commissioners* [2001] E.C.R. I-1027 (claim arising out of discriminatory tax provision that prevented subsidiaries of non-UK resident companies delaying the date of tax payment).

[764] *Garden Cottage Foods*, n.761 above; *Cutsforth v Mansfield Inns Ltd* [1986] 1 C.M.L.R. 1.

[765] e.g. *Van Duyn v Home Office* [1974] 1 W.L.R. 1107, Ch.D., and Case 41/74, [1985] Ch. 358 ECJ (action for a declaration); *R v Attorney-General, Ex p. I.C.I.* [1987] 1 C.M.L.R. 72 and *R v Intervention Board for Agricultural Produce, Ex p. The Fish Producers' Organisation Ltd* [1988] 2 C.M.L.R. 661 (applications for judicial review).

[766] European Communities (Greek Accession) Act 1979; European Communities (Spanish and Portuguese Accession) Act 1985; European Union (Accessions) Act 1994 (in respect of Austria, Finland and Sweden, and Norway (who subsequently did not join)) 2003 (the countries that joined in 2004) and 2006 (Bulgaria and Romania).

[767] European Communities (Finance) Acts 1985 and 2001.

[768] European Communities (Amendment) Act 1986.

[769] European Communities (Amendment) Act 1993. The process of enacting this Act was particularly fraught for the government: see discussion by P. Beaumont and G. Moir, *Current Law Statutes Annotated* (1993). A challenge to the legality of ratification of the Treaty by the government was rejected: *R v Secretary of State for Foreign and Commonwealth Affairs, Ex p. Rees-Mogg* [1994] Q.B. 552; R. Rawlings, [1994] P.L. 254, 367.

[770] European Communities (Amendment) Act 1998.

[771] European Communities (Amendment) Act 2002.

[772] e.g. the Companies Acts 1980 and 1981, which implemented directives on the harmonisation of company law; the Importation of Milk Act 1983, passed in response to a judgment of the European Court which held that UK restrictions on the importation of UHT milk were contrary to Community rules on the free movement of goods (Case 124/81, *Commission v United Kingdom* [1983] E.C.R. 203); the Sex Discrimination Act 1986.

[773] Sections 5 and 6 of the 1972 Act confer powers to make subordinate legislation concerning customs matters and the common agricultural policy. Statutory instruments implementing Community obligations have been made under other statutes.

[774] There is a power to make any order, rules, regulations or scheme "for the purpose of implementing any Community obligation of the United Kingdom, or enabling any such obligation to be implemented, or of enabling any rights enjoyed or to be enjoyed by the United Kingdom under or by virtue of the Treaties to be exercised" and a person exercising any statutory power or duty (including a power to give directions or legislate by means of orders, rules, regulations or other subordinate instrument) may have regard to the objects of the Communities and to any such obligation or rights: s.2(2), as amended by the Legislative Reform Act 2006, s.27(1).

[775] Note, however, the limits on such legislation in respect of Community regulations: above, para.5–049.

legislation; or (4) create any new criminal offence punishable with more than two years imprisonment, or three months on summary conviction, or a fine of more than level 5 on the standard scale, or £100 a day.[776] It is subject to the negative resolution procedure.[777] The power under s.2(2), taken in conjunction with subs.(4), may be exercised in respect of post-1972 as well as pre-1972 statutes.[778] Subordinate legislation made for a purpose mentioned in s.2(2) may, by express provision, state that a reference to a Community instrument or provision is to be construed as a reference to that instrument or provision as amended from time to time.[779] A statutory instrument can be made under both s.2(2) and another statutory power; all the provisions will be subject to the negative procedure.[780]

Arrangements have been made for the scrutiny of Community legislation by the Select Committee of the House of Lords on the European Union (between 1974 and 1999, the Select Committee on the European Communities) and the House of Commons European Scrutiny Committee (between 1974 and 1998, the Select Committee on European Legislation).[781] These committees consider draft Community legislation and other documents prepared by the Commission for submission to the Council of Ministers proposals under the second and third pillars, any other document published by one EU institution for submission to any other and any other document relating to EU matters deposited by a minister.[782] Detailed explanatory memoranda are prepared by the government. The Commons committee concentrates on the legal and political importance of each document, reporting also on the reasons for its opinion and on any matters of principle, policy or law which may be affected; the Lords deal more with technical legal and administrative implications.[783] The Lords committee has a number of sub-committees, including one customarily chaired by one of the Law Lords on law and institutions,[784] and each of the rest considering Community proposals within a particular subject area. The committees decide, *inter alia*, whether a particular proposal should be considered further by the respective Houses. In the Commons, a debate may be held on the floor of the House or in

---

[776] European Communities Act 1972, Sch.2(1), as amended by the Criminal Law Act 1977, s.32 and the Criminal Justice Act 1982, ss.37, 40, 46.

[777] *ibid.* Sch.2(2) See above para.5–027.

[778] *Thoburn v Sunderland City Council* [2002] EWHC 195 (Admin), above para.5–002.

[779] 1972 Act, Sch.2, para.1A, inserted by the Legislative and Regulatory Reform Act 2006, s.28, with effect from January 8, 2007.

[780] see *ibid.* Sch.2, paras 2A–2C, inserted by the 2006 Act, s.29.

[781] Established in 1974. See 1972–73 H.C. 143 and 463-I ("Foster Committee": Commons); 1972–73 H.L. 194 ("Maybray-King Committee": Lords). See also the Seventh Report of the Select Committee on Modernisation of the House of Commons (1997–98 H.C. 791, *The Scrutiny of European Business*); European Union Select Committee, First Report, 2002–03 H.L. 15, *Review of Scrutiny of European Legislation*; Thirty-Second Report, 2005–06 H.L. 179, *EU Legislation—Public Awareness of the Scrutiny Role of the House of Lords*; Modernisation of the House of Commons Select Committee, *Scrutiny of European Business*, Second Report, 2004–05 H.C. 465 (recommending a new Joint Grand Committee to consider matters related to the EU). E. Denza, "Parliamentary Scrutiny of European Legislation" [1993] Stat. L.R. 56; A. J. Cygan, *The United Kingdom Parliament and European Union Legislation* (1998) and "European legislation before the House of Commons—the work of the European Scrutiny Committee" in M. Adenas and A. Türk, *Delegated Legislation and the Role of Committees in the EC* (2000), Ch.9.

[782] The range of documents eligible for scrutiny has been extended over the lifetime of the committee following extensions in the range of EU activities.

[783] Joint meetings are occasionally held.

[784] The "legal eagles committee": E. Denza, [1993] Stat. L.R. 56, 59.

a standing committee. In 1990, two European Standing Committees were established in order to shift debates away from the floor of the House.[785] The Procedure Committee concluded that these committees functioned very well, making a useful contribution to effective scrutiny.[786] A third Committee was established in 1998. The government has undertaken that it will normally[787] provide time for such consideration where recommended by the Select Committee prior to a proposal being discussed by the Council of Ministers (the "scrutiny reserve"). However, the scrutiny of European secondary legislation is indirect in effect, given that Parliament can at best influence only one of the members of the Council, especially now that more Council decisions are reached by qualified majorities and that the legislative process is likely to be quicker.[788] Moreover, it can be difficult to keep abreast of changes in draft proposals as they progress through the Community legislative process.

6. VALIDITY OF EUROPEAN SECONDARY LEGISLATION

(a) Article 230 EC; the action for annulment

The validity of acts of Community institutions that are binding in law, and **5–061**
whether legislative or not, may be challenged directly by an *action for annulment*
brought in the European Court of Justice[789] under Art.230 EC[790]:

> "The Court of Justice shall review the legality of acts adopted jointly by the
> European Parliament and the Council, of acts of the Council, of the Com-
> mission and the ECB, other than recommendations and opinions,[791] and of

---

[785] See 1988–89 H.C. 622 and Cm. 1081; First Special Report from the Select Committee on European Legislation 1989–90 (1989–90 H.C. 512) and H.C. Deb., October 24, 1990, Vol.178, cols 375–401.

[786] First Report from the Select Committee on Procedure 1991–92 (1991–92 H.C. 31), *Review of European Standing Committees*; Third Report 1991–92 (1991–92 H.C. 331), *Government Response*. Debates "have been of a much more highly focused and objective quality": E. Denza, [1993] Stat. L.R 56, 58.

[787] The first formal resolution was made on October 30, 1980 (H.C. Deb., Vol.991, col. 844); it was replaced by one on October 24, 1990 (H.C. Deb., Vol.178, col.400) and by the current resolution on November 17, 1998 (H.C. Deb., Vol.319, cols 803–804). It provides that no minister should give agreement to any legislative proposal or any agreement under the second or third pillar which is still subject to scrutiny or awaiting consideration by the House; "agreement" includes agreement to a programme, plan or recommendation for EC legislation, political agreement, agreement to a common position under the co-decision or co-operation procedures and agreement to a joint text or confirmation of a common position under the co-decision procedure.

[788] See the reports on the Single European Act and Parlimentary Scrutiny: First Special Report from the Select Committee on European Legislation 1985–86 (1985–86 H.C. 533); Twelfth Report from the Select Committee on the European Communities 1985–86 (1985–86 H.L. 149).

[789] See above, paras 2–076—2–082: national courts may not rule acts of Community institutions invalid (Case 314/85, *Foto-Frost v Hauptzollamt Lübeck-Ost* [1987] E.C.R. 4199). The approach adopted by the European Court to the interpretation of Community law is considered below, paras 6–053—6–064.

[790] Formerly Art.173 of the EC Treaty, as amended by Art.G(53) TEU.

[791] This covers any act intended to have legal effect, and not merely regulations, directives and decisions: Case 22/70, *Commission v Council (ERTA)* [1971] E.C.R. 263 (action for annulment of a Council resolution concerning negotiations leading to an international agreement between the Member States and third countries); Case C-325/91, *France v Commission*, June 16, 1993 ("communication" intended to have legal effects annulled; commission should have adopted a directive or a decision).

acts of the European Parliament intended to produce legal effects *vis-à-vis* third parties.[792]

It shall for this purpose have jurisdiction in actions brought by a Member State, the Council or the Commission on grounds of lack of competence, infringement of an essential procedural requirement, infringement of this Treaty or of any rule of law relating to its application, or misuse of powers.

The Court shall have jurisdiction under the same conditions in actions brought by the European Parliament, by the Court of Auditors and by the ECB for the purpose of protecting their prerogatives.[793]

Any natural or legal person[794] may, under the same conditions, institute proceedings against a decision addressed to that person or against a decision which, although in the form of a regulation or a decision addressed to another person, is of direct and individual concern to the former.

The proceedings provided for in this Article shall be instituted within two months of the publication of the measure, or of its notification to the plaintiff, or, in the absence thereof, of the day on which it came to the knowledge of the latter, as the case may be."

Thus the range of acts that can be challenged by an individual is narrower than those that can be reviewed under the first three paragraphs of Art.230 EC. First, the act must be a "decision" in that it must have legal effect[795] and must not be a regulation, in the sense of an act which applies to objectively determined situations and has legal effects on classes of persons defined in a general and abstract manner.[796] Secondly, the act must be of "direct and individual concern" to the applicant.[797] If the action is successful, the act challenged is declared by the Court to be void,[798] and the matter is remitted to the institution concerned.

---

[792] The express reference to the Parliament was added by the Maastricht Treaty; acts of the Parliament had in any event previously been held to be subject to Art.173 of the EC Treaty (now Art.230 EC): Case 294/83, *Parti Ecologiste "Les Verts" v European Parliament* [1986] E.C.R. 1339.

[793] Prior to the changes effected by the Maastricht Treaty, the Court had held, initially, that the Parliament had no standing under Art.173 (Case 302/87, *European Parliament v Council* [1988] E.C.R. 5615) and then that it had standing to bring proceedings to safeguard its prerogatives (Case C-70/88, *European Parliament v Council* [1990] E.C.R. 1-2041); the ruling in the latter case is now enshrined in Art.230 EC.

[794] This term includes a Member State: Case 25/62 *Plaumann v Commission* [1963] E.C.R. 95.

[795] Cases 8–11/66, *Cimenteries v Commission* (the *Noordwijks Cement Accoord* case) [1967] E.C.R. 75: a notification by the Commission that certain agreements were prohibited under Art.85 of the EC Treaty which had the effect of removing a temporary immunity from fines, was held to be reviewable even though such fines could only be imposed if further steps were taken by the Commission.

[796] Collins *op. cit.* para.5–036, n.455, pp.232–234, 236–240. The Court looks to the substance and not the form; the fact that the act has been promulgated as a regulation is not conclusive. See, e.g. Cases 113, 118–121/77, *Japanese Ball Bearings Cases* [1979] E.C.R. 1185 where four Japanese ball-bearing manufacturers were held to be entitled to challenge a regulation imposing an import duty in general terms, but which on the facts was aimed at them. Individuals also do not have standing to challenge a directive (unless, presumably, it is a "disguised decision"): Cases T-172/98 and T-175–177/98, *Salamandar v Parliament* [2000] E.C.R. II-2487.

[797] There are a number of cases on this point, which are not always easy to reconcile: Collins, pp.234–256; Hartley (2003), Ch.12; R. Greaves, (1988) 11 E.L. Rev. 119. See e.g. Case C-321/95P, *Greenpeace International v Commission* [1998] All E.R. (EC) 620 (Greenpeace held not to have standing to challenge a decision authorising expenditure on a project to build power stations alleged to affect environmental rights).

[798] Art.231 EC. In the case of a regulation declared void, the Court can state which of its effects shall be considered as definitive; this enables the Court, for example, to declare that a regulation

Preliminary decisions can only be challenged if they affect the applicant's rights independently of the final decision: otherwise, the applicant must await the final decision and challenge that.[799]

The grounds for challenge are set out in Art.230 EC.[800] Although they are based upon the grounds for review in continental, particularly French, administrative law, arguments may be based on principles of administrative law derived from the legal systems of any Member State. The grounds may overlap in the sense that a particular set of facts may involve infringements under more than one heading.

Lack of competence corresponds to the English concept of substantive *ultra vires*[801] and the French concept of *excès de pouvoir* or *incompétence*. It may not be easily distinguishable from an allegation of *infringement of the Treaties or any rules of law relating to their application*. An example is *Meroni v High Authority*[802] where certain decisions under the Coal and Steel Treaty were held to be improperly delegated to certain subordinate bodies. Issues of competence also arise where subordinate legislation is challenged on the ground that the Treaty article(s) relied on as authority for the measure in fact do not provide an appropriate legal basis for it. The choice of legal basis must be based on objective factors which are amenable to judicial review, which include in particular the aim and content of the measure.[803] For example, in *Germany v Parliament and Council*; *R v Secretary of State for Health, Ex p. Imperial Tobacco Ltd*,[804] the Court annulled a directive[805] that prohibited tobacco advertising and sponsorship except at the point of sale. It had been adopted on the basis of Treaty provisions on the approximation of laws of Member States which had as their object the establishment and functioning of the internal market and the protection of the freedom to provide goods and services.[806] The Court held that these articles did not confer a general power to regulate the internal market; and that the directive did not actively contribute to eliminating obstacles to the free movement of goods and services or removing appreciable distortions of competition. The Court noted that the harmonisation of legislation of the Member States designed to protect and improve human health, which the applicants alleged was the "centre of gravity" of the direction, was expressly excluded by Art.129(4) of the EC Treaty (now Art.152(4)EC).

Infringement of an essential procedural requirement corresponds to the English doctrine of procedural *ultra vires* and the French concept of *vice de forme*. Only requirements of substantial importance are mandatory; for example,

---

remains effective until replaced by one adopted on a proper legal basis: see e.g. Cases C-164/97 and C-165/97, *Parliament v Council* [1999] E.C.R. I-1139.

[799] Compare Case 60/81, *IBM v Commission* [1981] E.C.R. 2639 (decision to institute proceedings for abuse of a dominant position not separately challengeable) *with* Case 53/85, *AKZO Chemie v Commission* [1986] E.C.R. 1965 (decision to show documents, claimed by the applicant to contain confidential information, to the complainant, challengeable).

[800] Hartley (2003), Ch.15.

[801] On the English *ultra vires* doctrine see below, Ch.18.

[802] Case 9/56, [1957–8] E.C.R. 133; see also Case 48/69, *ICJ v Commission (the Dyestuffs case)* [1972] E.C.R. 619.

[803] Case C-300/89, *Commission v Council* [1991] E.C.R. I-2867; Case C-271/94, *Parliament v Council* [1996] E.C.R. I-1689, para.14; Case 22/96, *Parliament v Council* [1998] E.C.R I-3231, para.23.

[804] Cases C-376/98 and C-74/99, [2000] E.C.R. I-8419.

[805] European Parliament and Council Directive (EC) 98/43.

[806] Arts 57(2), 66 and 100a of the EC Treaty (now Arts 47(2), 55 and 95 EC).

requirements to hold a hearing,[807] to consult the European Parliament,[808] to give reasons,[809] to state the provision under which the measure is adopted[810] and for a Commission decision to be properly authenticated.[811] Minor irregularities are ignored; for example, notification of a decision to a subsidiary rather than to the applicants where the latter had full knowledge of the decision in time to institute proceedings,[812] and the reporting of a decision in the *Official Journal* under an inaccurate title.[813]

Misuse of powers broadly corresponds to the abuse of discretion aspect of the *ultra vires* doctrine and the French concept of *détournement de pouvoir*. It covers, for example, the use of a power for an improper purpose.

(b) Article 241 EC: the plea of illegality[814]

5–062   Article 241 EC[815] provides that:

> "Notwithstanding the expiry of the period laid down in the fifth paragraph of Article 230, any party[816] may, in proceedings in which a regulation adopted jointly by the European Parliament and the Council, or a regulation[817] of the Council, of the Commission, or of the ECB is at issue, plead the grounds specified in the second paragraph of Article 230, in order to invoke before the Court of Justice the inapplicability of that regulation."

An individual may not challenge a *regulation* under Art.230 EC (above); if, however, he or she happens to be a party to proceedings before the Court of Justice he or she (and any other party) may do so under Art.241 EC. Article 241 EC may be invoked where proceedings are brought under some other provision of the Treaty which concern the party making the plea of illegality; it does not give that party an independent cause of action.[818]

---

[807] Case 41/69, *ACF Chemiefarma v Commission* [1970] E.C.R. 661; the challenge failed on the merits: see also the *Dyestuffs* case above. A hearing may be necessary even though it is not expressly required by Community legislation: Case 17/74, *Transocean Marine Paint Association v Commission* [1974] E.C.R. 1063.

[808] See above, para.5–050.

[809] See Art.253 EC above, para.5–038; Case 24/62, *Germany v Commission* [1963] E.C.R. 63. The reasons must be adequate: the act must "set out, in a concise, but clear and relevant manner, the principal issues of law and of fact upon which it is based and which are necessary in order that the reasoning which has led the Commission to its Decision may be understood" (*ibid.* p.69). See also Case 166/78, *Italy v Council* [1979] E.C.R. 2575. A Council directive was annulled where the statement of reasons was altered by the Council's secretariat, in a way that went beyond simple corrections of spelling and grammar: Case 131/ 86, *United Kingdom v Council* [1988] E.C.R. 905.

[810] Case 45/86, *Commission v Council* [1987] E.C.R. 1493; A. Arnull (1987) 12 E.L. Rev. 448. These cases may also raise questions of competence: see generally K. St. C. Bradley, "The European Court and the Legal Basis of Community Legislation" (1988) 13 E.L. Rev. 379.

[811] Case C-286/95P, *Commission v ICI plc* [2000] All E.R. (EC) 439.

[812] *Dyestuffs* case, *loc. cit.* n.802 above.

[813] Case 6/72, *Europemballage & Continental Can v Commission* [1973] E.C.R. 215.

[814] Hartley (2003), Ch.14.

[815] Formerly Art.184 of the EC Treaty as substituted by Art.G(58) TEU.

[816] This includes Member States: Case 32/65, *Italy v Council and Commission* [1966] E.C.R. 389.

[817] But not a *decision*: Case 156/77, *Commission v Belgium* [1978] E.C.R. 1881. The court again looks to substance rather than form: Case 92/78, *Simmenthal v Commission* [1979] E.C.R. 77.

[818] Case 31/62, *Wohrmann v Commission* [1962] E.C.R. 501.

(c) Article 232 EC: remedy against inaction[819]

Article 232 EC[820] provides that: **5–063**

> "Should the European Parliament, the Council or the Commission, in
> infringement of this Treaty, fail to act, the Member States and the other
> institutions of the Community[821] may bring an action before the Court of
> Justice to have the infringement established.
>
> The action shall be admissible only if the institution concerned has first
> been called upon to act. If, within two months of being so called upon, the
> institution concerned has not defined its position, the action may be brought
> within a further period of two months.
>
> Any natural or legal person may, under the conditions laid down in the
> preceding paragraphs, complain to the Court of Justice that an institution of
> the Community has failed to address to that person any act other than a
> recommendation or an opinion.
>
> The Court of Justice shall have jurisdiction, under the same conditions, in
> actions or proceedings brought by the ECB in the areas falling within the
> latter's field of competence and in actions or proceedings brought against
> the latter."

The Court of Justice has built in some limitations to actions under this article. An
action can only be brought where the institution in question has failed to define
its position within two months. In *Lütticke v Commission*[822] the Commission had
declined to take action against France on the ground that it had in fact complied
with the Treaty, and stated as much within the two month-period; the court held
that an action could therefore not be brought. An individual may not use Art.232
EC to circumvent the restrictions that prevent him bringing an action directly
against a Member State for breach of a Treaty provision,[823] or an action outside
the limits of Art.230 EC,[824] by attempting to bring an action against the Commission (respectively) (1) for failing to take action against the Member State, or (2)
failing to revoke a decision not in fact open to challenge under Art.230 EC.

(d) Articles 234 EC and 288 EC

The validity of Community legislation may also be considered by the European   **5–064**
Court of Justice on a reference under Art.234 EC,[825] or on an action for damages
under Art.288 EC.[826] In such cases the restrictions built into Art.230 EC do not
necessarily apply.

---

[819] Hartley (2003), Ch.13.
[820] Formerly Art.175 of the EC Treaty, as substituted by Art.G(54) TEU.
[821] This includes the Council, the Commission and the Parliament: Case 13/83, *European Parliament v Council* [1985] E.C.R. 1513: See P. Fennell, (1985) 10 E.L. Rev. 264.
[822] Case 48/65 [1966] E.C.R. 19.
[823] Under Arts 226 EC and 227 EC such actions can only be brought by a Member State or the Commission: See the *Lütticke* case, n.822 above.
[824] See above, para.5–061; Cases 10 and 18/68, *Eridania v Commission* [1969] E.C.R. 459.
[825] See below, Ch.18.
[826] See above, para.2–079, n.698.

STATUTORY INTERPRETATION

A. INTRODUCTION

While the enactment of a statute is the culmination of Parliament's legislative **6–001** process, it is merely the starting point for what may be many years of existence, in some cases posing problems for generations of users. If it is to have its proper effect it must be read and understood, although there are many other factors which govern the extent to which a particular measure is successful. There are various kinds of statute-user and many matters which may cause them difficulty.[1] It cannot realistically be assumed that all statutes are directed at the general public and are therefore designed to be understood by them. It is argued that statutes are complicated:

> " . . . because life is complicated. The bulk of the legislation enacted nowadays is social, economic or financial; the laws they [i.e. statutes] must express and the life situations they must regulate are in themselves complicated, and these laws cannot in any language or in any style be reduced to kindergarten level, any more than can the theory of relativity."[2]

The user tends to be the public official charged with the duty of implementation, the lawyer or the non-legal professional adviser, and statutes tend to be drafted accordingly: by experts for experts. Lay people[3] who wish to use statutes thus have to become acquainted with statute-handling techniques, or rely on explanatory material, such as textbooks or government leaflets, written by experts, or consult an expert personally. This is seen by some as a vicious circle: they doubt whether statutes need to be as complicated as experts who earn a living by explaining them to the rest of us would have us believe.

Some of the problems of the user, even the professional user, relate to the discovery of the relevant provisions and the establishment of an authentic, up-to-date text. Matters have, however, have been made easier as the result of the availability of a searchable online database of the original versions of all legislation from 1987 (statutory instruments) and 1988 (Acts) published by the Office of Public Sector Information, and the existence of unofficial databases of amended legislation.[4] A further problem is that provisions may be spread among a number of statutes and statutory instruments which have to be read together. The uninstructed lay person may well not accomplish even this stage. Once established, the text also has to be understood or "interpreted".[5] The task of

---

[1] See F. A. R. Bennion, *Statute Law* (3rd edn, 1990), Pt II (pp.83–205) and *Understanding Common Law Legislation* (2001); *cf.* W. Twining and D. Miers, *How To Do Things With Rules* (4th edn, 1999), Chs 7, 8.

[2] E. A. Dreidger, cited in Bennion (1990), pp.209–210.

[3] Or, indeed, lawyers and other professionals in matters outside their expertise.

[4] See para.5–022.

[5] The OED definitions of this term include both "to expound the meaning of" and "to make out the meaning of, explain to oneself".

interpretation may vary in difficulty. Some provisions can be understood automatically, without the conscious perception of any "problem" of interpretation:
some problems may be easy to solve after a moment's thought. At the other
extreme, a problem may be highly complex, enough to make the reader weep.
Printing or drafting errors can turn a provision into gibberish.

F. A. R. Bennion[6] has identified a number of factors that may cause doubt.
Some of these doubt-factors are inevitable and even desirable: others are avoida-
ble. First, there is what he terms the technique of *ellipsis*. Here, the draftsman
refrains from using certain words that he or she regards as necessarily implied:
the problem is that the users may not realise that this is the case. The unexpressed
words may normally be implied in statutes of a particular kind unless Parliament
expressly provides to the contrary: many of the principles of judicial review of
administrative action rest on this basis,[7] as do certain principles of criminal
liability.[8] Alternatively the implication may arise from the words that actually are
used. The judges on occasion exercise a limited power (in practice but not in
theory) to rewrite statutes, although it can be difficult to predict in any particular
case whether a judge will be prepared to act in that way.[9]

Secondly, the draftsman may use a *broad term* ("a word or phrase of wide
meaning") and leave it to the user to judge what situations fall within it. Most
words can be said to have a core of certain meaning surrounded by a penumbra
of uncertainty. A standard example is the term "vehicle". This clearly covers
motor cars, buses and motor cycles, but it is less clear whether it covers an
invalid carriage, a child's tricycle, a donkey-cart or a pair of roller-skates.[10]
Examples from decided cases include whether the routine oiling and maintenance
of points apparatus on the railway fell within the term "relaying or repairing" the
permanent way[11]; whether an accident arose "out of and in the course of [the
victim's] . . . employment"[12]; and whether a car from which the engine had been
stolen and a car which could not move under its own power as parts were missing
or rusted were "mechanically propelled vehicles" for which a licence was
required.[13] Sir Rupert Cross described this sort of case as "part of the daily bread
of judges and practitioners".[14] One difficulty here may be that the meaning of a
statutory expression may change with the passage of time.[15] A further technical
point that may arise when it has to be decided whether a set of facts conforms to

---

[6] *op. cit.* n.1 above, Chs 15–19.

[7] e.g. breach of natural justice, abuse of discretionary powers: see below, Ch.18.

[8] e.g. the effect of mistake and insanity on criminal liability. A major defect of the drafting of many
statutes creating offences is that they do not make it clear whether *mens rea* is a necessary
ingredient: see, e.g. *R v Warner* [1969] 2 A.C. 256. Another common defect is that statutes
imposing duties do not indicate whether breach of a duty can give rise to a civil action: see, e.g.
Lonhro Ltd v Shell Petroleum Co Ltd (No.2) [1982] A.C. 173.

[9] See below, para.6–015.

[10] Twining and Miers (1999), pp.194–200, *cf.* H. L. A. Hart, (1958) 4 J.S.P.T.L. (N.S.) 144–145.

[11] *London and North-Eastern Railway v Berriman* [1946] A.C. 278.

[12] See, e.g. *R v Industrial Injuries Commissioner, Ex p. A.E.U. (No.2)* [1966] 2 Q.B. 31. (accident
befalling an employee overstaying a tea-break). There have been many cases on this expression:
see N. J. Wikeley, *Wikeley, Ogus, and Barendt, The Law of Social Security* (5th edn, 2002),
pp.726–743.

[13] *Newberry v Simmonds* [1961] 2 Q.B. 345; *Smart v Allan* [1963] 1 Q.B. 291: the answers were,
respectively, yes and no, the main difference being that in the latter case there was no reasonable
prospect of the vehicle ever being made mobile again.

[14] J. Bell and Sir George Engle, *Cross, Statutory Interpretation* (3rd edn, 1995), pp.75–76. Another
good illustration is provided by the refusal of Parliament to define "disposal" and "disposition"
for the purposes of capital gains tax: see J. Tiley, *Revenue Law* (4th edn, 2000), para.35.1.

[15] See, for example, the "public good" defence in s.4 of the Obscene Publications Act 1959: *R v*

a statutory description is whether that decision is one of fact or one of law. This governs whether it should be decided by the jury (if there is one) or the judge, and the extent to which the decision can be upset by an appellate court.[16]

Third, there may be *politic uncertainty*: ambiguous words may be used deliberately, for example where a provision is politically contentious, or where departments wish to minimise the risk of legal challenge.[17]

Fourthly, there may be *unforeseeable developments*. These the draftsman cannot be expected to cover, although he or she may use language that is capable of extension. A well-known example of such extension is *Attorney-General v Edison Telephone Co*[18] where the Telegraph Act 1869, passed before the telephone was invented, was held to confer on the Postmaster General certain powers concerning telephone messages. However, extension may not be possible, and fresh legislation may be necessary. For example, new provisions of revenue law are regularly passed to meet novel tax avoidance schemes developed by smart lawyers and accountants precisely to exploit unforeseen loopholes.

Fifthly, there are many ways in which the wording may be inadequate. There may be a printing error.[19] There may be a drafting error such as the use of a word with two or more distinct meanings without a sufficient indication from the context or by a definition of which is meant, or grammatical or syntactic ambiguity. Examples of the latter include "ambiguous modification", where it is unclear which words are limited, restricted or described by a "modifier",[20] and the faulty reference of pronouns.[21] There may be an erroneous reference to another statute.[22] The draftsman may be mistaken about the law that is being altered[23] or the factual situation with which he or she is dealing. The statutory

6–002

Jordan [1977] A.C. 699, 718, *per* Lord Wilberforce: "[the phrase 'other objects of general concern'] is no doubt a mobile phrase; it may, and should, change in content as society changes." Cf. *Dyson Holdings Ltd v Fox* [1976] Q.B. 503 on whether the term "family" includes a "common law" spouse, criticised by D. J. Hurst, (1983) 3 L.S. 21; and *Fitzpatrick v Sterling Housing Association Ltd* [2001] 1 A.C. 27, where the House of Lords held that a partner in a stable and permanent homosexual relationship could be described as "a member of [the partner's] family" for the purposes of the Rent Act 1977, Sch.1, para.2(2). See also *R v Ireland*, below, para.6–029.

[16] See above, paras 1–011–1–013, and below, Ch.18.

[17] Bennion (1990), Ch.17; A. S. Miller, "Statutory language and the purposive use of ambiguity" 42 Va. L.Rev. 23 (1956); V. Sacks, "Towards Discovering Parliamentary Intent" [1982] Stat. L.R. 143, 157 (research on the background to a number of cases of interpretative difficulty showed that "unintelligible legislation was being added to the statute book because the Government either lacked clear objectives, or, had deliberately intended to obfuscate in order to avoid controversy").

[18] (1880) 6 Q.B.D. 244. Cf. *Royal College of Nursing v DHSS* [1981] A.C. 800.

[19] e.g. the presence of the word "upon" at the end of s.6 of the Statute of Frauds Amendment Act 1828: *Lyde v Barnard* (1836) 1 M. & W. 101; Local Government Act 1972, s.262(12) (reference to subs.(10) rather than subs.(9) in the Queen's Printer's copy, corrected in *Statutes in Force*); the presence of the word "convenient" in the Prescription Act 1832, s.8, apparently a misprint for "easement": C. Harpum, *Megarry and Wade, The Law Of Real Property* (6th edn, 2000), p.1134.

[20] G. C. Thornton, *Legislative Drafting* (3rd edn, 1987), pp.23–29. e.g. "public hospital or school" (does "public" modify "school" as well as "hospital"?). A statute of Charles II disqualified those who lacked certain property qualifications "other than the son and heir apparent of an esquire, or other person of higher degree." In *Jones v Smart* (1784) 1 Term Rep. 44 the court held that the words "son and heir apparent of" governed "person of higher degree" as well as "esquire".

[21] Thornton, pp.29–32. e.g. "and when they arose early in the morning, behold, they were all dead corpses": 2 Kings XIX 35.

[22] e.g. War Damage Act 1943, s.66(2)(b), corrected by the Universities and Colleges Estates Act 1964, s.4(1), Sch.3.

[23] e.g. *Inland Revenue Commissioners v Ayshire Employers' Mutual Insurance Association* [1946] 1 All E.R. 537.

provision may be narrower[24] or wider[25] than the object of the legislation. The provision may fail to indicate an important element, such as the time at which conditions of eligibility for some benefit are to be judged.[26] There may be the type of error described as "defective deeming, or asifism gone wrong".[27] There may be conflict within a statute or between different statutes. There may simply be a slip by the draftsman.[28] Overall, Bennion states that "it is extremely common for draftsmen to produce a text which raises doubt unnecessarily."[29]

As mentioned already, various people may have to interpret statutes for their own purposes. Some may take action based on their own view of a statutory provision. For example, in *R v Adams*[30] police officers decided that they could rely on a search warrant in respect of certain premises which had already been used once. The statute did not deal expressly with the question whether a warrant could be used more than once: the court held that it could not. Tax assessments may well be based on the Inland Revenue's interpretation of a doubtful provision of tax law: it will be for the Commissioners of Taxes or the courts to rule on the matter if the Revenue view is challenged. The courts stand in a rather different position from other statute users in that they have the power to resolve authoritatively disputes concerning the meaning of statutory provisions: their decisions are binding on the parties and may constitute binding precedents for the future.

It is notable that the general methods of statutory interpretation are not themselves regulated by Parliament, but have been developed by the judges. The Interpretation Act 1978, which from its title might seem to fulfil such a function, has the comparatively unambitious aim of providing certain standard definitions of common provisions,[31] and thereby enables statutes to be drafted more briefly than otherwise would be the case. Where Parliament or, more realistically, the executive has been dissatisfied with judicial interpretation of particular provisions the response has been to pay close attention to the future drafting of specific provisions in that area rather than to attempt to introduce legislation giving general directions to the judiciary. In the remainder of this chapter we consider the general approaches taken by judges to the interpretation of statutes, various internal and external aids to interpretation, the main presumptions which may be invoked and proposals for reform.

---

[24] e.g. *Adler v George* [1964] 2 Q.B. 7: the Official Secrets Act 1920, s.3 prohibited obstruction "in the vicinity of" a prohibited place; the Divisional Court held that this was to be read as "in or in the vicinity of".

[25] e.g. the Criminal Law Act 1977, ss.1 and 5, which on a literal interpretation preserved a much wider range of common law conspiracies than was obviously intended; in *R v Duncalf* [1979] 1 W.L.R. 918 the Court of Appeal declined to give a literal reading "when the effect of so doing would be so largely to destroy the obvious purpose of this Act" (*per* Roskill L.J. at p.923). *R v Duncalf* was approved by the House of Lords in *R v Ayres* [1984] A.C. 447. See now the Criminal Justice Act 1987, s.12.

[26] *Jackson v Hall* [1980] A.C. 854, concerning the Agriculture (Miscellaneous Provisions) Act 1976.

[27] Bennion (1990), pp.274–275; R. E. Megarry, *Miscellany-at-law* (1955), pp.361–362 ("there is too be much of this damned deeming": *per* (A. P. Herbert's) Lord Mildew).

[28] *cf. R v Moore* (1994) 159 J.P. 101, below, para.6–039, n.364.

[29] *ibid.* p.279.

[30] [1980] Q.B. 575.

[31] See above, para.5–020.

B. GENERAL APPROACHES TO STATUTORY INTERPRETATION

1. GENERAL APPROACHES OVER TIME

Judicial attitudes to legislation have changed with the passage of time. One of the **6–003** important factors has been the part played by statutes in the general scheme of the law: a related factor has been the conception held by judges as to the proper scope of the judicial function. Three so-called "rules" of statutory interpretation have been identified: the "mischief rule", the "golden rule" and the "literal rule", each originating at different stages of legal history. The "mischief rule" involved reading statutes as to address the "mischief" they were designed to "suppress"; the "literal rule" involved giving the words their ordinary and natural meaning; the "golden rule" involved giving words a different meaning from their ordinary and natural meaning to prevent absurdity.[32] To call them "rules" is, however, misleading: it is better to think of them as general approaches. They were analysed by Professor John Willis in his article "Statute Interpretation in a Nutshell".[33] He suggested that:

> "a court invokes whichever of the rules produces a result that satisfies its sense of justice in the case before it. Although the literal rule is the one most frequently referred to in express terms, the courts treat all three as valid and refer to them as occasion demands, but, naturally enough, do not assign any reasons for choosing one rather than another."[34]

Thus, on some occasions the "literal rule" would be preferred to the "mischief rule": on others the reverse would be the case. It was impossible to predict with certainty which approach would be adopted in a particular case.[35]

This analysis has been widely influential among the textbook writers but has had almost no impact on the English courts.[36] It is also potentially misleading in so far as it suggests that *in every case* there can be a live issue as to which of these three "rules" or approaches should be followed. The reality is very far from that. A helpful explanation of the relationship among them was given by Lord Scarman in *Stock v Frank Jones (Tipton) Ltd*[37] where he noted counsel's argument that the statutory words bore a meaning other the plain meaning, and continued[38]:

---

[32] These are discussed more fully at paras 6–005—6–007.

[33] (1938) 16 Can. Bar Rev. 1.

[34] *ibid.* p.16.

[35] This situation can be unkindly described as the "today's a day for the golden rule" approach. The tone of Professor Willis' article was one of scepticism.

[36] A LexisNexis search (28.1.07) reveals that the article has not been cited in an English court. The expression "there are three rules for the interpretation of statutes" appears in one case, decided by Mr P. H. Clarke FRICS in the Lands Tribunal: *Twinsectra Ltd v Jones* [1998] 2 E.G.L.R. 129. Discussion of the three as separate approaches appears in a tiny handful of judgments, e.g. Lloyd's L.J.'s dissenting judgment in *Dingmar v Dingmar* [2006] 2 F.C.R. 595; Lord Simon of Glaisdale's dissenting speech in *Cheng v Goverer of Pentonville Prison* [1973] A.C. 931; Watkin Williams J.'s judgment in *Harding v Preece* (1882) 9 Q.B.D. 281; Lord Blackburn's speech in *River Wear Commisoners v Adamson* (1877) 2 App. Cas. 743).

[37] [1978] 1 W.L.R. 231.

[38] At p.128.

"If the words used be plain, this is, I think, an illegitimate method of statutory interpretation unless it can be demonstrated that the anomalies are such that they produce an absurdity which Parliament could not have intended, or destroy the remedy established by Parliament to deal with the mischief which the Act is designed to combat."

More recently, Sir Rupert Cross suggested that the English approach involves not so much a choice between alternative "rules" as a progressive analysis in which the judge first considers the ordinary meaning of the words in the general context of the statute, a broad view being taken of what constitutes the "context", and then moves on to consider other possibilities where the ordinary meaning leads to an absurd result.[39] This unified "contextual" approach is supported by dicta in decisions of the House of Lords where general principles of statutory interpretation have been discussed. However, generalisations as to what judges actually do are difficult to substantiate: Sir Rupert Cross made it clear that his propositions were stated "with all the diffidence, hesitancy and reservation that the subject demands".[40]

It is important to appreciate that this analysis of the approach of judges to statutory interpretation operates at a high level of generality. It provides a framework for the solution of interpretative problems, but is not and cannot itself provide the solution. Where a problem of statutory interpretation comes before a court, counsel for each side will advance detailed arguments based on such matters as the nuances of language, the purpose of the statute, the particular aids and presumptions discussed below, and previously decided cases in the area. Different readings of the text will be examined to see which fits best into the statutory scheme. The practical consequences of the different possible interpretations will be compared. Indeed, the discussions in the House of Lords of general approaches to interpretation, on which Sir Rupert Cross's propositions were based, are not commonly cited in argument in decided cases.

6–004   The most recent major work on the subject is F. A. R. Bennion's *Statutory Interpretation*.[41] In his introduction, the author writes:

"The natural and reasonable desire that statutes should be easily understood is doomed to disappointment. Thwarted, it shifts to an equally natural and reasonable desire for efficient tools of interpretation. If statutes must be obscure, let us at least have simple devices to elucidate them. A golden rule would be best, to unlock all mysteries. Alas, . . . there is no golden rule. Nor is there a mischief rule, or a literal rule, or any other cure-all rule of thumb. Instead there are a thousand and one interpretative *criteria*. Fortunately, not all of these present themselves in any one case; but those that do yield factors that the interpreter must figuratively weigh and balance."[42]

The book comprises a Code, with a critical Commentary, in which various detailed interpretative criteria are enumerated, illustrated and criticised. It is a valuable source of the many kinds of detailed arguments that might be advanced

---

[39] The current editors of his book refer instead to "a result which is contrary to the purpose of the statute": see below, para.6–008.

[40] J. Bell and Sir George Engle, *Cross, Statutory Interpretation* (3rd edn, 1995), p.48.

[41] (4th edn, 2002, Supplement, 2005). For full reviews of the first edition, see D. R. Miers, [1986] P.L. 160; J. Bell, (1986) 6 O.J.L.S. 288.

[42] *ibid.* p.4.

before a court, and relies to a much greater extent than the established practitioners' manuals[43] on recent case law. This is particularly important "given the changes in judicial attitudes to statutory interpretation that have occurred in the past two-to-three decades . . . ".[44] There is a greater willingness to attempt to identify and to consider the purpose of the provision in question, and much less of (if ever there was) an inclination to adhere strictly to the supposed literal meaning of words irrespective of the context and the consequences of such a reading.[45] This point is strongly reinforced by the landmark decision of the House of Lords in *Pepper (Inspector of Taxes) v Hart*[46] that the courts are permitted in defined circumstances to consider Parliamentary material, including statements in debate, as an aid to statutory construction. One of the arguments in favour of relaxing the previous rule that excluded reference to such material was expressed as follows by Lord Griffiths[47]:

> "The days have long passed when the courts adopted a strict constructionist view of interpretation which required them to adopt the literal meaning of the language. The courts now adopt a purposive approach which seeks to give effect to the true purpose of legislation and are prepared to look at much extraneous material that bears upon the background against which the legislation was enacted. Why then cut ourselves off from the one source in which may be found an authoritative statement of the intention with which the legislation is placed before Parliament?"

It is often stated, as by Lord Griffiths in the passage just quoted, that the task of the judge is to discover the "intention of Parliament". This may be as to either the meaning or the scope of a particular word or phrase, or the general purpose that was to be achieved by the statute.[48] This concept causes difficulty for a number of reasons.[49] It cannot mean the intention of "all the members of both Houses" as some may not have been aware of the measure, and others may have opposed it. If it is taken to mean "all the members of both Houses who voted for it" there may be problems in that the majority "will almost certainly have been constituted by different persons at the different stages of the passage of the Bill",[50] and might have had different views as to its meaning or purpose. A vote in favour of a Bill may reflect loyalty to the party whip rather than an understanding or even half-hearted approval of the measure. Even assuming that there is a "collective intention" it is difficult to see how it could be ascertained. Would it be by reference to the debates or by canvassing the opinions of the legislators

---

[43] P. St. J. Langan, *Maxwell on the Interpretation of Statutes* (12th edn, 1969); S. G. G. Edgar, *Craies on Statute Law* (7th edn, 1971). These works have been regularly cited in court; Bennion (2002) is now cited with increasing frequency, usually in preference to the older works. There is a new edition of *Craies*: D. Greenburg, *Craies on Legislation* (8th edn, 2004).

[44] D. R. Miers, [1986] P.L. 160, 162.

[45] Below, para.6–006.

[46] [1993] A.C. 593; below, paras 6–037—6–041.

[47] [1993] A.C. 593, 617. *Cf.* Lord Browne-Wilkinson's reference to "the purposive approach to construction now adopted by the courts in order to give effect to the true intentions of the legislature" (p.635).

[48] Termed respectively "particular legislative intent" and "general legislative intent" by G. C. MacCallum Jr., (1966) 75 Yale L.J. 754.

[49] See Cross (1995), pp.23–31; M. Radin, (1930) 43 Harv. L.R. 863, 869–872; J. M. Landis, *ibid.* pp.886–893; D. Payne, (1956) 9 C.L.P. 96; R. Dworkin, "How to read the Civil Rights Act", *New York Review of Books*, December 20, 1979, pp.37–43.

[50] Cross (1995), p.24.

individually, possibly years after the event? The former would limit the "sample" to the minority who happened to speak: the latter would be a research task which might just produce usable results in respect of a provision requiring interpretation soon after enactment, but with the passage of time it would rapidly become hopeless. In any event it is questionable whether even if it is possible it would be appropriate for the meaning of a particular provision to be determined by an opinion poll of the original legislators. Given these difficulties, and the rule that prohibited reference to Parliamentary material,[51] it was stated that the best if not the only evidence of the "intention of Parliament" was the wording of the statute:

> "We often say that we are looking for the intention of Parliament, but that is not quite accurate. We are seeking the meaning of the words which Parliament used. We are seeking not what Parliament meant but the true meaning of what they said."[52]

The same point has been made by Lord Steyn in considering the view that "out of considerations of piety we frequently refer to the actual intentions of the draftsmen". In fact,

> "the subjective intention of the draftsmen is immaterial. The only relevant inquiry is as to the sense of the words in the context in which they are used."[53]

The meaning of the "intention of Parliament" must now be seen in the light of the decision in *Pepper (Inspector of Taxes) v Hart*.[54] Reference may now be made in specified circumstances to Parliamentary material that

> "clearly discloses the mischief aimed at or the legislative intention lying behind the ambiguous or obscure words."

In the case of statements made to Parliament,

> "as at present advised I cannot foresee that any statement other than the statement of the Minister or other promoter of the Bill is likely to meet these criteria."[55]

Thus, "an authoritative statement of the intention with which the legislation is placed before Parliament"[56] is taken to show which interpretation was "intended by Parliament".[57] The theory on which this inference is based is that:

> "If a Minister clearly states the effect of a provision and there is no subsequent relevant amendment to the Bill or withdrawal of the statement it

---

[51] See below, paras 6–037—6–041.
[52] *per* Lord Reid in *Black-Clawson International Ltd v Papierwerke Waldhof-Aschaffenburg A.G.* [1975] A.C. 591, 613.
[53] *R v Ireland* [1998] A.C. 147, 158. See also J. Steyn, (2001) 21 O.J.L.S. 59.
[54] [1993] A.C. 593; below, paras 6–037—6–041.
[55] *ibid.* p.634, *per* Lord Browne-Wilkinson (with whom five of the other six members of the House agreed).
[56] *ibid.* p.617G, *per* Lord Griffiths.
[57] *ibid.* p.617A, *per* Lord Bridge.

is reasonable to assume that Parliament passed the Bill on the basis that the provision would have the effect stated."[58]

This, together with the rejection of the possibility of "dredging through conflicting statements of intention" in order to establish "the true intention of Parliament",[59] confirms that the "intention of Parliament" is a notional device rather than something that actually exists. The House of Lords in *Pepper (Inspector of Taxes) v Hart*[60] was at pains to confirm the orthodox position as to the separation of powers whereby Parliament legislates and the judiciary interpret; the courts would still be interpreting the words of the Act, albeit with the assistance of a wider range of material.[61]

In *Wilson v Secretary of State for Trade and Industry*[62] Lord Nicholls of Birkenhead confirmed that

"when a court is carrying out its constitutional task of interpreting legislation it is seeking to identify the intention of Parliament expressed in the language used. This is an objective concept. In this context the intention the court reasonably imputes to Parliament in respect of the language used."

Finally, a helpful statement of the current approach is provided by Lord Bingham of Cornhill in *R (on the application of Quintavalle) v Secretary of State for Health*[63]:

"[8] The basic task of the court is to ascertain and give effect to the true meaning of what Parliament has said in the enactment to be construed. But that is not to say that attention should be confined and a literal interpretation given to the particular provisions which give rise to difficulty. Such an approach not only encourages immense prolixity in drafting, since the draftsman will feel obliged to provide expressly for every contingency which may possibly arise. It may also (under the banner of loyalty to the will of Parliament) lead to the frustration of that will, because undue concentration on the minutiae of the enactment may lead the court to neglect the purpose which Parliament intended to achieve when it enacted the statute. Every statute other than a pure consolidating statute is, after all, enacted to make some change, or address some problem, or remove some blemish, or effect some improvement in the national life. The court's task, within the permissible bounds of interpretation, is to give effect to Parliament's purpose. So the controversial provisions should be read in the context of the statute as a whole, and the statute as a whole should be read in the historical context of the situation which led to its enactment."

This confirms that the primary tasks centre on the true meaning of what Parliament has said and giving effect to what Parliament intended to achieve, but that

---

[58] *ibid.* p.633, *per* Lord Browne-Wilkinson, summarising the submissions of Anthony Lester Q.C. which he subsequently stated that he accepted (p.634).

[59] *ibid.* p.631, *per* Lord Browne-Wilkinson, referring to another of Mr Lester's arguments.

[60] *ibid.* pp.639–640, *per* Lord Browne-Wilkinson.

[61] This important constitutional point was emphasised by Lord Scarman in *Duport Steels Ltd v Sirs* [1980] I.C.R. 161, 189–190, above, para.5–023.

[62] [2004] 1 A.C. 816, at para.[56].

[63] [2003] 2 A.C. 687, at para.[8]. Lords Steyn, Hoffmann and Scott of Foscote expressly agreed with Lord Bingham's speech. This has been cited in many subsequent cases. See also Lord Steyn at para.[21].

there are limits ("permissible bounds") to what can be achieved by interpretation.

There are two final points. First, readers not interested in the historical so-called "rules" can skip straight to para.6–008. Secondly, the Human Rights Act 1998 authorises in cases concerning Convention rights a distinctively broader approach of interpretation than that discussed here.[64]

2. TRADITIONAL APPROACHES TO STATUTORY INTERPRETATION

(a) The "Mischief Rule"

6–005 The classic statement of the "mischief rule" is contained in the resolutions of the Barons of the Exchequer in *Heydon's Case*[65]:

> "that for the sure and true interpretation of all statutes in general (be they penal or beneficial, restrictive or enlarging of the common law), four things are to be discerned and considered:—
> 1st. What was the common law before the making of the Act.
> 2nd. What was the mischief and defect for which the common law did not provide.
> 3rd. What remedy the Parliament hath resolved and appointed to cure the disease of the commonwealth.
> And, 4th. The true reason of the remedy; and then the office of all the Judges is always to make such construction as shall suppress the mischief, and advance the remedy, and to suppress subtle inventions and evasions for continuance of the mischief, and *pro privato commodo*, and to add force and life to the cure and remedy, according to the true intent of the makers of the Act, *pro bono publico*."

These resolutions were the product of a time when statutes were a minor source of law by comparison with the common law, when drafting was by no means as exact a process as it is today[66] and before the supremacy of Parliament was firmly established. The "mischief" could often be discerned from the lengthy preamble normally included.[67]

The "mischief rule" was regarded by the Law Commissions, which reported on statutory interpretation in 1969,[68] as a "rather more satisfactory approach" than the other two established "rules". This was so even though the formulation in *Heydon's Case* was archaic in language, reflected a very different constitutional balance between the executive, Parliament and the people than would now be acceptable, failed to make clear the extent to which the judge should consider the actual language of the statute, assumed that statutes were subsidiary or supplemental to the common law and predated rules which prevented judges considering certain material which might throw light on the "mischief" and the

---

[64] See para.8–006.
[65] (1584) 3 Co. Rep. 7a, 7b.
[66] Some statutes were well drafted, such as the Statute of Uses 1535.
[67] *Black-Clawson International Ltd v Papierwerke Waldhof-Aschaffenburg A.G.* [1975] A.C. 591 *per* Lord Diplock at pp.637–638. See below, para.6–020.
[68] Law Com. No.21; Scot. Law Com. No.11.

"true reason of the remedy".[69] Seemingly, therefore, it was the best of a bad lot.

It came to be accepted that the "mischief rule" should only be applied where the words were ambiguous[70]; one of the improvements of the "contextual approach" discussed below is that the purpose of the statute should be considered as part of the context of the statutory words, and not merely as a last resort where the words are ambiguous.

(b) The "Literal Rule"

The eighteenth and nineteenth centuries saw a trend towards a more literal approach. Courts took an increasingly strict view of the words of a statute: if the case before them was not precisely covered they were not prepared to countenance any alteration of the statutory language. For example, in *R v Harris*[71] a statute[72] which made it an offence for someone "unlawfully and maliciously" to "stab, cut, or wound any person" was held not to apply where the defendant bit off the end of the victim's nose; the words indicated that for an offence to be committed some form of instrument had to be used.[73]

6–006

One of the leading statements of the "literal rule" was made by Tindal C.J. in advising the House of Lords in the *Sussex Peerage* case[74]:

> "My Lords, the only rule for the construction of Acts of Parliament is, that they should be construed according to the intent of the Parliament which passed the Act. If the words of the statute are in themselves precise and unambiguous, then no more can be necessary than to expound those words in their natural and ordinary sense. The words themselves alone do, in such case, best declare the intention of the lawgiver. But if any doubt arises from the terms employed by the Legislature, it has always been held a safe means of collecting the intention, to call in aid the ground and cause of making the statute, and to have recourse to the preamble, which, according to Chief Justice Dyer (*Stowel v Lord Zouch*, Plowden, 369) is 'a key to open the minds of the makers of the Act, and the mischiefs which they intended to redress.'"

This was taken to mean that the "mischief rule" was only applicable where the words were ambiguous.

The literal rule was favoured on a variety of grounds. It encouraged precision in drafting. Should any alternative approach be adopted, an alteration of the statutory language could be seen as a usurpation by non-elected judges of the legislative function of Parliament,[75] and other statute users would have the

---

[69] *ibid.* pp.19–20. See below, paras 6–037—6–041.

[70] See the *Sussex Peerage Case*, below, para.6–006.

[71] (1836) 7 C. & P. 446.

[72] 9 Geo. IV c. 31 s.12.

[73] The judge indicated that the defendant would be indicted for aggravated assault and thus "would not escape punishment if she was guilty." *Cf. Jones v Smart*, above, para.6–002, n.20.

[74] (1844) 11 Cl. & Fin. 85, 143.

[75] Conversely, it might be argued that a judge could conceal that his or her role was not as impersonal and objective as he or she would like it to appear by paying lip-service to the literal rule.

difficult task of predicting how doubtful provisions might be "rewritten" by the judges. On the other hand, judges were criticised on the ground that:

> "they have tended excessively to emphasise the literal meaning of statutory provisions without giving due weight to their meaning in wider contexts . . . .[76]
>
> To place undue emphasis on the literal meaning of the words of a provision is to assume an unattainable perfection in draftsmanship; . . . [and] ignores the limitations of language, which is not infrequently demonstrated even at the level of the House of Lords when Law Lords differ as to the so-called 'plain meaning' of words."[77]

Moreover, the literal approach is not helpful where the court is resolving a doubt as to the applicability of a "broad term".

Much has been made of a few post-war cases where literalism has perhaps been taken too far. For example, in *Bourne v Norwich Crematorium*[78] the question was whether a capital allowance could be claimed in respect of expenditure on a new furnace chamber and chimney tower of a crematorium, as expenditure on "buildings and structures" in use "for the purpose of a trade which consists of the manufacture of goods or materials or the subjection of goods or materials to any process". Stamp J. held that it could not: it would be "a distortion of the English language to describe the living or the dead as goods or materials".[79] However, it is unlikely that either the draftsman or Parliament thought specifically of cremation in connection with capital allowances and the policy of the provisions on capital allowances would seem to cover the "trade" of cremation.[80]

The "contextual approach" discussed below is based on the literal approach, but requires greater attention to be paid to the context in which the words appear.

(c) The "Golden Rule"

6–007   Some judges have suggested that a court may depart from the ordinary meaning where that would lead to absurdity. In *Grey v Pearson*[81] Lord Wensleydale said:

> "I have been long and deeply impressed with the wisdom of the rule, now, I believe, universally adopted, at least in the Courts of Law in Westminster Hall, that in construing wills and indeed statutes, and all written instruments, the grammatical and ordinary sense of the words is to be adhered to,

---

[76] Law Com. No.21; Scot. Law Com. No.11, p.5.

[77] *ibid.* p.17. For example, in *London and North Eastern Railway v Berriman* [1946] A.C. 278 (below para.6–012) members of the House of Lords who came to opposite conclusions on the meaning of "repairing" nevertheless each claimed to be applying the "fair and ordinary" (Lord Macmillan at p.295) or the "natural and ordinary" meaning (Lord Wright at p.301).

[78] [1967] 1 W.L.R. 691. See also *L.N.E.R. v Berriman*, below, para.6–012.

[79] *ibid.* p.695.

[80] See Law Com. No.21, pp.5–6; Cross (1995), p.70. The decision has not, however, been reversed by statute. See now the Capital Allowances Act 2001, s.274.

[81] (1857) 6 H.L. Cas. 61, 106 (a case concerning the construction of a will). *Cf.* the same judge when he was Parke B. in *Becke v Smith* (1836) 2 M. & W. 191, 195.

unless that would lead to some absurdity, or some repugnance or inconsistency with the rest of the instrument, in which case the grammatical and ordinary sense of the words may be modified, so as to avoid that absurdity and inconsistency, but no farther."

This became known as "Lord Wensleydale's golden rule" following a dictum of Lord Blackburn in *River Wear Commissioners v Adamson*[82]:

> "I believe that it is not disputed that what Lord Wensleydale used to call the golden rule is right, *viz.*, that we are to take the whole statute together and construe it all together, giving the words their ordinary signification, unless when so applied they produce an inconsistency, or an absurdity or inconvenience so great as to convince the Court that the intention could not have been to use them in their ordinary signification, and to justify the Court in putting on them some other signification, which, though less proper, is one which the Court thinks the words will bear."

One controversial aspect of this "rule" was whether it could only apply where the words were ambiguous, or whether it could also be used where the ordinary meaning was clear but "absurd". In so far as it was confined to the former situation it was a statement of the blindingly obvious: that where statutory words are ambiguous an interpretation that is not absurd is to be preferred to one that is. In so far as the "rule" could be applied in the latter situation it was clear that it should be used sparingly.[83] Some judges argued it could not be used in such a case at all. Lord Esher said[84]:

> "If the words of an Act are clear, you must follow them, even though they lead to a manifest absurdity. The Court has nothing to do with the question whether the legislature has committed an absurdity."

Another point of doubt was whether the concept of "absurdity" was confined to cases where a provision was "absurd" because it was "repugnant" to or "inconsistent" with other provisions of the statute, or whether it extended to "absurdity" for any reason. The Law Commissions noted that the "rule" provided no clear means to test the existence of the characteristics of absurdity, inconsistency or inconvenience, or to measure their quality or extent.[85] As it seemed that "absurdity" was in practice judged by reference to whether a particular interpretation was irreconcilable with the general policy of the legislature the "golden rule" turns out to be a less explicit form of the mischief rule.[86] The ideas behind the "golden rule" are reflected in the second and third aspects of the contextual approach discussed below.

---

[82] (1877) 2 App. Cas. 743, 764–765.

[83] Lord Mersey in *Thompson v Goold & Co* [1910] A.C. 409, 420; Lord Loreburn in *Vickers Sons, and Maxim Ltd v Evans* [1910] A.C. 444, 445.

[84] *R v Judge of the City of London Court* [1892] 1 Q.B. 273, 290. *Cf.* Lord Atkinson in *Vacher & Sons Ltd v London Society of Compositors* [1913] A.C. 107, 121–122.

[85] Law Com. No.21; Scot. Law Com. No.11, p.19.

[86] *ibid.* Sir Rupert Cross regarded the "golden rule" as a "gloss upon the literal rule": Cross, *Statutory Interpretation* (1976), p.170. *Cf.* E. A. Dreidger, (1981) 59 Can. Bar Rev. 781.

3. THE UNIFIED "CONTEXTUAL" APPROACH

6–008 Sir Rupert Cross set out a unified approach to statutory interpretation as follows[87]:

> "1. The judge must give effect to the [grammatical and][88] ordinary or, where appropriate, the technical meaning of words in the general context of the statute; he must also determine the extent of general words with reference to that context.
>
> 2. If the judge considers that the application of the words in their [grammatical and][89] ordinary sense would produce [a result which is contrary to the purpose of the statute],[90] he may apply them in any secondary meaning which they are capable of bearing.
>
> 3. The judge may read in words which he considers to be necessarily implied by words which are already in the statute and he has a limited power to add to, alter or ignore statutory words in order to prevent a provision from being unintelligible or absurd or totally unreasonable, unworkable, or totally irreconcilable with the rest of the statute.
>
> 4. In applying the above rules the judge may resort to [certain] aids to construction and presumptions. . . . "

(a) Rule 1

(i) *Context*

6–009 Under this approach a broader view is taken of the context than under previous approaches. The importance of context was discussed in *Attorney-General v Prince Ernest Augustus of Hanover*.[91] A statute of Queen Anne's reign[92] provided that Princess Sophia of Hanover "and the Issue of Her Body and all Persons lineally descending from Her born or hereafter to be born be and shall be . . . deemed . . . natural born Subjects of this Kingdom". The preamble recited that in order that they might be encouraged to become acquainted with the laws and constitutions of this realm "it is just and highly reasonable that they in Your Majesties Lifetime" be naturalised.[93] The respondent, who was born in 1914 and was a lineal descendant of Sophia, was granted a declaration that he was a British subject. The enacting words were clear and could not be restricted by the words in the preamble. Viscount Simonds said[94]:

---

[87] Cross (1976), p.43; third edition by J. Bell and Sir George Engle (1995), p.49. The label "contextual" was not attached by Cross, but is used here for convenience of reference. Rules 1 and 2 were expounded by Lord Simon in *Maunsell v Olins* [1975] A.C. 373, 391; rule 3 by Lord Reid in *Federal Steam Navigation Co Ltd v Department of Trade and Industry* [1974] 1 W.L.R. 505, 508–509. The "aids" and "presumptions" are discussed in Chs 5 to 7 of Cross's book.

[88] These words were added by the editors of the second and third editions of *Cross*.

[89] *ibid.*

[90] These words replace "an absurd result which cannot reasonably be supposed to have been the intention of the legislature" from the first edition. See pp.89–92 of the third edition for discussion of the change.

[91] [1957] A.C. 436. See A. Lyon, (1999) 20 Stat. L.R. 174.

[92] 4 & 5 Anne c.16.

[93] On the death of Queen Anne without issue the Crown of England would descend on Sophia and her heirs: Sophia's son became King George I.

[94] At pp.461, 463. Lord Tucker expressed his "complete agreement" with Viscount Simonds' opinion (p.472).

"[W]ords, and particularly general words, cannot be read in isolation; their colour and content are derived from their context. So it is that I conceive it to be my right and duty to examine every word of a statute in its context, and I use context in its widest sense which I have already indicated as including not only other enacting provisions of the same statute, but its preamble, the existing state of the law, other statutes *in pari materia*, and the mischief which I can, by those and other legitimate means, discern the statute was intended to remedy . . .

[N]o one should profess to understand any part of a statute or of any other document before he has read the whole of it. Until he has done so, he is not entitled to say that it, or any part of it, is clear and unambiguous."

Lord Normand said[95]:

"In order to discover the intention of Parliament it is proper that the court should read the whole Act, inform itself of the legal context of the Act, including Acts so related to it that they may throw light on its meaning, and of the factual context, such as the mischief to be remedied . . . It is the merest commonplace to say that words abstracted from context may be meaningless or misleading."

Even after the context had been considered it could not be said that the enacting words were unclear; the preamble itself was ambiguous; three of their Lordships also held that there was no inherent absurdity, judged at the time when the statute was passed, in the fact that all lineal descendants would be naturalised.[96]

(ii) *Purposive interpretation*

That the object of the statute is to be considered as part of the context was **6–010** emphasised in *Maunsell v Olins*.[97] The plaintiff owned the freehold of a farm. The farm's tenant had sublet a cottage to the Olins. If the cottage formed "part of premises which had been let as a whole on a superior letting" the Olins were entitled to the continued protection of the Rent Acts after the tenant's death. The House held by three to two[98] that the word "premises" was to be limited to dwelling-houses[99] and as the Olins were not the subtenants of part of premises in that limited sense they were not protected. Lord Wilberforce expressly endorsed Viscount Simonds' dictum in the *Hanover* case.[100] Lord Simon, with whom Lord Diplock entirely agreed, held that the term "premises" was to be construed more widely as in ordinary legal parlance "the subject-matter of a letting" or, more technically, as "the subject-matter of the habendum clause of the relevant lease".

---

[95] At p.465. See also Lord Somervell at pp.473–474.
[96] Most of the royal heads of Europe in the early twentieth century, including the German Kaiser, were lineal descendants of Sophia.
[97] [1975] A.C. 373. See also *Stock v Frank Jones (Tipton) Ltd* [1978] 1 W.L.R. 231, 236, and *Powdrill v Watson* [1995] 2 All E.R. 65, 79 (Lord Browne-Wilkinson).
[98] Lord Reid, Lord Wilberforce and Viscount Dilhorne; Lord Simon and Lord Diplock dissented.
[99] Viscount Dilhorne thought the term might mean "buildings".
[100] Above.

He did, however, make certain general observations as to interpretation, which were not controverted in the speeches of the majority[101]:

> "The rule in *Heydon's Case*, 3 Co. Rep. 7a itself is sometimes stated as a primary canon of construction, sometimes as secondary (i.e. available in the case of an ambiguity): *cf. Maxwell on the Interpretation of Statutes* (12th ed., 1969), pp. 40, 96, with *Craies on Statute Law*, 7th ed. (1971) pp. 94, 96. We think that the explanation of this is that the rule is available at two stages. The first task of a court of construction is to put itself in the shoes of the draftsman—to consider what knowledge he had and, importantly, what statutory objective he had—if only as a guide to the linguistic register. Here is the first consideration of the 'mischief'. Being thus placed in the shoes of the draftsman, the court proceeds to ascertain the meaning of the statutory language. In this task 'the first and most elementary rule of construction' is to consider the plain and primary meaning, in their appropriate register, of the words used. If there is no such plain meaning (*i.e.*, if there is an ambiguity), a number of secondary canons are available to resolve it. Of these one of the most important is the rule in *Heydon's Case*. Here, then, may be a second consideration of the 'mischief'."

In 1980, Lord Scarman said in a lecture in Australia that, "In London, no one would now dare to choose the literal rather than a purposive construction of a statute: and 'legalism' is currently a term of abuse."[102] Similar statements were made in *Pepper (Inspector of Taxes) v Hart,*[103] and by Lord Bingham of Cornhill in *R (on the application of Quintavalle) v Secretary of State for Health.*[104]

Reference is now frequently made by judges to the concept of "purposive"[105] statutory construction. Sometimes the term is used broadly to describe the general approach to the construction of statutes. As such, it is misleading as the legislative purpose is but one of the factors that should be considered as part of the context.[106] More commonly, it is used in a narrower sense, in the course of comparing readings based on the literal or grammatical meaning of words with readings based on a purposive approach. It may be used even more narrowly to denote a construction that involves straining the words of the statute in order to fulfil the legislative purpose.[107] The increased frequency in the use of the term by judges coincides with a discernible change in emphasis,[108] but the magnitude of the change should not be exaggerated.

---

[101] p.395. Other examples of interpretation in the light of the mischief include *Marshall v British Broadcasting Corporation* [1979] 1 W.L.R. 1071; *Maidstone B.C. v Mortimer* [1980] 3 All E.R. 552 and *Royal College of Nursing of the United Kingdom v DHSS* [1981] A.C. 800.

[102] (1981) 55 A.L.J. 175. *Cf.* Glanville Williams, "The Meaning of Literal Interpretation" (1981) 131 N.LJ. 1128, 1149, who argues that the primary question should be "What was the statute trying to do?" followed by "Will a particular proposed interpretation effectuate that object" and lastly, "Is the interpretation ruled out by the language?"

[103] [1993] A.C. 593; above, para.6–005 below, paras 6–037—6–041.

[104] See para.6–004.

[105] i.e. one that will "promote the general legislative purpose underlying the provisions": *per* Lord Denning M.R. in *Nothman v London Borough of Barnet* [1978] 1 W.L.R. 220, 228, based on the Law Commissions' Report: see below, para.6–052.

[106] See above, para.6–009.

[107] Bennion (1997), p.740 suggests that the term "purposive construction" is usually intended by judges to bear this meaning. *Sed quaere.*

[108] Lord Diplock in *Carter v Bradbeer* [1975] 1 W.L.R. 1204, 1206–1207; Laws L.J. in *Ashworth Ltd v Ballard Ltd* [1999] 2 All E.R. 791, 805 ("the difference between purposive and literal construction is in truth one of degree only").

First, it should not be assumed that a purposive approach will lead to a different result than a literal approach. Indeed, the opposite is normally the case:

"This correspondence is not surprising; indeed it is what we would expect. Parliament, having a certain purpose, naturally seeks to express this in the words used. If it did otherwise to any great extent, the legislature would be using an inefficient method."[109]

Accordingly, in a number of cases a purposive approach to construction has been adopted alongside a literal approach, each being regarded as leading to the same result.[110] The choice between different possible readings of the provision in question will commonly be influenced by a consideration of which reading best fulfils the legislative purpose.[111] On occasion, a purposive approach has been adopted where a literal approach would have led to absurdity or would have clearly defeated the purposes of the Act.[112] However, a purposive interpretation may only be adopted if judges "can find in the statute read as a whole or in material to which they are permitted by law to refer as aids to interpretation an expression of Parliament's purpose or policy".[113] Prior to *Pepper (Inspector of Taxes) v Hart*[114] there were cases where the judges found it impossible to discern the legislative purpose.[115] Recourse to parliamentary material may now help to establish the purpose of a particular provision,[116] but it must be recognised that usually it does not.[117] Furthermore, there are limits to the extent to which the courts are prepared to distort the statutory language in order to fulfil the legislative purpose.[118] This point may explain why statements are still made that while "purposive construction to resolve ambiguities of statutory language is often appropriate and necessary", the courts' "traditional approach to construction" gives "primacy to the ordinary, grammatical meaning of statutory language", it remaining the "golden rule of construction that a statute means exactly

---

[109] Bennion (2002) p.816.

[110] *Suffolk County Council v Mason* [1979] A.C. 705 (by both majority and minority judges): effect of designation of a footpath on a definitive map prepared under the National Parks and Access to the Countryside Act 1949; *Gardner v Moore* [1984] A.C. 548: Motor Insurers Bureau liable to compensate victim of international criminal act; *Leverton v Clwyd County Council* [1989] A.C. 706: woman and man employed at different establishments under the same collective agreement held to be employed under "common terms and conditions of employment".

[111] See, e.g. *Bank of Scotland v Grimes* [1985] Q.B. 1179; *In re Smalley* [1985] A.C. 622; *Greater London Council v Holmes* [1986] Q.B. 989; *Ferguson v Welsh* [1987] 1 W.L.R. 1553: see below.

[112] *R v Ayres* [1984] A.C. 447, modified in *R v Cooke* [1986] A.C. 909; *cf.* Lord Diplock in *Jones v Wrotham Park Settled Estates* [1980] A.C. 74, 105: *cf.* "rule 2" below.

[113] *per* Lord Scarman in *R v Barnet London Borough-Council, Ex p. Nilish Shah* [1983] 2 A.C. 309, 348 (the test was not satisfied here).

[114] [1993] A.C. 593: above, para.6–004, below, paras 6–037—6–041.

[115] Harman J. in *Re Potters Oil Ltd* [1985] BCLC 203, 207–208; Lloyd L.J. in *Hemens (Valuation Officer) v Whitsbury Farm and Stud Ltd* [1987] Q.B. 390, 401 (the House of Lords did not advert to this point on appeal [1988] A.C. 601); Lloyd L.J. in *I.R.C. v Mobil North Sea Ltd* [1987] 1 W.L.R. 389, 398, disapproved on appeal by Lord Templeman [1987] 1 W.L.R. 1065, 1071; Mann J. in *Hadley v Texas Homecare Ltd* and other cases (1987) 86 L.G.R. 577, 582 (list of items that may be sold on Sunday).

[116] See, e.g. *Pepper (Inspector of Taxes) v Hart* itself.

[117] See below, paras 6–037—6–041.

[118] *per* Lord Diplock in *Jones v Wrotham Park Settled Estates*, n.112 above; *cf.* "rule 3" below.

what it says and does not mean what it does not say."[119] It is also illustrated by the modern approach to the interpretation of taxing statutes. The House of Lords has confirmed that a purposive approach is to be adopted:

> "in determining the natural meaning of particular expressions in their context, weight is to be given to the purpose and spirit of the legislation."[120]

The previous approach whereby

> "the taxpayer was entitled to stand on a literal interpretation of the words used regardless of the purpose of the statute"

and

> "tax law was by and large left behind as some island of literal interpretation"

was no longer acceptable.[121] In *MacNiven v Westmoreland Investments*[122] Lord Hoffmann referred to the "valuable insights" of Lords Cooke and Steyn in *McGuckian*, but also stated that:

> "There is ultimately only one principle of construction, namely to ascertain what Parliament meant by using the language of the statute."

Accordingly, notwithstanding the fears of some, it is clear that the courts cannot ignore the statutory language in the course of furthering any supposed general statutory purpose that taxing statutes are designed to raise money from the taxpayer; and the extent to which statutory language will be strained to have that result is limited.[123]

(iii) *Application of statutory words to facts*

6–011   In a number of cases the task of the court is to determine whether a particular expression, often of some generality, applies to certain facts.[124] The decision may be reached as a matter of common sense, often with the assistance of dictionaries,[125] but here, as elsewhere, consideration of the legislative purpose may be

---

[119] *per* Lord Bridge of Harwich in *Associated Newspapers Ltd v Wilson* [1995] 2 A.C. 454, where a majority of the House of Lords held that giving a pay rise only to those employees who agreed to switch from collective bargaining to individual contracts was not "action . . . taken against" the others preventing or deterring them from being union members (contrary to the Employment Protection (Consolidation) Act 1978, s.23(l)); to extend the relevant provisions to cover omissions as well as action would require substantial recasting. See also his Lordship's remarks in *Holden & Co v C.P.S. (No.2)* [1994] 1 A.C. 22, 33.

[120] *IRC v McGuckian* [1997] 1 W.L.R. 991, 1005, *per* Lord Cooke of Thorndon. Endorsed by the House of Lords in *MacNiven v Westmoreland Investments* [2003] 1 A.C. 311. (See J.T., [2001] B.T.R. 153.)

[121] *ibid.* at p.1000, *per* Lord Steyn.

[122] [2003] 1 A.C. 311. Lords, Nicholls, Hope, Hutton and Hobhouse agreed with Lord Hoffmann. Both *McGuckian* and *MacNiven* were endorsed by the House in *Barclays Mercantile Business Finance Ltd v Mawson* [2005] 1 A.C. 684.

[123] See Editorial, "Interpreting Tax Statutes" (1997) 18 Stat. L.R. v (comment on *McGuckian*); N. Lee, "A purposive approach to tax statutes" (1999) 20 Stat. L.R. 124.

[124] See above, paras 1–011—1–013, 6–001.

[125] Below, para.6–030.

helpful. Examples include decisions that discrimination on the ground of nationality was not prohibited as being discrimination on the ground of "national origins",[126] that painting was "construction or maintenance work",[127] that a newspaper competition card was a "literary work",[128] that demolition work falls within the expression "work of construction" for the purposes of the Occupiers' Liability Act 1957,[129] that the provision of a daily continental breakfast constitutes "board" under the Rent Act 1977,[130] that a ship of any size provided by an employer for the purposes of his business constituted "equipment" under the Employer's Liability (Defective Equipment) Act 1969,[131] that a miscellaneous variety of items (including ceramic tiles, creosote, curtain railing, roofing felt and wallpaper) were not "motor accessories",[132] that the definition of "gypsies" as "persons of nomadic habit of life" included the requirement that there must be some recognisable connection between the travelling from place to place and the persons' livelihood[133] and that a "crane" is a machine that lifts objects, whether or not using the traditional means of a rope and pulley.[134]

(iv) *Choice between ordinary meanings*

Cases where a court has had to choose between different "ordinary meanings"   **6–012**
include *London and North Eastern Railway Co v Berriman*,[135] where the issue was whether a railwayman was "relaying or repairing" the permanent way while oiling and cleaning points apparatus. He had been knocked down and killed by a train. If he had been so engaged, his widow was entitled to damages and the company's failure to provide an adequate warning system would be a criminal offence. By three to two the House of Lords held that "relaying or repairing" involved putting right something that was wrong and not merely maintenance work of the kind the railwayman had been doing. The object of the statute seemed to cover workmen in this situation, but there was also a presumption that penal statutes should be strictly construed.[136]

Similarly, a narrow interpretation of the provision that a decision of the Crown Court on a matter "relating to trial on indictment" cannot be questioned by an appeal by case stated or on an application for judicial review[137] was preferred to

---

[126] *Ealing London Borough Council v Race Relations Board* [1972] A.C. 342.
[127] *Wilkinson v Doncaster Metropolitan Borough Council* (1985) 84 L.G.R. 257.
[128] *Express Newspapers v Liverpool Daily Post and Echo* [1985] 1 W.L.R. 1089.
[129] *Ferguson v Welsh* [1987] 1 W.L.R. 1553, 1560.
[130] *Otter v Norman* [1989] A.C. 129.
[131] *Coltman v Bibby Tankers Ltd* [1988] A.C. 276. This was so, notwithstanding a statutory definition of "equipment" to the effect that it "includes any plant and machinery, vehicle, aircraft and clothing" (1969 Act, s.l(3)): this was held to be "for the purpose of clarity" and not to cut down the general meaning of "equipment". The House of Lords could not think of any rational explanation for the exclusion of "ship" from the definition section (although this was probably deliberate: Sir Denis Dobson, [1988] Stat. L.R. 126).
[132] *Hadley v Texas Homecare Ltd* and other cases (1987) 96 L.G.R. 577.
[133] *R v South Hams District Council, Ex. p. Gibb* [1995] Q.B. 158. The duties towards gypsies in Pt II of the Caravan Sites Act 1968 could not have been intended to apply to those "whose moves are actuated not by need, but by caprice" (*per* Leggatt L.J. at p.173).
[134] *Nationwide Access Ltd v Commissioners of Customs and Excise, The Times,* March 22, 2000.
[135] [1946] A.C. 278.
[136] See further, below, para.6–048; *cf. Ealing London Borough v Race Relations Board* [1972] A.C. 342, where the House of Lords held by four to one that discrimination on the ground of *nationality* was not prohibited as being discrimination on the ground of "national origins".
[137] Supreme Court Act 1981, ss.28(2), 29(3).

a broad interpretation in *Re Smalley*.[138] It was not possible to discern any legislative purpose which would be served by giving the words any wider operation than in respect of decisions "affecting the conduct of"[139] the trial. An order estreating the recognisance of a surety for a defendant who failed to surrender to his bail at the Crown Court when committed for trial was not such a decision, and so could be challenged by judicial review. By contrast, in *Greater London Council v Holmes*,[140] a purposive approach to the interpretation of the right to a home loss payment, following compulsory acquisition of land, was held to be better served by a broad rather than a narrow interpretation. It should be noted that it has become increasingly common for judges to duck interpretative difficulties by classifying words as "ordinary English words".[141]

(v) *Technical words*

6–013   Examples of words used in a statute in a technical rather than an ordinary sense include "fettling" (trimming up of metal castings as they come from the foundry rather than "to put into good fettle" generally[142]); "crawling boards" (special boards with battens rather than simply boards for crawling on[143]); "offer for sale" (held not to cover the placing of a flick-knife in a shop window as this was in the law of contract merely an invitation to treat[144]); and "acceptance" (held to be used in its technical, commercial meaning, derived from the Bills of Exchange Act 1882, and not in its ordinary colloquial meaning).[145] Conversely, the majority in *Maunsell v Olins*[146] preferred what they regarded to be the popular meaning of "premises" to the technical legal meaning.

(vi) *An updating construction*

In determining the ordinary meaning of statutory words, the courts will normally find a meaning that accords with modern social conditions.[147] However, "this

---

[138] [1985] A.C. 622: see below, para.18–059. See also *Cooper v Motor Insurers Bureau* [1985] Q.B. 575. Contrast the statement by May L.J. in *R v Broadcasting Complaints Commission, Ex p. Owen* [1985] Q.B. 1153, 1174.

[139] *per* Lord Bridge at pp.642–645.

[140] [1986] Q.B. 989. See Oliver L.J. at p.995. *Cf. Att.-Gen's Reference (No.2 of 1994)* [1995] 1 W.L.R. 1579 (requirement that notice be give "on taking" a sample read as "on the occasion" of taking it); *R v Lynsey* [1995] 3 All E.R.654 ("common assault" in the Criminal Justice Act 1988, s.40, construed in broad sense to include battery).

[141] See above, para.1–012.

[142] *Prophet v Plan Brothers & Co Ltd* [1961] 1 W.L.R. 1130: See Harman L.J. at p.1133. The word "fettle" has other meanings, as in "Tom offered to . . . fettle him over the head with a brick" quoted in O.E.D.

[143] *Jenner v Allen West and Co Ltd* [1959] 1 W.L.R. 554.

[144] *Fisher v Bell* [1961] 1 Q.B. 394; *cf. Partridge v Crittenden* [1968] 1 W.L.R. 1204, *British Car Auctions v Wright* [1972] 1 W.L.R. 1519.

[145] *R v Nanayakkara* [1987] 1 W.L.R. 265.

[146] See above, para.6–010.

[147] According to Bennion (*Statutory Interpretation* (4th edn, 2002), pp.762–782), there is a presumption that Parliament intends to apply an "updating construction", treating the statute as "always speaking". See further, above, para.6–001, below, para.6–029; *R v Ireland* [1998] A.C. 147; *R v Westminster City Council, Ex p. A* (1997) 9 Admin. L.R. 504; *Cutter v Eagle Star Insurance Co Ltd* [1997] 2 All E.R. 311; *Victor Chandler International v Commissioners of Customs and Excise* [2000] 1 W.L.R. 1296; *R (on the application of Smeaton) v Secretary of State for Health* [2002] 2 F.L.R. 146 (term "miscarriage" in 1861 statute to be construed in accordance with modern usage to mean the termination of an established pregnancy, whatever the word was understood to mean in 1861).

does not mean that one can construe the language of an old statute to mean something conceptually different from what the contemporary evidence shows that Parliament must have intended".[148] A striking example is provided by *R (on the application of Quintavalle) v Secretary of State for Health*,[149] where the House of Lords held that live human embryos created by cell nuclear replacement (CNR) rather than fertilisation fell within the regulatory scope of the Human Fertilisation and Embryology Act 1990. The Act had defined "embryo" as "a live human embryo where fertilization is complete" given that at the time it was passed this was the only known way. The House held that the purpose of the Act was directed to live human embryos created outside the human body.

(b) Rule 2

A court may choose a "secondary meaning" where the primary meaning is **6–014** productive of injustice, absurdity, anomaly or contradiction or a result contrary to the purpose of the statute.[150] Thus, provisions giving a power of arrest in respect of an "offender" or "a person found committing an offence" have been held to cover *apparent* offenders[151]: police officers had to act on the facts as they appeared at the time and were not to be exposed to the risk of actions for damages merely because the suspect was subsequently acquitted. A provision of the Factories Act 1937 requiring the fencing of dangerous parts of a machine while the parts were "in motion" was held not to apply where a workman turned the machine by hand in order to repair it. The machine could not have been repaired while it was fenced.[152]

A court was held entitled to grant relief to a mortgagor under an endowment mortgage, notwithstanding that the words did not strictly apply to that form of mortgage.1[153] The legislative purpose of providing relief to mortgagors in temporary financial difficulties applied whatever the kind of mortgage. The notion of "absurdity" here seems not to be confined to cases where a provision is repugnant to or inconsistent with the rest of the statute.[154]

---

[148] *per* Lord Hoffmann in *Birmingham City Council v Oakley* [2001] 1 A.C. 617, 396 (where the House of Lords held by 3–2 that the layout of premises could not of itself give rise to a statutory nuisance); *cf. Goodes v East Sussex County Council* [2000] 1 W.L.R. 1356 (statutory duty to "maintain" highway does not entail duty to remove ice and snow).

[149] [2003] 2 A.C. 687. *Cf. R (on the application of Smeaton) v Secretary of State for Health* [2002] EWHC 610, [2002] 2 F.L.R. 146.

[150] *cf.* the "golden rule," above, para.6–007, *Stock v Frank Jones (Tipton) Ltd* [1978] 1 W.L.R. 231; *R v Pigg* [1983] 1 W.L.R. 6, below para.17–100; *R v Secretary of State for Health, Ex p. Hammersmith and Fulham London Borough Council* (1998) 31 H.L.R. 475 (noting that there has been some relaxation in the degree of absurdity or inconvenience required to justify departure from the ordinary meaning; "the more absurd or inconvenient the result, or the more obvious the failure of the Act to achieve its purpose . . . the clearer the language must be if it is to prevail": *per* Sir Christopher Staughton at p.480).

[151] *Barnard v Gorman* [1941] A.C. 378; *Wiltshire v Barrett* [1966] 1 Q.B. 312; *Wills v Bowley* [1983] 1 A.C. 57 (but note the strong dissenting speeches of Lord Elwyn-Jones and Lord Lowry, who took the view that it was not proper to depart from the literal interpretation of a statute where that would prejudice the liberty of the subject).

[152] *Richard Thomas and Baldwin's Ltd v Cummings* [1955] A.C. 321.

[153] *Bank of Scotland v Grimes* [1985] Q.B. 1179. See also *Paterson v Aggio* (1987) 19 H.L.R. 551.

[154] See Cross (1995), pp.93–105.

(c) Rule 3

6–015 A judge may read in words necessarily implied by the words actually used.[155] The line between cases of "necessary implication" and cases where the statutory language is modified to prevent an anomaly arising is, however, a fine one. It is clear that such modification should be a rare event. In *Stock v Frank Jones (Tipton) Ltd*[156] Lord Scarman said[157]:

> "If the words used by Parliament are plain, there is no room for the 'anomalies' test, unless the consequences are so absurd that, without going outside the statute, one can see that Parliament must have made a drafting mistake. If words 'have been inadvertently used,' it is legitimate for the court to substitute what is apt to avoid the intention of the legislature being defeated: *per* MacKinnon L.J. in *Sutherland Publishing Co. Ltd v Caxton Publishing Co. Ltd.*[158] This is an acceptable exception to the general rule that plain language excludes a consideration of anomalies, *i.e.* mischievous or absurd consequences. If a study of the statute as a whole leads inexorably to the conclusion that Parliament had erred in its choice of words, *e.g.* used 'and' when 'or' was clearly intended, the courts can, and must, eliminate the error by interpretation. But mere 'manifest absurdity' is not enough; it must be an error (of commission or omission) which in its context defeats the intention of the Act."

In the same case Lord Simon said that:

> "a court would only be justified in departing from the plain words of the statute were it satisfied that: (1) there is clear and gross balance of anomaly; (2) Parliament, the legislative promoters and the draftsman could not have envisaged such anomaly, could not have been prepared to accept it in the interest of a supervening legislative objective; (3) the anomaly can be obviated without detriment to such legislative objective; (4) the language of the statute is susceptible of the modification required to obviate the anomaly."[159]

There are a number of cases where the word "and" has been substituted for

---

[155] *Federal Steam Navigation Co v Department of Trade and Industry* [1974] 1 W.L.R. 505, 508–509. *Cf.* the concept of "ellipsis": above, para.6–001; *Adler v George*, above, para.6–002, n.24. *Wiltshire v Barrett, Barnard v Gorman*, and *Wills v Bowley*, n.151 above. Contrast *R v Brent London Borough Council, Ex p. Awua* [1996] A.C. 55, where the House of Lords held that the term "accommodation" for the purposes of the homelessness legislation should never have been read as meaning "settled" or "permanent" accommodation.

[156] [1978] 1 W.L.R. 231.

[157] At p.239.

[158] [1938] Ch. 174, 201.

[159] [1978] 1 W.L.R. 231, p.237. See also the similar remarks of Lord Diplock in *Jones v Wrotham Park Settled Estates* [1980] A.C. 74, 105, applied in *I.R.C. v Trustees of Sir John Aird's Settlement* [1984] Ch. 382 and *Inco Europe Ltd v First Choice Distribution (A Firm)* [2000] 1 W.L.R. 586, *per* Lord Nicholls at p.592 (criticised by D. Auchie, (2004) 25 Stat. L.R. 40 for going beyond the previous case law by correcting an error in the absence of ambiguity), and note the cautious remarks of Sir John Donaldson M.R. in *Carrington v Therm-A-Stor Ltd* [1983] 1 W.L.R. 138.

"or", and (? or) "or" for "and". *Federal Steam Navigation Co Ltd v Department of Trade and Industry*[160] concerned s.1(1) of the Oil in Navigable Waters Act 1955, which provided that where oil was discharged from a British ship in a prohibited sea area "the owner or master of the ship shall be guilty of an offence". The House of Lords held that where the owner and the master were separate persons both could be convicted, the provision being treated as if it read "the owner and/or the master". In *R v Oakes*[161] the Divisional Court treated s.7 of the Official Secrets Act 1920, which made it an offence where a person "aids or abets and does any act preparatory to the commission of an offence" under the Official Secrets Act as if it read "aids or abets *or* does any act preparatory". If read literally the result would have been "unintelligible".[162]

In *Re Lockwood*[163] Harman J. ignored certain words of a provision[164] which would have had the effect on an intestacy of preferring more distant relations to nephews and nieces. Conversely, in *Re DWS, Deceased*[165] the Court of Appeal[166] held that words should be read in that enabled relatives to inherit on an intestacy rather than the estate devolving to the Crown as *bona vacantia*.

In *R v Central Criminal Court, Ex p. Francis & Francis (A firm)*,[167] the House of Lords held that files of conveyancing documents in the possession of solicitors were "items held with the intention of furthering a criminal purpose" and therefore not "items subject to legal privilege"[168] protected from production to the police.[169] The solicitors had no such intention, but the majority of the House of Lords[170] held that it was sufficient that the documents were intended by a third party to be used to further the criminal purpose of laundering the proceeds of illegal drug-trafficking. This interpretation accorded with the purpose of the legislation. However, in the view of the minority[171] this could not be the grammatical meaning of the words, and such a widening of the ambit of the subsection could not be justified by any legitimate process of implication of terms.[172] Lord Bridge[173] regarded it as illegitimate to read into a statute a meaning which the language used will not bear in order to remedy a supposed

---

[160] [1974] 1 W.L.R. 505. *Cf. R. F. Brown & Co Ltd v T. & J. Harrison* (1927) 43 T.L.R. 394, 633, where the Court of Appeal suggested that "or" could sometimes be construed conjunctively; *cf.* MacKinnon L.J. at first instance and in *Sutherland Publishing Co Ltd v Caxton Publishing Co Ltd* [1938] Ch. 174, 201: "That is a cowardly evasion. In truth one word is substituted for another. For 'or' can never mean 'and'". See generally Sir Robert Megarry, "Andorandororand" in B. Rider (ed.), *Law at the Centre* (1999), Ch.6.

[161] [1959] 2 Q.B. 350.

[162] *per* Lord Parker C.J. at p.354. See also *R v Corby Juvenile Court, Ex p. M* [1987] 1 W.L.R. 55, where Waite J. indicated *obiter* that he would have been prepared in effect to rectify a drafting error, in the light of the legislation's manifest purpose; and *Gateshead Metropolitan Borough Council v L* [1996] Fam.55 (omission of word "ordinarily" before "reside" held to be a Parliamentary slip).

[163] [1958] Ch. 231.

[164] Administration of Estates Act 1925, s.47(5), as amended.

[165] [2001] Ch. 568.

[166] Aldous and Simon Brown L.JJ., Sedley L.J. dissenting.

[167] [1989] A.C. 346.

[168] Police and Criminal Evidence Act 1984, s.(10)(1), (2).

[169] Under the Drug Trafficking Offences Act 1986, s.27.

[170] Lords Brandon, Griffiths and Goff.

[171] Lords Bridge of Harwick and Oliver of Alymerton.

[172] *per* Lord Bridge at pp.371, 374.

[173] *ibid.* p.375.

defect or shortcoming which, if not made good, will make the statutory machinery less effective than the court believes it ought to be in order to achieve its
proper purpose.

Lord Oliver regarded the words as clear, concise, unequivocal and unambiguous: "there is no difficulty about giving the subsection a perfectly sensible
operation". It might be said to be "anomalous and incomplete" but was not
necessarily "absurd".[174] By contrast, Lord Griffiths regarded an interpretation
that confined the application of the exception to cases where the solicitors were
party to the requisite intention as "such an extraordinary result that I would only
adopt such a construction if driven to it."[175]

6–016   In some cases, however, defective statutory provisions are regarded as beyond
judicial redemption. For example, in *Inland Revenue Commissioners v Hinchy*[176]
s.55(3) of the Income Tax Act 1952 provided that a person who failed to submit
an accurate tax return should forfeit £20 plus "treble the tax which he ought to
be charged under this Act". Hinchy failed to declare some interest upon which
the tax due would have been £14 5s. The Commissioners claimed £438 14s. 6d.
(three times Hinchy's total tax bill for the year plus £20). The House of Lords
upheld their claim; their Lordships recognised that the result was absurd, but the
words actually used were not capable of a more limited interpretation. In
Canterbury City Council v Colley[177] the House of Lords gave effect to a
provision[178] that had the effect of requiring the compensation for revocation of
a planning permission to rebuild a house to be calculated on the assumption that
planning permission would be granted to rebuild the house. While this undoubtedly caused hardship to the owners, the words were "clear and express".[179]
Assuming this was an anomaly, it could only be dealt with by "substantially
rewriting the section".[180] This would involve "more than a mere purposive
construction" and fell outside the parameters laid down by Lord Simon of
Glaisdale in *Stock v Frank Jones (Tipton) Ltd.*[181]

It may be that judges are less inhibited in reading statutory provisions as if the
language were modified where they are contained in subordinate legislation. In
R. v Stratford-on-Avon District Council, ex p. Jackson,[182] the Court of Appeal
held that the words 'an application for judicial review shall be made promptly'
in R.S.C. Order 53, s.4(1) were to read as if they referred to the application for
leave to apply for judicial review. This was the 'only sensible construction'[183]
which could be given to the rule, and the construction that had been adopted in
practice.[184]

---

[174] *ibid.* p.389.
[175] *ibid.* p.383. For other examples of "rectification", see *Deria v General Council of British
Shipping* [1986] I.C.R. 172; *McMonagle v Westminster City Council* [1990] 2 A.C. 716 (words
regarded as surplusage to avoid absurd result); *X v Morgan Grampian Ltd* [1991] 1 A.C. 1, 55;
and *Powdrill v Watson* [1995] 2 All E.R. 65, 85–86.
[176] [1960] A.C. 748. See also *Inland Revenue Commissioners v Ayrshire Employers' Mutual Insurance Association Ltd* [1946] 1 All E.R. 637.
[177] [1993] A.C. 401.
[178] Town and Country Planning Act 1971, s.164(4).
[179] *per* Lord Oliver of Aylmerton at p.409.
[180] *per* Lord Oliver at p.406.
[181] *ibid.* and see para.6–015.
[182] [1985] 1 W.L.R. 1319. See also *R v Chief Adjudication Officer, Ex p. B* [1999] 1 W.L.R. 1695;
Pickstone v Freemans plc [1989] A.C. 66.
[183] *ibid.* p.1322.
[184] The drafting error was subsequently corrected by SI 1987/1423, r.63, Sch.

Finally, in *Porter v Honey*[185] the House of Lords held that the deemed consent conferred by regulations[186] for the display of one estate agent's sale board extended by necessary implication to cover the first board displayed notwithstanding the unlawful display of subsequent boards by other agents. The result suggested by the grammatical construction of the regulation was that the first agent would be guilty of an offence where another agent, without the former's knowledge or consent, placed a second board upon the same property. Such a result would be "unjust and absurd".[187]

> "We are dealing here with delegated legislation which does not receive the scrutiny of primary legislation and if in the interests of administrative convenience such an apparently unjust rule is to be introduced it should be in the clearest possible language so that the purport of the legislation can be readily recognised and the need for such a measure can be carefully considered before it is approved."[188]

On the other hand, a court may not be willing to alter statutory language where that would involve the creation of a new criminal offence.[189]

C. THE CONTEXT: INTERNAL AIDS TO INTERPRETATION

There is a wide range of material that may be considered by a judge both: (1) in determining the primary meaning of the statutory words; and (2) where there is ambiguity, in pointing the way to the interpretation that is to be preferred. Some of these aids may be found within the statute in question, or in certain "rules of language" commonly applied to statutory texts: others are external to the statute. We deal first with "internal aids".   **6–017**

It is commonly observed that statutes must be read as a whole.[190] It may perhaps be doubted whether every word of a long and complicated statute will be examined with care, but a judge may well be presented with arguments based on: (1) a comparison with enacting words elsewhere in the statute; or (2) one of the non-enacting parts of the statute listed in the previous chapter.[191] There is an important distinction between these two kinds of aid. Non-enacting words of a statute may be consulted as a guide to the meaning of the provision in question; however, if the words of the provision, considered in their context, are regarded as clear, any conflict between them and any of the non-enacting parts must be

---

[185] [1988] 1 W.L.R. 1420. Another example is *R (on the application of Confederation of Passenger Transport UK) v Humber Bridge Board* [2004] Q.B. 310 (increased tolls on the Humber Bridge held to be applicable to large buses notwithstanding their omission from the amending Orders as the result of a clear error by the draftsmen).

[186] The Town and Country Planning (Control of Advertisements) Regulations 1984 (SI 1984/421).

[187] *per* Lord Griffiths at p.1422.

[188] *ibid.* pp.1426–1427.

[189] *R (on the application of Haw) v Secretary of State for the Home Department* [2006] Q.B. 359, DC. But note that the Court of Appeal allowed an appeal on the basis that the words were clear.

[190] See, e.g. para.6–009 above.

[191] See above, paras 5–014—5–017.

disregarded. Where a conflict between enacting words cannot be resolved by interpretation, the later provision takes precedence.

1. OTHER ENACTING WORDS

6–018 An examination of the whole of a statute, or at least those Parts which deal with the subject matter of the provision to be interpreted, should give some indication of the overall purpose of the legislation. It may show that a particular interpretation of that provision will lead to absurdity when taken with another section.[192] Moreover, there is at least a weak presumption that a word or phrase is to be accorded the same meaning wherever it appears in the statute. For example, in *Gibson v Ryan*[193] the court had to decide whether an inflatable rubber dinghy and a fish basket came within the term "instrument" in s.7(1) of the Salmon and Freshwater Fisheries (Protection) (Scotland) Act 1951. It held that they did not in the light of s.10, which drew a distinction "between instruments on the one hand, boats on the other hand and baskets on, if there is such a thing, the third hand."[194] A court may, however, be satisfied that different meanings are intended.[195] There may, of course, be a definition section.[196]

2. LONG TITLE

6–019 It became established in the nineteenth century that the long title could be considered as an aid to interpretation,[197] once it was accepted that it could be amended as a Bill passed through Parliament. The long title should be read, as part of the context, "as the plainest of all the guides to the general objectives of a statute"[198] although "it will not always help as to particular provisions".[199] In *Fisher v Raven*[200] the House of Lords held that the term "obtained credit" in s.13 of the Debtors Act 1869 (which made it an offence to obtain credit under false pretences) was limited to the obtaining of credit in respect of the payment or repayment of money only and did not extend to cover the receipt of money on a promise to render services or deliver goods in the future. The Act's long title:

> "An Act for the Abolition of Imprisonment for Debt, for the Punishment of Fraudulent Debtors, and for other purposes"

[192] See, e.g. cases establishing that a court could not order the forfeiture of real property used in relation to the commission of criminal offences: *R v Beard (Graham)* [1974] 1 W.L.R. 1549 and *R v Khan (Sultan Ashraf)* [1982] 1 W.L.R. 1405.

[193] [1968] 1 Q.B. 250.

[194] Diplock L.J. at p.255.

[195] e.g. "whosoever being married, shall marry" in s.57 of the Offences Against the Person Act 1861, considered in *R v Allen* (1872) L.R. 1 C.C.R. 367: "being married" meant "being validly married" whereas "shall marry" meant "go through a marriage ceremony".

[196] Above, para.5–020.

[197] *Fielding v Morley Corporation* [1899] 1 Ch. 1, 34.

[198] Not all long titles are as helpful in this regard as Lord Simon's words suggest.

[199] *per* Lord Simon in *Black-Clawson International Ltd v Papierwerke Waldhof Aschaffenburg A.G.* [1975] A.C. 591, 647.

[200] [1964] A.C. 210. See also *Watkinson v Hollington* [1944] K.B. 16; *R v Wheatley* [1979] 1 W.L.R. 144.

was regarded as supporting the view that the Act concerned debtors in the ordinary sense of the word. However, in *Ward v Holman*[201] the Divisional Court held that s.5 of the Public Order Act 1936, which made it an offence to use in any public place or meeting, *inter alia*, insulting behaviour likely to cause a breach of the peace, was not restricted to conduct at public meetings, processions and the like, notwithstanding the Act's long title. The relevant part of the long title read:

"An Act to . . . make . . . provision for the preservation of public order on the occasion of public processions and meetings and in public places"

but the court regarded the enacted words as wide and "completely unambiguous"[202] and, accordingly, applicable to disputes between neighbours. The position appears to be that:

"once their full context is considered in the light of the purposes of the Act, it is the unambiguous words of a section which will prevail over the long title."[203]

3. PREAMBLE

The use of preambles[204] was considered in *Attorney-General v Ernest Augustus of Hanover*.[205] The position was summarised by Lord Normand[206]: **6–020**

"When there is a preamble it is generally in its recitals that the mischief to be remedied and the scope of the Act are described. It is therefore clearly permissible to have recourse to it as an aid to construing the enacting provisions. The preamble is not, however, of the same weight as an aid to construction of a section of the Act as are other relevant enacting words to be found elsewhere in the Act or even in related Acts. There may be no exact correspondence between preamble and enactment, and the enactment may go beyond, or it may fall short of the indications that may be gathered from the preamble. Again, the preamble cannot be of much or any assistance in construing provisions which embody qualifications or exceptions from the operation of the general purpose of the Act. It is only when it conveys a clear and definite meaning in comparison with relatively obscure or indefinite enacting words that the preamble may legitimately prevail."

Accordingly, the preamble cannot prevail over clear enacting words.[207]

---

[201] [1964] 2 Q.B. 580.
[202] *per* Lord Parker C.J. at p.587.
[203] Cross (1995), p.128; *R v Bates* [1952] 2 All E.R. 842, 844, *per* Donovan J.; *R v Galvin* [1987] Q.B. 862.
[204] The long title is on occasion referred to erroneously as the preamble.
[205] [1957] A.C. 436, see above, para.6–009.
[206] At p.467. See also Viscount Simonds at pp.462–464, and see *The Norwhale* [1975] Q.B. 589.
[207] *R (on the application of Jackson) v Attorney General* [2006] 1 A.C. 262, *per* Lord Steyn at para.[89].

4. Short Title

6–021   It seems that the short title should not be used to resolve a doubt as it is given
"solely for the purpose of facility of reference" or as a "statutory nickname".[208]
Some judges, however, have questioned whether it should always be
ignored.[209]

5. Headings

6–022   Unlike the previous three parts of a statute, headings, side-notes and punctuation
are not voted on in Parliament. They may nevertheless be considered as part of
the context. In *Director of Public Prosecutions v Schildkamp*[210] Lord Reid
said:

> "The question which has arisen in this case is whether and to what extent
> it is permissible to give weight to punctuation, cross-headings and side-
> notes to sections in the Act. Taking a strict view, one can say that these
> should be disregarded because they are not the product of anything done in
> Parliament . . .
>
> But it may be more realistic to accept the Act as printed as being the
> product of the whole legislative process, and to give due weight to every-
> thing found in the printed Act. I say more realistic because in very many
> cases the provision before the court was never even mentioned in debate in
> either House, and it may be that its wording was never closely scrutinised
> by any member of either House. In such a case it is not very meaningful to
> say that the words of the Act represent the intention of Parliament but that
> punctuation, cross-headings and side-notes do not. So, if the authorities are
> equivocal and one is free to deal with the whole matter, I would not object
> to taking all these matters into account, provided that we realise that they
> cannot have equal weight with the words of the Act. Punctuation can be of
> some assistance in construction. A cross-heading ought to indicate the scope
> of the sections which follow it but there is always a possibility that the scope
> of one of these sections may have been widened by amendment. But a side-
> note is a poor guide to the scope of a section, for it can do no more than
> indicate the main subject with which the section deals."

This case concerned s.332(3) of the Companies Act 1948, which makes it an
offence knowingly to be a party to the carrying on of a business with intent to

---

[208] Lord Moulton in *Vacher & Sons Ltd v London Society of Compositors* [1913] A.C. 107, 128.
Section 4(1) of the Trade Disputes Act 1906 was held to confer upon trade unions immunity from
tort actions generally and not just in trade dispute cases. See also *R v Crisp and Homewood* (1919)
83 J.P. 121, where Avory J. held that the broad enacting words of s.2 of the Official Secrets Act
1911 were not to be altered or limited by reference to the short title (*cf. R v Galvin* [1987] Q.B.
862).

[209] Scrutton L.J. in *Re Boaler* [1915] 1 K.B. 21 40; but *cf.* Buckley L.J. at p.27. In *British Amusement
Catering Trades Association v Westminster City Council* [1990] 1 A.C. 147, Lord Griffiths stated
(at p.157) that he had "given weight to the title of the [Cinematograph] Acts" in holding that a
video game was not a "cinematograph exhibition". Many other considerations pointed to the
same conclusion (see below, para.6–034).

[210] [1971] A.C. 1, 10.

defraud creditors or for a fraudulent purpose. However, it appeared among a group of sections grouped under the cross-heading "Offences Antecedent to and in course of Winding-Up", and s.332(1), a parallel provision making the officers of a company personally responsible for its debts in similar circumstances, included the words "in the course of the winding-up". The House of Lords held by a majority that an offence under s.332(3) could only be committed after a winding-up order had been made.[211]

It also seems that reference may be made to a heading to resolve a doubt where the enacted words are ambiguous. However, it may not be used to change the meaning of enacted words where they are regarded as clear. Thus, a woman was convicted of an indecent assault upon a boy notwithstanding that the relevant section appeared under the heading of "Unnatural Offences".[212] The words "any indecent assault" were not regarded as ambiguous so as to justify consideration of the heading.

6. SIDE-NOTES

It is now clear that side-notes (now section headings), although unamendable in Parliament, can be considered as part of the context in considering the meaning of provisions in the section.[213] However, where the enacting words of the section are clear, inconsistent words in the section heading will not prevail. In *Chandler v Director of Public Prosecutions*[214] the defendants were charged under s.1(1) of the Official Secrets Act 1911, which makes it an offence to approach a prohibited place for a purpose prejudicial to the safety of the state, in respect of a demonstration at a military airfield in favour of nuclear disarmament. The marginal note read "Penalties for spying" and it was accepted that the defendants had not engaged in "spying". Nevertheless, the House of Lords held that the defendants were rightly convicted.

6–023

7. PUNCTUATION

Punctuation in statutes was considered by Lord Reid in *Inland Revenue Commissioners v Hinchy*[215]:

6–024

> "[B]efore 1850 there was no punctuation in the manuscript copy of an Act which received the Royal Assent, and it does not appear that the printers had

---

[211] The effect of this decision was reversed by the Companies Act 1981, s.96 (now the Companies Act 1985, s.458): see *R v Kemp* [1988] Q.B. 645.

[212] Offences Against the Person Act 1861, s.62; *R v Hare* [1934] 1 K.B. 354. See also *R v Surrey (North-Eastern Area) Assessment Committee* [1948] 1 K.B. 28, 32–33.

[213] *R v Montila* [2004] 1 W.L.R. 3141, at paras [31]–[37]. See to similar effect Lord Reid in *Director of Public Prosecutions v Schildkamp* [1971] A.C. 1, 10.

[214] [1964] A.C. 763. Lord Reid's statement at p.789 that "side-notes cannot be used as an aid to construction" is not now authoritative in so far as it suggests that they cannot provide any guidance to interpretation.

[215] [1960] A.C. 748, 765.

any statutory authority to insert punctuation thereafter. So even if punctuation in more modern Acts can be looked at (which is very doubtful), I do not
think that one can have any regard to punctuation in older Acts."

In modern statutes, it does now seem that punctuation will be considered to the
same extent as non-enacting words, although it may be altered or ignored where
necessary to give effect to the purpose of the statute.[216] In *Hanlon v The Law
Society*[217] Lord Lowry said:

> "I consider that not to take account of punctuation disregards the reality that
> literate people, such as Parliamentary draftsmen, punctuate what they write,
> if not identically, at least in accordance with grammatical principles. Why
> should not literate people, such as judges, look at the punctuation in order
> to interpret the meaning of the legislation as accepted by Parliament."

D. THE CONTEXT: RULES OF LANGUAGE

6–025 There are a number of so-called "rules of language" commonly referred to in the
context of statutory interpretation by Latin tags. They are not legal rules, but
"simply refer to the way in which people speak in certain contexts".[218] Moreover, they are not as precise in their operation as would be expected from their
label as "rules".

1. EJUSDEM GENERIS

6–026 General words following particular ones normally apply only to such persons or
things as are *ejusdem generis*[219] (of the same *genus* or class) as the particular
ones. For example, the Sunday Observance Act 1677 provided that "no tradesman, artificer, workman, labourer or other person whatsoever, shall do or exercise any worldly labour, business, or work of their ordinary callings upon the
Lord's Day". In a series of cases the prohibition was held to be restricted to
"other persons" following callings of a similar kind to those specified.[220] There
must normally, and perhaps invariably, be more than one species mentioned to

---

[216] *Alexander v Mackenzie* 1947 J.C. 155, 166; *R v Brixton Prison Governor, Ex p. Naranjansingh*
[1962] 1 Q.B. 211; *Luby v Newcastle upon Tyne Corporation* [1965] 1 Q.B. 214.
[217] [1981] A.C. 124, 198. *Cf.* Lord Reid in *DPP v Schildkamp* above, para.6–022.
[218] Cross, (1995), p.134.
[219] If one is driven to an English translation of the principle it would be that "a provision in the
statute is, broadly speaking, to be including things of a like kind, but things not of a like kind":
see Newman J. in *R (on the application of Sissen) v Newcastle upon Tyne Crown Court* [2004]
EWHC 1905 (Admin). The Latin expression is still frequently used and is more convenient.
[220] Not, therefore, a coach proprietor (*Sandeman v Beach* (1827) 5 L.J. (O.S.) K.B. 298), farmer (*R
v Cleworth* (1864) 4 B. & S. 927) or barber (*Palmer v Snow* [1900] 1 Q.B. 725).

constitute a "genus",[221] and it must be possible to construct a "genus" out of the list of specific words. In *Allen v Emmerson*[222] it was held that the phrase "theatres and other places of entertainment" in s.33 of the Barrow-in-Furness Corporation Act 1872 did not constitute a genus. Accordingly, a fun fair required a licence under the section even though no charge was made for admission. There must be some "general words" if the principle is to apply.[223]

The *ejusdem generis* rule may be displaced where the general words should be interpreted widely to accord with the object of the statute. *Skinner v Shew*[224] concerned a provision which enabled a person to obtain an injunction against someone claiming to be the patentee of an invention who threatened him or her with any legal proceedings or liability "by circular advertisement or otherwise", unless he or she instituted those proceedings promptly. The Court of Appeal held that the desire of Parliament was "that threats of patent actions shall not hang over a man's head" and that it would be wrong to read the section as not applying to threats sent by private letter. In *Flack v Baldry*[225] the Divisional Court held that electricity, discharged[226] from an electric stun gun, fell within the description "any noxious liquid, gas or other thing" in the Firearms Act 1968.[227] Such a weapon as an electric stun gun came within the mischief of the Act.

2. *Noscitur a Sociis*

This tag refers to the fact that words "derive colour from those which surround   **6–027** them".[228] For example, the word "floors" in the expression "floors, steps, stairs, passages and gangways", which were required to be kept free from obstruction, was held not to apply to part of a factory floor used for storage rather than passage.[229] The wider context may, however, negative any such "colouration". The "*ejusdem generis* rule" can be regarded as an application of this wider principle.

3. *Expressio Unius est Exclusio Alterius*

"Mention of one or more things of a particular class may be regarded as   **6–028** silently excluding all other members of the class . . . Further, where a statute

---

[221] *Alexander v Tredegar Iron and Coal Co Ltd* [1944] K.B. 390; *Quazi v Quazi* [1980] A.C. 744, 807–808 (*per* Lord Diplock): the term "other" in the expression "judicial or other proceedings" was held not to be confined to quasi-judicial proceedings.

[222] [1944] K.B. 362.

[223] *Attorney General's Reference (No.2 of 1995)* [1996] 3 All E.R. 860 (offence to exercise "control, direction or influence" over a prostitute's movements, which words were to be read disjunctively, with persuasion or compulsion not necessary to establish "influence").

[224] [1893] 1 Ch. 413. *Cf.* Lord Scarman in *Quazi v Quazi*, above, at p.824.

[225] [1988] 1 W.L.R. 214.

[226] The House of Lords held, overruling the Divisional Court on this point, that the electricity was "discharged": [1988] 1 W.L.R. 393.

[227] s.5(1)(b).

[228] *per* Stamp J. in *Bourne v Norwich Crematorium Ltd* [1967] 1 W.L.R. 691.

[229] Factories Act 1961, s.28(1): *Pengelley v Bell Punch Co Ltd* [1964] 1 W.L.R. 1055.

uses two words or expressions, one of which generally includes the other, the more general term is taken in a sense excluding the less general one: otherwise there would have been little point in using the latter as well as the former."[230]

For example, a provision that imposed a poor rate on the occupiers of "lands", houses, tithes and "coal mines" was held not to apply to mines other than coal mines, although the word "lands" would normally cover all kinds of mine.[231] However, a court may be satisfied that the "exclusio" was accidental, particularly where an application of the maxim would lead to absurdity.[232] The maxim can rarely, if ever, be enough to exclude the common law rules of natural justice.[233]

E. THE CONTEXT: EXTERNAL AIDS TO INTERPRETATION

1. HISTORICAL SETTING

6–029   A judge may consider the historical setting of the provision that is being interpreted. In *Chandler v Director of Public Prosecutions*[234] the defendants sought to argue that disarmament "would be beneficial to the State", and that their purpose was thus not "prejudicial to the safety or interests of the State". Lord Reid said[235]:

> "Even in recent times there have been occasions when quite large numbers of people have been bitterly opposed to the use made of the armed forces in peace or in war. The 1911 Act was passed at a time of grave misgiving about the German menace, and it would be surprising and hardly credible that the Parliament of that date intended that a person who deliberately interfered with vital dispositions of the armed forces should be entitled to submit to a jury that Government policy was wrong and that what he did was really in the best interests of the country, and then perhaps to escape conviction because a unanimous verdict on that question could not be obtained."

The Victorian attitude of sympathy towards insurgents against continental governments has been considered as part of the background of the Extradition Act

---

[230] *Maxwell on Interpretation of Statutes* (12th edn, 1969), p.293. See J. M. Keyes, (1989) 10 Stat. L.R. 1.

[231] Poor Relief Act 1601, s.1: *R v Inhabitants of Sedgley* (1831) 2 B. & Ad. 65.

[232] *Colquhoun v Brooks* (1888) 21 Q.B.D. 52, 65; *Dean v Wiesengrund* [1955] 2 Q.B. 120.

[233] *R (on the application of West) v Parole Board* [2005] 1 W.L.R. 350, *per* Lord Bingham of Cornhill at para.[29].

[234] [1964] A.C. 763: see above, para.6–023.

[235] At p.791.

1870.[236] In some cases a statute is passed to deal with a particular grievance or problem, and should be historically interpreted; normally, however, it should be "deemed to be always speaking", with the courts "free to apply the current meaning of the statute to present day conditions".[237]

2. DICTIONARIES AND OTHER LITERARY SOURCES

Dictionaries are commonly consulted as a guide to the meaning of statutory words.[238] As words are to be read in their context, as already discussed, this should only be a starting point: **6–030**

> "Sentences are not mere collections of words to be taken out of the sentence, defined separately by reference to the dictionary or decided cases, and then put back into the sentence with the meaning which one has assigned to them as separate words so as to give the sentence or phrase a meaning which as a sentence or phrase it cannot bear without distortion of the English language."[239]

Textbooks may also be consulted.[240]

3. PRACTICE

The practice followed in the past may be a guide to interpretation. For example, the "uniform opinion and practice of eminent conveyancers has always had great regard paid to it by all courts of justice".[241] This is the case where the technical meaning of a word or phrase used in conveyancing is in issue.[242] Commercial usage may also be considered. In *United Dominions Trust Ltd v Kirkwood*[243] the   **6–031**

---

[236] *Schtraks v Government of Israel* [1964] A.C. 556, 582, 583: *R v Governor of Pentonville Prison, Ex p. Cheng* [1973] A.C. 931. See now the Extradition Act 1989. For other vivid examples where history has played a significant part see *R v Z* [2005] 2 A.C. 645 and *R (on the application of Jackson) v Attorney General* [2006] 1 A.C. 262.

[237] *per* Lord Steyn in *R v Ireland* [1997] 4 All E.R. 225, 233 (accordingly, "bodily harm" in the Offences Against the Person Act 1861 should be read to include psychiatric illness, notwithstanding that "psychiatry was in its infancy in 1861". See also above, para.6–013, n.147).

[238] See, e.g. *R v Peters* (1886) 16 Q.B.D. 636 (definitions of "credit" in Dr Johnson's and Webster's dictionaries); *Re Ripon (Highfield) Confirmation Order 1938, White and Collins v Minister of Health* [1939] 2 K.B. 838 (definition of "park" in O.E.D.); *Eglen (Inspector of Taxes) v Butcher* [1988] S.T.C. 782 (definitions of "infirmity" in O.E.D.: third definition, with connotations of illness or congenital defect, preferred to first, "a weakness or want of strength", with the result that a dependent relative allowance could not be claimed under income tax legislation in respect of a healthy infant).

[239] *per* Stamp J. in *Bourne v Norwich Crematorium Ltd* [1967] 1 W.L.R. 691, 696.

[240] e.g. *Re Castioni* [1891] 1 Q.B. 149 where Stephen J. referred to his own *History of the Criminal Law* on the meaning of "political crime"; a work by John Stuart Mill was also consulted.

[241] *per* Lord Hardwicke L.C. in *Bassett v Bassett* (1744) 3 Atk. 203, 208.

[242] See *Jenkins v Inland Revenue Commissioners* [1944] 2 All E.R. 491; *cf. Pilkington v Inland Revenue Commissioners* [1964] A.C. 612, 634.

[243] [1966] 2 Q.B. 431.

Court of Appeal had to apply the phrase "any person bona fide carrying on the business of banking".[244] Lord Denning M.R. said[245]:

> "In such a matter as this, when Parliament has given no guidance, we cannot do better than look at the reputation of the concern amongst intelligent men of commerce."

In these cases the usage or practice precedes the enactment of related technical legislation. The *subsequent* practice of those who are involved in the implementation of a statute is not generally regarded as a permissible aid.[246] A different view may be taken in respect of old statutes:

> "It is said that the best exposition of a statute . . . is that which it has received from contemporary authority . . . *Contemporanea expositio est fortissima in lege.* Where this has been given by enactment or judicial decision, it is of course to be accepted as conclusive. But, further, the meaning publicly given by contemporary or long professional usage is presumed to be the true one, even where the language has etymologically or popularly a different meaning."[247]

This principle cannot be applied to modern statutes.[248]

4. Other Statutes *In Pari Materia*

6–032   Related statutes dealing with the same subject matter as the provision in question may be considered both as part of the context and to resolve ambiguities.[249] A statute may indeed provide expressly that it should be read as one with an earlier statute or series of statutes. *Later* statutes *in pari materia* cannot be regarded as part of the context of the enactment but may be considered where a provision is

---

[244] Moneylenders Act 1900, s.6(d).

[245] At pp.454, 455.

[246] e.g. practice notes provided by the Central Land Board for the guidance of its staff in the administration of the Town and Country Planning Act 1947: *London County Council v Central Land Board* [1958] 1 W.L.R. 1296. Statements in a government circular may be "simply wrong": *R v Wandsworth London Borough Council, Ex p. Beckwith* [1996] 1 W.L.R. 60, 65, *per* Lord Hoffmann.

[247] *Maxwell on Interpretation of Statutes* (12th edn, 1969), p.264 cited in *R v Casement* [1917] 1 K.B. 98, where the court declined to take the Statute of Treasons 1351 "and read it as though we had seen it for the first time". See D. J. Hurst, "The problem of the elderly statute" (1983) 3 L.S. 21, 23–30, who notes that the term *contemporanea exposito* should (1) be confined to exposition by commentators at or near the time of enactment, and (2) be distinguished from continuous usage and custom.

[248] *Campbell College, Belfast (Governors) v Commissioners of Valuation for Northern Ireland* [1964] 1 W.L.R. 912 (strictly, a case concerning usage rather than *contemporanea expositio*: Hurst, *op. cit.*); *per* Lord Clyde in *Fitzpatrick v Sterling Housing Association Ltd* [1999] 4 All E.R. 705, 726.

[249] See Viscount Simonds in the *Hanover* case, above, para.6–009.

ambiguous, "to see the meaning which Parliament puts on the self-same phrase in a similar context, in case it throws any light on the matter".[250]

Occasionally an argument may be based on a comparison with a statute not *in pari materia*, although such a statute will not be considered as part of the context.[251]

Where a later Act amends an earlier Act the position as to interpretation is not clear. In *Lewisham London Borough Council v Lewisham Juvenile Court JJ.*,[252] Viscount Dilhorne stated[253] that it was wrong to construe an unamended section of the earlier Act in the light of amendments made by the later Act, unless there was an ambiguity. Lord Salmon, however, said[254] that:

> "the whole Act as amended should be taken into consideration when construing any section in the Act. A section of an Act, whether or not it is amended, must in my view be construed in the context of the whole Act as it stands."

The other judges did not express their views unequivocally on this point, although Lord Keith seemed to incline to Viscount Dilhorne's position and Lord Scarman to Lord Salmon's.[255] Lord Salmon's view may create difficulties for the draftsman of subsequent amendments if he or she is to be required to judge the effect of the amendments on the interpretation of unamended provisions.

Where a later Act inserts a new provision in an earlier Act, it may be held that this provision is to be interpreted by reference to the later Act.[256]

5. LEGISLATIVE ANTECEDENTS

A slightly different situation from those considered in the previous section arises 6–033 when the provision in question has been re-enacted in the same or similar form in a succession of statutes. For example, the origins of s.56 of the Law of Property Act 1925[257] were considered in *Beswick v Beswick*,[258] where the House of Lords held that the term "other property" did not apply to personalty. However, the legislative antecedents should not be considered as part of the

---

[250] *per* Lord Denning M.R. in *Payne v Bradley* [1962] A.C. 343, 357; *cf. Re MacManaway* [1951] A.C. 161; *Lewisham London Borough Council v Lewisham Juvenile Court JJ.* [1980] A.C. 273, 281–2, 291; *Mendip District Council v Glastonbury Festivals Ltd* (1993) 91 L.G.R. 447, 453.

[251] See, e.g. *R v Westminster Betting Licensing Committee, Ex p. Peabody Donation Fund* [1963] 2 Q.B. 750; *cf. Brown v Bennett (No.2)* [2002] 1 W.L.R. 713, 726, where it was held that it was in the circumstances illegitimate to found an argument on a comparison with a statute not in *pari materia*.

[252] [1980] A.C. 273.

[253] At pp.281–282.

[254] At p.291.

[255] See pp.302 and 310.

[256] *R v Secretary of State for the Home Department, Ex p. Margueritte* [1983] Q.B. 180; see A. Samuels, [1983] Stat. L.R. 111.

[257] "A person may take an immediate or other interest in land or other property, or the benefit of any condition, right of entry, covenant or agreement over or respecting land or other property, although he may not be named as a party to the conveyance or other instrument."

[258] [1968] A.C. 58. See also *Pierce v Bemis* [1986] Q.B. 384.

context of a consolidation measure; reference to them should only be made if the words are unclear,[259] this concept being broader than cases of "overt ambiguity".[260] In interpreting consolidation Acts there is a presumption that Parliament does not intend to alter the existing law.[261] As with all presumptions it may be rebutted by clear language.[262]

Where other statutes are considered, arguments may be based on similarities or dissimilarities in the statutory language itself, or on judicial decisions concerning provisions subsequently re-enacted. It is sometimes suggested that Parliament, or more realistically, the draftsman, must have had such decisions in mind during the preparation of consolidation legislation,[263] that there is at least a rebuttable presumption that re-enactment without alteration amounts to the Parliamentary endorsement of the decisions and that, for example, a decision of a High Court judge thus "endorsed" would have to be applied by the Court of Appeal and the House of Lords.[264] The theory of "Parliamentary endorsement" was doubted by Lord Wilberforce and Lord Simon in *Farrell v Alexander*.[265] Moreover, in *R v Chard*[266] the House of Lords held that while there might be such a presumption where the judicial interpretation is well settled and well recognised, it would yield to the fundamental rule that the ordinary sense of statutory words should be adhered to unless it led to some absurdity. In any event, the theory cannot apply when the authority supposedly "endorsed" is itself subsequently overruled by the House of Lords.[267] The re-enactment of words in a consolidation Act subject to

---

[259] *Farrell v Alexander* [1977] A.C. 59: Lord Wilberforce at pp.72–73, Lord Simon at pp.82–85 and Lord Edmund-Davies at p.97; *R v West Yorkshire Coroner, Ex p. Smith* [1983] Q.B. 335; *R v Heron* [1982] 1 W.L.R. 451; *Champion v Maughan* [1984] 1 W.L.R. 469; *Prior (Valuation Officer) v Sovereign Chickens Ltd* [1984] 1 W.L.R. 921; *Di Palma v Victoria Square Property Co Ltd* [1986] Ch. 150; *Morton v The Chief Adjudication Officer* [1988] I.R.L.R. 444 (construction of consolidating regulations); *Sheldon v R.H.M. Outhwaite (Underwriting Agencies) Ltd* [1995] 2 W.L.R. 570 (no ambiguity or difficulty); *Associated Newspapers Ltd v Wilson* [1995] 2 A.C. 454 (majority and minority in the House of Lords differed on whether there was a "difficulty" justifying recourse to legislative history and differed on the interpretation of that history); *R v Secretary of State for the Environment, Transport and the Regions, Ex p. Spath Holme Ltd* [2001] 2 A.C. 349; *British Waterways Board v Severn Trent Water Ltd* [2002] Ch. 25. Indeed, "it is particularly useful to have recourse to the legislative history if a real difficulty arises," whatever the form of the consolidation measure (see above, para.5–005) (*per* Lord Scarman in *R v Heron* [1982] 1 W.L.R. 451, 459, 460; *cf.* Lord Simon at p.455 who stressed the point that the statute in issue here was not (unlike that in *Farrell v Alexander*), a "modern consolidation Act", but was a "pure" consolidation, with verbatim reproduction of the existing enactment "with all its blemishes and imperfections"; accordingly, it was more likely to be necessary to look at the legislative history). See generally, A. F. Newhouse, "Constructing and Consolidating" [1980] B.T.R. 102; R. Bramwell, [1992] B.T.R. 69.

[260] *per* Lord Bingham in *R v Secretary of State for the Environment, Transport and the Regions, Ex p. Spath Holme Ltd* [2001] 2 A.C. 349, 388.

[261] *R v Governor of Brixton Prison, Ex p. De Demko* [1959] 1 Q.B. 268, affirmed [1959] A.C. 654.

[262] e.g. *Re A Solicitor* [1961] Ch. 491.

[263] See Lord Evershed in *Ex p. De Demko* [1959] 1 Q.B. 268, 281.

[264] *Re Cathcart, Ex p. Campbell* (1869) 5 Ch. App. 603, 706 (James L.J.); *Barras v Aberdeen Fishing and Steam Trawling Co Ltd* [1933] A.C. 402, 411–412 (Lord Buckmaster); *E.W.P. Ltd v Moore* [1992] Q.B. 460; *Lowsley v Forbes* [1998] 3 All E.R. 897, 906.

[265] [1977] A.C. 59, 74, 90–91. See also Denning L.J. in *Royal Crown Derby Porcelain Ltd v Raymond Russell* [1949] 2 K.B. 417, 429; *R v Bow Road JJ. (Domestic Proceedings Court), Ex p. Adedigba* [1968] 2 Q.B. 572, 583; E. A. Marshall, (1974) 90 L.Q.R. 170; C. J. F. Kidd, (1977) 51 A.L.J. 256.

[266] [1984] A.C. 279.

[267] *Southwark London Borough Council v Whillier* [2001] I.C.R. 142, EAT.

one of the special parliamentary procedures precluding debate on the merits would not have an effect on the construction of those words.[268]

In the case of *codifying* statutes,[269] "the proper course is in the first instance to examine the language of the statute and to ask what is its natural meaning, uninfluenced by any considerations derived from the previous state of law".[270] The application of any presumption that the law is unaltered would destroy the utility of codification. However, the previous state of the law may be considered where a technical expression is used or a provision of the code is ambiguous.

6. STATUTORY INSTRUMENTS

The extent to which a regulation may be used in interpreting a provision in the Act under which it was made was considered in *Hanlon v The Law Society*[271] where Lord Lowry formulated the following propositions[272]: **6–034**

"(1) Subordinate legislation may be used in order to construe the parent Act, but only where power is given to amend the Act by regulations or where the meaning of the Act is ambiguous.

(2) Regulations made under the Act provide a Parliamentary or administrative *contemporanea expositio* of the Act but do not decide or control its meaning: to allow this would be to substitute the rule-making authority for the judges as interpreter and would disregard the possibility that the regulation relied on was misconceived or *ultra vires*.

(3) Regulations which are consistent with a certain interpretation of the Act tend to confirm that interpretation.

(4) Where the Act provides a framework built on by contemporaneously prepared regulations, the latter may be a reliable guide to the meaning of the former.

(5) The regulations are a clear guide, and may be decisive, where they are made in pursuance of a power to modify the Act, particularly if they come into operation on the same day as the Act which they modify.

(6) Clear guidance may also be obtained from regulations which are to have effect as if enacted in the parent Act."

Propositions (3) and (4) were cited by Lord Griffiths in *British Amusement Catering Trades Association v Westminster City Council*,[273] in the course of holding that a video game was not a "cinematograph exhibition", and that,

---

[268] See also *Stubbings v Webb* [1993] A.C. 498, 506–507 (amendment of Limitation Act 1939 in 1975 and consolidation in 1980 no endorsement of Court of Appeal decision in *Letang v Cooper* [1965] 1 Q.B. 232.)

[269] See above, para.5–005.

[270] *Bank of England v Vagliano Brothers* [1891] A.C. 107, 144, 145 (Lord Herschell); applied in *R v Fulling* [1987] Q.B. 426 and *R v Smurthwaite* [1994] 1 All E.R. 898, in respect of the Police and Criminal Evidence Act 1984.

[271] [1981] A.C. 124.

[272] At pp.193–194.

[273] [1989] A.C. 147, 158.

accordingly, an amusement arcade did not have to be licensed under the Cinematograph Act 1909, s.1. His Lordship noted that relevant safety regulations[274]
only made sense

> "if the 'cinematograph exhibitions' referred to in the regulations are under-
> stood in the sense of a show to an audience; for example, there are frequent
> references to the auditorium . . . ."[275]

7. OFFICIAL REPORTS

6–035 Legislation may be preceded by a report of a Royal Commission, the Law
Commissions or some other official advisory committee. This kind of material
may be considered as evidence of the pre-existing state of the law and the
"mischief" with which the legislation was intended to deal. However, it has been
held that the recommendations contained therein may not be regarded as evidence of Parliamentary intention as Parliament may not have accepted the
recommendations and acted upon them.[276] The first of these propositions is
generally accepted: the second proposition only survived in the *Black-Clawson*
case by three to two. The question was whether a judgment in a German court
dismissing the plaintiff's claim for money due, on the ground that it was brought
out of time, barred such a claim in an English court. It did not have this effect at
common law,[277] and the House of Lords held by four to one that this had not been
altered by s.8 of the Foreign Judgments (Reciprocal Enforcement) Act 1933.
Section 8 had been enacted in a form identical to cl.8 of a draft Bill attached to
the report of a departmental committee of "eminent lawyers", and the report
indicated that the draft Bill was not thought to change the common law. Of the
majority, Lords Reid and Wilberforce held that the report could not be considered
as a guide to Parliament's intention. Lord Reid thought that the rule against the

---

[274] The Cinematography (Safety) Regulations 1955 (SI 1955/1129). In *Deposit Protection Board v
Dalia* [1994] 2 A.C. 367, 397, Lord Browne-Wilkinson stated that regulations can only be used
as an aid to construction if "roughly contemporaneous with the Act being construed". This is
inconsistent with the *British Amusement* case, which was not cited.

[275] [1989] A.C. 147, 158. *Cf.* the unwillingness of Wood J. in *R v Bolton Metropolitan Borough
Council, Ex p. B* (1985) 84 L.G.R. 78 to use the Code of Practice made under s.12G of the Child
Care Act 1980 as a guide to the meaning of ss.12A to 12G; and Potts J. in *R v Secretary of State,
Ex p. Greenpeace Ltd* [1994] 4 All E.R. 352, 365: "Primary legislation is not to be construed by
reference to general policy statements or departmental guidance".

[276] *Eastman Photographic Materials Co Ltd v Comptroller General of Patents* [1898] A.C. 571;
Assam Railways and Trading Co Ltd v Inland Revenue Commissioners [1935] A.C. 445; *Black-
Clawson International Ltd v Papierwerke Waldhof-Aschaffenburg A.G.* [1975] A.C. 591; *R v
Allen* [1985] A.C. 1029; *Arnold v Central Electricity Generating Board* [1988] A.C. 288;
Hampshire County Council v Milburn [1991] 1 A.C. 325 (Royal Commission); *R v Horseferry
Road Magistrates' Court, Ex p. Siadatan* [1991] 1 Q.B. 280 (Law Commission Report); *D.P.P. v
Bull* [1995] Q.B. 88 (Wolfenden Report on *Homosexual Offences and Prostitution*). *Cf. R v
Gomez* [1993] A.C. 442 where the refusal of the majority of the House to refer to the 8th Report
of the Criminal Law Revision Committee led to a decision on the law of theft that "flatly
contradicted the intention of Parliament", which had enacted legislation in all material respects
identical to the CLRC's draft Bill: Commentary by Sir John Smith, [1993] Crim.L.R. 305. See
also *R v Anderson* [1986] A.C. 27 (Commentary by J. C. Smith, [1985] Crim. L.R. 651). On
examination, the mischief identified in a report may turn out to be narrower than that dealt with
by Parliament: *R v Kemp* [1988] Q.B. 645.

[277] *Harris v Quine* (1869) L.R. 4 Q.B. 653.

citation of expressions of intention in Parliament excluded *a fortiori* such expressions in pre-Parliamentary reports. Lord Wilberforce stated that if reports were admissible as evidence of the meaning of the enacted words there would simply be two documents to construe instead of one, that it was the function of the courts to declare the meaning of enacted words, and that "it would be a degradation of that process if the courts were to be merely a reflecting mirror of what some other interpretation agency might say".[278] Viscount Dilhorne and Lord Simon of Glaisdale thought, however, that reports should be admissible as a guide to Parliament's intention; at least in a case such as this where a draft Bill had been enacted without material alteration.[279] To forbid this "would be to draw a very artificial line which serves no useful purpose".[280] "Why read the crystal when you can read the book? Here the book is already open; it is merely a matter of reading on."[281] Lord Diplock dissented as to the meaning of s.8 but agreed with Lords Reid and Wilberforce on the use of official reports. The *Black-Clawson* case must now be read in light of the decision in *Pepper (Inspector of Taxes) v Hart*[282] permitting recourse to Parliamentary materials. Reference to *Hansard* may now make it clear whether a report has been relied upon.

It is also clear that external aids generally are not only used for "identifying the mischief the statute is intended to cure" but more generally in identifying the purpose of legislation as part of a purposive approach to interpretation.[283] The House of Lords has held subsequently, without referring to either the *Black-Clawson* case or *Pepper v Hart*, that where a provision was enacted to give effect to a Law Commission recommendation, it was "permissible, and indeed desirable, for the courts to have regard to the view of the Law Commission" on the issue in question.[284] This straightforward approach is to be welcomed.

In *J.H. Rayner Ltd v Department of Trade*,[285] Staughton J. held that Cabinet and department documents from the 1950s, obtained from the Public Record Office under the 30-year rule,[286] were not admissible as an aid to the interpretation of Order in Council concerning the International Tin Council:

> "It would be quite extraordinary to construe either parliamentary or delegated legislation by reference to the secret deliberations of departmental officials or of the Cabinet. One cannot, after all, even look at the deliberations in Parliament recorded by Hansard, which ought at least in theory to be a more immediate guide to the meaning of legislation than the intentions of ministers and their officials."[287]

---

[278] p.629.

[279] pp.621–623 and 651–652 respectively.

[280] Viscount Dilhome at p.622.

[281] Lord Simon at p.652.

[282] Below, paras 6–037—6–041.

[283] Lord Nicholls of Birkenhead in *R v Secretary of State for the Environment, Transport and the Regions, Ex p Spath Holme Ltd* [2001] 2 A.C. 349, 397.

[284] *I. v D.P.P.* [2001] 2 All E.R. 583, *per* Lord Hutton at paras [22]–[24] (scope of the statutory offence of affray). See also *R v G* [2004] 1 A.C. 1034 (para.7–027) where one of the grounds for overruling *Caldwell* was that it was inconsistent with the approach of the Law Commission, whose report Parliament clearly intended to implement.

[285] [1987] B.C.L.C. 667.

[286] Public Records Act 1958, s.5.

[287] [1988] BCLC 667, 689, *per* Staughton J. The relaxation of the rule against citing Parliamentary material in *Pepper (Inspector of Taxes) v Hart* (below, paras 6–037—6–041) does not extend to departmental documents.

8. TREATIES AND INTERNATIONAL CONVENTIONS[288]

6–036 Problems of statutory interpretation relating to treaties (or international conventions) may arise in four main ways. In the background are two principles: first, that a treaty cannot have effect in English law unless incorporated by statute; and secondly, that there is a presumption that Parliament does not legislate in such a way that the United Kingdom would be in breach of its international obligations.

(1) An Act of Parliament may implement a treaty and expressly enact that it shall be part of English law. The text will normally be given in a schedule. Here, a broad purposive construction should be adopted rather than a literal one.[289] This does not, however, mean that the broadest possible interpretation is always the right one.[290] Textbooks, dictionaries, expert opinion and the judgments of foreign courts may be consulted[291]; *travaux peparatoires*, such as the proceedings of the conferences at which the treaty was prepared, may also be used, albeit with caution.[292]

(2) An Act of Parliament may implement a treaty by enacting substantive provisions of English law but without expressly incorporating the text of the treaty as part of English law. Three questions may arise concerning the use of the treaty as an aid to the interpretation of the statute.

(i) Can the treaty only be considered if it is expressly referred to in the Act? The intention to implement the treaty may, for example, be mentioned in the preamble or long title.[293] In *Salomon v Commissioners of Customs and Excise*[294] the Court of Appeal held that a relevant treaty could be consulted even if not expressly referred to in the statute. *Per* Diplock L.J.:

---

[288] See F. A. Mann, *Foreign Affairs in English Courts* (1986), Ch.5; R. Higgins in F. G. Jacobs and S. Roberts (eds), *The Effect of Treaties in Domestic Law* (1987), Ch.7; S. Fatima, *Using International Law in Domestic Courts* (2005); *Dicey, Morris and Collins on the Conflict of Laws* (14th edn, 2006), pp.12–18; D. L. Mendis, (1992) 13 Stat. L.R. 216; R. Gardiner, (1995) 44 I.C.L.Q. 620, criticising the lack of use by English judges of the rules for interpretation of treaties in the Vienna Convention on the Law of Treaties 1969.

[289] *Stag Line Ltd v Foscolo Mango & Co Ltd* [1932] A.C. 328, 350; *James Buchanan & Co Ltd v Babco Forwarding and Shipping (UK) Ltd* [1978] A.C. 141; *cf.* below, para.6–064, n.545 and R. J. C. Munday, (1978) 27 I.C.L.Q. 450; *Fothergill v Monarch Airlines Ltd* [1981] A.C. 251; *Rothmans Ltd v Saudi Airlines* [1981] Q.B. 368; *The Hollandia* [1983] 1 A.C. 565: see F. A. Mann, "Uniform Statutes in English Law" (1983) 99 L.Q.R. 376, who argued that the purposive approach had been carried too far.

[290] *Morris v KLM Royal Dutch Airlines* [2001] 3 All E.R. 126 ("bodily injury" in Art.17 of the Warsaw Convention 1929 held not to extend to mental injury or distress given that in 1929 claims for such injury or distress were not known in any of the jurisdictions of the parties to the Convention in 1929 and not mentioned in the *travaux preparatoires*).

[291] See, e.g. *Swiss Bank Corporation v Brink's MAT Ltd* [1986] Q.B. 853.

[292] See the *Fothergill* case, n.289 above; *Gatoil International Inc v Arkwright-Boston Manufacturers Mutual Insurance Co* [1985] A.C. 255, 263–265. The material must be "public and accessible" and "clearly and indisputably point to a definite legislative intention" (*ibid.*). "Only a bull's eye counts": Lord Steyn in *Effort Shipping Co Ltd v Linden Management S.A.* [1998] A.C. 605, 623. Reference to *travaux preparatoires* may not prove helpful: *Hiscox v Outhwaite (No.1)* [1992] 1 A.C. 562, 593; see R. Gardiner, (1995) 44 I.C.L.Q. 620, 624–626; *Re Deep Vein Thrombosis and Air Travel Group Litigation* [2003] 1 All E.R. 935; *R (on the application of Mullen) v Secretary of State for the Home Department* [2005] 1 A.C. 1, *per* Lord Steyn at paras [50]–[54].

[293] See, e.g. Recognition of Divorces and Legal Separations Act 1971; Arbitration Act 1975; State Immunity Act 1978.

[294] [1967] 2 Q.B. 116.

"If from extrinsic evidence it is plain that the enactment was intended to fulfil Her Majesty's Government's obligations under a particular convention, it matters not that there is no express reference to the convention in the statute. One must not presume that Parliament intends to break an international convention merely because it does not say expressly that it is intending to observe it."[295]

(ii) Can the treaty only be considered if the words of the statute are on their face ambiguous, or is the treaty to be read as part of the context of the statute *before* it is determined whether the words are ambiguous? The first, more restrictive, approach is supported by authority.[296] However, the courts have not been astute to hold statutory words to be clear, without consideration of the treaty,[297] and, in any event, the better view is that the treaty should be considered as part of the context of the enacting words.[298] This would be in conformity with the modern trend towards a broader view of "context" in statutory interpretation.[299]

(iii) If the enacted words are unambiguous, can they be read as if they were modified, by reference to the treaty? The answer here is clearly no. If the enacted words are unclear, but are reasonably capable of more than one meaning, a meaning that is consonant with treaty obligations is to be preferred to one that is not, in accordance with the presumptions mentioned above.[300] However,

"If the terms of the legislation are clear and unambiguous, they must be given effect to, whether or not they carry out Her Majesty's treaty obligations, for the sovereign power of the Queen in Parliament extends to breaking treaties (see *Ellerman Lines Ltd v Murray*[301]), and any remedy for such a breach of an international obligation lies in a forum other than Her Majesty's own courts."[302]

---

[295] *ibid.* p.144. *Cf.* Lord Denning M.R. (in more general terms) at p.141; Russell LJ. at p.152. *Re Westinghouse Uranium Contract* [1978] A.C. 547; *Re State of Norway's Application* [1987] Q.B. 433. The decision of the House of Lords in *Ellerman Lines Ltd v Murray* [1931] A.C. 126 had been thought to support a requirement of express reference, but Diplock L.J. in *Salomon* expressed the view that it was not authority for that proposition: [1967] 2 Q.B. 116, 144.

[296] Diplock L.J. in *Salomon v Commissioners of Customs and Excise* [1967] 2 Q.B. 116, 145. References to having recourse to the terms of a treaty as aids to the construction of provisions that are "ambiguous or vague" are frequent: e.g. *Quazi v Quazi* [1980] A.C. 744, 808 (Lord Diplock); *Fothergill v Monarch Airlines Ltd* [1984] A.C. 251, 299 (Lord Roskill); *Minister of Public Works v Sir Frederick Snow* [1984] A.C. 426, 435 (Lord Brandon). The principle has been formulated by Lord Diplock without *express* reference to "ambiguities" or "vagueness" but it is unlikely that he intended a different result: *The Eschersheim* [1976] 1 W.L.R. 430, 436; *Garland v British Rail Engineering Ltd* [1983] 2 A.C. 751, 771.

[297] Brandon J. in *The Annie Hay* [1968] P. 341; Lane J. in *The Banco* [1971] P. 137; Warner J. in *National Smokeless Fuels Ltd v I.R.C.* [1986] S.T.C. 300 (emphasising that a broad view is to be taken in this context of what constitutes an "ambiguity").

[298] I. Brownlie, *Principles of Public International Law* (6th edn, 2003, p.46); Bennion (2002) p.582. Lord Denning M.R. appeared to support this position in *Salomon v Commissioners of Customs and Excise* [1967] 2 Q.B. 116, 141.

[299] Above, paras 6–008—6–013.

[300] *per* Diplock L.J. in Salomon's case [1967] 2 Q.B. 116, 143; *Post Office v Estuary Radio Ltd* [1968] 2 Q.B. 740, 757.

[301] [1931] A.C. 126. It was not "proper to resort to the draft convention for the purpose of giving to the section a meaning other than that which . . . is its natural meaning" (*per* Lord Tomlin at p.147).

[302] *per* Diplock L.J. in *Salomon's* case [1967] 2 Q.B. 116, 143.

Statutory words cannot be interpreted in order to produce conformity with a treaty if the words are not reasonably capable of bearing that meaning.[303]

(3) It may be argued that a statute should be interpreted in the light of an international convention such as the European Convention on Human Rights. In *Birdi v Secretary of State for Home Affairs*[304] Lord Denning M.R. said that if an Act of Parliament contradicted the Convention "I might be inclined to hold it invalid". However, he retracted this in *Ex p. Bhajan Singh*.[305] In *R v Chief Immigration Officer, Ex p. Salamat Bibi*[306] it was said that a court could look to the Convention "if there is any ambiguity in our statutes, or uncertainty in our law".[307] It clearly cannot prevail over clear words in a statute.[308] However, it was also held (prior to implementation of the Human Rights Act 1998) that the Secretary of State was not under any legal obligation to take the Convention into account when exercising statutory discretionary powers,[309] and the fact that a right was protected by the Convention did not itself mean that it would be a "legitimate expectation" protected by principles of English administrative law.[310] It was difficult to square this restrictive approach with more positive dicta elsewhere.[311] The broader approach is now firmly reflected in the "principle of legality" recognised by the House of Lords as part of the common law[312] and interpretation so as to produce conformity with Convention rights is now required by s.3 of the Human Rights Act 1998.[313] Futhermore, the Court of Appeal has held more generally that a court is entitled to take account of the provisions of a treaty in interpreting a statute, even where the statute was not passed to *implement* any particular treaty obligation:

"The principle . . . requires that domestic legislation should be construed so as to be in conformity with an international obligation of this country if it is clear that the legislation was intended by Parliament to be in conformity with that obligation and if such a construction is one which is and was

---

[303] *cf.* Lord Diplock in *The Eschersheim* [1976] 1 W.L.R. 430, 436. However, it is not obvious that the courts should not be able in this context to employ their limited power to read statutes as if modified: above, para.6–015.

[304] Unreported, referred to in *R v Secretary of State for the Home Department, Ex p. Bhajan Singh* [1976] Q.B. 198.

[305] *ibid.*

[306] [1976] 1 W.L.R. 979.

[307] *ibid.* p.984 *per* Lord Denning M.R. See, to similar effect, Lord Fraser in *Attorney-General v BBC* [1981] A.C. 303, 352; Sir Robert Megarry V.-C. in *Trawnik v Lennox* [1985] 1 W.L.R. 532, 541; Lord Goff in *Attorney-General v Guardian Newspapers (No.2)* [1990] 1 A.C. 109, 283: " . . . I conceive it to be my duty, when I am free to do so, to interpret the law in accordance with the obligations of the Crown under this treaty"; *Waddington v Miah* [1974] 1 W.L.R. 683 and *R v Deery* [1977] Crim. L.R. 550, where the presumption against retrospective legislation was reinforced by prohibitions against the retrospective application of criminal penalties contained in the European Convention and the International Covenant on Civil and Political Rights.

[308] *R v Greater London Council, Ex p. Burgess* [1978] I.C.R. 991; *Kynaston v Secretary of State for Home Affairs* (1981) 73 Cr. App. R. 281.

[309] *Fernandes v Secretary of State for the Home Department* [1981] Imm. A.R. 1. *Cf.* the powerful argument that standards derived, *inter alia*, from the Convention should be used to structure the inherently vague concept of *Wednesbury* unreasonableness: J. Jowell and A. Lester, [1987] P.L. 368.

[310] *R v Immigration Appeal Tribunal, Ex p. Chundawadra* [1988] Imm. A.R. 161.

[311] See the cases cited in n.307 above.

[312] Below, para.6–043.

[313] Below, para.8–006.

properly applicable to the terms of the legislation when first enacted. International obligations cannot alter the clear meaning of statutes. They may, however, be permitted to make clear which of more than one reasonable meaning was intended by Parliament."[314]

(4) The special case of the interpretation of Community legislation is considered below.[315]

9. PARLIAMENTARY MATERIALS

(a) The traditional approach

It was reaffirmed by the House of Lords in *Davis v Johnson*[316] that a court may   **6–037** not refer to Parliamentary materials for any purpose whatsoever connected with the interpretation of statutes. The prohibition covered such materials as reports of debates in the House and in committee, the explanatory memoranda attached to Bills and successive drafts of Bills. A number of judges openly disagreed with the rule.[317] References were occasionally made to *Hansard* in the course of particular cases, apparently without objection from other parties and without reference to the prohibition.[318] Some judges admitted to consulting *Hansard* informally.[319] Relaxation of the prohibition was opposed by the Law Commissions in view of doubts as to the reliability and availability of legislative material.[320]

By contrast legislative materials were (and are) used in many foreign jurisdictions, including the United States and many European countries, where they tend to be more accessible and concise. There have, however, been criticisms that the practice of referring to legislative history has been abused.[321]

In *Pickstone v Freemans plc*[322] the House of Lords held that it is permissible to cite the terms in which delegated legislation is presented to Parliament by ministers as a guide to the intention of Parliament in approving the legislation in question, and thus as an aid to the interpretation of the legislation. The regulations in question,[323] as is almost universally the case,[324] were not subject to the

---

[314] *per* Ralph Gibson L.J. in *J. H. Rayner Ltd v Department of Trade* [1989] Ch. 72, 230–231; see to similar effect, Kerr L.J. at pp.164–166; with whom Nourse L.J. agreed on this point: p.222. The court approved a dictum of Scarman L.J. in *Pan-American World Airways Inc v Department of Trade* [1976] 1 Lloyd's Rep. 257, 261.

[315] paras 6–053—6–064.

[316] [1979] A.C. 264; *Hadmor Productions v Hamilton* [1983] 1 A.C. 191, 232–233.

[317] e.g. Lord Denning M.R. in the Court of Appeal *Davis v Johnson* [1979] A.C. 264, 276–277.

[318] e.g. *McVeigh v Beattie* [1988] Fam. 69, 84.

[319] e.g. Lord Denning M.R. in *Davies v Johnson* (n.316 above).

[320] Law Com. No.21, Scots Law Com. No.11 (1969), pp.31–37.

[321] *ibid.* pp.32–34. The rules against reliance on lesgislative materials have been relaxed in Australia (by statute: Acts Interpretation Act (Cwlth), s.15AB, added in 1984) and New Zealand (by the judges: see J. F. Burrows, [1989] N.Z.L.J. 94). See also G. Bale, (1995) 74 Can. Bar Rev. 1, 23–25; Bryson J, [1992] Stat. L.R. 187.

[322] [1989] A.C. 66, HL, followed in *R (on the application of Amicus) v Secretary of State for Trade and Industry* [2004] I.R.L.R. 430. See A. I. L. Campbell, 1989 S.L.T. 137. See also *Conerney v Jacklin* [1985] Crim. L.R. 234, where *Hansard* was cited as a guide to the purpose of regulations, as distinct from their interpretation.

[323] The Equal Pay (Amendment) Regulations 1983 (SI 1983/1794), amending s.1(2)(c) of the Equal Pay Act 1976, so as to comply with requirements of Community law.

[324] See above, para.5–027 on Parliamentary scrutiny.

Parliamentary process of consideration and amendment in Committee as a Bill would have been.

(b) Pepper v Hart

6–038   Then, in *Pepper (Inspector of Taxes) v Hart*[325] the House of Lords significantly relaxed the general prohibition as it related to Acts of Parliament. At issue was the interpretation of the Finance Act 1976, which stated that where a benefit was provided by an employer to higher-paid employees (or their families) the employees would have to pay income tax on the "cash equivalent" of that benefit.[326] The "cash equivalent" was the "cost of the benefit" less so much (if any) as was made good to those providing the benefit; the "cost of the benefit" was "the amount of any expense incurred in or in connection with its provision, and . . . includes a proper proportion of any expense relating partly to the benefit and partly to other matters".[327] The appellants were members of staff of a fee-paying school, Malvern College, whose sons were educated at the school under a concessionary scheme whereby they paid one-fifth of the standard fee charged for other parents. They were assessed on income tax on the basis that the "cost of the benefit" was the relevant proportion of the overall expenditure incurred in providing facilities to all the pupils (the "average cost" basis). The taxpayers claimed that the cost should be the *additional* expenditure incurred in respect of their sons (the "marginal cost" basis). As they were filling spare places at the school, this would come to a small amount in respect of equipment and food, itself more than covered by the concessionary fee paid.

The House of Lords held: (1) that without recourse to Parliamentary material, the proper interpretation of s.63 would have supported the "average cost" approach adopted by the Revenue[328]; but (2) the prohibition against reliance on Parliamentary material should be relaxed[329]; and (3) in the light of statements made by Robert Sheldon MP, the Financial Secretary to the Treasury, at the Committee stage, it was clear that the Bill had been passed on the basis that its effect was to assess such benefits on the marginal cost to the employer, and s.63 should be construed accordingly.[330] The leading speech was given by Lord

---

[325] [1993] A.C. 593. See above, paras 6–004, 6–005. Following argument before five Law Lords, a special Appellate Committee of seven Law Lords was convened under the chairmanship of the Lord Chancellor to hear argument on the exclusionary rule. The decision has spawned a vast literature: see, e.g. S. D. Girvin, (1993) 22 Anglo-Am. L.R. 475; D. Miers, (1993) 56 M.L.R. 695; D. Oliveil, [1993] P.L. 5; D. Davies, [1993] B.T.R. 172; T. St. J. Bates (1993) J.L.S.S. 251, (1993) 14 Stat. L.R. 46 and [1995] C.L.J. 127; B. J. Davenport, (1993) 109 L.Q.R. 149; F. A. R. Bennion, (1993) 14 Stat. L.R. 149; J. H. Baker [1993] C.L.J. 353; S. C. Styles, (1993) 14 J.L.S. 151; Sir Nicholas Lyell Q.C., (1994) 15 Stat. L.R. 1; Lord Lester, *ibid.* p.10; J. C. Jenkins, *ibid.* p.23; G. Bale, (1995) 74 Can. Bar Rev. 1; J. Steyn, (2001) 21 O.J.L.S. 59.

[326] s.61.

[327] s.63.

[328] Lords Browne-Wilkinson, Keith of Kinkel, Bridge of Harwich, Ackner and Oliver of Aylmerton. Lords Mackay of Clashfern and Griffiths disagreed on this point.

[329] All the members of the House of Lords except Lord Mackay of Clashfern L.C.

[330] Some commentators argue that the statement made late at night to a standing committee ("comprising some eleven future cabinet ministers": Sir Nicholas Lyell, (1993) 14 Stat. L.R. 1, 5) were "really describing the effects of pre-existing legislation as interpreted in practice by the Revenue rather than setting out the Government's express policy intentions with regard to new wording" (*ibid.* p.2); and see Bennion (1997), pp.472–487.

Browne-Wilkinson,[331] who stated[332] that "the exclusionary rule should be relaxed so as to permit reference to Parliamentary materials where (a) legislation is ambiguous or obscure, or leads to an absurdity; (b) the material relied upon consists of one or more statements by a Minister or other promoter of the Bill together if necessary with such other Parliamentary material as is necessary to understand such statements and their effect; (c) the statements relied upon are clear.[333] Further than this, I would not at present go."

This step was desirable:

"The courts should not deny themselves the light which Parliamentary materials may shed on the meaning of the words Parliament has used and thereby risk subjecting the individual to a law which Parliament never intended to enact."[334]

It would facilitate the modern purposive approach to statutory construction.[335] It was also logically indistinguishable from the position taken in *Pickstone v Freemans plc*.[336] There, the court was authorised to look at ministerial statements made in introducing regulations which *could not* be amended by Parliament; here the same would be permitted for statements "made in introducing a statutory provision which, though capable of amendment, was not in fact amended".[337] His Lordship rejected a series of arguments against the change. There was nothing constitutionally improper in relaxing the rule: the courts would still be interpreting Parliament's[338] words and would not be "questioning" the "freedom of speech and debates or proceedings" in Parliament contrary to Art.9 of the Bill of Rights.[339] Although the "practical reasons for the rule (difficulty of getting access to Parliamentary materials and the cost and delay in researching it)" were "not without substance", they could be "greatly exaggerated".[340] Experience in Commonwealth countries where the rule had been abandoned did not suggest that the drawbacks were substantial,

"provided that the court keeps a tight control on the circumstances in which references to Parliamentary material are allowed."[341]

Lord Mackay of Clashfern L.C. was alone in dissent on this point. He had no objection in principle to the change but was concerned at the "possibility at least **6–039**

---

[331] With whom all but Lord Mackay of Clashfern L.C. expressly agreed.
[332] p.640.
[333] i.e. "clearly discloses the mischief aimed at or the legislative intention lying behind the ambiguous or obscure words": *per* Lord Browne-Wilkinson at p.634. The statement should be "directed to the very point in question in the litigation": *per* Lord Browne-Wilkinson in *Melluish (Inspector of Taxes) v BMI (No.3) Ltd* [1996] A.C. 454, 481.
[334] Lord Browne-Wilkinson at p.638.
[335] See above, para.6–010.
[336] Above.
[337] Lord Browne-Wilkinson at p.635.
[338] *Cf.* above, para.6–004.
[339] See also *Prebble v Television New Zealand Ltd* [1995] 1 A.C. 321, PC.
[340] Lord Browne-Wilkinson at p.633.
[341] *ibid.*

of an immense increase in the cost of litigation".[342] The evidence from other jurisdictions did not justify the view that there had been no substantial increase in the cost of litigation there, and the Parliamentary processes involved were materially different from those in the United Kingdom.[343]

Much of the initial comment on *Pepper v Hart* was critical.[344] There were fears that the decision could, as predicted by Lord Mackay, generate a significant increase in ultimately unnecessary cost. Access to Parliamentary materials can be difficult,[345] as can identifying who are the relevant ministers or promoters and following clauses through changes in numbering in successive prints of a Bill. Lord Browne-Wilkinson himself accepted that in many, if not most, cases there would be no "crock of gold".[346] On the other hand, tables of debates on Bills have been published,[347] published annotations to Acts now commonly include relevant extracts from *Hansard*, and *Hansard* for recent sessions has become available on the internet (from 1988–89) and on CD-Rom.

Experience of the application of *Pepper v Hart* in subsequent cases has been mixed. In very few does reference to Parliamentary material appear to have been decisive in solving an interpretative difficulty. A rare example is *Sunderland Polytechnic v Evans*,[348] where the Employment Appeal Tribunal declined to follow one of its own previous decisions[349] on the interpretation of a provision of the Wages Act 1986, in the light of a reference to two ministerial statements in debate. Reference to *Hansard* may make clear the general purpose of a particular provision, while throwing little light on the meaning of particular words within it.[350] Help may also be gained from considering the context into which words have been added as an amendment,[351] or the absence from ministerial statements of support for a construction contended for by a party.[352]

---

[342] p.615.

[343] *ibid.*

[344] See, e.g. T.St.J. Bates, (1993) 14 Stat. L.R. 46 (welcoming the relaxation in principle but noting ambiguities in Lord Browne-Wilkinson's formulation and criticising the failure to relate it to other aids to interpretation); Miers, (1993) 56 M.L.R. 695 discussing, *inter alia*, the implications for parliamentary debate and the relationship between the legislature and the judiciary ("there is a real danger of the courts becoming too close to the executive's intentions" (p.708)); G. Marshall in D. Oliver and G. Drewry (eds), *The Law and Parliament* (1998), Ch.IX (arguing that the exclusory rule should have been maintained on the grounds that "citizens are governed by laws and not by the wishes of legislators" and constitutionalism and the separation of powers should not permit "members of the executive and legislative branches to interpret the law as well as make it"); R. Summers in D. Butler *et al.* (eds), *The Law, Politics and the Constitution* (1999), Ch.12.

[345] Only very few law libraries (including the Houses of Parliament and the Universities of Nottingham and London) hold complete series of Standing Committee debates: see G. Holborn, (1993) 24 *Law Librarian* 141. In the case of an old statute the *Hansard* record may be incomplete; see *R (on the application of Ashbrook) v Secretary of State for the Environment Food and Rural Affairs* [2005] 1 E.G.L.R. 99 (Law of Commons Amendment Act 1893).

[346] [1993] A.C. 593 at pp.634–635, 637. If, however, a clear statement in Parliament is found, that should obviate the need for further litigation.

[347] *Current Law Statutes Service*, Table of Parliamentary Debates (1950–2005).

[348] [1993] I.C.R. 392. Others are *R v Northumbrian Water Ltd, Ex p. Newcastle & North Tyneside Health Authority* [1999] J.P.L. 704; *A.E. Beckett & Sons (Lyndons) Ltd v Midland Electricity plc* [2001] 1 W.L.R. 281; *Haringey LBC v Marks & Spencer plc* [2004] L.L.R. 479; *R (on the application of National Grid Gas plc) v Environment Agency* [2006] EWHC 1083 (Admin).

[349] *Home Office v Ayres* [1992] I.C.R. 175.

[350] *Building Societies Commission v Halifax Building Society* [1995] 3 All E.R. 193, 209–210.

[351] *Grovedeck Ltd v Capital Demolition Ltd* [2000] Build. L.R. 181.

[352] *Re Blackspur Group plc, The Times*, July 5, 2001.

More frequently, a reference to *Hansard* merely confirms the view of a question of construction that the judge or court would reach independently,[353] although this confirmation may make a matter that is otherwise debatable "clear beyond peradventure".[354] In some cases, reference is made to a ministerial statement as making the matter clear without an express indication whether the same view would have been reached independently.[355] Conversely, the statements made in Parliament may not be helpful,[356] or sufficiently clear to require any different meaning to be given to the words.[357] There are also cases where reference to *Hansard* has not been regarded as justified, on the ground that there is no ambiguity, obscurity or absurdity,[358] which may be because the point is covered by binding precedent,[359] or where a judicial invitation to counsel to undertake a *Pepper v Hart* search has been resisted in view of the consequent delay.[360]

The conditions laid down by Lord Browne-Wilkinson have naturally been the subject of further consideration. Thus, ambiguity has been identified where the

---

[353] e.g. *R v Warwickshire County Council, Ex p. Johnson* [1993] A.C. 583, HL (misleading price indication by Dixons electrical goods store manager not given "in the course of a business of his" within the Consumer Protection Act 1987, s.20); *Chief Adjudication Officer v Foster* [1993] A.C. 754, HL (power to make regulations specifying circumstances in which persons were to be treated as being or not being severely disabled not confined to defining the degree of disability); *R v Secretary of State for the Home Department, Ex p. Mehari* [1994] Q.B. 474 (ministerial statement pointed to a particular construction which in any case was supported by other considerations); *Elf Enterprise Caledonia Ltd v I.R.C.* [1994] S.T.C. 785, 798; *Botross v London Borough of Hammersmith and Fulham* (1994) 27 H.L.R. 179; *Thomas Witter Ltd v TBP Industries Ltd* [1996] 2 All E.R. 573; *I.R.C. v Laird Group plc* [2001] S.T.C. 689; *Re Blackspur Group plc, The Times,* July 5, 2001; *Lewis v Eliades* [2004] 1 W.L.R. 692; *Rodway v South Central Trains Ltd* [2005] I.C.R. 1162; *Nickonosv v Governor of Brixton Prison* [2006] 1 All E.R. 927; *Harding v Wealands* [2007] 2 A.C. 1, HL. Curiously, reference to Parliamentary material to confirm an interpretation was initially proposed by counsel for the appellants in *Pepper v Hart* as one of the permitted grounds, but this was abandoned during argument: Lord Lester, (1994) 15 Stat. L.R. 10, 21. It rapidly crept into practice.

[354] *Stubbings v Webb* [1993] A.C. 498, HL, *per* Lord Griffiths at p.508 (three-year limitation for period from date of requisite knowledge for personal injury actions *inter alia* for "breach of duty" not applicable to trespass to the person; reference to *Hansard* made it clear that Parliament intended to implement a Committee report.) Oral argument in this and the *Johnson* and *Foster* cases (n.353 above) had been completed before the decision in *Pepper v Hart* was announced. Unfortunately, *Stubbings v Webb* has created clear anomalies that require legislation attention: *A v Hoare* [2006] EWCA Civ 395.

[355] e.g. *Chief Constable of Merseyside Police v Harrison* [2007] Q.B. 79 (civil not criminal standard of proof applicable to closure orders under the Anti-social Behaviour Act 2003).

[356] There are many examples, including *Massmould Holdings Ltd v Payne* [1993] S.T.C. 62; *Sheppard v I.R.C (No.2)* [1993] S.T.C. 240, 255; *Re Bishopsgate Investment Management Ltd* [1993] Ch. 481, 490, (also no ambiguity, obscurity or absurdity); *R v Registered Designs Appeal Tribunal, Ex p. Ford Motor Co Ltd* [1995] 1 W.L.R. 18; *Dennby v Yeldon* [1995] 3 All E.R. 624.

[357] *Macdougall v Wrexham Maelor Borough Council* (1993) 69 P.&C.R. 109, 122.

[358] *Islwyn Borough Council v Newport Borough Council, The Times,* June 28, 1993, CA; *R v Secretary of State for Foreign and Commonwealth Affairs, Ex p. Rees-Mogg* [1994] Q.B. 552, 556–557; *Busby v Co-operative Insurance Society* [1994] 1 E.G.L.R. 136; *R v Secretary of State for the Home Department, Ex p. Okello* [1994] Imm. A.R. 261; *DPP v Bull* [1995] Q.B. 88 (term "common prostitute" confined to women, as would have been confirmed by a reference to *Hansard); Petch v Gurney (Inspector of Taxes)* [1994] 3 All E.R. 731; *R v Singleton* [1995] Crim. L.R. 236; *R v Director General of Fair Trading, Ex p. Benham Ltd* [2001] 1 E.G.L.R. 21; *R v Richmond London Borough Council, Ex p. Watson* [2001] Q.B. 370.

[359] *Sheppard v I.R.C. (No.2)* [1993] S.T.C. 240, Aldous J.; *Dawkins v Department of the Environment* [1993] I.C.R. 517, CA; *National Rivers Authority v Alfred McAlpine Homes East Ltd* [1994] 4 All E.R. 286, 296–297, DC.

[360] *R v Dorset County Council, Ex p. Rolls* (1994) 26 H.L.R. 381.

meaning of a particular phrase is uncertain in its application,[361] or where various judges or courts have differed over a point of interpretation.[362] The rules apply to ambiguity in legislation affecting criminal proceedings, and not just civil proceedings.[363] The concept of ambiguity should also apply to the position that arises where there is an inconsistency between two statutory provisions, although a different view appeared to have been taken in *R v Moore*.[364] While most of the statements in Parliament referred to have been those of ministers, reference has also been made to statements by the successful mover of an amendment[365] and a Parliamentary Agent before a House of Commons Committee at the committee stage of a Private Bill.[366] The fact that a statement is made on the advice of a law officer is no reason for it to be excluded.[367] However, reference may not be made to a press release, which is a departmental and not a Parliamentary document.[368] Ministerial statements may cease to be of value where words are re-enacted following court decisions on their interpretation.[369] Reference may not be made to ministerial statements on *other* provisions.[370] The requirement that a statement be "clear" has not received separate attention, although statements cited may not be regarded as helpful.[371]

6–040   The decision in *Pepper v Hart* has led to changes in practice. Any party intending to refer to *Hansard* must, unless the judge otherwise directs, serve upon all other parties and the court copies of the extracts in question, with a brief summary of the argument intended to be based thereon.[372] It seems that extracts from *Hansard* will be cited in argument and decisions on whether the court is able and willing to rely on them are taken later.

As regards Parliamentary proceedings,

---

[361] *Sheppard v I.R.C. (No.2)* [1993] S.T.C. 624, referring to Lord Diplock in *I.R.C. v Joiner* [1975] 1 W.L.R. 1701, 1710; *I.R.C. v Laird Group plc* [2001] S.T.C. 689. But note the limitation introduced by the *Spath Holme* decision: below, para.6–041.

[362] *Doncaster Borough Council v Secretary of State for the Environment* (1992) 91 L.G.R. 459, 476–477; *Chief Adjudication Officer v Foster* [1993] A.C. 754, 772. But judicial disagreement does not *necessarily* let in *Pepper v Hart*: Longmore L.J. in *Re OT Computers Ltd* [2004] Ch. 317, paras [39]–[41].

[363] *Botross v London Borough of Hammersmith and Fulham* (1994) 27 H.L.R. 179, 186. But it would be wrong in principle to extend the ambit of an ambiguous criminal statute by reference to *Pepper v Hart*: see Lord Phillips C.J. in *Thet v DPP* [2006] EWHC 2701 (Admin), at para.[15]. Cf. para.6–048.

[364] (1994) 159 J.P.101, where the Court of Appeal (Criminal Division) solved a problem caused by defective drafting by refusing to apply the literal meaning of a provision as to do so would "frustrate the plain legislative intent", and reading the words "following provisions" as if they were "preceding provisions". It is difficult in any event to see that there was not "absurdity".

[365] *Chief Adjudication Officer v Foster* [1993] A.C. 754; *Botross v London Borough of Hammersmith and Fulham* (1994) 27 H.L.R. 179, 187 (amendment accepted by government minister).

[366] *London Regional Transport Pension Fund Trust Co Ltd v Hatt, The Times*, May 20, 1993. The statement was of no help to the court.

[367] *R v Secretary of State for Foreign and Commonwealth Affairs, Ex p. Rees-Mogg* [1994] Q.B. 552, 566, *per* Lloyd L.J.

[368] *Elf Enterprise Caledonia Ltd v I.R.C.* [1994] S.T.C. 785, 798. A press release was, however, mentioned by Lord Browne-Wilkinson in *Pepper v Hart* [1993] A.C. 593, 628 although the case turned on ministerial statements.

[369] *I.R.C. v Willoughby* [1995] S.T.C. 143, 174 *per* Morritt L.J.: "In these circumstances it must be assumed that the original intention, whatever it was, was superseded by acceptance of the decisions of the courts."

[370] *Melluish v B.M.I. (No.3) Ltd* [1996] A.C. 454, 481 *per* Lord Browne-Wilkinson.

[371] See above, n.356.

[372] *Practice Direction (Hansard: Citation)* [1995] 1 W.L.R. 192.

"If it proves necessary to correct any inadvertent ambiguity or error in a ministerial statement made during the passage of a Bill, the aim is to do this as promptly as possible at an appropriate point during the further consideration of the Bill. The best means of doing so and reading such a correction into the official record will depend on a number of factors, including the stage which the Bill has reached and the nature of the proceedings at that point."[373]

Corrections are no longer left to correspondence with Members.

(c) Attacks on *Pepper v Hart*

The first nine years of the operation of *Pepper v Hart* has largely borne out the **6–041** fears expressed by Lord Mackay of Clashfern.[374] Issues concerning the cost of litigation have been raised with the legal profession. The possibility of reference being made to Parliamentary material has been raised in over 600 cases to date.[375] In each of these, research will have been done at the client's expense; in very few indeed does a "crock of gold" appear to have made a difference to the outcome. What cannot be estimated is the extent to which awareness of that material has influenced the supposed "independent" approach of the judges to questions of interpretation.

The House of Lords considered *Pepper v Hart* at some length in *R v Secretary of State for the Environment, Transport and the Regions, Ex p. Spath Holme Ltd.*[376] The question was whether a general power to make regulations restricting or preventing increase of rent for dwellings was itself restricted to countering general inflation in the economy. The House held unanimously that it was not. All the members seemed concerned to a greater or lesser extent with the costs of frequent citation of *Hansard*, and agreed that it was exceptional for such citation to be helpful. Lords Bingham, Hope and Hutton were agreed that the conditions laid down in *Pepper v Hart* should be "strictly insisted upon".[377] Furthermore, a distinction was to be drawn between issues as to (1) the meaning of a statutory expression, and (2) the scope of a statutory power. The *Pepper v Hart* exception was available in respect of the former, but, as regards the latter, according to Lord Bingham, only

> "if a minister were, improbably, to give a categorical assurance to Parliament that a power would not be used in a given situation, such that Parliament could be taken to have legislated on that basis . . . "[378]

For Lord Hope,

> "it would be contrary to fundamental considerations of constitutional principle to allow it to be used to enable reliance to be placed on statements made

---

[373] Vol.239, H.C. Deb, March 14, 1994, written answer by the Parliamentary Secretary, Lord Chancellor's Department, John M. Taylor MP.

[374] See e.g. Lord Hohouse of Woodborough in *Wilson v Secretary of State for Trade and Industry* [2004] 1 A.C. 816, at para.[140], and Lord Hoffmann in *Robinson v Secretary of State for Northern Ireland* [2002] UKHL 32, [2002] N.I. 390 at para.[40].

[375] *LexisNexis* search (28.1.07).

[376] [2001] 1 All E.R. 195.

[377] *ibid.* pp.212, 227, 233.

[378] *per* Lord Bingham at p.392; Lord Hutton did not comment on this qualification; Lord Hope regarded it as a qualification applicable to both (1) and (2): see below.

in debate about matters of policy which have not been reproduced in the enactment."[379]

Furthermore, the *Pepper v Hart* exception was only ever available to prevent the executive seeking to place a meaning on words different from that which ministers attributed to those words when promoting the legislation in Parliament.[380] Lords Nicholls and Cooke did not accept this distinction and argued, persuasively, that (2) is really an example of (1).[381] All the members of the House were agreed that the particular *Hansard* statements relied on by *Spath Holme* did not provide clear and unequivocal support to the narrower interpretation of the power which they in fact rejected; Lord Cooke alone regarded them as helpful in confirming that adoption of a broader view would not thwart Parliament's intention. It is submitted that the doubtful distinction adopted by the majority in *Spath Holme* will have little impact in reducing the level of costs wasted in fruitless *Hansard* searches. A more fundamental reconsideration is required. Lord Steyn, writing extra-judicially,[382] has mounted a powerful attack on the decision:

> "It remains my view that *Pepper v Hart* has substantially increased the cost of litigation to very little advantage. Many appellate judges share this view."[383]

Furthermore, it was wrong in principle to treat ministerial policy statements as a source of law. There was a case for confining *Pepper v Hart* to "the admission against the executive of categorical assurances given by ministers to Parliament".[384] These views are echoed in *Spath Holme*, although Lord Steyn's proposed restriction on the scope of *Pepper v Hart* would be much more radical and was only taken up by Lord Hope.[385]

The House returned yet again to the scope of *Pepper v Hart* in *Wilson v Secretary of State for Trade and Industry*.[386] Here, the issue was whether a legislative provision[387] was incompatible with Convention rights under the Human Rights Act 1998. The Court of Appeal[388] was referred to the Parliamentary debates and concluded that they provided no answer to the question why the courts were denied the power to do what was just in such cases.[389] Neither was

---

[379] *ibid.* p.408. Lord Bingham's reservations centred more on the unlikelihood of a minister seeking to define the legal effect of the draftman's language (p.392).

[380] *ibid.*; repeated *obiter* in *R v A* [2001] UKHL 25, [2002] 1 A.C. 45 at para.[81]; *Wilson v First County Trust Ltd (No.2)* [2004] 1 A.C. 816 at para.[113]; and by Lord Steyn (judicially) in *R (on the application of Jackson) v Attorney General* [2006] 1 A.C. 262 at para.[97]

[381] Lord Nicholls at pp.398–399.

[382] (2001) 21 O.J.L.S. 59. Lord Millett regards *Petter v Hart* as a "regrettable decision": (1999) 20 Stat. L.R. 107, 110. Lord Hoffmann has stated that the difficulties discussed in Lord Steyn's article "were not in my view fully answered in *Pepper v Hart*": *Robinson v Secretary of State for Northern Ireland* [2002] N.I. 390 at para.[40]. For further criticism see A. Kavanagh, "*Pepper v Hart* and Matters of Constitutional Principle" (2005) 121 L.Q.R. 98.

[383] *ibid.* p.64.

[384] *ibid.* p.67.

[385] Above.

[386] [2004] 1 A.C. 816.

[387] That a creditor could not enforce a regulated loan agreement where the debtor had not signed a document containing all the prescribed terms: Consumer Credit Act 1974, s.127(3). This was so even where that omission had caused no prejudice to anyone.

[388] [2002] Q.B. 74.

[389] Sir Andrew Morritt V.-C. at paras [35]–[36]; "Indeed, such references as there are to the point tend to confuse rather than to illuminate.": *ibid.*

the Secretary of State able to explain this now.[390] The Court of Appeal held that the provision was incompatible with Art.6(1), ECHR and the First Protocol, Art.1. The House of Lords allowed an appeal,[391] holding: (1) that the Human Rights Act 1998 could not apply retrospectively and so was inapplicable; (2) that in any event s.127(3) was not incompatible with either Art.6 or the First Protocol, Art.1; and (3) that the Court of Appeal's approach to the use of *Hansard* was illegitimate. On (3), the House did not altogether rule out reference to *Hansard* where the issue was one of assessing compatibility with Convention rights.[392] However, this would be where a ministerial or other statement contained information throwing light on the rationale underlying the legislation. The courts would have to be careful not to treat the statement as indicative of the objective intention of Parliament and could not give a ministerial statement determinative weight. It would also be wrong for a lack of cogent justification in the course of debate to "count against" the legislation on issues of proportionality.[393] The Court of Appeal process of scrutinising *Hansard* to see whether it disclosed any justification for the relevant provisions was unacceptable.[394]

While the *Pepper v Hart* rule was not itself attacked by the parties, there were nevertheless some valuable comments on the constitutional difficulties some have identified. Lord Nicholls of Birkenhead emphasised[395] that the requirement that the statement to be relied on must be made by a minister or other promoter was one of a number of "practical safeguards" designed to keep references to *Hansard* within reasonable bounds. This did not encroach upon the court's constitutional task of determining objectively what was Parliament's intention in using the language in question.[396] A clear and ambiguous ministerial statement was "part of the background to the legislation" and "cannot control the meaning of an Act of Parliament". On this basis there would seem to be no fundamental constitutional objection to *Pepper v Hart* itself. On another point, only Lord Hope indicated (in his case continuing) support for the quasi-estoppel basis for *Pepper v Hart* put forward originally by Lord Steyn.[397] The argument was mentioned by others,[398] without comments on its merits. It may be that Lord Hobhouse was less enthusiastic about *Pepper v Hart* than Lord Nicholls; nevertheless he simply noted that the rule in *Pepper v Hart* was not itself challenged and stated unequivocally that it should not be extended.[399]

In conclusion, it is submitted that: (1) there is no substantial constitutional argument against *Pepper v Hart*, for the reasons given by Lord Nicholls in

---

[390] para.[37]

[391] [2004] 1 A.C. 816.

[392] As argued by counsel briefed to appear by the Speaker of the House of Commons and the Clerk of the Parliaments.

[393] Lord Nicholls of Birkenhead at paras [51]–[67]. See also Lord Hope of Craighead at paras [110]–[118] and Lord Hobhouse of Woodborough at paras [139]–[145]. On the *Hansard* issue, Lord Scott of Foscote expressly agreed with Lord Nicholls (para.[173]) and Lord Rodger of Earlsferry with Lord Hobhouse (para.[178]).

[394] Lord Hobhouse at para.[143].

[395] para.[58].

[396] Lord Hobhouse made the same point at paras [139]–[140].

[397] At para.[113].

[398] Lord Nicholls at para.[59] and Lord Hobhouse at para.[140]. Lord Nicholls' general justification for the core *Pepper v Hart* rule seems inconsistent with this position. This position does *not* "represent the law as it stands today" as argued by S. Vogenauer, (2005) 25 O.J.L.S. 629: see P. Sales, (2006) 26 O.J.L.S. 585.

[399] para.[140].

Wilson[400]; (2) that confining *Pepper v Hart* to the quasi-estoppel model put forward by Lord Steyn ultimately does not work conceptually,[401] and is not really needed given the general absence of "clear" statements that resolve problems; (3) that the *pragmatic* reasons for overruling or restricting *Pepper v Hart* are now very strong especially given the introduction of the practice that clear ministerial assurances given to Parliament should be incorporated in the Explanatory Note. The risk that in a particular case there is a "crock of gold" that has been missed from the Note is so small that it cannot justify the costs to the system as a whole of continuing to encourage *Hansard* searches. Possible, pragmatic, variants might be to restrict permissible citations to the period for which *Hansard* is available on the Internet or to the period before full Explanatory Notes became available.

(d) Other references to Parliamentary material; Explanatory Notes

6–042   It has been held that reference may be made, notwithstanding the *Pepper v Hart* restrictions, to Parliamentary material designed to throw light on whether the purpose and object of a statute was to enact an EC directive or introduce the provisions of an international convention, as distinct from any question of the construction of a particular statutory provision.[402] Furthermore, references have continued to be made without apparent objection in other situations that do not appear to fall within the restrictions.[403] It is submitted that the former, which builds on the position taken in *Pickstone v Freemans plc*,[404] is right and should be regarded as surviving *Spath Holme*; the latter cannot survive.

It is now established that the Explanatory Notes that now accompany every Bill and Act can be considered as part of the context when interpreting a provision, even where there is no ambiguity. They are admissible aids to construction in so far as they "cast light on the objective setting or contextual scene of the statute, and the mischief at which it is aimed". Indeed they may be more helpful than Committee reports and White Papers as the connection with the shape of the proposed legislation is closer. The *Pepper v Hart* difficulties do not arise.[405] Similarly, the Explanatory Note attached to a statutory instrument[406] can

---

[400] A full rebuttal of such objections is provided by S. Vogenauer, "A Retreat from *Pepper v Hart*?" (2005) 25 O.J. L.S. 629 and P. Sales, (2006) 26 O.J.L.S. 585.

[401] Compare the exclusion of estoppel from public law doctrine and the very restrictive circumstances in which a substantive legitimate expectation may arise.

[402] *Three Rivers District Council v Bank of England (No.2)* [1996] 2 All E.R. 363; *U v W (HM Attorney General, Intervener)* (unreported, November 27, 1996); such a point would probably now be made clear by reference to the explanatory note.

[403] See Bennion (2002), pp.578–579. Whether this is sufficient to constitute a "residual right" of the court to refer (*ibid.*) is, however, highly doubtful given the absence of discussion of the propriety of the reference and the strictures expressed in *Spath Holme*.

[404] Above, para.6–037.

[405] Lord Steyn in *R (on the application of Westminster City Council) v National Asylum Support Service* [2002] 1 W.L.R. 2956, paras [2]–[6] (the point was not mentioned by the other members. See R. Munday, (2006) 170 J.P. 124, who expresses concern on the ground, *inter alia*, that they may be misleading. The permissibility of referring to explanatory notes as part of the context was confirmed by the House in *R (on the application of Marper) v Chief Constable of South Yorkshire* [2004] 1 W.L.R. 2196: see Lord Steyn at para.[4], with whom the other members of the House agreed. Indeed "it has become common practice for their Lordships to ask to be shown the explanatory notes when issues are raised about the meaning of words used in an enactment": the Appellate Committee in *R v Mantila* [2004] 1 W.L.R. 3141, at para.[35].

[406] And presumably the Explanatory Memorandum prepared by the relevant government department. Reference was made to an EM in *R (on the application of British Waterways Board) v First Secretary of State* [2006] EWHC 1019 (Admin).

be referred to in identifying the mischief which it was attempting to remedy[407] and to help determine whether words were omitted from the instrument by mistake.[408]

A final thought is that the rarity of cases in which reference to *Hansard* solves the problem is itself disappointing, providing examples of situations where it would appear that those involved in the legislative process have not fully understood what they were doing.

F. PRESUMPTIONS

1. Presumptions of General Application; the Principle of Legality

There are various presumptions that may be applied in doubtful cases. These are **6–043** to be distinguished from the "presumptions of general application" whereby certain basic legal principles are presumed to apply unless excluded by express words or necessary implication.[409] These principles modify even unambiguous provisions. Examples include aspects of the *ultra vires* doctrine, such as natural justice and abuse of discretion, general principles of criminal liability, and the principle that no-one shall be allowed to gain an advantage from his or her own wrong. Striking illustrations of this last principle include *Re Sigsworth*,[410] where Clawson J. held that apparently unambiguous provisions as to the distribution of the residuary estate on an intestacy were not to be applied so as to enable a murderer to benefit from the victim's estate, and *R v Secretary of State for the Home Department, Ex p. Puttick*,[411] where Astrid Proll, who had achieved a marriage with a citizen of the UK and Colonies by the crimes of fraud, forgery and perjury, was held not to be entitled to registration as a United Kingdom citizen, notwithstanding the absolute terms of s.6(2) of the British Nationality Act 1948. She had entered the country under a false identity, and she had committed these crimes in satisfying the Registrar General that in her assumed identity she had been divorced and there was no impediment to the marriage, and in obtaining a marriage licence.

---

[407] See *Pickstone v Freemans plc* (above, para.6–037).

[408] *R (on the application of Confederation of Passenger Transport UK) v Humber Bridge Board* [2004] Q.B. 310. Although it was suggested in *Coventry and Solihull Waste Disposal Co Ltd v Russell (Valuation) Officer* [1999] 1 W.L.R. 2093, 2103, that this was only possible where the SI was ambiguous, it is submitted that the principle is not so limited.

[409] See above, para.6–001.

[410] [1935] Ch. 89.

[411] [1981] Q.B. 767. See also *R v Chief National Insurance Commissioners, Ex p. Connor* [1981] Q.B. 758 and the Forfeiture Act 1982. *Puttick* was held to be confined to a situation where the criminal behaviour achieved for the claimant the necessary precondition that entitled her to registration in *R (on the application of Hicks) v Secretary of State for the Home Department* [2005] EWHC 2818 (Admin): appeal dismissed, [2006] EWCA Civ 400. *Cf. R v Registrar-General, Ex p. Smith* [1991] 2 Q.B. 393, CA (similar principle applied where enforcement of an apparently clear statutory duty would facilitate crime resulting in danger to life); see A. P. Le Sueur, [1991] P.L. 326, noting that the decision ran counter to views expressed in standing committee on the provision in question.

In recent cases, many decided in the period running up to implementation of the Human Rights Act 1998, members of the House of Lords have sought to articulate a more general principle that explains and justifies this approach to the relationship between common law and statute. In *R v Secretary of State for the Home Department, Ex p. Pierson*[412] the House of Lords by a majority,[413] and on a variety of grounds, held that the Secretary of State had acted unlawfully in increasing the tariff element of a mandatory life sentence with retrospective effect. Lord Steyn noted that the Home Secretary's powers were wide and general; there was no ambiguity in the statutory language so as to engage the presumption against the invasion of common law rights.[414] However, a

> "broader principle applies. Parliament does not legislate in a vacuum. Parliament legislates for a European liberal democracy founded on the principles and traditions of the common law. And the courts may approach legislation on this initial assumption. But this assumption only has prima facie force. It can be displaced by a clear and specific provision to the contrary."[415]

This is the "principle of legality" and protects both procedural safeguards provided in the common law (such as natural justice) and substantive basic or fundamental rights (such as the right of access to the court[416]; the principle that a sentence may not retrospectively be increased[417]; the presumption that a statutory offence requires a mental element[418]; the right to family life[419] and the principle of equality[420]). "Unless there is the clearest provision to the contrary Parliament must be presumed not to legislate contrary to the rule of law."[421] Lord Steyn reiterated this approach in the context of subordinate legislation in *R v Secretary of State for the Home Department, Ex p. Simms*,[422] this time with the express concurrence of Lords Browne-Wilkinson and Hoffmann. The House held unanimously that a general ban on interviews between prisoners and journalists who refused to undertake not to publish any part of the interviews was unlawful. The principle of legality required an express indication to justify this interference with the fundamental and basic right asserted by the prisoners, here the right to seek through oral interviews to persuade a journalist to investigate the safety of the conviction and to publicise his or her findings in an effort to gain justice for the prisoner. There was no such indication.[423] Lord Hoffmann put it this way[424]:

---

[412] [1998] A.C. 539.
[413] Lords Steyn, Hope and Goff, Lords Browne-Wilkinson and Lloyd dissenting.
[414] See below, para.6–045.
[415] [1998] A.C. 539, 587–590, citing Cross (1995), pp.142–143. See also Lord Browne-Wilkinson at pp.573–576, relying on the presumption that Parliament does not intend to change the common law without clearly expressing that intention: below, para.6–045.
[416] *Raymond v Honey* [1983] 1 A.C. 1.
[417] [1998] A.C. 539.
[418] *B. (a minor) v DPP* [2000] 2 A.C. 428, 460 (*per* Lord Nicholls); *R v K* [2002] 1 A.C. 462.
[419] *R v Secretary of State for the Home Department, Ex p. Montana* [2001] 1 W.L.R. 552.
[420] *Matadeen v Pointu* [1999] 1 A.C. 98, PC; *Hall & Co v Simons* [2002] 1 A.C. 615.
[421] [1998] A.C. 539, 591.
[422] [2000] 2 A.C. 115.
[423] *ibid.* p.130.
[424] *ibid.* p.131.

"Parliamentary sovereignty means Parliament can, if it chooses, legislate contrary to fundamental principles of human rights. The Human Rights Act 1998 will not detract from this power. The constraints upon its exercise by Parliament are ultimately political, not legal. But the principle of legality means that Parliament must squarely confront what it is doing and accept the political cost. Fundamental rights cannot be overridden by general or ambiguous words. This is because there is too great a risk that the full implication of their unqualified meaning may have passed unnoticed in the democratic process. In the absence of express language or necessary implication to the contrary, the courts therefore presume that even the most general words were intended to be subject to the basic rights of the individual."

This principle is now regularly cited[425] and provides the approach to be adopted apart from reliance on the provisions of the Human Rights Act 1998,[426] although the view has also been expressed that it does not add much, if anything, to an individual's Convention rights.[427] It remains of particular significance, however, in so far as fundamental rights can be identified beyond those expressly dealt with in the European Convention. The concepts of "fundamental rights" and "Convention rights" are not coterminous.[428]

2. Presumptions for Use in Doubtful Cases

These have been termed "policies of clear statement"[429]; or "in effect announce-   **6–044** ments by the courts to the legislature that certain meanings will not be assumed unless stated with special clarity".[430] The courts have created a measure of protection for certain values by establishing a requirement that Parliament use clear words if they are to be compromised or overridden. There are many difficulties. The Law Commissions pointed out that there was no established order or precedence in the case of conflict between different presumptions; that the individual presumptions were often of doubtful status or imprecise in scope;

---

[425] See e.g. *B (a minor) v DPP* [2000] 2 A.C. 428; *McNally v Secretary of State for Education* [2001] EWCA Civ 332 (express right of education officer to attend disciplinary hearing to be regarded as subject to overriding requirements of natural justice: *per* Dyson L.J.); *R v Special Commissioner, Ex p. Morgan Grenfell Ltd* [2001] S.T.C. 497 (right to legal professional privilege a fundamental right but overridden by necessary implication); *R (on the application of Anufrijeva) v Secretary of State for the Home Department* [2004] 1 A.C. 604 (principle that a decision takes effect only on communication represents elementary fairness and can only be overridden expressly or by necessary implication); *R (on the application of Roberts) v Parole Board* [2005] UKHL 45, [2005] 2 A.C. 738.

[426] Below, Ch.8.

[427] *R v Secretary of State for the Home Department, Ex p. Montana* [2001] 1 W.L.R. 522 at para.[15]. Lord Hoffmann in *Ex p. Simms* regarded s.3 of the 1998 Act as the express enactment as a rule of construction of the principle of legality: [2000] 2 A.C. 115, 132.

[428] This point works both ways: a Convention right may not have a common law analogue: *R v Worcester County Council Ex p. SW* [2000] H.R.L.R. 702 (no common law right to private life).

[429] H. M. Hart and A. M. Sacks, cited in Law Com. No.21, p.21.

[430] Law Com. No.21, p.21.

that reference to a presumption was unnecessary where a court decided that the words are clear; and that there was no accepted test for resolving a conflict between a presumption, such as the presumption that penal statutes should be construed restrictively, and giving effect to the purpose of a statute, for example the purpose of factory legislation to secure safe working conditions.[431]

It is impossible to produce a definitive list of presumptions which may be applied. As the Law Commissions noted, particular presumptions may be "modified or even abandoned with the passage of time, and with the modification of the social values which they embody".[432] There is room for debate as to why certain values and not others are selected for protection, and differences of view among the judges as to the strength of the protection that ought to be accorded. For example, the presumptions concerned with protecting the existing property or money of individuals have been contrasted with the absence of any presumptions in favour of individuals claiming state benefits.[433] While there are authorities stressing in general terms the importance of protecting individual liberty,[434] and particular freedoms such as freedom of speech,[435] freedom of assembly[436] and freedom from physical restraint,[437] there have been comparatively few cases outside the last of these categories where full effect has been given to these factors.[438]

However, such cases would now be dealt with in accordance with the broader-based "principle of legality"[439] and the Human Rights Act 1998.[440] Some of the principles of interpretation that have already been mentioned are sometimes put in the form of a presumption, for example presumptions against "intending what is inconvenient or unreasonable" or "intending injustice or absurdity".[441] On the other hand, it has been suggested that now that there is a greater willingness to adopt a purposive approach to interpretation and that a wider view is taken of the context of particular provisions, "the role of presumptions in interpretation is necessarily less important than in the days of more literal interpretation".[442] Furthermore, the articulation in recent cases of an underlying principle of legality, applicable in all cases and not just cases of ambiguity, would seem to

---

[431] *ibid.* p.22.

[432] *ibid.* p.21. *Cf.* section (d) below.

[433] Cross (1995), p.194; *Presho v Department of Health and Social Security* [1984] A.C. 310; *Chief Adjudication Officer v Brunt* [1988] A.C. 711; *Riley v Chief Adjudication Officer (Note)* [1988] A.C. 746, CA.

[434] "Parliament is presumed not to enact legislation which interferes with the liberty of the subject without making it clear that this was its intention": *per* McCullough J. in *R v Hallstrom, Ex p. W* [1986] Q.B. 1090, 1104 (in the context of detention for treatment under the Mental Health Act 1983: see M. J. Gunn, [1986] J.S.W.L. 290)).

[435] e.g. Lord Reid in *Cozens v Brutus* [1973] A.C. 854, 862; Scarman L.J. in *Re F (orse A) (A Minor) (Publication of Information)* [1977] Fam. 58, 99.

[436] *cf. Beatty v Gillbanks* (1892) 9 Q.B.D. 308; Lord Denning M.R. (dissenting) in *Hubbard v Pitt* [1976] Q.B. 142, 178–179; *Hirst v Chief Constable of West Yorkshire* (1986) 85 Cr.App.R. 143.

[437] e.g. *R v Hallstrom, Ex. p. W,* n.434 above; *Collins v Wilcock* [1984] 1 W.L.R. 1172.

[438] Compare the above cases with, e.g., *Duncan v Jones* [1936] K.B. 218; *Thomas v Sawkins* [1935] 2 K.B, 249; *Liversidge v Anderson* [1942] A.C. 206.

[439] Above, para.6–043.

[440] Below, Ch.8. See for example *R (on the application of Laporte) v Chief Constable of Gloucestershire* [2006] UKHL 55, concerning freedoms of expression and assembly.

[441] See *Maxwell on Interpretation of Statutes* (12th edn, 1969), pp.199–212.

[442] Cross (1995), p.190.

occupy much (although not all) of the ground occupied by the specific presumptions set out in this section.[443]

(a) Presumptions against changes in the common law

This is one of the more controversial presumptions, given that modern legislation **6–045** may often be intended to change the common law or may deal with matters with which the common law was unconcerned, such as the "welfare state." Lord Reid formulated the presumption as follows in *Black-Clawson International Ltd v Papierwerke Waldhof-Aschaffenburg A.G.*[444]:

> "In addition to reading the Act you look at the facts presumed to be known to Parliament when the Bill which became the Act in question was before it, and you consider whether there is disclosed some unsatisfactory state of affairs which Parliament can properly be supposed to have intended to remedy by the Act. There is a presumption which can be stated in various ways. One is that in the absence of any clear indication to the contrary, Parliament can be presumed not to have altered the common law further than was necessary to remedy the 'mischief'. Of course it may and quite often does go further. But the principle is that if the enactment is ambiguous, that meaning which relates the scope of the Act to the mischief should be taken rather than a different or wider meaning which the contemporary situation did not call for."

In *Leach v R*[445] a provision that a spouse of a defendant "may" be called as a witness was held not to overturn the common law rule that a wife was not *compellable*; it merely made her a *competent* witness. In *Beswick v Beswick*[446] the House of Lords refused to interpret s.56 of the Law of Property Act 1925 in such a way as to overturn the doctrine of privity of contract. A more doubtful use of the presumption was made in *Chertsey Urban District Council v Mixnam's Properties Ltd*[447] where the House held that a power for a local authority to attach "such conditions as . . . [it] may think it necessary or desirable to impose" to a caravan site licence could only be used to impose conditions relating to the use of the land: conditions by which the authority sought to protect the interests of tenants were held to be *ultra vires*.

(b) Presumption against ousting the jurisdiction of the courts

The courts have generally looked with disfavour upon Parliament's attempts to **6–046** oust their jurisdiction. Such attempts have been particularly common in the administrative law context,[448] where "exclusion clauses" have been construed

---

[443] Particularly, for example, the presumption against interference with access to the courts or vested rights and against the retrospective operation of legislation.

[444] [1975] A.C. 591, 614.

[445] [1912] A.C. 305; Criminal Evidence Act 1898, s.4(1). See now the Police and Criminal Evidence Act 1984, s.80, as amended.

[446] [1968] A.C. 58, See above, para.6–033.

[447] [1965] A.C. 745.

[448] See de Smith, Woolf and Jowell, *Judicial Review of Administrative Action* (5th edn, 1995), pp.231–249; Sir William Wade and C. F. Forsyth, *Administrative Law* (9th edn, 2004), pp.712–727.

narrowly[449] or evaded.[450] It is notable that where the courts have given effect to an "exclusion clause" the clause has only purported to oust their jurisdiction after a six-week period.[451]

(c) Presumption against interference with vested rights

6-047 If there is any ambiguity it is presumed that, "the legislature does not intend to limit vested rights further than clearly appears from the enactment".[452] This is so whether the legislation is prospective or retrospective.[453] There is some uncertainty as to when rights are to be regarded as vested, and it has been suggested that "the courts have tended to attach the somewhat woolly label 'vested' to those rights which they conclude should be protected from the effect of the new legislation".[454] There is an associated presumption that proprietary rights are not to be taken away without compensation.[455] It has been suggested that where the words are ambiguous, they should be construed in such a way as will cause less interference with existing rights notwithstanding that there are indications that that Parliament intended a more "stringent" meaning.[456]

However,

> "judges are bound to administer the law as it is, not as they would like it to be. If Parliament, in its wisdom, chooses to legislate in a way which clearly does infringe individual rights, the court is bound to give effect, however unwillingly, to such legislation."[457]

(d) Strict construction of penal laws in favour of the citizen

6-048 Laws which impose criminal or other penalties are strictly construed, so that if the words are ambiguous and there are two reasonable interpretations, the more

---

[449] e.g. where a statute provides that a decision shall be "final", that is read as meaning only that there is no right of *appeal*: the remedy of certiorari is not excluded: *R v Medical Appeal Tribunal, Ex p. Gilmore* [1957] 1 Q.B. 574; *cf. Ex p. Waldron* [1986] Q.B. 824.

[450] e.g. a provision that a "determination by the Commission . . . shall not be called in question in any court of law" was held not to exclude proceedings for judicial review where the "determination" was *ultra vires* and a nullity, and thus not a "determination" at all: *Anisminic Ltd v Foreign Compensation Commission* [1969] 2 A.C. 147 (Foreign Compensation Act 1950, s.4(4)); *cf. Att.-Gen. v Ryan* [1980] A.C. 718.

[451] *Smith v East Elloe Rural District Council* [1956] A.C. 585; *R v Secretary of State for the Environment, Ex p. Ostler* [1977] Q.B. 122; Wade and Forsyth (2004), pp.727–739. Rather inconsistently, effect in excluding judicial review has been accorded to a "conclusive evidence" provision: *R v Registrar of Companies, Ex p. Central Bank of India* [1986] Q.B. 1114.

[452] *Per* Ungoed-Thomas J. in *Re Metropolitan Film Studios Application* [1962] 1 W.L.R. 1315, 1323.

[453] *Wilson v First County Trust Ltd (No.2)* [2004] 1 A.C. 816, *per* Lord Rodger of Earlsferry at para.[193]–[197]. As to the separate presumption against retrospective legislation, see para.6–049.

[454] *ibid.*

[455] *Belfast Corporation v O.D. Cars Ltd* [1960] A.C. 490; *cf. Westminster Bank Ltd v Beverley Borough Council* [1971] A.C. 509.

[456] *per* Winn L.J. *obiter* in *Allen v Thorn Electrical Industries Ltd* [1968] 1 Q.B. 487.

[457] *per* Sir Nicolas Browne-Wilkinson in *E.M.I. Records Ltd v Spillane* [1986] 1 W.L.R. 967, 973, in the course of holding that the Customs and Excise Commissioners had wide powers under the VAT legislation to require the production of documents, which powers were "distasteful to those trained in the law" (*ibid*). See also *Secretary of State for Defence v Guardian Newspapers Ltd* [1985] A.C. 339, *per* Lord Scarman at pp.362–363.

lenient one will be given.[458] Thus, the provision that "all lotteries are unlawful" was not interpreted as creating a criminal offence.[459] A provision penalising the personation at an election of "any person entitled to vote" was held not to apply to a person who personated a deceased voter.[460] Other examples are *R v Harris*[461] and *London and North Eastern Railway Co v Berriman*.[462] It has, however, been suggested that while the courts still pay lip service to this principle, it is rarely applied in practice if there are social reasons for convicting.[463] In *Anderton v Ryan*[464] the House of Lords adopted a restrictive, and purportedly "purposive", reading of s.1 of the Criminal Attempts Act 1981, so that it would not apply to some forms of impossible attempts. In so doing they took insufficient account of the Law Commission Report that led to the 1981 Act,[465] and introduced "confusion and uncertainty".[466] Their Lordships regarded some results of a broad reading of the section as absurd, and Lord Bridge found it surprising that Parliament, if intending to do so, "should have done so by anything less than the clearest express language".[467] Following devastating academic criticism,[468] the House of Lords overruled *Anderton v Ryan* in *R v Shivpuri*.[469]

A court will be particularly unwilling to exercise its limited power to alter the statutory language so as to give a purposive construction[470] where the statute is a penal one and the consequence the defendant's conviction.[471] Similarly, it will not normally (if ever) be appropriate to rely on *Pepper v Hart* to resolve an ambiguity in a penal statute against a citizen.[472]

Statutes giving the police a power of arrest are not regarded as "penal laws" for this purpose[473]:

---

[458] *per* Lord Esher in *Tuck & Sons v Priester* (1887) 19 Q.B.D. 629, 638; *R v Allen* [1985] A.C. 1029, 1034; *R v Clarke* [1985] A.C. 1037, 1048, 1053; but *cf. R v Caldwell* [1982] A.C. 341 where the House of Lords majority held that the word "reckless" was to be construed as an "ordinary English word" notwithstanding that this was contrary to: (1) the interests of the defendant; (2) the views of the Law Commission; and (3) established decisions of lower courts, and that it would cause great complexity in the law: see J. C. Smith, [1981] Crim. L.R. 393. *Caldwell* has now been overruled: para.7–027.

[459] Betting and Lotteries Act 1934: *Sales-Matic Ltd v Hinchcliffe* [1959] 1 W.L.R. 1005.

[460] Poor Law Amendment Act 1851, s.3: *Whiteley v Chappell* (1868) L.R. 4 Q.B. 147.

[461] Above, para.6–006.

[462] Above, para.6–012.

[463] Glanville Williams, *Textbook of Criminal Law* (2nd edn, 1983), pp.12–18; *cf. Fisher v Bell* (para.6–013 above); *R v Ottewell* [1970] A.C. 642, 649; *R v Bloxham* [1983] 1 A.C. 109, 114; *Attorney-General's Reference (No.1 of 1988)* [1989] A.C. 971, 991; *R v Z (Attorney General for Northern Ireland's Reference)* [2005] 2 A.C. 645 (principle did not prevent the House concluding that proscription of the "Irish Republican Army" under by the Terrorism Act 2000 extended to the "Real IRA").

[464] [1985] A.C. 560.

[465] Law Com. No.102.

[466] J. C. Smith, [1985] Crim. L.R. 504.

[467] [1985] A.C. 560, 583.

[468] Most notably by Glanville Williams, "The Lords and Impossible Attempts or *Quis Custodiet Ipsos Custodes?*" [1986] C.L.J. 33, acknowledged by Lord Bridge in *R v Shivpuri* [1987] A.C. 1, 23. See below, para.7–027.

[469] [1987] A.C. 1: see J. R. Spencer, [1986] C.L.J. 361; P. R. Glazebrook, [1986] C.L.J. 363 (noting that the decision in *Shivpuri* involved modification of the statutory language).

[470] See para.6–010.

[471] *R (on the application of Haw) v Secretary of State for the Home Department* [2006] Q.B. 359, DC. But note that the Court of Appeal allowed an appeal on the basis that the words in question when read in context were clear.

[472] *Massey v Boulden* [2003] 1 W.L.R. 1792, *per* Simon Brown L.J. at paras [18]–[20].

[473] See above, para.6–014.

"no one doubts that a prime factor in the process of construction [of statutes conferring arrest powers] is a strong presumption in favour of the liberty of the innocent subject. But it is clear from the authorities at least that a statute may be held to have rebutted the presumption by something falling short of clear express language."[474]

(e) Presumption against retrospective operation

6–049   In *Re Athlumney*, R.S. Wright J. stated:

"Perhaps no rule of construction is more firmly established than this—that a retrospective operation is not to be given to a statute so as to impair an existing right or obligation, otherwise than as regards matter of procedure, unless that effect cannot be avoided without doing violence to the language of the enactment. If the enactment is expressed in language which is fairly capable of either interpretation, it ought to be construed as prospective only."[475]

Furthermore,

"it seems to me entirely proper, in a case where some retrospective operation was clearly intended, equally to presume that the retrospective operation of the statute extends no further than is necessary to give effect either to its clear language or to its manifest purpose."[476]

In *L'Office Cherifien des Phosphates v Yamashita-Shinnihon Steamship Co Ltd*,[477] the House of Lords emphasised, however, that the basis of the rule was "simple fairness". The question to what degree, if any, a particular provision has retrospective effect was to be determined not by reference to "generalised presumptions or maxims" but considering

"whether the consequences of reading the statute with the suggested degree of retrospectivity is so unfair that the words used by Parliament cannot have been intended to mean what they might appear to say."[478]

This question in turn was to be answered by weighing a series of factors, including the degree of retrospectivity suggested; the value and nature of the rights affected on which the retrospective legislation will impinge; the clarity of the language; and the circumstances in which the legislation was enacted. The distinction between substantive and procedural rights was misleading,

---

[474] *per* Lord Bridge in *Wills v Bowley* [1983] 1 A.C. 57, 101. It is difficult to see how such a presumption can be regarded as either "strong" or even much of a "presumption".

[475] [1898] 2 Q.B. 547, 551–552. See above, para.5–019.

[476] *per* Lord Bridge in *Arnold v Central Electricity Generating Board* [1988] A.C. 228, 275, in the course of holding that while the Limitation Act 1975 modified retrospectively the position as to limitation in respect of actions governed by the Law Reform (Limitation of Actions, etc.) Act 1954, as amended, it did not apply so as to defeat a right to plead a time bar that had accrued under the Limitation Act 1939. See also *Pearce v Secretary of State for Defence* [1988] A.C. 755.

[477] [1994] 1 A.C. 486, HL.

[478] *per* Lord Mustill at pp.524–525. The other members of the House agreed with Lord Mustill's speech.

"since it leaves out of the account the fact that some procedural rights are more valuable than some substantive rights."[479]

Moreover, it was doubtful whether it was "possible to assign rights such as the present unequivocally to one category rather than another". On this approach,[480] s.13A of the Arbitration Act 1950,[481] which conferred a new power on an arbitrator to dismiss a claim for want of prosecution where there had been "inordinate and inexcusable delay", was to be interpreted as enabling an arbitrator to take account of delays before the section came into force.

In *Waddington v Miah*[482] the House of Lords held that certain offences created by the Immigration Act 1971 were not intended to operate retrospectively. Lord Reid stated[483] that in view of the prohibitions contained in the Universal Declaration of Human Rights and the European Convention on Human Rights,[484] "it is hardly credible that any government department would promote or that Parliament would pass retrospective criminal legislation". The presumption was also relied on by the House of Lords in *Wilson v Secretary of State for Trade and Industry*[485] in the course of holding that in general the principle of interpretation in s.3(1) of the Human Rights Act 1998 does not apply to causes of action accruing before the section came into force.

On the other hand, in *Chebaro v Chebaro*[486] the Court of Appeal held that the right conferred by the Matrimonial and Family Proceedings Act 1984, s.12(1), to apply for financial relief where a marriage "has been dissolved" by proceedings overseas, applied to a decree pronounced before the commencement of the Act. The meaning of the words used, importing a retrospective effect, was "plain and unequivocal".[487]

(f) Presumption that statutes do not affect the Crown

It is presumed that the Crown is not bound by a statute unless reference is made to it expressly or by necessary implication: **6–050**

"Since laws are made by rulers for subjects a general expression in a statute such as 'any person', descriptive of those upon whom the statute imposes

---

[479] *per* Lord Mustill at p.528. See also *Yew Bon Tew v Kenderaan Bas Maria* [1983] 1 A.C. 553, where the Privy Council noted that an apparently "procedural" alteration, such as a change in limitation period, could affect existing rights and obligations; retrospective effect was denied to an extension in limitation period so as to affect an accrued right to plead a time bar. For other examples of cases where retrospective effect has been denied, see *Bonning v Dodsley* [1982] 1 W.L.R. 279; *Lewis v Lewis* [1986] A.C. 828; *Plewa v Chief Adjudication Officer* [1995] 1 A.C. 249. Retrospective effect was given to procedural changes in *Thompson v Thompson* [1986] Fam. 38 and *R v Makanjuola* [1995] 1 W.L.R. 1348, and, in view of clear words in the statute, to restrictions on right of appeal against a deportation order in *R v Secretary of State for the Home Department, Ex p. Mundowa* [1992] 3 All E.R. 606.

[480] Applied in *Antonelli v Secretary of State for Trade and Industry* [1998] Q.B. 948 (new power under Estate Agents Act 1979 to prohibit persons from acting as estate agents if they have a conviction for fraud, dishonesty or violence, exercisable in respect of pre-commencement convictions); and *Westminster City Council v Haywood (No.2)* [2000] 2 All E.R. 634.

[481] Inserted by the Courts and Legal Services Act 1990, s.102; in force from January 1, 1992.

[482] [1974] 1 W.L.R. 683.

[483] At p.694.

[484] See para.4–042.

[485] [2004] 1 A.C. 816. See para.8–016.

[486] [1987] Fam. 127.

[487] *per* Balcombe L.J. at p.131. See also *Williams v Williams* [1971] P. 271; *Powys v Powys* [1971] P. 340; *Hewitt v Lewis* [1986] 1 W.L.R. 444; *Hager v Osborne* [1992] Fam. 94.

obligations or restraints is not to be read as including the ruler himself."[488]

Questions may arise as to whether a particular institution is a servant or agent of the Crown and so within the "shield of the Crown".[489]

(g) Others

6–051 Other presumptions that may be invoked include the presumption that Parliament does not intend to violate international law,[490] and that a statute does not apply to acts committed abroad.[491]

G. REFORM

6–052 As mentioned above,[492] Parliament has refrained from intervening to give general directions to the judges as to methods of statutory interpretation. The Law Commissions saw their report on *The Interpretation of Statutes*[493] as a contribution to the process of educating judges and practitioners, and only proposed a limited degree of statutory intervention. They appended draft clauses. The first[494] provided that in ascertaining the meaning of any provision of an Act, the matters which may be considered include: (a) all indications provided by the Act as printed by authority, including punctuation, side-notes and short title; (b) any relevant report of a body presented or made to Parliament; (c) any relevant treaty or other international agreement; (d) any other Command Paper bearing on the subject matter of the legislation; and (e) any other document declared by the Act to be a relevant document for the purposes of the section. The weight to be given is "no more than is appropriate in the circumstances". The second provided:

> "2.—The following shall be included among the principles to be applied in the interpretation of Acts, namely—
>
> > (a) that a construction which would promote the general legislative purpose underlying the provision in question is to be preferred to a construction which would not; and

---

[488] *per* Diplock L.J. in *BBC v Johns* [1965] Ch. 32, 78; *cf.* Wrottesley J. in *Att.-Gen v Hancock* [1940] 1 All E.R. 32, 34. *Lord Advocate v Dumbarton District Council* [1990] 2 A.C. 580 (noted by J. Wolffe, [1990] P.L. 14); O. Hood Phillips and P. Jackson, *Constitutional and Administrative Law* (8th edn, 2001), pp.318–320. The Crown may rely on any statutory defence that would be available to a private party: Crown Proceedings Act 1947, s.31(1). See generally, P. W. Hogg, *Liability of the Crown* (2nd edn, 1990); P. Jackson, [1990] Denning L.J. 45.

[489] See, e.g. *Tamlin v Hannaford* [1950] 1 K.B. 18; *Town Investments Ltd v Department of the Environment* [1978] A.C. 359; *British Medical Association v Greater Glasgow Health Board* [1989] A.C. 1211.

[490] See above, para.6–036.

[491] See above, para.5–018.

[492] para.6–002.

[493] Law Com. No.21; Scot. Law Com. No.11 (1969).

[494] Clause 3 provided for the application of the first two clauses to subordinate legislation; cl.4 provided for a presumption that breach of a statutory duty should be actionable at the suit of any person who sustains damage.

(b) that a construction which is consistent with the international obligations of Her Majesty's Government in the United Kingdom is to be
preferred to a construction which is not."

These were approved in part by the Renton Committee[495] but attempts by Lord
Scarman to introduce Bills based on the proposals failed.[496]

In so far as the proposed provisions reflect current practice they seem superfluous; the few that go beyond it, such as the use of official reports and White
Papers, have been controversial, but have been overtaken by the relaxation in the
prohibition against reference to Parliamentary materials achieved by the
judges.[497] Clause 1(c) would have the effect of disapproving the restrictive
approach adopted in *Ellerman Lines v Murray*,[498] and as such would be useful,
but that decision has been largely outflanked, and might well be reconsidered by
the House of Lords if the occasion were to rise. Overall, the enactment of these
proposals would make little difference in practice.

The Renton Committee's recommendation that the preparation of a new
Interpretation Act should be put in hand eventually led to the Interpretation Act
1978, a consolidation measure with minor changes incorporating Law Commission proposals. This is an aid to drafting rather than interpretation.[499] "At the
level of general principles ... the subject does not lend itself to
legislation".[500]

H. THE INTERPRETATION OF COMMUNITY LEGISLATION

1. METHODS OF INTERPRETATION

Close attention has been paid to the methods of interpretation of Community **6–053**
legislation adopted by the Court of Justice of the European Communities.[501] A
number of different techniques have been identified, to which commentators have
attached a variety of labels. The Court has consistently shown that it is more
likely to be influenced by the *context*[502] and *purposes*[503] of a legislative provision
than its exact *wording*[504] or the subjective intentions of those who promulgated

---

[495] Cmnd. 6053, 1975, pp.139–148. See above, para.5–009.
[496] See Miers and Page (2nd edn, 1990), pp.176–180.
[497] See above, paras 6–037—6–041.
[498] [1931] A.C. 126; above, para.6–035, n.295.
[499] Above, para.5–020.
[500] Cross (1995), p.191. Courts of Commonwealth countries where declarations of general principles
of interpretation have been enacted seem rarely to refer to them in practice: W. A. Leitch, [1980]
Stat. L.R. 5, 8.
[501] See the *Reports of the Judicial and Academic Conference*, Court of Justice of the European
Communities, September 27–28, 1976; A. Bredimas, *Methods of Interpretation and Community
Law* (1978); L. N. Brown and T. Kennedy, *The Court of Justice of the European Communities* (5th
edn, 2000), Ch.14; R. Plender, "The Interpretation of Community Acts by Reference to the
Intentions of the Authors" [1982] 2 Y.E.L. 57; T. Millett, [1989] Stat. L.R. 163; S. Weatherill and
P. Beaumont, *EU Law* (3rd edn, 1999), pp.184–201.
[502] "Contextual" or "Schematic" interpretation.
[503] "Purposive" or "teleological" interpretation.
[504] "Literal" interpretation.

the legislation.[505] The extent to which the Court's overall approach differs from the so-called "common law" approach of English judges is debatable. It has also probably been exaggerated.[506] Certainly the ideas underlying the various techniques of interpretation adopted by the Court are more familiar than some of the labels. It should also be noted that the techniques tend to be employed cumulatively rather than as alternatives.[507]

The process of interpretation must obviously commence with an analysis of the text. However, literal interpretation, in so far as that implies an exclusive or predominant concern with wording and grammar, is not favoured. The Court has shown little inclination to hold that words carry one "plain", "ordinary" or "clear" meaning so that considerations of context and purpose are rendered irrelevant. There are several reasons for this.

(a) The method of drafting

6–054   Many of the key provisions of the EC and Euratom Treaties are drafted in general terms, and with no "definition sections". For example, Art.23 EC (ex Art.9) refers to the prohibition between Member States of customs duties and "all charges having equivalent effect". Article 82 EC (ex Art.86) prohibits the "abuse by one or more undertakings of a dominant position within the common market or in a substantial part of it". It gives four examples of an "abuse" but no indication of what is meant by "dominant position". These concepts are left to be developed by the Community institutions, including the Court. The ECSC Treaty was and Community secondary legislation is in general more tightly drafted, but they still, inevitably, employ broad terms.

(b) Languages

6–055   The texts of the EC, Euratom and EU Treaties and all Community secondary legislation are published in several languages, each of which is equally authentic.[508] Arguments based on the exact wording of any one version are accordingly less compelling; it can never have been intended that Community law applies differently in different Member States. In cases of doubt it may be necessary to consider all the versions in the light, as ever, of context and purposes. For example, in *Stauder v City of Ulm*[509] the Court considered a decision of the Commission on the sale of butter at reduced prices to persons in receipt of welfare benefits. The German and Dutch versions provided that the butter had to be exchanged for a "coupon indicating [the recipients'] names". A German citizen argued that this was an infringement of fundamental rights. The Court found that the French and Italian versions referred to a "coupon referring to the person concerned", and preferred this more liberal wording. The objective of the decision could be achieved by methods of identification other than names.

---

[505] "Historical" or "subjective" interpretation.

[506] P. Dagtoglou, "The English Judges and European Community Law" [1978] C.L.J. 76.

[507] There is, for example, no place for a "today's the day for the teleological rule" approach.

[508] The only authentic text of the ECSC Treaty was French. The other two basic Treaties and the TEU are authentic in 23 languages (no separate language is specified for Austria, Belgium, Cyprus and Luxembourg) (see Arts 314 EC, 225 EAEC, 53 EU, as amended by the Accession Treaty for Bulgaria and Romania). Secondary legislation is authentic in all of these except Irish.

[509] Case 29/69, [1969] E.C.R. 419.

(c) The status of the Court

The Court is in a stronger position in relation to the other Community institutions **6–056** than a national court in relation to its national parliament. Legislation is not promulgated by an elected body alone, but by the nominated Commission and Council or by the Council and European Parliament acting jointly. The Court is expressly enjoined to "ensure that in the interpretation and application of this Treaty the law is observed"[510] and is expressly empowered to review the legality of acts of the Council and Commission.[511] It is placed on an equal footing with the other institutions in Art.7 EC (ex Art.4). Moreover, it has proved more difficult than expected for the Council to agree upon legislative proposals placed before it by the Commission. The resultant "legislative short-fall" has compelled the Court to determine questions of interpretation, and to fill gaps, in the light of the general aims of the Community and general principles of law. To an extent it has been forced to adopt a legislative role, and has not felt the need to disguise it.[512]

The Court's position in relation to the Member States is more problematic. There is an inevitable tension between the Community's harmonisation aims and the perceived interests of individual Member States. The Court could have adopted a position of neutrality; instead it has chosen to take a "partisan" line in favour of the achievement of the aims of the Community, as a kind of counter-weight to the Council of Ministers, which has tended more to reflect state interests. Member States are indeed expressly required by Art.10 EC (ex Art.5) to take all appropriate measures to fulfil obligations arising out of the Treaty or acts of Community institutions, to facilitate the achievement of the Community's tasks and to abstain from any measure that could jeopardise the attainment of the objectives of the Treaty.

(d) Community purposes

The freedom of the Court to adopt a purposive approach is naturally facilitated **6–057** by the express statement of the Community's aims and objectives included in the Treaties (including their preambles). Articles 2 and 3 EC (ex Arts 2 and 3)[513] provide:

"Article 2

The Community shall have as its task, by establishing a common market and **6–058** an economic and monetary union and by implementing common policies or activities referred to in Articles 3 and 4 to promote throughout the Community a harmonious, balanced and sustainable development of economic activities, a high level of employment and of social protection, equality between men and women, sustainable and non- inflationary growth, a high degree of competitiveness and convergence of economic performance, a high level of protection and improvement of the quality of the environment,

---

[510] Art.220 EC (ex Art.164).

[511] Art.230 EC (ex Art.173) Above, para.5–061.

[512] Note, for example, the enunciation of a rule with *prospective* effect only in the second *Defrenne* case: Case 43/75, [1976] E.C.R. 455.

[513] As substituted by Art.G (2), (3)/TEU and amended by the Treaty of Amsterdam. Art.4 provides for economic and monetary union.

the raising of the standard of living and quality of life, and economic and social cohesion and solidarity among Member States.

Article 3

6–059   (1) For the purposes set out in Article 2, the activities of the Community shall include, as provided in this Treaty and in accordance with the timetable set out therein:

(a) the prohibition, as between Member States, of customs duties and quantitative restrictions on the import and export of goods, and of all other measures having equivalent effect;

(b) a common commercial policy;

(c) an internal market characterized by the abolition, as between Member States, of obstacles to the free movement of goods, persons, services and capital;

(d) measures concerning the entry and movement of persons as provided for in Title IV;

(e) a common policy in the sphere of agriculture and fisheries;

(f) a common policy in the sphere of transport;

(g) a system ensuring that competition in the internal market is not distorted;

(h) the approximation of the laws of Member States to the extent required for the functioning of the common market;

(i) the promotion of co-ordination between employment policies of the Member States with a view to enhancing their effectiveness by developing a co-ordinated strategy for employment;

(j) a policy in the social sphere comprising a European Social Fund;

(k) the strengthening of economic and social cohesion;

(l) a policy in the sphere of the environment;

(m) the strengthening of the competitiveness of Community industry;

(n) the promotion of research and technological development;

(o) encouragement for the establishment and development of trans-European networks;

(p) a contribution to the attainment of a high level of health protection;

(q) a contribution to education and training of quality and to the flowering of the cultures of the Member States;

(r) a policy in the sphere of development cooperation;

(s) the association of the overseas countries and territories in order to increase trade and promote jointly economic and social development;

(t) a contribution to the strengthening of consumer protection;

(u) measures in the spheres of energy, civil protection and tourism:

(2) In all the activities referred to in this Article, the Community shall aim to eliminate inequalities, and to promote equality, between men and women."

Moreover, the reasons on which regulations, directives and decisions are based are stated in a preamble. The Court has attached much more importance to these express statements of purpose than to attempts to discern from other sources the subjective intentions of the authors of Community legislation.[514] Indeed, the details of the negotiations leading up to the Treaties and of debates within the Council and Commission concerning secondary legislation have not been published.[515] There have been occasional references by Advocates General to a statement made by the government of a Member State to the national parliament in the course of a ratification debate, but not to the exclusion of other considerations.[516]

In relation to purposive interpretation reference has been made to the so-called "rule of effectiveness" (*régle de l'effet utile*), a concept borrowed from international law. This means that, "preference should be given to the construction which gives the rule its fullest effect and maximum practical value".[517] This concept has been used as a justification for holding that the Community or one of its institutions has certain "implied powers", such as the power to require the repayment of a state aid granted in breach of the Treaty.[518] Similarly, in the *E.R.T.A. Case*[519] it was held that the Community had the implied power to establish treaty relations with non-Member States. The Court argued that it was the "necessary effect" or "consequence" of the making of a regulation on the harmonisation of provisions in the road transport field that the Community assume the exclusive right to conclude international agreements relating to the same subject matter.

(e) Context

References by the Court to the purposes of the Community are commonly closely **6–060** associated with arguments that seek to place the provision to be interpreted in the context of relevant rules of Community law. The Court may refer to the "general scheme of the Treaty", or to other treaty provisions in the relevant Part or to general principles of Community law. In the case of secondary legislation reference will be made to the enabling provisions in the Treaty.

(f) Examples

Striking examples of the Court's dynamic approach to interpretation are provided **6–061** by its decisions already discussed on the direct effectiveness of treaty provisions and secondary legislation, and the supremacy of Community law.[520] Another good example is the *Continental Can* case.[521] A New York company (Continental

---

[514] In Case 136/79, *National Panasonic (UK) Ltd v Commission* [1980] E.C.R. 2033, A. G. Warner argued that statements by individual members of the Council, the European Parliament, the Commission or the Commission's staff could not be relied upon for guidance as to the meaning of a Council Regulation (pp.2066–2067). See generally Plender (1982) *op. cit.* n.501 above.

[515] In Case C-292/89, *R v Immigration Appeal Tribunal, Ex p. Antonissen* [1991] E.C.R. I-745, the Court held that a declaration made by the Council at the time of adoption of certain secondary legislation, and disclosed by the Council for the purposes of litigation, could not be used for the purposes of interpretation as the content of the declaration was not referred to in the wording of the legislation.

[516] See e.g. Case 6/60, *Humblet v Belgium* [1960] E.C.R. 559.

[517] H. Kutcher, *Conference Reports* (see n.501 above), I–41.

[518] e.g. Case 70/72, *Commission v Germany* [1973] E.C.R. 829.

[519] Case 22/70, *Commission v Council* (E.R.T.A.) [1971] E.C.R. 263.

[520] The *van Gend en Loos* case, above, para.5–040 *Costa v E.N.E.L.*, above, para.5–054.

[521] Case 6/12, *Europemballage Corporation and Continental Can Co Inc v Commission* [1973] E.C.R. 215.

Can) held, through a German subsidiary (SLW), what the Commission determined to be a dominant position over a substantial part of the common market in meat tins, fish tins and metal closures for glass jars. Subsequently, acting through a Belgian subsidiary (Europemballage), Continental Can acquired a Dutch firm (TDV) which specialised in similar products. The Commission decided that the merger amounted to an abuse of the dominant position mentioned above, as the effect was practically to eliminate competition in the relevant products. The ECSC treaty expressly provided for merger control (Art.66); the EEC Treaty did not. Nevertheless, the Court held that a merger could in principle amount to an abuse of a dominant position contrary to Art.86 of the EC Treaty (now Art.82 EC), although it did not do so on the facts of the case. In so deciding the Court stated that it was necessary "to go back to the spirit, general scheme and wording of Art.86, as well as to the system and objectives of the Treaty".[522] It referred to the original version of Arts 2 and 3(f),[523] and to Art.85 of the EC Treaty (now Art.81 EC), which prohibited:

"all agreements between undertakings, decisions by associations of undertakings and concerted practices which may affect trade between Member States and which have as their object or effect the prevention, restriction or distortion of competition within the common market. . . . "

The Court observed[524]:

"[I]f Article 3(f) provides for the institution of a system ensuring that competition in the common market is not distorted, then it requires *a fortiori* that a competition must not be eliminated. This requirement is so essential that without it numerous provisions of the Treaty would be pointless. Moreover, it corresponds to the precept of Article 2 of the Treaty. . . .
    . . . Articles 85 and 86 seek to achieve the same aim on different levels, that is, the maintenance of effective competition within the common market. The restraint of competition which is prohibited if it is the result of behaviour falling under Article 85, cannot become permissible by the fact that such behaviour succeeds under the influence of a dominant undertaking and results in the merger of the undertaking concerned."

In other words, the prohibition of certain acts when done in concert by separate undertakings was not to be evaded by merger of those undertakings.
    It is a matter of debate whether the Court has gone too far in its willingness to "fill gaps".[525] It is clearly obliged to make policy decisions given the points already made as to the broad terms of many key Treaty provisions and secondary legislation. It is not so clear that decisions that recognise an inherent jurisdiction in the Court outside the express heads of jurisdiction set out in the EC Treaty[526]

---

[522] *ibid.* p.243.
[523] Art.3(f) is now 3(g): above, para.6–059.
[524] p.244.
[525] See, e.g. Weatherill and Beaumont (1999), pp.193–201; H. Rasmussen, *On Law and Policy in the European Court of Justice* (1986) and (1988) 13 E.L. Rev. 28.
[526] Case C-2/88 Imm., *Zvartveld* [1990] E.C.R. I-3367 and I-4405 (order to Commission to send reports to a national court).

that are reached "despite textual indications to the contrary"[527] are justifiable.[528] That there are limits is illustrated by the decisions confirming that directives are not directly effective between private individuals.[529]

(g) Restrictive interpretation

Interpretation in the light of purposes and context does not necessarily mean that **6–062** such interpretation is "broad" or "liberal". Exceptions to general Community rules and derogations to Treaty obligations are restrictively interpreted. For example, the principle of the free movement of workers is subject to "limitations justified on grounds of public policy, public security or public health".[530] These limitations are strictly construed.[531] Restrictions may not be imposed unless the person's presence or conduct "constitutes a genuine and sufficiently serious threat to public policy",[532] and the requirements of public policy must affect "one of the fundamental interests of society",[533] although it is for the national authorities to determine whether the facts of a particular case fall within these principles.

2. GENERAL PRINCIPLES OF LAW[534]

The Court often refers to "general principles of law" derived from the national **6–063** laws of Member States.[535] These are regarded as part of "the law" of which the Court is to ensure observance.[536] They can be employed in the interpretation of Treaty provisions but cannot override them. In relation to secondary legislation and other acts of the institutions they are not so confined: a challenge to the legality of a measure may be based on breach of one of these principles.[537]

Examples include:

---

[527] e.g. Case 294/83, *Les Verts v European Parliament* [1986] E.C.R.1339 (action under Art.173 of the EC Treaty (now Art.230 EC) to review legality of act of Parliament admissible notwithstanding the absence of any reference to Parliament in Art.173 in its original form; Case C-70/88, *European Parliament v Council* [1990] E.C.R. I-2041, above, para.5–061.

[528] Weatherill and Beaumont, pp.197–201.

[529] Above, paras 5–044, 5–045.

[530] Art.39(3) EC (ex Art.48(3)); Directive 64/221/EEC.

[531] Case 41/74, *Van Duyn v Home Office* [1974] E.C.R. 1337, above, para.5–044; Case 67/74, *Bonsignore v Oberstadtdirektor Cologne* [1975] E.C.R. 297; Case 36/75, *Rutili v French Minister of the Interior* [1975] E.C.R. 1219; Case 30/77, *R v Bouchereau* [1977] E.C.R. 1999.

[532] Case 36/75, *Rutili* [1975] E.C.R. 1219, 1231.

[533] Case 30/77, *R v Bouchereau* [1977] E.C.R. 1999, 2014.

[534] L. N. Brown and T. Kennedy, *The Court of Justice of the European Communities* (5th edn, 2000), Ch.15; A. Arnull *et al.*, *Wyatt and Dashwood's European Union Law* (5th edn, 2006). T. C. Hartley, *The Foundations of European Community Law* (5th edn, 2003), Ch.5.

[535] They may also be derived from Treaty provisions.

[536] Art.220 EC (ex Art.164) above, para.6–056. See also Art.230 EC (ex Art.173), above, para. 5–061, which provides expressly that a Community act may be annulled for infringement of "any rule of law relating to its application". *Cf.* Art.288(2) EC (ex Art.215(2).

[537] See above, para.5–061.

— the principle of *proportionality*, which requires that:"the individual should
not have his freedom of action limited beyond the degree necessary for the
public interest"[538];

— the *audi alteram partem* principle of natural justice, which requires that
persons affected by an adverse decision be given an opportunity to make
representations[539];

— the principle of non-discrimination:"whereby comparable situations must not
be treated differently and different situations must not be treated in the same
way, unless such treatment is objectively justified"[540];

— the related principles of *legal certainty* and *legitimate expectation*, which
require, respectively, that: "those subject to the law should not be placed in
a situation of uncertainty as to their rights and obligations" and "those who
act in good faith on the basis of the law as it is or seems to be should not be
frustrated in their expectations".[541]

These "general principles" include respect for "fundamental rights",[542]
derived from national constitutions or from international conventions concerning
human rights, such as the European Convention on Human Rights.[543] This does
not mean that the Convention is part of Community law and so directly enforceable under the European Communities Act 1972: "the European Court does not
deal with fundamental rights in the abstract; it only deals with them if they arise
under Treaties and have a bearing on Community law questions".[544]

---

[538] A. G. de Lamothe in Case 11/70, *Internationale Handelsgesellschaft v EVSt.* [1970] E.C.R. 1125,
1147; *cf.* the *Rutili* case, above (requirement of a *genuine and sufficiently serious* threat to public
policy to justify interference with freedom of movement). The proportionality doctrine has not
generally been part of English domestic law (*R v Secretary of State for the Home Department, Ex
p. Brind* [1991] 1 A.C. 696), but this is now subject to the important qualifications that it is
applicable within the spheres of EC law and the Human Rights Act 1998.

[539] Case 11/74, *Transocean Marine Paint Association v Commission* [1974] E.C.R. 1063; *cf.* Case
136/79, *National Panasonic Ltd v Commission* [1980] E.C.R. 2033 (no need to give prior warning
of an investigation by Commission inspectors).

[540] Wyatt and Dashwood (2006), pp.249–250. See Case 20/71, *Sabbatini v European Parliament*
[1972] E.C.R. 345 (Council Regulation concerning expatriation allowances for employees of the
Parliament held invalid on the ground of sex discrimination).

[541] Wyatt and Dashwood (2006), p.244.

[542] T. C. Hartley, (1975–76) 1 E.L. Rev. 54; M. Dauses, (1985) 10 E.L. Rev. 398; S. O'Leary, (1995)
32 C.M.L. Rev. 519; J. Weiler, (1995) 32 C.M.L. Rev. 579; the *International Handels* case (n.538,
above).

[543] Case 4/73, *Nold v Commission* [1974] E.C.R. 491; the *Rutili* Case (n.531 above); Case 118/75
Watson and Belmann [1976] E.C.R. 1185; Case 136/79, *National Panasonic (UK) Ltd v Commission* [1980] E.C.R. 2033 (no infringement of the right of privacy guaranteed by Art.8(1) of the
European Convention: an investigation of a company's books without prior warning was held to
be justified as "necessary in a democratic society in the interests of . . . the economic well-being
of the country," within the one of the exceptions specified in Art.8(2)); Case 63/83, *Kirk* [1984]
E.C.R. 2689 (application of the principle that penal provisions may not have retrospective effect):
see N. Foster, (1985) 10 E.L. Rev. 276; Case C-185/95P, *Baustahlgewebe GmbH v Commission*
[1998] E.C.R. I-8417 (right to legal process within a reasonable period (*cf.* Art.6(1), ECHR)
applicable to proceedings by the Commission and before the Court of First Instance concerning
the imposition of fines by the Commission on an undertaking for infringement of Community
law). Respect for fundamental rights is also enshrined in Art.6 EU (with a procedure for
addressing recommendations to Member States, on suspending rights, enshrined in Art.7 EU.

[544] *Kaur v Lord Advocate* 1980 S.C. 319, 333 (Lord Ross, Court of Session (Outer House)).

3. INTERPRETATION BY ENGLISH COURTS

The approach that should be taken by English judges was considered by Lord **6–064**
Denning M.R. in *Bulmer v Bollinger*[545]:

> "Beyond doubt the English courts must follow the same principles as the
> European court. Otherwise there would be differences between the countries
> of the nine. . . . It is enjoined on the English courts by section 3 of the
> European Community Act 1972 . . .
>
> No longer must they examine the words in meticulous detail. No longer
> must they argue about the precise grammatical sense. They must look to the
> purpose or intent. To quote the words of the European court in the *Da Costa*
> case,[546] they must deduce 'from the wording and the spirit of the Treaty the
> meaning of the community rules'. They must not confine themselves to the
> English text. They must consider, if need be, all the authentic texts. . . . They
> must divine the spirit of the Treaty and gain inspiration from it. If they find
> a gap, they must fill it as best they can. They must do what the framers of
> the instrument would have done if they had thought about it. So we must do
> the same. Those are the principles, as I understand it, on which the European
> court acts."

The dangers of applying a strict literal interpretation to provisions of Community law are illustrated by *R v Henn*.[547] Article 28 EC (ex Art.30) prohibits the imposition of "quantitative restrictions on imports and all measures having equivalent effect". The Court of Appeal (Criminal Division) held that the ban on the importation of indecent or obscene material imposed by s.42 of the Customs Consolidation Act 1876 did not fall within Art.30 as it imposed a total prohibition rather than a mere restriction "measured by quantity". This view was, not, however, relied upon by counsel on appeal to the House of Lords, or in argument before the Court of Justice, as it was clearly contrary to a number of earlier decisions of the Court of Justice, and inconsistent with the purposes of the Community. As a matter of common sense, a complete prohibition on the free movement of goods is likely to be more questionable under Community law than a partial restriction. Lord Diplock said that this showed "the danger of an English court applying English canons of statutory construction".[548] It is submitted that the Court of Appeal's interpretation was excessively "literalist" even by English standards.

---

[545] [1974] Ch. 401, 425–426. See also the similar views expressed by Lord Denning M.R. in *Buchanan & Co Ltd v Babco Forwarding & Shipping (UK) Ltd* [1977] Q.B. 208, 213–214. His Lordship's attempt to apply the "European Method" of "filling gaps" to the interpretation of an international convention on the carriage of goods by road was resisted by the House of Lords: [1978] A.C. 141, 153 (Lord Wilberforce), 156 (Viscount Dilhorne) and 160 (Lord Salmon); *cf.* above, para.6–036. See also the doubts as to the propriety of "gap-filling" expressed by Nolan J. in *Yoga for Health Foundation v Customs and Excise Commissioners* [1984] S.T.C. 630.

[546] [1963] C.M.L.R. 224, 237.

[547] [1978] 1 W.L.R. 1031, CA; [1981] A.C. 850, E.C.J., HL; Case 34/79 [1979] E.C.R. 3795.

[548] [1981] A.C. at p.914. See also *R v Licensing Authority, Ex p. Smith, Kline & French Laboratories Ltd* [1990] 1 A.C. 64, 75 (Dillon L.J.), 84 (Balcombe L.J.) and 87 (Staughton L.J.) (need to adopt a purposive and not a semantic approach to the interpretation of EC directives). An appeal to the House of Lords was dismissed, the matter being determined by reference to English law: [1990] 1 A.C. 64, 90. See to the same effect the House of Lords in *Litster v Forth Dry Dock & Engineering Co Ltd* [1990] 1 A.C. 546 and *Shanning International Ltd (In Liquidation) v Rasheed Bank* [2001] UKHL 31, [2001] 1 W.L.R. 1462.

JUDICIAL PRECEDENT

A. INTRODUCTION[1]

7–001 One of the hallmarks of any good decision-making process is consistency: like cases should be treated alike. Consistency is not, however, always appropriate,

---

[1] See generally Sir Rupert Cross and J. W. Harris, *Precedent in English Law* (4th edn, 1991); L. Goldstein (ed.), *Precedent in Law* (1987) (note the bibliography at pp.249–273); C. Manchester and D. Salter, *Exploring the Law* (3rd edn, 2006).

as, for example, where a case is seen with the passage of time and changes of circumstance no longer to offer a just solution to a recurring problem. Moreover, there are always difficulties in determining whether two cases are truly "like". Nevertheless, unjustifiable inconsistency may lead to a sense of grievance on the part of those affected and to a reasonable suspicion that the people making the decisions do not know what they are about. One of the main functions of the superior courts of law is the authoritative determination of disputed questions of law. A court's decision is expected to be consistent with decisions in previous cases and to provide certainty for the future so that the parties and others may arrange their affairs in reliance on the court's opinion. These considerations are reflected in the English system of judicial precedent.

The decisions of judges must be reasoned, and the reasons will include propositions of law. A judge in a later case is bound to consider the relevant case law and will normally accept the propositions stated as correct unless there is good reason to disagree; in some circumstances he or she is required to accept them even if they are in his or her view obviously wrong. So all relevant precedents are to a greater or lesser extent "persuasive", and some of them may be "binding" under what is termed the doctrine of *stare decisis*.[2] The characteristic that an individual precedent may be binding is distinctive of common law systems. In continental systems based upon codes that are theoretically complete, judicial decisions are not, technically, sources of legal rules. They may, however, carry great persuasive weight, particularly where there is a trend of cases to the same effect, and they have been of great importance in the development of certain areas of the law.[3]

Under the English system, a proposition stated in or derived from case A is binding in case B if: (1) it is a proposition of law; (2) it forms part of the *ratio decidendi* of case A (the reason or ground upon which the decision is based); (3) case A was decided in a court whose decisions are binding on the court that is deciding case B; and (4) there is no relevant difference between cases A and B which renders case A "distinguishable". A precedent which is not binding may nevertheless be persuasive. These points are developed below. As we shall see, judges faced with a precedent that they do not like have a number of possible escape routes to explore, and there is for the litigant who can afford it the possibility of recourse to a higher court for a bad precedent to be overruled. The system seeks to balance the general benefits of consistency and certainty against the requirement of justice in individual cases.

On one view judges are seen as picking their way through dusty old volumes of law reports and loyally following the precedents without too much regard for the justice of the case. On another they are seen as paying lip service to the system, and "loyally" following all the precedents that they agree with; those that they do not agree with are distinguished on spurious grounds, or just ignored. These views lie at the extremes and contain elements of caricature as well as

---

[2] "Keep to what has been decided previously": Cross and Harris (1991), p.3. The term is most commonly used to refer to the common law notion of *binding* precedent (Cross and Harris (1991), p.100: "the general orthodox interpretation of *stare decisis* . . . is *stare rationibus decidendis* ('keep to the *rationes decidendi* of past cases').") Alternative possible usages are (1) broader: referring to the general desirability of conformity with past precedents (*cf.* Cross (1977), p.4), and (2) narrower: referring to the obligation to follow the *decision* (i.e. order of the court) in a past case that is not reasonably distinguishable, as distinct from the principle of law on which the decision was based (Cross and Harris (1991), pp.100–101).

[3] *ibid.* pp.10–15. R. David and J. Brierley, *Major Legal Systems in the World Today* (3rd edn, 1985), pp.133–149; R. David, *English Law and French Law* (1980), pp.21–26.

truth. It is not possible to make a useful generalisation about judicial behaviour in practice; there are variations in approach from judge to judge, and the same judge may even vary his or her position according to the nature of the case to be decided.[4]

The notion that judges ought generally to abide by relevant precedents developed over several centuries.[5] Blackstone wrote in the eighteenth century that it was "an established rule to abide by former precedents, where the same points come again in litigation . . . unless flatly absurd or unjust",[6] and Parke J. said in 1833[7]:

> "Our common-law system consists in the applying to new combinations of circumstances those rules of law which we derive from legal principles and judicial precedent; and for the sake of attaining uniformity, consistency and certainty, we must apply those rules, where they are not plainly unreasonable and inconvenient, to all cases which arise; and we are not at liberty to reject them, and to abandon all analogy to them, in those to which they have not yet been judicially applied, because we think that the rules are not as convenient and reasonable as we ourselves could have devised."

The practice of relying on precedents in equity was also established by the eighteenth century. The modern strict rules whereby a single precedent can be binding, and precedents can be binding even if "unreasonable and inconvenient", developed in the nineteenth and twentieth centuries. Important factors were the regularisation of and improvements in law reporting following the establishment of the Incorporated Council of Law Reporting[8] and the reorganisation of the courts with a clear hierarchical structure in the latter part of the nineteenth century.[9] The rule that appellate courts are normally bound by their own previous decisions was clearly established for the House of Lords in 1898[10] and for the Court of Appeal in 1944.[11]

B. PROPOSITION OF "LAW"

7–002 Decisions on questions of fact may not be cited as precedents.[12] The line between "law" and "fact" may, however, be difficult to draw. An issue is one of fact where it turns on the reliability or credibility of direct evidence, or on inferences

---

[4] See further above, paras 4–41—4–44.

[5] See C. K. Alien, *Law in the Making* (7th edn, 1964), pp.187–235, 380–382; T. Ellis Lewis, (1930) 46 L.Q.R. 207, 341, (1931) 47 L.Q.R. 411, (1932) 48 L.Q.R. 230; W. H. D. Winder, (1941) 57 L.Q.R. 245 (precedent in equity); G. J. Postema, "Some roots of our notion of precedent" and J. Evans, "Changes in the doctrine of precedent during the nineteenth century" in Goldstein (1987), Chs 1, 2.

[6] *Blackstone's Commentaries* 69, 70.

[7] *Mirehouse v Rennell* (1833) 1 Cl. & F. 527, 546.

[8] See below, para.7–039.

[9] See above, para.2–003.

[10] See below, para.7–026. It was changed in 1966.

[11] See below, paras 7–014—7–024.

[12] *Qualcast (Wolverhampton) Ltd v Haynes* [1959] A.C. 743. Otherwise, "the precedent system will die from a surfeit of authorities" (*per* Lord Somervell at p.758), or the judges might be "crushed under the weight of our own reports" (*per* Lord Denning at p.761).

from circumstantial evidence. For example, the fact that someone was driving at a high speed may be established by the testimony of a witness, or by inference from such evidence as tyre marks. More difficult are cases which raise an issue whether the facts found conform to a legal description. Such issues are sometimes classified as issues of fact. For example, whether conduct is "unreasonable," and so a breach of the duty of care for the purposes of the tort of negligence, is a question of fact. In *Baker v E. Longhurst & Sons Ltd*[13] Scrutton L.J. stated[14] that "if a person rides in the dark he must ride at such a pace that he can pull up within the limit of his vision ... ". This was treated as a proposition of law until the Court of Appeal ruled that it was not.[15] In *Qualcast (Wolverhampton) Ltd v Haynes*[16] the House of Lords held that a county court judge could not be bound by precedent to hold that an employer who failed to give instructions to an employee as to the use of protective clothing had been negligent.

Where a legal description contained in a statute is "an ordinary word of the English language" its application to the facts found may be held to be a question of fact, and not to be the subject of judicial definition or interpretation.[17] The judges are particularly inclined to classify questions as questions of fact where they wish to avoid the proliferation of authorities.[18] However, where words are used in an unusual sense, or a statute has to be "construed" or "interpreted" before it can be applied, a question of law is raised.[19] The construction of particular words in a contract similarly does not give rise to a binding decision on a point of law.[20]

C. DETERMINING THE RATIO DECIDENDI

1. *Ratio* and *Dictum*

A proposition of law can only be binding if it forms part of the *ratio decidendi*[21] (commonly shortened to *ratio*) of the case. **7–003**

---

[13] [1933] 2 K.B. 461.

[14] At p.468.

[15] *Tidy v Battman* [1934] 1 K.B. 319; *Morris v Luton Corporation* [1946] 1 K.B. 114; Lord Greene hoped that this "suggested principle" would "rest peacefully in the grave" (p.116). *Cf. Worsfold v Howe* [1980] 1 W.L.R. 1175.

[16] [1959] A.C. 743.

[17] See above, para.1–011.

[18] e.g. *R v Industrial Injuries Commissioner, Ex p. A.E.U. (No.2)* [1966] 2 Q.B. 31, 45, 48–49, *per* Lord Denning M.R., in relation to the expression "arising out of and in the course of his employment".

[19] Denning L.J. in *British Launderers' Association v Borough of Hendon Rating Authority* [1949] 1 K.B. 462, 411–472; Lord Reid in *Cozens v Brutus*, above, para.1–011.

[20] *per* May L.J. in *Ashville Investments Ltd v Elmer Contractors Ltd* [1989] Q.B. 488, 495 (construction of an arbitration clause); *Clarke v Newland* (unreported, December 21, 1988) (interpretation of restrictive covenant in a partnership agreement). In *Customs and Excise Commissioners v Le Rififi Ltd* [1995] S.T.C. 103, the Court of Appeal held that the same principle applied to the construction of a VAT assessment form.

[21] Usually pronounced "rayshio", although variants may be encountered in practice.

Sir Rupert Cross and J. W. Harris, in the leading English monograph on precedent, gives this description[22]:

> "The *ratio decidendi* of a case is any rule of law expressly or impliedly treated by the judge as a necessary step in reaching his conclusion, having regard to the line of reasoning adopted by him, or a necessary part of his direction to the jury."[23]

They also point out that a judge may adopt more than one line of reasoning leading to the same result, in which case there may be more than one *ratio*. A proposition of law stated by a judge that is not necessary for his or her conclusion is termed an *obiter dictum* or *dictum*.[24] It may, for example, be a proposition wider than is necessary for the facts of the case, or a proposition concerning some matter not raised in the case. Statements of law on points which are fully argued by counsel and considered by the judge, but which do not technically play any part in determining the result, are sometimes termed "judicial *dicta*".[25]

Conversely, where a court *assumes* a proposition of law to be correct without addressing its mind to it, the decision of that court is not binding authority for that proposition.[26] However, this rule "must only be applied in the most obvious of cases and limited with great care".[27] It will normally only apply where the point has not been expressly raised before the court and there has been no argument on it; it may, however, be the case that a point has not been argued but "scrutiny of the judgment indicates that the court's acceptance of the point went beyond mere assumption. Very little is likely to be required to draw that latter conclusion; because a later court will start from the position, encouraged by judicial comity, that its predecessor did indeed address all the matters essential for the decision".[28]

---

[22] *Precedent in English Law* (4th edn, 1991), p.72. This formulation was expressly endorsed by the Court of Appeal in *R (Kadhim) v Brent London Borough Council Housing Benefit Review Board* [2001] Q.B. 955.

[23] *cf.* the narrower definition proposed by N. MacCormick (in L. Goldstein (ed.), *Judicial Precedent* (1987), Ch.6, p.170): "A *ratio decidendi* is a ruling expressly or impliedly given by a judge which is sufficient to settle a point of law put in issue by the parties' arguments in a case, being a point on which a ruling was necessary to his justification (or one of his alternative justifications) of the decision in the case." It is narrower in that it refers to a "ruling" by the judge (so as to cover the interpretation of a statute rather than the statute itself where one is involved), and a requirement that it be necessary for the *justification* for the decision, rather than the decision itself.

[24] Not "an *obiter*". The plural is *obiter dicta*. For examples of cases where it has been held that a particular proposition was not necessary for the decision, see *Penn-Texas Corporation v Murat Anstalt (No.2)* [1964] 2 Q.B. 647, 661 (Lord Denning M.R.); *Re State of Norway's Application (No.2)* [1988] 3 W.L.R. 603, 618–620 (May L.J.), 629–631 (Balcombe L.J.), 646–649 (Woolf L.J.); *Rickless v United Artists Corp.* [1988] Q.B. 40; *Dunnachie v Kingston-upon-Hull City Council* [2005] 1 A.C. 226.

[25] Megarry J. in *Brunner v Greenslade* [1971] Ch. 993, 1002–1003.

[26] *R (on the application of Kadhim) v Brent London Borough Council Housing Benefit Review Board* [2001] Q.B. 955; applied in *Scrivens v Ethical Standards Officer* [2005] EWHC 529 (Admin). This principle, however, has not always been observed, e.g. in respect of the *Havana case*: see below, para.7–021.

[27] *per* Buxton L.J. in *Kadhim* at para.[40].

[28] *ibid.* It had previously been suggested that the matter turns on whether the court in the earlier case had "turned its mind to the point" and not on whether the point has been argued: *R v Charles* (1975) 63 Cr.App. R. 252, 259 (Bridge L.J.); *Meer v London Borough of Tower Hamlets* [1988] I.R.L.R. 399, 402 (Balcombe L.J.).

2. The Principle Enunciated by the Judge

The task of determining the *ratio* of a case can be complicated, and writers on the subject are not agreed as to how that task is approached by the judges in practice, or how, in theory, it should be approached.[29] It is impossible to assert with confidence that there is any one method of approach which is invariably adopted by the judges. The obvious starting point is the wording of the judgment in question. A judge in giving the reasons for his or her decision will normally indicate the proposition[30] of law upon which he or she regards the decision as based. He or she will explain why he or she thinks this proposition is correct, usually by referring to earlier authorities and showing that it makes good sense. These "explanations" or "justifications" must be distinguished from the proposition of law which they support, as only the latter can be part of the *ratio*.[31]

7–004

The proposition as enunciated by the judge has a good claim to be regarded as the *ratio*. For example, the editor of a published law report who endeavours to state the *ratio* in the headnote to the case, will frequently use actual sentences from the judgment. A judge in a later case will commonly summarise the effect of a case by citing a passage from the judgment, and saying that a particular sentence or passage sets out "the *ratio*". In many cases, the judge will be content to leave the matter there. However, it may be necessary for the judgment in the earlier case to be subjected to careful analysis (by academic commentators, by counsel, and ultimately by the judge) for the *ratio* to be determined.

In some cases, the rulings are "so embedded in the reasoning as to require minor grammatical reconstruction in order to obtain more explicitly stated forms of them".[32] There may be differing views as to whether a particular ruling was "necessary for the decision".[33] It may be unclear, where a number of different reasons are given for a decision, whether each is to be regarded as a *ratio*.[34] Further difficulties may arise from the differing levels of generality of language that may be used in the formulation of propositions of law: the *ratio* may subsequently be restated in wider or narrower form.[35]

---

[29] See, e.g. Cross and Harris (1991) Ch.2; A. L. Goodhart, "Determining the *Ratio Decidendi* of a Case" in *Essays in Jurisprudence and the Common Law* (1931), pp.1–26; the somewhat acerbic dispute between J. L. Montrose and A. W. B. Simpson: (1957) 20 M.L.R. 124, 413, 587, (1958) 21 M.L.R. 155; A. L. Goodhart, (1959) 22 M.L.R. 117; Simpson, in A. G. Guest (ed.), *Oxford Essays in Jurisprudence* (1961), Ch.VI; N. H. Andrews, (1985) 5 L.S. 205, 209–222; N. MacCormick in L. Goldstein (ed.), *Judicial Precedent* (1987), Ch.6.

[30] There may be more than one relevant proposition; the singular is used here for convenience.

[31] *cf.* Goodhart (1931), pp.3–4: "A bad reason may often make good law".

[32] MacCormick (1987), p.180.

[33] A good example here is provided by a proposition stated by Lord Bridge in *R v Secretary of State for the Home Department, Ex p. Khawaja* [1984] A.C. 74, 117, to the effect that the Home Secretary could not base a "conducive to the public good" deportation order (Immigration Act 1971, s.3(5)(b)) on a ground arising from the circumstances of the original entry of the person concerned. Divergent views were subsequently expressed on: (1) what Lord Bridge meant; (2) whether it was necessary for the ultimate decision in *Khawaja*; (3) whether it should anyway be followed even if *obiter*: compare *In re Owusu-Sekyere* [1987] Imm. A.R. 425, C.A., with *R v Immigration Appeal Tribunal, Ex p. Patel* [1988] Imm. A.R. 35, CA. The matter was ultimately resolved by the House of Lords (through Lord Bridge) holding that the proposition was "simply mistaken": *Ex p. Patel* [1988] A.C. 910, 922.

[34] See below, para.7–007.

[35] See below, para.7–005.

Then, in "extreme cases, judges may do no more than indicate that it is because the facts of the case are certain facts viewed under certain fact-descriptions that the decision ought to be as it is".[36] Here, the method for determining the *ratio* suggested by A. L. Goodhart[37] can be employed: that is, by taking account of (a) the facts treated expressly or impliedly by the judge as material, and (b) the decision as based on them. Other features of Goodhart's theory were: (1) that the *ratio* was not found in the reasons given on the rule of law set forth in the opinion (although the opinion might furnish a guide for determining which facts the judge considered material and which immaterial); (2) the inclusion of a series of rules for finding which facts were and were not material; (3) that the judge's view on this question had to be accepted by subsequent courts. The theory was offered as being of general application, and, indeed, as "a guide to the method which I believe most English courts follow".[38] Both claims are doubtful, the first because of the downplaying of the principle as enunciated by the judge,[39] and the second simply because "there seems little or no evidence to support this".[40] Nevertheless, the method remains potentially helpful where, probably through faulty technique, the reasons given for a decision do not include an express indication of the relevant principle of law.

3. THE "INTERPRETATION" OF PRECEDENTS

7–005   The judge who is called upon to determine a disputed point of law chooses the generality of the language in which he or she expresses a conclusion. The proposition may be very general, it may be closely tailored to the facts of the case or it may be formulated at some intermediate level. Most, although not all, judges are reluctant to make general statements of law, and it is anyway well established that a judgment must be read in the light of the facts of the case in which it was given. In *Quinn v Leathem*,[41] the Earl of Halsbury L.C. said that:

> "every judgment must be read as applicable to the particular facts proved, or assumed to be proved, since the generality of the expressions which may be found there are not intended to be expositions of the whole law, but governed and qualified by the particular facts of the case in which such expressions are to be found."

This point is commonly made where the judge in case B wishes to hold that the *ratio* of case A is narrower than that apparently expounded by the judge or court in case A, and is accordingly not applicable. An example of this is given by the decision of the majority of the Privy Council in *Mutual Life and Citizens'*

---

[36] MacCormick (1987), p.180.

[37] Goodhart (1931), pp.1–26.

[38] A. L. Goodhart, (1959) 22 M.L.R. 117, 124.

[39] *Cf.* Cross and Harris (1991), pp.63–71, criticising Goodhart's "scanty regard to the way in which the case was argued and pleaded, the process of reasoning adopted by the judge and the relation of the case to other decisions" (*ibid.* p.67).

[40] Lord Lloyd and M. D. A. Freeman, *Lloyd's Introduction to Jurisprudence* (5th edn, 1985), p.1117 (omitted from the 6th edn, 1994).

[41] [1901] A.C. 495, 506. *Cf.* Diplock L.J. in *Miller-Mead v Minister of Housing and Local Government* [1963] 2 Q.B. 196, 235–236.

Assurance Co Ltd v Evatt,[42] which sought to restrict the scope of liability in tort for negligent misstatement to cases where the defendant was or claimed to be in the business of giving information or advice of the relevant kind. The speeches in the leading case, *Hedley Byrne & Co Ltd v Heller and Partners Ltd*[43] were interpreted to support the incorporation of such a condition, notwithstanding the dissent of Lord Reid and Lord Morris of Borth-y-Gest, who had taken part in the *Hedley Byrne* decision and who said that they were "unable to construe the passages from our speeches cited in the judgment of the majority in the way in which they are there construed".[44] Conversely, a proposition stated by a judge may be regarded as too restrictive. A well-known example is *Barwick v The English Joint Stock Bank*,[45] where Willes J. said:

> "The general rule is, that the master is answerable for every such wrong of the servant or agent as is committed in the course of the service and for the master's benefit, though no express command or privity of the master be proved."[46]

It had previously been doubted whether a master was vicariously liable in respect of the fraud, as distinct from the non-deliberate wrongdoing, of a servant. On the facts of the case the master had benefited, albeit unwittingly, from the fraud. Subsequently, in *Lloyd v Grace, Smith & Co*[47] the House of Lords held that an employer could be vicariously liable for the fraud of an employee committed in the course of employment, notwithstanding that the employer received no benefit. The reference to the "master's benefit" was not to be regarded as part of the *ratio* of *Barwick's* case in the light of Willes J.'s judgment when read as a whole and of judgments in other cases both before and after *Barwick*. These are examples of the *ratio* of a case being reformulated *by a court not bound by it*. It has indeed been doubted whether courts "exercise any power of correcting statements of law drawn from binding decisions".[48]

4. CASES WHERE NO REASONS ARE GIVEN

The report of an old case may simply contain a statement of the facts, the arguments of counsel and an order of the court based on those facts. Here, the *ratio* has, if possible, to be inferred, but its authority is understandably very weak.[49] It would be most unusual for such a case to be decisive in modern litigation.

7–006

---

[42] [1971] A.C. 793. On the Privy Council and precedent, see below, paras 7–022, 7–029.

[43] [1964] A.C. 465.

[44] [1971] A.C. 793, 813. The minority position has been preferred by several English judges: see *Esso Petroleum Co Ltd v Mardon* [1975] Q.B. 819, 830 (Lawson J.) and [1976] Q.B. 801, 827 (Ormrod L.J.); *Howard Marine and Dredging Co Ltd v Ogden & Sons Ltd* [1978] Q.B. 574, 591 (Lord Denning M.R.), 600 (Shaw L.J.).

[45] (1866) L.R. 2 Ex. 259.

[46] *ibid.* p.265.

[47] [1912] A.C. 716.

[48] See A. W. B. Simpson, (1959) 22 M.L.R. 453, 455–457.

[49] Cross and Harris (1991), p.47.

5. Judgments With More than one *Ratio*

7–007   A number of distinct points of law may be at issue in a case, each of which taken separately would be sufficient to determine the case in favour of one side (say the claimant). The judge may be content to take one point only, give judgment for the claimant, and decline to comment on the other points. Instead, he or she may express an opinion on these points, while making it clear that the decision is to rest on the first point and that the other remarks are *dicta*. Yet again, he or she may state a conclusion on each point without any distinction, resolving them all in favour of the claimant. In the third situation, each conclusion is a separate *ratio*, and in principle, each *ratio* is binding.[50]

6. The *Ratio Decidendi* of Appellate Courts[51]

7–008   Determining the *ratio* of the decision of an appellate court where separate judgments are given can be a difficult task. Some principles are reasonably clear. Where all the members of the court are agreed as to the result of the case, any *ratio* that commands the support of a majority is binding.[52] For example, in a three-member court where two judges support ground A and the third ground B, ground A is the *ratio*. If three judges support ground A and two ground B, there are two *rationes*. Where a judge dissents as to the result, his or her views must technically be disregarded for the purpose of ascertaining the *ratio* on the ground that his or her reasons cannot be "necessary" for a decision he or she opposes. Dissenting judgments may, however, carry persuasive weight. Where there is no majority in favour of any particular *ratio*, a later court may hold that the case has no discernible *ratio* which has to be followed, although it may not adopt any reasoning which would show the decision itself to be wrong.[53] In some cases there may be much time and effort spent in the search for a *ratio* which is as elusive as the holy grail.[54]

---

[50] *Jacobs v London County Council* [1950] A.C. 361, 369 (Lord Simonds); *Behrens v Bertram Mills Circus Ltd* [1957] 2 Q.B. 1, 24–25 (Devlin J.); *Miliangos v George Frank (Textiles) Ltd* [1975] Q.B. 487, 502–503 (Lord Denning M.R.); R. E. Megarry, (1958) 74 L.Q.R. 350; *City of Westminster v Clarke* (1991) 23 H.L.R. 506, *per* Dillon L.J. at p.515 and Balcombe L.J. at p.516 (the decision of the Court of Appeal was subsequently reversed by the House of Lords: [1992] 2 A.C. 288). On other occasions Lord Denning argued that the Court of Appeal is not necessarily bound by both or all the *rationes* of an earlier *Court of Appeal* decision: *Hanning v Maitland (No. 2)* [1970] 1 Q.B. 580; *Ministry of Defence v Jeremiah* [1980] 1 Q.B. 87. On this he stood alone: see Hazel Carty, (1981) 1 L.S. 68, 71–72.

[51] Cross and Harris (1991), pp.84–96; G. Paton and G. Sawer, (1947) 63 L.Q.R. 461; A. M. Honore, (1955) 71 L.Q.R. 196.

[52] e.g. *Amalgamated Society of Railway Servants v Osborne* [1910] A.C. 87. A statement "I agree" may simply indicate concurrence with the order proposed in the leading judgment and not necessarily all the reasoning: Lord Russell of Killowen (then Russell L.J.), Address to the Holdsworth Club of the University of Birmingham 1968–69, reprinted in B. W. Harvey (ed.), *The Lawyer and Justice* (1978).

[53] See the analysis of the decision of the House of Lords in *Central Asbestos Ltd v Dodd* [1973] A.C. 518 by the Court of Appeal in *Re Harper v National Coal Board (Intended Action)* [1974] Q.B. 614.

[54] See, for example, the decision of the House of Lords in *Chaplin v Boys* [1971] A.C. 356. First-year law students are not recommended to read this case; it should, however, be one of the party pieces of students of conflict of laws.

A further complication arises where the Court of Appeal bases a decision on point A, but the case proceeds to the House of Lords, which (1) dismisses the appeal, but (2) bases its decision on point B, (3) holds that on a proper analysis point A does not arise, and (4) expresses no view on the soundness of point A. In *R v Secretary of State for the Home Department, Ex p. Al-Mehdawi*[55] the Court of Appeal held that the previous decision of the Court of Appeal[56] is no longer binding authority for point A, although it remains of "powerful persuasive influence".[57] Counsel for the Secretary of State had argued that this was so either (1) because point A had been replaced by point B as the *ratio* of the decision, or (2) as an additional exception to the rule in *Young v Bristol Aeroplane Co Ltd.*[58] The Court of Appeal seemed to accept the first of these arguments, but did not expressly reject the second.

D. THE HIERARCHY OF THE COURTS AND THE RULES OF BINDING PRECEDENT

Broadly speaking, a court is only *obliged* to follow the decisions of courts at a higher or the same level in the court structure, and there are a number of exceptions even to that requirement. For the purposes of the following discussion it must be assumed that all the other factors mentioned in Section A above are present which combine to make a precedent binding in a particular case.

7–009

1. MAGISTRATES' COURTS AND COUNTY COURTS

Decisions of these courts are rarely reported outside the pages of local newspapers, but even if they were properly reported they would not constitute precedents binding on anyone. They do not bind themselves, although it is to be expected that an individual magistrate or county court judge will attempt to be consistent in his or her own decision making. A magistrates' court may also be reminded by the clerk of the practice of the local bench, and other benches in the area. The matter upon which a "local view" may develop will rarely be a point of law; more commonly it will relate to a procedural requirement or the exercise of discretion, as in sentencing or the granting of bail.[59] Magistrates' courts and county courts are bound by decisions of the High Court, Court of Appeal and House of Lords.

7–010

---

[55] [1990] 1 A.C. 876.
[56] Here, *R v Diggines, Ex p. Rahmani* [1985] Q.B. 1109, CA, on appeal: [1986] A.C. 475.
[57] *per* Taylor L.J. [1990] 1 A.C. 876, 883. Taylor L.J. had, indeed, been a party to the Court of Appeal decision in *Ex p. Rahmani*, and ultimately, here, remained of the same opinion. The decision on the point in question was, however, ultimately reversed by the House of Lords: *ibid.*
[58] [1944] K.B. 718. See below, paras 7–016—7–024.
[59] See, e.g. *R v Nottingham JJ., Ex p. Davies* [1981] 1 Q.B. 38 where the practice of the City of Nottingham bench of refusing to hear full argument on a third or subsequent application for bail, unless there were "new circumstances", was endorsed by the Divisional Court.

2. THE CROWN COURT

7–011 Decisions of judges in the Crown Court are reported rather more frequently than those of magistrates' and county courts. This is partly because the judge may be a High Court judge whose pronouncements are inevitably more authoritative, and partly because reports of cases on points of criminal law, even at this level, find an outlet in the pages of publications such as the Criminal Law Review and the Criminal Appeal Reports. However, there is no regular reporting, and it has been suggested that Crown Court decisions are merely persuasive authorities whatever the status of the judge.[60] The Crown Court is bound by decisions of the Court of Appeal and the House of Lords. It has been asserted that it is not bound by decisions of the Divisional Court,[61] but this is hard to square with the rule that Divisional Courts are normally bound by their own previous decisions.[62]

3. THE HIGH COURT

7–012 The decision of a High Court judge is binding on inferior courts, but not technically on another High Court judge, and certainly not on a Divisional Court (i.e. a court of two or more judges). High Court judges are reluctant to depart from the decisions of other High Court judges,[63] Chancery judges being particularly loath to disagree with their colleagues for fear of upsetting transactions affecting property rights and the like.[64] There are, however, examples of judicial disagreement, one of the most notable being on the question whether failure to wear a seat-belt in a car can amount to contributory negligence. This had to be settled by the Court of Appeal.[65] It has been suggested that a decision should be followed unless the later judge is convinced that it was wrong; and that a decision of a High Court judge should more readily be followed by a deputy High Court judge on the ground that the former possesses a higher status.[66] However, it has been stated that where there are conflicting decisions of judges of co-ordinate jurisdiction, the later decision should thereafter be preferred, provided that it was reached after full consideration of the first decision: the only, rare, exception would be where the third judge was convinced that the second judge was wrong

---

[60] A. Ashworth, "The Binding Effect of Crown Court Decisions" [1980] Crim. L.R. 402–403; *cf.* Cross and Harris (1991), pp.6, 123. Some cases are reported in the regular law reports: see, e.g. *R v Bourne* [1939] 1 K.B. 687, where the summing up of Macnaghten J. on the pre-Abortion Act 1967 law of procuring an abortion was generally accepted as authoritative (*cf.* [1938] 3 All E.R. 615).

[61] *R v Colyer* [1974] Crim. L.R. 243 (Judge Stinson).

[62] See below, para.7–013.

[63] See *Police Authority for Huddersfield v Watson* [1947] K.B. 842, 848, where it is explained by Lord Goddard C.J. to be a matter of "judicial comity". A similar approach is adopted by the Employment Appeal Tribunal in respect of its own previous decisions; "An EAT will normally treat an earlier decision as authoritative unless it is convinced that the decision is wrong": *per* Peter Gibson L.J. in *London Borough of Lambeth v Tunde Apelogun-Gabriels* [2001] EWCA Civ 1852.

[64] There are also many fewer Chancery judges than Queen's Bench judges and so they are more likely to meet each other; whether this boosts "judicial comity" is a matter for speculation.

[65] *Froom v Butcher* [1976] Q.B. 286 answered the question in the affirmative.

[66] *per* Sir Louis Blom-Cooper Q.C. in *R v Hertsmere Borough Council, Ex p. Woolgar* (1996) 27 H.L.R. 703; applied by Stephen Richards Q.C. in *R v London Borough of Southwark, Ex p. Bediako* (1997) 30 H.L.R. 22.

in not following the first, for example where some binding or persuasive authority had not been cited in either of the first two cases.[67] This view has been cited with approval on a number of occasions,[68] although it has been emphasised that the matter remains one of judicial comity: there is no new head of binding precedent.[69] Indeed, Lindsay J. in *In Re Saunders (A Bankrupt)*[70] pointed out that:

> "At my request I had my attention drawn to cases on the subject of judges of coordinate jurisdiction following each other. As none is strictly binding on me I am, entertainingly, not bound by the decisions as to how far I should regard myself as bound."

4. DIVISIONAL COURTS

A Divisional Court is bound by decisions of the Court of Appeal and the House **7–013** of Lords. In *Huddersfield Police Authority v Watson*[71] and *Younghusband v Luftig*,[72] Divisional Courts of the King's Bench Division, in each case presided over by Lord Goddard C.J., held that they were bound by previous Divisional Court decisions to the same extent that the Court of Appeal was bound by its own previous decisions.[73]

The matter was reconsidered by the Divisional Court in *R v Greater Manchester Coroner, Ex p. Tal*.[74] It was held that the position was different where a Divisional Court was exercising the supervisory jurisdiction of the High Court on an application for judicial review,[75] and was faced by a previous decision of the Divisional Court acting in the same capacity. Its position was analogous to that of a judge at first instance faced with a previous decision of another judge of first instance: here, the judge in the later case would follow the earlier decision

---

[67] *Colchester Estates (Cardiff) v Carlton Industries plc* [1986] Ch. 80.

[68] *Taylor Woodrow Property Co Ltd v Lonrho Textiles Ltd* [1985] 2 E.G.L.R. 120, B. Hytner Q.C., sitting as a deputy High Court judge (in respect of two conflicting decisions of the Court of Appeal); *Elite Investments Ltd v T. I. Bainbridge Silencers Ltd* [1986] 2 E.G.L.R. 43, Judge Paul Baker Q.C., sitting as a judge of the High Court; *Glofield Properties Ltd v Morley* [1988] 1 E.G.L.R. 113, Hutchison J.; *Re A. E. Fair Ltd* [1992] B.C.L. 333, where Ferris J. on this basis followed a decision of Vinelott J. in preference to an earlier decision of his own (thus taking judicial comity a long way); this course of action was subsequently commended by Dillon L.J. in *Bishopsgate Investment Ltd v Maxwell* [1993] Ch. 1, 14; the Court of Appeal in that case upholding Vinelott J.'s approach; *Chancery plc v Ketteringham, The Times*, November 23, 1993, David Neuberger Q.C. sitting as a deputy High Court judge. The later decision that is preferred may be one of the Court of Session: *Minister of Pensions v Highman* [1948] 2 K.B. 153; *Banks v Kokkinos* [1999] 3 E.G.L.R. 133.

[69] *Forsikringsaktieselskapet Vesta v Butcher* [1986] 2 All E.R. 488, Hobhouse J.

[70] [1997] Ch. 60, 79. Here, the judge declined to follow two High Court decisions where there had not been full argument on the relevant point. But then, in *Re Taylor (A Bankrupt)* [2007] Ch. 150, Judge Kershaw Q.C., sitting as a High Court judge, declined to follow the substantive ruling in *Re Saunders*!

[71] [1947] K.B. 842: on an appeal from quarter sessions in a civil case concerning police pensions.

[72] [1949] 2 K.B. 354: on an appeal by case stated from justices in a criminal case.

[73] Under *Young v Bristol Aeroplane Co Ltd*, below, paras 7–016—7–024. The possibility of the Divisional Court applying one of the *Young v Bristol Aeroplane* exceptions was acknowledged by Lord Goddard in the latter case: [1949] 2 K.B. 354, 361.

[74] [1985] Q.B. 67. See P. Jackson, (1985) 101 L.Q.R. 157.

[75] See below, paras 18–046—18–059.

> "unless he is convinced that that judgment is wrong, as a matter of judicial comity; but he is not bound to follow a judge of equal jurisdiction."[76]

The same principle of *stare decisis* was applicable where two Divisional Court decisions were involved:

> "We have no doubt that it will be only in rare cases that a divisional court will think it fit to depart from a decision of another divisional court exercising this jurisdiction."[77]

Ex p. Tal was one of these "rare cases",[78] the Divisional Court holding that any error of law made by an inferior court or tribunal caused it to act outside its jurisdiction.[79] It declined to follow *R v Surrey Coroner, Ex p. Campbell*,[80] where it had been held that this principle applied only to *tribunals*, and not *courts*, such as a coroner's court.[81] The court in *Ex. p. Tal*[82] also expressed doubts, *obiter*, as to whether the strict approach to precedent in cases where the Divisional Court was acting in an appellate capacity was still appropriate. Robert Goff L.J. noted that at the time of *Younghusband v Luftig*,[83] the Divisional Court was the final court of appeal in criminal cases tried summarily,[84] and the House of Lords, in most cases the final court of appeal, regarded itself as bound by its own previous decisions (subject to narrow exceptions).[85] Neither of these points remained true in 1984. In criminal cases at least, his Lordship[86] could see no reason why the Divisional Court should not adopt the more flexible approach of the Criminal Division of the Court of Appeal,[87] in preference to the narrower approach of the Civil Division based on *Young v Bristol Aeroplane Co Ltd*.[88]

In subsequent cases, the approach to precedent of the Divisional Court in *Ex p. Tal*[89] has been cited with approval on numerous occasions,[90] although some

---

[76] *ibid.* at p.81, *per* Robert Goff L.J., citing *Huddersfield Police Authority v Watson* [1947] K.B. 842, 848, *per* Lord Goddard C.J.

[77] [1985] Q.B. 67, 81, *per* Robert Goff L.J.

[78] Others are *R v Chief Metropolitan Stipendiary Magistrate, Ex p. Secretary of State for the Home Department* [1988] 1 W.L.R. 1204; *R v Governor of Brockhill Prison, Ex p. Evans* [1997] Q.B. 443.

[79] Under the principle of *Anisminic Ltd v Foreign Compensation Commission* [1969] 2 A.C. 147.

[80] [1982] Q.B. 661.

[81] In accordance with dicta of Lord Diplock in *Re Racal Communications Ltd* [1981] A.C. 374.

[82] n.74 above.

[83] n.72 above.

[84] See below. It had also been the final court of appeal under the police pensions legislation in *Huddersfield Police Authority v Watson*, n.71 above.

[85] See below.

[86] [1985] Q.B. 67, 78, 79.

[87] See below, para.7–025. A more flexible approach had also been adopted in two nineteenth-century Divisional Court cases, both concerning criminal appeals: *Fortescue v Vestry of St Matthew, Bethnal Green* [1891] 2 Q.B. 170; *Kruse v Johnson* [1898] 2 Q.B. 91. These cases were not cited in *Huddersfield Police Authority v Watson* and *Younghusband v Luftig*.

[88] Below, paras 7–016—7–024.

[89] n.71 above.

[90] *Hornigold v Chief Constable of Lancashire* [1986] Crim. L.R. 792 (appeal in a criminal case); *R v Chief Metropolitan Stipendiary Magistrate, Ex p. Secretary of State for the Home Department* [1988] 1 W.L.R. 1204 (application for judicial review); *R v Metropolitan Stipendiary Magistrate, Ex p. London Waste Regulation Authority* [1993] 3 All E.R. 113 (appeal by case stated and application for judicial review); *R v Hendon JJ., Ex p. DPP* [1994] Q.B. 167 (application for judicial review; DC disagreed with statement made in a previous case "without discussion" (Mann L.J. at p.179)).

judges seem happier to disregard a previous Divisional Court decision if this can be done by reference to a "*Young v Bristol Aeroplane Co* exception".[91] It has also been emphasised that *Ex p. Tal*:

> "was not intended to provide freedom to parties to re-argue points simply on the ground that they might persuade the Court to reach a different conclusion. Before a point may be re-argued, the party must be able to indicate, at the outset of the argument, specific material on the basis of which it might properly be submitted that the Court may be convinced that the previous decision was plainly wrong."[92]

Divisional Court decisions are binding on High Court judges sitting alone[93] and inferior courts, but not the Employment Appeal Tribunal.[94]

5. THE COURT OF APPEAL (CIVIL DIVISION)[95]

(a) The general position

Decisions of the Court of Appeal are binding on the Divisional Court, the **7–014** Employment Appeal Tribunal, High Court judges[96] and inferior courts. The Court of Appeal is bound to follow decisions of the House of Lords. On occasion, the House has felt it necessary to remind the Court of Appeal of this. In 1970, Captain Jack Broome R.N. (retd.) brought a libel action against David Irving and Cassell & Co Ltd, respectively author and publisher of a book entitled *The Destruction of Convoy P.Q.17*. The case was heard over 17 days by Lawton J. and a jury.[97] The jury awarded £15,000 "compensatory damages" and £25,000 "exemplary damages". The situations in which exemplary damages could be awarded had been listed by Lord Devlin in *Rookes v Barnard*,[98] a decision of the

[91] *R v Plymouth JJ., Ex p. Driver* [1986] Q.B. 95, 123–124 (*per incuriam*); *R v Plymouth JJ., Ex p. Hart* [1986] Q.B. 950 (conflicting decisions); *R v Weston-super-Mare JJ., Ex p. Shaw* [1987] Q.B. 640, 648 (conflicting decisions): all applications for judicial review; *Shaw v DPP* [1993] 1 All E.R. 918 (*per incuriam*).

[92] *Hornigold v Chief Constable of Lancashire* [1986] Crim. L.R. 792.

[93] *Huddersfield Police Authority v Watson* [1947] K.B. 842, 848; *Ettenfield v Ettenfield* [1939] P. 377, 380; *contra: Elderton v United Kingdom Totalisator Co Ltd* (1945) 61 T.L.R. 529 where a judge of the Chancery Division declined to follow the decision of a Divisional Court of the Queen's Bench Division.

[94] *Portec (UK) Ltd v Mogensen* [1976] I.C.R. 396, 400; *Breach v Epsylon Industries Ltd* [1976] I.C.R. 316, 320.

[95] See T. Prime and G. Scanlan, "Stare decisis and the Court of Appeal; Judicial confusion and judicial reform" (2004) 23 C.J.Q. 212, calling for the uncertainties in the doctrine to be remedied quickly.

[96] Even an *Ex parte* decision of the Court of Appeal: *The Alexandras P.* [1986] Q.B. 464. In *Lane v Willis* [1972] 1 W.L.R. 326, 332, Davies L.J. rebuked Lawson J. for expressing the opinion, though accepting he was bound by it, that a Court of Appeal decision was wrong.

[97] It survived an interruption by Welsh language demonstrators: *Morris v Crown Office* [1970] 2 Q.B. 114.

[98] [1964] A.C. 1129. The other members of the House expressly concurred with Lord Devlin's statement on exemplary damages.

House of Lords, and the principles subsequently applied by the Court of Appeal to the tort of defamation.[99] Not surprisingly, Lawton J. had directed the jury accordingly in the *P.Q.17* case. Both author and publisher appealed against the award of exemplary damages. The Court of Appeal, after a nine-day hearing, rejected the appeal.[100] The case fell within one of the situations in which Lord Devlin had held that exemplary damages could be awarded,[101] the judge's direction had been adequate and the jury's award was not perversely large. The Court of Appeal was not, however, content with that. The members of the court (Lord Denning M.R., Salmon and Phillimore L.JJ.) took the view that the law on exemplary damages as expounded by Lord Devlin was "unworkable". Lord Denning M.R. said that the common law on exemplary damages had been well settled before 1964, that there were two House of Lords cases[102] which had approved that settled doctrine and which Lord Devlin must have "overlooked" or "misunderstood", that *Rookes v Barnard* had not been followed in Commonwealth courts, and that the new doctrine was "hopelessly illogical and inconsistent". He concluded:

> "I think the difficulties presented by *Rookes v Barnard* are so great that the judges should direct the juries in accordance with the law as it was understood before *Rookes v Barnard*. Any attempt to follow *Rookes v Barnard* is bound to lead to confusion."[103]

Surprisingly, there was no discussion of the question whether Lord Devlin's statement formed part of the *ratio decidendi* of *Rookes v Barnard*.

7–015   Cassells appealed to the House of Lords; a 13-day hearing was held before seven Law Lords. The Court of Appeal's decision to uphold the jury's verdict was affirmed by a majority.[104] Lord Devlin's approach to exemplary damages was endorsed, with varying enthusiasm, by a majority. The approach of the Court of Appeal to *Rookes v Barnard* was roundly condemned. Lord Hailsham L.C.:

> "[I]t is not open to the Court of Appeal to give gratuitous advice to judges of first instance to ignore decisions of the House of Lords in this way and, if it were open to the Court of Appeal to do so, it would be highly undesirable. . . .
>
> The fact is, and I hope it will never be necessary to say so again, that, in the hierarchical system of courts which exists in this country, it is necessary for each lower tier, including the Court of Appeal, to accept loyally the decisions of the higher tiers. Where decisions manifestly conflict, the decision in *Young v Bristol Aeroplane Co Ltd* offers guidance to each tier in

---

[99] *McCarey v Associated Newspapers Ltd* [1965] 2 Q.B. 86; *Broadway Approvals Ltd v Odhams Press Ltd* [1965] 1 W.L.R. 805.

[100] *Broome v Cassell & Co Ltd* [1971] 2 Q.B. 354.

[101] See W. V. H. Rogers, *Winfield and Jolowicz on Tort* (17th edn, 2006), pp.939–952. See now *Kuddus v Chief Constable of Leicestershire* [2002] 2 A.C. 122.

[102] *E. Hulton & Co v Jones* [1910] A.C. 20 and *Ley v Hamilton* (1935) 153 L.T. 384.

[103] [1971] 2 Q.B. 354, 381, 384.

[104] *Cassell & Co Ltd v Broome* [1972] A.C. 1027. It has been described as "what may well be the most hostile *affirmation* of a Court of Appeal decision in our history": Julius Stone, "On the Liberation of Appellate Judges—How not to do it!" (1972) 35 M.L.R. 449.

matters affecting its own decisions. It does not entitle it to question considered decisions in the upper tiers with the same freedom."[105]

Other members of the House of Lords added their voices to the chorus of disapproval.[106] They pointed out that the parties had been put to much expense in litigating broad legal issues unnecessary for the disposal of their dispute.[107] Lord Devlin had not overlooked the two House of Lords cases (*Ley v Hamilton* was discussed at length in his speech) and, on proper analysis, they were not binding authorities on the award of exemplary damages.[108]

The House of Lords similarly found it necessary to assert its authority over the Court of Appeal in *Miliangos v George Frank (Textiles) Ltd.*[109]

Since the retirement of Lord Denning M.R., the general loyalty of the Court of Appeal to decisions of the House of Lords has not been in question. However, an exception was provided by the decision of the Court of Appeal in *JD v East Berkshire Community NHS Trust.*[110] Here the court held that the decision of the House of Lords in *X (Minors) v Bedfordshire County Council*[111] that local authorities do not owe a duty of care to children at risk of abuse or their parents[112] could not survive introduction of the Human Rights Act 1998; this provided new causes of action for breaches of Convention rights, the existence of which had undermined the policy consideration that had largely dictated the House of Lords' decision. A duty of care could accordingly be owed to the child. This approach to precedent attracted criticism,[113] but not by counsel or the House itself when the case proceeded to the House of Lords.[114] In *Lambeth LBC v Kay*[115] the House strongly reaffirmed the normal rule, while accepting *JD* as a "partial exception" albeit one where the facts were of an "extreme character".[116] The proposal that a lower court can (or must) depart from a decision that is "clearly inconsistent" with a later ruling of the ECtHR[117] would in practice be unworkable; there were often different views as to whether there was such inconsistency. Certainty was best achieved by adhering to the rules of precedent. In addition there was normally a "margin of appreciation" accorded to national courts and it was for them to set (initially at least) the domestic standards.[118] This seems, with respect, the right approach as it avoids extensive litigation in the lower court about this special precedent rule. Situations where cases are or have become inconsistent with the ECHR are likely to reach the higher courts in any event.

---

[105] [1972] A.C. 1027, 1054.
[106] See Lord Reid at pp.1084, 1091–1093; Lord Wilberforce at pp.1112–1113; Lord Diplock at pp.1131–1132; Lord Kilbrandon at pp.1132, 1135.
[107] *cf.* below, para.18–038, n.524.
[108] Viscount Dilhorne dissented on this last point: [1972] A.C. at pp.1109–1111.
[109] [1976] A.C. 443, discussed below, para.7–021.
[110] [2004] Q.B. 558.
[111] [1995] 2 A.C. 633.
[112] Except via the *Hedley Byrne* principle.
[113] J. Wright, (2004) 20 P.N. 58, 63.
[114] [2005] 2 A.C. 373, at [21], [30]–[36], [82], [119], [124]–[125]. The House was concerned only with appeal by the parents.
[115] [2006] 2 A.C. 465.
[116] Lord Bingham of Cornhill at para.[45]. The very children who lost in *X (Minors) v Bedfordshire* had subsequently succeeded before the ECtHR on the ground of a breach of Art.3: *Z v UK* (2001) 10 B.H.R.C. 384.
[117] Put forward in varying formulations by the parties and interveners (the First Secretary of State, JUSTICE and Liberty).
[118] See Lord Bingham at paras [40]–[44].

(b) Young v Bristol Aeroplane Co Ltd

7–016 In *Young v Bristol Aeroplane Co Ltd*[119] the Court of Appeal[120] held that it was bound by its own previous decisions, and by decisions of courts of co-ordinate jurisdiction such as the Courts of Exchequer Chamber. Three exceptions were identified. First, a decision of the Court of Appeal given *per incuriam* need not be followed. Secondly, where the court is faced by previous conflicting decisions of the Court of Appeal or a court of co-ordinate jurisdiction, it may choose which to follow. Thirdly, where a previous decision of the Court of Appeal, although not expressly overruled, cannot stand with a subsequent decision of the House of Lords, the decision of the House must be followed. Since *Young*'s case further light has been thrown on the scope of these three exceptions and suggestions have been made for additional ones. Lord Denning M.R. fought, almost single-handed, against the notion that the Court of Appeal should be bound by its own previous decisions at all. In addition, it has been unclear whether the grounds upon which the Court of Appeal may question one of its own decisions may be employed by a court lower in the hierarchy in respect of a decision of a higher court. These matters are considered in turn.

(c) Accepted exceptions to Young v Bristol Aeroplane Co Ltd

(i) *Decisions given per incuriam*

7–017 If interpreted and applied literally the *per incuriam* doctrine could be used to evade the effect of any decision thought to have been reached "through want of care". However, the term in this context is interpreted narrowly. A decision will not be regarded as *per incuriam* merely on the ground that another court thinks it wrongly decided, that it has been inadequately argued[121] or that the decision contains points which are not derived from the arguments of counsel.[122] In *Morelle v Wakeling*, Sir Raymond Evershed M.R. said that as a general rule the *per incuriam* doctrine could only apply to:

> "decisions given in ignorance or forgetfulness of some inconsistent statutory provision or of some authority binding on the court concerned: so that in such cases some part of the decision or some step in the reasoning on which it is based is found, on that account to be demonstrably wrong."[123]

---

[119] [1944] K.B. 718. See also *Condé Nast Productions Ltd v Customs and Excise Commissioners* [2006] S.T.C. 1721.

[120] A "full court" consisting of Lord Greene M.R., Scott, MacKinnon, Luxmoore, Goddard and du Parcq L.JJ. Note that it was held in this case a "full court" is bound by previous Court of Appeal decisions to the same extent as a court ordinarily constituted. See further below para.7–025. It has been suggested, obiter, by Beldam L.J. that the *Young* principles should be applied by the Employment Appeal Tribunal in respect of its own previous decisions: *Tracey v Crosville Wales Ltd* [1996] I.C.R. 237, 257–258. The point was left open by Waite and Otton L.JJ.; a different view was taken in *London Borough of Lambeth v Tunde Apelogun-Gabriels* [2001] EWCA Civ 1853: above, para.7–012, n.63.

[121] *Morelle v Wakeling* [1955] 2 Q.B. 379, 406; *Miliangos v George Frank (Textiles) Ltd* [1975] Q.B. 487, 503 (Lord Denning M.R.); *cf. Chief Adjudication Officer v Brunt* [1988] A.C. 711, 724, 726, CA.

[122] *per* Lord Diplock in *Cassell & Co Ltd v Broome* [1972] A.C. 1027, 1131.

[123] [1955] 2 Q.B. 379, 406. See generally, P. Wesley-Smith, (1980) 15 J.S.P.T.L.(N.S.) 58. In *Industrial Properties Ltd v A.E.I.* [1977] Q.B. 580 dicta in a Court of Appeal decision were held to have been made *per incuriam* on the ground that the court had misunderstood a decision of the Court of Exchequer Chamber; they had only been referred to an inadequate report of that decision.

In *Dixon v British Broadcasting Corporation*[124] a decision on the construction of a statutory provision was regarded as *per incuriam* on the ground that other relevant provisions which threw light on the words in question had not been brought to the attention of the court. A clearer example is *Bonulami v Home Secretary*.[125] An order was obtained under the Bankers' Books Evidence Act 1879 for the inspection of bank accounts to obtain evidence in criminal proceedings. The Court of Appeal (Civil Division) held that it had no jurisdiction to entertain an appeal as this was a "criminal cause or matter",[126] notwithstanding that in an earlier[127] case it had heard such an appeal. The point as to jurisdiction had not been taken or considered by counsel or any member of the court:

> "Failure to consider a statutory provision is one of the clearest cases in which, on the principles laid down in *Young v Bristol Aeroplane Co Ltd*, this court is not bound to follow its own decisions."[128]

The exact scope of the *per incuriam* doctrine has been thrown into some doubt by three judgments of Sir John (subsequently Lord) Donaldson M.R. In *Duke v Reliance Systems Ltd*[129] he put it in narrow terms, as applying where the court *must* (not *might*) have reached a different conclusion had a statute or binding precedent been drawn to its attention. In *Williams v Fawcett*,[130] the Court of Appeal disapproved one of the grounds of a number of decisions[131] in which it had been held that a notice to show cause why the respondent should not be committed to prison for breach of a non-molestation order had to be signed by the "proper officer" of the county court. There was no warrant for this requirement in the statute or procedural rules. Sir John Donaldson M.R. recognised the dangers of treating a decision as given *per incuriam* simply on the ground that it could be demonstrated to be wrong, but argued that this was an "exceptional" case for various reasons: (1) the clearness with which the growth of the error could be detected if the decisions were read consecutively; (2) the cases were concerned with the liberty of the subject[132]; (3) they were by no means unusual; and (4) they were "most unlikely to reach the House of Lords, which, if we do not act is alone able to correct the error which has crept into the law".[133]

Subsequently, in *Rickards v Rickards*[134] the Court of Appeal declined to follow its own previous decision in *Podbery v Peak*,[135] in which it had been held that the

---

[124] [1979] Q.B. 546.
[125] [1985] Q.B. 675. See also *White v Chief Adjudication Officer* [1986] 2 All E.R. 905; *Pearce v Secretary of State for Defence* [1988] A.C. 755, 785, CA; *Rakhit v Carty* [1990] 2 Q.B. 315; *R v Fennell (Peter)* [2000] 1 W.L.R. 2011 (decision *per incuriam* where relevant provisions, including the Interpretation Act 1978, had not been cited).
[126] Supreme Court Act 1981, s.18(1)(a): see below, para.18–022.
[127] *R v Grossman* (1981) 73 Cr.App.R. 302.
[128] *per* Stephenson L.J. at [1985] Q.B. 675, 682.
[129] [1988] Q.B. 108. See above, para.5–057.
[130] [1988] Q.B. 604. See also *M v P (contempt: committal); Butler v Butler* [1993] Fam. 167 and *Nicholls v Nicholls* [1997] 1 W.L.R. 314, confirming the breadth of the court's discretion to rectify technical defects in committal orders.
[131] *Lee v Walker* [1988] Q.B. 1191 and several unreported decisions.
[132] Although it was noted that the present decision would not be beneficial to the contemnors, who would be deprived of a technical ground of challenge to their imprisonment; *Williams v Fawcett* is therefore not to be equated with the "special exception" recognised in the Criminal Division of the Court of Appeal: see below, para.7–025.
[133] [1988] Q.B. 604, 616–617.
[134] [1990] Fam. 194.
[135] [1981] Ch. 344.

Court of Appeal had no jurisdiction to entertain an appeal against the refusal of a judge to grant leave to appeal out of time. The court in *Rickards*, which included Lord Donaldson M.R., was satisfied that the decision in *Podbery v Peak* was wrong, but noted that in practice it was unlikely that litigants would incur the cost of appealing to the House of Lords on this point.[136] Further considerations that justified treating *Podbery v Peak* as a decision given *per incuriam* were: (1) that it related to a procedural rule rather than substantive law (erroneous decisions as to procedural rules affecting only the parties engaged in the relevant litigation); and (2) that it involved the jurisdiction of the court, errors on matters of jurisdiction being "particularly objectionable".[137] It was stated that this extended approach to the *per incuriam* doctrine should only be adopted in "rare and exceptional" cases.[138]

In more recent cases, the narrowness of the scope of this extension to the *per incuriam* doctrine has been emphasised. In *Re Probe Data Systems (No.3)*[139] the Court of Appeal regarded these authorities as establishing that

> "in order to come within this category, it must be shown not only that the decision involved some 'manifest slip or error', but also that to leave the decision standing would be likely to produce serious inconvenience in the administration of justice, or significant injustice to citizens, or some equally serious consequences."[140]

However, in other cases, an apparently broader approach has been adopted. Thus, in *R v Parole Board, Ex p. Wilson*[141] the Court of Appeal departed from the decision in *R v Secretary of State for the Home Department, Ex p. Gunnell*[142] in holding that a discretionary life sentence prisoner was entitled to disclosure of the reasons, report or facts adverse to his request for release. This was justified, as "the liberty of the subject was in issue"[143] and he would in any event be entitled to see the information once s.34 of the Criminal Justice Act 1991 was brought into force.

---

[136] Leave was granted in *Bokhari v Mahmood* (unreported, 1988) for the point to be taken to the House of Lords, but the appeal was not pursued.

[137] "Either because it will involve an abuse of power if the true view is that the court has no jurisdiction or a breach of the court's statutory duty if the true view is that the court is wrongly declining jurisdiction": *per* Lord Donaldson M.R. at p.203.

[138] Lord Donaldson M.R. at p.203 Balcombe L.J. at p.206; Nicholls L.J. at p.210; *cf.* Lord Donaldson M.R. in *Langley v North West Water Authority* [1991] 1 W.L.R. 697, confirming that "any departure from previous decisions of this court is in principle undesirable and should only be considered if the previous decision is manifestly wrong. Even then it will be necessary to take account of whether the decision purports to be of general application and whether there is any other way of remedying the error, for example, by encouraging an appeal to the House of Lords." This proposition was endorsed by the Court of Appeal in *Limb v Union Jack Removals Ltd* [1998] 1 W.L.R. 1354 at paras 34, 35. However, the court confusingly seemed not to regard it as an aspect of the *per incuriam* doctrine itself. A further variant is provided by *Desnousse v Newham LBC* [2006] Q.B. 831, where the *Williams v Fawcett* line of authority was said to be "an exceptional residual category of cases which are not strictly *per incuriam*": *per* Lloyd L.J. at para.[75]. See further below, para.7–020.

[139] [1992] B.C.L.C. 405.

[140] *per* Scott L.J. at p.414.

[141] [1991] 1 Q.B. 740. See also *Jones v Vans Colina* [1996] 1 W.L.R. 1580, where it was asserted that a decision regarded as incorrect was *per incuriam*, without further analysis.

[142] *The Times*, November 7, 1984.

[143] Lord Taylor C.J. at p.755 citing only this factor from the many mentioned by Lord Donaldson M.R. in *Williams v Fawcett* [1986] Q.B. 604, 615 and 616.

Finally, it should be noted that in some cases the *per incuriam* doctrine has been regarded as confined to the narrow formulation of *Morelle v Wakeling*.[144] However, as *Williams v Fawcett*[145] and cases following it were not cited they are presumably *per incuriam* on this point.

(ii) Conflicting decisions

Decisions in the Court of Appeal may conflict. The decision in case A may not be cited to the court in case B, whereas both cases A and B are cited in case C[146]; case A may not have been reported,[147] or may simply have been overlooked. Cases A and B may be decided by different divisions of the Court of Appeal at roughly the same time. Case A may be cited in case B but, in the view of the court in case C, erroneously interpreted. The resulting confusion may be settled by the Court of Appeal choosing which case or line of cases to follow and overruling any cases that conflict.[148] It has been argued that the court should be bound by the earlier case, case A (as the court in case B was not entitled to depart from it[149]) and, alternatively, that it should follow case B (as the later case[150]) but neither argument has prevailed.

7–018

(iii) Decisions impliedly overruled by the House of Lords

In *Young v Bristol Aeroplane Co Ltd*[151] Lord Greene M.R. stated that the Court of Appeal was not bound by a previous decision which "although not expressly overruled, cannot stand with a subsequent decision of the House of Lords".[152] This principle was relied upon by Oliver J. in *Midland Bank Trust Co Ltd v Hett, Stubbs & Kemp*[153] where he declined to follow the decision of the Court of Appeal in *Groom v Crocker*[154] on the ground that it was inconsistent with the subsequent decision of the House of Lords in *Hedley Byrne & Co Ltd v Heller*

7–019

---

[144] See above. See e.g. *ACE Insurance SA-NV v Zurich Insurance Company* [2001] EWCA Civ 173, [2001] 1 Lloyd's L.R. 618.

[145] See above.

[146] See the cases discussed in *Fisher v Ruislip-Northwood Urban District Council* [1945] K.B. 584. The decision in case B may be regarded as given *per incuriam*: see *W. A. Sherratt Ltd v John Bromley Church Stratton Ltd* [1985] Q.B. 1038.

[147] e.g. *Cathrineholm A/S v Norequipment Trading Ltd* [1972] 2 Q.B. 314.

[148] *ibid.*; *Ross-Smith v Ross-Smith* [1961] P. 39; *Ashburn Anstalt v Arnold* [1989] Ch. 1; *cf. Midland Bank Trust Co Ltd v Hett, Stubbs & Kemp* [1979] Ch. 384; *Esselte AB v Pearl Assurance plc* [1997] 1 W.L.R. 891.

[149] A. L. Goodhart, (1947) 9 C.L.J. 349. This point was expressly left open by the Court of Appeal in *Dairy International Ltd v Tazzyman* [1997] 1 W.L.R. 1256.

[150] R. N. Gooderson, (1950) 10 C.L.J. 432. This was given as one reason for choosing between conflicting decisions in *Circuit Systems Ltd v Zuken-Redac (UK) Ltd* [1997] 1 W.L.R. 721. Conversely, it was expressly rejected as an argument in *Starmark Enterprises Ltd v CPL Distribution Ltd* [2001] EWCA Civ 1252, [2002] Ch. 306, the Court of Appeal holding that the later of two conflicting decisions had erroneously distinguished the earlier, and that the earlier should be followed.

[151] [1944] K.B. 718.

[152] *ibid.* p.722. Applied in *Huang v Secretary of State for the Home Department* [2006] Q.B. 1.

[153] [1979] Ch. 384. The case concerned the liability of a solicitor for negligence: see above, para.3–044.

[154] [1939] 1 K.B. 194. Authorities following *Groom v Crocker* and decided after *Hedley Byrne* were regarded as inconsistent with the decision of the Court of Appeal in *Esso Petroleum Co Ltd v Mardon* [1976] Q.B. 801.

& Partners Ltd.[155] It seems that the Court of Appeal is free to depart from the earlier decision but is not bound to do so.[156]

(iv) *Decisions on interlocutory appeals and applications for permission to appeal*

7–020   In *Boys v Chaplin*[157] the Court of Appeal held that it was not bound by a previous decision of the Court of Appeal where that court comprised two Lords Justices hearing an interlocutory appeal. It is the nature of the appeal that is crucial, not the number of members of the court. In *Langley v North Western Water Authority*[158] the Court of Appeal affirmed, *obiter*,[159] that "the authority of a two judge court should today be regarded as being the same as that of a three judge court". It was not clear whether this was intended to cast doubt on the reasoning of *Boys v Chaplin*.[160] Lord Donaldson M.R. noted that, in that case, Lord Denning M.R. and Diplock L.J.[161] relied on "the summary nature of the argument under the then existing practice in the case of interlocutory appeals heard by two judge courts"; he contrasted this with the "present practice", where the division of work between two and three-judge courts was not determined by whether there will be no need for other than brief argument or the point is of minimal importance other than to the "immediate parties."[162] Since *Langley*, the distinction between interlocutory and final appeals has been abolished, and it is difficult to see what remains of the *Boys v Chaplin* exception. In *Cave v Robinson Jarvis and Rolfe*[163] Potter L.J. stated[164]:

> "In a broad sense, the modern equivalent of the *Boys v Chaplin* paradigm of a decision reached under time constraints and on the basis of brief argument is the decision of a Lord Justice or Lords Justices upon an oral application for leave to appeal."

Such decisions are not binding on later substantive appeals or applications for leave.[165] In *Cave*, the Court of Appeal followed a previous decision[166] of a two-judge court on an interlocutory appeal, which though *ex tempore* had been carefully considered. Sedley L.J. suggested[167] that the decision not followed in *Boys v Chaplin* would today be overset

---

[155] [1964] A.C. 465. *Cf. Department for Transport, Environment and the Regions v Mott MacDonald* [2006] EWCA Civ 1089, holding that the decision in *Burnside v Emerson* [1968] 1 W.L.R. 1490 had not impliedly been overruled by the House of Lords in *Goodes v East Sussex CC* [2000] 1 W.L.R. 1356.

[156] *Woodward v Abbey National plc* [2006] I.R.L.R. 677, para.[63]. It chose to do so in this case.

[157] [1968] 2 Q.B. 1. Applied in *Welsh Development Agency v Redpath Dorman Long Ltd* [1994] 1 W.L.R. 1409, although the court there did not have its attention drawn to *Langley v North West Water Authority* [1991] 1 W.L.R. 697.

[158] [1991] 1 W.L.R. 697.

[159] *per* Lord Donaldson M.R. at p.710.

[160] [1968] 2 Q.B. 1.

[161] At pp.23 and 35 respectively.

[162] [1991] 1 W.L.R. at p.710.

[163] [2001] EWCA Civ 245, [2002] 1 W.L.R. 581. See T. Prime and G. Scanlan, (2004) 23 C.J.Q. 212.

[164] para.[24].

[165] *ibid.*; *Clarke v University of Lincolnshire and Humberside* [2000] 3 All E.R. 752, 761–762.

[166] *Brocklesby v Armitage & Guest (Note)* [2002] 1 W.L.R. 598.

[167] para.[31].

"not because it was an interlocutory decision of a two-judge court, but either because this court was satisfied that it was outdated, unjust and incontestably wrong or because, this court having had to leave it standing, the House of Lords overruled it."

The Court of Appeal decision in *Cave* was overturned by the House of Lords, but the House did not express a view on whether the lower court had been right to follow *Brocklesby*.

(d) Possible exceptions to Young v Bristol Aeroplane Co Ltd

(i) *Inconsistency with an earlier House of Lords decision*

Lord Greene M.R.'s summary of conclusions in the *Young*'s case and the head notes of most of the reports indicate that a Court of Appeal decision which is inconsistent with *any* House of Lords case, whether prior or subsequent, does not bind the Court of Appeal. The relevant passage from the main body of Lord Greene's judgment,[168] however, includes the word "subsequent". Moreover, in *Williams v Glasbrook Bros.*[169] Lord Greene expressly asserted that the exception was so limited; if the Court of Appeal misinterprets an earlier House of Lords decision "nobody but the House of Lords can put that mistake right".[170] This position has been supported by Lord Denning M.R.[171] and Lord Simon,[172] and is to be preferred "in the interests of certainty".[173] Against these authorities, and in favour of a more widely drawn exception to *Young*'s case, are the decision of the Court of Appeal in *Fitzsimons v The Ford Motor Co*[174] and the opinion of Lord Cross in *Miliangos v George Frank (Textiles) Ltd.*[175]

7–021

The *Miliangos* case illustrates some of the difficulties that can arise. In 1960 the House of Lords in the *Havana* case[176] made a decision which was based on the unchallenged assumption that a judgment in an English court could only be given in sterling. The actual point in issue was the date at which a debt payable in US dollars had to be converted to the equivalent in sterling for the purposes of proceedings in England to enforce payment. In *Schorsch Meier G.m.b.H. v Hennin*[177] the Court of Appeal[178] held (1) that the operation of the *Havana* case had been limited by Art.106 of the EEC Treaty (since repealed), which was regarded as enabling EEC nationals to obtain judgments in a foreign currency, and (2) (Lawton L.J. dissenting) that in any event the *Havana* rule could be disregarded as the fact that sterling was no longer a stable currency meant that the rationale behind the rule no longer stood. On the latter point, the majority founded themselves on the maxim *cessante ratione legis cessat ipsa lex* (if the reason for a law ceases to be valid the law itself ceases). In *Miliangos v George*

---

[168] Above, para.7–017.

[169] [1947] 2 All E.R. 884.

[170] *ibid.* p.885. If the House of Lords' decision had not been cited, the Court of Appeal decision would be *per incuriam*: see above.

[171] *Miliangos v George Frank (Textiles) Ltd* [1975] Q.B. 416, 502.

[172] *ibid.* [1976] A.C. 443, 478–479.

[173] Sir Rupert Cross, *Precedent in English Law* (3rd edn, 1977), p.143, a statement omitted from the 4th edition.

[174] [1946] 1 All E.R. 429. This was not cited in *Williams v Glasbrook Bros.*

[175] [1976] A.C. 443, 496.

[176] *Re United Railways of Havana and Regla Warehouses Ltd* [1961] A.C. 1007.

[177] [1975] Q.B. 416.

[178] Lord Denning M.R., Lawton L.J. and Foster J.

Franks (Textiles) Ltd a plaintiff who was not an EEC national sought to take advantage of the second *ratio* of *Schorsch Meier*. Bristow J.[179] held that he was obliged to follow the House of Lords' decision in *Havana* in preference to that of the Court of Appeal in *Schorsch Meier*, notwithstanding the fact that it had been cited to the court in *Schorsch Meier*. The *Havana* rule could only be altered by statute or another decision of the House. On appeal, the Court of Appeal[180] then held that *Schorsch Meier* was binding (1) on courts beneath the Court of Appeal in the hierarchy, and (2) on the Court of Appeal itself, the relevant exception to *Young v Bristol Aeroplane Co Ltd* being confined to inconsistent *subsequent* House of Lords' decisions. The House of Lords held (1) that the Court of Appeal had acted incorrectly in *Schorsch Meier* in failing to follow *Havana*, but (2) (Lord Simon dissenting) that the *Havana* case should be overruled. As to the dilemma facing the trial judge and the Court of Appeal in *Miliangos*, Lord Cross[181] took the view that *Schorsch Meier* should not have been followed (endorsing Bristow J.'s approach), Lord Simon[182] thought that the Court of Appeal in *Miliangos* had acted correctly, and the other members of the House of Lords expressed no definite opinion.[183] The position taken by Bristow J. and Lord Cross assumes that:

> "the *Schorsch Meier* majority decision was not law in any proper sense, since it was reached in total disregard of the proper law as it then existed in a rule of the House of Lords, and which . . . bound the Court of Appeal to reach a decision contrary to that actually reached."[184]

However, the analogous argument is not accepted in cases of "horizontal conflict" between decisions in the same court. Thus, where Court of Appeal decisions conflict, the Court of Appeal in a subsequent case may choose which to follow.[185]

More recently, in *Holden & Co v Crown Prosecution Service*[186] the Court of Appeal asserted a preference for the broader view, relying on a dictum of Lord Wright in *Noble v Southern Railway Co.*[187] However, none of the other relevant authorities on the point were cited (except *Young v Bristol Aeroplane Co Ltd* itself) and the decision on this point might therefore be open to challenge as reached *per incuriam*.

(ii) *Inconsistency with a Privy Council decision*

7–022 In *Worcester Works Finance Ltd v Cooden Engineering Co Ltd*[188] Lord Denning M.R. said[189]:

---

[179] [1975] Q.B. 487, 491.
[180] [1975] Q.B. 487, 499.
[181] [1976] A.C. 443, 496.
[182] [1976] A.C. 443, 470.
[183] Professor Cross thought the desirability of contradictory statements on this point to be "highly questionable" and that there was "something to be said for the discreet silence" of the other three members of the House: P. M. S. Hacker and J. Raz (eds), *Law, Morality and Society* (1977), p.153.
[184] C. E. F. Rickett, (1980) 43 M.L.R. 136, 141.
[185] See above, para.7–018.
[186] [1990] 2 Q.B. 261, *per* Lord Lane C.J. at p.272. Followed in *Great Peace Shipping Ltd v Tsavliris Salvage (International Ltd)* [2003] Q.B. 679.
[187] [1940] A.C. 583, 598.
[188] [1972] 1 Q.B. 210.
[189] At p.217.

"Although decisions of the Privy Council are not binding on this Court, nevertheless when the Privy Council disapproves of a previous decision of this Court or casts doubt on it, we are at liberty to depart from the previous decision."

This statement can be seen as part of Lord Denning's battle against the rule that the Court of Appeal is bound by its own previous decisions, and it has been held that this is not authoritative in the light of the strictures of the House of Lords in *Davis v Johnson*.[190]

The matter has received further attention in *R v James*.[191] Here the Court of Appeal (Criminal Division), in considering the true interpretation of the defence of provocation under the Homicide Act 1957, was presented with a conflict between the decisions of the House of Lords in *R v Smith (Morgan)*[192] and of the Privy Council in *Att-Gen for Jersey v Holley*.[193] *Smith* had been subject to considerable academic criticism; in the absence of a suitable appeal to the House, all nine Law Lords who constituted the Board in *Hallett* were agreed that the outcome should be regarded as settling the Law of England and not just the Law of Jersey. Six of the nine were agreed that *Smith* was wrongly decided; three dissented. In *James*, the Court of Appeal decided to follow *Hallett*. The exceptional features justifying this approach were: (i) that all nine of the Law Lords in *Hallett* were agreed that the decision would clarify the law definitively; (ii) the majority constituted half the Appellate Committee of the House; (iii) the result of any appeal on the issue on the House was a foregone conclusion. It was unlikely that the court would ever again be presented with such circumstances; the decision should not be taken as a licence to decline to follow a decision of the House in any other circumstances.[194] The outcome is pragmatic and the situation likely to remain rare.

(iii) *Other possibilities*[195]

In *B v B*[196] the Court of Appeal held that s.1(1) of the Domestic Violence and Matrimonial Proceedings Act 1976 did not give a county court jurisdiction to grant an injunction excluding a spouse[197] from the "matrimonial home" where that spouse had a proprietary interest in the home. A few days later this decision   **7–023**

---

[190] Below: *In re Spectrum Plus Ltd* [2004] Ch. 337, *per* Lord Phillips M.R. at para.[58] (see H. N. Bennett, (2005) 121 L.Q.R. 23). In *Darayden Holdings Ltd v Solland International Ltd* [2005] Ch. 119, Lawrence Collins J. expressed willingness in principle to apply a decision of the Privy Council in preference to a decision of the Court of Appeal, to save the expense of an appeal to the House of Lords: *cf.* the opposite view expressed by Richard Siberry Q.C. in *O'Kane v Jones* [2005] Lloyd's Rep. I.R. 169. In *Re Spectrum Plus Ltd* [2005] 2 A.C. 680, Baroness Hale at para.[163] made it clear that the decision in that case did not prevent this point being argued on a future occasion. See further M. D. G. Conaglen and R. C. Nolan, (2006) 122 L.Q.R. 349, preferring the approach in *James*; J. Elvin, (2006) 29 M.L.R. 819. On the Privy Council and precedent see further below, paras 7–029, 7–033.

[191] [2006] Q.B. 588.

[192] [2001] 1 A.C. 146. The House held that the jury was allowed to take into account personal characteristics of the accused that (1) were relevant to the gravity of the provocation, or (2) affected his powers of self-control.

[193] [2005] 2 A.C. 580. The Privy Council held that the jury could only take account of (1).

[194] Lord Phillips of Worth Matravers C.J. at paras [5]–[45].

[195] See also *R v Secretary of State for the Home Department, Ex p. Al-Mehdawi* [1990] 1 A.C. 876, above, para.7–008.

[196] [1978] Fam. 26, decided on October 13, 1977 by Bridge, Waller and Megaw L.JJ.

[197] Whether real, or for want of a better expression, "common law".

was followed by the Court of Appeal in *Cantliff v Jenkins*.[198] These cases caused some consternation, as the plain words of the statute seemed to give the county court that jurisdiction. The point was raised again in *Davis v Johnson*, and a five-member Court of Appeal was assembled.[199] Only Cumming-Bruce L.J. held that the earlier cases were correctly decided. Goff L.J. held that they were binding even though they were wrong. The other three members of the court held that they were wrong, and, on a variety of grounds, not binding. Lord Denning said that:

> "while the court should regard itself as normally bound by a previous decision of the court, nevertheless it should be at liberty to depart from it if it is convinced that the previous decision was wrong."[200]

Either the Court of Appeal should take for itself guidelines similar to those taken by the House of Lords,[201] or this should be regarded as an additional exception to *Young v Bristol Aeroplane Co Ltd*.[202] Lord Denning had long argued for such a change,[203] but had been unable to convince either his colleagues or the House of Lords. Sir George Baker P. and Shaw L.J. were prepared to contemplate a new, limited exception to *Young v Bristol Aeroplane Co Ltd*, Shaw L.J.'s formulation being the narrower.[204]

The House of Lords unanimously dismissed an appeal; *B v B* and *Cantliff v Jenkins* were overruled.[205] However, the House strongly reafffirmed the rule that the Court of Appeal was bound by its own previous decisions, subject to clearly defined exceptions which did not include those advanced in the Court of Appeal. The argument in favour of *Young*'s case was summarised by Lord Diplock[206]:

> "In an appellate court of last resort a balance must be struck between the need on the one hand for the legal certainty resulting from the binding effect of previous decisions, and, on the other side the avoidance of undue restriction on the proper development of the law. In the case of an inter-mediate appellate court, however, the second desideratum can be taken care of by appeal to a superior appellate court, if reasonable means of access to

---

[198] [1978] Fam. 47, decided on October 20, 1977 by Stamp, Orr and Ormrod L.JJ. The couple were joint tenants.

[199] [1979] A.C. 264. Lord Denning M.R., Sir George Baker P., Goff, Shaw and Cumming-Bruce L.JJ.: described by Lord Denning as "a court of all the talents" [1979] A.C. 264, 271.

[200] [1979] A.C. 264, 278–282.

[201] See below, paras 7–026, 7–027.

[202] [1944] K.B. 718.

[203] *The Discipline of Law* (1979), pp.297–300; *Gallie v Lee* [1969] 2 Ch. 17, 37; *Hanning v Maitland (No.2)* [1970] 1 Q.B. 580, 587; *Barrington v Lee* [1972] 1 Q.B. 326, 338. He temporarily conceded defeat in *Tiverton Estates Ltd v Wearwell Ltd* [1975] Ch. 146, 160–161, but raised the point again in *Davis v Johnson* and suffered a "crushing rebuff" (*The Discipline of Law* (1979), p.299).

[204] [1979] A.C. 204, 290, 308.

[205] Lord Diplock alone thought that *B v B* had been correctly decided, making the overall division of appellate judicial opinion eight all: [1979] A.C. 264, 323. That case had concerned the situation where the man was sole tenant. However, his Lordship held that an injunction could be awarded where both parties were joint tenants: as the facts of *Davis v Johnson* fell into that category he was in favour of dismissing the appeal.

[206] [1979] A.C. 264, 326. Viscount Dilhorne, Lord Kilbrandon, and Lord Scarman expressly agreed with Lord Diplock's views on precedent: [1979] A.C. 264, 336, 340, 349. See also Scarman L.J. in *Tiverton Estates Ltd v Wearwell Ltd* [1975] Ch. 146, 172–173 and in *Farrell v Alexander* [1976] Q.B. 345, 371.

it are available; while the risk to the first desideratum, legal certainty if the court is not bound by its own previous decisions grows even greater with increasing membership and the number of three-judge divisions in which it sits. . . ."

The argument against is that "the House of Lords may never have an opportunity to correct [an] error; and thus it may be perpetuated indefinitely, perhaps for ever".[207] Litigants may be unable to finance a further appeal; the case may be settled; an insurance company or big employer who wins in the Court of Appeal may " buy off an appeal to the House of Lords by paying ample compensation to the appellant".[208] Lord Diplock responded by pointing out that in view of *Cantliff v Jenkins* there had been no need for anything but the briefest of hearings in the Court of Appeal, and an appeal to the House could have been heard and decided quickly. The argument of delay and expense could also be used to justify any High Court or county court judge in refusing to follow a decision of the Court of Appeal that he thought was wrong. There is also the possibility of using the "leap-frog" procedure under the Administration of Justice Act 1969.[209]

Lord Salmon expressed some sympathy for Lord Denning's views, but said that "until such time, if ever, as all his colleagues in the Court of Appeal agree with those views, *stare decisis* must still hold the field".[210] In view of the large number of Lord Justices, keeping to *stare decisis* might be "no bad thing". He suggested that where the Court of Appeal gave leave to appeal from a decision it felt bound to make by authority and with which it disagreed, it should have the statutory power to order that the costs of the appeal be paid from public funds. This would be a very rare occurrence, and the cost minimal.

According to the Court of Appeal *stare decisis* does not prevent an English court giving effect to a change in a rule of international law notwithstanding the existence of English precedents based on the old rule.[211] It also seems that the Court of Appeal is not bound by its own previous decisions where it is the court of last resort, with no possible appeal to the House of Lords.[212]

(e) Can lower tiers rely on the exceptions to Young v Bristol Aeroplane Co Ltd?

This question was answered in the negative by Lord Hailsham L.C. in *Cassell & Co Ltd v Broome*,[213] but there have been cases where the Divisional Court or a trial judge has declined to follow a decision of the Court of Appeal on the ground

7–024

---

[207] *per* Lord Denning M.R. in *Davis v Johnson* [1979] A.C. 264, 278.
[208] *ibid.* p.278.
[209] See below, para.18–038. Lord Diplock [1979] A.C. 264, 324–325.
[210] [1979] A.C. 264, 344.
[211] *Trendtex Trading Corporation v Central Bank of Nigeria* [1977] Q.B. 529, 554 (Lord Denning M.R.), 579 (Shaw L.J.) (a case on the scope of the doctrine of state immunity). Stephenson L.J. dissented on this point. The Court of Appeal's decision was followed by Robert Goff J. and the Court of Appeal in *I Congreso del Partido* [1978] Q.B. 500 and [1981] 1 All E.R. 1092, and Lloyd J. in *Planmount Ltd v Republic of Zaire* [1981] 1 All E.R. 1110; but not by Donaldson J. in *Uganda Co (Holdings) Ltd v Government of Uganda* [1979] 1 Lloyd's Rep. 481. The House of Lords in *I Congreso del Partido* endorsed the general approach of the Court of Appeal in *Trendtex* but did not advert to the "precedent" aspect: [1983] 1 A.C. 244.
[212] Lord Denning M.R. in *Davis v Johnson* [1979] A.C. 264, 282.
[213] [1972] A.C. 1027, 1054; above, para.7–014. In *Baker v The Queen* [1975] A.C. 774, 788, Lord Diplock stated that a lower court could not rely on the *per incuriam* rule in relation to the decision of a higher court, but could choose between conflicting decisions.

that it was inconsistent with a House of Lords' decision,[214] and the point cannot be regarded as settled. It is difficult, for example, to see that a trial judge should follow a decision of a higher court given in ignorance of a binding statutory provision. According to Lord Denning M.R., where decisions of the same court conflict, lower courts should follow the later case[215]; Donaldson J. disagreed.[216]

6. The Court of Appeal (Criminal Division)[217]

7–025 This court is obviously bound by decisions of the House of Lords. It is also generally bound by its own previous decisions and those of its forerunners, the Court of Criminal Appeal and the Court for Crown Cases Reserved. However, as the liberty of the subject is involved, *stare decisis* is not applied with the same rigidity as in the Civil Division. A decision may not be followed if it falls within one of the established exceptions to *Young v Bristol Aeroplane Co Ltd*.[218] An example is *R v Gould*[219] where the Court of Appeal (Criminal Division) followed a decision of the Court of Crown Cases Reserved in 1889[220] in preference to a later conflicting decision of the Court of Criminal Appeal in 1921,[221] on the question whether *mens rea* was an essential ingredient of the offence of bigamy. In addition, Diplock L.J. stated in *Gould* that:

> "if upon due consideration we were to be of opinion that the law had been either misapplied or misunderstood in an earlier decision of this court or its predecessor, the Court of Criminal Appeal, we should be entitled to depart from the view as to the law expressed in the earlier decision notwithstanding that the case could not be brought within any of the exceptions laid down in *Young v Bristol Aeroplane Co Ltd.*"[222]

It has been uncertain whether this power is available wherever the court is convinced that the earlier decision is wrong, as this *dictum* suggests, or only

---

[214] *R v Northumberland Compensation Appeal Tribunal, Ex p. Shaw* [1951] 1 K.B. 711, where the Divisional Court declined to follow the decision of the Court of Appeal in *Racecourse Betting Control Board v Secretary for Air* [1944] Ch. 114 on the ground that it was inconsistent with the views expressed by the House of Lords in *Walsall Overseers v L.N.W. Ry Co* (1878) 4 App. Cas. 30 and the Privy Council in *R v Nat. Bell Liquors Ltd* [1922] 2 A.C. 128, which cases had not been cited. The *Shaw* case was not cited in *Cassell & Co Ltd v Broome*. See also *Midland Bank v Hen, Stubbs & Kemp*, above, para.7–019; *The Alexandros P.* [1986] Q.B. 464; *Hughes v Kingston upon Hull City Council* [1999] Q.B. 1193.

[215] *Davis v Johnson* [1979] A.C. 264, 279. See to the same effect *Taylor Woodrow Property Co Ltd v Lonrho Textiles Ltd* [1985] 2 EGLR 120, B. Hytner Q.C. (sitting as a deputy High Court judge); Warner J. in *Re Smith (a bankrupt)* [1988] Ch. 457; and the decision of the Employment Appeal Tribunal in *Langley v BURLO* [2006] I.C.R. 850.

[216] *Uganda Co (Holdings) Ltd v Government of Uganda* [1979] 1 Lloyd's Rep. 481, 485: a trial judge should "seek to anticipate how the Court of Appeal itself would . . . resolve the conflict".

[217] See G. Zellick, [1974] Crim. L.R. 222; R. Pattenden, [1984] Crim. L.R. 592.

[218] [1944] K.B. 718. See above, paras 7–016—7–023. For an example of an application of the *per incuriam* doctrine, see *R v Ewing* [1983] Q.B. 1039, disapproving *R v Angeli* [1979] 1 W.L.R. 26 on the ground that it could not stand with the decision of the House of Lords in *Blyth v Blyth* [1966] A.C. 643; and *R v El-Gazzar* (1986) 8 Cr.App.(S) 182.

[219] [1968] 2 Q.B. 65. Other examples are *R v Preece, R v Howells* (1976) 63 Cr.App.R. 28; *R v Maginnis* [1986] Q.B. 618.

[220] *R v Tolson* (1889) 23 Q.B.D. 168.

[221] *R v Wheat* [1921] 2 K.B. 119.

[222] [1968] 2 Q.B. 65, 69.

where overruling is in the interests of the defendant. The preponderance of authority supports the latter, narrower view. A clear statement was made by the court in *R v Spencer*[223]:

> "As a matter of principle we respectfully find it difficult to see why there should in general be any difference in the application of the principle of *stare decisis* between the Civil and Criminal Divisions of the Court, save that we must remember that in the latter we may be dealing with the liberty of the subject[224] and if a departure from authority is necessary in the interests of justice to an appellant, then this court should not shrink from so acting."[225]

This does not, however, extend to allowing a defendant to rely on a wrongly decided case to provide a technical defence.[226]

This restriction does not apply to decisions on matters of sentencing. In *R v Newsome, R v Browne*[227] the Court of Appeal (Criminal Division) overruled two earlier decisions of the court[228] to the effect that a judge could not increase a sentence of imprisonment once passed to ensure that it would not be suspended even if this were to be done immediately. Widgery L.J. said[229] that if a court of five members is constituted:

> "to consider an issue of discretion and the principles upon which discretion should be exercised, that court ought to have the right to depart from an earlier view expressed by a court of three, especially where it was a matter in which the court did not have the opportunity of hearing argument on both sides."

The view that a "full court"[230] has greater power to overrule than an ordinarily constituted court was also held by the Court of Criminal Appeal,[231] although it

---

[223] [1985] Q.B. 771. Followed in *R v Pope (Alan)* [2001] EWCA Crim 972 where no exception to *Young* was available.

[224] The defendant's "liberty" appears not to be at stake where he or she has been fined but not imprisoned: *R v Burke* [1988] Crim. L.R. 839, CA.

[225] *ibid.* p.779, *per* May L.J. See, to the same effect, Lord Goddard C.J. in *R v Taylor* [1950] 2 K.B. 368, 371 (Court of Criminal Appeal), referring to the "bounden duty" of the court to reconsider an erroneous decision, on the strength of which "an accused person has been sentenced and imprisoned"; Lord Diplock, *obiter*, in *DPP v Merriman* [1973] A.C. 584, 605: the liberty of the court "to depart from a precedent which it is convinced was erroneous is restricted to cases where the departure is in favour of the accused": this *dictum* was applied by the court in *R v Jenkins* (1983) 76 Cr.App.R. 313, 318 (the better view here is that the consideration was irrelevant as the court was choosing between conflicting decisions and not overruling a single decision: J. C. Smith, [1983] Crim. L.R. at pp.388–389), and in *R v Howe* [1986] Q.B. 626, 642.

[226] *per* Lord Woolf C.J. in *R v Simpson* [2004] Q.B. 118, at para.34. The court declined to apply a precedent that held that the court lacked jurisdiction to make a confiscation order where the notice served on the court was not in the required form.

[227] [1970] 2 Q.B. 711, decided in July 1970.

[228] *R v Corr, The Times*, January 16, 1970 and *R v Maylam* (unreported) decided on February, 26 1970. In *Newsome and Browne*, the actual sentences were suspended as it was "the only fair thing to do" (a form of prospective overruling: see below, para.7–028).

[229] At p.717. Endorsed by the court in *R v Simpson* [2004] Q.B. 118.

[230] A term which usually denotes a court of more than the usual number of judges (e.g. five or seven for the Divisional Court, five for the Court of Appeal and seven in the House of Lords) and not a court of all the judges eligible to sit.

[231] *R v Taylor* [1950] 2 K.B. 368.

has been rejected by the Divisional Court[232] and the Court of Appeal.[233] It seems in practice that a full court is not necessary where one of the exceptions to *Young v Bristol Aeroplane Co Ltd* is applied, but is thought appropriate where over-ruling is contemplated on wider grounds.[234] In *Newsome* Widgery L.J. stressed that the court would be more reluctant to depart from an earlier decision where guilt or innocence was involved as distinct from the exercise of the court's discretion.

It is uncertain whether the Court of Appeal (Criminal Division) is bound by decisions of the Court of Appeal (Civil Division), and *vice versa*. Before reorganisation the Court of Appeal and Court of Criminal Appeal seemed not to be bound by each other's decisions.[235]

A decision of the court is treated as a binding authority notwithstanding that the appellant who has won the argument on the point of law has had his or her appeal dismissed under the proviso to s.2 of the Criminal Appeal Act 1968.[236]

7. THE HOUSE OF LORDS

(a) Overruling previous House of Lords decisions

7–026   Decisions of the House of Lords are[237] binding on courts lower in the hierarchy, including, if not especially, the Court of Appeal. In *London Tramways v London County Council*[238] the House of Lords held that it was bound by its own previous decisions in the interests of finality and certainty in the law. It was accepted that a decision could be questioned where it conflicted with another decision of the House or was made *per incuriam*.[239] Other exceptions were suggested. However, as the House was the final court of appeal the correction of error was normally dependent on the vagaries of the legislative process. In 1966 Lord Gardiner L.C.

---

[232] *Younghusband v Luftig* [1949] 2 K.B. 354: curiously, a criminal case.

[233] In the exercise of its civil jurisdiction: *Young v Bristol Aeroplane Co Ltd* [1944] K.B. 718, 725.

[234] *Gould* was decided by a three-member court: see Zellick, [1974] Crim. L.R. 222, 231–232.

[235] See *Hardie & Lane v Chilton* [1928] 2 K.B. 306, CA versus *R v Denyer* [1926] 2 K.B. 258, CCA and the statement of Lord Hewart C.J. in the Court of Criminal Appeal at 20 Cr.App.Rep. 185.

[236] As originally enacted; see below, para.18–013. Here the distinction between *ratio* and *dictum* is "meaningless in practice": Cross and Harris (1991), p.80; above, paras 7–003—7–008.

[237] The dismissal by the House of Lords of a petition for leave to appeal against a decision of a lower court does not constitute implied approval of that decision by the House: *Re Wilson* [1985] A.C. 750, 756.

[238] [1898] A.C. 375: not "London Street Tramways" see the list of errata at the start of the [1898] A.C. volume (Cross and Harris (1991), p.102, n.22). See D. Pugsley, (1996) 17 *Legal History* 172.

[239] See above, para.7–017. For an example of a choice by the House of Lords between two conflicting decisions of its own, see *Moodie v Inland Revenue Commissioners* [1993] 1 W.L.R. 266 (following *Ramsay (W.T.) Ltd v I.R.C.* in preference to *I.R.C. v Plummer* [1980] A.C. 896). See J. Tiley, [1991] B.T.R. 402; D. Sandler, [1993] C.L.J. 399. Lord Templeman stated (at p.273): "Faced with conflicting decisions, the courts are entitled and bound to follow *Ramsay*'s case because in *Plummer*'s case this House was never asked to consider the effect of a self-cancelling scheme and because the principle of *Ramsay*'s case restores justice between individual taxpayers and the general body of taxpayers." It is submitted that these are substantive reasons for preferring *Ramsay*, rather than a rule that the later of two conflicting decisions must always be followed.

made the following statement on behalf of himself and the Lords of Appeal in Ordinary[240]:

> "Their Lordships regard the use of precedent as an indispensable foundation upon which to decide what is the law and its application to individual cases. It provides at least some degree of certainty upon which individuals can rely on the conduct of their affairs, as well as a basis for orderly development of legal rules.
>
> Their Lordships nevertheless recognise that too rigid adherence to precedent may lead to injustice in a particular case and also unduly restrict the proper development of the law. They propose, therefore, to modify their present practice and, while treating former decisions of this House as normally binding, to depart from a previous decision when it appears right to do so.
>
> In this connection they will bear in mind the danger of disturbing retrospectively the basis on which contracts, settlements of property and fiscal arrangements have been entered into and also the especial need for certainty as to the criminal law.
>
> This announcement is not intended to affect the use of precedent elsewhere than in this House."

A press notice issued at the same time[241] indicated that the statement was of great importance although it should not be supposed that it would frequently be applied. An example of a case where it might be used would be where an earlier decision was "influenced by the existence of conditions which no longer prevail, and that in modern conditions the law ought to be different". The change would also enable the House to pay greater attention to Commonwealth decisions critical of the House. As predicted the power has been used sparingly. Members of the House seem reluctant to state expressly that an earlier decision is "overruled" even where that appears to be the case.

The decision in *The Aello*[242] on a point of shipping law[243] was overruled in the *Johanna Oldendorff*.[244] As we have seen, the *Havana* case,[245] or at least the assumption upon which it was based, was overruled in *Miliangos v George Frank (Textiles) Ltd.*[246] The decision in *Congreve v Inland Revenue Commissioners*[247] was overruled in *Vestey v Inland Revenue Commissioners (Nos 1 and 2)*[248] on the

---

[240] *Practice Statement (Judicial Precedent)* [1966] 1 W.L.R. 1234. Lord Denning M.R. and Lord Parker C.J. were also present. See R. W. M. Dias, [1966] C.L.J. 153; R. Stone, [1968] C.L.J. 35; J. Stone, (1969) 69 Columbia L.R. 1162. The circumstances surrounding the introduction of the Statement and the way in which it has been used are examined by A. Paterson in *The Law Lords* (1982), Ch.6 and pp.154–169 and G. Maher, [1981] Stat. L.R. 85. See also below, para.7–032.

[241] See M. Zander, *The Law-Making Process* (4th edn, 1994), pp.192–193.

[242] [1961] A.C. 135.

[243] The test for determining when a ship has "arrived" in port. The expense of delay in discharging cargo from an "arrived" ship caused, for example, by congestion at the berths, normally falls on the charterer and not on the owners of the vessel.

[244] *E. L. Oldendorff v Tradax Export* [1974] A.C. 479. This was the first occasion when the statement was clearly used. It has been argued that it had already been used in *Conway v Rimmer* [1968] A.C. 910 and *British Railways Board v Herrington* [1972] A.C. 879: see Paterson (1982), p.164. On *Conway v Rimmer*, see J. Stone, *op. cit.* n.240 above.

[245] [1961] A.C. 1007: see above, para.7–021.

[246] [1976] A.C. 443. In the same year the Statement was used in the Scottish case of *Dick v Burgh of Falkirk* 1976 S.L.T. 21.

[247] [1948] 1 All E.R. 948.

[248] [1980] A.C. 1148.

ground that the earlier decision, on a point of construction of a Finance Act, had led to unforeseen results that were "arbitrary, potentially unjust and fundamentally unconstitutional".[249] The law as to the liability of the occupiers of land towards trespassers was restated by the House, with some differences of formulation among their Lordships, in *British Railways Board v Herrington*.[250] The law as expounded, more restrictively, by the House in *Robert Addie & Sons (Collieries) Ltd v Dumbreck*[251] was, according to the headnote in the Law Reports, "reconsidered".[252] Then, the House in *R v Secretary of State for the Home Department, Ex p. Khawaja*[253] overruled the decision in *R v Secretary of State for the Home Department, Ex p. Zamir*[254] holding that a person could only be removed as an "illegal immigrant" if the *court* was satisfied that the entry was illegal: it would no longer be sufficient that the *immigration officer* was satisfied and had some evidence for that belief. The issue concerned the liberty of the subject and did not fall into any of the categories in which the *Practice Statement* indicated the need for special caution.

7–027   Most spectacularly, the House of Lords in *R v Shivpuri*[255] overruled its earlier decision in *Anderton v Ryan*[256] which had misinterpreted the Criminal Attempts Act 1981 in holding that a defence of impossibility in the criminal law had to an extent survived the Act. *Anderton v Ryan* had been adversely criticised by almost all the academic commentators, most notably by Professor Glanville Williams in an article in the Cambridge Law Journal.[257] Among the grounds for Professor Williams' criticism were that the House disregarded (1) the bulk of the relevant academic literature, (2) the Law Commission report that led to the 1981 Act,[258] and (3) the plain words of the Act. Lord Bridge, who had been a party to the decision in *Anderton v Ryan*, delivered the main speech in *R v Shivpuri*. He acknowledged that the earlier decision was wrong, that there was no valid ground on which it could be distinguished, and that it should be overruled, notwithstanding the "especial need for certainty in the criminal law".[259] He was undeterred by the consideration that *Anderton v Ryan* was recent: "If a serious error is embodied in a decision of this House has distorted the law, the sooner it is corrected the better".[260] He could not see how anyone could have acted in reliance on *Anderton v Ryan* in the belief that he or she was acting innocently, and now find that, after all, he or she was to be held to have committed a criminal offence. A decision to follow *Anderton v Ryan* would "be tantamount to a declaration that the Act of 1981 left the law of criminal attempts unchanged

---

[249] *per* Lord Wilberforce at p.1176.

[250] [1972] A.C. 879.

[251] [1929] A.C. 358.

[252] Lord Reid's word at p.879. Lord Reid (p.898) and Lord Morris did, however, say that *Addie's* case was "wrongly decided". Lord Pearson regarded the *Addie* formulation as an "anomaly" which "should be discarded" (p.930). Lord Diplock rejected it "as amounting to an exclusive or comprehensive statement" of the duty owed to a trespasser (p.941). Lord Wilberforce spoke of "developing" the law in *Addie's* case (p.921). See now the Occupiers' Liability Act 1984.

[253] [1984] A.C. 74.

[254] [1980] A.C. 930.

[255] [1987] A.C. 1.

[256] [1985] A.C. 560.

[257] "The Lords and Impossible Attempts, or *Quis Custodiet Ipsos Custodes?*" [1986] C.L.J. 33.

[258] *Attempt, and Impossibility in relation to Attempt, Conspiracy and Incitement* (Law Com. No.102, 1980).

[259] A reference to the 1966 *Practice Statement*, above para.7–026.

[260] [1987] A.C. 1, 23.

following the decision in *R v Smith (Roger)*".[261] He concluded by referring to Professor Williams' article:

"The language in which he criticises the decision in *Anderton v Ryan* is not conspicuous for its moderation, but it would be foolish, on that account, not to recognise the force of the criticism and churlish not to acknowledge the assistance I have derived from it."[262]

Nine months later, in *R v Howe*[263] the House of Lords again departed from an earlier decision in a criminal law case, overruling *DPP for Northern Ireland v Lynch*.[264] In *Howe*, it was held that duress can never be a defence to murder: in *Lynch* it had been held that it could be raised as a defence by a principal in the second degree, albeit not the actual killer. Here, the arguments in favour of overruling were significantly weaker than in *R v Shivpuri*.[265] In *Murphy v Brentwood District Council*,[266] the House overruled its decision in *Anns v Merton London Borough Council*,[267] and held that a local authority owes no duty of care in tort to protect the purchaser of a house from economic losses caused by defects in the house. *Anns* was contrary to established principle, and overruling would restore certainty to the law. In *R v G*[268] the House of Lords departed from the decision in *R v Caldwell*[269] holding that foresight of consequences was an essential ingredient of "recklessness" in the Criminal Damage Act 1971. Reasons for overruling included that conviction of serious crime be based on a culpable state of mind; the rule could produce unfairness; the widespread criticism of *Caldwell* by academics, judges and practitioners; and the *Caldwell* approach was a misinterpretation of the Act. Finally, in *Horton v Sadler*[270] the House of Lords departed[271] from a decision that prevented a claimant seeking a discretionary disapplication of the ordinary limitation period in a personal injuries case where he or she had issued proceedings in respect of those injuries before that period had expired. The reasoning was unsound and had given rise to distinctions that were so fine as to reflect no credit.

Other invitations to the House to overrule a past decision have not been accepted. A remarkable example is *Jones v Secretary of State for Social Services*[272] where four out of seven members of the House held that the earlier

---

[261] [1975] A.C. 476, also known as *Haughton v Smith* [1973] 3 All E.R. 1109, HL. Criticism of this decision had led to the 1981 Act.

[262] [1987] A.C. 1, 23. Professor Williams' campaign on this issue stretched over decades: see P. S. Atiyah, *Pragmatism and Theory in English Law* (1987), pp.180–183. On *Shivpuri*, see J. R. Spencer, [1986] C.L.J. 361; P. R. Glazebrook, [1986] C.L.J. 363; [1986] Crim. L.R. 536, commentary by J. C. Smith; E. M. Clare Canton, (1987) 137 N.L.J. 491, also commenting on *Howe*, below.

[263] [1987] A.C. 417.

[264] [1975] A.C. 653.

[265] See [1987] Crim. L.R. 480, commentary by J. C. Smith; C. Gearty, [1987] C.L.J. 203; H. P. Milgate, "Duress and the Criminal Law: Another about turn by the House of Lords" [1988] C.L.J. 61; L. Walters, "Murder under duress and judicial decision-making in the House of Lords" (1988) 8 L.S. 61.

[266] [1991] 1 A.C. 398. See J. W. Harris, (1991) 11 O.J.L.S. 416.

[267] [1978] A.C. 728.

[268] [2004] 1 A.C. 1034.

[269] [1982] A.C. 341.

[270] [2007] 1 A.C. 307.

[271] *Walkley v Precision Forgings Ltd* [1979] 1 W.L.R. 606.

[272] [1972] A.C. 944. Alternatively entitled *R v National Insurance Commissioners, Ex p. Hudson*. See J. Stone, (1972) 35 M.L.R. 449, 469–477.

decision of the House in *Re Dowling*[273] on a point of national insurance law[274] was incorrect, but only three thought that *Re Dowling* should be overruled. The main "defector" was Lord Simon of Glaisdale, who stated[275] that the 1966 declaration should be used most sparingly; that a variation of view on a matter of statutory construction would rarely provide a suitable occasion for its use unless it could be convincingly shown that a previous, erroneous, construction was causing administrative difficulties or individual injustice; that the House should be reluctant to encourage litigants to reopen arguments once concluded; that there was much to be said for each side of this case; and that *Re Dowling* was not unworkable and could in any event be altered more appropriately by Parliament.[276] In *Fitzleet Estates Ltd v Cherry*[277] the House refused to review a 1965 majority decision on a point of tax law, in the absence of any new argument, any change of circumstances or any suggestion that it was productive of injustice. In *Hesperides Hotels Ltd v Muftizade*[278] the House declined to modify the long-established rule that the High Court has no jurisdiction to entertain an action for damages for trespass to land situated abroad.[279] The rule was accepted in other jurisdictions, a change might involve conflict with foreign jurisdictions and there had been no change of circumstances. In *President of India v La Pintada Compania Navigacion S.A.*[280] the House declined to depart from an earlier decision[281] that the common law does not award general damages for delay in payment of a debt. Much of the injustice caused by this decision had been removed by a combination of legislative and judicial intervention; Parliament had declined to accept a recommendation from the Law Commission[282] that would have covered the case here, while accepting other recommendations in the area; and reversal of the common law rule would have the effect of overriding restrictions in the statutory provisions that had been enacted. Perhaps the most

---

[273] *R v Deputy Industrial Injuries Commissioner, Ex p. Amalgamated Engineering Union, re Dowling* [1967] 1 A.C. 725.

[274] Whether a decision by a National Insurance Commissioner (adjudicating a claim for industrial injuries benefit) that injuries were caused by an industrial accident, was binding on a Medical Appeal Tribunal (adjudicating a subsequent claim for industrial disablement benefit).

[275] At pp.1024–1025. Lord Wilberforce would not have favoured overruling *Re Dowling* if its *ratio* had been narrowly interpreted (see pp.995–996). Lord Diplock was in favour of overruling but recognised he was in the minority and so he reluctantly agreed that the appeal should be allowed (p.1015). *Cf.* Lord Reid in *R v Knuller* [1973] A.C. 435, 455–456, where he expressed the view that the House should not overrule *Shaw v DPP* [1962] A.C. 220, notwithstanding that he had dissented in *Shaw* and still thought that it had been wrongly decided; *cf.* Lord Hailsham and Lord Edmund-Davies in *R v Cunningham* [1982] A.C. 566, 581, 582. See R. Brazier, [1973] Crim. L.R. 98.

[276] It was so altered: see N. J. Wikeley and others, *Ogus, Barendt and Wikeley's The Law of Social Security* (4th edn, 1995), p.331.

[277] [1977] 1 W.L.R. 1345. Similarly, in *Paal Wilson & Co v Partenreederei Hannah Blumenthal* [1983] 1 A.C. 854 the House declined to overrule the recent decision in *Bremer Vulkan v South India Shipping Corp.* [1981] A.C. 909, which had "provoked serious disquiet among the whole commercial community" (*per* Lord Goff in *Food Corporation of India v Antclizo Shipping Corporation (The Antclizo)* [1988] 1 W.L.R. 603, 606). One point was "the special need for certainty, consistency and continuity in the field of commercial law" (*per* Lord Brandon at p.913). See B. J. Davenport, (1988) 104 L.Q.R. 493. The House called for the matter to be considered by Parliament and this led to the Courts and Legal Services Act 1990, s.102.

[278] [1979] A.C. 508.

[279] *British South Africa Co v Companhia de Moçambique* [1893] A.C. 602.

[280] [1985] A.C. 104. See P.M.N., [1984] 3 L.M.C.L.Q. 365.

[281] *London, Chatham and Dover Railway Co v South Eastern Railway Co* [1893] A.C. 429.

[282] Law Com. 88 (Cmnd. 7229, 1978) Report on *Interest*: see the Administration of Justice Act 1982, Sch.1. The relevant recommendation had indeed been rejected by the government: see P.M.N., *op. cit.*, p.366.

remarkable recent decision of this kind has been that in *R v Kansal (No.2)*[283] where it was held[284] that the House should not depart from its previous decision in *R v Lambert*,[285] notwithstanding that a majority[286] regarded it as erroneous. *Lambert* was a recent decision, it represented a possible view that had not been shown to be unworkable and it related only to a point of transitional concern.[287]

In other cases, the House may simply be convinced that the earlier decision was correct.[288]

Harris[289] suggests that an analysis of the case law reveals certain underlying considerations. First, the House must be convinced that it is in a position to substitute a ruling which will make a "net improvement in the law"[290]; secondly, the House will normally decline to overrule a decision where there are no new arguments not considered in the earlier case and no material change in circumstances; thirdly, it is a reason not to overrule a decision that people have regulated their affairs in reliance on it; fourthly, importance may be attached to the fact that legislation appears to have been enacted on the assumption that the impugned decision represents the law; fifthly, there is some support for the view that the House should not overrule an earlier decision where the issue is moot, the ruling on it making no difference to the outcome of the present case. A further point is that weight can certainly be given to the extent and cogency of criticism a decision arouses.

(b) Prospective overruling

In *Jones v Secretary of State for Social Services*,[291] Lord Simon of Glaisdale   **7–028** suggested that consideration should be given to the introduction, preferably by statute, of a power for the House of Lords to overrule a decision "prospectively" (i.e. for future cases only). Such a power is exercised by the United States Supreme Court[292] and in several states in the USA. This involves the express recognition that the notion that judges do not make law is a fiction, but avoids the

---

[283] [2001] UKHL 62, [2002] 2 A.C. 69.

[284] Lords Slynn, Lloyd, Steyn and Hutton, Lord Hope dissenting.

[285] [2001] UKHL 37, [2002] 2 A.C. 545.

[286] Lords Lloyd, Steyn and Hope.

[287] For further discussion, see below, para.8–016.

[288] See, e.g. *Smoker v London Fire and Civil Defence Authority* [1991] 2 A.C. 502 (*Parry v Cleaver* [1970] A.C. 1), *R v Reid* [1992] 1 W.L.R. 793 (*R v Laurence* [1982] A.C. 510) *Rees v Darlington Memorial Hospital NHS Trust* [2004] A.C. 309 (*McFarlane v Tayside Board* [2000] 2 A.C. 59) (no claim for the costs of bringing up a child that would not have been born but for the defendant doctor's negligence; *McFarlane* was, however, controversially modified by a majority in holding that there should in such cases be a £15,000 conventional award).

[289] Cross and Harris (1991), pp.135–143, "Towards principles of overruling—when should a final Court of Appeal second guess?" (1990) 10 O.J.L.S. 135 and (1991) 11 O.J.L.S. 416. See also A. Paterson, *The Law Lords* (1982), pp.156–167, identifying criteria that reflected the dominant consensus of the Law Lords in the mid-1970s; and B. V. Harris, (2002) 118 L.Q.R. 408. The dangers for final appellate courts in overruling are discussed by Judge J. D. Heydon, (2006) 122 L.Q.R. 399.

[290] Cross and Harris (1991), p.138.

[291] [1972] A.C. 944, 1026–1027. See also his Lordship's statement in *Miliangos v George Frank (Textiles) Ltd* [1976] A.C. 443, 490, and Lord Diplock [1972] A.C. 944, 1015.

[292] See, e.g. *Mapp v Ohio* 367 U.S. 643 (1961); *Linkletter v Walker* 381 U.S. 618 (1965); *Miranda v Arizona* 384 U.S. 436 (1966).

undesirable consequences of retrospectively upsetting established arrangements.[293] There are difficulties in choosing the date of transition: for example,
should the litigant who has successfully argued that a case should be overruled
be entitled to the retrospective effect of that decision, notwithstanding the general
determination that the rule should be changed prospectively? If the answer is no,
litigants will have little incentive to mount the necessary arguments. Lord Devlin
opposed the general idea of prospective overruling on the ground that it "turns
judges into undisguised legislators".[294] The House of Lords changed a rule of
practice (as distinct from a rule of *law*) prospectively in *Connelly v DPP*.[295]

   More significantly, the issue was debated at some length by the House of Lords
in *Re Spectrum Plus Ltd*.[296] The House noted a number of objections in principle
and difficulties in practice but held they did not lead to the conclusion "that it can
never be justified as a proper exercise of judicial power".[297] For example, there
could be cases where a decision on an issue of law was unavoidable, but it would
have "such gravely unfair and disruptive consequences for past transactions or
happenings" that the House would be compelled to depart from normal principles. Indeed, given that the European Court of Human Rights at times interprets
and applies the ECHR with prospective effect only, it would be odd if a similar
approach could not be adopted by the House in interpreting and applying
Convention rights under the Human Rights Act 1998.[298] The present case was,
however, one where an earlier first instance decision was properly to be overruled
with retrospective effect. Lords Steyn and Scott, however, doubted that it could
be possible to permit prospective overruling in a dispute about the interpretation
of a statute.[299] The difficulty was that were the House to reach a conclusion as to
the correct meaning of a statute but then decline to apply to the case in hand the
statute thus construed, this would in effect involve the suspension of a law
without the consent of Parliament. Such action "by regall authority" is contrary
to s.1 of the Bill of Rights 1688. While this expression probably did apply to the
exercise of judicial authority there, it was unlikely that the promoters of the 1688
Act would have contemplated that the House of Lords had such a power. It is
submitted that this argument is not decisive. It is not at all surprising to
contemplate that the judicial branch might have a power not available to the
executive or to an individual component of the legislature. It would be odd if the

---

[293] See generally W. Friedmann, (1966) 29 M.L.R. 593; M. D. A. Freeman, (1973) 26 C.L.P. 166; A.
Nicol, (1976) 39 M.L.R. 542; Cross and Harris (1991), pp.228–232, M. Arden, (2004) 120 L.Q.R.
7; Lord Rodger of Earlsferry, (2005) 121 L.Q.R. 57.

[294] Lord Devlin, "Judges and Lawmakers" (1976) 39 M.L.R. 11, 20: reprinted in *The Judge* (1979),
p.12.

[295] [1964] A.C. 1254. See also Lord Goff in *Kleinwort Benson Ltd v Lincoln City Council* [1999] 2
A.C. 349.

[296] [2005] UKHL 41, [2005] 2 A.C. 680. Ian Glick Q.C. was appointed by the Attorney-General to
act as *amicus curiae*. See D. Sheehan and T. T. Arvind, (2006) 122 L.Q,R. 20.

[297] Lord Nicholls of Birkenhead at para.[39]. In *Barclays Bank plc v O'Brien* [1994] 1 A.C. 180, the
House laid down guidelines for the future as to the procedure to be followed if a bank is to rebut
an inference of undue influence where a wife gives a charge over her property to support her
husband's debts. This has been regarded (M. Arden, (2004) 120 L.Q.R. 7) as an example of
prospective overruling as some earlier cases were by implication no longer good law. The matter
was, however, dealt with in "a very low key way" (Arden, *op.cit.*).

[298] Lord Nicholls at para.[42], citing Lord Rodger, (2005) 121 L.Q.R. 57, 77. It is not obvious that
this argument would not also hold good for lower courts. This point was not reached in *R (on the
application of Wright) v Secretary of State for the Home Department* [2006] EWCA Civ 67, as
the ECtHR decision in question was regarded as retrospective.

[299] Lord Steyn at para.[45]; Lord Scott at para.[126].

transformation of the House of Lords into the Supreme Court of the UK would make any substantive difference.

In practice a decision of the House of Lords on an appeal from Scotland or Northern Ireland will be regarded as binding on English courts lower in the hierarchy on points where the law of the two countries is the same.[300]

8. THE PRIVY COUNCIL

Decisions of the Judicial Committee of the Privy Council are not technically binding on English courts except in respect of matters where an appeal lies from such a court to the Privy Council.[301] Nevertheless, in exceptional circumstances a Privy Council decision has been followed in preference to a decision of the House of Lords.[302] Furthermore, decisions of the Judicial Committee on devolution issues and issues of legislative competence are expressly made binding in all legal proceedings (other than proceedings before the Committee).[303] Apart from this, Privy Council decisions may still be highly persuasive.[304] The Privy Council will normally follow its own previous decisions, but is not bound to do so.[305] It is not bound to follow decisions of the House of Lords on common law issues, although the latter have great persuasive authority: the common law may develop differently in different parts of the Commonwealth.[306] A House of Lords' decision on the interpretation of recent legislation common to England and another part of the Commonwealth will, however, be treated as binding.[307]

7–029

9. THE COURT OF JUSTICE OF THE EUROPEAN COMMUNITIES AND THE EUROPEAN COURT OF HUMAN RIGHTS

The decisions of this court on matters of Community law are binding on English courts up to and including the House of Lords.[308] It tends to follow its own

7–030

---

[300] Cross and Harris (1991), p.22, *Heyman v Darwins Ltd* [1942] A.C. 356, 401 (Lord Porter); *Glasgow Corporation v Central Land Board* 1956 S.C. (HL) 1: where the law of "crown privilege" was held to be different in the two countries; *Re Tuck's Settlement Trusts, Public Trustee v Tuck* [1978] Ch. 49, 61 (Lord Denning M.R.).

[301] e.g. in ecclesiastical and prize matters: *Combe v Edwards* (1877) 2 P.D. 354. In *Port Line Ltd v Ben Line Steamers Ltd* [1958] 2 Q.B. 146, Diplock J. declined to follow a Privy Council decision that was in his view wrongly decided.

[302] Above, para.7–022.

[303] e.g. Scotland Act 1998, s.103(1); see further para.2–075.

[304] See, e.g. above, para.7–022, below, para.7–033.

[305] *Gideon Nkambule v R* [1950] A.C. 379; *Fatuma Binti Mohamed Bin Salim v Mohamed Bin Salim* [1952] A.C. 1; *Baker v The Queen* [1975] A.C. 774, 787–788; *Lewis v Attorney General of Jamaica* [2001] 2 A.C. 50 (prerogative of mercy in death penalty case to be exercised by procedures that were fair and amenable to judicial review); *Gibson v Government of USA* [2007] UKPC.

[306] e.g. on the right to punitive damages in tort: the Privy Council in *Australian Consolidated Press Ltd v Uren* [1969] 1 A.C. 590 did not follow the House of Lords' decision in *Rookes v Barnard* [1964] A.C. 1129; and on the liability of a local authority in respect of the inspection of buildings in the course of construction the Privy Council in *Invercargill City Council v Hamlin* [1996] 2 W.L.R. 367 did not follow the decision of the House of Lords in *Murphy v Brentwood District Council* [1991] 1 A.C. 398 (above, para.7–027).

[307] *de Lasala v de Lasala* [1980] A.C. 546.

[308] See above, paras 5–053—5–059; European Communities Act 1972, s.3(1).

previous decisions, although it is not bound to do so.[309] The Court of First Instance is expressly bound by decisions of the Court of Justice on points of law in cases referred back to the Court of First Instance.[310] Otherwise, it will regard itself as bound by decisions of the Court of Justice and will not lightly depart from its own previous decisions.[311]

The European Court of Human Rights usually follows its own previous precedents in the interests of legal certainty, but may depart if there are cogent reasons to do so.[312] Exceptionally it may declare that a judgment should only have prospective effect,[313] or give a "period of grace" for the state to bring its law into conformity with the ECHR.[314] The extent to which English courts must have regards to the jurisprudence of the Court under the Human Rights Act 1998 is dealt with below.[315]

10. TRIBUNALS

7–031   Where there is a hierarchy of tribunals, the decisions of the appellate tribunals will bind lower tribunals. For example, Social Security and Child Support Appeal Tribunals must follow decisions of the Social Security and Child Support Commissioners.[316] Tribunals are not permitted to lay down precedents binding on themselves,[317] the emphasis, in theory at least, being on deciding each case on its own facts. However, the case law of some tribunals is systematically reported[318] and general principles tend to become established,[319] and the "essential differences in practice from, say, the House of Lords or the Court of Appeal . . . are not

---

[309] Cases 2, 8, 29, 30/62, *Da Costa en Schaake NV v Nederlandse Belasting-administratie* [1963] E.C.R. 31; L. N. Brown and T. Kennedy, *The Court of Justice of the European Communities* (5th edn, 2000), Ch.16; T. Koopmans in D. O'Keefe and H. G. Schermers (eds), *Essays in European Law and Integration* (1982); A. G. Toth, "The authority of judgments of the European Court of Justice: binding force and legal effect" (1984) 4 Y.E.L. 1.

[310] Statute of the Court of Justice, Art.61, second para.

[311] Brown and Kennedy (2000), pp.375–377.

[312] See e.g. *Coster v UK*, judgment of January 18, 2001, (2001) 33 E.H.R.R. 479.

[313] *Marckx v Belgium*, judgment of June 13, 1979, (1979) 2 E.H.R.R. 330.

[314] *Walden v Liechtenstein*, judgment of March 16, 2000.

[315] para.8–003.

[316] *R.(I) 12/75* (Tribunal of Commissioners); N. J. Wikeley, *Wikeley, Ogus and Barendt*'s *The Law of Social Security* (5th edn, 2002), pp.204–205; T. Buck, *et al.*, *Making Social Security Law* (2005), Ch.5. A single Commissioner should follow a decision of a Tribunal of Commissioners on a point of legal principle unless there are compelling reasons why he should not: *ibid.*; *R.(U) 4/88(T)*; it has been held that tribunals and Commissioners are bound by decisions of the High Court and above: *ibid.*; but this is now subject to the qualification that the Commissioners now regard decisions of the High Court on substantive points of social security law made on judicial review as those of a court of co-ordinate jurisdiction, and so to be followed unless the Commissioner is convinced that they are wrong: *R.(IS) 15/99*. A decision of a Divisional Court and a decision on a challenge to a Commissioner's decision should, however, be followed: *ibid.* A decision given without reasons, made with the consent of the parties, cannot be cited as a precedent: *CSDLA/101/00*.

[317] *Merchandise Transport Ltd v British Transport Commission* [1962] 2 Q.B. 173, CA, in relation to the Transport Tribunal.

[318] In the context of social security, the Commissioners have emphasised that adjudicating officers and tribunals are bound by unreported Commissioners' decisions as well as reported: *R.(I) 12/75; R.(SB) 22/86.*

[319] J. A. Farmer, *Tribunals and Government* (1974), Ch.3, pp.171–180; T. Buck, (2006) 25 C.J.R.

as marked as one might think".[320] In the context of social security appeals, a Tribunal of Commissioners has held[321] that in determining whether to be bound by a decision of a previous Tribunal, it should adopt and adapt the principles laid down in the 1966 *Practice Statement*[322] concerning the House of Lords, and not the principles laid down in *Young v Bristol Aeroplane Co Ltd.*[323]

11. THE NATURE OF RULES OF BINDING PRECEDENT

Apart from the 1966 *Practice Statement*, propositions as to the binding effects of previous decisions have been contained in the judgments of decided cases. It has been pointed out that such propositions cannot form part of the *ratio* of a case as they are "necessarily irrelevant to the issues of law and fact that have to be decided by the court".[324] Professor Cross[325] argued that this only seems applicable to statements of higher courts about the way in which lower courts should behave,[326] but that in any event statements about the rules of precedent are statements about the courts' own practice which fall outside the *ratio-obiter* distinction. The 1966 *Practice Statement* owed its validity "to the inherent power of any court to regulate its own practice".[327] The possibility that the Court of Appeal might change the rule that it is bound by its own previous decisions by a similar practice statement has been mooted.[328] However, Lord Simon of Glaisdale asserted that any change would require legislation,[329] Cumming-Bruce L.J. accepted loyally that the constitutional functions of the House of Lords include that of declaring with authority the extent to which the Court of Appeal is bound by its previous decisions,[330] and Lord Denning in any event failed to persuade his colleagues that a change would be desirable.[331] The exceptional change to the statute as a precedent of a Privy Council decision recognised by the Court of Appeal in *R v James*[332] was certainly not based on legislation, but was

7–032

---

[320] *ibid.* p.175.
[321] *R.(U) 4/88.*
[322] Above, para.7–026.
[323] Above, paras 7–016—7–024.
[324] Glanville Williams, (1954) 70 L.Q.R. 469, 471; *cf.* Diplock L.J. in *Boys v Chaplin* [1968] 2 K.B. 1, 35.
[325] "The House of Lords and the Rules of Precedent" in P. M. S. Hacker and J. Raz (eds), *Law, Morality and Society* (1977), pp.144–160. For the contrary argument that pronouncements on precedent do indeed establish rules of law, see P. J. Evans, [1982] C.L.J. 162, criticised by L. Goldstein [1984] C.L.J. 88, with a reply by Evans, *ibid.* p.108. For the argument that they establish rules of *customary* law, see P. Aldridge, (1984) 47 M.L.R. 187. For the argument that the 1966 *Practice Statement* established, or modified, a constitutional convention, see Lord Simon of Glaisdale in *R v Knuller* [1973] A.C. 435, at p.485 and A. R. Blackshield, in L. Goldstein (ed.), *Judicial Precedent* (1987), Ch.5.
[326] *ibid.* p.154.
[327] *ibid.* p.157; Salmon L.J. in *Galli v Lee* [1969] 2 Ch. 17, 49; Lord Denning M.R. in *Davis v Johnson* [1979] A.C. 264, 281; Lord Salmon in *Davis v Johnson* (above para.7–023).
[328] *ibid.*
[329] *Miliangos v George Frank (Textiles) Ltd* [1976] A.C. 443, 470.
[330] *Davis v Johnson* [1979] A.C. 264, 311.
[331] See above, para.7–023.
[332] See para.7–022.

founded in part on the assertion by the Law Lords that comprised the Judicial Committee of the intention that it was to determine English law.

E. PERSUASIVE AUTHORITIES[333]

7–033   Precedents that are not technically binding may be cited as persuasive authorities. The extent to which a precedent will be persuasive may depend on a variety of factors including the status of the court, the country in which it was located, the reputation of the judge, whether the relevant proposition formed part of the *ratio*, whether the judgment was considered or *ex tempore*[334] and whether the judge in the later case agrees with it. Thus the attention of the court may be drawn to the *ratio* of a decision of an English court lower in the hierarchy, to *obiter dicta*, to a dissenting judgment, to a decision of the Privy Council or to a court abroad. A good example of a consideration of the advantages and disadvantages of the overruling by the House of Lords of an established line of authorities at the level of the Court of Appeal is provided by *Mannai Investment Co Ltd v Eagle Star Life Assurance Co Ltd.*[335] Here the House by 3 to 2[336] held that a notice to determine a lease that contained a minor misdescription would be effective provided that, construed against its contextual setting, it would unambiguously inform a reasonable recipient how and when it was to operate. The House overruled a Court of Appeal decision of some 50 years' standing[337] that had prescribed a stricter approach. The majority were satisfied that this contextual approach to the interpretation of notices was consistent with the modern approach to the construction of contracts and would not generate uncertainty or interfere with legitimate expectations, the stricter approach being one which allowed "one party to take unmeritorious advantage of another's verbal error".[338] The minority took the view that the existing law should not be disturbed as it was clear and well settled and disputes were rare.

Great weight will be attached to considered statements by the House of Lords whatever their technical standing. For example, in *Hedley Byrne & Co Ltd v Heller and Partners Ltd,*[339] the House of Lords held that the existence of a special relationship could give rise to a duty to take care in giving information or advice; breach of the duty could in turn lead to an action for damages in respect of purely economic losses. The Court of Appeal had held that such a duty could not arise, following its earlier decision in *Candler v Crane, Christmas & Co.*[340] The House overruled the *Candler* decision and endorsed the dissenting judgment

---

[333] See R. Bronaugh, "Persuasive precedent" in L. Goldstein (ed.), *Judicial Precedent* (1987), Ch.8.

[334] Lord Russell of Killowen has suggested that unreserved judgments should be approached with "great caution": *op. cit.* para.7–008, n.52; *cf.* Lord Reid in *Haley v London Electricity Board* [1965] A.C. 778, 792.

[335] [1997] A.C. 749. See P. V. Baker, (1998) 114 L.Q.R. 55. For another example, see *Sudbrook Trading Estate Ltd v Eggleton* [1983] 1 A.C. 444.

[336] Lords Steyn, Hoffmann and Clyde, Lords Goff and Jauncey dissenting.

[337] *Hankey v Clavering* [1942] 2 K.B. 326.

[338] *per* Lord Hoffmann at p.780.

[339] [1964] A.C. 465.

[340] [1951] 2 K.B. 164.

in that case by Denning L.J. Having found that a duty of care *did* arise as the plaintiffs claimed, the House nonetheless found for the *defendants* on the ground that they had effectively disclaimed responsibility for the statements in question. There was much debate on the issue whether the observations concerning the duty of care were *obiter*.[341] Cairns J. in *W. B. Anderson and Sons Ltd v Rhodes*[342] regarded such a suggestion as "unrealistic":

> "When five members of the House of Lords have all said, after close examination of the authorities, that a certain type of tort exists, I think that a judge of first instance should proceed on the basis that it does exist without pausing to embark on an investigation whether what was said was necessary to the ultimate decision."[343]

Similarly, it became accepted that solicitors acting as advocates were entitled to the same immunity from legal action as barristers, notwithstanding that the view had been expressed in decisions of the House of Lords concerning barristers.[344]

The "neighbour principle" expounded by Lord Atkin in *Donoghue v Stevenson*[345] can be regarded as part of the *ratio* of his speech, but not as part of the *ratio* of the House of Lords as a whole.[346] Nevertheless the principle was influential in subsequent decisions which extended the scope of the tort of negligence,[347] although the most recent decisions in the area have emphasised that it should be used, cautiously and is not the sole determinant of the existence of a duty of care.[348] By contrast, dicta of Lord Diplock[349] setting out a broader approach to the jurisdiction of a criminal court in respect of offences where elements take place abroad were adopted by the Privy Council (in respect of Hong Kong)[350] and the Supreme Court of Canada[351] but the Court of Appeal subsequently held that they could not be regarded sufficient to displace earlier, binding Court of Appeal authority to the contrary.[352]

Decisions of the Privy Council may be strongly persuasive, particularly now that membership of the Judicial Committee is mainly drawn from Lords of Appeal.[353] The Privy Council decision in *The Wagon Mound (No.1)*[354] is accepted to be the leading authority on remoteness of damage in the tort of

---

[341] See W. V. H. Rogers, *Winfield and Jolowicz on Tort* (13th edn, 1989), p.274, n.97.

[342] [1967] 2 All E.R. 850.

[343] *ibid.* p.857.

[344] For the present position, see above, para.3–044.

[345] [1932] A.C. 562, 580.

[346] Two of the five members dissented and the other two did not expressly concur with Lord Atkin's formulation: see R. F. v Heuston, (1957) 20 M.L.R. 1, 5–9.

[347] See, e.g. *Hedley Byrne & Co Ltd v Heller and Partners Ltd* [1964] A.C. 465.

[348] See, e.g. *Murphy v Brentwood District Council* [1991] 1 A.C. 398.

[349] *Treacy v DPP* [1971] A.C. 537.

[350] *Liangsiriprasert v US Government* [1991] 1 A.C. 225.

[351] *Libman v R* (1985) 21 D.L.R. (4th) 174.

[352] *R v Manning* [1999] Q.B. 980. The issues have from June 1, 1999 been dealt with by Pt 1 of the Criminal Justice Act 1993.

[353] Similarly, decisions of the House of Lords and Court of Appeal are of high persuasive authority in the courts of the Isle of Man, given that the Privy Council is the final court of appeal from a Manx court: *Frankland v The Queen* [1987] A.C. 576, PC.

[354] *Overseas Tankship (UK) Ltd v Morts Dock Engineering Co Ltd* [1961] A.C. 388.

negligence, and has been applied in preference to the decision of the Court of Appeal in *Re Polemis*.[355]

The desirability of uniformity between Scottish and English courts on points common to both systems has often been stressed, particularly on the construction of statutes and revenue and taxation matters.[356] The citation of overseas authorities seems to be increasingly common.[357] Lord Denning would not, however, in practice have followed a decision of the deputy magistrate of East Tonga in preference to six decisions of the House of Lords.[358] There have been complaints that counsel, particularly in busy appellate courts, cite too many authorities both English and foreign[359]; at the same time, counsel owes a duty to the court to cite all relevant authorities whether for or against him.

Textbooks may be cited as authorities although they can never be binding.[360] Some treatises have long been accepted as authoritative guides to the law in previous centuries, including the Abridgments of the Year Books[361] compiled by Fitzherbert and Brooke, the treatise known as "Glanvill" dating from the late twelfth century, Bracton's *De Legibus et Consuetudinibus Angliae* from the thirteenth, Littleton's *Tenures* from the fourteenth, Fitzherbert's *Nature Brevium*, Coke's *Institutes of the Laws of England* first published in 1628, eighteenth-century works on criminal law by Hale, Hawkins and Foster[362] and Blackstone's *Commentaries on the Laws of England* first published in 1765–69. These works are not cited often today, the ones on criminal law perhaps being referred to most commonly.[363] It used to be convention that living authors could not be cited as authorities, although their words could be adopted by counsel as part of his or her argument,[364] on the doubtful ground that while alive the author might change his or her mind.[365] This convention is no longer observed,[366] and books and articles by authors both living and dead are commonly cited.[367] In appropriate cases

---

[355] *Re Polemis and Furness, Withy & Co Ltd* [1921] 2 K.B. 560: see *Doughty v Turner Manufacturing Co Ltd* [1964] 1 Q.B. 518, CA; *Smith v Leech Brain & Co Ltd* [1962] 2 Q.B. 405, 415, where Lord Parker C.J. indicated *obiter* that the *Wagon Mound* case enabled a trial judge to follow other decisions of the Court of Appeal prior to *Polemis*. The test for remoteness is now whether the kind of damage was reasonably foreseeable: the former test was whether the damage was the direct consequence of the defendant's conduct. *Cf.* Robert Goff J. in *I Congreso del Partido* [1978] Q.B. 500, 517–519.

[356] See, e.g. *Abbott v Philbin (Inspector of Taxes)* [1960] Ch. 27, rvsd [1961] A.C. 352; *Westward Television Ltd v Hart (Inspector of Taxes)* [1969] 1 Ch. 201, 212; *Secretary of State for Employment and Productivity v Clarke, Chapman & Co Ltd* [1971] 1 W.L.R. 1094, 1102.

[357] See R. J. C. Munday, (1978) 14 J.S.P.T.L. (N.S.) 201, 203–207.

[358] See the (regrettably) fictional report of *Grenouille v National Union of Seamen* reproduced in Denning, *The Family Story* (1981), pp.219–220.

[359] See e.g. Lawton L.J. (1980) 14 L.T. 163, 166.

[360] *Cordell v Second Clanfield Properties Ltd* [1969] 2 Ch. 9, 16: Megarry J. in relation to Sir Robert Megarry and H. W. R. Wade, *The Law of Real Property*.

[361] See below, para.7–039.

[362] Sir Matthew Hale, *The History of the Pleas of the Crown*, published posthumously in 1736 but written in the previous century; William Hawkins, *Pleas of the Crown* (1716); Sir Michael Foster, *Crown Cases and Crown Law* (1762).

[363] See, e.g. *Button v DPP* [1966] A.C. 591; *R v Merriman* [1973] A.C. 584 (*Hale* and *Hawkins*).

[364] See, e.g. Vaughan Williams L.J. in *Greenlands Ltd v Wilmshurst* (1913) 29 T.L.R. 685, 687.

[365] Lord Reid (1972) 12 J.S.P.T.L. (N.S.) 22. This convention was the basis of somewhat leaden jokes to the effect that certain celebrated works were "fortunately" not works of authority.

[366] See *Halsbury's Laws of England* (4th edn) Vol.26, para.587.

[367] For example, in criminal law cases references to books by Glanville Williams and Sir John Smith and B. Hogan are frequent; in administrative law, Sir William Wade and C. F. Forsyth, *Administrative Law*, (9th edn, 2004) and de Smith, Woolf and Jowell, *Judicial Review of Administrative Action* (5th edn, 1995) are similarly authoritative. See the splendid story by A. Arden, [1980] Conv. 454, 458 (review of the 4th edn of *de Smith*).

reference may also be made to principles of Roman law, and especially, in that regard, Justinian's *Digest*.[368]

F. DISTINGUISHING

A precedent, whether persuasive or binding, need not be applied or followed if it can be "distinguished": i.e. there is a material distinction between the facts of the precedent case and the case in question. What counts as a "material" distinction is obviously crucial. The judge in the later case is expected to explain why the distinction is such as to justify the application of a different rule. If the distinction is spurious, the judge may be criticised or reversed or, if the case distinguished is generally regarded as a bad precedent, applauded for his or her boldness. There is no test or set of tests for whether a distinction is legally relevant; it all depends upon the circumstances of the case. **7–034**

An example is provided by *R v Secretary of State for the Environment, Ex p. Ostler*.[369] In 1956, the House of Lords in *Smith v East Elloe R.D.C.*[370] ruled that a provision[371] that the validity of a compulsory purchase order should not be questioned in any legal proceedings, other than a statutory application to quash made within six weeks, meant what it said: an action to impugn an order on the ground of fraud could not be brought some six years later. However, in *Anisminic Ltd v The Foreign Compensation Commission*[372] the House held that s.4 of the Foreign Compensation Act 1950, which provided that a determination by the Commission "shall not be called in question in any court of law", was not effective to render immune from judicial review a purported determination that was in truth a nullity and thus not a "determination" at all. The decision in *Smith v East Elloe R.D.C.* was adversely criticised but not overruled. In *Ostler* the Court of Appeal was faced with an ouster clause of the kind at issue in *Smith v East Elloe R.D.C.*, and it followed *Smith* in preference to *Anisminic*, which was distinguished on a variety of grounds. For example, the point was taken that s.4 of the 1950 Act purported to exclude judicial review altogether whereas the provision in *Ostler* was more akin to a limitation period in that it excluded review only after a six-week period. It was said that *Anisminic* concerned a "judicial" decision and *Ostler* an "administrative" one. Their Lordships were not, however, unanimous as to their reasons, and Lord Denning M.R. subsequently indicated extra-judicially that he no longer regarded most of his own as sound.[373]

---

[368] See, e.g. *Coggs v Bernard* (1703) 2 Ld. Raym. 909 and *Dalton v Angus* (1881) 6 App. Cas. 740.

[369] [1977] Q.B. 122.

[370] [1956] A.C. 736.

[371] Acquisition of Land (Authorisation Procedure) Act 1946, Sch.1, Pt IV, paras 15, 16.

[372] [1969] 2 A.C. 147.

[373] *The Discipline of Law* (1979), pp.108–109.

G. PRECEDENT AND STATUTORY INTERPRETATION

7–035   A decision on a question of the construction of a statute is binding to the same extent as a decision on other kinds of question.[374] Thus it is applicable in cases concerning the same words in the same Act and "in all cases which do not provide substantial relevant differences".[375] The same words appearing in a different statute may be interpreted differently, although a decision on the construction of a particular set of words may be used as a guide when other statutes dealing with the same or a similar subject-matter are considered.[376] If words which have been the subject of construction by a court are re-enacted by Parliament without alteration, a court will be very slow to overrule that decision but not always unwilling to do so.[377] Moreover, Lord Wilberforce has stated that[378]:

> "Self-contained statutes, whether consolidating previous law, or so doing with the amendments, should be interpreted, if reasonably possible, without recourse to antecedents,[379] and that recourse should only be had when there is a real and substantial difficulty or ambiguity which classical methods of construction cannot resolve."

H. RATIO DECIDENDI AND RES JUDICATA

7–036   In its wider meaning the term "judgment" is used to cover the whole of the judge's pronouncement after the arguments of each side have been heard (e.g. as in "I will deliver my judgment after lunch"). In its narrower meaning it is used to cover the order of the court as distinct from the reasons for it (e.g. "There will be judgment for the plaintiff for £500"). Assuming the order lies within the judge's jurisdiction it is binding on the parties (*res judicata*). They may not reopen the issue that has just been determined, unless a statute has provided for an appeal.[380] Thus the court's *order* is binding on the *parties* under the *res judicata* doctrine; the *ratio decidendi* is binding on other *courts* in accordance with the principles outlined above under the doctrine of binding precedent. A startling illustration of the distinction was provided by the following series of cases. A testator, John Arkle Waring, left annuities to Mr Howard and Mrs Louie

---

[374] *Per* Lord Reid in *Goodrich v Paisner* [1957] A.C. 65, 88 and *London Transport Executive v Betts* [1959] A.C. 211, 232.

[375] *Goodrich v Paisner, ibid.*

[376] *ibid.*; Lord Upjohn in *Ogden Industries Pty Ltd v Lucas* [1970] A.C. 113, 127; *R v Freeman* [1970] 1 W.L.R. 788 (meaning of "firearm" in successive Firearms Acts).

[377] *Royal Crown Derby Porcelain Ltd v Raymond Russell* [1949] 2 K.B. 417, 429, *per* Denning L.J.; *cf. R v Bow Road JJ., Ex p. Adedigba* [1968] 2 Q.B. 572.

[378] *Farrell v Alexander* [1977] A.C. 59, 73. Lord Simon and Lord Edmund-Davies agreed with this approach; *cf.* above, para.6–033.

[379] i.e. the history of the provisions and the cases decided on them.

[380] See Ch.18. In the case of courts and tribunals with a jurisdiction limited by statute there is also the possibility of judicial review under the *ultra vires* doctrine where the jurisdiction has been exceeded or abused.

Burton-Butler "free of income tax". In 1942 the Court of Appeal in *Re Waring, Westminster Bank Ltd v Awdry*,[381] on an appeal in which Howard was a party, held that income tax had to be deducted. Louie was not a party as she was in an enemy occupied country. Leave to appeal to the House of Lords was refused. Four years later the House of Lords in *Berkeley v Berkeley*[382] overruled the *Awdry* case. Subsequently, Jenkins J. held that the *Awdry* case was *res judicata* so far as Howard was concerned notwithstanding that its *ratio* had been overruled in *Berkeley v Berkeley* and that Louie's annuity would be dealt with in accordance with the latter case.[383]

I. LAW REPORTS[384]

(a) Introduction

Any legal system that is based to any significant extent upon judicial precedent **7–037** requires an effective system whereby those precedents are reported and indexed. In theory, a case may be cited as a precedent even it if has not been reported. In practice, comparatively few cases are referred to in textbooks or cited in court unless they have been reported in one of the series of published law reports, although such references are becoming more common.[385] Occasionally a judge has referred to an unreported case with which he was concerned as counsel or judge.[386] Indexed transcripts of all unreported cases in the Court of Appeal (Civil Division) are kept in the Supreme Court Library[387] and some are listed in *Current Law* and copies of unreported House of Lords' decisions are kept in the House of Lords Records Office. Transcripts of many decisions of the High Court, most of the Court of Appeal and all of the House of Lords and Privy Council are now available on the Internet.[388] Thousands of unreported cases decided since January 1, 1980, including all decisions of the House of Lords and Court of Appeal (Civil Division), are included on *LexisNexis*.

---

[381] [1942] Ch. 426.
[382] [1946] A.C. 555.
[383] *Re Waring, Westminster Bank v Burton-Butler* [1948] Ch. 221.
[384] See generally Sweet & Maxwell's *Guide to Law Reports and Statutes* (4th edn, 1962); P.A. Thomas, *Dare and Thomas, How to Use a Law Library* (4th edn, 2001), Ch.2; W. W. S. Breem, in E. M. Moys (ed.), *Manual of Law Librarianship* (2nd edn, 1987), Ch.4: "Primary sources: law reports"; P. Clinch, *Using a Law Library* (2nd edn, 2001); G. Holborn, *Butterworths Legal Research Guide* (2nd edn, 2001).
[385] R. J. C. Munday, (1978) 14 J.S.P.T.L. (N.S.) 201, 207–216.
[386] e.g. *Wilkinson v Downton* [1897] 2 Q.B. 57, 61; *Harling v Eddy* [1951] 2 K.B. 739, 746 (Denning L.J.).
[387] From 1951, an official note has been made of all Court of Appeal (Civil Division) decisions (see (1951) 95 S.J. 266). A microfiche edition of the transcripts 1951–1980 is available from HMSO (see V. Tunkel, (1986) 136 N.L.J. 1045). Transcripts of decisions of the Court of Appeal (Criminal Division) from 1960 are held by the Criminal Appeal Office in the Royal Courts of Justice (Breem, in Moys (1987), p.143). The arrangements for transcribing cases are considered by Breem, *op. cit.*, pp.144–146, and S. Cole, (1988) 19 *The Law Librarian* 89.
[388] See further, below para.7–039.

(b) A modern law report

7–038   A full law report today commonly includes the following information: the names of the parties[389]; the court in which the case was decided; the name of the judge or judges; the date or dates of the hearing; the headnote (a summary of the decision prepared by the reporter)[390]; lists of the cases discussed and cited; the previous history of the litigation, including a summary of the claims made and the result of proceedings in lower courts; the facts[391]; the names of counsel; the arguments of counsel[392]; an indication of whether judgment is reserved by the inclusion of the expression *Cur. adv. vult*[393]; the judgment or judgments[394]; the order of the court and an indication of whether leave to appeal is granted or refused; the names of the solicitors; the name of the barrister who reports the case.

(c) Law reporting[395]

7–039   The earliest law reports were contained in the "Year Books" compiled annually between the thirteenth and sixteenth centuries. These reports concentrated upon points of procedure and pleading rather than the final decisions of the courts, and were written first in Norman French and later in "law French" (an amalgam of English, French and Latin).[396] These are today mainly of interest to legal historians. Between the sixteenth and nineteenth centuries a large number of "private" or "nominate" reports appeared. Most were named after the reporter. They varied widely in their style and content, their accuracy and their reputation.[397] Some, such as those of Coke, Plowden and Saunders were of high authority. Others were regarded as of little value.[398] Some were in law French; most were in English. The focus of attention switched from the pleadings to the court's decision and the best reports included the full reasons. The first to be published in more or less the form we have today, although not verbatim reports, were Burrow's reports of the eighteenth century. The first that regularly published reports of newly decided cases were Durnford and East's "Term Reports". The private reports are cited by the name, usually abbreviated, of the reporter or

---

[389] Appeals to the House of Lords since 1974 carried the same title as in the court of first instance: *Procedure Direction* [1974] 1 W.L.R. 305. Previously, the name of the appellant appeared first.

[390] The headnote may be inaccurate (see, e.g. *Young v Bristol Aeroplane Co Ltd*, above, para.7–021) although modern headnotes are generally reliable. It may include a summary of the facts or simply be the reporter's version of the *ratio decidendi*.

[391] The facts stated in the judgments may be left unedited or the reporter may set out the facts separately.

[392] These are only regularly printed in a few sets of reports such as The Law Reports and Lloyd's Law Reports. Interjections from the bench may also be included. The original transcripts commonly record the post-judgment submissions of counsel (and rulings) on such matter as costs.

[393] *Curia advisari vult*: "the court wishes to consider the matter".

[394] In full reports these are printed verbatim, in some, such as in the Criminal Law Review and the Solicitors' Journal, only summaries are given.

[395] See J. H. Baker, *An Introduction to English Legal History* (4th edn, 2002), Ch.11; L. W. Abbott, *Law Reporting in England 1485–1585* (1973), reviewed by Baker, [1974] C.L.J. 156; P. Reeves, (1989) 86 L.S. Gaz. July 26; R. Munday, (2001) 165 J.P.N. 162.

[396] See J. H. Baker, *Manual of Law French* (1979).

[397] C. K. Allen, *Law in the Making* (7th edn, 1964), pp.221–232.

[398] e.g. Barnardiston: see R. G. Logan, (1987) 18 *The Law Librarian* 87.

the reports, the volume and the page.[399] The year is not technically part of the reference but is normally included.[400] Most of the cases in the private reports were reprinted in *The English Reports* published in 176 volumes between 1900 and 1930. There was also a series entitled *The Revised Reports* edited by Sir Frederick Pollock and included such cases reported between 1785 and 1865 as were "still of practical utility".[401]

The patchwork coverage of private enterprise law reports was seen to be unsatisfactory.[402] In 1865 a council consisting of the Attorney General, the Solicitor General, two barristers from each of the inns of court, two sergeants and two solicitors was formed; in 1870 it was incorporated as "The Incorporated Council of Law Reporting for England and Wales" with as its primary object:

> "the preparation and publication in a convenient form, at a moderate price, and under gratuitous professional control of Reports of Judicial Decisions of the Superior and Appellate Courts of England."

The Council is not funded by the state and is non-profit-making.[403] Its reports are semi-official in that judgments appearing in the Law Reports are revised by the judges, and that this series should be cited in preference to any alternative.[404] It is increasingly common for them to be referred to by the judiciary as "official" even through technically they are not.[405] The corrections may make the report conform to what was actually said; on occasion a report is changed to conform to what the judge meant to say, which is rather more controversial.[406] There have been three series of the Law Reports: the first from 1865 to 1875,[407] the second from 1875 to 1890[408] and the third from 1891 to date.[409] The Incorporated Council also publishes the (unrevised) "Weekly Law Reports" and the "Industrial Cases Reports". There are a number of series of specialist official reports including the "Reports of Tax Cases" published under the direction of the Inland Revenue, the "Reports of Patent, Design and Trade Mark Cases" published by the Patent Office and the "Immigration Appeal Reports" published by The Stationery Office. There are also a number of series associated more obviously with private enterprise, of which the "All England Law Reports" is a general

---

[399] e.g. *Coggs v Bernard* (1703) 2 Ld. Raym. 909 (Lord Raymond).

[400] In round brackets. Where the year is part of a reference it is given in square brackets.

[401] See R. G. Logan, (1982) 13 *The Law Librarian* 23.

[402] See W. T. S. Daniel, *The History and Origin of "The Law Reports"* [1884].

[403] *Incorporated Council of Law Reporting v Att.-Gen.* [1972] Ch. 73. The Court of Appeal held that the Council's purposes were charitable.

[404] *Westminster Bank Executors and Trustee Co (Channel Islands) Ltd v National Bank of Greece S.A. (Practice Note)* [1970] 1 W.L.R. 1400; *Bray v Best* [1989] 1 W.L.R. 167, 169; *Practice Direction (Law reports: Citation)* [1991] 1 W.L.R. 1; *Practice Direction (CCA: Citation of Authority)* [1995] 1 W.L.R. 1096; *Practice Direction (CA: Citation of Authorities)* [2001] 1 W.L.R. 1001.

[405] R. Munday, (2001) 165 J.P.N. 162.

[406] See, e.g. *Ghani v Jones* [1970] 1 Q.B. 693; R. M. Jackson, [1970] C.L.J. 1, 3; (1969) 119 N.L.J. 1011; (1970) 120 N.L.J. 423. See further R. Munday, (2001) 165 J.P.N. 162, 342.

[407] e.g. *Osgood v Nelson* (1872) L.R. 5 H.L. 636. A reference to this series normally includes the year of the decision (in round brackets as it is not technically part of the reference); the letters "L.R."; the volume number of the relevant series; the abbreviation for that series (there were 11 in all, running concurrently); and the page number.

[408] e.g. *Huth v Clarke* (1890) 25 Q.B.D. 391. A reference no longer includes the letters "L.R." and there are six series: one for Appeal Cases and one for each of the five divisions of the High Court (reduced to three in 1888).

[409] e.g. *Ridge v Baldwin* [1964] A.C. 40. A reference includes the year of the *report*, not the decision, in square brackets; the series (A.C.; Q.B.; Ch.; Fam.) and the page number.

series rivalling the Weekly Law Reports.[410] The trend is for an increasing number of cases to be reported and for new series of reports to be started,[411] with concomitant problems of expense for law libraries and practitioners, duplication[412] and pressure on research time. Brief law reports also appear in an increasing number of daily newspapers.[413] These are usually printed shortly after judgment has been given, and are compiled by barristers and are therefore citable in court.[414]

The system of law reporting was examined by a committee which reported in 1940.[415] The committee did not favour any radical change, such as giving the Incorporated Council a monopoly of reporting or the licensing of reporters. The majority rejected the proposals of A. L. Goodhart, who wrote a dissenting report, that a shorthand writer should take down the text of every judgment, that a transcript be sent to the judge for correction and that the corrected report be filed in the court records and made available to any reporter or member of the public for a small fee. The reasons put forward were the cost, the extra burden on the judges and the fact that almost every decision of importance was already reported: "What remains is less likely to be a treasure house than a rubbish heap in which a jewel will rarely, if ever, be discovered".[416] This position has, however, been reached by the widespread availability of databases of transcripts of cases,[417] coupled with the adoption, for ease of reference, of a neutral citation system for the House of Lords, both divisions of the Court of Appeal and the Administrative Court.[418] From January 11, 2001,[419] all judgments in the House of Lords, Court of Appeal and High Court have been issued with paragraph numbers in square brackets; and judgments in the House of Lords, Court of Appeal and Administrative Court have been numbered consecutively through the year.[420] From 2002, neutral citation numbering has been extended to all judgments given by the High Court in London, and, at the request of someone wishing to include it in a report, High Court judgments delivered outside London.[421] Once a case is reported, its neutral citation is to appear in front of the citation from the law report series.

---

[410] The criteria for the selection of cases for reporting in the Law Reports and the All England Law Reports are considered by N. H. Andrews, "Reporting Case Law" (1985) 5 L.S. 205, 225–231, based on information supplied by the editors of these series. See also F. D. Cumbrae-Stewart, "The aim and form of law reports" (1985) 59 A.L.J. 616.

[411] R. J. C. Munday, (1978) 14 J.S.P.T.L. (N.S.) 201–203. See also D. Milman, (1987) 8 Co. Law. 242, noting several new series of company law reports. The trend continued through the 1990s; see R. Munday, (2002) 166 J.P.N. 6, 29.

[412] A glance at Sweet & Maxwell's *Current Law Citator* will confirm this.

[413] The *Times* has printed law reports for over 100 years. It has been joined by the *Financial Times, Guardian, Independent and Daily Telegraph*: see M. Findlay, *The Law Magazine*, March 18, 1989, p.31.

[414] They must be distinguished from summaries of cases in the "news" pages of *The Sun* (etc.).

[415] Report of the Law Reporting Committee (HMSO, 1940).

[416] *ibid.* p.20.

[417] See below.

[418] See *Practice Direction (Sup. Ct: Form of Judgments, Paragraph Marking and Neutral Citation* [2001] 1 W.L.R. 194. See R. Munday, (2001) 165 J.P.N. 342. On the introduction of such a system in Canada, see M. Felsky, (1998) 29 *The Law Librarian* 159.

[419] From the first judgment in 2001 in the case of the House of Lords.

[420] i.e. [2001] UKHL 1, 2, 3 etc.; [2001] EWCA Civ 1, 2, 3 etc.; [2001] EWCA Crim 1, 2, 3 etc.; [2001] EWHC Admin 1, 2, 3 etc.

[421] *Practice Direction (HC: Neutral Citations)* [2002] 1 W.L.R. 346. The form is now [2002] EWHC 1, 2, 3 etc. followed by (Ch), (Pat), (QB), (Admin), (Comm), (Admlty), (TCC) or (Fam) as the case may be.

Decisions of the Court of Justice of the European Communities are reported in the *European Court Reports*, an official series, and in the *Common Market Law Reports*, a private enterprise series, which includes in addition reports of the decisions of national courts on Community law matters.

The most significant developments in recent years have been in the field of the computerisation of statutes, statutory instruments and law reports. *LexisNexis* Butterworths offer the *LexisNexis* system, which includes English, Scottish and American materials; as well as European and Commonwealth materials. A vast amount of material is now available on the Internet. It is now normal practice for there to be a fully searchable database of all judgments for each of the leading appellate courts in the United States and the Commonwealth, and international courts such as the Court of Justice of the European Communities and the European Court of Human Rights.[422] There are databases of decisions of the House of Lords and the Privy Council,[423] the SmithBernal database gives access to transcripts of decisions of the High Court and Court of Appeal,[424] and the British and Irish Legal Information Institute (BAILII)[425] covers a wide range of legislative material and case law across all jurisdictions of the UK.

(d) The citation of precedents

Until recently, the only condition for admission of a report has been that it has been vouched for by a barrister present during the whole time when the judgment was given.[426] However, in *Roberts Petroleum Ltd v Kenny Ltd*,[427] the House of Lords stated that in future it would decline to allow transcripts of unreported judgments of the Court of Appeal (Civil Division) to be cited in the House without leave; such leave would only be granted on counsel giving an assurance that the transcript contained some relevant principle of law that was binding on the Court of Appeal and of which the substance, as distinct from the mere choice of phraseology, was not to be found in any judgment of that court that appeared in one of the generalised or specialised series of reports. The Court of Appeal broadly followed suit.[428] In practice, the judges seem reluctant to prevent the citation of unreported cases.[429]

The expansion of the number of law reports and the revolution in the means of access to transcripts adds to the cost of preparing and arguing cases as the number of at least possibly relevant authorities that can be identified increases. This naturally conflicts with the policy of seeking to increase the efficiency of litigation. In an attempt to curb the citation of authorities, Lord Woolf C.J. issued

7–040

---

[422] *http://www.europa.eu.int/cj/en/index.htm*; *www.echr.coe.int*. Reports or transcripts of the courts of many overseas jurisdictions are available through a series of linked Legal Information Institutes: see *www.worldlii.org*, giving links to the others.

[423] *www.publications.parliament.uk/pa/ld/ldjudgmt.htm; www.privy-council.org.uk*.

[424] *www.casetrack.com*.

[425] *www.bailii.org*.

[426] See *Parkinson v Parkinson* [1939] P. 346, 348, 351–352; *Birtwistle v Tweedale* [1954] 1 W.L.R. 190n: *Estates Gazette* report not admitted. Cf. *Baker v Sims* [1959] 1 Q.B. 114 and *Smith v Wyles* [1959] 1 Q.B. 164. A report by a person who is a solicitor or has a Supreme Court qualification (i.e. a right of audience in relation to all proceedings in the Supreme Court) has the same authority as if it had been by a barrister: Courts and Legal Services Act 1990, s.115.

[427] [1983] 2 A.C. 192. See R. J. C. Munday, (1983) 80 L.S. Gaz. 1337; N. H. Andrews, (1985) 5 L.S. 205. Note the critical response of F. A. R. Bennion (*ibid.* p.1635) and N. Harrison (Managing Director of the company which marketed *Lexis*), (1984) 81 L.S. Gaz. 257.

[428] *Practice Statement (Court of Appeal: Authorities)* [1996] 1 W.L.R. 854.

[429] R. Munday, (2002) 166 J.P.N. 6, 9.

a Practice Direction[430] providing that a judgment in specified categories may not in future be cited before any court unless it clearly indicates[431] that it purports to establish a new principle or to extend the present law. The specified categories are: applications attending by one party only; applications for permission to appeal; decisions on applications that only decide that the application is arguable; and (subject to exceptions) county court cases. As regards other categories of judgment (including those of the Court of Justice of the European Communities and the European Court of Human Rights), the courts will in future pay particular attention to any indication given by the court delivering the judgment that it was seen as only applying decided law to the facts or otherwise not extending or adding to existing law. Advocates seeking to cite a judgment containing such indications will be required to justify their decision. Furthermore, advocates will be required to state (in any skeleton argument and appellant's or respondent's notices) in respect of each authority they wish to cite the proposition of law that it demonstrates and the parts of the judgment that support that proposition. Reasons must be given for citing more than one authority in favour of a given proposition. Authorities from other jurisdictions must not be cited without proper consideration of whether it does indeed add to the existing body of law. Where they are cited, the advocate must indicate what it adds that is not to be found in authority in this jurisdiction or the justification for adding to domestic authority. It remains to be seen how this will affect practice. There is always the risk that the time taken in the substantive citation of a case will simply be replaced by time arguing about whether it should be cited.

Both the High Court and Court of Appeal require that where a case has been reported in official law reports published by the Incorporated Council of Law Reporting for England and Wales it must be cited from that source. It is now permissible to cite a copy of a reproduction of a judgment in electronic form provided it is easily legible (12-point font preferred, 10 or 11 point acceptable), and the advocate presenting the report is satisfied that it has not been reproduced in a garbled form.[432]

---

[430] *Practice Direction (CA: Citation of Authorities)* [2001] 1 W.L.R. 1001. See R. Munday, (2002) 166 J.P.N. 6, 32.

[431] By an express statement to that effect in respect of judgments after April 8, 2001; by an indication from the language used in earlier judgments. Examples are the decision of the Court of Appeal in *London Borough of Lambeth v Tunde Apelogun-Gabriels* [2001] EWCA Civ 1853, [2002] I.C.R. 713 (settling conflict in earlier case law; *R (on the application of Ipsea Ltd) v Secretary of State for Education and Skills* [2003] EWCA Civ 07, [2003] E.L.R. 393 (novel point fully argued on an application of permission to appeal); Sullivan J. in *R (on the application of William Hill Organisation Ltd) v Batley and Dewsbury Betting Licensing Committee* [2004] EWHC 1201 (Admin), [2004] L.L.R. 536 (application attended by one party).

[432] *Practice Direction*, n.428 above.

THE HUMAN RIGHTS ACT 1998

A. INTRODUCTION[1]

The United Kingdom has been subject to the European Convention on Human **8–001** Rights (ECHR) since it came into force in 1953. Individuals have been able since 1966 to bring cases against the UK through the ECHR machinery, and the European Court of Human Rights has found violations in a series of cases.[2] There was also an extensive debate as to whether the European Convention should be incorporated into English law, so as to enable individuals who would otherwise have to pursue, usually over a number of years, a claim before the European Court of Human Rights, to have the issues addressed by an English court. Various models were proposed, including simple incorporation of the ECHR as it stands

---

[1] See generally on the Human Rights Act 1998, C. Baker (ed.), *Human Rights Act 1998: A Practitioner's Guide* (1998); M. Hunt, *Practitioner's Guide to the Human Rights Act 1998* (1998); R. Clayton and H. Tomlinson, *The Law of Human Rights* (2000); S. Grosz, J. Beatson and P. Duffy, *Human Rights: The 1998 Act and the European Convention* (2000); Lord Lester and D. Pannick, *Human Rights Law and Practice* (2nd edn, 2004); J. Wadham and H. Mountfield, *The Human Rights Act 1998* (4th edn, 2007); M. Amos, *Human Rights Law* (2006).

[2] See above, para.2–083.

and the enactment of a Bill of Rights with a text drawn as appropriate from a range of International treaties, including the ECHR, by which the UK is bound.[3] Further variants would see a Bill of Rights set in the context of a written constitution, with the fundamental elements of both entrenched as a higher form of law, which could not be amended by ordinary legislation, but only through some special process of constitutional amendment.[4] These variants would require modifications (to say the least) of the traditional doctrine of Parliamentary sovereignty.[5] Among the main political parties, the Liberal Democrats have tended to favour developments of this kind and the Conservatives have tended to oppose them. Traditionally, the Labour party has been opposed to moves that would enhance the powers of the (unelected and supposedly conservative) judiciary.[6] However, the policy of the Labour party changed in the 1990s[7] and a significant measure of incorporation of the European Convention on Human Rights became one of a series of constitutional measures[8] secured by the Labour government elected in 1997 early in its term of office. The White Paper, *Rights Brought Home: The Human Rights Bill*[9] placed the practical effect of non-compliance at the centre of its case:

> "It takes on average five years to get an action into the European Court of Human Rights once all domestic remedies have been exhausted; and it costs an average of £30,000. Bringing these rights home will mean that the British people will be able to argue for their rights in the British courts—without this inordinate delay and cost. It will also mean that the rights will be brought much more fully into the jurisprudence of the courts throughout the United Kingdom, and their interpretation will thus be far more subtly and powerfully woven into our law."[10]

The situation adopted respects the traditional doctrine of Parliamentary sovereignty in that the judges are not accorded power to strike down primary legislation that is incompatible with a Convention right; instead they may make a declaration of incompatibility (s.4) which in turn may pave the way for a special form of amending legislation (a remedial order) or amendment through some other route. Beyond that there is a new rule for the interpretation of legislation (s.3) and a new rule that it is unlawful for a public authority to act in a way incompatible with a Convention right (s.6). The provisions of the Human Rights Act can affect both the interpretation and application of legislation and the development of the common law, and can reach into most areas regulated or affected by law. One controversial matter is, however, the extent to which its provisions may regulate the relationship between two parties neither of whom is a public authority.[11]

---

[3] e.g. IPPR, *A Written Constitution for the United Kingdom* (2nd edn, 1993).
[4] See S. H. Bailey, D. J. Harris and B. L. Jones, *Civil Liberties: Cases and Materials* (4th edn, 1995), pp.14–26; M. Zander, *A Bill of Rights?* (4th edn, 1996).
[5] See above, para.5–002.
[6] Curiously, the objection more likely to be voiced by Labour ministers today is that judges are unduly liberal.
[7] *A New Agenda for Democracy*, adopted by the Labour Party Conference in 1993.
[8] Others were the devolution measures: the Scotland Act 1998 and the Government of Wales Act 1998.
[9] Cm. 3782, 1997.
[10] para.1.14.
[11] Below, para.8–014.

The basic purpose of the Act is stated to be "to give further effect to rights and freedoms guaranteed under the European Convention on Human Rights".[12]

B. KEY CONCEPTS AND PROVISIONS

1. CONVENTION RIGHTS

"Convention rights" are the rights and fundamental freedoms set out in Arts 2 to **8–002** 12 and 14 of the Convention, Arts 1 to 3 of the First Protocol and Art.1 of the Thirteenth Protocol, as read with Arts 16 to 18 of the Convention, but subject to any derogation or reservation.[13]

Convention rights are set out in Sch.1 to the Act and cover, respectively, the right to life (Art.2), the prohibition of torture (Art.3), the prohibition of slavery and forced labour (Art.4), the right to liberty and security (Art.5), the right to a fair trial (Art.6), no punishment without law (Art.7), the right to respect for private and family life (Art.8), freedom of thought, conscience and religion (Art.9), freedom of expression (Art.10), freedom of assembly and association (Art.11), the right to marry (Art.12), the prohibition of discrimination affecting the enjoyment of Convention rights and freedoms (Art.14), the protection of property (First Protocol, Art.1), the right to education (First Protocol, Art.2),[14] the right to free elections (First Protocol, Art.3), and the abolition of the death penalty (Thirteenth Protocol, Art.1).

Nothing in Arts 10, 11 and 14 is to be regarded as preventing the imposition of restrictions on the political activity of aliens; nothing in the Convention may be interpreted as implying any right to engage in any activity or perform any act

---

[12] *Human Rights Act* 1998, Long Title. For the purpose of the Act, " 'the Convention' means the Convention for the Protection of Human Rights and Fundamental Freedoms, agreed by the Council of Europe at Rome on November 4, 1950 as it has effect for the time being in relation to the United Kingdom": s.21(1).

[13] s.1(1), (2). As to derogations and reservations, see ss.14–17, as amended. A "designated derogation" is a derogation by the UK from an ECHR Article or Protocol designated by a derogation order made by the Secretary of State: s.14, as amended by SI 2001/1216, art.2, and SI 2003/1887, Sch.2, para.10. A derogation order (see the 1998 Act, Sch.3, Pt 1 (inserted by the Human Rights Act 1998 (Amendment No.2) Order 2001 (SI 2001/4032), Sch.) and the Human Rights Act 1998 (Designated Derogation) Order 2001 (SI 2001/3644)) in respect of the power under s.23 of the Anti-terrorism, Crime and Security Act 2001, authorising the extended detention of resident aliens suspected of terrorism who could not lawfully be deported, was quashed by the House of Lords on the ground that ss.21 and 23 were disproportionate: *A v Secretary of State for the Home Department* [2004] UKHL 56, [2005] 2 A.C. 68. The provisions did not rationally address the threat to the security of the UK presented by Al-Qaeda since they did not address the threat presented by UK nationals; they permitted suspected terrorists to pursue their activities abroad if there was any country to which they could go; and they permitted the detention of persons not suspected of presenting any threat to the security of the UK. There was also a violation of Art.14, ECHR. Sch.3, Pt 1 was repealed by the Human Rights Act 1998 (Amendment) Order 2005 (SI 2005/1071).

[14] The UK has entered a reservation to the second sentence of Art.2: "In the exercise of any function which it assumes in relation to education and to teaching, the State shall respect the right of parents to ensure such education and teaching in conformity with their own religious and philosophical convictions.' " This was accepted "only so far as it is compatible with the provision of efficient education and training, and the avoidance of unreasonable public expenditure": see 1998 Act, Sch.3, Pt III.

aimed at the destruction of Convention rights or their limitation to a greater extent than provided for in the Convention; and restrictions permitted under the Convention are not to be applied for any purpose other than those for which they have been prescribed.[15]

Some Convention rights are absolute. For example, Art.2 provides that:

> "No one shall be subjected to torture or to inhuman or degrading treatment or punishment."

Others are drafted with closely defined qualifications, exclusions or exceptions. For example, Art.5 provides that:

> "Everyone has the right to liberty and security of person. No one shall be deprived of his liberty save in the following cases and in accordance with a procedure prescribed by law."

It proceeds to list six situations of lawful arrest or detention, including lawful detention after conviction by a competent court, lawful arrest and detention effected for the purpose of bringing the person before the competent legal authority on reasonable suspicion of having committed an offence, detention of a minor by lawful order for the purpose of educational supervision and the lawful detention of persons for the purpose of the spreading of infectious diseases, of persons of unsound mind, alcoholics or drug addicts or vagrants.

Article 6(1) provides that:

> "In the determination of his civil rights and obligations or of any criminal charge against him, everyone is entitled to a fair and public hearing within a reasonable time by an independent and impartial tribunal established by law. . . . "

Judgment must be pronounced publicly but the press and public may be excluded from all or part of the trial in prescribed circumstances. The rest of Art.6 sets out specific rules applicable to those charged with criminal offences.

Yet other Articles are drafted subject to broadly drawn exceptions. One example is Art.8, concerning respect for private and family life.[16]

Articles 9, 10 and 11 provide, respectively, for the right to freedom of thought, conscience and religion, the right to freedom of expression and the "right to freedom of peaceful assembly and to freedom of association with others" subject to similarly worded exceptions. Some of these Articles are considered further in more detail below.[17]

The Secretary of State may by order make such amendments to the Human Rights Act 1998 as he considers appropriate to reflect the effect, in relation to the UK, of a Protocol to the Convention which the UK has ratified or signed with a view to ratification; no amendment may come into force before the Protocol concerned is in force in relation to the UK.[18]

---

[15] Arts 16 to 18.
[16] See below, para.8–023.
[17] See below, paras 8–017––8–026.
[18] 1998 Act, s.1(4)–(6), subs.(4) as amended by SI 2003/1887, Sch.2, para.10(1).

Convention rights for the purposes of the application of the ECHR in respect of the UK and the application of the Human Rights Act 1998 are not necessarily confined to those who are within the UK jurisdiction.[19]

2. THE AUTHORITY OF EUROPEAN COURT OF HUMAN RIGHTS JURISPRUDENCE

Any court or tribunal determining a question which has arisen under the Act in connection with a Convention right must take into account, so far as it is of the opinion that it is relevant, any judgment, decision or advisory opinion of the European Court of Human Rights; certain opinions and decisions of the European Commission or Human Rights[20]; and decisions of the Committee of Ministers taken under Art.46.[21] Evidence of any judgment, decision, declaration or opinion of which account may have to be taken under s.2 is to be given in proceedings before any court or tribunal in such manner as may be provided by rules of court or, in the case of proceedings before a tribunal, rules made for the purposes of s.2 by the Lord Chancellor or the Secretary of State.[22]   **8–003**

In *R (on the application of Alconbury Developments Ltd) v Secretary of State for the Environment, Transport and the Regions*[23] Lord Slynn said[24]:

> "Your Lordships have been referred to many decisions of the European Court of Human Rights on Article 6 of the Convention. Although the Human Rights Act 1998 does not provide that a national court is bound by these decisions it is obliged to take account of them so far as they are relevant. In the absence of some special circumstances it seems to be that the court should follow any clear and constant jurisprudence of the European Court of Human Rights. If it does not do so there is at least a possibility that the case will go to that court which is likely in the ordinary case to follow its own constant jurisprudence."

Lord Hoffmann said[25] that had the decisions of the Court "compelled a conclusion so fundamentally at odds with the distribution of powers under the British Constitution, I would have considerable doubts as to whether they should be followed". The other members of the House did not comment expressly on this point. All were agreed that there was no inconsistency between English law and the ECHR.[26]

---

[19] *R (on the application of Ullah) v Special Adjudicator* [2004] UKHL 26, [2004] 2 A.C. 323.

[20] i.e. opinions in a report under Art.31 of the Convention as to whether the facts found constitute a breach of the Convention; decisions by the Commission under Art.26 in connection with the exhaustion of domestic remedies and the requirement that it deal with a matter within six months from the date on which the final decision was taken; and decisions by the Commission under Art.27(2) that a petition is inadmissible as incompatible with the provisions of the Convention, manifestly ill-founded, or an abuse of the right of petition.

[21] 1998 Act, s.2(1).

[22] 1998 Act, s.2(2), (3), subs.(3) as amended by SI 2003/1887, Sch.2, para.10(2) and SI 2005/3429, Sch., para.3. By virtue of *ibid.* Art.3(2), the functions of the Secretary of State under s.2(3) are to be exercisable concurrently with the Lord Chancellor.

[23] [2001] UKHL 23, [2003] 2 A.C. 295.

[24] para.[26].

[25] para.[76].

[26] See further, para.8–022.

Lord Slynn's approach was echoed by the Court of Appeal in *R (on the application of Anderson and Taylor) v Secretary of State for the Home Department*.[27] Here, the court held that while it was of the view that the fixing of the tariff element of a mandatory life sentence by the Home Secretary should conform to the requirements of Art.6(1), ECHR, and did not do so, it should defer to the contrary view of the European Court of Human Rights, which was in any event about to reconsider the principles applicable in this area. The court took account of the other court's particular expertise as an international court in the interpretation of the ECHR and considerations of comity. By the time a further appeal was heard by the House of Lords,[28] the ECtHR had come to a different view,[29] which the House of Lords followed. Lord Bingham of Cornhill stated[30] that:

> "While the duty of the House under section 2(1)(a) of the Human Rights Act 1998 is to take into account any judgment of the European Court, whose judgments are not strictly binding, the House will not without good reason depart from the principles laid down in a carefully considered judgment of the court sitting as a Grand Chamber."

Even more will this be so where that is a recent judgment of the Grand Chamber.[31] Where there is a clear and consistent line of decisions of the Commission, not inconsistent with those of the ECtHR, good reasons are needed for them not to be followed by a UK court.[32]

The impact of rulings of the ECtHR on domestic precedents was considered by the House of Lords in *Kay v Lambeth LBC; Leeds City Council v Price*.[33] The House held that the normal domestic rules of precedent should be followed notwithstanding that a decision that is binding under those rules is inconsistent with a subsequent decision of the ECtHR. This was subject to one partial exception that had previously been recognised: the Court of Appeal in *D v East Berkshire Community NHS Trust*[34] had been entitled to conclude that the decision of the House of Lords in *X (Minors) v Bedfordshire County Council*[35] in relation to children could not survive the enactment of the Human Rights Act 1998. However, this was a "very exceptional case". Judgment in *X* had been given in 1995, well before the 1998 Act; no reference had been made to the ECHR in any of the opinions; and the very children whose claim in negligence had been rejected as unarguable succeeded before the ECtHR in establishing a breach of Art.3. Such an approach to precedent was not, however, permissible "save where the facts are of that extreme character".

---

[27] [2001] EWCA Civ 1698. Lord Slynn's dictum was relied on in argument by counsel for the Secretary of State but only referred to by one member of the court.

[28] [2003] 1 A.C. 837.

[29] *Stafford v UK* (2002) 35 E.H.R.R. 32.

[30] At para.[18].

[31] *per* Keene L.J. in *R (on the application of Harrison) v Secretary of State for the Home Department* [2003] EWCA Civ 432, para.[28].

[32] *R (on the application of Carson) v Secretary of State for Work and Pensions* [2002] EWHC 978 (Admin), [2002] 3 All E.R. 994, para.[38]. See also the comments of the Court of Appeal: [2003] EWCA Civ 797, [2003] 3 All E.R. 577, paras [40], [41]. The point did not arise in the House of Lords: [2005] UKHL 37, [2006] 1 A.C. 173.

[33] [2006] UKHL 10, [2006] 2 A.C. 465, *per* Lord Bingham of Cornhill at paras [40]–[45]. All the other six members of the House agreed on this matter.

[34] [2004] Q.B. 558.

[35] [1995] 2 A.C. 633

The fact that a decision of a UK court is to be challenged before the European Court of Human Rights is not of itself sufficient to justify ordering a stay on the enforcement of the judgment, although a stay might be ordered if there was a real probability of the enactment of legislation by the UK Parliament that would reverse the effect of the judgment.[36]

3. THE "MARGIN OF APPRECIATION", "DEFERENCE" AND PROPORTIONALITY

The jurisprudence of the European Court of Human Rights recognises that in **8–004** considering whether there has been compliance with the ECHR Member States are in some contexts accorded a "margin of appreciation". This takes account of the fact that the ECHR machinery is subsidiary to the national systems safeguarding human rights, leaving to those national systems in the first place the task of securing the Convention rights and freedoms.[37] Furthermore, some of the concepts enshrined in ECHR articles do not have a uniform European content.[38] Accordingly,

> "by reason of their direct and continuous contact with the vital forces of their countries, State authorities are in principle in a better position than the international judges to give an opinion on the exact content of these requirements as well as on the 'necessity' of a 'restriction' or 'penalty' intended to meet them . . . [I]t is for the national authorities to make the initial assessment of the reality of the pressing social need implied by the notion of 'necessity' in this context.
>
> Consequently, Article 10(2) leaves to the Contracting States a margin of appreciation."[39]

However, the power of appreciation is not unlimited, and the decisions of Member States are subject to "supervision" by the European Court, which must decide whether the reasons given by national authorities to justify measures of "interference" are relevant and sufficient, applying a test of proportionality.[40] The scope of the power of appreciation does, however, vary according to context. For example the concept of "maintaining the authority . . . of the judiciary", another justification found for interference with freedom of expression found in Art.10(2), has a "far more objective notion" than the protection of "morals", the domestic law and practice of Member States revealing "a fairly substantial measure of common ground". Here, "a more extensive European supervision corresponds to a less discretionary power of appreciation".[41] Contexts in which

---

[36] *Westminster City Council v Porter (No.1)* [2002] EWHC 1589 (Ch) (refusing a stay on enforcement against Dame Shirley Porter in respect of c.£26m certified as due under s.18(8) of the Audit Commission Act 1998, following the decision of the House of Lords in *Porter v Magill* [2002] 2 A.C. 357).

[37] *Handyside v UK* (1996) 1 E.H.R.R. 737, para.48.

[38] *ibid.*, giving as an example the absence of a "European conception of morals" for the purposes of consideration of one of the justifications for interferences with freedom of expression ("the protection of . . . morals") set out in Art.10(2).

[39] *ibid.*

[40] *ibid.* paras 49, 50.

[41] *Sunday Times v UK* (1979) 2 E.H.R.R. 245, para.59.

a margin of appreciation has been recognised include the establishment of justifications for interference with protected rights and freedoms under para.2 of Arts 8 to 11[42]; areas where the Article in question contains vague expressions[43]; and where the Court has to determine whether a state has failed to comply with a positive obligation to protect a Convention right.[44]

The "margin of appreciation" doctrine does not as such apply where an English court is reviewing decisions and acts of public authorities by virtue of the Human Rights Act 1998.[45] That doctrine itself comprises separate elements: first, the appropriate measure of deference by a court to a public authority and, secondly the deference of an international court to state authorities. Only the former could itself be relevant at the domestic level.[46] Nevertheless, in some contexts it will be appropriate for a reviewing court to recognise a "discretionary area of judgment". This point has been made by Lord Hope of Craighead[47]:

> "[I]n the hands of the national courts also the Convention should be seen as an expression of fundamental principles rather than as a set of mere rules. The questions which the courts will have to decide in the application of these principles will involve questions of balance between competing interests and issues of proportionality.
>
> In this area difficult choices may have to be made by the executive or the legislature between the rights of the individual and the needs of society. In some circumstances it will be appropriate for the court to recognise that there is an area of judgment within which the judiciary will defer, on democratic grounds, to the considered opinion of the elected body or person whose act or decision is said to be incompatible with the Convention. The point is well made at page 74, paragraph 3.21 of Lester and Pannick (eds) *Human Rights Law and Practice* (1999), where the area in which these choices may arise is conveniently and appropriately described as the 'discretionary area of judgment.' It will be easier for such an area of judgment to be recognised where the Convention itself requires a balance to be struck, much less so where the right is stated in terms which are unqualified. It will be easier for it to be recognised where the issues involve questions of social and economic policy, much less so where the rights are of high constitutional importance or are of a kind where the courts are especially well placed to assess the need for protection."

Examples of contexts in which an area of discretionary judgment has been recognised include decisions of the *executive*, such as the decision of the

---

[42] Above.

[43] e.g. determination by a Member State that the "life of the nation" is threatened by a "public emergency" so as to justify a derogation under Art.15: *Lawless v Ireland (No.3)* (1961) 1 E.H.R.R. 15, para.207.

[44] e.g. *X Y and Z v UK* (1997) 24 E.H.R.R. 143 and *TP and KM v UK*, judgment of May 10, 2001, below, para.8–019.

[45] *per* Lord Hope of Craighead in *R v DPP, Ex p. Kebilene* [2000] 2 A.C. 326, 375; *R (on the application of ProLife Alliance) v BBC* [2002] 2 All E.R. 756, para.[31], and, on appeal, [2003] UKHL 23, [2004] 1 A.C. 185, *per* Lord Walker of Gestingthorpe at para.[132].

[46] M. Fordham and T. de la Mare, "Identifying the Principles of Proportionality" in J. Jowell and J. Cooper, *Understanding Human Rights Principles* (2001), pp.54–55.

[47] *ibid.*

Secretary of State that the purposes behind a deportation order justified the consequential interference with family life[48]; decisions of planning inspectors on the balance between interference with private and family life (Art.8(1)) on the one hand and furtherance of the legitimate aims of the planning system on the other[49]; decisions to make or confirm a compulsory purchase order[50]; decisions of the Prison Service as to policies in the management of prisons[51]; the decision of the Secretary of State to exclude an alien in the light of risks of public disorder notwithstanding consequent interference with freedom of expression[52]; and decisions of local authorities concerning children who might be at risk.[53] Where the question arises of the compatibility of primary or secondary[54] legislation the *legislature's* area of discretionary judgment has been recognised in such areas as the arrangements for termination of shorthold and introductory tenancies,[55] the distribution of state benefits,[56] and the general prohibition on political advertising.[57] Particular difficulty has been caused by measures to deal with terrorism. The House of Lords concluded in a leading case that great weight should be given to the judgment of the Home Secretary and Parliament that there was a "public emergency threatening the life of the nation" within the meaning of Art.15(1), ECHR, one of the preconditions for exercise of the power to make a derogation order. However, even measures taken to deal with threats to national security were open to challenge on grounds that they were disproportionate and discriminatory, and while any decision of a representative democratic body commanded respect, "the degree of respect will be conditioned by the nature of the decision".[58]

---

[48] *R (on the application of Samaroo) v Secretary of State for the Home Department* [2001] EWCA Civ 1139; *R (on the application of Mahmood) v Secretary of State for the Home Department* [2001] 1 W.L.R. 840; *R v Secretary of State for the Home Department, Ex p. Isiko* [2001] H.R.L.R. 295.

[49] *Buckland v Secretary of State for the Environment, Transport and the Regions* [2001] EWHC Admin 524; *Clarke v Secretary of State for the Environment, Transport and the Regions* [2001] EWHC Admin 800 (citing the ECtHR decision in *Chapman v UK* (2001) 10 B.H.R.C. 48, para.92 and *Buckley v UK* (1997) 23 E.H.R.R. 101, para.75, referring to the wide margin of appreciation enjoyed by national authorities in planning cases).

[50] *Baker v First Secretary of State* [2003] EWHC 2511 (Admin) (cpo in respect of an unfit dwelling).

[51] *R (on the application of P, Q and QB), v Secretary of State for the Home Departments* [2001] EWCA Civ 1151, [2001] 1 W.L.R. 2002.

[52] *Farrakhan v Secretary of State for the Home Department* [2001] EWHC Admin 781; reversed on the facts by the Court of Appeal: [2002] EWCA Civ 606, [2002] Q.B. 1391 (held appropriate "to accord a particularly wide margin of discretion to the Secretary of State": para.[71]).

[53] *R (on the application of S) v Swindon Borough Council* [2001] EWHC Admin 334.

[54] Where approved by Parliament.

[55] *Donoghue v Poplar Housing and Regeneration Community Association Ltd* [2001] EWCA Civ 595, [2002] Q.B. 48; *R (on the application of McLellan) v Bracknell Forest BC* [2001] EWCA Civ 1510, [2002] Q.B. 1129.

[56] *Waite v London Borough of Hammersmith and Fulham* [2002] EWCA Civ 482; *R (on the application of Carson) v Secretary of State for Work and Pensions* [2002] EWHC 978 (Admin).

[57] *R (on the application of Animal Defenders International) v Secretary of State for Culture, Media and Sport* [2006] EWHC 3069 (Admin), [2007] H.R.L.R. 9.

[58] *A v Secretary of State for the Home Department* [2004] UKHL 56, [2005] 2 A.C. 68, *per* Lord Bingham at paras [29], [37]–[42]. *Cf.* Lord Hope at para.[107], stating that while the executive and legislature "are to be accorded a wide margin of discretion in matters relating to national security", "interference with the right to liberty must be accorded the fullest and most anxious scrutiny". For discussion, see D. Feldman, [2006] P.L. 364.

8–005   The approach to be adopted by the courts in reviewing decisions where the decision-maker is required to comply with the Convention as a matter of law[59] was summarised as follows by Lord Phillips of Worth Matravers M.R. in *R (on the application of Mahmood) v Secretary of State for the Home Department*.[60] First, even where human rights are at stake, the role of the court was supervisory; it did not substitute its own decision for that of the executive and was to bear in mind that there would often be an area of discretion permitted to the executive before a response could be demonstrated to infringe the Convention. Secondly, in conducting a review of a decision affecting human rights, the court should subject it to "the most anxious scrutiny". Thirdly, instead of merely applying the tests of *Wednesbury* unreasonableness, as modified as regards decisions affecting human rights,[61] the court should:

> "ask the question, applying an objective test, whether the decision-maker could reasonably have concluded that the interference was necessary to achieve one or more of the legitimate aims recognised by the Convention."

The third of these propositions was subject to modification by the House of Lords in *R (on the application of Daly) v Secretary of State for the Home Department*.[62] Here, the House of Lords held that a blanket rule requiring that on a cell search a prisoner was not to be present when prison officers examined his legally privileged correspondence was unlawful. Lord Steyn stated[63] that Lord Phillips M.R.'s third proposition needed "clarification" as it did not make sufficiently clear the distinction between even heightened scrutiny *Wednesbury* review and the test of proportionality required for the purposes of the ECHR and the Human Rights Act 1998. The proper approach in applying the proportionality test was set out by the Privy Council in *de Freitas v Permanent Secretary of Ministry of Agriculture, Fisheries, Lands and Housing*.[64] In determining whether a limitation (by an act, rule or decision) is arbitrary or excessive the court should ask itself:

> "whether: (i) the legislative objective is sufficiently important to justify limiting a fundamental right; (ii) the measures designed to meet the legislative objective are rationally connected to it; and (iii) the means used to impair the right or freedom are no more than is necessary to accomplish the objective."

Most cases would be decided in the same way under the *Wednesbury* and proportionality approaches,[65] but, "the intensity of review is somewhat greater

---

[59] This will normally arise in proceedings under s.7, in respect of an act made unlawful by s.6: see below, para.8–010.

[60] [2001] 1 W.L.R. 840 at paras [37]–[40].

[61] See *R v Ministry of Defence, Ex p. Smith* [1996] Q.B. 517, 554, below, para.18–050. The extent to which the proportionality principle differs from the recent flexible approach to *Wednesbury* review has been much discussed: see e.g. M. Fordham and T. de la Mare, "Identifying the principles of proportionality" in J. Jowell and J. Cooper (eds), *Understanding Human Rights Principles* (2001), pp.27–89; I. Leigh, [2002] P.L. 265.

[62] [2001] UKHL 26, [2001] 2 A.C. 532.

[63] paras [25]–[28]. The other members of the House expressly agreed with Lord Steyn.

[64] [1999] 1 A.C. 69, *per* Lord Clyde at p.80.

[65] The *Daly* case was itself an example of this as the policy was unlawful applying both common law (see Lord Bingham's speech) and Convention principles.

under the proportionality approach". Three concrete differences were, first, that:

"the doctrine of proportionality may require the reviewing court to assess the balance which the decision maker has struck, not merely whether it is within the range of rational or reasonable decisions."

Secondly,

"the proportionality test may go further than the traditional grounds of review in as much as it may require attention to be directed to the relative weight accorded to interests and considerations."

Thirdly, even the heightened scrutiny test developed in *Ex p. Smith* is not necessarily appropriate to the protection of human rights in view of the fact that the European Court of Human Rights in the same case found the approach to be inadequate given that it effectively excluded any consideration by domestic courts of the question whether the interference with the applicants' rights answered a pressing social need or was proportionate to the national security and public order aims pursued.[66] All this did not, however, mean that there had been a "shift to merits review".

In *R (on the application of Samaroo) v Secretary of State for the Home Department*[67] the Court of Appeal held that in deciding what proportionality requires in any particular case the issue will normally[68] have to be considered in two stages. The first question is "can the objective of the measure be achieved by means which are less interfering of an individual's rights?" At the second stage, it is assumed that the means employed are necessary in the sense that they are "the least intrusive of Convention rights that can be devised in order to achieve the aim". The question here is "does the measure have an excessive or disproportionate effect on the interests of affected persons?" The *Daly* case illustrated the application of the first question: the blanket policy was unlawful as the legitimate aim of maintaining security in prison would be met by a rule that entitled prison officers to examine privileged correspondence of an individual prisoner who was attempting to intimidate or disrupt a search, or whose past conduct had shown that he was likely to do so. The *Samaroo* case illustrated the application of the second question. It was clear that in general terms the objective of preventing crime and disorder was sufficiently important to justify limiting a fundamental right (here the right to family life) and that the deportation of those convicted of serious criminal offences (especially, as here, drug trafficking offences) was a measure rationally connected to that objective. The only issue here was whether a deportation had a disproportionate effect on the applicant's rights under Art.8(1). The task of the Secretary of State was within his discretionary area of judgment to "strike a fair balance" between the legitimate aim and the affected

---

[66] *Smith and Grady v UK* (1999) 29 E.H.R.R 493, para.138.
[67] [2001] EWCA Civ 1139, [2001] U.K.H.R.R. 1150, *per* Dyson L.J. at paras [14]–[23].
[68] But not invariably. The first stage does not apply in planning cases where the interests of parties other than the State have to be balanced: *Lough v First Secretary of State* [2004] EWCA Civ 905, [2004] 1 W.L.R. 2557; *R (on the application of Clays Housing Co-operative Ltd) v Housing Corp* [2004] EWCA Civ 1658, [2005] 1 W.L.R. 2229.

person's Convention rights. The task of the court in reviewing his decision was supervisory of that discretionary area of judgment. It had to decide:

> "whether the Secretary of State has struck the balance fairly between the conflicting interests of [the applicant's] right to respect for his family life on the one hand and the prevention of crime and disorder on the other. In reaching its decision, the court must recognise and allow to the Secretary of State a discretionary area of judgment."[69]

Factors relevant in determining to what extent (if at all) there should be deference to the decision maker, include[70]: (a) the nature of the Convention right; is it absolute or does it require a balance to be struck? The court is less likely to defer to the decision maker in the former case[71]; (b) the extent to which the issues require consideration of social, economic or political factors; the court will usually accord considerable deference in such cases because it is not expert in the realm of policy making, nor should it be because it is not democratically elected or accountable; (c) the extent to which the court has special expertise, for example in relation to criminal matters; (d) where the rights claimed are of especial importance (e.g. freedom of expression and access to the courts) a "high degree of constitutional protection" will be appropriate.[72] In the present case, a "significant margin of discretion" to the decision of the Secretary of State was appropriate. The Convention right was not absolute and the court did not have expertise in judging how effective the deportation policy was as a deterrent. It was for the Secretary of State to show that he had struck a fair balance. How much weight he gave to each factor would be the subject of careful scrutiny by the court and the court would interfere with the weight accorded by the decision maker

---

[69] Samanu, para.[35].

[70] Based on Lester and Pannick (eds), *Human Rights Law and Practice* (1999), para.3.26. See also Laws L.J.'s formulation of four principles stating how UK courts should approach the issue of deference: *R (on the application of International Transport Roth GmbH) v Secretary of State for the Home Department* [2003] Q.B. 728, paras [83]–[87]. These are that: (1) "greater deference is to be paid to an Act of Parliament than a decision of the Executive or subordinate measure"; (2) there is more scope for deference "where the Convention itself requires a balance to be struck much less where the right is stated in terms which are unqualified"; (3) "greater deference will be due to the democratic powers where the subject-matter in hand is peculiarly within their constitutional responsibility and less when it lies more particularly within the constitutional responsibility of the courts"; (4) "greater or lesser deference will be due according to whether the subject-matter lies more readily within the actual or potential expertise of the democratic powers or the courts." Laws L.J. dissented on the outcome of the case.

[71] As in the case of claims of breaches of Art.3, ECHR: *R (on the application of N) v Secretary of State for the Home Department* [2003] EWHC 207 (Admin), para.[65] (errors in processing asylum application leading to a delay of over 10 months during which the claimant had been treated as if the application had been rejected, leading to financial loss, serious worry and symptoms of major depressive disorder). The same position arises where there is a breach of Art.8(1) and no reliance is placed on the qualifications in Art.8(2): *ibid.* This was, however, reversed on the facts by the Court of Appeal, on the ground that the claimant's psychiatric vulnerability was unforeseeable: [2003] EWCA Civ 1406, [2004] Q.B. 1124.

[72] *cf. R (on the application of Roberts) v Parole Board* [2003] EWHC 3120 (Admin), [2004] 2 All E.R. 776 (where Maurice Kay J. reviewed "at a level of the utmost intensity" (para.[17]) the decision of the Parole Board in reviewing the case of a mandatory life sentence prisoner to appoint a "specially appointed advocate" to make representations in respect of material not disclosed to the prisoner or his lawyers; the decision was upheld). The Court of Appeal and House of Lords dismissed appeals on other grounds: [2004] EWCA Civ 1031, [2005] Q.B. 410, [2005] UKHL 45, [2005] 2 A.C. 738.

"if, despite an allowance for the appropriate margin of discretion, it concludes that the weight accorded was unfair and unreasonable."[73]

On the facts of *Samaroo*, the Secretary of State was entitled to regard Class A drug trafficking offences as very serious; to attach importance to his general policy of deporting those convicted of importation of Class A drugs to protect UK residents and to deter others; and to attach particular weight to the applicant's role as a "crucial part of the organisation". He recognised the serious interference with the applicant's right to family life under Art.8(1). Overall, the Secretary of State conclusion was a "fair and reasonable conclusion that he was entitled to reach".[74]

It should be noted that Lord Hoffmann has argued that the term "deference" is inappropriate:

"I do not think that its overtones of servility, or perhaps gracious concession, are appropriate to describe what is happening. In a society based upon the rule of law and the separation of powers, it is necessary to decide which branch of government has in any particular instance the decision-making power and what the legal limits of that power are. That is a question of law and must therefore be decided by the courts."[75]

This view was criticised extra-judicially by Lord Steyn,[76] who argued that deference is not a matter of law but a matter of discretion to be exercised according to the circumstances of the case, the true justification for which is "the relative institutional competence or capacity of the branches of government".[77] The House of Lords returned to the issue in *Huang v Secretary of State for the Home Department*.[78] This case concerned the right of a person who did not qualify for entry to the UK under the Immigration Rules to appeal against an adverse immigration decision (refusal of leave to remain) on the ground that the decision was unlawful under s.6(1) of the Human Rights Act 1998.[79] The House of Lords held, in a single opinion, first, that the role of the court on such an appeal in determining whether the decision was incompatible was to decide the matter for itself, on up-to-date facts, and not merely to review the decision

---

[73] para.[39].

[74] para.[41]. *Cf. Buckland v Secretary of State for the Environment, Transport and the Regions* and other cases [2001] EWHC Admin 524, para.[56] where Sullivan J. in respect of an appeal in a planning case against an inspector's decision rejected the submission that it was for the court to "satisfy itself that the right balance has been struck by the inspector that would be to embark on a merits review". Followed by Elias J. in *Gosbee v First Secretary of State* [2003] EWHC 770 (Admin) at paras [22]–[23].

[75] *per* Lord Hoffmann in *R (on the application of ProLife Alliance) v British Broadcasting Corp* [2003] UKHL 23, [2004] 1 A.C. 185, para.[75]; *cf.* Lord Walker of Gestingthorpe at para.[144]: deference "may not be the best word to use, if only because it is liable to be misunderstood". See also the comments in response by Laws L.J. in *R (on the application of Carson) v Secretary of State for Work and Pensions* [2003] EWCA Civ 797, [2003] 2 All E.R. 577, para.[73].

[76] "Deference: A Tangled Story" [2005] P.L. 346. See also R. Clayton, [2004] P.L. 33; J. Rivers, "Proportionality and Variable Intensity of Review" [2006] C.L.J. 174 (considering competing theories of proportionality and stressing the need for a cautious approach).

[77] *ibid.* p.352. See also Lord Bingham in *A v Secretary of State for the Home Department* [2004] UKHL 56, [2005] 2 A.C. 68, para.[29]: the question is better approached "as one of demarcation of functions or what Liberty in its written case called 'relative institutional competence'".

[78] [2007] UKHL 11.

[79] Immigration and Asylum Act 1999, s.65.

maker's conclusion that his own decision was compatible. Secondly, in performing that role the court will "consider and weigh all that tells in favour" of the
decision, including, in an immigration case, such matters as the desirability of
applying known rules if the system is to be workable, consistent, predictable and
fair, the need to discourage deliberate breaches of the law, and in some cases the
views on the particular case of the Secretary of State:

> "The giving of weight to factors such as these is not, in our opinion, aptly
> described as deference: it is performance of the ordinary judicial task of
> weighing up the competing considerations on each side and according
> appropriate weight to the judgment of a person with responsibility for a
> given subject matter and access to special sources of knowledge and
> advice."[80]

The House noted[81]

> "a tendency, both in the arguments addressed to the courts and in the
> judgments of the courts, to complicate and mystify what is not in principle,
> a hard task to define, however difficult the task is, in practice, to
> perform."

It is submitted that this helpfully confirms that there is no free-standing
doctrine of "deference" that prevents a court that is minded to conclude that a
particular decision is a disproportionate interference with a Convention right
from so holding, out of "deference" to Parliament or the elected executive.[82] It
is also submitted that the approach to what should apparently no longer be
labelled "deference"[83] is also[84] applicable in the class of cases where the court
is reviewing the decision of another decision maker, in judicial review proceedings, as the ultimate question of compatibility is one of law that the court must
determine under the 1998 Act.[85] There may well be a distinction of degree
between the two classes of case, it being more likely that significant weight will
be attached to, say, the view of a minister where he is also the primary decision
maker[86]; but not a distinction in kind. This would also fit well with the clear view
of the House that the extent to which the court will take account of the views of
others, including the decision maker, will be heavily context-specific. It is
notable that the House mentioned,[87] but without approval, the distinction drawn

---

[80] para.[16].
[81] para.[14].
[82] As powerfully argued by T. R. S. Allan, "Human Rights and Judicial Review: A Critique of 'Due
Deference'" [2006] C.L.J. 671, noting that such a doctrine would in effect be one of non-
justiciability.
[83] Unfortunately the House provided no substitute label.
[84] The House in *Huang* emphasised that its remarks were directed to appeals under s.65.
[85] It should not in any event be the view of the decision maker on the ultimate question whether the
decision is proportionate that carries weight; it should be the view on such matters as the
importance of the object to be achieved by the decision.
[86] "The judgment of the primary decision maker, on the same or substantially the same factual basis,
is always relevant and may be decisive": para.[12].
[87] At para.[14].

by the Court of Appeal[88] between cases where the court had to judge the weight or merits of a government policy and a "discretionary area of judgment" was accordingly to be recognised, and cases where the decision was not so based. Overall, *Huang* provides some reassurance that there is no principle, set at a high level of generality, which will prevent or discourage courts from acting appropriately to protect Convention rights. This is not to say that the task in individual cases is an easy one,[89] or that particular decisions will not attract criticism as being unduly "deferential".[90]

Cases where the public authority has failed to establish a justification for the interference with the applicant's rights and freedoms under the proportionality approach are relatively unusual. Illustrations include: *Daly*[91]; *R (on the application of Farrakhan) v Secretary of State for the Home Department*[92] (at first instance but reversed on appeal[93]); *Aston Cantlow and Wilmcote with Billesley Parochial Church Council v Wallbank*[94] (by the Court of Appeal, but reversed by the House of Lords)[95]; *R (on the application of Hirst) v Secretary of State for the Home Department*[96]; *A v Secretary of State for the Home Department*[97]; *R (on the application of Baiai) v Secretary of State for the Home Department*[98]; and *R (on the application of Wright) v Secretary of State for Health.*[99] In these cases, the court disagrees with the balancing of the relevant factors by the decision maker, by reference to the proportionality test, after taking due account of the extent of

---

[88] [2005] EWCA Civ 105, [2006] Q.B. 1.

[89] See n.62 above.

[90] The *Farrakhan* and *ProLife Alliance* decisions n.75, (upholding refusal to transmit party election broadcast judged by the BBC to be offensive) have attracted particular adverse comment: see e.g. Allan, [2006] C.L.J. 671, 681–682, 689–690; E. Barendt, [2003] P.L. 580 (*ProLife*); A. Scott, (2003) 66 M.L.R. 224 (*ProLife*).

[91] n.62, above.

[92] [2001] EWHC Admin 781. Held to be insufficient evidence that there was more than a nominal risk that community relations would be endangered if the ban on the applicant's entry to the UK for the limited purpose and duration sought were lifted.

[93] [2002] EWCA Civ 606, [2002] Q.B. 1391. Held that the Secretary of State had provided a sufficient explanation for a decision that turned on his personal, informed, assessment of risk to demonstrate that his decision was not disproportionate, although the merits of the appeal were "finely balanced".

[94] [2001] EWCA Civ 713, [2002] Ch. 51. Liability of particular owners of former glebe land to contribute to chancel repairs held to be arbitrary in its incidence (contrary to the First Protocol, Art.1) and unjustifiably discriminatory (contrary to Art.14) as it was not a proportionate means of maintaining historic buildings, and so lacked a reasonable and objective justification.

[95] [2003] UKHL 37, [2004] 1 A.C. 546. *Per* Lord Hope of Craighead, Lord Scott of Foscote and Lord Hobhouse of Woodborough: there was no violation of First Protocol, Art.1 as the liability was an incident of the ownership of the land in question and not deprivation of the claimants' possession or control over the use of their property.

[96] [2002] EWHC 602 (Admin), [2002] 1 W.L.R. 2929 (policy imposing blanket ban on prisoner having telephone contact with the media held unlawful by Elias J.).

[97] [2004] UKHL 56, [2005] 2 A.C. 68. See para.8–008.

[98] [2006] EWHC 823 (Admin), [2007] 1 W.L.R. 693 (the requirement for certain persons subject to immigration control who wished to marry to obtain a certificate of approval from the Secretary of State was directed to the legitimate objective of preventing "sham" marriages contracted as a means of avoiding immigration control; however, it was disproportionate in that it affected the Art.12 rights of very many more people than was necessary to achieve the legislative objective, it automatically regarded non C of E marriages as a sham, and arbitrarily failed to take into account many factors relevant in considering whether a proposed marriage was a sham; it was also disproportionate discrimination on the ground of nationality contrary to Arts 12 and 14). This was upheld by reference to Art.12: [2007] EWCA Civ 478.

[99] [2006] EWHC 2886 (Admin), [2007] 1 All E.R. 825 (procedure for placing a person provisionally on the Protection of Vulnerable Adults list unfair and disproportionate; person so listed had to wait nine months before being able to apply to a Care Standards Tribunal).

"deference" (for want of a better word) to the decision maker appropriate in the circumstances.

It has been held that intervention is more straightforwardly based where the decision maker has failed to analyse the issues in the manner required by the proportionality test; where a decision is made "without proper consideration by the decision maker of highly relevant proportionality issues", it never reaches "the point of refinement at which the judicial obligation of deference" crystallises.[100] There is in effect a failure to take account of relevant considerations. However, it is not clear whether this approach survives the decision of the House of Lords in *R (on the application of SB) v Governors of Denbigh High School*[101] that in considering a challenge to the proportionality of a challenged decision the court is not concerned with whether the decision is the product of a defective decision-making process[102] but whether Convention rights have been violated:

" . . . what matters in any case is the practical outcome not the quality of the decision-making process."[103]

It is submitted that the House was right to hold that the courts should not prescribe detailed decision-making structures for decision makers. However, it would also be odd if a conventional judicial review challenge[104] could not be mounted, at least in exceptional cases, where it is clear that the decision maker was unaware that its decision affected Convention rights.[105] It is also difficult to see that, in a borderline case, such a decision would deserve any significant "deference".

Finally, it should be noted that there are, exceptionally, some situations where it is *for the court itself* to determine whether the interference with the claimant's Convention rights is proportionate. Examples include an exercise of discretion by the High Court to grant injunctive relief to enforce planning legislation.[106]

---

[100] *per* Maurice Kay J. *in R (on the application of CD) v Secretary of State for the Home Department* [2003] EWHC 155 (Admin). For other examples, see *R (on the application of Madden) v Bury MBC* [2002] EWHC 1882 (Admin) (council's decision to close residential home quashed where there was no detailed evidence that Art.8 issues had been considered); *R (on the application of Baiai) v Secretary of State for the Home Department* [2006] EWHC 823 (Admin), [2006] 3 All E.R. 608, at paras [89], [151]. *Cf.* Silber J. in *R (on the application of N) v Secretary of State for the Home Department* [2003] EWHC 207 (Admin) at para.[62] (little justification for deference where the conduct of which complaint is made comprises failures to act arising not from a positive or conscious decision not to act but from administrative errors; reversed on other grounds: [2003] EWCA Civ 1406, [2004] Q.B. 1124).

[101] [2006] UKHL 15, [2007] 1 A.C. 100.

[102] The Court of Appeal ([2005] 1 W.L.R. 3372 at para.[75] *per* Brooke L.J.) set out six questions that the decision-making structure ought to have addressed.

[103] See Lord Bingham at paras [28]–[31].

[104] Which commonly can be based on defects in the approach to decision making.

[105] In *Denbigh*, the School "had taken immense pains to devise a uniform policy which respected Muslim beliefs" (*per* Lord Bingham at para.[34]). The House held that the school's decision not to admit a pupil while wearing a jilbab either did not interfere with her right to manifest her religious belief (Lords Bingham, Hoffmann and Scott) or did so interfere but was objectively justified (Lord Nicholls and Baroness Hale).

[106] *South Buckinghamshire District Council v Porter* [2003] UKHL 26, [2003] 2 A.C. 558. See also *R (on the application of Wilkinson) v Broadmoor Special Hospital Authority* [2001] EWCA Civ 1545, [2002] 1 W.L.R. 419 (decision to administer medical treatment to mental patient without consent); *Secretary of State for the Home Department v MB* [2006] EWCA Civ 1140 (non-derogating control orders under the Prevention of Terrorism Act 2005).

However, at the other end of the spectrum are cases where appropriate justification for interference with a protected right can be derived from the statutory scheme itself and need not always be demonstrated on a case-by-case basis.[107]

4. Interpretation of Legislation and Declarations of Incompatibility

(a) The boundary between interpretation and amendment

Section 3(1) of the 1998 Act provides that: 8–006

"So far as it is possible to do so, primary legislation[108] and subordinate legislation[109] must be read and given effect in a way which is compatible with Convention rights."

This provision applies to primary and subordinate legislation whenever enacted,[110] but does not affect the validity, continuing operation or enforcement of (1) any incompatible primary legislation, and (2) any incompatible secondary legislation if (disregarding any possibility of revocation) primary legislation prevents removal of the incompatibility.[111] In these cases a court,[112] in any

---

[107] *Wandsworth LBC v Michalak* [2002] EWCA Civ 271, [2003] 1 W.L.R. 617, *per* Brooke L.J. at paras [46], [47] citing *James v UK* (1986) 8 E.H.R.R. 123, para.68, *Di Palma v UK* (1988) 10 E.H.R.R. 149 at 155–156 and *Mellacher v Austria* (1989) 12 E.H.R.R. 391, paras 45, 52, 53. *Michalak* concerned the grant of a possession order in respect of a local authority flat against a person who did not qualify under the legislation as a successor to the secure tenancy. This position was endorsed, more strongly, by the House of Lords in *Harrow LBC v Qazi* [2003] UKHL 43, [2004] 1 A.C. 983, in the context of proceedings by a local authority seeking possession of premises where the claimant's tenancy had been terminated by the act of his spouse as joint tenant and in *Kay v Lambeth LBC; Leeds City Council v Price* [2006] UKHL 10, [2006] 2 A.C 465. See further, below, para.8–023.

[108] i.e. any public general, local and personal or private Act of Parliament, any measure of the Church Assembly or the General Synod of the Church of England; certain Orders in Council; and certain orders made under primary legislation bringing one or more provisions of that legislation into force or amending any primary legislation: s.21(1). An Order in Council made in the exercise of the royal prerogative is primary legislation: *Hopkins v Secretary of State for Defence* [2004] All E.R. (D) 362 (Feb).

[109] i.e. any Order in Council that does not qualify as primary legislation; any Act of the Scottish Parliament, the Parliament of Northern Ireland or the Northern Ireland Assembly; and any order, rules, regulations scheme, warrant, by-law or other instrument made under primary legislation, under an Act of any of the bodies just mentioned or an Order in Council applying only to Northern Ireland, or by a member of the Scottish Executive, a Northern Ireland minister or department in the exercise of prerogative or other executive functions on behalf of Her Majesty.

[110] s.3(2)(a).

[111] s.3(2)(b), (c). For the argument that s.3(2)(b) operates as a limit to the broad duty arising under s.3(1), so that s.3(1) may not be invoked to support a proposed reading that "would have the effect of so impairing the operation and/or effectiveness of the clause under scrutiny so as to render it for all practical purposes a dead letter, or close to a dead letter" see C. Gearty, (2002) 118 L.Q.R. 248, 250–258.

[112] i.e. the House of Lords, the Judicial Committee of the Privy Council, the Courts-Martial Appeal Court, the High Court of Justiciary sitting otherwise as a trial court, the Court of Session, the High Court and the Court of Appeal in England and Wales and in Northern Ireland: s.4(5).

proceedings where it determines whether a provision is compatible with a Convention right,[113] may make a *declaration of incompatibility*. Such a declaration does not affect the validity, continuing operation or enforcement of the provision and is not binding on the parties to the proceedings in which it is made.[114] Where a court is considering the possibility of a declaration of incompatibility, the Crown is entitled to notice in accordance with rules of court and a minister of the Crown (or his nominee), a member of the Scottish Executive, and a Northern Ireland minister or department is entitled, on giving notice in accordance with rules of court, to be joined as a party to the proceedings.[115]

Following a declaration of incompatibility or a finding by the European Court of Human Rights in proceedings against the UK that a provision is incompatible with an obligation of the UK arising from the Convention, a minister of the Crown may make a remedial order, subject to the approval of each House of Parliament, amending primary legislation or amending or revoking subordinate legislation.[116] It is of course also possible for other processes for amendment to be adopted, including fresh primary legislation. The fast-track order procedure is indeed only available if the minister considers there are "compelling reasons" for proceeding under s.10.

The obligation imposed by s.3(1) is not confined to any particular institution or person. Accordingly, as well as applying to courts and tribunals it will apply to government departments and local authorities and will govern their approach to the interpretation of legislation conferring functions upon them. Legislation is to be interpreted in such a way to be compatible "so far as it is possible to do so". The modern approach for statutory interpretation expects statutory provisions to be interpreted in their context, with the notion of "context" construed widely. It is accepted that judges may read in words necessarily implied and have a limited power to add to, alter or ignore statutory words in order to prevent a provision from being unintelligible or absurd or totally unreasonable, unworkable or totally irreconcilable with the rest of the statute.[117]

This approach includes the power to read statutory provisions as qualified by broad principles that reflect fundamental values of the common law and which Parliament is presumed to intend to be applicable unless the contrary is expressly

---

[113] This means that "interpretation of the legislation in accordance with s.3 is an essential preliminary step to making a declaration of incompatibility . . . because the court cannot be satisfied the legislation is incompatible until effect has been given to the interpretative obligation set out in s.3": *per* Lord Nicholls of Birkenhead in *Wilson v Secretary of State for Trade and Industry* [2003] UKHL 40, [2004] 1 A.C. 816, para.[14].

[114] s.4(1)–(4), (6).

[115] s.5.

[116] s.10 and Sch.2. A remedial order has been made following the decision in *R (on the application of H) v Mental Health Review Tribunal* [2002] Q.B. 1: see the Mental Health Act 1983 (Remedial Order 2001) (SI 2001/3712). A remedial order was made following the decision of the ECtHR in *Mark Grieves v UK* (App. No.57067/00) that there had been a violation of Art.6(1) in that the position of the judge advocate in the applicant's court-martial did not provide a sufficient guarantee of independence as he had been appointed by the Chief Naval Judge Advocate, a serving naval officer; the necessary changes were effected by the Naval Discipline Act 1957 (Remedial) Order 2004 (SI 2004/66) made under the "urgent" procedure prescribed in Sch.2, para.4. The Marriage Act 1949 (Remedial Order) 2007 (SI 2007/438) removed the prohibitions on the marriage of a person to the parent of his or her former spouse or to the former spouse of his or her child, following the ruling in *B and L v UK*, judgment of September 13, 2005, that these prohibitions contravened Art.12.

[117] Above, para.6–015.

stated, such as fundamental principles of human rights,[118] the substantive principles of judicial review,[119] the general principles of criminal liability such as the presumption in favour of a requirement of *mens rea* for criminal offences,[120] the principle that no person should be allowed to benefit from his own wrong,[121] and respect for legal professional privilege.[122]

Courts and tribunals required to determine an issue of compatibility will clearly be expected to use all legitimate techniques of statutory interpretation to read and give effect to a provision so as to be compatible with Convention rights. The same is presumably true of other persons and bodies to whom the obligation under s.3(1) applies, although it may well in practice prove difficult to criticise them should they decline to adopt an approach based on one of the more sophisticated judicial techniques of statutory interpretation (such as the power in limited circumstances to treat statutory language as modified). In any event, there will come a point where the words of a provision are so unequivocal that effect has to be given to them notwithstanding incompatibility. So much is assumed in the existence of the power of certain courts to grant a declaration of incompatibility.[123]

Nevertheless, it has been made clear that the enactment of s.3(1) does involve the addition of an extra dimension to the ordinary methods of interpretation. In *R v A*[124] the House of Lords considered the ambit of the statutory prohibition on the introduction at a trial for a sexual offence evidence of the complainant's

[118] *R v Secretary of State for the Home Department, Ex p. Simms* [2000] 2 A.C. 115.
[119] See Ch.18.
[120] See D. C. Ormerod, *Smith & Hogan Criminal Law* (11th edn, 2005), Chs 7 (crimes of strict liability) and 11 (general defences); *Sweet v Parsley* [1970] A.C. 132.
[121] See e.g. *R v Secretary of State for the Home Department, Ex p. Puttick* [1981] Q.B. 767; *R v Registrar-General, Ex p. Smith* [1991] 2 Q.B. 393.
[122] *R (on the application of Morgan Grenfell Ltd) v Special Commissioners of Income Tax* [2002] UKHL 21, [2003] 1 A.C. 563.
[123] Lord Hope in *R v Lambert* [2001] 3 W.L.R. 206, 233–235, paras [70]–[81]; Lord Nicholls in *Re S (Minors) (Care Order: Implementation of Care Plan)* [2002] UKHL 10, [2002] 2 A.C. 291 para.[38].
[124] [2001] UKHL 25, [2002] 2 A.C. 45. Other examples include *R v Lambert* [2002] 2 A.C. 545 (defence available to defendant charged with possession of drugs to prove that they neither believed nor suspected nor had reason to suspect that substance in their possession was a controlled drug interpreted as imposing evidential burden not a legal burden as otherwise there would be a violation of the presumption of innocence in Art.6(2)) (*cf. Sheldrake v DPP* [2004] UKHL 43, [2005] 1 A.C. 264); *Cachia v Faluyi* [2001] EWCA Civ 998, [2001] 1 W.L.R. 1966 (word "action" in the Fatal Accidents Act 1976, s.2(3) ("Not more than one action shall lie for and in respect of the same subject matter of complaint") to be interpreted as "served process" to protect claimant's right of access to the court); *Ghaidan v Ghodin-Mendoza* [2004] UKHL 30, [2004] 2 A.C. 557 (provision of the Rent Act 1977 conferring a right of succession on a person who was living with a deceased statutory tenant "as his or her wife or husband" was to be read as meaning "as if they were his or her wife or husband" so as to extend to persons in a same-sex relationship); *R (on the application of Middleton) v HM Coroner for the Western District of Somerset* [2004] UKHL 10, [2004] 2 A.C. 182 (new interpretation of Coroners Rules required); *R (on the application of Sim) v Parole Board* [2003] EWCA Civ 1845, [2004] Q.B. 1288 (provision that the Board "shall direct the prisoner's release if satisfied that it is no longer necessary for the protection of the public that he should be confined (but not otherwise)" to be interpreted so that the Board must conclude that it is no longer necessary to detain the recalled prisoner unless the Board is positively satisfied that the interests of the public require that he should be confined, so as to ensure compliance with Art.5(4)); *Secretary of State for the Home Department v MB* [2006] EWCA Civ 1140, [2006] H.R.L.R. 37 (procedural requirements of s.3(10) of the Prevention of Terrorism Act 2005 "read down" to secure compliance with Art.6(1); validity of order to be judged on the basis of the evidence available to the court, not limited to the evidence before the Secretary of State; court entitled to substitute its own judgment if required by Art.6(1)).

sexual behaviour unless one of a number of narrowly drawn exceptions applied. One of these was that there was an issue of consent and the behaviour was alleged to be so similar to any such behaviour which took place as part of the event in question or at or about the same time as that event that the similarity could not reasonably be explained as a coincidence.[125] The House held that this was to be interpreted as giving rise to a test for admissibility of whether the evidence was so relevant to the issue of consent that to exclude it would endanger the fairness of the trial under Art.6. Lord Steyn recognised that the "ordinary methods of purposive construction" of s.41(3)(c) could not cure the excessive breadth of s.41 so far as it related to previous sexual experience between a complainant and the accused. "Whilst the statute pursued desirable goals, the methods adopted amount to legislative overkill." However,

> "the interpretative obligation under section 3 of the 1998 Act is a strong one. It applies even if there is no ambiguity in the language in the sense of the language being capable of two different meanings. It is an emphatic adjuration by the legislature. . . . Section 3 . . . places a duty on the court to strive to find a possible interpretation compatible with convention rights. Under ordinary methods of interpretation a court may depart from the language of the statute to avoid absurd consequences: section 3 goes much further. Undoubtedly, a court must always look for a contextual and purposive interpretation: section 3 is more radical in its effect. . . . In accordance with the will of Parliament as reflected in secion 3 it will sometimes be necessary to adopt an interpretation which linguistically may appear strange. The techniques to be used will not only involve the reading down of express language in a statute but also the implication of provisions. A declaration of incompatibility is a measure of last resort."[126]

8-007   Accordingly, s.41 was to be read as subject to the implied provision that evidence or questioning required to ensure a fair trial under Art.6 should not be treated as inadmissible. It would seem that this extra dimension is closely analogous to the power to read statutory provisions as qualified by broad common law principles set out above. Interpretative techniques that may be permissible according to the circumstances include "reading up" or "reading down" (interpreting words, respectively, broadly or restrictively) or, more unusually, reading particular words in or out of a statute.[127]

In *Donoghue v Poplar Housing and Regeneration Community Association Ltd*,[128] the Court of Appeal indicated *obiter* that the court should always first ascertain whether, absent s.3, there would be any breach of the convention as, otherwise, s.3 could be ignored; if it had to rely on s.3 it should limit the extent of the modified meaning to that which is necessary to achieve compatibility; s.3 did not entitle the court to *legislate*, its task was one of *interpretation*; the views of the parties and of the Crown as to whether a "constructive" interpretation should be adopted could not modify the task of the court, which was under a duty

---

[125] Youth Justice and Criminal Evidence Act 1999, s.41(3).

[126] paras [43]–[45]. See to similar effect, Lord Slynn at paras [11]–[13], [15]; Lord Clyde at paras [136], [140]; Lord Hutton at paras [160]–[163]. Lord Hope of Craighead (paras [109]–[110]) took a narrower view holding that s.3 could not be used to imply a general provision of this nature but only to "read down" the actual words of s.41.

[127] D. Feldman, *English Publc Law* (2004), paras 7.70–7.80.

[128] [2001] EWCA Civ 595, [2002] Q.B. 48.

to adopt s.3 where it applied; where a compatible result could not be reached through interpretation, the court retained a discretion whether to grant a declaration of incompatibility, which would presumably be influenced by the usual considerations which apply to the grant of declarations.[129]

The boundary between interpretation and (impermissible) amendment was held by the House of Lords in *Re S (Minors) (Care Order: Implementation of Care Plan)*[130] to have been crossed in that case by the Court of Appeal.[131] The Court of Appeal had held that provisions of the Children Act 1989 concerning care orders should be subject to modifications that enhanced the role of the court. The House disapproved one of these, namely that the guardian ad litem or local authority had the right to apply to the trial court if starred milestones in the care plan were not achieved within a reasonable time of the date set at trial. This would depart from a "cardinal principle" of the Act "that the courts are not empowered to intervene in the way local authorities discharge their parental responsibilities under final care orders".[132] In ascribing a meaning by virtue of s.3(1), it was important for a court to identify clearly the particular statutory provision(s) whose interpretation led to that result; here, the Court of Appeal had not identified any such provision of the 1989 Act, and indeed there was none. The introduction of the starring system would have far reaching practical effects on the workload of local authorities and their allocation of scarce financial and other resources; "these are matters for decision by Parliament not the courts".[133] Furthermore, the starring system went much further than provide a judicial remedy to victims of actual or proposed conduct that would be unlawful under Arts 6 and 8.

Two points emerge. First, it would seem that the practical effects of a particular modification of statutory language by virtue of s.3(1) interpretation may properly be relevant in determining whether the boundary has been crossed. Nevertheless, it is submitted that it would be wrong to confine s.3(1) in all cases to the making of small changes. Secondly, it is also submitted that it would be wrong for s.3(1) to be confined to securing what would be effectively textual modifications to specified provisions. Such an approach would fail to take account of the powers of the courts to read statutes as modified (in the absence of clear words to the contrary) by fundamental, albeit broadly stated, principles.[134] That a broad rather than a narrow approach to s.3(1) should be adopted was confirmed by the House of Lords in *Ghaidan v Ghodin Mendoza*.[135]

The strength of the interpretative obligation under s.3(1) is confirmed by the point that it may require a court below the level of the House of Lords to

---

[129] *per* Lord Woolf C.J. at para.[75].
[130] [2002] UKHL 10, [2002] 2 A.C. 291. Other examples of cases where s.3(1) could not be used to support the reading contended for include: *R (on the application of Hooper) v Secretary of State for Work and Pensions* [2003] EWCA Civ 813, [2003] 11 W.L.R. 2623 (references in benefits legislation to the feminine gender could not be read by virtue of s.3(1) as including the masculine; the point was not raised before the House of Lords: [2005] UKHL 29, [2005] 1 W.L.R. 1681); *R (on the application of Wilkinson) v Inland Revenue Commissioners* [2005] UKHL 30, [2005] 1 W.L.R. 1718 ("widow" cannot be read to include "widower").
[131] *Re W & B (children); Re W (children)* [2001] EWCA Civ 757, [2001] H.R.L.R. 1120.
[132] para.[42].
[133] paras [43], [44].
[134] See above.
[135] [2004] UKHL 30, [2004] 2 A.C. 557, the House holding (Lord Millett dissenting) that the entitlement of a person living with the original tenant "as his or her wife or husband" to become statutory tenant by succession on the latter's death extended to persons in same-sex relationship. See R. Wintemute, [2003] P.L. 621; A. Kavanagh, [2005] P.L. 23.

disregard a decision of the House.[136] It does not, however, enable a court to change substantive law with effect retrospectively prior to commencement of the HRA 1998.[137]

Finally, in any case where a declaration of incompatibility is made, it will *ex hypothesi* have proved impossible to secure compatibility via s.3(1).[138] There is obviously tension between the two provisions. The essential dilemma is this. On the one hand, a remedy for the claimant in the particular case can only be guaranteed via s.3(1). The greater the violence that would do to the legislation, the stronger the argument that the matter should be dealt with by a declaration of incompatibility; this should lead to amending legislation, but this may well not be retrospective in effect so as to benefit the claimant. The early decision in *R v A*[139] was in fact one where the House was prepared to engage in significant rewriting; since then they have generally been rather more cautious in the use of s.3(1) and more inclined to make a declaration of incompatibility. Whichever way they go, there is likely in a difficult borderline case to be criticism from some quarter.[140]

(b) Declarations of incompatibility

8–008   Declarations of incompatibility have been made (and not challenged successfully on appeal) in a small number of cases, as follows. In *R (on the application of H) v Mental Health Review Tribunal*[141] the Court of Appeal found that the reversed burden of proof, in respect of matters justifying the detention of a mental patient, in s.73 of the Mental Health Act 1983 was incompatible with Art.5. In *R (on the application of International Transport Roth GmbH) v Secretary of State for the Home Department*[142] the Court of Appeal held that then penalty regime applicable to lorry drivers and haulage companies as persons responsible for clandestine entrants was incompatible with Art.6 and the First Protocol, Art.1. The penalty imposed under the scheme was disproportionate to its goal. In *R (on the application of Wilkinson) v Inland Revenue Commissioners*[143] Moses J. granted a declaration that provisions governing a bereavement allowance payable to "widows" constituted unjustifiable gender discrimination contrary to Art.14, taken with Art.8 or First Protocol, Art.1. In *R (on the application of Anderson) v Secretary of State for the Home Department*[144] the House of Lords held that

---

[136] *R (on the application of IH) v Secretary of State for the Home Department* [2002] EWCA Civ 646, [2003] Q.B. 320; *R (on the application of C) v Secretary of State for the Home Department* [2002] EWCA Civ 647 (powers of Mental Health Review Tribunal following order for conditional discharge of patient broader than held in *Campbell v Secretary of State for the Home Department* [1988] 1 A.C. 120). This approach was approved by the House of Lords in *IH* [2003] UKHL 59, [2004] 2 A.C. 253.

[137] *Wainwright v Home Office* [2001] EWCA Civ 2081, [2002] Q.B. 1334.

[138] See below.

[139] Above.

[140] For discussion, see A Kavanagh, (2004) 24 O.J.L.S. 259, [2004] P.L. 537 and [2005] P.L. 23 and D. Nicol, [2004] P.L. 273.

[141] [2002] Q.B. 1.

[142] [2002] EWCA Civ 158, [2003] Q.B. 728. Simon Brown and Jonathan Parker L.JJ., Laws L.J. dissenting. The statutory regime was amended by primary legislation.

[143] [2002] EWHC 182 (Admin), [2002] S.T.C. 347. The Court of Appeal dismissed an appeal: [2003] EWCA Civ 814, [2003] 1 W.L.R. 2683, holding that the Inland Revenue had no power to pay the equivalent allowance to a widower by way of concession. The House of Lords dismissed a further appeal: [2005] UKHL 30, [2005] 1 W.L.R. 1718. The allowance was abolished by primary legislation from 2000.

[144] [2002] UKHL 46, [2003] 1 A.C. 837.

involvement of the Home Secretary in fixing the tariff period for a convicted murder was incompatible with Art.6(1). In *R (on the application of D) v Secretary of State for the Home Department*[145] the absence of any power in s.74 of the Mental Health Act 1983 for the release of a prisoner in the circumstances of the claimant was held to be incompatible with Art.5(4).

In *Bellinger v Bellinger*[146] the House of Lords held that those parts of English law which failed to give legal recognition to the acquired gender of transsexual persons were incompatible with Arts 8 and 13. In *R (on the application of Morris) v Westminster City Council (No.3)*[147] Keith J. granted a declaration that a provision[148] that required a housing authority in determining whether a person had a priority need for accommodation to disregard a person from abroad who is not eligible for housing assistance[149] was incompatible with Arts 8 and 14, ECHR. The provision discriminated on the ground of nationality and was unlikely to achieve the legitimate aim of discouraging benefit tourism, given that there was nothing to prevent British citizens bringing dependent children to the UK simply to render themselves eligible for housing assistance under Pt VII of the 1996 Act. In *R (on the application of MH) v Secretary of State for Health*[150] the Court of Appeal held that ss.2 and 29(4) of the Mental Health Act 1983 were incompatible with Art.5(4), ECHR. In *A v Secretary of State for the Home Department*[151] the House of Lords held that s.23 of the Anti-terrorism, Crime and Security Act 2001, enabling the indefinite detention of suspected terrorists who could not lawfully be deported, was incompatible with Arts 5 and 14, ECHR. In *R (on the application of Baiai) v Secretary of State for the Home Department*[152] Silber J. held that s.19 of the Ayslum and Immigration (Treatment of Claimants, etc) Act 2004 was incompatible with Arts 12 and 14, ECHR; this required certain persons subject to immigration control who wished to marry (other than under the rites of the Church of England) to obtain a certificate of approval of the Secretary of State.

Most recently, in *R (on the application of Hindawi) v Secretary of State for the Home Department*,[153] the House of Lords held that provisions that prevented long-term prisoners liable for removal from the UK after serving their sentences from having their cases reviewed by the Parole Board in the same manner as long-term prisoners was incompatible with Arts 5 and 14.

Even where there is clear incompatibility, the court retains a discretion whether to grant a declaration. In *R (on the application of M) v Secretary of State for Health*,[154] Maurice Kay J. found that the provision in the Mental Health Act 1983 that prescribed who qualified to be the "nearest relative" of a detained person for

---

[145] [2002] EWHC 2805 (Admin), [2003] 1 W.L.R. 1315.
[146] [2003] UKHL 21, [2003] 2 A.C. 467.
[147] [2004] EWHC 2191 (Admin), [2005] 1 W.L.R. 865. The Court of Appeal dismissed an appeal: [2005] EWCA Civ 1184, [2006] 1 W.L.R. 505.
[148] s.185(4) of the Housing Act 1996.
[149] i.e. a person subject to immigration control not of a class prescribed by regulations: s.185(2). Here, this was the claimant's daughter.
[150] [2004] EWCA Civ 1609, [2005] 1 W.L.R. 1209.
[151] [2004] UKHL 56, [2005] 2 A.C. 68. The relevant provisions were not renewed, but replaced by a control order regime under the Prevention of Terrorism Act 2005.
[152] [2006] EWHC 823, [2006] 2 F.L.R 645.
[153] [2006] UKHL 54, [2007] H.R.L.R. 12.
[154] [2003] EWHC 1094 (Admin), [2003] U.K.H.R.R. 746. For further examples, see below.

the purpose of a number of safeguards in the Act was incompatible with Art.8(1). This was because there was no procedure by which a person unsuitable to discharge that role[155] could be replaced. Incompatibility was, indeed, conceded by the Secretary of State, following a friendly settlement of a case brought against the UK before the ECtHR,[156] and amending legislation was before Parliament. Maurice Kay J. rejected the Secretary of State's arguments that a declaration should not be granted as a matter of discretion. These included that a declaration was not needed as the government had undertaken to introduce amending legislation (but over three years had elapsed since the friendly settlement); the ECtHR had been content to approve a friendly settlement; the proposed Mental Health Bill would resolve the problem (it would be wrong to make assumptions about the form the Bill would take); by making a declaration the judge would be expressing a view about how the government and Parliament should go about its business (not so; it would be for the government to decide what steps to take in response to a declaration of incompatibility); it was preferable for reform to be effected by primary legislation rather than a remedial order (this would be a matter for the Minister not the court); a declaration would not help M, whose situation would not be changed until the legislation was amended (this would always be the case with declarations of incompatibility). On the other hand, there were good reasons for making a declaration: the incompatibility had to be identified a considerable time before and had not been removed; there was uncertainty now as to the form and commencement of such removal; the matter was important for M and for many others.

8–009   In the majority of cases where a declaration of incompatibility is sought the claim fails. There have also been a number of cases where a declaration of incompatibility is made by a lower court, but set aside on appeal. These include *Alconbury*[157]; *Matthews v Ministry of Defence*[158]; *Wilson v Secretary of State for Trade and Industry*[159]; *R (on the application of Hooper) v Secretary of State for Work and Pensions*[160]; *R (on the application of Uttley) v Secretary of State for the*

---

[155] M's "nearest relative" was her adoptive father, whom she alleged had sexually abused her as a child.

[156] *JT v UK*, App/26494/95, February 26, 1997, E Com HR; Judgment of ECtHR, March 30, 2000.

[157] See para.8–021; declaration granted by the Divisional Court set aside on appeal to the House of Lords.

[158] Declarations granted by Keith J. ([2002] EWHC 13, QB) set aside by the Court of Appeal: [2002] EWCA Civ 773, [2002] 1 W.L.R. 2621 (Crown Proceedings Act 1947, s.10, preventing claims in tort by servicemen against the Crown where death or injury is certified or attributable to service for the purposes of entitlement to a war pension, not incompatible with Art.6). An appeal to the House of Lords was dismissed: [2003] UKHL 4, [2003] 1 A.C. 1163.

[159] Court of Appeal ([2001] EWCA Civ 633, [2002] Q.B. 74) held that s.123(3) of the Consumer Credit Act 1974, in so far as it prevented a court from making an enforcement order unless a document containing all the prescribed terms had been signed by the debtor or hirer, was incompatible with Art.6(1) and the First Protocol, Art.1; this was reversed by the House of Lords, *sub nom., Wilson v Secretary of State for Trade and Industry* ([2003] UKHL 40, [2004] 1 A.C. 816). The House held that no declaration of incompatibility could be made so as to interfere with pre-commencement rights; but apart from that Art.6 was not applicable and the First Protocol, Art.1 not infringed.

[160] [2003] EWCA Civ 813, [2003] 1 W.L.R. 2623, setting aside a declaration granted by Moses J. ([2002] EWHC 191 (Admin)) that legislation providing for the payment of certain benefits to widows and not widowers was incompatible with Art.14, together with Art.8. The House of Lords allowed a further appeal, but the relevant provisions had by then been repealed and so a declaration was unnecessary: see Lord Hoffmann at para.[52].

Home Department[161]; *R (on the application of MH) v Secretary of State for Health*[162]; and *Secretary of State for the Home Department v MB*.[163]

The limits to the power to grant a declaration of incompatibility were explored by the House of Lords in *Re S (Minors) (Care Order: Implementation of Care Plan)*.[164] The House held that the Children Act 1989 provisions regulating care orders were not incompatible with Arts 8 and 6(1). If a local authority performed its duties in accordance with the legislation then in the ordinary course of events there should not be any infringement of the Art.8 rights of the child or the parent. The fact that the Act entrusted responsibility to the local authority was not itself such an infringement given that it was an experienced and responsible public authority. Neither did the fact that the court did not retain an ongoing supervisory role. If an authority failed to discharge its responsibilities under the Act, leading to an infringement of Art.8, a remedy would be available under ss.7 and 8 of the HRA 1998. Furthermore, the absence of an express remedial procedure from the Children Act 1989 could not *itself* constitute a breach of Art.8, or indeed of any Convention right (given that Art.13, ECHR, which provided that everyone whose Convention rights are violated "shall have an effective remedy" was not reproduced in the 1998 Act).[165] As regards the argument that the Children Act 1989 was inconsistent with Art.6(1), the House held that there were indeed some conceivable child care decisions where English law might not satisfy the requirements of Art.6(1). These included decisions affecting children with no parent or guardian able and willing to become involved in questioning a care decision by a local authority. However, the absence of provision for access to a court as guaranteed by Art.6 from a particular statute:

"does not, in itself, mean that the statute is incompatible with Article 6(1). Rather, this signifies at most the existence of a lacuna in the statute."[166]

A statutory lacuna is not statutory incompatibility. However, there were also some child care decisions made while a care order was in force where Art.6(1) might require access to a court, but where such access would be inconsistent with the underlying basic principle of the Children Act 1989, as distinct from any express provisions of that Act. The House left open the question which incompatibility of this kind was sufficient for the purpose of s.4.[167]

---

[161] [2004] UKHL 38, [2004] 1 W.L.R. 2278, setting aside a declaration that provisions in respect of the claimant's release from prison were incompatible with Art.7, ECHR granted by the Court of Appeal, [2003] EWCA Civ 1130, [2003] 1 W.L.R. 2590.

[162] [2005] UKHL 60, [2006] 1 A.C. 441, setting aside declarations that ss.2 and 29(4) of the Mental Health Act 1983 were incompatible with Art.5(4), ECHR granted by the Court of Appeal, [2004] EWCA Civ 1609, [2005] 1 W.L.R. 1209.

[163] [2006] EWCA Civ 1140, [2007] Q.B. 415, setting aside a declaration that the procedures in s.3 of the Prevention of Terrorism Act 2005, relating to the supervision by a court of non-derogating control orders made by the Secretary of State were incompatible with the right to a fair hearing under Art.6.

[164] [2002] UKHL 10, [2002] 2 A.C. 29.

[165] *per* Lord Nicholls at paras [52]–[64].

[166] *ibid.* paras [65]–[86].

[167] *ibid.* paras [87], [88]. See also Elias J. *obiter,* in *R (on the application of J) v Enfield LBC* [2002] EWHC 432, para.[67] (court must be satisfied that a particular statutory provision is incompatible with a Convention right; in the case of a failure to take positive steps it might be more appropriate "simply to state that there is a gap in the legal assistance provided which, in certain very limited circumstances, may lead to a breach of a Convention right, without making a formal section 4 declaration" (para.[69])).

Finally, it should be noted that the fact that existing incompatible legislation may, in the interests of legal certainty, be applied to a claimant pending necessary reform does not necessarily itself constitute a breach of the Convention.[168]

The standing necessary to be granted a declaration of incompatibility is not wholly clear. In *R (on the application of Rusbridger) v Attorney General*,[169] the House of Lords held that two *Guardian* journalists had "an interest and standing" to be awarded a declaration as to the interpretation of s.3 of the Treason Felony Act 1848 in the light of s.3 of the 1998 Act, and did not need to show they were "victims" under s.7 of the 1998 Act.[170] A literal interpretation of the 1848 Act would make encouragement of abolition of the monarchy, albeit without advocacy of the use of criminal violence, an offence, and *The Guardian* had published articles promoting republicanism. However, the House unanimously refused to grant a declaration in the exercise of its discretion on the ground that there was no live, practical issue. No prosecution had been, or would be, brought on such a basis, in view of s.3 of the 1998 Act, and it was not appropriate to use ss.3 and 4 as "an instrument by which the courts can chivvy Parliament into spring-cleaning the statute book".[171] Accordingly, it seems that while there is jurisdiction to grant a declaration of incompatibility to a person who is not a victim, the fact that a person is not affected may well lead to a refusal of a declaration as a matter of discretion. The Court of Appeal has held subsequently that a declaration of incompatibility will not be granted where the grounds raised do not apply to the party seeking it. In *Lancashire CC v Taylor*,[172] the Court of Appeal held that the tenant of an agricultural holding against whom an order of possession was sought on the ground that he was in breach of tenancy conditions, could not appropriately be granted a declaration that the statutory scheme was incompatible with the HRA 1998 on the ground that it discriminated unlawfully between two other categories of tenant.[173] Whether this was so as a matter of jurisdiction or discretion was, however, left unclear. Lord Woolf C.J. noted[174] that the tenant here was not a victim for the purposes of s.7, there was no realistic possibility that any remedial action taken after a declaration of incompatibility would benefit him in any way, and it was "doubtful in the extreme that a court would exercise its discretion in favour of Mr Taylor if he could not be affected by the breach of

---

[168] *R (on the application of Hooper) v Secretary of State for Work and Pensions* [2002] EWHC 191 (Admin), paras [120]–[129]; and see the Court of Appeal [2003] EWCA Civ 813, [2003] 1 W.L.R. 2633, paras [70]–[78], but then the doubts of Lord Hoffmann in the House of Lords: [2005] UKHL 29, [2005] 1 W.L.R. 1681, para.[62].

[169] [2003] UKHL 38, [2004] 1 A.C. 357.

[170] Lord Steyn at para.[21]. The parties were agreed on this point. Lords Scott of Foscote (para.[38]) and Walker of Gestingthorpe (para.[59]) expressly agreed with Lord Steyn. As to s.7, see para.8–012.

[171] See Lord Hutton at para.[36], Lord Rodger of Earlsferry at para.[58], Lord Walker of Gestingthorpe at para.[61]. Lord Rodger (at para.[55]) expressly concluded that there was no sign that the claimants had been affected in any way by the existence of s.3 of the 1848 Act and that the present proceedings were in substance an *actio popularis*.

[172] [2005] EWCA Civ 284, [2005] 1 W.L.R. 2668.

[173] Those facing eviction for failure to maintain the holding (following service of a notice requiring work or repairs to be done) and those facing eviction for failure to improve it (following service of a notice requiring compliance with an condition that such improvements be made). The former class had additional procedural protections, being entitled to have the notice to do work referred to arbitration before service of the notice to quit.

[174] Giving the judgment of the court (Lord Woolf C.J. and Sedley and Gage L.JJ.), at paras [37]–[44].

the Convention on which he was attempting to rely". However, he went on to say,[175] after citing Lord Steyn in *Rusbridger*,[176] that

> "This desirably flexible approach to the grant of declarations cannot appropriately be applied in the circumstances that exist here where Mr Taylor has not been and could not be personally adversely affected by the repealed legislation on which he seeks to rely. To allow him to do so would be to ignore section 7 of the HRA."

It is not clear whether this is intended to suggest that the court does not have jurisdiction to grant a declaration of incompatibility unless the applicant is a victim under s.7. It is submitted that this goes too far and does not follow from the terms of the 1998 Act. However, the refusal of a declaration can amply be justified as a matter of discretion.

5. Unlawful Action

(a) The scope of section 6

Section 6(1) provides that: **8–010**

> "It is unlawful for a public authority to act[177] in a way which is incompatible with a Convention right."

This does not apply to an act if as the result of one or more provisions of primary legislation the authority could not have acted differently,[178] or in the case of one or more provisions of, or made under, primary legislation which cannot be read or given effect in a way compatible with Convention rights, the authority was acting so as to give effect to or enforce those provisions.[179]

It has been held that as s.6(2)(a) exculpates a public authority that infringes a human right, it is to be narrowly construed. It accordingly only applies where legislation dictates the breach of the Convention right in question and not merely where it is said that the authority has no alternative as the result, for example, of the lack of resources.[180] The authority must be under a *duty* not to act in that way.[181]

---

[175] At para.[44].

[176] At para.[21].

[177] This includes a failure to act, but not a failure to introduce in or lay before Parliament a proposal for legislation or make any primary legislation or remedial order: s.6(6).

[178] s.6(2)(a).

[179] s.6(2)(b).

[180] *R (on the application of S) v Airedale NHS Trust* [2002] EWHC 1780 (Admin), paras [111]–[113] (in respect of the seclusion of the claimant under the Mental Health Act 1983; no breach of Art.5 found on the facts)

[181] *per* Lord Hope of Craighead in *R (on the application of Hooper) v Secretary of State for Work and Pensions* [2005] UKHL 29, [2005] 1 W.L.R. 1681, para.[71]. *Cf. R (on the application of Wilkinson) v IRC* [2005] UKHL 30, [2006] S.T.C. 270 (Inland Revenue Commissioners had no power to concede by way of extra statutory concession an allowance which Parliament could have granted but had not granted, on grounds of general equity between men and women; s.6(2)(a) accordingly applied).

By contrast, s.6(2)(b) applies where an authority has a *discretion* to give effect to or enforce provisions of or made under primary legislation which cannot be read or given effect to in a way which is compatible with Convention rights. The discretion may arise from one or more statutory provisions or at common law.[182] It has been held that s.6(2)(b) applies in any case where the *exercise* of a power conferred by legislation would necessarily involve incompatibility with a Convention right. It is no answer that compatibility could simply be achieved by refraining from exercising the power in question.[183] Section 6(2)(b) has also been held to apply to protect the Secretary of State's decision to refuse to exercise a common law power to make payments to widowers equivalent to payments to widows authorised by statute, where there was no objective justification for the differential legislative treatment.[184] On the other hand, s.6(2)(b) does not apply where regulations are incompatible with Convention requirements, unless the legislation requires the regulations to be made in that form (in the former circumstances the regulations can, and presumably should, be quashed).[185]

(b) "Public authority"

8–011   "Public authority" includes (a) a court or tribunal and (b) any person certain of whose functions are functions of a public nature,[186] but not either House of Parliament[187] or a person exercising functions in connection with proceedings in Parliament.[188] A government department or local authority would, for example, appear to be an obvious "public authority" without reference to (a) or (b) and so all of its acts would appear to be subject to s.6(1).[189]

---

[182] *ibid.* para.[72].

[183] *R v Kansal (No.2)* [2001] UKHL 62, [2002] 2 A.C. 69, *per* Lord Hope at para.[88]. *Cf.* cases where the power can legitimately be read down, but not extinguished, so as to secure conformity: *Friends Provident Life Office v Secretary of State for the Environment, Transport and the Regions* [2001] EWHC (Admin) 820, [2002] 1 W.L.R. 1450 (not every exercise of power to *refuse* to call-in a planning application would necessarily be incompatible with Art.6).

[184] *R (on the application of Hooper) v Secretary of State for Work and Pensions* [2005] UKHL 29, [2005] 1 W.L.R. 1681, *per* Lord Hoffmann at paras [41]–[52]: the Secretary of State did not have to show that the decision to refuse to make extra-statutory payments was "necessary" to give effect to the statutory provisions in question; he was giving effect to the incompatible provisions in that it was only if he made payments under them to widows could any complaint of discrimination arise on the part of the widowers. Otherwise, there would always be a duty to use common law powers to neutralise the effects of the legislation, and this would be contrary to the evident purpose of s.6(2) to preserve the sovereignty of Parliament. See to similar effect Lord Hope. Lord Brown doubted that s.6(2)(b) applied but held that s.6(2)(a) did. Lords Nicholls and Scott left open which subpara. applied but were clear that one did.

[185] *R (on the application of Bono) v Harlow District Council* [2002] EWHC 423 (Admin), [2002] 1 W.L.R. 2475.

[186] In relation to a particular act, a person is not a public authority by virtue only of (b) if the nature of the act is private: s.6(5). The purpose of this provision was said by Stanley Burnton J. in *R (on the application of Heather) v Leonard Cheshire Foundation* [2001] EWHC Admin 429, para.[91] to be "to exclude from the obligation of a hybrid authority to comply with Convention rights both its private functions and its acts of a private nature (such as the purchase of stationery) carried out in connection with the exercise of its public functions".

[187] Apart from the House of Lords in its judicial capacity: s.6(4).

[188] s.6(3).

[189] Confirmed by Lord Nicholls of Birkenhead in *Aston Cantlow and Wilmcote with Billesley Parochial Church Council v Wallbank* [2003] UKHL 37, [2004] 1 A.C. 546, at para.[7]. See further below.

The Court of Appeal has stated that the definition of who is a "public authority" and what is a "public function" should be given a "generous interpretation".[190] The court held that the role of a housing association which was a registered social landlord in providing accommodation for the defendant and then seeking possession was so closely assimilated to that of the local authority that it was performing public functions. Among the points made was that the mere fact that a body performed an activity which otherwise a public body would be under a duty to perform did not mean that such performance was necessarily a public function.[191] What can make an act, which would otherwise be private, public:

> "is a feature or a combination of features which impose a public character or stamp on the act. Statutory authority for what is done can at least help to mark the act as being public; so can the extent of control over the function exercised by another body which is a public authority. The more closely the acts that could be of a private nature are enmeshed in the activities of a public body, the more likely they are to be public. However, the fact that the acts are supervised by a public regulatory body does not necessarily indicate that they are of a public nature. . . . "[192]

Also of particular importance was the closeness of the relationship between the council (Tower Hamlets London Borough Council) and Poplar. Poplar had been created by Tower Hamlets to take a transfer of local authority housing stock; five of its board members were also Tower Hamlets councillors; Poplar was subject to the guidance of Tower Hamlets as to the manner in which it acted towards tenants. The defendant at the time of transfer was a sitting tenant of Tower Hamlets and it was intended that she would be treated no better and no worse than if she remained a tenant of Tower Hamlets. In a borderline case, such as this, it was very much a question of fact and degree.[193]

In *R (on the application of Heather) v Leonard Cheshire Foundation*[194] Stanley Burnton J. held that the expression "public function" was to be accorded the same meaning as under CPR Pt 54.[195] This could not involve a "purely functional" test as it would then apply, for example to the provision of education by private schools and of residential care to fee-paying patients. The adjective "public" in s.6 was used "in the sense of governmental".[196] Here, the judge held, distinguishing *Donoghue*, that a charitable foundation which ran a care home, the

---

[190] *Donoghue v Poplar Housing and Regeneration Community Association* [2001] EWCA Civ 595, [2001] 2 F.L.R. 284, para.[58], *per* Lord Woolf C.J. Other examples of bodies exercising a public function include a voluntary adoption agency exercising powers under the Adoption Act 1976 and regulations (*R (on the application of Gunn-Russo) v Nugent Care Society* [2001] EWHC Admin 566, [2001] U.K.H.R.R. 1320); and the head teacher and the governing body of a maintained school (*A v Head Teacher and the Governors of Lord Grey School* [2004] EWCA Civ 382, [2004] Q.B.1231, paras [36]–[38]). Bodies held not to be public authorities include Lloyd's (*Doll-Steinberg v The Society of Lloyd's* [2002] EWHC 419 (Admin)); *R (on the application of West) v Lloyd's of London* [2004] EWCA Civ 506, [2004] 3 All E.R. 251); and Network Rail Infrastructure Ltd (formerly Railtrack) (*Cameron v Network Rail Infrastructure Ltd* [2006] EWHC 1133 (QB), [2007] 1 W.L.R. 163).

[191] *ibid.*, giving as an example the provision by a small hotel of bed and breakfast accommodation as a temporary measure.

[192] *ibid.* para.[65].

[193] *ibid.* paras [65], [66].

[194] [2001] EWHC Admin. 429.

[195] See para.18–054.

[196] At para.[86].

majority of whose residents were funded by their local authority or health authority, was not exercising a public function. The foundation was established by private individuals, not the local authority; no purchasing authority was able to require the foundation to accept a particular person as a service user or resident; the statutory regulation was less extensive; there was no relationship with a statutory authority as integrated as that as that between Poplar and Tower Hamlets.[197] The Court of Appeal dismissed an appeal,[198] holding that the degree of public funding of the activities of an otherwise private body was relevant but not determinative; the Foundation was neither standing in the shoes of the local authorities nor exercising statutory powers.

The House of Lords provided guidance on the scope of the expression "public authority" in *Aston Cantlow and Wilmcote with Billesley Parochial Church Council v Wallbank*.[199] Unfortunately, neither *Donoghue* nor *Heather* were mentioned. The House held that a distinction is to be drawn between a "core" public authority and a "hybrid" public authority. A "core" public authority is one which falls within s.6 of the 1998 Act without reference to the inclusory words of s.6(3).[200] A "hybrid" public authority is one which exercises both public and non-public functions; however, by virtue of s.6(5)[201] it is not a public authority in respect of acts of a private nature. The term "public authority" is "essentially a reference to a body whose nature is governmental in a broad sense of that expression".[202] Similarly, the distinction between functions of a governmental nature and functions which are not of that nature is a useful guide in drawing the distinction between "public" and "private" for the purpose of s.6(3)(b) and (5).[203] There is no single test of universal application; factors to be taken into account

> "include the extent to which in carrying out the relevant function the body is publicly funded, or is exercising statutory powers, or is taking the place of central government or local authorities, or is providing a public service."[204]

A "non-governmental organization" for the purposes of Art.34, ECHR[205]

---

[197] The position was accordingly the same as pre-commencement, where it had been held that such a body was not subject to judicial review: *R v Servite Housing Association, Ex p. Goldsmith and Chatting* [2001] L.G.R. 55.

[198] [2002] EWCA Civ 366, [2002] 2 All E.R. 936.

[199] [2003] UKHL 37, [2004] 1 A.C. 546.

[200] See above. For Lord Hobhouse a core public authority is, by inference, "a person or body all of whose functions are of a public nature" (para.[85]). It is submitted that this overstates the position if intended to be the test for as distinct from the consequences of being a public authority.

[201] See above.

[202] *per* Lord Nicholls of Birkenhead at para.[7], Lord Hope of Craighead at para.[47], Lord Hobhouse of Woodborough at paras [87], [88].

[203] *per* Lord Nicholls at para.[10], Lord Hobhouse at para.[90].

[204] *per* Lord Nicholls at para.[12].

[205] This provides that the ECtHR may receive applications from "any person, non-governmental organisation or group of individuals claiming to be the victim of a violation" of the rights set out in the ECHR. The term "governmental organisation" does not refer only to the government or central organs of the state but, where powers are distributed along decentralised lines, it refers to any national authority which exercises public functions: *Ayuntamiento de Mula v Spain* 68 D.R. 209 (1991), at 215 (where the Commission held that a City Council could not make an application under the former Art.25 (now Art.34), ECHR). See also *Holy Monasteries v Greece* (1995) 20 E.H.R.R. 1 and *Hautanemi v Sweden* (1996) 22 E.H.R.R. CD 155, where respectively, monasteries part of the Greek Orthodox Church and the Church of Sweden were held to be non-governmental organisations.

ought not to be regarded as a core public authority as this would prevent it being able to claim as a victim under Art.34. The expression "non-governmental organization" has an autonomous meaning under the ECHR. The decided cases on the amenability of bodies to judicial review[206] are not determinative of whether a body is to be classed as a public authority, whether core or hybrid, but maybe of some assistance.[207] Applying these principles, the House of Lords held that a Parochial Church Council was not a core public authority, and (Lord Scott dissenting) that its act in seeking to enforce the defendants' liability to pay for chancel repairs was an act of a private nature.

In *R (on the application of Beer (trading as Hammer Trout Farm)) v Hampshire Farmers' Markets Ltd*,[208] the Court of Appeal rejected the argument that the decision in *Aston Cantlow* had overruled ("superseded") the decisions in *Donoghue* or *Heather*. Much of the discussion in *Aston Cantlow* was directed to whether the PCC was a core public authority; only Lord Nicholls[209] had given general guidance on hybrid authorities and what is a public function for the purposes of s.6(3). Accordingly, provided it was borne in mind that regard should be had to any relevant Strasbourg jurisprudence, then relevant passages from *Donoghue*[210] and *Heather*,[211] "will continue to be a source of valuable guidance", para.[12] of Lord Nicholls' speech being "redolent of the flavour of that guidance".[212] Indeed, on the facts of most cases, the questions whether a body is a hybrid public authority exercising a public function and is amenable to judicial review would receive the same answer, the Strasbourg jurisprudence being likely to be less helpful in relation to the former, fact-sensitive question than in relation to whether a body is a core public authority.[213] In this case, the Court of Appeal held that Hampshire Farmers Markets Ltd, a company limited by guarantee, set up by stall-holders with the county council's assistance to take over the council's role in organising farmers' markets, was both amenable to judicial review and a public authority for the purposes of s.6 of the HRA 1998. It had been conceded that had the decision challenged (to refuse to allow the applicant to participate in the market) been by the county council, it would have been subject to judicial review. The change in structure was insufficient to lead to a different conclusion. Key features were that the power in question was being exercised to control the right of access to a public market, which although not a statutory or charter market was held on publicly owned land to which the public had access; and the close relationship between HFML and the county council. HFML was set up and

---

[206] See Ch.18.

[207] See Lord Hope of Craighead at paras [47]–[52]. Lord Scott of Foscote agreed (at para.[129]) with Lord Hope in concluding that the PCC was not a core public authority; but, dissenting on this point, held that the PCC's act in enforcing chancel repair liability was not an act of a private nature (paras [130]–[132]). See to a similar effect as Lord Hope, Lord Hobhouse at paras [85]–[90] and Lord Rodger of Earlsferry at paras [157]–[172]. Only Lord Hope and Lord Hobhouse expressly commented on the case law on amenability to judicial review, noting respectively that the cases may provide "some assistance as to what does, and what does not, constitute a 'function of a public nature' within the meaning of s.6(3)(b)" (Lord Hope at para.[52]) and that references to the law of judicial review did not assist on the question whether the PCC was a core public authority (Lord Hobhouse at para.[87]).

[208] [2003] EWCA Civ 1056, [2004] 1 W.L.R. 233.

[209] Above.

[210] Lord Woolf C.J. at paras [65], [66].

[211] Lord Woolf C.J. at para.[35].

[212] *per* Dyson L.J. at paras [24], [25].

[213] *per* Dyson L.J. at paras [28], [29].

assisted by the council and had stepped into the council's shoes. The absence of any statutory underpinning was not a matter of great weight.

The Court of Appeal returned to the matter in *Johnson v Havering LBC*; *YL v Birmingham City Council*.[214] The question here was whether a private care home, when accommodating a person under arrangements made with a local authority for the implementation of the authority's functions under s.21 of the National Assistance Act 1948, was exercising a public function for the purposes of the HRA 1998. The Secretary of State for Constitutional Affairs was given permission to intervene, and presented an argument that the *Heather* decision was inconsistent with *Aston Cantlow* and should be overruled. The Court of Appeal held that *Heather* remained binding on the Court of Appeal, and granted leave to appeal to the House of Lords.[215]

(c) Proceedings under section 7

8–012 A person who claims that a public authority has acted (or proposes to act) in a way made unlawful by s.6(1) may, if he or she is (or would be) a "victim of the unlawful act", bring proceedings (including a counterclaim) against the authority under the Act in the appropriate court or tribunal (as determined in accordance with rules)[216] or rely on the Convention right(s) concerned in any legal proceedings.[217] If the proceedings are brought on an application for judicial review, the applicant is to be taken to have a sufficient interest in relation to the unlawful act only if he is, or would be, the victim of that act.[218] The concept of a "victim" is intended to reflect the approach of the European Court of Human Rights[219] and is narrower than the concept of "sufficient interest" which, as currently applied, accords standing to public interest groups as well as affected individuals.[220] Proceedings must be brought before the end of: (a) one year beginning with the date on which the act complained of took place; or (b) such longer period as the court or tribunal considers equitable having regard to all the circumstances, subject to any rule imposing a stricter time limit in relation to the procedure in question.[221]

---

[214] [2007] EWCA Civ 26.

[215] For criticism of the *Heather* approach see P. P. Craig, (2002) 118 L.Q.R. 551 and the Joint Committee on Human Rights (Seventh Report, 2003–04 H.L. 39, H.C. 382) (recommending a broader, functional rather than institutional approach; commended by M. Sunkin, [2004] P.L. 643); *cf.* D. Oliver [2002] P.L. 476 and [2004] P.L. 329 (broad approach not necessarily desirable).

[216] See s.7(9)–(12), subs.(9) as amended by SI 2003/1887, Sch.2, para.10(2) and SI 2005/3429, Sch., para.3. In England and Wales rules are made by the Lord Chancellor or Secretary of State or are rules of court. The functions of the Secretary of State under subs.(9)(a) and under subs.(11) by virtue of subs.(9)(a) are to be exercisable concurrently with the Lord Chancellor by virtue of SI 2005/3429, art.3(2). Such rules have been made in respect of the Proscribed Organisations Appeal Commission: see the Proscribed Organisations Appeal Commission (Human Rights Act Proceedings) Rules 2001 (SI 2001/127).

[217] s.7(1), (2) "Legal proceedings" includes (a) proceedings brought by or at the instigation of a public authority, and (b) an appeal against the decision of a court or tribunal: s.7(6).

[218] s.7(3)

[219] s.7(7). See Baker (*op. cit.*, n.1), pp.40–44. A local authority cannot be a "non-governmental organisation" and so a victim under Art.34, ECHR; *per* Owen J. in *R (on the application of the Mayor and Citizens of Westminster) v Mayor of London* [2002] EWHC 2440 (Admin), paras [52]–[54].

[220] See para.18–054.

[221] s.7(5).

(d) Judicial remedies

Where the court or tribunal finds that an act (or proposed act) of a public **8–013**
authority is (or would be) unlawful under s.6(1), it may grant such relief or
remedy, or make such order, within its powers as it considers just and appropriate. However, damages may be awarded only by a court which has power to
award damages, or to order the payment of compensation, in civil proceedings.
No award of damages is to be made unless, taking account of all the circumstances of the case, including any other relief or remedy granted or order made
in relation to the act in question by that or any other court, and the consequences
of any decision (of that or any other court) in respect of that act, the court is
satisfied that the award is necessary to afford "just satisfaction" to the person in
whose favour it is made. In determining whether to award damages or the amount
of an award, the court must take into account the principles applied by the
European Court of Human Rights in relation to the award of compensation under
Art.41 of the Convention.[222] A public authority against which damages are
awarded is to be treated for the purposes of the Civil Liability (Contribution) Act
1978, as liable in respect of damage suffered by the person to whom the award
is made.[223] Proceedings under s.7(1)(a) in respect of the judicial act of a court
(including an act done on the instructions or on behalf of a judge) may be brought
only by exercising a right of appeal, on an application for judicial review (unless
the court is not amenable to judicial review) or in such other forum as may be
prescribed by rules.[224]

The Court of Appeal has provided guidance on the award of damages under s.8
of the HRA 1998.[225] The code established by the HRA[226] has to be applied with
due regard to the Strasbourg jurisprudence, although the assistance to be derived
from it is limited. There are significant features which distinguish this code from
the approach to the award of damages in a private law contract or tort action.
Thus, the award of damages is confined to the class of unlawful acts of public
authorities identified by s.6(1); the court has a discretion whether to make an
award; the award must be necessary to achieve "just satisfaction", language
distinct from the approach at common law; the court must take account of the
principles applied by the ECtHR in awarding compensation; and exemplary
damages are not awarded. A balance has to be drawn between the interests of the
victim and the public as a whole. The principles applied by the ECtHR are that

[222] The Court under Art.41 may only award pecuniary compensation; this covers pecuniary and non-
pecuniary loss and costs and expenses, but not aggravated or exemplary damages.

[223] s.8. A claim for compensation may also be made under Art.5(5) ECHR, which provides that
"Everyone who has been the victim of arrest or detention in contravention of the provisions of
this Article shall have an enforceable right to compensation". This is district and separate from
claims under s.8 in respect of unlawful acts, and gives rise to a Convention right which may be
pursued in a UK court: *R (on the application of Richards) v Secretary of State for the Home
Department* [2004] EWHC 93 (Admin).

[224] s.9(1), (2). In proceedings in respect of a judicial act done in good faith, damages may not be
awarded beyond the extent required by Art.5(5) of the Convention; the award is made against the
Crown, and no award can be made unless the responsible minister (or his nominee) is joined as
a party: s.9(3)–(5). Direct proceedings under s.7(1)(a) in respect of the decision of a judge will
accordingly be struck out; *Branch v Department for Constitutional Affairs* [2005] EWHC 550,
QB.

[225] *Anufrijeva v Southwark LBC; R (on the application of N) v Secretary of State for the Home
Department; R (on the application of M) v Secretary of State for the Home Department* [2003]
EWCA Civ 1406, [2004] Q.B. 1124.

[226] ss.6–8.

the applicant should, in so far as this is possible, be placed in the same position as if his Convention rights had not been infringed. If the breach causes significant pecuniary loss, this is usually assessed and awarded. However, the ECtHR has not been consistent in awards where there is no financial loss, in particular for anxiety and distress. The UK courts should adopt a broad brush approach in dealing with claims for damages for maladministration, without a close examination of the authorities or an extensive and prolonged examination of the facts. Relevant factors include the scale and the manner of the violation. Where the consequences of the infringement of human rights is similar to that being considered in the comparators elected, rough guidance is provided by the levels of damages awarded in respect of torts as reflected in guidelines issued by the Judicial Studies Board, the levels of awards made the Criminal Injuries Compensation Board or recommended by the Parliamentary and Local Government Ombudsmen. Accordingly, in cases of maladministration outside the scope of any tort, Ombudsmen awards may be the only comparator. In the rare cases where there is through maladministration breach of a positive obligation under Art.8 to provide support, and damages are appropriate, the scale should be modest. Awards (if made at all) should also be modest in cases involving delays in processing asylum claims.[227] To ensure that the costs of obtaining damages are proportionate to the relief, the courts should look critically at any attempt to recover damages for maladministration by any procedure other than judicial review; the judge before granting permission to apply for judicial review should require the claimant to explain why an internal complaints mechanism or a complaint to an Ombudsman is not more appropriate.[228] The Court of Appeal upheld two decisions at first instance that there had been no violation of Art.8 and reversed a finding of a violation in a third case.[229] It also endorsed the general approach in two further cases at first instance concerning breaches of Art.5[230] and Art.8.[231]

The House of Lords[232] has given guidance on the proper approach to the award of damages for violations of Art.6, ECHR, noting that in the vast majority of cases in which the ECtHR finds such a violation, it treats the finding as, in itself, just satisfaction under Art.41, ECHR. Unlike violations of Arts 3, 4 or 8, it does not follow from a finding that the trial process has involved a breach of Art.6 that the outcome of the process was wrong or would have been otherwise had the

---

[227] *per* Lord Woolf C.J. in *Anufrijeva* at paras [49]–[78].

[228] *per* Lord Woolf C.J., *ibid.* at paras [79]–[81].

[229] Respectively *Anufrijeva v Southwark LBC* (unreported, December 4, 2002, Newman J.); *M v Secretary of State for the Home Department* (Richards J.); *R (on the application of N) v Secretary of State for the Home Department* [2003] EWHC 207 (Admin).

[230] *R (on the application of KB) v Mental Health Review Tribunal* [2003] EWHC 193 (Admin), [2004] Q.B. 936 (damages (£1,000, £1,000, £4,000, £1,000, £350 and £1,000 in respect of delays in release) awarded in six out of eight cases of claimants detained unlawfully under the Mental Health Act 1983 in breach of Art.5; in so far as complaints centred on unreasonable delays before a case was reviewed by a MHRT, no award was to be made on the basis of loss of a chance of a favourable decision: a claimant had to establish on the evidence that he would have had an earlier favourable decision; helpful guidance could be obtained from awards recommended by the Local Government Ombudsman.

[231] *R (on the application of Bernard) v Enfield LBC* [2002] EWHC 2282, [2003] H.R.L.R. 111 (£10,000 awarded to claimants in respect of breach of Art.8(1) arising from the "deplorable" nature of the accommodation made available to family where the mother was severely disabled.)

[232] *R (on the application of Greenfield) v Secretary of State for the Home Department* [2005] UKHL 15, [2005] 1 W.L.R. 673.

breach not occurred.[233] The ECtHR has ordinarily been willing to depart from this practice where it finds a causal connection between the violation found and the loss for which compensation is claimed, whether pecuniary or non-pecuniary, and awards have been modest.[234] Awards by the English courts should be similar to those made by the ECtHR; it was not right to suggest that awards under s.8 should not be on the low side as compared with tortious awards.[235] On the facts, no award of damages was made in respect of a disciplinary award by a prison governor, who was held not be an independent and impartial tribunal for the purposes of Art.6, ECHR. Furthermore, legal representation should have been permitted. Proceedings had been conducted with exemplary conscientiousness and it was inappropriate to speculate whether a legal representative might have persuaded the governor to take a different view.[236]

In practice, awards of damages have accordingly been unusual.[237]

(e) The effect of the Act on private relations

The extent to which the HRA 1998 can have effect between parties neither of **8–014** which is a public authority has generated considerable academic discussion. Much of the debate has been couched in terms of a question whether the Act has "horizontal effect" between private parties in addition to "vertical effect" between a private party and the state, language used in respect of the extent to which EU law has direct effect.[238] It has, however, been cogently argued that this terminology is unhelpful and misleading in that it assumes as valid a sharp distinction between the spheres of public and private law which is itself controversial.[239] There is "no such firm distinction, because the very presence of law introduces a public element: private relations are in part constituted by both statute and common law, and the State lurks behind both".[240] The real issue is the extent or degree to which the 1998 Act affects the law governing wholly private relations.

The first point to note is that the Act creates a new right to bring a direct claim for breach of Convention rights only against a public authority.[241] While the term "public authority" is to be interpreted autonomously and may extend to include bodies or persons who would not be so regarded for other purposes,[242] it remains the case that there is a significant "private sector" not subject to such claims. However, it is also significant that it is expressly made unlawful for a public

---

[233] Lord Bingham of Cornhill at paras [7], [8]. The other members of the House agreed with Lord Bingham.

[234] Lord Bingham at paras [11]–[17].

[235] Lord Bingham at para.[18].

[236] Lord Bingham at para.[28].

[237] A further example is *Van Colle v Chief Constable of Hertfordshire* [2007] EWCA Civ 325 (award of £25,000 in respect of breach of Art.2 by police through failure to prevent murder of prosecution witness; quantum reduced from £50,000 awarded at first instance in the light of the Strasbourg jurisprudence). *Cf.* cases where no awards were made: e.g. *R (on the application of Baiai) v Secretary of State for the Home Department* [2006] EWHC 1035 (Admin). For discussion, see Law Commission Report No.266, *Damages under the Human Rights Act 1998* (Cm. 4853, 2000); D. Fairgrieve, [2001] P.L. 695; R. Clayton, [2005] P.L. 429.

[238] See paras 5–044, 5–045.

[239] Sir Stephen Sedley, *Freedom, Law and Justice* (1999); M. Hunt, "The 'Horizontal Effect' of the Human Rights Act: Moving Beyond the Public-Private Distinction", in J. Jowell and J. Cooper (eds), *Understanding Human Rights Principles* (2001), pp.161–178.

[240] Hunt, *op. cit.*, p.173.

[241] ss.6, 7: above, paras 8–010—8–012.

[242] Above, para.8–011.

authority to act in a way which is incompatible with a Convention right.[243] A court is a "public authority". It is accordingly argued that in considering the application of the law (whether legislation or common law) in the determination of disputes between private parties, the court is *obliged* to produce a solution that conforms to Convention rights. Such rights therefore become enforceable between private parties.[244] This position has been resisted on two main grounds. First, there are a number of indications in both the terms and structure of the 1998 Act[245] and in debates on the passage of the Human Rights Bill through Parliament[246] that this was not the intention. Secondly, the "Convention rights" referred to in the 1998 Act are themselves under ECHR jurisprudence rights against the state and not against private individuals.[247] The latter point might not be decisive to the extent that a Convention right against the state might itself require the state (through the court) to create a private law right enforceable between private parties in order to dispose of the litigation in a way compatible with that Convention right. The fact that there was not a blanket intention automatically to achieve this result in the case of all Convention rights does not mean that such a result might not properly be reached in relation to some of them.

The opposite position would have been for the 1998 Act to have *no effect whatsoever* on legal relations between private parties. This was not the intention either. The point was explored in the context of the consideration of an amendment proposed by Lord Wakeham that would have provided specifically that a court had no duty to act compatibly with the Convention in a case where neither party before it was a public authority. The amendment was intended to make it clear that the Act did not itself create a private law right of privacy. Lord Irvine L.C., in resisting the amendment, said:

> "We . . . believe that it is right as a matter of principle for the courts to have the duty of acting compatibly with the Convention not only in cases involving other public authorities but also in developing the common law in decided cases between individuals. Why should they not? In preparing this Bill, we have taken the view that it is the other course, that of excluding Convention considerations altogether from cases between individuals, which would have to be justified. We do not think that that would be justifiable; nor, indeed, do we think that it would be practicable."[248]

---

[243] 1998 Act, s.6.

[244] Sir William Wade in J. Beatson *et al.* (eds), *Constitutional Reform in the United Kingdom: Principles and Practices* (1998), p.61, [1998] E.H.R.L.R. 520 and "Horizons of Horizontally" (2000) 116 L.Q.R. 217.

[245] In particular, the enactment of provisions dealing expressly with direct claims against public authorities.

[246] Lord Irvine L.C. (in discussing s.6(1)): "We decided first of all that a provision of this kind should apply only to public authorities . . . and not to private individuals. . . . The Convention had its origins in a desire to protect people from the misuse of power by the state, rather than from the actions of private individuals" (H.L. Deb., Vol.582, col.1232, November 3, 1997) and Jack Straw MP, H.C. Deb., Vol.314, col.406, June 17, 1998, cited by G. Phillipson, (1999) 62 M.L.R. 824, 826–827.

[247] Sir Richard Buxton, "The Human Rights Act and Private Law" (2000) 116 L.Q.R. 48. *Cf.* Wade, (2000) 116 L.Q.R. 217, arguing in response that the process of translation into domestic law has broadened their scope.

[248] H.L. Deb., Vol.583, col.783, November 24, 1997; a passage that "is rapidly becoming the best-known paragraph of the whole of *Hansard*" (Buxton, (2000) 116 L.Q.R. 48, 58).

This passage is itself ambiguous. It has naturally been cited by Wade in support of his position,[249] in that the development of the common law by the courts is said to flow from the duty to act compatibly.[250] In any event, it certainly does provide powerful confirmation that the Act was intended to have a significant measure of indirect effect on laws affecting private parties, and this is endorsed in varying terms by most commentators.[251] For example, Hunt's view is that the courts are under an obligation to act compatibly with the Convention in determining the outcomes of private law litigation by developing the common law,

> "but subject to the ultimate constraint that it must not create entirely new causes of action where nothing analogous previously existed."[252]

The courts have not fully resolved these arguments. In *Douglas v Hello! Ltd*[253] the Court of Appeal discharged an interim injunction granted to restrain the publication by *Hello!* magazine of photographs of the wedding of Michael Douglas and Catherine Zeta-Jones. Exclusive publication rights had been granted to the third claimant, the proprietors of *OK!* magazine. One issue was the effect of the HRA 1998 on the possible development of a right of privacy. Sedley L.J. concluded that this was not the place, at least without much fuller argument, to resolve the question

> "does [the 1998 Act] simply require the courts' procedures to be Convention-compliant, or does it require the law applied by the courts, save where primary legislation plainly says otherwise, to give effect to the Convention principles?"

However, if the step from the existing law of confidentiality to privacy

> "is not simply a modern restatement of the scope of a known protection but a legal innovation . . . then I would accept [counsel's] submission . . . that this is precisely the kind of incremental change for which the Act is designed: one which without underpinning the measure of certainty which is necessary to all law gives substance and effect to section 6. . . . "[254]

This point was reinforced by reference to s.12 of the 1998 Act, which provides that if a court is considering whether to grant any relief (which includes any

---

[249] (2000) 116 L.Q.R. 217, 222–223.

[250] A proposition inconsistent with earlier statements by Lord Irvine. Note Wade's comment that "it may be fair to assume that the Government, being alerted by Lord Wakeham's amendment to the prospect of horizontality, had decided to accept it" ((2000) 116 L.Q.R. 217, 223). It is submitted that the existence of such a crucial change of mind cannot be left to inference; given that Lord Irvine was arguing against a position under which Convention considerations would be *irrelevant*, it is equally, if not more plausible, to conclude that he merely sought to make it clear that Convention considerations were *relevant* in developing the common law, a proposition that most support.

[251] See M. Hunt, "The 'Horizontal Effect' of the Human Rights Act" [1998] P.L. 423 and *op. cit.*, n.239 above; Lester and Pannick, *Human Rights: Law and Practice* (1999), pp.31–32; S. Grosz, J. Beatson and P. Duffy, *Human Rights: the 1998 Act and the European Convention* (2000), pp.89–93; G. Phillipson, (1999) 62 M.L.R. 824 (Convention rights in this context "figure only as principles to which the courts must have regard" (p.848)); I. Leigh, (1999) 48 I.C.L.Q. 57.

[252] *op. cit.*, n.239, pp.177–178.

[253] [2001] H.R.L.R. 512, [2001] Q.B. 967. See A. Young, [2002] P.L. 232.

[254] *ibid.* paras [128], [129].

remedy or order other than in criminal proceedings and therefore extends to litigation between private parties) which, if granted, might affect the exercise of the Convention right to free expression, it must, *inter alia*, have particular regard to the importance of that right. Where the material in question is claimed or appears to be journalistic, literary or artistic material, the court must also have regard to the extent to which the material has, or is about to, become available to the public, or it is, or would be, in the public interest for the material to be published, and to any relevant privacy code. These requirements make clear,

> "the direct applicability of at least one article of the Convention as between one private party to litigation and another."[255]

Sedley L.J. concluded that

> "we have reached a point at which it can be said with confidence that the law recognises and will appropriately protect a right of personal privacy."[256]

Brooke L.J. noted this dilemma:

> "On the one hand, Article 8(1) . . . appears to create a right, exercisable against all the world, to respect for private and family life. On the other hand, Article 8(2) . . . , section 8 of the Act, and the general philosophy of both the Convention and the Act (namely that these rights are enforceable only against public authorities), all appear to water down the value of the right created by Article 8(1)."[257]

Nevertheless, his Lordship appeared to accept the position that

> "it is the judges who must develop the law so that it gives appropriate recognition to Article 8(1) rights."

Whether this would be by an extension of the law of confidence or by recognising the existence of new relationships which give rise to enforceable legal rights was not for the court on this occasion to predict.[258] Keene L.J. similarly held that the duty of the courts under s.6(1) of the 1998 Act

> "arguably includes their activity in interpreting and developing the common law, even where no public authority is a party to the litigation."

Whether this extended to creating a new cause of action was controversial, but did not fall to be determined as reliance here was placed on the law of confidence; the boundaries of that law were not immutable and the current state of English law was likely to protect the privacy of a purely private wedding.[259] Subsequently, in *Venables v News Group Newspapers Ltd*[260] Dame Elizabeth Butler-Sloss in the Family Division stated expressly that the s.6(1) obligation,

---

[255] *ibid.* paras [131]–[133].
[256] *ibid.* para.[110].
[257] *ibid.* para.[82].
[258] *ibid.* para.[88].
[259] *ibid.* para.[166].
[260] [2001] Fam. 430.

"does not seem to me to encompass the creation of a free-standing cause of action based directly upon the articles of the convention"

but does require the court,

"to act compatibly with Convention rights in adjudicating upon existing common law causes of action, and that includes a positive as well as a negative obligation. . . . "[261]

This seems to endorse the middle position. Subsequent case law has not provided a definitive answer to the question of the extent to which the courts are obliged by s.6 to give the HRA 1998 "horizontal effect". In the particular context of the right to privacy, there seems now to be general agreement as to the principles to be applied as part of English law. These are: (1) that there is at common law no general tort governing all forms of invasion of privacy and it is not open to the English courts to create one[262]; and (2) that there is a cause of action for breach of confidence where there is a wrongful disclosure of private information, however the information is acquired[263]; that a "duty of confidence" arises "wherever a person receives information he knows or ought to know is fairly and reasonably to be regarded as confidential"[264]; and that in deciding whether a disclosure is actionable it is necessary to balance the rights enshrined respectively in Arts 8 and 10, ECHR.[265] In *Campbell v MGN Ltd*,[266] it was accepted that there was no duty of confidence in respect of the fact that the celebrated model Naomi Campbell was a drug addict and undergoing treatment by Narcotics Anonymous. However, the House of Lords upheld by 3 to 2[267] that, applying these principles, there was a breach of such a duty in the publication of details of the therapy and of photographs, covertly taken, of her when leaving NA meetings. However, there has not necessarily been agreement on the questions (3) whether the English courts were obliged to come to that conclusion, and (4) if so, what was the source of that obligation. In *Campbell*, Lord Hoffmann[268] stated that Art.8 was "by virtue of s.6 of the 1998 Act, a guarantee of privacy only against public authorities". Nevertheless, there was no good reason why

[261] para.[27].

[262] *Wainwright v Home Office* [2003] UKHL 53, [2004] 2 A.C. 406 (no remedy for gross invasion of privacy arising out of (pre HRA) strip search of woman and her disabled son when visiting another son in prison; ECtHR subsequently found breaches of Arts 8 and 13, ECHR: *Wainwright v UK*, Judgment of September 26, 2006; Baroness Hale of Richmond in *Campbell v MGN Ltd* [2004] UKHL 22, [2004] 2 A.C. 257 at para.[133].

[263] The earlier law required that the information had originally been disclosed by one person to another in confidence: Lord Nicholls in *Campbell* at para.[13].

[264] Lord Nicholls at para.[14].

[265] Lord Nicholls at paras [16]–[17]. *Cf.* Lord Hoffmann at paras [47]–[48], [55]–[56] (considering "the relationship between the freedom of the press and the common law right of the individual to protect personal information" without referring to Arts 8 and 10); Lord Hope at paras [85]–[86] ("the jurisprudence of the ECtHR offers important guidance as to how these competing rights ought to be approached and analysed"; and Baroness Hale at paras [132]–[140] (expressly balancing the Convention rights under Arts 8 and 10).

[266] [2004] UKHL 22, [2004] 2 A.C. 457. See also *Douglas v Hello! Ltd* [2005] EWCA Civ 595, [2006] Q.B. 125, where the Court of Appeal upheld the decision of the judge at trial that the conduct of Hello! Constituted a breach of confidence or invasion of the claimant's privacy.

[267] Lords Hope and Carson and Baroness Hale, Lords Nicholls and Hoffmann dissenting.

[268] paras [49]–[51].

"a person should have less protection against a private individual than he would have against the state for the publication of personal information for which there is no justification."

This suggests that the English courts were *choosing* to incorporate the principles of Arts 8 and 10 into the common law but were not obliged to do so. Lord Nicholls agreed with the second point but preferred to leave open "the controversial question whether the European Convention itself has this wider effect".[269]

By contrast, Baroness Hale said[270]:

"The 1998 Act does not create any new cause of action between private persons. But if there is a relevant cause of action applicable, the court as a public authority must act compatibily with both parties' convention rights."

Subsequently, in *Douglas v Hello! Ltd (No.3)*[271] the Court of Appeal noted that, shortly after the decision in *Campbell*, the ECtHR had decided, in *von Hannover v Germany*,[272] that the state's obligations under Art.8 may include positive obligations to adopt measures designed to secure respect for private life even in the sphere of the relation of individuals between themselves. It also cited the views of both Lord Nicholls and Baroness Hale in *Campbell*, without apparently noticing any difference between them, and concluded that:

"in so far as private information is concerned, we are required[273] to adopt, as the vehicle for performing such duty as falls on the courts in relation to Convention rights, the cause of action formerly described as breach of confidence. As to the nature of that duty, it seems to us that ss.2, 3, 6 and 12 of the Human Rights Act all point in the same direction. The court should, in so far as it can, develop the action for breach of confidence in such a manner as will sure effect to both Art.8 and Art.10 rights."[274]

The source of this obligation remains obscure. One thing that *is* clear is that the courts have not espoused the "full, direct horizontal effect" argument advanced by Wade and others.[275] Beyond that, it is submitted that there has as yet been no effective answer to Lord Hoffmann's point in *Campbell* as to the scope of Convention rights. Accordingly, the proper basis for developing the law between private individuals should either be as a matter of choice for the English courts[276] or where a positive obligation is imposed on states by the jurisprudence of the ECtHR.[277]

---

[269] paras [16]–[18].

[270] para.[132]. Lord Hope said (at paras [85]–[86]) that the case raised no new issues of principle although incorporation of Arts 8 and 10 had changed the language. His view on the point that divided Lord Hoffmann and Baroness Hale is unclear. Lord Carswell agreed with Lord Hope and Baroness Hale.

[271] [2005] EWCA Civ 595, [2006] Q.B. 125.

[272] Judgment of June 24, 2004.

[273] But by what? The doctrine of precedent, s.6 of the HRA 1998 via the horizontal effect argument or s.6 via *von Hannover*?

[274] paras [51]–[53].

[275] Lord Phillips M.R. in *Douglas* at para.[50].

[276] Lord Hoffmann's position in *Campbell*.

[277] As in the *von Hannover* case, above.

Finally, it is not disputed that the interpretative obligation under s.3 may apply to legislation that regulates the relations of private parties, although not with retrospective effect.[278]

6. OTHER MATTERS

A person's reliance on a Convention right does not restrict any other right or freedom conferred on him by or under any law having effect in any part of the UK, or his right to make any claim or bring any proceedings which he could make apart from ss.7 to 9.[279] Special provisions apply where a court is considering granting any relief which might affect the exercise of the Convention right to freedom of expression or the exercise by a religious organisation of the Convention right to freedom of thought, conscience and religion.[280] A minister in charge of a Bill in either House of Parliament must, before the second reading, make a statement in writing either that in his or her view the provisions of the Bill are compatible with the Convention rights, or that, although he or she is unable to make such a statement, the government wishes the House to proceed with the Bill.[281]

8–015

7. COMMENCEMENT

The 1998 Act was brought fully into force on October 2, 2000.[282] Section 22(4) provides:

8–016

> "Paragraph (b) of subsection (1) of section 7 applies to proceedings brought by or at the instigation of a public authority whenever the act in question took place; but otherwise that subsection does not apply to an act taking place before the coming into force of that section."

Section 7(1)(b) is the provision that enables a victim of an unlawful act (by virtue of s.6(1)) to "rely on the Convention right or rights concerned in any legal

---

[278] *Wainwright v Home Office* [2001] EWCA Civ 2081, [2002] Q.B. 1334, paras [20]–[40], [61].

[279] s.11.

[280] ss.12, 13.

[281] s.19. This has been treated seriously within government, and there is detailed internal guidance as to the steps that must be taken: Cabinet Office, *The Human Rights Act 1998 Guidance for Departments* (2nd edn, 2000); and the *Guide to Legislative Procedures* (*www.cabinetoffice. gov.uk/legislation*), Pt 10. See Lester and Pannick, (*op. cit.*, n.1), paras 8.02–8.08. Thetre have been very few s.19(1)(b) statements.

[282] s.22(3); Human Rights Act 1998 (Commencement No.2) Order 2000 (SI 2000/1851). Sections 18 (effect of appointment of judge to ECtHR), 20 (supplemental power to make orders) and 21(5) (abolishing the death penalty under the Army Act 1955, the Air Force Act 1955 or the Naval Discipline Act 1957) came into effect on the passing of the Act.

proceedings". The meaning of these provisions has been considered in two decisions of the House of Lords. In *R v Lambert*[283] the House of Lords held by a majority[284] that s.22(4) prevents a person convicted at a criminal trial held before commencement from relying at an appeal brought after commencement on an argument that there was a breach of his Convention rights at the trial (here, that the imposition by the Misuse of Drugs Act 1971 of a reverse burden of proof violated the presumption of innocence enshrined in Art.6(2)). The majority held that the reference in s.22(4) to "proceedings brought by or at the instigation of a public authority" was intended to reflect the distinction drawn in s.7(6), which provides:

> "In subsection (1)(b) 'legal proceedings' includes—
>
> (a) proceedings brought by or at the instigation of public authority; and
> (b) an appeal against the decision of a court or tribunal."

Accordingly, an appeal by an unsuccessful defendant was not to be treated as a proceeding brought by or at the instigation of a public authority. Considerable confusion and uncertainty would be produced if the examination of pre-commencement trials could be opened up on post-commencement appeals. Given that this was the proper interpretation of ss.22(4) and 7(1)(b), it was not possible for the appellant to rely on ss.6[285] or 3(1), which had no express retroactive effect, as producing a different result.[286] A further point was that the wording of s.7(1)(a) by virtue of s.9 covered the bringing of an appeal and s.7(1)(a) clearly did not apply to any act taking place before commencement.[287] Lord Hope of Craighead held that the retrospective use of s.7(1)(b) was permitted at the stage of any appeal against the decision of a court in proceedings brought by or at the instigation of a public authority; however, an accused whose trial took place before commencement was only entitled to rely on an appeal after commencement on an alleged breach of Convention rights *by the prosecuting authority*. It did not enable him to challenge a ruling by the court itself.[288] Lord Steyn dissented, holding that the House of Lords was not entitled to act unlawfully now by upholding a conviction obtained in breach of a Convention right.[289]

The issues were reconsidered five months later by the House of Lords in *R v Kansal (No.2)*.[290] Here, the issue was whether the defendant in a post-commencement appeal by him could argue that his Convention rights had been breached by the prosecution in deciding to adduce evidence of answers obtained under compulsion in bankruptcy proceedings. The House comprised the same Law Lords with the substitution of Lord Lloyd for Lord Clyde. The House held

---

[283] [2001] UKHL 37; [2002] 2 A.C. 545. See G. Dingwall, (2002) 65 M.L.R. 450.

[284] Lords Slynn of Hadley, Hope of Craighead, Clyde and Hutton, Lord Steyn dissenting.

[285] i.e. the argument that the Court of Appeal as a "public authority" would act unlawfully now if it acted in a way incompatible with a Convention right.

[286] *per* Lord Slynn at paras [7]–[14]. Lord Clyde adopted the same approach at paras [140]–[142] and Lord Hutton at paras [169]–[176].

[287] *per* Lord Clyde at para.[139].

[288] paras [101]–[107].

[289] paras [27]–[31].

[290] [2001] UKHL 62, [2002] 2 A.C. 69.

that its previous decision in *Lambert*, reached after a full argument, should be followed. Lord Slynn was not persuaded that the decision in *Lambert* was wrong, and did not accept that a valid distinction could be drawn between acts of the judiciary and acts of the prosecution.[291] Lord Hutton considered the *Lambert* decision to be correct.[292] Lord Lloyd thought that the decision in *Lambert* was plainly erroneous but should be followed.[293] Lord Steyn reaffirmed his view that the majority in *Lambert* was mistaken; this view was reinforced by the considerations: (1) that the word "proceedings" covers both trials and appeals; (2) that the words "proceedings brought by or at the instigation of a public authority" in s.22(4) were "singled out for special treatment in recognition of the United Kingdom's international obligations" under the ECHR from the date of ratification by the UK in 1951 or the date of conferment of the right of petition in 1966; and (3) that the discretion of the Courts of Appeal to refuse to extend time for leave to appeal provided an effective filter in respect of old convictions. However, it would be wrong now to depart from the ratio of *Lambert*.[294] Lord Hope agreed that *Lambert* was wrongly decided and was the only member of the House to argue that it should now depart from it.[295] He identified a number of anomalies that arose if the majority were right. First, an appeal by the prosecution by way of case stated following an acquittal at trial held prior to commencement would be proceedings brought by a public authority. Secondly, a reference by the Attorney-General to the Court of Appeal under s.36 of the Criminal Justice Act 1988 for review of a sentence pronounced prior to commencement which he considered unduly lenient would also be a separate proceeding by a public authority. Thirdly, where a conviction was quashed on other grounds, the defendant would be able to rely on Convention rights at any retrial. Fourthly, the interpretation of s.22(4) as excluding appeals would apply in civil cases, and even where the decision at first instance was in the defendant's favour and an appeal was taken after commencement by the public authority.[296]

It is unfortunate that the matter was not made clearer in the 1998 Act and that the interpretation which a majority of the House in *Kansal (No.2)* thought to be wrong remains the law. Defendants in pre-commencement trials will of course be able to take Convention points to the European Court of Human Rights. The Court of Appeal has accepted that in consequence of the view of the majority in *Kansal (No.2)* that *Lambert* was wrongly decided, *Lambert* should not be applied beyond its strict *ratio*.[297]

In civil cases, the courts have consistently applied the general principle of *Lambert* that, apart from the limited exception in s.22(4), the 1998 Act does not

---

[291] paras [8]–[10].
[292] paras [101]–[109].
[293] paras [17]–[24].
[294] paras [25]–[27].
[295] paras [50]–[72].
[296] paras [73]–[74].
[297] *R v Lyons* [2001] EWCA Crim 2860, [2002] 2 Cr.App.R. 210, para.[45] (the court, however, rejected arguments: (1) that where a conviction at a pre-commencement trial was found by the ECtHR to be in breach of Art.6 of the Convention, the Court of Appeal was bound to quash the conviction; and (2) that contemporary standards of fairness required the convictions to be quashed where evidence had been admitted of answers given under compulsion. The admission of such evidence had been expressly authorised by Parliament and there was no ground prior to commencement for regarding the legislation as impliedly repealed).

apply to acts or decisions before October 2, 2000.[298] In *Wilson v Secretary of State for Trade and Industry*,[299] the House of Lords held that the 1998 Act is not to be held to apply retrospectively so as to interfere with existing rights and duties. A natural reading of the words of ss.6 to 9 was that they were directed to post-Act events; this was powerfully supported by the context: "One would not expect a statute promoting human rights values to render unlawful acts which were lawful when done."[300] Section 3 expressly applies to legislation whenever enacted and so may have the effect of changing the interpretation and effect of legislation already in force. However, this is subject to the general principle that:

> "Parliament is presumed not to have intended to alter the law applicable to past events and transactions in a manner which is unfair to those concerned in them, unless a contrary intention appears."[301]

The intention of Parliament must be identified in respect of the particular statutory provision in question, but in general the principle of s.3(1) will not apply to causes of action accruing before it came into force.[302] This is, however, a general and not universal principle.[303] On the facts of *Wilson*, s.3(1) could not be used to interfere with rights acquired under the Consumer Credit Act 1974.

As regards appeals in civil cases, the aspect of the *Lambert* reasoning that involved drawing a distinction between proceedings at first instance and on appeal has not been followed. In *MacDonald v Advocate-General for Scotland*,[304] the House of Lords held[305] that s.22(4) did not apply where the original proceedings in respect of discriminatory acts that took place pre-commencement

---

[298] *R (on the application of Langton) v Secretary of State for Environment, Food and Rural Affairs* [2001] EWHC Admin 1047, paras [62]–[68]; *Re McKerr* [2004] UKHL 12, [2004] 1 W.L.R. 807 and *R (on the application of Hurst) v Commissioner of Police for the Metropolis* [2007] UKHL 13 (modifications of coroners' rules necessary to secure compliance with Art.2 not applicable in respect of pre-commencement deaths). See also *Aston Cantlow and Wilmcote with Billesley Parochial Church Council v Wallbank* [2001] EWCA Civ 713, [2002] Ch. 51 where it was conceded that a person served with a chancel repairs notice pre-commencement could raise an argument based on breach of Convention rights on an appeal on a preliminary issue heard post-commencement; this seems difficult to square with *Lambert* but can be reconciled on the basis that there had been no final determination of liability pre-commencement; on appeal it was conceded by the defendant parish council that the 1998 Act applied in order to obtain a ruling on the substantive issues, which were resolved in its favour: [2003] UKHL 37, [2004] 1 A.C. 546. Lord Hope of Craighead (at paras [25]–[32]) regarded the concession as rightly made; no issue of retrospectivity arose as the proceedings had only been at a preliminary stage at the time of commencement. The point was expressly left open by Lord Nicholls of Birkenhead at para.[4], Lord Hobhouse of Woodborough at para.[80] (noting that the judgment of Ferris J. was a final judgment on the preliminary point at issue).

[299] [2003] UKHL 40, [2004] 1 A.C. 816.

[300] *per* Lord Nicholls of Birkenhead in *Wilson* at para.[12].

[301] Staughton L.J. in *Secretary of State for Social Services v Tunnicliffe* [1991] 2 All E.R. 712 at 724, cited by Lord Nicholls at para.[19].

[302] *per* Lord Nicholls at paras [20]–[23]; Mummery L.J. in *Wainwright v Home Office* [2001] EWCA Civ 2081, [2002] Q.B. 1334, para.[61].

[303] See Lord Hope of Craighead in *Wilson* at para.[99].

[304] [2003] UKHL 34, [2004] 1 All E.R. 339.

[305] *per* Lord Nicholls of Birkenhead at para.[23]. Neither could a different result be reached by arguing that prosecution of a post-commencement appeal by the public authority constituted an act prohibited by s.6(1): para.[24]. Lord Hope of Craighead (para.[50]), Lord Hobhouse of Woodborough (para.[105]), Lord Scott of Foscote (para.[112]) and Lord Rodger of Earlsferry (para.[151]) agreed with Lord Nicholls on these points.

were instigated by the claimant against a public authority, succeeded before the Employment Appeal Tribunal, leading to a post-commencement appeal by the public authority to the Court of Session, and then to an appeal by the claimant to the House of Lords. Here the appellate proceedings were to be regarded as part of the original proceedings instigated by the claimant, thus falling outside s.22(4). Curiously, the *Lambert* speeches were not analysed in *MacDonald*. By parity of reasoning it would seem that where the civil proceedings were instigated originally by a public authority, the respondent to those proceedings should be able to raise Convention points on a post-commencement appeal, whoever the appellant.[306]

The term "proceedings" for the purposes of s.22(4) does not in any event apply to the service of a notice on a person requiring work to be done[307] or to the holding of an inquest post-commencement in respect of a pre-commencement death.[308]

For the purpose of s.22(4), judicial review proceedings are to be regarded as proceedings brought by the applicant and not by the Crown (a public authority) as the Crown's involvement is nominal only.[309]

C. SPECIFIC CONVENTION RIGHTS

This section considers the major provisions of the ECHR applicable in the context of the administration of justice, as interpreted and applied by both the European Court of Human Rights[310] and English courts, the latter in particular in the period that has followed implementation of the HRA 1998. **8–017**

(a) Article 2

This provides generally that "everyone's right to life shall be protected by law". More specifically, "no one shall be deprived of his life intentionally save in the execution of a sentence of a court following his conviction of a crime for which **8–018**

---

[306] This position seems to be endorsed, *obiter*, by Lord Hope of Craighead in *Wilson*, above, at para.[90].

[307] *R (on the application of Langton) v Secretary of State for Environment, Food and Rural Affairs* [2001] EWHC Admin 1047, para.[66]. *Cf. Re Malcolm* [2004] EWHC 339 (Ch), [2004] 1 W.L.R. 1803, holding that the essence of M's complaint concerned the state of the law at the time, pre-commencement, when certain rights vested in his trustee in bankruptcy, and that the 1998 Act therefore did not apply; s.22(4) did not apply as the present proceedings were brought by him and not by a public authority (point conceded on appeal: [2004] EWCA Civ 1748, [2005] 1 W.L.R. 1238).

[308] *R (on the application of Hurst) v Commissioner of Police for the Metropolis* [2007] UKHL 13.

[309] *R (on the application of Ben-Abdelazziz) v Haringey London Borough Council* [2001] EWCA Civ 803, [2001] 1 W.L.R. 485.

[310] See generally D. J. Harris, M. O'Boyle and C. Warbrick, *The European Convention on Human Rights* (1995); A. Mowbray, *Cases and Materials on the European Convention on Human Rights* (2nd edn, 2007); J. Simor and B. Emerson, *Human Rights Practice*. See above, para.2–083.

this penalty is provided by law".[311] Furthermore, deprivation of life is not to be
regarded as a contravention of Art.2,

> "when it results from the use of force which is no more than absolutely
> necessary
>
> a   in defence of any person from unlawful violence;
> b   in order to effect a lawful arrest or to prevent the escape of a person
>   lawfully detained;
> c   in action lawfully taken for the purpose of quelling a riot or
>   insurrection."[312]

This "ranks as one of the most fundamental provisions in the Convention" and
is non-derogable in peacetime. Its provisions must be "strictly construed".[313] In
particular, the test of "absolute necessity" in Art.2(2) involves "a stricter and
more compelling test of necessity" than that normally applicable when determining whether state action is "necessary" under other articles of the Convention.
The force used (which may extend to non-intentional killings) "must be strictly
proportionate to the achievement of the aims set out in subparagraphs a, b and c".
The Court must subject deprivation of life to "the most careful scrutiny", taking
into consideration not only the actions of state agents who actually administer the
force but also the surrounding circumstances, including the planning and control
of the actions in question.[314] Accordingly, attention may be focused under Art.2
on the structure of the law regulating the use of force in (for example) the
prevention of crime; the planning of operations that may involve the use of force
by state agents; and the acts that involve the use of force.[315] An operation must
be "planned and conducted in such a way as to avoid or minimise, to the greatest
extent possible", any risk of the lives of innocent bystanders.[316]

The general obligation under Art.2(1) requires each state not only to have
appropriate provisions of substantive criminal law, but also in appropriate circumstances, to take positive operational measures to protect individuals at
risk.[317] A further implied requirement is that states must undertake effective
investigations into all killings (whether or not by stage agents), involving "some

---

[311] Art.2(1).

[312] Art.2(2).

[313] *McCann v UK* (1995) 21 E.H.R.R. 97, para.147.

[314] *ibid.* paras 149, 150.

[315] See e.g. *McCann v UK*, above which arose out of the killing of three unarmed suspected IRA
terrorists in Gibraltar by SAS soldiers. The ECtHR held that the applicable legal standard in the
law of Gibraltar (use of force must be reasonably justified) was sufficient as applied in practice
to comply with Art.2; that there was no premeditated plot to kill the suspects; that the actions of
the soldiers did not violate Art.2(2) as they honestly (although mistakenly) believed them to be
necessary to prevent detonation of a car bomb; but (by 10 votes to nine) that there was a violation
arising out of a lack of appropriate care in the control and organisation of the arrest operation.

[316] *Ergi v Turkey*, judgment of July 28, 1998, para.79.

[317] *Osman v UK* (1998) 29 E.H.R.R. 245 (no violation of Art.2(1) on the facts where police failed
to arrest a person who subsequently murdered Mr Osman and seriously injured his son; it must
be established "that the authorities knew or ought to have known at the time of the existence of
a real and immediate risk to the life of an identified individual or individuals from the criminal
act of a third party and that they failed to take measures within the scope of their powers which,
judged reasonably, might have been expected to avoid the risk" (para.120). *Cf. Kaya v Turkey*,
Judgment of March 28, 2000 (violation established); *Edwards v UK* (2002) 35 E.H.R.R. 487
(violation found in respect of killing of prisoner by cellmate); *Van Colle v Chief Constable of
Hertfordshire* [2007] EWCA Civ 325 (breach where police failed to prevent murder of prosecution witness).

form of independence and public scrutiny capable of leading to a determination of whether the force used was or was not justified".[318]

(b) Article 3

This provides that "no one shall be subjected to torture or to inhuman or **8–019** degrading treatment or punishment". It is the subject of no exceptions and cannot be the subject of a derogation. "Inhuman treatment" has been held to include such matters as the adoption of a practice of violence by police officers leading to intense suffering and physical injury[319] and the causing of severe mental distress and anguish[320]; "degrading treatment" to include actions "such as to arouse in their victims feelings of fear, anguish and inferiority capable of humiliating and debasing them and possibly breaking their physical or moral resistance"[321]; and "degrading punishment" to include judicial corporal punishment.[322] The assessment of whether the level reaches the minimum necessary for a finding that Art.3 has been violated depends on all the circumstances of the case, such as the nature and content of the treatment, its duration, its physical and mental aspects and, in some circumstances, the sex, age and state of health of the victim.[323] The ECtHR is imposing increasingly high standards.[324]

Apart from liability based on the actions of state officials themselves, the state is obliged by Art.3 to undertake an effective official investigation where an individual raises an arguable claim that he or she has been seriously ill-treated by state officials in breach of that Article.[325] Furthermore, the state must take

[318] *Kava v Turkey* (1998) 28 E.H.R.R. 1. The UK has been found to have violated this requirement in a series of cases arising out of killings in Northern Ireland: e.g. *Jordan v UK* (2001) 37 E.H.R.R. 52; *McKerr v UK* (2002) 34 E.H.R.R. 20; *Finucane v UK* (2003) 37 E.H.R.R. 29; *cf. R (on the application of Amin) v Secretary of State for the Home Department* [2003] UKHL 51, [2004] 1 A.C. 653; *R (on the application of Middleton) v West Somerset Coroner* [2004] UKHL 10, [2004] 2 A.C. 182 (inquest procedure not sufficient to meet Art.2 requirements); *Scholes v Secretary of State for the Home Department* [2006] EWCA Civ 1343, [2006] H.R.L.R. 44.

[319] *Ireland v UK* (1978) 2 E.H.R.R. 25, para.174 (interrogation techniques used in Northern Ireland in 1971); *Tomasi v France* (1992) 15 E.H.R.R. 1 (large number of blows inflicted on terrorist suspect).

[320] *Kurt v Turkey* (1998) 27 E.H.R.R. 91.

[321] *Ireland v UK*, above, para.167. The Court has to have regard to whether the objective of the treatment is to humiliate and debase the person concerned, but the absence of such an intention does not conclusively rule out a violation of Art.3: *Peers v Greece* (2002) 33 E.H.R.R. 51, para.74; *Price v UK* (2001) 34 E.H.R.R. 1285 (conditions of detention in prison of severely disabled person held to constitute degrading treatment, where she was dangerously cold, risked developing sores and was unable to go to the toilet or keep clean without the greatest of difficulty).

[322] *Tyrer v UK* (1978) 2 E.H.R.R. 1; *cf. Campbell and Cosans v UK* (1982) 4 E.H.R.R. 293 (no breach of Art.3 arising from risk of corporal punishment in state school); *Costello-Roberts v UK* (1993) 19 E.H.R.R. 112 (no breach of Art.3 arising from case of corporal punishment in non-state funded school).

[323] *A v UK* (1998) 27 E.H.R.R. 611 at para.20.

[324] *Selmoni v France* (2000) 29 E.H.R.R. 403.

[325] *Assenov v Bulgaria* (1998) 28 E.H.R.R. 652; *Salman v Turkey*, Judgment of June 27, 2000 (inadequate investigation of death in police custody. Obligation to investigate not confined to cases where it is apparent that the killing was caused by an agent of the state); *Jordan v UK*, Judgment of May 4, 2001 (lack of effective investigation into death of person shot by police officer); *R v DPP, Ex p. Manning* [2001] Q.B. 330 (coroner's inquest held to be full and effective inquiry into death of prison inmate); *R (on the application of Wright) v Secretary of State for the Home Department* [2001] EWHC Admin 520, [2002] H.R.L.R. 1 (inquest into death of prison inmate from asthma attack held not to be an effective official investigation as a key witness was not called although he was available and willing to attend, shortcomings in medical treatment were not explored and the claimants were not represented); *R (on the application of Green) v*

positive steps, including the enactment of appropriate criminal offences, to protect persons from being subject to Art.3 mistreatment by other private persons,[326] although there is a wide margin of appreciation.[327] It is a breach of the Art.3 to take action in relation to someone within the jurisdiction which carries the real risk that it will expose that person to infringement of his or her Art.3 rights outside the jurisdiction.[328] Where the risk arises from the actions of non-state actors it must also be shown that the state has failed to provide reasonable protection.[329] Furthermore, the principle may apply where the risk is of a flagrant infringement of other Articles.[330]

In *Z v UK*[331] the Court held that the failure of a local authority to take steps to protect four children in its area from severe neglect, deprivation and abuse at the hands of their parents constituted a breach of Art.3; the authorities had been aware of the serious ill-treatment and neglect suffered by the children for over four years. The government did not contest the Commission's findings of a breach of Art.3. On the other hand, the refusal by the Director of Public Prosecutions of proleptic immunity from prosecution to a husband whose wife was suffering from a progressive degenerative illness and who wished to assist her suicide has been held not to fall within Art.3. It did not constitute proscribed "treatment" and the state was not under a positive obligation to ensure that a competent, terminally ill person who wished but was unable to take her own life should be entitled to seek assistance of another without that person being exposed to the risk of prosecution.[332] Furthermore, the determination of priorities in the provision of healthcare[333] and delays in receiving medical treatment have been held not to give rise to a remedy under Art.3.[334]

Police Complaints Authority [2004] UKHL 6, [2004] 1 W.L.R. 725 (no requirement based on Arts 2 and 3 for PCA to disclose witness statements to victim prior to conclusion of any criminal proceedings).

[326] *A v UK* (1998) 27 E.H.R.R. 611 (caning of child by stepfather sufficiently serious to engage Art.3; criminal law that provided defence of reasonable chastisement to be disproved beyond reasonable doubt held to be inadequate protection). The law was changed by the removal of the defence of reasonable chastisement for assaults causing actual bodily harm or worse by the Children Act 2004, s.58. See H. Keating, (2006) 29 L.S. 394.

[327] *cf. Osman v UK* (1998) 29 E.H.R.R. 245, paras 115–116 (Art.2); *Rees v UK* (1986) 9 E.H.R.R. 56, para.37 (Art.8), cited by Lord Bingham in *R (on the application of Pretty) v Director of Public Prosecutions* [2001] UKHL 61, [2002] 1 A.C. 800, para.[15].

[328] *Soering v UK* (1989) 11 E.H.R.R. 439 (extradition to a country where there was a real risk that the person concerned would face a real risk of being subjected to torture or to inhuman or degrading treatment or punishment); *R (on the application of Ullah) v Special Adjudicator* [2002] EWCA Civ 1856, *per* Lord Phillips of Worth Matravers at para.[29].

[329] *R (on the application of Bagdanavicius) v Secretary of State for the Home Department* [2005] UKHL 38, [2005] 2 A.C. 668.

[330] *R (on the application of Ullah) v Special Adjudicator* [2004] UKHL 26, [2004] 2 A.C. 323; *R (on the application of Razgar)* [2004] UKHL 27, [2004] 2 A.C. 368.

[331] Judgment of May 10, 2001. *Cf. V v UK* (1999) 30 E.H.R.R. 121, where the Court held that the trial and sentence of two 11-year-old boys for the murder of a two-year-old (when they were 10) did not violate Art.3; *R (on the application of Limbuela) v Secretary of State for the Home Department* [2005] UKHL 66, [2006] 1 A.C. 396 (application of Art.3 threshold to asylum seeker refused support).

[332] *R (on the application of Pretty) v Director of Public Prosecutions* [2001] UKHL 61, [2002] 1 A.C. 800.

[333] *R v North West Lancashire Health Authority, Ex p. A* [2000] 1 W.L.R. 977 (decision not to fund gender reassignment surgery other than in exceptional circumstances; *per* Auld L.J. at 996: "It is plain, in my view, that Art.3 was not designed for circumstances of this sort of case where the challenge is as to a health authority's allocation of finite funds between competing demands".

[334] *R (on the application of Watts) v Bedford Primary Care Trust and the Secretary of State for Health*

(c) Article 5

Articles 5 to 7 contain a series of provision of importance for the administration **8–020** of justice. Article 5 provides as follows:

"**Article 5—Right to liberty and security**

1. Everyone has the right to liberty and security of person. No one shall be deprived of his liberty save in the following cases and in accordance with a procedure prescribed by law:

a   the lawful detention of a person after conviction by a competent court;

b   the lawful arrest or detention of a person for non-compliance with the lawful order of a court or in order to secure the fulfilment of any obligation prescribed by law;

c   the lawful arrest or detention of a person effected for the purpose of bringing him before the competent legal authority on reasonable suspicion of having committed an offence or when it is reasonably considered necessary to prevent his committing an offence or fleeing after having done so;

d   the detention of a minor by lawful order for the purpose of educational supervision or his lawful detention for the purpose of bringing him before the competent legal authority;

e   the lawful detention of persons for the prevention of the spreading of infectious diseases, of persons of unsound mind, alcoholics or drug addicts or vagrants;

f   the lawful arrest or detention of a person to prevent his effecting an unauthorised entry into the country or of a person against whom action is being taken with a view to deportation or extradition.

2. Everyone who is arrested shall be informed promptly, in a language which he understands, of the reasons for his arrest and of any charge against him.

3. Everyone arrested or detained in accordance with the provisions of paragraph 1.c of this article shall be brought promptly before a judge or other officer authorised by law to exercise judicial power and shall be entitled to trial within a reasonable time or to release pending trial. Release may be conditional by guarantees to appear for trial.

4. Everyone who is deprived of his liberty by arrest or detention shall be entitled to take proceedings by which the lawfulness of his detention shall be decided speedily by a court and his release ordered if the detention is not lawful.

5. Everyone who has been the victim of arrest or detention in contravention of the provisions of this article shall have an enforceable right to compensation."

Article 5 provides safeguards against arbitrary detention. For it to apply there must be a "deprivation" of physical liberty, and not merely a restriction on freedom of movement. The distinction is one of degree, and turns on such matters

[2003] EWHC 2228 (Admin) (*Ex p. A* followed; in addition nothing the claimant had to endure was so severe or so humiliating as to engage Art.3).

as the type, duration, effects and manner of implementation of the measure in question.[335] To be lawful, the deprivation must fall within one or more of the prescribed situations, which are to be narrowly interpreted, and be in accordance with a procedure prescribed by law. There are implied obligations that when the state detains a person, the authorities must "account for his or her whereabouts", and that the authorities "must take effective measures to safeguard against the risk of disappearance and to conduct a prompt effective investigation into an arguable claim that a person has been taken into custody and has not been seen since".[336]

For lawful detention after conviction under Art.5(1)(a) the punishment must not be arbitrary and disproportionate[337] and there has to be a sufficient connection between the order of the court following conviction and the detention in question.[338] This has been held to cover the exercise by the Home Secretary of power to recall a life sentence prisoner who committed further offences after his release.[339] Article 5(1)(b), *inter alia*, authorises detention in accordance with a court order, and is not violated merely because the order is set aside on appeal.[340] Article 5(1)(c) authorises the lawful exercise of police powers of arrest[341] provided there is on the facts "reasonable suspicion" or arrest or detention is "reasonably considered necessary" as the case may be. Where challenged, the government must "furnish at least some facts or information capable of satisfying the Court that the arrested person was reasonably suspected of having committed the alleged offence".[342]

For a person to be detained as a person of "unsound mind" under Art.5(1)(e), he or she must be "reliably shown to be of 'unsound mind'," the mental disorder "must be of a kind or degree warranting compulsory confinement" and the "validity of continued confinement depends upon the persistence of such a disorder".[343] Such a person must be detained in a hospital, clinic or other appropriate institution.[344]

---

[335] *Engel v Netherlands* (1976) 1 E.H.R.R. 647 (detention of soldier in locked cell fell within Art.5; confinement during off duty hours in an unlocked building in barracks did not); *Guzzardi v Italy* (1980) 3 E.H.R.R. 333 (confinement of Mafia suspect to small hamlet on island fell within Art.5); *R (on the application of Gillan) v Commissioner of Police of the Metropolis* [2006] UKHL 12, [2006] 2 A.C. 307 (police stop-search under s.45 of the Terrorism Act 2000 did not involve deprivation of liberty under Art.5, in the absence of special circumstances; the procedure was ordinarily relatively brief and the person would not be arrested, handcuffed, confined or removed to any different place). Restrictions on freedom of movement are covered by the Fourth Protocol, Art.2 (which has not been ratified by the UK).

[336] *Kurt v Turkey* (1998) 27 E.H.R.R. 91, para.124.

[337] *Engel* at para.58; *R v Lichniak* [2002] UKHL 47, [2003] 1 A.C. 903 (mandatory life sentence not arbitrary and disproportionate).

[338] *Van Droogenbroek v Belgium* (1982) 4 E.H.R.R. 443, para.39.

[339] *Weeks v UK* (1987) 10 E.H.R.R. 293.

[340] *Bentham v UK* (1996) 22 E.H.R.R. 293.

[341] See below, paras 14–006—14–013 on police arrest powers in England and Wales.

[342] *Fox, Campbell and Hartley v UK* (1980) 13 E.H.R.R. 157, para.34; the fact that F and C had previous convictions for terrorist acts connected with the IRA was insufficient on its own to constitute reasonable suspicion of the commission of terrorist offences seven years later. *Cf. Margaret Murray v UK* (1994) 19 E.H.R.R. 193.

[343] *Winterwerp v Netherlands* (1979) 2 E.H.R.R. 387, para.39; *Johnson v UK* (1997) 27 E.H.R.R. 296 (authorities entitled to a measure of discretion in deciding whether to order the immediate and absolute discharge of a person no longer suffering from the mental disorder which led to the confinement).

[344] *Aerts v Belgium* (1998) 29 E.H.R.R. 50.

Detention for the purposes of deportation or extradition under Art.5(1)(f) will not be justified where it exceeds a reasonable time[345] or where, in the absence of a power to extradite, a person is deported in circumstances that amount to disguised extradition.[346]

By virtue of Art.5(2):

> "any person arrested must be told, in simple, non technical language that he can understand, the essential legal and factual grounds for his arrest, so as to be able, if he sees fit, to apply to a court to challenge its lawfulness in accordance with paragraph 4. . . . "[347]

The information must be conveyed promptly, although not necessarily at the very moment of arrest. This echoes the requirement of the common law as to the exercise of arrest powers.[348]

Those arrested under Art.5(1)(c) must be brought before a judicial officer promptly (Art.5(3)). Review by a public prosecutor is likely to be insufficient.[349] Exercises of power to keep terrorist suspects in custody for up to five days without review by a judge have been held to violate this requirement.[350] Where persons arrested under Art.5(1)(c) are to be tried, they are also entitled to trial within a reasonable time or to release pending trial, the time requirement here being less onerous than the requirement of "promptness" as regards the review of detention. Neither the proceedings themselves nor the provisional detention of accused persons may be prolonged beyond a reasonable time, the former covering the whole period to the end of the trial.[351] What is reasonable naturally depends on the circumstances.[352] A provision automatically denying bail in specified circumstances is likely to be held to violate this requirement.[353]

Where a person is detained by a person or body which is not itself a "court", such as the police, he or she must be entitled to take proceedings by which the lawfulness of the detention is decided speedily by a court (Art.5(4)).[354] To be a court, a body must be independent of the executive and the parties, be able to consider all aspects of the justification for detention and able to make a binding

---

[345] *Quinn v France* (1995) 21 E.H.R.R. 529; *cf. Chahal v UK* (1996) 23 E.H.R.R. 413 (C had been detained for a considerable time but the authorities had acted with due diligence).

[346] *Bozano v France* (1986) 9 E.H.R.R. 297.

[347] *Fox, Campbell and Hartley v UK* (1990) 13 E.H.R.R. 157, para.40.

[348] See below, para.14–012.

[349] *Huber v Switzerland*, Judgment of October 23, 1990: *Assenov v Bulgaria* (1998) 28 E.H.R.R. 652.

[350] *Brogan v UK* (1988) 11 E.H.R.R. 117. The government subsequently derogated from the requirements of Art.5(3), and then withdrew the derogation following the introduction of revised arrangements under the Terrorism Act 2000: see Bailey, Harris and Jones (2001), pp.586–587. See further below. A decision not to extend a custody time limit (para.14–070) does not necessarily mean that there has been a breach of Art.5(3): *R (on the application of O v Crown Court at Harrow* [2006] UKHL 42, [2007] 1 A.C. 249.

[351] *Wemhoff v Federal Republic of Germany* (1968) 1 E.H.R.R. 55, paras 4–9.

[352] *Wemhoff*, paras 10–17 (W's detention between 1961 and his conviction in 1965 in exceptionally complicated fraud case held to be reasonable); *W v Switzerland* (1993) 17 E.H.R.R. 60.

[353] *Caballero v UK* (2000) 30 E.H.R.R. 643.

[354] See *R (on the application of H) v Secretary of State for Health* [2005] UKHL 60, [2006] 1 A.C. 441 (rejecting the argument that effective access required that where the person lacked capacity to take a case to MHRT there should be an automatic reference).

decision.[355] Where a person is detained indefinitely,[356] reviews must normally be available at reasonable intervals.[357]

A derogation order may be made in respect of the rights conferred by Art.5. In the landmark ruling in *A v Secretary of State for the Home Department,*[358] however, the House of Lords held that the regime for the indefinite detention of suspected foreign terrorists who could not lawfully be deported under s.23 of the Anti-terrorism, Crime and Security Act 2001, was disproportionate and discriminatory. This has been replaced by a new regime of control orders under the Prevention of Terrorism Act 2005. These fall into two classes. Where a derogation order has been made a "derogating control order" may be made by a court. In the absence of a derogation, a less intrusive "non-derogating control order" may be made by the Secretary of State. No derogation order has been made. The courts have held certain "non-derogating control orders" to be so restrictive of liberty as to contravene Art.5 and be unlawful.[359]

(d) Article 6

8–021   Article 6[360] provides:

> **"Article 6—Right to a fair trial**
>   1. In the determination of his civil rights and obligations or of any criminal charge against him, everyone is entitled to a fair and public hearing within a reasonable time by an independent and impartial tribunal established by law. Judgment shall be pronounced publicly but the press and

---

[355] *De Wilde, Ooms and Versyp v Belgium (the "vagrancy" cases)* (1971) 1 E.H.R.R. 373; *Chahal v UK* (1996) 23 E.H.R.R. 413 (judicial review and advisory panel ("Three Advisers") system insufficient for compliance in respect of detention in the context of deportation on national security grounds); *Benjamin and Wilson v UK*, Judgment of September 26, 2002; *R (on the application of Smith) v Parole Board* [2005] UKHL 1, [2005] 1 W.L.R. 350 and *R (on the application of Roberts) v Parole Board* [2005] UKHL 45, [2005] 2 A.C. 738 (Parole Board proceedings must be procedurally fair for there to be compliance with Art.5(4)).

[356] Not where the sentence of a court is determinate: see *R (on the application of Giles) v Parole Board* [2003] UKHL 42, [2004] 1 A.C. 1 (imposition by judge of extended sentence to protect the public from serious harm under s.2(2)(b) of the Criminal Justice Act 1991 did not attract requirement of further reviews).

[357] *Winterwerp*, para.55; *X v UK* (1981) 4 E.H.R.R. 188 (review by habeas corpus proceedings of detention under Mental Health Act 1959, following recall, insufficient for compliance with Art.5(4) as habeas corpus proceedings dealt only with the lawfulness of detention under domestic law; reviews by Mental Health Review Tribunals were also insufficient as their functions were advisory only, the position on this point subsequently being changed to secure compliance by the Mental Health Act 1983); *Weeks v UK* (1987) 10 E.H.R.R. 293 (role of Parole Board and judicial review in considering recall of discretionary life sentence prisoner and periodic examination of detention insufficient for compliance with Art.5(4)); *Thynne, Wilson and Gunnell v UK* (1990) 13 E.H.R.R. 666 (arrangements for review of continued detention of discretionary life sentence prisoner by the Parole Board and judicial review following completion of the "tariff" period (i.e. the indication by the trial judge of the period considered necessary to meet the requirements of retribution and deterrence) held to violate Art.5(4)); *cf. Wynne v UK* (1994) 19 E.H.R.R. 333 (no requirement for a continuing remedy in respect of mandatory life sentence prisoners); *Hussain v UK* (1996) 22 E.H.R.R. 1 (continuing remedy required after expiration of tariff period in respect of juvenile detained during Her Majesty's Pleasure); *T v UK, V v UK* (1999) 30 E.H.R.R. 121 (continuing remedy required during tariff period where tariff set by Home Secretary).

[358] [2004] UKHL 56, [2005] 2 A.C. 68. See (2005) 68 M.L.R. 654–676 (notes by T. Hickman, S. Tierney, D. Dyzenhaus, J. Hiebert).

[359] See e.g. *Secretary of State for the Home Department v JJ* [2006] EWCA Civ 1141, [2006] H.R.L.R. 38; *Secretary of State for the Home Department v Abu Rideh* [2007] EWHC 804 (Admin).

[360] See P. Craig, "The Human Rights Act, Art.6 and Procedural Rights" [2003] P.L. 753.

public may be excluded from all or part of the trial in the interests of morals, public order or national security in a democratic society, where the interests of juveniles or the protection of the private life of the parties so require, or to the extent strictly necessary in the opinion of the court in special circumstances where publicity would prejudice the interests of justice.

2. Everyone charged with a criminal offence shall be presumed innocent until proved guilty according to law.

3. Everyone charged with a criminal offence has the following minimum rights:

a   to be informed promptly, in a language which he understands and in detail, of the nature and cause of the accusation against him;

b   to have adequate time and facilities for the preparation of his defence;

c   to defend himself in person or through legal assistance of his own choosing or, if he has not sufficient means to pay for legal assistance, to be given it free when the interests of justice so require;

d   to examine or have examined witnesses against him and to obtain the attendance and examination of witnesses on his behalf under the same conditions as witnesses against him;

e   to have the free assistance of an interpreter if he cannot understand or speak the language used in court."

Key concepts that may give rise to issues under Art.6(1) include whether there is: (a) a "determination of civil rights and obligations"; (b) a "criminal charge"; (c) a "fair and public hearing"; (d) "within a reasonable time; (e) "by an independent and impartial tribunal". The applicable principles are as follows:

"Determination of civil rights and obligations"

Here, a broad view has been adopted. For this provision to apply to a case (or "contestation"[361]) it is not necessary that both parties be private persons. Furthermore, the character of the governing legislation, for example, as civil, commercial or administrative law, and whether the matter falls within the jurisdiction of an ordinary court or a specialist administrative body are of little consequence.[362] It must be shown that there is a genuine and serious dispute[363] and that its resolution has a direct effect (is "directly decisive for") a civil right or obligation.[364] In *Ringeisen v Austria*[365] it was held that Art.6 applied to the

---

[361] The words "contestation sur" appear in the French text of Art.6 (rather than "determination of") and thus has no direct counterpart in the English text. It should be given a substantive rather than a formal meaning: *Le Compte. Van Leuven and De Meyere v Belgium* (1981) 4 E.H.R.R. 1, para.45

[362] *Ringeisen v Austria* (1971) 1 E.H.R.R. 455, para.94.

[363] *Benthem v The Netherlands* (1985) 8 E.H.R.R. 1, para.32.

[364] *Le Compte, Van Leuven and De Meyere*, above, para.47. The expression of a view by the Secretary of State concerning a person's citizenship status is not a "determination" under Art.6(1) as this is not a matter for him to decide: *R (on the application of Harrison) v Secretary of State for the Home Department* [2003] EWCA Civ 432.

[365] Above. See also *König v Germany* (1978) 2 E.H.R.R. 170 (Art.6 applicable to decisions of administrative court to revoke authorisations to run clinic and to practise medicine; concept of "civil rights and obligations" must be interpreted autonomously and not solely by reference to the domestic law of the respondent state and is not confined to private law disputes in the traditional sense).

decision of an administrative Commission, applying administrative law principles, whether to approve a contract for sale of agricultural land for building as being in the public interest.

"Civil rights" may include entitlements to social insurance and welfare benefits provided by the state,[366] and issues concerning contributions to social insurance schemes,[367] but not situations where benefits may be provided by the state as a matter of discretion.[368]

In *R (on the application of Alconbury Developments Ltd) v Secretary of State for the Environment, Transport and the Regions*,[369] the House of Lords considered the application of these principles to the planning system, in particular the power of the Secretary of State to determine directly whether planning permission should be granted, where a particular planning application was called-in or an appeal "recovered" from final determination by a planning inspector, or the Secretary of State was the statutory decision maker. Lords Slynn, Hoffmann, Clyde and Hutton[370] rejected an argument, raised on an intervention by Scottish ministers, that these planning decisions did not involve the *determination* of civil rights and obligations but were simply the exercise of legal powers which affected, perhaps changed, such rights and obligations. A "dispute" or "contestation" arose at least from the time when a power was exercised and objection was taken to that exercise.[371] The members of the House were agreed that, in the light of the European Court's jurisprudence,[372] Art.6(1) clearly applied in this context.

Similarly, a decision to grant planning permission to X in respect of Y's land[373] and a decision to grant planning permission to X in respect of X's land for a development that will detrimentally affect both the enjoyment by Y of his home and its monetary value,[374] are determinations that affect Y's civil rights. However, a grant of planning permission is unlikely to be "directly decisive" of the civil rights of third parties living at some distance from the land in question.[375] Furthermore, a decision by a local authority to take steps required by an enforcement notice in default of compliance by the recipient of the notice does

---

[366] *Feldbrugge v Netherlands* (1986) 8 E.H.R.R. 425 and *Deumeland v Germany* (1986) 8 E.H.R.R. 448 (social insurance); *Salesi v Italy* (1993) 26 E.H.R.R. 187 (welfare benefits); the ECtHR found in *Feldbrugge* that the private law features of the arrangements (effect on claimant in her personal, economic capacity; close connection with the contract of employment; affinities with insurance under the ordinary law) outweighed the public law features (relevant rules enshrined in legislation; compulsory nature of the insurance; assumption by the state of responsibility for social protection).

[367] *Schouten and Meldrum v Netherlands* (1994) 19 E.H.R.R. 432.

[368] *Machatova v Slovak Republic* (1997) 24 E.H.R.R. CD44 (payment of a hardship allowance).

[369] [2001] UKHL 23, [2003] 2 A.C. 295.

[370] paras [27–]38, [131]–[135], [145]–[157], [181]–[184].

[371] *per* Lord Clyde at para.[147].

[372] Including *Bryan v UK* (1995) 21 E.H.R.R. 342; *Chapman v UK*, Judgment of January 18, 2001.

[373] *British Telecommunications plc v Gloucester City Council* [2001] EWHC Admin 1001.

[374] *R (on the application of Katho) v Rhondda Cynon Taff County Borough Council* [2001] EWHC Admin 527; *Friends Provident Life Office v Secretary of State for Transport, Local Government and the Regions* [2001] EWHC Admin 820, [2002] 1 W.L.R. 1450 (civil rights of owner of shopping centre held to be directly affected by proposed new large retail development); *R (on the application of Adlard) v Secretary of State for the Environment, Transport and the Regions* [2002] EWHC 7 (Admin) (the point was assumed on appeal: [2002] 1 W.L.R. 2515, at para.[14]).

[375] *R (on the application of Vetterlein) v Hampshire CC* [2001] EWHC Admin 560, [2002] 1 P.&C.R. 31. See also *R (on the application of Cummins) v London Borough of Camden* [2001] EWHC Admin 1116 (effect of proposed development on view from claimant's flat and on playground associated with the block of flats too remote); *R (on the application of Westminster City Council)*

not engage Art.6(1); the "civil right" in question will already have been determined by the procedures that led to the valid and effective enforcement notice in question.[376]

Further examples of situations involving the determination of civil rights and obligations include a decision of the Crown Court hearing an appeal from licensing justices[377]; the decision of a professional disciplinary tribunal that a person was not fit to practise[378]; the determination under regulations whether a person was to be treated as possessing capital of which he had deprived himself for the purpose of decreasing the amount that he might be liable to pay for his residential care[379]; the decision of a review panel in respect of the termination of an introductory tenancy[380]; a decision of the Secretary of State to withdraw support provided under Pt VI of the Immigration and Asylum Act 1999 from a destitute asylum-seeker,[381] or to refuse support on the ground that he was not satisfied that asylum was claimed as soon as reasonably practicable after arrival in the UK[382]; and proceedings on an application (on notice) for an Anti-social Behaviour Order under s.1 of the Crime and Disorder Act 1998.[383]

Interim or provisional measures normally do not involve the determination of civil rights and obligations, but may do so if they have a "clear and decisive" impact on such rights or obligations.[384]

A person's right to express a preference to which school his child should attend is not a "civil right".[385] Similarly, there is no private right for a person to receive education suitable to his needs, which would be engaged, for example, by a decision concerning exclusion of that person from a school.[386] Furthermore, the

---

v Mayor of London [2002] EWHC 2440 (Admin) (evidence of impact on property values of introduction of road congestion charges insufficient to establish interference with civil rights).

[376] R (on the application of M) v Horsham DC [2003] EWHC 234 (Admin). See also St Brice v Southwark LBC [2002] 1 W.L.R. 1537 (issue of warrant of possession required to give effect to a possession order, itself accepted to have been determined in accordance with Art.6(1), held to be an administrative process which did not determine civil rights).

[377] R (on the application of Smith) v Lincoln Crown Court [2001] EWHC Admin 928, [2002] 1 W.L.R. 1332.

[378] R (on the application of Fleurose) v Securities & Futures Authority [2001] EWCA Civ 2015, [2002] I.R.L.R. 297.

[379] R (on the application of Beeson) v Dorset County Council [2002] EWCA Civ 1812 (on the basis that the case was "concerned with the question, what premises [the claimant] will occupy as his home and upon what terms": per Laws L.J. at para.[28]).

[380] R (on the application of McLellan) v Bracknell Forest BC [2001] EWCA Civ 1510, [2002] Q.B. 1129.

[381] R (on the application of Husain) v Asylum Support Adjudicator [2001] EWHC Admin 832.

[382] R (on the application of Q) v Secretary of State for the Home Department [2003] EWHC 195 (Admin).

[383] R (on the application of McCann) v Manchester Crown Court [2003] 1 A.C. 787. However, proceedings without notice for an interim ASBO do not involve the determination of civil rights: R (on the application of Kenny) v Leeds Magistrates' Court; R (on the application of M) v Secretary of State for Constitutional Affairs [2003] EWHC 2963 (Admin), [2004] 1 W.L.R. 2298.

[384] Zlínsat, spol.s.r.o. v Bulgaria, Judgment of June 15, 2006; applied by Stanley Burnton J. in R (on the application of Wright) v Secretary of State for Health [2006] EWHC 2886 (Admin), [2007] 1 All E.R. 825 (process of provisional listing on the Protection of Vulnerable Adults list unfair and disproportionate; provisional listing would have a clear and decisive impact on the contract of employment as a care worker).

[385] Re JC (unreported, July 31, 2000); cf. Simpson v UK (1989) 64 DR 188.

[386] R (on the application of B) v Head Teacher of Alperton Community School and other cases [2001] EWHC Admin 229, [2002] B.L.G.R. 132, where it was held that the right to sue in negligence recognised in Phelps v Hillingdon London Borough Council [2000] 2 A.C. 619 did not constitute such a private right.

decision of an Independent Appeal Panel whether to reinstate an excluded pupil does not engage Art.6(1) by virtue of its effect on the civil right to enjoy a fair reputation; the proceedings are not directly decisive of reputation and the potentiality for damage is recognised through the requirement that natural justice be observed in those proceedings.[387] Whether the duty of a local housing authority, in specified circumstances, to secure accommodation for a homeless person gives rise to a "civil right" has not been resolved.[388] Whether a hearing by a Parole Board as to whether a prisoner's release on licence should be revoked involves determination of a civil right has also been left open.[389]

"Criminal charge"

This too must be given an autonomous interpretation and a matter may be classified as "criminal" for the purposes of Art.6 that would not be so classified in domestic law.[390] Relevant factors include the type of national law embodying the offence (and how such conduct is dealt with in other jurisdictions), the nature of the conduct prohibited and the severity of the punishment.[391] The administration of a reprimand or warning under s.55 of the Crime and Disorder Act 1998 does not involve the determination of a criminal charge[392]; neither do proceedings on an application (on notice) for an Anti-Social Behaviour Order,[393] or a hearing as to whether a prisoner's release on licence should be revoked.[394] Disciplinary proceedings may or may not fall within Art.6 according to the circumstances.[395] For example, Art.6(1) does not apply to proceedings of an Independent Appeal Panel concerning exclusion of a pupil from a state school on disciplinary grounds, notwithstanding that the misconduct alleged constituted a criminal offence. Although expulsion was significant it did not lead to a denial of

---

[387] *ibid.* considering *Golder v UK* (1975) 1 E.H.R.R. 524, *Helmers v Sweden* (1993) 15 E.H.R.R. 285 and *Fayed v UK* (1994) 18 E.H.R.R. 393.

[388] This question was left open by the House of Lords in *R (on the application of Runa Begum) v Tower Hamlets LBC* [2003] UKHL 5, [2003] 2 A.C. 430.

[389] *R (on the application of Smith) v Parole Board* [2005] UKHL 1, [2005] 1 W.L.R. 350, *per* Lord Bingham of Cornhill at paras [42]–[44]. Lord Walker of Gestingthorpe (para.[90]) and Lord Carswell (para.[91]) agreed with Lord Bingham. Lords Hope of Craighead (at paras [76]–[81]) and Slynn (paras [58]–[60]) held that Art.6(1) did not apply. Lord Carswell (para.[91]) also agreed with Lord Hope.

[390] *Engel v The Netherlands* (1976) 1 E.H.R.R. 647; *Attorney General's Reference (No.2 of 2001)* [2001] 1 W.L.R. 1869 (in general the term "charge" corresponds to the sense used in English criminal procedure, and does not in the ordinary way extend to interrogation or interview).

[391] *ibid.* para.82.

[392] *R (on the application of R) v Durham Constabulary* [2005] UKHL 21, [2005] 1 W.L.R. 1184 (no determination of a criminal charge was involved once there had been a decision that R should not be prosecuted for an offence).

[393] *R (on the application of McCann) v Manchester Crown Court* [2002] UKHL 39, [2003] 1 A.C. 787. Accordingly, they did not attract the specific obligations set out in Art.6(2), (3); however, they involved the determination of civil rights and obligations and so engaged Art.6(1).

[394] *R (on the application of Smith) v Parole Board* [2005] UKHL 1, [2005] 1 W.L.R. 350 (decision cannot "lead to punishment": *per* Lord Bingham of Cornhill at para.[40]).

[395] *ibid.*: military disciplinary offences leading to liability only to light punishment not within Art.6; other, more serious, disciplinary offences were. *Cf. Campbell and Fell v UK* (1984) 7 E.H.R.R. 165 (prison disciplinary proceedings attracting serious loss of remission subject to Art.6); *Ezeh and Connors v UK* (2002) 35 E.H.R.R. 691, (2003) 39 E.H.R.R. 1 (prison disciplinary proceedings that had attracted the award of 40 and seven additional days, did not constitute proceedings on criminal charges) followed by the house of Lords in *R (on the application of Greenfield) v Secretary of State for the Home Department* [2005] UKHL 14, [2005] 1 W.L.R. 673; *R (on the application of Fleurose) v Securities and Futures Authority* [2001] ECWA Civ 2015 (proceedings before the disciplinary appeal tribunal of the Securities and Futures Authority not criminal); *Han*

access to the educational system or constitute the determination of a criminal charge. The relevant provisions were not part of the general law applicable to persons generally; the sanction was not criminal and not disproportionate to the disciplinarian objective it existed to achieve.[396] Similarly, it does not apply to internal disciplinary mechanisms whereby an employer decides whether or not to trust an employee and whether he has been guilty of a fundamental breach of contract,[397] or to the imposition of a surcharge on a councillor in respect of losses caused to the local authority by wilful misconduct.[398]

"Fair and public hearing"

This may include a right of effective access to a court,[399] and "equality of arms" including adequate disclosure of relevant evidence[400] and the right of a defendant to participate effectively in his or her criminal trial.[401] Courts must give reasons for their judgments, although the extent of this obligation depends on the circumstances and a detailed answer to every argument is not necessarily required.[402]

The right of access may be held to have been denied where there is a broad blanket rule excluding civil liability where competing public policy arguments cannot be evaluated,[403] but not merely where domestic law after the proper and fair examination of the claim determines that no remedy is available in a given situation.[404] Similarly, the imposition of a fixed penalty regime disproportionate

& Yau v Commissioners of Customs and Excise [2001] EWCA Civ 1048, [2001] 1 W.L.R. 2253; Official Receiver v Stern (No.1) [2001] 1 W.L.R. 2230; R (on the application of Thompson) v Law Society [2004] EWCA Civ 167, [2004] 1 W.L.R. 2230; (decision to impose a reprimand in solicitors' disciplinary proceedings did not determine civil rights).

[396] R (on the application of B) v Head Teacher of Alperton Community School and other cases [2001] EWHC Admin 229.

[397] R (on the application of H) v Hertfordshire County Council [2002] EWCA Civ 146.

[398] Porter v UK (2003) 37 E.H.R.R. CD8 (the surcharge was compensatory not punitive). The case arose out of Porter v Magill, above, para.4–040.

[399] Golder v UK (1975) 1 E.H.R.R. 524 (rights of access to a court by prisoner for determination of civil claim); Airey v Ireland (1979) 2 E.H.R.R. 305 (rights of access must be practical and effective).

[400] Rowe and Davis v UK (2000) 30 E.H.R.R. 1. Cf. the common law of natural justice, below, para.18–051.

[401] Stanford v UK. Judgment of February 23, 1994 (implicit right to hear and follow proceedings not violated by use of glass screens in front of the dock which caused a minimal loss of sound); V v UK (1999) 30 E.H.R.R. 121 (violation of Art.6(1) where 11-year-old defendant was tried for murder in adult court (with modifications); the fact the was represented by skilled counsel was not sufficient given his immaturity and disturbed emotional state).

[402] Hiro Balani v Spain (1995) 19 E.H.R.R. 566; Garcia Ruig v Spain (2001) 31 E.H.R.R. 222. This does not require magistrates to give reasons for rejecting submissions of no case: Moran v DPP [2002] EWHC 89 (Admin); professional judges must, however, give reasons: Flannery v Halifax Estate Agencies Ltd [2000] 1 W.L.R. 377 (pre-HRA); English v Emery Reimbold & Strick Ltd [2002] EWCA Civ 605.

[403] Osman v UK (1999) 1 L.G.L.R. 431.

[404] Z v UK, Judgment of May 10, 2001; T.P. and K.M. v UK, Judgment of May 10, 2001. There may, however, be a breach of Art.13 (absence of effective remedy, see para.8–025). See also Matthews v Ministry of Defence [2003] UKHL 4, [2003] 1 A.C. 1163 (bar to tort claim by servicemen held to be a substantive and not a procedural limitation and so not in violation of Art.6(1) (see T. Hickman [2004] P.L. 122; Wilson v Secretary of State for Trade and Industry [2003] UKHL 40, [2004] 1 A.C. 816 (provision that a regulated agreement under s.8 of the Consumer Credit Act 1974 is not enforceable unless a document containing all the prescribed terms is signed by the debtor held not to be a procedural bar but a limitation on the substantive scope of a creditor's rights).

to the object to be achieved may be held to infringe the applicant's right to have the appropriate level of penalty determined by an independent tribunal.[405] The right of access may require the Civil Procedure Rules to be interpreted in such a way (via s.3(1) of the 1998 Act) as to remove an unjustifiable hindrance to a litigant's right to proceed.[406] On the other hand, the six-week time-limit on appeals under s.288 of the Town and Country Planning Act 1990 and the requirement of promptness for a claim for judicial review do not constitute a disproportionate restriction on the right of access.[407] The right to a public hearing is subject to exceptions where exclusion "from all or part of the trial" is "in the interests of morals, public order or national security in a democratic society, where the interests of juveniles or the protection of the private life of the parties so require, or to the extent strictly necessary in the opinion of the court in special circumstances where publicity would prejudice the interests of justice".[408]

"Within a reasonable time"

Each case must be assessed according to its circumstances, including the complexity of the case, the applicant's conduct and the manner in which the matter was dealt with by the administrative and judicial authorities.[409] The reasonable time may begin to run before the formal launch of proceedings.[410] While the state's failure to hold a trial within a reasonable time constitutes a breach of the Convention, it does not follow that holding a trial after the expiry of a reasonable time necessarily constitutes a breach; a stay on proceedings will only be proportionate to the breach where there can no longer be a fair hearing or it would otherwise be unfair to try the defendant.[411]

"Independent and impartial tribunal"

This requirement echoes the common law *nemo judex* principle.[412] "Independent" and "impartial" are separate, but closely related requirements. As to the former, regard must be had to the manner of the appointment of the tribunal members, their terms of office, the existence of guarantees against outside

---

[405] *R (on the application of International Transport Roth GmbH) v Secretary of State for the Home Department* [2002] EWCA Civ 158, [2003] Q.B. 728 (Simon Brown and Jonathan Parker L.JJ., Laws, L.J. dissenting).

[406] *Goode v Martin* [2001] EWCA Civ 1899, [2002] 1 W.L.R. 1828.

[407] See *Matthews v Secretary of State for the Environment, Transport and the Regions* [2001] EWHC Admin 815 (s.288); *Lam v UK* (App. No.41671/98) noted by Stanley Burnton J. in *R (on the application of Elliott) v Electoral Commission* [2003] EWHC 395 (Admin) (judicial review).

[408] Art.6(1). See *Re Trusts of X Charity* [2003] EWHC 1462 (Ch), [2003] 1 W.L.R. 2751; *Pelling v Bruce-Williams* [2004] EWCA Civ 845, [2004] Fam. 155.

[409] *König v Germany* (1978) 2 E.H.R.R. 170, para.99 (delays of over 10 years in administrative proceedings that were still not concluded and a delay of over five years in separate proceedings each held to breach Art.6(1)). *Mellors v UK* (App. No.57836/00, Judgment of July 17, 2003) (period of over three years to resolve appeal held to violate Art.6(1)).

[410] *ibid.* para.98.

[411] *Att-Gen's Reference (No.2 of 2001)* [2003] UKHL 68, [2004] 2 A.C. 72 (Lords Bingham of Cornhill, Nicholls of Birkenhead, Steyn, Hoffmann, Hobhouse of Woodborough, Millett and Scott of Foscote, Lords Hope of Craighead and Rodger of Earlsferry dissenting). A different view has been taken on this issue by the Privy Council in respect of Scotland: *H.M. Advocate v R* [2004] 1 A.C. 462 (Lords Hope of Craighead, Clyde and Rodger of Earlsferry, Lords Steyn and Walker of Gestingthorpe dissenting).

[412] See paras 4–040, 18–051.

pressure and the question whether the tribunal presents an appearance of independence.[413] There are two aspects to the question of "impartiality": first, "the tribunal must be subjectively free of personal prejudice or bias"; secondly, "it must also be impartial from an objective viewpoint, that is, it must offer sufficient guarantees to exclude any legitimate doubt in this respect. . . . "[414] These requirements have led to the reintroduction of a more subjective approach in applying the *nemo judex* principle.[415]

The tribunal must also be "established by law". A *de facto* judge, that is a person who is believed, and believes himself, to have the necessary judicial authority, is regarded in law as possessing that authority[416]; such a person falls within the Art.6(1) requirement that the tribunal be established by law.[417]

The absence of an independent and impartial tribunal may, however, be cured if the proceedings before it are subject to "subsequent control by a judicial body that has full jurisdiction and does provide the guarantees of Art.6(1)."[418] It has been accepted that this does not require a full appeal on the merits of every administrative decision taken by the executive that affects private rights.[419] The extent to which judicial review or a statutory application to quash provides "full jurisdiction" has been considered in a number of cases by the European Court and Commission.[420] In *Bryan v UK*[421] the Court held that because the appointment of an inspector to hear an appeal against an enforcement notice could be revoked by the executive where the executive's own policies might be in issue, the inspector's appointment did not satisfy Art.6(1) requirements as to the appearance of independence. However, the High Court's powers of review were sufficient for compliance with Art.6(1) overall. The Court stated that in making this assessment, it was necessary to have regard to matters such as the subject matter of the decision appealed against, the manner in which it was arrived at and

---

[413] *Findlay v UK* (1997) 24 E.H.R.R. 221, para.73. It is not necessary that the "guarantees" "must as a matter of law be formal, in some way cast in stone" (*per* Laws L.J. in *R v Spear* [2001] 2 W.L.R. 1692, para.[35]); the question is whether a reasonable man apprised of the relevant facts available to the "persistent, even dogged inquirer as a member of the public" would conclude that there was a real doubt as to the tribunal's impartiality or independence (*Scanfuture UK Ltd v Secretary of State for Trade and Industry* [2001] I.R.L.R. 416, EAT; *R (on the application of Husain) v Asylum Support Adjudicator* [2001] EWHC Admin 832).

[414] *ibid.* See *McGonnell v UK* (2000) 30 E.H.R.R. 289 (sufficient doubt for breach of Art.6(1) as to Guernsey judge's impartiality when participating in planning appeal arose from his previous act in presiding over Guernsey's parliament when it considered the detailed development plan for the land in question); *V v UK* (1999) 30 E.H.R.R. 121 (breach of Art.6(1) in role of Home Secretary in determining tariff for juvenile murderers; independent means, inter alia, "independent . . . of the executive"); *R (on the application of Anderson and Taylor) v Secretary of State for the Home Department* [2003] 1 A.C. 837 (HL held that the Home Secretary's role in relation to mandatory life sentence prisoners was incompatible with Art.6(1), following *Stafford v UK* (2002) 35 E.H.R.R. 32, ECtHR).

[415] Above, para.4–040.

[416] *Fawdry and Co (a firm) v Murfitt (Lord Chancellor intervening)* [2002] EWCA Civ 643, [2003] Q.B. 104.

[417] *Coppard v Customs and Excise Commissioners* [2003] EWCA Civ 511, [2003] Q.B. 1428.

[418] *Albert and Le Compte v Belgium* (1983) 5 E.H.R.R. 533, para.29.

[419] European Commission of Human Rights in *Kaplan v UK* (1980) 4 E.H.R.R. 64, para.161.

[420] *ISKCON v UK*; App. No.20490/92, March 8, 1994 (Commission) (no violation of Art.6(1) in determination by inspector of appeal against enforcement notice); *Bryan v UK* (1995) 21 E.H.R.R. 342; *Chapman v UK* (2001) 10 B.H.R.C. 48 (no violation of Art.6(1) in determination by inspector of appeal against enforcement notice); *Howard v UK* App. No.10825/84, July 16, 1987 (Commission); *Varey v UK* App. No.26662/95, October 27,1999 (Commission) (no violation of Art.6(1) in determination of Secretary of State to dismiss appeals against refusal of planning permission, contrary to inspectors' recommendations).

[421] Above.

the content of the dispute, including the desired and actual grounds of appeal. Here, the court noted the quasi-judicial character of the proceedings before the inspector, the inspector's duty to exercise independent judgment, the requirement that inspectors must not be subject to any improper influence, and the stated mission of the inspectorate to uphold the principle of openness, fairness and impartiality. Any shortcomings in these respects could have been reviewed by the High Court. The High Court was able to deal with most of the points in fact raised by the appellant. As to the facts and planning merits, the High Court did not have jurisdiction to substitute its view for that of the inspector, but could intervene if the inspector had taken into account irrelevant factors or had omitted to take account of relevant factors or if the evidence was not capable of supporting a finding of fact or if the decision was perverse or irrational. Such an approach by an appeal tribunal on questions of fact could reasonably be expected in specialised areas of the law such as this, particularly where the facts had already been established in the course of a quasi-judicial procedure governed by many of the Art.6(1) safeguards.[422]

8–022   *Bryan v UK* has been applied in respect of the decision of an inspector to dismiss an appeal against a discontinuance notice[423] and in determining a planning appeal.[424] However, in *R (on the application of Alconbury Developments Ltd) v Secretary of State for the Environment, Transport and the Regions*[425] the Divisional Court granted a declaration that provisions enabling the Secretary of State to call-in planning applications, to direct that a planning appeal should be determined by himself rather than his inspector (a "recovered appeal") and to approve compulsory purchase and highway orders were incompatible with Art.6(1). This was on the ground that the Secretary of State was not independent and impartial and that the processes in question were not saved by the possibility of challenge before the High Court by a statutory application to quash. The court held that *Bryan v UK* was distinguishable and that it was impossible to read the relevant provisions in such a way (for example by enlarging the permissible grounds of appeal) as to comply with Art.6(1).

The House of Lords unanimously allowed an appeal[426] on the ground that, while the Secretary of State could not be seen objectively as independent and impartial (and this was accepted by him), the powers of the High Court were in fact sufficient.[427] Furthermore, this overall conclusion applied even to decisions where the financial interests of other government departments were engaged, although particular points might arise in subsequent proceedings. It was noted that decisions were taken by ministers who so far as possible had no connection with the area from which the case came, assisted by a decision officer who worked separately from other civil servants involved in casework. There would also have been an inquiry conducted by an inspector, who would report to the Secretary of State. The situation whereby, in practice in rare and controversial

[422] paras 40–47.
[423] *O'Brien v Department of the Environment, Transport and the Regions* (unreported, January 28, 2001).
[424] *Bhamjee v Secretary of State for the Environment, Transport and the Regions* (unreported, January 23, 2001).
[425] [2001] H.R.L.R. 10. See to the same effect the decision of the Court of Session in *County Properties Ltd v The Scottish Ministers* [2000] H.R.L.R. 677.
[426] [2001] UKHL 23, [2003] 2 A.C. 295.
[427] Applying *Bryan v UK* and *Zumtobel v Austria* (1993) 17 E.H.R.R. 116.

cases, decisions on planning policy could be made by a democratically accountable member of the executive was well entrenched in UK constitutional practice
and the House expressed itself satisfied that this conformed to Art.6(1):

> "To substitute for the Secretary of State an independent and impartial body
> with no central electoral accountability would not only be a recipe for chaos:
> it would be profoundly undemocratic."[428]

Lord Hoffmann noted[429] that a distinction was to be drawn between matters of
fact and matters of planning policy or expediency. It was only in relation to the
former that the additional safeguards identified in *Bryan v UK* in respect of the
inspector's involvement were needed to justify the limited review of findings of
fact by the High Court. It was separately accepted by the European Court of
Human Rights in *Zumtobel v Austria* that:

> "respect must be accorded to decisions taken by administrative authorities
> on grounds of expediency"[430]

and as regards these matters

> "there has never been a single voice in the Commission or the European
> Court to suggest that our provisions for judicial review are inadequate to
> satisfy Article 6."[431]

The distinction between matters of policy and matters of fact was applied in
subsequent cases, with, where the decision maker was not independent and
impartial, judicial review being recognised as an adequate remedy in respect of
the former but not the latter.[432] However, the significance of the distinction was
reduced by the decision of the House of Lords in *Runa Begum v Tower Hamlets
LBC*.[433] Here the House held that the possibility of review by the county court of
determinations by a local housing authority, including decisions on matters of
fact, as to whether it owed a duty under Pt VII of the Housing Act 1996 to secure
accommodation for a homeless person, was sufficient for compliance with
Art.6(1). The review mechanism, an appeal under s.204 of the 1996 Act, applied
conventional judicial review principles. The House held that there was no
necessity for an appeal on the merits on factual issues, although it left open the
question whether the county court should apply a greater intensity of review on
factual issues. The House, furthermore, indicated that review on conventional
judicial review grounds would generally be sufficient in cases of administrative

---

[428] *per* Lord Nolan at para.[60].

[429] paras [98]–[117].

[430] (1993) 17 E.H.R.R. 110, para.[32].

[431] para.[122].

[432] e.g. *British Telecommunications plc v Gloucester City Council* [2001] EWHC 1001; *Friends
Provident Life Office v Secretary of State for Transport, Local Government and the Regions*
[2001] EWHC 820, [2002] 1 W.L.R. 1450 (assessment of likely impact of proposed development
to be regarded for this purpose as planning judgment rather than "an issue of fact and the
evaluation of fact"); *R (on the application of McLellan) v Bracknell Forest BC* [2001] EWCA Civ
1510, [2002] Q.B. 1129 (review panel not independent and impartial as regards decision to
proceed with termination of introductory tenancy but judicial review adequate remedy where
issue was reasonableness of termination decision); *cf. Adan v London Borough of Newham* [2001]
EWCA Civ 1916, [2002] 1 W.L.R. 2120.

[433] [2002] UKHL 5, [2003] 2 A.C. 430.

decision-making, as in discharging regulatory functions (such as licensing or granting planning permission) or administering schemes of social welfare.[434] Accordingly, in a number of situations previously considered by the lower courts[435] the distinction between policy and fact would no longer be significant, judicial review being sufficient in all cases. It should be noted, however, that the decision in *Runa Begum* concerned a matter where it was assumed that a "civil right" was engaged and recognised that a decision that it was so engaged would involve an extension of the Strasbourg jurisprudence. It is submitted that the more clearly a situation falls within the core of the "civil right" concept, the less likely it is where facts are in issue that the right to an independent and impartial tribunal will be satisfied by recourse to a court equipped only with the conventional powers of judicial review.

Non-compliance overall with the requirement of access to an independent and impartial tribunal has been found in respect of housing benefit review boards[436]; part-time sheriffs in Scotland appointed by the Lord Advocate with a limited term of office[437]; the Crown Court when constituted (in accordance with the rules) to hear an appeal from licensing justices so as to include other members of the licensing committee to which those justices belonged[438]; and disciplinary adjudications by prison governors leading to additional days in prison.[439]

Article 6(2) and (3) impose particular requirements, including the presumption of innocence, in respect of persons "charged with a criminal offence". These are also applicable to disciplinary proceedings that fall within Art.6(1).[440]

(e) Article 8

8–023 This provides:

> **"Article 8—Right to respect for private and family life**
>
> 1. Everyone has the right to respect for his private and family life, his home and his correspondence.
>
> 2. There shall be no interference by a public authority with the exercise of this right except such as is in accordance with the law and is necessary in a democratic society in the interests of national security, public safety, or the economic well-being of the country, for the prevention of disorder or

---

[434] See Lord Hoffmann at paras [42], [59]. At para.[41] his Lordship distinguished *Bryan v UK*, above, on the ground that it concerned an appeal against an enforcement notice where the inspector's decision on an appeal would be binding in subsequent criminal proceedings.

[435] Including those summarised at n.432, above.

[436] *R (on the application of Bewry) v Norwich City Council* [2001] EWHC Admin 657, [2002] H.R.L.R. 21 (councillor membership of Board determining issue involving credibility; breach of common law requirement equivalent to that comprised in Art.6); distinguished in *R (on the application of Bibi) v Housing Benefit Review Board of Rochdale MBC* [2001] EWHC Admin 967 (councillor membership of Board meant that it could not be independent or expert in the *Alconbury* sense, but judicial review was a sufficient remedy given that most of the facts were not substantially in issue and that the councillors had no personal interest in their finding that a tenancy was not on a commercial basis and so did not enable a claim to be made for housing benefit).

[437] *Starrs v Ruxton* 2000 J.C. 208.

[438] *R (on the application of Smith) v Lincoln Crown Court* [2001] EWHC Admin 928, [2002] 1 W.L.R. 1332 (judicial review of the Crown Court held to be an inadequate remedy).

[439] *R (on the application of Greenfield) v Secretary of State for the Home Department* [2005] UKHL 14, [2005] 1 W.L.R. 673.

[440] *Albert and Le Compte v Belgium* (1983) 5 E.H.R.R. 533, para.39.

crime, for the protection of health or morals, or for the protection of the rights and freedoms of others."

Engagement of Article 8(1)

"Private life" is a concept that is not confined to "an 'inner circle' in which the individual may live his own personal life as he chooses and to exclude therefrom entirely the outside world" but extends to cover, to a degree, the right to establish and develop relationships with other human beings, and activities of a professional or business nature,[441] but without extending the notion of "private" to the whole of an individual's business or professional life.[442] It covers "the physical and moral integrity of the person, including his or her sexual life".[443] It applies, *inter alia*, to the collection of secret information concerning individuals,[444] the disclosure of medical records and information concerning patients[445] and children,[446] and the disclosure to the media of the CCTV footage by a local authority of the events following a suicide attempt by a person in a public street.[447] It does not, however, apply to confer a right to die,[448] or to the mere communication to a person by a public authority of its decision to take a step that is a precursor to enforcement action,[449] or (probably) to the retention by the police of fingerprints and DNA samples lawfully taken by them.[450]

The notion of "family life" is not confined solely to families based on marriage and may encompass other de facto relationships; when deciding whether a relationship can be said to amount to "family life" relevant factors may include whether the couple live together, the length of their relationship and whether they have demonstrated their commitment to each other by having children together or by other means.[451] The family life of adult siblings living together may engage Art.8(1),[452] But it does not at present recognise that the

---

[441] *Niemietz v Germany* (1992) 16 E.H.R.R. 97, para.29 (search of applicant's office covered by Art.8); *Amann v Switzerland*, Judgment of February 16, 2000 (interception of a private telephone call concerning a business matter covered by Art.8).

[442] *R v Worcester County Council, Ex p. SW* [2000] H.R.L.R. 702, 717–718.

[443] *X and Y v Netherlands* (1985) 8 E.H.R.R. 235, para.22. *Cf. Smith and Grady v UK* (1999) 29 E.H.R.R. 493; *Lustig-Prean and Beckett v UK* (1999) 29 E.H.R.R. 548 (breaches of Art.8 in respect of investigations into and administrative discharges of homosexual members of the armed forces). *Cf. X v Y* [2004] EWCA Civ 662 (Art.8 not engaged where X was dismissed following his conviction for an offence of gross indecency committed in a toilet which was open to the public).

[444] *Leander v Sweden* (1987) 9 E.H.R.R. 433.

[445] *Z v Finland* (1995) 25 E.H.R.R. 371 *Cf. Campbell v MGN Ltd* [2004] UKHL 22, above para.8–014.

[446] See *X v SO* [2003] EWHC 1101 (QB); *Re S (a child)* [2004] UKHL 47, [2005] 1 A.C. 593; *In re a Local Authority* [2003] EWHC 2746 (Fam), [2004] 1 Fam. 96.

[447] *Peck v UK* (2003) 36 E.H.R.R. 41.

[448] *R (on the application of Pretty) v Director of Public Prosecutions* [2001] UKHL 61, [2002] 1 A.C. 800.

[449] *R (on the application of Denson) v Child Support Agency* [2002] EWHC 154 (Admin), [2002] 1 F.L.R. 938 (Art.8(1) might be engaged if the person was in a vulnerable category).

[450] *R (on the application of S) v Chief Constable of South Yorkshire* [2004] UKHL 39, [2004] 1 W.L.R. 2196 (Lords Steyn, Rodger of Earlsferry, Carswell and Brown of Eaton-under-Heywood, Baroness Hale of Richmond dissenting on the point).

[451] *X, Y and Z v UK* (1997) 24 E.H.R.R. 143 (de facto family ties held to link a (female to male) transsexual and a woman (who had lived together for over 10 years) and their child (by AID)).

[452] *Senthuran v Secretary of State for the Home Department* [2004] EWCA Civ 950, [2004] 4 All E.R. 365.

"family life" guarantee is applicable to the relationship between a same-sex couple.[453] Article 8(1) has been held to be applicable in a range of cases concerning the decision making of local authorities concerning children in care[454] and adoption,[455] and the policy of the Prison Service with respect to the length of time babies would be permitted to live with their mothers in prison.[456]

The right to respect for private and family life has been held to give rise to an obligation for the state to facilitate access to information about an individual's past[457] and about hazardous activities that have exposed the applicants to health risks,[458] and to carry out a sufficiently specific and complete study of the impact of night flights on the private and family lives of residents very close to Heathrow airport.[459] On the other hand, Art.8(1) does not given rise to a right to receive financial assistance to support a person's family life or to ensure that individuals may enjoy family life to the full or in any particular manner.[460]

The term "home" is to be construed broadly. It is an autonomous concept which does not depend on classification under domestic law; whether a particular habitation constitutes a "home" which attracts the protection of Art.8(1) "will depend on the factual circumstances, namely, the existence of sufficient and continuous links".[461] The factor of "unlawfulness" is relevant rather to the reference in Art.8(2) to "in accordance with law" and to the balancing exercise undertaken in assessing the necessity of any interference.[462] Accordingly, the term "home" is not confined to a residence legally established in accordance with national law but extends to long-term residence on land in caravans albeit contrary to planning law.[463] (Conversely, it will not apply where travellers trespass upon land and possession proceedings are started two days later by the owner.[464])

---

[453] *Estevez v Spain*, Judgment of May 10, 2001, applied by Lord Nicholls and Lord Mance in *M v Secretary of State for Work and Pensions* [2006] UKHL 11, [2006] 2 A.C. 91, paras [21]–[30], [132]–[151]. The matter will in due course be reconsidered by the ECtHR: see Lord Mance at para.[152].

[454] See *TP and KM v UK*, Judgment of May 10, 2001.

[455] *In re B (a child)* [2001] UKHL 70, [2002] 1 W.L.R. 258 where the House of Lords held that the balancing exercise required by Art.8 does not differ in substance from the balancing exercise undertaken by a court when deciding under English law whether adoption would be in the best interests of the child.

[456] *R (on the application of P. Q and QB) v Secretary of State for the Home Department* [2001] EWCA Civ 1151 (it was held that the policy that children should leave at 18 months should be applied more flexibly).

[457] *Gaskin v UK* (1989) 12 E.H.R.R. 36.

[458] *McGinley and Egan v UK* (1998) 27 E.H.R.R. 1 (no infringement found).

[459] *Hatton v UK* (2002) 34 E.H.R.R. 1.

[460] *Vaughan v UK*, App. No.12639/87; *Petrovic v Austria* (2001) 33 E.H.R.R. 14, para.26.

[461] *Buckley v UK* (1996) 23 E.H.R.R. 101, para.63, where the Commission's view was quoted by the Court.

[462] *ibid.*

[463] *Buckley v UK* (1996) 23 E.H.R.R. 101. See also *Harrow LBC v Qazi* [2003] UKHL 43, [2001] 1 A.C. 983 (council house that claimant had lived in for eight years and then continued to occupy following termination of joint tenancy by claimant's spouse continued to be his "home" notwithstanding that his right to occupy it had ended). Occupation of a plot as a trespasser by a traveller for a fortnight was insufficient to make it a "home"; eviction nevertheless engaged Art.8 as the result of the effect on private and family life: *Ward v Hillingdon LBC* [2001] EWHC Admin 91, [2001] H.R.L.R. 825.

[464] See Lord Scott of Foscote in *Kay v Lambeth LBC; Leeds City Council v Price* [2006] UKHL 10, [2006] 2 A.C. 465, para.[129]; for Lord Bingham of Cornhill, para.[48], the point was "all but unarguable".

The interest protected is the "right to respect" for the home. It follows that enforcement action under planning law[465] and eviction from a home[466] may engage Art.8(1). However, it does not impose a general obligation on local authorities to remedy problems caused by a design defect,[467] or to provide a home.[468] The right to respect for a home may be infringed by causing, or allowing others to create, severe environmental pollution[469] and failing to warn of environmental risks.[470] A person's loss of amenity in his home arising from flooding from public sewers or from the grant of planning permission for a development on neighbouring land must accordingly be balanced against the other interests involved, including where relevant those of other landowners and the general public.[471]

Overall, states are accorded a wide margin of appreciation, particularly in respect of arguments that they should take positive steps in support of the rights protected by Art.8(1).[472] In the case of a claim that the state is under a positive obligation,

> "regard must be had to the fair balance that has to be struck between the general interest and the interests of the individual."[473]

---

[465] *Buckley v UK*, above (no infringement found).

[466] *Harrow LBC v Qazi* [2003] UKHL 43, [2004] 1 A.C. 983; *Kay v Lambeth LBC*; *Leeds City Council v Price* [2006] UKHL 10, [2006] 2 A.C. 465. The significance of this is much reduced by the approach to Art.8(2): see below.

[467] *Lee v Leeds City Council; Ratcliffe v Sandwell MBC* [2002] EWCA Civ 6, [2002] 1 W.L.R. 1488 (a violation of Art.8(1) may, however, arise on the facts of a particular case); *cf. R (on the application of Erskine) v Lambeth LBC* [2003] EWHC 2479 (Admin) (no breach of Art.8 arising from layout of kitchen).

[468] *Mazari v Italy* 28 E.H.R.R. CD 175; *Chapman v UK* (2001) 33 E.H.R.R. 18, para.99; *R (on the application of Morris) v Newham LBC* [2002] EWHC 1262 (Admin); *R (on the application of W) v Lambeth LBC* [2002] EWCA Civ 613, *per* Brooke L.J. at para.[85]. A failure to provide suitable accommodation may, however, in exceptional circumstances amount to a lack of respect for private and family life: *R (on the application of Bernard) v Enfield LBC* [2002] EWHC 2282 (Admin), [2003] H.R.L.R. 111.

[469] *Lopez Ostra v Spain* (1994) 20 E.H.R.R. 277; *cf. Powell and Rayner v UK* (1980) 12 E.H.R.R. 355 (no infringement found) and *Hatton v UK* [2002] 34 E.H.R.R. 1 (aircraft noise generated by flights at Heathrow: infringement found); *R (on the application of Vetterlein) v Hampshire CC* [2001] EWHC Admin 560 (applicants' "generalised environmental concerns" in respect of proposed incinerator held too remote to engage Art.8(1)).

[470] *Guerra v Italy* (1998) 26 E.H.R.R. 357.

[471] See respectively, *Marcic v Thames Water Utilities Ltd* [2003] UKHL 66, [2004] 2 A.C. 42 (statutory scheme under the Water Industry Act 1991 held to strike a reasonable balance between the interests of customers whose properties were prone to sewer flooding and the interests of all the other customers of the sewerage undertaker (see Lord Nicholls of Birkenhead at paras [37]–[46])); *Lough v First Secretary of State* [2004] EWCA Civ 905, [2004] 1 W.L.R. 2557 (claimants' loss of amenity, comprising as claimed here loss of privacy, overlooking, loss of light, loss of a view and interference with television reception, to be balanced against interests of prospective developing landowner).

[472] See e.g. *X, Y and Z v UK* (1997) 24 E.H.R.R. 143 (no obligation for UK to recognise parental rights for transsexual who was not the biological father, in absence of generally shared approach among the contracting states); *Rees v UK* (1986) 9 E.H.R.R. 56 (no obligation to amend birth registration system to alter recorded sex of post-operative transsexual); *Sheffield v UK* (1998) 27 E.H.R.R. 163; *Botta v Italy* (1998) 26 E.H.R.R. 241; *Anufrijeva v Southwark LBC* [2003] EWCA Civ 1406, [2004] Q.B. 1124 (breach of positive obligations under domestic law to provide welfare support may provide the element of culpability necessary to give rise to a breach of Art.8(1): *per* Lord Woolf C.J. at para.[45]).

[473] *Botta v Italy* (1998) 26 E.H.R.R. 241, para.33.

Where a positive obligation arises it commonly comprises both the introduction
of a legislative or administrative scheme and a requirement that it be operated
competently so as to achieve its aim.[474]

Justification under Art.8(2)

For an interference with rights protected by Art.8(1) to be justified by reference
to Art.8(2), it must be: (a) "in accordance with the law"; (b) "necessary in a
democratic society"; and (c) for a legitimate aim. To be "in accordance with the
law", the interference must have some basis in domestic law (such as primary
and delegated legislation but not internal instructions); the law must be "adequately accessible: the citizen must be able to have an indication that is adequate,
in the circumstances, of the legal rules applicable to a given case"; and a norm
to be regarded as "law" must be "formulated with sufficient precision to enable
the citizen to regulate his conduct: he must be able—if need be with appropriate
advice—to foresee, to a degree that is reasonable in the circumstances, the
consequences which a given action may entail".[475] As regards what is "necessary
in a democratic society", it has been stated that:

> "(a) the adjective 'necessary' is not synonymous with 'indispensable',
>   neither has it the flexibility of such expressions as 'admissible',
>   'ordinary', 'useful', 'reasonable or desirable' . . .
> (b) the Contracting States enjoy a certain but not unlimited margin of
>   appreciation in the matter of the imposition of restrictions, but it is for
>   the Court to give the final ruling on whether they are compatible with
>   the Convention.
> (c) The phrase 'necessary' in a democratic society means that, to be
>   compatible with the Convention, the interference must, inter alia,
>   correspond to a 'pressing social need' and be 'proportionate to the
>   legitimate aim pursued.'
> (d) Those paragraphs of Articles of the Convention which provide for an
>   exception to a right guaranteed are to be narrowly interpreted
>   . . . ."[476]

Justifications under Art.8(2) have been found in a wide variety of situations.
For example, decisions to take children into care may be justified as pursuing the
legitimate aims of protecting health or morals and the rights and freedoms of the
child, the state having wide margin of appreciation in deciding whether removal
is necessary; stricter scrutiny is, however, appropriate for further limitations on
family life, such as restrictions on parental access, and the decision-making
process has to be fair.[477] The English courts have held various aspects of
domestic child law to reflect the requirements of Art.8.[478] A compulsory purchase order can be justified as necessary to protect the environment[479] and
enforcement action in planning law as necessary for the well-being of the country

---

[474] *Anufrijeva*, para.[16].
[475] *Silver v UK* (1983) 5 E.H.R.R. 347, paras 85–88, applying the principles developed in respect of
Art.10 by the Court in *Sunday Times v UK* (1979) 2 E.H.R.R. 245.
[476] *ibid.* para.[97].
[477] *TP v UK* (2002) 34 E.H.R.R. 2.
[478] See e.g. *Re B (a child)* [2001] UKHL 70, [2002] 1 W.L.R. 258 (confirmation of adoption orders);
Re v (a child) [2004] EWCA Civ 54, [2004] 1 W.L.R. 1433 (Pt IV of the Children Act 1989).
[479] *Baker v First Secretary of State* [2003] EWHC 2511 (Admin).

and for public safety.[480] It will only be in exceptional circumstances that the enforcement of a right to possession of a home in accordance with domestic property law is incompatible with Art.8; in the vast majority of cases, the right of a public landowner to enforce such a right will automatically supply the justification required by Art.8(2). It will not be necessary to provide individual justification in each case, the court being entitled to assume that domestic law has struck the right balance, although this would not prevent the defendant (in a rare case) from being able to show that the balance struck by the general law in his or her type of case is non-compliant.[481] Indeed, the ECtHR had held (prior to *Kay*) that the summary procedure for the eviction of gypsies in breach of licence conditions at a local authority caravan site violated Art.8.[482]

A final example is that the retention by the police of fingerprints and DNA samples of individuals not convicted of criminal offences does not contravene Arts 8 or 14.[483]

(f) Article 10

This provides: 8–024

> **"Article 10—Freedom of expression**
> 1. Everyone has the right to freedom of expression. This right shall include freedom to hold opinions and to receive and impart information and ideas without interference by public authority and regardless of frontiers. This article shall not prevent States from requiring the licensing of broadcasting, television or cinema enterprises.
> 2. The exercise of these freedoms, since it carries with it duties and responsibilities, may be subject to such formalities, conditions, restrictions or penalties as are prescribed by law and are necessary in a democratic society, in the interests of national security, territorial integrity or public safety, for the prevention of disorder or crime, for the protection of health or morals, for the protection of the reputation or rights of others, for preventing the disclosure of information received in confidence, or for maintaining the authority and impartiality of the judiciary."

The structure of Art.10, conferring a right to freedom of expression, is similar to that of Art.8. It brings into play a wide range of laws that impinge on that freedom, including those, for example, that protect the reputation of individuals (defamation), protect the administration of justice from prejudicial press comment (contempt of court), and prohibit the publication of indecent or obscene material. Most of the cases turn on the question whether the restriction can be justified under Art.10(2). For example, in *Handyside v UK*[484] it was held that the conviction of the publisher of the *Little Red Schoolbook* under the Obscene Publications Act 1959 and associated seizures of copies did not breach Art.10. The interferences with expression were prescribed by law and had an aim that

---

[480] *Buckley v UK* (1996) 23 E.H.R.R. 101; *Lough v First Secretary of State* [2004] EWCA Civ 905, [2004] 1 W.L.R. 2557 (planning authority must conduct appropriate balancing exercise).

[481] *Kay v Lambeth LBC; Leeds City Council v Price* [2006] UKHL 10, [2006] 2 A.C. 465.

[482] *Connors v UK* (2004) 40 E.H.R.R. 189 (the law was disproportionate in that gypsies on local authority sites received less legal protection than those on private sites).

[483] *R (on the application of S) v Chief Constable of South Yorkshire Police* [2004] UKHL 39, [2004] 1 W.L.R. 2196.

[484] (1976) 1 E.H.R.R. 737.

was legitimate under Art.10(2) ("the protection of morals in a democratic society"); the national authorities had been entitled to conclude, within their margin of appreciation, that the interferences were necessary for that purpose, in that they were a necessary response to a pressing social need. This decision may be compared with that in *Sunday Times v UK*[485] where the Court held that an injunction granted to restrain publication of an article setting out evidence and argument relevant to civil actions against the distributors of thalidomide, a drug which caused babies to be born with deformities, violated Art.10. The interference with free expression was prescribed by law (the common law of contempt of court), had a legitimate aim (maintaining the authority of the judiciary), but was not a proportionate response to a social need sufficiently pressing to outweigh the public interest in freedom of expression. The main problem was that the common rule applied constituted an absolute prohibition on the prejudgment of issues in pending cases. The exceptions in Art.10(2) are to be interpreted narrowly.

(g) Article 13

8–025 This article, which does not appear in the HRA 1998, provides:

> **"Article 13—Right to an effective remedy**
>   Everyone whose rights and freedoms as set forth in this Convention are violated shall have an effective remedy before a national authority notwithstanding that the violation has been committed by persons acting in an official capacity."

Accordingly, where an individual has an arguable claim to be the victim of a violation of ECHR rights, he or she should have a remedy before a national authority (not necessarily judicial) to have the claim decided and, if appropriate, to obtain redress; the aggregate of remedies under domestic law may be sufficient.[486] The requirements of Art.13 are less onerous than those of Art.6(1) (which is applicable in a narrower range of circumstances).[487] The police complaints system does not provide an effective remedy in respect of alleged abuses of authority contrary to the ECHR by police officers.[488] In *Z v UK*,[489] the European Court of Human Rights held that child victims of ill-treatment and abuse by their parents did not have an effective remedy for the damage they had suffered as a result of the failure of the local authority to protect them (contrary to Art.3). The government accepted that the availability of compensation from the Criminal Injuries Compensation Board (which covered only criminal acts), the possibility of complaining to the Local Government Ombudsman (whose recommendations were not legally enforceable) and the complaints procedure under the Children Act 1989 was insufficient alone or cumulatively to satisfy the requirements of Art.13. The Court noted that the decision of the House of Lords

---

[485] (1979) 2 E.H.R.R. 245.
[486] *Silver v UK* (1983) 5 E.H.R.R. 347.
[487] *ibid.* para.[109].
[488] *Khan v UK* (2000) 8 B.H.R.C. 310, paras [45]–[47].
[489] [2002] 34 E.H.R.R. 97. See also *Peck v UK* (2003) 36 E.H.R.R. 41 (breach of Art.13 arising from absence of effective remedy for breach of Art.8(1) arising out of disclosure of CCTV footage; judicial review, recourse to media commissions, and the law of breach of confidence did not provide such a remedy); *McGlinchey v UK*, judgment of April 29, 2003 (breach of Art.13 arising from lack of remedy for breach of Art.8(1) arising out of medical treatment of prisoner).

in *X (Minors) v Bedfordshire County Council*[490] barred proceedings in negligence, and the government's submission that in the future under the HRA 1998 victims of human rights breaches would be able to bring proceedings in courts empowered to award damages. It did not consider it appropriate

> "to make any findings as to whether only adversarial court proceedings could have finished effective redress, though judicial remedies indeed furnish strong guarantees of independence, access for the victim and family and enforceability of awards in compliance with the requirements of Article 13,"[491]

A breach of Art.13 was found on a similar basis in *TP and KM v UK*.[492] An English court should "strive to avoid" a risk that the UK be in breach of Art.13.[493]

(h) Article 14

This article provides: 8–026

"Article 14—Prohibition of discrimination

The enjoyment of the rights and freedoms set forth in this Convention shall be secured without discrimination on any ground such as sex, race, colour, language, religion, political or other opinion, national or social origin, association with a national minority, property, birth or other status."

This does not constitute a free-standing prohibition of discrimination on the stated grounds (which are themselves given as examples)[494]; complaints must be concerned with one of the substantive protected rights and freedoms taken in conjunction with Art.14.[495] The facts at issue must accordingly "fall within the ambit of one or more" of the substantive provisions of the ECHR.[496] This will be the case, for example, where legislation is introduced to promote a Convention right or freedom or affects the way in which it is organised.[497] The House of

---

[490] [1995] 2 A.C. 633.

[491] paras [105]–[111].

[492] Judgment of May 10, 2001, paras [104]–[110] (in respect of breach of Art.8). This arose out of *M v Newham London Borough Council*, heard with *X (Minors) v Bedfordshire County Council*, above.

[493] *R v Canterbury Crown Court, Ex p. Regentford Ltd* [2001] H.R.L.R. 362, para.19, *per* Waller L.J.

[494] This matter is addressed in Protocol 12, which will come into force when ratified by 10 states in respect of those states and any subsequent states to ratify. Other impermissible grounds of discrimination under Art.14 include sexual orientation: *Salgueiro da Silva Mouta v Portugal* (2001) 31 E.H.R.R. 47 at paras 28 and 36; *Ghaidan v Godin-Mendoza* [2004] 2 A.C 557: *R (on the application of Amicus) v Secretary of State for Trade and Industry* [2004] EWHC 860 (Admin), para.[193].

[495] *Belgian Linguistic case (No.2)* (1968) 1 E.H.R.R. 252, para.9. It is not necessary to establish breach of the substantive right of freedom in question: *Abdulaziz, Cabales and Balkandali v UK* (1985) 7 E.H.R.R. 471, para.71; it is sufficient that "a personal group is treated, without proper justification, less favourably than another, even though the more favourable treatment is not called for by the Convention": *ibid.*, para.82.

[496] *Rasmussen v Denmark* (1984) 7 E.H.R.R. 371, para.29, followed in *Abdulaziz*, above, para.71.

[497] *Petrovic v Austria* (2001) 33 E.H.R.R. 14, paras 26–29 (payment of parent leave allowance not required by Art.8 but intended to promote family life and affecting its organisation by enabling one parent to stay at home and look after the children).

Lords has confirmed that a tenuous link with another provision of the ECHR is not sufficient to bring Art.14 into play.[498]

The next point is that the reference among the prohibited grounds to "other status" is not interpreted as precluding discrimination on any ground, but only on the ground of a "personal characteristic".[499] A status does not have to be immutable.[500] However, it is for example merely historical fact and not a personal characteristic that distinguishes those who have lawfully had finger-prints and samples taken from them in the course of an investigation and those who have not provided fingerprints and samples.[501]

Then, Art.14 does not prohibit every difference in treatment, but only those differences where "other persons in an analogous or relevantly similar situation enjoy preferential treatment" and "there is no objective and reasonable justifica-tion".[502] The existence of such a justification must be "assessed in relation to the aims and effects of the measure under consideration, regard being had to the principles which normally prevail in democratic societies". A difference in treatment must pursue a "legitimate aim" and there must be a "reasonable relationship of proportionality between the means employed and the aim sought to be realised".[503]

So far as the English courts are concerned, there have been some differences of view as to the approach to be adopted. Some have articulated a series of (admittedly overlapping) questions to be addressed. Others have preferred a more general approach.

---

[498] *M v Secretary of State for Work and Pensions* [2006] UKHL 11, [2006] 2 A.C. 91 (regulations had the effect that M, a person now living with a same sex partner, had to pay more in child support than if her current partner were male; this was held not to fall within the ambit of the right to respect for the family relationship between M and her two children, and to have only a tenuous link with respect for family life of the new family unit consisting of M, her new partner and their children by their former marriages (assuming that should be regarded as a family). See also *R (on the application of Erskine) v Lambeth LBC* [2003] EWHC 2479 (Admin) (principal purpose of Pt 6 and s.189 of the Housing Act 1985 was the promotion of public health and not the rights, such as those under Art.8, of individuals).

[499] *Kjeldsen v Denmark* (1976) 1 E.H.R.R. 711 at 732–733, applied by Lord Steyn in *R (on the application of S) v Chief Constable of South Yorkshire* [2004] UKHL 39, [2004] 1 W.L.R. 2196, paras [46]–[52].

[500] Accordingly, there is discrimination on the basis of a personal characteristic where a person has parental responsibility for a child by virtue of a residence order as distinct from an adoption order: *Francis v Secretary of State for Work and Pensions* [2005] EWCA Civ 1303, [2006] 1 All E.R. 748. Such an order gave rise to a continuing relationship.

[501] *R (on the application of S) v Chief Constable of South Yorkshire*, above (in respect of a challenge to the Chief Constable's policy to retain such fingerprints and samples unless there were exceptional circumstances). Differential treatment is not based on a personal characteristic where it arises out of objectively different statutory regimes with different arrangements as to cases to an independent appeal tribunal: *R (on the application of Beeson) v Dorset CC* [2001] EWHC Admin 986 (appeal allowed on other grounds: [2002] EWCA Civ 1812; differences between the county court and High Court in rules governing litigation: *St Brice v Southward LBC* [2001] EWCA Civ 1138, [2002] 1 W.L.R. 1537; the application of different procedures for the recovery of possession from tenants according to the nature of the breach of conditions alleged: *Lancashire CC v Taylor* [2005] EWCA Civ 284, [2005] 1 W.L.R. 2668; membership of the hunting community: *Countryside Alliance v Att.-Gen.* [2005] EWHC 1677 (Admin) (rejecting challenges to the Hunting Act 2004); the fact that a person lacks accommodation: *R (on the application of M) v Secretary of State for Work and Pensions* [2006] EWHC 1761 (Admin); or has a tort claim: *Re T&N Ltd* [2005] 2870 (Ch), [2006] 3 All E.R. 697.

[502] *Belgian Linguistic case (No.2)*, para.10; *Stubbings v UK* (1996) 23 E.H.R.R. 213, para.70.

[503] *ibid.* para.10.

The relevant principles were summarised as a series of four questions by Brooke L.J. in *Wandsworth LBC v Michalak*.[504] The court:

"should ask itself the four questions I set out below. If the answer to any of the four questions is No, then the claim is likely to fail, and it is in general unnecessary to proceed to the next question. These questions are: (i) Do the facts fall within the ambit of one or more of the substantive Convention provisions . . . ?; (ii) If so, was there different treatment as respects that right between the complainant on the one hand the other persons put forward for comparison ('the chosen comparators') on the other? (iii) Were the chosen comparators in an analogous situation to the complainant's situation? (iv) If so, did the difference in treatment have an objective and reasonable justification: in other words, did it pursue a legitimate aim and did the differential treatment bear a reasonable relationship of proportionality to the aim sought to be achieved? The third test addresses the questions whether the chosen comparators were in a sufficiently analogous situation to the complainant's situation for the different treatment to be relevant to the question whether the complainant's enjoyment of his Convention right has been free from Art.14 discrimination."

It was recognised in subsequent cases that a fifth question also had to be asked, namely whether the proscribed treatment was on one or more of the proscribed grounds under Art.14.[505] However, in *R (on the application of Carson) v Secretary of State for Work and Pensions*[506] all the members of the House of Lords stated that the revised *Michalak* approach was not always appropriate. Lord Nicholls stated[507] that he preferred to keep the formulation of the relevant issues in these cases as simple and non-technical as possible:

"Article 14 does not apply unless the alleged discrimination is in connection with a Convention right and on a ground stated in Art.14. If this prerequisite is satisfied, the essential question for the court is whether the alleged discrimination, that is the difference in treatment of which complaint is made, can withstand scrutiny. Sometimes the answer to this question will be plain. There may be such an obvious, relevant difference between the claimant and those with whom he seeks to compare himself that their situations cannot be regarded as analogous. Sometimes, where the position is not so clear, a different approach is called for. Then the court's scrutiny

---

[504] [2002] EWCA Civ 271, [2003] 1 W.L.R. 617, para.[20], adopting the structure suggested by Grosz, Beatson and Duffy, *Human Rights: The 1998 Act and the European Convention* (2002). This approach has been followed in many cases, including *R (on the application of Amicus) v Secretary of State for Trade and Industry* [2004] EWHC 860 (Admin), paras [192]–[199] and *R (on the application of Morris) v Westminster City Council (No.3)* [2004] EWHC 2191 (Admin), [2005] 1 W.L.R. 865.

[505] See Baroness Hale in *Ghaidan v Mendoza* [2004] UKHL 30, [2004] 2 A.C. 557, para.[134]; Lord Steyn in *R (on the application of S) v Chief Constable of South Yorkshire* [2004] UKHL 39, [2004] 4 All E.R. 193, para.[42].

[506] [2005] UKHL 37, [2006] 1 A.C. 173.

[507] At para.[2]. See also Lord Hoffmann at paras [28]–[33], Lord Rodger of Earlsferry at paras [42], [43], Lord Walker of Gestingthorpe at paras [61]–[70], and Lord Carswell at para.[97]. Lord Nicholls' approach was adopted by Sir Mark Potter P in *Wilkinson v Kitzinger* [2006] EWHC 2002 (Fam).

may best be directed at considering whether the differentiation has a legitimate aim and whether the means chosen to achieve the aim is appropriate and not disproportionate in its adverse impact."

A particular concern in preferring a broader and simpler approach was to avoid the development of a detailed jurisprudence about comparisons and the identification of comparators.[508] Questions whether two situations are analogous, and whether there is an objective justification for differential treatment commonly overlap.

Different legislative provision may be made for the different countries of the UK "to take account of regional differences and characteristics of an objective and reasonable nature".[509] An illustration of an objective and reasonable justification for a difference based on national origin is provided by *R (on the application of Mitchell) v Coventry University*[510] where regulations that classified a British citizen born and brought up in Hong Kong as an "overseas" student for the purpose of liability to pay university fees, while classifying former British dependent territory citizens resident in Hong Kong, within three years before September 1, 2000, and who emigrated to the UK, as "home" students, were upheld. Classification as a home student primarily depended on three years' ordinary residence in the UK subject to exceptions for recent immigrants; these exceptions had been withdrawn other than for former BDT citizens in Hong Kong for a transitional period following the change of status of Hong Kong. There was not a "relevant similarity" as the claimant had never fallen within the exceptions in the regulations; the suggested comparators had always done so, in both their broad and narrow form.[511]

D. PRACTICAL IMPLEMENTATION OF THE ACT

8–027 Distinctive features of the implementation process have been an extensive training exercise for the judiciary, superintended by the Judicial Studies Board[512] and a full programme for guidance and training for government departments and other public bodies and the general public, overseen by a Human Rights Unit formerly located in the Home Office but now transferred to the Lord Chancellor's Department/DCA/MoJ.[513] Parliament has established a Joint Committee on Human Rights to scrutinise Bills and report on other matters related to human rights, which has produced a series of valuable reports.[514]

---

[508] See e.g. Lord Carswell at para.[97].

[509] *Magee v UK*, Judgment of June 6, 2000.

[510] [2001] EWHC Admin 167. *Cf. R (on the application of Hooper) v Secretary of State for Work and Pensions* [2003] EWCA Civ 813, [2003] 1 W.L.R. 2363 (no objective justification for government's timetable for introducing changes to regime for widow's pension so as to secure equality), reversed by HL: [2005] UKHL 29, [2005] 1 W.L.R. 1681.

[511] The court assumed for the purposes of argument but did not decide that Art.2 of Protocol 1 extended to govern access to higher education.

[512] See above, para.4–033.

[513] See MoJ website.

[514] See e.g. Seventh Report, 2001–02 H.L. 58, *Making of Remedial Orders*; reports on all remedial orders, regular reports on the implementation of changes following adverse ECtHR rulings reports on the scrutiny of particular Bills, and reports on particular matters such as the 32nd Report, 2005–06 H.L. 278, H.C. 1716, *The Human Rights Act: the DCA and Home Office Reviews*; D.J. Feldman, "Parliamentary Scrutiny of Legislation and Human Rights" [2002] P.L. 323.

E. IMPACT OF THE ACT

A number of features can be identified from the first five years in which the HRA **8–028** 1998 has been in operation.[515] The Act has certainly been cited and discussed in a large number of decided cases, although the caseload has not been as great as originally anticipated.[516] In some, a bad HRA point is taken as the last resort of the desperate. In many, points have required extended analysis as the jurisprudence of the Act settles down and the undoubted difficulties of interpretation and application are addressed.

The House of Lords and Court of Appeal have decided landmark cases that provide guidance on important issues such as the proper approach to interpretation under s.3(1), the proportionality test, the discretionary area of judgment to be accorded to decision makers and the extent to which the Act operates retrospectively. The extent to which the Act has made a difference to the *outcomes* of decided cases is in fact relatively limited. The principles applied under the Act commonly lead to the same result as the common law and the ordinary processes of statutory interpretation and judicial review, particularly with the development of the principle of legality and the more flexible approach to *Wednesbury* review. There have been few cases where there has been a declaration of incompatibility, the use of s.3(1) to provide a reading for a statutory provision that could not have been achieved through other processes of statutory interpretation, or a finding that legislation or a decision is not a proportionate response to a legitimate objective. A number of such cases have, indeed, been overturned on appeal. Nevertheless, there are a number of areas where a significant impact can be discerned, including aspects of the criminal process, prisoners' rights, issues arising from the requirement of independence and impartiality for those who determine civil rights and obligations, developments in the area of privacy and measures concerning terrorism.

Curiously, but predictably, the Act has generated a full spectrum of views. There are those who criticise decisions in particular cases as excessively cautious in protecting rights,[517] those who defend the generally relatively cautious approach as the right one[518] and some who argue stridently for the Act's amendment or repeal on the basis, usually, that too much weight is given to the human rights of individuals perceived in some way to be a threat to society. The leading proponents of the third position have tended to be sections of the media, commonly seizing on comments by politicians on particular cases. A vivid example was provided by contrasting comments on the decision of Sullivan J. in *R (on the application of GG) v Secretary of State for the Home Department.*[519]

---

[515] See generally, P. Craig, "The Courts, the Human Rights Act and Judicial Review" (2001) 117 L.Q.R. 589; F. Klug and K. Starmer [2001] P.L. 654; A. Ashworth, [2001] Crim. L.R. 855; F. Klug and C. O'Brien, [2002] P.L. 649; F. Klug and K. Starmer, [2005] P.L. 728; C. Harvey (ed.), *Human Rights in the Community* (2005). For a review of HRA decisions in the House of Lords, see B. Dickson (2006) 26 L.S. 329.

[516] Statistics were provided by the Human Rights Unit on the LCD website but have not been maintained.

[517] C. Gearty, *Can Human Rights Survive?* (2006).

[518] See e.g. above, para.8–004; K. Ewing, "The Futility of the Human Rights Act" [2004] P.L. 829 (noting significant judicial deference in the face of increasingly illiberal legislature responses to terrorism; this pre-dated the HL decision in *A v Secretary of State for the Home Department*); S. Harris-Short, "Family Law and the Human Rights Act 1998: judicial restraint or revolution?" (2005) 17 C.F.L.Q 329.

[519] [2006] EWHC 1111 (Admin).

This concerned armed Afghans who hijacked an aeroplane and had it flown to Stansted airport. They were subsequently convicted of hijacking and other offences, but could not be deported back to Afghanistan as there was a risk that their Art.3 Convention rights would be infringed there by the Taliban.[520] Sullivan J. held that the grant to them some years later of temporary admission status rather than discretionary leave to enter was unlawful without a change in primary legislation. The Prime Minister in response to the judgment said that it was an "abuse of common sense" that they could not be deported[521]; the Home Secretary, Mr Reid, said:

> "when decisions are taken which appear inexplicable or bizarre to the general public, it only reinforces the perception that the system is not working to protect or in favour of the vast majority of ordinary decent hard-working citizens in this country."

The next day, the *Sun* started a campaign to persuade the government to "rip up" the Act.[522] Reviews of the Act were launched by the DCA and the Home Office on this and other cases. The Court of Appeal[523] upheld Sullivan J.'s judgment, describing it as "impeccable".[524] The Joint Committee on Human Rights subsequently agreed with the findings of the reviews that the Act "has not significantly impeded the Government's objectives on crime, terrorism or immigration".[525] It noted that "unfounded criticism" by ministers only served to perpetuate misunderstandings and misperceptions about the Act among the wider public.[526] The government has accordingly accepted that there is no case for amendment or repeal of the Act. Instead, it has taken steps to improve guidance and promote a human rights culture with public service,[527] and to challenge myths and misconceptions about the Act. Indeed, the significance of the Act cannot to be judged solely by reference to outcomes in litigation. Much will also turn on the success or otherwise of a culture within public and private organisations that understands human rights issues and takes them seriously.

---

[520] The ECtHR decision in *Chahal v UK* (1997) 23 E.H.R.R. 413 makes it clear that such deportation by the UK would itself violate Art.3. It is this principle that has caused most difficulty for the government. It has intervened in a case before the ECtHR, *Ramzy v The Netherlands*, seeking an exception to the *Chahal* principle in national security cases. (*Cf. Third party submissions by Liberty and Justice*, drafted by Rabinder Singh Q.C. and Alex Bailin, November 22, 2005.)

[521] Which wasn't the issue.

[522] Cited by the Joint Committee on Human Rights, 32nd Report, 2005–06 H.L. 278, H.C. 1716, p.9.

[523] *S v Secretary of State for the Home Department* [2006] EWCA Civ 1157.

[524] para.[50].

[525] Government Responses to the 32nd Report, Cm. 7011, 2007, p.3.

[526] 32nd Report, p.12.

[527] In 2006, it held a series of events to launch new publications, including *Human Rights: Human Lives—A Handbook for Public Authorities: A Guide to the Human Rights Act 1998* (3rd edn), along with the DCA *Review of the implementation of the Human Rights Act* (see www.dca.gov.uk/peoples-rights/publications.htm).

PART II

SOLVING LEGAL PROBLEMS

PROBLEMS ABOUT PROBLEMS

In this part of the book we focus on resolution of "legal problems". How should **9–001** such problems be defined? Are there distinctions to be drawn between legal problems and social problems? Are lawyers the only people, or even the best people, to solve legal problems? What is a problem?

These are issues which have been the subject of much research and discussion reflecting the growing awareness of the existence of an unmet need for legal assistance and the development of agencies both in the public sector (such as law centres) and in the private sector (such as claims management companies) to meet it. A more recent potential manifestation of the opposite situation is what is described as a "compensation culture" where individuals are said to be encouraged to pursue frivolous or false claims.

This chapter explores some of these issues whilst Ch.10 assesses the strengths and weaknesses of the major public sector agencies currently involved in giving advice and solving problems. Throughout both chapters we shall be particularly concerned with the role of lawyers although we will also note the potential effect of current government policy[1] that "new ways of delivering" legal services might expand the range of advice and assistance provided by non-lawyers and the private sector.[2]

We tend to focus on the courts as the principal forum for resolving disputes and books on the English and Welsh legal system (including ours) usually devote a considerable amount of space to litigation. Court procedure tends to individualise grievances and tailor them to the adversarial model.[3] Yet it remains true that only a tiny fraction of legal matters end up in court.[4] If it were otherwise the court system would simply collapse under the strain.

---

[1] Department for Constitutional Affairs (October 2005) *The Future of Legal Services: Putting Consumers First*; the Legal Services Bill and, regulating commercial claims management organisations, the Compensation Act 2006.

[2] In anticipation of the Bill becoming law, the Co-Operative Group is, at the time of writing, establishing a range of legal services. See J. Parker, "Co-op extends post-Legal Services Bill offering", *The Lawyer,* January 17, 2007.

[3] Whilst the individual action has been the only source of litigation in the past, there is an increasing recognition of the importance of group actions, see below, para.11–016.

[4] See below, para.11–025.

This is partly explained by the ability of lawyers or other advisers to negotiate a mutually acceptable resolution to many disputes.[5] In addition, both government policy[6] and, as we will see in subsequent chapters, the procedural rules of the civil courts, now actively encourage the use of alternatives to litigation.[7] Further, some matters are intrinsically non-contentious and rarely involve recourse to the courts.[8] Other matters may "go away" once the individual has been provided with information or advice on the law.

However, many issues do not emerge into the realm of legal assistance at all, because they are never identified as legal problems by the sufferers; never reach lawyers, or, having reached lawyers, are not recognised as problems within the lawyer's or the law's purview.[9] This situation is unacceptable and any scheme to provide legal services, whether in the public or the private sector, must be judged on its ability to bridge this gap.[10]

A. WHAT IS A PROBLEM?

9–002   This may appear to be an odd question to pose, but it has a bearing on our approach to the provision of legal services and the involvement of lawyers. Does a situation only become a problem when a sufferer identifies it as something with a potential solution? If the individual's mood is one of resigned acceptance of one of life's difficulties, or a belief that help with the issue is not realistically available,[11] should we consider that such a person has a problem? If an individual seeks legal assistance with something that they do not perceive negatively—buying a house; starting a new business venture or a new job—should we consider that such a person does *not* have a problem?

This is not confined to legal or "justiciable"[12] problems (although in many situations there may be an unrecognised legal problem) but has its effects in other

---

[5] See below, paras 11–025—11–031. Note, however, that Genn *et al.*, *Understanding Advice Seeking Behaviour: Further Findings from the LSRC Survey of Justiciable Problems* (LSRC, 2004) found that solicitors were also the most likely category of adviser to suggest mediation although rates for suggesting mediation were low overall (*ibid.*, fig.8); CABx and other advisers being more likely to advise that the client contact their opponent direct.

[6] DCA, *Annual Report 2005/06; Monitoring the Effectiveness of the Government's Commitment to using Alternative Dispute Resolution.*

[7] See below, paras 11–032—11–040.

[8] This is generally true of conveyancing, wills and probate and agreeing contractual relationships, all of which often, though not always or necessarily, involve a lawyer.

[9] This general difficulty has been termed "unmet legal need". See, e.g. R. Abel-Smith, M. Zander and R. Brooke, *Legal Problems and the Citizen* (1973); P. Morris, R. White and P. Lewis, *Social Needs and Legal Action* (1973); A. Byles and P. Morris, *Unmet Need: The Case of the Neighbourhood Law Centre* (1977); H. Genn, *Meeting Legal Needs?* (1982); D. Harris *et al.*, *Compensation and Support for Illness and Injury* (1984); The Committee on the Future of the Legal Profession, *A Time for Change* (1988), Chair: Lady Marre, Ch.7 [hereafter, the Marre Committee]; P. Robertshaw, *Rethinking Legal Need: The Case of Criminal Justice* (1991); Legal Action Group, *A Strategy for Justice* (1992); R. Smith (ed.), *Shaping the Future* (1995); Lord Chancellor's Department, *Legal Aid—Targeting Need* (Cm. 2854, 1995); H. Genn, *Paths to Justice* (1999); Pleasance *et al.*, *Local Legal Need* (2001); Pleasance *et al.*, *Causes of Action: Civil Law and Social Justice* (LSC, 2004); Genn *et al.* (2004); DCA, *Getting Earlier, Better Advice to Vulnerable People* (March 2006).

[10] For the Government's approach to this problem as a matter of social exclusion, see below, para.10–001 and DCA, *Getting Earlier, Better Advice to Vulnerable People* (2006).

[11] Genn (1999), identified these people as "lumpers", see below, para.9–008.

[12] See Pleasance, *et al.* (2004), below.

areas as well. The failure on the part of the sufferer to appreciate that solutions might exist may be the result of a combination of factors. Genn *et al.* in 2004[13] found that those in temporary accommodation, men and black and ethnic minority respondents were more likely to do nothing to resolve "justiciable problems" than others and reasons given for taking no action included "the feeling that nothing could be done" (comprising both lack of knowledge[14] about the availability of redress and "a sense of powerlessness"[15]); fear; and, in accident cases, a belief that the accident was no-one's fault. Concern as to expense was also a factor inhibiting individuals from approaching solicitors in particular. When the individual fails even to recognise a need for assistance, it is, of course, very difficult for an advice agency to provide it to them. The role of the lawyer or other adviser in taking the initiative in identifying problems with which help can be provided becomes important and it is in this type of work that the law centres have been particularly successful. In the private sector, advertising by claims management companies has highlighted, not without controversy, the availability of redress, particularly for personal injury.[16] The identification of the problem then is made by the adviser rather than the sufferer and the relationship between the *need* for legal services and the *demands* actually made by clients is exposed.[17]

If the provision of legal services was to be limited to circumstances in which individuals perceived themselves to have a "justiciable problem", it would be relatively limited. However, law centres and the Citizens Advice Bureaux have long existed to meet a greater need. Amongst the objectives of the Legal Services Bill, as well as of current governmental and Legal Services Commission strategy, is a commitment to improvement of access to justice by individuals and increasing public understanding of legal rights.[18]

B. WHEN IS A PROBLEM "LEGAL"?

It is by no means every problem which requires a lawyer's assistance in its resolution, or, increasingly, can or will only be addressed by a lawyer who is   **9–003**

---

[13] *Understanding Advice Seeking Behaviour: Further Findings from the LSRC Survey of Justiciable Problems* (Legal Services Research Centre, 2004). In Pleasence, *et al.*, *Causes of Action: Civil Law and Social Justice* (LSC, 2004), based on the same data, reported reasons for inaction were given as nothing could be done; insufficient importance; no dispute; others taking action; a desire to preserve a relationship; scared to act; would take too long; and cost (p.52). Greater levels of inaction were seen in relation to problems relating to mental health, clinical negligence, police treatment, personal injury and discrimination (*ibid.* p.54). See also H. Genn, "Who Claims Compensation: Factors Associated with Claiming and Obtaining Damages" in Harris *et al.* (1984), esp. pp.70–76.

[14] An objective of current government policy in this area is to "increase public understanding of the citizen's legal rights": see *Putting Consumers First*, p.26.

[15] *Op. cit.*, p.15.

[16] See para.9–011 below.

[17] For an early analysis of this particular problem, see Adamsdown Community Trust, *Community Need and Law Centre Practice* (1978), pp.36–37.

[18] *Putting Consumers First, op. cit.*, pp.25–26; see also Legal Services Commission, *Making Legal Rights a Reality*, 2006–2011, p.15. DCA, *Getting Earlier, Better Advice to Vulnerable People* (2006), p.15 and the website of the Public Legal Education and Support Task Force at *http://www.pleas.org.uk/*.

formally qualified in the sense discussed in Ch.3. Equally, not every problem with which a lawyer is asked to deal is a legal one. Traditionally, lawyers have been proud of their reputation as advisers on general financial and property matters.[19] In any event, it would be pointless to define as legal problems only those which are *actually* dealt with by lawyers or even by other legal services providers, for that would exclude all those problems which never reach them, but which should.[20]

Would it be realistic to define legal problems as those with which private practitioners normally deal? However, this is a very restrictive definition. If a client does not identify a particular issue as a matter with which a private sector lawyer could or should help or if a solicitor viewed it as outside her or his field, it would not be a legal problem. If solicitors in private practice as a group withdrew from certain types of activity because of competition from another sector or because they could not carry it out economically,[21] equally those matters would cease to be legal problems. This cannot be right.[22]

There is often, therefore, a narrow perception of the circumstances in which it is appropriate to approach a solicitor.[23] There have been criticisms of the narrow nature of the work of most solicitors and it is true that the legal advice and assistance scheme (now falling within the Community Legal Service scheme) was introduced in 1973 to extend the range of their work. Business needs will drive solicitors to expand their areas of work or, on the other hand, to withdraw from other areas, such as will drafting or domestic conveyancing.

Another approach is objectively to define a problem as legal against categories of types of problem. This emphasises the problems with which a solicitor *could* deal but the categories will tend to fluctuate over time as law and society

---

[19] Their traditional role is affected by regulation in certain areas, introduced for the benefit of clients, e.g., under the Financial Services and Markets Act 2000, and by the increasing difficulty of being able to justify non-fee-paying activity, such as counselling.

[20] Genn *et al., op. cit.* (2004) p.26 report that "although solicitors were the most likely to be advising on the respondent's legal position, CABx were also apparently advising very frequently as were a substantial minority of 'other' types of adviser. Thus advice about an individual's position in relation to their problem is being offered by a relatively wide range of initial sources and not simply by legal professionals".

[21] There is the potential for this to be the case even where the work is ostensibly publicly funded if remuneration is not seen to be sufficient or authorisation too restrictive. At the time of writing, proposals to reform public funding from a market-based perspective including fixed fees to suppliers (see DCA, *Legal Aid Reform: the Way Ahead*, Cm. 6993, November 2006), particularly in the criminal sector were being said to threaten provision of publicly funded assistance by solicitors such that there was said to be "a real risk that legal aid solicitors will soon be rarer than NHS dentists", Law Society Press release, *Opposition to legal aid reforms grows*, January 17, 2007. See also *Legal Aid Recruitment Survey—results* (Law Society, 2006) for challenges surrounding the recruitment of young solicitors into this area of practice.

[22] Acceptance of this approach would, by definition, mean that there was no unmet legal need.

[23] See, e.g. Abel-Smith, Zander and Brooke (1973), pp.156–160; J. Jenkins, E. Skordaki and C. F. Willis, *Public Use and Perception of Solicitors* (1989), Ch.5; Research Surveys of Great Britain, *Report on Awareness, Usage and Attitudes towards the Professional Services and Advice Provided by Solicitors* (1986); G. Chambers and S. Harwood, *Solicitors in England and Wales: Practice, Organisation and Perceptions—First Report: The Work of Solicitors in Private Practice* (1990); G. Chambers and S. Harwood, *Solicitors in England and Wales: Practice, Organisation and Perceptions—Second Report: The Private Practice Firm* (1991); J. Jenkins and V. Lewis, *Client Perceptions: Existing and Potential Clients; Experiences and Perceptions of Using a Solicitor for Personal Matters* (1995), Ch.2; Genn (1999); R. Craig, M. Rigg, R. Briscoe and P. Smith, *Clients' Experiences of Using a Solicitor for Personal Matters* (Law Society Research Study No.40, 2001); Genn *et al.* (2004); Pleasance *et al.* (2004).

change,[24] and the very fact of normatively including some categories and excluding others may tend to restrict our thinking rather than allowing us to accept that any situations to which the law pertains can give rise to a legal problem even if there is no immediately available legal framework for its solution. If lawyers define the categories, their approach would be different to that of clients, so that the "felt and expressed need" of the demand side of the equation would not be represented in any determination of "legal need".[25]

A definition of a legal problem as "an unresolved difficulty to which the law **9–004** is relevant" may appear to be too vague and begging too many questions.[26] This is, however, ultimately the approach taken by the Legal Services Bill. Part 3 first regulates "reserved legal activity"[27]—advocacy in court; conduct of litigation; "reserved instrument activity"[28]; probate and notarial activities and the administration of oaths—and defines "legal activity", which includes reserved legal activity but also:

> "12(3)(b) Any other activity which consists of one or both of the following:
>
> (i) the provision of legal advice or assistance in connection with *the application of the law* or with any form of *resolution of legal disputes*; [our italics]
>
> (ii) the provision of representation in connection with any matter concerning the application of the law or any form of resolution of legal disputes
>
> (5) For the purposes of subsection (3) "legal dispute" includes a dispute as to any matter of fact, the resolution of which is relevant to determining the nature of any person's legal rights or liabilities."

It will be instructive to see whether the statutory enshrinement of this approach will encourage lawyers and other regulated advisers not to seek to establish the legal nature of the problem and then find the relevant law, but to establish the nature of the problem and then contemplate whether any part of the law might be relevant.[29] "Legal activity" may be later brought into the regulatory system as

---

[24] For example, taking a lease, repairs undone, attempted eviction of the client (a tenant), attempted eviction by the client (a landlord), buying a house, defective goods, instalment arrears, unpaid debt owed, taken to court for debt, death in the family, making a will, accidents, social security benefits, employment problems, matrimonial problems, court proceedings, and juvenile court proceedings: Abel-Smith, Zander and Brooke (1973), Ch.8. This list, however, is very much of its time and focused on the private individual, omitting all business and company law activity and matters of more recent development, such as immigration issues; inclusion of civil partnership within the definition of "matrimonial" or claims arising out of the Disability Discrimination Act 1995.

[25] This is the taxonomy developed by J. S. Bradshaw in *Problems and Progress in Medical Care* (1972) and discussed in P. Robertshaw, *Rethinking Legal Need: The Case of Criminal Justice* (1991). Felt need is limited because it is what the client may want without any idea of what may be available, whereas expressed need is "'felt' need translated into action, or economic demand".

[26] See Royal Commission on Legal Services, *Report, Vol.1* (1978), para.2.2 and the Marre Committee (1988), para.7.3.

[27] cl.12. Further definitions appear in Sch.2.

[28] Generally, documents relating to the transfer and registration of land.

[29] Categorisation is essential for initial teaching, but is not determinative of what the law can do.

"reserved legal activity" and one can imagine advisory organisations, not authorised under the new system, pragmatically determined to categorise an ambivalent
problem as outside the ambit of Pt 3 in order to keep the client's business.[30]

The advantages of this broad approach are: first, there is less of a risk of
inappropriately distinguishing legal and, say, social problems which may, of
course, overlap for some clients.[31] Secondly, there is an encouragement to clients
to make use of legal services, because they can identify lawyers or other
regulated advisers as one of the "correct" agencies to approach. The task for
lawyers (as opposed to other advisers) under this new regime will, then, be to
demonstrate that in breadth of areas of work, in accessibility, price and particularly in quality, they can compete with other regulated providers of legal
services. One of the objectives of the Legal Services Bill in providing for
authorisation of other providers of legal services and alternative business structures for lawyers is to "encourage competition in legal services and the promotion of choice".[32] Thirdly, a new remedy or novel application of the law may
result from the approach, because of the need for imagination on the part of the
lawyer or other adviser.

In recent research by the Legal Services Research Centre,[33] following on from
Genn's major study five years earlier,[34] 5,611 respondents to an initial screening
interview were asked about their experiences of problems in a number of
categories.[35] They were also asked about involvement in court proceedings. Of
the respondents 1,623 then proceeded to a face-to-face interview where they
were asked, *inter alia*, about advice and information: outcomes, resolution
processes and sources of financial assistance in relation to one problem that they
had identified. Of those participating in the screening interview, 37 per cent
identified that they had had at least one justiciable problem falling within those
categories in the relevant period[36]:

	Percentage
Consumer	13.3
Neighbours	8.4
Money/debt	8.3
Employment	6.1

---

[30] Note that the activities of claims management companies are now regulated under the Compensation Act 2006.

[31] For an early criticism of this dichotomy, see P. Morris, R. Cooper and A. Byles, "Public Attitudes
to Problem Definition and Problem Solving: A Pilot Study" (1973–74) 3 Brit. J. Social Work 301.
Issues about linked problems and "cycles of decline" entered by those would are ground down
by and cannot resolve, multiple problems, ultimately leading to additional use of NHS, police and
benefits resources is addressed in DCA, *Getting Earlier, Better Advice to Vulnerable People*
(2006), p.7.

[32] *Putting Consumers First, op. cit.* p.26.

[33] Pleasence *et al.*, *Causes of Action: Civil Law and Social Justice* (2004, Legal Services Commission). See also Genn *et al.* (2004).

[34] Genn (1999).

[35] Pleasence *et al.*, *op.cit.* p.4.

[36] *ibid.*, table 2.1, p.14. Perhaps not surprisingly, 52 per cent of respondents to a parallel survey of
120 people in temporary accommodation identified problems relating to rented accommodation;
ibid., p.30.

	Percentage
Personal injury	3.9
Rented housing	3.8
Owned housing	2.4
Welfare benefits	2.3
Relationship breakdown	2.2
Divorce	2.2
Children	1.9
Clincial negligence	1.6
Domestic violence	1.6
Discrimination	1.4
Unfair treatment by the police	0.7
Homelessness	0.6
Mental health	0.5
Immigration	0.3

We have indicated what we consider to be the best working definition of a legal problem, as well as that shortly to be imposed by regulatory legislation, but the discussion will be redundant unless there is an effective means of ensuring that those who have legal problems, however defined, secure legal assistance. It is this problem that we go on to address.

C. THE COMMUNITY LEGAL SERVICE AND THE MEETING OF NEED

One reason for the introduction of the Community Legal Service (CLS) was to endeavour to ensure that there was a meeting of legal need by reorganising the way in which legal assistance was funded in civil cases. The CLS Development Fund provides funds to assist CLS Regional Offices to address local need. The current five-year strategy of the CLS,[37] *Making Legal Rights a Reality*, launched in March 2006, draws on the research of Pleasence *et al.*, and proposes "an increased focus on the needs of the client" (in principle the individual, rather than, for example, the small business client) as well as working in partnership

9–005

---

[37] Following consultation in *Making Legal Rights a Reality* (Legal Services Commission, 2005). See also the Legal Services Commission *Annual Report 2005/6* (2006).

with other funding providers, particularly local authorities.[38] Among the methods
by which this objective is to be met is the creation of Community Legal Advice
Centres and Networks to deliver assistance in relation to a broad range of social
welfare issues, and to take "legal services to groups of people that currently do
not access mainstream services . . . and to clients that are particularly vulnerable . . . "[39] as well as expansion of the existing CLS Direct telephone information service.[40]

D. LEGAL PROBLEMS AND THE USE OF LAWYERS

9–006 The best people to assist with legal problems are not always lawyers. So, for
example, trading standards departments in local authorities have always been
highly skilled in handling consumer problems and Citizens Advice Bureaux have
been and continue to be a major source of advice on a wide range of problems.[41]
The current strategy of the CLS is to "provide access to a service which ranges
from basic advice to legal representation in the full range of social welfare
problems as well as children and family problems".[42] As we have seen, the Legal
Services Bill is intended to broaden the range of individuals and bodies providing
regulated legal services.

1. WHO USES SOLICITORS?

9–007 A person may use a solicitor for a variety of purposes. Large corporations, to the
extent that they do not employ in-house lawyers, have the ability either to employ
their own lawyers and/or to set criteria for the engagement of independent firms
of lawyers to deliver the services that they require on a privately funded basis. In
these cases, the client can be the powerful player in the lawyer/client relationship.
However, where individuals or small or medium-sized enterprises are the clients,
then the position may be and often is very different and, since public CLS
funding is not available to businesses, the small or medium-sized business
enterprise may experience unmet legal need on economic grounds, except to the
extent that it is able to rely on third party funding by its directors or shareholders
or through private sector insurance, whether specifically for legal expenses or
otherwise. Thus, individuals and small businesses may use solicitors for a
relatively narrow range of work and, as we shall see, may be wary of using them

---

[38] *Making Legal Rights a Reality* (LSC, March 2006) and endorsed by *Getting Earlier, Better Advice
to Vulnerable People* (DCA, March 2006).
[39] *ibid.* p.8.
[40] *ibid.* p.6.
[41] See below, para.10–008. In the further discussion of the data used by Pleasence *et al.*, in Genn
et al. (2004), p.21 "about one in four of those who obtained advice went directly to a solicitor for
advice and just under one-fifth went directly to a CAB". Other first advisers reported included
local authorities, other advice agencies, trades unions, employers, the police, insurance companies, social workers, ombudsmen, housing associations, health professionals, court staff,
barristers, religious bodies, social security offices, the media and other consultants.
[42] *Making Legal Rights a Reality, op. cit.*, p.2.

for a variety of reasons including ignorance of their value and concerns over cost and accessibility.

A 2000 survey of clients' experience of using a solicitor for personal matters largely confirmed the result of earlier studies:[43] 16 per cent of adults had consulted a solicitor within the previous 12 months. The most common reason for consulting a solicitor was conveyancing or other issues related to buying and selling a home (28 per cent), with divorce; matrimonial[44] and child care matters; will-making; compensation for personal injury or medical accident and probate being the next most common.[45] This survey also revealed that the clients who used a solicitor "were more likely to be male, aged 25–54 and in social grades ABC1 (professional, managerial and non-manual workers), compared with the general population. Conveyancing clients tended to be aged 25–44, while clients seeking help with wills and probate were typically at the older end of the age range".[46] This is not surprising given the ages at which people are likely to be able to afford their own accommodation and at which they consider their own mortality or become the potential beneficiaries of a deceased relative. Clients from social grade E (dependent on state benefits) were a relatively large proportion of those seeking advice in relation to divorce.[47] "Injury compensation clients were typically in the youngest age groups and were the only group skewed towards social grade C2 (skilled manual workers)."[48] Provision of legal advice on such matters by trade unions may be part of the explanation for this.[49] Indeed, some of the explanations may well lie in the awareness of the availability of legal advice within certain groups of the community or, in the case of personal injury claims in particular, aggressively marketed claims management activity.

Having ruled out trivial problems, Pleasance *et al.* (2004) found that, of those respondents who took any action to try to resolve their problem, 63 per cent sought formal advice (25 per cent of first advisers being solicitors)[50]; the remainder, with or without informal assistance from books, the Internet or friends and family, most often contacted their opponent and sought to negotiate a resolution, only 2 per cent of these people then going on to issue proceedings; 2

---

[43] R. Craig, M. Rigg, R. Briscoe and P. Smith, *Clients' Experiences of Using a Solicitor for Personal Matters* (Law Society Research Study No. 40, 2001). M. Zander (1969) 66 L.S. Gaz. 174; Morris, Cooper and Byles (1973–74); Adamsdown Community Trust (1978); R.C.L.S., Vol.2, s.8, pp.173–198; Research Surveys of Great Britain (1986); Jenkins, Skordaki and Willis (1989), Ch.5; J. Jenkins and V. Lewis, *Client Perceptions—Existing and Potential Clients: Experience and Perceptions of Using a Solicitor for Personal Matters* (1995). For a survey of client perceptions of non-lawyer advisers, see J. Johnstone and J. Mason, *Advice Agencies, Advisors and their Clients; Perceptions of Quality* (DCA Research Series 10/05, December 2005). See also T. Hilton and S. Migdal, "Why clients need, rather than want, lawyers" (2005) 12 (1) Int. J. Legal Prof. 145.

[44] Pleasence *et al.*, *op. cit.*, p.53, suggest, in reporting that 18 per cent of those who failed to take action on relationship breakdown did so because of costs concerns, that "cost concerns in relation to problems ancillary to relationship breakdown reflect a general perception that such problems should be dealt with through a solicitor".

[45] *ibid.*. para.1.2.

[46] *ibid.*

[47] *ibid.*

[48] *ibid.*

[49] See below, para.10–011. The claims management organisations who entered this market at about the same time as this survey had probably had too little impact at this point to have had a significant effect but see the Blackwell report, below at para.9–011.

[50] *op. cit.*, p.72.

per cent using an ombudsman and 1 per cent a mediation provider.[51] However, of those who took formal advice, 11 per cent approached their opponent; 3 per cent used an ombudsman and 7 per cent a mediation provider. The likelihood of individuals who took any action seeking formal advice was tied strongly to the type of problem. So, for example, whilst action was less likely than inaction in domestic violence cases, of those who took action, the vast majority sought formal advice. Consumer, mental health and debt problems frequently prompted action, but action without formal legal advice; whereas homelessness, relationship breakdown and divorce were more likely to prompt the taking of formal legal advice.[52] Factors relating to the individual, his or her employment status and educational background also affected whether or not formal advice was taken; as was the importance and monetary value of the dispute.

Where someone did not take action, the reason for doing so was also tied to the type of problem, a belief that nothing could be done being prevalent in mental health and discrimination claims but much less so in personal injury claims, which Pleasance *et al.* suggest might be the result of the proliferation of advertisement by claims management companies and others offering "no win; no fee" arrangements in that sector.[53] Personal injury claims were, however, the most likely to be thought of as insufficiently important to be worth acting on, whilst no respondent gave that as a reason for a failure to act in a divorce matter (where action was often thought to be unnecessary because it was being taken by the other party). This reflects the prevalence of undefended, effectively consensual divorce. Concerns about the length of time it might take to resolve a problem were most frequently reported in consumer and money cases.[54]

Where someone did seek advice (usually after attempting to resolve the matter themselves), solicitors were most likely to be the first port of call in divorce, relationship breakdown and housing; whilst the police were the most frequent resort in cases of domestic violence. Some types of problem, particularly consumer, employment, money, personal injury, benefits and children showed a very broad spread of initial contacts including local councils, employers,[55] insurers and "other" advice agencies.[56]

However, many respondents—15 per cent of the respondents who sought advice being unsuccessful in doing so[57]—sought advice subsequently from other agencies, whether through referral (e.g. by a CAB to a solicitor[58]) or as a result of confusion about the plethora of advice agencies in operation, described by

---

[51] Mediation providers in non-commercial cases may be provided through a court-annexed scheme or through a specialist local provider such as Bristol Mediation or Bristol Family Mediation.

[52] This information is taken from Pleasance *et al.* (2004), Ch.3.

[53] It was also found that no respondents reported failing to take action in personal injury cases because of the length of time likely to be involved. This might also be the result of advertising over-simplifying the procedure required to pursue a claim in this sector.

[54] Information in *ibid.* Ch.3.

[55] 22 per cent of those seeking advice about disputes with their employer first obtained advice from that employer, *ibid.* p.71.

[56] *ibid.* Figure 3.9.

[57] *ibid.* p.62. Pleasance *et al.* identify that what unsuccessful might mean (at least when not related simply to an inability to make contact or obtain a convenient appointment, particularly for those in employment) will differ according to the individual concerned: "[a] n adviser being unable to help potentially covers a range of possibilities: that the adviser was not in a position to give advice about the respondent's problem; that they did not know the answer to the respondent's questions; or, that they did not think there was anything that could be done about the respondent's problem", *ibid.* p.62.

[58] Genn *et al.* (2004) p.29 report that trades unions, insurers and CABx were the most likely first advisers to refer clients on to a solicitor.

Pleasence *et al.* as "the advice maze".[59] The Legal Services Commission strategy for 2006–11 seeks to promote integration of advice provision and links between different providers in an attempt to alleviate this problem.[60]

2. IGNORANCE AND APATHY

Genn discovered in some of her early work that ignorance of the law did dissuade **9–008** some potential claimants from seeking legal advice in relation to personal injuries, and legal advice was often only sought after other sources of advice, which often was ill-informed, had been accessed.[61] The Marre Committee was subsequently convinced that ignorance was a major cause of people not seeking legal advice even when it was appropriate.[62] Further, some people take the view that "it's not worth pursuing it" or "let's just forget about it" or "it's just one of those things".

This type of apathy is a major reason in explaining why people do not seek legal advice.[63] This was confirmed by subsequent work undertaken by Professor Genn.[64] A fifth of the problems reported to Pleasence *et al.*[65] were not acted on, that inaction most frequently being founded on:

> "[a] belief that nothing could be done, indicating a lack of knowledge about obligations, rights, remedies and procedures on the part of the general public. Of even more concern, respondents sometimes reported having taken no action because they were too scared[66] to act. This was as common

[59] *ibid.* p.68. Genn *et al.* (2004), considering the same point, comment "[g]iven the lack of fit between some of the choices of first adviser with the type of problem being experienced, this finding suggests that there is considerable scope for improving public consciousness about appropriate sources of advice for particular types of problems". *Ibid.* p.20. As an example of the breadth of such provision in the social welfare context, see Michael Bell Associates *A Strategy for Advice Services in Nottingham* (2005) commissioned by Nottingham City Council and available on its website at *http://www.nottinghamcity.gov.uk/sitemap/reports_and_guides*. This identifies, *inter alia*, sources of funding for advice services ranging from the local authority, Legal Services Commission and other central government (including regeneration funding available to particularly disadvantaged areas) through the European Social Fund, the private sector and charities. Agencies participating in the review and providing free assistance in the field of social welfare law included the law centres and CABx but also local community advice centres and charities such as Shelter and the Deaf Society. Student advice services were also identified as providers of such advice and it was recommended that as "there is also likely to be information and advice being provided by many community support organisations . . . it would be useful to map the level and type of provision and ensure that these groups are provided with the appropriate level of advice and support to ensure they provide quality information services and can make appropriate referrals to other legal advice providers when necessary" *ibid.* p.29.

[60] See also DCA, *Getting Earlier, Better Advice to Vulnerable People* (2006), pp.9–11.

[61] H. Genn, "Who Claims Compensation: Factors Associated with Claiming and Obtaining Damages" in D. Harris *et al.*, *Compensation and Support for Illness and Injury* (1984), esp. pp.75–76, 65–67.

[62] The Committee on the Future of the Legal Profession, *A Time for Change* (1988), Chair: Lady Marre [hereafter, the Marre Committee], paras 7.17–7.39.

[63] Genn (1984).

[64] *Paths to Justice* (1999).

[65] This proportion was higher in the more socially excluded group surveyed in a parallel study of those in temporary accommodation where it rose to 28% (Genn *et al.* 2004), p.14.

[66] Genn *et al.* (2004) give a figure of about 25% of those with a domestic violence problem and 14% of those with problems with neighbours being in this category, p.15.

a reason for inaction as concerns about the time it can take to resolve problems, and a more common reason than concerns about costs."[67]

Whilst ignorance may sometimes be a problem,[68] Genn *et al.* (2004) report that "[a]bout one-quarter of respondents said that there were advisers that they had considered contacting, but in the end did not do so".[69] They also found a degree of "referral fatigue" as the more clients were referred on by one adviser to a different adviser; the less likely they were actually to make contact with the second and subsequent source of assistance.[70]

Recommendations for dealing with the problem of legal apathy, connected to the current government's agenda on social exclusion[71] appear in both Department for Constitutional Affairs (DCA) (from May 9, 2007, Ministry of Justice) and Legal Services Commission current strategies. A Public Legal Education And Support Task Force has been created by the DCA under the chairmanship of Professor Genn[72] and the Legal Services Commission strategy includes "information and education about legal rights and responsibilities" amongst its priority areas of work.[73]

3. The Public Image

9–009 The image of an advice-giving agency is crucial because it is at the stage of identifying an appropriate agency that most people are obstructed in solving their problem.[74] A repeat player's impression of his or her first contact with a solicitor will be telling. Where the client is a first time player, identifying an agency with a strong image will assist. In a 2000 survey of clients' experiences of using a solicitor for personal matters, it was reported that most clients used smaller firms of solicitors. Forty per cent used firms with 2–4 partners and approximately 33 per cent used firms with 5–10 partners, whereas only 10 per cent used a large firm (which is hardly surprising since many large firms increasingly offer little to private clients and may well be intimidating or impossible to access off the street)

---

[67] *op. cit.* p.86.

[68] Genn's research in 1999also revealed "a depth of ignorance about the legal system and a widespread inability to distinguish between criminal and civil courts:" *ibid.* p.247.

[69] *op. cit.* p.16

[70] *ibid.* p.31

[71] For earlier suggestions, see The Marre Committee (1988), paras 7.20–7.39; R. Smith (ed.), *Shaping the Future* (1995), Pt III and Genn (1999), p.255

[72] The remit of public legal education being stated as working "to ensure that people:
   • are aware of their legal rights and responsibilities and can recognise where the law can provide a remedy;
   • understand key legal issues and processes;
   • have the confidence and skills [to] deal with their problems;
   • and know where to go to get help": PLEAS website: *http://www.pleas.org.uk.*

[73] LSC, *Making Legal Rights a Reality 2006–2011* (2006), p.4. The other two priorities are stated as "individual acts of advice and representation" and "strategic action to address the need for advice and representation".

[74] The Marre Committee (1988), paras 7.48–7.93. See also DCA, *Getting Earlier, Better Advice to Vulnerable People* (2006) p.9: "people need clear, well-known brands to help them navigate the range of services available . . . ".

and 5 per cent used a sole practitioner.[75] Further, it was reported that the most important reason for choosing a law firm was a recommendation from someone else, followed by previous experience of the firm, the good reputation of the firm and convenient offices.[76] Small and medium-sized business clients, however, routinely sought advice on legal matters from advisers such as accountants, auditors, surveyors, architects and employment consultants, one reason for doing so being that other professionals were seen as better informed and more up to date than solicitors.[77]

The 2000 clients' experiences survey reported that:

"more than half of all those seeking legal advice in the last 12 months felt that their law firm had been very good overall, and well over three-quarters felt that it had been good or very good. At the other end of the scale, one in ten rated the firm as poor or very poor, and a similar proportion rated it fair. Clients involved in wills or probate cases were the most likely to give positive ratings, whereas for conveyancing and particularly divorce or injury cases, views were slightly less favourable. The key reasons given for a positive rating were that the people handling their case had been very experienced and professional, that they did everything the client wanted, were efficient and provided a good service. Poor ratings were most often put down to generally poor service, with further mentions of inefficiency, things taking longer than necessary, not showing an interest in the client and not keeping the client informed . . . 83 per cent of clients rated their solicitor[78] good or very good overall, the majority saying that he/she was very good (60 per cent). Only 7 per cent of clients rated their solicitor poor; divorce clients were the most likely to do this."[79]

The Marre Committee indicated that there are two particular problems with the image of lawyers. First, there is a fear of lawyers. They are unapproachable because of the inaccessibility of their premises and their unwelcoming nature, their work methods do not tie in with client needs and they show a poor response to the needs of linguistic minorities. The Committee recommended greater use of shop premises, innovative work practices, use of interpreters and that people from cultural and ethnic minorities be supported, by the professional bodies, in entering the legal profession.[80] Secondly, there is dissatisfaction with lawyers.[81] It seems fairly clear that the Law Society's initiatives in client care are having some impact[82] and other work may be making a difference.[83] Also, Genn et al.

---

[75] R. Craig, M. Rigg, R. Briscoe and P. Smith, *Clients' Experiences of Using a Solicitor for Personal Matters* (Law Society Research Study No.40, 2001), para.1.2. A parallel study of 250 business clients, J. Hall, *Client Views: Small and Medium-sized Enterprises*, was published by the Law Society in 2004.

[76] R. Craig, M. Rigg, R. Briscoe and P. Smith, *op. cit.*

[77] J. Hall, *Client Views: Small and Medium-sized Enterprises* (Law Society, 2004).

[78] As opposed to the firm.

[79] R. Craig, M. Rigg, R. Briscoe and P. Smith, *Clients' Experiences of Using a Solicitor for Personal Matters* (Law Society Research Study No.40, 2001), paras 1.4 and 1.7.

[80] The Marre Committee (1988), paras 7.40–7.47. As to the recruitment of lawyers from ethnic minorities, see above, para.3–051 and such measures as the Law Society's Diversity Access Scheme.

[81] *ibid.* paras 7.48–7.93.

[82] See above, para.3–036, but note the comments of the Legal Services Ombudsman, at para.3–043.

[83] See above, Ch.3

in 2004 found that more than 60 per cent of their respondents who had used a solicitor would definitely recommend that solicitor to others, and a further 20 per cent would probably do so.[84] Nevertheless, government has seen fit to create legislation—the Legal Services Bill—one of whose objectives is to supervise the regulation of the profession to "protect and promote consumers' interests".[85] Traditionally law centres have not suffered from the problems associated with solicitors' firms, but they have a different attitude and agenda.

4. COST, ACCESSIBILITY AND BARRIERS

9–010   Genn, in her 1999 study, identified cost as a noticeable barrier to accessing legal advice. In Genn *et al.* (2004), where clients were dissatisfied with solicitors, reasons given were "not giving the kind of help needed (45%), . . . the quality of advice offered (49%) . . . being too expensive (29%)".[86] 75 per cent of that sample is reported by Pleasence *et al.*, using the same data, as not having had to pay for the advice received, either because no charge was made at all (e.g. police, local authority, advice centre or CAB) or because fees were covered by LSC funding, trade unions, employers, legal expenses insurers, friends and family or some form of conditional fee agreement[87] and none of the sample paid for advice in full.[88] Outside the remit of the LSC, however, cost, the management of costs and keeping the client informed about costs were identified as problems by some clients in the 2004 small and medium-sized enterprise study; and although reasonableness of fees was placed only sixth on the list of factors involved in choosing a law firm; of the 51 interviewed clients, 86 per cent indicated that reasonableness of fees was excellent or very good. A frequent reason given by these clients for seeking advice from other sources such as banks or accountants was, however, that of cost.[89]

The cost of legal advice will continue to be a problem, because professional services are expensive. However, advice to individuals is available through the CLS and there continues to be a commitment to a range of means of paying for legal services within the private sector (particularly representation through the so-called "no win, no fee" system)[90] and a commitment to driving the costs of the various aspects of the legal system down wherever possible. Of course, perception of cost as well as actual cost may be a problem. Genn's 1999 research revealed that, in the main survey, "about three out of four respondents disagreed or strongly disagreed with the suggestion that lawyers' charges were reasonable for the work that they do (72 per cent)".[91] When advice had been received, there was some increase in the feeling that the charges were reasonable.[92] It is also

---

[84] Genn *et al.* (2004) *op. cit.* p.33. CABx, overall, had similar results in the category "definitely" and slightly better results in the category "probably".

[85] DCA, *The Future of Legal Services: Putting Consumers First* (2005, Cm. 6679), p.20.

[86] Genn *et al.* (2004) *op. cit.* p.34.

[87] *ibid.* p.80.

[88] *ibid.* p.82.

[89] J. Hall, *op. cit.* The most important factor in choice of law firm was "willingness to keep you up to date with progress".

[90] This is the conditional fee system, see below, para.11–007.

[91] Genn (1999), p.236.

[92] "About 18% agreed or strongly agreed that lawyers' charges were reasonable for the work that they do as compared with only 11% of those who had obtained non-legal advice about their problem and 14% of those who had handled their problem without advice:" *ibid.* p.238.

important to note that this research revealed a view that "the legal system works better for the rich than the poor".[93] However, there was some evidence in 1999 that there was a perception that legal aid was gradually being withdrawn,[94] which would have raised concerns about costs. Nevertheless, Pleasance *et al.* also report that "[w]ith solicitors, respondents were most likely to abandon a strategy of obtaining advice because of concerns about cost, although these concerns appeared to be based more on assumptions about the cost of solicitors' services than estimates provided by solicitors themselves".[95]

As regards the geographical aspect of accessibility, Pleasence *et al.*, although reporting complaints about accessibility of advice services because of, for example, difficulties in getting through on the telephone, comment that "[o]nly rarely did respondents complain that they had been unable to obtain advice because an adviser had been too far away".[96] Nevertheless, respondents more often reported actually being successful in obtaining advice from solicitors and insurance companies: "[t]his reflects the ease of use of insurance companies' legal help lines and the geographical distribution of solicitors' firms, as well as the commercial nature of both of these types of adviser".[97] Local authorities and insurances companies, however, whilst more accessible than, for example, CABx, were less likely to be able to provide any actual assistance.[98] Much information is, of course, now available on the Internet, although the DCA noted difficulty in finding government-funded advice websites and their complexity once found.[99]

A fundamental barrier to the obtaining of advice remains at present, however, the plethora of advice agencies in existence and the lack of consistency and communication between them. So, for example, the DCA in its 2006 paper *Getting Earlier, Better Advice to Vulnerable People* comments that:

> "the majority of the independent advice sector is made up of a large number of small providers. This means that a key barrier to people obtaining independent advice is being unaware of where to go, which often results in people not seeking advice at all, or seeking it from the wrong provider. Those who try to obtain advice from the wrong place are rarely signposted elsewhere and, even if they are, the suggested alternative is often still unsuitable ... we believe that this low awareness and lack of effective referral between advice providers is a result of the uncoordinated way that Government funds and commissions these services. The result is a fragmented and uncoordinated provider base, which is confusing for the public, and where resources for awareness raising activity are spread thinly."[100]

Current strategy of both the DCA (now Ministry of Justice) and the Legal Services Commission is, therefore, directed to consistency by, *inter alia*, the creation of Community Legal Advice Centres and better communication between providers.

---

[93] "Almost three-quarters of respondents agreed or strongly agreed with [that] proposition": *ibid.* p.234.
[94] *ibid.* p.235.
[95] *op. cit.* p.66.
[96] *ibid.* p.65.
[97] *ibid.* p.65.
[98] *ibid.* p.66.
[99] DCA, *Getting Earlier, Better Advice to Vulnerable People* (2006), p.8.
[100] *ibid.* p.9.

E. OVERMET LEGAL NEED—THE "COMPENSATION CULTURE"?

9–011 Particularly where the private sector is involved in the meeting of legal need, the possibility arises that individuals who might not otherwise have pursued legal claims might be actively recruited to do so inappropriately; the recruiter having a financial interest in the business of recruiting claimants (sometimes described as "claims farming") and managing the claims at least to a negotiated result if not into litigation.[101] Clearly, if an individual has a legitimate claim with prospects of success in court, he or she should not be precluded from pursuing it and such activity is a way of meeting a perceived legal need at least in some[102] sectors, particularly that of personal injury work. There is, however, concern in the media and in the current government of the development of a

> "'compensation culture' where people believe that they can seek compensation for any misfortune that befalls them, even if no-one else is to blame. This mis-perception undermines personal responsibility and respect for the law and creates unnecessary burdens through an exaggerated fear of litigation."[103]

In fact, as we will see in Ch.12, the number of claims proceeding through the courts has dropped substantially in recent years, but this does not prevent the potential development of a public perception to the contrary. For example, research commissioned by the DCA and the Advertising Standards Authority found 50 per cent of respondents to a survey assuming that the number of false claims for personal injury had increased over the previous five years, an assumption perhaps based on the amount of advertising on television, in the press and elsewhere (as in GPs' or hospital waiting rooms,[104] for example) by commercial claims management companies.[105] Such advertising, it was found, sometimes tended to over-estimate the simplicity of making a claim; did not necessarily

---

[101] Such organisations may act as referral organisations so that claims are then passed on to solicitors on the organisation's "panel" but in some cases the organisation will deal with the initial stages, seeking to negotiate a result for the client, with the claim only being passed on to solicitors (who may pay a "referral fee") if negotiation fails and litigation is the next result. Referral fees, governed from July 1, 2007 by the Solicitors *Code of Conduct 2007*, Rules 8 and 9 (replacing the Solicitors Introduction and Referral Code 1990), are also currently controversial. See, for example, Anon, "The ins and outs of referral fees" (2006) 103(3) L.S.G. 31.

[102] *Effects of Advertising in Respect of Compensation Claims for Personal Injuries* (DCA, 2006)

[103] DCA, *Tackling the Compensation Culture: Government Response to the Better Regulation Task Force Report: "Better Routes to Redress"* (November 2004), p.1. A Constitutional Affairs Select Committee was formed in December 2005 to address issues surrounding the existence or prevention of a compensation culture: see *Government Response to the Constitutional Affairs Select Committee's Reports: "Compensation culture" and "Compensation culture: NHS Redress Bill"* (May 2006, Cm. 6784).

[104] The Better Regulation Task Force, *Better Routes to Redress*, (May 2004) recommended that the NHS regulate what was permitted to be advertised on their premises.

[105] Another source of misleading expectations identified in *Better Routes to Redress*, p.13 is the media, both as to the ease of pursuing apparently frivolous claims and the amount of compensation claimed or awarded. One might recall that awards of damages in the USA in particular are calculated on a different basis to the approach taken in this jurisdiction, and are frequently awarded by a jury (see the discussion of the effect of a jury on damages awards in Ch.15). In addition, the facts of a case are more complex than the urban myth it has generated, *see Liebeck v McDonald's Restaurants PTS Inc*, 1995 WL 360309, not fully reported but discussed in P. Ryan, "Revisiting the United States Application of Punitive Damages: Separating Myth from Reality" (2003) 10(1) ILSA J. of Int'l and Comp. Law 69 and in *Better Routes to Redress* at p.13.

make the link between the existence of a claim and the possibility of having to pursue it through the courts; did not necessarily make it clear that someone had to be at fault before compensation would be awarded; and were not always clear about the meaning of the so-called "no win, no fee" funding arrangements being offered.[106] Concern about the activities of claims management organisations, which had swelled to take advantage of the shift from legal aid to private sector funding of personal injury cases in particular,[107] were raised in 2000 in the *Report of the Lord Chancellor's Committee to Investigate the Activities of Non-Legally Qualified Claims Assessors and Employment Advisers* ("The Blackwell Report")[108] which suggested that although it was at that time premature to regulate such organisations by legislation, some form of quality control might be advisable. Two substantial players in the sector subsequently failed rather dramatically.[109] Whilst the Claims Standards Federation (previously the Claims Standards Council) was suggested as a potential regulator for the sector, it is consistent with the move towards more active central regulation of legal services seen in the Legal Services Bill that, ultimately, following recommendations in the Better Regulation Task Force paper *Better Routes to Redress* in May 2004, a legislative solution was devised which now appears in Pt 2 of the Compensation Act 2006, regulating the provision of "advice or other services in relation to the making of a claim", including:

"(i) the provision of financial services or assistance,

(ii) the provision of services by way of or in relation to legal representation,

(iii) referring or introducing one person to another, and

(iv) making inquiries [other than in the context of giving evidence as, for example, an expert witness]."[110]

The compensation culture is, however, thought to be more a creature of the media and public fear than an actual impediment to the resolution of well-founded claims, although there remains a Parliamentary Under-Secretary of State at the time of writing with this topic within her official remit.[111]

---

[106] Consumers, naturally, tended to notice the "no fee" part of this description. Whilst in some cases it may be the case that in the absence of a failure to recover, no payment will be required, in some cases the client is still expected to pay expenses such as court fees and experts' fees. Note also that the statement says nothing about the kind of fee that will be charged in the event of the client *winning*. Where litigation has not been commenced, that fee may be assessed as a percentage of the compensation awarded (see the Blackwell Report and *Better Routes to Redress, op. cit.* pp.20 *et seq.*). The complexity of some payment arrangements can be seen clearly in *In The Matter Of Claims Direct Test Cases* [2003] EWCA Civ 136 and *Accident Group Test Cases (No.2)* [2004] EWCA Civ 575.

[107] *Better Routes to Redress*, p.21.

[108] LCD, February 2000.

[109] Claims Direct, see "Insult added to injury as Claims Direct gives in", *The Independent*, August 11, 2001 and The Accident Group, see "This disaster was no Accident", *telegraph.co.uk*, June 11, 2003.

[110] s.4.

[111] See, for example the statement in DCA, *Making a Difference: Taking Forward Our Priorities* (May 2005), p.7: "[w]e will tackle any practices that encourage people to make spurious claims against people or organisations that are not to blame for other people's actions or misfortune . . . We will clamp down on advertising that creates false expectations about the chances of making a successful claim or excessive compensation, particularly in the public sector . . . Where there is no blame, there should be no claim."

F. MEETING UNMET LEGAL NEED

9–012 Legal aid was the traditional means of meeting otherwise unmet need. The Labour government has taken the view that unmet need is a problem of social exclusion and so has put the requirement to meet the need high on its list of priorities. "Social exclusion is what happens when people or areas suffer from a combination of linked problems such as lack of access to services, unemployment, poor skills, low incomes, poor housing, crime, poor health and family breakdowns".[112] Pleasance *et al.* suggest that, whilst there was a wide range of government and government-funded agencies, "public investment needs to be co-ordinated to reduce duplication of effort, to prevent initiative being at odds and to best bring about government objectives" and that, on the basis of their findings, resources could be more accurately targeted at those who felt that nothing could be done or were scared to take action, and to "those advisers who people naturally gravitate towards" as well as pointing out the potential for expansion of and liaison within the private sector.[113] Current government strategy, as expressed by the DCA (now Ministry of Justice), seeks to address such problems in the public sector by promoting co-ordination and consistency of advice under three heads:

- "advice is people focused—dealing with the many problems and disputes that individuals may face, rather than dealing with each problem in isolation;
- Advice is right first time—so that wherever people go to get advice, they are able to access the advice they need to resolve their problems and disputes; and
- We learn from our mistakes—people's needs for advice are a detailed indication of where services fail to deliver."[114]

---

[112] Lord Chancellor's Department, *Social Exclusion* (2001), *www.lcd.gov.uk.* using the Social Exclusion Unit's definition from July 2000.

[113] *op. cit.* p.117

[114] DCA, *Getting Earlier, Better Advice to Vulnerable People* (2006), p.12. In related moves to simplify claims in other ways, the NHS Redress Act 2006 provides for a compensation system that would allow "redress to be provided without recourse to civil proceedings" in claims against the NHS, for example low value clinical negligence claims. On a similar model there is at present a Consumers, Estate Agents and Redress Bill 2006–07 requiring some suppliers to have consumer complaints systems. Streamlined processes are also being suggested in debt claims (DCA, *Debt Programme: Position Paper*, March 2005), including a "pre-action notice" to be sent by creditors to debtors prior to resorting to court proceedings which explicitly encourages the debtor to seek the help of CABx or specialist debt advice organisations.

INFORMATION AND ADVICE SERVICES

By discussing in the preceding chapter the ways in which the public may **10–001** perceive a problem as a "legal" problem and the steps which the profession might take to assist in the identification of problems requiring legal advice for their solution, we have already indicated that we are concerned, in the main, with the provision of information and advice by lawyers. However, legal advice has never been provided solely by lawyers; the Community Legal Service (CLS) is not established on the basis that lawyers will be the only source of legal advice and information and, as we have seen, the Legal Services Bill allows for and promotes the provision of legal services by other means. Further, the focus has been on individuals accessing legal information and advice. When it is companies or other businesses, particularly large organisations, different factors apply. Here there are fewer problems associated with ignorance or concerns over cost. Many business clients require law firms to bid for business in so-called "beauty parades" and in so doing the firms must convince their prospective clients that they will provide quality and value for money. It is only when we turn back to individuals that we see the problems arising. Indeed, the government elected in May 1997 sees access to legal services as one strand in its desire to tackle social exclusion[1] and has continued to express that view.[2]

---

[1] Lord Chancellor's Department, *Social Exclusion* (2001), *www.lcd.gov.uk.*
[2] In, for example, *Getting Earlier, Better Advice to Vulnerable People.*

The Legal Services Commission (LSC) is the organisation responsible from 2000 for "legal aid".[3] It does so through two arms: the Criminal Defence Service for criminal cases and the CLS for civil and family cases.[4] The "core objective" of the CLS is to "protect and promote people's rights"[5] with a particular current focus on "those threatened with loss of liberty; vulnerable children; those suffering domestic violence; those suffering from "maladministration or challengeable lack of service by public authorities" and the socially excluded. Its core objective is sought to be attained through three priority areas of work: individual acts of advice and representation; "strategic action to address the need for advice and representation" and public legal education. The CLS is a network of organisations "which funds, provides and promotes civil legal services".[6] Funding is provided to organisations by entering into contracts with such suppliers, provided they have attained the relevant quality assurance standards recognised as "quality marks".

The best means of approaching the organisation of the CLS is to look to the quality marks since these vary according the service provided by the organisation in question. The three main quality marks available are Information Services, General Help and Specialist Help.[7]

Information Services

10–002   This level is for information points that rely on the public accessing information themselves rather than on advice being provided on action a specific client might take. Services are sub-divided into "self-help information" and "assisted information".

Self help information points would include places—such as local councils and libraries—providing access to leaflets and directories (such as the CLS Legal Adviser Directory) and/or websites (including CLS Direct[8]).

10–003   *Assisted information* is for organisations that have a dedicated information service, although this does not have to be the sole purpose of the organisation. There should be staff who are able to help clients access information, to identify where a client needs further information or advice and help clients select an appropriate service where they will be able to receive this. The service will not provide advice.[9]

---

[3] Access to Justice Act 1999. For a comparative view of current provision, see J. Flood, A. Whyte, "What's wrong with legal aid? Lessons from outside the UK" (2006) 25(Jan) C.J.Q. 80.

[4] Its research arm, the Legal Services Research Centre, is responsible for much of the material referred to in Ch.9.

[5] LSC, *Making Legal Rights a Reality, The Legal Services Commission's Strategy for the Community Legal Service 2006–2011* (2006) at p.4. See also DCA and LSC, *Legal Aid Reform: the Way Ahead*, (November 2006, Cm. 6993).

[6] LSC, *Annual Report 2005–06*, p.5.

[7] Other quality marks are Quality Mark for the Bar; Mediation Quality Mark; Quality Mark for Websites; Telephone Standards and Specialist Support. The latter was, however, terminated as a discrete service in January 2006 although that decision is currently under re-consideration: LSC *Annual Report 2005–06*, p.15.

[8] *http://www.clsdirect.org.uk*. A telephone service and series of leaflets are also provided under the same brand. In 2005/6 the telephone helpline received more than 509,000 calls; specialist telephone advisers completed 73,625 cases and the website had 2,108,755 visitors: LSC *Annual Report 2005–06*, p.16.

[9] In Nottingham, for example, holders of this mark at the time of writing include the public libraries; the courts, a number of ethnic minority community organisations and specialist groups including the Alcohol Problems Advisory Service.

General Help

The Quality Mark defines General Help as services that provide the following **10–004**

- diagnosing clients' problems;

- giving information and explaining options;

- identifying further action the client can take; and

- giving basic assistance, e.g. filling in forms, contacting third parties to seek information.

This will generally be done in one interview although there may be some follow-up work. The client then retains responsibilities for further action.[10]

The service may also provide a *General Help with Casework* service, i.e. **10–005** taking action on behalf of clients in order to move the case on. This may include negotiation and advocacy on the client's behalf to third parties of the telephone, by letter or face-to-face. By definition, most cases will involve follow-up work with the service provider retaining responsibility for this.

The current Casework categories are as follows:

- Subject-based: welfare benefits; housing; debt; consumer/general contract; employment; immigration; and nationality.

- Client-based: disability; younger people; older people; race equality; asylum seekers; and refugees.

Organisations certified in this category should have at least one person working in the relevant field for at least 12 hours per week.

Specialist Help[11]

Specialist Help refers to the provision of legal advice and representation "on **10–006** complex matters in specific areas of law" provided by legally qualified persons.[12] Law firms wishing to obtain a CLS contract allowing them to undertake "legal aid work" are unable to do so without first obtaining the Specialist Quality Mark pending development by the CLS of a "preferred supplier" scheme, the intention being that, by 2009, the LSC will be working only with preferred suppliers.[13]

At the time of writing, that part of CLS strategy designed to co-ordinate provision of face-to-face advice including social welfare services through CLS

[10] In Nottingham, for example, at the time of writing this mark was held by the Trading Standards Advice Centre, Nottingham Trent University Student Advice Centre, a number of housing groups and local community advice centres.

[11] CLS, *Quality Mark Standard* (2000), at pp.4–5, and available on the CLS website: *www.justask.org.uk.*

[12] At the time of writing those listed for Nottingham in this category were several firms of solicitors, Shelter and the CAB.

[13] LSC, *Annual Report 2005–06*, p.26. A Unified Contract is in the course of finalisation at the time of writing although, as we will see, proposals for fee structures are controversial within the profession. Preferred suppliers will benefit from a greater proportion of powers devolved from the LSC: *http://www.legalservices.gov.uk/civil/preferred_supplier.asp.*

Networks and Centres[14] was said to be in some difficulty through difficulties in tendering.[15]

A. THE SPECIAL FEATURES OF INFORMATION AND ADVICE PROVISION

10–007   The Quality Marks that the CLS demands provide clients accessing organisations with minimum guarantees.

Further, there is a considerable and increasing amount of information available. With the development of various media, legal information has been much more readily available to those who access the various types of media. For example, television has found that consumer programmes have been a valuable source of audience figures. These programmes often deal with the provision of legal advice, especially when something has gone wrong with a purchase. With the growth of the Internet, there has been an explosion in the availability of such information. Many law firms feel that it is obligatory not only to advertise their services on their own website, but also to provide a service for readers free of charge. The latter may be regarded as a more sophisticated form of marketing by encouraging clients to approach the firm for further information, advice and representation as required.

B. AGENCIES OFFERING LEGAL ADVICE

1. CITIZENS' ADVICE BUREAUX[16]

10–008   The CAB Service owes its existence to wartime necessity, having its origins in the combined operation by the Ministry of Health, the National Council for Social Service and the Family Welfare Association in 1938 to provide advice and information in the war emergency. Government assistance terminated with the war's end and local Bureaux were left to scrape along on what they could glean from local authorities and other sources. The service was revived at the beginning of the 1960s by the injection of government funding and was stimulated by mention in two major inquiries (the Molony Committee on Consumer Protection in 1962 and the Royal Commission on Legal Services in 1980). When the central body, the National Association of Citizens' Advice Bureaux (NACAB), was reviewed in 1984, the CAB service was described as " . . . an invaluable national asset".[17]

---

[14] *Making Legal Rights a Reality*, p.8.
[15] See S. Willman, "Access to justice or Tesco Law?" (2006) 156(7244) N.L.J. 1537; S. Hynes, "Is there life after CLACs?" (2007) *Legal Action*, 10.
[16] J. Citron, *Citizens Advice Bureaux: For the Community, by the Community* (1989); J. Richards, *Inform, Advise and Support: 50 Years of the Citizens Advice Bureau* (1989).
[17] *Review of the National Association of Citizens' Advice Bureaux* (the Lovelock Report: Cmnd. 9139, 1984).

"The aims of the Citizens Advice Service are:

- to ensure that individuals do not suffer through lack of knowledge of their rights and responsibilities or of the services available to them, or through an inability to express their needs effectively;
- to exercise a responsible influence on the development of social policies and services, both locally and nationally."[18]

As the Citizens Advice *Annual Report and Accounts 2005/06* states "462 member bureaux regularly delivered advice from over 3,000 locations including: 834 bureaux locations, 1054 health care settings, 625 community centres, 217 legal settings and also by email, phone, online, in people's homes, via interactive kiosks and DigiTV. Our online advice website *adviceguide.org.uk* received 4.3 million visits, an increase of 83 per cent from 2004/5".[19] [20] The main categories of client problems with which CABx help are[21]: benefits (1,500,000 queries in 2005/06); debt (1,437,000); employment (473,000); housing (402,000); legal (294,000); relationships (288,000); consumer (157,000); utilities (57,000); tax (52,000); and other (588,000).[22] Clearly the CAB service meets a real need. Much of the CAB information and advice is provided by trained volunteers. In 2005/06 there were 20,264 volunteers, of whom 12,734 worked as advisers, 4,444 as trustees and 3,086 as volunteer administrators, social policy co-ordinators, IT support and fundraisers. At the same time, there were only 408 paid staff and 18 trustees in the CAB service.[23]

Different strategies will be adopted according to the nature of the queries and the resources available to any individual CAB. Advisers are at least trained to provide information and advice. They will be at least able to provide appropriate information and sign-posting, where appropriate, to a more suitable service. In some cases, a particular CAB may be able to provide a more specialised service. For example, some CABx can provide significant support in preparing for legal cases, such as Employment Tribunal hearings.

Even though very significant costs are saved through the support of volunteers, the service is still expensive, not least because of the provision, by NACAB, of an essential information system. In 2005/06 Citizens Advice cost £37,515,000 and received funding of £37,637,000, principally (£30,774,000) from government grants.[24] Funding of £133,147,000 for bureaux largely came from local authorities (£63,728,000) and the Legal Services Commission (£29,170,000).[25]

2. Other Not-for-profit Agencies

There is a wide range of other agencies. Many of them are members of Advice[UK]   **10–009**
(formerly the Federation of Independent Advice Centres, founded in 1979). The mission of Advice[UK] and, therefore, of its members is that "people's rights have

---

[18] *Citizens Advice, Annual Report and Accounts 2005/6*, p.3.
[19] e.g. the CAB at the Royal Courts of Justice in London.
[20] *ibid.* at p.5.
[21] Not including adviceguide online enquiries.
[22] *ibid.* at p.5.
[23] *ibid.*
[24] Other donors included financial institutions, law firms, utilities and charities.
[25] *ibid.* p.5.

no meaning without the means to enforce them . . . providing free information and advice [is] a vital contribution to helping individuals and communities in need to enforce their rights and improve their quality of life".[26] Advice[UK] is itself a member of the Advice Services Alliance (ASA UK).[27] ASA UK is an umbrella body for not-for-profit advice organisations, promoting "the development of high quality advice services and co-operation between advice organisations". Its members include Citizens Advice and the Law Centres Federation as well as Shelter, DIAL UK and Age Concern and associate members include the Child Poverty Action Group, Liberty, National Debtline, the Refugee Council and RNIB.

C. SPECIALIST AGENCIES OFFERING LEGAL ADVICE TO MEMBERS AND CLIENTS

10–010   One of the benefits of membership of some organisations is that legal advice may be made available. The advice may be connected to the main business of the organisation. Legal advice may be made available either through the employment of lawyers within the organisation[28] or by the engagement of lawyers in private practice at the expense of the organisation.

1. TRADES UNIONS

10–011   Legal services provided through a trades union have been, and remain, a significant factor in the recruitment and retention of members. It appears that most, if not all, trades unions offer some form of legal advice service to members. The offering may be limited to employment related matters,[29] it may be extensive[30] or it may provide an employment plus service.[31] The latter appears increasingly to be the norm. An employment plus service is likely not only to provide free legal advice on employment law issues, but also a service to deal with injuries as

---

[26] http://www.adviceuk.org.uk.

[27] http://www.asauk.org. ASA UK also operates Advicenow.org.uk and ADRnow.org.uk. For discussion of some ASA activities, see also N. Ardill, "A route map for legal education" (2005) (Jul) Legal Action, 8; A. Griffith, "Causes of Action and the CLS strategy: is this really evidence-based policy making?" (2006) (Dec) Legal Action, 6. See also the Advisers Institute which acts as a professional body for advisers in all fields: http://www.advisersinstitute.org.uk.

[28] But account must be taken of the limits on practice of employed solicitors, see above, paras 3–013 and 03–027.

[29] e.g. the GMB provides legal assistance to members as follows: "on employment matters, including occupational accidents and diseases, unfair dismissal and redundancy, discrimination and equal pay, working time and national minimum wage. Through GMB and its solicitors, our members recover over £1 million each week in compensation. Social security awards, especially in relation to disability, are also substantial. We also provide legal support to members and/or their families for non-work personal injuries: http://www.gmb.org.uk.

[30] e.g. BECTU's legal services include employment law, accidents, wills, conveyancing and a 24-hour legal helpline on all non-employment issues: http://www.bectu.org.uk. See also UCATT: http://ucatt.org.uk.

[31] e.g. TGWU: http://www.tgwu.org.uk.

a result of accidents and to provide a wills and conveyancing service.[32] Whilst claims management companies are now regulated under Compensation Act 2006, trades unions acting in such a capacity are exempted from the authorisation regime.[33]

2. MOTORING ORGANISATIONS

The original motoring organisations, the Automobile Association and the Royal **10–012** Automobile Club, provide a variety of benefits to their members, including legal advice. Understandably, their legal services are limited to matters relating to motoring (but e.g. the RAC includes legal expenses insurance in its insurance services[34]) covering primarily advice on general motoring law, disputes with garages, and claims arising out of accidents.[35]

3. THE CONSUMERS' ASSOCIATION

The Consumers Association (CA) began in 1957 as a small group publishing a **10–013** magazine with the results of the comparative testing of aspirins and kettles and has since become a multi-million pound organisation with influence over manufacturers and retailers as well as those responsible for the formulation of consumer policy. Its reports on solicitors in particular have underpinned the regulation aspects of the Legal Services Bill.[36]

The information function is performed through the magazine *Which?* available to subscribers, but having a general impact because of its availability in libraries and the extent to which it is referred to and talked about in the media. Unfavourable mention in *Which?* is regarded as a major problem for manufacturers and service providers.

On the legal advice side, the CA operates a legal service for individual members. Legal advice, in the form of answers to readers' questions, is also contained in the magazine and there are statements of law in other CA publications.

4. CLAIMS MANAGEMENT COMPANIES AND PRIVATE SECTOR ADVISERS

As we have seen in Ch.9, some legal services are provided, not through the LSC **10–014** but through the private sector. The nature of such activity varies but frequently

---

[32] See the various trades union websites accessible through the website of the Trades Union Congress: *http://www.tuc.org.uk.*

[33] See DCA *Code of Practice for the Provision of Regulated Claims Management Services by Trade Unions* (November 2006); Compensation (Exemptions) Order 2007, SI 2007/209.

[34] This is an increasingly important means of funding litigation, see below, para.11–007.

[35] For the AA, see *www.theaa.com*; for the RAC, see *http://www.rac.co.uk.*

[36] See, for example, J. Farrar, 2001, "Arrogant, incompetent, negligent and unprofessional . . . ", (August 2001) *Which?*, 8. Other consumer organisations may hold similar views, see, for example, National Consumer Council, *Legal Services Bill: the consumer interest* (November 2006).

involves the negotiation of an individual's claim with a potential defendant or a potential defendant's insurer. If the claim is disputed, the matter is then referred to a solicitor. Claims management organisations are now required to obtain specific authorisation and are regulated under the Compensation Act 2006.[37]

5. STUDENT CLINICS

10–015 There has been increased interest in recent years[38] in exposing law students to "real" clients and "real problems" through pro bono work. Such clinical legal education activity may extend to a full-scale legal advice centre under the supervision of a solicitor with suitable experience[39]; involve students in innocence projects[40]; or in other forms of pro bono work such as streetlaw work.[41] Sometimes advice is made available only to other students but in other cases services are extended, perhaps in specific fields, such as employment or landlord and tenant advice, to the general public. Clearly there is a potential tension between the educational objectives of the activity and the interests of the, frequently disadvantaged, clients and supervision must be carefully provided.[42]

D. LAW CENTRES[43]

10–016 One of the most significant developments in the provision of legal help in the last part of the twentieth century was the emergence of law centres. Drawing some inspiration from the American system of neighbourhood law firms but adapting themselves to local conditions and the rules of the legal profession in this

---

[37] See *http://www.claimsregulation.gov.uk*.

[38] In many cases under the aegis of the Clinical Legal Education Organisation, see the UK Centre for Legal Education website at *http://www.ukcle.ac.uk*. According to LawWorks (previously the Solicitors' Pro Bono Group), 53% of law schools and law faculties are now involved in some form of pro bono activity: *LawWorks' Research Shows Increase In Demand For Pro Bono Work Among Students* (2006), *http://lawworks.org.uk*.

[39] Work may extend even to taking cases to court under the supervision of the clinic's solicitor: see, for example, J. Parker, "Kent Law School goes up against DLA Piper in Tesco worker pay case" *The Lawyer*, 26 February 2007.

[40] See *http://www.innocencenetwork.org.uk*.

[41] Public legal education in schools or in the community on subjects such as, for example, human rights.

[42] For some discussion, see J. Marson, A. Wilson and M. van Hoorebeek, "The necessity of clinical legal education in university law schools: a UK perspective" (2005) Aug. *International Journal of Clinical Legal Education*, 29; D. Nicholson, "Legal Education or community service? The extra-curricular student law clinic" (2006) Web J.C.L.I. 3 and J. Parker, "Good Practice" (2007) 21(3) *The Lawyer*, 16.

[43] For a comprehensive survey of the origins and development of the law centre movement, see M. Zander, *Legal Services for the Community* (1978), Chs 2 and 3; Royal Commission on Legal Services *Report, Vol.1* (1979), Ch.8; Law Centres Federation, *The Case for Law Centres* (1989); R. Widdison, (1988) L.S. Gaz. March 16, pp.35–37; JUSTICE, *Law Centres* (1995); E. Davidson, "Three Triumphant Decades of Law, Politics, and Campaigns at Camden" (2003) 153(7108) N.L.J. Supp. 26; P. Heron, "Why I joined . . . a law centre" (2005) 32(May/Jun) YSG Mag. 12; G. Sharp, "Touring Law Centres", (2006) *Legal Action*, 10; the Law Centres Federation website: *http://www.lawcentres.org.uk*.

country, law centres provide a local base for the dissemination of legal services outside the legal profession.

1. THE BEGINNINGS[44]

Some provision was made for the giving of legal advice by salaried solicitors **10–017** outside the ambit of private practice in the Legal Aid and Advice Act 1949, but the part of the Act (s.7) which would have established full-time paid solicitors located at Legal Aid Area Headquarters and travelling to smaller places was never brought into force. An alternative scheme for the provision of advice was proposed and adopted after 10 years of pressure had failed to get the original scheme implemented.

The real origins of the law centre movement are usually attributed to the publication of pamphlets by the lawyers of the Conservative and Labour parties and the individual initiative of pioneers who became impatient at the slowness of official bodies in responding to the pressure for change. *Justice for All*[45] analysed the unmet need for professional legal services and proposed the establishment of local legal centres in places of deprivation, to be staffed by salaried lawyers and to exist with and be supplemental to the private profession. It was suggested that the type of work undertaken by the centres should be restricted but that they should be free of those rules of professional etiquette that then existed (e.g. advertising and touting for business) which would inhibit their work. It is not, perhaps, surprising that the solution of the Conservative lawyers in their pamphlet, *Rough Justice*,[46] to the same problem was the introduction of subsidies for practitioners operating privately in deprived areas and an extension of the assistance given by lawyers to voluntary advice agencies. However, they were prepared to countenance the appointment of salaried lawyers as a last resort.

The Law Society moved from implacable opposition to the salaried lawyers proposal in the 1949 Act and *Justice for All* to acceptance of salaried solicitors as part of its own proposals for an Advisory Liaison Service.[47] This Service would provide legal help to CABx and other agencies; would establish close liaison between the local profession and CABx and other relevant services; would provide oral advice for the public in cases that could be readily disposed of; would maintain permanent advisory centres where necessary, offering advice and assistance short of proceedings or representation in court; and would set up permanent local centres offering representation in magistrates' courts and county courts and the conduct of litigation where this could not be undertaken by solicitors' firms.

Part II of the Legal Advice and Assistance Act 1972 appeared to be designed to give the Law Society the power to carry out these proposals. But it was then frustrated by the failure of successive governments to bring Pt II into force.

---

[44] See also "Significant Dates in the Development of Law Centres" at *http://www.lawcentres.org.uk*.

[45] A report of the Society of Labour Lawyers in the Fabian research series, no.273 (1968).

[46] Society of Conservative Lawyers, *Rough Justice* (1968).

[47] *Legal Advice and Assistance*, Memorandum of the Council of the Law Society (1969).

2. DEVELOPMENT

10–018   Impatient of the slow progress being made officially, local lawyers and community workers set up a law centre in North Kensington in 1970.[48] A variety of other centres emerged in 1973–74; by October 1982 there were 38 centres around the country,[49] by 1987–88 there were 61,[50] by 1995 there were 55,[51] and in 2007 there were 56.[52] In order to be a Law Centre, properly so called, the organisation must be a member of the Law Centres Federation.

The struggle for most of the centres has always been for funds.[53] Traditionally, the sources of funds has been grant-aid from public or charitable funds, with major sponsors being the local council. Funding sources "emerged and [grew] in . . . uncoordinated, sporadic fashion in response to local initiatives".[54] The introduction of block contracting for legal aid raised the prospect of more secure funding for law centres, and this is confirmed by the funding approach under the CLS,[55] but that does not contain a guarantee of funding for law centres. Law centres will qualify for funding if they go through the same procedures as solicitors in the private sector, which requires the obtaining of a contract for the provision of certain legal work and the maintenance of the Specialist Quality Mark and will, under current proposals, require law centres to acquire preferred supplier status to secure funding.[56]

3. WORK

10–019   "Law Centres provide their local communities with a comprehensive legal service that puts the legal and human rights of individuals first. Law Centres help to overcome the obstacles faced by people who need access to the legal system. . . .

Law Centres are a valuable community resource that empowers and supports local people. . . . Managed democratically by individuals from their local area, Law Centres compliment the services of other community groups, advice agencies and solicitors in the area to ensure that there is no duplication of work. They regenerate local areas by ensuring that public services reach those most in need."[57]

In consequence, they prioritise their areas of work and specialise in

---

[48] C. Robinson *et al.*, *Coming of Age: North Kensington Law Centre 1970–88.*
[49] 31st *Legal Aid Annual Reports* (1980–81), pp.128–129. And see M. Zander and P. Russell, "Law Centres Survey" (1976) L.S. Gaz. 208 and the Royal Commission on Legal Services, Vol.2, Pt B, Section 3.
[50] *38th Legal Aid Annual Reports* (1987–88), pp.102–103.
[51] JUSTICE, *Law Centres* (1995), p.4 and App.2.
[52] *http://www.lawcentres.org.uk*, "Complete list of law centres".
[53] It is this which explains the fluctuation in membership of the Law Centres Federation.
[54] JUSTICE, *Law Centres* (1995), p.17.
[55] See below. In 2005–06, £209, 744 of total income of £842,493 was received from the Legal Services Commission: *Equality through Justice, Law Centres Federation Annual Report 2005/6*, p.25.
[56] See below, at para.10–021.
[57] "What do Law Centres do?" at *http://www.lawcentres.org.uk*.

"welfare rights; disability rights; immigration and asylum; housing and homelessness; employment rights; community care; and all forms of discrimination. Other areas of work vary according to local need and may include public law, mental health, education rights and young people and children's rights."[58]

Law Centres work by employing

"solicitors, barristers, legal advisers and community workers . . . in addition to dealing with individual cases (including test cases, judicial reviews and representation), they also:

- Take on cases that clarify and extend rights for the public.
- Provide legal education, training and information about the law and people's rights.
- Propose improvements in the law as it affects their clients.
- Work with local providers of public services, such as local authorities to meet community needs.
- Provide legal advice and services for voluntary and community sector organisations."[59]

To become a law centre and a member of the Law Centres Federation, an organisation must meet minimum requirements for membership[60]:

- democratic and non-profit-making, accountable to the community and independent of funders, the professions and other "non-consumer interests" whilst serving a particular catchment area;

- with a normal staff of at least six workers, two of whom are solicitors;

- providing free legal advice and assistance at no cost to its users, including court and tribunal representation as well as training and education;

- working with oppressed people and groups to make them aware of what their rights are and how they can be used to improve their lives;

- committed to social action to combat deprivation and discrimination as an integral part of delivering legal services to the community;

- reporting to the Law Centres Federation; co-operating with other groups with similar interests and striving for change in unjust laws and the inaccessible legal system.[61]

4. The Future

Client satisfaction with law centres has always been high. For example, it was reported in 1992 that law centre workers are approachable and accessible.[62] **10–020**

---

[58] *ibid.*
[59] *ibid.*
[60] "Minimum criteria for LCF Membership" at *http://www.lawcentres.org.uk.*
[61] JUSTICE (1995), p.4 taking the information from the guidelines for membership of the LCF. See also "Setting up a Law Centre" at *http://www.lawcentres.org.uk.*
[62] L. Hiscock and G. Cole, "Law centre client perceptions of the service they received at the Centres they visited" (1992).

Many organisations, including political parties, are supportive of the work of law centres.[63] The government sees the law centres as contributing to the amelioration of social exclusion.[64] Law Centres have played a significant part in the provision of legal advice. Whether their future is any more certain than it has been in writing previous editions of this book still remains to be seen and the LCF itself has raised concerns about proposals for change to CLS funding arrangements.[65] It is dependent upon the continuing willingness of funders to provide the necessary resources.

E. SOLICITORS IN PRIVATE PRACTICE

10–021 Whilst there are many different sources of legal advice and many of these will form part of the CLS, it is still lawyers who are the major purveyors of legal advice.[66] This is true, even if we discount the role of the lawyer and big business. In providing legal advice, even to big business, two questions arise, and they are in relation to cost and availability. As regards legal advice to big business, the lawyer has to be available as the client requires and cost will have been a factor in determining whether the lawyer's firm got the client's business.

Evidence that the cost of a solicitor's advice, or fear of that cost, and the relative inaccessibility of many offices led to the original speculation about the degree of unmet legal need.[67] In consequence, there was a substantial growth in alternative provision of legal advice, not least through the expansion of the CABx and the creation of Law Centres. Lawyers, working within those organisations have responded, as have those in private practice, whether from personal motivation or in order to obtain or retain business following the introduction of the CLS.

If clients (or their insurers or trades union) are able to pay the bill, they can get advice from a solicitor of their choice as often as they desire and on whatever topic they choose. If they cannot pay the bill, they must rely on the services provided voluntarily by solicitors and barristers; or a law centre or similar advisor, including a claims manager operating on a no win no fee arrangement; or come within the CLS; or use another agency or service; or, in the absence of some agreement such as a conditional fee arrangement, do without.[68] Within the context of the objectives of the CLS, doing without is unacceptable and the government sees access to legal advice as one means of addressing social exclusion.[69]

---

[63] JUSTICE (1995), p.13.

[64] Lord Chancellor's Department, *Social Exclusion* (2001), at *www.lcd.gov.uk*. See also LCF and DCA, *Legal and Advice Services: A Pathway out of Social Exclusion* (November 2001); *Legal and Advice Services: A Pathway to Regeneration* (February 2004); LCF, *Working with Local Government* (November 2005).

[65] "The Government's plans to reform legal aid threatens access to justice and the future of Law Centre services", *http://www.lawcentres.org.uk*.

[66] See also above, Ch.8.

[67] See above, para.9–010.

[68] As Genn discovered, there is a large proportion of the population who will indeed "lump it" and take no action when presented with a problem to which there might be a legal solution, see above, para.9–008.

[69] *Social Exclusion* (2001), and see above, para.9–012.

1. Voluntary Schemes

Many lawyers have been involved in the provision of free legal advice, being **10–022** generous with their time and talents, to the extent that some of the larger firms have personnel engaged in pro bono activity on a full time basis or introducing targets for pro bono work by individual lawyers. This has built upon a number of initiatives, not least the poor persons' procedure in litigation[70] and other initiatives identified by the Rushcliffe Committee in 1944.[71] At the time of writing, LawWorks (before 2006 the Solicitors' Pro Bono Group),[72] is undertaking a "million hours' project" seeking to identify how much pro bono activity is being undertaken by the profession. Barristers, similarly, may agree to represent clients without payment.[73]

A typical means whereby lawyers offer their services free is through the CAB service or a LawWorks clinic. A CAB will establish a system of advisory sessions by local solicitors or trainees, operating on a rota basis, giving free legal advice to clients on an appointments basis. The purpose might be either to resolve a problem at that interview or to provide initial advice that will lead to further advice either through that or another solicitor's firm.

In other cases, lawyers may provide initial advice to clients without recouping the cost (e.g. the "first free interview"), which, of course, may also act as a means of recruiting clients; or offer their services as mediators on a volunteer basis. A LawWorks Community Groups project offers free business law advice to not-for-profit organisations. In addition, some firms become involved with community projects that do not involve the provision of legal advice.

2. The Community Legal Service

(a) Background

The CLS has taken over all aspects of the original Legal Aid service. One aspect **10–023** of the old scheme was the provision of limited amounts of legal advice and information under the "Green Form" scheme originally instituted under the Legal Advice and Assistance Act 1972. A solicitor could give 90 minutes' of oral or written advice and "assistance" (which might include, for example, writing a letter of complaint on behalf of the client).[74] Whilst there were extensions, notably the advice by way of representation scheme that enabled representation at some tribunals, and duty solicitor schemes at courts and police stations, the

---

[70] A formal procedure was instituted in 1914 and was described as " . . . the first regular scheme for legal aid in the Supreme Court": H. Kirk, *Portrait of a Profession* (1976), p.164. It was put under the control of the Law Society in 1923 as a result of the proposals of the Lawrence Committee, *The Report of the Poor Persons' Rules Committee* (Cmd. 2358, 1925). It could not cope with the increasing pressure of work in the 1930s and ultimately was overtaken by the Legal Aid Scheme in 1949.

[71] *Report of the Committee on Legal Aid and Advice* (Cmd. 6641, 1945), pp.17–21.

[72] *http://lawworks.org.uk*.

[73] See the Bar Pro Bono Unit at *http://barprobono.tribalforge.net*. Barristers joining the panel commit to a minimum of three days' work on a pro bono basis instructed through the Bar's Direct Access scheme, although some do much more.

[74] Legal Aid Act 1988, s.2(2).

scheme, as with the entire Legal Aid service, was under severe pressure and government determined that reform was necessitated. The major criticisms of the scheme appear to have been five-fold and in the following areas:

(a) as it was administered by solicitors, it was limited to work solicitors were prepared to undertake;

(b) the financial and hourage limits were too low so that delay was caused in awaiting extensions[75];

(c) the limits for eligibility were lower than for legal aid proper and the scheme was, therefore, available only to a very small number of people;

(d) the level of public awareness of the scheme was low;

(e) the system was susceptible of abuse by unscrupulous solicitors.[76]

When examining the CLS it can be seen that many of its aspects are clearly intended to meet some of these criticisms without losing the strengths of the Green Form scheme.

(b) Solicitors and the CLS

10–024   The involvement of solicitors is with the specialist help aspect of CLS provision, as well as the provision of advice and information, that is, in "the provision of help by the giving of advice as to how the law applies in particular circumstances"; "the provision of help in preventing, or settling or otherwise resolving, disputes about legal rights and duties"; "the provision of help in enforcing decisions by which disputes are resolved", and "the provision of help in relation to legal proceedings not relating to disputes".[77] In providing such services, the provider is obliged, in so far as is reasonably practicable, to:

"(a) promote improvements in the range and quality of services provided as part of the Community Legal Service and in the ways in which they are made accessible to those who need them,

(b) secure that the services provided in relation to any matter are appropriate having regard to its nature and importance, and

(c) achieve the swift and fair resolution of disputes without unnecessary or unduly protracted proceedings in court."[78]

In order to be a provider of relevant services, a solicitors' firm must obtain a contract with the CLS entitling it to receive funding from the CLS Fund. Similar arrangements apply in respect of the Criminal Defence Service (CDS). At the time of writing, in order to obtain a contract, the provider must acquire the "specialist quality mark" described in outline above.[79]

---

[75] J. Baldwin and S. Hill, *The Operation of the Green Form Scheme in England and Wales* (1988), p.62, Table 14.

[76] See, for an example, H. Muir and C. Dyer, "Lawyer ran multi-million pound legal aid scam", *Guardian*, October 30, 2004.

[77] Access to Justice Act 1999, s.4(2)(b), (c), (d) and (e).

[78] *ibid.* s.4(4).

[79] A "Unified Contract for Civil Legal Aid providers" was intended to replace the existing "General Contract" in March 2007 but was successfully challenged in court by the law society: "Law society secures court win on legal aid" press release July 27, 2007. As indicated on its website, however, the CLS is moving towards a position where it will devolve greater powers to those with "Preferred Supplier" status.

The obtaining of a quality mark is a crucial element of the CLS or the CDS for whatever involvement the organisation requires. The standards for each quality mark cover seven key quality areas[80]:

Access to Service:	This covers access "for the public to legal services providers on the basis of local needs and priorities" in the case of the CLS and "to ensure that every person suspected or accused of a crime has access to appropriate quality criminal defence services" in the case of the CDS.
Seamless Service:	This covers signposting and referral to other agencies.
Running the Organisation:	This covers the roles and responsibilities of key staff and financial management.
People Management:	This covers equal opportunities for staff, ensuring that "staff either possess, or are enabled to acquire the skills and knowledge required to meet the clients' needs", as well as supervision.
Running the Service:	This covers "efficient and effective file management".
Meeting Clients' Needs:	This covers information to clients including costing information, confidentiality, privacy and fair treatment and maintaining quality where someone else delivers part of the service.
Commitment to Quality:	This covers complaints, other user feedback and maintaining quality procedures.

In auditing an applicant for one of the quality marks (and in auditing organisations that already have such a mark), the auditor will look for   **10–025**

"objective evidence on the files of the following:

- the information gained from the client and other sources;
- the advice given based on that information;
- the steps taken following that advice"[81]

in conjunction with a set of "transaction criteria"[82] for the particular type of work conducted by the organisation (including a specific set for criminal work). Compliance with these criteria is a necessary precursor to obtaining or maintaining a quality mark.

Possession of a quality mark, however, does not entitle an organisation to receive CLS or CDS funding by way of a contract. The CLS awards two main types of contract: for "controlled work" and for "licensed work" and, exceptionally, a Very High Cost Case contract. The CDS also awards a General Criminal Contract.

---

[80] Information taken from LSC, *Step by Step Guide to the Quality Mark* available on both CLS and CDS websites.

[81] *http://www.legalservices.gov.uk/civil/how/cdg_transaction_criteria.asp*.

[82] *ibid.*, where copies of all transaction criteria booklets currently available can be found.

(c) Funding of legal advice—controlled work

10–026   A controlled work contract covers "general Legal Advice" in one or more
specific categories of law: "[i]t covers legal advice and assistance—referred to as
Legal Help, as well as Help at Court[83] and Legal Representation in front of
Mental Health Review Tribunals and the Asylum and Immigration Tribunal. This
is usually the first stage of legal aid that clients require".[84] It is important to be
aware that separate funding ("General Family Help", "Family Mediation" and
"Help with Mediation") is available in connection with family law litigation,
although we do not, in general, examine it further.

> " '*Legal Help*' is a level of service the grant of which authorises services
> falling within Section 4(2) of the Access to Justice Act 1999 other than:
>
> (i) The provision of general information about the law and legal system
>   and the availability of legal services (except where such provision is
>   incidental to the provision of help in a specific case).
> (ii) Issuing or conducting court proceedings.
> (iii) Advocacy or instructing an advocate in proceedings.
> (iv) The provision of mediation or arbitration (but this does not prevent
>   legal help being given in relation to mediation or arbitration or cover-
>   ing payment of a mediator's or arbitrator's fees as a
>   disbursement)."[85]

Consequently it would cover initial advice, some investigation and correspondence short of becoming involved in litigation or court work.

> " '*Legal Representation*' is a level of service the grant of which authorises
> legal representation for a party to proceedings or for a person who is
> contemplating taking proceedings. This includes the following:
>
> (i) Litigation services.
> (ii) Advocacy services.
> (iii) All such help as is usually given by a person providing representation
>   in proceedings, including steps preliminary or incidental to
>   proceedings.
> (iv) All such help as is usually given by such a person in arriving at or
>   giving effect to a compromise to avoid or bring to an end any
>   proceedings.
>
> Legal representation does not include the provision of mediation or arbitra-
> tion (but this does not prevent help being given in relation to mediation or
> arbitration, or the payment of a mediator's or arbitrator's fees as a
> disbursement)".[86]

In March 2006, 6,725 controlled work contracts were in place across England
and Wales.[87]

---

[83] "*Help at Court*" is a level of service the grant of which authorises help and advocacy for a client
in relation to a particular hearing, without formally acting as legal representative in the proceedings, unless this is authorised by the Commission, *ibid.*
[84] Legal Services Commission *Annual Report 2005/06*, p.17.
[85] LSC *Funding Code 2005*, para.3A–004.
[86] *ibid.*
[87] Legal Services Commission *Annual Report 2005/06*, p.18.

In 2005/06 CLS Controlled Work, that is, assistance provided under the Legal Help scheme, not including representation at court, was provided as follows[88]:

Group providing assistance	Number of acts of assistance
Solicitors	449,890
Not-for-profit organisations	163,140
CLS Direct telephone advice	73,625
Other (such as pilots or projects)	21,855
Total acts of assistance	708,510

(d) Funding of advice—licensed work

Licensed work covers all other civil Legal Representation other than that which might be covered in a separate Very High Cost Case contract. Here an application is made for funding in each case on an individual basis and assessed separately. A controlled work contract incorporated licensed work although there were, in 2006, 227 contracts in place for licensed work only.[89] **10–027**

CLS Licensed Work, covering all civil legal representation other than Legal Help, and Help at Court and Legal Representation before Mental Health Review Tribunals and the Asylum and Immigration Tribunal were recorded as follows in 2005/06 and 2004/05.[90]

	Funding applications received	Certificates issued	Final bills paid	Substantive benefit to client
Family	160,826	130,598	139,375	57
Non-family	33,969	24,467	36,161	45
Total 2005/6	194,795	155,065	175,536	54
Total 2004/5	193,329	154,648	180,033	56

(e) Funding of advice in criminal cases and the duty solicitor schemes

The CDS, which came into operation on April 2, 2001, also awards contracts to approved suppliers for criminal defence work.[91] In addition, there are at present **10–028**

---

[88] LSC *Annual Report 2005/06*, Table 3.
[89] *ibid.*
[90] *ibid.*, Table 4.
[91] The General Criminal Contract, holders of which are also expected to have a Specialist Quality Mark in criminal work. In 2005/06 2,608 such contracts were in place: LSC *Annual Report and Accounts 2005/06*, p.22.

in seven centres[92] across the country, Public Defence Services whose personnel are directly employed by the LSC. Under the Criminal Defence Act 2006, responsibility for the provision of legal aid in criminal cases was transferred from the courts to the LSC. In 2005, the CDS also piloted CDS Direct: providing advice on the telephone to those detained in police stations for minor offences, intended to save money on duty solicitor schemes.[93]

For many years, there have been duty solicitor schemes, allowing individuals to receive advice from a solicitor either at the police station or at court. The Duty Solicitors Arrangements 2001 (last amended in October 2006)[94] provide for the two duty solicitor schemes; at the magistrates' court and at the police station. The CDS is obliged to establish local schemes in each identified region (the regions being: London South, London East, London West, South Eastern, Southern A, Southern B, South Western A, South Western B, South Wales, North Wales, West Midlands A, West Midlands B, West Midlands C, East Midlands A, East Midlands B, Eastern A, Eastern B, North Western A, North Western B, North Eastern A, North Eastern B, Yorkshire and Humberside A, Yorkshire and Humberside B, and Merseyside).[95] The LSC is "responsible for ensuring that all members of Local Schemes are competent to undertake Duty Solicitor work".'[96]

The first such scheme was initiated by the Bristol Law Society in 1972 to provide legal advice to defendants appearing at the local magistrates' court,[97] which provided the model for others which followed. By mid-1975 there were 29 duty solicitor schemes[98] and the Law Society felt it necessary to prepare and publish a guide for the assistance of local law societies.[99] Consistency was introduced by s.1 of the Legal Aid Act 1982, enabling the Law Society to act under powers that had appeared in s.15 of the Legal Aid Act 1974. The first statutory scheme was the Legal Aid (Duty Solicitor) Scheme 1983.[100]

There are two duty solicitor schemes. One is that available to provide free legal advice and assistance at a police station to anyone questioned about an offence, whether arrested or not. There is no means test for this advice and no payment has to be made. In some serious circumstances the police can delay a person's access to legal advice under s.58 of the Police and Criminal Evidence Act 1984.[101] The scheme means that a duty solicitor is available 24 hours a day, although sometimes availability may be restricted to advice on the telephone. Of course, any given person being questioned could, alternatively, either ask to see a list of local solicitors or contact their own solicitor.

The other scheme provides free legal advice and assistance at a magistrates' court. Whilst it will clearly be preferable for an individual to have arranged legal representation before arriving at court, this scheme ensures that it is possible to avoid defendants being unrepresented. All courts have a duty solicitor scheme[102]

---

[92] Birmingham, Cheltenham, Chester, Darlington, Liverpool, Pontypridd and Swansea.

[93] See the CDS website under "duty solicitor": *http://www.legalservices.gov.uk/criminal.asp.*

[94] Available on the CDS website. The arrangements are made under Access to Justice Act 1999, s.3(4). Duty Solicitor Arrangements 2001 (as amended), para.3.2.

[95] *ibid.* Sch.1.

[96] *ibid.* para.4.3.

[97] (1972) L.S. Gaz. 819.

[98] *25th Legal Aid Annual Reports* [1974–75], pp.6–7.

[99] (1975) 72 L.S. Gaz. 577–579. For comment on the schemes at this time, see Royal Commission on Legal Services, *Report Vol.1* (1979), p.93.

[100] *34th Legal Aid Annual Reports* [1983–84], pp.185–197 and 37–43.

[101] See below, para.14–022.

[102] Legal Aid Board, *Annual Report 1999–2000* (HC 664, 2000), para.4.3.

at which advice and assistance, including advocacy assistance, are provided.[103] From 2004, a court duty solicitor can only, with some limited exceptions, advise those in custody or charged with an imprisonable offence.[104]

Not all those detained at police stations will, of course, take up the offer of a duty solicitor. Some suspects have a predisposition to seek advice which others lack, some perceive that advice would be of little benefit (which is bound to be true in many minor offences), some are confident that they can do as well without advice as with it, some believe that nothing can help, some trust the police to act fairly, some wish to get out of the station as quickly as possible and believe that advice will delay the process, some have a low opinion of the quality of advice that they are likely to receive and of the scheme itself.[105] Some of the problems for suspects accessing legal advice are the product of police practices,[106] but some are the product of the practices of solicitors. Some suspects have previous experience of the scheme which was poor.[107] Sanders and Young in 2000 discovered that, at least in the early stages of duty solicitor schemes, problems created by solicitors included the following[108]:

(1) The unavailability of solicitors, even when the request was to have the advice of someone from the duty solicitor scheme. The problems were identified as either being that the schemes did not require someone always to be on duty; or that the scheme was simply over stretched by demand.[109]

(2) Often legal advice was provided not by a solicitor but by a paralegal, who was not always trained properly for the task. One study identified the possible problems of using non-qualified and untrained staff as being: lack of legal expertise; lack of confidence; role conflict; and over-identification with the police.[110]

(3) Often advice would be given over the telephone rather than in person, which, except in very clear cases, could lead to poor, inaccurate or detrimental advice.[111]

---

[103] Note, however, that Criminal Defence Act 2006 inserts s.3B into Access to Justice Act 1999 imposing a means test on representation in the magistrates' court.

[104] *Duty Solicitor Manual* (May 2006) para.2.5(2), For some research on usage of such schemes, see T. Bucke and D. Brown, *In Police Custody: Police Powers and Suspects' Rights Under the Revised Pace Codes of Practice* (Home Office Research Study no.174, 1997) and A. Sanders and R. Young, *Criminal Justice* (2nd edn, 2000); L. Bridges, E. Cape, A. Abubaker and C. Bennett, *Quality in Criminal Defence Services* (2000).

[105] Sanders and Young (2000), pp.221–222.

[106] *ibid.* pp.223–228.

[107] "Duty solicitors are crap anyway, they work for the fucking police and the courts" *ibid.* p.222, quoting Choongh (1993).

[108] Sanders and Young (2000), pp.229–237.

[109] The LSC reports 100% coverage in duty solicitor schemes in 2005/06; *Annual Report and Accounts 2005/06 op. cit.*

[110] M. McConville and J. Hodgson, *Custodial Legal Advice and the Right to Silence* (Royal Commission on Criminal Justice Research Study no. 16, 1993), pp.30–34. Such advisers were sometimes former police officers, specifically employed by solicitors' firms for their familiarity with police procedure.

[111] Whilst there was improvement in consequence of changes in the obligations of duty solicitors in the mid-1990s, a subsequent study still discovered that about 20% of suspects secured advice by telephone: Sanders and Young (2000), pp.232–233. Clearly the CDS pilot for telephone advice in the police station approves assistance being given in this way.

(4) Often there were doubts about the quality of the advice and assistance. In origin this centred on some confusion as to the role of the legal adviser. Some did very little, being both passive and compliant. The failure of legal advisers to act is most starkly seen in the case of the "Cardiff Three", where the Court of Appeal commented that "the solicitor appears to have been gravely at fault for sitting passively through this travesty of an interview" which clearly contravened the rules against oppression.[112]

Many of these criticisms were taken seriously. The Royal Commission on Criminal Justice recommended that steps be taken to improve the quality of the legal advice made available:

(1) The guidance to solicitors (the Law Society's *Advising Clients at the Police Station*) on their roles should be made more widely known, be better understood, and more consistently acted upon. Specifically, it was recommended that the Law Society actively progress its production of a training video.[113]

(2) Steps should be taken to ensure that the client's own solicitor and their representatives should meet the same standards as duty solicitors. This should be the case even where the solicitor is not working under the legal aid scheme.[114]

(3) The training education, supervision and monitoring of all legal advisers who operate at police stations should be reviewed.[115]

Important steps have been taken to address many of the concerns.

(1) Tightening the appointment process for duty solicitors and their representatives. Thus improvements were made in the quality and commitment of the persons appointed to duty solicitor schemes.[116] The current criteria determining appoint to a duty solicitor scheme require the Legal Services Commission to appoint only those solicitors who are "competent to undertake Duty Solicitor work"[117] and normally someone is appointed to both a police station and a magistrates' court scheme.[118] So the applicant must provide evidence of that competence, either through membership of a

---

[112] *R v Paris, Abdullahi and Miller* (1993) 97 Cr. App. R., p.104.
[113] Royal Commission on Criminal Justice, *Report* (Cm. 2263, 1993), p.38.
[114] *ibid.*
[115] *ibid.*
[116] The person to be appointed would have to hold a current practising certificate, be willing to act personally and to undertake the majority of the rota duties allocated, have a regular criminal practice, have comprehensive experience of defence work, and adequate experience of providing advice to persons arrested and held in custody, and to act in a non-discriminatory way. S/he must have attended an advocacy training course, unless sufficiently experienced, and a police station advice course, unless substantially experienced. The applicant must agree not to provide money or other gifts to suspects, except food, drink and smoking material for immediate consumption. The applicant then went through a rigorous selection process, including an interview. The appointment would last for five years, during which time certain aspects would be monitored: Duty Solicitor Arrangements 1994, paras 32–48.
[117] *Duty Solicitor Arrangements 2001* (amended 2006), para.4.3.
[118] *ibid.* para.4.19.

previous scheme or by accreditation.[119] Applicants must have "comprehensive experience of criminal defence work, including the provision of advice in the Police Station and advocacy in the Crown Court or magistrates' court throughout the 12 months prior to the application . . . ".[120] A member of a scheme must hold a current practising certificate, not be a special constable, not be suspended or excluded from membership of another scheme, not be facing a criminal charge or have been convicted of a non-rehabilitated criminal offence, and not be the subject of an adverse finding through the professional misconduct bodies.[121]

(2) Tightening the requirements for continued membership of a scheme.[122] A duty solicitor must[123]: undertake "at least two hours of continuing professional development annually on issues relevant to the law, practice and procedure in the Police Station or magistrates' courts"[124]; undertake personally a set minimum number of rota turns in magistrates' courts and rota cases at the police station[125] and continue to do evidenced general criminal defence work and police station work.[126]

(3) Clarifying the obligations upon duty solicitors.[127] Thus the suspect was more likely to receive at least advice.[128] The current clarification of the obligations is backed by the possibility of suspension from the scheme.[129] Suspension may occur where a duty solicitor: unreasonably failed to attend a police station; sent a representative when he or she should have attended personally; failed to accept a reasonable number of calls; failed to accept rota cases; unreasonably failed to carry out duties or comply with requirements of the scheme; is under criminal investigation or has been convicted of a crime or is being investigated by the Office for the Supervision of Solicitors[130]; does not demonstrate the necessary level of competence; no longer complies with the location rules; is no longer a fee earner within a

---

[119] *ibid.*, paras 4.4 and 4.6. On accreditation, see also Legal Aid Board, *Annual Report for 1999–2000* (HC Papers 664, 2000), paras 4.9–4.11.

[120] *Duty Solicitor Arrangements 2001* (amended 2006), para.4.5. Certain periods are disregarded, e.g. maternity leave and sickness: para.4.5(b).

[121] *ibid.* para.4.18. As to refusal of membership and appeals, see paras 4.21–4.23.

[122] Where a member's circumstances change, s/he is under an obligation to notify the Legal Services Commission: *Duty Solicitor Arrangements 2001* (amended 2006), para.5.10.

[123] Failure to comply with these requirements may lead to suspension from the scheme: *ibid.* paras 5.2 and 5.3.

[124] *ibid.* para.5.1(a).

[125] *ibid.* para.5.1(b).

[126] *ibid.* para.5.1(c). The evidence is that the solicitor must have accepted at least 12 police station cases annually involving attendance at the police station, or all cases where fewer were offered.

[127] See the Legal Aid Board Duty Solicitor Arrangements 1994 and the Legal Aid Board Legal Advice and Assistance at Police Stations Register Arrangements 1994 in the *Legal Aid Handbook 1995*, pp.457–486.

[128] The duty solicitor was under an obligation to accept the case and to provide initial advice on the telephone: Duty Solicitor Arrangements 1994, para.53. Also s/he was under an obligation to attend the police station where the crime was an arrestable offence and where the suspect was to be interviewed, go through an identification process or complained of serious maltreatment by the police: *ibid.* para.54.

[129] *Duty Solicitor Arrangements 2001* (amended 2006), para.5.4.

[130] Now undertaken by the Solicitors' Regulation Authority.

firm that is a CDS supplier with a contract; or some other good reason.[131]

(4) The gradual move towards a rota scheme means that it is highly likely that a duty solicitor will be available unless the scheme is swamped with business at a particular time. This is also contributed to by the contracting scheme imposing clearer burdens upon the solicitors gaining a General Criminal Contract.

(5) Improving quality assurance, which does not necessarily mean that the advice and assistance must be provided by a solicitor, as many paralegals are as well qualified and skilled in this particular area. What has been achieved is a clearer position as to who can be a non-solicitor providing advice and assistance.[132]

(6) It is for the LSC to decide what scheme to adopt.[133] The difficulty with this is that if a rota scheme is not adopted, there is less of a guarantee of availability of a duty solicitor. However, it would seem that there is a preference for rota schemes.[134]

(7) Being aware of a scheme makes it more likely that a suspect will request advice and assistance, and the LSC is required to "take steps to ensure that potential clients are made aware of the availability of the Duty Solicitor at Police Stations and magistrates' court".[135]

(8) Improving contact between the police station and the duty solicitors through the use of the Duty Solicitor Call Centre Service.

10–029 It is possible that there will still be some problems with the schemes. Whilst considerable effort has been made to address many of the problems, and they have clearly had their impact, the cause of some of the problems may not be addressed at least fully by these changes. Sanders and Young have suggested three reasons why the scheme, and the Police and Criminal Evidence Act 1984, have been ineffective and which may not be addressed by such changes:

(1) Enforcement is in the hands of those same officers and solicitors who may not have a vested interest in adhering to the rules. As regards solicitors, this is compounded by the poor rate of pay and the frequently unsociable hours.

(2) Police stations are police territory, but the main suspects for breach of the rules (the police) are also the gatekeepers.

(3) The rules themselves have allowed for bending.

The current set of figures for the work of the CDS are to be found in the LSC *Annual Report* for 2005/06.[136] These figures reveal the number and type of defendant assisted by the duty solicitor scheme[137]:

---

[131] *ibid.* para.5.4. As to the period of suspension, appeals, etc. see paras 5.5–5.9 and 7.13–7.22. Local instructions on the operation of the scheme may be issued under paras 6.13–6.15.

[132] Non-solicitors may obtain the right to advise in the police station through the Law Society's Police Station Representatives Accreditation Scheme.

[133] *ibid.* para.6.2.

[134] *ibid.* paras 6.1–6.8.

[135] *ibid.* para.6.12.

[136] Legal Services Commission, *Annual Report 2005/06* (HC 1215).

[137] *ibid.* Table 6.

Advice or representation	Type of service	Numbers	Total claimed £000
Police station: suspects not yet charged	Free standing advice and assistance	13,954	1,526
	Police station advice and assistance	756,101	172,794
Lower courts: defendants who have been charged	Court Duty Solicitor sessions	86,069	19,782
	Representation orders	581,307	295,235
	Advice, assistance and advocacy where no representation order granted	52,733	14,823
Higher courts: defendants who have been charged	Very High Cost Criminal Case contracts let	414	103,187
	Representation orders	121,483	592,306

3. The Future

At the time of writing, public funding of legal services is again controversial. In **10–030** 2005, in response to concerns about the proportion of the budget spent on criminal proceedings, the Department for Constitutional Affairs (DCA) (from May 2007 Ministry of Justice) published *A Fairer Deal for Legal Aid*,[138] the conclusions of a Fundamental Legal Aid Review commenced in 2004, concluding that "[f]urther short-term tinkering of the current system for buying and providing publicly funded legal advice and representation will no longer guarantee that the finite legal aid budget will continue to meet the needs of our society. Only fundamental reform can achieve this".[139] Recommendations involved, in particular, a focus on encouraging individuals to resolve their disputes otherwise than through litigation, and a review of procurement methods by the LSC. This review of procurement was carried out by Lord Carter of Coles in 2006.[140] In parallel with this, the LSC published its strategy for the CLS in the period 2006–11[141] and both were followed at the end of 2006 by the joint DCA and LSC paper *Legal Aid Reform: the Way Ahead*[142] in which it was indicated that the Carter proposals would be accepted. Consequently, the basis on which LSC contracts will be awarded in the future will one of "best value competition, based on quality, capacity and price", albeit with transitional provisions.[143] In addition,

---

[138] Cm. 6591, July 2005.

[139] *ibid.* p.39.

[140] *Legal Aid: A Market-Based Approach to Reform* (DCA, July 2006). Consultation on the proposals was contained in DCA and LSC, *Legal Aid: A Sustainable Future* (CP 13/06, July 2006).

[141] *Making Legal Rights a Reality* (March 2006).

[142] Cm. 6993, November 2006. Other consultations on the Legal Services Commission appear on the DCA website at *http://www.dca.gov.uk/laid/laidfr.htm*.

[143] *ibid.* p.7.

particular control, including tariffs of fixed and graduated fees, will be introduced for criminal work, as a preliminary to competitive tendering.

Whilst emphasis is placed in the proposals on contracts being awarded not on the basis of price but also of quality, the proposals remain, at the time of writing, controversial, the Law Society, for example, commenting that "[i]f implemented, the government's plans to reform legal aid could lead to hundreds of legal aid practitioners giving up legal aid work. This will leave many vulnerable clients unrepresented".[144] If the new contracting arrangements do result either in a reduction in the number of advisers able or prepared to offer advice under the scheme, or a reduction in their geographical spread, it remains to be seen whether, for example, newly authorised organisations entering the sector in the wake of the Legal Services Bill will be in a position to fill the gap.

---

[144] *http://lawsociety.org.uk*, "What Price Justice Campaign". A similar campaign is underway at the Law Centres Federation: "Support Our Campaign to Protect Legal Aid and Law Centres", *http://www.lawcentres.org.uk* and the Director of Citizens Advice has commented "[l]egal aid is essential to enable people on limited means to get access to justice. However, the Government's proposed system, with limited exceptions, will pay the same per case whether it requires one hour or eight to resolve. There will therefore be pressure on all legal aid suppliers to cherry-pick simple cases. Many of the people that bureaux help are vulnerable and have very complicated cases that take a lot of assistance. If those people cannot come to us for help, there may be nowhere else for them to go": *http://www.citizensadvice.org.uk/press_20070111.*

PART III

PRE-TRIAL PROCEDURE

CHAPTER 11

FEATURES OF LITIGATION AND OTHER METHODS OF DISPUTE RESOLUTION

In Pt II we looked at advice and information. Now we begin a Part called Pre-trial **11–001** Procedure and it may appear that we are progressing inexorably towards the courtroom. Yet between the recognition of a dispute which may end in a trial and its actual arrival before the judge lies a lengthy period of negotiation before or during the operation of the formal pre-trial procedure. An understanding of the significance of these negotiations, which may sometimes more accurately be described as bargaining, and the resulting settlements is fundamental to civil litigation. We concentrate on civil matters, even though in the criminal context there is the analogous feature of "plea bargaining". The other two topics we consider in this chapter, costs and delay, have significance in both civil and criminal litigation, and are interrelated with pre-trial negotiations. Finally, in the civil context, we consider the increasingly important topic of resolving disputes by methods other than litigation.

Influencing both civil and criminal procedure before and at trial, the English adversarial approach permits the parties to dictate the issues to be resolved and—to a limited extent—to settle the pace of the action. In a previous edition of this book the following statement appeared at this point:

> "In civil cases, the court has had no role in directing the course of the proceedings except on the application of one or other party. It has always been able to impose penalties on parties who break the rules without permission, by the award of costs against them, but it has not been able to enforce the rules of its own volition."

It is indicative of the extent of the so-called "Woolf reforms" (more accurately: the Civil Procedure Rules 1998[1] (the CPR)—completely changing the face of civil procedure in England and Wales from April 26, 1999—that that simple statement must now be wholly revised. In addition, although the rules themselves are a statutory instrument, the accompanying forms and "practice directions" (PDs) which must be read alongside the rules are not, not all amendments require a statutory instrument. For an up-to-date set of rules and practice directions, the reader is best advised to use the Department for Constitutional Affairs (DCA) website (from May 9, 2007, renamed the Ministry of Justice)[2] and for forms, the website of HM Courts Service.[3] This chapter is believed to be up to date to the 43rd update to the Civil Procedure Rules.

In civil cases, as we will see in Chs 12 and 15, the court is responsible for the "active management" of cases.[4] Except where positively prohibited from so doing, it may exercise its powers on an application or on its own initiative.[5]

The parties select the issue or issues on which to fight—although the court may narrow them—and the evidence—although the court may limit the types and extent of evidence—with which to support their case. Whilst it might be thought to be in the interests of the parties to conceal what they know so that negotiation, in the form of bargaining, can proceed more effectively through a process of bluff and ambush, the court will, in pursuit of its objective of dealing with cases justly, demand that as much as possible be disclosed in the early stages so that the matters really in dispute can be identified and the strength of the evidence assessed. As we will see in Ch.12, the parties have positive obligations to assist in that process.[6]

A. COSTS

1. CIVIL CASES

11–002 The costs involved in civil litigation are of the utmost importance to the parties—they may prevent an action ever being brought, they may render a victory in court

---

[1] SI 1998/3132. The many subsequent amendments to the rules are listed on the Ministry of Justice website.

[2] http://www.justice.gov.uk/civil/procrules_fin/index.htm.

[3] http://www.hmcourts-service.gov.uk.

[4] CPR Pt 1.

[5] CPR r.3.3.

[6] See CPR r.1.3 and Courts and Legal Services Act 1990 ss.27 and 28, inserted by Access to Justice Act 1999, s.42 and to be replaced by Legal Services Bill, cl.180.

Pyrrhic when damages are swallowed up in costs, they may prevent a meritorious appeal, and they will always be a factor in the risk of litigation.

Lawyers are familiar with the concept that the costs in a case can easily be greater than the amount actually in dispute between the litigants. For many people the costs of litigation are difficult, impossible, or off-putting. When litigation is necessary, it is important, if a system of civil justice is to be fair, that litigants must "have an equal opportunity, regardless of their resources, to assert or defend their legal rights".

In his Interim Report, Lord Woolf concluded that the then level of costs was not an inevitable or necessary feature of litigation and that the then current attitudes to litigation were a major factor in creating high costs and costs uncertainty.

In parallel with Lord Woolf's investigations, however, was a political initiative that HM Courts Service should be self-funding.[7] This had already resulted in a vast increase in court fees over a short period: for example, it cost £55 to issue a writ in 1993, but £500 to issue the same claim in 1998.[8] This, of itself, acted as a disincentive to the issue of court proceedings, particularly in the small claims track where a further fee of £80 payable by the claimant on allocation was particularly contentious and later withdrawn although retained for all other cases (at £100 in the county court and £200 in the High Court).[9] The Woolf reforms have been in operation for seven years at the time of writing and there is a growing body of research on aspects of their effectiveness.[10] The extent to which they can be said to have been successful in the field of costs as elsewhere is considered in Ch.12.

Costs have to be looked at in two respects, first the costs which may be ordered to be paid by one of the parties to the other in litigation, and, secondly, the costs which a client is obliged to pay his or her own lawyer. It is not necessarily the case that the amount recovered by the successful party from the losing party will cover the whole of the successful party's solicitor's bill.

(a) Costs payable in litigation

"There is no other system of justice where litigants devote so much time, effort and money to litigation over who should bear the costs of

---

[7] In 2005/06, of HM Courts Service gross fee income for civil services was £437.2 million, of which £408 million was recouped from civil fees: HM Courts Service, *Working for You: Annual Report & Accounts 2005/06*, p.35.

[8] Fees are scaled in accordance with the value of the case: these are maxima It might be noted that the current maximum fee, for issue of a claim of more than £300,000 in the High Court, is £1,700. Fees in civil proceedings are now contained in the Civil Proceedings Fees (Amendment) Order 2006 (SI 2006/719).

[9] The question of court fees remains contentious. The responses to the Law Society's *Sixth Woolf Questionnaire* in September 2003 suggested that 33 per cent of solicitor respondents had known clients to be discouraged from pursuing claims because of court fees. The full response to this and other "Woolf Questionnaires" are available on the Law Society website.

[10] See, for example, the Lord Chancellor's Department paper, *Emerging Findings* (March 2001); and its second paper *Further Findings* (August 2002); the Law Society's *Sixth Woolf Questionnaire* (September 2003); J. Peysner and M. Seneviratne, *The Management of Civil Cases: the courts and the post-Woolf landscape* (DCA Research Series 9/05, November 2005). Other research papers can be found on the DCA/Ministry of Justice website.

proceedings. There is no other system where the courts at all levels are called upon to adjudicate as many disputes over costs. . . . ."[11]

11–003   In deciding whether to begin or continue litigation, one major factor is whether a party will have to pay the costs or be able to recover them from the other party.

The principles applying to the assessment of costs after a trial (previously "taxation of costs") do not prevent the parties reaching their own agreement about costs where a settlement is effected before trial. Indeed, in the majority of cases, costs are agreed between the parties.[12] Nevertheless, the assessment rules remain significant in providing the framework within which the parties can negotiate.

The steps are, first, that the judge must decide who should pay costs and on what basis.[13] The judge may award costs of different issues to different parties.[14] Secondly, a costs judge (previously a "taxing officer") must determine exactly what costs are to be paid (this is now known as "detailed assessment of costs"). If the trial lasts no more than one day, the trial judge will probably do this him or herself on the basis of schedules of costs submitted by the parties in advance of the trial. This procedure, which is also adopted in relation to the costs of any short pre-trial hearing, is known as "summary assessment of costs".[15]

Lord Woolf, in his Interim Report, considered the argument that the rule that costs normally follow the result can induce a "win at all costs mentality [which] is supported by some research which indicates that the existing rule has the tendency to increase expenditure on cases when compared with a system where each party bears its own costs".[16] However, the rule tends only to support meritorious cases where there are greater expectations of success. The arguments in favour of the rule were identified in the Interim Report: (1) "it is fairer that a party who has succeeded in litigation should at least be able to recover the major proportion of his [or her] own costs from his [or her] unsuccessful opponent." (2) "the rule deters unmeritorious litigation and encourages earlier settlement." It also identified the arguments against the rule. (1) "It may deter meritorious as well as unmeritorious claims." (2) "It favours the wealthy litigant over the less wealthy." (3) "It can so increase the costs at stake that parties feel impelled to go on, thus making it impossible to reach a settlement."[17] No person bringing

---

[11] A. A. S. Zuckerman, "An Unseemly Squabble Amongst Public Authorities Over Costs" (2006) 25(JAN) C.J.Q. 1.

[12] If the parties are in the opposite position: having agreed on the substantive issues but not on how much the recoverable costs should be, an application can be made to the court to resolve the amount payable under CPR r.44.12A ("cost-only proceedings").

[13] Interim Report, p.201. See A. A. S. Zuckerman, "Reform in the Shadow of Lawyers' Interests" in Zuckerman and Cranston (eds) *Reforming Civil Procedure* (1995).

[14] See, for example, *BCT Software Solutions Ltd v C. Brewer & Sons Ltd* [2003] EWCA Civ 939.

[15] CPR r.43.3, 44.7; PD 43–48 paras 3, 13 and 14. *A Guide to Summary Assessment* can be found on HM Courts Service website. The effectiveness or otherwise of summary assessment, as a pragmatic method of assessing and awarding costs is one of the more contentious areas of the reforms: The Law Society's *Sixth Woolf Questionnaire, op. cit.*, in September 2003, asking, *inter alia*, "Are you still experiencing inconsistent summary costs assessment orders?" found that 44 per cent of respondents answered "yes".

[16] Interim Report, pp.202–203.

[17] Final Report, Ch.4. See also Sir Peter Middleton's *Review of Civil Justice and Legal Aid* ("the Middleton Report", September 1997); the Lord Chancellor's Department research paper *Solicitors' fixed costs in civil claims* (1998) and Goriely, Butt and Sherr, *Costing Fast Track Procedures Through Hypothetical Studies* (Lord Chancellor's Department research paper, 1998).

litigation should be immune from the financial risk factor, because of the burdens imposed on society and the courts of taking such a step, and so Lord Woolf concluded that the rule should stay, but recommended that the rule be made more effective, particularly to encourage co-operative and discourage unco-operative conduct by the parties.

Lord Woolf ultimately proposed that the recoverable costs in fast track cases should be limited to a maximum of £2,500, banding cases according to their value and allowing for a percentage of the fixed costs[18] to be recoverable if the case settled prior to trial.[19] Whilst this regime did not ultimately find its way into the CPR, the recoverable costs of the *trial* in the fast track[20] are limited by CPR Pt 46; more recently, specific fixed recoverable costs schemes have been imposed for some aspects of road traffic and employers' liability claims[21]; pre-emptive "costs capping" has been used in some cases to limit possible exposure to payment of the opponent's costs[22]; and in any case the court may predetermine the amount of a jointly-appointed expert's fees that will be recoverable from the losing party.

Nevertheless, the basic rule remains that "costs follow the event", that is to say the successful party can expect the judge to order the loser to pay some or all of his or her solicitor's bill.[23] It was stated in *AEI Rediffusion Music Limited v Phonographic Performance Limited (Costs)*[24] by Lord Woolf M.R. (as he then was) that:

"I draw attention to the new Rules because, while they make clear that the general rule remains, that the successful party will normally be entitled to costs, they at the same time indicate the wide range of considerations which will result in the court making different orders as to costs. From April 26, 1999 the 'follow the event principle' will still play a significant role, but it

---

[18] Disbursements (i.e. expenses over and above the solicitors' fees) were to be recoverable separately.

[19] Continued debate about costs can be found on the Civil Justice Council website at *http://www.costsdebate.civiljusticecouncil.gov.uk*. See in particular the CJC report *Improved Access to Justice—Funding Options and Proportionate Costs* (August 2005).

[20] The usual way of dealing with claims worth between £5,000 and £15,000. See para.12–005 *et seq.* See also DCA consultation paper *Part 46 of the Civil Procedure Rules: fast track trial costs* (April 2007).

[21] CPR Pt 45, PD 43–48, s.25A; *Nizami v Butt* [2006] EWHC 159, QBD; K. Underwood, *Fixed Costs*, (2nd edn, 2006, Butterworths Law); P. Fenn and N. Rickman, *Monitoring the Fixed Recoverable Costs Scheme* (2007, Civil Justice Council).

[22] Using CPR r.44.3 to cap the recoverable costs pre-emptively at an early stage in the proceedings; *Solutia v Griffiths* [2001] EWCA Civ 736; *R v The Prime Minister, Ex p. CND* [2002] EWHC 271; *A v Leeds Teaching Hospital NHS Trust* [2003] EWHC 1034; *King v Telegraph Group Ltd* [2004] EWCA Civ 613; *R (on the application of Corner House Research) v Secretary of State for Trade and Industry* [2005] EWCA Civ 192; *Goodson v HM Coroner for Bedfordshire and Luton (Protective Costs)* [2005] EWCA Civ 1172; *Henry v BBC (Costs Capping)* [2005] EWHC 2503. For comment on this concept and on the extent to which costs can be pre-emptively estimated, see J. Peysner, "Predictability and Budgeting", [2004] 23 C.J.Q. 15 and A. A. S. Zuckerman, "Cost capping orders in CFA cases improve costs control but raise questions about the CFA legislation and its compatibility with Art.6 of the European Convention on Human Rights" (2005) 24(JAN) C.J.Q. 1.

[23] See CPR r.44.3(2): "If the court decides to make an order about costs—(a) the general rule is that the unsuccessful party will be ordered to pay the costs of the successful party; but (b) the court may make a different order".

[24] [1999] 1 W.L.R. 1507; CA. For some other early expressions of intent as to the "loser pays" principle, see *Liverpool C.C. v Rosemary Chavasse Ltd (Costs)* [2000] C.P. Rep. 8, Ch D; *Scholes Windows Ltd v Magnet Ltd (No.2)* [2000] E.C.D.R. 266, Ch D.

will be a starting point from which a court can readily depart. . . . The most significant change of emphasis of the new Rules is to require courts to be more ready to make separate orders which reflect the outcome of different issues."

Other factors to be considered[25] are:

(a) the conduct of the parties, including:

    (i) conduct before and during proceedings including the extent of compliance with any pre-action protocol[26];

    (ii) whether or not it was reasonable for a party to pursue or contest a particular issue within the case;

    (iii) the manner in which a party has conducted the case[27];

    (iv) whether a successful claimant has exaggerated the claim.

(b) partial success;

(c) any offer to settle drawn to the court's attention (this will normally have been made under CPR Pt 36).

The court[28] has a great deal of flexibility in the order it makes and might, for example, order a party[29] to pay:

(a) a proportion of the opponent's costs (e.g. 50 per cent);

(b) a stated amount (e.g. £5,000) towards the opponent's costs;

(c) the opponent's costs from or until a certain date;

(d) the opponent's costs incurred prior to the issue of proceedings;

(e) the opponent's costs relating to particular steps in proceedings;

(f) the opponent's costs of a distinct part of the proceedings (e.g. liability), an approach known as an "issue-based" costs order;

(g) interest on the opponent's costs.[30]

---

[25] CPR rr.44.3 (4) and (5).

[26] A stage of procedure acting as a precursor to the formal issuing of court proceedings. See Ch.12. As we will see, an unreasonable failure to attempt to resolve the dispute by alternative dispute resolution is also a factor currently taken into account in determining costs.

[27] For an application of this rule where one party had instructed a comparatively small regional firm of solicitors whilst the other had instructed a very large City firm, see *Mars UK Ltd v Teknowledge (No.2)*, [1999] 2 Costs L.R. 44; Ch D.

[28] Other conventional types of order frequently used in interim hearings (i.e. hearings prior to the trial) are set out in PD 43–48 para.8.5.

[29] It is sometimes possible to make costs orders for or against non-parties under the Supreme Court Act 1981, s.51: CPR r.48.2. The non-party may be the legal representative of one of the parties to the litigation: see CPR r.48.7, PD 43–48 section 53; *Ridehalgh v Horsefield* [1994] Ch. 205; *Persaud v Persaud* [2003] EWCA Civ 394.

[30] Judgments Act 1838, s.17; County Courts Act 1984, s.74. See *Powell v Hertfordshire Health Authority* [2002] EWCA Civ 1786; *Nova Productions Ltd v Mazooma Games Ltd (Interest on Costs)* [2006] EWHC 189, Ch D.

However, if the form of the order, whether it relates to the whole costs of the winning party or not, is expressed as anything other than an order for payment of a stated amount, the next stage is to calculate the amount payable. At a short hearing, where summary assessment is appropriate, the court will carry out this evaluation immediately by way of "summary assessment". Alternatively, a judge may order that costs are to be subjected to detailed assessment. In either case, assessment will be on one of two bases[31]:

(a) The standard basis, where the court will consider whether:

    (i) costs were "proportionately and reasonably incurred", or

    (ii) "were proportionate and reasonable in amount"

(b) The indemnity basis, where the court will consider whether costs were "unreasonably incurred; or unreasonable in amount".[32]

Historically, the two bases contained a difference of emphasis—on the standard basis costs were recoverable only if *reasonable*, whereas on the indemnity basis, costs were irrecoverable only if *unreasonable*. However, the editors of the White Book (the principal practitioner reference in civil litigation) now suggest that the test for each basis is "whether or not the costs have been reasonably incurred or are reasonable in amount" and the difference between the two is confined to the requirement, when assessing costs under the standard basis, also to consider proportionality.[33]   **11–004**

From the point of view of the receiving party, the indemnity basis is the preferred basis, as even disproportionate costs are, at least in principle, recoverable. Aside from the specific power to award indemnity costs where a claimant's Pt 36 offer has been rejected,[34] costs may be awarded on the indemnity basis where the paying party's conduct of the litigation has been "unreasonable" at least if this is to a high degree.[35]

The subsequent procedure is for the solicitor for the receiving party—generally within a time limit of three months from the making of the costs

---

[31] CPR r.44.4.

[32] CPR r.44.5.

[33] Brooke L.J. (gen. ed.), *Civil Procedure 2006* (Sweet & Maxwell), p.1157. An assessment of proportionality has been held to involve a two stage test: (a) a "global approach" deciding whether the total claimed is proportionate taking into account the factors listed in CPR r.44.5(3) and (b) if the total claimed is not disproportionate, the costs judge will then go on to consider the recoverability of individual items claimed: *Home Office v Lownds* [2002] EWCA Civ 365. The Law Society's *Sixth Woolf Questionnaire*, *op. cit.*, in September 2003, found 77 per cent of respondents confirming that "the authorities on proportionality" had had an impact (the questionnaire did not ask whether the impact was positive or negative). An attack on a costs order as being disproportionate by virtue of Art.10 ECHR failed in *Campbell v Mirror Group Newspapers Ltd (Costs)* [2005] UKHL 61.

[34] CPR r.36.21. See *Reid Minty v Taylor* [2001] EWCA Civ 1723, CA; *McPhilemy v Times Newspapers Ltd (No.2)* [2001] EWCA Civ 933. As to Pt 36 offers and payment generally, see below, para.12–028. and I. R. Scott, "Indemnity Costs" (2002) 21 C.L.Q. 183.

[35] The test no longer requires unconscionable behaviour: *Reid Minty (a firm) v Taylor* [2001] EWCA Civ 1723; *Kiam v MGN Ltd (Costs)* [2002] EWCA Civ 66; *Bim Kemi AB v Blackburn Chemicals Ltd (Costs)* [2003] EWCA Civ 889; *Balmoral Group Ltd v Borealis (UK) Ltd (Indemnity Costs)* [2006] EWHC 2531. Indemnity costs can be awarded as a sanction for failure to comply with rules, practice directions or court orders: *Biguzzi v Rank Leisure Plc* [1999] 1 W.L.R. 1926, CA; *Petrotrade Inc. v Texaco Ltd* [2001] C.P. Rep. 29, CA.

order[36]—to compile a "notice of commencement" and a bill of costs[37] and send it to the paying party together with any supporting documents.[38] If the parties are unable to agree the amount of costs, the receiving party will then request a "detailed assessment hearing". The preparation of a bill of costs for detailed assessment is a very skilled and detailed task. Specialists ("costs draftsmen"[39]) exist who undertake the drafting of the bill, usually for a commission calculated on the total amount of the bill or for a salary if employed by a large firm of solicitors. This payment is allowable on assessment and so may be recoverable from the losing party.

The costs judge hears the parties and decides any issues in dispute, either allowing each item in the bill to stand or disallowing or reducing it. The total arrived at by this process (the "assessed costs") is the amount to be paid by the party ordered to pay. The costs awarded are, however, if awarded on the standard basis, unlikely to cover all the work the receiving party's solicitor has carried out for his or her client but a proportion closer to 60 or 70 per cent.[40]

There are some circumstances, other than those set out in CPR r.44.5, in which costs are not awarded to the successful party. One is CPR Pt 36. Another is that the party who is ultimately successful at trial might nevertheless have been unsuccessful in a pre-trial hearing (for example to have his or her opponent's case struck out as having "no real prospect of success" under CPR Pt 24) and to have been penalised at that time by the award of the costs of that pre-trial hearing against him or her. Costs of such hearings will normally be summarily assessed at the time of the hearing and must be paid within 14 days of assessment.[41] Further, in order to ensure that the client, who often will not have attended the hearing, is aware of the way in which the action is being conducted on his or her behalf, the solicitor must inform the client in writing of the adverse costs order within 7 days of its having been made.[42]

Three other related matters should be mentioned. First, where the successful party is a party to a conditional fee agreement with his or her solicitors (and counsel) the success fee and insurance premium (described as "additional liabilities") are *prima facie* recoverable from the losing party at the conclusion of the proceedings in addition to the ordinary costs.[43] Secondly, the successful unassisted party in an action where the opponent has legal aid may be awarded costs against the Legal Services Commission where certain statutory conditions are met.[44] Finally, people who conduct their own litigation are entitled to costs in respect of their own time and effort spent preparing and presenting the case.[45]

---

[36] CPR r.47.14, PD 43–48 para.40.

[37] CPR r.47.6, PD 43–48 para.32. Where the receiving party has the benefit of a conditional fee agreement (see below, para.11–008), these details will include details of the success fee and insurance premium.

[38] If the receiving party is claiming a sum more than 20% greater than was set out in a costs estimate filed during the course of proceedings (see Ch.12) an additional explanation of the increase must be given, and the paying party can claim that he or she reasonably relied on the earlier estimate.

[39] The Association of Law Costs Draftsmen has a website at *http://www.alcd.org.uk/index1.htm*.

[40] For a review of the contribution of the solicitors' "hourly rate" to this discussion, see M. Cook, "Solicitors' Hourly Rates" (2005) 24(JAN) C.J.Q. 142.

[41] CPR r.44.8.

[42] CPR r.44.2.

[43] CPR rr.44.3A, 44.3B, PD 43–49 paras 9, 10, 11,14, 19.

[44] Community Legal Service (Cost Protection) Regulations 2000 as amended (SI 2000/824), reg.5.

[45] CPR r.48.6, PD 43–48 para.52

(b) Costs payable to solicitor (private funding)

As indicated above, whilst the successful party will often receive payment **11–005** towards his or her legal costs from the losing party, this will not necessarily cover the whole of the solicitor's bill.

Solicitors are obliged to present their bills within a reasonable time of concluding the work.[46] The client's contractual obligation is to pay the bill presented by the solicitor. Ultimately the solicitor is entitled to sue the client for "proper costs". What costs are proper may ultimately be determined independently by detailed assessment,[47] but this is a highly unusual step for a solicitor to take; the better approach would be a simple debt action, or, in appropriate circumstances, insolvency proceedings against the client.

The concern for the client is whether the solicitor is overcharging. It is difficult for the client to assess whether the costs are appropriate for the service received.[48] Until July 1, 2007, a solicitor was obliged to provide information as to costs as soon as instructed by the client under the Solicitors' Costs Information and Client Care Code 1999.[49] The main object of the 1999 Code was "to make sure that clients are given the information they need to understand what is happening generally and in particular on (i) the cost of legal services both at the outset and as a matter progresses; and (ii) responsibility for clients' matters". Although many firms used standard letters and internal systems intended to ensure that the code was followed, it is a fact that the Code was reissued in 1999 in a more precise and directive format than its predecessor in an attempt to reduce problems with clients and was again tightened up in 2006 as a result of the consumer-focused impetus of the Clementi review[50] discussed in Ch.3. If solicitors had always complied with the Code, many of their problems with clients would have disappeared. Prior to the introduction of the 1999 Code, the Legal Services Ombudsman stated that "full compliance with the written professional standard is . . . an absolutely essential safeguard for clients, and very much in the interests of solicitors themselves if they are to avoid complaints about costs".[51] The National Association of Citizens' Advice Bureaux had noted in 1995 that complaints about costs were a major area of CAB work and that there was poor compliance with the previous standard.[52] Research sponsored by the National

---

[46] *The Guide to the Professional Conduct of Solicitors*, principle 14.06: *http://www.lawsociety. org.uk/professional/conduct/guideonline.law*. From July 1, 2007 this is replaced by *Solicitors' Code of Conduct 2007*, which contains no explicit equivalent provision. For some background on this topic, see M. Zander, "Where are we heading with the Funding of Civil Litigation" (2003) 22 C.J.Q. 23.

[47] This procedure is also available to determine a reasonable amount of costs payable by a client to his or her own solicitor as well as between opposing parties. See, for example, CPR r.48.8, PD 43–48 para.54.

[48] This is true for commercial as well as for private clients.

[49] This was last amended in June 2006 to include some of the information previously contained in Practice Rule 15 (Solicitors' Practice Rules 1990, also amended in June 2006).

[50] See, for some pre-Clementi concerns, J. Farrar, "Arrogant, incompetent, negligent and unprofessional . . . " *Which?*, August 2001, p.8. For the Law Society's position on these issues, see *Law Society Addresses . . . " Which? Concerns*, Law Society Press Release August 2, 2001 and the more wide-ranging *Blueprint for Change* published on March 23, 2001.

[51] N. Harris, *Solicitors and Client Care* (1994), p.22.

[52] *"Modernising Justice" . . . Modernising regulation?* (1998/1999) Annual Report of the Legal Services Ombudsman, p.29.

Consumer Council then concluded that "a significant minority [of clients] do not always receive the kind of information on costs required by the ... standards".[53]

Did the 1999 Code made any difference? In 1998, 11 per cent of cases referred to the Legal Services Ombudsman involved a failure to inform about costs.[54] In 1999/2000, 4 per cent of cases involved "excessive costs" and 3 per cent inadequate costs information.[55] Failure to provide proper costs information continues to be a source of complaint to the Legal Complaints Service.[56]

The *Solicitors' Code of Conduct 2007* rule 2, client relations, now covers the relevant ground. Paragraph 2.03 requires that the solicitor should give "the best information possible about the likely overall cost of a matter both at the outset and, when appropriate, as the matter progresses". In particular solicitors must "advise the client of the basis and terms of [their] charges; (b) advise the client if charging rates are to be increased; (c) advise the client of likely payments which [they or their] client may need to make to others; (d) discuss with the client how the client will pay, in particular: (i) whether the client may be eligible and should apply for public funding; and (ii) whether the client's own costs are covered by insurance or may be paid by someone else such as an employer or trade union; (e) advise the client that there are circumstances where [the solicitor] may be entitled to exercise a lien for unpaid costs; (f) advise the client of their potential liability for any other party's costs; and (g) discuss with the client whether their liability for another party's costs may be covered by existing insurance or whether specially purchased insurance may be obtained". This provision does not explicitly, as did its predecessor, require a breakdown to be shown between fees, VAT and disbursements[57]; or the time likely to be spent on the matter if an hourly rate is being charged; although the information must be "clear and confirmed in writing". Additional information to be provided to clients under conditional fee agreements (colloquially "no win: no fee" arrangements) and those with the benefit of public funding appear in paras 2.03(2) and (3).

Failure to provide such information, or to provide it in writing, if it was "inappropriate in the circumstances" to do so, does not amount to a breach of the rule (para.2.03(7)).[58]

---

[53] *Demanding Progress* (1999/2000) Annual Report of the Legal Services Ombudsman, p.36.

[54] *Reflecting Progress* (2000/2001) Annual Report of the Legal Services Ombudsman, p.37.

[55] Legal Services Ombudsman's *Annual Report 1999/2000*. We have already seen, in Ch.3, some of the results of what was perceived as a failure by solicitors and by the Law Society to deal with client complaints effectively. See also Allen and Clarke, "Keeping the Client Happy" (2000) 97(16) L.S.G. 26–28, 30–33; Seneviratne, "Consumer Complaints and the legal profession: making self regulation work?" (2000) 7(1) I.J.L.P.,39–58.

[56] See J. Saville, "Client Expectations and Complaints" (2007) 1 J.P.I.L. 86. The Legal Services Ombudsman's *Annual Report and Accounts 2005/06* does not separate out grounds of complaint in this way but still retains "not adequately informed" amongst the top 10 reasons for complaint against all lawyers.

[57] Although these would fall within category (c) above.

[58] The notes to Rule 2 make it clear that breaches of these provisions will not necessarily mean that the solicitor is unable to recover costs from the client although a material breach might amount to "inadequate professional services", a finding of which by the Legal Complaints Service might result in the bill being unenforceable. See also *Garbutt v Edwards* [2005] EWCA Civ 1206, where the opponent argued that if the solicitor's own client was not obliged to pay the solicitor as a result of a breach of the 1999 Code, those costs were not, therefore, recoverable from the opponent in litigation.

It has been said that solicitors "must not take unfair advantage of the client by   **11–006**
overcharging for work done or to be done".[59] Whilst there is no specific
reference to overcharging in the *Solicitors' Code of Conduct 2007*, the notes to
rule 2 point out that solicitors must "act in the client's best interests . . . and
[they] must not abuse or exploit the relationship by taking advantage of a client's
age, inexperience, ill health, lack of education or business experience, or emotional or other vulnerability". Deliberate overcharging—which might in some
cases amount to a criminal offence in any event—would, it is suggested, also
result in disciplinary action through the Solicitors' Disciplinary Tribunal, as
described in Ch.3.

Assessing the propriety of costs will depend on whether they relate to a
contentious matter (i.e. where litigation has been commenced).[60] If a client
objects to the bill submitted by the solicitor in a contentious matter, an application can be made for its detailed assessment.[61] If granted,[62] assessment is carried
out on the "indemnity basis" but it is presumed that the costs: (a) have been
reasonably incurred, if they were incurred with the express or implied approval
of the client; (b) have been reasonable in amount, if their amount was expressly
or impliedly approved by the client; (c) have been unreasonably incurred, if they
are of an unusual nature or amount and the solicitor failed to inform the client
that, as a result, they might be irrecoverable from the opponent. It should be
noted that, unless the order for assessment was made on the application of the
solicitor and the client failed to attend or a court order provided otherwise, then,
if the bill is reduced by one-fifth or more on assessment, the solicitor will pay the
costs of the assessment, otherwise the client will do so.[63]

In non-contentious civil matters, the client may, provided the bill does not
exceed £50,000, seek a remuneration certificate through the Law Society Legal
Complaints Service Remuneration Scheme.[64] Normally, the client must pay the
disbursements, VAT and 50 per cent of the costs sought by the solicitor prior to
seeking the certificate.[65] The client may then be charged such sum as is determined by the Legal Complaints Service to be "fair—based on our assessment of
the work completed by your solicitor".[66] If still unsatisfied, the client has the
right to apply to the High Court for an order to have the bill assessed.[67] If
granted, the costs judge assesses the costs on the same basis as in a contentious
case.

---

[59] Law Society Gazette, March 18, 1998, quoted in *Professional Conduct, op cit.*, at 30.02.
[60] An order must be granted if the request is made within one calendar month of delivery of the bill,
    otherwise the court has a discretion: Solicitors' Act 1974, s.70.
[61] CPR r.48.8
[62] Solicitors' Act 1974, ss.7(9) and (10).
[63] Solicitors' (Non Contentious Business) Remuneration Order 1994 (SI 1994/2616), art.11(1).
[64] *ibid.* Art.4(1). A client may not seek a remuneration certificate after the expiry of one month from
    the date on which the client was given information under art.8 as to his or her entitlement to seek
    such a certificate (in many cases this will be pre-printed on the solicitor's invoice), after a bill has
    been delivered and paid, or after a court order for assessment of costs, *ibid.*, art.9.
[65] *ibid.*, art.3(2). See also the description of the procedure on the Legal Complaints Service website:
    http://www.legalcomplaints.org.uk.
[66] *http://www.legalcomplaints.org.uk.* See, for discussion of this procedure, Fennell (1992).
[67] Solicitors' (Non-Contentious Business) Remuneration Order 1994, art.5(1): if the costs judge
    allows less than half of the sum originally charged to the client, this will be reported to the
    Solicitors' Regulation Authority.

(c) Costs payable to solicitor (insurance)

11–007   It is possible that a litigant may have legal expenses insurance which is "payment of an annual premium to carry cover, in given categories of cases, for a claimant's[68] legal costs (including any costs awarded against him [*sic*]) up to a limit of indemnity". A policy is either personal or commercial and is either a "stand-alone" policy or an "add-on policy" (that is added on to household or motor insurance).[69] Its take-up is comparatively small in the stand-alone format, "[a]lthough free-standing policies have not proved successful, legal expenses insurance, in the form of cheap but limited add-on policies to car or house insurance is probably more widespread in this country than generally believed".[70] Very many individuals, however, remain simply unaware that they have such cover in its "add-on" format.[71] This form of insurance is frequently described as "before-the-event" insurance.

A second form of insurance is "after the event insurance", where an individual does not purchase the policy until *after* the cause of action has arisen. The risk insured against is, therefore, not, as in legal expenses insurance, the risk of *litigation*, but the risk of *losing* the actual or contemplated litigation. The most common usage of after-the-event policies is in conjunction with conditional fee agreements. The premium paid for an after the event policy, as opposed to that for a before the event policy, is potentially recoverable from a losing opponent in litigation.[72]

(d) Costs payable to solicitor (conditional fee agreements)[73]

11–008   The conditional fee agreement (CFA), often, and somewhat misleadingly called a "no win: no fee" agreement, was developed in the context of a proposed reduction in public funding for civil litigation.

The common law "indemnity principle" prescribed that a losing party could not be asked to pay to the successful party any *more* than the successful party was obliged to pay to his or her own solicitor. In a "no win: no fee agreement" the client and solicitor have, in effect agreed that, the client having been successful,

---

[68] Here used in the technical sense of a person claiming under a policy: potential defendants may have and use legal expenses insurance.

[69] V. Prais, "Legal Expenses Insurance" in Zuckerman and Cranston (1995), p.434. See also Prais, "A question of insurance" (1999) 149 N.L.J. 1372; Greer, "Legal Expenses Insurance—have they really got you covered?" (1999) 149 N.L.J. 781; Samuels, "Legal Expenses or Litigation Insurance" (1998) 17 C.J.Q. 16.

[70] Middleton Report, *op. cit.*, para.5.51, further quoting an expenditure on premiums in 1995 in the region of £25 million.

[71] For an indication of the extent to which the advising solicitor must ask the client to search for previously unsuspected insurance cover, see *Sarwar v Alam* [2001] EWCA Civ 1401, CA, where the claimant, a car passenger, was, unknown to him, covered by the insurance policy of the *defendant* driver. See also, Allen, "After-the event insurance failure highlighted" (2000) 97(30), L.S.G. 4 and Marshall, "Making a Good Recovery" (2001) 151 N.L.J. 1856.

[72] See below, para.11–008. See also the Middleton Report, *op. cit.*

[73] For some background and evaluative information, see KPMG, *Conditional Fees—a Business Case* (1998, report to the Lord Chancellor's Department); *Access to Justice with Conditional Fees* (1998, Lord Chancellor's Department consultation paper); *Conditional Fees—Sharing the Risk of Litigation* (September 1999, Lord Chancellor's Department consultation paper); NACABx, *Conditional Fees—Sharing the risk of Litigation: A response by the CAB service* (2001).

the amount the client will pay to the solicitor in respect of the solicitor's work on the case is nought. Consequently, it was thought, the losing party could not be compelled to pay any of the successful party's costs at all.[74] At one time, such agreements amounted to the common law offence of champerty,[75] but from the time of the Criminal Law Act 1967, s.13 until 1995,[76] such agreements were not an offence but were unenforceable contracts and were contrary to the professional rules of conduct.[77]

Consequently, the CFA is a creature of statute: Courts and Legal Services Act 1990, s.58.[78] Initially, the availability of CFAs was confined to personal injury,

---

[74] The position was further complicated by a number of cases in which unconventional charging arrangements that apparently contravened the indemnity principle and/or were void for champerty were considered and sometimes permitted: *Hodgson v Imperial Tobacco Ltd (No. 1)* [1998] 1 W.L.R. 1056, CA; *Thai Trading Co v Taylor* [1998] Q.B. 781, CA; *Bevan Ashford v Geoff Yeandle (Contractors) Ltd* [1999] Ch. 239, Ch D; *Hughes v Kingston-upon-Hull City Council*, [1999] Q.B. 1193, QBD; *Awwad v Geraghty & Co*, [2001] Q.B. 570, CA. The effect of *Thai Trading* (where a solicitor acting in litigation for his wife agreed to restrict his own charges to anything recovered from the opponent) in particular can now be achieved by a "conditional fee agreement without a success fee" under statute. For a historical review, see J. Peysner, "A revolution by degrees: from costs to financing and the end of the indemnity principle" [2001] Web J.C.L.I., 1.

[75] See *Factortame Ltd v Secretary of State for the Environment, Transport and the Regions (Costs) (No.2)* [2002] EWCA Civ 932. Professional funding companies do exist within the current statutory framework, but must take the risk of being ordered to bear some part of the costs liability: *Arkin v Borchard Lines Ltd (Costs Order)* [2005] EWCA Civ 655.

[76] The Conditional Fee Agreements Regulations 1995 (SI 1995/1675).

[77] As strict contingency fees remain in contentious work: Solicitors' Practice Rules 1990 (as amended), rule 8, re-enacted in *Solicitors' Code of Conduct 2007*, para.2.04(1): "You must not enter into an arrangement to receive a contingency fee for work done in prosecuting or defending any contentious proceedings before a court of England and Wales, a British court martial or an arbitrator where the seat of the arbitration is in England and Wales, except as permitted by statute or the common law". The "contingency fee" is common in the USA but can only be used in England and Wales for non-contentious (or pre-contentious) work. In a strict contingency fee situation, the lawyer becomes entitled to a percentage of a successful client's damages awarded at trial or recovered by negotiation or mediation, irrespective of the amount of work done by the lawyer on the case. In principle, this is less likely to result in under-compensation of the client as damages in the USA are likely to be awarded by a jury and often therefore are considerably larger than equivalent awards in England (although frequently reduced on appeal). An extreme and dramatic example of the effect of a contingency fee on US lawyers undertaking a large case (bearing all the costs of investigation and the pre-trial procedures themselves in anticipation of a substantial percentage of a large award of damages) is provided in J. Harr, *A Civil Action* (1995, Arrow Books Limited) and the Paramount Pictures feature film of the same title.

For further discussion of the distinction, see J. Peysner, "What's wrong with contingency fees?" (2001) 10(1) Nott. L.J. 22 and A. Walters, "Contingency fee arrangements at common law" (2000) 116 L.Q.R., 371. As contingency fees are not prohibited until or unless court proceedings or arbitration is commenced, they are frequently used as a means of funding by claims management companies and claims assessors who seek to negotiate a settlement without recourse to the courts. See further the report of the Blackwell Committee, *The investigation of non-legally qualified claims assessors and employment advisers who act for reward* (February 2000), p.105, the Compensation Act 2006, which provides for the regulation of claims management services and para.9–011.

[78] The many statutory instruments governing the field from the Conditional Fee Agreements Regulations 2000 (SI 2000/692) onwards have now been revoked by the Conditional Fee Agreements (Revocation) Regulations 2005 (SI 2005/2305) following the consultation carried out by the DCA through the consultation paper *Simplifying CFAs* (June 2003) responses to which appear in *Making Simple CFAs a Reality* (June 2004) and in *New Regulation for Conditional Fee Agreements* (2005). A considerable and technical case law had developed (see n.90 below) such that, when the Law Society's *Fifth Woolf Questionnaire* (2002) asked "Do you consider conditional fee arrangements to be working?" 75% of respondents had answered "no". From November 1, 2005, therefore, CFAs are reliant entirely on the primary legislation and the rules of professional conduct for their effect. The Solicitors Practice (Client Care) Amendment Rule 2005,

insolvency and human rights cases. Subsequently virtually all civil proceedings were brought into the ambit of the scheme.[79]

The detail of the CFA is a complex subject beyond the scope of this book.[80] Put at its simplest, the solicitor and client agree that if the client loses the case—and in a complex case they may have to define in advance what "win" or "lose" actually mean—the client will not pay any costs to the solicitor.

The arguments in favour of a conditional fee system include: it allows litigation which would not otherwise be brought; the lawyers involved act more conscientiously on behalf of their client and it is a simpler method of payment.[81] The arguments against such systems include: it is an open invitation to unprofessional conduct; lawyers will refuse to take on weaker cases; there is increased pressure to win and so accept an early settlement (when costs are relatively low) rather than run the risk, at heavier cost, of going to trial.[82]

It is important to note, however that disbursements such as court fees, expert's fees and counsel's fees[83] are in principle still payable by the client to his or her own solicitor if the client loses, unless they are written off or covered by insurance. In addition, as a losing party, the client will normally expect to have to pay the opponent's costs, but this risk is frequently—and invariably in personal injury cases—provided for by an after the event insurance policy taken out at the same time as the CFA.

In the absence of such a policy, the client will have to pay the opponent's costs out of his or her own funds[84]: the principal reason why "no win: no fee" is a misnomer.

---

amending the 1999 Code to effect this change is superseded by the *Solicitors' Code of Conduct 2007*, para.2.03(2). Collective CFAs, also referred to in the regulations, might be used by, for example, a trades union: see *Thornley v Lang* [2003] EWCA Civ 1484.

[79] Work done in contemplation of litigation (or, as with many claims management organisations, with a view to settling the claim without litigation) does not fall within the statutory scheme: *Gaynor v Central West London Buses Ltd* [2006] EWCA Civ 1120.

[80] For a detailed discussion of the operation of the conditional fee agreement, see K. Underwood, *No Win, No Fee, No Worries* (2001, EMIS Professional Publishing) and *Conditional Fees: a Guide to Funding Litigation* (ed. G. Wignall and M. Napier) (2006, Law Society). For the information required to be given by a solicitor to a client about to embark on a CFA, see *Solicitors' Code of Conduct 2007*, para.2.03(2).

[81] R.C.L.S. Report, p.176.

[82] For discussion prior to Courts and Legal Services Act 1990, s.58, see R.C.L.S. Report, at p.77; the majority in *Wallersteiner v Moir (No.2)* [1975] Q.B. 373 (Lord Denning M.R., in the minority, put in a strong plea for the contingency fee in a particular type of company law action brought by a shareholder); M. Zander, *Legal Services for the Community* (1978), p.218; R. White, "Contingent Fee: A Supplement to Legal Aid?" (1978) 41 M.I.R. 286; *Civil Justice Review* (1989), para.389. For a review of client experience, see J. Sandbach, *No Win, No Fee, No Chance* (2004, Citizens' Advice).

[83] If a barrister is also engaged in the case, he or she may enter into a separate CFA (sometimes called a "conditional retainer agreement" or "CRA") with the client in respect of his or her fees; see CFA Guidance (amended September 2006) on the Bar Council website. See also Wignall, "CFAs and the Bar" (2001) 151 N.L.J. 355. For concern about the potential effects of CFAs on barristers' chambers (when members of those chambers might sit as judges), see *Smith v Kvaerner Cementation Foundations Ltd* [2006] EWCA Civ 242.

[84] In some cases the lack of such cover might be grounds for the making of a pre-emptive cost-capping order: *King v Telegraph Group Ltd* [2004] EWCA Civ 613; *Knight v Beyond Properties Pty Ltd* [2006] EWHC 1242, Ch D. The solicitor may, of course, be aware from the outset that the client is unlikely to be able to pay in the event of losing and this does not of itself render the agreement champertous: *Times Newspapers Ltd v Burstein (Costs: Champertous Retainer)* [2002] EWCA Civ 1739.

If the client wins the case, however, the client agrees to pay not only the solicitor's normal rate, but normally also a "success fee"[85] calculated as a percentage of those normal fees.[86] Originally this success fee was deducted from damages, potentially causing under-compensation of the client. It also made the CFA less attractive to defendants who, in the absence of a counterclaim, did not expect to receive damages and would have to pay any success fee out of their own funds. Consequently, Access to Justice Act 1999, s.29 amended Courts and Legal Services Act 1990, s.58 to allow both the success fee[87] and the insurance premium to be recoverable from the losing party.[88] That this amendment was not *ultra vires* was confirmed by the Court of Appeal in *Callery v Gray (No.1)*.[89]

The agreement must be in writing.[90] The information to be explained to the client in advance in addition to the normal minima is now contained in *Solicitors' Code of Conduct 2007*, para.2.03(2): "(a) the circumstances in which [the] client

---

[85] The main distinction in concept, therefore, between a conditional fee agreement with a success fee and a US-style contingency fee, is that the amount paid by the winning client under a CFA remains calculated on the basis of the amount of work done by the lawyer on the case. The uplift cannot exceed 100% of the normal charge: Courts and Legal Services Act 1990, s.58(4)(c). A further restriction that in no circumstances should the success fee amount to a figure equivalent to more than 25% of the damages awarded was originally imposed voluntarily and, in the House of Lords, *Callery v Gray (No.2)* [2002] UKHL 28, [2002] 1 W.L.R. 2000 by the Law Society. The amount of the success fee should represent the risk of losing the case, a strong case should have a lower success fee than a weak case. The firm of solicitors, as a whole, should, of course, seek to ensure that the number of cases lost (no charge) is no greater than the number of cases won (up to twice normal charge) to ensure that the firm continues to operate at a profit. As a guide, an appropriate percentage for a claimant in a straightforward road accident case is apparently 20%, *Callery v Gray (No.1)* [2001] EWCA Civ 1117; and in a "straightforward case" generally, 5%: *Halloran v Delaney* [2002] EWCA Civ 1258. See also *Atack v Lee* [2004] EWCA Civ 1712, where a 20% success fee was awarded based on the knowledge of the solicitor about the case at the time of entering into the CFA. A success fee of 70% where the risk of losing was low was criticised by the Court of Appeal and reduced to 15% in *Begum v Klarit (Costs)* [2005] EWCA Civ 210 and a 100% success fee reduced to 50% in *U (A Child) v Liverpool City Council* [2005] EWCA Civ 475. An attempt to recover what amounted to a success fee of 120% necessarily failed in *Jones v Caradon Catnic Ltd* [2005] EWCA Civ 1821.

[86] CPR rr.43. 2, 44.3A, 44.3B. The existence of the CFA (but not the amount of the success fee) is notified to the opponent as early as possible in the proceedings and ideally as part of the pre-action protocol: CPR r.44.15. The court can reduce the success fee recoverable on assessment of costs if its amount is unreasonable: PD 43–48 para.11.8.

[87] Or at least that of part it representing the risk of losing the case as opposed to recompensing the solicitor for delayed payment: CPR r.44.3B (1)(a). An attempt to resist an order to pay a winning opponent's success fee was as an infringement of Art.10 ECHR failed in *Campbell v Mirror Group Newspapers Ltd (Costs)* [2005] UKHL 61.

[88] See, for example, the Law Society model conditional fee agreement for personal injury cases reproduced on its website. A 2003 survey of a sample of firms identified that, across all sizes of firm in the sample, 5% of work was carried out on a CFA basis: *Solicitors' Firms 2003*, Table 11.

[89] See also *Callery v Gray (No.2)* [2001] EWCA Civ 1246; CA approved by the House of Lords [2002] UKHL 28, dealing specifically with the recoverability of an after the event insurance premium of £350. The criteria on the basis of which the court will decide whether the premium is recoverable are set out in PD 43–48 para.11.10. Test cases on recoverability of premia were consolidated as *re Claims Direct Test Cases* [2003] EWCA Civ 136. See also *Sharratt v London Central Bus Co Ltd (No.2)*, [2004] EWCA Civ 575.

[90] Courts and Legal Services Act 1990, s.58. A number of technical issues about CFAs, including notification to the opponent, were dealt with in *Hollins v Russell* [2003] EWCA Civ 718; *Spencer v Wood (t/a Gordon's Tyres)* [2004] EWCA Civ 352; *Montlake v Lambert Smith Hampton Group Ltd (Costs)*, [2004] EWHC 1503; *Holmes v Alfred McAlpine Homes (Yorkshire) Ltd* [2006] EWHC 110, QBD; *Myatt v National Coal Board* [2006] EWCA Civ 1017. It should, however, be noted that these cases pre-date the revocation of many technical rules relating to CFAs in an effort to simplify and avoid such satellite litigation: see n.78 above.

may be liable for [the solicitor's] costs and whether [the solicitor] will seek payment of these from the client if entitled to do so; (b) if [the solicitor intends] to seek payment of any or all of [the solicitor's] costs from [the] client [the solicitor] must advise [the] client of their right to an assessment of those costs; and (c) where applicable the fact that [the solicitor is] obliged under a fee-sharing arrangement[91] to pay to a charity any fees which [the solicitor receives] by way of costs from the client's opponent or other third party". Nevertheless, the CFA has come to be the principal method of funding personal injury claims in particular.[92]

Now that the insurance premium and success fee are potentially recoverable from a losing opponent, it is essential that the opponent is aware of the additional risk, especially as the maximum success fee is a 100 per cent uplift on the solicitor's normal fees. Consequently, specified information about the CFA must be notified to the opponent although this does not include the amount of the success fee or how it is to be calculated.[93]

(e) Costs payable to solicitor (public funding)

(i) *Development of the current regime of public funding of civil litigation*

11–009   The modern Legal Services Commission scheme for civil cases—the Community Legal Service Fund—which still provides financial assistance (subject to eligibility) in connection with some types of proceedings in most of our civil courts, has come a long way since 1495 when statute provided for poor people, at the discretion of the Lord Chancellor, to sue without payment to the Crown, and to have lawyers assigned to them without fee.[94] More formal Poor Persons Procedure was established in 1914[95] and was put under the control of the Law Society in 1925.[96] The Law Society provided the necessary administrative structure. Further, its involvement made more likely the necessary free provision by solicitors of their services. Government money was only made available to meet the costs of the administrative work involved.

The Poor Persons Procedure, dependent upon the charity of the legal profession, could not cope with the increasing pressure of work in the 1930s and was supplemented in 1942 by a Services Divorce Department. This department, consisting of salaried solicitors employed by the Law Society with government funds, dealt with the matrimonial problems occasioned by the Second World War. The Committee was set up, with Lord Rushcliffe in the chair, in 1944, to review the provision of professional help for those who were unable to afford it, in both civil and criminal matters, and must have had the Services Divorce Department model in mind. The Committee's report[97] provided the basis upon which the Law

---

[91] See *Solicitors' Code of Conduct 2007*, rule 8.

[92] See P. Fenn, A, Gray, N. Rickman and Y. Mansur, *The funding of personal injury litigation: comparisons over time and across jurisdictions* (DCA Research Series 2/06, 2006).

[93] CPR r.44.15; PD 43–48, s.19. Where the CFA is entered into prior to the issue of proceedings, this notification should take place during the "pre-action protocol" period: PD. Protocols, para.4A.

[94] An Act to admit such persons as are poor to sue *in forma pauperis*.

[95] Described as " . . . the first regular scheme for legal aid in the Supreme Court": H. Kirk, *Portrait of a Profession* (1976), p.164.

[96] After it had fallen into complete chaos and on the recommendation of a committee under Mr Justice P. O. Lawrence (The Poor Persons' Rules Committee (Cmd. 2358, 1925)).

[97] *Report of the Committee on Legal Aid and Advice* (Cmd. 6641, 1945). This report also contains a good review of the then existing facilities for legal aid and advice.

Society was invited by the Lord Chancellor to undertake the task of organising a legal aid scheme, which resulted in the Legal Aid and Advice Act 1949, later amended by the Legal Aid Act 1974. Subsequently, the first major concern perceived with the system of legal aid was that confusions and inefficiency were created by too many people having the ability to decide whether or not to grant help.[98] Consequently, the administration of the scheme was removed from the Law Society and placed in the hands of the Legal Aid Board by the Legal Aid Act 1988.

So matters remained until the 1990s when both Conservative and Labour administrations had proposals to reduce the Legal Aid budget. In parallel with the Woolf Inquiry, Sir Peter Middleton reviewed public funding.[99] The reduction in availability of public funding eventually apparent in the Access to Justice Act 1999, implemented for civil cases in April 2000, was consciously effected in parallel with the development and expansion of the conditional fee agreement. So, for example, whilst personal injury cases are, in the main, now exempt from public funding, they are precisely the type of case in which the conditional fee agreement was initially developed and has proved most popular.

The Legal Services Commission (LSC),[100] created by Access to Justice Act 1999, ss.1–3 oversees both the Community Legal Service (CLS),[101] in respect of civil proceedings and the Criminal Defence Service (CDS) in respect of criminal proceedings. Whilst the CPR use the term "LSC funding",[102] the more familiar "legal aid" appears to be the preferred expression in government and Legal Services Commission publications at present.[103]

Whilst only "suppliers" (soon to be restricted to "preferred suppliers") with a specific contract with the LSC are now permitted to deal with publicly funded disputes,[104] it should be borne in mind that the modern system of funding is not intended to be confined to solicitors and barristers. The CLS is, by statute, committed to "promoting the availability of and "securing (within the resources made available, and priorities set . . .) . . . that individuals have access to services that effectively meet their needs".[105] These services are defined to include "general information about the law" and "advice". As we have seen in Ch.10, law centres and other advisers also provide assistance under the scheme.

---

[98] See *Legal Aid Efficiency Scrutiny* (Lord Chancellor's Department, 1986), followed by the White Paper, *Legal Aid in England and Wales: A New Framework* (Cm. 118, 1987).

[99] *Review of Civil Justice and Legal Aid* (the Middleton Report), September 1997. For other material demonstrating policy in the context of civil public funding at that time, see the Lord Chancellor's Department, May 1999 consultation paper *The Community Legal Service* and its 2001 report *Social Exclusion*.

[100] Much information about the LSC can be obtained from its website: *http://www.legalservices.gov.uk.*

[101] Access to Justice Act 1999, s.6(3) and Community Legal Service (Funding) Order 2000 (SI 2000/627), as amended. For a review of the testing of the new procedures, see Moorhead, *Pioneers in Practice, The Community Legal Service Pioneer Project Research Report* (2000). Note also the existence of CLS Direct which runs a publicly funded telephone advice service and maintains a website for lay enquirers at *http://www.clsdirect.org.uk.*

[102] CPR r.43.2(1)(i).

[103] See, for example, DCA, *Legal Aid: the Way Ahead* (Cm. 6993, November 2006).

[104] Access to Justice Act 1999, s.4(2). As described in Ch.10, the LSC is now developing a system where contractors are required to obtain "preferred supplier" status.

[105] Access to Justice Act 1999, s.4(1). For a recent comparative review of provision, see J. Flood and A. Whyte, "What's Wrong with Legal Aid? Lessons from Outside the UK" (2006) 25(JAN) C.J.Q. 80. Note also EU Directive 2002/8, intended to improve access to justice in cross-border disputes by establishing common minimum rules for legal aid in such cases.

(ii) *The scope of the scheme in respect of civil litigation*

11–010   Public funding for the conduct of litigation (i.e. "specialist help") is not available[106] in the following categories of case: negligence cases involving death or personal injury[107] (other than clinical negligence cases) or involving damage to property; boundary disputes, trusts, defamation and malicious falsehood; matters of company or partnership law or matters arising out of a business carried on by the applicant.[108] In addition, public funding is not available for conveyancing or will-making.[109] The Lord Chancellor has, however, a general discretion under the Access to Justice Act, s.6.8(b) to fund individual cases that would otherwise be excluded.[110]

Where funding is available for litigation, it is only available to those who fall within certain financial limits (with some exceptions[111]) and whose cases satisfy the merits test and other requirements of the CLS Funding Code 2005.

However, in the kinds of civil dispute where funding is available, a number of different levels of funding are available in mainstream (i.e. non-family or immigration and asylum) cases:

Legal Help—This is equivalent to what used to be known as the "green form" or "Claim 10" scheme. The solicitor is allowed to conduct a limited amount of preliminary work only[112] (such as an initial interview or compliance with a pre-action protocol) where the client is in receipt of some specific benefits (such as income support, income-based job seeker's allowance, etc.) or has a monthly gross income not exceeding £2,350[113] and capital not exceeding £8,000.

Help at Court—This is equivalent to what used to be known as "ABWOR" (assistance by way of representation). A solicitor who is present in the court building at the relevant time is allowed to represent a litigant at a particular hearing even though he or she is not more formally instructed by the litigant, to the same financial threshold and subject to the same financial limits as for "Legal Help".[114]

---

[106] Subject to certain exceptions currently set out in *Scope of the Community Legal Service Fund* (updated from 2001).

[107] Some very expensive personal injury claims may, as an exception, still be eligible for funding.

[108] Access to Justice Act 1999, s.6(6) and Sch.2, as amended by the Community Legal Service (Scope) Regulations 2000 (SI 2000/822). Funding is not normally available in cases involving foreign law, including that of Scotland and Northern Ireland; Access to Justice Act 1999, s.19.

[109] Subject to certain exceptions authorised by Access to Justice Act 1999, s.6(8) and currently set out in *Scope of the Community Legal Service Fund* (updated from 2001).

[110] This discretion is used, for example, to permit representation at inquests, in particular those concerning deaths in police custody (*Legal Services Commission Annual Report 2005/06*, Table 5).

[111] Set out in Community Legal Service (Financial) Regulations 2000 (SI 2000/516) as amended, reg.3 and including amongst others, children cases and Mental Health Review Tribunal representation as well as advice provided by an advice centre such as a law centre.

[112] Payment rates differ for different types of work and appear in the Payment Annex to the supplier's contract. The basic limit is, however, at present around £100 to £200.

[113] As from April 2006. If the client has more than four dependent children the level is increased. If disposable income exceeds £649 a month, funding will be refused: the Community Legal Service (Financial) Regulations 2000 as currently amended by the Community Legal Service (Financial) (Amendment) Regulations 2006 (SI 2006/713). Some not-for-profit organisations may be authorised to provide this level of help without a means test. Contributions are not required in respect of either legal help or help at court.

[114] Some not-for-profit organisations may be authorised to provide this level of help without a means test. Extensions are possible.

Legal Representation—this is available in the following courts and tribunals in non-family or immigration and asylum cases: House of Lords, Court of Appeal, High Court, county court, Employment Appeal Tribunal, Mental Health Review Tribunal, and in some instances in certain tax tribunals.

As described in Ch.10, it may be "Full Representation" in which case it will cover the full conduct of litigation for a client, including advocacy and settlement negotiations.[115] Alternatively, "Investigative Help" may be provided.[116] This will normally provide support only in investigation of the strength of a claim. Again, the client's gross monthly income must not exceed £2,350, with disposable monthly income not exceeding £649 although if disposable monthly income exceeds £279 a contribution will be charged. Capital must not exceed £8,000 (with specific disregards for pensioners). Where capital exceeds £3,000, the surplus will be levied as a contribution.[117]

(iii) *Making an application*

Applications for Legal Help and Help at Court[118] are processed immediately by **11–011** the solicitor in possession of the appropriate CLS contract by completion of a form. If the applicant is eligible for assistance no contribution is payable.

In applications for Legal Representation, the applicant will need to complete a detailed form CLS APP1 (requiring, in the case of applications for Full Representation, an indication in percentage terms of the likely prospects of success in the case) and also a financial application form CLS MEANS1 unless in receipt of the relevant benefits. The assessment of the applicant's resources, which determines financial eligibility for representation, and of the merits of the case is in most cases undertaken by an "assessment officer" in the appropriate LSC regional office.

If the applicant is potentially eligible on financial grounds, the assessment officer will go on to consider whether the merits test is made out. The assessment of the merits of the case, as defined by the *Funding Code*, is complex. Initial considerations are that funding will be refused if alternative funding is available,[119] alternative means of dispute resolution have yet to be tried and exhausted[120] or if the case will be allocated to the small claims track.[121] In the absence of such bars to public funding, then, using as we did in Ch.10, Full Representation as an example. Full Representation is not available if:

1. prospects of success are unclear; or

2. prospects of success are "borderline" (i.e. it is not possible to say that they exceed 50 per cent) and there are no additional factors of "significant wider public interest" or "overwhelming importance to the client"; or

3. prospects of success do not exceed 50 per cent; or

---

[115] In 2005/06, 18,711 full representation certificates were issued in non-family cases: LSC, *Statistical Information 2005/06*, Table CLS 8.
[116] In 2005/06, 5,756 investigative help certificates were issued in non-family cases: *ibid.*
[117] Access to Justice Act 1999, s.10 and Community Legal Service (Costs) Regulations 2000 (SI 2000/441) as amended.
[118] And for certain immigration and family assistance.
[119] *Funding Code*, paras 5.4.2 and 5.7.1.
[120] *ibid.* para.5.4.3.
[121] *ibid.* para.5.4.6. For the small claims track, see Ch.15, para.12–005.

4. prospects of success exceed 50 per cent, the claim is for damages and has no factors of "wider public interest" but the relevant additional criterion cannot be satisfied:

(a) prospects of success exceed 80 per cent and likely damages exceed likely costs; or

(b) prospects of success are 60–80 per cent and likely damages exceed likely costs by 2:1; or

(c) prospects of success are 50–60 per cent and likely damages exceed likely costs by 4:1; or

(d) the claim is not for damages, has no factors of "wider public interest" but "the likely benefits to be gained from the proceedings justify the likely costs".[122]

(iv) *The funding certificate and the applicant's contribution*

11–012   If, where not processed by the supplier, the application is approved by the regional director,[123] a certificate is issued, subject to the acceptance by the applicant of any conditions attached to it.[124] The certificate will set out the level of service to be provided[125] and may be limited to the taking of particular steps in the action. So, for example, in the first instance the certificate may be limited to the taking of counsel's initial opinion so that a second application will be required to amend the certificate for further action if counsel's opinion appears to warrant it. All certificates will set out the maximum amount of costs that may be incurred.[126]

If the application is successful and no contribution is payable, the regional director issues a certificate to the applicant's solicitor, and a copy is sent to the client.[127] If the applicant is successful but there is a contribution to pay, an offer of a certificate, with a requirement to make arrangements to pay the contribution, is made. The applicant has 14 days in which to signify acceptance and to pay any contribution or, if permitted to do so, to provide an undertaking to pay.[128] Contributions from income, it should be noted, are payable every month during the period of funding.

The contributions payable are significant financial burdens, particularly for an applicant towards the top end of the financial eligibility range. Once a certificate has been issued there are wide powers vested in the regional director to amend it.[129] The regional director also has power to discharge or revoke it upon the happening of specified events, including failure by the client to provide information, abuse or misrepresentation by the client, or where the applicant's financial position improves so that he or she is able to fund legal action.[130] In the case of refusal to grant a certificate or upon discharge or revocation of a certificate there

---

[122] *ibid.* para.5.7.
[123] If actual or likely costs exceed £25,000 or, if the case proceeds to trial, £75,000, or the claim is a multi-party action, the application will be referred to the Special Cases Unit: *ibid.* para.C23.
[124] *ibid.* paras C14 and C15.
[125] Investigative Help, Full Representation, etc.
[126] *Funding Code, op. cit.*, para.C33.3.
[127] *ibid.* paras C14 and C16.1.
[128] *ibid.* para.C15.
[129] *Funding Code*, para.C36. Alternatively, a solicitor authorised by a contract with the LSC to do so may amend the certificate, *ibid.* para.C37.
[130] *ibid.* para.C51 ff.

are various rights of review by the regional director and by a separate Funding Review Committee.[131]

Obviously there may be circumstances in which the normal procedure of application and issue cannot be followed because of the urgency of the matter and a procedure exists for obtaining an emergency certificate in such cases.[132]

(v) *The liabilities of the legally aided civil client*

When the provision of legal services for those who could not afford the normal fees was dependent upon the charity of the profession, the relationship between client and lawyer must have been somewhat awkward. The object of the scheme is to ensure that the relationship between solicitor and legally aided client is on exactly the same basis as that between solicitor and private client.[133] To that end, a client's financial obligations are to the CLS Fund and the solicitor receives payment out of the Fund.[134]   **11–013**

The full financial obligations of a legally aided client will, inevitably, depend upon the outcome of the case. As will be seen below, the legally aided client is usually under no obligation to pay any costs to the solicitor whatever the result; but may be under a liability to pay costs to a successful opponent.

If the legally aided client is *successful*, costs may be payable by the opponent in the normal way.[135] These costs are paid into the CLS Fund and go to pay the bills rendered to the Fund by solicitors and counsel acting for the legally aided client. If the costs recovered are *not* sufficient to cover the costs to the Fund, the difference is recouped from the contribution made by the legally aided client. Any balance remaining from the contribution is returned.[136]

However, where the contribution, if any, is not sufficient to make up the difference, the LSC has a first charge on any property, including money, recovered or preserved by the legally aided client in the proceedings.[137] This is the "statutory charge". The charge means that the LSC is entitled to recover the shortfall on expenditure from the CLS Fund out of the property that has been recovered or preserved by the legally aided client in the proceedings. Consequently, the legally aided client will not receive the full amount of a money award, the LSC retaining sufficient to cover the shortfall, or other property will become subject to a charge that may be enforced by the LSC. However, the charges on both money and other property may be postponed or other property substituted provided the LSC considers it unreasonable for the client to repay,[138] especially where the money or property is required to provide somewhere for the legally aided client to live.[139] It is, therefore, very important to establish whether the property was recovered or preserved in the proceedings, since only then does

[131] *ibid.* paras C57, C58 and para.5.5.
[132] *ibid.* s.3.
[133] Access to Justice Act, s.22.
[134] Access to Justice Act 1999, s.5. The rates of payment to suppliers of legal services are governed by the Community Legal Service (Funding) Order 2000 (SI 2000/627), as amended but note, however, the currently controversial proposals for replacement by fixed fees discussed at para.10–030 above.
[135] For an explanation of costs, see para.11–003.
[136] Access to Justice Act 1999, s.10(5). Community Legal Service (Financial) Regulations 2000 (SI 2000/516), as amended, reg.40(1).
[137] Access to Justice Act, s.10(7) and Community Legal Service (Financial) Regulations 2000 (SI 2000/516) as amended, regs 42 to 53.
[138] Community Legal Service (Financial) Regulations 2000 (SI 2000/516) as amended, reg.52A.
[139] Community Legal Service (Financial) Regulations 2000 (SI 2000/516) as amended, reg.52.

the statutory charge apply. The LSC will be concerned to resist any attempt to defeat the charge.[140] Further, there are certain exceptions to the charge, including, in normal circumstances, the client's clothes, furniture or tools of his or her trade.[141]

The charge helps to reduce the cost to the Exchequer of public funding.[142] Indeed, the statutory charge, along with costs recovery, may be more significant, for funding purposes, than contributions.[143] The statutory charge can be harsh in its impact on a claimant who sees a large proportion of his or her damages disappear into repayment of the costs of obtaining those damages in the first place.[144]

If the legally aided client is *unsuccessful*, his or her liability to the LSC is limited to the amount of his or her contribution and, in that respect, the LSC bears the financial risk of litigation. However, it is possible for the court to order a legally aided client to pay the opponent's costs in the action. The court must first consider, whether, on normal grounds, an award for costs should be so made.[145] If an award should be made it can only order the legally aided client to pay an amount in respect of the opponent's costs "which shall not exceed the amount (if any) which is a reasonable one for him to pay having regard to all the circumstances including (a) the financial resources of all parties to the proceedings, and (b) their conduct in connection with the dispute to which the proceedings relate".[146] This is not likely to be an especially serious problem for the funded party since if no contribution has been expected, he or she is not likely to be able to pay much in the way of costs to the opponent. This leaves successful unassisted parties in a rather unfortunate position.

(vi) *The costs of successful unassisted parties*

11–014   It is only since 1964 that a successful party not in receipt of public funding has been able to obtain costs from the body responsible for public funding at all. It is not easy to obtain such an award. Section 11(4)(d) of the Access to Justice Act

---

[140] As to whether property has been recovered or preserved, see *Hanlon v Law Society* [1981] A.C. 124 (property is recovered or preserved if it was in issue in the proceedings, recovered by the claimant if the subject of a successful claim, preserved by the respondent if the claim fails); *Curling v Law Society* [1985] 1 W.L.R. 470 (property recovered where possession of property obtained through proceedings); see also *Van Hoorn v Law Society* [1985] Q.B. 106. As to the castigation by the court of any attempts to defeat the charge, see *Manley v Law Society* [1981] 1 W.L.R. 335. In limited circumstances, however, the statutory charge may be waived: Community Legal Service (Financial) Regulations 2000 (SI 2000/516) as amended, regs 46–47.

[141] Community Legal Service (Financial) Regulations 2000 (SI 2000/516) as amended, reg.44.

[142] The overall budget for legal aid is a prime factor in current proposals for change. So, for example, "Since 1997 the cost of legal aid has increased from £1.5 billion to £2.1 billion" (DCA, *Legal Aid: A sustainable future*, July 2006, para.1.1); "However legal aid, like the rest of the public sector, needs to live within a finite budget: the increase in spending over the last decade (£1.5 billion in 1997 to over £2 billion now), is unsustainable. We want a system that is fair to clients, fair to the taxpayer, and fair to practitioners. We want a legal aid system that will be sustainable, and is suited to the needs of the 21st century. We want a system that will safeguard the future provision of legal aid for those who really need it" (DCA, *Legal Aid Reform: the Way Ahead*, November 2006, p.3).

[143] Lord Chancellor's Department, *Legal Aid—Targeting Need* (Cm. 2854, 1995), para.12.4.

[144] See, e.g. National Consumer Council, *Ordinary Justice* (1989), pp.92–94.

[145] See above, para.11–003.

[146] Access to Justice Act 1999, s.11(1). This costs protection does not apply to the extent that the LSC funding is Help at Court, Investigative Help and, in most cases, Legal Help: Community Legal Service (Cost Protection) Regulations 2000 (SI 2000/824), as amended, reg.3.

1999 and regs 5 to 7 of the Community Legal Service Regulations 2000 (as amended) permit a court, on the application of a successful party not in receipt of public funding, to award costs to be paid by the LSC if, under reg.5:

(i) the unsuccessful funded party has the benefit of costs protection[147];

(ii) the proceedings are finally determined in favour of the non-funded party;

(iii) the court has ordered the party in receipt of funding to pay costs but these do not cover the full costs;

(iv) the non-funded party has applied to the LSC within three months of the costs order (unless there is a good reason for the delay);

(v) it is just and equitable that the costs should be paid out of public funds;

(vi) if the proceedings were in a court of first instance, the legally aided client instituted the proceedings and the non-funded party (who must be an individual) will suffer financial hardship unless an order is made.

However, it remains perilous to be sued by a person in receipt of public funding as the risk of failing to recover the costs of defending must be weighed against the merits of the defence and the amount of damages sought from the defendant. Lawyers representing commercial concerns in particular may often be forgiven, therefore, for advising on an entirely pragmatic basis that it is not worth defending a claim brought by a legally aided individual.

(vii) *Critique*

There is little, if any, current support for litigation to be financed from public **11–015** funds irrespective of the means of the parties. Whilst there are obvious objections on the grounds of overall cost and whether it is fair that public moneys should be used to support people who can readily afford litigation, it is the case that there is some litigation which is unavoidable, albeit expensive and which should be supported. The current system seeks to balance rationing of available resources whilst avoiding the stifling of unmeritorious claims, all in the context of the parallel conditional fee system in the private sector. In the context of the current controversy about rates of payment to suppliers, outlined in Ch.10, despite government objectives to increase access to appropriate legal advice,[148] whilst simultaneously constraining expenditure on legal aid overall,[149] a concern must be the extent to which suppliers, both in the private and the public sector,[150] can provide the good quality service demanded, across a good geographical spread, for the rates of payment available.

(f) Costs payable to solicitor (organisational support)

Some clients may be able to obtain financial support for litigation through the **11–016** support of an organisation. The typical organisations which provide such support

---

[147] See para.11–013, above.
[148] DCA, *Getting Earlier, Better Advice to Vulnerable People* (2006).
[149] LSC and DCA, *Legal Aid: The Way Ahead* (Cm. 6993, 2006).
[150] See Law Centres Federation press release, "Law Centres call on Government for a new funding settlement", March 8, 2007.

are trades unions, which often provide general legal support, and pressure groups which usually provide support for a particular issue and will support litigation where it furthers the objectives of the group. In appropriate cases, organisations such as the Equal Opportunities Commission[151] or the Commission for Racial Equality[152] will support litigation.

(g) Costs payable to solicitor (multi-party actions)

11–017   Multi-party actions may receive public funding.[153] These claims, which may be subjected to a Group Litigation Order under CPR rr.19.10 to 19.15, generally fall into two categories, that is, claims arising out of a specific event, such as a disaster, and claims based on a common cause, such as a harmful drug.[154]

(h) Costs payable to solicitor (other proposed methods)

11–018   Two further methods of funding have been suggested in the past but are yet to be adopted. The first is a fixed costs scheme, proposed by the Law Society in 1987.[155] Zander describes this scheme as meaning that solicitors would pay a premium to an insurance company and the client would pay a fixed amount to cover the costs in the event of the case being lost.[156]

An alternative is the suggestion that a contingency legal aid fund might be established.[157] The fund would be financed by contributions from successful litigants. It would pay lawyers on a normal basis but recoup costs on a contingency basis. The lawyer, therefore, would be paid whatever the outcome of the case.[158] Zander, whilst seeing some merit in the proposal, indicated that the major problem would be the initial funding, particularly if the Fund were to be established on a voluntary basis.[159] The idea remained a possibility in the Middleton Report: " . . . it might be particularly appropriate for very expensive cases where it was not practicable for even a large firm to bear the amount of risk involved"[160] conducting such a case under a conditional fee agreement. A filling of this lacuna by a category of legal aid known as "Support Funding" has subsequently been abolished. The debate as to alternative means of funding continues, however, most recently in the 2005 Civil Justice Council (CJC) paper

---

[151] *http://www.eoc.org.uk.*
[152] *http://www.cre.gov.uk.*
[153] *Funding Code,* Part D and Legal Services Commission Multi-Party Action Arrangements 2000.
[154] See also Woolf Issue Paper, *Multi-party actions* (1996) and Final Report, Ch.17.
[155] Law Society's Contentious Business Committee, *Improving Access to Justice* (1987), see M. Zander, *Matter of Justice* (1989), pp.56–57.
[156] *ibid.* p.57.
[157] *Legal Aid—Targeting Need* (Cm. 2854, 1995), para.3.34. See also the Middleton Report, *op. cit.*
[158] Such a fund was proposed by JUSTICE in *Trial of Motor Accident Cases* (1966), criticised by R.C.L.S., Report, pp.177–178. JUSTICE reiterated the call in its *Memoranda on the Green Papers issued by the Lord Chancellor's Department: Contingency Fees* (1989). See also N.C.C., *Ordinary Justice* (1990), pp.191–193. The Law Society's Contentious Business Committee put forward a similar proposal: *Improving Access to Justice* (1987).
[159] Zander (1989), p.56.
[160] *Op. cit.,* para.5.56.

Improved Access to Justice—Funding Options and Proportionate Costs suggesting a reduced transactional cost scheme for the less complex, lower value injury claims, where the vast majority of claims are likely to succeed (95 per cent are settled before court proceedings are issued). Some recommendations are focused on areas where there are greater difficulties in obtaining funding to start legitimate claims. In these areas the CJC suggests a number of more imaginative, perhaps radical, solutions, based on a principle of "funding of last resort".[161] The Better Regulation Task Force, on the other hand, approved of regulated contingency fees.[162] Clearly the debate will continue.[163]

(i) Costs and settlement

A litigant's doubts whether costs will be recovered at all, or, if recovered, **11–019** whether the amount received will cover the amount expended, may have been assuaged to some extent by the availability of the CFA but otherwise will be powerful factors in the decision whether and, if so, when to settle.

Another procedure, contained in CPR Pt 36, which may place either party in further difficulties is that of a formal offer of settlement, which can be made by either party and can be made prior to the issue of proceedings. The defendant may make an offer in purported satisfaction of the claimant's claim.[164] Alternatively, or in addition, the claimant may make an offer to accept a certain sum in satisfaction of his or her claim. On notification of the offer, the offeree may accept the offer or may continue the action. Offers may be made under CPR Pt 36 in respect of non-monetary issues, such as the percentage of liability. Further discussion of the implications of this encouragement to make and to accept offers, including the potential costs penalties for failure to do so and, having rejected an offer but failing to achieve a better result at the eventual trial, are discussed below at para.12–028.

2. CRIMINAL CASES

To what extent can the "loser pays costs" rule apply in criminal matters? This **11–020** rule is of lesser significance because of the existence of public funding through

---

[161] See *Improved Access to Justice—Funding Options and Proportionate Costs* (CJC, 2005).

[162] *Better Routes to Redress* (2004).

[163] In this context it is instructive to note the responses to a question appearing in the Law Society's *Sixth Woolf Questionnaire* (2003). Asked whether they had ever had to turn away clients with cases with greater than 50% chances of success (or where the chances were unknown), 60% of respondents answered "yes". Reasons for the lack of funding were unavailability of after the event insurance; solicitors being unwilling to take the claim on a CFA basis and a lack of funding to investigate the merits to decide whether or not to take the risk. A form of legal aid designed to help with the latter issue ("Support") is no longer available.

[164] A number of cases on this topic involving defendants of significant means but limited cash flow have led to an amendment in the 44th amendment to the CPR removing, at least in some circumstances, the obligation on a defendant actually to make a payment. For other cases on Pt 36, see Ch.15.

the Criminal Defence Service and because prosecutions brought by the Crown Prosecution Service are funded by government. Further, the defendant does not have the option of minimising costs by deciding not to go ahead with the case! The defendant does, though, have the right to plead guilty and/or to bargain about charge and plea, either of which might reduce the costs involved in a trial. Criminal courts, though, have powers to make orders about costs in various circumstances.[165]

A defendant's costs order may be made in favour of an acquitted defendant by the Crown Court or a magistrates' court.[166] These costs are awarded out of central funds. The award covers what the court considers is reasonably sufficient to compensate the party for expenses properly[167] incurred in the proceedings and directly related to them. The order should normally be made unless there are positive reasons for not doing so: an example suggested by the relevant practice direction being where the defendant's own conduct brought suspicion on him- or herself.[168] A defendant's costs order may be made by (a) a magistrates' court where an information has been laid but not proceeded with, or where the court decides not to commit the accused for trial, or where, on summary trial, the court dismisses the information; (b) the Crown Court where a person is not tried for an offence for which he or she was indicted or sent for trial, or has been acquitted. It may exercise its discretion where a person is convicted on some counts but not others (in which case only part of the costs may be ordered to be paid), and it may also make an order in favour of a successful appellant.[169] There are also circumstances in which the Administrative Court and the Court of Appeal may make defendant's costs orders.[170]

Costs may be awarded to a successful private prosecutor[171] out of central funds[172] in relation to proceedings for an indictable offence and before the Divisional Court in respect of a summary offence.[173] The costs awardable are those which are just and reasonable.[174]

An award of costs may be made against a convicted defendant.[175] The court may also order costs between the parties, in particular where there has been

---

[165] The award of costs to a successful defendant (Prosecution of Offences Act 1985, s.16); to a private prosecutor both out of central funds and against an unsuccessful defendant (ss.17 and 18); between the parties (s.19 and Costs in Criminal Cases (General) Regulations 1986 (SI 1986/1335)) and as "wasted costs orders" (s.19A). As pointed out in the Practice Direction on Costs in Criminal Proceedings, para.I.2.3 there is an inherent jurisdiction to order solicitors personally to pay costs "thrown away" by wasteful activity and the court may also make orders in relation to CDS funding and "recovery of defence costs orders".

[166] Prosecution of Offences Act 1985, s.16(1), (2).

[167] A requirement of the Prosecution of Offences Act 1985, s.16(6). Costs not properly incurred include those in respect of work unreasonably done, or costs wasted by failure to conduct proceedings with reasonable competence and expedition (note that in such cases a wasted costs order may be made, see *ibid.* s.19A and Practice Direction on Costs in Criminal Proceedings, Pts VIII and IX.

[168] Practice Direction on Costs in Criminal Proceedings, para.II.1.1.

[169] *ibid.* Pt II.

[170] *ibid.* Pt II.3 and II.4.

[171] i.e. not a public authority or a person acting on behalf of a public authority: Prosecution of Offences Act 1985, s.17(2).

[172] Prosecution of Offences Act 1985, s.17.

[173] Practice Direction on Costs in Criminal Proceedings, Pt III.

[174] Prosecution of Offences Act 1985, s.17(2).

[175] *ibid.*, s.18, Practice Direction on Costs in Criminal Proceedings, Pt VI.

"unnecessary or improper act or omission".[176] Similarly, where a defendant is legally aided, the judge may, in effect, indicate that a proportion of costs should not be recoverable by the solicitor from the CDS.[177] By virtue of Criminal Defence Service Act 2006, imposing means testing on criminal legal aid, "contribution orders" may be made requiring a defendant to pay towards his or her defence costs.[178]

3. TRIBUNALS

We shall repeat elsewhere that it is difficult to generalise about tribunals. Broadly the parties to a dispute which is settled by a tribunal will bear their own costs, subject to any specific rules applicable to a particular tribunal. We can merely give a number of examples. **11–021**

In the case of Social Security and Child Support Tribunals under the Social Security Act 1998, the claimant can claim a contribution to expenses, such as for loss of earnings (if any), travelling and childcare. These are payable whatever the outcome of the hearing. No costs can be awarded against the claimant. Expenses can also be claimed for the representative, if not paid for by the organisation they represent, and witnesses.

In Employment Tribunals, s.13(1) of the Employment Tribunals Act 1996[179] permits the award of costs or expenses in principle. The tribunal will not normally, however, make an award of costs as, under the Employment Tribunal (Constitution and Rules of Procedure) Regulations 2004,[180] an award will be made only where the party or a party's representative has acted vexatiously, abusively, disruptively or unreasonably, or the bringing or conducting of the proceedings by a party was misconceived, and in other specified circumstances. This may be a fixed sum not exceeding £10,000 award by the tribunal, a fixed sum agreed by the parties or an order for costs to be subject to detailed assessment. A preparation time order can also be made under similar conditions. A wasted costs order may now be made against a representative personally.

In the Lands Tribunal, costs are within the discretion of the tribunal[181] and it is interesting to note that of the four Lands Tribunals bills taxed in 2005, the average amount allowed on taxation was £41,126.[182]

The last example is highly unusual. LSC funding is not generally available for tribunals (the exceptions include the Employment Appeal Tribunal, Mental Health Review Tribunal, Asylum and Immigration Tribunal and in some

---

[176] Prosecution of Offences Act 1985, s.19; Practice Direction on Costs in Criminal Proceedings, Part VII; Criminal Procedure Rules 2005, Pt 78.

[177] Practice Direction on Costs in Criminal Proceedings, Pt X.

[178] The Criminal Defence Service Act 2006 replaces Access to Justice Act 1999, s.17, which had provided for "recovery of defence costs orders, dealt with in Practice Direction on Costs in Criminal Proceedings, Pt XI and in Criminal Procedure Rules 2005, Pt 77 (which is, at the time or writing, blank).

[179] As amended by the Employment Rights (Dispute Resolution) Act 1998.

[180] SI 2004/861.

[181] Lands Tribunal Rules 1996 (SI 1996/1022).

[182] *Judicial Statistics 2005*, table 11.1 p.141. A further 162 bills were taxed in the Queen's Bench Division from other tribunals, the average amount claimed being £25,353. The figure is quite startling in comparison with the much lower figure for claims in the Queen's Bench Division.

instances certain tax tribunals); they are intended to be cheap and both sides are clearly expected to bear their own costs.[183]

4. CIVIL PROCEEDINGS—WHAT DO THEY ACTUALLY COST

11–022   It was one of the earliest conclusions of Lord Woolf's inquiry[184] into the civil litigation system that "excessive cost deters people from making or defending claims" and that the "problem of disproportionate cost occurs throughout the system. It is most acute in smaller cases where the costs of litigation, for one side alone, frequently equal or exceed the value of what is at issue."[185] Initially, the Woolf Inquiry requested research by the Supreme Court Taxing Office with the assistance of Professor Hazel Genn, which gave information about average costs, confirmed the view that disproportionate cost was a significant problem and provided fascinating information as to the components of the costs in a sample of 673 cases.[186] Further research was carried out by the Supreme Court Taxing Office on a sample of 2,184 cases ranging in value from £5 to £660m, for the purposes of the Final Report.

In this latter research, there was a difference in average costs allowed by the taxing office between different types of case: medical negligence cases had a mean average of costs allowed at £29,380; personal injury cases at £19,382; professional negligence at £32,866 and official referees' cases[187] at £35,844.

> "There is a lack of proportionality between costs and claim value at the lower end of the claim value scale. . . . in 40 per cent of the lowest value claims,[188] the costs on one side alone were close to, or exceeded, the total value of the claim. By way of contrast, in 60 per cent of claims over £250,000, costs represented less than 20 per cent of the value of the claim."[189]

Following the implementation of the Woolf reforms, it is more difficult to see whether Lord Woolf's desire to make the cost of litigation "more affordable, more predictable and more proportionate to the value and complexity of individual cases" has been achieved, or if so, to what extent. In March 2001, the Lord Chancellor's Department, in its paper *Emerging Findings*, considered it "too early to provide a definitive view on costs"[190] but had convened a Costs Working Group and commissioned a report on the possible benchmarking of costs in civil cases.[191]

There is some support for the contention that, the CPR demanding that a great deal of the preparatory work is done prior to the issuing of court proceedings, there is in fact an *increase* in costs overall: more costs being incurred in the early

---

[183] See Ch.12, n.7 and n.8.
[184] *ibid.* p.9.
[185] *ibid.* pp.252 *et seq.*
[186] Final Report, Annex II gives a summary of the main findings of this subsequent research.
[187] Now the Technology and Construction Court, CPR Pt 60.
[188] Less than £12,500.
[189] Final Report, Annex III, para.16.
[190] *Emerging Findings, op. cit.*, para.7.1.
[191] Following a recommendation in Final Report, Ch.7.

stages of the case prior to any possible settlement.[192] This is supported, in particular, by a study carried out by Professors Peysner and Seneviratne in 2005, concluding that "case management . . . is effective in cutting delay but it is ineffective in cutting costs or, indeed, may increase costs. Lord Woolf's aspiration that case management would achieve his aims in relation to costs has not been achieved. Rules alone cannot achieve proportionality, economy, certainty and predictability of costs: policy solutions are required".[193]

B. DELAY

Delay causes problems in both civil and criminal matters despite the existence of **11–023** time-limits which are intended to expedite cases. The reasons for delay differ in civil and criminal procedure, not least because of the temptation in civil matters—which the Woolf reforms sought to frustrate—for the parties to agree through their lawyers to delays in proceedings.

1. CIVIL MATTERS

"There are four areas in which delay or a lengthy timescale is a matter for **11–024** concern:

1. the time taken to progress a case from the initial claim to a final hearing;

2. the time taken to reach settlement;

3. delay in obtaining a hearing date; and

4. the time taken by the hearing itself."[194]

---

[192] *Emerging Findings, op. cit.*, para.7.7, a view maintained in the subsequent *Further Findings* (2002). See also the Law Society *Response to the Third Woolf Questionnaire* (February 2001) in which 45% of respondents identified this "frontloading" of cases as being a problem. In the *Fifth Woolf Questionnaire* (2002) 70% of respondents were experiencing difficulty justifying and recovering front loaded costs when cases settled but 66% thought the problems of front loading were outweighed by the benefits of earlier settlement. *Judicial Statistics 2005*, Table 11.1 shows figures for detailed assessment of bills (whether for the purposes of recovery from an opponent, for legal aid or under the Solicitors' Act).

[193] J. Peysner and M. Seneviratne, *The Management of Civil Cases: the courts and the post-Woolf landscape* (DCA Research Series 9/05, 2005), p.71.

[194] Interim Report, p.13. The earlier *Civil Justice Review* (1989), para.49, identified delay occurring "at three main stages, namely: (i) before proceedings are commenced; (ii) between the commencement of proceedings and the point where the case is either settled or is ready for trial; and (iii) between readiness for trial and the trial itself." One study prior to the Woolf reforms showed that in cases where writs or summons (now claim forms) were issued, the major component of elapsed time was the period between issue of writ or summons and the settlement or trial: Incubon (1986), para.4.2. That study also revealed that in personal injury litigation at that time the three principal causes of delay were: (i) the medical circumstances of the case; (ii) the long wait for trials in the Royal Courts of Justice; and (iii) a lack of clear or prompt response from the other side: *ibid.* para.4.8.1. Further analysis of delay appears in Final Report, Annex III; is a factor considered in the Middleton Report and is discussed in Peysner and Seneviratne, *op. cit.*, at p.14.

The reasons for the slow progress of actions at these stages were diverse. At the outset, then as now, the plaintiff (now claimant) might be slow to contact a solicitor[195]; later, negotiations for a settlement might drag on[196]; where relevant, the extent of the plaintiff's (now claimant's) injuries might not become clear until the end of a lengthy period of treatment[197]; investigations might have to be carried out to ascertain the evidence[198]; expert opinions may have to be obtained; communication and action by both sides might be slow; the advice of counsel might be taken; the length of time spent waiting for the trial to begin could, prior to the Woolf reforms, be substantial[199]; errors might be made by the professionals involved[200]; the developing litigation ethos might, historically, have necessitated the lengthening of the process before trial for tactical reasons.[201]

[195] The time taken for an incident causing personal injury to advice first being sought was found in the Incubon Study to be, expressed as medians (that is half the cases took more than the time and half took less), 3.4 months for cases ultimately at the Royal Courts of Justice, 1.6 months for cases ultimately at District Registries (for provincial High Court cases) and 1.9 months for county court cases: Incubon (1986), Appendix 1. The figures only relate to those cases where proceedings were actually issued. The reasons why people may take so long to see a solicitor are, in part, explored in Ch.9 above. It is, however, thought that the period of delay in seeking legal advice is, generally, decreasing: Final Report, Annex III, para.36.

[196] The Incubon Study showed that the median period from incident to settlement, where proceedings were issued, for the various types of case, were 43.7 months (Royal Courts of Justice), 37.5 months (District Registry cases), 22 months (county court cases): Incubon (1986), App.1. In his Interim Report, Lord Woolf noted that settlement often occurred at a very late stage of the proceedings, involving the parties in substantial additional costs. At that time, personal injury cases often took 4–6 years to settle: Interim Report, p.13. Additional research carried out on a sample of 2,184 cases for the Final Report showed that medical negligence cases were the longest (an average of 65 months from first instruction of solicitor to resolution); followed by personal injury cases (56 months) and professional negligence claims at (41 months). Unsurprisingly, cases without such a high investigative and evidential element, such as Companies Court cases, took much less time (approximately 13 months): Final Report, Annex III, para.21. The CPR allow (r.26.4 and PD 26 para.3) for a formal stay (a pause) to be granted in ongoing proceedings so that the building-up of solicitors' costs can be halted whilst the parties attempt settlement.

[197] This was often said to be a good reason for delay, but, as Lord Woolf pointed out in the Interim Report, "even in such cases it should be possible to dispose of issues of liability, and to award interim damages": Interim Report, p.13. The award of an interim payment (i.e. a sum on account of damages) was available prior to the Woolf reforms and is now to be found in CPR rr.25.6 to 25.9 and PD 25b.

[198] The modern régime, however, assumes that such investigations are carried out prior to issue of proceedings in the pre-action protocol stage. The effect seems to be that early investigation and exchange of information may make early settlement more likely. However, where the case does go to court, an enforced period in the region of three or four months before proceedings can be issued adds to the delay and to the expense of the trial. The effect of weight and complexity on delayed issue of proceedings was, however, apparent even at the time of the Final Report: Annex III, paras 31–33.

[199] Lord Woolf noted that, in part because of late settlement of cases, and thus late withdrawal, there was overlisting at the courts in order to ensure full use of the judges' time; this of necessity produced wastage. The Winn Committee on Personal Injuries Litigation had drawn attention to this problem as early as 1968 (Cmnd. 3691) and regarded it as deplorable. In 1986 the Incubon Study found that the mean waiting periods from setting down (the stage at which the parties indicated that they had completed the pre-trial procedure and were ready for trial) until trial were 10.2 months for Royal Courts of Justice cases, 5.1 months for District Registry cases and 1.9 months for county court cases: Incubon, (1986), App.1.

[200] See J. Hern, "Court v solicitor errors" (1990) *Law Society Gazette*, May 2, p.32.

[201] Historically, at least, delay could easily be compounded by high usage of interim procedures which could be of doubtful appropriateness, such as applications for wide disclosure of documents, for interim injunctions or the pursuing of unmeritorious appeals from interim orders, see the Interim Report, pp.14 and 150–179 and Cranston "'The Rational Study of the Law': Social Research and Access" in Zuckerman and Cranston (1995). The impact of CPR Part 1, the overriding objective which places the management of cases to trial in the hands of the judge, as

Delay created by these reasons, both human and procedural, could prove to be extremely frustrating to the parties, particularly to the plaintiff (now the claimant) who might feel that delay amounted to a denial of justice.[202]

The complexities of the law itself can add to the amount of time taken to resolve a case. *Saif Ali v Sydney Mitchell and Co*[203] provides an example of a remarkably prolonged action under the pre-CPR regime, complicated by the expiry of the limitation period.[204] It is clearly an unusual case, but there was still a considerable lapse of time whilst what were then the normal procedures were being followed. The timetable was as follows[205]:

March 26, 1966	Mr Saif Ali, a passenger in a car driven by his friend Mr Akram, was injured in a collision with a car driven by Mrs Sugden.
October 16, 1966	Mrs Sugden was convicted of driving without due care and attention.
1967	Mr Ali and Mr Akram consulted a solicitor with a view to making a claim. The solicitor took counsel's opinion.
October 1968	The solicitor instructed the barrister to draft the pleadings[206] and advise.
November 14, 1968	A writ[207] and statement of claim[208] was issued claiming damages against Mr Sugden only, alleging that his wife was driving as his agent at the time of the accident. Mr Sugden was the owner of the car and he had insured it.[209]
Later	A meeting was held between Mr Ali's solicitor and the insurance company at which the company indicated that the agency question might be disputed and that contributory negligence might be alleged against Mr Akram.

well as the reduction in the scope of civil appeals in CPR Pt 52, is intended to frustrate such tactics, particularly when, as was often the case, they were employed by the wealthier of the parties (who could afford the costs of making such unnecessary applications) to place pressure on the less wealthy.

[202] Note Art.6 of the European Convention on Human Rights, given direct effect by Human Rights Act 1998, entitling litigants to "a fair and public hearing *within a reasonable time* by an independent and impartial tribunal established by law" (our italics).

[203] [1978] Q.B. 95, CA; [1980] A.C. 198, HL.

[204] Jacob states that the Limitation Acts have "operated in a sort of blind, mathematical way without regard to the merits of the claim or the circumstances of the parties or any other consideration": Jacob (1987), p.268. He makes certain recommendations for reform: *ibid.* pp.269–270. In April 2001 the Law Commission also recommended simplification, particularly in the context of the Human Rights Act 1998: *Limitation of Actions* (Report No.270).

[205] The timetable is culled from the judgments in both the Court of Appeal and the House of Lords. There are, unfortunately, some discrepancies in the dates given in the two courts—naturally, the House of Lords' version has been accepted!

[206] Now "statement of case".

[207] Now "claim form".

[208] Now "particulars of claim".

[209] Under the CPR, however, a further delay of several months would have occurred here prior to the issue of the claim, whilst the parties complied with the Personal Injury Pre-Action Protocol. Whilst this procedure lengthens the delay at this stage, it might well have resulted in settlement or at least in information becoming available to both parties that would reduce the delay at later stages in the action. See *More Civil Justice? The impact of the Woolf reforms on pre-action behaviour* (2002, IALS and University of Westminster).

674 CHAPTER 11

March 26, 1969	The limitation period expired[210] without any amendment to the writ, and without Mr Ali issuing proceedings against either Mr Akram or Mrs Sugden, the actual drivers in the collision.[211]
August 29, 1969	The writ was served on Mr Sugden.[212]
October 16, 1969	Mr Sugden entered a defence denying his wife's agency.[213]
November 1969	The barrister advised that Mr Ali should be separately represented.[214]
June 24, 1971	Mr Sugden amended his defence and admitted that his wife *was* acting as his agent.
January 21, 1972	Mr Sugden applied to the court for leave[215] to withdraw his admission of agency with consent of the plaintiff's solicitors. Leave was granted.
May 9, 1972	The House of Lords decision in *Launchbury v Morgans*[216] led Mr Ali's advisers to believe that it was impossible to continue the action.
April 22, 1974	The action against Mr Sugden was discontinued and Mr Ali's impregnable claim had disappeared.
September 19, 1974	Freshly advised, Mr Ali issued a writ against the solicitors who had represented him until November 1969 alleging negligence.[217]
May 29, 1975	The defendant solicitors issued a third party notice against the barrister whose advice they had taken,[218] asking that he should indemnify them on the grounds that they had acted on his advice.
July 26, 1976	The barrister successfully applied to have the third party notice struck out on the grounds that it disclosed no cause of action.

[210] In a personal injury action such as this, proceedings must be issued within three years of the cause of action arising.

[211] There would appear to have been good cases against both the actual drivers—presumably Mr Ali was advised to proceed against Mr Sugden because he was the insured person, and was reluctant to proceed against Mr Akram who was his friend.

[212] At this time, a writ remained valid for a year after its issue. Now a claim form normally remains valid only for four months after issue: CPR r.7.5.

[213] It is now at this stage that the court becomes actively involved in the management of the case to trial. It is highly unlikely that a modern court would have permitted the subsequent four-year delay in the personal injury action.

[214] It was perceived too late that Mr Ali's interests and Mr Akram's interests were not identical!

[215] Now "permission".

[216] [1973] A.C. 127: a case in which the House of Lords held that a husband who had borrowed his wife's car to go on a "pub-crawl" was not her agent for the purpose of fixing her with liability for his negligent driving.

[217] This would now have been preceded by a full exchange of information over weeks or months under the Professional Negligence Pre-Action Protocol.

[218] Now an "additional claim" under CPR Pt 20, i.e. a document joining the barrister in Mr Ali's action.

| February 24, 1977 | The solicitors successfully appealed to Kerr J. and the third party notice was restored. The barrister successfully appealed to the Court of Appeal and the third party notice was again struck out.[219] |
| November 2, 1978 | The solicitors successfully appealed to the House of Lords and the third party notice was restored.[220] *NB*: The third party action between the solicitors and the barrister did not decide that he *was* negligent, merely that *if* he had been negligent, he *would* be liable to the solicitors. The question whether he was negligent remained for trial if disputed by the barrister. |

Prior to Lord Woolf's investigations, a number of attempts had been made to address problems of delay, including the distribution of cases between High Court and county courts.[221] Lord Woolf's approach to dealing with delay was to increase the role of the courts in the management of litigation, and this lay at the heart of his proposals in the Interim Report (1995). This was refined in the Final Report, which contains in App.III a detailed analysis of the cost and delay before trial in a sample of over 2,000 cases selected by the Supreme Court Taxing Office:

"It is unreasonable in my view to expect clients to wait on average two to three years for the resolution of a dispute . . . The way to achieve [reduction in that delay] is for the court to determine an appropriate timetable to bring cases to final disposition."[222]

As we have indicated, it is unlikely that such a degree of delay as demonstrated in *Saif Ali* would be permitted under the current regime, although one must nevertheless realise that the pre-trial stages are by no means instantaneous. The pre action protocol procedure which we will examine in Ch.12, whilst encouraging settlement, can, if no settlement is reached by means of the protocol, add several months before formal court proceedings can be issued. The relevant figures for 2005/06 not being available at the time of writing, we refer to those for 2004, where the average time between issue of proceedings (following completion of any pre-action protocol) and requesting a trial date was, in the Queen's Bench Division, 43 weeks.[223] A further 54 weeks elapsed, on average, before the start of the trial.[224] In 2005, Peysner and Seneviratne found "mixed views" about whether the CPR had in fact reduced problems of delay, including difficulties in identifying who was responsible for any delay: solicitors, clients or

---

[219] [1978] Q.B. 95. The court relied heavily on *Rondel v Worsley* [1969] A.C. 191. Under the current, limited, appeal system it is unlikely this appeal would have proceeded this far, let alone to the House of Lords: see CPR Pt 52 and PD 52.

[220] [1980] A.C. 198.

[221] *Report of the Committee on Personal Injuries Litigation* (Cmnd. 3691, 1968), Chair, Winn L.J.; *Report of the Personal Injuries Litigation Working Party* (Cmnd. 7476, 1979), Chair Cantley J.; *Civil Justice Review, Report of the Review Body on Civil Justice* (Cm. 394, 1989).

[222] Final Report, Ch.2, para.31.

[223] *Judicial Statistics*, 2004, Table 3.8. It is worth comparing the London figures with those for the rest of England and Wales. In London, the average was 23 weeks to request for a trial date (70 elsewhere) and 58 weeks to the start of the trial (48 elsewhere).

[224] *ibid.*

expert witnesses with full diaries.[225] Addressing issues of delay in both civil and criminal proceedings is, however, within the current business plan of HM Courts Service.[226]

2. Criminal Matters

11–025　Although the delay in criminal cases is of a different order of magnitude, it still gives rise to concern. The concern is expressed on behalf of defendants in custody because they may ultimately be acquitted or given non-custodial sentences, and on behalf of defendants on bail because of the uncertainty and unpleasantness of a pending criminal trial. In addition there are difficulties associated with trials relating to incidents that happened in times long gone by. Witnesses forget.

There is, in theory, an eight-week time limit between committal and trial on indictment,[227] but that rule may be dispensed with by the Crown Court and the following figures indicate the present position. In England and Wales in 2005, of the 76,328 defendants committed for trial, 36.4 per cent were dealt with in less than eight weeks[228]; of the 49,390 who pleaded guilty, 46.9 per cent were dealt with in less than eight weeks; and of the 26,938 who pleaded not guilty, only 14.7 per cent were dealt with in less than eight weeks.

Delays for defendants in trials on indictment were giving cause for concern as long ago as 1975, when the James Committee reported, but at that stage over 70 per cent of cases were disposed of within eight weeks.[229] The matter has attracted further attention[230] and continues to do so.[231] A number of steps were implemented to seek to reduce overall delay.[232] Nevertheless, the overall figure for 2005 shows, as we have seen, less than 50 per cent of cases being disposed of within eight weeks.

Those defendants awaiting trial in custody might seem to be the most seriously disadvantaged by delay and they do tend to take priority. In 2005, 37.1 per cent of this group waited less than eight weeks for trial, and 69 per cent less than 16 weeks. The figures for those defendants on bail were 34.8 per cent and 62.3 per cent respectively.[233]

The situation differs around the country and the *average* length of time between committal and trial for those pleading not guilty varies from 13.8 weeks

---

[225] *Op. cit.* at p.14.

[226] *HM Courts Service Business Plan* 2006/07.

[227] See below, para.14–065.

[228] *Judicial Statistics 2005*, Tables 6.15 and 6.16.

[229] *The Distribution of Criminal Business between the Crown Court and the Magistrates' Courts*, Cmnd. 6323 (1975), para.23.

[230] For example, Narey, *Review of Delay in the Criminal Justice System* (1997), *Modernising Justice* (December 1998); the Crime and Disorder Act 1998, *Time Intervals for Criminal Procedure in the Magistrates' Courts—October 2000* (Lord Chancellor's Department Information Bulletin April 2000); the Auld review: *Criminal Justice: The Way Ahead*, Cm. 5074 (February 2001).

[231] See, for example, the plans of HM Courts Service in its *Business Plan 2006/07*.

[232] For a summary of steps taken following the Crime and Disorder Act 1998, see Ernst & Young, *Reducing Delay in the Criminal Justice System: Evaluation of the Pilot Schemes* (Home Office, August 1999). See also *Evaluation Report of the Joint Performance Management Pilot Scheme on Cracked Ineffective and Vacated Trials* (Lord Chancellor's Department, October 2001).

[233] *Judicial Statistics 2005*, Table 6.17.

in Wales and Chester to 24.4 weeks in the South East.[234] The national average for those pleading not guilty is 21.3 weeks. For those pleading guilty, the *average* length of time varies from 8.3 weeks in Wales and Chester to 13.2 weeks in the South East. The national average for those pleading guilty is 12 weeks.[235]

One of the problems with trial at Crown Court is with producing lists of cases which are accurate enough to enable prediction of the timing of the case for the benefit of the defendant and advocate and the most efficient use of judicial and court time. The Royal Commission on Criminal Justice had "no solution to the listing problem and despite all the complaints made to us about it, no different system was suggested to us that was obviously better than the present case".[236] The *Criminal Statistics 2005 (England and Wales)*,[237] show an average waiting time for trial in the Crown Court (from committal to the beginning of the trial) as 15.3 weeks in 2005.[238]

As regards delay at magistrates' courts, further reference can be made to the *Criminal Statistics 2005*. As regards indictable offences (including offences triable either way), in 2005 the average number of days from offence to completion was 122 days, an increase on 2004 attributed to "a rise in the average time it took from offence to charge or laying of information".[239] The implementation of the Criminal Procedure Rules 2005, introducing case management powers similar to those already in operation in the civil courts, is intended to help to assist with issues of delay.[240]

C. SETTLEMENT

Cost and delay are just two of the factors which persuade the great majority of those involved in civil disputes to effect a compromise and settle their differences before trial. Increasingly they do so before issuing court proceedings at all. The then Lord Chief Justice in 1980 commented that, "If it were not that a high proportion of cases are compromised long before they reach court the administration of justice would soon grind to a halt; the courts would be overwhelmed by the volume of work."[241] This sentiment is still true and posits a fundamental dilemma in civil procedure: are settlements fair? The courts now have a positive obligation to encourage them.[242] **11–026**

---

[234] *ibid.*, Table 6.18.

[235] *ibid.*

[236] The Royal Commission on Criminal Justice, *Report* (Cm. 2263, 1993), para.40. See also J. Plotnikoff and R. Woolfson, *From Committal to Trial: Delay at the Crown Court* (1993).

[237] Published by the Home Office (November 2006).

[238] *ibid.* para.1.16.

[239] *ibid.* para.1.13.

[240] See, however, *Judicial Statistics 2005*, p.82 "While the time that indictable only cases spend in the Crown Court has increased, it is hoped that the overall time from arrest to sentence will decrease".

[241] In the course of the foreword to the first edition (1980) of D. Foskett, *The Law and Practice of Compromise*. See also the 6th edn of 2005.

[242] CPR Pt 1. See below, para.12–002. Previously the court's role was limited to ratifying settlements involving children and patients under the Mental Health Act and this active jurisdiction is retained in CPR Pt 21 and PD 21.

1. WHO SETTLES WHEN?

11–027   The settlement of a dispute is achieved by an agreement between the parties to abandon any further claim in respect of the subject of the dispute. It takes the form of a legally binding contract and the normal rules of contract apply to establish the existence, meaning and effect of the agreement. In general the parties are completely free to negotiate the terms of the settlement.[243] A settlement may be arrived at more usually before proceedings have begun—a result encouraged by the pre-action protocols—but may also be arrived at during the course of proceedings, including during the course of a stay of those proceedings specifically arranged to allow the parties to attempt to compromise, or during the course of the trial.[244] Once agreement is reached, the settlement is just as final as a judgment[245] and, unless the agreement has been improperly procured, the issues of fact and law raised in the original claim may not be the subject of further litigation.[246]

(a) Information from the judicial statistics

11–028   The judicial statistics inevitably provide an incomplete picture since the only information available relates to matters where proceedings have been issued and many disputes may already have been settled by then.

The following figures are taken from the *Judicial Statistics* for 2005 and relate to the Queen's Bench Division. A total of 14,317 claim forms were issued in 2005. Of these, 3,841 were issued by the Royal Courts of Justice in London and 11,476 by district registries.[247] One might compare the pre-Woolf 1994 figures quoted in a previous edition of this book, referring to a total of 153,624 writs and originating summonses issued. The substantial decrease since 1999 reflects not only the increasing role of the county courts and of alternative dispute resolution but also the significant deterrent effect of the CPR.[248] As, at the time of writing, complete figures were not available for 2005, we consider the 2004 figures to indicate the proportion of claims leaving the court process after issue. In 2004, in the Royal Courts of Justice, 4,292 claims were issued; 692 claims were disposed of by judgment given either by default or under CPR Pt 24; 1,963 cases reached the point of requesting a trial date of which 31 per cent were determined after a trial, and 60 per cent were settled, struck out or withdrawn before trial.[249] Clearly these figures are not entirely comparable because they relate to cases at different stages in the procedure.

---

[243] There are some exceptions, e.g. settlements involving children and patients: see CPR Pt 21 and PD 21.

[244] The court should be informed of the fact of settlement: see, for example, the rider to that effect on the allocation questionnaire. If the case is settled within 7 days of filing the pre-trial checklist that makes final arrangements for trial, the relevant fee (£600 in the High Court) is refundable, presumably as an incentive.

[245] The settlement should be recorded in a "consent order" sealed by the court: CPR r.40.6.

[246] Foskett (1985) Pt I.

[247] *ibid.* Table 3.1

[248] See para.12–035.

[249] *Judicial Statistics 2004*, pp.38–40.

A surprisingly high number of cases are settled "at the door of the court" with the parties in attendance ready for trial.[250] A number of settlements require the formal approval of the court.[251] The DCA/Ministry of Justice's most recent figures suggest that, on average, only 20 per cent of claims issued now reach trial.[252] What is perhaps more significant, assuming that the number of civil causes of action remains roughly the same, is the dramatic decrease in the number of claims being issued, even when the redistribution of work to the county courts is taken into account: from 153,624 Queen's Bench Division claims in 1994[253] to 14,317 in 2005.[254] A huge proportion of disputes, it seems, are settled without recourse to the courts at all.[255]

(b) Research information

Research prior to the Woolf reforms[256] was, however, consistent in demonstrat-   **11–029** ing that the vast majority of claims settle without recourse to trial; perhaps the most dramatic being that of the Pearson Commission that 86 per cent of cases settled without proceedings being started. In March 2001 the Lord Chancellor's Department[257] reported that "[a]necdotal evidence suggests that pre-action protocols are working well to promote settlement before issue and to reduce the number of ill-founded claims". Of respondents to the Law Society's *Fifth Woolf Questionnaire* in 2002, 66 per cent felt that the problems of frontloading of activity under the CPR were outweighed by the benefits of early settlement.

As we have already seen, there is empirical evidence that far fewer cases are reaching the point of issue of proceedings, and of those that enter the court system, late settlements at the door of the court are reducing.[258] Where disputes reached the stage of formal court proceedings being issued, Peysner and Seneviratne, in 2005, were told of settlement rates of 80 per cent in some courts.[259]

We should now have demonstrated to your satisfaction the enormous importance of the process of settlement. It is the normal procedure in the vast majority of cases. Is it fair?

---

[250] The prospect of immediate trial concentrates the minds of the parties and their advisers wonderfully. In its paper, *Emerging Findings* (March 2001), the Lord Chancellor's Department concluded that, of cases settling prior to trial, fewer were now doing so at the door of the court (i.e. literally on the morning of the trial or otherwise very close to the trial date) as opposed to earlier in the pre-trial procedure, in fast track cases from 50% settling early in 1998/99 to 70% in 1999/2000 (para.4.3) and in multi-track cases from 63% to 72%.

[251] See CPR Pt 21.

[252] *Emerging Findings, op. cit.*

[253] *Judicial Statistics 1995*, Cm. 3290, Ch.3.

[254] *Judicial Statistics 2005*.

[255] Possibly by use of one of the many methods of alternative dispute resolution ("ADR"), see para.11–033 below.

[256] Including that of the Winn Committee: *Report of the Committee on Personal Injuries Litigation* (Cmnd. 3691,1968); the Pearson Commission (1978, Cmnd. 7054) and the Oxford Study: D. Harris *et al.*, *Compensation and Support for Illness and Injury* (1984).

[257] *Emerging Findings, op. cit.*, paras 3.12 *et seq.* See also the later paper *Further Findings* (2002) para.3.13 referring to the research study *More Civil Justice? The impact of the Woolf reforms on pre-action behaviour, op. cit.*, finding that 85% of cases in the sample settled "without recourses to the courts".

[258] *Emerging Findings, op. cit.*, para.4.1 *et seq.* Note, however, that Peysner and Seneviratne, *op. cit.*, p.40 considered there still to be a problem of late settlement, specifically on the day bvefore the trial.

[259] *Op. cit.*, p.35.

2. NEGOTIATIONS FOR A SETTLEMENT

11–030   The settlement process is very much a matter of bargaining, and it is bargaining
of a difficult and expensive character. As economists would say, the case involves
a bilateral monopoly, since the claimant has to "sell" his claim to one potential
buyer—the insurer—and the insurer has to "buy" the claim from only one
potential seller—the plaintiff [claimant]."[260]

Having taken pains in Pt II to point out that there are a number of non-legal
sources of advice and assistance, we do not now wish to give the impression that
the negotiation of settlements is exclusively the province of lawyers. Other
agencies are quite heavily involved, some in the capacity of e.g. mediator or
arbitrator,[261] others commercially[262] or representing the interests of members in
a more specialised field.[263]

Settlements can be examined by considering personal injury claims, in which
they play a major role, and which have been the subject of research and critical
assessment.[264] It is clear that the analysis in the first paragraph holds good,
whoever the parties actually are. The claimant cannot shop around for the best
offer, the two parties must deal with each other and strike an acceptable bargain
through their own negotiating skill.

The defendant in a personal injury action is likely to be represented by an
insurance company, which takes complete control of and financial responsibility
for the claim. If the defendant is not insured, he or she is not likely to be worth
suing.[265] The staff in the claims department of an insurance company will be
skilful and experienced negotiators, with adequate resources to deal with
claims.[266]

The claimant in a personal injury claim is the person hurt as a result of an
accident. He or she is unlikely to have any skill or previous experience in seeking
compensation for injury and is, therefore, largely dependent on the legal advice
sought and received.[267]

Once the claimant has found a solicitor, the problems that may face the
claimant in the initial stages of negotiation must be discussed. Two questions
arise: first the liability question, i.e. is the defendant liable in law? Secondly the

---

[260] Cane (1993), p.226. A "plaintiff" is now a "claimant".

[261] See below para.11–033.

[262] Such as the private sector claims assessors and claims management companies. For further
information about claims assessors see the report of the Blackwell Committee: *The investigation
of non-legally qualified claims assessors and employment advisors who act for reward* (February
2000) and provision for their regulation in the Compensation Act 2006.

[263] Primarily the trades unions, but also the motoring organisations, see above para.11–016 and Cane
(1993), p.219. Advice agencies also involve themselves on behalf of clients, from time to time
taking an active part in negotiation and settlement.

[264] See, in particular, Harris *et al.* (1984); H. Genn, *Hard Bargaining* (1987); see also Cane (1993).
We consider claims by individuals, but group actions are becoming increasingly significant and
present different issues, see Cane (1993), pp.227–230.

[265] Unless rich, either personally or because the defendant is a large company or other organisation
(e.g. considerable sums of health service finance fund the defence of legal actions brought against
health authorities and their employees). In road traffic accident cases, however, the Motor
Insurers' Bureau provides a potential remedy in respect of untraced or uninsured defendant
drivers.

[266] See Genn (1988), pp.7–8 and 50–52, 63.

[267] See H. Genn, "Who Claims Compensation: Factors associated with Claiming and Obtaining
Damages" in Harris *et al.* (1984), p.76.

quantum question, i.e. if the defendant is liable, how much should the damages be?[268]

Proving liability will depend, if it is denied by the defendant, upon three factors. First, the information which the client has about the accident. It is likely that the client will see the solicitor some time after the accident, when memory may already have begun to fade. Indeed there is some evidence which shows that the longer the delay in seeing a solicitor, the less likely damages will be obtained.[269] Secondly, more may be discovered about the accident. Prior to the Woolf reforms, research indicated that it was often the case that a plaintiff's solicitor either did not have the resources to undertake investigations or was loath to seek out all available reports even though much was and is available in terms of police accident reports, health and safety reports and so on.[270] The effect of the reforms, however, is to impose on both parties an obligation to carry out investigations prior to the issue of proceedings and to communicate the results of those investigations to each other, with copies of appropriate documents under e.g. the Personal Injury Pre-Action Protocol.[271] The aims of the Personal Injury Pre-Action Protocol are explicitly (our italics):

> "more pre-action contact between the parties; better and earlier exchange of information; better pre-action investigation by both sides; *to put the parties in a position where they may be able to settle cases fairly and early without litigation*; to enable proceedings to run to the court's timetable and efficiently, if litigation does become necessary; to promote the provision of medical or rehabilitation treatment (not just in high value cases) to address the needs of the claimant."

As we have seen in discussion above, there is evidence that use of the protocols has significantly reduced the number of claims issued in the courts.

Thirdly, there is the question of how good the witnesses will be when, and if, **11–031** it comes to establishing a case in court. Any witnesses will need to be contacted and the quality of their evidence assessed. Overall, it is not a simple—and therefore not an inexpensive—process to discover whether there is enough evidence to pursue a claim. If a possible claim does emerge from the evidence available, an attempt will be made to put a monetary value on the injuries suffered by the claimant. At this stage negotiations and other forms of dispute resolution other than court proceedings are likely to begin and are encouraged by the protocols:

> "2.16 The parties should consider whether some form of alternative dispute resolution procedure would be more suitable than litigation, and if so,

---

[268] The separateness of these issues is reflected in the fact that it is possible for split trials to be ordered so that, e.g. liability can be established whilst waiting for the medical condition of the claimant to be diagnosed adequately and before the quantum issue is determined: PD 26 para.9.1; PD 29 para.5.3(7) Whilst awaiting determination of quantum, the claimant can apply for interim payments on account of damages: CPR rr.25.6 to 25.9, PD 25b. Indeed, some insurance companies will offer voluntary interim payments to, for example, allow the claimant to undertake medical treatment privately and therefore more quickly, recognising that the more quickly the claimant is treated, the more quickly he or she will be, for example, back at work, thus reducing the overall claim for damages for comparatively small outlay.

[269] D. Harris, "Claims for Damages: Negotiating, Settling or Abandoning" in Harris *et al.* (1984), p.104 and Table 3.7.

[270] Genn (1987), pp.67–69.

[271] Described further in Ch.12. See also Final Report, Ch.10.

endeavour to agree which form to adopt. Both the claimant and defendant may be required by the court to provide evidence that alternative means of resolving their dispute were considered. The courts take the view that litigation should be a last resort, and that claims should not be issued prematurely when a settlement is still actively being explored. Parties are warned that if the protocol is not followed (including this paragraph) then the court must have regard to such conduct when determining costs.

2.17 It is not practicable in this protocol to address in detail how the parties might decide which method to adopt to resolve their particular dispute. However, summarised below are some of the options for resolving disputes without litigation:

- Discussion and negotiation.
- Early neutral evaluation by an independent third party (for example, a lawyer experienced in the field of personal injury or an individual experienced in the subject matter of the claim).[272]
- Mediation—a form of facilitated negotiation assisted by an independent neutral party.[273]

2.18 The Legal Services Commission has published a booklet on 'Alternatives to Court', CLS Direct Information Leaflet 23 (www.clsdirect.org.uk/legalhelp/leaflet23.jsp), which lists a number of organisations that provide alternative dispute resolution services.

2.19 *It is expressly recognised that no party can or should be forced to mediate or enter into any form of ADR."*[274]

To establish the possible quantum of damages, it is necessary to obtain as much information as possible about the injuries which the client suffered, and the future effect of such injuries, in particular upon the client's earning capacity. The client will, therefore, need a medical report.[275] Evaluating quantum is particularly difficult. In an American experiment, 20 pairs of practising lawyers negotiated on identical information about a case. The highest outcome was $95,000; the lowest $15,000; and the average was just over $47,000![276] Most solicitors will refer to the Judicial Studies Board Guidelines[277]— a publication giving "tariffs" for different kinds of injury, as well as one of the publications giving reports of recent awards.[278] Use of these resources can, however, only provide a range of appropriate awards and the parties must negotiate within that range to reach a settlement. Normally the result will be payment of one lump sum in the same way that damages consequent on a successful court action are also paid in a lump sum,[279] although interim awards[280] and awards of provisional

---

[272] See para.11–038 below.
[273] See para.11–040 below.
[274] Personal Injury Pre-action Protocol.
[275] Which, if proceedings are issued, must be attached to the particulars of claim: PD 16 para.4.3.
[276] G. R. Williams, *Legal Negotiation and Settlement* (1983) referred to in Genn (1987), p.77.
[277] Judicial Studies Board *Guidelines for the Assessment of General Damages in Personal Injury Cases* (8th edn, 2006, OUP).
[278] Such as *Kemp & Kemp on Quantum*. A typical report describes the injuries suffered by the claimant and the amounts awarded under the various heads of damage.
[279] See below para.15–010.
[280] CPR rr.25.6 to 25.9 and PD 25b.

damages[281] can be made. It is, however, possible for the injured party and the insurance company to agree on a "structured settlement". Under such a scheme sums of money are paid over periodically either for a fixed period or until the death of the injured party. These sums can then be varied over time to reflect changes consequent upon the damage caused to the injured party.[282]

The orthodox view of civil pre-trial procedure, and that which underlies Lord Woolf's thinking,[283] is that the more the two parties know about the real issues between them, the more likely it is that a "realistic" settlement can be reached.[284] A careful balance must be struck, however, between providing information in accordance with an early request or under a pre-action protocol,[285] and protecting one's client's interests. Whilst negotiations are conducted in an atmosphere of pressure, the danger of an over aggressive, adversarial approach is that it is often inimical to the interests of the parties[286] and an approach that resists revealing much information to the other side was easily identified[287] as a major reason for delay in the civil justice system.

Thus, the quality of the negotiators and their approach play a significant role in the settlement that is achieved. Insurance company representatives are almost invariably skilled, but the levels of skill and experience of the claimant's solicitor may vary considerably and the research evidence suggests that this is a highly significant factor in the settlement process.[288] Individual negotiators will differ in their approach from the combative and confrontational to the co-operative and may have differing views as to the effectiveness of such different approaches, particularly in the context of the spirit of co-operation enshrined in the CPR.[289]

Clearly there is considerable pressure on the various parties to the negotiation. Since the claimant is a prime contributor, it must be realised that it is important

---

[281] i.e. awards made now on the basis that a specified further medical condition (such as epilepsy or ostheoarthritis) will not develop within a specified period, the claimant having the right to apply for additional damages if the condition does develop within the period. Jurisdiction to make such an order is provided by Supreme Court Act 1981, s.32A and County Courts Act 1984, s.51 and implemented by CPR Pt 41 and PD 41.

[282] The payments are financed by the purchase of an annuity by the liability insurer, and, by an Inland Revenue concession, are not taxable as income. See R. Lewis (1988) 15 J.L.S. 392; D. K. Allen (1988) 104 L.Q.R. 448. Procedure is provided in PD 40c.

[283] Final Report, Ch.10.

[284] This is the especial function of the pre-action protocols, see below, para.12–010, of statements of case, see below, para.12–015; disclosure, see below, para.12–026; requests for further information under CPR Pt 18, see below, para.12–017 and exchange of witness statements and experts' reports, see below para.15–005. All these procedures except for the pre-action protocol take place well after the start of the action and all, as we have already seen, a considerable time after the accident.

[285] The requirement that some indication must be given in advance—of the method of funding may provide material for the opponent to draw inferences as to the client's financial position, even if this information is not explicitly revealed.

[286] Interim Report.

[287] See above, para.11–029, n.13.

[288] See Genn (1987). It is perhaps ironic in this context that skills training in negotiation (contentious and non-contentious) no longer forms part of the curriculum of the Legal Practice Course undertaken by intending solicitors.

[289] See Genn (1987), esp. pp.46–50, 53. For an analysis of the co-operative approach, see Fisher, Ury, Patton and Guyer, *Getting to Yes* (2004, Simon & Schuster). See also Fisher and Shapiro, *Beyond Reason: Using Emotions as You Negotiate* (2006, Penguin) Considerable work has been done on negotiation strategies and approaches by the Harvard Negotiation Project: *http://www.pon. harvard.edu/hnp*.

to utilise what advantages are possessed, consequently there is considerable pressure on him or her as well.

3. PRESSURES

11–032   The pressure to conclude a settlement is almost always on the claimant who can be placed at a considerable disadvantage against the skilled defendant.[290] Broadly, the pressures are attributable to delay, cost and the risk of litigation.

We have considered the delay that, even after the Woolf reforms, is likely to occur in a personal injury claim which goes to trial in the High Court.[291] The incentive to settle and clear the matter up quickly is significant. The claimant may be urgently in need of the money. It is he or she who will be incurring additional expenses as a result of the accident and whose earning power may have been impaired. Social security payments are unlikely to be adequate compensation for loss of earnings and injuries. Interest is payable on damages from the date of the cause of action to the date of judgment in all personal injury cases (unless there are special reasons to the contrary) and the court may order interest on that basis in other cases,[292] but the claimant may prefer to have the money in hand. An interim payment may be awarded by the court on application, but an order will only be made when it is clear that the defendant will be held liable at trial.[293]

---

[290] A claimant in a personal injury claim is, unless particularly unlucky, likely to be a first-time user of the system. An insurance company is, of course, in the business of dealing with such claims.

[291] See above para.11–024.

[292] Supreme Court Act 1981, s.35A; County Courts Act 1984, s.69. Claimants in debt cases may be entitled to rely on a more advantageous rate of interest under Late Payment of Commercial Debts (Interest) Act 1998, s.1.

[293] Supreme Court Act 1981, s.32. An order may be made under CPR r.25.7 at an interim hearing if: " . . . any of the following conditions are satisfied—(a) the defendant against whom the order is sought has admitted liability to pay damages or some other sum of money to the claimant; (b) the claimant has obtained judgment against that defendant for damages to be assessed or for a sum of money (other than costs) to be assessed; (c) it is satisfied that, if the claim went to trial, the claimant would obtain judgment for a substantial amount of money (other than costs) against the defendant from whom he is seeking an order for an interim payment whether or not that defendant is the only defendant or one of a number of defendants to the claim; (d) the following conditions are satisfied—(i) the claimant is seeking an order for possession of land (whether or not any other order is also sought); and (ii) the court is satisfied that, if the case went to trial, the defendant would be held liable (even if the claim for possession fails) to pay the claimant a sum of money for the defendant's occupation and use of the land while the claim for possession was pending; or (e) in a claim in which there are two or more defendants and the order is sought against any one or more of those defendants, the following conditions are satisfied—(i) the court is satisfied that, if the claim went to trial, the claimant would obtain judgment for a substantial amount of money (other than costs) against at least one of the defendants (but the court cannot determine which); and (ii) all the defendants are either—(a) a defendant that is insured in respect of the claim; (b) a defendant whose liability will be met by an insurer under section 151 of the Road Traffic Act 1988 or an insurer acting under the Motor Insurers Bureau Agreement, or the Motor Insurers Bureau where it is acting itself; or (c) a defendant that is a public body.
(4) The court must not order an interim payment of more than a reasonable proportion of the likely amount of the final judgment.
(5) The court must take into account—(a) contributory negligence; and (b) any relevant set-off or counterclaim".

There is some evidence that delay and associated anxiety can cause a recognisable psychological state of "litigation neurosis",[294] a complaint which disappears on the resolution of the dispute. It is almost inevitable that the circumstances associated with a legal dispute will cause worry and upset, but long delays weaken the spirit as well as the claim.[295]

The claimant has little to gain by delay. It may be that the injuries are such that their full effects will not become apparent for some time and a hasty settlement might lead to an underestimation of the damage,[296] but generally any attempts to delay—even if ultimately frustrated by the case management powers of the court—are on the side of the defendants.[297] Lord Woolf explicitly recognised the risks of delay:

"Delay before the start of proceedings is just as undesirable (and can be just as expensive) as delay in the course of litigation. There would be no point in offering a fast track timetable of 20 or 30 weeks to a claimant who has spent two or three years in fruitless negotiations before bringing the case to court at all. What is needed is a system which enables the parties to a dispute to embark on meaningful negotiation as soon as the possibility of litigation is identified, and ensures that as early as possible they have the relevant information to define their claims and make realistic offers to settle."[298]

D. ALTERNATIVE DISPUTE RESOLUTION (ADR)

"In future, government departments will only go to court as a last resort. . . . Instead, government legal disputes will be settled by mediation or arbitration whenever possible."[299]

As this quotation indicates, methods of resolving disputes other than going **11–033** through a process of adjudication by the courts have become increasingly

---

[294] See the material cited by P. Cane, *Atiyah's Accidents, Compensation and the Law* (4th edn, 1987) p.151 and the footnotes thereto. The converse may also be true: many solicitors have encountered clients for whom the litigation forms their principal interest in life.

[295] The circumstances of the claimant are also important. An elderly, infirm person might want to receive money quickly in order to enjoy it.

[296] The power to award provisional damages is unlikely to assist the *settlement* process, since it only applies to judgments. Indeed, it could conceivably encourage claimants to go to court to take advantage of the power. It will not be possible to reopen settlements on this account so that the claimant will now have an additional choice to make in deciding on settlement or litigation. On the other hand, it may give the claimant greater bargaining power with the defendant, since a settlement may now be in the defendant's interests.

[297] A modern example of delay on the part of the defendant is the alleged tendency of some defendants to wait out the maximum three months for a full response to the claimant under the Personal Injury Pre-Action Protocol. See further Law Society *Response to Third Woolf Questionnaire* in which 15% of respondents said that pre-action protocols were not generally complied with, defendants, insurers and loss adjusters being identified as classes of parties that did not comply. 68% of respondents said that courts did not impose sanctions for breach of protocols. See also *Fifth Woolf Questionnaire* on the effectiveness of the approach to be taken in cases without a specific protocol: PD Protocols, para.4.

[298] Final Report, Ch.10, para.4.

[299] Lord Chancellor's Department press release, March 23, 2001.

popular.[300] Organisations designed to support this approach have become well established in the last 10 years.[301] Whilst the courts cannot compel the parties to attempt an alternative method of resolution prior to engaging in litigation,[302] a number of initiatives are already in place encouraging the use of mediation in particular[303] and judges are specifically directed to encourage use of an ADR procedure "if the court considers that appropriate and [to facilitate] the use of such procedure".[304] Settlement by simple negotiation between the parties or their representatives can be seen as a form of ADR since it avoids the necessity of adjudication by a court. Settlement by negotiation also indicates some of the problems that, potentially, face all forms of ADR. In the past there has been a dichotomy between those who advocated a "litigation first" approach to negotiation and those who advocated a more conciliatory approach designed to achieve a compromise.[305] The modern paradigm, however, in accordance with the dictates of the CPR, is to regard litigation as a last resort and only one amongst a bouquet of different methods of dispute resolution.[306] It is no accident that an increasing number of firms of solicitors no longer have a "Litigation Department" but rather a "Dispute Resolution Department."

[300] A booklet produced for the general public by the Lord Chancellor's Department: *Resolving Disputes without Going to Court* is available on the Ministry of Justice website and another, *Alternatives to Court*, can be found on the LSC website.

[301] For example, the ADR group and CEDR.

[302] *Emerging Findings* (March 2001), para.4.11 suggests that there is a "clear view" in this jurisdiction that ADR should not be made compulsory and this is repeated in PD Protocols, para.4.7: "It is expressly recognised that no party can or should be forced to mediate or enter into any form of ADR." See further R. Ingelby, "Court Sponsored Mediation: The case against Mandatory Participation" (1993) 56 M.L.R. 441. The practice in the Commercial Court of making "ADR orders" (*Admiralty and Commercial Court Guide 2006*, section G and App.7) is persuasive rather than mandatory in nature: "The parties shall take such serious steps as they may be advised to resolve their disputes by ADR procedures . . . "

[303] See, for example, the power to stay litigation for a month or more to allow the parties to seek to resolve the claim otherwise than by litigation: CPR r.26.4; the pilot mediation scheme for small claims in the Central London County Court described in H. Genn, *The Central London County Court Pilot Mediation Scheme* (1998) Lord Chancellor's Department research paper; and the power of the Commercial Court, now contained in the Commercial Court Guide, (section G and App.7) to make "ADR orders". According to *Emerging Findings, op. cit.*, para..4.13, over 130 ADR orders were made in the first year of the CPR contrasted with 43 in the preceding year. There is also a mediation scheme in the Court of Appeal.

[304] CPR r.1.4.

[305] For examples prior to the Woolf reforms, see A. Boon, "Ethics and Strategy in Personal Injury Litigation" (1995) 22 J.L.S. 353; C. Menkel-Meadow, "Lawyer Negotiations: Theories and Realities—What we can learn from mediation" (1993) 56 M.L.R.

[306] A CEDR survey quoted in *Emerging Findings, op. cit.*, para.4.12 showed a 141% increase in the number of commercial mediations since the introduction of the new regime. For a discussion of ADR in this context, see further *ADR Discussion Paper* (1999) and *ADR Discussion Paper: summary of responses* (2000), both available on the Ministry of Justice website which now contains a section devoted to ADR and includes a number of research papers on the subject: *http://www.justice.gov.uk/civil/adr/index.htm*. See also the European Judicial Network in Civil and Commercial Matters setting out not only EU Commission policy but also describing methods of alternative dispute resolutoin available in different member states: *http://ec.europa.eu/civiljustice/adr/adr_gen_en.htm*.

There are various forms of ADR in addition to negotiation,[307] for example:

(a) arbitration;

(b) ombudsmen;

(c) expert determination;

(d) mediation-arbitration (med-arb.);

(e) early neutral evaluation (ENE);

(f) conciliation;

(g) mediation; and

(h) online dispute resolution (ODR).

We can only provide a brief description of each of these in this text. Those wishing to pursue the topic of ADR further are advised to consult the increasing numbers of specialist texts on the individual forms of ADR.[308]

(a) Arbitration[309]

Arbitration has a long and dignified history and is frequently used in, for **11–034** example, the resolution of construction disputes. The case is evaluated by an arbitrator or panel of arbitrators, who may be experts in the relevant field rather than lawyers.[310] The decision, which is legally binding, is, however, made on the basis of the relevant substantive law. Procedure may be very similar to that used in litigation: the filing of statements of case; examination of witnesses; and so on. Consequently, although arbitration may have the benefit of privacy, it may not be less expensive or less formal than litigation.

A related procedure available in construction cases is that of "adjudication", the principal feature of which is the speed by which a decision is made available: generally within 28 days of referral to the adjudicator.[311]

(b) Ombudsmen

Ombudsmen exist in a number of fields, generally in relation to public (e.g. the **11–035** Local Government Ombudsman) or quasi-public bodies (e.g. the Banking Ombudsman or the Legal Services Ombudsman). Their function is to deal with

---

[307] Some theorists do not include negotiation as a form of ADR. According to *ADR Discussion Paper: summary of responses, op. cit.*, para.5, others do not include the comparatively formalistic arbitration.

[308] For example, Brown and Marriott, *ADR: Principles and Practice* (1999, 2nd edn, Sweet & Maxwell); Kendall, *Expert Determination* (3rd edn, 2001, Sweet & Maxwell, a new edition due in May 2008), Boulle and Nesic, *Mediation, Principles, Process, Practice* (2001, Butterworths); Tweedale and Tweedale, *A Practical Approach to Arbitration Law* (1999, Blackstone Press).

[309] See the consolidating Arbitration Act 1996. It is a peculiarity of arbitration in England and Wales that, unless the parties agree to exclude it in advance, there is the possibility of an appeal from the arbitral award on a question of law, as well as in respect of irregularity (CPR Pt 62).

[310] Many are, however, members of the Chartered Institute of Arbitrators.

[311] Housing Grants, Construction and Regeneration Act 1996, s.108; Scheme for Construction Contracts (England and Wales) Regulations 1998 (SI 1998/649).

complaints in the relevant sector and they may have powers to award compensation or only to make recommendations to the body against whom the complaint is made out.

(c) Expert determination

11–036   A straightforward example of this method of ADR is sometimes used in boundary disputes. The parties agree to be bound by the decision of an independent expert, in the example, a surveyor who comes to a conclusion as to the correct siting of the boundary.

(d) Mediation-arbitration (med-arb.)

11–037   As its name suggests, this is a combination of mediation and arbitration. The parties begin by mediating, but if they fail to resolve the dispute by mediation, have agreed in advance to submit the dispute to binding arbitration.

(e) Early neutral evaluation (ENE)

11–038   In this form of ADR, the parties consult an independent third party, often a lawyer, who provides his or view of the merits of the case on the basis of short submissions from each side. This view is not binding on the parties but, if it is, for example, a view on whether or not a clause in a contract is likely to be enforceable as a matter of law, allows the parties to seek an informed resolution of the dispute by other means, such as negotiation. The Commercial Court offers a "without prejudice, non-binding" early neutral evaluation service by a commercial judge who, following the evaluation, takes no further part in the case.[312]

(f) Conciliation

11–039   Conciliation, often confused with mediation, is used in particular in the resolution of industrial disputes by the Advisory, Conciliation and Arbitration Service (ACAS). Of the two, conciliation often involves more active work on the part of the conciliator.

(g) Mediation

11–040   Mediation has become the archetypal form of ADR to the extent that the expression "ADR" is sometimes casually assumed to *mean* mediation. It shares many factors with conciliation, the distinguishing factor being that the mediator is less likely to become actively involved in the resolution but is more likely to take a "facilitative" role, possibly by using the technique of "shuttle diplomacy", assisting the parties to find means of moving forwards to a resolution. The result (if any) of a mediation will, therefore, be a compromise, as in negotiation. Consequently, it is not suitable for cases where a determination on the merits is required, in "test cases" where a precedent must be set and where specific legal remedies (such as injunctions) are required. It does, however, seek to empower the parties into resolving their own dispute and focuses on common

---

[312] *Admiralty and Commercial Court Guide 2006*, G2, p.121.

interests and goals rather than the narrow issues of legal dispute and can be very significant where, for instance, a continuing relationship between the parties is desirable (as, for example, in children cases and in some kinds of business dispute). Clearly, where a co-operative and non-adversarial response is desirable, mediation can assist parties who, perhaps because of entrenched positions or an imbalance of articulacy, may have difficulty in reaching a compromise by negotiation alone. It can also frequently be both quicker and substantially cheaper than court proceedings. Mediation will normally be conducted under the aegis of one or other of the mediation organisations such as CEDR or the ADR Group and its results will be binding if the parties agree in advance that that is to be the case.[313] If the mediation fails, then the content of the discussion at the mediation is not admissible at any subsequent trial.[314] A number of court-based mediation schemes have been established in recent years, such that a National Mediation Helpline now exists to refer county court users to appropriate means of assistance and a Civil Mediation Council has been formed.[315] In the European context, a Green Paper of 2002[316] treats the establishment of effective means of ADR across the Community as "a political priority" and invites consideration of a method of making the results of mediation enforceable across the Community in the same way as court judgments and arbitral awards.

Whilst ADR is now positively encouraged by the CPR and pre-action protocols, as well as by the provision in the Commercial Court of a mechanism known as an "ADR" order,[317] it remains the case that there are no official proposals at present to render attempts at ADR (usually mediation) mandatory, as is the position in some other jurisdictions.[318] However, the "encouragement" offered by the courts in this jurisdiction has been fairly direct, the current position being that a party who "unreasonably" refuses to engage in ADR risks a contrary award of costs at the trial.[319]

ADR has significant consequences not only for procedure but also for the substantive law. The more disputes, and the more difficult they are, which are resolved by ADR, the less those disputes are resolved in a publicly accountable environment or on the basis of their legal merits. As ADR has meant that fewer cases come before the courts, so the courts have reduced opportunities to develop the law and to create the precedent that is crucial to a common law system. So ADR is not a side-effect free cure-all. We end this section where we began, with the governmental initiative advocating the use of ADR to resolve its own

---

[313] The Law Society's Training Standards (June 2000) for civil/commercial mediation are available on its website and provide a straightforward guide to the structure and procedures of a mediation conducted under the Law Society's Code of Practice for Civil/Commercial Mediation (*Professional Conduct, op. cit.*, Ch.22).

[314] See *Hall v Pertemps Group Ltd* [2005] EWHC 3110, Ch D.

[315] *http://www.civilmediation.org.*

[316] COM (2002) 196 final. See also the draft directive COM (2004) 718 final.

[317] See *Admiralty and Commercial Court Guide 2006*, section G and App.7 and H. Genn, *Court Based ADR Initiatives for Non-Family Civil Disputes: the Commercial Court and the Court of Appeal* (2002).

[318] See, for example, the Florida Rules, r.44.102.

[319] *Dunnett v Railtrack Plc* [2002] EWCA Civ 303; *Reed Executive Plc v Reed Business Information Ltd (Costs: Alternative Dispute Resolution)* [2004] EWCA Civ 887; *Halsey v Milton Keynes General NHS Trust* [2004] EWCA Civ 576; *Burchell v Bullard*, [2005] EWCA Civ 358; *Hickman v Blake Lapthorn (Costs)* [2006] EWHC 12, QBD. See also I. Grainger, "The costs consequences of a failure to mediate" (2004) 23(OCT) C.J.Q. 244; S. Shipman, "Court Approaches to ADR in the Civil Justice System" (2006) 25 (APR) C.J.Q. 181; B. Tronson "Mediation Orders: Do the Arguments Against Them Make Sense" (2006) 25 (JUL) C.J.Q. 412.

disputes. " ... there will still be cases which are not suitable for ADR such as those involving intentional wrongdoing, abuse of power, public law, human rights and vexatious litigants. There will also be disputes where a legal precedent is needed to clarify the law or where it would not be in the public interest to settle".[320]

---

[320] LCD press release, March 23, 2001.

PRE-TRIAL CIVIL PROCEDURE

12–001   At this stage we move from a comparative approach, taking account of civil, tribunal and criminal procedure, and concentrate on civil procedure. The procedures that must be followed before a trial in the High Court or county court, and indeed even before initiating the court process,[1] should be used by the parties to expose the real area of difference between them and concentrate attention upon it. Issues not in dispute should be eliminated and the scope of the disagreement narrowed. If the parties are not able or prepared to narrow the issues in this way, increasingly the court will step in to narrow the issues of its own volition. Using the procedures, and particularly the pre-action protocols, in this way has the dual effect of preparing the case as precisely as possible for trial and of encouraging a settlement by revealing to the parties the exact nature of their dispute. As we saw in Ch.11, the parties are increasingly encouraged to seek to resolve the dispute outside the litigation process by use of ADR techniques.

In any consideration of civil procedure, however, it is important to understand the major shift in approach enshrined in the Civil Procedure Rules 1998,[2] brought into force on April 26, 1999 and often colloquially referred to as "the Woolf Reforms". The Civil Procedure Rules 1998 (CPR) are divided into "Parts", each of which contains a number of rules. Almost all Parts are accompanied by one or more practice directions (PDs) giving more precise details of procedure. Further, at the date of writing, the CPR still had annexed to it Schs 1 and 2, these being the diminishing remnant of the old rules[3] yet to be incorporated into the CPR. A continuous process of review is gradually bringing the matters covered by the Schedules within the ambit of the main rules as well as introducing new matter: so, for example, October 2005 brought into force Pt 76 of the CPR in respect of proceedings under the Prevention of Terrorism Act 2005. The CPR themselves are updated and corrected at regular intervals and the 41st update, in particular, placed emphasis on the use of methods of ADR techniques.[4] (At the date of writing (March 2007) the CPR had received their 43rd update.[5]) This chapter is believed to be up to date to that point.

---

[1] Pre-action protocols.

[2] SI 1998/3132 under the power conferred by Civil Procedure Act 1997, s.2. For a list of amending statutory instruments up to and including Civil Procedure (Amendment No.3) Rules 2006, SI 2006/3435 the Ministry of Justice website.

[3] Sch.1 contains the remainder of the Rules of the Supreme Court (RSC) governing the High Court and Sch.2 contains the equivalent remainder of the County Court Rules (CCR).

[4] See, for example, PD. Protocols, para.4.7.

[5] These updates have in the past been made on a (roughly) monthly basis and now appear approximately quarterly. Consequently, for effective use of the CPR it is essential to consult the most up-to-date version available. Given the regularity of updates, this will frequently not be a textbook or even such practitioners' texts as the widely used White Book *(Civil Procedure 2006,* Sweet & Maxwell*)*, but the Ministry of Justice website: *http://www.justice.gov.uk.* Similarly the most up-to-date information about fees and court forms is generally found on HM Courts Service website: *http://www.hmcourts-service.gov.uk/.* Another useful reference is A. A. S. Zuckerman, *Civil Procedure* (LexisNexis, 2003).

The Woolf reforms are the latest manifestation of a long-standing dissatisfaction with the process of judicial resolution of civil disputes.[6] The complexity of pre-trial procedure, particularly in the High Court, had been said to act not only as a deterrent to all but the most determined litigant but also as a weapon for the recalcitrant defendant who might manipulate it so as to place pressure upon the plaintiff (now known as the "claimant").

Lord Woolf's review of the system comprised an interim report (the Interim Report), published in June 1995[7] and a final report (the Final Report) in July 1996[8] accompanied by a set of draft civil procedure rules. Following a period of consultation, redrafting and testing[9] the new rules, enacted as a statutory instrument in 1998[10] were brought into force in England and Wales on April 26, 1999.[11]

Lord Woolf's starting point was perhaps best expressed in the Interim Report when he identified the adversarial culture, for which lawyers and the system were responsible, as creating an environment in which "questions of expense, delay, compromise and fairness may have only low priority. The consequence is that expense is often excessive, disproportionate and unpredictable; and delay is frequently unreasonable".[12] Further, the problems of delay, cost and complexity remained "the key problems facing civil justice to-day".[13]

During the consultation process, steps were taken to implement some of the proposals contained in the Interim Report, such as the appointment of the then Vice-Chancellor of the Chancery Division as the Head of Civil Justice.[14]

---

[6] Prior to the two Woolf Reports, for example, came the *Report of the Review Body on Civil Justice* (Cm. 394, 1989); *Civil Justice on trial—the case for change: Report by the Independent Working Party set up by the General Council of the Bar and the Law Society* (1993) (Chair H. Heilbron, Vice Chair: H. Hodge). In addition the courts had sought to move towards a more "managed" system: *Practice Direction* [1995] 1 All E.R. 385—in introducing this practice direction the Lord Chief Justice said "The aim is to try to change the whole culture, the ethos, applying in the field of civil litigation". See also J. Rozenberg, *The Search for Justice* (1995) pp.171–182 and C. Glasser, *Solving the Litigation Crisis* (1994) quoted in the Interim Report at p.5.

[7] Lord Woolf, *Access to Justice: An Interim Report* (1995) (hereafter the Interim Report).

[8] Lord Woolf: *Final Report on Access to Justice* (1996) (hereafter the Final Report).

[9] As, for example, the following Lord Chancellor's Department research papers: Goriely, Butt and Sherr, *Costing Fast Track Procedures through Hypothetical Studies*, (1998); Peysner, Unell, Scott, McLachlan, *Report of the Fast Track Simulation Project* (1998).

[10] SI 1998/3132.

[11] A sudden rise in the issue of civil proceedings in the months immediately prior to April 26, 1999 is commonly attributed to a misconceived belief amongst practitioners that claims brought before "Woolf-Day" would proceed under the familiar old rules. See the Lord Chancellor's Department paper *Emerging Findings* (March 2001) at 3.3. In fact, Pt 51 of the CPR contained transitional provisions which brought all pending cases within the ambit of the new rules within a year of grace expiring in 2000.

[12] Interim Report, p.7.

[13] *ibid.*

[14] Others listed in the Final Report, p.2 include the involvement of the Judicial Studies Board in training judges in their new role of managers of cases; the encouragement of ADR in a Lord Chancellor's Department publication *Resolving Disputes without Going to Court* and proposals for a unified rule making committee. The Civil Justice Council, an advisory body formed in response to the recommendation in the Interim Report that a body should be formed "with responsibility for overseeing and co-ordinating the implementation of Lord Woolf's proposals" first met in 1998, having been constituted under Civil Procedure Act 1997, s.6. Summaries of its meetings and the subjects of its discussion can be found on its website at *http://www.civiljustice council.gov.uk.* A White Paper, *Modernising Justice*, setting out the government's objectives at this time was published in December 1998.

Finally, however, Lord Woolf's proposals were grouped under the following series of objectives:[15]

(a) litigation will be avoided wherever possible;

(b) litigation will be less adversarial and more co-operative[16]:

(c) litigation will be less complex;

(d) the timescale of litigation will be shorter and more certain;

(e) the cost of litigation will be more affordable, more predictable, and more proportionate to the value and complexity of individual cases;

(f) parties of limited financial means will be able to conduct litigation on a more equal footing;

(g) there will be clear lines of judicial and administrative responsibility for the civil justice system;

(h) the structure of the courts and the deployment of judges will be designed to meet the needs of litigants;

(i) judges will be deployed effectively so that they can manage litigation in accordance with the new rules and protocols; and

(j) the civil justice system will be more responsive to the needs of litigants.

Whether and, if so, to what extent the regime meets these objectives[17] will be considered at the end of this chapter, once we have examined pre-trial procedure in more detail.

A. THE OVERRIDING OBJECTIVE

12–002   A useful guide to the ethos of the current regime can be obtained from Pt 1 of the CPR (otherwise known as the "overriding objective"). This is the governing principle to be employed by the courts in exercising their powers of case management.[18] Consequently, we set it out here in full:

---

[15] Final Report, section 1, para.9.

[16] It is an objective of the Community Legal Service's strategy to 2011 to work with the Ministry of Justice to "support . . . changes to court and tribunal systems and procedures to make them less adversarial and more user friendly": *Making Legal Rights a Reality* (Legal Services Commission, March 2006), p.2.

[17] Much anecdotal evidence could be found in the legal press in the early years of the current regime. The Ministry of Justice has, however, conducted some evaluation of its own, the initial findings of which are contained in its paper *Emerging Findings* (March 2001) and more recently in its second report *Further Findings* (August 2002). See also J. Peysner and M. Seneviratne, *The Management of Civil Cases: the Courts and the Post-Woolf Landscape* (DCA Research Series 9/05, November 2005).

[18] For some examples of its application, see *Maltez v Lewis, The Times*, May 4, 1999, Ch D; *Jenkins v Grocott* [2001] C.P. Rep. 15, QBD; *GKR Karate UK Ltd v Yorkshire Post Newspapers* [2000] 1 W.L.R. 2571, CA; *Law v St. Margarets Insurances Ltd* [2001] EWCA Civ 30, CA; *Holmes v SGB Services plc* [2001] EWCA Civ 354, CA; *Tasyurdu v Immigration Appeal Tribunal* [2003] EWCA Civ 447, CA; *Hampshire Waste Services Ltd v Intending Trespassers upon Chineham Incinerator Site* [2003] EWHC 1738, Ch D; *Campbell v Mirror Group Newspapers Ltd (Costs)* [2005] UKHL 61, HL; *Pastouna v Black* [2005] EWCA Civ 1389, CA.

"1.1 (1) These Rules are a new procedural code with the overriding objective of enabling the court to deal with cases justly.

(2) Dealing with a case justly includes, so far as is practicable

(a) ensuring that the parties are on an equal footing;
(b) saving expense;
(c) dealing with the case in ways which are proportionate

    (i) to the amount of money involved;
    (ii) to the importance of the case;
    (iii) to the complexity of the issues; and
    (iv) to the financial position of each party;

(d) ensuring that it is dealt with expeditiously and fairly; and
(e) allotting to it an appropriate share of the court's resources, while taking into account the need to allot resources to other cases.

1.2 The court must seek to give effect to the overriding objective when it

(a) exercises any power given to it by the Rules; or
(b) interprets any rule.

1.3 The parties are required to help the court to further the overriding objective.[19]

1.4 (1) The court must further the overriding objective by actively managing cases.

(2) Active case management includes

(a) encouraging the parties to co-operate with each other in the conduct of the proceedings;
(b) identifying the issues at an early stage;
(c) deciding promptly which issues need full investigation and trial and accordingly disposing summarily of the others;
(d) deciding the order in which issues are to be resolved;
(e) encouraging the parties to use an alternative dispute resolution procedure if the court considers that appropriate and facilitating the use of such procedure;
(f) helping the parties to settle the whole or part of the case;
(g) fixing timetables or otherwise controlling the progress of the case;
(h) considering whether the likely benefits of taking a particular step justify the cost of taking it;
(i) dealing with as many aspects of the case as it can on the same occasion;
(j) dealing with the case without the parties needing to attend at court;
(k) making use of technology; and
(l) giving directions to ensure that the trial of a case proceeds quickly and efficiently."

The court's powers in respect of these obligations are set out in CPR Pt 3 and include the following:

---

[19] For practical examples, see *Tasyurdu v Immigration Appeal Tribunal* [2003] EWCA Civ 447; *Thames Trains Ltd v Adams* [2006] EWHC 3291, QB.

"3.1(2) Except where these Rules provide otherwise, the court may:

(a) extend or shorten the time for compliance with any rule, practice direction or court order (even if an application for extension is made after the time for compliance has expired);

(b) adjourn or bring forward a hearing;

(c) require a party or a party's legal representative to attend the court;

(d) hold a hearing and receive evidence by telephone or by using any other method of direct oral communication;

(e) direct that part of any proceedings (such as a counterclaim) be dealt with as separate proceedings;

(f) stay the whole or part of any proceedings or judgment either generally or until a specified date or event;

(g) consolidate proceedings;

(h) try two or more claims on the same occasion;

(i) direct a separate trial of any issue;

(j) decide the order in which issues are to be tried;

(k) exclude an issue from consideration;

(l) dismiss or give judgment on a claim after a decision on a preliminary issue;

(ll) order any party to file and serve an estimate of costs;

(m) take any other step or make any other order for the purpose of managing the case and furthering the overriding objective.

(3) When the court makes an order, it may:

(a) make it subject to conditions, including a condition to pay a sum of money into court; and

(b) specify the consequence of failure to comply with the order or a condition.

(4) Where the court gives directions it may take into account whether or not a party has complied with any relevant pre-action protocol.

(5) The court may order a party to pay a sum of money into court if that party has, without good reason, failed to comply with a rule, practice direction or a relevant pre-action protocol.

(6) When exercising its power under paragraph (5) the court must have regard to:

(a) the amount in dispute; and

(b) the costs which the parties have incurred or which they may incur. . . .

3.3 (1) Except where a rule or some other enactment provides otherwise, the court may exercise its powers on an application or of its own initiative.
. . .
3.4 (2) The court may strike out a statement of case if it appears to the court:

(a) that the statement of case discloses no reasonable grounds for bringing or defending the claim;

(b) that the statement of case is an abuse of the court's process or is otherwise likely to obstruct the just disposal of the proceedings; or

(c) that there has been a failure to comply with a rule, practice direction or court order . . . "

1. RELEVANCE OF EARLIER DECISIONS

The words "a new procedural code" were inserted into CPR Pt 1 at a compar- **12–003**
atively late stage. The intention seemed to be to create a *tablua rasa*, a blank page
unsullied by the laxities of the past. The effect of this was, however, to create
uncertainty in the professions, particularly where there were well-established
precedents on rules that appeared in identical words in the new canon. After
seven years, procedural case law specific to the current rules is now in place, but
the approach to the relevance of old decisions has been by no means consistent.[20]
Inevitably case law decided under the old rules has been used to inform current
judgment, frequently in the case of lacunae in the CPR.[21] Perhaps the most
significant statement of intent in this respect, however, comes from Lord Woolf
sitting in *Biguzzi v Rank Leisure plc*[22]:

> "The whole purpose of making the CPR a self-contained code was to send
> the message[23] which now generally applies. Earlier authorities are no longer
> generally of any relevance once the CPR applies."

Where old case law can be relied on, then, it must be viewed through the mirror
of the overriding objective, as well as the obligation of procedural fairness and
independence in Art.6 ECHR, either of which may well produce a different
result.[24]

2. TERMINOLOGY

Even if older cases on procedural matters have ceased to be relevant, the CPR are **12–004**
only a "procedural code" and do not seek to supplant the whole corpus of
English substantive law. Lawyers had to become bilingual for a period, understanding pre-1999 terminology such as "plaintiff"; "writ"; "default summons"
and "*ex parte*" when reading older cases, whilst using the modern equivalents in
their day-to-day practice. For current purposes, however, the most significant

---

[20] For some examples, see *Purdy v Cambran* [2000] CP Rep. 67, CA; *Lombard Natwest Factors Ltd
v Arbis, The Times*, December 10, 1999, Ch D; *Mattel Inc. v RSW Group plc* [2004] EWHC 1610,
Ch D.

[21] As, for example, in *South Tyneside MBC v Wickes Building Supplies Ltd* [2004] EWHC 2428,
QBD and *Global Multimedia International Ltd v ARA Media Services, The Times*, August 1,
2006, Ch D.

[22] [1999] 1 W.L.R. 1926; [1999] 4 All E.R. 934; [2000] C.P. Rep. 6; *The Times*, October 5, 1999, CA.
Further reinforcement appears in *Reid Minty v Taylor* [2001] EWCA Civ 1723, CA, refined in
Kiam v MGN Ltd (Costs) [2002] EWCA Civ 66, CA.

[23] That the court is in control and that time limits are now more important than ever.

[24] Peysner and Seneviratne, in *The Management of Civil Cases: The Courts and the Post-Woolf
Landscape* (November 2005, DCA Research Series 9/05) report views on this subject ranging
from a feeling that the new system, with its greater focus on case-by-case discretion, created
uncertainty to a "liberation" that problem-solving was no longer constrained by pre-existing case
law.

changes in terminology were those replacing "plaintiff" with "claimant" and "writ" or "county court (default) summons" with "claim form".

B. TRACKS

12–005 Prior to 1999, this text had to cover substantial differences in procedure between the county court (governed by the County Court Rules) and the High Court (governed by the Rules of the Supreme Court). The effect of the Woolf reforms was not, however, to amalgamate the two courts as well as to merge their rules of operation, and some minor differences of jurisdiction remain. However, the unification of the High Court and county courts into a single Civil Court is now proposed following a Department of Constitutional Affairs consultation in 2005.[25] Whether or not separate courts survive, however, it is important to understand the "track" system, summarised here.

The *small claims track* occupies the territory formerly occupied by the small claims court in the county court. Its jurisdiction is confined to, for the most part, claims not exceeding £5,000. A European Small Claims Procedure,[26] allowing a simplified cross-border procedure in cases worth less than €2000, is in the process of finalisation at the time of writing.

The *fast track* occupies the majority of the remainder of defended civil cases, being the "normal track" for claims above the small claims limit but whose value does not exceed £15,000.[27] Most fast track claims proceed in the county court.

Cases not fulfilling the criteria for the small claims track or the fast track are allocated to the *multi track*, the "hallmarks" of which are expressed to be "(1) the ability of the court to deal with cases of widely differing values and complexity, and (2) the flexibility given to the court in the way it will manage a case in a way appropriate to its particular needs".[28]

Alongside the continuing evolution of the pre-trial process after 1999, the Human Rights Act 1998, brought into force in October 2000, rendered the European Convention on Human Rights (ECHR) of direct effect in England and Wales. The impact is largely twofold: the civil courts have become a forum for those seeking remedies in respect of infringement of their human rights by public authorities and, as public authorities themselves, the courts have an obligation to uphold the human rights of individual litigants, both in their right under Art.6 to a fair and public trial but also in other areas including the rights to freedom of expression and the right to privacy.[29]

Despite the stated intention of the regime to make the procedure easier for the layperson to understand, procedural complexities remain and generally speaking continue to necessitate the services of a lawyer or other legal adviser.

---

[25] *A Single Civil Court?* (DCA, February 2005) and DCA press release 19 October 2005.
[26] See *Proposal for a Regulation of the European Parliament and of the Council establishing a European Small Claims Procedure* (Commission, 2005/0020(COD)).
[27] Increased from the recommendation in the Final Report of £10,00. At the time of writing consultation is taking place on raising the limit in personal injury claims to £25,000: *Case track limits and the claims process for personal injury claims* (DCA, April 2007). Such claims will only under CPR r.26.6(5) proceed in the fast track procedure if the trial "is likely to last for no longer than one day" and only limited (or no) expert evidence will be required.
[28] PD 29 para.3.2.
[29] For a case where the court acknowledged that the result would have been different in the absence of the Human Rights Act, see *Goode v Martin* [2001] EWCA Civ 1899, CA.

C. THE COUNTY COURT

The jurisdiction of the county court is now synonymous with that of the High **12–006** Court in many instances.[30] Most of the claims in the county court are based upon contract and tort. In 2005, 1,870,374 claims were issued,[31] 1,610,347 (86 per cent) of which were "money" claims.[32] Sixty-one per cent of the money claims were for amounts less than £1,000.[33]

Despite the Woolf reforms, there are still jurisdictional questions to be assessed in determining in which court to commence an action—set out conveniently in PD 7 para.2—but there are wide provisions for transfer.[34] Nevertheless, sanctions may be applied against the claimant who has issued proceedings in the wrong court.[35]

Since almost all county court cases will be proceeding in the small claims or fast track,[36] HM Courts Service has a commitment to provide a trial date within 20 weeks of allocation,[37] which may be quicker than in the High Court.

D. THE HIGH COURT

Unless a specific enactment (such as the Human Rights Act 1998) requires **12–007** proceedings to be brought in the High Court, claims whose value does not exceed £15,000 cannot be brought in the High Court.[38] Consequently, the vast majority of claims are handled by the county court.

During 2005, the total number of claims issued in the Queen's Bench Division of the High Court was 15,317, a slight rise on 2004.[39] This is, however, to be compared with the last figures immediately preceding the Woolf reforms, a figure

---

[30] As a consequence of recommendations in the *Civil Justice Review* (1989) introduced by the High Court and County Courts Jurisdiction Order 1991 (SI 1991/724).

[31] *Judicial Statistics 2005*, Table 4.1. In the light of the expressed aim of the Woolf reforms to avoid litigation where possible, the issue statistics have shown a steady decrease since 1999.

[32] *ibid.*

[33] *Judicial Statistics* 2005, p.43.

[34] CPR Pt 30 and PD 30.

[35] CPR r.30.2(2).

[36] Examples of exceptions are personal injury cases worth less than £50,000 and claims proceeding in the London county courts where by PD 29 para.2, claims brought in the Royal Courts of Justice (the London office of the High Court) of a value less than £50,000 "will generally" be transferred to one of the London county courts.

[37] The process of allocating a claim to a track once the statements of case of both parties have been filed. For definitions of "allocation" and "statement of case" see paras 12–015 and 12–021. Allocation should take place approximately a month to two months after issue of the claim form. It should, however, be noted that the pre-action protocol may take up to three months to complete and that even once the action has been formally commenced, the statements of case stage may take another month or two. Consequently the whole period from initial letter of claim to fast track trial may still be in the region of a year. *Judicial Statistics 2005* indicates at Table 4.17 that the average period between issue and trial in the county court is 52 weeks and between allocation and trial 28 weeks.

[38] High Court and County Courts Jurisdiction Order 1991 (SI 1991/724), amended by subsequent statutory instruments up to and including SI 2001/1387. There will be some exceptions under specific enactments, as, for example, the Human Rights Act 1998 which provides at s.4 that claims arising from judicial acts can only be brought in the High Court or above.

[39] *Judicial Statistics 2005*, Table 3.1.

closer to 100,000.[40] A large proportion of the reduction may reasonably be attributed to the effect of the Woolf reforms in encouraging disputants to resolve their differences in ways other than litigation.

E. COURT PROCEDURE GENERALLY

12–008   A distinction more significant than that between the High Court and county court is, however, between small claims track, fast track and multi-track case management models. Whilst, as we have seen, in fact, small claims and most fast track cases will be dealt with in the county court and most multi-track claims in the High Court, the distinctions between the tracks are not necessarily co-extensive with the distinction between the two courts.

1. COURT MANAGEMENT OF LITIGATION

12–009   It was a fundamental tenet of Lord Woolf's thinking[41] that the courts should wrest control of the procedure from the parties; the parties (or perhaps more correctly, their legal representatives) being perceived as in large part responsible for delay and the running up of large fees. Consequently, as we have seen, CPR Parts 1 and 3 confer significant powers on the court to control the progress of a claim towards trial and to impose sanctions on any party impeding that progress. In particular, although it may be regarded as a sanction of last resort a party's claim or defence may be struck out for failure to comply with rules or court orders.

Further, as a result of the Human Rights Act 1998, the court, as a "public authority" within the meaning of the Act has been subjected to sanction if it permits breaches of human rights.[42] The obvious human right with which the court will be concerned is that guaranteeing a fair and public trial within a reasonable time (Art.6). It is as a direct result of the High Court and County Courts Jurisdiction (Amendment) Order 1999,[43] implementing Art.6, that arrangements were made for all hearings, even short procedural pre-trial hearings, to take place in public.[44] As to the "fairness" of the trial, it was thought, prior to implementation of the Act, that it might become commonplace for

---

[40] See *Judicial Statistics* 2005, p.35 for a graphic demonstration of the decrease in issue of Queen's Bench claims since 1999.

[41] Earlier attempts had been made to seek to increase the efficiency of the system, such as *Practice Direction* [1995] 1 All E.R. 385. The aim of this practice direction was, according to the then Lord Chief Justice, "to try and change the whole culture, the ethos, applying in the field of civil litigation".

[42] Principally in respect of the parties to litigation before the court, but also in respect of others, such as witnesses.

[43] SI 1999/1014.

[44] This has had a particular impact, following *Scarth v UK* (1999) Application no.33745/96, ECHR, on small claims track hearings. These had previously been not only informal, but also by way of arbitration and held in private. The holding of hearings in public is now the invariable case at least in principle, subject to predictable exceptions (such as the need to protect a child): CPR r.39.2. In practice the rooms normally used by district judges and masters for pre-trial hearings are not of a size to accommodate large numbers of the interested public.

appeals to include, automatically or by way of afterthought, an allegation that the appellant had been deprived of a fair trial. Lord Woolf, sitting in the Court of Appeal, announced the approach the courts would take to such allegations:

> "In my judgment, cases such as this, do not require any consideration of human rights issues, certainly issues under article 6. It would be highly undesirable if the consideration of those issues was made more complex by the injection into them of article 6 style arguments. I hope that judges will be robust in resisting any attempt to introduce those arguments. . . . When the 1998 Act becomes law, counsel will need to show self restraint if it is not to be discredited."[45]

The court must also ensure that orders it makes do not cause breaches of human rights and this will often involve the court in seeking to strike a fair balance between two competing rights.[46] Where one of the rights involved is that of freedom of expression, s.12 of the Human Rights Act 1998 imposes further obligations on the court.[47]

2. Prior to Commencing an Action: the Pre-action Protocols

Although prior to April 26, 1999 it was considered good practice for the claimant **12–010** (through his or her legal representatives) to write a "letter before action" to the proposed defendant, outlining the nature of the claim and, in a liquidated claim, inviting payment within, say, seven days, this was regarded perhaps as a warning at most, with the added potential benefit that it might provoke payment or meaningful negotiations.

As Lord Woolf had recomemnded that litigation should be avoided wherever possible,[48] he suggested that "pre-action protocols" should be developed to govern the pre-issue stages of litigation. It was intended that these should:

(a) encourage the use of alternative dispute resolution (ADR);

(b) promote "economy" in the use of expert witnesses—the parties are encouraged to make consensual arrangements for expert evidence, in particular to agree to the use of a single expert witness between them rather than one each;

---

[45] *Daniels v Walker* [2000] 1 WLR 1382, CA.

[46] A number of recent cases involving injunctions give good examples of the way in which the courts seek to achieve this balancing act, e.g. *Douglas and Zeta-Jones v Hello! Ltd* [2001] 2 WLR 992.

[47] See *Cream Holdings Ltd v Banerjee* [2004] UKHL 44, HL; *Greene v Associated Newspapers* [2004] EWHC 2322, QBD. The court may also need to mediate between two competing human rights, such as privacy and freedom of expression: *Douglas and Zeta Jones v Hello! Ltd, op. cit.*; *Campbell v Mirror Group Newspapers Ltd* [2004] UKHL 22.

[48] It is thought that the use of pre-action protocols has been a contributing factor in the decrease in the number of civil claims being issued: *Emerging Findings op. cit.*, paras 3.12 to 3.16 inclusive.

(c)   enable parties to obtain and exchange information (such as, for example, information about the likely value of the claim);

(d)   assist parties to comply with the tight timetable likely to be set by the court for the pre-trial stages once (if at all) court proceedings were issued.

At the date of writing there are nine approved pre-action protocols for: personal injury claims; defamation claims; construction and engineering disputes; clinical negligence; professional negligence; judicial review cases; disease and illness claims; housing disrepair cases; and possession claims based on rent arrears.[49] Whilst each contains matters specific to the nature of the type of claim under discussion, the essential structure of a protocol is a timetable for letters setting out, in the claimant's case, the nature and details of the claim (and proposals for expert evidence) and in the defendant's case, a reasoned response setting out the extent to which the claim is disputed. There are sanctions for failure to comply with the appropriate protocol.[50] Further, in the light of our discussion of methods of ADR in Ch.11, it should be noted that in both protocol and non-protocol cases, the parties are strongly encouraged to seek to resolve their dispute outside the litigation system, with potential penalties in the litigation if they do not.

> "The parties should consider whether some form of alternative dispute resolution procedure would be more suitable than litigation, and if so, endeavour to agree which form to adopt. Both the Claimant and Defendant may be required by the Court to provide evidence that alternative means of resolving their dispute were considered. The Courts take the view that litigation should be a last resort, and that claims should not be issued prematurely when a settlement is still actively being explored. Parties are warned that if this paragraph is not followed then the court must have regard to such conduct when determining costs."[51]

---

[49] In the specialist Technology and Construction Court all parties are normally expected to comply with the protocol for construction and engineering disputes: *Technology and Construction Court Guide* (2nd edn, 2005).

[50] In the words of PD Protocols, para.2.3:

> "(1) an order that the party at fault pay the costs of the proceedings, or part of those costs, of the other party or parties;
>
> (2) an order that the party at fault pay those costs on an indemnity basis;
>
> (3) if the party at fault is a claimant in whose favour an order for the payment of damages or some specified sum is subsequently made, an order depriving that party of interest on such and in respect of such period as may be specified, and/or awarding interest at a lower rate than that at which interest would otherwise have been awarded;
>
> (4) if the party at fault is a defendant and an order for the payment of damages or some specified sum is subsequently made in favour of the claimant, an order awarding interest on such sum and in respect of such period as may be specified at a higher rate, not exceeding 10% above base rate (*cf.*, CPR r.36.21(2)), than the rate at which interest would otherwise have been awarded."

The extent to which a protocol has been complied with must also be indicated to the court at the allocation stage and the extent of compliance or non-compliance will be a factor when the court is considering the award of costs: CPR r.44.3(5).

[51] PD Protocols, para.4.7.

In cases other than those to which an approved protocol applies, the parties must, however, engage in very similar behaviour,[52] subject again to sanctions for failure to do so.

3. COMMENCING AN ACTION

To begin a claim, the claimant must file a number of documents, including a **12–011** cheque for the appropriate issue fee,[53] the claim form and any notice of funding,[54] at the court office.[55] In some county court cases this can be done over the internet.[56]

The particulars of claim may be filed at this stage or alternatively filed within 14 days after the claim form (once "issued" by the court) has been served on the defendant.[57] The claim form is a prescribed form requiring information to be given as to the nature of the claim and its value (to establish that the court has jurisdiction).[58] There is no specific form for the particulars of claim (although it must comply with the requirements of CPR Part 16 and PD. 16[59]) and must inform the defendant with sufficient particularity of the claim against him or her. In certain types of case (such as personal injury claims) additional prescribed documents must accompany the particulars of claim.[60] There is, however, a general discretion to add to or include in the particulars of claim any or all of the following:

(a) any point of law on which the claim is based;

(b) the name of any witness the claimant intends to call; and

(c) any document "necessary to" the claim.[61]

---

[52] PD Protocols, para.4.1:

> "In cases not covered by any approved protocol, the court will expect the parties, in accordance with the overriding objective and the matters referred to in CPR 1.l(2)(a), (b) and (c), to act reasonably in exchanging information and documents relevant to the claim and generally in trying to avoid the necessity for the start of proceedings."

[53] It often surprises litigants to know the amount of the fee, which, depending on the value of the claim, can be up to £1,700. See the Civil Proceedings Fees Order 2004 (SI 2004/3121), Sch.1, as substituted by the Civil Proceedings Fees (Amendment) Order 2005 (SI 2005/3445). Guides to court fees also appear on HM Courts Service website. See also a current consultation paper on the civil fee structure: *A consultation by the Department for Constitutional Affairs: Civil Court Fees* (DCA, April 2007).

[54] Such as a conditional fee agreement.

[55] CPR r.7.2 (1).

[56] See PD 7e for the issue of some types of county court claims through "Money Claim Online".

[57] CPR r.7.4.

[58] CPR r.16.2, 16.3, PD 16 para.2 and PD 7 para.3. Note that in suitable cases proceedings can be issued against "persons unknown", see *Bloomsbury Publishing Group Plc v News Group Newspapers Ltd (Continuation of Injunction)* [2003] EWHC 1205, [2003] 1 W.L.R. 1633.

[59] See, for example, the list of contents of the particulars of claim at CPR r.16.4 and the further details required by PD 16 paras 3 to 9 inclusive.

[60] In a personal injury claim, a medical report setting out the claimant's injuries and a "schedule of past and future expenses and losses" ("special damages"): see PD 16 para.4. Additional requirements for fatal accident claims, recovery of land, hire purchase, Competition Act 1998 and human rights claims are also set out in PD 16.

[61] PD 16 para.13.3.

The claim form, and, if separate, the particulars of claim, must contain a "statement of truth".[62] This statement is in the words "I believe/the claimant believes that the facts stated in this claim form/these particulars of claim are true". It is normally signed by the actual claimant rather than by his or her legal representative[63] and the sanction for signing without an honest belief in the truth of the document is a penalty for contempt of court.[64]

On payment of the appropriate fee,[65] the claim form (with or without the particulars of claim) is sealed by the court. This is the official commencement of the court proceedings ("issue").[66] The sealed claim form is then sent to the defendant, usually by the court but sometimes by the claimant.[67] The process of transmitting the sealed claim form to the defendant is known as "service" and may be carried out in a number of ways including facsimile transmission and, in limited circumstances, e-mail.[68]

Generally, proceedings are brought under CPR Pt 7. However, in cases where the claimant "seeks the court's decision on a question which is unlikely to involve a substantial question of fact",[69] such as judicial review, the alternative Pt 8 procedure is available. The Pt 8 procedure omits most of the normal stages of exchange of evidence and proceeds to an early hearing of the merits of the dispute.

(a) County court/High Court: which court for issue?

12–012   As we have seen, a claim form cannot normally be issued in the High Court unless the value of the claim exceeds, at the time of writing, £15,000.[70] This is is the same financial limit as for the "multi-track" case management model, so that for all practical purposes, all High Court cases will be multi-track. If the claim is for personal injuries, however, the claim cannot be started in the High Court unless its value exceeds £50,000. This does not, however, prevent claims whose value exceeds either figure being issued in the county court, perhaps for reasons of convenience. Aside from merely financial considerations, claims should be begun in the High Court if their complexity or importance in the

---

[62] PD 7 para.7 and CPR r.22 (l)(a).

[63] Although it can be signed by the legal representative: PD 22 para.3.8.

[64] CPR r.32.14. See also *Malgar v R. E. Leach (Engineering) Ltd* [2000] C.P. Rep. 39, Ch D, *per* Scott V.C.: "it is important that flagrant breaches of the obligation to be responsible and truthful in verifying statements of case and in verifying witness statements should be policed and enforced if necessary by committal proceedings". *Malgar* was relied on in support of a finding of contempt in *Kabushiki Kaisha Sony Computer Entertainment Inc. v Ball (Application for Permission to Bring Proceedings)* (2004) 27(9) I.P.D. 27098, Ch D.

A claim form, particulars of claim or any other statement of case from which the statement of truth has been omitted altogether is not a nullity, but is vulnerable to being struck out: PD 22 para.4.

[65] At the date of writing, fees range from £30 for a claim worth less than £300 issued in the county court, to £1,700 for a High Court claim for £300,000: see Civil Proceedings Fees (Amendment) Order 2006 (SI 2006/719).

[66] PD 7 para.5.1.

[67] CPR Pt 6 and PD 6.

[68] See generally CPR Pt 6 and PD 6.

[69] CPR r.8.1(2) and PD 8 para.1.1.

[70] PD 7 para.2.1 and High Court and County Courts Jurisdiction Order 1991 (SI 1991/724), amended by High Court and County Courts Jurisdiction (Amendment) Order 1999 (SI 1999/1014). However, if the claim is issued in the Royal Courts of Justice in London, PD 29, para.2 provides for the transfer of some categories of case worth less than £50,000 to a county court in the London area.

context of public interest demand it.[71] After issue, however, claims may be transferred, not only between High Court and county court, but also to the specialist courts such as the Technology and Construction Court, the Commercial Court or the Mercantile Court.[72] Statutes and individual provisions of the CPR may, however, regulate the jurisdiction of the courts. So, for example, whilst Human Rights Act claims can be brought in either court, if the subject of the complaint is a judicial act, the claim must be commenced in the High Court.[73]

(b) County court: fast track

A claim form in the (imaginary) case of *Wilkinson v Walkertronic Super Hi-Fi-Vid Ltd* follows, with the basic particulars of claim and the response pack. Where the claimant is a litigant in person, the style of the documentation will be less formal (although if it is not compliant with CPR Pts 7 and 16 and their accompanying practice directions, it may be vulnerable to being struck out[74]) but the information on which the claim is based must appear clearly so that the defendant knows what is the case against him or her. This claim is likely to be allocated to the fast track and has been issued in the county court.

12–013

---

[71] PD 7 para.2.4.

[72] Proceedings may also be started in the specialist courts, some of which, such as the Commercial Court, treat all claims as multi-track. For these specialist courts, see CPR Pts 58, 59 and 60.

[73] PD 7 para.2.10. For specific jurisdictional provisions, particularly as to the jurisdiction of masters and district judges to make certain types of order, see PD 2B Allocation of Cases to Levels of Judiciary.

[74] CPR r.3.4(2)(a).

Claim Form

In the
NOTTINGHAM COUNTY COURT

	for court use only
Claim No.	
Issue date	3rd October 2006

SEAL

Claimant

CYRIL JACK WILKINSON

24 YEW DRIVE
LENTON
NOTTINGHAM
NG 7 1SS

Defendant(s)

WALKERTRONIC SUPER HI-FI-VID LIMITED
TRADING ADDRESS:UNIT 17 THE LAURELS SHOPPING PRECINCT
NOTTINGHAM
NG1 Y77

Brief details of claim

The Claimant's claim is for damages estimated at £6,210.00 and interest arising form
the Defendant's supply, in breach of a contract of 1st February 2006, made between
the Claimant and the Defendant, of a defective computer game.

Value

I expect to recover more than £5,000 but less than £10,000.

		£
Defendant's name and address	WALKERTRONIC SUPER HI-FI-VID LIMITED TRADING ADDRESS:UNIT 17 THE LAURELS SHOPPING PRECINCT NOTTINGHAM NG1 Y77	

Amount claimed	to be determined
Court fee	£250.00
Solicitor's costs	£100.00
Total amount	£350.00

The court office at Nottingham County Court
60 Canal Street, Nottingham NG1 7EJ
is open between 10 am and 4 pm Monday to Friday. When corresponding with the court, please address forms or letters to the Court Manager and quote the claim number.

N1 Claim form (CPR Part 7)(01.02)   N1/1

	Claim No.	

Does, or will, your claim include any issues under the Human Rights Act 1998?   ☐ Yes   ☒ No

Particulars of Claim (attached)(to follow):

Statement of Truth

*(I believe)(The Claimant believes) that the facts stated in these particulars of claim are true.

* I am duly authorised by the Claimant to sign this statement.

Full name   CYRIL JACK WILKINSON

Name of Claimant's solicitor's firm   POPP, LEES AND STONE

signed   *C J Wilkinson*   position or office held

*(Claimant)(Litigation friend)(Claimant's solicitor) (if signing on behalf of firm or company)

*delete as appropriate

Popp, Lees and Stone
Haltergate
Nottingham
NG1 6FF
DX Nottingham 1

Claimant's or Claimant's solicitor's address to which documents or payments should be sent if different from overleaf including (if appropriate) details of DX, fax or e-mail.

Notes for claimant on completing a claim form

Before you begin completing the claim form

- You must think about whether alternative dispute resolution (ADR) is a better way to reach an agreement before going to court. The leaflet 'Making a claim? - Some questions to ask yourself' explains more about ADR and how you can attempt to settle your claim.

- Please read all of these guidance notes. The notes follow the order in which information is required on the form.

- If you are filling in the claim form by hand, please use black ink and write in block capitals.

- Copy the completed claim form and the defendant's notes for guidance so that you have one copy for yourself, one copy for the court and one copy for each defendant. Send or take the forms to the court office with the appropriate fee. The court will tell you how much this is.

- Court staff can help you fill in the claim form and give information about procedure once it has been issued. But they cannot give legal advice. If you need legal advice, for example, about the likely success of your claim or the evidence you need to prove it, you should contact a solicitor or a Citizens Advice Bureau.

Further information may be obtained from the court in a series of free leaflets.

Notes on completing the claim form

Heading

You must fill in the heading of the form to indicate the name of the court where you want the claim to be issued.

The claimant and defendant

As the person issuing the claim, you are called the 'claimant'; the person you are suing is called the 'defendant'. Claimants who are under 18 years old (unless otherwise permitted by the court) and patients within the meaning of the Mental Health Act 1983, must have a litigation friend to issue and conduct court proceedings on their behalf. Court staff will tell you more about what you need to do if this applies to you.

Providing information about yourself and the defendant

full address including postcode

You should provide the full address including postcode for yourself and the defendant. The postcode for any address in the United Kingdom may be obtained free from the Royal Mail Address Management Guide, or their website at www. royalmail.com.

If an address does not have a postcode you will need to ask the judge for permission to serve the claim with this information missing. There is no additional fee for this, but if you omit a postcode and fail to ask permission of the judge the court will not allow your claim to be served on the defendant until you supply the missing postcode or a judge permits service without it.

You must provide the following information about yourself and the defendant according to the capacity in which you are suing and in which the defendant is being sued.

When suing or being sued as:-

an individual:

You must enter his or her full unabbreviated name where known, including their first name and any middle name, their last name and the title by which she or he is known (i.e. Mr., Mrs., Ms., Dr., etc.) and residential address (including postcode and telephone number). Where the defendant is a proprietor of a business, a partner in a firm or an individual sued in the name of a club or other unincorporated association, the address for service should be the usual or last known place of residence or principal place of business of the company, firm or club or other unincorporated association.

Where the individual is:

trading under another name

you must enter his or her full unabbreviated name where known, and the title by which he or she is known and the full name under which he or she is trading, e.g. 'Mr. John Smith trading as Smith's Groceries'.

suing or being sued in a representative capacity

you must say what that capacity is e.g. 'Mr Joe Bloggs as the representative of Mrs Sharon Bloggs (deceased)'.

suing or being sued in the name of a club or other unincorporated association

add the words 'suing/sued on behalf of' followed by the name of the club or other unincorporated association.

an unincorporated business - a firm

In the case of a partnership (other than a limited liability partnership) you must enter the full name of the business followed by the suffix 'a firm'.

Enter the name of the firm followed by the words 'a firm' e.g. 'Bandbox - a firm' and an address including postcode for service. This may either be one of the partners residential addresses or the principal or last known place of business of the firm.

a company registered in England and Wales or a Limited Liability Partnership

In the case of a registered company or limited liability partnership, you must enter the full name of the company or partnership followed by the appropriate suffix, i.e. Ltd, Plc, LLP. You must provide an address, including postcode which is either the company's registered office or any place of business in England and Wales that has a real, or the most, connection with the claim e.g. a shop where goods were bought.

a corporation (other than a company)

enter the full name of the corporation and any suffix if appropriate and the address including postcode in England and Wales which is either its principal office or any other place where the corporation carries on activities and which has a real connection with the claim.

an overseas company (defined by s744 of the Companies Act 1985)

You must enter the company's full name and any suffix if appropriate and address including postcode. The address must either be the registered address under s691 of the Act or the address of the place of business having a real, or the most, connection with the claim.

under 18 write '(a child by Mr Joe Bloggs his litigation friend)' after the name. If the child is conducting proceedings on their own behalf write '(a child)' after the child's name.

a patient within the meaning of the Mental Health Act 1983 write '(by Mr Joe Bloggs his litigation friend)' after the patient's name.

Brief details of claim

You must set out under **this** heading:
- a concise statement of the nature of your claim
- the remedy you are seeking e.g. payment of money;

Value

If you are claiming a **fixed amount of money** (a 'specified amount') write the amount in the box at the bottom right-hand corner of the claim form against 'amount claimed'.

If you are <u>not</u> claiming a fixed amount of money (an 'unspecified amount') under 'Value' write "I expect to recover" followed by whichever of the following applies to your claim:

- 'not more than £5,000' **or**
- 'more than £5,000 but not more than £15,000' **or**
- 'more than £15,000'

If you are **not able** to put a value on your claim, write 'I cannot say how much I expect to recover'.

Personal injuries
If your claim is for 'not more than £5,000' and includes a claim for personal injuries, you must also write 'My claim includes a claim for personal injuries and the amount I expect to recover as damages for pain, suffering and loss of amenity is' followed by either:

- 'not more than £1,000' **or**
- 'more than £1,000'

Housing disrepair
If your claim is for 'not more than £5,000' and includes a claim for housing disrepair relating to residential premises, you must also write 'My claim includes a claim against my landlord for housing disrepair relating to residential premises. The cost of the repairs or other work is estimated to be' followed by either:

- 'not more than £1,000' **or**
- 'more than £1,000'

If within this claim, you are making a claim for other damages, you must also write:

'I expect to recover as damages' followed by either:
- 'not more than £1,000' **or**
- 'more than £1,000'

Defendant's name and address

Enter in this box the title, full names, address and postcode of the defendant receiving the claim form (ie. one claim form for each defendant). If the defendant is to be served outside England and Wales, you may need to obtain the court's permission.

Particulars of claim

You must set out under this heading:
- a concise statement of the facts on which you rely
- a statement (if applicable) to the effect that you are seeking aggravated damages or exemplary damages
- details of any interest which you are claiming
- any other matters required for your type of claim as set out in the relevant practice direction

Statement of truth

This must be signed by you, or by your solicitor or your litigation friend, if appropriate.

Where the claimant is a registered company or a corporation the claim must be signed by either the director, treasurer, secretary, chief executive, manager or other officer of the company or (in the case of a corporation) the mayor, chairman, president or town clerk.

Address for documents

Insert in this box the address at which you wish to receive documents and/or payments, if different from the address you have already given under the heading 'Claimant'. The address must be in England or Wales. If you are willing to accept service by DX, fax or e-mail, add details.

Notes for defendant on replying to the claim form

Please read these notes carefully - they will help you decide what to do about this claim. Further information may be obtained from the court in a series of free leaflets

- If this claim form was received with the particulars of claim completed or attached, you must reply within 14 days of the date it was served on you. If the words 'particulars of claim to follow' are written in the particulars of claim box, you should not reply until after you are served with the particulars of claim (which should be no more than 14 days after you received the claim form). If the claim was sent by post, the date of service is taken as the second day after posting (see post mark). If the claim form was delivered or left at your address, the date of service will be the day after it was delivered.

- You may either:
  - pay the total amount i.e. the amount claimed, the court fee, and solicitor's costs (if any)
  - admit that you owe all or part of the claim and ask for time to pay or
  - dispute the claim

- If you do not reply, judgment may be entered against you.
- The notes below tell you what to do.
- The response pack will tell you which forms to use for your reply. (The pack will accompany the particulars of claim if they are served after the claim form).

- Court staff can help you complete the forms of reply and tell you about court procedures. But they cannot give legal advice. If you need legal advice, for example about the likely success of disputing the claim, you should contact a solicitor or a Citizens Advice Bureau immediately.

Registration of Judgments: If this claim results in a judgment against you, details will be entered in a public register, the Register of Judgments, Orders and Fines. They will then be passed to credit reference agencies which will then supply them to credit grantors and others seeking information on your financial standing. **This will make it difficult for you to get credit.** A list of credit reference agencies is available from Registry Trust Ltd, 173/175 Cleveland Street, London W1T 6QR.

Costs and Interest: Additional costs and interest may be added to the amount claimed on the front of the claim form if judgment is entered against you. In a county court, if judgment is for £5,000 or more, or is in respect of a debt which attracts contractual or statutory interest for late payment, the claimant may be entitled to further interest.

Your response and what happens next

How to pay

Do not bring any payments to the court - they will not be accepted.

When making payments to the claimant, quote the claimant's reference (if any) and the claim number.

Make sure that you keep records and can account for any payments made. Proof may be required if there is any disagreement. It is not safe to send cash unless you use registered post.

Admitting the Claim

Claim for specified amount

If you admit all the claim, take or send the money, including the court fee, any interest and costs, to the claimant at the address given for payment on the claim form, within 14 days.

If you admit all the claim and you are asking for time to pay, complete Form N9A and send it to the claimant at the address given for payment on the claim form, within 14 days. The claimant will decide whether to accept your proposal for payment. If it is accepted, the claimant may request the court to enter judgment against you and you will be sent an order to pay. If your offer is not accepted, the court will decide how you should pay.

If you admit only part of the claim, complete Form N9A and Form N9B (see 'Disputing the Claim' overleaf) and send them to the court within 14 days. The claimant will decide whether to accept your part admission. If it is accepted, the claimant may request the court to enter judgment against you and the court will send you an order to pay. If your part admission is not accepted, the case will proceed as a defended claim.

Claim for unspecified amount

If you admit liability for the whole claim but do not make an offer to satisfy the claim, complete Form N9C and send it to the court within 14 days. A copy will be sent to the claimant who may request the court to enter judgment against you for an amount to be decided by the court, and costs. The court will enter judgment and refer the court file to a judge for directions for management of the case. You and the claimant will be sent a copy of the court's order.

If you admit liability for the claim and offer an amount of money to satisfy the claim, complete Form N9C and send it to the court within 14 days.

The claimant will be sent a copy and asked if the offer is acceptable. The claimant must reply to the court within 14 days and send you a copy. If a reply is not received, the claim will be stayed. If the amount you have offered is **accepted** -

- the claimant may request the court to enter judgment against you for that amount.
- if you have requested time to pay which is not accepted by the claimant, the rate of payment will be decided by the court.

If your offer in satisfaction is **not accepted** -

- the claimant may request the court to enter judgment against you for an amount to be decided by the court, and costs; and
- the court will enter judgment and refer the court file to a judge for directions for management of the case. You and the claimant will be sent a copy of the court's order.

Disputing the claim

If you are being sued as an individual for a specified amount of money and you dispute the claim, the claim may be transferred to a local court i.e. the one nearest to or where you live or carry on business if different from the court where the claim was issued.

If you need longer than 14 days to prepare your defence or to contest the court's jurisdiction to try the claim, complete the Acknowledgment of Service form and send it to the court within 14 days. This will allow you 28 days from the date of service of the particulars of claim to file your defence or make an application to contest the court's jurisdiction. The court will tell the claimant that your Acknowledgment of Service has been received.

If the case proceeds as a defended claim, you and the claimant will be sent an Allocation Questionnaire. You will be told the date by which it must be returned to the court. The information you give on the form will help a judge decide whether your case should be dealt with in the small claims track, fast track or multi-track. After a judge has considered the completed questionnaires, you will be sent a notice of allocation setting out the judge's decision. The notice will tell you the track to which the claim has been allocated and what you have to do to prepare for the hearing or trial. **Leaflets telling you more about the tracks are available from the court office.**

Claim for specified amount

If you wish to dispute the full amount claimed or wish to claim against the claimant (a counterclaim), complete Form N9B and send it to the court within 14 days.

If you admit part of the claim, complete the Defence Form N9B and the Admission Form N9A

and send them both to the court within 14 days. The claimant will decide whether to accept your part admission in satisfaction of the claim (see under 'Admitting the Claim - specified amount'). If the claimant does not accept the amount you have admitted, the case will proceed as a defended claim.

If you dispute the claim because you have already paid it, complete Form N9B and send it to the court within 14 days. The claimant will have to decide whether to proceed with the claim or withdraw it and notify the court and you within 28 days. If the claimant wishes to proceed, the case will proceed as a defended claim.

Claim for unspecified amount/return of goods/non-money claims

If you dispute the claim or wish to claim against the claimant (counterclaim), complete Form N9D and send it to the court within 14 days.

Personal injuries claims:

If the claim is for personal injuries and the claimant has attached a medical report to the particulars of claim, in your defence you should state whether you:

- agree with the report **or**
- dispute all or part of the report **and** give your reasons for doing so **or**
- neither agree nor dispute the report **or** have no knowledge of the report

Where you have obtained your own medical report, you should attach it to your defence.

If the claim is for personal injuries and the claimant has attached a schedule of past and future expenses and losses, in your defence you must state which of the items you:

- agree **or**
- dispute **and** supply alternative figures where appropriate **or**
- neither agree nor dispute or have no knowledge of

Address where notices can be sent

This must be either your solicitor's address, your own residential or business address in England and Wales or (if you live elsewhere) some other address within England and Wales.

Statement of truth

This must be signed by you, by your solicitor or your litigation friend, as appropriate.

Where the defendant is **a registered company or a corporation** the response must be signed by either the director, treasurer, secretary, chief executive, manager or other officer of the company **or** (in the case of a corporation) the mayor, chairman, president or town clerk

N1(N1C)/6

Please read these notes carefully - they will help you decide what to do about this claim. You will have received a notice of hearing telling you when and where to come to court with the claim form. A leaflet is available from the court office about what happens when you come to a court hearing.

- You must reply to the claim form within 14 days of the date it was served on you. If the claim form was
  - sent by post, the date of service is taken as the second day after posting (see post mark)
  - delivered or left at your address, the date of service will be the day after it was delivered
  - handed to you personally, the date of service willl be the day it was given to you
- You may either
  - pay the amount claimed
  - admit liability for the claim and offer to make payments to keep the goods
  - dispute the claim
- If you do not reply or attend the hearing, judgement may be entered against you.
- The notes below tell you what to do.
- Court staff can help you complete the forms of reply and tell you about court procedure. But they cannot give legal advice. If you need legal advice, for example about the likely success of disputing the claim, you should contact a solicitor or a Citizens Advice Bureau immediately.

Registration of Judgments: If this claim results in a judgement against you, details will be entered in a public register, the Register of Judgments, Orders and Fines. They will then be passed to credit reference agencies which will then supply them to credit grantors and others seeking information on your financial standing. **This will make it difficult for you to get credit** A list of credit reference agencies is available from Registry Trust Ltd, 173/175 Cleveland Street, London W1T 6QR.

Costs and Interest: Additional costs and interest may be added to the amount claimed on the front of the claim form if judgment is entered against you. In a county court, if judgment is for £5,000 or more, or is in respect of a debt which attracts contractual or statutory interest for late payment, the claimant may be entitled to further interest.

Your response and what happens next

How to pay

Do not bring any payments to the court - they will not be accepted.

When making payments to the claimant, quote the claimant's reference (if any) and the claim number.

Make sure that you keep records and can account for any payments made. Proof may be required if there is any disagreement. It is not safe to send cash unless you use registered post.

Admitting the Claim

If you admit liability for the claim and offer to make payments in order to keep the goods. Complete Form N9C and send it to the court within 14 days. **Remember** to keep a copy for yourself. The court will send a copy of your admission to the claimant and ask if your offer is acceptable.
If the claimant **accepts your offer** and asks the court to
enter judgment before the date of the hearing, you will be sent a copy of the judgment and need not come to the hearing. If you do not hear from the court it is in your interests to attend the hearing.
If your offer is **not accepted**, you should attend the hearing. The court will treat your admission as evidence so remember to bring a copy of your admission with you to the hearing.

Disputing the claim

If you dispute the claim or wish to claim aginst the claimant (counterclaim), complete Form N9D and send it to the court within 14 days. **Remember** to keep a copy for yourself and to bring it with you to the hearing. The court will send a copy of your defence to the claimant. At the hearing the court may make a final order or judgment in the claim. If the court agrees that you have a valid defence (or counterclaim), it will tell you and the claimant what to do to prepare for a future hearing. If you send your defence to the court after the 14 days has expired, and you want to rely on it at the hearing, the court may take your failure to file it on time into account when deciding what order to make in respect of costs.

Statement of truth

This must be signed by you, by your solicitor or your litigation friend, as appropriate.
Where the defendant is a **registered company or a corporation** the response must be signed by either the director, treasurer, secretary, chief executive, manager or other officer of the company **or** (in the case of a corporation) the mayor, chairman, president or town clerk.

N1(FD) Consumer Credit Act claim (04.06)

IN THE NOTTINGHAM COUNTY COURT   CLAIM NO. NG0178943

BETWEEN

Cyril Jack Wilkinson

Claimant

– and –

Walkertronic Super Hi-Fi-Vid Limited

Defendant

PARTICULARS OF CLAIM

---

1   By a written contract[75] made on 1st February 2006 the Claimant purchased from the Defendant for the sum of £150.00 a Magivid electronic football game ("the Game") for use in conjunction with a computer owned by the Claimant ("the Agreement").

2   The Defendant entered into the Agreement in the course of its business as a general electrical retailer.

3   Consequently it was an implied term of the Agreement that the Game should be of satisfactory quality.[76]

4   Further or alternatively, on 1st February 2006 at the Defendant's premises, the Claimant made known to Mr. Evans of the Defendant, the particular purpose for which the Game was being bought, that is, for use in conjunction with the Claimant's computer, the gist of the Claimant's words being "I'm going to use this with an Apple Mac".

5   It was therefore an implied term of the Agreement that the Game would be fit for that purpose.[77]

6   The Claimant used the Game on three occasions, but whilst in use on 5th February 2006 it exploded ("the Explosion") causing damage to the Claimant's computer and setting fire to a pair of curtains. Structural damage was caused to the door and window and decorations in the same room were damaged by smoke and scorching.

7   The Explosion was caused by the Defendant's breach of contract.

8   In breach of the terms set out in paragraphs 3 and 4 above the Game was not of satisfactory quality and/or was not fit for its purpose.

---

[75] Note that a copy of this contract must be attached to the particulars of claim: PD 16 para.7.3.
[76] Sale of Goods Act 1979, as amended, s.14(2).
[77] Sale of Goods Act 1979, as amended, s.14(3).

PARTICULARS

The Game was liable to overheat when used more than once in the same day.

The Game overheated within 10 minutes of being connected to the Claimant's computer.

9   As a result of the matters set out above the Claimant has suffered loss and damage:

PARTICULARS OF LOSS AND DAMAGE

Refund of price paid	£150.00
Value of the computer	£2,000.00
Replacement of curtains	£60.00
Redecoration and structural repairs	£4,000.00
TOTAL ESTIMATED LOSSES	£6,210.00

10   Further the Claimant claims interest under s.69 of the County Courts Act 1984 on such damages as may be awarded to him at such rate and for such period as the Court thinks fit.

AND THE CLAIMANT CLAIMS

1   Damages

2   Interest under s.69 of the County Courts Act 1984

Popp, Lees and Stone

Statement of truth[78]

I believe that the facts stated in these Particulars of Claim are true

C J Wilkinson

Cyril Jack Wilkinson
Claimant

Dated 3rd October 2006

Popp, Lees and Stone
Solicitors
Haltergate
Nottingham
NG1 6FF
Solicitors for the Claimant

---

[78] See CPR Pt 22 and PD 22 for statements of truth generally.

(c) High Court: multi track

We will also consider the (equally imaginary) case of *George and Hacker v Reliable Nag Supply Stables (a firm)*, a claim worth in excess of £65,000. This claim will be issued in the High Court and is likely to be allocated to the multi-track.

12–014

4. STATEMENTS OF CASE (PREVIOUSLY "PLEADINGS")

Since the adversarial system depends upon the two parties selecting the issues for resolution and acquiring the evidence to support them, it is necessary that the parties should communicate to each other the elements of their case. The system of statements of case (which includes the claim form and the particulars of claim as well as the defence which we discuss below) amounts to a formal exchange of allegations so as to define the matters that are in dispute. In combination with the pre-action correspondence, they also reduce, in furtherance of the overriding objective, the possibility of either party being surprised by the other at trial. The format and to a large extent the content of statements of case is prescribed by the CPR, particularly Pts 7, 15, 16 and 20 and their accompanying practice directions.[79]

12–015

If the claimant has served a claim form not accompanied by the particulars of claim, the next document to be prepared and served is the particulars of claim (which will be accompanied by the response pack).[80] In the particulars of claim the claimant's claim against the defendant must be set out, with the facts that will be relied on for support, the injury/loss that has been suffered and the remedy being sought. The document should be "concise"[81] but sufficiently full to allow the defendant to ascertain the case against him or her and to prepare a defence.

The art of drafting statements of case is therefore very important. Statements of case should state facts only, although matters of law or evidence may optionally be included in accordance with PD 16 para.13.3. They must state only the material facts and those material facts must be set out with sufficient detail but without excessive detail. Drawing that latter balance is where the real skill lies.

Finally and fundamentally, each statement of case must be capable of having a statement of truth attached to it.

In *George and Hacker v Reliable Nag Supply Stables (a firm)* the particulars of claim could be set out as follows:

---

[79] These Parts do not apply to some specialist claims such as those brought under Pt 8, defamation claims (Pt 53), possession proceedings (Pt 55) and probate claims (Pt 57): PD 16, para.1.

[80] Note variations to this sequence in the Commercial Court.

[81] CPR r.16.2.

IN THE HIGH COURT OF JUSTICE   CLAIM NO. G0167234

QUEEN'S BENCH DIVISION

NOTTINGHAM DISTRICT REGISTRY

BETWEEN

PETER GEORGE (1)

MARTIN HACKER (2)

Claimants

– and –

RELIABLE NAG SUPPLY STABLES (a firm)

Defendant

PARTICULARS OF CLAIM

1   The Claimants and the Defendant entered into an oral contract ("the Contract") on 25th June 2006 for the sale by the Defendant to the Claimants of a piebald gelding known as Skipper ("the Horse") for the price of £65,000, paid by the Claimants to the Defendant on 25th June 2006.

PARTICULARS[82]

At approximately 3pm on 25th June 2006, at a meeting held on the premises of the Defendant, the First Claimant said to Mrs. Wooldbridge of the Defendant words to the effect "Is Skipper still on the market? We're still looking for something for general hacking and jumping at local gymkhana level." Mrs. Wooldbridge replied that he was still available and that his price had been reduced to £65,000. The First Claimant replied "Then we'll take him".

2   The Defendant sold the Horse in the course of its business as horse traders.

3   Consequently it was an implied term of the Contract that the Horse would be of satisfactory quality, specifically sound and in good health.[83]

4   Further or alternatively, as set out in paragraph 1 above, the Claimants made known to the Defendant a specific purpose for which the Horse would be required, namely general hacking and for jumping at the local gymkhanas. Consequently it was an implied term of the Contract that the Horse would be fit for such purposes.[84]

---

[82] PD 16 para.7.4.

[83] Sale of Goods Act 1979, as amended, s.14(2).

[84] *ibid.* s.14(3).

5   The Claimants took delivery of the Horse from the Defendant on 26th June 2006.

6   In breach of the terms set out in paragraphs 3 and 4 above, the Horse was not of satisfactory quality and/or was not fit for its purpose.

PARTICULARS

The Horse was found to be suffering from Bastard Strangles and was therefore entirely useless and worthless to the Claimants.

7   As a result of the matters set out above the Claimants have suffered loss and damage.

PARTICULARS

Cost price of Horse	£65,000.00
Fees paid to Sutton Riding Enterprises for the care of alternative horse from 1st July to 20th August	£290.00
TOTAL ESTIMATED LOSS	£65,290.00

8   Further the Claimants claim interest under s.35A Supreme Court Act 1981 on the amount found due to them at such rate and for such period as the Court thinks fit.

AND THE CLAIMANTS CLAIM

(1) Damages

(2) Interest under statute

Popp, Lees and Stone

Statement of truth

I believe that the facts stated in these Particulars of Claim are true

Peter George   *Martin Hacker*

Peter George   Martin Hacker

Claimants

Dated 10th November 2006

Popp, Lees and Stone
Solicitors
Haltergate
Nottingham
NG1 6FF
Solicitors for the Claimant

In both county court and High Court cases, together with the claim form and particulars of claim,[85] the defendant receives a "response pack"[86] containing forms on which to acknowledge service of the claim, admit the claim, or to deny it, or to counterclaim. An admission, acknowledgment or defence must be returned to the court within 14 days. If the defendant merely acknowledges service (perhaps because he or she needs more time to investigate and set out a defence) then a defence must also be filed within 28 days.[87]

If the claim form is served on its own with particulars of claim to follow, the defendant need not respond until the particulars of claim arrive.[88] Failure to submit an acknowledgement or defence on time will permit the claimant, normally on submission of the appropriate form and without a hearing, to have a judgment entered against the defendant immediately.[89]

The response pack for the *Walkertronic* case follows.

---

[85] If the two are served separately, the response pack accompanies the later particulars of claim.
[86] CPR r.7.8(1).
[87] CPR r.15.4.
[88] CPR r.9.1(2). The position is different in the Commercial Court for which the separate Admiralty and Commercial Court Guide and CPR Pt 58 and PD 58 should be consulted.
[89] CPR Pt 12.

Response Pack

You should read the 'notes for Defendant' attached to the claim form which will tell you when and where to send the forms.

Included in this pack are:

- either **Admission Form N9A**
  (if the claim is for a specified amount)
  or **Admission Form N9C**
  (if the claim is for an unspecified amount
  or is not a claim for money)
- either **Defence and Counterclaim Form N9B** (if the claim is for a specified amount)
  or **Defence and Counterclaim Form N9D**
  (if the claim is for an unspecified amount
  or is not a claim for money)
- **Acknowledgment of service** (see below)

Complete

If you admit the claim or the amount claimed and/or you want time to pay	the admission form
If you admit part of the claim	the admission form and the defence form
If you dispute the whole claim or wish to make a claim (a counterclaim) against the Claimant	the defence form
If you need 28 days (rather than 14) from the date of service to prepare your defence, or wish to contest the court's jurisdiction	the acknowledgment of service
If you do nothing, judgment may be entered against you	

Acknowledgment of Service

Defendant's full name if different from the name given on the claim form

In the	
NOTTINGHAM COUNTY COURT	
Claim No.	NG 06787878
Claimant (including ref.)	CYRIL JACK WILKINSON
Defendant	WALKERTRONIC SUPER HI-FI-VID LIMITED

Address to which documents about this claim should be sent (including reference if appropriate)

	if applicable
fax no.	
DX no.	DX
Ref. no.	
e-mail	

DX

Tel. no.   Postcode

Tick the appropriate box

1. I intend to defend all of this claim ☐

2. I intend to defend part of this claim ☐

3. I intend to contest jurisdiction ☐

(My) (Defendant's) date of birth is D D M M Y Y Y Y

If you file an acknowledgment of service but do not file a defence within 28 days of the date of service of the claim form, or particulars of claim if served separately, judgment may be entered against you.

If you do not file an application to dispute the jurisdiction of the court within 14 days of the date of filing this acknowledgment of service, it will be assumed that you accept the court's jurisdiction and judgment may be entered against you.

Signed

(Defendant)(Defendant's solicitor)(Litigation friend)

Position or office held
(if signing on behalf of firm or company)

Date

The court office at   Nottingham County Court
60 Canal Street, Nottingham NG1 7EJ
is open between 10 am and 4 pm Monday to Friday. When corresponding with the court, please address forms or letters to the Court Manager and quote the claim number.

N9 Response Pack (04.06)

2006 Edition 04.2006

N9

5093018

Admission (specified amount)

- You have a limited number of days to complete and return this form
- Before completing this form, please read the notes for guidance attached to the claim form

When to fill in this form
Only fill in this form if:
- you are admitting all of the claim **and** you are asking for time to pay; or
- you are admitting part of the claim. (You should also complete form N9B)

How to fill in this form
- Tick the correct boxes and give as much information as you can. **Then sign and date the form.** If necessary provide details on a separate sheet, add the claim number and attach it to this form.
- Make your offer of payment in box 11 on the back of this form. **If you make no offer the Claimant will decide how much and when you should pay.**
- If you are not an individual, you should ensure that you provide sufficient details about the assets and liabilities of your firm, company or corporation to support any offer of payment made in box 11.
- You can get help to complete this form at **any** county court office or Citizens Advice Bureau.

Where to send this form
- **If you admit the claim in full**
Send the completed form to the address shown on the claim form as one to which documents should be sent.
- **If you admit only part of the claim**
Send the form **to the court** at the address given on the claim form, together with the defence form (N9B).

How much of the claim do you admit?

☐ I admit the full amount claimed as shown on the claim form **or**

☐ I admit the amount of   £ _____

1 Personal details

Surname	
Forename	

☐ Mr   ☐ Mrs   ☐ Miss   ☐ Ms

☐ Married   ☐ Single   ☐ Other (specify) _____

Date of birth   D D M M Y Y Y Y

Address _____

Postcode _____

Tel. no. _____

Name of court	
	NOTTINGHAM COUNTY COURT
Claim No.	NG 06787878
Claimant (including ref.)	CYRIL JACK WILKINSON
Defendant	WALKERTRONIC SUPER HI-FI-VID LIMITED

2 Dependants *(people you look after financially)*

Number of children in each age group

under 11 ☐   11-15 ☐   16-17 ☐   18 & over ☐

Other dependants
(give details) _____

3 Employment

☐ I am employed as a _____
My employer is _____

Jobs other than main job *(give details)* _____

☐ I am self employed as a _____
Annual turnover is   £ ____

☐ I **am not** in arrears with my national insurance contributions, income tax and VAT

☐ I **am** in arrears and I owe   £ ____

Give details of:
(a) contracts and other work in hand _____
(b) any sums due for work done _____

☐ I have been unemployed for ____ years ____ months

☐ I am a pensioner

4 Bank account and savings

☐ I have a bank account
   ☐ The account is in credit by   £ ____
   ☐ The account is overdrawn by   £ ____

☐ I have a savings or building society account
The amount in the account is   £ ____

5 Residence
I live in   ☐ my own house   ☐ lodgings
     ☐ my jointly owned house   ☐ council accommodation
     ☐ rented accommodation

N9A Form of admission (specified amount) (04.06)   N9A/1

6 Income

My usual take home pay *(including overtime, commission, bonuses etc)*	£	per
Income support	£	per
Child benefit(s)	£	per
Other state benefit(s)	£	per
My pension(s)	£	per
Others living in my home give me	£	per
Other income *(give details below)*		
	£	per
	£	per
	£	per
Total income	**£**	**per**

8 Priority debts *(This section is for arrears only. Do not include regular expenses listed in box 7.)*

Rent arrrears	£	per
Mortgage arrears	£	per
Council tax/Community Charge arrears	£	per
Water charges arrears	£	per
Fuel debts: Gas	£	per
Electricity	£	per
Other	£	per
Maintenance arrears	£	per
Others *(give details below)*		
	£	per
	£	per
Total priority debts	**£**	**per**

7 Expenses

(Do not include any payments made by other members of the household out of their own income)

I have regular expenses as follows:

Mortgage *(including second mortgage)*	£	per
Rent	£	per
Council tax	£	per
Gas	£	per
Electricity	£	per
Water charges	£	per
TV rental and licence	£	per
HP repayments	£	per
Mail order	£	per
Housekeeping, food, school meals	£	per
Travelling expenses	£	per
Children's clothing	£	per
Maintenance payments	£	per
Others *(not court orders or credit debts listed in boxes 9 and 10)*		
	£	per
	£	per
	£	per
Total expenses	**£**	**per**

9 Court orders

Court	Claim No.	£	per

Total court order instalments	**£**	**per**

Of the payments above, I am behind with payments to *(please list)*

10 Credit debts

Loans and credit card debts *(please list)*

	£	per
	£	per
	£	per

Of the payments above, I am behind with payments to *(please list)*

11 Offer of payment

☐ I can pay the amount admitted on _____

or

☐ I can pay by monthly instalments of £ _____

If you cannot pay immediately, please give brief reasons below

12 Declaration

I declare that the details I have given above are true to the best of my knowledge

Signed _____

Date _____

Position or office held *(if signing on behalf of firm or company)* _____

Oyez 7 Spa Road London SE16 3QQ © Crown copyright.   N9A   04.06 5093026 N9A/2

Defence and Counterclaim (specified amount)

Name of court	
NOTTINGHAM COUNTY COURT	

- Fill in this form if you wish to dispute all or part of the claim and/or make a claim against the Claimant (counterclaim).
- You have a limited number of days to complete and return this form to the court.
- Before completing this form, please read the notes for guidance attached to the claim form.
- Please ensure that all boxes at the top right of this form are completed. You can obtain the correct names and number from the claim form. The court cannot trace your case without this information.

How to fill in this form

- Complete sections 1 and 2. Tick the correct boxes and give the other details asked for.
- Set out your defence in section 3. If necessary continue on a separate piece of paper making sure that the claim number is clearly shown on it. In your defence you must state which allegations in the particulars of claim you deny and your reasons for doing so. **If you fail to deny an allegation it may be taken that you admit it**.
- If you dispute only some of the allegations you must
  - specify which you admit and which you deny; and
  - give your own version of events if different from the Claimant's.

Claim No.	NG 06787878
Claimant (including ref.)	CYRIL JACK WILKINSON
Defendant	WALKERTRONIC SUPER HI-FI-VID LIMITED

- If you wish to make a claim against the Claimant (a counterclaim) complete section 4.
- Complete and sign section 5 before sending this form to the court. Keep a copy of the claim form and this form.

Community Legal Service Fund (CLSF) *Community Legal Service*
You may qualify for assistance from the CLSF (this used to be called 'legal aid') to meet some or all of your legal costs. Ask about the CLSF at any county court office or any information or help point which displays this logo.

1. How much of the claim do you dispute?

☐ I dispute the full amount claimed as shown on the claim form

or

☐ I admit the amount of   £ _____

If you dispute only part of the claim you must **either:**

- pay the amount admitted to the person named at the address for payment on the claim form (see How to Pay in the notes on the back of, or attached to, the claim form). Then send this defence to the court

or

- complete the admission form **and** this defence form and send them to the court.

  ☐ I paid the amount admitted on *(date)* _____
  or
  ☐ I enclose the completed form of admission
  (go to section 2)

2. Do you dispute this claim because you have already paid it? *Tick whichever applies*

☐ **No** *(go to section 3)*

☐ **Yes** I paid £ _____ to the Claimant
on _____ *(before the claim form was issued)*

Give details of where and how you paid it in the box below *(then go to section 5)*

3. Defence

Defence (continued)

Claim No.

4. If you wish to make a claim against the Claimant (a counterclaim)

If your claim is for a specific sum of money, how much are you claiming? £

I enclose the counterclaim fee of £

My claim is for *(please specify nature of claim)*

- To start your counterclaim, you will have to pay a fee. Court staff can tell you how much you have to pay.

- You may not be able to make a counterclaim where the Claimant is the Crown (e.g. a Government Department). Ask at your local county court office for further information.

What are your reasons for making the counterclaim?
If you need to continue on a separate sheet put the claim number in the top right hand corner

5. Signed
(To be signed by you or by your solicitor or litigation friend)

*(I believe)(The Defendant believes) that the facts stated in this form are true. *I am duly authorised by the Defendant to sign this statement

*delete as appropriate

Position or office held
(if signing on behalf of firm or company)

Defendant's date of birth, if an individual

D D M M Y Y Y Y

Date

Give an address to which notices about this case can be sent to you

Postcode

Tel. no.

if applicable

fax no.

DX no. DX

e-mail

Oyez 7 Spa Road London SE16 3QQ
© Crown copyright.

N9B

2006 Edition 4.2006
5093034
N9B/2

Admission (unspecified amount, non-money and return of goods claims8)

In the
NOTTINGHAM COUNTY COURT

Claim No.	NG 06787878
Claimant (including ref.)	CYRIL JACK WILKINSON
Defendant	WALKERTRONIC SUPER HI-FI-VID LIMITED

- Before completing this form please read the notes for guidance attached to the claim form. If necessary provide details on a separate sheet, add the claim number and attach it to this form.

- If you are not an individual, you should ensure that you provide sufficient details about the assets and liabilities of your firm, company or corporation to support any offer of payment made.

In non - money claims only
☐ I admit liability for the whole claim
(Complete section 11)

In return of goods cases only
Are the goods still in your possesion?
☐ Yes   ☐ No

Part A Response to claim (tick one box only)
☐ I admit liability for the whole claim but want the court to decide the amount I should pay / value of the goods

OR

☐ I admit liability for the claim and offer to
pay [   ] in satisfaction of the claim
(Complete part B and sections 1-11)

Part B How are you going to pay the amount you have admitted? (tick one box only)

☐ I offer to pay on (date) [   ]

OR

☐ I cannot pay the amount immediately because (state reason)

[   ]

AND

I offer to pay by instalments of [£   ]
per (week)(month)
starting (date) [   ]

1 Personal details

Surname [   ]

Forename [   ]

☐ Mr   ☐ Mrs   ☐ Miss   ☐ Ms
☐ Married   ☐ Single   ☐ Other (specify) [   ]

Date of birth   D D M M Y Y Y Y [   ]

Address [   ]
Postcode [   ]
Tel. no. [   ]

2 Dependants (people you look after financially)

Number of children in each age group

under 11 [ ]   11-15 [ ]   16-17 [ ]   18 & over [ ]

Other dependants (give details) [   ]

3 Employment

☐ I am employed as a [   ]
My employer is [   ]
Jobs other than main job (give details) [   ]

☐ I am self employed as a [   ]
Annual turnover is [£   ]

☐ I am not in arrears with my national insurance contributions, income tax and VAT

☐ I am in arrears and I owe [£   ]

Give details of:
(a) contracts and other work in hand [   ]
(b) any sums due for work done [   ]

☐ I have been unemployed for [years] [months]

☐ I am a pensioner

4 Bank account and savings

☐ I have a bank account
☐ The account is in credit by [£   ]
☐ The account is overdrawn by [£   ]

☐ I have a savings or building society account
The amount in the account is [£   ]

5 Residence
I live in
☐ my own property   ☐ lodgings
☐ jointly owned house   ☐ rented property
☐ council accommodation

N9C/1

6 Income

My usual take home pay *(including overtime, commission, bonuses etc)*	£	per
Income support	£	per
Child benefit(s)	£	per
Other state benefit(s)	£	per
My pension(s)	£	per
Others living in my home give me	£	per
Other income *(give details below)*		
	£	per
	£	per
	£	per
Total income	£	**per**

8 Priority debts

(This section is for arrears only. Do not include regular expenses listed in section 7.)

Rent arrrears	£	per
Mortgage arrears	£	per
Council tax/Community Charge arrears	£	per
Water charges arrears	£	per
Fuel debts: Gas	£	per
Electricity	£	per
Other	£	per
Maintenance arrears	£	per
Others *(give details below)*		
	£	per
	£	per
Total priority debts	£	**per**

7 Expenses

(Do not include any payments made by other members of the household out of their own income)

I have regular expenses as follows:

Mortgage *(including second mortgage)*	£	per
Rent	£	per
Council Tax	£	per
Gas	£	per
Electricity	£	per
Water charges	£	per
TV rental and licence	£	per
HP repayments	£	per
Mail order	£	per
Housekeeping, food, school meals	£	per
Travelling expenses	£	per
Children's clothing	£	per
Maintenance payments	£	per
Others *(not court orders or credit debts listed in boxes 9 and 10)*		
	£	per
	£	per
	£	per
Total expenses	£	**per**

9 Court orders

Court	Claim No.	£	per

Total court order instalments	£	**per**

Of the payments above, I am behind with payments to *(please list)*

10 Credit debts

Loans and credit card debts *(please list)*

	£	per
	£	per
	£	per

Of the payments above, I am behind with payments to *(please list)*

11 Declaration

I declare that the details I have given above are true to the best of my knowledge

Signed	
Date	

Position or office held (if signing on behalf of firm or company)

2006 Edition 04.2006
5093042
N9C/2

Defence and Counterclaim (unspecified amount, non-money and return of goods claims)

In the
NOTTINGHAM COUNTY COURT

Claim No.	NG 06787878
Claimant (including ref.)	CYRIL JACK WILKINSON
Defendant	WALKERTRONIC SUPER HI-FI-VID LIMITED

- Fill in this form if you wish to dispute all or part of the claim and/or make a claim against the Claimant (a counterclaim).
- You have a limited number of days to complete and return this form to the court.
- Before completing this form, please read the notes for guidance attached to the claim form.
- Please ensure that all the boxes at the top right of this form are completed. You can obtain the correct names and number from the claim form. The court cannot trace your case without this information.

How to fill in this form

- Set out your defence in section 1. If necessary continue on a separate piece of paper making sure that the claim number is clearly shown on it. In your defence you must state which allegations in the particulars of claim you deny and your reasons for doing so. **If you fail to deny an allegation it may be taken that you admit it.**
- If you dispute only some of the allegations you must
  - specify which you admit and which you deny; and
  - give your own version of events if different from the Claimant's.

- If the claim is for money and you dispute the Claimant's statement of value, you must say why and if possible give your own statement of value.
- If you wish to make a claim against the Claimant (a counterclaim) complete section 2.
- Complete and sign section 3 before returning this form.

Where to send this form

- Send or take this form immediately to the court at the address given on the claim form.
- Keep a copy of the claim form and the defence form.

Community Legal Service Fund (CLSF)

You may qualify for assistance from the CLSF (this used to be called 'legal aid') to meet some or all of your legal costs. Ask about the CLSF at any county court office or any information or help point which displays this logo.

1. Defence

Defence (continued)

Claim No. [   ]

2. If you wish to make a claim against the Claimant (a counterclaim)

If your claim is for a specific sum of money, how much are you claiming? £ [   ]

- To start your counterclaim, you will have to pay a fee. Court staff can tell you how much you have to pay.

I enclose the counterclaim fee of £ [   ]

My claim is for (please specify)

[   ]

- You may not be able to make a counterclaim where the Claimant is the Crown (e.g. a Government Department). Ask at your local county court office for further information.

What are your reasons for making the counterclaim?
If you need to continue on a separate sheet put the claim number in the top right hand corner

3. Signed

(To be signed by you or by your solicitor or litigation friend)

*(I believe)(The Defendant believes) that the facts stated in this form are true. *I am duly authorised by the Defendant to sign this statement

* delete as appropriate

Position or office held (if signing on behalf of firm or company)

Defendant's date of birth, if an individual

D D M M Y Y Y Y

Date

Give an address to which notices about this case can be sent to you

Postcode

Tel. no.

if applicable

fax no.

DX no. DX

e-mail

N9D

2006 Edition 4.2006

5093050
N9D/2

(a) The defence and Part 18 requests

12–016   Having been given the necessary information about the claimant's case (whether in the statements of case or during the pre-action stage), the defendant must settle on his or her tactics. In defence, he or she may choose to refute the whole of the claimant's claim and the facts on which it is based, or may admit the whole claim whilst pleading an explanation which allows liability to be avoided, may admit the whole case but object that it discloses no cause of action, may admit part of the claim, may make a counterclaim or may adopt a combination of these approaches or adopt them as alternatives.[90] The forms within the response pack permit all these possibilities. It is not necessary to use the forms to serve a defence or a counterclaim and most legal representatives will draw up a separate document by way of defence, if only because the space to give details on the form is rather limited. Whichever option is used, the content of the defence must comply with CPR rr.16.5 and 16.6 and PD 16 paras 10 to 13 inclusive.

There are specified time limits for the filing of statements of case, including the defence and there are limits to the extent that these can be dispensed with by the consent of the parties[91] without the court's prior permission. The court may extend time by order but will consider the effect of any delay on the overall timetable and the imperatives of the overriding objective.

For the purpose of the later case management of the claim, it should be noted that it is the filing of a defence that triggers the distribution by the court of allocation questionnaires.[92] Where a claim is not to be defended, then default judgment will normally be entered and the only issue for discussion will be the means and method of payment. Consequently there is no need for the court to become involved in any management of the claim towards a hypothetical trial of the merits.

Where a defence is drafted, then, the defendant will need to respond to each of the allegations set out by the claimant. The choice of responses[93] to any particular allegation is to:

(a) Admit. So, for example, Walkertronic is likely to admit paragraph 1: that there was a contract between itself and Mr Wilkinson.

(b) Deny. If the defendant denies an allegation it must give reasons for the denial. This is a deliberate change to the old rules where it was often sufficient for the defendant to say simply "Paragraph 4 is denied" thus requiring the claimant to guess whether the reason for the denial was, for example, a dispute as to the facts or a fundamental difference as to the legal principles involved. Consequently, Walkertronic may deny the allegation of breach, giving as its "reason" that the game was operating satisfactorily when tested shortly before sale.

---

[90] Defences in the alternative can sometimes appear extremely confusing. In relying on alternatives, issues might arise about the propriety of the statement of truth, apparently verifying contradictory facts: see *Clarke v Marlborough Fine Arts (London) Ltd (Amendments)* [2002] 1 W.L.R. 1731, Ch D; *Binks v Securicor Omega Express Ltd* [2003] EWCA Civ 993, CA. Those relying on a multiplicity of alternative defences will also have to be prepared to meet a court determined to reduce the case to its essentials under CPR r.1 4(2)(b) and (c).

[91] For example, the period for filing a defence can be extended by the parties for a maximum of 28 days, thereafter the permission of the court will have to be sought: CPR r.15.5.

[92] CPR r.26.3.

[93] CPR r.9.2.

(c) "The defendant is unable to admit or deny and requires the claimant to prove . . . ." This middle route allows the defendant to deal with matters to which he or she cannot respond *because* he or she does not have the information. So, for example, Walkertronic may take this approach towards the allegations of loss.[94]

As with the particulars of claim, PD 16 may prescribe particular contents in particular types of case[95] and there is the option under PD 16 para.13.3 to include:

(a) any point of law on which the defence is based;

(b) the name of any witness the defendant intends to call; and

(c) any document "necessary to" the defence.

The defence must also contain a statement of truth.[96]

Naturally, the wider the defence, the wider the issues that remain for resolution at the trial, the greater must be the claimant's preparations and the greater the likelihood that a pro-active judge applying CPR r.1.4(2)(b) and (c)—which, it should be remembered, the parties are under a duty to assist the court in furthering—will require the defendant to narrow its case before those preparations begin. This is because if the defendant is not prepared to admit any of the facts pleaded by the claimant they may all have to be proved in court with a consequent increase in the length and costs of the case. However, in addition to the powers of the judge to narrow the issues, either party may serve notice under CPR r.32.18 requiring the admission of facts with a penalty in costs for unjustified refusal. If the defendant does make substantial admissions in the defence, it will have the effect of disclosing and narrowing the issues between the parties so that—however effective the pre-action stages have been in this respect—both parties are now aware of precisely what remains in dispute. In order that the statements of case should disclose clearly what remains in dispute, any issue of fact in a statement of case must be specifically denied or it will normally be deemed to have been admitted.[97] The court will send a copy of the defence to the claimant.[98]

The defendant may consider that the information given in the particulars of **12–017** claim is defective or insufficient to allow a defence to the claim to be prepared. In an extreme case, the defendant may seek to have the claim struck out under CPR r.3.4 on the basis that it "discloses no reasonable grounds for bringing . . . the claim" or to apply for summary judgment against the claimant under CPR Pt 24 on the basis that the claimant has "no real prospect of succeeding . . . and there is no other compelling reason why the case . . . should be disposed of at a trial". Alternatively, the defendant is entitled to request "further information" from the claimant under CPR Pt 18.[99] In the case of George and Hacker, the defendant wishes to know more:

---

[94] PD 16 para.13.3.

[95] For example, in a personal injury case, the defendant must respond specifically to the medical report and schedule of losses attached to the particulars of claim: PD 16 para.12.

[96] PD 15 para.2, PD 16 para.11; CPR r.22.1(1)(a).

[97] CPR r.16.5(3).

[98] CPR r.26.3.

[99] As is the claimant from the defendant if the defence is worthy of being struck out under CPR r.3.4; judgment being given against the defendant under CPR Pt 24 or a request for further information under Pt 18 is justified.

IN THE HIGH COURT OF JUSTICE   CLAIM NO. NG0167234

QUEEN'S BENCH DIVISION

NOTTINGHAM DISTRICT REGISTRY

BETWEEN

PETER GEORGE (1)

MARTIN HACKER (2)

Claimants

– and –

RELIABLE NAG SUPPLY STABLES (a firm)

Defendant

REQUEST UNDER CPR PART 18 BY THE CLAIMANT FOR
FURTHER INFORMATION FROM THE DEFENDANT MADE ON
18th FEBRUARY 2006[100]

QUESTION 1

Of paragraph 6

6   In breach of the terms set out in paragraphs 3 and 4 above, the Horse was not
of satisfactory quality and/or was not fit for its purpose.

PARTICULARS

The Horse was found to be suffering from Bastard Strangles and was therefore
entirely useless and worthless to the Claimants.

PLEASE STATE

At which time it is alleged the Horse was discovered to be suffering from Bastard
Strangles and how long it is alleged that the condition had existed.

QUESTION 2

Of paragraph 7

7   As a result of the matters set out above the Claimants have suffered loss and
damage.

---

[100] See PD 18 para.1.6.

PARTICULARS

Cost price of Horse	£65,000.00
Fees paid to Sutton Riding Enterprises for the care of alternative horse from 1st July to 20th August	£290.00
TOTAL ESTIMATED LOSSES	£65,290.00

PLEASE STATE

Full particulars of the stabling provided for the alternative horse at Sutton Riding Enterprises and a detailed analysis of the fees charged.

The Claimant expects a response to this request by 4pm on 1st December 2006.

Martin Martinson[101]

Dated 18th November 2006

Furlong & Co
43 Bridle Lane
Nottingham
NG7 5RR
Solicitors for the Defendant.

(b) The counterclaim

So far we have omitted detailed consideration of one important possibility. The **12–018** defendant may wish to make a claim against the claimant in addition to defending the claimant's claim. It is not necessary to bring a separate claim. It is possible to add a *counterclaim*[102] to the defence. Set out below is the defence and counterclaim of the Reliable Nag Supply Stables.

---

[101] Note that it is possible to detect from the nature of the signature that the request was drafted by a barrister or solicitor-advocate ("counsel"). Whilst all court documents "drafted by a legal representative" must bear the signature of that legal representative, documents drafted by solicitors will be "signed" in the name of their firm (except in the Commercial Court): PD 5 para.2.1. Documents drafted by barristers and solicitor-advocates, on the other hand, are "signed" in the name of the individual barrister or solicitor-advocate.

[102] CPR r.20.2(l)(a), 20.4 and PD 20 para.6. Note that an issue fee equivalent to that payable on issue of a claim fee is normally payable by the defendant on raising a counterclaim.

IN THE HIGH COURT OF JUSTICE   CLAIM NO. NG0167234

QUEEN'S BENCH DIVISION

NOTTINGHAM DISTRICT REGISTRY

BETWEEN

PETER GEORGE (1)

MARTIN HACKER (2)

Claimants

– and –

RELIABLE NAG SUPPLY STABLES (a firm)

Defendant

DEFENCE AND COUNTERCLAIM

DEFENCE

1   Except that it is denied that the First Claimant made any statement as to the intended purpose for which the Horse was required, no such statement having been made paragraph 1 of the Particulars of Claim is admitted.

2   Paragraphs 2 and 3 of the Particulars of Claim are admitted.

3   Paragraph 4 of the Particulars of Claim is denied for the reasons set out in paragraph 1 above.

4   Paragraph 5 of the Particulars of Claim is admitted.

5   Paragraph 6 of the Particulars of Claim is denied.

REASONS

The Horse underwent a veterinary inspection on 24th June 2006 and was not suffering from Bastard Strangles or from any other infection at that time.

6   The Defendant is unable to admit or deny but wishes the Claimants to prove the amount of the losses set out in paragraph 7 of the Particulars of Claim.[103]

7   Further or alternatively, it was an express term of the Contract that the Defendant would exchange the Horse for another if the Horse should within 14 days prove unsuitable to the Claimant.

---

[103] The award of interest being in the discretion of the court, it is not normally regarded as necessary to respond to it specifically.

8   By a further agreement made at or about the beginning of July 2006 ("The
     Second Contract") between the Defendant and the Claimants under the
     express term referred to in paragraph 7 above, the Claimants agreed to
     exchange the Horse for another and to take delivery of a suitable bay mare
     ("the Mare") owned by the Defendant pending their decision to retain the
     Horse or the Mare.

9   In breach of the Second Contract, the Claimants failed to make any decision
     as to which of the horses they would retain and, on or about 21st August
     2006, returned the Mare to the Defendant thereby repudiating the
     Contract.

10   If and to the extent, if at all, which is denied for the reasons set out above,
     that the Defendant is liable to the Claimants, it will seek to set off the
     damages and sums counterclaimed below to extinguish or diminish such
     liability.

COUNTERCLAIM

11   The Defendant repeats paragraphs 8 and 9 of the Defence.

12   It was an implied term of the Second Contract that the Claimants would take
     reasonable care of the Mare whilst in their custody.

13   In breach of the term set out in paragraph 11 above, the Claimants failed to
     take reasonable care of the Mare:

PARTICULARS

When the Claimants returned the Mare to the Defendant its ribs were
protruding, its hooves were broken, its coat was dull and ungroomed, 3 shoes
were missing and it was in poor health.

14   As a result of the breaches set out in paragraph 13 above, the Defendant
     suffered loss and damage.

PARTICULARS

1 Loss of profit on the sale of a horse	£15,000
2 Transport costs on delivery and collection	£500
3 Veterinary costs for the Mare	£2,000
4 Farrier's fees for the Mare	£1,000
5 Loss of value of the Mare	£10,000
TOTAL ESTIMATED LOSSES	£28,500

15   Further the Defendant claims interest under s.35A Supreme Court Act 1981
     on the amount found to be due to the Defendant at such rate and for such
     period as the Court thinks fit.

AND the Defendant counterclaims

1   Damages under paragraph 14 above

2   Interest under statute

Furlong & Co

Statement of truth

I believe that the facts stated in this Defence and Counterclaim are true

Patricia Wooldbridge

Patricia Wooldbridge, Partner

Dated 21ˢᵗ November 2006

Furlong & Co
43 Bridle Lane
Nottingham
NG7 5RR
Solicitors for the Defendant

(c) The reply to defence and the defence to counterclaim

12–019   Where a defence raises new facts, the claimant may wish to file a reply[104] and where a counterclaim has been made it is usual for the claimant to file a defence.[105] These should be combined into a single document[106] and will usually be the final documents in the statements of case. Although in theory the defendant might file a *rejoinder*, the claimant a *surrejoinder*, the defendant a *rebutter* and the claimant a *surrebutter*, doing so requires the express permission of the court[107] and they are rare to the point of near extinction.

Below, we set out a reply to defence and defence to counterclaim in *George and Hacker's* case.

---

[104] CPR r.16.7.
[105] Indeed, the claimant risks a default judgment being entered for the amount of the counterclaim if no defence is filed: CPR Pt 12, applied to counterclaims by CPR r.20.3(3).
[106] PD 15 para.3.2.
[107] CPR r.15.9.

IN THE HIGH COURT OF JUSTICE   CLAIM NO. NG0167234

QUEEN'S BENCH DIVISION

NOTTINGHAM DISTRICT REGISTRY

BETWEEN

PETER GEORGE (1)

MARTIN HACKER (2)

Claimants

– and –

RELIABLE NAG SUPPLY STABLES (a firm)

Defendant

REPLY TO DEFENCE AND DEFENCE TO COUNTERCLAIM

REPLY TO DEFENCE

1   For the reasons set out below, the Claimants join issue with the Defendant except insofar as paragraphs 2, 4 and 7 of the Defence and Counterclaim are concerned.

DEFENCE TO COUNTERCLAIM

2   It is admitted that the Second Contract described in paragraph 8 of the Defence and Counterclaim was made, but it is denied that the Defendant offered a suitable horse in exchange, the Mare being in poor condition at the time of its delivery to the Claimants.

3   The Claimants paid employees of Sutton Riding Enterprises to attend to the Mare and informed the Defendant at all times of the poor condition of the Mare.

4   Consequently, whilst it is admitted that the Claimants returned the Mare to the Defendant on or about 21st August 2006, it is denied that the Claimants repudiated the Contract as alleged in paragraph 9 of the Defence and Counterclaim or in any other way.

5   For the reasons set out above, paragraph 10 of the Defence and Counterclaim is denied.

6   Paragraph 11 of the Defence and Counterclaim is admitted.

7   Whilst it is admitted that the Mare was ill when returned to the Defendant, that illness was the direct result of the Mare's having been in poor condition at the time of its delivery to the Defendant.

8   Consequently it is denied that the Claimants are in breach of the term set out in paragraph 13 of the Defence and Counterclaim or in any other way.

9   For the reasons set out above, paragraph 14 of the Defence and Counterclaim is denied.

Popp, Lees and Stone

Statement of truth

I believe that the facts stated in this Reply to Defence and Defence to Counter-claim are true

Peter George   *Martin Hacker*

Peter George   Martin Hacker

Claimants

Dated 30th November 2006

Popp, Lees and Stone
Solicitors
Haltergate
Nottingham
NG1 6FF
Solicitors for the Claimant

(d) Statements of case—the consequences of failure

12–020   If the defendant fails to file an acknowledgement of service in time, or files an acknowledgement of service but then fails to file a defence in time; or if a claimant fails to file a defence to the defendant's counterclaim in time then the opponent is entitled to enter a "default" judgment against him or her.[108] If the claim is for a specified sum, then the judgment will be a final judgment for the amount claimed, interest and fixed costs. If the claim is not for a specified sum then judgment will be entered on liability only and there will then be a "disposal hearing"[109] at which the parties will be able to appear and dispute the amount of damages prior to final judgment being entered.

5. Allocation

12–021   As we have seen, once a defence has been filed, the court begins the process that will lead it to be in a position to manage the case. Both (or in more complex cases, all) parties are sent an allocation questionnaire by the court.[110] This must be completed and returned to the court within 14 days, the claimant paying a fee

---

[108] CPR Pt 12. There are limited circumstances in which default judgment is not permitted and a hearing must be convened.

[109] PD 26 para.12.8.

[110] Procedure in some of the more specialist courts such as the Commercial Court, is different: see, for example, *the Admiralty and Commercial Court Guide* and CPR Pt 58 and PD.

of £200 in the High Court and £100 in the county court.[111] If the questionnaires are not returned in time, the parties risk the claim being struck out.[112] The parties may not agree between themselves to alter the date for return of the questionnaires.[113]

A copy of the questionnaire (which should, unless the claim falls within the small claims limits, be accompanied by an estimate of costs incurred to date and to be incurred in the future running of the claim[114]) follows:

---

[111] Following representations by such institutions as the Civil Justice Council and the National Association of CABx, the fee is not payable in what will be small claims money cases under £1,500. Otherwise, although a short form allocation questionnaire is used for potential small claims cases, the full county court fee is payable unless the paying party successfully obtains exemption for fees as a result of a means test.

[112] PD 26 para.2.5.

[113] CPR r.26.3(6A).

[114] PD 26 para.2.1(2); PD 43–48, s.6. A second estimate is required to be filed at pre-trial checklist stage in cases outside the small claims track and the court has power to require a party to file one at any stage in the proceedings. See *Leigh v Michelin Tyre plc* [2003] EWCA Civ 1766. Note, however, that this requirement is widely ignored by litigants and not enforced by the courts: Peysner and Seneviratne, *The Management of Civil Cases: the courts and the post-Woolf Landscape*, (DCA Research Series 9/05, November 2005). Where estimates are provided (even if only given as a total in the relevant section of the allocation questionnaire), a difference of more than 20% between the estimate and the sum later claimed on detailed assessment may be difficult to recover: PD 43–48, para.6.5A.

Allocation questionnaire

To be completed by, or on behalf of,

| RELIABLE NAG SUPPLY STABLES (A FIRM) |

who is [1st] [2nd][3rd] [x][Claimant] [Defendant] [Part 20 claimant] in this claim

In the
HIGH COURT OF JUSTICE
QUEEN'S BENCH DIVISION
NOTTINGHAM DISTRICT REGISTRY

Claim No. NG06232323

Last date for filing 4PM 25TH NOVEMBER
with court office 2006

Please read the notes on page five before completing the questionnaire.

You should note the date by which it must be returned and the name of the court it should be returned to since this may be different from the court where the proceedings were issued.

If you have settled this claim (or if you settle it on a future date) and do not need to have it heard or tried, you must let the court know immediately.

Have you sent a copy of this completed form to the other party(ies)?   x Yes   No

A Settlement

Do you wish there to be a one month stay to attempt to settle the claim, either by informal discussion or by alternative dispute resolution?   x Yes   No

B Location of trial

Is there any reason why your claim needs to be heard at a particular court?   Yes   x No

If Yes, say which court and why?

C Pre-action protocols

If an approved pre-action protocol applies to this claim, complete **Part 1** only. If not, complete **Part 2** only. If you answer 'No' to the question in either Part 1 or 2, please explain the reasons why on a separate sheet and attach it to this questionnaire.

Part 1	The* protocol applies to this claim.
*please say which protocol	Have you complied with it? Yes No

Part 2	No pre-action protocol applies to this claim.
	Have you exchanged information and/or documents (evidence) with the other party in order to assist in settling the claim? x Yes No

D Case management information

What amount of the claim is in dispute?   £ [   ]

Applications

Have you made any application(s) in this claim?   ☐ Yes ☒ No

If Yes, what for?   [   ]   For hearing on [   ]
(e.g. summary judgment,
add another party)

Witnesses

So far as you know at this stage, what witnesses of fact do you intend to call at the trial
or final hearing including, if appropriate, yourself?

Witness name	Witness to which facts

Experts

Do you wish to use expert evidence at the trial or final hearing?   ☒ Yes ☐ No

Have you already copied any experts' report(s) to the other
party(ies)?   ☒ None yet ☐ Yes ☐ No
obtained

Do you consider the case suitable for a single joint expert in any field?   ☐ Yes ☒ No

Please list any single joint experts you propose to use and any other experts you
wish to rely on. Identify single joint experts with the initials 'SJ' after their name(s).

Expert's name	Field of expertise (e.g. orthopaedic surgeon, surveyor, engineer)

Do you want your expert(s) to give evidence orally at the trial or final hearing?   ☐ Yes ☒ No

If Yes, give the reasons why you think oral evidence is necessary:

continue over)))➡

N150/2

Track

Which track do you consider is most suitable for your
claim? Tick one box

☐ small   ☐ fast   ☒ multi-
claims   track   track
track

If you have indicated a track which would not be the normal track for the claim, please
give brief reasons for your choice

E   Trial or final hearing

How long do you estimate the trial or final hearing will
take?

| 2 | days | hours | minutes |

Are there any days when you, an expert or an essential witness will
not be able to attend court for the trial or final hearing?

☐ Yes   ☒ No

If Yes, please give details

Name	Dates not available

F   Proposed directions *(Parties should agree directions wherever possible)*

Have you attached a list of the directions you think appropriate
for the management of the claim?

☒ Yes   ☐ No

If Yes, have they been agreed with the other party(ies)?

☒ Yes   ☐ No

G   Costs

*Do **not** complete this section if you have suggested your case is suitable for the small
claims track **or** you have suggested one of the other tracks and you do not have a solicitor
acting for you.*

What is your estimate of your costs incurred to date?

£ 5,000

What do you estimate your overall costs are likely to be?

£ 20,000

In substantial cases these questions should be answered in compliance with CPR Part 43

N150/3

H Other information

Have you attached documents to this questionnaire?   [x] Yes   [ ] No

Have you sent these documents to the other party(ies)?   [x] Yes   [ ] No

If Yes, when did they receive them?   6TH OCTOBER 2006

Do you intend to make any applications in the immediate future?   [ ] Yes   [x] No

If Yes, what for?

In the space below, set out any other information you consider will help the judge to manage the claim.

Signed   Date

[Counsel][Solicitor][for the][1st][2nd][3rd][   ]
[Claimant] [Defendant][Part 20 claimant]

Please enter your firm's name, reference number and full postal address including (if appropriate) details of DX, fax or e-mail

		if applicable	
		fax no.	
		DX no.	DX
Tel. no.	Postcode		e-mail

Your reference no.

Notes for completing an allocation questionnaire

- If the claim is not settled, a judge must allocate it to an appropriate case management track. To help the judge choose the most just and cost-effective track, you must now complete the attached questionnaire.
- If you fail to return the allocation questionnaire by the date given, the judge may make an order which leads to your claim or defence being struck out, or hold an allocation hearing. If there is an allocation hearing the judge may order any party who has not filed their questionnaire to pay, immediately, the costs of that hearing.
- Use a separate sheet if you need more space for your answers marking clearly which section the information refers to. You should write the claim number on it, and on any other documents you send with your allocation questionnaire. Please ensure they are firmly attached to it.
- The letters below refer to the sections of the questionnaire and tell you what information is needed.

A Settlement

If you think that you and the other party may be able to negotiate a settlement you should tick the 'Yes' box. The court may order a stay, whether or not all the other parties to the claim agree. You should still complete the rest of the questionnaire, even if you are requesting a stay. Where a stay is granted it will be for an initial period of one month. You may settle the claim either by informal discussion with the other party or by alternative dispute resolution (ADR). ADR covers a range of different processes which can help settle disputes. More information is available in the Legal Services Commission leaflet 'Alternatives to Court' free from the LSC leaflet line Phone: 0845 3000 343.

B Location of trial

High Court cases are usually heard at the Royal Courts of Justice or certain Civil Trial Centres. Fast or multi-track trials may be dealt with at a Civil Trial Centre or at the court where the claim is proceeding. Small claim cases are usually heard at the court in which they are proceeding.

C Pre-action protocols

Before any claim is started, the court expects you to have exchanged information and documents relevant to the claim, to assist in settling it. For some types of claim e.g. personal injury, there are approved protocols that should have been followed.

D Case management information

Applications

It is important for the court to know if you have already made any applications in the claim, what they are for and when they will be heard. The outcome of the applications may affect the case management directions the court gives.

Witnesses

Remember to include yourself as a witness of fact, if you will be giving evidence.

Experts

Oral or written expert evidence will only be allowed at the trial or final hearing with the court's permission. The judge will decide what permission it seems appropriate to give when the claim is allocated to track. Permission in small claims track cases will only be given exceptionally.

Track

The basic guide by which claims are normally allocated to a track is the amount in dispute, although other factors such as the complexity of the case will also be considered. A leaflet available from the court office explains the limits in greater detail.

Small Claims track	Disputes valued at not more than £5,000 except - those including a claim for personal injuries worth over £1,000 and - those for housing disrepair where either the cost of repairs or other work exceeds £1,000 or any other claim for damages exceeds £1,000
Fast track	Disputes valued at more than £5,000 but not more than £15,000
Multi-track	Disputes over £15,000

E Trial or final hearing

You should enter only those dates when you, your expert(s) or essential witness(es) will not be able to attend court because of holiday or other commitments.

F Proposed directions

Attach the list of directions, if any, you believe will be appropriate to be given for the management of the claim. Agreed directions on fast and multi-track cases should be based on the forms of standard directions set out in the practice direction to CPR Part 28 and form PF52.

G Costs

Only complete this section if you are a solicitor and have suggested the claim is suitable for allocation to the fast or multi-track.

H Other Information

Answer the questions in this section. Decide if there is any other information you consider will help the judge to manage the claim. Give details in the space provided referring to any documents you have attached to support what you are saying.

N150/5

On receipt of the completed questionnaires, the court then begins the process of allocation. Allocation is the process whereby, acting on information provided by the parties in their allocation questionnaires, the court allocates the claim to one of the three tracks.[115] The criteria for the decision are set out in CPR r.26.8:

(a) the financial value (if any) of the claim (excluding interest, costs, admitted amounts, any potential deductions for contributory negligence);

(b) the nature of the remedy sought;[116]

(c) the likely complexity of facts, law or evidence;

(d) the number of parties;

(e) the value and complexity of any Pt 20 claim (such as a counterclaim);

(f) the amount of oral evidence required to decide the case;

(g) the importance of the case to those not directly involved with it (such as the general public or others in the process of bringing similar claims);

(h) the views of the parties (expressed in their allocation questionnaires); and

(i) the circumstances of the parties.

The parties are encouraged to co-operate with each other when completing their questionnaires. If the court is unable to make a decision about the appropriate track on the basis of the responses to the questionnaires, it may convene an allocation hearing.[117]

Following the decision as to allocation, a notice of allocation will be sent to the parties.[118] The court may also be able to provide some directions to progress the case towards trial, either because it is able to approve a list of suggested directions submitted by the parties (section F) or because the case can be managed without any further information from the parties. The court may well at this stage be able to give the parties a trial date or a trial "window". Alternatively (section A) the court may halt the progress of the case towards trial, normally for up to a month, to allow the parties to try to resolve their dispute by ADR or negotiation.[119]

The parties are therefore expected to be able to say at this comparatively early stage of the proceedings, for example which witnesses they propose to call or how long they think the trial should last. The fact that failure to file the allocation questionnaire within the time limit may lead to one's case being struck out is intended to concentrate the parties' minds.[120]

---

[115] CPR r.26.5.
[116] County court judges cannot, for example, at present make declarations of incompatibility under the Human Rights Act 1998, s.4. Similarly, there are restrictions on the level of judge who can grant an injunction: PD 2B.
[117] CPR r.26.5(4).
[118] CPR r.26.9.
[119] CPR r.26.4. See also Ch.11, paras 11–033 et seq.
[120] PD 26 para.2.5.

(a) The small claims track

12–022   The small claims track[121] (see CPR Pt 27 and PD 27) is reserved for claims of £5,000 or less, with variations for personal injury claims (where the global value must not exceed £5,000 but the personal injury element must not be worth more than £1,000)[122] and housing disrepair claims (where the cost of repairs must not exceed £1,000 and any additional claim must not exceed a further £1,000). Raising the jurisdictional limit was seen to be important to maintain access to this system and the limit has steadily risen over the years from £20 in 1846, to £1,000 as a consequence of the Civil Justice Review in 1989 and to £3,000 in 1996 as a result of Lord Woolf's Interim Report.[123] The limit was extended to its current position in 1999.[124]

To summarise the scale of the court's involvement in small claims cases, in 2005, approximately 48 per cent of all defended claims brought in the county court were allocated to the small claims track and in 2005, 47,521 small claims hearings were held.[125] Whilst the hearing remains informal, it is a "trial" and must therefore also normally take place in public.

The claimant must follow the common procedure outlined above up to the point of the allocation questionnaire, when the court will allocate the claim to the small claims track in accordance with the jurisdictional limits set out above and the normal criteria in CPR r.26.8.

Many of the more complex rules about evidence, expert and other witnesses and Pt 36 offers and payments do not apply in the small claims track. Following allocation the court will impose directions, normally without a directions hearing, and give a date for the final hearing. A number of standard directions are set out in an appendix to PD 27 but in summary the parties will not normally be permitted to rely on expert evidence (whether given orally or in writing) and the parties must supply each other, not less than 14 days before the hearing, with copies of all documents on which they intend to rely at the hearing. The strict rules of evidence will not apply to the hearing. In particular, there will be limits on the amount of cross-examination that will be permitted.

Legal Services Commission funding is not normally available for representation at small claims hearings although both parties may have received some initial assistance or advice that is covered by the scheme. It is expected that the parties will appear in person although there is no prohibition on appearing by a lawyer or by a lay representative.[126] Normally, no costs order is made except for the costs of issuing the claim and any further costs awarded against a party who has behaved unreasonably.[127]

---

[121] For a recent research study on usage of the small claims track, see P. Lewis, "The Consumer's Court? Revisiting the Theory of the Small Claims Procedure" (2006) 25(JAN) C.J.Q. 52. See also N. Madge, "Small Claims in the County Court" (2004) 23(Jul) C.J.Q. 201.

[122] CPR r.26.6(1).

[123] For background, see the following consultation papers: *Access to Justice—The Small Claims Procedure: Small Claims Appeals—Proposed New Procedures* (2000).

[124] The limits are under reconsideration. See *The Courts: Small Claims, Government Response to the Constitutional Affairs Select Committee Report* (DCA, February 2006, Cm. 6754). See also J. Baldwin, *Lay and Judicial Perspectives on the Expansion of the Small Claims Regime* (DCA Research, 2002).

[125] *Judicial Statistics 2005*, Tables 4.8 and 4. 9; 77,687 small claims were defended and allocated to the track, the remainder being resolved other than by hearing. *Ibid.*, Table 4.7.

[126] PD 27 para.3.

[127] CPR r.27.14

(b) The fast track

The fast track rules (CPR Pt 28 and PD 28) envisage that, on or following **12–023** allocatoin to the fast track, the court will be able to impose directions without seeing the parties.[128] This may be optimistic, especially where one or both parties do not have legal representation. If this is the case then, in a potential fast track case, the court may convene an "allocation and directions hearing".

A list of possible directions appears in the appendix to PD 28. However, for present purposes it is sufficient to set out the "typical timetable" given by way of example in PD 28 para.3.12:

Disclosure	within 4 weeks from the making of the order
Exchange of statements of witnesses of fact	within 10 weeks from the making of the order
Exchange of expert's reports	within 14 weeks from the making of the order
Distribution of pre-trial checklists by the court	within 20 weeks from the making of the order
Return of completed pre-trial checklists	within 22 weeks from the making of the order
Trial (1 day)	within 30 weeks from the making of the order

If a party wishes to vary the timetable, then the dates can be varied by consent, unless the date sought to be altered is that of (a) the return of the pre-trial checklist, the trial or trial period, or (b) a date for completion of another task, variation in which will make it necessary to alter any of those dates.[129] In any of those cases, the court's express permission must be obtained. Failure to comply with directions potentially attracts a number of sanctions, from striking out of the defaulter's claim or defence to costs.[130]

Should the dispute remain unresolved by the time all the directions have been completed, further directions for the immediate preparation of and course of events at trial will be made at listing when the parties are required to file pre-trial checklists to assist the court. There are limits to recoverable costs in the fast track, specifically the costs of the trial advocate (CPR Pt 46) but also in road traffic and employer's liability claims (CPR Pt 45).

(c) The multi-track

As in the fast track, it is possible that the court might be able to give directions **12–024** simply by reading the allocation questionnaires and material submitted with those questionnaires (which, as can be seen from the questionnaire, may include a list of directions agreed between the parties) and without seeing the parties. However, as multi-track cases (CPR Pt 29 and PD 29) are likely to include

---

[128] PD 28 para.2.2.
[129] CPR r.28.4.
[130] *Biguzzi v Rank Leisure plc* [1999] 1 W.L.R. 1926, CA; *Baron v Lovell* [1999] C.P.L.R. 630, [2000] P.I.Q.R. P20, CA; *Woodward v Finch* [1999] C.P.L.R. 699, CA; *Cank v Broadyard Associates Ltd* [2001] C.P. Rep. 47, CA; *Carlco Ltd v Chief Constable of Dyfed Powys* [2002] EWCA Civ 1754, CA.

complexities of law or evidence,[131] there is specific provision in the multi track for one or more case management hearings described as "case management conferences" or, for those specifically concerned with the immediate preparation for and conduct of the trial, "pre-trial reviews".[132] The court has express power to convene such hearings "whenever it appears necessary or desirable to do so".[133]

The case management conference, in particular, is a significant expression of "the flexibility given to the court in the way it will manage a case in a way appropriate to its particular needs".[134] For that reason it is required that, where there is legal representation, a person "familiar with the case and with sufficient authority to deal with any issues that are likely to arise" should attend any case management conference or pre-trial review.[135]

The format of the hearing may be less formal than other hearings, taking the form of a business meeting or discussion rather than following the normal structure for interim hearings of applicant's submissions followed by respondent's submissions. Case management conferences are now frequently held over the telephone.

The topics of discussion at a case management conference are almost limitless (although if the court wishes to impose a single expert instructed jointly by the parties or an assessor, this must be done at a case management conference).[136] However, one of the court's principal concerns will be to narrow the areas in dispute under CPR r.1.4(2)(b) and (c). Consequently the court might order the preparation of a case summary, or the parties might themselves decide that a case summary would be of assistance.[137] A case summary is simply a short document setting out the issues of fact that are agreed or in dispute and the evidence the parties consider will be needed to resolve those areas of dispute.

Other matters that may be considered at a case management conference include:

(a) whether the claimant's claim is clear (i.e. should further information be provided under CPR Pt 18?);

(b) whether any statements of case require amendment;

(c) disclosure of documentary evidence;

(d) expert evidence[138];

(e) factual evidence (i.e. arrangements for exchange of witness statements);

---

[131] For an unusual case in which allocation to the multi-track was in dispute, see *Kearsley v Klarfeld* [2005] EWCA Civ 1510.

[132] CPR r.29.2 and 29.4, PD 29 para.3.3.

[133] PD 29 para.3.6.

[134] PD 29 para.37; the other "hallmark" being "the ability of the court to deal with cases of widely differing values and complexity".

[135] CPR r.29.3(2) and PD. 29 para.5.2. The parties should consider bringing their clients in any event: PD 29 para.5.6. See also *Matthews v Tarmac Bricks & Tiles Ltd* [1999] C.P.L.R. 463, CA.

[136] PD 29 para.4.13.

[137] PD 29 paras 5.6(3), 5.7.

[138] Note PD 29 para.5.5: the court will expect to be able to identify the experts to be used by name (or at least by field) and to order whether or not the expert will appear at the trial to give oral evidence. If a party has pre-empted a direction about experts, that party is at risk that the costs already incurred in instructing an expert who may not be permitted by the court, will be irrecoverable even if that party is successful at trial.

(f) clarification of expert evidence and questions to experts;

(g) whether it will be appropriate to order a split trial (e.g. that liability is resolved before the parties incur the additional costs of proving quantum);[139]

(h) whether to direct the parties to consider ADR.[140]

The distribution and submission of pre-trial checklists will proceed as in the fast track. There may at this stage be a hearing to set a timetable for trial and to fix the trial date if these matters have not already been resolved at earlier hearings.[141]

If a party wishes to vary the timetable, then the dates can be varied by consent, unless the date sought to be altered is that of (a) the case management conference or pre-trial review; the return of the pre-trial checklist; the trial or trial period, or (b) a date for completion of another task, variation in which will make it necessary to alter any of those dates.[142] In any of those cases, the court's express permission must be obtained. Failure to comply with directions potentially attracts the same range of sanctions, from striking out of the defaulter's claim or defence to costs as in the fast track.

6. OTHER PRE-TRIAL MATTERS

(a) Summary judgment

It would obviously be an unacceptable delaying tactic for a defendant to indicate an intention to defend when there was no real defence, thus gaining time in which to pay a debt or damages which could not seriously be disputed. Consequently, there is a procedure, originally available only to plaintiffs, but extended by the CPR to both parties, allowing for early resolution of claims with limited prospects of success at trial.   **12–025**

The test is set out as follows:

"The court may give summary judgment against a claimant or defendant on the whole of a claim or on a particular issue if:

---

[139] PD 29 para.5.3.

[140] This was a response to a recommendation by the Better Regulation Taskforce, seeking to address the preception of a "compensation culture" in its May 2004 paper *Better Routes to Redress*, responded to by the government in its November 2004 response *Tackling the Compensation Culture*. See now PD 29 para.4.10(9):

> "Such directions may be, for example, in the following terms:
> 'The parties shall by [date] consider whether the case is capable of resolution by ADR. If any party considers that the case is unsuitable for resolution by ADR, that party shall be prepared to justify that decision at the conclusion of the trial, should the judge consider that such means of resolution were appropriate, when he is considering the appropriate costs order to make.
>   The party considering the case unsuitable for ADR shall, not less than 28 days before the commencement of the trial, file with the court a witness statement without prejudice save as to costs, giving reasons upon which they rely for saying that the case was unsuitable'."

[141] CPR r.29.7, 29.8.

[142] CPR r.29.5 PD 29 para.6.1. See also *Rollinson v Kimberly Clark Ltd* [2000] C.P. Rep. 85, CA.

(a) it considers that:

   (i) that claimant has no real prospect of succeeding on the claim or issue; or

   (ii) that defendant has no real prospect of successfully defending the claim or issue; and

(b) there is no other compelling reason why the case or issue should be disposed of at trial."[143]

Consequently, either party may apply to the court for a hearing to decide whether judgment should be given on the whole or part of a claim if the application can be supported by evidence stating that the applicant believes that their opponent has no real prospect of succeeding on the claim or issue or defending it, as appropriate.[144] Indeed, the court has power to convene such a hearing of its own initiative.[145] The opponent has the opportunity to adduce evidence[146] in response. At the hearing (although the court has power to deal with this or any other pre-trial hearing on the papers without any oral representations and, in fact, hearings are frequently conducted by telephone)[147] the master or district judge has the task of balancing the rights of the claimant and the defendant, applying a test described by Lord Woolf in *Swain v Hillman*[148] in the following terms:

"The words 'no real prospect of being successful or succeeding' [*sic*] do not need any amplification, they speak for themselves. The word 'real' distinguishes fanciful prospects of success. . . . "

There are a number of options open to the court, but, perhaps where the claim or defence does have a real prospect of success, but not a strong one, the court may make a conditional order, requiring payment of a sum of money into court as a condition of that party being permitted to continue with the claim or with the defence.[149] Such conditions, which can be applied in other circumstances, particularly as a sanction for failure to comply with rules, orders or pre-action protocols,[150] may have the effect of discouraging the party with the weak case, or at least inducing careful consideration of the strength of the case. The master or district judge may, however, decide in favour of the applicant, granting judgment on the claim where the applicant is a claimant or striking out or

---

[143] CPR r.24.2. The court can convene such a hearing of its own motion but in practice is likely to be reluctant to do so: Peysner and Seneviratne, *The Management of Civil Cases: The Courts and the Post-Woolf Landscape* (DCA Research Series 9/05, November 2005).

[144] PD 24 para.2.3(b).

[145] CPR r.3.3; *Orford v Rasmi Electronics Ltd.* [2002] EWCA Civ 1672; Anon., "Summary Judgment at Trial" (2003) 22(MAR) C.J.Q. 104. In practice the court will rarely do so.

[146] It is unusual to allow oral examination of the parties at this or any other pre-trial hearing: CPR r.32.6.

[147] CPR r.3.1(d); PD 23 para.2.

[148] [2001] 1 All E.R. 91, CA. See also *Three Rivers District Council v Bank of England (No.3)* [2001] UKHL 16; *Royal Brompton Hospital NHS Trust v Hammond (No.5)* [2001] EWCA Civ 550, CA; *ED&F Man Liquid Products Ltd v Patel* [2003] EWCA Civ 472, CA; *HRH Prince of Wales v Associated Newspapers Ltd* [2006] EWHC 522, Ch D; *Skipper v Calderdale MBC* [2006] EWCA Civ 238, CA. Part 24 is also frequently used to "enforce" decisions of adjudicators, see Ch.11.

[149] PD 24 para.5. See also *Anglo-Eastern Trust v Kermanshahchi (No.2)* [2002] EWCA Civ 198, [2002] C.P. Rep. 36, CA.

[150] CPR r.3.1(3) and (5).

dismissing the claim if the applicant is a defendant, thus greatly speeding up the process of litigation in accordance with the overriding objective.

(b) Disclosure and inspection

So that each party may be aware of documents[151] relating to issues in the case, **12–026** rules requiring "disclosure"[152] of those documents place an obligation on the litigant to disclose their existence and, possibly, to allow inspection of their content. Where there is a pre-action protocol, then, as we have seen, much disclosure should take place even before the court becomes involved in the dispute. Even where there is not a protocol, then similar behaviour should involve disclosure of many documents in advance. Further, documents may be and in some cases must be attached to the particulars of claim. To assist in this process, either party may call on the court to intervene by making an order for disclosure prior to issue of the claim form.[153]

Nevertheless, as the real areas of dispute may not become apparent until the final statement of case has been filed, there is further provision for disclosure as part of the case management directions.

The parties and ultimately the court will have to decide on matters including:

(a) The scope of search—how far should the parties search in archives and obscure storage facilities, as well as in electronic sources such as computers, BlackBerrys and mobile telephones[154] for documents that might be of only tangential relevance to the case?

(b) The scope of disclosure. The default provision is for "standard disclosure", that is, disclosure of documents that are of direct probative value. Documents falling within standard disclosure are those:

   (i) on which the disclosing party relies;

  (ii) which adversely affect the case of the disclosing party; adversely affect the case of another party; or which support the case of another party; and

 (iii) which the disclosing party is required to disclose by a relevant practice direction.[155]

---

[151] A "document" is defined as "anything in which information of any description is recorded", CPR r.31.4 and therefore includes electronic media, videotapes, photographs and DVDs.

[152] Known as "discovery" prior to 1999.

[153] s.33 Supreme Court Act 1981, s.52 County Courts Act 1984 and CPR r.31.16. The statutory restriction of this procedure to personal injury claims was removed on implementation of the CPR by the Civil Procedure (Modification of Enactments) Order 1998 (SI 1998/2940). For the approach of the courts to this jurisdiction, see for example: *Burrell's Wharf Freeholds Ltd v Galliard Homes Ltd* [2000] C.P. Rep. 4, TCC; *Bermuda International Securities Ltd v KPMG* [2001] EWCA Civ 269, CA; *Black v Sumitomo Corp.* [2001] EWCA Civ 1819, CA; *Three Rivers DC v Bank of England (Disclosure) (No.1)* [2002] EWCA Civ 1182, CA; *Baron Jay v Wilder Coe (A Firm)* [2003] EWHC 1786, QBD; *Rose v Lynx Express Ltd* [2004] EWCA Civ 447, CA; *Briggs & Forrester Electrical Ltd v Southfield School for Girls* [2005] EWHC 1734, TCC; *BSW Ltd v Balltec Ltd* [2006] EWHC 822, Ch D. Peysner and Seneviratne, *op. cit.*, found evidence of such applications being treated as "the norm" where insufficient material had been provided at the protocol stage.

[154] See PD 31, para.2A.

[155] CPR r.31.6.

The parties and/or the court may, however, consider that disclosure could be limited to a smaller category of documents. What is unlikely to be permitted, however, in a normal case, is more wide-ranging disclosure.[156]

Once the extent of the search and the scope of the disclosure obligation have been defined, then each party must normally produce a list of documents in proper form within the deadline imposed by the court. The documents are divided into three categories: those which the claimant or defendant has in his or her control[157] and is willing to produce; those which he or she has but is not willing to produce; and those which he or she has had in his or her control but has no longer. Objections to the production of documents for inspection will be based either on the documents no longer being in the disclosing party's control, or on one or more of the privileges to which a litigant is entitled.[158] Note that the list must contain a "disclosure statement" equivalent to a statement of truth.[159] A copy of the list of documents in *George and Hacker v Reliable Nag Supply Stables* is set out on the pages that follow:

---

[156] Such as that permitted, under the old regime, by the principles set out in *Compagnie Financière et Commercials du Pacifique v Peruvian Guano Co* (1882) L.R. 11 Q.B.D. 55, CA. From March 2002, however, such disclosure (of any documents that will "enable the party applying for disclosure either to advance his own case or to damage that of the party giving disclosure; or lead to a train of enquiry which has either of those consequences") again became available, in appropriate cases, by application to the court for "specific disclosure" under CPR r.31.12: PD 31, para.5.5.

[157] CPR r.31.8.

[158] There are certain recognised privileges—legal professional privilege, privilege against self-incrimination; "without prejudice" documents; Crown privilege or public interest immunity. See *Three Rivers DC v Bank of England (Disclosure) (No.4)* [2004] UKHL 48, HL; N. Andrews, "Legal Advice Privilege's Broad Protection—The House of Lords in Three Rivers (No. 6)" (2005) 24(APR) C.J.Q., 185. Note, however, CPR r.35.10 removing privilege from instructions to an expert witness and PD 21 para.6.3 which requires production to the court in certain circumstances of instructions to counsel that would otherwise attract legal professional privilege (although there must presumably be some doubt whether a mere practice direction is capable of removing privilege). See *Lucas v Barking, Havering and Redbridge Hospitals NHS Trust* [2003] EWCA Civ 1102, CA; *Jackson v Marley Davenport Ltd* [2004] EWCA Civ 1225, CA; *Vasiliou v Hajigeorgiou* [2005] EWCA Civ 236, CA. The section of CPR r.48.7 containing a similar provision in relation to wasted costs orders, was declared ultra vires: *General Mediterranean Holdings S.A. v Patel* [2000] 1 W.L.R. 272; [1999] 3 All. E. R. 673, QBD. Further, but only where the documents in question come under CPR r.31.6(b) (i.e. those that adversely affect the disclosing party's case, adversely affect another party's case or support another party's case), inspection can be withheld on the ground that it would be "disproportionate" (CPR r.31.3(2)). See *Punjab National Bank v Jain* [2004] EWCA Civ 589, CA.

[159] CPR rr.31.10(5); 31.23 and PD 31, para.8.

List of Documents:
Standard Disclosure

In the	
	HIGH COURT OF JUSTICE
	QUEEN'S BENCH DIVISION
	NOTTINGHAM DISTRICT REGISTRY
Claim No.	NG06232323
Claimant (including ref)	PETER GEORGE (1)
	MARTIN HACKER (2)
Defendant (including ref)	RELIABLE NAG SUPPLY
	STABLES (A FIRM)
Date	16TH FEBRUARY 2007

Notes

- The rules relating to standard disclosure are contained in Part 31 of the Civil Procedure Rules.

- Documents to be included under standard disclosure are contained in Rule 31.6

- A document has or will have been in your control if you have or have had possession, or a right of possession, of it **or** a right to inspect or take copies of it.

Disclosure Statement

I, the above named

   [x] Claimant   [ ] Defendant

   [ ] Party (if party making disclosure is a company, firm or other organisation identify here who the person making the disclosure statement is and why he is the appropriate person to make it)

state that I have carried out a reasonable and proportionate search to locate all the documents which I am

required to disclose under the order made by the court on (date of order) | 12TH FEBRUARY 2007 |

[x] I did not search for documents:-

   [x] pre-dating | JUNE 2005 |

   [x] located elsewhere than

      | AT MY HOME OR THAT OF THE SECOND CLAIMANT |

   [x] in categories other than

      | CONTRACTUAL DOCUMENTS AND CARE RECORDS OF HORSES |

   [ ] for electronic documents

[x] I carried out a search for electronic documents contained on or created by the following:
(list what was searched and extent of search)

| ON MY HOME COMPUTER AND BLACKBERRY AND THOSE OF THE SECOND CLAIMANT |

☐ I did not search for the following:-

   ☒ documents created before   JUNE 2005

documents contained on or created by the ☒ Claimant   ☐ Defendant

☐ PCs	☐ portable data storage media
☐ databases	☐ servers
☐ back-up tapes	☐ off-site storage
☒ mobile phones	☐ laptops
☐ notebooks	☐ handheld devices
☐ PDA devices	

documents contained on or created by the ☐ Claimant   ☐ Defendant

☐ mail files	☐ document files
☐ calendar files	☐ web-based applications
☐ spreadsheet files	☐ graphic and presentation files

documents other than by reference to the following keyword(s)/concepts
(delete if your search was not confined to specific keywords or concepts)

I certify that I understand the duty of disclosure and to the best of my knowledge I have carried out that duty. I further certify that the list of documents set out in or attached to this form, is a complete list of all documents which are or have been in my control and which I am obliged under the order to disclose.

I understand that I must inform the court and the other parties immediately if any further document required to be disclosed by Rule 31.6 comes into my control at any time before the conclusion of the case.

☐ I have not permitted inspection of documents within the category or class of documents (as set out below) required to be disclosed under Rule 31(6)(b)or (c) on the grounds that to do so would be disproportionate to the issues in the case.

Signed _____   **Date**   16th February 2007

(Claimant)(Defendant)('s Litigation Friend)

N265/2

List and number here, in a convenient order, the documents (or bundles of documents if of the same nature, e.g. invoices) in your control, which you do not object to being inspected. Give a short description of each document or bundle so that it can be identified, and say if it is kept elsewhere i.e. with a bank or solicitor

I have control of the documents numbered and listed here. I do not object to you inspecting them/producing copies.

1 Defendant's receipt for £65,000	25th June 2005
2 Care logbook for the Horse	Various dates
3 Account of Sutton Riding Enterprises	20th August 2005
4 Care logbook for the Mare	Various dates
5 Letter Claimants' solicitors to Defendant	20th October 2006
6 Correspondence, including emails, and copy correspondence, including e-mails between Claimants' solicitors and Defendants' solicitors	Various dates
7 Claim form, statements of case, applications and orders common to the parties	Various dates

List and number here, as above, the documents in your control which you object to being inspected. (Rule 31.19)

I have control of the documents numbered and listed here, but I object to you inspecting them:

1 All notes, electronic documents, memoranda, drafts and witness statements not previously filed in interim applications prepared solely for the purpose of the conduct of the Claimants' case or in the contemplation thereof which fall within standard disclosure.

2 All communications of whatsoever nature passing between the Claimants and their solicitors or counsel which fall within standard disclosure.All communications of whatsoever nature passing between the Claimants, their solicitors or counsel and their expert witness or witnesses which fall within standard disclosure.

3 Instructions to, opinions of counsel and drafts, including electronic documents, produced by counsel which fall within standard disclosure.

4 All notes, electronic documents, proofs, reports or expert memoranda called into existence for the purpose of assisting the Claimants or their solicitors or counsel in the conduct of the action or in contemplation thereof which fall within standard disclosure.

N265/3

Say what your
objections are

I object to you inspecting these documents because:

Other than the instructions to an expert witness within category 2 above,
they are by their very nature privileged. I object to you inspecting any
such instructions to an expert witness which may fall within standard
disclosure under CPR r. 35.10(4).

List and number
here, the documents
you once had in your
control, but which
you no longer have.
For each document
listed, say when
it was last in your
control and where it
is now.

I have had the documents numbered and listed below, but they are no longer in my control.

N/A

Oyez 7 Spa Road, London SE16 3QQ
      © Crown Copyright.

N265

2005 Edition 10.2005
N265/4

5093335

Further information to assist in proving one's case can be obtained through the Pt 18 procedure described above. In addition, a power currently contained in the Supreme Court Act 1981, s.34 and the County Courts Act 1984, s.53 allowing orders for post-commencement disclosure against non-parties to the claim (such as, for example, the claimant's employer in a personal injury case) was in 1999 extended to all cases.[160]

(c) Exchange of witness statements

As a result of proposals in the Civil Justice Review, from 1992 it became the **12–027** practice for the court to order exchange of written statements of the oral evidence which each party intends to use at trial. This provision is now contained in CPR Pt 32. Those statements are required to be in a standard format (PD 32), in the witness' own words "as far as practicable"[161] and to contain a statement of truth.[162] Generally speaking, an adjunct to the order for exchange will be that the statements stand as evidence-in-chief at the trial: i.e. that after the witness has confirmed that the statement is his or her own, the court will proceed straight to cross-examination.

If a statement is not served in respect of a witness, then *prima facie* that witness cannot be called to give evidence at trial.[163] This of course causes difficulties with a useful but unco-operative witness whose attendance at trial can be compelled by use of a witness summons but to little effect if the evidence is inadmissible because of the failure to exchange a statement. To deal with this deadlock, the CPR provide for use, subject to the court's permission, of a "witness summary" to replace the unobtainable witness statement.[164] We will discuss witnesses of fact further in Ch.15.

(d) Expert witnesses

See Ch.15.

---

[160] Civil Procedure (Modification of Enactments) Order 1998 (SI 1998/2940). The relevant rules appear in CPR r.31.17.

[161] A cautionary tale is provided in *Alex Lawrie Factors Ltd v Morgan* [2001] C.P. Rep. 2; *The Times*, August 18, 1999, CA. Here, the written evidence of a party who wished to set aside a transaction on the grounds of undue influence had been drafted by her lawyers, who included such matters as technical comment on the relevant cases on the topic. Reading this document, the court was forced to conclude that the party appeared to be so knowledgeable that she could hardly have been acting under undue influence! For an example of a judge's concern at the *manner* in which the statement was obtained, see *Aquarius Financial Enterprises Jnc v Certain Underwriters at Lloyd's* (2001) 151 N.L.J., QBD, Commercial Court. See also *E D & F Man Liquid Products Ltd v Patel* [2002] EWHC 1706, QBD, *Co-operative Group Ltd (formerly Co-operative Wholesale Society Ltd) v International Computers Ltd* [2003] EWHC 1, TCC reversed on its merits (but not on the comments relating to witness statements) at [2003] EWCA 1955, CA; *Wreford-Smith v Airtours Holidays Ltd* [2004] EWCA Civ 453, CA.

[162] The penalty for signing without an honest belief in the truth of the facts so verified is contempt of court. See *MBNA American Bank N.A. v Freeman* [2000] All E.R. (D) 1743, Ch D; *Daltel Europe Ltd (In Liquidation) v Makki (Committal for Contempt)* [2006] EWCA Civ 94, CA.

[163] CPR r.32.10. Conversely, if the statement is exchanged but the witness is not called, any other party may rely on the statement as hearsay: CPR r. 32.5(5) and *Society of Lloyd's v Jaffray, The Times*, August 3, 2000, QBD.

[164] CPR r.32.9.

(e) CPR Pt 36

12–028   Prior to 1999 it was possible for a defendant, at any time after issue of proceedings, to pay money into court in attempted satisfaction of the plaintiff's claim. The plaintiff could then choose whether to accept the amount paid in and discontinue the action, or carry on the action in the hope of obtaining a greater sum at trial. The penalty for the plaintiff was that he or she would normally bear all the costs of the action from the date the payment in could have been accepted (normally 21 days after payment was made) unless awarded a sum in excess of the amount the defendant had paid in. Under the 44th update to the CPR, the defendant has been relieved of obligation actually to make payment in court.[165] However the penalty for the claimant is retained in CPR r.36.14(2).

This useful procedure allowed a defendant to use it to protect himself or herself from a zealous plaintiff who wanted to have the "day in court" or to apply pressure to accept a sum in settlement rather than risk a heavy bill in costs and it has been incorporated into Pt 36 of the CPR. It is important to stress two points. First that the plaintiff could not and the claimant cannot now both accept the sum and continue the action. Secondly, the judge is not told of the offer until the questions of liability and damages have been settled.

So useful a procedure is it, indeed, that it was extended under the CPR in a number of ways. First, and most significantly, the procedure was opened to claimants. A claimant may use the Pt 36 procedure to say, for example, "I am prepared to accept £20,000 in settlement of my claim ostensibly valued at £30,000". If the offer is accepted, that is the end of the claim. If the defendant does not accept the offer then, it is kept secret from the trial judge. If the defendant does not at trial obtain a better result than the offer (e.g. in this case an award of damages against the defendant of less than £20,000), the defendant will be penalised. The question is, of course, how to penalise a defendant in this situation. The defendant will have lost the case, have to pay the claimant's damages and a large part if not all of the claimant's costs irrespective of the Pt 36 offer. The answer imposed by CPR r.36.14(3) is that the court will, unless it is unjust, require the defendant to pay additional interest of up to 10 per cent above base rate on damages and costs from the last date the defendant could have accepted the offer as well as the claimant's costs on an indemnity basis. If the offer was made very early in the proceedings, this additional interest can amount to a very large sum.[166]

---

[165] Suggestions for streamlining the system, in particular for removing the requirement for the defendant to support the offer by making an actual payment, appeared in the August 2001 Lord Chancellor's Department consultation paper *Payments into Court in Satisfaction of Claims* and were implemented in the 44th amendment to the CPR. See also, for the rationale behind the change, *Crouch v King's Healthcare NHS Trust* [2004] EWCA Civ 1332 and *Stokes Pension Fund Trustees v Western Power Distribution (South West) Plc* [2005] EWCA Civ 854.

[166] For example: *All-In-One Design and Build Ltd v Motcomb Estates Ltd*, *The Times*, April 4, 2000, TCC; *Dew Pitchmastic plc v Birse Construction Ltd (No.2)*, *The Times*, June 21, 2000, TCC; *Petrotrade Inc. v Texaco Ltd* [2001] C.P. Rep. 29, CA; *Amber v Stacey* [2001] 2 All E.R. 88; CA; *Scammell v Dicker*, [2001] 1 W.L.R. 631, CA; *McPhilemy v Times Newspapers Ltd* [2001] EWCA Civ 933, CA; *Reid Minty v Taylor* [2001] EWCA Civ 1723, CA; *Quorum A/S v Schramm (Costs)* [2002] 2 All E.R. (Comm) 179, QBD, Commercial Court; *Kiam v MGN Ltd (Costs)* [2002] EWCA Civ 66, CA; *Huck v Robson* [2002] EWCA Civ 398, CA; *Excelsior Commercial & Industrial Holdings Ltd v Salisbury Hamer Aspden & Johnson (Costs)* [2002] EWCA Civ 879; *Mitchell v James (Costs)* [2002] EWCA Civ 997; *Budgen v Andrew Gardner Partnership* [2002] EWCA Civ 1125; *Dyson Appliances Ltd v Hoover Ltd (Costs)* [2002] EWHC 2229; *KR v Bryn Alyn Community (Holdings) Ltd (In Liquidation) (Part 36 Appeal: Joinder of Parties)* [2003] EWCA Civ 783; *Ali Reza-Delta Transport Co Ltd v United Arab Shipping Co SAG (Costs)* [2003]

Secondly, for both claimants and defendants the procedure is extended beyond simple offers of money. So, for example, in a tort claim, the defendant might offer under Pt 36 to accept 60 per cent liability, suggesting that the claimant was 40 per cent contributorily negligent.

Finally the CPR allow Pt 36 to be used prior to the issue of proceedings[167] as well as in respect of appeals.

F. INTERIM REMEDIES

Interim remedies are "designed to deal with the position of the parties pending the trial, to maintain as far as possible the status quo ante and to preserve, protect and where necessary enhance the rights and interests of the parties in the inevitable interval between the start of the proceedings and the trial". There are many remedies available, a non-exclusive list of which appears in CPR r.25.1, but perhaps the three most significant are the interim injunction, the freezing injunction and the search order. **12–029**

(a) Interim injunction

The significance of the interim injunction is not only that it is a speedy and effective method of preserving the status quo ante prior to a trial, but also that the decision of the judge on the granting of an injunction is often taken by the parties as an indication of what the trial judge would do and therefore the proceedings may go no further. **12–030**

An interim injunction is usually negative in form, that is to restrain the defendant from doing something, rather than mandatory, that is, requiring an act to be done. It is effective because a breach of an injunction is a contempt of court which is punishable by imprisonment, fine and sequestration of property, as appropriate. Further, the injunction does not just affect the parties to the action, it also applies to anyone knowing of it and its terms. Third parties then are under an obligation to observe its terms at least so that steps amounting to a breach are not taken, under the penalty of sanctions for contempt of court.

Such an injunction can be granted in either High Court or county court proceedings. It is usually applied for on the basis of the other party being informed and thus able to challenge the granting of the injunction ("with notice"). However, in an emergency it may be applied for and granted without

---

EWCA Civ 811; *Johnson v Gore Wood & Co (No.3)* [2004] EWCA Civ 14; *Garratt v Saxby* [2004] EWCA Civ 341; *Flynn v Scougall* [2004] EWCA Civ 873; *Blackham v Entrepose UK* [2004] EWCA Civ 1109; *Read v Edmed* [2004] EWHC 3274; *Capital Bank Plc v Stickland* [2004] EWCA Civ 1677; *HSS Hire Services Group Plc v BMB Builders Merchants Ltd (Costs)* [2005] EWCA Civ 626; *Daniels v Commissioner of Police of the Metropolis* [2005] EWCA Civ 1312; *Decoma UK Ltd (formerly Conix UK Ltd) v Haden Drysys International Ltd (Costs)* [2005] EWHC 2429; *Hawley v Luminar Leisure Plc* [2006] EWCA Civ 30; *Day v Day (Costs)* [2006] EWCA Civ 415; *Brennan v ECO Composting Ltd* [2006] EWHC 3153; *Lahey v Pirelli Tyres Ltd* [2007] EWCA Civ 91. See also A. A. S. Zuckerman "CPR 36 offers" (2005) 24(APR) C.J.Q. 167.

[167] CPR r.36.3(2) *op. cit.*, n.166. See *Huck v Robson, op. cit.*, n.58.

notice to the other side.[168] In appropriate circumstances an injunction can be obtained prior to the issue of proceedings.[169]

An interim injunction will be granted if the principles laid down in *American Cyanamid Co v Ethicon Ltd.*[170] are satisfied. First, the applicant must establish that there is a good arguable claim to the right that is to be protected. Secondly, the applicant must show that there is a serious question to be tried. Thirdly, the grant depends on which way the balance of convenience lies. Further, and since the implementation of the Human Rights Act 1998, the court may have to consider whether or not the grant of the injunction infringes the respondent's human rights, particularly when the injunction, if granted, might prevent the respondent exercising his or her right of freedom of expression.[171]

(b) Freezing injunction

12–031   The freezing injunction—known prior to 1999 as a *Mareva* injunction[172]—is a specialised form of interim injunction used to prevent not only a foreign defendant transferring assets abroad and thus out of the jurisdiction so as to defeat—or at least complicate—enforcement of any award of damages, but also to prevent a defendant within the jurisdiction transferring assets abroad or concealing them in England and Wales. It is an interim remedy falling within the ambit of Pt 25 of the CPR.

The injunction is effective because it is swift and secret and not only does it act against the defendant who would be in contempt of court for breach but also against innocent third parties. The main advantage of this is that it applies to banks through which transfer of assets is most likely to take place, especially in an age of the computerised transfer of funds.[173] The third party has a right to be paid all reasonable expenses and costs, thus having a right of set-off in connection with an account which has become the subject of a freezing injunction.

Such an injunction is normally granted in the High Court.[174] A standard form order is attached to PD 25 and variations from this order must be brought to the specific attention of the court when the application is made.[175] A freezing injunction is usually applied for without notice to the respondent, so that the opponent cannot defeat its effect consequent upon notice of an application. The claimant must then show a good arguable case,[176] must make full and frank disclosure of all the facts that the judge will need to know, including in particular information of the existence of assets that are desired to be the object of the injunction, and must make clear the grounds for believing that without an injunction there is a real risk of any judgment in his or her favour not being satisfied as well as demonstrating compliance with CPR r.25.3 and, if the application is prior to the issue of proceedings, CPR r.25.2(2)(b). As with all injunctions, the claimant must normally provide an undertaking as to damages,

---

[168] CPR rr.25.2(2)(b).

[169] CPR r.25.2, 25.3.

[170] [1975] A.C. 396, HL.

[171] See especially Human Rights Act 1998, s.12.

[172] *Mareva Companiera Naviera v International Bulk Carriers* [1980] 1 All E.R. 213, CA.

[173] However, if the bank fails to implement the order, see *Customs and Excise Commissioners v Barclays Bank Plc* [2006] UKHL 28.

[174] But see *Schmidt v Wong* [2005] EWCA Civ 1506.

[175] *Memory Corporation plc v Sidhu* [2000] 1 W.L.R. 1443, CA; *Interoute Communications UK Ltd v Fashion Gossip Ltd, The Times,* November 10, 1999, Ch D.

[176] See *Fourie v Le Roux* [2007] UKHL 1.

that is, the ability to cover the expenses of the defendant should the claimant's case ultimately fail.[177] Further and as with any order the court is asked to make, the court must consider whether granting the order will further the overriding objective as well as its obligations under the Human Rights Act 1998. The order can also be granted in aid of foreign proceedings[178] or arbitrations,[179] for example freezing assets in this jurisdiction and, exceptionally, on a worldwide basis.[180]

(c) Search order

The search order—known prior to 1999 as an *Anton Piller* order[181]—is a special **12–032** form of mandatory injunction derived initially from the inherent power of the court to make an order for the detention or preservation of property which is the subject matter of a cause, and of documents and articles relating to it. It was placed on a statutory footing by Civil Procedure Act 1997, s.7 and is an interim remedy within the ambit of CPR Pt 25. The order often empowers the claimant to enter the defendant's premises and search for and seize material documents and articles ("execution of the order"), but, as it is not a search warrant, no force may be used in entering premises. A large number of caveats intended to protect the interests of the defendant—including the requirement allowing the defendant to claim legal privilege[182] in respect of documents; allowing the defendant a period within which to take legal advice; and most significantly, providing for the search to be supervised by an independent solicitor ("the supervising solicitor") who subsequently provides a written report to the court on the way in which the search was carried out—are contained in the standard order attached to PD 25. As with the freezing injunction, any variation from the standard order must be drawn to the court's attention when the application is made.[183]

The application is without notice to the defendant, for obvious reasons, and consequently the applicant must give full disclosure of all facts the judge is likely to need to know.[184] The claimant must provide evidence describing the premises and the relevant property or documents and show some strong evidence that serious harm or serious injustice will be done if the order is not made and that there is a real risk of the evidence being destroyed or hidden. As usual, the claimant must provide an undertaking as to damages and, as with any order the court is asked to make, the court must consider whether granting the order will further the overriding objective as well as its obligations under the Human Rights Act 1998.[185]

---

[177] See *Eliades v Lewis (No.9)* [2005] EWHC 2966, QBD.

[178] Civil Jurisdiction and Judgments Act 1982, s.25. For an example, see *Motorola Credit Corp v Uzan (No.6)* [2003] EWCA Civ 752.

[179] See *Cetelem S.A. v Roust Holdings Ltd (Application for Further Freezing Order)* [2005] EWHC 300, QBD.

[180] See, for example, *Dadourian Group International Inc. v Simms* [2006] EWCA 399.

[181] *Anton Piller A.G. v Manufacturing Process Ltd* [1976] 1 Ch. 55; [1976] 2 W.L.R. 162.

[182] For some problems in this respect, see *C Plc v P* [2006] EWHC 1226, Ch D.

[183] As can other relevant factors of which the judge should be made aware: *Elvee Ltd v Taylor* [2001] EWCA Civ 1943, CA.

[184] Failure to do so can lead to the discharge of the order: *Gadget Shop Ltd v The Bug.com* [2001] C.P. Rep. 13, CA and *St. Merryn Meat Ltd v. Hawkins* [2001] C.P. Rep. 116, Ch D.

[185] The order is not, intrinsically, a breach of human rights: *Chappell v UK* [1990] 12 E.H.R.R 1; ECHR. The way in which it is obtained or executed might, however, lead to such a breach: see *St Merryn Meat Ltd v Hawkins, op. cit.*

(d) Other pre-trial remedies

12–033   Other remedies include the High Court power to make interim receivership orders, the High Court and county court power to make interim orders relating to property relevant to an action, the limited power to prevent a defendant leaving the jurisdiction, and the High Court or county court power to make an order requiring an interim payment on account of any damages, debt or other sum which a defendant may be held liable to pay.[186] A remedy exclusive to defendants (including defendants to counterclaims), obliged to defend a claim brought by a claimant who may be discovered to have insufficient funds to reimburse the defendant his or her costs when he or she is vindicated at trial, is that of security for costs[187]: an order whereby the claimant must pay into court for safekeeping an amount of money representing the defendant's costs in defending the claim.

G. HAVE THE WOOLF REFORMS ACHIEVED THEIR OBJECTIVES?

12–034   A great deal of ink has been spilt over the last seven years in seeking to evaluate the real effect of the reforms on the court, the practitioner and on the client. Certain effects were immediately apparent from such empirical studies as the 1999 and 2000 *Judicial Statistics*,[188] showing a remarkable drop in the number of civil claims issued. Otherwise evidence of the effect of the reforms in more anecdotal form is overwhelming but useful sources of information on the effect of the reforms can be found in the March 2001 Lord Chancellor's Department paper *Emerging Findings*; the Department for Constitutional Affairs August 2002 paper *Further Findings*; and a research project carried out by Professors John Peysner and Mary Seneviratne for the Department of Constitutional Affairs in November 2005: *The Management of Civil Cases: The Courts and post-Woolf Landscape*.[189] One must also take into account the increasing effect of the drive towards use of ADR procedures in place of litigation.

a. Litigation will be avoided wherever possible[190]

12–035   As we have seen from examination of the judicial statistics, there has been a startling drop in the number of civil claims issued since the introduction of the reforms. If one assumes that the number of litigatable disputes has not decreased then, to that extent, litigation as a process has been avoided. What is yet to be explored is the real rationale for the reduction.

A possible rationale is, of course, one of cost. Whilst a litigant in person may incur no lawyer's fees, he or she is generally obliged to pay the prescribed court

---

[186] CPR rr.25.6 to 25.9 inclusive and PD 25B. See also: *South West Water Services Ltd v International Computers Ltd* [2001] Lloyd's Rep. P.N. 353, QBD, TCC; *Parry v North West Surrey Health Authority, The Times*, January 5, 2000, QBD; *Harmon CFEM Facades (UK) Ltd v The Corporate Officer of the House of Commons* [2001] C.P. Rep. 20, TCC.

[187] CPR rr.25.12 to 25.15 inclusive. An alternative ground is that, the claimant being resident abroad, an order for costs would be difficult to enforce against their assets, wherever situated.

[188] *Op. cit.*

[189] DCA Research Series 9/05.

[190] See *Cowl v Plymouth City Council* [2001] EWCA Civ 1935.

fees of up to £1,700 (in the High Court) on issue and further fees on filing allocation questionnaires and pre-trial checklists. The fees alone, then, can, especially in a small claims track case, rapidly approach the value of the claim.

The initial fall in the number of issued cases identified in *Emerging Findings* was almost certainly a result of the concern of lawyers and their clients about entering an unfamiliar and untried procedure. A survey by the firm Lovells, quoted in *Emerging Findings*, suggested that 7 per cent of that firm's clients were consciously treating litigation as a last resort. Nevertheless, the trend away from issuing proceedings has continued, identified both in *Further Findings* and in the 2005 *Judicial Statistics*.

In *Further Findings*, the effect of the pre-action protocols in requiring the potential parties to litigation to clarify what is in dispute and to exchange information prior to the issue of proceedings was also identified as contributing to the decline in issue of proceedings: 85 per cent of cases in a survey quoted[191] having settled prior to issue. An additional contributory factor towards the compromise of cases is the tactical use of CPR Pt 36.[192] A CEDR Civil Justice Audit is quoted in *Emerging Findings* to the effect that 74 per cent of the lawyers surveyed felt CPR Pt 36 had made settlement easier and this sentiment is echoed by the compilers of *Further Findings*.

b. Litigation will be less adversarial and more co-operative

Emerging Findings located evidence that claims were becoming compromised earlier in the life of the litigation rather than—literally—at the door of the court on the day of trial. It reported that 70 per cent of fast track cases (during the period November 1999 to December 2000) settled prior to the day of trial.[193] In *Further Findings*, it was identified that the percentage of issued fast track cases that proceeded to trial had fallen by late 2001 to 23 per cent. Only 8 per cent of cases in both fast and multi-tracks were settling as late as the day of the trial. Logically, the emphasis of the CPR on earlier and earlier disclosure of evidence and identification of the issues in dispute should contribute to this effect—the earlier the real nature of the dispute and the strengths and weaknesses of the case are revealed, the earlier the parties are able to identify areas of potential compromise. The fact that much or all of this process may take place prior to the issue of proceedings will also contribute to the reduction in the number of claims issued—the impact of the pre action protocols and similar behaviour acting as an incitement to compromise the dispute instead of issuing proceedings. Peysner and Seneviratne, finding that judges are now taking a much more pro-active role in the management of cases, suggest that this additional call on limited judicial resources may only be possible because of the reduction in the number of claims issued.[194] In terms of co-operation, however, they do identify a clear change in culture inculcated by the new procedure: greater co-operation and less opportunity, particularly by defendants, to manipulate the system:

12–036

---

[191] Goriely, Moorehead and Abrams, *More Civil Justice? The impact of the Woolf Reforms on pre-action behaviour* (2002, Law Society and Civil Justice Council Research Study 43).

[192] See para.12–028.

[193] A similar, but much less significant, drop in settlements close to trial was also identified in multi-track cases.

[194] *Op. cit.* at 9.

" . . . co-operation between the parties has improved. Indeed, it was observed by judges that when disputes arise, it is usually between the judge and the parties, rather than inter-party disagreement. This was borne out by solicitors, who claimed that judges can be 'obstructive' at case management conferences, and that there are many cases where the court intervenes too much. Practitioners agreed that there was more co-operation with each other and that this was necessary to maximise whatever flexibility there was in the system."[195]

It is, of course, entirely possible to argue that the pragmatic settlement of cases outside the formal court system detracts from the concept of "justice"—a pragmatic result, particularly where a settlement is reached in the shadow of the risk of a penalty under CPR Pt 36 if the offer were not "beaten" at trial, is not a "just" result.

As we have seen in Ch.11, ADR is now not only a serious alternative to litigation but actively promoted not only by ADR professionals but also by the courts themselves[196] and by the government. In *Further Findings* it was suggested that there was a significant increase in recourse to mediation in particular immediately after the introduction of the reforms, but that this has levelled off.[197] Peysner and Seneviratne found limited use of ADR (specifically mediation), particularly in boundary and family disputes and other types of dispute being dealt with in the fast track. In commercial cases, however, mediation was regarded as more useful, particularly in the absence of a pre-action protocol affecting the generality of commercial claims. Nevertheless, with the potential for sanction against parties who do not engage in ADR in cases where it is appropriate to do so, and increasing access to and flexibility of ADR mechanisms, the potential for an effect on the litigation statistics is inevitable.

Further Findings also comments on the contribution of single joint experts under this head. A Court Service examination of available data suggested that in 46 per cent of county court trials where any expert evidence was adduced, that evidence was adduced by a single joint expert.

c. *Litigation will be less complex;*

12–037   Clearly, the fact that the rules are now (almost entirely) unified, removes a level of complexity from civil litigation. Set against this, however, is the proliferation of specialist guides for individual courts: the Queen's Bench Division Guide (for the Royal Courts of Justice); the Mercantile Court Guide; and the Admiralty and Commercial Court Guide. Any person new to civil procedure who attempts to comprehend the mysteries of Pts 20 or 36 would be forgiven for a belief that the new rules are, in places at least, significantly more complex than the old. The authors of *Emerging Findings* commented only that "the Civil Procedure Rules are developing to meet these criteria". It was clearly anticipated in *Emerging Findings* that the court's ability to narrow the issues and to control the evidence adduced to prove or disprove those issues, powers typically exerted at the case

---

[195] *Op. cit.* at 12.

[196] See the cases cited in Ch.11 on the subject of costs penalties being imposed for an unreasonable failure to try to resolve the dispute by ADR.

[197] ADR orders have been available in the Commercial Court since 1993. For a discussion of usage of ADR in that court, see H. Genn, *Court Based ADR Initiatives for Non-family Civil Disputes: The Commercial Court and the Court of Appeal* (LCD Research 1/2002).

management conference would be a "key factor" towards the simplification of litigation. By *Further Findings*, it was anticipated that the incorporation of the remainder of the "rump" of the old Rules of the Supreme Court and County Court Rules into the CPR would be complete by 2004, although, at the time of writing, this is yet to be the case. That report did, however, cite a Court User Satisfaction Survey in November 2001 suggesting that, whilst 70 per cent of the public found the procedures easy to understand, only 51 per cent of "professional" users agreed.

The pro-activity of judges in engaging in efficient case management is also a contributing factor in simplifying litigation and reducing the need for additional applications. Peysner and Seneviratne, looking at the role of the case managing judge, consider the case management conference, as "the venue which brings together the legal advisers and the procedural judge, who then shapes the future conduct of the matter" as "one of the major successes of the CPR".[198]

d. The timescale of litigation will be shorter and more certain;

The average period between issue of proceedings and trial in the county court is now 52 weeks.[199] In addition, it is important to realise that the pre-action protocols may add a further 3 to 4 months prior to issue. *Emerging Findings* discovered that the waiting time for small claims hearings rose shortly after the implementation of the CPR but had settled to a generally lower figure.[200] *Further Findings* identified an ongoing decline in waiting times for trial, although noting that personal injury and negligence cases tend to take longer than the average. The question remains, however, whether, particularly for an individual litigant, a period of a year before trial and the potential of recovery, is adequate.[201] Peysner and Seneviratne found "mixed views" amongst their interviewees as to the CPR having reduced delay in the system, some participants suggesting that active case management intervention by judges could in fact be the cause of additional delay. They also found concern that timescales set by the court should be realistic, difficulties being identified in the listing for hearing of interim applications in particular.

12–038

Is the timescale more certain? The court is encouraged to fix a trial date or trial window comparatively early in the process.[202] Timetabling decisions should be worded in terms giving a date (and sometimes a time of day) by way of deadline. However, whilst a solicitor or barrister will be accustomed to, for example, a hearing starting late or being held over to a second day, as an inconvenience, any

---

[198] *Op. cit.* at 25. Equivalent figures are not provided for the High Court. A. A. S. Zuckerman, however, sees the availability of and attitude of the courts to relief from sanctions for breaches of the CPR as undermining the scheduling of claims: "Civil Litigation: A Public Service for the Enforcement of Civil Rights" (2007) 26(JAN) C.J.Q. 1. An audit spanning the last years of the old regime and the first years of the new is reported in J. Shapland, "The Need for Case Management? Profiles of Liquidated and Unliquidated Cases" (2003) 22(Oct) C.J.Q. 324.

[199] *Judicial Statistics 2005*, Table 4.17. This compares favourably with the average waiting period for a county court trial described in *Judicial Statistics 1995*, Cm. 3290, p.35, of 79 weeks.

[200] 522 days in 2000 as against 663 in 1997.

[201] As we will see in Ch.15, however, judgment in one's favour by no means guarantees recovery. It should also be noted that there are means by which the claimant can obtain payments on account of damages to ameliorate the wait: CPR rr.25.6 to 25.9 and PD 25b.

[202] On allocation in the small claims track (CPR r.27.4); "as soon as practicable after the date specified for filing a completed pre-trial checklist" in the fast track (giving the parties at least three weeks' notice of the actual date) (CPR r.28.6); "as soon as practicable after" filing of the pre-trial checklist, the listing hearing or pre-trial review in the multi-track (CPR r.29.8).

vagary in the timetable may be devastating to a litigant in person who has taken time off work.[203]

e. The cost of litigation will be more affordable, more predictable, and more proportionate to the value and complexity of individual cases

12–039   The compliers of both *Emerging Findings* and *Further Findings* considered it too early to be definitive about costs. The reforms have changed the shape of expenditure on litigation, demanding considerable front-loading in order to comply with pre-action protocol requirements—incurred even if the case then settles[204]—whether or not overall costs have decreased. The charges of solicitors and expert witnesses were thought in *Further Findings* to have obscured the issue and some constituencies, such as insurers, were reported to be of the view that costs had increased.

Peysner and Seneviratne considered the effect of the reforms on the cost of litigation in some detail in their study. They endorse the suggestion that, because of the front-loading effect of the protocols, a case settling early will have cost more than it might have done prior to the reforms, when much of the investigatory work could be postponed until it became clear that the case was "a runner". In a case proceeding to trial, however, the question is whether overall costs have reduced since the reforms. Peysner and Seneviratne found that "most opinion suggests an increase in unit costs"[205] but that this view was not universal; some practitioner respondents being of the opinion, for example, that claimants' costs had increased but defendants' costs decreased as more defendant work was being dealt with on a bulk "commodity" basis. Judges, however, seemed to be of the opinion that costs had increased overall. In any event, however, Peysner and Seneviratne also found there to be a view amongst judges in particular that costs were frequently still disproportionate to the value of the claim.

f. Parties of limited financial means will be able to conduct litigation on a more equal footing

12–040   The litigant in person is perhaps the most obviously potentially disadvantaged person in the civil litigation system. *Emerging Findings* located anecdotal evidence that the new system was thought to be more friendly to litigants in person than to lawyers. Where lawyers were retained, *Emerging Findings* quoted a number of surveys conducted by lawyers and allied organisations such as CEDR. The consensus of clients surveyed was generally in favour of the reforms.[206] Lawyers, especially those schooled under the old regime, may have been more

---

[203] For a discussion of the perspective of the litigant in person, see Gibb, "When the Quest for Justice sours", *The Times*, November 28, 2000.

[204] Costs of complying with a pre-action protocol can be recoverable as costs incidental to subsequent proceedings but this does not apply to the defendant's costs of issues dealt with at preaction protocol stage but not pursued in the subsequent litigation (i.e. issues that the preaction protocol process has itself disposed of in narrowing the issues in dispute): *McGlinn v Waltham Contractors Ltd* [2005] EWHC 1419.

[205] *Op. cit.* at 60.

[206] Wragge & Co had found 89% of their clients to be in favour, Eversheds 54% and CEDR 80%.

cautiously accepting.[207] *Further Findings* endorses findings that litigants in person in the county courts found the procedures and helpfulness of court staff satisfactory but does to some extent leave open a complaint that sanctions are not routinely applied for non compliance, particularly non compliance with pre action protocol requirements.

g. There will be clear lines of judicial and administrative responsibility for the civil justice system

This aspect of the reforms was not covered in *Emerging Findings.*[208] *Further Findings*, however, reported on the appointment of a Head of Civil Justice; designated civil judges at each civil trial centre; the creation of the Civil Justice Council; and the Judicial Technology Board. **12–041**

h. The structure of the courts and the deployment of judges will be designed to meet the needs of litigants;

i. Judges will be deployed effectively so that they can manage litigation in accordance with the new rules and protocols; and

j. The civil justice system will be more responsive to the needs of litigants.

All of these factors are related to the infrastructure of the court system. The litigant, particularly the litigant in person, is overwhelmed by sources of information, particularly on the internet.[209] A Court Service consultation, reported as *Modernising the Civil and Family Courts* (May 2002) resulted in a new model with the objectives of: **12–042**

(a) increasing choices for court users;

(b) reducing social exclusion; and

(c) improving the use of technology in the courts.[210]

---

[207] For example, Allen, "Inconsistent Judges plague Woolf Reforms", 2001 98(13) L.S.G. referring to a Law Society survey of 50 firms of solicitors, 80% of which were in favour of the reforms but 62% of which referred to problems caused by inconsistency between judges, to difficulties with the process of summary assessment of costs (see para.11–003) and generally to difficulty in recovering, even when successful, costs incurred during the substantial pre-action stages encouraged by the CPR.

[208] Each civil court or group of civil courts had, for example, from a very early stage in the reforms, a designated judge responsible for overseeing implementation (Lord Chancellor's Department press release October 27, 1998). Within the more public arena, publicity was given to the individual areas of responsibility of named parliamentary secretaries within the Lord Chancellor's Department: Lord Chancellor's Department press release June 18, 2001.

[209] See for example, HM Courts Service website (*http://www.hmcourts-service.gov.uk/*) which includes, as well as a complete set of court forms, a series of advice leaflets designed for litigants in person; Just Ask!, a website of the Legal Services Commission (*http://www.justask.org.uk*) designed for use by lay members of the public and the Ministry of Justice website (*http://www.justice.gov.uk/index.htm*) less ostensibly designed for the lay court user but nevertheless containing a complete set of court rules; and the Civil Justice Council website (*http://www.civiljusticecouncil.gov.uk*).

[210] A number of initiatives are in progress in this respect. See HM Courts Service *National Business Plan 2006–07*.

By way of example of such activity, one might note the possibility of issuing proceedings online through Money Claim online,[211] and the prevalence of hearings conducted by telephone. There is a pilot scheme for filing of documents and communication with the court by email in some courts.[212] Nevertheless, Peysner and Seneviratne found respondents to their survey commenting unfavourably on:

(a) judges' workload and lack of time for reading and "boxwork"[213];

(b) failures in the IT systems available to the courts;

(c) court administration workload resulting in problems of administration, listing of hearings and lost documents.

Within HM Courts Service, work is ongoing to improve service provision, albeit in the context of a reduced overall budget. Strategy at present is focused, according to HM Courts Service *National Business Plan 2006–2007* on seven key areas encompassing both civil and criminal courts:

- "improved use of our buildings
- removal of high volume bulk work from our courts
- centralisation of some back office administration
- improved take-up of telephone and e-services
- new ways of administering the £20bn of money we handle each year
- consolidation of fines and enforcement activity in the national enforcement service;
- improved electronic management of documents and case files".[214]

Litigants, lawyers and researchers will, no doubt, monitor progress closely.

---

[211] PD 7e and *http://www.hmcourts-service.gov.uk/onlineservices/mcol/index.htm*. A parallel Possession Claim Online to deal with rent and mortgage arrears is in its early stages: HM Courts Service, *Working for You: Annual Report and Accounts 2005/6*, p.29 and can be found at *http://www.hmcourts-service.gov.uk/onlineservices/pcol/index.htm*.

[212] PD 5b.

[213] Procedural matters dealt with on the papers, as, for example, most allocation decisions.

[214] HM Courts Service *National Business Plan 2006–2007*, p.5.

CHAPTER 13

PRE-HEARING: TRIBUNALS

In the preceding chapter we used the actions in the county court and the Queen's **13–001** Bench Division as examples of civil procedure. For this chapter there is no standard model. Generalisation about tribunal procedure is almost impossible in the face of divergent practice in different tribunals[1] and there is no accepted pattern. However, there are certain common principles and objectives in tribunal adjudication and there are common procedural problems to be solved. Furthermore, the establishment of a (largely) unified tribunal system under the Tribunals, Courts and Enforcement Act 2007 is to be accompanied by the establishment of Tribunal Procedural Rules.[2] This chapter sets out to examine these objectives and the way in which they influence procedure prior to a tribunal hearing; the common problems which procedural rules must attempt to solve; the amount of legal advice or help which is available; and finally, the pre-hearing procedure adopted in two particular tribunals as illustrative of the various solutions designed to meet the needs of individual claimants and individual tribunals.

A. THE COMMON OBJECTIVES

The starting point of any discussion must be the Franks Report[3] and its assertion **13–002** that tribunals should display three common characteristics: openness, fairness and impartiality.[4] It is clear that the attainment of each of these objectives will have implications for the procedural rules adopted.

---

[1] The various types of tribunal and their jurisdiction are discussed above, paras 2–007—2–017, 2–019.
[2] Made under Sch.5.
[3] Report of the Committee on Administrative Tribunals and Enquiries (Cmnd. 218, 1957).
[4] *ibid.* In particular, paras 23–25, 41–42. The characteristic of impartiality is reinforced by the requirements of Art.6(1), ECHR (above, para.8–021).

In requiring that tribunals should be open, the Committee intended that the proceedings should be given sufficient publicity so that they were known to those who might need to make use of them. In addition, it was stated that the essential reasoning underlying decisions should be made known to the parties.[5] Openness means more than the adoption of a rule of procedure that, save where the personal interests of the claimant (or some public interest such as national security) would be prejudiced, tribunal hearings should be conducted in public. It signifies rather a notion of availability or accessibility—that tribunal adjudication is open to all those who might have a problem lying within the jurisdiction of a particular tribunal. In order that a tribunal is *accessible* to the public, each citizen needs to be aware of his or her right to use the tribunal where appropriate[6]; the information given in official publications and forms must be comprehensible; tribunal hearings need to be conveniently located; advice and assistance needs to be available either through the Community Legal Service or through other agencies; and the procedure to be followed both prior to and during the hearing should be sufficiently clear that the claimant can follow it and understand the implications of seeking a tribunal hearing. Establishing the right procedural rules is but one aspect of making tribunals accessible to the public.

The objectives of fairness and impartiality are closely linked, and are especially important to a system which does not have the weight and authority enjoyed by the courts in the public esteem. Naturally, the claimant must be assured that the adjudication is even-handed or he or she will dismiss the whole process as unfair, but the procedure to be followed is also crucial. Procedural fairness—the feeling induced in the claimant that he or she has had "a fair crack of the whip"—is absolutely essential and according to the Franks Committee depends upon, " . . . the adoption of a clear procedure which enables parties to know their rights to present their case fully and to know the case which they have to meet".[7]

As well as displaying these three characteristics, tribunals are also expected to offer informal, cheap and quick adjudication, providing a contrast to the procedures of the High Court.[8] The problem lies in achieving an acceptable standard of decision making based on adequate information and argument, without rendering tribunals as formal, expensive and slow as the civil courts. In practice, the reforms to civil procedure on the one hand, particularly in so far as they affect the handling of smaller claims, the introduction of unified Tribunal Procedure rules on the other, and the growing emphasis on ADR in both is leading to the blurring of the distinction between the two.[9] Increasingly, the procedures of both courts and many tribunals are subject formally to the "overriding objective" that cases be dealt with "justly", with some variations in formulation.[10]

---

[5] *ibid.* para.98.
[6] This goes back to the question of ensuring that problems are recognised and identified accurately; see Ch.9.
[7] Franks Report (1957), para.42.
[8] For a comparison between courts and tribunals, see R. E. Wraith and P. G. Hutchesson, *Administrative Tribunals* (1973), Ch.10. *Cf.* above, para.2–015.
[9] See paras 11–033—11–040, Ch.12 and para.13–009.
[10] See e.g. para.13–008 (Employment Tribunals); Asylum and Immigration Tribunal (Procedure) Rules 2005 (SI 2005/230), r.4; Residential Property Tribunal Procedure Regulations 2006 (SI 2006/831), reg.4.

Before a tribunal case reaches a hearing it must be prepared for adjudication and the parties must be in a position to participate fully at the hearing. There are, broadly, three stages in pre-hearing procedure which might be termed, "knowing your rights", "knowing the ropes", and "knowing the case". There is now considerable research evidence on the factors that may motivate or deter members of the public from seeking redress for tribunal relevant grievances.[11] Key factors reported by focus group respondents as most likely to inhibit taking action were lack of knowledge about avenues of redress, and the consequent assumption that there was no legal remedy or that it would be necessary to go to court; and concerns about accessing the legal system (the perception that it would be costly, time-consuming and complicated; for some, that there would be significant cultural and communication barriers; for some, that skin tone, social class or educational ability might affect chances of succeeding). Such factors could, however, be overcome where some of a number of factors were present: a strong sense of principle; a feeling that the issue at stake was critical to resolve; knowledge of how to resolve the grievance; and fulsome and extensive advice and support provided by an advice agency or legal representative. Accordingly, key factors in determining use of tribunals were: "seriousness of the grievance or the principles involved"; "perceptions of personal entitlement to dispute a grievance"; "confidence and familiarity with the process and legal system as a whole"; and "access to fulsome and extensive advice".[12] The position as regards access to pre-hearing advice is clearly a crucial factor.

B. "KNOWING YOUR RIGHTS"—IDENTIFYING THE TRIBUNAL

Courts do not have to advertise. There is a general awareness that civil courts are **13–003** the venue for settling disputes (although there may be some difficulty for individuals in perceiving that they have a problem capable of legal settlement), and as to criminal courts, defendants have little choice about whether they wish to avail themselves of the court's jurisdiction. In respect of tribunals, the first difficulty for the parties may lie in realising that there is a body with jurisdiction over their grievance whose assistance might be invoked. The various tribunals need to be sufficiently well publicised so as to alert people to their existence and powers.

In general, individuals may take their case to a tribunal as a result of a decision of a Government department which affects them (a citizen/state dispute), or as a result of experiencing an event or series of events which the law places within the jurisdiction of a particular tribunal (normally a citizen/citizen dispute). Into the former category would fall appeals to the Social Security and Child Support

---

[11] See H. Genn, B. Lever and L. Gray, *Tribunals for Diverse Users* (DCA Research Series 1/06, January 2006), Ch.3.

[12] *ibid.* pp.113–116. Only the last two of the key factors were related to ethnicity, the relationship being more to do with cultural familiarity and language barriers than experience or fear of discrimination.

Appeal Tribunals[13]; the General Commissioners of Income Tax[14]; the Asylum and Immigration Tribunal[15]; and many others. Into the latter category would fall applications to an Employment Tribunal[16] or to a Rent Assessment Committee.[17] This division is significant because in citizen/state dispute the individual concerned may be notified of the existence of the tribunal and of the right of appeal at the time that the decision is notified. Thus, the claimant should know of the right of appeal and how to make an application. He or she may not know what are the implications of an appeal or precisely how to go about preparing the case, but he or she is given a start.[18]

In respect of citizen/citizen disputes it is for the applicant to realise that, if he or she is unfairly dismissed or the rent is too high, that there is an opportunity to pursue the grievance in a tribunal. Some tribunals must, therefore, give special consideration to how they can make the public aware of their jurisdiction.

In a survey of published research,[19] Adler and Gulland note that there are two types of ignorance which can prevent an appellant from making an appeal: of the fact that there may be grounds for appealing and of the procedures which need to be followed. The general conclusion, supported by much of the research evidence, is that the former is often more important, although some potential appellants may not realise they have a right of appeal at all.[20] For example, as regards the (former) Appeals Service tribunals, most users received information about the right to appeal, although most appellants did not really understand the appeals process.[21]

1. The Availability of Legal Advice

13–004   With very limited exceptions, legal aid and now funding for legal representation under the Legal Services Commission Funding Code has not been available for *representation* at tribunal hearings.[22] The green form legal advice scheme was

[13] Where the original decision is made by an officer of the Benefits Agency, see above, para.2–038.

[14] Against an income tax assessment, the tribunal being arranged in accordance with the Taxes Management Act 1970.

[15] Against an immigration decision or in certain circumstances the rejection of an asylum claim by the Home Office (e.g. refusal of leave to enter the UK, a deportation order), under the Nationality, Immigration and Asylum Act 2002, ss.82, 83, as amended.

[16] See above, paras 2–031, 2–032.

[17] See para.13–008.

[18] The effectiveness of which should not be overstated: A study of three tribunals showed that only 53% of Appeals Service tribunal users interviewed obtained information about appeal from this source; the figures for SENDIST and CICAP were 45% and 33%. It was nevertheless the commonest source. The next commonest was an adviser: Genn, Lever and Gray, *Tribunals for Diverse Users* (2006), pp. 124–125.

[19] M. Adler and J. Gulland, *Tribunal Users' Experiences, Perceptions and Expectations: A Literature Review* (Council on Tribunals, November 2003).

[20] *ibid.* p.3.

[21] *ibid.* pp.3, 4.

[22] Legal representation is available for cases in the Employment Appeal Tribunal, Mental Health Review Tribunals, the Proscribed Organisations Appeal Commission, the Asylum and Immigration Tribunal, and some cases before Care Standards Tribunals or concerning penalties classed as criminal in ECHR terms before the VAT and Duties Tribunal and the General and Special Commissioners of Income Tax; this is subject to financial and merits criteria (except that representation at a MHRT is available regardless of financial resources but subject to a reasonableness test). See further below, para.16–015.

intended to provide a source of advice for the public on matters relating to tribunals and how to use them.[23] It was, however, a source of regret to the Lord Chancellor's Advisory Committee on Legal Aid that the scheme was not used more extensively for that purpose.[24]

It was difficult to quantify precisely the number of tribunal cases dealt with by solicitors under the green form scheme. The study by Genn and Genn of representation at tribunals found that solicitors were consulted by 4 per cent of appellants before Social Security Appeal Tribunals, 27 per cent of appellants to Immigration Adjudicators, 36 per cent of applicants to Industrial Tribunals and over 60 per cent of patients applying to Mental Health Review Tribunals.[25] It was Social Security Appeal Tribunals that had by far the highest case load, and the contribution of solicitors here under the green form scheme or otherwise was clearly very limited.

The replacement of the legal aid and advice schemes by the Community Legal Service established by the Access to Justice Act 1999 was in part driven by a policy that increased emphasis in public funding should be given to social welfare law.[26] As at March 31, 2006, Controlled Work contracts had been issued to solicitors' offices and not for profit organisations in a number of categories potentially relevant to tribunal work.[27] Among the high priority areas for funding were social welfare issues, such as housing, debt, employment rights and benefit advice. As regards Controlled Work[28] the three largest numbers of completed matters reported for 2005–06 were immigration, housing and welfare benefits.[29] It is difficult to assess how far these arrangements meet needs, although the information available has been improving.[30]

2. Other Sources of Advice

The agencies discussed in Ch.10 (CABx,[31] independent advice centres, law **13–005** centres, trade unions, etc.) are available to offer help to individuals, but their work has been supplemented by the growth of specialist groups. Some of these are attached to large, generalist agencies, some exist independently.[32] Many

---

[23] In 1969, the Law Society asserted that the introduction of a legal advice scheme would encourage solicitors to operate in areas of unmet legal need and ensure that adequate legal services would be provided.

[24] See, e.g. *26th Legal Aid Annual Reports* [1975–76], p.58.

[25] H. Genn and Y. Genn, *The Effectiveness of Representation at Tribunals* (LCD, 1989), pp.15, 30, 39, 56. See further on this study, below, paras 13–006, 16–013, 14.

[26] See *Annual Report of the Legal Services Commission, 2005–06*, Statistical Information, p.3.

[27] Mental health 283, Employment 216, Housing 587, Welfare benefits 459, and Immigration 367: *ibid.*

[28] i.e. Work covering legal advice and assistance (Legal Help), Help at Court, and Legal Representation in front of MHRTs and the AIT.

[29] 121,032, 104,605 and 94,368, respectively out of a total of 786,522; the figures for mental health and employment were respectively 34,111 and 20,966. The corresponding figures for licensed work (Legal Representation other than work covered by Controlled Work or Very High Cost Cases) final bills paid were 2,232; 13,872 (which would include a large number of cases in the county court); 76; 166; 122: *ibid.* p.6.

[30] See P. Pleasance, *Causes of Action: Civil Law and Social Justice* (2nd edn, 2006), Legal Services Research Centre Research Paper No.14, reporting on periodic English and Welsh Civil and Social Justice Surveys. See paras 9–004, 9–010, 9–012.

[31] On the role of CABx in tribunal representation, see para.16–012.

[32] A survey of some of these specialist groups is contained in R. Lawrence, *Tribunal Representation, The Role of Advice and Advocacy Services* (1980).

sources of advice and information are now available on the Internet. This includes Community Legal Service Direct,[33] funded by the CLS, which aims to provide "free high-quality legal information to help you deal with your legal problems". This comprises leaflets and factsheets, a facility to search for a "high-quality local legal adviser or solicitor"; links to the "best advice websites in the UK"; and access to the CLS Direct Legal Calculator to see if the inquirer is eligible for legal aid. If a person qualifies for legal aid, it is possible to call a national helpline for free advice about benefits, tax credits, housing, employment, education or debt problems.

The Free Representation Unit[34] is an independent group, now based at 289–293 High Holborn, London, which offers an advocacy service in cases referred to it by advice agencies. In fact, this Unit may not be involved at the pre-hearing stage and may rely heavily on the referring agency for the initial advice to the claimant and preparation of the case. The Unit employs a director, two administrators, and two salaried case workers, one for social security cases and one for employment cases. The funding comes from the Bar Council, the Inns of Court, particular chambers and solicitors' firms, individual barristers, referral agencies, who pay a small annual income, and training days. These support 100 or so volunteer representatives, many of whom are Bar students or pupil barristers.[35] They represent in 65–70 per cent of the 1,400 cases referred to them each year.

Other independent groups[36] have based themselves in advice centres, offering a service to clients of that centre and those referred by other statutory or voluntary agencies. Finally, there is a growing number of welfare rights and advice units provided by local authority social service departments offering advice and advocacy services[37] and advice centres attached to University Students' Unions.[38]

The advice available is, therefore, dependent partly upon local initiatives and there has been no systematic national coverage. Some steps to address the variability of coverage are now being taken by the CLS with the establishment in deprived areas of new Community Legal Advice Centres, designed to bring together civil legal aid, funded by the LSC, and social welfare advice services provided by local authorities. Initially, the centres are likely to cover debt, housing, welfare benefits, employment, community care and family issues.[39]

---

[33] See *www.clsdirect.org.uk/index.jsp*.

[34] *www.freerepresentationunit.org.uk*; Westgate, *Counsel*, Vol.2, No.1, Michaelmas/Autumn 1986, p.12; H. Brooke Q.C. and T. Leaver, *ibid.* p.13; General Council of the Bar, *Quality of Justice: The Bar's Response* (1989), pp.72–76 (indicating the Bar Council's wish for FRU services to be expanded); N. Lieven, *Counsel.* February 1991, p.22; D. Conn, *Legal Action*, December 1993, p.9; M. Pennycook, *Counsel*, March/April 1994, pp.23–24. FRU work has also been developed in Birmingham.

[35] A Bar Pro Bono Unit, was established in 1996: *www.barprobono.tribalforge.net*; and a Solicitors Pro Bono Group, now LawWorks, was formed in 1997 to support, promote and encourage pro bono work across the solicitors' profession (*http://lawworks.org.uk*).

[36] These have included the Birmingham Tribunal Representation Unit; Walsall Advice and Representation Project; South Wales Anti-Poverty Action Centre; the London Advice Services Alliance representation service (LASA). It seems that only LASA is currently in existence.

[37] See e.g. Harlow Welfare Rights and Advice, the Nottinghamshire Welfare Rights Service, Manchester Advice's Welfare Rights Service.

[38] e.g. Advice and Representation Centres at Birmingham and Brunel.

[39] Community Legal Service Newsletter, *directions* 02, June 2006. Centres are to be established, after a tendering process. The first are in Leicester, Gateshead and Derby. See further the DCA Report, *Getting Earlier, Better Advice to Vulnerable People* (2006); *CLS Strategy 2006–2011, Making Legal Rights a Reality* (CLS, 2006), pp.8–10.

There are also to be Community Legal Advice Networks of existing CLS supported organisations. The joining-up of separate services is obviously a step forward; the success of the strategy will be monitored.

3. SEEKING ADVICE

A study of tribunal representation conducted for the Lord Chancellor's Depart- **13–006** ment[40] looked at the proportion of appellants before four tribunals (Social Security Appeal Tribunals, Immigration Adjudicators, Industrial Tribunals and Mental Health Review Tribunals) who sought advice before the hearing. From information drawn from case files,[41] it appeared that only 22 per cent[42] of SSAT appellants sought advice before the hearing.[43] The corresponding figures for the other three were much higher: 80 per cent for Immigration Adjudicators,[44] 70 per cent for Industrial Tribunals,[45] and 64 per cent for MHRTs,[46] again with regional and other variations. The study suggested that failure to seek advice (or representation) often stemmed from ignorance about the nature of appeals (ranging from over-confidence to bewilderment). In other cases, appellants who recognised a need for advice either did not know where to go or could not obtain or pay for representation.[47] A more recent study in respect of Appeals Service tribunals, Criminal Injuries Compensation Appeals Panels, and Special Educational Needs and Disability Tribunals (SENDIST), found respectively that 63 per cent, 65 per cent and 88 per cent of users attending hearings had had pre-hearing advice or help with their appeal. There was no significant difference between White and Minority Ethnic users in the extent to which such advice had been obtained. The percentages advised by solicitors were respectively 11 per cent, 70 per cent and 63 per cent.[48]

C. "KNOWING THE ROPES"—MAKING APPLICATION TO A TRIBUNAL

Rules of procedure begin to take effect when an applicant decides to invoke the **13–007** jurisdiction of the tribunal by making an application for a hearing. Prior to that he or she may have tried to effect a settlement of the grievance in the same way

---

[40] H. Genn and Y. Genn, *The Effectiveness of Representation at Tribunals* (LCD, 1989), discussed by R. Young, (1990) 8 C.J.Q. 16 and T. Mullen, (1990) 53 M.L.R. 230.

[41] Likely to understate the position.

[42] Of these, 31% went to a CAB, 16% to a solicitor, and the rest went to a wide variety of sources including trade unions, tribunal units, law centres, welfare rights centres, social workers, general advice centres, unemployment centres, pressure groups and church groups.

[43] Genn and Genn (1989), pp.13–15. There were considerable variations according to region and type of case: *ibid.* pp.15–18.

[44] *ibid.* pp.29–32; the main sources were UKIAS and solicitors.

[45] *ibid.* pp.38–43; the main sources were solicitors and trade unions (appellants), outside or in-house lawyers (respondents).

[46] *ibid.* pp.56–57; dominated by solicitors.

[47] *ibid.* pp.59–62, 221–222.

[48] H. Genn, B. Laver and L. Gray, *Tribunals for Diverse Users* (DCA Research Series 1/06, January 2006), pp.126–127. A wide variety of sources of advice were identified: see Table 4.2 on p.129.

as would have been done in a civil matter, but because a significant proportion of tribunal matters concern the correctness of a decision made by a government department or agency the scope for settlement may be fairly limited.[49] However, it is increasingly common for there to be express provision for seeking review of a decision by the decision maker.[50] In other cases, particularly where an application to an Employment Tribunal may be in prospect, there are pre-hearing procedures expressly designed to secure a mutually acceptable resolution of the problem.[51]

In relation to the making of an application there are three procedural aspects to be considered. What form should the application take? What information should it contain? Within what time limit, if any, should it be made? These are questions which have been considered and answered in the civil courts, and they are obviously questions which are common to all tribunals. It would be tempting to assume that a Code of Procedure could be devised to encompass all tribunals and make specific provision for these and other points. The Franks Committee[52] moved towards this position with a recommendation that a Council on Tribunals should formulate the procedural rules for each tribunal, based on principles common to all tribunals but tailored to suit the needs of the particular tribunal.[53] In the event, the Tribunals and Inquiries Act 1958 merely provided that the Council on Tribunals (established by the Act) should be consulted when procedural rules were made in respect of certain specified tribunals.[54] This matter is to be revisited by the development of Tribunal Procedure Rules under the Tribunals, Courts and Enforcement Act 2007.[55]

What form should an application to a tribunal take? Many tribunals[56] encourage or require the completion of a printed form, a method of application which can either assist or hinder the applicant. He or she may be deterred from pursuing the case by the complexity or unintelligibility of the questions, but will at least be shown the information required and sometimes directed towards a source of help and advice.[57] Again, the nature of the dispute may have an effect on procedure in that in citizen/state disputes the jurisdiction is likely to be automatic

---

[49] This is dependent upon the procedures of the Department concerned. In social security matters an application to a tribunal ensures an initial review of the decision by an officer, and there is some evidence to suggest that the intervention of an advice agency can get "mistakes" straightened out without recourse to a tribunal: Genn and Genn (1989), pp.136–137; J. Baldwin, N. Wikeley and R. Young, *Judging Social Security* (1992), Ch.3.

[50] See e.g. the Social Security and Child Support (Decisions and Appeals) Regulations 1999 (SI 1999/991), Pt II, Ch.I (revisions) and Ch.II (supersessions); M. Harris, "The place of formal and informal review in the administrative justice system" in M. Harris and M. Partington (eds), *Administrative Justice in the 21st Century* (1999), Ch.2, criticising a move from formal review to informal revision arrangements.

[51] In the Employment Tribunal procedure, emphasis is placed upon conciliation and the mediating role of the Advisory Conciliation and Arbitration Service, although this usually occurs after the application has been made.

[52] Report of the Committee on Administrative Tribunals and Enquiries (Cmnd. 218, 1957).

[53] *ibid.* paras 63–64.

[54] Now Tribunals and Inquiries Act 1992, s.8. Procedural rules are normally contained in a statutory instrument made by the Minister whose Department is responsible for the particular tribunal. The Council has published Model Rules of Procedure (Cm. 1434, 1991) for the guidance of those who draft such rules.

[55] See para.13–009.

[56] For example, the use of Forms ET1 and ET3 for Employment Tribunals (below para.13–008) is (from October 1, 2005) mandatory.

[57] e.g. the Employment Tribunal claims form states that a Trade Union or Citizens Advice may be able to help. Department of Work and Pensions leaflets include similar advice.

and the applicant will not have to show the grounds which bring the matters within the tribunal's jurisdiction. In citizen/citizen disputes the applicant's first job will be to establish that the case falls within the tribunal's jurisdiction and a printed form with appropriate questions will be helpful both to tribunal and applicant.

In many cases the applicant has the opportunity of including matters for the consideration of the tribunal in the application, or in a subsequent statement. Ultimately, he or she may make representations at the hearing (if one is held)[58] and it is likely to be the style and conduct of the hearing which determines how much advance information is required by the tribunal.

It has inevitably been found necessary to impose time limits within which a tribunal application must be submitted, and some have limits on later stages of the procedure.[59] The balance has to be struck between allowing a tribunal to make a speedy determination in a dispute (based on evidence which is not too far distant in time) and ensuring that an applicant is not unduly prejudiced by the limit. The Council on Tribunals has taken a particular interest in this matter and has welcomed the extension of time limits in some tribunals.[60] In addition, it is desirable that there should be a procedural rule allowing for applications to be made out of time where there is good cause.[61]

D. "KNOWING THE CASE"—THE PRE-HEARING EXCHANGE OF INFORMATION

" . . . citizens should know in good time the case which they will have to **13–008** meet, whether the issue to be heard by the tribunal is one between citizen and administration or citizen and citizen. . . . We do not suggest that the procedure should be formalised to the extent of requiring documents in the nature of legal pleadings. What is needed is that the citizen should receive in good time beforehand a document setting out the main points of the opposing case. It should not be necessary . . . to require the parties to adhere

---

[58] Not all tribunals will hold an oral hearing.

[59] An application to a Social Security and Child Support Appeal Tribunal must be made within one month of the date of notification of the decision against which the appeal is brought or, where a written statement of reasons is requested, within 14 days of the expiry of that period or, if provided outside one month, within 14 days of the date on which the statement is provided: SI 1999/991, reg.31, as amended; an application to an Employment Tribunal in respect of unfair dismissal within three months of dismissal; Employment Rights Act 1996, s.111(2). There are no time limits on the hearings and the Council on Tribunals has regularly expressed disquiet at the long backlog of cases awaiting hearing by various tribunals.

[60] Annual Report of the Council on Tribunals, 1980–81, at p.23.

[61] e.g. for SSCSATs, time can be extended for up to a year where it was not practicable because of special circumstances (such as serious illness) for an application to be made within the time limit: SI 1999/991, reg.32, as amended; for Employment Tribunals, the claim can be presented "within such further period as the tribunal considers reasonable in a case where it is satisfied that it was not reasonably practicable for the complaint to be presented before the end of that period of three months": Employment Rights Act 1996, s.111(2). See, e.g. *Palmer v Southend-on-Sea Borough Council* [1984] I.C.R. 372 (question what is reasonably practicable essentially one of fact for the tribunal); *Machine Tool Industry Research Association v Simpson* [1988] I.C.R. 558 (not reasonably practicable to bring complaint until employee has knowledge of fundamental fact that made the dismissal unfair); *Marks & Spencer plc v Williams-Ryan* [2005] I.C.R. 1293.

rigidly at the hearing to the case as previously set out, provided always that the interests of another party are not prejudiced by such flexibility."[62]

The amount of pre-hearing activity and the precision with which the parties are required to formulate and disclose their respective cases can vary from tribunal to tribunal. Before 1984, the applicant was given the greatest latitude in Social Security Appeal Tribunals. He or she was not required to produce any specific grounds of appeal or indicate what his or her argument might be. This was then changed, and an appeal to a Social Security and Child Support Appeal Tribunal now must "contain particulars of the grounds on which it is made".[63] It is not clear how much detail is necessary.[64] The applicant will receive from the relevant Agency a full statement of facts, submissions, statutory authorities and Commissioner's decisions. This document ("the appeal submission") will also be sent to members of the tribunal and is likely to form the basis of the hearing. There is a power for the tribunal chairman to require the applicant to furnish such further particulars as may reasonably be required.[65]

The parties before a Rent Assessment Committee are more likely to have had a full opportunity of finding out about the case.[66] Where the issue concerns the determination of a fair rent for a protected tenancy, before the matter can come before a Rent Assessment Committee, application must be made to a rent officer. This application can be made by either landlord or tenant or both jointly, but if the application is not joint, the other party is invited to take part in consultations with the rent officer and the applicant to consider what rent should be registered.[67] Only if one party is dissatisfied with the rent which is registered can he or she appeal to the Rent Assessment Committee, who then invite both parties to make written or oral representations. By the time of the hearing, both parties will have had the opportunity to familiarise themselves with all the circumstances and the representations made by each of them. Subject to a few exceptions, no new protected tenancies can be granted after the commencement of the Housing Act 1988. The Rent Assessment Committee does, however, have jurisdiction under Pt I of the Act to fix the rent of an assured tenancy or assured shorthold tenancy where the landlord proposes a rent increase.[68] Here, the tenant applies directly to the committee, and the committee then serves a notice on both parties specifying a period of not less than seven days during which either written representations or a request to make oral representations may be made by that party to the

---

[62] Report of the Committee on Administrative Tribunals and Enquiries (Cmnd. 218, 1957), at pp.17–18.

[63] Social Security and Child Support (Decisions and Appeals) Regulations 1999 (SI 1999/991), reg.33(1). It must also include sufficient particulars to enable the decision appealed against to be identified: *ibid.*

[64] Where the Secretary of State is satisfied that the form, although not completed in accordance with the instructions, includes sufficient information to enable the appeal or application to proceed, he may treat the form as satisfying these requirements: reg.33(4); similarly if a letter is sent rather than the approved form: reg.33(5). If it does not the Secretary of State may request further information in writing; if this is not forthcoming, the form or letter is placed before a legally qualified panel member: reg.33(8).

[65] 1999 Regulations, reg.38(2).

[66] See generally R. E. Megarry, *The Rent Acts* (1988), Vol.1, Chs 24 and 25, Vol.3, Chs 16 and 17; J. E. Martin, *Residential Security* (2nd edn, 1995), Chs 10 and 14.

[67] Rent Act 1977, Sch.11, para.3, as amended.

[68] Housing Act 1988, s.13(4)(a), 14. There are certain other matters also within its jurisdiction under Pt I.

committee. The committee may make such inquiry (if any) as it thinks fit.[69] The tenant must complete an application form providing factual details about the premises,[70] but there is no requirement for the tenant to indicate why he or she objects to the proposed rent increase. Accordingly, the parties here may be less well-informed by the time of the hearing than in cases where the committee's function is that of reviewing the decision of a rent officer.

A third approach is adopted in the Employment Tribunal.[71] Employment Tribunal proceedings are now subject to the "overriding objective". The overriding objective of the relevant regulations[72] and procedural rules[73] is to enable tribunals and chairmen to deal with cases justly. This includes, so far as is practicable: (a) ensuring that the parties are on an equal footing; (b) dealing with the cases in ways which are proportionate to the complexity or importance of the issues; (c) ensuring that it is dealt with expeditiously and fairly; and (d) saving expense. A tribunal or chairman must seek to give effect to this when exercising power under or interpreting the regulations or rules, and the parties must assist them to further the overriding objective.[74] A claim must be brought by the claimant presenting the "details of the claim" in writing, using the form prescribed by the Secretary of State (the ET1 form) and giving the "required information". The Secretary of State must not accept the claim if the form is not used or all or part of the claim if all the relevant required information is not provided. Similarly, if the respondent wishes to respond to the claim it must respond within 28 days, again using the prescribed form (the ET3 form). This must state, *inter alia*, whether the respondent wishes to respond to the claim in whole or in part, and if so, "on what grounds".[75] This ensures at the outset that both sides will have some idea of the case to be met. Thereafter there are opportunities for both formal and informal exchange of information.

The tribunal has wide powers of case management. The chairman may at any time, on the application of a party or on his or her own motion, make such an order as he or she thinks fit in relation to any matter which appears to him or her to be appropriate. Examples of such orders include an order as to the manner in which proceedings are to be conducted, including any time limit; that a party provide additional information; requiring the attendance of a witness, the disclosure of a document or the provision of written answers to questions put by the tribunal or chairman; and a wide variety of other matters.[76] If a party does not comply with an order or a practice direction,[77] a chairman or tribunal may make

---

[69] Rent Assessment Committee (England and Wales) Regulations 1971 (SI 1971/1065), reg.2A, inserted by SI 1988/2200, and amended by SI 1997/3007.

[70] Prescribed by the Assured Tenancies and Agricultural Occupancies (Forms) Regulations 1997 (SI 1997/194).

[71] For procedure in Employment Tribunals generally see, I. T. Smith and G. Thomas, *Smith and Wood's Industrial Law* (8th edn, 2003), Ch.8, pp.494–530; J. McMullen *et al.*, *Employment Tribunal Procedure* (LAG, 2004); D. Sneath, *Employment Tribunals* (2005); *Employment Tribunal Practice and Procedure* (I.D.S. 2006 edition).

[72] Employment Tribunals (Constitution and Rules of Procedure) Regulations 2004 (SI 2004/1861)).

[73] The Employment Tribunals Rules of Procedure (Sch.1 to the Regulations, Schs 2 to 6 set out rules for particular classes of case).

[74] reg.3, as amended by SI 2004/2351, reg.2.

[75] Rules of Procedure, rr.1–6. In specified circumstances where there is no or no acceptable response, the chairman may issue a default judgment: r.8. Copies of the forms are available at *www.employmenttribunals.gov.uk/publications/publications.htm*.

[76] Rules of Procedure, r.10.

[77] Issued under reg.13.

a costs order, or strike out the whole or part of the claim or response and, where appropriate, order that a respondent be debarred from responding to the claim altogether.[78] In race and sex discrimination cases there is a "question-and-answer procedure", analogous to interrogatories in civil procedure.[79] Standard questionnaires are available for the purposes of this procedure.[80]

A new procedure was introduced in 1980 which had the effect of disclosing information to the parties. The "pre-hearing assessment" was an attempt to reduce the number of cases going to a hearing by bringing the parties together, without witnesses, to undergo a review of the application. This operated to expose the case to both sides and although there was no power to strike out an unworthy case there was a possible penalty on costs at the hearing if the tribunal indicated, at the pre-hearing assessment, that there was no reasonable prospect of a successful application or defence.[81] These procedures owed more to the High Court and county court than to other tribunals, but overall did not prove to be a success.[82] They were replaced by "pre-hearing reviews" which include a power for the tribunal conducting the review to require a party to pay a deposit of £150 (now an amount not exceeding £500) if he or she wishes to continue the proceedings, in respect of contentions that have little (previously "no") reasonable prospect of success.[83] This last step was opposed by the Council on Tribunals, without success.[84] Amongst the orders that may be made (only a a pre-hearing review or a hearing if one of the parties has so requested) as an order striking out or amending all or part of a claim or response on the grounds that it is scandalous, or vexatious, or has no reasonable prospect of success; striking out any claim or response on the ground that the manner in which the proceedings have been conducted has been scandalous, unreasonable or vexatious; or striking out a claim which has not been actively pursued, or where it is no longer possible to have a fair hearing.[85]

Informally, there may be an exchange of information because of the involvement of conciliation officers. All applications and subsequent documents are sent to ACAS[86] and a conciliation officer is under an obligation to attempt a conciliation either at the request of one of the parties, or of his or her own volition.[87] This conciliation may be rejected by the parties but it is likely to lead to some informal exchange of information unless the conciliation officer never even gets his foot in the door.

These examples of pre-hearing procedure, necessarily selective, are intended to illustrate three different approaches to the objective set out by the Franks

[78] r.13.

[79] Sex Discrimination Act 1975, s.74, as amended; Race Relations Act 1976, s.65, as amended.

[80] Sex Discrimination (Questions and Replies) Order 1975 (SI 1975/2048); Race Relations (Questions and Replies) Order 1977 (SI 1977/842).

[81] Rules of Procedure, r.6.

[82] See Smith and Wood, (2003), p.521. There was a decline in their use; they could make conciliation more difficult.

[83] Employment Act 1989, s.20, giving the Secretary of State power to make regulations for pre-hearing reviews; see now Rules of Procedure, r.20.

[84] Annual Report of the Council on Tribunals for 1987–88 (1988–89 H.C. 102), pp.36–38; Annual Report for 1988–89 (1988–90 H.C. 114), pp.33–34.

[85] Rules of Procedure, r.18.

[86] The Advisory Conciliation and Arbitration Service.

[87] Employment Tribunals Act 1996, ss.18, 19, as amended. See Smith and Wood (2003), pp.529–530. L. Dickens et al., Dismissed (1985), Ch.6. In 2005–06, 71% of applications notified to conciliation officers were settled or withdrawn without a hearing: ACAS Annual Report 2005–06.

Committee. Full obligatory disclosure by one side; opportunity to disclose by both sides, but no obligation and no penalty for non-disclosure; limited obligatory disclosure by both sides, with opportunities for further disclosure supported by sanctions.

E. TRIBUNAL PROCEDURE RULES

Schedule 5 to the Tribunals, Courts and Enforcement Act 2007[88] makes provision about the content of the Tribunal Procedure Rules, which are to be made by the Tribunal Procedure Committee.[89] Among matters in respect of which provisions may be made are time limits; repeat applications; a tribunal acting of its own initiative; hearings (including dealing with matters without a hearing); proceedings without notice; representation ("additional rights of audience"); evidence, witnesses and attendance; the use of information; costs and expenses; set-off and interest; arbitration, the correction of errors and the setting-aside of decisions on procedural grounds.[90]   **13–009**

[88] In force from a day to be appointed.
[89] See Pt 2 of Sch.5 as to its composition, and Pt 3 as it the process by which the rules are to be made.
[90] Sch.5, Pt 1.

CHAPTER 14

PRE-TRIAL CRIMINAL PROCEDURE

14–001 In this chapter we consider the stages in the process before the trial for those suspected of having committed criminal offences.[1]

One must recognise from the outset that there is a wide variation of bodies within the criminal justice system that are seeking to satisfy their own differing objectives. Auld L.J. observed that there is no true criminal justice "'system' worthy of the name, only a criminal justice process to which a number of different government departments and agencies and others make separate and sometimes conflicting contributions".[2] The players within the criminal process have their own priorities.

Nevertheless, it is worth outlining the government's overarching aims for the criminal process as these have represented an attempt from the centre to ensure a more coordinated approach to criminal justice matters.[3] The aims also provide some insight into the motives for the changes that have been made in recent years as well as the future reform agenda. The stated aims are: reducing "crime and the fear of crime and their social and economic costs" and dispensing "justice fairly and efficiently and to promote confidence in the law".[4] These general aims have been given further detail in a series of more specific objectives, and these include: reducing the level of actual crime and disorder; reducing the adverse impact of crime and disorder on people's lives; reducing the economic costs of crime; ensuring that there is a just and effective outcome to criminal investigations; dealing with cases with appropriate speed; meeting the needs of victims, witnesses, jurors; respecting the rights of defendants and to treat them fairly; and

---

[1] For detailed consideration of the increasingly complex procedures, see J. Sprack, *Criminal Procedure* (11th edn, 2006); *Archbold* (2007); *Blackstone's Criminal Practice* (2007).

[2] Chapter 8, para.1, and see A. Ashworth and M. Redmayne, *The Criminal Process* (3rd edn, 2005), pp.16–18.

[3] See for example, Home Office, *Justice For All*, (2002) Cm. 5563, para.0.26, "We must bring the component parts of the CJS together to form a coherent whole." See also, Home Office, *Delivering Simple, Speedy, Summary Justice* (2006) which is designed to foster cooperation between the different agencies involved in the trial in order to speed up the process.

[4] See *Criminal Justice System: Strategic Plan 1999–2002*, para.1.3.

promoting confidence in the criminal justice system. In its second strategic plan the government has outlined further objectives:

> "the public will have confidence that the criminal justice system is effective and that it serves all communities fairly; victims and witnesses will receive a consistent high standard of service from all criminal justice agencies; we will bring more offences to justice through a more modern and efficient justice process; rigorous enforcement will revolutionise compliance with sentences and orders of the court; criminal justice will be a joined up, modern and well run service, and an excellent place to work for people from all backgrounds."[5]

The objectives are broadly based but in seeking to fulfil them the government has ensured that the criminal process remains the focus for constant reform.

In addition to constant reform and amendment, the rules of the pre-trial criminal process are also frequently challenged in the courts with the resulting complexity that such volatility produces. The most obvious reason for this is the potential conflict behind the different objectives that the rules are designed to achieve: an efficient process, which maximises fairness and reliability for the suspect and protects his other rights. The tension between securing optimal efficiency and respecting fundamental rights has become particularly acute in recent years as successive governments' initiatives to combat crime have relied on changes in the rules of procedure and evidence rather than the substantive law. A further explanation for the complexity of the pre-trial procedural rules is that they are, by and large, rules made by lawyers for lawyers, and as such, there is no pressure for them to be as accessible to the layman as should the substantive law. A final reason for the degree of complexity of the rules is that many of these regulations can be altered with greater ease than for example substantive criminal law, because many of the rules derive from secondary legislation only. The result is that they are repeatedly amended without consolidation, adding to their inaccessibility and complexity.

Throughout this chapter the reader should bear in mind that pre-trial criminal procedure should not be regarded as simply a means to an end. The application of the procedures affect the manner of investigation, the rights afforded to the suspect, and, most significantly, has a considerable impact on the criminal trial itself.

> "There are few who would now propound the view that the centrepiece of the English criminal process is the trial, and that the few earlier procedures are merely designed to ensure that no one is put on trial unless there is a good case against them and that dangerous people are kept in custody before trial."[6]

The change of view described in this quotation has resulted from research into the operation of the criminal justice system, which has developed particularly

---

[5] See Office for Criminal Justice Reform, *Cutting Crime, Delivering Justice: A Strategic Plan for Criminal Justice 2004–08* (2004) Cm. 6288. See also, Home Office, *Confident Communities in a Secure Britain: The Home Office Strategic Plan 2002–08* (2004) Cm. 6287.

[6] A. Ashworth, "Criminal Justice and the Criminal Process" (1988) 28 Brit. J. Crim. 111 at 112.

strongly from the 1970s onwards.[7] In particular, attention has been paid to the various pressures that lead to pleas of guilty and the avoidance of contested trials before a jury. "It has become commonplace that early decisions in the criminal process seem strongly associated with and determinative of later decisions . . . ".[8] For example, a confession made by a suspect to the police may well be crucial, given the difficulties that will thereafter arise in challenging it or explaining it away in court. Similarly, a defendant who is remanded in custody will have to overcome a host of practical problems in the organisation of a defence that do not arise if bail is granted. Moreover, the whole system would break down were it not that a very high proportion of those who are prosecuted for an offence plead guilty. In 2005, there were guilty pleas in 66 per cent of cases in the Crown Court.[9] Accordingly the outcome of the vast majority of cases is determined by the processes considered in the present chapter, and only a minority by the trial process considered in Ch.17. In truth this reflects only a fraction of all crime that occurs. Research has indicated that in 2005–06 there was an estimated 10.9 million crimes against adults.[10] The rate of attrition is considerable. During the same period 5.6 million crimes were recorded by the police,[11] and the detection rate for crimes was 27 per cent[12] (the rate has been dropping since the 1960s when it was around 45 per cent), with 1.78 million offenders ultimately found guilty or cautioned.[13] The incredible pressures on the criminal justice system take their toll. The recognition in the 1990s that miscarriages of justice had occurred in a series of high profile cases[14] has led to a wealth of discussion of the aspects of the system that had contributed to them. Many related to the pre-trial stages, including the fabrication of evidence by the police, mistaken identification, unreliable work by forensic scientists, unreliable confessions, and non-disclosure of evidence.[15] These matters were the subject of consideration by the Royal Commission on Criminal Justice (hereafter RCCJ)[16] which was appointed in 1991. However, by the time the Commission reported in 1993 the government's

---

[7] For general surveys see especially A. Ashworth and M. Redmayne, *The Criminal Process* (3rd edn, 2005); A. Sanders and R. Young, *Criminal Justice* (3rd edn, 2007); K. Doolin, S. Uglow, D. Cheney, L. Dickson, *Criminal Justice* (2nd edn, 2002); N. Padfield, *Text and Materials on the Criminal Justice Process* (3rd edn, 2003); M. Davies, H. Croall and J. Tyrer, *Criminal Justice: An Introduction to the Criminal Justice Process in England and Wales* (3rd edn, 2005).

[8] Ashworth (1988) *op. cit.* p.113.

[9] *Criminal Statistics for England and Wales 2005* (2006), Table 2.10. In 2005, 1.78 million offenders were found guilty or cautioned. *ibid.* para.1.10.

[10] *ibid.* para.1.2.

[11] *ibid.*

[12] *ibid.* para.1.8.

[13] *ibid.* para.1.10.

[14] See C. Walker, "Chronology of *Causes Celebres*" in C. Walker and K. Starmer (eds), *Justice in Error* (1993), pp.6–13, including references to the Guildford Four, the Maguire Seven, the Birmingham Six, Judith Ward, the Tottenham Three (Silcott, Raghip and Braithwaite), Stefan Kiszko, the Darvell bothers, and the Cardiff Three (Paris, Abdullahi and Miller), and cases arising out of the activities of the West Midlands Police Serious Crimes Squad. See also J. Rozenburg, "Miscarriages of Justice" in E. Stockdale and S. Casale (eds), *Criminal Justice Under Stress* (1992) and C. Walker and K. Starmer (eds), *Miscarriages of Justice: A Review of Justice in Error* (1999). Miscarriages continue to come to light. See for example the murder conviction of Stephen Dowling overturned after 27 years. The Criminal Cases Review Commission increases the opportunity for such cases to come to light, including those from some time ago, as, e.g. in *R v Bentley* [1999] Crim. L.R. 330. See below, Ch.18, para.18–018.

[15] Walker (1993) pp.13–15. Other issues concern the conduct of the trial, the presentation of the accused in a prejudicial manner and appeal procedures (*ibid.*). See also the JUSTICE *Report on Miscarriages of Justice* (1989).

[16] (1993) Cm. 2263.

central concern appeared to have reverted from the prevention of miscarriages of justice to the control of crime; and the RCCJ's Report itself, influenced as it was by the terms of reference drafted by government, did not have the prevention of miscarriages as its central organising theme.[17] Its recommendations have been heavily criticised,[18] and they certainly "favoured the interests of the police and prosecution agencies more than those of suspects".[19] Nevertheless, its proposals were influential in government legislation such as the Criminal Procedure and Investigation Act 1996.

As criminal justice has entered a new millennium, so reform has continued to be driven by efficiency and crime control values.[20] Even taking account of the wide range of diverse influences now brought to bear on the process, Packer's classic exposition of the two competing models of criminal justice—crime control and due process—serve a useful mechanism for evaluating the process. These and other, more sophisticated models, have been developed in an attempt to explain more effectively the interrelationships of the policies and principles at stake[21] and will be considered later in the chapter (section K).

As noted, criminal procedure is constantly evolving and is the subject of relentless scrutiny and review. Readers should be aware that the specific provisions referred to in this chapter are subject to continuing change, for example through the staggered introduction of the Criminal Justice Act 2003, and the on-going review of the Police and Criminal Evidence Act Codes of Practice.[22]

The material in this chapter is divided into three broad parts. First, we consider the process of investigation of offences (section A); secondly, the process whereby a decision is taken whether a prosecution should be instituted (sections B and C); and thirdly, the pre-trial procedures in criminal cases (sections D to J). We conclude with an attempt to evaluate some of the basic features of the system (section K).

A. INVESTIGATION

1. INVESTIGATIVE AGENCIES

A number of very diverse organisations are empowered to conduct investigations **14–002** which are primarily designed to lead to (or have at least as a possible outcome) criminal prosecution. The most important, in terms of the volume and seriousness of cases dealt with, is of course the police, and therefore the discussion in this chapter will focus on their activity.

---

[17] The Commission was heavily criticised for its very limited conclusions and for its methodology—see, e.g. L. Bridges, "Normalizing Injustice: The RCCJ" (1994) 21 J. Law and Soc. 20.

[18] See, e.g. Sanders and Young (2007), pp.16–19.

[19] *ibid.* p.17.

[20] e.g. Home Office, *Rebalancing the Criminal Justice System in Favour of the Law-Abiding Majority: Cutting Crime, Reducing Reoffending and Protecting the Public* (2006).

[21] A. Bottoms and J. McLean, *Defendants in the Criminal Process* (1976).

[22] See, e.g. Home Office Consultation Paper, *Modernising Police Powers: Review of the Police and Criminal Evidence Act 1984* (2007). The Home Office website provides a *Register of Suggested Changes to the PACE Codes*, which contains a list of all proposed changes to the Codes that are under consideration, at: *http://police.homeoffice.gov.uk/news-and-publications/publication/operational-policing/Register_of_All_Changes_04_06*. See also M. Zander, "The Joint Review of PACE: a deplorable report" (2003) N.L.J. 204.

2. THE ROLE OF THE POLICE

14–003 Only a small proportion of the criminal offences committed lead ultimately to a criminal prosecution and fewer still lead to a conviction. In 2005–06 the British Crime Survey estimated that there were 10.9 million offences committed against adults (8.4 million fewer than in 1995).[23] Many of these offences are not reported to the police, and of those that are, not all are recorded. In 2005–06 there were 5.6 million crimes recorded by the police,[24] which is just over half the number of offences committed according to the British Crime Survey. Morgan and Newburn,[25] estimated that only about 7 per cent of all crime (about 20 per cent of that reported to the police) is detected and less than half of those lead to a conviction or caution.[26] In 2005–06 the picture is slightly different. Around 27 per cent of recorded crime is detected,[27] but the point remains valid that many offences will be undetected, or if detected not reported to the police, or if reported not recorded as an offence by the police.[28] This has been termed the "justice gap" by the Government who have subsequently directing some of their reforms towards closing this gap.[29]

Despite the fall in the rate of crime the public perception remains that crime is actually increasing.[30] Of the offences that do come to the attention of the police, it seems that the overwhelming majority are reported by members of the public and only a fraction discovered by the police themselves.[31] About a third of the "members of the public" quoted in these surveys are in fact organisations, store detectives or security firms.[32] These figures reflect the well-established fact that the police are not primarily employed in detecting crime, but in a vast range of other peace-keeping activities.[33]

Some indication of the pressures on police forces can be gleaned from the figures in the Home Office paper *Criminal Justice: The Way Ahead*,[34] which reveals that in an average day, the police receive 25,500 "999" calls, make 5,000 arrests, and conduct 2,200 stops and searches.

Once offences have come to the attention of the police,

---

[23] Home Office, *Crime in England and Wales 2005–6* (2006) H.O.S.B. 12/06, para.2.1.

[24] *ibid.* para.2.2. For more detail about police measures of crime see para.4.2.

[25] R. Morgan and T. Newburn, *The Future of Policing* (1997).

[26] *ibid.* p.37.

[27] *Crime in England and Wales 2005–6* (2006) para.8.1.

[28] Comparing figures of recorded crime and detected crime can be problematic. See, *ibid*, para.8.2. It has been suggested that the average police officer clears up less than one crime per month: Home Office, *Crime in England and Wales 2004–5* (2005) H.O.S.B. 11/05 p.115, quoted in Sanders and Young (2007), p.54.

[29] Home Office, *Narrowing the Justice Gap* (2002).

[30] *Crime in England and Wales 2005–6* (2006) para.3.1.

[31] See Ashworth and Redmayne (2005), p.140 and for earlier statistics see A. Ashworth, *The English Criminal Process: a Review of Research* (1984), p.12, based, *inter alia*, on D. Steer, *Uncovering Crime* (RCCP Research Study No.7, HMSO, 1980); A. K. Bottomley and C. Coleman, *Understanding Crime Rates* (1981); J. Burrows, "How Crimes Come to Police Notice" (Home Office Research Bulletin No.13, 1982), pp.12–15. A 1992 survey found that only 5% of recorded crimes come to notice as a result of police patrols or observations: M. Maguire and C. Norris, *The Conduct and Supervision of Criminal Investigations* (RCCJ Research Study No.5, 1992), p.8 above, n.5. See also J. Shapland and J. Vagg, *Policing by the Public* (1988).

[32] Burrows, *op. cit.*

[33] See Sanders and Young (2007), p.54; R. Morgan and T. Newburn, *op. cit.*, n.3.

[34] (2001), p.9.

"the clear message that emerges from practically all recent empirical studies ... is that the police are rarely faced with the classic situation of detective fiction, that of the search for the unidentified perpetrators of known offences."[35]

In most cases the process of detection is straightforward as the offender is, for example, caught red-handed, identified by the victim or other witnesses or found by the police at or near the scene of the crime, or is one of a few people with ready access to the crime or an obvious motive, or gives himself or herself up.[36] In a significant number of cases an offence is admitted during an interview concerning other offences,[37] or the offender is identified as such following a search of his or her property, or of his person when taken into police custody.[38] In only a minority of cases[39] are special detection skills used (e.g. involving informants, fingerprint search, DNA profiles, local police knowledge, police records). Research by Phillips and Brown[40] found that of the 4,250 arrests they examined, in 71 per cent of cases the arresting officer claimed that the basis of his reasonable suspicion was from only one source of evidence. In 40 per cent of all cases the main ground for the suspicion derived from "a police observation of the offence".[41] Given the limitations on police manpower it is unsurprising that most efforts are focused on investigations where a result is most likely, and on the more serious cases.[42] It should also be noted that the increasing use of surveillance and undercover policing as an element of intelligence-led policing strategies mean that the potential offender has often been identified by the police at an earlier stage in the criminal conduct.

The arrangements for the supervision of police investigations were one of the matters specified in the RCCJ's terms of reference.[43] The RCCJ were "less satisfied" with arrangements for supervising routine police inquiries than those in major investigations; indeed research found that supervision as such scarcely applied in most of the cases studied.[44] A "new approach to supervision" was

---

[35] Bottomley and Pease, (1986), p.46, based on R. Mawby, *Policing the City* (1979) and Steer (1980). See further the articles collected in R. Reiner, *Policing I* (1996), Pt II, "The Role of the Police in Practice"; R. Reiner, *The Future of Policing* (2000). For an illustration of the diversity see Home Office, *Diary of a Police Officer* (2001). This involved a report on a "typical shift" of a police officer in an attempt to identify ways in which to "free up" time so that officers could perform more "reassurance policing" (p.v): *www.homeoffice.gov.uk.*

[36] In Steer's study (1980) of indictable offences dealt with by the Oxford police, these accounted for 47% of a random sample and 71% of a sample of serious cases: p.73, Table 3.4. See generally pp.71–78, 96–116.

[37] Many offences thereby come to the attention of the police for the first time. Such admissions may be made with a view to the other offences being "taken into consideration" (TIC) during sentencing.

[38] Steer, *op. cit.,* 41% and 20% respectively: *ibid.*

[39] Steer, *op. cit.,* 13% and 11% respectively: *ibid.*

[40] *Entry into the Criminal Justice System: A Survey of Arrests and their Outcomes* (HORS No.49, 1998); see also Sanders and Young (2007), p.59.

[41] *ibid.* p.41.

[42] *ibid.* pp.71–72.

[43] Cm. 2263, pp.18–23.

[44] J. Baldwin and T. Moloney, *The Supervision of Police Investigations in Serious Criminal Cases* (RCCJ Research Study No.4, HMSO, 1992); M. Maguire and C. Norris, *The Conduct and Supervision of Criminal Investigations* (RCCJ Research Study No.5, HMSO, 1992); B. Irving and C. Dunningham, *Human Factors in the Quality Control of CID Investigations* (RCCJ Research Study No.21, HMSO, 1993).

recommended throughout the police service, with improved training in supervision at all levels, detective training and training in investigation to be overhauled. Part IV of the Criminal Justice and Police Act 2001 created a Central Police Training and Development Authority as a non-departmental public body to oversee such matters.[45]

One fundamental point emphasised by the RCCJ was that:

> "the police should see it as their duty when conducting investigations to gather and consider all the relevant evidence, including any which may exonerate the suspect. . . . A greater emphasis, such as the police service now advocates, on thorough investigation will not only help to ensure that innocent people are not convicted of crimes which they did not commit but also that fewer guilty people are acquitted because the evidence against them fails when tested in court."[46]

The adoption, once the view is taken that a particular suspect is guilty, of a blinkered approach that concentrates on the construction of a case against him or her and which downplays (or conceals) evidence that points to a different conclusion, has been a recurrent criticism of the police approach to investigations.[47]

Part II of the Criminal Procedure and Investigation Act 1996 provides statutory definitions of the duties of police investigators in relation to the collection, storage and disclosure of information and other material in an investigation.[48] An important feature of the 1996 Act is that, in the course of defining the duties and responsibilities of the police in respect of disclosure, it provides a definition of criminal investigation, and makes it clear that the police are under a duty to investigate the crime not the individual suspect, so that all lines of inquiry must be pursued. The European Court of Human Rights has also recognised the duty to carry out effective investigation into crime.[49] Despite reform, many commentators claim that the police, by the nature of their profession, continue to structure cases against individual suspects.[50]

To facilitate the process of investigation, the law provides the police with a series of powers to interfere with the legal rights of members of the public: powers of arrest and detention, powers to enter and search land and buildings and to search persons, and powers to seize property and conduct surveillance. The law also establishes a framework for controlling the exercise of such powers by setting conditions as to who may exercise the power and the circumstances in which they may be exercised, and by providing for supervision or periodic reviews. It also provides remedies for a breach of legal requirements. Given that most police powers authorise the commission of what would otherwise be torts or crimes (e.g. assault, false imprisonment, trespass to land, trespass to goods), exceeding the limits of a particular power may well expose the officers concerned (and the Chief Constable, who is vicariously responsible in tort) to an action for

---

[45] See, Centrex, *Helping to Develop Policing: Annual Report and Accounts 2006* (2006) HC1340. Centrex will be replaced by the National Policing Improvement Agency under the Police and Justice Act 2006.

[46] Cm. 2263, p.10.

[47] M. McConville, *et al., The Case for the Prosecution* (1991).

[48] The statute is supplemented by a Code of Practice issued by the Home Secretary under powers in s.23.

[49] See especially *Osman v UK* (1998) 29 E.H.R.R. 245; *Aydin v Turkey* (1997) 25 E.H.R.R. 251.

[50] See Sanders and Young (2007), Ch.5.

damages or a criminal prosecution. This is a reflection of the fundamental guarantee that the police are subject to the rule of law and must justify contraventions of the law by reference to a statutory or common law power.[51] In addition to breaches of the law, officers are also subject to disciplinary regulations which may be contravened even where no tort or crime is committed. The internal accountability of the police has been a controversial area, and was the subject of considerable change when the Police Reform Act 2002 introduced a new complaints process known as the Independent Police Complaints Commission which began operations in 2004.[52] It is hoped that the introduction of this body, coupled with the increasingly close scrutiny of operations and thematic reviews by Her Majesty's Inspectorate of Constabulary, will assuage the public fears that the police operate without adequate checks.[53] Police powers are not usually subject to a requirement of prior independent judicial supervision, and some leave considerable discretion in the hands of the individual officer.

The key statute regulating police powers over the citizen is the Police and Criminal Evidence Act 1984 (PACE)[54] although this has been supplemented by many others including the Criminal Justice and Public Order Act 1994, the Crime and Disorder Act 1998, the Regulation of Investigatory Powers Act 2000, the Criminal Justice and Police Act 2001, the Criminal Justice Act 2003, the Serious Organised Crime and Police Act 2005, and the Police and Justice Act 2006.

PACE extended the formal powers of the police in certain significant respects but narrowed them in others. It also strengthened the controls over the exercise of police powers in general and clarified and strengthened the rights of defendants in custody. Many of these controls are, however, found not in the Act itself but in Codes of Practice made by the Secretary of State.[55] As the foreword to the original Code noted, these were intended to provide clear and workable guidelines for the police, balanced by safeguards for the public. The sanctions for

---

[51] See T. Jones, T. Newburn and D. Smith, "Policing and the Idea of Democracy" (1996) 36 B.J. Crim. 182.

[52] See, *www.ipcc.gov.uk/index.htm*. See also, Sanders and Young (2007), pp.612–630; D. Ormerod and A. Roberts, "The Police Reform Act 2002: Increasing Centralisation, Maintaining Confidence and Contracting Our Crime Control" [2003] Crim. L.R. 141; G. Smith, "Rethinking Police Complaints" (2004) 44 B.J. Crim. 15; G. Smith, "A Most Enduring Problem: Police Complaints Reform in England and Wales" (2006) 35 J. Soc. Pol. 121.

[53] See *http://inspectorates.homeoffice.gov.uk/hmic/*. In 2005–06, there were 26,268 complaints received by the police, 46% were dealt with through local resolution, 28% required investigation, 14% were dispensed and 12% withdrawn. See, Independent Police Complaints Commission, *Police Complaints: Statistics for England and Wales 2005–6*, (2006) IPCC Research and Statistics Series Paper 5.

[54] This followed the Report of the Royal Commission on Criminal Procedure, Cmnd. 8092 (1981) but differed in some important matters from its recommendations. See also, Home Office Consultation Paper, *Modernising Police Powers: Review of the Police and Criminal Evidence Act 1984* (2007).

[55] Under ss.66, 67. There are at present eight Codes: Code A on Powers of Stop and Search; Code B on Search and Seizure; Code C on the Detention, Treatment and Questioning of Persons; Code D on the Identification of Persons; Code E on Tape Recording; Code F on visual recording with sound of interviews; Code G deals with powers of arrest; and Code H deals with detention and questioning in relation to terrorist suspects. There have been a number of revisions to the Codes and the latest set of Codes came into effect on 31 December 2005. See also, Home Office, *PACE Review: Review of the Joint Home Office/Cabinet Office Review of the Police and Criminal Evidence Act 1984* (2002); E. Cape, "The Revised PACE Codes of Practice: A Further Step Towards Inquisitorialism" [2003] Crim. L.R. 355. A further review of PACE is anticipated in 2007, as outlined in, Home Office, *Rebalancing the Criminal Justice System in Favour of the Law-Abiding Majority: Cutting Crime, Reducing Reoffending and Protecting the Public* (2006).

breach of a Code tend to be more indirect than for breach of the substantive law.[56] The intention was to strike a satisfactory balance between police powers and the rights of subjects, but it remains open to question whether that has been achieved.[57] However, Brown, reviewing 10 years of research into PACE, concluded that it had "introduced a greater element of fairness into pre-trial procedures" with suspects being more aware of their rights, and that there were benefits for the police in terms of clearer and more certain powers.[58]

There is not the space here for more than a brief survey of the police powers.[59] One important general point to note throughout is that the structure of police powers is such that the police officer at the lowest level of the organisation, i.e. those dealing with suspects, have the greatest amount of discretion. This is not typical of an organisational structure; usually the level of discretion increases further up the hierarchy. This breadth of discretion renders it all the more important that the powers are carefully prescribed by the statutes and narrowly interpreted by the courts.

3. POLICE POWERS

14–004   It is necessary to provide a brief explanation of a number of recurring expressions found in police powers. Many of the police powers depend on the presence of reasonable "suspicion", "cause" or "belief" in the existence of a state of affairs. There is a spectrum with reasonable suspicion at the lower end.[60] It "arises at or near the starting point of an investigation of which the obtaining of prima facie proof is the end . . . Prima facie proof consists of admissible evidence. Suspicion can take into account matters that could not be put in evidence at all."[61] It does not presuppose that the police should have obtained sufficient evidence to bring charges. The Strasbourg Court has confirmed that "reasonable suspicion presupposes the existence of facts or information which would satisfy an objective observer that the person concerned may have committed a criminal offence.

---

[56] Other persons who investigate offences must have regard to any relevant provision (See *R v Twaites and Brown* (1990) 92 Cr.App.R. 106 (Ladbrokes investigators); *R v Bayliss* (1993) 98 Cr.App.R. 235 (store detective), but not for example teachers investigating pupils offences (*G v DPP* [1989] Crim. L.R. 150), and the Codes are admissible in evidence and if relevant to civil or criminal proceedings, are to be taken into account by the court or tribunal. However, breach of a Code by a person does not of itself render him or her liable to any civil or criminal proceedings (ss.67(8)–(11)). Breach of a Code may give rise to exclusion of evidence.

[57] For a sceptical view, see A. Sanders, "Rights, Remedies and the Police and Criminal Evidence Act" [1988] Crim. L.R. 802.

[58] D. Brown, *PACE Ten Years On: A Review of the Research* (HORS 155).

[59] For fuller treatment see J. English and R. Card, Police Law (9th edn, 2005); K. Starmer, M. Strange, Q. Whitaker and A. Jennings, *Criminal Justice, Police Powers and Human Rights* (2001); E. Cape and J. Luqmani, *Defending Suspects at Police Stations: The Practitioners Guide to Advice and Representation* (5th edn, 2006); M. Zander, *The Police and Criminal Evidence Act 1984* (5th edn, 2006); R. T. H. Stone, *Entry, Search and Seizure* (4th edn, 2005); L. Jason-Lloyd, *An Introduction to Policing and Police Powers* (2005).

[60] On definitions of reasonable suspicion see *Shaaban Bin Hussein v Hong Fook Kam* [1970] A.C. 942.

[61] *ibid., per* Lord Devlin at 948.

What may be regarded as 'reasonable' will however depend on all the circumstances."[62] The English courts have adopted a compatible definition,[63] and officers rely on the specific guidance provided in the Code of Practice A. Despite efforts in the Codes of Practice, accompanying PACE, to guard against the abuse of powers based on such a low threshold, Home Office research has confirmed that officers' suspicions (at least as regards stop and search) are aroused as a result of appearance (including youth; type of vehicle; incongruence; "in some cases" ethnicity); being known to the police; and fitting the suspect description.[64]

A further general threshold test worth noting is the statutory power for a constable to use reasonable force wherever it is necessary in the exercise of any power under PACE.[65]

(a) Stop and search

Prior to PACE, the powers to stop and search people were haphazard and **14–005** unsatisfactory. PACE extended the general powers of the police to stop and search persons and vehicles. They are used extensively. In 2004–05 there were 839,977 recorded stops of people/vehicles.[66]

Under s.1 of PACE a constable may stop and search a person or vehicle in a public place if he or she has reasonable grounds to suspect he or she will find stolen or prohibited articles. "Prohibited" articles include offensive weapons (made or adapted for causing injury or intended by the person having it with him for such use), articles adapted for use in burglary, theft, obtaining by deception or taking a vehicle without authority, a knife or other bladed or sharply pointed article, articles made, adapted or intended for use in criminal damage, and prohibited fireworks.[67] There are similar powers under other statutes authorising searches, for example for drugs, for firearms and for intoxicating liquor on those at, or travelling to, sporting events.[68] Sanders and Young have argued that at some point in the future, the argument will no doubt be pressed that it would be less confusing for the police to be given the power to stop and search for evidence of *any* crime.[69]

---

[62] *Fox, Campbell and Hartley v UK* (1990) 13 E.H.R.R. 157; *Guzzardi v Italy* (1980) 3 E.H.R.R. 333; *Brogan v UK* (1988) 11 E.H.R.R. 117.

[63] See *O'Hara v Chief Constable of the RUC* [1997] A.C. 286 and *Castorina v Chief Constable of Surrey* (1988) N.L.J.R. 180.

[64] See, *inter alia*, P. Quinton, N. Bland and J. Miller, *Police Stops, Decision-making and Practice* (HORS Paper No.130, 2000).

[65] 1984 Act, s.117. The use of handcuffs does not breach safeguards in Art.3 of the ECHR: *Rainien v Finland* (1997) 26 E.H.R.R. 543.

[66] *Statistics on Race and the Criminal Justice System 2005* (2006). Of the recorded stops and searches, 14% were of black people, 7% were Asian people. The figures represent a rise in the use of stop and search from the previous year of 14% though this is partly explained by the possible increase in the level of recording following the implementation of recommendation 61 of *The Stephen Lawrence Inquiry* (1999) Cm. 4262. For a consideration of the impact of the Lawrence Inquiry see, J. Foster, T. Newburn and A. Souhami, *Assessing the Impact of the Stephen Lawrence Inquiry*, (2005) Home Office Research Study 294.

[67] PACE, s.1, as amended by the Criminal Justice Act 1988, s.140; Criminal Justice Act 2003 s.1; Serious Organised Crime and Police Act 2005, s.115. Note also Home Office Consultation Paper, *Modernising Police Powers: Review of the Police and Criminal Evidence Act 1984* (2007) Ch.3.

[68] See the list in Annex A to the *Code of Practice for the Exercise by Police Offices of Statutory Powers of Stop and Search* (2006) (Code A).

[69] Sanders and Young (2007) p.74, footnote 99.

All these powers are now subject to the safeguards set out in s.2 of PACE, which, *inter alia*, require the constable, before commencing a search, to give his or her name[70] and that of his or her police station the object of the proposed search, the grounds for the search, and, if out of uniform, documentary evidence that he or she is a constable. A failure to comply with these requirements will render the search unlawful and the officer will not be acting in the execution of his duty.[71] The search, if conducted, is to be proportionate to what the person is suspected of having done/possessing, and the length of time for detention must not extend beyond the time taken for the search and must in all the circumstances be reasonable.[72] The courts are, however, unlikely to exclude evidence obtained by an illegal search.[73]

The person searched may not be required to remove any clothing in public other than an outer coat, jacket or gloves,[74] and only a constable in uniform may stop a vehicle. A record must be made of the search stating the object of the search, the grounds for it, and the time, place and result. The suspect must be provided with a copy of the written record.[75] In 2003 Code A introduced the requirement to record stops which although occurring with a view to search, the search was not carried out due to suspicion being eliminated as a result of questioning the suspect.[76]

Quinton and Bland[77] found that some forces used the power to stop the same individuals repeatedly as a means of monitoring the whereabouts of "known criminals". This was considered to be an effective use of the power, with improved targeting of searches increasing arrest rates.[78] Miller, Bland and Quinton,[79] found substantial variation between forces in the extent to which searches are used,[80] but that searches appear to have a "minor role" in detecting offenders for the range of all crimes involved, and a "relatively small role" in detecting offenders.[81]

Section 60 of the Criminal Justice and Public Order Act 1994 contains the power to "stop and search *in anticipation* of violence". Where a senior officer reasonably believes that incidents involving serious violence may take place and that it is expedient to do so to prevent their occurrence, he or she may authorise that the s.60 powers shall be exercisable "at any place within the locality for a period not exceeding twenty four hours".[82] These powers enable a uniformed constable to stop any pedestrian or vehicle and search for offensive weapons or dangerous instruments.[83] What is significant here is that the constable need not

---

[70] Unless he or she believes that to do so would place him or her in danger, in which case the warrant number should be given, see Code A, para.3.8(b).

[71] *Osman v DPP* (1999) 163 J.P. 725.

[72] PACE Code A, para.3.3.

[73] See *R v McCarthy* [1996] Crim. L.R. 818; *cf. R v Fennelly* [1989] Crim. L.R. 142.

[74] PACE Code A, para.3.5. Except under CJPOA, s.60AA (above) in relation to disguises and s.45(3) of the Terrorism Act 2000 which empowers the officer to demand the removal of headgear or footwear.

[75] PACE, s.2(3)(d) and s.3. See also Code A, para.4.

[76] PACE Code A, para.4.12.

[77] *Modernising the Tactic* (Police Research Series Paper No.128, 1999).

[78] See the further research on information gathering, P. Quinton, N. Bland and J. Miller, *Police Stops, Decision-making and Practice* (Police Research Series Paper No.130, 2000).

[79] *The Impact of Stops and Searches on Crime and the Community* (Police Research Series Paper No.127, 2000).

[80] *ibid.* p.12.

[81] *ibid.* p.27.

[82] This may be extended for a further 24 hours by a superintendent.

[83] i.e. instruments which have a blade or are sharply pointed.

reasonably suspect that the pedestrian or vehicle is carrying such an item. The power is intended to allow the police to stop and search "*before* they have a reasonable suspicion against a person".[84] Section 60AA of the Criminal Justice and Public Order Act extends the powers of the officer conducting a stop and search further by providing a power to demand the removal of disguises worn to conceal the wearer's identity.[85] The Terrorism Act 2000 contains similar powers whereby an area can be designated in which searches may be carried out without reasonable suspicion for items connected with terrorism.[86]

The police also have a power to carry out general road checks on the written authority of a police superintendent.[87] The aim must be to find a person who has committed or is intending to commit an offence, a witness to an offence or a person unlawfully at large.[88] In each case the relevant offence must be an indictable one, replacing the previous need for the relevant offence to be a "serious arrestable" one, and therefore increasing the scope of the power.[89]

The exercise of stop and search powers remains very controversial. One of the most recurring concerns is the fact that black people are more likely to be stopped and searched than white.[90] Code of Practice A emphasises, *inter alia*, that a person's race, age or appearance can never itself be a reasonable ground for suspicion,[91] but it is still doubted whether the reasonable ground standard is generally met.[92] Quinton, Bland and Miller[93] in their review of the concept of reasonable suspicion and its application concluded that there needs to be further clarification of the concept, since generalisations are still used by police officers in practice. Stone and Pettigrew[94] concluded that a disproportionate number of searches could be due to: ethnic bias in officers; a larger proportion of ethnic groups in the population available to be stopped and searched; and a higher concentration of minority groups in the areas targeted.[95]

Stone and Pettigrew[96] also explored public experiences of stop and search, reporting that "there was a very strong perception that the way in which stops

---

[84] M. O'Brien, Under Secretary of State for the Home Office, Commons Standing Committee B, June 9, 1998, col.788.

[85] PACE, s.4A. See *DPP v Avery* [2002] 1 Cr.App.R. 31.

[86] PACE, ss.44–47. See *R (on the application of Gillan and Another) v Commissionmer of Police for the Metropolis* [2005] U.K.H.L. 12.

[87] PACE, s.4.

[88] These are specified in Sch.5 and include, *inter alia*, treason, murder, manslaughter, rape, kidnapping, certain sexual offences, certain firearms offences and causing death by dangerous driving. They also include drug trafficking offences: see the Drug Trafficking Act 1994, ss.l(3)(a) to (f), as amended.

[89] The change was made by the Serious Organised Crime and Police Act 2005.

[90] C. F. Willis, *The Use, Effectiveness and Impact of Police Stop and Search Powers* (H. O. Research and Planning Unit Paper 15, 1983); M. McConville [1983] Crim. L.R. 605; B. Bowling and C. Phillips, *Racism, Crime and Justice* (2002) Ch.5; *The Stephen Lawrence Inquiry: Report of an Inquiry by Sir William MacPherson of Cluny* (1999) Cm. 4262, para.45.8.

[91] PACE, s.66; Code A para.2.2. Discrimination in the exercise of these powers may give rise to an action under the Race Relations (Amendment) Act 2000.

[92] D. Dixon *et al.*, "Reality and Rules in the Construction and Regulation of Police Suspicion" (1989) Int. J. Sociology of Law 185. D. Dixon *et al.*, "Reality and Rules in the Construction and Regulation of Police Suspicion" (1989) Int. J. Sociology of Law 185.

[93] *Police Stops, Decision-making and Practice* (Police Research Series Paper No.130, 2000).

[94] V. Stone and N. Pettigrew, *The Views of the Public on Stops and Searches* (Police Research Series Paper No.129, 2000).

[95] See also, P. Waddington, K. Stenson and D. Don, "In Proportion: Race and Police Stop and Search", (2004) 44 Brit. J. Crim. 889.

[96] Stone and Pettigrew (2000).

and searches are currently handled causes more distrust, antagonism, and resentment than any of the positive effects they can have". However, despite this, all ethnic groups felt that stops and searches should remain if fundamental changes were made in the ways the powers are used (especially as regards the police attitude and the provision of reasons for the search).

Miller[97] also examined the ethnicity of those stopped and searched and explored the complexity behind these oft-cited statistics on racial bias. The findings of the research did not suggest a general pattern of bias against those from minority ethnic backgrounds.[98] However, one must recognise that regardless of the arguments suggesting a racial bias or otherwise, stop and search powers remain a serious infringement of personal liberty and must be carried out with the utmost sensitivity if the police are to maintain fruitful community relations. Code of Practice A confirms that the Act and Code do not "affect the ability of an officer to speak to or question a person in the ordinary course of his duties without detaining him or exercising any element of compulsion".[99] Such a course of action may reduce the tensions surrounding a formal search, though it would appear that it not necessarily the formal powers of stop and search that are viewed as problematic by those subjected to them, but the attitudes and behaviour of those carrying them out.[100]

(b) Arrest[101]

14–006 An arrest amounts to a deprivation of liberty and as such must comply with Art.5 of the ECHR, by being in accordance with law, and fulfilling one of the specified purposes listed—the most pertinent being that in Art.5(1)(c) of bringing a person before the competent legal authority on reasonable suspicion of having committed an offence.

(i) Arrest with a warrant[102]

14–007 In some cases an arrest is authorised by a warrant issued by a magistrate under s.1 of the Magistrates' Courts Act 1980, as an alternative to the issue of a summons. The issue of an arrest warrant or a summons follows the laying of an information on oath to the effect that the person named has, or is suspected of having, committed an offence. A warrant should not be issued where a summons would be equally effectual, but may, for example, be employed where the defendant fails to answer to a summons. Using a summons as a way of initiating the prosecution process is preferable to the more intrusive alternative of arrest. The trend in English law is, however, to move towards a wider use of the arrest powers, and increasingly to use powers of arrest without a warrant, and consequently, over which there is no prior judicial supervision.

---

[97] *Profiling Populations Available for Stops and Searches* (Police Research Series Paper No.131, 2000).

[98] *ibid.* p.84.

[99] Code A, Notes for Guidance, para.1.

[100] Home Office, *Stop and Search Action Team: Strategy 2004–5* (2004) p.8.

[101] See generally, *Blackstone's Criminal Practice* (2007) D1.7–1.36; Sanders and Young (2007), Ch.3; A. Keogh, "Police State or Proportionate Response" (2006) N.L.J. 81.

[102] The other warrants to arrest including, for example, those for extradition, are not examined here.

A further basis for arrest with a warrant exists with the European Arrest Warrant, whereby each state in the European Union agrees to enforce an arrest warrant issued in any other Member State.[103]

(ii) *Arrest without a warrant: constables*

Powers of arrest without warrant under PACE were originally confined to a range **14–008** of "arrestable" offences. Under the Serious Organised Crime and Police Act 2005 (SOCPA) arrest powers are "rationalised" to the extent that all offences are now arrestable subject to a necessity criterion. Thus, despite the name of the legislation, someone committing the most minor of offences, littering for example, could be arrested if deemed "necessary".[104]

The amendment to s.24 of the PACE[105] gives the police powers to arrest anyone who is in the act of committing an offence or whom he or she has reasonable grounds for suspecting to be committing or about to commit such an offence. Where an offence has been committed, a constable may arrest anyone who is guilty of it, or whom he or she has reasonable grounds for suspecting to be guilty. (Here, the offence must have been committed by someone.) Where a constable has reasonable grounds for suspecting that an offence has been committed, he or she may arrest anyone whom he or she has reasonable grounds for suspecting to be guilty of it. A constable may arrest anyone who is about to commit an offence or whom he or she has reasonable grounds for suspecting to be about to commit such an offence.[106] The power of summary arrest is exercisable only if the constable has reasonable grounds for believing that for any of the following reasons, it is "necessary" to arrest the person in question:

(a) to enable the name of the person in question to be ascertained (in the case where the constable does not know, and cannot readily ascertain, the person's name, or has reasonable grounds for doubting whether a name given by the person as his name is his real name);

(b) correspondingly as regards the person's address;

(c) to prevent the person in question:

  (i) causing physical injury to himself or any other person;
  (ii) suffering physical injury;
  (iii) causing loss of or damage to property;
  (iv) committing an offence against public decency; or
  (v) causing an unlawful obstruction of the highway;

(d) to protect a child or other vulnerable person from the person in question;

(e) to allow the prompt and effective investigation of the offence or of the conduct of the person in question;

---

[103] S. De Mas, "Protecting the Legal Rights of the Travelling Citizen: Easier Said than Done" [2003] Crim. L.R. 865.

[104] See Home Office, *Policing: Modernising Police Powers to Meet Community Needs* (2004), section 2.

[105] Serious Organised Crime and Police Act 2005 s.110. A new code relating to the statutory power of arrest has also been introduced: PACE Code of Practice G.

[106] On the difficulties created by this being too premature for even a charge of attempt, see *R v Geddes* [1996] Crim. L.R. 894.

(f)   to prevent any prosecution for the offence from being hindered by the disappearance of the person in question.

Whilst the necessity test is designed as a limit upon the power of summary arrest, the above list is extensive (though exhaustive) and, it is suggested, the necessity criterion will almost always be satisfied.[107]

(iii) *Arrest without a warrant: other persons*

14–009   The power of arrest by anyone other than a constable is now dealt with in a separate section of PACE, namely s.24A. Such an arrest can only be made where the offence is indictable. A person may arrest without warrant anyone who is in the act of committing an indictable offence, or anyone he or she has reasonable grounds for suspecting to be committing such an offence. Where such an offence has been committed a person may arrest anyone who is guilty of the offence, or whom he or she has reasonable grounds for suspecting to be guilty. The power of arrest is only exercisable if it appears to the person that it is not reasonably practicable for a constable to make the arrest, and there are reasonable grounds for believing that it is necessary to prevent the person in question:

(a)   causing physical injury to himself or any other person;

(b)   suffering physical injury;

(c)   causing loss of or damage to property; or

(d)   making off before a constable can assume responsibility for him.

It can be seen that the powers of the police are wider than those of private citizens. The powers of citizens to effect arrests were, historically, no different from police, but now it is clearly much more limited. The increasing trend towards private security (in shopping centres and other public places), will mean that the "citizens' arrest" powers come under closer scrutiny.

(iv) *Arrest without warrant under specific statutory powers*

14–010   PACE repealed many specific statutory powers of arrest available to the police, while preserving powers under numerous Acts listed in Sch.2. These include powers under the Immigration Act 1971 and the Mental Health Act 1983. Other specific powers of arrest have been created since PACE.[108] There is, in particular, a very broad power of arrest under the Terrorism Act 2000, s.41. However, given the wide arrest powers available since the reforms introduced by SOCPA, specific statutory powers of arrest are less likely to be introduced.

---

[107] J. R. Spencer, "Extending the Police State" (2005) 155 N.L.J. 477.

[108] e.g. Sporting Events (Control of Alcohol, etc.) Act 1985, s.7(2); Public Order Act 1986, s.3(6) (affray), s.4(4) (fear or provocation of violence), s.5(4) (harassment, alarm or distress) (see in particular on these very extensively used powers the research paper by D. Brown and T. Ellis, *Policing Low Level Disorder: the Use of section 5 of the Public Order Act 1986* (HORS, 1994 No.135), ss.12(7), 13(10) and 14(7) of the Public Order Act 1986 (processions and assemblies); Criminal Justice and Public Order Act 1994, s.61 (power to remove trespassers from land), s.63 (raves) and s.68 (aggravated trespass).

(v) *Arrest at common law*

At common law, there is a power to arrest for breach of the peace where a breach **14–011** of the peace is taking place or reasonably anticipated.[109] This power is not confined to constables and was not modified by PACE. Arrest powers for breach of the peace have been clarified to ensure compatibility with Art.5 of the ECHR.[110]

(vi) *Common requirements*

There are a number of conditions that must be fulfilled for an arrest to be valid, **14–012** apart from the existence of a relevant power of arrest. Some are derived from the common law and some from statute. Very commonly, the arrestor is required to have "reasonable suspicion" to believe or suspect the arrested person has committed, is committing, or is about to commit an offence. If the validity of the arrest is challenged in legal proceedings the onus lies on the arrestor to establish to the satisfaction of the court that objectively reasonable grounds existed: it is insufficient that the arrestor honestly believed that he or she had such grounds.[111] The concept of reasonable suspicion lies between that of suspicion without any proof and that of prima facie proof based on admissible evidence (i.e. evidence that if not controverted would be sufficient for a conviction).[112] Whether it exists in a particular case is a question of fact not law, and it is unusual for an arrest to be held unlawful for lack of reasonable grounds.[113] This is a low threshold test and there is a danger that it will be abused by officers.

If the arresting officer has made a reasonable but erroneous interpretation of the law, he will not have a reasonable suspicion and the arrest will be unlawful.[114] The reasonableness of the officer's decision is to be based on the information available to him at that time.[115] The courts have accepted that reasonable suspicion can be founded on the basis of information provided and does not require the police to believe a suspect to be guilty.[116] In *O'Hara v Chief*

---

[109] *Bibby v Chief Constable of Essex* (2000) 164 J.P. 297; *Austin and Saxby v Commissioner of Police for the Metropolis* [2005] H.R.L.R. 20; See also D. Nicholson and K. Reid, "Arrest for Breach of the Peace and the ECHR" [1996] Crim. L.R. 764; *R v Howell (Erroll)* [1982] Q.B. 416, DC; *Albert v Lavin* [1982] A.C. 546. The court in *Howell* stated that "there is a breach of the peace whenever harm is actually done or is likely to be done to a person or in his presence to his property or a person is in fear of being so harmed through an assault, an affray, a riot, unlawful assembly or other disturbance" (*per* Watkins L.J. at 427).

[110] See *Foulkes v Chief Constable of Merseyside* [1998] 3 All E.R. 705; *Bibby v Chief Constable of Essex* (2000) 164 J.P. 297; on the ECHR interpretation of breach of the peace see *Steel v UK* (1999) 28 R.H.R.R. 603.

[111] *R v Inland Revenue Commissions, Ex p. Rossminster Ltd* [1980] A.C. 952 at 1011, *per* Lord Diplock.

[112] *Dumbell v Roberts* [1944] 1 All E.R. 326; *Hussein v Chong Foot Kam* [1970] A.C. 942.

[113] See generally S. H. Bailey and D. J. Birch [1982] Crim. L.R. 475. An arrest may be based on hearsay evidence: *Erskine v Holland* [1971] R.T.R. 199; *R v Evans* [1974] R.T.R. 232. See also *Doorson v Netherlands* (1996) 22 E.H.R.R. 330. The ECtHR adopts a similar view to the UK courts on the requirements for a lawful arrest.

[114] *Todd v DPP* [1996] Crim. L.R. 344.

[115] *Redmond-Bate v DPP* (1999) 163 JP 789.

[116] *Castorina v Chief Constable of Surrey* [1988] N.J.L.R. 180; this can be from a police national computer check: *Hough v Chief Constable of Staffordshire, The Times*, February 14, 2001. See also *Murray v UK* (1994) 19 E.H.R.R. 193; *Brogan v UK* (1988) 11 E.H.R.R. 117.

Constable of the RUC, the House of Lords confirmed that reasonable suspicion could be founded on information from senior officers, but not merely on an instruction to arrest.[117] The ECtHR has emphasised that it is necessary for the officer to have formed a suspicion based on objective grounds.[118]

The arrestor, or another officer,[119] must make it clear that the arrestee is under compulsion either by physical means, such as taking him or her by the arm, or by using words of compulsion to which the arrestee accedes.[120] The use of reasonable force is sanctioned by PACE, s.117.[121] The arrestee must be informed that he or she is under arrest, and of the ground for arrest, at the time of the arrest or as soon as practicable thereafter.[122]

An arrest is unlawful if the person arrested is not told the ground of arrest in compliance with s.28(3); however, the arrest becomes lawful once the ground is given.[123] The degree of information that it is necessary for the officer to provide has been the subject of dispute. It has been held, for example, that when arresting a suspect for drug dealing, it is not necessary to specify the class of drugs involved. To do so would be to require undue technicality.[124] This requirement of adequate information was an important common law requirement, and it is also found in Art.5(2) of the ECHR—a suspect must be informed properly in a language he understands of the reason for his arrest.[125] The need to explain the grounds for the arrest are not necessary where the arrestor is a private citizen and the fact or ground of arrest is obvious. There is a further, general exception where it is not reasonably practicable to impart the information before the arrestee escapes from arrest.[126]

More controversially, in *R v Chalkley and Jeffries*[127] the court confirmed that it is acceptable for the police to inform the suspect of one reason for the arrest that would be technically applicable even if they are in fact investigating him or her for another more serious offence that is not disclosed. The danger with this concession to the police for the use of holding charges is that the suspect will not perceive the seriousness of his or her situation and will, for example, decline legal assistance.

The arrestor must regard his or her action of arrest in the sense of a possible first step in the criminal process: if, for example, he or she simply detains

---

[117] [1997] A.C. 286.

[118] *O'Hara v UK* [2002] Crim. L.R. 493, acknowledging the difficulty in being able to prove this when the investigation involved reliance on informers.

[119] See *Dhesi v Chief Constable of West Midlands* (*The Times*, May 9, 2000).

[120] *Alderson v Booth* [1969] 2 Q.B. 216.

[121] See also the Criminal Law Act 1967, s.3.

[122] *DPP v Hawkins* [1988] 1 W.L.R. 1166 (arrest not retrospectively unlawful if the ground is not given when it first becomes practicable); *Abbassy v Commissioner of Police of the Metropolis* [1990] 1 W.L.R. 385 (no need to specify a particular crime or give a technical definition of the offence; sufficient to use commonplace language). See *Fox, Campbell and Hartley v UK* (1990) 13 E.H.R.R. 157. There is no need for the reasons to be provided in writing: *X v Netherlands* (1966) 9 Y.B. 474.

[123] *Lewis v Chief Constable of the South Wales Constabulary* [1991] 1 All E.R. 206.

[124] *Clarke v Chief Constable of North Wales*, *The Independent*, May 22, 2000, CA (Civ. Div.), *per* Brooke L.J., with whom Sir Christopher Staughton agreed; Sedley L.J. dissented.

[125] *Murray v UK* (1994) 19 E.H.R.R. 193.

[126] PACE, s.28. The requirements as to giving the ground of arrest were based on the common law: *Christie v Leachinsky* [1947] A.C. 573. See also *Gelberg v Miller* [1961] 1 W.L.R. 153; *R v Telfer* [1976] Crim. L.R. 562.

[127] [1998] 2 Cr.App.R. 79.

someone for questioning with no thought of arrest it cannot be a valid arrest.[128] In addition, to ensure compliance with Art.5 the arrest must be "for the purpose of securing [the] fulfilment [of an obligation prescribed by law] and not, for instance, punitive in character".[129]

Finally, as the power of arrest is a statutory discretion exercisable (normally) by a public official, a particular exercise may be challenged as an *ultra vires* abuse of discretion.[130] In practice, the police officer may well exercise the discretion not to arrest but to turn a blind eye, particularly given the bureaucracy involved in his or her processing an arrestee. This has been estimated at an average three-and-a-half hours spent per arrestee.[131]

(vii) *The effects of PACE*

The potential benefits of the PACE arrest regime are that it provides a relatively **14–013** comprehensive code and does incorporate safeguards such as the requirement of reasonable suspicion in most cases and that the suspect must be cautioned after arrest. On the negative side, the threshold of reasonable suspicion is very low, and in some cases the powers can be exercised even without reasonable suspicion. More recent changes have arguably eroded the safeguards of PACE still further. The ability to arrest for any offence where "necessary", introduced under the SOCPA, places a considerable burden on the individual officer to make a swift decision in potentially challenging circumstances, and it is suggested that further guidance is needed from the courts on the scope of the power if it is not a power used simply because it can be used.[132]

Research on the immediate effects of PACE suggested that the level of initial evidence on which arrests were based had become stronger, with a greater emphasis on independent evidence, although there was still a proportion of suspects who were arrested on limited evidence.[133]

More recent research has been conducted reviewing the impact of PACE.[134] In one extensive survey, Phillips and Brown found that 87 per cent of people arrested had been arrested on the basis of suspicion of committing an offence.[135] They reviewed the procedures following arrest and provided a comprehensive socio-demographic breakdown of arrests and the circumstances leading to

---

[128] *Kenlin v Gardiner* [1967] 2 Q.B. 510; *R v Brown* (1976) 64 Cr.App.R. 231.

[129] *McVeigh v UK* (1981) 25 D.R. 15, Euro Comm.

[130] *Holgate-Mohammed v Duke* [1984] A.C. 437 (where the challenge failed on the merits); *Plange v Chief Constable of South Humberside Police, The Times*, March 23, 1992 (arrest where officer knew that there was no possibility of a charge would be unlawful as the officer had acted on an irrelevant consideration or for an improper purpose).

[131] See the *Diary of a Police Officer* (2001), p.vi: *www.homeoffice.gov.uk*.

[132] See Code G, para.1.3.

[133] B. L. Irving and I. K. McKenzie, *Police Interrogation: the Effect of the Police and Criminal Evidence Act 1984* (1989), pp.64–66, 145–147, 193. Here, Irving's 1979 study of practice in Brighton (RCCP Research Study No.2, 1980) was replicated in 1986 and again in 1987. *Cf.* K. Bottomley, *et al., The Impact of PACE: Policing in a Northern Force* (1991), Ch.4, where research in the period 1987–88 suggested that the changes in arrest powers had comparatively little effect on day-to-day policing on the streets, although the view of most police officers was that there had been a significant reduction in the previous practice of arresting suspects "on a hunch".

[134] e.g. D. Brown, *PACE Ten Years On: A Review of the Research* (1997), above.

[135] *Entry into the Criminal Justice System: A Survey of Police Arrests and their Outcomes* (Home Office Research and Statistics Paper 185, 1998), p.27.

arrest.[136] As with stop and search, there are concerns that arrests are not founded on reasonable suspicion, and that there are disproportionate arrest rates of members of ethnic groups.[137]

The broader concerns with the arrest powers in England are that there is a greater move towards depriving individuals of their liberty earlier in the investigative process based on a low threshold of suspicion, and without judicial supervision.[138]

(c) Entry, search and seizure

14–014 The police[139] have a wide variety of powers to enter and search premises, and seize property, either with or without a warrant. A large number of statutes enable a judge or magistrate to issue a warrant authorising the entry to and search of specified premises. For example, warrants may be granted to search for stolen goods, obscene publications, drugs and a host of other items.[140]

Article 8 of the ECHR protects against infringements of privacy, in the home or workplace, unless prescribed by law and necessary and proportionate to a legitimate aim. The most pertinent legitimate aim here is that of the prevention and detection of crime. The European Court has emphasised repeatedly the importance of adequate safeguards against abuse, notwithstanding the margin of appreciation,[141] especially if the search is conducted otherwise than with judicial supervision.[142]

PACE introduced a new general power for justices of the peace to issue warrants authorising entry and search for evidence relating to an indictable offence,[143] other than "items subject to legal privilege",[144] "excluded mate-

---

[136] 85% of arrestees were male; 15% were juveniles (under 17); 54% were unemployed, 27% employed; and 14% pupils or students; 78% were white, 13% black and 7% Asian (96% of whom were male); over 60% of those arrested had previous convictions; 10% were known to be subject to a court order at the time of arrest. Phillips and Brown's study "was not designed to explore the links between unemployment and crime, but it does provide striking evidence of the high level of unemployment among criminal suspects" (p.18). The reason for disproportionate numbers is described as "complex" (p.13). Whether suspects had a criminal history varied considerably according to the offence for which they had been arrested. Figures were higher for those arrested for prostitution, burglary, vehicle related crime and public order, but lower for shoplifting, criminal damage, other theft, and offences of sex and violence (p.20).

[137] Home Office, *Statistics on Race and the Criminal Justice Stysem*, 2004 (2005). See also; M. Fitzgerald and R. Sibbitt, *Ethnic Monitoring in Police Forces* HORS 173, 1997; Philips and Brown, (1998); S. Holdaway, *The Racialisation of British Policing* (1996) pp.84–104.

[138] See P. Hillyard and D. Gordon, "Arresting Statistics and the Drift to Informal Justice in England and Wales" (1999) 26 J.L.S. 502.

[139] We do not consider here the powers of the security services nor the specific statutory powers of various regulatory bodies.

[140] Theft Act 1968, s.26; Obscene Publications Act 1959, s.3; Misuse of Drugs Act 1971, s.23; Human Tissue Act 2004, Sch.5, para.3; for a full account, see R. T. H. Stone, *Entry, Search and Seizure* (4th edn, 2005).

[141] See *Niemitz v Germany* (1992) 16 E.H.R.R. 97; *Funke v France* (1993) 16 E.H.R.R. 297.

[142] See *Camenzind v Switzerland* (1999) 28 E.H.R.R. 458, para.45.

[143] PACE, s.8 referred to a serious arrestable offence and was amended by the Serious Organised Crime and Police Act 2005. On the endorsement of warrants between UK jurisdictions see *R v Manchester Stipendiary Magistrates, Ex p. Granada* [2000] 1 W.L.R. 1. See generally, C. Walker [1997] C.L.J. 114.

[144] PACE, s.10. For comprehensive analysis see J. Auburn, *Legal Professional Privilege: Law and Theory* (2000), Ch.8.

rial"[145] or "special procedure material".[146] The magistrate must be satisfied that it is not practicable to communicate with a person who could consent to entry; or although a person could permit entry, it is not practicable to communicate with a person who could permit access to the evidence; or entry to the premises will be denied unless a warrant is produced; or the purposes of the search might be frustrated or seriously prejudiced unless entry could be gained immediately under warrant. Existing powers to grant search warrants were thereafter also subject to the restriction that they could not authorise searches for such material.[147] Instead, an order granting access to excluded material or special procedure material may be granted by a Circuit judge, in limited circumstances. The first set of conditions is that there are reasonable grounds for belief that an indictable offence has been committed, special procedure material which is likely to be relevant evidence and of substantial value to the investigation will be present, alternative methods of securing the evidence have failed or would be futile, and that it is in the public interest to permit access to the material. The second set of conditions are that there are reasonable grounds for believing that excluded material or special procedure material is on the premises and otherwise a search would be permissible within an existing search warrant power.[148] In *R v Central Criminal Court, Ex p. Bright*,[149] the Divisional Court stressed that the judge had to be satisfied that the statutory requirements for such an order had been established. The judge was not simply asking himself whether the decisions of the constable making the applications were reasonable. If the judge was satisfied that the access conditions existed, he or she was not bound to make the order, but had a discretion to refuse. The judge could take account of factors such as the impact on third parties, the antiquity of matters, the potentially nominal sentence that might be passed, the potential stifling of public debate and the risk of requiring a person to incriminate himself.

In the last resort, a Circuit judge may issue a warrant authorising a constable to enter and search for such material.[150]

---

[145] *ibid.* s.11. This covers confidential personal records, human tissue or tissue fluid taken for medical purposes and confidential journalistic material ("personal records" and "journalistic material" being further defined in ss.12 and 13). Excluded material can, however, be disclosed voluntarily by the holder: *R v Singleton* [1995] 1 Cr.App.R. 431 (dental records). Hospital records of patients' admission to and discharge from a mental hospital are "personal records" within PACE, s.12, as they are records "relating to" their mental health: *R v Crown Court at Cardiff, Ex p. Kellam* (1993) 16 B.M.L.R. 76, DC.

[146] *ibid.* s.14. This covers confidential and journalistic material falling outside the definition of "excluded material".

[147] *ibid.* s.9(2).

[148] *ibid.* s.9(1) and Sch.1. Excluded material is more sensitive than special procedure material and only accessible under (2): see *R v Central Criminal Court, Ex p. Brown, The Times*, September 7, 1992. Non-compliance with an order is a contempt of court. The application is made *inter partes*, prior notice being given to the person holding the material. The material in question must be specified, either in the notice of application or otherwise: *R v Central Criminal Court, Ex p. Adegbesan* [1986] 1 W.L.R. 1292; *R v Manchester Crown Court, Ex p. Taylor* [1988] 1 W.L.R. 705; but the evidence on which the application is based need not: *R v Inner London Crown Court, Ex p. Baines & Baines* [1988] Q.B. 579. The suspect need not be notified if he or she is not the holder of the material: *R v Leicester Crown Court, Ex p. DPP* [1987] 1 W.L.R. 1371. The judge may hold the hearing in open court or in chambers: *R v Central Criminal Court, Ex p. DPP, The Times*, April 1, 1988. See generally R. T. Stone [1988] Crim. L.R. 498 and A. A. S. Zuckerman [1990] Crim. L.R. 472.

[149] [2001] 2 All E.R. 244, DC.

[150] *ibid.* Sch.1, paras 12–14. This is available, e.g. where use of the order procedure might seriously prejudice the investigation.

In a series of cases it was acknowledged that PACE presented practical difficulties when large volumes of disputed material were stored on premises.[151] Section 15(5) of PACE, authorises only one entry in pursuit of a warrant, so that it was impossible to complete a search of a large volume of material with a single warrant. The Criminal Justice and Police Act 2001 remedied the problem by providing the power to remove material to be examined elsewhere, and by allowing for the removal of intrinsically linked material (e.g. on a computer hard disk). The extended powers allow for seizure even where it may be legally privileged.[152] Specific protection is, however, provided to legally privileged material which can be seized.[153] The 2001 Act requires that notice is given to the occupier specifying what has been seized and the grounds on which it has been seized. The information must include the notification of a right to apply to a judge for the return of seized material and an explanation of how to apply to be present at any examination of the material seized.[154] The occupier or some other person with an interest in the property has an opportunity to be present at the examination.[155] There is a right to apply to the appropriate judicial authority to challenge the use of the powers. The court, on a successful application can order the return of material or, *inter alia*, order that it be examined by an independent third party. There is a duty to secure the material seized pending the hearing of such applications. In limited circumstances, the police may now seek a warrant for multiple entries to the same premises, or to multiple premises controlled or occupied by a specified person. This change, enacted by the SOCPA,[156] was in response to a Home Office Consultation Paper[157] which noted that repeated applications for warrants relating to the same premises "can cause delay and impede investigations".[158]

PACE clarified and strengthened the safeguards governing the issue and execution of *all* search warrants.[159] For example, entry and search had to be within one month of the date of the warrant, subsequently extended to three months in 2005[160] it must be at a reasonable hour[161] and the officer in charge must first attempt to communicate with the occupier, unless it appears that would frustrate the object of the search; before the search commences,[162] the officer must identify him or herself and state the purpose of the search and the grounds for undertaking it; the warrant must be shown and a copy of the warrant must be

---

[151] *R v Chesterfield Justices, Ex p. Bramley* [2001] 1 All E.R 411, DC; *R v HM Customs and Excise, Ex p. Popely* [2000] Crim. L.R. 388, DC; *R v Inland Revenue Commissioners, Ex p. Tamosius Partners (a firm)* [2000] Crim. L.R. 390, DC.

[152] See ss.50–70.

[153] s.54. Section 55 provides protections similar to those in PACE for special procedure material but does not apply where the underlying power of seizure is found in legislation where such protection is not afforded.

[154] s.52.

[155] s.53(4).

[156] Now contained in PACE, s.8(1A).

[157] Home Office, *Modernising Police Powers to Meet Community Needs* (2004).

[158] *ibid.* para.3.3.

[159] PACE, ss.15, 16. See also the *Code of Practice for the Searching of Premises by Police Officers and the Seizure of Property found by Police Officers on Persons or Premises* (2006) (Code B).

[160] SOCPA extended the period to three months following the assertion in the Consultation document that one month was arbitrary *Modernising Police Powers to Meet Community Needs*, para.3.9.

[161] *Kent Pharmaceuticals Ltd v Director of the Serious Fraud Office* [2002] E.W.H.C. 3023.

[162] Not before entry: *R v Longman* (1988) 88 Cr.App.R. 148.

given to the occupier or left at the premises.[163] Searches are only to be conducted to the extent necessary to achieve the object of the search.[164] Breach of these last requirements renders the search and seizure unlawful.[165] Compliance with these requirements is also vital to ensure ECHR compatibility. Courts have been strict in requiring that relevant documentation must be completed, but generous in interpreting when the documents should be made available to the accused. A full record must be kept of searches[166] and a search register must be maintained at each sub-divisional police station with copies of all records required by Code B.[167]

The apparent safeguard of judicial supervision for many PACE searches by the requirement of a warrant being obtained under s.8 may in practice be illusory. In a survey of two city forces, it was found that s.8 had been rarely used.[168] The example of 860 searches of premises disclosed that 12 per cent were conducted under a judicial warrant and 87 per cent under post-arrest powers (75 per cent under s.18, 2 per cent under s.32, and 6 per cent following and entry to arrest under s.17).[169] In addition, it has been argued that the judiciary have failed to provide adequate protection for material when issuing warrants.[170]

Aside from searches under s.8, searches under s.18 have been widely used[171]: in the case of indictable offences, a constable may be authorised by an officer of the rank of inspector or above to enter and search any premises occupied or controlled by a person under arrest if the constable has reasonable grounds to suspect that there is evidence relating to the offence in question or a similar or related indictable offence.[172] Requirements for officers to notify occupants of the reasons for searches are applicable when entry is being effected under s.18.[173] It remains possible for the police to conduct searches by consent, provided this is given in writing.[174]

PACE also provides a series of powers for the police to enter premises without a warrant; to execute an arrest warrant; to arrest for an indictable offence or certain other specified offences which list is regularly added to; including to pursue[175] and recapture a person unlawfully at large; to save life or limb or

---

[163] The occupier may ask a friend or third party to be present unless it would seriously hinder the investigation: Code B, para.6.11.

[164] s.16(8), Code B, para.6.9. Premises must be left secure: Code B, para.6.13.

[165] *R v Chief Constable of Lancashire, Ex p. Parker* [1993] Q.B. 577. See also, *Kent Pharmaceuticals Ltd v Director of the Serious Fraud Office* [2002] E.W.H.C. 3023.

[166] Code B, para.8.

[167] Code B, para.9.1.

[168] K. Lidstone and C. Palmer, *The Investigation of Crime: A Guide to Police Powers* (2nd edn, 1996), p.99.

[169] *ibid.* p.98.

[170] e.g. for journalists material: R. Costigan, "Fleet Street Blues; Police Seizure of Journalists Material" [1996] Crim. L.R. 231.

[171] *Lidstone*, p.98.

[172] *ibid.* s.18. This power, unlike s.32, is not limited to cases where the person was there at the time of or immediately before arrest. The authorisation must be contained in an independent document (a record of oral authority included in a notebook is insufficient): *R v Badham* [1987] Crim. L.R. 202 (Wood Green Crown Court).

[173] e.g. in *Lineham v DPP* [2000] Crim. L.R. 861 where officers refused to slide a warrant under the door and the occupier refused to view the warrant pressed to the window. The officers failed to explain the reason for the search.

[174] Consent by a purported victim of crime does not render inadmissible evidence discovered when the "victim" is prosecuted relying on evidence discovered: *R v Sanghera* [2001] 1 Cr.App.R. 299.

[175] Pursuit must be almost contemporaneous with entry: *D'Souza v DPP* [1992] 4 All E.R. 545.

prevent serious damage to property.[176] The constable must have reasonable grounds for believing that the person sought is there. The constable exercising this power must, unless it is impracticable or undesirable, give the occupier a legitimate reason for doing so (not merely that he wants to speak to the occupier).[177] All common law powers of entry were abolished, save that of entry to deal with or prevent a breach of the peace.[178]

Powers of seizure under s.19 are very wide, with a requirement that the officer lawfully on premises reasonably believes that the item was obtained in connection with the commission of an offence or as a consequence of a commission of an offence, that it is not legally privileged, and that it is necessary to seize the item to avoid concealment, loss or destruction.[179] Powers of seizure have been interpreted broadly, and it has been held that the police even have powers under ss.18 and 19 to seize the premises themselves where they are mobile.[180]

For entry to premises to be justified by reference to s.17(1)(b) to arrest a person for an indictable offence, the police officer entering must have reasonable grounds to suspect the person sought to be guilty of the offence in question; the provision cannot justify entry to effect an unlawful arrest.[181]

Where a person is arrested by a constable away from a police station, that person may be searched on arrest if the constable has reasonable grounds to believe that he or she may present a danger to self or others, or has something which might be used to assist an escape, or which might be evidence relating to an offence. In addition, the constable may enter and search any premises in which the person was at the time of or immediately before the arrest, for evidence relating to the offence in question, if he or she has reasonable grounds to believe that such evidence is there.[182]

Although PACE provides a comprehensive code of search powers, adequate protection against an unjustifiable invasion of privacy is only secured by the strict interpretation adopted by the courts.

(d) Police/state surveillance

14–015 Policing has become increasingly reliant on forms of surveillance of suspects that fall short of arrest and do not involve overt entry and seizure from the premises of the individual.[183] Initially such activities were pursued only by the intelligence agencies, but they now form a significant part of everyday policing. There is little doubt that the reliance on undercover policing will continue to increase as technology develops to permit this, as criminal activity diversifies in more

---

[176] s.17. See the court's stay of proceedings when the police had entered, without statutory authority, the premises of an unconscious person to check for the identity of relatives and had discovered quantities of drugs: *R v Veneroso* [2002] Crim. L.R. 306 (April).

[177] See *O'Loughlin v Chief Constable of Essex* [1998] 1 W.L.R. 374; see also *Linehan v DPP* [2000] Crim. L.R. 685.

[178] See *Thomas v Sawkins* [1935] 2 K.B. 249; *Friswell v Chief Constable of Essex Police* [2004] E.W.H.C. 3009 (QB) the police officer does not have the power to enter premises to investigate whether a further breach of the peace would occur.

[179] s.19(2).

[180] *Cowan v Metropolitan Police Comr.* [2000] 1 W.L.R. 254, CA (Civ. Div.).

[181] *Kynaston v DPP* (1987) 87 Cr.App.R. 200, DC.

[182] PACE, s.32.

[183] Overt surveillance is also playing an increasing role in everyday policing activity, for example see *Plymouth Head Camera Project: Body Worn Digital Recording System Interim Report* (2007) available at *www.homeoffice.gov.uk*.

sophisticated ways, and as policing becomes more intelligence led and targeted.[184] It is necessary for the law to have clear regulation on the process of the authorisation for operation of, and remedies against, such intrusive policing activities. Surveillance, particularly when carried out covertly, raises human rights concerns, and it is arguably the case that it is only the presence of the Human Rights Act that has been the spur towards comprehensive regulation of surveillance techniques.

Under Art.8 of the ECHR, secret surveillance must be prescribed by law, as well as being necessary and proportionate to achieve a legitimate aim identified in Art.8(2).[185] As the European Court has forcefully explained, state surveillance "can undermine or even destroy democracy on the ground of defending it".[186] There is no doubt that state surveillance is an interference with the private life of the citizen,[187] and that Art.8 will be applicable to police surveillance; the main question will be as to whether the interference is in accordance with law,[188] is necessary and proportionate to a legitimate aim,[189] and is sufficiently accessible and precise to prevent arbitrary application.

The absence of adequate domestic safeguards to regulate the action of the police in fitting covert listening devices to a suspect's house was described by the House of Lords in *Khan*[190] as "astonishing". The Police Act 1997 sought to provide regulation in this area.

Part III of the Police Act provides limited regulation of surveillance involving entry on/interference with property, and provides immunity from civil and criminal liability for those acting under its terms of authorisation.[191] Supervision of the procedures is carried out by "Surveillance Commissioners"[192] appointed by the Prime Minister from the ranks of senior judiciary, and a Code of Practice is issued under s.71 of the Regulation of Investigaory Powers Act 2000. The Act was, however, merely another example of a piecemeal approach to the regulation of surveillance.

The Regulation of Investigatory Powers Act 2000 (RIPA)[193] seeks to introduce a more comprehensive code of surveillance measures including surveillance of internet data, and the types of communication not dealt with in the Police Act 1997: pagers, e-mails, mobile phones, etc. All forms of covert surveillance other than those involving covert entry upon or interference with property or wireless telegraphy are now regulated by RIPA. The Act aims to ensure compliance with

---

[184] See generally HMIC, *Policing with Intelligence* (1997); Justice, *Under Surveillance* (1998); S. Davies, *Big Brother: Britain's Web of Surveillance and the New Technological Order* (1996).

[185] *Kopp v Switzerland* (1998) 27 E.H.R.R. 91; *Klass v Germany* (1978) 2 E.H.R.R. 24. S. Uglow "The Human Rights Act 1998: Part 4: Covert Surveillance and the European Convention on Human Rights" [1999] Crim. L.R. 287; N. Taylor, "State Surveillance and the Right to Privacy" (2002) Surveillance and Society 1(1).

[186] *Klass v Germany* (1979–80) 2 E.H.R.R. 214.

[187] *Kopp v Switzerland* (1998) 27 E.H.R.R. 91; *Valenzuela v Spain* (1999) 28 E.H.R.R. 483; *Khan v UK* [2000] Crim. L.R. 684. See *Amann v Switzerland* (2000) 30 E.H.R.R. 843, which seems to adopt a strict approach in interpreting Art.8.

[188] See *Valenzuala v Spain* (1999) 28 E.H.R.R. 483.

[189] See N. Taylor, "Policing, Privacy and Proportionality" [2003] *E.H.R.L.R* Special Issue 86.

[190] [1997] A.C. 558. See further, *Khan v UK* [2000] Crim. L.R. 684; (2001) 31 E.H.R.R 45.

[191] s.92. See generally ss.91–108.

[192] Regulation of Investigatory Powers Act 2000, s.81(1).

[193] See also the following comprehensive discussions of the provisions: Y. Akdeniz, N. Taylor, and C. Walker "Regulation of Investigatory Powers Act 2000: Bigbrother.gov.uk: State Surveillance in the Age of Information and Rights" [2001] Crim. L.R. 73; H. Fenwick, *Civil Liberties and Human Rights* (3rd edn, 2002), pp.670–726; C. Harfield and K. Harfield, *Covert Investigation* (2005).

the Human Rights Act 1998, and this is apparent from its structure: each
authorisation must be based on necessity and proportionality, and the list of
specified aims reflects those in Art.8(2).[194]

Part I of the 2000 Act regulates surveillance over post and telecommunications.[195] The Secretary of State is responsible for authorising all intercepts
(which can only be requested by senior officers).[196] The warrants are for limited
duration,[197] and the authorisation is reviewed by the independent Interception
Commissioner. Although authorisation can be justified on very wide grounds,
including the prevention and detection of crime, these provisions represent an
improvement on those contained in the now repealed Interception of Communications Act 1985, since, for example, they extend to private telephone networks
that are connected to public telecommunications systems.[198]

Part II of RIPA provides a regulatory framework for the use of three types of
covert surveillance,[199] namely, directed surveillance, intrusive surveillance and
the use and conduct of covert human intelligence sources. The distinction
between "directed"[200] and "intrusive" surveillance[201] is crucial, but is argued by
many to be flawed. "Directed surveillance" is defined as covert surveillance that
is undertaken in relation to a specific investigation or a specific operation which
is likely to result in the obtaining of private information about a person.[202]
"Intrusive surveillance" is defined as covert surveillance carried out in relation
to anything taking place on residential premises.[203] Greater protection is afforded
against intrusive surveillance than in respect of directed surveillance; with
intrusive surveillance requiring authorisation from the Home Secretary or specified senior officers.[204] Similarly, the purposes for which intrusive surveillance
can be granted are more limited, and, in addition to the grounds of national
security and economic well being of the country, include that the surveillance be
necessary and proportionate to the detection/prevention of serious crime.[205] The
authorisation procedure for directed surveillance is much less rigorous, being
satisfied by a designated person—in the police, a superintendent. Although the
Code specifies that authorising officers should not "ideally be responsible for

---

[194] The supervision of covert police activities is governed by Pt IV of RIPA which provides powers
for the appointment of interception of communications commissioners. Provision is also made for
the appointment of intelligence service commissioners and chief surveillance commissioners and
a tribunal to consider complaints (see s.65). This is less satisfactory than a requirement of full
judicial supervision in every case, and the prior authorisation of the Commissioners is not
required for every act of surveillance.
[195] Prompted by *Halford v UK* [1997] 24 E.H.R.R. 523.
[196] RIPA, s.6(2).
[197] Usually three months: s.9(6).
[198] See *R v Allan* [2001] Crim. L.R. 739.
[199] For a discussion of the meaning of "covert", see *R v Rosenburg* [2006] Crim. L.R. 540.
[200] s.26(2).
[201] s.26(3)–(5).
[202] Private information is defined as being "any information relating to a person's private or family
life or personal relationships with others". See Covert Surveillance Code of Practice (2005),
para.4.3. This clearly ensures that private information extends beyong the traditional public/
private spheres. Further, see: *P.G. and J.H. v United Kingdom*, No.44787/98; *Perry v United
Kingdom* (2004) 39 E.H.R.R. 3. A wide range of public authorities are empowered to carry out
directed surveillance, and these are listed in the Schedule to RIPA. For intrusive surveillance, see
RIPA, s.32(6).
[203] As defined in s.48.
[204] See RIPA 2000 (Prescription of Officers, Ranks and Positions) Order 2000 (SI 2000/2417).
[205] s.81(3).

authorising their own activities",[206] the procedure lacks sufficient independent supervision and has been heavily criticised. For directed surveillance the authorizing officer must apply two tests before granting an authorization, namely, he or she must believe the authorization is proportionate to what is sought to be achieved and that the action is necessary for one of the purposes specified in s.28(3).[207] Only conduct specified plainly in the authorisation will be lawful, and therefore applications should be clear and comprehensive. Lack of attention to the wording of applications has been a common deficiency highlighted by the Office of the Surveillance Commissioner.[208]

The distinction between intrusive and directed surveillance will obviously affect the likelihood of the authorisation being granted and the degree of scrutiny the request receives, and yet the distinction rests on the place being investigated and not on the person affected or the degree of privacy in the individual circumstances.[209]

Part II of the Act also provides for the regulation of "covert human intelligence sources" (informants and other undercover sources). These are defined as people who "establish or maintain a personal relationship with a person for the covert purpose of using the relationship to obtain information or provide access to information to another person or covertly disclosing information obtained by the use of such a relationship or as a consequence of the existence of such a relationship".[210] Given the increased use of such individuals in the era of intelligence-led policing, regulation is essential, but it is regrettable that the authorisation procedure is limited to that for directed surveillance. There is no offence of failure to obtain an authorisation, but such a failure will amount to an unlawful act under the Human Rights Act 1998.[211]

One of the most controversial aspects of RIPA was the introduction in Pt III of powers to compel the compulsory disclosure of encryption keys (or a plain text copy) for electronically-held material. The fear that criminals would be able to exploit the internet and electronic communications systems and that their activities would not be capable of effective investigation and detection led to these far-reaching provisions. Despite these powers, which were introduced in the face of considerable opposition, the Act has in fact been criticised for failing to keep pace with technology.[212] Despite the pronouncements that such powers were a necessary addition to RIPA, Pt III has yet to be brought into force.[213]

An individual aggrieved by the use of any of the powers in RIPA or Pt III of the Police Act has redress only to the tribunal established under RIPA.

---

[206] Covert Surveillance Code of Practice, para.3.10.

[207] This is explained by the Office of the Surveillance Commissioner, *Annual Report 2000–2001*, (2001) para.4.13. See also the problems highlighted in *R v Grant* [2005] EWCA Crim 1089; D. Ormerod and A. Waterman, "Abusing a Stay for Grant?" [2005] Covert Policing Review.

[208] Office of the Surveillance Commissioner, *Annual Report 2003–2004*, (2004) para.12.

[209] e.g. see *R v Rosenburg* [2006] Crim. L.R. 540.

[210] s.26(8). Further, see B. Fitzpatrick, "Covert Human Intelligence Sources as Offenders: The Scope of Immunity from the Criminal Law" [2005] Covert Policing Review 15.

[211] s.65. Challenges to the legitimacy of surveillance should be made through the tribunal established for this purpose.

[212] See Y. Akdeniz, N. Taylor, and C. Walker "Regulation of Investigatory Powers Act 2000: Bigbrother.gov.uk: State Surveillance in the Age of Information and Rights" [2001] Crim. L.R. 73.

[213] Office of the Surveillance Commissioners, *Annual Report 2005–06* (2006) H.C. 1298, para.2.5.

(e) Detention[214]

14–016 PACE greatly improved the position of the suspect in police detention. Prior to the Act the Judges' Rules offered the only protections and these were not of statutory status, were confusing and did not offer comprehensive protection. PACE introduced for the first time detailed arrangements regulating the length of time persons may be kept in custody by the police before a court appearance. Under these arrangements, a person arrested by a constable must either be taken to a police station as soon as practicable,[215] or be released under what is termed "street bail", and required to attend a station at a later date.[216] If the suspect is taken to a station, this should normally be a "designated police station" (i.e. one of the stations designated by the chief officer of police as having enough accommodation for detained prisoners).[217] In some circumstances any station may be used, but no-one may be kept longer than six hours at a non-designated station.

Under s.29 of PACE an individual may be present at the police station without being arrested. The volunteer is free to leave at any time unless he is arrested.[218] If a person is not arrested, but is cautioned, the officer who cautions him must also inform him that he is not under arrest, that he is not obliged to remain, but that if he does he is entitled to free legal advice.[219]

(i) *The custody officer*

14–017 An important feature of the arrangements for protection during detention is the division of function between the custody officer (CO) and the officers concerned with the investigation. One or more COs (of at least the rank of sergeant) must be appointed for each designated police station[220] and a variety of duties are imposed directly on that officer once a person has been brought to the station. Subject to a few exceptions, the CO must not be involved in the investigation,[221] as he or she is supposed to provide independent scrutiny of the suspect's position in detention. Under the Police Reform Act 2002 the police are able to appoint civilian custody officers,[222] who are able to perform certain of the functions of the police CO. Such appointments are open to the criticism that civilians will not be sufficiently able to uphold suspects' rights in the face of pressure from investigating officers. However, in the alternative it may be that such civilians,

---

[214] See generally Sanders and Young (2007), Ch.4; *Blackstone's Criminal Practice* (2007) D1.36–1.68. Note also Home Office Consultation Paper, *Modernising Police Powers: Review of the Police and Criminal Evidence Act 1984* (2007) Ch.3.

[215] PACE, s.30. Any delay in taking the suspect to the station must not be used to circumvent the procedural guarantees in relation to questioning. See *R v Khan* [1993] Crim. L.R. 54; *R v Raphaie* [1996] Crim. L.R. 812.

[216] *ibid.* s30A, as inserted by the Criminal Justice Act 2003, Pt 2.

[217] *ibid.* s.35.

[218] See on the abuse by the police of this situation J. McKenzie, R. Morgan and R. Reiner, "Helping the Police with their Inquiries" [1990] Crim. L.R. 22.

[219] PACE Code C: *Detention, Treatment and Questioning of Persons by Police Officers* (2006), para.3.21.

[220] There is a *duty* to appoint one and a *discretion* (which must be exercised reasonably) to appoint more: *Vince v Chief Constable of the Dorset Police* [1993] 2 All E.R. 321.

[221] *ibid.* s.36. An officer of any rank may perform the functions of a custody officer if such an officer is not readily available: s.36(4).

[222] Sch.4.

unaffected by deep rooted police culture, might be able to cast a more objective eye over the detention regime.

COs have been very heavily criticised. McConville, Sanders and Leng describe officers in their research who were "complicitous in the creation of [an] off-the-record interview by permitting the case officer to visit the suspect in the cells or by authorising his release to the interviewroom without recording it".[223] However, in research for the Home Office, Brown[224] found that "custody officers show considerable independence in the way they carry out their job although practical constraints limit their examination of the evidence against a suspect when considering whether to authorise detention".[225] It is important that there is no detention without adequate justification, as Art.5(i)(c) of the ECHR requires.[226]

The range of important responsibilities falling on the CO includes the evaluation of whether the person arrested was lawfully arrested. The CO is entitled to assume, in the absence of any evidence to the contrary, that the arrest is lawful.[227]

The CO must determine, as soon as practicable, whether there is sufficient evidence to charge the person arrested (D).[228]

If in the CO's view there is sufficient evidence to charge, D must be (i) charged or (ii) released without charge, either with or without bail.[229] Philips and Brown, in research for the Home Office, found that 52 per cent of those arrested in their survey were charged, 17 per cent cautioned, and in 20 per cent of cases there was no further action. Around 17 per cent of suspects were initially bailed for further inquiries, but 44 per cent of these led to no further action.[230]

Once D is charged with an offence, the CO must order his or her release (with or without bail[231]). Bail will be be granted in most cases[232] unless: (1) D's name and address cannot be ascertained satisfactorily; or the CO has reasonable grounds for believing (2) that D will fail to appear in court to answer to bail; or (3) that where D is arrested for an imprisonable offence, D's detention is necessary to prevent him or her from committing an offence; or (4) that where D is arrested for a non-imprisonable offence, D's detention is necessary to prevent him or her causing physical injury to another or loss or damage to property; or (5) that D's detention is necessary to prevent him or her from interfering with the administration of justice or the investigation of offences (or an offence); or (6) that D's detention is necessary for his or her own protection. In any of these circumstances, the CO may authorise D to be kept in police detention.[233] Bucke

---

[223] *The Case for the Prosecution* (1991), p.58.

[224] *Pace Ten Years On* (1997).

[225] *ibid.* p.2.

[226] *Punzelt v Czech Republic* (2001) 33 E.H.R.R. 49; *Jecius v Lithuania* (2002) 35 E.H.R.R. 16.

[227] *DPP v L* [1999] Crim. L.R. 752.

[228] s.37. The custody officer must determine whether there is sufficient evidence on which to charge D and if there is the case must be passed to the Crown Prosecution Service for a charging decision to be made. See below.

[229] *ibid.* s.37.

[230] Black and Asian suspects were more likely to be bailed than White suspects: p.82.

[231] For analysis see J. Raine and M. Willson, "Police Bail with Conditions" (1997) 37 Brit. J. Crim. 593.

[232] Criminal Justice and Public Order Act 1994, s.25. See generally Sanders and Young (2007), p.175.

[233] PACE, s.38, as amended by the 1994 Act, s.28(2). In the case of an arrested juvenile (generally persons between 10 and 17) there is a further ground; i.e. that the CO has reasonable grounds for believing that D ought to be detained in his or her own interests: s.38(1)(b).

and Brown found that 20 per cent of defendants were refused bail and that 63 per cent were granted unconditional bail.[234] Under the Criminal Justice Act 2003, COs have been given the new power to bail detained persons for the purpose of allowing time for the Crown Prosecution Service to decide whether they are to be charged.[235] Unlike where bail is granted pending further investigation, conditions can be attached.[236]

If in the CO's view there is not sufficient evidence,[237] D must be released (with or without bail), unless the CO has reasonable grounds for believing that D's detention without charge is necessary to secure or preserve evidence relating to an offence for which D is under arrest, or to obtain such evidence by questioning him or her.[238] In that case the CO may authorise D to be kept in police detention, and, if this is done, must open a "custody record" in respect of D, i.e. a written record of the various stages and incidents of the period in detention.

If at any time the CO becomes aware that the grounds of detention have ceased to apply, and he or she is not aware of any other grounds on which continued detention under the Act could be justified, he or she must order D's immediate release.[239] This is to be without bail unless it appears to the CO (1) that there is need for further investigation of any matter in connection with which D was detained, or (2) that proceedings may be taken against D in respect of any such matter.[240]

The CO also has general responsibilities for the welfare of those in detention including ensuring that the requirements of the Act and the Code of Practice governing detention are observed.[241] The CO has a vital role in ensuring that D is informed of his rights from the moment of detention. Under Code C, where a person arrives at a police station under arrest, or is arrested there, the CO must tell him clearly of: (1) his right to have someone informed of the arrest; (2) his right to consult privately with a solicitor, and the fact that independent legal advice is available free of charge; and (3) his right to consult the Codes of Practice.[242] He must be given: (1) a written notice setting out these rights including his right to a copy of the custody record, the terms of the caution (see below), and the arrangements for obtaining legal advice; and (2) an additional notice setting out his entitlements while in custody.[243] Whether the provision of the information is of effective use to the suspect in such circumstances is debatable.[244]

The CO also has a very important role to play in ensuring that vulnerable suspects are adequately protected with the special safeguards relating to the presence of appropriate adults. Special arrangements apply where the person appears to be deaf, or there is doubt about his hearing, or is juvenile, or is mentally handicapped or suffering from a mental disorder, or is blind or seriously

---

[234] (1997), Ch.7.

[235] PACE, s.37(7).

[236] Criminal Justice Act 2003 Sch.2, para.6(3).

[237] Phillips and Brown (1998), found that in 61% of cases the evidence on arrest was reported to be sufficient to charge: p.43.

[238] PACE, s.37(2).

[239] s.39.

[240] ibid.

[241] PACE, s.39. See the Code of Practice for the Detention, Treatment and Questioning of Persons by Police Officers (HMSO, 1995) (Code C).

[242] Code C.3.1.

[243] Code C.3.2.

[244] See Sanders and Young (2007), p.170.

visually handicapped or unable to read.[245] These normally require the involvement of an independent third party such as an interpreter, an approved social worker or an "approved adult" as the case may be.

A custody record must be opened as soon as it is practicable for each person who is brought to a police station under arrest or who is arrested at the police station having attended there voluntarily.[246] The CO is responsible for the accuracy and completeness of the custody record and for ensuring that it accompanies the detained person on any transfer to another station.[247] Where the person leaves police detention, or is taken before a court, he or she, and his/her legal representative or appropriate adult is entitled, on request, to be given a copy of the record and, on giving reasonable notice, to inspect the original.[248] The custody record will prove crucial if a challenge is made to the detention of the suspect in an attempt to have evidence excluded. As elsewhere in PACE, one of the main safeguards for the suspect is the provision of records of all police action.

These various responsibilities may lead a CO into conflict with an officer of higher rank involved in the investigation. Such matters must be referred to an officer of the rank of superintendent or above.[249]

(ii) *Periodic reviews*

Provision is made for there to be periodic reviews of a person's continued **14-018** detention in custody. Thus a "review officer" (the CO if D has been arrested and charged, otherwise an inspector or above not directly involved in the investigation) must carry out a review not later than six hours after the detention was first authorised, and then at intervals not longer than nine hours, although these can in some circumstances be postponed.[250] If D has not been charged by the time of the review, the review officer considers again the matters considered by the CO when initially processing D. Before authorising D's continued detention the review officer must give D (unless asleep), or any solicitor representing D who is available, an opportunity to make representations about the detention.[251]

Compliance with these time limit requirements can be important in subsequent false imprisonment actions. For example, in *Roberts v Chief Constable of Cheshire Constabulary*,[252] R was arrested on suspicion of burglary at 10.50 p.m. and taken to a police station where detention was authorised at 11.25 p.m. At 1 a.m. he was transferred to another station and continued detention was authorised at 1.45 a.m. The first review was conducted at 7.45 a.m., and thereafter at 4.20 p.m. before R was released without charge at 6.55 p.m. R claimed that the first review should have occurred earlier. The Court of Appeal held that the police failure to comply with mandatory provisions in s.34 rendered the detention unlawful and that it was irrelevant that the detention would have been lawfully continued had the review in fact taken place when it should have. The review

---

[245] Code C.3.12–C.3.20.
[246] Code C.2.1.
[247] Code C.2.3.
[248] Code C.2.4, C.2.5.
[249] *ibid*. s.39(6).
[250] *ibid*. s.40(4).
[251] *ibid*. s.40.
[252] [1999] 2 All E.R. 326, CA (Civ. Div.).

should have occurred at 5.25 a.m. and the continued detention after that time was a false imprisonment (even though R was unaware of that at the time).

The Criminal Justice and Police Act 2001[253] allows for reviews to be conducted by telephone or by video-link where necessary. In addition, it provides the opportunity to make custody decisions regarding charging, detention and bail by video-link where the CO is at a different station.

(iii) *Time limits for detention without charge*

14–019   As to the periods of detention under PACE, a person could not be kept in police detention for more than 24 hours without being charged. The Criminal Justice Act 2003 extended the position to allow a further 12 hours to be approved by a superintendent in relation to any arrestable offence. SOCPA has further allowed detention up to 96 hours for any indictable offence. These represent significant extensions of the law.

The "detention clock" normally starts (the "relevant time") when D arrives at the first police station to which he or she is taken after arrest, or, if D is arrested at a police station after attending voluntarily, at the time of arrest. There are special provisions governing persons brought from another police area or outside England and Wales. After the 24-hour period, a person who is not charged must be released, either with or without bail, unless the station superintendent authorises a further 12 hours detention.[254] The superintendent or above must have reasonable grounds for believing that D's continued detention is necessary to secure or preserve evidence relating to the offence for which D is under arrest, or to obtain such evidence by questioning him or her; that the offence in question is an indictable offence; and that the investigation is being conducted diligently and expeditiously. Authorisation cannot be given by the superintendent after the expiry of the 24-hour period or before the second review.[255]

Detention can only be extended beyond the 36-hour period on the authority of a warrant of further detention granted by a magistrates' court.[256] The criteria for the grant of a warrant are the same as for authorisation of continued detention by a superintendent. D must be brought before the court and is entitled to legal representation. The application must be made within the 36-hour period, or, if it is not practicable for a court to sit at the expiry of 36 hours, within six hours thereafter.[257] The warrant may extend the detention for such period as the court thinks fit, up to a maximum of 36 hours.[258] Fresh applications may be made to the court, on the same basis, for the warrant to be extended for further periods not exceeding 36 hours, up to a maximum of 96 hours.[259] The application must be in

---

[253] s.73 inserting into PACE ss.40A and 45A. Regulated by Code C paras 15.9–15.11.

[254] PACE, s.41.

[255] In 2004–05, 1,132 people were detained for more than 24 hours before being released without charge, taken from M. Ayres and L. Murray, *Arrests for Recorded Crime (Notifiable Offences) and the Operation of Certain Police Powers Under PACE* (Home Office Statistical Bulletin 21/05, 2005).

[256] i.e. a court of two or more justices sitting otherwise than in open court: s.45(1).

[257] If an application is made after the 36-hour period, the court will dismiss it if it appears that it would have been reasonable for the police to make it within that period: s.43(7); see *R v Slough Magistrates' Court, Ex p. Stirling* (1987) 151 J.P. 603.

[258] PACE, s.43.

[259] *ibid.* s.44.

writing and explain the progress of the investigation and the reason that an extension is sought. If an application for a warrant or an extension is refused, and in any event at the expiry of the 96-hour period, D must be charged or released, with or without bail. Release may, however, be postponed until the expiry of any period of detention that has already been authorised.[260] Full details of the various steps involved in extending periods of detention must be entered in the custody record. Home Office statistics reveal that warrants for detention are rarely refused.[261]

Statistics on detention times and the influences drawn from them have been controversial since the original studies conducted for the RCCP. The RCCP found that about 75 per cent of suspects were dealt with within six hours and about 95 per cent within 24 hours. A survey conducted by the Metropolitan Police for three months in 1979 showed that only 0.4 per cent of 48,343 persons had been held for over 72 hours without charge or release.[262] Brown[263] in a review of 10 forces found considerable variations from station to station in the length of detention without charge, this being strongly linked with the seriousness of the crime in question, but also perhaps with differences in the CO's approach to PACE. The RCCJ did not think any changes in detention limits were necessary although recommended that further national statistics should be maintained.[264] Given recent changes which allow for extended detention for any indictable offence, close scrutiny of detention statistics must be maintained.

(iv) Detention after charge

Article 6(3) of the ECHR requires that, on being charged, D must be informed, **14–020** "in a language which he understands and in detail, of the nature and cause of the accusation against him".[265]

Where D is kept in detention after charge, he or she must be brought before a magistrates' court as soon as is practicable. If this is to be a local court this must be on the day D is charged or the following day; if this is to be a court in a different petty sessions area, D must be removed to that area as soon as practicable and brought before the court on the day of his or her arrival in the area or the following day. If necessary, the clerk to the justices must make special arrangements for a court to sit.[266] A magistrates' court having power to remand a person in custody may, if the remand is for a period not exceeding three clear

---

[260] For example, by a superintendent where a warrant of further detention is refused (see s.43(15), (16)), or by a warrant if an extension is refused (see s.44(7)(8)).

[261] M. Ayres and L. Murray, *Arrests for Recorded Crime (Notifiable Offences) and the Operation of Certain Police Powers Under PACE* (Home Office Statistical Bulletin 21/05, 2005). In 2004–05, 423 warrants of further detention were applied for and only eight of the applications were refused.

[262] RCCP Report, para.3.96.

[263] D. Brown, *Detention at the Police Station under the Police and Criminal Evidence Act 1984* (Home Office Research Study 104, 1989).

[264] Cm. 2263 (1993), p.30.

[265] Art.6(3). See *Brozick v Italy* (1989) 12 E.H.R.R. 37 and *Pelissier v France* (1999) 30 E.H.R.R. 715.

[266] PACE, s.46. The clerk has a discretion to arrange for a local court or for a court in another division, in accordance with the wishes of the local justices: *R v Avon Magistrates' Courts Committee, Ex p. Brooms* [1988] 1 W.L.R. 1246.

days, commit him to police detention for the purposes of inquiries into other offences.[267]

(v) *The effects of PACE*

14–021   Commentators noted dramatic falls in the levels of complaints about treatment by the police in the charge room or cells[268] and improvements in arrangements for the welfare of suspects.[269] However, there are specific problems with the scheme of PACE protection for detainees revealed by researchers. The initial authorisation of detention by the CO has been found to be, in practice, a formality.[270] Phillips and Brown found it to be exceptional for the CO to refuse detention. Of the 4,250 cases examined, only one case was refused.[271]

Furthermore, it has been claimed that the review process (at least at six and 15 hours) tends to become routinised, with little heed paid to any representations,[272] and it must be questioned whether video review will improve the position.[273] Phillips and Brown in their research for the Home Office found that the average time spent without charge was six hours 40 minutes. The average time for those who sought legal advice was just over nine hours; while for those who did not it was five and a half hours.

The RCCJ[274] noted that the police were "not entirely comfortable with the custody officer role" and that "performance of it, though improving, still leaves something to be desired". They recognised that it might also be unrealistic to expect a CO to take an independent view of a case investigated by colleagues.[275] Nevertheless, the role was recommended to remain with the police rather than be handed to the CPS or an independent body. The CJA 2003 has provided for the appointment of civilian COs. The RCCJ recommended that steps should be taken to develop and strengthen performance of the role, including the delegation of clerical and administrative tasks to civilians under the CO's control; refresher-training; the centralisation of CO functions within forces wherever practicable and their provision as a separate specialist service; the introduction of computerisation of the custody record process to a national standard; and continuous video-recording (including sound-track) of all the activities in the custody office, the passages and stairways leading to the cells and, if feasible, the cell passage and doors of individual cells.

Improvements in custody suite safeguards have also been prompted by a desire to reduce the number of deaths in custody.[276] The improvements have included:

---

[267] Magistrates' Court Act 1980, s.128(7), (8), as inserted by the 1984 Act, s.48.

[268] M. Maguire (1988) 28 Brit. J. Crim. 19, 41.

[269] *ibid.* B. L. Irving and I. K. McKenzie, *Police Interrogation: the effects of the Police and Criminal Evidence Act 1984* (1989), pp.196–198 (replicating the RCCP Research Study No.2, 1980).

[270] I. McKenzie, R. Morgan and R. Reiner [1990] Crim. L.R. 22 at 22–27.

[271] (1998), p.49.

[272] Bottomley, *et al.*, (1991), pp.91–92.

[273] PACE, s.40A and s.45A which effectively reveresed the decision in *R v Chief Constable of Kent, Ex p. Kent Police Federation* [2000] Crim. L.R. 854.

[274] Cm. 2263, pp.30–34.

[275] Researchers have, however, observed instances of conflict between custody and investigating officers over detention before charge and other matters: Bottomley *et al.* (1991), Ch.V.

[276] See Home Office, *Deaths During or Following Police Contact, April 2004 to March 2004* (2004), confirm that in 2003–4, 100 people died in police custody or otherwise in the hands of the police.

in-cell CCTV; life signs monitors; keeping cell hatches closed but ensuring adequate ventilation in cells; evaluation using nurses and community psychiatric nurses in cell suites; introducing the Association of Police Surgeons' medical forms; and recommending that forces consider establishing "custody users groups".[277]

(f) Treatment of persons in custody

Part V of PACE and the Code of Practice on Detention (Code C) give the police certain powers to obtain evidence from persons in custody but, more importantly, make detailed provisions as to the conditions in which such persons are kept. It is important to note that the suspect in police custody, is, at that stage of the proceedings, only held on the basis of—at the minimum—a reasonable suspicion; no charges have been laid.

14–022

The ECHR is significant in offering protection under Art.5 and Art.3 also protects against torture or inhumane or degrading treatment or punishment. There are occasions on which excessive force used by police officers in the course of detention will amount to a breach of Art.3.[278] If the suspect enters police custody without injury and later suffers such, it is incumbent on the State to provide an explanation for the injury.[279] In extreme cases Art.2's protection of a right to life might also have a role to play, particularly as regards deaths in custody.[280]

As a further safeguard against maltreatment, the custody suite of every police station is subject to an inspection, without warning, from the Independent Custody Visitors (formerly Lay Visitors). These are people selected from the local community who have the right to enter the custody suite to check on the well-being of its occupants.[281]

As noted, one of the main safeguards in the PACE system is the CO who has the many responsibilities for the welfare of the suspect as outlined above.[282] The CO must make a record of everything the person detained (D) has with him or her and if necessary D may be searched to enable this to be done.[283] A more

---

[277] See, for example, T. Newburn and S. Hayman, *Policing, Surveillance and Social Control: CCTV and police monitoring of suspects* (2001); *PCA Annual Report 1998–99*. T. Newburn, "The Introduction of CCTV into a Custody Suite: Some Reflections on Risk, Surveillance and Policing", in A. Crawford (ed.) *Crime and Insecurity: The Governance of Safety in Europe* (2002). For a medical review of the problems, see Sir Montague Levine (1998) Medico-Legal Journal 97. See also Home Office, *Drunks and Disorder: Processing Intoxicated Arrestees in Two City Centre Custody Suites* (2002).

[278] See *Rubitsch v Austria* (1995) 21 E.H.R.R. 573; *Assenov v Bulgaria* (1998) 28 E.H.R.R. 65; *Selmouni v France* (1999) 29 E.H.R.R. 403. See also *R v DPP, Ex p. Treadaway* (1994) (1997) July 31, DC.

[279] See *Aksoy v Turkey* (1996) 23 E.H.R.R. 553.

[280] For a comprehensive consideration of deaths in custody, see Joint Committee on Human Rights, *Deaths in Custody*, Third Report of Session 2004–5 (2004) H.C. 137.

[281] The website of the Independent Custody Visiting Association can be seen at: *www.icva.org.uk/*. From this site there is access to Annual Reports and the Code of Practice on Custody Visiting issued pursuant to s.51(6) of the Police Reform Act 2002.

[282] Note also the special responsibilities as regards the child or young person detained in the station (see s.37 as amended) and the responsibilities regarding those with disabilities.

[283] PACE, s.55, as amended by the Criminal Justice Act 1988, Sch.15, para.99. Items may be seized on the same grounds as those set out in s.54(4): s.55(12).

intrusive "*strip search*"—a search involving the removal of more than outer clothing—may be necessary to achieve this.[284] Strip searches are conducted in around 3 per cent of detentions.[285]

An officer of the rank of inspector[286] or above may authorise an *intimate search* if he or she has reasonable grounds for believing D may have concealed on him or her anything which he or she could use to cause physical injury, or a Class A drug (possessed with criminal intent).[287] In 2003–04 there were 93 intimate searches, 81 of which were for drugs, with 11 leading to the discovery of Class A drugs. Of the 93 searches, 13 were carried out by a police officer, 12 in the presence of a suitably qualified person, and 68 by a suitably qualified person.[288]

D's *fingerprints*[289] can be taken, where possible with his or her consent, but they can be taken without consent if D is detained in connection with a recordable offence.[290] The taking of fingerprints is now almost a matter of course, particularly since the need for the approval of an inspector to exercise the power was removed by the Criminal Justice Act 2003. Further changes in 2005 will allow the taking of fingerprints at a place other than a police station where the identity of the suspect is in doubt.[291] If fingerprints are taken then D should be told of the reasons for so doing[292] and that the prints may be checked against existing police records (a "speculative search").[293]

A *non-intimate sample*[294] can be taken without consent,[295] and reasonable force can be used if necessary.[296] Before it is taken the suspect must be warned of its potential use in speculative searches and told of the reasons why the sample

---

[284] See *Wainwright v Home Office* [2003] 4 All E.R. 696 in which the House of Lords rejected a claim that strip searches which did not follow the approved procedure under the Prison Rules breached Arts 3 and 8 of the ECHR.

[285] T. Bucke and D. Brown, *In Police Custody: Police Powers and Suspects' Rights under the Revised PACE Codes of Practice* (1997), p.48.

[286] Formerly the requirement was for a superintendent: see s.78, CJPA 2001.

[287] PACE, s.55, as amended by the 1988 Act, Sch.15, para.99. Items may be seized on the same grounds as those set out in s.54(4): s.55(12).

[288] M. Ayres and L. Murray, *Arrests for Recorded Crime (Notifiable Offences) and the Operation of Certain Police Powers Under PACE* (Home Office Statistical Bulletin 21/05, 2005).

[289] s.78(8) of the CJPA 2001 extends the definition of fingerprints to "a record of the skin pattern and other physical characteristics or features of the fingers or palms", and s.78(7) allows for electronic fingerprinting. Note that the National Automated Fingerprints Identification System gives all forces access to a full national database of convicted criminals' fingerprints on their use at trial. See also *R v Buckley* (1999) 163 J.P. 561.

[290] PACE, s.61(2A). A recordable offence is an offence specified in SI 2000/1139 National Police Records (Recordable Offences) Regulations 2000 (SI 1985/1941).

[291] Serious Organised Crime and Police Act 2005 s.117.

[292] PACE, s.61(7)(a).

[293] PACE, s.61(7A)(a).

[294] i.e. sample of hair other than pubic hair; a sample taken from or from under a nail; a swab taken from any part of the body including the mouth but not any other body orifice; saliva; or a footprint or similar impression of any part of the body other than a part of the hand: s.65, definitions substituted by the Criminal Justice and Public Order Act, ss.58, 59(1). The definition of non-intimate sample is amended by the CJPA 2001, s.81 so that "skin impressions' " may be taken (previously footprints were the only listed non-intimate sample of this nature). The 1994 Act reclassified samples from mouth swabs as non-intimate, in accordance with a recommendation by the RCCJ (Cm. 2263, pp.14–15). This assists DNA profiling: see B. Steventon (1995) 59 Brit. J. Crim. Law 411.

[295] PACE, s.62(3A).

[296] Code D, para.6.7.

is being taken. In most cases, non-intimate samples are taken after charge, rather than as a part of the investigation itself.[297]

An *intimate sample*[298] may only be taken if there is *both* authorisation by an inspector[299] *and* written consent.[300] Authorisation need not precede consent.[301] Under PACE, the authorising officer had to have reasonable grounds to suspect involvement in a recordable offence. The definition of an intimate sample was extended by the Criminal Justice and Public Order Act 1994 Act,[302] with dental impressions now included, but mouth swabs relegated to the non-intimate category.[303] Suspects should be cautioned in accordance with Code D before a sample is taken. Home Office researchers found that intimate samples are taken "very rarely",[304] with blood being the most common form of sample.

The protections in the PACE scheme for taking samples have been eroded by successive statutes. Formerly, an intimate sample other than a sample of urine could only be taken by a registered medical practitioner (or registered dentist in the case of dental impressions).[305] Under the Criminal Justice and Police Act 2001, the taking of an intimate sample can now be taken by a registered nurse. Section 62(1A) of PACE allows for intimate samples to be taken when a person is not in police detention, if the person's previous two non-intimate samples have been taken in the course of the investigation and they have proved insufficient.[306]

The creeping extension of the national DNA database has caused some recent controversy.[307] Non-intimate samples (which includes material from which DNA can be extracted) can now be taken, without consent, from anyone arrested for a recordable offence and detained in a police station, irrespective of whether the sample is relevant to the crime being investigated. DNA samples and profiles may now be retained and the latter held on the national DNA database for comparison with other profiles, irrespective of whether the person is cleared of the offence or not prosecuted. Section 82 of the Criminal Justice and Police Act 2001 removed the obligation to destroy samples and prints where the suspect was cleared of an earlier offence.[308] The retention of samples and private data is

---

[297] T. Bucke and D. Brown (1997), p.45.

[298] i.e. a sample of blood, semen or any other tissue fluid, urine or pubic hair, a dental impression, or a swab taken from a person's body orifice other than the mouth: s.65, definitions substituted by the 1994 Act, s.58. The reference to dental impressions was added on the recommendation of the RCCJ (Cm. 2263, p.15).

[299] Formerly the requirement was of a superintendent.

[300] PACE, s.62, as amended by the 1994 Act, s.54. A court or jury may draw such inferences as appear proper from a refusal without good cause, and a refusal may constitute corroboration: s.62(10).

[301] *R v Butt* [1999] Crim. L.R. 414.

[302] s.58.

[303] The latter change was effected in Northern Ireland by the Criminal Justice Act 1988, Sch.14; for criticism see M. Gelowitz [1989] Crim. L.R. 198 and C. Walker and I. Cram [1990] Crim. L.R. 479.

[304] Bucke and Brown (1997), p.46.

[305] PACE, s.62(9), as amended by the 1994 Act, s.54(5).

[306] An inspector must authorise such a sample and the suspect must consent.

[307] N. Taylor and A. Roberts, "Genes on Record: One Size Fits All?" (2006) N.L.J. 1354; M. Redmayne, "The DNA Database: Civil Liberty and Evidentiary Issues" [1998] Crim. L.R. 437.

[308] This puts the decision of the House of Lords in *Attorney-General's Reference No.3 of 1999* on a statutory footing. A new s.64(3AA) is substituted for the old s.3(A) and (B) and also allows for samples from volunteer mass screenings to be retained if the person is convicted or has given consent (which cannot be withdrawn).

subject to the safeguards in Art.8 of the ECHR.[309] The English courts have held that the retention of DNA samples and fingerprint evidence after a suspect has been cleared of the offence is not incompatible with Art.8.[310]

The use of intimate samples at trial will not constitute a breach of the privilege against self-incrimination. As the ECtHR noted in *Saunders v UK*,[311] the right not to incriminate oneself does not extend to the use in criminal proceedings of material "which may be obtained from the accused through the use of compulsory powers but which has an existence independent of the will of the suspect such as, *inter alia*, documents acquired pursuant to a warrant, breath, blood and urine samples, and bodily tissues for the purpose of DNA testing".[312] Art.8 privacy issues could arise however.

Other important rights provided for the suspect by PACE include the right to have someone informed[313] when arrested and to have access on request to legal advice.[314] Currently, around one-fifth of suspects exercise the right to have a person contacted to inform them of the detention.[315] This right is recognised by the ECHR[316] and is regarded as particularly important for contact with the family of detainees.[317] Under PACE Code C, if the third party chosen cannot be contacted, D may choose up to two alternatives; attempts beyond these may be allowed as a matter of discretion.[318] D must be informed that any letter, call or "message (other than to a solicitor) may be read or listened to as appropriate and may be given in evidence; a telephone call may be terminated if abused; the costs can be at public expense at the discretion of the custody officer".[319] D may receive visits at the CO's discretion.[320] If a friend, etc., makes inquiries about D's whereabouts, the information must be given if D agrees, provided there has been no decision to delay D's right to communicate.[321] D's communication with others may be denied or delayed by an officer of the rank of inspector or above

---

[309] See A. Roberts and N. Taylor, "Privacy and the DNA Database" [2005] E.H.R.L.R 373; *Murray v UK* (1994) 19 E.H.R.R. 193; *X v Germany* (1976) 3 D.R. 1024.

[310] *R (on the application of Marper) v Chief Constable of South Yorkshire* [2004] 4 All E.R. 193; see commentary [2005] Crim. L.R. 136. See generally Victoria Parliament Law Reform Committee, *Forensic Sampling and DNA Databases in Criminal Investigations* (2004: Melbourne VPLRC); Law Reform Commission of Ireland, *Consultation Paper on The Establishment of a DNA Database*, Consultation Paper No.29 (2004); *On the Record: A Thematic Inspection Report* (2000: HMIC) and *Under the Microscope—Refocused* (2002: HMIC). For a sceptical view of the operation of the National DNA Database, see C. McCartney, "Forensic DNA Sampling and the England and Wales National DNA Database: A Sceptical Approach" (2004) 12 *Critical Criminology*, 157.

[311] (1997) 23 E.H.R.R. 313.

[312] *ibid.*, para.69.

[313] PACE, s.56.

[314] *ibid.* s.58. This express legal right replaced the much weaker statement in the Preamble to the Judges Rules that a person under investigation should be able to consult a solicitor privately, even if he or she was in custody, provided no unreasonable delay or hindrance was caused to the investigation or the administration of justice. This was not a legal requirement: in practice few suspects asked to see a solicitor and many requests were refused. In *R v Chief Constable of South Wales, Ex p. Merrick* [1994] 1 W.L.R. 663, DC, the court recognised a common law right of access to a lawyer of a person on remand in custody at a magistrates' court (s.58 of PACE was not applicable).

[315] D. Brown, *PACE Ten Years On* (1997), p.3.

[316] See *McVeigh, O'Neill, and Evans v UK* (1981) 5 E.H.R.R. 71.

[317] See *Cicek v Turkey* February 27, 2001.

[318] Code C.5.1.

[319] Code C.5.7.

[320] Code C.5.4.

[321] Code C.5.5.

if he considers that they may result in either of the conditions in s.56(5)(a) or (b) (in the case of a person detained for an indictable offence).[322]

Even more important is the right to consult a solicitor[323] privately[324] at any time. The right of access to a solicitor vests in the detainee alone, so that a solicitor has no right of access to a client in the custody area.[325] Code C provides that all people in police detention must be informed that they may at any time consult and communicate privately, whether in person, in writing or on the telephone, with a solicitor and that independent legal advice is available free of charge from the duty solicitor.[326] A poster advertising the right to legal advice must be prominently displayed in the charging area of every police station.[327] No police officer must at any time do or say anything with the intention of dissuading a person in detention from obtaining legal advice.[328] D is reminded of the right to legal advice at the beginning of each interview.[329]

The right of access to a solicitor is backed by a statutory 24-hour duty solicitor scheme. Research on the operation of the PACE arrangements indicated that initially there was a significant increase in the number of suspects seeking legal advice, although they still only constituted a minority; that a variety of ploys were used by the police to discourage exercise of the right; that only a small proportion of suspects had a lawyer with them during police interrogation; and that there might have been a rise in the number of suspects who refused to make admissions.[330] In 2001 a new Public Defender Service was established under-taking, *inter alia*, defence work in police stations. Assessments are mixed, with some suggesting that the quality of advice is an improvement on the previous position but that the Service is ultimately similar to that provided by a private

---

[322] The officer must have reasonable grounds for believing that exercise of the right will lead to interference with evidence connected with an indictable offence; interference with or injury to other persons; or the alerting of others suspected of such an offence but not yet arrested; or will hinder the recovery of any property obtained as the result of such an offence, or the value of the suspect's proceeds of drug trafficking; where there are reasonable grounds for believing that D has benefited from the indictable offence and the recovery of that benefit will be hindered by telling the named person of the arrest (Proceeds of Crime Act 2002).

[323] This extends to cover a trainee solicitor, a duty solicitor representative or an accredited repre-sentative on a register maintained by the Legal Services Commission; other representatives are to be admitted unless an officer of the rank of inspector or above considers that such a visit will hinder the investigation of crime: Code C.6.12. See *R v Chief Constable of the Avon and Somerset Constabulary, Ex p. Robinson* [1989] 1 W.L.R. 793. There can be no blanket ban on a particular solicitor's representative: *R (Thompson) v C.C. of Northumbria* [2001] EWCA Civ 321.

[324] See *S v Switzerland* (1992) 14 E.H.R.R. 670 and Art.6(3)(c); *R (La Rose) v Commissioner of Police for the Metropolis* [2001] EWHC Admin 553; *PG and JH v UK* [2002] Crim. L.R. 308, finding a breach of Art.8 where police cells were bugged. The Terrorism Act 2000, Sch.8, para.9 provides that an Assistant Chief Constable can, in specified circumstances, direct that consulta-tion will be in the sight and hearing of an independent officer.

[325] *Rixon v Chief Constable of Kent, The Times*, April 11, 2000, CA (Civ. Div.).

[326] Code C.6.1. On ECHR guarantees of free legal representation, see Art.6 and *Pakelli v FRG* (1984) 6 EHRR 1.

[327] Code C.6.3.

[328] Code C.6.4.

[329] Code C.11.2.

[330] See Sanders and Young (2007), pp.194–214; D. Brown, *Detention at the Police Station under the Police and Criminal Evidence Act 1984* (HORS No.104, 1989), Ch.3 and HORPU Bulletin 26; A. Sanders *et al., Advice and Assistance at Police Stations and the 24 Hour Duty Solicitor Scheme* (LCD, 1989) and A. Sanders and L. Bridges [1990] Crim. L.R. 494; B. L. Irving and I. K. McKenzie, *Police Interrogation* (1989), pp.53–59, 113–115, 157–164, 199–200; A. Sanders and L. Bridges in C. Walker and K. Starmer, Miscarriages of Justice (1999).

firm,[331] whilst the Legal Services Commission has stated that it "provides a better quality of service than private practitioners, according to independent research".[332]

Phillips and Brown confirmed early research findings that those who might benefit most from legal advice "often did not request it because they were anxious not to delay their time in custody or because they were told that they probably would not be charged".[333] Their research also revealed that requests for legal advice varied significantly depending on the offence, and the station at which the suspect was held. In addition, "significant predictors of demand for legal advice [included] ethnic[ity], employment status; previous convictions; condition on arrival at the station; and whether answering police bail".[334]

The improper denial of the right to legal advice is likely to lead to exclusion under s.78 of PACE of any confession.[335] Denial of the right to legal advice might also constitute a breach of Art.6 of the ECHR. The ECtHR has repeatedly emphasised the importance of "prompt" access to legal advice.[336] The right is recognised as important under the Convention; it is not absolute but it is of "paramount importance" when inferences from silence are in issue.

Delay in the exercise of these rights can only be authorised by an officer of the rank of superintendent or above: the officer must have reasonable grounds for believing that exercise of the right will lead to interference with evidence connected with an offence; interference with or injury to other persons; or the alerting of others suspected of such an offence but not yet arrested; or will hinder the recovery of any property obtained as the result of such an offence; or the value of the suspect's proceeds of drug trafficking, or that D has benefited from the indictable offence and the recovery of that benefit will be hindered.[337] In any event, D must be allowed to exercise these rights within 36 hours of the "relevant time".[338] Phillips and Brown[339] found no instance of delay in their survey of 4,250 cases. In one research study, there was no such finding in a sample of 12,500 cases, and previous research has found the percentage of cases to be less than 1 per cent.[340]

---

[331] Sanders and Young (2007), pp.211–212. See, Legal Services Commission, *Public Defender Service: first year of operation* (2002) available at *www.legalservices.co.uk*.

[332] G. Langdon-Down, "Public Defender Service: Staunch Defence" (2007) L.S. Gaz. 22. For a comprehensive review of the Public Defender system, see: L. Bridges, E. Cape, P. Fenn, A. Mitchell, R. Moorhead and A. Sherr, *Evaluation of the Public Defender Service in England and Wales* (2006), available at: *www.legalservices.gov.uk*.

[333] (1998), p.59.

[334] *ibid.* p.62.

[335] See *R v Samuel* [1998] Q.B. 615.

[336] *Imbroscia v Switzerland* (1993) 17 E.H.R.R. 444; *Murray v UK* (1996) 22 E.H.R.R. 29; *Condron v UK* (2001) 31 E.H.R.R. 1; [2000] Crim. L.R. 679; *Magee v UK* [2000] Crim. L.R. 681; *Averill v UK* [2000] Crim. L.R. 682. See also the UN *Basic Principles on the Role of Lawyers* (1990) principles 5 and 8.

[337] "Will" not "might": *R v Samuel* [1988] Q.B. 615: on the ECHR dimension, see *Bonzi v Switzerland* (1978) D.R. 185.

[338] PACE, ss.56(2)–(9), 58(5)–(11), as amended by the Drug Trafficking Offences Act 1986, s.32; Code C, Annex B(A). Access may not be delayed on the ground that the solicitor might advise the person not to answer any questions: *ibid.* Pt (A)3. Access may only be delayed by reference to the specific circumstances of the case: general fears that solicitors will unwittingly carry out messages, etc., will not be sufficient: *R v Samuel*, above; *cf. R v Alladice* (1988) 87 Cr.App.R. 380; *R v Davison* [1988] Crim. L.R. 442.

[339] (1998), p.281.

[340] T. Bucke and D. Brown (1997), p.23.

Where a person is permitted to consult a solicitor, who is available when the interview begins or is in progress, the solicitor must be allowed to be present at the interview.[341] The solicitor may only be required to leave if his conduct is such that the investigating officer is unable properly to put questions, and on the authority of an officer not below the rank of superintendent.[342]

The quality of legal advice remains controversial. A report by Sanders et al.[343] was critical of the quality of service provided by duty solicitors, with a high proportion relying on telephoned advice rather than attendance in person. Phillips and Brown's research confirms that telephone advice is still much more likely from a duty solicitor than a suspect's own.[344] In the last few years there has been a rise in the number of face-to-face consultations, with a decline in telephone advice.[345] Nevertheless, reliance on advice by telephone appears to be relatively commonplace under the new Public Defender Service.[346] Bridges et al. discovered that in some areas of police station practice both the Public Defender Service and private practice performed poorly. "The most notable of these was in the failure to record the advice offered to suspects in police stations regarding their legal position."[347] Research indicates that the length of the consultation lasted, on average, 15 minutes, which represents a considerable increase than that revealed in earlier research.[348]

Research was also critical of the quality of legal advice made available.[349] The RCCJ found the evidence on the quality of legal advice to be "disturbing" but, rather weakly, thought the answer lay in improved training, supervision and monitoring.[350] Research concerning the Public Defence Service revealed that whilst the police service generally thought that the quality of advice given by Public Defence Service lawyers was about the same as private practice lawyers, no one in the survey felt that the quality was better.[351]

Brown's review, in *PACE Ten Years On*, found that around 38 per cent of suspects now request legal advice and that the figure is rising. By 1997, Bucke and Brown reported that the figure was 40 per cent.[352] Of those who request legal advice, around 80 per cent receive it.[353] Custody officers were successful in contacting advisers in 88 per cent of cases in Phillips and Brown's study. Nevertheless commentators claim that: "whether by accident or design, many officers discourage recourse to legal advice much of the time".[354]

---

[341] Code C.6.8.

[342] If readily available, and otherwise an officer not below the rank of inspector who is not connected with the investigation: Code C.6.9, C.6.10.

[343] A. Sanders and L. Bridges in C. Walker and K. Starmer (1999).

[344] Phillips and Brown *op. cit.* p.66.

[345] T. Bucke and D. Brown (1997), p.24.

[346] Sanders and Young (2007) p.212.

[347] Bridges *et al.*, *Evaluation of the Public Defender Service in England and Wales* (2006), p.180.

[348] Bucke and Brown (1997), p.28.

[349] See J. Baldwin, *The Role of Legal Representation at the Police Station* (RCCJ Research Study No.3, HMSO, 1992); M. McConville and J. Hodgson, *Custodial Legal Advice and the Right to Silence* (RCCJ Research Study No.16, HMSO, 1993).

[350] pp.37–39.

[351] Bridges *et al.*, *Evaluation of the Public Defender Service in England and Wales* (2006), p.237.

[352] On the legal profession's attitude to duty solicitor schemes, see Sanders and Young (2007), p.198.

[353] D. Brown, *PACE Ten Years On* (1997), p.2.

[354] Sanders and Young (2007), p.204. On the poor quality of legal advice, see L. Bridges and S. Choongh, *Improving Police Station Legal Advice* (1998) and L. Bridges, E. Cape, A. Abubaker

PACE Code C sets out in some detail many other requirements as to the physical conditions in which detainees are kept[355]; the handling of any complaints[356] about treatment in custody and medical treatment,[357] the welfare of detainees being the basic responsibility of the CO. Concerns about the care and welfare of the suspect in detention have increased in recent years.[358] Phillips and Brown found that 4 per cent of arrestees were too drunk to be dealt with on arrival, 1 per cent were violent and 1 per cent were totally unco-operative with the CO.[359] There have been suggestions to "divert" these people from the police custody suite into other facilities, e.g. "detoxification facilities".[360]

Soon after PACE came into force, Maguire reported that the levels of complaints about treatment by the police in the charge room or cells had fallen dramatically in three of the four areas studied, and that conditions in charge rooms and cells, although not fully satisfactory, had clearly improved. He was surprised by the relaxed and even polite manner in which the procedures were often carried out.[361] Irving and McKenzie noted that the CO role and the record-keeping requirements "have, in Brighton at least, eliminated casual infringement of suspects' welfare rights". Moreover, "the system is now so constituted that if a serious breach of the rules governing the welfare of prisoners does occur, a serious conspiracy would now be necessary to avoid its detection".[362] Despite these early indications the safeguards in PACE do not always protect the suspect adequately against police impropriety, and yet, in successive amendments to the Act, the protections have been eroded by Parliament.

(g) Questioning

14–023 Detailed provision is made in PACE Code C governing the questioning of persons in custody. This replaced the non-statutory Judges' Rules and Administrative Directions to the Police, which had previously provided guidance as to the proper conduct of interrogations.[363] As noted at the beginning of the chapter, the pre-trial process has an enormous impact on the trial process. The significance of the interview in securing confessions and incriminating evidence

---

and C. Bennett, *Quality in the Criminal Defence Service* (2000); Bridges *et al.*, *Evaluation of the Public Defender Service in England and Wales* (2007).

[355] Code C.5, covering, e.g. visits, provision of writing materials, and giving an additional right to make one telephone call; C.8., covering, e.g. the heating, cleanliness and ventilation of cells, bedding, toilet facilities, clothing, meals, exercise and hourly visits.

[356] Code C.9.2. Complaints must be dealt with by an officer of at least the rank of inspector not connected with the investigation.

[357] Code C.9.5.

[358] See, *Napier v The Scottish Ministers* [2004] U.K.H.R.R. 881.

[359] *op. cit.* p.51. See also HORS Paper No.183, *Drugs and Crime: The Results of Research on Drug Testing and Interviewing Arrestees* (2001) HORS No.183. See also A. Sondhi *et al.*, *Statistics from the Arrest Referral Monitoring Programme* (Home Office, 2001).

[360] See further, Independent Police Complaints Commission, *Deaths Following Police Contact Statistics 2004/5* (2005).

[361] (1988) 28 Brit. J. Crim. 19 at 41.

[362] B. L. Irving and I. K. McKenzie, *Police Interrogation: the Effects of the Police and Criminal Evidence Act 1994* (1989), pp.196–198.

[363] The Judges' Rules originated in 1906, with revised versions issued in 1964 and 1978 together with related Administrative Directions from the Home Office. Compliance with the Rules would tend to ensure that a confession was admissible. Breach of a particular Rule or Direction might, but in practice normally did not, render the confession inadmissible.

cannot be underestimated. We offer an outline of the most important aspects of the regulation of questioning.[364]

When introduced, the PACE scheme of regulating questioning represented a clear improvement on the previous procedures. Since then, its effectiveness in protecting the suspect has been undermined in a number of ways: successive parliamentary amendments to PACE have diluted the protections on offer, and, particularly in the case of the right to silence, have undermined the policy behind the scheme. In addition, the protection that PACE offered has been recognised to be defective, for example, in its failure to offer adequate remedies for the breaches of the protections and because some of the key protections are contained only in the Codes of Practice and not in the statute itself. Since PACE, there has however also been an increased awareness of the dangers of false confessions from all suspects in custody not just those in specific categories of vulnerability. The RCCJ did not make any substantial recommendations to improve the position, and although the Human Rights Act 1998 has in some areas led to strengthening of protections, the scheme still has the potential to allow miscarriages of justice.

(i) *The right to silence*

In general, the police may ask any person such questions as they think appropriate.[365] However, the person asked is normally under no duty to answer.[366] A mere refusal to answer cannot constitute the offence of obstructing a police officer in the exercise of his or her duty.[367] The position at common law was that the jury at trial could not normally be expressly invited to draw any adverse inferences from the silence of the accused before the trial (although they could not be stopped from doing so in the privacy of the jury room). In practice, only a minority of suspects questioned by the police relied on their right of silence.[368] Indeed, commentators noted the considerable psychological pressures on suspects:

14–024

---

[364] See Sanders and Young (2007), Chs 4 and 5 and Ashworth and Redmayne (2005), Ch.4 for excellent reviews.

[365] For the contrary historical position see Sanders and Young (2007), Ch.5.

[366] There are some exceptions where a refusal to give information is itself an offence: e.g. the Companies Act 1985, ss.434–436 (investigation of the affairs of a company); and see the non-exhaustive list in Sch.3 to the Youth Justice and Criminal Evidence Act 1999. The ECtHR has found convictions based on evidence secured by these compulsory powers to be contrary to Art.6 of the ECHR: *Saunders v UK* (1997) 23 E.H.R.R. 313.

[367] If the refusal is combined with positive acts that obstruct the police, such as abuse, threats or misleading answers the position may be different: e.g. *Ricketts v Cox* (1981) 74 Cr.App.R. 298.

[368] This was confirmed in the Report of the Royal Commission on Criminal Procedure, Cmnd. 8092 (1981), pp.83–84, based on research it had commissioned: see P. Softley, Research Study No.4 (confession or admission made by 61% of the 187 suspects in the study); B. Irving, Research Study No.2 (admissions made by 65% of the 60 suspects observed). See also J. Baldwin and M. McConville, Research Study No.5 (*Confessions in Crown Court Trials*) and *Courts, Prosecution and Conviction* (1981), Ch.6; J. Vennard, Research Study No.6 (*Contested Trials in Magistrates' Courts*) and H.O. Research Study No.71 (1982); M. Zander [1979] Crim. L.R. 203; B. Mitchell [1983] Crim. L.R. 5.

"To remain silent in a police interview room in the face of determined questioning by an officer with legitimate authority to carry on this activity requires an abnormal exercise of will."[369]

It was a matter of some debate how important confessions or admissions were in establishing the prosecution case. The police certainly regarded interrogation as a central feature of their work, a very high proportion of suspects who made confessions subsequently pleaded guilty, with, *inter alia*, a consequent saving of police time, and only a very small proportion of those who confessed were ultimately acquitted.[370] On the other hand, the research concerning Crown Court cases conducted by Baldwin and McConville for the RCCP indicated that the prosecution's case would only have been fatally weakened had the accused's statement not been adduced in about 20 per cent of cases.[371] Furthermore, false confessions and police misconduct, usually in the form of the inventing of confessions, were identified by JUSTICE as two of the five common threads through most of the allegations of miscarriages of justice made over the years.[372]

In various ways, the arrangements under the 1984 Act were designed to encourage exercise of the right of silence and to improve the reliability of confessions. Thus, a person who asks for legal advice may not be interviewed[373] until he or she has received it unless:

- exercise of the right of access to such advice can properly be delayed; or

- an officer of the rank of superintendent or above has reasonable grounds for believing that; delay will involve an immediate risk of harm to persons or serious loss of or damage to property,[374] or awaiting the arrival of the solicitor would cause unreasonable delay to the process of investigation; or

---

[369] Irving, *op. cit.* p.153. On the psychology of the interrogation process, see B. Irving and L. Hilgendorf, Research Study No.1 (*Police Interrogation: The Psychological Approach*); B. Irving and I. K. McKenzie, *Police Interrogation: the Effect of the Police and Criminal Evidence Act 1984* (1989), pp.17–25, 235–240; G. H. Gudjonsson, *The Psychology of Interrogation and Confessions* (2003); G. H. Gudjonsson, *The Psychology of Interrogations* (2006).

[370] M. McConville and J. Baldwin, *Courts, Prosecutions, and Convictions* (1981), Ch.5, *esp.* pp.106–114.

[371] *ibid.* Ch.6. Evaluations of case papers were made by independent assessors. Research concerning contested magistrates' court cases suggested that confession evidence was most influential in cases based on circumstantial rather than direct evidence: Vennard (1980) and (1982).

[372] JUSTICE, *Miscarriages of Justice* (1989), p.4. The point is reinforced by the presence of unreliable confessions at the heart of many of the high profile miscarriage of justice cases: Walker in C. Walker and K. Starmer (eds), *Justice in Error* (1993), p.14, citing the Guildford Four, the Birmingham Six, Judith Ward, the Tottenham Three and Cardiff Three cases. See also K. Starmer and M. Woolf in C. Walker and K. Starmer (1999).

[373] The definition of "interview" has caused particular difficulty (see H. Fenwick [1993] Crim. L.R. 174; S. Field (1993) 13 L.S. 254). The current definition is "the questioning of a person regarding his involvement in a criminal offence or offences which . . . is required to be carried out under caution" (Code C.11.1A).

[374] It is only on this ground that a person heavily under the influence of drink or drugs can be interviewed at all or an arrested juvenile or a person who is mentally ill or mentally handicapped, a person who has difficulty in understanding English or a hearing disability can be interviewed in a police station in the absence, respectively, of an appropriate adult or of an interpreter: Code C.11.15, 12.3, 13.2, 13.5, and Annex C. Interviews outside the police station are permitted in limited circumstances: Code C.11.1. See *DPP v Blake* [1989] 1 W.L.R. 432 (estranged father of juvenile not an "appropriate adult": see Note for Guidance 1C). On the role of the "appropriate adult" in investigations, see: B. Littlechild, "Reassessing the Role of the Appropriate Adult" [1995] Crim. L.R. 540; J. Hodgson, "Vulnerable Suspects and Appropriate Adults" [1997] Crim. L.R. 785; C. Palmer, "Still Vulnerable After All These Years" [1996] Crim. L.R. 633; H.

- the solicitor nominated cannot be contacted or refuses to attend (and D declines to ask for a duty solicitor or the duty solicitor is unavailable); or

- D agrees in writing or on tape that the interview may be started at once.

In the third and fourth situations above, an officer of the rank of inspector or above must agree for the interview to proceed.

As noted, if D is allowed to consult a solicitor, and the solicitor is available, D must be allowed to have him or her present during the interview. The solicitor may only be required to leave the interview if his or her conduct is such that the investigating officer is unable properly to put questions to the suspect, and then only on the authority of an officer of the rank of superintendent or above.[375] Research suggests that the legal representative is rarely likely to be anything like so interventionist as to present this problem.

Ten years after PACE had been enacted, the government took the view that the safeguards it had introduced were sufficient to justify inroads on the "right of silence" to the extent of permitting the jury or magistrates in certain circumstances to draw adverse inferences from a suspect's silence. This was despite the fact that one year before the changes were introduced, a majority of the RCCJ had concluded that no change should be made to the right to silence in the police station.[376] They believed that:

> "the possibility of an increase in the convictions of the guilty is outweighed by the risk that the extra pressure on suspects to talk in the police station and the adverse inferences invited if they do not may result in more convictions of the innocent."

They recognised the frustration of the police caused by exercise of the right to silence, but thought that experienced professional criminals who wished to remain silent were likely to continue to do so and to justify their position by stating at trial that their solicitors had advised them to say nothing until the allegations against them had been fully disclosed.

The government rejected the majority's view and introduced legislation to permit adverse inferences to be drawn at trial from silence in specified circumstances. The Criminal Justice and Public Order Act 1994 provides that "such inferences as appear proper" may be drawn at various stages of the trial process by a court or jury (and in some circumstances, a judge) in four situations.[377] First, inferences may be drawn from silence at trial: s.35 (these are discussed in Ch.17 below). As regards the pre-trial process, there are three situations to consider.

Section 34(1), provides:

> "where, in any proceedings against a person for an offence, evidence is given that the accused—

Pierpoint, "A Survey of Volunteer Appropriate Adult Services in England and Wales" (2004) 4 Y.J. 32; See also, *www.appropriateadult.org.uk.*

[375] Code C.6.9–6.11. The Notes for Guidance (6D) state that a solicitor may challenge an improper question or the manner in which it is put or advise the client not to reply to particular questions.

[376] *ibid.* pp.50–55, endorsing the position of the RCCP on this point (see Cmnd. 8092, para.4.50).

[377] See I. Dennis [1995] Crim. L.R. 4, 9–18; R. Pattenden [1995] Crim. L.R. 602; P. Mirfield [1995] Crim. L.R. 612.

(a) at any time before he was charged with the offence, on being questioned under caution by a constable trying to discover whether or by whom the offence had been committed, failed to mention any fact relied on in his defence in those proceedings; or

(b) on being charged with the offence or officially informed that he might be prosecuted for it, failed to mention any such fact, being a fact which in the circumstances existing at the time the accused could reasonably have been expected to mention when so questioned, charged or informed. . . . "

In consequence of the introduction of s.34, the caution was changed to the following[378]:

"You do not have to say anything. But it may harm your defence if you do not mention when questioned something which you later rely on in court. Anything you do say may be given in evidence."

It will be noted that while this caution has to be administered, *inter alia*, on arrest,[379] the questioning of a suspect should normally only take place in a police station, where the safeguards of access to legal advice and recording requirements apply.

The second provision affecting the pre-trial process and incrimination is s.36 under which adverse inferences can be drawn from the failure of an accused to account for objects, substances or marks found on arrest on him or his clothing or footwear[380] or in his possession or in any place in which he is at the time of arrest. The arresting or investigating officer must reasonably believe that the object, etc., may be attributed to the suspect's participation in the commission of an offence specified by the officer, who must inform the suspect that he so believes. The constable must also inform the suspect in ordinary language of the effect of the section should he fail to comply with the constable's request. Similar provisions apply to an accused's failure to account for his presence at a place at or about the time the offence for which he was arrested is alleged to have been committed (s.37). The special warnings that must be given to the suspect under Code C: 10.11 explain the offence that is being investigated, what the suspect is to account for, the officer's belief that the fact may be due to the suspect's involvement in the offence, that a court may draw an inference from a refusal to account for the fact and that a record of the interview will be available as evidence. Research reveals that the warning is given in 39 per cent of cases in which a suspect has remained silent,[381] but that the warning is often not understood by the suspect.[382]

The European Court of Human Rights' jurisprudence has proved to be extremely important in restricting the impact of these abrogations of the right to silence in domestic law. Although there is no express right to silence on the face of Art.6, the court found such a right to be embodied in the Art.6 right to a fair

---

[378] PACE, Code C.10.5.
[379] Code C. 10.4.
[380] Or the condition of the clothing or footwear.
[381] T. Bucke *et al.* (2000), p.39.
[382] *ibid.* pp.39–40.

trial.[383] In construing the Northern Irish legislation on which the current English provisions were constructed, the ECHR held in *Murray v United Kingdom*[384] that drawing inferences from silence:

> "is a matter to be determined in the light of all the circumstances of the case, having particular regard to the situations where inferences may be drawn, the weight to be attached to them by the national courts and their assessment of the evidence and the degree of compulsion inherent".[385]

The provisions in ss.34–37 were amended to ensure compliance with this ruling from the ECtHR. Under s.34(2A) no adverse inferences can be drawn from silence or a failure to explain substances, etc., unless the accused has been allowed an opportunity to consult a solicitor prior to being questioned, charged, or informed as mentioned.[386]

In another extremely important decision, *Saunders v United Kingdom*[387] the European Court examined the use of compulsory questions—those backed by a sanction for a failure to answer *per se*. The majority decision is important for the right to silence generally:

> "the right not to incriminate oneself, in particular, presupposes that the prosecution in a criminal case seek to prove their case against the accused without resort to evidence obtained through means of coercion or oppression in defiance of the will of the accused. In this sense the right is closely linked to the presumption of innocence contained in article 6(2)."

This also led to English legislation being amended to ensure compliance.[388]

In *Condron v United Kingdom*,[389] the ECtHR held that the jury must be properly directed to consider the suspect's reasons for silence and that adverse references could not form the sole or main basis for conviction.[390]

In *R v Argent*[391] Lord Bingham laid down the criteria to be met at trial before the jury may draw an inference under s.34. The conditions are that: there must be proceedings against a person for an offence; the alleged failure to mention facts must occur before charge; the alleged failure must occur during questioning under caution by a constable; the questioning must be directed to trying to discover whether or by whom the alleged offence had been committed; the alleged failure must be to mention any fact relied on in his defence; the failure to mention a fact which in the circumstances existing at the time was a fact the

---

[383] In *Murray v UK* (1996) 22 E.H.R.R. 29 the court accepted that the right to remain silent under police questioning and the privilege against self-incrimination were generally recognised international standards which lay at the heart of the notion of a fair procedure under Art.6. However, the drawing of adverse inferences from the defendant's refusal, at arrest, during police questioning and at trial to explain his presence at a house where an IRA informer had been held captive was held not to infringe Art.6; these were reasonable inferences to draw in all circumstances of the case.

[384] [1996] 22 E.H.R.R. 29.

[385] para.61.

[386] As inserted by the Youth Justice and Criminal Evidence Act 1999, ss.58(1), (4).

[387] (1997) 23 E.H.R.R. 313.

[388] See Youth Justice and Criminal Evidence Act 1999, s.59.

[389] (2001) 31 E.H.R.R. 1; See also *Chenia* [2003] 2 Cr.App.R. 83.

[390] See: *Beckles v United Kingdom* [2002] 36 E.H.R.R. 162; *Petkar* [2004] 1 Cr.App.R. 270.

[391] [1997] 2 Cr.App.R. 27.

accused could reasonably have been expected to mention when so questioned.[392] These conditions now form the basis of the Judicial Studies Board specimen direction and have been accepted by the European Court.[393]

Adverse inferences cannot be drawn under s.34 unless the accused relies on a fact at trial that he could have been expected to mention; merely putting the prosecution to proof is not sufficient to trigger the inferences,[394] nor will a defendant's admission of an element of the prosecution case be sufficient.[395] However, s.34 does not apply only where the accused gives evidence, but the "fact relied upon" may come from a witness called by the accused or elicited from a prosecution witness.[396] In any case in which the section does not apply, the jury must be warned that they should not draw any adverse inferences.[397] Where the jury are invited to draw adverse inferences they must be provided with clear judicial guidance on the task.[398] No adverse inferences are to be drawn if the accused has remained silent in response to interviews conducted beyond the point at which it has been established that there is sufficient evidence to charge.[399] No adverse inferences will be drawn unless there exists a prima facie case against the accused without relying on such evidence.[400] Silence cannot form the sole or main element of evidence against the accused.[401]

However, adverse inferences that can be drawn are not limited to the fact that the defendant must have lied in fabricating the new line of defence, but can also include that the defendant refused to reveal his defence earlier because his explanation would not stand up to scrutiny.[402] Most importantly, the provision of legal advice to remain silent cannot in itself prevent adverse inferences being drawn. In *Condron* the Court of Appeal stated that if legal advice to remain silent acted as a bar to adverse inferences being drawn, s.34 would be rendered meaningless.[403] Thus, the jury would have to consider whether the reasons for advice were reasonable. In *Betts*[404] the Court of Appeal moved their position, stating that adverse inferences should not be drawn when the reliance on legal advice to remain silent was genuine. The question of whether that reliance was reasonable was not relevant. *Howell*[405] provided a further twist, however. Here the defendant relied on legal advice to remain silent though he claimed he had

---

[392] His lordship emphasised that the time referred to is the time of questioning, and account must be taken of all the relevant circumstances existing at that time. Matters to be taken into account include the time of day, the defendant's age, experience, mental capacity, state of health, sobriety, tiredness, knowledge, personality and legal advice.

[393] *Beckles v United Kingdom* [2002] 36 E.H.R.R. 162.

[394] *R v Moshaid* [1998] Crim. L.R. 420.

[395] *R v Belts and Hall* [2001] 2 Cr.App.R. 257.

[396] *R v Webber* [2004] 1 W.L.R. 404.

[397] *R v McGarry* [1998] 3 All E.R. 805.

[398] See *R v Birchall* [1999] Crim. L.R. 311; *R v Gill* [2001] 1 Cr.App.R. 61; *Condron v UK* [2001] 31 E.H.R.R. 1. See the guidance provided by the Judicial Studies Board at *www.jsboard.co.uk*. See also *R v Salami* [2003] EWCA Crim 3831.

[399] *R v McGuiness* [1999] Crim. L.R. 318; *R v Pointer* [1997] Crim. L.R. 676; *R v Gayle* [1999] Crim. L.R. 502; *R v Ioannou* [1999] Crim. L.R. 586.

[400] See *R v Hart* [1998] 6 *Arch News* 1; *R v Gill* [2001] 1 Cr.App.R. 61.

[401] s.38(3); *Condron* (above).

[402] *R v Daniel* [1998] 2 Cr.App.R. 373; *Beckles and Montague* [1999] Crim. L.R. 148; *R v Taylor* [1999] Crim. L.R. 77.

[403] *R v Condron* [1997] 1 Cr.App.R. 185, at 191; *Condron v UK* [2001] 31 E.H.R.R. 1.

[404] [2001] Cr.App.R. 257.

[405] [2003] Crim. L.R. 405; see also *R v Knight* [2004] 1 Cr.App.R. 117; *R v Hoare and Pierce* [2005] 1 Cr.App.R. 355. See also E. Cape, "Sidelining Defence Lawyers Police Station Advice After Condron" (1997) 4 E. & P. 386.

wanted to explain himself. What was crucial to the court was not whether reliance was genuine, but whether it was reasonable. This clear conflict was addressed in *Beckles*,[406] where the Court of Appeal adopted a position that requires the reliance on legal advice to be both genuine and reasonable. This places both the client and the legal adviser in a difficult position and perhaps "indicates the difficulty of operating a workable regime of drawing inferences from silence while at the same time promoting the importance of legal advice".[407]

The inroads into the so-called right to silence remain controversial[408] especially given the continuing concern over the effectiveness of safeguards for suspects at the police station and the lack of research data to support police claims that the exercise of the right to silence in a significant number of cases seriously impedes the investigation of offences. Bucke *et al.* conclude that: "whatever philosophical standpoint is adopted, it seems clear that the change in the law has not led to undue practical disadvantages to the defendant".[409] However, academic commentators have argued that the sections produce undue complexity at trial and are too costly in terms of the number of collateral issues and appeals that they generate.[410]

Bucke *et al.* found that, since the 1994 Act, there has been no significant rise in the proportion of suspects requesting legal advice. The figure remained stable at around 40 per cent.[411] The percentage of suspects exercising their right to silence has not altered dramatically since the Act. Those who obtained legal advice were "far more likely to refuse" all questions than those who had not.[412] More serious allegations were more likely to lead to silence as was a suspect having a previous record (13 per cent as opposed to 5 per cent). Bucke *et al.*[413]

---

[406] [2005] 1 All E.R. 705. See also *Beckles v UK* (2003) 36 E.H.R.R. 13.

[407] Ashworth and Redmayne (2005) p.97. See also *R v Loizou* [2006] EWCA Crim 1719 on the loss of legal professional privilege once the defendant provided evidence which related to the advice given to her by her solicitor to remain silent. See also *Archbold News* (2006) 2.

[408] See S. Easton, "Legal Advice, Common Sense and the Right to Silence" (1998) 2 E. & P. 109; S. Seabrooke, "More Caution Needed on Section 34 of the Criminal Justice and Public Order Act 1994" (1999) 3 E. & P. 209; R. Pattenden, "Silence: Lord Taylor's Legacy" (1998) 2 E. & P. 141. See also the excellent review by Dennis: "Silence in the Police Station: the Marginalisation of Section 34" [2002] Crim. L.R. 25; B. Malik, "Silence on Legal Advice: Clarity But Not Justice? *R v Beckles*" (2005) 9 E. & P. 211; A. Choo, "Prepared Statements, Legal Advice and the Right to Remain Silent: *R v Knight*" (2004) 8 E. & P. 62; A. Samuels, "Say nothing or tell them everything? What advice should the lawyer give to theclient charged with a crime?" (2006) 170(8) J.P. 133.

[409] T. Bucke *et al.* (2000), p.73.

[410] See D. Birch, "Suffering in Silence: A Cost-Benefit Analysis" [1999] Crim. L.R. 769.

[411] "Before the Act, 10% of suspects refused to answer all questions, 13% refused to answer some, and 77% answered all. Under the Act, 6% refused to answer all questions, 10% refused to answer some, and 84% answered all." T. Bucke *et al.*, p.31.

[412] *ibid.* p.78.

[413] Of those who received legal advice before the Act, 20% refused to answer all questions, 19% refused to answer some, and 61% answered all. After the Act those figures are 13%, 9% and 78%. For those who did not receive legal advice, the figures before the 1994 Act were: 3% refused to answer all: 9% refused to answer some; and 88% answered all questions. After the Act, the figures are 2%, 6%, and 92%. The Act seems to have had the greatest impact on black suspects far fewer of whom now refuse to answer questions. See Sanders and Young (2007), pp.229; Ashworth and Redmayne (2005), pp.93–99. J. Jackson, M. Wolfe and K. Quinn, *Legislating Against Silence: The Northern Ireland Experience* (2000) after reviewing NI provisions concluded was that "whereas terrorism suspects had not greatly changed their approach to interviews, they were more likely to testify after the 1988 Order"—54% in 1991 compared with 6% in 1987, *ibid.*, p.33.

also assert that there is no reported "miscarriage of justice" resulting from a vulnerable suspect losing his right to silence.

(ii) *Interviewing*[414]

14–025   Code C prescribes that an accurate record must be made of each interview with a suspect.[415] Interviews must normally take place at a police station[416] and the record must normally be made during the course of the interview, which implies either tape-recording the interview or making contemporaneous notes. These were regarded as essential safeguards for the suspect if false confessions were to be avoided and yet were not incorporated as specific statutory criteria with appropriate remedies.

Defining the time at which an interview occurs has proved problematic. The constant conflict is between, on the one hand, treating any dialogue between the police and the suspect as an interview so that the caution is issued and the PACE safeguards are triggered, and on the other, seeking to allow the police to engage in limited initial exchanges which may serve to dispel suspicion and thus avoid escalating the confrontation with the individual. The correct time to caution is when there are grounds for suspicion (objectively assessed) but insufficient evidence to support a prima facie case of guilt. Similarly, it is important that the definition of interview extends to those conversations occurring after charges have been laid, or should have been laid, so that the suspect is not denied the PACE protections.[417] Research for the Home Office[418] found that "little supervision or monitoring of interviews occurs ... [and] some unregulated interviewing continues to occur outside the interview room".

In addition to regulating the interviews, PACE governs the general welfare and environment of the suspect throughout his time in the police station, and this is important because of the potential impact on interview vulnerability. In any period of 24 hours eight hours must normally be free from questioning, travel or other interruptions, if possible at night. Interview rooms must be adequately heated, lit or ventilated. Breaks must normally be made at recognised meal times and at two-hour intervals. Full details must be recorded of the periods and of incidents of the interrogation. Written statements under caution must be taken in accordance with Annex D to the Code.

14–026   All interviews by police officers at police stations with a person suspected of an indictable offence must be tape-recorded in accordance with the *Code of*

---

[414] See Sanders and Young (2007), Ch.5 and Ashworth and Redmayne (2005), Ch.4.

[415] Code C.11. The Code makes it clear that a written record must be kept of all interviews and other comments by suspects, and, unless impracticable, shown to the suspect.

[416] Following a decision to arrest, the suspect may not be interviewed about the relevant offence except at a police station unless the consequent delay would be likely to lead to interference with or harm to evidence or other people or lead to the alerting of other suspects not yet arrested; here, interviewing must cease once the relevant risk has been averted or the necessary questions put: Code C.11.1. Research studies for the RCCJ showed that questioning outside the police station still occurred in a significant proportion of cases (10% in one study, 8% in another); it was, however, impossible to estimate the frequency of pre-interview "discussions" between police and suspect, possibly with the use of inducements or threats: Cm.2263, pp.26–27. On the recommendation of the RCCJ any "significant" statement or silence which occurred before arrival at the station must be put to the suspect at the start of any interview there: Code C.11.4.

[417] See *R v Pointer* [1997] Crim. L.R. 676.

[418] *PACE Ten Years On* (1997), p.30.

Practice on Tape Recording (PACE Code E).[419] The RCCJ noted Baldwin's finding that there were additional benefits to video over audio-taping in some 20 per cent of the cases studied, although showing such recordings to jurors and magistrates might have some prejudicial effect, for example symptoms of nervousness might be mistaken for symptoms of guilt; a powerful visual impact might distract from what was said. The RCCJ majority recommended further research.[420] The Criminal Justice and Police Act 2001 makes provision for the video-taping of interviews, but this is not a statutory requirement.[421] Whilst this offers better protection for the suspect, it must be remembered that the video can only record what occurs in the police interview room and only when it is switched on.

Question marks over the effectiveness of the PACE regime in protecting the interests of suspects under interrogation, and in minimising the risk of false confessions[422] remain. The formal position of the suspect is now considerably enhanced by comparison with the pre-PACE position. However, effectiveness of the formal structure is undermined by such factors as the poor quality of much legal advice in the police station. Furthermore, access to taped records of interviews has demonstrated the very poor quality of much of the interviewing conducted by police officers.[423] In response, "the police service, on an official level at least, has been stressing that questioning a suspect is only part of the process of investigation—and a decreasingly important part".[424]

A Home Office circular[425] laid down principles of investigative interviewing, emphasising, *inter alia*, the points that the role of interviewing should be to obtain accurate and reliable information in order to discover the truth about matters under police investigation, that interviewing should be approached with an open mind, that when questioning anyone a police officer must act fairly and that vulnerable people must be treated with particular consideration at all times. These developments were welcomed by the RCCJ.[426] The RCCJ (by a majority) rejected proposals that a conviction should never be based solely on an uncorroborated confession, and (unanimously) rejected proposals that no confession should be admissible unless made or confirmed in the presence of a solicitor.

---

[419] Police and Criminal Evidence Act 1984 (Tape-recording of Interviews) (No.1) Order 1991 (SI 1991/2687) and (No.2) Order 1992 (SI 1992/2803 as amended by the Police and Criminal Evidence Act 1984 (Tape-recording of Interviews) (Amendment) Order 2001 (SI 2001/2480).

[420] See further A. Leonard (1991) 141 N.L.J. 1512; M. McConville [1992] Crim. L.R. 532 and (1992) 142 N.L.J. 960 and 1120; J. Baldwin (1991) 141 N.L.J. 1512 and (1992) 142 N.L.J. 1095. See RCCJ, Cm. 2263, pp.39–40. See also on the risks of video evidence at trial: D. W. Elliott, "Video-Tape Evidence and the Risk of Overpersuasion" [1998] Crim. L.R. 159.

[421] s.76, inserting s.60A into PACE. See PACE Code F on visual recording with sound of interviews with suspects.

[422] See Sanders and Young (2007), pp.275–278.

[423] J. Baldwin, "Police Interview Techniques" (1993) 33 Brit. J. Crim. 325, *cf.* the observations of the Court of Appeal in *R v Paris, Abdullahi and Miller* (1993) 97 Cr.App.R. 99.

[424] *ibid.* pp.325–326.

[425] 22/1992. H.O. Circular 7/1993 announced a new national training package for basic interviewing skills. See Sanders and Young (2007), pp.263–269.

[426] Cm. 2263, pp.11–14. T. Williamson, "Reflections on Current Police Practice" in D. Morgan and G. M. Stephenson, *Suspicion and Silence* (1994), Ch.7, noting (at p.111) that the principles of investigative interviewing were not yet widely understood. See also T. Newton, "The Place of Ethics in Investigative Interviewing by Police Officers" (1998) Howard Jnl. 52. See also E. Shepherd and R. Milne, "Full and Faithful: Ensuring Quality Practice and Integrity of Outcome in Witness Interviews" in A. Heaton-Armstrong, E. Shepherd and D. Wolchover (eds), *Analysing Witness Testimony* (1999) and see B. Clifford and A. Memon, "Obtaining Detailed Testimony: The Cognitive Interview" *ibid.*

However, they did recommend (unanimously) that the judge at trial should warn the jury that great care is needed before convicting on the basis of a confession alone.[427] The recommendation was ignored.

In addition to these changes to the regime of police interrogation, PACE led to important changes in the law governing the admissibility of confessions and admissions in evidence.[428] The key provisions are s.76 of PACE, which relates to confessions, and s.78, which concerns the exclusion of all kinds of evidence. The basic test is found in s.76(2):

> "(2) If, in any proceedings where the prosecution proposes to give in evidence a confession[429] made by an accused person, it is represented to the court that the confession was or may have been obtained
>
> (a) by oppression[430] of the person who made it; or
> (b) in consequence of anything said or done which was likely, in the circumstances existing at the time, to render unreliable any confession which might be made by him in consequence thereof, the court shall not allow the confession to be given in evidence against him[431] except in so far as the prosecution proves to the court beyond reasonable doubt that the confession (notwithstanding that it may be true) was not obtained as aforesaid."[432]

Section 78(1) provides:

> "In any proceedings the court may refuse to allow evidence on which the prosecution proposes to rely to be given if it appears to the court that, having regard to all the circumstances including the circumstances in which the evidence was obtained, the admission of the evidence would have such an adverse effect on the fairness of the proceedings that the court ought not to admit it."

This is applicable to confessions as well as other kinds of evidence.[433]

---

[427] Cm. 2263, pp.57–68. On corroboration and confessions see R. Pattenden, "Should Confessions be Corroborated" (1991) 107 L.Q.R. 319; Sanders and Young (2007), pp.273–275.

[428] See generally: P. Mirfield, *Silence and Improperly Obtained Evidence* (1997); I. H. Dennis, *The Law of Evidence* (2nd edn, 2002); A. Keane, *The Modern Law of Evidence* (6th edn, 2006), Ch.13; A. Choo, *Evidence* (2006) Ch.2; D. J. Birch, "The Pace Hots Up: Confessions and Confusions under the 1984 Act" [1989] Crim. L.R. 95.

[429] This "includes any statement wholly or partly adverse to the person who made it, whether made to a person in authority or not and whether made in words or otherwise" (s.82(1)); it therefore covers any admission, not just a full confession.

[430] This "includes torture, inhuman or degrading treatment, and the use or threat of violence (whether or not amounting to torture)": s.76(8). Note also the protections in Art.3 of the ECHR as outined above.

[431] If a confession is put before the jury and the judge subsequently has doubts about oppression or reliability, it is too late for exclusion under s.76, although the judge could discharge the jury or direct the jury to disregard the statement under the common law: *R v Sat-Bhambra*, above.

[432] The court may require this to be proved of its own motion: s.76(3).

[433] *R v Mason* [1988] 1 W.L.R. 139. The court's common law powers to exclude evidence were preserved by s.82(3). The ambit of these powers was uncertain, although they clearly included power to exclude evidence whose probative value was outweighed by its prejudicial effect: *R v Sang* [1980] A.C. 402. In *Matto v Wolverhampton Crown Court* [1987] R.T.R. 337, Woolf L.J. (as he then was) indicated that s.78 was if anything wider than the common law (p.346).

The courts have employed these sections to exclude confession evidence rather more vigorously than had been anticipated. The first hurdle is that of "oppression", to which the Court of Appeal in *R v Fulling*[434] accorded its dictionary meaning as the "exercise of authority or power in a burdensome, harsh or wrongful manner; unjust or cruel treatment of subjects, inferiors etc., the imposition of unreasonable or unjust burdens".

The court noted, with apparent approval, a quotation in the dictionary under this definition: "There is not a word in our language which expresses more detestable wickedness than oppression", and continued: "We find it hard to envisage any circumstances in which such oppression would not entail some impropriety on the part of the interrogator."[435] This definition is narrower than the concept of "oppression" at common law,[436] but wider than that suggested by the definition section in the Act.[437] There have been few cases in which a confession has been excluded on this ground.[438] In *R v Fulling*[439] itself, D confessed while (so she claimed) in distress following the revelation by the interrogator that her boyfriend had for some three years been having an affair with the woman currently held in the next cell: this was held not to constitute oppression. The most notorious case where oppression has been found is *R v Paris, Abdullahi and Miller*[440] (the "Cardiff Three"), where the Court of Appeal (Criminal Division) quashed the convictions of the three appellants for murder. Miller had been interviewed for some 13 hours. Having denied involvement over 300 times, he was finally persuaded to make admissions. Lord Taylor C.J. stated that each member of the court had been "horrified" by what they heard in the tape recording of one interview:

> "Miller was bullied and hectored. The officers . . . were not questioning him so much as shouting at him what they wanted him to say. Short of physical violence, it is hard to conceive of a more hostile and intimidating approach by officers to a suspect."[441]

Moreover, Miller's solicitor

> "appears to have been gravely at fault for sitting passively through this travesty of an interview".[442]

---

[434] [1987] Q.B. 426. The decision is criticised for its ambiguity in Sanders and Young (2007), p.251.

[435] *ibid.* p.432. See also *R v Hughes* [1988] Crim. L.R. 545, CA (no police misconduct, so not oppression where, through a misunderstanding, D did not see the Duty Solicitor).

[436] "something which tends to sap, and has sapped, that free will which must exist before a confession is voluntary" (*per* Sachs L.J. in *R v Priestly* (1967) 51 Cr.App.R. 1); *cf.* Edmund Davies L.J. in *R v Prager* [1972] W.L.R. 260 at 266.

[437] The term "includes" in the definition suggests that it was not intended to be exhaustive.

[438] To date there are very few decisions: *R v Davison* [1988] Crim. L.R. 442 (Central Criminal Court) and commentary, *R v Ismail* [1990] Crim. L.R. 109; *R v Beales* [1991] Crim. L.R. 118 (Norwich Crown Court) (officer deliberately misstated evidence in order to pressurise suspect).

[439] See [1987] Q.B. 426.

[440] (1992) 97 Cr.App.R. 99. *Cf. R v Emmerson* (1990) 92 Cr.App.R. 284; *R v Heaton* [1993] Crim. L.R. 593; *R v L* [1994] Crim. L.R. 839, where pressure applied (e.g. raised voice) did not amount to oppression. Moreover, officers are "not required to give up after the first denial or even after a number of denials": *per* Lord Taylor C.J. in *Paris* at 104.

[441] p.103.

[442] p.104.

14–027   Attempts have subsequently been made to address the defects of interviewing
techniques illustrated by cases such as this. To date, there are very few decisions
in which a confession has been excluded on this ground. Breaches of the law or
codes will not necessarily constitute oppression, nor[443] will a failure to allow D
to see a duty solicitor owing to a misunderstanding,[444] nor will the use by a police
officer of a raised voice and bad language, expressing impatience and irritation,
for a short time during an otherwise low-key interview, amount to oppression.[445]
Counsel for the defendant in *R v Samuel*[446] felt unable to argue that "the conduct
of the police in delaying access to a legal representative amounted to oppression". The distinction between oppressive and non-oppressive conduct is a
matter of degree. Interviews that were constructed in a tendentious, persistent,
aggressive and prurient manner would be excluded,[447] and oppression in one
interview may taint subsequent interviews and lead to their exclusion.[448]

Section 76(2)(a), in requiring the prosecution to prove the absence of oppression may in fact be of greater symbolic rather than practical significance. Any
confession excluded under this head could also be excluded under the category
of unreliability (below—s.76(2)(b)), or under s.78. It could be argued, in light of
the interpretation in *Fulling*, that the section is used by the courts to exclude
evidence of confessions as a means of disciplining the police. The courts deny
that they have such a disciplinary function, but despite the explicit statements to
this effect,[449] some cases suggest otherwise.[450]

The second hurdle to the admissibility of a confession under PACE is that of
"unreliability" and this has been invoked more frequently. Under s.76(2)(b) the
prosecution have to prove that the confession was not unreliable. The word
"unreliable" . . . means "cannot be relied upon as being the truth".[451] Moreover,
the question is whether *any* confession which the accused might make in
consequence of anything said or done was likely to be rendered unreliable, not
whether the confession made was unreliable.[452] The question is as to the reliability of "any" confession made in "such" circumstances as those alleged.[453]

Section 76(2)(b) has been invoked in a diverse range of circumstances,
including, for example, where a child has been interviewed in the absence of an
"appropriate adult"[454]; where there have been doubts about the reliability of a
confession by a person of low intelligence[455]; where proper records of the

---

[443] *R v Parker* [1995] Crim. L.R. 233; *Re Proulx* [2001] 1 All E.R. 57.

[444] *R v Hughes* [1988] Crim. L.R. 545.

[445] *R v Emmerson* (1990) 92 Cr.App.R. 284.

[446] [1988] Q.B. 615.

[447] *R v Ridley*, December 17, 1999, unreported, CA (Crim. Div.).

[448] *Burut v Public Prosecutor* [1995] 2 A.C. 579, PC (manacled and hooded suspects being
interrogated suffered oppression).

[449] See, e.g. *R v Chalkley and Jeffries* [1998] 2 Cr.App.R. 78.

[450] See, e.g. *R v Mason* [1988] 1 W.L.R. 139.

[451] *per* Stuart-Smith L.J. in *R v Crampton* (1990) 92 Cr.App.R. 369 at 372; *R v Cox* [1991] Crim.
L.R. 276.

[452] *ibid.*

[453] *R v Bow Street Magistrates, Ex p. Proulx* [2001] 1 All E.R. 57; [2000] Crim. L.R. 997 and
commentary.

[454] *DPP v Blake* [1989] 1 W.L.R. 432, CA.

[455] *R v Harvey* [1988] Crim. L.R. 241 (Central Criminal Court): (psychopathic woman of low
intelligence may have confessed after hearing her lover confess in order to protect her); *R v
Everett* [1988] Crim. L.R. 826, CA (man of 42 with mental age of eight: judge had taken no
account of his mental condition); *R v Delaney* (1988) 88 Cr.App.R. 338, CA (D educationally
subnormal and proper records not kept); *R v Raghip*, *The Times*, December 9, 1991 (psychological evidence of mental condition admissible and court not bound by whether D's IQ was

confession have not been kept[456]; where there has been an improper inducement[457]; where there has been denial of access to a solicitor[458]; where, in one case, a drug addict was held in custody for 18 hours without being allowed the prescribed rest periods[459]; and even because of the solicitor's interventions.[460]

In principle, this hurdle is not limited to breaches of the law or of the Codes, but as most of the requirements are designed to promote reliability, breaches of them are a common factor to many of the cases. One controversial limitation is that the unreliability must arise from something "said or done", and this has been held not to include anything said or done by D himself,[461] although this has been doubted.[462]

As with the claim of oppression under s.76(2)(a) if an interview is improperly conducted this may lead to the exclusion of subsequent interviews even though they are conducted according to the rules.[463] This is a question of fact and degree. The extent to which the factors which led to the exclusion of the first interview impact on the others will be crucial, as will the extent to which the suspect had an opportunity to exercise informed and independent choice regarding the subsequent interview.[464] The opportunity to seek legal advice before the subsequent interview is also very important.[465]

Section 76(4)(a) of PACE allows for the admissibility of material discovered as a result of inadmissible confessions—e.g. where a confession has been excluded on grounds of oppression, but the confession revealed the whereabouts of the weapon involved in the crime, the weapon can be admitted but no reference can be made by the prosecution as to the inadmissible confession. This follows the common law.[466] Section 76(4)(b) also follows the common law by

---

above an arbitrary figure for the mentally defective); *R v Kenny* [1994] Crim. L.R. 284. In a number of cases, the confessions of mentally handicapped suspects have been quashed by the Court of Appeal as unsafe and unsatisfactory, irrespective of any question as to their admissibility: see *R v Moss* (1990) 91 Cr.App.R. 371; *R v Mackenzie* (1992) 96 Cr.App.R. 98; *R v Brine* [1992] Crim. L.R. 122; *R v Wood* [1994] Crim. L.R. 222. If the accused's mental state is in issue, expert evidence should be called: *R v O'Brien* [2000] Crim. L.R. 676. See also *R v Blackburn* (2005) *The Times* June 10.

[456] *R v Doolan* [1988] Crim. L.R. 747; *R v Waters* [1989] Crim. L.R. 62 (W was also wrongly questioned after charge); *R v Chung* (1990) 92 Cr.App.R. 314, CA; *R v Joseph* [1993] Crim. L.R. 205, CA. In the absence of a proper record, the prosecution may be unable to discharge its onus of proving reliability beyond reasonable doubt: *R v Delaney* [1989] Crim. L.R. 139 and commentary.

[457] *R v Phillips* (1987) 86 Cr.App.R. 18, CA (statement that if D confessed, offences could be taken into consideration rather than prosecuted); *R v Howden-Simpson* [1991] Crim. L.R. 49 (threat to pursue more than two charges); *R v M.P.C., Ex p. Thompson* [1997] Crim. L.R. 211 (formal offer of caution for confession); *R v Barry* (1991) 95 Cr.App.R. 384, CA (prosecution unable to prove beyond reasonable doubt that statement was not made in response to offer of assistance in obtaining bail).

[458] *R v Gerald* [1999] Crim. L.R. 315.

[459] *R v Trussler* [1988] Crim. L.R. 446 (Reading Crown Court).

[460] *R v M* [2000] *Arch News* 2.

[461] *R v Goldenberg* (1988) 88 Cr.App.R. 285, (D's argument that his confession was unreliable as his motive was to obtain bail, or credit for helping the police, held not to fall within s.76(2)).

[462] *R v Crampton* (1990) 92 Cr.App.R. 369 (doubtful whether merely holding an interview with a suspect undergoing withdrawal symptoms is "something done" within the meaning of s.76(2)); *R v Walker* [1998] Crim. L.R. 211.

[463] *R v Ismail* [1990] Crim. L.R. 109, CA; *R v McGovern* (1990) 92 Cr.App.R. 228; *R v Glaves* [1993] Crim. L.R. 685; *R v Neil* [1994] Crim. L.R. 441. See generally, P. Mirfield, "Successive Confessions and the Poisonous Tree" [1996] Crim. L.R. 554.

[464] *R v Nelson and Rose* [1998] 2 Cr.App.R. 399.

[465] See *Prouse v DPP* (1999) All E.R. (D) 748.

[466] *R v Warwickshall* (1783) 1 Leach 263.

allowing the prosecution to adduce evidence of the manner in which a suspect expresses himself even if the confession in which that is revealed is inadmissible.[467]

Confessions are also liable to be excluded under the very broad discretion in s.78 of PACE.[468] The court in exercising that discretion is to have regard to the manner in which the evidence was obtained. Examples of the diverse range of cases in which evidence has been excluded include: where the police have denied access to a solicitor in breach of s.58[469]; where a suspect is not told that a solicitor has come to the police station at another person's request[470]; where D has not been advised of the right to legal advice[471]; where a proper record of the interview was not made[472]; where there was a breach of Code C. 11.3 relating to inducements[473]; where there is a breach of a requirement to caution.[474]

Where the allegation is that there has been a breach of the Code of Practice, the courts will not necessarily exclude the evidence, even if there is a "significant or substantial" breach.[475] The court will consider the nature rather than the number of breaches,[476] and the court will be influenced by whether the police

---

[467] e.g. suspect's unusual spelling ("Blady Belgiam") identical to that used by the offender: *R v Voisin* [1918] 1 K.B. 531.

[468] On the history of exclusion, see D. Ormerod and D. Birch "The Evolution of the Discretionary Exclusion of Evidence" [2004] Crim. L.R. 766. For cogent analysis of way in which the section has been utilised in excluding unfairly obtained evidence, see A. Choo and S. Nash, "What's the Matter with Section 78?" [1999] Crim. L.R. 929. See also K. Grevling, "Fairness and the Exclusion of Evidence" (1997) 113 L.Q.R. 606 on the imprecision of the section.

[469] *R v Samuel* (1988) 87 Cr.App.R. 232; *R v Parris* (1988) 89. Cr.App.R. 68 (superintendent's order that D to be kept incommunicado under s.56 wrongly assumed to exclude access to a solicitor under s.58); *R v Walsh* (1989) 91 Cr.App.R. 161. Exclusion is not, however, automatic, and may not follow where D is aware of his rights: *R v Alladice* (1988) 87 Cr.App.R. 380 (D admitted he was well able to cope with the interviews, that he understood the caution and was aware of his rights); *R v Dunford* (1990) 91 Cr.App.R. 150 (D had a record and was aware of his right not to answer questions); *R v Oliphant* [1992] Crim. L.R. 40 (presence of a solicitor would have added nothing to what O knew of his legal rights); *R v Anderson* [1993] Crim. L.R. 447 (even if a solicitor had been present and advised silence, A would not have acted on such advice).

[470] Contrary to Code C, Annex B, para.3: *R v Franklin, The Times*, June 16, 1994 (proviso applied).

[471] *R v Absolam* (1988) 88 Cr.App.R. 332 (no caution before questioning; no proper record); *R v Beycan* [1990] Crim. L.R. 185.

[472] *R v Keenan* [1990] 2 Q.B. 54 (officers unaware of Code C); *R v Canale* [1990] 2 All E.R. 187 (where the breaches were described as "flagrant", "deliberate", and "cynical"); *R v Bryce* [1992] 4 All E.R. 567 (interview after tape recorder switched off at B's request; no fresh caution and no contemporaneous record); *R v Cox* (1992) 96 Cr.App.R. 464 (questioning before arrival at police station held to be "interview" to which Code C.11 requirements applied). In *R v Keenan*. Hodgson J. emphasised the importance of these provisions as safeguards against "verballing" by the police (i.e. "the police inaccurately recording or inventing the words used in questioning a detained person"). *Cf. R v Matthews, Dennison, Voss* (1989) 91 Cr.App.R. 43 where the Court of Appeal declined to interfere with the trial judge's exercise of discretion to admit a confession notwithstanding breach of the recording requirements (the confession included correct details as to where the victim's clothes were found); and *R v Dunn* (1990) 91 Cr.App.R. 237 where there were breaches of the recording requirements but a confession was held to be admissible as D's solicitor's clerk was present at the interview and so able to protect his interests.

[473] *R v Howden-Simpson* [1991] Crim. L.R. 49 (the police indicated they would proceed on only two of a series of charges if D admitted one).

[474] *R v Absolam* (1988) 88 Cr.App.R. 332; *R v Hunt* [1992] Crim. L.R. 582 (H seen by a police officer to have a flick knife and asked what it was for; it was held that there was ample evidence to suspect commission of an offence and he should have been cautioned).

[475] "The task of the court is not merely to consider whether there would be an adverse effect on the fairness of the proceedings, but such an adverse effect that justice requires the evidence to be excluded, *per* Saville J., in *R v Walsh* (1989) 91 Cr.App.R. 161 at 163.

[476] *R v Stewart* [1995] Crim. L.R. 500.

acted in bad faith.[477] The courts will also be especially vigilant where the suspect is a vulnerable person.[478] Unlike s.76, s.78 is a very open ended discretion,[479] but there is no clear guidance as to which party must establish the potential unfairness.[480]

There is also the opportunity for the courts to exclude evidence under any common law power, since s.82(3) of PACE expressly preserves these powers.

One problem that has presented a particular difficulty for the courts is that **14–028** which arises when the police carry out deliberate deceptions on the suspect in order to secure evidence.[481] The courts have been most troubled by those cases in which the deception has involved not only lies made to the suspect, but also where his legal representative has been duped. For example, in *R v Mason (Carl)*,[482] D confessed to arson after the interrogators falsely told him, and his solicitor, that they had found at the scene a fragment of a bottle which had contained inflammable liquid and that D's fingerprint was on the fragment. This was described as "reprehensible":

> "We hope never again to hear of deceit such as this being practised on an accused person, and more particularly possibly on a solicitor whose duty it is to advise him, unfettered by false information from the police."[483]

There are, however, tricks and stratagems that the police may legitimately use in securing evidence where they suspect that the crime has been committed. Thus, in *R v Christou and Wright*[484] the Court of Appeal declined to exclude evidence of transactions concerning stolen property conducted at a "shady" jeweller's shop ("Stardust Jewellers") run for three months by undercover police officers. The transactions were recorded by cameras and sound-recording equipment. The court noted that "the trick was not applied to the appellants; they

---

[477] *per* Lord Lane C.J. in *R v Alladice* (1988) 87 Cr.App.R. 380 at 386. As I. Dennis points out in his article "Reconstructing the Law of Criminal Evidence" [1989] C.L.P. 21 at 34, if the courts are protecting rights and not disciplining the police, the question of good faith or bad is immaterial.

[478] In *R v Aspinall* [1999] 2 Cr.App.R. 115, there had been a clear breach of the Code when a schizophrenic had been interviewed without an appropriate adult or solicitor. The trial judge had been wrong to deny the need for an appropriate adult, and should have asked whether the fairness of the trial was affected by the police interview, bearing in mind that the suspect might appear normal to a layperson. The court also acknowledged that there had been a breach of Art.6 because the denial of access to a legal adviser was particularly important in a vulnerable suspect case.

[479] As to whether there is in truth any discretion once a court has determined that the reception of the evidence would have an adverse effect on the fairness of the proceedings, see *R v Chalkley and Jeffries* [1998] 2 Cr.App.R. 79.

[480] See *R v Anderson* [1993] Crim. L.R. 447. In *R (on the application of Saifi) v Governor of Brixton Prison* [2001] 4 All E.R. 168 the Court of Appeal doubted whether there was truly a "burden of proof issue".

[481] Ashworth offers a thorough examination of the many arguments that can be advanced for and against deceptive police practices (1998) 114 L.Q.R. 108. These include arguments that: criminals deserve reduced rights only, so no harm is done to them by police deception; the criminal relies on deception, so it is not unfair for him to be treated in similar fashion; entrapment and deception might be wrong in general, but in the specific context they will benefit the community. On the other hand, by deceiving suspects, the police infringe the integrity principle, they abuse the power of the state, and reduce confidence in the criminal justice system.

[482] [1988] 1 W.L.R. 139.

[483] *ibid.* p.144.

[484] [1992] Q.B. 979. *Cf. R v Smurthwaite, R v Gill* [1994] 1 All E.R. 898 where the Court of Appeal declined to exclude the evidence of recordings of conversations in which the defendants solicited police officers posing as contract killers to kill their respective spouses.

voluntarily applied themselves to the trick",[485] and held that admission of the evidence was not unfair. Furthermore, the requirements of Code C did not apply as the appellants were not being questioned by police officers acting as such. While the undercover officers had asked questions about the areas to be avoided in selling the goods, this was at least partly to maintain their cover. However, where it is established that undercover officers have used their pose in order to circumvent the requirements of the Code, the evidence will be excluded.[486] Similarly, the police cannot use an informer to effectively circumvent the relevant rules.[487] The line is not necessarily easy to draw.[488]

The courts' willingness to exclude confessions for breaches of the Act or the Codes does much to make their requirements effective. However, evidence obtained involving a breach of individual rights under the European Convention does not of itself lead to the exclusion of evidence. The crucial question is whether the particular breach leads to unfairness.[489]

These and many other issues regarding the exclusion of confession evidence obtained improperly remain difficult to interpret because there appear to be so many possible (often conflicting) principles upon which the decisions are based.[490]

---

[485] *per* Lord Taylor C.J. at 989.

[486] *R v Bryce* [1992] 4 All E.R. 567 (court excluded answers to questions that were not necessary to maintain cover and were not contemporaneously recorded). See also *R v MacLean and Koosten* [1993] Crim. L.R. 687; *R v Cadette* [1995] Crim. L.R. 229; *R v Edwards* [1997] Crim. L.R. 348.

[487] See *R v Allen* [2004] EWCA Crim 2236; *Allan v United Kingdom* (2002) 13 B.H.R.C. 652: the police coached the informer and instructed him to "draw out" the suspect in the cell they were sharing.

[488] See discussion by G. Robertson Q.C., "Entrapment Evidence" [1994] Crim. L.R. 805. Covertly-recorded conversations to which police officers are not party, but in situations set up by them, have been admitted in a number of cases. In addition to *R v Allen* above, see *R v Jelen, R v Katz* (1989) 90 Cr.App.R. 456; *R v Ali (Shaukat), The Times*, February 19, 1991; *R v Bailey and Smith* [1993] 3 All E.R. 513 (conversation between B and S placed together in a police cell, with connivance of custody officer, after charge and remand by magistrates). A case that goes even further is *R v Roberts* [1997] 1 Cr.App.R. 217 where R and a fellow suspect, C, were charged with robbery. C then asked to be placed in a cell with R in the hope that R would admit the offence and exculpate C. R made incriminating remarks, which were recorded in this bugged cell. The Court of Appeal upheld the trial judge's decision to admit the recordings since proper authorisation had been obtained to bug the cell and the trial judge had found that there had been no deception by the police, because C was a suspect and not a police informer. See generally, G. Morgan, (2002) 152 N.L.J. 453.

[489] *Khan v United Kingdom* (2001) 31 E.H.R.R. 45. *R v P* [2001] 2 W.L.R. 463. See, D. Ormerod "The European Convention on Human Rights and the Exclusuion of Evidence: Trial Remedies for Article 8 Breaches" [2003] Crim. L.R. 60; B. Fitzpatrick and N. Taylor "Human Rights and the Discretionary Exclusion of Evidence" (2001) 65(4) J. Crim. Law 349.

[490] See especially P. Mirfield, *Silence and Improperly Obtained Evidence* (1997). The relevant principles themselves have been helpfully analysed by commentators, and include, apart from reliability and fairness, the protection of rights and the deterrence of police misconduct. See also A. Ashworth, "Excluding Evidence as Protecting Rights" [1977] Crim. L.R. 723.

B. THE RESPONSIBILITY FOR INSTITUTING PROSECUTIONS[491]

The historical development of the English prosecution process placed emphasis **14–029** upon the role of the private individual as prosecutor. As the police forces grew so they began to assume the responsibility for bringing prosecutions (but only exercising individual rather than statutory rights); and practice diverged from that in Scotland where a public prosecutor (the procurator fiscal) became established and the right of private prosecution diminished.[492] In fact, for many years the theory of the private prosecution in England no longer matched the reality of the situation, not only because of the powers of the Director of Public Prosecutions, but also because of restrictions placed by statute upon private prosecutions for many offences.[493] In practice, the majority of prosecutions were brought by the police and almost all the balance by other public agencies. Truly private prosecutions were highly unusual. Furthermore, from 1986 the conduct of most classes of criminal proceedings has been taken over by the Crown Prosecution Service (CPS) established by the Prosecution of Offences Act 1985. The fiction that the prosecution is acting in a private capacity is not maintained. This has taken on a special significance in the human rights era, since there have been attempts to argue that the CPS acts directly on behalf of the victim. The House of Lords has rejected this argument: the CPS should not be seen as the representative of the victim in the criminal trial.[494] The English courts have confirmed that although there are many diverse bodies that might wish to represent the interests of the victims in a case they should only be allowed to intervene in a trial on behalf of the victim in an exceptional case and on overwhelming grounds.[495]

The CPS is of course a public body and as such is bound to act in accordance with the ECHR,[496] although, in fact, the ECHR has not provided a very clear obligation on the prosecuting authorities to prosecute, rather there is an obligation to act fairly and to provide an adequate *process* for the prosecution.[497]

---

[491] See generally, Sanders and Young (2007), Ch.7; Sprack, *A Practical Approach to Criminal Procedure* (2006), Ch.4; Ashworth and Redmayne (2005), Chs 6 and 7; I. Sigler, "Public Prosecution in England and Wales" [1974] Crim. L.R. 642; *The Royal Commission on Criminal Procedure* (Cmnd. 8092, 1980); JUSTICE, *The Prosecution Process in England and Wales* (1970); P. Devlin, *The Criminal Prosecution in England* (1960); M. McConville, "Prosecuting Criminal Cases in England and Wales: Reflections of an Inquisitorial Adversary" (1984) VI(1) Liverpool L.R. 15; K. de Gama, "Police Powers and Public Prosecutions: Winning by Appearing To Lose?" (1988) 6 Int. J. Sociology of Law 339.

[492] For favourable comment on which see the Auld Report (2001), Ch.10, para.12.

[493] By requiring the consent of the DPP, the Attorney-General, a High Court judge or some other authority, to the proposed prosecution.

[494] See *R v Weir* [2001] Crim. L.R. 653.

[495] See *Re Pinochet Ugarte (No.2)* [1999] 2 W.L.R. 272, HL.

[496] Human Rights Act, s.6.

[497] See *R v DPP, Ex p. Manning* [2000] 3 W.L.R. 463; *R (Amin) v Home Secretary* [2002] EWCA Crim 390.

1. Prosecution Arrangements before the Prosecution of Offences Act 1985[498]

(a) Police prosecutions

14–030   Prior to the establishment of the CPS, the responsibility of deciding whether or not to prosecute suspects and the conduct of proceedings for less serious offences were regarded as two of the main functions of the police, as aspects of their general duty to enforce the law.[499]

The procedure adopted varied according to the practice of the force concerned but the initial steps were normally taken in the name of the officer who had decided on the prosecution. Sometimes in the name of the Chief Constable, more often in the name of the head of the appropriate division or subdivision. If there was any legal difficulty, for example in deciding the appropriate charge or assessing the weight of the evidence on a particular charge, the police were able to take advice either from a prosecuting solicitors' department established by the police authority or from a private firm employed for that purpose.

By the 1980s, 31 of the 43 police forces in England and Wales were able to draw on the expertise of their own prosecuting solicitors' department for legal advice and for representation in court.[500] It was clear that a prosecuting solicitor acted on instructions from the police and was merely an adviser in a solicitor/client relationship, but the line of authority, the budgetary controls, the amount of advocacy undertaken and the degree of "independence" enjoyed varied greatly from force to force.[501]

If the police *did* decide on a prosecution it was quite possible for a police officer to present the case in the magistrates' court. The Royal Commission on the Police suggested that it was undesirable for police officers to act as prosecutors save in minor cases.[502] In practice, the police could not conduct cases in the Crown Court and only prosecuted in the magistrates' court in straightforward cases.[503] In some areas, *all* prosecutions were undertaken by prosecuting solicitors. In serious cases, a measure of control was exerted by the Director of Public Prosecutions and the Law Officers.

(b) The Director of Public Prosecutions and the Law Officers

14–031   The basic functions of the DPP have always included those of undertaking prosecutions of particular importance or difficulty and advising chief officers of police. Indeed, prior to the establishment of the CPS and the DPP's new role as head of the service, these were his main functions. Additionally, many statutes provided (and many still do) that prosecutions could only be brought in respect

---

[498] Sanders and Young (2007), Ch.7.

[499] *Final Report of the Royal Commission on the Police* (Cmnd. 1782, 1962), para.59.

[500] The Metropolitan Police and the City of London force had their own special arrangements, leaving 10 forces to rely on private practitioners to provide the necessary service. See *Royal Commission on Criminal Procedure, The Investigation and Prosecution of Criminal Offences in England and Wales: The Law and Procedure* (hereafter RCCP I) (Cmnd. 8092-1, 1980), App.22.

[501] An analysis of the system is to be found in *The Prosecution System, Survey of Prosecuting Solicitors, Departments*, RCCP Research Study No.11 (HMSO, 1980).

[502] Cmnd. 1782, para.381.

[503] RCCP I, paras 144–145.

of certain offences with the consent of the DPP. This had become a popular provision where the offence was controversial, or the statutory provision slightly ambiguous, or public policy considerations were involved, or mitigating factors might be present or where vexatious or trivial private prosecutions might be brought.[504]

A further power strengthening the DPP's position was a general power to take over criminal proceedings and then to deal with them as he wished, including the offering of no evidence if he so chose. This power was equally applicable to private prosecutions and was used, for example, to discontinue a private prosecution brought against a person to whom the DPP had given a promise of immunity from proceedings in return for giving evidence for the prosecution at another trial.[505] In that case it was held that the court had no power to interfere with the Director's exercise of discretion in how he conducted proceedings taken over by him or her. These powers taken together gave the DPP a significant amount of control over prosecution policy in relation to serious criminal offences.

The two important provisions relating to the Attorney-General[506] were his power to enter a *nolle prosequi* in proceedings on indictment[507] and the requirement of his consent to the prosecution of certain offences.[508] These remain after the Prosecution of Offences Act 1985. The grant of a *nolle prosequi* by the Attorney-General stops proceedings on indictment immediately. It does not actually amount to an acquittal, so the accused may be indicted again on the same charge,[509] but another *nolle prosequi* may then be granted. A request for such a grant may be made by any person and the exercise of the power is equivalent to the DPP taking over proceedings and offering no evidence or a prosecutor offering no evidence, except that in both the latter cases the effect would formally be an acquittal.

The categories of offences for which the Attorney-General's consent was required for prosecution indicated that his primary responsibility in deciding whether to give consent was to weigh factors of national and public significance, conscious that he was the Minister answerable in Parliament for all matters connected with the conduct of criminal proceedings. However, it was clearly established that the Attorney-General's decision should be made on quasi-judicial and not on political grounds.[510]

(c) Criticisms

These arrangements were subjected to close scrutiny, first by JUSTICE in 1970, **14–032** and then by the Royal Commission on Criminal Procedure in 1981. JUSTICE[511] argued that the responsibility for prosecutions in all but trivial cases should be

---

[504] See the evidence of the DPP to the RCCP, part of which is reproduced at RCCP I, para.159.

[505] *Turner v DPP* (1978) 68 Cr.App.R. 70.

[506] On the work of the Attorney-General see Lord Steyn, "The Weakest and Least Dangerous Department of Government" [1997] P.L. 84.

[507] This is a common law power not subject to any control by the courts: *R v Comptroller of Patents* [1899] 1 Q.B. 909.

[508] *cf.* the powers of the DPP referred to earlier. The manner in which the Att.-Gen.'s consent is to be provided and the degree of detail necessary are considered in *R v Cain* [1976] Q.B. 496.

[509] *Goddard v Smith* (1704) 3 Salk. 245. See also *Ridpath* (1713) 10 Mod 152.

[510] Statement by the Prime Minister to the House of Commons, February 16, 1959 (HC Deb, Vol.600, col.31), part of which is cited in RCCP I, para.164.

[511] *The Prosecution Process in England and Wales* (1970). See also J. Sigler [1974] Crim. L.R. 642; A. S. Bowley [1975] Crim. L.R. 442.

taken out of the hands of the police and given to a national prosecuting authority. In support of this recommendation it was said that:

(a) a police officer might convince himself of the guilt of a suspect and become psychologically committed to a prosecution;

(b) public policy and the circumstances of the individual were relevant considerations in the decision to prosecute;

(c) the English system was unique in Europe in allowing the whole process from interrogation to prosecution to be effectively under the control of the police in the majority of cases;

(d) investigators found it difficult to achieve the necessary detachment in taking what is essentially a "judicial-type" decision whether or not to prosecute;

(e) police involvement might influence the conduct of the prosecution in deciding appropriate charges or otherwise "bargaining" with a suspect, or in putting pressure on counsel at trial to take a particular line;

(f) police officers were not trained as lawyers or advocates and those tasks involving the expertise of lawyers or advocates should not be undertaken by the police.

The RCCP's approach was to analyse and establish the standards for judging the adequacy of a prosecution system; to measure the existing system by those standards; and then to recommend any changes necessary to achieve the standards. Put briefly, the RCCP decided that the system should be judged on fairness, openness and accountability, and efficiency.

In considering the question of *fairness* in the existing arrangements the Commission concentrated on the issues of whether the "right" people were brought to trial, and in a way which demonstrated "consistency" in policy and practice in the various police forces. The RCCP considered the evidence of acquittal statistics which indicated that a high proportion of acquittals ordered and directed by the judge at the Crown Court were the result of insufficient prosecution evidence.[512] The failure of prosecution witnesses at trial accounted for many of these cases, but there were clearly some cases where it should have been foreseen that the evidence would be inadequate. The lack of fairness demonstrated by such cases was only mitigated by their relative infrequency.[513]

Statistics contained in the Report showed that there was, indeed, a degree of inconsistency in prosecution policy and practice,[514] and that there was no effective machinery for achieving conformity. Although this created unfairness, the RCCP concluded that it was not the main focus of public concern and that the solution, the strengthening of central control or a national prosecution service,

---

[512] RCCP Report, para.6.19. See also M. McConville and J. Baldwin, *Courts Prosecution and Conviction* (1981).

[513] The RCCP Report suggested that one-fifth of directed acquittals might fall into this category. However, directed acquittals only formed 7% of all cases disposed of by the Crown Court and the Crown Court only dealt with approximately 15% of all indictable offences. See RCCP Report, para.6.22.

[514] *ibid.* para.6.40. Inconsistency was primarily evident in the statistics relating to the use of the caution for both adults and juveniles.

could find better justification on the ground of openness and accountability than on the ground of improved fairness.

The question of *accountability* was complicated because of the implications for the defendant of any public scrutiny of the exercise of the discretion to prosecute. Questioning the decision of the prosecutor after an acquittal might amount to a "retrial" if the prosecutor attempted to defend the decision. If the prosecutor was required to defend a decision not to institute proceedings, unwarranted doubts might be cast on the suspect without the suspect having an opportunity to defend himself.

However, the RCCP considered that those problems could be overcome by generalising the issue involved, and that accountability in the "explanatory and co-operative mode" to a local supervisory authority was desirable. Additionally, a prosecution agency would clearly be accountable to the body providing it with funds for its economic efficiency and organisation.

The *efficiency* of a prosecuting system was not to be judged solely in terms of the efficient use of resources. Delays in preparation causing adjournments and inadequate preparation causing the collapse of cases certainly cost money, but could also cause injustice, inconvenience and frustration to all those concerned in the process.

At the same time, the concept of efficiency was notoriously difficult to use in relation to the criminal justice system; objectives were hard to define in precise terms and it was accordingly difficult to measure whether they had been achieved. The best the RCCP could propose was uniformity in prosecution arrangements, which would make possible the detection of inefficiencies in the system, and assist in achieving nationally such consistency in the application of general prosecution policies as was thought desirable.[515]

The RCCP concluded that " . . . there is a case for some change. Indeed, not a single witness who has addressed this part of our terms of reference in detail has argued that there should be absolutely no change made. The areas of debate are on the direction and extent of change".[516]

2. PROSECUTION ARRANGEMENTS UNDER THE PROSECUTION OF OFFENCES ACT 1985[517]

(a) The Crown Prosecution Service[518]

The 1985 Act established the CPS headed by the DPP.[519] The DPP and the   **14–033**
headquarters staff are based in three centres in London, Birmingham and York.

---

[515] RCCP Report, para.6.64.
[516] *ibid.* para.6.65.
[517] See the symposium in [1986] Crim. L.R. 3–44; K. W. Lidstone, (1987) 11 Crim. L.J. 296. For comparative material on public prosecutors see J. Fionda, *Public Prosecutors and Discretion: A Comparative Study* (1993); Special Issue of (2000) European Journal of Crime, Criminal Law and Criminal Justice.
[518] See generally *www.cps.gov.uk.*
[519] 1985 Act, s.2. The DPP must possess a 10-year general qualification under the Courts and Legal Services Act 1990, s.71 (i.e. a right of audience in any part of the Supreme Court or all proceedings in county courts or magistrates' courts).

England and Wales are divided by the DPP into 42 areas based on police areas,[520] with a "virtual" 43rd area known as CPS Direct which provides out-of-hours charging advice to the police. Staff are appointed by the DPP. Any member of the CPS who has a "general qualification" may be designated by him or her as a Crown Prosecutor. The DPP must designate a Chief Crown Prosecutor for each area, who is responsible to him or her for supervising the operation of the Service in that area.

The CPS employs around 8,184 people[521] including barristers and solicitors, and these members of the service are accorded the limited rights of audience enjoyed by solicitors holding practising certificates. A number of CPS lawyers are qualified to appear in Crown Court and other higher courts. This means that employed solicitors with Higher Rights qualifications are able to appear in some cases in the Crown Court, and other higher courts. Concerns have, however, been raised about the desirability of the CPS lawyers prosecuting cases in the Crown Court without the intervention of an independent barrister in private practice. By 2006, there were 604 Higher Court Advocates employed by the CPS.[522]

The Narey Report[523] recommended that the CPS should attempt to free up resources by allowing the DPP to confer on non-qualified staff the power to review files and to conduct less contentious cases in the magistrates' court. Following these recommendations, s.7A of the Prosecution of Offenders Act 1985[524] provided that CPS designated caseworkers may undertake certain work, such as straightforward guilty pleas in the magistrates' court. Their role has expanded, and now includes conducting contested bail hearings and pre-trial reviews. Serious concerns have been raised about the use of administrators to make decisions affecting prosecution, even in these limited circumstances.[525] The decision is one that is crucial to the defendant, the victim and also has the potential to affect relations with the police. Whilst promoting the "freeing up" of resources it remains contentious that laypeople are increasingly carrying tasks originally designed for fully trained lawyers.

---

[520] There were originally 31 Areas, grouped in four Regions (Northern, Midland, London and South East, South and West): see *Crown Prosecution Service Annual Report for 1987–88* (1987–88 H.C. 563), p.45. These were reduced to 13 in 1993, including a new unified London area. The aim was to enhance the role and responsibilities of Chief Crown Prosecutors and to provide a shorter and more direct means of communication and accountability: *Annual Report of the CPS for 1993–94* (1993–94 H.C. 444), Ch.2. This proved to be an unsatisfactory arrangement which led to an over-centralised and over-bureaucratised service. In 1997 the CPS was reorganised into 42 areas coterminous with the police areas: see Attorney-General's Written Answer HC, Vol.294, cols 73–74, May 21, 1997. This was a move that was approved by the Glidewell Report, Cm. 3960 (1998), *The Review of the CPS*. Many of that Report's recommendations were designed to rationalise the management of the CPS, with the introduction of a Chief Executive at H.Q. and attempts to decentralise the structure. The Report estimated that the top 400 lawyers in the CPS spent less than one-third of their time on casework and advocacy, illustrating the over bureau-cratisation of the service.

[521] Figures correct up to March 2006. For updated information see: *www.cps.gov.uk.*

[522] See *Crown Prosecution Service Annual Report and Resource Accounts for 2005–6* (2006) at p.7. The CPS is also introducing an Advocacy Strategy whereby the Service routinely conducts its own advocacy in all courts. The Strategy will build on the Pilots in Hertfordshire and Hampshire & Isle of Wight, which were established in June 2004. In March 2005, the CPS recorded its highest level of HCA activity conducting 830 Crown Court sessions and advocating on 2,330 cases.

[523] M. Narey, *Review of Delay in the Criminal Justice System* (1997).

[524] As inserted by s.53 of the Crime and Disorder Act 1998, s.53.

[525] R. Robins, "Laying Down the Law" (2005) 102.41 L.S. Gaz. 20.

(b) Functions of the Crown Prosecution Service

The CPS's declared aim is "to deliver a high quality prosecution service that brings offenders to justice, helps reduce both crime and the fear of crime and thereby promote public confidence in the rule of law through the consistent fair and independent review of cases and through their fair, thorough and firm presentation at court".[526] **14–034**

More specific legal requirements on the functioning of the CPS are imposed by the 1985 Act. In truth this Act is phrased in terms of a set of functions conferred on the DPP, acting under the superintendence of the Attorney-General, however, it is also provided that every Crown Prosecutor shall have all the powers of the DPP as to the initiation and conduct of proceedings, acting under his or her direction.[527] Section 3(2) of the 1985 Act lists the duties of the DPP, and includes the following:

- to take over the conduct of all criminal proceedings, other than specified proceedings, instituted on behalf of a police force;

- to institute and conduct criminal proceedings in any case where it appears to him that the importance or difficulty of the case makes it appropriate for him to do so, or it is otherwise appropriate for proceedings to be instituted by him;

- to take over the conduct of all binding over proceedings instituted on behalf of a police force;

- to give, to such extent as he considers appropriate, advice to police forces on all matters relating to criminal offences;

- to appear for the prosecution, when directed by the court to do so, on any appeal under—

  (i) s.1 of the Administration of Justice Act 1960 (appeal from the High Court in criminal cases);
  (ii) Pt I or Pt II of the Criminal Appeal Act 1968 (appeals from the Crown Court to the criminal division of the Court of Appeal and thence to the House of Lords); or
  (iii) s.108 of the Magistrates' Courts Act 1980 (right of appeal to Crown Court) as it applies, by virtue of subs.(5) of s.12 of the Contempt of Court Act 1981, to orders made under s.12 (contempt of magistrates' courts);

- to appear, if he thinks it appropriate to do so, to apply for discharge or variation of an anti social behaviour order under the Crime and Disorder Act 1998 s.1C;

- to discharge such other functions as may from time to time be assigned to him by the Attorney-General.

(i) Statutory charging

Under the 1985 reforms the role of the CPS was to take over a case once a person had been charged by the police. Significant changes have been made to this **14–035**

---

[526] *CPS Annual Report, 2005–2006* (2006).
[527] 1985 Act, s.1(6). Similarly, where the consent of the DPP is required by statute, that consent can be expressed by a Crown Prosecutor: s.1(7). It need not be in writing: *R v Jackson* [1997] Crim. L.R. 755.

relationship as a result of the Criminal Justice Act 2003,[528] implementing recommendations contained in the Auld Report[529] that the CPS should be involved in the process of actually charging a suspect. The DPP has noted that statutory charging "is the single most significant development in the handling of criminal casework since the establishment of the CPS".[530]

A concern under the preceding system of charging was the substantial gap between the number of offences recorded by the police and the considerably lower number of convictions that followed.[531] By bringing about a closer working relationship between the police and the CPS it is the aim that the gap is reduced and a more efficient process follows. Brownlee outlines the aims of the new "statutory charging scheme":

"[T]he elimination at the earliest opportunity of hopeless cases, the production of more robust prosecution cases, the elimination of unnecessary or unwarranted delays in the period between charge and disposal, and the reduction of the number of trials that crack through the offering and acceptance of guilty pleas to reduce charges at a late stage in the process."[532]

Prior to statutory charging it was argued that the police, using a different test to that used by the CPS, too often preferred the most serious of the charges open to it in a particular case.[533] This would result in the CPS having to modify charges often late in the process. For example, the *CPS Annual Report 1999–2000* revealed that 22 per cent of police charges for assault, public order and road traffic cases were incorrect.[534] As recognised by Brownlee, this had the knock-on effect of encouraging defendants to plead not guilty to the original charge for tactical reasons, namely, in the hope that the CPS would reduce the charge.

Following a successful pilot the Criminal Justice Act 2003 transferred the responsibility for the charging decision from the police to local Crown Prosecutors for the majority of offences.[535] The custody officer still plays the vital "gatekeeping" role of deciding whether to release a suspect without charge, bail him pending further investigation, or put the suspect's case to the duty prosecutor to consider the charge. If the case is put to the duty prosecutor he or she must determine the charge taking into account the evidential and public interest tests as set out in the CPS Code.[536] The duty prosecutor can agree to prosecute immediately, take no further action against the suspect, or order that the custody

---

[528] See, I. Brownlee, *The Statutory Charging Scheme in England and Wales: Towards a Unified Prosecution System?* [2004] Crim. L.R. 896.

[529] Auld (2002) Ch.10, para.12.

[530] *CPS Annual Report, 2005–2006* (2006), p.2.

[531] For a consideration of the relationship between the CPS and the police see: J. Baldwin and A. Hunt, "Prosecutors Advising in Police Stations" [1998] 521 Crim. L.R.

[532] Brownlee [2004] 896 at 897.

[533] HM Crown Prosecution Service Inspectorate, *Thematic review of attrition in the prosecution process* (2003).

[534] Cited in Auld Report (2001), Ch.10, para.37.

[535] Statutory charging was introduced in all 42 CPS areas by March 2006, one year ahead of the original schedule, see, *CPS Annual Report, 2005–2006* (2006), p.2.

[536] Considered below.

officer bail the suspect where more evidence is required to make a decision as to the appropriate charge.[537]

Other than for relatively minor offences, Crown Prosecutors will take charging decisions in all cases. This represents a major shift in the relationship between the police and the CPS and its success to a large extent will be dependent upon how that relationship develops (see below).

(ii) Conditional caution

The CJA 2003 also introduced the conditional caution, defined as "a caution which is given in respect of an offence committed by the offender and which has conditions attached to it".[538] If the offender fails without excuse to comply with the conditions then criminal proceedings for the original offence can be instituted. The relevant offender must have admitted the offence before the option of a conditional caution is made available; this is to ensure that it is not the caution that has induced the admission.[539] The "relevant prosecutor"[540] must decide that there is sufficient evidence to charge the offender. Conditions that are attached to the caution must facilitate the offender's rehabilitation or ensure that he makes reparation for the offence.[541] The Police and Justice Act 2006 proposes that punitive conditions might be attached to a caution[542] and it has been suggested that Art.6 of the European Convention will thus be engaged and the procedures adopted for issuing such cautions will be more closely scrutinised.[543]

14–036

(iii) Private Prosecutions

The 1985 Act preserves the right of private prosecution by providing that nothing in Pt I shall preclude any person from instituting any criminal proceedings, or conducting any proceedings which the DPP is not under a duty to take over.[544] The DPP does, however, still have power to take over private prosecutions at any stage.[545] The CPS will take over and discontinue a prosecution where, on the evidence, there is no case to answer, which involves a different test from that applied when deciding whether to initiate a prosecution. If a prosecution is taken over, the prosecutor may of course exercise the power to discontinue under s.23.

14–037

---

[537] Criminal Justice Act 2003 Sch.2, para.6(3) amending PACE, s.47. This new power allows the custody officer to attach bail conditions, which can be contrasted with the position regarding bail pending further investigation where no conditions can be imposed (PACE, s.34(5)).

[538] Criminal Justice Act 2003 s.22(2).

[539] Code of Practice on Conditional Cautions (2004) para.4.1. The Code is issued under CJA 2003, s.25.

[540] CJA 2003, s.23(4): the term includes Crown Prosecutors.

[541] ibid. s.22(3). This may involve, for example, treatment for drink or drug dependency, anger management courses, cleaning graffiti and suchlike: see para.5.2 of the Code.

[542] Police and Justice Act 2006, s.17.

[543] I. Brownlee, "Conditional cautions and fair trial rights in England and Wales: form versus substance in the diversionary agenda?" [2007] Crim. L.R. 127.

[544] Thus a private prosecution may be brought where the DPP has decided not to exercise the power under s.3(2)(b) of the 1985 Act (text above): Bow Street Stipendiary Magistrate, Ex p. South Coast Shipping [1993] Q.B. 645 (private prosecution for manslaughter arising out of the collision (between the Bowbelle and the Marchioness on the River Thames in 1989).

[545] 1985 Act, s.6. On when it is appropriate for the DPP to take over proceedings see R v DPP, Ex p. Duckenfield [2000] 1 W.L.R. 55.

(c) Relationship between the Crown Prosecution Service and the police

14–038   Arguably, the decision to prosecute is a trial-related matter (and quasi judicial) rather than an investigative matter. As such, it could be seen to be more appropriate for the CPS to take the principal responsibility. It is hoped that through the statutory charging scheme earlier involvement of the CPS could lead to the collection of better quality evidence that is more focused on the needs of the trial. It had been argued that there was a natural tendency for the police, once satisfied as to who was responsible, to consider as mistaken any material that points in another direction,[546] this tendency being present in a number of notorious miscarriages of justice.[547] The prosecutor would be constrained by the information provided by the police, and

> "it would be irrational and indefensible in most cases if the prosecutor did *not* endorse police action, because the file is constructed in order to leave this as the only proper option."[548]

This placed the CPS in a difficult position. The question whether to discontinue a case is a pivotal one in the prosecution process, and it is particularly important for the CPS since the number of non-jury acquittals of cases is often used as a measure of the CPS's success. This increased the pressure to drop cases that are only marginally likely to succeed, but that action was a major source of conflict with the police.

Co-operation between the police and prosecutors under the new arrangements ought to ensure the problem is reduced. Indeed, pilot projects associated with the statutory charging scheme showed that under the new charging arrangements not only did conviction rates increase but discontinuance rates decreased.[549] If such progress can be seen across the country then the chances of an harmonious relationship between the CPS and the police will be improved despite the latter having lost some considerable responsibility. However, when considering very early pilot schemes of CPS lawyers in the police station, Baldwin and Hunt failed to detect a particularly efficient working relationship.[550] Sanders and Young also point out that the decisions taken by the CPS still rely wholly on the evidence presented to them by the police, and for the latter to actively seek and take advice from prosecutors will require a change in their culture.[551] Without such a change, Brownlee argues that a danger to be avoided is Crown Prosecutors being exposed to police culture and being "seduced by policing rather than prosecutorial priorities".[552] Efficient cooperation must not dilute the independence of the prosecutor.

---

[546] McConville, *op. cit.* pp.28–32; A. Sanders, "Constructing the Case for the Prosecution" (1987) 14 J.I.S. 229.

[547] The *Evans, Virag and Dougherty* and *Confait* cases: see L. Kennedy, *Ten Rillington Place* (1961); Devlin Report on the *Evidence of Identification in Criminal Cases* (HMSO, 1976); Fisher Report on the Confait Case (HMSO, 1977).

[548] McConville, *op. cit.* p.30. *Cf.* A. Sanders [1986] Crim. L.R. 16 at 27, who argues that the structure gives the prosecutors power to drop cases but little incentive to do so; and K. W. Lidstone, (1987) 11 Crim. L.J. 296 at 310–312.

[549] *CPS Annual Report, 2003–2004*, p.6.

[550] Baldwin and Hunt [1998] Crim. L.R. 521.

[551] Sanders and Young (2007), p.334.

[552] Brownlee [2004] 896 at 906.

(d) Crown Prosecution Service operations[553]

The workload of the CPS is substantial. In 2005–06, the CPS dealt with **14–039**
1,176,112 defendants in the magistrates' court and Crown Court.[554] There is no
question that the organisation operates under incredible pressure.

It is generally agreed that the CPS got off to a bad start, many of its problems
stemming from a lack of resources.[555] Its official complement for staff was
inadequate for the work it had to do and it was unable to recruit up to its
complement. Private practice lawyers were employed as agents in a higher
proportion of cases than planned or thought desirable, and this added to the
expense of the operation as a whole. A recurrent theme in the criticism of the
service was the inadequate preparation of cases, particularly less important cases
being handled by inexperienced staff, leading to the late service of papers, delays
and the unnecessary discontinuance of cases. Relations between the CPS and the
police were too often strained, the former criticising the quality and late delivery
of files, the latter complaining that cases were discontinued unnecessarily and
that the CPS demanded a higher standard of file preparation than had been the
norm.[556] Others drew attention to instances both of the dropping of winnable
cases and of the continuation of cases doomed to failure.

Throughout the 1990s steps were taken in response to these difficulties. A
combination of higher salaries, major recruitment initiatives and the recession
enabled the CPS to recruit substantially to its complement and reduce reliance on
agents. A number of initiatives supported and improved liaison at national and
local levels.[557] The RCCJ endorsed "the unambiguous separation of the roles of
investigator and prosecutor".[558] They were encouraged by what they saw as the
"improving performance of the CPS, although noting that it may still remain
patchy in some areas".[559]

Nevertheless, the Labour Government, newly elected in 1997, recognised that
a wholesale review of the CPS was necessary.[560] The Glidewell Review[561] was
established to "examine the organisation and structure of the CPS together with
the CPS policies and procedures and to consider whether and if so what changes

---

[553] See A. Ashworth, "Developments in the Public Prosecutor's Office in England" (2000) Euro
Journal of Crime, Criminal Law and Criminal Justice for an accessible review of CPS. See
generally on the CPS, Ashworth and Redmayne (2005), Chs 6 and 7; Sanders and Young (2007),
Ch.7; A. Sanders, "From Suspect to Trial" in M. Maguire, R. Morgan and R. Reiner (eds),
Oxford Handbook of Criminology (2nd edn, 1997).

[554] CPS Annual Report 2005–2006 (2006), p.7.

[555] See the Glidewell Report (1998), Chs 8, 10; National Audit Office, Review of the Crown
Prosecution Service (1988–89 H.C. 345); Second Report of the Committee of Public Accounts,
Review of the Crown Prosecution Service (1989–90 H.C. 164); Fourth Report of the Home
Affairs Committee (1989–90 H.C. 118). The story of the establishment of the CPS is told from
the point of view of its first head in Sir Thomas Hetherington, Prosecution and the Public Interest
(1989); cf. J. Rozenberg, The Case for the Crown (1987), Ch.4.

[556] Only 42% of adult fines are "perfect" (fully satisfactory and on time): HM Crown Prosecution
Service Inspectorate, Thematic Review of Attrition in the Prosecution Process (2003)
para.9.25.

[557] Including trilateral meetings with the LCD and the Home Office, participation in the work of the
Working Group on Pre-Trial Issues and the Standing Commission on Efficiency (Annual Report
of the CPS, 1990–91, pp.17, 19–20). On the proposed restructuring of the Criminal Justice
Agencies, see Auld Report (2001), Ch.8.

[558] Cm. 2263, p.69.

[559] ibid. p.70.

[560] On poor morale in the CPS see F. Bawdon (1998) N.L.J. 491, and see F. Davies (1997) 161 J.P.N.
207 for a description of media attacks at the time.

[561] The Review of the CPS Cm 3960, (1998).

are necessary in order to provide for the more effective and efficient prosecution of crime through local public prosecutors". Its recommendations were generally well received, although it did draw criticism for its focus on management and administration rather than legal issues.[562]

14–040   The CPS remains a target for heavy criticism. In 2001, for example, the Denman Report on Racial Discrimination in the CPS found that there was "institutional" racism in the Service.[563] The ease with which criticism can be levelled at the CPS is increased by the availability of targets and performance indicators which are continually being imposed.[564] These include aims of: improving the delivery of justice by increasing the number of offences for which an offender is brought to justice to 1.25 million for 2007–08; increasing the level of public confidence in the criminal justice system to more than the baseline figure of 39 per cent; reducing the number of people in ethnic minority communities who believe the criminal justice system would treat them worse than people of other races; increase the satisfaction of victims and witnesses.[565] The Service also has to produce efficiency savings of £34 million by 2008.[566] The programme of continual reform of the CPS continues unabated.

3. OTHER AGENCIES[567]

14–041   There is little doubt that police have greatest impact on the number of criminal prosecutions (even when road traffic cases are taken out of the equation). Despite this, and the greater symbolic significance of the police role in investigation of crime, nevertheless, the non-police agencies play an important role in investigating a wide range of (sometimes very serious) criminal offences. Government departments, local authorities, nationalised industries and other public bodies may all have cause to institute prosecutions within their particular field. A survey was undertaken on behalf of the Royal Commission on Criminal Procedure[568] which concentrated on particular courts and identified the Post Office, British Transport Police, the Department of the Environment and local authorities as contributing almost 70 per cent of the non-police prosecutions in those courts.[569]

4. PRIVATE PROSECUTIONS

14–042   "This historical right which goes right back to the earliest days of our legal system, though rarely exercised in relation to indictable offences, and

---

[562] See, e.g. comments at (1998) N.L.J. 824 at 861.

[563] para.3.2.1. See also B. Mhalanga, *Race and the CPS* (1997). The Inquiry's principal findings, were that: "for a large public employer, the CPS responded slowly to modern equal opportunities legislation and practices; although ethnic minority staff are well represented overall, they are seriously under-represented in both the higher administrative grades and the higher lawyer grades. This pattern cannot simply be attributed to historical factors" (para.3.2.1).

[564] See, for example, Home Office, *Justice for All* (2002) Cm. 5563, Ch.1.

[565] *CPS Annual Report 2005–2006*, p.10.

[566] *ibid.* p.12.

[567] See Sanders and Young (2007), pp.360–372.

[568] *Prosecutions by Private Individuals and Non-Police Agencies*, RCCP Research Study No.10 (HMSO, 1980). See also A. Samuels [1986] Crim. L.R. 33.

[569] RCCP Research Study No.10 *op. cit.* Table 2.3 at p.15.

though ultimately liable to be controlled by the Attorney-General (by taking over the prosecution and, if he thinks fit, entering a *nolle prosequi*) remains a valuable constitutional safeguard against inertia or partiality on the part of authority."[570]

Lord Wilberforce thus stated the traditional view of the private prosecution.

In fact, the growing practice of requiring the consent of the DPP or Attorney-General to prosecution, the establishment of the CPS and the considerable cost of mounting a private prosecution now combine to minimise the significance of this historical right. We have already noted the requirement of consent but cost is an even more discouraging factor. Legal aid is not available to a private prosecutor who must meet the cost of investigation, preparation and representation[571] out of his or her own pocket. A court may award costs to a successful private prosecutor[572] but he or she also runs the risk of having them awarded against him or her if he or she is not successful. In addition, if the prosecution was vindictive, the prosecutor risks the possibility of an action in malicious prosecution.[573] A private prosecutor has no right of access to documents, such as police statements, reports and photographs, held by the CPS.[574] There have, of course, been some notable private prosecutions,[575] but in general, they are confined to offences of shoplifting and common assault.[576]

C. THE EXERCISE OF DISCRETION IN PROSECUTIONS

Not every criminal offence is prosecuted. The courts could not possibly cope with the workload and, in any event, prosecution may not always be the most effective means of dealing with a violation of the criminal law. If some offenders are to be "let off" whilst others are brought before the courts it is important to

14–043

---

[570] *Gouriet v Union of Post Office Workers* [1978] A.C. 435 at 477.

[571] The Crown Court can allow a private prosecution to be conducted in person: *R v Southwark Crown Court, Ex p. Tawfick* (1995) 7 Admin. L.R. 410 (by virtue of the Courts and Legal Services Act 1990, s.27(2)(c)).

[572] Prosecution of Offences Act 1985, s.17: costs can only be awarded in respect of proceedings for an indictable offence, and proceedings in the Divisional Court or the House of Lords in respect of a summary offence. They cannot cover investigation expenses.

[573] e.g. *R v Belmarsh Magistrates' Court, Ex p. Watts* [1999] 2 Cr.App.R. 188.

[574] *R v Director of Public Prosecutions, Ex p. Hallas* (1987) 87 Cr.App.R. 340.

[575] e.g. the prosecution of the men accused of the murder of Stephen Lawrence mounted by the victim's family following the dropping of charges by the CPS: see E. Saunders (1995) 145 N.L.J. 1423, noting the successful outcome of committal proceedings, and rehearsing the difficulties of such prosecutions. See also the case involving the officers on duty at Hillsborough: *R v DPP, Ex p. Duckenfield* and see *R v DPP, Ex p. Camelot* (1998) 10 Admin. L.R. 93 (private prosecution rather than judicial review appropriate means of challenge). Two cases brought by Mrs Mary Whitehouse aroused interest: *R v Lemon* [1979] A.C. 617, where the accused was convicted of blasphemous libel and the Crown subsequently took over the case on appeal; and *Whitehouse v Bogdanov*, where the accused was acquitted on a charge of procuring an act of gross indecency between males contrary to s.13 of the Sexual Offences Act 1956 which resulted from his producing a play (*The Romans in Britain*), containing a scene of intercourse between males (one non-consenting). The prosecution was discontinued after the judge had ruled that there was no case to answer and the Attorney-General eventually entered a *nolle prosequi*. See [1982] P.L. 165.

[576] RCCP Research Study No.10 *op. cit.*, Ch.5. Further, see A. Samuels "Non-Crown Prosecutions: Prosecutions by Non Police Agencies and by Private Individuals" [1986] Crim. L.R. 33. L. H. Leigh, "The Seamless Web? Diversion from The Criminal Process and Judicial Review" (2007) 70(4) M.L.R. 654.

know when such a decision may be made, by whom and on what principles. The
exercise of this particular discretion has attracted considerable attention.[577]

1. THE POLICE

14–044 A choice exists as soon as a police officer discovers that a criminal offence may
have been committed. Should an investigation be started if the situation is
unclear? If the facts are already clear should action be taken to ensure that the
offence is formally considered for prosecution? This problem is faced by every
police officer present at an incident and it must be resolved on individual
initiative and or in accordance with instructions received from a superior officer.
Although it may be the officer's inclination to warn a motorist driving without
lights not to repeat the offence, the Chief Constable may have decided, as a
matter of policy, to prosecute all such offenders and issued instructions accordingly. The discretion exercised in this way by the officer concerned is otherwise
generally uncontrolled, except where failure to take action may itself amount to
a criminal offence or neglect of duty.[578] As noted earlier, the police service is
unusual in organisational terms, in that those lower in the hierarchy have a great
deal of discretion.

The courts have examined the exercise of discretion at a senior level which
would affect the way that the officer on the spot carries out his or her duties.[579]
In *R v Metropolitan Police Commissioner, Ex p. Blackburn (No.1)*,[580] Mr Raymond Blackburn applied for an order of mandamus directed to the Commissioner
requiring him to enforce the provisions of the Betting, Gaming and Lotteries Act
1963 in London gaming clubs. It appeared that the Commissioner had sanctioned
a force order which effectively stopped observation in gaming clubs by the police
and prevented any attempt to enforce the Act.[581] The Court of Appeal held that,
whilst the police had a discretion not to prosecute, it was not proper to take a
policy decision that certain offences would *never* be prosecuted since that was to
negate the exercise of discretion and would amount to a failure in their duty to
enforce the law. However, the courts will not interfere in cases where it is alleged
that the police are not paying *enough* attention to particular offences or prosecuting in sufficient numbers. Mr Blackburn again sought an order of mandamus in
R v Metropolitan Police Commissioner, Ex p. Blackburn (No.3)[582] this time in
respect of the Obscene Publications Act 1959, but the court would not grant it.
Whereas in the first case the police had deliberately decided not to prosecute, in

---

[577] See Ashworth and Redmayne (2005) Ch.6.

[578] *R v Dytham* [1979] Q.B. 722 (criminal offence of wilful neglect of duty).

[579] See Sanders and Young (2007), pp.323–327.

[580] [1968] 2 Q.B. 118. As to judicial review of CPS decisions not to discontinue proceedings, see
below.

[581] The terms of the relevant instructions are set out in the judgment of Lord Denning M.R. at
134–135. In the event, the instructions in question were withdrawn before the appellate hearing
and the Commissioner, through counsel, gave an undertaking to that effect.

[582] [1973] Q.B. 241. For a further instalment in the drama see *R v Metropolitan Police Commissioner, Ex p. Blackburn, The Times*, March 6, 1980. Mr Blackburn referred to the Master of Rolls
in the course of that case as, "the greatest living Englishman" Lord Denning is reported to have
replied, "Tell that to the House of Lords".

this case they were hampered by lack of resources and the uncertainty of the law. "It is no part of the duty of this court to presume to tell the (Commissioner) how to conduct the affairs of the Metropolitan Police, nor how to deploy his all too limited resources."[583] The courts have also acknowledged that the *efficient* use of resources is a proper matter for the police to consider when deploying its officers,[584] and this could have a clear impact on the manner in which policies are created and implemented and how individual officers respond to given circumstances.

Given that an individual officer may be under instructions about how to deal with particular offences and will also have received training for this task, what considerations are likely to be taken into account in the exercise of discretion? Naturally, the gravity of the offence is likely to be uppermost but the officer may also think about the evidence likely to be available in a prosecution; the degree of certainty that the offence has been committed; the attitude of the victim; the personal circumstances of the offender; and the efficacy of a prosecution compared with other ways of dealing with the problem. These are, on a local level, not dissimilar to the considerations appropriate to the decisions of the CPS on whether to continue a prosecution.[585] In this case, however, the decision will need to be taken quickly and often without the help and advice of colleagues. If the officer decides not to arrest or report for prosecution he or she might take no further action (NFA),[586] issue an informal warning to the offender or attempt a conciliation between offender and victim.

Aside from these relatively informal actions, an officer may decide to invoke formal measures short of recommending prosecution. A formal warning, or simple caution, can be issued by the police in circumstances where they are satisfied that the offence is capable of proof but do not intend to prosecute. In 2005 revised National Standards for cautioning were issued.[587] The main features are that there must be evidence of guilt sufficient to give a realistic prospect of conviction; the offender must admit the offence[588] and the offender must understand the significance of a caution and give informed consent to being cautioned.[589] Consideration should be given to whether a caution is in the public interest, taking account of the public interest principles set out in the *Code for Crown Prosecutors*.[590]

The utility of the simple caution is that it enables less serious offenders to be dealt with simply and speedily and diverts them away from the courts. However, one might question the extent to which defendants feel pressured into admitting the offence and accepting a caution in order to avoid the possibility of prosecution.[591] Furthermore, concern has also been voiced over the wide variations in the

---

[583] *per* Roskill L.J. at p.262.

[584] *R v Chief Constable of Sussex, Ex p. Independent Traders Ferry Ltd* [1998] 3 W.L.R. 1260, HL.

[585] See below.

[586] Philips and Brown (1998) found that one-fifth of all arrests ended in no further action, p.83.

[587] Home Office, *The Cautioning of Offenders* (2005) Home Office Circular 30/2005.

[588] *R v Metropolitan Police Commissioner, Ex p. P* [1995] T.L.R. 305.

[589] A caution costs a defendant his good character in a subsequent trial: see *R v Martin* [2000] Crim. L.R. 615; see further and R. May, "The Legal Effect of a Police Caution" [1997] Crim. L.R. 491.

[590] See below.

[591] *R v Metropolitan Police Commissioner, Ex p. Thompson* [1997] 1 W.L.R. 1519.

cautioning rates in different police areas.[592] Whilst the National Standards represent an attempt to alleviate such inconsistency, Sanders and Young argue,
"Official public interest criteria are replaced in practice by unofficial police
interest criteria. These working criteria may, however, lead to undesirable patterns of decision making".[593]

In addition to the simple caution, the CJA 2003 introduced the conditional
caution though this can only be authorised by a prosecutor.[594] It should be noted,
however, that the presentation of the case to the prosecutor is largely dependent
upon the police and their interpretation/construction of it.

Assuming that an officer has arrested an offender or reported him or her for
prosecution, a decision about whether to prosecute is made initially by the
custody officer. The way in which the custody officer has exercised this gatekeeping role has been the subject of much criticism. It has been argued that the
role lacks necessary independence in that the officer is subject to the same
working culture as the investigating officers. As a result cases were put forward
for prosecution on the basis of weak evidence or in relation to charges that were
simply too high. Reforms in the CJA 2003 introducing statutory charging have
attempted to alleviate this problem somewhat. Whilst the custody officer still
makes a decision on whether the case is appropriate for prosecution, if he or she
believes that prosecution should follow then the case is passed to the duty
prosecutor (the prosecutor based in the police station) who takes the final
decision, possibly after further consultation with the investigating officers. It
must be recognised however, that though police discretion has reduced considerably in this area by the statutory charging system, the CPS, in making its
decision, still depends heavily upon the information that is provided for it by the
police. The latter have the ability to present the case (consciously or otherwise)
in the way they wish it to be viewed,[595] which can have a major impact upon the
way in which the CPS reached its decision.[596]

2. THE CODE FOR CROWN PROSECUTORS

14–045   Prior to the establishment of the CPS, as we have seen, the decision to prosecute
would in most cases be taken by the police, in some cases with the advice of a
prosecuting solicitor, or by a member of the DPP's office. It was clear that the
police did not adopt a blanket policy of prosecutions, and did take other factors
into account, but there was comparatively little formal evidence of what those

---

[592] R. Evans and R. Ellis, *Cautioning in the 1990s* (HORF No.52, 1997); D. Crisp and D. Moxon,
Case Screening by the CPS: How and Why Cases are Terminated (HORS 137, 1995), Ch.4; G.
Hughes, A. Pilkington, and R. Leistein, "Diversion in the Culture of the Severity" (1998) 37
Howard J.C.J. 16; G. Laycock and R Tarling, "Police Force Cautioning: Policy and Practice" in
Moxon (ed.) (1985), Ch.6; C. Harding and G. Dingwall, *Diversion in the Criminal Process*
(1998), Ch.7.

[593] Sanders and Young (2007) p.355.

[594] See above. See also, Code for Crown Prosecutors (2004), pp.15–16.

[595] For further details about case construction more widely, see: M. McConville, A. Sanders and R.
Leng, *The Case for the Prosecution* (1991).

[596] Sanders and Young (2007) pp.329–344.

factors were.[597] In 1983, the Attorney-General issued *Criteria for Prosecution*,[598] setting out the approach of the Attorney-General and the DPP to the institution of prosecutions in cases for which they were responsible. The intention was, however, that they be taken into account by all those responsible for prosecutions. The *Criteria* subsequently formed the basis of the *Code for Crown Prosecutors* issued by the DPP.[599] There have been five versions of the Code, the latest one being in 2005.[600]

The Code is to be applied by the CPS "so that it can make fair and consistent decisions about prosecutions"[601] reflecting the duty of the CPS "to make sure that the right person is prosecuted for the right offence".[602] Crown Prosecutors must be "fair, independent and objective".[603] Their key task is to determine whether a case meets the tests set out in the Code and thus should proceed to court. This is a continuing process so that prosecutors can take account of any change of circumstances.[604] The CPS is a public authority for the purposes of the Human Rights Act 1998, and Crown Prosecutors must apply the ECHR principles in accordance with the Act.[605] The decision to prosecute is approached in two stages: (1) the *evidential test*; and (2) the *public interest test*. As to the first stage, Crown Prosecutors must be satisfied that there is enough evidence to provide a "realistic prospect of conviction" against each defendant on each charge, taking account of what the defence case may be. This is difficult test to apply at such an early stage of proceedings. There is a "realistic prospect of conviction" where a properly directed jury or bench of magistrates is more likely than not to convict. Crown Prosecutors must consider whether the evidence can be used and is reliable. Relevant considerations are whether any evidence may be excluded by the court, for example, because of the way it was gathered; whether it is likely that a confession is unreliable, for example, because of the defendant's age, intelligence or lack of understanding; what explanation the defendant has given and the weight a court is likely to attach to it; whether a witness's background is likely to weaken the prosecution case, as where he or she has a dubious motive or relevant previous conviction; and whether evidence of identification is strong enough (if identity is in issue). Crown Prosecutors should not ignore evidence because they are not sure on these points; they should, however, "look closely at it when deciding if there is a realistic prospect of conviction".[606]

---

[597] See, however, the account by a former chief constable: A. F. Wilcox, *The Decision to Prosecute* (1972), and the research project conducted by A. Sanders between 1980 and 1983: Sanders [1985] Crim. L.R. 4, and "The Prosecution Process" in D. Moxon (ed.), *Managing Criminal Justice* (1985), Ch.7.

[598] (1983) 147 J.P.N. 223; Home Office Circular 26/1983. See A. Sanders, "Prosecution Decisions and the Attorney-General's Guidelines" [1985] Crim. L.R. 4: he doubted that the *Criteria* would generally have much effect in reducing "inconsistency, weak cases and shady practice", but noted that they had led to changes in at least two forces (*ibid.* pp.17, 18).

[599] The Code is available on the CPS website.

[600] See, J. Rogers, "Restructuring the Exercise of Prosecutorial Discretion in England" (2006) O.J.L.S. 775.

[601] Code, para.1.1.

[602] Code, para.2.3.

[603] Code, para.2.2.

[604] Code, para.4.2.

[605] Code, para.2.6.

[606] Code, para.5.5.

If the evidential test is passed, Crown Prosecutors must then consider if a prosecution is needed in the public interest.[607] A prosecution will usually take place unless there are public interest factors tending against prosecution which clearly outweigh those tending in favour. These must be balanced "carefully and fairly" and those that can affect the decision to prosecute "usually depend on the seriousness of the offence or the circumstances of the offender".[608] The Code provides non-exhaustive lists of common public interest factors for and against prosecution. As regards factors in favour, it is noted that "the more serious the offence, the more likely it is that a prosecution will be needed in the public interest". A prosecution is likely to be needed if:

(a) a conviction is likely to result in a significant sentence;

(b) a conviction is likely to result in a confiscation or any other order;

(c) a weapon was used or violence was threatened during the commission of the offence;

(d) the offence was committed against a person serving the public (e.g. a police or prison officer or a nurse);

(e) the defendant was in a position of authority or trust;

(f) the evidence shows that the defendant was a ringleader or an organiser of the offence;

(g) there is evidence that the offence was premeditated;

(h) there is evidence that the offence was carried out by a group;

(i) the victim of the offence was vulnerable, has been put in considerable fear, or suffered personal attack, damage or disturbance;

(j) the offence was committed in the presence of, or in close proximity to, a child;

(k) the offence was motivated by any form of discrimination against the victim's ethnic or national origin, sex, religious beliefs, political views or sexual orientation, or the suspect demonstrated hostility towards the victim based on any of those characteristics;

(l) there is a marked difference between the actual or mental ages of the defendant and the victim, or if there is any element of corruption;

(m) the defendant's previous convictions or cautions are relevant to the present offence;

(n) the defendant is alleged to have committed the offence whilst under an order of the court;

(o) there are grounds for believing that the offence is likely to be continued or repeated, for example, by a history of recurring conduct;

---

[607] The DPP, and now the CPS, are guided by a statement made by a former Attorney-General, Lord Shawcross, in the course of a House of Commons debate. "It has never been the rule in this country. I hope it never will be that suspected criminal offences must automatically be the subject of prosecution": HC Deb, Vol.483, col.681, January 29, 1951 (para.6.1).

[608] Code, para.5.8.

(p)   the offence, although not serious in itself, is widespread in the area where it was committed; or

(q)   a prosecution would have a significant positive impact on maintaining community confidence.[609]

A prosecution is less likely to be needed if:

(a)   the court is likely to impose a nominal penalty;

(b)   the defendant has already been made the subject of a sentence and any further conviction would be unlikely to result in the imposition of an additional sentence or order, unless the nature of the particular offence requires a prosecution;

(c)   the offence was committed as a result of a genuine mistake or misunderstanding (these factors must be balanced against the seriousness of the offence);

(d)   the loss or harm can be described as minor and was the result of a single incident, particularly if it was caused by a misjudgement;

(e)   there has been a long delay between the offence taking place and the date of the trial, unless:

   (i)   the offence is serious;
   (ii)   the delay has been caused in part by the defendant;
   (iii)   the offence has only recently come to light; or
   (iv)   the complexity of the offence has meant that there has been a long investigation;

(f)   a prosecution is likely to have a bad effect on the victim's physical or mental health, always bearing in mind the seriousness of the offence;

(g)   the defendant is elderly or is, or was at the time of the offence, suffering from significant mental or physical ill health, unless the offence is serious or there is a real possibility that it may be repeated. The CPS, where necessary, applies Home Office guidelines about how to deal with mentally disordered offenders. Crown Prosecutors must balance the desirability of diverting a defendant who is suffering from significant mental or physical ill health with the need to safeguard the general public;

(h)   the defendant has put right the loss or harm that was caused (but defendants must not avoid prosecution solely because they can pay compensation); or

(i)   details may be made public that could harm sources of information, international relations or national security.[610]

While the Code lists these competing factors, it is also made clear that prosecutors must not simply add up the number of factors on each side: they "must decide how important each factor is in the circumstances of each case and go on to make an overall assessment".[611]

[609] Code, para.5.9.
[610] Code, para.5.10.
[611] Code, para.5.11.

They must also always take account of the consequences for the victim of the decision whether to prosecute. "It is important that a victim is told about a decision which makes a significant difference to the case in which he is involved." It is difficult for the CPS to strike a balance between meeting the victim's needs and not being placed under inappropriate pressure in individual cases to pursue a case which is not in the public interest because of the victim's circumstances.[612] At the same time the CPS must be careful to respect the confidentiality of material when disclosing reasons to the victims.

Where the defendant is a youth, prosecutors must also consider his or her interests; the stigma of a conviction can cause very severe harm to his or her prospects and young offenders can sometimes be dealt with without going to court. However, prosecutors "should not avoid prosecuting simply because of the defendant's age. The seriousness of the offence or the youth's past behaviour may make prosecutions necessary."[613]

Crown Prosecutors should also consider alternatives to prosecution including simple and conditional cautions. As to the former, the prosecutor should tell the police it they think a caution would be more suitable than a prosecution so that the police can administer it.[614] With a conditional caution the prosecutor should also give an indication as to what conditions would be appropriate.[615]

As to charges,[616] Crown Prosecutors should select charges which: (a) reflect the seriousness of the offending; (b) give the court adequate powers to sentence and impose appropriate post conviction orders; and (c) enable the case to be presented in a clear and simple way. Thus they may not always continue with the most serious charge and should not continue with more charges than are necessary. Indeed, they should never go ahead with more charges than are necessary, or a more serious charge, in order to encourage a defendant to plead guilty to some, or a less serious charge. They should not change the charge simply because of the venue in which the case will be heard.

As to mode of trial,[617] Crown Prosecutors must apply the national guidelines. Speed must never be the only reason for asking for summary trial, but prosecutors should consider the effect of any likely delay if a case is sent to the Crown Court and any possible stress on victims and witnesses if the case is delayed.

Crown Prosecutors should only accept a guilty plea if they think the court is able to pass a sentence that matches the seriousness of the offending, and never just because it is convenient. Care must be taken when considering pleas that would enable the accused to avoid the mandatory minimum sentence.[618]

If the CPS tells a suspect or defendant that there will not be a prosecution or that the prosecution has been stopped, that is normally the end of the matter. However, a prosecution may be re-started: (a) in rare cases where the original decision was clearly wrong; (b) where the prosecution has been stopped so that more evidence which is likely to become available in the fairly near future can be collected (here, the prosecution will tell the defendant that the prosecution may well start again); or (c) in other cases where more significant evidence is

---

[612] On this see Sanders and Young (2007) pp.375–379.

[613] Code, para.8.8. This is much weaker than the provisions in the 2nd Code that "the youth of the offender" was a public interest factor against prosecution and that juveniles should not be prosecuted unless exceptional circumstances dictated otherwise.

[614] Code, para.8.3.

[615] Code, para.8.7.

[616] Code, para.7.

[617] Code, para.9.

[618] Code, para.10.5.

discovered later.[619] Furthermore, the CJA 2003 provides that following an acquittal for a serious offence the Crown Prosecutor may, with the consent of the DPP, apply to the Court of Appeal for an order quashing the acquittal and requiring the defendant to be retried.[620]

Quality of decision

The rate of discontinuance has been a thorn in the side of the CPS since its **14–046** inception. It should be recognised that some cases of discontinuance may in fact be a reflection of improper charges applied by the police before the case reached the CPS. Nevertheless, there has always been a concerted effort on the part of the CPS to reduce the overall number. In recent years the number of discontinuances in the magistrates' court has been steadily declining. In 2001–02 the figure was 16.2 per cent. In 2003–04 the figure had dropped to 13.8 per cent and by 2005–06 had dropped still further to 11.6 per cent.[621] If rates of discontinuance reflect a criticism of the CPS then it is fair to say that there is improvement. Furthermore, the move to statutory charging ought to bring about more accurate charging of the defendant from the outset and thus discontinuance rates should drop further still. However, care must be taken to recognise the multitude of reasons for discontinuance rather than merely striving to meet targets of apparent "success".

In 2000 Her Majesty's Crown Prosecution Service Inspectorate was established as a statutory body[622] tasked with promoting effectiveness, efficiency and fairness of the prosecution process. A recurring problem identified by the Inspectorate has been the poor quality of endorsements on files prepared by the CPS. The Inspectorate's 2003 Thematic Report on "the Justice Gap" suggested that some lawyers were failing to take a robust and proactive approach to the important task of continuing review.[623] Furthermore, the overall approach to file endorsement was unsatisfactory. In 20 per cent of the charge attrition cases considered the reason for the charged being dropped or changed was not endorsed in sufficient detail.[624] Ashworth and Redmayne comment that "while it remains possible that all these decisions were correctly taken and these are merely failures of record keeping, the two reports suggest strongly that this was not the case".[625]

The decisions taken by the CPS are dependent almost entirely on the information they receive from the police and this, in turn, affects the quality of those decisions. The move to statutory charging may bring about a closer working relationship between the police and the CPS. The consequence of this might be that the police are better advised on how to prepare a case for prosecution and the CPS are better placed to make a fully informed decision as to what charges

---

[619] Code, para.12.2. On stays of proceedings for abuse of process where the prosecution have reneged on promises see below, Ch.17.

[620] See below, Ch.17.

[621] CPC *Annual Report 2005–6*, Annex A. For further details on CPS performance against qualitative measures see, *HM Chief Inspector's Annual Report 2004–5* (2005) H.C. 129, Annex 6.

[622] Crown Prosecution Service Inspectorate Act 2000.

[623] HM Crown Prosecution Service Inspectorate, *Thematic Review of Attrition in the Prosecution Process* (2003) para.8.8.

[624] *ibid.* para.8.16. Similar problems are identified in HMCPSI, *Report of a Joint Inspection into the Investigation and Prosecution of Cases Involving Allegations of Rape* (2002) para.8.48; HMCPSI, *Violence at Home* (2004) para.7.18.

[625] Ashworth and Redmayne (2005) p.191.

should be preferred. On the other hand, a closer working relationship might compromise what independence currently exists, leading to the CPS being subsumed by the very strong occupational culture of the police service. Analysis of this new relationship will be one of the keys to recognising the future progress and performance of the CPS, a recognition which cannot come solely through the analysis of centrally set targets.

3. Prosecutions by Other Agencies

14–047 The CPS prosecutes around 95 per cent of Crown Court and 25 per cent of magistrates' court cases. Most of the prosecutions brought by non-police agencies arise out of the enforcement of regulatory legislation in the context of business, including legislation concerning protection of the health and safety of employees,[626] trading standards[627] and protection of the environment.[628] Those who enforce this kind of legislation tend to prefer other methods of securing compliance, such as advice, negotiation and warning, with prosecution as a last resort.[629] The internal decision-making arrangements tend to make prosecution more difficult than non-prosecution.[630] It has been noted that the potential defendants tend to be middle class (companies, managers, self-employed) rather than working class (who comprise the majority of those dealt with by the police).[631] However, it has been argued that the class bias exhibited by the prosecution patterns arises not from deliberate bias on the part of the law enforcers, but reflects more fundamental economic and social differences between different types of "crime" and "criminal".[632]

A similar contrast can be drawn between the rarity of prosecutions for tax evasion and the much more common use of prosecutions for social security frauds.[633] Other agencies to compare include the Commissioners for Customs

---

[626] See W. G. Carson, "White Collar Crime and the Enforcement of Factory Legislation" (1970) 10 Brit. J. Crim. 383, and *The Other Price of Britain's Oil* (1982); D. Kloss [1978] Crim. L.R. 280.

[627] R. Cranston, *Regulating Business* (1979) (enforcement of trading standards); B. Hutter, *The Reasonable Arm of the Law* (1988) (environmental health officers); H. Croall (1988) 15 J.L.S. 293 and (1989) 29 Brit. J. Crim. 157.

[628] See G. Richardson, A. Ogus and P. Burroughs, *Policing Pollution* (1982); K. Hawkins, *Environment and Enforcement* (1984); M. Weatt (1989) 29 Brit. J. Crim. 57.

[629] See generally, The Hampton Report, *Reducing Adminstrative Burdens: Effective Inspection and Enforcement* (2005).

[630] See A. Sanders, "Class Bias in Prosecution" (1985) 24 Howard Journal 176, comparing the "institutional propensity to prosecute" of the police with the "propensity not to prosecute" of the Factory Inspectorate.

[631] Sanders, *op. cit.*

[632] *ibid.* pp.194–197.

[633] See the Grabiner Report Into the Informal Economy (1999). See M. Levi [1982] B.T.R. 36; Report of the Keith Committee on the *Enforcement Powers of the Revenue Departments* (Cmnd. 8822, 1983); S. Uglow, "Defrauding the Public Purse" [1984] Crim. L.R. 128; R. Smith, "Who's Fiddling? Fraud and Abuse" in S. Ward (ed.), *DHSS in Crisis* (1985); D. Cook, *Rich Law, Poor Law* (1989); D. Cook, *Poverty, Crime and Punishment* (1997). The approach of both the police and other agencies to the investigation and prosecution of fraud is considered by M. Levi, *Regulating Fraud* (1987).

and Excise,[634] the Board of the Inland Revenue,[635] the Health and Safety Executive,[636] the DSS.[637]

The powers of such organisations give rise to two distinct problems. First, there is the question to what extent they should be permitted to conduct both investigative and prosecutorial functions, given the importance of the separation of these functions in relation to the mainstream criminal process. Secondly, there is the question of maintaining consistent standards in the prosecution policies themselves. Commentators have drawn attention to the fact that the regulatory authorities are often more compliance orientated in their outlook.[638] With such a diverse range of authorities, each protecting their own interests, it is inevitable that different prosecution policies evolve. This is unobjectionable provided certain minimum criteria are met: the prosecution policy must not be capricious or arbitrary or discriminatory; it must be published and accessible to the public; and the courts must exercise the power of review of its execution and application. The Codes should strive to match the level of protection that is afforded to the criminal suspect investigated by the police and prosecuted by the CPS. Occasionally, prosecution policies have clashed.[639]

One argument that is commonly relied upon to justify the right of the organisations to conduct prosecutions is that there is no restriction placed on the individual bringing a purely private prosecution (see above). It is not clear that the right of a private prosecution necessarily justifies other agencies' activities. A distinction could be drawn between truly private prosecutions and those brought on behalf of the "state" (perhaps any central government departments). It might be considered advantageous if *all* prosecutions other than those taken by private individuals were taken over by the CPS. There would be greater consistency, and separation from the investigation, which might be desirable provided that the prosecuting authority acknowledged the necessary differences of policy between departments.[640]

---

[634] For criticism of Customs and Excise prosecutions see G. McFarlane (1999) 149 N.L.J. 1123. See also Customs and Excise, the Gower-Hammond Report (2001) on prosecution and investigation policies.

[635] The overwhelming acceptance of the IRC's power to prosecute was accepted by the Court of Appeal, despite there being no express statutory power: *R (on the application of Hunt) v CCRC* [2001] Crim. L.R. 324; *R v W* [1998] S.T.C. 550. Its policy of selective enforcement was accepted in *R v IRC, Ex p. Mead and Cook* [1992] S.T.C. 482; *R v IRC, Ex p. Alien* [1997] S.T.C. 1141. See J. Roording [1996] Crim. L.R. 240.

[636] On the HSE see the protocol with the CPS for work-related deaths (1998) 148 N.L.J. 911. See D. Bergman (1999) 149 N.L.I. 1656 questioning the HSE failure to prosecute in thousands of cases.

[637] See recently on the new DSS powers, G. McKeeva, "Detecting, Prosecuting and Punishing Benefit Fraud: The Social Security Administration (Fraud) Act 1997", (1999) 62 M.L.R. 261.

[638] On other agencies see A. Reiss "Styles of Regulatory Justice" in K. Hawkins and J. Thomas (eds), *Enforcing Regulation* (1984); on prosecutions of regulatory offences see S. Antrobus and I. Cooper (2001) Sol. J. June 8, pp.520, 553, 574. See also G. Richardson, *Strict Liability for Regulating Crime: the Empirical Research* [1987] C.L.R. 295. The different policies of prosecution have also been highlighted by, e.g. the Grabiner Report into the Informal Economy (1999).

[639] See, e.g. *R v W* [1998] (CPS and Inland Revenue policies on tax evasion). But, see the written answer of the Attorney-General in *Hansard* April 8, 1998, col.231, on the strengthened arrangements for liaison between the prosecuting authorities of the Inland Revenue and the CPS. See S. Lewis and R. Clutterbuck, [1998] Crim. L.R. 139.

[640] Obviously there would have to be a clarification of what was a private as opposed to a state prosecution, and drawing this distinction could be difficult in some cases.

4. JUDICIAL REVIEW AND THE DECISION TO PROSECUTE[641]

14–048   Decisions of the CPS to initiate a prosecution are open to challenge on an application for judicial review in limited circumstances. The possibility of judicial review of police decisions was recognised (as regards a decision not to prosecute) in *R v Metropolitan Police Commissioner, Ex p. Blackburn (No.1)*[642] and (as regards a decision to prosecute and not caution a juvenile) in *R v Chief Constable of the Kent County Constabulary, Ex p. L.*[643] The House of Lords has, however, subsequently held that in the absence of dishonesty, *mala fides* or some exceptional circumstance, a decision to prosecute cannot be challenged by way of judicial review.[644] Arguments that the prosecution amounts to an abuse of process should be raised in the course of the trial itself.[645] A decision not to prosecute remains reviewable because no other remedy is available.

In *R v DPP, Ex p. C*,[646] the Divisional Court quashed a decision of the CPS to *discontinue* a prosecution where it was shown that the CPS had failed to have regard to material matters. The matter was remitted to the CPS for reconsideration. In general, the DPP is not under an obligation to provide reasons for his or her decision not to prosecute. The position may be different where there has been a death in custody. Where a suspect has died in custody and an inquest jury has returned a verdict of unlawful killing, implicating an officer against whom there was prima facie evidence, any failure to prosecute must at least be explained.[647]

Decisions of the Attorney-General not to prosecute are not open to judicial review, because of his or her "unique constitutional position".[648]

D. THE CLASSIFICATION OF OFFENCES

14–049   If a decision is taken to prosecute an offender, the Crown Prosecutor, or relevant prosecuting agency, must decide on the appropriate charge. The selection of the charge is important because it may determine the court in which the case will be tried and, hence, the mode of trial. We have already recorded that both the magistrates' court and the Crown Court have original criminal jurisdiction and

---

[641] M. Burton, "Reviewing CPS Decisions not to Prosecute" [2001] Crim. L.R. 374; C. Hilson [1993] Crim. L.R. 739.

[642] [1968] 2 Q.B. 118.

[643] [1993] 1 All E.R. 756.

[644] *R v DPP, Ex p. Kebilene* [2000] 2 A.C. 326.

[645] See *R (Pepushi) v CPS (2004) The Times* May 21, 2004. As to the factors to be taken into account when determining if an abuse of process has arisen, see *R v Mulla* [2004] 1 Cr.App.R. 72.

[646] [1995] 1 Cr.App.R. 136.

[647] *R v DPP, Ex p. Manning* [2001] Q.B. 330. Burton [2001] Crim. L.R. 374.

[648] *R v Att.-Gen., Ex p. Taylor, The Independent*, August 3, 1995 (application by T and her sister for judicial review of the Attorney-General's decision not to prosecute certain newspapers for contempt of court in respect of prejudicial coverage of their murder trial, following the quashing of their convictions).

the work is divided between them according to the seriousness of the charge. In the Crown Court, the trial is "on indictment" with a judge and jury, and in the magistrates' court the trial is summary and conducted by the magistrates. Criminal offences are classified according to the way in which they are to be tried and the number of categories was reduced to three by the Criminal Law Act 1977,[649] which was based upon the report of the James Committee on the *Distribution of Criminal Business between the Crown Court and the Magistrates' Courts.*[650]

Section 14 of the 1977 Act provided that there should be offences triable only on indictment; offences triable only summarily; and offences triable either way.[651] A fourth category has been added by s.40 of the Criminal Justice Act 1988, which provides that, in certain circumstances, a summary offence may be added to an indictment tried at the Crown Court.

1. Offences Triable only on Indictment

All offences at common law were triable on indictment. The other two categories are creatures of statute and, therefore, in the absence of any specific provision an offence will be triable on indictment. In practice, this category is reserved for the most serious offences including murder, manslaughter, rape, robbery, causing grievous bodily harm with intent, blackmail and riot. Some offences were "downgraded" by the Criminal Law Act 1977, Sch.2[652] so as to be triable either way, and the trend has been to reserve indictable offences for the most serious circumstances and most new offences are triable either way or summarily.   **14–050**

Section 51 of the Crime and Disorder Act 1998 removed the requirement for committal proceedings for offences triable *only* on indictment.[653] Offenders charged with such offences must be "sent" to the Crown Court for trial without committal. These "indictable only procedures" are clearly designed to speed up the process of such cases.

Section 51 of and Sch.3 of the 1998 Act result in the following rather complex procedures.

The court *shall* send the following to the Crown Court:

(a)   D, charged with an indictable only offence to be tried for that offence.

---

[649] The pertinent parts of this Act were re-enacted in the Magistrates' Courts Act 1980.

[650] (Cmnd. 6323, 1975). The Committee was chaired by James L.J.

[651] Section 14 was repealed by the Magistrates' Courts Act 1980, s.154 and *not* re-enacted but it is a convenient statement of the three categories. Sections 17–25 of the 1980 Act adopted the same tripatrite system. The Interpretation Act 1978, Sch.1 defines each of the three categories. The procedures hereafter stated apply to adults. In the case of juveniles, summary trial is almost always the mode of trial, even for indictable offences: see Magistrates' Courts Act 1980, s.24. In the exceptional cases in which juveniles are tried in the Crown Court, English law has adopted a special procedure in light of the ECHR ruling in *T. v UK* (2000) 30 E.H.R.R. 121, see *The Consolidated Criminal Practice Direction: Further Directions Applying in the Crown Court* (2005) Pt IV.39.

[652] Now to be found in Magistrates' Courts Act 1980, Sch.1.

[653] See generally, R. Leng, R. Taylor and M. Wasik, *Blackstone's Guide to the Crime and Disorder Act 1998* (1998), Ch.5.

(b) D, charged with an indictable only offence and any either way or summary offence where that offence is related[654] to the indictable only offence.

(c) E, jointly charged on a related either way offence with D who faces an indictable only offence (or related either way or other relevant offence) and D is, *at this hearing*, sent to the Crown Court on that indictable only charge.

(d) E, who has been sent to the Crown Court to face an either way offence (with which he or she is jointly charged with D) must also be sent to the Crown Court on any related either way or summary offences with which he or she is charged.

Magistrates *may* send the following:

(a) D, who has already been sent to the Crown Court for an indictable only offence and who now appears charged with any either way or summary offence (which carries a sentence of imprisonment/driving disqualification) where that offence is related to the indictable only offence.

(b) E, jointly charged on a related either way offence with D who faces an indictable only offence where D has already been sent to the Crown Court on that indictable only charge.

(c) F, a child or young person jointly charged with an adult charged with an indictable only offence where F faces a related either way or summary offence (for which the penalty is imprisonment or disqualification), may be sent whether D has been previously sent for trial or is being sent for trial at this hearing.

Related either way offences[655] are included in the indictment and tried in the Crown Court in the normal way. If by the time of the Crown Court trial the indictable only offence has been dropped, the Crown Court applies the plea before venue procedure and conducts a mode of trial hearing (both discussed below).

2. OFFENCES TRIABLE ONLY SUMMARILY

14–051 Magistrates actually deal with the vast majority of trials in this country (around 95 per cent) and they have exclusive jurisdiction in summary trial. Summary offences must be created by statute and the designation of an offence as summary prevents a jury trial. It was the proposed reclassification of certain offences as triable only summarily which caused much heated criticism of the James Report.[656] The Criminal Law Act 1977 made provision for the "down-grading"

---

[654] By s.50(12)(c) and (d), an offence is related to an indictable-only offence if it "arises out of circumstances which are the same as or connected with those giving rise to the indictable-only offence".

[655] s.51(12)(c).

[656] *The Distribution of Criminal Business between the Crown Court and Magistrates' Courts* (Cmnd. 6323, 1975).

of certain offences which might previously have come before a jury.[657] The pressure to reclassify other offences, such as small thefts, as summary only has continued.[658] In more recent times proposals to remove the right of election for mode of trial have similarly generated concerns.

3. Offences Triable Either Way[659]

This category is now comprised of: (1) those offences specifically mentioned in **14–052** the Sch.1 to the Magistrates' Courts Act 1980; (2) all other offences which prior to the Criminal Law 1977 Act were triable either on indictment or summarily and which were not redesignated in 1980[660]; and (3) all offences established since 1977 as triable either way. Amongst the important offences triable either way are all indictable offences under the Theft Acts 1968 and 1978 (save for robbery, blackmail, assault with intent to rob and some burglaries); most of the offences under the Criminal Damage Act 1971, including arson; and certain offences under the Perjury Act 1911.

In respect of offences triable either way it is, of course, necessary to provide a procedure for determining the mode of trial. The relevant procedure has been the subject of repeated amendment. In 1995 substantial changes were enacted which oblige the defendant to enter a plea before the mode of trial decision is made. The "plea before venue", which was designed to maximise the opportunity to keep the greatest number of cases possible in the magistrates' court,[661] operates as follows.[662]

(i) The charge is written down and read to the accused.[663]

(ii) It is explained to the accused that if he or she indicates a guilty plea, the trial will be dealt with summarily, but that the case may be committed for

---

[657] 1977 Act, s.15 and Sch.1.

[658] See e.g. D. Wolchover, "The Right to Jury Trial" (1986) 136 N.L.J. 530 at 576; N. A. McKittrick, "Curbing the Right to Jury Trial" (1988) 152 J.P.N. 515. The Practice Direction on mode of trial decision making is now drafted so as to create a presumption in favour of a summary only trial.

[659] For a good historical account of the problem with either way offences, see Auld Report (2001), Ch.10, paras 123–127.

[660] Magistrates' Courts Act 1980, s.17.

[661] See A. Edwards [1997] Crim. L.R. 321; R. Leng and R. Taylor, *The Blackstone's Guide to the CPIA 1996* (1996); S. Enright (1997) 147 N.L.J. 1691. The hearing can occur before a lone magistrate: s.18(5). On the problems of the process, see, A. Herbert, "Mode of Trial and Magistrates' Sentencing Powers: Will increased powers inevitably lead to a reduction in the committal rate?" [2003] Crim. L.R. 314.

[662] Magistrates' Courts Act 1980, ss.19–21 as heavily amended by the Criminal Procedure and Investigations Act 1996, s.49 and the Powers of Criminal Courts (Sentencing) Act 2000, s.165. Magistrates are obliged to follow the procedure strictly otherwise their decision will be liable to be quashed as *ultra vires*.

[663] Who should be present unless: it impracticable owing to his or her disorderly behaviour; or, provided there is legal representation, the accused consents to being absent and there is a good reason for the absence; or, where there is a live link from a remand facility: see Crime and Disorder Act 1998, s.57. See further on live links the Learmont Report, *Review of Prison Service Security and Escape from Parkhurst Prison on Tuesday 3rd January 1995*, Cm. 3020 (1996).

sentence in the Crown Court if the magistrates are of the opinion that their sentencing powers are inadequate.[664]

(iii) Following the explanation, the accused is asked to indicate a plea.[665]

(iv) If the indication is guilty, the court proceeds as if this was a guilty plea received at a summary trial.[666] If the magistrates wish to keep open the option of committing to the Crown Court for sentencing they should make that explicit to the accused to prevent any misunderstanding and any legitimate expectation arising.[667]

(v) If the indication is one of not guilty, the court listens to any representations from the prosecutor and the accused about the most suitable mode of trial.

(a) Mode of trial

14–053 The court proceeds to decide on the more suitable mode of trial, taking into account the nature of the case, whether the circumstances make the offence one of a serious character, whether the limited powers of punishment of a magistrates' court would be adequate, and any other relevant circumstances. The ability to inflict an adequate punishment in the circumstances as presented is perhaps the most influential factor which shapes the decision of the magistrates.

If the court considers summary trial more appropriate, that should be explained to the accused, as should the fact that he or she need not consent to summary trial but can opt for trial by jury, and that after a summary trial the magistrates have power to send him or her to the Crown Court for sentence.[668] If the accused consents to summary trial, the case proceeds. If the accused elects trial on indictment, the magistrates proceed with committal proceedings. If the court considers that trial on indictment is more appropriate it will proceed with committal proceedings and the accused effectively has no choice in the matter.[669]

Where the examining justices are faced with the decision on mode of trial, they must never base their decision on the grounds of convenience, but must give proper consideration to all relevant factors and should not be persuaded by the accused (or prosecutor)[670] to allow a summary trial where the offence ought really to be tried on indictment. There are a number of examples of magistrates'

---

[664] See Powers of Criminal Courts (Sentencing) Act 2000, s.3. If the defendant pleads not guilty, and the magistrates accept jurisdiction, then the power to commit to the Crown Court for sentence will be abolished by the CJA 2003.

[665] The Magistrates' Courts Act 1980, s.17A(5).

[666] If the court adjourns for sentencing reports having indicated an intention to deal with the case without committing the case to the Crown Court for sentencing, then in the absence of further information affecting the gravity of the case, a decision to commit for sentence will be subject to judicial review: *R v Norwich Magistrates Court, Ex p. Elliott* [2000] 1 Cr.App.R. (S) 152.

[667] *R v Wirral Magistrates Court, Ex p. Jermyn* [2001] Crim. L.R. 45 (can commit without new information but dangers of false expectation of D cannot be ignored); see also *R v Feltham Justices, Ex p. Rees* [2001] Crim. L.R. 47.

[668] Under the Powers of Criminal Courts (Sentencing) Act 2000, s.3.

[669] The Magistrates Courts Act 1980, s.21.

[670] The court should presume that the prosecution's version of the facts is correct. *See Practice Direction (Criminal Proceedings Consolidation)* [2002] 1 W.L.R. 2870, para.51.

courts being severely criticised for allowing serious cases to be tried summa-rily.[671] The justices are aided somewhat by a provision that they may, during a trial[672] (before the conclusion of the prosecution evidence[673]), decide to dis-continue the summary trial and proceed as examining justices if the prosecution case reveals the offence to be more serious than might at first have appeared.[674] The reverse change is possible, from committal proceedings to summary trial, subject, in this case, to the consent of the accused.[675]

The defendant should be permitted to change his or her election if he or she has not properly understood the nature and significance of the choice of the mode of trial,[676] similarly, if he or she has made a decision on the wrong view of the facts.[677] To minimise the risk of misinformed pleas, the prosecution is obliged, on the defence requesting it, to provide a summary of the case and/or copies of the written statements prior to the mode of trial decision,[678] and prior to the plea before venue. Unless the court is satisfied that no injustice will result, there should be an adjournment to allow for consideration of the material.[679] The court should not exercise the power to alter the mode of trial because it disagrees with the original determination of the mode of trial made by a different bench.[680]

In the absence of bad faith on the part of the prosecutor or of unfairness or prejudice to the accused, the prosecutor may substitute a summary offence for an either way offence even if the purpose is to deprive the accused of the "right" to jury trial[681]; in effect denying an opportunity to a greater chance of acquittal. The prosecution can in many cases dictate the venue by charging summary only offences or an either way offence and a summary only in the alternative. If the

---

[671] See, e.g. *R v Coe* [1968] 1 W.L.R. 1950; *R v Northamptonshire Magistrates' Court, Ex p. Customs and Excise Commissioners, The Independent*, February 23, 1994 (decision to try £200,000 VAT fraud summarily quashed); *R v Horseferry Road Magistrates Court, Ex p. DPP* [1997] C.O.D. 89 (possession of 114 ecstasy tablets); *cf. R v Derby JJ., Ex p. DPP, The Times*, August 17, 1999 (banging victims head on wall—not using a weapon).

[672] But not on the basis of pleading only: see *R v St Helens Magistrates Court, Ex p. Critchley* [1988] Crim. L.R. 311; *cf. R v Newham Juvenile Court, Ex p. F (A Minor)* (1984) 84 Cr.App.R. 81.

[673] Not after a plea of guilty has been accepted: *R v Dudley JJ., Ex p. Gillard* [1986] A.C. 442, HL; *R v Telford JJ., Ex p. Darlington* (1987) 87 Cr.App.R. 194; *R v Bradford Justices, Ex p. Grant* (1999) 163 J.P. 717; and not prior to the commencement of summary trial: *R v Southend Magistrates' Court, Ex p. Wood* (1986) 152 J.P. 97; *R v St. Helens Magistrates' Court, Ex p. Critchley* (1987) 152 J.P. 102. See Stevens, (1987) 151 J.P.N. 848. This includes hearing submissions on a preliminary point: *R v Horseferry Road Magistrates Court, Ex p. K* [1997] Q.B. 23. See *Archbold* (2007), para.1–75.

[674] Magistrates' Courts Act 1980, s.25(2), as amended by the Criminal Procedure and Investigation Act 1996, s.47. But not merely because co-accused have been committed for trial: *R v Charley Magistrates' Court, Ex p. Darbyshire* [1994] C.L.Y. 997; *R v Wigan Magistrates' Court, Ex p. Layland* (1995) 160 J.P. 223.

[675] *ibid.* s.25(3), (3A), (4), as amended by the Prosecution of Offences Act 1985, s.31(5)(6), Schs 1, 2. See *R v Liverpool JJ., Ex p. CPS* (1989) 90 Cr.App.R. 261. No power exists other than under the statute: *R v Herefordshire JJ., Ex p. J.*

[676] *R v Birmingham JJ., Ex p. Hodgson* [1985] Q.B. 1131, DC (unrepresented defendants had been under the misapprehension that they had no defence; earlier authorities considered); see B. Gibson (1985) 149 J.P.N. 67. See also *R v Forest Magistrates' Court, Ex p. Spicer* (1988) 153 J.P. 81; *R v Bourne JJ., Ex p. Cope* (1988) 153 J.P. 161. The magistrates have a broad discretion in this application: *R v Southampton Justices, Ex p. Briggs* [1972] 1 W.L.R. 277.

[677] See *R v Isleworth Crown Court and Uxbridge Magistrates Court, Ex p. Buda* [2000] 1 Cr.App.R. (S) 538.

[678] See Magistrates' Court (Advance Information) Rules 1985 (SI 1985/601).

[679] *R v Calderdale Justices, Ex p. Donaghue and Cutler* [2001] Crim. L.R. 141.

[680] *R v Birmingham Stipendiary Magistrate, Ex p. Webb* (1995) 95 Cr.App.R. 75.

[681] *R v City of Liverpool Stipendiary Magistrate, Ex p. Ellison* (1988) 153 J.P. 433; *Cooke v DPP* (1992) 156 J.P. 497.

accused elects trial at the Crown Court, the CPS could drop the either way charge leaving the summary trial. In the converse situation the court must be careful not to allow the prosecutor to add an indictable only charge as a way of overruling the magistrate's earlier decision to try the defendant summarily.[682] If the prosecutor disagrees with the magistrate's decision to try the accused summarily, judicial review may be sought.

The advantages of the plea before venue system are that it reduces delay and relieves the congestion in the Crown Court, reduces the number of cracked trials (those in which a guilty plea is made at the last minute), and saves money.[683] The obvious effect is that fewer cases will be committed to the Crown Court for trial, but this is partially offset by an increase in numbers of committals for sentence.[684] The increase in the number of guilty pleas made at the plea before venue stage is inevitable because it gives the accused the opportunity to maximise any sentencing discount[685]; but this carries with it the danger that innocent people will indicate a guilty plea earlier to secure a lesser sentence rather than risk defending the accusation with a potentially higher sentence if convicted.

In the 1980s there was a steady increase in the number and proportion of triable either way cases committed for trial in the Crown Court.[686] This led to higher costs and greater numbers being imprisoned. Home Office research indicated that a high proportion, over 60 per cent, were committed at the discretion of the magistrates rather than at the insistence of the defendant, and that there were considerable variations in practice among the courts surveyed.[687] Guidelines were formulated in some areas to enhance consistency[688] and magistrates were encouraged to retain more cases within their jurisdiction.[689] National guidelines were published in October 1990. They were updated in 1995 and were re-examined[690] in light of the changes introduced by plea before venue, which has reduced the pressure on magistrates.

---

[682] *R v Redbridge Justices, Ex p. Whitehouse* (1992) 94 Cr.App.R. 332.

[683] See for comment G. Bavidge and K. Kerrigan, "Plea Before Venue" (1998) 148 N.L.J. 62; P. Tain, "Plea Before Venue" (1998) S.J. 156.

[684] Whilst there has 15,000 fewer cases per year committed to the Crown Court for trial, there has been a rise of 10,000 cases a year committed to the Crown Court for sentence: *Criminal Statistics, England and Wales* 2002, Figure 3.2.

[685] *R v Rafferty* [1999] 2 Cr.App.R. (S) 449; *R v Barber* [2001] 1 Cr.App.R. 548.

[686] From 55,000 to 93,500 between 1979 and 1987, an increase from 15% to 21% of all defendants proceeded against for either-way offences: *Criminal Statistics 1979*, Table 4.5; *1989*, Table 6.4.

[687] C. Hedderman and D. Moxon, *Magistrates' Court or Crown Court? Mode of Trial Decisions and Sentencing* (Home Office Research Study No.125, HMSO, 1992). See also studies by A. E. Bottoms and J. D. McClean, *Defendants in the Criminal Process* (1976), Ch.4; C. R. Searle, (1989) 153 J.P.N. 526; and D. Riley and J. Vennard, *Triable Either Way Cases: Crown Court or Magistrates' Court?* (Home Office Research Study No.98, 1988); J. Gregory, *Crown Court or Magistrates' Court* (1976).

[688] N. A. McKittrick, "Considerations in Determining Mode of Trial" (1987) 151 J.P.N. 468, setting out guidelines formulated by the liaison judges in the East Midlands. A revised version is set out at (1989) 153 J.P.N. 314. *Cf.* the study by Searle, *op. cit.*, of cases in Nottingham.

[689] *cf.* letter from the Home Office to the Magistrates' Association summarising the research and suggesting that it was unlikely that the increase in committal rates was accounted for by an increase in the level of the seriousness of offences: (1989) 45 The Magistrate 65. Note that the cost of proceedings in the magistrates' court is around £500 compared with around £8,600 in the Crown Court (*Digest 4* (1998) *op. cit.*); Sanders and Young (2007), p.446 suggest that a fairer comparison of prices is of guilty pleas in each court: magistrates' courts cost around £210, Crown Court, £1,400.

[690] *R v Warley Magistrates Court, Ex p. DPP* [1998] 2 Cr.App.R. 307.

The National Guidelines set out some general considerations,[691] based on the case law, but concluding with the proposition that, in general, either way offences should be tried summarily unless the court considers that one or more of the features specified in the guidelines for particular offences is present and that its sentencing powers are insufficient. The guidelines also state directly that some offences should generally be committed for trial: these include violent disorder and supply or possession with intent to supply a Class A drug.[692] Where cases involve complex questions of fact or difficult questions of law, the court should consider committal for trial.

(b) Mode of trial decisions and the Criminal Justice Act 2003

Before the plea before venue scheme was introduced, research into defendants' reasons for choosing between summary trial and trial by jury (where a choice is permitted) suggested that the major factor was the intended plea: defendants intending to contest the case commonly regarded trial by jury in the Crown Court as offering a fairer hearing and a better chance of acquittal, in comparison with the magistrates' courts which were said to be biased in favour of the prosecution.[693] A significant number of defendants intending to plead guilty also wished to be dealt with in the Crown Court, notwithstanding larger sentencing powers, given their confidence in sentencing by a judge rather than by magistrates.[694] Reasons cited most frequently for those choosing summary trial were to get the case to court quickly, the chance of a lighter sentence, to avoid lengthy court proceedings and the triviality of the case.[695] In addition, defendants elect Crown Court trial for tactical reasons including taking the opportunity to maximise their time on remand. There is also the heavy influence of legal advice on election to be borne in mind.[696]

14-054

Research in the early 1990s highlighted the apparent oddities in the exercise of choice by both defendants and magistrates.[697] For example, magistrates' sentencing powers would have been sufficient to deal with the majority of cases where they had declined jurisdiction; most defendants who elected Crown Court trial were influenced by the prospects of acquittal, but 82 per cent ended up pleading guilty to all charges on which they were convicted[698]; while more than half of

---

[691] The most recent version of the guidelines can be found at: *The Consolidated Criminal Practice Direction*, Pt V.51: Mode of Trial. These can be found as part of the Criminal Procedure Rules and are available at the website of the Department for Constitutional Affairs/Ministry of Justice: *www.dca.gov.uk*.

[692] Crime (Sentences) Act 1997, s.3 introduced a further problem for charges of Class A drug trafficking, because automatic sentences flow from a defendant having two previous convictions for drugs offences. See comment at (1998) 162 J.P.N. 238.

[693] But see P. Darbyshire [1997] Crim. L.R. 861 at 869.

[694] Another factor was to elect for trial in the Crown Court in order to gain access to the prosecution case against the defendant. This incentive was removed by the Magistrates' Court (Advance Information) Rules 1985 (SI 1985/601), requiring the prosecution, on request, to provide the accused with either copies of the prosecution witness statements or with a summary of the facts (r.4). There remains disquiet as to the disparity of compliance in different CPS areas.

[695] Hedderman and Moxon (1992) and Riley and Vennard (1988), confirming earlier surveys by Bottoms and McClean (1976) and J. Gregory, *Crown Court or Magistrates' Court?* (HMSO, 1976).

[696] See Ashworth and Redmayne (2005), Ch.10.

[697] Hedderman and Moxon (1992).

[698] P. Tague, "Tactical Reasons for Recommending Trials Rather than Guilty Pleas in the Crown Court", [2006] Crim. L.R. 23.

those who elected jury trial said that the possibility of a lighter sentence influenced their decision, in fact the Crown Court made far more use of custody than the magistrates, court irrespective of area.[699]

The RCCJ recommended that in the light of the early research, changes should be made to introduce a more rational division of either way cases between magistrates' courts and the Crown Court. The Commission noted that "trial in a magistrates' court is many times cheaper". Beliefs that trial in the Crown Court would be fairer or offer a better chance of acquittal were not relevant. As to the first point, magistrates' courts "conduct over 93 per cent of all criminal cases and should be trusted to try cases fairly".[700] The RCCJ appeared undisturbed by the absence of research on the quality of criminal justice in the magistrates' court.

In 1999 and again in 2000 the Government unsuccessfully introduced Criminal Justice (Mode of Trial) Bills into Parliament. The measures would remove the right to elect jury trial in either way cases with the intention of improving efficiency and reducing costs. There was tremendous opposition from many quarters. The proposals were based on the RCCJ recommendations, despite these having been the subject of very cogent criticism.[701]

In light of the defeat of these measures in Parliament, the Government sought a different method of reducing the number of cases proceeding to the Crown Court. The Criminal Justice Act 2003 has made a number of changes to the allocation procedure, though the main provisions of the procedure are still awaiting implementation in early 2007. The Act increases the sentencing powers of magistrates from a maximum of six months to twelve months for any single offence.[702] Schedule 3 to the CJA states that the court is to be informed about, and can take account of a defendant's previous convictions when considering whether its sentencing powers are adequate. Before jurisdiction is determined, the defendant is entitled to ask the magistrates for an indication as to whether, if he pleaded guilty, the sentence would be a custodial one. The magistrates have discretion whether to give such an indication but if they do so the defendant can reconsider his original indication (plea before venue) as to his plea. If the defendant then decides to plead guilty the magistrates will proceed to sentence but can only give a custodial sentence where it was indicated. If the magistrates indicated a non-custodial sentence would be imposed then this presents a real incentive to the defendant to then plead guilty as the magistrates are bound by their indication. If the defendant pleads not guilty and the magistrates accept jurisdiction, the option of a committal to the Crown Court for sentence will not be available. If the defendant pleads guilty but the magistrates do not accept jurisdiction then they can commit to the Crown Court. The committal for trial is abolished and where the court decides that trial on indictment is suitable the case is sent straight to the Crown Court under s.51 of the Crime and Disorder Act 1998. The CJA will also impact upon the ability to switch from summary trial to committal proceedings. This is replaced with a new power for the prosecution to apply for an either way case which has been allocated for summary trial to be

---

[699] On the additional danger of racially discriminatory elements in the mode of trial procedures see I. Brown and R. Hullin, "A Study of Sentencing in the Leeds Magistrates Court: The Treatment of Ethnic Minority and White Offenders" (1992) 32 Brit. J. Crim. 41.

[700] Cm. 2263, pp.85–89.

[701] See A. Ashworth [1993] Crim. L.R. 830; L. Bridges (1993) 143 N.L.J. 1542; L. Bridges (2000) Legal Action, July 6, p.8; M. Zander, "Why Jack Straw's Jury Reform Has Lost the Plot" (2000) 150 N.L.J. 723.

[702] A. Herbert, "Mode of Trial and Magistrates' Sentencing Powers: Will increased powers inevitably lead to a reduction in the committal rate?" [2003] Crim. L.R. 314.

tried on indictment instead, but this application must be made before the summary trial begins.

Ashworth and Redmayne query whether magistrates should be entrusted with increased powers over the liberty of individuals.[703] Magistrates are after all lay people and there have been doubts expressed about the overall quality of justice in the magistrates' courts. Zander suggests that the available research evidence indicates that "increasing magistrates' sentencing powers is doomed to fail".[704] One argument is that mode of trial decisions are generally seen as being straightforward and thus increased sentencing powers will not alter this outlook. The result will be a small reallocation of business. Alternatively, the reforms may result in magistrates handing down longer sentences to defendants that are above what they might have received had their case gone to the Crown Court as previously. This might have an overall inflationary effect upon sentences handed down by magistrates.

(c) Committal for sentence

The Court of Appeal has emphasised that those who plead guilty before the venue is determined should receive the maximum discount for so doing.[705] It has also emphasised that great care must be taken not to give an accused the belief that committal for sentence has been ruled out.[706] If there are disputes about the facts, it may be necessary to conduct a *Newton* hearing to decide whether to commit for sentence.

14–055

Following the introduction of the plea before venue system, there was a marked increase in the number of committals for sentence to the Crown Court. However, research has shown that the magistrates often commit cases for sentence which result in sentences well within the magistrates' own powers, with 62 per cent of all those committed for sentence receiving a penalty that could have been imposed by the magistrates.[707] The Auld Report estimated that 55 per cent of defendants convicted by the Crown Court after committal for trial receive sentences which lie within the magistrates' power.[708] The problem of whether to commit for sentence is exacerbated by the plea before venue scheme because the magistrates are acting on less information when committing for sentence, and are much less likely to have access to all mitigating information.

4. SUMMARY OFFENCES IN THE CROWN COURT

The present pre-trial process is further complicated by ss.40 and 41 of the Criminal Justice Act 1988.[709] Under s.41 where a magistrates' court commits a

14–056

---

[703] Ashworth and Redmayne (2005) p.303.

[704] M. Zander, "Why oh why do magistrates commit so many cases to the Crown Court?" (2003) 153 N.L.J. 689.

[705] *R v Barber* [2002] Cr.App.R. 548. See also *R v Rafferty* [1999] 1 Cr.App.R. 235.

[706] *R v Horseferry Road Magistrates' Court, Ex p. Rugless* (2000) 164 J.P. 311. See also *R (White) v Barking Magistrates' Court* [2004] E.W.H.C. 417. An adjournment in itself is not enough to give rise to a legitimate expectation: *R v Norwich Magistrates' Court, Ex p. Elliott* [2000] 1 Cr.App.R. (S) 152.

[707] See C. Flood-Page and A Mackie, *Sentencing Practice: an Examination of Decisions in Magistrates' Courts and the Crown Court in the Mid-1990s* (HORS No.180, 1998).

[708] (2001), Ch.10, para.150.

[709] ss.40 and 41 of the Magistrates' Courts Act 1980 are described by Auld as "a muddle": Ch.7, para.39.

person to the Crown Court for trial of an either way offence, it may also commit him or her for trial of any summary offence which is (a) punishable with imprisonment or disqualification from driving, and (b) arises out of circumstances which appear to be the same as or connected with those giving rise to the either way offence. If the summary offence relates to an indictable only offence it must be sent to the Crown Court under the indictable only initiative discussed above. If the defendant is convicted on the indictment, and then pleads guilty to the summary offence, the Crown Court can deal with it then and there, although it can only exercise the sentencing powers that the magistrates' court would have had. If the defendant pleads not guilty, the matter has to be remitted for trial in the magistrates' court, unless the prosecution state that they would not wish to offer evidence in which case the Crown Court must dismiss the charge. If the Court of Appeal allows an appeal against conviction for the associated either way offence, it must set aside the conviction for the summary offence, and it may direct that no further proceedings be taken in relation to it.

The sections provide a more convenient procedure for dealing with cases involving both summary and indictable offences but at the cost of adding significantly to the complexity of the law.

E. GETTING THE ACCUSED INTO COURT

14–057   If an accused is to be prosecuted for an offence, he or she must actually be brought before a court to have the charge tried or at least to have it determined how and when the trial process should begin. As we have already seen there are two basic methods by which this can be done: by arrest (without warrant) and charge, or by summons. An information is merely a statement of the suspected offence and offender, either written or verbal, in terms specified by Pt 7 of the CPR 2005, which is placed before a magistrate or the justices' clerk so that a summons or warrant may be issued. An information will be sufficient if it describes the offence with which the accused is charged in ordinary language, avoiding technical terms, and gives such particulars as may be necessary to provide reasonable information about the nature of the charge.[710]

On the grant of a summons, which is a judicial matter, the magistrate, the clerk or the clerk's delegate should satisfy himself that the offence is known to the law; that it is not out of time; that the court has jurisdiction and that the informant has the requisite authority to prosecute.[711] A warrant should only be issued if it appears that a summons will be ineffective. The summons, if issued, will not look very different from the information.

The summons should be signed and served on the accused. The accused should then respond to the summons and attendance at court on a specified day has therefore been secured. If he or she fails to respond, a warrant may then be appropriate. In general, magistrates cannot try a summary offence unless the information was laid within six months from the time when the offence was committed.[712]

---

[710] Crim. P.R. r.7.2(1)(a) and (b).
[711] *R v Metropolitan Stipendiary Magistrate, Ex p. Klahn* [1979] 1 W.L.R. 933.
[712] Magistrates' Courts Act 1980, s.127.

When s.29 of the CJA 2003 comes into force the laying of an information and the issue of a summons will no longer be used by public prosecutors to commence prosecutions.[713] Instead a 'written charge' will be issued to the person charged with the offence, and a 'requisition' will require him or her to appear before the magistrates court to answer the charge. The written charge and the requisition must be served on the accused and a copy of both documents sent to the court.[714] This means that the requirement to attend court will come from the prosecutor rather than the court. The magistrates' court will have no involvement until the accused makes his first appearance before the court.

F. BAIL OR CUSTODY?[715]

Introduction

To deprive an accused of liberty pending trial may be to keep in custody an **14–058** innocent person or one who, though convicted, ultimately receives a non-custodial sentence. The presumption of liberty is a strong one and is endorsed by the ECHR, Art.5,[716] and recognised as fundamental in key constitutional statutes in English law including the Habeas Corpus Act 1679 and the Bill of Rights 1688. However, to allow an accused liberty pending trial may be to permit him or her to disappear, commit further offences, or interfere with witnesses and obstruct the course of justice. The refusal or grant of bail is a difficult decision, raising "some of the most acute conflicts in the whole criminal process"[717] calling for the very clearest safeguards to be in place before a defendant who has not yet faced trial is detained.[718] The European Court emphasised the importance of the guarantee under Art.5(3) for trial within a reasonable time as well as the

---

[713] See Auld Report Ch.10, para.57.

[714] CJA 2003, s.29(3).

[715] See generally, Ashworth and Redmayne (2005), Ch.8; Sanders and Young (2007) Ch.9; Sprack (2006), Ch.7; A. Hucklesby, "Bail in Criminal Cases", in M. McConville and G. Wilson, *The Handbook of The Criminal Justice Process* (2002) Ch.7; Law Commission, *Bail and the Human Rights Act*, Report No.269 (2000); N. Corre and D. Wolchaker, *Bail in Criminal Proceedings* (1999); R. Morgan and S. Jones, "Bail or Jail?" in E. Stockdale and S. Casale, *Criminal Justice under Stress* (1992), Ch.2; P. Cavadino and B. Gibson, *Bail: The Law, Best Practice and the Debate* (1993); M. King, *Bail or Custody* (Cobden Trust, 1971); A. K. Bottomley, *Decisions in the Penal Process* (1973), pp.93–105, and "The Granting of Bail: Principles and Practice" (1968) 31 M.L.R. 40; M. Zander, "Bail: A Reappraisal" [1967] Crim. L.R. 25 at 100, 128; M. Winfield, *Lacking Conviction* (1984); C. Chatterton, *Bail: Law and Practice* (1986).

[716] Under Art.5(3) every person detained should be brought promptly before a judge or other officer authorised by law to exercise judicial power and by Art.5(4) he or she is entitled to take proceedings by which the lawfulness of his detention shall be decided speedily by a court and his release ordered if the detention is not lawful. On the impact of the Human Rights Act 1998 on bail see *Bail and the Human Rights Act 1998*, Report No.269 (2000). See also Lord Bingham's comments on the fundamental presumption of liberty in *R v Manchester Crown Court, Ex p. McDonald* [1999] 1 All E.R. 805.

[717] Ashworth and Redmayne (2005), p.207.

[718] *ibid.* p.209. See also U. Raifeartaigh, "Reconciling Bail Law with the Presumption of Innocence" (1997) 17 O.J.L.S. 1.

right to be released pending trial.[719] The Law Commission has considered the domestic position and provided a comprehensive examination of the ECHR and English bail in its Report No.269.[720]

The issue of bail is raised as soon as a person is arrested and remains live until trial and, indeed, between conviction and appeal. The procedure by which the accused is released subject to a requirement to surrender to custody again at a specified time and place is termed the "granting" of bail. Bail may be granted by the police, the magistrates' court, the Crown Court, the High Court and the Court of Appeal under a variety of extremely complex statutory provisions and common law decisions, but the granting of bail in all criminal proceedings must be in accordance with the principles set out in the Bail Act 1976. Bail may be granted unconditionally, subject to conditions, subject to a surety or be denied and the accused remanded in custody.

Before considering the general principles it is helpful to define two important terms. A *surety* is a person who is willing to undertake to secure the surrender of the accused to custody. The grant of bail may be made conditional upon the accused finding a suitable surety or sureties.[721] Whoever is willing to be a surety must enter into a *recognisance*, which is a formal acknowledgement that he or she will owe the Crown a specified sum of money if the accused fails to surrender to custody. No money is payable by the surety unless the accused actually absconds.[722] The use of sureties has been accepted by the European Court as compatible with the Art.5.[723]

The imposition of sureties has been found to operate in practice in a discriminatory fashion against the poor, effectively excluding their chances of bail.[724] Statutory criteria are now fixed for determining the suitability of persons who may offer to be sureties where the grant of bail is conditional upon finding sureties.[725] In considering the suitability of a proposed surety, regard may be had,

---

[719] *Wemhoff v Germany* (1979) 1 E.H.R.R. 55. See also, *McDonald v Procurator Fiscal*, *The Times* (2003) April 17, in which the High Court of Justiciary held that whilst a bail condition required a defendant to remain in his dwelling at all times, except between 10 a.m. and noon, this amounted to a restriction on liberty, and not a deprivation of liberty, such as would engage Art.5.

[720] *Bail and the Human Rights Act 1998*, Report No.269 (2000).

[721] Bail Act 1976, s.3(4). Personation of bail is an offence under the Forgery Act 1861, s.34. On the procedures for taking sureties and ensuring that the surety is suitable, see Bail Act 1976, s.8.

[722] The recognisance may not be forfeited if the surety has made every effort to secure the appearance of the accused and acted with all due diligence, but the obligation is upon the surety to satisfy the court that all or part of the sum should not be forfeited. A surety who acts on legal/ professional advice should not be penalised merely because the court disagrees with that advice: *R v Bristol JJ., Ex p. Nisar Ahmed* [1997] C.O.D. 12 (where surety became aware of D's absconding and on legal advice did not notify the court). The court reviewed the principles of forfeiture in *R v Maidstone Crown Court, Ex p. Lever and Connell* [1996] 1 Cr.App.R. 524, and emphasised that any reductions in the sum payable by the surety would be exceptional. In general, only in exceptional cases will the court order that the recognisance should not be forfeited: Magistrates' Courts Act 1980, s.120 (as amended); *R v Southampton JJ., Ex p. Green* [1976] Q.B. 11; *R v Waltham Forest JJ., Ex p. Palfrey* (1980) 2 Cr.App.R.(S.) 208; *R v Knightsbridge Crown Court, Ex p. Newton* [1980] Crim. L.R. 715; *R v Ipswich Crown Court, Ex p. Reddington* [1981] Crim. L.R. 618; *R v Wells Street Magistrates' Court, Ex p. Albanese* [1982] Q.B. 333; *R v Uxbridge JJ., Ex p. Heward-Mills* [1983] 1 W.L.R. 56; *R v Inner London Crown Court, Ex p. Springall* (1986) 85 Cr.App.R. 214; *R v York Crown Court, Ex p. Coleman and How* (1987) 86 Cr.App.R. 151.

[723] *Schertentleib v Switzerland* (1980) D.R. 137.

[724] See Cavadino and Gisbson, pp.40–46. On the potentially discriminatory impact of bail decisions on racial groups and between sexes, see Ashworth and Redmayne (2005), pp.230–232.

[725] Bail Act 1976, s.8(2). See generally J. Morton, "Sureties" (1985) 135 N.L.J. 981.

inter alia, to financial resources, character and any previous convictions, and "proximity" to the accused.[726]

1. GENERAL PRINCIPLES RELATING TO THE GRANT OF BAIL

The Bail Act introduced a general right to bail for accused persons and certain **14–059** others subject to exceptions specified in a Schedule to the Act. In fact, the exceptions are substantial and this has led commentators to speak of a "presumption in favour of bail" rather than a "right to bail". In addition, the Act focused attention upon the need for information about the accused to be available to the court so that the bail decision could be an informed one, and required reasons to be given to the accused where bail was not granted so that he or she might more effectively conduct an appeal against the decision.

Section 4 of the Bail Act 1976 creates the *right to bail*:

"(1) A person to whom this section applies shall be granted bail except as provided in Schedule 1 to this Act.

(2) This section applies to a person who is accused of an offence when

(a) he appears or is brought before a magistrates' court or the Crown Court in the course of or in connection with proceedings for the offence, or

(b) he applies to a court for bail [or for a variation of the conditions of bail] in connection with the proceedings."

This does not create a right to bail for those convicted who are seeking bail pending appeal. Similarly, where the magistrates have summarily convicted an offender and he or she is committed to the Crown Court for sentencing there is no right to bail. By virtue of s.25 of the Criminal Justice and Public Order Act 1994 bail will not be granted where a person is charged with murder, attempted murder or manslaughter or rape or attempted rape[727] after having previously been convicted of such an offence or culpable homicide unless there are exceptional circumstances to justify the grant of bail. The original form of s.25 was to *prohibit* bail in such cases, and the European Court confirmed that this breached Art.5.[728] The compatibility of s.25 with Art.5 was confirmed by the House of Lords in *R (O) v Harrow Crown Court*.[729]

Schedule 1 to the Act creates the *exceptions to the right to bail*, and distinguishes between defendants accused or convicted of offences punishable with imprisonment[730] and those not punishable with imprisonment.[731] In respect of the imprisonable offences the accused need not be granted bail if:

(a) the court is satisfied that there are substantial grounds for believing[732] that the accused would, if released on bail:

---

[726] "Proximity" to the accused includes consideration of kinship, place of residence or other matters.

[727] See also the list of serious sexual offences added by the Sexual Offences Act 2003 Sch.6 para.32.

[728] *Carballero v UK* [2000] Crim. L.R. 587; *SBC v UK* (2002) 34 E.H.R.R. 619.

[729] *R (O) v Harrow Crown Court* [2006] U.K.H.L. 42. See, P. Tain (2006) S.J. 1219.

[730] Sch.1, Pt I.

[731] Sch.1, Pt II.

[732] See *R v Mansfield JJ., Ex p. Sharkey* [1985] Q.B. 613.

(i) fail to surrender to custody,[733] or

(ii) commit an offence while on bail,[734] or

(iii) interfere with witnesses or otherwise obstruct the course of justice,[735] whether in relation to himself or any other person.

The accused also need not be granted bail if:

(b) it appears to the court that he was on bail in criminal proceedings on the date of the offence (this has been amended by s.13 of the CJA 2003, as yet not in force, so that bail *must* be refused to an adult defendant on bail at the date of the offence unless the court is satisfied that there is no significant risk that he would commit an offence if released on bail);

(c) the court is satisfied that he or she should be kept in custody for his or her own protection;

(d) he or she is already serving a custodial sentence or has been bailed and arrested for absconding; or

(e) the court is satisfied that, owing to lack of time since the commencement of the proceedings, it has not been practical to obtain sufficient information for the purposes of taking the decisions required to be taken in relation to (a)–(c) above.

This last point emphasises that the court must have access to information about the defendant because it is required to have regard to specified matters (as far as they appear relevant) including (and these are not exhaustive):

(a) the nature and seriousness of the offence (and the probable method of dealing with it);

(b) the character, antecedents, associations and community ties of the defendant;

(c) the defendant's record in respect of any previous grants of bail;

(d) the strength of the evidence against him or her, except in the case of an accused whose case is adjourned for inquiries or a report.

These issues require little further explanation other than, aside from CJPOA 1994, s.25, the gravity of the charge should not be an automatic reason for refusing bail.[736]

In respect of non-imprisonable offences the defendant may only be denied bail if it appears to the court that he or she has previously failed to surrender to bail and that the court believes that, if released, he or she would again fail to surrender

---

[733] On the fear of absconding and the ECHR see *Lettellier v France* (1991) 14 E.H.R.R. 83; *Clooth v Belgium* (1991) 14 E.H.R.R. 717.

[734] The fear of offending on bail is recognised as a relevant factor in granting bail in ECHR case law: *Toth v Belgium* (1991) 14 E.H.R.R. 551. For criticism of this as a legitimate ground for consideration see Sanders and Young (2007), p.467; Ashworth and Redmayne (2005), pp.208–213. See also U. ni Raifeartaigh, "Reconciling Bail Law with the Presumption of Innocence" (1997) 17 O.J.L.S. 1, questioning why granting bail should be a significant problem given the realisation that there are many convicted criminals released from prison who may pose a threat.

[735] Sch.1, Pt I, para.2.

[736] *Hurnam v State of Mauritius* [2006] 1 W.L.R. 857.

to custody.[737] The court, if it is to refuse bail, must be "satisfied that there are substantial grounds for believing" that one of the specified situations exists.

Bail conditions

If bail is refused by the court or conditions are imposed on the grant of bail in respect of anyone to whom s.4 of the Act applies; the court must make a record and give reasons for withholding bail or imposing the conditions with a view to enabling the accused to make application to another court.[738] The court has a duty to inform an unrepresented accused of his right to challenge or make further application to other courts.[739] This is a logical requirement, given that the courts are directed towards examining specific considerations in the refusal of bail. The accused is entitled to know in what respect he or she is considered unsuitable for bail. Furthermore, reasons must now be given where the court grants bail to an accused when the prosecution opposed it.[740] The court having heard a full argument on bail must issue a certificate confirming this.[741]   **14–060**

The court may attach conditions to bail necessary to secure that the accused:

(a) surrenders to custody;

(b) does not commit an offence while on bail;

(c) does not interfere with witnesses or otherwise obstruct the course of justice;

(d) makes him or herself available for the purposes of enabling inquiries, or a report to be made to assist the court in dealing with him or her for the offence[742];

(e) before the time appointed for him or her to surrender to custody, he or she attends an interview with an authorised advocate or authorised litigator.

In this context, it is not necessary that the court has "substantial grounds" for its conditions: it is sufficient that it perceives "a real and not fanciful risk" of, for example, an offence being committed.[743] The CJA 2003 also adds that the court may impose further conditions, namely, to protect the accused or, if he or she is a young person, for his or her welfare.[744]

---

[737] Sch.1, Pt II, para.2, or that he or she is kept in custody for his own protection, that he is already serving a custodial sentence, or that he has been arrested under s.7.

[738] Bail Act 1976, s.5(3), as amended by the Criminal Justice and Police Act 2001 s.129(1) inserting a new (2A) and (2B) in s.5. The European Court has explained the need for reasons to be provided: *Tomasi v France* (1992) 15 E.H.R.R. 1; *Neumeister v Austria* (1968) 1 E.H.R.R. 91; *Sabita v Italy*, April 6, 2000.

[739] s.5(6).

[740] Bail Act 1976, Sch.1, Pt I, para.9A, inserted by the Criminal Justice Act 1988. This provision was passed in view of public concern about bail being too readily granted in cases of serious alleged violence.

[741] Bail Act 1976, ss.5(6A)–(6C).

[742] Bail Act 1976, s.3(6), Sch.1, para.8(1). The power to attach conditions extends to both imprisonable and non-imprisonable offences (see *R v Bournemouth Magistrates' Court, Ex p. Cross* (1988) 89 Cr.App.R. 90). For the argument that a surety of good behaviour might be imposed as a condition of bail under the court's binding-over powers, see N. Corre [1986] Crim. L.R. 162. See also B. P. Block (1990) 154 J. P. N. 83; P. W. H. Lydiate, *ibid.*, p.132.

[743] *R v Mansfield JJ., Ex p. Sharkey* [1985] Q.B. 613.

[744] CJA 2003 s.13(1).

The imposition of conditions on the grant of bail can be a very serious matter.[745] It is not uncommon for the magistrates to require the accused to report regularly to a police station as a condition of bail, or to observe a curfew, or to reside[746] in or keep away from particular places. The most common conditions imposed are the requirement to be resident at a specified address, a prohibition on contacting a specified individual, and a requirement to report to a police station. In serious matters the accused may be required to surrender his or her passport.[747] It is arguable that the conditions attached ought to relate primarily to securing the attendance of the accused in court but they can also be used to curtail potentially criminal activities pending the trial of the alleged offence.[748]

2. APPLICATION OF THE PRINCIPLES

14–061 An issue which initially concerned the courts was the procedure to be adopted on successive applications for bail. The magistrates' court is given power, prior to the commencement of the hearing, to remand an accused person in custody for a period not exceeding eight clear days[749] and this may be appropriate where the prosecution are not yet ready to proceed with the case. In complex cases this meant a court appearance occurring every eight days for a considerable length of time.[750] At every appearance the accused was entitled to request bail and would normally appear before differently constituted courts each time.[751] In Nottingham, the City justices adopted a policy under which after a second application[752] for bail they would not consider on subsequent applications matters previously

---

[745] See J. Raine and M. Willson "The Imposition of Conditions in Bail Decisions" (1996) 35 Howard Jnl. 256. Conditions might be suggested by the defence in the hope of securing bail.

[746] On the legitimacy of curfews on bail conditions see A. Gillespie, "Curfew and Bail" (2001) 151 N.L.J. 465.

[747] Raine and Willson (1996) Guidance was given by the Home Office in Circular 206/1977 of November 18, 1977. Courts were, e.g. requested to be especially selective in requiring regular reporting to a police station as this can be burdensome for the police and also raise identification problems.

[748] During the 1984–85 miners' strike, striking miners charged with criminal offences were frequently granted bail subject to conditions prohibiting picketing at premises other than the defendant's own place of work: the practice was controversial (see S. McCabe and P. Wallington, *The Police, Public Order, and Civil Liberties* (1988), pp.97–98), but held to be lawful by the Divisional Court (*R v Mansfield JJ., Ex p. Sharkey* [1985] Q.B. 613). See also *R v Bournemouth Magistrates' Court, Ex p. Cross* (1988) 89 Cr.App.R. 90 (bail conditions prohibiting defendants charged with disturbing a fox hunting meet from attending another hunt meeting held valid).

[749] Magistrates' Courts Act 1980, s.128(6), subject to ss.128A and 129. Section 129 empowers the court to make further remand in the accused's absence in specified circumstances (illness, etc.). Where an accused has been bailed from a police station following charge, the court has power to appoint a later date for appearance: s.43(1).

[750] This can clearly be oppressive since the accused is being held in custody without trial, but it is well established that an unreasonable delay on the part of the prosecution will be a good reason for granting bail: *R v Nottingham Justices, Ex p. Davies* [1981] Q.B. 38 at 44.

[751] At the time of Davies' application (see note above) the Nottingham bench consisted of 320 justices, with up to 25 courts sitting each day. The chance of getting the same justices two weeks running was negligible. On the proportion of defendants who did not seek bail on their first appearance see B. Brink and C. Stone, "Defendants Who Do Not Ask for Bail" [1999] Crim. L.R. 152.

[752] After the *second* application, because the first is usually made by a duty solicitor who may not be fully briefed so as to make a proper application. On the second application the accused will normally be legally aided and represented by his or her own solicitor who should then be in a position to place all relevant matters before the court.

before the court unless there had been a change in circumstances.[753] In effect, remand in custody became automatic. In *R v Nottingham JJ., Ex p. Davies*[754] it was argued on behalf of Davies that he had a right to bail which was only defensible on the specified grounds; that the court has a duty to consider the grant of bail on every occasion on which the accused appears; and that the fact of a previous remand could not, of itself, satisfy the justices that one of the specified grounds still existed. The court did not accept the argument. The finding of the original court that Sch.1 circumstances existed,

> " . . . is to be treated like every other finding of the court. It is res judicata or analogous thereto . . . It follows that on the next occasion when bail is considered the court should treat, as an essential fact, that at the time when the matter of bail was last considered, Schedule 1 circumstances did indeed exist. Strictly speaking, they can and should only investigate whether that situation has changed since then."[755]

This decision excited both favourable[756] and unfavourable[757] comment, and was in certain respects in need of retirement.[758] It has now been codified by s.154 of the Criminal Justice Act 1988.[759] This provides:

> "(1) If the court decides not to grant the defendant bail, it is the court's duty to consider, at each subsequent hearing while the defendant . . . remains in custody, whether he ought to be granted bail.
> (2) At the first hearing[760] after that at which the court decided not to grant the defendant bail[761] he may support an application for bail with any argument as to fact or law that he desires (whether or not he has advanced that argument previously).
> (3) At subsequent hearings the court need not hear arguments as to fact or law which it has heard previously."

This makes it clear that while the court is not obliged to hear repeated arguments, it has a discretion to do so; the position is, accordingly, a little more flexible than

---

[753] A policy apparently inspired by certain remarks made by Ackner J. to a meeting of justices' clerks and reported in (1980) 36 *The Magistrate* 34, 97. The actual wording of the Nottingham policy is contained in the report of *Davies* [1981] Q.B. 38 at 41.

[754] [1981] Q.B. 38.

[755] [1981] Q.B. 38 at p.44.

[756] Anon., "Bail Applications" (1980) 144 J.P.N. 319; editorials in (1980) 36 *The Magistrate* 97 at 135; K. Polak, "Applications for Bail" (1980) 144 J.P.N. 525.

[757] M. Hayes, "Where Now the Right to Bail" [1981] Crim. L.R. 20. In "Bail—a Suitable Case for Treatment" (1982) 132 N.L.J. 409, J. Burrow analyses other less predictable effects of the decision.

[758] See S. Holdham, (1985) 135 N.L.J. 471; P. W. H. Lydiate, "Bail Procedure in Magistrates' Courts: Basic Procedures" (1987) 151 J.P.N. 164, 181. See also *R v Reading Crown Court, Ex p. Malik* [1981] Q.B. 451 and *R v Slough JJ., Ex p. Duncan and Embling* (1982) 75 Cr.App.R. 384 (different views expressed on whether as a general rule reaching the stage of committal for trial would constitute a change in circumstances: Donaldson L.J. in the *Reading* case indicated *obiter* that it would; Ormrod L.J. in the *Slough* case that it would not necessarily do so).

[759] Inserting a new Pt IIA in Sch.1 to the Bail Act 1976.

[760] Occasions when a person is remanded in his or her absence (see below) are not "hearings": *R v Dover and East Kent JJ., Ex p. Dean* (1991) 156 J.P. 357.

[761] A decision that it has not been practicable to obtain sufficient information to decide to grant bail is not a "decision not to grant bail" for these purposes: *R v Calder JJ., Ex p. Kennedy* (1992) 156 J.P. 716.

that suggested by Donaldson L.J. in *Ex p. Davies*. The Law Commission concluded that this was compatible with the ECHR but recommended that the
passage of time might be a sufficient reason in a given case to require a full
argument to be heard by the court.[762]

The position has also been affected to some extent by the provisions of s.59 of
and Sch.9 to the Criminal Justice Act 1982.[763] This enables the court to remand
an accused in his or her absence for up to three successive remand hearings
provided that he or she consents and is legally represented. This alleviates the
problem of constant weekly journeys for the accused who does not wish to
contest the remand, but *Ex p. Davies* still applies to prevent the non-consenting
accused from seeking bail on every remand appearance. Section 155 of the
Criminal Justice Act 1988[764] authorised the introduction of a new power for the
court to remand in custody for a period up to 28 days without the accused's
consent. This is exercisable where the accused has previously been remanded in
custody for the same offence and the court has set a date for the next stage in the
proceedings.[765]

The Auld Report questioned the quality of bail decisions, particularly since 24
per cent of a sample of 1,283 alleged offenders granted bail were subsequently
convicted or cautioned for an offence whilst on bail.[766] The average length of a
bail hearing in London Magistrates' Court was also found to be a mere six
minutes.[767] The Auld Report also commented on the inconsistency of bail
decision-making, particularly in the magistrates,[768] and recommended that bail
decisions be given greater scrutiny.[769] The Law Commission in its Report No.269
also proposed appropriate training and guidance on the bail decision making
process for magistrates and judges.[770]

3. POLICE BAIL

14-062 The CJA 2003 introduced "street bail" whereby police officers are enabled to
bail suspects at the scene of an arrest and thus prior to their arrival at the police

---

[762] Report No.269, para.12.9 and para.12.23. See also *Bezicheri v Italy* (1989) 12 E.H.R.R. 210.

[763] Inserting s.128(1A)–(1C), (3A)–(3E) of the Magistrates' Courts Act 1980, as amended by the
Criminal Procedure and Investigations Act 1996. See C. May, *Remands in the Absence of the
Accused* (1985), (HORPU Paper No.34, 1985).

[764] Inserting s.128A of the Magistrates' Courts Act 1980.

[765] Magistrates Courts Act 1980, s.128A(2). The provision was first introduced experimentally in
specified areas, but now extends to all petty sessions areas: Magistrates' Courts (Remands in
Custody) Order 1991 (SI 1991/2667). This followed a Home Office report which concluded that
there was "little evidence" to support the concerns expressed during the passage of the 1988 Act
that this "would cause an increase in the time spent in custody": P. F. Henderson and P. Morgan,
Remands in Custody for up to 28 days: the Experiments (HORPU Paper No.62, 1991). The Prison
Reform Trust was, however, critical of this conclusion: see Cavadino and Gibson (1993),
Ch.11.

[766] Ch.10, para.76.

[767] Auld Report, (2001), Ch.10, para.78.

[768] Ch.10, para.79–80. ACPO have criticised the CPS for failing to take bail hearings seriously (Auld
Report (2001), Ch.10, para.81). See the Law Commission's *Guide for Bail Decision Takers*
(2001).

[769] (2001), p.430.

[770] The Law Commission, Bail and the Human Rights Act 1998, Report No.269, Pt IV. See also its
Guidance for Bail Decision Takers and their Advisers (2001).

station.[771] However, this new form of bail has been described as "ill-thought out and misconceived", given that decisions concerning bail require considered assessments that have real and potentially damaging implications for the suspect.[772] "It is difficult to see how informed and proportionate decisions will be made by police officers in the environment of the street where the situation may be heated, the circumstances of the offence unclear and/or disputed, victims may be present and information is likely to be limited".[773]

Before granting bail officers need to be satisfied that they have the correct name and address for the suspect; that the suspect will answer bail; that the suspect is not a danger to themselves or the public; and that the suspect understands the nature of street bail process. No conditions can be attached other than that the suspect must attend a police station. If evidence subsequently comes to light he can be re-arrested without warrant. Furthermore, if the suspect fails to attend the police station as required he can be arrested.[774] It is advantageous in allowing officers to remain on patrol without having to return to the station immediately, allowing them to plan more effectively when the person should attend the station for an interview.[775] However, as Hucklesby argues "it enables the police simply to keep track of suspects even where there is not enough existing evidence to charge under the guise of collecting further evidence".[776] Whilst the more efficient use of police time is undoubtedly a major bonus the fact that such a significant discretion is exercised outside of the police station environment must bring with it concerns relating to the circumvention of individual rights and the potential for discriminatory practice.

Once the suspect has arrived at the station PACE establishes a number of situations in which a person in police custody may be released on bail. The decision in most cases is taken by the custody officer. Where the custody officer orders a person's release under s.34 (in that detention can no longer be justified), this must be without bail unless it appears to the custody officer (1) that there is need for further investigation of any matter in connection with which he or she was detained, or (2) that proceedings may be taken against him or her in respect of any such matter: if it does so appear, the person must be released on bail. In other situations, there is a discretion to release with or without bail, where a person is released before charge (s.37); after charge (s.38); after 24 hours' detention (s.41); after 36 hours detention (s.42); or where a warrant for further detention is refused or expires (ss.43, 44).[777] In each case a release on bail "shall be a release on bail granted in accordance with sections 3, 3A, 5 and 5A of the Bail Act 1976 as they apply to bail granted by a constable"[778] and shall be subject to a duty to appear before a magistrates' court on the date of the next available court sitting[779] or to return to the police station as directed by the

---

[771] CJA 2003 s.4 which amends s.30A–D of PACE. This came into force in January 2004. See also, Home Office, *Criminal Justice Act 2003: Bail Elsewhere than at a Police Station*, (2003) Circular 61/2003 Part C.

[772] A. Hucklesby "Not Necessarily a Trip to the Police Station: The Introduction of Street Bail" [2004] Crim. L.R. 803 at 808.

[773] *ibid.*

[774] PACE, s.30D(1).

[775] See, Home Office, *Justice for All* (2002) Cm. 5563, para.3.10.

[776] Hucklesby [2004] p.804.

[777] See PACE, ss.37(2), (7)(b), 38(1); 41(7); 42(10); 43(15)(18); 44(7).

[778] PACE, s.47(1), as amended by the Criminal Justice and Public Order Act 1994, s.27(1)(a). These sections comprise general provisions (s.3), conditions of police bail (s.3A) and supplementary provisions (ss.5, 5A).

[779] PACE, s.47(3A).

custody officer, who must specify the time and place.[780] The option of requiring the accused to return to the police station can be employed to give the police time to continue their inquiries.

Following the development of statutory charging, whereby the duty prosecutor determines the charge to be laid against the suspect, the custody officer, who has determined that there is sufficient evidence to charge, has the power to release on bail pending the decision by the prosecutor on whether a charge ought to follow.[781] Furthermore, the Crown Prosecutor may choose to order that the custody officer bail the suspect where more evidence is required to make a decision as to the appropriate charge.[782]

Where an accused is released on police bail after being charged, the custody officer has the power to attach conditions (other than a condition requiring residence in a bail hostel or that the accused makes himself available for enabling inquiries or a report to be made).[783] Where the custody officer has granted police bail, he or she or another custody officer at the same police station may vary the conditions at the request of the person on bail, and may impose conditions or more onerous conditions.[784] Conditions may only be imposed (or varied) if it appears to the officer necessary to do so for the purpose of preventing that person from failing to surrender to custody, committing an offence while on bail or interfering with witnesses or otherwise obstructing the course of justice.[785] The custody officer must give reasons for imposing or varying conditions, and these must be included in the custody record.[786] Where a custody officer grants bail and imposes conditions, or varies conditions, a magistrates' court on the application by or on behalf of the person on bail may grant bail or vary the conditions.[787] The police have an express power of arrest for failure to answer to police bail.[788] As Raine and Willson observe, the police are really exercising a judicial function in imposing such conditions. The new power to attach conditions was felt "not to have delivered the efficiency advantages that its advocates had anticipated".[789] Hardly any change in the working pattern of the courts was recorded to have resulted.[790]

In the case of indictable or either way offences, the prosecution may apply to the appropriate magistrates' court for the grant of police bail to be reconsidered, and the court may vary or impose conditions or withhold bail. An application must be based on information not available to the custody officer when the

---

[780] PACE, s.47(3).

[781] PACE s.37(7).

[782] Criminal Justice Act 2003 Sch.2, para.6(3) amending PACE s.47. This new power allows the custody officer to attach bail conditions, which can be contrasted with the position regarding bail pending further investigation where no conditions can be imposed (PACE, s.34(5)).

[783] PACE, s.47(1A), inserted by the Criminal Justice and Public Order Act 1994, s.27(1)(b); Bail Act 1976, ss.3(6), 3A, as amended and inserted by ibid. s.27(2)(3). The introduction of this power was recommended by the RCCJ, Report, para.5.22. Section 3A applies s.3 with modifications to conditions in the case of police bail. Research suggests that these are being used when previously unconditional bail would have been granted: J. Raine and M. Willson, "Police Bail with Conditions" (1997) 37 Brit. J. Crim. 593.

[784] Bail Act 1976, s.3A(4), applying s.3(8) in different terms to cases of police bail.

[785] ibid. s.3(A)(5); cf. s.3(6), above.

[786] ibid. s.5A(2), (3), inserted by the 1994 Act, Sch.3, para.2, applying s.5(3),(4), in different terms to cases of police bail.

[787] Magistrates' Courts Act 1980, s.43B, inserted by the 1994 Act, Sch.3, para.3. See also Crim. P.R. r.19.1(1).

[788] PACE, s.46A, inserted by the 1994 Act, s.29.

[789] J. Raine and M. Willson, "Police Bail with Conditions" (1997) 37 Brit. J. Crim. 593, at 602.

[790] See also R. Raine and J. Willson, (1996) Howard J.C.J. 256; (1995) J.L.S. 22.

decision was taken.[791] This applies only to offences triable on indictment or either way.

If the accused is in police custody as the result of a warrant issued by a magistrate or the Crown Court, then the warrant itself will dictate the granting of bail and the previous provisions will not apply. Either the warrant will be "endorsed for bail"[792] in terms which must be observed by the police, or it will require the police to bring the accused before the court immediately.[793] In this case, of course, the grant of bail is, strictly speaking, made by the court and not the police.

The use of police bail is substantial. In general, the more serious the type of offence, the higher the proportion of those arrested who are held in custody. Research in the 1980s found that the highest proportion was in respect of robbery (57 per cent); and burglary, sexual offences and criminal damage all exceeded the average.[794]

4. Bail from the Magistrates' Court

If the accused has been arrested without warrant, and has not been bailed by the police, or arrested with a warrant which is not endorsed for bail, he or she must be brought before a magistrates' court and will then have an opportunity to request bail. Indeed, the court is under an obligation to consider the question of bail even if no application is made.[795] Only comparatively minor cases can be disposed of at one appearance in the magistrates' court. The court accordingly has express power to adjourn:

14–063

(1) an inquiry as examining justices, either before or during the inquiry[796];

(2) a summary trial, either before or during the trial[797];

(3) proceedings to determine mode of trial in the case of offences triable either way.[798]

---

[791] Bail Act 1976, s.5B, inserted by the 1994 Act, s.30. if the court grants bail in the face of prosecution opposition it must give reasons: ss.8A–8C as inserted by the Criminal Justice and Police Act 2001, s.129.

[792] Magistrates' Court Act 1980, s.117. The magistrate issuing the warrant will state on the warrant that the person arrested is to be released subject to a duty to appear at a specified court and time: s.117(2)(a).

[793] See the form of warrant set out as Form 4, the Magistrates' Courts (Forms) Rules 1981 (SI 1981/553).

[794] See R. Tarling, P. Jones and A. Sanders, "Police Bail" (1986) 21 HORB 52, Table 2, based on 1980 figures.

[795] Because of the provision in the Bail Act 1976, s.4(1) that a person to whom the Act applies *shall* be given bail except where Sch.1 applies. See J. N. Spencer (1986) 150 J.P.N. 724; P. H. W. Lydiate (1987) 151 J.P.N. 25.

[796] Magistrates' Courts Act 1980, s.5(1).

[797] *ibid.* s.10(1). This power may be exercised after conviction and before sentence, to enable inquiries to be made: s.10(3). There is also a power to adjourn a trial to enable a medical examination and report to be made; this power is available where the offence is punishable with imprisonment and the court is satisfied that the accused did the act or made the omission charged: s.30.

[798] *ibid.* s.18(4).

On these occasions, the court may, and sometimes must, remand the accused, which simply means a direction that he or she should be held in custody for a specified period, or that he or she should be released on bail with an obligation to appear again before the court on a specified date.[799] In deciding whether to remand on bail or in custody the magistrates must have regard to the provisions of the Bail Act but may take advantage of s.154 of the Criminal Justice Act 1988 to lessen the burden of continuing applications. The position is further eased by the provision for extended remands in custody.[800] The most significant factors influencing remand decisions in the magistrates' courts are whether the police have granted bail,[801] the seriousness of the offence and court policy.

Although magistrates make the formal remand decisions, it has been argued that there are various professional decision-makers involved in the remand process and that many decisions are taken prior to the formal hearing.[802] In her research, Hucklesby discovered that that in 85 per cent of cases the CPS did not request a remand, and in only 9 per cent of *all* cases was there a contested remand hearing in court. The major influences on the remand decision were the police, CPS, defence lawyers (who sometimes withhold the right to make effective bail applications from clients). In only 12 per cent of all cases did the CPS actually provide a rationale to the court for its request for remand/conditional bail.

5. BAIL FROM THE CROWN COURT

14–064   The Crown Court may grant bail to an accused who is in custody pending a hearing in the Crown Court (after committal for trial or sentence); or being "sent" to the Crown Court under s.51 of the Crime and Disorder Act; or pending an appeal against conviction or sentence by the magistrates; or pending the completion of the hearing in the Crown Court; or pending the statement of a case for the High Court or the outcome of an application for judicial review; or pending an appeal to the Court of Appeal where the Crown Court has given a certificate under the Criminal Appeal Act 1968.

If, in any of those cases, the accused is actually before the court then application is made orally to the judge, otherwise the application is in writing in a specified form and the accused is not entitled to be present at the hearing.

---

[799] *ibid.* s.128(1).

[800] Adjournments under ss.10(3) and 30 (see above) may be for not more than four weeks at a time (if the accused is on bail) or three weeks at a time (if he or she is in custody); or three weeks for a medical examination where the court is satisfied that the accused performed the act or omission and requires medical reports on his or her mental or physical condition (Powers of Criminal Courts (Sentencing) Act 2000, s.11) and the accused may be remanded for the period of the adjournment: s.128(6)(b). Remands on bail may be for longer than eight days if the accused and the other party consent: s.128(6)(a). The accused may be further remanded if he or she is unable to appear by reason of illness or accident: s.129(1): see *R v Liverpool City JJ., Ex p. Grogan* (1990) 155 J.P. 450 (magistrates must have solid grounds for finding this to be established). See, A. Hucklesby, "Court Culture: An Explanation of the Variations in the Use of Bail by Magistrates" (1997) 36 Howard Jnl. 129; P. Jones, "Remand Decisions in Magistrates' Courts" in D. Moxon (ed.), *Managing Criminal Justice* (1985), Ch.10. See also P. M. Morgan and R. Pearce, *Remand Decisions in Brighton and Bournemouth* (1989) (HORPU Paper 53); P. M. Morgan, (1990) 29 H.O.R.B. 18.

[801] See A. Hucklesby, "Remand Decision-Makers" [1997] Crim. L.R. 269, who found that in almost half of the cases where the CPS opposed bail, the defence did not contest it.

[802] A. Hucklesby [1997] Crim. L.R. 269.

An important addition to the powers of the Crown Court is the power to grant bail on an application by a person who has been refused bail by a magistrates' court. The application may only be made where the magistrates have heard full argument before refusal.[803] Some conditions attached to bail by the magistrates may be challenged under CJA 2003, s.16.[804]

Furthermore, by virtue of the Bail (Amendment) Act 1993, the prosecution has the right to appeal to the Crown Court against a decision by a magistrates' court to grant bail. This only arises where: (1) the accused is charged with or convicted of an offence punishable by imprisonment; (2) the prosecution is conducted by the CPS; and (3) the prosecution made representations against bail before it was granted. The matter is reheard and the Crown Court judge may remand the accused in custody[805] or grant bail with or without conditions. The CPS must give oral notice of the appeal at the conclusion of the proceedings[806] and the notice must be confirmed in writing, and Crown Court hearing must occur within 48 hours.[807]

6. Bail from the High Court

Following s.17 of the CJA 2003 the High Court can hear an application for bail, or vary its conditions under s.22 of the Criminal Justice Act 1967 only if the accused is appealing by way of case stated against conviction or sentence and the magistrates have withheld or granted conditional bail.

14-065

7. Breach of Bail

In 2005 around 12 per cent of those bailed at the magistrates' court or Crown Court failed to appear.[808] There were 157,000 prosecutions for failure to surrender to bail in 2005, a reduction of some 23,000 on the previous year.[809] Over the last decade the number of people remanded in custody by magistrates has fallen steadily.

14-066

The Bail Act 1976 replaced the defendant's personal recognisance with a new criminal offence of failing to surrender to custody without reasonable cause.[810] If

---

[803] For the certification procedure to be adopted see Criminal Justice Act 1982, s.60(3), inserting new subss.5(6A), (6B), (6C) in the Bail Act 1976 (s.5(6A), as amended by the Criminal Justice and Public Order Act 1994, Sch.4, Pt II, para.23(b)).

[804] These include electronic monitoring, curfew, residence, contact or the provisions of a surety.

[805] The judge should indicate that the period of remand in custody should not exceed eight days from the date when the applicant last appeared before the magistrates: *Re Bone* [1995] C.O.D. 94.

[806] Which is satisfied if five minutes late: *R v Isleworth Crown Court, Ex p. Clarke* [1998] 1 Cr.App.R. 257.

[807] i.e. the prosecution must commence the appeal within that time: *R v Middlesex Guildhall, Ex p. Okoli* [2001] 1 Cr.App.R. 1.

[808] *Criminal Statistics* (2006) Table 4.5.

[809] *ibid.*

[810] Bail Act 1976, s.6(1). Appearance at the arraignment necessarily involves surrendering to custody: *R v Central Criminal Court, Ex p. Guney* [1996] 2 W.L.R. 675, HL (in respect of the departure to Northern Cyprus of Asil Nadir). *Cf. DPP v Richards* [1988] Q.B. 701 (compliance with court's procedure requiring D to report to inquiry counter sufficient to surrender to bail); *R (Hart) v Bow Street Magistrates' Court, The Times*, January 17, 2002.

a defendant has reasonable cause for failure to surrender to custody at the appointed time and place, he or she must surrender as soon as reasonably practicable thereafter, or be guilty of an offence.[811] The burden of showing reasonable cause is on the defendant.[812] Powers of arrest are attached to the offence.[813] The accused may be fined or imprisoned on summary conviction, or by the Crown Court, where the offence is dealt with as if it were a criminal contempt of court.[814] Where the accused has failed to surrender to bail granted by a magistrates' court, proceedings are initiated by the court by its own motion, following an invitation by the prosecutor, the proceedings then being conducted by the prosecutor.[815] Where the accused has failed to surrender to police bail, proceedings should be commenced by charge or the laying of an information.[816]

In the event of failure to surrender, any personal security given by the accused[817] may be forfeited, as may the sums of money promised by the sureties—"estreating a surety's recognizance". Normally those sums would be forfeited in full, but the court must exercise a proper discretion as to whether any part of the sum should be remitted on account of the sureties' behaviour, responsibility or means. There are also controversial powers of arrest for anticipated breach of bail, which may be exercised whenever an officer has reasonable grounds for believing that the accused is *not likely* to surrender or that bail is *about to be* broken or has been broken.[818] The accused must be taken before a court within 24 hours.[819] The court is empowered to remand the person in custody or to alter the conditions of bail, or re-impose existing conditions.[820]

Provisions in the CJA 2003 will change this position when they are brought into effect. Section 15 states that the court must refuse bail to an adult defendant who failed to surrender to custody in answer to bail (in the same proceedings) unless satisfied that there is no significant risk of this if he or she were released.

The frequency of offending while on bail was examined by Hucklesby and Marshall,[821] who found that the provisions of s.26 of the Criminal Justice and Public Order Act 1994 had had little effect on the numbers who committed offences on bail. The main impact was the shift to imposing conditional bail (finding a 17 per cent increase in use since 1994 Act).

---

[811] *ibid.* s.6(2).

[812] s.6(3). Errors of legal representatives may be a reasonable cause: see *DPP v Speede* [1998] 2 Cr.App.R. 108.

[813] *ibid.* s.7.

[814] The maximum penalties are three months' imprisonment or a fine not exceeding level 5 on the standard scale; 12 months imprisonment or a fine at the Crown Court. Bail Act offences should be dealt with separately from the other substantive matters and put clearly to the defendant: *R v Boyle* [1993] Crim. L.R. 40; *R v How* [1993] Crim. L.R. 201.

[815] See, *Consolidated Criminal Practice Direction* para.I.13.8.

[816] *ibid.* para.I.13.6.Failure to surrender here is not tantamount to defiance of a court order.

[817] i.e. any security taken where it appears likely that the accused will leave Great Britain: Bail Act 1976, s.3(5).

[818] Or that a surety has given written notice to the police that the bailed person is unlikely to surrender to custody and that the surety wishes to be relieved of the obligation. See s.7(3).

[819] Section 7(4)(a); see also *R v Governor of Glen Parva Young Offenders Institution, Ex p. G (A Minor)* [1998] 2 Cr.App.R. 349.

[820] See *R v Liverpool JJ., Ex p. DPP* [1993] Q.B. 233.

[821] "Tackling Offending on Bail" (2000) Howard J.C.J. 150.

8. Numbers of Remand Prisoners

The large numbers of prisoners held on remand is problematic for a number of **14–067**
reasons. First, it should be remembered that many prisoners held on remand have
yet to be tried and thus are innocent until proven guilty yet they have had their
liberty taken away. Secondly, statistically, most remand prisoners are ultimately
given a custodial sentence by the court. This is not a surprise of itself as
the reasons why the person has been given a custodial sentence will often be the
same reasons that led to remand in custody in the first instance. However, the
impact that the period on remand has on the ultimate sentence must be considered. For example, the presentation of mitigating factors before sentence is
more difficult for an accused that has spent time on remand.[822] Thirdly, it has
been recognised that remand prisoners suffer some of the worst conditions within
the prison system. In 2005 figures revealed that of the 804 people who had
committed suicide in prison in the preceding decade, 55 per cent of those were
on remand, despite remandees only comprising 19 per cent of the total prison
population.[823] The large number of remand prisoners has caused severe problems
of overcrowding,[824] sometimes involving detention in police, rather than prison,
custody.[825] In 2007 the Annual Report from the Chief Inspector of Prisons stated
that "all the prisons inspected were operating at the limits of capacity: as a
consequence, accommodation that was not fit for use, or for its present occupation levels, was being used."[826]

In November 2006 13,099 people were being held on remand. Of these, 8,201
were untried prisoners, with the remaining being convicted but awaiting sentence.[827] The *Criminal Statistics for England and Wales 2005*[828] report that
59,000 people were remanded in custody by magistrates in 2005, this represented
10 per cent of all those remanded.[829] Thirty per cent of those committed for trial
at the Crown Court in 2005 were remanded.[830] Fifty-nine per cent of those
committed on bail to the Crown Court for trial and 71 per cent of those
committed in custody eventually pleaded guilty.[831] Seventy-six per cent of those
pleading guilty, after having been committed in custody to the Crown Court for
trial and 37 per cent of those pleading guilty after having been so committed on
bail were sentenced to immediate custody.[832] Fifty per cent of those remanded in

---

[822] See A. Ashworth, *Sentencing and Criminal Justice* (4th edn, 2005), p.285.
[823] Howard League for Penal Reform, *Briefing Paper on Prison Overcrowding and Suicide* (2005)
p.4.
[824] For details on the effects of overcrowding see, Joint Committee on Human Rights, *Deaths in
Custody*, Third Report of Seesion 2004–05 (2005) HC 137, Ch.4. Prison overcrowding may be
a relevant factor for the court to take into account where a case falls on the borderline between
a non-custodial and a custodial sentence: *Attorney General's Reference (No.11 of 2006) (R v
Scarth)* [2006] Crim. L.R. 775.
[825] Authorised for periods not exceeding three clear days by the Magistrates' Courts Act 1980,
s.128(7), (8). See (1987) 151 J.P.N. 433.
[826] HM Chief Inspector of Prisons for England and Wales, *Annual Report 2005–2006* (2007) H.C.
210, at p.21.
[827] National Offender Management Service, *Population in Custody Monthly Tables: November 2006*
(2006) see Table 1. For updated statistics see *www.homeoffice.gov.uk*.
[828] Home Office, *Criminal Statistics for England and Wales 2005* (2006).
[829] *ibid.* Table 4.4.
[830] *ibid.* Table 4.7.
[831] *ibid.*
[832] *ibid.*

custody before trial at magistrates' courts or the Crown Court were sentenced to custody.[833]

It is clear that with the rises in prison population the conditions for the remand prisoner are unlikely to significantly improve in the short term. The Chief Inspector of Prisons has commented that at the same time as increases in the prison population, "there are resource constraints on public spending, which are likely to affect the quality of life in prisons both directly and indirectly. This is an alarming and potentially extremely damaging combination".[834]

G. COMMITTAL PROCEEDINGS

14–068 In recent years there has been a considerable reduction in the circumstances in which committal proceedings are held. Section 51 of the Crime and Disorder Act 1998 requires that cases involving offences triable only on indictment are sent to the Crown Court without committal. The CJA 2003 will overhaul the way in which cases triable either way reach the Crown Court. Schedule 3 to the Act will remove such offences from the committal procedure and see that they are governed by the procedure under s.51 as above. The procedure to be followed by magistrates under this process will be firstly to conduct the plea before venue. If a not guilty plea is indicated the mode of trial procedure will follow. If the accused elects trial on indictment or the magistrates decline jurisdiction the case will be transferred to the Crown Court. The CJA will also streamline the process for cases of serious fraud and cases involving child witnesses.[835] Until the reforms are implemented, likely to be 2007, two types of committal procedure will continue to be used.

1. Committals under the Magistrates' Courts Act

14–069 Under s.6(1) of the Magistrates' Courts Act 1980, the examining magistrates consider the documentary evidence to decide whether an accused should be sent to the Crown Court. Under s.6(2) of the 1980 Act, there can be a committal without consideration of the evidence.[836]

Section 6(1) committals (with consideration of the evidence)[837] apply to all unrepresented defendants and in those cases in which the legal representative requests it. Obviously, the hearings will only be necessary where the accused has pleaded not guilty to an offence which is triable either way. Indictable only offences are sent to the Crown Court immediately under s.51 of the Crime and Disorder Act 1998 and summary offences and guilty pleas are dealt with in the magistrates' court or committed for sentence.

---

[833] *ibid.*
[834] *Annual Report 2005–2006* (2007) H.C. 210, p.6.
[835] CDA 1998 s.51B and s.51C respectively.
[836] See s.6(1) and (2) as substituted by the Criminal Procedure and Investigations Act 1996, s.47, Sch.1, para.4.
[837] Crim. P. R. r.103.

The magistrates hear an outline of the case from the prosecutor who adduces the prosecution evidence (all in documentary form). The types of evidence that can be adduced by the prosecution are carefully prescribed in the Magistrates' Courts Act 1980. These are limited to documents and exhibits, and the conditions for each type of statement are found in ss.5B–5E of the 1996 Act.

The defence do not have an opportunity to adduce evidence, but can make a submission of no case to answer.[838] Note that ss.76 and 78 of PACE have no application in committal proceedings, and so there is no opportunity for objection to evidence in an attempt to exclude it.[839] The prosecutor responds to any defence submission. The standard of proof required is very low for the court to be satisfied—there needs only to be a prima facie case. Cases will be rejected where no evidence is available to prove an essential element of the offence and where prosecution evidence is so manifestly unreliable that no reasonable tribunal could convict on it. If the submission of no case is rejected the bench has the charges read to the accused and formally announces the decision to commit to a specified Crown Court.

If the accused is discharged by the magistrates at the end of the committal proceedings this is not the equivalent of an acquittal at trial. He or she may be charged again with the same offence, and be required to undergo committal proceedings again, whereas an acquittal at trial effectively prevents any further proceedings for the same offence.[840]

Committals without Consideration of the Evidence occur under s.6(2).[841] The examining justices can commit without considering any evidence against the accused if he or she is represented and consents to this procedure. Defence representatives should seek a s.6(1) committal if the evidence served does not disclose a prima facie case. As Sprack notes "committals without consideration of the evidence are a pure formality, and may take 5 minutes or less to accomplish".[842] The prosecution simply presents a bundle of papers to be transmitted to the Crown Court. If the magistrates are satisfied that the evidence tendered by the prosecution falls within s.5A(3) of the Act they may commit the accused for trial for the offence without consideration of the evidence.

If in the course of a summary trial the case appears to be more suitable for Crown Court, the magistrates shall adjourn the hearing and recommence committal proceedings.[843]

The place of the trial is determined mainly by the nature of the charge on which the accused is committed. Criminal offences triable on indictment are divided into classes according to their seriousness and the classes are distinguished by stipulations about the seniority of the judge required to try the case. In the light of these, the magistrates must specify the most convenient location

---

[838] See *R v Barking Justices, Ex p. DPP* (1995) 159 J.P. 353.

[839] Magistrates' Courts Rules 1981, r.70(5) provides for parts of documents to be treated as inadmissible. See also *R v Highbury Magistrates Court, Ex p. Boyce* (1984) 79 Cr.App.R. 132.

[840] If he or she is discharged after committal proceedings the plea of *autrefois acquit* (below) is not available because there has been no trial for the offence. The prosecutor will have to choose whether to abandon the prosecution, or seek further evidence with a view to beginning proceedings again, or invoke the voluntary bill procedure, repeated use of committal proceedings may in an appropriate case be restrained as vexatious or an abuse of process: *R v Manchester City Stipendiary Magistrate, Ex p. Snelson* [1977] 1 W.L.R. 911.

[841] The procedure is set out in the CPR 2005, r.10.2.

[842] Sprack (2006), p.224.

[843] Magistrates' Courts Act 1980, s.25.

of the Crown Court. In practice, each magistrates' court is informed by the presiding judge for the circuit of the location to which proceedings should normally be transferred.

An accused or the prosecutor may make an application to a High Court judge to substitute another place of trial[844] and such applications are usually made in cases where it is feared that local prejudice and hostility will endanger the prospects of a fair trial.[845] Reporting restrictions apply to committal proceedings.[846] In all cases, certain and basic items of information are exempt from the restrictions, including the identity of the court and the names of the justices; the names, and occupations of the parties and witnesses and the ages of the accused and witnesses; the charges (or a summary); the court's decision; the names of legal representatives; the date and place to which proceedings are adjourned; arrangements as to bail and legal aid.[847] Breach of the restrictions is a summary offence.[848] These restrictions are in addition to any other restrictions imposed by an enactment.[849]

The Criminal Procedure Rules provide that the trial should not normally begin before the expiration of 14 days or after the expiration of eight weeks from transfer.[850] Home Office statistics reveal that the average time taken in 2005 from committal to a start of the hearing in the Crown Court was 15.3 weeks.[851]

2. CUSTODY TIME LIMITS

14–070   A complex scheme of time limits for the "preliminary stages" of proceedings for an offence is established by regulations made under s.22 of the Prosecution of Offences Act 1985.[852] Custody time limits may be imposed to govern the period for which a defendant may be kept in custody before the start of summary trial; and, in cases of trial on indictment, for specified "preliminary stages" before arraignment in the Crown Court. Overall time limits may be set for the same stages. These rules have been the subject of a considerable amount of case law and have been repeatedly amended.

The principles applicable in custody time limit extension cases were reviewed by the Lord Chief Justice in *R v Manchester Crown Court, Ex p. Macdonald*[853]

---

[844] Supreme Court Act 1981, s.76.

[845] For example, the trial of Brady and Hindley, the Moors Murderers, was held in Chester rather than the more likely location in Manchester, and the trial of those convicted of the Birmingham pub bombings was held in Lancaster.

[846] Crime and Disorder Act 1998 s.52A. See *Blackstone's* (2007) para.9.13–9.16.

[847] CDA 1998 s.52A(7).

[848] CDA 1998 s.52B.

[849] It is possible for magistrates to lift reporting restrictions but forbid publication of particular matters under s.4(2) of the Contempt of Court Act 1981: *R v Horsliam JJ., Ex p. Farquaharson* [1982] Q.B. 762. However, it has been held that magistrates should be slow to impose restrictions under s.4(2) *in addition* to those applicable to committal proceedings: *R v Beaconsfield JJ., Ex p. Westminster Press Ltd, The Times*, June 28, 1994.

[850] Crim. PR (2005), r.39.1 which sets out the relevant periods under the Supreme Court Act 1981, s.77. This requirement is, however, directory and not mandatory: in an appropriate case the Crown Court may grant an extension of time, even after the eight-week period has expired: *R v Governor of Spring Hill Prison, Ex p. Sohi and Dhillon* (1987) 86 Cr.App.R. 382.

[851] *Criminal Statistics for England and Wales 2005* (2006), Table 2B.

[852] See Corbett and Korn, "Custody Time Limits in Serious and Complex Cases: Will they Work in Practice" [1987] Crim. L.R. 737.

[853] [1999] 1 Cr.App.R. 409.

in which the presumption of liberty and the significance of Art.5 of the ECHR were emphasised.[854] The overriding purpose of custody time limits is to ensure that periods in custody for unconvicted defendants are as short as practically possible; to oblige the prosecution to prepare diligently for trial, and to give the courts power to control extensions.

The effect of expiry of a custody time limit is release on bail; and of an overall time limit that the proceedings are stayed.[855] However, the court may extend a time limit if it is satisfied that there is a good and sufficient cause for doing so,[856] *and*, the prosecution has acted with all due diligence and expedition.[857] However, the judge may extend the custody time limit even when the prosecution has not acted with due diligence if the prosecution's failure was not itself the cause for the extension.[858]

The standard limits to be met are 70 days between first appearance and commencement of committal proceedings or summary trial in either way offences and 112 days between committal and trial; 70 days between first appearance and summary trial for an either way offence (56 days if the decision for summary trial taken within 56 days) 112 days between committal for trial and arraignment.[859] For indictable only offences under s.51 of the Crime and Disorder Act 1998, the time limit is 182 days including time spent in custody in the magistrates' court.[860] For summary offences the time limit is 56 days from the accused's first appearance until the start of the summary trial.[861] The trial starts when a guilty plea is taken or the prosecution present evidence. Where an accused is already held in custody at the time of the imposition of the custody time limits, the same limits apply.[862] The time limits do not apply to the period between trial and retrial.[863] Under the ECHR, reasonable time guarantees in Art.6 apply from the moment of charge until the determination of a final appeal.[864]

---

[854] See in particular the European Court's decisions in *Wemhoff v Germany* (1968) 1 E.H.R.R. 55; *Stögmuller v Austria* (1969) 1 E.H.R.R. 155; *Zimmerman v Switzerland* [1983] 6 E.H.R.R. 17.

[855] See *R v Croydon Youth Court, Ex p. DPP* (2000) 165 J.P. 181.

[856] Which may include the defence's need for time: *McKay White v DPP* [1989] Crim. L.R. 375; a desire for specific counsel: *McDonald* (above); or the lack of a court or a trial judge: *R v Norwich Crown Court, Ex p. Cox* (1992) 97 Cr.App.R. 145; *cf. R v Norwich Crown Court, Ex p. Stiller* (1992) 156 J.P. 624; such cases are to be approached with great caution: *R v C.C.C., Ex p. Abu-Wardeh* [1997] 1 W.L.R. 1083; *R v Birmingham C.C., Ex p. Cunningham*, March 13, 2002. Neither the seriousness nor complexity of the offence, nor the shortness of the period of the extension are good and sufficient reasons: *R v Governor of Winchester Prison, Ex p. Roddie* [1991] 1 W.L.R. 303; *R v Leeds C.C., Ex p. Briggs* [1998] 1 Cr.App.R. 413; and nor is the protection of the public: *R v C.C.C., Ex p. Abu-Wardeh* [1997] 1 W.L.R. 1083; or the fact that the accused would be otherwise entitled to bail: *R v Guildford Crown Court, Ex p. Fraser* [1995] C.O.D. 316; matters relevant to the granting of bail are not relevant: *R v Sheffield Crown Court, Ex p. Headley* [2000] 2 Cr.App.R. 1. Absconding by D not in itself sufficient: *R v Blair*, October 7, 1998; pending extradition can be sufficient: *R v Woolwich Crown Court, Ex p. Gilligan* [1998] 2 All E.R.

[857] s.22(3), as amended. The need for due expedition is not a disciplinary provision: *R v Leeds Crown Court, Ex p. Bagoutie*, The Times, May 31, 1999; *R v Kingston Crown Court, Ex p. Bell* (2000) 164 J.P. 633.

[858] *R (Gibson) v Winchester Crown Court* [2004] 1 W.L.R. 1623.

[859] Prosecution of Offences (Custody Time Limits) Regulations 1987 (SI 1987/299), as amended by SI 1988/164, SI 1989/767 and 1107, SI 1995/555 and SI 2000/3284.

[860] See Prosecution of Offences (Custody Time Limits) (Modification) Regulations 1998.

[861] reg.4A of the Prosecution of Offences (Custody Time Limits) Regulations 1987, as amended. See also Prosecution of Offences (Custody Time Limits) (Amendment) Regulations 1999 (SI 1999/2744).

[862] *R v Peterborough Crown Court, Ex p. L* [2000] Crim. L.R. 470.

[863] *R v Leeds C.C., Ex p. Whitehead* [1998] 7 *Archbold News* 1.

[864] *Neumeister v Austria* (1979–80) 1 E.H.R.R. 91.

More rigorous standards of time-keeping must apply where the defendant is in custody.[865] The English time limits fall well within the periods considered to be reasonable by the ECHR when interpreting the right to trial within a reasonable period.[866]

Where a defendant is charged on different dates with more than one offence, a separate limit applies in respect of each offence, even if they arise from the same facts and could be included as alternatives.[867] There will be no new custody time limit triggered if the new offence introduced merely restates the one charged. If the prosecution introduce a new charge which amounts to an allegation of a new offence, a new time limit will be triggered,[868] and if an accused absconds the time limit may be suspended.[869]

The European Court has reiterated that the persistence of a reasonable suspicion is critical to the legality of continued pre-trial detention. The Court will examine whether domestic courts have required special diligence in the pre-trial preparations.[870]

3. THE VOLUNTARY BILL PROCEDURE[871]

14–071   It is convenient to deal with the voluntary bill procedure at this point since it is a way of getting an indictable offence tried *without* committal by the magistrates. A bill of indictment must be preferred against a defendant as a preliminary to the trial. A bill may only be preferred if proceedings against the defendant have been committed for trial, or as directed by the Court of Appeal (e.g. where ordering a new trial) or by a High Court judge.[872]

A written application to a High Court judge for consent to the preferring of a bill of indictment must state reasons for the application, whether there have been previous applications and the application must be accompanied by the bill of indictment. If committal proceedings have been taken, the application must be accompanied by copies of the documents identifying relevant materials.[873] The

---

[865] *Abdoella v Netherlands* (1992) 20 E.H.R.R. 585.

[866] See: Art.5(3), *Wemhoff v Germany* (1968) 1 E.H.R.R. 55, see also, e.g. the excessive delay in some jurisdictions: *Ferrantelli and Santangelo v Italy* (1996) 23 E.H.R.R. 288 (16yrs!).

[867] *R v Wirral District Magistrates' Court, Ex p. Meikle* (1990) 154 J.P. 1035; *R v Waltham Forest Magistrates' Court, Ex p. Lee* (1993) 157 J.P. 811. The preferral of new charges solely to defeat custody time limits will, however, be an abuse of process (*ibid.*; *cf. R v Great Yarmouth Magistrates, Ex p. Thomas, Davis and Darlington* [1992] Crim. L.R. 116).

[868] *R (Wardle) v Crown Court at Leeds* [2001] 2 W.L.R. 865; [2001] Crim. L.R. and commentary.

[869] Prosecution of Offenders Act 1985 s.22(5).

[870] See *Punzelt v Czech Republic* (2001) 33 E.H.R.R. 49. See also S. Trechsel, *Human Rights in Criminal Proceedings* (2005) Ch.19.

[871] See C. M. Chatterton and P. K. Brown, *Committals for Trial to the Crown Court* (1988), pp.232–241; C. Lewis (1981) 78 L.S. Gaz. 1442; *Consolidated Criminal Practice Direction* para.IV.35.

[872] Administration of Justice (Miscellaneous Provisions) Act 1933, s.2(2), as amended by the Criminal Procedure and Investigations Act 1996, Sch.1.

[873] The Indictments (Procedure) Rules 1971 (SI 1971/2084), rr.6–10, as amended by the Crime and Disorder Act 1998 govern the procedure. To be valid, the bill must be signed by a proper officer of the court certifying compliance with the requirements: *R v Morais* (1988) 87 Cr.App.R. 9. However, it would appear that the court's approach to procedural failures such as this has changed following *R v Ashton* [2006] EWCA Crim 794. The court must consider the interests of justice generally and whether there is a real possibility that either the defence or the prosecution will suffer prejudice on account of the procedural failure.

defendant has no right to a hearing, although the judge, may in the exercise of discretion, entertain written or, perhaps, in very exceptional circumstances, oral representations.[874] The decision of a judge to issue a voluntary bill is not susceptible to challenge on an application for judicial review.[875]

This procedure allows an accused to be put on trial at the discretion of a High Court judge and is rarely used, but could be effective in circumventing committal proceedings where unusual problems arose.[876] The procedure should not be used as a means of depriving the accused of an opportunity to seek dismissal of a charge under s.51 of the Crime and Disorder Act 1998.[877]

The preferment of a voluntary bill is an exceptional procedure. Consent should only be granted where good reason to depart from the normal procedure is clearly shown and only where the interests of justice, rather than considerations of administrative convenience, require it.

H. DISCLOSURE OF EVIDENCE [878]

In a civil case, the pre-trial procedure can be operated so as to allow each party **14–072** to discover the essentials of the case to be met and to discover the basic issues in dispute between the parties. In a criminal matter, despite the introduction of the plea and directions hearing (now plea and case managment hearing) and the pre-trial review mechanisms, the two sides have less scope for selecting the ground on which they wish to fight and many issues may be intentionally left in dispute until the trial.[879] However, it can be a considerable advantage to the prosecution, defence and to the court if by the time of the trial the two sides have some indication of the evidence to be given and the arguments to be raised. It is important to recall that non-disclosure of evidence by the police and others to the prosecutor, or the prosecutor to the defence have been recurrent themes in many of the high-profile miscarriage of justice cases.[880]

---

[874] *R v Raymond* [1981] Q.B. 910, criticised by G. Harrison, (1986) J. Crim. Law 383, but approved by the Privy Council in *Brooks (Lloyd) v DPP of Jamaica* [1994] 1 A.C. 568. See *Archbold* (2007), para.1–213.

[875] *R v Manchester Crown Court, Ex p. Williams and Simpson* (1990) 154 J.P. 589; *contra, R v IRC, Ex p. Dhesi, The Independent*, August 14,1995.

[876] e.g. where the defendant disrupted committal proceedings (*R v Paling* (1978) 67 Cr.App.R. 299); or to prefer an indictment against two defendants, one of whom has already been committed for trial.

[877] See *R v X and Y* [1999] 5 *Archbold News* 4. The procedure may be used where there have been deliberate attempts by the defence to frustrate the committal by a technical objection: *R v DPP, Ex p. Moran* [1999] 3 *Archbold News* 3.

[878] J. Plotnikoff and R. Woolfson, *"A Fair Balance?" Evaluation of the Operational Disclosure Law* (HORDS Occasional Paper No.76, 2001); Andrews and Hirst, *Criminal Evidence* (4th edn, 2001), pp.125–135; T. Owen in K. Starmer *et al.* (2001); Emmerson and Ashworth (2001), Ch.14, Pt G. Ashworth and Redmayne (2005) Ch.9.

[879] Although there is a procedure whereby formal admissions can be made under the Criminal Justice Act 1967, s.10, thereby eliminating the need for undisputed evidence to be given at trial orally.

[880] See C. Walker in C. Walker and K. Starmer, *Justice in Error* (1993), p.14, referring to, *inter alia*, the Guildford Four, the Maguire Seven, the Darvell brothers and Judith Ward in particular. Other examples include Stefan Kiszko. See also J. Niblett, *Disclosure in Criminal Cases* (1997); B. Fitzpatrick in Walker and Starmer (1999). Chs 1, 3.

The RCCJ made proposals for greater disclosure by the defence, with some restriction on the prosecution's disclosure duties. The Criminal Procedure and Investigations Act 1996 (CPIA) introduced these reforms but unfortunately they have since proved to be extremely unsatisfactory, with further guidelines having to be issued to render the scheme workable and to ensure compatibility with the ECHR. The CPIA has been extremely heavily criticised by many commentators and practitioners. The CPS Inspectorate Report, *The Thematic Review of the Disclosure of Unused Material*[881] concluded that "the Criminal Procedure and Investigations Act 1996 is not at present working as Parliament intended, nor does its present operation command the confidence of criminal practitioners".

Plotnikoff and Woolfson found that many respondents regarded the statutory scheme as so unsatisfactory that practitioners had returned to the common law principles.[882] The disclosure procedure came under greater pressure because of the changes introduced in the Crime and Disorder Act to speed up pre-trial hearings. One of the conclusions of Plotnikoff and Woolfson's report was that: "88 per cent of barristers, 87 per cent of defence solicitors, 84 per cent of CPS respondents, 61 per cent of judges and 44 per cent of justices' clerks were dissatisfied with the way the Criminal Procedure and Investigations Act 1996 was operating".[883] As a result a series of important changes to the disclosure regime were introduced by the Criminal Justice Act 2003, which became effective in 2005.[884]

The obligation on the prosecution to disclose matters to the defence is one of the most onerous, and a failure to comply is likely to render the trial unfair. Article 6 of the ECHR has helped to shape the current disclosure obligations. There is no right to disclosure expressed in the Convention, but the European Court has recognised that it is fundamental to ensure the "equality of arms". The defendant's right to adequate time to prepare his defence[885] and the requirement of equality of arms[886] are both important principles which place obligations on the prosecuting authority. The accused must have access to as much material as possible if the adversarial trial is to remain fair.

---

[881] (2000) For surveys and reports commenting (almost universally in negative terms) see: ACPO and the National Crime Faculty, *Disclosure and the CPIA: Implementation in Practice* (1998); *The Annual Report of the Chief Inspector of the CPS* (1998–9); Criminal Bar Association, *Disclosure Provisions Survey*; H. Hallett (1998) *Counsel*, Dec.; LCD, *Draft Attorney-General's Guidelines on Disclosure: A Consultative Document* (2000); Crown Prosecution Service Inspectorate, The Inspectorate's Report on the Thematic Review of the Disclosure of Unused Material (CPSI, 2000); J. Plotnikoff and R. Woolfson, *"A Fair Balance"?: Evaluation of the Operation of Disclosure Law* (HORDS Occasional Paper No.176, 2001); Butterfield Review, *Review of Criminal Investigations and Prosecutions conducted by HM Customs and Excise* (2002), Ch.12, especially 12.28, describing the regime as "the worst of all worlds".

[882] Plotnikoff and Wolfson (2001) para.1.6. In response to concerns from all branches of the profession and agencies involved in the criminal justice system, the Home Office established a steering group to conduct research into the effectiveness of the Criminal Procedure Investigations Act. See C. Clarke, "HO/Government Perceptions, Past and Present Proposals for Future Strategy" (2000) Med. Sci. 103.

[883] Plotnikoff and Wolfson (2001) p.121.

[884] In addition to the statutory regime under the Criminal Procedure and Investigations Act 1996 and the Criminal Justice Act 2003, there is a Code of Practice issued under the 1996 Act and the Attorney-General's Guidelines *Disclosure of Information in Criminal Proceedings* (2005). Further to this is the Court of Appeal's *Protocol for the Control and Management of Unused Material in the Crown Court* (2006), which should be applied by trial judges, see *R v K* [2006] EWCA Crim 724. See also, Crim. P.R. (2005) Pt 25. See also, M. Zander, "Mission Impossible" (2006) N.L.J. 618.

[885] *Edwards v UK* (1992) 15 E.H.R.R. 417.

[886] *Jespers v Belgium* (1981) 27 D.R. 61.

1. Disclosure by the Prosecution

It is a fundamental principle of a fair trial that the defendant must know the case **14–073** against him and have an opportunity to prepare his defence. Clearly, the prosecution are under a duty to disclose to the defence the whole of the evidence on which they propose to rely.[887] This aspect of disclosure is not generally controversial. Article 6(3)(b) of the ECHR requires the accused to have "at his disposal, for the purposes of exonerating himself, or of obtaining a reduction in his sentence, all relevant elements that have been or could be collected by the competent authorities".[888] What is more controversial is the extent to which the prosecution have to disclose to the defence any material that is not used for the prosecution case, where the unused material might undermine the prosecution case or assist the defence.[889]

(a) Background

The extent to which the prosecution has to disclose information has developed **14–074** rapidly over recent years. Some requirements were clear at common law, including that of notifying the defence of, at least, the name and address of a witness who could give material evidence but would not be called by the prosecution[890]; making expert and technical evidence available; giving the defence a copy of any statements made by a prosecution witness which conflict with the evidence given at trial[891]; making known any convictions affecting the credibility of prosecution witnesses.[892] In 1981, the Attorney-General issued guidelines setting out the additional material which must be made available to the defence, with exceptions for especially prejudicial or sensitive information.[893] The guidelines were overtaken by cases reconsidering the extent to which the common law requires

---

[887] It may be necessary to have full disclosure at a very early stage so that a defendant can make an informed choice regarding his plea before venue (*R v Calderdale Magistrates' Court, Ex p. Donahue and Cutler* [2001] Crim. L.R. 141) and even earlier, so that he can make an informed choice about consenting to a caution. See J. Appozardi, "Disclosure at the Police Station" [2002] Crim. L.R. 295, discussing the decision in *DPP v Ara* [2001] 4 All E.R. 559. See also *R v DPP, Ex p. Lee* [1997] 2 All E.R. 737, considering the possible need to disclose early to assist with bail applications or motions to stay proceedings, or other material assisting the defendant's preparation for trial.

[888] *Jespers*, para.58.

[889] Recall that the forensic capabilities of the defence are severely limited when compared to those of the State. In addition, the prosecution are not desperately seeking a conviction, they are acting as ministers of justice and should not abuse the process. See for further discussion the speech of Lord Hope in *R v Brown* [1998] A.C. 367, and the opinion of the committee in *H and C* [2004] U.K.H.L. 3 at para.13.

[890] There was disagreement between Lord Denning M.R. and Diplock L.J. in *Dallison v Caffery* [1965] 1 Q.B. 348 on the extent of the obligation. The Master of the Rolls was of the opinion that prosecuting counsel should make the witness' statements available to the defence. Diplock L.J. thought it was enough to make the witness available by notifying a name and address (*cf. R v Bryant and Dickson* (1946) 31 Cr.App.R. 146; *R v Lawson* (1989) 90 Cr.App.R. 108).

[891] *R v Howes*, March 27, 1950, CCA (unreported), cited in Archbold, *Criminal Pleading, Evidence and Practice* (43rd edn), para.4–179.

[892] *R v Collister and Warhurst* (1955) 39 Cr.App.R. 100; *R v Paraskeva* (1982) 76 Cr.App.R. 162. The same principle applies to disciplinary findings against police officers: *R v Edwards* [1991] 1 W.L.R. 207, and the request by a prosecution witness for a reward: *R v Rasheed, The Times*, May 20, 1994. See also *R v Guney* [1998] 2 G.App.R. 242.

[893] *Practice Note* [1982] 1 All E.R. 734.

disclosure.[894] The leading case was *R v Ward*[895] where the Court of Appeal on a reference from the Home Secretary quashed the convictions of Judith Ward for complicity in a series of bombings in the 1970s. The Court of Appeal found that the non-disclosure of a series of items of evidence[896] constituted material irregularities and that the prosecution were under a duty to disclose to the defence "material evidence"—that which tends either to weaken the prosecution case or to strengthen the defence case.[897] Some elements of the scheme adopted in *Ward* were refined in subsequent cases, in particular, in *R v Davies, Johnson and Rowe*,[898] and *R v Keane*[899] and some of these aspects of the common law are still important under the present statutory scheme for disclosure.

The common law expansion of disclosure obligations met with considerable criticism from the police, who claimed that the balance between defence access to material and preserving sensitive sources had swung too far towards the accused, and noted that vast quantities of information now had to be examined and disclosed.[900] The RCCJ[901] thought that the arrangements as to sensitive material were satisfactory.[902] It was recommended that such cases should be dealt with by High Court judges or nominated Circuit judges. However, they accepted that, otherwise, the burden on the prosecution had gone "beyond what is reasonable", and they made recommendations for change. The government subsequently published a consultation document[903] setting out a more detailed scheme that in its view would reduce the burdens on the prosecution to a greater extent than proposed by the RCCJ. The government claimed that the scheme would significantly reduce the volume of material that must be disclosed for no good purpose but not increase the risk of a miscarriage of justice. Critics suggested that it would merely "accept the risk of further miscarriages as the cost of achieving economy".[904]

---

[894] The guidelines did not have legal force and conflicted with the case law: see *R v Brown (Winston)* [1994] 1 W.L.R. 1599.

[895] [1993] 1 W.L.R. 619. See also *R v Reilly* [1994] Crim. L.R. 279; *R v McCarthy* (1994) 158 J.P. 283.

[896] Including material experimental data that might have cast doubt on the evidence of forensic scientists called by the prosecution; statements made to police officers withdrawing confessions made to other officers; other statements by W which cast doubt on her reliability as a witness.

[897] The test was *materiality not admissibility: R v Preston* [1994] 2 A.C. 730. "Material" documents are those which are: (1) relevant or possibly relevant to an issue in the case; or (2) raise or possibly raise a new issue whose existence is not apparent from the evidence the prosecution proposes to use; and (3) hold out a real (as opposed to fanciful) prospect of providing a lead on evidence which goes to (1) or (2): *R v Melvin* (unreported, December 20, 1993), approved by the Court of Appeal in *R v Keane* [1994] 1 W.L.R. 746 at 752. The term "issues in the case" was given a "broad interpretation": *R v Brown (Winston)* [1994] 1 W.L.R. 1599, 1606.

[898] [1993] 1 W.L.R. 613.

[899] [1994] 1 W.L.R. 746.

[900] See, e.g. C. Pollard [1994] Crim. L.R. 42 (Mr Pollard was Chief Constable of the Thames Valley Police).

[901] Cm. 2263, pp.91–97. These recommendations are considered by J. Glynn [1993] Crim. L.R. 841.

[902] On the understanding that the procedure outlined in *Davies* did indeed extend to sensitive material falling outside the scope of public interest immunity (contrary to the subsequent decision in *R v Brown (Winston)* [1994] 1 W.L.R. 1599.

[903] *Disclosure: A Consultation Document* (Cm. 2864, 1995).

[904] R. Leng [1995] Crim. L.R. 704 at 708. The CPS estimates that it spends £6 million per annum complying with the disclosure requirements, but that examinations by CPS lawyers of all unused material would cost £30 million extra. The cost to police forces in terms of disclosure officers' time to comply with disclosure was estimated to be £5.8 million: Plotnikoff and Woolfson (2001), pp.109–110.

(b) The current law

Provisions on disclosure are now contained in the Criminal Procedure and **14–075**
Investigations Act 1996 (as amended by the Criminal Justice Act 2003).[905] The
scheme places obligations on both the prosecution and defence.

Recognising the significance of the need for a complete record of information
to be maintained as a prerequisite to adequate disclosure, the Act places a
statutory duty on those charged with investigating offences to record and retain
information[906] and a Code of Practice provides further detail on the manner of the
collation and recording.[907] The Code makes detailed provision for the retention[908] of crime reports, final versions of witness statements (draft versions if
inconsistent), interview records and tapes and forensic and expert evidence, as
well as material calling into question the veracity of a witness. The officer has to
prepare a schedule of relevant material and specify on it any "sensitive material".[909] If there is a large volume of material which has not been examined
because it is presumed to be irrelevant, the defence should be alerted to its
existence. The investigator has a duty to alert the prosecutor to material which
might undermine the case.[910]

The police interviewed by Plotnikoff and Woolfson agreed that the disclosure
officer's role was of critical importance, especially in serious crime. The Act
clearly places a considerable burden on the investigator, and the success of the
scheme turns on the bona fides and proficiency of this officer. Once the police
have assembled the schedule, the obligation passes to the prosecutor.

(c) Prosecution disclosure

The prosecutor must review the schedule of material[911] and disclose to **14–076**
the accused that which "might reasonably be considered capable of undermining
the case for the prosecution against the accused, or of assisting the case for the

---

[905] Part 1. On the implementation of the CPIA scheme for disclosure see J. Sprack, "The Criminal
Procedure Investigations Act 1996: The Duty of Disclosure" [1997] Crim. L.R. 308; A. Edwards,
"The Procedural Aspects" [1997] Crim. L.R. 321. For an analysis of the amendments made by
the CJA 2003, see M. Redmayne, "Criminal Justice Act 2003: Disclosure and Its Discontents"
[2004] Crim. L.R. 441.

[906] Criminal Procedure and Investigations Act 1996, s.23.

[907] Criminal Procedure and Investigations Act 1996, s.26. Paragraph 5.1 of the Code makes the
investigator responsible for ensuring that any information relevant to the investigation is recorded
and retained, whether it is gathered in the course of the investigation (e.g. documents seized in
the course of searching premises) or generated by the investigation (e.g. interview records). If
there is any doubt about the relevance of material, the investigator should retain it. The *Attorney
General's Guidelines* (2005) suggest that the disclosure officer should not be someone whose role
is likely to result in a conflict of interest (para.25).

[908] See P. Plowden and K. Kerrigan, "Cards on the Table?" (2001) N.L.J. 735 at 820, discussing
cases in which evidence that might have been valuable to the defence was inadvertently
destroyed. See also, S. Martin, "Lost and Destroyed Evidence: The Search for a Principled
Approach to Abuse of Process" (2005) 9 E. & P. 158.

[909] i.e. that which it is not in the public interest to disclose (para.6.12 provides examples). The
Attorney-General's Guidelines (2005) emphasise that descriptions by disclosure officers in non-
sensitive schedules should be detailed, clear and accurate.

[910] Code, para.7.2.

[911] i.e. material in the prosecutor's possession acquired in connection with the case or which he or
she has been allowed to inspect.

accused".[912] The decision is one to be made by the prosecutor and cannot be abdicated to a judge.[913]

However, primary disclosure will not apply if the court upholds a public interest immunity (PII) claim or where disclosure is otherwise prohibited (e.g. by the RIPA 2000, s.17). The prosecutor must also at this stage serve on the defence a document indicating the nature of other prosecution material prescribed by the Code of Practice and which has not been disclosed, other than material covered by PII. In relation to the material that is primary disclosure material, the prosecutor alerts the defence to the existence of the material and allows them access to it or copies of it depending on what is most suitable and practicable. The duty of disclosure arises as soon as is reasonably practicable.[914] The prosecutor has a duty to review disclosure schedules to ensure that they are accurate and complete. If the prosecutor considers that because of an omission or because certain material cannot be disclosed, it would be impossible for a fair trial to occur, he or she should discontinue the case.[915]

The key element of this procedure is the prosecutor's decision as to what might "undermine" the case. The use of this expression was designed to narrow the scope of disclosure from that imposed at common law.[916] In the course of the debates on the Criminal Procedure Investigations Act 1996, the Home Office Minister, Mr David McLean, explained that the word undermine "is not confined to material raising a fundamental question about the prosecution . . . the disclosure scheme is aimed at undisclosed material that might help the accused notwithstanding the fact that there is enough evidence to provide a realistic prospect of conviction".[917] The *Attorney-General's Guidelines* (2005) which were introduced to clarify some of the problems with the 1996 Act, and have been updated in light of subsequent amendments, provide further guidance.[918] The explanation of the key terms "undermine" and "potentially undermine" which are central to the decision that the prosecutor must make, are explained

---

[912] Criminal Procedure Investigations Act 1996, s.3(1)(a) as amended by the Criminal Justice Act 2003 s.32. The decision of the prosecutor is reviewable. The wording in the CPIA 1996, which has been repealed, spoke of disclosing evidence which "in the prosecutor's opinion" undermined the prosecution case.

[913] *R v B* [2000] Crim. L.R. 50.

[914] Criminal Procedure and Investigations Act 1996, s.13. Plotnikoff and Woolfson (2001), p.71, found that primary disclosure was served at, or just, after committal in most cases (90% according to the CPS; 60% according to the defence). Many respondents from all areas of the criminal justice system felt that non-sensitive unused material was often withheld from the accused (including 15% of judges being of this opinion).

[915] *Attorney-General's Guidelines* (2005), para.41.

[916] See *R v Keane* [1994] 1 W.L.R. 746 where the court held that the correct test was whether it was evidence that was relevant or which might raise a new issue or hold out a real prospect of providing a lead on such evidence. Note that a wide interpretation of "undermine" is supported by the decision of the European Court in *Rowe and Davis v UK* (2000) 30 E.H.R.R. 1. The European Court emphasised that the right to a fair trial means that the prosecution authorities should disclose to the defence all material evidence in their possession for and against the accused to ensure the "equality of arms". This suggests that the current obligations of primary disclosure may be too narrow, and that *all* evidence which is material to the case ought to be disclosed, not merely that which *might* tend to undermine the prosecution case: B. Emmerson, "Prosecution Disclosure in Criminal Cases: The ECHR and the Human Rights Act 1998" (2000) Med. Sci. Law 125.

[917] H.C. Standing Committee B, May 14, 1996, col.34.

[918] The Crown Prosecution Code for Crown Prosecutors (2004) also states at para.2.5: "It is the duty of Crown Prosecutors to review, advise on and prosecute cases, ensuring that the law is properly applied, that all relevant evidence is put before the court and that obligations of disclosure are complied with . . . "

as "anything that tends to show a fact inconsistent with the elements of the case . . . ".[919]

Although there is no explicit statutory provision dealing with previous convictions of prosecution witnesses, the Court of Appeal have made it clear that these should be disclosed as potentially undermining the prosecution case.[920] Following the common law position explained in *R v Mills*,[921] the prosecution are obliged to supply the defence with copies of *any* witness statements from unreliable witnesses that the prosecution do *not* propose to call.

A number of problems with primary disclosure remain. For example, it presumes that the schedule of material will have been accurately recorded by the police,[922] and that it will have been accurately and comprehensively disclosed to the prosecutor for him or her to make a decision on disclosure.[923] Plotnikoff and Woolfson found that primary disclosure decisions are rarely included in the brief to the prosecuting barrister, with 75 per cent of barristers suggesting that their instructions rarely contain an adequate account of the reasons for primary disclosure. The danger is not just that the police will deliberately withhold material from the prosecutor, but that this will occur despite the police officer's best efforts.[924] The respondents to Plotnikoff and Woolfson's survey emphasise that the drawing up of the schedules of material is an onerous task.[925] The CPS and other legal advisers found that unused material was commonly omitted from schedules/wrongly listed, especially in high volume crimes such as burglary, but also in serious drugs and sexual offence cases.[926] The CPS described the quality of descriptions by disclosure officers as poor in a large number of cases.[927] In a long and complex investigation the volume of material produced will run to tens of thousands of pages of material.[928] Plotnikoff and Woolfson found that 72 per cent of defence barristers, but only 45 per cent of prosecution barristers often

---

[919] *Attorney-General's Guidelines* (2005), paras 36–38.

[920] See *R v Vasilou* [2000] Crim. L.R. 845 and commentary; *cf. R v Ecclestone*, July 10, 2001, CA; *R v Jamil* [2002] Crim. L.R. Information adverse to a police witness should be disclosed: *R v Guney* [1998] 2 Cr.App.R. 242. Plotnikoff and Woolfson's research (p.46) revealed that only one of 39 CPS areas in the survey kept a record of the adverse judicial comments relating to police officers, as required by *R v Guney* (1998) 2 Cr.App.R. 242. See also on the disclosure of adverse information on the prosecution witness Plotnikoff and Woolfson (2001), Ch.5. Similarly, where reliance is placed on a witness turning Queen's evidence it is necessary for the prosecution to offer to disclose the witness's convictions to the jury unless the defence request otherwise: *R v Taylor; R v Goodman* [1999] Crim. L.R. 407. In their research Plotnikoff and Woolfson (2001), Ch.3, found that the procedures for checking on adverse information on prosecution witnesses was poor, with checks not always performed, and entries recorded in only 24% of relevant cases. The results on criminal record checks on prosecution witnesses were revealed to the defence as primary disclosure in only 4% of all cases.

[921] [1998] 2 A.C. 382.

[922] For an example of a case in which the police failed to record the details of an alleged offence see *R v Abbassi* discussed at (2000) 150 N.L.J. 1666.

[923] See, M. Redmayne, "Criminal Justice Act 2003: Disclosure and Its Discontents" [2004] Crim. L.R. 440.

[924] On the continued dependence on the police in the disclosure regime see *R v Jackson* [2000] Crim. L.R. 377.

[925] Plotnikoff and Woolfson (2001), Ch.4.

[926] *ibid.* Fig. 4, p.27.

[927] Over 60% in some categories, *ibid.* Fig. 5. p.29. On routine revelation to the CPS see Plotnikoff and Woolfson (2001), Ch.7.

[928] Plotnikoff and Woolfson found that the average size of the file of unused material studied by the CPS in a serious case was 54.6 inches deep: Table 12, p.35.

discussed disclosure matters when instructed.[929] There was considerable disparity between the CPS claims about their processing of unused material and the less positive experience of the barristers instructed by them. Further, there is the problem of the inevitable delay in disclosing material to the defence, particularly where there is a large volume of material.[930]

(d) Public interest immunity (PII)[931]

14–077   Material which would be subject to primary disclosure but which is believed to be protected by PII is subject to special procedures which have proved very controversial in a number of cases. The investigator will produce, in the course of the investigation, a schedule of sensitive material (e.g. relating to informers and covert human intelligence sources).[932] This information is passed to the prosecutor who must apply to the court for PII if he or she thinks that it is necessary to do so.[933] At common law the Court of Appeal in *Ward* held that the prosecution should disclose the material to the court for its decision as to whether the public interest was against the defence having access to the material. The Court of Appeal refined these requirements in *R v Davis, Johnson and Rowe*[934] and the Criminal Procedure Investigations Act 1996 preserves these common law rules in relation to PII.[935]

The procedure for a PII application has undergone some significant developments in recent years. The European Court has repeatedly emphasised the significance in the adversarial trial of the concept of equality of arms whereby the State has an obligation to "gather evidence against and for the accused and to allow access to all relevant material before trial".[936]

In *R v Davis, Johnson and Rowe*, the Court of Appeal[937] adopted a tripartite model for PII applications. In most cases there would be a hearing for PII with the defence being notified of the hearing, the type of material involved, and the defence having an opportunity to make representations. In exceptional cases where even to reveal the application to the defence could be contrary to the

---

[929] p.52.
[930] See the discussion by R. Toney, "Disclosure of Evidence and Legal Assistance at Custodial Interrogation: What does the ECHR Require" (2001) 5 E. & P. 39, considering the potential breaches of the Convention under existing English law; see also Emmerson and Ashworth (2001), para.14–114.
[931] The procedure is outlined in Crim. P.R. (2005) rr.25.1–25.5.
[932] D. Corker, "The Criminal Procedure Investigations Act 1996 Disclosure Regime; PII and Third Party Disclosure, The Defence Perspective" (2000) Med. Sci. Law 116, noting that the effectiveness of the Act is dependent on the conscientiousness of the investigator.
[933] Prosecution counsel should also be meticulous in ensuring that all potential PII material has been reviewed: *R v Menga* [1998] Crim. L.R. 58.
[934] (1993) 97 Cr.App.R. 110.
[935] s.21(2). *Rowe and Davis v UK* [2000] 30 E.H.R.R. 1; [2000] Crim. L.R. 584 confirms that the pre-*Ward* disclosure rules in England were in breach of Art.6 because they allowed prosecutors to withhold evidence (even from the judge if it related to PII) which might have undermined their case. The decision also casts doubt on the compatibility of the 1996 procedure for secondary disclosure being delayed until after the defence disclosure. See further the commentary by A. Ashworth [2000] Crim. L.R. 584; and C. Walker and G. Robertson in Walker and Starmer (1999).
[936] *Jespers v Belgium* (1981) 27 D.R. 61; *Edwards v UK* (1993) 15 E.H.R.R. 417; *Benendoun v France* (1994) 18 E.H.R.R. 54. On *Edwards v UK* in the ECtHR see the comment by S. Field and J. Young, "Disclosure, Appeals, and Procedural Traditions: *Edwards v. U.K.*" [1994] Crim. L.R. 264.
[937] [1993] 1 W.L.R. 613.

public interest, the prosecution would not be obliged to disclose the category of material held and there would be an *ex parte* hearing. In the most extreme cases, the prosecution need not even alert the defence to the proposed *ex parte* hearing.[938]

In determining PII, the judge is not restricted to considering only admissible evidence.[939] The court has an obligation to review whether the level of secrecy from the defence remains necessary.[940] The court is also under a duty throughout the trial to keep under review the decisions made as to PII.[941] The obligations on trial judges with a PII application can be onerous; in one case it was reported that the judge spent 11 days reading material before being able to rule on disclosure.[942]

This tripartite PII scheme was examined by the ECtHR in *Rowe and Davis v United Kingdom*[943] where the European Court held there was a legitimate need in some cases for public interest immunity certificates to attach to certain prosecution material, but that this category should be narrowly construed. The procedure must involve the judicial decision as to whether the material was strictly necessary as PII. In *Jasper v United Kingdom*,[944] the ECtHR held, by a bare majority, that the exceptional procedure whereby an *ex parte* PII application can be made without notification to the defence of the category of material was compatible with Art.6,[945] in spite of the claims that judicial bias or error would go undetected.[946] A minority of the Court thought that the appointment of special counsel to represent the interests of the defence in the PII hearing was the appropriate solution to the issue.[947] The European Court returned to the issue in *Edwards and Lewis v United Kingdom*.[948] Information was kept from the defence on PII grounds, but the trier of fact in the case was not a jury but the judge himself. It was held to be unfair that the judge was to determine the case whilst

---

[938] There is no need for an *ex parte* application where there was nothing to be said which could not be said in the presence of defence counsel: *R v Smith* [1998] 2 Cr.App.R. 1 (adequate records must always be kept of such *ex parte* application hearings).

[939] *R v Law, The Times*, August 15, 1996.

[940] The procedure was incorporated in the Crown Court (Criminal Procedure Investigations Act 1996) (Disclosure) Rules 1997 (SI 1997/698).

[941] s.15. On PII see Plotnikoff and Woolfson (2001), Ch.10 recognising that it is difficult to monitor PII work but that in general it was felt by practitioners that the number of applications for PII had risen since 1996. Approximately 36% of PII applications in the cases examined were successful.

[942] *R v W* [1997] 1 Cr.App.R. 166 at 168. In *R v W* the judge had relied on counsel to sift the disputed material and discard the irrelevant before the judge ruled on it. This practice was endorsed by the Court of Appeal.

[943] (2000) 30 E.H.R.R. 1, [2000] Crim. L.R. 584. In *Rowe and Davis v UK*, the European Court did not address the fairness of the *ex parte* procedure under the Criminal Procedure and Investigations Act 1996 and Crown Court (Criminal Procedure and Investigation Act 1996) (Disclosure) Rules 1997. See the subsequent decisions of the English Court of Appeal: *R v Davis, Rowe and Johnson (No.2), The Times*, April 24, 2000; *(No.3)* [2001] 1 Cr.App.R. 8.

[944] (2000) 30 E.H.R.R. 441; [2001] Crim. L.R. 586. An *ex parte* application may not be made by the defence: *R v Turner* [1995] 1 W.L.R. 264 at 267. In *Jasper v UK* and *Fitt v UK* [2000] Crim. L.R. 586, the European Court accepted that where the trial judge had reviewed the PII application and the defence were notified, there was no breach of Art.6.

[945] The decision was by a bare majority of 9. See further the commentary on this case by A. Ashworth, [2001] Crim. L.R. 586.

[946] The *Attorney General's Guidelines* (2005) provide further guidance for the PII application in paras 20–22.

[947] See also the Auld Report, Ch.10, paras 191–197, *cf.* discussion by Owen (2001), p.148 and see *Chahal v UK* (1997) 23 E.H.R.R. 413.

[948] *Edwards and Lewis v United Kingdom* (2003) 15 B.H.R.C. 189.

being in possession of information about which the defence were unaware and therefore no ability to challenge. A possible answer to this problem was again the suggestion of the appointment of special counsel. The House of Lords considered the issue in *R v H and C*.[949] The judgment is interesting in itself for its attempt to reassert the principles of the 1996 regime, emphasising perhaps that the system was not working. However, the House of Lords did provide a checklist for PII cases which is worth detailing in full.

> "When any issue of derogation from the golden rule of full disclosure comes before it, the court must address a series of questions: (1) What is the material which the prosecution seek to withhold? This must be considered by the court in detail. (2) Is the material such as may weaken the prosecution case or strengthen that of the defence? If No, disclosure should not be ordered. If Yes, full disclosure should (subject to (3), (4) and (5)) be ordered. (3) Is there a real risk of serious prejudice to an important public interest (and, if so, what) if full disclosure of the material is ordered? If No, full disclosure should be ordered. (4) If the answer to (2) and (3) is Yes, can the defendant's interest be protected without disclosure or disclosure be ordered to an extent or in a way which will give adequate protection to the public interest in question and also afford adequate protection to the interests of the defence? This question requires the court to consider, with specific reference to the material which the prosecution seek to withhold and the facts of the case and the defence as disclosed, whether the prosecution should formally admit what the defence seek to establish or whether disclosure short of full disclosure may be ordered. This may be done in appropriate cases by the preparation of summaries or extracts of evidence, or the provision of documents in an edited or anonymised form, provided the documents supplied are in each instance approved by the judge. In appropriate cases the appointment of special counsel may be a necessary step to ensure that the contentions of the prosecution are tested and the interests of the defendant protected. In cases of exceptional difficulty the court may require the appointment of special counsel to ensure a correct answer to questions (2) and (3) as well as (4). (5) Do the measures proposed in answer to (4) represent the minimum derogation necessary to protect the public interest in question? If No, the court should order such greater disclosure as will represent the minimum derogation from the golden rule of full disclosure. (6) If limited disclosure is ordered pursuant to (4) or (5), may the effect be to render the trial process, viewed as a whole, unfair to the defendant? If Yes, then fuller disclosure should be ordered even if this leads or may lead the prosecution to discontinue the proceedings so as to avoid having to make disclosure. (7) If the answer to (6) when first given is No, does that remain the correct answer as the trial unfolds, evidence is adduced and the defence advanced? It is important that the answer to (6) should not be treated as a final, once-and-for-all, answer but as a provisional answer which the court must keep under review."[950]

The House declined to suggest that special counsel should always be appointed but that it might be a necessary step in appropriate cases. The Court of Appeal[951]

---

[949] *R v H and C* [2004] U.K.H.L 3.
[950] *ibid.*
[951] [2004] 1 Cr.App.R. 17.

provided some indication as to when those appropriate circumstances might be, namely, when the material is relevant to a preliminary determinative ruling such as an application to stay the proceedings where the judge will benefit from adversarial argument.[952]

In *R v Templar*[953] the Court warned against frequent meeting in chambers between the judge and prosecuting counsel in the absence of the defendant or his legal representatives.

(e) Defence disclosure

It should be noted that defence disclosure relates to material that the defence *will* use, as opposed to the prosecution duty regarding unused material. Prior to the 1996 Act the defence was able to avoid revealing its case (apart from in alibi and in certain other exceptional situations). The RCCJ[954] felt that there were "powerful reasons for extending the obligations on the defence to provide advance disclosure". This would encourage earlier and better preparation of cases, and might result in the prosecution being dropped in the light of defence disclosure, an earlier resolution through a plea of guilty, or an earlier trial date. The length of the trial could be more readily estimated, leading to a better use of time both of the court and of those involved in the trial. Cases where the defendant withholds the defence to the last possible moment "in the hope of confusing the jury and evading investigation of a fabricated defence" ("ambush defences"[955]) would be kept to a minimum. Michael Zander dissented from these recommendations[956] on the ground that it was "contrary to principle for the defendant to be made to respond to the prosecution's case until it has been presented at the trial". Given that the burden of proof lies throughout on the prosecution, "it is not the job of the defendant to be helpful either to the prosecution or to the system. His task, if he chooses to put the prosecution to the proof, is simply to defend himself." Furthermore, ambush defences were in fact rare and when they occur "usually do not pose much of a problem".[957] The majority's proposals would in fact "cause extra delay, cost and general inefficiency in the system—to little, if any, purpose", given the general nature of the defence disclosure requirement. The government subsequently accepted the majority's diagnosis of the "problem" and legislated for defence disclosure under the CPIA. The extent of defence disclosure has been expanded further by the Criminal Justice Act 2003.

14–078

Under CPIA s.5 following prosecution disclosure and the committal of the case to the Crown Court, the accused must present a defence statement to the court and the prosecution. This must be a written statement which includes details of any defence, issues of fact that are disputed and why, and any points of law he or she wishes to raise.[958] In addition, the defence must disclose the particulars of any alibi and a list of the names and addresses of any alibi

---

[952] C. Taylor, "What Next for Public Interest Immunity?" (2005) J. Crim. L. 75.

[953] *R v Templar* [2003] EWCA Crim 3186.

[954] pp.97–100.

[955] The Crown Court Study (RCCJ Research Study No.19 by M. Zander and P. Henderson) showed that "ambush defences" were considered by prosecution counsel to have occurred in 7% of contested cases, by the CPS in 10% and by the police in 26%. They were considered by the CPS to have caused "serious problems" in 3% of contested cases and by the police in 8%.

[956] Cm. 2263, pp.221–223.

[957] *ibid.*

[958] CPIA 1996, s.6A. For problems related to a lack of detail accompanying a defence statement, see: *R v Bryant* [2005] EWCA Crim 2079 *per* Judge L.J. at para.12.

witnesses and the details of any experts that have been consulted.[959] Amendments introduced in 2003 will ensure that the defence must notify the prosecution and the court of *any* witness it intends to call and provide their details.[960] A code of practice to govern police interviews with such witnesses is required under CPIA, s.21A.

The thrust of these requirements is to further "encourage" the cooperation of the defence in the prosecution process, but, following *Gleeson*,[961] it is fair to say that the law has been clarified. In *Gleeson*, the accused had a technical defence to the charge specified in the indictment, and waited until the end of the prosecution case before advancing a submission of no case to answer. Whilst the judge agreed that the accused had forwarded a sound defence the prosecution were given the opportunity to correct the indictment. The Court of Appeal commented that it was no longer acceptable for defence advocates to seek to take advantage of errors by deliberately delaying the identification of the error until the last moment.[962] The extent of the co-operation required here amounts to the defence positively helping the prosecution case. The uncertain scope of this decision is at least clarified by the wide-ranging requirements of defence disclosure as modified by the Criminal Justice Act 2003.[963]

Comments may be made at trial and inferences may be drawn by the tribunal of fact if the defence does not serve a statement (at all or in time[964]) or sets out inconsistent defences.[965] There can be no conviction on an adverse inference alone.[966] Where an adverse inference is allowed, the judge must warn the jury of the appropriate uses they can make of the evidence.[967]

The most significant objection to the defence disclosure provisions is that they pose a threat to the presumption of innocence.[968] However, English courts have acknowledged that there is a need for extreme caution before allowing any adverse inferences to be drawn, particularly where the allegation is that there is an inconsistency between the defence at trial and that made in an advance

---

[959] CPIA 1996, s.6D. See also: M. Zander, *Consultation on Proposals for Advance Disclosure of Defence Witness Lists and Unused Defence Expert Reports* (2002).

[960] CPIA 1996, s.6C.

[961] [2004] 1 Cr.App.R. 406; [2004] Crim. L.R. 579.

[962] See also, *Malcolm v DPP* [2007] E.W.H.C. 363.

[963] P. Wilcock and J. Bennathan, "New Disclosure Rules for 2005", (2004) N.L.J. 918.

[964] The defence statement must be served within 14 days of the primary disclosure: Criminal Procedure and Investigations Act 1996 (Defence Disclosure Time Limits) Regulations 1997: SI 1997/684.

[965] CPIA 1996, s.11. On inferences, Plotnikoff and Woolfson found that 43% of judges would initiate legal argument on adverse inferences ((2001), p.72). A tactic might have been to keep defence statements relatively vague with only sufficient information to avoid adverse inferences being drawn. However, para.35 of *Disclosure: A Protocol for the Control and Management of Unused Material in the Crown Court*, (2006) states that the defence statement "must identify the matters of fact upon which the accused takes issue with the prosecution, and the reason why, in relation to each disputed matter of fact. It must further identify any point of law (including points as to the admissibility of evidence, or abuse of process) which the accused proposes to take, and identify authorities relied on in relation to each point of law. Where an alibi defence is relied upon, the particulars given must comply with [s.6(2) CPIA 1996]. Judges will expect to see defence case statements that contain a clear and detailed exposition of the issues of fact and law in the case."

[966] CPIA 1996, s.11(10). On the potential uses for the defence statement of disclosure, see S. Thompson, "Defence Statements—Weighting the Scales or Tipping the Balance on a Submission of No Case" [1998] Crim. L.R. 802.

[967] See also *R v Burge and Pegg* [1996] 1 Cr.App.R. 163.

[968] See R. Leng, "Losing Sight of the Defendant" [1995] Crim. L.R. 704.

statement.[969] One problem was that the earlier statement may not have been that of the accused but of the defence solicitors. This has been dealt with by CPIA, s.6E[970] which deems that a statement made by a solicitor purportedly on behalf of the accused will be deemed to on his or her behalf unless proved to the contrary.[971]

(f) The continuing duty on the prosecution

The prosecution must ensure that the question of disclosure remains under continuous review.[972] Therefore, if the prosecution is of the opinion that it has any material which might undermine the prosecution case or might be reasonably expected to assist the accused's defence it must disclose it as soon as is practicable. Limitations in respect of PII and statutorily protected material apply here as with primary disclosure.[973] This replaces the previous position whereby in response to defence disclosure the prosecution had to make secondary disclosure. This requirement, under CPIA, s.7, has not been abolished but it is difficult to see what relevance it has now that there is a continuous duty to disclose.

14–079

(g) Third party material[974]

Where the material, which might undermine the prosecution case or assist the defence, is in the possession of a third party (e.g. social services or an education department) special problems arise.[975] If the material has been used by the police in the investigation, it will be held by the prosecution and the usual rules of disclosure will apply. The prosecutor is under an obligation to inform relevant agencies,[976] and to make efforts to secure the information, especially if it is likely to undermine the prosecution case or assist the defence.

14–080

If material is not within the prosecution possession but the defence is aware of its existence and seeks to obtain it, a witness summons under the Criminal Procedure Attendance of Witnesses Act 1965, ss.2–4 must be sought.[977] The witness summons procedure has been examined by the courts and in *H(L)*[978] the very limited purpose of s.2 and s.97 was noted to be to produce documents "likely to be material evidence".[979] An application must be made in writing

---

[969] *R v Wheeler* [2001 Cr.App.R. 10: See also *R v Tibbs* [2000] 2 Cr.App.R. 309.

[970] As inserted by CJA 2003, s.36.

[971] See *R (Sullivan) v Crown Court at Maidstone* [2002] 1 W.L.R. 2747 in which a local practice direction requiring that all defence statements should be signed by the accused before being passed to the prosecution and the judge was declared unlawful.

[972] CPIA 1996, s.7A. See *Attorney General's Guidelines* (2005) paras 17–19.

[973] s.7(5). See also Regulation of Investigatory Powers Act 2000, s.17.

[974] For a reflection on the problems associated with third party disclosure see the judgment of Longmore L.J. in *R v Alibhai* [2004] EWCA Crim 681. See also *Disclosure: A Protocol for the Control and Management of Unused Material in the Crown Court* (2006) paras 53–63.

[975] See also D. A. H. Rodwell, "Applications for Third Party Material Where PII is Likely to be Claimed" [1998] Crim. L.R. 332.

[976] See *Attorney General's Guidelines* (2005) para.47 and see Home Office, *Giving Evidence or Information About Suspected Crimes: Guidance for Departments and Investigations* (Home Office, 1997).

[977] Magistrates' Courts Act 1980, s.97, and see Criminal Procedure Investigations Act 1996, s.66. See also the guidance in *Attorney-General's Guidelines* (2005), paras 51–54.

[978] [1997] 1 Cr.App.R. 176 (Reading Crown Court, Sedley J.).

[979] If the defence insist on calling the witness and the department/agency resists disclosure costs may be awarded against the defence.

specifying why the material is sought and why it is believed to be material evidence. There must be a supporting affidavit.[980] The court, in considering whether to compel the third party to disclose the material will balance the potential damage to confidentiality against the potential benefit to the defendant.[981] Research has found that there are few applications for disclosure of material from agencies but they can be onerous and costly.[982] Mackie and Burrows report that most requests were from social services and education departments. The defence application for third party disclosure must not be a fishing expedition and must state why a summons is required. The obligation on third parties is much less than that on the prosecution.[983]

(h) The Court of Appeal and disclosure

14–081   Challenges to the PII procedure and decisions not to disclose material to the defence are often raised in appeals to the Court of Appeal (Criminal Division). Its obligation is to ensure that the trial was fair and that the conviction is safe. With questions of disclosure this means that the Court of Appeal will be obliged to consider whether the trial judge would have been likely to order disclosure and whether the reasonable jury would have been likely to come to a different conclusion on the evidence disclosed.[984] The European Court has accepted that the Court of Appeal is capable, in such cases, of rectifying errors of disclosure at trial by undertaking its own review of the disputed material.[985] If no opportunity for consideration of the material at the appeal is possible, a breach of Art.6 would occur.[986]

(i) Summary trials

14–082   The prosecution duty of primary disclosure is applicable whenever the accused pleads not guilty. Once the primary disclosure has been complied with, the accused may voluntarily provide a defence statement. The statute allows for adverse comment and inferences to be drawn as in the trial on indictment.

The *Attorney-General's Guidelines* make it clear that the prosecutor should, in addition to complying with the obligations under the CPIA 1996, provide to the defence all evidence upon which the Crown proposes to rely in a summary trial. "Such provisions should allow the accused or their legal advisers sufficient time properly to consider the evidence before it is called".[987]

PII applies in the magistrates' court.[988] If the court orders that the material is to be withheld the accused may apply for a review of that ruling. One practical

---

[980] For comment on the procedural rules see D. Corker, "Third Party Disclosure" (1999) 149 N.L.J. 1006 at 1063. The article reviews tactical approaches to defence disclosure.

[981] Under para.3.6 of the Criminal Procedure Investigations Act 1996 Code of Practice, the investigator should ask the third party to retain the material and inform the prosecutor of its existence. Material viewed by the officer even though not obtained by him or her must be recorded under para.4.4 of the Code of Practice; Owens (2001), p.141.

[982] Mackie and Burrows *A Study of Requests for Disclosure of Evidence to Third Parties in Contested Trials* (HORS 134, 2000).

[983] *R v Brushett* [2001] Crim. L.R. 471.

[984] *R v Botmeh* [2002] Crim. L.R. 209.

[985] *Edwards v UK* (1992) 15 E.H.R.R. 417.

[986] See *Rowe and Davis v UK* (2000) 30 E.H.R.R. 1; *IJL, GMR v UK* [2001] Crim. L.R. 133.

[987] *Attorney-General's Guidelines* (2005) para.57.

[988] s.14.

difficulty of the PII system in the magistrates' court arises because the applications are made *ex parte* and are heard by the bench that will have to adjudicate the issues.[989]

The ECtHR has recognised the importance of disclosure in guaranteeing a fair trial even at the summary trial level.[990] Plotnikoff and Woolfson found that primary disclosure occurred in around two-thirds of summary trials, but that defence statements were very rarely served.[991] In the vast majority of cases primary disclosure was made more than two weeks before trial.[992]

(j) Critical review[993]

The CPIA 1996 has been subjected to close critical examination, and it has been **14–083** claimed that the Act is so defective and leaves so much power in the hands of the police that it presents a real risk of future miscarriages of justice.[994] There have been many calls for independent supervision.[995] Ede[996] describes the results of national CPS surveys in which police completion of disclosure schedules was identified as inadequate, unreliable and incomplete. The pattern of failure is described as "horrifying". The profession's own ad hoc surveys found over 200 separate examples of non-disclosure. Not only is the pattern of unreliable police scheduling, but the lack of confidence in the system is startling. 70 per cent of those surveyed reported that "the disclosure provisions of the Criminal Procedure Investigations Act 1996 are unworkable in the interests of justice".[997] The examples of non-disclosure included all varieties of material including statements by complainants that directly contradicted their earlier statement. The survey also revealed that there was a lack of knowledge on the part of disclosure officers as to what type of material ought to be disclosed as listed and listed on the schedule.[998]

In short, the disclosure regime places too much power in the hands of the police officer who: is potentially biased, will be likely to construct a case against the accused, and has inadequate knowledge of what is likely to be useful for the

---

[989] See *R v South Worcester JJ., Ex p. Lilley* [1995] 1 W.L.R. 1595; *R v Stipendiary Magistrate for Norfolk* (1997) 161 J.P. 773: *R (on the application of DPP) v Acton Youth Court* [2001] 1 W.L.R. 1828. Section 14 of the Criminal Procedure Investigations Act 1996 does not require the bench to review the PII applications; *cf.* the Crown Court procedure. See also Plotnikoff and Woolfson (2001), p.84.

[990] *Foucher v France* (1998) 25 E.H.R.R. 234.

[991] Plotnikoff and Woolfson (2001) p.65.

[992] *ibid.*

[993] For criticism of the practical operation of the Criminal Procedure Investigations Act 1996 see the special issue of Med. Sci. Law (2000), Vol.40; D. Ormerod, "Improving the Disclosure Regime" (2003) 7 E. & P. 102; For a critique of the CJA reforms see Redmayne "Criminal Justice Act 2003: Disclosure and Its Discontents" [2004] Crim. L.R. 440.

[994] See C. Taylor, "Advance Disclosure: Reflections on the Criminal Procedure Investigations Act 1996" (2001) 40 Howard J.C.J. 114.

[995] S. Sharpe (1999) J. Crim. Law 67; [1999] Crim. L.R. 273: in advance of the 2003 reforms, suggested an independent commissioner with the power to review cases and monitor the accuracy of disclosure by the police.

[996] R. Ede, "The CPIA in Practice—The Legal Profession's Experience" (2000) 40 Med. Sci. Law 97.

[997] *ibid.* at 98.

[998] See for graphic examples of failings in disclosure the catalogue in R. Ede (2000), pp.99–101.

defence if disclosed.[999] It is also argued that the some of these problems form part of the culture of the police service[1000] and as such are unlikely to be rectified by relatively minor modifications in the law. Further deficiencies include the problem that schedules are not scrutinised with sufficient care by the CPS and the defence ends up with only a partial disclosure. Miscarriages of justice are inevitable. Even the DPP is recorded as noting that there are dangers of innocent people being convicted.[1001]

In an empirical study of the operation of the 1996 Act, and the *Attorney General's Guidelines*, Plotnikoff and Woolfson examined 193 prosecutor files and interviewed all those involved in the criminal justice agencies.

As far as the police operation was concerned, they found that the officer in charge of the investigation was very likely to be the disclosure officer with a member of the investigative team performing the task in serious cases. Disturbingly in 21 per cent of police forces, responsibility for "schedule completion" did not lie with the officer in charge nor, in many cases, with any single individual.[1002] Barristers, the CPS, defence solicitors and justices' clerks complained of police failure to include material on an unused material schedule.[1003] The authors also found that there were many instances of undated schedules (37 per cent); that descriptions of items on schedules were "poor" in 73 per cent of cases; that good reasons for sensitivity were given in only 43 per cent of cases; only 14 per cent of forces had special provisions to deal with sensitive material; separate schedules were prepared for multiple defendants cases in only 9 per cent of such cases; 43 per cent of disclosure officers thought better training was needed; and 28 per cent thought better guidance on categorisation of unused material was needed.[1004]

Without doubt there is no simple solution to the problems associated with disclosure and Redmayne warns against looking back to the common law position as though it represented the halcyon days.[1005] Disclosure has always caused problems and by its very nature, will continue to do so. However, the problems can be alleviated to an extent through training and education which seeks to address the cultural problems of prosecution reluctance to disclose, and the structural problems involved in what the legislative regime demands. "The statutory regime requires the culturally adversarial police to fulfil an effectively inquisitorial function; prosecutors to view material from a defence perspective; the defence to act in the interests of the administration of the justice system rather

---

[999] See C. Taylor (2001) Howard Jnl. 114; J. Epp (2000) E. & P. 188. Plotnikoff and Woolfson found that 82% of judges, 38% of CPS respondents, 30% of senior police officers, and 27% of disclosure officers felt that it was unrealistic to expect police officers to identify undermining material (p.121). Eighty-two per cent of judges had criticised officers on their disclosure role (p.73). Significant numbers of cases were reported as stayed for abuse of process as a result of disclosure failings. See generally Ch.12.

[1000] H. Quirk, "The significance of culture in criminal procedure reform: why the revised disclosure regime cannot work" (2006) E. & P. 42.

[1001] (2000) 40 Med. Sci. Law at 101. See, e.g. *R v Higgins* [2002] EWCA Crim 336 (failure to disclose inconsistent identification statements). In 2000 the Criminal Cases Review Commission ranked non-disclosure as the third most common reason for referral of cases (*Annual Report 1999–2000*). Disclosure was again referred to in the 2004 Report (*Annual Report 2003–2004*). Its absence in 2006 represents a welcome change.

[1002] Plotnikoff and Woolfson (2001), p.20.

[1003] *ibid.* p.26.

[1004] See generally Plotnikoff and Woolfson (2001), Ch.3.

[1005] Redmayne, [2004] Crim. L.R. 441 at 460.

than of their clients; and defendants to cooperate with proceedings against themselves".[1006]

I. A PRE-TRIAL REVIEW

As in the civil process there have been a number of reforms in recent years designed to aid the management of a trial before the hearing itself begins.[1007] In the Crown Court the Criminal Procedure and Investigations Act 1996 ss.39 to 43 give statutory form to the various procedures that have been developed.

14–084

Plea and Case Management Hearings in the Crown Court[1008] apply to all cases (other than serious fraud). At a plea and case management hearing (PCMH), pleas are taken, and in contested cases the prosecution and defence are expected to assist the court in identifying the key issues. The advocate briefed in the case should appear in the PCMH whenever practicable. Before the PCMH, where the defendant intends to plead guilty to all or part of the indictment, the defence must notify the probation service, the prosecution and the court as soon as this is known. This will enable the defendant to be sentenced at the PCMH whenever possible. In contested cases, prosecution and defence are expected to inform the court of a series of matters including the number of witnesses and the order in which they will be called, admitted facts, exhibits and schedules, expert evidence being called, points of law and evidence expected to arise, the estimated length of the trial, witness and advocate availability. The judge can make such orders as lie within his power as appear to be necessary to secure the proper and efficient trial of the case. A standard questionnaire should be completed by both parties and given to the judge to enable him to effectively set the timetable and issue appropriate directions. These hearings are typically short. The hearing should take place within seven weeks of the committal for trial, and within 14 weeks of the accused being sent for trial under the Crime and Disorder Act 1998, s.51 if the accused is in custody, and within 17 weeks if on bail.[1009] The CIPA 1996 allows judges to make binding rulings at the PCMH or any other preliminary hearing. The rulings may follow an application or be of the judge's own motion, and may relate to any question as to admissibility or any question of law arising.[1010] The ruling has binding effect until the case is disposed of—by a jury verdict, or the case being dropped. The judge may discharge or vary the ruling if it is in the interests of justice to do so.

1. PREPARATORY HEARINGS

Preparatory hearings were initially available only in serious fraud cases, but now judges have the power to make binding rulings in all cases on any question as to

14–085

[1006] H. Quirk, (2006) 10 E. & P. 42.
[1007] The importance of active case management has been emphasised by the Court of Appeal: *R v Jisl* (2004) *The Times*, April 19, 2004.
[1008] *Consolidated Criminal Practice Direction* IV.41.8.
[1009] *Consolidated Criminal Practice Direction* IV.41.5 and IV.41.6.
[1010] Criminal Procedure and Investigations Act 1996, s.40.

the admissibility of evidence and any other question of law, at any point after the
a case is sent for trial in the Crown Court.

These powers were introduced by the CPIA 1996.[1011] The procedures follow
very closely those of the fraud trial scheme on which they were based.[1012] A
preparatory hearing is an opportunity to resolve legal issues before a jury is
sworn. An application may be made by either party, or the court may, of its own
motion, initiate one. The trial judge may make an order for a preparatory hearing
at any time prior to the jury being sworn. This type of hearing should be held
where the judge believes that the indictment reveals "a case of such complexity
or a case whose trial is likely to be of such length that substantial benefits are
likely to accrue".[1013]

The purpose of the hearing is to identify material issues for the jury,[1014] assist
the jury to understand, expedite proceedings, and help the judge manage the trial.
The judge may order the prosecution to prepare its evidence and any explanatory
material in such form as appears to the judge likely to aid comprehension by the
jury. The judge may also order the prosecution to provide the defence with a case
statement of principal facts, witnesses, etc., and may order the defence to disclose
the principal issues of its case. Failure to comply with the disclosure orders will
result in adverse inferences being capable of being drawn, as in a case where the
defence depart from the disclosure at trial. This is subject to the judge giving
leave to draw such inferences.[1015] The judge will make rulings on points of law
and on the admissibility of evidence.[1016] The pre-trial rulings made *must* be those
within the purposes of the preparatory hearing—identifying material issues for
the jury, assisting them to understand the issues, expediting proceedings before
them, and helping the judge to manage the trial. Reporting restrictions apply to
preparatory hearings.[1017]

The Act also introduced the opportunity to appeal from the judge's ruling at
the preparatory hearing[1018] and this route to securing the opinion of the appellate
courts has proved particularly useful in resolving difficult questions of law before
the trial commences.[1019]

There is also a system of pre-trial hearings in the magistrates' courts. Where
the defendant is charged with an either way offence, pleads not guilty and
consents to a hearing in the magistrates' court, a date for a pre-trial review is set
if it is thought to be necessary. As above, such pre-trial reviews are aimed at
ensuring the parties are ready for the trial, and magistrates can make appropriate
directions. Under the Courts Act 2003, s.45 binding rulings can be made, and the
court may decide questions as to issues of admissibility or other questions of
law.[1020]

[1011] ss.28–38. See R. Leng, and R. Taylor, *Blackstone's Guide to the CPIA 1996* (1996), Ch.3.
[1012] See Criminal Procedure and Investigations Act 1996 (Preparatory Hearings) Rules 1997 (SI
1997/1052).
[1013] Criminal Procedure Investigations Act 1996, s.29(1).
[1014] *ibid.* s.29(1).
[1015] *ibid.* s.34(2), (3), (4).
[1016] *ibid.* s.31(2).
[1017] *ibid.* s.37, names, addresses, etc., can be published. The court may lift restrictions: s.37(3).
[1018] ss.35–36.
[1019] See, e.g. *R v Z* [2000] 2 A.C. 483; see also *R v Claydon* [2004] 1 W.L.R. 1575, where the CA
accepted that the judge had the power to determine at a preparatory hearing questions of
excluding evidence under s.78 of PACE.
[1020] Magistrates' Courts Act 1980, s.8A as inserted by the Courts Act 2003, Sch.3.

J. OBTAINING LEGAL ADVICE AND REPRESENTATION[1021]

Legal advice and professional assistance may be required by defendants at two **14–086** quite different stages. They will initially have to deal with the police and face interrogation by them, the results of which are likely to have a considerable influence on their case at trial. They may wish to be advised how to conduct themselves to the best advantage at this stage of the procedure, particularly in light of the significance of the answers they provide or the silence they adopt. As has been noted above, the interview stage of the pre-trial criminal process is taking on an increasing significance in the outcome of cases. If charged, the accused will want assistance in the preparation and presentation of his or her case at and before the trial. The extent to which lawyers are involved in these two distinct situations is different. Almost all those charged with serious offences are represented at trial, many fewer are "represented" during interrogation at the police station.

The importance of access to effective legal representation as a human right cannot be ignored.[1022] Article 6(3)(b) of the ECHR provides that a person charged with a criminal offence must be provided with "adequate time and facilities for the preparation of his defence". In addition, Art.6(3)(c) provides that everyone charged with a criminal offence has the right to "defend himself in person or through legal assistance of his own choosing or, if he has not sufficient means to pay for legal assistance, to be given it free when the interests of justice so require". The legal representation must be effective, and as such the state will be obliged to intervene in the event of the legal service provided to an accused being manifestly unsatisfactory. The Auld Report also emphasised that it was "critical" to the provision of a fair trial that there existed a scheme for just and efficient working of defence lawyers.[1023]

In practical terms what the ECHR guarantees mean is that the representative must be appointed early enough to be able to deal effectively with the case.[1024] In general, the accused will be able to select his own representative, but this is not an unlimited right,[1025] and the state may select an appropriate counsel for him or her irrespective of his wishes, where that is relevant and there are sufficient grounds for doing so.[1026] In some circumstances the defendants' right to represent himself or his desire not to be represented can be overridden and appropriate counsel appointed to act on his behalf.[1027] Once selected, the lawyer does not have to supply unlimited services to the accused; it is legitimate to have regard to the budgets imposed on him or her by the state funding system.[1028]

The other important aspect of the ECHR and the European Court's case law in this area is that it recognises the need for the accused to be offered *free* legal

---

[1021] *Archbold* (2007) Ch.6; *Blackstone's Criminal Practice* (2007) D.29; See www.legalservices.gov.uk.

[1022] See Ashworth, "Legal Aid, Human Rights and Criminal Justice" in Young and Wall (eds) (1996).

[1023] Ch.10, pp.400–404.

[1024] *X and Y v Austria* (1978) D.R. 160.

[1025] See *R v Mills* [1997] 2 Cr.App.R. 206; *Goddi v Italy* (1984) 6 E.H.R.R. 457.

[1026] See *Croissant v Germany* (1992) 16 E.H.R.R. 135, para.129.

[1027] *Croissant; Imbroscia v Switzerland* (1994) 17 E.H.R.R. 441.

[1028] See *M v UK* (1984) 36 D.R. 155. See also *R v Oates* [2002] 1 W.L.R. 2833, holding that Art.6(3) does not require legal aid to allow the appellant to renew her appeal against conviction.

assistance if it is in the interests of justice to do so.[1029] There is not an unfettered right to "legal aid", but in determining whether a case is one in which it is in the interests of justice to require assistance, the European Court has adopted a strict stance.[1030]

1. Legal Advice at the Police Station

14–087   As we have seen, PACE strengthens the right of those being interviewed by the police to have access to legal advice, and the courts have emphasised the importance of these rights in excluding evidence of confessions obtained in breach of them.

The duty solicitor advice scheme can be used for the purpose of securing the services of a solicitor at the police station.[1031] The duty solicitor must be accredited with the Criminal Defence Service. The suspect can of course rely on his or her own private legal adviser. If the suspect selects his own private representative, it will be permissible for advice to be provided at the station by a solicitor, or a probationary representative.

In theory, the accused has the opportunity, the means and the motive to ensure that he or she is properly advised on the most advantageous way to conduct him or herself at the police station. In practice, only a minority of accused persons receive that advice.

2. Advice and Representation after Charge

14–088   The Legal Aid scheme adopted in 1988 was severely criticised. In short, the means test for eligibility rendered the scheme unfair and it was in general an inefficient scheme prone to delay and abuse.[1032] In addition, the Legal Aid bill had spiralled. In 1992–93 the cost was £507 million and in 1997–98 that had grown to £733 million. In the Crown Court, spending went from £221 million in 1992–93 to £349 million in 1997–98.[1033] The framework under which the fees were paid was outdated and inflexible with inappropriately financed incentives. These encouraged delay and adjournments.[1034] The costs were extremely high in the Crown Court, with 94 per cent of defendants making no contribution.[1035] The system of means testing for contributions cost almost as much to administer as it recouped. The public had lost confidence in the system with so much being spent on some very high cost cases. The government sought to introduce a

---

[1029] *Pakelli v Germany* (1984) 6 E.H.R.R. 31.

[1030] See *Granger v UK* (1990) 21 E.H.R.R. 469; *Benham v UK* (1996) 22 E.H.R.R. 293.

[1031] See above. This is free of charge irrespective of the suspect's means.

[1032] See the discussion above in Ch.10. See also T. Goriely, "The Development of Criminal Legal Aid in England and Wales" in Young and Wall (eds) (1996).

[1033] See LCD, *Modernising Justice: the Government's Plans for Reforming Legal Services and the Courts*, (1998) Cm. 4155, para.6.6. On the statistics provided, see A. Tunkel (1997) 147 N.L.J. 1020, see also LCD, *Striking the Balance* (1996).

[1034] *Modernising Justice*, para.6.7.

[1035] *ibid*.

system that was better focused on quality and value for money,[1036] and which would keep to a minimum delay.[1037]

As a result of these problems substantial reforms were implemented. The provision of public funding for criminal cases is now dealt with by the Access to Justice Act 1999 (AJA 1999). Under this Act the Criminal Defence Service (CDS) was established in 2001 (functioning under the Legal Services Commission (LSC)). The purpose of the CDS is defined in AJA 1999, s.12(1) as "securing that individuals involved in criminal investigations or criminal proceedings have access to such advice, assistance and representation as the interests of justice require". The CDS complies with this duty by contracting solicitors in private practice to carry out publicly funded criminal defence work. In addition, the LSC has also piloted its own Public Defender Service with the aim of providing an additional option to enable the provision of quality criminal defence services in areas where existing provision is low or of a poor standard.

(a) Advice and assistance

Under the Criminal Defence Service (General) (No.2) Regulations 2001[1038] the **14–089** LSC shall fund advice and assistance, including advocacy assistance, to any individual who is the subject of a criminal investigation or is the subject of legal proceedings. Irrespective of the means of the accused, Regulation 5 sets out the occasions when advice and assistance (other than by way of legal representation) may be granted, and this includes advice to an individual held in custody following arrest and all advocacy assistance before a magistrates' court or Crown Court. Advice and assistance covers general help from a solicitor including giving general advice, writing letters, negotiating, getting a barrister's opinion and preparing a written case.[1039] *Advocacy Assistance* covers the cost of a solicitor preparing a case and initial representation in certain proceedings in both the magistrates' court and the Crown Court.

(b) Representation

Representation[1040] covers the cost of a solicitor or barrister to prepare and **14–090** represent the accused in any criminal proceedings.[1041] Representation can also cover advice on appeal against a verdict or sentence of the magistrates' court or the Crown Court (or a decision of the Court of Appeal) and preparing the notice of appeal itself. Representation is not available to bring a private prosecution.

To obtain legal representation a defendant must make an application to the court. In the magistrates' court the application may be made orally or in writing to the justices' clerk and in the Crown Court to the Court or the court manager. If the application is turned down the applicant must be provided with reasons and the details of the appeal process.[1042] In order to find greater consistency in the

---

[1036] *ibid.* para.6.11.
[1037] See also the recommendations in Narey (1997), Ch.4, noting that 50% of adjournments were due to legal aid issues.
[1038] Criminal Defence Service (General) (No.2) Regulations 2001 (SI 2001/1437).
[1039] See Access to Justice Act 1999, s.13. The full definition is provided in Criminal Defence Service (General) (No.2) Regulations 2001 (SI 2001/1437), r.4.
[1040] Access to Justice Act 1999, s.14.
[1041] See generally the Criminal Defence Service (General) (No.2) Regulations 2001 (SI 2001/1437).
[1042] Criminal Defence Service (Representation Order Appeals) Regulations 2001.

grant or refusal of legal representation the Criminal Defence Service Act 2006 has taken the decision away from courts and placed it in the hands of the LSC. Decision making will still rest with the courts in practice though the LSC will lay down procedures to be followed.[1043] This Act has also re-introduced a means test in relation to an application for representation, supplementing the existing merits test.

The merits test means that a representation order is made by the court if the court feels that it is in the "interests of justice" that the accused should be represented.[1044] The interests of justice require the court to take into account: (a) whether the accused would be at risk of losing his liberty, or livelihood or suffering serious damage to his reputation[1045]; (b) whether the case will involve consideration of a substantial question of law; (c) whether the individual may be unable to understand the proceedings or to state his own case[1046]; (d) whether the case will involve tracing, interviewing, or expert cross-examination of witnesses and whether it is in the interests of another person that the accused be represented.[1047]

The Criminal Defence Service Act 2006 re-introduces the means test to ensure that those who can pay for their own legal representation do so. Financial eligibility for representation is calculated on the basis that certain individuals are automatically eligible—those on job seeker's allowance, income support, those under 16, or under 18 but in full time education etc.—and for others the calculation turns on their income and capital. The "simple" test stipulates that if an individual's gross annual income is below £11,590 they qualify for assistance. Those earning above £20,740 do not qualify. Those in between are subject to the "full" means test whereby ultimately, if the applicant's annual disposable income is less than £3,156 they will qualify for assistance. As yet this only applies to representation in the magistrates' court though the aim is that the scheme will be applied to representation in the Crown Court later in 2007.

The degree of choice of legal representation that should be available for the accused has been a controversial issue.[1048] The ECHR, as noted above, supports the right to choose, but does not give an unfettered right. The CDS scheme allows for the accused to choose from the accredited representatives, but there is a strong expectation of continued representation so that one solicitor will follow the case from start to finish. In particular, there is a desire to prevent the tactic of the accused dismissing his legal team on the eve of the trial thereby securing a further delay in the proceedings.[1049] It is necessary to strike the balance between

---

[1043] See in particular A. Wilcox and R. Young, *Understanding the Interests of Justice* (2006).

[1044] Access to Justice Act 1999, Sch.3, para.5.

[1045] See under previous law, *R v Liverpool City Magistrates Court, Ex p. McGhee* [1993] Crim. L.R. 609 (community service order is not a deprivation of liberty); and see *R v Highgate JJ., Ex p. Lewis* [1977] Crim. L.R. 611; *R. Chester Magistrates, Ex p. Ball* (1999) 163 J.P. 757 (the court failed to take reputation into account).

[1046] *R (Matara) v Brent Magistrates' Court* (2005) 169 J.P. 576. The presence of an interpreter during the proceedings did not answer the point that the claimant did not understand what was said to him at the point of arrest. The decision to refuse legal representation was quashed.

[1047] Access to Justice Act 1999, Sch.3, para.5(2). See also *R v Scunthorpe Justices, Ex p. S, The Times*, March 5, 1998 (16-year-old not able to conduct cross-examination of the police officer).

[1048] See the LCD Paper, *CDS: Choice of Representation* (2000) and J. Epp and D. O'Brien, (2000) 150 N.L.J. 1664.

[1049] *R v Smith (Henry Paul)* [2006] EWCA Crim 2307; See further the LCD Consultation Paper, *Establishing a Salaried Defence Service and Draft Code of Conduct for Salaried Defenders Employed by the LSC* (2000) and Access to Justice Act 1999, s.15(2).

the defendant's right to choose and to feel confident in the legal representation he or she receives and the need to ensure efficiency in the system.

(c) Recovery of defence costs orders (RDCOs)[1050]

The Crown Court may order that costs are recovered from a defendant who has **14–091** been granted representation. The court will assess whether it is reasonable to impose such an order having regard to all the circumstances including the defendant's means.[1051] An RDCO can be made for the full amount of the costs incurred in representing the accused, but is not available if the accused has only appeared in the magistrates' court, is committed for sentence, is appealing to the Crown Court against sentence, or, other than in exceptional circumstances, has been acquitted. The RDCO is not to be regarded as part of the sentence and is not dependent on a conviction.

(d) The Public Defence Service

The LCD in its Consultation Paper[1052] developed the idea that was introduced in **14–092** the White Paper *Modernising Justice*, in which the government claimed that properly funded salaried defenders can be more cost-effective and provide a better service than lawyers in private practice.[1053] It was felt that a system with Public Defenders would be cheaper, easier to monitor, more flexible and because it lacked a profit motive would be more focused on securing justice. Criticisms of the public defenders scheme are that it lacks independence from the government and that it is perceived as such. There is also the danger that it will be overloaded with work and that it will fail to secure high quality staff.[1054] Furthermore, it could lead to less choice for the accused, by reducing access to the private sector, and this could reduce overall quality through lost competition. The service exists alongside the private providers, reflecting the government's aim to optimise the balance between the public and private sectors. However, its performance to date has been mixed.[1055] In an extensive survey carried out by Bridges *et al.*,[1056] it was established that Public Defender Offices were "not performing less well in their police station work than private practice and in some

---

[1050] Defence costs are recovered under the RDCO scheme set up under s.17 of the Access to Justice Act 1999. See also the CDS (Recovery of Defence Costs Orders) Regulations Order 2001 (SI 2001/856 and the CDS (Recovery of Defence Costs Orders) (Amendment) Regulations 2002 (SI 2002/713) as amended by SI 2005/2783.

[1051] *ibid.* rr.11 and 12.

[1052] See further the LCD Consultation Paper, *Establishing a Salaried Defence Service and Draft Code of Conduct for Salaried Defenders Employed by the LSC* (2000); see also comment at (2000) 150 N.L.J. 923.

[1053] The Government reviewed schemes in USA, Canada, Australia and concluded that a mixed scheme with public defenders and private representatives available was the most effective solution. The Canadian research quoted refers to the high quality of the work provided with no effect on the outcomes of cases and the respect and confidence of the profession and the judiciary. See C. Frazer (2000) 150 N.L.J. 670 casting doubt on the claims about the Canadian experience.

[1054] The difficulty of attracting and retaining high quality practioners into low paid legal aid work has been a long standing one: R. Smith, "Resolving the Legal Aid Crisis" (1991) Law Soc. Gaz. 27.

[1055] See the Report available at: *www.legalservices.gov.uk/criminal/pds/evaluation.asp*.

[1056] L. Bridges, E. Cape, P. Fenn, A. Mitchell, R. Moorhead and A. Sherr, *Evaluation of the Public Defender Service in England and Wales* (2006), available at: *www.legalservices.gov.uk;* See also, E. Cape, "The Rise (and fall?) of a Criminal Defence Profession" [2004] Crim. L.R. 401.

respects better".[1057] Furthermore, "although there were some significant differences in performance between the [Public Defender Offices] and private practice
in the Crown Court, again with [Public Defender Offices] for the most part
performing better, in general such differences were greater at the investigation
and magistrates' court stages of cases".[1058] Considering the perceptions of other
criminal justice professionals the overwhelming conclusion was that the Public
Defender Office performs at a similar level of quality and in a similar way to
private practice, but where there was a perceived difference (albeit from a small
minority) it was that the Public Defender was poorer.[1059] In conclusion, the
research team could "envisage a wider role for the [Public Defence Service] as
an essential guarantor of quality standards, minimum costs and client choice of
representative in a more managed market for such services".[1060]

K. EVALUATIONS

14–093   As a conclusion to this chapter it is valuable to place some of the detailed
analysis of the complex legal structure in a broader theoretical context.

1. THEORETICAL APPROACHES

14–094   Major official reviews in the area of criminal procedure were undertaken by the
Royal Commission on Criminal Procedure[1061] (RCCP), the Royal Commission
on Criminal Justice[1062] (RCCJ) and the Auld Review. The RCCP's terms of
reference were to examine whether changes were needed in England and Wales,
in:

> "(i) the powers and duties of the police in respect of the investigation of
> criminal offences and the right and duties of suspects and accused persons,
> including the means by which these are secured;
>   (ii) the process of and responsibility for the prosecution of criminal
> offences; and
>   (iii) such other features of criminal procedure and evidence as relate to
> the above".

The RCCJ's terms of reference were:

[1057] *ibid.* p.180.
[1058] *ibid.* p.182.
[1059] *ibid.* p.263.
[1060] *ibid.* p.306.
[1061] *The Investigation and Prosecution of Criminal Offences in England and Wales: The Law and Procedure* (Cmnd. 8092–1, 1981). Twelve Research Studies were commissioned.
[1062] Report (Cm. 2263, 1993). The extensive literature on the RCCJ includes the following: M.McConville and L.Bridges (eds), *Criminal Justice in Crisis* (1994); S. Field and P. Thomas (eds), "Justice and Efficiency? The Royal Commission on Criminal Justice" (1994) 21 J.L.S. 1–164 (special issue); Symposium [1993] Crim. L.R. 808 *et seq.*; L. Bridges and M. McConville (1994) 57 M.L.R. 75; M. Zander, *ibid.* p.264; reply by Bridges and McConville, *ibid.* p.267; R. Young and A. Sanders (1994) 14 O.J.L.S. 435.

"to examine the effectiveness of the criminal justice system in England and Wales in securing the conviction of those guilty of criminal offences and the acquittal of those who are innocent, having regard to the efficient use of resources"

and in particular to consider whether changes were needed in eight specific areas.[1063]

The Auld Review was established to report on the

"practices and procedures of, and the rules of evidence applied by, the criminal courts at every level, with a view to ensuring that they deliver justice fairly, by streamlining all their processes, increasing their efficiency and strengthening the effectiveness of their relationships with others across the whole of the criminal justice system, and having regard to the interests of all parties including victims and witnesses, thereby promoting public confidence in the rule of law."[1064]

As we have seen, many features of pre-trial criminal procedure and practice flow from the recommendations of these bodies although, often significantly, modified by the government. The RCCP Report led to the Police and Criminal Evidence Act 1984 and the Prosecution of Offences Act 1985. The RCCJ Report led to changes introduced by the Criminal Justice and Public Order Act 1994, the Criminal Appeal Act 1995 and the Criminal Procedure and Investigations Act 1996. The Auld Report has led to the enourmous scope of materials covered in the Criminal Justice Act 2003. At the same time many changes have been introduced simply as a matter of government policy. The approach of adopting reform following reviews provides the opportunity for fundamental theoretical issues to be addressed in a way that altering criminal procedure as a basic matter of government policy does not. Whether the opportunity is seized is a separate matter.

The reform of criminal procedure is often explained in terms of striking a "balance", although this concept of balancing is used without adequate elaboration.

(a) The "fundamental balance" in the criminal process

In formulating its recommendations—in respect of the matters within its terms of reference—the RCCP was required to have regard "both to the interests of the community in bringing offenders to justice and to the rights and liberties of persons suspected of crime", and to take into account the "need for the efficient and economical use of resources". **14–095**

The RCCP regarded the task of reviewing the criminal process with what it termed the "fundamental balance" between the interests of the community, and the rights and liberties of individual citizens as the "central challenge" which

---

[1063] (i) the conduct and supervision of police investigations; (ii) the role of the prosecutor and the disclosure of material to the defence; (iii) the role of experts; (iv) the arrangements for the defence of accused persons, access to legal advice and expert evidence; (v) the "right to silence"; (vi) the powers of the court in directing proceedings and the court's duty in considering evidence; (vii) the role of the Court of Appeal; and (viii) arrangements for considering and investigating allegations of miscarriages of justice.

[1064] Report, (2001), para.1.

faced it.[1065] Previous official reports on aspects of criminal justice[1066] had made no, or only passing, reference to the concept, although the debate that followed the Eleventh Report of the Criminal Law Revision Committee had revealed the main schools of thought on the nature, and role of, a possible balance in pre-trial criminal procedure. The most controversial of the recommendations in the Eleventh Report involved the restriction of the suspect's right of silence when interrogated by the police. The supporters of the change took a utilitarian approach: "the law should be such as will secure as far as possible that the result of the trial is the right one".[1067] The many improvements in criminal law, procedure and trial over the previous century justified the removal of safeguards that appeared to unduly favour the defence. Leading opponents took a libertarian stance, and argued that:

> " ... in reality the right of silence formed a vital issue in the whole constitutional relationship in a free society between the individual and the state. ... Each step in the criminal process, ... including the right of silence, must be judged not only as a means to the goal of reaching a reliable verdict, but also, and equally important, for its coherence with a liberal understanding of how free persons, including suspects in the police station, at all stages ought to be treated."[1068]

A third, distinct, approach was to regard some, although not necessarily all, of the individual's rights in pre-trial procedure as negotiable, provided that appropriate checks and safeguards were introduced. Thus a minority of the Criminal Law Revision Committee was prepared to modify the right of silence only if statutory provision was made for the use of tape recorders.[1069] In general terms it was the third approach that the RCCP purported to adopt, although not simply as a series of compromises between the other main schools of thought. Some commentators on the Report took the view that an appropriate balance had not been struck[1070]; others were less sceptical.[1071]

By contrast with the RCCP, the RCCJ did not even attempt to explore theoretical issues in any depth. The approach of the RCCJ was to examine the separate elements set out in the terms of reference, and make such detailed, practical recommendations as they thought appropriate. They noted that it could be argued that "there is a potential conflict between the interests of justice on the one hand and the requirement of fair and reasonable treatment for everyone involved, suspects and defendants included, on the other".[1072]

They accepted that these would not be reconcilable throughout the system in the eyes of all those involved. However,

---

[1065] RCCP Rep., p.4.

[1066] Royal Commission on Police Powers and Procedure (Cmd. 3297, 1929); Royal Commission on the Police (Cmnd. 1728, 1962); Eleventh Report of the Criminal Law Revision Committee on Evidence (General) (Cmnd. 4991, 1972).

[1067] Eleventh Report, p.15.

[1068] RCCP Rep., pp.9, 10.

[1069] ibid. pp.10, 11.

[1070] e.g. D. McBarnet [1981] Crim. L.R. 445 (noting the wider powers to be given to the police, the removal of traditional safeguards, the weakness and vagueness of the safeguards proposed in their place, and that the research was heavily dependent on police sources, and even then selectively ignored); M. McConville and J. Baldwin, (1982) 10 Int. J. Sociology of Law 287.

[1071] Albeit with particular reservations: L. H. Leigh (1981) 44 M.L.R. 296; B. Smythe [1981] P.L. 184 at 481.

[1072] Cm. 2263, p.8.

"we do believe that the fairer the treatment which all the parties receive at the hands of the system the more likely it is that the jury's verdict, or where appropriate the subsequent decision of the Court of Appeal, will be correct."[1073]

This discussion is both curious and revealing. The Commission's conception of the "interests of justice" was not explained, but the contrast drawn with the fair treatment of individuals suggests that it is "the conviction of those guilty of criminal offences and the acquittal of those who are innocent" (taking words from the terms of reference). This suggests a return to utilitarianism. The possibility that an individual's right to fair treatment might itself be a fundamental value that requires respect in its own terms, irrespective of whether it promotes or diminishes the "correctness" of verdicts is not recognised or explored. Ultimately the Commission attempted to by-pass the issue with its claim that

"when taken as a whole our recommendations serve the interests of justice without diminishing the individual's right to fair and reasonable treatment."[1074]

However, the cautionary "when taken as a whole" suggests that the Commission accepted that some particular recommendations might be prejudicial to individual rights.

Both the RCCJ's refusal to address theoretical issues directly, and the implicit theoretical approach that was discerned from its recommendations were the subject of much adverse comment.[1075] Commentators criticised the RCCJ's elevation of the resources issue to "coequal status" with the traditional concerns of convicting the guilty and acquitting the innocent[1076] and its

"uncritical acceptance of the theory of criminal justice implicit in a liberal reading of its terms of reference—terms which place efficiency on all fours with justice, and which construct the conviction of the innocent as no more important than the acquittal of the guilty."[1077]

In the event, its recommendations seemed mostly to be directed at improvements in the efficient management of the system at the expense of the presumption of innocence. Most had

"no bearing whatsoever on the cultural and structural features of the system which led to miscarriages of justice, and some of those which do are likely to exacerbate those underlying causes rather than the reverse."[1078]

Lord Justice Auld in his Review also recognised the need for a "balance of some sort to be struck between the community's interest in providing an efficient and

---

[1073] *ibid.*

[1074] *ibid.*

[1075] See M. McConville and L. Bridges (eds), *Criminal Justice in Crisis* (1994), Pt I, esp. Chs 1–5 by, respectively, L. Bridges and M McConville, N. Lacey, D. Nobles and R. Schiff and C. Wells. *Cf.* the defence of the RCCJ on this point by one of its members, M. Zander (1993) 143 N.L.J. 1364.

[1076] Bridges and McConville, *op. cit.* p.11.

[1077] Lacey, *op. cit.* n.86.

[1078] *ibid.* pp.40–41.

economic system for administering justice, bearing in mind also its many other commitments, and the manner of fair trial that it provides for offences of different seriousness".[1079]

The greater and more explicit emphasis in the Auld Review on the efficiency of the system further complicates the idea that there can be any true objectivity in the exercise of "balance" in this context. In particular, the community's interest is recognised to comprise separate interests in protection against crime and also in the swift administration of justice. Although the concept of efficiency in the process might at first appear neutral, in reality, introducing procedures designed to streamline the system and reduce delay is seldom an exercise in which the defendant's interests are promoted.

The Auld Review refrained from adopting any general theoretical model, favouring a pragmatic approach. The validity of this approach has been questioned, particularly since, in the most part, Lord Justice Auld refrained from commissioning any empirical work from which to draw these pragmatic conclusions.

Any discussion of a "balancing of interests" between two opposing factions is over simplistic. In reality there are many groups and individuals each with competing interests none of which can be assigned precise values, and some of which are so fundamental that they should not feature in any such exercise.

(b) Theoretical models

14–096   An evaluation of the merits of a "balancing exercise" can be more effectively achieved when viewed in the context of opposing theoretical models.

The Royal Commission on Criminal Procedure, for example, characterised the "two main opposing groups" in the right of silence debate as "those who gave paramountcy to the principles of the presumption of innocence and the burden of proof, and those who saw the purpose of the criminal justice system as being a means to the end of bringing the guilty to justice".[1080] The identification by the Royal Commission of these two major schools of thought echoes the two theoretical models of the criminal process proposed by Herbert L. Packer as an aid to the evaluation of the criminal justice system in the United States, the Due Process Model and the Crime Control Models.[1081] These models represented

> "an attempt to abstract two separate value systems that compete for priority in the operation of the criminal process. Neither is presented as either corresponding to reality or representing the ideal to the exclusion of the other."[1082]

Moreover, they did not represent the difference between the law as it should be ("law in the books") and the law as in fact it operated ("law in action"). They were extremes, and reality lay at some point on the spectrum between them. Indeed, there was some common ground in the two models' assumptions: (1) that the functions of defining conduct that may be treated as criminal is separate from,

---

[1079] Ch.2, para.18.
[1080] RCCP Rep., p.11.
[1081] H. L. Packer, *The Limits of the Criminal Sanction* (1969), Pt II.
[1082] *ibid.* p.153.

and prior to, the process of identifying and dealing with persons as criminals; (2) that when it appears that a crime has been committed and that there is a reasonable prospect of apprehending and convicting its perpetrator, criminal process ought ordinarily to be invoked; (3) that there are limits to the powers of government to investigate and apprehend persons suspected of committing crimes (e.g. the security and privacy of the individual may not be invaded at will); (4) that accused persons may, if they wish, force the operators of the process to demonstrate to an independent authority (the court) that they are guilty. Differences between the models lay in part in the strength and content of these assumptions, particularly the fourth.

Under the Crime Control Model, the most important function of the criminal process is the repression of criminal conduct. To fulfil this purpose, the system must operate efficiently. It must have the capacity to apprehend, try, and convict a high proportion of offenders whose offences become known, and to do so with speed and finality. This leads to an emphasis on informality and uniformity, and on minimising the occasions for challenge. Extra-judicial processes are preferred to judicial: the expertise of police and prosecutors is relied upon to screen out those who are probably innocent; those who are left in should be processed as speedily as possible, preferably with a plea of guilty at the trial stage.

> "The image that comes to mind is an assembly-line conveyor belt down which moves an endless stream of cases, never stopping, carrying the cases to workers who stand at fixed stations and who perform on each case as it comes by the same small but essential operation that brings it one step closer to being a finished product. . . . "[1083]

By contrast, the Due Process Model resembles an obstacle course. "Each of its successive stages is designed to present formidable impediments to carrying the accused any further along in the process."[1084] This model stresses the dangers of error in informal, non-adjudicative fact finding: people are notoriously unreliable observers of disturbing events and confessions to the police may be induced by physical or psychological coercion. Formal, adjudicative, adversary fact-finding processes, in which the case is heard by an impartial tribunal and the accused has a full opportunity to challenge the case against him or her, are necessary to reduce the dangers of error. Mistakes (convicting the innocent, setting the guilty free) should be eliminated to the fullest extent possible. (Under the Crime Control Model, such mistakes are acceptable in so far as they do not interfere with the repression of crime (e.g. by allowing too many guilty people to escape).) Apart from the question of reliability, there is also a concern to prevent official oppression of the individual, and emphasis on the presumption of innocence and on securing compliance with the procedural rules governing the criminal process, perhaps with the exclusion of illegally obtained evidence or reversal of convictions where the rules are breached. On the assumption that the resources made available for the operation of the criminal process are limited, a preference for Due Process values over Crime Control values will lead to a reduction in the quantitative output of the system.

[1083] *ibid.* p.159.
[1084] *ibid.* p.163.

Writing in the late 1960s, Packer concluded that the criminal process as it actually operated in the large majority of cases in the United States probably approximated to the Crime Control Model. On the other hand, judicial decisions based on the US Constitution were pushing the law nearer to the Due Process Model.[1085] For McConville and Baldwin, writing in 1981, the English system too in many ways conformed to the Crime Control Model. Although the police-suspect encounter was one of the key exchanges in the criminal process, the safeguards available to suspects in custody were virtually non-existent. Similarly, there was a lack of Due Process safeguards surrounding pleas of guilty, and connected procedures such as plea bargaining; almost 90 per cent of all defendants charged with serious offences pleaded guilty, and trial by jury (the epitome of the Due Process Model) was used by only 5 per cent of those eligible to be so tried. The function of the jury was thus "largely symbolic—to uphold due process values in the occasional show trial".[1086] Another commentator, McBarnet, stressed the point that it would not be correct to regard the substance of the law as reflecting Due Process values which are then subverted "by policemen bending the rules, by lawyers negotiating adversaries out of existence, by out-of-touch judges or biased magistrates . . . ". In reality "the law governing the production, preparation and presentation of evidence does not live up to its own rhetoric . . . Police and court officials need not abuse the law to subvert the principles of justice; they need only use it".[1087]

Developments since then have, like the system as a whole, reflected both Due Process and Crime Control values. However, the latter have tended to predominate.[1088] Thus as regards pre-trial procedure, the introduction of the PACE regime has seen the significant extension of police powers of arrest, stop-search, detention and evidence-gathering. While many of these powers are comparatively rarely used, the numbers of arrest and stop-searches have rocketed.[1089] The requirement of "reasonable suspicion" does not seem to be a practical constraint, supervision of police officers on the street is minimal, and powers are used disproportionately against "the young, male, working class and black".[1090]

[1085] *ibid.* p.239. Major cases included *Miranda v Arizona* 384 U.S. 436 (1966) (suspects in custody must be advised of their rights, which include the right of access to a lawyer before interrogation); *Mapp v Ohio* 367 U.S. 643 (1961) (rule excluding illegally obtained evidence applicable to state as well as federal prosecutions); *Gideon v Wainwright* 372 U.S. 325 (1963) (state must provide counsel for defendants financially unable to provide their own). See more recently *US v Leon* (1984) 104 S Ct. 3405.

[1086] M. McConville and J. Baldwin, *Courts, Prosecution and Conviction* (1981), pp.3–7.

[1087] *ibid.*; (1981), pp.154–157. See also D. McBarnet, "False Dichotomies in Criminal Justice Research" in J. Baldwin and A. K. Bottomley, *Criminal Justice: Selected Readings* (1978), Ch.2. *Cf.* McConville *et al., The Case for the Prosecution* (1991), Ch.9, criticising McBarnet's approach in so far as it would focus attention on the law (and the judicial and political elites who made it) and regard the practice of "the system's low-level officials such as the police" as relatively unimportant; and for its assumption that legal rhetoric does not form part of the law itself.

[1088] See, generally, Sanders and Young (2007).

[1089] *ibid.* See Table 2.1 and Table 2.4.

[1090] A. Sanders and R. Young, "The Rule of Law, Due Process and Pre Trial Criminal Justice" (1994) C.L.P. 125 at 137. *Cf.* R. Reiner in R. Morgan and R. Reiner (eds), *The Oxford Handbook of Criminology* (1994), p.727 (cited by Sanders and Young) referring to a study that confirmed "that the weight of adversarial policing falls disproportionately on young men in the lower socio-economic and least powerful social group".

Little has been done to restrict or regulate the use of the very broad discretion in operational policing. More effective schemes of monitoring have been implemented, but these bring with them further problems, as, e.g. with the stop and search powers discussed above. Similarly, attempts to regulate the use of police powers for surveillance which have become so common in this era of intelligence-led policing have, arguably, been inadequate. In particular there is a lack of independent scrutiny of authorisations for covert police operations which have the potential to infringe the suspects most personal privacy.

Crime control values can also be clearly identified in the continual expansions to police powers (e.g. to take samples, to retain samples, to take overt and covert video footage of suspects, to bail suspects away from the station). At the same time, the safeguards of the suspect in custody are diluted (e.g. with lower ranks of officer authorising action, and samples being retained indefinitely).

In contrast, the increased regulation of the interrogation process, including the right of access to legal advice, and the enforcement of that regulation by judicial decisions to exclude confession evidence certainly reflects both the rhetoric and practice of Due Process. However, the limits must be noted: many suspects are interrogated without a lawyer present; the quality of much of the legal advice is poor; and there is no rule that illegally obtained evidence is inadmissible. These Due Process-based developments have nevertheless been used to justify attenuation of the "right of silence", itself an embodiment of Due Process values. The inherently coercive interrogation process remains in police hands and convictions may still be based solely on a confession. While interrogations in serious cases are tape-recorded, confessions may be influenced by off-the-record deals made outside the police station, in police cells or while the tape-recorder is switched off. The crucial need for a change in attitude so that the police approach investigations (and interviews) with an open mind is to be addressed only as a matter for police (re) training. Additionally, the quality of legal advice needs to be improved, and it may be desirable to prescribe that a legal adviser should be present at all interviews. Such reforms will be resisted, in part at least because of the pressures of economy and efficiency, as well as on the now popular mantra that the "balance" in criminal procedure already weighs too heavily in the suspect's favour.

Arguably, the significance of the exchanges that occur in the police station are now so great for the defendant throughout the rest of the criminal process, that the safeguards need to be substantially increased, not reduced.

Another Due Process development, the disclosure requirements imposed by the courts, has been modified by the CIPA 1996 and the Criminal Justice Act 2003. The government's Crime Control objective, seeking to maximise the efficiency with which cases are despatched, is clearly reflected in the legislation, with, for example, the most crucial role being performed by the police, and the obligation on the accused to issue a defence statement which clearly outlines the details of his case if he is to avoid adverse inferences being drawn at the trial. The system has in fact proved to be tremendously controversial and a major source of potential miscarriages of justice.

The effect of the CPS as an antidote to these trends is uncertain, given its undoubted dependence on the case as presented to it by the police. The fragile relationship of the CPS and the police will be thoroughly tested by recent reforms which ensure greater CPS involvement at an earlier stage of the process.

Finally, while evaluation of the criminal justice process from the standpoints of Due Process and Crime Control is in our view helpful, it should be noted both that the dichotomy has its critics[1091] and that other models have been proposed.[1092]

2. HUMAN RIGHTS

14–097   The trend towards Crime Control summarised in the preceding section has arguably been countered to some degree by the influence of the Human Rights Act 1998.

The effect of the Act is difficult to gauge. It should be remembered that the European Convention on Human Rights represents a minimum standard of rights and thus one would expect that the effect of such rights on substantive law would be less than their impact upon the culture of those public authorities that are subject to it. The Act, nevertheless, has had a significant impact on many aspects of the criminal process including: the regulation of the police conduct[1093]; the circumstances in which adverse inferences from silence might be drawn at trial[1094]; the amendment of pre-trial procedures such as bail[1095]; and, on the preparation for trial generally, especially in relation to the disclosure of evidence.[1096]

It is of some concern that in some areas where the Act has potentially acted as a brake upon substantially crime control oriented measures, it has been depicted as an obstacle to public safety. Both the Government and the Conservative

---

[1091] See Ashworth and Redmayne (2005), pp.38–40, criticising: (1) a lack of a clear explanation of the relationship between the two models; (2) the assumption that there was a significant relationship between the system of pre-trial justice and the crime rate; (3) the underestimation of the importance of resource management; (4) the absence of allowance for victim-related matters; and (5) internal inconsistencies (e.g. the emphasis on speed in only the Crime Control model). See also Sanders and Young (2007), Ch.1, in which the authors discuss their "freedom" model. This seeks to evaluate the freedoms of potential and actual victims against harm with the due process freedoms of suspects and defendants. They argue that a human rights approach is not a sufficient answer to the problem of balancing crime control and due process. The ultimate goal of their system is to ensure the optimum protection of freedom overall.

[1092] See, in addition to Ashworth and Redmayne (2005) and Sanders and Young (2007), A. Bottoms and J. D. McClean, *Defendants in the Criminal Process* (1976), pp.226–232, and M. King. *The Framework of Criminal Justice* (1981), Ch.2. Bottoms and McClean identify a third, Liberal Bureaucratic Model, based on the viewpoint of the "enlightened courts administrator": this purports to prefer Due Process values to Crime Control values, but imposes pressures (e.g. in support of summary trials and guilty pleas) to make the system workable, and in so doing in practice reinforces Crime Control. King analyses models, three based on the perspectives of typical participants: (i) Due Process (defence lawyers), (ii) Crime Control (police), and (iii) Medical (probation officers: emphasis on reabilitation); and three based on the work of social theorists: (iv) Bureaucratic (emphasising the management of crime and criminals), (v) Status Passage (emphasising the public degradation of the defendant) and (vi) Power (emphasising the maintenance of class domination).

[1093] See especially the introduction of RIPA 2000 and the House of Lords decision in *R v Looseley* [2001] U.K.H.L. 53 on entrapment.

[1094] See especially, the decisions of *Condron and Condron v UK* [2001] E.H.R.R. 1 and the amendments made by the Youth Justice and Criminal Evidence Act 1999.

[1095] See Law Commission, *Bail and the Human Rights Act 1998* (1999) No.269; see also, *R (O) v Harrow Crown Court* [2006] U.K.H.L. 42.

[1096] See, for example, *Rowe and Davies v United Kingdom* (2000) 30 E.H.R.R. 1; *Edwards and Lewis v United Kingdom* (2005) 40 E.H.R.R. 893; *Atlan v United Kingdom* (2002) 34 E.H.R.R. 833.

opposition have spoken of the need to amend or replace the Act.[1097] However, following reviews of the operation of the Act, the Home Office has accepted "that the HRA has not impeded in any way the Government's ability to protect the public against crime".[1098] The Government has also given some backing to the HRA, stating that the European Convention, "sets out the rights that represent the basic principles of human decency, but also contains provisions which permit exactly the sort of balanced approach that allows the courts to weigh up the freedom of the individual against the right of the public to be protected".[1099] Though it accepts that a balanced approach can be taken, the Government questions whether the balance drawn by the European Court has been in the appropriate place. "We will be robust in addressing the areas where the European Court of Human Rights in Strasbourg interprets the Convention in a way that stops us applying a proper balance effectively".[1100]

The ECHR should serve as an important bulwark against the increasing pressure for reform based on Crime Control values. This will be aided by the fostering of a more pervasive human rights culture within public authorities, and a greater understanding of the effects of the HRA based on the correction of the negative myths surrounding the legislation and clearer guidance on its operation.[1101]

There remains a constant tension between the interests identified above, but in recent years, there has been a growing recognition and exploration of other important interests influencing the criminal justice process.

3. THE ROLE OF THE VICTIM

In recent years increased attention has been paid to the role of the victim.[1102] In **14–098** the White Paper, *Justice for All,* the Government stated that it would, "put victims and witnesses at the heart of the CJS and ensure they see justice done

---

[1097] In May 2006 there was public controversy over the HRA following three high-profile cases. It was suggested that the Act was preventing the Government from ensuring public safety, and that it should be repealed or amended. The Prime Minister asked the Home Office and the Department for Constitutional Affairs to conduct reviews of the impact of the HRA; see, Department for Constitutional Affairs, *Review of the Implementation of the Human Rights Act* (2006); Government Response to the Joint Committee on Human Rights' Thirty-second Report of Session 2005–06 (2007) Cm. 7011. See also, R. Clayton, "The Human Rights Act Six Years On: Where Are We Now?", [2007] E.H.R.L.R 11.

[1098] Government Response to the Joint Committee on Human Rights' Thirty-second Report of Session 2005–06 (2007) Cm. 7011, para.16.

[1099] Home Office, *Rebalancing the Criminal Justice System in Favour of the Law-Abiding Majority: Cutting Crime, Reducing Reoffending and Protecting the Public* (2006) para.2.12.

[1100] *ibid.* para.2.13.

[1101] *ibid.* paras 2.14–2.17. See also, Joint Committee on Human Rights' Thirty-second Report of Session 2005–06, *The Human Rights Act: The DCA and Home Office Reviews* (2006) H.C. 1716, Chs 5 and 7.

[1102] See especially, J. Dignan, *Understanding Victims and Restorative Justice* (2005); R. Elias, *The Politics of Victimization: Victims, Victimology, and Human Rights* (2006); J. Goodey, *Victims and Victimology: Research, Policy and Practice,* (2004); T. Newburn, Crime and Criminal Justice Policy (2nd edn, 2003), Ch.9; C. Hoyle and A. Sanders, "Restorative Justice: Assessing the Prospects and Pitfalls", in M. McConville and G. Wilson, *The Handbook of the Criminal Justice Process* (2002); A. Crawford and J. Goodey (eds), *Integrating a Victim Perspective within Criminal Justice* (2000).

more often and more quickly."[1103] If this rhetoric is borne out in concrete reform it may, to some extent, tackle the paradoxes that have been noted.[1104] First, there is the contradiction that the victim has a crucial role to play in reporting the offence to the police and as the major agent in detecting the offender, but that little account is taken of the victim's attitudes and experiences by the professionals involved in the criminal justice system. Secondly, initially at least, "major projects aimed at fulfilling victims' needs have been set up without regard to, or even investigation into, victims' expressed needs".[1105]

The greater awareness of the plight of the victim and the desire to regain public confidence in the criminal justice system indicate a growing influence for the victim in pre-trial process.

In 2003 the Government established the Victims' Advisory Panel designed to allow representatives of victims' organisations to comment directly to relevant ministers on policy developments.[1106] Under the Domestic Violence, Crime and Victims Act 2004 the Government has introduced a Code of Practice for victims of crime.[1107] Through it a range of services appropriate to each victim are made available, including, for example, the local victim support service. Victims appearing in criminal proceedings should be given the opportunity to attend a pre-trial court familiarisation visit. The police should keep victims informed of decisions such as the arrest of a suspect and his subsequent release if he has been bailed. Likewise the CPS should inform the victim of the charging decisions that have been taken. Other bodies have similar requirements to fulfil under the Code. The need for victims to be kept informed about the progress of their case is important and in this sense the Code represents a positive move. However, it should be recognised that the rights contained in the Code are not enforceable in court and thus if the various bodies concerned are unable to deliver what is in the Code this will leave the victim with a greater sense of grievance. This raising of victims' expectations is also seen in the use of victim personal statements. It has been claimed that such statements are useful in providing the victim with a voice when otherwise they are largely ignored. However, as with many measures directed towards victims, the rhetoric is good but there is little real substance to follow.[1108]

As noted by Dignan and Cavadino, only a victim centred model of criminal justice could really put the victim's interests at the heart of the system.[1109] Though aspects of the Crime Control or Due Process models can enhance

---

[1103] Home Office, *Justice for All*, (2002) Cm. 5563, esp. Ch.2. See also Department for Constitutional Affairs, *Hearing the Relatives of Murder and Manslaughter Victims: The Government's Plans to Give Bereaved Relatives of Murder and Manslaughter Victims a Say in Criminal Proceedings* (2005); J. Jackson, "Justice for All: Putting Victims at the Heart of Criminal Justice" (2003) 30 J. Law & Soc. 309; P. Rock, *Constructing Victims' Rights* (2004).

[1104] J. Shapland, J. Willmore and P. Duff, *Victims in the Criminal Justice System* (1985), Ch.10. See, generally, S. Walkate, *Victimology* (1989).

[1105] *ibid.* p.178.

[1106] DVCVA 2004, s.55.

[1107] Domestic Violence, Crime and Victims Act 2004, s.32. The Code can be seen on the Home Office website at: *www.homeoffice.gov.uk/documents/victims-code-of-practice?view=Binary*. R. Ward, "Protecting the Victims of Crime" (2005) N.L.J. 1150.

[1108] I. Edwards, "A Genuine Voice?" (2005) N.L.J. 1341.

[1109] J. Dignan and M. Cavadino, "Towards a Framework for Conceptualising and Evaluating Models of Criminal Justice from a Victim's Perspective", (1996) Int. R. Victimology 153; see also I. Edwards, "An Ambiguous Participant" (2004) 44 Brit. J. Crim. 967.

victims' rights in certain specific instances, ultimately these are merely by products of the different goals those models are seeking to achieve.

4. THE (RE) EMERGENCE OF TERRORISM

There is not the scope within this text to do justice to a comprehensive analysis **14–099** of recent legislation directed towards the prevention and detection of offences of terrorism.[1110] The issue is raised because one should not underestimate its importance to the criminal process more widely. The concern surrounding legislation directed towards terrorism is that it tends to include powers that severely curtail individual rights, and that such draconian measures might become either a part of the general policing landscape, or at least change the landscape so that general police powers become more extensive.

Contradictory as it may seem, "emergency" anti terrorism legislation has been a part of the British legal landscape for many years.[1111] The Terrorism Act 2000 represented an effort to break the cycle of such reactive legislation in this field and presented a more comprehensive code. However, the events of September 11, 2001 changed the context once more and again the legislature has responded through a series of reactive measures. The Anti-terrorism, Crime and Security Act 2001[1112] introduced detention without trial, subsequently held to be incompatible with human rights[1113] and replaced by control orders in the Terrorism Act 2005.[1114] The Terrorism Act 2006, arguably a reaction to the London bombings, has introduced further controversial measures directed at the "encouragement" of terrorism, and has extended the police powers of detention in terrorist cases from a maximum of 14 days to 28 days.[1115] This latter reform came about after Parliament rejected a Government proposal to extend the period of detention to up to 90 days. The concern is summed up by Lord Hoffman:

> "The real threat to the life of the nation, in the sense of people living in accordance with its traditional laws and political values, comes not from terrorism but from laws such as these."[1116]

The extension of special provisions into the general criminal justice landscape should be avoided, but equally the state must be alive to the possibility that excessive powers might alienate sections of the public on which the success of everyday policing relies.

[1110] See, C. Walker, *A Guide to the Anti-terrorism Legislation* (2002); C. Walker, "Terrorism and Criminal Justice—Past, Present and Future" [2004] Crim. L.R. 55; C. Walker and J. Broderick, *The Civil Contingencies Act 2004: Risk, Resilience and the Law in the United Kingdom* (2006); C.Walker, "Clamping Down on Terrorism in the United Kingdom" (2006) J. Int'l Crim. Just. 1137.

[1111] D. Bonner, "Responding to Crisis: Legislating Against Terrorism" (2006) L.Q.R. 602.

[1112] C. Walker and Y. Akdeniz, "Anti-terrorism laws and data retention: War is Over?" (2003) N.I.L.Q. 159.

[1113] *A v Secretary of State for the Home Department* [2004] U.K.H.L. 56; See also M. Elliott, "United Kingdom: Detention Without Trial and the War on Terror" (2006) Int'l. J. Const. L. 553.

[1114] M. Zander, "The Prevention of Terrorism Act 2005" (2005) N.L.J. 438.

[1115] A. Naseem Bajwa, "Pre-Charge Detention in Terrorism Cases" (2006) N.L.J 1578.

[1116] *A v Secretary of State for the Home Department* [2004] U.K.H.L. 56, para.97.

L. FUTURE DEVELOPMENTS

14–100   The pressure for further reform of the pre-trial criminal process continues unabated. Many changes are still being effected by the Criminal Justice Act 2003, including for example, the use of judge only trials in cases of serious fraud, and the Serious Organised Crime and Police Act 2005. Such is the huge scope of both pieces of legislation that their effect will be felt for some time to come.[1117] In the short term the Government has committed itself to "rebalancing" the criminal justice system. This will include measures such as ongoing reviews of PACE coupled with a reduction in police bureaucracy; expanding the use of punitive conditional cautions; and bulk processing of regulatory offences to free up the courts from non-serious cases.

There are clearly identifiable themes in the future reform proposals.

1. Efficiency, Managerialism and Consumerism

14–101   Many of the most recent legislative changes have been introduced solely in an attempt to speed up the process or to save money, with little apparent concern for the protections of the suspect.[1118] When viewed in combination some of these reforms appear to have as their sole objective the securing of the earliest possible guilty plea. Attempts to improve efficiency are clearly at the forefront of the proposals to "speed up magistrates' courts", "reduce the length and cost of . . . cases in the Crown Court", and develop bulk processing of regulatory offences. The aim of the 2007 review of PACE is explicitly to "raise the efficiency and effectiveness of the police service".[1119] The extent to which any changes made to PACE will impact negatively on suspects' rights will require close scrutiny given that the areas for consideration include, for example, looking "to provide processes for dealing with the person on the street which minimizes both the processes and procedures which an officer needs to complete and the level of contact and inconvenience for the individual".[1120] Other areas for review include: detention and the custodial process; bail; the use of biometric information and the removal of operational constraints on the use of fingerprints; and questioning after charge. That PACE should be reviewed in light of changing circumstances is not doubted, but one must hope that the desire for increased efficiency is not the overriding objective.

As elsewhere in the legal system, the criminal process has felt the effects of the growing importance of managerialism. In the pre-trial process this can be seen in the greater significance accorded to monitoring, protocols, and performance targets of the agencies, and of the desire to improve the "service" provided to clients in the criminal justice system. The Police and Justice Act 2006 establishes the National Policing Improvement Agency which is designed to assist police forces in delivering their national "mission critical" priorites.

[1117] The Criminal Justice Act 2003 contains 339 sections, and The Serious Organised Crime Act 2005 contains 179 sections.

[1118] See, for example, the controversial mode of trial reforms.

[1119] Home Office Consultation Paper, *Modernising Police Powers: Review of the Police and Criminal Evidence Act 1984* (2007) p.2.

[1120] *ibid.* para.3.1.

As for consumerism, there is a danger that as "crime" is such a political issue, every government will respond to popular (mis)conceptions about crime rates. This can lead to over hasty reactions to issues given an over inflated significance as a result of particular headline cases. In the long run these can seriously diminish the protection afforded to the suspect in the pre-trial process.[1121] This is a particularly pernicious threat, because the trial process, and especially the paradigm of the seldom used jury trial, will remain largely unscathed as the inroads are made into fundamental safeguards arising before trial. These processes are, as we have seen, as important in protecting against miscarriages of justice as those at trial, and yet they are more readily sacrificed without public concern.

Retaining public confidence in the criminal justice system is important; but responding to public satisfaction surveys by amending the criminal process will not always serve to promote public confidence in the long term. Whilst the Government speaks of rebalancing the criminal justice system in favour of the law-abiding majority, Sanders and Young have argued that "from the suspect's point of view, the system is now icily unbalanced".[1122] Research has shown that those who have the poorest knowledge of the system "tend to have lower opinions of the courts and sentences".[1123] This carries with it a much broader and often unrecognised danger of relying on statistics which can be manipulated as easily in this area as elsewhere.[1124]

[1121] See the report by Walker, Kershaw and Nicholas, *Crime in England and Wales 2005–6*, (2006) which found that one in three people thought there was a "lot more" crime now compared to two years ago.

[1122] Sanders and Young (2007), p.651.

[1123] See J. Mattinson and C. Mirrlees-Black, "Attitudes to Crime and Criminal Justice: Findings from the BSC" (2000), HORS 200, p.8. D. Smith, *Confidence in the Criminal Justice System: What Lies Beneath*, Ministry of Justice Research Series 7/07 (2007).

[1124] On changes to crime statistics methodology see Home Office, *Review of Crime Statistics: A Discussion Document* (2000). For a comparison of criminal statistics across jurisdictions, see G. Barclay, G. Tavares and A. Siding, *International Comparisons of Criminal Justice Statistics 1999* (Home Office 6/01, 2001). See also Home Office, *Improving Public Attitudes to the Criminal Justice System: The Impact of Information* (2002) HORS No.245.

PART IV

THE HEARING

CHAPTER 15

THE CIVIL TRIAL

From the variety of different civil proceedings we shall again take the action in **15–001** the Queen's Bench Division as our example.[1] However we shall also make reference to the county court, both in its fast track and in its small claims jurisdictions.

It is arguable that very little time should be spent considering the civil trial, since so much effort is expended on resolving the case prior to that stage.[2] Indeed discussion of the trial stage is almost incidental to the Woolf reports and CPR Pt 39 "Miscellaneous Provisions relating to hearings" and its practice direction occupy only 11 pages out of the three-volume Civil Procedure Rules. The resolution of disputes by other means was not only promoted by the Woolf reforms[3] but is of increased significance in practice, as we saw in Ch.11. However, the civil trial is important not only in being the final point for the resolution of disputes, but as a means of creating the precedent that is crucial to a common law system.[4]

---

[1] See Ch.11.

[2] See above, para.12–036.

[3] See for example CPR r.1.4(2)(e).

[4] Subject to the court's ability to depart from precedent in pursuit of the higher obligation to protect human rights. See also N. Armstrong, "Making Facts", in A. A. S. Zuckerman and R. Cranston (eds), *Reforming Civil Procedure* (1995), pp.99–100 and S. S. Juss, "Constitutionalising rights without a constitution: the British Experience under article 6 of the Human Rights Act 1998" (2006) 27 Statute L. Rev. 29.

A. ADVERSARIAL PROCEDURE

15–002   Adversarial procedure is the fundamental, characteristic feature of English civil justice.[5]

> "You have two adversaries in every civil dispute—someone asserting a right, someone denying it. Someone contending for one thing, someone contending against it."[6]

Lord Woolf, whilst not recommending the abandonment of the adversarial principle, identified it as a major cause of many of the problems associated with the civil justice system. He recommended the retention of the best aspects of the adversarial approach combined with a more interventionist management role by the courts. This has, as we have seen in Ch.12, most significance for the pre-trial stage, but has implications also for the trial stage.

PD 28 para.8 indicates that, at least in the fast track "the judge will generally have read the papers in the trial bundle". The number of cases proceeding through the courts having decreased dramatically since the Woolf reforms, judges should now have more time to read into the case although in their recent study, Peysner and Seneviratne found that judges did not have sufficient allocated reading time and frequently had to read into cases the night before the hearing. It is the function of the parties, normally through counsel or solicitor-advocate[7] to bring the evidence and argue the law that will win the case, subject to case management constraints placed on them by the procedural judge.

Reforms to civil procedure as a result of Lord Woolf's reforms and otherwise have streamlined the trial stage, particularly in the fast and small claims tracks. Excessive use of documents[8] and expert witnesses[9] was controlled, oral examination-in-chief was almost entirely replaced by submission of written witness

---

[5] Sir Jack I. H. Jacob, *The Fabric of English Civil Justice* (1987), p.5. Adversarial procedure can be compared with the inquisitorial system, see *ibid.* pp.5–19. See also N. Andrews, *Principles of Civil Procedure* (1994), Ch.3 and Interim Report p.29.

[6] Sir Jack I. H. Jacob, "The Adversary System of Civil Litigation" (1983) City of London Law Review 17, 18. See also J. A. Jolowicz, "Adversarial and Inquisitorial Models of Civil Procedure", 52 I.C.L.Q. 281; A. J. Cannon, "Effective Fact Finding" (2006) 25 (Jul) C.J.Q. 327.

[7] As a result of the numbers of solicitors obtaining rights of audience in the higher courts (and indeed members of other professions, such as patent attorneys and costs draftsmen) the word "advocate" will be used hereafter as a generic term. There are, however, limitations: a solicitor may not act as advocate if, *inter alia*, he or she is likely to be called as a witness or where his or her connection with the client would mean that it was difficult for them to maintain professional independence; he or she is a company director and the company is a party to the proceedings; or, more significantly in this context, if the solicitor has been responsible for deciding on a course of action and the legality of that action is in dispute in the proceedings, *Solicitors' Code of Conduct 2007*, Rule 11. A potentially significant difference between the barrister and the solicitor-advocate is that a solicitor-advocate may be the same solicitor who has managed the case in all its detail throughout the pre-trial procedure. A barrister is perhaps more likely to have been brought in, either in the final stages with a view to conducting the trial, or for specific tasks, such as the drafting of statements of case.

[8] CPR r.31.6.

[9] CPR r.35.1.

statements[10] and hearsay ceased to be inadmissible in civil proceedings.[11] The latter reflects the reality that "the rules of evidence play an almost insignificant part in the civil trial process".[12]

Consequently, cases should now be much better prepared for trial.[13] The consequences of this assumption are particularly noticeable in the fast track where:

(a)   The trial will not last more than four hours (i.e. a single court "day").

(b)   There will not normally be an opening speech.

(c)   Written witness statements will stand as evidence-in-chief.[14]

(d)   Time allowed for presentation of evidence, for cross-examination and for closing submissions may be limited in advance.

(e)   Expert evidence at trial will normally be submitted in writing rather than orally.

(f)   The recoverable costs of the fast track trial will not exceed £350 if the claim is for a sum of up to £3,000; £500 for a claim of £3,000 to £10,000 and £750 for a claim of more than £10,000.[15]

Similar directions may also be given in the multi-track where the case management conference[16] and pre-trial review[17] will involve the parties in clearly identifying issues for trial and those which can be resolved before trial. In addition, advocates are limited as to the citation of legal authorities.[18] Fixed dates or fixed "trial windows" are now the norm.

At the beginning of a multi-track trial, an *opening speech* is made on behalf of the claimant. The object of the opening speech is to outline the case with reference to the evidence that is to be called. The opening may be briefer—and indeed, subject to a time limit by the judge—in a civil case than in a criminal case since there will not normally be a jury and the advocate will not have to explain such matters as the burden and standard of proof.

---

[10] CPR r.32.5(2).

[11] Civil Justice Review (1989), paras 266–270, Law Commission, The *Hearsay Rule in Civil Proceedings* (L.C. Consultation Paper No.117, 1991) and Civil Evidence Act 1995, s.1 (also CPR rr.33.1 to 33.5 inclusive). It should, however, be remembered that the court has express authority (although presumably subject to the obligation to provide a fair trial under Art.6) to "exclude evidence that would otherwise be admissible" CPR r.32.1.

[12] Jacob (1987), p.266.

[13] See above para.12–002.

[14] See CPR r.32.5(2): the "witness statement shall stand as [the witness'] evidence in chief unless the court orders otherwise".

[15] CPR Pt 46. Lord Woolf in fact recommended that the total recoverable costs of a fast track case (that is, both the trial and the pre-trial activity) should be restricted (Final Report, Ch.4)). Limits on recovery of pre-trial costs or success fees in cases such as road traffic accident and employer's liability cases now appear in CPR Pt 45. See K. Underwood, "Current Issues—Fixed Costs and Conditional Fees" (2005) 24(JUL) C.J.Q. 388.

[16] See CPR r.29.3 and PD 29 para.5.

[17] CPR r.29.3. It is not unknown for judges to set a timetable for the trial including the length of time each advocate may spend on examining each witness and in making closing submissions.

[18] Practice Direction (Citation of Authorities) [2001] 2 All E.R. 510, CA.

15–003   Normally any agreed reports[19] or other documentary evidence are put in evidence in the opening speech. If the judge has had the opportunity to read the papers, he or she may indicate to the advocate that there is no need to cover all the points in the opening speech or that the opening speech may be dispensed with altogether.[20] This is an advantage of trial by judge alone: the judge can move the advocates on where matters are understood or undisputed without having to ensure that the jury has grasped the issue, and, if the judge is prepared and the issues have been effectively narrowed during the pre-trial stages, considerable time and costs can be saved during the trial. At the conclusion of the opening speech, if any, for the claimant, the first witnesses are called.

It is no accident that there are, except in the case of single joint experts, witnesses for the claimant and witnesses for the defendant. The parties are, within the constraints of CPR r.32.1[21]—which may be used to limit the number of witnesses called and/or the amount of time any individual witness spends in the witness box—free to choose the people to give evidence to support their contentions.[22]

The claimant's advocate will begin by calling each claimant's witness in turn. Evidence may be given by videolink.[23] It is comparatively rare in modern practice[24] that the oral questioning of a witness by the advocate "on the same side" is permitted by the court, but when it is available it is termed *examination-in-chief*.[25] If there is no oral examination-in-chief, the witness may be asked no more than to identify him or herself and to confirm the accuracy of the witness statement that has been exchanged on his or her behalf, before being handed over to examination by the advocate for the other side. It is essential, therefore, that those who draw up witness statements do so in the knowledge that, in effect, they are producing in written form the evidence-in-chief[26] at the trial, it being unlikely that the witness will be permitted to amplify the statement simply to remedy omissions made by the person who took down the statement.

Where there is any examination-in-chief, the advocate must observe two rules. Leading questions[27] must not be asked and the witness' oral evidence given in

---

[19] e.g. medical reports or those of other experts, particularly those of single joint experts.

[20] A direction that opening speeches are not required may have been made at the pre-trial stage, as, for example, at a pre-trial review.

[21] Note that CPR r.32.1 is the only section of CPR Pt 32 to apply in the small claims track.

[22] The single joint expert, however, occupies the middle ground. Although such an expert witness has been instructed by both parties, if he or she appears to give oral evidence at the trial (which is by no means certain), the expert may be be subject to cross-examination by both parties. See *Austen v Oxford City Council*, Lawtel AC0103346, April 17, 2002, QBD and Experts' Protocol, para.17.15. As we will see, cross-examination of one's own witnesses is not normally permitted. Other variations to the normal rules appear in the Civil Evidence Act 1995, s.3 (implemented by CPR r.33.3) under which a party who has tendered evidence as hearsay can be required by their opponent to produce the witness at trial for cross-examination by that opponent.

[23] CPR r.32.3. Videolink evidence may be allowed even if the reason the witness is not present in court is to avoid arrest or extradition (*Polanski v Conde Nast Publications Ltd* [2005] UKHL 10) or tax liability (*McGlinn v Waltham Contractors Ltd* [2006] EWHC 2322, TCC).

[24] CPR r.32.5(2)

[25] As to the judge's role in examining witnesses for both the claimant and the defence see para.15–009 below.

[26] See PD. 32 at para.18.1 "The witness statement must, if practicable, be in the intended witness's own words . . . ". For further discussion on this topic, see 12–027.

[27] A leading question is one which suggests to the witness the answer which the advocate expects. "What time did the accident occur?" is a proper question. "The accident occurred at 7.30pm, did it not?" is a leading question if the timing of the accident is in dispute in the case and is, therefore, prohibited. It is commonly agreed between the advocates and the judge that, if oral examination-in-chief is to take place at all a witness may be "led" on non-contentious issues to save time.

court must not be contradicted by the witness' written statement.[28] Neither a solicitor (including a solicitor-advocate) nor a barrister is, any longer, prohibited from merely discussing the case or the evidence to be given with a potential witness, but, as there remain stringent prohibitions against "coaching" or "rehearsing" witnesses,[29] it is quite possible that there may be variations in testimony when the witness is under examination.[30]

At the conclusion of the oral evidence-in-chief, if any, the advocate for the defendant is given the opportunity to cross-examine in an attempt to shake the testimony of the witness or to extract information useful to the defendant's case. In cross-examination the advocate is at liberty to exploit contradictory statements made by the witness using the written statement exchanged on behalf of the witness.[31] After the defence evidence has been heard in the same way the defendant's advocate may make a *closing speech* summarising his or her view of the evidence and the law, to which the claimant's advocate may reply. Again, the judge may indicate to the advocates that argument on a particular point which may already have been decided or which is irrelevant is not necessary. At any point in the proceedings the judge may decide to look at the place in which the events in issue took place. The judge would normally be accompanied at a "view" by the parties and their legal representatives but may order instead that he or she be accompanied only by, say, the parties' expert witnesses.

15–004

Ultimately the judge is required to give a reasoned judgment, stating the conclusions on the factual issues in dispute and the legal implications of those findings of fact.[32]

---

[28] It is, of course, open to the advocate to ask a witness to think again about an answer, but the discrepancy between the answer and the earlier statement may not be suggested. In an extreme case, the advocate might seek to have the earlier statement put in as evidence at the end of the examination-in-chief: Civil Evidence Act 1968, s.2(2). As oral examination-in-chief is disappearing, the scope for such discrepancies arising in examination-in-chief are, of course, diminishing.

[29] A current issue is whether "witness familiarisation" or "witness preparation" training is impermissible on this basis. See *R v Momodou (Henry)* [2005] EWCA Crim. 177; *R v Salisbury* [2005] EWCA Crim. 3107; *Ultraframe (UK) Ltd v Fielding (No.2)* [2005] EWHC 1638 (Ch.); P. Cooper, "Witness Preparation; Play it Safe" (2005) 155 N.L.J. 1753; "Witness Preparation" (2005) 155(7165) N.L.J. 275; "Witness Preparation: staying within the Rules" (2004) 154(7154) N.L.J. 1768 and the Bar Council *Guidance on Witness Preparation* (2005).

[30] Before 2007, the *Law Society Code for Advocacy* prescribed at 6.5: "Advocates must not when interviewing a witness out of court: (a) place witnesses who are being interviewed under any pressure to provide other than a truthful account of their evidence; (b) rehearse, practise or coach witnesses in relation to their evidence or the way in which they should give it." The *Solicitors' Code of Conduct 2007* now merely at note 11.01 (12f) lists "seeking to persuade a witness to change their evidence" as an example of misleading the court. Other regulation on contact with witnesses from the solicitor's perspective appear in *Solicitors' Code of Conduct 2007* at rule 10.04.

The *Code of Conduct of the Bar of England and Wales* (8th edn) adds to the two principles originally adopted by solicitors the further requirement at para.705 that a barrister "except with the consent of the representative for the opposing side or of the court, (may not) communicate directly or indirectly about a case with any witness, whether or not the witness is his lay client, once that witness has begun to give evidence until the evidence of that witness has been concluded". Whilst there is no longer any bar on barristers having contact with witnesses otherwise, the Bar's *Guidance on Preparation of Witness Statements, Preparing Witness Statements for use in Civil Proceedings, Dealings with Witnesses* (2001) indicates at para.9 that barristers should "exercise [their] discretion and consider very carefully whether and to what extent such contact is appropriate, bearing in mind in particular that it is not the barrister's function . . . to investigate and collect evidence".

[31] CPR r.32.4

[32] There is an entitlement to a reasoned judgment even in the much more informal small claims track hearing: CPR r.27.8(6).

There are variations to the above procedure. First, the judge may sit with assessors. Secondly, there are a few cases where the judge may sit with a jury. Thirdly, the court may order separate trials of liability and quantum of damages.[33] Finally, preliminary questions of fact or law can be heard before the main trial.[34]

B. WITNESSES AND EXPERT EVIDENCE

15–005 Lay witnesses may well be under considerable pressure in giving evidence. The pressures on an expert witness will be less in one respect, as such a witness will have had time to reflect on the evidence to be given and may, as a "professional" witness, even have received training in his or her role.[35] However, although the expert may have immunity from civil suit[36] in respect of his or her activities as expert, an expert who fails adequately to perform may have costs awarded against him or her,[37] or be reported to and disciplined by his or her professional body.[38] However, as we have seen and particularly in the fast track, expert evidence will be given by way of written report instead of oral evidence during the trial. Even in a multi-track case the general principle is that "expert evidence is to be given in a written report unless the court directs otherwise".[39] In the small claims track, the court's express permission is required to rely on expert evidence at all.[40] Expert evidence is opinion evidence and opinion evidence is admissible from an expert, though not from an ordinary witness. Experts are not limited to giving opinion evidence. They may:

> "(a) assist a party to establish the facts and to assess the merits of a case and with its preparation; (b) give to the court, as evidence, their expert opinion where opinion evidence apart from that of an expert would not be strictly admissible; (c) give factual evidence on a subject, where, because of their expertise, their evidence will have greater weight than that of an unqualified witness. Evidence as to foreign law will fall into this category. So does the

---

[33] See, for example, PD 29 para.5.3(7).

[34] An alternative method of resolving a preliminary issue of fact but perhaps more particularly of law (such as the proper construction of a document) would be to use the summary judgment procedure in CPR Pt 24.

[35] This is not to suggest that the witness will have been "coached" in relation to this particular case but that those who regularly appear as expert witnesses may seek generic training in presenting themselves in court. However, see n.29 above on the care to be taken by the providers of such training to avoid inappropriately "coaching" witnesses.

[36] *Stanton v Callaghan* [2000] 1 Q.B. 75. The immunity does not extend to perjury or contempt by the expert.

[37] *Phillips v Symes (A Bankrupt) (Expert Witnesses: Costs)* [2004] EWHC 2330.

[38] *Pearce v Ove Arup Partnership Ltd* (2002) I.P.D. 25011; *Meadow v GMC* [2006] EWCA Civ 1390.

[39] CPR r.35.5(1).

[40] CPR r.27.5. One should note that the only provisions of CPR Pt 35 that apply in the fast track are rr.35.1, 35.3, 35.7 and 35.8.

evidence which surveyors sometimes give, in addition to their opinion evidence, as to measurements they have made or examinations which they have carried out; (d) conduct enquiries on behalf of the court and report to the court as to their findings; and (e) sit as assessors with judges to assist the court to understand the technical evidence which the court has to consider."[41]

The right of the parties to adduce expert evidence is somewhat restricted by the Civil Evidence Act 1972[42] and to a much greater extent by the CPR both explicitly[43] and by judges in the exercise of their case management function.[44] In addition, the expert's duties, rights, obligations and even the format of his or her report are closely prescribed by CPR Pt 35 and its practice direction. After some discussion with the two main organisations representing expert witnesses—the Academy of Experts[45] and the Expert Witness Institute[46]—the Protocol for the Instruction of Experts to Give Evidence in Civil Claims (the Experts' Protocol) produced under the ambit of the Civil Justice Council now appears as an annex to PD 35, superseding to some extent the codes of practice of those two organisations.[47]

A party will not be allowed to call expert evidence at trial unless both the court's prior permission has been obtained to adduce expert evidence in respect of a particular issue[48] and—even if the expert is to give oral evidence[49]—a report containing the expert's evidence is exchanged in advance of the trial.[50] The disclosure (by simultaneous exchange if the parties each have their own expert on the same issue) of reports also allows for technical issues to be further narrowed by submitting clarificatory questions to experts[51] and/or by having the experts for the opposing parties meet to see if they can reach areas of agreement.[52]

The fundamental tenets of the new regime, identified in the Final Report[53] are:

---

[41] Interim Report p.181.

[42] s.2

[43] See, for example, CPR rr.35.1, 35.4 and 35.5.

[44] See, for example, *Matthews v Tarmac Bricks & Tiles Ltd, The Times*, July 1, 1999, CA; *Baron v Lovell, The Times*, September 14, 1999, CA, *Daniels v Walker*, [2000] 1 W.L.R. 1382, CA; *Cosgrove v Pattison* [2000] C.P. Rep. 68; Ch D; *R (Factortame) v Transport Secretary (No.8)* [2002] 3 W.L.R. 1104, CA. For examples of a refusal to admit expert evidence, see *Clarke (Executor of the Will of Francis Bacon) v Marlborough Fine Art (London) Ltd* [2002] EWHC 11, and *J.P. Morgan Chase Bank (Formerly Chase Manhattan Bank) v Springwell Navigation Corporation* [2006] EWHC 2755 (Comm).

[45] http://www.academy-experts.org/default.htm.

[46] http://www.ewi.org.uk.

[47] A review of the protocol from the perspective of an expert appears in M. Hall, "Expert Witnesses: Standing Independent" *Legal Week* 22 September 2005.

[48] CPR r.35.4.

[49] See *Kearsley v Klarfeld* [2005] EWCA Civ 1510 for circumstances in which it was decided that oral evidence was required.

[50] CPR r.35.13.

[51] CPR r.35.6. For an example of such questions, see *Mutch v Allen* [2001] C.P. Rep. 77, CA.

[52] CPR r.35.12. See Experts' Protocol paras. 18.3 and 18.6 and *Hubbard v Lambeth, Southwark and Lewisham Health Authority* [2001] EWCA Civ 1455, CA; *Stallwood v David* [2006] EWHC 2600, QBD.

[53] Final Report, Ch.13. Many of these principles in fact only restated the existing law: *National Justice Compania Naveria SA v Prudential Assurance Co Ltd (The Ikarian Reefer) (No.1)* [1995] 1 Lloyd's Rep. 455, CA. They are, however, now stated explicitly in PD 35 para.1.

(a) A statement that "the expert's function is to assist the court". His or her duty is more explicitly defined as a duty on the expert to "help the court impartially on matters within his expertise".[54]

(b) The court is to have "complete control" over the use of expert evidence, including:

  (i) ordering that no expert evidence is required at all (either in relation to the whole dispute or to a particular issue)[55];
  (ii) limiting the number of experts to be called by each party[56];
  (iii) ordering that expert evidence should be given by a jointly instructed expert[57];
  (iv) receiving expert evidence in written form only.[58]

(c) Requiring experts for the parties (assuming separate experts) to meet to see whether they can narrow the areas of dispute.[59]

15–006   Lord Woolf had, in his Interim Report, proposed that it should be the norm that, rather than each party instructing, for example, an expert accountant to calculate the amount of the claimant's losses, each coming to different results between which the court had to choose, a single expert should be appointed jointly by the parties to make a neutral calculation. There was in fact already a limited power to appoint a "court expert" on the application of one or both parties in RSC Ord. 40, but it was little used.

A particular fear at the time was that the imposition of a single joint expert on a case would increase, rather than decrease costs,[60] as each party would then feel the need to instruct its own "shadow" or "advice" expert to comment on the findings of the joint expert: three experts then becoming involved in the case rather than two.[61]

---

[54] See CPR, r.35.3 which adds the rider that this obligation "overrides any obligation to the person from whom [the expert] has received instructions or by whom he is paid". Exceptionally, this rule also applies to small claims track cases. See also on the question of independence, Experts' Protocol, para.15.2.

[55] See CPR rr.35.1 (which also applies in the small claims track) and 35.4. Note in particular that expert evidence will normally be adduced in writing rather than orally in the fast track (CPR r.35.5(2)) and that in the small claims track express permission must be obtained to rely on expert evidence at all (CPR r.27.5).

[56] For an unusual approach to the numbers of experts permitted, see *ES v Chesterfield and North Derbyshire Royal Hospital NHS Trust* [2003] EWCA Civ 1284, CA.

[57] CPR rr.35.7 and 35.8. Exceptionally, both these rules also apply to small claims track cases. It should be noted that the court can limit the recoverable fees of the joint expert, thus requiring the parties to be economical in their choice of expert, or to bear the risk of the expenditure on expert witnesses: CPR r.35.4(4).

[58] As with witness statements, it is the invariable practice that written reports of experts are exchanged prior to trial. CPR r.35.5 adds the rider that the provision of written-only expert evidence will be the norm in the fast track.

[59] CPR r.35.12.

[60] The use of the single joint expert must be proportionate to the case. For a case in which the expert ran into difficulties with the fee limit imposed by the court, see *Kranidiotes v Paschali* [2001] EWCA Civ 357, PC.

[61] See the DCA paper *Further Findings* (August 2002) and D Hall, "Under Scrutiny" (2001) 145(47) *Solicitors' Journal, Expert Witness Supplement*, 18. The Experts' Protocol, para.17, acknowledges that shadow experts might be used but warns "the costs of such expert advisers may not be recoverable".

Lord Woolf, however, persisted: "[a]s a general principle, I believe that single experts should be used wherever the case (or the issue) is concerned with a substantially established area of knowledge and where it is not necessary for the court directly to sample a range of opinions".[62] The Department for Constitutional Affairs estimated that by 2000/01, where expert evidence was relied on at all, 46 per cent of county court cases involved single joint experts.[63] Peysner and Seneviratne[64] found single joint experts being regarded as the norm in fast-track cases in particular and this mirrors the findings of the Law Society in responses to the *Fourth Woolf Questionnaire* (2002), where 38 per cent of respondents thought single joint experts were appropriate in fast-track cases, but opinion was much more evenly divided as to their utility in multi-track cases.

The report of the "single joint expert", where the procedure is used is only a preliminary step. In *Daniels v Walker*,[65] where one of the parties objected to the findings of the single joint expert and sought permission from the court to call an expert witness of his own, Lord Woolf in the Court of Appeal said:

> "In a substantial case such as this, the correct approach is to regard the instruction of an expert jointly by the parties as the first step in obtaining expert evidence on a particular issue. It is to be hoped that in the majority of cases it will not only be the first step but the last step. If, having obtained a joint expert's report, a party, for reasons which are not fanciful, wishes to obtain further information before making a decision as to whether or not there is a particular part (or indeed the whole) of the expert's report which he or she may wish to challenge, then they should, subject to the discretion of the court, be permitted to obtain that evidence."

The obligations of the expert witness are perhaps best considered by examining the prescribed content of the written report for multi-track and fast-track cases[66] which will frequently, especially in the fast track, be the only way in which the expert evidence is presented at trial. PD 35 requires the following format[67]:

(a) details of qualifications[68];

---

[62] Final Report, Ch.13, para.19.

[63] *Emerging Findings, op. cit.* para.4.20. For an example of attempts to meet the joint expert in the absence of the other party, see *Peet v Mid Kent Healthcare NHS Trust* [2001] EWCA Civ 1703; CA. The Experts' Protocol provides at para.17.12 that: "[s]ingle joint experts should not attend any meeting or conference which is not a joint one unless all the parties have agreed in writing or the court has directed that such a meeting may be held and who is to pay the experts' fees for the meeting".

[64] *Op. cit.*

[65] [2000] 1 W.L.R. 1382, CA. See also *Cosgrove v Pattison* [2000] C.P. Rep. 68, *The Times*, February 13, 2001, Ch D; *Alderson v Stillorgan Sales Ltd* [2000] EWCA Civ 1060, 2001 WL 825127, Ch D; *Austen v Oxford City Council* April 17, 2002, QBD (unreported) *Mosedale v Lapwith* [2004] C.L.Y. 346, County Court; *Ighani v R&H Electrical Limited* May 26, 2005, County Court (unreported) and, for the European perspective on a similar issue, *Mantovanelli v France* (1997) E.H.R.R. 370.

[66] PD 35, para.1. Variations or additions to it may be required by specialist courts (such as the Commercial Court or by the professional body to which the expert belongs.

[67] The codes of expert witness organisations or professional bodies may require additional content. For some pragmatic views, see P. Cooper, "Telling it like it is" (2005) 155 N.L.J. 1765; S. Burn, "Expert Witnesses—making an Impression" (2006) 156 N.L.J. 308.

[68] See Experts' Protocol para.13.6 for an indication of the level of detail.

(b)   literature and other material relied on[69];

(c)   a statement "setting out the substance of all facts and instructions given to the expert which are material to the opinions expressed in the report or upon which those opinions are based";

(d)   identification of facts that are within the expert's own knowledge (as opposed, for example, to those which the expert has been told or which the expert has been asked to assume)[70];

(e)   details of tests and experiments carried out, including whether or not they were undertaken under the expert's supervision[71];

(f)   where there is a range of opinion on the issue, a summary of the range of opinion and the expert's reasons for adopting his or her position[72];

(g)   a summary of conclusions;

(h)   if the expert's opinion is qualified in any way, details of the qualification;

(i)   a statement that the expert understands his or her duty to the court,[73] has complied and will continue to comply with it;

(j)   a statement of truth: "I confirm that insofar as the facts stated in my report are within my own knowledge I have made clear which they are and I believe them to be true, and that the opinions I have expressed represent my true and complete professional opinion".[74]

Item (c) on the list bears some explanation. Lord Woolf had expressed concern that pressure was placed on experts to adopt a particular view.[75] After consultation, he remained of the view that transparency of instructions was vital.[76] Many experts will satisfy their obligations in this respect by simply attaching a copy of

---

[69] *ibid.* para.13.8.

[70] *ibid.* para.13.9 as to the level of detail and separation of matters of fact and opinion.

[71] *ibid.* para.13.7.

[72] *ibid.* paras 13.12 and 13.1.3.

[73] In the Commercial Court the statements are expanded to include reference to the Commercial Court Guide.

[74] In *Toth v Jarman* [2006] EWCA Civ. 1028, it was suggested by the Court of Appeal that an additional declaration might usefully be added:

> "(a) That the expert has no conflict of interest (e.g. financial, personal, by way of obligation as an office of an organisation etc) other than those disclosed in the report.
> (b) That any interest disclosed does not affect his or her suitability as an expert.
> (c) That if there is any change in this position between report and trial the expert will notify those by whom he or she is instructed."

[75] It is and always was highly unethical to require an expert to alter his or her opinion: *National Justice Compania Naviera S A v Prudential Assurance Co Ltd (The Ikarian Reefer) (No.1)* [1995] 1 Lloyd's Rep. 455, CA.

[76] Final Report Ch.13 paras 31 to 33 inclusive. Where a single joint expert is ordered, the instructions are jointly drafted by the parties (and therefore the content is known to both) or, if the expert is sent separate instructions by each party, those instructions are copied to the opponent: CPR r.35.8(2).

the letter of instruction to their reports but the nature of this obligation is also discussed in the Experts' Protocol.[77]

The expert witness may be different from an "ordinary" witness in that opinion evidence is being given on matters within a technical field and about investigations carried out by the expert. However, where permission is given for the expert to give oral evidence, he or she is examined and cross-examined in just the same way. Where the parties are permitted to have separate, individually instructed experts, those experts are just as much the "property" of one party as are lay witnesses, subject to the experts' overriding duty "to help the court on the matters within [their] expertise".[78]

An additional power, which could be useful, is contained in the Supreme Court Act 1981, s.70 and County Courts Act 1984, s.63 and now implemented by CPR r.35.15 which allows the appointment of assessors or scientific advisers to assist in the hearing and disposal of the action. These are people who sit with the judge at the trial of the action and their role is considered more fully later in this chapter.

C. THE USE OF THE JURY IN CIVIL CASES

Jury trial is wholly exceptional in civil cases in this jurisdiction and confined to a handful of circumstances. The erosion in the use of juries has been gradual. It appears to have begun with the introduction of the discretionary use of juries in all but six causes of action in 1833[79] and was continued by the temporary

15–007

---

[77] PD 35, para.2.2(3). See Experts' Protocol, para.13.15: "[t]he mandatory statement of the substance of all material instructions should not be incomplete or otherwise tend to mislead". The imperative is transparency. The term "instructions" includes all material which solicitors place in front of experts in order to gain advice. The omission from the statement of "off-the-record" oral instructions is not permitted. . . . " See, for example, *Morris v Bank of India*, November 15, 2001, Ch D, (unreported); *Salt v Consignia plc* [2002] 12 C.L. 51, Bow County Court; *Lucas v Barking, Havering and Redbridge Hospitals NHS Trust* [2003] EWCA Civ 1102, CA. For the application of this rule to draft reports, see *Jackson v Marley Davenport Limited* [2004] EWCA Civ 1225, CA. Where parties disinstruct an expert and seek to rely on a different one, it may be a condition of doing so that the draft or other report of the original expert is disclosed to the opponent: *Beck v Ministry of Defence* [2003] EWCA Civ 1043, and *Vasiliou v Hajigeorgiu* [2005] EWCA Civ 236, CA. See also A. A. S. Zuckerman, "Disclosure of Expert Reports" (2005) 24 (Jul) C.J.Q. 293–297; P. Tracey, "Has privilege been lost post-CPR?" (2005) 155 N.L.J. 1169; B. Mahendra, "Expert Witness evidence: a case law update" (2005) 155 N.L.J. 1762; S. Lindsay, "Civil Procedure—Expert Evidence—Expert Reports" (2005) 3 J.P.I.L. C113–114; A. Edis, "Privilege and Immunity: Problems of Expert Evidence" (2007) 26(JAN) C.J.Q. 40; D. M. Dwyer, "The Effective Management of Bias in Civil Expert Evidence" (2007) 26(JAN) C.J.Q. 57.

[78] CPR r.35.3.

[79] Rules of the Supreme Court 1883, Ord.XXXVI. The causes of action in which there was a right to jury trial were: libel, slander, malicious prosecution, false imprisonment, seduction and breach of promise of marriage. These provisions formed the basis of the statutory reform in 1933. An analysis of the decline in the use of the jury, on the basis of statistics then available, is contained in R. M. Jackson, "The Incidence of Jury Trial during the Past Century" (1937) 1 M.L.R. 132. Jackson does not advance the view that the 1833 Rules were significant in reducing the number of jury trials, but the figures seem to support that contention. See also, M. G. Buckley, "Civil Trial by Jury" (1966) 19 C.L.P. 63. A good chronological account is provided by Bankes L.J. in *Ford v Blurton* (1922) 38 T.L.R. 801 at 802–803.

suspension of jury trial beginning during the First World War and ending in
1925.[80]

The current position, now found in s.69 of the Supreme Court Act 1981, was
first established in 1933.[81] Section 69 provides, first, for a qualified right to jury
trial in some cases, and, secondly, for a discretion to order jury trial in other
cases.

The qualified right to jury trial applies in cases of fraud,[82] libel,[83] slander,
malicious prosecution[84] and false imprisonment.[85] Jury trial is to be granted
unless "the court is of the opinion that the trial requires any prolonged examination of documents or accounts or any scientific or local examination which
cannot conveniently be made with a jury. . . . "[86] This qualified right is exercised
most frequently in defamation actions (that is, libel and slander).[87] After considerable debate about the outcome of a number of celebrated libel actions, the
Court of Appeal now has the power either to order a new trial on the ground that
damages awarded by the jury are excessive or inadequate or, without the agreement of the parties, to substitute for the sum awarded by the jury such sum as
appears to the court to be proper.[88] As the jury's control over awards of damages
has lessened, jury trial might become less attractive to claimants.[89]

---

[80] The Juries Act 1918 provided for trial by judge alone unless the court ordered otherwise, subject
to the right to jury trial in a category of cases slightly wider than that in the 1883 Rules. This
provision was continued by the Administration of Justice Act 1920 but repealed by the Administration of Justice Act 1925

[81] The Administration of Justice (Miscellaneous Provisions) Act 1933, s.6. The number of jury trials
declined sharply after 1933.

[82] The meaning of fraud in this context was considered by Sir Robert Megarry V.-C. in *Stafford
Winfield Cook v Winfield* [1981] 1 W.L.R. 45. For a more recent example, see *Inland Revenue
Commissioners v Kingston Crown Court*, July 24, 2001, Lawtel C0101706, DC.

[83] Although it may not be appropriate for preliminary issues in a defamation case to be tried before
a jury: *Turkot v Global G.O.L.D. Holding GmbH* [2006] EWHC 3361, (QB).

[84] For recent examples, see *Isaac v Chief Constable of the West Midlands Police* [2001] EWCA Civ
1405 CA and *Morrison v Chief Constable of the West Midlands Police* [2003] EWCA Civ
271.

[85] Or any other questions or issues prescribed: Supreme Court Act 1981, s.69(1)(c). County Courts
Act 1984, s.66 provides the equivalent for the county courts. Any application for a claim to be
tried by a jury is made within 28 days of filing a defence: CPR r.26.11. Queen's Bench Division
Guide (applying to the Royal Courts of Justice in London) provides the following at para.8.3.1:
"Claims for libel and slander (defamation), fraud, malicious prosecution and false imprisonment
will be tried by a judge and jury unless the court orders trial by a judge alone."

[86] Supreme Court Act 1981, s.69(l).

[87] *Beta Construction Ltd v Channel Four Television Co Ltd* [1990] 1 W.L.R. 1042. The national
importance of the issues may render jury trial appropriate even if there is considerable documentary evidence: *Rothermere v Times Newspapers* [1973] 1 W.L.R. 448. However, due care
must be taken not to overburden the jury, as may have occurred in *Orme v Associated Newspapers
Group*, March 31, 1981, (unreported) (QBD); December 20, 1982 (unreported) (CA), where the
trial, involving alleged defamation of the Unification Church, lasted more than five months and
117 witnesses were called. *McDonald's Corporation v Steel and Morris* [1997] EWHC (QB) 366
(the "McLibel trial") in 1996, a trial occupying 313 hearing days, was heard without a jury.
Lawyers are required to take great care in estimating the length of trial so as to avoid "hardship
and inconvenience" to jurors: Queen's Bench Division Guide, para.8.3.2.

[88] Courts and Legal Services Act 1990, s. 8; *Grobbelaar v. News Group Newspapers Ltd* [2001]
EWCA Civ 33, CA and [2002] UKHL 40, HL.

[89] A number of factors have conspired to reduce the number of defamation cases coming to trial and
hence to a jury: the Defamation Act 1996 and CPR Pt 53 contain new defences (innocent
dissemination) and a new regime allowing for summary disposal of defamation claims. In
addition, the pre-action protocol for defamation claims is also intended to reduce the number of
claims that come to trial. However, in the Royal Courts of Justice in 2005, 252 defamation claims
were nevertheless issued: *Judicial Statistics 2005*, Table 3.2.

The discretion to order a jury trial in other cases should be ordered only exceptionally.[90] The factors, over and above those imposed by CPR Pt 1, to be taken into account are: the need for uniformity in the award of damages in personal injury cases, the jury being ignorant of the conventional figures in comparable cases[91]; that in such cases the severity[92] or unusual[93] nature of the injuries are not exceptional circumstances, but if they are unique or nearly so,[94] jury trial may be appropriate; the possibility of dishonesty[95] or deliberate lying; the fact that the honour and integrity of the person applying for jury trial may be at stake[96]; the fact that trial without a jury is speedier and less expensive[97]; the proposition that, in the circumstances, trial by judge alone is "more likely to achieve a just result than trial by jury".[98] Further, Lord Diplock indicated that jury trial should not be ordered either simply because there might be a conflict of evidence, since many cases will involve issues of credibility and that is not a sufficient reason to depart from the "usual rule" of trial by judge alone[99] or simply because a party has the "mistaken belief . . . that judges as a class are likely to be biased against him or in favour of his opponent" since to decide on that basis would provide such beliefs with credence, whereas the system is based upon "an impartial judiciary."[100]

If a jury trial does take place it, as in criminal proceedings, is controlled by the provisions of the Juries Act 1974. The qualification for service of jurors, the procedure for summoning, the compilation of panels, the ballot and swearing of jurors, and the right to challenge for cause are all exactly the same for civil and criminal trials.[101] Majority verdicts may be accepted in civil cases, although there is greater flexibility than in criminal matters since the parties to the action may proceed by agreement with an incomplete jury.[102] The discretion to exclude a juror from service which may be exercised by the appropriate officer or by the court[103] is likely to be exercised more freely in civil matters where there may be considerable hardship or inconvenience caused by a long trial.

D. SHOULD THE JURY BE RETAINED IN CIVIL CASES?

In some earlier editions of this book, it was considered that, if the debates on the Supreme Court Bill 1981 (now the Supreme Court Act 1981) were any guide, **15–008**

---

[90] Supreme Court Act 1981, s.69(3). *Ward v James* [1966] 1 Q.B. 273, *per* Lord Denning M.R. at p.303. In the event this case was sent for jury trial but the court was influenced by factors peculiar to it. The point was emphasised in *Williams v Beasley* [1973] 1 W.L.R. 1295, *per* Lord Diplock at 1299H.

[91] *Ward v James* [1966] 1 Q.B. 273, *per* Lord Denning M.R. at pp.296–300, 303.

[92] *Sims v William Howard and Son Ltd* [1964] 2 Q.B. 409.

[93] *Watts v Manning* [1964] 1 W.L.R. 623.

[94] *Hodges v Harland and Wolff Ltd* [1965] 1 W.L.R. 523. The observations of Davies L.J. at pp.1087–1088 are helpful in setting out the difficulties of jury trial.

[95] *Sims v William Howard and Son Ltd* [1964] 2 Q.B. 409 *per* Pearson L.J. at p.419.

[96] *Ward v James* [1966] 1 Q.B. 273, *per* Lord Denning M.R. at p.295; *Williams v Beasley* [1973] 1 W.L.R. 1295, *per* Lord Diplock at p.1298H.

[97] *Williams v Beasley* [1973] 1 W.L.R. 1295, *per* Lord Diplock at p.1299H.

[98] *ibid. per* Lord Diplock at p.1299H.

[99] *ibid. per* Lord Diplock at pp.1298–1299.

[100] *ibid.* at p.1299H.

[101] See below Ch.17.

[102] Juries Act 1974, s.17.

[103] *ibid.* ss.9 and 9A.

that this was already an academic question. Parliament at that time showed itself unwilling to countenance any further restriction on the right to jury trial, let alone its abolition.[104] The debate about jury trials in general raised its head again more recently in the context of the results of Auld L.J.'s review of the criminal courts,[105] and extended to the civil context particularly in the context of a spate of well-publicised libel trials in 2001[106] as well as the introduction of the Defamation Act 1996, implemented by Pt 53 of the CPR and supplemented by a specific pre-action protocol for defamation cases.

The disadvantages of jury trial appear to be the additional time, and consequential additional expense of a jury trial; the variability of jury verdicts; the potential hardship and inconvenience suffered by individual jurors in lengthy cases; the unrealistic expectation that lay people[107] should listen to and comprehend complex and extensive evidence; the unpredictability of jury verdicts and the reluctance of the Court of Appeal to interfere with jury awards[108]; and the additional burden which may be placed on advocates and judge where complex questions of law are in issue.[109]

These reasons are sound pragmatic grounds for the proposition that jury trial is not the "best" mode of trial for all civil claims and that trial by judge alone would normally be preferable. But are any of the reasons sufficiently strong to support the view that civil juries should be abandoned altogether?

The Faulks Committee on Defamation[110] recommended restrictions on the use of juries in defamation actions whilst rejecting arguments for their total abolition. The Committee concluded that in defamation cases the court should have the same discretion to order jury trial as in other civil cases and that the function of the jury should be limited to deciding issues of liability, leaving the assessment of damages to the judge.[111]

Various distinguished judges have, however, declared the constitutional importance of the right to jury trial. For example, Atkin L.J. in *Ford v Blurton* described jury trial as "the bulwark of liberty, the shield of the poor from the rich

---

[104] Jacob (1987), pp.156–160.

[105] *A Review of the Criminal Courts of England and Wales* (September 2001), Ch.5.

[106] *Grobbelaar v News Group Newspapers Ltd op. cit.*, thought to be the first case in more than 100 years in which a jury's award of damages was set aside as "perverse" (Scott-Bayfield, "Defamation Update" (2001) Sol. J. 145 (21), p.501). Although the jury's award was reinstated by the House of Lords ([2002] UKHL 40), it was reduced to £1, which can hardly have been a great deal of comfort to the claimant. See also *Loutchansky v. Times Newspapers Ltd* [2001] E.M.L.R. 933, QBD; *McPhilemy v Times Newspapers Ltd* [2001] EWCA Civ 871, CA; *Berezovsky v Forbes Inc.* [2001] EWCA Civ 1251, CA; *Hamilton v Al Fayed* [2001] 1 A.C. 395, HL (affirming decisions below); *Irving v Penguin Books Ltd* [2001] EWCA Civ 1197.

[107] Note, however, that as a result of the report of Auld L.J., *op. cit.* many bars to eligibility for jury service were removed, so allowing lawyers, including judges, to sit on juries, Criminal Justice Act 2003, s.321 amending Juries Act 1974, s.1.

[108] See *Grobbelaar v News Group Newspapers Ltd* [2002] UKHL 40, HL.

[109] These defects of the jury as a mode of trial are culled from various sources including: M. G. Buckley, "Civil Trial by Jury" (1966) 19 C.L.P. 63; W. R. Cornish, *The Jury* (1968), Ch.8; P. Devlin, *Trial by Jury* (1956), pp.130–135; *Hodges v Harland and Wolff Ltd* [1965] 1 W.L.R. 523; *Ward v James* [1966] 1 Q.B. 273; and the *Report of the Committee on Defamation* (Cmnd. 5909, 1975) (The Faulks Committee). Other examples of concern about costs and the use of juries in libel trials under the CPR are cited in Hickman, "The Press Gang", L.S.G., June 19, 2001 and in Melville-Brown, "Media Law", (2000) 97(16) L.S.G.38 discussing *Irving v Penguin Books Ltd, op. cit.*

[110] *Report of the Committee on Defamation, op. cit.*

[111] *ibid.* paras 455–457.

and the powerful".[112] Although this argument may appear to be more suited to criminal trials, there is some truth in it in relation to civil trials, particularly in, for example, some kinds of professional negligence claim. However, if judges are independent of the state and other vested interests,[113] that argument may be weak. A different suggestion is that it is desirable to involve as many people as possible in the administration of justice[114] and that the jury stands between the judges and the person in the street to ensure that ordinary standards are applied in the doing of justice.[115]

E. THE ROLE OF THE JUDGE

In civil matters, therefore, the judge normally sits alone to determine the outcome of the action. The incidence of jury trial has already been explained, but there are a number of situations in which the judge may have the assistance of others sitting with him or her. The composition of the Employment Appeal Tribunal, with lay members and High Court judges, exemplified the formal introduction of lay expertise into the judicial process, but there is a general power[116] to call in the aid of one or more assessors or scientific advisers in particular cases.   **15–009**

Assessors are used especially in certain types of admiralty proceedings in the Queen's Bench Division,[117] but there is nothing to prevent a judge, provided it is consistent with CPR Pt 1 and the obligations of Art.6, ECHR to do so, using an assessor in other cases.[118] One would expect that the need for an assessor would be identified during the case management stages prior to the trial, rather than the trial judge adjourning the trial in order to obtain expert assistance.[119] The decision at trial, however, remains that of the judge; the assessors merely advise.[120]

It may prove difficult for the judge to refrain from intervening with questions and observations during the course of the trial. Trial procedure is relatively flexible in a civil trial and the absence of the jury enables the judge to take a more robust line in dealing with matters that are irrelevant or uncontentious. However,

---

[112] (1922) 38 T.L.R. 801 at 805. See also, to similar effect, Bankes L.J. in the same case. The same point was made by Mr Frank Dobson M.P. in the debates on the Supreme Court Bill when he said: "Jury service is more important to the preservation of individual liberty and the preservation of our judicial system than all the scurvy race of lawyers put together."

[113] See above, Ch.4.

[114] See, e.g., the evidence of Sir Peter Rawlinson Q.C. and Viscount Dilhorne given to the Faulks Committee (1975), para.477.

[115] On a pragmatic level, Lord Denning M.R. supported the jury for the protection of a person's honour and integrity or to discover when one party may be lying; *Ward v James* [1966] 1 Q.B. 273 at 295.

[116] Supreme Court Act 1981, s.70; County Courts Act 1984, s. 63. See also CPR r.35.15 and PD 35 para.6.

[117] Where the assessor is normally one or more of the Elder Brethren of Trinity House: CPR r.61.13.

[118] In *Ahmed v University of Oxford* [2002] EWCA Civ 1907, for example, assessors were appointed under Race Relations Act 1976, s.67(4).

[119] Devlin J. suggested adjournment as preferable to obtaining such advice after the trial but before judgment in *Esso Petroleum Co Ltd v Southport Corporation* [1956] A.C. 218 at 222–223. His view was supported by the House of Lords in the same case.

[120] For guidance on the role of assessors and the interelationship between the judge and the assessor, see *Ahmed v University of Oxford, op. cit.*

the judge must not take such an active part in the case that it appears that the
advocates are deprived of the conduct of the trial. As a result of the positive
obligations imposed on the trial judge by CPR Pt 1 and Art.6 ECHR, an
interventionist role is now justifiable.[121]

If sitting alone, the judge may take time to decide where the truth lies, or, more
accurately, whether the claimant has satisfied the burden of proof,[122] and give a
reserved judgment at a later date, or an extempore judgment may be given at the
conclusion of the hearing. If sitting with a jury, the judge must sum up the
evidence and direct on the law as would be done in a trial on indictment.
Ultimately judgment will be given.

F. THE JUDGMENT AND REMEDIES

15–010   A judgment is a reasoned decision in which the judge will normally set out the
facts of the case as found by him or her, and provide conclusions on the law
applicable to the facts. Some of the arguments put by the advocates may be
repeated so as to set the decision in context,[123] and an opinion is likely to be
given on all matters relating to the action that might be relevant if the losing party
appealed. In particular, there may be findings of fact which are not crucial to the
first instance judgment but which might become relevant if the Court of Appeal
were to take a different view. The trial judge will attempt to avoid the expense
and difficulty of a new trial if the appellate court changes a part of the
judgment.[124]

There is an important adage worthy of repetition: where there is a legal right
there is, or ought to be, a legal remedy and, where there is no remedy, there is no
right. There is an extensive range of remedies, which may be added to or
varied[125] by judicial decision or by legislation. By s.3 of the Courts and Legal
Services Act 1990, county courts may generally award the same remedies as the
High Court.[126] Damages are the most likely remedy sought in the Queen's Bench
but readers should be aware that other remedies are available. In particular, the
claimant may be seeking the recovery of property, one of the many equitable

---

[121] *Demarco Almeida v Opportunity Equity Partners Ltd* [2006] UKPC 44. For the position where a
   judge has to withdraw from a case because of an inability to provide a fair trial, see, *R v Bow
   Street Magistrates, Ex p. Pinochet (No.2)* [2001] 1 A.C. 119, HL; *Locabail (UK) Ltd v Bayfield
   Properties Ltd* [2000] Q.B. 451, CA.
[122] i.e. whether the claimant has proved his or her case on a balance of probabilities.
[123] Because it is the responsibility of the parties—within the constraints of the judicial case
   management applied to the case—to advance argument on the issues they wish to be decided, it
   is always important to know whether a particular line of argument has been canvassed or not
   when assessing a judgment. In respect of appellate decisions reported in the Law Reports series,
   the major arguments of the advocates are normally set out as part of the report.
[124] e.g. although a judge may find against a claimant on the question of the defendant's liability in
   negligence, the quantum of damages may be determined lest the Court of Appeal reverses on the
   liability point (unless it has already been arranged that there should be a split trial). If no finding
   had been made on quantum the issue would have to be the subject of another trial.
[125] If a new remedy affects the substantive law, it can only be created by Act of Parliament.
[126] County courts do not have the power to order certain kinds of injunctions, declarations of
   incompatibility under the Human Rights Act 1998 or orders of kinds to be prescribed by the Lord
   Chancellor.

remedies, such as an order for specific performance,[127] an injunction,[128] or a declaration.

Damages is the common law term for an order requiring payment of money by way of compensation. An award of damages may be made in relation to a vast range of wrongs and indebtedness.[129] The traditional division of damages is into liquidated and unliquidated damages: liquidated where the claimant specifies a set sum of money as owed at law in the original claim (described in the CPR as "claims for a specified sum"); unliquidated ("claims for an unspecified sum") where the court must calculate the sum to be paid if liability is established, unless the parties agree the quantum of damages.

Where the parties do not agree, the basis for awarding damages will be slightly different dependent upon the cause of action. The basic theory of damages for contract is that they should put the claimant in the position he or she would have been in, financially at least, had the contract been properly performed. The basic theory of tort damages is that the claimant, so far as money can, should be returned to the position he or she would have been in had the tort not occurred.

Judges are, for example, frequently called upon to assess damages in cases where the defendant has negligently inflicted personal injuries upon the claimant. There are normally two aspects of such an award: (i) compensation for non-pecuniary losses; and (ii) compensation for pecuniary or economic losses. Under the first head there may be damages for pain and suffering and loss of amenity[130] or, where the part of a body injured has no apparent function, the injury itself.[131] Damages for loss of amenity are awarded roughly in accordance with a tariff dependent on the seriousness of the injury or injuries.[132] Under the second head fall damages for such items as lost earnings[133] and medical expenses.

For example, in *Lim Poh Choo v Camden and Islington Area Health Authority*[134] the plaintiff (in the terminology then current), an NHS registrar, suffered serious brain damage after a minor operation. She was ultimately awarded £229,298.64. This included £20,00 for pain and suffering and loss of amenities; £3,956 for expenses to the date of trial; £16,500 for the costs of care in Malaysia; £1,923 for travelling expenses; £4,226.64 for the costs of care in the United Kingdom to date; £14,213 for loss of earnings to the date of trial; £76,800 for the

---

[127] Available to enforce contractual obligations.

[128] The most common form of injunction is prohibitory since it forces a defendant to desist from wrongful conduct or forbids wrongful conduct when it has not even started, i.e. the *quia timet* injunction. A mandatory injunction requires the doing of some act.

[129] Whilst this chapter concentrates on claims in contract and tort, damages can be awarded in quasi-contract, in certain equity claims, e.g. where recission is allowed for innocent misrepresentation, or where a trustee commits a breach of trust. Further, certain tribunals may also award compensation, e.g. an Employment Tribunal for unfair dismissal.

[130] e.g. damages for the loss of a leg, which may be increased where the claimant was a keen sports player whose enjoyment of life is thus substantially impaired.

[131] e.g. a spleen, *Forster v Pugh* [1955] C.L.Y. 741.

[132] Details of damages given in personal injury cases are given in *Kemp and Kemp on the Quantum of Damages* (looseleaf and CD Rom). The "tariff" is set out in the Judicial Studies Board *Guidelines for the Assessment of General Damages in Personal Injury Cases* (8th edn, Oxford University Press).

[133] In the most serious cases there will be the difficult task of estimating the loss of earnings in the future.

[134] [1980] A.C. 174.

costs of future care; and £92,000 for the loss of future earnings including pension rights.[135]

At the end of the judgment, the successful party's advocate must ask formally for judgment to be entered in the terms which the judge has indicated. The advocate may ask for, for example, "judgment for the claimant for £229,298.64" or "judgment for the defendant and that the claimant's claim be dismissed". At this stage the question of any interest payable on a money judgment will be raised by the advocate, who will also ask for costs.[136] It is at this stage that the trial judge is made aware of the details of any Pt 36 offer[137] and can decide whether or not to impose any penalising orders on a party who has failed to do better than the opponent's offer.[138]

Traditionally, money judgments were expressed in sterling, but since 1975 it has been possible for a court to give judgment in a foreign currency.[139]

By CPR r.40.3, the order containing the judgment will normally be drawn up by the court.[140] Having obtained judgment, the successful party must go on to enforce it. We can now refer to the successful party as the "judgment creditor" and the unsuccessful party as the "judgment debtor".

G. ENFORCING JUDGMENT[141]

1. INTRODUCTION

15–011 If judgment is obtained, the order of the court may be declaratory or con-stitutive[142] and nothing more need be done. In most instances, however, the order will require the performance or non-performance of some further act or acts. The

---

[135] Liability and damages in mesothelioma cases are now governed by the Compensation Act 2006.

[136] See para.11–003.

[137] See para.12–028.

[138] See CPR r.36.14.

[139] Practice Direction (QBD: Judgment: Foreign Currency) (No.1), [1976] 1 W.L.R. 83, PD 40, para.10; *Miliangos v George Frank (Textiles) Ltd* [1976] A.C. 443, and, more recently, *Carnegie v Giessen* [2005] EWCA Civ 191.

[140] Unless the court orders one of the parties to draw it up, or one of the parties agrees to draw it up, the court dispenses with the need to draw up the order or the order is a consent order. Where the order is drawn up by one of the parties, sufficient copies of it for all the parties must be filed with the court no later than seven days later for sealing by the court. CPR rr.40.3 and 40.4 and PD 40B para.1.

[141] Recognition and enforcement of judgments with EU countries (other than Denmark) is governed by Council Regulation (EC) No.44/2001 and with some other countries by the Administration of Justice Act 1920, Pt II or the Foreign Judgments (Reciprocal Enforcement) Act 1933. Enforcement of judgments as between different parts of the UK is governed by Civil Jurisdiction and Judgments Act 1982, Pt 11. See CPR Pt 74. Regulation 805/2004 provides for a European Enforcement Order in undefended cases: C. Crifo, "First steps towards the harmonistaion of civil procedure: the regulation creating a European enforcement order for uncontested claims" (2005) 24(APR) C.J.Q. 200.

[142] "Constitutive" orders are extremely various and extend across many areas of law. Examples in the civil law are adoption and legitimation orders, award of guardianship, divorces, appointment of trustees, dissolution of partnerships, liquidation of companies, adjudication in bankruptcy. Sometimes the order merely records a fact, an example being the declaration that a seeming marriage was always null and void.

form of the court order will frequently demonstrate this: thus the normal order in an action for damages requires the defendant to pay the claimant the specified figure.

Many defendants obey court orders out of law-abiding motives.[143] Others will be influenced by the fact that practical procedures exist to secure performance or obedience. These procedures might be said to form a system of enforcement, which Jacob, however, has described as being

> "an unplanned, unsystematic, haphazard, complex system. It operates, especially in relation to money judgments, largely on a hit-or-miss basis. In relation to both money and non-money judgments, it is in part effective, but in part it is ineffective, inefficient, somewhat random and sometimes oppressive."[144]

These sentiments were shared by the Lord Chancellor's Department in 2000: "[t]he picture that emerges is of an enforcement system that is not particularly effective, difficult to understand and prone to excessive delay".[145]

Parts 70 to 73 inclusive were incorporated into the CPR in March 2002 in order to deal with enforcement in a more consistent and coherent way. This is the end result of a process commenced in March 1998 and culminating in July 2001[146] with a report containing 40 proposals seeking to: (1) make the process more straightforward and comprehensible; (2) improve recovery rates; (3) achieve fairness for both debtors (who may genuinely not have the means to pay) and creditors; and finally (4) to speed up the process. In July 2001 a Green Paper[147] was issued; followed by a White Paper in March 2003[148] and, at the time of writing, a Tribunals, Courts and Enforcement Bill ("the Bill").

At present, however, the procedures that exist are variously derived from the common law, equity and statute. They are primarily aimed at specific forms of judgment, but they are capable of being used for any type of judgment if they can be effective. Thus sequestration, authorising the seizure of all or any property of the defendant within the jurisdiction, imposition of a fine, and committal to prison are all drastic sanctions suitable for flagrant breaches of orders such as injunctions, but in extreme circumstances they can be used to enforce other types of judgment where there has been a civil contempt of court. Imprisonment for a few civil debts may also be imposed, separately from a finding of contempt of court.

A brief description of the main enforcement orders available follows, together with an indication of the proposed amendments under the Bill, but, as the

---

[143] However, in the report of the *First Phase of the Enforcement Review* (July 2001) (hereafter Enforcement Review) it was suggested that at least £600 million a year was lost in unpaid judgments.

[144] Jacob (1987) p.188.

[145] Enforcement Review, *op. cit.*

[146] It is worth noting that the review itself commented on the paucity of statistical information about the effectiveness of the enforcement process but that, for example, the Court Service had provided figures suggesting that only approximately 35% of county court warrants of execution result in payment.

[147] *Towards Effective Enforcement: A Single Piece of Bailiff Law and a Regulatory Structure for Enforcement*, Lord Chancellor's Department, July 2001 (Cmd. 5096).

[148] *Effective Enforcement: Improved methods of recovery for civil court debt and commercial rent and a single regulatory regime for warrant enforcement agents* (DCA, March 2003 (Cm.5744)). Abolition of the common law right to distrain for rent arrears and a new procedure for commercial rent arrears recovery appear in Pt 3 of the Bill.

different enforcement orders are targeted at different kinds of assets, it may be necessary, before moving to seek such an order, to find out more about the judgment debtor's means. This can be achieved by an order under CPR Pt 71 (previously "oral examination" of the judgment debtor) that the debtor attend court, on pain of committal, to provide information about his or her means or any other information required for enforcement of the order. This will normally take place in the judgment debtor's local county court.[149] Part 4 of the Bill allows for the judgment creditor to apply for disclosure of information about the debtor held by, for example, a government department or HM Revenue and Customs Commissioners or, as an "information order" against any other person, such as, in principle, the debtor's employer.

It should also be noted that the Bill contains, in Pt 5, substantial provisions designed to assist debtors manage their indebtedness, including both debt management schemes and "enforcement restriction orders". A National Enforcement Service, launched in March 2005 for implementation in 2007/08 to improve recovery of criminal fines may also ultimately take civil judgments within its remit.

2. Enforcement of Money Judgments

(a) Fieri Facias or warrant of execution

15–012   These forms of enforcement operate against the debtor's movable property. The High Court form is the writ of *fieri facias*.[150] This writ is, by Courts Act 2003, s.99, no longer issued to the sheriff of the county where the defendant's goods are located but to the relevant "enforcement officer" and the enforcement officer enforces the writ by seizing goods sufficient to cover in value the amount owed under the judgment, the costs of execution and expenses.

The county court form is the warrant of execution,[151] which requires the court bailiff to carry out the order. The seized goods must be expected to cover only the amount owed under the judgment and the costs of execution.

Where the sum to be enforced is £5,000 or more, enforcement proceedings must be taken in the High Court, regardless of in which court the trial was heard. Where the sum is less than £600, enforcement must be through the county court. For sums in between, enforcement may be through either court.[152]

The exercise of this concurrent jurisdiction is vast. In 2005, 36,039 writs of fieri facias and 339,262 warrants of execution were issued.[153] Part 3 of the Bill renames writs of fieri facias "writs of control" and warrants of execution "warrants of control" and prescribes a new procedure for execution in Sch.12. Following some concern expressed in the Green Paper about the quality control of those carrying out execution, Pt 3 also provides for certification of "enforcement agents".

---

[149] PD 71 para.2.1.
[150] CPR Sch.1, RSC Ord. 46 and PD RSC 46.
[151] CPR Sch.2, CCR Ord. 26 and PD RSC 46.
[152] High Court and County Courts Jurisdiction Order 1991 (SI 1991/724) as amended, art.8.
[153] *Judicial Statistics 2005*, Table 3.11 and p.55 respectively.

(b) Third Party Debt Orders (previously "garnishee proceedings")

Here, the judgment creditor obtains payment by attaching a debt (such as a **15–013** commercial debt, or the contents of a bank account) owed to the judgment debtor by a third party so that it is paid to the judgment creditor instead. The procedure is governed by CPR Pt 72 and PD 72 implementing suggestions made in the Enforcement Review,[154] including the provision that a judgment debtor can obtain a "hardship payment order". In 2005, 28 third party debt orders were issued in the Queen's Bench Division of the High Court[155] and 6,593 in the county courts.[156]

(c) Attachment of earnings

A third party debt order cannot be obtained over wages. The Attachment of **15–014** Earnings Act 1971 empowers the county court[157] to oblige employers to make deductions from the judgment debtor's wages to satisfy the judgment (provided the judgment or the unsatisfied portion of it exceeds £50). In 2005, 41,666 orders were made.[158]

The Enforcement Review proposed a "substantial overhaul" of this procedure, suggesting amongst other proposals: (1) a fixed tariff of deductions rather than individual calculations in each individual case, themselves reliant on the debtor's ability and willingness to complete the appropriate forms; (2) finding a mechanism to track debtors on change of job; and (3) introducing a national register of orders. Clauses 83 and 84 of the Bill amend the 1971 Act to implement points (1) and (2). As to point (3), a national register of Judgments, Orders and Fines replaced the register of county court judgments in April 2006.[159]

(d) Charging orders

Charging orders under the Charging Orders Act 1979 allow charges to be created **15–015** on property. The procedure is governed by CPR Pt 73 and PD 73. The judgment creditor becomes in effect an equitable chargee with rights to recoup his or her debt from the income of the property or from its later sale. Consequently, the debtor cannot, for example, sell the property without satisfying the debt or having the order transferred to other property. The principal type of property so chargeable is land or any interest in land, and the charge is registrable under the Land Charges Act 1972. Government and company stocks, dividends and interest on such stock and moneys in court may also be subjected to a charging order.[160] An application for a charging order must be made in the county court unless the judgment debt exceeds £5,000 in which case the application may be made in the High Court.[161] In 2005, 170 charging orders were issued in the Queen's Bench

---

[154] *op. cit.*, s.6.
[155] *Judicial Statistics 2005*, Table 3.11.
[156] *ibid.* Table 4.19.
[157] CPR Sch.2, CCR Ord. 27. The High Court only has power to attach for payment of maintenance orders; Attachment of Earnings Act 1971, s.1.
[158] *Judicial Statistics 2005*, Table 4.21.
[159] Courts Act 2003, s.98(1)(a) and Register of Judgments, Orders and Fines Regulations 2005 (SI 2005/3595). The Register can be inspected at *http://www.registry-trust.org.uk.*
[160] See CPR r.73.6.
[161] Charging Orders Act 1979, s.1(2).

Division of the High Court and applications were made for 65,676 orders in the county court, the latter a 44 per cent increase on 2004.[162] Clauses 85 and 86 of the Bill amend the 1979 Act to regulate the way in which the charging order can be enforced when the judgment debtor defaults on agreed instalment payments as well as allowing for a minimum financial threshold below which a charging order cannot be made or cannot be enforced by sale.

(e) Equitable execution: appointment of a receiver

15–016 Where none of the other means of execution is likely to be effective, it is possible for a receiver to be appointed to take income due to the judgment debtor and apply it towards the debt owed to the judgment creditor.[163] Because of the effectiveness of the other means of execution and since it is cumbersome, this is a rarely used means of enforcement.

3. POSSESSION ORDERS

(a) Land

15–017 The procedure governing the procedure for possession claims is found in CPR Pt 55 and its practice direction.[164] The means of enforcement remains a writ of possession in the High Court[165] and a warrant for possession in the county court.[166] In 2005, enforcement proceedings were issued in respect of 22 possession claims in the High Court and 131,505 in the county court.[167]

(b) Goods

15–018 Judgments for delivery of goods may allow the judgment debtor the option of paying the value of the goods rather than giving them up. Otherwise, execution is by way of writ of delivery in the High Court[168] instructing the enforcement officer to cause the goods to be delivered to the claimant. In the county court, a similar procedure is undertaken through a warrant of delivery.[169] In 2005, the High Court issued a single writ for delivery but in the county courts, 2,380 warrants for delivery of goods were issued.[170]

---

[162] *Judicial Statistics 2005*, Tables 3.11 and 4.20 respectively.
[163] CPR Sch.1, RSC Ord. 30.
[164] Civil Procedure (Amendment) Rules 2001. Note there is now a pre-action protocol for possession claims based on rent arrears and that new provision is made for rent arrears recovery generally under Pt 3 of the Bill.
[165] CPR Sch.1, RSC Ord. 45, r.3 and PD.
[166] CPR Sch.2. CCR Ord. 26, r.17 and PD.
[167] *Judicial Statistics 2005*, Tables 3.11 and 4.20.
[168] CPR Sch.1, RSC Ord. 45, r.4.
[169] CPR Sch.2, CCR Ord. 26, r.16 and PD.
[170] *Judicial Statistics 2005*, Tables 3.11 and 4.20.

4. MANDATORY AND PROHIBITORY ORDERS

(a) Specific performance

A failure by a seller to execute an instrument in response to a judgment for specific performance may be overcome by the appointment of someone else (e.g. a Chancery master) to execute it in the seller's stead.[171] **15–019**

(b) Injunction

The injunctions that may be imposed as a means of execution are the same as those that may be imposed as a remedy consequent upon the trial.[172] **15–020**

5. CONCLUSION

Such enforcement procedures form the largest component of the work of the civil courts, accounting for a substantial proportion of their resources.[173] This is reflected in the figures quoted above from the *Judicial Statistics 2005*. For this reason, as we have seen, debt enforcement procedures were examined as a part of the Civil Justice Review in 1988,[174] by the Enforcement Review from 1998 and continue to be the subject of vigorous examination at the date of writing.[175] **15–021**

---

[171] CPR Sch.1, RSC Ord. 45, r.8.

[172] See above, para.15–010.

[173] Civil Justice Review (1988), para.534(i).

[174] *ibid.* Ch.9. "Debt enforcement" is not limited to the enforcement of judgment debts: *ibid.* para.534.

[175] See Enforcement Review (July 2000); the Green Paper *Towards Effective Enforcement—a single piece of bailiff law and a regulatory structure for enforcement* (July 2001), the White Paper *Effective Enforcement* (March 2003) and the Tribunals, Courts and Enforcement Bill, 2006. An Advisory Group on Enforcement Service Delivery was formed in September 2001 and presented its final report in December 2003.

THE TRIBUNAL HEARING

At the hearing, the chairman of the tribunal has the difficult task of ensuring that **16–001** a sufficient level of informality is achieved so that the parties do not feel inhibited in putting their respective cases, whilst maintaining some procedural and evidentiary safeguards so that the rights of the parties are not prejudiced in an unacceptable way.

We made the point in the previous chapter on tribunals that it is scarcely possible to choose a "typical" tribunal and the observations hereafter draw on a variety of sources. However, just as there are common problems to be solved in devising an appropriate pre-hearing procedure, so there are common problems in the conduct of hearings. What procedural rules, if any, should be followed? What role should the chairman play and what responsibilities does he or she have? What sort of representation, if any, should be permitted or encouraged, and how should it be funded?

A. PROCEDURE

Differing approaches to the achievements of procedural fairness may be **16–002** observed, but in most tribunals much is left to the chairman in determining the form of the hearing. Three illustrations may demonstrate that the amount of guidance given by the appropriate rules is often minimal.

1. Social Security and Child Support Appeal Tribunals

Where an appeal is made to an appeal tribunal the appellant and any other party must notify the clerk to the tribunal, on a form approved by the Secretary of State, whether he or she wishes to have an oral hearing or is content for the matter to proceed without (a "paper hearing"[1]). This must be done with 14 days of receipt of the form, otherwise the appeal may be struck out. If an oral hearing is requested, one must be held unless the appeal is struck out. In any event, the chairman may of his or her own motion direct that an oral hearing be held if satisfied that such a hearing is necessary to enable the tribunal to reach a decision.[2] The chances of success are likely to be greater where the appellant opts for an oral hearing.

The procedural regulations provide that:

> "Subject to the following provisions of this Part,[3] the procedure for an oral hearing shall be such as the chairman, or in the case of an appeal tribunal which has only one member, such as that member, shall determine."[4]

This general power is qualified in certain respects by other provisions. Fourteen days' notice of an oral hearing must be given, unless waived. Representation is permitted[5]; witnesses may be called[6]; every person who has the right to be heard shall be given an opportunity of putting questions directly to any witnesses called at the hearing and of addressing the tribunal[7]; an oral hearing must be in public except where the chairman is satisfied that it is necessary to hold the hearing (or part of a hearing) in private in the interests of national security, morals, public order or children, for the protection of the private or family life of one or more parties, or in special circumstances because publicity would prejudice the interests of justice[8]; any party to the proceedings is entitled to be present and to be heard.[9]

It is the chairman (or single member) who decides how these requirements should be fulfilled and it is to be expected that there will be variations in procedure from chairman to chairman. The Social Security and Child Support

---

[1] Note Wikeley's comment that it is difficult to reconcile this with the inquisitorial philosophy of social security tribunals: *Wikeley, Ogus and Barendt's The Law of Social Security* (5th edn, 2002), p.196.

[2] Social Security and Child Support (Decisions and Appeals) Regulations 1999 (SI 1999/991), reg. 39, as amended by SI 2004/3368, reg.2(5).

[3] i.e. Ch.IV (oral hearings), V (Decisions of Appeal Tribunals and Related Matters) of Pt VI (Appeal Tribunals for Social Security Contracting Out of Pensions, Vaccine Damage and Child Support).

[4] SI 1999/991, reg.49(1).

[5] *ibid.* reg.49(8).

[6] *ibid.* reg.49(11), as substituted by SI 2002/1379, reg.14(a).

[7] *ibid.* reg.49(11).

[8] *ibid.* reg.49(6)

[9] *ibid.* reg.49(7), as substituted by SI 2002/1379, reg.14(b). A party, representative or tribunal member (other than the chairman) may be present by means of a live television link. "Party to the proceedings" is defined in reg.1(3), and in the case of appeals to an appeal tribunal mean the Secretary of State (or Board of Inland Revenue or an officer of the Board in contributions cases), and any other person who is one of the principal parties for the purpose of ss.13 and 14 of the Social Security Act 1998 (redetermination of appeals by tribunal; appeal from tribunal to Commissioner) or who has a right of appeal under other specified provisions.

Commissioners[10] may correct procedural irregularities on appeal, but it will be apparent that the provisions are so widely drafted that such an irregularity will have to be very serious before it will be regarded as material.[11]

A "possible model"[12] is for there to be: a brief introduction by the chairman; a question to the presenting officer if he or she has anything further to say about the submission (for example enabling a concession to be made); a brief statement by the appellant's representative outlining arguments but not giving evidence; questions to the appellant by the tribunal, the appellant's representative, and the presenting officer[13]; further points arising from the evidence by the representative and the presenting officer; and the appellant is asked if there is anything else he or she wants to tell the tribunal. The tribunal has a discretion to proceed with the hearing in the absence of the appellant.[14] At the conclusion of the hearing, the members of the tribunal consider their decision in private.[15]

Every decision must be recorded in summary by the chairman (or single member); this must be included in a decision notice in such written form as has been approved by the President of appeal tribunals.[16] Copies of the notice must be sent or given to every party to the proceedings as soon as may be practicable after the appeal has been decided.[17] A party may apply to the clerk for a statement of the reasons for the tribunal's decision within one month of the sending or giving of the decision notice. The statement must be prepared by the chairman (or single member). If the decision is not unanimous, the notice must indicate that one member dissented and the statement of reasons must include the reasons given for the dissent.[18]

The role of the presenting officer in the procedure of an SSCSAT is interesting in that he or she is expected to put forward the view of the officer who made the decision against which the claimant is appealing, but is also expected to exercise

---

[10] See above, para.2–039. The Commissioners constitute an appeal body from the decisions of SSCSATs.

[11] In practice the most important ground of appeal is failure to state the reasons for a decision adequately: N. J. Wikeley, *Wikeley, Ogus and Barendt's The Law of Social Security* (5th edn, 2002), p.201.

[12] Suggested in *The Benchbook* (8th edn, 2006), pp.84–85 (available on the Tribunals Service Website). However, it is not just the order of events which is significant but the attitude and appearance of the tribunal members. One of the original authors, representing a nervous claimant at a NILT had been at pains to explain in advance the informality of the procedure and distinguish it from court procedure as seen in "Crown Court" on television. The opening remarks of the chairman of the tribunal were, "Good afternoon, I must warn you, Mrs X, that you must tell the truth in these proceedings—we are just like a court." If the claimant had been unrepresented, the niceties of procedure would have mattered little after that!

[13] The presenting officer is an officer of the DWP specifically assigned to present cases before tribunals. Some presenting officers, therefore, become very experienced "advocates" and well known to their local tribunal. Presenting officers are, however, becoming more and more rare: *Benchbook*, para.44.

[14] SI 1999/991, reg.49(4), (5). If an appellant who has been given due notice at the last known address fails to attend without giving any explanation "it will usually be right to proceed in his absence": *Benchbook*, p.8.

[15] The clerk to the tribunal (but not the presenting officer) is permitted to remain with the members during their deliberations: SI 1999/991, reg.49(12).

[16] SI 1999/991, reg.53(1)–(3).

[17] The prescribed form no longer includes a space where there may be written summary grounds for the decision: there were conflicting Commissioner's decisions on whether a failure to state such grounds was a breach of procedure: CIB/4497/98; CSDLA/551/1999: see D. Bonner (ed), *Social Security Legislation 2006* Vol. III (Commentary by R. White and M. Rowland), p.633.

[18] SI 1999/991, reg.53(4)–(5), as amended by SI 2002/1379, reg.16 and SI 2005/337 reg.2(10), see Bonner, *op. cit.*, pp.633–639.

individual judgment and assist the tribunal in reaching a proper resolution of the case.[19] This may require him or her to advance arguments on behalf of the appellant if he or she thinks that they should be brought to the attention of the tribunal, although there have been differing views expressed about the enthusiasm with which presenting officers have fulfilled that function.[20] The tribunal and the claimant may be assisted insofar as it is unlikely that a presenting officer will be defending at a hearing his or her own decision on an original claim and objectivity may be easier to display in those circumstances.[21] The unusual practice of allowing decision-makers to defend their own decisions as presenting officers is likely to emphasise the adversarial nature of the proceedings at the expense of the inquisitorial.

It is legitimate to ask to what extent an inquisitorial mode is adopted in the hearing. It is true that the tribunal members are more involved in the direct questioning of both sides than a judge would be, and the informal structure of the proceedings allows particular points, once raised, to be followed through to a conclusion immediately if that appears convenient.[22] The functions of the statutory authorities (decision-maker, tribunal, Commissioner) have been described as

"investigatory or inquisitorial. A social security appeal tribunal is exercising quasi-judicial functions and forms part of the statutory machinery for investigating claims. . . . Its investigatory function has as its object the ascertainment of the facts and the determination of the truth. . . . "[23]

As an aspect of this

"It is open to a tribunal and indeed it is the members' duty, whenever they identify a point in favour of the claimant, notwithstanding that it has not

[19] For a lawyer's analysis of this role, see Diplock L.J. in *R v Deputy Industrial Injuries Commissioner, Ex p. Moore* [1965] 1 Q.B. 456 at 486. A claimant would not necessarily take the same view, even if he knew what was meant by *lis inter partes* and *amicus curiae*. See also *Benchbook*, pp.75–76.

[20] M. Herman, *Administrative Justice and Supplementary Benefits* (1972); K. Bell, *Research Study on Supplementary Benefit Appeal Tribunals, Review of Main Findings: Conclusions: Recommendations* (DHSS 1975). The *Decision Makers Guide* (Vol.1, para.06429) states that "The role of the presenting officer is that of *amicus curiae* . . . rather than an advocate. The presenting officer should not 1. put questions to any appellant or witness in a hostile manner 2. think in terms of 'winning' the case." Despite this, during observations of hearings for the study by Genn and Genn (1989) "many Presenting Officers were seen to argue their cases forcefully and to display pleasure when their decision was ultimately confirmed" (p.161). Baldwin, Wikeley and Young (*Judging Social Security* (1992), Ch.7), found that while most of the POs interviewed seemed to have a reasonable grasp of the *amicus curiae* concept, the role adopted most often in practice was neutral and reactive (in 20 per cent of cases, the PO appeared to adopt the full *amicus curiae* role; in 8 per cent an adversarial position was taken) (pp.184–185)

[21] The *Decision Makers Guide* states (Vol. 1, para.06420) that "The DM who made the decision under appeal can attend the hearing and present the case personally. However, the DM is usually represented by the presenting officer." Cases where there has been no PO have attracted criticism of the Social Security Commissioner: CI/1524/2000; CI/5972/1999. Nevertheless their attendance is "more and more rare": *The Benchbook*, para.44. The Legally Qualified Panel member can require attendance of a PO: para.06415.

[22] One of the original authors experienced an NILT in which he was interrupted in the midst of representations by comments from the claimant's husband who was attending the hearing as a "member of the public" and was sitting at the back of the room. The chairman encouraged him to speak up and proceeded to deal with the point he raised by questioning both the claimant and the insurance officer. Having dealt with it to his satisfaction the chairman asked if the husband had any further observations . . .

[23] R(S) 1/87, pp.6–7 (Commissioner V. G. H. Hallett). That an inquisitorial approach should be adopted was confirmed in *Kerr v DSD* [2004] 1 W.L.R. 1372.

been taken by the claimant, to consider it and to reach their decision in the light of it."[24]

Moreover, the presenting officer should attempt to present a balanced view. However, there are limits. A tribunal is not expected to question facts presented by a claimant just in case after further investigation they might prove to be materially different in the claimant's favour, especially where there is no suggestion that the claimant is unsure of the facts as presented.[25]

" . . . [T]he primary duty for making out his case falls on the claimant, and he must not expect to rely on the tribunal's own expertise. We would be slow to convict a tribunal of failure to identify an uncanvassed factual point in favour of the claimant in the absence of the most obvious and clear cut circumstances."[26]

Moreover, exhortations that an inquisitorial approach should be adopted do not necessarily reflect the actual practice.[27]

2. EMPLOYMENT TRIBUNALS

The rules of procedure for a hearing at an Employment Tribunal are, in some **16–003** respects, more explicit. The objectives to be attained at the hearing are included as part of the rules. In respect of the SSCSAT, we noted that the normal provision is simply for the chairman (or single member) to determine the procedures; for the Employment Tribunal, the procedural rules provide:

"(2) So far as it appears appropriate to do so, the chairman or tribunal shall seek to avoid formality in his or its proceedings and shall not be bound by any enactment or rule of law relating to the admissibility of evidence in proceedings before the courts.

(3) The chairman or tribunal . . . shall make such enquiries of persons appearing before him or it and of witnesses as he or it considers appropriate and shall otherwise conduct the hearing in such a manner as he or it considers most appropriate for the clarification of the issues and generally for the just handling of the proceedings."[28]

---

[24] R(SB) 2/83, p.557 (Tribunal of Commissioners). This includes a duty to ensure that all relevant questions have been asked of a claimant, although not necessarily to adjourn to enable a claimant who has chosen not to appear to deal with the matter: R(IS)11/99, paras 31, 32. Furthermore, where the claimant does not appear, the matter should be mentioned in the full statement of reasons: *ibid.* paras 37, 38.

[25] *ibid.* p.558. It was contended on behalf of the claimant that the local tribunal should, of its own motion, have investigated the origin and nature of funds in a personal account in a building society, in order to determine whether they truly represented business assets and not personal monies. That contention was rejected.

[26] R(SB) 2/83, p.558.

[27] The study by Genn and Genn (1989) found that while SSAT chairs consistently expressed the belief that proceedings were inquisitorial, this was denied by many experienced representatives, whose views were "often based on the perception that tribunals did not have the time to delve in sufficient detail into appellants' cases": pp.159–163.

[28] The Employment Tribunals (Constitution and Rules of Procedure) Regulations 2004 (SI 2004/1861), Rules of Procedure, r.14(2),(3).

Although those may be the implicit objectives of other tribunals, it is interesting that they should be explicit for the Employment Tribunal, and consequently ironic that the Employment Tribunal is generally reckoned to be one of the more formal and legalistic of the tribunals. It is also now provided that the overriding objective of the procedural rules is "to enable tribunals to deal with cases justly".[29]

A chairman or tribunal, depending on the relevant rule, may hold: (a) a case management discussion; (b) a pre-hearing review; (c) a hearing; or (d) a review hearing.[30] Case management discussions are interim hearings, deal with matters of procedure and management, and are held in private by a chairman.[31] Pre-hearing reviews are also interim hearings, are conducted by a chairman or tribunal, and take place in public. The chairman or tribunal may carry out a preliminary consideration of the proceedings, and may determine interim or preliminary matters, issue an order under r.10, require a deposit, consider oral or written representations or evidence, and deal with interim relief. Judgment can be given on preliminary issues of substance, and the proceedings then be struck out or dismissed.[32] A hearing is held by a tribunal in public for the purpose of determining outstanding procedural or substantive issues or disposing of the proceedings.[33] A review hearing is held by a chairman in public to review a default judgment[34]; or by a chairman or tribunal to review other decisions.[35] Where a hearing is required to be in public, it may nevertheless be held in private to hear evidence from a person which he or she could not disclose without contravening a legislative prohibition, acting in breach of confidence, or whose disclosure would cause substantial injury to any undertaking of his or her or in which he or she works.[36] A party is entitled to give evidence, call witnesses, question any witness and address the tribunal.[37] If a party has failed to attend the hearing, the tribunal must consider the information made available to it by the parties but subject to that provision, the tribunal may dismiss or dispose of the proceedings or adjourn.[38]

The order of events at a hearing is likely to differ with the nature of the claim.[39] In the ordinary unfair dismissal case the burden of proof lies with the employer to show that the dismissal was not unfair and the employer will normally be called on first. If the employee alleges constructive dismissal, or the employer otherwise disputes the fact of dismissal, then it will be for the employee to begin and make out his or her case. Whoever has the first word, the

---

[29] See para.13–008.

[30] r.14(1). Under, respectively, rr.17, 18, 26 or 33 or 36. A case management discussion or pre-hearing review may be conducted by use of electronic communication: r.15.

[31] r.17(1). Any determination of a person's civil rights and obligations cannot be dealt with here: r.17(2).

[32] rr.18–20.

[33] r.26.

[34] r.33.

[35] r.36.

[36] *ibid.* r.16. Breach of the requirement to sit in public renders the decision unlawful: *Storer v British Gas plc* [2001] 1 W.L.R. 1237 (hearing held in regional chairman's office protected by coded security lock not a hearing in public, notwithstanding that no member of the public was actually prevented from attending).

[37] *ibid.* r.27(2). Subject to r.14(3).

[38] *ibid.* r.27(5),(6).

[39] For Employment Tribunal procedure generally, see I. T. Smith and G. Thomas, *Smith and Wood's Industrial Law* (8th edn, 2003), pp.511–530).

procedure thereafter is, in form, similar to court procedure with the calling, examination and cross-examination of witnesses leading to final statements on both sides. The chairman and members of the tribunal may ask more questions and become more involved in the proceedings than a judge would, and the rules about the correct form of examination and cross-examination are relaxed along with the rules of evidence, but an observer at a hearing would receive a strong impression of adversarial procedure and formality. It has also been emphasised that it would not be helpful to describe the role of the tribunal as "inquisitorial" or "pro-active" in disability discrimination cases. It is not the tribunal's duty to obtain evidence or ensure that adequate medical evidence is obtained by the parties, although the parties would no doubt be reminded at the directions hearing of the need in most cases for qualified informed medical evidence of the claimed impairment to be obtained.[40]

3. RENT ASSESSMENT COMMITTEES

The Rent Assessment Committee (RAC)[41] exercises jurisdiction of three main kinds. It receives and determines objections against the fixing and registration (or confirmation) of a fair rent by a rent officer[42]; it fixes the rent of an assured tenancy where the landlord proposes a rent increase[43]; and, when exercising the powers of a rent tribunal, it controls rent and security of tenure in respect of "restricted contracts".[44] Some potential confusion was created by the Housing Act 1980 in the abolition of the rent tribunal and the reallocation of its functions to an RAC.[45] However, since the Housing Act 1988[46] no new restricted contracts can be created and there are now very few applications under the old Rent Tribunal jurisdiction.[47] A number of matters can now be referred to rent assessment committees constituted as leasehold valuation tribunals.[48] These include

16–004

---

[40] *McNicol v Balfour Beatty Rail Maintenance Ltd* [2002] I.C.R. 1498, para.[26], *per* Mummery L.J.

[41] See generally R. E. Megarry, *The Rent Acts* (1988), Vol.1, Chs 24 and 25, Vol.3, Chs 16 and 17; J. C. Martin, *Residential Security* (2nd edn, 1995), Chs 10 and 14; S. Blandy, [2001] J.H.L. 43 and S. McGrath, [2001] J.H.L. 53 (LVTs).

[42] Under the provisions of the Rent Act 1977, Pt. IV.

[43] Under the Housing Act 1988, Pt. I.

[44] As defined in Rent Act 1977, ss.19–21.

[45] s.72. The provisions of the section are, at first sight, so startling that they may properly be set out in full:

> "(1) Rent tribunals, as constituted for the purposes of the 1977 Act, are hereby abolished and section 76 of the 1977 Act (Constitution, etc. of rent tribunals) is hereby repealed.
>
> (2) As from the commencement of this section the functions which, under the 1977 Act, are conferred on rent tribunals shall be carried out by rent assessment committees.
>
> (3) A rent assessment committee shall, when constituted to carry out functions so conferred, be known as a rent tribunal."

The object appears to be to achieve a uniformity of appointment for the two bodies, without altering their functions.

[46] s.36.

[47] See P. Sparkes, *A New Landlord and Tenant* (2001), pp.164–165, 238.

[48] Commonhold and Leasehold Reform Act 2002, s.173.

jurisdiction concerning leasehold enfranchisement,[49] the determination of matters relating to service charges,[50] the determination of questions concerning a tenant's right to buy the landlord's interest when it has been disposed to a third party,[51] the appointment of a manager for flats,[52] the determination of the terms on which a landlord's interest can be required compulsorily,[53] and the determination of questions concerning rights of collective enfranchisement and lease renewal conferred on the tenants of flats,[54] and various matters under the Commonhold and Leasehold Reform Act 2002.[55] A further range of appeals lie to committees constituted as Residential Property Tribunals; these matters tend to concern disputes with local housing authorities and not citizen-citizen disputes.[56]

The RAC does not need to hold a hearing. The obligation lies on the landlord and the tenant to request the opportunity to make oral representations and there are provisions for the disposal of the matter on written representations in the absence of an application for a hearing.[57] It should be emphasised that the absence of a hearing does not relieve the tribunal of considering the matter, indeed it points up the inquisitorial role because the committee then have an obligation to make such inquiry as they think fit and consider any information supplied or representation made by the parties.[58] This demonstrates the necessity for procedural safeguards throughout the determination of an issue—they are not confined to a hearing. Leasehold Valuation Tribunals may determine an application without an oral hearing where it has given the applicant and respondent not les than 28 days' notice in writing and neither makes a request to be heard.[59]

The RAC rules provide that " . . . the parties shall be heard in such order, and . . . the procedure shall be such as the committee shall determine" and "a party may call witnesses, give evidence on his own behalf and cross-examine any witnesses called by the other party".[60] Each party may be heard in person "or by a person authorised by him in that behalf," whether or not a solicitor or barrister.[61] The rules specify that the hearing shall be in public unless the committee decide otherwise "for special reasons".[62]

---

[49] Leasehold Reform Act 1967, Pt I.

[50] Landlord and Tenant Act 1985, s.27A, inserted by the 2002 Act, s.155. See also s.20C (limitation of service charges: costs of proceedings) and Sch., para.8 (right to challenge landlord's choice of insurers).

[51] Landlord and Tenant Act 1987, ss.11–13, substituted by the Housing Act 1996, Sch.6, Pt II.

[52] 1987 Act, Pt II, ss.21–24.

[53] 1987 Act, s.31.

[54] Leasehold Reform, Housing and Urban Development Act 1993, Pt I, s.91.

[55] ss.84, 85, 94, 99, 159, 168.

[56] Housing Act 2004, ss.229–231, Sch.13. These include appeals against action taken by local authorities to enforce housing standards under Pt 1 of the Act. Appeals under the equivalent previous arrangements lay to the county court.

[57] Rent Act 1977, Sch.11, paras 6, 7(1)(b), 9 and Rent Assessment Committee (England and Wales) Regulations 1971 (SI 1971/1065), reg.6 (RACs). Where there is no hearing, each party must have the opportunity to comment on the other's case.

[58] 1977 Act, Sch.11, paras 7(1)(a), 9(1) (RACs).

[59] Leasehold Valuation Tribunals (Procedure) (England) Regulations 2003 (SI 2003/2099), reg.13, as amended by SI 2004/3098, reg.5.

[60] SI 1971/1065, reg.4. Similar rules apply to LVTs: SI 2003/2099, reg.14(7)(a), (c).

[61] Rent Act 1977, Sch.11, para.8; SI 2003/2099, reg.14(7)(b).

[62] SI 1971/1065, reg.3(1); SI 2003/2099, reg.14(b) ("in the particular circumstances of the case").

B. THE ROLE OF THE CHAIRMAN

The references to the chairman earlier in this chapter will already have demon- **16–005**
strated the significance of his or her role. The task of any chairman, whatever the
nature of the tribunal, is to ensure that:

" . . . the proceedings are conducted with scrupulous fairness to all parties
and that the proper balance is struck between formality and informality. In
particular, he must make sure at the outset that the parties fully understand
the issue, especially when they are not legally represented; and he must
ensure that they have an opportunity to present their cases adequately."[63]

Different chairmen may quite properly take different views about how to conduct
tribunal hearings whilst pursuing the objectives referred to in the preceding
paragraph, and the chairman's discretion is substantial. Since so much depends
on the chairman it is important briefly to examine three issues—the appointment
and qualification of chairmen; training provision; and the adequacy of judicial
and other safeguards intended to ensure procedural fairness.

1. APPOINTMENT AND QUALIFICATION

The formal position on appointment and qualification is set out in Ch.4.[64] The **16–006**
involvement of the Lord Chancellor in the appointment of the majority of
tribunal chairmen has been intended to demonstrate, and preserve, their independence of the relevant government department. As to qualification, the controversy is over the desirability of requiring that a chairman should be legally
qualified.

The inherent difficulty in tribunal adjudication will by now have become
apparent. It is desirable to achieve a high standard of decision-making coupled
with demonstrable procedural fairness, whilst retaining the informality, cheapness and speed which are meant to be the hallmarks of the tribunal. Lawyer-
chairmen seem to have less difficulty in achieving the former than the latter. Two
examples will suffice.

When the Industrial Tribunal was created, the procedural rules specifically
required the chairman, in setting the procedure, to seek to avoid formality so far
as it was appropriate to do so.[65] All chairmen of Employment Tribunals are
lawyers of not less than seven years' standing[66] and the appellate body is
presided over by a High Court judge.[67] The Employment Tribunal has become
formal, with predictable procedure and a large body of case-law. That can hardly
be a coincidence.[68]

---

[63] *Report of the Council on Tribunals 1959*, p.6.
[64] Above, para.4–016.
[65] See above, para.16–003.
[66] Above, para.4–016, n.214.
[67] For the composition of the Employment Appeal Tribunal, see above, para.2–033.
[68] It has attracted both judicial and academic criticism on that account. The criticism reflects a
particular view of the functions of an ET. See the observations of Lord Denning M.R. in *Walls
Meat Co. Ltd v Khan* [1979] 1 I.C.R. 52 at 56; Lawton L.J. in *Clay Cross (Quarry Services) Ltd
v Fletcher* [1979] I.C.R. 1 at 8; Ormrod L.J. in *National Vulcan Engineering Insurance Group Ltd
v Wade* [1978] I.C.R. 800 at 808; Dunn L.J. in *Methven v Cow Industrial Ltd* [1980] I.C.R. 463
at 470.

The Supplementary Benefit Appeal Tribunal was accustomed to non-lawyer chairmen. There was no prohibition on the appointment of lawyers but by 1980, after 14 years of existence,[69] only one chairman in four was legally qualified.[70] Kathleen Bell's research,[71] published in 1975, was not especially complimentary to the existing chairmen:

> " . . . generally speaking, they did not fully comprehend the complexities of the work . . . too often proceedings were unsystematic, inconsistent and over-influenced by sympathy or otherwise. Separate deliberations were frequently non-existent when the appellant was absent, and in other instances were quite often somewhat rambling and of rather poor quality. We examined a large number of official Reports of Proceedings, the majority of which did not adequately record a reasoned decision."[72]

This view was supported by other commentators.[73] Following the Bell Report there was a determined effort to appoint more lawyers as SBAT chairmen. Following the merging of SBATs and NILTs into Social Security Appeal Tribunals,[74] now SSCSATS, the chairmen are all lawyers of at least five years' standing,[75] and a regional and national structure of full-time chairmen has been created.[76]

SSCSATs are obviously more closely modelled on the NILT than the SBAT. The NILT certainly achieved a reputation as one of the best models of an informal tribunal with a qualified chairman.[77] In the view of Professor Lewis, who had some harsh criticism of SBATs, NILTs [were] " . . . usually a model of balancing informal expertise with order and legality".[78]

The debate over the desirability of lawyer-chairmen involves many of the same arguments that are deployed in respect of legal representation at tribunals.[79] The skills of the lawyer are thought to lie in order, objectivity and procedure rather than speed, informality and expertise. The Franks Committee were early advocates of the legally-qualified chairman. "Objectivity in the treatment of cases and the proper sifting of facts are most often best secured by having a legally qualified chairman."[80] The Committee also noted that there had been substantial agreement on this matter among witnesses. Later writers have

[69] SBATs were created by the Ministry of Social Security Act 1966 as the successor to national assistance appeal tribunals.

[70] N. Harris, "The Appointment of Legally Qualified Chairmen for SBATs" (1982) 132 N.L.J. 495.

[71] *Research Study on Supplementary Benefit Appeal Tribunals, Review of Main Findings: Conclusions: Recommendations* (HMSO, 1975).

[72] *ibid.* p.6.

[73] A. Frost and C. Howard, *Representation and Administrative Tribunals* (1977); M. Herman, *Administrative Justice and Supplementary Benefits* (1972); N. Lewis, "Supplementary Benefits Appeal Tribunals" [1973] P.L. 257.

[74] Above, para.2–036. These arrangements came into effect in April 1984 and there were transitional provisions which eliminated all non-lawyer chairmen.

[75] *ibid.* The period was formerly seven years.

[76] There is a President of SSCSATs and a number of Regional Chairmen with supervisory and training responsibilities.

[77] There appears to have been no specific requirement that chairmen of NILTs should be qualified lawyers, but it was an almost unbroken rule of practice.

[78] N. Lewis, "Supplementary Benefit Appeal Tribunals" [1973] P.L. 275.

[79] See below, paras 16–010—16–015.

[80] Report of the Committee on Administrative Tribunals and Enquiries (Cmnd. 218, 1957), para.55.

advanced further arguments[81]: the ability of lawyers to uphold basic legal principles in the field of administrative adjudications[82]; the maintenance of firm control over tribunals bred out of confidence and expertise[83]; the natural inclination of lawyers to control bias and prejudice in the presentation of cases; and the grasp of legal questions which is relevant in most areas of tribunal work.[84]

These views have not gone unopposed,[85] and even the advocates of lawyer-chairmen have not usually gone so far as to suggest that chairmanship should be the exclusive province of lawyers,[86] yet the recent developments have been along that line. It is unfortunate that other very suitable people may be excluded from chairmanship. The presence of a lawyer-chairman is certainly no guarantee of good chairmanship; a survey found that in one of every six SSAT hearings observed, "the chairman's conduct of the case was in our view open to serious criticism", citing particular examples of cases where the chairman was "accusatory in approach", "too dominant" or "maintained a severe, stern tone of voice throughout".[87]

2. TRAINING

For many years, arrangements for training were recognised to be inadequate. **16–007**
More recently, significant steps have been taken to improve the position.[88]

3. CORRECTION OF PROCEDURAL IRREGULARITIES

In the major tribunals we have so far considered there is a provision for a right **16–008**
of appeal to an appellate body who have the power to correct procedural irregularities.[89] Where there is no appellate body or where the appeal does not properly deal with the defect alleged judicial review may be sought. That remedy is considered in Ch.18.[90] Both the existence of the appellate body and the ultimate oversight of the courts provide the safeguard against the wrongful exercise of a chairman's considerable discretion.

---

[81] They are collected and analysed by J. Fulbrook, *Administrative Justice and the Unemployed* (1978), pp.215–219.

[82] H. W. R. Wade, *Towards Administrative Justice* (1963), p.43.

[83] H. L. Elcock, *Administrative Justice* (1969), pp.50–53.

[84] Especially in the Employment Tribunals, and in the determination of claims in respect of industrial injuries.

[85] R. M. Titmuss, "Welfare 'Rights', Law and Discretion" (1971) 42 *Political Quarterly*, pp.113–132.

[86] The Franks Committee (above, n.63.) recommended that, " ... the appointment of persons without legal qualification should not be ruled out when they are particularly suitable". (para.55).

[87] Baldwin, Wikeley and Young, *Judging Social Security* (1992), pp.115–119.

[88] See above, para.4–018.

[89] The Employment Appeal Tribunal for Employment Tribunals, and the Social Security and Child Support Commissioners for SSCSATs.

[90] paras 18–046—18–059.

C. THE ROLE OF THE "WING" MEMBERS

16–009   It is a distinctive feature of the tribunal system that has given considerable scope for lay participation in adjudication. Some of the alleged disadvantages of lawyer-chairmen may be moderated by the presence of lay people as members of the tribunal.

The appointment of the lay members has already been described,[91] and there is comparatively little in the way of research work into how the laymen approach their task and the nature of their relationship with the chairman.[92] In relation to social security tribunals there was doubt about the extent of their participation in the hearing and the adjudication, although it was recognised that a lack of participation might result from the absence of training and guidance. Indeed, a survey found that few wing members said very much, that two-thirds of those members who remained silent were entirely passive and that many "can be said to have given the appearance of being seriously out of their depth". Furthermore, it appeared that members frequently failed to participate actively in the deliberations.[93] The role of lay members in SSCSATs has now been reduced.[94]

The White Paper, *Transferring Public Services: Complaints, Redress and Tribunals*[95] noted the need for a review of the role of non-legal members as a whole. There were three issues. First, what precisely should the role of non-legal members be; was it to add balance to the panel or to ensure that particular interests are represented? Secondly, was it in any event desirable for an expert to be a *member* of a tribunal rather than a *witness*. Thirdly, what role could non-legal members play in the new alternatives to hearings that the new service should develop. If anything, it is likely that the role of non-legal members will be further diminished, as the first-tier of tribunals comes to look more and more like that of a District judge in the magistrates' or county courts.

D. REPRESENTATION BEFORE TRIBUNALS

16–010   " . . . it is desirable that every applicant before any tribunal should be able to present his case in person or to obtain representation."[96]

In order to achieve this objective, the Royal Commission on Legal Services asserted that tribunal procedure would need to be simplified wherever possible; the existing schemes for representation by lay persons would need to be developed and funded; and legal aid would need to be made available for certain cases.[97] These findings were based on a significant amount of evidence received by the Commission[98] which was in addition to the published research already

---

[91] Above, para.4–016.
[92] See J. Fulbrook, *Administrative Justice and the Unemployed* (1978), pp.226–229; J. Baldwin, N. Wikeley and R. Young, (1992), pp.143–153.
[93] Baldwin, Wikeley and Young (1992), pp.146–147.
[94] See above, para.2–038.
[95] Cm. 6243, p.34.
[96] R.C.L.S. Vol.1, para.15.11, p.169.
[97] *ibid.*
[98] The Commission received evidence from both lawyers and non-lawyers active in the tribunal representation field. Its own research is contained in Vol.2. Section 4, pp.91–101.

available.[99] An important study was subsequently commissioned by the Lord Chancellor's Department, covering Social Security Appeal Tribunals, Industrial Tribunals, Mental Health Review Tribunals and Immigration Adjudicators.[100] The whole question of tribunal representation is one which has continued to attract much attention, especially because of the large numbers of cases currently being determined by tribunals.[101]

In this section we consider six related issues, the first three relating to the present position and the second three to possible future provision of representation. What are the rules about representation? Who are the representatives? What do they do? Should lawyers be involved in representation less often, more often, or not at all? Should legal involvement be publicly funded?

1. THE RULES

Article 6(2) of the ECHR provides that everyone charged with a criminal offence **16–011** has the right to defend himself in person or through legal assistance of his own choosing; a person who does not have sufficient means has the right to free legal assistance when the interests of justice so require. "Criminal charge" for this purpose has to be given an autonomous meaning and accordingly some cases determined by a tribunal and not by a criminal court may be covered by Art.6(2).[102] In *R (on the application of Fleurose) v Securities and Futures Authority Ltd*[103] the Court of Appeal held that the determination by the SFA's Disciplinary Appeal Tribunal of an appeal under the SFA's code applicable to traders in securities did not constitute the determination of a criminal charge. The offence was restricted to a specified group rather than the public at large and the penalty, although serious in that it would involve loss of livelihood, could not involve loss of liberty.[104] That did not conclude the question of the right to (free) legal assistance as such a right could in appropriate circumstances be regarded as inherent in the right to a fair hearing in Art.6(1). Mr Fleurose had legal representation before the first instance Disciplinary Tribunal but not the Appeal Tribunal. The Appeal Tribunal had been presided over by a former Law Lord (Lord Bridge), who was "at pains to take points on Mr Fleurose's behalf". There was no additional point that could have been advanced at the appeal hearing for which representation by a trained lawyer was needed. There was accordingly no unfairness resulting from the lack of legal representation. The court left open the

---

[99] Notably the studies carried out by Professor Kathleen Bell, *Research Study on Supplementary Benefit Appeal Tribunals, Review of Main Findings: Conclusions: Recommendations* (DHSS 1975): "National Insurance Local Tribunals," *Journal of Social Policy*, Vols 3.4 and 4.1 (1974/5). Other studies include R. Lawrence, *Tribunal Representation* (1980); E. Kessler *et al.*, *Combatting Poverty: C.A.Bx., Claimants and Tribunals* (NACAB Occasional Paper No.11, 1980); R. Lawrence, "Solicitors and Tribunals" [1980] J.S.W.L. 13; *Tribunal Assistance, the Chapeltown Experience* (NACAB Occasional Paper, No.14, 1982).

[100] H. Genn and Y. Genn, *The Effectiveness of Representation at Tribunals* (LCD, 1989), discussed by R. Young, (1990) 9 C.J.Q. 16 and T. Mullen, (1990) 53 M.L.R. 230.

[101] See Ch.2.

[102] See above, para.8–021.

[103] [2001] I.R.L.R. 297.

[104] The court applied principles set out in *Han & Yau v Commissioners of Customs and Excise* [2001] 1 W.L.R. 2253 and *Official Receiver v Stern* [2001] 1 W.L.R. 2230.

question "whether in this class of case, the Convention ever requires that free legal representation be provided".[105]

The situation here may be contrasted with the position with respect to matters referred to the Financial Services and Markets Tribunals by individuals against whom the Financial Services Authority have decided to take action in respect of alleged market abuse.[106] Here the sanctions that may be applied extend to members of the general public and are not confined to particular groups such as securities traders. Accordingly, the government agreed that a special legal assistance scheme should be established on the assumption that proceedings would be classified for Convention purposes as involving the determination of a criminal charge.[107]

Apart from the ECHR, and whether or not there is an absolute right to legal representation protected by the principles of natural justice,[108] it is rare for such a right to be specifically denied by tribunal rules.[109] However, a right to legal representation is only useful if the applicant has sufficient funds to pay a lawyer[110]; can find one who is competent in the field; and if the case is one in which the skills of a lawyer will be significant. As we shall see, representation by lawyers in tribunals is not generally common.

Some tribunals place restrictions on representation by persons other than lawyers,[111] but the usual provision is for an unfettered right to representation.[112] The ability of the applicant to select an appropriate representative has resulted in the appearance before tribunals of a wide variety of representatives.

2. WHO ARE THE REPRESENTATIVES?

16–012 Some distinctions must be made between the different tribunals in that they attract different representatives.

The study by Genn and Genn showed that Citizens Advice Bureaux were the most frequent representatives at SSATs (closely followed by family or friends);

---

[105] para.23. The issue appears to have centred on the right to *free* legal assistance as distinct from the right to have such assistance at all.

[106] Financial Services and Markets Act 2000, s.127(4).

[107] *ibid.* ss.134, 135; Financial Services and Markets Tribunal (Legal Assistance) Regulations 2001 (SI 2001/3632). See further, below, para.16–015.

[108] See Sir William Wade and C. F. Forsyth, *Administrative Law* (9th edn, 2004), at pp.520–521.

[109] The only exception seems to be Health Authority or Primary Care Trust discipline committees. Before that tribunal paid representation by a lawyer is not permitted; a lawyer may only appear as a "friend" and not address the Committee or put questions to witnesses: National Health Service (Service Committees and Tribunal) Regulations 1992 (SI 1992/664), Sch.4, para.5(3), substituted by SI 1996/703, reg.13. See further below, para.16–014.

[110] Save in exceptional circumstances, see para.16–015 below.

[111] For example, representation by non-lawyers is only permitted at the discretion of the Lands Tribunal (Lands Tribunal Rules 1996 (SI 1996/1022), r. 37(1)); *cf.* the General Commissioners of Income Tax, where a party may be represented by any person, subject in a particular case to refuse permission to a non-lawyer for "good and sufficient reasons" (General Commissioners (Jurisdiction and Procedure) Regulations 1994 (SI 1994/1812), reg.12); the AIT, where an appellant may be represented by any person not prohibited by s.84 of the Immigration and Asylum Act 1999 (Asylum and Immigration Tribunal (Procedure) Rules 2005 (SI 2005/230), r.48). No limits are placed on representation at SSCSATs and ETs.

[112] See the procedural rules of the tribunals considered, above.

the UKIAS before Immigration Adjudicators; lawyers and trade unions at Industrial Tribunals; and solicitors at MHRTs.[113] The proportion of all appellants represented at the hearing varied considerably. 16 per cent of SSAT, appellants were represented, but only 12 per cent by agencies or individuals with experience of representation or with any special expertise.[114] In contrast, 90 per cent of appellants at immigration hearings, 58 per cent of applicants and 73 per cent of respondents at Industrial Tribunals, and 61 per cent of applicants at MHRTs were represented by someone other than a relative or friend.[115] By 2000–01, figures for the extent of representation at tribunals included (with, where known, the percentages of representatives legally qualified in brackets): MHRTs 99 per cent (99); immigration adjudicators 90 per cent; Lands Tribunal 90 per cent (100); Social Security Commissioners 63 per cent (15); Employment Tribunal 58 per cent (33); SENT 51 per cent (17); Social Security and Child Support Appeals Tribunals (40 per cent); and Rent Assessment Panels (5 per cent).[116]

Although there will always be some who defy categorisation, it is possible to discern five groupings from amongst those people who undertake representation. First, there are those who represent at tribunals as a result of a *professional interest in their members or clients*. We are referring here principally to trade union representatives, employers' organisation representatives and social workers who go to a tribunal with a client. Representation has been a significant feature of the legal services supplied by trade unions to their members,[117] and this is particularly marked in the field of national insurance, industrial injuries and employment issues. This has resulted in the trade unions taking a cautious view over the future development of lay or legal representation. They have appeared not to be anxious to have competitors providing alternative services to their members.[118] Social workers have been involved in the work of social security tribunals. This group of representatives should be in a position to offer effective representation as a result of skill and experience acquired in particular tribunals.

The second group consists of representatives provided by *voluntary organisations* for the benefit of their members. The Benson Commission noted the work done by the Royal British Legion in Pensions Appeal Tribunals,[119] and the Claimants' Unions have specialised in the area of social security tribunals.[120]

---

[113] Genn and Genn (1989), pp.19, 33, 46, 58. R.C.L.S. Vol.2, Section 4, Table 4.7; Bell, *Research on S.B.A.T.s*, pp.15–16 (see n.99, above).

[114] Genn and Genn (1989), pp.19–22.

[115] *ibid.* pp.32–35, 43–53, 56–59.

[116] M. Adler and J. Gulland, *Tribunal Users' Experiences, Perceptions and Expectations: A Literature Review* (Council on Tribunals, 2003), p.18. A further survey in respect of Appeals Service tribunals, SENDIST and CICAP found no statistically significant difference in the rate of representation between different ethnic groups within the sample as a whole: Genn, Lever and Gray, *Tribunals for Diverse Users* (2006), p.261. As to the types of representative, see *ibid.*, pp.261–264.

[117] G. Latta and R. Lewis, "Trade Union Legal Services" (1974) *XII British Journal of Industrial Relations* 561; R. Lewis and G. Latta, "Union Legal Services" (1973) 123 N.L.J. 386; TUC's annual *Trade Union Trends Survey, Focus on Employment Tribunals*.

[118] See G. Bindman, "Trade Unions and Legal Services" *LAG Bulletin*, March 1979, 56.

[119] R.C.L.S., Vol.1, para.15.16. R.C.L.S., Vol.1, para.15.16.

[120] On the role of the Claimants' Unions, see H. Rose, "Who can de-label the claimant", in M. Adler and A. Bradley, *Justice, Discretion and Poverty* (1976). *Cf.* Nottingham Claimants Action: *www.geocities.com/ncajsa*.

The third group consists of representatives provided by *generalist or specialist advice agencies* for the benefit of anyone who wishes to consult the agency and accept an offer of help. The Citizens Advice Bureaux has provided such a service to the public,[121] and there are other examples of advice agencies becoming involved in representation as an incidental part of their general service. Specialist agencies, like the Child Poverty Action Group, provide representation in their own field.[122] The United Kingdom Immigrants Advisory Service (UKIAS) provided an interesting example of a specialist agency set up with public funds to deal with enquiries on a particular topic. It was described by the Benson Commission as " . . . a unique counselling and advocacy service dealing with one field of tribunal work and manned by a full time salaried staff".[123] In 1992 its responsibilities were split between the Refugee Legal Centre and the Immigration Advisory Service.[124] The fourth group consists of representatives provided by various specific *tribunal representation projects*. The CAB service has over the years been associated with major schemes in Birmingham, Leeds, Sheffield, Newcastle and Wolverhampton and has also provided the stimulus for other local initiatives. The Free Representation Unit provides representation before tribunals in London.[125]

The fifth group consists of *lawyers*. We have already noted that lawyers do provide some representation in tribunals, but this is normally paid for by the client. Very few tribunals have rules as to costs which would allow the recovery of legal expenses.[126] Some representation is funded publicly but it is exceptional. Funding for Legal Representation is available for a small number of tribunals; Legal Help may be available in respect of preparatory work.[127] Assistance short of representation can no doubt prove very irritating for the tribunal and it appears that solicitors may have been remunerated for assistance which has spilled over into representation.

There must inevitably be a composite group of "everybody else". Particularly in SBATs, the category of friends and relatives as representatives was significant. As we shall shortly demonstrate, the role of a "representative" can be very restricted, and it may be sufficient that his attendance has ensured the attendance of the applicant. That job can be done as well (possibly better) by a friend as by an advocate.

---

[121] Although it is fair to point out that much has depended on the ability and willingness of volunteers in a particular bureau to undertake the task of representation, and there is considerable pressure and CABx resources. The coverage has consequently been patchy. A majority of CABx provide a representation service of some sort, although not necessarily for more than the occasional case: interview with a NACAB representative cited by J. Baldwin (1989) 8 C.J.Q. 24, 36. By 1995, in 86 per cent of bureaux, advisers undertook representation themselves: NACAB Annual Report 1994–95, p.21. A 2000–01 survey showed that 475 of 501 bureaux which responded offered representation at SSATs, 443 at Employment Tribunals, with smaller numbers for others: NACAB response to LCD Consultation on the Leggatt Report (2001).

[122] This is confined to a small number of test cases: *www.cpag.org.uk.*

[123] R.C.L.S. Vol.1 para.15.17.

[124] *www.refugee-legal-centre.org.ukww.iasuk.org.uk.* They are now funded under the Immigration and Asylum Act 1999, s.81. Other providers of immigration advice and representation (other than solicitors and barristers) are now regulated by an Immigration Services Commissioner and Tribunal under Pt V of the 1999 Act (see *Legal Action*, April 2001, p.9).

[125] See above, para.13–005.

[126] See above, para.11–021.

[127] See above, paras 10–023—10–027.

3. WHAT DO REPRESENTATIVES DO?

This may seem to be an odd question. However, we use it to demonstrate that the **16–013** assistance offered by a representative may range more widely than simply putting the applicant's case at a hearing.

From the outset, the representative is likely to be involved in an advice-giving role whether he or she is an expert in the field or not.[128] It is obvious that those experienced representatives who have gained a thorough knowledge of their subject are able to evaluate the merits, and likely success, of the applicant's case and can act accordingly. This advisory role is significant because it may operate to exclude the weak and unmeritorious cases at an early stage.[129] If the effect of this screening is to allow the representative only to pursue those cases believed to be worthwhile, he or she gains an enhanced reputation with the tribunal in respect of the cases that are pursued through to a hearing. Moreover, the scarce resources of advice agencies and the like should not be used to support hopeless cases.

There are some reservations expressed about the validity of this advisory role, not least because the adviser may be constituting him or herself as the adjudicator rather than the tribunal, and coming between the applicant and the tribunal. It is argued that applicants should be given the confidence and expertise to use the system themselves rather than experience the "interference" of another expert who would come to some tidy arrangement with the tribunal leaving the claimant as isolated as ever.[130] This is a minority view, however, and most of the representation schemes that have been established place emphasis on the provision of advice by an "expert" at an early stage.[131] There is also the reservation expressed by some about

> "doing the Government's job for them. You are telling someone to leave the country or not to . . . claim a benefit. You are the soft police."[132]

A second function of a representative may be to act as a negotiator on behalf of the applicant with a view to effecting a settlement of the problem.[133] We noted the importance of settlements in the civil process in Ch.11[134]—they also have their place in the tribunal process. The intervention of a third party on behalf of an applicant may produce a change in the decision which satisfies the claimant. This might be called anti-representation since it has the effect of preventing a tribunal hearing, but it benefits both the applicant and the tribunal.[135] A third

---

[128] Even the next-door neighbour might be asked whether or not to appeal!

[129] See Genn and Genn (1989), pp.134–135.

[130] The Claimants' Union recognised a "right" to be represented whatever the merits of the case might appear to be. See generally, R. Lawrence, *Tribunal Representation* (1980), p.18; H. Rose, "Who Can De-Label the Claimant?" in M. Adler and A. Bradley, *op. cit.*

[131] Some of the tribunal representation schemes operate on a "consultancy" basis whereby volunteer lay representatives themselves receive help and guidance at the early stages of a possible appeal (see, for example, the West Midlands project—*Combatting Poverty*, n.99 above). Others give a direct service to the claimant but rely heavily on the expertise of the representatives.

[132] Quotation from a Law Centre, cited by Genn and Genn (1989), pp.134–135.

[133] *ibid.* pp.135–138.

[134] Above, paras 11–026—11–032.

[135] One of the arguments advanced in favour of the extension of representation is its effect in diminishing the caseload of tribunals.

function of representation may be simply to ensure the attendance of the applicant. This is sometimes referred to as a "hand-holding exercise".[136] The published figures demonstrate that an applicant has a higher chance of success at a tribunal if he or she attends, whether or not represented, than if he or she does not attend.[137] Claimants who receive an unfavourable decision on their claim may immediately give notice of appeal without giving thought to how to pursue the appeal.[138] On receipt of the appeal papers they decide not to go along to the hearing because the case is not arguable, or they are frightened, or ignorant of the process, or no longer interested. If they seek advice at all, they may simply need the reassurance that someone will attend the tribunal with them and help them through the procedure—not necessarily as an advocate but as a friend. Once at the hearing, with the presence of a supporter they are able to respond sufficiently to the tribunal to allow the case fully to be considered.

A fourth function is that of preparing the case for the hearing, good preparation being fundamental to the success of appeals. This includes interviewing the client, collecting documentary evidence, arranging for witnesses to attend and researching the law. Most appellants and applicants are likely to have difficulty in identifying the facts relevant to the case and securing the necessary evidence.[139]

This may seem quite a late stage to be arriving at the representative's job of representing. At the hearing, the function of the representative is to put forward the applicant's case without coming completely between the applicant and the tribunal. The representative should not forget that the tribunal will be interested to hear from the applicant directly.[140] The need to marshal the arguments for the benefit of the tribunal will be dictated partly by the complexity of the subject matter and partly by the procedure adopted.[141] The skills required are not necessarily those of the advocate—but it helps the tribunal if the representative can present a logical, orderly, relevant analysis of the issues and the evidence. Statistics show that the represented claimant is better off at a tribunal.[142] This point is confirmed by the study by Genn and Genn,[143] which also indicates that specialist representatives have the greatest effect on the probability of success.[144] Finally, the expertise gained by the representative and his or her familiarity with the system may be used for the benefit of others in the exchange of information and pressure for reform. In the informal world of tribunals the shared experience

---

[136] Particularly by the Citizens Advice Bureaux. See the NACAB Administrative Circular (1974), cited in R. Lawrence, *Tribunal Representation* (1980), p.59. This circular is no longer current, but the function remains the same.

[137] K. Bell, *op. cit.* (above, n.99); Genn and Genn (1989), p.68 (SSATs); this is not a surprising finding. Attendance at least allows the tribunal the possibility of questioning the claimant.

[138] This does not mean that a high proportion of the recipients of adverse DSS (now DWP) decisions appeal: see Genn and Genn (1989), pp.130–134.

[139] Genn and Genn (1989), pp.138–147.

[140] The Social Security Commissioner has, on occasion, criticised a representative who appears to have dominated the hearing to the exclusion of the applicant. (See R(I) 36/61.)

[141] In the Employment Tribunal, for example, the representative has his or her job defined by the adoption of a fairly standard, adversarial procedure. See above.

[142] Although there are some reservations about the interpretation of the evidence: R. Lawrence, *Tribunal Representation* (1980), pp.19–20.

[143] Genn and Genn (1989), Ch.3. Other factors independently associated with success were the type of case, number of witnesses, geographical location (SSATs) and the identity of the chair or the adjudicator (SSATs, ITS, Immigration hearings). See also Genn, Lever and Gray, *Tribunals for Diverse Users* (2006), pp.264–267.

[144] Welfare rights centres, tribunal units and law centres for social security appeals, UKIAS and lawyers for immigration hearings.

is invaluable. This sharing may be formal, through publications,[145] or informal, through word of mouth but it is undoubtedly a factor in the increasing success of lay representatives.

Much of this section has been directed towards the less formal tribunals and the experience of the Employment Tribunal is somewhat different. There, the actual representation at the hearing takes on the major significance and the other functions are consequently diminished.[146] It is not surprising that with considerable lawyer representation the emphasis has been placed upon advocacy.

Overall it was the clear conclusion of the study by Genn and Genn that representation of appellants and applicants increases the accuracy of tribunal decision-making and improves the fairness of the process by which decisions are reached.[147] Arguments that tribunals proceedings are informal and simple, and that representation is accordingly unnecessary and undesirable, are ill-founded.[148] The view of tribunals, representatives and presenting officers in the four areas studied

> "was that much of the law with which they were concerned was complex and the adjudicative function of tribunals was often a highly technical forensic process."[149]

Moreover,

> "the experience of unrepresented appellants and applicants indicates that, even in the most informal hearings, they have difficulty in expressing themselves; they do not understand the relevance of the rules and regulations that are quoted to them; and when they lose, frequently leave in a state of disappointment and frustration."[150]

It was the unanimous belief of representatives interviewed that "no matter how well-intentioned tribunals might be, it was impossible to compensate for lack of representation"; on the other hand, the majority of chairs of SSATs and industrial tribunals believed that they could compensate for lack of representation. The observation of hearings for the purpose of the study tended to confirm the former view.[151] Finally, some fears have been expressed about the extent to which an involvement with representation will inevitably result in a commitment to reform of the system, an over-identification with the position of the applicants, or an engagement in political activity.[152] How objective/disinterested can a representative remain? This anxiety has been examined and answered effectively by David

---

[145] For example, information is disseminated through NACAB and CPAG literature (e.g., respectively, through *The Adviser* and the *Welfare Rights Bulletin*), and other periodicals.

[146] The negotiation function is, to some extent, undertaken by the conciliation officers of ACAS, see above, para.13–008.

[147] Genn and Genn (1989), pp.247–248.

[148] *ibid.*

[149] *ibid.* p.244; and generally Ch.4.

[150] *ibid.* pp.246–247; and generally Ch.7.

[151] *ibid.* pp.215–216.

[152] This has been a particular fear of NACAB who have been very sensitive about allegations of political involvement and campaigning.

Bull, whose analysis of the range of advocacy and its implications for the representatives is very convincing.[153]

4. SHOULD LAWYERS BE INVOLVED MORE? LESS? AT ALL?

16–014 The answer to this particular question depends upon the skills which lawyers bring to tribunal representation and the effect that the deployment of those skills is likely to have on the style and procedure of tribunals. It further depends upon the objectives which a system of tribunals seeks to achieve, and upon the complexity of the law which is being administered, the nature of the particular tribunal under consideration and upon the nature of the particular case under consideration, for there may be especial circumstances which warrant the attention of a lawyer.

Given all these variables it is difficult to formulate a single answer. Perhaps the convenient starting-point is to ask whether lawyers have a place in tribunal representation at all. Against the proposition that a citizen should have a right to legal representation in all forms of judicial or quasi-judicial proceedings[154] may be put the assertion that lawyers "spoil" tribunal adjudication by detracting from those qualities which tribunals are alleged to display, namely speed, informality, cheapness and expertise.[155] In particular, it has been argued that, in respect of areas in which discretion is an important element, the introduction of "legalism" is likely to hinder the operation of discretion to the disadvantage of the claimant.[156] These arguments have not prevailed[157] and there is, apparently, only one example of a tribunal which positively prohibits legal representation.[158] It would certainly be difficult now to make a case for a blanket prohibition on legal representation, and it is generally accepted that lawyers have *some* part to play.

The more difficult question is the *extent* to which lawyer-representation is desirable. In practice, this question is closely linked with the possibility of

---

[153] D. Bull, "The Anti-Discretion Movement in Britain: Fact or Phantom?" [1980] J.S.W.L. 65.

[154] See above, para.16–011.

[155] For the virtues (alleged) of tribunal adjudication, see above, para.2–015. It is interesting to note that in the small claims track (see above, para.12–022) legal representation is not prohibited but it is discouraged because of the limitation of the recovery of costs.

[156] R. M. Titmuss, "Welfare 'Rights', Law and Discretion" (1971) 42 *Political Quarterly*, pp.113–132. The subject is discussed fully in J. Fulbrook, *Administrative Justice and the Unemployed* (1978), pp.275–293.

[157] Indeed, in the social security field benefits (first supplementary benefit, now income support) have become rule—rather than discretion-based and there is no longer a right of appeal to a tribunal in respect of the main remaining discretion-based benefit (social fund payments).

[158] Discipline Committees of Health Authorities and PCTs: see the National Health Service (Service Committees and Tribunals) Regulations 1992 (SI 1992/664), as amended by SI 1996/703. These replaced Service Committees of Family Health Service Authorities from April 1, 1996, with a jurisdiction now confined to claims by an authority that the practitioner is in breach of his or her terms of service, and matters concerning overpayments. Since 1996 there has been a separate procedure for complaints by patients. Contrast the procedure under which a practitioner may be removed from the list of practitioners undertaking to provide family health service on grounds of efficiency, fraud or unsuitability; here, decisions are made by the Health Authority with an appeal lying to the Family Health Services Appeal Authority (superseding, from 2001, the National Health Service Tribunal); legal representation is expressly permitted before the Authority (Family Health Service Appeal Authority (Procedure) Rules 2001 (SI 2001/3750), r.11), as was the case before the Tribunal.

providing public funds for such representation, for without funding the likelihood that an applicant will be able to pay for the services of a lawyer is slim.[159] However, until a positive case has been made for legal representation, funds will not be made available. What is the strength of the case?

There has been comparatively little evidence of the extent to which lawyers are involved in tribunal work or, incidentally, of their likely response if money were to be made available to allow them to undertake more.[160] Statistics from the research studies that have been done demonstrate the very low proportion of cases in social security tribunals which have lawyer representatives,[161] although the proportion is much higher in other tribunals such as Employment Tribunals.[162] If the Employment Tribunal is any guide the presence of lawyer representatives is likely to formalise procedure and reinforce the adversarial style of the proceedings. This fear has been expressed also in respect of social security tribunals, not least because the criticisms levelled at such tribunals by lawyers tend to focus on the failure to follow a consistent and clear judicial process in adjudication.[163] The lawyers' response to such a failure is normally to formulate procedural rules and safeguards to be operated by lawyers.

The research conducted by Professor Bell indicated that there was no great enthusiasm amongst appellants for professional advocates; rather they were anxious to see the tribunal play a more *enabling* role thereby improving the opportunity for appellants to put their own case.[164] Few among the tribunals and representatives interviewed for the study by Genn and Genn believed that lawyers were necessarily best equipped to conduct tribunal representations; the most common view was that specialisation and experience were the most important qualifications.[165] Despite fears that lawyerly skills may frustrate some of the objectives of tribunal adjudication, the prevailing view is that legal representation is desirable in particular circumstances. This view is based mainly upon the combined arguments of legal complexity in certain fields and the importance of the issues to the individual claimant. The study by Genn and Genn concluded that while the main development should be in the direction of increased funding to lay agencies, this would not provide the complete answer. There might be a need for skilled legal representation before the explicitly adversarial Industrial Tribunals, and to fill gaps left by the uneven geographical coverage of lay advice and representation agencies.[166]

It is of course difficult to disentangle the issue of whether lawyers should be involved, and that of whether their contribution should be supported by public funding, to which we now turn.

---

[159] This is especially the case in social security tribunals where there is likely to be only a relatively small amount of money at stake. Costs are not normally awarded by tribunals, see para.11–021 above.

[160] R. Lawrence, "Solicitors and Tribunals" [1980] J.S.W.L. 13; N. Harris, "Solicitors and Supplementary Benefit Cases" (1983) 34 N.I.L.Q. 144.

[161] K. Bell, *op. cit.* below n.163; R.C.L.S. Vol.2 Section 4; Genn and Genn (1989), p.20.

[162] R.C.L.S. Vol.2, Section 4, Tables 4.7, 4.8; Genn and Genn (1989), pp.44–45, 50; above, para.16–012.

[163] K. Bell, *Research Study on Supplementary Benefit Appeal Tribunals. Review of Main Findings: Conclusions: Recommendations* (DHSS, 1975), pp.19–20.

[164] *ibid.* p.18.

[165] Genn and Genn (1989), p.245; generally pp.171–178, 193–198, 210–215.

[166] Genn and Genn (1989), pp.249–250.

5. WHEN SHOULD FUNDING FOR LEGAL REPRESENTATION BE AVAILABLE FOR TRIBUNALS?

16–015   There is no serious dispute that it would be impossible for funding for legal representation to be made available for all cases in all tribunals. Different reasons would be given by different people. The expense,[167] the inappropriateness, the availability of skilled lay representation, and the possible lack of interest amongst the solicitors' profession[168] would all be reasons used to reject the extension of funding to all cases. There is an equal measure of agreement about the need to extend such funding to *some* tribunal cases, but two difficulties arise. First, it is difficult to agree the criteria which would establish eligibility; secondly, the advocates of the development of lay representation would not wish the extension of legal aid to be viewed as an alternative to funding better organised and more comprehensive schemes of lay representation.

Over the years, there have been many calls for the extension of legal aid to more if not all tribunals, at least for complex or test cases or those with a significant point of law or affecting individual liberty on livelihood.[169] These have had relatively little impact, but it is at least now recognised that public funding for legal representation will be needed where required by Art.6 of the ECHR.

The current position is that the Access to Justice Act 1999 provides that funding for legal representation may not be provided except in specified proceedings, and the only tribunals mentioned are the Employment Appeal Tribunal, Mental Health Review Tribunals, the Asylum and Immigration Tribunal and the Special Immigration Appeals Commission and the Proscribed Organisations Appeal Commission.[170] The Lord Chancellor may by direction require or authorise that funding be provided for excluded services, and he has done so in respect of Legal Help, Help at Court and Legal Representation in all proceedings before the Protection of Children Act Tribunal (now part of the work of the Care Standards Tribunal), in specified proceedings[171] before the General and Special

---

[167] Particularly given the steady (and controversial) erosion of public funding for proceedings before courts.

[168] See R. Lawrence, "Solicitors and Tribunals" [1980] J.S.W.L. 13 at 19–25.

[169] See the previous edition of this book, para.16–021, referring to the views of the Franks Committee, the Council on Tribunals, the Lord Chancellor's Advisory Committee on Legal Aid, the Benson Commission, Presidents of Tribunals and other bodies.

[170] Sch.2, para.2(1), as amended by the Community Legal Service (Scope) Regulations 2000 (SI 2000/822) and the Terrorism Act 2000, Sch.14, para.19. Advocacy before the Lands Tribunal and the Commons Commissioner was excluded for the first time "because they do not have sufficient priority to justify public funding": *Lord Chancellor's Revised Guidance* on *Applications for Exceptional Funding* (applying from November 1, 2001), para.5. See also *LSC Funding Code: Criteria*, Section 12—Mental Health (no financial test but an application may be refused if it is unreasonable in the particular circumstances of the case for LR to be granted); *LSC Funding Code:—Criteria*, Section 13—Immigration (most of the normal financial and merits criteria apply; LR will be refused if the prospects of achieving a successful outcome are unclear or borderline (save where the case has a significant wider public interest, is of overwhelming importance to the client or raises significant human rights issues) or poor; save where the case has a significant wider public interest, LR will be refused unless the likely benefits justify the likely costs, such that a reasonable private paying client would be prepared to take the proceedings).

[171] i.e. where it is in the interests of justice for the client to be legally represented and the proceedings concern penalties declared by the courts to be criminal in ECHR terms or where an appeal reasonably seeks to argue that they are such criminal penalties.

Commissioners of Income Tax and VAT and Duties Tribunals. Also covered are appeals from those tribunals to the superior courts in the same circumstances. Cases are eligible even where they arise out of the running of a business.[172]

Cases may also qualify by reference to the Lord Chancellor's authority to the LSC to fund excluded services in Legal Representation (or Legal Help or Help at Court) in proceedings which have a significant wider public interest,[173] other than proceedings arising out of the carrying on of the client's business.[174] Examples of particular cases where a significant WPI has been found to exist have included representation before the Pensions Appeal Tribunal to consider whether schizophrenia could arise from military service,[175] and before the Social Security Commissioner to consider whether certain elements of jobseeker's allowance benefit were discriminatory against men.[176] He may also authorise the funding of individual cases on the request of the LSC,[177] but this will be in "extremely unusual" cases.[178] The client must be financially eligible for Legal Representation; relevant Funding Code criteria must be satisfied; no alternative means of funding must be available; and there is either a significant wider public interest, or the case is of "overwhelming importance"[179] to the client, or there is convincing evidence that there are other exceptional circumstances such that without public funding for representation it would be practically impossible for the client to bring or defend the proceedings, or the lack of public funding would lead to obvious unfairness in the proceedings. However, the Lord Chancellor has noted that the mere fact the opponent was represented does not necessarily make the proceedings unfair; "most tribunals are designed to be accessible to unrepresented clients". He will use "as a benchmark" those very exceptional cases where the ECtHR had indicated that the right of access to the court had effectively been denied because of the lack of public funding.[180] It is clear that tribunal representation through either of these routes will be rare.[181]

The ECHR also lies behind the establishment of a separate legal assistance scheme specifically for market abuse cases before the Financial Services and

---

[172] Lord Chancellor's Direction, *Tribunal Funding*, April 2, 2001, reproduced in the LSC's *The Funding Code: Guidance*, Pt 22, Tribunal Representation.

[173] i.e. "the potential of the proceedings to produce real benefit for individuals other than the client (other than benefits to the public at large which normally flow from proceedings of the type in question)": *LSC Funding Code: Criteria*, para.2.4.

[174] Lord Chancellor's Direction, *Scope of the Community Legal Service Fund: Exceptions to the Exclusions*, April 2, 2001, para.10.

[175] Public Interest Advisory Panel Report 01/62 (LSC, *Focus* 37. p.13): rating "significant".

[176] PIAP/01/56 (*Focus 36*, p.32): rating "significant;" *cf.* PIAP/01/66 (*ibid* p.34): no SWPI on the facts.

[177] Access to Justice Act 1999, s.6(8)(b); *Lord Chancellor's Revised Guidance on Applications for Exceptional Funding* (applying from November 1, 2001) (LSC, *Focus 36*, pp.25–28). Reproduced in LSC, *The Funding Code: Guidance* Pt C27.

[178] *Revised Guidance*, para.2.

[179] i.e. "a case which has exceptional importance to the client, beyond the monetary value (if any) of the claim, because the case concerns life, liberty or physical safety of the client or his or her own family, or a roof over their heads": *LSC Funding Code: Criteria*, para.2.4.

[180] *Revised Guidance*, paras 8, 9, 10. The guidance was revised following judicial review proceedings in *R (on the application of Jarrett) v LSC* [2001] EWHC Admin 389 and it incorporates the principles set out in *X v UK* (1984) 6 E.H.R.R. 136; see A. Lockley, *Legal Action*, August 2001. pp.18–19.

[181] In 2005/06, 16 applications for exceptional funding in individual inquiry/tribunal cases had been refused by the LSC, and 34 had been referred to the Lord Chancellor (28 granted, 4 pending): LSC Annual Report, 2005/06, *Statistical Information*, p.13.

Markets Tribunal.[182] Applications for funding are made to the Tribunal. The Tribunal must grant assistance to an individual if satisfied that it is in the interests of justice to do so and the applicant's financial resources are such that he or she requires assistance in meeting the legal costs in relation to proceedings before the Tribunal. The Tribunal must take account of specified factors including whether an adverse decision would be likely to cause the individual to lose his or her livelihood or suffer serious damage to reputation; whether a substantial question of law might arise; whether the individual might be unable to understand the proceedings or state his or her own case; whether the proceedings might involve the tracing, interviewing or cross-examination of witnesses on behalf of the individual; and whether it is in the interests of another person that the individual be represented. A contribution may be payable in accordance with detailed rules set out in the regulations. These criteria echo a number of those recommended in the past by the Council or Tribunals and might be applied in other analogous cases. The costs of the scheme are met by a levy on the community regulated by the Financial Services Authority.[183]

The Leggatt Report[184] noted that Professor Genn's research in the 1980s showed that appellants benefited significantly from representation.[185] However, it concluded (without the support of any research evidence) that representation

> "not only often adds unnecessarily to cost, formality and delay, but it also works against the objective of making tribunals directly and easily accessible to the full range of potential users."

It asserted that implementation of its recommendations overall

> "should radically reduce the need for representation whilst meeting human rights requirements."[186]

Where appellants were still in need of representation, the remit of the CLS should be extended, on an exceptional basis, to specific cases or classes of cases rather than to particular tribunals. Cases would have to have a reasonable prospect of success, and representation should be provided where required because the appellants' personal circumstances (such as inadequate knowledge of English or mental or physical disability) or the complexity of the case in fact or law make it unreasonable to expect the case to be presented by themselves. The LSC should set tribunal-specific criteria, under the Lord Chancellor's direction where appropriate, against which applications for public funding would be tested. There should be pilot studies in specific tribunals.[187]

---

[182] See above, para.16–011 and the Financial Services and Markets Tribunal (Legal Assistance) Regulations 2001 (SI 2001/3632), made under the Financial Services and Markets Act 2000, ss.134, 135.

[183] 2000 Act, s.136.

[184] Above, para.2–010.

[185] See above, para.16–013. Supported by research on legal representation in unfair dismissal cases in employment tribunals: A. Sinclair, N. Botten and S. Cahill, "Unfair Dismissal, Representation and Compensation" [2000] 5 Web JCLI (legal representation appeared to be a significant determinant of both success and compensation).

[186] LCD, 2001, para.4.21.

[187] *ibid.* paras 4.22–4.26.

This overall approach is open to criticism[188] on a variety of grounds. First, the assumption that accessibility to the unrepresented can be achieved in the vast majority of cases is unsupported by research evidence and, indeed, runs counter to the research by Professor Genn. Secondly, the failure to consider the possibility of developing lay representation services is disappointing.[189] The approach does, however, chime in with the consistent reluctance of successive governments to extend publicly funded tribunal representation, an approach that is only really explicable on grounds of cost.

The ensuing White Paper, *Transforming Public Services: Complaints, Redress and Tribunals* noted[190] that a "key principle" of Leggatt was that tribunals should operate so that there are few exceptions to the principle that tribunal users should be able to prepare and present their cases themselves. It acknowledged that that "some have argued differently",[191] citing the Law Society's argument that legal aid should be extended to Employment and Social Security tribunals. The government rejected the view that the blanket availability of legal aid should be extended in this way. For tribunals where public funding for representation was not already available its intention was to reduce the need for representation by the provision of alternative approaches to dispute resolution, by improved assistance for the preparation of cases and better trained panel members. Where there was still a need, funding was available for exceptional cases under s.6(8)(b) of the Access to Justice Act 1999.[192]

E. EXPERIENCES OF TRIBUNALS

Increasing attention is being paid to the experiences of users of tribunals. This is **16–016** an important theme of the reforms currently in progress following the Leggatt Report.[193] An observational study[194] concerning three tribunals[195] reported favourably on the "generally high levels of professionalism and care on the part of tribunal judiciary".[196] Most users interviewed after the end of the hearing and before the decision claimed to have felt comfortable during hearings, subject to some evidence of a slightly lower level of comfort expressed by South Asian users. The vast majority expressed high levels of trust. One in five, though, mentioned concerns about unfairness or lack of respect shown during the hearing, through failing to listen, asking questions interpreted as hostile or appearing to have made their minds up. Post-decision interviews indicated that about a quarter of the users who were unsuccessful had not understood the reason for the

---

[188] M. Adler, "Self-help is no substitute" (2001) 8(2) *Tribunals* 19; *Legal Action*, October 2001, p.3; NACAB response to the LCD consultation on the Leggatt Report (2001).

[189] Possible models that have been employed include tribunal units that accept referrals from other agencies, that are based within advice centres, and that concentrate on the provision of training and advice to other representatives: see R. Lawrence, *Tribunal Representation* (1980).

[190] Cm. 6243, 2004, pp.50–51.

[191] This is disingenuous: the overwhelming expert view in this area is sceptical of the Leggatt position.

[192] But in practice this provides funding in a very small number of cases.

[193] See para.2–010.

[194] H. Genn, B. Lever, L. Gray, *Tribunals for diverse users* (DCA Research Series 1/06, January 2006).

[195] Appeals Service Tribunals; SENDIST; Criminal Injuries Appeals Panels.

[196] p.190. See generally Ch.5.

decision. The unsuccessful users were very likely to say that the decision was unfair; among Minority Ethnic users about one-third said they thought the decision had been influenced by their ethnicity.[197]

F. ALTERNATIVES TO ORAL HEARINGS

16–017   One of the themes of the White Paper, *Transforming Public Services: Complaints, Redress and Tribunals*[198] was the determination to explore alternatives to the traditional oral hearing. The ombudsmen services had shown that sound decisions fully respecting the rights of parties could be made without formal hearings. While steps had been taken with telephone and video-conferencing, "we need to go further and to re-engineer processes radically so that just solutions can be found without formal hearings at all". It would be a task for the new Tribunals Service to develop new ways of operating, in conjunction with departments, and users and representatives. These would have to be piloted. The Service's priorities and objectives for 2006–07 include that of reducing the volume of appeals reaching a full tribunal hearing and to dispose of those that do in more efficient and effective ways. In 2006–07, two separate pilots were to be undertaken, one to provide customers with enhanced advice and one to cover early neutral evaluation, mediation and other ADR materials. There would also be research on potential and existing tribunal users to ascertain why some do not use the system, to consider how tribunals can be made more attractivce, to increasing understanding of attitudes and explore other options to resolve disputes going before tribunals.[199]

Responses to a consultation exercise by the Council on Tribunals on the use and value of oral hearings in the administrative justice system gave rise to a number of common themes. These included that oral hearing can play a valuable role in terms of both effectiveness and the perception of fairness; that in some situations ultimate access to an oral hearing was essential to the pursuit of justice; the form and style of an oral hearing can significantly affect the user's experience; some groups of respondents had relatively little knowledge and experience of ADR; and that the need for advice and assistance remains significant whichever form of dispute resolution is adopted.[200]

---

[197] pp.243–246. See generally Ch.6. The latter points in particular pose challenges for tribunals: pp.245, 246.
[198] Cm.6243, pp.27–28.
[199] *Tribunal Service Business Plan 2006–07*, pp.11, 19. See T. Wall, "Tribunals Service Early Dispute Resolution Project", Council on Tribunals *Adjust* Newsletter, February 2007.
[200] *www.council-on-tribunals.gov.uk/publications/628.htm*.

CHAPTER 17

THE CRIMINAL TRIAL

17–001   This chapter examines the criminal trial. It should be read taking a critical approach, bearing in mind the many competing values at stake, which are described in outline by Packer's two models of criminal justice.[1] Without necessarily agreeing with either of Packer's models, or suggesting that they represent an accurate or exhaustive account of the criminal process, Packer's models provide a useful mechanism for evaluating the objectives of the trial process and the extent to which the present trial rules, principles and policies fulfil these objectives.[2] Packer's "crime control model" emphasises the importance of the repression of criminal behaviour in the most efficient manner. There is a requirement for high rates of arrest and conviction, and a major interest in promoting speed and finality in the criminal justice system. There is, therefore, an emphasis on informal, routine procedures, relying heavily on the work of the police to determine guilt. Consequently, whatever procedures are used presume guilt. The "due process model" stresses the need to protect the accused against error. Whereas the crime control model looks like a conveyor-belt approach to criminal justice, the due process model looks more like an obstacle course. Every stage in the due process model assumes the innocence of the accused and requires formidable impediments to be overcome to establish guilt. The trial stage is, therefore, essential to the due process model.

The rhetoric of the English criminal justice process reflects the due process model, particularly in the period immediately following the enactment of the Human Rights Act 1998. Obvious examples include the presumption of innocence, reflected in the prosecution bearing the burden of proof in a criminal trial, and the "fair trial" guarantees of Art.6 of the ECHR and the impact these have on the interpretation of the rules relating to the admissibility of evidence. The impact of the Human Rights Act 1998 and the ECHR is particularly keenly felt in the criminal trial owing to the very broad guarantees in Art.6 and their expansive interpretation by the European Court. The impact on evidence and procedural law is far more marked than with the substantive law. Article 6(1) of the European Convention on Human Rights provides:

> "In the determination of . . . any criminal charge against him, everyone is entitled to a fair and public hearing within a reasonable time by an independent and impartial tribunal established by law. Judgment shall be pronounced publicly but the press and public may be excluded from all or part

---

[1] See H. L. Packer, *The Limits of the Criminal Sanction* (1968). Packer's models are discussed more fully in relation to pre-trial criminal procedure above, where also attention is drawn to the "fundamental balance" between the interests of the community and the rights and liberties of individual citizens considered by the Royal Commission on Criminal Procedure. M. King, *The Framework of Criminal Justice* (1981) provides a method of examining the criminal justice system by building more models on to those created by Packer. See also M. Wasik, T. Gibbons and M. Redmayne, *Criminal Justice Text and Materials* (1999).

[2] For a detailed critique of Packer's models see A. Sanders and R. Young *Criminal Justice* (3rd edn, 2007), pp.19–35. Attempts have been made to reinterpret Packer's models as not being in conflict, but rather, that the due process goals qualify those of the crime control model: see A. Ashworth and M. Redmayne, *The Criminal Process* (3rd edn, 2005), Ch.2 generally, and "Criminal Justice and the Criminal Process" (1988) 28 B.J. Crim. 111. Ashworth's reinterpretation of Packer is criticised by Sanders and Young (2007), pp.22–25. See also D. Smith, "Case Construction and the Goals of Criminal Process" (1998) 37 B.J. Crim. 319; P. Duff, "Crime Control Due Process and 'the Case for the Prosecution' " (1998) 38 B.J. Crim. 611.

of the trial in the interests of morals, public order, or national security in a democratic society, where the interests of juveniles or the protection of the private life of the parties so require, or to the extent strictly necessary in the opinion of the court in special circumstances where publicity would prejudice the interests of justice."[3]

The impact of the ECHR on domestic law is so significant that it has already generated a domestic human rights jurisprudence[4] in criminal justice. Commentators have offered interesting rights-based models by which the criminal justice process can be evaluated.[5] As an example, we will consider Ashworth and Redmayne's critique of Packer's model on a human rights-based approach later in the chapter. Other alternatives for evaluation of the system that have been proposed will also be examined.[6]

Because of the impact of the Human Rights Act 1998, due process guarantees perhaps appeared, in the immediuate aftermath of the legislation, to be more substantial than they really are. The flurry of cases in the wake of the Act emphasised existing protections and extended the scope of some. However, it should not be forgotten that there has been a relentless legislative drive towards improving efficiency in the criminal process. This has not always attracted the same high profile as when "human rights" arguments have triumphed in the courts. The efficiency driven initiatives in the process usually demonstrate a clear "crime control" leaning. As many commentators observe, it is inappropriate to dismiss the crime control model too quickly. Examples of practices that reflect the crime control model in the English process include the many cases being diverted from trial, the channelling of cases into the magistrates' courts, the police occasionally violating the rules governing their powers and many, perhaps too many, guilty pleas being entered. In addition, the threats posed by terrorism have in some respects brought about a political backlash against the rhetoric of human rights, and the value of the Human Rights Act itself has been questioned.[7] As a result, the crime control model plays a greater role in the English criminal justice system than would at first appear.

It may be of some value in reading this chapter to consider the differences between processes designed to establish the truth of events and procedures adopted in the English criminal trial.[8] At the criminal trial, it is for the prosecution to establish its case against the accused to the satisfaction of the magistrates

---

[3] See C. Ovey and R. White, *European Convention on Human Rights* (2006); M. Amos, *Human Rights Law* (2006); S. Trechsel, *Human Rights in Criminal Proceedings* (2005).

[4] For studies of the impact of the Human Rights Act, see Department for Constitutional Affairs, *Review of the Implementation of the Human Rights Act* (2006); R. Clayton, "The Human Rights Act Six Years On: Where Are We Now?" [2007] E.H.R.L.R 11; F. Klug and K. Starmer, "Standing Back from the Human Rights Act: how effective is it five years on?" [2005] P.L. 716; Lord Steyn 2000–2005, "Laying the Foundations of Human Rights Law in the Kingdom" [2005] E.H.R.L.R. 349; Joint Committee on Human Rights' Thirty-second Report of Session 2005–06, *The Human Rights Act: the DCA and Home Office Reviews* (2006) Cm. 1716; Government Response to the Joint Committee on Human Rights' Thirty-second Report of Session 2005–06 (2006) Cm. 7011.

[5] See especially Ashworth and Redmayne (2005).

[6] See, e.g. the "freedom" model: Sanders and Young (2007).

[7] Home Office, *Rebalancing the Criminal Justice System in favour of the law-abiding majority: Cutting crime, reducing reoffending and protecting the public* (2006) p.4.

[8] See, further Z. Bankowski, "The Jury and Reality" in M. Findlay and P. Duff (eds), *The Jury Under Attack* (1988) and works referred to therein.

or jury beyond a reasonable doubt through an adversarial procedure. Considerable efforts are made to ensure "fairness" in the procedure, so the court cannot
take account of all possible forms of evidence. The trial procedures are also
firmly bedded in the oral tradition with witnesses being called to give oral
testimony on oath and be subjected to cross-examination in full view of the
accused and the trier of fact. Moves to protect vulnerable witnesses and to
enhance the quality of the evidence received demonstrate an increasing willingness to move away from the strict oral tradition.[9]

17–002   Outside the criminal trial, judgments as to the truth of a matter are likely to be
made, not by adversarial methods, but inquisitorially; not so as to be satisfied
beyond reasonable doubt, but as more likely than not; not by evidence which
passes the rules of legal admissibility, but on any reliable evidence.[10] It is not the
objective of the criminal trial to establish the truth of what happened, although
it is presumably believed that the criminal trial will produce results that closely
resemble the truth of the matter. The merits of the adversarial system and the
potential advantages of an inquisitorial approach[11] are frequently called into
question, particularly when the current criminal trial process is perceived as
being under acute stress. The adversarial trial process has frequently been
criticised for inhibiting "a problem solving approach".[12] Some aspects of English criminal trial process might be regarded as shifting towards a more inquisitorial process,[13] and evidence of a general convergence of inquisitorial and
adversarial systems has also been suggested.[14] Many might regard the emphasis
on the full panoply of adversarial trial processes as being of greater symbolic
than practical significance bearing in mind that so few cases reach the Crown
Court, and so few of those result in a full jury trial. Nevertheless, the jury trial
still represents the paradigm of the criminal trial in England and Wales.

It is important also to record at the outset that the criminal trial process is
constantly evolving. There is a continual pressure for change, both to improve the
procedures in principled legal terms and to improve efficiency. This occurs not
only from the natural evolution of the common law which is particularly volatile
in this area, but also from successive government reviews and policy initiatives.
These all too often lead to over-hasty legislation.

In recent years the criminal trial has also come under pressure to recognise the
significance of other interests and objectives peripheral to the determination of

---

[9] See the reforms in Pt II of the Youth Justice and Criminal Evidence Act 1999. On orality, see
  generally J. Spencer [1994] Crim. L.R. 628. But note *Luca v Italy* [2001] Crim. L.R. 747.
[10] See J. McEwan, "Adversarial and Inquisitorial Proceedings" and J. Jackson, "Evidence: Legal
  Perspectives" in R. Bull, and D. Carson (eds), *Handbook of Psychology in Legal Contexts* (1995).
  "Trial Procedures" in C. Walker and K. Starmer, *Miscarriages of Justices: A Review of Justice
  in Error* (1999). On the many different systems falling within the general classification as
  inquisitorial, see M. Damaska, "Evidential Barriers to Conviction and 2 Models of Criminal
  Process: A Comparative Study" (1973) 121 U. Penn. L.R. 506.
[11] Note that the Auld Report states that the criminal trial is an investigation for the truth. Ch.1,
  para.12.
[12] C. Pollard, "Public Safety, Accountability and the Courts" [1996] Crim. L.R. 152.
[13] As for example with enhanced disclosure regimes and a diminution of the orality principles.
[14] See N. Jorg, S. Field and C. Brants in C. Hardin, P. Fennell, N. Jorg, and B. Swart, *Criminal
  Justice in Europe* (1995). J. Hodgson, "Suspects, Defendants And Victims in the French Criminal
  Process: The Context Of Recent Reform" (2002) 51(3) I.C.L.Q. 781. For comparisons with the
  English procedure see L. H. Leigh and L. Zedner, *A Report of the Administration of Criminal
  Justice in the Pre-trial Phase in England and Germany* (RCCJ Research Study No.1, 1992). For
  a brief but accessible account of the French system, see S. Wesley, "A Glimpse of French
  Criminal Justice" (1998) N.L.J. 326; R. Jones, "Criminal Procedure in France" (1999) J.P.N.
  592.

guilt or innocence. The most prominent influences have included an increased recognition of the victim's role in the criminal justice system.[15] In addition, there is a discernible trend towards consumerism in which "users" of the criminal justice system must be satisfied by the "service" they receive.[16] There are also the obvious signs of the impact of managerialism,[17] with more monitoring, protocols, performance indicators and processes to guarantee efficiency being implemented.[18]

The constant pressures within criminal justice are made stark by the objectives established in the *Criminal Justice: The Way Ahead* wherein the criminal justice system should be "effective at preventing offending and reoffending; efficient in the way it deals with cases; responsive at every stage to the needs of the victims and the law-abiding community; and accountable for the decisions it takes".[19] It is under constant pressure to achieve these aims, and this generates an incredible internal pressure on the process because the objectives are not always in harmony. These pressures become most acute in the trial process where under close public scrutiny "results" and final determinations have to be made.

The trial process and the number of defendants involved can be illustrated by the diagram below, taken from the Criminal Statistics for England and Wales 2005.

---

[15] See Department for Constitutional Affairs, *Hearing the Relatives of Murder and Manslaughter Victims: The Government's Plans to Give Bereaved Relatives of Murder and Manslaughter Victims a Say in Criminal Proceedings* (2005), available at *www.dca.gov.uk;* JUSTICE, *Victims in Criminal Justice* (1998). Some have fashioned approaches to the criminal process which focus on the victim: see J. Dignan, and M. Caradino, "Towards a Framework for Conceptualising and Evaluating Models of Criminal Justice from a Victim Perspective" (1996) 4 Int. R. Victimology 153; J. Shapland, "The Criminal Justice System and the Victim" (1985) 10 Victimology 585.
[16] See A. Walker, C. Kershaw and S. Nicholas, *Crime in England and Wales 2005–6* (12/06 HOSB, 2006) available at *www.homeoffice.gov.uk;* 80% of people are confident that the system respects the rights of the accused and treats them fairly; 44% that it is effective in bringing people who commit crime to justice; 36% that it meets the needs of victims.
[17] See N. Lacey, "Government as Manager, Citizen as Consumer" (1994) 57 M.L.R. 534; Sanders and Young (2007), pp.35–38.
[18] For example, see Home Office, *Delivering Simple, Speedy, Summary Justice* (2006).
[19] *Criminal Justice: The Way Ahead* (2001) p.5.

Figure 1.1   **Flows through the Criminal Justice System, 2005**

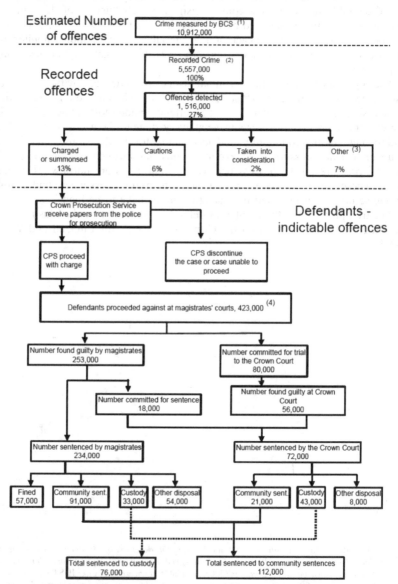

1. Covers crimes against households and individuals, reported in the 2005/06 British Crime Survey interviews, that were not necessarily reported to the police. This set of offences is not strictly comparable to recorded crime.

2. Covers all indictable, including triable either way, offences plus a few closely associated summary offences.

3. Includes formal warnings for cannabis possession, penalty notices for disorder and non-sanction detections

A. SUMMARY TRIAL[20]

"*No country in the world relies on magistrates as we do.*"[21]

There are almost 500 magistrates' courts around England and Wales and the bulk   **17–003**
of their work concerns minor offences, their powers of sentencing are limited and
their decisions create no legal precedents. Nevertheless they do deal with the vast
majority of criminal cases[22] (around 95 per cent) and they constitute the tribunal
most likely to be encountered by the "ordinary" person.[23] Despite this, there is
surprisingly little public awareness of their functioning or even of the composition of the magistrates' court. In recent years the work of the magistrates has
come under very close academic and government scrutiny, largely because of the
attempts to maximise efficiency in the criminal justice process by channelling
more cases into the cheaper and quicker magistrates' court process. Recent
research has indicated that the government's objectives of fostering greater
co-operation between the parties involved in magistrates' courts hearings has led
to cases being dealt with even more swiftly.[24] In the first three months of the
government's pilot project under the "Simple, Speedy, Summary Justice"[25]
banner, 60 per cent of guilty pleas were dealt with on the day. There was a 70 per
cent reduction in cases being adjourned at the first hearing and, interestingly, a 30
per cent increase in guilty pleas at the first hearing.

We have already considered the ways in which the appearance of a person
accused of a summary offence or an offence triable either way can be secured in

---

[20] The body of literature on the summary trial is expanding. For an accessible account see J. Sprack, *Criminal Procedure* (11th edn, 2006). The practitioners' works are *Stone's Justices Manual* and *Blackstone's*, both published annually. The Auld Report also provides an excellent overview of the subject in Ch.3. The other sources relied on Flood-Page and Mackie, *An Examination of the Decisions in Magistrates' Courts and the Crown Courts in the Mid-1990s* (HORS 1998). E. Burney, *J.P., Magistrate, Court and Community* (1979); P. Carlen, *Magistrates' Justice* (1976); A. P. Carr, *Criminal Procedure in Magistrates' Court* (1983); P. Darbyshire, *The Magistrates' Clerk* (1984); J. Gregory, *Crown Court or Magistrates' Court?* Office of Population Censuses and Surveys (HMSO, 1976); B. Harris, *The Criminal Jurisdiction of Magistrates* (11th edn, 1988); H. Parker, M. Sumner and J. Jarvis, *Unmasking the Magistrates* (1989); J. W. Raine, *Local Justice* (1989); P. J. Rowe and S. J. Knapp, *Evidence and Procedure in Magistrates' Courts* (3rd edn, 1989); R. Tarling, *Sentencing Practice in Magistrates' Courts* HORS (No.56, 1981); J. Vennard, *Contested Trials in Magistrates' Courts*, RCCP Research Study No.6, 1980); J. Vennard, *Contested Trials in Magistrates' Courts*, HORS No.71, 1981); C. Hedderman and B. Noxon, *Magistrates' Courts or Crown Court? Mode of Trial Decisions and Sentencing* (Home Office Research Study No.125, 1992). For a brief summary of the work of the Home Office Research and Planning Unit, see D. Moxon, "Current Research Bearing on the Work of Magistrates' Courts" (1984) 148 J.P.N. 634.

[21] Auld Report (2001), Ch.3, para.1. Comparison with other European systems reveal that England and Wales is the only jurisdiction in which there is such a high proportion of criminal cases, including serious cases decided by lay people (p.xiii).

[22] In 2005 there were 1,895,000 defendants proceeded with in the magistrates' court: Home Office Statistical Bulletin, *Criminal Statistics for England and Wales 2005* (2006), Table 1.1). The number of proceedings for summary non-motoring offences fell by 4%. There were falls for indictable offences (of 7%) and summary motoring offences (8%) para.1.12.

[23] This Chapter does not deal in detail with the special rules and procedures governing the trial of juveniles and young people. The Youth Court structure is similar to that of the magistrates' court, with the magistrate presiding. The most significant differences are in the limitations on reporting and open access to the courts and in the range of disposal powers available.

[24] *Delivering Simple, Speedy, Summary Justice: An Evaluation of the Magistrates' Court Tests* (2007).

[25] Home Office, *Delivering Simple, Speedy, Summary Justice* (2006).

the magistrates' court. In short, this will be because the offence is one that is triable summarily only or because it is an either way offence and it has been determined that it should be tried in the magistrates' court. We have also explained the procedure adopted by the court in selecting the mode of trial of an offence triable either way. If summary trial is the appropriate way of determining guilt or innocence for the offence charged, the first formal step is for the magistrates' clerk to read the information to the accused or the defendant (these terms are used inter-changeably), and secure a plea to that information.

1. THE INFORMATION[26]

17–004 The information is the formal document containing the allegation(s) against the accused. Unlike an indictment it does not contain a separate statement of the alleged offence and then the particulars alleged to constitute the offence. It merely contains a statement that combines the essential facts and the alleged offence. Each information should allege one offence only.[27] It is sufficient if the accused is given reasonable notice of the charge to be met and the way in which it is alleged the offence was committed.[28] The use of plain, non-technical language is intended to simplify matters for the accused. This is consistent with the broader principle of a fair trial that the accused must know the case against him and be able to understand the accusations.[29] This is particularly important in summary proceedings where there is a greater chance that the accused will be unrepresented. The magistrates' court can allow for defective informations to be corrected by granting an adjournment.[30] Specimen informations relating to criminal damage, theft and carrying an offensive weapon follow:

(i) Henry Frederick Smailey on the 1st day of March 2007 did without lawful excuse damage a motor vehicle, namely a Ford Focus number Y123 ABC, belonging to John Smith intending to damage the property or being reckless as to whether that property would be damaged; contrary to section 1(1) of the Criminal Damage Act 1971.

(ii) Henry Frederick Smailey on the 1st day of March 2007 stole £15 belonging to John Smith; contrary to sections 1 and 7 of the Theft Act 1968.

(iii) Henry Frederick Smailey on the 1st day of March 2007 without lawful authority or reasonable excuse had with him in a public place, namely the Headrow Shopping Centre, Leeds, an offensive weapon, namely a bayonet; contrary to section 1(1) of the Prevention of Crime Act 1953.[31]

---

[26] Criminal Procedure Rules (2005) r.7.3.

[27] For the difficulty in deciding whether the information alleges more than one information (and thereby infringes the rule against duplicity), see *Blackstone's* (2007), D19.5. The question is essentially one of degree and it is possible to cure defects in the course of the trial: see Magistrates' Courts Act 1980, s.123.

[28] The rules relating to the drafting of an information are contained in the CPR r.7.2(1). See further the comments of Watkins L.J. in *Rubin v DPP* [1990] 2 Q.B. 80 at 86.

[29] See especially the explicit guarantee in *Pelissier v France* (2000) 30 E.H.R.R. 715.

[30] On a lack of specificity in the information see generally *Hunter v Coombs* [1962] 1 W.L.R. 573.

[31] Note that these are all statutory offences and as such there is a mandatory requirement to refer to the statute creating the offence; see *Atterton v Browne* [1945] K.B. 122.

For a summary offence the information must be laid within six months of the time when the offence was committed.[32] Even if a previous information has been laid in time, that will be insufficient unless the one the defendant actually faces is also laid within the six-month period.[33] The time limit on laying of the information is obviously designed to ensure a speedy resolution to the prosecution.[34] However, this absolute time limit could be seen as denying a victim the opportunity to obtain justice, particularly if there has been undue delay in investigating the complaint.[35] The average time from offence to completion for defendants in indictable cases in the magistrates' court in 2005 was 122 days.[36]

(a) Lay and professional magistrates

Lay justices are appointed for the whole of England and Wales but are assigned to a particular "justice area"[37] by the Lord Chancellor. That area will usually be the one in which they live or work in order to enhance the local knowledge that can be brought to bear on a case.[38] A District Judge who is a professional and salaried member of the judiciary is, by virtue of his or her office, a justice of the peace for every commission area.[39] District Judges tend to be allocated cases involving complex areas of law or evidence, those cases involving inter-linked or lengthy issues, and those involving considerations of public safety, public interest immunity and extradition.

17–005

2. PRESENCE OF THE ACCUSED

At a trial on indictment, the accused must be in court to enter a plea and is normally present through the whole trial.[40] Summary trial is different in that provision is made for guilty pleas to be made by post and also, where the accused

17–006

---

[32] Magistrates' Courts Act 1980, ss.127(1),(2)(a). See also, *Atkinson v DPP* [2005] 1 W.L.R. 96.

[33] *R v Network Sites Ltd, Ex p. London Borough of Havering* [1997] Crim. L.R. 595.

[34] On the discretion not to proceed in circumstances of delay see *R v Newcastle-upon-Tyne Justices Ex p. John Bryce Contractors Ltd* [1976] 1 W.L.R. 517 and *R v Brentford Justices, Ex p. Wong* [1981] O.B. 445. The accused can challenge a prosecution on grounds of unconscionable delay if there has been prosecution inefficiency which has created prejudice for the accused: *R v Gateshead, JJ., Ex p. Smith* (1982) 75 Cr.App.R. 200. For an example see *R v Watford JJ., Ex p. Outrim* [1983] R.T.R. 26 (22-month delay in drink driving summons).

[35] This problem might arise, for example, where the offence alleged is summary only and is a complaint against a police officer. For a proposal to require 14 days' notice of a potential case to be served and extension of time limit to three years, see Anon., "Summary Time-Limits and Police Protection" (1998) 162 J.P.N. 259.

[36] See *Criminal Statistics* (2005), para.1.12.

[37] Courts Act 2003 s.8.

[38] This does not allow magistrates to make assumptions without hearing evidence: see *Carter v Eastbourne BC* (2000) 164 J.P. 273. Difficulties also arise because of knowledge of local repeat offenders. This has the potential to conflict with the right to a fair trial under Art.6. See *R v Altrincham JJ., Ex, p. Pennington* [1975] Q.B. 549; *Brown v UK* (1986) 8 E.H.R.R. 272.

[39] The appointment and removal of District Judges is contained in the Courts Act 2003 ss.22 to 26. See generally on the locality of justice in the magistrates' court and the effect of the evolution of the District Judges, P. Seago, C. Walker and D. Wall, [2000] Crim. L.R. 631 at 648–651. See also, *Sitting as a District Judge in the Magistrates' Court* (2006) available at *www.jsboard.co.uk*.

[40] Trials in *absentia* are not incompatible with the ECHR: *Colozza v Italy* (1985) 7 E.H.R.R. 516.

fails to appear at the appointed time and place, for trial in the absence of the accused.[41] Both these procedures are designed to spare the time and expense of the participants where there is no real intention to defend the charge, but they are hedged with certain safeguards to ensure that injustice does not result.

Section 11 of the Magistrates' Courts Act 1980 allows for proceedings to continue in the accused's absence, but if proceedings have begun by summons, the case should not proceed unless the summons has been proved to have been served on the accused within a reasonable time of the hearing or the court is satisfied that the accused has appeared on a previous occasion to answer the information.[42] If the accused is ignorant of the proceedings, he can, under s.14 of the Magistrates' Courts Act 1980 make a statutory declaration that he was unaware of the summons/proceedings. This must be served on the justices' clerk within 21 days. The effect of this is to render all proceedings void, and a differently constituted bench must then try the information afresh.

If the prosecution does not appear for the hearing, and the accused does, the magistrates may dismiss the information. If evidence has previously been received on an earlier occasion, they may proceed in the absence of the prosecution.[43] Great care must be taken not to infringe fundamental guarantees of natural justice where there is a decision to continue in the absence of a party rather than to adjourn.[44] This is particularly important in view of the need to respect the guarantees found in Art.6 of the ECHR including an opportunity for the accused to be represented, to have witnesses against him examined and to a "fair trial" in the broadest sense. There is also the need to maintain open justice in the summary trial and to be seen to be doing so.

Written pleas of guilty made by post may be entered only if the offence is a summary offence. A written plea of guilty is retractable in writing until the date of the hearing.[45] The safeguards to ensure that no injustices result from this procedure are that the accused must be served with a statement of the facts alleged by the prosecution and an explanatory note in addition to the usual summons; a wish not to be present must be made clear by the accused in writing; the statement of facts, the plea and anything which the accused has written in relation to mitigation or personal financial circumstances must be read out in court by the clerk; and no information is given to the court by the prosecution other than that contained in the documents.[46] This court procedure is very strict and any deviation will result in the proceedings being a nullity.[47] An amended version of this procedure may be used even when the defendant is present, provided he or she consents.[48] If the accused pleads guilty by post, there is no need for him to attend in person. If he pleads not guilty by post, the court will usually adjourn in his absence and fix a date for trial. If the accused does not respond or fails to appear, there will usually be a further adjournment before,

---

[41] See Magistrates' Courts Act 1980, s.11(1).
[42] See also Magistrates' Courts Act 1980, s.55(3).
[43] Magistrates' Courts Act 1980, ss.15, 56.
[44] See *R v Swansea Justices and Davies, Ex p. DPP* (1990) 154 J.P. 709.
[45] Magistrates' Courts Act 1980, s.12(6).
[46] Magistrates' Courts Act 1980, s.12; Magistrates' Courts (Procedure) Act 1998, s.1(2). The option is made available at the discretion of the prosecution: *Blackstone's* (2007), paras D19.24–19.26.
[47] See *R v Epping and Ongar JJ., Ex p. Breach* [1987] R.T.R. 233 and *Blackstone's* (2007), para.D19.24.
[48] Magistrates' Courts Act 1980, s.12A and see *Blackstone's* (2007), para.D19.25. The use of this procedure was scrutinised in the Auld Report (2001).

finally, the prosecution occurs in his absence. The accused must be given a fair opportunity to be present, but this is not an unlimited one.[49] A magistrates' court has a general discretion to proceed with a trial in the absence of the accused,[50] including where the right to be present has been voluntarily waived by the accused, for example, by abusing it as a consequence of indecent, outrageous or unseemly behaviour, or ceasing to claim it by deliberately jumping bail. In such cases, a plea of not guilty is entered on behalf of the accused. In any case, the court must be cautious in the exercise of its discretion ensuring that the convenience of the parties does not override the interests of the administration of justice.[51] It is important that magistrates retain a discretion to require physical presence of the accused for the hearing and/or for sentencing. The Divisional Court has emphasised that convenience and expedience in the system should not outweigh the need for the presence of the accused in serious cases.[52]

The Magistrates' Courts (Procedure) Act 1998 introduced a procedure that is further designed to speed up the process of summary hearings. The accused is issued with a summons, but rather than that being a simple statement of facts of no evidential status, the summons is accompanied by a witness statement. This procedure is designed to reduce the administrative burden on the police. If the accused pleads guilty, the court clerk can summarise the witness statements[53] for the bench for sentencing. If the accused pleads not guilty, there is a normal hearing and if the defendant does not respond, a prosecution is required but reliance on the witness statements is permissible

3. THE PLEA[54]

The substance of the information will be explained to the accused, if present in the magistrates' court, and he or she will be asked to plead. A plea is usually only sought to the general issue, that is, the accused is asked to plead guilty or not guilty. However, preliminary points may be raised; for example, whether the court has jurisdiction to try the accused or whether the information charges more than one offence. If these points are successfully raised, the trial cannot continue.[55] The magistrates have the jurisdiction to stay proceedings for an abuse of process as recognised by the House of Lords in *R v Horseferry Road Magistrates*

17–007

---

[49] *R v Ealing Magistrates' Court, Ex p. Burgess* [2000] Crim. L.R. 855.

[50] Magistrates' Courts Act 1980, s.11. The accused may show, within 21 days after finding out about the proceedings, that he or she did not know of the summons or proceedings until after their commencement in which case the conviction would be set aside under the Magistrates' Courts Act 1980, s.14. See J. Sprack, *Criminal Procedure* (11th edn, 2006), p.172.

[51] See H. Brayne, (2002) 152 N.L.J. 373.

[52] *R v Dewsbury Magistrates' Court, Ex p. K, The Times*, March 16, 1994.

[53] Usually contained in a statement admissible under s.9 of the Criminal Justice Act 1967.

[54] See Ashworth and Redmayne (2005), Ch.10.

[55] Special pleas may be entered as those in response to an indictment (see below) although technically the pleas of *autrefois acquit* and *autrefois convict* only apply to indictments. The same effect is achieved in magistrates' courts by dealing with the matter on a plea of not guilty: see *Connelly v DPP* [1964] A.C. 1254. The prosecution can, with leave of the court, withdraw the summons, but this does not equate to a plea of guilty: the prosecution may be instituted by a fresh summons at a later date. See *R v Grays JJ., Ex p. Low* [1990] 1 O.B. 54; *London Borough of Islington v Michalaeides* [2001] Crim. L.R. 843. The repeat prosecution will often not be regarded as oppressive because the accused will not have been in jeopardy at the first hearing: see *N. Yorkshire Trading Standards v Coleman* (2001) 166 J.P. 76; *Holmes v Campbell* (1998) 162 J.P. 655.

Court, Ex p. Bennett.[56] This power can be exercised where there has been unconscionable delay, or where the prosecution have manipulated or misused the process of the court so as to deprive the accused of the opportunity of a fair trial.[57] The power is to be exercised sparingly.[58] It is often safer for the magistrates to decline to stay proceedings and leave the matter to be dealt with by the High Court on an application for judicial review.[59]

In a summary trial where the accused is present, the magistrates' clerk reads out the information. The accused is asked to plead guilty or not guilty. The accused's plea must be freely made and unambiguous, and should normally be made personally.[60] The accused's response determines the remainder of the procedure. The court has a discretion to allow a change of plea at any time before sentence.[61]

There is, however, no specific procedure to deal with the situation where the accused does not reply to the information. The procedure available in the Crown Court to consider fitness to plead is not available to a magistrates' court.[62] The full insanity plea is, however, available in the magistrates' court.[63] In the event of a defendant appearing unfit, the possibilities are either to discontinue the proceedings, and perhaps contact the social services department; or to commit the accused for trial in the Crown Court if the offence can be tried on indictment[64]; or to enter a plea of not guilty, and then determine whether the accused did the act or made the omission charged and, if so, adjourn pending medical reports as a result of which the court may order hospitalisation without convicting the accused.[65]

Where the offence is triable either way and the accused is unfit to give consent to a summary trial, the magistrates' court has the exceptional power to proceed as if he has consented, provided that the accused is represented. This enables the court to use the power in s.37 of the Mental Health Act 1983 to hospitalise

---

[56] [1994] 1 A.C. 42. On abuse where there is a loss of evidence in the magistrates' court see *R (Ebrahim) v Feltham Magistrates' Court* [2001] Crim. L.R. 741, [2001] 1 All E.R. 831. See also, S. Martin, "Lost and Destroyed Evidence: The Search for a Principled Approach to Abuse of Process" (2005) I.J.E.P. 158.

[57] *R v Willesden JJ., Ex p. Clemmings* (1987) 87 Cr.App.R. 280.

[58] *R v Oxford City JJ., Ex p. Smith*, (1982) 75 Cr.App.R. 200.

[59] *R v Belmarsh Magistrates', Ex p. Watts* [1999] 2 Cr.App.R. 188, DC. On the difficulties of the same bench of magistrates hearing abuse claims and conducting the full hearing, see *R v Worcester JJ., Ex p. Bell* (1993) 157 J.P. 921.

[60] *R v Wakefield JJ., Ex p. Butterworth* [1970] 1 All E.R. 1181; *R v Gowerton JJ., Ex p. Davies* [1974] Crim. L.R. 253; *R v Kingston upon Thames Magistrates' Court, Ex p. Davey* (1985) 149 J.P. 744.

[61] *S (an infant) v Manchester City Recorder* [1971] A.C. 481.

[62] *R v Metropolitan Stipendiary Magistrate Tower Bridge, Ex p. Aniifowosi* (1985) 149 J.P. 748.

[63] On any charge involving *mens rea*: see *R v Horseferry Road Magistrates' Court, Ex p. K* [1997] Q.B. 23.

[64] This raises separate problems regarding the accused's ability to consent to a summary trial.

[65] Mental Health Act 1983, s.37(3); Powers of Criminal Courts (Sentencing) Act 2000, s.11; see *R v Lincoln (Kesteven) JJ., Ex p. O'Connor* [1983] 1 W.L.R. 335; M. Wasik, "Hospital Orders without Trial" (1983) 147 J.P.N. 211 and *Blackstone's* (2007), paras D19.39 to D19.41. See J. Evans and A. Tomison, "Assessment of the Perceived Need for a Psychiatric Service to a Magistrates Court" (1997) 37(1) Med. Sci. Law 161 (4.9% of cases of suspects held overnight in police custody needed psychiatric help). See also, C. Chambers and K. Rix, "A Controlled Evaluation of Assessment by Doctors and Nurses in a Magistrates Court Mental Health Assessment and Diversion Scheme" (1999) 39(1) Med. Sci. Law 38 (assessments by doctors/nurses enabled magistrates to reduce remands in custody of people suspected of suffering mental illness and to grant bail in more cases). See also T. Exworthy and J. Parrott, "Evaluation of a Diversion from Custody Scheme at Magistrates' Courts" (1993) J. For. Psych. 497.

without convicting.[66] Section 11 of the Powers of Criminal Courts (Sentencing) Act 2000 allows the magistrates to adjourn for medical reports. If the court adjourns under s.11, and bails the accused, it must order a medical examination of the accused. There is no power under this procedure to impose a custodial sentence on an absent accused.

The other options open to the prosecution before the plea is made are to withdraw a summons or to offer no evidence. Magistrates have no discretion not to try an information, except in cases of an abuse of process.

4. THE GUILTY PLEA

If, as is most common, the accused enters a guilty plea,[67] the court can convict **17–008** him without hearing evidence. (In the magistrates' court, the incidence of guilty pleas is very high, and often approaches 90 per cent.[68]) Alternatively, the court can proceed to hear the facts of the case from the prosecution, including any further offences that the accused wishes to have taken into consideration and any previous convictions. These facts are not usually elicited from witnesses unless there is some substantial disagreement,[69] but are presented by the prosecutor concerned. The procedure before sentence is considered below.

In certain circumstances social inquiry reports are required, for example, before community punishments can be imposed, and it is normal for a case to be adjourned if such a report is necessary or desirable.[70] The probation service is responsible for compiling a report and it will be available to the bench at the adjourned hearing, when the defence will have the opportunity of seeing and commenting upon it. With or without a report, the bench will listen to anything that may be said by the defence by way of mitigation of sentence.

Where the defendant pleads guilty, there is a sentencing discount. There is very strong evidence that quite explicit charge bargaining occurs in the magistrates' court whereby the prosecution offer to accept a guilty plea to a lesser charge than that originally laid, to encourage the accused to plead guilty.[71]

5. THE NOT GUILTY PLEA

A plea of not guilty normally results in an immediate adjournment to an agreed **17–009** date so that the prosecution and defence can assemble their witnesses and court

---

[66] See *R v Lincoln (Kesteven) JJ., Ex p. O'Connor* [1983] 1 W.L.R. 335.

[67] It is unclear whether this can come unilaterally from a legal representative: *R v Williams* [1978] Q.B. 373; *Blackstone's* (2007), para.D19.33.

[68] See D. Riley and J. Vennard, HORS 98, p.6. See *Criminal Statistics* (2005): 62% of defendants in summary cases pleaded guilty, (para.1.14), and proof in absence, where the defendant has not entered a plea, amounted to 16%. In only 4.8% of cases is there a conviction after trial in the magistrates' court: *Crown Prosecution Service Annual Report 2006–6* (2006) Annex A. p.86.

[69] Magistrates' Courts Act 1980, s.9(3).

[70] Magistrates' Courts Act 1980, s.10(3).

[71] See Ashworth and Redmayne (2005), pp.269–273; Sanders and Young (2007), pp.409–417 and A. Mulcahy, "The Justifications of Justice: Legal Practitioners Accounts of Negotiated Case Settlement in Magistrates Courts" (1994) 34 Brit. J. Crim. 411. Note the CPS Code, para.10, which stipulates that convienience should not be a suffcient reason to amend charges.

time can be allocated.[72] The prosecution can of course offer no evidence in which case that is the end of the matter and there can be no retrial of the same offence.[73] At the recommencement of the adjourned hearing the procedure will follow the normal adversarial lines. The prosecution is entitled to address the court through an opening speech[74] and will then lead evidence through witnesses who will be subject to examination-in-chief, cross-examination and, perhaps, re-examination.[75] If the case is not especially difficult, the prosecution will often start with witnesses immediately, since, with an experienced bench, there is no need to stress general points which might be necessary at a trial on indictment.[76] If the case has been adjourned after the prosecution witnesses have testified, the bench is permitted to seek a refresher of their testimony from the prosecutor, with the defence having the right to respond to it.[77] Magistrates do not have the power to dismiss a case on grounds of perceived unfairness without hearing any evidence except where there is unconscionable delay or where because of an abuse of the process the accused is unable to receive a fair trial and the proceedings are stayed.

At the close of the prosecution case, the defence may submit that there is no case to answer. The magistrates stop the hearing if they find that no reasonable tribunal could convict on the prosecution evidence, either because an essential element of the offence has not been proved or because the evidence has been discredited on cross-examination.[78] The magistrates must not say whether *they* would convict on the evidence so far presented, merely whether a reasonable bench *could* convict. Prosecution advocates are permitted to address the bench on a submission of no case if it relates to points of law, but this creates problems by comparison with the procedure in the Crown Court since magistrates will hear the arguments about the disputed item of evidence as a question of law, and then later go on to decide the issues of fact. If the submission of no case is accepted, the accused is discharged. There is no obligation for the magistrates to provide reasons for the rejection on a submission of no case.[79] If it is rejected, the right of the defence to call witnesses and build a defence is not prejudiced. The defence then calls evidence, with the accused as the first witness.[80] The accused is not obliged to give evidence.

At the close of the defence case, the defence is entitled to make a closing speech to the bench. Exceptionally, the prosecution may be permitted to speak

---

[72] See M. Wasik and A. Turner, "Sentencing Guidelines for Magistrates' Courts" [1993] Crim. L.R. 345 at 355. For a review of the use of adjournments in Scotland and calls for more proactive intervention from justices see F. Leverick and P. Duff, "Court Culture and Adjournment in Criminal Cases: A Tale of Four Courts" [2002] Crim. L.R. 39. There is no opportunity to challenge by judicial review a refusal to adjourn: *North Somerset District Council v Richards* [2002] EWHC 1336 (Admin).

[73] *R v Pressick* [1978] Crim. L.R. 377.

[74] On securing the presence of witnesses in the magistrates' court see Magistrates' Courts Act 1980, s.97, and the Justices' Clerks Rules 2005 (SI 2005/545) para.2 of the Schedule.

[75] The order of proceedings is similar to that in trial on indictment (see below).

[76] e.g. the burden and standard of proof, the need to listen carefully to the evidence, etc.

[77] *L and B v DPP* [1998] 2 Cr.App.R. 69.

[78] The criteria were contained in a *Practice Note* [1962] 1 All E.R. 448 (criticised by E. C. J. McBride, (1990) 154 J.P.N. 99). This Practice Note was revoked by the Practice Direction (*Criminal Proceedings: Consolidation*) but nothing was put in its place. See *Blackstone's* (2007), para.D20.22.

[79] See *Moran v DPP* [2002] EWHC 89 (Admin). See also *Steward v DPP* [2003] 1 W.L.R. 952.

[80] PACE, s.79.

again and, if so, the defence will be given a second opportunity.[81] The defence is always entitled to the last word.

The clerk should take a note of the evidence throughout the hearing.[82] The summary trial is in open court reflecting the importance of the principle of open justice, but the magistrates may, under their inherent jurisdiction, hear representations in chambers during the trial.[83] All parties should be present on such occasions and the clerk should take appropriate notes of such hearings.

Concern has been expressed at the scope and frequency of the reporting restrictions used in magistrates' courts.[84] It has been emphasised that the "public nature of the proceedings deters inappropriate behaviour on the part of the court. It also maintains the public confidence in the administration of justice. It enables the public to know that justice is being administered impartially. It can result in evidence becoming available".[85] Undoubtedly, public confidence in the criminal justice system is important, and public hearings do serve to promote that confidence.

The rules of evidence are very similar for summary trial as for trials on indictment. The crucial differences that do exist flow from the fact that magistrates make the decisions arising in the trial on points of law and are also the tribunal of fact. The strict division of the functions between judge and jury in the Crown Court is impossible in the magistrates' court. The problem is most acute where the defence challenges prejudicial evidence that the prosecution seek to rely on.[86] Magistrates have a discretion as to when they choose to deal with challenges to admissibility[87]; but should be alert to the dangers of the accused tactically leaving the challenge to the end of the prosecution case.[88] As a classic example of the dilemma, it is for the magistrates to decide, for example, whether a confession is admissible in accordance with the Police and Criminal Evidence Act 1984 (PACE).[89] They must obviously be informed of the accused's confession. If they decide it is not admissible they must attempt to determine the guilt of the accused without taking account of the confession.[90] Such a task is extraordinarily difficult, but is nevertheless essential where the deciders of fact

---

[81] CPR r.37.1

[82] Practice Direction (*Criminal Proceedings: Consolidation*) para.V.55.4.

[83] *R v Nottingham Magistrates' Court, Ex p. Furnell* (1996) 160 J.P. 201. See also *R v Birmingham Magistrates' Court, Ex p. Ahmed* [1995] Crim. L.R. 503.

[84] See M. Dodd, "Lifting the Veil of Secrecy: Reporting Restriction Orders" (2001) J.P.N. 498, discussing widespread use of orders under ss.4(2) and 11 of the Contempt of Court Act 1981 to prohibit information about the defendant. On open hearing generally, see also the very important statements in *R v Central Independent TV plc* (1994) 2 F.L.R. 151.

[85] *per* Lord Woolf M.R. in *R v Legal Aid Board, Ex p. Kaim Toder (A firm)* [1998] 3 All E.R. 541 at 549.

[86] See *Blackstone's* (2007), para.D20.9–20.11.

[87] *F v Chief Constable of Kent* [1982] Crim. L.R. 682.

[88] The power to deal with challenges as preliminary issues was approved in *A v DPP* (2000) 164 J.P. 317, DC (facts revealing prima facie defence of duress).

[89] In magistrates' courts the dual function of the justices as judges of both fact and law generally renders the "trial within a trial" an unnecessary sophistication, though one must be held where the admissibility of a confession is in issue: *R v Liverpool Juvenile Court, Ex p. R* [1988] Q.B. 1. See *Blackstone's* (2007), para.D20.9.

[90] It is not necessary for the bench to refer the case to another bench to conduct the hearing of the trial proper.

and law are one (or three) and the same.[91] Wasik[92] has examined the principled and practical difficulties of the magistrates operating as triers of law and fact and has identified a number of grounds on which risks of bias and evidential regimes in magistrates' and Crown Courts differ. In particular, these arise because the evidential regime in the magistrates' court is more "relaxed" with some points of evidence not being taken and the defendant being unrepresented.[93]

As far as public confidence in the summary trial system and the perception of bias is concerned, the problems of magistrates having prior knowledge of the regular offenders in their area in particular also produces a significant problem.

6. The Unrepresented Defendant

17–010   It has so far been assumed that the accused who appears at a magistrates' court is represented by either a barrister or a solicitor. The availability of legal aid and the existence of duty solicitor schemes at magistrates' courts means that representation is more readily available than in the past. Nevertheless, many defendants in magistrates' courts are unrepresented. At least when pleading not guilty, the lack of representation is a major disadvantage. There is an inherent inequality of resources in a criminal trial where "the State" brings a legal action against an individual (even against a corporation). This inequality is at its most acute when the accused is unrepresented. The difficulties for an unrepresented defendant include ignorance of procedure and of legal rules of evidence and substantive criminal law; the pressure imposed by a bewildering situation; an inability to understand, or even hear, what is going on; and the difficulty of putting forward one's own case sensibly, clearly and intelligibly. The principal safeguard is that the clerk is under a duty to assist an unrepresented defendant in the presentation of his or her case.[94] Other safeguards exist, including, fundamentally, that the charge must be explained to an unrepresented accused in straightforward language.[95] These obligations and the other willing efforts of the clerk may ameliorate, but cannot eliminate these difficulties. Any inequality of resources between prosecution and defence strikes deep at the heart of an adversarial system: when a significant imbalance exists, the system does not work fairly.[96]

---

[91] There is no requirement that a magistrate who has led a public interest immunity hearing should be compelled to disqualify himself from hearing the case proper: *R v Stipendiary Magistrate for Norfolk, Ex p. Taylor* [1998] Crim. L.R. 276.

[92] M. Wasik, "Magistrates: Knowledge of Previous Convictions" [1996] Crim. L.R. 851.

[93] See also P. Darbyshire, "Previous Misconduct at Magistrates' Courts—Some Tales from the Real World", [1997] Crim. L.R. 105.

[94] Practice Direction (*Criminal Proceedings: Consolidation*) para.V.55.9.

[95] Magistrates' Courts Rules 1981, r.13A.

[96] See S. Trechsel, *Human Rights in Criminal Proceedings* (2005) Ch.4, Pt III; J. Jackson, "Trial Procedures" in C. Walker and K. Starmer (eds), *Justice in Error* (1993), p.131. See also Art.6 of the ECHR, and the discussion of the "equality of arms" principle in Emmerson and Ashworth, *Human Rights and Criminal Justice* (2001).

7. THE VERDICT

The magistrates normally retire to consider their decision. Where the trial is **17–011**
before a bench of lay magistrates, rather than a District Judge, a majority[97] must
be satisfied beyond reasonable doubt that the charge is proved before they can
convict.

The magistrates decide questions of both fact and law and they will have the
benefit of advice from their clerk, which, in practice, they accept.[98] The clerk has
a duty to advise on matters of law including ECHR and Human Rights Act 1998
jurisprudence, questions of mixed fact and law, practice and procedure, penalties
available, relevant decisions of superior courts and other guidelines, other relevant matters and appropriate decision-making structures and by assisting the
court as to the formulation of reasons. The clerk is also able to offer advice on
sentencing, but should be careful not to be perceived as advocating a particular
disposal power. The clerk must not appear to be influencing the magistrates'
decision on the facts when giving legal advice. This is a very difficult line to
tread.

The appellate courts have been at pains to emphasise that justice must be seen
to be done in magistrates' courts. In particular, it is improper for a third party to
be with the magistrates in the retiring room whilst they consider their verdict.
Even the briefest of interventions may raise doubts about what has transpired
between an outsider and the magistrates, and so is strictly forbidden.[99] A similar
rule is imposed to preserve the inviolability of the deliberations of a jury.

There is, however, a difference between a jury engaged in fact-finding and the
position of magistrates. The jury have already received instruction on the law
from the judge in a summing-up. The magistrates will receive advice if they ask
for it from the clerk, which they may seek in the course of their deliberations. The
influence a clerk has over the magistrates is a matter of conjecture. Speculation
that the clerk may have played too substantial a role in the verdict can be fuelled
by his or her presence in the retiring room for a substantial period. The courts
will quash a conviction if the clerk visits the retiring room where there is no good
reason for doing so.[100] The best approach is for legal advice, including not only
advice on questions of law and practice and procedure but also refreshing the
magistrates' memory as to matters of evidence and principles of sentencing, to be
given in open court, when the advocates on both sides can contribute to the
advice being proffered. However, if it is thought that the magistrates have retired
to consider their verdict having been misinformed as to the law, the clerk may
inform them of the correct position.[101] Such advice given in the retirement room
is provisional and should be explained in open court.[102]

---

[97] Which is the reason why magistrates normally sit in threes. The chairperson has no casting vote
so that if a two-person court is divided the case must be retried: *R v Redbridge JJ., Ex p. Ram*
[1992] Q.B. 384.

[98] The advice from the clerk is regulated by the Practice Direction *(Criminal Proceedings: Consolidation)* para.V.55. s.28. As to the practice of accepting that advice, see *R v Jones-Nicks* [1977]
R.T.R. 72 and see *Blackstone's* (2007), para.D19.48.

[99] *R v Stratford upon Avon JJ., Ex p. Edmonds* [1973] R.T.R. 356.

[100] In *R v Guildford JJ., Ex p. Harding* (1981) 145 J.P. 174 the conviction was quashed because the
clerk had retired with the magistrates to advise them when the case was absolutely
straightforward.

[101] See *R v Uxbridge JJ., Ex p. Smith* [1985] Crim. L.R. 670.

[102] See *R (Murchison) v Southend Magistrates' Court* (2006) 170 J.P. 230, where the clerk, in
assisting the justices with compiling their reason for their verdict made them aware of the

On returning to court, the magistrates give their verdict of guilty or not guilty with some limited provision of reasons. Although the ECHR requires that as an element of the fair trial, the court should provide reasons for its judgment, there is at present no obligation on a magistrates' court to provide reasons.[103]

If the verdict is guilty the procedure will follow the same course as after a plea of guilty. If not guilty, the accused will be discharged. There is no opportunity for the magistrates to use alternative verdicts as can occur in the Crown Court where the accused might be found guilty of a lesser offence under the Criminal Law Act 1967, s.3.[104] There is an important and extremely wide power in s.142 of the Magistrates' Courts Act 1980 which allows magistrates to set aside a decision where it is in the interests of justice to do so.[105] This is regarded as a "slip rule" to rectify errors and not a power to be used to order a rehearing where the right of appeal to the Crown Court has been lost (e.g. by pleading guilty).[106] The magistrates may order a rehearing by a differently constituted bench having made a s.142 order.

8. Sentencing[107]

17–012   Not only is it the function of the magistrates to determine guilt, but they must also impose a sentence upon the offender. The magistrates have a power to adjourn after convicting but before sentencing in order to enable inquiry to be made about the accused.[108] The magistrates will hear reports, antecedents and mitigation before pronouncing sentence.[109] The decision as to sentence must be made by at least a majority. The magistrates are obliged under the Criminal Justice Act (CJA) 2003[110] to give reasons for a custodial sentence. Maximum sentences are laid down in respect of each offence. Some offences can be punished by imprisonment (with or without a fine); some by a fine or lesser sentence alone. Where the offence is one triable summarily only, magistrates may not at present impose a term of imprisonment greater than six months for any single offence or the maximum provided in the relevant statute whichever is the lower. When Sch.26 to the CJA 2003 is brought into force, the penalty for a

---

defendant's antecedents before the verdict had been given in open court, the decision was subject to judicial review. The Divisional Court dismissed the appeal on the facts but stated that the verdict should always be given in open court before advice is sought or given as to the defendant's antecedents.

[103] See, *R (McGowan) v Brent Justices* (2002) 166 J.P. 29. It is enough for the bench to indicate the basis of their decision without providing a detailed judgment. See also *McKerry v Teesdale & Wear Valley Justices* (2000) 164 J.P. 355. The essence of the exercise is to inform the accused why he has been found guility. This can usually be achieved in a few sentences.

[104] There is a fear that such a power would be misused in the magistrates' court. See *R v Liverpool Youth Court, Ex p. H* [2001] Crim. L.R. 487.

[105] See *R v Gwent Magistrates' Court, Ex p. Carey* (1996) 160 J.P. 613; *R v Ealing JJ., Ex p. Sahota* (1998) 162 J.P. 3.

[106] See *R v Croydon Youth Court, Ex p. DPP* [1997] 1 Cr.App.R. 411.

[107] For detailed consideration of sentencing in the magistrates' court see *Blackstone's 2007* Ch.D. 21.

[108] Magistrates' Courts Act 1980, s.10(3).

[109] See J. Shapland, *Between Conviction and Sentence* (1981).

[110] s.174(1).

number of summary offences will be raised to 51 weeks. The maximum fine is laid down by reference to the standard scale of fines that was introduced in 1982. It has five levels. Currently level 1 imposes a maximum fine of £200, level 2 a maximum fine of £500, level 3 a maximum fine of £1,000, level 4 a maximum fine of £2,500 and level 5 (otherwise known as the statutory maximum) a maximum fine of £5,000.[111]

Where the offence is triable either way and is being tried summarily, magistrates still cannot impose a term of imprisonment more than six months, and the maximum fine they may impose is that specified in the statute and may be greater than £5,000. There is no maximum aggregate fine that can be imposed on conviction for a number of offences dealt with together. When s.154 of the CJA 2003 comes into force magistrates will be empowered to impose a sentence of up to twelve months for a single offence and s.282 will increase the maximum penalty on summary conviction for an either way offence from six to 12 months.[112] The maximum aggregate term for two or more offences will be increased to 65 weeks.[113]

It is not necessarily the case that imprisonment will be imposed when it is available as a sentencing option. If imposed it can run consecutively or concurrently to existing sentences or those contemporaneously imposed. Indeed a major question for the magistrates is whether to impose a custodial sentence or not. The range of non-custodial sentences available include, not only imposing a fine, but also placing someone on probation, ordering attendance at an attendance centre, suspending or partially suspending a sentence of imprisonment, ordering someone to make payment of a compensation order,[114] sentencing someone to undertake a community punishment or granting an absolute or conditional discharge, as well as specific (options available for young people).[115] As an indication of the proportion of different sentences issued in the magistrates' court, in 2005 there were 1.89 million defendants proceeded against in the magistrates' court (of which 423,400 were for indictable offences).[116] There were 1,426,100 defendants found guilty in the magistrates, of which 252,900 involved indictable offences.[117] The number proceeded against in the magistrates' courts by type of offence also revealed 637,000 summary non-motoring cases and 834,700 summary motoring cases.[118] A total of 182,000 were given community sentences (which include: community rehabilitation orders; supervision orders; community punishment orders; attendance centre orders; community punishment and rehabilitation orders; reparation orders; curfew orders; action plan orders and detention and training orders).[119]

Whilst the sentencing power of magistrates is limited, they do have the very **17–013** important power to commit a case to the Crown Court for sentencing when the offence is triable either way and they are of the opinion that the offence is so serious that the punishment warranted lies beyond their power, or the custodial

---

[111] The Magistrates' Court Sentencing Guidelines (2004) provide guideline fines.
[112] See A. Samuels (1999) 163 J.P. 993.
[113] CJA 2003, s.155.
[114] Powers of Criminal Courts (Sentencing) Act 2000, s.131.
[115] As to sentencing in magistrates' courts, see *Blackstone's* (2007), Section D21.
[116] *Criminal Statistics for England and Wales 2005* (2006), Table 2.1.
[117] *ibid.* (2006), Table 2.3.
[118] *ibid.*
[119] *ibid.* (2006), Table 4.5.

sentence is greater than that which the magistrates can impose and is needed to protect the public where the accused is convicted of an offence of violence or sex.[120] The power to commit has been used frequently but with over half those cases sent to the Crown Court, the sentence actually imposed could have been imposed by the magistrates themselves. Flood-Page and Mackie found this to be true in 62 per cent of cases.[121] Since 1997 there has been an increase in the number of committals for sentence as a direct result of the plea before venue provisions. It is now common for an accused to indicate a guilty plea at the plea before venue but thereafter to be committed for sentence to the Crown Court. The new allocation procedure and increased sentencing powers available to magistrates under the CJA 2003, Sch.3 reflect a further attempt to redistribute business and keep more cases in the magistrates' court. Before the accused elects the venue he is able to request an indication from the magistrates whether, if he pleads guilty before jurisdiction is determined, the sentence will be custodial or not. If he then pleads guilty the magistrates proceed to sentence and can only impose a custodial sentence if one was indicated. If the magistrates have accepted jurisdiction then their power to commit to the Crown Court for sentence will be removed. However, there has been concern expressed that increased sentencing powers might result in those cases that are currently dealt with by magistrates simply receiving longer sentences, with no overall increase in the number of cases retained by magistrates. Thus, longer sentences may result but without a corresponding redistribution of business.[122]

The indication of sentence in return for a guilty plea is a considerable incentive for a defendant. Linked to this incentive is the knowledge that a guilty plea will attract a sentencing discount. However, the propriety of the application of the sentencing discount for early guilty pleas being applied in the magistrates' court has been called into question. Flood-Page and Mackie found "attempts to predict sentences on the basis of case factors were not particularly successful",[123] and that the average custodial sentence in the magistrates' court for those pleading guilty was 3.7 months as compared to a sentence of 3.8 months for those pleading not guilty.[124] Henham[125] found that in 90 per cent of cases sentencers indicated that they had taken account of the early plea, but concluded that the discount scheme had "done little to regulate the pragmatic nature of decision making in sentence discounts".[126] The Sentencing Guidelines Council issued guidance in 2004 designed to "promote consistency in sentencing by providing clarity for courts, court users and victims so that everyone knows exactly what to expect".[127]

---

[120] Powers of Criminal Courts (Sentencing) Act 2000, s.3.

[121] C. Flood-Page and A. Mackie, Sentencing Practice (HORS No.180, 1998), p.89.

[122] M. Zander, "Why do magistrates commit so many cases to the Crown Court?" (2003) 153 N.L.J. 689. See also S. Cammiss, "I Will in a Momant Give You the Full History: Mode of Trial, Prosecutorial Control and Partial Accounts" [2006] Crim. L.R. 38; A. Herbert, "Mode of Trial and Magistrates' Sentencing Powers: Will Increased Powers Inevitably Lead to a Reduction in the Committal Rate?" [2003] Crim. L.R. 314.

[123] C. Flood-Page and A. Mackie, Sentencing Practice (HORS No.180, 1998), p.34.

[124] ibid.

[125] R. Henham, "Reconciling Process and Policy: Sentence Discounts in the Magistrates' Court" [2000] Crim. L.R. 436.

[126] p.450. For criticism of the methodology see Sanders and Young, (2007), pp.391–396.

[127] Sentencing Guidelines Council, Reduction in Sentence for a Guilty Plea: Guideline" (2004) available at: *www.sentencing-guidelines.gov.uk*.

9. Do Magistrates Reach The Right Result?

The answer to this question, as with the question whether juries arrive at the right **17–014** result, depends upon what is meant by "right result" and must inevitably be impressionistic. Care must be taken with assertions either that magistrates or that juries acquit too many people. Comparing the statistics on rates of acquittal in the magistrates' courts and Crown Courts is apt to mislead since there are a number of factors that may influence the venue of the trial and the not guilty plea in that venue. In 2005, of those pleading not guilty 66 per cent in the Crown Court were acquitted; 33 per cent were found not guilty in the magistrates' court.[128] Even so, there are many different beliefs about summary trial, including that an accused has a greater chance of acquittal before a jury, that magistrates' impose lighter sentences in circumstances where the Crown Court and magistrates have the same sentencing powers, that judges impose lighter sentences in the same circumstances, and that magistrates' courts are biased in favour of the prosecution.[129] Further, there is some evidence that the criminal fraternity lack confidence in magisterial decision-making[130]: "Defendants do not expect justice to be done in the magistrates' court."[131] It is unclear whether that is because they believe magistrates get decisions wrong, or because they get them right. As the Auld Report recognised: "it is impossible for outside researchers and reviewers to evaluate the relative 'correctness of juries' verdicts and magistrates' courts' decisions".[132] The Auld Report was clear in its message that reliance for reform of the magistrates and assessment of the effectiveness of the magistrates' work ought not to be based on public opinion.[133]

In assessing the quality of justice dispensed in the magistrates' court, what is important above all else is that magistrates' courts provide trials that are fair and in accordance with principles of due process. There must be accountability and consistency in their decision-making whatever the pressures of efficiency in the process.

The debate as to the comparable quality of justice in the magistrates' court and the Crown Court has persisted for decades. Vennard's early study of contested trials in the magistrates' court[134] gives some support to the view that magistrates do weigh evidence carefully and reach a verdict that is broadly in line with identifiable features of the evidence heard. The criticism most frequently made of magistrates is that they place too much credibility on the evidence of police officers and are generally too "prosecution-minded".[135] This criticism emanates not only from the accused who opts for trial by jury because it is "fairer", or because magistrates are amateurs who cannot be expected to get it right, or

---

[128] See *Criminal Statistics for England and Wales 2005* (2006), Table 2.10.

[129] Bottoms and McLean (1976), Ch.4; Parker, Sumner and Jarvis (1989), p.60; and D. Riley and J. Vennard, "Triable-Either-Way Cases: Crown Court or Magistrates' Court?" (1988) 25 *Home Office Research Bulletin* 31 at 34.

[130] Riley and Vennard (1988), p.34. See *R v Highgate JJ., Ex p. Riley* [1996] R.T.R. 150 (JP reprimanding D for calling police officer a liar).

[131] Sanders and Young (2007), p.485

[132] Ch.3, para.24.

[133] p.105.

[134] Vennard (1980) Vennard (1981) and J. Vennard, "Acquittal Rates in Magistrates' Courts" (1981) 11 *Home Office Research Bulletin* 21.

[135] See e.g. evidence to the James Committee, *The Distribution of Criminal Business Between the Crown Court and the Magistrates' Court*, Cmnd. 6323, (1975); B. Wootton, *Crime and Penal Policy* (1978).

because they estimate that there is a better chance of acquittal,[136] but also from amongst those individuals and organisations who gave evidence to the James Committee.[137] The research study undertaken by Vennard had as its aims:

(i) to appraise and itemise for contested cases the substance of the evidence presented by the prosecution and the defence, and attempt to quantify weaknesses and[138] strengths in that evidence—such as whether or not the credibility of witnesses was impugned; and

(ii) to attempt to explain the trial outcome in contested cases in relation to the type of evidence presented by both parties and to criteria pertaining to witness credibility.

On somewhat limited evidence, Vennard concluded that her findings indicated that " . . . magistrates' decisions whether to convict or acquit are strongly associated with a few quantifiable indices of the evidence adduced by the parties and the credibility of witnesses".[139] Strong associations were detected between direct evidence implicating the accused given by the prosecution witnesses whose credibility was not impugned, and conviction. Conversely there was a strong association between acquittal, the prosecution witnesses' lack of credibility, and the lack of direct evidence. These findings are not startling but they may reassure critics that magistrates are generally operating along rational lines.

For another slightly more recent view, which relies partly upon different work by Vennard on acquittal rates, one may look at King's response[140] to proposals by the Justices' Clerks Society[141] that more trials should be diverted into the magistrates' court. King was dismissive of claims that magistrates offer a better quality of justice than juries and argued vigorously against proposals to reduce the right to jury trial.

Further, even more recently, Sanders and Young's review of the research evidence, leads them to conclude that the defendants perception as to the unfairness of magistrates' court trial are accurate.[142] They identify a number of possible explanations for the higher acquittal rates in the Crown Court compared with magistrates' court: (a) more people have to be convinced in the Crown Court (at least 10 out of 12 rather than two out of three)[143]; (b) the social composition of the magistrates compared with juries militates more in favour of conviction in a magistrates' court; (c) magistrates become "case-hardened" whereas juries come fresh to the criminal justice system (case hardening is offset, according to the Auld Report, by the infrequency of the magistrates' sitting, their training, the changing constitution of each panel, the presence of a clerk and their obligation to explain their decisions); (d) magistrates' court procedures place

---

[136] Gregory (1976).
[137] See *The Distribution of Criminal Business Between the Crown Court and the Magistrates' Court* (1975) Cm. 6323.
[138] Vennard (1981), p.4.
[139] *ibid.* p.20.
[140] M. King, "Against Summary Trial" *L.A.G. Bulletin*, April 1982, p.14.
[141] "A Case for Summary Trial-Proposals for a Redistribution of Criminal Business" published by the Justices' Clerks Society.
[142] Sanders and Young (2007), pp.480–494.
[143] On the question of whether magistrates are properly regarded as surrogate jurors, see the Auld Report (2001), p.l04.

defendants at a greater disadvantage because of the lack of disclosure requirements; the magistrates are aware of inadmissible evidence (e.g. confessions), and
justices' clerks have a significant impact. They conclude that it "is no exaggera-
tion to say that magistrates' courts are crime control courts overlaid with a thin
layer of due process icing. At every twist and turn in the process, defendants are
saddled with handicaps which undermine their willingness or ability to stand for
their rights in court."[144] In consequence, they express surprise that the RCCJ in
1993 wished to reduce the right to jury trial, especially since no research was
commissioned to examine justice in the lower courts.[145]

There is no question that the magistrates' court offers a swifter, cheaper
criminal process. The pressure to channel more and more cases into the magistrates has been increasing over the years, as exemplified when the government
twice introduced a Bill to remove the defendant's right to jury trial at his own
election and empowering the magistrates to make the decision as to venue. The
Criminal Justice (Mode of Trial) Bill 2000 was twice defeated in the House of
Lords and it is expected that the issue has been put to one side for the foreseeable
future.

There is no doubt that the government is anxious to maximise the use that can **17–015**
be made of the more efficient process in the magistrates' court. The questions that
remain are whether the magistrates are sufficiently accountable,[146] socially representative,[147] and whether they offer a lesser form of justice or one that is merely
different from that in the Crown Court. Research has shown that although the
magistracy is not wholly representative, they command respect.[148] "Magistrates
are not wholly reflective of the communities from which they are drawn, but
nevertheless they have an important symbolic effect of lay participation in the
system which should not be undervalued."[149] There are many aspects to these
difficult questions that cannot be addressed here. Fundamentally, it has to be
questioned what the primary purpose of the magistrates' court is. Is it a diluted
form of (swifter) justice? Are magistrates surrogate jurors? Are magistrates
community representatives in the criminal justice system?

A more specific interest involves not just comparing the quality of justice
dispensed by the magistrates as compared with the Crown Court, but that of the
lay magistrates compared with the District Judges (Magistrates' Court) the old
"Stipendiary". The research demonstrates that while District Judges are capable
of dealing with a greater volume of cases more quickly than the lay magistrates,[150] they are more expensive than lay magistrates (not least because they
convict more people thereby adding to the prison costs!).[151] Other research

---

[144] Sanders and Young (2007), p.493.

[145] *ibid.* (2007), p.491.

[146] See S. Doran and R. Glenn, *Lay Involvement in Ajudication: Review of the Criminal Justice
System in Northern Ireland* (Criminal Justice Review Research Report No.11, 2000).

[147] See P. Darbyshire [1997] Crim. L.R. 681.

[148] The Auld Report p.95, citing Morgan and Russell.

[149] The Auld Report, p.98.

[150] See also R. Morgan and N. Russell, *The Judiciary in the Magistrates' Court* (R.D.S. No.66,
2000). The Auld Report detailed criticism that is made of Morgan and Russell's costings based
on their failure to allow for the various factors involved in the cases District judges hear (p.97).
See also Auld (2001), p.95.

[151] For a criticism of the costings and calculations used by in Morgan and Russell's study see Auld
(2001), pp.96–97 where the question of principle regarding different sentencing practice is
examined. On the differences between the two branches see P. Seago, C. Walker and D. Wall,
"The Development of the Professional Magistracy in England and Wales" [2000] Crim. L.R.
631.

conducted recently by Flood-Page and Mackie[152] found that professional magistrates are more likely than lay magistrates to impose custodial sentences. Morgan and Russell in their research found that there was nothing to suggest that any differences in decision-making patterns were attributable to the professional magistrates who tended to be dealing with more serious cases.[153] Auld recommended no significant change in the numbers of lay or professional magistrates.[154]

Morgan and Russell[155] considered the balance between lay and professional magistrates and how the system can utilise both to maximum effect. The research was conducted into the opinions of the public and opinions of magistrates and court users. The efficiency of the lay and professional magistrates studied reveals that professional magistrates deal with more cases more swiftly[156]: estimates were that they would deal with 30 per cent more cases than lay magistrates. The professional magistrates took fewer adjournments and were more likely to inspire greater confidence in court users with greater consistency, efficiency, confidence, and by providing better reasons.[157] Sanders'[158] research has also questioned the extent to which the magistrates' court "embodies the core values which underlie serious crimes". His radical suggestion to improve the system was for three tiers of tribunal with District Judges sitting alone to hear controversial cases, a mixed court comprising lay members and District Judges to try contested cases and either way sentencing cases and the judge and jury to deal with the most serious crimes. Sanders' proposal for a District Judge to sit alone in cases in which legal issues arise and with lay magistrates when "social skills" are necessary was designed to maximise the opportunity for respective skills of the branches to be deployed and to create a closer parallel with the paradigm judge and jury.[159] The Auld Report rejected Sanders' approach describing it as "depriving summary justice of the best features of professional lay judges sitting separately".[160] It was regarded as prohibitively expensive.

Research into the magistrates' courts has also revealed an astonishing ignorance on the part of the general public as to how summary justice is delivered. Seventy-three per cent of the public were unaware of the difference between the lay and professional magistrates.[161] Lay magistrates were felt to represent the views of the public better than professional judges and were felt to be more likely to be sympathetic to the defendant's circumstances. It was, however, felt that professional magistrates were better at assessing guilt and managing the case more efficiently. The research revealed that the public felt that summary offences of a non-serious nature could be dealt with by a single magistrate. However, these

---

[152] (1998), Ch.7.
[153] p.49.
[154] Auld (2001), p.102. See also R. Morgan, "Magistrates: The Future According to Auld" (2002) 29 J.L.S. 308; A. Sanders, "Core Values, the Magistracy and the Auld Report" (2002) 29 J.L.S. 324.
[155] *The Judiciary in the Magistrates Courts* (2000).
[156] Average time per trial by lay magistrates is 34 minutes and 24 minutes by the District Judge (p.42). See Morgan and Russell, pp.34–43.
[157] Ch.2. For detailed qualitative assessment of the magistrates' performance—including attentiveness, courtesy, avoidance of jargon—see p.45.
[158] *Community Justice and Modernising the Magistracy in England and Wales* (2001) and see A. Sanders, (2002).
[159] See *Community Justice: Modernising the Magistracy in England and Wales* (2001); the Auld Report, p.104.
[160] p.105.
[161] Morgan and Russell, p.xi.

often illogical and certainly ill-informed views expressed by the public were dismissed as "valueless" and "uninformed opinion" on the relative strengths of the branches of the magistracy.[162]

Efforts to maintain and enhance public confidence in the magistracy have included a greater emphasis on selection and training of magistrates. Morgan and Russell found that the magistracy, whilst not representative of the community as a whole, did command confidence. However, Auld concluded that there was "scope for improvement" in the recruitment of magistrates, so as to better reflect national and local communities and to develop fairer and more efficient and consistent procedures and sentencing.[163] It was also recommended that the selection and appointment procedures for magistrates should also be improved to better reflect the community.[164] A National Recruitment Strategy began in 2003 with the aim of recruiting and retaining magistrates from under-represented groups. The Judicial Studies Board has also taken on a much stronger role in the training of magistrates to ensure greater standards of consistency across the country.[165]

An important point echoed throughout the Auld Report[166] is that "[p]ublic confidence is not an end in itself; it is or should be an outcome of a fair and efficient system".[167] Certainly recent reforms have reflected a desire to increase efficiency but the need for fairness should not be downplayed on the assumption that magistrates only deal with trivial issues.

B. TRIAL ON INDICTMENT[168]

A trial on indictment (that is one that takes place in the Crown Court), most commonly arises when an adult defendant has been charged with an offence that is triable only on indictment, or has been charged with an either way offence and has elected to be tried on indictment.[169] The pre-trial procedures that will be applicable before a case reaches the Crown Court have been discussed above. In an attempt to expedite the most serious cases more efficiently, the Crime and Disorder Act 1998, s.51, introduced a scheme whereby offences triable only on indictment are not dealt with by committal proceedings but proceed directly to

17–016

[162] Auld (2001), p.96.

[163] ibid., p.98.

[164] National Strategy for the Recruitment of Lay Magistrates (2003) available at www.dca.gov.uk. The Department for Constitutional Affairs states that "significant progress has been made on the recruitment of magistrates, some of which has taken place under the Magistrates' National Recruitment Strategy", Judicial Appointments 7th Annual Report 2004–5 (2006) Cm. 6731.

[165] www.jsboard.co.uk—see the Strengthened Role Project. See also Arrangements for the Organisation and Management of Magistrates' Training in the Unified Courts Administration (2005) J.S.B. 1.0/2005.

[166] p.105.

[167] p.106.

[168] The leading practitioner work, Archbold deals with all aspects of the trial on indictment: Archbold is published annually and updated by supplements throughout the year.

[169] Other methods by which the trial on indictment may arise include preferment of a voluntary bill, see above. See also the Practice Direction (Criminal Proceedings: Consolidation) para.IV.35.

the Crown Court, following a preliminary ruling by the magistrates. When Sch.3 to the CJA 2003 comes into force this will take the reforms a step further by applying s.51 to include offences triable either way.

If proceedings are transferred from a magistrates' court for trial in the Crown Court, those proceedings are begun by the "preferment of a bill of indictment". This procedure simply involves sending the bill of indictment[170] to the appropriate officer of the Crown Court for signature. Once it is signed, the accused may be brought before the court. Then the accused must be asked to plead to the indictment, in a process known arraignment. The bill of indictment must be preferred (delivered) to the appropriate officer in the Crown Court within 28 days of the date on which the case was transferred.[171]

In *Morais*[172] the Court of Appeal quashed the conviction and ordered a retrial where the bill of indictment was not signed, stating that the signature was not a formality but a "necessary condition precedent to the existence of a proper indictment". However, this has been superseded by the potentially far-reaching decision in *Ashton*.[173] In that case the court stated:

> "whenever a court is confronted by failure to take a required step, properly or at all, before a power is exercised (a procedural failure), the court should first ask itself whether the intention of the legislature was that any act done following that procedural failure should be invalid. If the answer to that question is no, then the court should go on to consider the interests of justice generally, and most particularly whether there is a real possibility that either the prosecution or the defence may suffer prejudice on account of the procedural failure. If there is such a risk, the court must decide whether it is just to allow the proceedings to continue. On the other hand, if a court acts without jurisdiction if, for instance, a magistrates' court purports to try a defendant on a charge of homicide then the proceedings will usually be invalid."[174]

Thus, the case has much wider ramifications than solely for bills of indictment. To what extent it represents a sea change of attitude is yet to be discovered but it certainly suggests a more flexible approach to procedural errors which is less likely to result in a successful defence submission for the case to be discharged or stayed as an abuse of process.[175]

The indictment is the formal statement of the charge(s) against the accused and should contain the statement of the offence (a description of the offence), and the particulars of the offence, that is a brief statement of the essential facts that

---

[170] Ultimate responsibility for this lies with counsel for the prosecution: *Blackstone's* (2007), para.D10.4. See also *R v Newland* [1988] Q.B. 402. Once counsel has been instructed he or she becomes responsible for the propriety of the indictment: *R v Moss* [1995] Crim. L.R. 828.

[171] The 28-day limit can be extended by a further 28 days initially, and then further still by a Crown Court judge. From April 2007, r.14.1(2) permits the Crown Court to extend the limit even after it has expired. See also: *R v Urbanowski* (1976) 62 Cr.App.R. 229, CA; *R v Soffe* (1982) 75 Cr.App.R. 133, CA.

[172] *R v Morais* (1988) Cr.App.R. 9.

[173] *R v Ashton* [2006] EWCA Crim 794. See also *R v Clarke* [2006] EWCA Crim 1196.

[174] *ibid.* at para.4.

[175] See also *Malcolm v DPP* [2007] EWHC 363, which suggests that a discernable change is occurring.

constitute the offence.[176] The statement of the offence should be precise, using the recognisable common law name,[177] the statutory name and derivation,[178] or sufficient details of a statutory offence.[179] The particulars must give "reasonable information as to the nature of the charge",[180] so that the accused knows the details of the charge and the prosecution may not shift its ground during the trial. The fair trial guarantees in Art.6 include that the accused must know the charges against him.[181] In addition, Art.7 guarantees that there should be no retrospective criminalisation (which has been interpreted to mean that the offence must be drafted with sufficient precision that the citizen is able to regulate his behaviour). At a minimum, it is essential that the counts of the indictment are drafted with sufficient detail to meet the requirements of the ECHR and to ensure that the accused has sufficient information to prepare his defence and challenge the prosecution case.[182]

It is vital that the counts of an indictment are specific. If, for example, a count alleges different types of conduct it will be important for the jury to be directed so that they must be unanimous as to the type of conduct they find proved.[183]

Three specimen indictments follow: a common law offence, a precise statutory description and a statutory offence for which there is no short description. They are taken from decided cases and reflect particular difficulties of those cases. Simpler cases will produce simpler indictments.

(i) *Shaw v DPP*[184]

Statement of offence: Conspiracy to corrupt public morals **17–017**
Particulars of offence: Frederick Charles Shaw on diverse days between the 1st day of October 1959 and the 23rd day of July 1960 within the jurisdiction of the Central Criminal Court, conspired with certain persons who inserted advertisements in issues of a magazine entitled "Ladies' Directory" numbered 7, 7 revised, 8, 9, 10 and a supplement thereto, and with certain other persons whose names are unknown, by means of the said magazine and the said advertisements

---

[176] See, for example, Sprack (2006) paras 15.01–15.03.
[177] e.g. murder; manslaughter; blasphemy; conspiracy to corrupt public morals.
[178] e.g. theft, contrary to s.1 of the Theft Act 1968; robbery, contrary to s.8(1) of the Theft Act 1968; arson, contrary to s.1(1) and (3) of the Criminal Damage Act 1971. See the Indictment Rules 1971 (SI 1971/1253), r.6.
[179] For example, removing an article from a place open to the public, contrary to s.11(1) of the Theft Act 1968.
[180] The Crown is not obliged to prove every particular: *R v Hancock* [1996] 2 Cr.App.R. 554; Indictment Rules 1971 (SI 1971/1253), r.3(1).
[181] For studies of the impact of the Human Rights Act, see Department for Constitutional Affairs, *Review of the Implementation of the Human Rights Act* (2006); F. Klug and K. Starmer, "Standing Back from the Human Rights Act: how effective is it five years on?" [2005] P.L. 716; Lord Steyn 2000–2005, "Laying the Foundations of Human Rights Law in the Kingdom" [2005] E.H.R.L.R. 349. "Criminal charge" in Art.6 has an autonomous convention meaning, and will be determined by reference to the classification of the offence in domestic law, the nature of the offence and the severity of the penalty: *Engel v Netherlands* (1979–80) 1 E.H.R.R. 647, para.82.
[182] See generally *Pelissier v France* (2000) 30 E.H.R.R. 715; Trechsel (2005) Ch.8. On the desirability of clear and comprehensive indictments see Bowes, "The Form of Indictments" [1995] Crim. L.R. 114.
[183] *R v D* [2001] Crim. L.R. 160 and commentary.
[184] [1962] A.C. 220.

to induce readers thereof to resort to the said advertisers for the purposes of
fornication and of taking part in or witnessing other disgusting and immoral acts
and exhibitions, with intent thereby to debauch and corrupt the morals as well of
youth as of divers other liege subjects of Our Lady the Queen and to raise and
create in their minds inordinate and lustful desires.

(ii) *R v Miller*[185]

17–018   Statement of offence: Arson, contrary to section 1(1) and (3) of Criminal Damage
Act 1971.
  Particulars of offence: James Miller on a date unknown between August 13
and 16, 1980, without lawful excuse, damaged by fire a house known as No. 9,
Grantham Road, Sparkbrook, intending to do damage to such property or reck-
less as to whether such property would be damaged.

(iii) *R v Markus*[186]

17–019   Statement of offence: Conniving at a corporation fraudulently inducing the
investment of money contrary to sections 13(l)(b) and 19 of the Prevention of
Fraud (Investments) Act 1958.
  Particulars of offence: Edward Jules Markus between August 25, 1970, and
January 15, 1971, within the jurisdiction of the Central Criminal Court being a
director of Agricultural Investment Corporation S.A. of the First National Invest-
ment Corporation S.A. and of Agri-International S.A. and of Agri-International
(U.K.) Ltd connived at the fraudulent inducement of Agricultural Investment
Corporation S.A., through its agents First National Investment Corporation S.A.
and Agri-International S.A. and Agri-International (U.K.) Ltd of Dr Hermann
Schlick and Mrs Theodoline Schlick to take part in an arrangement to invest
$1038.32 in Agri-Fund (the said investment being an arrangement with respect
of property other than securities, the purpose or pretended purpose of which was
to enable the said Dr Hermann Schlick and the said Mrs Theodoline Schlick to
participate in the profits alleged to be likely to arise from the holding of Agri-
Fund) by representations that Agricultural Investment Corporation S.A. was
genuinely carrying on an honest business and that moneys invested in Agri-Fund
were immediately redeemable at the option of the investor which representations
both he and the said corporation knew to be misleading false and deceptive.
  These examples satisfy the requirements that an indictment should include
such information as to the time and place of the offence so as to indicate to the
accused the acts which are alleged to constitute the offence,[187] a reasonably clear
description of any property involved,[188] the identity of any "victim" or a

---

[185] [1983] 2 A.C. 161.
[186] The offence in question has since been repealed, but the indictment is a good example of the types
    of offence that lack clear succinct definition.
[187] An allegation as to time may be made in ordinary language, and the dates between which the
    offence may be quite a long way apart, as in Shaw's indictment. It is only in a few cases that either
    time or place is of the essence of the offence (e.g. the victim's age), in which case greater
    particularity is required.
[188] In Miller's indictment, No.9, Grantham Road, Sparkbrook. The name of the owner of the property
    is unnecessary in most cases.

description reasonable so as to be identifiable, any factual circumstances necessary to the offence,[189] and any special mental element required by the offence which is not inherent in the statement of the offence.[190]

Indictments may contain more than one offence provided they are founded on the same facts or for in part of a series of offences of the same or a similar character, but the charges must be separated and are then known as "counts".[191] Whenever the trial involves more than one count of an offence, there are difficulties in guaranteeing that the accused knows precisely what is alleged in each count, and for the jury in being agreed in their verdict on the same facts in each relevant count. In addition, the judge must be clear on which facts are proved against the accused for the purposes of determining sentence. It is important that the prosecutor does not overload the indictment with charges such that it does not fairly and accurately reflect the alleged criminality of the defendant.

Three particular difficulties that arise in the context of the contents of the indictment are: the danger of duplicity, the use of specimen counts and the joinder of indictments.

The rule against duplicity is easy to state, but can cause problems in practice. In short, the rule is designed to guarantee that "no one count of the indictment should charge the defendant with having committed two or more separate offences".[192] This is particularly difficult in cases where the accused's conduct continues over a long period of time.

The use of specimen counts can also be difficult in practice. A specimen count is laid against a defendant as a typical example of the conduct alleged. In such cases it is imperative that the count is drafted with great care to ensure that the accused knows the extent of the accusation against him.[193]

The rules on joinder (i.e. when different offences with different counts can be joined together for the one trial) are governed by the Indictment Rules 1971[194] which provide that charges may be joined together if founded on the same facts, they are part of a series of offences or are of similar character.[195] The indictment

---

[189] For example, in an indictment for theft, the particulars must state that the property in question belonged to another, but does not have to state who that other was.

[190] For example, the particulars on an indictment for an offence under s.18 of the Offences Against the Person Act 1861 should allege an intent to do grievous bodily harm to the victim or to resist or prevent lawful apprehension, as appropriate. The particulars of an indictment for arson under s.l(1) and (3) of the Criminal Damage Act 1971 must allege either an intent to destroy or damage another's property, or recklessness as to whether such property would be destroyed or damaged. On the specific necessity to spell out the *mens rea* of the charge in the indictment, see *R v Ike* [1996] Crim. L.R. 515.

[191] On the purpose of the provision of particulars see *R v Hancock* [1996] 2 Cr.App.R. 554. The court must avoid the possibility that the particulars lack sufficient specificity to inhibit the defendant preparing the case.

[192] Indictment Rules 1971, r.4(2).

[193] *R v Rackham* [1997] 2 Cr.App.R. 222. Where D pleads not guilty the jury try the sample counts but it is possible for the judge sitting alone to try the remaining counts: see, Domestic Violence, Crimes and Victims Act 2004, s.17.

[194] r.9. See *R v Christou* [1997] A.C. 117, [1996] Crim. L.R. 911, in which the House of Lords confirmed the discretion of the judge to order counts to be tried together. See also *R v Lockley and Sainsbury* [1997] Crim. L.R. 455, recognising that technical points should not prevail to nullify the whole indictment where there was a misjoinder, provided there was no possible prejudice to the accused.

[195] The trial judge has the power to sever them in the interests of justice. See r.5(3) and *R v Christou* [1997] A.C. 117. For evidence that jurors are confused by joinder, see Darbyshire, Maughan and Stewart, "What Can We Learn from Published Jury Research? Findings for the Criminal Courts Review" [2001] Crim. L.R. 970 at p.973.

may join two or more accused (rather than joining counts) either if they are both named in the same count in the indictment or in separate counts which would legitimately lie on one indictment.[196] Joining offenders and offences is a pragmatic issue which involves balancing the additional burden on the parties and the trier of fact and the broader issues of the interests of justice.

Indictments may be amended provided that no risk of injustice results, and this includes the possibility of new counts being added to the indictment,[197] but indictments should not be overloaded with counts that render the trial unduly complex and place an unfair burden on the accused and/or the jury.

1. Hearing in Open Court

17–020   It is regarded as essential to the administration of justice that hearings take place in open court. A public hearing protects litigants against the administration of justice occurring in secret without adequate scrutiny,[198] and reflects the importance of the interest society has in, literally, seeing that justice is fairly administered. It is endorsed by the guarantees in Art.6 and by the Strasbourg Court's jurisprudence.[199] Public trials and media reporting are essential to the administration of justice.[200] Nevertheless, there are some occasions on which either or both may be restricted, and allowance for this is made in Art.6 (of the ECHR):

> "the press and public may be excluded from all or part of the trial in the interests of morals, public order, or national security in a democratic society, where the interests of juveniles or the protection of the private life of the parties so require, or to the extent strictly necessary in the opinion of the court in special circumstances where publicity would prejudice the interests of justice."[201]

Concern about the number of cases taking place out of the eye of the public became so great that a right of appeal against orders restricting or preventing reports of or restricting access to trials on indictment was introduced by s.159 of the Criminal Justice Act 1988.[202] A distinction has been recognised between the

---

[196] *R v Assim* [1996] 2 Q.B. 249.

[197] See J. C. Smith, "Adding Counts to the Indictment" [1996] Crim. L.R. 889, criticising the decision in *R v Osieh* [1996] 2 Cr.App.R. 144 that it was permissible for a judge to add a count to the indictment which was not founded on the facts found by the examining magistrates. On the rules governing the amendment of the indictment see *Blackstone's* (2007) para.D10.63–10.70. It is important that amendments to the indictment are fair to the accused by not significantly changing the nature of the prosecution case against the defendant: *R v O'Connor* [1997] Crim. L.R. 516.

[198] See *Pretto v Italy* (1984) 6 E.H.R.R. 182, para.21; *Riepan v Austria*. [2001] Crim. L.R. 231.

[199] See *Werner v Austria; Szuces v Austria* (1998) 26 E.H.R.R. 310. See generally, Treschel (2005) Ch.5. The English courts have long-accepted that criminal proceedings should occur in the presence of the accused: *R v Agar* (1990) 90 Cr.App.R. 318; *R v Preston* [1994] 2 A.C. 130.

[200] See *Attorney-General v Leveller Magazine* [1979] A.C. 440; Art. 6(1) of the European Convention on Human Rights (emphasising the need for a "fair and public hearing" and that judgment is to "be pronounced publicly"); *Blackstone's* (2007) para.D2.93.

[201] See also Art.10 and I. Cram, "Automatic Reporting Restrictions in Criminal Proceedings and Article 10 of the ECHR" [1998] E.H.R.L.R. 742.

[202] An "aggrieved" person may appeal and this has been held to include both media representatives and the accused: *Re A* [2006] 1 W.L.R. 1361. Much of the credit for the creation of s.159 is due to Tim Crook and the National Union of Journalists, see, e.g. *R v Central Criminal Court, Ex p. Crook, The Times*, November 8, 1984.

general public and the media having unlimited access to trials. For example, it is necessary for the media to be present at an obscenity trial to report on the nature of the allegedly obscene material, but there is no such necessity for the public to be present.

Both the Crown Court and the magistrates' Courts[203] can sit *in camera* where (a) there is the possibility of disorder, (b) a witness would refuse to testify publicly, (c) the effect of a public hearing on possible future prosecutions would be too damaging.[204] In addition, there are statutory powers under the Official Secrets Act 1920[205] and the Children and Young Persons Act 1933[206] relating to the removal of the public from the courtroom. As regards media reporting, the media has a general freedom to report, subject primarily to liability for contempt of court.[207] Section 4 of the Contempt of Court Act 1981 allows for postponing reporting where that is necessary to avoid "a substantial risk of prejudice to the administration of justice". This does not extend to protecting the welfare of the accused.[208]

Saturation media coverage and interest in serious crimes has created significant difficulty in exceptionally high profile cases such as the killing of Jill Dando, the retrial of Michael Stone for the murder of members of the Russell family,[209] and the Soham murders. In such cases it is difficult to ensure that the prior press coverage has not rendered a fair trial impossible.

2. THE ORDER OF PROCEEDINGS

We shall consider the proceedings at trial in some detail in this chapter and see them from the point of view of the various parties to the trial: the accused, counsel, witnesses, the judge and the jury. At the outset it is useful to set out the chronology of the trial from the first appearance of the accused until he or she leaves the court.

17–021

---

[203] Even though s.121(4) of the Magistrates' Courts Act 1980 obliges magistrates' courts to sit in open court; see *Blackstone's* (2007), paras D2.49; D2.106. On privacy and the administration of justice more widely, see M. Tugendhat and I. Christie, *The Law of Privacy and the Media* (2002) Ch.12.

[204] Sprack (2006) para.20.90.

[205] Official Secrets Act 1920 s.8.

[206] Children and Young Persons Act 1933 s.36–39.

[207] See *Blackstone's* (2007), para.14.59. C.J. Miller, *Contempt of Court* (3rd edn, 2000); H. Fenwick and G. Phillipson, *Media Freedom Under the Human Rights Act* (2006) Ch.6. Reporting is also limited by the need to comply with general rules relating to contempt of court to protect the trial from being prejudged or prejudiced and also by other statutory rules, such as s.11 of the Contempt of Court Act 1981 on withholding of names and various provisions to protect the identity of children and victims of sexual offences.

[208] *R v Newton Abbey JJ., Ex p. Belfast Telegraph Newspapers Ltd, The Times*, August 27, 1197; *R v Sherwood, Ex p. The Telegraph* (2001) unreported, May 3, 2001.

[209] See, e.g. *R v Taylor* (1994) 98 Cr.App.R. 361; *R v Stone* [2001] Crim. L.R. 465 and commentary; *R v Croydon Magistrates' Court, ex p. Simmons*, unreported January 26, 1996. On publicity and its effects on the jury see N. Steblay, J. Beservic, S. Fulero, B. Jiminez-Lorente, "The Effects of Pre-Trial Publicity on Jurors Verdicts: A Meta Analytical Review" (1999) 23 Law and Human Behaviour 219. The Court of Appeal in *R v Andrews (Tracy)* [1999] Crim. L.R. 156, sanctioned the use of questionnaires to ascertain the jury's knowledge in exceptional circumstances. See generally, D. Corker and M. Levi, "Pre-Trial Publicity and its Treatment in English Courts" [1996] Crim. L.R. 622.

(a) The arraignment[210]

17–022 The accused is brought to the bar of the court and the indictment is read out and a plea in respect of each count is sought separately. Requirements of a fair trial include an expectation that the accused will be present throughout the hearing unless there has been a clear and unequivocal waiver.[211] The plea may be to the "general issue", that is a plea of "guilty" or "not guilty". If a defendant fails to plead to an indictment, the court must decide whether this is due to mental or physical incapacity or whether wilful silence. The arraignment of an individual must occur within a reasonable time of his being committed. This is not a right recognised formally by the ECHR, but has been supported by much of the Strasbourg Court's jurisprudence on trial within a reasonable time.

The arraignment is the point of the trial where issues such as double jeopardy, the jurisdiction of the court to try the accused and errors in the indictment may be raised.

(i) Double jeopardy

17–023 A basic principle is that no person should be tried twice for the same offence. Consequently "the unwarranted harassment of the accused by multiple prosecutions" is avoided.[212] There are two major exceptions to this principle, namely, where a retrial is available following a "tainted acquittal" and the more recent reform to permit appeals in serious cases where new evidence has emerged. These will be considered below.

The basic principle is established in English law by the availability of the special pleas in bar: the pleas of *autrefois acquit*; of *autrefois convict*; and of pardon.[213] These pleas are rarely used in practice, because the accuracy of court records ensures that people are rarely prosecuted for the same offence twice. The philosophy underlying the double jeopardy protection is encapsulated in this succinct statement:

> "the State with all its resources and power should not be allowed to make repeated attempts to convict an individual for an alleged offence thereby subjecting him to embarrassment, expense and ordeal, and compelling him to live in a continuing state of anxiety and insecurity."[214]

The significance of double jeopardy is also recognised in the ECHR, where Art.4 of Protocol 7 provides that "no one shall be liable to be tried or punished

---

[210] See *Archbold* (2007) para.4–97; *Blackstone's* (2007), section D11.

[211] See *R v Hayward; R v Jones; R v Purvis* [2003] 1 A.C. 1, where the House of Lords catalogued the relevant principles to be applied in deciding whether to try the accused in his absence. The judicial discretion to try the defendant in his absence must be exercised with great care, and fairness to the defendant was of prime importance. See also *R v Smith* [2006] EWCA Crim 2307; *R v O'Hare* [2006] EWCA Crim 471, [2006] Crim. L.R. 950.

[212] See M. L. Friedland, *Double Jeopardy* (1969), pp.3–4.

[213] The possibility of similar questions arising through issue estoppel must be recognised, although such an argument is probably inapplicable to the criminal law: *DPP v Humphrys* [1977] A.C. 1, except in habeas corpus applications: *R v Governor of Brixton Prison, Ex p. Osman* [1991] 1 W.L.R. 281. The more likely method of raising these questions is through the inherent power of the judges to prevent oppression of an accused where there is an abuse of process. Abuse of process is a claim being considered by the courts much more frequently in recent years.

[214] Stevens J. In the US Supreme Court in *Hudson v US* (1997) 118 S.Ct. 488 at 499.

again in criminal proceedings under the jurisdiction of the same State for an offence for which he has already been finally acquitted or convicted in accordance with the law and the penal procedure of that State".[215] A derogation exists for a fundamental defect in the first trial or for new evidence coming to light.[216] As Emmerson and Ashworth observe, the root of the problem in double jeopardy is the difficulty in attaching precise weight to the "valves of accuracy and finality in the criminal justice system".[217]

The question of whether a defendant is facing a double jeopardy trial can be complex, but ultimately the question is whether the accused is "in jeopardy" of conviction for the "same offence" on more than one occasion. The concept of the "same offence" has been construed narrowly by the Court of Appeal.[218]

As stated above, Parliament has already made inroads into the protection against double jeopardy. The first exception appears in the Criminal Procedure and Investigations Act 1996[219] which allows for a second prosecution of an acquitted person where the accused has been convicted of an offence of witness or juror intimidation, and the court convicting the accused of that intimidation offence specifies that in its opinion there is a "real possibility" that but for such intimidation there would not have been an acquittal on the principal trial. The second prosecution for the main offence can only take place when the High Court grants an order quashing the first acquittal if satisfied that it is likely that but for the interference or intimidation the accused would not have been acquitted, that it does not appear to be contrary to the interests of justice to take proceedings again, that the accused has had an opportunity to make representations to the High Court, and that the conviction for intimidation will still stand.

The second exception applies to new evidence retrials as was introduced under the CJA 2003.[220] Schedule 3 includes a list of qualifying offences, all of which are serious. Under s.76 a prosecutor can, with the written consent of the DPP, apply to the Court of Appeal for an order to quash an acquittal for a qualifying offence. The DPP must be satisfied that the evidence is new[221]; that it is in the public interest to proceed; and that the trial does not run counter to the UK's obligations under the Treaty of the European Union and its equivalent double jeopardy rule.[222] The Court of Appeal will order the retrial if the evidence is new

---

[215] See e.g. *Sailer v Austria* [2002] ECHR 382 37/97. See also Art.14 of the International Covenant on Civil and Political Rights.

[216] See *Gradinger v Austria*, October 23, 1995, A 328-C; *Oliveira v Switzerland* (1998-V), p.1990.

[217] B. Emerson and A. Ashworth (2001), p.313.

[218] *R v Beedie* [1998] Q.B. 356. The Court of Appeal declined to interpret Lord Morris's statements in *Connelly*, which had been regarded as expressing the views of the majority, as requiring a broad approach to the problem. B charged with manslaughter having been already been convicted in an earlier prosecution for a specific statutory offence brought by the Health and Safety Executive in relation to the same facts—the death of the tenant from the faulty gas fire in B's premises.

[219] ss.54–57. For consideration of their compatibility with Protocol 7 see Emmerson and Ashworth (2001), p.309.

[220] See, Law Commission Consultation Paper No.156, *Double Jeopardy* (1999) Law Commission Report No.267, *Double Jeopardy and Prosecution Appeals* (2001); I. Dennis, "Rethinking Double Jeopardy: Justice and Finality in Criminal Process" [2000] Crim. L.R. 933; B. Fitzpatrick, "One Idea and Two Myths From The Criminal Justice Bill 2002" (2003) J. Crim. L. 149; P. Roberts, "Double Jeopardy Law Reform: a Criminal Justice Commentary" (2002) 65 M.L.R. 393;

[221] CJA 2003, s.78.

[222] CJA 2003, s.76(4).

and compelling and that the retrial would be in the interests of justice. This includes a consideration of issues such as any prejudicial publicity about the accused and the length of time since the offence took place.[223]

There are concerns that the relaxation of the double jeopardy rule might result in prosecutions being pursued less meticulously than might previously have been the case, the prosecution bodies being subconsciously influenced by the potential availability of a second bite of the cherry should the case fail. However, the legislation seeks to ensure that the availability of the retrial is tightly controlled and in 2006 the conviction of William Dunlop illustrated the utility of the reform.[224] In 1991 Dunlop was acquitted of the murder of Julie Hogg. Despite a subsequent confession that he had indeed committed murder, Dunlop could only be charged with perjury in relation to the original trial, but could not face the murder charge again. This clear miscarriage of justice proved to be a major catalyst prompting the relaxation of the double jeopardy rule.[225]

It is important to note that the discussion in this part of the chapter has considered the position of the accused relying on his earlier acquittal to bar any future prosecution. There is, in addition, the separate issue of the prosecution use of previous *acquittals* in the criminal trial. In *R v Z*,[226] the House of Lords ruled that evidence of previous acquittals is admissible on behalf of the prosecution where the accused later faces charges for other conduct.[227]

(ii) *Autrefois acquit and autrefois convict*[228]

17–024   The appropriate plea, depending upon whether the accused has already been acquitted (*autrefois acquit*) or convicted (*autrefois convict*) of the same offence, or substantially the same offence, is normally made in writing before the beginning of the trial, although it may be made at any stage. There must be a valid conviction; other findings bringing proceedings to an end do not qualify. After such a plea, it is for the judge without a jury to decide whether the plea is successful.[229] The burden of proof is on the accused to establish this on the balance of probabilities.[230]

The circumstances in which either plea will be available were explored in *Connelly v DPP*.[231] The House of Lords, mainly through the speech of Lord Morris, indicated that the pleas are not limited to circumstances where an accused has been charged with exactly the same offence arising out of the same set of circumstances. A person previously acquitted or convicted of an offence cannot be tried again for that same offence or a substantially similar offence or

[223] CJA 2003, s.79.

[224] *R v Dunlop* [2007] 1 W.L.R. 1657; see also [2007] Crim. L.R. 390.

[225] J. Scott, "Double Jeopardy: Two Stabs at Justice" (2006) L.S.G. 103. A further significant trigger for the reappraisal of the rule was the Inquiry into the Murder of Stephen Lawrence: *The Stephen Lawrence Inquiry: Report of an Inquiry by Sir William Macpherson of Cluny*, Cm. 426–I (1999).

[226] [2000] 3 W.L.R. 117, HL. On *R v Z* see P. Roberts, "Acquitted Misconduct Evidence" [2000] Crim. L.R. 952.

[227] cf. *Sambasivam v Public Prosecutor of Malaysia* [1950] A.C. 458.

[228] *Archbold* (2007) para.4–16; *Blackstone's* (2007) paras D11.52–11.70.

[229] Criminal Justice Act 1988, s.122.

[230] *R v Cologhan* (1976) 63 Cr.App.R. 33.

[231] [1964] A.C. 1254.

an offence that was a proper alternative.[232] A proper alternative offence is one of which the accused could have been found guilty at the earlier trial instead of that named in the indictment. So, for example, if Fred is acquitted of murdering Ann, he cannot later be charged with her murder (subject to the new evidence retrial discussed above), nor can he be charged with her manslaughter or causing her death by reckless driving or causing her grievous bodily harm with intent. The decision of the Court of Appeal in *Beedie* has construed *Connolly* narrowly.[233] Further, if the accused has previously been acquitted of an offence that, as a matter of fact, is essential to establish guilt of the offence charged, he or she cannot be tried for that lesser offence later.[234] This can give rise to difficulties in interpreting clusters of related offences.[235]

However, the plea of *autrefois convict* does not operate to prevent a person being tried on a charge which is more serious than the one of which he or she has originally been convicted. So, for example, if Dorothy attacks and seriously injures Michael she may be convicted of causing grievous bodily harm with intent. If Michael dies after the trial from the injuries, Dorothy may be tried for murder.[236] Note also that there is no strict rule that the Crown should not seek a third trial if the jury fails to agree on two previous occasions.[237]

(iii) *Jurisdiction*

The plea is that the court has no jurisdiction to try the accused for the relevant offence. The plea is concerned with the territorial jurisdiction of the court. The Crown Court can, as a general rule, only try crimes committed in England and Wales. **17–025**

(iv) *Errors in the indictment*

There are many technical rules about the drafting of indictments, primarily concerned with the requirements that indictments must be (a) positive and (b) not duplicitous. The rules are discussed in the works on criminal procedure.[238] Such errors as perceived by the accused may be raised for consideration through a number of avenues, but primarily by applying to the judge to quash the indictment, whereby no further proceedings would take place on the indictment, or through an abuse of process claim. These are not technically pleas as such. It is also possible at this stage to challenge a criminal charge by asserting that the legislation under which the offence is charged is *ultra vires*. This need not be entered as a formal plea.[239] **17–026**

---

[232] The power to enter an alternative verdict is provided by the Criminal Law Act 1967, s.6, which has been widely interpreted by the House of Lords in *R v Wilson; R v Jenkins* [1984] A.C. 242.

[233] In *R v Beedie* [1998] Q.B. 356, Rose L.J. quoted Lord Devlin in *Connolly* "for the doctrine to apply it must be the same offence both in fact and law".

[234] Consequently, an earlier acquittal of theft precludes a trial for robbery on the same facts, because theft is an essential element in proving robbery, see Theft Act 1968, ss.1 and 8.

[235] See, e.g. *R v G* [2001] Crim. L.R. 898 relating to assault and s.47 of the Offences Against the Person Act 1861.

[236] See the Law Reform (Year and A Day Rule) Act 1996.

[237] *R v Henworth* [2001] Crim. L.R. 505.

[238] *Archbold* (2007), para.1–236; *Blackstone's* (2007), D10.

[239] See *Boddington v British Transport Police* [1998] 2 All E.R. 210.

(v) *Abuse of process*

17–027   Although not technically a plea in bar, it is worth considering at this stage the
motion to stay proceedings for an abuse of process[240] which has the same effect
if pleaded successfully. This is an area in which the law has developed rapidly in
recent years. The court has an inherent jurisdiction to prevent its own process
being abused.[241] The trial judge in a criminal case does not have the responsibility for instituting a prosecution, nor to prevent one being brought which is in his
opinion undesirable, but he has the power to stay proceedings if they constitute
an abuse of process. The accused who seeks a stay must prove, on the balance of
probabilities, that it is either impossible for him to receive a fair trial, or that it
would be unfair to try him. The usual basis of the claim is that the prosecution
has manipulated the process or misused the powers of the court,[242] reneged on a
promise to the accused's detriment,[243] lost or destroyed evidence,[244] contributed
to the commission of the offence,[245] or there has been excessive delay.[246] The
power to stay for abuse is a broad power, but it is vital that the courts have that
power to maintain the integrity of the criminal justice process, and ensure that the
executive action is conducted within the rule of law. The discretion is to be
exercised sparingly because there is a very strong public interest in people who
are alleged to have committed crimes facing trial.[247]

(b) The empanelling and swearing of the jury

17–028   If a plea of not guilty is entered, a jury of 12 people will be empanelled and, after
an opportunity for challenges, sworn. The indictment will be read to the jury that
will be told of its obligation to listen to the evidence and to determine guilt or
innocence. The precise order in which speeches are delivered will depend on
whether the accused is represented and whether he chooses to testify.

---

[240] See D. Corker and D. Young, *Abuse of Process and Fairness in Criminal Proceedings* (2002);
Choo, *Abuse of Process and Judicial Stay of Proceedings* (1993).

[241] See *Connelly v DPP* [1964] A.C. 254; *DPP v Humphreys* [1977] A.C. 1; *R v Horseferry Road
Magistrates' Court, Ex p. Bennett* [1994] 1 A.C. 42; *R v Derby Crown Court, Ex p. B* [1996] A.C.
487; *R v Mullen* [1999] 2 Cr.App.R. 143.

[242] See, e.g. *R v Dean* [1998] 2 Cr.App.R. 177; *R. (Wardle) v Leeds Crown Court* [2002] 1 A.C.
754.

[243] On prosecutors reneging on promises not to prosecute see also *R v Townsend, Dearsley and
Bretscher* [1998] Crim. L.R. 126; *R v Thomas* [1995] Crim. L.R. 938; *R v Bloomfield* [1997] 1
Cr.App.R. 135; *R v Drury* [2001] Crim. L.R. 847; *Jones v Whalley* [2006] U.K.H.L. 41; *cf. R v
Mulla* [2004] 1 Cr.App.R. 6.

[244] *R (Ebrahim) v Feltham Magistrates' Court* [2001] 2 Cr.App.R. 23; see also, S. Martin, "Lost and
Destroyed Evidence: The search for a principled approach to abuse of process" (2005) I.J.E.P.
158.

[245] It is for the trial judge, in the exercise of his discretion, to decide whether there had been an abuse
of process which amounted to an affront to the public conscience and thereby required proceedings to be stayed: *Latif and Shahzad*, [1996] Crim. L.R. 414, HL. See also *R v Mullen (No.2)*
[1999] 3 W.L.R. 777; *R v Hardwicke and Thwaites* [2001] Crim. L.R. 220.

[246] There have been prosecutions after a delay of 33 years (*R v King* [1997] Crim. L.R. 298) and 56
years (*R v Sawoniuk* [2000] Crim. L.R. 456). On delay and the implications of Art.6 see *Attorney
General's Reference (No.2 of 2001)* [2004] 2 A.C. 72; *R v S* [2006] EWCA Crim 756.

[247] *R v B* [1996] Crim. L.R. 406. (19-year delay). On the need for the trial judge to warn the jury
about difficulties in cases of delay see *R v J* [1997] Crim. L.R. 297 and *R v Jenkins* [1998] Crim.
L.R. 411 (30 years). Applications based on delay should still be exceptional: *R v Smolinski* [2004]
2 Cr.App.R. 40.

(c) The opening speech[248]

Counsel for the prosecution addresses the jury. The function of the opening is to **17–029** explain to the jury the basic elements of the prosecution case, the evidence that is to be called and the burden and standard of proof. Even allowing for the fact that any mistakes may ultimately be corrected by the judge in the summing-up, it is vital that prosecution counsel does not claim more than can be proved for it may eventually be difficult for the jury to remember whether allegations made in the speech were actually substantiated by the evidence.[249] Equally counsel must not refer to any evidence that is inadmissible,[250] or which defending counsel has indicated will be challenged as inadmissible. Counsel should avoid using emotive language that is likely to prejudice the jury against the accused.

(d) The prosecution case

Witnesses called by the prosecution give their evidence in turn (examination- **17–030** in-chief) and may be subjected to questioning by the defence (cross-examination). Counsel for the prosecution may have the final word with each witness (re-examination) but must ask questions only on matters raised in the course of cross-examination. The way in which and the sort of questions counsel asks and whether evidence is admissible are both decided upon by the judge alone.

(e) Defence submission of no case to answer

At the close of the prosecution case the defence may ask the trial judge to direct **17–031** the jury to acquit the accused because there is no case to answer.[251] The power is used sparingly, but a failure properly to halt a case on a submission can constitute an abuse of process.[252] If this submission is accepted, the trial ends and the accused is acquitted. This submission and the judge's deliberation on the matter occur in the absence of the jury. If the submission fails the trial continues, and no reference to the submission should be made in the presence of the jury. If at the conclusion of the evidence, the trial judge is of the opinion that no reasonable jury properly directed could safely convict, he should raise the matter with counsel, even if no submission of no case to answer had been made.[253] It is possible to halt the trial on the same basis at any point after the submission.

---

[248] See *Blackstone's* (2007), paras D14.1–14.6.

[249] A particular example of the dangers is to be found in the trial of James Hanratty, where a vital piece of evidence was referred to in the opening speech but never proved in evidence; see L. Blom-Cooper, *The A6 Murder*. In any event, it may be tactically more sensible to pitch the opening on a relatively low key lest the jury should later be disappointed with the prosecution witnesses.

[250] The opening of such evidence will not automatically lead to the quashing of a subsequent conviction: *R v Jackson* [1953] 1 W.L.R. 591. The normal course would be for the judge to discharge the jury and recommence the trial if the defendant has been seriously prejudiced.

[251] See *R v Galbraith* (1980) 73 Cr.App.R. 124; *R v Shippey* [1988] Crim. L.R. 767; *Archbold* (2007), para.4–292.

[252] *R v Smith* [2000] 1 All E.R. 263.

[253] This was more desirable than the practice of judges writing to the Court of Appeal expressing concern at the verdict of a jury: *R v Brown (Jamie)* [1998] Crim. L.R. 196. See also, *R v Brown* [2002] 1 Cr.App.R. 46.

(f) Defence opening speech

17–032 Defence counsel is only entitled to make an opening speech to the jury if at least one witness (other than the accused) is to be called as to the *facts* of the case. Otherwise, counsel must simply start to call evidence.[254]

(g) The defence case

17–033 Witnesses called by the defence are examined. If the accused is called as a witness he or she should be the first defence witness so that he gives his testimony before hearing that of all the other witnesses.[255] They may be cross-examined by prosecution counsel and re-examined by defence counsel. The defence may again raise a submission of no case to answer.[256]

(h) Re-opening

17–034 In an exceptional case the prosecution will be allowed to re-open the case to rebut matters that have arisen. This should arise only where the evidence could not have been foreseen as likely to arise, or where evidence unexpectedly becomes available to the prosecution after the close of its case or the evidence is of a formal nature and has been inadvertently omitted from the prosecution case. Similarly, the defence may in an exceptional case be allowed to re-open its case if new material comes to light. It is worth noting at this point that, theoretically at least, the judge has the power to call a witness of his own accord. This is an exceedingly rarely exercised power. A witness so called may be cross-examined by both parties with leave of the judge.[257] There are cogent proposals for this power to be exercised more frequently, provided it is commensurate with the judge remaining impartial and being seen to be such.

(i) Closing speeches

17–035 Both counsel may address the jury at the close of the evidence. The prosecution goes first and the defence has the last word.[258] In the closing speech prosecution counsel may review the evidence and emphasise alleged strengths in the prosecution case and weaknesses in the defence.[259] The length of the speeches is a matter for judicial discretion.[260] Neither counsel should refer to matters that have not been adduced in evidence. The jury is likely to be reminded once again of the burden and standard of proof.

(j) Prosecution Appeals

17–036 Until the summing up the prosecution has a right of appeal against points of law determined by the trial judge.

---

[254] See the Criminal Evidence Act 1898, s.2.
[255] See PACE, s.79.
[256] *R v Anderson, The Independent*, July 3, 1998.
[257] *R v Roberts* (1984) 80 Cr.App.R. 89.
[258] On the content appropriate of the defence closing see *R v Tuegel* [2000] 2 Cr.App.R. 361.
[259] For an example of an improper closing speech leading to a successful appeal see; *Ramdhanie v The State* [2005] U.K.P.C. 47.
[260] *R v Haggard* [1995] Crim. L.R. 347.

Prosecution appeal rights were traditionally very restricted, and this was based on a number of reasons, including, that it was more important for the scarce resources available in the appeals system to be centred upon rectifying mistakes in terms of wrongful conviction rather than wrongful acquittal. However, it must be recognised that if the purpose of an appeal is about maximising accuracy then there are persuasive arguments for allowing appeals irrespective of which party is involved. Equally, whilst finality is seen as an important feature of an appeals system so to is accuracy. Ashworth and Redmayne also comment that the "structure of the appeals process reveals a marked asymmetry between prosecution and defence appeal rights".[261] In light of the Government's strategic objective to rebalance the criminal justice system, then the issue of prosecution appeal rights was ripe for change.

Part 9 of the CJA 2003,[262] influenced by a number of reports,[263] extended the appeal rights of prosecutors to challenge points of law made by trial court judges in the Crown Court at any time up until the summing up.[264] The rights of appeal introduced under the Act apply only to trials on indictment[265] and allow for an appeal to the Criminal Division of the Court of Appeal.[266] The prosecution require the leave of the judge or the Court of Appeal. Two rights of appeal are introduced. Section 58 allows for appeals to be made against terminating rulings, whilst s.62 allows for appeals against evidentiary rulings.

Initially part of the Bill, the expression "terminating" was dropped during the Third Reading. It remains in common currency given that the rulings to which the expression has been applied are in fact terminating, or have the effect of bringing proceedings for the offence charged to an end.[267] As a condition of its appeal, s.58(8) states that if the prosecution informs the court of their intention to appeal then they must also inform the court of their agreement that if leave to appeal is refused or if the prosecution abandons the appeal the defendant is acquitted. This is a heavy price for the prosecution to pay and thus will only be exercised by the prosecution where, in absence of the right of appeal, they would offer no evidence.

Inevitably, interlocutory appeals cause delay and disruption to the main proceedings. Thus, the appeal may be expedited or non-expedited as determined by the judge after hearing representations from the parties.[268]

The Court of Appeal can confirm, reverse or vary the ruling.[269] Where the Court confirms the ruling then the defendant is acquitted. Where the ruling is varied or reversed the proceedings must be resumed or a fresh trial ordered if it

---

[261] Ashworth and Redmayne (2005), p.360.

[262] For an overview of the reforms see I. Dennis, "Prosecution Appeals and Retrial for Serious Offences" [2004] Crim. L.R. 619.

[263] The Report of the Royal Commission on Criminal Justice (1993) Ch.10; Law Commission Consultation Paper No.158 *Prosecution Appeals Against Judges' Rulings* (2000); Law Commission Report No.267, *Double Jeopardy and Prosecution Appeals* (2002) Pt VII; *The Criminal Courts Review* (2001) Ch. 12; *Justice for All* (2002) Cm. 5563.

[264] CJA 2003, s.58(13).

[265] CJA 2003, s.57(1).

[266] CJA 2003, s.57(3).

[267] These include, for example, a stay of proceedings; successful plea of *autrefois acquit* or *autrefois convict*; a ruling on unfitness to plead; a ruling of no case to answer. It does not apply to the Attorney-General's grant of a *nolle prosequi*; unsolicited jury verdicts; rulings made during the summing up; a ruling to discharge the jury; quashing a count on the indictment: *R v Thompson* [2006] EWCA Crim 2849.

[268] CPR 2005 (SI 2005/384) r.66.4(1).

[269] CJA 2003, s.61(1).

is necessary in the interests of justice, or the defendant is acquitted for the offences under appeal.

As a late introduction to the Act, s.62 provides for a right of appeal against evidentiary rulings that significantly weaken the prosecution case. This appeal route has not as yet been brought into operation. It is a separate process from that described above and an evidentiary ruling that has the effect of terminating the case can also be the subject of a s.58 termination ruling. An appeal against an evidentiary ruling can only be made in relation to a qualifying offence[270] and before the defence case opens.[271] The ruling must relate to prosecution, not defence evidence. Leave to appeal is required but unlike with termination rulings, the prosecution do not have to concede that the defendant must be acquitted if the appeal is lost or abandoned.

The evidentiary ruling must "seriously weaken the prosecution case"[272] and this question is to be determined by the court (though of course the weakening need not to be so as to require the prosecution to be abandoned as that would be covered by s.58). This means that a number of evidentiary rulings can be the subject of appeal if their combined effect is to significantly weaken the case. The types of ruling to which this appeal route are likely to apply include the exclusion of evidence under PACE s.78 and s.76.

Expedited and non-expedited appeal routes exist and the proceedings may continue in respect of any offence which is not the subject of appeal. The Court of Appeal can confirm, vary or reverse the decision. If the ruling is confirmed there is no obligation on the Court to acquit the defendant.

Whilst the new prosecution appeals process has been broadly welcomed there are some concerns as to how it might affect the workload of the already overburdened Court of Appeal.

(k) The summing-up

17–037   The trial judge must sum up the evidence to the jury, directing it as to the law and explaining its function. It is usual for the judge to discuss with counsel, in the absence of the jury, the proposed content of his summing-up before delivering it. The value of this exercise has become crucial in relation to a number of offences. In all cases it has the potential to clarify the issues which should therefore render the summing-up more helpful for the jury, and it should serve to prevent unmeritorious appeals on the minutae of the summing-up.

The summing-up must contain a direction on the burden and standard of proof, a review of the facts and should provide adequate guidance on the elements of the offence. The judge will adopt standard "specimen directions" issued by the Judicial Studies Board.[273]

(l) The verdict

17–038   The jury retires to consider its verdict. The jury remain together in the custody of the bailiff in the court precincts. The jury is incommunicado except for essential communications from the jury bailiff. Only very exceptionally is evidence admitted after the retirement of the jury. A unanimous verdict is the first

---

[270] The appeal can only be made against an evidentiary ruling in a qualifying offence: see Sch.4.
[271] CJA 2003, s.62(8).
[272] CJA 2003, s.63(2).
[273] See *www.jsboard.org.uk*.

objective, but a majority verdict may eventually be acceptable. The verdict of the jury is announced by the person known as the "foreman" in open court.

(m) Information for sentencing

Since not all the necessary information is provided during the trial to enable an **17–039** appropriate sentence to be imposed, after conviction an information gathering exercise is often undertaken, which includes the possibility of a plea in mitigation being made by either defence counsel or the accused in person.

(n) Sentence

The judge passes sentence on the accused.   **17–040**

(o) Appeal

The defendant can appeal against conviction and/or sentence with the leave of the **17–041** judge or of the Court of Appeal. The prosecution can, in exceptional cases, appeal against what it considers to be an unduly lenient sentence. The procedures for appeals are considered below in Ch.18. The defendant may further pursue an unsuccessful appeal via the Criminal Cases Review Commission. Appeals from either party from decisions of the Court of Appeal or the Divisional Court lie to the House of Lords subject to leave and strict compliance with procedures.

3. The Accused

Historically, the accused laboured under a considerable disadvantage in the **17–042** criminal trial. The Criminal Law Revision Committee (CLRC), considering the rules of evidence in criminal cases, identified the following difficulties that had hindered the accused[274]: the "indecent haste" with which trials were conducted[275]; the severe restrictions upon legal representation; the accused was not permitted to give evidence on oath in all cases; there was only rarely a right to appeal against conviction.

  Since all these obstacles to a fair trial have been removed, and, according to the CLRC, because of the improved quality of juries and magistrates, it has been suggested that the accused is in a very strong position in the criminal trial.[276] This view has not been accepted by all commentators. McBarnet,[277] on completion of a critical examination of the criminal justice system, concluded that the "process of conviction is easier than the rhetoric of justice would have us expect—and easier still the lower the status of the defendant".[278] Whilst the law appears to provide considerable protection for the accused, there are many exceptions, which reduce the protection in reality.

---

[274] Criminal Law Revision Committee, *Eleventh Report, Evidence (General)* (Cmnd. 4991, 1972), pp.10–12. The recommendations of this comprehensive yet controversial report were implemented in part by PACE and by the Criminal Justice and Public Order Act 1994.

[275] Mr Justice Hawkins described one 1840s Old Bailey Trial which lasted 2 minutes 53 seconds as "a high example of expedition", and stated that trials after dinner lasted on average 4 minutes: Hawkins, *Memoirs*, cited in the CLRC 11th Report (1972), p.11.

[276] CLRC 11th Report (1972), pp.10–12.

[277] D. J. McBarnet, *Conviction: Law, the State and the Construction of Justice* (1981).

[278] *ibid.* p.155.

The implementation of the Human Rights Act 1998 reinvigorated the debate about the accused's position in the English criminal trial. In 2006 the Government stated its desire to "rebalance" the criminal justice system in order to counter the "increasing public concern that it gives the wrongdoer better protection than the law-abiding".[279] This rebalancing would include challenging decisions of the European Court of Human Rights "which stop us applying a proper balance effectively".[280] The protections for the accused in the criminal trial have rarely strengthened or endorsed in recent legislation, and this looks unlikely to change.

The first procedural question relating to the attendance of the accused concerns the attendance at the Crown Court. There is a fundamental requirement to a fair trial. If in custody, the accused is brought to court from prison; if on bail the accused is informed of the time and date of the trial and told when to attend. The accused *must* attend court so as to answer in person when the indictment is put, because no one else may enter a plea.[281]

Whilst needing to be present at the arraignment, the accused may be absent for the trial, although that will happen only in exceptional cases, because the accused needs to be present in order to "hear the case against him and have the opportunity . . . of answering it".[282] This important safeguard of requiring the physical presence of the accused is echoed in Art.6 of the ECHR, which implies a right to be present to participate in the proceedings.[283] The defendant may waive his right by conduct or failing to attend.[284] Such cases include those where the accused is violent or disorderly,[285] is ill,[286] absconds from the trial,[287] or remains absent having informed the court of his belief that no fair trial would occur.[288]

The Court of Appeal reaffirmed the principles dictating when a trial can occur in the absence of the accused.[289] A defendant has a general right to attend and be

---

[279] Home Office, *Rebalancing the Criminal Justice System in favour of the law-abiding majority: Cutting crime, reducing reoffending and protecting the public* (2006), p.3.

[280] *ibid.* p.4.

[281] *R v Heyes* [1951] 1 K.B. 29. In some circumstances, the failure of the accused to plead personally to the indictment results in a mistrial: *R v Boyle* [1954] 2 Q.B. 292; *R v Ellis* (1973) 57 Cr.App.R. 571. However, if the trial had proceeded as though a "not guilty" plea had been recorded no material irregularity had necessarily occurred: *R v Williams* [1978] Q.B. 373.

[282] *R v Lee Kun* (1916) 11 Cr.App.R. 293, 300, *per* Lord Reading. *R v Howson* (1982) 74 Cr.App.R. 172 and G. Zellick, "The Criminal Trial and the Disruptive Defendant" (1980) 43 M.L.R. 121 at 284.

[283] See *Ekbatani v Sweden* (1991) 13 E.H.R.R. 504, para.25.

[284] See, e.g. *Colozza v Italy* (1985) 7 E.H.R.R. 516.

[285] It is possible to handcuff or restrain an accused, but only if there is a danger of escape or violence, and whether such restraint is justified should be investigated in court without the jury, see *R v Vratsides* [1988] Crim. L.R. 251; *R v Rollinson* (1997) 161 J.P. 107. See also *R v Berry* (1897) 104 L.T.J. 110, where the accused performed an impromptu striptease on the clerk's table. On the use of handcuffs see *R v Mullen* [2000] Crim. L.R. 873 accepting that the potential prejudice to the accused of his being seen in handcuffs is ameliorated by a suitable warning to the jury from the judge.

[286] *R v Pearson, The Independent*, February 25, (1998); *R v Howson* (1981) 74 Cr.App.R. 172, where it was indicated that the discretion must not be exercised if the accused's defence could be prejudiced by his or her absence.

[287] *R v Jones (No.2)* [1972] 1 W.L.R. 887; *R v Charles and Tucker* [2001] Crim. L.R. 732 and commentary; [2001] 2 Cr.App.R. 209.

[288] *R v Donnelly* [1998] Crim. L.R. 1311, CA.

[289] See *R v Hayward* [2001] Q.B. 862. See also *R v Smith* [2006] EWCA Crim 2307; *R v O'Hare* [2006] EWCA Crim 471, [2006] Crim. L.R. 950.

represented, but those rights can be waived wholly or in part. The decision to proceed in the absence of a defendant (or his legal representatives) falls within the discretion of the trial judge. That discretion is to be used in rare and exceptional cases, particularly if the defendant is unrepresented. In exercising the discretion the judge must consider fairness to both defence and prosecution and all the relevant circumstances, especially: whether the absence is voluntary; whether an adjournment might be appropriate or sufficient to deal with the problem; the likely length of any adjournment; whether there is an unequivocal waiver of the right to representation; whether instructions could still be proffered; the potential disadvantage to the defendant in continuing; the risk of the jury reaching an improper conclusion from speculating about the defendant's absence; the effect of delay on the memories of witnesses; the general public interest, the interest of the victims and the witnesses; and the undesirability, in joint trials, of severing trials. These principles were commended by the House of Lords with the addition that the seriousness of the offence should not be a consideration, and, even if the accused has absconded voluntarily it is desirable that he should be represented.[290]

The problem of whether the accused has a right to "confront his accuser" has been an issue for the English courts. The most acute difficulties have arisen in relation to vulnerable witnesses, particularly child sexual abuse victims who are in fear of seeing the alleged abuser in person. The law's response has been to prevent the accused from cross-examining the witness directly, thereby reducing the degree of confrontation, and by allowing witnesses to give evidence by live link, from behind screens and in the most serious cases by video-recorded testimony under the special measures provisions of the Youth Justice and Criminal Evidence Act 1999.[291] Whether the inability visually to confront an accuser inhibits the accused from having a fair trial in any meaningful sense is doubtful.[292] Outside of the 1999 Act the court may exercise common law powers to allow witnesses to give evidence anonymously provided that a fair trial can still take place.[293]

The second procedural question relates to the accused's response on arraignment after the indictment has been read. The accused is required to answer to every count on the indictment and each plea will be recorded. In the great majority of cases the plea will be "guilty" or "not guilty", although there are several other possibilities.

It is worth noting that the prosecution does not always have to proceed to trial but could (a) offer no evidence or (b) let counts lie on the file.

---

[290] *R v Jones* [2003] 1 A.C. 1. See also P. Ferguson, "Trial in Absence and Waiver of Human Rights" [2002] Crim. L.R. 554; Where the accused has absconded the conduct of counsel is covered by the Code of Conduct of the Bar: Written Standards for the Conduct of Professional Work paras 15.3.1–15.3.2. Further, see: *R v O'Hare* [2006] Crim. L.R. 950.

[291] ss.16–35. See L. Hoyano, "Variations on a Theme by Pigot: Special Measures Directions for Child Witnesses" [2000] Crim. L.R. 250; D. Birch, "A Better Deal for Vulnerable Witnesses" [2000] Crim. L.R. 223; L. Hoyano, "Striking a Balance Between the Rights of Defendants and Vulnerable Witnessesill Special Measures Contravene Guarantees of a Fair Trial" [2001] Crim. L.R. 948.

[292] *R (D) v Camberwell Green Youth Court* [2003] 2 Cr.App.R. 257 where the court held that Art.6 did not require that vulnerable witnesses must give evidence in the same room as the accused and thus the provisions of the YJCEA were not incompatible with the Convention.

[293] *R v Davis* [2006] EWCA Crim 1155.

(a) The plea of guilty

17–043   The defendant's acknowledgment of guilt must be unmistakable. It must be made freely by the accused in person, who must have knowledge of the elements of the offence.[294] The accused must not be under undue pressure from counsel or the court. A plea entered under the threat of withdrawal of legal representation would, for example, vitiate the plea. It is quite proper for defence counsel to advise the accused, perhaps in very forceful terms, that a plea of guilty could be advantageous in securing a lesser sentence and/or that the evidence seems to point strongly to guilt. Counsel must also stress that a guilty plea should only be entered if the accused has actually committed the alleged offence.[295]

Plea bargaining

17–044   The importance attached to the accused's freedom to enter the plea desired is reflected in the "plea bargaining" cases where it was suspected that unfair pressure had been placed on the accused.[296] "Plea bargaining . . . describes the practice whereby the accused enters a plea of guilty in return for which he will be given some consideration that results in a sentence concession."[297] There are a number of ways in which this problem arises.

The first method can be accurately described as charge bargaining: a plea arrangement made between prosecution and defence counsel whereby a plea of guilty to a lesser charge on the indictment is accepted in return for the prosecution not proceeding with the more serious charge(s). The second method by which the sentence concession is obtained is a plea of guilty to the offence charged. A guilty plea attracts a lighter sentence.[298]

The value of a guilty plea in the criminal process is that it reduces the time and money spent on achieving convictions, it obviates the need for a trial and the

---

[294] *R v Golathan* (1915) 11 Cr.App.R. 79. For the dangers of pleas entered by counsel, see *R v Ellis* (1973) 57 Cr.App.R. 571.

[295] *R v Goodyear* [2005] 3 All E.R. 117.

[296] The particular pressure that gave rise to concern was where it appeared to the accused that the judge had indicated to counsel that an unsuccessful plea of not guilty would attract a heavier sentence: *R v Turner* [1970] 2 Q.B. 321.

[297] J. Baldwin and M. McConville, *Negotiated Justice* (1977), p.19. This early research study is a prerequisite for any detailed study of the subject of plea bargaining. See also, P. Thomas, "Plea Bargaining and the *Turner* Case" [1970] Crim. L.R. 559; A. Davis, "Sentences for Sale: A New Look at Plea Bargaining in England and America" [1970] Crim. L.R. 150 and 218; R. Purves, "That Plea-Bargaining Business" [1971] Crim. L.R. 470; S. McCabe and R. Purves, *By-Passing the Jury* (1972); Bottoms and McLean (1976); J. Baldwin and M. McConville, "Plea Bargaining: Legal Carve-Up or Legal Cover-Up" (1978) 5 B.J.L.S. 228; "Plea Bargaining and the Court of Appeal" (1979) 6 B.J.L.S. 200; "The Influence of the Sentencing Discount in Inducing Guilty Pleas" in J. Baldwin and A. K. Bottomley (eds), *Criminal Justice: Selected Readings*, "Preserving the Good Face of Justice: Some Recent Plea Bargain Cases" (1978) 128 N.L.J. 872 and *Court, Prosecution and Conviction* (1981); S. Moody and J. Tombs, "Plea Negotiations and Scotland" [1983] Crim. L.R. 297; S. Moody and J. Tombs, *Prosecution in the Public Interest* (1982); Wasik, Gibbons and Redmayne (1999), pp.375–388; M. McConville, "Plea Bargaining, Ethics and Politics" (1998) 25 J. Law and Soc. 562; G. Fisher, "Plea Bargaining's Triumph" (2000) Yale L.J. 857; J. Morton, "Behind Closed Doors" (2000) 150 N.L.J. 1843; M. McConville and M. Mirsky, *Jury Trials and Plea Bargaining* (2005); Sanders and Young (2007), Ch.8; Ashworth and Redmayne (2005) Ch.10. J. Morton, "Please Please Me" (2005) 69(4) J. Crim. L. 277.

[298] See Sentencing Guidelines Council, *Reduction in Sentence for a Guilty Plea: Guideline* (2004) available at: *www.sentencing-guidelines.gov.uk.*

inherent difficulties of proof, it spares the witnesses an experience which can be both unpleasant and distressing,[299] and it is alleged to demonstrate an attitude of contrition and remorse on the part of the accused.[300] The advantages to the prosecution of offering concessions or inducements to persuade the accused to plead guilty are the certainty and economy thereby secured. These advantages must be balanced against the need to ensure that offenders are convicted of offences only when they are actually guilty and which properly represent the seriousness of their behaviour. The danger of the accused pleading guilty under pressure to obtain the maximum sentencing discount or failing to make a free informed decision about his plea should not be underestimated.

Sentence discount is maximised where the accused admits his guilt at the first opportunity.[301] This will attract a discount on a sliding scale from a maximum of one-third. Exceptions apply to those convicted of murder who must serve a "minimum term" starting at 15 years as a minimum, and those offences where Parliament has indicated that a minimum custodial sentence applies.[302] In some cases the discount will operate not only to reduce the severity of a particular form of sentence but also to alter the type of sentence from, for example, custodial to non-custodial. The prosecution are not obliged to accept a plea of guilty to a lesser alternative offence. If the prosecution do reject such a plea, the prosecution can call evidence of it in the trial.[303]

For the truly guilty defendant and the prosecution, a plea bargain represents a mutually beneficial compromise. A guilty plea is obtained and so is a sentence concession. However, these concessions also operate (intentionally) as inducements and create enormous pressure on the accused who is at his/her most vulnerable in facing this most difficult of decisions in the criminal process. There are significant problems both with charge bargaining and with the sentence discount.

Although the early research of McCabe and Purves suggested that the guilty pleas obtained were justified in the light of the evidence and the benefit to the criminal justice system,[304] subsequent research has largely demonstrated that defendants' changes of plea, especially when late, are contrary to the actual wishes of the accused, being based upon the advice of the lawyers,[305] resulting in the supposed imprisonment of innocent people.[306] The need to avoid delay and unnecessary hearings under the Criminal Procedure Rules 2005 coupled with the potential desire for a high case turnover in an era of fixed case fees places increased pressure on defence lawyers to bring about a guilty plea.

---

[299] See: Sentencing Guidelines Council (2004), para.2.1.
[300] For example, see *R v Karim* [2005] EWCA Crim 533 at para.31. This rationale is doubted by Sanders and Young (2007) p.387.
[301] Sentencing Guidelines Council (2004), para.4.3.
[302] For example, Criminal Justice Act 2003, s.287, a minimum of five years must be served by an adult guilty of possessing firearms.
[303] See *R v Hazeltine* [1967] 2 Q.B. 857.
[304] S. McCabe and R. Purves, *By-passing the Jury* (1972) and see Sanders' and Young (2007), p.424.
[305] See Sanders and Young (2007) p.396; see also, E. Cape, "The Rise (and Fall) of a Criminal Defence Profession" [2004] Crim. L.R. 401.
[306] A. Bottoms and J. McClean, *Defendants in the Criminal Process* (1976) and J. Baldwin and M. McConville, *Negotiated Justice* (1977). However, the Crown Court Survey discovered that few innocent people were persuaded to plead guilty; see M. Zander and P. Henderson (1993), pp.96–98.

Advance indications from the court regarding the sentence have long been seen as restricting the defendant's choice over his plea. Following *Turner*,[307] it was held that the only acceptable indications as to sentence would be as to the type of sentence imposed, and this would be regardless of the defendant's plea. However, it was widely accepted that these rules were widely ignored and judges and barristers would often meet prior to the trial to discuss a bargain over the sentence.[308] The Royal Commission on Criminal Justice considered the issue but merely stated that it could "see no objection to such discussions, but the earlier they take place the better; consultation between counsel before the trial would often avoid the need for the case to be listed as a contested trial".[309] The concern of the Commission was with the wastage of resources of the "cracked trial", that is the trial which was believed to be contested, but at which the accused pleads guilty.[310]

As discussed earlier the CJA 2003 has changed the position in the magistrates' courts. A defendant in a triable either way case in which the magistrates have accepted jurisdiction can seek an indication as to sentence from the court if he were to plead guilty.

If a guilty plea is made in error by the accused, it may be withdrawn, and the trial judge may permit, at his discretion, a change of plea at any time before sentence.[311]

(b) The plea of not guilty

17–045   This plea occasions little difficulty. It constitutes a denial of the prosecution's allegations and requires them to prove all the elements of their case, except those facts admitted by the defence.[312] The plea must be entered by the accused personally.

A plea of not guilty may be changed during the trial with the leave of the judge.[313] There are many reasons for a change of plea, such as the possibility of an unwelcome outcome of the trial if the plea of not guilty is maintained.[314] It has been held that if a not guilty plea is changed to guilty, it is not necessary for the judge to require the jury formally to return a verdict since the plea is a public

---

[307] *R v Turner* [1970] 2 W.L.R. 1093.

[308] Sanders and Young (2007), pp.401–402.

[309] RCCJ, Report (1993), p.114.

[310] In fact not all parties are disappointed; the CPS, whilst recognising the resources wastage, also appreciated the guilty plea, especially when the prosecution was not convinced that it would get a conviction: Zander and Henderson (1993), p.156.

[311] *S (an infant) v Manchester Recorder* [1971] A.C. 481. Late changes of plea may well be made when the accused indicates that his or her original plea was made as a result of threats. See, e.g. *R v Dodd, Pack* (1982) 74 Cr.App.R. 50. Where the allegation of the threat was that it was made when the accused was represented by counsel, it is unlikely that the change of plea will be allowed.

[312] Admissions may be made at various stages of criminal proceedings in accordance with the Criminal Justice Act 1967, s.10: see Sprack (2006), p.336.

[313] The judge also has a discretion to allow an accused to alter his plea back to not guilty: *R v Drew* [1985] 1 W.L.R. 914. As to the procedure to be adopted on change of plea, see *R v Ellis* (1973) 57 Cr.App.R. 571.

[314] In *R v Sullivan* [1984] A.C. 156 the accused changed his plea to guilty, because when he raised the claim that he assaulted someone when in an epileptic fit it was made clear that he was raising the defence of insanity which would result in his being sent to a mental hospital.

admission.[315] The ordinary practice is, however, for the jury to return a verdict whenever the accused is in their charge, even in cases of a formal change of plea to guilty.

(c) The accused not pleading

The expectation is that the accused will be able, with legal representation, to plead. However, the accused may "stand mute", that is make no reply or no intelligible reply, when the charge is put. A jury must then be empanelled to determine whether the accused is "mute of malice" or "mute by visitation of God". The issue is tried like any other jury matter by the bringing of evidence, examination of witnesses, summing-up and verdict. An adjournment may be necessary to provide facilities by which the accused can communicate. If the accused is found to be mute of malice (the prosecution having proved it beyond a reasonable doubt[316]) a plea of not guilty is formally entered on behalf of the accused.[317] If found to be mute by visitation of God the question arises as to whether the accused is fit to plead to the charge at all. **17–046**

(d) Fitness to plead[318]

The question of fitness to plead may arise not only where the accused has remained silent on arraignment and been found mute by visitation of God, but also where there is a defence submission of unfitness or the prosecution bring the matter to the judge's attention.[319] The question is "whether the accused is under a disability, that is to say under any disability such that . . . it would constitute a bar to his being tried . . . ".[320] This issue used to be determined by a jury but is now determined by a judge alone.[321] **17–047**

Because it is desirable that a person charged with a criminal offence should stand trial if possible and should have the chance to show that the prosecution case is inadequate, the question of fitness to plead may be deferred until the opening of the defence case, at the discretion of the trial judge.[322] The onus of proving the question of fitness lies with the party raising it. If raised by the defence it must be proved on a balance of probabilities; if raised by the prosecution it must be proved beyond reasonable doubt.[323] In deciding whether the accused is unfit, he or she has to have sufficient ability in relation to: understanding the charges; understanding the plea; challenging jurors; instructing

---

[315] *R v Poole* [2002] Crim. L.R. 242.

[316] *R v Sharp* [1960] 1 Q.B. 357, CA.

[317] Criminal Law Act 1967, s.6(1).

[318] See D. Ormerod, *Smith and Hogan: Criminal Law* (11th edn, 2005) pp.250–256.

[319] See *O'Donnell* [1996] Crim. L.R. 121 on the correct procedure to be adopted. See also R. Mackay and G. Kearns, "An Upturn in Unfitness to Plead? Disability in Relation to the Trial under the 1991 Act" [2000] Crim. L.R. 532, assessing the impact of the 1991 Act. See generally R. D. Mackay, *Mental Condition Defences in the Criminal Law* (1995).

[320] Criminal Procedure (Insanity) Act 1964, s.4(1), as substituted by the Criminal Procedure (Insanity and Unfitness to Plead) Act 1991, s.2.

[321] Criminal Procedure (Insanity) Act 1964 s.4A as amended by the Domestic Violence, Crime and Victims Act 2004.

[322] Criminal Procedure (Insanity) Act 1964, s.4(2). The same process then applies: s.4A(5).

[323] The question of the onus and standard of proof is considered in *R v Podola* [1960] 1 Q.B. 325, which is of general interest on the question of fitness to plead.

counsel; understanding the course of the trial; and giving evidence.[324] If the accused is found to be unfit to plead, the court must then determine whether he or she "did the act or made the omission charged against him as the offence" and, if so, make such a finding.[325] If the court is satisfied that the accused is unfit and did perform the act or omission it will make an appropriate disposal order in accordance with s.5 of the Act.[326] If not so satisfied, the jury must acquit the accused.

(e) Right to silence[327]

17–048   We consider here the problems of the defendant's silence and its effect at trial.[328] The so called "right to silence" was predicated on the propositions that the accused should not be required to provide any evidence which might be incriminating and is entitled to make the prosecution prove its case without answering questions before or at the trial. Where the accused failed to testify, the accepted comment was that established by Lord Parker C.J. in *R v Bathurst*[329]:

> " . . . the accused is not bound to give evidence, he can sit back and see if the prosecution have proved their case, and that, whilst the jury have been deprived of the opportunity of hearing his story tested in cross-examination, the one thing that they must not do is to assume that he is guilty because he has not gone into the witness box."

---

[324] *R v M* [2003] EWCA Crim 3452.

[325] Criminal Procedure (Insanity) Act 1964, s.4A(2) and (3). *R v Omara* [2004] EWCA Crim 431. There is no power to reverse the decision on unfitness.

[326] As amended by the Domestic Violence, Crime and Victims Act 2004, s.24.

[327] See the major textbooks on the law of evidence and for more detailed reviews of the issues surrounding the right to silence; see K. Starmer and M. Woolf, in C. Walker and K. Starmer (1999) S. Greer and R. Morgan (eds), *The Right of Silence Debate* (1990); S. M. Easton, *The Right to Silence* (1998); S. C. Greer, (1990) 53 M.L.R. 709; R. Leng, *The Right to Silence in Police Interrogation: A Study of Some of the Issues Underlying the Debate* (RCCJ Research Study No.10, HMSO, 1993); D. Morgan and G. M. Stephenson, *Suspicion and Silence* (1994); I. Dennis [1995] Crim L.R. 4 at 9–18. On the implementations of the silence provisions and the history see J. Wood and A. Crawford, *The Right to Silence* (1989); A. Zuckerman, [1989] Crim. L.R. 855; J. Coldrey (1991) 20 Anglo-Am. L.R.; D. Morgan and G. Stephenson (eds), *Suspicion or Silence: the Right to Silence in Criminal Investigations* (1994). For academic comment on the implementation and operation of the sections, see P. Mirfield, *Silence Confessions and Improperly Obtained Evidence* (1998). See also I. Dennis, (1995) 54 C.L.J. 342, [1995] Crim. L.R. 4; S Easton [1998] 2 Int. J.F. & P.; J. Jackson [1993] 44 N.I.L.O. 103; R. Pattenden [1995] Crim. L.R. 602; Pattenden [1998] 2 E. & P. 141; D. Birch [1999] Crim. L.R. 769; Sir Stephen Sedley, "Wringing Out the Fault: Self Incrimination in the 21st Century" [2001] N.J.L.O. 107. For a summary of the debate preceding enactment, see the Home Office Research Study by T. Bucke, R. Street, and B. Brown, *The Right to Silence: The Impact of the Criminal Justice and Public Order Act 1994* (2000), Ch.1. On the right to silence provisions in Northern Ireland, see the review by J. Jackson, M. Wolfe and K. Quinn, *Legislating Against Silence: The NI Experience* (2000), revealing that terrorist suspects were more likely to testify after the 1988 Order (the equivalent of the s.34 provision). Their conclusion was that the order had, generally, the contrary effect to that expected and that there had been a marked "decline in convictions in those cases which have been contested" see (p.144). On the constitutionality of the right to silence, see P. J. Shwikkard, "Is it Constitutionally Permissible to Infringe the Right to Remain Silent" (2001) 5 E. & P. 32.

[328] Exercising the right to silence in the face of police questioning is covered in the chapter on pre-trial criminal procedure.

[329] [1968] 1 All E.R. 1175 at 1178. See also *R v Martinez-Tobon* [1994] 1 W.L.R. 388.

Though only limited changes were recommended by the Royal Commission on Criminal Justice,[330] major changes were introduced by ss.34–38 of the Criminal Justice and Public Order Act 1994. The right to keep silent was not *abolished* but greater risks are now run by the accused who maintains that position, before or at trial.[331] Much has been written of the extremely controversial reforms though it remains unclear whether they have been successful in securing more convictions of defendants (particularly hardened criminals).[332]

Bucke *et al.*[333] found that since the 1994 Act, the percentage of suspects exercising their right to silence has not altered dramatically. Before the Act, 10 per cent of suspects refused to answer all questions, 13 per cent refused to answer some, and 77 per cent answered all. Under the Act, six per cent refused to answer all questions, 10 per cent refused to answer some, and 84 per cent answered all.[334] Those who obtained legal advice were "far more likely to refuse" all questions than those who had not. More serious allegations were more likely to lead to silence as was a suspect having a previous record (13 per cent as opposed to five per cent). Of those who received legal advice before the Act, 20 per cent refused to answer all questions, 19 per cent refused to answer some, and 61 per cent answered all. After the Act those figures are 13 per cent, nine per cent and 78 per cent respectively. For those who did not receive legal advice, the figures before the 1994 Act were: three per cent refused to answer all; nine per cent refused to answer some; and 88 per cent, answered all questions. After the Act, the figures are two per cent, six per cent and 92 per cent respectively.[335]

Following the enactment of the 1994 Act, the common law position relating to the right to silence still pertains when the statutory provisions are inapplicable, and in such circumstances, it is incumbent on the trial judge to direct the jury that they should not draw adverse inferences from silence.[336]

---

[330] RCCJ, Report (1993), pp.54–55. The majority recommended that "it is when but only when the prosecution has been fully disclosed that defendants should be required to offer and answer to the charges made against them at the risk of adverse comment at trial on any new defence they then disclose or on any departure from the defence which they previously disclosed". See also the recommendations of the Home Office Working Group (1989). For powerful adverse criticism of the proposals, see A. A. S. Zuckerman, [1989] Crim. L.R. 855; J. Wood and A. Crawford, *The Right of Silence: The Case for Retention* (1989); S Greer, (1990) 53 M.L.R 709; B. Irving and I. McKenzie (1990) 1 J. Foresenic Psychiatry 167. For arguments in favour of change, see G. Williams, "The Right of Silence and the Mental Element" [1988] Crim. L.R. 97.

[331] It is important to note also that adverse inferences can be drawn against a defendant who fails adequately to disclose a defence later relied on at trial: Criminal Procedure and Investigation Act 1996, s.11. On the potential to draw adverse inferences from the failure to make adequate defence disclosure, see S. Thompson, "Defence Statements—Weighting the Scales or Tipping the Balance on a Submission of No Case" [1998] Crim. L.R. 802.

[332] See D. J. Birch, "Suffering in Silence; A Cost-Benefit Analysis of Section 34 of the Criminal Justice and Public Order Act 1994" [1999] Crim. L.R. 769. T. Bucke, R. Street and B. Brown, *The Right to Silence: The Impact of the Criminal Justice and Public Order Act 1994* (2000) conclude that: "whatever philosophical standpoint is adopted, it seems clear that the change in the law has not led to undue practical disadvantages to the defendant" (p.73). See also the excellent review by I. Dennis "Silence in the Police Station: The Marginalisation of Section 34" [2002] Crim. L.R. 25.

[333] T. Bucke, R. Street and B. Brown, *The Right to Silence: The Impact of the Criminal Justice and Public Order Act 1994* (2000).

[334] *ibid.* p.31.

[335] *ibid.* p.33.

[336] *R v McGarry* [1999] 1 W.L.R. 1500.

As Lord Bingham C.J. observed in *Bowden*[337] ss.34–38 "restrict rights recognized at common law as appropriate to protect defendants against the risk of injustice [and as such] should not be construed more widely than the statutory language requires".

This common law protection against incrimination from silence is supported by Art.6 of the ECHR which although it does not expressly provide a "right to silence" has been interpreted expansively by the European Court as implicitly providing a protection against self-incrimination and providing a "right to silence" as part of the fundamental guarantees of the fair trial.[338] In *Funke v France*,[339] the ECtHR recognised: "the right of anyone charged with a criminal offence, within the autonomous meaning of the expression in Art.6, to remain silent and not to contribute to incriminating himself." Particularly important are the ECHR guarantees against drawing adverse inferences where the accused has not had an opportunity to seek legal advice or from convicting a person exclusively on his silence.[340]

It is important to note that there is often confusion as to the precise ambit of the protections regarding silence, and this confusion is exacerbated by misleadingly using the expression interchangeably with the "privilege against self-incrimination". The privilege against self-incrimination is a different issue arising, *inter alia*, when the accused is questioned under powers that are backed by sanctions for failure to reply. Domestic law has been heavily influenced by the ECtHR decision in *Saunders v UK*,[341] where the defendant had been convicted of offences in relation to the Guinness-Distillers take-over. His conviction rested in part on the answers he provided to questions under compulsion—i.e. where the failure to answer is itself an offence. The Strasbourg Court held that this constituted an infringement of the privilege against self-incrimination. The majority stated: "the right not to incriminate oneself, in particular, presupposes that the prosecution in a criminal case seek to prove their case against the accused without resort to evidence obtained through means of coercion or oppression in defiance of the will of the accused. In this sense the right is closely linked to the presumption of innocence contained in article 6(2)."[342]

The statutory scheme

17–049 Section 34 of the Criminal Justice and Public Order Act 1994[343] provides that where an accused, before charge, when questioned under caution or after charge, "failed to mention any fact relied on in his defence" in criminal proceedings and

---

[337] [1999] 2 Cr.App.R. 176 at 181.
[338] See *Saunders v UK* (1996) 23 E.H.R.R. 313; *Murray v UK* (1996) 22 E.H.R.R. 29; *Condron v UK* [2000] Crim. L.R. 679.
[339] (1993) 16 E.H.R.R. 297.
[340] See e.g. *Condron v UK* [2000] Crim. L.R. 679; *Heaney and McGuiness v Ireland* [2001] Crim. L.R. 481; see further Ashworth [2001] Crim. L.R. 855 at 866.
[341] [1997] 23 E.H.R.R. 313.
[342] The European Court has vacillated between strong and weak approaches to this: compare *Funke v France* (1993) 16 E.H.R.R. 297 with *J.B. v Switzerland* [2001] Crim. L.R. 748. High profile cases on self-incrimination were some of earliest applications of the ECHR in argument in domestic criminal cases soon after implementation of the Human Rights Act 1998: *Brown v Stott* [2001] E.H.R.R. 78 (see R. Pillay, "Self-Incrimination and Article 6: The Decision of the Privy Council in *Procurator Fiscal v Brown*" [2001] E.H.R.R. 78). See also *R v Hertfordshire County Council, Ex p. Green Environmental Industries Ltd* [2000] 2 W.L.R. 373; *Attorney-General's Reference No.7 of 2000* [2001] EWCA Crim. 888.
[343] Note also ss.36 and 37 are concerned with the failure to account for objects, substances, marks and presence.

that fact was one "which in the circumstances existing at the time the accused could reasonably have been expected to mention when so questioned, charged or informed" then the judge (or magistrates) may "draw such inferences from the failure as appear proper."[344] There can be no conviction on silence alone,[345] and juries must be reminded of this in any case to which s.34 applies.[346] Section 34(2A) was added to bring English law into compliance with the Art.6.[347] As a result, no adverse inferences may now be drawn from the accused's silence unless he or she had an opportunity to consult with a legal adviser.[348]

The Court of Appeal has emphasised that there are numerous hurdles to overcome before the jury can begin drawing inferences from silence.[349] In addition to the requirement that proceedings have been instituted, the alleged failure to mention facts, which must have taken place before the defendant was charged, has to have occurred while the accused was undergoing questioning under caution, the objective of which was to establish whether or by whom the alleged offence was committed.[350] Furthermore, the alleged failure has to be to mention any fact which the defendant relies on in his defence. In *Knight*,[351] the Court of Appeal held that where the accused refused to answer questions under caution but prepared a full statement to the police which matched his later testimony in court, no adverse inferences could be drawn. The statute speaks of a failure to mention facts rather than a failure to answer police questions. However, in *Turner*[352] the Court spoke of the potential dangers of relying upon a statement which the defendant realises at trial was not full or which he or she contradicts.

Finally, the relevant fact[353] has to be one which, in the circumstances, the defendant could reasonably have been expected to mention, taking account of that particular defendant's characteristics, such as age, health and mental capacity, and legal advice as relevant circumstances.[354] Whilst the issue requires appropriate jury directions, the matter should then be left for the jury to decide. The directions given will clearly be of crucial importance and the Court of Appeal provided some clarification as to the nature of the direction in *Petkar*.[355] The burden of proof remains on the prosecution throughout.[356]

---

[344] Criminal Justice and Public Order Act 1994, s.34(1) and (2).

[345] *ibid.* s.38.

[346] *R v Abdullah* [1999] 3 Arch. News 2.

[347] *Murray v UK* (1996) 22 E.H.R.R. 29. See R. Munday, "Inferences from Silence and European Human Rights Law" [1996] Crim. L.R. 370, discussing the implications of *Murray*, which held that M's right to a fair trial had been violated because he did not have access to a lawyer in the first 48 hours of detention.

[348] On the need to have access to a legal adviser before adverse inferences can be drawn, see also A. Jennings, "Resounding Silence" (1996) 146 N.L.J. 725 at 746, 821.

[349] See especially *R v Argent* [1997] 2 Cr.App.R. 27.

[350] *R v Johnson* [2005] EWCA Crim 971. If the suspect refuses to leave his cell for questioning then the section cannot apply.

[351] [2004] 1 W.L.R. 340. See also, A. Keogh, "The Right to Silence—Revisted Again" (2003) 153 N.L.J. 1352; A. Choo, "Prepared Statements, Legal Advice and the Right to Silence: *R v Knight*" (2004) 8 I.J.E. & P. 62.

[352] [2004] 1 All E.R. 1025.

[353] The House of Lords has stated that "fact" should be given a broad meaning: *R v Webber* [2004] 1 W.L.R. 404.

[354] *R v Argent* [1997] 2 Cr.App.R. 27. On the vexed problem of relying upon legal advice to remain silent, see the chapter on pre trial criminal procedure.

[355] *R v Petkar* [2004] 1 Cr.App.R. 22.

[356] *R v Gowland-Wynn* [2002] 1 Cr.App.R. 569. See also, *R v Parchment* [2003] EWCA Crim 2428.

Section 34 only comes into play if the accused relies on a fact at trial that it is reasonable to expect him previously to have mentioned. It is clear that if the accused remains silent at trial and offers no evidence by way of a defence—i.e. simply puts the prosecution to proof—the section has no part to play.[357] Difficulties arise if the accused puts forward a theory or proposition that is not "a fact".[358] In these cases the section should have no part to play and no adverse inferences should be drawn.

Inferences can only be drawn from a failure to mention such "facts" where, if in the circumstances at the time, the accused could reasonably be expected to mention them. As such, the personal characteristics of the accused must be considered (and this should not be done in a restrictive manner[359]) including age, experience, mental capacity, health, sobriety, tiredness and personality and the extent of the accused's knowledge of the case against him. Where the accused remains silent on legal advice that reliance must be both genuine and reasonable.[360] This may result in the accused waiving his lawyer client privilege at trial in order to explain why he was silent.

Research has revealed a list of no fewer than 25 factors that lead practitioners to advise no comment in interview. The most common reason is insufficient police disclosure, followed by insufficient evidence and, third, the "physical or mental condition of the client". Other factors included a fear of incriminating other people, the implausibility of the statement, and the police already being poised to charge.[361] On the factors that led advisers to recommend that clients answer questions, the most important was the category of the defence followed by fear of adverse inferences being drawn and a belief that the police would be less likely to charge the accused if he or she had an explanation.

If there was silence at the investigative stage, and a fact is relied on at trial and it is reasonable to have expected the accused to have mentioned it, the section allows inferences to be drawn. Under s.34 the prosecution have to establish a prima facie case against the accused before reliance on the silence can be made. The jury must be reminded of this obligation.[362] Many inferences *might* be drawn: that the accused is guilty, that he was unwilling to expose his defence to scrutiny, that the accused is turning on his co-accused, etc.[363] The jury must be directed with great care as to what permissible uses may be made of the accused's pre-trial silence.

The silence provisions continue to provoke controversy, not only as to their efficiency, but as to the more pernicious effects they have on the criminal process. Jackson has argued that the loss of the right to silence has transformed parts of what were purely investigative activities of the police into a formal part of the

---

[357] *R v Moshaid* [1998] Crim. L.R. 420.

[358] See *R v Nickolson* [1999] Crim. L.R. 61; *R v B (MT)* [2000] Crim. L.R. 181. The "facts" relied upon should be explicitly identified in the course of the direction to the jury: *R v Chenia* [2003] 2 Cr.App.R. 6.

[359] *R v Argent* [1997] 2 Cr.App.R. 27.

[360] See *R v Hoare* [2005] 1 Cr.App.R. 22; *R v Beckles* [2005] 1 All E.R. 705. See the discussion in chapter covering pre-trial criminal procedure.

[361] The problem still remains where adverse inferences are drawn or the defendant has been asked questions beyond the point at which there was sufficient evidence to charge him with an offence (in breach of PACE Code C C.11.4; 16.1). See *R v Pointer* [1997] Crim. L.R. 676; *R v Gayle* [1999] Crim. L.R. 502; *R v Elliott.* [2002] EWCA Crim. 931.

[362] *R v Milford* [2001] Crim. L.R. 330.

[363] *R v Mountford* [1999] Crim. L.R. 575: The status of this decision is now doubted. See *R. v Gowland-Wynn* [2002] 1 Cr.App.R. 569; *R v Chenia* [2003] 2 Cr.App.R. 6.

proceedings against the accused. The danger of this shift is that unlike other legal proceedings the safeguards for the accused at that early stage are minimal.[364]

Silence at trial[365]

As regards the failure to testify at trial, s.35 of the Criminal Justice and Public Order Act 1994 provides that at a trial[366] and at the conclusion of the prosecution case (the matter does not arise where there is no case to answer) if the accused does not give evidence or then answer questions (without good cause, e.g. physical or mental condition[367]), "it will be permissible for the court or jury to draw such inferences as appear proper from his failure to give evidence or his refusal, without good cause, to answer any question". Whilst the accused is not compelled to give evidence,[368] the risks in failing to give evidence are enhanced, since the inference that the court may draw is that the accused is guilty of the offence charged.[369] However, the accused cannot be convicted solely, or mainly,[370] on an inference drawn from silence,[371] and inferences of guilt will not be drawn where the prosecution has a weak case.[372] If the defence seek to rely on good cause for failing to testify, they must adduce evidence on the *voir dire*. On the *voir dire*, the judge may take account of expert evidence, and the conduct of the accused before and after the offence.

17–050

The Court of Appeal provided clear guidance in *R v Cowan* as to how the judge should direct the jury. A jury must find that there was a case to answer on the prosecution evidence before drawing an adverse inference from the defendant's silence, and they must be reminded that the burden of proof remained on the prosecution. They should also be told that the defendant is entitled to remain silent and an inference from failure to give evidence cannot on its own prove guilt. Judges should warn the jury that the condition for holding a defendant's silence against him is that the only sensible explanation for that silence is that he has no answer to the case or none that could stand up to cross-examination.[373] Without these directions the jury may attach undue importance to the defendant's absence from the witness box.

The drawing of inferences may be regarded as a significant infringement in the existing rights of the accused to a fair trial, and may reflect a move towards the crime control model.[374] This is echoed by the further extension of existing

---

[364] See J. Jackson, "Silence and Proof: Extending the Boundaries of Criminal Proceedings in the U.K." [2001] E. & P. 145.

[365] See Practice Direction (*Criminal Proceedings: Consolidation*) para.IV.44.

[366] If the accused's guilt is not in issue or "it appears to the court that the physical or mental condition of the accused makes it undesirable for him to give evidence", the provisions do not apply: s.35(1).

[367] *R v Friend* [1997] 1 W.L.R. 1433. See E. Cape, "Mentally Disordered Suspects and the Right to Silence" (1996) 146 N.L.J. 80; S. Sharpe "Vulnerable Defendants and Inferences from Silence" (1997) 147 N.L.J. 842.

[368] *R v Cowan* [1996] Q.B. 373; s.35(4).

[369] s.35(3). See *Murray v DPP* [1994] 1 W.L.R. 1.

[370] Following the decision of the European Court in *Murray v UK* (1996) it is necessary to warn the jury that they should not convict "mainly" on silence. *R v Burchill* [1999] Crim. L.R. 311.

[371] s.38.

[372] *Murray v DPP* [1994] 1 W.L.R. 1; *Waugh v The King* [1950] A.C. 203.

[373] Counsel should be consulted as to be the appropriate directions: *R v Gough* [2002] Crim. L.R. 526.

[374] See further below.

powers to take and retain samples and specimens from suspects considered in Ch.14 above.

4. Representation and the Obligations of Counsel

17–051 The availability of legal assistance ensures that it is very unusual to find an unrepresented accused in the Crown Court. Those who are unrepresented have normally chosen to conduct their own defence. If the accused dismisses counsel, the judge must warn the defendant of the dangers in proceeding without counsel, and may adjourn for new counsel to be instructed unless of the opinion that this is not in the interests of justice (e.g. because it is likely that the accused will dismiss him also or will be mute of malice offering no instruction[375]). Ultimately, the defendant may insist on proceeding without counsel.[376] Both prosecution and defence counsel are under obligations to behave in accordance with professional standards and in a particular manner in the course of the trial.

So far as is reasonably practicable, a defendant is entitled to choose his representative.[377] The overriding question is of meeting the requirements of justice for both the prosecution and the defence in the circumstances of the particular case.[378] It is also worth noting that under Art.6(3)(c) of the ECHR, everyone charged with a criminal offence has a minimum right "to defend himself through legal assistance of his own choosing or, if he has not sufficient means to pay for the legal assistance, to be given it for free when the interests of justice so require".[379] This includes the right to have adequate opportunity to organise his defence in an appropriate way and without restriction as to the possibility to put all relevant defence arguments before the trial court.[380]

The ethical dimension to the representation of the accused in a criminal trial and to the role of the prosecutor is often overlooked. Ashworth and Blake[381] in their illuminating study identified six key ethical issues for the defence: defending a person believed to be guilty; where the advocate believes that perjury has been or will be committed; where the defence lawyer knows of an error of law in the proceedings which favours the defence; where the defence lawyer knows of an error of fact in the proceedings which favours the defence, where the defence lawyer offers advice to a cheat who wishes to plead not guilty; where the defence lawyer and the defendant disagree on the conduct of the defence. Ethical difficulties for the prosecutor were described as including: where the prosecutor realises that the court or the defence has made an error which favours the

---

[375] *Ricketts v R.* [1998] 1 W.L.R. 1017, PC.

[376] *R v Mills* [1997] 2 Cr.App.R. 206.

[377] D. O'Brien and J. Arnold, "Defending the Right to Choose: Legally Aided Defendants and Choice of Legal Representative" [2001] E.H.R.L.R. 409. See also the LCD Paper, *Criminal Defence Service: Choice of Representation* (1999); R. Moorhead, "Third Way Regulation: Community Legal Service Partnerships" (2001) 64 M.L.R. 543.

[378] *R v De Oliveira* [1997] Crim. L.R. 600.

[379] *Imbrioscia v Switzerland* (1993) 17 E.H.R.R. 441. See generally, Emmerson and Ashworth, Ch.4. In English law, "criminal charge" remains largely undefined. See generally, H. Grant "Commissions of Inquiry—Is There a Right to be Legally Represented" [2001] P.L. 377.

[380] *Can v Austria* (1985) Com.Rep A/96.

[381] See M. Blake and A. Ashworth, "Some Ethical Issues in Prosecuting and Defending Criminal Cases" [1998] Crim. L.R. 16. The authors also consider the appropriate ethical limits of cross-examination. See L. Ellison, "The Mosaic Art?: Cross-examination and the Vulnerable Witness" (2001) 21 L.S. 353.

prosecution; where the prosecutor realises that certain evidence may have been obtained unfairly; where the prosecutor enters into a plea negotiation despite doubts about the charges being sustainable; where the prosecutor makes representations in favour of a custodial remand, at the instigation of the police, even though the legal requirements are not strictly fulfilled.[382] Counsel must be careful to avoid appearing for the Crown against defendants whom they have previously defended,[383] and it is important that counsel avoid any conduct that might give rise to a perception of bias generally.[384]

Counsel should always act in accordance with the rules and etiquette of the Bar.[385] "A barrister has an overriding duty to the court to act with independence in the interests of justice: he must assist the court in the administration of justice and must not deceive or knowingly or recklessly mislead the court."[386] The latter principle is of the utmost importance and impinges upon the task of counsel at several points in the trial.

There can be little doubt that the increasingly consumerist attitude to criminal justice will result in a greater number of complaints and appeals against conviction being brought on the basis of alleged incompetence of counsel.[387]

(a) Prosecuting counsel

The Standards Applicable to Criminal Cases annexed to the Code of Conduct for the Bar of England and Wales state that: **17–052**

> "Prosecuting counsel should not attempt to obtain a conviction by all means at his command. He should not regard himself as appearing for a party. He should lay before the Court fairly and impartially the whole of the facts which comprise the case for the prosecution and should assist the Court on all matters of law applicable to the case."[388]

A distinguished Old Bailey judge, who had been Senior Prosecuting Counsel at that court, warned a prosecutor against feeling pride or satisfaction in the mere fact of success, or boasting of the percentage of convictions secured over a period

---

[382] See also the interesting comparative work by Kai Ambos, "The Status, Role and Accountability of the Prosecutor of the International Criminal Court: A Comparative Overview on the Basis of 33 National Reports" (2000) Euro. J. Crime, Crim. Law and Crim. Justice, 89, reviewing very different roles and responsibilities of prosecuting counsels in domestic proceedings.

[383] *R v Dann* [1997] Crim. L.R. 46.

[384] See e.g. the decision in *R v Batt* [1996] Crim. L.R. 910 that cohabiting barristers ought not to appear against each other in the same trial.

[385] *Code of Conduct for the Bar of England and Wales* (8th edn, 2004), as amended. Paragraph 4 states: "The general purpose of this Code is to provide the requirements for practice as a barrister and the rules and standards of conduct applicable to barristers which are appropriate in the interests of justice in England and Wales ... ". The Code can be accessed at *www.barcouncil.org.uk.*

[386] *ibid.* para.302.

[387] *Blackstone's* (2007) paras D24.37–24.40. See *Boodram v The State* [2002] Crim. L.R. 524 and commentary. See generally R. Shiels, "Blaming the Lawyer" [1997] Crim. L.R. 740. Examples might include failing to serve an alibi notice—see *R v Nangle* [2001] Crim. L.R. 507. Errors in the criminal trial are not always attributable to incompetence; counsel often have incredibly short periods of time in which to prepare cases.

[388] *Code of Conduct for the Bar of England and Wales: Written Standards for the Conduct of Professional Work*, section 3 para.10.1. (hereinafter, *Standards in Criminal Cases*).

of time. It is, he said, " . . . no rebuff to his prestige if he fails to convince the tribunal of the prisoner's guilt".[389] It is highly undesirable for prosecuting counsel to use unnecessarily emotive language that can only excite sympathy for the victim or prejudice against the accused. What is required of prosecuting counsel is an element of objectivity in conducting the trial process. This will often be difficult to achieve.

Three broad areas require careful consideration and the exercise of judgment by counsel: the desirability and propriety of a plea arrangement; the nature and presentation of the prosecution case at trial; the amount of assistance which needs to be given to the defence or the judge.

(i) *The plea arrangements*

17–053   As noted, where there are a number of counts in the indictment or where one count contains alternative charges or where the jury might convict of a lesser charge, it is not uncommon for the defence to offer or the prosecution to seek a plea of guilty to a lesser charge in return for an agreement from the prosecution to offer no evidence on the more serious charge. This is a form of plea-bargaining. In a sense, there is a double advantage in these circumstances. Assume that the accused is charged on one indictment containing two separate counts of rape and one count of indecent assault. If, in return for an agreement to accept not guilty pleas to the counts of rape, the accused agrees to plead guilty to the other count of indecent assault he will render himself liable to a less severe sentence on the lesser charge and also receive credit for a guilty plea. Clearly, the offer of a plea arrangement creates a certain amount of pressure on the accused. Sanders and Young review the arguments that barristers acting for the prosecution have a number of reasons, other than the client's best interests, for seeking to settle a case. These include that they are expected to seek bargains since that is in the interests of the administration of justice, and the comity of the Bar; and the fact that a barrister may do both prosecution and defence work which encourages agreements.[390] Note also that given the methods by which barristers are paid for a case, it is not in their interest to persuade the accused to plead guilty too early.

The advantages of a guilty plea for the prosecution are obvious: there is a saving of time and money; witnesses are spared the experience of testifying; the inevitable uncertainty of the trial is exchanged for the certainty of a plea. On the other hand, "a Crown Prosecutor must never accept a guilty plea just because it is convenient".[391]

The award of an automatic sentencing discount for a plea of guilty is clearly driven by a desire to maximise efficiency in the system with more people pleading guilty at the earliest possible stage of the proceedings.[392] The other saving is that a trial resulting in conviction would lead to a longer sentence than

---

[389] C. Humphreys, "The Duties and Responsibilities of Prosecuting Counsel" [1955] Crim. L.R. 739.
[390] Sanders and Young (2007), Ch.8.
[391] *Code for Crown Prosecutors* (2004), para.10.1.
[392] The average hearing time for a contested case in the Crown Court is 9.8 hours compared to 1.3 for non-contested cases: Department for Constitutional Affairs, *Judicial Statistics 2005* (2006), Table 6.21.

is imposed under the discount system, leading to greater costs incurred in the prison service.[393]

Based on empirical research, Henham argues that sentencing discounts are objectionable from the point of view of due process because they conflict with the presumption of innocence by removing the need for the prosecution to prove its case.[394] Henham has also shown that the relationship between the plea, the discount, the timing and the type of offence is important.

The arrangement of pleas is a common feature of the trial on indictment and it is alleged that it can be improperly facilitated by the CPS "overcharging" the accused at the outset. If more serious charges are included on the indictment when the evidence is, at best, equivocal, prosecuting counsel has more to bargain with. The Code for Crown Prosecutors discourages a proliferation of charges and prohibits proceeding with a more serious charge "just to get a defendant to plead guilty to a less serious one".[395] The Attorney-General has issued guidelines on the procedure for the acceptance of pleas,[396] which refers to the Code for Crown Prosecutors, and considers the circumstances in which a plea is to be reduced or fewer charges are to be offered. The guidelines emphasise the need for records to be kept of any exchanges. It is also important that, if a case has been listed for trial but a plea to a lesser offence is accepted or no evidence is offered, the views of the victim (or family of the bereaved) should be taken into account, and they should be kept informed of the developments. Guidelines on the responsibilities of counsel include advice on the appropriate role in the plea bargaining exercise.[397] The prosecution advocate may ask the defence if a plea will be forthcoming, but should not indicate that a particular plea will be acceptable before that has been offered (para.6.1). Where the defence offers a plea, the prosecution advocate may discuss this with a view to establishing that it is acceptable, i.e. "that it reflects the defendant's criminality and provides the court with sufficient powers to sentence appropriately" (para.6.2). The plea should be put in writing and the document should be passed to the CPS (para.6.6). The prosecution advocate is under a duty to discuss matters with the victim/victim's family if a plea is to be accepted or no evidence is to be offered (para.6.3). There is also an obligation to check the acceptability of the plea with the CPS (para.6.5).

No bargain is directly permissible about the length of sentence on particular charges, but is permissible about the charges to be proceeded with. However, if the prosecution have agreed or acquiesced in a bargain struck between defence and the judge as to sentence, they should then be estopped from referring the sentence to the Court of Appeal as unduly lenient.[398] Even if not openly seeking a longer sentence, the prosecution will influence the sentence passed by the selection of charges at the outset, and by influencing the mode of the trial. In addition, the prosecution must inform the court of the minimum sentence possible and inform the court of the accused's antecedents. Finally, If it appears to the Attorney-General that a sentence in an indictable only offence or a certain specified indictable offence is unduly lenient, he may refer the sentence to the Court of Appeal.

---

[393] See R. Henham, "Bargain Justice and Justice on Demand? Sentence Discounts and the Criminal Process" (1999) 62 M.L.R. 515.

[394] For criticism of the methodology see Sanders and Young (2007), p.392.

[395] *Code for Crown Prosecutors* (2004), para.7.2.

[396] *Attorney-General's Guidelines on the Acceptance of Pleas* [2001] 1 Cr.App.R. 425.

[397] *Farquarson Committee Guidelines* (2002) available at: *www.cps.gov.uk/publications/prosecution/ farqbooklet.html.*

[398] See *Attorney General's Reference No.44 of 2000* [2001] 1 Cr.App.R. 416.

(ii) *The presentation of the prosecution case*

17–054   Apart from planning the general strategy of the prosecution case, counsel has four specific tasks in its presentation. Opening and closing speeches are made, prosecution witnesses are examined and defence witnesses are cross-examined. In each of these tasks rules of conduct as well as rules of procedure and evidence must be observed.

The *opening speech* to the jury is of the utmost importance.[399] The greatest level of concentration and understanding is likely to be exhibited at the beginning and end of a trial. It is highly undesirable that prosecuting counsel should open the case with unnecessarily emotive language, and where the offences charged are likely to excite particular sympathy for the victim or prejudice against the accused. Counsel should warn the jury not to be influenced by such emotions in weighing the evidence.[400]

In *examination-in-chief* of prosecution witnesses, counsel must obey the golden rule of sticking to the facts in issue. Counsel should not use leading questions[401] (except on uncontentious matters and with the agreement of the defence) and there are certain other constraints on the lines of questioning.[402] Whether a question is a leading one is a matter for the judge to decide.

In *cross-examination* of defence witnesses, prosecuting counsel is entitled to test their evidence fully and fairly subject to the normal constraints on the line of questioning.[403] Counsel may ask leading questions.

As a matter of practice, the prosecution must present all the evidence on which they intend to rely before the close of their case.[404] However, further evidence may, exceptionally, be called, at the discretion of the trial judge where it was not previously available, was omitted inadvertently, or used to rebut matters arising *ex improviso*.[405]

Counsel will also have an opportunity to make a closing speech.

(iii) *Assisting the other participants—the defence and the judge*

17–055   Prosecuting counsel has an obligation to assist the defence by the disclosure of certain evidence. The disclosure provisions are considered more fully elsewhere,[406] but in brief the prosecution must consider whether all witness statements in the possession of the prosecution have been properly served on the defence.[407]

---

[399] See the comments by Judge L.J. in *R v Lashley* [2005] EWCA Crim 2016 at para.13. Jurors involved in the Jubille Line case, interviewed in 2005, spoke of the utility of the opening speech in providing them with an important overview of the case. See S. Lloyd-Bostock, *Report on the Interviews with Jurors in the Jubilee Line Case* (2006), available at: *www.hmcpsi.gov.uk.*

[400] *Blackstone's* (2007), para.D.14.6.

[401] i.e. a question which by its form suggests the desired answer. "You saw the defendant take the jewellery and put it in his pocket, didn't you?"

[402] e.g. questions about previous inconsistent statements may not generally be put (unless the witness is hostile), nor questions impugning the witness's credit. Counsel must not vilify, insult or annoy any witness: *Code of Conduct*, para.5.10(e). For suggestion that counsel should adopt cognitive interviewing skills, see P. Davies, "Cognitive Interviewing" (1997) N.L.J. 1705. This allegedly produces better accounts because the story the witness tells is his own.

[403] That is it should be directed to an issue in the case or to the credit of a witness.

[404] *Blackstone's* (2007), para.F.6.1.

[405] See *Jolly v DPP* [2000] Crim. L.R. 471 for a summary of the position.

[406] See Ch.14.

[407] See *Standards in Criminal Cases*, paras 10.4(c) and (d).

The obligation to assist the judge is made clear in the Code of Conduct. Not only must counsel assist by arguments on point of law or procedure arising during the trial, but it is also "the duty of prosecuting counsel to assist the court at the conclusion of the summing-up by drawing attention to any apparent errors or omissions of fact or law".[408] Needless to say, this duty has to be discharged with considerable tact.

Influencing the court with regard to sentence is not part of the duties of prosecuting counsel, although the prosecution may now request that the Attorney-General seek a review by the Court of Appeal of a sentence believed to be unduly lenient.[409]

(b) Defence counsel

Counsel defending a client in a criminal case may face conflict between the duty to the court and the duty to the client. It may be asked how counsel can act as advocate for someone who is "obviously guilty", or put forward a defence or a mitigation which appears to be based on the slenderest of evidence. The answer given by the Bar Council is that, consistent with counsel's duty not knowingly to deceive or mislead the court,[410] every accused person has a right to have the prosecution case tested and their own case put. In a statement following the case of *R v McFadden*,[411] in which the trial judge had criticised counsel for wasting time, the Chairman of the Bar said[412]:

> "It is the duty of counsel when defending an accused on a criminal charge to present to the court, fearlessly and without regard to his personal interests, the defence of that accused. It is not his function to determine the truth or falsity of that defence, nor should he permit his personal opinion of that defence to influence his conduct of it. . . . Counsel also has a duty to the court and to the public. This duty includes the clear presentation of the issues and the avoidance of waste of time, repetition and prolixity. In the conduct of every case counsel must be mindful of this public responsibility."[413]

Counsel must " . . . endeavour to protect his client from conviction except by a competent tribunal and upon legally admissible evidence sufficient to support a conviction for the offence charged".[414] Counsel should "ensure that the defendant is never left unrepresented at any stage of his trial".[415] Counsel's opinion of the weight of evidence and the credibility of any defence being

17–056

---

[408] *Standards in Criminal Cases*, para.10.7.

[409] *ibid.* para.10.8.(b) As to the review of sentencing, see the Criminal Justice Act 1988, s.36.

[410] *Code of Conduct*, para.302.

[411] (1976) 62 Cr.App.R. 187.

[412] Melford Stevenson J. had taken a very dim view of the length of the trial in which the evidence had occupied over 30 days, and the closing speeches for the defence six-and-a-half days. There were seven defendants, but the judge thought that counsel had behaved improperly and took the unusual course of inviting the taxing master to look carefully at the fees allowed counsel on legal aid taxation.

[413] (1976) 62 Cr.App.R. 193. The complaints against defending counsel were investigated by the Professional Conduct Committee of the Bar, and rejected.

[414] *Standards in Criminal Cases*, para.11.1.

[415] *ibid.* para.15.2.1.

suggested by the client will obviously be factors in the advice which defence
counsel gives.

(i) Advising on plea and the accused's confession

17–057 It must be made clear to the accused that there is complete freedom of choice of
plea and that the accused has complete responsibility for it. In practice the advice
and attitude of defence counsel can be crucial, as the study by Baldwin and
McConville[416] demonstrates. For example, 48 per cent accused people gave as
their reason for changing their plea the advice that they had received from
counsel. It is difficult to offer advice which will inevitably carry great weight
whilst leaving the accused free to make up his or her mind. In 21 out of 121
studied cases there was evidence that the advice given was not fair or
proper.[417]

Counsel may give the accused an assessment of the strength of the prosecution
case and the likelihood of acquittal, the details of any plea arrangement which
has been or might be negotiated, the credibility of any defence which may be
advanced, and the dangers of attempting to discredit prosecution witnesses,
especially the police. If the accused is misled by counsel into pleading guilty (e.g.
where counsel assures the accused that such pleas will not affect other charges)
a fair trial is jeopardised. The court always has the discretion to allow a plea to
be withdrawn.[418]

Counsel must not "devise" facts for his client, e.g. by suggesting a defence
that is more plausible than that claimed.[419] Also important is counsel's attitude
and demeanour. If the accused is given the impression that counsel has no hope
or confidence of an acquittal or appears indifferent to the accused's protestations
of innocence, the pressure on the accused will be further increased.

The Court of Appeal, in considering defence counsel's obligations to advise a
client, has observed that if need be the advice may be in strong terms, but that
counsel must emphasise that the accused should only plead guilty if actually
guilty.[420] If defence counsel deprives the accused of the freedom of plea, a guilty
plea would be a nullity.[421] However, such cases are rare since the advice needs
to be couched in extreme terms to contravene the guidelines. If an innocent client
decides to plead guilty, counsel must continue to represent the client, "but only
after he has advised what the consequences will be and that what can be
submitted in mitigation can only be on the basis that the client is guilty".[422]

Sanders and Young suggest that the barrister may not always be acting in the
best interests of her or his client. This, they suggest, is because of the barrister's
obligation to the court and the administration of justice as well as to the client
(although this is not as significant as prosecution counsel's responsibilities), and
the low standard fees for legal aid work encourage the barrister to seek late guilty
pleas. Barristers are under considerable pressure of work often receiving briefs
shortly before seeing the client so they are often "ill-prepared and ill-disposed to

---

[416] *Negotiated Justice* (1977), Ch.3.
[417] See also Sanders and Young (2007), pp.413–421.
[418] *R v W (AG)* [1999] Crim. L.R. 87.
[419] See *Written Standards*, para.5.8. See A. Hutchinson, "The Perjury Problem" (2001) 151 N.L.J.
160.
[420] *R v Turner* [1970] 2 Q.B. 321 at 326. See A. Ashworth and M. Blake, "Some Ethical Issues in
Prosecuting and Defending Criminal Cases" [1998] Crim. L.R. 16 at 25.
[421] *R v Peace* [1976] Crim. L.R. 119; *R v Inns* (1975) 60 Cr.App.R. 231.
[422] *Standards in Criminal Cases*, para.11.5(a).

fight on a defendant's behalf", and many criminal barristers are not of particularly high quality.[423]

Counsel may discover that the client is guilty of the offence charged. This may emerge from the client in clear terms in the form of a confession or as a result of inconsistent statements or from supposition on the part of counsel. A conflict then arises between the duty to the client and the duty to the court. If the discovery is based upon inconsistent statements or counsel's suspicions or speculations, no general guidance is provided by the Code of Conduct since it all depends on the actual circumstances of the particular case.[424] If the discovery is based upon a confession, it is made clear that counsel is not prevented from appearing in the accused's defence, nor does it release counsel from "his imperative duty to do all that he honourably can for his client".[425] However, a confession limits what counsel may do. Counsel "must not assert as true that which he knows to be false". He may not connive at, much less attempt to substantiate, a fraud.[426] Counsel may not suggest that someone else committed the crime or call any evidence known to be false. Counsel may take objections to the competency of the court, to the form of the indictment, to the admissibility of evidence and to the evidence admitted. "In other words, a barrister must not . . . set up an affirmative case inconsistent with the confession made to him."[427] Further, since the issue in a criminal trial is whether or not the accused is guilty and the burden of proof lies on the prosecution, counsel may test the prosecution evidence and may argue that the case against the accused has not been established.[428]

(ii) Correcting defects

The conflict between the duty to the client and the duty to the court may also arise **17–058** with regard to defence counsel's obligations in respect of procedural error, or factual or legal errors made by the court, not noticed by the prosecution. One view, proceeding partly from the conception of the trial as a game in which the underdog (the accused) is entitled to the benefit of any errors, is that defence counsel is under no obligation to correct the judge. The Code of Conduct, however, requires counsel to bring all authorities, (that is all relevant statutes and cases, including those unfavourable to the defence) and any procedural irregularity to the attention of the court before the summing up has begun.[429] It would also appear that the Criminal Procedure Rules 2005 demand a less adversarial approach. In *Malcolm*, the court, taking the Rules into account stated, "Criminal trials are no longer to be treated as a game . . . It is the duty of the defence to make its defence and the issues it raises clear to the prosecution and to the court

---

[423] Sanders and Young (2007), pp.417–425. In the USA, questions have been raised on numerous occasions about the standard of advocacy and representation afforded to indigent defendants. See R. E. Priehs, "Appointed Counsel for Indigent Criminal Appellants: Does Compensation Influence Effort?" (1999) The Justice System Journal 73.

[424] *Standards in Criminal Cases* para.12.6.

[425] *ibid.* para.12.2. It is also important to bear in mind: "(a) that every punishable crime is a breach of common or statute law committed by a person of sound mind and understanding; (b) that the issue in a criminal trial is always whether the defendant is guilty of the offence charged, never whether he is innocent; (c) that the burden of proof rests on the prosecution."

[426] *ibid.* para.12.3.

[427] *ibid.* para.12.4.

[428] *ibid.* para.12.5.

[429] *Code of Conduct*, para.708(c).

at an early stage".[430] Points of procedural irregularity must not be reserved so as to form the basis of an appeal.[431]

(iii) *The conduct of the defence*

17–059   If, at the end of the prosecution presentation, defence counsel believes that a case has not been established against the accused, a submission of no case to answer may be made which, if successful, results in the acquittal of the accused. The judge must decide whether or not the prosecution have adduced evidence on which a jury, properly directed, could convict in accordance with the law.[432] Ordered acquittals occur where the judge orders an acquittal before the trial commences. Directed acquittals are those in which the judge directs the jury to acquit once the trial has formally commenced.

If the CPS considers with due care whether or not to prosecute there should be relatively few successful submissions of no case unless, for example, the prosecution witnesses fail to appear or do not support the case for the prosecution. In the years since the CPS was introduced the number of directed acquittals in the Crown Court increased dramatically, and it is claimed that most of these (70–80 per cent) non-jury acquittals were foreseeable at an early stage.[433] This has called into question the effectiveness of the CPS function of reviewing charges,[434] and it might be expected that fewer cases will lead to acquittals in this way now that the CPS are responsible for determining the charge in the majority of cases.

In his study of non-jury acquittals, Baldwin[435] discovered that 44 per cent of ordered acquittals were attributable to the failure of a witness to attend or because the witness retracted the statement; 3.2 per cent were due to witnesses proving untrustworthy prior to trial; 15.9 per cent were as a result of the judge concluding that there was no realistic prospect of conviction or that the evidence was insufficient; 14.3 per cent were attributable to the successful conviction of others in the case; 11.1 per cent due to a legal problem or questions about the conduct of the investigation. Directed acquittals occurred usually where a key witness had not come up to proof (34 per cent) or with other evidential problems (32 per cent) or insufficient evidence (12 per cent). Baldwin concluded that a lack of experience in CPS workers and their working very closely with the police were very important reasons for the CPS pursuing charges that were rejected at trial. These pressures flow in part from a lack of true independence,[436] and from internal inadequacies in CPS funding and management. As stated above, the statutory charging scheme whereby it is now the responsibility of the CPS to determine the relevant charge ought to alleviate this problem somewhat. Further reasons for the

---

[430] *Malcolm v DPP* [2007] EWHC 363, at para.31.
[431] *ibid.* para.708(d).
[432] *R v Galbraith* [1981] 1 W.L.R. 1039.
[433] See J. Baldwin, "Understanding Judge Ordered and Directed Acquittals" [1997] Crim. L.R. 536.
[434] See further A. Ashworth, "Developments in the Public Prosecutor's Office in England and Wales" (2000) Eur. J. of Crime, Criminal Law and Criminal Justice, pp.257–275. See also A. Hoyano, L. Hoyano, G. Davis and S. Goldie, "A Study of the Impact of the Revised Code for Crown Prosecutors" [1997] Crim. L.R. 556.
[435] J. Baldwin [1997].
[436] Sanders and Young (2007), pp.496–501.

high proportion of directed/ordered acquittals include the unwillingness of counsel to drop a case[437] and in many cases the very late briefing of counsel leaving no real opportunity for them to advise the CPS to discontinue a weak case.

The problem is one that is unlikely ever to be conclusively resolved since as Baldwin observed, the "task of establishing whether there is a realistic prospect of conviction is a largely subjective evaluation".[438]

If the case proceeds, the formal procedure for the defence will be the same as for the prosecution, with an opening speech, witnesses and a closing speech. Counsel is not restricted to commenting only on the evidence led, but should not ask the jury to make a recommendation of mercy.[439]

(iv) *After the verdict*

Defence counsel, after a plea or verdict of guilty, will usually make a plea in mitigation of sentence on behalf of the client. As favourable a view as possible is put on the client's circumstances and suggestions may be made as to why particular sentences would or would not be appropriate. Save in exceptional circumstances, it is defence counsel's duty to see the client after conviction and sentence.[440] Counsel may give initial advice on appeal or the existence of grounds of appeal.[441]   **17–060**

5. WITNESSES

In most contested trials, witness evidence will be called by the prosecution and the defence.[442] People who might be witnesses may be unwilling to appear or there may be some doubt about their capacity to give evidence. Whether a witness satisfies the legal requirements to give evidence (i.e. is a "competent" witness) is a matter of law for the judge. Prosecuting and defence counsel exercise considerable discretion in who they will call. They must bear in mind not only the legal requirements but also the practical consideration that there is no point in calling someone who will not "come up to proof", that is, someone who will not be able to provide a convincing and consistent story in court, particularly under cross-examination. In certain cases it may be necessary to call expert witnesses. Counsel is permitted to communicate with witnesses whom he expects to call. In the case of the defendant, character and expert witnesses, counsel may interview them.[443] In the case of other witnesses the communication is limited to explaining the court's procedure and putting the witness at ease.[444] Counsel must not coach any witness as to the substance of his evidence or the manner in which to testify.[445]   **17–061**

---

[437] For a response to Baldwin's article see P. Lewis, "The CPS and Acquittals by Judge: Finding the Balance" [1997] Crim. L.R. 653.

[438] Baldwin [1997], p.540.

[439] *R v Black* (1964) 48 Cr.App.R. 52.

[440] *Standards in Criminal Cases*, para.17.2.

[441] As to appeals in criminal cases, See Ch.18.

[442] Some cases, e.g. can be proved on scientific evidence alone.

[443] *Written Standards*, para.6.3.2.

[444] *ibid.* para.6.1.3.

[445] See *Momodou (Practice Note)* [2005] 1 W.L.R. 3442.

(a) Competence of witnesses

17–062   The primary question for determining "competence" is whether a person will be capable of giving intelligible evidence. Under s.53(3) of the Youth Justice and Criminal Evidence Act 1999 "all persons are (whatever their age) competent to give evidence". The crucial issue is whether the witness is able to give intelligible testimony. Issues of competence may arise, e.g. where the witness is a child or someone suffering from a mental disorder. Where there is some doubt, the matter should be raised before the witness begins testifying.[446]

The 1999 Act places the burden on a party calling a witness to satisfy the judge (on the balance of probabilities) that the witness will be able to give intelligible evidence. In determining this question, in the absence of the jury, the judge should have regard to any special measures or directions that may be available to the witness (e.g. live link TV, communication aids, etc.), and may receive expert evidence if necessary.[447]

"Competence" also raises potential problems whether the accused and the accused's spouse can testify. The accused has been allowed to give evidence on his or her own behalf since the Criminal Evidence Act 1898,[448] but a spouse only became generally competent for the prosecution by virtue of s.80 of the PACE 1984.[449]

The accused is not competent for the prosecution. A co-accused may give evidence for the prosecution if he has ceased to be on trial—i.e. he has pleaded guilty, or has been acquitted or a *nolle prosequi* has been entered by the Attorney-General.

(b) Compellability of witnesses

17–063   Most people can be compelled to be witnesses, with the exception of the accused and the accused's spouse. However, the accused's spouse is compellable on behalf of the accused generally,[450] and for the prosecution[451] and co-accused in respect of specified offences. There are many other miscellaneous categories of individuals over whom special claims of incompellability may arise (e.g diplomats, judges). Once a witness is compellable, he or she must answer questions posed in the proceedings, and a failure to do so is a contempt of court.[452]

---

[446] See Youth Justice and Criminal Evidence Act 1999, ss.53–56 on the procedure for competence. Expert evidence may be necessary, especially where the issue is whether a mentally ill person can given intelligible testimony. See *R v Deakin* [1994] 4 All E.R. 769; *R v Barratt* [1996] Crim. L.R. 495.

[447] s.54(5)

[448] s.1. The accused's spouse has been competent for the defence since the 1898 Act, see PACE, s.80, as amended by the Youth Justice and Criminal Evidence Act 1999, s.53.

[449] PACE, s.80 as amended. He or she is not competent if a co-accused is charged in the proceedings. As to the many difficulties in interpreting the section regarding both the competence and compellability of spouses, see P. Creighton, "Spouse Competence and Compellability" [1990] Crim. L.R. 34. This applies to married couples and civil partners: Civil Partnership Act 2004 s.84(1), but not cohabitees: *Pearce* [2002] 1 W.L.R. 1553.

[450] PACE, s.80(2A). See J. R. Spencer, "Spouses as Witnesses: Back to Brighton Rock?" [2003] C.L.J. 250.

[451] s.80(2A).

[452] See, e.g. *R v Bird* (1997) 161 J.P. 96; *R v Maguire* [1996] Crim. L.R. 833.

(c) Oaths

As a general rule, the oral testimony of every witness must be given on oath.[453]   **17–064**
Witnesses who do not wish to testify on a religious text may affirm instead.
Practical advice on which holy books are used for different religious and the way
in which religions may wish to, e.g. wash, cover heads, remove shoes is provided
to the judiciary.[454] Prior to the Youth Justice and Criminal Evidence Act 1999
children could only give evidence unsworn. Under the 1999 Act, all those aged
under 14 give unsworn evidence. Witnesses over that age may give sworn or
unsworn evidence. Section 55(2) provides that a witness who has a sufficient
"appreciation of the solemnity of the occasion" should give sworn evidence.
There have been suggestions that the jury attaches little weight to the witness
taking oath.

(d) Giving evidence

A witness gives evidence initially in response to questions from counsel by   **17–065**
whom he or she was called. "Leading" questions must be avoided. The witness
is then available to counsel for the other side for cross-examination, where the
object will be to elicit evidence favourable to the cross-examiner's case and to
discredit unfavourable evidence. The judge has the power to ask questions of a
witness, but should exercise caution in doing so, particularly with the defendant
as a witness. Finally, counsel who called the witness is entitled to re-examine the
witness, but must not raise any new issues.[455]

   A witness appearing at trial to give their remembered account of events that
may have occurred many months ago may seem like an unlikely way to get the
best evidence of what happened. The significance placed on such a procedure
rather than on documentary evidence illustrates the importance of the principle of
orality which still underpins the English criminal trial: all evidence is best
delivered orally by the person with direct knowledge of events. This pays little
heed to the evidence from psychological research which reveals how fragile are
witness' memories, how suggestible they are in questioning and how weak are
juror's perceptions/judgments based on witness demeanour.[456] Nor does it pay
adequate attention to the fact that the witness will be allowed to read earlier
witness statements in order to refresh his/her memory before going into the
witness box. The jury is surely misled if they think that the witness is really
recalling details from months before.

   Giving evidence in court is a trying experience.[457] Consequently, counsel has
to be aware of the possibility of the witness not coming up to proof, i.e. the
capacity of the witness not only to retell the story convincingly when responding
to examination-in-chief, but also to be able to stick to that story when subject to
cross-examination.

---

[453] On the form and procedure of the administration of the oath, see Oaths Act 1978.
[454] See *R v Mehrban* [2002] Crim. L.R. 439.
[455] *R v Harman* [1985] Crim. L.R. 326.
[456] See G. Millar and J. Burgoon, "Factors Affecting Assessments of Witness Credibility" in L. Kerr
    and R. Bray (eds), *The Psychology of the Courtroom* (1982); Jeremy A. Blumenthal, "A Wipe of
    the Hands. A Lick of the Lips: The Validity of Demeanor Evidence in Assessing Witness
    Credibility" (1993) 72 Nebraska Law Review 1157; M. Stone, "Instant Lie Detection: Demean-
    our and Credibility in Criminal Trials" [1991] Crim. L.R. 821.
[457] See Royal Commission on Criminal Justice, *Report* Cm. 2263 (1993), p.128.

In recent years much has been done to improve the support and guidance provided to those who are to give evidence. The Court of Appeal has emphasised that whilst familiarising witnesses with the court is legitimate it must be carefully regulated to ensure it does not overstep the boundary and become witness "coaching" into how they ought to testify.[458]

The Witness Service[459] provides help to all witnesses in the Crown Court ensuring that the witness has advance information and by answering non-legal questions. Introduced in 1996, the Service has been acknowledged anecdotally to play a significant role in reducing the ordeal of appearing as a witness. However, independent academic research has suggested that the Service does "little to ameliorate" the unpleasant experience of giving evidence in a Crown Court.[460] Research findings[461] reveal that 76 per cent of witnesses were very or fairly satisfied with their overall treatment in the criminal justice system. The witnesses' satisfaction with court officials was high. Moreover, levels of satisfaction were strongly related to provision of information to witness.[462] Almost 20 per cent of witnesses felt intimidated by the process and 25 per cent by an individual person (the figure rose to 57 per cent with child witnesses).[463] Thirty-nine per cent of witnesses said they would not be happy to be a witness again.[464]

For some witnesses, the trauma of a court appearance will be particularly severe. Part II of the Youth Justice and Criminal Evidence Act 1999 contains special measures that may be ordered by the judge to assist witnesses. The Act categorises those witnesses who are eligible by reason of age (under 17) or incapacity, or fear or distress. Further special protection is afforded to child witnesses and those giving evidence in sexual and other specified cases. In those cases in which the special measures are not automatic, the judge must assess which of the special measures are to be ordered, focusing on the extent to which they might enhance the *quality* of the witnesses' evidence. The measures that can be ordered include the use of screens to shield the witness (s.23), the use of live link television (s.24) the possibility of giving evidence in a private chamber (s.25), the removal of wigs and gowns (s.26), the use of video-recorded evidence-in-chief (s.27) and cross-examination recorded on video before the trial (s.28), the use of intermediaries to communicate with witnesses or conduct the examination (s.29) and other aids to communication. The aim of the Act is to maximise the opportunity for all witnesses who can give an intelligible account to give the best account possible.[465] The CJA 2003 will, when the relevant sections come into force, permit the video recording of an interview with a witness other than

---

[458] *R v Momodou (Practice Note)* [2005] 1 W.L.R. 3442; [2005] Crim. L.R. 588.

[459] See: *www.victimsupport.org.uk.*

[460] A. Riding, "The Crown Court Witness Service: Little Help in the Witness Box" (1999) 38 Howard Jnl 411.

[461] E. Whitehead, *Key Findings from the Witness Satisfaction Survey 2000* (HORSD No.133, 2001).

[462] 80% of prosecution witnesses and 72% of defence witnesses received helpful information.

[463] 42% of those reported the incident to police.

[464] 87% were satisfied with the CPS; 67% with the defence; and an impressive 95% with the judge. Most concerned were women (68%) and children (69%). Problems identified by witnesses included delay in court (17% waited four hours; 37% in magistrates' courts waited at least one hour). The separation of defence and prosecution witnesses in waiting was preferred, and treatment in cross-examination was very influential in the overall satisfaction ratings. Witness Services exist in Crown Court centres and in 1997/98 offered support to 120,550 people: *Digest IV*, p.17.

[465] On the increased use of IT in court rooms to facilitate the giving of evidence and its comprehension by the jury see Auld, Ch.11.

the accused to be admitted as evidence-in-chief.[466] Furthermore, evidence from witnesses other than the accused will be permitted in certain circumstances to provide evidence via a "live link".[467]

In every case, the witness will be subjected to examination not only regarding his or her testimony relating to the facts in issue in the trial on which he or she has given evidence-in-chief, but also on his or her credibility. In particular, questioning as to previous convictions, bias or a general reputation for untruthfulness will be likely. In recent years concerns have arisen in a number of trials with the payments to witnesses by the media.[468] These matters can be explored in cross-examination, but there is a danger that the witness will be so tainted as to cause the trial to be unfair.

All such questioning must comply with the Code of Conduct of the Bar, by which each barrister is bound to show courtesy and respect to witnesses. The judge can also question the witnesses, but this must be done cautiously.

(e) Expert witnesses

The function of an expert witness in a criminal trial is to assist the jury in matters **17–066** outside the jury's competence or normal knowledge.[469] For example an expert may prove, from scientific tests, that the accused has handled explosives[470] or, from DNA testing, that the accused had sexual intercourse with the victim,[471] or, from examining a vehicle, that a road traffic accident was caused by brake failure. Expert evidence will not be admitted to resolve a question on which the jury can bring their own experience to bear, for example on a defence of provocation, the effect on an ordinary man of discovering that his girlfriend was pregnant by another man,[472] on a prosecution for publishing an obscene book, the effect it may have on an ordinary person likely to read it.[473] There is no limit to

---

[466] CJA 2003, s.137.

[467] CJA 2003, s.51.

[468] see *R v West* (1996) 2 Cr.App.R. 374. Lord Chancellor's Department Consultation Paper, *Payments to Witnesses: A proposed criminal offence of making, or agreeing to make, or receiving, payments to witnesses or potential witnesses in criminal proceedings* (2002); see also, *The Response to the Consultation Paper* (2003), both available at *www.dca.gov.uk*.

[469] See *R v Turner* [1975] Q.B. 834. See generally, M. Redmayne, *Expert Evidence and Criminal Justice* (2000). As to the work of such experts, see I. R. Freckleton, *The Trial of the Expert* (1987); D. J. Gee, "The Expert Witness in the Criminal Trial" [1987] Crim. L.R. 307; P. Roberts and C. Willmore, *The Role of Forensic Science Evidence in Criminal Proceedings* (RCCJ Research Study No.11 1993); RCCJ Report, Ch.9; R. Stockdale and C. Walker, "Forensic Evidence" in C. Walker and K. Starmer (eds), *Justice in Error* (1993) and C. Walker and R. Stockdale, "Forensic Evidence" in C. Walker and K. Starmer (eds), *Miscarriges of Justice: A Review of Justice in Error* (1999).

[470] Care must, of course, be taken in what tests are used and what they establish and in presenting the evidence accurately, reliably, fairly and credibly. Failure in these respects was part of the reason for the interim report on the Maguire case concluding that their convictions for taking part in IRA explosions were unsafe, see Sir John May, *Interim Report on the Maguire Case* (1990). The Court of Appeal quashed the convictions.

[471] See K. F. Kelly, J. J. Rankin and R. C. Wink, "Method and Application of DNA Finger-printing: A Guide for the Non-Scientist" [1987] Crim. L.R. 105; R. M. White and J. J. D. Greenwood, "DNA Fingerprinting and the Law" (1988) 51 M.L.R. 145; and T. Burke *et al.* (eds), *DNA Fingerprinting: Approval and Applications* (1991). On the dangers of the use of the prosecutor's fallacy in DNA evidence see *R v Doheny* [1997] Crim. L.R. 669. See generally, M. Krawczak, *DNA Fingerprinting* (2nd edn, 1998).

[472] See *R v Turner* [1975] Q.B. 834.

[473] See *R v Anderson* [1972] 1 Q.B. 304. By contrast, if the question was the effect a publication would have on a child, expert evidence might be admissible, see *DPP v A & BC Chewing Gum Ltd* [1968] 1 Q.B. 159.

the subjects on which the courts are prepared to receive expert evidence.[474] The jury are not bound by the views of the expert.[475]

The precise definition of who constitutes an "expert" remains unclear. The traditional rule is that an expert is one proved to the satisfaction of the court to have such qualification by reason of study or experience: *R v Silverlock*.[476] The courts have taken an overly generous attitude to who might qualify as an expert, with "ad hoc" experts being accepted where their expertise derived from the investigation into the case, e.g. where a police officer had viewed a film repeatedly, he was treated as an expert witness on the events.[477] Similarly, confusion remains over the scope of expert evidence, with a lack of precise definition of which matters fall outside the knowledge and experience of the jury. The present test tends to lead to an inquiry into whether the subject matter is abnormal or not, when a more useful test might be to question whether the evidence would be helpful to the jury irrespective of their understanding of the subject matter.[478] There are very few additional safeguards against the English courts admitting controversial novel forms of evidence (e.g. facial mapping, video-super imposition,[479] voice identification evidence,[480] ear prints,[481] etc). This is in stark contrast to most other jurisdictions where the judiciary undertake a gatekeeping function to prevent evidence of dubious relevance or reliability from being admitted. In particular, the US Supreme Court has imposed an obligation that any novel scientific or technical evidence must be demonstrated to be reliable, and in answering that question the court will consider the falsifiability of the technique or science in question, whether it has been subjected to peer review and/or publication, whether the technique or science has a known potential error rate, to what extent the discipline is subject to standards and controls, and whether there is support of a body of the scientific community for the technique.[482]

Problems with forensic science and other expert evidence have been partly to blame for some of the recently identified miscarriages of justice in England and Wales. The Royal Commission on Criminal Justice reporting in 1993 made a number of recommendations to address some of the identified problems. A major problem had been that the forensic laboratory services have been available largely only to the prosecution and have become prosecution-minded, such that there can be a failure to exercise true scientific objectivity in dealing with the evidence and a failure to pass on information and interpretations of value to the defence rather than the prosecution.[483] In consequence, the Royal Commission recommended that the forensic science facilities should become available to the

---

[474] *R v Robb* (1991) Cr.App.R. 161.

[475] *R v Stockwell* (1993) 97 Cr.App.R. 260.

[476] [1894] 2 Q.B. 766.

[477] *R v Clare and Peach* [1995] 2 Cr.App.R. 333.

[478] See generally, M. Redmayne, *Expert Evidence and Criminal Justice* (2000).

[479] *R v Clark* [1995] 2 Cr.App.R. 425; *Stockwell* (1993) 97 Cr.App.R. 260; *R v Robb* (1991) 93 Cr.App.R. 161.

[480] D. Ormerod, "Sounds Familiar? Voice Identification Evidence" [2001] Crim. L.R. 595; D. Ormerod, "Sounding Out Expert Voice Identification" [2002] Crim. L.R. 771.

[481] *R v Kempster* [2003] All E.R (D) 215; *R v Dallagher* [2003] 1 Cr.App.R. 195.

[482] *Daubert v Merrett Dow* 125 R. v. Ed. 2d. 469 (1993). For discussion see Slovenko (1998) 2 E. & P. 190; Graham (1998) 2 E. & P. 211. And see generally, Redmayne (2000), and S. J. Odgers and J. T. Richardson "Keeping Bad Science Out Of The Courtroom—Changes in American and Australian Expert Evidence Law" (1995) U.N.S.W. Law Journal.

[483] See J. Rozenberg, "Miscarriages of Justice" in E. Stockdale and S. Casale (eds), *Criminal Justice Under Stress* (1992) and P. Roberts and C. Willmore (1993).

defence as well as the prosecution.[484] The efficacy of the scheme depends upon legal aid being available for the purpose.[485] Quality control was also obviously a contributory factor to the errors in earlier cases, and the Royal Commission made a raft of proposals intended to address this problem.[486] At the end of the day, of course, quality control relies upon the individuals wishing and being able to act independently and honestly and not wishing to assist in "case construction" rather than case assessment.

6. THE ROLE OF THE JUDGE[487]

"The Judge is not an advocate. Under the English and Welsh system of criminal **17–067** trials he is more like the umpire at a cricket match, he is certainly not the bowler whose business it is to try to get the batsman out."[488] The characterisation of the judge as the umpire or referee in our adversarial system is not entirely appropriate in the context of the trial on indictment.[489] It is true that the judge should apply the rules, allow counsel to present the case without undue hindrance, not intervene unduly and that ultimately the decision on matters of fact belongs to the jury. However, it is equally true that the judge exercises a very considerable discretion in respect of many aspects of the trial and it is reasonably clear that the way in which that discretion is exercised may have a significant bearing on the outcome. Indeed, in certain circumstances, the judge's ruling will determine the case. The judge's impartiality must, of course, be beyond doubt.[490] The Human Rights Act 1998 and the increased awareness of the ECHR[491] that it has engendered has served to underline the significance of impartiality. The independence of members of the judiciary was also brought sharply into focus in the course of the *Pinochet* litigation.[492]

In considering the extent of the judge's discretion and the possible effects of its exercise we should bear in mind the relationship between judge and jury.

In simple terms, the separation of functions between the judge and the jury is that the judge is to deal with matters of law and the jury with matters of fact. It is the judge's function to determine certain procedural matters; to consider any plea-bargaining; to decide upon the admissibility of evidence; to sum up on the law and the evidence for the benefit of the jury; and to pass sentence. It will be

---

[484] RCCJ Report, p.149.

[485] See Sanders and Young (2007), p.314

[486] RCCJ Report, Ch.9.

[487] See *Jones v National Coal Board* [1957] 2 Q.B. 55, discussed by Lord Denning in *The Due Process of Law* (1980), pp.58–62. See P. Devlin, *The Judge* (1979) and, for a unique account by the judge of a criminal trial, P. Devlin, *Easing the Passing* (1985). See also R. Pattenden (1990); A. Samuels, "Judicial Misconduct and the Criminal Trial" [1982] Crim. L.R. 221; J. Jackson, "Judicial Responsibility in Criminal Proceedings" (1997) C.L.P. 59; C. Walker in Walker and Starmer (1999).

[488] *per* Cumming-Bruce L.J. in *R v Gunning*, July 7, 1980, unreported.

[489] See M. E. Frankel, "The Search for the Truth: An Umpireal View" (1975) 123 U. Penn. L.R. 1031.

[490] The ECtHR has emphasised the importance of the impartiality of the judiciary. See *Castillo Algar v Spain* (2000) 30 E.H.R.R. 827.

[491] The ECHR jurisprudence on impartiality is contained in number of cases, principal ones being *Piersack v Belgium* (1983) 5 E.H.R.R. 169; *Le Compte v Belgium* 4 (1982) E.H.R.R. 1.

[492] *R v Bow St. Magistrates' Court, Ex p. Pinochet Ugarte (No.2)* [1999] 1 All E.R. 577 and see *Locabail v Bayfield Properties* [2000] Q.B. 45. See generally above.

seen that the distinction between matters of law and matters of fact is often blurred, and that the judge, in any case, has considerable influence in the determination of matters of fact.

Whilst the judge has a significant impact in some areas, in other areas, he or she has very little influence. For example, in relation to plea-bargaining, the judge is not a key player, and yet it might be thought that greater judicial involvement would be more likely to protect the interests of the defendant, as well as paying adequate respect to the administration of justice. There is clearly a dilemma in considering to what extent to involve the judge in such matters. At the same time, there is a clear desire to see jury involvement, although their role in the criminal justice system is in fact minimal. There does not appear to be a public desire to see judicially controlled criminal justice, if only because of suspicions about what judges might do. Set against this is the ability of the judge to exercise independent judgment. A further dimension to this debate was added by the Human Rights Act 1998 whereby the judiciary are more specifically empowered as the guardians of human rights. Although they do not have the power to strike down legislation as incompatible with the ECHR, they are capable of reading down legislation, and in some cases this has involved such extensive reinterpretation as to amount to judicial legislating, even in relation to Acts passed after the Human Rights Act 1998.[493]

The Criminal Procedure Rules 2005[494] arguably reflect a lack of confidence in the parties' ability adequately to progress a case.[495] The Rules have laid down explicit case management powers upon the court. The "overriding objective" of the new code[496] is that cases be dealt with justly, and the court must seek this objective by "actively managing the case".[497] This includes early identification of the issues and the setting of the timetable. The danger of making such changes is that the delicate balance necessitated within an adversarial approach is affected without due consideration given to whether it has had an inappropriate effect upon the rights of the defendant.

(a) Procedural matters

17–068   From the outset, the judge has control over the progress of the trial and the administrative and procedural problems that may arise. The judge must decide questions relating to the form of the indictment and any necessary amendment to it; the taking of the plea from the accused and its acceptability; whether a special plea of *autrefois acquit* or *autrefois convict* has been successfully raised by the accused; whether to stay proceedings for abuse; the determination of preliminary

---

[493] See, e.g. the decision of the HL in *R v A* [2001] U.K.H.L. 25. See also *Ghaidan v Godin-Mendoza* [2004] U.K.H.L. 30; A. Kavanagh "Statutory Interpretation and the Human Rights Act After Anderson: A More Contextual Approach" [2004] P.L. 537.

[494] SI 2005/384.

[495] See, RCCJ Report (1993), p.142: The Commission recommended that "wherever practicable in complex cases judges should take on responsibility for managing the progress of a case, securing its passage through the various stages of pre-trial discussion to preparatory hearing and trial and making sure that the parties have fulfilled their obligations both to each other and to the court".

[496] CPR, r.1.1.

[497] *ibid.* r.3.2.1. See also *R v Jisl* [2004] All E.R. (D) 31.

points raised by counsel; and the desirability of separate trials.[498] Whilst these may be classed as procedural questions, their importance should not be underestimated. In some cases the determination of the procedural point may settle the whole issue.

The empanelling and swearing of the jury is subject to judicial control. The judge will settle any question over challenges. Once sworn, with the case proceeding, the jury may be discharged by the judge for a variety of reasons. The effect of discharging the jury is not to acquit the accused—he or she may be remanded for a second trial.[499]

It is also the judge's responsibility to maintain order in court. The judge has powers of punishment for contempt where there is misbehaviour.[500] Similarly, the judge has the power to protect the proceedings from publicity that would inhibit a fair trial.

Although counsel for the prosecution and the defence must conduct their respective cases in accordance with the Code of Conduct, the judge has a significant role in controlling the questioning of witnesses by counsel[501] and in restraining counsel from improper practices. Control should be discreet and the judge must resist the temptation to take over the questioning or to criticise counsel's conduct to such an extent that the jury might thereby be prejudiced.[502] The judge must be, and be seen to be, scrupulously fair.[503] Judicial interruptions to cross-examination of the defence may result in an unfair trial if they deprive the accused of a chance to put his or her case and/ or otherwise give an appearance of bias.[504]

---

[498] The practice is to join several charges together on one indictment where they are founded on the same facts or form part of a series of offences of the same or similar character and so have one trial: Indictment Rules 1971, r.9. See C. Yates, "How Many Counts to an Indictment?" [1976] Crim. L.R. 428.

[499] *R v Randall* [1960] Crim. L.R. 435. In this case the jury was discharged after returning verdicts of not guilty, which were then stated to be majority verdicts. (Majority verdicts were not at that time acceptable.) The plea of *autrefois acquit* at the second trial was rejected.

[500] There is a summary power to punish contempts "in the face of the court" which exists to maintain the dignity and authority of the judge and to ensure a fair trial and which applies in a magistrates' court: Contempt of Court Act 1981, s.12. See *Balogh v Crown Court at St Albans* [1975] 1 Q.B. 73, discussed in Lord Denning, *The Due Process of Law* (1980), pp.12–18. The accused was apprehended before he livened up court proceedings by introducing "laughing gas" into the ventilating system at St Albans Crown Court. See also, *Morris v Crown Office* [1970] 2 Q.B. 114 (group of students breaking up a libel trial); *R v Aquarius* [1974] Crim. L.R. 373 (disruptive behaviour of defendant); *R v Logan* [1974] Crim. L.R. 609 (outburst by defendant after sentence); *Lecointe v Courts Administrator of the Central Criminal Court* (1973, unreported) (distribution of leaflets at the Old Bailey inciting people to picket the court); *R v Powell* (1994) 98 Cr.App.R. 224 (member of public wolf-whistled at a female juror from the public gallery). See generally H. Fenwick and G. Phillipson, *Media Freedom Under the Human Rights Act* (2006) Pt II. Judge Pickles sentenced a witness to five days imprisonment for her failure to give evidence against her ex-boyfriend, the Court of Appeal quashed the finding of contempt because the trial was not fair, but made clear that a person who refuses without adequate excuse to give evidence to the court may be punished, which will usually mean imprisonment: *R v Renshaw* [1989] Crim. L.R. 811.

[501] The line of questioning must be relevant and material and witnesses should be treated courteously.

[502] *R v McFadden* (1976) 62 Cr.App.R. 187, and see Samuels (1982), p.223.

[503] It is not appropriate to indicate to counsel that the accused's hope of acquittal is almost gone: *R v Alves* [1996] Crim. L.R. 599. See recently *Randell v the Queen* [2002] U.K.P.C. 19. See also *R v Lashley* [2005] EWCA Crim 2016 in which the trial judge had shown inappropriate personal animosity towards defence counsel.

[504] See, e.g. *R v Frixou* [1998] Crim. L.R. 352 where the judge asked the accused 106 of the total 189 questions!

(b) Plea bargaining

17–069 Following the case of *Turner*,[505] a principle was established whereby the judge should only give an advance indication as to the *type* of sentence that the defendant might face, and should not engage in sentence bargaining. It was widely recognised that this principle was regularly ignored by barristers and judges meeting in advance of, or during the trial to bargain over the sentence.[506] The Runciman Commission recommended[507] that the practice be made legitimate but this was not acted upon. In 2005, the Court of Appeal in *Goodyear*[508] looked beyond the *Turner* principle and formally recognised sentence bargaining.

The defendant, usually at the plea and case management hearing, can seek an indication as to sentence but that indication reflects the situation at the time and is not binding if the defendant does not plead guilty. The judge should indicate the maximum sentence should a guilty plea follow, but should not go further in suggesting what the sentence would be for a contested trial. However, it remains open for a judge to indicate that the sentence will be unaffected by the plea. Any indication binds the judge. Further, the defendant must be aware that the sentence might be the subject of an appeal should it be considered to be too lenient. Sanders and Young argue that the *Goodyear* principles are open ended and contradictory and as such do not provide a stable framework.[509]

The rules ultimately encourage guilty pleas and whilst the defendant should be told that he must only plead guilty if he is so, it must be recognised that this does not always reflect reality.[510]

(c) Admissibility of evidence

17–070 One of the functions of the trial judge is to control the input of material upon which the jury will ultimately base its decision. This the judge does by applying the complex body of rules that make up the law of evidence.[511]

(i) *Relevance and admissibility*

17–071 The evidence a jury hears must be both relevant and admissible. Evidence is relevant if it is logically probative or disprobative of some matter that requires proof, i.e. if it makes that matter more or less probable.[512] Thus when a person is accused of murder it is relevant to prove that he or she had a motive to kill the victim, that he or she was seen in possession of the murder weapon, and that he or she was unwilling to account for his or her movements at the time the murder was committed. None of these matters would, standing alone, be likely to establish beyond reasonable doubt that the accused committed the offence, but the proof of each tends to render guilt more probable, which is all that is required.

---

[505] *R v Turner* [1970] 2 W.L.R. 1093.
[506] For example, see: *R v Nazham* [2004] EWCA Crim 491.
[507] RCCJ (1993) p.112.
[508] *R v Goodyear* [2005] 3 All E.R. 117.
[509] Sanders and Young (2007), p.404.
[510] *ibid.* pp.402–405.
[511] See generally, A. Choo, *Evidence* (2006) Ch.5; A. Keane, *The Modern Law of Evidence* (2006), Ch.3.
[512] *per* Lord Simon in *DPP v Kilbourne* [1973] A.C. 729 at 756, HL.

Not all evidence that is relevant is also admissible. Relevant evidence may have various deficiencies, the most common of which are that it may be unreliable or prejudicial to a fair trial, it may be privileged material or it may have been unfairly obtained. An array of technical rules of exclusion has therefore developed to prevent such evidence being given.

The rules of exclusion of evidence of any type are seldom absolute and the judge must be familiar with the various exceptions which exist and under which evidence may be received. Exceptions are frequently made in respect of evidence that is not subject to the deficiency against which the rule of exclusion is designed to guard. This is a consequence of the evolutionary nature of the subject and the absence of any attempt to codify the general rules of criminal evidence.[513] Thus a confession made by an accused person, though hearsay (and thus generally inadmissible), may be given in evidence, as it is a statement that goes against the interest of the person making it and so is unlikely to be unreliable. Exceptions to the rules of exclusion are generally hedged about with conditions to prevent the admission of undesirable and/or unreliable evidence. Thus, for example, where it is proposed to rely upon a confession made by an accused person, the prosecution must, by virtue of s.76 of PACE 1984, be able to prove beyond reasonable doubt that it was not obtained either:

"(a) by oppression of the person who made it; or
 (b) in consequence of anything said or done which was likely, in the circumstances existing at the time, to render unreliable any confession which might be made by him in consequence thereof."[514]

(ii) *Determining admissibility*

Where the admissibility of an item of evidence, such as a confession, is contested, it would obviously be inadvisable for argument to take place in front of the jury, who would then hear that a confession had been made, even if it were subsequently ruled to be inadmissible. There is therefore a special procedure whereby matters relating to the admissibility of evidence may be determined in the absence of the jury, and this is known as the trial within a trial or *voire dire*. Witnesses may be called in the usual way,[515] and legal argument heard, after which the judge makes his or her ruling.[516]   **17–072**

(iii) *Discretionary exclusion*

Where the strict rules of evidence might operate unfairly, a trial judge has various discretionary powers to exclude from the jury's consideration evidence that is   **17–073**

---

[513] *Cf.* the Australian position.

[514] PACE, s.76(2).

[515] Although a special oath is used, which is known as the "*voire dire*", and from which the procedure takes its name: "I swear I will true answer make to all such questions as the court shall demand of me."

[516] The trial within a trial may form a significant, and sometimes lengthy, part of the proceedings. When the "Birmingham Six" came to trial, a "trial within a trial" was held to determine the admissibility of confessions made by the accused, which lasted eight days, at the end of which the statements were admitted by the judge, Bridge J., who gave a reasoned decision covering 15 pages: *McIllkenny v Chief Constable of West Midlands Police Force* [1980] Q.B. 283 at 314, *per* Lord Denning M.R.

both relevant and otherwise admissible.[517] The best known and most frequently exercised power is to be found in s.78 of PACE, which provides that the judge:

> "may refuse to allow evidence on which the prosecution proposes to rely to be given if it appears to the court that, having regard to all the circumstances, including the circumstances in which the evidence was obtained, the admission of the evidence would have such an adverse effect on the fairness of the proceedings that the court ought not to admit it."

An example of the use of this power might be in respect of a confession, which, though it was not obtained in circumstances rendering it inadmissible under s.76 of PACE, was nevertheless procured in breach of the rules governing interrogation in such a way that it would be unfair to admit it.[518] Other examples of the exclusion of evidence under this discretion include evidence obtained in breach of the Codes relating to identification evidence and evidence obtained in breach of other Codes of Practice relating to search and seizure. In addition to the power conferred by s.78,[519] the trial judge may exclude evidence by virtue of the discretion vested in him or her by the common law.[520] There is also the power to stay proceedings for abuse of process which is exercised in some situations in which the evidence has been obtained unfairly such that it is unfair to try the accused or where he cannot have a fair trial.[521]

In *Latif & Shahzad*,[522] Lord Steyn acknowledged a "considerable overlap" between the s.78 principles and those applicable to abuse of process.

The abuse of process doctrine meant that the trial judge must:

> "weigh in the balance the public interest in ensuring that those that are charged with grave crimes should be tried and the competing public interest in not conveying the impression that the court will adopt the approach that the end justifies any means."

In *R v P*,[523] Lord Hobhouse pointed out that a defendant is not entitled to have unlawfully obtained evidence excluded simply because it has been so obtained. Lord Hobhouse also emphasised that the English courts would not adopt a

---

[517] See generally R. Pattenden (1990), Ch.7.

[518] See, e.g. *R v Samuel* [1988] Q.B. 615 in which the accused confessed to robbery after having been denied access to his solicitor in breach of s.58 of PACE. The court regarded this denial of "one of the most important and fundamental rights of a citizen" as sufficient justification for exclusion of the confession under s.78.

[519] The section is not applicable in committal proceedings: s.78(3), as inserted by the Criminal Procedure and Investigations Act 1996, s.47. Some confusion has arisen as to the applicability of the section in extradition proceedings, but it is clear that it should apply: *Re Proulx* [2000] Crim. L.R. 997 and commentary. *Cf.* the dictum of Lord Hoffmann in *R v Governor of Brixton Prison, Ex p. Levin* [1997] A.C. 714.

[520] The judge has power at common law to exclude evidence at his or her discretion where the prejudicial effect of prosecution evidence outweighs its probative value, and (in certain cases) where evidence has been improperly obtained, see *R v Sang* [1980] A.C. 402.

[521] For an excellent discussion of the narrow approach to s.78 and comparisons with the abuse of process doctrine see A. Choo and S. Nash, "What's the Matter with Section 78" [1999] Crim. L.R. 729.

[522] [1996] 1 W.L.R. 104 at 109.

[523] [2001] 2 W.L.R. 463.

scheme of mandatory exclusion of evidence obtained in breach of a Convention right.[524]

The ECtHR influence cannot be ignored; in certain areas it has a profound effect on domestic law. For example, in *Teixiera de Castro v Portugal*,[525] the Court found a breach of Art.6 where undercover officers incited the offender to commit an offence which he would not otherwise have committed. The House of Lords, as a result, re-addressed English law on the propriety of undercover operations involving enticement. *Looseley*[526] confirmed that English law is not in conflict with the ECHR jurisprudence, but that evidence obtained as a result of undercover enticement will be liable to be excluded from the trial,[527] though in principle the grant of a stay of proceedings as as an abuse of the court's process might be more appropriate.

(d) Summing-up[528]

The other major matters of law which are the responsibility of the judge are those which must be explained to the jury so that it can reach a proper decision.[529] The judge will deal with these matters in the summing-up, telling the jury that it must accept his or her direction on issues of law. Summing up is of particular significance since the jury, conscious of the impending duty to decide the fate of the accused, will be particularly attentive and because of this the material they hear, as the last information before they retire, will have a greater impact. **17–074**

Lord Hailsham, at the time the Lord Chancellor, emphasised the judge's obligations in summing up:

> "The purpose of a direction to a jury is not best achieved by a disquisition on jurisprudence or philosophy or a universally applicable circular tour round the area of law affected by the case. The search for universally applicable definitions is often productive of more obscurity than light. A direction is seldom improved and may be considerably damaged by copious recitations from the total content of a judge's notebook. A direction to a jury should be custom-built to make the jury understand their task in relation to a particular case. Of course, it must include references to the burden of proof and the respective role of jury and judge. But it should also include a succinct but accurate summary of the issues of fact as to which a decision is required, a correct but concise summary of the evidence and arguments on both sides and a correct statement of the inferences which the jury are entitled to draw from their particular conclusions about the primary facts."[530]

Achieving such a summing up may well be difficult, especially in the case of long and complex trials. It is common and approved practice for the trial judge to discuss with counsel the precise details of the summing-up before it is

---

[524] See *R v Khan* [1997] A.C. 587; *Khan v UK* [2000] Crim. L.R. 508; *P.G. v UK* [2002] Crim. L.R. 308; *R v Button* [2005] EWCA Crim 516.

[525] (1998) 28 E.H.R.R. 101.

[526] *R v Looseley* [2001] 1 W.L.R. 2060.

[527] See further, A. Ashworth [2002] Crim. L.R. 161.

[528] *Archbold* (2007), para.4–368.

[529] On the dangers of juries being ill informed after summing-up see I. Francis, "Mystical Reverance for the Jury" (2001) 151 N.L.J. 63.

[530] *R v Lawrence* [1982] A.C. 510. See also *R v McVey* [1988] Crim. L.R. 127.

delivered. It would seem proper to suggest that many of the problems might be avoided if judges were careful to ensure that the language they use is that which a jury is likely to understand[531] and that the length of time taken to deliver a summing-up is as little as possible consistent with clarity.[532] Madge has argued for the greater use of written directions to juries.[533] As the House of Lords pointed out: a judge should not be compelled to give meaningless or absurd directions.[534]

A summing-up usually consists of the following elements.

(i) *A direction as to the respective tasks of judge and jury*

17–075   The jury is told that it is for the judge to decide upon matters of law and for it to decide upon matters of fact and that it should not be influenced by any judicial opinions expressed about the evidence[535]; it is for the jury to decide what facts have been proved.[536] It would be naive to think, however, that the views of the judge, if expressed, have no bearing on the jury's decision.[537]

(ii) *A direction as to the burden and standard of proof*

17–076   The judge should tell the jury about the burden and standard of proof.[538] Prosecuting counsel may have done so in the opening speech and it may have

---

[531] The point is made, e.g. by R. Harding, "Jury Performance in Complex Cases" in Findlay and Duff (1988), Ch.5; by M. Levi, "The Role of the Jury in Complex Cases" in Findlay and Duff (1988), Ch.6; and by E. Griew, "Summing Up the Law" [1989] Crim. L.R. 768, who supports his argument, at p.773, with American research which suggests "that a good many vocabulary items freely used in jury instructions are incomprehensible to an alarming percentage of jurors . . . ". In the Crown Court Survey, it was found that most jurors perceived no difficulties with legal jargon in understanding their case: Zander and Henderson (1993), p.212. Very few jurors had difficulty with the judge's direction on the law: *ibid.* pp.216–217. For research which demonstrates how incompetent most jurors are when presented with complex material in the course of a fraud trial, see T. Honess, M. Levi and E. Charman, "Juror Competence in Processing Complex Information: Implications from a Simulation of the Maxwell Trial" [1998] Crim. L.R. 763. The authors conclude that with some screening and more assistance, 80% of jurors are competent to deal with complex trials.

[532] Many jurors, in the Crown Court Survey, were of the view that they could have coped without the judge summing up on the facts, although fewer took this view with the longer cases: *ibid.* pp.214–215. See on the virtue of brevity in summing up *R v Farr* (1999) 163 J.P. 193. A two-minute summing up was upheld in *R v Brown* [1995] Crim. L.R. 746.

[533] See N. Madge, "Summing Up: A Judge's Perspective" [2006] Crim. L.R. 817.

[534] See *R v Aziz* [1996] 1 A.C. 41.

[535] See also Darbyshire *et al.* (2001), p.39 for the impact on the jury of these directions.

[536] *R v Bradbury* (1920) 15 Cr.App.R. 76; *R v Mason* (1924) 18 Cr.App.R. 131. The jury may decide upon a verdict which may appear to be "perverse" despite this statement, provided it realises it has that opportunity.

[537] At its lowest, the position of the summing-up at the end of the trial must give it significance. Add to that the respect accorded to a professional's view by lay people and their natural tendency to rely on the judge's analysis and the judge's influence is clear.

[538] *R v Bentley* [1999] Crim. L.R. 330; [2000] 1 Cr.App.R. 307. If a case gets to the stage of a summing-up, Griew has doubted whether talk of the burden of proof is appropriate, since the prosecution must by then have established a *prima facie* case, otherwise a submission of no case to answer would have succeeded; and, in reality, the jury must rely on all the evidence, not just that provided by the prosecution, but also that provided by the defence: Griew (1989). If the jury ask for further guidance, the judge should use similar words to that used in the original direction: *R v Milligan, The Times*, March 11, 1989. See generally, B. Shapiro, *Reasonable Doubt and Probable Cause* (1991).

been referred to during the trial. The judge tells the jury that the burden of proving the guilt of the accused lies on the prosecution save in the case of the common law defence of insanity and subject to any statutory exception. This is echoed by Art.6 and the jurisprudence of the Strasbourg Court.[539]

The standard that must be satisfied is proof beyond a reasonable doubt.[540] So if, for example, Vera, a defendant, raises the issue by stating that an apparent attack was carried out in self-defence, it is for the prosecution to prove beyond reasonable doubt that she was not acting in self-defence, rather than on Vera to prove on a balance of probabilities that she was so acting. The judge directs that the jury must be satisfied so that they are sure of the accused's guilt.[541] Until recently this has not been thought to create many problems. Montgomery[542] surveyed responses by potential English jurors to the English direction on the burden and standard of proof as compared to the US directions. Earlier research had shown that jurors set the "beyond reasonable doubt" formula as lying between 51 per cent–92 per cent.[543] Montgomery applied a strict US test "proof precluding every reasonable hypothesis" compared with the English "satisfied so that you are sure" test. The results of the small sample (with some question marks as to methodology) was that the less defined and more subjective English test led to fewer convictions. Very few would, under either test, convict on less than 75 per cent certainty. Montgomery's conclusions are challenged by Zander,[544] who argues that on the basis of empirical research conducted for the *Review Auld Report*, 51 per cent of the general public would require themselves to be 100 per cent sure before convicting. Thirty-one per cent of magistrates would share this view. Approximately 75 per cent of both samples would need to be at least 90 per cent sure before convicting.

The summing-up and the simple direction on the burden of proof has been observed, however, to cause greatest difficulties in cases where the crime can be established on the basis of a number of different, mutually exclusive grounds. If, for example, six jurors are satisfied that the accused committed the offence according to one of the bases alleged by the prosecution, and the other six on an alternative mutually exclusive ground, how can the jury really be satisfied as to

---

[539] *Barbara v Spain* (1989) 11 E.H.R.R. 360. For the decisions of the HL on the burden of proof and the Human Rights Act 1998 see *R v DPP, Ex p. Kebilene* [2000] 3 W.L.R. 972; [2000] Crim. L.R. 486; *R v Lambert* [2001] 1 Cr.App.R. 205; *Sheldrake v DPP; Attorney General's Reference* (No.4 of 2002) [2004] 3 W.L.R. 976. See also, N. Padfield "The Burden of Proof Unresolved" [2005] Cambridge L.J. 17; C. Wells, "Reversing the Burden" (2005) N.L.J. 183.

[540] If the burden lies upon the defence, the standard is the lower one of the balance of probabilities: *R v Carr-Briant* (1943) 29 Cr.App.R. 76. As to the prosecution standard, the actual formulation of the direction to the jury has varied. "Satisfied so that you feel sure" has its supporters: *Walters v The Queen* [1960] 2 A.C. 26; *R v Summers* (1952) 36 Cr.App.R. 14. So does, "satisfied beyond all/any/a reasonable doubt": *DPP v Woolmington* [1935] A.C. 462; *R v Lawrence* [1982] A.C. 510. For the judge who wishes to be doubly safe, the direction, " . . . satisfied beyond reasonable doubt so that you feel sure of the defendant's guilt" has also been approved: *Fergusan v The Queen* [1979] 1 W.L.R. 94.

[541] The expression is lacking in clarity—and deliberately so. In *R v Wickramaratne* [1998] Crim. L.R. 565 where the jury expressed concern at what weight should be given to their "feelings", the Court of Appeal recommended that the judge should remind them of the direction on the burden of proof and advise to put feelings aside. See also, *R v Bentley* [2001] 1 Cr.App.R. 21.

[542] "The Criminal Standard of Proof" (1998) N.L.J. 582.

[543] R. Hastie (ed.), *Inside the Juror: The Psychology of Juror Decision-making* (1993), pp.100–106.

[544] M. Zander, "The Criminal Standard of Proof—How Sure is Sure?" (2000) 150 N.L.J. 1517.

the guilt of the accused?[545] This also raises the important question whether the case has been put in such a way that the accused can be said to have had a fair opportunity to know the case against him.

The problem of inconsistent verdicts—where the jury return acquittals on some counts and guilty verdicts on others which suggests a logical inconsistency in their decision-making—is also a difficult one. The Court of Appeal must consider whether there is a rational way in which verdicts can be explained.[546] It is not sufficient that the jury have, for example, merely demonstrated by their verdicts that the victim's credibility was in doubt on some counts.[547] For a successful appeal, it is necessary to show not only that there is a logical inconsistency in the verdict, but also that it is not possible to postulate a legitimate claim of reasoning which could explain the inconsistency.[548] The courts seem to allow for a conviction where a "legitimate train of reasoning" by the jury leads to a "logical inconsistency".

(iii) *Alternative verdicts returned by the jury*

17–077   The judge should put alternative verdicts to the jury where appropriate,[549] but the judge is to ensure that the defendant has a fair trial on the evidence presented and there is no improper prejudice to the accused, ensuring also that the jury are not distracted from the main issue. It may be preferable to amend the indictment rather than leave alternatives to the jury. Before returning an alternative verdict the jury must acquit on the more serious charge or be discharged from returning a verdict. This can render the selection of the appropriate charge for the offence extremely important.[550] On hearing an appeal, the Court of Appeal has the power to substitute an alternative verdict justified by the evidence as found at trial.

(iv) *A direction as to the definition of the offence charged and the facts which have to be proved before there can be a conviction*

17–078   The judge must explain to the jury the legal requirements of the offence charged and the facts of which the jury must be convinced before they can convict. This often is not easy. In a case of theft, for example, the judge should say that the property stolen must have belonged to someone else and must have been appropriated by the accused, who must have been dishonest and intending to deprive the other person permanently of the property.[551] Even that seemingly straightforward statement creates difficulties. What is an appropriation? What amounts to dishonesty? What if the property has been "borrowed", to be returned at some (distant) future date? Some difficulties may be resolved by judges relying on model directions created by the courts and specimen directions produced by

---

[545] See J. C. Smith, "Satisfying the Jury" [1988] Crim. L.R. 335. See also the decision in *R v D* [2000] 8 Arch. News 2; *R v Gianaetto* [1997] 1 Cr.App.R. 1; *R v Brown* (1983) 79 Cr.App.R. 115. On the *Brown* problem of jury inconsistentcy see P. Robertshaw, "The Conjunctive or Disjunctive Jury" (1999) J. Crim. L. 231.

[546] *R v IK* [1999] Crim. L.R. 740It.

[547] *R v Hayward* [2000] Crim. L.R. 189.

[548] *R v G* [1998] Crim. L.R. 483 and commentary by JCS, and *R v Fielder-Beech* [1998] Crim. L.R. 503.

[549] *R v Bergman* [1996] 2 Cr.App.R. 399.

[550] On the tactics of prosecuting counsel selecting the correct charge or overcharging, see *R v Fernandez* [1997] 1 Cr.App.R. 123.

[551] Theft Act 1968, s.1.

the Judicial Studies Board with the approval of the Lord Chief Justice.[552] On the other hand, it might be questioned whether use of such directions may not introduce excess rigidity[553] and, in particular, whether it might not confuse the jury both by using overly complex (lawyerly) language and by introducing superfluous elements of law.[554]

The judge should not direct the jury on matters not raised in the case, but may be obliged to raise alternative defences not relied on explicitly by the accused (e.g. provocation as a defence to murder where the accused has alleged that he was acting in self-defence and would not wish to undermine the chances of that defence by also pleading provocation which, by definition, admits that he lost his temper).[555]

A simple example of theft raises starkly the problem of the distinction between matters of law and matters of law and fact when considering what to say about words like "dishonesty". The judge must direct the jury on issues of law. The problem that arises is the tendency, increasingly exhibited by the courts, to have to regard at least with some words appearing in the definition of criminal offences as words of the ordinary English language whose meaning is not, therefore, a question of law.[556] This was the approach taken with regard to "dishonesty" by the Court of Appeal in *R v Feely*,[557] which was trenchantly criticised largely on the ground that it was leaving to the jury a decision which was properly that of the judge.[558] This approach is still adopted in the interpretation of some words, although judges usually provide definitions where possible.[559] Of course, the greater the number of issues of law upon which the judge gives a direction, the fewer the opportunities for the exercise of discretion or common sense by the jury and the greater is the control of the judge.[560]

The failure to provide clear definitions precludes a citizen from predicting with any certainty whether his conduct will be regarded as criminal. The ECHR guarantees in Art.7 that there should not be retrospective criminalisation. If a common law offence or definition of an element of the offence is too vague or depends substantially on the jury's definition (on a case by case basis) it may conflict with Art.7.[561]

---

[552] See *www.jsboard.co.uk*.

[553] See Lord Hailsham's statement in *R v Lawrence*, above.

[554] Griew (1989), who points out that there may be a temptation amongst trial judges to provide too much legal information in order to make their directions appeal-proof.

[555] See, e.g. *R v Johnson* [1989] 1 W.L.R. 740 and S. Doran, "Alternative Defences and the Invisible Burden on the Trial Judge" [1991] Crim. L.R. 878.

[556] See Lord Reid in *Brutus v Cozens* [1973] A.C. 854 (on the meaning of the word "insulting" in the Public Order Act 1936, s.5, since repealed by the Public Order Act 1986, s.40(3)); Lawton L.J. in *W v L* [1974] Q.B. 711 (on the meaning of "mental illness" in the Mental Health Act 1959).

[557] [1973] Q.B. 530.

[558] See, e.g. D. W. Elliott, "Law and Fact in Theft Act Cases" [1976] Crim. L.R. 707; G. Williams, "Law and Facts" [1976] Crim. L.R. 472 at 537; E. J. Griew, *Dishonesty and the Jury* (1974); A. Briggs, "Judges, Juries and the Meaning of Words" (1985) 5 L.S. 314.

[559] No *definition* (as opposed to explanation) of the meaning of "intention" has been provided by the courts in a series of cases, see D. Ormerod, *Smith and Hogan: Criminal Law* (11th edn, 2005), pp.93–102. The most recent decision is that of the HL in *R v Woolin* [1998] 4 All E.R. 103.

[560] The jury will usually follow such a direction by the judge, and thus the exercise of discretion is limited. The jury is, of course, permitted to exercise discretion outside the judge's direction, which some might describe as not legitimate or perverse.

[561] See *Kokkinakis v Greece* (1994) 17 E.H.R.R. 397; *CR v UK* at (1995) 21 E.H.R.R. 363; *Mattocia v Italy* [2001] E.H.R.L.R. 89.

(v) *A direction as to evidential points*

17–079   It may be necessary for the judge to give directions about the evidence which the jury has heard. The judge should remind the jury that speeches by counsel do not form part of the evidence. The jury may have to be warned of the legal requirements in relation to certain evidence lest they rely upon that evidence too readily in deciding questions of fact. The judge again exercises control over the jury.

An example is where the defence is one of mistaken identity, since eyewitness evidence may be based on a fleeting glimpse. Rarely, for example, would a by-passer have more than a swift glimpse of the bank robber running out of a bank to the getaway car. In such circumstances it is possible for witnesses genuinely and honestly to be convinced that they are right. They may, in fact, be mistaken. The jury must be informed of the problems which can arise. Before the summing-up, the judge may withdraw the evidence from the jury if it is "poor" and the prosecution should inform the defence of any material discrepancies between the description originally given and the accused's actual appearance. In the summing-up, the judge should warn the jury of the need for caution; the circumstances in which the identification took place should be drawn to the attention of the jury, in particular the length of time the observation could have lasted and the conditions; the judge should remind the jury of any weaknesses that have become apparent and point out to the jury that evidence of recognition of someone known can be relied upon more satisfactorily than identification of a stranger.[562]

Other important discussions on issues of evidence will include the uses that can be made of a defendant's failure to disclose an item of evidence before trial or his failure to testify. The Judicial Studies Board provides a specimen direction for the judge to deliver when a defendant has failed to testify.[563] Similarly, the judge will give a special warning when the defendant has lied about issues peripheral to the main ones in the case,[564] or where evidence of a particular witness carries a special hazard (e.g. a co-defendant or someone who may be tainted by an improper motive[565]). It is also important that the judge gives a direction as to the "good" character of the accused (where he has one).[566] The judge ought not to refer to the defendant's failure to call any witness, lest this confuse the jury as to the burden of proof.[567] The judge must be careful not to make improper comments on the defendant's testimony, which is not to say that he cannot comment in strong terms where necessary.[568] The judge should also

---

[562] *R v Turnbull* [1977] 2 Q.B. 224. For a comprehensive listing of the rules relating to evidence of identification, see *Blackstone's* (2007) Section F18.

[563] See [1995] 2 Cr.App.R. 192. See also, the website of the Judicial Studies Board: *www.jsboard.co.uk*—the relevant direction is at para.39 of the criminal law specimen directions.

[564] See *R v Lucas* [1981] Q.B. 720; *R v Burge and Pegg* [1996] 1 Cr.App.R. 163. See also, L. Connor "Lies, Lying and Lucas" (2004) J.P. 168; *R v Nash* [2004] EWCA Crim 164.

[565] See *R v Spencer and Smails* [1987] A.C. 128; *R v Makunjuola* [1995] 2 Cr.App.R. 469.

[566] See *R v Vye* (1993) 97 Cr.App.R. 134. *Teeluck v The State* [2005] 1 W.L.R. 2421. And this must not be done sarcastically: *R v Lloyd* [2000] 2 Cr.App.R. 355.

[567] See *R v Wright* [2000] Crim. L.R. 510; *R v Khan* [2001] Crim. L.R. 673.

[568] *R v Winn-Pope* [1996] Crim. L.R. 521. Though the judge must be careful not to attack counsel's professional integrity such that it would damage the accused's confidence in the administration of justice in that case: *R v Lashley* [2005] EWCA Crim 2016.

avoid making adverse comment in front of the accused, even where the jury are absent.[569]

(vi) A summary of the evidence in the case

It is for the judge to put the case before the jury by reviewing the facts and a **17–080** failure to do so is a procedural irregularity. In a complex case, this will involve a substantial amount of the evidence being rehearsed for the jury's benefit.[570] Whether this is really an appropriate function is doubtful, especially as it may be unnecessary, may provide the judge with too much influence over the jury, and may make it appear as though the prosecution is being supported by the judge.[571]

Whilst the determination of matters of fact is for the jury, the judge is entitled to comment on matters arising out of the evidence,[572] including the strength of the respective cases[573] the demeanour and quality of witnesses,[574] the credibility of evidence and the quality of any argument. Comment may be in strong terms provided that, overall, it is not unfair[575] and the jury are reminded clearly and forcefully that they have the ultimate responsibility for deciding issues of fact.[576] It is vital that the judge puts the defence to the jury[577] no matter how ridiculous it seems.[578] It is not incumbent on a judge to repeat the whole of the defendant's lengthy statements in interviews provided he refers to the salient passages.[579]

Comments may be other than verbal[580]: gesture, tone of voice and facial expression can all speak volumes in indicating the judge's view of the merits, and

---

[569] *R v Roncali* [1998] Crim. L.R. 584.

[570] The judge keeps a note of the evidence—a process which has a significant effect on the speed of the criminal trial—and will remind the jury of it in the summing-up. However, merely reading out such notes, especially in complex cases, was criticised by the Court of Appeal in *R v Charles* (1979) 68 Cr.App.R. 334, see Sprack (2006), p.349. The judge must also be careful to put the defence case fully and properly, see *R v Tillman* [1962] Crim. L.R. 261; *R v Hamilton* [1972] Crim. L.R. 266. For an incisive consideration of the function of summing-up, see Griew (1989).

[571] D. Wolchover, "Should Judges Sum Up on the Facts?" [1989] Crim. L.R. 781 and the findings of the Crown Court Survey for the Royal Commission on Criminal Justice (1993).

[572] See *R v Evans* (1990) 91 Cr.App.R. 173. For an interesting account of the summing-up in the *Oz* case, see T. Palmer, *The Trials of Oz* (1971). There was a great deal of comment contained in that summing-up which was later the subject of appeal: *R v Anderson* [1972] 1 Q.B. 304.

[573] "[I]n *O'Donnell* (1917) 12 Cr.App.R. 219 a conviction was upheld where the judge said that the prisoner's story was a 'remarkable' one and contrary to previous statements he had made, but in *Canny* (1945) 30 Cr.App.R. 143 repeatedly telling the jury that the defence was 'absurd' and that there was no foundation for defence allegations amounted to a direction to find the case against the accused proved. The conviction was therefore quashed.": Sprack (2006), p.349.

[574] "I thought he was a jolly good witness. He wasn't prepared to whitewash all of *Oz* like some of the other so-called experts and I can't say fairer than that": *per* Judge Argyle, quoted in Palmer (1971), p.252.

[575] *R v Middlesex Justices, Ex p. DPP* [1952] 2 Q.B. 758; *R v O'Donnell* (1917) 12 Cr.App.R. 219; *R v Canny* (1945) 30 Cr.App.R. 143.

[576] *R v West* (1910) 4 Cr.App.R. 179; *R v Beeby* (1911) 6 Cr.App.R. 138; *R v Frampton* (1917) 12 Cr.App.R. 202. The following is an example of such a direction: " . . . if I now express an opinion and you agree, well, that's alright. If not, you can disagree. You do not have to do what I tell you. What I think is irrelevant. *You* have to decide": *per* Judge Argyle, Palmer (1971), p.239.

[577] *R v Curtin* [1996] Crim. L.R. 831; *R v Akhtar* [2000] 1 Arch. News 2.

[578] e.g. *R v Marr* (1989) 90 Cr.App.R. 154, where the accused claimed to have tripped and to prevent himself from falling had grasped the female victim by the crotch to support himself.

[579] *R v Soames-Waring* [1999] Crim. L.R. 89.

[580] On the use of language in judicial statements see the following US research: S. Philips, *Ideology in the Language of Judges: How Judges Practice Law, Politics and Courtroom Control* (1998).

such matters do not appear in the transcript.[581] The Court of Appeal appears to be unwilling to interfere with a conviction on the ground that the judge has overstepped the permissible limits of comment unless the summing-up is very defective.[582] The judge must not become or appear to become a prosecutor.[583] An informal constraint on the extent of judicial comment is the possibility that the jury will react against a very strong direction to convict and, out of perversity or sympathy for the accused or some other motivation, bring in a verdict of acquittal. A direction that the jury must convict should never be given.[584]

In the event that the judge realises that he or she has given an erroneous direction in summing up, or an error has been drawn to his attention by counsel, he may recall the jury and re-direct. Both prosecution and defence counsel are obliged to seek rectification of errors of which they become aware.[585]

The Judicial Studies Board has, through the production of specimen directions,[586] reduced the number of appealable errors made in summing up. The Judicial Studies Board was established in 1979 to provide training for the judiciary in criminal law. Its activities now cover wider aspects of judicial training. In addition to its issuing of model directions, its continuing training and induction programmes for the judiciary and its monitoring and evaluation objectives, the Judicial Studies Board produces other important practical guides.

(e) Sentencing[587]

17–081 Once the jury have found the accused to be guilty of an offence or after the accused has pleaded guilty, it is for the judge to pass sentence on the offender. The judge must have the necessary information available about the offence and the offender. If this is available, sentencing may occur immediately; if not, there may be an adjournment.

(i) *Information for sentencing*

17–082 The judge must be provided with the facts of the offence. Where the accused has pleaded guilty, these facts will not as yet have been set out. They are now given by the prosecutor, who might also make reference to the impact the offence has had upon the victim. So called "victim impact statements" have been considered

---

[581] See Wolchover (1989).

[582] *cf. R. v Anderson* [1972] 1 Q.B. 304. Such defects will occur where the judge usurps the jury's function, as in *R v Canny* (1945) 30 Cr.App.R. 143, see n.573 above. This issue may also overlap with the question of whether a judge can direct a conviction, see text below.

[583] See the guidance given by Simon Brown L.J. in *R v Nelson* [1997] Crim. L.R. 234.

[584] *R v Wang* [2005] 1 W.L.R. 661; *R v Caley-Knowles* [2006] EWCA Crim 1611; see also, *R v Kelleher* [2003] EWCA Crim 3525.

[585] *R v Langford, The Times*, January 12, 2001.

[586] There were complaints that the Judicial Studies Board directions were not publicly available and yet were being relied upon by judges as authoritative texts: see R. Munday, "The Bench Books: Can the Judiciary Keep a Secret?" [1996] Crim. L.R. 296. The directions are now published on the website. See also the published correspondence between Kennedy L.J. and Roderick Munday at [1996] Crim. L.R. 529. See also R. Munday (2002) J. Crim. Law 158 criticising an unduly rigid adherence to specimen directions.

[587] See A. Ashworth, *Sentencing and Criminal Justice* (2005); *Blackstone's* (2007) Part E; A. Ashworth and A. von Hirsch, *Proportionate Sentencing: Exploring the Principles* (2005); Sprack (2006) Pt 4.

by the Court of Appeal where it has been stated that the sentencer should not make assumptions not supported by evidence about the impact on the victim; if the offence was particularly distressing for the victim then the court should be informed; evidence as to the impact on the victim should be by way of a proper witness report and served on the defence; the evidence of the victim should be approached with care; and the opinions of the victim's close relatives should not be considered.[588]

The prosecutor provides the facts which, if disputed, may lead to a "Newton" hearing at which the prosecutor is obliged to prove them.[589] This hearing follows a normal adversarial format with strict rules of evidence applying and the judge directing himself or herself as if he or she were a jury.

The prosecutor will then provide evidence as to the offender's "antecedents". This includes such things as previous convictions, educational history, employment record, home circumstances and resources. The evidence should be produced in accordance with the relevant Practice Direction.[590] The defence may challenge the evidence, in which case the prosecutor must prove it. Further information may be contained in a variety of reports, in particular a social inquiry report, prepared by either a probation officer or a social worker, considering the factors leading to the offence and a recommendation as to appropriate sentence.[591] Section 156 of the CJA 2003 requires the court to obtain a pre-sentence report when it is considering a custodial or community sentence.

The courts also rely on risk assessments, with a recognition that these can provide better information qualitatively and quantitatively than antecedents thereby producing a greater likelihood of the optimal disposal. This should also lead to a more effective use of the limited resources of the criminal justice system, and provide better protection for the victim and the public.[592] Other reports that will be offered to the court include medical and psychiatric reports and reports from places where a person has been held, such as a remand centre or prison when on remand in custody. The court has the power to remand a person to hospital for the preparation of medical reports.[593]

There is therefore an ever greater requirement of vigilance on criminal practitioners to be aware of criminal records.[594] There is also a greater need for caution in the recording and transcription of records and in their being kept up to date. Counsel has a duty to inform himself or herself of the court's sentencing powers, and to correct the judge should he or she fall in to error.[595]

---

[588] *R v Perks* [2001] 1 Cr.App.R. 66.
[589] So-called after the decision of the Court of Appeal in *R v Newton* (1983) 77 Cr.App.R. 13. See also, *R v Ahmed* (1984) 6 Cr.App.R. (S) 391; *R v Gandy* (1989) 11 Cr.App.R. (S) 564. On what to do with disputed Newton hearings see K. Browne, "Handling an Unexploded Newton Bomb" (1998) 142 S.J. July 24, 742.
[590] *Practice Direction (Criminal Proceedings: Consolidation)* [2002] 1 W.L.R. 2870.
[591] R. Horn and M. Evans, "The Effect of Gender on Pre-Sentence Reports" (2000) 39 Howard Jnl. 184 reveal in their empirical research that PSRs were often written by someone of the same gender as the offender and that motivations for male and female offenders were explained differently. The main motivations for women to offend were identified as money and drugs; for men, they were money, drugs and alcohol.
[592] See C. Clarkson and R. Morgan (eds), *The Politics of Sentencing Reform* (1995).
[593] See Mental Health Act 1983, s.35.
[594] See M. Wasik, "The Vital Importance of Certain Previous Convictions" [2001] Crim. L.R. 363.
[595] *R v Brown* [1996] Crim. L.R. 134.

(ii) *Plea in mitigation*

17–083   Once the court has received reports and material for sentencing, the defence may then make a plea in mitigation. Defence counsel should be restrained in the presentation of mitigation and should not impugn the character of witnesses. If the defence seek to rely on evidence in the course of the plea, they bear the burden of proving it.[596] The plea of mitigation will usually be made by the advocate, and it is important to note the protection in s.83 of the Powers of Criminal Courts (Sentencing) Act 2000 (PCC(S)A) whereby a court shall not impose a custodial sentence on an adult who has not previously been imprisoned or accused unless he or she is legally represented.

Prosecution counsel should monitor defence claims and, if necessary, request a Newton hearing to resolve disputes. The prosecution's role in sentencing is a neutral one and there is no objective in seeking a heavier sentence. The judge is entitled to seek the assistance of prosecution counsel whenever necessary. Even if not openly seeking a longer sentence, the prosecution will influence the sentence passed by the selection of charges at the outset, and by influencing the mode of the trial. In addition, the prosecution must inform the court of the minimum sentence possible and inform the court of the accused's antecedents.

It is worth remembering that the prosecution can appeal unduly lenient sentences. The Court of Appeal's power has prompted questions about whether the courts will be unduly influenced by public opinion. Only cases from Crown Court may be referred, apart from exceptional other cases.[597] Shute[598] in his review of the power notes that sometimes sentences have been doubled in length by the Court of Appeal.[599]

Finally, as an aspects of the plea in mitigation an offender may have other cases taken into consideration. This clears up outstanding offences and the offender is likely to get a substantial sentencing reduction for those offences so as to reward honesty. The offender is still only liable for the maximum sentence available for the offence to which he pleaded guilty or was convicted, not for the those offences taken into consideration as well. The scheme whereby courts take into consideration other offences raises very difficult issues regarding the presumption of innocence and the fair trial guarantees. Ashworth, for example, argues that sentencing discounts generally conflict with the presumption of innocence.[600]

Sentencing may be deferred for up to six months to allow the court to take account of the offender's post-conviction behaviour and any other relevant circumstances.[601] The court will make clear to the offender that sentence is deferred and explain why. The court passing sentence at the end of the period of

---

[596] *R v Guppy* [1994] Crim. L.R. 614. The burden is on a balance of probabilities, though, generally, the sentencer would accept the accuracy of defence counsel's statement.

[597] e.g. indecent assault; s.14, Offences Against the Person Act 1861.

[598] On the References see S. Shute, "Who Passes Unduly Lenient Sentences? How Were They Listed?: A Survey of Attorney-General's Reference Cases, 1989–1997" [1999] Crim. L.R. 603.

[599] See also S. Shute, "Prosecution Appeals Against Sentence: The First Five Years" (1994) 57 M.L.R. 745. Between 1989 and 1997 there were 367 reviews.

[600] See A. Ashworth, "The Impact on Criminal Justice" in B. Markesinis (ed.), *The Impact of the Human Rights Bill on English Law* (1998), p.141.

[601] Powers of Criminal Courts (Sentencing) Act 2000, s.1.

deferment should be appraised of the reasons for deferring so as to assess whether the accused has complied with any relevant obligations.[602]

(iii) *Sample counts*[603]

If the offending has been committed repeatedly over time, the prosecution might choose to prosecute for one specific example of this offending at an identifiable point in the period of time. If this course is adopted and the accused is convicted, he should not be sentenced for offences other than that for which he has been found guilty.[604] If the accused pleads guilty to the sample count, sentencing occurs on that understanding.[605]

17–084

(iv) *What sentence is imposed?*

A sentence is laid down for each offence.[606] For a very limited range of offences the penalty is fixed by law. Murder is the main example, since the judge is obliged to impose a sentence of life imprisonment.[607] If the offence is a common law offence, the sentence is a maximum of life imprisonment or a fine. If the offence is a statutory offence, the statute will lay down the punishment.

17–085

The CJA 2003[608] introduced a new framework for "dangerous offenders".[609] These are individuals who have been assessed as dangerous and who have committed one of the specified offences.[610] If the offender is 18 or over, is convicted of one of the serious offences defined in Sch.15, and the court believes that there is a risk to the public of serious harm, the court must impose a life sentence if the offence carries that sentence as its maximum and the court believes it to be justified.[611] Under s.227 "extended sentences" may be imposed on a "dangerous offender" for offences other than serious offences with a maximum penalty of between two and 10 years.[612] The applicability of these

---

[602] See *R v George* [1984] 1 W.L.R. 1082.

[603] M. Chapman, "Specimen Counts and Sentencing: A Principled Approach and the Proper Procedure" (1997) J. Crim. L. 315 reviewing English decisions and warning of the danger of infringement of a fair trial and the presumption of innocence.

[604] *R v Canavan* [1998] 1 Cr.App.R. 79.

[605] *R v Huchison* [1972] 1 W.L.R. 398.

[606] If the offender has been committed by the magistrates to trial on indictment for an offence triable either way and also a related summary offence within s.41 of the Criminal Justice Act 1988, the Crown Court has the sentencing powers which the magistrates' court would have had on conviction at summary trial.

[607] Murder (Abolition of Death Penalty) Act 1965, s.1. Powers of Criminal Courts (Sentencing) Act 2000, s.93. The Home Secretary is no longer involved in amending the minimum term imposed by the judiciary: see *R. (Anderson) v Secretary of State for the Home Department* [2003] 1 A.C. 837, and Criminal Justice Act 2003 Sch.37, Pt 8. See also, *R. (Hammond) v Secretary of State for the Home Department* [2006] 1 A.C. 603; S. Shute, "Punishing Murderers: Release Procedures and the Tariff" [2004] Crim. L.R. 873; *Practice Direction* [2002] 3 All E.R. 904; *R v Lichniak (Daniella Helen)* [2003] 1 A.C. 903. Guidance on setting the minimum term for mandatory life sentences is found in *R v Jones* [2006] 2 Cr.App.R. 19; see also, Practice Direction (*Criminal Proceedings: Consolidation*), para.IV.49.

[608] D. Thomas, "The Criminal Justice Act 2003: Custodial Sentences" [2004] Crim. L.R. 702.

[609] CJA 2003, ss.224–236. See A. Gillespie, "The Spider's Web" (2006) 156 N.L.J 1153.

[610] CJA 2003, Sch. 15. All the specified offences carry a penalty of two years' imprisonment or more. In addition some offences are defined as either violent, sexual or serious.

[611] For similar provisions relating to those under 18 see CJA 2003, s.226.

[612] *ibid.*, s.228.

sections turns on the interpretation of "dangerousness". If the offender has no previous convictions relating to a specified offence then the court must consider the nature and circumstances of the offence; any pattern of behaviour surrounding the offence; and any information about the offender. If the offender has a previous conviction for a specified offence then the court must consider the same factors, but begins from a position of assuming that the offender poses a significant risk to the public.[613]

The Powers of Criminal Courts (Sentencing) Act 2000 introduced minimum custodial sentences for certain specified offences. Subject to a discretion, an adult offender convicted of a Class A drug trafficking offence and who has been convicted of the offence on two previous occasions must receive a minimum custodial sentence of seven years.[614] Similar provisions apply in relation to domestic burglary[615] (a minimum term of three years), and firearms offences[616] (a minimum term of five years), though the latter can apply even to a first offence.

The CJA 2003 also introduces a scheme known as "custody plus",[617] which is due to be implemented in 2007. This replaces all prison sentences up to 12 months in length with a two part sentence. The first part will consist of a custodial sentence of between two and 13 weeks followed by release on licence under supervision in the community for at least 26 weeks. Conditions may be attached to the licence such as a curfew. Intermittent custody has also been introduced under the same legislation.[618] Where the offender is given a sentence of between 28 and 51 weeks an order can be passed whereby the number of days that the offender must spend in custody is specified and intermittent periods of release on licence are provided for. The aim of such an order is to ameliorate the harsh consequences that prison can lead to, such as loss of employment and family problems.

The judge has a wide range of other possible sentences available. These include: absolute discharge; conditional discharge; parental bind-overs; fines; compensation orders; restitution orders; forfeiture orders; community sentences; community rehabilitation orders; community punishment orders; curfew orders; attendance centre orders; supervision orders; action plan orders; drug treatment and testing orders; suspended prison sentences; anti-social behaviour orders; and registration under the Sex Offenders Act 1997.[619] Analysis of these, and others is beyond the scope of this text but are covered in detail in practitioners texts such as Archbold and Blackstone's.[620]

---

[613] See *R v Lang* [2006] 2 All E.R. 410; [2007] Crim. L.R. 177, in which the Court of Appeal set out a list of factors to consider when assessing dangerousness. See also *R v O'Brien* [2006] EWCA Crim 1741.

[614] PCC(S)A 2000, s.110

[615] PCC(S)A 2000, s.111.

[616] CJA 2003, s.287.

[617] CJA 2003, s.181. See also Home Office, *Making Punishments Work; Report of a Review of the Sentencing Framework in England and Wales* (2001); M, Gullick, "Sentencing and Early Release of Fixed Term Prisoners" [2004] Crim. L.R. 653.

[618] CJA 2003, s.183.

[619] Under the CJA 2003 many of these sentences will become separate orders available to the judge if the court determines that a generic community sentence should be passed.

[620] *Blackstone's* (2007), E1; *Archbold* (2007) Ch.5; See also J. Sprack, *Criminal Procedure* (11th edn, 2006) Pt 4.

(iv) *Imposing a particular sentence*

The judge must choose an appropriate sentence. Under the CJA 2003 any court **17–086** dealing with an offender must have regard to the purposes of sentencing identified in s.142. These are:

(a)   the punishment of offenders;

(b)   the reduction of crime (including its reduction by deterrence)[621];

(c)   the reform and rehabilitation of offenders;

(d)   the protection of the public;

(e)   the making of reparation by offenders to those affected by their offences.

The sentencer must determine the importance of each principle in light of the facts of the case.[622]

For many years, the Court of Appeal had been developing a sophisticated tariff approach to sentencing by the setting of guidelines in an endeavour to ensure consistency in sentencing. In an effort to improve the appropriateness of sentencing powers generally the Sentencing Advisory Panel was established under ss.80–81 of the Crime and Disorder Act 1998 as an independent non-departmental public body reporting annually to the Home Office and the Lord Chancellor's Department. It provided views on appropriate sentencing guidelines to the Court of Appeal. In the wake of the CJA 2003 the Sentencing Guidelines Council was established and the Advisory Panel's role is now linked to the Council. The Sentencing Guidelines Council receives the advice of the Advisory Panel and uses it to formulate sentencing guidelines on the subject. Final sentencing guidelines are then issued to be used by sentencers.[623]

(v) *Changes in sentencing approach*

The Powers of Criminal Courts (Sentencing) Act 2000 consolidated a number of **17–087** statutes in an area in which there has been a great deal of confusion.[624] This period of stability was to be very short lived however. The CJA 2003 makes considerable changes to the sentencing framework.[625] The gradual implementation of this legislation means that it is too difficult to consider its overall impact at this stage, not least because not only are many of its provisions not yet in force but recent history suggests some of the provisions may never be brought into force. It is fair to say that the area of sentencing remains a complicated one.

From a political standpoint sentencing is a difficult area. The idea that tougher sentencing is linked to public confidence in the criminal justice system appears to be an important factor in successive governments ignoring the research on

---

[621] See *R v Oosthuizen* [2006] 1 Cr.App.R. 73.

[622] Sentencing Guidelines Council, *Overarching Principles: Seriousness* (2004) para.1.2.

[623] The relevant guidelines can be seen at: *www.sentencing-guidelines.gov.uk/guidelines/ index.html.*

[624] D. Thomas, "Sentencing Legislation: the case for consolidation" [1997] Crim. L.R. 406.

[625] The sentencing provisions in the Act resulted from the Halliday Review, see Home Office, *Making Punishments Work: Report of a Review of the Sentencing Framework for England and Wales* (2001); E. Baker and C. Clarkson, "Making Punishments Work? An Evaluation of the Halliday Report" [2002] Crim. L.R. 81.

sentencing and crime rates. "The simple notion that increasing sentences will have a kind of hydraulic effect in reducing criminality is unsustainable."[626] In general terms it would appear that the Government are pursuing a policy of reserving custodial sentences for the more serious offenders. Whether this emanates from a position of principle or a realisation that prisons are full is debateable. Recently, the Government has reached the conclusion that, "We know that catching people is a good way to deter people from offending—figures show that the likelihood of getting caught is a more important deterrent than how tough sentences are."[627] Its five-year sentencing strategy aims to protect the public through tough sentences for dangerous criminals, but also seeks strategies beyond prison and looks to the rehabilitation of offenders.[628]

In 2005, 1.48 million offenders were sentenced in courts in England and Wales.[629] The number of people given immediate custodial sentences at all courts was 101,236, representing a downward trend from an 80-year high in 2002.[630] Statistics demonstrate that in the decade 1995–2005 the average custodial sentence received in the Crown Court for indictable offences increased by 25 per cent to 25.5 months, whilst sentences issued by the magistrates' court remained relatively stable.[631] The prison population in 2007 is just over 80,000.[632] This expanding figure remains a major concern,[633] and as a response the Government has considered "transitional home leave" for low risk offenders,[634] Home Office advice to judges to jail only the most dangerous or persistent offenders,[635] and in early 2007 consideration has been given to plans to build new prisons to ease the problem of overcrowding.[636]

Public opinion on sentencing and prisons is often ill-informed. There is considerable public debate (academic and otherwise) as to sentencing policy generally. Ashworth and Hough,[637] identify numerous problems with taking heed of public opinion in view of the inadequate knowledge on which such opinions are based,[638] and the confusion between general sentencing policy and sentences in particular cases.

---

[626] A. Ashworth, *Sentencing and Criminal Justice* (4th edn, 2005), p.381.

[627] Home Office, *A Five Year Strategy for Protecting the Public and Reducing Re-offending* (2006) Cm. 6717, para.1.5.

[628] *ibid.*, Ch.3. See J. Broadhead, "More Effective or More of the Same?" (2006) N.L.J 293.

[629] *Home Office Statistical Bulletin* (2007) 03/07, para.1.12. Available at: *www.homeoffice.gov.uk/ rds/pdfs07/hosb0307.pdf.*

[630] *ibid.* Table 2.3.

[631] *Ibid.* Table 2.5 and Table 2.14.

[632] HM Prison Service (2007) Population Bulletin March 2007. Monthly prison population figures are available at *www.hmprisonservice.gov.uk.*

[633] See the concerns expressed by Anne Owers, the Chief Inspector of Prisons, *HM Chief Inspector of Prisons Annual Report 2005/6* (2007) H.C. 210 at p.5; see also R. Morgan, "What's the Problem" (2007) N.L.J. 305.

[634] *The Times* August 17, 2007, p.8.

[635] *The Times* January 25, 2007, p.4.

[636] *The Times* February 16, 2007, p.24. This follows the commitment outlined in Home Office, *Rebalancing the Criminal Justice System in Favour of the Law-Abiding Majority: Cutting Crime, Reducing Reoffending and Protecting the Public* (2006) p.4.

[637] A. Ashworth and M. Hough "Sentencing and the Climate of Opinion" [1996] Crim. L.R. 776,

[638] See generally, S. Shute, "The Place of Public Opinion in Sentencing Law" [1998] Crim. L.R. 465, concluding that there are a number of cases in which it has been made clear that judges are "at the very-least" bound to consider the relevance of public opinion, without letting it take an overriding weight. One of the problems identified by Shute is that the public's opinion on sentencing is ill-informed.

(vi) *Victims and sentencing*

A controversial issue of sentencing policy relates to the increased significance in **17–088** the court's consideration of the use of victim impact statements. The Court of Appeal has emphasised that judges should not make unsupported assumptions about the effect of an offence on a victim, but should take account of particularly damaging effects if known and proved in a proper form and served on the accused. The statement of the victim himself or herself should be approached with caution but should be received by the court.[639]

The victim input to the sentencing process can be defended on grounds of proportionality and as a move towards restorative justice and can be seen as a way of making the system more efficient by providing better information. It could also be defended on the ground that the process will benefit the victim and act in a therapeutic fashion.[640] There is a value inherent in participation of all parties in the legal process. The danger is that such a system raises the expectations of the victim who perceives their input as more significant than it really is.

There are also significant practical problems in accepting victim statements, including: defining who constitutes a victim for these purposes (e.g. does it include the relatives of the deceased victim?); regulating the content of the statement (is it to be limited to the views of the victim as to what happened? their views on appropriate sentence?); and what form the statements are to take. Some argue that the victim input is useful for the purposes of fulfilling the restoration/ compensation of victims.

The effectiveness of the victim impact statements (VIS) scheme has been scrutinised by a number of researchers. Erez's review of research in Australia and in the USA demonstrates that VIS do not generate significant practical difficulties in operation; moreover, the claim is that VIS provide therapeutic benefits for the victim and enlightens the sentencer.[641] Other researchers conclude that VIS fail not only the victim but also the courts.[642] Sanders *et al.* identify six common purposes of victim participation: (1) giving victims a "voice" for therapeutic purposes; (2) for enabling the interests and views of victims to be taken into account in decision-making; (3) ensuring that victims are treated with respect by criminal justice agencies; (4) reducing the stress for victims of criminal proceedings; (5) increasing victim satisfaction with the criminal justice system; (6) increasing victim co-operation, as a result of any of the above objectives being fulfilled.[643]

Ashworth has also been extremely critical of the use of the victim impact statement. He argues that the victims' procedural rights (increased involvement in the system) and substantive rights (which include being given information and treated fairly) can be achieved without relying on VIS. He suggests that it would

[639] *R v Perks* [2001] 1 Cr.App.R. (S.) 19; I. Edwards, "The Place of Victims' Preferences in the Sentencing of 'Their Offenders' " [2002] Crim. L.R. 689.

[640] In Home Office Research conducted in 1998, R. C. Hoyle, E. Cope, R. Morgan and A. Sanders, *Evaluation of the One Stop Shop and Victim Statement Pilot Projects* (Home Office 1998) assessed the feelings of victims about the process of completing the report.

[641] E. Erez, "Who's Afraid of the Big Bad Victim? Victim Impact Statements on Victim Empowerment and Enhancement of Justice" [1999] Crim. L.R. 545.

[642] A. Sanders, C. Hoyle, R. Morgan and E. Cape, "Victim Impact Statements: Don't Work, Can't Work" [2001] Crim. L.R. 477.

[643] *ibid.* p.448

be preferable to empower victims by use of substantive rights without the disadvantages attaching to procedural rights.[644] Ashworth[645] observes that:

> "once the idea of victims' rights is closely scrutinised, however, the strength of its appeal becomes diluted. It is one thing to argue for the right of victims to compensation, support and sympathetic treatment both from law enforcement agencies and in court. It is quite another thing to argue that they should have the right to be represented in court, to submit a victim impact statement, or to be allowed to voice an opinion on sentence."[646]

Under the 1996 Victims' Charter a requirement was included that the police and the CPS take the victim's interests into account. The victim personal statement (VPS) detailed issues such as the emotional, financial and medical harm suffered by the victim.[647] The problem associated with the VPS, as with the VIS above, is that expectations are raised above what can be delivered. Sanders *et al.* discovered that only around one-third of victims claim to feel better for having made a personal statement, with 18 per cent feeling worse.[648] Nevertheless, despite (at best) ambiguous evidence about the efficacy of the VPS trials, they are now an accepted part of the criminal process, and can be taken into account by the court in sentencing.[649]

The position of the victim is taking on a more central position in the criminal justice system. In 2003 the Government established the Victims' Advisory Panel designed to allow representatives of victims' organisations to comment directly to relevant ministers on policy developments.[650] The Domestic Violence, Crime and Victims Act 2004 requires the Secretary of State to issue a code of practice setting out the duties of criminal justice agencies in relation to victims and witnesses,[651] and establishes a Commissioner for Victims and Witnesses to investigate complaints about failures to fulfil those duties. From 2006 a pilot scheme was introduced whereby "victims' advocates" can be appointed to make statements on behalf of the victim in certain murder and manslaughter cases.[652] This can be a lawyer or even a friend acting on behalf of the victim.

However, despite this clearly more central position for victims in the criminal justice system, the problem remains whether such moves are rhetoric or reality.[653] As Sanders and Young comment, "in one sense there is no stopping the trend towards the provision of victim information to criminal justice officials and the courts. This is partly because, in the political sphere, no one dares argue against victims' rights".[654]

---

[644] See Ashworth, "Victim Impact Statements and Sentencing" [1993] Crim. L.R. 498.

[645] "Crime, Community and Creeping Consequentialism" [1996] Crim. L.R. 220.

[646] *ibid.* p.224.

[647] See, J. Graham, K. Woodfield, M. Tibble and S. Kitchen, *Testaments of harm: a qualitative evaluation of the Victim Personal Statements Scheme* (National Centre for Social Research, 2004) L. McGowan, "When Victims Attack" (2006) N.L.J. 574.

[648] A. Sanders *et al.* [2001] Crim. L.R. 447 at 450

[649] See, Practice Direction (*Criminal Proceedings: Consolidation*) para.III.28.

[650] DVCVA 2004, s.55.

[651] DVCVA 2004, s.32.

[652] See, Department for Constitutional Affairs, *Hearing the Relatives of Murder and Manslaughter Victims: The Government's Plans to Give Bereaved Relatives of Murder and Manslaughter Victims a Say in Criminal Proceedings* (2005), available at *www.dca.gov.uk*; see also, J. Spencer, "Victim Advocates and Victim Care—the Place of the Victim in the Criminal Process" (2006) 10(4) Mags. C.P. 10.

[653] See I. Edwards, "A Genuine Voice?" (2005) N.L.J. 1341.

[654] Sanders and Young (2007), p.667.

7. THE JURY[655]

(a) Historical background[656]

The decision of the Fourth Lateran Council in 1215 to withdraw the support of **17–089**
the Roman Catholic Church from the process of trial by ordeal is generally
recognised as the factor which prompted the adoption of the jury system for the
determination of criminal cases. That the jury was in existence before 1215 is
undisputed, since it would have been almost the only means of collecting
information in administrative as well as judicial matters.[657] In addition to determining issues which were relevant to the king, juries came to be used for
determining issues of interest to private individuals and were available to replace
trial by battle.[658] When trespass was alleged, including the allegation of a breach
of the king's peace, a writ of *venire facias* went to the sheriff who summoned a
group of 12[659] men to meet and give a verdict on the allegation. On the demise
of trial by ordeal the jury was used to determine the guilt of alleged
criminals.[660]

In the beginning, the role of the jury was unclear.[661] Were the 12 individuals
to deliberate and deliver a verdict to the judge, or was the judge to treat them as
witnesses, examine them and then come to a decision? The resolution of this
question shaped the future of the jury and the future of criminal procedure.[662] In
the event, the collective deliberative role of the jury prevailed and the transition
from knowledge to ignorance as the primary characteristic of a juror began. The
landmarks are well known. By 1367 it had become established that the verdict
had to be unanimous.[663] Witnesses began to give evidence and the jury were

---

[655] Vast amounts of material are available. Some to which we shall particularly be referring in this
section includes: P. Darbyshire, A. Maughan and A. Stewart, *What Can the English Legal System
Learn From Jury Research Published up to 2001?* (2001), www.criminal-courts-review.org.uk; W.
R. Cornish, *The Jury* (1971); Lord Devlin, *Trial by Jury* (1956); N. Walker with A. Pearson (eds),
The British Jury System (1975); J. Baldwin and M. McConville, *Jury Trials* (1979); M. McCon-
ville and J. Baldwin, *Courts, Prosecution and Conviction* (1981); M. D. A. Freeman, "The Jury
on Trial" (1981) 34 C.L.P. 65; M. Findlay and P. Duff (eds), *The Jury Under Attack* (1988); S.
Enright and Morton, *Taking Liberties: The Criminal Jury in the 1990s* (1990); N. Vidmar, *World
Jury Systems* (2000); *Auld Report* (2001), Ch.5.

[656] Sir Frederick Pollock and F. W. Maitland, *History of English Law* (2nd edn, 1898), Vol.II,
pp.618–650; W. S. Holdsworth, *History of English Law* (3rd edn, 1922), Vol.1, pp.312–350; J. H.
Baker, *An Introduction to English Legal History* (3rd edn, 1990), Ch.5. For an account of the
function of the grand jury see A. Watson, "The Grand Jury in England's Past and America's
Present" (1998) 162 J.P.N. 839. For the recent history of the jury see, P. Thornton "Trial by Jury:
Fifty Years of Change" [2004] Crim. L.R. 633; *Archbold* (2007) para.4–199.

[657] The practice of getting a group together and putting them under oath to tell the truth had been
highly effective for the Normans.

[658] Under Henry II two assizes existed: the grand assize and the petty assize. It was the petty assize
which evolved into the jury.

[659] Why twelve? The answer is unknown, although it is the same number as the Apostles of Christ
and the ancient tribes of Israel. Psychological evidence suggests that this is not the optimal size
for the decision-making. See N. Fay, S. Garrod and J. Carletta, "Group Discussions Interactive
Dialogue or as Serial Monologue" (2000) 11 Psy. Science 41. See generally, Darbyshire *et al.*,
(2001) p.40.

[660] C. Wells, "Instructions Given by Henry III to Itinerant Justices 1219" (1914) 30 L.Q.R. 97.

[661] Pollock and Maitland (1898), pp.622 *et seq.*

[662] Guiding procedure into the adversarial system and away from the inquisitorial system with its
emphasis on judicial involvement.

[663] Baker (1990), p.90.

prevented from talking to any outsider until they reached a verdict.[664] In *Bushell's* case it was established that the jury had the right to give a verdict according to its conscience.[665] By the eighteenth century it was finally established that a juror should not take part in a case of which he had personal knowledge.

(b) The role of the jury

17–090   Discussing the role of the jury in the modern trial has become controversial since it is argued by many that it is impossible to conduct any meaningful examination of the role until we are aware of the way that juries actually function. At present, there is little modern research into the working of the English jury. There is a mass of other material (largely from the USA).[666]

The jury has been described as having three functions.[667] First, it is the jury that is to decide the facts and it is on those facts which it then determines guilt. The jury is to arrive at its verdict by considering whether it is satisfied that the prosecution has proved its case solely on the evidence presented at the trial and in accordance with the direction of the judge as to the law. Secondly, the jury adds certainty to the law, since it gives a general verdict. The jury merely states that the accused is either guilty or not guilty, and gives no reasons. The decision is not open to dispute. Thirdly, the jury represents the "just face" of the criminal justice system, since it can arrive at its unchallengeable decision on any basis it chooses. In particular, it is proper for the jury to arrive at an acquittal according to its conscience,[668] even if a conviction is clearly required according to the relevant law.

Whilst the jury has these functions, it is not all that should be said about its role, particularly since they could be performed by other bodies. Jury service is described as an important public duty.[669] It has been suggested that the jury satisfies the constitutional role that no-one should be tried apart from judgment by one's peers. Whilst this claim is frequently made, however, it does not follow that the phrase "judgment by one's peers" has a consistent meaning. Marshall suggests that it can mean one, or more, of the following:

> "1. A claim to the judgment of one's peers, or equals or neighbours
> 2. A claim to the judgment of a body of fair-minded persons
> 3. A claim to the judgment by an independent or impartial body of persons
> 4. A claim to the judgment of a randomly chosen body of persons

---

[664] *ibid.* p.89.

[665] *R v Sheriffs of London, Ex p. Bushell* (1670) Vaughn 135.

[666] On research generally see P. Robertshaw, "Method and Ethics in Advancing Jury Research" (1998) 38 Med. Sci. Law 328; and Darbyshire *et al.*, (2001).

[667] See P. Duff and M. Findlay, "The Jury in England: Practice and Ideology" (1982) 10 International Journal of the Sociology of Law 253. See also, M. Findlay, "The Role of the Jury in a Fair Trial" in Findlay and Duff (1988), Ch.10. See Lord Steyn, "The Role of the Bar, The Judge and the Jury: Winds of Change" [1999] P.L. 51; "the jury is an integral and indispensable part of our constitutional arrangements".

[668] As established in *Bushell's Case*. See also T. A. Green, *Verdict According to Conscience, 1200–1800* (1985) for a history of the jury in this role.

[669] Practice Direction (*Criminal Proccedings: Consolidation*) para.IV.42.

5. A claim to the judgment of a representative body of persons."[670]

In fulfilling its functions and its constitutional role, there are a number of qualities which enable a jury to perform effectively. Thus a jury, it is said, should be independent, impartial and representative, and it should be randomly selected. It is not the case that these qualities are always consistent; for example, a representative jury may be partial[671] and random selection does not necessarily produce fairness in the trial.[672]

(c) Qualification for jury service and selection

To *qualify* for selection as a juror, a person must be aged between 18 and 70, **17–091** registered as a parliamentary or local government elector, and have been ordinarily resident in the United Kingdom for any period of at least five years since the age of 13.

A person selected will not be permitted to serve as a juror if he or she falls into the categories of people disqualified or ineligible under Sch.1 to the Juries Act 1974.[673]

The people *disqualified* are those who: (1) are on bail in criminal proceedings; or (2) at any time have been sentenced in the United Kingdom to life imprisonment or custody for life; (3) or have been sentenced to detention during Her Majesty's pleasure; or (4) have been imprisoned or detained for public protection; or (5) have been given an extended sentence[674]; or (6) have been sentenced to imprisonment or detention for five years or more.

Until the CJA 2003 wider categories of people were *ineligible* for jury service, including: (1) the judiciary, (2) others concerned, or in the last 10 years concerned with the administration of justice, including barristers (and their clerks), solicitors and trainees, the staff of the Crown Prosecution Service, authorised advocates or litigators, court staff, prison officers and prison custody officers, police officers and forensic scientists, (3) the clergy. The Auld Report recommended that the categories of ineligibility be abolished,[675] and this was given effect in CJA 2003, s.321.[676] The aim was to take advantage of the skills and experience of a wide range of professional people and counter the idea that "jury service is only for those not important or clever enough to get out of it".[677] The objective of ineligibility for those concerned with the administration of justice was presumably on the basis either that a jury with lawyers on it will not decide according to the judge's direction but might use its own superior knowledge of the law, or that current or previous involvement in the criminal justice system

---

[670] G. Marshall, "The Judgement of One's Peers: Some Aims and Ideal of Jury Trial" in Walker with Pearson (1975), p.5.

[671] See M. Findlay with P. Byrne, "Introduction" in Findlay and Duff (1988).

[672] See Darbyshire *et al.* (2001); S. Lloyd-Bostock and C. Thomas, "Decline of the Little Parliament: Juries and Jury Reform in England and Wales" (1999) 62 Law and Contemporary Problems 7. This is a particular problem when faced with the issue of the racial mix of a jury; see below.

[673] As amended by the Criminal Justice Act 2003, s.321.

[674] Under CJA 2003, ss.227–228.

[675] Auld Report (2001), pp.144–149. See also Darbyshire *et al.* (2001),

[676] See *R v Abdroikov* [2005] EWCA Crim 1986.

[677] Auld Report (2001) Ch.5 para.14.

will deprive the jury of its impartiality. Such concerns have not disappeared[678] but the potential effects of the reforms cannot be evaluated fully due to the secrecy afforded to jury deliberations.

In 1972,[679] the requirement that a juror should be an occupier of a house with a prescribed rateable value was abolished, and the electoral register adopted as the basis of qualification. Since 1981, jurors have been selected by computer.[680] A number is allotted to every person on the electoral register, and a random number programme is then run through the computer to produce the jury list. As selection is made from the register of electors there is the potential for under-representation of certain groups.[681]

The precise representations of socio-economic groups and ethnic groups on juries is unclear. There is evidence that juries are less middle class[682] and much younger than before,[683] but there is still an under-representation of women and members of ethnic minorities.[684] The most significant challenges to the composition of the jury remains that relating to race: two-thirds of all juries are white.[685] The failure to ensure a representative jury has been explained by Bohlander as being that "there exists the distinct possibility that the different lifestyle, mentality and experience arising from membership of an ethnic minority will not be taken sufficiently into account in trials where members of such a minority are the defendants".[686] Daly and Pattenden more recently have expressed concern about the effects of a jury's unconscious racial bias when assessing issues such as witness credibility.[687]

The Auld Report made a controversial recommendation to allow a judge to empanel up to three jurors from an ethnic minority in a case in which race is

---

[678] P. Thornton "Trial by Jury: Fifty Years of Change" [2004] Crim. L.R. 633.

[679] By the Criminal Justice Act 1972, which implemented some of the recommendations of the Morris Committee (1965).

[680] See R. Tarling, "The Random Selection of Jurors", Home Office Research Bulletin No.13 (1982) and Lord Chancellor's Department, *The Crown Court: A Guide to Good Practice for the Courts* (1990), paras 9.1–9.2.

[681] See R. May, "Jury Selection in the USA: Are there lessons to be learned?" [1998] Crim. L.R. 270. On the jury summons and the way in which a more diverse pool can be gathered than by the use of an electoral register, see D. Schreckhise and C. H. Sheldon, "The Search for Greater Jury Diversity: The Case of the US DC System for the Eastern District of Washington" (1998) 20 The Justice System Journal 95. The sample, when gathered from a range of sources, was found to be more diverse, younger, less well-educated, more likely to include racial minorities and to bear a greater resemblance to the population. The problem of jurors being reluctant to serve seems to be universal; see e.g. in the USA. R. Seltzer, "The Vanishing Juror: Why There Are Not Enough Available Jurors" (1999) 20 Justice System Journal 203. See Darbyshire *et al.*, p.4.

[682] *Jury Trials* Table 10, p.95. See Sanders and Young (2007), p.501.

[683] *ibid.* Table 11, p.96. 27% of jurors empanelled in Birmingham in 1975 and 1976 were under 30.

[684] The Crown Court Survey discovered that more men than in the general population serve on juries (53% on juries and 48% in the general population); that most juries had a wide spread of ages; that most jurors were working full-time (69%); that there was a slight over-representation of clerical workers and under-representation of skilled manual workers; and that there were more people who left school later than in the general population: Zander and Henderson (1993), pp.234–241. Ethnic mix is considered in the text following. See for a critical survey Darbyshire *et al.* (2001), pp.3–10.

[685] Zander and Henderson (1993), p.241; C. Thomas and N. Balmer, Ministry of Justice, *Diversity and Fairness in the Jury System*, Ministry of Justice Research Series 2/07 (2007).

[686] M. Bohlander, "'By a jury of his peers'—The Issue of Multi-racial Juries in a Polyethnic Society" (1992) XIV(1) Liverpool L.R. 67. Sanders and Young (2007), p.507.

[687] G. Daly and R. Pattenden, "Racial Bias and the English Criminal Trial Jury" (2005) 64(3) Camb. L.J. 678.

likely to be an important issue. This model is based on American research.[688] It has been criticised because it rests on the assumption that a randomly selected jury will not be capable of hearing a case without racial bias. Moreover, the selected jurors might well regard themselves as second-class jurors,[689] and there has been little evidence to suggest that this will produce greater public confidence in the system.[690] However, research carried out in six Crown Court centres between 2001 and 2002 was able to draw the explicit conclusion that:

"The most important reported factor that had a positive influence on juror confidence in this study was the perceived benefits of having a diverse group of people from different social and economic backgrounds with different viewpoints and experiences. Diversity was seen as an essential component in deciding guilt and innocence in all trials ranging from the minor cases to the most serious."[691]

The Court of Appeal in *R v Ford*[692] decided that a trial judge has no power to interfere with the composition of the jury or the jury panel in order to produce a multi-racial jury and that there is no principle that a jury should be racially balanced. Attempts to construct a jury (for reasons other than race) by selecting on the basis of their post codes has been rejected.[693] The argument in favour of racially balancing the jury is to avoid partiality.

The damage done to the criminal justice system by the perception of racist juries is demonstrated by cases such as *Sanders v UK*[694] where the ECtHR found a breach of Art.6 when the trial judge had failed to discharge a jury having discovered that they had made racist jokes.

It is not possible to challenge the summoning officer on the basis that the jury panel is not representative, because no black person is on the panel, although if bias or other impropriety could be shown then a challenge could be founded.[695]

(d) Summons, empanelling and vetting

The people selected for jury service receive a summons requiring them to attend at the Crown Court at a specified time. Accompanying the summons are a form, **17–092**

---

[688] pp.156–159. See Darbyshire *et al.* (2001), pp.16–18. The results extrapolated from research by L. Bridges, S. Choongh and M. McConville, *Ethnic Minority Defendants and the Right to Elect Jury Trial* (2000) could suggest that there are lower conviction rates in some instance where a greater proportion of the jury shares D's ethnicity.

[689] See J. Abramson, *We, The Jury*, (1994), Ch.3.

[690] See generally N. King, "The effects of Race Conscious Jury Selection on Public Confidence in the Fairness of Jury Proceedings: An Empirical Puzzle" (1994) 31 American Crim. L.R. 1177.

[691] R. Matthew, L. Hancock, and D. Briggs, *Jurors' Perceptions, Understanding, Confidence and Satisfaction in the Jury System: a study in six courts* (2004) p.3. Online Report 05/04 available at: *www.homeoffice.gov.uk/rds/*.

[692] [1989] 3 All E.R. 445. The court's reasons for rejecting the power were that it would interfere with random selection, that the power would have to be granted by statute and that it interferes with the responsibility of the Lord Chancellor's Department to summon jurors, *ibid.* pp.448–449. The Court of Appeal has held that the decision in Ford is not affected by the Human Rights Act 1998: *R v Smith* [2003] 1 W.L.R. 2229.

[693] See *R v Tarrant* [1998] Crim. L.R. 342; and also, *R v Smith (Lance Percival)* [2003] 1 W.L.R. 2229.

[694] *Sanders v UK* [2000] Crim. L.R. 767.

[695] *R v Ford* [1989] 3 All E.R. 445 at 450.

which is intended to identify those ineligible or disqualified, and a set of notes,[696] which explains something of the procedure of jury service and the functions of the juror.[697] A failure to attend the Crown Court can result in a fine, as can unfitness for service through drink or drugs after attendance.[698] Again, the implicit assumption is that a person must be competent in order to act as a juror. This principle, in the circumstances, permits derogation from the requirement that the jury be randomly selected. Darbyshire *et al.*, found that up to one in six people did not attend, and that there was no sanction ever imposed on such individuals.[699]

Those summoned for service constitute the jury panel for that court and from that panel the jury for an individual case will be selected. The panel may be divided into parts relating to different days or sittings.[700] The jury list contains the names, addresses and dates for attendance of the panel. The parties to the case and their lawyers are entitled to inspect the list before or during the trial.[701] Such information may assist counsel in deciding whether to challenge any of the jurors but, since the occupation of jurors is no longer provided, there is very little on which defence counsel may rely for a challenge for cause without further investigation into the individual's life.

The controversial subject of *jury vetting* surfaced in 1978 as a result of the trial of a soldier and two journalists (Aubrey, Berry and Campbell) on charges under the Official Secrets Act 1911. It became apparent during the trial that the jury panel had been investigated by the prosecuting authority, and, in the ensuing public debate, the Attorney-General published the guidelines under which the vetting had been carried out.[702]

The guidelines make clear that vetting may involve the search of criminal records for the purpose of ascertaining whether or not a member of the panel is a disqualified person,[703] or the limited further investigation of members of the panel (a) in security or terrorist cases[704] with the object of revealing political beliefs which are so biased that they might interfere with the juror's fair

---

[696] The information that is presented to prospective jurors can be found at *www.courtservice.gov.uk/*

[697] The notes assist the juror in the task by dealing with the swearing-in and challenges, trial procedure, the verdict, secrecy, taking notes, etc.

[698] Juries Act 1974, s.20, as amended by the Criminal Justice and Public Order Act 1994, Sch.10, para.28. The person summonsed must attend and not someone standing in for them. In response to claims of juror impersonation see S. Enright, "Britain's Reluctant Jurors" (1989) 138 N.L.J. 538), the Lord Chancellor's Department has emphasised that it is a criminal offence for any person to impersonate a juror, and as a matter of routine court staff will check on identity: (1989) 138 N.L.J. 758. A failure to comply with security procedures to enter the court and a failure to be available for service: *R v Dodds* [2003] 1 Cr.App.R. 3.

[699] On the Imposition of fines see the procedure to be adopted as outlined in *R v Dodds* [2003] 1 Cr.App.R. 3.

[700] Juries Act 1974, s.5.

[701] *ibid.* s.5(2), (3).

[702] The current full text is to be found at (1989) 88 Cr.App.R. 124.

[703] The Annex to the Guidelines contains the Recommendations of the Association of Chief Police Officers with regard to the carrying out of checks on the previous convictions of the jury panel to ensure that disqualified persons do not sit on a jury. For the full text, see (1989) 88 Cr.App.R. 124.

[704] These are cases described as being exceptional types of cases of public importance for which the provisions as to majority verdicts and the disqualification of jurors may not be sufficient to ensure the proper administration of justice. Jury vetting is thus a further safeguard in (a) security cases, defined as cases in which national security is involved and part of the evidence is likely to be heard in *camera*, and (b) terrorist cases, of which no definition is provided: *Attorney-General's Guidelines* (1989) 88 Cr.App.R. 124.

assessment of the facts or lead a juror to exert improper pressure on fellow jurors, or (b) in security cases alone with the object of discovering whether a juror might be in danger of making improper use of evidence given *in camera*.[705] A further investigation is made, on the personal authority of the Attorney-General, using the records of Police Special Branches and, with regard to the cases in (b), the security services, and is known as an "authorised check". No checks other than with these sources and no general inquiries may be made except to the limited extent that they may be needed to confirm the identity of a juror. The information gleaned from an authorised check is sent to the Director of Public Prosecutions, who decides what information ought to be provided to prosecuting counsel. Consequently, a juror may be asked to stand by for the Crown provided it is appropriate to exercise that power in the circumstances,[706] but the prosecution is under a duty to ask a juror to stand by where he or she might be biased against the defendant.[707]

(e) Excusal and discretionary deferral

Any member of a jury panel may be excused service at the discretion of the appropriate officer, for good reason,[708] in addition to those who may be excused as of right because they have recently served or are members of the armed services. The latter two provisions are straightforward, but the discretion to excuse from service is not one which is widely known. A person's attendance may be deferred once if it is shown to the appropriate officer that there is good reason for it.[709] **17–093**

Concern has been expressed at the ease with which some people are excused jury service with little or no scrutiny of the reasons provided. The danger is that juries will come to be constituted almost exclusively of the elderly and unemployed. There are numerous reasons for the seeking excusal with medical reasons, childcare commitments, employment, holidays, etc., all playing a part.[710]

---

[705] *ibid.*

[706] As to the guidance on the exercise of the power of stand by as a consequence of jury vetting, see the *Attorney-General's Guidelines*, paras 9, 10, 11 and 12.

[707] The prosecution is only obliged to give a (general) indication of why a juror may be inimical to their interests: *Attorney-General's Guidelines*, para.11.

[708] Juries Act 1974 s.9(2). If the appropriate officer refuses to excuse a person from jury service an appeal to the court may be made, see Criminal Procedure Rules 2005 (S.I. 2005 No.384), r.39.2. Any person who so appeals must be given an opportunity to make representations in support of the appeal. See *R v Guildford Crown Court, Ex p. Siderfin* [1990] 2 Q.B. 683.

[709] See Derbyshire *et al.* (2001), pp.3–10, and A. Shaw and J. Airs, *Jury Excusal and Deferral* (H.O. RDS No 102, 1999); H. Fukurai, "The Representative Cross-Section Requirement: Jury Representativeness and Cross-Sectional Participation from the Beginning to the End of the Jury Selection Process" (1999) 23 Int. J. Comp. and Applied Crim. J. 56.

[710] See Matthew, Hancock, and Briggs (2004): in their study in six Crown Court centres 36% of jurors applied for deferral, many citing work or domestic pressures. On jurors' negative attitudes to service see Darbyshire *et al.*, p.44. The Crown Court Study carried out for the Runciman Royal Commission included jury questionnaires. Jurors were asked "How interesting have you found being on jury service?" The majority said they found it either "Very interesting" (74%), or "Fairly interesting" (22%). Only 4% were negative about the experience. Jurors were asked to rate the jury system overall. One third (33%) thought it was a "Very good system" and 47% thought it was a "Good system". 15% had no particular view. Only 3% thought it a "Poor system" and 2% a "Very poor system".

(f) Ballot, challenges and swearing in

17–094   From the jury panel, the jury for a particular case is selected by ballot in open court.[711] The clerk of the court has the names of all members of the panel. The names are put on cards, the cards are shuffled and the clerk reads out the names from the pile of cards. Hence, a random selection should be achieved from a randomly-selected panel. It is legitimate to call by numbers in the event that there is a fear of jury intimidation.[712]

On entering the jury box to be sworn, each juror may be challenged by the prosecution or the defence.[713] The defence has only the right to challenge for cause. The prosecution has the right to challenge for cause or to require a juror to stand by.

Challenge for cause has been fairly unusual,[714] but the abolition of peremptory challenge and the imposition of restrictions on the prosecution's right to stand by "have given new practical importance to what had been thought to be [this] largely obsolescent institution".[715] It is possible to challenge the panel,[716] but the most likely use of challenge is to individual jurors. Challenge can be on statutory grounds, that is on the basis of ineligibility or disqualification, or common law grounds. There are four possible forms of common law challenge: privilege of peerage; past criminal conviction; lack of requisite qualification; and presumed or actual bias in the juror.

Of these grounds of challenge, the first three are relatively straightforward, since they refer back to ineligibility and disqualification.[717] Bias requires further consideration. In this context it means "whether the individual juror will be able to, and will, be loyal to his oath to give a true verdict according to the evidence".[718] Buxton classifies bias into three headings:

(a) connection with the case[719] or with the parties,[720] and if there is a connection, bias is in effect assumed;

(b) knowledge of the accused's character[721] and if there is knowledge, bias is also in effect assumed;

(c) general hostility,[722] in this case, bias is not assumed but must be established.

---

[711] Juries Act 1974, s.11.

[712] See *R v Comerford* [1998] 1 Cr.App.R. 235.

[713] See R. Buxton, "Challenging and Discharging Jurors—1" [1990] Crim. L.R. 225.

[714] In a survey of 3,165 cases the defence challenged for cause in 39 cases, i.e. 1% and the prosecution challenged for cause in 25 cases, i.e. 1%: J. Vennard and D. Riley, "The Use of Peremptory Challenge and Stand by of Jurors and their Relationship to Trial Outcome" [1988] Crim. L.R. 731.

[715] Buxton (1990), p.225.

[716] *ibid.* pp.225–226.

[717] See Buxton (1990), pp.228–229. Buxton, p.228, points out that, whilst not all criminal convictions can ground a challenge for cause as such, nevertheless a criminal conviction might ground a challenge on some other basis such as bias, as indicated by the Court of Appeal in *R v Mason* [1981] Q.B. 881.

[718] Buxton (1990), pp.229–230.

[719] e.g., that the juror is personally connected with the facts of the particular case, see *ibid.* p.230.

[720] e.g. that the juror is related to one of the parties, see *ibid.*

[721] Personal knowledge is intended here, not that gained through the media, which may, though, in exceptional circumstances be sufficient, see *ibid.* pp.231–232.

[722] e.g. the holding of political opinions. The court in *R v Swain* (1838) 2 M. & Rob. 112 emphasised the need to establish more than mere general hostility. In that case two jurors' active opposition to the Poor Law Act 1834 founded such a challenge, see Buxton (1990), p.232.

It follows from the meaning of bias that the fact that a juror is of a particular race or holds a particular religious belief cannot be the basis of a challenge for cause on the grounds of bias (or any other ground).[723]

Jurors cannot be questioned before being challenged to ascertain whether there is ground for bias, consequently basing a challenge on lack of requisite qualification or bias may be particularly difficult, especially since the defence only has information as to the juror's name and address and not as to occupation.[724] If a challenge is made, it is tried by the trial judge.[725] The burden of proof lies on the party challenging. Witnesses may be called to support or defeat the challenge, but a prima facie case must be made before the challenged juror may be cross-examined, upon which fairly stringent limits are placed. The question of bias is assessed according to the test described in *In re Medicaments and Related Classes of Goods (No.2).*[726] The House of Lords has subsequently approved this ECHR-compatible test of bias[727]: would a fair minded and informed observer conclude that there was a real possibility, or real danger, the two being the same, that there was bias.

The prosecution still retains the right to stand by for the Crown.[728] The prosecution has the right (without providing a reason) to require someone not to sit on the jury (stand by) unless there are not enough members of the panel left from which to produce a jury. Any challenges thereafter have to be for cause. Whilst this right of standing by still exists, its use has been limited through the issuing of guidelines by the Attorney-General which specifically state that the abolition of the peremptory challenge means that "the Crown should assert its right to stand by only on the basis of clearly defined and restrictive criteria".[729] These criteria do not include the right to influence the overall composition of the jury nor should the right be exercised with a view to tactical advantage,[730] but the right may be used in connection with jury vetting or where a juror is manifestly unsuitable and the defence agree with the exercise of the power.[731] The judge has a residual power to exclude a juror at his discretion, as for example where the juror is infirm and counsel has not challenged.[732]

A juror, having entered the jury box and remained unchallenged, is then sworn[733] in. When 12 have been sworn the accused may be "given in charge" to

---

[723] *R v Ford* [1989] 3 All E.R. 445 at 449.

[724] The restriction on questioning is imposed by *R v Dowling* (1845) 7 St. Tr. (N.S.) 381; *R v Stewart* (1845)1 Cox C.C. 174; Buxton (1990), p.226. See *R v Andrews* [1999] Crim. L.R. 156 on the questioning of potential jurors to ascertain whether they had an interest in the case (e.g. knowledge of adverse publicity). Compare the very different position in the United States where potential jurors may be questioned to ascertain whether they might be prejudiced. In one case it took four months to question 1,035 people before a jury could be sworn. See Harman and Griffith (1979), pp.26–27 and M. George, "Jury Selection, Texas Style" (1988) 138 N.L.J. 438. Buxton (1990), p.227, n.15 points out that the recommendation of the Roskill Committee on Fraud Trials to re-instate the provision of a juror's occupation has not been implemented.

[725] Juries Act 1974, s.12(l). The judge may order that the hearing of a challenge for cause be *in camera* or in chambers: Criminal Justice Act 1988, s.118(2).

[726] [2000] 1 W.L.R. 700.

[727] *Porter v Magill* [2002] 2 A.C. 357.

[728] The constitutionality of the right to stand by was confirmed in *R v McCann* (1991) 92 Cr.App.R. 239.

[729] (1989) 88 Cr.App.R. 123, para.3.

[730] *ibid.* para.1.

[731] The power, therefore, can be used where it becomes apparent that a juror selected to try a complex case is illiterate: *ibid.* para.5.

[732] See e.g. *R v Mason* [1981] Q.B. 881, 887.

[733] See Practice Direction (*Criminal Proceedings: Consolidation*) para.IV.42.4.

the jury and the trial can begin.[734] Each jury should, save in exceptional circum-stances hear only one case as a group. Therefore the members are distributed back in the pool from which future jury groups will be selected.[735]

(g) Discharge[736]

17–095   The judicial power to discharge[737] the entire jury or individual jurors once the trial has begun is closely related to the challenge for cause considered above. Consequently, there is no power to discharge a jury because of its racial mix.[738] A judge's decision to discharge a jury or juror is unchallengeable, whereas if the judge decides not to discharge, that decision may be challenged on appeal against conviction by the accused on the basis that the conviction is to be regarded as unsafe because there was no discharge.[739]

If doubt arises about the capacity to act as a juror because of physical disability or insufficient understanding of English, an individual juror may be discharged. It may also be appropriate to accommodate a juror where necessary by exercising the discharge power, for example, on the death of a relative.[740]

The discharge power enables the judge to deal with irregularities and impropri-eties before and after the retirement of the jury to consider its verdict. If something untoward might have happened the judge has the power to investigate by questioning the jurors.[741] Before retirement, the sort of matters which may lead the judge to discharge a juror are: drunkenness; inattention to the proceed-ings; frivolous behaviour; acquisition of information which ought not to be available to a juror, such as existing knowledge of the accused's bad character; or contact with someone outside the jury which in the circumstances is an irregularity rather than acceptable conduct and which may interfere with the course of justice.[742] In view of the nexus between challenge and discharge, an important ground for discharge is bias in a juror becoming apparent later than the time for challenge. In some cases the bias of an individual juror may lead to the discharge of the jury as a whole, since the accused's right to a fair trial has been prejudiced.[743] The trial judge ought not to make inquiry into the eligibility of a juror on the basis of a jury note or question save to ensure that adequate inquiry was made of the juror before the trial commenced.[744]

---

[734] This is not an essential part of trial procedure. At the end of the swearing-in, the clerk may read the indictment to the jury and tell them that it is their "charge" to say whether the accused is guilty or not.

[735] See Juries Act 1974, s.11.

[736] See R. Buxton, "Challenging and Discharging Jurors—2" [1990] Crim. L.R. 84.

[737] Juries Act 1974, s.16.

[738] *R v Ford* [1989] 3 All E.R. 445. See H. Fukurai, E. W. Butler and R. Krooth, *Race and the Jury: Racial Disenfranchisement and the Search for Justice* (1993).

[739] Juries act 1974, s.18. See *R v Panayis* [1999] Crim. L.R. 84; Buxton, (1990–91), pp.284–285.

[740] *ibid.* p.285. The power must be exercised by a High Court or Circuit judge or recorder.

[741] *R v Appiah* [1998] Crim. L.R. 134.

[742] *ibid.* pp.286–287. See also *Putnam* (1991) 93 Cr.App.R. 281 and *Thorpe* [1996] 1 Cr.App.R. 269. The judge can investigate by questioning the jury or jurors to ascertain whether there has been any interference: see *R v Appiah* [1998] Crim. L.R. 134.

[743] *ibid.* pp.287–288, commenting on *R v Spencer* [1987] A.C. 128 where the House of Lords decided that the failure to discharge the jury after three of them had been in discussion with a biased, discharged juror who may well have influenced them, meant that the conviction had to be quashed as being unsafe. Caution must be exercised: *R v Doherty* [1997] 1 Cr.App.R. 274. On the test for bias see: *Porter v Magill* [2002] A.C. 357.

[744] *R v Obellim* [1997] 1 Cr.App.R. 355.

A long trial can place a considerable strain on the jury and there are provisions which allow the discharge of individual jurors in the course of a trial in the event of illness or other good reason.[745] So long as the jury does not fall below nine members, the trial can proceed.[746]

It is not always necessary for a judge to discharge a jury even where there have been attempts to influence or intimidate them.[747] The integrity of the jury is what matters and the trial judge is the master of his or her court, and is entitled to question members of the public regarding "seemingly untoward conduct" in the court. In considering discharging the jury, the cost of a retrial is not a factor for the judge to consider.[748] The trial judge retains the power to set aside the discharge of the jury where that was ordered on a mistaken belief that they were unable to reach a verdict provided the jury had not dispersed or communicated with others.[749]

After retirement, the jury must not separate or speak to anyone. If there is any such separation or communication the jury will normally be discharged.[750] A single juror may be discharged after the jury have retired if the judge exercises his discretion to do so.[751]

(h) The trial, the summing-up and the deliberations

During the course of the trial the members of the jury sit together in the jury box and listen to the evidence and the speeches of counsel. Jurors are entitled to take notes if they wish.[752] Such notes taken are subject to the same restrictions of secrecy as the jurors' deliberations. Jurors may also ask questions.[753] At an early stage of the trial, probably at the first adjournment, the jurors will be warned not to discuss the case with anyone except amongst themselves, and then only in the jury room. This instruction is designed to prevent outside influences on jurors[754] and may be reinforced by a reminder not to come to a view about the case until

17–096

---

[745] Juries Act 1974, s.16, provides that a juror can be discharged when incapable of continuing to act through illness or for any other reason. The power to discharge should be exercised generously. Trial by jury depends upon the willing co-operation of the public and, in any event, an aggrieved and inconvenienced juror is not likely to be a good one: *R v Hambery* [1977] Q.B. 924.

[746] Juries Act 1974, s.16(1). The number required for a majority verdict is adjusted accordingly.

[747] *R v Thorpe* [1996] Crim. L.R. 273 (suspicious liaison between member of public and juror (her fiancee)).

[748] *R v Blackwell* [1996] Crim. L.R. 428. See also *R v Walker* [1996] Crim. L.R. 752, the court should not take account of early aborted trial and length of present trial.

[749] *R v Aylott* [1996] 2 Cr.App.R. 169.

[750] Buxton, (1990–91), pp.288–291. Permission may be granted under the Juries Act 1974, s.13, which, since the amendment of the Criminal Justice and Public Order Act 1994, includes the period after retirement of the jury.

[751] *R v Wood* [1997] Crim L.R. 229.

[752] Although some have doubted the value of this (see Cornish (1971), pp.50–51), the Royal Commission has recommended that the judge should explain in the opening remarks that they may make notes: RCCJ, Report (1993), p.134. This was based upon the discovery that jurors frequently found notes helpful: Zander and Henderson (1993), pp.201–212. Jurors interviewed following the Jubilee Line case expressed that they would have appreciated more advice at the beginning of the trial on procedures such as taking notes: S. Lloyd-Bostock, *Report on Interviews with Jurors in the Jubilee Line Case* (HMCPSI, 2006) at p.5.

[753] They rarely do so: Zander and Henderson (1993), pp.213–214.

[754] Not necessarily sinister influences: the juror must give a verdict according to the evidence adduced in court and not on any other basis.

all the evidence and arguments have been heard.[755] Research confirms that the most important factor in the jury's decision-making is the evidence in the case.[756] There has been a growing concern about the impact of pre-trial publicity and the potential prejudice to jurors,[757] particularly in high-profile cases.

The contents of the summing up have been noted in the preceding section, as well as the significant place it has in the sequence of the trial. Prichard,[758] suggests that the judge should give the jury a *pro forma* to assist in their decision-making, but questions whether this would add to delay and intimidate the jury thereby preventing "principled acquittals". It would provide a more structured debate in the jury room and would render appeals more easily processed, and could enhance respect for the jury.[759] The Auld Report[760] has recommended that juror's be provided with better information on decision-making and also encouraged more effective summings-up with questionnaires to focus the jury on the right inquiries.[761]

The initial direction on verdict will be that unanimity should be achieved, and although the jurors will know from the notes provided that a majority verdict is possible, the object of the deliberations should be unanimity.[762] The jury will be instructed to appoint a foreman when they retire. At the end of the summing up the jury retires to the jury room to consider its verdict and are kept together privately until a verdict is reached or it is discharged.[763] It will only be in an exceptional case that the trial judge asks the jury to consider the verdict without retiring to the jury room.[764] In a complex case the jury may be provided with written instructions to assist their deliberations.[765] Darbyshire *et al.* discovered that, on average, three jurors per average jury are responsible for 50 per cent of the discussion.[766]

The judge must be careful not to put the jury under pressure to reach a verdict, in particular, he or she should avoid indicating a particular time by which they should return a verdict,[767] and must be cautious in the words chosen to encourage

---

[755] This instruction may not always be heeded. The anonymous juror in the Thorpe trial revealed that the jury had decided on acquittal on the first day of the trial: see "Thorpe's Trial: How the Jury Saw It" *New Statesman*, July 27, 1979.

[756] See Darbyshire *et al.* (2001), p.12; but note also the reports that jurors do not follow the warnings against reasoning from propensity: V. Hans and A. N. Doob, "Section 12 of the Canadian Evidence Act and the Deliberation of Simulated Juries" (1976) 18 Crim. L.Q. 235.

[757] See D. Corker and M. Levi, "Pre-trial Publicity and its Treatment in the English Courts" [1996] Crim. L.R. 622 considering the relationship between pre-trial publicity, prejudice, and a willingness to exercise powers of contempt.

[758] "A Reform of the Jury Trial" (1998) 148 N.L.J. 475.

[759] For disturbing evidence of how poor jurors' grasp of the directions is, see Darbyshire *et al.* (2001), p.26 and on how significant the direction is for the deliberation see N. Finkel, *Commonsense Justice: Juror's Notions of the Law* (1995).

[760] Auld, pp.532–538.

[761] On written instructions to the jury see Darbyshire *et al.* (2001), pp.35–36. See also Lloyd-Bostock (2006): jurors expressed that they would have appreciated guidance on what to expect from the summing up and directions.

[762] See *R v Daly* [1999] Crim. L.R. 88.

[763] Circumstances are now somewhat less primitive than when juries were locked up without refreshment to encourage them to concentrate. Juries are now allowed refreshment at their own expense: Juries Act 1974, s.15.

[764] *R v Rankine* [1997] Crim. L.R. 757. The jury dealt with the case without retiring, but although the conviction was quashed, the Court of Appeal approved the practice on the facts of that case. For criticism see I. Khan and C. Thatcher, "Justice on a Show of Hands" (1997) N.L.J. 1182.

[765] *R v McKechnie* (1992) 94 Cr.App.R. 51. See also, Lloyd-Bostock (2006).

[766] p.31.

[767] See *R v Buttle* [2006] Crim. L.R. 840; *R v, Duffin* [2003] EWCA Crim 3064.

a jury to reach a verdict without undue pressure.[768] The judge is under a continuing duty to assist the jury.[769]

The jury bailiff must ensure that no one comes into contact with the jury except by leave of the court.[770] In particularly difficult cases it may be necessary to provide overnight hotel accommodation for the jurors under the close supervision of the court. If the jury are allowed to separate during their consideration of the verdict, the trial judge should remind them of the need to decide the case on the evidence and not to talk to anyone about the case other than in the jury room and not to allow others to talk to them about the case.[771]

If the jury requires further information from the judge to explain a point in the summing-up, or if guidance is required, the normal practice is for counsel to be consulted and the jury, if necessary, brought back into court.

The judge then tries to resolve the problem and may, if appropriate, remind the jury of the evidence. The jury should not receive any further evidence once they have begun their deliberations.[772] The jury can and do ask questions of the judge as they are entitled to do. The correct procedure is for their questions to be relayed to the judge who, except when responding to questions unconnected with the trial, should deal with the question in open court so that counsel are present.[773] This reduces the risk that the judge will be perceived as influencing the jury one way or another. It is arguable that defence counsel ought to be informed of all communications from the jury. The only exception to this policy of openness with jury communications is that the trial judge ought never to reveal jury voting figures if these have been revealed to him. Matters drawn to the judges' attention which relate to "domestic" matters of the jury and those relating to the trial are distinguishable; it is necessary always to inform counsel of jury communications relating to the trial and desirable though not essential with "domestic" matters.[774] Once a verdict has been received and the court concludes that it is unambiguous it cannot investigate further.[775]

Jury communications to the judge can create considerable difficulty. In *Schot and Barclay*,[776] a juror's note to the judge explaining the absence of a verdict on the "conscious" beliefs (*sic*) of the juror had led the judge to ask for an explanation which then led him to discharge the jury. The judge initiated contempt proceedings against *Schot and Barclay* (the jurors). S claimed that she just did not understand the case, and B refused to take part. The judge found both in contempt and sentenced them to 30 days' imprisonment. On appeal, the Court quashed the convictions holding that it was incorrect for the judge to investigate

17–097

---

[768] See *R v Watson* [1988] Q.B. 690 at 700. *R v Baker* [1998] Crim. L.R. 351.

[769] *R v Naway, The Times*, June 8, 1999.

[770] Juries Act 1974, s.13. This rule is enforced very strictly and any breach of it is likely to lead to the discharge of the jury or the later quashing of any conviction: *R v Prime* (1973) 57 Cr.App.R. 632; *R v Goodson* [1975] 1 W.L.R. 549; *R v Davis* (1960) 44 Cr.App.R. 235.

[771] *R v Oliver* [1996] 2 Cr.App.R. 514. see e.g. juror making mobile phone calls; *R v Farooq* [1995] Crim. L.R. 169. On using the internet for private research during the trial see; *R v Karakaya* [2005] 2 Cr.App.R. 5; *R v Marshall* [2007] EWCA Crim 35.

[772] *R v Owen* [1952] 2 Q.B. 362 (oral evidence); *R v Davies* (1975) 62 Cr.App.R. 194 (documentary); *R.v McNamara* [1996] Crim. L.R. 750 (requesting the defendant to turn to provide a profile view).

[773] See *R v Gorman* [1987] 1 W.L.R. 545.

[774] *R v Brown and Stratton* [1998] Crim. L.R. 505; *R v Conroy and Glover* [1997] 2 Cr.App.R. 285. On the desirability for the judge to keep defence counsel informed of any inquiry into the jury's proceedings see *R v Obellim* [1996] Crim. L.R. 601.

[775] *R v Hart* [1998] Crim. L.R. 418; *Ramstaed v The Queen* [1999] 2 A.C. 92.

[776] (1997) 161. J.P. 473

the circumstances, and finding that the judge should have given a majority verdict direction in those circumstances.

Jurors will not be permitted to take tools into the jury room to conduct experiments relevant to the case (e.g. scales for weighing drugs).[777] The jury may be provided with exhibits if requested, but in the case of tapes they should be replayed if at all in open court.[778] A jury should not be allowed, e.g. a knife after retiring. In the event that the jury have any materials in the retiring room, the judge must warn them as to their legitimate uses.[779] No new evidence may be received at this stage, so that if an exhibit is tampered with the trial may be unfair.[780]

The jurors will select a person known as a "foreman" to speak for the jury on all matters and, ultimately, to deliver the verdict. An important aspect of the role of the foreman is to chair the jury's deliberations. Consequently, he or she has the possibility of significantly influencing the decision.[781] The method of selection is a matter for the jury.[782] In some other jurisdictions, juries select a foreman at the outset, and their judges have suggested that not to do so would be "disastrous".[783]

The deliberations of the jury are kept secret. Jurors are told that what is said in the jury room should not be disclosed to anyone even after the trial is over.[784] There have been examples of this instruction being ignored and some of what is known about the jury and the way in which it approaches its task emanates from the published experiences of individual jurors.[785] Statute makes it contempt of court to obtain, disclose or solicit any particulars of statements made, opinions expressed, arguments advanced or votes cast by members of a jury in the course of their deliberations in any legal proceedings.[786]

The sacrosanct principle of the privacy of the jury deliberations does not extend to events occurring with the jury outside the jury room. In *Young*[787] the Court of Appeal were able to conduct an inquiry into the incidents of a jury in a hotel during their deliberations where the jury had sought to contact, via a ouija board, the victim of the alleged murder they were trying.

The confidentiality of jury deliberations has been considered by the House of Lords. In *Mirza*[788] and *Connor* the House of Lords considered conjoined cases where, in the first instance, a letter had been written to the trial judge by a juror claiming that there had been racial prejudice against the defendant during the

---

[777] See *Stewart* (1989) 89 Cr.App.R. 273.

[778] *R v Riaz* (1991) 94 Cr.App.R. 339; *R v Hagan* [1999] 1 Cr.App.R. 464.

[779] *R v Crees* [1996] Crim. L.R. 830.

[780] See *R v Kaul* [1998] Crim. L.R. 135; *cf. R. v Abrar, The Times*, May 26, 2000, where the new evidence was revealed only by an examination of the exhibit.

[781] J. Baldwin and M. McConville, "Juries, Foremen and Verdicts" (1980) 20 Brit. J. Crim. 35.

[782] The question apparently often put is, "Has anybody been on a jury before?" A juror who admits to experience often becomes foreman.

[783] See the N.Z. research below.

[784] As they are informed in the notes accompanying the jury summons.

[785] E. Devons, "Serving as a Juryman in Britain" (1965) 28 M.L.R. 561; D. Barber and G. Gordon (eds), *Members of the Jury* (1976).

[786] Contempt of Court Act 1981, s.8(1). Such proceedings for contempt may only be brought by, or with the permission of, the Attorney-General, or on the motion of a competent court: s.8(3). A competent court for this purpose is one which has jurisdiction to deal with the alleged contempt. This includes attempts by the defence to investigate matters: *Mickleburgh* [1995] 1 Cr.App.R. 297; *McCluskey* (1994) 98 Cr.App.R. 216; *Schot* [1997] 2 Cr.App.R. 383.

[787] *R v Young* [1995] Q.B. 324. See J. Spencer [1995] Camb. L.J. 519.

[788] *R v Mirza; R. v Connor* [2004] 1 All E.R. 925.

jury's deliberations.[789] In the second case, a juror claimed that the jury had been anxious to reach a verdict quickly and had not given sufficuent consideration to the case. The Court of Appeal had dismissed both appeals on the basis that jury deliberations were sacrosanct and what had been said in private was inadmissible as evidence. The House of Lords agreed. The common law rule prohibiting evidence of jury deliberations was compatible with the right to a fair trial under Art.6 of the European Convention on Human Rights. Indeed, it was stated that the common law rule actually buttressed Art.6 in allowing the jury to operate effectively.[790]

The House of Lords returned to the issue in *Smith*,[791] where a juror wrote to   **17–098**
the trial judge during the trial to state that other jurors were ignoring the directions they had been given. The trial judge had sought to repeat his directions in more forceful terms though the House of Lords allowed the appeal on the basis that the trial judge's directions had not been robust enough to ensure that the jury carried out their task appropriately for the remainder of the trial. Lord Carswell set out six scenarios relating to how the common law rule operates where the propriety of the jury verdict is in issue:

(1) The general rule is that the court will not investigate, or receive evidence about, anything said in the course of the jury's deliberations while they are considering their verdict in their retiring room.[792]

(2) An exception to the above rule may exist if an allegation is made which tends to show that the jury as a whole declined to deliberate at all, but decided the case by other means such as drawing lots or tossing a coin. Such conduct would be a negation of the function of a jury and a trial whose result was determined in such a manner would not be a trial at all.[793]

(3) There is a firm rule that after the verdict has been delivered evidence directed to matters intrinsic to the deliberations of jurors is inadmissible.[794]

(4) The common law has recognised exceptions to the rule, confined to situations where the jury is alleged to have been affected by what are termed extraneous influences, e.g. contact with other persons who may have passed on information which should not have been before the jury.[795]

---

[789] See, G. Daly and R. Pattenden, "Racial Bias and the English Criminal Trial Jury" (2005) 64(3) C.L.J. 678.

[790] Lord Steyn dissented, concluding that a verdict involving a racial element was unfair and the European Court would place this issue above the need for privacy in jury deliberations. See *Remli v France* (1996) 22 E.H.R.R 253 on the need to ensure an impartial tribunal. See also Department for Constitutional Affairs, *Jury Research and Impropriety* (2005) CP04/05, available at *www.dca .gov.uk*; K. Quinn, "Jury bias and the European Convention on Human Rights: a well-kept secret?" [2004] Crim. L.R. 998; P. R. Ferguson, "The criminal jury in England and Scotland: the confidentiality principle and the investigation of impropriety" (2006) 10(3) E. & P. 180; L. McGowan, "Trial by jury: still a lamp in the dark? (2005) 69(6) J. Crim. L. 518; N. Haralambous, "Investigating Impropriety in Jury Deliberations: A Recipe for Disaster" (2004) J. Crim. L. 411.

[791] *R v Smith (Patrick)*; *R v Mercieca* [2005] 2 Cr.App.R. 10.

[792] *R v Miah* [1997] 2 Cr.App.R. 12 at 18, *per* Kennedy L.J

[793] *R v Mirza* at para.123, *per* Lord Hope of Craighead.

[794] *Ellis v Deheer* [1922] 2 K.B. 113.

[795] *R. v Blackwell* [1995] 2 Cr.App.R. 62.

(5) When complaints have been made during the course of trials of improper behaviour or bias on the part of jurors, judges have on occasion given further instructions to the jury and/or asked them if they feel able to continue with the case and give verdicts in the proper manner. This course should only be taken with the whole jury present and it is an irregularity to question individual jurors in the absence of the others about their ability to bring in a true verdict according to the evidence.[796]

(6) Section 8(1) of the Contempt of Court Act 1981 is not a bar to the court itself carrying out necessary investigations of such matters as bias or irregularity in the jury's consideration of the case. The members of the House who were in the majority in *Mirza* all expressed the view that if matters of that nature were raised by credible evidence the judge can investigate them and deal with the allegations as the situation may require.

In *Scotcher*,[797] the situation arose whereby a juror wrote to the mother of the defendant the day after the trial had concluded to express his opinion that the verdict was unsafe based upon the way the jury had deliberated. The juror was prosecuted under s.8 of the Contempt of Court Act. By contacting a third party he had committed a contempt. Had he attempted to contact the clerk of the court or another member involved in the administration of justice he would not have been vulnerable to prosecution.[798]

Jury secrecy clearly remains a well established principle. Reasons against allowing research into the jury's deliberations include: the need to maintain finality and certainty in a case; the need to protect the jury; the need to prevent friction between jurors. The secrecy of the jury room is said to be the basis on which trial by jury continues to exist. The arguments in favour of secrecy have been stated extra-judicially by Mr Justice McHugh[799]: (1) it is necessary to ensure freedom of discussion in the jury room; (2) it protects jurors from outside influences; (3) if the public knew how juries reached decisions, the jury would lose its place in the public esteem; (4) without it citizens would be reluctant to serve as jurors; (5) it is necessary to ensure the finality of the verdict; (6) it protects the community satisfaction which flows from a unanimous verdict; (7) it enables juries to bring in unpopular verdicts; (8) it prevents unreliable disclosures by jurors and prevents verdicts being misunderstood; (9) it protects the privacy of the individual juror and prevents harassment; (10) it protects jurors from pressure to explain their reasons for a verdict; (11) it prevents vendettas against jurors; (12) it prevents enormous public pressures being placed on jurors.

The arguments against secrecy and in favour of disclosure have been stated by the same author[800]: (1) it will make juries more accountable; (2) it will enable injustices to be cured; (3) it could lead to inquiries into the reliability of convictions; (4) it could lead to worthwhile reforms of the legal system; (5) it may have an educational effect on the public; (6) it is necessary to ensure that

---

[796] *R v Orgles* (1994) 98 Cr.App.R. 185.

[797] *Attorney General v Scotcher* [2005] 1 W.L.R. 1867.

[798] For an overview of these cases see D. Corker, "Jury Malpractice" (2005) N.L.J. 946. See also, P. Ferguson, "Whistleblowing Jurors" (2004) N.L.J. 370.

[799] "Jurors' Deliberations, Jury Secrecy, Public Policy and the Law of Contempt" in Findlay and Duff (1988), pp.62–65.

[800] *ibid.* pp.65–67.

jury trial can be properly examined to see if it is working[801]; (7) it is required by each juror's freedom of expression.

As far as academic research into the jury is concerned, "[t]he one recommendation of the [Royal] Commission that has received almost unequivocal support from the academic community is that s.8 of the Contempt of Court Act 1981 should be amended so as to permit proper research into jury decision-making".[802] The limited examples of research and shadow jury research have proved extremely enlightening.[803] The majority of responses to the Department for Constitutional Affairs' *Jury Research and Impropriety Consultation Paper* also favoured a limited degree of research to be allowed, though this would fall short of allowing access to the actual deliberations.[804] The Government stated that more research should be carried out within the confines of the existing law before changes to s.8 of the Contempt of Court Act are made.

(i) The verdict

The jury returns its verdict in open court with the foreman answering the questions posed. A verdict is given on each count, save that where the counts are in the alternative, a verdict is only taken on one, and the jury are discharged from returning a verdict on the other (this leaves the Court of Appeal open to substitute such a verdict if necessary[805]). The jury is entitled to return verdicts in relation to alternative offences[806] and the judge will have explained this to them if it is appropriate, after having warned counsel of his intention to do so. Care must be taken to ensure that the accused's right to a fair trial is not jeopardised by this course of action.[807] There are procedures to deal with the situations where the jury returns verdicts which are ambiguous or inconsistent or where the verdict returned is for an offence less than that charged in the indictment where that has been left to the jury.

17–099

If the jury's verdict is misunderstood, it can be corrected immediately, provided the jury has not been discharged[808] and if performed promptly so that the jury has not had an opportunity to hear further prejudicial material against the accused or discuss the case with others. If a verdict is given in the sight and

---

[801] Jury research is not made impossible, but is made much harder, by the secrecy requirement; see S. McCabe, "Is Jury Research Dead"? in Findlay and Duff (1988), Ch.2.

[802] Sanders and Young (2007), p.545.

[803] See, e.g. the Oxford Centre for Socio-Legal Studies Research into the impact on juries of knowing that the accused has a previous conviction. The findings were that recent convictions for offences similar to that now charged and convictions for child sex offences were particularly prejudicial. See Law Commission Consultation Paper No.141 (1996); S. Lloyd-Bostock, "Decline of the Little Parliament: Juries and Jury Reform in England and Wales" (1999) 62 Law and Contemporary Problems 7. See also S. Lloyd-Bostock "The Jury in the UK: Juries and Jury Research in Context" in G. Davies, S. Lloyd- Bostock, M. McMurran and C. Wilson, *Psychology, Law and Criminal Justice—International Developments in Research and Practice* (1996).

[804] Department for Constitutional Affairs, *Jury Research and Impropriety: Summary of Responses* (2005) CP04/05, available at *www.dca.gov.uk*. See also, J. Holroyd, "Judging the Jury" (2005) N.L.J 398.

[805] See Criminal Appeal Act 1968, s.3.

[806] See Criminal Law Act 1967, s.6(3).

[807] See *Pelissier v France* (2000) 30 E.H.R.R. 715.

[808] *R v Andrews* (1985) 82 Cr.App.R. 148. Where a jury foreman unambiguously reports a unanimous verdict the Court of Appeal is not permitted to interfere, even where the juror raised the point with the judge: *Millward* [1999] Crim. L.R. 164. If the error is recognised at once, the problem can be rectified at that time: *Maloney* [1996] Cr.App.R. 303.

hearing of the whole jury and there is no dissent then there is a rebuttable presumption that they have all consented to it.[809]

The judge is obliged to accept the jury's verdict unless it is one on which the indictment cannot be lawfully returned, or is ambiguous, or is inconsistent.[810] The judge ought not to seek clarification of the basis for the verdict except in cases of voluntary manslaughter where the judge needs to know for sentencing purposes whether the jury are concluding that the verdict is one of killing under provocation or diminished responsibility, rather than involuntary manslaughter. In any case the jury may make a recommendation of leniency but will never be invited to do so by the judge or counsel, even if they expressly ask permission to do so.[811]

If the jury cannot agree on a verdict they are discharged and the accused may be retried. By convention, where two juries cannot return a verdict, an accused is not prosecuted a third time.[812]

There is little doubt that jurors can find the exercise a harrowing task and there have been suggestions that more debriefing and even counselling should be provided in traumatic cases.[813]

Majority verdicts

17–100 The requirement that the verdict be unanimous, which had stood since the thirteenth century, was abandoned by the Criminal Justice Act 1967, which introduced the majority verdict. The governing provision is now the Juries Act 1974, s.17:

> "(1) . . . the verdict of a jury in proceedings in the Crown Court or the High Court need not be unanimous if
>
> (a) in a case where there are not less then eleven jurors, ten of them agree on a verdict; and
>
> (b) in a case where there are ten jurors, nine of them agree on a verdict.
>
> . . .
>
> (3) The Crown Court shall not accept a verdict of guilty by virtue of subsection (1) above unless the foreman of the jury has stated in open court the number of jurors who respectively agreed to and dissented from the verdict.
>
> (4) No court shall accept a verdict by virtue of subsection (a) . . . unless it appears to the court that the jury have had such period of time for deliberation as the court thinks reasonable having regard to the nature and complexity of the case; and the Crown Court shall in any event not accept such a verdict unless it appears to the court that the jury have had at least two hours for deliberation."

---

[809] *R v Austin* [2003] Crim. L.R. 426.
[810] See *R v Robinson* [1975] Q.B. 508.
[811] *R v Langham* [1996] Crim. L.R. 430.
[812] On hung juries, see New Zealand Law Commission, Juries in Criminal Trials (2001) Report No.69, Ch.13.
[813] See Darbyshire *et al.* (2001) p.42.

At the outset the jury is directed to reach an unanimous verdict[814] and no mention should normally be made of the majority verdict procedure.[815] However, as has been mentioned, the jurors know of the procedure from the notes accompanying the jury summons.

A *Practice Direction*[816] sets out the procedure which ensures that the safeguards contained in the Act (a minimum period of deliberation and a statement in open court of the majority) are observed. The stages are as follows:

1. If the jury returns[817] within two hours,[818] only a unanimous verdict is acceptable. If there is no unanimity the jury is sent back for further deliberation.

2. If the jury returns after two hours ten minutes[819] have elapsed it is asked if a verdict has been reached. If it is not unanimous and the judge considers that the jury has had a reasonable time for deliberation and having regard to the nature and complexity of the case the judge will direct it that a majority verdict is acceptable, although they should still try to reach unanimity.

3. When the jury finally returns, a precise set of questions is asked:

    (i) Have at least ten (or nine as the case may be) of you agreed upon your verdict? If "Yes",
    (ii) What is your verdict? Please answer only "Guilty" or "Not Guilty".
    (iii) (a) If "Not Guilty," accept the verdict without more ado.
        (b) If "Guilty," is that the verdict of you all or by a majority?
    (iv) If "Guilty" by a majority, how many of you agreed to the verdict and how many dissented?

The foreman must state in open court the number of jurors who agreed to and dissented from the verdict before the judge can properly accept a guilty verdict, but there is no requirement that the precise words of the *Practice Direction* be used so long as it is clear to the ordinary person how the jury divided.[820] The formulation of the questions in the *Practice Direction* is intended to prevent anyone (other than the jurors) knowing whether a not guilty verdict was reached

---

[814] See *R v Daly* [1999] Crim. L.R. 88.

[815] *R v Thomas* [1983] Crim. L.R. 745. The fact that the judge told the jury in the summing-up that he was entitled to take a majority verdict after at least two hours was held not to be such a significant irregularity that there was the risk of a miscarriage of justice. The fear is of "inviting" the jury to disagree from the start: see also *R v Modeste* [1983] Crim. L.R. 746. *R v Porter* [1996] Crim. L.R. 126.

[816] Practice Direction (Crime: Majority Verdict) [1970] 1 W.L.R. 916. These are directory, not mandatory in nature: *Shields* [1997] A.C. 758. See Practice Direction (*Criminal Proceedings: Consolidation*) para.IV.46.

[817] "Returns" in the context of the *Practice Direction* includes being sent for by the judge who may be wondering how the deliberations are progressing.

[818] The statutory requirement that not less than two hours should be allowed for the initial deliberation is mandatory: *R v Barry* [1975] 1 W.L.R. 1190. The initial period may be such longer time as the judge thinks reasonable. A complicated case is an instance where a longer period is to be expected: Juries Act 1974, s.17(4); *R v Bateson* (1969) 54 Cr.App.R. 11; *R v Thornton, R. v Stead* (1989) 89 Cr.App.R. 54.

[819] *Practice Direction* [1970] 1 W.L.R. 916. The period that has elapsed since the last member of the jury left the jury box must be stated in open court before the jury is asked for its verdict. The extra 10 minutes allows for the practical necessities of electing a foreman and returning from the jury room to the court room.

[820] *R v Pigg* [1983] 1 W.L.R. 6.

by a majority.[821] Even the Court of Appeal will not look behind the verdict that was read out, even in the face of a letter from the foreman stating that the wrong figures were read out.[822]

Before the introduction of the majority verdict, it was the case that if a jury failed to reach a unanimous verdict it was discharged and the accused might or might not be retried at the discretion of the prosecution. The majority verdict was introduced because fears of jury "nobbling" (i.e. intimidation) had been expressed and it was argued that the unanimity rule made it too easy for professional criminals to threaten or intimidate one member of a jury into holding out for a not guilty verdict.[823] However, the evidence in favour of these arguments put forward by the government to support the majority verdict was at best scanty.[824] The government relied also on the argument of efficiency that the reform would save resources in avoiding the consumption of time for the police and others involved in a second trial, although little importance was attached to this argument.[825]

Very strong arguments against the use of majority verdicts have been advanced.[826] The unanimity principle rather than the majority verdict reduces the risk of convicting the innocent. Unanimous verdicts command greater community acceptance and thus the public has greater confidence in the criminal justice system, and the evidence suggests that the rate of hung juries, that is where the jury is discharged after being unable to agree, has not been much affected by the introduction of the majority verdict.[827] Further, Freeman has argued that the introduction of the majority verdict weakens the effect of the requirement that the prosecution must prove its case beyond a reasonable doubt, since if one member of a jury of 12 people is not satisfied of the guilt of the accused that is a clear indication that there is a reasonable doubt as to the prosecution's case and so the accused should be acquitted.[828] Maher has pointed out that this argument rather assumes that proof beyond a reasonable doubt is a concept which can be described in terms of probability. However,

> "it can be said that insisting on an unanimity rule is not always necessary in order to show that the principle of proof of the guilt of the accused beyond reasonable doubt is being taken seriously. For if a jury is large in size and is also representative of the community or society in general, then some relaxation of the rule may not frustrate the purpose of the principle which is to give the accused a right not to be convicted of a charge unless the case against him has been made out at a level of practical certainty. The rule of unanimity may also be relaxed where this right receives adequate protection by other means . . . . But it can be said that if no such safeguards

---

[821] Thus avoiding a sort of second-class acquittal. See *R v Adams* [1969] 1 W.L.R. 106.

[822] *R v Millward* [1999] 1 Cr.App.R. 61. See *R v Tantram* [2001] Crim. L.R. 824 where the conviction was quashed after the jury sought to correct a verdict error 27 minutes after the trial.

[823] See P. Duff and M. Findlay, "The Politics of Jury Reform" in Findlay and Duff (1988), Ch.13, pp.212–215 and N. Blake in *ibid*, p.143. See also, P. Byrne, "Jury Reform and the Future" in *ibid*. Ch.12, p.191.

[824] See, e.g. Blake *op. cit.*

[825] See Duff and Findlay in Findlay and Duff (1988), p.213.

[826] See Sanders and Young (2007), pp.510–513.

[827] D. Brown and D. Neal, "Show Trials: The Media and the Gang of Twelve" in *ibid*. Ch.8, p.134.

[828] Freeman (1981). See also Brown and Neal in Findlay and Duff (1988), p.134.

exist for an accused then jury verdicts must be unanimous, or be near to unanimity, if the accused's right to proof of his guilt at the level of practical certainty is to be upheld."[829]

The introduction of majority verdicts and the consequent debate can be usefully elucidated by referring back to Packer's models of criminal justice. The government appears to have been aware that most of its arguments in favour of majority verdicts were crime control model arguments, which may be why emphasis was also placed on the claim of improving fairness to the accused by preventing jury nobbling (emphasising values of the due process model).[830] Further, Maher's argument for accepting the majority verdict is conditional upon true respect being granted to the principles of due process.

(j) Is the jury competent to make decisions?

It has been asserted that the jury acquits too many people,[831] but the evidence supporting such a claim is, at best, equivocal.[832] Darbyshire et al. extrapolate from US research that there are approximately 225 wrongful convictions and 4,000 wrongful acquittals per annum.[833]

17–101

The question of competence is unanswerable, depending as it does on a series of assumptions about the jury that cannot be tested in the absence of permission to conduct jury research. In particular, questions arise as to whether it is proper for juries to decide cases on whatever grounds it chooses, regardless of the direction on the law by the judge, and, secondly, whether the jury is capable of understanding the evidence and making decisions in complex cases.[834] These doubts may be regarded as an attack on the independence of the jury since some would argue that the very arbitrariness and prejudice of which complaint is made proves that independence.[835] There are a series of more complex questions such as whether the public expects the jury to "get the result right" or to act as a guardian of certain standards of due process.

The New Zealand Law Commission[836] conducted extensive research, led by Warren and Young at the University of Wellington, into all aspects of jury selection, excisal, decision-making, secrecy, etc. Their conclusions were that:

> "in the great majority of cases, jurors are conscientious and their decisions are sound. The virtual absence of criticism of the conduct of juries in even the most controversial cases, is striking. The essentially anonymous verdict of ordinary citizens chosen at random given to the process the legitimacy of

---

[829] G. Maher, "The Verdict of the Jury" in *ibid.* Ch.3, pp.45–49, esp. p.49.

[830] Duff and Findlay in *ibid.* pp.212–215.

[831] See Sanders and Young (2007), pp.535–542 for a particularly telling critique.

[832] See the statistics referred to above, which do not distinguish between pleas of guilty and not guilty; S. Butler, "Acquittal Rates" and J. Vennard, "The Outcome of Contested Trials" in D. Moxon (ed.), *Managing Criminal Justice* (1985); Zander (1993), pp.475–476. Sir Robert Mark's other grounds of complaint such as the professional criminal being let off too frequently, and the activities of crooked lawyers are responded to by Zander (1993), pp.475–478. See for a vigorous critique of Mark's argument: Sanders and Young (2007), pp.520–521.

[833] p.32.

[834] See also J. Cooper *et al.*, "Complex Scientific Testimony: How Do Jurors Make Decisions" (1996) 20 Law and Human Behaviour 379.

[835] See e.g. Brown and Neal in Findlay and Duff (1988); and Mr Justice McHugh in *ibid.*

[836] Report No.69, *Juries in Criminal Trials* (2001) available in full from *www.lawcom.govt.nz*.

total independence; they are indeed the 'little parliament' to which community decision making is delegated."[837]

The Report also recognises one further important function of the jury as "educating the public about the workings of the criminal justice system".

(i) *Do juries arrive at "perverse" verdicts?*[838]

17–102 There are two aspects of the question whether juries reach "perverse" verdicts:
first, whether a jury's decisions according to conscience should be permitted,
and, secondly, what the function of the jury is when matters of conscience are not
raised.

(1) *"Perverse" verdicts and the conscience of the jury*

If the value of trial by jury lies in the involvement of the public in the criminal
process, thus permitting the exercise of "community conscience" and providing
the "just face" of the law, the jury, it can be argued, must be entitled to arrive at
decisions which appear to be contrary to the law. Thus the jury's acquittal of
Clive Ponting of charges under s.2 of the Official Secrets Act 1911 may be
viewed as the jury exercising its constitutional role to arrive at a decision
according to its conscience.[839]

Ponting had passed to Tam Dalyell MP documents relating to the sinking of
the Argentinian battleship, the *General Belgrano*, by a British submarine during
the Falklands War in 1982. These documents were clearly covered by s.2, and the
judge directed the jury that, on his understanding of s.2, Ponting had no authorisation to pass them to someone such as Dalyell and there was no other lawful
justification for Ponting's act. Nevertheless the jury acquitted him.

On the other hand, it can be argued that permitting juries to decide according
to their conscience is completely inappropriate in "enlightened times".[840] Thus,
the acquittal of Ponting may be regarded as wholly improper. If the law is wrong,
the proper means of challenge and change is through the democratic process. As
Blom-Cooper has argued, "it cannot be for a single jury, unelected and chosen at
random from one tiny corner of the nation, to thwart the democratic process
either by disapplying the Act of Parliament or determining that a prosecution is
official persecution of the accused".[841]

(2) *"Perverse" verdicts and jury decision-making*

Whatever view is taken as to the acceptability of the jury acting according to its
conscience, there may be an argument about "perverse" verdicts in a different

---

[837] p.81. *Cf.* the calls for abolition of jury. See A. Bell, "Twelve Good Men and True! Bah Humbug"
(1997) 147 N.L.J. 1857, by a juror who was disgusted by what he found.
[838] See T. A. Green, *Verdict According to Conscience 1200–1800* (1985).
[839] C. Ponting, *The Right to Know: The Inside Story of the Belgrano Affair* (1985). See also N.
MacCormick, "The Interest of the State and the Rule of Law" in P. Wallington and R. M. Merkin,
Essays in Memory of Professor F. H. Lawson (1986). See recently the acquittal of the GM crop
protestors.
[840] The phrase is that of Jeremy Bentham in *Draft of a Code for the Organisation of the Judicial
Establishment in France* (1790), quoted in G. Marshall, "The Judgement of One's Peers: Some
Aims and Ideal of Jury Trial" in Walker with Pearson (1975), p.1. On perverse verdicts see V.
Bethell's campaign, discussed by J. Morton, "A Propos" (2001) 151 N.L.J. 142.
[841] L. Blom-Cooper, "Article 6 and Modes of Criminal Trial" [2001] E.H.R.L.R. 1 at 6.

sense. Whether juries' verdicts may be described as "perverse" on a more general basis depends upon what the role of the jury in decision-making is perceived to be.[842] If a narrow approach is taken, a verdict is right if it is reached by the jury after an honest, careful and reasonable attempt to apply the law (as explained by the judge in the summing-up) to the facts as it finds them, taking no other circumstances into account.[843] Then both greater certainty in the outcome of trials and greater consistency in juries' decisions is achieved.[844] A broad approach might perceive a verdict to be right where it is a verdict of acquittal, say, after a consideration of the evidence which indicated guilt or even without any consideration of the evidence at all, provided it nevertheless results from a reasonable exercise of discretion in favour of the accused reflecting the jury's sympathy, clemency or disapproval of the prosecution.

The narrow approach will view more acquittals as perverse verdicts and hence leads to the argument that reform of the jury is necessary. Jury research has been undertaken to attempt to consider whether juries do arrive at "perverse verdicts". Because of the limitations imposed upon researchers, the methods employed to analyse and explain the decision-making process and the verdicts reached in particular cases have necessarily been indirect.[845] One approach has been to compare the verdict of the jury in selected cases with the "verdict" of the professional participants in the trial; the other has been to arrange for a "mock" or "shadow" jury to listen to a case and then observe its deliberations when required to give a verdict. Both methods have their drawbacks but the results are illustrative of different features of jury decisions.

Major English research studies have been conducted which take account of the views of the professionals.[846] The first, by McCabe and Purves,[847] dealt with 475 accused tried on indictment over a two-year period, concentrating solely on the 115 who were acquitted by the jury. The second, by Baldwin and McConville,[848] dealt with 2,406 accused who appeared in the Birmingham Crown Court over an 18-month period, concentrating on the 500 accused who contested their cases. The latter study is, therefore, of wider significance since it looks at all jury verdicts and not solely acquittals. There were some differences of methodology but both studies sought to explain the relevant verdicts by reference to the views of counsel,[849] solicitors, the judge and police officers.[850]

The first study attempted to categorise the 115 acquittals[851] according to the views of the professionals. It appeared that only 15 of the 115 acquittals were based on a deliberate decision to go against the evidence. All the others were

---

[842] The House of Lords clarified in *R v. Wang* [2005] 1 W.L.R. 661 that there are no circumstances in which a judge is entitled to direct the jury to return a guilty verdict. See also *R v Kelleher* [2003] EWCA Crim 3525; *R v Caley-Knowles* [2006] EWCA Crim 1611, [2007] Crim. L.R. 61.

[843] The argument is not denying the jury's function to be the decider of the facts.

[844] See, e.g. on the general point about consistency, Lord Devlin, *The Judge* (1979), Ch.5; also E. J. Griew, *Dishonesty and the Jury* (1974) and G. Williams, *The Proof of Guilt* (1963), Ch.10.

[845] See McCabe in Findlay and Duff (1988). See also R. Eldin, "A Juror's Tale" (1988) 138 N.L.J. 37.

[846] Reference should also be made to M. Zander, "Are Too Many Professional Criminals Avoiding Conviction—A Study of Britain's Two Busiest Courts" (1974) 37 M.L.R. 28.

[847] S. McCabe and R. Purves, *The Jury at Work* (1972).

[848] J. Baldwin and M. McConville, *Jury Trials* (1979).

[849] The Bar did not co-operate in the Birmingham survey.

[850] The police did not co-operate in the Oxford survey.

[851] In the Oxford study there were a further 58 cases in which the accused was acquitted on the direction of the judge.

explicable on the grounds of weakness in the prosecution case, the failure of prosecution witnesses or the credibility of the accused's explanation. Many of the acquittals were regarded as correct by the professionals and the proportion of perverse verdicts was established as low in relation to acquittals[852] and very low in relation to all contested cases.[853]

In the second study, Baldwin and McConville concluded that it was not possible to determine an overall pattern in the cases where the outcome was regarded as questionable. Those cases included convictions as well as acquittals and so doubts are raised about the conventional wisdom that the accused gets the benefit of the doubt from the jury. A similar proportion of wayward verdicts occurred in this study[854] and the authors agreed that it was a tiny fraction of all cases that pass through the criminal courts, yet they pointed out the serious nature of the cases tried by the jury and concluded that trial by jury is " . . . an arbitrary and unpredictable business".[855] The authors recognised that the significance of their research was limited to an assessment of the accuracy of verdicts and that the political and constitutional issues were also very important. They believed, however, that the political and constitutional debate should be informed by as much knowledge as possible about the veracity of jury verdicts.

In sum, the English evidence[856] demonstrates that there is an identifiable, if relatively small, number of cases in which juries reach perverse verdicts, although views differ on whether these deviations can be explained on any particular basis.

In the course of the Oxford study,[857] McCabe and Purves also utilised the "shadow" jury technique. In 30 cases, a second "jury" was installed in the court to listen to the proceedings and then to deliberate and reach a verdict. This method has the drawback that the degree of pressure which exists when a jury is dealing with the fate of an accused is lacking in mock deliberations, but the main conclusions pointed to the care and determination of the jurors to go about their task methodically, discount their prejudices and look for evidence on which to base their verdict.[858] This would suggest that in real cases the jury is likely to display the same, or an even greater, degree of conscientiousness and application. On the other hand, some evidence suggests that jury trial is a lottery when considering the competence of jurors to follow and remember evidence and think through the issues raised logically and carefully.[859]

The New Zealand Law Commission has undertaken valuable research in the area, which if the ban on research was lifted could be replicated in England and Wales.[860] The conclusion of the study was that to assist in decision-making, jurors should receive more information in the style in which it would be

---

[852] One verdict in eight amongst the jury acquittals, and one verdict in 11 amongst all acquittals.
[853] One verdict in 32 amongst the accused dealt with in the period of the study.
[854] *Jury Trials* Chs 4 and 5.
[855] *ibid.* p.132.
[856] There has been more extensive research in America, starting with H. Kalven and H. Zeisel, *The American Jury* (1966) (The Chicago Jury Project); see McCabe in Findlay and Duff (1988). In England, Zander's conclusions are broadly in line with the other studies.
[857] S. McCabe and R. Purves, *The Shadow Jury At Work* (1974). See also, A. P. Sealy, "What Can Be Learned from the Analysis of Simulated Juries?" in Walker with Pearson (1975).
[858] *ibid.* p.61.
[859] See *The Times*, October 24, 1988. See also, S. Lloyd-Bostock, *Report on Interviews with the Jurors in the Jubilee Line Case* (HMCPSI, 2006).
[860] Report No.69, *Juries in Criminal Trials* (2001) available in full from *www.lawcom.govt.nz.*. See also, W. Young, N. Cameron and Y. Tinsley, Juries in Criminal Trials: A Summary of the Research Findings (New Zealand Law Commission, 1999): available at: *www.lawcom.govt.nz.*

presented in everyday life. In particular, they should be provided with a glossary of terms, a set of detailed notes, visual aids, and decision trees and flow charts. The research also suggested that there should be more attempt for the parties to agree more of the issues and to settle common ground before the trial proper. This would enable the jury to focus more clearly on the contentious issues. The research recommended that "streamlining the evidence for the jury is one valid objective of case flow management, and the focus of this should be the elimination of irrelevant or repetitious evidence, but that it must be done cautiously and with regard for the circumstances of each case".[861] To a limited degree the Criminal Procedure Rules attempt to forward this through active case management, which involves early identification of the issues.[862] Maximising the information available to the jury (e.g. by providing copies of the judge's notes) is not just about saving money and time but also about better equipping the jury to make their decision. The New Zealand research also concluded that the jury should be actively encouraged to ask questions during the trial. The jury should be encouraged to review evidence before they take the first vote amongst themselves.[863]

(ii) The jury in complex cases

A similar debate about the ability of the jury to cope with the information and how it is possible to monitor their use of the information has been encountered when considering the role of the jury in complex cases. The debate relies more upon the nature of the trials, such as fraud trials and trials involving scientific evidence,[864] which, it is suggested, means that the jury cannot competently arrive at proper decisions. The inherent complexity of some cases was part of the argument that led to the abolition of the jury in most civil cases.[865] In the context of criminal cases, the Roskill Committee on Fraud Trials concluded that "we do not find trial by a random jury a satisfactory way of achieving justice in cases as long and complex as [many fraud trials]. We believe that many jurors are out of their depth".[866]

A decade ago the Home Office/Lord Chancellor's Department Consultation Document[867] also questioned whether an alternative to the jury trial should be available in cases of serious and complex fraud. The paper considered the arguments for alternatives to the traditional jury trial and examined how suitable cases for an alternative trial would be identified and segregated from the mainstream. However, research on the decision-making of juries[868] suggests that juries are competent to make decisions, including decisions in complex cases. It

17–103

---

[861] On the N.Z. research see I. Francis, "A Beginning a Middle and an End . . . but not Necessarily in that Order" (2001) 151 N.L.J. 229. See also, I. Francis, "Jury Trial: Evolution or Extinction" (2001) N.L.J. 414.

[862] CPR, r.3.2(1).

[863] Report No.69 (2001) para.335.

[864] See, e.g. Harding in Findlay and Duff (1988), pp.82–90, concentrating on the Australian criticism of jury performance in such cases as the *Chamberlain* case. See also the criticisms of jury competence considered in M. Levi, "The Role of the Jury in Complex Cases" in Findlay and Duff (1988), Ch.6; and Lord McCluskey, *Law, Justice and Democracy* (1986) (Reith Lectures).

[865] See above.

[866] *Fraud Trials Committee: Report*; Chair: Lord Roskill (1986), para.8.35.

[867] *Juries in Serious Fraud Trials* (1998).

[868] See above.

has been suggested that the real fault in complex cases lies not with the jury, but rather with other participants in the criminal trial.[869]

Interviews with jurors involved in the Jubilee Line case reveal that "the jury taken as a whole did not appear to have difficulty understanding the evidence or the essentials of the case presented to it".[870] Rather, what was more problematic in a case of such apparent complexity was the difficulties jurors had in spending so much time away from their work and domestic lives.[871] The *Woolmer Report* into the collapse of the Jubilee Line case stated that, "[T]he size and nature of the case was not such as to make it intrinsically unmanageable before a jury. The fundamental reason the trial had to be terminated was because it had gone on too long".[872]

Nevertheless, despite this evidence, cases involving serious or complex fraud may in future take place before a judge sitting alone when s.43 of the CJA 2003 is brought into force.[873] At the hearing the prosecution would have to apply to the court for such a trial, which would be granted on the basis that the length or complexity of the trial would make it so burdensome that the interests of justice require consideration to be given to conducting the trial without a jury. What exactly does "burdensome" encompass? The research above suggests that complexity is not a real issue for juries but the length of trials can be. Thus, if juries are to be replaced in certain trials because of the possible length of the case then this suggests a more appropriate response would be to attempt to ensure a shorter trial through more effective case management. The Criminal Procedure Rules attempt to introduce greater judicial case management but little time has been given to consider the efficacy of these measures before the introduction of s.43 and the replacement of juries.

Given that the jury has been so central to the Crown Court trial, s.43 has been controversial and as such will only be brought into effect by a positive resolution of each House of Parliament.[874] The human rights group *Liberty* has expressed the concern that judge-only trials might be extended to other areas of the law despite assurances to the contrary from the Government.[875]

(k) Replacing the jury?[876]

17–104 Questions continue to be raised about the role and efficacy of the jury. Judge-only trials are a clear possibility in the case of serious fraud trials discussed above, and there are further provisions in the CJA 2003 to allow the prosecution to apply for a judge-only trial in cases of jury tampering.[877] The court must be satisfied that there is evidence of a clear and present danger that jury tampering will take place;

---

[869] As pointed out by both Harding in Findlay and Duff, and Levi in *ibid.*
[870] S. Lloyd-Bostock (2006) p.17.
[871] *ibid.* p.13.
[872] HMCPSI (The Woolmer Report), *Review of the Investigation and Criminal Proceedings Relating to the Jubilee Line Case* (2006) para.5, available at: *www.hmcpsi.gov.uk/reports/JubileeLineReponly.pdf.*
[873] G. Jones, "Descent into Darkness" (2006) N.L.J 1893.
[874] See, Fraud (Trials Without a Jury) Bill 2006–7.
[875] Liberty, *Liberty's briefing on the Fraud (Trials without a Jury) Bill for 2nd reading in the House of Commons* (2006) available at *www.liberty-human-rights.org.uk.*
[876] See, W. R. Cornish, *The Jury* (1968), Ch.10. See on reform I. Francis, "Juries: the Worst Form of Trial, Except for all the Rest" (2001) 151 N.L.J. 582. See also I. Francis, "The Best or All Possible Worlds" (2001) 151 N.L.J. 63 on the comparisons between the way jurors and magistrates perform their functions and the support they are offered.
[877] CJA 2003, s.44.

and that the risk of jury tampering is so substantial that it is necessary in the interests of justice for the trial to be conducted without a jury. If the judge discharges a jury due to evidence of tampering he can continue the trial without a jury or order a retrial without a jury.[878] Both the prosecution and defence can appeal against such a ruling.[879]

The Domestic Violence, Crimes and Victims Act 2004 opens up a further possibility of trial on indictment without a jury. Under s.17, the prosecution may apply for trial by jury of sample counts. Where the jury convicts on a sample count, the other counts relating to the sample may be tried by the judge alone.[880]

The Government's attempts to restrict the ability to elect jury trial in 1999 and 2000 both failed.[881] Instead a number of reforms have followed that seek to retain as many cases in the magistrates' court as possible. Although not overtly suggested as a policy objective in criminal cases generally, replacement of the jury by some other method of determining facts in criminal matters must be considered. There would appear to be four options.[882]

(i) *The single judge*[883]

Most civil trials are conducted by a judge alone deciding both fact and law. In criminal matters the District Judge magistrate has the same function. The advantages of this option include time-saving at trials[884] through the District Judge not having to explain so many matters to the jury, the reduction in the likelihood of decision-making being affected by outside influences,[885] and the reduction in the likelihood of verdicts not in accordance with the law. It may also increase confidence in the system by professional users. Reviews and monitoring of the system are easier and more effective because of the obligation on the judge provide reasons. The consistency of decision-making is also enhanced by the judge applying pre-arranged professional guidelines.

17–105

The disadvantages of this option include the lack of community participation, the loss of the independence and impartiality of the jury, and the possibility that the judge would become case-hardened or prosecution-minded. Further, there would be little protection against eccentricity, and decisions on guilt being taken by one person might be too onerous a burden.[886]

---

[878] CJA 2003, s.45.

[879] CJA 2003, s.47.

[880] This seeks to reverse the decision in *R v Kidd* [1998] 1 All E.R. 42. This has not yet been brought into force.

[881] I. Francis, "Will it All End in Middle Tiers" (2001) N.L.J. 1700; J. Morton, "First of All, Let's Kill All Juries" (2001) N.L.J 1509.

[882] Assuming that we are considering alternative types of tribunal rather than adjustment to the jury, such as the reduction of the number of jurors.

[883] See J. Jackson and S. Doran, *Judge without Jury* (1995).

[884] See the importance of the District Judge in the magistrates' court.

[885] The judge may be more immune to threats. This line of reasoning lay behind the introduction of single judge courts in certain trials in Northern Ireland in 1973 as a result of the Diplock Report (*Report of the Commission to Consider Legal Procedures to Deal with Terrorist Activities in Northern Ireland*, Cmnd. 5185 (1972)), see now, the Northern Ireland (Emergency Provisions) Act 1978.

[886] See, e.g. S. Greer and A. White, "Restoring Jury Trial to Terrorist Offences in Northern Ireland" in Findlay and Duff (1988), Ch.11.

The most comprehensive treatment of the issue of the single judge in recent years has been by Jackson and Doran.[887] Drawing upon experience and research into the Diplock Courts in Northern Ireland, the authors argue that the task of jury fact-finding ought not to be considered in isolation from the context of the judicial control, and that there ought to be a re-division of the tasks between judge and jury to utilise their respective strengths.

They conclude that it is not possible to compare in any meaningful sense judges and jurors since jurors have the freedom to ignore the law.[888] Judges, however, are better equipped to deal with evidence that requires intellectual exercises; are more likely to arrive at the correct conclusion (although it is acknowledged that that is a very legalistic non-holistic way of looking at the trial[889]); do more than decide questions of law, they filter the evidence heard by the jury[890]; are not case hardened, but rather "hard logicians" preferred by counsel because they will not respond emotively[891]; are trained to approach cases more atomistically. Jury absence would allow for judges to question witnesses more vigorously,[892] and allow the judge to intervene in closing speeches.[893] As far as the jury is concerned, the authors conclude that juries should be left to deal with cases on credibility—that is what society wants the jury to be doing.[894] The jury is chosen to arbitrate between the individual and the state because it is impartial and independent.[895] A jury trial is to be viewed as a trial on the merits and not on only the legal considerations.[896]

(ii) *The bench of judges*

17–106   Some of the disadvantages of the single judge option, such as the possibility of becoming prosecution-minded or making eccentric decisions, might be avoided by a bench of three or five judges. The disadvantages of this option include that it would be enormously expensive and recruitment might be difficult and that the nature of the judiciary would be transformed because a considerable increase in the number of judges would allegedly weaken the bench. There would be considerable implications for the legal profession if a career judiciary were necessitated.

Many of the disadvantages associated with decision-making by professionals would remain, in particular the absence of community participation in trial. The willingness of benches of judges of the Court of Appeal to permit convictions to stand where new evidence has emerged after the trial which might cause a jury to entertain reasonable doubt serves to increase the distrust of such decision-making tribunals.[897]

---

[887] "Judge and Jury: Towards a New Division of Labour in Criminal Trials" (1997) 60 M.L.R. 759.

[888] *ibid.* p.764.

[889] p.766.

[890] p.767.

[891] p.764. In case of a submission of no case, the judge is more interventionist and leaves no room for the jury to do any work.

[892] p.774.

[893] p.774.

[894] p.769.

[895] p.760.

[896] p.772.

[897] A development initiated by the decision of the House of Lords in *Stafford v DPP* [1974] A.C. 878. It is heavily criticised in Lord Devlin, *The Judge* (1979) pp.148–176.

(iii) *The composite tribunal*

On certain appeals from the magistrates' court, a Crown Court judge sits with **17–107**
two lay magistrates.[898] Some European jurisdictions[899] rely heavily upon the
composite tribunal of lay people and judge and one observer, at least, has
professed himself to be impressed by the system.[900]

The advantages would include the probability that trials would be speedier
because the judge would be involved in all discussions, and that the lay people
involved would be able to outvote the judge thus maintaining the overriding
influence of representatives of the community.

Possible disadvantages would include whether the judge would have too
significant a say in most cases and whether decision-making would still be
independent and impartial so as to preserve a fair trial. Furthermore, the lay
people might have to be trained which could mean that they would no longer be
representatives of the community.

(iv) *The special jury*

The special jury is an option which seeks to satisfy the demand for community **17–108**
participation and independence, but to ensure competence through training. Thus
a jury is still selected from non-lawyers, but the only people eligible to serve on
such a jury are those who have been trained for jury service. Consequently, the
objective of random selection may be defeated and trial would be in the hands of
a select group of people, albeit not all lawyers.

C. EVALUATIONS

Critical analysis of all aspects of the criminal trial is essential. It may be that **17–109**
Packer's two-model system[901] will help readers to think through the many issues
in relation to the criminal trial. For example, it might be suggested that the crime
control model, emphasising the necessity to reduce criminal conduct and requiring that the system operate efficiently, helps to explain why it has been proposed
that more offences be tried summarily where the accused does not need to be
present, why plea bargaining is permitted and why proposals for jury reform are
made. On the other hand, it could be suggested that the due process model helps
to explain certain developments with regard to the criminal trial, for example, the
developments as to the exclusion of evidence under PACE.

However, Packer's models are intended to be extremes, recognising that
systems actually adopt a compromise or balance, as the Royal Commission on
Criminal Procedure set out to achieve in its "fundamental balance" and which
the Royal Commission on Criminal Justice recognised.[902] It is also necessary,

---

[898] It used to be possible for lay magistrates to sit with a judge at a trial on indictment, but that was
     unusual and they did not take part in the decision: Supreme Court Act 1981, s.8(1).
[899] Described in Cornish (1968).
[900] Cornish was particularly complimentary about the Scandinavian system: *ibid.* Ch.10.
[901] For a description of these models, see Ch.14.
[902] The Royal Commission was, however, required to pay significant attention to efficiency and cost
     and it failed to make clear its basic approach for which it has been criticised, see, e.g. Sanders and
     Young (2007), Ch.1.

therefore, to consider whether that balance is actually being achieved, or whether too much emphasis is being placed on the desire to control crime or on the desire to ensure that the accused gets a fair trial.

Packer's model might be regarded as overly simplistic with the two conflicting positions advanced. This has caused some to offer more sophisticated explanations of the process, reinterpreting Packer's model. Ashworth is very critical of the ubiquitous balancing in the criminal justice system,[903] with the danger that balancing involves an unacceptable disguise for weight being attached to incomparable factors in an exercise with apparent transparency. Ashworth is concerned to identify the principles that should serve to protect the rights of the suspect throughout the criminal process.

Five main criticisms of Packer's model are advanced. First, that Packer's model does not explain the relationship between due process and crime control albeit accepting that they are not absolutely polar. Secondly, Packer assumes that the crime control model is capable of affecting crime rates. Thirdly, Packer underestimates the resource management in the process. Fourthly, the models make no allowance for the victim in the system. Finally, there are internal critiques, e.g. delay is bad for both crime control and due process. On this basis, it is argued that Packer's two models are no longer satisfactory for interpreting the tendencies of the criminal justice model.

A further alternative approach is that advanced by Sanders and Young, who argue that the freedom of the individual to be free from injury/damage/ harm is a primary purpose of the criminal law while the procedural laws of criminal process are designed to ensure freedom of suspect. The authors seek to evaluate the existing criminal process by assessing the extent to which rules/procedures maximise relative freedoms. Their aim is to protect against a net loss of freedom overall. The problem with the approach, as acknowledged by the authors, is that the model requires some sort of calculation of freedom which is not readily susceptible to objective evaluation.

An evaluation on the basis of these models or the fundamental balance can be undertaken on any of the topics in this chapter.

There are a number of aspects of the criminal trial that warrant very detailed critical analysis and we have selected a few with whom to conclude the discussion of the trial.

(a) Magistrates' court or Crown Court trial?

17–110   There is a long history of attempting to increase the summary jurisdiction and restricting the number of cases being heard in the Crown Court.[904] This history has continued in the reforms enacted through the CJA 2003. The arguments in favour tend to be largely based upon efficiency, since magistrates' trials will be cheaper and will be shorter,[905] there is the possibility of written pleas of guilty, the trial may proceed in the absence of the accused and magistrates may be less likely to acquit.

These appear to be arguments founded on the concept of crime control. However, that does not necessarily make them bad or wrong, provided that adequate protections for the accused are provided. It is this side of the balance

---

[903] Ashworth and Redmayne (2005), p.40.

[904] S. Cammiss, "I Will In a Moment Give You the Full History: Mode of Trial, Prosecutorial Control and Partial Accounts" [2006] Crim. L.R. 38.

[905] See further, Home Office, *Delivering Simple, Speedy, Summary Justice* (2006).

which may be missing, in view of the poor levels of legal representation and the need for the magistrates to decide matters of both law and fact.

A move towards magistrates' court trial may, of course, be thought to be fundamentally inappropriate if, for example, there is a belief that jury trial is an essential element in a fair trial or that only jury trial represents the essential requirement of community participation.

(b) Plea bargaining[906]

In the course of this chapter two forms of plea bargaining have been considered   **17–111** from the perspective of the various participants in the criminal trial, not least the accused. They are the plea arrangement between counsel for the accused to plead guilty to a lesser charge, otherwise known as charge bargaining, and the sentencing discount available on a plea of guilty by the accused. Some would argue that there are really three types of bargain: the charge bargain, the fact bargain, and the plea bargain proper where the accused changes his plea to accept a low sentence and avoid trial.

Plea bargaining has much to say for it in terms of efficiency by encouraging the guilty to plead guilty at the earliest possible opportunity, and in saving considerable resources by having fewer contested trials. However, it seems generally to be accepted that the inducements to plead guilty should not be such that they create a substantial danger of the innocent pleading guilty. The pressures exerted by defence counsel giving advice to the accused "in strong terms" are long established, having been identified by Baldwin and McConville in their research study which concentrated on 121 Crown Court defendants who made late changes of plea from not guilty to guilty.[907] The criticisms made of the attitude and performance of counsel caused the publication of the research to be surrounded with controversy, but the conclusions of the study were that the sentencing discount and the rules governing the interrogation of suspects by the police were primarily responsible for any deficiencies exposed, rather than the conduct of the participants in the criminal process.[908]

Although lip-service is paid to the notion that the sentencing discount is based on the expression of remorse, the primary justification for the inducements to plead guilty is administrative expediency. The Sentencing Guidelines explicitly state that the maximum discount will only be available where the defendant indicated guilt at the earliest possible opportunity.[909] In a system which places so

---

[906] See Sanders and Young (2007). M. E. Vogel, "The Social Origins of Plea Bargaining: Conflict and the Law in Process of State Formation 1830–1860" (1999) Law and Society Rev. 161 discusses the early use of plea bargaining in the USA and demonstrates that it was used as a tool of the advocates who were politically ambitious. See also A. Alschuler, "Plea Bargaining and its History" (1979)13 Law and Society Rev. 211; J. H. Langbein, "Understanding the Short History of Plea Bargaining" (1979) 13 Law and Society Rev. 261; L. M. Mather, "Comments on the History of Plea Bargaining" (1979) 13 Law and Society Rev. 281; D. D. Guidorizzi, "Should We Really Ban Plea Bargaining? The Core Concerns of Plea Bargaining Critics" (1998) 47 Emory L.R. 753.

[907] *Negotiated Justice* (1977). The research technique involved detailed interviews with defendants accused of serious crimes. The interviews were conducted soon after the trial had finished and it is inevitable that the particular sample might be inclined to protest innocence and exaggerate the pressures involved. Nevertheless, it would appear that the number of people wrongly convicted after a guilty plea may be underestimated.

[908] *ibid.* Ch.6.

[909] Sentencing Guidelines Council, *Reduction in Sentence for a Guilty Plea: Guideline* (2004) para.4.3.

much emphasis upon the assumed innocence of the accused and the right to require the prosecution to prove their case, the existence of strong pressures to plead guilty may appear quite contradictory. The evidence currently available allows no complacency and suggests that more attention needs to be focused on those who plead guilty and, as a result, do not participate in the elaborate procedures described in the rest of this chapter.[910]

Sentence bargaining, whereby an advance indication is given as to what discount might be available in return for a guilty plea has now gained legitimacy and a degree of accountability through the decison in *Goodyear*.[911] The Court of Appeal laid down a number of guidelines that one might hope brings some regulation into an area previously dominated by informal discussions in judges' chambers.[912] However, Sanders and Young argue "that the guidelines are too open-ended and self contradictory to provide a stable legal framework".[913] For example, the guidelines do not rule out the type of private discussions that used to occur.

There have been some very forceful criticisms of plea bargaining, including Darbyshire's[914] catalogue of the problems identified from the many research projects in this area. These include the fact that discount rewards: are racially divisive; punish those who elect trial; reward the guilty; are efficiency based rules at the cost of the defendant's rights; increase the likelihood of induced confessions; lead to the not guilty pleading guilty; encourage lazy prosecuting and defending; assume a defendant has adequate knowledge and is well informed of his rights and the options available to him; ignores the principle of open justice; and marginalise the victim. It is unlikely that recent reforms have answered these problems.

(c) Jury reform

17–112   If crime control were the dominant motive in jury reform, arguments for abolition of the jury would be anticipated, since juries are inefficient and may acquit too many people, their decisions are unpredictable, and there is no appeal against an acquittal. In fact, proposals for the abolition of the jury are very rarely put forward, perhaps because of the popular support the jury receives through an ingrained belief that it is a constitutional protection against improper action by the State or simply that it is every person's right to be tried by one's peers.

The arguments are actually concerned with what crimes should be tried by the jury. Many advocates of the jury are firmly of the view that it is under attack, but that the attack is not direct or frontal against the institution of the jury itself.[915] Some advocates take the view that the attack is predicated on the basis of the crime control model. Arguably, the changes proposed for judge-only trials in cases of complex fraud and jury tampering are not based on principle but rather on administrative efficiency. The evidence suggests that long trials are a burden

---

[910] See further, S. Dell, *Silent in Court* (1971); S. McCabe and R. Purves, *By-Passing the Jury* (1972); Bottoms and McClean (1976). See also McBarnet (1981).

[911] *R v Goodyear* [2005] 1 W.L.R. 2532.

[912] See, M. Zander, "Please m'lud, how long will I get?" (2005) N.L.J. 677.

[913] Sanders and Young (2007), p.404.

[914] "The Mischief of Plea Bargaining and Sentencing Rewards" [2000] Crim. L.R. 894.

[915] See, e.g. P. Duff and M. Findlay, "The Politics of Jury Reform" in Findlay and Duff (1988), Ch.13; Freeman (1981); Lord Devlin, *Trial by Jury* (1956); Lord Devlin, "Trial By Jury for Fraud" (1986) 6 O.J.L.S. 311.

for juries in personal terms but there is less evidence to suggest that legal complexities are a real concern for juries.

(d) Victims

Until relatively recently victims were not regarded as important players in the full **17–113** criminal justice process. The prosecution (unless a private prosecution) is not brought on behalf of any individual victim, but by the State. More recently the victim's role has come to be recognised in the criminal justice system as a central one—see, for example, the Department for Constitutional Affairs Consultation Paper on Hearing the Relatives of Murder and Manslaughter Victims.[916] Many might regard this move to recognise victims' rights as a move back to the position of the last century where victims occupied a central role in the criminal justice system.[917] Arguments for victims' rights are usually associated with ensuring better crime control, with the criminal justice system being seen to avoid victimising those who are already the victims of crime. There are difficult issues raised above including the extent to which victims should have a say in charge bargaining and in sentencing. There needs to be great caution in ensuring that victims are given an appropriate opportunity to contribute to the process, whilst not being bound by the victim's requests.

(e) Case Management

The overriding objective of the Criminal Procedure Rules is that "cases be dealt **17–114** with justly". One can scarcely find fault with that, and the interpretation of the term "justly" gives due prominence to individual rights. Indeed, the Criminal Procedure Rules in general are a welcome exercise in consolidation and move a step closer towards codification of the law.[918] However, one must be careful to ensure that the need to deal with a case "efficiently and expeditiously",[919] whilst avoiding "unnecessary hearings"[920] is not at the expense of defendants' rights, for example, through inappropriate encouragement of guilty pleas, or acceptance of similarly inappropriate charge bargains.

The decision in *Ashton*[921] whereby procedural errors may be more readily rectified by the court emphasises the extent to which the overriding objective is influencing the law and the approach of the Court of Appeal. The decision has been the subject of criticism. Richardson comments, "[T]he unpalatable truth is that the overriding objective in the Criminal Procedure Rules (convict the guilty and acquit the innocent), taken together with the obligation imposed upon each participant in the conduct of a case to prepare and conduct the case in accordance with the overriding objective is incompatible with an adversarial system of justice."[922] This potential sea change in the traditionally adversarial nature of

---

[916] Department for Constitutional Affairs, *Hearing the Relatives of Murder and Manslaughter Victims: The Government's Plans to Give Bereaved Relatives of Murder and Manslaughter Victims a Say in Criminal Proceedings* (2005), available at *www.dca.gov.uk.* See also, J. Spencer, "Victim Advocates and Victim Care—the Place of the Victim in the Criminal Process" (2006) Mags. C.P. 10.

[917] Fenwick (1997), p.318.

[918] See J. R. Spencer, "Codifying Criminal Procedure" [2006] Crim. L.R. 279.

[919] CPR, r.1.1(2)(e).

[920] CPR, r.3.2.

[921] *R v Ashton* [2006] EWCA Crim 794.

[922] J. Richardson, Criminal Law Week 06/43/06.

criminal proceedings is further emphasised in *Malcolm*, where the court stated:

> "Criminal trials are no longer to be treated as a game, in which each move is final and any omission by the prosecution leads to its failure. It is the duty of the defence to make its defence and the issues it raises clear to the prosecution and to the court at an early stage. That duty is implicit in rule 3.3 of the Criminal Procedure Rules, which requires the parties actively to assist the exercise by the court of its case management powers, the exercise of which requires early identification of the real issues."[923]

(f) Managerialism

17–115   Many of the changes implemented to the criminal process in the last decade in particular have been directed towards improving efficiency in the system.[924] This has led, inevitably, to the adoption of managerial ideas—processes, monitoring, performance standards and protocols. The real concern should be to ensure that the management of the process is efficient without diminishing the quality of justice delivered. Rationalising the infrastructure of the institutions and agencies responsible for criminal process should serve to improve the criminal trial process itself but it must be ensured that such changes do not conflict with a fair trial.[925]

---

[923] *Malcolm v DPP* [2007] EWHC 363, para.31.

[924] See, for example, Home Office, *Delivering Simple, Speedy, Summary Justice* (2006).

[925] See C. Pollard, "Public Safety, Accountability and the Courts" [1996] Crim. L.R. 151. In response, A. Ashworth, "Crime, Community and Creeping Consequentialism" [1996] Crim. L.R. 220, considers a rights-based focus to the question of reform, asking what "foundation" many of the so-called rights in the trial process have.

CHAPTER 18

APPEALS AND JUDICIAL REVIEW

A. INTRODUCTION

18–001 In this chapter we consider the various mechanisms for correcting errors in, and otherwise reviewing, the decisions of courts and tribunals. There are two basic kinds of legal procedure that are available for these purposes. An *appeal* may be provided by statute: indeed it will only be available if a statute has so provided, as the common law does not recognise any rights of appeal as such. The common law has provided only for the *review* of decisions either on the ground that the body which made the decision had no jurisdiction in the matter, or on the ground that the formal record of proceedings revealed that there had been some error of law. Where the body was an inferior body of limited jurisdiction, the appropriate remedy was a writ of certiorari to remove the proceedings into the Court of King's Bench: if the decision was shown to be defective it would be quashed. If such a body was proposing to act outside the jurisdiction in the future, a writ of prohibition would lie to prevent it from so acting; if it failed to perform a duty, the appropriate remedy was a writ of mandamus. These "prerogative" remedies would be available to challenge, for example, the decisions of justices of the peace in summary criminal proceedings or in civil cases. Where, however, the decision was that of one of the superior courts, or followed a criminal trial on indictment at the assizes or quarter sessions, the remedy was a writ of error, closely analogous to certiorari.[1] There were also informal devices whereby matters could be adjourned so that the views of other judges could be obtained[2] and special procedures for the review of decisions in the Court of Chancery.[3]

In the nineteenth and early twentieth centuries, writs of error were replaced by statutory appeals. The prerogative writs continued to be available in respect of the courts of summary jurisdiction, but now in parallel to statutory appeals. They were also increasingly used to correct the decisions of local authorities, government departments and statutory tribunals. In 1938 they became prerogative "orders" rather than writs,[4] and in 1978 they came to be exclusively available on a new procedure termed an "application for judicial review".[5]

Apart from these basic options there are various other avenues for the redress of grievances, some of which are enshrined in statute (e.g. references by the Criminal Cases Review Commission to the Court of Appeal (Criminal Division)), some dependent on an exercise of the royal prerogative (e.g. the prerogative of mercy) and some informal.

There are two basic functions fulfilled by mechanisms for appeal or review. The first is that of the correction of errors of fact, substantive law or procedure made by the court or tribunal below. The second is that of the harmonious development of the law. Appellate courts commonly comprise a number of judges whereas trial courts and tribunals normally have a single judge or legally qualified chairman, sitting alone or with a jury or lay members. Appellate judges tend to be of greater experience and seniority than trial judges and their case load tends to be smaller, giving greater time for consideration; these factors become more pronounced the higher one moves up the courts hierarchy. In limited circumstances fresh evidence may be admitted before the reviewing court.

---

[1] See above, para.2–005.
[2] *ibid.*
[3] *ibid.*
[4] Administration of Justice (Miscellaneous Provisions) Act 1938, s.7.
[5] See below, paras 18–046—18–059.

Appellate courts may also correct divergences of approach among different courts of first instance.[6] Finally, appellate structures will only work optimally where there is a harmonious working relationship between the appeal body and the body supervised. This involves a suitable measure of deference to at least aspects of the latter's decisions.[7]

B. VARIABLE FACTORS IN APPEAL AND REVIEW MECHANISMS

There are a number of factors which must be taken into account when consider- **18–002**
ing any legal procedure for redressing a grievance:

(1) Who can institute an appeal?[8]

(2) Can the appeal be brought as of right or only by the permission of a court or other body?

(3) What are the permissible grounds for an appeal?

(4) What is the time limit within which an appeal must be brought?

(5) To which court or tribunal does the appeal lie?

(6) What material may the appellate body consider?

(7) Who may appear as parties on the appeal?

(8) What are the powers of the appellate court?

C. APPEALS

In this section we consider appeals from courts and tribunals.[9] We concentrate on **18–003**
appeals in basic civil and criminal cases: in addition a vast number of rights of appeal have been created in special cases which cannot be covered in detail.[10]
The appeals are presented in four groups:

---

[6] e.g. the Court of Appeal in *Froom v Butcher* [1976] Q.B. 286 settled the difference between judges who held that failure to wear a seat belt in a car would normally constitute contributory negligence and those who did not: the former approach was approved.

[7] See R. Nobles and D. Schiff, "The Right to Appeal and Workable Systems of Justice" (2002) 65 M.L.R. 676. Consider, for example, the role of appellate courts in reviewing questions of fact or the exercise of discretion, below.

[8] For convenience this is to be taken here to include "seek review".

[9] As to the constitution and functions of appellate courts, see Ch.2.

[10] A list may be found in D. Price, *Appeals* (1982).

(1) summary criminal proceedings and civil proceedings originating in magistrates' courts;

(2) criminal proceedings on indictment;

(3) civil cases originating in a county court or the High Court;

(4) appeals in administrative law matters.

The basic principles governing rights of appeal from a court seem to be that: (1) there should be one chance to appeal on the facts or merits and a series of opportunities to take points of law up the hierarchy of the courts; (2) there should be one chance to appeal as of right, with further appeals being dependent upon obtaining leave; and (3) that an acquittal by a jury in a criminal case should normally be regarded as final. Appeals from tribunals or public authorities tend to be limited to points of law. The ECHR does not provide a right of appeal in Art.6, but Protocol 7, Art.2 does provide such a right in respect of both conviction and sentence. Protocol 7 has not been incorporated into domestic law by the Human Rights Act 1998. ECHR protections do nevertheless apply, because the European Court applies Art.6 guarantees to the appeal proceedings where they exist in domestic law.[11]

1. Appeals from Magistrates' Courts

18–004   A person aggrieved by a decision of a magistrates' court in a criminal case, or in certain civil cases, has the option of (1) appealing on fact or law to the Crown Court, or (2) appealing on a point of law alone direct to the High Court, by way of "case stated". If the first option is chosen, an appeal lies thereafter to the High Court as in (2). In family cases, the appeal lies only to the High Court.

Once a case reaches the High Court, further appeals in criminal cases lie only to the House of Lords, and further appeals in civil cases lie on the same basis as in other civil cases determined by the High Court. In a criminal case, where the magistrates commit a convicted person to the Crown Court for sentence, the appeal thereafter lies to the Court of Appeal (Criminal Division).[12] The Auld Report in 2001 commented that the present appeal system in English law is "mixed and overlapping", with "procedural impediments to its ability both to do justice in individual cases and adequately to protect the public interest". The main recommendation was to streamline the process so that there would be similar bases for appeal in each level of jurisdiction, to replace the existing duplication with a single procedure and to improve the matching of the tribunal to the complexity of the case.[13]

---

[11] See *Delcourt v Belgium* (1969) 1 E.H.R.R. 355; *Tolstoy v UK* (1995) 20 E.H.R.R. 442. See generally M. Strange, in K. Starmer *et al.*, *Criminal Justice, Police Powers and Human Rights* (2001), Ch.19; B. Emmerson and A. Ashworth, *Human Rights and Criminal Justice* (2001), Ch.17.

[12] Criminal Appeal Act 1968, s.10: see below, para.18–016.

[13] Ch.12, para.4.

(a) Appeals from magistrates' courts to the Crown Court[14]

The defendant in a criminal case may appeal to the Crown Court, as of right (a) **18–005**
if he or she pleaded guilty[15] against sentence; or (b) if he or she did not plead
guilty, against the conviction or sentence.[16] "Sentence" includes any order made
on conviction other than an order for costs and certain other orders.[17] Similarly,
a person may appeal against an order for contempt of a magistrates' court[18] or an
order binding him or her over to keep the peace or to be of good behaviour.[19] The
prosecutor or complainant may not appeal against an acquittal or a refusal to
make or vary an order.[20] This right to appeal does not preclude a challenge by
way of judicial review if the complaint is of any impropriety or denial of a fair
trial.[21] The Criminal Cases Review Commission can refer to the Crown Court
any conviction of the magistrates' court.[22] There has been less detailed academic
scrutiny of the operation of the appellate jurisdiction of the Crown Court than of
the Court of Appeal.

Notice of appeal must be given within 21 days after the day on which the
decision or sentence appealed against was given.[23] The notice must state the
grounds for appeal. The Crown Court may extend the time for giving notice of

---

[14] See *Blackstone's Criminal Practice 2007*, Pt D-27; A. Keogh, *Criminal Appeals and Review Remedies for Magistrates' Court Decisions* (1999); Sprack (2004), Ch.25. In 2000 there were 13,902 appeals received against magistrates' courts decisions, with 5,341 against conviction, 7,691 against sentence and 870 other (e.g. licences): *Judicial Statistics 2000*, and see K. Malleson and S. Roberts, [2002] Crim. L.R. 274, n.9. In 2005 there were 12,843 appeals received: *Judicial Statistics 2005*.

[15] There is no opportunity to appeal against conviction from a guilty plea: *R v Birmingham Crown Court, Ex p. Sharma* [1988] Crim. L.R. 741; see A. Keogh, (1999), Ch.5. If the plea of guilty was "equivocal" the defendant may appeal to the Crown Court to set aside the conviction and remit the case to the magistrates with a direction to enter a plea of "not guilty" and try the case summarily: the magistrates' court is obliged to comply with the direction provided that there has been a proper inquiry by the Crown Court and sufficient evidence from which it could find that the plea had been equivocal: *R v Plymouth JJ., Ex p. Hart* [1986] Q.B. 950. A plea is equivocal where something emerges during the trial which throws doubt on it, e.g. in theft, "guilty, but I took it by mistake". See *R v Durham Quarter Sessions, Ex p. Virgo* [1952] 2 Q.B. 1. The Crown Court should seek affidavit evidence from the chairman of the bench or the clerk before sending it back: *R v Rochdale JJ., Ex p. Allwork* [1981] 3 All E.R. 433. The Crown Court may also remit a case where it subsequently transpires that a plea of guilty was made under duress: *R v Huntingdon Crown Court, Ex p. Jordan* [1981] Q.B. 857.

[16] Magistrates' Courts Act 1980, s.108(1). The power of the magistrates' court to reopen any order made by them which has not been subsequently determined by a higher court has been extended by Criminal Appeal Act 1995, s.26, leaving a very broad discretion in the magistrates' hands. See *Collett v Bromsgrove DC* [1997] Crim. L.R. 206.

[17] *ibid.* s.108(3). Probation orders and orders for conditional discharge were formerly excluded: see now the Powers of Criminal Courts (Sentencing) Act 2000, s.14. See further the catalogue of orders in *Archbold* (2007), paras 2–161—2–172a.

[18] Contempt of Court Act 1981, s.12(5).

[19] Magistrates' Courts (Appeals from Binding Over Orders) Act 1956, s.1; *Hughes v Holley* (1986) 86 Cr.App.R. 130.

[20] *Lee v Leeds Crown Court* [2006] EWHC 2550 (Admin) (refusal to vary a restraining order). Such a right may be expressly conferred, e.g. the Customs and Excise Management Act 1979, s.147: offences under the Customs and Excise Acts.

[21] See *R v Hereford Magistrates' Court, Ex p. Prussia* [1997] 2 Cr.App.R. 340 (doubting *R v Peterborough JJ., Ex p. Dowler* [1996] 2 Cr.App.R. 561). See further *Archbold* (2007), para.2–160.

[22] Criminal Appeal Act 1995, s.11.

[23] Crown Court Rules 1982 (SI 1982/1109), r.7, as amended by SI 2001/614; Criminal Procedure Rules 2005 (SI 2005/384), Pt 63. See *Archbold* (2007), para.2–180.

appeal either before or after it expires.[24] The appellant may abandon the appeal by giving notice in writing up to three days before the hearing of the appeal.[25]

The appeal is treated as a complete rehearing,[26] and the procedure is exactly the same as at a summary trial in the magistrates' court. Appeals are heard by a circuit judge or recorder who must normally sit with two magistrates.[27] The appeal can be heard notwithstanding the absence of the appellant,[28] even where he or she has not instructed counsel to appear on his or her behalf.[29] The relevant witnesses will attend the court and give evidence as at the original trial. The parties are not, however, confined to the evidence placed before the magistrates. The Crown Court may find the case proved on a basis other than that found by the magistrates' court.[30] Where the appeal is against sentence only, it is usual for the prosecution merely to put forward facts which had been admitted or found by the magistrates, although there is no technical reason why sworn evidence should not be given.[31] The Crown Court can pass sentence on a different factual basis than that found in the magistrates' court.[32]

The powers of the Crown Court are as follows.[33] It may correct any error or mistake in the order or judgment against which the appeal is brought, and at the end of the hearing may:

(a) confirm, reverse or vary any part of the decision appealed against, including a determination not to impose a separate penalty in respect of an offence[34];

(b) remit the matter with its opinion thereon to the authority whose decision is appealed against; or

---

[24] *ibid.*

[25] Crown Court Rules 1982, r.11; Criminal Procedure Rules 2005, Pt 63; Magistrates' Courts' Act 1980, s.109.

[26] See *Drover v Ragman* [1951] 1 K.B. 380; *Northern Ireland Trailers v Preston Corporation* [1972] 1 W.L.R. 203; *Hughes v Holley* (1986) 86 Cr.App.R. 130: these cases show that the court must, however, consider the state of affairs existing at the time the order was appealed against. Appeals against binding-over orders are to be conducted as a rehearing: *Shaw v Hamilton* [1982] 1 W.L.R. 1308.

[27] See Supreme Court Act 1981, s.74; Crown Court Rules 1982, r.3, as amended; *Criminal Practice Direction*, para.33.5.

[28] *R v Croydon Crown Court, Ex p. Clair* [1986] 1 W.L.R. 746 (the Crown Court had refused to hear the appeal in the appellant's absence: mandamus was granted requiring them to do so). The Crown Court cannot quash a decision on the basis that the defendant was denied the opportunity to have his case heard owing to his representatives' error, if the magistrates have acted correctly: *R v Secretary of State for Home Department, Ex p. Al Mehdawi* [1990] 1 A.C. 876.

[29] *R v Crown Court at Guildford, Ex p. Brewer* (1987) 87 Cr.App.R. 265 (the appellant's counsel was present, but, following refusal of an application for an adjournment, took no further part in the proceedings as he had no instructions to do so). Persistent absence from an appeal should not be taken to constitute abandonment of the appeal: *R (on the application of Hayes) v Chelmsford Crown Court* [2003] EWHC 73 (Admin), [2003] Crim. L.R. 400.

[30] *Hingley-Smith v DPP* [1998] 1 Arch. News 2, DC; *R (on the application of Graves) v Islington LBC* [2003] EWHC 2817 (Admin).

[31] *Paprika Ltd v Board of Trade* [1944] K.B. 327; *Shaw v Hamilton* [1982] 1 W.L.R, 1308; *Williams v R* (1983) 77 Cr.App.R. 329; *R v Telford JJ., Ex p. Darlington* (1987) 87 Cr.App.R. 194.

[32] *Bussey v DPP* [1999] 1 Cr.App.R.(S) 125 (departure from facts to be explained to accused).

[33] Supreme Court Act 1981, s.48, as amended. See *Archbold* (2007), para.2–178.

[34] Prior to the enactment of s.156 of the 1988 Act, the subsection merely referred to a power to vary "the decision appealed against". The Divisional Court in *Dutta v Westcott* [1987] Q.B. 291 gave the words a strained interpretation in holding that the Crown Court was empowered to vary the penalty imposed for another offence dealt with by the magistrates on the same occasion, but which was not appealed against: the amendment gave express authority for this.

(c) make any order in the matter as it thinks just and exercise any power which that authority might have exercised.

These powers are subject to any limit or restriction imposed by any other enactment. A punishment in a criminal case may be more or less severe than that awarded by the magistrates' court, provided that it could have been imposed by that court.[35] The court must give reasons for its decision.[36] Costs may be awarded against an unsuccessful appellant[37] and may be awarded to a successful appellant out of central funds.[38]

In civil matters, appeals lie to the Crown Court in respect of a variety of licensing and other matters.[39]

(b) Appeals from magistrates' courts to the High Court by "case stated"

Any person who was party[40] to any proceedings before a magistrates' court or who is "aggrieved"[41] by its decision may question the decision on the ground that it is wrong in law or in excess of jurisdiction by applying to the justices for them to state a case for the opinion of the High Court.[42] An application may not be made following committal proceedings,[43] at an interlocutory stage in a summary hearing,[44] to challenge a decision by the magistrates declining jurisdiction,[45] where there is otherwise a right of appeal to the High Court or where the decision is said by an enactment to be "final".[46] The application must be made within 21 days, and any right to appeal to the Crown Court is lost when this is done.[47] The justices may refuse to state a case if they are of opinion that the

18–006

---

[35] Supreme Court Act, s.48. See *Arthur v Stringer* (1986) 84 Cr.App.R. 361.

[36] *R v Harrow Crown Court, Ex p. Dave* [1994] 1 W.L.R. 98; *R v Inner London Crown Court, Ex p. London Borough of Lambeth Council* [2000] Crim. L.R. 303; failure to do so could render the Crown Court's decision invalid: *R v Kingston Crown Court, Ex p. Bell* (2000) 64 J.P. 633; *R (on the application of Taylor) v Maidstone Crown Court* [2003] EWHC 2555 (Admin) (decision quashed where insufficient reasons were given).

[37] Prosecution of Offences Act 1985, s.18(1)(b).

[38] Prosecution of Offences Act 1985, s.16(3); see also *Johnson v RSPCA* (2000) 164 J.P. 345.

[39] See, e.g. Licensing Act 2003, s.166.

[40] e.g. defendant *or prosecutor* in a criminal case: *R v Newport (Salop) JJ., Ex p. Wright* [1929] 2 K.B. 416.

[41] This covers a person who is not a party but whose legal rights are affected by the decision: *Drapers Company v Holder* (1892) 57 J.P. 200, e.g. the owner of stolen goods who seeks a restitution order.

[42] Magistrates' Courts Act 1980, s.111(1).

[43] *Atkinson v United States Government* [1971] A.C. 197; *Cragg v Lewes District Council* [1986] Crim. L.R. 800.

[44] *Streames v Copping* [1985] Q.B. 920 (to challenge a disputed ruling that the magistrates had jurisdiction). *Cf. Loade v DPP* [1990] 1 Q.B. 1052 (Divisional Court has no jurisdiction in a criminal case to entertain an appeal by case stated at an interlocutory stage of an appeal to the Crown Court); there is such a jurisdiction in civil cases, but justices should exercise their power only in exceptional circumstances (*R v Chesterfield JJ., Ex p. Kovacs* [1992] 2 All E.R. 325).

[45] *Pratt v A. A. Sites Ltd* [1938] 2 K.B. 459: the remedy here is to apply for judicial review: see *Streames v Copping, per* May L.J. at 928.

[46] 1980 Act, s.111(1). See *Liverpool City Council v Worthington, The Times,* June 16, 1998.

[47] *ibid.* s.111(4). See *P. & M. Supplies (Essex) Ltd v Hackney London Borough Council* (1990) 154 J.P. 814. An appeal by case stated against conviction will not debar an appeal to the Crown Court against sentence, and vice versa: an appeal by case stated on both matters debars the appeal to Crown Court completely: *R v Winchester Crown Court, Ex p. Lewington* [1982] 1 W.L.R. 1277.

application is "frivolous",[48] but may not do so where the application is made by or under the direction of the Attorney-General. If they do exercise their power to refuse, the applicant may seek an order of mandamus from the High Court to compel them to state a case, and the High Court has a discretion whether to make an order.[49]

The procedure for stating a case is regulated by the Magistrates' Courts Rules 1981.[50] The application is made to designated officer for the magistrates' court whose decision is questioned. Unless the application is refused, a draft case must be sent to the parties, and it may be amended by the justices in the light of any representations received. The case must state the facts found and the questions of law or jurisdiction on which guidance is sought. It must specify any finding of fact which is claimed to be unsupported by evidence, but it may not otherwise contain a statement of evidence.[51] In practice it is normally prepared by the clerk. An appeal by way of case stated may be withdrawn by the appellant without leave.[52]

In criminal cases the appeal is normally heard by a Divisional Court of the Queen's Bench Division; otherwise, it is normally heard by a single judge. Where the appeal relates to the enforcement of a maintenance order, the appeal lies by case stated.[53] The appellant must file the appellant's notice, the stated case and a copy of the order in the Crown Office or the Principal Registry of the Family Division within 10 days of receiving the case, and must serve a copies on the respondent within four days of so lodging it. The High Court may return the case for amendment.[54]

On an appeal, the High Court may reverse, affirm or amend the decision or remit it to the justices for their reconsideration in the light of the court's opinion, or make such other order as the court thinks fit.[55] Apart from the obvious power to correct errors of law, such as the misinterpretation of a statute, the court will treat any decision unsupported by the evidence, or otherwise one which no reasonable magistrates could reach, as erroneous in law.[56] The court may take the view that in the light of its ruling on the law in a criminal case the defendant is clearly guilty or clearly innocent, in which event it will direct the magistrates to convict or acquit as the case may be. Otherwise the matter will be left to the magistrates. The Divisional Court may order the magistrates' court to make an appropriate order or otherwise to complete unfinished proceedings; or to conduct a rehearing before the same or a different bench. The rehearing should only be

---

[48] This term includes cases where the argument on the point of law cannot succeed, e.g. where the law has been authoritatively stated in a superior court. "Frivolous" has been interpreted as meaning "futile, misconceived, hopeless or academic": *R v Mildenhall Magistrates' Court, Ex p. Forest Heath D.C.* (1997) 161 J.P. 401. Or a "try-on": Sedley L.J. in *R (on the application of Murra) v Horseferry Road Magistrates' Court* [2002] EWHC 1238 (Admin).

[49] On the procedure where magistrates refuse to state a case see *R v Blackfriars Crown Court, Ex p. Sunworld* [2000] 1 W.L.R. 2102. See generally Keogh, (1999), Ch.11.

[50] SI 1981/552, as amended, rr.76–81. In criminal cases, the applicable rules are the Criminal Procedure Rules 2005, Pt 64.

[51] See *Turtington v United Cooperatives Ltd* [1993] Crim. L.R. 376.

[52] *Collett v Bromsgrove District Council* (1996) 160 J.P. 593.

[53] *Berry v Berry* [1987] Fam 1; *R v Bristol JJ., Ex p. Hodge* [1997] Q.B.974. Such appeals have in the past been made to the Family Division, but may be heard by a judge of the Family Division sitting in the Administrative Court.

[54] Supreme Court Act 1981, s.28A, inserted by the Statute Law (Repeals) Act 1993, Sch.2, para.9, and then substituted by the Access to Justice Act 1999, s.61.

[55] *ibid.*

[56] *Bracegirdle v Oxley* [1947] 1 K.B. 349. This is significantly narrower than the appeal on the merits to the Crown Court: see section (a) above.

ordered if it will not deny the accused a fair trial.[57] Appeal against sentence should normally be directed to the Crown Court.[58] The Auld Report made the radical recommendation that in criminal cases there should be no right of appeal to the High Court by an appeal by way of case stated, and no right to challenge the magistrates' decision by way of judicial review.[59] This is currently a rarely used avenue of appeal; in 2000 there were 125 appeals by way of case stated in criminal cases and 336 claims for judicial review.[60] Malleson and Roberts pointed out that the proposals would nevertheless reduce the efficiency of the system.[61]

Subject to a possible appeal to the House of Lords in a criminal case, the decision of the High Court is final.[62]

(c) Appeals from magistrates' courts to the High Court in family cases

In certain family matters an appeal lies to the Family Division of the High Court. **18–007** These include the making or refusal of orders under the Domestic Proceedings and Magistrates' Courts Act 1978[63] and variations of maintenance orders.[64] The appeal can raise matters of fact or law and is not by case stated. A notice of motion must be served and the appeal entered within six weeks of the decision challenged.[65]

Appeals from the making of or refusal to make an order under the Children Act 1989 also lie from the magistrates' court to the Family Division.[66] Notice of appeal must normally be served within 14 days. Appeals are heard by a judge of the Family Division at the nearest convenient High Court centre.[67] On an appeal the High Court may make such orders as may be necessary to give effect to its determination of the appeal.[68] Similar rules apply to appeals in respect of orders concerning family homes and domestic violence.[69]

---

[57] *Griffith v Jenkins* [1992] 2 A.C. 76, *cf.* the Divisional Court decisions in *Maydew v Flint* (1984) 80 Cr.App.R. 49; *Rigby v Woodward* [1957] 1 W.L.R. 250.

[58] *R v Ealing JJ., Ex p. Scrafield* [1994] R.T.R. 195 (application for judicial review rejected).

[59] Ch.12, para.35.

[60] Ch.12, para.16.

[61] [2002] Crim. L.R. 272.

[62] Supreme Court Act 1981, s.28A(4); below, para.18–009.

[63] s.29. Other than interim maintenance orders, against which no appeal lies. Appeals are heard by a Divisional Court. Appeals as to the *enforcement* of maintenance orders lie by case stated: see section (b), above.

[64] Maintenance Orders Act 1958, s.4(7). Appeals are head by a Divisional Court. See *Hackshaw v Hackshaw* [1999] 3 F.C.R. 51.

[65] Family Proceedings Rules 1991 (SI 1991/1247, as amended), r.7.28, r.8.2, as amended. This appeal regime is distinct from that under the Children Act 1989 (see below): *P v P (Periodical Payments)* [1995] 1 F.L.R. 563.

[66] Children Act 1989, s.94, as amended by the 2002 Act, s.100. See Family Proceedings Rules 1991 (SI 1991/1247), r.4.22, as amended; Family Procedure (Adoption) Rules 2005 (SI 2005/2795), rr.171–183. See *Re O (Family Appeals: Management)* [1998] F.L.R. 431.

[67] *Practice Direction (Appeals from Magistrates' Courts)* [1992] 1 W.L.R. 261.

[68] e.g. 1978 Act, s.29(2); 1989 Act, s.94(4); 1996 Act, s.61(2). The principles of *G v G (Minors: Custody Appeal)* [1985] 1 W.L.R. 647 (below, para.18–026) broadly apply to appeals under s.94: *Re M (Section 94 appeals)* [1995] 1 F.L.R. 546, CA and see *Re W* [1999] 3 F.C.R. 337. Fresh evidence will only be received in exceptional circumstances: *Croydon London Borough Council v A* [1992] Fam. 169; *cf. S v Merton London Borough Council* [1994] 1 F.C.R. 186.

[69] Under Pt IV of the Family Law Act 1986. See s.61 and the Family Proceedings Rules 1991, r.8.1A.

Proposals have been made for rationalising the details of arrangements for appeals in family cases.[70] Elements would include the abolition of case stated appeals, provision for appeals from magistrates' courts to lie to the county court, and generally the introduction of new Family Procedure Rules harmonised with the CPR.

(d) Appeals from the Crown Court to the High Court

18–008　　Where there has been an appeal from a magistrates' court to the Crown Court, any party to the proceedings[71] may appeal by case stated on a point of law or jurisdiction to the High Court.[72] The procedure is similar to that for such appeals from the magistrates' court direct to the High Court.[73] The same right of appeal is available in respect of any other decision of the Crown Court[74] except one relating to trial on indictment and in certain licensing matters.[75] Subject to a possible appeal to the House of Lords in a criminal case the decision of the High Court is final.[76]

(e) Appeals from the High Court to the House of Lords[77]

18–009　　In civil cases which have reached the High Court on appeal, further appeals lie on the same bases as in other civil matters determined by the High Court.[78] Until 1960 there was, however, no further right of appeal in a criminal case, and the Divisional Court of the Queen's Bench Division was the final authority on many matters concerning summary offences.[79] Under the Administration of Justice Act 1960[80] either the prosecutor or the defendant may appeal to the House of Lords on a point of law of public general importance. Leave must be obtained from either the Divisional Court or the House of Lords: the Divisional Court must certify that a point of law of general public importance is involved,[81] and it must

---

[70] See Family Justice Council Response to the *HMCS Consultation Paper on Family Procedure Rules* (CP 19/06) (December 2006), referring to Reports of the Family Appeals Review Group (July 1998) and the Family Procedure Rules Committee (July 2005). Annex 1 lists 12 routes of appeal in total. For judicial concern, see *Re L (Family Proceedings Court) (Appeal: Jurisdiction)* [2005] 1 F.L.R. 210, paras [55]–[61].

[71] i.e. in a criminal case, either prosecutor or defendant.

[72] Supreme Court Act 1981, s.28, as amended. For powers of disposal, see s.28A, substituted by the Access to Justice Act 1999, s.61.

[73] Crown Court Rules 1982 (SI 1982/1109), r.26; Criminal Procedure Rules 2005, r.64.7, and *cf.* above para.18–006. For the procedure on applications see *DPP v Coleman* [1998] 1 All E.R. 912.

[74] e.g. matters such as firearms licensing where an appeal lies direct to the Crown Court: see P. J. Clarke and J. W. Ellis, *The Law Relating to Firearms* (1981), pp.104–111; *Kavanagh v Chief Constable of Devon and Cornwall* [1974] Q.B. 624.

[75] Supreme Court Act 1981, s.28(2) *cf.* s.29(3), As to appeals in relation to trials on indictment, see below, para.18–010 and on the relationship between appeals by case stated and applications for judicial review, see below para.18–059. The Law Commission (Law Com. No.226, 1994), has recommended that no new case stated appeals be created and that appeals on a point of law are to be preferred: p.106.

[76] 1981 Act, s.28A(4). See para.18–009.

[77] See A. Keogh, (1999), Ch.12.

[78] See below, para.18–022. Decisions on case stated appeals are, however, final: para.18–023.

[79] For example, there was no right to appeal against the unsatisfactory decisions in *Thomas v Sawkins* [1935] 2 K.B. 249 and *Duncan v Jones* [1936] K.B. 218: see S. H. Bailey, D. J. Harris and B. L. Jones, *Civil Liberties: Cases and Materials* (4th edn, 1995), pp.248–251, 259–264.

[80] ss.1–9, s.2 as amended by the Courts Act 2003, s.88.

[81] There is no right to appeal against the refusal of a certificate: *Gelberg v Miller* [1961] 1 All E.R. 618n. HL.

appear either to that court or to the House of Lords[82] that the point ought to be considered by the House. On the appeal, the House may exercise any of the powers of the Divisional Court or may remit the case to it. The House is not confined to answering the certified question and may dispose of the proceedings on any grounds which appear to be appropriate.[83]

2. APPEALS FOLLOWING TRIAL ON INDICTMENT[84]

(a) Appeals from the Crown Court to the Court of Appeal (Criminal Division)

Persons convicted[85] of an offence on indictment may appeal to the Court of Appeal (Criminal Division). The powers of the Court of Appeal were remodelled by Pt I of the Criminal Appeal Act 1995, following recommendations of the Royal Commission on Criminal Justice.[86] The powers of the Court of Appeal have been the subject of continuing controversy following this reform, and as a result of the Human Rights Act 1998 which has caused a re-focusing of the inquiry from safety to broader concerns of fairness.[87]   **18–010**

(i) Appeals against conviction

(1) *Grounds and procedure.* The person convicted may only appeal if either (a) a certificate from the trial judge that the case is fit for appeal[88] or (b) leave of the Court of Appeal (Criminal Division) is obtained.[89]   **18–011**

The appellant must either serve the trial judge's certificate on the appropriate officer of the Crown Court with a notice of appeal, or serve notice of application for leave to appeal.[90] The notice must be served within 28 days of conviction, although the time limit may be extended by the court.[91] The grounds of the

---

[82] The application for leave is made first to the Divisional Court and only if that court refuses to the House of Lords. See the 1960 Act, s.2, as amended.

[83] *R v Jones* [2006] 2 W.L.R. 772, *per* Lord Hoffmann at para.[69].

[84] See *Archbold* (2007) Ch.7; *Blackstone's Criminal Practice* (2007) D24.

[85] This includes a person who pleaded guilty: *R. v Lee (Bruce)* [1984] 1 W.L.R. 578; *R. v Swain* [1986] Crim. L.R. 480; and where a verdict has been returned, but the judge has postponed sentence: *R. v Drew* [1985] 1 W.L.R. 914.

[86] Cm. 2263, 1993, Ch.10. See Sir John Smith, [1995] Crim. L.R. 920.

[87] See, Office for Criminal Justice Reform, *Quashing Convictions: Report of a Review by the Home Secretary, Lord Chancellor and Attorney General* (2006).

[88] *The Consolidated Criminal Practice Direction* V.50.4; Crim. P.R. (2005) r.68.2.

[89] 1968 Act, s.1(2), as substituted by the Criminal Appeal Act 1995, s.l. Prior to this change, the person convicted could appeal as of right on any ground which involved a question of law alone.

[90] *ibid.* s.18(1).

[91] 1968 Act, s.18(2). Leave may be granted some years later. See, e.g. *R. v Foster* [1985] Q.B. 115, where F was convicted of rape in 1977, following a plea of guilty. Another man confessed to and was convicted of the offence in 1981. F was granted a free pardon in 1982 and leave to appeal in 1984, when the conviction was quashed. The court has rejected a claim that to deny an extension of time when the basis of the appeal is a change in the law is contrary to Art.7 of the ECHR: *R. v Jones (Beatrice)* [1999] Crim. L.R. 820. The European Court has accepted that reasonable time limits can be imposed on appeals: *Vacher v France* (1996) 24 E.H.R.R. 482. The restrictions on appeal must not be such as to destroy the essence of the right: *Omar v France* (1998) 29 E.H.R.R. 210.

appeal or application must be stated,[92] but may be varied or amplified within such time as the court may allow. The appellant may apply for bail,[93] and be present at the hearing.[94]

If it appears to the Registrar of Criminal Appeals that the notice of appeal or application for leave to appeal does not show any substantial ground he or she may refer the appeal or application to the court for summary determination, and the court, if it considers the appeal to be frivolous[95] or vexatious, may dismiss the appeal summarily.[96]

The defendant at the trial should be seen by his solicitor and counsel in the event of conviction or sentence and advised on whether there appear to be reasonable grounds for an appeal.[97] The defendant may only pursue an appeal under ss.1 and 2 of the 1968 Act once, even where he seeks to adduce fresh evidence on the second occasion.[98]

The Criminal Appeal Act does not discriminate between those who pleaded guilty at trial and those who were convicted after a hearing. However, the Court of Appeal has restricted the availability of appeals to those who pleaded guilty. If the accused has pleaded guilty he will only be able to pursue an appeal against conviction if his plea was a result of a ruling which was erroneous and left him with no legal escape from a verdict of guilty. If the ruling of the judge was such as to lead to the admission of damaging evidence against the accused, and he pleaded guilty recognising the case was hopeless, the plea would be treated as an acknowledgement of the truth of the facts.[99]

Applications for leave to appeal are normally dealt with by a single judge who examines the papers and may grant leave, refuse it, or refer the case to the court.[100] If leave is refused an application may be renewed to the court within 14 days.[101]

---

[92] *Consolidated Criminal Practice Direction* II.15.1. *Criminal Procedure Rules* 2005 r.68.3. If leave is limited to only specified grounds of appeal, the Court of Appeal will not hear argument on other grounds without granting leave: *R. v Jackson* [1999] 1 All E.R. 572; *R. v Cox* [1999] 2 Cr.App.R. 6.

[93] Criminal Appeal Act 1968, s.19.

[94] Criminal Appeal Act 1968 s.22.

[95] e.g. the ground of appeal could not possibly succeed on argument: *R. v Taylor* [1979] Crim. L.R. 649.

[96] Criminal Appeal Act 1968, s.20.

[97] *Guide to Proceedings in the Court of Appeal Criminal Division* (1997) available at *www.hmcourts-service.gov.uk/index.htm*. See also M. Zander, [1972] Crim. L.R. 132, [1975] Crim. L.R. 364 and *Practice Note* [1974] 2 All E.R. 805. The RCCJ was very critical of the quality of legal advice given at this stage, and the arrangements for access to advice from prison: Cm. 2263, pp.164–167, based on J. Plotnikoff and R. Woolfson, *Information and Advice for Prisoners about Grounds for Appeal and the Appeals Process* (RCCI Research Study No.18, 1993).

[98] *R. v Pinfold* [1988] Q.B. 462; *R. v Berry* [1991] 1 W.L.R. 125: there are two apparent exceptions: where the decision on the original appeal is a nullity and where, owing to some defect in procedure, the appellant on the first appeal being dismissed suffered an injustice, (e.g. the appellant has not been notified of the hearing of the appeal, or counsel has been unable to attend (*ibid.*)). A case may also be referred back to the Court of Appeal by the Criminal Cases Review Commission whereupon the rule in *Pinfold* does not apply: see *R. v Thomas* [2002] Crim. L.R. 912.

[99] *R. v Kennedy* [1998] Crim. L.R. 739, *R. v Chalkley and Jeffries* [1998] 2 All E.R. 155; *R. v P* [2005] 2 Cr.App.R. 21.

[100] On the difficulties in achieving this preparation see Auld Report (2001), Ch.12, paras 79– 86.

[101] See *Criminal Procedure Rules* 2005 r.68.6.

A representation order may be granted for further advice and assistance and for representation before the single judge or the court.[102] The single judge and the court have power, when refusing an application for leave to appeal, to direct that part of the time during which a person has been in custody after lodging his application should not count towards sentence.[103] In both 1970 and 1980 the then Lord Chief Justice issued a reminder of the existence of this power in view of the delay caused to the hearing of meritorious appeals by the lodging of huge numbers of hopeless applications.[104] In the two years after 1970 the number of applications for leave to appeal was cut by a half, although the problem subsequently recurred. In the 1980 Direction, it was stated a direction for loss of time "will normally be made unless the grounds are not only settled and signed by counsel, but also supported by the written opinion of counsel". Counsel should only so act where he or she considers that the proposed appeal is properly arguable. Moreover, a direction will also normally be made where an application is renewed to the court after the single judge has refused it as wholly devoid of merit: here, whether or not the grounds have been settled and signed by counsel.[105] The European Court has accepted this practice.[106]

The administrative tasks in relation to appeals are performed by the Criminal Appeal Office, headed by the Registrar of Criminal Appeals. The documents in the case, including, if appropriate, a transcript, are assembled by the office. Skeleton arguments must be lodged with the Registrar and served on the prosecuting authority within 14 days of receipt by the advocate of leave. Similarly the skeleton argument of the prosecuting advocate must be lodged within 14 days.[107] If leave is granted, a lawyer on the staff of the office then prepares a descriptive "summary" of the facts and grounds of appeal to assist the full court.[108] This should usually be available to counsel.

The Auld Report recommended that academic lawyers should be able to sit as ad hoc judges of the court or to supply written briefs to the court or points of law.[109] The Report also called for measures to allow the Court of Appeal to "slow down" to allow more time for preparation and judgment writing.[110]

(2) *Evidence*.[111] The court, under s.23(1) and (3) of the Criminal Appeal Act 1968,[112] *may* "if they think it necessary or expedient in the interests of justice": (a) order the production of any document, exhibit or other thing connected with the proceedings; (b) order the examination of any witness who would have been a compellable witness at the trial, whether or not he or she was called; and (c) receive any evidence which was not adduced in the proceedings from which the appeal lies.[113]

18–012

---

[102] On the obligation to comply with Art.6, see the decisions of the European Court in *Grainger v UK* (1990) 12 E.H.R.R. 469; *Maxwell v UK* (1994) 19 E.H.R.R. 197.

[103] Criminal Appeal Act 1968, s.29; See also *Consolidated Criminal Practice Direction*, para. II.16.

[104] Lord Parker C.J., (1970) 54 Cr.App.R. 280; Lord Widgery C.J., (1980) 70 Cr.App.R. 186.

[105] *R. v Gayle, The Times*, May 28, 1986.

[106] *Monnell and Morris v UK* (1987) 10 E.H.R.R. 205.

[107] See *Consolidated Criminal Practice Direction* para.II.17.

[108] *ibid.* para.II.18.

[109] Ch.12, para.89.

[110] Ch.12, para.95.

[111] See R. Pattenden, *Judicial Discretion and Criminal Litigation* (2nd edn, 1990), pp.355–358.

[112] As amended by the Criminal Appeal Act 1995, s.41.

[113] The court may examine such material as it thinks fit in deciding whether to order production of documents or the attendance of witnesses at the hearing of the appeal; it is not confined to material

In considering whether to receive any evidence, the Court of Appeal must have regard in particular to

> "(a) whether the evidence appears to the court to be capable of belief[114];
> (b) whether it appears to the court that the evidence may afford any ground for allowing the appeal;
> (c) whether the evidence would have been admissible in the proceedings from which the appeal lies on an issue which is the subject of the appeal[115]; and
> (d) whether there is a reasonable explanation for the failure to adduce the evidence in those proceedings".[116]

Between 1966 and 1995, s.23(2) of the 1968 Act provided for a *duty* of the court to receive evidence which was "likely to be credible", and which would have been admissible in the proceedings from which the appeal lay on an issue which was the subject of the appeal, and the court was satisfied that there was a reasonable explanation for the failure to adduce it at trial. The RCCJ thought that the "likely to be credible" test, which was interpreted as "evidence well capable of belief",[117] imposed too high a threshold.[118]

In *R. v Lattimore and others*[119] the Court of Appeal emphasised that the conditions limiting the old s.23(2) duty were not to be read as limiting the discretion under s.23(1).[120] This case arose out of the killing of Maxwell Confait, which was shortly followed by a fire at the house where he lived. Two youths were convicted of killing him (one for murder, one manslaughter) and those two and another were convicted of arson, solely on the basis of their own confessions. Three years later the Home Secretary referred the cases to the Court of Appeal (Criminal Division). The court, acting under s.23(1), received the evidence of three expert witnesses who had given evidence at the trial (two fire experts and a pathologist) and two further medical witnesses who gave evidence as to the time of death. However, they refused to admit evidence of persons who sought to throw light on the killer's identity, as they doubted its credibility and admissibility and in any event did not need to rely upon it. In addition, the Crown was permitted to call a fire expert and a forensic pathologist who had given evidence at the trial. The court held that this evidence showed that the lapse of time between the killing and the fire was much greater than had originally been

---

relating to the trial and the documents placed before the court by the parties: *R. v Callaghan* [1988] 1 W.L.R. 1, a pre-appeal review in the Birmingham pub bombers' case. The appellants sought to prevent the judges reading documents relating to other litigation and police inquiries arising out of the case, unless raised by the parties; the court held that its jurisdiction was not so confined, but acceded to the appellants' request in the exercise of its discretion. See also *Callaghan v UK* (1989) 60 D.R. 296.

[114] *R. v O'Hare* [2006] EWCA Crim 2512.
[115] i.e. the issue must have been raised first at the trial: *R. v Melville* [1976] 1 W.L.R. 181.
[116] 1968 Act, s.23(2), as substituted by the Criminal Appeal Act 1995, s.41. Under (d) the test is whether evidence could with "reasonable diligence" have been obtained for use at the trial: *R. v Beresford* (1971) 56 Cr.App.R. 143: B had failed to mention his presence at the "Poco a Poco Club" until he sought leave to introduce an alibi witness on the appeal. The court held that he had not used reasonable diligence and in any event disbelieved the witness. See also *R. v Haynes* [2002] EWCA Crim. 1855; *R. v Hampton* (2004) *The Times* October 13, 2004.
[117] *per* Edmund Davies L.J. in *R. v Stafford and Luvaglio* (1968) 53 Cr.App.R. 1 at 3.
[118] Cm. 2263. p.174.
[119] (1975) 62 Cr.App.R. 53.
[120] *ibid.* p.56.

thought and it threw sufficient doubt on the confessions for the homicide and arson convictions to be quashed. Scarman L.J. stated that the medical evidence was presented to the Court of Appeal "in a much sharper focus than it was at the trial".[121] In other cases under the original version of section 23 fresh evidence was admitted where another person confessed to the crime for which the appellant was convicted,[122] where prosecution witnesses subsequently made statements inconsistent with their testimony[123] or had subsequently been found to have fabricated confessions attributed to suspects in other cases,[124] and where it was claimed that there was an irregularity at the trial.[125] Exceptionally, fresh evidence could be admitted following an unequivocal plea of guilty,[126] or where an arguable line of defence was not pursued at trial.[127] As Lord Bingham C.J. has emphasised, there is "a crucial obligation on a defendant in a criminal case to advance his whole defence and any evidence on which he relies before the jury trial. He is not entitled to hold evidence in reserve and then seek to introduce it on appeal following conviction."[128]

Under the current version of s.23, the discretion under s.23(1) is now structured by reference to the conditions set out in subsection (2) and there is no longer a *duty* to receive evidence in specified circumstances. However, it will be noted that the court ultimately retains a discretion to receive evidence even where there is no reasonable explanation for the lack of adduction at trial. The RCCJ urged "that in general the court should take a broad, rather than a narrow, approach" to their powers to receive evidence.[129]

In *Hanratty*,[130] the Court of Appeal made it clear that in appropriate cases, fresh evidence could be admitted on behalf of the prosecution. The appellant has a right to be present when issues of fact are decided by the Court of Appeal. This is supported by the European Court's interpretation of Art.6.[131]

---

[121] (1975) 62 Cr.App.R. 53 at 60. The events were subsequently the subject of an Inquiry by Sir Henry Fisher: 1977–78 H.C. 90, which concluded that "on a balance of probabilities" all three were involved in the arson and that two (excluding one of the two originally convicted for it) were involved in the killing. The report made a number of recommendations concerning the interrogation process and other aspects of the case.

[122] *R. v Ditch* (1969) 53 Cr.App.R. 627.

[123] *R. v Conway* (1979) 70 Cr.App.R. 4.

[124] *R. v Williams, The Times,* January 27, 1994.

[125] *R. v Leggett and others* (1969) 53 Cr.App.R. 51: interruptions by the Chairman of Quarter Sessions (e.g. when it appeared that an address by counsel to the jury would be protracted "he observed in a loud voice, 'Oh, God,' and then laid his head across his arm and made groaning noises": p.56). Appeal dismissed.

[126] *R. v Lee (Bruce)* [1984] 1 W.L.R. 578; *R. v Foster* [1985] Q.B. 115 (F. had received a free pardon for offences of which another had now been convicted); *R. v Swain* [1986] Crim. L.R. 480 (evidence that there was a risk that D's mind was affected by LSD when he changed his plea to guilty).

[127] *R. v Ahluwalia* [1992] 4 All E.R. 889. The court did, however, emphasise that it required much persuasion to allow a defence to be raised for the first time on appeal if the option had been exercised at trial not to pursue it; here a contemporary report on D stated that she suffered from "endogenous depression" at the time she killed her husband: D was not consulted about the report and it was unclear why it had not been pursued as the basis of a diminished responsibility defence. The court ordered a retrial.

[128] *R. v Jones* [1997] 1 Cr.App.R. 86 at 93; *R. v Borthwick* [1998] Crim. L.R. 274; *R. Neaven* [2006] EWCA Crim 955; *R. v Gay* [2006] EWCA Crim 820.

[129] Cm. 2263, p.174. See, *R. v Cairns* [2000] Crim. L.R. 473.

[130] *R. v Hanratty* [2002] EWCA Crim 1141.

[131] *Ektabani v Sweden* (1988) 13 E.H.R.R. 504; *Pelissier v France* (2000) 30 E.H.R.R. 715. For consideration of whether English law complies see Strange (2001), p.241.

18–013   (3) *Disposition.* Section 2 of the Criminal Appeal Act 1968 as originally enacted provided that:

> "2(1)—Except as provided by this Act, the Court of Appeal shall allow an appeal against conviction if they think—
>
> (a) that the verdict of the jury should be set aside on the ground that under the circumstances of the case it is unsafe or unsatisfactory; or
>
> (b) that the judgment of the court of trial should be set aside on the ground of a wrong decision of any question of law; or
>
> (c) that there was a material irregularity in the course of the trial, and in any other case shall dismiss the appeal:
>
> Provided that the Court may, notwithstanding that they are of the opinion that the point raised in the appeal might be decided in favour of the appellant, dismiss the appeal if they consider that no miscarriage of justice has actually occurred.
>
> (2) In the case of an appeal against conviction the Court shall, if they allow the appeal, quash the conviction."

These grounds for intervention were somewhat wider than those that were open to the Court of Criminal Appeal under the Criminal Appeal Act 1907.[132] The RCCJ criticised the drafting of s.2 as "confusing".[133] For example, the grounds overlapped in that an error of law or an irregularity at trial might cause the court to think that the original conviction was unsafe or unsatisfactory; it was doubtful whether there was any difference between "unsafe" and "unsatisfactory"; the wording of the proviso appeared difficult to reconcile with (a) and (b). Accordingly, they recommended (by a majority) that s.2 be redrafted to provide a single broad ground of appeal, that a conviction "is or may be unsafe". If it was unsafe, the appeal would be allowed outright; if it might be, the conviction would be quashed and (normally) a retrial ordered.

Section 2 now provides that

> "(1) Subject to the provisions of this Act, the Court of Appeal—
>
> (a) shall allow an appeal against conviction if they think that the conviction is unsafe; and
>
> (b) shall dismiss such an appeal in any other case."

Under the original version of section 2, verdicts were set aside as unsafe and unsatisfactory where, for example, there had been a misdirection as to the ingredients of the offence charged or the burden of proof, the judge had improperly withdrawn an issue from the jury or failed to put a line of defence to them, evidence was wrongfully admitted or excluded or, exceptionally, where counsel's decision not to call the defendant "was taken either in defiance of or without proper instructions, or when all the promptings of reason and good sense pointed

---

[132] The court could allow an appeal if they thought that the verdict was unreasonable, or could not be supported by the evidence or otherwise there was an error of law or a miscarriage of justice. The wider grounds were first enacted in the Criminal Appeal Act 1966.

[133] Cm. 2263, pp.167–169. See also R. J. Buxton, (1993) 109 L.Q.R. 66.

the other way".[134] Decisions on some of these points could also amount to a wrong decision on a point of law under s.2(1)(b). The "material irregularity" ground in s.2(1)(c) was designed to cover procedural irregularities,[135] although other defects were sometimes so described. Under this head the Court of Appeal could interfere with an exercise of discretion[136] by the judge where he or she had "erred in principle or there is no material on which he could properly have arrived at his decision",[137] or the court thought that the judge's ruling might have resulted in injustice to the defendant.[138]

The approach to s.2(1)(a) was described as follows by Widgery L.J. in *R. v Cooper*[139]:

> "[I]n cases of this kind the court must in the end ask itself a subjective question, whether we are content to let the matter stand as it is, or whether there is not some lurking doubt in our minds which makes us wonder whether an injustice has been done. This is a reaction which may not be based strictly on the evidence as such; it is a reaction which can be produced by the general feel of the case as the court experiences it."

Indeed, a conviction could be quashed as unsafe and unsatisfactory where the specific grounds of appeal were rejected.[140]

The new single ground of appeal was criticised for covering only part of one **18–014** of the original grounds specified in s.2[141] Parliament was assured by the Home Secretary that

> "in substance it restates the existing practice of the Court of Appeal and I am pleased to note that the Lord Chief Justice has already welcomed it."[142]

According to the Minister of State, the Lord Chief Justice and the senior judiciary believed that "the new test re-states the existing practice of the Court of

---

[134] *R. v Clinton* [1993] 4 All E.R. 998 at 1005. The question was not the extent of counsel's ineptitude but the effect on the trial according to the (then) terms of the 1968 Act, s.2(1)(a). *Cf. R. v Goutam* [1988] Crim. L.R. 109 and *R. v Ensor* [1989] 1 W.L.R. 497, discussed in *Clinton*. In suggesting in *Ensor* that the court would only intervene in cases of "flagrantly incompetent advocacy", the court was only giving "general guidelines" as to the correct approach and was not intending to derogate from the wording of s.2(1)(a). There remains confusion over whether the test is based solely on the effect of counsel's errors on the fairness of the trial and the safety of the conviction, or whether it is necessary also to demonstrate "flagrant incompetence" (*R. v Donnelly* [1998] Crim. L.R. 131) or "*Wednesbury*— unreasonableness" (*R. v Ullah* [2000] 1 Cr.App.R. 351). See *Boodram v The State* [2002] Crim. L.R. and commentary and *R. v Nangle* [2001] Crim. L.R. 506. See also the Bar Council guidance on such appeals.

[135] *per* Lord Salmon in *DPP v Shannon* [1975] A.C. 717 at 773.

[136] e.g. to sever counts in an indictment, to permit cross-examination of a defendant on his or her previous convictions or to discharge a jury.

[137] Devlin J. in *R. v Cook* (1959) 43 Cr.App.R. 138 at 147.

[138] *R. v McCann* (1991) 92 Cr.App.R. 239: the court held that the trial judge should have ordered a retrial of the three charged with conspiracy to murder Mr Tom King, following public statements made by Mr King and Lord Denning concerning the proposal to change the law on the right to silence.

[139] [1969] 1 Q.B. 267 at 271. The case was one of alleged mistaken identification and another man of similar appearance had admitted to a witness that he had committed the crime: even though all the evidence had been before the jury, the conviction was quashed. For other examples of "lurking doubts" see *R. v Pattinson* (1973) 58 Cr.App.R. 417; *R. v Spencer* [1987] A.C. 128.

[140] *R. v Bracewell* (1978) 68 Cr.App.R. 44.

[141] See Sir John Smith, [1995] Crim. L.R. 920 at 923–925.

[142] Vol.256, H. C. Deb. col.24 March 6, 1995, cited by Smith, *ibid*.

Appeal".[143] Accordingly, the RCCJ's unanimous view that the Court of Appeal "should be readier to overturn jury verdicts that it has shown itself to be in the past"[144] did not appear to have been reflected in the new drafting of s.2.[145]

Section 2 should have been an innocuous provision, being intended merely to restate the Court's powers in hearing appeals against conviction.[146] However, the over-economical drafting[147] cast doubt on whether the Court of Appeal retained any power to quash convictions of those who were considered to be factually guilty. Under the 1968 Act there was no doubt that such convictions could be quashed, although the practice was rare and confusing[148] (and made rarer still by the opportunity to apply the proviso).[149]

Commentators on the 1995 Act immediately highlighted the s.2 drafting problem,[150] and it was not long before this surfaced in the case law. Initially, there was a raft of inconsistent cases serving only to confuse the position.[151] One strong decision, which took a clear stance, was Auld L.J.'s comprehensive treatment of the issues in *Chalkley and Jeffries*[152] which adopted a distinctly narrow interpretation of s.2.[153]

In *Chalkley*, the accuracy of the verdict rather than any conclusion as to the overall fairness of the process became the primary consideration for determining safety.[154] The removal of the formula "unsafe *and* unsatisfactory" from the 1968 Act appeared therefore to represent the major change in the Court's approach to appeals that had been anxiously anticipated by academics. *Chalkley* proved to be an unpopular decision in academic circles,[155] largely because it went against the formula and established practice of the 1968 Act and the intention of Parliament. A second, more principled reason for the lack of popularity with the decision flowed from its implicit rejection of the broader notion of justice and the

---

[143] Standing Committee B, March 21, 1995, col.26, cited by Smith, *ibid.*
[144] Cm. 2263, p.162.
[145] The words "or may be" in the RCCJ's recommendation for s.2 were thought by some to send this signal; however, given that a conviction is "unsafe" if there is merely a "lurking doubt" (see above), it is difficult to see what of substance was added by those words: see Smith, [1995] pp.921–922.
[146] See the statements in the HC debates, cited in Smith, [1995] at p.924.
[147] Although following the majority recommendation of the RCCJ (1993), pp.167–169.
[148] *ibid.*, pp.167–169. See also Buxton, (1993) 109 L.Q.R. 66.
[149] As examples of cases in which the Court of Appeal quashed convictions despite being confident as to guilt of the appellant, see *R. v Algar* [1954] 1 Q.B. 279; *R. v Llewellyn* (1978) 67 Cr.App.R. 149; *R. v Mason* (1988) 86 Cr.App.R. 349.
[150] J. C. Smith, [1995]; A. Clarke, "Criminal evidence safety or supervision? The unified ground of appeal and its consequences in the law of abuse of process and exclusion of evidence" [1999] Crim. L.R. 108; P. Taylor, *Taylor on Appeals* (2000), paras 6.015–6.031.
[151] *R. v Hickmet* [1996] Crim. L.R. 588, *cf. R. v Graham* [1997] 1 Cr.App.R. 302.
[152] *R. v Chalkley and Jeffries* [1998] 2 Cr.App.R. 79.
[153] See N. Taylor and D. Ormerod, "Mind the Gaps: Safety, Fairness and Moral Legitimacy", [2004] Crim. L.R. 266; I. Dennis, "Fair Trials and Safe Convictions", (2003) C.L.P. 211.
[154] This position is also one favoured in the Consultation Paper from the Office for Criminal Justice Reform, *Quashing Convictions: Report of a Review by the Home Secretary, Lord Chancellor and Attorney General* (2006) available at: *www.homeoffice.gov.uk;* see also, S. Ireland, "Defective Justice" (2006) N.L.J. 1733; I. Dennis, "Convicting the Guilty: Outcomes, Process and the Court of Appeal", [2006] Crim. L.R. 955; JUSTICE, *Response to OCJR consultation Quashing Convictions: Report of a review by the Home Secretary, Lord Chancellor and Attorney General* (2006) available at: *www.justice.org.uk*; Liberty, *Liberty's response to the Office for Criminal Justice Reform: "Quashing Convictions"* (2006) available at: *www.liberty-human-rights.org.uk.*
[155] Sir John Smith was clearly against it: see commentary on *Chalkley* [2000] Crim. L.R. 214. See also Henry Blaxland [1999] *Archbold News* 4. Other eminent commentators including James Richardson, the editor of *Archbold*, were in favour. See *Archbold* (1999) para.7–46(a).

responsibility of the Court of Appeal to be (and be seen to be) maintaining the moral legitimacy of the process. If confidence in the accuracy of the verdict is the sole determinant of safety there is no room for deliberation about the impact on the morality of the verdict resulting from any discovered unfairness.

Despite these criticisms, *Chalkley* was followed in a number of subsequent cases.[156] Smith drew attention to the resulting illogicality[157]: Trial courts might be required to exclude evidence, which, ultimately, would have no effect on the validity of the resulting conviction. If the Court of Appeal were satisfied as to factual guilt, the conviction itself was safe regardless of the genesis of the evidence in question.

The next phase in the Court's struggle to resolve the scope of its powers stemmed from the controversial case of *Mullen*.[158] The Court dealt directly with the question whether an abuse of process at trial could render unsafe a factually correct guilty verdict. In the earlier case of *McDonald*[159] Auld L.J. had questioned whether the Court retained such a power under s.2. In *Martin*,[160] members of the House of Lords had delivered conflicting opinions on this issue. This uncertainty enabled the Court of Appeal in *Mullen* to seek recourse to parliamentary statements recorded in *Hansard* (under the rule in *Pepper v Hart*[161]) interpreting the amended s.2. Although the debates on the 1995 Act revealed no express reference to whether the concept of "unsafe" extended to factually correct verdicts, such cases had provided grounds for quashing convictions prior to the amendment, and thus fell within the 1995 "restatement" of the existing law.

In *Mullen* the Court reasserted its supervisory role, though given the gravity of the attack on the lawful administration of justice in that case—executive kidnapping and extradition of the suspect—it was not universally accepted that the Court had signalled a full return to the pre-amendment practice in all cases. Adopting this approach, despite Mullen being found guilty in a trial that was not unfair of itself, the Court of Appeal quashed his conviction on the basis that the holding of the trial constituted an abuse of process.[162]

A further complicating factor in the interpretation of s.2 has been the influence of the ECHR jurisprudence on Art.6, particularly following the enactment of the Human Rights Act 1998. Art.6 guarantees a fair trial in the determination of a criminal charge, and this includes appeals.

In a domestic context, the Court of Appeal began to explore the relationship between fairness and safety in *Davis*,[163] concluding that a breach of Art.6 would *not* inexorably lead to a conclusion that a conviction was unsafe. "The effect of any unfairness upon the safety of the conviction will vary according to its nature and degree".[164] Although the broader approach (*Mullen*) of s.2 was now being

[156] *R. v Kennedy* [1999] 1 Cr.App.R. 54; [1998] Crim. L.R. 739; *R. v Rajcoomar* [1999] Crim. L.R. 728; *R. v Callaghan* [1999] 5 *Archbold News* 2; *R. v Doldur* (1999) *The Times*; *R. v Clarke and Hewins* [1999] 6 *Archbold News* 2; *R. v Blackwood* [2000] 6 *Archbold News* 1.

[157] *R. v. Chalkley* [2000] Crim. L.R. 214.

[158] *R. v Mullen* [1999] 2 Cr.App.R. 143.

[159] *R. v McDonald* [1998] Crim. L.R. 808.

[160] *R. v Martin* [1998] 1 Cr.App.R. 347.

[161] *Pepper v Hart* [1993] A.C. 593.

[162] See *Quashing Convictions: Report of a Review by the Home Secretary, Lord Chancellor and Attorney General* (2006) in which it is proposed that the Court of Appeal should not quash convictions on "purely" technical grounds.

[163] [2001] 1 Cr.App.R. 115.

[164] *R. v Davis, Johnson and Rowe* [2000] All E.R. Rev. 169.

preferred to the narrow approach of *Chalkley*, it was still open to the Court to uphold a conviction as safe in the absence of overall fairness. Such a conclusion continued to draw criticism. One very compelling objection was that the European Convention deals with suspect's minimum rights, and therefore, "the only way to give effect to the right to a fair trial is to quash a conviction following a trial where those minimum rights have not been accorded to the accused."[165]

The next stage of the Court's struggle with these issues arose in *Togher, Parsons and others*,[166] where the Court of Appeal appeared to provide greater clarity on the inter-relationship between safety and fairness. The Court favoured a wide interpretation of s.2 so that a conviction could be regarded as unsafe on grounds unrelated to the issue of guilt.[167] This broader approach reverted *almost* back to the pre-1995 position.[168]

> " . . . [E]ven if there was previously a difference of approach, that since the 1998 Act came into force, the circumstances in which there will be room for a different result before this Court and before the ECHR because of unfairness based on the respective tests we employ will be rare indeed. Applying the broader approach identified by Rose L.J., [in *Mullen*] we consider that if a defendant has been denied a fair trial it will almost be inevitable that the conviction will be regarded as unsafe."[169]

The question then is, does unfairness require or merely allow a conviction to be overturned as being unsafe?

Initially, the House of Lords seemed to accept that unfairness (at least in Art.6 terms) equated with a lack of safety. In *Forbes*,[170] it was suggested that any significant breach of Art.6 ought to be enough to render the conviction unsafe. This is what Dennis has called an "absolutist" stance.[171] Similarly, in *R. v A.*,[172] Lord Steyn stated that it is:

> "well established that a guarantee of a fair trial under Article 6 is absolute: a conviction obtained in breach of it cannot stand. The only balancing permitted is in respect of what the concept of a fair trial entails: here account may be taken of the familiar triangulation of interests of the accused, the victim and society."[173]

Eminent human rights specialists such as Emmerson and Ashworth interpreted this to mean that the relative importance of the trial defect could be taken into account when considering whether the proceedings as a whole were unfair. If

---

[165] See the commentary by J. Richardson in *Criminal Law Week* (2000) 00/28/01.

[166] [2001] 3 All E.R. 463; [2001] 1 Cr.App.R. 457. See also; [2001] Crim. L.R. 124; R. Nobles and D. Schiff, "Due process and Dirty Harry dilemmas: criminal appeals and the Human Rights Act" [2001] M.L.R. 64(6), 911; B. Emmerson and A. Ashworth, *Human Rights and Criminal Justice* (2001), Ch.17.

[167] *Mullen* [1999] 2 Cr.App.R. 143.

[168] See the detailed analysis by A. Clarke, [1999] Crim. L.R. 108.

[169] *R. v. Togher* [2001] 3 All E.R. 463 at 471.

[170] [2001] 1 A.C. 473, para.23 *per* Lord Bingham. See also *R. v Francom* [2001] 1 Cr.App.R. 17; [2000] Crim. L.R. 108.

[171] See, Dennis (2003) C.L.P. 211.

[172] [2001] UKHL 25.

[173] *ibid.*, para.38. Though one should be alert to this "familiar triangulation" of interests being skewed so as to give undue weight to the interests of the state, thereby breathing new life into *Chalkley*.

unfairness was established then the conviction was necessarily unsafe. Such an approach had the advantage of greater clarity and simplicity.

However, subsequent cases in which plainly "guilty" individuals would have walked free on such an interpretation caused the House to retreat rapidly from the proposition that fairness and safety were synonymous. Taken to its logical conclusion equating fairness with safety could, it was realised, produce unpalatable results. For example, in Lambert[174] three Law Lords recoiled from this "absolutist" proposition:

> " . . . an unfairness is not always fatal to a conviction . . . . If there is doubt about guilt then the conviction must be held to be unsafe. But if there is no doubt about guilt it is not every case where an unfairness can be identified that will necessarily and inevitably lead to a quashing of the conviction."[175]

Sanders and Young comment that it is "deplorable that there should have been such judicial vacillation for several years over a matter as important as this".[176] Whilst it could be argued that the over-simplified legislation has caused the problem, Schiff and Nobles[177] have argued that the Court of Appeal has always interpreted its own powers as it sees fit. Such a pragmatic approach might allow for flexibility in its response to appeals but has produced "an unstable and unpredictable body of appellate case-law."[178]

The 1995 version of s.2 and the challenges to trial procedures based on Art.6 arguments have also caused the courts to reconsider the "lurking doubt" test adopted in R. v Cooper (above).[179] However, Leigh argues[180] that in any event, the lurking doubt test was never one which applied to situations in which the Court of Appeal felt generally uneasy about a verdict rendering it unsafe. He states that for a verdict to be unsafe there has always had to be a combination of circumstance and evidence that has led to the use of the phrase "lurking doubt".[181] Whilst the phrase has passed into accepted jurisprudence Leigh argues that there is little case law to justify the position.[182]

Where fresh evidence is admitted, the question for the court is still whether in the light of the evidence overall, the verdict is unsafe (formerly, unsafe and unsatisfactory[183]). This point was made by the House of Lords in Stafford v

---

[174] [2001] 3 W.L.R. 206, para.43 (Lord Steyn), para.159 (Lord Clyde) and paras 199–200 (Lord Hutton).

[175] ibid., at para.159. See also Skuse [2002] EWCA Crim 991, where, at [63] Rix L.J. stated: "had we held that there had been a breach of Art.6(1), we consider that we would not have been bound to hold the conviction to be unsafe".

[176] Sanders and Young (2007) p.570.

[177] D. Schiff and R. Nobles, "Criminal Appeal Act 1995: the semantics of jurisdiction" (1996) 59 M.L.R. 573, p.578.

[178] Sanders and Young (2007) p.571.

[179] The courts had originally held that following the 1995 Act, the "lurking doubt" test was no longer appropriate: R. v. F. [1999] Crim. L.R. 306 and commentary.

[180] L. H. Leigh, "Lurking Doubt and the Safety of Convictions", [2006] Crim. L.R. 809.

[181] ibid. Leigh argues that the leading case of Cooper itself can be viewed as being an appeal based on a reasoned analysis of the evidence and not simply a general impression. See also Leigh's analysis of the apparent cases of lurking doubt: R. v Bell [2003] 2 Cr.App.R. 13; R. v Smolinski [2004] 2 Cr.App.R. 661.

[182] See, R. (Pearson) v Criminal Cases Review Commission [2000] 1 Cr.App.R. 141; R. v Heron [2005] N.I.C.A. 34; R. v Pollock [2004] N.I.C.A. 34.

[183] The fresh evidence would not reveal an error of law or constitute a "material irregularity" under s.2(1)(b) and (c) of the Criminal Appeal Act 1968 as originally drafted.

DPP.[184] After referring to the concept of the "lurking doubt" mentioned in *R. v Cooper* Viscount Dilhorne continued, "That this is the effect of section 2(1)(a) is not to be doubted",[185] although he also emphasised that the Court of Appeal should not place any fetter or restriction on its power under s.2. The court was not bound to ask in a case where new evidence was admitted whether that evidence "might . . . have led to the jury returning a verdict of not guilty?": if it was satisfied that there was no reasonable doubt about the guilt of the accused the conviction should not be quashed even though the jury might have come to a different view.

In *Pendleton*,[186] the House of Lords emphasised that the test was whether the conviction was unsafe, not whether the appellant was guilty. The safety of the conviction was to be determined by the Court of Appeal and the effect the new evidence had upon the minds of the court, not its presumed effect upon the original jury. However, it would usually be the case for the court to test its provisional view by asking whether the fresh evidence might reasonably have affected the decision of the trial jury. If it would then the verdict should be considered to be unsafe.

This approach to "fresh evidence" cases has been roundly criticised by Lord Devlin[187] on the basis that it is wrong in principle for judges rather than juries to determine whether the appellant is guilty; the proper course of action where the fresh evidence *could* have made a difference to the verdict[188] would be for the court to order a new trial.[189] The first verdict should be regarded as unsatisfactory simply on the ground that it was not given upon the whole of the evidence.[190] Given that the appeal in *Stafford v DPP* was dismissed, the appellants were thereafter imprisoned on the basis of the verdict of the judges.

Given that the matter is to be tested by reference to the views of the appeal court judges rather than the views of a hypothetical jury, a further question arises whether that is so in all fresh evidence cases. In particular, should the judges determine issues as to whether the oral testimony of a new or re-examined witness is credible?[191] In a number of cases the court has ordered a new trial,[192] but in *R. v Cooper and McMahon*[193] the court determined such a question itself. The case is one of the most publicised examples of a miscarriage of justice, and came before the Court of Appeal on no less than five occasions. Three men, Cooper, McMahon and Murphy, were convicted of the murder of a Luton subpostmaster during an unsuccessful robbery. They were identified by a professional criminal, Mathews, who admitted taking part in the robbery but denied involvement in the murder. He turned Queen's evidence and the men were convicted solely on his testimony. They appealed without success to the Court of Appeal. Mathews subsequently received part of the reward offered by the Post

---

[184] [1974] A.C. 878. Followed in *R. v Callaghan* (1988) 88 Cr.App.R. 40 (the first reference to the Court of Appeal in the Birmingham pub bombing case); *R. v Byrne* (1988) 88 Cr.App.R. 33.

[185] [1974] A.C. p.892.

[186] *R. v Pendleton* [2002] 1 W.L.R. 72; *R. v Hakala* [2002] 578; Crim. L.R. *R. v Poole and Mills* [2004] Crim. L.R. 60.

[187] *The Judge* (1979), pp.133–135, 148–176.

[188] This was in effect the same test as that for applying the proviso: see *Stirland v DPP* (1944) 30 Cr.App.R. 40 at 46–47.

[189] See below. Indeed, until 1989 the court could only order a new trial in fresh evidence cases.

[190] See counsel's argument in *Stafford v DPP* [1974] A.C. 878 at 884C. See also *R. v Craven* [2001] Crim. L.R. 464.

[191] The test for admissibility is merely whether the fresh evidence is capable of belief: see above.

[192] See Devlin (1979), pp.165–166.

[193] *ibid.*, pp.166–173; L. Kennedy (ed), *Wicked Beyond Belief* (1980).

Office. In 1973 Murphy's conviction was quashed by the Court of Appeal following the discovery of a fresh alibi witness. This naturally threw doubt on Mathews' identification of Cooper and McMahon and the Home Secretary referred the case to the Court of Appeal on three further occasions. On the first of these in 1975, the court refused to permit Mathews to be recalled for further cross-examination, indicated that the jury "could" have acquitted Murphy and convicted the others, and dismissed the appeal. The court refused leave to appeal to the House of Lords, reaffirming that in the light of *Stafford v DPP*[194] it was "not a necessary function of this Court, when considering fresh evidence, to evaluate the effect which it would have on the jury at the trial".[195] On the second, in 1976, Mathews was recalled and cross-examined: the judges concluded from their observations that he was telling the truth on the "vital part of his story" although other parts were discredited (a "cock and bull story"). This self-evidently surprising result did not inspire confidence in trial (or at least partial trial) by judges alone. The final reference by the Home Secretary (of the case of McMahon alone) was unsuccessful on the ground that the fresh alibi evidence sought to be tendered was not likely to be credible, and even if believed would be insufficient to afford a ground for allowing the appeal.[196] In 1980, following the publication of a book on the case edited by Ludovic Kennedy (*Wicked Beyond Belief*), the Home Secretary, William Whitelaw, ordered the release of Cooper and McMahon[197]: the case was "wholly exceptional" and there was a "widely felt sense of unease about it" which he shared. He was not to be taken as criticising his predecessors, who had "acted with scrupulous regard to the constitutional conventions in referring each piece of alleged new evidence to the Court of Appeal and in acting in accordance with the court's judgment. Any general departure from that rule would clearly be disastrous." His action was not to be taken as a precedent.

The RCCJ[198] endorsed Lord Devlin's criticism insofar as it concerned a decision by the court to hear and evaluate itself the fresh evidence and despite it to reject the appeal. In their view, the proper approach once the court has decided to receive fresh evidence that is relevant and capable of belief, and which could have affected the outcome of the case, is that it should quash the conviction and order a retrial. However, if a retrial was not practicable or desirable, the court should decide the matter itself in accordance with *Stafford*, and not simply allow the appeal automatically. The Criminal Appeal Act 1995 did not address this question.

A further problem in determining the safety of a conviction is that the Court of Appeal is now faced with an increasing number of appeals from convictions of many years standing. The Court has decided that in conducting the appeal, the present law of evidence and procedure should be applied to the case (including major changes in suspect protection such as PACE) but that the substantive criminal law should remain as at the time of the conviction.[199] This presents problems where the law has made radical changes regarding, e.g. identification evidence, disclosure, character evidence, etc. It also creates anomalies because

---

[194] [1974] A.C. 878.
[195] (1975) 61 Cr.App.R. 215.
[196] *R. v McMahon* (1978) 68 Cr.App.R. 18: criticised in Kennedy (1980), pp.132–135.
[197] Written Answer, H.C. Deb. Vol.988, cols 719–720, July 18, 1980.
[198] Cm. 2263, p.175.
[199] See *R. v O'Brien* [2000] Crim. L.R. 676; *R. v Bentley* [1999] Crim. L.R. 330; *R. v King* [2000] Crim. L.R. 835; *R. v Hussain* [2005] EWCA Crim 31; *R. v Steele* [2006] EWCA Crim 195.

changes in legal attitude to offences are ignored whilst changes to procedure are taken into account. Sir John Smith pointed out the danger that the courts could be swamped with applications from cases in which convictions were perfectly proper at the time,[200] though the Court of Appeal has resisted some attempts to challenge convictions on this basis.[201]

The Auld Report recommended that when hearing appeals on a reference from the Criminal Cases Review Commission, the Court of Appeal should apply the law in force at the time of conviction/sentence.[202]

The Human Rights Act introduced further difficulties with arguments arising as to its potential retrospectivity.[203] The House of Lords confirmed that the Human Rights Act does not permit an appellant to make a retrospective challenge to a decision which was lawfully correct at the time but which would be regarded as breaking the 1998 Act.[204] In addition the Human Rights Act 1998 raised the question of whether the Court of Appeal could remedy defects in the trial procedure. Since Art.6 of the ECHR applies to the whole of the criminal proceedings, it is accepted that in some circumstances the Court of Appeal's scrutiny of a piece of evidence will be sufficient to cure a defect at trial.[205] The Court usually gives reasons for its decision, bit it can decline to do so where the public interest demands secrecy.[206]

As alternatives to quashing a conviction, other possibilities that may be open to the Court of Appeal are the substitution of a conviction for an alternative offence, where the jury would have found the defendant guilty of that offence and it appears to the court that the jury must have been satisfied of facts which proved him or her guilty of it,[207] and the substitution of a finding of insanity or of unfitness to plead.[208]

---

[200] See commentary on *R. v Bentley* [1999] Crim. L.R. 330 at 331 and *R. v Johnson* [2001] Crim. L.R. 125.

[201] See for example Rose L.J. expressing surprise that a case had been referred by the CCRC without new evidence, on the basis of changes to the law relating to legal advice in police stations: *R. v Gerald* [1999] Crim. L.R. 315.

[202] Ch.12, para.l06.

[203] See K. Kerrigan [2000] Crim. L.R. 71.

[204] *R. v Lambert* [2001] 3 W.L.R. 206. The majority held that an appellant could not rely on the provisions of Sch.1 of the the Human Rights Act 1998 in respect of a conviction before the Act came into force. In *R. v Kansal (No.2)* [2001] UKHL 6, the House confirmed this approach although doubting the reasoning in *Lambert*, which had been decided only months before. The House of Lords in *Kansal (No.2)* held that the Human Rights Act 1998 would not apply to an appellant who had been tried before the Act came into force, even if the appeal was occurring after the Act was in force. See also *R. v Benjafield* [2002] UKHL 2 in which the House of Lords confirmed that the Human Rights Act 1998 would not apply to an appeal against a confiscation order imposed before October 2, 2000.

[205] See, e.g. *Edwards v UK* (1992) 15 E.H.R.R. 417; *R. v Botmeh and Alami* [2002] 1 W.L.R. 531; *R. v. Craven* [2001] Crim. L.R. 464; [2001] 2 Cr App R. 181; *cf. Condron v UK* (2000) 31 E.H.R.R.

[206] *R. v Doubtfire* [2001] 2 Cr.App.R. 209 (secrecy of information involved).

[207] Criminal Appeal Act 1968, s.3. The sentence may not be higher than that originally passed. The power is a discretionary one: *R. v Peterson* [1997] Crim. L.R. 339. It is not sufficient that the Court of Appeal is of the opinion that the defendant is guilty, on the facts found by the jury, of another equally serious offence, and on that basis that his original conviction can be upheld: *R. v Graham* [1997] Crim. L.R. 340. The imposition of an alternative offence is not incompatible with Art.6 of the ECHR: *Pelissier v France* (2000) 30 E.H.R.R. 715. An alternative verdict can be substituted by the Court of Appeal even where the defendant pleaded guilty in the Crown Court: Criminal Appeal Act 1968 s.3A (as inserted by CJA 2003 s.316).

[208] Criminal Appeal Act 1968, s.6, Sch.1.

Ultimately, the Court of Appeal's task is a difficult one in which it must strive to direct the law and offer coherent precedent for the trial courts whilst at the same time being prepared to rectify errors in the trial process without jeopardising the finality of the system.[209]

(4) *New Trials*. Where the Court of Appeal allows an appeal against conviction, it may order that the appellant be retried where it appears that this is required by the interests of justice.[210] The appellant may only be retried for the offence in respect of which the appeal was allowed, an offence of which he or she could have been convicted at the original trial on an indictment for that offence or an offence charged in an alternative count of the indictment at the trial on which the jury were discharged from giving a verdict.[211] **18–015**

In ordering a retrial, considerations must include the question whether the accused can have a fair trial given the delay since the original trial[212] and to the danger that adverse publicity following the original conviction will render a fair retrial impossible.[213]

Where a retrial is ordered, arrangements must normally take place within two months.[214] Thereafter, if the prosecution wishes to proceed, it must apply to the Court of Appeal for leave; conversely, the defendant may apply to the Court of Appeal to set aside the retrial order and enter a verdict of acquittal of the offence for which he or she was ordered to be retried. On either application, the court may grant leave, but may only do so if it is satisfied that the prosecution has acted with due expedition,[215] and that there is a good and sufficient cause for a retrial in spite of the lapse of time since the retrial order was made.

There are many well established categories on which appeals are based.

(ii) *Appeals against sentence and reviews of sentencing*

A person who has been convicted of an offence on indictment may appeal to the Court of Appeal (Criminal Division) against any sentence passed on him or her for the offence, except a mandatory life sentence.[216] Leave to appeal must be obtained from the Court of Appeal, or the judge who passed the sentence must certify that the case is fit for appeal,[217] and the procedure is essentially the same **18–016**

---

[209] See K. Malleson, "Appeals Against Conviction and the Principle of Finality" in Field and Thomas (eds), *Justice and Efficiency? The Royal Commission on Criminal Justice* (1994). For criticism of the judiciary sitting in the Court of Appeal as to their awareness of the scope of their powers, see K. Malleson, *Review of the Appeal Process* (Research Study 17, 1993). For an analysis of the Court of Appeal's work in terms of due process and crime control modes (as used in Chs 14 and 17 evaluations of the trial process) see S. Greer, "Miscarriages of Criminal Justice Reconsidered" (1994) 57 M.L.R. 58.

[210] 1968 Act, s.7(1), as amended by the Criminal Justice Act 1988, s.43(2). See Pattenden (1990), pp.366–370. For the procedure on retrial see s.8 and Sch.1. Any sentence passed after a retrial may not be longer than the original one.

[211] *ibid.*, s.7(2). For the analogous power to award a *venire de novo*, see below, para.18–020. This can only be done where the original trial is a nullity.

[212] *R. v Graham* [1997] 1 Cr.App.R. 302.

[213] *R. v Stone* [2001] Crim. L.R. 465 (Subsequent retrial and reconvention for murder).

[214] In *R. v Kimber* [2001] Crim. L.R. 897, it was held that there could be an extension in exceptional cases.

[215] See *R. v Jones* [2003] 1 Cr.App.R. 313.

[216] Criminal Appeal Act 1968, s.9(1A) as inserted by CJA 2003, s.271. The offender can appeal against the minimum term set by a court in a murder case.

[217] 1968 Act, s. 11(1).

as in appeals against conviction.[218] The court, if it considers that the appellant should be sentenced differently, may quash any sentence or order which is the subject of the appeal and substitute any other sentence or order that it thinks appropriate, provided that it would have been within the jurisdiction of the court below. The appellant may not, however, be dealt with more severely than by the court below,[219] except that the court may bring a suspended sentence into effect.

The court will interfere with an exercise of discretion as to sentence where the sentence is not justified by law, where matters are improperly taken into account or improperly ignored, where fresh matters are to be taken into account, or where the sentence is manifestly excessive or wrong in principle.

Under the Criminal Justice Act 1988[220] the Attorney-General may refer certain sentences to the Court of Appeal (Criminal Division). It is available in respect of cases of a description specified by statutory instrument made by the Secretary of State, or in which sentence is passed on a person for an offence triable only on indictment or for an offence of a description specified by statutory instrument.[221] The power may be exercised where "it appears to the Attorney-General that the sentencing of a person in a proceeding in the Crown Court has been unduly lenient". In addition to this safeguard the Court of Appeal has emphasised that before any increase in sentence can be made the Attorney General must exercise his discretion to refer the case to the Court, and the Court of Appeal must consider whether to grant leave for the reference, and whether the sentence was indeed too lenient.[222]

The Court of Appeal may quash any sentence passed on the defendant, and in place of it pass such sentence (including a heavier sentence[223]) as it thinks appropriate and as the court below had power to pass when dealing with him or her. The Court considers the reference on the facts proved at trial or admitted.[224] When the Court of Appeal has concluded its review, the Attorney-General or the defendant may refer a point of law to the House of Lords. The Court of Appeal must certify that it is a point of law of general public importance, and the leave of either the Court of Appeal or the House of Lords is necessary.

The arguments in favour of the reference procedure were marshalled by J. R. Spencer,[225] who wrote that under-sentencing: (i) blunts the deterrent effect of the criminal law; (ii) causes outrage to the victim; (iii) is demoralising to the police; (iv) causes injustice to those who were appropriately sentenced; (v) undermines public confidence in the administration of justice and the authority of the courts; (vi) may cause public danger; and (vii) hinders development of a rational sentencing policy by the Court of Appeal. The main[226] contrary argument is that

---

[218] On granting bail pending appeal see, *Consolidated Criminal Practice Direction*, para.IV.50.

[219] 1968 Act s.11(3). A hospital order with an indefinite restriction order was held not to be more severe than a sentence of three years' imprisonment in *R. v Bennett* [1968] 1 W.L.R. 980.

[220] ss.35, 36.

[221] 1968 Act, s.35(3)–(5). There have been a number of extensions over the years and these are included in the Criminal Justice Act 1988 (Reviews of Sentencing Order 2006 (SI 2006/1116), Sch.1. For an argument that the scheme should extend to either way offences see S. Shute, (1994) 57 M.L.R. 745.

[222] *Attorney General's Reference (No.14 of 2003)* (2003) *The Times* 18 April 2003.

[223] *Attorney-General's Reference (No.4 of 1989)* [1990] 1 W.L.R. 41.

[224] *Attorney General's Reference (No.95 of 1998)*, *The Times*, April 21, 1999. The increase of sentence will not necessarily breach Art.6 of the ECHR: *De Salvador Torres v Spain* (1996) 23 E.H.R.R. 601.

[225] "Do We need a Prosecution Appeal Against Sentence?" [1987] Crim. L.R. 724.

[226] Others are summarised, and dismissed by Spencer, *ibid.* pp.729–736.

the procedure offends the principle against double jeopardy, in particular the need "to prevent the state . . . abusing its power and control over the prosecution process in order to harass and oppress an individual or minority".[227] While it is "virtually unthinkable" that the government would seek to abuse its powers in this way, the risk should nevertheless be recognised.[228]

As the offender has to face the prospect of being sentenced twice over the Court of Appeal may make allowance and take this into account in the revised sentence.[229]

The Court of Appeal has stated that an application will not be granted unless there was some error of principle in the judge's sentence and that public confidence would be damaged if the sentence was not altered.[230]

Shute has examined the use of the reference procedure from 1989–1997.[231] His research reveals that between 1989 and the end of 1997, 367 sentences were reviewed as unduly lenient. The most common offences appealed were robbery and offences of causing grievous bodily harm. The majority of the referrals are from circuit judges (71 per cent) with assistant recorders (6.5 per cent), High Court judges (7.5 per cent) and full recorders (15 per cent) significantly lower. The success rate for the Attorney-General remained high and pretty constant for each group (over 80 per cent), except High Court judges (61 per cent). Twelve per cent of all cases reviewed were tried at the Old Bailey. The research also revealed a number of problems of misallocation of cases to judges not authorised for that class of offence. The *Auld Report* recommended that there should be less "tinkering" with sentences by the Court of Appeal.[232]

As discussed on the chapter on the criminal trial, under the Criminal Justice Act 2003, the prosecution can now appeal against some rulings of the trial judge. These refer to so called "termination" rulings and evidentiary rulings.[233] Furthermore, the 2003 Act introduces a major exception to the double jeopardy principle for qualifying offences for which there is new and compelling evidence.[234]

(iii) *Appeals against findings of insanity*

A person in whose case a verdict of not guilty by reasons of insanity[235] is returned may appeal to the Court of Appeal on the same grounds as against a conviction.[236] The powers of the court are similar. In appropriate cases, the court

18–017

---

[227] S. Seabrooke, "Two-timing the Double Jeopardy Principle" [1988] Crim. L.R. 103 at 104. Spencer takes a narrower view of the double jeopardy principle: [1987] Crim. L.R. 724 at 735, as meaning (1) that it is wrong to punish a person twice for the same offence; and (2) that a person must not be put in peril of conviction twice.

[228] Seabrooke, [1988] Crim.L.R, 103.

[229] *Attorney-General's Reference (No.1 of 1991)* [1991] Crim. L.R. 725. See also, CJA 2003 s.272 where the Court of Appeal shall not make any allowance where the minimum term for murder is considered too lenient. See also, *Attorney-General's Reference (Nos 14 and 15 of 2006)* [2006] EWCA Crim 1335.

[230] *Attorney-General's Reference (No.5 of 1989) (R. v HW-Trevor)* (1990) 90 Cr.App.R. 358 (custodial sentence substituted for a fine for causing death by reckless driving).

[231] S. Shute, [1999] Crim. L.R. 603.

[232] Ch.12, para.101.

[233] CJA 2003 ss.57–61 and ss.62–66.

[234] CJA 2003 ss.75–97.

[235] "Insanity" here means insanity under the *M'Naghten* rules, which do not cover all cases of mental disorder and do cover some situations where there is no mental disorder: see generally D. Ormerod, *Smith and Hogan: Criminal Law* (11th edn, 2005), pp.250–271.

[236] 1968 Act, ss.12, 13, as amended by the Criminal Appeal Act 1995, s.2.

may substitute a conviction for an offence, or a verdict of acquittal[237]: in the former case it has power to pass an appropriate sentence or make a hospital or other order, in the latter it may order that the appellant be admitted to hospital for assessment.[238]

(iv) *References by the Criminal Cases Review Commission*

18–018   Where a person was (1) convicted on indictment or (2) tried on indictment and found not guilty by reason of insanity or (3) found by a jury to be under a disability, the Home Secretary formerly had power to refer the case to the Court of Appeal.[239] Two kinds of reference were possible. The first was a reference of the whole case, in which event the reference was treated as an appeal.[240] The court was not limited to the grounds mentioned in the Home Secretary's letter of reference.[241] A further appeal could then lie to the House of Lords. The other possibility was that a particular point might be referred for the opinion of the court.[242] The court gave what was essentially only an advisory opinion, with any further action to be taken by the Home Secretary.[243] This form of reference was uncommon.[244]

The Home Secretary preferred to refer a case to the Court of Appeal rather than to recommend the exercise of the prerogative to grant a pardon or remit a sentence[245]: it was thought that persistent use of the power to recommend a pardon would undermine the distinction between the functions of the executive and of the judiciary.[246] Indeed it was, in part, dissatisfaction with the review by the Home Office of criminal convictions that led to the establishment of the Court of Criminal Appeal. The Home Secretary's approach was summarised in a memorandum to the Home Affairs Committee[247]:

"In considering convictions on indictment, the Home Secretary . . .

(a)   will not normally intervene where normal avenues of appeal to the Court of Appeal have not been exhausted;

(b)   will, where the normal avenues are not available and intervention seems justified, consider using his power of reference to enable the Court to hear the case;

(c)   will consider recommending the exercise of the Royal Prerogative where intervention seems justified but for some reason (e.g. lapse of

---

[237] *ibid.* s.13(4).

[238] *ibid.* ss.14, 14A, as substituted by the Criminal Procedure (Insanity and Unfitness to Plead) Act 1991, s.4, and Sch.1 to the 1991 Act.

[239] 1968 Act, s.17.

[240] *ibid.* s.17(1)(a).

[241] *R. v Chard* [1984] A.C. 279; followed in *R. v Callaghan* [1988] 1 W.L.R. 1.

[242] 1968 Act, s.17(1)(b).

[243] See *Thomas (Arthur) v The Queen* [1980] A.C. 125, where the Privy Council held that advice given to the Governor-General under an identically worded provision was not binding on him, and could not be the subject of an appeal to the Privy Council.

[244] See, e.g. *R. v O'Neill* (1948) 33 Cr. App.R. 19; *R. v McCartan* (1958) 42 Cr.App.R. 262; *R. v McMahan* (1978) 68 Cr.App.R. 18.

[245] See below, para.18–070.

[246] 1981–82 H.C. 421, 6th Report on *Miscarriages of Justice*, p.2.

[247] *ibid.*

time, inadmissibility as evidence of salient new facts) a resort to the
judicial appeal process would not be appropriate."

However, the Home Secretary would not intervene on the basis of evidence
already considered by the courts. A case would only be referred where there was
some new evidence or new consideration of substance which had not been before
the courts and which appeared to cast doubt on the safety of the conviction.[248]
Moreover, if a case was referred to the Court of Appeal and the conviction was
upheld, the Home Secretary would only intervene thereafter if the case was
wholly exceptional.[249]

A further point is that it is only the Court of Appeal that can quash a
conviction: a pardon does not have that effect.[250] Thus, in a number of cases the
reference procedure was used to secure the formal quashing of a conviction[251] or
a sentence[252] that fell outside the powers of the trial court, often for reasons of
some technicality. Indeed, it was uncommon for the Court of Appeal to quash a
conviction, following a reference, on the basis of its doubts about the merits of
the conviction.[253] "Judicial distaste for the whole reference procedure has verged
at times upon open hostility."[254] A decision of the Home Secretary to refuse to
refer a case to the Court of Appeal following investigation by the Criminal Cases
Unit (CCU) could be challenged on an application for judicial review; such
challenges were generally unsuccessful.[255] However, in *R. v Secretary of State
for the Home Department, Ex p. Hickey (No.2)*[256] the Divisional Court held that
where the Secretary of State ordered inquiries to be made following receipt of a
petition, he was obliged as a matter of fairness to disclose the outcome of those
inquiries to the petitioner before deciding whether to refer a case under s.17.

[248] *ibid.* In a number of cases the courts rejected applications for judicial review of decisions not to
make s.17 references, holding that this policy was not applied inflexibly: *R. v Secretary of State
for the Home Department, Ex p. Pegg (Kenneth Stephen)* [1991] C.O.D. 47; *R. v Secretary of State
for the Home Department, Ex p. McCallion* [1993] C.O.D. 148.

[249] e.g. *R. v Cooper and McMahon*, above, para.18–014. The previous Home Secretaries had firmly
taken the view that they should not override the court's decision: see L. Kennedy; (ed.), *Wicked
Beyond Belief* (1980), pp.130, 159–160, 169.

[250] *R. v Foster* [1985] Q.B. 115: see above, para 18–012, below, para.18–070.

[251] *R. v Davies* (1981) 76 Cr.App.R. 120 (following D's extradition, a new count was added to the
indictment with D.'s agreement, but contrary to the Extradition Act 1870, s.19).

[252] e.g. *R. v Bardoe* [1969] 1 W.L.R. 398 (youth of 17 wrongly sentenced to life imprisonment); *R.
v McKenna* (1985) 7 Cr.App.R.(S.) 348; *R. v Seafietd, The Times*, May 17, 1988 (suspended
sentence supervision order wrongly attached to six-month and three-month sentences, neither
being a sentence of "more than six months").

[253] Widely publicised rejections of appeals included the Cooper and McMahon case, above,
para.18–014; the Birmingham pub bombing case (*R. v Callaghan* (1988) 88 Cr.App.R. 40; C.
Mullin, *Error of Judgment* (rev. edn., 1990); the Carl Bridgwater murder case (see P. Foot,
Murder at the Farm (1988)). By contrast, the Court of Appeal allowed an appeal in case of the
Guildford Four (*R. v Richardson, The Times*, October 20, 1989) although here the prosecution felt
itself unable to support the convictions (see G. McKee and R. Franey, *Time Bomb* (1988); S.
Edwards (1989) 139 NLJ 1449). It also ultimately allowed an appeal in the case of the
Birmingham Six: *R. v Mcllkenny* [1992] 2 All E. R. 417 and the Maguire Seven: *R. v Maguire*
[1992] 2 All E.R. 433. See more generally C. Walker, and K. Starmer (eds), *Miscarriages of
Justice* (1999).

[254] P. O'Connor, [1990] Crim. L.R. 615 at 617.

[255] *R. v Secretary of State for the Home Department, Ex p. Cleeland* (unreported, October 8, 1987);
R. v Same, Ex p. Ewing (unreported, July 28, 1988): *R. v Same, Ex p. Garner* [1989] C.O.D. 461;
the cases cited in above, *R. v Secretary of State for the Home Department, Ex p. Ram* [1995]
C.O.D. 250.

[256] [1995] 1 W.L.R. 734.

The exercise of the s.17 reference power, particularly in the context of the high profile miscarriage of justice cases, generated much controversy.[257] The RCCJ found that the power was not often exercised,[258] noting the self-imposed limitations adopted by the Home Office. It concluded that the Home Secretary's role was "incompatible with the proper separation of powers as between the courts and the executive" and recommended the establishment of a new independent Criminal Cases Review Authority to consider alleged miscarriages of justice, to supervise further inquiries (if needed) and to refer cases to the Court of Appeal.[259] This recommendation was implemented by Pt II (ss.8–25) of the Criminal Appeal Act 1995.

The 1995 Act established the Criminal Cases Review Commission[260] (CCRC) as a body corporate, independent of the Crown, with not fewer than 11 members appointed by the Queen on the recommendation of the Prime Minister.[261] Members may be full-time or part-time and are appointed for five years (renewable to a maximum of 10 years). At least one-third of the members must be legally qualified, and at least two-thirds must be persons who appear to the Prime Minister to have knowledge or experience of any aspect of the criminal justice system. Where a person has been convicted of an offence on indictment, the Commission may at any time refer the conviction to the Court of Appeal and (whether or not they refer the conviction) any sentence (not fixed by law) imposed in relation to the conviction. The reference is to be treated as an appeal under ss.1 or 9 of the 1968 Act. On a reference, the Commission may give notice that any other conviction on the indictment in question is to be treated as also referred. The Commission also has power to refer summary convictions and sentences to the Crown Court.[262] References may not be made unless

> "(a) the Commission consider that there is a real possibility that the conviction, verdict, finding or sentence would not be upheld were the reference to be made,
>   (b) the Commission so consider—
>
>> (i) in the case of a conviction, verdict or finding, because of any argument, or evidence, not raised in the proceedings which led to it or on any appeal or application for leave to appeal against it, or
>> (ii) in the case of a sentence, because of an argument on a point of law, or information, not so raised, and
>
>   (c) an appeal against the conviction, verdict, finding or sentence has been determined or leave to appeal against it has been refused."[263]

---

[257] See, M. Mansfield and N. Taylor, "Post Conviction Procedures", in C. Walker and K. Starmer, *Justice in Error*, (1993). For an examination of miscarriages of justice throughout the century and a theoretical analysis of the reforms introduced to address miscarriages see R. Nobles and D. Schiff, *Understanding Miscarriages of Justice* (2000). For an examination of the history of appeals see R. Pattenden, *English Criminal Appeals, 1844–1994: Appeals Against Conviction and Sentence in England and Wales* (1996).

[258] 36 cases (48 appellants) between 1981 and 1988, 28 (49 appellants) between 1989 and 1992. The Home Office received between 700 and 800 "petitions" each year: Cm. 2263, p.181.

[259] *ibid.* pp.182–187. See K. Malleson, (1994) 21 J.L.S. 151.

[260] See; *www.ccrc.gov.uk/index.htm*

[261] Appointed in accordance with the Office for the Commissioner for Public Appointments' Code of Practice: see, *www.ocpa.gov.uk/*

[262] *ibid.* s.11. K. Kerrigan, "Miscarriages of Justice in the Magistrates' Court: The Forgotten Power of the Criminal Cases Review Commission", [2006] Crim. L.R. 124.

[263] *ibid.* s.13(1).

However this is not to prevent the making of a reference

"if it appears to the Commission that there are exceptional circumstances which justify making it".[264]

Notwithstanding the view of the RCCJ that the approach of the Home Office was unduly restrictive, these provisions appear to enshrine the previous policy. Nobles and Schiff comment, "the CCRC's mandate could reasonably be interpreted as, do what the CCU did, but do it more often".[265] The Commission should only refer a case if it considers that there is a "real possibility" that the conviction will not be upheld because of new evidence or information or an argument not advanced at trial. The case should also only be referred if an appeal has been unsuccessful or an application to appeal refused.[266] A "real possibility" has been interpreted as meaning that there has to be a "reasonable prospect" of a conviction not being upheld. Lord Bingham described it as "imprecise, but plainly denotes . . . more than an outside chance or a bare probability".[267]

Nobles and Schiff highlight the fact that the Commission cannot escape a position of deference to the Court of Appeal so long as its objective is to investigate cases with a view to referring them to the Court of Appeal.[268] In part this stems from the Commission being compelled to second guess, by use of the "real possibility" test, whether the Court of Appeal would allow the appeal.[269] Similarly, Duff,[270] examining the English and Scottish Commissions, concludes that the Commissions are less effective than they should be because they are bound to show deference to the Court of Appeal on this basis.

The Chairman of the CCRC has sought to emphasise that whilst the CCRC and the Court of Appeal exercise mutual respect, the CCRC is very much an independent body;

"The responsibility for deciding whether to refer a case rests exclusively with us. If we make a reference, the court has no option but to hear it. The court cannot take a preliminary look and say: "We have better things to do with our time. This reference is misconceived and we do not propose to deal with it"."[271]

Nevertheless, he has further commented;

"What is absolutely essential, it seems to me, is that, whatever statutory test Parliament . . . imposed, it has to be one that articulates with the test that the

---

[264] *ibid.* s.13(2). *R. v Gerald* [1999] Crim. L.R. 315.

[265] R. Nobles and D. Schiff, "The Criminal Cases Review Commission: Establishing a Workable Relationship with the Court of Appeal", [2005] Crim. L.R. 173. See also, R. Nobles and D. Schiff, "A Reply to Graham Zellick" [2005] Crim. L.R. 195.

[266] *R. v Criminal Cases Review Commission, ex p. Pearson* [2000] 1 Cr. App.R. 141.

[267] *ibid.*

[268] See R. Nobles and D. Schiff, [2005] Crim. L.R. 173. See also, Ashworth and Redmayne (2005) p.359.

[269] On "real possibility" as the appropriate test, for criticism of the use of this test see Nobles and Schiff, [2001] 64 M.L.R. 280 at p.284. See also Home Affairs Committee Report, paras 20–24, recommending a review of the test after the Commission has been in operation for five years.

[270] [2001] Crim. L.R. 341.

[271] G. Zellick, "The Criminal Cases Review Commission and The Court Of Appeal: The Commission'sPerspective", [2005] Crim. L.R. 937, at 940. Echoed by the Divisional Court in *R. (on the application of the Director of Revenue and Customs Prosecutions) v Criminal Cases Review Commission* [2006] EWHC 3064 (Admin).

Court of Appeal itself has to apply. If you break that link and you establish an asymmetry between the two tests, you would be creating an absurd situation. It would create tension between the Court of Appeal and the Commission, it would raise expectations, it would cause confusion, and it is difficult to see what possible public interest could be served by referring cases on a basis that had no relationship to the test employed by the Court itself."[272]

Despite this, the difficulty of asymmetry has been highlighted in relation to cases referred on the basis that there has been a change in the common law between conviction and application to the CCRC. Naturally, defendants convicted under one interpretation of the law will feel rightly hard done by if they suffer in prison when others who have committed identical acts are acquitted because the courts have subsequently adopted a more generous interpretation of the offence. Nevertheless, if those cases led to successful appeals then the appeals system would grind to a halt under the workload. Such cases will almost always be out of time, and though the Court of Appeal has discretion to extend the notice for appeal,[273] they will only exercise the discretion where the defendant would suffer a "substantial injustice" as a result.[274] However, the Court of Appeal must deal with cases referred by the CCRC but the CCRC is not similarly prohibited from referring cases out of time. If the CCRC were to take account of the Court of Appeal's policy then they would not refer cases out of time which do not satisfy the latter's interpretation of its discretion. This would result in a symmetrical approach. However, in *R. (on the application of the Director of Revenue and Customs Prosecutions) v Criminal Cases Review Commission*,[275] the Divisional Court held that the CCRC was under no obligation to have regard to, still less to implement, a practice of the Court of Appeal which operated at a stage with which the CCRC was not concerned. The CCRC could refer a case at any time.[276] It has been commented that the "practical consequences are potentially overwhelming for the CCRC."[277] As was recognised by the CCRC chairman, coherence between the tests operated by both bodies is required if confusion is to be avoided.

References to the Court of Appeal from the CCRC are to be treated as ordinary appeals except that the Court is not bound by its previous determinations on the merits of an appeal.[278]

Other points to note are that references may be made with or without an application having been made by the person to whom it relates; the Commission must take account of any application or representations made to it by or on behalf of the person concerned, any other representations made to it and any other matters which appear to it to be relevant; the Commission may refer a particular

---

[272] Home Affairs Select Committee, *The Work of the Criminal Cases Review Committee* (2004) HC. 289-I. Professor G. Zellick, Chairman of the CCRC, giving oral evidence to the committee in response to Q.28; available at: *www.publications.parliament.uk/pa/cm200304/cmselect/cmhaff/289/4012703.htm.*

[273] Criminal Appeal Act 1968 s.18(3).

[274] See *R. v Ramsden* [1972] Crim. L.R. 547; *R. v Hawkins* [1997] 1 Cr.App.R. 234.

[275] *R. (on the application of the Director of Revenue and Customs Prosecutions) v Criminal Cases Review Commission* [2006] EWHC 3064 (Admin).

[276] Criminal Appeal Act 1995, s.9(1)(a).

[277] See the commentary on *R. (on the application of the Director of Revenue and Customs Prosecutions) v Criminal Cases Review Commission* [2007] Crim. L.R. 383.

[278] *R. v Thomas* [2002] EWCA Crim. 941.

point to the Court of Appeal for its opinion; where a reference is treated as an appeal, the appeal may be on any ground whether or not related to the Commission's reason for making the reference provided that leave has been obtained by the appellant to add to the grounds stated by the CCRC[279]; where an application is made for a reference, the Commission must give reasons to the applicant for deciding not to make one.[280] The Commission is entitled to make evaluative judgments when referring a case and making its report under s.15 to the Court.[281] The Commission may be directed to make an investigation by the Court of Appeal and may be asked by the Home Secretary to consider a matter arising in the consideration of whether to recommend the exercise of the prerogative of mercy.[282] The Commission has powers to obtain documents and to require the appointment of investigating officers from a police force or (if appropriate) another public body, who must undertake such inquiries as the Commission may from time to time reasonably direct. There is also a general power to take any steps which they consider appropriate for assisting them in the exercise of any of their functions, including undertaking or arranging for others to undertake inquiries, and obtaining, or arranging for others to obtain, statements, opinions and reports.[283]

The process for assessment of a case is as follows.[284] At stage one, consideration is given to whether a case is eligible for review. This involves assessing the scope of the Commission's jurisdiction, and ensuring that normal appeals processes have been exhausted. This process is greatly assisted where the application is based on legal advice, as is now occurring in a greater proportion of applications.[285] A decision is made whether to pursue the case. The case is then allocated to an individual caseworker who conducts a screen review. In 2005–06, 51 per cent of cases were closed at this stage.[286] At stage two the investigation is focussed as a caseworker works alongside a Commissioner. This is often the most time consuming and resource intensive aspect of the process. A further 11 per cent of cases fell at this stage in 2005–06. Stage three is when an investigating officer might be appointed, particularly if the investigation is complex. In cases that are investigated, the CCRC gather evidence, interviews witnesses, seeks expert advice, (particularly forensic advice), liaises with other agencies (especially the Court Service, Prison Service, CPS, police, Customs and Excise,

---

[279] This follows CJA 2003 s.315, which amends the Criminal Appeal Act 1995, s.14: "(4A) Subject to subsection (4B), where a reference under section 9 or 10 is treated as an appeal against any conviction, verdict, finding or sentence, the appeal may not be on any ground which is not related to any reason given by the Commission for making the reference. (4B) The Court of Appeal may give leave for an appeal mentioned in subsection (4A) to be on a ground relating to the conviction, verdict, finding or sentence which is not related to any reason given by the Commission for making the reference." See also, *R. v Smith (Wallace Duncan) (No.3)* [2003] 1 W.L.R. 1647.
[280] 1995 Act, s.14.
[281] *R. v Coles and Bradley* [1999] 8 *Archbold News* 3.
[282] *ibid.* ss.15, 16. The Commission statement is conclusive of the matter referred. The Commission may also give a reasoned opinion to the Home Secretary that he or she should consider whether to recommend exercise of the prerogative of mercy.
[283] *ibid.* ss.17–22. For restrictions on the disclosure of information by members or employees of the Commission, see ss.23–25.
[284] For an account of the Commission's procedure see *CCRC Annual Report 2005–06* (2006) p.16; see also, J. MacKeith, (1999) 67(2) Medico-Legal Journal 47; L. Jason-Lloyd, (2000) 164 J.P.N. 791; B. Capon, (1998) 162 J.P.N. 659; S. O'Doherty, (1999) 163 J.P.N. 844.
[285] From around one in ten in 1997 to 60% in 2005-6.
[286] *CCRC Annual Report 2005-6* (2006) p.17.

etc. Once the investigation has occurred, a commissioner decides whether refer a case to the Court of Appeal or not.[287]

The applicant is kept informed of the progress of the case and of the decision and the reasons for that decision. A decision of the Commission not to refer a case because the matters relied on had been considered by the court already should not be challenged by way of judicial review except in rare cases. The judicial review procedure should be used only to ensure that the Commission has acted in a lawful manner and not to invite the courts to act as an appellate body in respect of the Commission's decision.[288]

Concerns have been raised regarding the Commission's prioritising of cases. It has been questioned whether it would be more desirable to devote resources to those more recent alleged miscarriages where the applicants are still detained, rather than review the admittedly serious, but not pressing, cases of miscarriages where offenders were hanged, or those where there are no living individuals with a direct link to the case in question.[289] In *Hanratty*[290] the Court of Appeal recognised that there were public interest factors in the case albeit that the accused had been hanged some forty years previously. The Court were less sympathetic to the references in *Ellis*[291] and *Knighton*,[292] claiming in the latter that "[W]e have studied all the material drawn to our attention by the CCRC. Having done so, we are troubled that this conviction was referred at all. William Knighton has been dead for 75 years . . . There are here no issues of exceptional notoriety, and therefore public interest, as in *Bentley*[293] or *Hanratty*."[294]

There have also been concerns about the number of applicants who lack legal representation. Although a considerable improvement upon the position prior to the establishment of the CCRC, whereupon applicants received very little assistance,[295] it remains the case that around forty per cent of applicants lack potentially crucial legal assistance.[296]

Inadequate resources has also been a constant feature of the CCRC. In 2005–06 the Commission claims to have fewer case review managers than it needs.[297] The number of cases referred to the Commission means that it is barely able to deal with the new cases referred each year. By 2006 the CCRC had received 8,540 applications since its inception.[298] There has been a backlog of cases throughout the short history of the CCRC though in 2005–06 it closed more

---

[287] In complex cases this requires a committee of at least three Commission members.

[288] *R. v CCRC, ex p. Pearson* [1999] Crim. L.R. 732.

[289] See for example, See, Zellick, [2005] Crim. L.R. 937 at 942–943; Nobles and Schiff, [2005] Crim. L.R. 173 at 179–80;

[290] *R. v Hanratty* [2002] 2 Cr.App.R. 30.

[291] *R. v Ellis* [2003] EWCA Crim 3556.

[292] *R. v Knighton* [2002] EWCA Crim 2227.

[293] *R. v Bentley* [2001] 1 Cr.App.R. 307.

[294] Zellick, [2005] Crim. L.R. 937 at 943.

[295] See, M. Mansfield and N. Taylor, "Post Conviction Procedures", in C. Walker and K. Starmer, *Justice in Error*, (1993).

[296] In 2004–05 62% of applicants were legally represented. In 2005–06 this figure had dropped to 60%. See, *CCRC Annual Report 2004–5* (2005) p.38, and *CCRC Annual Report 2005–6* (2006) p.46.

[297] *CCRC Annual Report 2005–6* (2006) p.49. The problem of lack of resources has been a constant feature, see, A. James, N. Taylor and C. Walker, "The Criminal Cases Review Commission: Economy, Effectiveness and Justice", [2000] Crim. L.R. 140 at 145.

[298] *CCRC Annual Report 2005–6* (2006) HC 1290 p.20, available at: *www.ccrc.gov.uk*

cases than it received. Nevertheless, there were still 247 cases waiting at the end of March 2006.[299]

Nevertheless, despite problems, the Commission has been generally well received.[300] Initial fears about the Commission's independence and ability to investigate cases have not materialised, but concerns regarding its workload have been a persistent problem. The Commission will always be in a position whereby it stands to suffer from its own success: the more appeals referred by the Commission to the appeal court, and the more that lead to a conviction being quashed, the more likely there will be an increase in the number of applications made by defendants. The CCRC itself recognises that "the long term trend suggests that there will continue to be a high level of applications."[301]

(vi) *Attorney-General's references*[302]

Section 36 of the Criminal Justice Act 1972 introduced a procedure whereby the **18–019** Attorney-General may refer a point of law to the Court of Appeal where the defendant in a trial on indictment has been acquitted. The point must actually have arisen in the case. The court gives its opinion and may thereafter refer the point to the House of Lords. The Attorney-General may appear in person or be represented by counsel: the acquitted person may be represented by counsel, or with leave may appear in person.[303]

The reference has no effect on the trial or the acquittal. No mention must be made in the reference of the proper name of any person or place which is likely to lead to the identification of the acquitted person. His or her identity must not be disclosed during the proceedings except with consent.

The aim of this procedure is to ensure that an erroneous direction by a trial judge on the law is corrected at the earliest opportunity and without the need for legislation. Whereas the defendant may appeal where such a direction leads to an erroneous conviction, the prosecution has (as yet) no right to appeal against an erroneous acquittal in a trial on indictment. The sanctity of an acquittal by a jury is maintained by the provisions designed to secure that the reference procedure cannot operate to the detriment of the person acquitted.

---

[299] *ibid.* at p.15. For earlier reviews of its performance see; R. Nobles and D. Schiff, "The Criminal Cases Review Commission: Reporting Success?" [2001] 64 M.L.R. 280; A. James, N. Taylor and C. Walker, "The Criminal Cases Review Commission: Economy, Effectiveness and Justice", [2000] Crim. L.R. 140

[300] See K. Malleson, [1995] Crim. L.R. 929; The Chairman of the CCRC has stated: "I know from my own contacts with the judges, as from relevant judgments, that our work is valued and respected, and for that I pay tribute to the judges." See, G. Zellick, [2005] Crim. L.R. 937; See also, *R. v Mattan* (1998) *The Times*, March 5, 1998, in which Rose LJ commented: "the Criminal Cases Review Commission is a necessary and welcome body, without whose work the injustice in this case might never have been identified."; A. James, N. Taylor and C. Walker, [2000] Crim. L.R. 140; Home Affairs Select Committee Report, *The Work of the Criminal Cases Review Commission* (1999): The Committee was "impressed by the overwhelmingly positive tone of the opinions on the Commission's work" from lawyers (para.18); see also, *R. v Azam* [2006] EWCA Crim 161 at para.60.

[301] *ibid.* at p.20.

[302] See J. Jaconelli, [1981] Crim. L.R. 543.

[303] In practice, however, the defendant is normally not represented and counsel for the Attorney-General is opposed by counsel appearing as an advocate to the court, instructed by the Treasury Solicitor. In *Attorney-General's References (Nos.1 and 2 of 1979)* [1980] Q. B. 180, the Law Commission, who had instigated the references in order to secure clarification of the law concerning conditional intention to steal, submitted a memorandum for the assistance of the court.

In general, judges have resisted the introduction of procedures whereby matters may be referred to them for an advisory opinion.[304] One of the grounds for
refusing in the exercise of their discretion to grant a declaration on a disputed
matter of law is that the dispute is hypothetical rather than real.[305] However, the
opinions under the reference procedure relate to a real case, and, moreover, one
in which an opinion has already been expressed by the trial judge. The exact
status of the opinions as precedent is, however, uncertain: as they have no actual
effect on the outcome of the case as far as the defendant is concerned, it is
arguable that they are not binding, either on trial judges or on the Court of Appeal
itself; however, they are obviously of strong persuasive force.

The reference procedure has been characterised as "problematic"[306] in view of
the doubts as to precedental status and the fact that the defendant often has little
interest in contesting the case.[307] Nevertheless, the procedure has been of value
in providing authoritative guidance in a number of areas of criminal law, most
notably that of conditional intention to steal, where the Court of Appeal's
decision on a reference put an end to a line of argument that had led to a large
number of undeserved acquittals.[308]

(vii) *Venire de novo*

18–020 Where there has been a "mis-trial", in the sense either that the trial has never
been validly commenced or the jury has not validly returned a verdict, the Court
of Appeal may order the issue of a writ of *venire de novo* for a "new" trial: the
first "trial" is treated as a nullity.[309] This may be done, for example,[310] where
proceedings have not been properly instituted,[311] where the court is not properly
constituted,[312] where the defendants although separately indicted are tried
together,[313] where there is an equivocal plea of guilty which should not have been
accepted as such,[314] where the jury is not properly constituted,[315] where the jury

---

[304] There was weighty judicial opposition to clause 4 of the Rating and Valuation Bill 1928, which
would have enabled the Minister of Health to seek advisory opinions from the High Court on
questions of rating law: the clause was dropped: see Lord Hewart, *The New Despotism* (1929)
Ch.7; E. C. S. Wade, (1930) 46 L.Q.R. 169 and (1931) 47 L.Q.R. 58; C. K. Allen, (1931) 47
L.Q.R. 43 at 60. But note the introductory appeal procedure discussed above, para.14–081.

[305] e.g. *Blackburn v Att.-Gen.* [1971] 1 W.L.R. 1037, where the court declined to make a declaration
on the hypothetical question whether by signing the Treaty of Rome, Her Majesty's Government
would irreversibly surrender in part the sovereignty of Parliament.

[306] J. Jaconelli, *op. cit.*

[307] The Supreme Court of the United States refuses to consider "moot" points even where they arise
out of real and not hypothetical situations.

[308] *Attorney-General's References (Nos 1 and 2 of 1979)* [1980] Q.B. 180. See *R. v Bayley and
Easterbrook* [1980] Crim. L.R. 503.

[309] This jurisdiction, formerly exercised by the Court for Crown Cases Reserved, was preserved for
the Court of Criminal Appeal (*Crane v DPP* [1921] 2 A.C. 299) and is now exercised by the Court
of Appeal under the Supreme Court Act 1981, s.53(2).

[310] See R. B. Cooke, (1955) 71 L.Q.R. 100 (now Lord Cooke of Thorndon); M. Knight, *Criminal
Appeals* (1970), pp.216–219.

[311] *R. v Angel* (1968) 52 Cr.App.R. 280: the consent of the DPP was necessary but had not been
obtained *R. v Newland* [1988] Q.B. 402: the indictment was a nullity as it joined disparate
offences (*cf. R. v O'Reilly* (1989) 90 Cr.App.R. 40).

[312] *R. v Cronin* (1940) 27 Cr.App.R. 179: trial presided over by a person unqualified to act as a deputy
recorder.

[313] *Crane v DPP* above.

[314] See, e.g. *R. v Baker* (1912) 7 Cr.App.R. 217 at 252.

[315] e.g. where a juror was personated by his bailiff, who was neither on the jury panel nor qualified
to be so: *R. v Wakefield* (1918) 13 Cr.App.R. 56 or where the defendant is denied his right of
challenge: *R. v Williams* (1925) 19 Cr.App.R. 67; *R. v Gash* (1967) 51 Cr.App.R. 37.

is improperly discharged before giving a verdict,[316] or the verdict is ambiguous.[317] It is open to the Court of Appeal simply to quash a conviction without ordering a retrial.[318] Moreover, there may be a rule that the court may not order a *venire de novo* where the "mis-trial" led to an acquittal.[319]

In *R. v Rose*[320] the House of Lords emphasised that the power to order a *venire de novo* was not available where there was an irregularity in the course of the trial occurring between the time that it had been validly commenced and the discharge of the jury after returning a verdict. Here, the judge had applied improper pressure on the jury to reach a verdict by imposing a time limit: the House held that the Court of Appeal had no alternative but to quash the conviction under s.2 of the Criminal Appeal Act 1968, and had no jurisdiction to order a *venire de novo*.[321]

The court of trial may direct a *venire de novo* where the jury is discharged before giving a verdict, for example where they fail to agree or there is an irregularity in the conduct of proceedings.[322]

(b) Appeals from the Court of Appeal (Criminal Division) to the House of Lords

An appeal lies from the Court of Appeal (Criminal Division) to the House of Lords at the instance of either the defendant or the prosecutor.[323] The Court of Appeal must certify that a point of law of general public importance is involved.[324] In addition, leave must be obtained from either the Court of Appeal or the House of Lords and this can only be granted where it appears that the point is "one which ought to be considered by the House".[325] If leave is granted, the   **18–021**

---

[316] *R. v Hancock* (1931) 100 L.J.K.B. 419: the defendant changed his pleas from not guilty to guilty, but the jury did not formally return a guilty verdict; *cf. R. v Poole* [2002] Crim. L.R. 242.

[317] *R. v Lewis* (1988) 87 Cr.App.R. 270: the way the verdicts were taken left it unclear whether they were unanimous or majority.

[318] See, e.g. *R. v Golathan* (1915) 11 Cr.App.R. 79; *R. v Lewis* (1988) 87 Cr.App.R. 270. It is not clear whether it is open to the prosecution to recommence proceedings: if the court is simply regarded as holding the decision of the "first" trial to be a nullity, it seems that there could be such proceedings; if, however, the conviction is quashed under the Criminal Appeal Act 1968, s.2, the position is as if there had been a judgment and verdict of acquittal and fresh proceedings could be met by a plea of *autrefois acquit.*

[319] *R. v Middlesex Quarter Sessions, Ex p. DPP* [1952] 2 Q.B. 758. An alternative ground for the decision was that the irregularity was not such as to cause a mistrial. There may be exceptions to the supposed rule where the defendant is party to the irregularity or is tried by a court with no jurisdiction over charges of the kind in question: R. B. Cooke, (1955) 71 L.Q.R. 100 at 116.

[320] [1982] A.C. 822; see also *R. v O'Donnell* [1996] 1 Cr.App.R. 286.

[321] The position is the same where the defendant changes his or her plea to guilty in reliance on the judge's ruling on a point of law that is subsequently shown to be erroneous: *R. v Hunt* [1986] Q.B. 125 at 132 (an appeal was allowed by the House of Lords, but this point was not dealt with: [1987] A.C. 352.)

[322] See R. B. Cooke, *op. cit.* pp.120–125; Juries Act 1974, s.21(4).

[323] Criminal Appeal Act 1968, s.33(1). Where a point of law is referred to the Court of Appeal by the Attorney-General under the Criminal Justice Act 1972, s.36 (see above) the court may thereafter refer the point to the House of Lords. If the Court of Appeal had certified a point but refused leave, and then failed to inform the prosecution—thereby rendering it impossible for the prosecution to petition the House of Lords for leave within 14 days—the Court of Appeal could relist the matter: *R. v Cadman-Smith* [2001] Crim. L.R. 644.

[324] The RCCJ recommended that this requirement be dropped: Cm. 2263, p.178.

[325] 1968 Act, s.33(2).

House may in its discretion allow a point to be argued that is not connected with the point certified.[326]

An application for leave to appeal is normally made immediately after the Court of Appeal's decision, but may be made in writing within 14 days.[327] The point is normally formulated by counsel for the applicant, sometimes with the assistance of counsel for the other side. If a certificate is refused the matter may not be taken any further: the refusal is not itself a decision that may be subject to appeal.[328] Reasons are not normally given for refusing a certificate.[329] Where a certificate is granted, the application for leave should be made first to the Court of Appeal, and only if leave then is refused by that court, to the House of Lords, within 14 days.[330] The Court of Appeal may grant bail.[331]

Where the prosecutor is granted leave to appeal or gives notice of intention to apply for leave, and but for the decision of the Court of Appeal the defendant would be liable to be detained, the Court of Appeal may make an order for his or her detention or direct that he or she is not to be released except on bail so long as the appeal is pending.[332]

The House in disposing of an appeal may exercise any of the powers of the Court of Appeal or remit the case to that court.[333] Any sentence substituted by the House of Lords runs from the time when the other sentence would have begun to run, unless the House otherwise directs.[334] Any time spent on bail pending hearing of the appeal does not count towards the sentence.[335]

3. APPEALS IN CIVIL CASES

18–022   In this section we consider appeals in civil cases originating in the county court or the High Court. Appeals in civil cases originating in the magistrates' court or Crown Court have already been discussed.[336]

---

[326] *Att.-Gen. for Northern Ireland v Gallagher* [1963] A.C.349. Where, however, the certificate relates to conviction only the House will not deal with matters of sentence: *Jones v DPP* [1962] A.C. 635.
[327] Criminal Appeal Act 1968, s.34. The time limit may be extended for applications by the defence only. There is no power to extend prosecution time limits: *R. v Weir* [2001] 1 W.L.R. 421.
[328] *cf.* in relation to appeals to the House of Lords from the Divisional Court, *Gelberg v Miller* [1961] 1 W.L.R. 459.
[329] *R. v Jones* (1975) 61 Cr.App.R. 120; *R. v Cooper, R. v McMahon* (1975) 61 Cr.App.R. 215.
[330] Criminal Appeal Act 1968, s.34. The time limit may be extended for defendants.
[331] *ibid.* s.36.
[332] Criminal Appeal Act 1968, s.37(2). The order ceases to have effect if leave is refused, or the application for leave is not made within the due time, or the appeal is determined, or the liability for detention otherwise ceases, as the case may be: *ibid.* ss.34(3), 37(3).
[333] Criminal Appeal Act 1968, s.35(3). Where the House of Lords hears an appeal, but it turns out that points not disposed of by the Court of Appeal are relevant to whether a conviction should stand, the House may remit the matter to the Court of Appeal or itself exercise the powers of the Court of Appeal in relation to those points: *R. v Mandair* [1995] 1 A.C. 208, H.L. The Court of Appeal may not otherwise itself re-list the case to consider the unresolved grounds: *R. v Berry (No.2)* [1991] 1 W.L.R. 125 and *R. v Berry (No.3)* [1995] 1 W.L.R. 7, CA.
[334] *ibid.* s.43(2).
[335] *ibid.* s.43(1).
[336] See above, paras 18–005—18–009.

(a) Appeals in the county court, High Court and Court of Appeal

The structure of appeals in civil cases originating in the county court or High Court has been remodelled as part of the Woolf reforms.[337] The aim has been to enable appeals to be directed to the most appropriate level, to require permission for most appeals, to restrict second and further appeals, and to reduce the proportion of appeals dealt with by re-hearing rather than review. A single structure has been created covering appeals to and within county courts, the High Court and the Court of Appeal. Amendments to the legislative structure were made by the Access to Justice Act 1999[338] and the main provisions are now to be found in the CPR Pt 52 and the associated Practice Direction. Appeal proceedings are subject to the "overriding objective" in CPR r.1.1 "of enabling the court to deal with cases justly".

(i) *When is an appeal available?*

18–023

It is provided generally that, subject to an order made by the Lord Chancellor,[339] any party to any proceedings in the county court dissatisfied with the determination of the judge or jury may appeal to the Court of Appeal[340]; and that the Court of Appeal has jurisdiction to hear and determine appeals from any judgment or order of the High Court.[341] However, in a number of situations, appeals to the Court of Appeal are expressly excluded:

(a) in respect of questions of fact arising in certain actions by a landlord for possession of the premises[342];

(b) where the parties have agreed in writing that the judge's decision shall be final[343];

(c) from any judgment of the High Court in any criminal cause or matter[344];

(d) from any order of the High Court or any other court or tribunal allowing an extension of time for appealing from a judgment or order[345];

---

[337] See *Access to Justice* (HMSO, 1996), Ch.14; *Report of the Review of the Court of Appeal (Civil Division)* (Bowman Report) (LCD, 1997). The changes have been described as "the most significant changes in the arrangements for appeals in civil proceedings in this country for 125 years": Brooke L.J. in *Tanfern Ltd v Cameron MacDonald (Practice Note)* [2000] 1 W.L.R. 1311. See generally N. Andrews, [2000] C.L.J. 464 and *English Civil Procedure* (2003), Ch.38; A. Zuckerman, *Zuckerman on Civil Procedure* (2nd edn, 2006), Ch.23; R. Nobles and D. Schiff, (2002) 65 M.L.R. 676.

[338] ss.54–57.

[339] Under s.56(1) of the Access to Justice Act 1999 as amended, which enables the Lord Chancellor, after consulting the LCJ and other senior judges, to provide that appeals which would otherwise lie to a county court, the High Court or the Court of Appeal shall lie instead to another of those courts.

[340] County Courts Act 1984, s,77(1), as amended.

[341] Supreme Court Act 1981, s.16(1), as amended.

[342] County Courts Act 1984, s.77(6) (excluding the appeal under s.77(1)).

[343] *ibid.* s.79(1).

[344] Supreme Court Act 1981, s.18(1)(a). Here, the appeal lies to the House of Lords under the Administration of Justice Act 1960: see above, para.18–009.

[345] s.18(1)(b). An appeal lies from a refusal to make such an order: *cf. Rickards v Rickards* [1990] Fam. 194.

(e) from any decision expressed by statute to be final[346];

(f) from a decree absolute of divorce or nullity of marriage, by a party who, having had time and opportunity to appeal from the decree nisi, has not done so[347];

(g) from a divorce order[348];

(h) from a final dissolution order, nullity order or presumption of death order under Ch.2 of Pt 2 of the Civil Partnership Act 2004, by a party who, having had time and opportunity to appeal from the conditional order on which that final order was founded, has not appealed from the conditional order[349];

(i) from any decision of the High Court under Pt I of the Arbitration Act 1996, except as provided by that Act[350];

(j) from a judgment or order of the High Court sitting as a Prize Court[351];

(k) from an order refusing leave to a vexatious litigant to institute or continue legal proceedings.[352]

In some circumstances, an appeal lies directly from the High Court to the House of Lords.[353]

The Court of Appeal also has a residual jurisdiction to reopen proceedings in order to avoid real injustice in exceptional circumstances where there is no other effective remedy; this may include cases where an order has been procured by fraud or evidence has arisen that suggests that there is a real possibility that the trial judge was biased.[354] The jurisdiction can also be exercised by the High Court[355] and is now regulated, in restrictive terms[356] by CPR r.52.17. This states that the Court of Appeal or the High Court[357] will not re-open a final determination of any appeal unless

(a) it is necessary to do so to avoid real injustice;

(b) the circumstances are exceptional and make it appropriate to reopen the appeal; and

---

[346] s.18(1)(c). For example a decision of the High Court on an appeal by case stated in a non-criminal case is final: 1981 Act, s.28A(4). This means what it says: *Westminster City Council v O'Reilly (Leave to appeal: Jurisdiction)* [2004] 1 W.L.R. 195; *Farley v Secretary of State for Work and Pensions (No.2)* [2005] 2 F.L.R. 1075 (holding that the decision of the Court of Appeal in *Farley (No.1)* [2005] 2 F.L.R. 1059 in a case concerning child support maintenance was not a valid order as it followed an appeal by case stated; the Court, however, came to the same outcome as in *No.1* through a judicial review procedural route).

[347] s.18(1)(d), as amended by the Family Law Act 1996, Sch.10.

[348] s.18(1)(dd), inserted by the Family Law Act 1996, Sch.8, para.30, from a day to be appointed.

[349] s.18(1)(fa), inserted by the 2004 Act, Sch.27, para.68.

[350] s.18(1)(g), substituted by the 1996 Act, Sch.3, para.37.

[351] *ibid.* s.l6(2). An appeal lies to the Privy Council.

[352] *ibid.* s.42(4).

[353] See below, para.18–038.

[354] *Taylor v Lawrence* [2003] Q.B. 528. The permission of the Court of Appeal is necessary for a case to be reopened.

[355] *Seray-Wurie v Hackney LBC* [2003] 1 W.L.R. 257.

[356] As intended in *Taylor*, although in the year after *Taylor* was decided, there were over 200 applications to re-open appeals, all without merit: *White Book 2006*, para.52.17.1.

[357] The county court has no such jurisdiction: *Gregory v Turner* [2003] 1 W.L.R. 1149; r.52.17(3). Neither has the EAT: *Asda Stores Ltd v Thompson (No.2)* [2004] I.R.L.R. 598.

(c) there is no alternative effective remedy.[358]

A successful application for permission was made in *Couwenbergh v Valkova*.[359]

(ii) *When is permission required?*

The Access to Justice Act 1999 introduced a general provision whereby rules of **18–024** court may provide that any right of appeal to a county court, the High Court or the Court of Appeal (other than a right of appeal in a criminal cause or matter) may be exercised only with permission.[360] No appeal can be made against a decision of a court under this provision to give or refuse permission, although this does not affect any right under rules of court to make a further application for permission,[361] or, in the case of the county court, exclude the right to apply for judicial review on the ground of lack of jurisdiction (in a narrow sense) or a complete denial of a right to a fair hearing.[362] CPR r.52.3 provides that an appellant or respondent requires permission to appeal where the appeal is from the decision of a judge in the county court or the High Court, except where the appeal is against a committal order,[363] a refusal to grant habeas corpus or a secure accommodation order made under s.25 of the Children Act 1989, or as provided by Practice Direction 52. The Practice Direction provides that the permission of the Court of Appeal or, where the lower court's rules allow, the lower court is required for all appeals except as provided for by statute or CPR r.52.3.[364] These general provisions are not to be construed as introducing a general requirement for permission to appeal across specific statutory appeals which are not otherwise subject to any restriction.[365]

---

[358] See also *Practice Direction 52*, para.25, and Zuckerman (2006), pp.906–908.

[359] [2004] EWCA Civ 676: there was a real prospect that an appeal would succeed in meeting the *Taylor* criteria on the basis that a deceit had been practised on the Court. See further [2005] EWCA Civ 145, where the Court of Appeal remitted the case for rehearing in the Chancery Division. Cf. *Re Uddin (A Child)* [2005] 1 W.L.R. 2398: the "integrity of the earlier litigation process" has to have been "critically undermined" (para.[18]). Another successful application was made in *Feakins v Intervention Board for Agricultural Produce* [2006] EWCA Civ 699 (court misled).

[360] Access to Justice Act 1999. s.54(1)(2).

[361] *ibid.* s.54(4). *Tanfern Ltd v Cameron-Macdonald* [2000] 1 W.L.R. 1311.

[362] Permission to apply for judicial review will only be granted in exceptional circumstances: *R (on the application of Sivasubramaniam) v Wandsworth County Court* [2003] 1 W.L.R. 475; *Gregory v Turner* [2003] 1 W.L.R. 1149; *R (on the application of Sinclair Gardens Investments (Kensington) Ltd) v Lands Tribunal* [2006] 3 All E.R. 650; *R (on the application of Strickson) v Preston Crown Court* [2006] EWHC 3300 (Admin).

[363] Permission is not needed whether the appeal is by the person who is committed to prison, or the person who sought the committal order and who wishes to appeal on the ground that the sentence of committal was unduly lenient: *Wood v Collins* [2006] EWCA Civ 743. Permission *is* needed where no order of committal is made: *Barnet LBC v Hurst* [2003] 1 W.L.R. 722; *M v M (Breaches of Orders: Committal)* [2006] 1 F.L.R. 1154.

[364] para.4.2.

[365] *Colley v Council for Licensed Conveyancers* [2002] 1 W.L.R. 160 (statutory right of appeal under the Administration of Justice Act 1985, s.26(7)); *Re B (a patient) (Court of Protection: appeal)* [2006] 1 All E.R. 978 (High Court judge nominated under Pt VII of the Mental Health Act 1983, dealing with the management of property and affairs of patients, not sitting as a "judge of the High Court" and so r.52.3 not applicable).

(iii) *Routes of appeal*

18–025   These are now prescribed by an order made by the Lord Chancellor[366]:

(1) an appeal from the decision[367] of a District judge or deputy District judge of a county court lies to a Circuit judge[368];

(2) subject to (1), an appeal from a decision of a county court lies to the High Court[369];

(3) an appeal from a registrar, master, District judge of the High Court or deputy lies to a High Court judge.[370]

(1) to (3) are subject to the following:

(4) an appeal lies to the Court of Appeal where the decision to be appealed is a final decision[371] in a claim under CPR Pt 7 allocated to the multi-track or made in specialist proceedings[372]; and

(5) where an appeal is made to a county court or the High Court (other than from a decision of a court officer authorised to assess costs) and on hearing the appeal the court makes a decision, an appeal lies only to the Court of Appeal.[373] An appeal lies from the decision of a High Court judge to the Court of Appeal.[374]

Family proceedings and appeals against a decision of an authorised court officer in detailed costs assessment proceedings are subject to different arrangements.[375] Where a decision in a multi-track case or specialist proceedings is not a final decision,[376] the route of appeal depends on the type of judge who made

---

[366] Access to Justice Act 1999 (Destination of Appeals) Order 2000 (SI 2000/1071), made under the 1999 Act, s.56(1) and (3).

[367] This includes any judgment, order or direction of the High Court or a county court: para.1(2)(a).

[368] SI 2000/1071, art.3(2).

[369] *ibid.* art.3(1). Until 1934 the appeal lay first to a Divisional Court and thereafter to the Court of Appeal. In bankruptcy cases an appeal lies to a Divisional Court of the Chancery Division; an appeal lies from that Court to the Court of Appeal and the latter's decision is final: Insolvency Act 1986, s.375(2), as amended by the 1999 Act, Sch.15.

[370] *ibid.* art.2.

[371] i.e. a decision of a court that would finally determine (subject to any possible appeal or detailed assessment of costs) the entire proceedings (or part of a hearing or trial which has been split into parts) whichever way the court decided the issues before it: *ibid.* para.1 (2)(c), (3). It does not include a decision only on the detailed assessment of costs: *Dooley v Parker* [2002] EWCA Civ 96.

[372] *ibid.* art.4, as amended by SI 2003/490. Specialist proceedings are admiralty and arbitration proceedings, commercial and mercantile actions, Patents Court and Technology and Construction Court business proceedings under the Companies Acts and probate and inheritance.

[373] *ibid.* art.5.

[374] By virtue of the Supreme Court Act 1981, s.16(1).

[375] In family proceedings, appeals lie from a District judge in the county court to a Circuit judge; District judge in the High Court or the Principal Registry to a High Court judge of the Family Division; Circuit judge or High Court judge to Court of Appeal. (The position in respect of adoption orders is now governed by the Access to Justice Act 1999 (Destination of Appeals) (Family Proceedings) Order 2005 (SI 2005/3276)). Appeals from an authorised Court officer lie to a costs judge (taxing master) or a District judge of the High Court (CPR, rr.47.21–47.26).

[376] e.g. a case management decision, the grant or refusal of interim relief, an order striking out proceedings or an order giving summary judgment under CPR, Pt 24.

the order, the appeal lying to the next judge in the hierarchy.[377] The same applies to decisions in claims allocated to the small claims track and fast track, and to claims under the CPR Pt 8 procedure.

Where in any proceedings in a county court or the High Court a person appeals, or seeks permission to appeal, to a court other than the Court of Appeal or the House of Lords, the Master of the Rolls, or the court from which or to which the appeal is to be made, or from which permission to appeal is sought, may direct that the appeal shall be heard instead by the Court of Appeal.[378] Furthermore, where a relevant court (i.e. the court from or to which an appeal is made or from which permission to appeal is sought) considers that an appeal which is to be heard by a county court or the High Court would raise an important point of principle or practice, or there is some other compelling reason for the Court of Appeal to hear it, the relevant court may order the appeal to be transferred to the Court of Appeal, the Master of the Rolls or the Court of Appeal may remit it.[379]

(iv) Grounds of appeal and the powers of the appeal court

Every appeal is limited to a review of the decision of the lower court unless a **18–026** practice direction makes different provision for a particular category of appeal; or the court considers that in the circumstances of an individual appeal it would be in the interests of justice to hold a re-hearing.[380] There is not, however, a sharp distinction between "review" and "re-hearing", more a "spectrum shaded between the one and the other".[381] Unless it orders otherwise, the appeal court will not receive oral evidence or evidence which was not before the lower court.[382] The appeal court will allow an appeal where the decision of the lower court was (a) wrong, or (b) unjust because of a serious procedural irregularity or other irregularity in the proceedings of the lower court.[383] It may draw any

---

[377] Practice Direction 52, para.2A1: District judge of a county court to Circuit judge; Master, District judge of the High Court or Circuit judge to High Court judge; High Court judge to Court of Appeal.

[378] Access to Justice Act 1999, s.57. Referred to as a "leapfrog appeal". This does not enable the application for *permission* to appeal to be transferred: *Re Claims Direct Test Cases* [2002] EWCA Civ 428, para.[22]. An example of the use of s.57 is *R (on the application of McLellan) v Bracknell Forest BC* [2002] Q.B. 1129.

[379] CPR r.52.14. This power should be used sparingly and if the lower court is in doubt the matter can be referred to the Master of the Rolls: *Clark (Inspector of Taxes) v Perks* [2001] 1 W.L.R. 17.

[380] CPR r.52.11(1). The hearing is a re-hearing if the appeal is from the decision of a Minister, person or other body and that Minister, etc., did not hold a hearing to come to that decision or held a hearing but the procedure adopted did not provide for the consideration of evidence: Practice Direction 52, para.9.1.

[381] May L.J. in *Yorkshire Water Services Ltd v Taylor Woodrow Construction Northern Ltd* [2005] EWCA Civ 894; 104 Con. L.R. 76, at para.[22], referring to his own judgment in *EI Du Pont De Nemours & Co v ST Dupont* [2004] I.P.&T. 559.

[382] CPR r.52.11(2). Where the court at first instance has failed to provide reasons for its decision, an appellate court should not accede to a request for a re-hearing unless the lower court had refused to provide reasons when asked to do so or there was good reason for not asking it to do so: *Secretary of State for Trade and Industry v Lewis* [2001] 2 B.C.L.C. 597; as a general rule, appeals should proceed by way of review and there are no set criteria for determining when proceeding by way of re-hearing is appropriate, the court having a wide discretion according to the circumstances of the case: *Audergon v La Baguette Ltd* [2002] EWCA Civ 10.

[383] CPR r.52.11(3).

inference of fact which it considers justified on the evidence.[384] At the hearing a party may not rely on any matter not contained in the appeal notice unless the appeal court gives permission.[385]

A decision will be wrong where the court erred in law or fact or there was an error in the exercise of discretion sufficient for the appeal court to intervene.[386] On the last of these the principle stated by Lord Fraser of Tullybelton in *G v G (Minors: Custody Appeal)*[387] has been held[388] to be relevant:

> " . . . the appellate court should only interfere when it considers that the judge of first instance has not merely preferred an imperfect solution which is different from an alternative imperfect solution which the Court of Appeal might or would have adopted, but has exceeded the generous ambit within which a reasonable disagreement is possible."

This approach will not, however, apply where the appeal is by way of re-hearing as there the discretion will be exercised afresh. Ground (b) may apply where the decision is not itself "wrong".[389]

On an appeal, the appeal court has all the powers of the lower court, unless restricted by statutory provisions, and has express power: (a) to affirm, set aside or vary any order or judgment; (b) refer any claim or issue for determination by the lower court; (c) order a new trial or hearing; (d) make orders for the payment of interest; and (e) make a costs order. In an appeal from a claim tried with a jury, the Court of Appeal may instead of ordering a new trial: (a) make an order for damages; or (b) vary an award of damages made by the jury.[390]

A judge must give sufficient reasons for his or her decision to enable the parties and any appellate tribunal readily to analyse the reasoning that was essential to that decision.[391] For example, if the expert evidence of one witness is preferred to that of another, the judge must explain why.[392] However, it is not necessary to deal with every argument presented by counsel.[393]

---

[384] CPR r.52.11(4). Prior to the changes, the tests for accepting fresh evidence were set out in *Ladd v Marshall* [1954] 1 W.L.R. 1489: (1) the evidence could not have been obtained with reasonable diligence for use at the trial; (2) the evidence must be such that, if given, it would probably have an important influence on the result of the case, though it need not be decisive; (3) the evidence must be such as is presumably to be believed; it must be apparently credible, though it need not be incontrovertible. These tests remain of persuasive authority when the court exercises its discretion under the new rules: *Hertfordshire Investements Ltd v Bubb* [2000] 1 W.L.R. 2318; *Hamilton v Al Fayed (No.4)* [2001] E.M.L.R. 15; *Gillingham v Gillingham* [2001] EWCA Civ 906; but the application of the principles in a particular case may require modification in the light of the overriding objective.

[385] CPR r.52.11(5).

[386] *White Book 2006*, para.52.11.3.

[387] [1985] 1 W.L.R. 647 at 652.

[388] By Brooke L.J. in *Tanfern Ltd v Carmeron MacDonald* [2000] 1 W.L.R. 1311, para.[32].

[389] *White Book 2006*, para.52.11.3.

[390] CPR r.52.10.

[391] *English v Emery Reimbold & Strick Ltd and other cases* [2002] 1 W.L.R. 2409. If a well-founded application for permission to appeal on the ground of inadequate reasons is made to the trial judge, the judge should consider whether additional reasons should be given; if it is made to the appeal court, it should consider adjourning the application and remitting the case to the trial judge: *ibid.* This approach is applicable in family cases: *Re B (Appeal: Lack of reasons)* [2003] 2 F.L.R. 1035.

[392] *Flannery v Halifax Estate Agencies Ltd* [2000] 1 W.L.R. 377.

[393] *Eagil Trust Co Ltd v Pigott-Brown* [1985] 3 All E.R. 119 at 121, *per* Griffiths L.J.; approved in *English* at para.[17], subject to the general principle set out above.

(v) *Second appeals*

Where an appeal is made to the county court or the High Court in relation to any **18–027**
matter (other than a criminal cause or matter), no appeal may be made to the
Court of Appeal from that decision unless the Court of Appeal considers that the
appeal would raise an important point of principle or practice, or there is some
other compelling reason for the Court of Appeal to hear it.[394]

(vi) *Applications for permission to appeal*

An application for permission to appeal may be made: (a) to the lower court at **18–028**
the hearing at which the decision to be appealed was made; or (b) to the appeal
court in an appeal notice. There is no requirement to raise the matter with the
lower court, although this is encouraged.[395] Where the lower court refuses
permission, a further application for permission may be made to the appeal court.
Applications are normally dealt with on paper. If that court refuses permission
without a hearing the applicant may within seven days request the decision to be
reconsidered at a hearing.[396] Permission will only be given where: (a) the court
considers that the appeal would have a real prospect of success[397]; or (b) there is
some other compelling reason why the appeal should be heard.[398] An order
giving permission may: (a) limit the issues to be heard; and (b) be made subject
to conditions.[399] Reasons must be given for refusing permission.[400] If permission
is refused, no further appeal is available.[401] Permission to appeal will be granted
more sparingly in respect of case management decisions[402] and second

---

[394] Access to Justice Act 1999, s.55; CPR r.52.13. See *Uphill v BRB (Residuary) Ltd* [2005] 1 W.L.R.
2070 (anything less than very good prospects of success will rarely suffice; but this will not
necessarily be enough, as in a case where the intended appellant has contributed to the court's
mistake; and only a real prospect of success may in some circumstances be enough as in cases
where the intended appellant has not had a fair hearing); *Cramp v Hastings BC* [2005] 4 All E.R.
1014 (*Uphill* guidance not exhaustive; also may be relevant to consider the provenance of the
appeal).

[395] *Re T (A Child: Contact)* [2003] 1 F.L.R. 531 at paras [12]–[13].

[396] *Practice Direction 52*, para.4.15 provides that notice of a permission hearing will be given to the
respondent, who is not required to attend unless this is requested by the court. In most cases,
applications for permission are determined without the court requesting written submissions or
attendance at an oral hearing (if there is one) by the respondent; in the absence of such a request,
costs will not normally be allowed to a respondent who volunteers submissions on attendance; if
there is such a request, the court will normally allow the respondent his or her costs if permission
is refused: *ibid.* paras 4.22–4.24. See further *Jolly v Jay* [2002] EWCA Civ on which some
changes to the PD were based.

[397] i.e. a realistic as opposed to a fanciful prospect of success: Lord Woolf M.R. in *Swain v Hillman*
[2001] 1 All E.R. 91, cited by Brooke L.J. in *Tanfern*, above, para.[21].

[398] The *White Book* 2006, para.52.3.6 states that (b) provides a "valuable reserve power" for use in
cases, for example, where the law requires clarification; it may be appropriate for permission to
be granted on condition that the appellant pays both parties' costs in any event. However, in the
case of junior appellate courts only (a) should be applied; such a court is "hardly the forum" to
address questions of public interest or general policy.

[399] CPR r.52.3(2)–(7). If limited or conditional permission is granted by an appellate judge after a
hearing, the issue cannot be re-opened at the full hearing: *Fieldman v Markovitch, The Times*, July
31, 2001.

[400] *Hyams v Plender* [2001] 1 W.L.R. 32, para.[17].

[401] Access to Justice Act 1999, s.54(4); *Rineker v University College London* [2001] 1 W.L.R. 13
(Court of Appeal has no jurisdiction to entertain appeal against refusal of High Court judge to
grant permission to appeal against an order of a costs judge). See also para.18–024.

[402] *Practice Direction 52*, paras 4.4, 4.5 (specifying as relevant considerations the significance of the
issue, the practical consequence of an appeal and whether it would be more convenient to
determine the issue at or after trial).

appeals.[403] The Court of Appeal is particularly reluctant to grant permission to appeal in respect of complex findings of fact made by judges in the Technology and Construction Court.[404] Where an appellant or respondent seeks permission from the appeal court it must be requested in the appellant's or respondent's notice as the case may be.

(vii) *The appeal process*

18–029   The appellant must file an "appellant's notice" setting out the grounds of appeal at the appeal court within: (a) such period as may be directed by the lower court; or (b) where there is no such direction, 21 days after the date of the decision that the appellant wishes to appeal. Unless the appeal court orders otherwise, an appellant's notice must be served on each respondent[405] as soon as practicable and in any event not later than seven days, after it is filed.[406] If the appellant is represented, a skeleton argument must accompany or be included in the appellant's notice; if that is impracticable it must be lodged and served within 14 days of filing the notice. An appellant who is not represented is encouraged to lodge a skeleton argument but is not required to do so.[407]

Unless the court otherwise directs, a respondent need not take any action when served with an appellant's notice until notified that permission to appeal has been granted.[408] A respondent may file and serve a respondent's notice; and must file a notice if seeking permission from the appeal court to appeal or wishing to ask that court to uphold the order for reasons different from or additional to those of the lower court. The notice must be filed within: (a) such period as may be directed by the lower court; or (b) where there is no such direction, 14 days after the date he or she is served with the appellant's notice, or notification that the appeal court has given the appellant permission to appeal or notification that the application for permission to appeal and the appeal itself are to be heard. Unless the appeal court otherwise orders, a respondent's notice must be served on the appellant and any other respondent as soon as practicable and, in any event, not later than seven days after it is filed.[409] Similar requirements apply to respondent's notices as for appellant's notices. The respondent must supply a skeleton

---

[403] See para.18–027.

[404] *Yorkshire Water Services Ltd v Taylor Woodrow Construction Northern Ltd* [2005] EWCA Civ 894.

[405] i.e. a person other than the appellant who was a party to the proceedings in the lower court and who is affected by the appeal; and a person who is permitted by the appeal court to be a party to the appeal: CPR r.52.1(3)(e).

[406] CPR r.52.4. Form Nl61 is to be used. Specified documents, and any others which the appellant reasonably considers necessary to enable the appeal court to reach its decision must also be filed then, or reasons given why they are not currently available (Practice Direction 52, paras 5.6–5.7). A more limited set is needed for the small claims track (*ibid.* para.5.8). If permission has been given by the lower court or is not required, the documents must also be served on the respondents at this stage (*ibid.* para.5.24); if permission is obtained from the appeal court, they must be served within seven days of receiving the order granting permission (*ibid.* para.6.2).

[407] *Practice Direction 52*, para.5.9. Such skeleton arguments should contain a numbered list of points stated as concisely as the nature of the case allows which should both define and confine the areas of controversy; each point should be followed by references to any documentation on which the appellant proposes to rely. Other information needed may include glossaries, a chronology of relevant events and authorities on points of law: Practice Direction 52, paras 5.10, 5.11.

[408] *ibid.* para.5.22.

[409] CPR r.52.5. Form N162 is to be used.

argument in all cases where he or she proposes to address arguments to the court, or may do so in the case of the small claims track.[410]

The appeal court may extend or shorten time.[411] Unless the appeal court or the lower court orders otherwise, or the appeal is from the Immigration Appeal Tribunal, an appeal does not operate as a stay of any order or decision of the lower court.[412] An appeal notice may not be amended without the permission of the appeal court.[413] The appeal court has power, where there is a compelling reason, to strike out the whole or part of an appeal notice, to set aside permission to appeal in whole or in part, or to impose or vary conditions upon which an appeal may be brought.[414]

If permission is granted, the appeal court will send the parties notification of the date of the hearing or the period of time (the "listing window") during which the appeal is likely to be heard and, in the Court of Appeal, the "hear by date", a copy of any order giving permission to appeal and any other directions given by the court.[415] The appellant will also be sent an Appeal Questionnaire, to be returned within 14 days. This will include, if the appellant is legally represented, the advocate's time estimate for the hearing and confirmation of other matters.[416]

(viii) *Who may exercise the powers of the Court of Appeal*

A court officer assigned to the Civil Appeals Office who is a barrister or solicitor **18–030** may, with the consent of the Master of the Rolls, exercise the jurisdiction of the Court of Appeal with regard to: matters incidental to any proceedings in the Court of Appeal, any other matter where there is no substantial dispute between the parties, and the dismissal of any appeal or application for non-compliance with an order, rule or practice direction. However, such an officer may not decide an application for permission to appeal, bail pending on appeal, an injunction, or (normally) a stay of proceedings. A party may request any decision of a court officer to be reviewed by the Court of Appeal.[417]

(ix) *Effect of new authorities and legislation*

The court should take account of any new authorities and of any relevant, **18–031** retrospective legislation. For example, in *Attorney-General v Vernazza*,[418] Mr Vernazza was declared to be a vexatious litigant and prohibited by the High Court from *instituting* legal proceedings without leave. By the time his appeal was heard by the Court of Appeal, the High Court had been given a new statutory power to prohibit vexatious litigants from *continuing existing* proceedings without leave. The House of Lords held that the new legislation, as it affected

---

[410] *Practice Direction 52*, paras 7.6, 7.7, 7.7A. It should, where appropriate, answer the arguments set out in the appellant's skeleton argument: *ibid.* para.7.8.

[411] CPR rr.3.1(2)(a) and 52.6. An appeal may lie, with permission, against a decision that time should not be extended: *Foenander v Bond Lewis & Co* [2002] 1 W.L.R. 525.

[412] CPR r.52.7. See *Hammond Suddard Solicitors v Agrichem International Holdings Ltd* [2001] EWCA Civ 2065.

[413] CPR r.52.8

[414] CPR r.52.9.

[415] *Practice Direction 52*, para.6.3.

[416] *ibid.* para.6.5.

[417] CPR r.52.16.

[418] [1960] A.C. 965.

procedural and not substantive rights, was retrospective, should have been applied to Mr Vernazza by the Court of Appeal, and should be applied to him now. Where there are new authorities or legislative provisions which are relevant to a decision of the High Court, leave to appeal out of time will be granted if it is just to do so.[419]

Similarly, the court should take account of any material changes in the facts since the trial. For example, in *Murphy v Stone-Wallwork (Charlton) Ltd,*[420] an action was brought by an employee against his employers for breach of statutory duty. The judge and the Court of Appeal assessed the damages on the assumption that the plaintiff would continue to be employed by the defendants on lighter work. A fortnight after the decision in the Court of Appeal, the plaintiff was dismissed because of his incapacity. The House of Lords[421] held that even though it did not appear that the employers had acted in bad faith or oppressively, evidence of the change of circumstances was admissible, as the basis on which the case had been conducted on both sides had been suddenly and materially falsified. It should, however, be noted that the change occurred within the time limit for appealing: it is unlikely that a leave to appeal out of time would be granted in such circumstances, in view of the need for finality in litigation, unless, perhaps, there was bad faith or oppression. A more restrictive approach is adopted in respect of the admission of fresh evidence.[422]

The Court of Appeal similarly adopts a restrictive approach to points not taken at the trial and presented for the first time in the Court of Appeal. The court will not decide in favour of an appellant on a new point unless it is satisfied beyond doubt (1) that it has before it all the facts bearing upon the new contention as completely as if it had been raised at the trial, and (2) that no evidence could have been adduced at the trial which by any possibility could prevent the point from succeeding.[423] Accordingly, it may permit a new question to be raised on the construction and application of a regulation where the facts are not disputed.[424]

(x) *Decision-making in the Court of Appeal*

18–032   The approach of the Court of Appeal varies according to whether the appeal concerns: (1) questions of fact; (2) awards of damages; (3) exercises of judicial

---

[419] *In Re Earl of Berkeley, Borrer v Berkeley* [1945] Ch. 1; *Anns v Walcroft Property Co Ltd* [1976] Q.B. 882; *Property and Reversionary Investment Corporation Ltd v Templar* [1977] 1 W.L.R. 1223.

[420] [1969] 1 W.L.R. 1023. See also *Mulholland v Mitchell* [1971] A.C. 666; *Hughes v Smith, The Times,* April 21, 1989. Evidence concerning post-hearing developments is "readily admitted" in cases concerning the welfare of children: *G v G (Minors: Custody Appeal)* [1985] 1 W.L.R. 647 at 654, *per* Lord Eraser. See, e.g. *M v M (Minor: Custody Appeal)* [1987] 1 W.L.R. 404; *A v A (Custody Appeal: Role of Appellate Court)* [1988] 1 F.L.R. 193; *Re A (A Minor) (Abduction)* [1989] 1 F.L.R. 365.

[421] The same principle would have applied by the Court of Appeal if the change had occurred after the trial.

[422] See above, para.18–026.

[423] See Lord Herschell in *The Tasmania* (1890) 15 App.Cas. at 225 and Jessel M.R. in *Ex p. Firth, re Cowburn* (1882) 19 Ch.D. 419, 429; *Ashcroft v Mersey Regional Health Authority* [1985] 2 All E.R. 96; *Transcontainer Express Ltd v Custodian Security Ltd* [1988] 1 Lloyd's L.R. 128; *Khan v National Union of Rail Maritime and Transport Workers* [2001] EWCA Civ 959.

[424] *Donaghey v P. O'Brien & Co* [1966] 1 W.L.R. 1170 at 1180; on appeal: *Donaghey v Boulton & Paul Ltd* [1968] A.C. 1 at 14, 23, 31; *cf. Jones v Department of Employment* [1989] Q.B. 1 (Court of Appeal willing to entertain a new argument on a point of law on an appeal against striking out, where the facts are assumed).

discretion; (4) questions of law; and (5) a new trial. The principles set out in this section were developed before the recent changes to appeals. It remains fully to be seen how far they may be modified in applying the new formulation of the grounds of appeal.[425]

(1) *Questions of fact.* In the vast majority of cases, the trial will have been **18–033** conducted by a judge sitting without a jury. The findings of fact will be set out in the judgment. On an appeal, a distinction will be drawn by the Court of Appeal between findings of "primary fact" and inferences of fact drawn from those primary facts (sometimes termed "secondary facts").[426] The Court of Appeal is most reluctant to disturb findings of primary fact where they are based on the testimony of witnesses who have been seen by the judge, and who, in accordance with the practice of the Court of Appeal, will not be seen in person on the appeal.[427] The judge's findings will normally have been based, at least in part, on his or her observations of manner and demeanour, and this advantage is denied to the Court of Appeal. In exceptional cases, the court may find that the trial judge has "failed to use or has palpably misused his advantage".[428] The judge's impression of the witnesses' demeanour "should be carefully checked by a critical examination of the whole of the evidence".[429] A judgment:

" . . . may be demonstrated . . . to be affected by material inconsistencies and inaccuracies or [the trial judge] may be shown to have failed to appreciate the weight or bearing of circumstances admitted or proved or otherwise to have gone plainly wrong".[430]

The court is a little less reluctant to interfere with findings based upon expert evidence.[431]

On the other hand, the Court of Appeal is much more willing to draw inferences from the primary facts different from those drawn by the trial judge, provided that it is in as good a position as the judge to draw such inferences.[432]

This dichotomy is echoed in the modern case law, although the most recent cases emphasise the need for flexibility whether the Court of Appeal is considering primary facts or inferences. This does not, however, involve a change of approach by comparison with the pre-CPR era.[433] In *Assicurazioni Generali SpA v Arab Insurance Group (BSC)*[434] Clarke L.J. noted the cases in which the courts

---

[425] Above, para.18–026.

[426] See above, paras 1–011—1–013.

[427] *SS. Hontestroom (Owners) v SS. Sagaporack (Owners)* [1927] A.C. 37; *Powell v Streatham Manor Nursing Home* [1935] A.C. 243; *Watt or Thomas v Thomas* [1947] A.C. 484.

[428] *per* Lord Summer in *SS. Hontestroom v SS. Sagaporack*, above, at 47. Cf. *Whitehouse v Jordan* [1981] 1 W.L.R. 246.

[429] *per* Lord Greene M.R. in *Yuill v Yuill* [1945] P. 15 at 22.

[430] *per* Lord Macmillan in *Watt or Thomas v Thomas* [1947] A.C. 484 at 491.

[431] *Joyce v Yeomans* [1981] 1 W.L.R. 549 (medical witnesses).

[432] *Benmax v Austin Motor Co Ltd* [1955] A.C. 370; *Biogen Inc v Medeva plc* [1997] R.P.C. 1 at 45, *per* Lord Goff: "It would . . . be wrong to treat *Benmax* as authorising or requiring an appellate court to undertake a *de novo* evaluation of the facts in all cases in which no question of the credibility of witnesses is involved. Where the application of a legal standard such as negligence . . . involves no question of principle but is simply a matter of degree, an appellate court should be very cautious in differing from the judge's evaluation."

[433] Waller L.J. in *Black v Davies* [2005] EWCA Civ 531, at para.[17].

[434] [2003] 1 W.L.R. 577. The comments of Clarke and Ward L.JJ. (paras [12]–[23] and [195]–[197] respectively) have frequently been cited since.

would only interfere with a judge's findings of fact which depended on his or her view of the credibility of witnesses if satisfied that he or she was "plainly wrong".[435] However, while in some cases the judge's conclusions will be based almost entirely on oral evidence, in most cases, the position is more complex. In many, conclusions will be reached as a result partly of the view formed of the oral evidence and partly from an analysis of the documents. In others they will be based entirely or almost entirely on the document. Accordingly,

> "In appeals against conclusions of primary fact the approach of an appellate court will depend upon the weight to be attached to the findings of the judge and that weight will depend upon the extent to which, as the trial judge, the judge has an advantage over the appellate court; the greater that advantage the more reluctant the appellate court should be to interfere."[436]

On the other hand,

> "some conclusions of fact are not conclusions of primary fact of the kind to which I have just referred. They involve an assessment of a number of different factors which have to be weighed against each other. This is sometimes called an evaluation of the facts and is often a matter of degree upon which different judges can legitimately differ. Such cases may be closely analogous to the exercise of a discretion and, in my opinion, appellate courts should approach them in a similar way."[437]

Accordingly,

> "so far as the appeal raises issues of judgment on unchallenged primary findings and inferences, this court ought not to interfere unless it is satisfied that the judge's conclusion be outside the bounds within which reasonable disagreement is possible."[438]

But even here, there is room for variability:

> " . . . the standards applied by the law in different contexts vary a great deal in precision and generally speaking, the vaguer the standard and the greater the number of factors which the court has to weigh up in deciding whether the standards have been met, the more reluctant an appellate court will be to interfere with the trial judge's decision."[439]

Overall therefore,

> " . . . there is no single standard which is appropriate in every case. The most important variables include the nature of the evaluation required, the

---

[435] para.[12], citing *National Justice Cia Naviera SA v Prudential Assurance Co Ltd* [1995] 1 Lloyd's Rep. 455, *per* Stuart-Smith L.J. at 458–459.

[436] para.[15].

[437] para.[16].

[438] Mance L.J. in *Todd v Adam* [2002] 2 All E.R. (Comm) 97 at [129], cited by Clarke L.J. at para.[17].

[439] Buxton L.J. in *Norowzian v Arks Ltd (No.2)* [2000] F.S.R. 363, 370, cited by Clarke L.J. at para.[18].

standing and experience of the fact-finding judge or tribunal, and the extent to which the judge or tribunal had to assess oral evidence."[440]

A further point is that where the appeal court finds that the judge's findings of primary fact are unsustainable, it must carry out its own evaluation and is not to be inhibited by the judge's evaluation.[441]

Where the trial is conducted with a jury, the powers of the Court of Appeal are more limited. A verdict will be set aside if the evidence was such that no jury properly directed could reasonably have returned it.[442]

(2) *Awards of damages.* The Court of Appeal will not vary an award of **18–034** damages merely because the judges sitting on the appeal would have awarded a different figure. It will only do so:

" . . . if satisfied that the judge has acted on a wrong principle of law or has misapprehended the facts, or has, for those or other reasons, made a wholly erroneous estimate of the damage suffered."[443]

In practice, the Court of Appeal is much more likely to interfere with an award of damages than a finding of fact, especially where, as with large personal injuries awards, complex calculations are necessary.

Where damages were assessed by a jury, the Court of Appeal was only prepared to interfere with an award where it was "so excessive or so inadequate that no 12 reasonable jurors could reasonably have awarded it".[444] The consequence of this cautious approach was that awards of significantly different amounts in similar cases were permitted to stand. This was one of the factors in the move away from trial by jury in civil cases.[445] In *Ward v James*,[446] Lord Denning M.R. said[447]:

"In future this court will not feel the same hesitation as it formerly did in upsetting an award of damages by a jury. If it is out of all proportion to the circumstances of the case (that is, if it is far too high or far too low), this court will set it aside."

This approach appears to bring the position closer to that applied to awards by judges. In *Sutcliffe v Pressdram Ltd*[448] the Court of Appeal set aside a libel award of £600,000 to the wife of the so-called "Yorkshire Ripper". The traditional approach was followed, and it was not regarded as having been changed by *Ward v James*.[449]

---

[440] *per* Robert Walker L.J. in *Bessant v South Cone Incorporated* [2003] R.P.C. 101, at para.[12] (should be a real but not the highest degree of reluctance to interfere with decision of hearing officer in complex patents case).
[441] Dyson L.J. in *Collier v Williams* [2006] EWCA Civ 20, at para.[94].
[442] See below, para.18–037.
[443] *per* Morris L.J. in *Scott v Musial* [1959] 2 Q.B.
[444] *ibid.* pp.437–438.
[445] See above, para.15–007.
[446] [1966] 1 Q.B. 273.
[447] *ibid.* p.301.
[448] [1991] 1 Q.B. 153.
[449] *op. cit.* n.446. A majority of the Court of Appeal regarded the jury in the *Sutcliffe* case as having wrongly included an award of exemplary damages. Mrs Sutcliffe settled the case for £60,000.

The Court of Appeal may substitute an award of damages for that made by a judge. If the award was made by a jury the position formerly was that the Court of Appeal could only vary an award with the consent of the parties[450]: otherwise it had to order a new trial, which could be by judge alone. However, there is now power to make rules of court enabling the Court of Appeal in specified cases to substitute an award for that made by the jury.[451] Accordingly, it was provided that in any case where the Court of Appeal has power to order a new trial on the ground that damages awarded by a jury are excessive or inadequate, the court may instead of so ordering substitute such sum as appears to it to be proper.[452]

18–035   (3) *Exercises of discretion*. On many matters, a decision may be left to an exercise of the judge's discretion. Where the matter is then taken to the Court of Appeal, that court will only interfere with the judge's exercise of discretion if he or she has erred in law, applied an incorrect principle, misapprehended the facts, taken irrelevant matters into consideration or ignored relevant considerations, or if the court is satisfied that the decision was wrong.[453] This is not regarded as enabling the Court of Appeal to interfere merely because the judges sitting on the appeal would have exercised the discretion differently.[454] An example is *Charles Osenton & Co v Johnston*,[455] where the House of Lords reversed an order for trial by an official referee on the ground that the judge had not given sufficient weight to the point that the professional reputation of surveyors was at stake.

In addition, modern statutes commonly leave decisions on substantive as distinct from procedural matters to the discretion of judges. Examples include awards under the Inheritance (Provision for Family and Dependants) Act 1975, financial provision after divorce and decisions concerning custody of and access to children. The same principles have been applied to the role of the Court of Appeal here,[456] and it has been stressed that the court should be particularly unwilling to interfere where the exercise of discretion is based on the impression made by a person in the witness box.[457]

However, in custody cases there has been a difference between: (1) those who take the view that the appellate court should only interfere where the judge has erred in law, taken some irrelevant matter into account or failed to take some relevant matter into account, or where the decision is "plainly wrong" in the

---

[450] RSC Ord.59, r.11(4).

[451] Courts and Legal Services Act 1990, s.8.

[452] Ord.59, r.11(4), as substituted by SI 1990/2599; see now CPR r.52.10(3). See *Rantzen v Mirror Group Newspapers Ltd* [1994] Q.B. 670, where the CA reduced a libel award from £250,000 to £110,000, the court noting that it should scrutinise large awards of damages more closely than hitherto in the context of the protection of freedom of expression by Art.10, ECHR; *John v Mirror Group Newspapers Ltd* [1997] Q.B. 586, where the CA reduced an award of £350,000 to £75,000, and held that in future juries could be referred by way of comparison to the conventional compensation scales in personal injury cases, as well as previous libel awards, and both judge and counsel could indicate to the jury the level of award they thought appropriate; *Kiam II v MGN Ltd* [2003] Q.B. 281.

[453] *Evans v Bartlam* [1937] A.C. 473. This is regarded as broader than the tests applied by the court in reviewing exercises of administrative discretion under the principles stated in the *Wednesbury* case (see below, para.18–050): *Tsai v Woodworth, The Times*, November 30, 1983.

[454] *per* Viscount Simon L.C. in *Charles Osenton & Co v Johnston* [1942] A.C. 130 at 138.

[455] *ibid.*

[456] See, e.g. *In re Thornley, Deed* [1969] 1 W.L.R. 1037; *Preston v Preston* [1982] Fam. 17.

[457] *B v W (Wardship: Appeal)* [1979] 1 W.L.R. 1041.

sense that no reasonable judge could have so decided[458]; and (2) those who take the view that, in addition, the appellate court may interfere on the ground that the judge's decision is "plainly wrong" as a consequence of erring in the course of balancing the relevant factors.[459] The House of Lords in *G v G (Minors: Custody Appeal)*[460] clearly endorsed the second school of thought. It expressly rejected as too narrow the "no reasonable judge" formulation: this was based on the "*Wednesbury* unreasonableness" principle[461] applicable to judicial control over the decision of an administrative body, and was not the appropriate test here. The distinction between the tests was admittedly "a fine one".[462] Furthermore, it was clear that even under the less restricted approach approved by the House of Lords, the Court of Appeal would only exceptionally interfere with a decision where it could not point to an error of law or to a particular factor that should (or should not) have been taken into account: i.e. only in a case where the judge had "exceeded the generous ambit within which a reasonable disagreement is possible".[463] Another formulation that is increasingly being cited frequently is that of Lord Woolf M.R. in *AEI Rediffusion Music Ltd v Phonographic Reformers Ltd*[464]:

> "Before the court can interfere it must be shown that the judge has either erred in principle in his approach or has left out of account or has taken into account some feature that he should, or should not, have considered, or that his decision was wholly wrong because the court is forced to the conclusion that he has not balanced the factors fairly in the scale."

A further point made by the House of Lords in *G v G (Minors: Custody Appeal)* was that the principles set out are generally applicable to all judicial exercises of discretion: appeals concerning the welfare of children do not form a special category.[465] The principles have subsequently been cited in connection with financial provision after divorce,[466] the award of costs[467] and the grant of injunctions,[468] and have been held to be relevant under the CPR.[469] The adherents of both schools were agreed that the Court of Appeal may not interfere merely

---

[458] Stamp L.J. dissenting, in *Re F (A Minor) (Wardship: Appeal)* [1976] Fam. 238 at 249–255; Sir John Arnold P. in *Clode v Clode* (1982) 3 F.L.R. 360 at 363.

[459] *Re O (Infants) (Wardship: Appeal)* [1971] Ch. 748; Browne and Bridge L.JJ. in *Re F (A Minor) (Wardship: Appeal)* [1976] Fam. 238; *B v W (Wardship: Appeal)* [1979] 1 W.L.R. 1041; *D v M (Minor: Custody Appeal)* [1983] Fam. 33.

[460] [1985] 1 W.L.R. 647. See J. Eekelaar, (1985) 48 M.L.R. 704; C. Forder and R. Ward, "Child Custody Appeals: the Search for Principle" [1987] C.L.J. 489; S. P. de Cruz, (1986) 130 S.J. 563.

[461] Below, para.18–050.

[462] [1985] 1 W.L.R. 647 at 656, *per* Lord Bridge.

[463] *per* Lord Fraser at 652, based on Asquith L.J. in *Bellenden (formerly Satterthwaite) v Satterthwaite* [1948] 1 All E.R. 343 at 345. The point that this formulation should not apply where there is an error of law or principle is emphasised by Eekelaar, and by Forder and Ward, *op. cit.* n.460 above. Most of the post-*G v G* cases in which an appeal has been allowed have been characterised as involving errors of principle, rather than errors in balancing the relevant factors.

[464] [1999] 1 W.L.R. 1507, 1523.

[465] *ibid.* at 651, *per* Lord Fraser.

[466] *Morris v Morris* [1985] 1 F.L.R. 1176; *Mason v Mason* [1986] 2 F.L.R. 212; *Allen v Allen* [1986] 2 F.L.R. 265; *Whiting v Whiting* [1988] 1 W.L.R. 565.

[467] *Hawkins v Dhawan* (1987) 19 H.L.R. 232.

[468] *Att.-Gen. v Guardian Newspapers Ltd* [1987] 1 W.L.R. 1248.

[469] See above, para.18–026.

because the members of that court would have exercised the discretion differently.[470]

If an appellate court wishes to vary a discretionary order, it may either substitute an appropriate order, remit the case to the judge (or to another judge) or, in exceptional cases, hear evidence in order to resolve any doubts.[471]

18–036   (4) *Questions of law.* Here, the Court of Appeal may simply substitute its opinion for that of the court below.

18–037   (5) *New trial.* Section 17 of the Supreme Court Act 1981 provides that applications for a new trial of any matter tried in the High Court must normally be directed to the Court of Appeal. However, rules of court may prescribe cases or classes of cases where applications are to be made to the High Court: such cases can only be those where trial was by a judge alone and no error of the court at the trial is alleged.[472]

Where a case is tried by judge alone, the proper course for a dissatisfied party is normally[473] to appeal. On an appeal, the Court of Appeal may, as we have noted, correct any error of fact or law and may vary the judgment. However, in some cases it may be appropriate for the Court of Appeal to order a new trial.[474] This may be so where, for example, the essence of the complaint is that there has not been a fair trial. For example, a party may be "taken by surprise" where a case is called on for hearing unexpectedly, or develops in a wholly unexpected manner. Similarly, a new trial may be ordered where fresh evidence is discovered,[475] or a witness confesses that his or her evidence was false,[476] or in cases of misconduct by the judge[477] or counsel.

Where a case is tried by a judge sitting with a jury, the proper course for a party dissatisfied is again to appeal and, where appropriate, apply for a new trial.[478] The grounds for such applications mentioned above in relation to trial by judge alone will also be relevant here. In addition, there are a number of grounds related particularly to jury trial, including misdirection of the jury, the improper admission or rejection of evidence, and claims that there was no evidence to go to the jury, that the verdict was against the weight of evidence or that the damages are excessive or inadequate.[479] There will, however, be no new trial if the court is satisfied that the jury, if rightly directed, would still have returned the same verdict.[480]

---

[470] *Re F (A Minor)*, n.459 above, at 250 (Stamp L.J.); 257–258 (Browne L.J.); *Clarke-Hunt v Newcombe* (1983) 4 F.L.R. 482 at 486–487 (Cumming-Bruce L.J.).

[471] *per* Lord Scarman in *B v W*, n.457 above, at p.1055, in relation to custody orders.

[472] e.g. where judgment has been obtained in the absence of a party: CPR r.39.3(3), (5).

[473] i.e. unless an application must be made to the High Court: n.472 above.

[474] Jurisdiction to do so is recognised by CPR r.52.10(2)(c).

[475] See above, para.18–026. *Meek v Fleming* [1961] 2 Q.B. 366 (court misled by concealment of material evidence).

[476] *Piotrowska v Piotrowski* [1958] 1 W.L.R. 798.

[477] *Jones v National Coal Board* [1957] 2 Q.B. 55, above, para.4–028, n.446.

[478] Under the CPR, applications for a new trial appear to have been subsumed into appeals. See, e.g. *McPhilemy v Times Newspapers Ltd* [2001] EWCA Civ 871. For the purposes of the rules requiring permission to be obtained, a right of appeal includes a right to apply for a new trial or to set aside a verdict, finding or judgment in any matter in the High Court tried by a jury: Access to Justice Act 1999, s.54(6).

[479] See above, para.18–034.

[480] *Rowell v Pratt* [1938] A.C. 101, 116.

A verdict supported by no evidence is regarded as erroneous in law: if it is claimed, however, that a verdict is against the weight of evidence, it will only be set aside if it was perverse in the sense that it was one that no reasonable jury could have found.[481]

A new trial may be ordered on one particular aspect of a case, without affecting the other aspects. For example, there may be a new trial on a question of damages without prejudice to a finding of liability.

(b) Appeals from the High Court to the House of Lords

In certain circumstances an appeal in a civil case may be taken directly from the **18–038** High Court (whether a single judge or a Divisional Court) to the House of Lords, "leap-frogging" the Court of Appeal. The conditions are prescribed by Pt II of the Administration of Justice Act 1969.[482]

Any of the parties to civil proceedings[483] in the High Court may apply to the trial judge[484] for a certificate to the effect that he is satisfied:

(1) that the "relevant conditions" are fulfilled in relation to his decision in the proceedings;

(2) that a sufficient case for a "leap-frog" appeal has been made out to justify an application for leave to appeal; and

(3) that all the parties consent to the grant of a certificate.[485]

Where apart from the provisions of Pt II of the 1969 Act no appeal would lie to the Court of Appeal without the leave of the trial judge or the Court of Appeal, the judge is not to grant a certificate unless it appears to the judge that apart from those provisions "it would be a proper case for granting leave".[486] The "relevant conditions" are:

(1) that a point of law of general public importance is involved in the decision; and

(2) that the point of law either—

"(a) relates wholly or mainly to the construction of an enactment or of a statutory instrument, and has been fully argued in the proceedings and fully considered in the judgment of the judge in the proceedings, or

---

[481] *Metropolitan Ry Co v Wright* (1886) 11 App. Cas. at 152; *Mechanical and General Inventions Co Ltd v Austin* [1935] A.C. 346; *Grobbelaar v News Group Newspapers Ltd* [2001] 2 All E.R. 437 (on the appeal the House of Lords held that the Court of Appeal had misinterpreted the verdict, which was therefore not perverse; an award of £1 was substituted for one of £85,000: [2002] 1 W.L.R. 3024). If it is obvious that no verdict for the plaintiff on all the available evidence could be supported, the court may save the waste of time in ordering a new trial by ordering judgment to be entered for the defendant: *Mechanical Inventions Co Ltd v Austin, ibid.*

[482] This possibility was recommended by the Evershed Committee on Supreme Court Practice and Procedure, Final Report (Cmd. 8878, 1953), paras 483–503. The Law Lords at the time were not in favour of the proposal, but attitudes had changed by the late 1960s. See L. Blom-Cooper and G. Drewry, *Final Appeal* (1972), pp.149–151.

[483] i.e. "proceedings other than proceedings in a criminal cause or matter": Administration of Justice Act 1969, s.12(8).

[484] Or Divisional Court, as the case may be: *ibid.*

[485] 1969 Act, s.12(1).

[486] *ibid.* s.15(3).

(b) is one in respect of which the judge is bound by a decision of the
Court of Appeal or of the House of Lords in previous proceedings,
and was fully considered in the judgments given by the Court of
Appeal or the House of Lords (as the case may be) in those previous
proceedings."[487]

No certificate can be granted if by virtue of any enactment no appeal would lie
from the High Court to the Court of Appeal or from the Court of Appeal to the
House of Lords, or if the decision or order of the judge was made in the exercise
of jurisdiction to punish for contempt of court.[488]

Otherwise, the judge has a discretion whether to grant a certificate,[489] and no
appeal lies from a grant or refusal.[490] The application for a certificate should
normally be made at the hearing but may be made within 14 days.[491]

If a certificate is granted any party may apply within one month to the House
of Lords for leave to appeal directly.[492] No hearing is held. The House may grant
leave "if . . . it appears . . . to be expedient to do so", whereupon no appeal will
lie to the Court of Appeal.[493] Moreover, no appeal will lie to the Court of Appeal
once a certificate is granted until either the time for an application for leave has
expired or, where an application is made, until it has been determined by the
House.[494]

The "leap-frog" procedure is used in comparatively few cases,[495] although it
does enable there to be a significant saving in time and expense if a case is
destined for the House of Lords. One of the problems is that it may be difficult
for a trial judge to perceive that a case is so destined: it may only become so in
the light of the decision in the Court of Appeal.[496]

(c) Appeals from the Court of Appeal to the House of Lords

18–039   An appeal lies from any judgment or order of the Court of Appeal to the House
of Lords, provided that leave is obtained from either court.[497] No appeal lies from
a decision of the Court of Appeal to refuse leave for an appeal to itself; such a
refusal does not constitute a "judgment or order".[498] An application for leave is

---

[487] *ibid.* s.12(3).

[488] *ibid.* s.15(1), (2), (4).

[489] *IRC v Church Commissioners for England* [1975] 1 W.L.R. 1383.

[490] 1969 Act, s.12(5).

[491] *ibid.* s.12(4).

[492] The House may grant an extension of time: *ibid.* s.13(1).

[493] *ibid.* s.13(2). The limitation only applies to a decision *or that part of a decision* on which leave
is given: *R (on the application of Jones) v Ceredigion CC* [2007] UKHL 14; [2007] 1 W.L.R.
1400.

[494] *ibid.* s.13(5).

[495] The early practice is reviewed by G. Drewry in "Leapfrogging—And a Lord Justices' Eye View
of the Final Appeal" (1973) 89 L.Q.R. 260. A recent example is *Alconbury*, above
para.8–021.

[496] e.g. as in *Cassell & Co Ltd v Broome* [1972] A.C. 1027: see above, para.1–015. The Lord
Chancellor suggested that in view of the doubts raised about the direction in *Rookes v Barnard*
[1964] A.C. 1129, the proper course would have been to wait for a case in which the point was
directly raised and suggest that the parties take *that* case directly to the House of Lords: *ibid.*
p.1053.

[497] Appellate Jurisdiction Act 1876, s.3; Administration of Justice (Appeals) Act 1934, s.1.

[498] *Lane v Esdaile* [1891] A.C. 210; *Whitehouse v The Board of Control* [1960] 1 W.L.R. 1093; *R v
Secretary of State for Trade and Industry, Ex p. Eastaway* [2000] 1 W.L.R. 2222. *Cf. Geogas S.A.
v Trammo Gas* [1991] 1 W.L.R. 776 (no appeal against grant of leave by CA).

made first to the Court of Appeal, normally immediately after judgment. It is only if leave is refused that a petition for leave may be made to the House.

Among grounds commonly given by the Court of Appeal for refusing leave to appeal are that the point concerns an interlocutory matter, the point is one of fact rather than law, the subject matter is trivial, the matter has become of academic interest only to one or both of the parties[499] and that the Court of Appeal was unanimous and not divided. On the other hand, leave is normally granted in revenue cases.[500]

Petitions to the House of Lords for leave are heard by an Appeal Committee of three Law Lords,[501] and must be lodged within one month from the date of the order of which complaint is made.[502] If the committee determines that a petition is inadmissible in that it relates to a matter outside the jurisdiction of the House,[503] it may refuse leave on that ground alone and not consider the content. If a petition is admissible, the Appeal Committee considers whether leave should be given. The test applied is whether a petition raises "an arguable point of law of general public importance which ought to be considered by the House at that time, bearing in mind that the matter will already have been the subject of judicial decision and may have already been reviewed on appeal". If it is unanimously of the opinion that leave should be refused, it is dismissed without a hearing. If the Committee is unanimous that a petition should be allowed without further proceedings, it grants leave outright. Other options are to invite the respondent to lodge written objections to the petition, and to give leave on terms. Having considered those objections, the Appeal Committee may grant leave without a further hearing. In any case in which the members are not unanimous, or where further argument is required, the petition is referred for an oral hearing by the committee.[504] The parties may appear in person or may be represented by solicitors (known as "agents" on appeals to the House) or counsel. In the case of "leap-frog" appeals from the High Court[505] the petition for leave must be lodged within one month from the date on which the necessary certificate was granted: the time can be extended. The petition is considered by the Appeal Committee without a hearing.[506] Brief reasons are given for refusing leave, but the committee does not otherwise explain its decisions.[507] Conditions may be attached to a grant of leave: this is commonly done on appeals by the Inland Revenue in tax cases, where leave is only granted if the Revenue undertake to pay the costs of the appeal for the respondent in any event. If a

---

[499] cf. *Ainsbury v Millington* [1987] 1 W.L.R. 379, where the House refused to hear arguments on this ground in a case in which leave had been granted.

[500] See L. Blom-Cooper and G. Drewry, *Final Appeal* (1972), pp.146–149.

[501] See above, para.2–073. and L. Blom-Cooper and G. Drewry, *Final Appeal* (1972), Ch.VII.

[502] House of Lords Practice Directions applicable to Civil Appeals (2007 edn), Dir.2. Petitions for leave to appeal out of time are, however, admissible, and an extension of time may be granted: *ibid.*

[503] Exclusions from jurisdiction are listed in Dir.1.14, 1.18, 1.19–1.20.

[504] *ibid.* Dir.4.

[505] See above, para.18–038.

[506] Practice Directions applicable to Civil Appeals, Dir.6.

[507] *ibid.*, Dir.4.7; Appeal Committee, 38th Report, 2002–03 H.L. 89, *Petitions for leave to appeal: reasons for the refusal of leave.* This is a change of practice; this was necessary as a matter of Community law where a question of such law was involved, and it was not thought right to discriminate between petitions that raised such questions and those that did not: *ibid.* para.8. Failure to give reasons did not violate Art.6(1), ECHR: *Nerva v UK* (Application No.42295/98), July 11, 2000: see Andrews (2003), para.38.74.

condition is imposed by the Court of Appeal, the applicant may treat this as a refusal and apply for leave to the House of Lords.

Where an application for leave to appeal has been refused, it is nevertheless possible, in exceptional cases, for a fresh application to be made and granted.[508]

An appeal must be lodged in the House of Lords within three months of the date of the order appealed from, unless the House or the court below otherwise orders, or a different period is fixed by statute.[509] Leave to appeal out of time may be obtained. Unless a certificate of public funding or legal aid certificate has been granted, or the appellant is in an appeal under the Child Abduction and Custody Act 1985 or a Minister or government department, or the respondent agrees to waive the requirement, the appellant must give security for costs in the sum of £25,000.[510]

The appeal is normally considered by an Appellate Committee of five Law Lords.[511] The parties may appear in person or be represented by counsel. Wherever possible, a "statement of the facts and issues" involved in the appeal should be agreed by the parties; disputed material should be removed from the Statement and included instead in each party's case. An Appendix of documents should also be prepared. The Statement and Appendix must be lodged within six weeks of the presentation of the appeal.[512] The parties must also each lodge a "case", being "the statement of the party's argument in the appeal", in the form of the heads of argument counsel proposes to submit.[513] All members of the Appellate Committee will have read the statement(s) and case and the judgments in the court below in advance of the hearing.

The House has noted and deprecated a tendency to expand the written cases to incorporate and develop in them detailed written arguments, supported by lengthy citations and references to numerous authorities:

> " . . . much on the same lines as the written 'briefs' submitted by the parties in appeals to appellate courts in the United States, which have resulted in oral argument playing a relatively insignificant role in the decision-making process adopted by appellate courts in that country."[514]

The pre-reading was, it was emphasised, not intended to reduce the part played by oral argument in the decision-making process. Cases should include the *heads* of argument on each issue, and only *key* authorities should be mentioned.

It has, however, been doubted whether all members of the Committee do always read all the papers in advance, and whether all the members always come

---

[508] See *Buttes Gas v Hammer* [1982] A.C. 888 (leave to appeal from [1975] Q.B. 557 in the light of related proceedings: but note the criticisms of F. A. Mann (1983) 2 C.J.Q. 320 at 325–326); *R v Home Secretary, Ex p. Khera* [1984] A.C. 74 (the House of Lords invited the appellant to re-apply for leave following their Lordships' decision to review *R v Home Secretary, Ex p. Zamir* [1980] A.C. 930).

[509] Practice Directions applicable to Civil Appeals, Dir.7. The court below can only abridge the time not extend it.

[510] *ibid.* Dir.10; Standing Order V.

[511] See above, para.2–073.

[512] *ibid.* Dirs 11–13. There should be a "succinct account of the main facts, including an account of the judicial proceedings up to that point and an account of the issues raised by the appeal".

[513] See above, para.2–073. *Practice Directions applicable to Civil Appeals*, Dir.15.

[514] *M.V. Yorke Motors v Edwards* [1982] 1 W.L.R. 444 at 446–448; reaffirmed in *G v G (Minors: Custody Appeal)* [1985] 1 W.L.R. 647. These principles now apply to the statement(s) of facts and issues: Dir.11.

to a hearing without at least a provisional conclusion in mind.[515] It would obviously be undesirable for preconceived opinions to be based on limited information. Indeed, it has been suggested that changes in the practice of both the Court of Appeal[516] and the House of Lords may inevitably transform the nature of oral argument:

" . . . which is bound to lose its force where it is no longer a dialogue in the traditional sense, but an attempt to dislodge or fortify an existing impression, however provisional it may be said to be . . . . [T]he introduction of radical changes under the heading of practice and procedure is outside the province of judges."[517]

The respective approaches of the House to question of fact, discretion and law are similar to that taken by the Court of Appeal.[518] The House "may determine what of right, and according to the law and custom of this realm, ought to be done" in relation to the appeal. Where the House reverses or varies an order of the court below, or orders anything to be done by the court below, the order of the House of Lords must be made an order of the High Court[519]: the House itself has no machinery for enforcement.

The House also has inherent jurisdiction to correct any injustice caused by an earlier order of the House, although it will not reopen any appeal save in circumstances where, through no fault of a party, he or she has been subjected to an unfair procedure. There is no question of an order being reopened just because it is thought that the first decision is wrong.[520]

4. APPEALS IN ADMINISTRATIVE LAW MATTERS

(a) Introduction

No neat classification is possible of the vast range of functions performed by **18–040** administrative authorities. Neither is it possible to discern any clear pattern in the availability of rights of appeal from administrative decisions.[521]

The Franks Committee[522] noted that:

" . . . over most of the field of public administration no formal procedure is provided for objecting or deciding on objections. . . . Of course the aggrieved individual can always complain to the appropriate administrative

---

[515] F. A. Mann, (1983) 2 C.J.Q. 320 at 327–328, 334–335.
[516] See above, paras 2–071, 18–029.
[517] F. A. Mann, above.
[518] See above, paras 18–032—18–037.
[519] See CPR *Practice Direction 40B*, para.13.
[520] *R v Bow Street Metropolitan Stipendiary Magistrate, Ex p. Pinochet Ugarte (No.2)* [1999] 1 All E.R. 577, *per* Lord Browne-Wilkinson at pp.585–586.
[521] See S.A. de Smith and R. Brazier, *Constitutional and Administrative Law* (8th edn, 1998), pp.513–514; *Law Commission Report, Administrative Law: Judicial Review and Statutory Appeals* (Law Com. No.226), Pt XII.
[522] See above, para.2–008.

authority, to his Member of Parliament, to a representative organisation or to the press. But there is no formal procedure on which he can insist. . . . It may be thought that in these cases the individual is less protected against unfair or wrong decisions [than where there is provision for a formal procedure involving a tribunal or inquiry]."[523]

Such decisions were outside the committee's terms of reference, although it did express "much sympathy" with the proposal by Professor W. A. Robson that there should be a general administrative appeal tribunal, with jurisdiction to hear not only appeals from tribunals and from Ministers after a public inquiry, "but also appeals against harsh or unfair administrative decisions in that considerable field of administration in which no special tribunal or enquiry procedure is provided".[524] The committee, however, felt that it had to consider the proposal in relation to its limited terms of reference, and that, viewed from that standpoint, the proposal was to be rejected.

Since then, the problem noted by the Franks Committee has been partly met by the establishment of "Ombudsmen" of various kinds. The Parliamentary Commissioner for Administration and Local Commissioners have power to investigate complaints that there has been injustice consequent on "malad-ministration" in central and local government.[525] The concept of "maladminis-tration" covers such matters as corruption, bias, unfair discrimination, giving misleading advice, failure to explain the reasons for a decision, losing correspon-dence and unreasonable delay. The relevant defects are mostly procedural, although where a decision is "thoroughly bad in quality" maladministration may be inferred, and in certain circumstances authorities may be required to recon-sider a rule that has caused hardship. The commissioners may not, however, question the merits of a discretionary decision taken without maladministra-tion,[526] and may not entertain a complaint in respect of which there is a right of appeal to a tribunal or a remedy by way of proceedings in a court of law, unless it is not reasonable to expect the complainant to utilise those possibilities.[527]

As to the availability of statutory appeals against administrative decisions, the late Professor de Smith noted[528] that there is in general no appeal against discretionary decisions of central government involving questions of national policy or the allocation of scarce resources, against decisions of public corpora-tions or against most discretionary decisions of local authorities on the allocation of limited resources.

However, in certain other areas of public administration, particularly where no sensitive issue of policy is involved, where questions of law may loom large or where a decision has a significant impact on individual rights of liberty or property there may be provision for an appeal.

---

[523] Cmnd. 218, pp.2–3.

[524] Cmnd. 218, p.28.

[525] See generally, de Smith and Brazier (1998), Ch.30; Sir William Wade and C. F. Forsyth, *Administrative Law* (9th edn, 2004), pp.83–108, 125–127; P. P. Craig, *Administrative Law* (5th edn, 2003). pp.233–252. There is also an office of National Health Service Commissioner (held by the PCA) and there are separate Commissioners in Northern Ireland and Wales.

[526] Parliamentary Commissioner Act 1967, s.12(3); Local Government Act 1974, s.34(3).

[527] *ibid.* ss.5(2) and 26(6) respectively.

[528] de Smith and Brazier (1998), pp.513–514.

(b) Particular areas

(i) *Regulatory functions*

Many activities are subjected to state regulation for such purposes as the protec- **18–041**
tion of public health and welfare. Certain activities are prohibited by law. Others
are permitted provided that those who participate in them register with a public
authority.[529] Yet others require a specific permission or licence from a public
authority: the ease with which a licence may be obtained, and the grounds upon
which a licence may be refused are almost infinitely variable.

Control may also be exerted by procedures for inspection. For example, health
and safety inspectors may inspect factory premises, offer advice on safety
matters, issue notices requiring the cessation of dangerous activities, and, in the
last resort, bring criminal proceedings for breaches of the law.

Decisions made in the course of regulatory procedures of this kind are
commonly subject to a statutory right of appeal to a tribunal,[530] the Crown
Court,[531] a county court[532] or, most commonly, a magistrates' court.[533]

In a small number of cases, such as decisions of the Office of Fair Trading
concerning consumer credit licensing and the supervision of estate agency work,
an appeal lies to a Minister, in these examples the Secretary of State for Trade
and Industry, who appoints a panel of independent persons to hear such
appeals.[534]

It is normal for it to be possible on such appeals to challenge a decision on the
merits as well as on any point of law. This may be so even where it is expressly
stated that the decision is "at the discretion" of the authority in question. For
example, a grant of a permit for amusements with prizes,[535] is "at the discretion
of the local authority".[536] An appeal lies to the Crown Court. In *Sagnata Ltd v
Norwich Corporation*,[537] the Court of Appeal held that the recorder at quarter
sessions (now the Crown Court) had been correct to go into the merits of a refusal
of a permit afresh on appeal, although this did not mean that he "ought not to pay
great attention to the fact that the duly constituted and elected local authority

---

[529] Registration requirements may also be imposed to raise revenue.

[530] e.g. appeals to an Employment Tribunal against an improvement or prohibition notice served by
a health and safety inspector.

[531] e.g. decisions of a chief officer of police in relation to firearms certificates and the registration of
firearms; refusal of a permit for the commercial provision of amusements with prizes; and many
decisions of justices of the peace in administrative matters: see D. Price, *Appeals* (1982),
pp.37–40.

[532] e.g. a person aggrieved by a notice requiring him or her to carry out works of repair, by a demand
for the recovery of expenses where the authority has acted in default or by a demolition or closing
order: Housing Act 1985, ss.191, 269, and Sch.10, para.6: Price (1982), pp.46–49.

[533] e.g. revocation of a LGV licence (Road Traffic Act 1988, s.119), refusal of a zoo licence (Zoo
Licensing Act 1981, s.18) or a pet shop licence (Pet Animals Act 1951, s.1).

[534] From November 2, 2000, the Secretary of State has automatically accepted the panel's recommendation, unless they have reached a conclusion that is wrong in law or new evidence comes
to light; panel members can now only be removed from office on the ground of misbehaviour or
incapacity; the changes reflecting implementation of the ECHR: *Changes to Appeals System
under the Consumer Credit Act and the Estate Agents Act* (DTI Statement, November 2, 2000);
and see DTI, *Consumer Credit Act 1974. Guide to Appeals from Licensing Decisions of the OFT*
(2003).

[535] e.g. fruit machines.

[536] Lotteries and Amusements Act 1976, Sch.3. para.7(1)(a).

[537] [1971] 2 Q.B. 614.

have come to an opinion on the matter, and ought not lightly to reverse their opinion".[538]

(ii) *Welfare benefits*

18–042   Another important sphere of state activity is that of the provision of many kinds of welfare benefits. Here, it is common for rights of appeal to be granted to a tribunal.[539]

(iii) *Tribunals*

18–043   Where a decision-making function has been entrusted to a tribunal, it is normal for there to be a further appeal on points of law, either to a special appellate tribunal such as the Social Security and Child Support Commissioners or the Employment Appeal Tribunal,[540] to the High Court or to the Court of Appeal.[541] For example, the Tribunals and Inquiries Act 1992 provides[542] for a right of appeal on a point of law to the High Court from the decisions of over 10 tribunals,[543] and there are several others for which similar provision is made by specific statutes. Appeals from tribunals to the High Court on points of law may be required to be made by means of a case stated procedure. Most lie to the Queen's Bench Division, but some, such as those against decisions of the Commons Commissioners and the Special and General Commissioners of Income Tax, lie to the Chancery Division. Appeals are generally heard by a single judge.[544] The establishment of a unified tribunal system will bring some regularity to the appellate structure.[545]

(iv) *Land use*

Given the traditional concern of the law for the protection of property rights it is perhaps not surprising that statutory rights to appeal figure prominently in respect of governmental decisions that infringe or affect property rights. Two kinds of procedure require special mention here. First, planning permission is generally necessary for "the carrying out of building, engineering, mining or other operations in, on, over or under land" or "the making of any material change in the use" of buildings or land.[546] Applications for permission are made to the local planning authority and an appeal on merits, fact or law lies against a refusal to

---

[538] *per* Lord Goddard C.J. in *Stepney Borough Council v Joffe* [1949] 1 K.B. 599 at 603, endorsed by Edmund Davies L.J. in *Sagnata, ibid.* at 637. See also *Darlington Borough Council v Paul Wakefield* (1988) 153 J.P. 481.

[539] See above, paras 2–034—2–038.

[540] See above, para.2–033.

[541] e.g. from the Lands Tribunal and the Foreign Compensation Commission.

[542] s.11. The appeal must be brought by a "party" to proceedings: i.e. a litigant and not merely a beneficiary of the litigation: *S. (a minor) v Special Educational Needs Tribunal* [1996] 1 W.L.R. 382.

[543] e.g. Employment Tribunals (for certain matters), Rent Assessment Committees and Pension Appeal Tribunals.

[544] See RSC, Ord.94, rr.8,9. (CPR Sch.1); CPR *Practice Direction Pt 52*, para.18.

[545] Above, para.2–017.

[546] Town and Country Planning Act 1990, s.55.

the Secretary of State.[547] An appeal may involve a hearing by way of a public local inquiry conducted by an inspector appointed by the Secretary of State, unless the appellant wishes simply to make written representations. The inspector may make the decision personally, except in the 30 per cent or so of larger-scale applications, where the decision is taken by the Secretary of State. An appeal thereafter lies on a point of law to the Queen's Bench Division.[548]

Secondly, there are many powers which authorise the compulsory acquisition of land. The typical procedure provides for a compulsory purchase order to be made by a local authority, subject to confirmation by a Minister. If there are objections, a hearing before an inspector must be held on behalf of the Minister. If the Minister confirms the order, the typical provision[549] governing further appeals enables a person aggrieved by the order to apply within six weeks to the High Court for the order to be quashed on the ground either:

(1) that it is "not within the powers of the Act"; or

(2) that the applicant has been substantially prejudiced by failure to comply with a requirement of the Act.

The order may not otherwise be challenged: thus the person aggrieved may not, for example, seek to challenge an order by applying for judicial review[550] whether within the six-week period or not.[551]

The first limb of the grounds of challenge purports to approximate to judicial review under the *ultra vires* doctrine,[552] although it has been given a wider interpretation by the courts. The correct approach was stated as follows by Lord Denning M.R. in *Ashbridge Investments Ltd v Minister of Housing and Local Government*[553]:

> "The court can only interfere on the ground that the Minister has gone outside the powers of the Act or that any requirement of the Act has not been complied with. Under this section it seems to me that the court can interfere with the Minister's decision if he has acted on no evidence; or if he has come to a conclusion to which on the evidence he could not reasonably come; or if he has given a wrong interpretation to the words of the statute; or if he has taken into consideration matters which he ought not to have taken into account, or vice versa; or has otherwise gone wrong in law. It is identical with the position when the court has power to interfere with the decision of a lower tribunal which has erred in point of law."

[547] Successively, the Secretary of State for the Environment, the Secretary of State for Transport, Local Government and the Regions, the Deputy Prime Minister, and the Secretary of State for Communities and Local Government.

[548] Similar arrangements apply in respect of enforcement notices issued following a breach of planning control. As to compliance with Art.6(1) of the ECHR see above, para.8–021.

[549] e.g. Acquisition of Land Act 1981, ss.23–25; Housing Act 1985, Sch.22, para.7; Town and Country Planning Act 1990, ss.287, 288. See RSC, Ord.94, rr.12, 13.

[550] See below, paras 18–046—18–059.

[551] See *Smith v East Elloe R.D.C.* [1956] A.C. 736; *R v Secretary of State for the Environment, Ex p. Ostler* [1977] Q.B. 122.

[552] See below, paras 18–047—18–050.

[553] [1965] 1 W.L.R. 1320 at 1326. Applied by the Court of Appeal in *Coleen Properties Ltd v Minister of Housing and Local Government* [1971] 1 W.L.R. 433, and subsequent cases.

This would appear to extend the grounds of challenge to include errors of law not of a kind to cause the authority to act *ultra vires*.

(v) *Appeals from Ministers*

18–044   In a small number of situations where Ministers have to determine questions which may have a significant legal content, there is a further right of appeal on a point of law (or analogous grounds) to the High Court. These include the procedures mentioned in the previous section, decisions of the Secretary of State for Trade and Industry on appeals from the Director-General of Fair Trading, and deportation decisions.[554]

(vi) *Immigration*

18–045   The impact on individual liberty of decisions to refuse entry to or to deport persons who have no legal right to enter or remain in the United Kingdom is such that a special appellate structure has been established.[555] The decisions of immigration officers or the Home Secretary, whether discretionary or not, may normally be the subject of an appeal to the Asylum and Immigration Appeal Tribunal.[556] A party to certain appeals may apply to the High Court for an order, on the ground that the AIT had made an error of law, requiring the AIT to reconsider its decision; and after reconsideration, an appeal lies, to the Court of Appeal. The permission of the AIT, or if refused the Court of Appeal, is needed.[557]

D. APPLICATIONS FOR JUDICIAL REVIEW

18–046   An appeal will only lie if expressly provided by statute. Apart from, but parallel to, any appellate structure is the control exercised by the High Court over the decisions of any statutory authority[558] with a limited jurisdiction or area of power. This "judicial" control is exercised on the basis of two doctrines. The only significant doctrine today is the *ultra vires* doctrine. The other is the power of the High Court to quash any decision within the reach of the prerogative order of certiorari if an error of law is apparent on the face of the decision-making body's record of proceedings: for this purpose it is immaterial whether the error of law is such as to cause the body to act *ultra vires*.[559] There is not the space here

---

[554] See below.
[555] Nationality, Immigration and Asylum Act 2002, Pt 5.
[556] In specified cases involving national security an appeal lies to the Special Immigration Appeals Commission under the Special Immigration Appeals Commission Act 1997, as amended.
[557] 2002 Act, ss.103A, 103B, inserted by the Asylum and Immigration (Treatment of Claimants, etc) Act 2004, s.26(6).
[558] Or bodies established under the royal prerogative: *R v Criminal Injuries Compensation Board, Ex p. Lain* [1967] 2 Q.B. 864; or otherwise performing public functions: *R v Panel on Take-Overs and Mergers, Ex p. Datafin plc* [1987] Q.B. 815.
[559] *R v Northumberland Compensation Appeal Tribunal, Ex p. Shaw* [1952] 1 K.B. 338. This doctrine is in practice obsolete.

to give more than a very brief account of the *ultra vires* doctrine, and the procedures for seeking judicial review.[560]

1. The Ultra Vires Doctrine

Public authorities are normally given a circumscribed area of authority by Parliament. The function of the courts is to ensure that such authorities, whether inferior courts, tribunals, ministers or local authorities, do not exceed any of the limits expressly set by Parliament, and that they perform any statutory duties. If that were all to be done, the *ultra vires* doctrine would simply be an exercise in statutory interpretation, and more or less straightforward as the case might be. However, the courts have in addition read certain implied limitations into governmental powers aimed at ensuring that those powers are not abused, and that decision-making processes are fair procedurally. It is assumed that these limitations are to be observed unless Parliament expressly provides otherwise.

18–047

If express or implied limits are exceeded, the body in question is said to have acted *"ultra vires"*, i.e. beyond its powers: if they are not, the body has acted *"intra vires"*. Where a decision is judicial rather than administrative[561] the term "jurisdiction" is used rather than "power", but the difference is one of terminology rather than substance. For convenience of exposition a number of different *ultra vires* situations are commonly distinguished.

The principles of judicial review are applied to bodies exercising public functions even where there is no statutory background. The theoretical foundations for judicial intervention here cannot be the *ultra vires* doctrine as such. It is then argued, first, that the substantive principles of judicial review as applied in such cases are the product of the common law (which is relatively uncontroversial) and, secondly, that this is also true when those principles are applied in areas with a statutory background (which is hotly contested).[562] The *ultra vires* theory may be easier to reconcile with parliamentary sovereignty and seems to have significant, although not universal, judicial support.[563] However, both theories recognise that the principles of judicial review may be modified or excluded from operation where Parliament legislates with the necessary specific intent to do so.

---

[560] The leading works include de Smith, Woolf and Jowell, *Judicial Review of Administrative Action* (5th edn, 1995); Sir William Wade and C. F. Forsyth, *Administrative Law* (9th edn, 2004); P. P. Craig, *Administrative Law* (5th edn); J. Goudie, M. Supperstone and P. Walter (eds), *Judicial Review* (3rd edn, 2005). For a briefer account see S. A. de Smith and R. Brazier. *Constitutional and Administrative Law* (4th edn, 1998), Chs 26, 27. On the application for judicial review, see C. Lewis, *Judicial Remedies in Public Law* (3rd edn, 2004); M. Fordham, *Judicial Review Handbook* (4th edn, 2004).

[561] These categories represent each end of a spectrum rather than two discrete categories.

[562] See, e.g. C. Forsyth (ed.), *Judicial Review and the Constitution* (2000); M. Elliott, *The Constitutional Foundations of Judicial Review* (2001) (setting out a modified *ultra vires* theory), critically reviewed by P. P. Craig and N. Bamforth, [2001] P.L. 763 (exponents of the common law theory).

[563] Lord Irvine, [1999] E.H.R.L.R. 350 at 368; Lord Steyn's exposition of the principle of legality in the context of statutory interpretation, *contra*: Lord Woolf M.R., [1995] P.L. 65; Sir John Laws, [1995] P.L. 72 at 79.

(a) Straightforward situations

18–048   In some cases a question may arise whether a particular activity falls within the scope of existing statutory authority. For example, in *Attorney-General v Fulham Corporation*[564] the establishment of a municipal laundry was held not to be within the corporation's statutory powers to provide wash-houses. The courts, however, accept that authority may be "reasonably implied" from the express provisions of a statute,[565] and, furthermore, that matters "reasonably incidental" to activities expressly or impliedly authorised will also be held to be *intra vires*.[566]

(b) Jurisdiction over fact and law

18–049   In many situations, a body may only act where it is first established that a given state of affairs exists. For example, a court or tribunal may only have jurisdiction over a certain geographical area; a rent tribunal may only have jurisdiction in respect of "leases" of "furnished" premises; there may be a monetary limit to jurisdiction. In these examples, the "preliminary", "collateral" or "threshold" question is clearly distinguishable from the "main" question the court or tribunal has to determine. Moreover, the former is determinable at the commencement of that body's hearing. The superior courts have taken the view that inferior courts and tribunals may not extend their jurisdiction by erroneous determinations of these "preliminary", "collateral" or "jurisdictional" issues, whether or not the error is one of fact or law.[567] If challenged, decisions on these points will be redetermined by the High Court on an application for judicial review.

In other cases, however, the distinction between "preliminary" and "main" questions is less easy to draw. This is particularly so where it is alleged that a tribunal with jurisdiction at the commencement of an inquiry has "wandered outside its designated territory" by misconstruing the statute which gives it power to act. This area of administrative law has been the subject of much sophisticated analysis: it has, however, been doubted whether there is any clear-cut or convincing test to distinguish "jurisdictional" questions from others. It may be that in the last resort the classification applied by a reviewing court turns more on whether that court wishes to intervene than on the application of any clear principle.

The decision of the House of Lords in *Anisminic Ltd v Foreign Compensation Commission*[568] was widely regarded as broadening significantly the range of errors of law that would be regarded as causing a tribunal to exceed its jurisdiction.

In *Pearlman v Keepers and Governors of Harrow School*[569] Lord Denning M.R. said that the traditional distinction between jurisdictional and non-jurisdictional errors should be discarded and replaced by a rule that all errors of law, as distinct from errors of fact, should be regarded as jurisditional. This view has

---

[564] [1921] 1 Ch. 440.
[565] *Baroness Wenlock v River Dee Co* (1885) 10 App.Cas.354 at 362.
[566] *Att.-Gen. v Great Eastern Railway Co* (1880) 5 App.Cas. 473 at 478.
[567] See, e.g. *R v City of London, etc. Rent Tribunal, Ex p. Honig* [1951] 1 K.B. 641.
[568] [1969] 2 A.C. 147.
[569] [1979] Q.B. 56.

been broadly endorsed by certain members of the House of Lords, but not in respect of courts whose decisions are in law "final".[570]

The Court of Appeal has recently held that unfairness arising from an error of fact can in limited circumstances give rise to a discrete ground of challenge.[571]

(c) Discretion

The courts under the *ultra vires* doctrine ensure that bodies entrusted with a discretion do not fetter it unlawfully by developing rigid rules which preclude a genuine consideration of each case on its merits or by entering contracts or other agreements incompatible with a proper exercise of discretion. Similarly, a body may not be estopped from exercising a statutory discretion and may not delegate the exercise of a discretion without express or implied statutory authority.

18–050

Furthermore, an administrative body may not "abuse" its discretion by exercising powers in bad faith or for an improper purpose, by taking account of irrelevant considerations or ignoring relevant considerations, or by making a decision that is so unreasonable that no reasonable authority could make it.[572] This last principle is sometimes termed one of "irrationality".[573] In recent years, this has been applied flexibly according to context so that:

> "the more substantial the interference with human rights, the more the court will require by way of justification before it is satisfied that the decision is reasonable"

in this sense.[574] Conversely,

> "the greater the policy content of a decision, and the more remote the subject matter of a decision from ordinary judicial experience, the more hesitant the court must necessarily be in holding a decision to be irrational".[575]

Finally, the Court of Appeal has recognised a further ground of challenge in circumstances where a public authority acts or seeks to act inconsistently with a person's legitimate expectation, and this gives rise or would give rise to substantive unfairness.[576]

(d) Natural justice

There are two basic principles of natural justice. The first, the *nemo judex in sua causa* rule, provides that no person should be a judge in his or her own cause. It

18–051

---

[570] *In Re Racal Communications Ltd* [1981] A.C. 374, *per* Lord Diplock and Lord Keith; *R v Hull University Visitor, Ex p. Page* [1993] A.C. 682. See further para.18–024 on judicial review of decisions of the county court.

[571] *E v Secretary of State for the Home Department; R v Secretary of State for the Home Department* [2004] Q.B. 1044.

[572] These principles were expounded by Lord Greene M.R. in *Associated Provincial Picture Houses Ltd v Wednesbury Corporation* [1948] 1 K.B. 223.

[573] Lord Diplock in *Council of Civil Service Unions v Minister for Civil Service* [1985] A.C. 374 at 410–414.

[574] Submission of David Pannick Q.C., approved by the Court of Appeal in *R v Ministry of Defence, Ex p. Smith* [1996] 2 W.L.R. 305 at 336, 346.

[575] Sir Thomas Bingham M.R. in *ibid.* at 337–338.

[576] *R v North and East Devon Health Authority, Ex p. Coughlan* [2001] Q.B. 213.

is applied to judicial or quasi-judicial decision and may extend beyond.[577] The rule is breached where the adjudicator has a direct financial interest[578] or is a party or associated with a party,[579] or where there is a real possibility of bias.[580]

The other, the *audi alteram partem* rule, applies to a wider range of decision-making functions and requires prior notice to be given of a decision adverse to individual interests together with an opportunity to make representations. The detailed content of this rule varies from the rigorous procedural standards expected of courts to the minimal standards of "fairness" required in respect of purely administrative decisions: the content in any given case will depend on the court's appraisal of what is appropriate in the circumstances.[581]

(e) Procedural ultra vires

18–052 The procedure to be adopted for a particular decision-making process may be expressly prescribed by statute or statutory instrument. However, the consequences of failure to observe a particular step are not commonly spelled out. The courts have traditionally drawn a distinction between *mandatory* and *directory* requirements: failure to observe a mandatory step renders the ultimate decision *ultra vires*; failure to observe a directory step does not have this effect, although in some cases "substantial compliance" may be necessary. Important safeguards such as an obligation to consult[582] or to inform a person of rights of appeal[583] are normally held to be mandatory: trivial typographical errors which do not mislead[584] are normally regarded as directory matters, although the distinction is not always easy to draw.[585] In more recent cases, the courts have emphasised that these issues do not turn simply on a generic analysis of the nature of different kinds of requirement but on the examination of the facts and context of the particular case. Key questions are: (1) Is substantial compliance sufficient and has there been substantial compliance? (2) Is the non-compliance capable of being waived? (3) If it is not capable of being waived or has not been waived, what have the consequences of non-compliance been?[586] In most cases, the courts will only quash a decision where the applicant has been prejudiced;

---

[577] See Sedley J. in *R v Secretary of State for the Environment, Ex p. Kirkstall Valley Campaign Ltd* [1996] 3 All E.R. 304.

[578] e.g. *Dimes v Grand Junction Canal Proprietors* (1852) 3 H.L. Cas. 759 (decision of Lord Cottenham L.C. set aside by the House of Lords on the ground that he held shares in the plaintiff company).

[579] *R v Bow Street Magistrate, Ex p. Pinochet Ugarte (No.2)* [2000] 1 A.C. 119, above, para.4–040.

[580] See above, para.4–040.

[581] See, e.g. *Ridge v Baldwin* [1964] A.C. 40 (dismissal of a chief constable without prior notice and a proper hearing held to be void); *R v Commission for Racial Equality, Ex p. Cottrell and Rothon* [1980] 1 W.L.R. 1580 at 1586–87 (emphasising the variable content of the *audi alteram partem* rule and the duty to act fairly); *R v Secretary of State for the Home Department, Ex p. Doody* [1994] 1 A.C. 531 (fairness may require reasons to be given for a decision).

[582] *Agricultural etc. Training Board v Aylesbury Mushrooms Ltd* [1972] 1 W.L.R. 190.

[583] *London & Clydeside Ltd v Aberdeen District Council* [1980] 1 W.L.R. 182.

[584] e.g. *R v Dacorum Gaming Licensing Committee* [1971] 3 All E.R. 666.

[585] Lord Hailsham in the *London & Clydeside* case, *op. cit.* n.611 at 183; his Lordship also suggested *obiter* that the courts should adopt a more flexible approach to this issue: this view is beginning to find favour: see, e.g. the Court of Appeal in *R v Lambeth Borough Council, Ex p. Sharp* [1987] J.P.L. 440.

[586] *R v Immigration Appeal Tribunal, Ex p. Jeyeanthan* [2000] 1 W.L.R. 354.

however, there remain some situations where this may happen without evidence of prejudice.

2. The Methods of Obtaining Judicial Review

(a) Introduction

Judicial review of judicial and administrative decisions and delegated legislation **18–053** may be sought "directly" or "collaterally". A direct challenge may be made either:

(1) by a claim for judicial review in the Queen's Bench Division where the court may award one or more of a number of remedies: namely, a quashing order (formerly certiorari), a mandatory order (formerly mandamus), a prohibiting order (formerly prohibition),[587] an injunction, a declaration, damages, restitution or the recovery of a sum due; or

(2) in an ordinary claim in the Queen's Bench or Chancery Divisions for an injunction, a declaration, or damages.

A challenge is made collaterally where the argument that an act or decision, such as a byelaw, is *ultra vires* is raised as a defence to enforcement proceedings or prosecution.[588]

A new, unified, procedure for an application for judicial review was introduced in 1978.[589] It was remodelled as part of the Woolf reforms and is now governed by the CPR Pt 54.[590] In 1982, the House of Lords held that as a general rule it would be contrary to public policy and an abuse of the process of the court for a plaintiff complaining of a public authority's infringement of his or her "public law rights" to seek redress by an ordinary action rather than an application for judicial review.[591] Private law claims against public authorities, such as actions for damages, might still be brought by ordinary proceedings.[592] The distinction between public law and private law matters was, however, very difficult to draw. After some hesitation,[593] it was held that the principle of *O'Reilly v Mackman*[594] did not prevent a defendant in criminal proceedings for breach of a byelaw raising the validity of the byelaw collaterally by way of defence at the trial.[595] Similarly, in a civil case, matters of *vires* could be raised in defence of private law

---

[587] The English labels have been introduced as part of the drive against the use of Latin terms as part of the Woolf reforms; whether this break with history will add to the general public's understanding of judicial review remedies is doubtful.

[588] See, e.g. *Kruse v Johnson* [1898] 2 Q.B. 91.

[589] RSC, Ord.53; Supreme Court Act 1981, s.31.

[590] Introduced following Sir Jeffrey Bowman's *Review of the Crown Office* (2000), with effect from October 2, 2000 (also implementation date for the Human Rights Act 1998).

[591] *O'Reilly v Mackman* [1983] 2 A.C. 237.

[592] *Davy v Spelthorne Borough Council* [1984] A.C. 262.

[593] *Quietlynn Ltd v Plymouth City Council* [1988] Q.B. 114, DC (pet.dis. [1987] 1 W.L.R. 1090, HL).

[594] *op. cit.* n.619.

[595] *R v Reading Crown Court, Ex p. Hutchinson* [1988] Q.B. 384, DC (pet.dis. [1988] 1 W.L.R. 308). The challenge was ultimately successful: *DPP v Hutchinson* [1990] 2 A.C. 783.

rights, where those rights were not dependent upon a public law decision.[596] These difficulties have now been much diminished by the reduction in the differences between ordinary procedure and judicial review procedure under the CPR.[597]

(b) Procedure on applications for judicial review

18–054   The procedure on applications for judicial review is prescribed by s.31 of the Supreme Court Act 1981 and CPR Pt 54. A "claim for judicial review" is a claim to review the lawfulness of an enactment, or of "a decision, action or failure to act in relation to a public function". The "judicial review procedure" is the procedure under CPR Pt 8, modified by Pt 54.[598] The judicial review procedure *must* be used in a claim for judicial review where the claimant is seeking a mandatory, prohibiting or quashing order or an injunction under s.30 of the Supreme Court Act 1981 restraining a person from acting in any office in which he or she is not entitled to act.[599] The judicial review procedure *may* be used in a claim for judicial review where the claimant is seeking a declaration or injunction (other than under s.30 of the 1981 Act), although it must be used if a declaration or injunction is sought in addition to one of the remedies listed in r.54.2.[600] The court may grant the declaration or injunction claimed if it considers that it would be just and convenient to do so, having regard to the nature of the matters in respect of which, and the persons and bodies against whom, mandatory, prohibiting and quashing orders may be granted, and all the circumstances of the case.[601] On a claim for judicial review the claimant may seek any of the remedies mentioned above in respect of the same matter; he or she may also claim and be awarded damages, restitution or recovery of a sum due if there is a good cause of action, although this procedure may not be used to seek damages alone.[602]

The procedure is in two stages. The claimant must first obtain permission from a High Court judge by filing a claim form in the Administrative Court Office, which must be served on the defendant and other interested parties. The application for permission is dealt with on paper, although if permission is refused (or granted on terms) the claimant may request an oral hearing.[603] The test for the grant of permission is whether the claimant has a reasonable or arguable case to

---

[596] *Wandsworth London Borough Council v Winder* [1985] A.C 461 (council tenant entitled to raise in defence to an action for arrears of rent that the council's decision to raise the rent was an *ultra vires* abuse of discretion under the *Wednesbury* principles: the argument ultimately failed: *Wandsworth London Borough Council v Winder (No.2)* (1988) 20 H.L.R. 400). In *Roy v Kensington and Chelsea and Westminster Family Practitioner Committee* [1992] 1 A.C. 624, the House of Lords held that a doctor was entitled to enforce his private law rights to remuneration (whether contractual or statutory) by an ordinary action. In *Mercury Communications Ltd v Director General of Telecommunications* [1996] 1 W.L.R. 48, Lord Slynn emphasised that flexibility should be retained in determining the limits of "public law" and "private law".

[597] Lord Woolf C.J. in *Clark v University of Lincolnshire and Humberside* [2000] 1 W.L.R. 1988.

[598] CPR r.54.1.

[599] Supreme Court Act 1981, s.31(1); CPR r.54.2.

[600] CPR r.54.3(1).

[601] 1981 Act, s.31(2).

[602] CPR r.54.3(2) as amended by SI 2003/3361, rr.13, 54.6; Supreme Court Act 1981, s.31(4), as amended by SI 2004/1033.

[603] *ibid.* r.54.12(3). A respondent who chooses to attend is unlikely to be awarded costs notwithstanding that the application for permission is rejected: *Practice Direction 54*, paras 8.4–8.6.

put forward.[604] If permission is refused after a hearing, the person seeking permission may in a civil case[605] apply to the Court of Appeal within seven days for permission to appeal. On such an application, the Court of Appeal may, instead of giving permission to appeal, give permission to apply for judicial review, and the case then proceeds in the High Court unless the Court of Appeal otherwise orders.[606] If the Court of Appeal refuses permission to appeal, there is no further appeal to the House of Lords,[607] although if the Court of Appeal does grant permission to appeal, but then refuses permission to apply for judicial review, an appeal does lie to the House of Lords.[608]

The claim form must state the remedy or remedies sought and include or be accompanied by a detailed statement of the claimant's grounds for bringing the claim, a statement of the facts relied on, and other specified documents.[609] Any person who wishes to take part in the judicial review must file an acknowledgement of service within 21 days.[610] The court may not grant permission unless it considers that the applicant has a "sufficient interest" in the matter (*locus standi* or standing): it is not necessary, however, for it to be shown that his or her legal rights are affected, and a broad rather than narrow approach is normally adopted.[611]

Once permission is granted, the case normally proceeds to a hearing in the Administrative Court, although it may with the consent of the parties be determined without a hearing.[612] A defendant and any other person served with a claim form who wishes to contest the claim or support it on additional grounds must file and serve detailed grounds and any written evidence within 35 days.[613] Furthermore, any person may apply for permission to file evidence or make representations at the hearing.[614] Evidence is normally presented in written form; cross-examination of a witness may exceptionally be permitted.[615] Interim remedies may be granted and (again exceptionally) disclosure of documents.[616]

The claim form must be filed promptly and in any event not later than three months after the grounds to make the claim first arose. The time limit may not be extended by agreement. These rules do not apply when any other enactment

---

[604] *per* Lord Diplock in *IRC v National Federation of Self-Employed and Small Businesses Ltd* [1982] A.C. 617 at 644. Permission may be refused in the exercise of the court's discretion.

[605] There is no further appeal in a criminal case (Supreme Court Act 1981, s.18(1)(a)), but the High Court may chose to grant permission, dismiss the substantive application, and certify that a question of general public importance arises, leaving the claimant to seek leave to appeal from the House of Lords: *White Book 2006*, para.54.12.4.

[606] CPR r.52.15.

[607] *Re Poh* [1983] 1 W.L.R. 2; *R v Secretary of State for Trade and Industry, Ex p. Eastaway* [2000] 1 W.L.R. 2222.

[608] *R v London Borough of Hammersmith and Fulham, Ex p. Burkett* [2002] UKHL 23; [2002] 1 W.L.R. 1593.

[609] CPR r.54.6; *Practice Direction 54*, para.5.

[610] CPR r.54.8.

[611] *IRC v National Federation of Self Employed and Small Businesses Ltd* [1982] A.C. 617; *R v H.M. Inspectorate of Pollution, Ex p. Greenpeace (No.2)* [1994] 4 All E.R. 329; *R v Secretary of State for Foreign Affairs, Ex p. World Development Movement Ltd* [1995] 1 W.L.R. 386.

[612] CPR r.54.18.

[613] CPR r.54.14.

[614] CPR r.54.17.

[615] CPR r.54.16. This disapplies CPR r.8.6(1). The court retains an inherent jurisdiction to order cross-examination in an appropriate case.

[616] CPR, Pt 25 and r.31.6.

specifies a shorter time limit.[617] The time limit may be extended by the court.[618] Where the High Court considers there has been undue delay in making a claim for judicial review, the court may refuse to grant permission on any relief sought if it considers that granting the relief sought would be likely to cause substantial hardship to, or substantially prejudice the rights of, any person, or would be detrimental to good administration.[619] A remedy may also be refused in the exercise of the court's discretion on other grounds.[620]

Where substantive judicial review proceedings are determined (one way or the other) by the High Court or the Court of Appeal, further appeals lie as in other cases.

(c) The remedies

(i) *Mandamus (mandatory order)*

18–055   The prerogative[621] order of mandamus[622] (now a mandatory order) lies to compel performance of a public (not necessarily statutory) duty. For example, it may be granted where a tribunal wrongfully declines to hear a matter that does in fact lie within its jurisdiction, or, where there has been an *ultra vires* abuse of discretion, to ensure that the matter is reconsidered according to law.[623]

(ii) *Prohibition (prohibitory order) and certiorari (quashing order)*

18–056   The prerogative orders of prohibition and certiorari[624] are similar in scope. Prohibition lies to restrain a tribunal or other authority where it is about to act *ultra vires* or to complete an *ultra vires* act already begun. Certiorari lies to quash[625] a decision already made where:

    (1) it is *ultra vires*; or

    (2) it has been obtained by fraud[626]; or

---

[617] CPR r.54.5. A claim is not necessarily made promptly when it is brought within three months: *R v Greenwich Borough Council, Ex p. Cedar Transport Group Ltd* [1983] R.A. 173. There is, however, no standard expectation that challenges to grants of planning permission be brought within six weeks, mirroring the time limit available for appeals against refusal of planning permission: *R v Hammersmith and Fulham London Borough Council, Ex p. Burkett* [2002] UKHL 23; [2002] 1 W.L.R. 1593.

[618] CPR r.3.1(2)(a).

[619] Supreme Court Act 1981, s.31(6). In *R v Diary Produce Quota Tribunal For England and Wales, Ex p. Caswell* [1990] 2 A.C. 738, the House of Lords held that where an application was not brought promptly or within three months within RSC, Ord.53, r.4, there was "undue delay" even if an extension of time had been granted, and so s.31(6) was brought into play. A decision to extend time cannot itself be reopened at the substantive hearing, although s.31(6) may be applied: *R v Criminal Injuries Compensation Board, Ex p. A* [1999] 2 A.C. 330 (in respect of Ord.53); *R v Lichfield District Council, Ex p. Lichfield Securities Ltd* [2001] EWCA Civ 3014.

[620] e.g. where the applicant is actuated by improper motives or there is another equally convenient and beneficial remedy.

[621] So called because the writ replaced by the modern order was thought to be especially associated with the Crown.

[622] Normally pronounced "mandaymus".

[623] e.g. *Padfield v Minister of Agriculture* [1968] A.C. 997.

[624] Normally pronounced "sersheeorair'eye".

[625] Not "squash," "quosh" or "gnash" (*cf. R v Pressick* [1978] Crim. L.R. 377).

[626] See *R v Wolverhamptom Crown Court, Ex p. Crofts* [1983] 1 W.L.R. 204.

(3) there is an error of law apparent on the face of the record of proceedings.

These orders were formerly confined to decisions in respect of which there was a duty to act judicially, but they may now be sought in respect of any judicial or administrative[627] (but not legislative) act.

(iii) *Declarations and injunctions*

A person may obtain a declaration on a disputed matter of law, or an injunction, whereby a party to an action is required to do or refrain from doing a particular thing.[628] These were in origin private law remedies but are today frequently sought in respect of the decisions of public authorities.

18–057

(iv) *Habeas corpus*[629]

The prerogative writ of *habeas corpus ad subjiciendum* lies to secure a person's release from wrongful imprisonment. An *ex parte* application for a writ must be made to a single judge of any Division of the High Court,[630] or to a Divisional Court of the Queen's Bench Division if the court so directs, and takes precedence over other business. In an emergency, an application may be made to a judge out of court, for example, at home at night. If *prima facie* grounds are shown by an affidavit by or on behalf of the prisoner the matter is normally adjourned for a full hearing. In exceptional cases the writ may be issued forthwith to the custodian, requiring that the prisoner be produced to the court at the time specified for the full hearing. It either event, the burden of justifying the detention lies on the custodian: if he or she fails, the prisoner's release is ordered.

18–058

The grounds for granting a writ of habeas corpus are essentially the same as for an application for judicial review. An appeal lies in civil cases as of right to the Court of Appeal and then with leave to the House of Lords. In criminal cases an appeal lies from the High Court to the House of Lords, with the leave of either.[631] An appeal may be taken from a refusal to discharge the prisoner or grant an order of release: in the latter event the person's right to remain at large cannot be affected by the outcome of the appeal.[632] After a refusal to grant habeas corpus no further application may be made on the same grounds and evidence.[633]

An application for habeas corpus is the standard method of challenging extradition decisions.

(d) Relationship between claims for judicial review and appeals

The remedies available on a claim for judicial review are discretionary, and will not be awarded if there is some equally convenient and beneficial remedy such

18–059

---

[627] *R v Hillingdon London Borough Council, Ex p. Royco Homes Ltd* [1974] Q.B. 720.

[628] See Zamir and Woolf, *The Declaratory Judgment* (3rd edn, 2002).

[629] See R. J. Sharpe, *The Law of Habeas Corpus* (2nd edn, 1989); de Smith, Woolf and Jowell, *Judicial Review of Administrative Action* (5th edn, 1995), pp.672–681; RSC Ord.54.

[630] An application by a parent or guardian in respect of the custody, care or control of a child lies to the Family Division: RSC, Ord.54, r.11.

[631] Administration of Justice Act 1960, ss.1, 15(3).

[632] *ibid.* s.15(1)(4), as amended by the Access to Justice Act 1999, s.65(2)(a). In criminal cases an order may be made providing for the continued detention as amended by *ibid.* of the defendant or directing that he or she shall not be released except on bail: *ibid.* s.5.

[633] *ibid.* s.14(2).

as a right of appeal. However, an appeal to a Minister against a planning condition will not, for example, be regarded as convenient as certiorari where the issue is purely one of law.[634] Indeed, it has sometimes been stated that a claim for judicial review must be made where a challenge is based on the *ultra vires* doctrine, rather than exercising a right to appeal on a point of law.[635]

Conversely, a claim for judicial review will be less appropriate than an appeal by case stated where complicated findings of fact are involved,[636] and will not be entertained in respect of points arising in the course of trials or committal proceedings[637]: such proceedings must be concluded before any challenge can take place, whether by appeal or application for judicial review.

Statutory provisions may purport to exclude or restrict judicial review. For example, the Crown Court is made amenable to the supervisory jurisdiction of the High Court in respect of matters other than those relating to trial on indictment.[638]

A claim for judicial review may be made to challenge a sentence or order on the ground that it is harsh or oppressive,[639] this being regarded as a sentence that is so much greater than normal standards as to constitute an excess of jurisdiction or an error of law.[640]

E. REFERENCES TO THE EUROPEAN COURT OF JUSTICE[641]

18–060   One of the major functions of the Court of Justice of the European Communities[642] is that of ensuring consistency in the decision-making of national courts

---

[634] *R v Hillingdon London Borough Council, Ex p. Royco Homes Ltd* [1974] Q.B. 720.

[635] *Metropolitan Properties Co v Lannon* [1968] 1 W.L.R. 815; *Chapman v Earl* [1968] 1 W.L.R. 1315; *Henry Moss Ltd v Customs and Excise Commissioners* [1981] 2 All E.R. 86 at 90 (*per* Lord Denning M.R.), criticised by A. W. Bradley, [1981] P.L. 476; *contra, Elliott v Brighton Borough Council* (1980) 79 L.G.R. 506.

[636] *R v Crown Court at Ipswich, Ex p. Baldwin* [1981] 1 All E.R. 596.

[637] *R v Wells Street Stipendiary Magistrate, Ex p. Seillon* [1978] 1 W.L.R. 1002 (committal proceedings); *R v Rochford JJ., Ex p. Buck* (1978) 68 Cr.App.R. 114 (summary trial).

[638] Supreme Court Act 1981, s.29(3); *R v Sheffield Crown Court, Ex p. Brownlow* [1980] Q.B. 530 (jury vetting order held to relate to trial on indictment); J. Kodwo Bentil, (1988) 152 J.P.N. 323.

[639] *R v St Albans Crown Court, Ex p. Cinnamond* [1981] Q.B. 480; *R v Tottenham JJ., Ex p. Joshi* [1982] 1 W.L.R. 631. It has been suggested that *Cinnamond* was wrongly decided (Watkins L.J. in *Arthur v Stringer* (1986) 84 Cr.App.R. 361 at 368), or should at least be confined to cases where the sentence is "truly astonishing" (Watkins L.J. in *R v Crown Court at Croydon, Ex p. Miller* (1986) 85 Cr.App.R. 152 (decided before *Arthur v Stringer*)). The court may, however, refuse in the exercise of its discretion to entertain an application for judicial review if a right to appeal against sentence has not been exercised: *R v Battle Magistrates' Court, Ex p. Shepherd* (1983) 5 Cr.App.R.(S) 124.

[640] *R v DPP, Ex p. McGeary* [1999] Crim. L.R. 430.

[641] D. W. K. Anderson *et al.*, *References to the European Court* (2nd edn, 2002); L. Collins, *European Community Law in the United Kingdom* (4th edn, 1990), Ch.3; T. C. Hartley, *The Foundations of European Community Law* (5th edn, 2003), Ch.9; L. N. Brown and T. Kennedy, *The Court of Justice of the European Communities* (5th edn), Ch.10; H. G. Shermers, *et al.* (eds), *Art.177 EEC: Experiences and Problems* (1987); A. Arnull, "The Use and Abuse of Art.177 EEC" (1989) 52 M.L.R. 622, "References to the European Court" (1990) 15 E.L. Rev. 375 and (1993) 18 E.L. Rev. 129; C. Barnard and E. Sharpston, (1997) 34 C.M.L. Rev. 1113; D. O'Keefe, (1998) 23 E.L. Rev. 509; L. Heffernan, (2003) 52 I.C.L.Q. 907.

[642] See above, paras 2–076—2–082.

in community law matters. The governing provision in the EC Treaty is Art.234 EC (ex Art.177):

> "(1) The Court of Justice shall have jurisdiction to give preliminary rulings concerning:
>
> (a) the interpretation of this Treaty;
> (b) the validity and interpretation of acts of the institutions of the Community and of the European Central Bank;
> (c) the interpretation of the statutes of bodies established by an act of the Council, where those statutes so provide.
>
> (2) Where such a question is raised before any court or tribunal of a Member State, that court or tribunal may, if it considers that a decision on the question is necessary to enable it to give judgment, request the Court of Justice to give a ruling thereon.
> (3) Where any such question is raised in a case pending before a court or tribunal of a Member State, against whose decisions there is no judicial remedy under national law, that court or tribunal shall bring the matter before the Court of Justice."

It should be noted that the reference procedure is not strictly an appeal: the decision to refer is taken by the national court and not a party and the court will only rule on the point of Community law raised and remit the case to the national court to apply the law to the facts of the case. Once the ruling has been made, full effect must be given to it by the English court, and if necessary a party must be allowed to argue a point not previously raised that arises from the ruling.[643] In some cases new issues arising from a ruling may necessitate a second reference.[644] We now examine the elements of Art.234 EC in more detail.

1. THE MATTERS THAT MAY BE REFERRED

The Court may give rulings concerning: (1) the interpretation of Treaty provisions[645]; and (2) the interpretation and validity of acts of the Community **18–061**

---

[643] *Astley v North Wales Training and Enterprise Council Ltd (trading as Celtec Ltd)* [2006] UKHL 29, [2006] I.C.R. 992.

[644] *Marks and Spencer plc v Customs and Excise Commissioners* [2005] UKHL 53, [2005] S.T.C. 1254.

[645] Art.177(l)(a) (now Art.234(1)(a)) EC covers the EC Treaty and all Treaties amending or supplementing it: subsidiary conventions are not covered: Case 44/84, *Hurd v Jones (Inspector of Taxes)* [1986] E.C.R. 29 (agreement between the Member States setting up European Schools in Community Countries not within Art.177): see L. N. Brown, (1986) 23 C.M.L. Rev. 895; Case 152/83, *Demouche v Fonds de Garantie Automobile* [1987] E.C.R. 3833 (agreement between national bureaux of motor vehicle insurers not within Art.177, notwithstanding that it implemented a Council Directive). The Court may also interpret the final provisions of the Maastricht Treaty Arts 46 to 53, and those parts that amend other treaties (Art.46 of the EU Treaty); see further below.

institutions (certainly the Council[646] and Commission and probably the Parliament and the Court itself[647]). Where, however, the act of the Council in question is the "statute" regulating the operation of an institution or body established by the Council, the court may only give a ruling if the statute so provides, and the ruling may only concern interpretation, not validity.[648] The task of "interpretation" is taken to include that of determining whether a provision is directly effective.[649] A question of validity *must* be referred as the European Court has the exclusive jurisdiction to rule on such a question.[650]

An additional jurisdiction to give preliminary rulings has been conferred on the Court by Art.68 EC (ex Art.73p) in respect of Title IV (ex Title IIIa) of the EC Treaty (visas, asylum, immigration and other policies related to free movement of persons).[651] Questions on the interpretation of Title IV or on the validity or interpretation of acts of Community institutions based on Title IV raised in a case pending before a final court or tribunal within Art.234(3) EC (ex Art.177(3)) can be referred by that court on the same basis as for other references. Lower courts cannot refer these matters. Furthermore, the Court of Justice is expressly excluded from ruling on any measure or decision taken pursuant to Art.62(1) relating to the maintenance of law and order and the safeguarding of internal security.[652] Finally, the Council, Commission or a Member State may request the Court to give a ruling on a question of interpretation of Title IV or the acts of Community institutions based on Title IV. Such a ruling is not to apply to judgments of courts or tribunals of the Member States which have become *res judicata*. These provisions do not, however, apply to the UK or Ireland.[653]

A further jurisdiction to give preliminary rulings arises in respect of Title VI of the Treaty of European Union (third pillar of the Treaty, narrowed by the Treaty of Amsterdam to cover only criminal issues). This, however, only arises where a Member State accepts that jurisdiction. The ruling may be on the validity and interpretation of framework decisions and decisions on the interpretation of conventions established under Title VI, and on the validity and interpretation of the measures implementing them.[654]

---

[646] The Court has asserted jurisdiction under Art.177 to interpret agreements between the Community and non-Member States, concluded on behalf of the Community by the Council: Case 181/73, *Haegeman v Belgium* [1974] E.C.R. 449 (Association Agreement between the EEC and Greece); or even agreements involving Member States to which the Community is not formally a party: Cases 267–269/81, *SPI* [1983] E.C.R. 801 (General Agreement on Tariffs and Trade). For criticism, see Hartley (2003), pp.273–276.

[647] Although a preliminary ruling is not itself an act that can be questioned on an application for a further preliminary ruling: Case 69/85, *Wunsche Handelsgesellschaft v Germany* [1986] E.C.R. 947: see G. Bebr (1987) 24 C.M.L. Rev. 719; this does not prevent the national court making a subsequent reference in the same proceedings: *ibid.*; Case 14/86, *Pretore di Salo v Persons Unknown* [1989] 1 C.M.L.R. 71.

[648] Art.234(1)(a) EC (ex Art.177(1)(c)).

[649] See above, paras 5–043—5–045.

[650] This was expressly provided by Art.41 ECSC, and the same position has been reached as regards the EC by the Court in Cases 314/85, *Firma Foto Frost v Haupzollant Lübeck-Ost* [1988] 3 C.M.L.R. 57, applied in *R v Ministry of Agriculture, Fisheries and Food, Ex p. FEDESA* [1988] 3 C.M.L.R. 661.

[651] Articles 61–69EC (ex Art.73i–73q). This was added by the Treaty of Amsterdam and contains material transferred from the Justice and Home Affairs Cooperation pillar of the EU.

[652] "This seems an extraordinary departure from the rule of law": Weatherill and Beaumont (1999), p.658.

[653] Protocol on the position of the United Kingdom and Ireland annexed by the Treaty of Amsterdam to the Treaty on European Union and the EC Treaty.

[654] Art.35(l)–(4) (ex K.7) of the EU Treaty. There is also a jurisdiction under Title VII (provisions

2. "ANY COURT OR TRIBUNAL"

Article 234(2) EC (ex Art.177(2)) provides that "any court or tribunal" may refer **18–062** a question if the conditions stated are applicable. In the United Kingdom, procedural rules have been made governing references from the county court, the High Court and the Court of Appeal (Civil Division),[655] the Court of Appeal (Criminal Division),[656] the Crown Court,[657] Employment Tribunals,[658] and the Competition Appeal Tribunal.[659] However, it is clear that magistrates' courts[660] and statutory tribunals[661] have power to refer matters to the Court of Justice even though no procedural rules have been made. The meaning of the expression "court or tribunal" will in the last resort be determined by the Court of Justice, and the title of an institution and its status in national law is not decisive.[662] It seems that any institution which exercises judicial or quasi-judicial functions and which has at least "a measure of official recognition"[663] will be included, and not, therefore, bodies whose functions are advisory,[664] investigatory, conciliatory, legislative or executive,[665] and not arbitrators[666] or (probably) domestic tribunals which exercise jurisdiction solely by virtue of a contractual arrangement between the parties.[667] The Court takes account of a number of factors

> "such as whether the body is established by law, whether it is permanent, whether its jurisdiction is compulsory, whether its procedure is *inter partes*, whether it applies rules of law and whether it is independent."[668]

on closer co-operation of Member States that wish to use EU mechanisms to do so): Art.46(C) of the EU Treaty).

[655] CPR Pt 68 and *Practice Direction 68*.

[656] Criminal Procedure Rules 2005 (SI 2005/384), r.75.1.

[657] Crown Court Rules 1982 (SI 1982/1109), r.29; CPR r.75.1.

[658] Employment Tribunals (Constitution and Rules of Procedure) Regulations 2004 (SI 2004/1861), r.58.

[659] Competition Appeal Tribunal Rules 2003 (SI 2003/1372), r.60.

[660] See, e.g. *R v Plymouth JJ., Ex p. Rogers* [1982] Q.B. 863.

[661] e.g. references have been made by the Employment Appeal Tribunal, a National Insurance Commissioner, Social Security Commissioners, Special Income Tax Commissioners, Value Added Tax Tribunals, a Northern Ireland industrial tribunal, an immigration adjudicator and an appointed person under the Trade Marks Act 1994.

[662] See W. Alexander and E. Grabandt, (1982) 19 C.M.L. Rev. 413; Case 61/65 *Vaassen* [1966] E.C.R. 261; Case 36/73 *Nederlandse Spoorwegen* [1973] E.C.R. 1299; Case 138/80 *Borker* [1980] E.C.R. 1975; Case 246/80 *Broekmeulen* [1981] E.C.R. 2311; Case 102/81 *Nordsee v Reederei Mond* [1982] E.C.R. 1095.

[663] e.g. supervision or regulation by a Minister: *Vaassen* and *Broekmeulen*, above.

[664] The fact that functions are technically advisory will not prevent the institution from being regarded as a "court or tribunal" if in reality it operates as a judicial body; accordingly, the Dutch *Road van State* (Council of State), in practice the supreme administrative court, has been held to be within Art.177: *Nederlandse Spoorwegen*, n.690 above. By contrast, the *commissione consultiva per la infrazioni valutarie* (Consultative Commission for Currency Offences), which gives reasoned opinions to the Italian Treasury on sanctions to be imposed for foreign exchange violations, was held not to fall within Art.177 in Case 318/85 *Criminal Proceedings Against Undterweger* [1986] E.C.R. 955: its opinions were not binding on the Treasury Minister.

[665] e.g. the professional association of the Paris Bar: *Borker*, n.662 above.; or the Luxembourg Director of Taxation: Case C–24/92 *Corbiau v Administration des Contributions* [1993] E.C.R. I–1227 (although entertaining a complaint against tax authorities, the Director was not an independent third party).

[666] *Nordsee*, n.690 above: See G. Bebr, (1985) 22 C.M.L. Rev. 489; C. M. Schmitthoff, (1987) 24 C.M.L. Rev. 143.

[667] Hartley (2003), pp.278–282.

[668] Case C–54/96, *Dorsch Consult Ingenieurgesellschaft mbH v Bundesbaugesellschaft Berlin mbH*

The approach of the Court seems to be becoming stricter, particularly by reference to the need for independence.[669]

Where a court or tribunal performs both judicial and non-judicial functions in respect of particular proceedings (e.g. as examining magistrate and public prosecutor), the Court of Justice will accept a reference from it in the first of those capacities.[670] The expression "court or tribunal of a Member State" extends to the courts of dependent territories to which at least the general institutional provisions (and possibly any provisions) of the EC Treaty apply.[671]

3. THE POWER TO REFER

18–063 Where any "question" within the scope of the preliminary rulings procedure is "raised before" any national court or tribunal that body may, "if it considers that a decision on the question is necessary to enable it to give judgment", refer the question to the European Court.

(a) "Question . . . raised before"

18–064 The question can be raised by a party or by the court itself.[672] Moreover, it is immaterial that the parties take the same position on the point of Community law.[673] The question for reference will be formulated by the national court, although the Court of Justice will confine itself to ruling on matters of *interpretation* and *validity*: it will not rule on the *application* of Community law to the facts or the compatibility of national law with Community law even if requested to do so. The Court will reformulate questions put too widely, and may even formulate the question for itself if the national court fails to do so.[674]

(b) "A decision on the question is necessary to enable it to give judgment"

18–065 This wording makes it clear that the material issue is whether a *decision* on the point of Community law is necessary and not whether a *reference* is necessary.

[1997] E.C.R. 1–4961, para.23 (holding that the German Federal Public Procurement Awards Supervisory Board, which made binding decisions, although not after *inter partes* hearings, on appeals from lower bodies concerning public procurement procedures, was able to make a reference); *cf.* Case C–516/99, *Schmid* [2002] E.C.R. I–4573, (appeal chamber of regional finance authority held to be insufficiently independent to be a court or tribunal); Case C–182/00 *Lutz GmbH* [2002] E.C.R. I–547 (Austrian commercial court exercising function of maintaining a register of companies not dealing with a dispute and so not exercising a judicial function or a court or tribunal).

[669] See A.G. Ruiz-Jarabo Colomer in Case C–259/04, *Emanuel v Continental Shelf 128 Ltd*, Opinion delivered on January 19, 2006, at para.26, citing *Schmidt* (below) and Case C–53/03, *Syfait* [2005] E.C.R. I–4609 (reference from Greek Competition Commission declared inadmissible).

[670] Case 14/86 *Pretore di Salo v Persons Unknown* [1987] E.C.R. 2545.

[671] Case C–355/89 *Barr and Montrose Holdings* [1991] E.C.R. I–3479 (courts of the Isle of Man).

[672] See, e.g. CPR r.68.2(1).

[673] Advocate-General Slynn in Case 244/801 *Foglia v Novello (No.2)* [1981] E.C.R. 3045 at 3071–3072.

[674] This was done in Case 6/64, *Costa v E.N.E.L.* [1964] E.C.R. 585; however, the Court may be unable to do so: Case 14/86, *Pretore di Salo v Persons Unknown* [1987] E.C.R. 2545, where the Court could not make anything of a very general question posed by the Italian court.

The Court of Justice will not normally review the decision of the national court that a reference should be made,[675] although in exceptional circumstances it may decline to accept a reference on the ground that the matter has not arisen in real, genuine, litigation: it is not willing to render advisory opinions, of academic interest only, on "general or hypothetical questions".[676] Accordingly, the Court has now said that the national court should state in its order for reference the reasons for which it considers it necessary to obtain a preliminary ruling, unless these can be clearly deduced from the file on the case,[677] and some explanation of the reasons for the choice of the Community provisions of which it requests an interpretation and their relationship to the applicable national law.[678] Furthermore, the Court will not rule on questions clearly irrelevant to the issues before the national court.[679]

Essentially, the decision to refer is for the national court or tribunal. However, in the *Rheinmuhlen* cases the Court of Justice held that: (1) "a rule of national law whereby a court is bound on points of law by the rulings of a superior court cannot deprive the inferior courts of their power to refer... questions" to the Court,[680] but that (2) Art.177 does not preclude a decision of an inferior court to refer a question "from remaining subject to the remedies normally available under national law".[681] This suggests that any attempt to fetter the discretion of a court under Art.234(2) EC (ex Art.177(2)) will be contrary to Community law. Nevertheless, in *Bulmer v Bollinger*[682] Lord Denning M.R. laid down certain "guidelines", which have been relied upon in a number of cases since, but which have also, in some respects, been the subject of widespread criticism, not least on the basis that they may constitute "fetters" which are contrary to Community law.[683] His Lordship set out the guidelines in two groups: (1) guidelines as to whether a decision is "necessary"; and (2) guidelines as to the exercise of the "discretion" to refer. He regarded the question of "necessity" as a condition precedent to the exercise of the discretion and, presumably, as raising matters of law or jurisdiction rather than discretion.[684] However, it seems that his Lordship

---

[675] *ibid.*; Cases 98, 162 and 258/85, *Bertini v Regione Lazio* [1986] E.C.R. 1885.

[676] Case 104/79, *Foglia v Novello (No.1)* [1980] E.C.R. 745; Case 244/80 *Foglia v Novello (No.2)* [1981] E.C.R. 3045: see A. Barav, (1980) 5 E.L. Rev. 443, G. Bebr, (1980) 17 C.M.L. Rev. 525 (*Foglia No.1*); D. Wyatt, (1981) 6 E.L. Rev. 449, G. Bebr, (1982) 19 C.M.L. Rev. 421 (*Foglia No.2*). It should be noted that this litigation was between private parties in Italy but was in reality directed at the alleged incompatibility of a French law with Community law. *Cf.* Cases 98, 162 and 258/85, *Bertini*, above.

[677] *Foglia v Novello (No.2)*, above, at 3062.

[678] Case C–167/94R, *Grau Gomis* [1995] E.C.R. I–1023. The Court has issued an *Information Note on references from national courts for a preliminary ruling* (2005/C 143/01).

[679] Case C–83/91, *Meilicke* [1992] E.C.R. 1–4871 and Case 343/90, *Lourenço Dias v Director da Alfândega do Porto* [1992] E.C.R. I–4673 see T. Kennedy, (1993) 18 E.L. Rev. 121.

[680] Case 166/73, *Rheinmühlen-Düsseldorf v EVSt (No.1)* [1974] E.C.R. 33: the lower court was, under German law, bound on points of law by decisions of a superior court; the Court of Justice held that this could not take away the lower court's power to refer under Art.177(2). See also Case 106/77, *Italian Minister for Finance v Simmenthal (No.2)* [1978] E.C.R. 629.

[681] Case 166/73, *ibid. (No.2)* [1974] E.C.R. 139. The court rejected the suggestion by A. G. Warner that the existence of a right to appeal against an order referring a question to the Court was contrary to Community law: see [1974] E.C.R. 33 at 43–44.

[682] [1974] Ch. 401 at 422–425.

[683] See, e.g. F. G. Jacobs, (1974) 90 L.Q.R. 486; J. D. B. Mitchell, (1974) 11 C.M.L. Rev. 351; E. Freeman, [1975] C.L.P. 176; Collins (1990), pp.176–183. In *Bulmer v Bollinger*, Stephenson L.J. (with whom Stamp L.J. agreed) stated that judges should "bear in mind" the considerations set out by Lord Denning M.R. ([1974] Ch. 401 at 430) but was also conscious of the requirement that the discretion must not be fettered (*ibid.* at 431).

[684] Collins (1990), p.179.

erroneously thought that it was the *reference* that had to be "necessary," whereas Art.234(2) EC (ex Art.177(2)) makes it clear that the significant point is whether a *decision* by the national court on the point is "necessary".[685] Accordingly, two of the matters mentioned by Lord Denning M.R. in relation to "necessity" should have been placed with the other group: the presentation here has been revised accordingly.

(i) *Jurisdiction to refer: is a decision "necessary"?*

18–066   (1) *"The point must be conclusive"* and (2) *"find the facts first"*. According to Lord Denning M.R. the point must be conclusive in the sense that a decision one way must lead to judgment for one party and a decision the other way to judgment for the other. Where the point would only be conclusive if decided one way, and the trial would have to go its full course in respect of the contested issues of fact or of English law if decided the other, then, according to Lord Denning M.R., a reference might be "desirable" or "convenient" but could not be "necessary". Moreover, "[a]s a rule you cannot tell whether it is necessary to decide a point until all the facts are ascertained. So in general it is best to decide the facts first".[686]

It seems to be generally agreed that this is too narrow, and that the correct view is that it may be appropriate to refer a point where there are still matters outstanding which will have to be determined should the decision of the Court of Justice go one way rather than another.[687] This broader view has been adopted by Ormrod L.J. in the Court of Appeal,[688] by the Divisional Court[689] and by Bingham J. in the High Court.[690] These cases suggest, however, that while there is jurisdiction to refer at an early stage, the facts should normally be found first.[691] A difficulty here is that it may not be clear which facts are relevant for the purposes of Community law until after the reference has been made. On the other hand, it has also been stressed by English courts that it may be impossible to formulate the questions to be referred until after a case has been argued.[692]

A further point is that it is not necessary that the whole of a case be affected by Community law for a decision to be necessary: it is sufficient if a particular aspect, such as the measure of damages or the terms of a court order, should be so affected.

---

[685] *ibid.* p.177.

[686] [1974] Ch. 401 at 422, 423.

[687] CPR r.68 provides that an order for reference may be made at any stage.

[688] *Polydor Ltd v Harlequin Record Shops Ltd* [1980] 2 C.M.L.R. 413 at 428: "necessary" to mean "reasonably necessary" and not "unavoidable".

[689] *R v Plymouth JJ., Ex p. Rogers* [1982] Q.B. 863 at 867–870.

[690] *Customs and Excise Commissioners v ApS Samex* [1983] 1 All E.R. 1042 at 1054.

[691] Templeman L.J. in *Polydor*, at 426; Lord Lane C.J. in *R v Plymouth JJ.*, above, at 182; Bingham J. in *Samex*, at 1056c. See also Lord Diplock in *R v Henn and Darby* [1981] A.C. 850 *ibid.* at 904. In *R v Plymouth JJ.* and *Samex* the matters outstanding were not significant in extent; a reference was, however, made at an early stage by Taylor J., with the agreement of both sides, in *R v Ministry of Agriculture, Fisheries and Food, Ex p. Agegate Ltd* [1987] 3 C.M.L.R. 939, and by Henry J. in *R v Ministry of Agriculture, Fisheries and Food, Ex p. FEDESA* [1988] 3 C.M.L.R. 661; a reference was made notwithstanding that there was an unresolved conflict on some factual matters, and over the objections of one party, by the Court of Appeal in *R v Pharmaceutical Society of Great Britain, Ex p. Association of Pharmaceutical Importers* [1987] C.M.L.R. 951.

[692] *Church of Scientology v Customs and Excise Commissioners* [1981] 1 All E.R. 1035 at 1039 (Brightman L.J.); *Lord Bethell v SABENA* [1983] 3 C.M.L.R. 1 (Parker J.).

The move away from Lord Denning M.R.'s attempt to formulate a narrow, clear-cut rule in this context means that the matter is so much one for the appreciation of the court itself that it would be artificial to seek to perpetuate the supposed distinction between "necessity" and "discretion": the approach of an appellate court is in practice likely to be similar in each case.

(ii) *Exercise of the discretion to refer*

(1) *Previous ruling. In Da Costa v Nederlandse Belastringadministratie*[693] the **18–067** Court of Justice stated that where it has given a ruling on a particular question of interpretation, and the same question arises in a subsequent case before a national court of last resort, the earlier ruling may "deprive the obligation [under Art.177(3)] of its purpose and thus empty it of its substance".[694] There would thus be no *obligation* to refer, although the Court also stressed that a national court still had a *discretion* to refer the question. In *Bulmer v Bollinger*[695] Lord Denning M.R. noted that the Court of Justice was not bound by its own previous decisions and said that an English court should only refer a case in such circumstances if it thinks the earlier ruling to be wrong or if there are new factors which ought to be brought to the notice of the Court of Justice.

(2) *Acte clair.* It has been a matter of much controversy whether a national court, whether a court of last resort or not, may decline to refer a question to the Court of Justice on the ground that, notwithstanding the absence of any prior ruling on the point by the Court of Justice, the point is clear and so no "question" arises. Commentators, both academic and judicial, have argued against the *acte clair* doctrine on the basis that there is a real risk that the national courts of different countries may each regard a question as "clear" but in fact decide it differently.[696] Conversely, national courts in several Member States have endorsed and relied upon the doctrine. In *Bulmer v Bollinger*[697] Lord Denning M.R. stated that there was no need to refer a question if the point is considered to be "reasonably clear and free from doubt".[698] Rather to everyone's surprise, in *CILFIT v Ministry of Health*[699] the Court of Justice approved the doctrine, although not in nearly so broad a formulation as Lord Denning's: thus, there is no *obligation* to refer if:

> " . . . the correct application of Community law is so obvious as to leave no scope for any reasonable doubt. The existence of such a possibility must be

---

[693] Cases 28, 29 and 30/62, [1963] E.C.R. 31.

[694] *ibid.* at 38. The same effect may be produced where previous decisions of the court have already dealt with the point of law in question "irrespective of the nature of the proceedings which led to those decisions, even though the questions at issue are not strictly identical": Case 283/81, *CILFIT v Ministry of Health* [1982] E.C.R. 3415 at 3429. The point is even stronger where "the question raised is substantially the same as a question which has already been the subject of a preliminary ruling in the same national proceedings": Case C–337/95, *Parfums Christian Dior* [1997] I–E.C.R. 6013, para.25.

[695] [1974] Ch. 401 at 422.

[696] See, e.g. Judge Pescatore in M. E. Bathhurst *et al.* (eds), *Legal Problems of an Enlarged European Community* (1972), pp.27–46 (but *cf.* M. Lagrange (1971) 8 C.M.L. Rev. 313); A. G. Capotorti in Case 283/81 at *CILFIT v Ministry of Health* [1982] E.C.R. 3415; G. Bebr, (1981) 18 C.M.L. Rev. 475 at 484–489.

[697] [1974] Ch. 401. See also the decision of the Conseil d'Etat in *Cohn-Bendit* [1980] 1 C.M.L.R. 543; G. Bebr, (1983) 20 C.M.L. Rev. 439.

[698] *ibid.* p.423.

[699] [1982] E.C.R. 3415, para.21. See D. Wyatt, (1983) 8 E.L. Rev. 179; N. P. Gravells, (1983) 99 L.Q.R. 518; H. Rasmussen, (1984) 9 E.L. Rev. 242.

assessed in the light of the specific characteristics of Community law, the particular difficulties to which its interpretation gives rise and the risk of divergences in judicial decisions within the Community."

In practice in UK courts the *acte clair* issue has arisen in courts other than of last resort, which accordingly have a discretion to refer.[700] There appears to have been a variation in approach depending on the context. Thus, the unwillingness of judges to refer possible defences arising under Community law to actions for breach of intellectual property rights has been contrasted with an apparent willingness to refer questions concerning equal pay and sex discrimination in employment law.[701] Points regarded by judges as clear turn out on closer examination by commentators to be at least arguable. The dangers of a reluctance to refer questions have been stressed by the House of Lords in *R v Henn and Darby*,[702] where Lord Diplock noted the different approaches to statutory interpretation adopted respectively by the Court of Justice and English courts[703] and the point that each of the (then) six texts of Community law was of equal authority. His Lordship said that English judges should not be "too ready to hold that because the meaning of the English text . . . seems plain to them no question of interpretation can be involved".[704] However, where the point was one "to which an established body of case law plainly applies" an English court might properly take the view that no real question of interpretation was involved.[705]

Lord Diplock's views were echoed by Sir Thomas Bingham M.R. in *R v International Stock Exchange of the UK and the Republic of Ireland Ltd, Ex p. Else (1982) Ltd*[706]:

"I understand the correct approach in principle of a national court (other than a final court of appeal) to be quite clear: if the facts have been found and the Community law issue is critical to the court's final decision, the appropriate course is ordinarily to refer the issue to the Court of Justice unless the national court can with complete confidence resolve the issue

---

[700] But *cf. S.A. Magnavision v General Optical Council (No.2)* [1987] 2 C.M.L.R. 262, below, para.18–068.

[701] A. Arnull, "Art.177 and the Retreat from Van Duyn" (1983) 8 E.L. Rev. 365. See also A. Dashwood and A. Arnull, "English Courts and Art.177 of the EEC Treaty" (1984) 4 Y.E.L. 255; L. W. Gormley, "The Application of Community Law in the United Kingdom, 1976–1985" (1986) 23 C.M.L. Rev 287 at 288–303.

[702] [1981] A.C. 850.

[703] See above, Ch.6.

[704] [1981] A.C. 850 at 906. See also Lord Diplock's speech in *Garland v British Rail Engineering Ltd* [1983] 2 A.C. 751; *cf.* Bingham J. in *Customs and Excise Commissioners v Ap S Samex* [1983] 1 All E.R. 1042: on three of four points the judge held clear views, but accepted that each was not so clear as to be *acte clair*; the Court of Appeal in *R v Pharmaceutical Society of Great Britain, Ex p. Association of Pharmaceutical Importers* [1987] 3 C.M.L.R. 951, *per* Kerr L.J. at 969–970; and McCullough J. in *R v Dairy Produce Quota Tribunal, Ex p. Hall & Sons (Dairy Farmers) Ltd* [1988] 1 C.M.L.R. 592 (discussed by A. Arnull, (1989) 52 M.L.R. 622 at 628–631).

[705] [1981] A.C. 850 at 906. Lord Diplock thought that the interpretation of Art.30 was clear in this sense, but as the Court of Appeal had taken a different view, the point was referred to the Court of Justice. See also *R v Secretary of State for Social Services, Ex p. Bomore Medical Supplies Ltd* [1986] 1 C.M.L.R. 228 (and other cases, discussed by A. Arnull, (1989) 52 M.L.R. 622 at 631–636).

[706] [1993] Q.B.534 at 545: see Walsh, (1993) 56 M.L.R. 881 and E. Szyszczak, (1995) 20 E.L. Rev. 214. The judge's decision to refer was set aside on the ground that the matter was *acte clair*. Applied by Leggatt L.J. in *R v Secretary of State for the National Heritage, Ex p. Continental Television BV* [1993] 2 C.M.L.R. 333 at 346.

itself. In considering whether it can with complete confidence resolve the issue itself the national court must be fully mindful of the differences between national and Community legislation, of the pitfalls which face a national court venturing into what may be an unfamiliar field, of the need for uniform interpretation throughout the Community and of the great advantage enjoyed by the Court of Justice in construing Community instruments. If the national court has any real doubts, it should ordinarily[707] refer."

While this should "no more be read as a statute than Lord Denning's original guidelines"[708] this does reflect a "*communitaire* approach consistent with the spirit of judicial co-operation that is needed if the Art.234 EC (ex Art.177) system is to do its job of ensuring uniform interpretation of Community law throughout the Community".[709]

More recently, however, the Court of Appeal[710] has expressed caution, picking up on concerns expressed by A.G. Jacobs as to the caseload of the Court of Justice. A.G. Jacobs suggested that references under Art.234(2) EC (ex Art.177(2)).

"will be most appropriate where the question is one of general importance and where the ruling is likely to promote the uniform application of the law throughout the European Union. A reference will be least appropriate where there is an established body of case law which could readily be transposed to the facts of the instant case; or where the question turns on a narrow point considered in the light of a very specific set of facts and the ruling is unlikely to have any application beyond the instant case."[711]

The Court of Appeal held that the court should bear these observations in mind and that there was no "real doubt" on the substantive point in issue.[712] Even in cases arising under Art.234(3) EC (ex Art.177(2)),[713] the Court's body of case law had developed to the extent that, particularly in technical fields such as customs and VAT, it

"now provides sufficient guidance to enable national courts and tribunals— and in particular specialised courts and tribunals—to decide many cases for themselves without the need for a reference."[714]

(3) *Other points*. Other factors identified by Lord Denning M.R. in *Bulmer v Bollinger*[715] as relevant to the exercise of a court's discretion included: (1) the

---

[707] Not *necessarily*: see *R v Ministry of Agriculture, Fisheries and Food, Ex p. Portman Agrochemicals Ltd* [1994] 3 C.M.L.R. 18, where while the judge did have doubts as to the meaning of Community law, the issue would become academic by the time the response to an Art.177 reference would be received.
[708] S. Weatherill and P. Beaumont, *EU Law* (3rd edn, 1999), p.336.
[709] *ibid.*
[710] *Trinity Mirror plc v Commissioners of Customs and Excise* [2001] S.T.C. 192 *Littlewoods Organisation plc v Commissioners of Customs and Excise* [2001] S.T.C. 1568.
[711] Case C–338/95, *Wiener S.I. GmbH v Hauptzollamt Emmerich* [1997] E.C.R. I–6495, para.20 of A.G. Jacobs' opinion.
[712] para.[52].
[713] Below, para.18–068.
[714] para.61 of A.G. Jacobs' opinion.
[715] [1974] Ch. 401 at 423–425.

time to get a ruling; (2) the need not to overload the Court of Justice; (3) the need to formulate the question clearly, which was another reason for finding the facts first; (4) "Unless the point is really difficult and important, it would seem better for the English judge to decide it himself"; (5) expense; and (6) the wishes of the parties:

> "If both parties want the point to be referred to the European Court, the English court should have regard to their wishes, but it should not give them undue weight. The English court should hesitate before making a reference against the wishes of one of the parties, seeing the expense and delay which it involves."

The tenor of Lord Denning's judgment was obviously restrictive: references should only be made in exceptional cases, and (possibly) only by the House of Lords. The possibility that the guidelines may, to an extent, conflict with Community law has already been noted.[716] However, the breadth of the discretion to refer has also been noted:

> "The matters referred to by Lord Denning are specifically stated only to be guidelines and, as Lord Denning himself said, when referring to the guidelines laid down by the House of Lords in *The Nema*,[717] with reference to applications for leave to appeal in matters of arbitration, 'guidelines may be stepped over, and are flexible'. I take it that he would apply the same standard to his own guidelines. At all events, it is perfectly clear that, where a discretion is conferred upon the court, that discretion cannot be fettered."[718]

One point not stressed expressly in *Bulmer v Bollinger*[719] is whether references should normally only be made by appellate courts. It has since been suggested that references should only exceptionally be made by trial judges in the Crown Court[720] and by magistrates' courts.[721] It is, however, often argued that an early reference may save time and expense. It is wrong in principle for the Court of Appeal to refer a point where it is known that the House of Lords in another case is to be invited to refer the same point.[722]

4. THE OBLIGATION TO REFER

18–068   Article 234(3) EC (ex Art.177(3)) provides that where a decision on a question of Community law is necessary to enable a court or tribunal to give judgment in

---

[716] See above, para.18–065.

[717] [1980] 2 Lloyd's Rep. 83.

[718] *per* Parker J. in *Lord Bethell v SABENA* [1983] 3 C.M.L.R. 1 at 4. *Cf.* Sir Thomas Bingham in *Ex p. Else (1982) Ltd*, n.706 above.

[719] [1974] Ch. 401.

[720] *R v Henn and Darby* [1981] A.C. 850 at 906: Lord Diplock regarded this as equivalent to referring before the facts are found. The Crown Court is presumably not so inhibited when dealing with an appeal from the magistrates in a summary criminal case: *cf. Charles Robertson (Developments) Ltd v Caradon District Council* [1988] 1 C.M.L.R. 293.

[721] *R v Plymouth JJ., Ex p. Rogers* [1982] Q.B. 863 at 870–871.

[722] *Condé Nast Publications Ltd v Customs and Excise Commissioners* [2006] EWCA Civ 976, [2006] S.T.C. 1721.

a pending case, and that court or tribunal is one "against whose decisions there is no judicial remedy under national law", an *obligation* to refer arises. The points discussed above concerning "necessity", previous rulings and the *acte clair* doctrine[723] are equally applicable here: indeed the decision in *CILFIT v Ministry of Health*[242] arose in respect of Art.177(3). Accordingly, there is no obligation to refer if the court establishes

> "that the question raised is irrelevant or that the Community provision in question has already been interpreted by the Court or that the correct application of Community law is so obvious as to leave no scope for any reasonable doubt."[725]

In addition, there is the question as to which courts are covered by Art.234(3) EC (ex Art 177(3)). The wording of the paragraph suggests that it applies only to courts from which an appeal never lies.[726] The view more widely favoured, however, is that it applies to any court from which an appeal or other "judicial remedy" does not lie in the case in question.[727] One difficulty that has not been settled is whether the remedy has to be available as of right. In *Hagen v Fratelli D. & G. Moretti S.N.C.*[728] Buckley L.J. stated that the "ultimate court of appeal" in this country "is either [the Court of Appeal] if leave to appeal to the House of Lords is not obtainable, or the House of Lords".[729] It is not clear whether "obtainable" means "obtainable ever" or "obtainable in the particular case" but the latter interpretation seems more likely. In *S.A. Magnavision NV v General Optical Council (No.2)*,[730] it was argued that once the Divisional Court, on an appeal by case stated from a magistrates' court in a criminal matter, had refused to certify a point of law of general public importance, it fell within Art.177(3). The refusal of the certificate would block any further appeal (to the House of Lords) and could not itself be challenged on appeal.[731] The Divisional Court sidestepped the argument, holding: (1) that as it had already dismissed the appeal, it was *functus officio*,[732] notwithstanding that the order had not yet been drawn up; and (2) that in any event the point of Community law was clear and the *acte*

---

[723] e.g. *Three Rivers District Council v Governor of the Bank of England* [2003] 2 A.C. 1.

[724] Above, para.18–067.

[725] Case C-495/03, *Intermodal Transport BV v Staatssecretaris van Financien*, Judgment of September 15, 2005.

[726] This was stated to be the correct view by Lord Denning M.R. *obiter* in *Bulmer v Bollinger* [1974] Ch. 401: the other members of the Court of Appeal expressed no view on the matter.

[727] See the Court of Justice, *obiter*, in Case 6/64, *Costa v E.N.E.L.* [1964] E.C.R. 585 at 592 and Case C–99/000, *Lyckeskog* [2002] E.C.R. I–4839. (Swedish court from which appeal could lie to supreme court if that court declared it admissible if important for guidance or there were special grounds, held not to be a final court or tribunal.)

[728] [1980] 3 C.M.L.R. 253.

[729] *ibid.* p.255, *cf.* Kerr L.J. (for a unanimous Court of Appeal) in *R v Pharmaneutical Society of Great Britain, Ex p. Association of Pharmaceutical Importers* [1987] 3 C.M.L.R. 951 at 969: "A court or tribunal below the House of Lords can only fall within [Art.177(2)] where there is no possibility of any further appeal from it." In *Chiron Corp v Murex Diagnostics (No.3)* [1995] F.S.R. 309 the Court of Appeal held that an application to the House of Lords for leave to appeal constituted a "judicial remedy" for the purposes of Art.177.

[730] [1987] 2 C.M.L.R. 262.

[731] See above, para.18–009.

[732] "having performed his function": i.e. the function of the judge is exhausted: D. M. Walker, *The Oxford Companion to Law* (1980), p.508. *Cf. Chiron Corp v Murex Diagnostics*, n.729 above.

clair doctrine applicable. It is also uncertain whether the availability of the remedy of certiorari (now quashing on order), which may only be sought if leave to apply is obtained, counts as a "judicial remedy".[733]

The fact that an interlocutory order may not be the subject of an appeal does not render it final for the purposes of Art.234(3) EC (ex Art.177(3)) provided that the decision is subject to review in the main or subsequent proceedings from which a reference may be made.[734-5]

A failure of a court obliged to refer a cause under Art.234(3) EC may with other facts give rise to a claim for damages.

5. Procedure

18-069 As mentioned above, procedural rules have been made for county courts, the Crown Court, the High Court and the Court of Appeal.[736] All references from these courts must be channelled through the Senior Master of the Queen's Bench Division.

An appeal lies against a decision or refusal to refer in the ordinary way.[737] Unless the court orders otherwise, the order is not sent to the European Court until the time for appealing against the order has expired, or an application for permission to appeal has been refused, or any appeal has been determined.

F. THE ROYAL PREROGATIVE OF MERCY[738]

"Mercy is not the subject of legal rights. It begins where legal rights end."[739]

---

[733] It was so held by Mr J. G. Monroe in *Re a Holiday in Italy* [1975] 1 C.M.L.R 184 (decision of a National Insurance Commissioner) but see F. G. Jacobs (1977) 2 E.L. Rev. 119.

[734-5] Case 107/76, *Hoffman-La Roche v Cemrafarm* [1977] E.C.R. 957: see F. G. Jacobs (1977) 2 E.L. Rev. 354; Cases 35 and 36/82, *Morson v Netherlands: Jhanjan v Netherlands* [1982] E.C.R. 3723: see N. P. Gravells (1983) 8 E.L. Rev. 250.

[736] See above, para.18–062. As to practice in the House of Lords as regards references, see *Practice Directions Applicable to Civil Appeals* (2007), Dir.34, and *Practice Directions Applicable to Criminal Appeals* (2007), Dir 32. Where a reference is refused, reasons will be given reflecting the CILFIT criteria: *ibid.*

[737] See *R v International Stock Exchange of the UK and the Republic of Ireland Ltd, Ex p. Else (1982) Ltd* [1993] Q.B. 534, where the Court of Appeal set aside a reference by the High Court.

[738] See generally P. Taylor, *Taylor on Appeals* (2001), Ch.13; N. Walker, *Aggravation, Mitigation and Mercy in English Criminal Justice* (1999), Ch.14; N. Taylor and J. Wood, "Victims of Miscarriages of Justice" in C. Walker and K. Starmer (eds), *Miscarriages of Justice: A Review of Justice in Error* (1999); on the history, particularly during the transition when the death penalty was being abolished, see R. F. V. Heuston, *Essays in Constitutional Law* (2nd edn, 1964), p.7.

[739] *per* Lord Diplock in *de Freitas v Benny* [1976] A.C. 239 at 247.

The Crown has retained certain of its prerogative powers as "fountain of justice" **18–070** in the field of the administration of justice. One such area is the prerogative of mercy exercised by the Crown on the advice of the Home Secretary.[740] This may take one of three forms[741]:

> "(i) *A Free Pardon*, the effect of which is that a conviction is to be disregarded, so that, so far as is possible, the person is relieved of all penalties and other consequences of the conviction; or
>
> (ii) *A Conditional Pardon*, which excuses or varies the consequences of the conviction subject to conditions—this power was used primarily to commute a sentence of death to one of life imprisonment[742] or
>
> (iii) *Remission* of all or part of the penalty imposed by the Court."

The power to recommend special remission is normally used for reasons unconnected with the merits of the conviction, for example, to reward assistance to the prison authorities[743] or to release a dying prisoner. Occasionally it may be used where new information casts doubt on the rightness of a conviction but the case is not suitable for reference to the Court of Appeal.[744]

---

[740] Section 9 of the Criminal Law Act 1967 deems a pardon signed by the Home Secretary to be "of like effect" as a pardon under the great seal. There may be a pardon by Act of Parliament: see *R.v Crosby* (1695) 12 St. Tr. 1291; *R. v Rookwood* (1696) 13 St. Tr. 139 at 186.

[741] "*Sixth Report from the Home Affairs Committee of the House of Commons* (1981–82, H.C. 421). Home Office Memorandum, p.1. The Criminal Cases Review Commission (previously the Home Secretary) may refer cases to the Court of Appeal (Criminal Division): see above. The following summary is based on this Memorandum. See also the comprehensive survey by A. T. H. Smith, [1983] P.L. 398, and the works cited therein; C. H. Rolph, *The Queen's Pardon* (1978): C. H. W. Gane, 1980 J.R. 18.

[742] On the Privy Council's approach to the exercise of the prerogative of mercy and the right of appeal on capital cases from territories over which it has jurisdiction, see *Linsberth Logan v The Queen* [1996] 2 W.L.R. 711 (emphasising the distinction between appeal and prerogative processes). The Privy Council has held that the exercise of the prerogative of mercy is not sufficient mechanism in itself to legitimate the otherwise cruel and unusual punishment of imposing mandatory death penalties in murder cases: *The Queen v Hughes* [2002] UKPC 12; see also *Reyes v The Queen* [2002] UKPC 11. The Privy Council has also emphasised that although there is there is no legal rights to mercy, the exercise of the prerogative must be conducted according to procedures which are fair, proper and amenable to judicial review, and which comply with State's international obligations. The condemned person therefore has a right information about the procedure: *Lewis v Attorney-General of Jamaica* [2001] 2 A.C. 50.

[743] Jack Straw, then Home Secretary, granted remission of the remainder of the sentences of imprisonment of two prisoners who saved the life of a prison worker who was attacked by a wild boar when working at the prison farm: *The Times*, June 19, 2001. See also reward of a prisoner who saved a suicidal cellmate, leading to a challenge over whether the remission led to his being recategorised as a short term prisoner (and therefore eligible for earlier release): *R. (on the application of Ghartley) v Home Secretary* [2001] EWHC Admin 199. More controversially, early release under the Good Friday Agreement was granted to a number of convicted terrorists, including those serving sentences for murder. In total, 428 prisoners were freed early: *The Times*, July 29, 2000. See also Lord Laird's question on the procedure adopted in the grant of the prerogative in these cases: *Hansard*, H.L., April 17, 2002, col.WA164. Mr Charles Clarke MP, Minister for the Home Office confirmed that the use of the royal prerogative was a "very rare" occurrence, to be used in "exceptional circumstances". The Minister reported that he had commissioned a review of the exercise of the power. See *Hansard*, H.C., May 8, 2001, col. 82W.

[744] *Home Office Memorandum*, pp.2–3.

The fact that an offender is terminally ill is not seen by the courts as a reason to interfere with an otherwise appropriate sentence.[745]

A free pardon[746] is normally only recommended when there are not merely doubts about the defendant's guilt but convincing grounds for thinking that he was innocent"; and this means morally as well as technically innocent. This "clean hands" doctrine implies that the Home Secretary must be satisfied . . . "that in the incident in question the defendant had no intention of committing an offence and did not in fact commit one."[747]

In practice the prerogative is more freely used in respect of cases tried summarily than tried on indictment.

A person who is acquitted on a criminal charge or whose conviction is quashed on appeal normally has no legal right to compensation.[748] However, for many years it was the normal practice of the Home Secretary to offer *ex gratia* compensation where a person was granted a free pardon, or, following the emergence of new evidence, had his or her conviction quashed on appeal out of time or after the Home Secretary had referred the case to the Court of Appeal.[749] A payment could also be made where there had been misconduct or default by the police or some other agency of the criminal justice system and in other, exceptional, cases. Payments were not, however, made simply because there had been an acquittal or a quashed conviction.[750] The amount of compensation was fixed on the recommendation of an independent assessor (in practice the chairman of the Criminal Injuries Compensation Authority whose advice was always accepted).[751] The assessor took account of pecuniary losses, damage to character

---

[745] *R. v Bernard* [1997] 1 Cr.App.R.(S.) 135; [1996] Crim. L.R. 673 and commentary.

[746] There is much confusion over the exact implications of a "free pardon": see A. T. H. Smith, *op. cit.*, pp.417–422. It seems to depend on the exact terms of the pardon in question. The terminology is clearly inappropriate where a person has been pronounced to be innocent. In New Zealand it has been held to be technically no more than an indication that the person concerned was wrongfully convicted: *Re Royal Commission on Thomas* [1980] 1 N.Z.L.R. 602, and in *R. v Foster* [1985] Q.B. 115, the Court of Appeal (Criminal Division) held that the effect of a free pardon was to remove from the subject of the pardon all pain, penalties and punishments ensuing from the conviction but not to eliminate the conviction. (The court proceeded to quash the conviction: see A. Wolfgarten and A. N. Khan, (1986) 130 S.J. 157).

[747] Home Office Memorandum p.3. In *R. v Secretary of State for the Home Department, Ex p. Bentley* [1993] 4 All E.R. 442. the Divisional Court invited the Home Secretary to reconsider his decision not to recommend a posthumous free pardon for Derek Bentley, who was hanged in 1953 for the murder of a police officer; his decision was flawed in that he had failed to consider the possibility of a posthumous conditional pardon reflecting not that B was "morally and technically innocent" (the criteria for a full (or free) pardon, which in the Home Secretary's view were not fulfilled), but simply that B ought to have been reprieved. Michael Howard, then Home Secretary, recommended the grant of a pardon and eventually the Court of Appeal overturned the conviction criticising heavily Lord Goddard's actions as trial judge in the case: [1999] Crim. L.R. 330.

[748] See N. Taylor, "Compensating the Wrongfully Convicted", Jo. Crim. L., (2003) 67(3), 220.

[749] See especially N. Taylor and J. Wood (1999) *op. cit.*, discussing the costs—financial, psychological and physical—to the wrongly convicted and their families. As an example, see the discussion in P. Foot, *Murder at the Farm* (1998) (the Carl Bridgewater case). See also R. Brandon and C. Davies, *Wrongful Imprisonment* (1973).

[750] There is no legitimate expectation created by the existence of the scheme: *R. (Mullen) v Secretary of State for the Home Department* [2004] 3 All E.R. 65, [2004] Crim. L.R. 837. On the exercise of ex gratia payments and their ECHR compatibility; see also *Secretary of State for Home Department, Ex p. Chahal* [1999] E.H.R.L.R, (payments only in case of fault in administration not incompatible). The ECtHR does not *require* a financial remedy: *Masson and Van Zon v Netherlands* [1996] 22 E.H.R.R. 491.

[751] The procedure was set out in H.C. Deb., July 29, 1976. written answers, cols 328–330.

or reputation and physical hardship. The offer was made without admission of liability, and while the claimant was free to accept or refuse, if he or she accepted then subsequent any legal claim was waived.[752] The Home Secretary also stated that he would regard any recommendation as to amount made by the assessor as binding upon him.[753]

A further step was taken by s.133 of the Criminal Justice Act 1988, which enacted a statutory right to compensation in situations following the terms of Art.14.6[754] of the International Covenant on Civil and Political Rights, except that it must be shown "beyond reasonable doubt" (not "conclusively") that there has been a miscarriage of justice. The compensation is paid to the accused person or, if he or she is dead, to the personal representatives. Whether there is a right to compensation is determined by the Secretary of State; the amount by an assessor appointed under Sch.12 to the 1988 Act.[755] The assessor must in particular have regard to the seriousness of the offence and the severity of the punishment, the conduct of the investigation and prosecution and any other conviction of the person and any punishment resulting from them.[756] There must be a "quashing" of the conviction for the purposes of s.133. Thus, where a claimant was successful on his third appeal against a murder conviction to the extent only that the Court of Appeal substituted a conviction for a lesser offence, there could be no compensation order.[757] The Divisional Court has concluded that the section requires proof of more than a quashed conviction and a "newly discovered fact". There had to be proof beyond reasonable doubt that there had been a miscarriage of justice. "In short, a miscarriage of justice in the context of section 133 means, in my judgment, the wrongful conviction of an innocent accused. Compensation goes only to those ultimately proved innocent, not to all those whose convictions are adjudged unsafe."[758] This can be a substantial burden on the victim of injustice.

---

[752] Between 1972 and 1981 there were 47 *ex gratia* payments: 16 of £10,000 or more and three of £20,000 or more: *Home Office Memorandum*. Appendix A(4). In 1983, £77,000 was paid to a man convicted of murder in 1973 on the basis of evidence of a Home Office scientist subsequently discredited. In 1984 Patrick Meehan accepted an offer of £50,500 after seven years in prison: he had previously rejected an offer of £7,500 and the amount was reassessed by an Edinburgh advocate: *Daily Telegraph*, February 2, 1984.

[753] Vol.87, H.C. Deb., November 29, 1985, written answers, cols.691–692: see P. Ashman, (1986) 136 N.L.J. 497.

[754] Art.14.6 of the International Covenant on Civil and Political Rights provides: "When a person has by a final decision been convicted of a criminal offence and when subsequently his conviction has been reversed or he has been pardoned on the ground that a new or newly discovered fact shows conclusively that there has been a miscarriage of justice, the person who has suffered punishment as a result of such conviction shall be compensated according to law, unless it is proved that the nondisclosure of the unknown fact in time is wholly or partly attributable to him."

[755] An assessor must be a lawyer who possesses a seven-year general qualification under the Courts and Legal Services Act 1990, s.71, or an advocate or solicitor in Scotland or a Northern Ireland barrister or solicitor of seven years standing, a person who holds or has held judicial office in any part of the United Kingdom, or the chairman or a member of the Criminal Injuries Compensation Board: Criminal Justice Act 1988, Sch.6, para.2, as amended by the 1990 Act, Sch.10, para.72(1).

[756] 1988 Act, s.133,(4A), added by the Criminal Appeal Act 1995, s.28. See, *O'Brien and Others v Independent Assessor* [2007] UKHL 10. A company cannot recover under s. 133: *R. v Secretary of State for the Home Department, Ex p. Atlantic Commercial UK Ltd*, *The Times*, March 10, 1997.

[757] *R. v Secretary of State for the Home Department, Ex p. Christofides* [2002] 1 W.L.R. 2769. It was also noted that the Secretary of State's scheme of compensation did not have to parallel the ECHR jurisprudence regarding just satisfaction.

[758] *per* Simon Brown L.J. in *R (on the application of Mullen) v Secretary of State* February 21, 2002.

The JUSTICE Committee considered the issue of compensation. It thought that persons given a free pardon and those whose convictions are quashed after a reference by the Home Secretary should have a *right* to compensation. Other persons whose convictions are quashed on appeal should be entitled to apply for compensation although that compensation could be refused or reduced in the light of the claimant's conduct or if the conviction was quashed on a technicality. In certain circumstances compensation should be paid to persons committed for trial in custody and acquitted or discharged, and persons who have had part of their sentence remitted. Claims should be dealt with by an Imprisonment Compensation Board established on the lines of the Criminal Injuries Compensation Board. The introduction of statutory compensation constituted only a partial move in this direction.[759]

Without doubt the system of compensation is not generous in scope or the level of awards made.[760] Somewhat strict constructions placed on both the *ex gratia* and statutory schemes by the Home Office and the courts have reflected a very cautious approach to recognising eligibility. Whilst no amount of monetary compensation can fully make amends for a wrongful conviction it can ease the burden for the applicant. What is undoubtedly lacking for those who have wrongfully suffered a loss of liberty, especially for an extended period, is any form of rehabilitation programme. For prisoners who have rightly served long sentences there are retraining schemes to help them find employment, somewhere to live and generally readjust into society. For the wrongfully convicted there is very little from the state beyond mere financial recompense.

Despite the substantial limitations of the two schemes, the *ex gratia* scheme was stopped with immediate effect following a statement by the Home Secretary in April 2006.[761] It was claimed that the *ex gratia* compensation scheme was not cost effective and could not therefore be justified. Future claims would only be considered under the statutory scheme. Though the latter does satisfy international requirements it is pertinent to state that those requirements set a minimum level. In addition, the Home Secretary also announced that changes would be brought to the statutory scheme. Under the guise of modernisation and simplification, it was announced that reforms to the scheme would introduce time limits for applications; permit the assessor to take greater account of applicants'

The conviction of M was quashed following a decision that the proceedings should have been stayed as an abuse of process owing to the police methods in securing his extradition to the UK. The court went on: "the quashing of the claimant's conviction in this case was a vindication of the rule of law, not the righting of a mistaken verdict". In *R. (Mullen) v Secretary of State for the Home Department* [2004] 3 All E.R. 65, the House of Lords overturned the payment made to the applicant but did not resolve the issue of whether an applicant need prove innocence. See further, S. Roberts, "Unsafe Convictions: Defining and Compensating Miscarriages of Justice", (2003) 66 M.L.R. 441; R. Nobles and D. Schiff, "Guilt and Innocence in the Criminal Justice System: A Comment on *R. (Mullen) v Secretary of State for the Home Department*", (2006) 69 M.L.R. 90. See also *R (Cliberry) v Secretary of State for the Home Department* [2007] EWHC Admin 1855.

[759] JUSTICE described the details of the scheme as "disappointing": 31st Annual Report of JUSTICE, pp. 27–28.

[760] See, *O'Brien and Others v Independent Assessor* [2007] UKHL 10 in which the House of Lords held that the Independent Assessor was justified in reducing the amount of compensation awarded to cover the living expenses that would have been incurred had the men not been in prison.

[761] Hansard, Written Ministerial Statement April 19 2006, col.15WS; See also, P. Ferguson, "Cut-Price Justice", (2006) N.L.J. 778; T. Fowles and D. Wilson, "Compensation for miscarriages of justice", Howard Journal 2006, 45(4), 427.

convictions when deciding the level of awards for non-pecuniary loss; take greater account of conduct by applicants which contributed to the circumstances leading to the miscarriage of justice; provide for an upper limit on the overall amount of compensation; and enable the assessor to reduce an award of compensation to zero in exceptional cases.

The proposals are said to reflect the Government's overarching theme of rebalancing the criminal justice system, and bring about a better balance with the treatment of victims of crime. However, there are clear differences between the two cases. Whilst victims of crime may be under compensated at present, the potentially devastating losses *caused* by the state to victims of miscarriages of justice are too easily overlooked.[762] Ferguson has argued:

> "It is impossible to avoid a lurking doubt that these changes are not about efficiency or equality of treatment but are motivated by an unworthy sentiment that criminals are benefiting from a windfall bounty."[763]

Undoubtedly, there have been cases which are somewhat unpalatable, but it is unfortunate that these, rather than real cases of substantial hardship, that are driving the agenda for reform.

[762] For example, in 1976, at the age of 23, Stefan Kiszko was convicted of the murder of a schoolgirl. The conviction was quashed in 1992 following the discovery of evidence (available at the original trial) that he could not have been the murderer. Less than two years after his release Mr Kiszko died at the age of 41. A family friend commented, "After being released, Stefan could not rouse himself and never recovered from what happened . . . . He could not face the world." (Sanders and Young, *Criminal Justice*, 1994. p.185). See also, *The Times*, March 16, 2007, following the death of Sally Clark, released in 2003 following wrongful imprisonment for the murder of her two sons, a family statement read that "she never fully recovered from the effects of this appalling miscarriage of justice".

[763] P. Ferguson, "Cut-Price Justice", (2006) N.L.J. 778. See also, P. Ferguson, "Lost Years", (2007) 539.

INDEX

This index has been prepared using Sweet & Maxwell's Legal Taxonomy. Main index entries conform to keywords provided by the Legal Taxonomy except where references to specific documents or non-standard terms (denoted by quotation marks) have been included. These keywords provide a means of identifying similar concepts in other Sweet & Maxwell publications and online services to which keywords from the Legal Taxonomy have been applied. Readers may find some minor differences between terms used in the text and those which appear in the index. Suggestions to *sweet&maxwell.taxonomy@ thomson.com*.

(All references are to paragraph number)